The
PRENTICE-HALL
UNIVERSAL ATLAS

The
PRENTICE-HALL
UNIVERSAL ATLAS

Prentice-Hall, Inc., Englewood Cliffs, New Jersey 07632

Library of Congress Cataloging in Publication Data
Main entry under title:
The Prentice-Hall universal atlas.
   Includes index.
   1. Atlases. I. Fullard, Harold. II. Prentice-Hall, inc.

G1201.P688 1983
ISBN 0-13-697094-X

This book is available at a special discount when ordered
in bulk quantities. Contact Prentice-Hall Inc., General
Publishing Division, Special Sales, Englewood Cliffs, N.J. 07632

Printed in Hong Kong.

1 2 3 4 5 6 7 8 9 10

ISBN 0-13-697094-X

Prentice-Hall International, *London*
Prentice-Hall of Australia Pty. Limited, *Sydney*
Prentice-Hall Canada Inc., *Toronto*
Prentice-Hall of India Private Limited, *New Delhi*
Prentice-Hall of Japan, Inc. *Tokyo*
Prentice-Hall Southeast Asia Pte. Ltd., *Singapore*
Whitehall Books Limited, Wellington, *New Zealand*
Editora Prentice-Hall do Brazil Ltda., *Rio de Janeiro*

**Acknowledgement is made to the following for providing the photographs used
in this atlas.**
Air India; Australian Information Service; Brazilian Embassy, London; British Aircraft
Corporation; British Airways; British Leyland; British Petroleum; British Rail; British
Steel Corporation; British Tourist Authority; Central Electricity Generating Board;
D. Chanter; Danish Embassy, London; Egypt Air; Fiat (England) Ltd.; Finnish Tourist
Bureau; Freightliners Ltd.; H. Fullard; M. H. Fullard; Gas Council Exploration Ltd.;
Commander H. R. Hatfield/Astro Books; H. Hawes; Israeli Govt. Tourist Office; Japan
Air Lines; Lufthansa; M.A.T. Transport Ltd.; Meteorological Office, London; Moroccan
Tourist Office; N.A.S.A. (Space Frontiers); National Coal Board, London; National
Maritime Museum, London; Offshore Co.; Pan American World Airways; Royal
Astronomical Society London; Shell International Petroleum Co. Ltd.; Swan Hunter
Group, Ltd.; Swiss National Tourist Office; B. M. Willett; Woodmansterne Ltd.

Preface

Within this book of over 400 pages there are a number of parts and indeed each part is paged separately. The main section is of course the collection of maps and its partner the index. To these are added economic, climate and population statistics and illustrations about the physical Earth and its economic and human affairs. It is hoped that in one way the work will be a reference source to which the reader can go when answers are required to specific questions, but in another sense that the reader can browse and find satisfaction in the illustrated part, the statistics and the maps themselves.

The maps are organized by continent. Each continent begins with a physical and a political map of the whole continent, together with maps showing climate and population. There are maps on these themes for the World and more detailed ones for the British Isles. Each contintent is broken down into regions with maps at a larger scale. For example, all of Western Europe is covered at a scale of 1:2.5M while Great Britain is at a scale of 1:1M; all of the United States is covered at scales of 1:6M with enlargements of the East and California at 1:3M

The place name forms are those that are used locally. The English conventional form often appears on the map and in the index this name is cross referenced to the locally spelled version. In the case of areas that do not use a Roman script the names have been transcribed according to the accepted systems of transcription. In the case of China, the maps and index use the Wade-Giles system and a list appears at the end of the index relating the Wade-Giles to the Pinyin system; the latter is coming into increasing use in the West. In the Pinyin system, to quote one example, Peking appears as Beijing.

International boundaries are drawn to show the *de facto* situation. This does not signify international recognition of that boundary but shows the limits of adminstration on either side of the line. Cease-fire lines are shown and specially labelled.

Rather than flicking through the book to find a particular map the reader is encouraged to consult the contents where the page number and title and, more importantly, the areas covered by the large scale maps are covered by an outline map of each continent. If he or she knows the place name then the index gives the map page number and the geographical co-ordinates.

The illustrated section which precedes the maps gives with maps, diagrams, photographs and brief text, a background to the physical, human and economic geography of the World. The economic section which has been revised for this edition gives the main statistical data for all the principal countries of the World. The climatic statistics show the average monthly rainfall and temperature for places to reflect the variety of climates of the World.

Contents

The Universe, Earth & Man 1-48

Maps 1-176

World

Europe & the British Isles

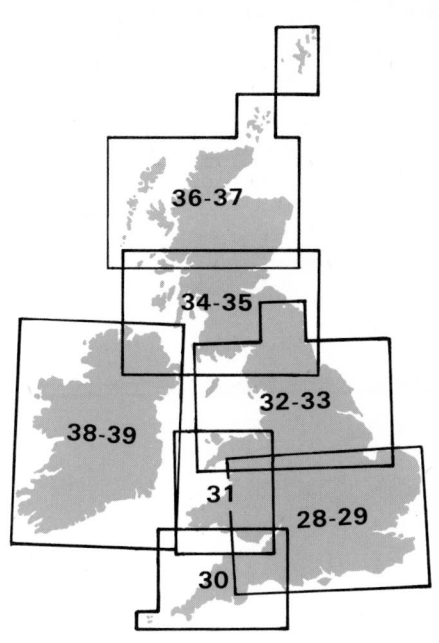

36-37
34-35
32-33
38-39
31
28-29
30

Europe

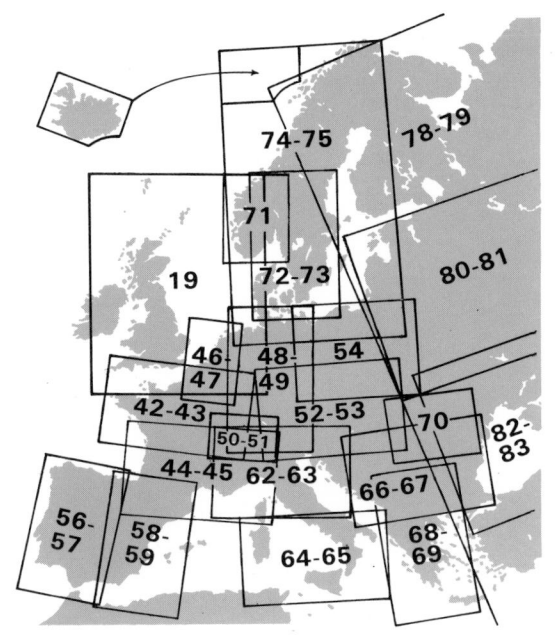

74-75
78-79
71
19
72-73
80-81
46-
47
48-
49
54
42-43
52-53
70
82-
83
50-51
44-45
62-63
66-67
56-
57
58-
59
64-65
68-
69

Asia

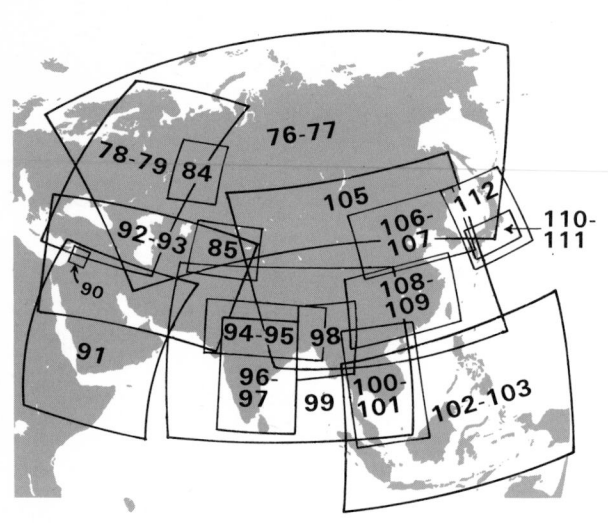

76-77
78-79
84
105
112
110-111
106-107
92-93
85
90
108-109
94-95
98
91
96-97
99
100-101
102-103

Africa

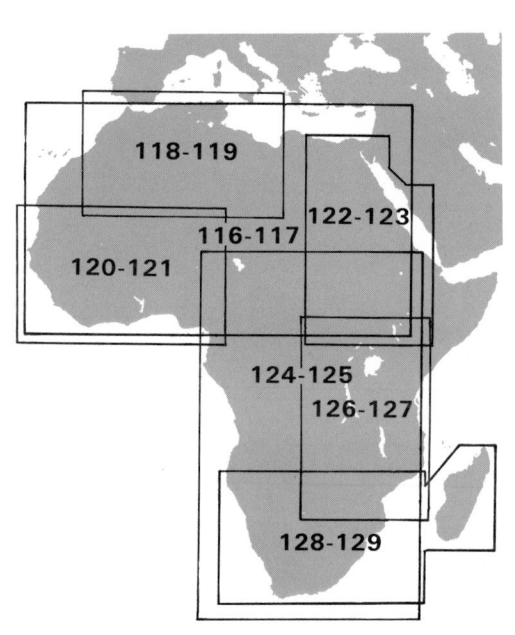

118-119
116-117
122-123
120-121
124-125
126-127
128-129

Australasia

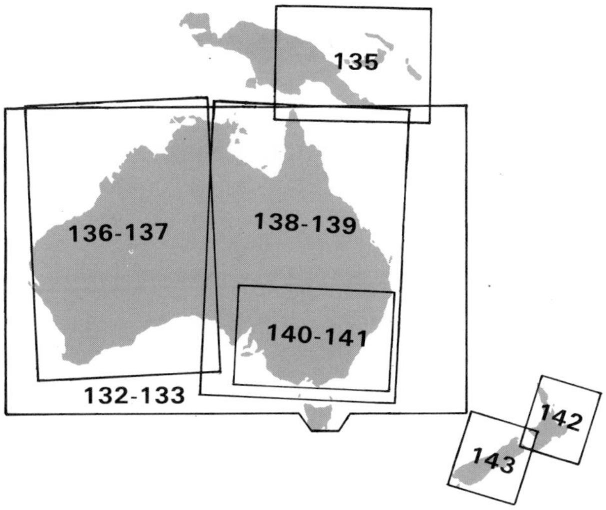

The Americas

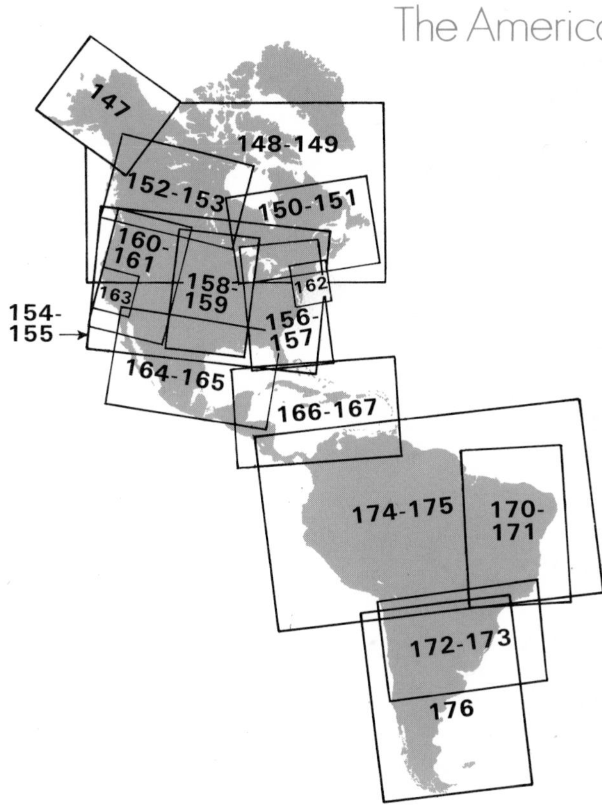

Index

State by State Statistics

Below is given basic population data by state together with totals for the whole of the U.S.A. The land area figure does not include lakes. All the population figures are from the 1970 or 1980 censuses except for the final column which comes from official estimates.

State	Capital	Land Area (sq. miles)	1970 Population in thousands	1980 Population in thousands	1970-1980 Percent Change	1980 Population Density	1980 Percent Resident in Metropolitan Areas	1982 Population Estimates
Alabama	Montgomery	50 767	3 444	3 891	12·9	76·6	62·0	3 943
Alaska	Juneau	570 833	303	400	32·4	0·7	43·2	438
Arizona	Phoenix	113 508	1 775	2 718	53·1	23·9	75·0	2 860
Arkansas	Little Rock	52 078	1 923	2 285	18·8	43·9	39·1	2 291
California	Sacramento	156 299	19 971	23 669	18·5	151·4	94·9	24 724
Colorado	Denver	103 595	2 210	2 890	30·7	27·9	80·9	3 045
Connecticut	Hartford	4 872	3 032	3 107	2·5	637·9	88·3	3 153
Delaware	Dover	1 932	548	596	8·6	308·0	67·0	602
District of Columbia	Washington	63	757	638	-15·7	10 127·0	100·0	631
Florida	Tallahassee	54 153	6 791	9 739	43·4	179·9	87·9	10 416
Georgia	Atlanta	58 056	4 588	5 464	19·1	94·1	60·0	5 639
Hawaii	Honolulu	6 425	770	965	25·3	150·2	79·1	994
Idaho	Boise	82 412	713	945	32·4	11·5	18·3	965
Illinois	Springfield	55 645	11 110	11 419	2·8	205·2	81·0	11 448
Indiana	Indianapolis	35 932	5 195	5 491	5·7	152·8	69·8	5 471
Iowa	Des Moines	55 965	2 825	2 914	3·1	52·1	40·1	2 905
Kansas	Topeko	81 778	2 249	2 363	5·1	28·9	46·8	2 408
Kentucky	Frankfort	39 669	3 221	3 661	13·7	92·3	44·5	3 667
Louisiana	Baton Rouge	44 521	3 645	4 203	15·3	94·4	63·4	4 362
Maine	Augusta	30 995	994	1 125	13·2	36·3	33·0	1 133
Maryland	Annapolis	9 837	3 924	4 216	7·5	428·6	88·8	4 265
Massachusetts	Boston	7 824	5 689	5 737	0·8	733·3	85·3	5 781
Michigan	Lansing	56 954	8 882	9 259	4·2	162·8	82·7	9 109
Minnesota	Minnesota	79 548	3 806	4 077	7·1	51·3	64·6	4 133
Mississippi	Jackson	47 233	2 217	2 520	13·7	53·4	27·1	2 551
Missouri	Jefferson City	68 945	4 678	4 917	5·1	71·3	65·3	4 951
Montana	Helena	145 388	694	787	13·3	5·4	24·0	801
Nebraska	Lincoln	76 644	1 485	1 570	5·7	20·5	44·2	1 586
Nevada	Carson City	109 894	489	799	63·5	7·3	82·0	881
New Hampshire	Concord	8 993	738	921	24·8	102·4	50·7	951
New Jersey	Trenton	7 468	7 171	7 364	2·7	986·1	91·4	7 438
New Mexico	Santa Fe	121 335	1 017	1 299	27·8	10·7	42·4	1 359
New York	Albany	47 377	18 241	17 557	-3·8	370·6	90·1	17 659
North Carolina	Raleigh	48 843	5 084	5 874	15·5	120·3	52·7	6 019
North Dakota	Bismarck	69 300	618	654	5·6	9·4	35·9	670
Ohio	Columbus	41 004	10 657	10 797	1·3	263·3	80·3	10 791
Oklahoma	Oklahoma City	68 655	2 559	3 026	18·2	44·1	58·5	3 177
Oregon	Salem	96 184	2 092	2 632	25·9	27·4	64·9	2 649
Pennsylvania	Harrisburg	44 888	11 801	11 867	0·6	264·4	81·9	11 865
Rhode Island	Providence	1 055	950	948	-0·3	897·6	92·2	958
South Carolina	Columbia	30 203	2 591	3 119	20·4	103·3	59·7	3 203
South Dakota	Pierre	75 952	666	690	3·6	9·1	15·9	691
Tennessee	Nashville	41 155	3 926	4 591	16·9	111·6	62·8	4 651
Texas	Austin	262 017	11 199	14 228	27·1	54·3	80·0	15 280
Utah	Salt Lake City	82 073	1 059	1 461	37·9	17·8	79·0	1 554
Vermont	Montpelier	9 273	445	512	15·0	55·1	22·3	516
Virginia	Richmond	39 704	4 651	5 346	14·9	134·6	69·6	5 491
Washington	Olympia	66 511	3 413	4 130	21·0	62·1	80·4	4 245
West Virginia	Charleston	24 119	1 744	1 950	11·8	80·8	37·1	1 948
Wisconsin	Madison	54 426	4 148	4 706	6·5	86·4	66·8	4 765
Wyoming	Cheyenne	96 989	332	471	41·6	4·9	15·3	502
United States	**Washington D.C.**	**3 539 289**	**203 302**	**226 505**	**17·6**	**64·0**	**74·8**	**231 534**

Large Metropolitan Areas

The table shows in alphabetical order those standard metropolitan areas (SMSA's) of over 200 000 inhabitants in size. An SMSA is broadly defined as an area comprising a central nucleus of over 50 000 inhabitants which together with its adjacent, dependent communities has a population of over 100 000 inhabitants.

Metropolitan Area	1980 Population in thousands	Rank	Percent change, 1970-1980
Akron *Ohio*	660	57	-2.8
Albany-Schenectady-Troy *N.Y.*	795	50	2.2
Albuquerque *N. Mex.*	454	86	36.4
Allentown-Bethlehem-Easton *Pa.-N.J.*	637	62	7.1
Anaheim-Santa Ana-Garden Grove *Calif.*	1 932	18	35.9
Ann Arbor *Mich.*	265	145	13.1
Appleton-Oshkosh *Wis.*	291	129	5.2
Atlanta *Ga.*	2 030	16	27.2
Augusta *Ga.-S.C.*	327	113	18.7
Austin *Tex.*	536	70	48.8
Bakersfield *Calif.*	403	97	22.1
Baltimore *Md.*	2 174	14	5.0
Baton Rouge *La.*	494	80	31.5
Beaumont-Port Arthur-Orange *Tex.*	375	104	8.0
Binghamton *N.Y.-Pa.*	301	126	-0.4
Birmingham *Ala.*	847	45	10.4
Boston *Mass.*	2 763	10	-4.7
Bridgeport *Conn.*	395	98	-1.6
Brownsville-Harlingen-San Benito *Tex.*	210	166	49.4
Buffalo *N.Y.*	1 243	31	-7.9
Canton *Ohio*	404	96	2.7
Charleston-North Charleston *S.C.*	430	91	28.0
Charleston *W. Va.*	270	142	4.8
Charlotte-Gastonia *N.C.*	637	61	14.2
Chattanooga *Tenn.-Ga.*	427	92	15.0
Chicago *Ill.*	7 102	3	1.8
Cincinnati *Ohio-Ky.-Ind.*	1 401	27	1.0
Cleveland *Ohio*	1 899	19	-8.0
Colorado Springs *Colo.*	317	120	32.7
Columbia *S.C.*	408	95	26.4
Columbus *Ga.-Ala.*	239	156	0.3
Columbus *Ohio*	1 093	35	7.4
Corpus Christi *Tex.*	326	114	14.5
Dallas-Ft. Worth *Tex.*	2 975	8	25.1
Davenport-Rock Is.-Moline *Iowa-Ill.*	384	100	5.9
Dayton *Ohio*	830	47	-2.6
Daytona Beach *Fla.*	259	149	52.7
Denver-Boulder *Colo.*	1 620	22	30.7
Des Moines *Iowa.*	338	111	7.8
Detroit *Mich.*	4 353	5	-1.9
Duluth-Superior *Minn.-Wis.*	267	143	0.5
El Paso *Tex.*	480	82	33.6
Erie *Pa.*	280	135	6.1
Eugene-Springfield *Oreg.*	275	138	27.8
Evansville *Ind.-Ky.*	309	123	8.6
Fayetteville *N.C.*	247	153	16.6
Flint *Mich.*	522	77	2.5
Fort Lauderdale-Hollywood *Fla.*	1 014	37	63.5
Fort Myers-Cape Coral *Fla.*	205	168	95.1
Fort Smith *Ark.-Okla.*	203	169	26.7
Fort Wayne *Ind.*	383	101	5.8
Fresno *Calif.*	515	78	24.6
Gary-Hammon-East Chicago *Ind.*	643	58	1.5
Grant Rapids *Mich.*	602	64	11.6
Greensboro-Winston-Salem-High Point *N.C.*	827	48	14.3
Greenville-Spartanburg *S.C.*	569	68	20.1
Hamilton-Middletown *Ohio*	259	148	14.4
Harrisburg *Pa.*	446	88	8.7
Hartford *Conn.*	726	54	0.8
Honolulu *Hawaii*	763	52	21.0
Houston *Tex.*	2 905	9	45.3
Huntington-Ashland *W. Va.-Ky.-Ohio*	311	122	8.5
Huntsville *Ala.*	309	124	9.3
Indianapolis *Ind.*	1 167	34	5.0
Jackson *Miss.*	320	117	23.8
Jacksonville *Fla.*	738	53	18.6
Jersey City *N.J.*	557	69	-8.4
Johnson City-Kingsport-Bristol *Tenn.-Va.*	434	90	16.1
Johnstown *Pa.*	265	146	0.6
Kalamazoo-Portage *Mich.*	279	137	8.3
Kansas City *Mo.-Kans.*	1 327	29	4.2
Killeen-Temple *Tex.*	215	164	34.3
Knoxville *Tenn.*	477	83	16.4
Lakeland-Winter Haven *Fla.*	322	116	40.8
Lancaster *Pa.*	362	108	13.2
Lansing-East Lansing *Mich.*	468	84	10.4
Las Vegas *Nev.*	462	85	69.0
Lawrence-Haverhill *Mass.-N.H.*	282	133	9.1
Lexington-Fayette *Ky.*	318	119	19.3
Lima *Ohio*	218	162	3.9
Little Rock-North Little Rock *Ark.*	393	99	21.7
Long Branch-Asbury Park *N.J.*	503	79	8.9
Lorain-Elyria *Ohio*	275	139	7.0
Los Angeles-Long Beach *Calif.*	7 478	2	6.2
Louisville *Ky.-Ind.*	906	43	4.5
Lowell *Mass.*	233	157	6.9
Lubbock *Tex.*	212	165	18.0
Macon *Ga.*	255	150	12.3
Madison *Wis.*	324	115	11.5
McAllen-Pharr-Edinburg *Tex.*	283	132	56.0
Melbourne-Titusville-Cocoa *Fla.*	273	140	18.7
Memphis *Tenn.-Ark.-Miss.*	913	42	9.4
Miami *Fla.*	1 626	21	28.3
Milwaukee *Wis.*	1 397	28	-0.5
Minneapolis-St. Paul *Minn.-Wis.*	2 114	15	7.6
Mobile *Ala.*	443	89	17.6
Modesto *Calif.*	266	144	36.7
Montgomery *Ala.*	273	141	20.7
Nashville-Davidson *Tenn.*	851	44	21.6
Nassau-Suffolk *N.Y.*	2 606	11	2-0
Newark *N.J.*	1 965	17	-4.5
New Brunswick-Perth Amboy-Sayreville *N.J.*	596	65	2.1
Newburgh-Middletown *N.Y.*	260	147	17.1
New Haven-West Haven *Conn.*	418	93	1.5
New London-Norwich *Conn.-R.I.*	249	152	2.8
New Orleans *La.*	1 187	33	13.4
Newport News-Hampton *Va.*	364	107	9.4
New York *N.Y.-N.J.*	9 120	1	-8.6
Norfolk-Virginia Beach-Portsmouth *Va.-N.C.*	807	49	10.1
Northeast *Pa.*	640	60	3.0
Oklahoma City *Okla.*	834	46	19.3
Omaha *Nebr.-Iowa*	570	67	5.1
Orlando *Fla.*	701	55	54.6
Oxhard-Simi Valley-Ventura *Calif.*	530	75	40.0
Paterson-Clifton-Passaic *N.J.*	448	87	-2-9
Pensacola *Fla.*	290	131	19.2
Peoria *Ill.*	366	106	7.0
Philadelphia *Pa.-N.J.*	4 717	4	-2.2
Phoenix *Ariz.*	1 508	26	55.3
Pittsburgh *Pa.*	2 264	13	-5.7
Portland *Oreg.-Wash.*	1 242	32	23.3
Poughkeepsie *N.Y.*	245	155	10.2
Providence-Warwick-Pawtucket *R.I.-Mass.*	919	41	1.1
Provo-Orem *Utah*	218	163	58.3
Raleigh-Durham *N.C.*	531	73	26.6
Reading *Pa.*	313	121	5.4
Richmond *Va.*	632	63	15.4
Riverside-San Bernardino-Ontario *Calif.*	1 557	25	36.7
Roanoke *Va.*	225	161	10.5
Rochester *N.Y.*	972	39	1.1
Rockford *Ill.*	280	136	2.7
Sacramento *Calif.*	1 014	38	26.2
Saginaw *Mich.*	228	160	3.8
Salem *Oreg.*	250	151	33.9
Salinas-Seaside-Monterey *Calif.*	290	130	17.4
Salt lake City *Utah*	936	40	32.7
San Antonio *Tex.*	1 072	36	20.7
San Diego *Calif.*	1 862	20	37.1
San Francisco-Oakland *Calif.*	3 253	6	4.6
San Jose *Calif.*	1 295	30	21.6
Santa Barbara-Santa Maria-Lompoc *Calif.*	299	128	13.0
Santa Rosa *Calif.*	300	127	46.3
Sarasota *Fla.*	202	170	68.0
Savannah *Ga.*	231	158	10.9
Seattle-Everett *Wash.*	1 607	23	12.8
Shreveport *La.*	377	103	12.1
South Bend *Ind.*	281	134	0.3
Spokane *Wash.*	342	110	18.9
Springfield-Chicopee-Holyoke *Mass.-Conn.*	531	74	-2.0
Springfield *Mo.*	208	167	23.6
St. Louis *Mo.-Ill.*	2 355	12	-2.3
Stockton *Calif.*	347	109	19.3
Syracuse *N.Y.*	642	59	0.9
Tacoma *Wash.*	486	81	17.8
Tampa-St. Petersburg *Fla.*	1 569	24	44.2
Toledo *Ohio-Mich.*	792	51	3.8
Trenton *N.J.*	308	125	1.2
Tucson *Ariz.*	531	72	51.1
Tulsa *Okla.*	690	56	25.6
Utica-Rome *N.Y.*	320	118	-6.0
Vallejo-Fairfield-Napa *Calif.*	334	112	33.2
Visalia-Tulare-Porterville *Calif.*	246	154	30.5
Washington *D.C.-Md.-Va.*	3 060	7	5.2
Waterbury *Conn.*	228	159	5.2
West Palm Beach-Boca Raton *Fla.*	573	66	64.2
Wichita *Kans.*	411	94	5.6
Wilmington *Del.-N.J.-Md.*	524	76	4.9
Worcester *Mass.*	373	105	0.2
York *Pa.*	381	102	15.7
Youngstown-Warren *Ohio*	531	71	-1.1

Cities and Towns

The list below gives those incorporated settlements as defined in the 1980 U.S. census with over 10 000 inhabitants. Where a dagger appears alongside an entry in Connecticut, Maine, Massachusetts, New Hampshire, Rhode Island and Vermont, it indicates that the town is a minor civil division and may include rural or other population. At the time of compilation 1980 population figures for unincorporated places had not been published, so these settlements are given in italics and figures are for 1970.

Alabama

Albertville 12 039
Alexander City 13 807
Andalusia 10 415
Anniston 29 523
Athens 14 558
Auburn 28 471
Bessemer 31 729
Birmingham 284 413
Bluff Park 12 372
Center Point 15 675
Cullman 13 084
Decatur 42 002
Dothan 48 750
Enterprise 18 033
Eufaula 12 097
Fairfield 13 040
Florence 37 029
Fort Payne 11 485
Fort Rucker 14 242
Gadsden 47 565
Homewood 21 271
Hoover 15 064
Hueytown 13 309
Huntsville 142 513
Jasper 11 894
Mobile 200 452
Montgomery 178 157
Mountain Brook 17 400
Northport 14 291
Opelika 21 896
Ozark 13 188
Phenix City 26 928
Prattville 18 647
Prichard 39 541
Scottsboro 14 758
Selma 26 684
Sheffield 11 903
Sylacauga 12 708
Talladega 19 128
Troy 12 587
Tuscaloosa 75 143
Tuskegee 12 716
Vestavia Hills 15 733

Alaska

Anchorage 173 017
Fairbanks 22 645
Juneau 19 528
Kenai Peninsula 25 282
Spenard 18 089

Arizona

Casa Grande 14 971
Chandler 29 673
Douglas 13 058
Flagstaff 34 641
Glendale 96 988
Lake Havasu City 15 737
Mesa 152 453
Nogales 15 683
Paradise Valley 10 832
Peoria 12 251
Phoenix 764 911
Prescott 20 055
Scottsdale 88 364
Sierra Vista 25 968
Sun City 13 670
Tempe 106 743
Tucson 330 537
Yuma 42 433

Arkansas

Arkadelphia 10 005
Benton 17 437
Blytheville 24 314
Camden 15 356
Conway 20 375
El Dorado 26 685
Fayetteville 36 604
Forrest City 13 803
Fort Smith 71 384
Hope 10 290
Hot Springs 35 166
Jacksonville 27 589
Jonesboro 31 530
Little Rock 158 461
Magnolia 11 909
Malvern 10 163
North Little Rock 64 419
Paragould 15 214
Pine Bluff 56 576
Rogers 17 429
Russellville 14 000
Searcy 13 612
Sherwood 10 586
Southwest Little Rock 13 231
Springdale 23 458
Stuttgart 10 941
Texarkana 21 459
Van Buren 12 020
West Helena 11 367
West Memphis 28 138

California

Alameda 63 852
Alamo-Danville 14 059
Albany 15 130
Alhambra 64 615
Alondra Park 12 193
Altadena 42 415
Alum Rock 18 355
Anaheim 221 847
Antioch 43 559
Arcadia 45 994
Arcata 12 338
Arden-Arcade 82 492
Arroyo Grande 11 290
Artesia 14 301
Ashland 14 810
Atascadero 15 930
Atwater 17 530
Azusa 29 380
Bakersfield 105 611
Baldwin Park 50 554
Banning 14 020
Barstow 17 690
Bell 25 450
Bellflower 53 441
Bell Gardens 34 117
Belmont 24 505
Benicia 15 376
Berkeley 103 328
Beverly Hills 32 367
Bloomington 11 957
Brawley 14 946
Brea 27 913
Broderick-Bryte 12 782
Buena Park 64 165
Burbank 84 625
Burlingame 26 173
Calexico 14 412
Camarillo 37 732
Campbell 27 067
Carlsbad 35 490
Carmichael 37 625
Carpinteria 10 835
Carson 81 221
Castro Valley 44 760
Ceres 13 281
Cerritos 52 756
Chico 26 601
China Lake 11 105
Chino 40 165
Chula Vista 83 927
Citrus Heights 21 760
Claremont 30 950
Clovis 33 021
Colton 27 419
Commerce 10 509
Compton 81 286
Concord 103 251
Corona 37 791
Coronado 16 859
Costa Mesa 82 291
Covina 33 751
Cudahy 17 984
Culver City 38 139
Cupertino 25 770
Cypress 40 391
Daly City 78 519
Davis 36 640
Del Aire 11 930
Delano 16 491
Diamond Bar 10 576
Downey 82 602
Duarte 16 766
Dublin 13 641
East La Mirada 12 339
East Los Angeles 104 881
East Palo Alto 18 727
Edwards 10 331
El Cajon 73 892
El Centro 23 996
El Cerrito 22 731
El Monte 79 494
El Segundo 13 752
Enterprise 11 486
Escondido 62 480
Eureka 24 153
Fairfield 58 099
Fair Oaks 11 256
Florence-Graham 42 900
Folsom 11 003
Fontana 37 109
Foster City 23 287
Fountain Valley 55 080
Fremont 131 945
Fresno 218 202
Fullerton 102 034
Gardena 45 165
Garden Grove 123 351
Gilroy 21 641
Glendale 139 060
Glendora 38 654
Hacienda Heights 35 969
Hanford 20 958
Hawaiian Gardens 10 548
Hawthorne 56 447
Hayward 94 167
Hemet 23 211
Hermosa Beach 18 070
Highland 12 669
Hillsborough 10 451
Hollister 11 488
Huntington Beach 170 505
Huntington Park 46 223
Imperial Beach 22 689
Indio 21 611
Inglewood 94 245
Irvine 62 134
Isla Vista 13 441
La Canada-Flintridge 20 153
La Crescenta-Montrose 19 620
Lafayette 20 879
Laguna Beach 17 860
Laguna Hills 13 676
La Habra 45 232
Lakeside 11 991
Lakewood 74 654
La Mesa 50 342
La Mirada 40 986
Lancaster 48 027
La Palma 15 663
La Puente 30 882
Larkspur 11 064
La Verne 23 508
Lawndale 23 460
Lemon Grove 20 780
Lennox 16 121
Livermore 48 349
Lodi 35 221
Loma Linda 10 694
Lomita 17 191
Lompoc 26 267
Long Beach 361 334
Los Alamitos 11 529
Los Altos 25 769
Los Angeles 2 966 763
Los Banos 10 341
Los Gatos 26 593
Lynwood 48 548
Madera 21 732
Manhattan Beach 31 542
Manteca 24 925
Marina 20 647
Martinez 22 582
Maywood 21 810
Menlo Park 25 673
Merced 36 499
Millbrae 20 058
Mill Valley 12 967
Milpitas 37 820
Mission Viejo 11 933
Modesto 106 105
Monrovia 30 531
Montclair 22 628
Montebello 52 929
Monterey 27 558
Monterey Park 54 338
Moraga 15 014
Morgan Hill 17 060
Mountain View 58 655
Napa 50 879
National City 48 772
Newark 32 126
Newport Beach 63 475
Norco 21 126
North Highlands 31 854
Norwalk 85 232
Novato 43 916
Oakland 339 288
Oceanside 76 698
Oildale 20 879
Ontario 88 820
Orange 91 788
Orangevale 16 493
Otay-Castle Park 15 445
Oxnard 108 195
Pacifica 36 866
Pacific Grove 15 755
Palmdale 12 277
Palm Desert 11 801
Palm Springs 32 271
Palo Alto 55 225
Palos Verdes Estates 14 376
Paradise 22 571
Paramount 36 407
Parkway-Sacramento South 28 574
Pasadena 119 374
Pendleton North 11 803
Pendleton South 13 692
Petaluma 33 834
Pico Rivera 53 459
Piedmont 10 498
Pinole 14 253
Pittsburg 33 034
Placentia 35 041
Pleasant Hill 25 124
Pleasanton 35 160
Pomona 92 742
Porterville 19 707
Port Hueneme 17 803
Rancho Cordova 30 451
Rancho Cucamonga 55 250
Rancho Palos Verdes 35 227
Redding 41 995
Redlands 43 619
Redondo Beach 57 102
Redwood City 54 965
Reedley 11 071
Rialto 35 615
Richmond 74 676
Ridgecrest 15 929
Riverside 170 876
Rohnert Park 22 965
Rosemead 42 604
Roseville 24 347
Rossmoor 12 922
Rowland Heights 16 881
Rubidoux 13 969
Sacramento 275 741
Salinas 80 479
San Anselmo 11 927
San Bernardino 118 057
San Bruno 35 417
San Carlos 24 710
San Clemente 27 325
San Diego 875 504
San Dimas 24 014
San Fernando 17 731
San Francisco 678 974
San Gabriel 30 072
Sanger 12 558
San Jose 636 550
San Juan Capistrano 18 959
San Leandro 63 952
San Lorenzo 24 633
San Luis Obispo 34 252
San Marcos 17 479
San Marino 13 307
San Mateo 77 561
San Pablo 19 750
San Rafael 44 700
Santa Ana 203 713
Santa Barbara 74 542
Santa Clara 87 746
Santa Cruz 41 483
Santa Fe Springs 14 559
Santa Maria 39 685
Santa Monica 88 314
Santa Paula 20 552
Santa Rosa 83 205
Santee 21 107
Saratoga 29 261
Seal Beach 25 975
Seaside 36 567
Selma 10 942
Sierra Madre 10 837
Simi Valley 77 500
South El Monte 16 623
South Gate 66 784
South Lake Tahoe 20 681
South Pasadena 22 681
South San Francisco 49 393
South San Jose Hills 12 386
South Whittier 46 641
Spring Valley 29 742
Stanton 21 144
Stockton 149 779
Suisun City 11087
Sunnyvale 106 618
Temple City 28 972
Thousand Oaks 77 797
Torrance 131 497
Tracy 18 428
Tulare 22 475
Turlock 26 291
Tustin 32 073
Tustin-Foothills 26 699
Ukiah 12 035
Union City 39 406
Upland 47 647
Vacaville 43 367
Valinda 18 837
Vallejo 80 188
Vandenburg 13 193
Ventura 74 474
Victorville 14 220
View Park-Windsor Hills 12 268
Visalia 49 729
Vista 35 834
Walnut Creek 53 643
Watsonville 23 543
West Athens 13 311
West Carson 15 501
West Covina 80 094
West Hollywood 34 622
Westminster 71 133
Westmont 29 310
West Puente Valley 20 733
West Sacramento 12 002
West Whittier-Los Nietos 20 845
Whittier 68 872
Willowbrook 28 705
Woodland 30 235
Yorba Linda 28 254
Yuba City 18 736
Yucaipa 19 284

Colorado

Arvada 84 576
Aurora 158 588
Boulder 76 685
Brighton 12 773
Broomfield 20 730
Canon City 13 037
Colorado Springs 215 150
Commerce City 16 234
Denver 491 396
Derby 10 206
Durango 11 426
Englewood 30 021
Fort Carson 19 399
Fort Collins 64 632
Golden 12 237
Grand Junction 28 144
Greeley 53 006
Lakewood 112 848
Littleton 28 631
Littleton Southeast 22 899
Longmont 42 942
Loveland 30 244
Northglenn 29 847

Pueblo 101 686
Security-Widefield 15 297
Sherrelwood ... 18 868
Sterling 11 385
Thornton 40 343
Westminster ... 50 211
Wheat Ridge ... 30 293

Connecticut

Ansonia 19 039
†Avon 11 201
†Berlin.......... 15 121
†Bethel 16 004
†Bloomfield 18 608
†Branford 23 363
Bridgeport..... 142 546
Bristol 57 370
†Brookfield 12 872
†Cheshire 21 788
†Clinton 11 195
†Cromwell 10 265
Danbury 60 470
Darien 18 892
Derby.......... 12 346
†East Hartford ... 52 563
†East Haven 25 028
†East Lyme...... 13 870
†Enfield......... 42 695
†Fairfield....... 54 849
†Farmington..... 16 407
†Glastonbury 24 327
†Greenwich 59 578
†Groton......... 41 062
Groton Borough 10 086
†Guilford........ 17 375
†Hamden 51 071
Hartford 136 392
†Killingly....... 14 519
†Ledyard 13 735
†Madison 14 031
†Manchester 49 761
†Mansfield 20 634
Meriden 57 118
Middletown 39 040
Milford 50 898
†Monroe 14 010
†Montville 16 455
Naugatuck 26 456
New Britain 73 840
†New Canaan ... 17 931
†New Fairfield ... 11 260
New Haven ... 126 109
†Newington 28 841
New London 28 842
†New Milford 19 420
†Newtown 19 107
†North Branford 11 554
†North Haven 22 080
Norwalk 77 767
Norwich 38 074
†Orange 13 237
†Plainfield....... 12 774
†Plainville 16 401
†Plymouth 10 732
†Ridgefield 20 120
†Rocky Hill 14 559
†Seymour 13 434
Shelton 31 314
†Simsbury 21 161
†Southbury 14 156
†Southington 36 879
†South Windsor 17 198
Stamford...... 102 453
†Stonington 16 220
Storrs 10 691
†Stratford 50 541
Torrington...... 30 987
†Trumbull 32 989
†Vernon 27 974
†Wallingford 37 274
Waterbury 103 266
†Waterford 17 843
†Watertown 19 489
†West Hartford .. 61 301
West Haven 53 184
†Westport 25 290
†Wethersfield ... 26 013
Willimantic..... 14 652
†Wilton 15 351
†Winchester..... 10 841
†Windham 21 062
†Windsor 25 204
†Windsor Locks .. 12 190
†Wolcott 13 008

Delaware

Dover.......... 23 512
Newark 25 247
Wilmington 70 195
Wilmington Manor-Chelsea-Leedom 10 134

District of Columbia

Washington ... 637 651

Florida

Altamonte Springs 22 028
Bartow 14 780
Belle Glade..... 16 535
Boca Raton..... 49 505
Boynton Beach 35 624
Bradenton 30 170
Brandon 12 749
Browardale..... 17 444
Browns Village 23 442
Cape Coral 32 103
Carol City 27 361
Casselberry 15 247
Cedar Hammock-Bradenton South........ 10 820
Clearwater 85 450
Cocoa 16 096
Cocoa Beach ... 10 926
Cooper City..... 10 140
Coral Gables ... 43 241
Coral Springs ... 37 349
Cutler Ridge 17 441
Dania.......... 11 811
Davie 20 877
Daytona Beach 54 176
Deerfield Beach 39 193
De Land........ 15 354
Delray Beach ... 34 325
Dunedin 30 203
Fort Lauderdale .. 153 256
Fort Myers 36 638
Fort Pierce 33 802
Fort Walton Beach 20 829
Gainesville 81 371
Gulfport 11 180
Haines City..... 10 799
Hallandale 36 517
Hialeah 145 254
Hollywood 117 188
Homestead..... 20 668
Jacksonville ... 540 898
Jacksonville Beach 15 462
Kendall 35 497
Key West 24 292
Kissimmee 15 487
Lakeland 47 406
Lake Worth 27 048
Largo 58 977
Lauderdale Lakes........ 25 426
Lauderhill 37 271
Leesburg....... 13 191
Lighthouse Point 11 488
Longwood...... 10 029
Margate 36 044
Melbourne 46 536
Merritt Island ... 29 233
Miami 346 931
Miami Beach ... 96 298
Miami Springs .. 12 350
Miramar 32 813
Myrtle Grove ... 16 186
Naples......... 17 581
New Port Richey 11 196
New Smyrna Beach 13 557
North Lauderdale ... 18 479
North Miami.... 42 566
North Miami Beach 36 481
North Palm Beach 11 344
Norwood 14 973
Oakland Park ... 21 939
Ocala 37 170
Opa-Locka 14 460
Orlando....... 128 394
Ormond Beach 21 378
Palatka 10 175
Palm Bay....... 18 560
Palm Beach Gardens 14 407
Panama City.... 33 346
Pembroke Pines........ 35 776
Pensacola 57 619
Perrine 10 257
Pine Hills 13 882
Pinellas Park ... 32 811
Plant City 19 270
Plantation 48 501
Pompano Beach 52 618
Port Charlotte .. 10 769
Port Orange 18 756
Port St Lucie.... 14 690
Riviera Beach... 26 596
Rockledge...... 11 877
St. Augustine... 11 985
St. Petersburg .. 236 893
Sanford........ 23 176
Sarasota 48 868
South Miami ... 10 884
South Miami Heights 10 395
South Patrick Shores 10 313
Sunrise 39 681
Sweetwater Creek........ 19 453
Tallahassee 81 548
Tamarac 29 142
Tampa 271 523
Tarpon Springs 13 251
Temple Terrace 11 097
Titusville 31 910
University (Hillsborough) 10 039
Venice 12 153
Vero Beach..... 16 176
Warrington..... 15 848
West Palm Beach 62 530
West Pensacola 20 924
Westwood Lakes........ 12 811
Wilton Manors 12 742
Winter Haven... 21 119
Winter Park 22 314
Winter Springs 10 475

Georgia

Albany......... 73 934
Americus 16 120
Athens 42 549
Atlanta 425 022
Augusta 47 532
Bainbridge 10 553
Brunswick 17 605
Carrollton 14 078
College Park 24 632
Columbus 169 441
Cordele 10 914
Covington 10 586
Dalton 20 743
Decatur 18 404
Douglas........ 10 980
Dublin 16 083
East Point 37 486
Fitzgerald 10 187
Forest Park 18 782
Fort Benning ... 27 495
Fort Gordon 15 589
Gainesville 15 280
Griffin 20 728
Hinesville 11 309
La Grange...... 24 204
Macon 116 860
Marietta 30 805
Midway-Hardwick 14 047
Milledgeville ... 12 176
Moultrie 15 708
Newnan 11 449
Rome 29 654
Roswell 23 337
Savannah 141 634
Smyrna 20 312
Statesboro 14 866
Thomasville 18 463
Tifton 13 749
Valdosta 37 596
Vidalia 10 393
Warner Robins 39 893
Waycross 19 371

Hawaii

Ewa 190 037
Hilo 37 017
Honolulu 365 048
Kahului 13 026
Koolauloa 14 195
Koolaupoko ... 109 373
Lahaina 10 284
Makawao-Paia 10 361
North Kona 13 748
Wahiawa 41 562
Waianae 32 810
Wailuku 10 674

Idaho

Blackfoot....... 10 065
Boise City 102 451
Caldwell 17 699
Coeur D'Alene...... 20 054
Idaho Falls 39 590
Lewiston 27 986
Moscow 16 513
Nampa......... 25 112
Pocatello 46 340
Rexburg 11 559
Twin Falls 26 209

Illinois

Addison........ 28 836
Alsip 17 134
Alton 34 171
Arlington Heights 66 116
Aurora......... 81 293
Bartlett 13 254
Batavia 12 574
Belleville 42 150
Bellwood 19 811
Belvidere 15 176
Bensenville 16 124
Berwyn 46 849
Bloomingdale... 12 659
Bloomington ... 44 189
Blue Island 21 855
Bolingbrook 37 261
Bourbonnais ... 13 280
Bradley 11 008
Bridgeview 14 155
Brookfield 19 395
Buffalo Grove... 22 230
Burbank 28 462
Cahokia 18 904
Calumet City ... 39 673
Canton 14 626
Carbondale..... 27 194
Carol Stream ... 15 472
Carpentersville 23 272
Centralia 15 126
Champaign..... 58 133
Charleston 19 355
Chicago 3 005 072
Chicago Heights 37 026
Chicago Ridge .. 13 473
Cicero 61 232
Collinsville 19 613
Country Club Hills 14 676
Crestwood 10 712
Crystal Lake 18 590
Danville........ 38 985
Darien 14 968
Decatur 94 081
Deerfield....... 17 430
De Kalb 33 099
Des Plaines 53 568
Dixon 15 659
Dolton 24 766
Downers Grove 39 274
East Moline 20 907
East Peoria 22 385
East St. Louis ... 55 200
Edwardsville ... 12 460
Effingham...... 11 270
Elgin 63 798
Elk Grove Village 28 907
Elmhurst....... 44 251
Elmwood Park .. 24 016
Evanston....... 73 706
Evergreen Park 22 260
Fairview Heights 12 414
Forest Park 15 177
Franklin Park ... 17 507
Freeport 26 406
Galesburg...... 35 305
Glendale Heights 23 163
Glen Ellyn 23 649
Glenview 30 842
Glenwood 10 538
Granite City 36 815
Hanover Park ... 28 850
Harvey......... 35 810
Hazel Crest..... 13 973
Herrin 10 040
Hickory Hills 13 778
Highland Park .. 30 611
Hinsdale 16 726
Hoffman Estates 38 258
Homewood..... 19 724
Jacksonville 20 284
Joliet 77 956
Justice 10 552
Kankakee 30 141
Kewanee 14 508
La Grange...... 15 681
La Grange Park.......... 13 359
Lake Forest..... 15 245
Lansing........ 29 039
La Salle 10 347
Libertyville 16 520
Lincoln 16 327
Lincolnwood ... 11 921
Lisle........... 13 625
Lombard 37 295
Loves Park 13 192
Macomb 19 632
Marion 14 031
Markham 15 172
Matteson 10 223
Mattoon 19 787
Maywood 27 998
McHenry....... 10 908
Melrose Park ... 20 735
Midlothian 14 274
Moline......... 45 709
Monmouth 10 706
Morton 14 178
Morton Grove .. 23 747
Mount Prospect 52 634
Mount Vernon 16 995
Mundelein 17 053
Naperville 42 330
Niles 30 363
Normal 35 672
Norridge 16 483
Northbrook 30 735
North Chicago .. 38 774
Northlake 12 166
North Park 15 679
Oak Forest 26 096
Oak Lawn 60 590
Oak Park 54 887
O'Fallon 10 217
Orland Park 23 045
Ottawa 18 166
Palatine 32 166
Palos Heights... 11 096
Palos Hills...... 16 654
Park Forest..... 26 222
Park Ridge 38 704
Pekin 33 967
Peoria 124 160
Peru........... 10 886
Pontiac 11 227
Prospect Heights 11 808
Quincy......... 42 352
Rantoul 20 161
Riverdale 13 233
River Forest 12 392
River Grove 10 368
Rock Falls 10 624
Rockford 139 712
Rock Island..... 47 036
Rolling Meadows 20 167
Romeoville 15 519
Roselle 16 948
Round Lake Beach 12 921
St Charles...... 17 492
Sauk Village.... 10 906
Schaumburg ... 52 319
Schiller Park.... 11 458
Skokie 60 278
South Holland .. 24 977
Springfield 99 637
Sterling 16 273
Streamwood ... 23 456
Streator 14 769
Summit 10 110
Taylorville 11 386
Tinley Park 26 171
Urbana 35 978
Villa Park 23 185
Washington 10 364
Waukegan 67 653
Westchester.... 17 730
West Chicago... 12 550
Western Springs 12 876
Westmont...... 16 718
Wheaton 43 043
Wheeling 23 266
Wilmette 28 229
Winnetka 12 772
Wood Dale 11 251
Woodridge 22 322
Wood River 12 449
Woodstock 11 725
Worth 11 592
Zion 17 861

Indiana

Anderson 64 695
Bedford 14 410
Beech Grove ... 13 196
Bloomington ... 51 646
Carmel 18 272
Clarksville...... 15 164
Columbus 30 292
Connersville.... 17 023
Crawfordsville .. 13 325
Crown Point ... 16 455
East Chicago ... 39 786
Elkhart......... 41 305
Elwood 10 867

Evansville 130 496
Fort Wayne 172 196
Frankfort 15 168
Franklin 11 563
Gary 151 953
Goshen 19 665
Greenfield 11 439
Greenwood 19 327
Griffith 17 026
Hammond...... 93 714
Highland 25 935
Hobart 22 987
Huntington 16 202
Indianapolis .. 700 807
Jeffersonville ... 21 220
Kokomo 47 808
Lafayette 43 011
Lake Station 14 294
La Porte 21 796
Lawrence 25 591
Lebanon 11 456
Logansport 17 899
Madison 12 472
Marion 35 874
Martinsville 11 311
Merrillville 27 677
Michigan City .. 36 850
Mishawaka ... 40 224
Muncie 77 216
Munster 20 671
New Albany ... 37 103
New Castle 20 056
Noblesville 12 056
Peru 13 764
Portage 27 409
Richmond 41 349
Schererville 13 209
Seymour 15 050
Shelbyville 14 989
South Bend ... 109 727
Speedway...... 12 641
Terre Haute ... 61 125
Valparaiso 22 247
Vincennes 20 857
Wabash 12 985
Warsaw 10 647
Washington 11 325
West
   Lafayette..... 21 247

Iowa
Ames......... 45 775
Ankeny 15 429
Bettendorf 27 381
Boone 12 602
Burlington 29 529
Cedar Falls 36 322
Cedar Rapids .. 110 243
Clinton 32 828
Council Bluffs .. 56 449
Davenport..... 103 264
Des Moines ... 191 003
Dubuque....... 62 321
Fort Dodge 29 423
Fort Madison ... 13 520
Indianola....... 10 843
Iowa City 50 508
Keokuk 13 536
Marion 19 474
Marshalltown ... 26 938
Mason City 30 144
Muscatine 23 467
Newton 15 292
Oskaloosa...... 10 629
Ottumwa 27 381
Sioux City 82 003
Spencer 11 726
Urbandale..... 17 869
Waterloo 75 985
West Des
   Moines 21 894

Kansas
Arkansas City .. 13 201
Atchison 11 407
Chanute 10 506
Coffeyville 15 185
Dodge City 18 001
El Dorado 10 510
Emporia 25 287
Garden City 18 256

Great Bend 16 608
Hays.......... 16 301
Hutchinson..... 40 284
Independence ... 10 598
Junction City ... 19 305
Kansas City ... 161 087
Lawrence 52 738
Leavenworth ... 33 656
Leawood 13 360
Lenexa 18 639
Liberal 14 911
McPherson 11 753
Manhattan 32 644
Merriam 10 794
Newton 16 332
*North Fort
   Riley* *12 469*
Olathe 37 258
Ottawa 11 016
Overland Park .. 81 784
Parsons 12 898
Pittsburg 18 770
Prairie Village .. 24 657
Salina 41 843
Shawnee 29 653
Topeka 115 266
Wichita 279 272
Winfield 10 736

Kentucky
Ashland 27 064
Bowling
   Green 40 450
Covington 49 013
Danville 12 942
Elizabethtown ... 15 380
Erlanger 14 433
Florence 15 586
*Fort Campbell
   North* *13 012*
Fort Knox *37 608*
Fort Thomas 16 338
Frankfort 25 973
Georgetown ... 10 972
Glasgow 12 958
Henderson 24 834
Hopkinsville ... 27 318
Jefferson-
   town 15 795
Lexington-
   Fayette 204 165
Louisville 298 451
Madisonville ... 16 979
Mayfield 10 705
Middles-
   borough 12 251
Murray 14 248
Newport 21 587
Nicholasville ... 10 400
Okolona *17 643*
Owensboro 54 450
Paducah 29 315
*Pleasure Ridge
   Park* *28 566*
Radcliff 14 519
Richmond 21 705
St. Matthews ... 13 354
Shively 16 819
Somerset 10 649
Valley Station .. *24 471*
Winchester..... 15 216

Louisiana
Abbeville 12 391
Alexandria 51 565
Baker 12 865
Bastrop 15 527
Baton Rouge .. 219 486
Bogalusa 16 976
Bossier City ... 49 969
Crowley....... 16 036
De Ridder 11 057
Eunice 12 479
Gretna 20 615
Hammond..... 15 043
Harahan 11 384
Houma 32 602
*Jefferson
   Heights* *16 489*
Jennings 12 401
Kenner 66 382

Lafayette....... 81 961
Lake Charles ... 75 051
Little Farms *15 713*
Marrero........ 29 015
Metairie 136 477
Minden 15 074
Monroe 57 597
Morgan City 16 114
Natchitoches ... 16 664
New Iberia ... 32 766
New Orleans .. 557 482
Opelousas 18 903
Pineville 12 034
Ruston........ 20 585
Scotlandville ... *22 599*
Shreveport ... 205 815
Slidell 26 718
*South Fort
   Polk* *15 600*
Sulphur 19 709
Tallulah 10 392
Terry *13 382*
Thibodaux..... 15 810
West Monroe ... 14 993
Westwego 12 663

Maine
Auburn 23 128
Augusta 21 819
Bangor 31 643
Bath.......... 10 246
Biddeford 19 638
*Brunswick
   Center* *10 867*
†Brunswick 17 366
†Gorham 10 101
Lewiston 40 481
†Orono 10 578
Portland 61 572
Presque Isle ... 11 172
Saco 12 921
*Sanford
   Center* *10 457*
†Sanford 18 020
†Scarborough ... 11 347
*South
   Portland* *22 712*
Waterville 17 779
Westbrook 14 976
†Windham 11 282

Maryland
Aberdeen 11 533
Annapolis 31 740
Arbutus *22 745*
Aspen Hill *16 887*
*Avenel-
   Hillandale* *19 520*
Baltimore 786 775
Bethesda *71 621*
*Birchwood
   City* *13 514*
Bowie 33 695
Brooklyn *13 896*
Cambridge 11 703
Camp Springs .. *22 776*
Catonsville *54 812*
Chevy Chase ... *16 424*
Chillum *35 656*
College Park ... 23 614
Cumberland 25 933
Dundalk *85 377*
Edgemere *10 352*
Essex......... *38 193*
Forestville *16 188*
Fort Meade *16 699*
Frederick 27 557
Gaithersburg ... 26 424
Glen Burnie ... *38 608*
Good Luck *10 584*
Greenbelt 16 000
Hagerstown ... 34 132
*Hillcrest
   Heights* *24 037*
Hyattsville...... 12 709
Kemp Mill *10 037*
Langley Park ... *11 564*
*Lanham-
   Seabrook* *13 244*
*Lansdowne-Baltimore
   Highlands* *17 770*

Laurel 12 103
*Lutherville-
   Timonium* *24 055*
Middle River ... *19 935*
*New Carroll-
   ton* *12 632*
*North
   Potomac* *12 784*
Overlea *13 124*
Oxon Hill *11 974*
Parkville 33 589
Pikesville *25 395*
Randallstown... *33 683*
Randolph *13 215*
Reisterstown ... *12 568*
Rockville 43 811
Rosedale *19 417*
Salisbury 16 429
Severna Park ... 16 358
Silver Spring ... *77 411*
*South
   Kensington* .. *10 289*
South Laurel ... *13 345*
*Suitland-Silver
   Hills* *30 355*
Takoma Park ... 16 231
Towson *77 768*
Wheaton....... *66 280*
White Oak *19 769*
*Woodlawn-
   Woodmoor* ... *28 821*

Massachusetts
†Abington 13 517
†Acton 17 544
Adams Center .. *11 256*
†Adams 10 381
†Agawam 26 271
*Amesbury
   Center* *10 088*
†Amesbury 13 971
*Amherst
   Center* *17 926*
†Amherst 33 229
†Andover 26 370
†Arlington 48 219
†Athol 10 634
Attleboro 34 196
†Auburn 14 845
†Barnstable 30 898
†Bedford 13 067
†Bellingham 14 300
†Belmont 26 100
Beverly 37 655
†Billerica 36 727
Boston 562 994
†Bourne 13 874
†Braintree 36 337
†Bridgewater 17 202
Brockton 95 172
†Brookline 55 062
†Burlington 23 486
Cambridge 95 322
†Canton 18 182
†Chelmsford.... 31 174
Chelsea........ 25 431
Chicopee 55 112
†Clinton 12 771
†Concord 16 293
†Danvers 24 100
†Dartmouth 23 966
†Dedham 25 298
†Dennis 12 360
†Dracut 21 249
†Duxbury 11 807
†Easthampton ... 15 580
†East
   Longmeadow .. 12 905
†Easton 16 623
Everett 37 195
†Fairhaven 15 759
Fall River 92 574
†Falmouth 23 640
Fitchburg 39 580
Fort Devens ... *12 915*
†Foxborough ... 14 148
†Framingham ... 65 113
†Franklin 18 217
Gardner 17 900
Gloucester 27 768
†Grafton 11 238

*Greenfield
   Center* *14 642*
†Greenfield 18 436
†Hanover 11 358
†Harvard 12 170
Haverhill 46 865
†Hingham 20 339
†Holbrook 11 140
†Holden 13 336
†Holliston 12 622
Holyoke 44 678
*Hudson
   Center* *14 283*
†Hudson 16 408
†Ipswich 11 158
Lawrence 63 175
Leominster 34 508
†Lexington 29 479
†Longmeadow ... 16 301
Lowell 92 418
†Ludlow 18 150
Lynn........ 78 471
†Lynnfield 11 267
Malden 53 386
†Mansfield 13 453
†Marblehead ... 20 126
Marlborough ... 30 617
†Marshfield 20 916
†Medfield 10 220
Medford 58 076
Melrose 30 055
†Methuen 36 701
†Middle-
   borough 16 404
Milford Center .. *13 740*
†Milford 23 390
†Millbury 11 808
†Milton 25 860
†Natick 29 461
†Needham 27 901
New Bedford ... 98 478
Newburyport ... 15 900
Newton 83 622
North Adams ... 18 063
Northampton ... 29 286
†North
   Andover 20 129
†North Attle-
   borough 21 095
†Northborough ... 10 568
†Northbridge ... 12 246
†North Reading .. 11 455
†Norton 12 690
†Norwood 29 711
†Oxford 11 680
†Palmer 11 389
Peabody 45 976
†Pembroke 13 487
Pittsfield 51 974
†Plymouth 35 913
Quincy....... 84 743
†Randolph 28 218
†Reading 22 678
Revere 42 423
†Rockland 15 695
Salem 38 220
†Saugus 24 746
†Scituate 17 317
†Seekonk 12 269
†Sharon 13 601
†Shrewsbury ... 22 674
†Somerset 18 813
Somerville 77 372
*Southbridge
   Center* *14 261*
†Southbridge ... 16 665
†South Hadley ... 16 399
†Spencer 10 774
Springfield ... 152 319
†Stoneham 21 424
†Stoughton 26 710
†Sudbury 14 027
†Swampscott ... 13 837
†Swansea 15 461
Taunton 45 001
†Tewksbury ... 24 635
†Wakefield 24 895
†Walpole 18 859
Waltham 58 200
†Wareham 18 457
†Watertown ... 34 384

†Wayland 12 170
*Webster
   Center* *12 432*
†Webster 14 480
†Wellesley 27 209
†Westborough ... 13 619
Westfield 36 465
†Westford 13 434
†Weston 11 169
†Westport 13 763
†West
   Springfield.... 27 042
†Westwood 13 212
†Weymouth ... 55 601
†Whitman 13 534
†Wilbraham ... 12 053
†Wilmington ... 17 471
†Winchester.... 20 701
†Winthrop 19 294
Woburn 36 626
Worcester ... 161 799
†Yarmouth 18 449

Michigan
Adrian 21 186
Albion 11 059
Allen Park 34 196
Alpena 12 214
Ann Arbor ... 107 316
Battle Creek ... 35 724
Benton
   Harbor 14 707
Berkley 18 637
Beverly Hills ... 11 598
Big Rapids 14 361
Birmingham ... 21 689
Burton 29 976
Cadillac 10 199
Clawson 15 103
Dearborn 90 660
Dearborn
   Heights 67 706
Detroit 1 203 339
*Drayton
   Plains* *16 462*
East Detroit ... 38 280
*East Grand
   Rapids* *10 914*
East Lansing ... 48 309
Ecorse 14 447
Escanaba 14 355
Farmington ... 11 022
Farmington
   Hills 58 056
Ferndale 26 227
Flint 159 611
Fraser 14 560
Garden City ... 35 640
Grand Haven ... 11 763
Grand
   Rapids 181 843
Grandville 12 412
Grosse Pointe
   Farms 10 551
Grosse Pointe
   Park 13 639
Grosse Pointe
   Woods 18 886
Hamtramck ... 21 300
Harper Woods .. 16 361
Hazel Park ... 20 914
Highland Park .. 27 909
Holland 26 281
Inkster 35 190
Jackson 39 739
Jenison *11 266*
Kalamazoo ... 79 722
Kentwood 30 438
Lakeview *11 391*
Lansing 130 414
Lincoln Park ... 45 105
Livonia 104 814
Madison
   Heights 35 375
Marquette ... 23 288
Melvindale 12 322
Menominee ... 10 099
Midland........ 37 250
Monroe 23 531

Michigan (continued)

Mount Clemens 18 806
Mount Pleasant 23 746
Muskegon 40 823
Muskegon Heights 14 611
Niles 13 115
Norton Shores 22 025
Novi 22 525
Oak Park 31 537
Owosso 16 455
Pontiac 76 715
Portage 38 157
Port Huron 33 981
River Rouge 12 912
Riverview 14 569
Romulus 24 857
Roseville 54 311
Royal Oak 70 893
Saginaw 77 508
St. Clair Shores 76 210
Sault Ste. Marie 14 448
Southfield 75 568
Southgate 32 058
Sterling Heights 108 999
Taylor 77 568
Traverse City 15 516
Trenton 22 762
Troy 67 102
Walker 15 088
Warren 161 134
Wayne 21 159
Westland 84 603
Westwood 41 343
Woodhaven 10 902
Wyandotte 34 006
Wyoming 59 616
Ypsilanti 24 031

Minnesota

Albert Lea 19 190
Anoka 15 634
Apple Valley 21 818
Austin 23 020
Bemidji 10 949
Blaine 28 558
Bloomington 81 831
Brainerd 11 489
Brooklyn Center 31 230
Brooklyn Park 43 332
Burnsville 35 674
Cloquet 11 142
Columbia Heights 20 029
Coon Rapids 35 826
Cottage Grove 18 994
Crystal 25 543
Duluth 92 811
Eagan 20 532
Eden Prairie 16 263
Edina 46 073
Fairmont 11 506
Faribault 16 241
Fergus Falls 12 519
Fridley 30 228
Golden Valley 22 775
Hastings 12 827
Hibbing 21 193
Hopkins 15 336
Inver Grove Heights 17 171
Lakeville 14 790
Mankato 28 651
Maple Grove 20 525
Maplewood 26 990
Marshall 11 161
Minneapolis 370 951
Minnetonka 38 683
Moorhead 29 998
Mounds View 12 593
New Brighton 23 269
New Hope 23 087
New Ulm 13 755
Northfield 12 562
North St. Paul 11 921
Oakdale 12 123
Owatonna 18 632
Plymouth 31 615
Ramsey 10 093
Red Wing 13 736
Richfield 37 851
Robbinsdale 14 422
Rochester 57 855
Roseville 35 820
St. Cloud 42 566
St. Louis Park 42 931
St. Paul 270 230
Shoreview 17 300
South St. Paul 21 235
Stillwater 12 290
Virginia 11 056
West St. Paul 18 527
White Bear Lake 22 538
Willmar 15 895
Winona 25 075
Woodbury 10 297
Worthington 10 243

Mississippi

Biloxi 49 311
Brookhaven 10 800
Canton 11 116
Clarksdale 21 137
Cleveland 14 524
Clinton 14 660
Columbus 27 383
Corinth 13 839
Greenville 40 613
Greenwood 20 115
Grenada 12 641
Gulfport 39 676
Hattiesburg 40 829
Jackson 202 895
Laurel 21 897
McComb 12 331
Meridian 46 577
Moss Point 18 998
Natchez 22 015
Ocean Springs 14 504
Pascagoula 29 318
Pearl 20 778
Picayune 10 361
Starkville 15 169
Tupelo 23 905
Vicksburg 25 434
Yazoo City 12 426

Missouri

Affton *24 264*
Arnold 19 141
Ballwin 12 750
Bellefontaine Neighbors 12 082
Belton 12 708
Berkeley 16 146
Blue Springs 25 927
Bridgeton 18 445
Cape Girardeau 34 361
Carthage 11 104
Clayton 14 219
Columbia 62 061
Concord *21 217*
Crestwood 12 815
Creve Coeur 12 694
Excelsior Springs 10 424
Ferguson 24 740
Florissant 55 372
Fort Leonard Wood *33 799*
Fulton 11 046
Gladstone 24 990
Grandview 24 502
Hannibal 18 811
Hazelwood 12 935
Indepen- dence 111 806
Jefferson City 33 619
Jennings 17 026
Joplin 38 893
Kansas City 448 159
Kennett 10 145
Kirksville 17 167
Kirkwood 27 987
Lee's Summit 28 741
Lemay *40 529*
Liberty 16 251
Maplewood 10 960
Marshall 12 781
Mexico 12 276
Moberly 13 418
Overland 19 620
Poplar Bluff 17 139
Raytown 31 759
Richmond Heights 11 516
Rolla 13 303
St. Ann 15 523
St. Charles 37 379
St. Joseph 76 691
St. Louis 453 085
St. Peters 15 700
Sappington *10 603*
Sedalia 20 927
Sikeston 17 431
Spanish Lake *15 647*
Springfield 133 116
University City 42 738
Warrensburg 13 807
Webster Groves 23 097

Montana

Anaconda-Deer Lodge County 12 518
Billings 66 798
Bozeman 21 645
Butte-Silver Bow 37 205
Great Falls 56 725
Havre 10 891
Helena 23 938
Kalispell 10 648
Missoula 33 388

Nebraska

Beatrice 12 891
Bellevue 21 813
Columbus 17 328
Fremont 23 979
Grand Island 33 180
Hastings 23 045
Kearney 21 158
Lincoln 171 932
Norfolk 19 449
North Platte 24 479
Omaha 311 681
Scottsbluff 14 156

Nevada

Carson City 32 022
Henderson 24 363
Las Vegas 164 674
North Las Vegas 42 739
Paradise *24 477*
Reno 100 756
Sparks 40 780
Winchester *13 981*

New Hampshire

Berlin 13 084
Claremont 14 557
Concord 30 400
†Derry 18 875
Dover 22 377
†Durham 10 652
†Exeter 11 024
†Goffstown 11 315
†Hampton 10 493
†Hudson 14 022
Keene 21 449
Laconia 15 575
Lebanon 11 134
†Londonderry 13 598
Manchester 90 936
†Merrimack 15 406
Nashua 67 865
Portsmouth 26 254
Rochester 21 560
†Salem 24 124
Somersworth 10 350

New Jersey

Asbury Park 17 015
Atlantic City 40 199
Bayonne 65 047
Belleville 35 367
Bellmawr 13 721
Bergenfield 25 568
Berkeley Heights 12 549
Bloomfield 47 792
Brick 53 629
Bridgeton 18 795
Burlington 10 246
Camden 84 910
Carteret 20 598
Cedar Grove 12 600
Cherry Hill 68 785
Cinaminson 16 072
Clark 16 699
Cliffside Park 21 464
Clifton 74 388
Collingswood 15 838
Cranford 24 573
Delran 14 811
Denville 14 380
Deptford 23 473
Dover 14 681
Dumont 18 334
East Brunswick 37 711
East Orange 77 025
East Windsor 21 041
Eatontown 12 703
Edison 70 193
Elizabeth 106 201
Elmwood Park 18 377
Englewood 23 701
Evesham 21 659
Ewing 34 842
Fair Lawn 32 229
Fairview 10 519
Fort Dix 26 290
Fort Lee 32 449
Freehold 10 020
Garfield 26 803
Glassboro 14 574
Glen Rock 11 497
Gloucester City 13 121
Hackensack 36 039
Haddon 15 875
Haddonfield 12 337
Hammonton 12 298
Hanover 11 846
Harrison 12 242
Hasbrouck Heights 12 166
Hawthorne 18 200
Hazlet 23 013
Highland Park 13 396
Hillsdale 10 495
Hillside 21 440
Hoboken 42 460
Hopatcong 15 531
Hopewell 10 893
Irvington 61 493
Jackson 25 644
Jersey City 223 532
Keansburg 10 613
Keamy 35 735
Lake Hiawatha *11 389*
Lakewood *17 874*
Linden 37 836
Lindenwold 18 196
Little Falls 11 496
Livingston 28 040
Lodi 23 956
Long Branch 29 819
Lyndhurst 20 326
Madison 15 357
Mahwah 12 127
Manville 11 278
Maple Shade 20 525
Maplewood 22 950
Marlboro *17 560*
Marlton *10 180*
McGuire 10 933
Mercerville-Hamilton Square *24 465*
Metuchen 13 762
Middlesex 13 480
Middletown 62 574
Milburn 19 543
Millville 24 815
Monroe 21 639
Montclair 38 321
Montville 14 290
Moorestown-Lenola *14 179*
Morristown 16 614
Mount Holly 10 818
Neptune 28 366
Newark 329 248
New Brunswick 41 442
New Hanover 14 248
New Milford 16 876
New Providence 12 426
North Arlington 16 587
North Bergen 47 019
North Brunswick 22 220
North Plainfield 19 108
Nutley 28 998
Oakland 13 443
Ocean City 13 949
Old Bridge 51 515
Orange 31 136
Palisades Park 13 732
Paramus 26 474
Passaic 52 463
Paterson 137 970
Pennsauken 33 775
Pennsville Center *11 014*
Pequannock 13 776
Perth Amboy 38 951
Phillipsburg 16 647
Piscataway 42 223
Plainfield 45 555
Pleasantville 13 435
Point Pleasant 17 747
Pompton Lakes 10 660
Princeton 12 035
Rahway 26 723
Ramsey 12 899
Randolph 17 828
Red Bank 12 031
Ridgefield 10 294
Ridgefield Park 12 738
Ridgewood 25 208
Ringwood 12 625
River Edge 11 111
Roselle 20 641
Roselle Park 13 377
Rutherford 19 068
Saddle Brook 14 084
Sayreville 29 969
Scotch Plains 20 774
Secaucus 13 719
Somers Point 10 330
Somerville 11 973
South Orange Village 15 864
South Plainfield 20 521
South River 14 361
Sparta 13 333
Springfield 13 955
Summit 21 071
Teaneck 39 007
Tenafly 13 552
Totowa 11 448
Trenton 92 124
Union 50 184
Union City 55 593
Ventnor City 11 704
Verona 14 166
Vineland 53 753
Waldwick 10 802
Wallington 10 741
Wanaque 10 025
Wayne 46 474
Weehawken 13 168
West Caldwell 11 407
Westfield 30 447
West Milford 22 750
West New York 39 194
West Orange 39 510
West Paterson 11 293
Westwood 10 724
White Horse-Yardville *18 680*
Willingboro 39 912
Winslow 20 034
Woodbridge 90 074
Woodbury 10 353
Wyckoff 15 500

New Mexico

Alamogordo 24 024
Albuquerque 331 767
Artesia 10 385
Carlsbad 25 496
Clovis 31 194
Farmington 30 729
Gallup 18 161
Grants 11 451
Hobbs 28 794
Las Cruces 45 086
Las Vegas 14 322
Los Alamos *11 310*
North Valley *10 366*
Roswell 39 676
Santa Fe 48 899
South Valley *29 389*

New York

Albany 101 727
Amsterdam 21 872
Arlington *11 203*
Auburn 32 548
Babylon 12 388
Baldwin *34 525*
Batavia 16 703
Bay Shore *11 119*
Beacon 12 937
Bellmore *18 431*
Bethpage *18 555*
Binghamton 55 860
Brentwood *28 327*
Buffalo 357 870
Canandaigua 10 419
Central Islip *36 391*
Cohoes 18 144
Commack *24 138*
Copiague *19 632*
Corning 12 953
Cortland 20 138
Deer Park *32 274*
Depew 19 819
DeWitt *10 032*
Dix Hills *10 050*
Dobbs Ferry 10 053
Dunkirk 15 310
Eastchester *23 750*
East Massapequa *15 926*
East Meadow *46 290*
East Northport *12 392*
East Rockaway 10 917
East Vesta *10 472*
Elmira 35 327
Elmont *29 363*
Elwood *15 031*
Endicott 14 457
Endwell *15 999*
Fairmount *15 317*
Floral Park 16 805
Franklin Square *32 156*
Fredonia 11 126
Freeport 38 272
Fulton 13 312
Garden City 22 927
Geneva 15 133
Glen Cove 24 618
Glens Falls 15 897
Gloversville 17 836
Half Hollow Hills *12 081*
Hamburg 10 582
Harrison 23 046
Hartsdale *12 226*

Hauppauge 13 957
Hempstead 40 404
Hicksville 49 820
Holbrook
Holtsville 12 103
Hornell 10 234
Huntington 12 601
Huntington
Station 28 817
Ithaca 28 732
Jamestown 35 775
Jericho 14 010
Johnson City ... 17 126
Kenmore 18 474
Kingston 24 481
Lackawanna ... 22 701
Lancaster 13 056
Levittown 65 440
Lindenhurst 26 919
Lockport 24 844
Locust Grove ... 11 626
Long Beach 34 073
Lynbrook 20 431
Mamaroneck ... 17 616
Massapequa ... 26 821
Massapequa
Park 19 779
Massena 12 851
Merrick 25 904
Middletown 21 454
Mineola........ 20 757
Mount
Vernon 66 713
Nanuet 10 447
Nesconset 10 048
Newark 10 017
Newburgh 23 438
New City 27 344
New Rochelle... 70 794
New York ... 7 071 030
Niagara Falls ... 71 384
North
Amityville ... 11 936
North Babylon .. 39 526
North
Bellmore 22 893
North Great
River 12 080
North Linden-
hurst 11 117
North
Massapequa .. 23 123
North Merrick .. 13 650
North New Hyde
Park 18 154
North
Tonawanda ... 35 760
North Valley
Stream 14 881
North
Wantagh..... 15 053
Oceanside 35 372
Ogdensburg 12 375
Lean........... 18 207
Oneida 10 810
Oneonta 14 933
Ossining 20 196
Oswego 19 793
Patchogue 11 291
Pearl River 17 146
Peekskill 18 236
Plainedge 10 759
Plainview 31 695
Plattsburg 21 057
Port Chester 23 565
Port
Washington ... 15 923
Potsdam 10 635
Poughkeepsie .. 29 757
Rochester 241 741
Rockville
Centre 25 405
Rome 43 826
Roosevelt 15 008
Rotterdam 25 214
Rye 15 083
St. James 10 500
Saratoga
Springs 23 906
Sayville 11 680
Scarsdale 17 650

Schenectady ... 67 972
Seaford 17 379
Selden 11 613
South
Farmingdale .. 20 464
South Stony
Brook 15 329
South
Westbury 10 978
Spring Valley ... 20 537
Suffern 10 794
Syosset 10 084
Syracuse ... 170 105
Tarrytown 10 648
Thornwood 6 874
Tonawanda 18 693
Troy 56 638
Uniondale 22 077
Utica 75 632
Valley Stream .. 35 769
Wantagh 21 783
Watertown 27 861
Watervliet...... 11 354
West Babylon ... 12 893
Westbury 13 871
West
Hempstead ... 20 375
West Islip 17 374
White Plains ... 46 999
Woodmere 19 831
Wyandach 15 716
Yonkers....... 195 351

North Carolina

Albemarle 15 110
Asheboro 15 252
Asheville 53 281
Boone 10 191
Burlington 37 266
Camp Le Jeune
Central 34 549
Cary 21 612
Chapel Hill 32 421
Charlotte 314 447
Cherry Point 12 029
Concord 16 942
Durham....... 100 831
Eden 15 672
Elizabeth City .. 13 784
Fayetteville..... 59 507
Fort Bragg...... 46 995
Gastonia 47 333
Goldsboro 31 871
Greensboro ... 155 642
Greenville...... 35 740
Havelock 17 718
Henderson 13 522
Hickory 20 757
High Point...... 64 107
Jacksonville 17 056
Kannapolis 36 293
Kinston 25 234
Laurinburg 11 480
Lenoir 13 748
Lexington 15 711
Lumberton 18 340
Monroe 12 639
Morganton 13 763
New Bern 14 557
North
Belmont 10 672
Raleigh 149 771
Reidsville 12 492
Roanoke
Rapids 14 702
Rocky Mount ... 41 283
Salisbury 22 677
Sanford 14 773
Shelby 15 310
Statesville..... 18 622
Thomasville ... 14 144
Wilmington 44 000
Wilson 34 424
Winston-
Salem 131 885

North Dakota

Bismarck..... 44 485
Dickinson 15 924
Fargo 61 308
Grand Forks ... 43 765

Grand Forks
Base......... 10 474
Jamestown 16 280
Mandan 15 513
Minot 32 843
Minot Base.... 12 077
West Fargo 10 099
Williston 13 336

Ohio

Akron......... 237 177
Alliance........ 24 315
Amherst 10 638
Ashland 20 326
Ashtabula 23 449
Athens 19 743
Austintown 29 393
Avon Lake 13 222
Barberton 29 751
Bay Village 17 846
Beavercreek ... 31 589
Bedford 15 056
Bedford
Heights 13 214
Bellefontaine ... 11 888
Berea 19 567
Bexley 13 405
Boardman 30 852
Bowling
Green 25 728
Brecksville 10 132
Bridgetown..... 13 352
Broadview
Heights 10 920
Brooklyn 12 342
Brook Park 26 195
Brunswick 27 689
Bucyrus 13 433
Cambridge 13 573
Campbell 11 619
Canton 94 730
Centerville 18 886
Chillicothe 23 420
Cincinnati 385 457
Circleville 11 700
Cleveland 573 822
Cleveland
Heights 56 438
Columbus 564 871
Conneaut 13 835
Coshocton 13 405
Cuyahoga
Falls 43 710
Dayton....... 203 588
Defiance 16 810
Delaware 18 780
Dover 11 526
East
Cleveland ... 36 957
Eastlake 22 104
East Liverpool .. 16 687
Elyria 57 504
Englewood 11 329
Euclid 59 999
Fairborn 29 702
Fairfield....... 30 777
Fairview Park ... 19 311
Findlay 35 594
Forest Park 18 675
Fort McKinley .. 11 536
Fostoria 15 743
Franklin 10 711
Fremont 17 834
Gahanna....... 18 001
Galion 12 391
Garfield
Heights 33 380
Girard 12 517
Greenville..... 12 999
Grove City 16 793
Hamilton 63 189
Huber Heights .. 18 943
Ironton 14 290
Kent 26 164
Kenwood 15 789
Kettering 61 186
Lakewood 61 963
Lancaster 34 953
Lima......... 47 381
Lincoln
Village 11 215

Lorain 75 416
Lyndhurst 18 092
Mansfield 53 927
Maple Heights .. 29 735
Marietta 16 467
Marion 37 040
Massillon 30 557
Maumee 15 747
Mayfield
Heights 21 550
Medina 15 268
Mentor 42 065
Miamisburg ... 15 304
Middleburg
Heights 16 218
Middletown ... 43 719
Montgomery ... 10 088
Mount Vernon .. 14 380
Newark 41 200
New
Philadelphia .. 16 883
Niles 23 088
North Canton .. 14 228
North College
Hill 10 990
North
Olmsted 36 486
Northridge 10 084
North
Ridgeville ... 21 522
North
Royalton 17 671
Norton 12 242
Norwalk 14 358
Norwood 26 342
Oregon 18 675
Overlook-Page
Manor 19 719
Oxford........ 17 655
Painesville 16 391
Parma 92 548
Parma
Heights 23 112
Perrysburg 10 215
Piqua 20 480
Portsmouth ... 25 943
Ravenna 11 987
Reading 12 879
Reynoldsburg.. 20 661
Richmond
Heights 10 095
Rocky River ... 21 084
Salem 12 869
Sandusky 31 360
Seven Hills 13 650
Shaker
Heights 32 487
Sharonville 10 108
Sheffield Lake .. 10 484
Shiloh 11 368
Sidney 17 657
Solon 14 341
South Euclid ... 25 713
Springdale.... 10 111
Springfield 72 563
Steubenville ... 26 400
Stow 25 303
Strongsville 28 577
Struthers 13 624
Sylvania 15 527
Tallmadge 15 269
Tiffin 19 549
Toledo 354 635
Troy 19 086
University
Heights 15 401
Upper
Arlington.... 35 648
Urbana 10 762
Vandalia 13 161
Van Wert 11 035
Vermilion 11 012
Wadsworth ... 15 166
Warren 56 629
Warrensville
Heights 16 565
Washington ... 12 682
West
Carrollton ... 13 148
Westerville.... 23 414
Westlake....... 19 483

Whitehall 21 299
Wickliffe 16 790
Willoughby 19 329
Willowick 17 834
Wilmington ... 10 431
Wooster 19 289
Worthington... 15 016
Wright-
Patterson..... 10 151
Xenia 24 653
Youngstown... 115 436
Zanesville 28 655

Oklahoma

Ada 15 902
Altus 23 101
Ardmore 23 689
Bartlesville 34 568
Bethany 22 130
Broken Arrow .. 35 761
Chickasha 15 828
Claremore 12 085
Del City 28 424
Duncan 22 517
Durant 11 972
Edmond........ 34 637
El Reno 15 486
Enid 50 363
Fort Sill 21 217
Guthrie 10 312
Lawton 80 054
McAlester 17 255
Miami 14 237
Midwest City ... 49 559
Moore 35 063
Muskogee...... 40 011
Norman 68 020
Oklahoma
City 403 213
Okmulgee 16 263
Ponca City 26 238
Sand Springs ... 13 246
Sapulpa....... 15 853
Shawnee 26 506
Stillwater 38 268
The Village 11 049
Tulsa 360 919
Woodward 13 610
Yukon 17 112

Oregon

Albany 26 546
Altamont....... 15 746
Ashland 14 943
Beaverton 30 582
Bend 17 263
Coos Bay 14 424
Corvallis 40 960
Eugene 105 624
Forest Grove ... 11 499
Grants Pass ... 14 997
Gresham....... 33 005
Hillsboro 27 664
Keizer 11 405
Klamath Falls... 16 661
La Grande 11 354
Lake Oswego .. 22 868
Lebanon 10 413
McMinnville ... 14 080
Medford 39 603
Milwaukie 17 931
Newberg 10 394
Oregon City ... 14 673
Pendleton 14 521
Portland 366 383
Roseburg 16 644
Salem 89 233
Springfield 41 621
The Dalles 10 820
Tigard 14 286
West Linn 12 956
Woodburn 11 196

Pennsylvania

Aliquippa 17 094
Allentown ... 103 758
Altoona 57 078
Baldwin 24 598
Beaver Falls ... 12 525
Bellevue 10 128
Berwick 12 189

Bethel Park 34 755
Bethlehem 70 419
Bloomsburg ... 11 717
Bradford 11 211
Brandywine
Village 11 411
Brentwood 11 907
Bristol 10 867
Butler 17 026
Canonsburg .. 10 459
Carbondale 11 255
Carlisle 18 314
Carnegie 10 099
Carnot-Moon ... 13 093
Castle
Shannon 10 164
Chambers-
burg 16 174
Chester 45 794
Clairton 12 188
Coatesville 10 698
Columbia 10 466
Connellsville ... 10 319
Darby 11 513
Dormont 11 275
Dunmore 16 781
Duquesne 10 094
Easton 26 027
Emmaus 11 001
Ephrata 11 095
Erie 119 123
Glenside 17 353
Greensburg ... 17 558
Hanover 14 890
Harrisburg ... 53 264
Hatboro West .. 14 278
Hazleton 27 318
Indiana 16 051
Jeannette 13 106
Jefferson-
Trooper 13 901
Johnstown 35 496
Kingston 15 681
Lancaster 54 725
Lansdale 16 526
Lansdowne ... 11 891
Latrobe 10 799
Lebanon 25 711
Lower Burrell .. 13 200
McKeesport ... 31 012
Meadville 15 544
Middletown ... 10 122
Monessen 11 928
Monroeville ... 30 977
Munhall 14 532
Murrysville ... 16 036
Nanticoke 13 044
New Castle ... 33 621
New
Kensington ... 17 660
Norristown 34 684
North Hills-
Ardsley 13 096
Oil City 13 881
Oreland......... 9 349
Penn Sq.-Plymouth
Valley 20 255
Philadelphia . 1 688 210
Phoenixville 14 165
Pittsburgh 423 938
Plum 25 390
Pottstown 22 729
Pottsville 18 195
Reading....... 78 686
Roslyn 18 811
Scranton 88 117
Shamokin 10 357
Sharon 19 057
State College ... 36 130
Sunbury 12 292
Swissvale 11 345
Uniontown ... 14 510
Warren 12 146
Washington ... 18 363
West Chester .. 17 435
West Mifflin ... 26 279
Whitehall 15 206
Wilkes-Barre ... 51 551
Wilkinsburg ... 23 669
Williamsport ... 33 401
Willow Grove ... 16 194

Yeadon 11 727
York 44 619

Rhode Island
†Barrington 16 174
†Bristol 20 128
†Burrillville 13 164
Central Falls ... 16 995
†Coventry 27 065
Cranston 71 992
†Cumberland ... 27 069
†East
Greenwich ... 10 211
East
Providence ... 50 980
†Johnston 24 907
†Lincoln 16 949
†Middletown ... 17 216
†Narragansett ... 12 088
Newport 29 259
Newport East ... 10 285
†North
Kingstown ... 21 938
†North
Providence ... 29 188
Pawtucket 71 204
†Portsmouth ... 14 257
Providence 156 804
†Smithfield 16 886
†South
Kingstown ... 20 414
†Tiverton 13 526
†Warren 10 640
Warwick 87 123
†Westerly 18 580
*Westerly
Center* 13 654
†West
Warwick ... 27 026
Woonsocket 45 914

South Carolina
Aiken 14 978
Anderson 27 313
Cayce.......... 11 701
Charleston 69 510
*Charleston
Yard* 13 565
Columbia 99 296
Conway 10 240
Easley 14 264
Florence 30 062
Gaffney 13 453
Gantt 11 386
Georgetown 10 144
Goose Creek ... 17 811
Greenville...... 58 242
Greenwood 21 613
Greer 10 525
Hanahan....... 13 224
Laurens........ 10 587
Mount
Pleasant 13 838
Myrtle Beach ... 18 758
North
Augusta 13 593
North
Charleston ... 65 630
Orangeburg 14 933
Rock Hill 35 344
Spartanburg.... 43 968
Sumter 24 890
Union 10 523
*Wade-
Hampton* 17 152
West
Columbia 10 409

South Dakota
Aberdeen 25 956
Brookings 14 951
Huron 13 000
Mitchell........ 13 916
Pierre.......... 11 973
Rapid City 46 492
Sioux Falls 81 343
Watertown 15 649
Yankton 12 011

Tennessee
Athens 12 080

Bartlett 17 170
Bristol 23 986
Chattanooga .. 169 565
Clarksville...... 54 777
Cleveland 26 415
Columbia 25 767
Cookeville 20 350
Dyersburg 15 856
East Ridge 21 236
Elizabethton ... 12 431
Franklin........ 12 407
Gallatin 17 191
Germantown ... 20 459
Greater Hendersonville ... 11 996
Greeneville..... 14 097
Hendersonville 26 561
Humboldt 10 209
Jackson 49 131
Johnson City ... 39 753
Kingsport 32 027
*Kingsport
North* 13 118
Knoxville...... 183 139
Lawrenceburg .. 10 175
Lebanon 11 872
McMinnville ... 10 683
Maryville 17 480
Memphis 646 356
Millington 20 236
Morristown ... 19 683
Murfreesboro... 32 845
Nashville-
Davidson 455 651
Oak Ridge 27 662
Paris 10 728
Red Bank White
Oak......... 13 297
Shelbyville 13 530
Springfield 10 814
Tullahoma 15 800
Union City 10 436

Texas
Abilene 98 315
Alice 20 961
Alvin 16 515
Amarillo 149 230
Andrews 11 061
Angleton 13 929
Arlington 160 123
Athens 10 197
Austin 345 496
Balch Springs .. 13 746
Bay City 17 837
Baytown 56 923
Beaumont..... 118 102
Bedford 20 821
Beeville 14 574
Bellaire 14 950
Belton 10 660
Benbrook 13 579
Big Spring 24 804
Borger 15 837
Brenham 10 966
Brownfield 10 387
Brownsville ... 84 997
Brownwood ... 19 203
Bryan 44 337
Burkburnett ... 10 668
Burleson 11 734
Canyon 10 724
Carrolton 40 591
Cleburne 19 218
College
Station 37 272
Conroe 18 034
Copperas
Cove........ 19 469
Corpus
Christi 231 999
Corsicana 21 712
Dallas 904 078
Deer Park 22 648
Del Rio 30 034
Denison 23 884
Denton 48 063
De Soto 15 538
Dumas 12 194
Duncanville ... 27 781

Eagle Pass 21 407
Edinburg 24 075
El Campo 10 462
El Paso 425 259
Ennis 12 110
Euless 24 002
Farmers
Branch 24 863
Forest Hill 11 684
Fort Bliss 13 288
Fort Hood 32 597
Fort Sam
Houston 10 553
Fort Worth 385 141
Freeport 13 444
Friendswood ... 10 719
Gainesville 14 081
Galveston 61 902
Garland 138 857
Grand Prairie .. 71 462
Grapevine 11 801
Greenville 22 161
Groves 17 090
Haltom City.... 29 014
Harlingen 43 543
Henderson ... 11 473
Hereford 15 853
Houston ... 1 594 086
Huntsville 23 936
Hurst 31 420
Irving 109 943
Jacksonville ... 12 264
Kerrville 15 276
Kilgore 10 968
Killeen 46 296
Kingsville 28 808
Lackland 19 141
Lake Jackson ... 19 102
La Marque 15 372
Lamesa 11 790
Lancaster 14 807
La Porte 14 062
Laredo 91 449
League City ... 16 578
Levelland 13 809
Lewisville 24 273
Longview 62 762
Lubbock 173 979
Lufkin 28 562
McAllen 67 042
McKinney 16 249
Marshall 24 921
Mercedes 11 851
Mesquite 67 053
Midland....... 70 525
Mineral Wells .. 14 468
Mission 22 589
Missouri City .. 24 533
Mount
Pleasant 11 003
Nacogdoches .. 27 149
Nederland..... 16 855
New
Braunfels 22 402
North Richland
Hills 30 592
Odessa 90 027
Orange 23 628
Palestine 15 948
Pampa 21 396
Paris 25 498
Pasadena 112 560
Pearland 13 248
Pecos........ 12 855
Pharr 21 381
Plainview 22 187
Plano 72 331
Port Arthur ... 61 195
Portland 12 023
Port Lavaca ... 10 911
Port Neches ... 13 944
Richardson 72 496
Robstown 12 100
Rosenberg 17 995
Round Rock ... 11 812
San Angelo ... 73 240
San Antonio .. 785 410
San Benito 17 988
San Marcos ... 23 420
Seguin........ 17 854
Sherman....... 30 413

Snyder 12 705
South
Houston 13 293
Stephenville ... 11 881
Sulphur
Springs 12 804
Sweetwater ... 12 242
Taylor 10 619
Temple 42 483
Terrell 13 225
Texarkana ... 31 271
Texas City 41 403
The Colony ... 11 586
Tyler 70 508
Universal City .. 10 720
University
Park 22 254
Uvalde 14 178
Vernon 12 695
Victoria 50 695
Vidor 12 117
Waco 101 261
Watauga 10 284
Waxahachie ... 14 624
Weatherford... 12 049
Weslaco 19 331
West University
Place 12 010
White Settlement 13 508
Wichita Falls ... 94 201

Utah
American
Fork 12 417
Bountiful....... 32 877
Brigham City .. 15 596
Cedar City 10 972
Clearfield 17 982
East Millcreek .. 26 579
Holladay 23 014
Kearns 17 247
Layton 22 862
Logan 26 844
Midvale 10 144
Murray 25 750
Ogden 64 407
Orem 52 399
Pleasant
Grove 10 669
Provo 73 907
Roy 19 694
St. George 11 350
Salt Lake
City 163 033
Sandy City 51 022
South Ogden .. 11 366
South Salt
Lake 10 561
Springville 12 101
Tooele 14 335
West Jordan.... 26 794

Vermont
†Bennington ... 15 815
†Brattleboro ... 11 886
Burlington 37 712
†Colchester ... 12 629
†Essex 14 392
Rutland 18 436
†South
Burlington ... 10 679
†Springfield ... 10 190

Virginia
Alexandria 103 217
Annandale 27 405
Arlington 174 284
Blacksburg 30 638
Bon Air 10 771
Bristol 19 042
Charlottesville .. 45 010
Chesapeake ... 114 226
Christiansburg 10 345
Colonial
Heights 16 509
Dale City 13 857
Danville 45 642
Fairfax 19 390
Fort Belvoir 14 591

Fort Hunt 10 415
Fort Lee 12 435
Fredericksburg 15 322
Front Royal ... 11 126
Groveton....... 11 761
Hampton 122 617
Harrisonburg .. 19 671
Herndon 11 449
Hopewell 23 397
Jefferson 25 432
Lake Barcroft ... 11 605
Lakeside 11 137
Lincoln 10 761
Long Branch ... 21 634
Lynchburg 66 743
Manassas 15 438
Martinsville ... 18 149
McLean 17 698
Newport
News 144 903
Norfolk 266 979
Petersburg 41 055
Portsmouth ... 104 577
Pulaski 10 106
Radford 13 225
Richmond 219 214
Roanoke 100 427
Rose Hill 14 492
Salem 23 958
Springfield 11 613
Staunton....... 21 857
Suffolk........ 47 621
Vienna 15 469
Virginia
Beach 262 199
Waynesboro ... 15 329
West
Springfield ... 14 143
Winchester.... 20 217
*Woodbridge-
Marumsco* ... 25 412

Washington
Aberdeen 18 739
Auburn 26 417
Bellevue 73 903
Bellingham ... 45 794
Bremerton ... 36 208
Centralia 10 809
Edmonds....... 27 526
Ellensburg ... 11 752
Everett 54 413
Fort Lewis 38 054
Kelso 11 129
Kennewick ... 34 397
Kent 23 152
Kirkland 18 779
Lacey 13 940
Lakes District ... 48 195
Longview 31 052
Lynnwood..... 21 937
Mercer Island... 21 522
Moses Lake ... 10 629
Mountlake
Terrace 16 534
Mount
Vernon 13 009
Oak Harbor ... 12 271
Olympia 27 447
Opportunity ... 16 604
Parkland 21 012
Pasco 17 944
Port Angeles ... 17 311
Pullman 23 579
Puyallup 18 251
Redmond 23 318
Renton 30 612
Richland 33 578
Seattle........ 493 846
Spokane 171 300
Tacoma 158 501
*University
Place* 13 230
Vancouver 42 834
Walla Walla ... 25 618
Wenatchee ... 17 257
Yakima 49 826

West Virginia
Beckley 20 492

Bluefield 16 060
Charleston 63 968
Clarksburg 22 371
Fairmont 23 863
Huntington ... 63 684
Martinsburg ... 13 063
Morgantown ... 27 605
Moundsville ... 12 419
Parkersburg ... 39 967
St. Albans 12 402
South
Charleston ... 15 968
Vienna 11 618
Weirton 24 736
Wheeling 43 070

Wisconsin
Allouez 13 753
Appleton 59 032
Ashwaubenon 14 486
Beaver Dam 14 149
Beloit 35 207
Brookfield 34 035
Brown Deer ... 12 921
Chippewa
Falls 11 845
Cudahy 19 547
De Pere 14 892
Eau Claire 51 509
Fond Du Lac 35 863
Franklin........ 16 871
Germantown ... 10 729
Glendale 13 882
Green Bay 87 899
Greendale 16 928
Greenfield 31 467
Janesville 51 071
Kaukauna 11 310
Kenosha 77 685
La Crosse 48 347
Madison 170 616
Manitowoc 32 547
Marinette 11 965
Marshfield 18 290
Menasha 14 728
Menomonee
Falls 27 845
Menomonie ... 12 769
Mequon 16 193
Middleton 11 779
Milwaukee 636 212
Monroe 10 027
Muskego 15 277
Neenah 23 272
New Berlin ... 30 529
Oak Creek 16 932
Oshkosh 49 678
Racine 85 725
St. Francis 10 066
Sheboygan 48 085
Shorewood..... 14 327
South
Milwaukee ... 21 069
Stevens Point... 22 970
Sun Prairie 12 931
Superior 29 571
Two Rivers 13 354
Watertown ... 18 113
Waukesha 50 319
Wausau 32 426
Wauwatosa ... 51 308
West Allis 63 982
West Bend ... 21 484
Whitefish Bay .. 14 930
Whitewater ... 11 520
Wisconsin
Rapids 17 995

Wyoming
Casper 51 016
Cheyenne 47 283
Gillette 12 134
Green River ... 12 807
Laramie 24 410
Rawlins 11 547
Rock Springs ... 19 458
Sheridan....... 15 146

Population of Cities

The population figures used are from censuses or more recent estimates and are given in thousands for towns and cities over 200 000 (over 500 000 in China and 250 000 in Japan, U.S.A. and U.S.S.R.). Where possible the population of the metropolitan areas is given e.g. Greater London. In the U.S.A. standard metropolitan statistical areas (S.M.S.A.) are used.

AFRICA

ALGERIA (1974)
Algiers ... 1 503
Oran ... 485
Constantine ... 350
Annaba ... 313
Tizi-Ouzou ... 224

ANGOLA (1970)
Luanda ... 475

CAMEROON (1976)
Douala ... 458
Yaoundé ... 314

CANARY ISLANDS (1974)
Las Palmas ... 328

CONGO (1975)
Brazzaville ... 290

EGYPT (1976)
Cairo ... 5 084
Alexandria ... 2 319
El Giza ... 1 247
Shubra el Kheima ... 394
El Mahalla el Kubra ... 293
Tanta ... 285
Port Said ... 263
El Mansura ... 258
Asyut ... 214
Zagazig ... 203

ETHIOPIA (1979)
Addis Abeba ... 1 210
Asmera ... 414

GABON (1976)
Libreville ... 186

GHANA (1970)
Accra ... 738
Kumasi ... 345

GUINEA (1972)
Conakry ... 526

IVORY COAST (1976)
Abidjan ... 850
Bouaké ... 318

KENYA (1979)
Nairobi ... 835
Mombasa ... 312

LIBYA (1973)
Tripoli ... 551
Benghazi ... 282

MADAGASCAR (1978)
Antananarivo ... 400

MALAWI (1977)
Blantyre ... 229

MALI (1976)
Bamako ... 404

MOROCCO (1973)
Casablanca ... 1 753
Rabat-Salé ... 596
Marrakesh ... 436
Fès ... 426
Meknès ... 403
Oujda ... 349
Kénitra ... 341
Tétouan ... 308
Safi ... 215
Tanger ... 208

MOZAMBIQUE (1970)
Maputo ... 384

NIGERIA (1975)
Lagos ... 1 477
Ibadan ... 847
Ogbomosho ... 432
Kano ... 399
Oshogbo ... 282
Ilorin ... 282
Abeokuta ... 253
Port Harcourt ... 242
Zaria ... 224
Ilesha ... 224
Onitsha ... 220
Iwo ... 214
Ado-Ekiti ... 213
Kaduna ... 202

SENEGAL (1976)
Dakar ... 799

SIERRA LEONE (1974)
Freetown ... 214

SOMALI REP. (1980)
Mogadishu ... 400

SOUTH AFRICA (1970)
Johannesburg ... 1 433
Cape Town ... 1 097
Durban ... 843
Pretoria ... 562
Port Elizabeth ... 469
Germiston ... 281

SUDAN (1973)
Khartoum ... 334

TANZANIA (1978)
Dar-es-Salaam ... 757

TUNISIA (1976)
Tunis ... 944
Sfax ... 475
Sousse ... 255

UGANDA (1975)
Kampala ... 331

ZAIRE (1974)
Kinshasa ... 2 008
Kananga ... 601
Lubumbashi ... 404
Mbuji Mayi ... 337
Kisangani ... 311

ZAMBIA (1980)
Lusaka ... 538
Kitwe ... 315
Ndola ... 282

ZIMBABWE (1978)
Harare ... 633
Bulawayo ... 366

ASIA

AFGHANISTAN (1976)
Kabul ... 588

BANGLADESH (1974)
Dacca ... 1 730
Chittagong ... 890
Khulna ... 437

BURMA (1977)
Rangoon ... 2 276
Mandalay ... 458

CAMBODIA (1973)
Phnom Penh ... 2 000

CHINA (1970)
Shanghai ... 10 820
Peking ... 7 570
Tientsin ... 4 280
Shenyang ... 2 800
Wuhan ... 2 560
Canton ... 2 500
Chungking ... 2 400
Nanking ... 1 750
Harbin ... 1 670
Luta ... 1 650
Sian ... 1 600
Lanchow ... 1 450
Taiyuan ... 1 350
Tsingtao ... 1 300
Chengtu ... 1 250
Changchun ... 1 200
Kunming ... 1 100
Tsinan ... 1 100
Fushun ... 1 080
Anshan ... 1 050
Chengchow ... 1 050
Hangchow ... 960
Tangshan ... 950
Paotow ... 920
Tzepo ... 850
Changsha ... 825
Shihkiachwang ... 800
Tsitsihar ... 760
Soochow ... 730
Kirin ... 720
Suchow ... 700
Foochow ... 680
Nanchang ... 675
Kweiyang ... 660
Wusih ... 650
Hofei ... 630
Hwainan ... 600
Penki ... 600
Loyang ... 580
Nanning ... 550
Huhehot ... 530
Sining ... 500
Wulumuchi ... 500

HONG KONG (1971)
Kowloon ... 2 195
Victoria ... 849
Tsuen Wan ... 272

INDIA (1971)
Calcutta ... 7 031
Bombay ... 5 971
Delhi ... 3 647
Madras ... 3 170
Hyderabad ... 1 796
Ahmedabad ... 1 742
Bangalore ... 1 654
Kanpur ... 1 275
Pune ... 1 135
Nagpur ... 930
Lucknow ... 749
Jaipur ... 615
Agra ... 592
Varanasi ... 584
Madurai ... 549
Indore ... 543
Allahabad ... 491
Patna ... 473
Surat ... 472
Vadodara ... 467
Cochin ... 439
Jabalpur ... 426
Tivandrum ... 410
Amritsar ... 408
Srinagar ... 403
Ludhiana ... 398
Sholapur ... 398
Gwalior ... 385
Hubli-Dharwar ... 379
Jamshedpur ... 357
Coimbatore ... 356
Mysore ... 356
Visakhaptnam ... 353
Calicut ... 334
Jodhpur ... 318
Vijaywada ... 317
Salem ... 309
Tiruchurapaili ... 307
Rajkot ... 301
Bhopal ... 298
Bareilly ... 296
Jullundur ... 296
Meerut ... 271
Guntur ... 270
Ajmer ... 263
Kolhapur ... 259
Algarh ... 252
Gorakhpur ... 231
Bhavnagar ... 225
Saharanpur ... 225
Chandigarh ... 219
Kota ... 213
Warangul ... 208
Durgapur ... 207
Ujjain ... 203
Jamnagar ... 200

INDONESIA (1971)
Jakarta ... 4 576
Surabaya ... 1 556
Bandung ... 1 202
Semarang ... 647
Medan ... 636
Palembang ... 583
Ujung Pandang ... 435
Malang ... 422
Surakarta ... 414
Yogyakarta ... 342
Banjarmasin ... 282
Pontianak ... 218

IRAN (1976)
Tehran ... 4 496
Esfahan ... 672
Mashhad ... 670
Tabriz ... 599
Shiraz ... 416
Ahvaz ... 329
Abadan ... 296
Qahremanshahr ... 291
Qom ... 247

IRAQ (1970)
Baghdad ... 2 969
Basra ... 371
Mosul ... 293
Kirkuk ... 208

ISRAEL (1977)
Tel Aviv-Jaffa ... 1 220
Jerusalem ... 376
Haifa ... 367

JAPAN (1980)
Tokyo ... 8 349
Yokohama ... 2 774
Osaka ... 2 648
Nagoya ... 2 088
Kyoto ... 1 473
Sapporo ... 1 402
Kobe ... 1 367
Fukuoka ... 1 089
Kitakyushu ... 1 065
Kawasaki ... 1 041
Hiroshima ... 899
Sakai ... 810
Chiba ... 746
Sendai ... 665
Okayama ... 546
Kumamoto ... 526
Amagasaki ... 524
Higashiosaka ... 522
Kagoshima ... 505
Hamamatsu ... 491
Funabashi ... 479
Niigata ... 458
Shizuoka ... 458
Nagasaki ... 447
Himeji ... 446
Sagamihara ... 439
Yokosuka ... 421
Kanazawa ... 418
Gifu ... 410
Nishinoyama ... 410
Kurashiki ... 404
Toyonaka ... 403
Matsuyama ... 402
Matsudo ... 401
Wakayama ... 401
Hachioji ... 387
Kawaguchi ... 379
Utsunomiya ... 378
Ichikawa ... 364
Oita ... 360
Urawa ... 358
Omiya ... 354
Asahikawa ... 353
Hirakata ... 353
Fukuyama ... 346
Iwaki ... 342
Takatsuki ... 341
Suita ... 332
Nagano ... 324
Hakodate ... 320
Takamatsu ... 317
Toyama ... 305
Toyohashi ... 304
Kochi ... 301
Fujisawa ... 300
Nara ... 298
Naha ... 296
Machida ... 295
Aomori ... 288
Koriyama ... 286
Akita ... 285
Toyota ... 282
Yao ... 273
Shimonoseki ... 269
Maebashi ... 265
Miyazaki ... 265
Fukushima ... 263
Okazaki ... 262
Kawagoe ... 259
Neyagawa ... 256
Akashi ... 255
Yokkaichi ... 255
Ichinomiya ... 253
Sasebo ... 251

JORDAN (1977)
Amman ... 712
Az Zarqa ... 263

KOREA, NORTH (1967-70)
Pyongyang ... 1 500
Chongjin ... 265

KOREA, SOUTH (1975)
Seoul ... 6 879
Pusan ... 2 450
Taegu ... 1 309
Inchon ... 797
Kwangju ... 606
Taejon ... 506
Masan ... 372
Chonju ... 311
Seongnam ... 272
Utsan ... 253
Suweon ... 224

KUWAIT (1975)
Kuwait ... 775

LEBANON (1971)
Beirut ... 702

MACAU (1975)
Macau ... 260

MALAYSIA (1970)
Kuala Lumpur ... 452
Georgetown ... 270
Ipoh ... 248

MONGOLIA (1977)
Ulan Bator ... 400

NEPAL (1971)
Katmandu ... 210

PAKISTAN (1972)
Karachi ... 3 499
Lahore ... 2 165
Faisalabad ... 822
Hyderabad ... 628
Rawalpindi ... 615
Multan ... 542
Gujranwala ... 360
Peshawar ... 268
Sialkot ... 204
Sargodha ... 201

PHILIPPINES (1975)
Manila ... 1 438
Quezon City ... 995
Davao ... 516
Cebu ... 419
Caloocan ... 364
Iloilo ... 248
Pasay ... 241
Zamboanga ... 240

SAUDI ARABIA (1974)
Riyadh ... 667
Jedda ... 561
Mecca ... 367
Taif ... 205

SINGAPORE (1977)
Singapore ... 2 308

SRI LANKA (1981)
Colombo ... 1 412

SYRIA (1978)
Damascus ... 1 142
Aleppo ... 878
Homs ... 306
Latakia ... 204

TAIWAN (1973)
Taipei ... 3 050
Kaohsiung ... 1 115
Tainan ... 513
Taichung ... 497
Chilung ... 341
Sanchung ... 260
Chiai ... 247
Hsinchu ... 205

THAILAND (1977)
Bangkok ... 4 702

TURKEY (1980)
Istanbul ... 2 854
Ankara ... 2 204
Izmir ... 754
Adana ... 569
Bursa ... 466
Gaziantep ... 371
Konya ... 309
Ekisehir ... 326
Kayseri ... 273
Diyarbakir ... 233
Mersin ... 215

UNITED ARAB EMIRATES (1976)
Abu Dhabi ... 236
Dubai ... 207

VIETNAM (1973-79)
Ho Chi Minh City ... 3 420
Hanoi ... 2 571
Haiphong ... 1 279
Da-Nang ... 492
Nha-trang ... 216
Qui-Nhon ... 214
Hué ... 209

YEMEN, SOUTH (1977)
Aden ... 285

AUSTRALASIA

AUSTRALIA (1977)
Sydney ... 3 122
Melbourne ... 2 694
Brisbane ... 995
Adelaide ... 923
Perth ... 844
Newcastle ... 372
Canberra ... 227
Wollongong ... 220

NEW ZEALAND (1981)
Auckland ... 770
Wellington ... 321
Christchurch ... 290

EUROPE

AUSTRIA (1978)
Vienna ... 1 587
Graz ... 249
Linz ... 203

BELGIUM (1976)
Brussels ... 1 042
Antwerp ... 662
Liège ... 433
Gent ... 219
Charleroi ... 210

BULGARIA (1978)
Sofia ... 1 032
Plovdiv ... 333
Varna ... 279

CZECHOSLOVAKIA (1977)
Prague ... 1 176
Brno ... 363
Bratislava ... 350
Ostrava ... 317

DENMARK (1977)
Copenhagen ... 1 251
Århus ... 246

FINLAND (1979)
Helsinki ... 893
Tampere ... 243
Turku ... 240

FRANCE (1975)
Paris ... 9 863
Lyon ... 1 152
Marseille ... 1 004
Lille ... 929
Bordeaux ... 591
Toulouse ... 495
Nantes ... 438
Nice ... 433
Rouen ... 389
Grenoble ... 389
Toulon ... 379
Strasbourg ... 355
St-Etienne ... 335
Lens ... 313
Nancy ... 279
Le Havre ... 264
Grasse-Cannes ... 255
Tours ... 235
Clermont-Ferrand ... 225
Valenciennes ... 224
Mulhouse ... 219
Rennes ... 213
Montpellier ... 205
Orléans ... 205
Dijon ... 203
Douai ... 203

GERMANY, EAST (1977)
East Berlin ... 1 111
Leipzig ... 565
Dresden ... 511
Karl-Marx-Stadt ... 309
Magdeburg ... 281
Halle ... 233
Rostock ... 219
Erfurt ... 206

GERMANY, WEST (1978)
West Berlin ... 1 910
Hamburg ... 1 664
München ... 1 297
Cologne ... 977
Essen ... 658
Frankfurt am Main ... 631
Dortmund ... 613
Düsseldorf ... 600
Stuttgart ... 584
Duisburg ... 563
Bremen ... 559
Hannover ... 549
Bochum ... 406
Wuppertal ... 396
Bielefeld ... 313
Gelsenkirchen ... 310
Mannheim ... 303
Bonn ... 285
Karlsruhe ... 274
Wiesbaden ... 271
Münster ... 267
Braunschweig ... 263

Mönchengladbach .. 258
Kiel .. 254
Augsburg .. 245
Aachen .. 243
Oberhausen .. 231
Lübeck .. 225
Krefeld .. 224
Hagen .. 222

GREECE (1971)
Athens .. 2 101
Thessaloniki .. 557
Piraeus .. 439

HUNGARY (1980)
Budapest .. 2 060
Miskolc .. 207

IRISH REPUBLIC (1981)
Dublin .. 525

ITALY (1977)
Rome .. 2 898
Milano .. 1 706
Napoli .. 1 225
Torino .. 1 182
Genova .. 795
Palermo .. 679
Bologna .. 481
Firenze .. 464
Catánia .. 400
Bari .. 387
Venézia .. 360
Verona .. 271
Messina .. 267
Trieste .. 265
Táranto .. 245
Cágliari .. 242
Padova .. 242
Bréscia .. 215

NETHERLANDS (1978)
Rotterdam .. 1 017
Amsterdam .. 965
s'Gravenhage .. 673
Utrecht .. 472
Eindhoven .. 363
Arnhem .. 284
Heerlen-Kerkrade .. 266
Enschede-Hengelo .. 241
Haarlem .. 229
Nijmegen .. 216
Tilburg .. 212
Groningen .. 200

NORWAY (1978)
Oslo .. 645
Bergen .. 211

POLAND (1978)
Warsaw .. 1 543
Łódz .. 824
Kraków .. 719
Wrocław .. 599
Poznań .. 538
Gdańsk .. 448
Szczecin .. 384
Katowice .. 352
Bydgoszcz .. 342
Lublin .. 295
Bytom .. 237
Gdynia .. 234
Częstochowa .. 228
Białystok .. 210
Sosnowiec .. 208
Zabrze .. 203
Gliwice .. 201

PORTUGAL (1975)
Lisbon .. 1 612
Oporto .. 1 315

ROMANIA (1978)
Bucharest .. 1 934
Iaşi .. 279
Timişoara .. 278
Cluj .. 273
Braşov .. 268
Constanţa .. 268
Galaţi .. 253
Craiova .. 231
Ploieşti .. 206
Brăila .. 200

SPAIN (1974)
Madrid .. 3 520
Barcelona .. 1 810
Valencia .. 713
Sevilla .. 569
Zaragoza .. 547
Bilbao .. 458
Malaga .. 403
Valladolid .. 275
Palma de Mallorca .. 267
Córdoba .. 250
Hospitalet .. 242
Murcia .. 241
Alicante .. 213
Granada .. 203

SWEDEN (1978)
Stockholm .. 1 380
Göteborg .. 694
Malmö .. 454

SWITZERLAND (1979)
Zürich .. 708
Basel .. 368
Genève .. 325
Berne .. 282
Lausanne .. 227

U.S.S.R. (1979)
Moscow .. 8 011
Leningrad .. 4 588
Kiyev .. 2 144
Tashkent .. 1 779
Baku .. 1 550
Kharkov .. 1 444
Gorkiy .. 1 344
Novosibirsk .. 1 312
Minsk .. 1 276
Kuybyshev .. 1 218
Sverdlovsk .. 1 211
Dnepropetrovsk .. 1 066
Tbilisi .. 1 066
Odessa .. 1 046
Chelyabinsk .. 1 031
Donetsk .. 1 021
Yerevan .. 1 019
Omsk .. 1 014
Perm .. 999
Kazan .. 993
Ufa .. 969
Rostov .. 934
Volgograd .. 929
Alma-Ata .. 910
Saratov .. 856
Riga .. 835
Krasnoyarsk .. 796
Voronezh .. 783
Zaporozhye .. 781
Lvov .. 667
Krivoy Rog .. 650
Yaroslavl .. 597
Karaganda .. 572
Krasnodar .. 560
Irkutsk .. 550
Vladivostok .. 550
Izhevsk .. 549
Novokuznetsk .. 541
Barnaul .. 533
Frunze .. 533
Khabarovsk .. 528
Tula .. 514
Kishinev .. 503
Zhdanov .. 503
Togliatti .. 502
Dushanbe .. 493
Penza .. 483
Vilnius .. 481
Samarkand .. 476
Kemerovo .. 471
Ivanovo .. 465
Ulyanovsk .. 464
Voroshilovgrad .. 463
Astrakhan .. 461
Orenburg .. 459
Ryazan .. 453
Nikolayev .. 441
Makeyevka .. 436
Tallinn .. 430
Tomsk .. 421
Kalinin .. 412
Magnitogorsk .. 406
Nizhniy Tagil .. 398
Lipetsk .. 396
Bryansk .. 394
Kirov .. 390
Arkhangelsk .. 385
Gomel .. 383
Murmansk .. 381
Groznyy .. 375
Kursk .. 375
Kaunas .. 370
Tyumen .. 359
Kaliningrad .. 355
Gorlovka .. 337
Chimkent .. 321
Kherson .. 319
Vinnitsa .. 313
Ashkhabad .. 312
Kurgan .. 310
Cheboksary .. 308
Orel .. 305
Chita .. 302
Simferopol .. 302
Naberezhnyye Chelny 301
Sevastopol .. 301
Ulan Ude .. 300
Vitebsk .. 297
Vladimir .. 296
Mogilev .. 290
Sochi .. 287
Semipalatinsk .. 283
Ordzhonikidze .. 279
Poltava .. 279
Taganrog .. 277
Smolensk .. 276
Ust-Kamenogorsk .. 274
Pavlodar .. 273
Tambov .. 270
Cherepovets .. 266
Prokopyevsk .. 266
Kaluga .. 265
Dzhambul .. 264
Komsomolsk-na-Amur .. 264
Saransk .. 263
Stavropol .. 258
Dzerzhinsk .. 257
Kostroma .. 255
Dneprodzerzhinsk .. 250
Makhachkala .. 250

UNITED KINGDOM (1981)
London .. 6 696
Birmingham .. 920
Glasgow .. 762
Liverpool .. 510
Sheffield .. 477
Leeds .. 449
Manchester .. 449
Edinburgh .. 419
Bristol .. 388
Belfast .. 374
Coventry .. 314
Bradford .. 281
Leicester .. 280
Cardiff .. 274
Nottingham .. 271
Hull .. 268
Wolverhampton .. 252
Stoke-on-Trent .. 252
Plymouth .. 244
Derby .. 216
Southampton .. 204

YUGOSLAVIA (1971)
Belgrade .. 775
Zagreb .. 602
Skopje .. 388
Sarajevo .. 271
Ljubljana .. 213

NORTH AMERICA

CANADA (1981)
Toronto .. 2 999
Montréal .. 2 828
Vancouver .. 1 268
Ottawa .. 718
Edmonton .. 657
Calgary .. 593
Winnipeg .. 585
Québec .. 576
Hamilton .. 542
St. Catherines .. 304
Kitchener .. 288
London .. 284
Halifax .. 278
Windsor .. 246
Victoria .. 233

COSTA RICA (1978)
San José .. 563

CUBA (1975)
Havana .. 1 861
Santiago de Cuba .. 316
Camaguey .. 222

DOMINICAN REPUBLIC (1978)
Santo Domingo .. 1 103
Santiago de los Caballeros .. 242

EL SALVADOR (1974)
San Salvador .. 366

GUATEMALA (1979)
Guatemala City .. 793

HAITI (1979)
Port-au-Prince .. 791

HONDURAS (1974)
Tegucigalpa .. 274

JAMAICA (1971)
Kingston .. 573

MEXICO (1978)
Mexico City .. 13 994
Guadalajara .. 2 343
Netzahualcóyotl .. 2 068
Monterrey .. 1 923
Puebla de Zaragoza .. 678
Ciudad Juárez .. 597
León de los Aldamas .. 590
Acapulco .. 421
Torreón .. 397
Tampico .. 375
Chihuahua .. 370
Mexicali .. 338
San Luis Potosi .. 315
Culiacán .. 302
Hermosillo .. 300
Veracruz Llave .. 295
Mérida .. 253
Aguascalientes .. 248
Saltillo .. 246
Morelia .. 239
Cuernavaca .. 227
Toluca .. 223
Durango .. 219
Reynosa .. 219
Nuevo Laredo .. 214

NICARAGUA (1974)
Managua .. 500

PANAMA (1980)
Panama .. 546

PUERTO RICO (1976)
San Juan .. 515
Bayamón .. 204

UNITED STATES (1980)
New York .. 9 120
Los Angeles .. 7 428
Chicago .. 7 104
Philadelphia .. 4 717
Detroit .. 4 353
San Francisco .. 3 251
Washington .. 3 061
Dallas .. 2 975
Houston .. 2 905
Boston .. 2 763
Nassau-Suffolk .. 2 606
St. Louis .. 2 356
Pittsburgh .. 2 264
Baltimore .. 2 174
Minneapolis-St Paul 2 114
Atlanta .. 2 030
Newark .. 1 966
Anaheim .. 1 933
Cleveland .. 1 899
San Diego .. 1 862
Miami .. 1 626
Denver .. 1 621
Seattle .. 1 607
Tampa-St Petersburg .. 1 569
San Bernardino .. 1 558
Phoenix .. 1 509
Cincinnati .. 1 401
Milwaukee .. 1 397
Kansas City .. 1 327
San Jose .. 1 295
Buffalo .. 1 243
Portland .. 1 243
New Orleans .. 1 187
Indianapolis .. 1 167
Columbus .. 1 093
San Antonio .. 1 072
Fort Lauderdale .. 1 018
Sacramento .. 1 014
Rochester .. 971
Salt Lake City .. 936
Providence .. 919
Memphis .. 913
Louisville .. 906
Nashville .. 851
Birmingham .. 847
Oklahoma .. 834
Dayton .. 830
Greensboro .. 827
Norfolk .. 807
Albany .. 795
Toledo .. 792
Honolulu .. 763
Jacksonville .. 738
Hartford .. 726
Orlando .. 700
Tulsa .. 689
Akron .. 660
Syracuse .. 643
Gary .. 643
N.E. Pennsylvania .. 640
Charlotte .. 637
Allentown .. 635
Richmond .. 632
Grand Rapids .. 602
New Brunswick .. 596
West Palm Beach .. 577
Omaha .. 570
Greenville .. 569
Jersey City .. 557
Austin .. 537
Youngstown .. 537
Tucson .. 531
Raleigh .. 531
Springfield .. 531
Oxnard .. 529
Wilmington .. 523
Flint .. 522
Fresno .. 515
Long Branch .. 503
Baton Rouge .. 494
Tacoma .. 486
El Paso .. 480
Knoxville .. 477
Lansing .. 472
Las Vegas .. 463
Albuquerque .. 454
Paterson .. 448
Harrisburg .. 447
Mobile .. 444
Johnson City .. 434
Charleston, S.C. .. 430
Chattanooga .. 427
New Haven .. 418
Wichita .. 411
Columbia .. 410
Canton .. 404
Bakersfield .. 403
Bridgeport .. 395
Little Rock .. 394
Davenport .. 384
Fort Wayne .. 383
York .. 381
Shreveport .. 377
Beaumont .. 375
Worcester .. 373
Peoria .. 366
Newport News .. 364
Lancaster .. 362
Stockton .. 347
Spokane .. 342
Des Moines .. 338
Vallejo .. 334
Augusta .. 327
Corpus Christi .. 326
Madison .. 324
Lakeland .. 322
Jackson .. 322
Utica .. 320
Lexington .. 318
Colorado Springs .. 317
Reading .. 313
Huntingdon .. 311
Evansville .. 309
Huntsville .. 309
Trenton .. 308
Binghamton .. 301
Santa Rosa .. 300
Santa Barbara .. 299
Appleton .. 291
Salinas .. 290
Pensacola .. 290
McAllen .. 283
Lawrence .. 282
South Bend .. 281
Erie .. 280
Rockford .. 280
Kalamazoo .. 279
Eugene .. 275
Lorain .. 275
Melbourne .. 273
Montgomery .. 273
Charleston, W. Va. .. 270
Duluth .. 267
Modesto .. 266
Ann Arbor .. 265
Johnstown .. 265
Newburgh .. 260
Hamilton .. 259
Daytona Beach .. 259
Macon .. 254
Salem .. 250

SOUTH AMERICA

ARGENTINA (1975)
Buenos Aires .. 8 436
Rosario .. 807
Córdoba .. 791
La Plata .. 479
Mendoza .. 471
San Miguel de Tucuman .. 366
Mar del Plata .. 300
Santa Fé .. 245
San Juan .. 218

BOLIVIA (1976)
La Paz .. 655
Santa Cruz .. 237

BRAZIL (1975)
São Paulo .. 7 199
Rio de Janeiro .. 4 858
Belo Horizonte .. 1 557
Recife .. 1 250
Salvador .. 1 237
Fortaleza .. 1 110
Pôrto Alegre .. 1 044
Nova Iguaçu .. 932
Belém .. 772
Curitiba .. 765
Brasilia .. 763
Duque de Caxias .. 537
São Gonçalo .. 534
Goiania .. 518
Santo André .. 515
Campinas .. 473
Santos .. 396
Manaus .. 389
Osasco .. 377
Niterói .. 376
São João de Meriti .. 366
Natal .. 344
Campos .. 337
São Luiz .. 330
Maceió .. 324
Guarulhos .. 311
Teresina .. 290
João Pessoa .. 288
Juiz de Fora .. 284
Londrina .. 284
São Bernardo do Campo .. 267
Jaboatao .. 259
Ribeirão Preto .. 259
Olinda .. 251
Campina Grande .. 236
Pelotas .. 232
Feira de Santana .. 227
Aracaju .. 226
Petrópolis .. 217
Sorocaba .. 208
Jundiai .. 205

CHILE (1978)
Santiago .. 3 692
Valparaiso .. 620
Concepción .. 519
Viña del Mar .. 262
Talcahuano .. 204

COLOMBIA (1973)
Bogotá .. 2 855
Medellin .. 1 159
Cali .. 990
Barranquilla .. 692
Cartagena .. 355
Bucaramanga .. 323
Cucuta .. 279
Manizales .. 232
Pereira .. 227
Ibagué .. 223

ECUADOR (1978)
Guayaquil .. 1 022
Quito .. 743

PARAGUAY (1974)
Asunción .. 565

PERU (1972)
Lima .. 3 303
Arequipa .. 302
Callao .. 297
Trujillo .. 240

URUGUAY (1975)
Montevideo .. 1 230

VENEZUELA (1976)
Caracas .. 2 576
Maracaibo .. 792
Valencia .. 439
Barquisimeto .. 430
Maracay .. 301
Barcelona-Puerto La Cruz .. 242

Population of Countries

Country	Area in thousands of square km	Population in thousands	Density of population per sq. km.	Capital Population in thousands
Afghanistan	647	15 540	24	Kabul (588)
Albania	29	2 734	94	Tiranë (192)
Algeria	2 382	18 594	8	Algiers (1 503)
Angola	1 247	7 078	6	Luanda (475)
Argentina	2 767	26 863	10	Buenos Aires (8 436)
Australia	7 687	14 727	2	Canberra (227)
Austria	84	7 507	89	Vienna (1 587)
Bangladesh	144	88 656	616	Dacca (1 730)
Belgium	31	9 859	318	Brussels (1 042)
Belize	23	145	6	Belmopan (4)
Benin	113	3 567	32	Porto-Novo (104)
Bhutan	47	1 298	28	Thimphu (60)
Bolivia	1 099	5 600	5	Sucre (63)
				La Paz (655)
Botswana	600	819	1	Gaborone (37)
Brazil	8 512	119 099	14	Brasilia (763)
Brunei	6	213	37	Bandar Seri
				Begawan (37)
Bulgaria	111	8 862	80	Sofia (1 032)
Burma	677	35 289	52	Rangoon (2 276)
Burundi	28	4 512	161	Bujumbura (157)
Cambodia	181	8 872	49	Phnom Penh (2 000)
Cameroon	475	8 503	18	Yaoundé (314)
Canada	9 976	23 343	2	Ottawa (718)
Central African Rep.	623	2 370	4	Bangui (187)
Chad	1 284	4 524	4	Ndjamena (179)
Chile	757	11 104	15	Santiago (3 692)
China	9 597	982 550	102	Peking (7 570)
Colombia	1 139	27 520	24	Bogota (2 855)
Congo	342	1 537	5	Brazzaville (290)
Costa Rica	51	2 245	44	San José (563)
Cuba	115	9 833	86	Havana (1 861)
Cyprus	9	629	68	Nicosia (147)
Czechoslovakia	128	15 312	120	Prague (1 176)
Denmark	43	5 124	119	Copenhagen (1 251)
Djibouti	22	119	5	Djibouti (62)
Dominican Republic	49	5 431	111	Santo Domingo (1 103)
Ecuador	284	8 354	29	Quito (743)
Egypt	1 001	41 995	42	Cairo (5 084)
El Salvador	21	4 813	229	San Salvador (366)
Equatorial Guinea	28	363	13	Rey Malabo (37)
Ethiopia	1 222	31 065	25	Addis Abeba (1 210)
Fiji	18	631	35	Suva (118)
Finland	337	4 788	14	Helsinki (893)
France	547	53 788	98	Paris (9 863)
French Guiana	91	64	1	Cayenne (25)
Gabon	268	551	2	Libréville (186)
Gambia	11	601	55	Banjul (48)
Germany, East	108	16 737	155	East Berlin (1 111)
Germany, West	249	61 658	248	Bonn (285)
Ghana	239	11 450	48	Accra (738)
Greece	132	9 599	73	Athens (2 101)
Greenland	2 176	50	0.02	Godthåb (9)
Guatemala	109	7 262	67	Guatemala (793)
Guinea	246	5 014	20	Conakry (526)
Guinea-Bissau	36	777	22	Bissau (109)
Guyana	215	884	4	Georgetown (187)
Haiti	28	5 009	179	Port-au-Prince (791)
Honduras	112	3 691	33	Tegucigalpa (274)
Hong Kong	1	5 068	4 827	Victoria (849)
Hungary	93	10 711	115	Budapest (2 060)
Iceland	103	228	2	Reykjavik (83)
India	3 288	683 810	208	Delhi (3 647)
Indonesia	2 027	7 383	73	Jakarta (4 576)
Iran	1 648	37 447	23	Tehran (4 496)
Iraq	435	13 084	28	Baghdad (2 969)
Irish Republic	70	3 440	49	Dublin (525)
Israel	21	3 871	184	Jerusalem (376)
Italy	301	57 140	190	Rome (2 898)
Ivory Coast	322	7 973	25	Abidjan (850)
Jamaica	11	2 192	199	Kingston (573)
Japan	372	117 057	315	Tokyo (8 349)
Jordan	98	2 779	28	Amman (712)
Kenya	583	16 402	28	Nairobi (835)
Korea, North	121	17 914	148	Pyongyang (1 500)
Korea, South	98	37 449	382	Seoul (6 879)
Kuwait	18	1 356	75	Kuwait (775)
Laos	237	3 721	16	Vientiane (177)
Lebanon	10	3 161	316	Beirut (702)
Lesotho	30	1 339	45	Maseru (29)
Liberia	111	1 873	17	Monrovia (172)
Libya	1 760	2 977	2	Tripoli (551)
Luxembourg	3	364	140	Luxembourg (78)
Madagascar	587	8 742	15	Antananarivo (400)
Malawi	118	5 968	51	Lilongwe (103)
Malaysia	330	13 436	41	Kuala Lumpur (452)
Mali	1 240	6 906	6	Bamako (404)
Malta	0.3	369	1 153	Valletta (14)
Mauritania	1 031	1 634	2	Nouakchott (135)
Mauritius	2	959	480	Port Louis (141)
Mexico	1 973	71 911	36	Mexico (13 994)
Mongolia	1 565	1 595	1	Ulan Bator (400)
Morocco	447	20 242	45	Rabat (596)
Mozambique	783	12 130	15	Maputo (384)
Namibia	824	852	1	Windhoek (61)
Nepal	141	14 010	99	Katmandu (210)
Netherlands	41	14 220	347	Amsterdam (965)
New Zealand	269	3 176	12	Wellington (321)
Nicaragua	130	2 703	21	Managua (500)
Niger	1 267	5 305	4	Niamey (130)
Nigeria	924	77 082	83	Lagos (1 477)
Norway	324	4 092	13	Oslo (645)
Oman	212	891	4	Muscat (25)
Pakistan	804	82 441	103	Islamabad (77)
Panama	76	1 837	24	Panama (546)
Papua New Guinea	462	3 082	7	Port Moresby (113)
Paraguay	407	3 067	8	Asunción (565)
Peru	1 285	17 780	14	Lima (3 303)
Philippines	300	48 400	161	Manila (1 438)
Poland	313	35 815	114	Warsaw (1 543)
Portugal	92	9 933	108	Lisbon (1 612)
Puerto Rico	9	3 188	358	San Juan (515)
Romania	238	22 201	93	Bucharest (1 934)
Rwanda	26	5 046	194	Kigali (90)
Saudi Arabia	2 150	8 367	4	Riyadh (667)
Senegal	196	5 661	29	Dakar (799)
Sierra Leone	72	3 474	48	Freetown (214)
Singapore	0.6	2 391	4 122	Singapore (2 308)
Somali Republic	638	3 645	6	Mogadishu (400)
South Africa	1 221	29 285	24	Pretoria (562)
				Cape Town (1 097)
Spain	505	37 430	74	Madrid (3 520)
Sri Lanka	66	14 738	223	Colombo (1 412)
Sudan	2 506	18 681	8	Khartoum (334)
Surinam	163	352	2	Paramaribo (151)
Swaziland	17	547	32	Mbabane (24)
Sweden	450	8 320	18	Stockholm (1 380)
Switzerland	41	6 329	154	Berne (282)
Syria	185	8 979	49	Damascus (1 142)
Taiwan	36	17 479	486	Taipei (3 050)
Tanzania	945	17 982	19	Dar-es-Salaam (757)
Thailand	514	46 455	90	Bangkok (4 702)
Togo	56	2 699	48	Lomé (135)
Trinidad and Tobago	5	1 156	227	Port of Spain (63)
Tunisia	164	6 363	39	Tunis (944)
Turkey	781	45 218	58	Ankara (2 204)
Uganda	236	13 225	56	Kampala (331)
United Arab Emirates	84	1 040	12	Abu Dhabi (236)
U.S.S.R.	22 402	265 542	12	Moscow (8 011)
United Kingdom	245	55 945	228	London (6 696)
United States	9 363	229 805	25	Washington (3 061)
Upper Volta	274	6 908	25	Ouagadougou (169)
Uruguay	178	2 899	16	Montevideo (1 230)
Venezuela	912	13 913	15	Caracas (2 576)
Vietnam	330	52 742	160	Hanoi (2 571)
Western Samoa	3	156	55	Apia (32)
Yemen, North	195	5 926	30	Sana (448)
Yemen, South	288	1 969	7	Aden (285)
Yugoslavia	256	22 471	88	Belgrade (775)
Zaïre	2 345	28 291	12	Kinshasa (2 008)
Zambia	753	5 680	8	Lusaka (538)
Zimbabwe	391	7 360	19	Harare (633)

Climatic Statistics

These four pages show temperature and precipitation statistics for over 80 stations. This page presents information for the stations in the United States, and the other three pages are devoted to the rest of the world. These two lists are divided into the broad climatic regions following the classification of Köppen (see World map on page 9).

The height above sea level of each station is stated beneath its name. The average monthly temperature, in degrees Fahrenheit, and the average monthly precipitation, in inches, is given. To the right, the average yearly rainfall, the average yearly temperature, and the annual range of temperature (the difference between the warmest and the coldest months) are also stated. The month with the highest temperature and the heaviest rainfall is shown in bold figures, and the month with the lowest temperature and the least rainfall in light figures.

		Jan.	Feb.	Mar.	Apr.	May	June	July	Aug.	Sept.	Oct.	Nov.	Dec.	Year	Annual range
Tropical rainy climate with rain at all seasons															
Miami, Florida	Precipitation	2·8	2·1	2·5	3·2	6·8	7·0	6·1	6·3	8·0	**9·2**	2·8	2·0	58·8	
25 ft. a.s.l.	Temperature	68	69	71	74	78	80	**82**	81	81	76	72	69	75	14
Desert climate															
Greenland Ranch (Death Valley), California	Precipitation	0·1	<0·1	0·1	0·1	0·2	0·1	**0·3**	**0·3**	0·2	<0·1	0·1	<0·1	1·6	
178 ft. b.s.l.	Temperature	52	58	66	75	84	94	101	98	92	75	58	53	76	49
Las Vegas, Nevada	Precipitation	**0·7**	0·5	0·3	0·3	0·2	0·2	0·5	0·5	0·3	0·3	0·2	0·4	4·4	
2,000 ft. a.s.l.	Temperature	45	50	55	63	70	80	**86**	84	76	66	54	46	65	41
Steppe climate															
Cheyenne, Wyoming	Precipitation	0·4	0·6	1·0	1·9	**2·4**	1·6	2·1	1·6	1·2	1·0	0·5	0·5	14·8	
6,139 ft. a.s.l.	Temperature	26	27	33	41	50	60	**67**	66	57	45	35	28	45	41
Warm mid-latitude climate with a dry summer															
Los Angeles, California	Precipitation	**3·1**	3·0	2·8	1·0	0·4	0·1	<0·1	<0·1	0·2	0·6	1·2	2·6	15·0	
312 ft. a.s.l.	Temperature	56	57	58	60	63	66	70	**71**	70	65	61	57	62	15
San Francisco, California	Precipitation	**4·7**	3·8	3·1	1·5	0·7	0·1	<0·1	<0·1	0·3	1·0	2·5	4·4	22·1	
52 ft. a.s.l.	Temperature	50	53	55	56	57	59	59	59	**62**	61	57	52	57	12
Warm mid-latitude climate with rain at all seasons and a long summer															
Atlanta, Georgia	Precipitation	4·9	4·8	**5·5**	3·7	3·6	3·7	4·7	4·3	3·2	2·6	3·1	4·5	48·6	
1,054 ft. a.s.l.	Temperature	43	46	52	61	70	72	**79**	78	73	63	52	44	61	36
Houston, Texas	Precipitation	3·5	3·0	3·3	3·6	**4·7**	4·6	3·9	3·9	4·1	3·7	3·5	4·3	46·1	
41 ft. a.s.l.	Temperature	53	56	63	69	75	81	83	**84**	79	71	61	54	69	31
New Orleans, Louisiana	Precipitation	4·6	4·2	4·7	4·8	4·5	5·5	**6·6**	5·8	4·8	3·5	3·8	4·6	57·4	
8 ft. a.s.l.	Temperature	54	58	63	69	76	81	82	**83**	79	71	62	56	69	29
St. Louis, Missouri	Precipitation	2·3	2·5	3·5	3·8	**4·6**	4·5	3·5	3·4	3·2	2·9	2·8	2·5	39·5	
568 ft. a.s.l.	Temperature	32	34	45	56	66	75	**80**	78	71	59	46	35	57	48
Oklahoma City, Oklahoma	Precipitation	1·3	1·0	2·2	3·3	**5·1**	3·5	2·9	2·7	3·0	3·0	2·0	1·6	31·6	
1,254 ft. a.s.l.	Temperature	37	40	50	60	63	77	**82**	81	74	64	50	40	60	45
Washington, D.C.	Precipitation	3·4	3·0	3·6	3·3	3·7	3·9	**4·4**	4·3	3·7	2·9	2·6	3·1	41·9	
72 ft. a.s.l.	Temperature	35	36	44	54	65	73	**78**	75	68	58	46	37	55	43
Cool mid-latitude climate with rain at all seasons and a severe winter															
Albany, New York	Precipitation	2·3	2·4	2·7	2·6	2·9	3·5	3·5	**3·6**	3·1	2·8	2·7	2·4	34·5	
97 ft. a.s.l.	Temperature	23	24	34	46	59	68	**73**	71	63	51	40	28	48	49
Bismark, North Dakota	Precipitation	0·4	0·4	0·9	1·5	2·3	**3·4**	2·2	1·8	1·2	0·9	0·6	0·6	16·2	
1,670 ft. a.s.l.	Temperature	8	11	25	43	54	64	**70**	68	58	45	29	16	36	62
Chicago, Illinois	Precipitation	1·9	2·0	2·6	2·8	3·4	**3·5**	3·3	3·2	3·1	2·6	2·4	2·0	32·8	
823 ft. a.s.l.	Temperature	25	27	36	48	58	68	**73**	72	61	54	40	30	49	48
Minneapolis, Minnesota	Precipitation	1·0	1·0	1·6	2·3	3·4	**4·4**	3·4	3·4	3·4	2·1	1·4	1·2	28·6	
830 ft. a.s.l.	Temperature	14	16	30	46	58	72	**73**	70	62	50	33	20	45	59
Portland, Maine	Precipitation	**4·0**	3·9	**4·0**	3·5	3·3	3·3	3·3	3·2	3·2	3·2	3·5	3·9	42·0	
103 ft. a.s.l.	Temperature	23	24	33	43	53	62	**73**	66	60	50	39	27	46	50
Polar climate															
Point Barrow, Alaska	Precipitation	0·2	0·1	<0·1	0·1	0·1	0·3	**0·9**	0·8	0·5	0·5	0·3	0·2	4·1	
22 ft. a.s.l.	Temperature	−15	−18	−15	−1	19	34	**40**	39	30	16	1	−11	10	58

		Jan.	Feb.	Mar.	Apr.	May	June	July	Aug.	Sept.	Oct.	Nov.	Dec.	Year	Annual range

Tropical rainy climate with rain at all seasons

		Jan.	Feb.	Mar.	Apr.	May	June	July	Aug.	Sept.	Oct.	Nov.	Dec.	Year	Annual range
Colombo, Ceylon	Precipitation	3·5	2·7	5·8	9·1	14·6	8·8	5·3	4·3	6·3	13·7	12·4	5·8	93·1	
24 ft. a.s.l.	Temperature	79	79	81	83	83	81	81	81	81	80	79	79	80	4
Entebbe, Uganda	Precipitation	2·6	3·6	6·3	10·1	9·6	4·8	3·0	2·9	2·9	3·7	5·2	4·6	59·3	
3,878 ft. a.s.l.	Temperature	72	72	72	72	71	70	68	69	70	71	72	72	71	4
Georgetown, Guyana	Precipitation	8·0	4·5	6·9	5·5	11·4	11·9	10·0	6·9	3·2	3·0	6·1	11·3	88·7	
6 ft. a.s.l.	Temperature	79	79	79	81	80	80	80	81	82	82	81	80	80	3
Manaus, Brazil	Precipitation	9·8	9·1	10·3	8·7	6·7	3·3	2·3	1·5	1·8	4·2	5·6	8·0	71·3	
144 ft. a.s.l.	Temperature	81	81	81	81	81	81	81	82	82	83	82	82	81	2
Monrovia, Liberia	Precipitation	1·2	2·2	3·8	8·5	20·3	38·3	39·2	14·7	29·3	30·4	9·3	5·1	202·3	
75 ft. a.s.l.	Temperature	80	79	80	80	79	77	76	77	77	78	79	80	78	4
Rio de Janeiro, Brazil	Precipitation	4·9	4·8	5·1	4·2	3·1	2·1	1·6	1·7	2·6	3·1	4·1	5·4	42·6	
201 ft. a.s.l.	Temperature	78	78	77	74	71	70	69	70	70	71	74	76	74	9
San Juan, Puerto Rico	Precipitation	4·3	2·7	2·9	4·1	5·9	5·4	5·7	6·3	6·2	5·6	6·3	5·4	60·8	
82 ft. a.s.l.	Temperature	75	75	75	77	79	80	80	80	80	80	79	77	78	5
Suva, Fiji	Precipitation	11·4	10·7	14·5	12·2	10·1	6·7	4·9	8·3	7·7	8·3	9·8	12·5	117·1	
20 ft. a.s.l.	Temperature	80	80	80	79	77	76	75	75	76	77	79	79	77	5
Tamatave, Madagascar	Precipitation	14·4	14·8	17·8	15·7	10·4	11·1	11·9	8·0	5·2	3·9	4·6	10·3	128·2	
20 ft. a.s.l.	Temperature	80	80	79	78	77	72	70	70	72	74	77	79	75	10

Tropical rainy climate with a dry season

		Jan.	Feb.	Mar.	Apr.	May	June	July	Aug.	Sept.	Oct.	Nov.	Dec.	Year	Annual range
Bombay, India	Precipitation	0·1	0·1	0·1	<0·1	0·7	19·1	24·3	13·4	10·4	2·5	0·5	0·1	71·2	
37 ft. a.s.l.	Temperature	75	76	79	83	86	84	81	80	80	83	81	78	81	11
Darwin, Australia	Precipitation	15·2	12·3	10·0	3·8	0·6	0·1	<0·1	0·1	0·5	2·0	4·7	9·4	58·7	
97 ft. a.s.l.	Temperature	83	83	84	84	82	78	77	80	83	85	86	85	83	9
Kano, Nigeria	Precipitation	<0·1	<0·1	0·1	0·4	2·7	4·6	8·1	12·2	5·6	0·5	<0·1	0·0	34·2	
1,533 ft. a.s.l.	Temperature	70	76	83	88	87	84	79	78	79	81	77	72	80	18
Kinshasa, Zaïre	Precipitation	5·3	5·7	7·7	7·7	6·2	0·3	<0·1	0·1	1·2	4·7	8·7	5·6	53·3	
1,066 ft. a.s.l.	Temperature	79	80	80	81	80	76	73	75	78	79	79	78	78	8
Mazatlan, Mexico	Precipitation	0·2	0·3	<0·1	0·0	<0·1	1·2	6·6	10·6	11·9	1·2	0·7	0·7	33·4	
256 ft. a.s.l.	Temperature	66	67	68	70	75	80	81	82	81	81	76	70	75	16
Parana, Brazil	Precipitation	11·3	9·3	9·4	4·0	0·5	<0·1	0·1	0·2	1·2	5·0	9·0	12·2	62·3	
853 ft. a.s.l.	Temperature	74	74	74	74	72	75	75	77	80	76	75	74	75	8
Saigon, South Vietnam	Precipitation	0·6	0·1	0·5	1·7	8·7	13·0	12·4	10·6	13·2	10·6	4·5	2·2	78·1	
30 ft. a.s.l.	Temperature	80	81	83	85	84	82	82	82	81	81	80	79	82	6
San José, Costa Rica	Precipitation	0·6	0·2	0·8	1·8	9·0	9·5	8·3	9·5	12·0	11·8	5·7	1·6	70·8	
3,760 ft. a.s.l.	Temperature	67	67	69	70	71	71	70	70	70	69	69	67	69	2

Desert climate

		Jan.	Feb.	Mar.	Apr.	May	June	July	Aug.	Sept.	Oct.	Nov.	Dec.	Year	Annual range
Antofagasta, Chile	Precipitation	0·0	0·0	0·0	<0·1	<0·1	0·1	0·2	0·1	<0·1	0·1	<0·1	0·0	0·5	
308 ft. a.s.l.	Temperature	69	68	66	64	61	59	58	56	59	61	64	66	63	13
Karachi, Pakistan	Precipitation	0·5	0·4	0·3	0·1	0·1	0·7	3·2	1·6	0·5	<0·1	0·1	0·2	7·7	
13 ft. a.s.l.	Temperature	66	69	76	81	86	87	86	83	82	76	75	69	78	21
Kazalinsk, Kazakhstan, U.S.S.R.	Precipitation	0·4	0·4	0·5	0·5	0·6	0·2	0·2	0·3	0·3	0·5	0·4	0·6	4·9	
207 ft. a.s.l.	Temperature	11	13	26	42	64	73	78	73	62	46	30	20	45	67
Timbuktu, Mali	Precipitation	<0·1	<0·1	0·1	<0·1	0·2	0·9	3·1	3·2	1·5	0·1	<0·1	<0·1	9·1	
988 ft. a.s.l.	Temperature	71	76	83	90	94	95	90	86	90	88	82	73	85	24
Walvis Bay, South Africa	Precipitation	<0·1	0·2	0·3	0·1	0·1	<0·1	<0·1	0·1	<0·1	<0·1	<0·1	<0·1	0·9	
24 ft. a.s.l.	Temperature	66	67	66	65	63	61	59	57	58	59	63	65	63	10
Warburton Ranges, Australia	Precipitation	1·0	1·2	1·8	1·3	1·0	0·7	0·3	0·4	0·1	0·6	1·0	1·2	10·6	
1,200 ft. a.s.l.	Temperature	84	83	79	71	61	56	55	59	65	71	77	82	70	29

	Jan.	Feb.	Mar.	Apr.	May	June	July	Aug.	Sept.	Oct.	Nov.	Dec.	Year	Annual range

Steppe climate

Alice Springs, N.T., Australia

| Precipitation | 1·7 | 1·3 | 1·1 | 0·4 | 0·6 | 0·5 | 0·2 | 0·3 | 0·3 | 0·7 | 1·2 | 1·5 | 9·9 | |
| Temperature | 84 | 82 | 77 | 68 | 60 | 54 | 53 | 58 | 65 | 73 | 79 | 81 | 68 | 31 |

1,901 ft. a.s.l.

Kabul, Afghanistan

| Precipitation | 1·2 | 1·4 | 3·7 | 4·0 | 0·8 | 0·2 | 0·1 | 0·1 | <0·1 | 0·6 | 0·8 | 0·4 | 13·3 | |
| Temperature | 27 | 31 | 44 | 55 | 65 | 72 | 76 | 75 | 68 | 58 | 48 | 37 | 54 | 49 |

5,955 ft. a.s.l.

Khartoum, Sudan

| Precipitation | <0·1 | <0·1 | <0·1 | <0·1 | 0·1 | 0·3 | 2·1 | 2·8 | 0·7 | 0·2 | <0·1 | 0·0 | 6·2 | |
| Temperature | 75 | 77 | 83 | 89 | 92 | 93 | 89 | 87 | 90 | 90 | 83 | 77 | 85 | 18 |

1,279 ft. a.s.l.

Saskatoon, Saskatchewan, Canada

| Precipitation | 0·9 | 0·5 | 0·7 | 0·7 | 1·4 | 2·6 | 2·4 | 1·9 | 1·5 | 0·9 | 0·5 | 0·6 | 14·6 | |
| Temperature | −1 | 3 | 17 | 38 | 51 | 55 | 65 | 62 | 51 | 39 | 22 | 7 | 35 | 66 |

1,690 ft. a.s.l.

Ulan Bator, Mongolia

| Precipitation | <0·1 | 0·1 | 0·1 | 0·2 | 0·4 | 1·1 | 3·0 | 2·0 | 0·9 | 0·2 | 0·2 | 0·1 | 8·2 | |
| Temperature | −14 | −6 | 9 | 26 | 42 | 57 | 61 | 58 | 46 | 32 | 9 | −8 | 26 | 75 |

4,347 ft. a.s.l.

Warm mid-latitude climate with a dry summer

Beirut, Lebanon

| Precipitation | 7·5 | 6·2 | 3·7 | 2·2 | 0·7 | 0·1 | <0·1 | <0·1 | 0·2 | 2·0 | 5·2 | 7·3 | 35·1 | |
| Temperature | 57 | 58 | 60 | 65 | 71 | 76 | 80 | 82 | 80 | 75 | 68 | 60 | 69 | 25 |

111 ft. a.s.l.

Cape Town, South Africa

| Precipitation | 0·6 | 0·3 | 0·7 | 1·9 | 3·1 | 3·3 | 3·5 | 2·6 | 1·7 | 1·2 | 0·7 | 0·4 | 20·0 | |
| Temperature | 69 | 70 | 67 | 63 | 58 | 56 | 56 | 55 | 57 | 61 | 65 | 66 | 62 | 15 |

56 ft. a.s.l.

Gibraltar

| Precipitation | 5·4 | 4·5 | 4·6 | 2·3 | 0·8 | 0·1 | <0·1 | 0·1 | 1·1 | 1·6 | 5·0 | 4·9 | 30·4 | |
| Temperature | 55 | 56 | 59 | 63 | 67 | 72 | 76 | 77 | 73 | 68 | 62 | 57 | 65 | 22 |

400 ft. a.s.l.

Perth, Australia

| Precipitation | 0·3 | 0·4 | 0·8 | 1·7 | 5·1 | 7·1 | 6·7 | 5·7 | 3·4 | 2·2 | 0·8 | 0·5 | 34·7 | |
| Temperature | 74 | 74 | 71 | 67 | 61 | 57 | 56 | 56 | 59 | 62 | 67 | 71 | 64 | 18 |

197 ft. a.s.l.

Rome, Italy

| Precipitation | 2·7 | 2·3 | 1·5 | 1·7 | 2·0 | 1·0 | 0·6 | 0·9 | 2·7 | 3·7 | 3·8 | 2·8 | 25·7 | |
| Temperature | 47 | 48 | 52 | 57 | 65 | 71 | 76 | 77 | 72 | 58 | 55 | 49 | 61 | 30 |

377 ft. a.s.l.

Santiago, Chile

| Precipitation | <0·1 | 0·1 | 0·2 | 0·5 | 2·5 | 3·3 | 3·0 | 2·2 | 1·2 | 0·6 | 0·3 | 0·2 | 14·1 | |
| Temperature | 69 | 68 | 65 | 59 | 53 | 48 | 49 | 51 | 54 | 58 | 63 | 67 | 59 | 21 |

1,706 ft. a.s.l.

Tunis, Tunisia

| Precipitation | 2·5 | 2·0 | 1·6 | 1·4 | 0·7 | 0·3 | 0·1 | 0·3 | 1·3 | 2·0 | 1·9 | 2·4 | 16·5 | |
| Temperature | 51 | 53 | 56 | 60 | 66 | 74 | 79 | 80 | 76 | 68 | 60 | 52 | 65 | 29 |

217 ft. a.s.l.

Warm mid-latitude climate with a dry winter

Addis Ababa, Ethiopia

| Precipitation | 0·5 | 1·5 | 2·6 | 3·4 | 3·4 | 5·4 | 11·0 | 11·8 | 7·5 | 0·8 | 0·6 | 0·2 | 48·7 | |
| Temperature | 59 | 62 | 63 | 64 | 64 | 61 | 59 | 59 | 60 | 60 | 58 | 57 | 60 | 7 |

8,038 ft. a.s.l.

Asuncion, Paraguay

| Precipitation | 5·5 | 5·1 | 4·3 | 5·2 | 4·6 | 2·7 | 2·2 | 1·5 | 3·1 | 5·5 | 5·9 | 6·2 | 51·8 | |
| Temperature | 83 | 82 | 76 | 74 | 68 | 63 | 64 | 68 | 71 | 74 | 78 | 82 | 74 | 20 |

456 ft. a.s.l.

Brisbane, Australia

| Precipitation | 6·4 | 6·3 | 5·7 | 3·7 | 2·8 | 2·6 | 2·2 | 1·9 | 1·9 | 2·5 | 3·7 | 5·0 | 44·7 | |
| Temperature | 77 | 76 | 74 | 70 | 65 | 60 | 59 | 60 | 65 | 70 | 73 | 76 | 69 | 18 |

137 ft. a.s.l.

Chungking, China

| Precipitation | 0·6 | 0·8 | 1·5 | 3·9 | 5·6 | 7·1 | 5·6 | 4·8 | 5·9 | 4·4 | 1·9 | 0·8 | 43·0 | |
| Temperature | 45 | 50 | 59 | 67 | 74 | 79 | 84 | 86 | 77 | 66 | 57 | 51 | 66 | 41 |

755 ft. a.s.l.

Mexico City, Mexico

| Precipitation | 0·5 | 0·2 | 0·4 | 0·8 | 2·1 | 4·7 | 6·7 | 6·0 | 5·1 | 2·0 | 0·7 | 0·3 | 29·4 | |
| Temperature | 54 | 56 | 61 | 64 | 66 | 65 | 63 | 64 | 64 | 60 | 59 | 55 | 60 | 12 |

7,575 ft. a.s.l.

New Delhi, India

| Precipitation | 0·9 | 0·7 | 0·5 | 0·3 | 0·5 | 2·9 | 7·1 | 6·8 | 4·6 | 0·4 | 0·1 | 0·4 | 25·2 | |
| Temperature | 57 | 61 | 72 | 82 | 92 | 93 | 89 | 86 | 84 | 79 | 68 | 60 | 77 | 36 |

714 ft. a.s.l.

Warm mid-latitude climate with rain at all seasons and a long summer

Buenos Aires, Argentina

| Precipitation | 3·1 | 2·8 | 4·3 | 3·5 | 3·0 | 2·4 | 2·2 | 2·4 | 3·1 | 3·4 | 3·3 | 3·9 | 37·4 | |
| Temperature | 74 | 73 | 70 | 63 | 56 | 49 | 50 | 52 | 55 | 60 | 66 | 72 | 61 | 25 |

89 ft. a.s.l.

Durban, South Africa

| Precipitation | 4·3 | 4·8 | 5·1 | 3·0 | 2·0 | 1·3 | 1·1 | 1·5 | 2·8 | 4·3 | 4·8 | 4·7 | 39·7 | |
| Temperature | 75 | 74 | 74 | 71 | 66 | 63 | 62 | 64 | 66 | 69 | 71 | 74 | 69 | 13 |

16 ft. a.s.l.

Shanghai, China

| Precipitation | 1·9 | 2·3 | 3·3 | 3·7 | 3·7 | 7·1 | 5·8 | 5·6 | 5·1 | 2·8 | 2·0 | 1·4 | 44·7 | |
| Temperature | 40 | 41 | 48 | 58 | 68 | 74 | 82 | 81 | 74 | 66 | 54 | 45 | 61 | 42 |

23 ft. a.s.l.

Sydney, Australia

| Precipitation | 3·5 | 4·0 | 5·0 | 5·3 | 5·0 | 4·6 | 4·6 | 3·0 | 2·9 | 2·8 | 2·9 | 2·9 | 46·5 | |
| Temperature | 71 | 72 | 69 | 65 | 59 | 54 | 53 | 56 | 59 | 63 | 67 | 70 | 63 | 19 |

138 ft. a.s.l.

Tokyo, Japan

| Precipitation | 1·9 | 2·9 | 4·2 | 5·3 | 5·8 | 6·5 | 5·6 | 6·0 | 9·2 | 8·2 | 3·8 | 2·2 | 61·6 | |
| Temperature | 38 | 40 | 45 | 54 | 63 | 70 | 76 | 79 | 72 | 62 | 52 | 42 | 58 | 41 |

19 ft. a.s.l.

	Jan.	Feb.	Mar.	Apr.	May	June	July	Aug.	Sept.	Oct.	Nov.	Dec.	Year	Annual range

Warm mid-latitude climate with rain at all seasons and a cool summer

Ankara, Turkey

	Jan.	Feb.	Mar.	Apr.	May	June	July	Aug.	Sept.	Oct.	Nov.	Dec.	Year	Annual range
Precipitation	1·3	1·2	1·3	1·3	1·9	1·0	0·5	0·4	0·7	0·9	1·2	1·9	13·6	
2,825 ft. a.s.l. Temperature	31	34	41	54	61	66	72	73	65	57	47	36	53	24

Bordeaux, France

Precipitation	2·7	2·8	2·9	2·6	2·5	2·3	2·0	1·9	2·2	3·0	3·8	3·9	32·6	
157 ft. a.s.l. Temperature	42	44	49	53	59	64	69	68	65	57	48	43	55	27

Christchurch, New Zealand

Precipitation	2·2	1·7	1·9	1·9	2·6	2·6	2·7	1·9	1·8	1·8	1·9	2·2	25·2	
0 ft. a.s.l. Temperature	62	61	58	54	48	44	42	44	48	53	57	60	52	20

Hanover, Germany

Precipitation	1·7	1·4	1·6	1·5	2·0	2·7	3·0	2·7	1·8	1·9	1·7	1·9	23·9	
561 ft. a.s.l. Temperature	33	35	40	47	56	61	64	63	58	49	41	36	49	31

London, U.K.

Precipitation	2·0	1·5	1·4	1·8	1·8	1·6	2·0	2·2	1·8	2·3	2·5	2·0	22·9	
149 ft. a.s.l. Temperature	39	40	44	48	54	60	64	63	59	51	44	41	51	25

Melbourne, Australia

Precipitation	1·9	1·8	2·2	2·3	2·1	2·1	1·9	1·9	2·3	2·6	2·3	2·3	25·7	
115 ft. a.s.l. Temperature	68	67	65	60	55	51	49	51	55	58	61	64	58	19

Paris, France

Precipitation	1·5	1·3	1·5	1·7	2·0	2·1	2·1	2·0	2·0	2·2	2·0	1·9	22·3	
164 ft. a.s.l. Temperature	37	39	44	51	57	63	66	65	60	52	44	38	51	29

Prince Rupert, B.C., Canada

Precipitation	9·8	7·6	8·4	6·7	5·3	4·1	4·8	5·1	7·7	12·2	12·3	11·3	95·3	
170 ft. a.s.l. Temperature	34	37	39	44	48	53	56	58	54	48	42	36	46	24

Shannon, Eire

Precipitation	3·8	3·0	2·0	2·2	2·4	2·1	3·1	3·0	·3·0	3·4	4·2	4·3	36·5	
8 ft. a.s.l. Temperature	37	42	45	48	53	58	60	61	58	51	46	43	51	24

Stanley, Falkland Is.

Precipitation	2·9	2·3	2·5	2·6	2·6	2·1	2·0	2·0	1·5	1·6	2·0	2·8	26·9	
6 ft. a.s.l. Temperature	49	48	47	43	39	36	35	36	39	41	45	47	42	14

Stavanger, Norway

Precipitation	4·1	2·9	2·4	2·4	1·9	2·5	3·2	4·6	4·7	5·1	4·6	4·3	42·7	
220 ft. a.s.l. Temperature	35	36	38	43	51	55	59	60	55	48	42	38	47	25

Valdivia, Chile

Precipitation	2·6	2·9	5·2	9·2	14·2	17·7	1F·5	12·9	8·2	5·0	4·9	4·1	102·4	
16 ft. a.s.l. Temperature	63	62	59	54	50	47	46	47	50	54	56	60	54	17

Cool mid-latitude climate with rain at all seasons and a severe winter

Arkhangelsk, U.S.S.R.

Precipitation	1·2	1·1	1·1	0·7	1·3	1·9	2·6	2·7	2·2	1·9	1·6	1·3	19·8	
22 ft. a.s.l. Temperature	5	6	16	29	40	51	58	55	45	33	20	9	31	53

Churchill, Manitoba, Canada

Precipitation	0·5	0·6	0·9	0·9	0·9	1·9	2·2	2·7	2·3	1·4	1·0	0·7	16·0	
43 ft. a.s.l. Temperature	−19	−16	−6	14	30	43	54	53	40	27	6	−11	18	73

Fort Nelson, B.C., Canada

Precipitation	0·8	1·1	0·6	0·5	1·4	2·5	2·4	1·3	1·3	1·1	1·4	0·9	15·3	
1,230 ft. a.s.l. Temperature	−6	2	18	38	50	58	62	60	50	36	7	−5	30	68

Moscow, U.S.S.R.

Precipitation	1·5	1·4	1·1	1·9	2·2	2·9	3·0	2·9	1·9	2·7	1·7	1·6	24·8	
505 ft. a.s.l. Temperature	15	16	25	39	55	57	66	62	52	40	27	18	40	51

Cool mid-latitude climate with a severe dry winter

Harbin, China

Precipitation	0·2	0·2	0·4	0·9	1·7	3·7	4·4	4·1	1·8	1·3	0·3	0·2	19·2	
526 ft. a.s.l. Temperature	−1	6	23	42	56	67	72	70	58	40	22	4	38	73

Irkutsk, U.S.S.R.

Precipitation	0·5	0·4	0·3	0·6	1·3	2·2	3·1	2·8	1·7	0·7	0·6	0·6	14·9	
1,532 ft. a.s.l. Temperature	−6	−1	14	31	45	56	60	58	46	31	11	−4	29	66

Polar climate

Angmagssalik, Greenland

Precipitation	2·9	2·4	2·6	2·1	2·0	1·8	1·5	2·1	3·3	4·7	3·0	2·7	31·1	
96 ft. a.s.l. Temperature	17	14	19	26	35	42	45	44	38	30	23	19	30	31

Cape Zhelanya, U.S.S.R.

Precipitation	0·2	0·1	0·1	0·1	0·2	0·5	1·0	1·3	0·7	0·3	<0·1	0·1	4·6	
26 ft. a.s.l. Temperature	1	3	−5	2	18	30	35	36	32	24	9	0	16	41

Resolute, N.W.T., Canada

Precipitation	<0·1	0·1	0·2	0·2	0·5	0·8	0·9	1·0	0·8	0·5	0·3	0·1	5·5	
56 ft. a.s.l. Temperature	−29	−31	−23	−8	16	34	40	37	23	5	−9	−21	3	71

Wrangel Island, U.S.S.R.

Precipitation	0·2	0·2	0·2	0·2	0·2	0·4	0·6	0·9	0·5	0·4	0·1	0·2	4·1	
10 ft. a.s.l. Temperature	−11	−14	−10	1	17	33	37	35	29	16	1	−6	11	51

Economic Section

Introduction

It is the aim of these statistics to present for various countries a picture of their character and position in the world in such a way that comparisons between countries may be made and a wide variety of basic questions answered.

The information includes both the sophisticated and the elementary. At all times it was thought more satisfactory to be specific about few items rather than general about many. Those chosen items are the most important within the general categories of area and demography, natural resources, industrial production and trade. The arrangement of columns corresponds to these categories. The first column is general and the rest refer to the four categories.

In case some of the terms are unfamiliar, explanations are given below in the appropriate part of the General Notes.

Table Arrangement

Country
1. Form of Government
2. Language(s).
3. Currency.
4. Average exchange rate, May 1983

Area and population
1. Area, sq. mi.
2. Population and density (Estimates June 1981)
3. Birth & Death rates per 000 Average annual rate of change (1970–77).
4. Urban population, 000's. Percentage of total population.
5. Capital population, 000's

Production
1. GDP (million $) for l.a. year & annual growth rate for l.a. 5 year period; GDP per capita for l.a. year & annual growth rate for l.a. 5 year period; Industrial origin of GDP, % distribution.
2. Agricultural production, 000 tons.
3. Livestock, 000 head
4. Fish caught, 000 tons 1980.
5. Roundwood 1980, million cu. ft.
6. Minerals mined, 000 tons. (Gas in teracalories).

Manufactures
1. Production/Consumption of all energy, million tons of coal equivalent, 1980. Electricity production, million kWh. (% Hydro-electricity, nuclear, geothermal).
2. Manufactures, 000 tons.
   (a) Agricultural, l.a. year.
   (b) Industrial, l.a. year.
   (Sawnwood, where given, is in 000 cu. ft.).
3. Communications: telephones & cars in use (000's), l.a. year Railways, passenger-mi. & ton-mi. (millions). Airlines, passenger-mi. & ton-mi. (millions). Sea cargo, loaded & unloaded 000 tons.

Trade
Export and Import totals, millions $.
List of major items.
Main trading partners.
Invisible trade balance. million $, 1981
Revenue from tourism, million $, 1978
Aid given (l.a. year) or received (average 1976–8) & source, miliion $

General Notes

As far as possible the figures refer to 1981. When they are for different years or periods the appropriate date is mentioned in the table description shown above. For the urban and capital populations the most recent estimates or figures from the latest censuses are given; these may be 5–10 years old.

Column One

The exchange rates for the U.S. $ are shown.

The C.F.A. franc is the unit of currency used throughout the African territories associated with France. (C.F.A. = Communauté Financière Africaine.)

Column Two

The area figure is for the total area of the country, including inland water bodies.

The birth and death rates are the latest figures that are available. The annual rate of change in the population is expressed as an average for the years 1975–79. The figure includes the net balance of births, deaths and migration.

Column Three

The GDP in line 1 is the Gross Domestic Product. In Communist countries the best similar measure is the NMP, the Net Material Product.

The Gross Domestic Product is a measure of a country's total production of goods and services. The figures are expressed in 'purchaser's values' which means the cost in the market of goods and services on delivery to the purchaser; that is the cost of materials, production, trade and transport charges. Imported goods and services are excluded.

The Net Material Product is not comparable to the GDP; it is the total net value of goods and production services, including taxes, in one year. Excluded are public administration, defence, personal and professional services. The conversion into dollars is based on the commercial import/export rate. The resulting figure should be used with great caution and treated as a general indicator.

The second figure is given for the GDP expressed per capita, and an annual average (over the latest available 5 year period) rate of increase is added after both. The differences between rates of increase are most illuminating.

The Industrial Origin of the GDP comes in the next line and is divided into three categories, Agriculture, Industry and Other. The percentage figures show which part of the GDP is contributed by each category.

Roundwood refers here to the forest output of wood whether for use as fuel, sawnwood or other products. The weight is without bark.

Column Four

The production and consumption of various types of energy is given as the coal equivalent. The equivalent is the conversion of the total calorific content of all energy sources into terms of the calorific value of 1 ton of coal. The production figure is based on the home production of coal, lignite, crude petroleum, natural gas and hydro- and nuclear electricity. Imported energy sources are not included, hence the apparent discrepancy between production and consumption of energy.

Synthetic fibres refer to non-cellulosic continuous and discontinuous fibres. They include textile, glass and spun fibres. The filaments are either natural polymers or synthetic polymers. The most familiar trade names for some of these are nylon, terylene, orlon, saran etc.

Petroleum products include particular products obtained from crude petroleum and shale oil. These products are liquefied petroleum gas, naphtha motor spirit, aviation gasoline, kerosene, white spirit, jet fuel, distillate fuel oils, residual fuel oils, lubricating oils, bitumen and paraffin wax.

Vehicles refer to passenger cars and commercial vehicles and heavy trucks, but not to agricultural machinery or tractors.

Rail traffic refers to all traffic within the borders of the country, but air traffic includes domestic and international flights.

Column Five

Exports are f.o.b. and imports c.i.f.

Invisible trade concerns the provision of services to people abroad and dividends from overseas assets. The invisible trade balance is the net balance of private earnings from, and expenditure on, this exchange of non-physical ('invisible') goods. The most important activities are international banking, insurance, shipping and tourism. Government activity is not accounted for, although this may significantly alter the overall balance.

The revenue from tourism is the total income, and not a net balance.

Aid is a general term for all planned assistance to the developing countries. Aid comes from governments ('official aid') and from private organisations ('private aid'). In 1978 net total aid from the developed market economies to the developing countries was $24 535 million and the private equivalent was $40 002 million. A second distinction can be made between bilateral and multilateral aid. Bilateral aid is arranged between two governments according to their own arrangements; this method accounts for over 85% of all aid. Multilateral aid is given through institutions such as the World Bank, the E.E.C., regional institutions like the Colombo plan and other U.N. institutions.

The principal sources used in the preparation of these tables were the Yearbooks of the U.N. (Statistical, Demographic, National Accounts and International Trade), the Monthly Bulletin of Statistics of the U.N. and the Yearbooks of the F.A.O.

Abbreviations

. . .: *data not available*	cu: *cubic*	c: *carats (thousand)*	sq: *square*	hydr: *hydro-electric*	T: *thousand*
t: *tons*	ft/ft²: *feet (square) (thousand)*	grt: *gross registered tons (thousand)*	kWh: *kilowatt-hour*	geo: *geothermal*	nucl: *nuclear*
lb.: *pounds*	gall: *gallon*	mi.: *mile*	l.a.: *latest available*	M: *million*	

Country	Area and Population	Production	Manufactures	Trade
AFGHANISTAN 1. Republic 2. Pashto, Persian 3. Afghani 4. $1=61.64	1. 250 000 sq. mi. 2. 16 363 000; 65 per sq. mi. 3. Br 45; DR 21; AI 2.5% 4. Urb. pop.: 2 134 (14.5%) 5. Kabul 588	1. GDP $2 669 (. . .); $190 (. . .) Agric. 53%, Indust. 20%, Others 27% 2. Wheat 3 000 Maize 798 Cottonseed 52 Cotton lint 28 3. Sheep 23 000 Cattle 3 980 Goats 3 000 5. Roundwood 282 6. Coal 170 Natural Gas 23 905 Salt 85	1. 2.72/0.97; 970 kWh (74 hydr.) 2a. Sugar 4 Sawnwood 14 120 Meat 242 b. Cement 126 Cotton woven 80 3. Telephones 31; Cars 37 Air: 180 pass.-mi.; 9 ton-mi.	Exports $729 Imports $924 Cotton Food Natural Gas Textiles Dried fruit Petroleum products Fresh fruit Machinery Exports to: U.S.S.R., U.K. and Pakistan Imports from: U.S.S.R., Japan and Iran Aid received (net): $73 from West, $164 from East
ALBANIA 1. Republic 2. Albanian 3. Lek 4. $1=6.27	1. 11 100 sq. mi. 2. 2 671 000; 233 per sq. mi. 3. BR 33; DR 8; AI 2.9% 4. Urb. pop.: 740 (34%) 5. Tirana 192	1. NMP . . . (9.2%); . . . (6.2%) 2. Wheat 510 Maize 250 Cottonseed 17 Cotton lint 9 3. Sheep 1 170 Goats 670 5. Roundwood 71 6. Lignite 1 020 Crude petroleum 2 800 Chrome 390 Copper 11.5 Nickel 8	1. 5.00/3.2; 2 450 kWh (78% hydr.) 2a. Sugar 40 Beer 3.2 T gall b. Cement 800 Copper 10 Cotton woven . . . Wool, woven . . .	Exports . . . Imports . . . Fuels and minerals Machinery Exports to: India, Czechoslovakia, Poland and E. Germany Imports from: India, Czechoslovakia, Poland and E. Germany
ALGERIA 1. Republic 2. Arabic, French 3. Algerian Dinar 4. $1=4.53	1. 919 595 sq. mi. 2. 19 590 000; 21 per sq. mi. 3. BR 47; DR 14; AI 3.4% 4. Urb. pop.: 8 467 (52%) 5. Algiers 1 503	1. GDP $17 931 (. . .); $1 001 (. . .) Agric. 8%, Indust. 39%, Others 53% 2. Wheat 1 400 Barley 750 Grapes 462 Oranges 300 3. Sheep 12 500 Goats 2 850 4. Fish 39 5. Crude petroleum 39 528 Natural Gas 158 474 Iron ore 1 927 Phosphates 997 Lead 2	1. 116.3/15.0; 6 216 kWh (5% hydr.) 2a. Wine 284 Meat 168 b. Cotton yarn 9 Cement 3 768 Petroleum products 4 610 3. Telephones 346; Cars 400 Rail: 901 pass.-mi.; 1 251 ton-mi. Air: 1 069 pass.-mi.; 6 ton-mi. Sea: 49 824 loaded; 13 500 unloaded	Exports $11 684 Imports $10 811 Crude petroleum Machinery Wine Iron and steel Natural Gas Food Exports to: France, W. Germany, U.S.A. and Italy Imports from: France, W. Germany, Italy and U.S.A. Aid received (net): $136 from West; $265 from East
ANGOLA 1. Republic 2. Portuguese 3. Kwanza 4. $1=30.31	1. 481 353 sq. mi. 2. 7 262 000; 16 per sq. mi. 3. BR 48; DR 23; AI 2.5% 4. Urb. pop.: 1 035 (15%) 5. Luanda 475	1. GDP $2 512 (. . .); $401 (. . .) 2. Coffee 60 Sugar cane 410 Maize 250 Palm oil 40 3. Cattle 3 209 Goats 935 4. Fish 78 5. Roundwood 282 6. Crude petroleum 7 277 Diamonds 400 c	1. 13.12/1.03; kWh (73 hydr.) 2a. Sugar 35 b. Cement 600 Cotton yarn 3 3. Telephones 28; Cars 75 Rail: 259 pass.; 3 391 ton-mi. Sea: 10 044 loaded; 3 984 unloaded	Exports $1 227 Imports $625 Coffee Machinery Diamonds Metals Crude petroleum Exports to: Portugal, Canada and Japan Imports from: Portugal, W. Germany, South Africa and U.S.A. Aid received (net): $41 from West; $76 from East
ARGENTINA 1. Republic 2. Spanish 3. Argentinian Peso 4. $1=47 213	1. 1 072 162 sq. mi. 2. 28 085 000; 26 per sq. mi. 3. BR 26; DR 9; AI 1.3% 4. Urb. pop.: 19 540 (83%) 5. Buenos Aires 8 436	1. GDP $35 227 (2.4%); $1 388 (1.0%) Agric. 12%, Indust. 36%, Others 52% 2. Wheat 7 900 Maize 13 500 Linseed 598 Citrus fruits 1 418 Wool 165 Grapes 2 700 3. Cattle 54 235 Sheep 30 000 4. Fish 384 5. Roundwood 353 6. Coal 434 Zinc 35 Crude petroleum 25 512 Lead 34 Natural gas 81 000 Silver 78 t	1. 51.2/49.2; 35 268 kWh (37% hydr., 6% nucl.) 2a. Meat 3 822 Wine 2 075 Sugar 1 624 b. Cotton yarn 74 Steel 2 196 Petroleum Vehicles: products 22 190 pass. 144; comm. 29 Cement 6 912 Iron 1 176 3. Telephones 2 404; Cars 3 000 Rail: 7 474 pass.-mi.; 6 789 ton-mi. Air: 4 307 pass.-mi.; 134 ton-mi. Sea: 30 156 loaded; 10 536 unloaded	Exports $8 016 Imports $10 544 Meat Machinery Cereals Iron and steel Wool Non-ferrous metals Exports to: Italy, Netherlands, Brazil and U.S.A. Imports from: U.S.A., W. Germany, Brazil and Japan Invisible trade balance: −$4 968 Revenue from tourism: $213 Aid received (net): $29 from West
AUSTRALIA 1. Commonwealth 2. English 3. Australian Dollar 4. $1=1.03	1. 2 967 893 sq. mi. 2. 14 927 000; 5 per sq. mi. 3. BR 16; DR 7; AI 1.2% 4. Urb. pop.: 11 650 (86%) 5. Canberra 227	1. GDP $92 290 (3.0%); $6 559 (1.5%) Agric. 5%, Indust. 25%, Others 70% 2. Wheat 16 400 Barley 3 430 Oats 1 530 Wool 700 Citrus fruits 476 Other fruits 2 000 3. Sheep 133 396 Cattle 25 177 4. Fish 136 5. Roundwood 565 6. Coal 100 872 Lead 393 Crude petroleum 18 623 Zinc 504 Manganese 1 033 Gold 18 Iron ore 60 480 Nickel 75 Bauxite 25 876 Copper 223 Silver 723t	1. 114.7/88.2; 103 200 kWh (18% hydr.) 2a. Meat 2 628 Sugar 3 450 Sawnwood 116 984 Butter & cheese 216 b. Wool yarn 20 Cement 5 736 Steel 7 956 Radios 38 Petroleum Vehicles: products 23 429 pass. 359; comm. 40 3. Telephones 62 663; Cars 5 799 Rail: . . .; 19 869 ton-mi. Air: 15 224 pass.-mi.; 378 ton-mi. Sea: 187 776 loaded; 26 220 unloaded	Exports $16 642 Imports $23 768 Wool Machinery Cereals Vehicles Metals Textiles Meat Crude petroleum Exports to: Japan, U.S.A. and N.Z. Imports from: U.S.A., Japan, U.K. and W. Germany Invisible trade balance: −$5 547 Revenue from tourism: $395 Aid given (net): $677
AUSTRIA 1. Federal Republic 2. German 3. Austrian Schilling 4. $1=16.91	1. 32 374 sq. mi. 2. 7 510 000; 233 per sq. mi. 3. BR 13; DR 12; AI 0.0% 4. Urb. pop.: 3 867 (52%) 5. Vienna 1 516	1. GDP $50 014 (3.8%); $6 660 (3.6%) Agric. 5%, Indust. 33%, Others 62% 2. Wheat 1 025 Barley 1 220 Potatoes 1 200 Rye 320 Pears 97 3. Pigs 3 706 Cattle 2 538 5. Roundwood 494 6. Lignite 3 076 Iron ore 945 Crude petroleum 1 344 Magnesite 1 003 Natural gas 12 781 Antimony 601 t Salt 542 Lead 6	1. 9.42/31.2; 42 900 kWh (69% hydr.) 2a. Wine 268 Sugar 490 Sawnwood 23 940 b. Cotton yarn 18 Wool yarn 9 Steel 5 076 Aluminum 142 Petroleum products 7 419 3. Telephones 2 443; Cars 2 247 Rail: 4 538 pass.-mi.; 6 409 ton-mi. Air: 768 pass.-mi.; 11 ton-mi.	Exports $15 845 Imports $21 048 Machinery Machinery Iron and steel Food Textiles Textiles Sawnwood Vehicles Chemical products Exports to: W. Germany, Italy, Switzerland and U.K. Imports from: W. Germany, Switzerland, Italy and France Invisible trade balance: +$3 168 Revenue from tourism: $4 509 Aid given (net): $226
BANGLADESH !. Republic 2. Bengali 3. Taka 4. $1=24.16	1. 55 598 sq. mi. 2. 89 655 000; 1 613 per sq. mi. 3. BR 47; DR 18; AI 2.4% 4. Urb. pop.: 8 759 (10%) 5. Dacca 1 730	1. GDP $9 376 (. . .); $112 (. . .) Agric. 52%, Indust. 7%, Others 41% 2. Rice 20 422 Bananas 625 Tea 40 Jute 868 3. Cattle 35 000 Goats 11 800 4. Fish 650 5. Roundwood 353	1. 1.78/4.06; 2 400 kWh (24% hydr.) 2a. Jute 868 Sugar 155 b. Cotton yarn 46 Cement 312 3. Telephones 101; Cars 22 Rail: 2 736 pass.-mi.; 459 ton-mi. Sea 972 loaded; 7 500 unloaded	Exports $791 Imports $2 594 Exports to: U.S.A., Pakistan, U.S.S.R. and U.K. Imports from: Japan, U.S.S.R. and U.K. Aid received (net): $681 from West; $50 from East

Country	Area and Population	Production	Manufactures	Trade
BELGIUM 1. Kingdom 2. French, Flemish, German 3. Belgian Franc 4. $1 = 46.95	1. 11 781 sq. mi. 2. 9 861 000; 836 per sq. mi. 3. BR 13; DR 11; AI 0.1% 4. Urb pop.: 9 286 (95%) 5. Brussels 1 042	1. GDP $88 807 (3.7%), $9 025 (3.4%) Agric. 2%, Indust. 30%, Others 68% 2. Wheat 943 Barley 823 Potatoes 1 426 Apples 131 3. Pigs 5 099 Cattle 3 116 4. Fish 46 5. Roundwood 95 6. Coal 6 590 Lead 102 Iron ore 13	1. 7.48/59.5; 53 640 kWh (2% hydr., 23% nucl.) 2a. Sugar 1 100 Sawnwood 24 180 b. Cotton yarn 41 Wool yarn 79 Steel 12 288 Copper 418 Coke oven coke 5 747 Plastics 1 943 Petroleum Vehicles: products 23 663 pass. 864; comm. 36 Iron 9 792 3. Telephones 3 271; Cars 3 159 Rail: 4 397 pass.-mi.; 4 665 ton-mi. Air: 3 227 pass.-mi.; 276 ton-mi. Sea: 42 804 loaded; 69 504 unloaded	Exports $55 641 Imports $62 123 (incl. Luxembourg) (incl. Luxembourg) Iron and steel Machinery Vehicles Vehicles Machinery Non-ferrous metals Non-ferrous metals Diamonds Textiles Petrol Trade is principally with: W. Germany, France, Netherlands and U.K. Invisible trade balance (incl. Luxembourg): + $1 596 Revenue from tourism: $1 300 Aid given (net): $2 605
BENIN 1. Republic 2. French 3. C.F.A. Franc 4. $1 = 339.82	1. 43 484 sq. mi. 2. 3 640 000; 83 per sq. mi. 3. BR 49; DR 19; AI 2.8% 4. Urb. pop.: 483 (14%) 5. Porto-Novo 104	1. GDP $503 (2.2%); $162 (−0.5%) Agric. 38%, Indust. 7%, Others 55% 2. Cassava 975 Palm oil 34 Maize 349 Cottonseed 15 Groundnuts 60 3. Goats 926 Cattle 771 4. Fish 25 5. Roundwood 106	1. −/0.12; 5 kWh 2a. Sawnwood 317 3. Telephones 10; Cars 14 Rail: 83 pass.-mi.; 94 ton-mi. Air: 86 pass.-mi.; 8 ton-mi. Sea: 73 loaded; 982 unloaded	Exports $26 Imports $267 Palm oil Manufactured products Oilseeds Machinery Cotton, Cocoa Exports to: France, Netherlands and U.K. Imports from: France, W. Germany Netherlands and U.K. Aid received (net): $53 from West
BOLIVIA 1. Republic 2. Spanish 3. Bolivian Peso 4. $1 = 44.0	1. 424 164 sq. mi. 2. 5 755 000; 13 per sq. mi. 3. BR 47; DR 18; AI 2.7% 4. Urb. pop.: 1 926 (42%) 5. La Paz 655, Sucre 63	1. GDP $2 334 (6.0%); $477 (3.2%) Agric. 17%, Indust. 25%, Others 58% 2. Maize 250 Barley 55 Potatoes 730 Citrus fruit 167 3. Sheep 8 750 Goats 3 050 5. Roundwood 141 6. Antimony 13 019 Crude petroleum 1 044 Tin 29 Silver 205 t Tungsten 3 997 t Zinc 47 Natural Gas 41 627 Copper 3 Lead 17	1. 5.04/1.68: 1 150 kWh (71% hydr.) 2a. Sugar 266 b. Cement 257 Tin 19 3. Telephones 49; Cars 35 Rail: 247 pass.-mi.; 368 ton-mi. Air: 596 pass.-mi.; 28 ton-mi.	Exports $909 Imports $825 Tin ore Cars Crude petroleum Flour Exports to: U.K., Argentina and U.S.A. Imports from: U.S.A., Japan, Argentina and Brazil Invisible trade balance: −$436 Aid received (net): $102 from West; $31 from East
BRAZIL 1. Federal Republic 2. Portuguese 3. New Cruzeiro 4. $1 = 248.82	1. 3 286 487 sq. mi. 2. 121 547 000; 36 per sq. mi. 3. BR 35; DR 9; AI 2.8% 4. Urb. pop.: 78 153 (64%) 5. Brasilia 1 306	1. GDP $175 807 (9.2%); $1 523 (6.2%) Agric. 9%, Indust. 26%, Others 65% 2. Maize 21 098 Rice 8 261 Cassava 25 050 Soya beans 15 000 Bananas 6 696 Oranges 11 399 Cottonseed 1 206 Tobacco 362 3. Cattle 93 000 Pigs 35 000 4. Fish 850 5. Roundwood 7 660 6. Coal 4 132 Crude petroleum 10 692 Iron ore 44 137 Natural Gas 28 700 Manganese 1 000 Asbestos 95 Gold 9 833 lb. Tin 8 Bauxite 6 714	1. 34.2/93.6; 137 388 kWh (92% hydr.) 2a. Meat 4 784 Sugar 8 500 Sawnwood 496 671 b. Cotton fabric 1 076 Iron 11 244 Steel 13 116 Aluminum 293 Cement 24 864 Radios 759 Petroleum Vehicles: products 45 987 pass. 662; comm. 97 3. Telephones 5 525; Cars 7 500 Rail: 7 421 pass.-mi.; 39 768 ton-mi. Sea: 123 996 loaded; 64 068 unloaded Air: 6 684 pass.-mi.; 328 ton-mi.	Exports $23 172 Imports $24 007 Coffee Machinery Cotton Crude petroleum Iron ore Cereals Machinery Non-ferrous metals Exports to: U.S.A., W. Germany, Netherlands, and Japan Imports from: U.S.A., W. Germany, Japan, Saudi Arabia and Iraq Invisible trade balance: −$13 128 Revenue for tourism: $108 Aid received (net): $100 from West. $600 from East
BULGARIA 1. Republic 2. Bulgar 3. Lev 4. $1 = 0.88	1. 42 823 sq. mi. 2. 8 890 000; 207 per sq. mi. 3. BR 16; DR 11; AI 0.7% 4. Urb. pop.: 5 503 (62%) 5. Sofia 1 032	1. NMP $15 965 (7.8%); $1 814 (7.2%) Agric. 18%, Indust. 51%, Others 31% 2. Wheat 4 429 Maize 2 477 Tobacco 133 Grapes 1 200 3. Sheep 10 433 Pigs 3 808 4. Fish 126 5. Roundwood 141 6. Coal 273 Crude petroleum 243 Lignite 28 980 Zinc 65 Iron ore 578 Lead 96	1. 16.9/50.3; 36 960 kWh (11% hydr., 17% nucl.) 2a. Meat 650 Sawnwood 51 749 Wine 510 Sugar 150 b. Cotton yarn 85 Iron 1 512 Steel 2 484 Cement 5 448 Petroleum products 11 436 3. Telephone 1 032; Cars 480 Rail: 4 322 pass.-mi.; 11 207 ton-mi. Air: 344 pass.-mi.; 4.4 ton-mi. Sea: 2 878 loaded; 19 094 unloaded	Exports $10 372 Imports $9 650 Cigarettes Machinery Alcoholic drinks Ferrous metals Clothing Petroleum products The principal trade is with U.S.S.R. Then: E. Germany Revenue from tourism: $230 Aid given (net): $15
BURMA 1. Republic 2. Burmese 3. Kyat 4. $1 = 8.13	1. 261 790 sq. mi. 2. 36 166 000; 137 per sq. mi. 3. BR 39; DR 14; AI 2.2% 4. Urb. pop.: 5 137 (24%) 5. Rangoon 2 276	1. GDP $3 563 (3.0%); $113 (0.8%) Agric. 46%, Indust. 11%, Others 48% 2. Rice 14 636 Groundnuts 476 Tobacco 55 Jute 35 3. Cattle 8 600 Buffaloes 1 950 4. Fish 585 5. Roundwood 918 6. Crude petroleum 1 460 Zinc 3 Lead 4 Silver 25 t	1. 2.96/2.22; 1 080 kWh (61% hydr.) 2a. Sugar 44 Sawnwood 14 649 b. Steel 4 Cotton yarn 13 3. Telephones 34; Cars 35 Rail: 2 019 pass.-mi.; 350 ton-mi. Air: 111 pass.-mi.; 1 ton-mi. Sea: 732 loaded; 408 unloaded	Exports $386 Imports $332 Sawnwood Machinery Rice Textiles Exports to: Japan, Indonesia and Vietnam Imports from: Japan, China, W. Germany, U.K. and Singapore Invisible trade balance: −$68 Aid received (net): $148 from West
CAMBODIA 1. Republic 2. French, Cambodian 3. Riel 4. $1 = 1 200	1. 69 898 sq. mi. 2. 8 718 000; 124 per sq. mi. 3. BR 46.0; DR 17.0; AI 2.9 4. Urb. pop.: 867 (10%) 5. Phnom Penh 2 000	1. GDP $881 (. . .) $125 (. . .) Agric. 41%, Indust. 17%, Others 42% 2. Rice 1 160 Maize 98 Rubber 10 Bananas 67 3. Cattle 956 Pigs 223 4. Fish 21 5. Roundwood 177	1. −/0.13; 150 kWh 2a. Sawnwood 1 517 3. Telephones 71; Cars 25 Rail: 33 pass.-mi.; 6.2 ton-mi. Air: 26 pass.-mi.; 1 ton-mi. Sea: 50 loaded; 583 unloaded	Exports $10 Imports $101 Rubber Machinery Rice Textiles Cattle Iron and Steel Exports to: Vietnam, Hong Kong and Singapore Imports from: France, Japan, China, Thailand and U.S.A.
CAMEROON 1. Republic 2. French, English 3. C.F.A. Franc 4. $1 = 339.82	1. 183 569 sq. mi. 2. 8 650 000; 46 per sq. mi. 3. BR 42; DR 19; AI 2.8% 4. Urb. pop.: 2 392 (29%) 5. Yaoundé 314	1. GDP $3 309 (3.7%); $427 (1.8%) Agric. 31%, Indust. 12%, Others 57% 2. Coffee 105 Groundnuts 120 Cocoa 110 Palm oil 80 3. Goats 2 340 Cattle 3 200 4. Fish 69 5. Roundwood 318	1. 0.16/0.64; 1 346 kWh (95% hydr.) 2a. Sawnwood 17 438 b. Aluminum 65 3. Telephones 22; Cars 55 Rail: 171 pass.-mi.; 439 ton-mi. Air: 194 pass.-mi.; 4 ton-mi. Sea: 924 loaded; 2 616 unloaded	Exports $1 384 Imports $1 602 Cocoa Manufactured goods Coffe Exports to: France, Netherlands and W. Germany Imports from: France, W. Germany and U.S.A. Aid received (net): $160 from West

Country	Area and Population	Production	Manufactures	Trade
CANADA 1. Commonwealth 2. English, French 3. Canadian Dollar 4. $1=1.23	1. 3 560 247 sq. mi. 2. 24 231 000; 8 per sq. mi. 3. BR 16; DR 7; AI 1.1% 4. Urb. pop.: 17 367 (76%) 5. Ottawa 718	1. GDP $177 947 (4.4%); 7 572 (3.1) Agric. 4%, Indust. 25%, Others 71% 2. Wheat 24 519 — Barley 13 384 Oats 3 570 — Maize 6 214 3. Cattle 12 468 — Pigs 9 585 4. Fish 1 305 5. Roundwood 5 683 6. Iron ore 24 367 — Crude petroleum 64 275 Coal 25 568 — Natural Gas 655 656 Copper 718 — Zinc 1 096 Nickel 130 — Asbestos 1 542 Gold 49 635 — Salt 6 222 Lead 332	1. 280.0/245.2; 378 648 kWh (69% hydr., 10% nucl.) 2a. Sawnwood 1 480 093 — Wood pulp 19 295 Paper 13 789 — Sugar 125 b. Iron 9 744 — Steel 15 024 Aluminum 1 183 — Copper 465 Radios 819 — Vehicles: Petroleum — pass. 803; comm. 520 products 71 140 — Cement 9 492 3. Telephones 15283; Cars 10 367 Rail: 1 795 pass.-mi.; 141 662 ton-mi. Air: 19 501 pass.-mi.; 481 ton-mi. Sea: 134 640 loaded; 67 416 unloaded	Exports $69 635 — Imports $65 622 Vehicles — Machinery Machinery — Vehicles Paper and cardboard — Iron and steel Non-ferrous metals — Textiles Wood pulp — Crude petroleum Sawnwood — Fruit and vegetables Crude petroleum Wheat Trade is principally with: U.S.A., U.K. and Japan Invisible trade balance: −$12 383 Revenue from tourism: $1 722 Aid given (net): $2 001
CENTRAL AFRICAN REPUBLIC 1. Republic 2. French 3. Franc C.F.A. 4. $1=364	1. 240 535 sq. mi. 2. 2 349 000; 10 per sq. mi. 3. BR 44; DR 23; AI 2.2% 4. Urb. pop.: 392 (27%) 5. Bangui 302	1. GDP $391 (1.3%); $218 (...) Agric. 31%, Indust. 18%, Others 51% 2. Maize 40 — Cassava 1 021 Bananas 144 — Coffee 17 Groundnuts 125 — Cottonseed 14 3. Goats 873 — Cattle 1 000 5. Roundwood 106 6. Diamonds 301 c	1. 0.01/0.07; 64 kWh (94% hydr.) 2a. Meat 41 — Sawnwood 2 576 3. Telephones 5; Cars 14 Air: 95 pass.-mi.; 9 ton-mi.	Exports $116 — Imports $81 Diamonds — Machinery Cotton, Coffee — Vehicles Exports to: France, Belgium and Lux. Imports from: France, W. Germany and Japan Aid received (net): $43 from West
CHAD 1. Republic 2. French 3. C.F.A. Franc 4. $1=364	1. 495 755 sq. mi. 2. 4 547 000; 10 per sq. mi. 3. BR 44; DR 24; AI 2.3% 4. Urb. pop.: 792 (18%) 5. N'Djamena 242	1. GDP $665 (3.3%); $165 (1.3%) Agric. 41%, Indust. 13%, Others 46% 2. Millet 580 — Groundnuts 110 Cottonseed 45 — Cotton 26 3. Cattle 3 800 — Goats 2 300 4. Fish 115 5. Roundwood 247	1. −/0.10; 64 kWh 2a. Meat 53 3. Telephones 7; Cars 10 Air: 100 pass.-mi.; 8 ton-mi.	Exports $59 — Imports $118 Cotton — Petroleum products Meat — Machinery Exports to: France, Nigeria and Cameroon Imports from: France, Nigeria and Netherlands Aid received (net): $86 from West, $3 from East
CHILE 1. Republic 2. Spanish 3. Chilean Peso 4. $1=73	1. 292 258 sq. mi. 2. 11 294 000; 39 per sq. mi. 3. BR 32; DR 8; AI 1.6% 4. Urb. pop.: 9 006 (81%) 5. Santiago 3 853	1. GDP $4 319 (0.8%); $421 (−1.0%) Agric. 10%, Indust. 27%, Others 63% 2. Wheat 686 — Grapes 980 Wool 22 — Tobacco 6 3. Sheep 6 800 — Cattle 3 745 4. Fish 2 817 5. Roundwood 388 6. Coal 1 115 — Iron ore 5 952 Crude petroleum 819 — Copper 1 081 Natural Gas 14 108 — Moybdenum 13	1. 6.31/10.94; 11 880 kWh (65% hydr.) 2a. Meat 381 — Sawnwood 77 059 Sugar 250 — Wood pulp 3 056 Wine 585 b. Iron 684 — Steel 624 Cotton yarn 23 — Copper 954 Fertilizers 139 — Cement 1 584 3. Telephones 467; Cars 300 Rail: 1 006 pass.-mi.; 1 073 ton-mi. Air: 1 378 pass.-mi.; 64 ton-mi. Sea: 9 947 loaded; 6 188 unloaded	Exports $3 952 — Imports $6 379 Copper — Machinery Iron ore — Food Fishmeal — Manufactured products Saltpetre — Chemical products Exports to: Japan, W. Germany, U.K., Argentina, U.S.A. and Brazil Invisible trade balance: −$2 316 Aid received (net): $49 from West
CHINA 1. Republic 2. Chinese and others 3. Yuan 4. $1=1.99	1. 3 691 521 sq. mi. 2. 1 007 755 000; 272 per sq. mi. 3. BR 21; DR 7; AI 1.4% 4. Urb. pop.: 188 169 (24%) 5. Peking 9 231	1. GDP ... (56%); ... (3.2%) Agric. 48%, Indust. 42%, Others 10% (1956) 2. Rice 146 292 — Wheat 58 493 Soya beans 13 050 — Groundnuts 3 513 Citrus fruits 1 100 — Tobacco 872 Tea 354 — Cotton lint 2 968 Cottonseed 6 000 3. Pigs 310 251 — Sheep 105 200 4. Fish 4 240 5. Roundwood 7 907 6. Coal 618 000 — Manganese 300 Crude petroleum 101 220 — Tungsten 11 Iron ore 32 500 — Tin 17 Salt 19 530 — Lead 160 Bauxite 1 750 — Copper 150	1. 614.2/565.5; 306 000 kWh 2a. Meat 23 112 — Sawnwood 747 124 Sugar 4 031 b. Iron 34 000 — Steel 35 600 Aluminum 350 — Cement 80 000 Cotton yarn 1 500 3. Telephones ...; Cars 50 Rail: ...; 354 715 ton-mi. Air: ...;... Sea: 18 200 loaded; 17 000 unloaded	Exports $22 280 — Imports $18 625 Agricultural prods. — Grain Textiles — Cotton products Minerals — Machinery Crude petroleum — Primary materials — Petrol Exports to: Hong Kong, U.S.S.R., Japan and Singapore Imports from: Japan, Australia, U.S.S.R. and Canada Aid given (net): $163
COLOMBIA 1. Republic 2. Spanish 3. Columbian Peso 4. $1=74.54	1. 439 737 sq. mi. 2. 28 776 000; 65 per sq. mi. 3. BR 32; DR 8; AI 2.8% 4. Urb. pop.: 13 410 (60%) 5. Bogotá 2 855	1. GDP $20 591 (5.7%); $803 (2.8%) Agric. 30%, Indust. 23%, Others 47% 2. Maize 880 — Rice 1 799 Cassava 2 150 — Bananas 3 555 Coffee 808 — Cottonseed 160 Tobacco 49 — Cotton lint 87 3. Cattle 24 251 — Pigs 2 245 4. Fish 65 5. Roundwood 1 483 6. Coal 4 000 — Silver 3 t Natural gas 20 900 — Gold 18 724 lb. Crude petroleum 6 754 — Iron ore 454	1. 20.5/21.2; 18 756 kWh (67% hydr.) 2a. Meat 834 — Paper 330 Sugar 1 185 — Sawnwood 31 169 b. Iron 492 — Steel 264 Petroleum products 7 148 — Cement 4 464 3. Telephones 1 410; Cars 454 Rail: 193 pass.-mi.; 551 ton-mi. Air: 2 615 pass.-mi.; 130 ton-mi. Sea: 8 040 loaded; 7 272 unloaded	Exports $2 956 — Imports $5 199 Coffee — Machinery Crude petroleum — Vehicles Cotton — Iron and Steel Bananas — Organic chemicals Sugar and Honey Exports to: U.S.A., W. Germany and Venezuela Imports from: U.S.A., W. Germany and Venezuela Invisible trade balance: −$397 Revenue from tourism: $295 Aid received (net): $66 from West, $290 from East
CONGO 1. Popular Republic 2. French 3. C.F.A. Franc 4. $1=364	1. 132 047 sq. mi. 2. 1 578 000; 13 per sq. mi. 3. BR 45; DR 19; AI 2.6% 4. Urb. pop.: 278 (29%) 5. Brazzaville 290	1. GDP $693 (...); $514 (...) 2. Cassava 530 — Palm oil 9 3. Goats 123 — Cattle 71 4. Fish 21 5. Roundwood 71 6. Gold 8 lb. — Diamonds ... Crude petroleum 3 096	1. 4.23/0.34; 120 kWh (50% hydr.) 2a. Sugar 22 — Sawnwood 2 259 3. Telephones 13; Cars 20 Rail: 171 pass.-mi.; 290 ton-mi. Air: 95 pass.-mi.; 9 ton-mi. Sea: 2 796 loaded; 708 unloaded	Exports $510 — Imports $291 Timber — Manufactured products Exports to: France, Italy, U.S.A., Brazil and Spain Imports from: France, U.S.A., Gabon and W. Germany Aid received (net): $61 from West
CUBA 1. Republic 2. Spanish 3. Cuban Peso 4. $1=0.86	1. 44 218 sq. mi. 2. 9 766 000; 220 per sq. mi. 3. BR 15; DR 6; AI 1.2% 4. Urb. pop.: 5 169 (60%) 5. Havana 1 861	1. NMP $8 943 (5.4%); $943 (4.8%) 2. Rice 518 — Cassava 328 Coffee 24 — Oranges 360 Sugar Cane 67 000 — Tobacco 34 3. Cattle 5 900 — Pigs 1 950 4. Fish 186 5. Roundwood 35 6. Chrome 10 — Nickel 37 Copper 3 — Crude petroleum 360	1. 0.42/13.1; 10 332 kWh (1.1% hydr.) 2a. Meat 284 — Sawnwood 3 953 Sugar 7 359 b. Petroleum products 6 212 Cotton, woven 156 Mm^2 — Cement 3 288 3. Telephones 321; Cars 80 Rail: 1 140 pass.-mi.; 1 631 ton-mi. Air: 506 pass.-mi.; 5 ton-mi. Sea: 2 316 loaded; 2 400 unloaded	Exports $3 967 — Imports $4 509 Sugar — Machinery Minerals — Cereals Tobacco — Fertilizers — Petroleum products Exports to: U.S.S.R., Japan and Spain Imports from: U.S.S.R. and Japan

Country	Area and Population	Production	Manufactures	Trade
CYPRUS 1. Republic 2. Greek, Turkish and English 2. Cypriot Pound 4. $1=1.95	1. 3 572 sq. mi. 2. 637 000; 179 per sq. mi. 3. BR 20; DR 9; AI 0.1% 4. Urb. pop.: 270 (42%) 5. Nicosia 147	1. GDP $1 364 (0.3%); $2 200 (0.1%) Agric. 11%, Indust. 19%, Others 70% 2. Barley 101 Potatoes 216 Grapes 213 Oranges 123 3. Sheep 515 Goats 360 6. Copper 5 Asbestos 35 Chrome 7	1. —/1.20; 1 056 kWh 2a. Wine 55 Sawnwood 2 118 b. Cement 1 032 3. Telephones 92; Cars 86 Air: 529 pass.-mi.; 11 ton-mi. Sea: 1 572 loaded; 2 376 unloaded	Exports $562 Imports $1 166 Vegetables Machinery Citrus fruits Textiles Copper Vehicles Exports to: U.K., Saudi Arabia and Lebanon Imports from: U.K., W. Germany, Italy, Iraq and Greece Revenue from Tourism: $273
CZECHOSLOVAKIA 1. Socialist Republic 2. Czech, Slovak 3. Koruna 4. $1=6.15	1. 49 370 sq. mi. 2. 15 314 000; 311 per sq. mi. 3. BR 16; DR 12; AI 0.7% 4. Urb. pop.: 9 795 (67%) 5. Prague 1 193	1. NMP $68 559 (5.1%); $4 561 (4.3%) Agric. 9%, Indust. 60%, Others 31% 2. Barley 3 500 Wheat 5 000 Oats 400 Potatoes 3 850 Apples 170 Tomatoes 82 3. Pigs 7 894 Cattle 5 002 5. Roundwood 635 6. Coal 29 150 Silver 36 t Lignite 94 879 Crude petroleum 84 Iron ore 558 Antimony 480 t Natural gas 5 268	1. 66.7/99.3; 74 064 kWh (6% hydr., 6% nucl.) 2a. Meat 1 444 Sawnwood 173 075 Sugar 870 Butter & cheese 308 Beer 527 T gall. b. Iron 10 080 Steel 15 264 Aluminum 32 Plastics 913 Wool yarn 63 Petroleum Cotton yarn 137 products 15 107 3. Telephones 2 981; Cars 1 950 Rail: 11 207 pass.-mi.; 44 875 ton-mi. Air: 909 pass.-mi.; 8 ton-mi.	Exports $14 887 Imports $14 650 Machinery Machinery Manufactured goods Petroleum Iron and steel Non-ferrous metals Vehicles Iron and steel Main trade is with: U.S.S.R., E. Germany, Poland and Hungary Aid given (net): $273
DENMARK 1. Kingdom 2. Danish 3. Danish Krone 4. $1=8.61	1. 16 629 sq. mi. 2. 5 122 000; 308 per sq. mi. 3. BR 10; DR 11; AI 0.3% 4. Urb. pop.: 4 191 (83%) 5. Copenhagen 1 382	1. GDP $50 334 (2.8%); $9 869 (2.4%) Agric. 6%, Indust. 21%, Others 73% 2. Barley 6 010 Oats 165 Wheat 792 Potatoes 880 Apples 80 Rape seed 310 3. Pigs 9 856 Cattle 2 933 4. Fish 2 027 5. Roundwood 71 6. Crude petroleum 756	1. 0.44/26.8; 18 204 kWh 2a. Pork 995 Beef 245 Butter & cheese 327 Sugar 522 b. Cotton yarn 1.9 Steel 800 Petroleum products 5 649 Ships (grt.) 364 3. Telephones 2 907; Cars 1 428 Rail: 2 079 pass.-mi.; 789 ton-mi. Air: 1 795 pass.-mi.; 81 ton-mi. Sea: 7 068 loaded; 31 836 unloaded	Exports $15 390 Imports $17 578 Machinery Machinery Pork Manufactured products Other meat Iron and steel Fish Textiles Exports to: Sweden, U.K. and W. Germany Imports from: W. Germany, Sweden and U.K. Invisible trade balance: −$787 Revenue from tourism: $1 120 Aid given (net): $566
ECUADOR 1. Republic 2. Spanish 3. Sucre 4. $1=81.40	1. 109 483 sq. mi. 2. 8 644 000; 78 per sq. mi. 3. BR 42; DR 10; AI 3.6% 4. Urb. pop.: 3 485 (43%) 5. Quito 808	1. GDP $4 056 (10.5%); $574 (6.8%) Agric. 20%, Indust. 29%, Others 51% 2. Maize 246 Rice 402 Bananas/Plantains 3 050 Oranges 530 Cocoa 96 Coffee 88 3. Cattle 2 366 Sheep 2 313 4. Fish 671 5. Roundwood 212 6. Crude petroleum 10 182 Gold 203 lb.	1. 15.4/4.99; 3 155 kWh (30% hydr.) 2a. Meat 222 Sawnwood 31 946 Sugar 359 b. Petroleum products 4 207 3. Telephones 240; Cars 65 Rail: 40 pass.-mi.; 21 ton-mi. Air: 357 pass.-mi.; 5 ton-mi. Sea: 9 372 loaded; 3 828 unloaded	Exports $2 481 Imports $2 253 Bananas Machinery Coffee Vehicles Cocoa Chemical products Exports to: U.S.A., Panama, Colombia and Chile Imports from: U.S.A., W. Germany and Japan Invisible trade blance: −$1 325 Aid received (net): $58 from West
EGYPT 1. Republic 2. Arabic 3. Egyptian Pound 4. $1=1.21	1. 386 661 sq. mi. 2. 43 465 000; 111 per sq. mi. 3. BR 38; DR 10; AI 2.6% 4. Urb. pop.: 18 097 5. Cairo 5 084	1. GDP $11 450 (3.9%); $308 (1.6%) Agric. 24%, Indust. 23%, Others 53% 2. Maize 3 308 Wheat 1 938 Rice 2 236 Tomatoes 2 632 Oranges 895 Dates 428 Cotton lint 500 Cottonseed 800 3. Cattle 2 040 Buffaloes 2 379 4. Fish 137 6. Iron ore 888 Salt 755 Crude petroleum 31 800 Phosphates 639	1. 48.2/20.8; 18 520 kWh (52% hydr.) 2a. Meat 449 Sugar 679 b. Cotton yarn 245 Iron 720 Wool yarn 10 Steel 612 Fertilizers 357 Cement 3 432 Petroleum products 13 630 3. Telephones 473; Cars 350 Rail: 5 775 pass.-mi.; 1 499 ton-mi. Air: 2 026 pass.-mi.; 25 ton-mi. Sea: 8 820 loaded; 11 496 unloaded	Exports $3 233 Imports $8 839 Cotton, Rice Machinery Cotton lint Manufactured products Fruit and vegetables Wheat, Vehicles Exports to: U.S.S.R., Italy and Netherlands Imports from: U.S.A., France, Italy, U.K. and W. Germany Invisible trade balance: −$206 Revenue from tourism: $701 Aid received (net): $1 421 from West, $36 from East
ETHIOPIA 1. Republic 2. Amharic 3. Ethiopian Birr 4. $1=2.04	1. 471 778 sq. mi. 2. 32 158 000; 67 per sq. mi. 3. BR 50; DR 25; AI 2.6% 4. Urb. pop.: 4 225 (14%) 5. Addis-Ababa 1 277	1. GDP $2 495 (. . .); $91 (. . .) Agric. 46%, Indust. 11%, Others 43% 2. Barley 750 Millet 190 Coffee 198 Maize 1 100 3. Cattle 26 100 Sheep 23 350 4. Fish 27 5. Roundwood 847 6. Gold 686 lb. Salt 80	1. 0.05/0.89; 675 kWh (71% hydr.) 2a. Sugar 165 Sawnwood 3 530 b. Cotton yarn 8 Cement 103 3. Telephones 80; Cars 40 Rail: 96 pass.-mi.; 129 ton-mi. Air: 469 pass.-mi.; 14 ton-mi. Sea: 378 loaded; 1 250 unloaded	Exports $418 Imports $567 Coffee Machinery Hides Manufactured products Exports to: U.S.A., Djibouti and Saudi Arabia Imports from: Japan, W. Germany, Kuwait, Italy and Saudi Arabia Aid received (net): $128 from West, $46 from East
FINLAND 1. Republic 2. Finnish, Swedish 3. Markka 4. $1=5.41	1. 130 119 sq. mi. 2. 4 801 000; 36 per sq. mi. 3. BR 13; DR 9; AI 0.3% 4. Urb. pop.: 2 846 (60%) 5. Helsinki 483	1. GDP $28 926 (2.9%); $6 090 (2.5%) Agric. 8%, Indust. 28%, Others 64% 2. Wheat 235 Barley 1 080 Oats 1 008 Potatoes 478 3. Cattle 1 766 Pigs 1 375 4. Fish 14 5. Roundwood 1 659 6. Iron ore 570 Chrome 187 Titanium 120 Copper 38 Zinc 53 Gold 880 kg	1. 2.62/24.6; 39 264 kWh (26% hydr., 17% nucl.) 2a. Meat 328 Butter & cheese 148 Sawnwood 362 707 Wood pulp 7 440 b. Paper 5 923 Newsprint 1 556 Iron 1 968 Steel 2 424 Cotton yarn 8 Ships (grt) 303 Petroleum products 9 327 3. Telephones 2 127; Cars 1 170 Rail: 2 034 pass.-mi.; 5 208 ton-mi. Air: 1 550 pass.-mi.; 34 ton-mi. Sea: 18 420 loaded; 30 180 unloaded	Exports $14 021 Imports $14 202 Paper and cardboard Machinery Wood pulp Crude petroleum Sawnwood Petroleum products Machinery Iron and steel Ships and boats Textiles Clothing Vehicles Exports to: U.K., Sweden, U.S.S.R. and W. Germany imports from: Sweden, W. Germany, U.S.S.R. and U.K. Invisible trade balance: −$904 Aid given (net): $127
FRANCE 1. Republic 2. French 3. French Franc 4. $1=7.27	1. 211 208 sq. mi. 2. 53 963 000; 254 per sq. mi. 3. BR 13; DR 9; AI 0.4% 4. Urb. pop.: 38 388 (73%) 5. Paris 9 863	1. GDP $421 359 (3.7%); $7 908 (3.1%) Agric. 5%, Indust. 30%, Others 65% 2. Wheat 22 782 Barley 10 180 Oats 1 754 Maize 9 100 Potatoes 6 400 Sugarbeet 31 800 Apples 1 840 Grapes 8 800 Tomatoes 800 Pears 435 Tobacco 46 Wool 22 Rape seed 1 023 3. Cattle 25 553 Pigs 11 629 Sheep 11 629 Goats 1 241 Horses 317 4. Fish 765 5. Roundwood 1 059 6. Coal 18 588 Iron ore 14 240 Crude petroleum 1 680 Lead 19 Natural Gas 66 528 Zinc 37 Salt 6 255 Potash 1 969 Bauxite 1 828	1. 50.2/233.8; 260 760 kWh (27% hydr., 24% nucl.) 2a. Meat 5 506 Butter & cheese 1 810 Wine 5 791 Beer 481 T gall. Sugar 5 600 Sawnwood 356 988 b. Iron 17 916 Steel 21 264 Aluminum 605 Cement 28 224 Plastics 2 842 Paper 5 121 Synthetic Petroleum fibres 202 products 68 442 Cotton yarn 240 Wool yarn 138 Ships (grt) 252 Radios 3 019 Vehicles: pass. 2 953; comm. 473 3. Telephones 19 870; Cars 19 150 Rail: 34 666 pass.-mi.; 39 987 ton-mi. Air: 22 668 pass.-mi.; 1 390 ton-mi. Sea: 59 400 loaded; 196 200 unloaded	Export $100 497 Imports $102 448 Machinery Machinery Vehicles Petrol Iron and Steel Iron and Steel Textiles Non-ferrous metals Wheat Vehicles Organic chemical Textile fibres products Meat Non-ferrous metals Fruits Petroleum products Petrol Wine Exports to: W. Germany, Belgium-Luxembourg, Italy and U.K. Imports from: W. Germany, Italy, Belgium-Luxembourg and U.S.A. Invisible trade balance: +$5 915 Revenue from tourism: $4 794 Aid given (net): $6 910

Country	Area and Population	Production	Manufactures	Trade

FRENCH GUIANA

1. French colony
2. French
3. Franc
4. $1=7.27

1. 35 135 sq. mi.
2. 69 000; 3 per sq. mi.
3. BR 25; DR 8; AI 3.4%
4. Urb. pop.: 29 (67%)
5. Cayenne 33

2. Cassava 8   Bananas 3
3. Pigs 7   Cattle 6
6. Gold 100 kg

1. −/0.17; 108 kWh
2a. Sugar . . .   Sawnwood 670
3. Telephones 13; Cars 17
Sea: 36 loaded; 228 unloaded

Exports $25   Imports $255
Timber   Machinery
Exports to: France, U.S.A. and Japan
Imports from: France, Trinidad and Tobago
Aid received (net): $76 from West

GABON

1. Republic
2. French, Bantu
3. C.F.A. Franc
4. $1=364

1. 103 347 sq. mi.
2. 555 000; 5 per sq. mi.
3. BR 31; DR 21; AI 1.1%
4. Urb. pop.: 160 (32%)
5. Libreville 186

1. GDP $2 012 (. . .); $3 725 (. . .)
Agric. 6%, Indust. 41%, Others 53%
2. Cassava 100   Bananas 71
Cocoa 4
3. Goats 90   Sheep 100
4. Fish 27
5. Roundwood 71
6. Crude petroleum 7 656   Gold 110 lb.
Manganese 1 175   Uranium 1 000 t

1. 13.4/1.02; 450 kWh (78% hydr.)
2a. Sawnwood 3 812   Beer 11.2 T gall.
b. Petroleum products 1 174
3. Telephones 7; Cars 22
Air: 80 pass.-mi.; 5 ton-mi.
Sea: 12 555 loaded; 1 382 unloaded

Exports $1 477   Imports $532
Petrol   Manufactured products
Sawnwood   Machinery
Manganese ores   Vehicles
Export to: France, U.S.A. and Argentina
Imports from: France, U.S.A. and Japan
Aid received (net): $35 from West

GERMANY (East)

1. Republic
2. German
3. Ostmark
4. $1=2.43

1. 41 766 sq. mi.
2. 16 736 000; 401 per sq. mi.
3. BR 14; DR 12; AI −0.2%
4. Urb. pop.: 12 749
5. Berlin (East) 1 146

1. NMP $72 190 (4.8%); $4 034 (5.1%)
Agric. 10%, Indust. 62%, Others 28%
2. Barley 3 800   Rye 1 800
Wheat 3 000   Potatoes 10 378
Apples 522   Rapeseed 330
3. Pigs 12 871   Cattle 5 722
Sheep 2 038
4. Fish 235
5. Roundwood 318
6. Lignite 267 000   Natural gas 28 122
Iron ore 19   Potash 3 422
Salt 2 741

1. 83.8/124.0; 98 796 kWh (11% nucl., 1.4% hydr.)
2a. Meat 1 919   Butter 281
Sugar 740   Beer 528 T gall.
Sawnwood 86 696
b. Cotton yarn 136   Wool yarn 36
Iron 2 436   Steel 7 464
Ships (grt) 354   Petroleum
Vehicles: products 19 000
pass. 180; comm. 41   Radios 1 103
Telephones 2 956; Cars 2 533
Rail: 14 300 pass.-mi.; 34 666 ton-mi.
Air: . . .; . . .
Sea: 3 504 loaded; 11 940 unloaded

Exports $19 398   Imports 20 888
Machinery   Machinery
Vehicles   Crude petroleum
Consumer goods   Iron ore
Coal
Fuels
The principal trade is with: U.S.S.R., Czechoslovakia,
W. Germany and Poland
Aid given (net): $57

GERMANY (West)

1. Federal Republic
2. German
3. Deutschmark
4. $1=2.43

1. 95 886 sq. mi.
(including W. Berlin)
2. 61 666 000; 642 per sq. mi.
3. BR 10; DR 12; AI 0.2%
4. Urb. pop.: 47 534 (77%)
5. Bonn 286

1. GDP $568 815 (2.4%); $9 278 (2.4%)
Agric. 3%, Indust. 42%, Others 55%
2. Barley 8 687   Wheat 8 314
Rye 1 729   Potatoes 7 800
Apples 750   Grapes 1 000
3. Pigs 22 553   Cattle 15 069
4. Fish 297
5. Roundwood 1 165
6. Coal 88 464   Zinc 110
Lignite 130 620   Natural gas 161 320
Iron ore 515   Crude petroleum 4 464
Salt 15 346   Potash 2 701

1. 160.0/352.5; 368 772 kWh (5% hydr., 11% nucl.)
2a. Meat 4 701   Butter & cheese 1 363
Sugar 3 600   Sawnwood 374 321
Wine 750   Beer 1 933 T gall.
b. Cotton yarn 146   Wool yarn 60
Iron 31 872   Steel 42 144
Aluminum 1 126   Radios 4 611
Vehicles: Petroleum
pass. 3 590; comm. 312   products 65 867
Ships (grt) 669   Synthetic fibres 789
3. Telephones 24 443; Cars 23 236
Rail: 25 806 pass.-mi.; 38 526 ton-mi.
Air: 13 435 pass.-mi.; 983 ton-mi.
Sea: 40 332 loaded; 96 576 unloaded

Exports $176 043   Imports $163 934
Machinery   Machinery
Vehicles   Non-ferrous metals
Iron and steel   Crude petroleum
Textiles   Iron and steel
Organic chemicals   Textiles
   Food
Exports to: France, Netherlands, U.S.A.
Belgium-Luxembourg and Italy
Imports from: Netherlands, France, Belgium-
Luxembourg, Italy and U.S.A.
Invisible trade balance: −$119 400
Revenue from tourism: $4 806
Aid given (net): $5 934

GHANA

1. Republic
2. English
3. Cedi
4. $1=2.75

1. 92 100 sq. mi.
2. 12 063 000; 132 per sq. mi.
3. BR 48; DR 17; AI 3.5%
4. Urb. pop.: 3 017 (31%)
5. Accra 738

1. GDP $4 277 (−0.4%); $433 (−3.2%)
Agric. 51%, Indust. 15%, Others 34%
2. Cassava 1 850   Cocoa 230
Groundnuts 90   Millet 73
3. Sheep 1 700   Goats 2 100
4. Fish 224
5. Roundwood 318
6. Bauxite 252   Manganese 129
Gold 23 369 lb.   Diamonds 1 950 c

1. 1.16/1.32; 4 764 kWh (99% hydr.)
2a. Sawnwood 13 449   Beer 22 T gall.
3. Telephones 65; Cars 64
Rail: 267 pass.-mi.; 189 ton-mi.
Air: 201 pass.-mi.; 2 ton-mi.
Sea: 2 433 loaded; 3 344 unloaded

Exports $1 096   Imports $993
Cocoa   Manufactured goods
Aluminium   Machinery
Exports to: U.K., U.S.A., W. Germany, U.S.S.R. and
Netherlands
Imports from: U.S.A., U.K., W. Germany and
Nigeria
Invisible trade balance: −$307
Aid received (net): $84 from West

GREECE

1. Republic
2. Greek
3. Drachma
4. $1=83.85

1. 50 944 sq. mi.
2. 9 707 000; 192 per sq. mi.
3. BR 15; DR 9; AI 1.1%
4. Urb. pop.: 5 686 (65%)
5. Athens 3 027

1. GDP $30 040 (4.7%); $3 209 (3.9%)
Agric. 15%, Indust. 19%, Others 66%
2. Wheat 2 750   Potatoes 986
Olives 1 350   Tomatoes 1 669
Grapes 1 603   Tobacco 122
3. Sheep 7 920   Goats 4 650
4. Fish 106
5. Roundwood 71
6. Iron ore 547   Bauxite 3 185
Lignite 27 720   Chrome 16
Magnesite 1 065

1. 4.80/20.5; 20 652 kWh (17% hydr.)
2a. Olive oil 280   Wine 540
Butter & cheese 182
b. Cotton yarn 110   Steel 1 000
Cement 13 260   Aluminum 148
Petroleum products 14 563
3. Telephones 2 487; Cars 880
Rail: 938 pass.-mi.; 432 ton-mi.
Air: 3 226 pass.-mi.; 47 ton-mi.
Sea: 21 420 loaded; 33 336 unloaded

Exports $4 292   Imports $8 677
Tobacco   Machinery
Iron and steel   Ships and boats
Raisins   Vehicles
Aluminium   Iron and steel
Cotton   Crude petroleum
Exports to: W. Germany, Italy, France and
Saudi Arabia
Imports from: W. Germany, Italy and Japan
Invisible trade balance: +$2 261
Revenue from tourism: $1 326

GUINEA

1. Republic
2. French
3. Syli
4. $1=22.76

1. 94 926 sq. mi.
2. 5 147 000; 54 per sq. mi.
3. BR 46; DR 21; AI 2.6%
4. Urb. pop.: 437 (11%)
6. Conakry 526

1. GDP $687 (. . .); $155 (. . .)
2. Cassava 600   Rice 330
Coffee 15   Bananas 327
Sweet potatoes 73   Palm oil 42
3. Sheep 437   Goats 405
5. Roundwood 106
6. Iron ore 1 000   Bauxite 12 838
Diamonds 80 c

1. 0.01/0.42; 500 kWh
2a. Sawnwood 3 177
3. Telephones 10; Cars 10
Air: 16 pass.-mi.; 1 ton-mi.
Sea: 1 300 loaded; 550 unloaded

Exports $70   Imports $100
Bauxite and aluminium   Machinery
Iron ore   Manufactured goods
Coffee   Foods
Main trade is with: Portugal and Sweden
Aid received (net): $26 from West, $1 from East

HAITI

1. Republic
2. French, Creole
3. Gourde
4. $1=5.00

1. 10 714 sq. mi.
2. 5 104 000; 477 per sq. mi.
3. BR 42; DR 16; AI 1.8%
4. Urb. pop.: 1 378 (28%)
5. Port-au-Prince 863

1. GDP $1 298 (4.3%); $269 (2.6%)
Agric. 41%, Indust. 15%, Others 44%
2. Bananas 510   Sisal 10
Cocoa 3   Coffee 33
3. Pigs 2 000   Goats 995
5. Roundwood 177
6. Bauxite 539

1. 0.03/0.27; 312 kWh (70% hydr.)
2a. Meat 58   Sugar 52
3. Telephones 18; Cars 25
Sea: 850 loaded; 646 unloaded

Exports $148   Imports $266
Coffee   Foods
Bauxite   Textiles
Sugar   Machinery
Sisal   Mineral oils
Exports to: U.S.A., France and Belgium-Luxembourg
Imports from: U.S.A., Neth., Antilles, Japan and Canada
Aid received (net): $83 from West

Country	Area and Population	Production	Manufactures	Trade
HONG KONG 1. British colony 2. English, Chinese 3. Hong Kong Dollar 4. $1=6.75	1. 399 sq. mi. 2. 5 154 000; 12 911 per sq. mi. 3. BR 17; DR 5; AI 1.9% 4. Urb. pop.: 4 017 (96%) 5. Victoria 849	1. GDP $7 036 (8.0%); $1 699 (5.9%) Agric. 15%, Indust. 24%, Others 75% 2. Rice 1 3. Pigs 600 Cattle 10 4. Fish 195 6. Iron ore . . .	1. —/7.27; 11 796 kWh 2b. Cotton yarn 128 Wool yarn 6 Woven natural silk 5.4 M ft.[2] 3. Telephones 1 251; Cars 160 Rail: 238 pass.-mi.; 37 ton-mi. Sea: 9 168 loaded; 26 400 unloaded	Exports $21 761 Imports $24 816 Clothing Textiles Textiles Machines Toys and games Diamonds Radios Cotton Exports to: U.S.A., U.K., Japan and W. Germany Imports from: Japan, China, U.S.A., U.K., and Singapore Revenue from tourism: $786
HUNGARY 1. Republic 2. Hungarian 3. Forint 4. $1=41.62	1. 35 919 sq. mi. 2. 10 711 000; 298 per sq. mi. 3. BR 13; DR 14; AI 0.4% 4. Urb. pop.: 5 679 (53%) 5. Budapest 2 060	1. NMP $56 310 (6.1%); $5 288 (5.6%) Agric. 15%, Indust. 47%, Others 38% 2. Maize 6 500 Wheat 4 800 Potatoes 1 600 Tobacco 15 Apples 1 100 Grapes 850 3. Pigs 8 330 Sheep 3 090 4. Fish 34 5. Roundwood 212 6. Coal 3 065 Bauxite 2 914 Lignite 22 878 Manganese 126 Natural gas 54 320 Crude petroleum 2 028	1. 21.3/41.2; 27 204 kWh (0.6% hydr.) 2a. Sugar 587 Sawnwood 40 665 Wine 550 b. Iron 2 220 Steel 3 648 Aluminum 74 Cotton yarn 59 Wool yarn 13 Petroleum products 8 193 3. Telephones 1 143; Cars 839 Rail: 7 683 pass.-mi.; 14 814 ton-mi. Air: 653 pass.-km; 5.5 t-km	Exports $8 712 Imports $9 128 Machinery Machinery Vehicles Vehicles Fruit and vegetables Iron and steel Iron and steel Crude petroleum Medicinal products Petroleum products Chemical products Main trade is with: U.S.S.R., W. Germany, E. Germany and Czechoslovakia Invisible trade balance: $98 Revenue from tourism: $415 Aid given (net): $52
ICELAND 1. Republic 2. Icelandic 3. Icelandic Krona 4. $1=21.00	1. 39 769 sq. mi. 2. 231 000; 5 per sq. mi. 3. BR 19; DR 7; AI 1.1% 4. Urb. pop.: 194 (87%) 5. Reykjavik 83	1. GDP $1 846 (4.9%); $8 392 (3.7%) 2. Potatoes 9 3. Sheep 797 4. Fish 1 515 Whaling 536	1. 0.36/1.09; 3 228 kWh (97% hydr., 1.4% geo.) 2a. Meat 25 Salt fish 42 b. Aluminum 75 3. Telephones 100; Cars 80 Air: 707 pass.-mi.; 13 ton-mi. Sea: 496 loaded; 1 279 unloaded	Exports $859 Imports $980 Fish, frozen and Machinery fresh Petroleum Fish, salted and products smoked Textiles Fish meal Iron and Steel Aluminum Paper and cardboard Cod liver oil Exports to U.S.A., U.K. and W. Germany Imports from: W. Germany, U.K., U.S.S.R., Denmark and Sweden
INDIA 1. Federal Republic 2. Hindi, English 3. Indian Rupee 4. $1=9.98	1. 1 261 816 sq. mi. 2. 683 810 000; 541 per sq. mi. 3. BR 33; DR 14; AI 2.8% 4. Urb. pop.: 145 261 (22%) 5. Delhi 3 647	1. GDP $93 870 (3.1%); $150 (1.0%) Agric. 36%, Indust. 17%, Others 47% 2. Wheat 36 460 Millet 10 500 Rice 82 000 Tea 565 Coffee 131 Tobacco 456 Rubber 150 Jute 1 450 Cotton lint 1 360 Cottonseed 2 720 3. Cattle 182 000 Goats 72 144 4. Fish 2 423 5. Roundwood 7 554 6. Coal 123 012 Manganese 600 Iron ore 25 953 Chrome 266 Bauxite 1 898 Crude petroleum 14 916 Copper 26 Lead 15 Zinc 31	1. 100.9/126.4; 72 116 kWh (40% hydr., 3% nucl.) 2a. Sugar 5 587 Butter & cheese 2 085 Sawnwood 128 456 b. Iron 9 756 Steel 10 632 Aluminum 213 Zinc 59 Cement 20 772 Cotton yarn 1 058 Radios 1 919 Petroleum products 20 982 3. Telephones 2 096; Cars 870 Rail: 132 287 pass.-mi.; 96 876 ton-mi. Air: 7 511 pass.-mi.; 278 ton-mi. Sea: 36 153 loaded; 28 989 unloaded	Exports $7 693 Imports $14 855 Jute products Machinery Tea Wheat Iron ore Petrol Iron and steel Cotton Cotton goods Iron and steel Exports to: U.S.A., Japan, U.S.S.R. and U.K. Imports from: U.S.A., U.K., Japan and W. Germany Revenue from tourism: $403 Invisible trade balance: $227 Aid received (net): $1 129 from West, $340 from East
INDONESIA 1. Republic 2. Bahasa Indonesia 3. Rupiah 4. $1=971	1. 735 271 sq. mi. 2. 150 520 000; 205 per sq. mi. 3. BR 34; DR 16; AI 2.4% 4. Urb. pop.: 23 246 (18%) 5. Jakarta 4 576	1. GDP $44 171 (7.7%); $304 (5.1%) Agric. 31%, Indust. 28%, Others 41% 2. Cassava 13 726 Groundnuts 855 Rice 32 776 Copra 1 254 Coffee 265 Tea 95 Tobacco 85 Rubber 937 3. Cattle 6 435 Goats 7 925 4. Fish 1 853 5. Roundwood 5 542 6. Coal 348 Tin 35 Bauxite 1 204 Natural gas 175 857 Nickel 29 Crude petroleum 78 852	1. 134.2/33.3; 7 140 kWh (36% hydr.) 2a. Meat 452 Sawnwood 120 267 Sugar 1 449 b. Cement 5 256 Tin 33 Petroleum products 23 140 3. Telephones 347; Cars 577 Rail: 2 772 pass.-mi.; 625 ton-mi. Air: 3 666 pass.-mi.; 78 ton-mi. Sea: 86 160 loaded; 18 696 unloaded	Exports $22 259 Imports $13 271 Crude petroleum Machinery Petroleum products Textiles Rubber Iron and steel Coffee Vehicles Tin Rice Spices Exports to: Japan, Singapore, U.S.A., Trinidad and Tobago Imports from: U.S.A., W. Germany, Japan, and Singapore Aid received (net): $584 from West
IRAN 1. Islamic Republic 2. Persian 3. Rial 4. $1=84.90	1. 636 296 sq. mi. 2. 39 320 000; 62 per sq. mi. 3. BR 43; DR 12; AI 2.8% 4. Urb. pop.: 17 342 (49%) 5. Teheran 4 496	1. GDP $52 835 (10.2%); $1 600 (7.4%) Agric. 9%, Indust. 48%, Others 43% 2. Wheat 5 800 Cottonseed 175 Rice 1 400 Cotton lint 87 Dates 301 Tea 22 Raisins 50 Tobacco 24 3. Sheep 4 196 Goats 13 709 5. Roundwood 212 6. Natural gas 155 980 Crude petroleum 65 988 Chrome 165 Zinc 35 Lead 20 Salt 700	1. 138.2/46.7; 17 150 kWh (18% hydr.) 2a. Sugar 400 b. Cotton yarn 65 Wool yarn 38 Cement 6 500 Petroleum products 27 750 3. Telephones 829; Cars 1 400 Rail: 1 851 pass.-mi.; 2 535 ton-mi. Air: 998 pass.-mi.; 25 ton-mi. Sea: 220 320 loaded; 14 532 unloaded	Exports $14 279 Imports $12 247 Crude petroleum Machinery Petroleum products Iron and steel Carpets Vehicles Textiles Exports to: U.S.S.R., W. Germany, U.S.A., Italy and Saudi Arabia Imports from: W. Germany, U.S.A., Japan, and U.K. Invisible trade balance: −$3 442 Revenue from tourism: $224 Aid received (net): $42 from West, $664 from East
IRAQ 1. Republic 2. Arabic 3. Iraq Dinar 4. $1=0,31	1. 167 925 sq. mi. 2. 13 527 000; 80 per sq. mi. 3. BR 47; DR 13; AI 3.5% 4. Urb. pop.: 7 646 (64%) 5. Bagdad 2 969	1. GDP $18 591 (. . .); $1 561 (. . .) Agric. 7%, Indust. 63%, Others 30% 2. Barley 600 Rice 250 Wheat 1 100 Dates 405 Cottonseed 11 Cotton lint 5 3. Sheep 11 650 6. Natural gas 14 912 Crude petroleum 44 892	1. 195.5/7.9; 8 000 kWh (9% hydr.) 2b. Cotton yarn 1 Petroleum products 7 790 3. Telephones 320; Cars 180 Rail: 494 pass.-mi.; 1 399 ton-mi. Air: 797 pass.-mi.; 31 ton-mi. Sea: 35 960 loaded; 4 103 unloaded	Exports $10 529 Imports $4 213 Crude petroleum Manufactured goods Dates Machinery, Food Exports to: India, China and Kuwait Imports from: U.K., W. Germany and Japan Revenue from tourism: $84 Aid received (net): $42 from West, $45 from East
IRELAND 1. Republic 2. Irish, English 3. Irish pound 4. $1=1.30	1. 27 136 sq. mi. 2. 3 440 000; 124 per sq. mi. 3. BR 19; DR 7; AI 1.5% 4. Urb. pop.: 1 556 (52%) 5. Dublin 525	1. GDP $8 647 (3.4%); $2 711 (2.3%) Agric. 14%, Indust. 30%, Others 56% 2. Barley 1 425 Wheat 320 Potatoes 1 050 Apples 10 Wool 9 Tomatoes 27 3. Cattle 6 696 Sheep 1 082 4. Fish 149 6. Lead 29 Zinc 117 Coal 36	1. 1.15/10.2; 10 908 kWh (11% hydr.) 2a. Meat 556 Sawnwood 5 047 Butter & cheese 166 b. Wool yarn 12 Petroleum Cotton yarn 4 products 1 951 3. Telephones 554; Cars 682 Rail: 625 pass.-mi.; 402 ton-mi. Air: 1 356 pass.-mi.; 53 ton-mi. Sea: 8 466 loaded; 16 379 unloaded	Exports $7 787 Imports $10 603 Cattle Machinery Beef Textiles Dairy products Vehicles Non-ferrous metals Iron and steel Machinery Crude petroleum Main trade is with U.K. Exports to: U.S.A., France, W. Germany, Netherlands and Belgium-Lux. Imports from: U.S.A., W. Germany, France, Italy and Japan Invisible trade balance: −$394 Revenue from tourism: $421

Country	Area and Population	Production	Manufactures	Trade

ISRAEL

1. Republic
2. Hebrew, Arabic
3. Shekel
4. $1=40.60

1. 7 992 sq. mi.
2. 3 954 000; 495 per sq. mi.
3. BR 24; DR 7; AI 2.3%
4. Urb. pop.: 3 327 (88%)
5. Jerusalem 398

1. GDP $12 295 (5.0%); $3 332 (2.1%)
   Agric. 6%, Indust. 27%, Others 67%
2. Wheat 215   Cottonseed 152
   Oranges 920   Cotton lint 92
   Grapefruits 536   Tomatoes 268
3. Cattle 301   Sheep 230
4. Fish 26
6. Phosphates 2 216   Potash 790
   Salt 100   Crude petroleum 12

1. 0.22/9.16; 12 432 kWh
2a. Meat 225   Butter & cheese 60
    Wine 33
b. Cotton yarn 14   Wool yarn 7
   Cement 2 304
3. Telephones 993; Cars 403
   Rail: 137 pass.-mi.; 394 ton-mi.
   Air: 2 988 pass.-mi.; 187 ton-mi.
   Sea: 6 024 loaded; 6 012 unloaded

Exports $5 416   Imports $7 777
Diamonds   Machinery
Fruit   Diamonds
Clothing   Iron and steel
Exports to: U.S.A., W. Germany, U.K.
and Hong Kong
Imports from: U.S.A., W. Germany, U.K.,
Netherlands and Switzerland
Invisible trade balance: −$688
Revenue from tourism: $596
Aid received (net): $780 from West

ITALY

1. Republic
2. Italian
3. Italian Lira
4. $1=1 445

1. 116 304 sq. mi.
2. 57 197 000; 492 per sq. mi.
3. BR 11; DR 10; AI 0.5%
4. Urb. pop.: 28 442 (52%)
5. Rome 2 898

1. GDP $173 655 (2.9); $3 076 (2.1%)
   Agric. 8%, Indust. 35%, Others 57%
2. Wheat 8 921   Maize 7 250
   Tomatoes 4 457   Grapes 10 888
   Olives 2 800   Tobacco 123
   Oranges 1 751   Apples 1 750
   Pears 1 160   Citrus 2 695
3. Cattle 8 734   Sheep 9 277
4. Fish 445
5. Roundwood 282
6. Lignite 1 950
   Natural gas 127 837 Zinc 44
   Crude petroleum 1 464 Asbestos 144
   Iron ore 53   Bauxite 18
   Lead 21

1. 26.4/189.3; 185 016 kWh (26% hydr.,
   1.2% nucl., 1.4% geo.)
2a. Meat 3 554   Butter & cheese 670
    Sugar 2 170   Wine 7 650
    Olive 680   Sawnwood 95 910
b. Iron 12 372   Steel 24 768
   Aluminum 524   Woven silk 16
   Cotton yarn 161   Wool yarn 146
   Radios 1 540   Ships (grt) 233
   Petroleum   Vehicles:
   products 78 770   pass. 1 256; comm. 175
   Synthetic Fibres 595
3. Telephones 17 088; Cars 17 750
   Rail: 24 517 pass.-mi.; 10 328 ton-mi.
   Air: 7 496 pass.-mi.; 305 ton-mi.
   Sea: 35 004 loaded; 225 432 unloaded

Exports $75 215   Imports $91 022
Machinery   Machinery
Vehicles   Petroleum
Textiles   Non-ferrous metals
Clothing   Iron and steel
Petroleum products   Textile fibres
Shoes   Cereals
Iron and steel   Vehicles
Fruit   Meat
Exports to: France, W. Germany, U.S.A. and U.K.
Imports from: W. Germany, France and U.S.A.
Invisible trade balance: +$1 518
Revenue from tourism: $4 762
Aid given (net): $3 025

IVORY COAST

1. Republic
2. French
3. C.F.A. Franc
4. $1=364

1. 124 504 sq. mi.
2. 8 298 000; 16 per sq. mi.
3. BR 48; DR 18; AI 4.2%
4. Urb. pop.: 2 174 (32%)
5. Abidjan 850

1. GDP $6 896 (8.6%); $906 (4.2%)
   Agric. 25%, Indust. 13%, Others 62%
2. Rice 550   Coffee 350
   Cassava 780   Cocoa 430
3. Sheep 1 200   Goats 1 250
4. Fish 77
5. Roundwood 388
6. Diamonds 48 c

1. 0.32/1.29; 1 836 kWh (67% hydr.)
2a. Sawnwood 23 651
   Petroleum products 968
3. Telephones 67; Cars 100
   Rail: 752 pass.-mi.; 372 ton-mi.
   Air: 104 pass.-mi.; 8 ton-mi.
   Sea: 4 356 loaded; 5 976 unloaded

Exports $2 515   Imports $2 493
Cocoa   Machinery
Coffee   Vehicles
Exports to: France, U.S.A., Italy and Netherlands
Imports from: France, W. Germany and U.S.A.
Invisible trade balance: −$1 285
Aid received (net): $115 from West

JAMAICA

1. Commonwealth
2. English
3. Jamaica Dollar
4. $1=1.78

1. 4 232 sq. mi.
2. 2 220 000; 526 per sq. mi.
3. BR 27; DR 6; AI 1.4%
4. Urb. pop.: 690 (37%)
5. Kingston 573

1. GDP $2 833 (5.3%); $1 349 (3.8%)
   Agric. 9%, Indust. 32%, Others 59%
2. Bananas 118   Copra 7
   Oranges 33   Sugar cane 2 453
3. Goats 380   Cattle 300
4. Fish 10
6. Bauxite 11 606

1. 0.02/2.76; 2 328 kWh (5% hydr.)
2a. Meat 51   Sugar 203
b. Petroleum products 865
3. Telephones 111; Cars 60
   Rail: 51 pass.-mi.; 115 ton-mi.
   Air: 640 pass.-mi.; 6 ton-mi.
   Sea: 5 424 loaded; 2 628 unloaded

Exports $974   Imports $1 473
Bauxite and aluminium Machinery
Sugar   Textiles
Bananas   Petroleum
Exports to: U.S.A., U.K., Canada and Norway
Imports from: U.S.A., Venezuela and U.K.
Revenue from tourism: $148
Aid received (net): $60 from West

JAPAN

1. Constitutional Monarchy
2. Japanese
3. Japanese Yen
4. $1=238

1. 143 660 sq. mi. (incl. Ryukyu Arch.)
2. 117 645 000; 818 per sq. mi.
3. BR 13; DR 6; AI 0.9%
4. Urb. pop.: 84 967 (76%)
5. Tokyo 11 695

1. GDP $821 875 (5.0%); $7 153 (3.7%)
   Agric. 5%, Indust. 32%, Others 63%
2. Rice 12 824   Potatoes 3 435
   Tomatoes 1 000   Apples 847
   Pears 522   Oranges/mandarines
   Tea 103   3 216
   Tobacco 143
3. Pigs 10 065   Cattle 4 385
4. Fish 110
5. Roundwood 1 200
6. Coal 17 688   Lead 47
   Natural gas 22 944 Manganese 29
   Crude petroleum 396 Zinc 242
   Iron ore 239   Gold 8 333 lb.
   Copper 52

1. 42.8/408.0; 521 868 kWh (15% hydr., 14% nucl.)
2a. Meat 3 022   Sugar 770
    Beer 973 T gall.   Sawnwood 1 311 818
    Wood pulp 9 975
b. Iron 81 684   Steel 101 676
   Aluminum 1 585   Plastics 5 911
   Cotton yarn 486   Wool yarn 113
   Woven silk 1 668 M ft.[2] Newsprint 2 566
   Synthetic Fibres 1 369 Petroleum
   Vehicles: products 156 461
   pass. 6 978   Radios 18 781
   comm. 4 206   T.V. Receivers 13 927
   Ships (grt) 7 288
3. Telephones 48 646; Cars 23 659
   Rail: 196 360 pass.-mi.; 24 412 ton-mi.
   Air: 20 463 pass.-mi.; 1 265 ton-mi.
   Sea: 83 532 loaded; 612 720 unloaded

Exports $152 016   Imports $143 287
Iron and steel   Crude petroleum
Electrical machinery   Machinery
Textiles   Sawnwood
Other machinery   Iron ore
Vehicles   Textile fibres
Ships and boats   Non-ferrous metals
                       Cereals
Exports to: U.S.A., S. Korea and
W. Germany
Imports from: U.S.A., Australia, Saudi Arabia
and Indonesia
Invisible trade balance: −$13 570
Revenue from tourism: $470
Aid given (net): $8 593

KENYA

1. Republic
2. Bantu, English
3. Kenyan Shilling
4. $1=12.96

1. 224 960 sq. mi.
2. 17 148 000; 75 per sq. mi.
3. BR 54; DR 14; AI 3.6%
4. Urb. pop.: 1 080 (10%)
5. Nairobi 835

1. GDP $2 892 (4.6%); $216 (1.1%)
   Agric. 34%, Indust. 13%, Others 53%
2. Maize 2 250   Cottonseed 28
   Coffee 87   Tea 91
3. Cattle 11 500   Goats 4 530
4. Fish 48
5. Roundwood 953
6. Salt 20   Soda ash 153

1. 0.13/1.78; 1 488 kWh (71% hydr.)
2a. Sugar 440
b. Cement 1 272   Petroleum products 2 027
3. Telephones 156; Cars 198
   Rail: 5 384 pass.-mi.; 2 197 ton-mi.
   (inc. Tanzania and Uganda)
   Air: 503 pass.-mi.; 14 ton-mi.
   Sea: 1 056 loaded; 4 584 unloaded

Exports $1 172   Imports $2 068
Coffee   Machinery
Tea   Vehicles
Petroleum products   Petroleum
Pyrethrum   Iron and steel
Exports to: U.K., W. Germany and Uganda
Imports from: U.K., Japan, W. Germany,
U.S.A. and Iran
Revenue from tourism: $158
Aid received (net): $189 from West

KOREA (NORTH)

1. Republic
2. Korean
3. Won
4. $1=0.94

1. 46 540 sq. mi.
2. 18 317 000; 391 per sq. mi.
3. BR 33; DR 8; AI 2.5%
4. Urb. pop.: 5 292 (37%)
5. Pyongyang 1 500

2. Rice 4 900   Maize 2 200
   Potatoes 1 620   Tobacco 46
3. Pigs 2 100   Cattle 950
4. Fish 1 400
5. Roundwood 177
6. Coal 35 000   Zinc 130
   Lead 110   Tungsten 3.8
   Iron ore 4 525   Copper 17

1. 44.8/48.5; 35 000 kWh (64% hydr.)
2b. Coal . . .   Lead 110
    Steel 4 000   Zinc 130
    Iron 3 500   Fertilizers 500
    Petroleum
    products 1 235
3. Sea: 1 300 loaded; 2 000 unloaded

Exports . . .   Imports
Minerals   Machinery
Metal products
Main trade is with the U.S.S.R.

KOREA (SOUTH)

1. Republic
2. Korean
3. Won
4. $1=765

1. 38 022 sq. mi.
2. 38 723 000; 1 018 per sq. mi.
3. BR 25; DR 8; AI 1.8%
4. Urb. pop.: 21 441 (57%)
5. Séoul 8 367

1. GDP $43 942 (10.4%); $1 187 (8.4%)
   Agric. 22%, Indust. 30%, Others 48%
2. Rice 7 032   Barley 771
   Potatoes 554   Cottonseed 3
3. Pigs 2 843   Cattle 1 715
4. Fish 2 091
5. Roundwood 2 400
6. Coal 19 980   Gold 2 967 lb.
   Iron ore 282   Tungsten 3.3

1. 14.8/54.3; 40 248 kWh (5% hydr., 9% nucl.)
2a. Meat 440   Sawnwood 107 417
b. Cotton yarn 245   Steel 5 892
   Radios 4 768   Iron 8 088
   Petroleum products 21 234
3. Telephones 2 387; Cars 249
   Rail: 13 190 pass.-mi.; 6 602 ton-mi.
   Air: 7 563 pass.-mi.; 580 ton-mi.
   Sea: 26 292 loaded; 79 020 unloaded

Exports $21 254   Imports $26 131
Clothing   Machinery
Plywood   Rice
Textiles   Petrol
Exports to: U.S.A., Japan and Saudi Arabia
Imports from: Japan, U.S.A. and Saudi Arabia
Invisible trade balance: −$2 008
Revenue from tourism: $408
Aid received (net): $198 from West

Country	Area and Population	Production	Manufactures	Trade

LAOS

1. Democratic Republic
2. Laotian, French
3. Kip
4. $1 = 10.00

1. 91 429 sq. mi.
2. 3 811 000; 41 per sq. mi.
2. BR 44; DR 20; AI 2.4%
4. Urb. pop.: 466 (15%)
5. Vientiane 177

1. GDP $285 (. . .); $86 (. . .)
2. Rice 1 115   Coffee 5
   Cottonseed 10   Tobacco 5
3. Pigs 1 176   Buffaloes 879
5. Roundwood 106
6. Tin 6

1. 0.11/0.23; 775 kWh (94% hydr.)
2a. Sawnwood 1 447
 b. Woven silk . . .
3. Telephones 7; Cars 15
   Air: 6 pass.-mi.; 1 ton-mi.

Exports 7   Imports 114
Sawnwood   Agricultural products
Tin   Petroleum products
Exports to: Thailand, Malaysia and Hong Kong
Imports from: Thailand, Japan, France and W. Germany
Aid received (net.): $40 from West, $20 from East

LEBANON

1. Republic
2. Arabic, French
3. Lebanese pound
4. $1 = 4.14

1. 4 015 sq. mi.
2. 2 688 000; 668 per sq. mi.
3. BR 30; DR 9; AI 2.5%
4. Urb. pop.: 1 278 (60%)
5. Beirut 702

1. GDP $3 198 (. . .); $1 142 (. . .)
   Agric. 10%, Indust. 16%, Others 74%
2. Wheat 28   Oranges 238
   Apples 115   Grapes 145
   Tomatoes 76   Tobacco 5
3. Goats 380   Sheep 280
6. Salt 35

1. 0.11/2.54; 1 800 kWh (47% hydr.)
2a. Sugar 12   Sawnwood 1 164
 b. Cotton yarn 5   Petroleum products 1 795
3. Telephones 192; Cars 315
   Rail: 1.2 pass.-mi.; 26 ton-mi.
   Air: 894 pass.-mi.; 291 ton-mi.
   Sea: 2 004 loaded; 1 296 unloaded

Exports $436   Imports $1701
Fruit   Machinery
Machinery   Textiles
Vegatables   Vehicles
Eggs   Petroleum products
Exports to: Saudi Arabia, Syria Libya and Kuwait
Imports from: U.S.A., W. Germany, France Italy and U.K.
Revenue from Tourism: $65
Aid received (net.): $46 from West

LIBYA

1. People's Republic
2. Arabic
3. Libyan Dinar
4. $1 = 0.296

1. 679 362 sq. mi.
2. 3 096 000; 5 per sq. mi.
3. BR 42; DR 13; AI 4.1%
4. Urb. pop.: 668 (30%)
5. Tripoli 551

1. GDP $17 421 (15.9%); $6 335 (12.1%)
   Agric. 2%, Indust. 58%, Others 40%
2. Barley 79   Tomatoes 238
   Dates 88   Olives 162
   Tobacco 1   Groundnuts 13
3. Sheep 6 000   Goats 1 500
6. Crude petroleum 55 116   Natural gas 46 600

1. 138.3/6.50; 3 096 kWh
2a. Olive oil 16
 b. Petroleum products 5 030
3. Telephones 41; Cars 400
   Air: 304 pass.-mi.; 4 ton-mi.
   Sea: 91 536 loaded; 7 356 unloaded

Exports $22 128   Imports $6 836
Crude petroleum   Machinery
                         Vehicles
Exports to: W. Germany, Italy, U.S.A. France and Spain
Imports from: Italy, U.K., W.Germany, France and Japan
Aid received (net): $10 from West

LUXEMBOURG

1. Grand Duchy
2. Luxembourgeois, French, German
3. Luxembourg Franc
4. $1 = 48.31

1. 998 sq. mi.
2. 364 000; 365 per sq. mi.
3. BR 12; DR 11; AI 0.3%
4. Urb. pop.:243 (68%)
5. Luxembourg 80

1. GDP $3 614 (2.4%); $10 040 (1.6%)
   Agric. 3%, Indust. 33%, Others 64%
2. Barley 72   Wheat 24
   Oats 33   Grapes 16
3. Cattle 224   Pigs 75
6. Iron ore 125

1. 0.03/5.41; 1 212 kWh (25% hydr.)
2a. Meat 21   Wine 97
    Beer 17 130 gall.   Sawnwood 917
 b. Iron 2 889   Steel 3 790
3. Telephones 192; Cars 164
   Rail: 186 pass.-mi.; 365 ton-mi.
   Air: 117 pass.-mi.; 1 ton-mi.

Exports   Imports
(see Belgium)   (see Belgium)

MADAGASCAR

1. Republic
2. Malagasy, French
3. Malagasy Franc
4. $1 = 385

1. 226 658 sq. mi.
2. 8 955 000; 39 per sq. mi.
3. BR 45; DR 19; AI 2.6%
4. Urb. pop.: 950 (14%)
5. Antananarivo 400

1. GDP $1 744 (. . .); $227 (. . .)
   Agric. 41%, Indust. 15%, Others 44%
2. Rice 1 999   Cassava 1 745
   Bananas 280   Sisal 20
   Coffee 95   Groundnuts 38
3. Cattle 10 150   Goats 1 600
4. Fish 54
5. Roundwood 212
6. Graphite 13   Gold 11 lb.
   Chrome 50   Titanium . . .

1. 0.02/0.62; 366 kWh (30% hydr.)
2a. Sugar 112   Sawnwood 8 260
 b. Cotton yarn 6   Cement 60
3. Telephones 29; Cars 57
   Rail: 171 pass.-mi.; 134 ton-mi.
   Air: 193 pass.-mi.; 11 ton-mi.
   Sea: 372 loaded; 984 unloaded

Exports $402   Imports $600
Coffee   Manufactured goods
Spices
Exports to: France, U.S.A. and Indonesia
Imports from: France, W. Germany and China
Invisible trade balance: −$243
Aid received (net.): $71 from West

MALAWI

1. Republic
2. Bantu, English
3. Kwacha
4. $1 = 1.12

1. 45 747 sq. mi.
2. 5 123 000; 135 per sq. mi.
3. BR 49; DR 25; AI 3.2%
4. Urb pop.: 471 (9%)
5. Lilongwe 103

1. GDP $627 (. . .); $119 (. . .)
   Agric. 49%, Indust. 11%, Others 40%
2. Maize 1 600   Groundnuts 180
   Tea 32   Tabacco 52
   Cottonseed 23   Cotton lint 9
3. Goats 630   Cattle 823
4. Fish 60
5. Roundwood 353

1. 0.05/0.29; 384 kWh (93% hydr.)
2a. Sawnwood 1 200   Beer 10 533 gall.
3. Telephones 27; Cars 13
   Rail: 52 pass.-mi.; 139 ton-mi.
   Air: 52 pass.-mi.; 1 ton-mi.

Exports $284   Imports $362
Tobacco   Machinery
Tea   Textiles
Groundnuts   Vehicles
Exports to: U.K., U.S.A., W. Germany and Netherlands
Imports from: U.K., Japan and South Africa
Invisible trade balance: −$159
Aid received (net.) $81 from West

MALAYSIA

1. Federation
2. Malay, Chinese, English and others
3. Ringgit
4. $1 = 2.30

1. 128 426 sq. mi.
2. 14 415 000; 111 per sq. mi.
3. BR 33; DR 8; AI 2.8%
4. Urb. pop.: 2 525 (29%)
5. Kuala Lumpur 452

1. GDP $8 491 (9.3%); $714 (6.6%)
   Agric. 28%, Indust. 23%, Others 49%
2. Rice 2 147   Palm oil 2 822
   Copra 30   Bananas 460
   Pineapples 206   Rubber 1 590
3. Pigs 1 188   Cattle 430
4. Fish 737
5. Roundwood 1 518
6. Iron ore 295   Tin 71
   Bauxite 701   Tungsten 100
   Crude petroleum 13 152   Gold 197 kg

1. 20.9/11.3; 9 540 kWh (14% hydr.)
2a. Meat 235   Sawnwood 185 219
 b. Cement 2 832
    Petroleum products 653
    Tin 70
3. Telephones 434; Cars 600
   Rail: 1 020 pass.-mi.; 700 ton-mi.
   (incl. Singapore)
   Air: 2 533 pass.-mi.; 72 ton-mi.
   Sea: 10 512 loaded; 16 476 unloaded

Exports $12 884   Imports $13 132
Rubber   Machinery
Tin   Crude petroleum
Sawnwood   Vehicles
Fish   Textiles
Palm oil   Rice
                         Iron and steel
                         Foods
Exports to: Singapore, Japan, U.S.A., U.K., and Netherlands
Imports from: Japan, U.K., Singapore, Australia and W. Germany
Aid received (net): $65 from West

MALI

1. Republic
2. French, Arabic
3. Mali Franc
4. $1 = 727

1. 478 766 sq. mi.
2. 7 150 000; 16 per sq. mi.
3. BR 43; DR 18; AI 2.7%
4. Urb. pop.: 1 077 (17%)
5. Bamako 404

1. GDP $546 (. . .); $94 (. . .)
2. Millet 980   Rice 142
   Groundnuts 190   Cottonseed 70
3. Sheep 6 127   Cattle 4 422
5. Roundwood 1 024

1. 0.01/0.20; 110 kWh (46% hydr.)
2a. Sugar 20   Meat 120
3. Telephones 5; Cars 20
   Rail: 96 pass.-mi.; 81 ton-mi.
   Air: 45 pass.-mi.; 1 ton-mi.

Exports $149   Imports $354
Cattle   Manufactured goods
Fish   Machinery
Cotton   Vehicles
Exports to: France, Ivory Coast, China and U.K.
Imports from: France, Ivory Coast, China and Senegal
Aid received (net): $112 from West, $1 from East

Country	Area and Population	Production	Manufactures	Trade

MALTA

1. Commonwealth
2. Maltese, English
3. Maltese Pound
4. $1 = 2.38

Area and Population
1. 122 sq. mi.
2. 366 000; 2 999 per sq. mi.
3. BR 15; DR 9; AI 1.4%
4. Urb. pop.: 296 (94%)
5. Valetta 14

Production
1. GDP $692 (11.1%); $2 036 (11.0%)
   Agric. 5%, Indust. 38%, Others 57%
2. Potatoes 22 — Wheat 3
   Tomatoes 16 — Grapes 3
3. Pigs 26 — Goats 7

Manufactures
1. –/0.46; 552 kWh
2a. Wine 1 — Wheat flour 36
3. Telephones 73; Cars 67
   Air 380 pass.-mi.; 3 ton-mi.
   Sea: 171 pass.-mi.; 856 ton-mi.
   Sea: 276 loaded; 1 380 unloaded

Trade
Exports $441 — Imports $853
Clothing — Foods
Textiles — Manufactured goods
Exports to: U.K., Libya and W. Germany
Imports from: U.K., Italy, W. Germany and U.S.A.
Revenue from tourism: $81

MAURITANIA

1. Republic
2. Arabic, French
3. Ouguiya
4. $1 = 53.55

Area and Population
1. 397 955 sq. mi.
2. 1 681 000; 5 per sq. mi.
3. BR 50; DR 22; AI 2.8%
4. Urb. pop.: 328 (23%)
5. Nouakchott 135

Production
1. GDP $375 (. . .); $264 (. . .)
   Agric. 25%, Indust. 18%, Others 57%
2. Millet 14 — Dates 14
3. Sheep 5 200 — Cattle 1 200
4. Fish 34
6. Iron ore 5 593 — Copper 3

Manufactures
1. –/0.29; 102 kWh
3. Telephones . . .; Cars 8
   Air: 99 pass.-mi.; 9 ton-mi.
   Sea: 7 022 loaded; 294 unloaded

Trade
Exports $259 — Imports $265
Iron ore — Machinery
Fish — Foods
Exports to: France, U.K., W. Germany, Spain, Italy and Belgium
Imports from: France, U.S.A., U.K. and Senegal
Aid received (net): $73 from West

MEXICO

1. Federal Republic
2. Spanish
3. Mexican Peso
4. $1 = 109

Area and Population
1. 761 604 sq. mi.
2. 71 193 000; 93 per sq. mi.
3. BR 38; DR 6; AI 3.0%
4. Urb. pop.: 45 796 (66%)
5. Mexico 14 750

Production
1. GDP $81 440 (5.0%); $1 244 (1.6%)
   Agric. 10%, Indust. 31%, Others 59%
2. Maize 14 766 — Copra 143
   Bananas 1 562 — Wheat 3 189
   Tomatoes 1 370 — Oranges 1 600
   Coffee 217 — Pineapples 568
   Cottonseed 530 — Tobacco 66
3. Cattle 31 784 — Pigs 12 900
4. Fish 1 240
5. Roundwood 424
6. Crude petroleum 105 948 — Lead 157
   Natural gas 255 169 — Zinc 212
   Coal 6 756 — Silver 1 655 t
   Iron ore 5 292 — Gold 12.7 T lb.
   Copper 110 — Mercury 76

Manufactures
1. 204.9/127.3; 73 068 kWh (25% hydr., 1.4% geo.)
2a. Meat 1 709 — Sugar 2 518
   Sawnwood 35 123
b. Iron 5 508 — Steel 7 452
   Aluminum 43 — Radios 1 126
   Cotton yarn 158 — Cement 17 844
   Petroleum — Vehicles:
   products 51 477 — pass. 358; comm. 172
3. Telephones 4 140; Cars 4 000
   Rail: 3 256 pass.-mi.; 25 664 ton-mi.
   Air: 9 136 pass.-mi.; 88 ton-mi.
   Sea: 62 712 loaded; 19 032 unloaded

Trade
Exports $20 033 — Imports $24 167
Cotton — Machinery
Sugar — Vehicles
Tomatoes — Organic chemical
Coffee — products
Cattle — Iron and steel
Machinery — Paper and cardboard
— Petroleum products
Exports to: U.S.A., Spain, Japan, W. Germany and Brazil
Imports from: U.S.A., W. Germany, Japan and France
Invisible trade balance: –$9 792
Revenue from tourism: $1 117
Aid received (net): $44 from West

MONGOLIA

1. People's Republic
2. Mongol
3. Tugrik
4. $1 = 3.36

Area and Population
1. 604 250 sq. mi.
2. 1 710 000; 3 per sq. mi.
3. BR 37; DR 8; AI 3.0%
4. Urb. pop.: 836 (51%)
5. Ulan-Bator 419

Production
1. NMP $. . . (5.3%); . . . (2.4%)
2. Wheat 240 — Potatoes 55
3. Sheep 14 400 — Goats 4 715
5. Roundwood 71
6. Coal 3 350
   Lignite 3 087 — Flourine . . .
   Copper 12 — Molybdenum . . .

Manufactures
1. 1.77/2.67; 1 650 kWh
2a. Wool . . . — Meat 232
   Sawnwood 16 591
b. Cement 166
3. Telephones 38; Cars . . .
   Rail: 152 pass.-mi.; 1 700 ton-mi.

Trade
Exports $343 — Imports $506
Livestock — Consumer goods
Wool — Machinery
Meat — Raw materials

MOROCCO

1. Kingdom
2. Arabic, French Spanish
3. Dirham
4. $1 = 6.56

Area and Population
1. 172 414 sq. mi.
2. 20 646 000; 119 per sq. mi.
3. BR 45; DR 14; AI 3.6%
4. Urb. pop.: 7 670 (41%)
5. Rabat 596

Production
1. GDP $10 224 (. . .); $555 (. . .)
   Agric. 16%, Indust. 23%, Others 61%
2. Barley 1 039 — Wheat 892
   Oranges 685 — Grapes 210
   Dates 105 — Olives 350
3. Sheep 16 100 — Goats 6 070
4. Fish 298
5. Roundwood 35
6. Coal 708 — Cobalt 7
   Iron ore 28 — Lead 168
   Antimony 504 — Phosphates 18 562
   Copper 24

Manufactures
1. 1.05/6.87; 4 692 kWh (32 hydr.)
2a. Meat 268 — Wine 80
   Olive oil 38 — Sawnwood 4 518
   Sugar 352
b. Petroleum — Wool yarn 2.6
   products 3 798 — Cement 3 564
3. Telephones 216; Cars 425
   Rail: 573 pass.-mi.; 2 414 ton-mi.
   Air: 968 pass.-mi.; 19 ton-mi.
   Sea: 20 808 loaded; 10 164 unloaded

Trade
Exports $2 249 — Imports $4 185
Phosphates — Machinery
Oranges — Manufactured goods
Vegetables
Exports to: France, W. Germany, Italy and Spain
Imports from: France, U.S.A., W. Germany, Italy and Spain
Revenue from tourism: $434
Aid received (net): $200 from West

MOZAMBIQUE

1. People's Republic
2. Portuguese, Bantu
3. Metica
4. $1 = 29.72

Area and Population
1. 302 329 sq. mi.
2. 10 757 000; 36 per sq. mi.
3. BR 45; DR 19; AI 2.6%
4. Urb. pop.: 442 (6%)
5. Maputo 384

Production
1. GDP $2 545 (. . .); $277 (. . .)
2. Cassava 2 850 — Maize 200
   Copra 70 — Groundnuts 80
   Cottonseed 37 — Sisal 12
3. Cattle 1 399 — Goats 335
5. Roundwood 388
6. Coal 456

Manufactures
1. 2.10/1.02; 14 000 kWh (97% hydr.)
2a. Sugar 185 — Sawnwood 4 765
   Beer 144 galls.
b. Petroleum products 365
3. Telephones 49; Cars 110
   Rail: 245 pass.-mi.; 2 111 ton-mi.
   Sea: 8 988 loaded; 3 540 unloaded

Trade
Exports $129 — Imports $278
Cotton — Machinery
Cashew nuts — Vehicles
Sugar — Iron and steel
Tea — Petroleum
Exports to: Portugal, S. Africa, U.K. and U.S.A.
Imports from: Portugal, S. Africa, W. Germany and U.K.
Aid received (net): $82 from West

NAMIBIA (South West Africa)

1. Mandated Territory
2. English, African dialects
3. Rand
4. $1 = 1.09

Area and Population
1. 318 261 sq. mi.
2. 1 200 000; 3 per sq. mi.
3. BR 44; DR 15; AI 2.9%
4. Urb. pop.: 200 (27%)
5. Windhoek 61

Production
1. (incl. with South Africa)
2. Maize 30 — Millet 15
3. Sheep 5 170 — Cattle 3 024
4. Fish 213
5. Roundwood . . .
6. Copper 39 — Zinc 37
   Lead 47 — Diamonds 1 898
   Tin 1 — Vanadium 462

Manufactures
2a. Meat 64
b. Copper 50 — Lead 46
3. Telephones 46; Cars . . .
   Rail: see South Africa

Trade
Exports . . . — Imports . . .
(Trade included with South Africa)

NEPAL

1. Kingdom
2. Nepalese Hindu
3. Nepalese Rupee
4. $1 = 13.20

Area and Population
1. 54 362 sq. mi.
2. 15 020 000; 277 per sq. mi.
3. BR 44; DR 21; AI 2.2%
4. Urb. pop.: 462 (4%)
5. Katmandu 210

Production
1. GDP $1 452 (3.3%); $114 (0.9%)
   Agric. 62%, Indust. 11%, Others 27%
2. Rice 2 407 — Maize 720
   Wheat 477 — Jute 43
3. Cattle 6 900 — Goats 2 500
5. Roundwood 459

Manufactures
1. 0.02/0.16; 220 kWh (74% hydr.)
2a. Sugar 7
3. Telephones 9; Cars . . .

Trade
Exports $97 — Imports $163
Food grains — Textiles
Livestock — Petroleum products
Jute — Iron and steel
Timber — Machinery, Tea
The main trade is with India
Aid received (net): $67 from West

Country	Area and Population	Production	Manufactures	Trade

NETHERLANDS

Country
1. Kingdom
2. Dutch
3. Gilder
4. $1=2.73

Area and Population
1. 13 004 sq. mi.
2. 14 246 000; 1 096 per sq. mi.
3. BR 13; DR 8; AI 0.7%
4. Urb. pop.: 12 368 (88%)
5. Amsterdam 958
   The Hague 673

Production
1. GDP $118 622 (3.2%); $8 509 (2.4%)
   Agric. 5%, Indust.30%, Others 65%
2. Barley 249   Wheat 822
   Tomatoes 400   Apples 300
   Pears 75   Potatoes 6 400
3. Pigs 10 315   Cattle 5 100
4. Fish 340
5. Roundwood 35
6. Crude petroleum 1332   Natural gas 638 825
   Salt 3 580

Manufactures
1. 98.0/87.8; 64 056 kWh (7% nucl.)
2a. Meat 2 020   Sugar 1 139
    (Pork 1 100)   Butter & Cheese 640
    Sawnwood 11 896
b. Iron 4 596   Steel 5 472
   Wool yarn 7   Cotton yarn 16
   Petroleum   Vehicles:
   products 38 565   Pass. 78; comm. 12
   Plastics 2 393   Ships (grt) 183
3. Telephones 6 341; Cars 4 350
   Rail: 5 738 pass.-mi.; 2 056 ton-mi.
   Air: 9 516 pass.-mi.; 683 ton-mi.
   Sea: 74 868 loaded; 245 244 unloaded

Trade
Exports $68 756   Imports $66 117
Machinery   Machinery
Textiles   Crude petroleum
Chemical products Textiles
Petroleum   Vehicles
Meat   Iron and steel
Iron and steel   Clothing
Vegables   Non-ferrous metals
Exports to: West Germany, Belgium-Luxembourg,
France, U.K., Italy and U.S.A.
Imports from: W. Germany, Belguim-Luxembourg,
U.S.A., France, U.K. and Italy
Invisible trade balance: + $592
Revenue from tourism: 1 260
Aid given (net.): $2 528

NEW ZEALAND

Country
1. Commonwealth
2. English
3. New Zealand Dollar
4. $1=1.52

Area and Population
1. 103 736 sq. mi.
2. 3 125 000; 31 per sq. mi.
3. BR 16; DR 8; AI 1.4%
4. Urb. pop.: 2 593 (83%)
5. Wellington 321

Production
1. GDP $16 628 (. . .); $5 346 (. . .)
   Agric. 10%, Indust. 25%, Others 65%
2. Barley 187   Pears 17
   Apples 222   Wheat 368
   Tomatoes 60   Wool 385
3. Sheep 71 200   Cattle 8 581
4. Fish 98
5. Roundwood 318
6. Coal 1 944   Lignite 216
   Natural gas 10 886   Gold 481 lb.
   Crude petroleum 408

Manufactures
1. 607/10.7; 22 704 kWh (74% hydr., 6% geo.)
2a. Meat 1 181   Butter & cheese 349
    Sawnwood 67 140   Wood pulp 1 043
    Wine 50
b. Petroleum   Vehicles:
   products 2 485   pass. 63; comm. 13
   Cement 756   Wool yarn 18
3. Telephones 1 715; Cars 1 307
   Rail: 252 pass.-mi.; 1 952 ton-mi.
   Air: 3 524 pass.-mi.; 126 ton-mi.
   Sea:10 236 loaded; 9 792 unloaded

Trade
Exports $5 563   Imports $5 684
Meat   Machinery
Wool   Textiles
Butter   Vehicles
Cheese   Iron and steel
                  Petroleum products
Exports to: U.K., Japan and Australia
Imports from: U.K., Australia, U.S.A. and Japan
Invisible trade balance: − $1 352
Revenue from tourism: $166
Aid given: (net): $73

NICARAGUA

Country
1. Republic
2. Spanish
3. Cordoba
4. $1=10.05

Area and Population
1. 50 193 sq. mi.
2. 2 824 000; 57 per sq. mi.
3. BR 47; DR 12; AI 5.2%
4. Urb. pop.: 1 404 (53%)
5. Managua 608

Production
1. GDP $1 980 (5.9%); $825 (2.4%)
   Agric. 23%, Indust. 21%, Others 56%
2. Maize 250   Rice 65
   Bananas 252   Coffee 63
   Cottonseed 115   Cotton lint 75
3. Cattle 2 401   Pigs 500
5. Roundwood 106
6. Copper 100   Gold 41.8 T lb.

Manufactures
1. 0.05/0.91; 988 kWh (40% hydr.)
2a. Sugar 193   Meat 61
    Sawnwood 14 190
b. Cement 161
3. Telephones 43; Cars 40
   Rail: 10 pass.-mi.; 603 ton-mi.
   Air: 47 pass.-mi.; 1 ton-mi.
   Sea: 725 loaded; 1 423 unloaded

Trade
Exports $448   Imports $883
Cotton   Machinery
Meat   Textiles
Coffee   Iron and steel
Exports to: U.S.A., Japan, Costa Rica and
W. Germany
Imports from: U.S.A., Guatemala, Costa Rica,
W. Germany, Japan and Venezuela
Aid received (net): $39 from West

NIGER

Country
1. Republic
2. Arabic, French
3. C.F.A. Franc
4. $1=364

Area and Population
1. 489 191 sq. mi.
2. 5 479 000; 10 per sq. mi.
3. BR 51; DR 22; AI 2.9%
4. Urb. pop.: 315 (8%)
5. Niamey 130

Production
1. GDP $699 (. . .); $152 (. . .)
   Agric. 51%, Indust. 7%, Others 42%
2. Groundnuts 100   Millet 1 117
3. Goats 7 318   Cattle 3 206
5. Roundwood 106
6. Tin 96   Uranium 3 700

Manufactures
1. . . ./0.3; 52 kWh
2a. Meat 71
3. Telephones 8; Cars 26
   Aviation: 90 pass.-mi.; 9 ton-mi.

Trade
Exports $160   Imports $196
Groundnuts   Manufactured goods
Exports to: France, Italy and Nigeria
Imports from: France, Ivory Coast and W. Germany
Aid received (net): $118 from West

NIGERIA

Country
1. Federal Republic
2. English,
   W. African
3. Naira
4. $1=0.71

Area and Population
1. 356 669 sq. mi.
2. 79 680 000; 223 per sq. mi.
3. BR 50; DR 18; AI 3.2%
4. Urb. pop.: 12 535 (19%)
5. Lagos 1 477

Production
1. GDP $47 683 (. . .); $682 (. . .)
   Agric. 26%, Indust. 38%, Others 36%
2. Cassava 11 000   Millet 3 230
   Rubber 43   Cocoa 160
   Groundnuts 580   Cottonseed 57
3. Goats 25 000   Cattle 12 500
4. Fish 480
5. Roundwood 3 495
6. Coal 168   Natural gas 5 167
   Tin 3   Crude petroleum 71 184

Manufactures
1. 153.1/11.1; 5 004 kWh (60% hydr.)
2a. Meat 813   Sugar 60
    Sawnwood 95 415
b. Petroleum products 6 465
   Cement 1 536
3. Telephones 128; Cars 400
   Rail: 487 pass.-mi.; 603 ton-mi.
   Aviation: 1 430 pass.-mi.; 10 ton-mi.
   Sea: 101 220 loaded; 5 000 unloaded

Trade
Exports $17 331   Imports $10 991
Petroleum   Machinery
Cocoa   Textiles
Groundnuts   Vehicles
Tin   Iron and steel
Exports to: Bermuda, U.S.A. and Netherlands
Imports from: U.K., W. Germany, U.S.A. and Japan
Invisible trade balance: $3 944
Aid received (net): $43 from West

NORWAY

Country
1. Kingdom
2. Norwegian
3. Norwegian
   Krone
4. $1=7.14

Area and Population
1. 125 182 sq. mi.
2. 4 100 000; 37 per sq. mi.
3. BR 13; DR 10; AI 0.4%
4. Urb. pop.: 1 779 (44%)
5. Oslo 624

Production
1. GDP $32 275 (4.7%); $7 949 (4.1%)
   Agric. 5%, Indust. 28%, Others 67%
2. Barley 650   Apples 47
   Oats 417   Potatoes 452
3. Sheep 2 040   Cattle 983
4. Fish 2 398
5. Roundwood 282
6. Coal 312   Molybdenum . . .
   Iron ore 2 644   Vanadium 460
   Copper 28   Zinc 28
   Titanium 827   Natural gas 264 634
   Crude petroleum 23 580
   Lead 3

Manufactures
1. 31.4/21.2; 93 516 kWh (99.4% hydr.)
2a. Butter & cheese 91   Sawnwood 86 943
    Canned fish 32   Wood pulp 1 602
    Fish meal 10
b. Iron 1 296   Steel 852
   Magnesium 39   Aluminum 638
   Paper 1 373   Wool yarn 4
   Ships (grt) 268   Petroleum
                      products 6 525
3. Telephones 1 636; Cars 1 234
   Rail: 1 505 pass.-mi.; 1 602 ton-mi.
   Air: 2 526 pass.-mi.; 85 ton-mi.
   Sea: 34 344 loaded; 18 324 unloaded

Trade
Exports $18 220   Imports $15 652
Non-ferrous metals Machinery
(mainly aluminium) Ships and boats
Ships and boats   Vehicles
Machinery   Iron and steel
Paper and cardboard Textiles
Fish   Non-ferrous metals
Iron and steel   Petroleum products
Exports to: U.K., Sweden, W. Germany,
Denmark and U.S.A.
Imports from: Sweden, W. Germany, U.K.
U.S.A. and Denmark
Invisible trade balance: − $127
Aid given (net): $575

PAKISTAN

Country
1. Republic
2. Urdu, English
3. Pakistan Rupee
4. $1=12.91

Area and Population
1. 309 425 sq. mi.
2. 84 579 000; 275 per sq. mi.
3. BR 43; DR 15; AI 3.2%
4. Urb. pop.: 16 558 (26%)
5. Islamabad 77

Production
1. GDP $12 889 (4.7%); $183 (1.9%)
   Agric. 29%, Indust. 16%, Others 55%
2. Rice 5 093   Wheat 11 340
   Dates 205   Maize 1 004
   Tobacco 67   Rapeseed 252
   Cotton lint 750   Cottonseed 1 500
3. Cattle 15 084   Sheep 28 468
4. Fish 279.
5. Roundwood 635
6. Coal 1 692   Salt 620
   Natural gas 77 905   Crude petroleum 480
   Antimony 69 t   Chrome 5

Manufactures
1. 12.3/18.0; 17 148 kWh (64% hydr., 1 nucl.)
2a. Meat 752   Sugar 928
    Sawnwood 2 118   Jute 1
b. Petroleum   Cotton yarn 389
   products 3 663   Cement 3 540
3. Telephones 259; Cars 347
   Rail: 10 753 pass.-mi.; 5 290 ton-mi.
   Air: 3 763 pass.-mi.; 157 ton-mi.
   Sea: 3 588 loaded; 11 484 unloaded

Trade
Exports $2 880   Imports $5 348
Textiles   Machinery
Cotton   Iron and steel
Leather   Fertilizer
Rice   Crude petroleum
                  Vehicles
Exports to: China, Japan, Iran and U.K.
Imports from: U.S.A., U.K., Japan and W. Germany
Invisible trade balance: − $545
Aid received (net): $513 from West, $226 from East

PANAMA

Country
1. Republic
2. Spanish
3. Balboa
4. $1=1.0

Area and Population
1. 29 209 sq. mi.
2. 1 940 000; 67 per sq. mi.
3. BR 27; DR 6; AI 3.1%
4. Urb. pop.: 963 (51%)
5. Panama 546

Production
1. GDP $2 043 (3.3%); $1 116 (0.2%)
   Agric. 17%, Indust. 18%, Others 65%
2. Rice 192   Bananas 1 185
   Coffee 6   Oranges 69
3. Cattle 1 525   Pigs 195
4. Fish 195
5. Roundwood 35

Manufactures
1. 0.10/1.22; 1 896 kWh (41% hydr.)
2a. Meat 62   Sugar 187
    Sawnwood 423
b. Petroleum products 2 239
3. Telephones 155; Cars 90
   Sea: 1 183 loaded; 3 419 unloaded

Trade
Exports $315   Imports $1 540
Bananas   Manufactured goods
Petroleum products Petroleum
                Machinery
Exports to: U.S.A. and W. Germany
Imports from: U.S.A., Ecuador, Venezuela and
Saudi Arabia
Invisible trade balance: + $677
Aid received (net): $35 from West

Country	Area and Population	Production	Manufactures	Trade
PERU 1. Republic 2. Spanish 3. Sol 4. $1 = 1 253	1. 496 224 sq. mi. 2. 18 279 000; 36 per sq. mi. 3. BR 40; DR 12; AI 2.8% 4. Urb. pop.: 11 980 (67%) 5. Lima 4 279	1. GDP $9 586 (3.4%); $586 (0.5%) Agric. 12%, Indust. 35%, Others 53% 2. Maize 587 / Rice 712 Oranges 152 / Coffee 95 Cottonseed 165 / Potatoes 1 627 3. Sheep 14 671 / Cattle 3 895 4. Fish 2 731 5. Roundwood 141 6. Iron ore 3 398 / Gold 1 800 Antimony 768 / Silver 1 318 t Copper 328 / Zinc 497 Lead 186 / Tungsten 549 Molybdenum 729 / Crude petroleum 9 552	1. 16.1/11.0; 8 805 kWh (78% hydr.) 2a. Meat 375 / Fish Meal Sugar 493 / Sawnwood 20 650 b. Cotton yarn ... / Copper 274 3. Telephones 420; Cars 312 Rail: 402 pass.-mi.; 380 ton-mi. Air: 840 pass.-mi.; 21 ton-mi. Sea: 10 284 loaded; 2 688 unloaded	Exports $3 364 / Imports $2 542 Copper / Machinery Fish Meal / Chemical products Iron ore / Wheat Cotton / Iron and steel Exports to: U.S.A., Japan and Italy Imports from: U.S.A., Ecuador and Venezuela Invisible trade balance: −$1 154 Revenue from tourism: $126 Aid received (net): $104 from West
PHILIPPINES 1. Republic 2. Tagalog, English 3. Philippine Peso 4. $1 = 9.84	1. 115 831 sq. mi. 2. 49 530 000; 427 per sq. mi. 3. BR 36; DR 9; AI 3.2% 4. Urb. pop.: 11 678 (32%) 5. Manila 1 479	1. GDP $21 204 8.3%); $457 (3.3%) Agric. 27%, Indust. 27%, Others 46% 2. Maize 3 176 / Rice 7 720 Bananas 4 280 / Pineapples 1 200 Coffee 140 / Copra 2 275 Tobacco 50 3. Pigs 7 590 / Buffaloes 2 760 4. Fish 1 558 5. Roundwood 1 236 6. Coal 360 / Copper 923 Iron ore 2 / Gold 52 T lb. Chrome 200 / Silver 63 t	1. 2.69/15.3; 15 948 kWh (20% hydr., 11% geo.) 2a. Meat 762 / Sawnwood 53 973 Salted fish 48 / Sugar 2 394 b. Plastics 63 / Petroleum Cotton yarn 38 / products 9 170 Cement 4 008 / Copper 291 3. Telephones 600; Cars 400 Rail: 156 pass.-mi.; 22 ton-mi. Air: 4 150 pass.-mi.; 96 ton-mi. Sea: 14 652 loaded; 19 008 unloaded	Exports $5 722 / Imports $7 946 Wood / Machinery Sugar / Petroleum Copra / Vehicles Copper / Iron and steel Exports to: U.S.A., Japan and Netherlands Imports from: Japan, U.S.A. and Saudi Arabia Invisible trade balance: −$543 Revenue from tourism: $356 Aid received (net): $205 from West
POLAND 1. People's Republic 2. Polish 3. Złoty 4. $1 = 86.85	1. 120 725 sq. mi. 2. 35 902 000; 298 per sq. mi. 3. BR 19; DR 9; AI 0.9% 4. Urb. pop.: 20 185 (58%) 5. Warsaw 1 543	1. NMP $87 150 (8.1%); $2 512 (7.1%) Agric. 16%, Indust. 52%, Others 32% 2. Barley 3 575 / Wheat 4 203 Rye 6 731 / Oats 2 731 Potatoes 42 600 / Apples 800 Tobacco 81 / Rapeseed 486 3. Pigs 18 487 / Cattle 11 801 4. Fish 640 5. Roundwood 741 6. Coal 163 020 / Nickel 2 Lignite 35 556 / Zinc 201 Copper 295 / Natural gas 51 189 Lead 44 / Salt 4 393	1. 211.9/198.8; 115 008 kWh (2.0 hydr.) 2a. Meat 2 357 / Sawnwood 260 690 Butter & cheese 623 / Sugar 1 872 Salted fish 18 2b. Iron 9 348 / Steel 15 720 Aluminum 66 / Plastics 591 Cotton yarn 196 / Wool yarn 89 Petroleum products 10 650 / Vehicles: Woven silk 4 592 T ft. / pass. 240; comm. 48 Ships (grt) 489 3. Telephones 3 095; Cars 2 270 Rail: 29 957 pass.-mi.; 68 208 ton-mi. Air: 1 326 pass.-mi.; 11 ton-mi. Sea: 38 761 loaded; 27 175 unloaded	Exports $13 249 / Imports $15 475 Coal / Dairy products Ships and boats / Iron ore Meat / Crude petroleum Dairy products / Cotton, Wheat Machinery / Iron and steel Clothing / Petroleum products / Machinery Main trade is with: U.S.S.R., W. Germany, Czechoslovakia and E. Germany Revenue from tourism: $224 Aid given (net): $103
PORTUGAL 1. Republic 2. Portuguese 3. Escudo 4. $1 = 97.35	1. 35 553 sq. mi. 2. 9 981 000; 279 per sq. mi. 3. BR 16; DR 10; AI 1.1% 4. Urb. pop.: 2 276 (26%) 5. Lisbon 1 612	1. GDP $15 349 (4.5%); $1 577 (3.4%) Agric. 13%, Indust. 34%, Others 53% 2. Wheat 310 / Maize 417 Grapes 900 / Olives 220 Tomatoes 670 / Wool 9 3. Sheep 5 200 / Pigs 2 500 4. Fish 265 5. Roundwood 282 6. Coal 180 / Tin 269 Iron ore 18 / Tungsten 1 392 Copper 3 / Gold 961 lb.	1. 1.16/11.0; 14 268 kWh (53% hydr.) 2a. Meat 461 / Sawnwood 78 719 Canned fish 47 / Salted fish 15 Wine 640 / Olive oil 33 b. Iron 348 / Steel 348 Petroleum / Vehicles: products 7 225 / pass. 32; comm. 38 Cotton yarn 97 / Wool yarn 14 3. Telephones 1 175; Cars 920 Rail: 3 636 pass.-mi.; 618 ton-mi. Air: 2 488 pass.-mi.; 67 ton-mi. Sea: 4 500 loaded; 23 976 unloaded	Exports $4 179 / Imports $10 182 Textiles / Machinery Clothing / Vehicles Wine / Iron and steel Diamonds / Cotton Machinery / Diamonds Fish / Cereals Cork / Crude petroleum Exports to: U.K., France and W. Germany Imports from: W. Germany, U.K., U.S.A. and France Invisible trade balance: −$41 Revenue from tourism: $600
ROMANIA 1. Socialist Republic 2. Romanian 3. Leu 4. $1 = 4.47	1. 91 699 sq. mi. 2. 22 457 000; 246 per sq. mi. 3. BR 18; DR 10; AI 1.0% 4. Urb. pop.: 10 626 (47%) 5. Bucharest 1 934	1. NMP $26 450 (10.8%); $1 240 (9.8%) Agric. 15%, Indust. 58%, Others 27% 2. Barley 2 500 / Wheat 5 800 Grapes 1 755 / Tomatoes 1 600 Tobacco 39 / Sunflower seed 824 3. Sheep 15 865 / Pigs 11 542 4. Fish 174 5. Roundwood 741 6. Coal 8 196 / Lead 20 Lignite 28 800 / Manganese 28 Iron ore 605 / Natural gas 365 549 Bauxite 688 / Crude petroleum 11 604	1. 86.9/102.3; 67 500 kWh (18% hydr.) 2a. Meat 1 824 / Sawnwood 165 557 Sugar 640 / Butter & cheese 278 b. Iron 8 856 / Steel 13 020 Petroleum products 22 624 / Cotton yarn 175 Woven silk 1 076 T ft² / Wool yarn 71 Fertilizers 2 383 / Aluminium 231 3. Telephones 1 196; Cars 235 Rail: 14 166 pass.-mi.; 45 792 ton-mi. Air: 775 pass.-mi.; 7 ton-mi. Sea: 4 257 Loaded; 4 859 unloaded	Exports $12 610 / Imports $12 458 Machinery / Machinery Consumer goods / Iron ore Petroleum products / Coke Cereals / Vehicles / Iron goods Exports to: U.S.S.R., E. Germany and W. Germany Imports from: U.S.S.R., E. Germany and W. Germany Aid given (net): $241
SAUDI ARABIA 1. Kingdom 2. Arabic 3. Rial 4. $1 = 3.45	1. 829 999 sq. mi. 2. 9 319 000; 10 per sq. mi. 3. BR 46; DR 14; AI 3.1% 4. Urb. pop.: 1 829 (23%) 5. Ar Riyãd 667	1. GDP $43 723 (...); $6 089 (...) Agric. 1%, Indust. 61%, Others 38% 2. Wheat 150 / Millet/Sorghum 112 Dates 429 / Tomatoes 170 3. Sheep 4 000 / Goats 1 974 6. Crude petroleum 490 800 / Natural gas 90 000	1. 729.9/12.4; 9 000 kWh 2b. Petroleum products 23 660 Cement 1 800 3. Telephones 185; Cars 400 Rail: 44 pass.-mi.; 40 ton-mi. Air: 2 202 pass.-mi.; 73 ton-mi. Sea: 410 000 loaded; 9 259 unloaded	Exports $120 240 / Imports $35 244 Crude petroleum / Machinery Petroleum products / Vehicles / Food Exports to: Japan, Italy, France and U.S.A. Imports from: U.S.A., Japan and W. Germany Invisible trade balance: −$24 618
SENEGAL 1. Republic 2. French, West African 3. C.F.A. Franc 4. $1 = 364	1. 75 750 sq. mi. 2. 5 811 000; 78 per sq. mi. 3. BR 55; DR 22; AI 2.6% 4. Urb. pop.: 1 149 (32%) 5. Dakar 799	1. GDP $1 704 (...); $342 (...) 2. Millet 750 / Rice 120 Bananas 2 / Groundnuts 900 3. Cattle 2 789 / Goats 890 4. Fish 359 5. Roundwood 71 6. Phosphates 1 501 / Salt 147 Titanium ... / Zirconium ...	1. −/1.41; 700 kWh 2a. Sawnwood 388 b. Petroleum products 745 / Cement 372 3. Telephones 42; Cars 65 Rail: 111 pass.-mi.; 101 ton-mi. Air: 99 pass.-mi.; 9 ton-mi. Sea: 3 240 loaded; 2 772 unloaded	Exports $536 / Imports $931 Groundnut oil / Food Groundnuts / Manufactured goods / Machinery Main trade is with: France Aid received (net): $149 from West
SINGAPORE 1. Republic 2. English, Chinese, Malay, Tamil 3. Singapore Dollar 4. $1 = 2.10	1. 224 sq. mi. 2. 2 443 000; 10 890 per sq. mi. 3. BR 17; DR 5; AI 1.2% 4. Urb. pop.: 2 363 (100%) 5. Singapore 2 391	1. GDP $5 128 (8.6%); $2 279 (7.0%) Agric. 2%, Indust. 27%, Others 71% 2. Cassava 1 3. Pigs 1 166 / Cattle 9 4. Fish 16 Granite 2 235	1. −/10.1; 7 440 kWh 2a. Meat 109 / Sawnwood 13 484 b. Manufacturing Industries ... 3. Telephones 475; Cars 208 Rail: see Malaysia Air: 10 730 pass.-mi.; 414 ton-mi. Sea: 34 236 loaded; 55 476 unloaded	Exports $20 993 / Imports $27 571 Rubber / Machinery Petroleum products / Textiles Machinery / Rubber Exports to: Malaysia, U.S.A. and Japan Imports from: Japan, Malaysia, U.S.A. and Saudi Arabia Invisible trade balance: +$4 594 Revenue from tourism: $524 Aid received (net): $11 from West

Country	Area and Population	Production	Manufactures	Trade
SOUTH AFRICA 1. Republic 2. English, Afrikaans 3. Rand 4. $1=1.09	1. 471 445 sq. mi. 2. 30 131 000; 65 per sq. mi. 3. BR 38; DR 10; AI 2.8% 4. Urb. pop.: 11 018 (48%) 5. Pretoria 562; Cape Town 1 097	1. GDP $37 136 (3.5%); $1 296 (0.9%) Agric. 8%; Indust. 41%, Others 51% 2. Maize 14 645 / Wheat 2 090 Oranges 569 / Pineapples 225 Grapes 1 275 / Cottonseed 100 Tobacco 34 / Wool 111 3. Sheep 31 650 / Cattle 12 200 4. Fish 640 5. Roundwood 565 6. Coal 131 184 Iron 18 408 / Manganese 5 040 Copper 199 / Asbestos 249 Chrome 2 870 / Antimony 9 700 Gold 1 445 T lb. / Nickel 25 Diamonds 7 726 c	1. 92.4/85.4; 95 016 kWh (2.8% hydr.) 2a. Meat 1 008 / Sugar 2 050 Wine 550 / Beer 495 T gall. Sawnwood 54 891 b. Iron 7 248 / Steel 8 940 Copper 185 / Cotton yarn 52 Wool yarn 21.1 / Petroleum Vehicles: / products 12 705 pass. 335; comm. 31 / Cement 7 128 3. Telephones 2 320; Cars 2 400 Rail: . . .; 60 092 ton-mi. Air: 5 767 pass.-mi.; 207 ton-mi. Sea: 47 160 loaded; 1 848 unloaded	Exports $9 618 / Imports $8 336 Diamonds / Machinery Fruit / Vehicles Wool / Textiles Copper / Crude petroleum Iron and steel / Petroleum products Machinery / Chemical products Cereals Exports to: U.K., Japan, U.S.A. and W. Germany Imports from: U.K., U.S.A., W. Germany and Japan Invisible trade balance: −$4 323 Revenue from tourism: $321
SOUTH YEMEN 1. People's Republic 2. Arabic 3. South Yemen Dinar 4. $1=0.345	1. 128 537 sq. mi. 2. 1 838 000; 16 per sq. mi. 3. BR 48; DR 23; AI 1.9% 4. Urb. pop.: 529 (33%) 5. Aden 285	1. GDP $242 (. . .); $147 (. . .) Agric. 19%, Indust. 27%, Others 54% 2. Millet 70 / Wheat 15 Dates 43 / Cottonseed 9 3. Goats 1 350 / Sheep 980 4. Fish 75	1. −/0.57; 180 kWh 2b. Petroleum products 1 845 3. Telephones 9; Cars 11 Sea: 1 426 loaded; 2 204 unloaded	Exports $248 / Imports $393 Petroleum products / Petroleum Cotton / Cotton fabric Cereals Exports to: U.K., Yemen and South Africa Imports from: Iran, Kuwait and Japan Aid received (net): $72 from West
SPAIN 1. Monarchy 2. Spanish 3. Spanish Peseta 4. $1=135	1. 194 897 sq. mi. 2. 37 654 000; 192 per sq. mi. 3. BR 14; DR 8; AI 1.1% 4. Urb. pop.: 23 556 (64%) 5. Madrid 3 159	1. GDP $133 325 (4.5%); $3 625 (3.4%) Agric. 9%, Indust. 28%, Others 63% 2. Barley 4 701 / Wheat 3 356 Tomatoes 2 074 / Oranges 1 500 Grapes 5 239 / Olives 1 348 Cottonseed 100 / Cotton lint 65 Tobacco 38 / Wool 21 3. Sheep 14 887 / Pigs 10 692 4. Fish 1 240 5. Roundwood 388 6. Coal 14 268 / Lead 83 Lignite 20 676 / Tungsten 390 Iron ore 4 206 / Mercury 1 070 t Copper 45 / Zinc 176 Crude petroleum 1 380	1. 25.2/95.0; 110 700 kWh (28% hydr., 5% nucl.) 2a. Meat 2 538 / Sugar 1 054 Olive oil 513 / Wine 3 331 Sawnwood 72 365 b. Cotton yarn 94 / Wool yarn 35 Silk fabric 2 712 T ft.[2] / Copper 108 Iron 6 528 / Steel 13 176 Aluminum 431 / Ships (grt.) 509 Radios 363 / Vehicles petroleum / pass. 862; comm. 127 products 31 265 / Cement 28 752 3. Telephones 10 311; Cars 7 556 Rail: 8 778 pass.-mi.; 7 787 ton-mi. Air: 9 933 pass.-mi.; 282 ton-mi. Sea: 48 672 loaded; 104 532 unloaded	Exports $20 337 / Imports $32 159 Machinery / Machinery Fruits / Crude petroleum Vegetables / Iron and steel Footwear / Organic chemicals Petroleum products / Maize Textiles / Soya Ships and boats / Sawnwood Olive oil / Copper Exports to: U.S.A., W. Germany, France and U.K. Imports from: U.S.A., W. Germany, France and Saudi Arabia Invisible trade balance: +$4 553 Revenue from tourism: $5 488
SRI LANKA 1. Republic 2. Sinhalese, English, Tamil 3. Sri Lanka Rupee 4. $1=22.95	1. 25 332 sq. mi. 2. 14 988 000; 591 per sq. mi. 3. BR 28; DR 6; AI 2.2% 4. Urb. pop.: 2 848 (22%) 5. Colombo 1 412	1. GDP $2 379 (4.5%); $168 (2.8%) Agric. 34%, Indust. 14%, Others 52% 2. Rice 2 229 / Cassava 537 Tea 210 / Copra 123 Rubber 133 / Tobacco 8 3. Cattle 1 623 / Buffaloes 850 4. Fish 186 5. Roundwood 247 6. Graphite 9 / Salt 152 Titanium 70	1. 0.18/1.54; 1 872 kWh (89% hydr.) 2a. Meat 32 / Sawnwood 917 b. Cotton yarn 8 / Petroleum products 1 415 3. Telephones 74; Cars 105 Rail: 2 384 pass.-mi.; 121 ton-mi. Air: 894 pass.-mi.; 18 ton-mi. Sea 1 188 loaded; 2 496 unloaded	Exports $1 036 / Imports $1 803 Tea / Machinery Rubber / Rice Copra / Sugar Coconuts / Flour Coconut fibre / Textiles Petroleum products Exports to: U.K., Pakistan, China, and U.S.A Imports from: Saudi Arabia, Iran and U.S.A. Aid received (net): $217 from West, $60 from East
SUDAN 1. Republic 2. Arabic, Hamitic, English 3. Sudanese Pound 4. $1=0.76	1. 967 500 sq. mi. 2. 18 901 000; 21 per sq. mi. 3. BR 46; DR 18; AI 3.2% 4. Urb. pop.: 3 288 (20%) 5. Khartoum 334	1. GDP $4 775 (. . .); $304 (. . .) Agric. 34%, Indust. 10%, Others 56% 2. Millet/sorghum 2 340 / Wheat 180 Dates 119 / Groundnuts 800 Cottonseed 187 / Cotton lint 99 3. Cattle 18 791 / Sheep 18 125 5. Roundwood 1 200 6. Chrome 24 / Salt 92	1. 0.06/1.22; 1 000 kWh (50% hydr.) 2a. Meat 427 / Sugar 235 b. Cement 140 / Petroleum Cotton fabrics 1 108 M ft.[2] / products 988 3. Telephones 62; Cars 55 Rail: . . .; 1 420 ton-mi. Air: 342 pass.-mi.; 6 ton-mi. Sea: 1 308 loaded; 2 220 unloaded	Exports $658 / Imports $1 529 Cotton / Machinery Gum Arabic / Cotton fabrics Sesame / Petrol products Groundnuts Exports to: Saudi Arabia, China, Japan and Italy Imports from: U.K., W. Germany, Japan and India Aid received (net): $170 from West, $21 from East
SWEDEN 1. Kingdom 2. Swedish 3. Krona 4. $1=7.47	1. 173 649 sq. mi. 2. 8 323 000; 47 per sq. mi. 3. BR 11; DR 11; AI 0.3% 4. Urb. pop.: 6 789 (83%) 5. Stockholm 1 384	1. GDP $76 788 (1.6%); $9 274 (1.2%) Agric. 4%, Indust. 27%, Others 69% 2. Oats 1 732 / Barley 2 510 Wheat 1 034 / Apples 92 Potatoes 1 112 / Rapeseed 353 3. Pigs 2 800 / Cattle 1 935 4. Fish 237 5. Roundwood 1 871 6. Iron ore 15 093 / Lead 85 Copper 51 / Zinc 181 Gold 8 926 lb. / Silver 169 t	1. 10.3/43.8; 99 960 kWh (64 hydr., 22% nucl.) 2a. Meat 545 / Butter & cheese 165 Sugar 374 / Sawnwood 398 960 Wood pulp 8 699 b. Iron 1 776 / Steel 3 768 Aluminum 84 / Copper 74 Paper 6 182 / Ships (grt) 338 Petroleum / Vehicles: products 12 592 / pass. 229; comm. 60 3. Telephones 6 160; Cars 2 883 Rail: 4 307 pass.-mi.; 9 061 ton-mi. Air: 2 772 pass.-mi.; 122 ton-mi. Sea: 33 420 loaded; 48 996 unloaded	Exports $28 632 / Imports $28 824 Machinery / Machinery Iron and steel / Petroleum products Paper and cardboard / Vehicles Wood pulp / Textiles Vehicles / Iron and steel Sawnwood / Non-ferrous metals Ships and boats / Clothing Iron ore / Crude petroleum Exports to: U.K., W. Germany, Denmark and Norway Imports from: W. Germany, U.K., U.S.A. and Denmark Invisible trade balance: −$1 941 Aid given (net): $1 250
SWITZERLAND 1. Federal Republic 2. German, French, Italian 3. Swiss Franc 4. $1=2.05	1. 15 941 sq. mi. 2. 6 473 000; 407 per sq. mi. 3. BR 12; DR 9; AI −0.3% 4. Urb. pop.: 3 423 (55%) 5. Bern 284	1. GDP $78 669 (0.1%); $12 408 (−0.1%) Agric. 6%, Indust. 40%, Others 54% 2. Potatoes 1 048 / Apples 240 Wheat 391 / Pears 55 3. Cattle 1 954 / Pigs 2 071 5. Roundwood 141 6. Salt 391	1. 5.8/23.7; 47 976 kWh (70% hydr., 28% nucl.) 2a. Meat 471 / Butter & cheese 160 Wine 1 803 gall. / Beer 88 T gall. Sawnwood 61 633 b. Iron 35 / Steel 784 Aluminum 82 / Cotton yarn 42 Petroleum / Silk fabrics 194 M ft.[2] products 3 613 3. Telephones 4 292; Cars 2 247 Rail: 5 648 pass.-mi.; 4 441 ton-mi. Air: 7 220 pass.-mi.; 304 ton-mi.	Exports $27 043 / Imports $30 696 Machinery / Machinery Watches / Vehicles Textiles / Iron and steel Medicines / Textiles Organic chemical / Petroleum products products Exports to: W. Germany, France, U.S.A., Italy and U.K. Imports from: W. Germany, France, Italy, U.S.A. and U.K. Invisible trade balance: +$6 934 Revenue from tourism: $2 446 Aid given (net): $3 502

Country	Area and Population	Production	Manufactures	Trade
SYRIA 1. Republic 2. Arabic 3. Syrian Pound 4. $1 = 3.95	1. 71 498 sq. mi. 2. 9 314 000; 129 per sq. mi. 3. BR 45; DR 9; AI 3.2% 4. Urb. pop.: 4 141 (48%) 5. Damascus 1 156	1. GDP $5 161 (9.8%); $702 (6.1%) Agric. 20%, Indust. 21%, Others 59% 2. Barley 1 406 Wheat 2 086 Grapes 359 Olives 297 Tomatoes 521 Tobacco 17 Cottonseed 213 3. Sheep 8 800 Goats 1 000 6. Crude petroleum 8 496 Salt 62 Natural gas 1 864 Phosphate 800	1. 12.9/9.4; 4 428 kWh (70% hydr.) 2a. Meat 178 Sugar 19 Olive oil 51 b. Cement 1 812 Petroleum Cotton, woven 355 products 8 454 3. Telephones 212; Cars 65 Rail: 238 pass.-mi.; 6 ton-mi. Air: 493 pass.-mi.; 6 ton-mi. Sea: 15 612 loaded; 7 392 unloaded	Exports $2 103 Imports $5 040 Cotton Machinery Livestock Iron and steel Crude petroleum Vehicles Vegetables Textiles Wheat Crude petroleum Exports to: France, Italy, Greece and U.S.A. Imports from: W. Germany, Italy, France, Iraq and Romania Aid received (net): $74 from West, $131 from East
TAIWAN 1. Republic 2. Chinese 3. New Dollar 4. $1 = 40.03	1. 13 892 sq. mi. 2. 18 135 508; 1 298 per sq. mi. 3. BR 26; DR 5; AI 2.1% 4. Urb. pop.: 8 211 (51%) 5. Tai-pei 3 050	1. GDP $32 337 (9.7%); $1 869 (7.7%) Agric. 11%, Indust. 46%, Others 43% 2. Rice 2 375 Bananas 185 Groundnuts 86 Citrus fruits 399 Pineapples 245 Tea 25 Soya beans 16 3. Pigs 8 781 Cattle 143 4. Fish 912 5. Roundwood 28 6. Coal 2 720 Gold 3 527 lb. Copper . . .	1. . . ./. . .; 40 192 kWh (12% hydr., 27% nucl.) 2a. Sugar 797 Sawnwood 23 086 Meat . . . b. Steel 4 244 Aluminum 31 Cotton yarn 157 Radios 8 721 Petroleum products 18 367 3. Telephones 2 566; Cars 325 Rail: 4 550 pass.-mi.; 1 669 ton-mi. Air: 538 pass.-mi.; 2 ton-mi. Sea: 36 887 loaded; 62 440 unloaded	Exports $22 611 Imports $21 199 Textiles Machinery Electrical goods Crude petroleum Timber products Iron and steel Plastics Chemicals Exports to: U.S.A., Japan and Hong Kong Imports from: Japan, U.S.A. and Kuwait
TANZANIA 1. Federal Republic 2. Swahili 3. Tanzanian Shilling 4. $1 = 9.65	1. 364 900 sq. mi. 2. 18 510 000; 52 per sq. mi. 3. BR 46; DR 16; AI 2.8% 4. Urb. pop.: 2 329 (13%) 5. Dar-es-Salaam 757	1. GDP $4 564 (. . .); $254 (. . .) Agric. 44%, Indust. 10%, Others 46% 2. Maize 750 Cassava 4 650 Bananas 1 580 Coffee 68 Cottonseed 110 Cotton lint 57 Tobacco 21 Sisal 81 3. Cattle 12 673 Goats 5 686 4. Fish 247 5. Roundwood 1 200 6. Gold 4 kg Diamonds 293 c	1. 0.06/1.07; 695 kWh (75% hydr.) 2a. Meat 189 Sawnwood 2 541 Sugar 124 Beer 165 galls. 3. Telephones 66; Cars 45 Rail: see Kenya Air: 22 pass.-mi.; 1 ton-mi. Sea: 1 080 loaded; 3 180 unloaded	Exports $508 Imports $1 226 Coffee Machinery Cotton Vehicles Diamonds Textiles Sisal Petroleum products Cashew nuts Iron and steel Exports to: U.K., W. Germany, U.S.A. and Italy Imports from: U.K., Japan, Netherlands and W. Germany Aid received (net): $341 from West, $12 from East
THAILAND 1. Kingdom 2. Thai 3. Baht 4. $1 = 23.00	1. 198 456 sq. mi. 2. 48 125 000; 243 per sq. mi. 3. BR 32; DR 9; AI 2.5% 4. Urb. pop.: 4 553 (13%) 5. Bangkok 4 702	1. GDP $20 030 (6.9%); $444 (4.1%) Agric. 27%, Indust. 22%, Others 51% 2. Maize 4 000 Rice 19 000 Bananas 2 021 Pineapples 2 000 Jute 219 Rubber 510 Cottonseed 153 Tobacco 87 Cassava 17 900 3. Buffaloes 6 299 Cattle 5 062 4. Fish 1 650 5. Roundwood 1341 6. Lignite 1 680 Tungsten 3 780 Iron ore 35 Tin 30 Antimony 3 548 Manganese 25 Lead 41	1. 0.94/17.2; 5 336 kWh (25% hydr.) 2a. Meat 639 Sawnwood 43 454 Sugar 1 641 b. Cotton yarn 90 Petroleum Cement 6 288 products 7 980 Tin 33 3. Telephones 409; Cars 271 Rail: 5 499 pass.-mi.; 1 743 ton-mi. Air: 4 687 pass.-mi.; 175 ton-mi. Sea: 12 456 loaded; 18 552 unloaded	Exports $7 001 Imports $9 914 Rice Machinery Maize Vehicles Rubber Iron and steel Fruit and vegetables Crude petroleum Tin Exports to: Japan, U.S.A., Singapore, Netherlands and Indonesia Imports from: Japan, U.S.A., W. Germany and Saudi Arabia Invisible trade balance: −$660 Revenue from tourism: $400 Aid received (net): $156 from West
TOGO 1. Republic 2. Bantu, Hamitic, French 3. C.F.A. Franc 4. $1 = 364	1. 21 925 sq. mi. 2. 2 705 000; 124 per sq. mi. 3. BR 48; DR 19; AI 2.6% 4. Urb. pop.: 330 (15%) 5. Lomé 135	1. GDP $626 (. . .); $266 (. . .) Agric. 28%, Indust. 12%, Others 60% 2. Cassava 470 Cocoa 15 Coffee 9 Groundnuts 35 Palm oil 20 3. Goats 750 Sheep 840 5. Roundwood 35 6. Phosphates 2 927	1. −/0.25; 75 kWh (15% hydr.) 2. Food industries . . . 3. Telephones 10; Cars 20 Rail: 56 pass.-mi.; 23 ton-mi. Air: 95 pass.-mi.; 9 ton-mi. Sea: 2 796 loaded; 774 unloaded	Exports $335 Imports $550 Cocoa Cotton fabric Phosphates Machinery Coffee Food Vehicles Exports to: France, W. Germany and Netherlands Imports from: France, W. Germany, U.K. and U.S.A. Aid received (net): $69 from West
TRINIDAD & TOBAGO 1. Commonwealth 2. English 3. Trinidad and Tobago Dollars 4. $1 = 2.41	1. 1 980 sq. mi. 2. 1 185 000; 598 per sq. mi. 3. BR 25; DR 7; AI 0.2% 4. Urb. pop.: 460 (49%) 5. Port of Spain 66	1. GDP $2 942 (. . .); $2 638 (. . .) Agric. 3%, Indust. 51%, Others 46% 2. Rice 22 Bananas 9 Oranges 3 Grapefruits 4 Cocoa 2 Coffee 2 Copra 2 3. Cattle 78 Pigs 59 6. Natural gas 22 949 Crude petroleum 9 780	1. 19.4/5.83; 1 836 kWh 2a. Sugar 90 Beer 5 431 gall. b. Petroleum products 8 262 3. Telephones 75; Cars 132 Air: 938 pass.-mi.; 11 ton-mi. Sea: 20 832 loaded; 14 856 unloaded	Exports $3 725 Imports $3 115 Petroleum products Crude petroleum Petroleum Manufactured goods Exports to: U.S.A., Netherlands and Surinam Imports from: U.S.A., U.K., Saudi Arabia and Indonesia Revenue from tourism: $91 Aid received (net): $5 from West
TUNISIA 1. Republic 2. Arabic, French 3. Dinar 4. $1 = 0.65	1. 63 170 sq. mi. 2. 6 513 000; 104 per sq. mi. 3. BR 35; DR 11; AI 2.5% 4. Urb. pop.: 2 205 (43%) 5. Tunis 944	1. GDP $5 641 (8.5%); $934 (6.3%) Agric. 16%, Indust. 18%, Others 66% 2. Wheat 963 Tomatoes 295 Oranges 141 Olives 700 Grapes 141 Dates 53 3. Sheep 4 967 Cattle 914 4. Fish 60 5. Roundwood 71 6. Lead 6 Crude petroleum 5 412 Iron ore 210 Zinc 8 Phosphates 4 925 Natural gas 4 352	1. 8.75/3.41; 2 676 kWh (0.8% hydr.) 2a. Sugar 8 Wine 70 Meat 102 Olive oil 140 b. Petroleum products 1 367 3. Telephones 158; Cars 102 Rail: 625 pass.-mi.; 1 065 ton-mi. Air: 894 pass.-mi.; 7 ton-mi. Sea: 4 380 loaded; 8 148 unloaded	Exports $2 189 Imports $3 479 Petroleum Machinery Olive oil Wheat Phosphates Textiles Fertilizer Iron and steel Exports to: France, Italy, Greece and W. Germany Imports from: France, W. Germany and Italy Revenue from tourism: $415 Aid received (net): $212 from West, $16 from East
TURKEY 1. Republic 2. Turkish 3. Lira 4. $1 = 205	1. 301 382 sq. mi. 2. 46 375 000; 153 per sq. mi. 3. BR 35; DR 10; AI 2.5% 4. Urb. pop.: 18 774 (45%) 5. Ankara 2 204	1. GDP $35 230 (6.9%); $873 (4.1%) Agric. 25%, Indust. 22%, Others 53% 2. Barley 5 900 Wheat 17 040 Apples 1 479 Oranges 723 Grapes 3 700 Tomatoes 3 900 Cottonseed 785 Cotton lint 488 Wool 62 Tobacco 200 3. Sheep 48 630 Goats 19 043 4. Fish 430 5. Roundwood 812 6. Coal 3 600 Zinc 41 Lignite 9 504 Crude petroleum 2 388 Iron ore 1 728 Antimony 835 t Chrome 259 Mercury 7 Bauxite 473 Copper 34	1. 12.2/29.8; 20 565 kWh (42% hydr.) 2a. Meat 858 Sawnwood 123 585 Sugar 1 300 Wine 30 Olive oil 112 b. I.on 324 Steel 1 799 Cotton yarn 166 Wool yarn 7 Petroleum Copper 26 products 13 986 Cement 15 041 3. Telephones 1 379; Cars 659 Rail: 3 487 pass.-mi.; 3 524 ton-mi. Air: 1 184 pass.-mi.; 5 ton-mi. Sea: 6 672 loaded; 20 520 unloaded	Exports $4 721 Imports $8 944 Cotton Machinery Nuts Vehicles Tobacco Fertilizer Raisins Crude petroleum Iron and steel Exports to: W. Germany, U.S.A., Italy and France Imports from: W. Germany, U.S.A., Iran, Italy and France Revenue from tourism: $230 Aid received (net): $706 from West

Country	Area and Population	Production	Manufactures	Trade

UGANDA

Country
1. Republic
2. English, Bantu
3. Ugandan Shilling
4. $1=277

Area and Population
1. 91 134 sq. mi.
2. 13 620 000; 150 per sq. mi.
3. BR 45; DR 14; AI 3.4%
4. Urb. pop.: 747 (7%)
5. Kampala 331

Production
1. GDP $2 407 (0.1%); $208 (−3.1%)
   Agric. 53%, Indust. 10%, Others 37%
2. Cassava 1 420 / Millet/sorghum 980
   Coffee 130 / Tea 1
   Cottonseed 11 / Groundnuts 150
3. Cattle 5 500 / Goats 2 155
5. Roundwood 177
6. Tin 120 / Tungsten 139
   Copper 8

Manufactures
1. 0.08/0.37; 648 kWh (99% hydr.)
2a. Meat 142 / Sugar 5
   Sawnwood 847 / Beer 4 860 gall.
3. Telephones 49; Cars 35
   Rail: see Kenya
   Air: 122 pass.-mi.; 5 ton-mi.

Trade
Exports $345 / Imports $293
Coffee / Manufactured goods
Cotton / Machinery
Copper / Vehicles
Exports to: U.K., U.S.A., Spain and France
Imports from: U.K., W. Germany, Kenya and Brazil
Aid received (net): $18 from West

UNITED KINGDOM

Country
1. Kingdom
2. English
3. English Pound
4. $1=0.623

Area and Population
1. 94 516 sq. mi.
2. 55 833 000; 591 per sq. mi.
3. BR 13; DR 12; AI −0.0%
4. Urb. pop.: 42 716 (76%)
5. London 6 696

Production
1. GDP $276 578 (2.1%); $4 955 (2.0%)
   Agric. 2%, Indust. 31%, Others 67%
2. Barley 10 149 / Wheat 8 465
   Oats 622 / Potatoes 6 400
   Apples 245 / Wool 52
3. Sheep 32 282 / Cattle 13 109
4. Fish 824
5. Roundwood 141
6. Coal 127 788 / Natural gas 359 655
   Iron ore 190 / Crude petroleum 87 036
   Tin 2 802 t / Salt 7 310
   Lead 2

Manufactures
1. 275.4/276.2; 277 716 kWh (2% hydr., 12% nucl.)
2a. Meat 2 989 / Sawnwood 60 751
   Butter & cheese 401 / Sugar 1 200
   Beer 1 461 T gall.
b. Iron 9 696 / Steel 10 620
   Aluminum 370 / Lead 333
   Copper 137 / Plastics 2 050
   Cotton yarn 52 / Wool yarn 183
   Synthetic fibres 552 / Silk fabric 7 984 M ft.[2]
   Paper 3 791 / Radios 891
   Petroleum / Vehicles:
   products 65 697 / pass. 955; comm. 229
   Ships (grt) 608 / Cement 12 828
3. Telephones 23 182; Cars 15 532
   Rail: 19 688 pass.-mi.; 10 872 ton-mi.
   Air: 31 432 pass.-mi.; 943 ton-mi.
   Sea: 100 836 loaded; 132 540 unloaded

Trade
Exports $105 588 / Imports $100 882
Machinery / Machinery
Vehicles / Crude petroleum
Textiles / Non-ferrous metals
Diamonds / Fruit and vegetables
Non-ferrous metals / Diamonds
Iron and steel / Minerals
Alcoholic drinks / Cereals
Aircraft / Butter
/ Meat
/ Textiles
Exports to: U.S.A., W. Germany, France, Ireland, Belgium-Luxembourg and Netherlands
Imports from: U.S.A., W. Germany, France and Netherlands
Invisible trade balance: + $10 648
Revenue from tourism: $4 010
Aid given (net): $10 273

UNITED STATES

Country
1. Federal Republic
2. English
3. U.S. Dollar

Area and Population
1. 3 618 770 sq. mi.
2. 229 805 000; 65 per sq. mi.
3. BR 16; DR 9; AI 0.8%
4. Urb. pop.: 149 325 (74%)
5. Washington 3 061

Production
1. GDP $1 877 983 (3.0%); $8 612 (2.2%)
   Agric. 3%, Indust. 29%, Others 68%
2. Barley 10 414 / Oats 7 375
   Maize 208 314 / Wheat 76 026
   Oranges 9 547 / Grapefruit 2 503
   Wine 1 450 / Soya Beans 55 260
   Cottonseed 5 673 / Tobacco 929
   Rice 8 408
3. Cattle 114 321 / Pigs 64 512
4. Fish 3 635
5. Roundwood 11 367
6. Coal 700 908 / Nickel 10
   Iron ore 54 223 / Tungsten 4 300
   Bauxite 1 812 / Vanadium 3 875 t
   Copper 1 529 / Natural gas 4 993 616
   Gold 66 488 lb. / Crude petroleum 421 308
   Lead 444 / Potash 2 052
   Molybdenum 13 / Phosphates 50 037
   Zinc 343

Manufactures
1. 2 090.4/2 369.7; 2 368 224 kWh (12% hydr., 11% nucl., 0.2 geo.)
2a. Meat 25 031 / Butter & cheese 2 514
   Sugar 5 771 / Wine 1 450
   Sawnwood 2 659 466 / Wood pulp 45 835
b. Cotton yarn 1 120 / Wool yarn 56
   Synthetic / Silk fabric 83 863 M ft.[2]
   fibres 3 340 / Paper 59 131
   Copper 1 317 / Magnesium 127
   Iron 66 564 / Steel 108 876
   Aluminum 6 090 / Plastics 12 418
   Petroleum / Vehicles:
   products: 532 019 / pass. 6 238; comm. 1 690
   Radios 10 300 / Ships (grt) 558
   Textiles
3. Telephones 164 027; Cars 123 467
   Rail: 12 000 pass.-mi.; 932 000 ton-mi.
   Air: 233 240 pass.-mi.; 6 315 ton-mi.
   Sea: 369 132 loaded; 422 700 unloaded

Trade
Exports $228 961 / Imports $271 269
Machinery / Vehicles
Vehicles / Machinery
Aircraft / Iron and steel
Cereals / Non-ferrous metals
Chemical products / Crude petroleum
Iron and steel / Petroleum products
Non-ferrous metals / Clothing
Soya / Paper and cardboard
Metals / Textiles
Coal / Metals
Textiles
Exports to: Canada, Japan, U.K., W. Germany and Mexico
Imports from: Canada, Japan, W. Germany, U.K. and Mexico
Invisible trade balance: + $39 470
Revenue from tourism: $7 284
Aid given (net): $14 323

UPPER VOLTA

Country
1. Republic
2. French
3. C.F.A. Franc
4. $1=364

Area and Population
1. 105 869 sq. mi.
2. 7 094 000; 67 per sq. mi.
3. BR 48; DR 22%; AI 2.6%
4. Urb. pop.: ... (8%)
5. Ouagadougou 169

Production
1. GDP $507 (...); $84 (...)
   Agric. 42%, Indust. 12%, Others 46%
2. Millet/sorghum 1 150 / Maize 100
   Rice 29 / Groundnuts 77
3. Cattle 2 760 / Goats 2 800
5. Roundwood 212
6. Gold ...

Manufactures
1. −/0.2; 120 kWh
2a. Meat 63
3. Telephones 8; Cars 12
   Air: 95 pass.-mi.; 96 ton-mi.

Trade
Exports $75 / Imports $338
Livestock / Manufactured goods
Cotton / Foods
Exports to: Ivory Coast, France and China
Imports from: France, U.S.A. and Ivory Coast
Aid received (net): $116 from West

URUGUAY

Country
1. Republic
2. Spanish
3. Uruguayan Peso
4. $1=33.88

Area and Population
1. 68 536 sq. mi.
2. 2 927 000; 41 per sq. mi.
3. BR 18; DR 10; AI 0.6%
4. Urb. pop.: 2 308 (83%)
5. Montevideo 1 230

Production
1. GDP $4 660 (1.6%); $1 612 (1.4%)
   Agric. 10%, Indust. 27%, Others 63%
2. Maize 196 / Wheat 400
   Grapes 53 / Oranges 58
   Linseed 21 / Wool 71
3. Sheep 19 980 / Cattle 10 952
4. Fish 120
5. Roundwood 71

Manufactures
1. 0.28/2.74; 3 331 kWh (68% hydr.)
2a. Meat 474 / Sawnwood 3 494
   Sugar 79
b. Petroleum products 1 564
3. Telephones 270; Cars 168
   Rail: 306 pass.-mi.; 188 ton-mi.
   Air: 31 pass.-mi.; 1 ton-mi.
   Sea: 430 loaded; 1 451 unloaded

Trade
Exports $1 215 / Imports $1 599
Beef / Machinery
Wool / Vehicles
Hides and skins / Crude petroleum
Exports to: W. Germany, Brazil and U.S.A.
Imports from: Argentina, Brazil, U.S.A. and Iraq
Aid received (net): $10 from West

U.S.S.R.

Country
1. Socialist Republic
2. Russian and others
3. Rouble
4. $1=0.73

Area and Population
1. 8 649 534 sq. mi.
2. 267 697 000; 31 per sq. mi.
3. BR 19; DR 10; AI 0.9%
4. Urb. pop.: 163 586 (62%)
5. Moscow 8 099

Production
1. NMP $540 214 (5.7%); $2 086 (4.8%)
   Agric. 17%, Indust. 51%, Others 32%
2. Barley 43 000 / Wheat 88 000
   Potatoes 83 000 / Grapes 6 500
   Tomatoes 6 150 / Cottonseed 5 879
   Tobacco 300
3. Sheep 141 573 / Cattle 115 057
4. Fish 9 412
5. Roundwood 12 567
6. Coal 510 000 / Tungsten 10 700 t
   Iron ore 145 202 / Zinc 1 010
   Bauxite 6 400 / Natural gas 3 879 080
   Chrome 960 / Crude petroleum 609 000
   Copper 1 140 / Phosphates 24 800
   Lead 570 / Potash 6 635
   Manganese 2 945 / Salt 14 500
   Molybdenum 17 / Asbestos 2 470
   Nickel 170 / Diamonds 9 500

Manufactures
1. 1 939.2/1 485.7; 1 325 004 kWh (14% hydr., 5% nucl.)
2a. Meat 15 367 / Sawnwood 3 515 880
   Butter & cheese 3 000 / Sugar 6 100
   Wine 3 200
b. Iron 107 760 / Steel 149 004
   Aluminum 2 400 / Copper 1 140
   Magnesium 70 / Paper 9 236
   Cotton yarn 1 624 / Wool yarn 426
   Synthetic fibres 1 089 / Silk fabric 491 T ft.[2]
   Linen 870 / Radios 8 728
   Petroleum / Vehicles:
   products 304 708 / pass. 1 314; comm. 874
3. Telephones 20 943; Cars 7 000
   Rail: 206 211 pass.-mi.; 2 177 847 ton-mi.
   Air: 6 200 pass.-mi.; 197 ton-mi.
   Sea: 150 916 loaded; 43 521 unloaded

Trade
Exports $76 449 / Imports $68 522
Machinery / Machinery
Iron and steel / Clothing
Crude petroleum / Ships
Non-ferrous metals / Iron and steel
Petroleum products / Minerals
Sawnwood / Railway rolling
Cotton / stock
Vehicles / Shoes
Main trade is with: E. Germany, Poland, Czechoslovakia, Bulgaria and Hungary
Aid given (net3m$3 327

Country	Area and Population	Production	Manufactures	Trade

VENEZUELA
1. Republic
2. Spanish
3. Bolivar
4. $1=4.29
	1. 352 144 sq. mi.
	2. 14 313 000; 41 per sq. mi.
	3. BR 37; DR 6; AI 3.0%
	4. Urb. pop.: 10 584 (76%)
	5. Caracas 2 849
		1. GDP $36 366 (5.8%); 2 772 (2.6%)
		   Agric. 6%, Indust. 36%, Others 58%
		2. Maize 415 Bananas 1 495
		   Oranges 430 Tomatoes 180
		   Cocoa 14 Coffee 62
		   Cottonseed 14 Sesame 30
		3. Cattle 10 939 Pigs 2 287
		4. Fish 172
		5. Roundwood 318
		6. Iron ore 10 061 Natural gas 135 907
		   Gold 1 903 lb. Crude petroleum 111 576
		   Diamonds 763 c Phosphates 109
		                         Coal 100
			1. 192.5/47.0; 31 000 kWh (47% hydr.)
			2a. Meat 691 Sawnwood 12 319
			   Sugar 291
			b. Iron 689 Steel 1 824
			   Cotton yarn 16 Synthetic fibres 17
			   Cement 3 426 Vehicles:
			   Petroleum pass. 97; comm 66
			   products 41 289
			3. Telephones 847; Cars 1 300
			   Rail: 24 pass.-mi.; 12 ton-mi.
			   Air: 2 190 pass.-mi.; 93 ton-mi.
			   Sea: 131 316 loaded; 8 568 unloaded
				Exports $20 950 Imports $10 655
				   Crude petroleum Machinery
				   Petroleum products Vehicles
				   Iron ore Iron and steel
				   Coffee Cereals
				                         Manufactured goods
				Exports to: U.S.A., Netherlands, Antilles
				and Canada
				Imports from: U.S.A., W. Germany and Japan
				Invisible trade balance: −$3 059

VIETNAM
1. Democratic Republic
2. Vietnamese
3. Dông
4. $1=2.18
	1. 128 402 sq. mi.
	2. 54 968 000; 427 per sq. mi.
	3. BR 40; DR 14; AI 2.4%
	4. Urb. pop.: 8 149 (18%)
	5. Hanoi 2 571
		1. Agric. 29%, Indust. 7%; Others 64%
		2. Rice 12 570 Cassava 3 400
		   Groundnuts 80 Tea 23
		   Maize 540 Tobacco 28
		3. Cattle 1 450 Buffaloes 2 200
		4. Fish 1 014
		5. Roundwood 2 259
		6. Coal 5 900 Phosphates 1 200
		   Salt 375
			1. 6.39/7.76; 3 900 kWh (18% hydr.)
			2a. Sawnwood 18 356
			b. Cotton yarn 10 Cement 544
			3. Telephones 47; Cars 66
			   Rail: 2 510 pass.-mi.; 608 ton-mi.
			   Air: 242 pass.-mi.; 3 ton-mi.
			   Sea: 198 loaded; 4 875 unloaded
				Exports $440 Imports $1 210
				Main trade is with U.S.S.R. and other
				Communist countries and Japan,
				France, Singapore and Hong Kong

YEMEN
1. Republic
2. Arabic
3. Riyal
4. $1=4.59
	1. 75 289 sq. mi.
	2. 5 940 000; 78 per sq. mi.
	3. BR 49; DR 24; AI 2.3%
	4. Urb. pop.: 331 (6%)
	5. Sana 448
		1. GDP 1 122 (. . .); $212 (. . .)
		   Agric. 61%, Indust. 3%, Others 36%
		2. Millet 70 Wheat 70
		   Coffee 4 Cottonseed 3
		3. Sheep 3 200 Cattle 950
			1. −/0.45; 75 kWh
			3. Telephones 4; Cars . . .
			   Sea: 25 loaded; 500 unloaded
				Exports $14 Imports $1 492
				Exports to: China, S. Yemen, Italy and Saudi Arabia
				Imports from: Saudi Arabia, Japan and India
				Aid received (net): $42 from West

YUGOSLAVIA
1. Federal Republic
2. Croatian, Serbian
3. Yugoslavian Dinar
4. $1=77.66
	1. 98 766 sq. mi.
	2. 22 516 000; 228 per sq. mi.
	3. BR 17; DR 9; AI 0.9%
	4. Urb. pop.: 7 914 (39%)
	5. Belgrade 775
		1. NMP $27 637 (5.8%); $1 294 (4.8%)
		   Agric. 16%, Indust. 40%, Others 44%
		2. Maize 9 800 Wheat 4 270
		   Grapes 1 330 Wool 10
		   Tobacco 70
		3. Sheep 7 388 Pigs 7 869
		4. Fish 58
		5. Roundwood 564
		6. Coal 384 Gold 7 880 lb.
		   Lignite 51 864 Lead 119
		   Iron ore 1 676 Silver 138 t
		   Antimony 1 724 Zinc 87
		   Bauxite 3 252 Chrome 2
		   Copper 111 Crude petroleum 4 380
		   Natural gas 16 367
			1. 28.6/45.8; 60 072 kWh (48% hydr.)
			2a. Meat 1 428 Sawnwood 149 636
			   Sugar 850 Wine 670
			b. Iron 3 072 Steel 2 352
			   Copper 93 Lead 86
			   Cotton yarn 118 Wool yarn 51
			   Synthetic fibres 97 Ships (grt) 284
			   Petroleum products 11 101
			3. Telephones 1 556; Cars 2 417
			   Rail: 6 468 pass.-mi.; 15 798 ton-mi.
			   Air: 1 691 pass.-mi.; 18 ton-mi.
			   Sea: 5 244 loaded; 23 400 unloaded
				Exports $10 929 Imports $15 757
				   Machinery Machinery
				   Non-ferrous metals Iron and steel
				   Ships and boats Vehicles
				   Clothing Textile fibres
				   Meat Textiles
				   Textiles Non-ferrous metals
				   Iron and steel Chemical products
				   Shoes Crude petroleum
				Exports to: Italy, U.S.S.R. and W. Germany
				Imports from: W. Germany, Italy and U.S.S.R.
				Invisible trade balance: +$1 753
				Revenue from tourism: $841

ZAÏRE
1. Democratic Republic
2. Kiswahili, etc.
3. Zaïre
4. $1=5.86
	1. 905 567 sq. mi.
	2. 26 377 000; 28 per sq. mi.
	3. BR 46; DR 19; AI 2.9%
	4. Urb. pop.: 7 997 (30%)
	5. Kinshasa 2 008
		1. GDP $3 158 (3.8%); $127 (1.0%)
		   Agric. 19%, Indust. 22%, Others 59%
		2. Cassava 13 000 Maize 520
		   Coffee 75 Groundnuts 320
		   Palm oil 155 Rubber 28
		   Bananas 1 790 Cottonseed 19
		3. Goats 2 722 Cattle 1 170
		4. Fish 115
		5. Roundwood 353
		6. Cobalt 11 Tin 3 450 t
		   Copper 505 Zinc 76
		   Manganese 21 Diamonds 6 100 c
		   Gold 3 678 lb. Tungsten 181 t
		   Crude petroleum 996
			1. 2.13/1.84; 4 360 kWh (99% hydr.)
			2a. Sugar Beer 110 T gall.
			   Sawnwood 3 177
			b. Copper 468 Zinc 58
			   Petroleum Cement 475
			   products 340
			3. Telephones 26; Cars 40
			   Rail: 290 pass.-mi.; 1 368 ton-mi.
			   Air: 514 pass.-mi.; 21 ton-mi.
			   Sea 464 loaded; 715 unloaded
				Exports $662 Imports $672
				   Copper Machinery
				   Diamonds Vehicles
				   Cobalt Petroleum products
				   Coffee Cotton fabric
				   Palm oil Cereals
				Exports to: Belgium-Luxembourg, U.K. and U.S.A.
				Imports from: Belgium-Luxembourg, U.S.A., France and
				W. Germany
				Aid received (net): $253 from West

ZAMBIA
1. Republic
2. English
3. Kwacha
4. $1=1.18
	1. 290 585 sq. mi.
	2. 5 961 000; 21 per sq. mi.
	3. BR 49; DR 17; AI 3.2%
	4. Urb. pop.: 2 280 (40%)
	5. Lusaka 538
		1. GDP $2 263 (3.2%); $414 (0.0%)
		   Agric. 16%, Indust. 29%, Others 55%
		2. Maize 1 000 Tobacco 4
		   Millet/sorghum 100 Groundnuts 30
		3. Cattle 2 151 Goats 310
		4. Fish 51
		5. Roundwood 177
		6. Coal 504 Tin . . .
		   Cobalt 5 Gold 545 lb.
		   Copper 588 Silver 33
		   Lead 16 Zinc 40
			1. 1.61/2.77; 9 792 kWh (99% hydr.)
			2a. Meat 69 Sugar 102
			   Sawnwood 1 482
			b. Copper 572 Zinc 42
			   Lead 10 Cement 144
			3. Telephones 57; Cars 105
			   Air: 342 pass.-mi.; 11 ton-mi.
				Exports $1 402 Imports $1 090
				   Copper Machinery
				   Zinc Vehicles
				   Lead Textiles
				   Cobalt Iron and steel
				   Tobacco Petroleum products
				Exports to: Japan, U.K., W. Germany and U.S.A.
				Imports from: U.K., Saudi Arabia and U.S.A.
				Aid received (net): $117 from West

ZIMBABWE
1. Republic
2. English
3. Zimbabwe Dollar
4. $1=0.97
	1. 150 804 sq. mi.
	2. 7 600 000; 49 per sq. mi.
	3. BR 47; DR 14; AI 3.2%
	4. Urb. pop.: 1 396 (20%)
	5. Harare 633
		1. GDP $2 999 (3.5%); $477 (0.1%)
		   Agric. 15%, Indust. 29%, Others 56%
		2. Maize 2 814 Millet/sorghum 327
		   Groundnuts 239 Tobacco 70
		3. Cattle 5 000 Goats 1 350
		5. Roundwood 282
		6. Coal 2 868 Gold 25 439 lb.
		   Iron ore 1 092 Nickel 15
		   Chrome 300 Tin 600
		   Copper 25 Asbestos 260
			1. 3.70/4.55; 4 512 kWh (88% hydr.)
			2a. Meat 146 Sugar 390
			   Sawnwood 5 718
			b. Iron 350 Steel 650
			   Copper 25
			3. Telephones 197; Cars 215
			   Rail: . . .; 3 278 ton-mi.
				Exports $1 423 Imports $1 322
				   Tobacco Machinery
				   Asbestos Textiles
				   Copper Vehicles
				   Gold Mineral fuels
				Main trade with U.K., W. Germany and U.S.A.
				Aid received from West

Chart of the Stars

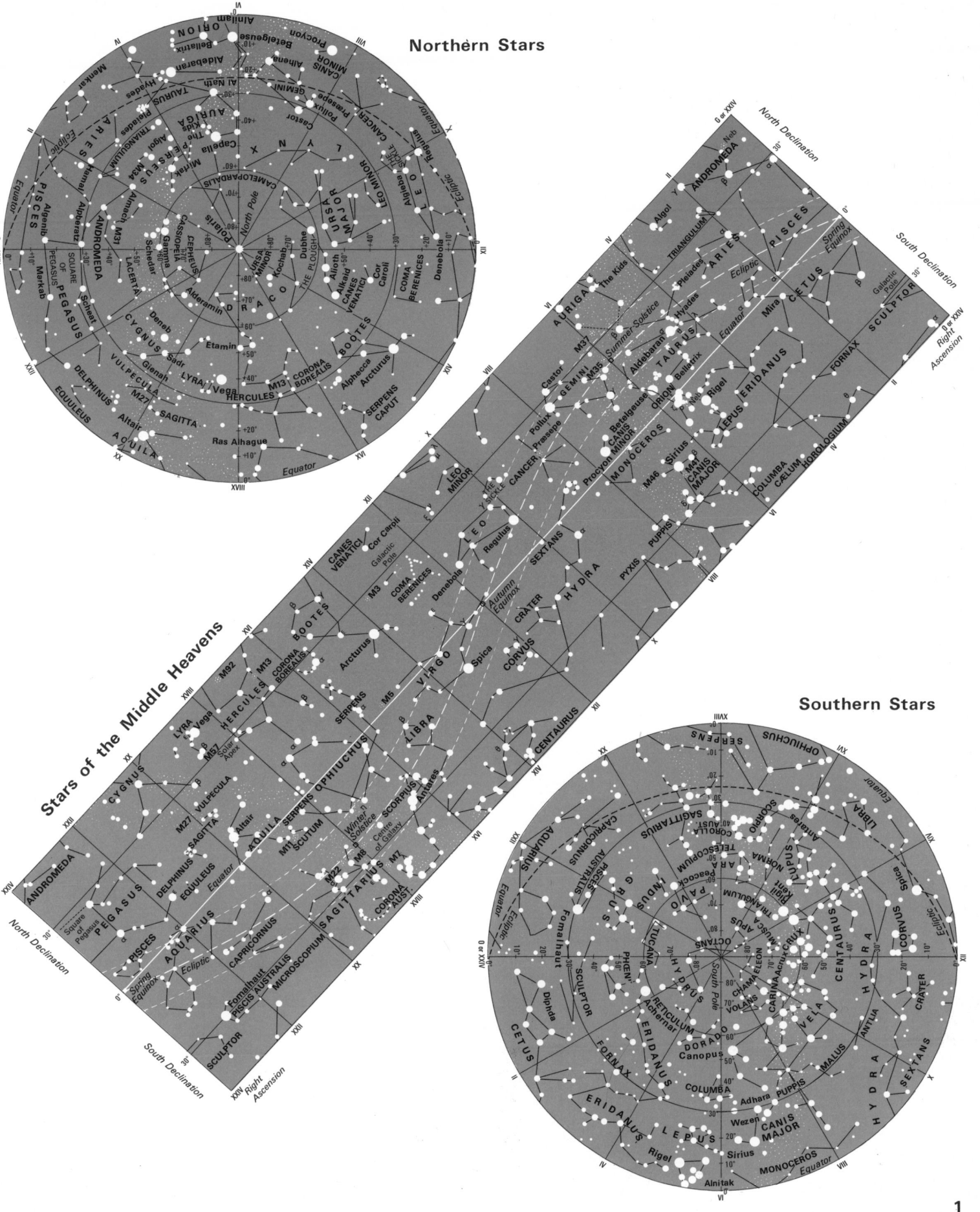

Northern Stars

Stars of the Middle Heavens

Southern Stars

1

The Solar System

The Solar System is a minute part of one of the innumerable galaxies that make up the universe. Our Galaxy is represented in the drawing to the right and The Solar System (S) lies near the plane of spiral-shaped galaxy, but 27 000 light-years from the centre. The System consists of the Sun at the centre with planets, moons, asteroids, comets, meteors, meteorites, dust and gases revolving around it. It is calculated to be at least 4 700 million years old.

The Solar System can be considered in two parts: the Inner Region planets- Mercury, Venus, Earth and Mars - all small and solid, the Outer Region planets - Jupiter, Saturn, Uranus and Neptune - all gigantic in size, and on the edge of the system the smaller Pluto.

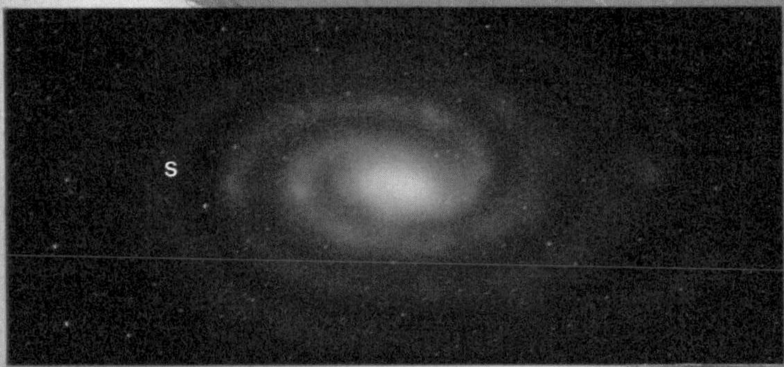

Our galaxy

Inner region planets

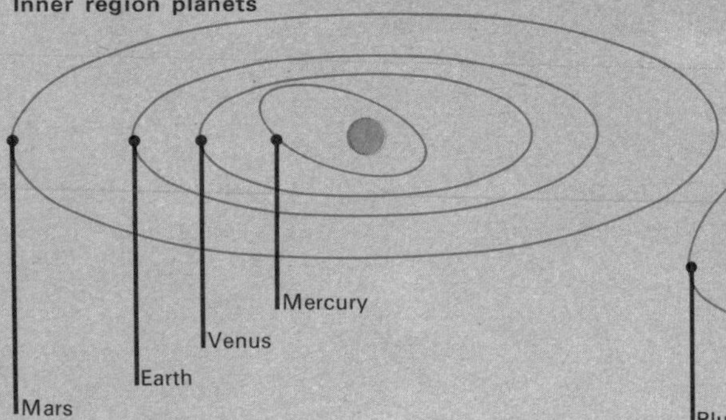

Outer region planets

Mercury

Venus

Earth

Mars

Pluto

Neptune

Uranus

Saturn

Jupiter

Mars

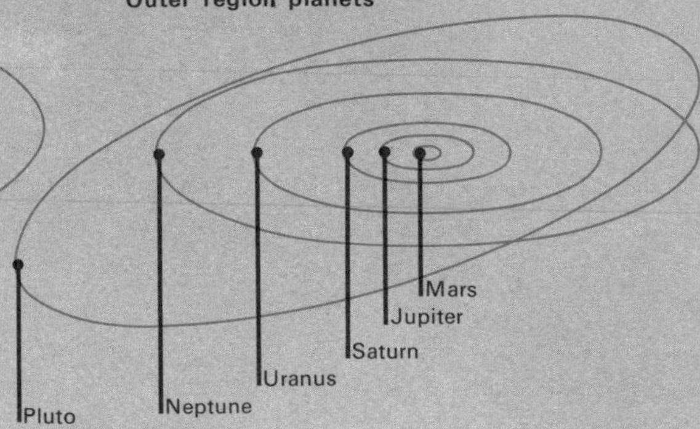

The planets
All planets revolve round the Sun in the same direction, and mostly in the same plane. Their orbits are shown (left) - they are not perfectly circular paths.

The table below summarizes the dimensions and movements of the Sun and planets.

The Sun
The Sun has an interior with temperatures believed to be of several million °F brought about by continuous thermo-nuclear fusions of hydrogen into helium. This immense energy is transferred by radiation into surrounding layers of gas the outer surface of which is called the chromosphere. From this "surface" with a temperature of many thousands °F "flames" (solar prominences) leap out into the diffuse corona which can best be seen at times of total eclipse (see photo right). The bright surface of the Sun, the photosphere, is calculated to have a temperature of about 11 000 °F and when viewed through a telescope has a mottled appearance, the darker patches being called sunspots - the sites of large disturbances of the surface.

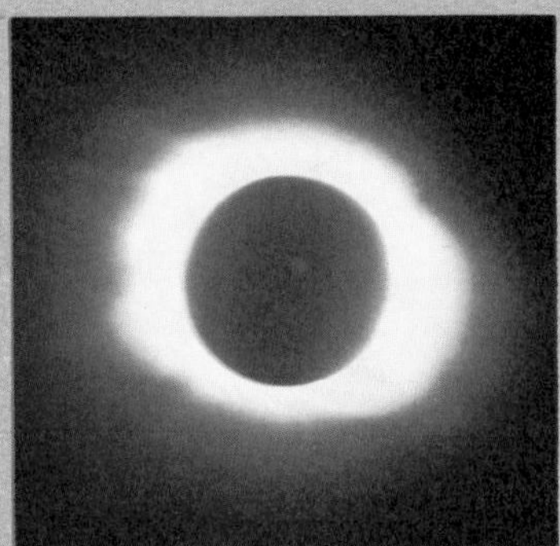

Total eclipse of the sun

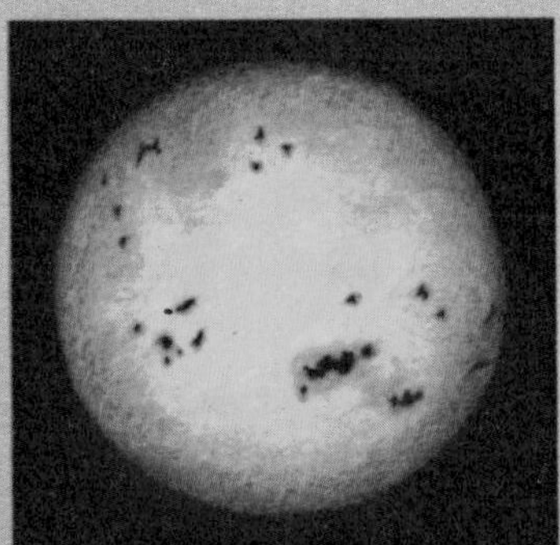

The sun's surface

	Equatorial diameter in mi.	Mass (earth=1)	Mean distance from sun in millions mi.	Mean radii of orbit (earth = 1)	Orbital inclination	Mean sidereal period (days)	Mean period of rotation on axis (days)	Number of satellites
Sun	864 432	332 946	—	—	—		25.38	—
Mercury	3 029	0.05	35.9	0.38	7°	87.9	58.6	0
Venus	7 517	0.81	67.2	0.72	3°23'	224.7	243	0
Earth	7 921	1.00	92.9	1.00	—	365.2	0.99	1
Mars	4 219	0.10	141.5	1.52	1°50'	686.9	1.02	2
Jupiter	88 679	317.9	483.3	5.20	1°18'	4332.5	0.41	14?
Saturn	74 520	95.1	886.2	9.53	2°29'	10759.2	0.42	11
Uranus	32 292	14.5	1781.6	19.17	0°46'	30684.8	0.45	5
Neptune	30 056	17.2	2 792	30.05	1°46'	60190.5	0.67	2
Pluto	1 863?	0.001	3663.9	39.43	17°1'	91628.6	6.38	1?

The Sun's diameter is 109 times greater than that of the Earth.

Distances from sun in millions mi.

5·9 — Mercury
7·2 — Venus
2·9 — Earth
1·5 — Mars

3·3 — Jupiter

886 — Saturn

782 — Uranus

792 — Neptune

664 — Pluto

Mercury is the nearest planet to the Sun. It is composed mostly of high density metals and probably has an atmosphere of heavy inert gases.

Venus is similar in size to the Earth, and probably in composition. It is, however, much hotter and has a dense atmosphere of carbon dioxide which obscures our view of its surface.

Earth is the largest of the inner planets. It has a dense iron-nickel core surrounded by layers of silicate rock. The surface is approximately $\frac{2}{5}$ land and $\frac{3}{5}$ water, and the lower atmosphere consists of a mixture of nitrogen, oxygen and other gases supplemented by water vapour. With this atmosphere and surface temperatures usually between −60°F and +100°F life is possible.

Mars, smaller than the Earth, has a noticeably red appearance. Photographs taken by the Mariner probes show clearly the cratered surface and polar ice caps, probably made from frozen carbon dioxide.

The Asteroids orbit the Sun mainly between Mars and Jupiter. They consist of thousands of bodies of varying sizes with diameters ranging from yards to hundreds of miles.

Jupiter is the largest planet of the Solar System. Photographs taken by Voyager I and II have revealed an equatorial ring system and shown the distinctive Great Red Spot and rotating cloud belts in great detail.

Saturn, the second largest planet consists of hydrogen, helium and other gases. The equatorial rings are composed of small ice particles.

Uranus is extremely remote but just visible to the naked eye and has a greenish appearance. A faint equatorial ring system was discovered in 1977. The planet's axis is tilted through 98° from its orbital plane, therefore it revolves in a retrograde manner.

Neptune, yet more remote than Uranus and larger. It is composed of gases and has a bluish green appearance when seen in a telescope. As with Uranus, little detail can be observed on its surface.

Pluto. No details are known of its composition or surface. The existence of this planet was firstly surmised in a computed hypothesis, which was tested by repeated searches by large telescopes until in 1930 the planet was found. Latest evidence seems to suggest that Pluto has one satellite, provisionally named Charon.

3

The Earth

Seasons, Equinoxes and Solstices

The Earth revolves around the Sun once a year and rotates daily on its axis, which is inclined at $66\frac{1}{2}°$ to the orbital plane and always points into space in the same direction. At midsummer (N.) the North Pole tilts towards the Sun, six months later it points away and half way between the axis is at right angles to the direction of the Sun (right).

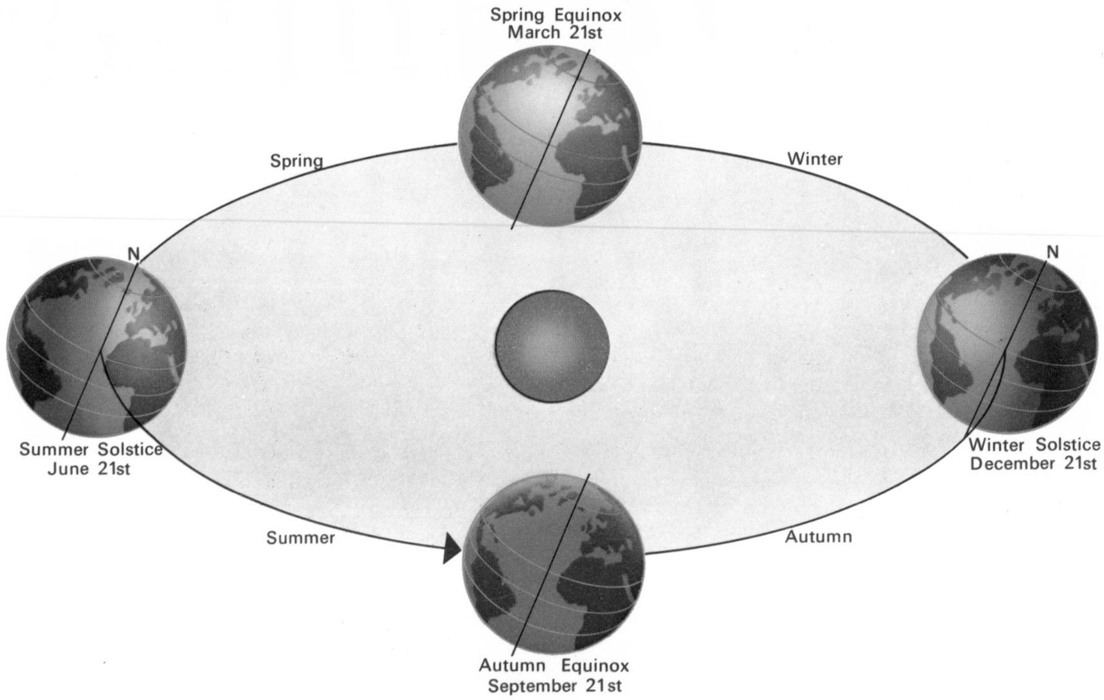

Earth data

Maximum distance from the Sun (Aphelion) 94 396 356 mi.
Minimum distance from the Sun (Perihelion) 91 287 515 mi.
Obliquity of the ecliptic 23° 27' 08"
Length of year - tropical (equinox to equinox) 365.24 days
Length of year - sidereal (fixed star to fixed star) 365.26 days
Length of day - mean solar day 24h 03m 56s
Length of day - mean sidereal day 23h 56m 04s

Spring Equinox March 21st

Spring

Winter

Summer Solstice June 21st

Winter Solstice December 21st

Summer

Autumn

Autumn Equinox September 21st

Arctic Circle

Sun's rays

Equator

Antarctic Circle

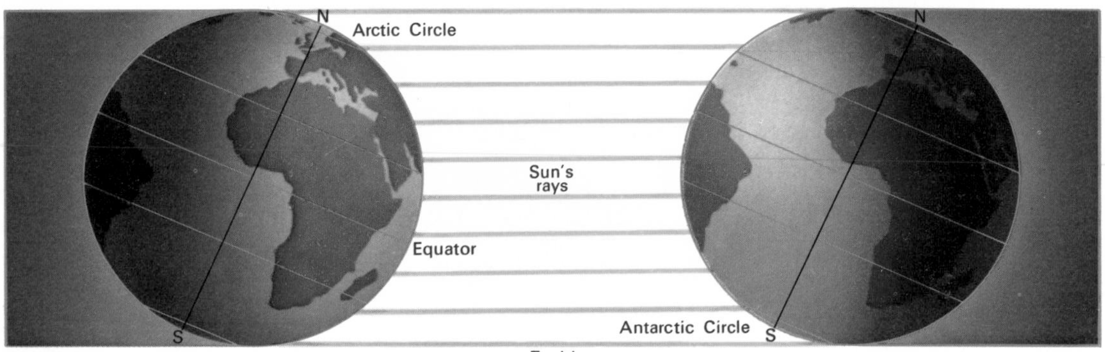

Length of day and night

At the summer solstice in the northern hemisphere, the Arctic has total daylight and the Antarctic total darkness. The opposite occurs at the winter solstice. At the equator, the length of day and night are almost equal all the year, at 30° the length of day varies from about 14 hours to 10 hours and at 50° from about 16 hours to 8 hours.

Apparent path of the Sun

The diagrams (right) illustrate the apparent path of the Sun at A the equator, B in mid latitudes say 45°N, C at the Arctic Circle $66\frac{1}{2}°$ and D at the North Pole where there is six months continuous daylight and six months continuous night

(A) Equator

(B) 45° North

(C) Arctic circle

(D) North pole

Equator 0°

45°N

Arctic Circle $66\frac{1}{2}°$N

4

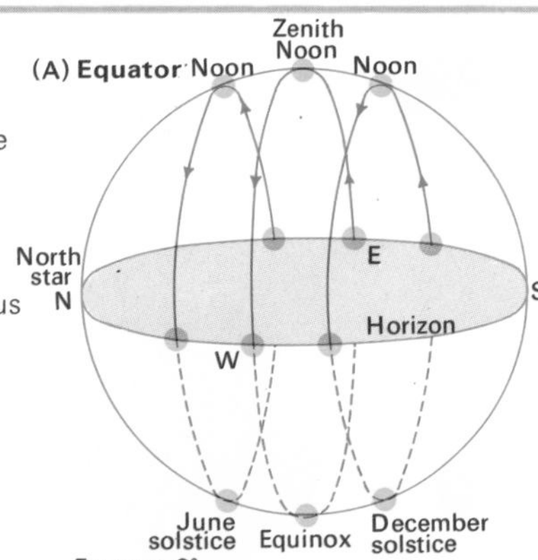

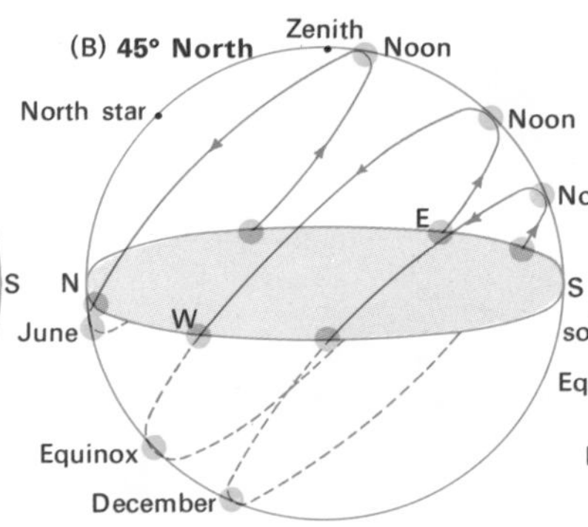

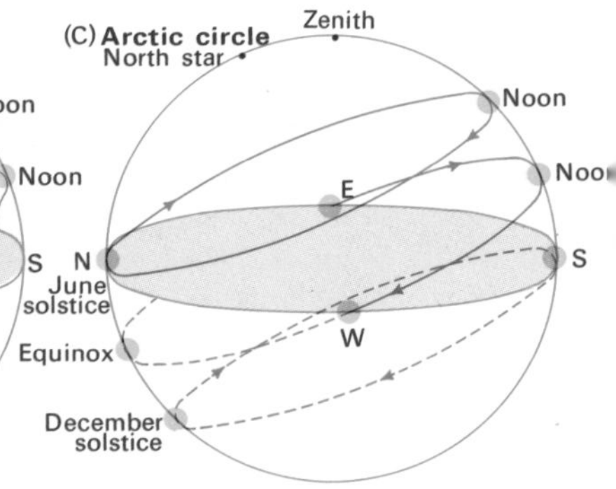

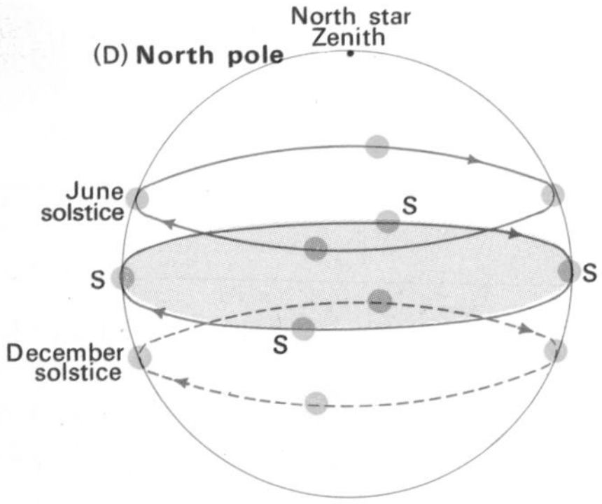

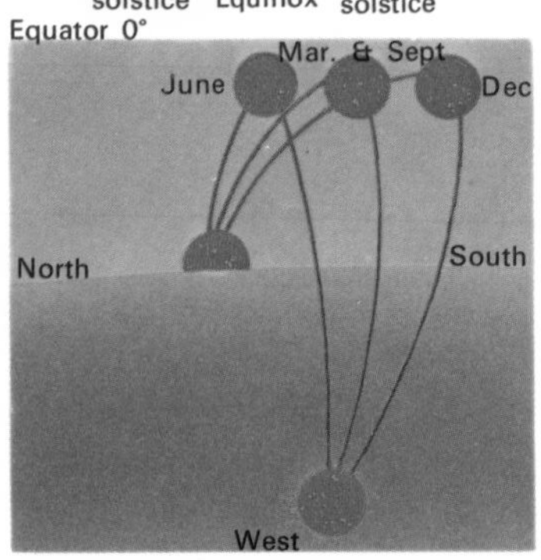

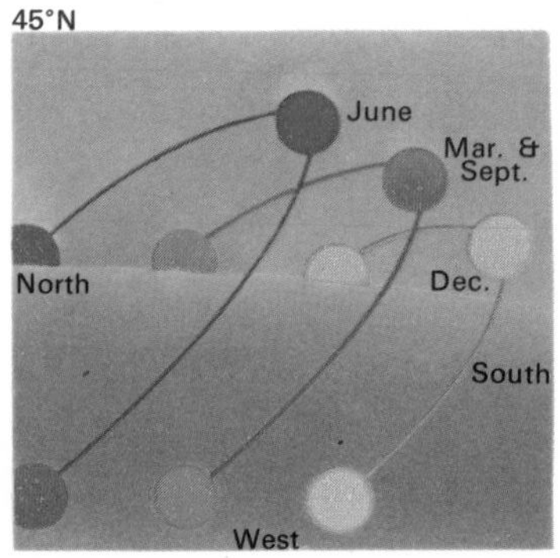

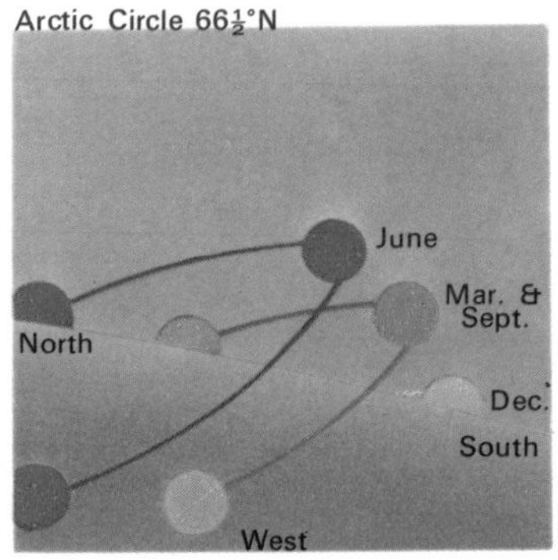

The Moon

The Moon rotates slowly making one complete turn on its axis in just over 27 days. This is the same as its period of revolution around the Earth and thus it always presents the same hemisphere ('face') to us. Surveys and photographs from space-craft have now added greatly to our knowledge of the Moon, and, for the first time, views of the hidden hemisphere.

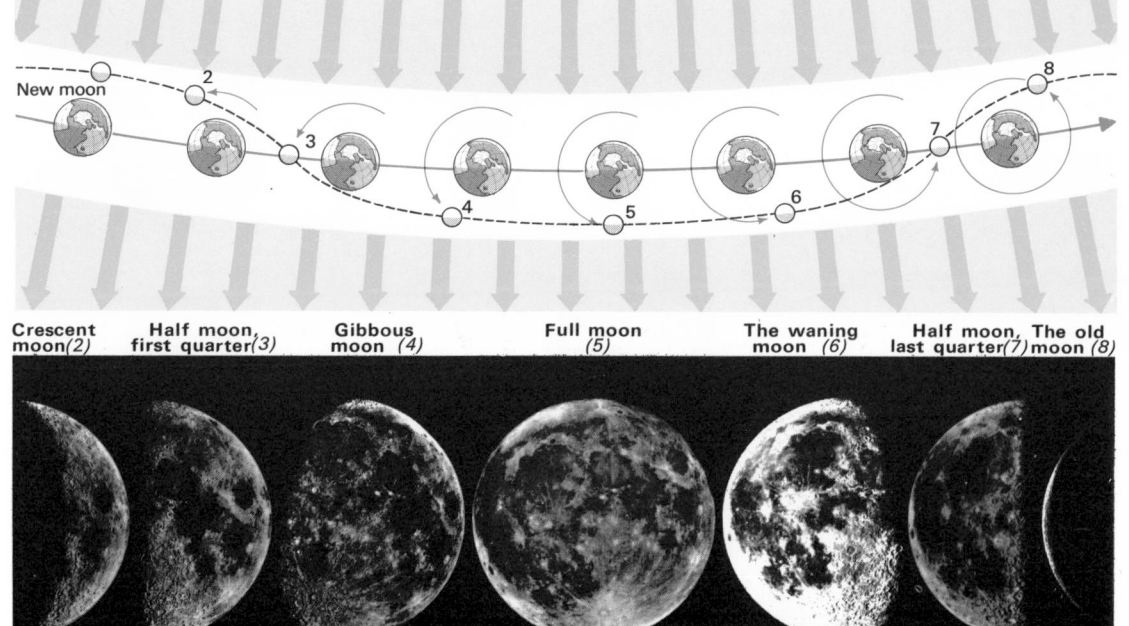

Phases of the Moon

The interval between one full Moon and the next is approximately $29\frac{1}{2}$ days - thus there is one new Moon and one full Moon every month. The diagrams and photographs (right) show how the apparent changes in shape of the Moon from new to full arise from its changing position in relation to the Earth and both to the fixed direction of the Sun's rays.

| Crescent moon(2) | Half moon, first quarter(3) | Gibbous moon (4) | Full moon (5) | The waning moon (6) | Half moon, last quarter(7) | The old moon (8) |

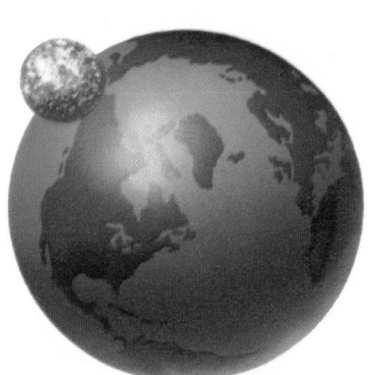

Moon data
Distance from Earth 221 330 mi.
to 252 551 mi.
Mean diameter 2 157 mi.
Mass approx. $\frac{1}{81}$ of that of Earth
Surface gravity $\frac{1}{6}$ of that of Earth
Atmosphere - none, hence no clouds, no weather, no sound.
Diurnal range of temperature at the Equator +400°F

Landings on the Moon
Left are shown the landing sites of the U.S. Apollo programme.
Apollo 11 Sea of Tranquility (1°N 23°E) 1969
Apollo 12 Ocean of Storms (3°S 24°W) 1969
Apollo 14 Fra Mauro (4°S 17°W) 1971
Apollo 15 Hadley Rill (25°N 4°E) 1971
Apollo 16 Descartes (9°S 15°E) 1972
Apollo 17 Sea of Serenity (20°N 31°E) 1972

Eclipses of Sun and Moon
When the Moon passes between Sun and Earth it causes a partial eclipse of the Sun *(right 1)* if the Earth passes through the Moon's outer shadow *(P)*, or a total eclipse *(right 2)*, if the inner cone shadow crosses the Earth's surface.

In a lunar eclipse, the Earth's shadow crosses the Moon and gives either total or partial eclipses.

Tides
Ocean water moves around the Earth under the gravitational pull of the Moon, and, less strongly, that of the Sun. When solar and lunar forces pull together - near new and full Moon - high spring tides result. When solar and lunar forces are not combined - near Moon's first and third quarters - low neap tides occur.

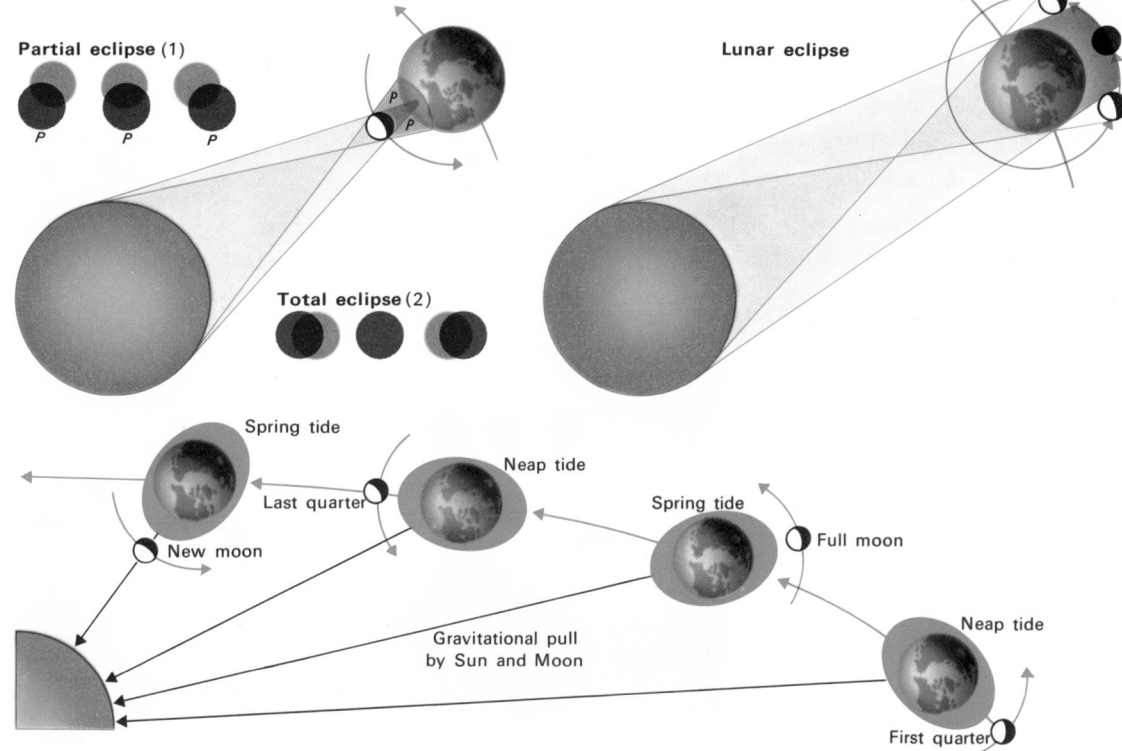

Time

Time measurement
The basic unit of time measurement is the day, one rotation of the earth on its axis. The subdivision of the day into hours and minutes is arbitrary and simply for our convenience. Our present calendar is based on the solar year of $365\frac{1}{4}$ days, the time taken for the earth to orbit the sun. A month was anciently based on the interval from new moon to new moon, approximately $29\frac{1}{2}$ days - and early calendars were entirely lunar.

Rotation of the Earth
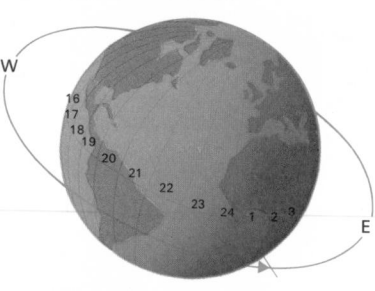

Greenwich Observatory

Prime Meridian

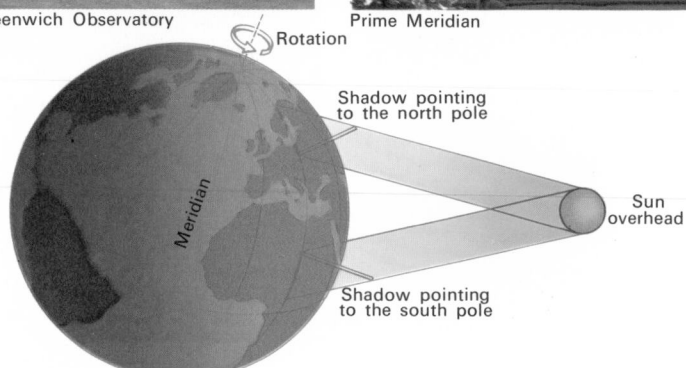

The International Date Line
When it is 12 noon at the Greenwich meridian, 180° east it is midnight of the same day while 180° west the day is only just beginning. To overcome this the International Date Line was established, approximately following the 180° meridian. Thus, for example, if one travelled eastwards from Japan (140° East) to Samoa (170° West) one would pass from Sunday night into Sunday morning.

Time zones
The world is divided into 24 time zones, each centred on meridians at 15° intervals which is the longitudinal distance the sun appears to travel every hour. The meridian running through Greenwich passes through the middle of the first zone. Successive zones to the east of Greenwich zone are ahead of Greenwich time by one hour for every 15° of longitude, while zones to the west are behind by one hour.

Night and day
As the earth rotates from west to east the sun appears to rise in the east and set in the west: when the sun is setting in Shanghai on the directly opposite side of the earth New York is just emerging into sunlight. Noon, when the sun is directly overhead, is coincident at all places on the same meridian with shadows pointing directly towards the poles.

Solar time
The time taken for the earth to complete one rotation about its own axis is constant and defines a day but the speed of the earth along its orbit around the sun is inconstant. The length of day, or 'apparent solar day', as defined by the apparent successive transits of the sun is irregular because the earth must complete more than one rotation before the sun returns to the same meridian.

Sidereal time
The constant sidereal day is defined as the interval between two successive apparent transits of a star, or the first point of Aries, across the same meridian. If the sun is at the equinox and overhead at a meridian on one day, then the next day the sun will be to the east by approximately 1°; thus the sun will not cross the meridian until about 4 minutes after the sidereal noon.

Astronomical clock, Delhi

Sundials
The earliest record of sundials dates back to 741 BC but they undoubtedly existed as early as 2000 BC although probably only as an upright stick or obelisk. A sundial marks the progress of the sun across the sky by casting the shadow of a central style or gnomon on the base. The base, generally made of stone, is delineated to represent the hours between sunrise and sunset.

Kendall's chronometer

Chronometers
With the increase of sea traffic in the 18th century and the need for accurate navigation clockmakers were faced with an intriguing problem. Harrison, an English carpenter, won a British award for designing a clock which was accurate at sea to one tenth of a second per day. He compensated for the effect of temperature changes by incorporating bi-metallic strips connected to thin wires and circular balance wheels.

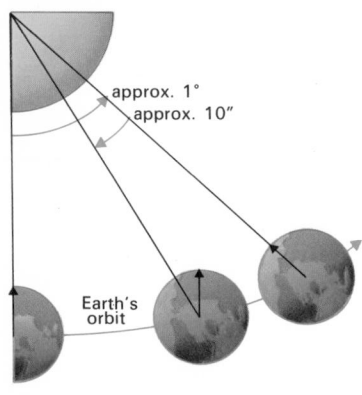

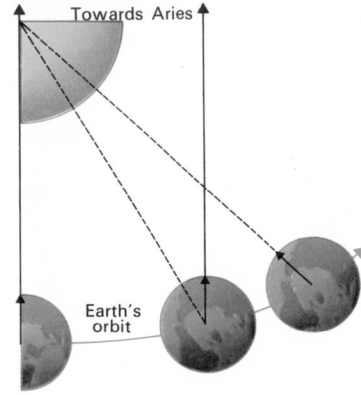

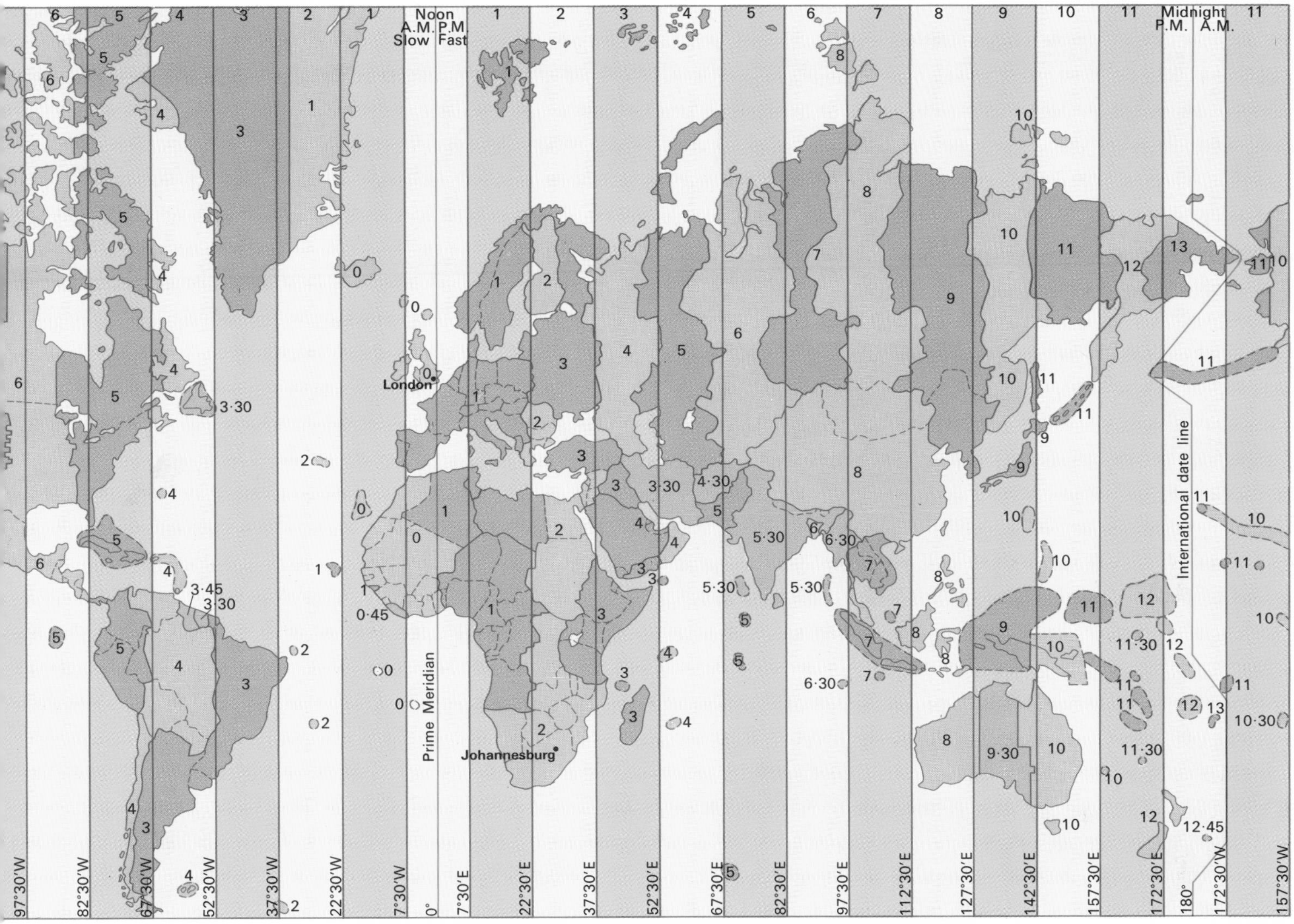

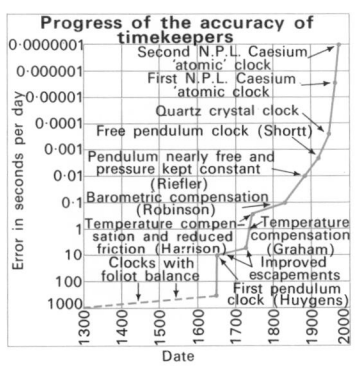

The top portion is a world time zone map with longitude markings. Header across the top:

6 5 4 3 2 1 Noon A.M. P.M. 1 2 3 4 5 6 7 8 9 10 11 Midnight 11
Slow Fast P.M. A.M.

Labeled places: London, Johannesburg, Prime Meridian, International date line

Longitude markings along the bottom:
97°30'W 82°30'W 67°30'W 52°30'W 37°30'W 22°30'W 7°30'W 0° 7°30'E 22°30'E 37°30'E 52°30'E 67°30'E 82°30'E 97°30'E 112°30'E 127°30'E 142°30'E 157°30'E 172°30'E 180° 172°30'W 157°30'W

Progress of the accuracy of timekeepers

Error in seconds per day (vertical axis): 0·0000001, 0·000001, 0·00001, 0·0001, 0·001, 0·01, 0·1, 1, 10, 100, 1000

Date (horizontal axis): 1300 1400 1500 1600 1700 1800 1900 2000

Labels on chart:
- Second N.P.L. Caesium 'atomic' clock
- First N.P.L. Caesium 'atomic' clock
- Quartz crystal clock
- Free pendulum clock (Shortt)
- Pendulum nearly free and pressure kept constant (Riefler)
- Barometric compensation (Robinson)
- Temperature compensation and reduced friction (Harrison)
- Temperature compensation (Graham)
- Improved escapements
- Clocks with foliot balance
- First pendulum clock (Huygens)

Vibration of quartz ring

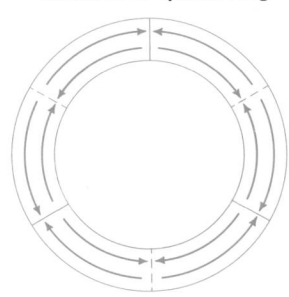

Time difference when travelling by air

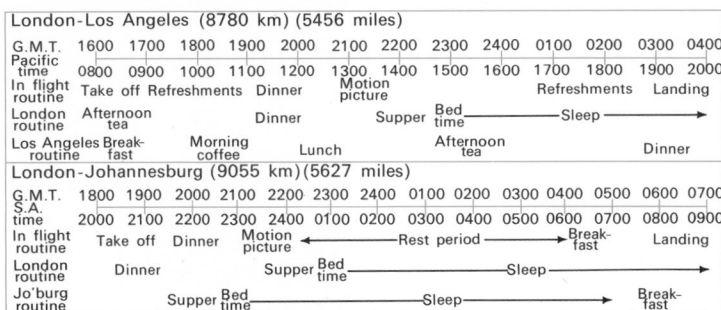

London–Los Angeles (8780 km) (5456 miles)

G.M.T.	1600	1700	1800	1900	2000	2100	2200	2300	2400	0100	0200	0300	0400
Pacific time	0800	0900	1000	1100	1200	1300	1400	1500	1600	1700	1800	1900	2000
In flight routine	Take off	Refreshments	Dinner		Motion picture						Refreshments	Landing	
London routine	Afternoon tea			Dinner			Supper	Bed time	Sleep				
Los Angeles routine	Break-fast		Morning coffee		Lunch			Afternoon tea			Dinner		

London–Johannesburg (9055 km) (5627 miles)

G.M.T.	1800	1900	2000	2100	2200	2300	2400	0100	0200	0300	0400	0500	0600	0700
S.A. time	2000	2100	2200	2300	2400	0100	0200	0300	0400	0500	0600	0700	0800	0900
In flight routine	Take off	Dinner	Motion picture		Rest period					Break-fast		Landing		
London routine	Dinner		Supper	Bed time		Sleep								
Jo'burg routine		Supper	Bed time		Sleep					Break-fast				

Chronographs

The invention of the chronograph by Charles Wheatstone in 1842 made it possible to record intervals of time to an accuracy of one sixtieth of a second. The simplest form of chronograph is the stop-watch. This was developed to a revolving drum and stylus and later electrical signals. A recent development is the cathode ray tube capable of recording to less than one ten-thousandth of a second.

Quartz crystal clocks

The quartz crystal clock, designed originally in America in 1929, can measure small units of time and radio frequencies. The connection between quartz clocks and the natural vibrations of atoms and molecules mean that the unchanging frequencies emitted by atoms can be used to control the oscillator which controls the quartz clock. A more recent version of the atomic clock is accurate to one second in 300 years.

International date line

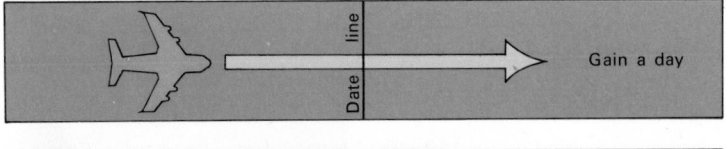

Gain a day

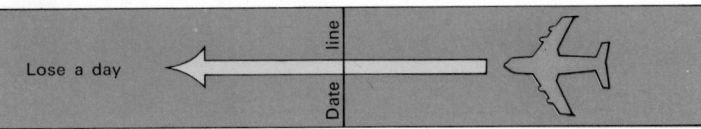

Lose a day

The Atmosphere and Clouds

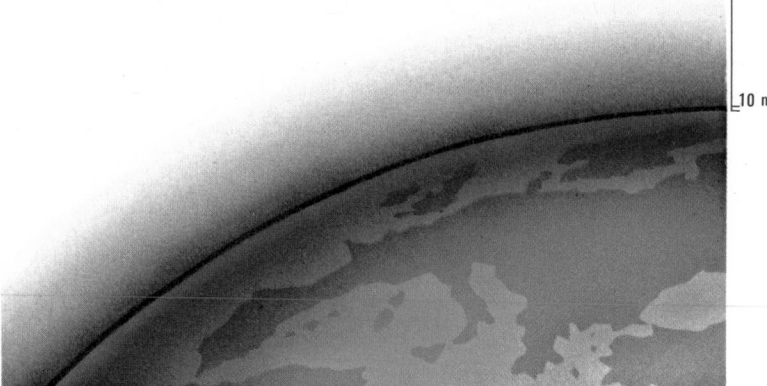

Earth's thin coating *(right)*
The atmosphere is a blanket of protective gases around the earth providing insulation against otherwise extreme alternations in temperature. The gravitational pull increases the density nearer the earth's surface so that 5/6ths of the atmospheric mass is in the first 10 mi. It is a very thin layer in comparison with the earth's diameter of 7 921 mi., like the cellulose coating on a globe.

Exosphere *(1)*
The exosphere merges with the interplanetary medium and although there is no definite boundary with the ionosphere it starts at a height of about 400 miles. The rarified air mainly consists of a small amount of atomic oxygen up to 400 miles and equal proportions of hydrogen and helium with hydrogen predominating above 1500 mi.

Ionosphere *(2)*
Air particles of the ionosphere are electrically charged by the sun's radiation and congregate in four main layers, D, E, F1 and F2, which can reflect radio waves. Aurorae, caused by charged particles deflected by the earth's magnetic field towards the poles, occur between 40 and 60 miles above the earth. It is mainly in the lower ionosphere that meteors from outer space burn up as they meet increased air resistance.

Stratosphere *(3)*
A thin layer of ozone contained within the stratosphere absorbs ultra-violet light and in the process gives off heat. The temperature ranges from about −65°F at the tropopause to about −75°F in the upper part, known as the mesosphere, with a rise to about 35°F just above the ozone layer. This portion of the atmosphere is separated from the lower layer by the tropopause.

Troposphere *(4)*
The earth's weather conditions are limited to this layer which is relatively thin, extending upwards to about 5 miles at the poles and 10 miles at the equator. It contains about 85% of the total atmospheric mass and almost all the water vapour. Air temperature falls steadily with increased height at about 1°F for every 150 feet above sea level.

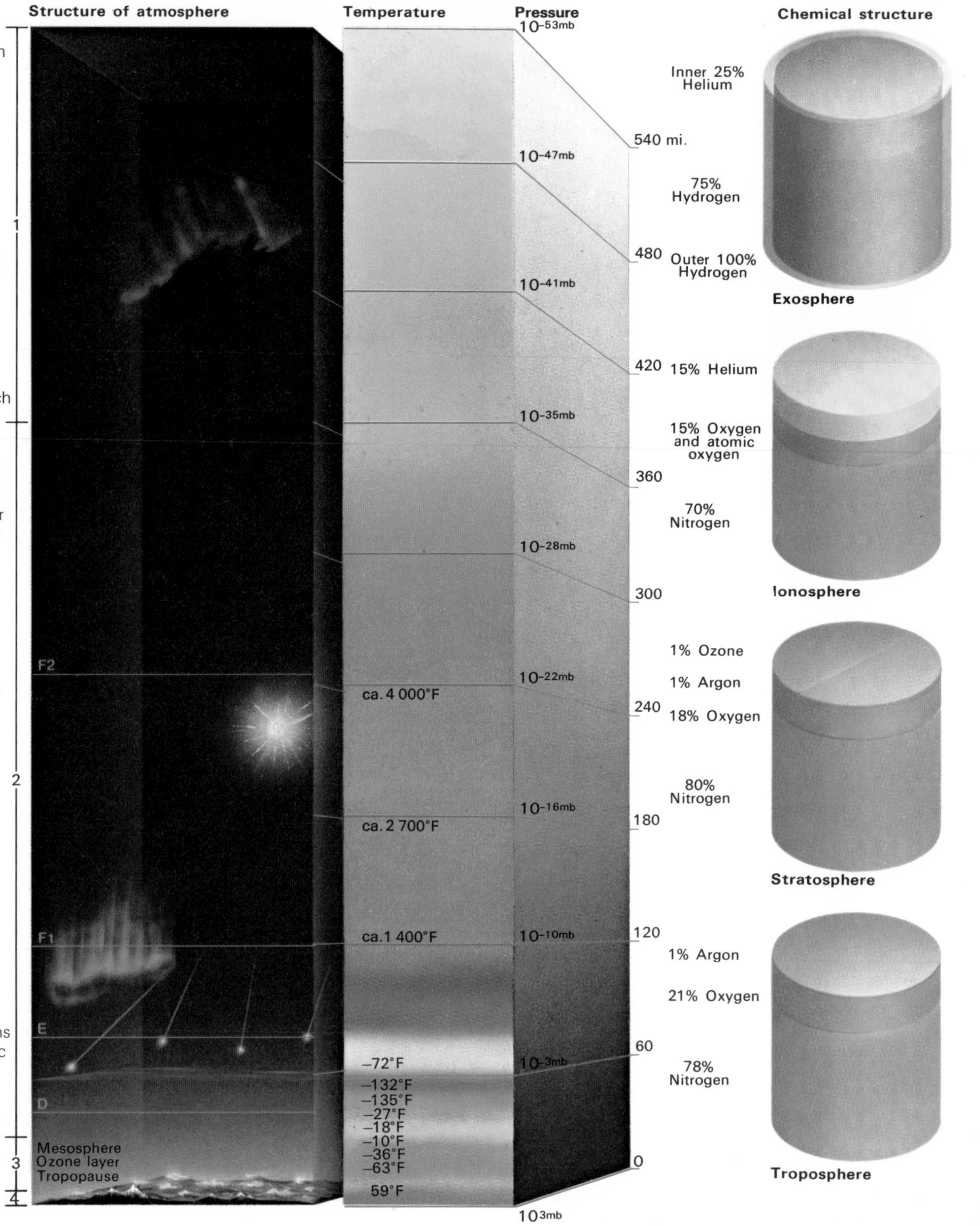

8

Structure of atmosphere

- 400 mi
- 10 mi

1

2

F2

F1

E

D

3
4
Mesosphere
Ozone layer
Tropopause

Temperature

ca. 4 000°F

ca. 2 700°F

ca. 1 400°F

−72°F
−132°F
−135°F
−27°F
−18°F
−10°F
−36°F
−63°F
59°F

Pressure

- 10^{-53}mb
- 540 mi.
- 10^{-47}mb
- 480
- 10^{-41}mb
- 420
- 10^{-35}mb
- 360
- 10^{-28}mb
- 300
- 10^{-22}mb
- 240
- 10^{-16}mb
- 180
- 10^{-10}mb
- 120
- 10^{-3}mb
- 60
- 0
- 10^{3}mb

Chemical structure

Inner 25% Helium

75% Hydrogen

Outer 100% Hydrogen

Exosphere

15% Helium

15% Oxygen and atomic oxygen

70% Nitrogen

Ionosphere

1% Ozone

1% Argon

18% Oxygen

80% Nitrogen

Stratosphere

1% Argon

21% Oxygen

78% Nitrogen

Troposphere

Pacific Ocean
Cloud patterns over the Pacific show the paths of prevailing winds.

Circulation of the air

30°N

Equator

30°S

Circulation of the air
Owing to high temperatures in equatorial regions the air near the ground is heated, expands and rises producing a low pressure belt. It cools, causing rain, spreads out then sinks again about latitudes 30° north and south forming high pressure belts.

High and low pressure belts are areas of comparative calm but between them, blowing from high to low pressure, are the prevailing winds. These are deflected to the right in the northern hemisphere and to the left in the southern hemisphere (Corolis effect). The circulations appear in three distinct belts with a seasonal movement north and south following the overhead sun.

Cloud types

Clouds form when damp air is cooled, usually by rising. This may happen in three ways: when a wind rises to cross hills or mountains; when a mass of air rises over, or is pushed up by another mass of denser air; when local heating of the ground causes convection currents.

Cirrus *(1)* are detached clouds composed of microscopic ice crystals which gleam white in the sun resembling hair or feathers. They are found at heights of 20 000 to 40 000 feet.

Cirrostratus *(2)* are a whitish veil of cloud made up of ice crystals through which the sun can be seen often producing a halo of bright light.

Cirrocumulus *(3)* is another high altitude cloud formed by turbulence between layers moving in different directions.

Altostratus *(4)* is a grey or bluish striated, fibrous or uniform sheet of cloud producing light drizzle.

Altocumulus *(5)* is a thicker and fluffier version of cirro cumulus, it is a white and grey patchy sheet of cloud.

Nimbostratus *(6)* is a dark grey layer of cloud obscuring the sun and causing almost continuous rain or snow.

Cumulus *(7)* are detached heaped up, dense low clouds. The sunlit parts are brilliant white while the base is relatively dark and flat.

Stratus *(8)* forms dull overcast skies associated with depressions and occurs at low altitudes up to 5 000 feet.

Cumulonimbus *(9)* are heavy and dense clouds associated with storms and rain. They have flat bases and a fluffy outline extending up to great altitudes.

High clouds

Middle clouds

Low clouds

Thousands of feet

1 Cirrus

2 Cirrostratus

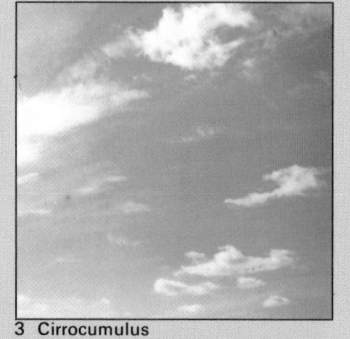

3 Cirrocumulus

4 Altostratus

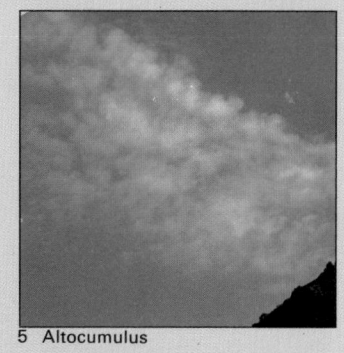

5 Altocumulus

6 Nimbostratus

7 Cumulus

8 Stratus

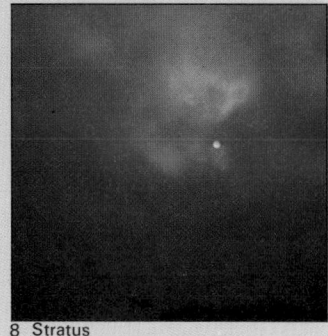

9 Cumulonimbus

Climate and Weather

All weather occurs over the earth's surface in the lowest level of the atmosphere, the troposphere. Weather has been defined as the condition of the atmosphere at any place at a specific time with respect to the various elements: temperature, sunshine, pressure, winds, clouds, fog, precipitation. Climate, on the other hand, is the average of weather elements over previous months and years.

Climate graphs *right*
Each graph typifies the kind of climatic conditions one would experience in the region to which it is related by colour to the map. The scale refers to degrees Fahrenheit for temperature and inches for rainfall, shown by bars. The graphs show average observations based over long periods of time, the study of which also compares the prime factors for vegetation differences.

Development of a depression *below*
In an equilibrium front between cold and warm air masses (i) a wave disturbance develops as cold air undercuts the warm air (ii). This deflects the air flow and as the disturbance progresses a definite cyclonic circulation with warm and cold fronts is created (iii). The cold front moves more rapidly than the warm front eventually overtaking it, and occlusion occurs as the warm air is pinched out (iv).

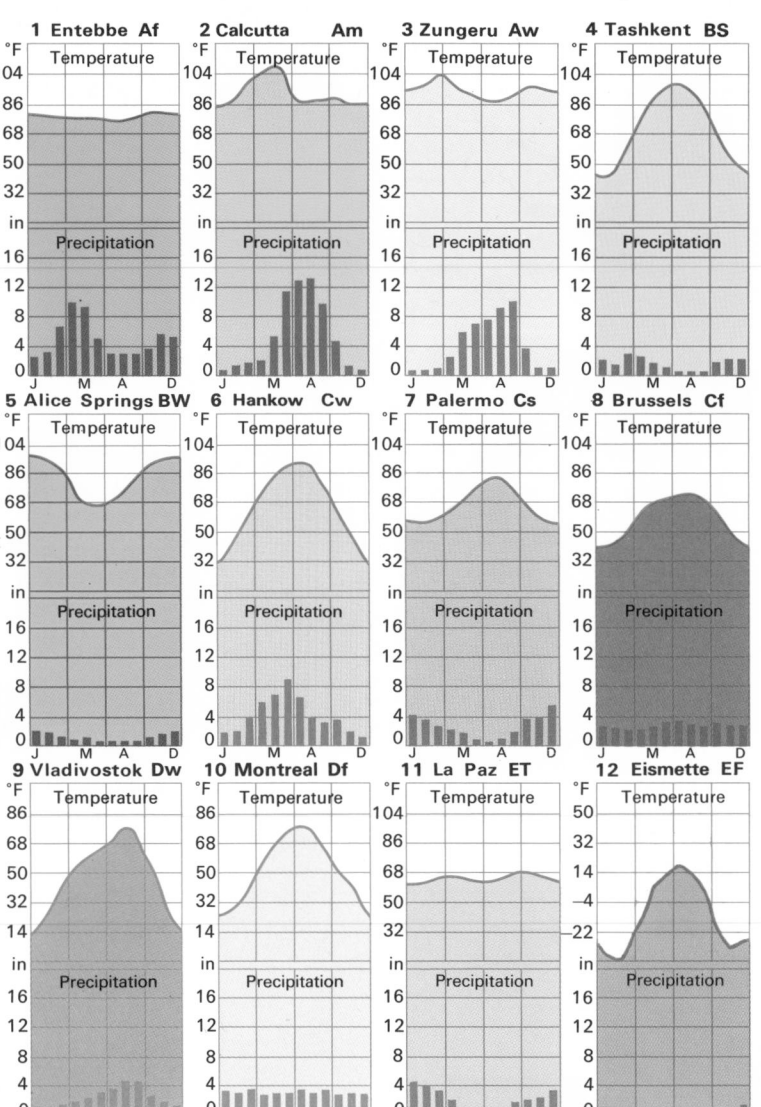

Af   Equatorial forest
Am   Monsoon forest
Aw   Savanna

Tropical climates

Af	Am	Aw

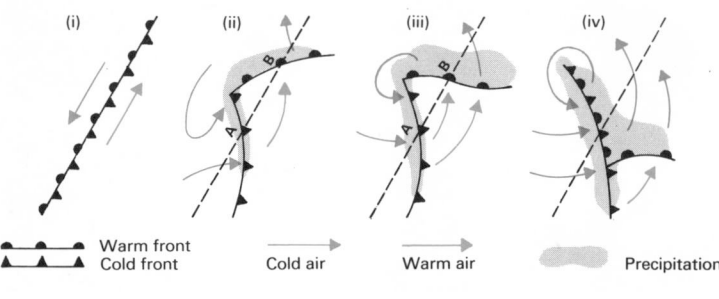

Warm front
Cold front   Cold air   Warm air   Precipitation

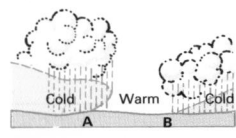 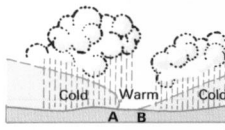 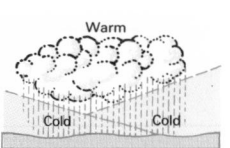

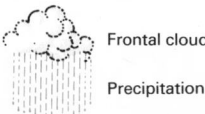
Frontal cloud

Precipitation

The upper diagrams show in plan view stages in the development of a depression.
The cross sections below correspond to stages (ii) to (iv).

Kinds of precipitation
Rain The condensation of water vapour on microscopic particles of dust, sulphur, soot or ice in the atmosphere forms water particles. These combine until they are heavy enough to fall as rain.

Hail Water particles, carried to a great height, freeze into ice particles which fall and become coated with fresh moisture. They are swept up again and refrozen. This may happen several times before falling as hail-stones.

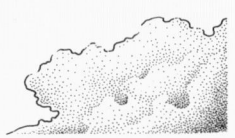 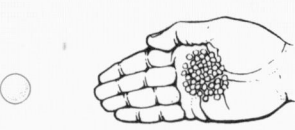

Frost Hoar, the most common type of frost, is precipitated instead of dew when water vapour changes directly into ice crystals on the surface of ground objects which have cooled below freezing point.

Snow is the precipitation of ice in the form of flakes, or clusters, of basically hexagonal ice crystals. They are formed by the condensation of water vapour directly into ice.

10

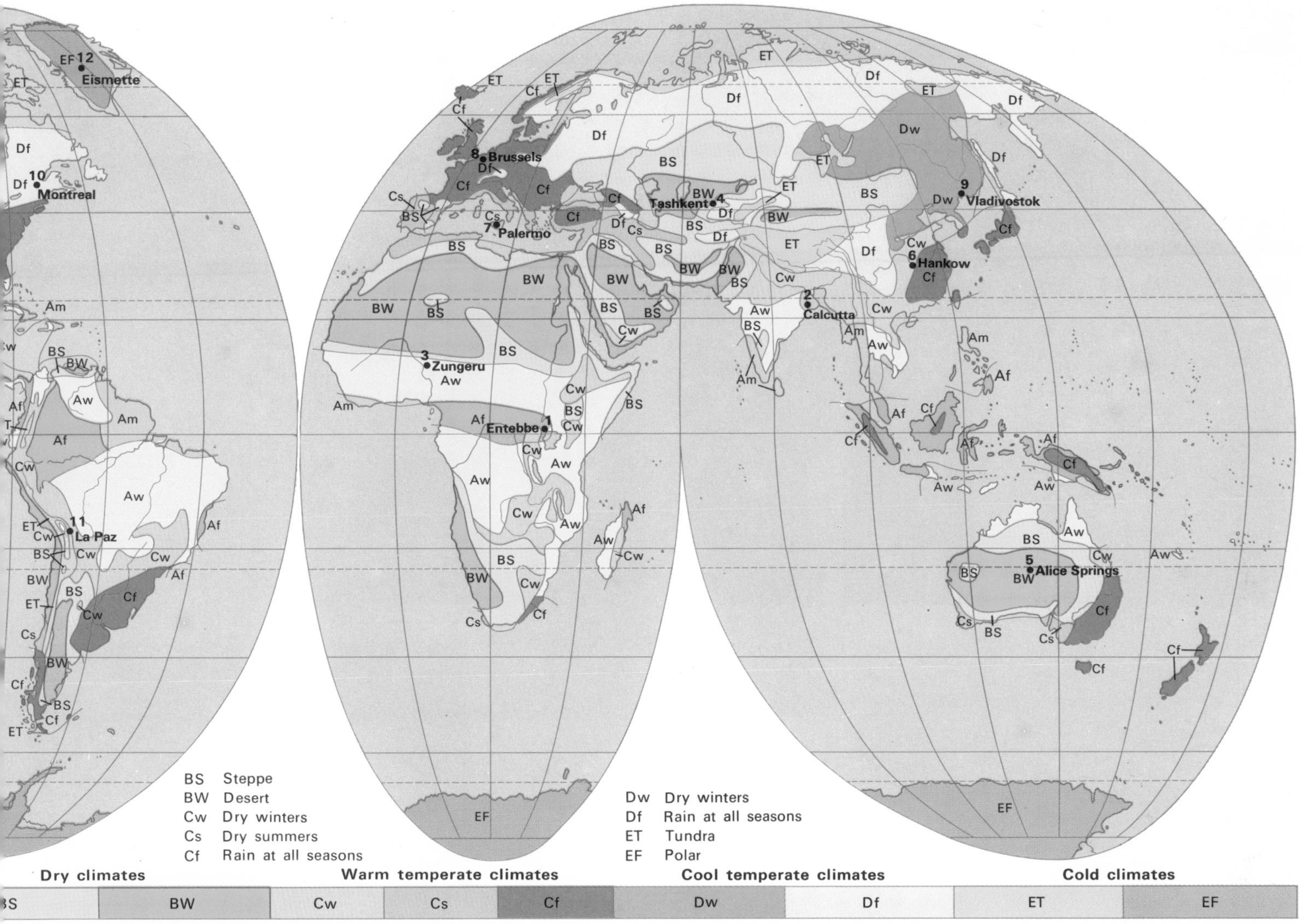

EF12 Eismette
ET
Df
Df 10 Montreal

ET ET Cf
Cf
Df
8 Brussels
Df
Cs Cf Cf
BS
Cs Cf
7 Palermo
Df
BS
Cf
BW
BS
BW
BS BW
3 Zungeru
Aw
Af
BS
Af Cw
1 Entebbe
Cw
Aw
Aw
Cw
Af
BS
BW Cw
Cs Cf

ET
Df
Cf
BS ET BS
Tashkent 4 BW
BW Df
Df Cs BS
Df
BS BW
BS
BW BS Cw
2 Calcutta
Aw
BS
Am

ET
Dw
Df
ET
BS
Df
Cw 9 Vladivostok
Dw
Cw
6 Hankow Cf
Cf
Am
Aw
Af
Af
Cf
Am
Af
Cf
Af
Cf
Aw
BS Aw
5 Alice Springs
BW Cw
Aw
Cs
BS Cs
Cf
Cf
Cf

EF

EF

BS Steppe
BW Desert
Cw Dry winters
Cs Dry summers
Cf Rain at all seasons

Dw Dry winters
Df Rain at all seasons
ET Tundra
EF Polar

Dry climates **Warm temperate climates** **Cool temperate climates** **Cold climates**

BS	BW	Cw	Cs	Cf	Dw	Df	ET	EF

Tropical storm tracks *below*
A tropical cyclone, or storm, is designated as having winds of gale force (40 mph) but less than hurricane force (75 mph) It is a homogenous air mass with upward spiralling air currents around a windless centre, or eye. An average of 65 tropical storms occur each year, over 50% of which reach hurricane force. They originate mainly during the summer over tropical oceans.

Extremes of climate & weather *right*
Tropical high temperatures and polar low temperatures combined with wind systems, altitude and unequal rainfall distribution result in the extremes of tropical rain forests, inland deserts and frozen polar wastes. Fluctuations in the limits of these extreme zones and extremes of weather result in occasional catastrophic heat-waves and drought, floods and storms, frost and snow.

Hurricane devastation

Hot desert

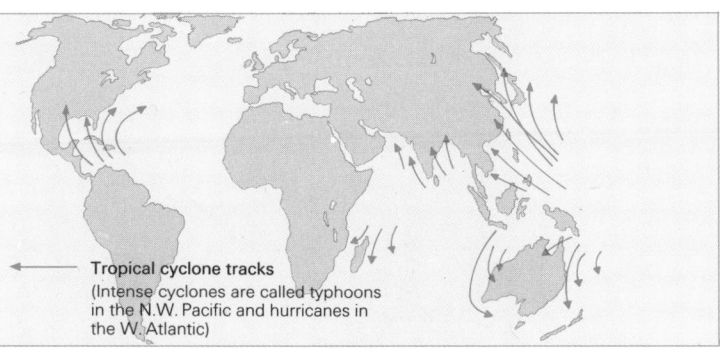
→ Tropical cyclone tracks
(Intense cyclones are called typhoons in the N.W. Pacific and hurricanes in the W. Atlantic)

Tornado

Arctic dwellings

The Earth from Space

Mount Etna, Sicily *left*
Etna is at the top of the photograph, the Plain of Catania in the centre and the Mediterranean to the right. This is an infra-red photograph; vegetation shows as red, water as blue/black and urban areas as grey. The recent lava flows, as yet with no vegetation, show up as blue/black unlike the cultivated slopes which are red and red/pink.

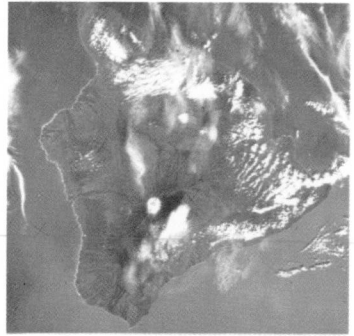

Hawaii, Pacific Ocean *above*
This is a photograph of Hawaii, the largest of the Hawaiian Islands in the Central Pacific. North is at the top of the photograph. The snowcapped craters of the volcanoes Mauna Kea (dormant) in the north centre and Mauna Loa (active) in the south centre of the photograph can be seen. The chief town, Hilo, is on the north east coast.

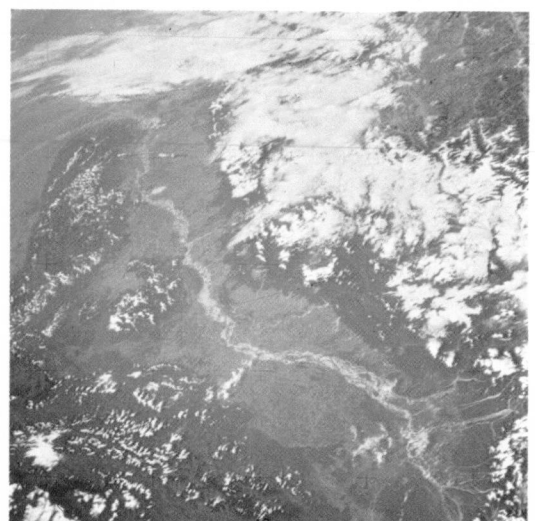

River Brahmaputra, India *left*
A view looking westwards down the Brahmaputra with the Himalayas on the right and the Khasi Hills of Assam to the left.

Szechwan, China *right*
The River Tachin in the mountainous region of Szechwan, Central China. The lightish blue area in the river valley in the north east of the photograph is a village and its related cultivation.

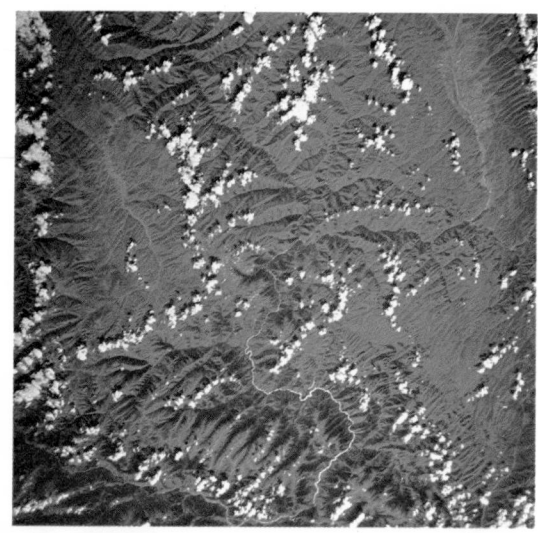

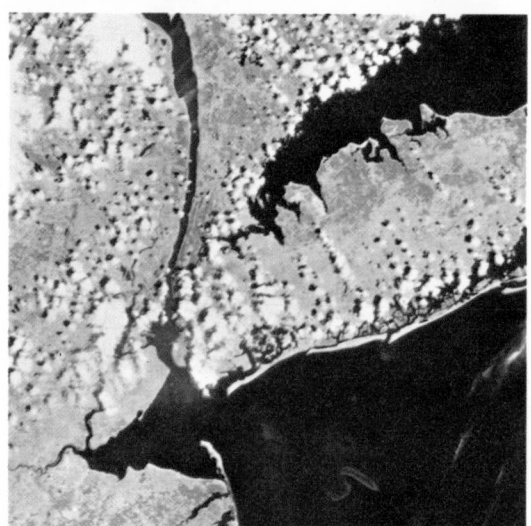

New York, U.S.A. *left*
This infra-red photograph shows the western end of Long Island and the entrance to the Hudson River. Vegetation appears as red, water as blue/black and the metropolitan areas of New York, through the cloud cover, as grey.

The Great Barrier Reef, Australia *right*
The Great Barrier Reef and the Queensland coast from Cape Melville to Cape Flattery. The smoke from a number of forest fires can be seen in the centre of the photograph.

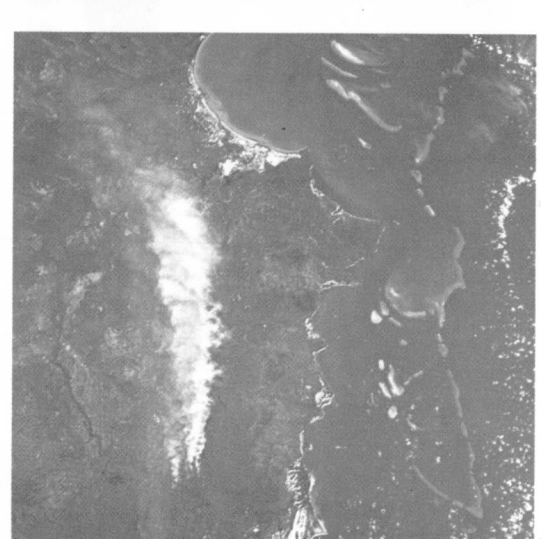

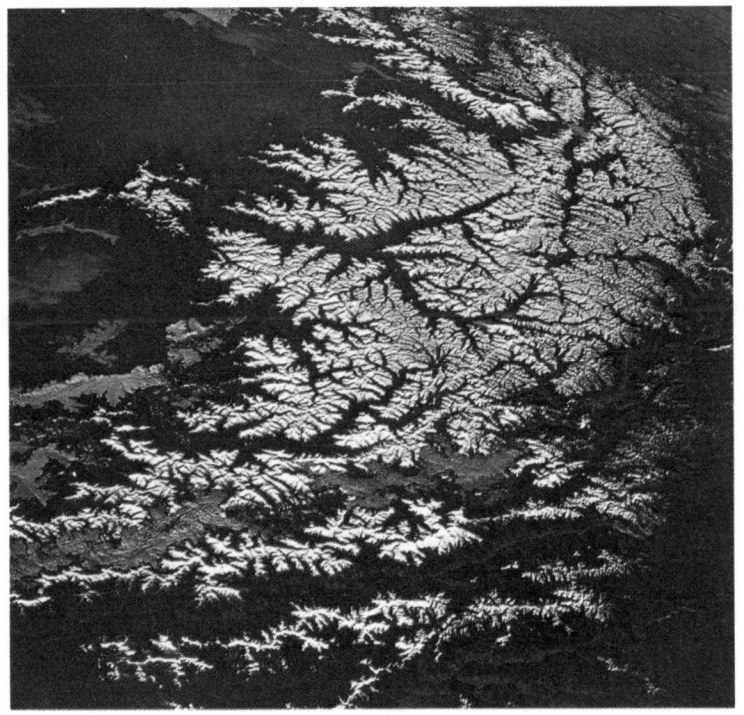

Eastern Himalayas, Asia
above left
A view from Apollo IX looking
north-westwards over the
snowcapped, sunlit mountain
peaks and the head waters of
the Mekong, Salween,
Irrawaddy and, in the distance,
with its distinctive loop, the
Brahmaputra.

Atacama Desert, Chile
above right
This view looking eastwards
from the Pacific over the
Mejillones peninsula with the
city of Antofagasta in the
southern bay of that peninsula.
Inland the desert and salt-pans
of Atacama, and beyond, the
Andes.

The Alps, Europe *right*
This vertical photograph shows
the snow-covered mountains
and glaciers of the Alps along
the Swiss-Italian-French
border. Mont Blanc and the
Matterhorn are shown and, in
the north, the Valley of the
Rhône is seen making its sharp
right-hand bend near Martigny.
In the south the head waters
of the Dora Baltea flow
towards the Po and, in the
north-west, the Lac d'Annecy
can be seen.

The Evolution of the Continents

The origin of the earth is still open to much conjecture although the most widely accepted theory is that it was formed from a solar cloud consisting mainly of hydrogen. Under gravitation the cloud condensed and shrank to form our planets orbiting around the sun. Gravitation forced the lighter elements to the surface of the earth where they cooled to form a crust while the inner material remained hot and molten. Earth's first rocks formed over 3500 million years ago but since then the surface has been constantly altered.

Until comparatively recently the view that the primary units of the earth had remained essentially fixed throughout geological time was regarded as common sense, although the concept of moving continents has been traced back to references in the Bible of a break up of the land after Noah's floods. The continental drift theory was first developed by Antonio Snider in 1858 but probably the most important single advocate was Alfred Wegener who, in 1915, published evidence from geology, climatology and biology. His conclusions are very similar to those reached by current research although he was wrong about the speed of break-up.

The measurement of fossil magnetism found in rocks has probably proved the most influential evidence. While originally these drift theories were openly mocked, now they are considered standard doctrine.

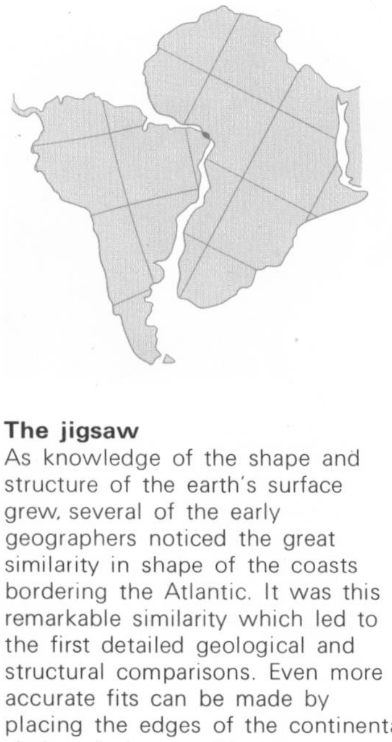

The jigsaw
As knowledge of the shape and structure of the earth's surface grew, several of the early geographers noticed the great similarity in shape of the coasts bordering the Atlantic. It was this remarkable similarity which led to the first detailed geological and structural comparisons. Even more accurate fits can be made by placing the edges of the continental shelves in juxtaposition.

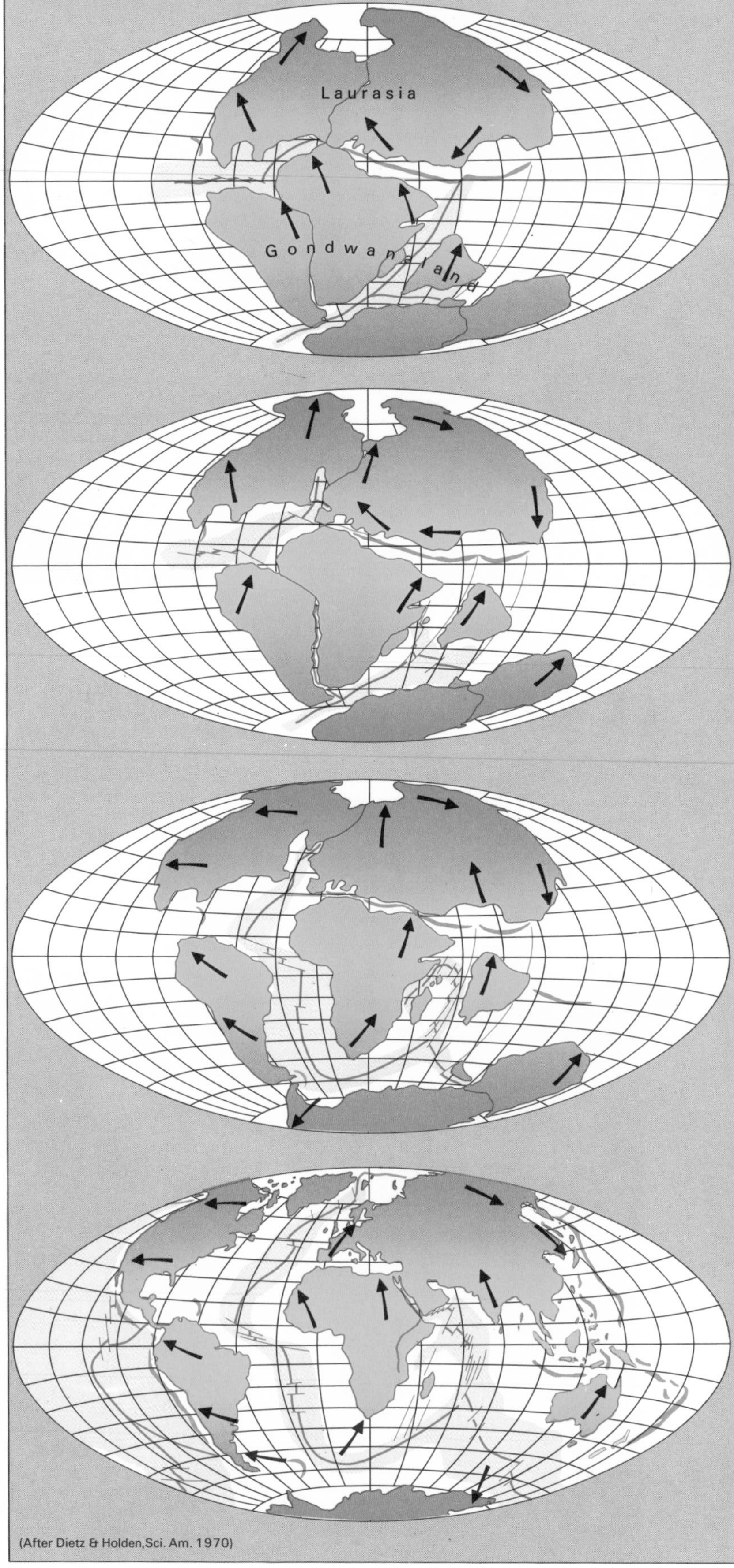

14

(After Dietz & Holden, Sci. Am. 1970)

180 million years ago.
The original Pangaea land mass had split into two major continental groups. The southern group, Gondwanaland, had itself started to break up, India and Antarctica-Australia becoming isolated. A rift had begun to appear between South America and Africa and, in the East, Africa was closing up the Tethys Sea.

135 million years ago.
Both Gondwanaland and Laurasia continued to drift northwards but the widening of the splits in the North Atlantic and Indian Oceans persisted. The South Atlantic rift continued to lengthen and a further perpendicular rift appeared which will eventually separate Greenland from North America. India continues heading northward towards Asia.

65 million years ago.
South America, completely separated from Africa, moved quickly north and westwards. Madagascar broke free from Africa but, as yet, there is no sign of the Red Sea Rift which will split Africa from the Arabian Peninsula. The Mediterranean sea is recognizable. In the south, Australia is still connected to Antarctica.

Today.
India has moved northwards and is colliding with Asia, crumpling up the sediments to form the folded mountain range of the Himalayas. South America has rotated and moved west to connect with North America. Australia has separated from Antarctica.

	Trench
	Rift
	New Ocean Floor
	Zones of slippage

Plate tectonics

The original debate about continental drift was only a prelude to a more radical idea; plate tectonics. The basic theory is that the earth's crust is made up of a series of rigid plates which float on a soft layer of the mantle and are moved about by convection currents in the earth's interior. These plates converge and diverge along margins marked by earthquakes, volcanoes and other seismic activity. Plates diverge from mid-ocean ridges where molten lava pushes upwards and forces the plates apart at a rate of up to 1 in. a year. Converging plates form either a trench, where the oceanic plate sinks below the lighter continental rock, or mountain ranges where two continents collide. This explains the paradox that while there have always been oceans none of the present oceans contain sediments more than 150 million years old.

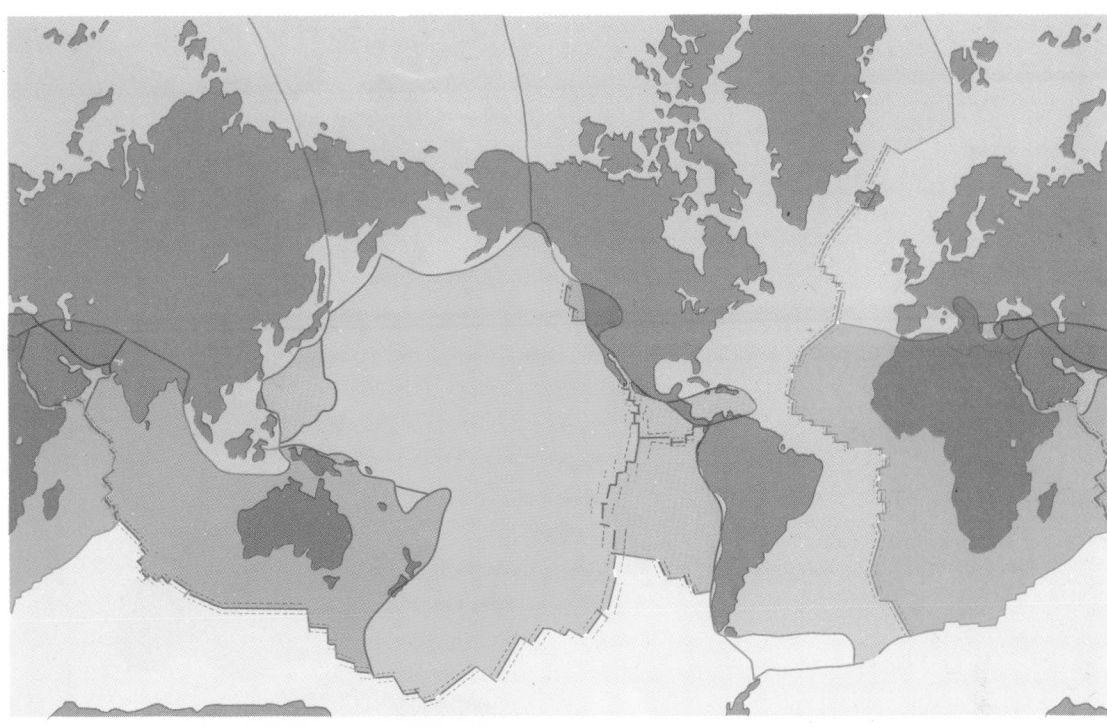

Trench boundary

The present explanation for the comparative youth of the ocean floors is that where an ocean and a continent meet the ocean plate dips under the less dense continental plate at an angle of approximately 45°. All previous crust is then ingested by downward convection currents. In the Japanese trench this occurs at a rate of about 5 in. a year.

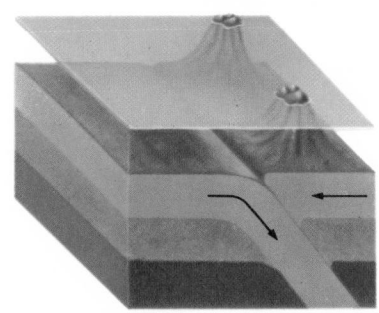

Transform fault

The recent identification of the transform, or transverse, fault proved to be one of the crucial preliminaries to the investigation of plate tectonics. They occur when two plates slip alongside each other without parting or approaching to any great extent. They complete the outline of the plates delineated by the ridges and trenches and demonstrate large scale movements of parts of the earth's surface

Ridge boundary

Ocean rises or crests are basically made up from basaltic lavas for although no gap can exist between plates, one plate can ease itself away from another. In that case hot, molten rock instantly rises from below to fill in the incipient rift and forms a ridge. These ridges trace a line almost exactly through the centre of the major oceans.

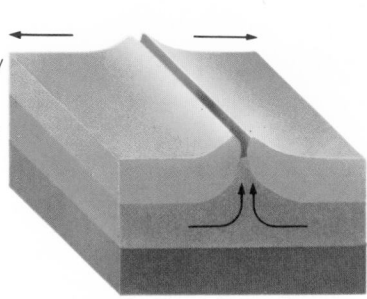

Destruction of ocean plates.

As the ocean plate sinks below the continental plate some of the sediment on its surface is scraped off and piled up on the landward side. This sediment is later incorporated in a folded mountain range which usually appears on the edge of the continent, such as the Andes. Similarly if two continents collide the sediments are squeezed up into new mountains.

Sea floor spreading

Reversals in the earth's magnetic field have occured throughout history. As new rock emerges at the ocean ridges it cools and is magnetised in the direction of the prevailing magnetic field. By mapping the magnetic patterns either side of the ridge a symmetrical stripey pattern of alternating fields can be observed (see inset area in diagram). As the dates of the last few reversals are known the rate of spreading can be calculated.

The Unstable Earth

The earth's surface is slowly but continually being rearranged. Some changes such as erosion and deposition are extremely slow but they upset the balance which causes other more abrupt changes often originating deep within the earth's interior. The constant movements vary in intensity, often with stresses building up to a climax such as a particularly violent volcanic eruption or earthquake.

The crust *(below and right)*
The outer layer or crust of the earth consists of a comparatively low density, brittle material varying from 3 mi. to 30 mi. deep beneath the continents. This consists predominately of silica and aluminium; hence it is called 'sial' Extending under the ocean floors and below the sial is a basaltic layer known as 'sima', consisting mainly of silica and magnesium.

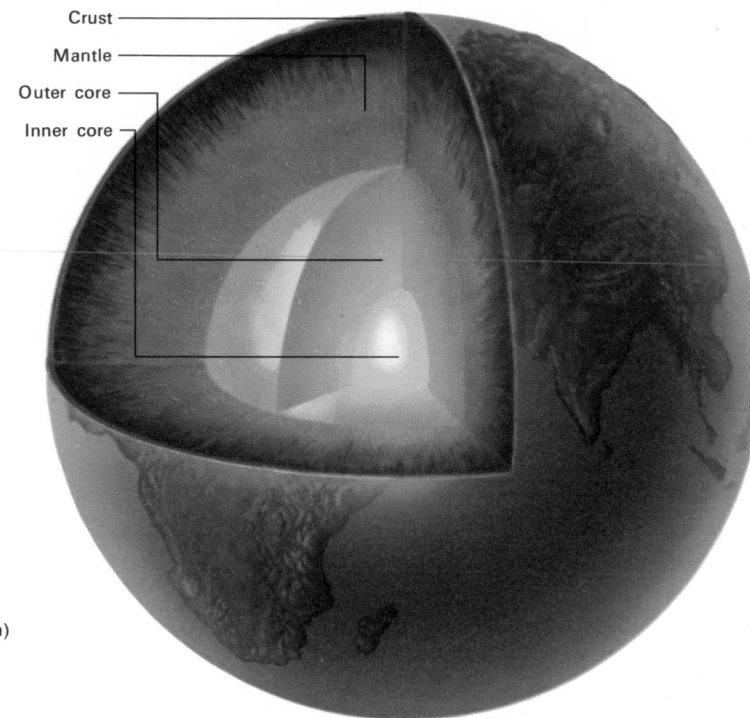

Crust
Mantle
Outer core
Inner core

Continental crust   Ocean crust

Sediment
Granite rock (sial)
Basaltic layer (sima)
Mantle

Volcanoes *(right, below and far right)*
Volcanoes occur when hot liquefied rock beneath the crust reaches the surface as lava. An accumulation of ash and cinders around a vent forms a cone. Successive layers of thin lava flows form an acid lava volcano while thick lava flows form a basic lava volcano. A caldera forms when a particularly violent eruption blows off the top of an already existing cone.

The mantle *(above)*
Immediately below the crust, at the mohorovicic discontinuity line, there is a distinct change in density and chemical properties. This is the mantle - made up of iron and magnesium silicates - with temperatures reaching 3 000°F The rigid upper mantle extends down to a depth of about 600 mi. below which is the more viscous lower mantle which is about 1 200 mi. thick.

The core *(above)*
The outer core, approximately 1 300 mi. thick, consists of molten iron and nickel at 3 500°F to 9 000°F possibly separated from the less dense mantle by an oxidised shell. About 3 000 mi. below the surface is the liquid transition zone, below which is the solid inner core, a sphere of 1 700 mi. diameter where rock is three times as dense as in the crust.

Shield volcano   **Cinder cone**   **Hornit cone**   **Caldera**

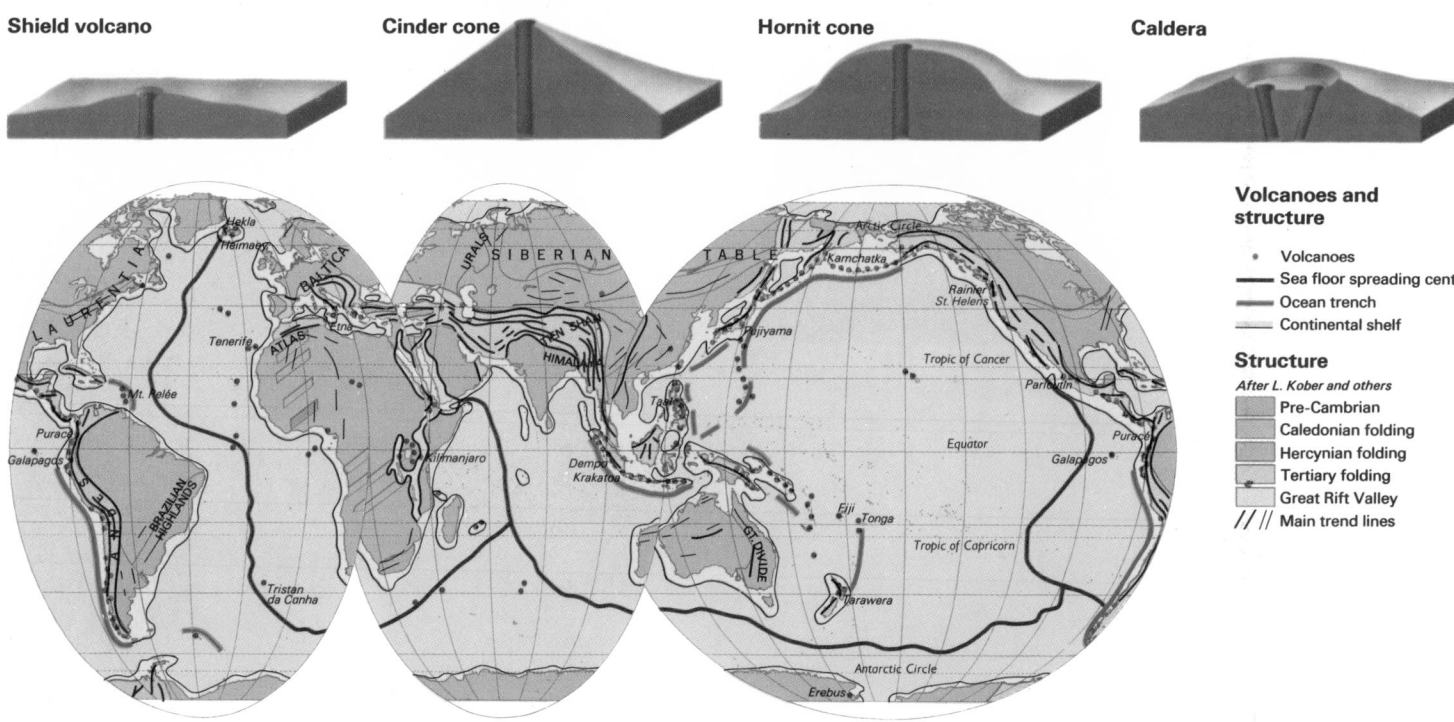

Volcanoes and structure

- • Volcanoes
- ── Sea floor spreading centre
- ━━ Ocean trench
- ─ Continental shelf

Structure
After L. Kober and others

- Pre-Cambrian
- Caledonian folding
- Hercynian folding
- Tertiary folding
- Great Rift Valley
- // // Main trend lines

Major earthquakes in the last 100 years and numbers killed

Year	Location	Killed	Year	Location	Killed	Year	Location	Killed	Year	Location	Killed
1896	Japan (tsunami)	22 000	1923	Japan, Tokyo	143 000	1939/40	Turkey, Erzincan	30 000	1966	U.S.S.R., Tashkent	destroyed
1906	San Francisco	destroyed	1930	Italy, Naples	2 100	1948	Japan, Fukui	5 100	1970	N. Peru	66 800
1906	Chile, Valparaiso	22 000	1931	New Zealand, Napier	destroyed	1956	N. Afghanistan	2 000	1972	Nicaragua, Managua	7 000
1908	Italy, Messina	77 000	1931	Nicaragua, Managua	destroyed	1957	W. Iran	10 000	1974	N. Pakistan	10 000
1920	China, Kansu	180 000	1932	China, Kansu	70 000	1960	Morocco, Agadir	12 000	1976	China, Tangshan	650 000
			1935	India, Quetta	60 000	1962	N.W. Iran	10 000	1978	Iran, Tabas	11 000
			1939	Chile, Chillan	20 000	1963	Yugoslavia, Skopje	1 000	1980	Algeria, El Asnam	20 000

World distribution of earthquakes

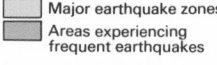

- Major earthquake zones
- Areas experiencing frequent earthquakes

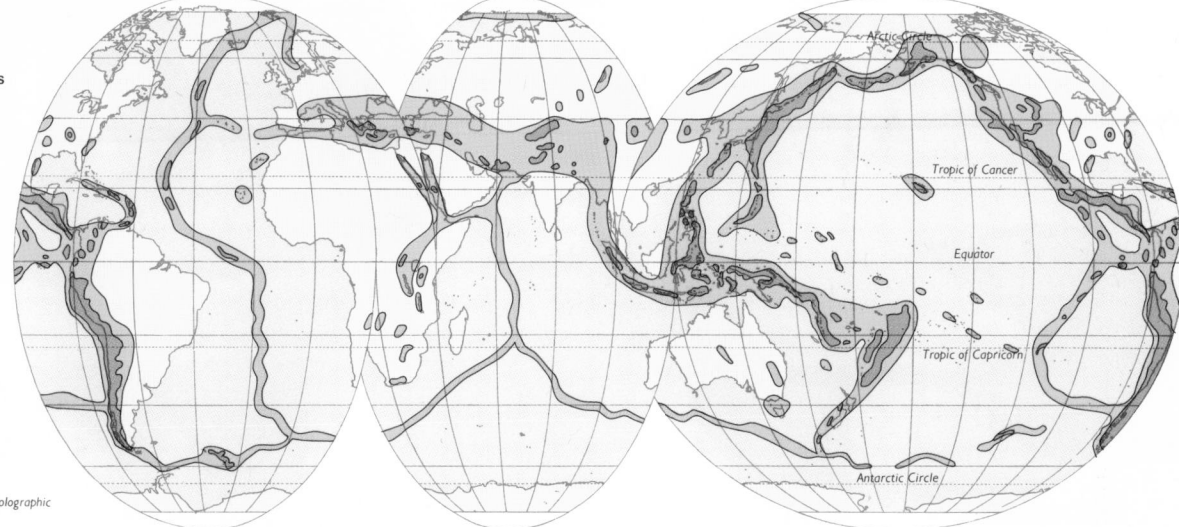

Projection: Interrupted Mollweide's Homolographic

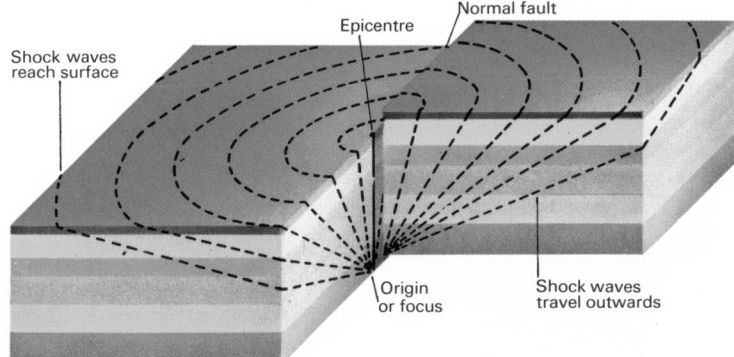

Earthquakes *(right and above)*

Earthquakes are a series of rapid vibrations originating from the slipping or faulting of parts of the earth's crust when stresses within build up to breaking point. They usually happen at depths varying from 5 mi. to 18 mi. Severe earthquakes cause extensive damage when they take place in populated areas destroying structures and severing communications. Most loss of life occurs due to secondary causes i.e. falling masonry, fires or tsunami waves.

Alaskan earthquake, 1964

Seismic Waves *(right)*

The shock waves sent out from the focus of an earthquake are of three main kinds each with distinct properties. Primary (P) waves are compressional waves which can be transmitted through both solids and liquids and therefore pass through the earth's liquid core. Secondary (S) waves are shear waves and can only pass through solids. They cannot pass through the core and are reflected at the core-mantle boundary taking a concave course back to the surface. The core also refracts the P waves causing them to alter course, and the net effect of this reflection and refraction is the production of a shadow zone at a certain distance from the epicentre, free from P and S waves. Due to their different properties P waves travel about 1,7 times faster than S waves. The third main kind of wave is a long (L) wave, a slow wave which travels along the earth's surface, its motion being either horizontal or vertical.

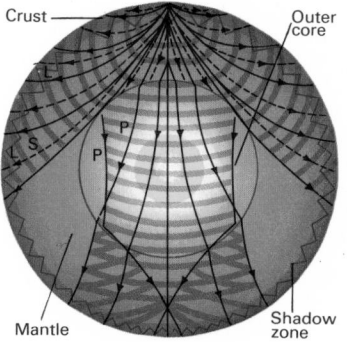

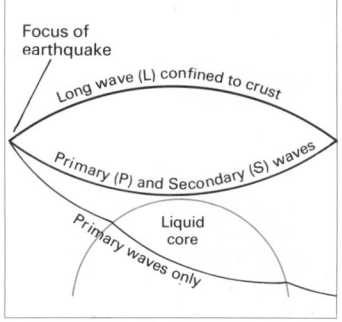

Tsunami waves *(left)*

A sudden slump in the ocean bed during an earthquake forms a trough in the water surface subsequently followed by a crest and smaller waves. A more marked change of level in the sea bed can form a crest, the start of a Tsunami which travels up to 370 mph with waves up to 200 ft high. Seismographic detectors continuously record earthquake shocks and warn of the Tsunami which may follow it.

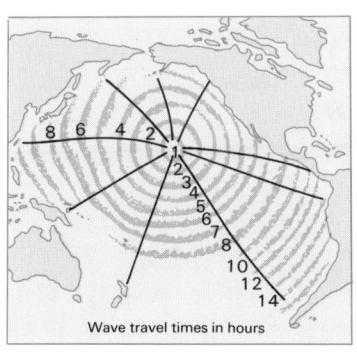

Wave travel times in hours

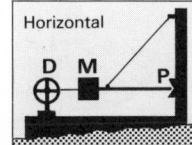

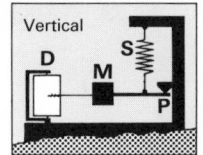

Principles of seismographs (left)

M = Mass
D = Drum
P = Pivot
S = Spring

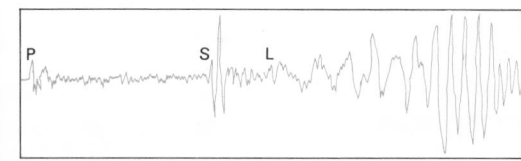

Seismographs

Seismographs are delicate instruments capable of detecting and recording vibrations due to earthquakes thousands of kilometres away. P waves cause the first tremors. S the second, and L the main shock.

The Making of Landscape

The making of landscape

The major forces which shape our land would seem to act very slowly in comparison with man's average life span but in geological terms the erosion of rock is in fact very fast. Land goes through a cycle of transformation. It is broken up by earthquakes and other earth movements, temperature changes, water, wind and ice. Rock debris is then transported by water, wind and glaciers and deposited on lowlands and on the sea floor. Here it builds up and by the pressure of its own weight is converted into new rock strata. These in turn can be uplifted either gently as plains or plateaux or more irregularly to form mountains. In either case the new higher land is eroded and the cycle recommences.

A Peneplain

Uplifted peneplain

Rivers

Rivers shape the land by three basic processes: erosion, transportation and deposition. A youthful river flows fast eroding downwards quickly to form a narrow valley (1) As it matures it deposits some debris and erodes laterally to widen the valley (2). In its last stage it meanders across a wide flat flood plain depositing fine particles of alluvium (3).

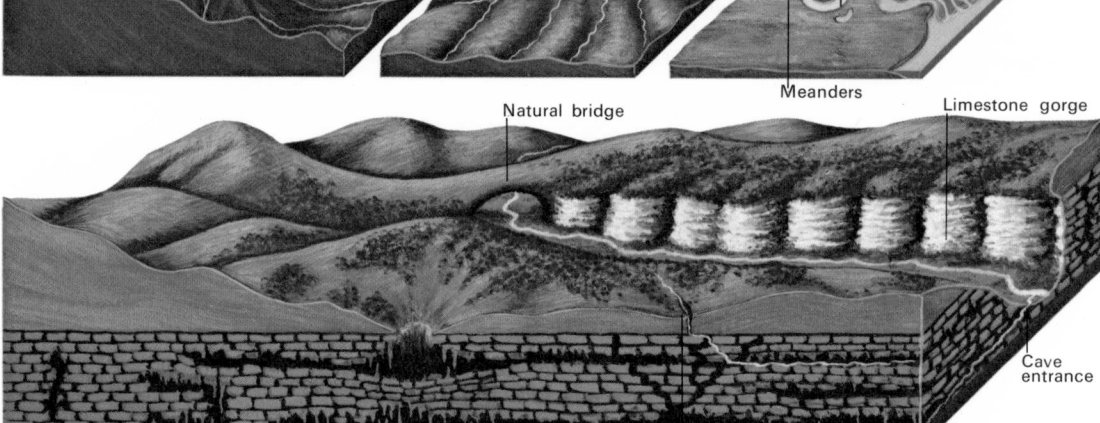

Youthful stage

Mature stage

Ox-bow

Old age stage

Meanders

Underground water

Water enters porous and permeable rocks from the surface moving downward until it reaches a layer of impermeable rock. Joints in underground rock, such as limestone, are eroded to form underground caves and caverns. When the roof of a cave collapses a gorge is formed. Surface entrances to joints are often widened to form vertical openings called swallow holes.

Natural bridge

Limestone gorge

Cave entrance

Impermeable rocks

Cave with stalactites and stalagmites

River disappears down swallow hole

Wind

Wind action is particularly powerful in arid and semi-arid regions where rock waste produced by weathering is used as an abrasive tool by the wind. The rate of erosion varies with the characteristics of the rock which can cause weird shapes and effects (right). Desert sand can also be accumulated by the wind to form barchan dunes (far right) which slowly travel forward, horns first.

Wind

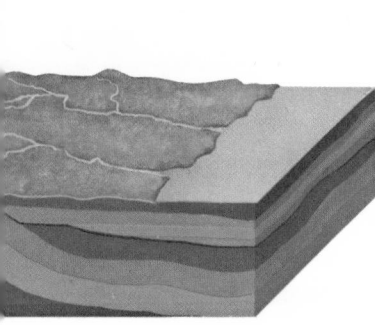

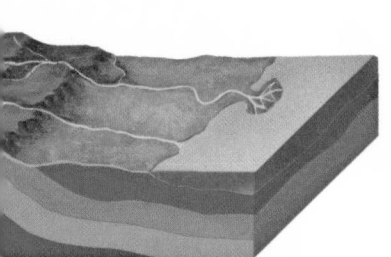

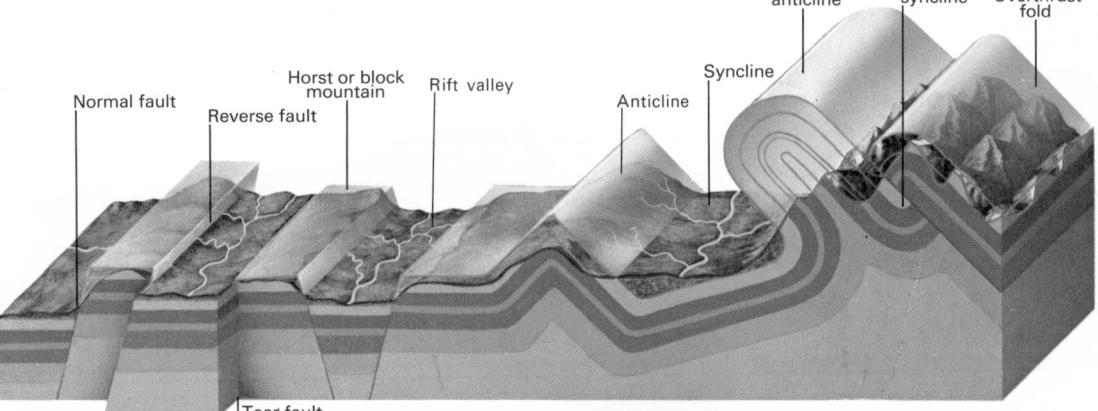

Folding and faulting

A vertical displacement in the earth's crust is called a fault or reverse fault; lateral displacement is a tear fault. An uplifted block is called a horst, the reverse of which is a rift valley. Compressed horizontal layers of sedimentary rock fold to form mountains. Those layers which bend up form an anticline, those bending down form a syncline : continued pressure forms an overfold.

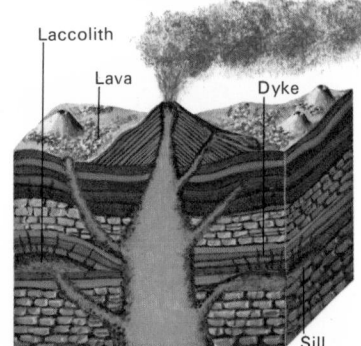

Volcanic activity

When pressure on rocks below the earth's crust is released the normally semi-solid hot rock becomes liquid magma. The magma forces its way into cracks of the crust and may either reach the surface where it forms volcanoes or it may collect in the crust as sills dykes or lacoliths. When magma reaches the surface it cools to form lava.

Waves

Coasts are continually changing, some retreat under wave erosion while others advance with wave deposition. These actions combined form steep cliffs and wave cut platforms. Eroded debris is in turn deposited as a terrace. As the water becomes shallower the erosive power of the waves decreases and gradually the cliff disappears. Wave action can also create other features (far right).

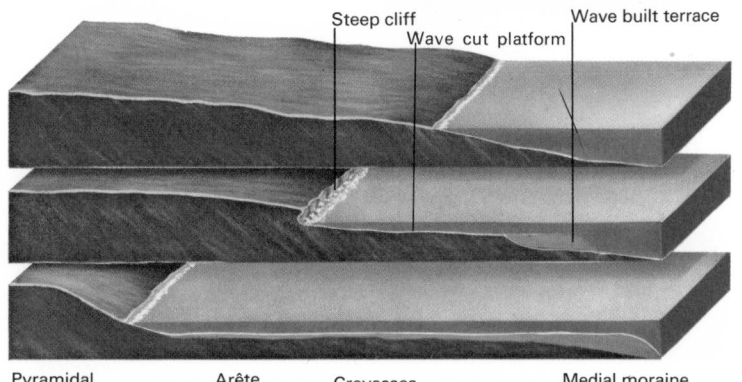

Ice

These diagrams *(right)* show how a glaciated valley may have formed. The glacier deepens, straightens and widens the river valley whose interlocking spurs become truncated or cut off. Intervalley divides are frost shattered to form sharp aretes and pyramidal peaks. Hanging valleys mark the entry of tributary rivers and eroded rocks form medial moraine. Terminal moraine is deposited as the glacier retreats.

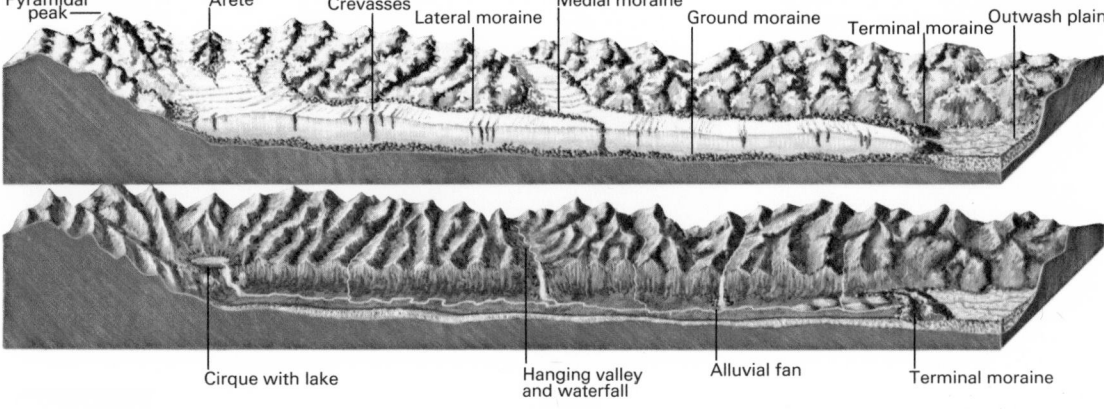

Subsidence and uplift

As the land surface is eroded it may eventually become a level plain - a peneplain, broken only by low hills, remnants of previous mountains. In turn this peneplain may be uplifted to form a plateau with steep edges. At the coast the uplifted wave platform becomes a coastal plain and in the rejuvenated rivers downward erosion once more predominates.

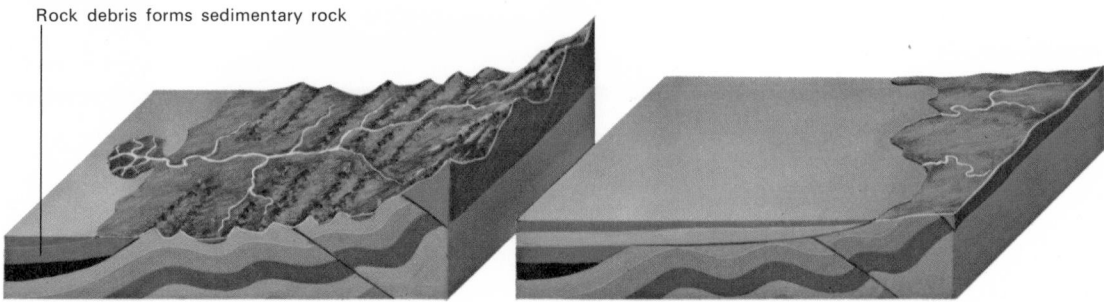

The Earth: Physical Dimensions

Its surface

Highest point on the earth's
surface: Mt. Everest, Tibet -
Nepal boundary   29 029 ft
Lowest point on the earth's
surface: The Dead Sea,
Jordan   below sea level 1296 ft
Greatest ocean depth :
Challenger Deep, Mariana
Trench   36 161 ft
Average height of land   2 756 ft
Average depth of seas
and oceans   12 493 ft

The Figure of Earth

An imaginary sea-level surface is
considered and called a geoid. By
measuring at different places the
angles from plumb lines to a fixed
star there have been many
determinations of the shape of parts
of the geoid which is found to be an
oblate spheriod with its axis along
the axis of rotation of the earth.
Observations from satellites have
now given a new method of more
accurate determinations of the
figure of the earth and its local
irregularities.

Land and Sea Hemispheres.

About 85% of the total land area
is contained in the hemisphere
centred on a point between
Paris and Brussels.

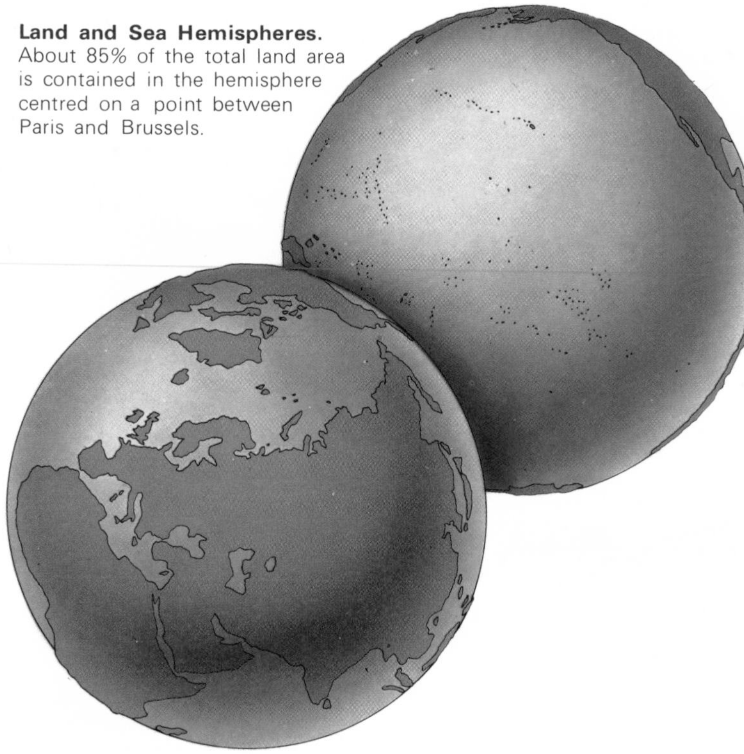

Dimensions

Superficial area	197 000 000 mi²
Land surface	57 000 000 mi²
Land surface as % of total area	29·2 %
Water surface	139 000 000 mi²
Water surface as % of total area	70·8 %
Equatorial circumference	24 888 mi.
Meridional circumference	24 845 mi.
Equatorial diameter	7 922 mi.
Polar diameter	7 895·2 mi.
Equatorial radius	3 960·9 mi.
Polar radius	3 947·6 mi.
Volume of the Earth	672 686 x 10⁶mi³
Mass of the Earth	5·9 x 10²¹ tonnes

Volume of the Earth $672\,686 \times 10^6$ mi³
Mass of the Earth 5.9×10^{21} tonnes

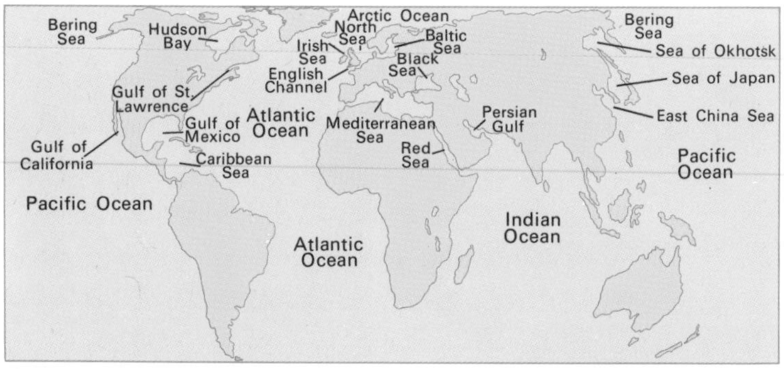

Oceans and Seas
Area in 1000 mi²

Pacific Ocean	63 985	North Sea	222
Atlantic Ocean	31 529	Black Sea	173
Indian Ocean	28 356	Red Sea	170
Arctic Ocean	5 541	Baltic Sea	163
Mediterranean Sea	1 145	Persian Gulf	92
Bering Sea	878	St. Lawrence, Gulf of	91
Caribbean Sea	750	English Channel & Irish Sea	69
Mexico, Gulf of	700	California, Gulf of	62
Okhotsk, Sea of	590		
East China Sea	482		
Hudson Bay	475		
Japan, Sea of	405		

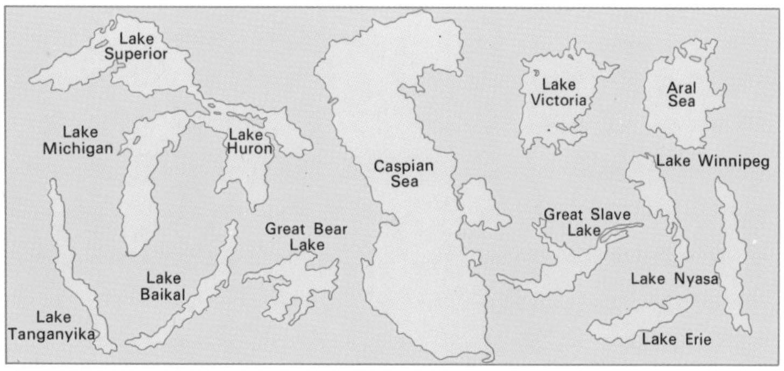

Lakes and Inland Seas
Areas in 1000 mi²

Caspian Sea, Asia	163·8	Lake Ontario, N.America	7·5
Lake Superior, N.America	31·8	Lake Ladoga, Europe	7·1
Lake Victoria, Africa	26·8	Lake Balkhash, Asia	6·7
Aral Sea (Salt), Asia	24·6	Lake Maracaibo, S.America	6·3
Lake Huron, N.America	23·0	Lake Onega, Europe	3·8
Lake Michigan, N.America	22·4	Lake Eyre (Salt), Australia	3·7
Lake Tanganyika, Africa	12·7	Lake Turkana (Salt), Africa	3·5
Lake Baikal, Asia	12·2	Lake Titicaca, S.America	3·2
Great Bear Lake, N.America	12·0	Lake Nicaragua, C.America	3·1
Great Slave Lake, N.America	11·2	Lake Athabasca, N.America	3·0
Lake Nyasa, Africa	11·0	Reindeer Lake, N.America	2·4
Lake Erie, N.America	9·9	Issyk-Kul, Asia	2·4
Lake Winnipeg, N.America	9·4	Lake Torrens (Salt), Australia	2·3
Lake Chad, Africa	8·0	Koko Nor (Salt), Asia	2·3
		Lake Urmia, Asia	2·3
		Vänern, Europe	2·2

Longest rivers

	mi.
Nile, Africa	4 155
Amazon, S.America	3 900
Mississipi - Missouri, N.America	3 895
Yangtze, Asia	3 900
Zaïre, Africa	2 900
Amur, Asia	2 740
Hwang Ho (Yellow), Asia	2 700
Lena, Asia	2 645
Mekong, Asia	2 600
Niger, Africa	2 600
Mackenzie, N.America	2 510
Ob, Asia	2 485
Yenisei, Asia	2 360

0   500   1 000   1 500   2 000   2 500   3 000   3 500   4 000 mi.

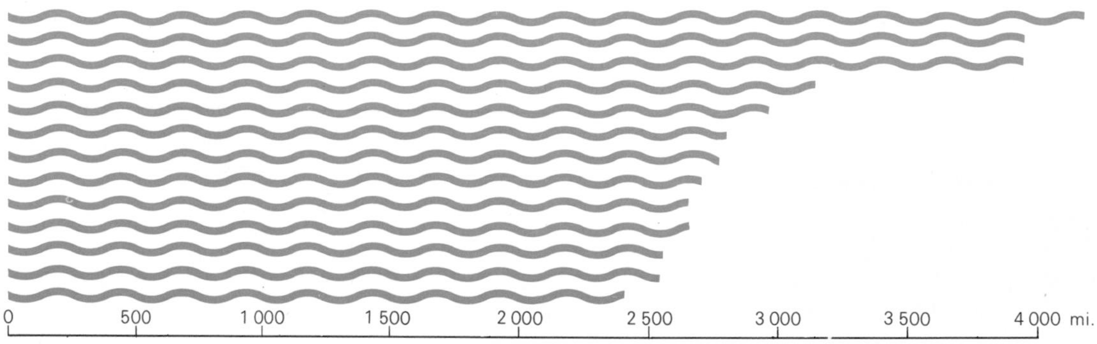

The Highest Mountains and the Greatest Depths.

Mount Everest defied the world's greatest mountaineers for 32 years and claimed the lives of many men. Not until 1920 was permission granted by the Dalai Lama to attempt the mountain, and the first successful ascent came in 1953. Since then the summit has been reached several times. The world's highest peaks have now been climbed but there are many as yet unexplored peaks in the Himalayas some of which may be over 25 000 ft

The greatest trenches are the Puerto Rico deep (30 184 ft). The Tonga (35 505 ft) and Mindanao (34 439 ft) trenches and the Mariana Trench (36 161 ft) in the Pacific. The trenches represent less than 2% of the total area of the sea-bed but are of great interest as lines of structural weakness in the Earth's crust and as areas of frequent earthquakes.

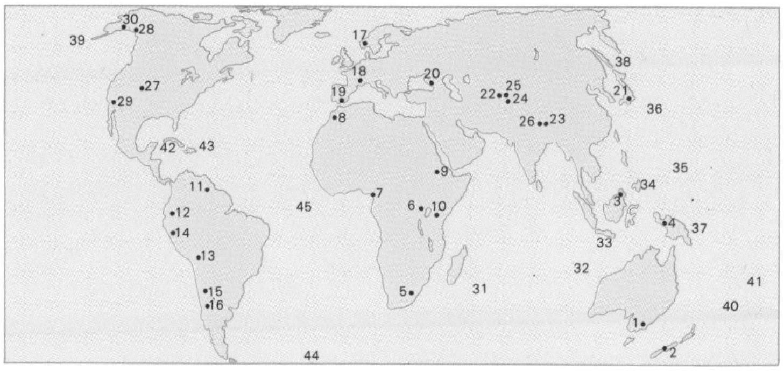

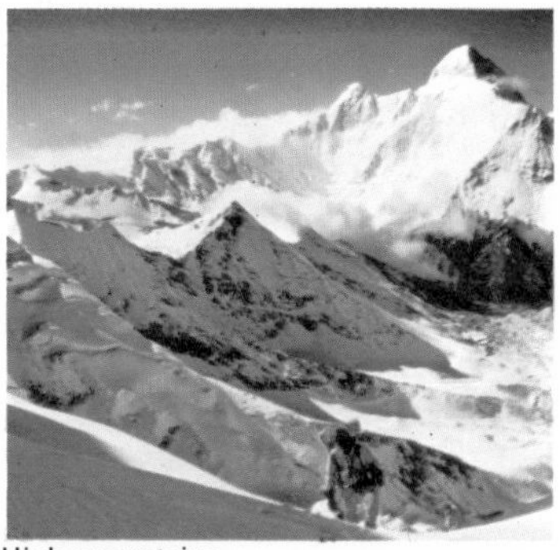

High mountains

Bathyscaphe

Waterfall

Dam

Mountain heights in metres   See table below

E. India & Oceania — Africa — South America — Europe and Asia — North America

1 Kosciusko 2 230 / 2 Mt. Cook (N.Z.) 3 764 / 3 Kinabalu 4 101 / 4 Jaya (Irian) 5 029 / 5 Mt. aux Sources 3 299 / 6 Ruwenzori 5 109 / 7 Cameroon peak 4 070 / 8 Dj. Toubkal 4 165 / 9 Ras Dashen 4 620 / 10 Kilimanjaro 5 895 / 11 Roraima 2 810 / 12 Chimborazo 6 267 / 13 Illimani 6 462 / 14 Huascaran 6 768 / 15 Ojos del Salado 6 863 / 16 Aconcagua 6 960 / 17 Galdhøpiggen 2 469 / 18 Mont Blanc 4 807 / 19 Mulhacen 3 478 / 20 Elbrus 5 633 / 21 Fujiyama 3 776 / 22 Communism peak 7 495 / 23 8 598 Kanchenjunga / 24 K2 8 611 / 25 Muztagh 7 723 / 26 Everest 8 848 / 27 Mt. Elbert 4 399 / 28 Mt. Logan 6 050 / 29 Mt. Whitney 4 418 / 30 Mt. McKinley 6 194

Ocean depths in metres   See table below

Indian Ocean — Pacific Ocean — Atlantic Ocean

Sea level

31 Mauritius basin 6 400 / 32 W. Australian basin 6 459 / 33 Java trench 7 450 / 34 Mindanao trench 10 497 / 35 Mariana trench 11 022 / 36 Japan trench 10 554 / 37 Bougainville deep 9 140 / 38 Kuril trench 10 542 / 39 Aleutian trench 7 822 / 40 Kermadec trench 10 047 / 41 Tonga trench 10 822 / 42 Cayman trough 7 680 / 43 Puerto Rico trough 9 200 / 44 S. Sandwich trench 8 428 / 45 Romanche deep 7 758

Notable Waterfalls heights in feet

Angel, Venezuela	3 215
Tugela, S. Africa	2 798
Mongefossen, Norway	2 539
Yosemite, California	2 421
Mardalsfossen, Norway	2 149
Cuquenan, Venezuela	2 001
Sutherland, N.Z.	1 899
Reichenbach, Switzerland	1 798
Wollomombi, Australia	1 699
Ribbon, California	1 611
Gavarnie, France	1 384
Tyssefallene, Norway	1 358
Krimml, Austria	1 214
King George VI, Guyana	1 200
Silver Strand, California	1 168
Geissbach, Switzerland	1 148
Staubbach, Switzerland	981
Trümmelbach, Switzerland	951
Chirombo, Zambia	879
Livingstone, Zaïre	849
King Edward VIII, Guyana	840
Gersoppa, India	830
Vettifossen Norway	820
Kalambo, Zambia	787
Kaieteur, Guyana	741
Maletsunyane, Lesotho	630
Terui, Italy	590
Kabarega, Uganda	400
Victoria, Zimbabwe-Zambia	351
Cauvery, India	318
Boyoma, Zaïre	200
Niagara, N.America	167
Schaffhausen, Switzerland	98

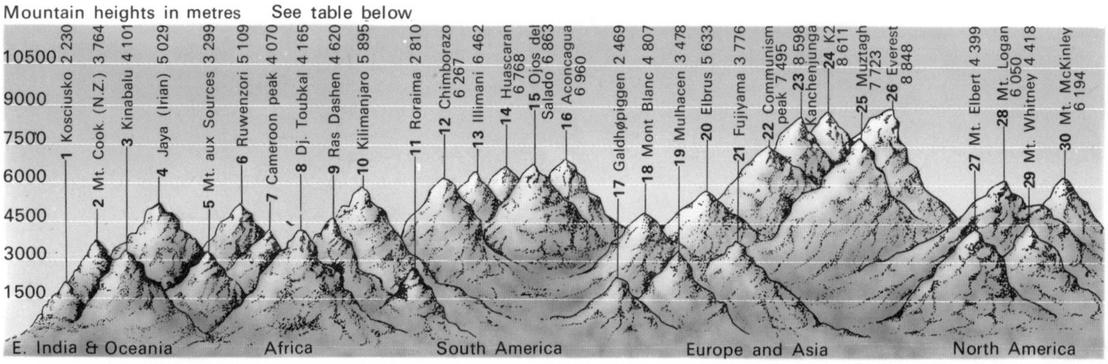

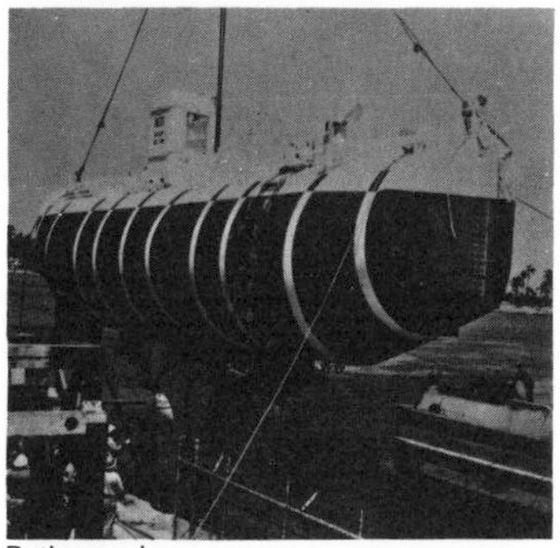

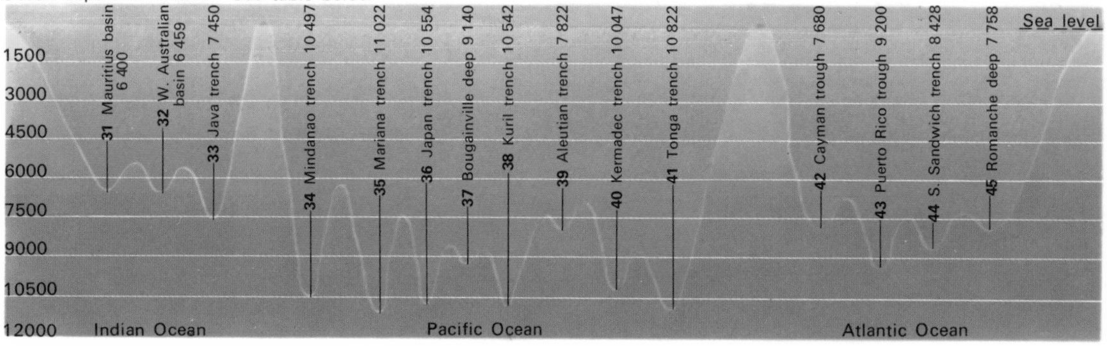

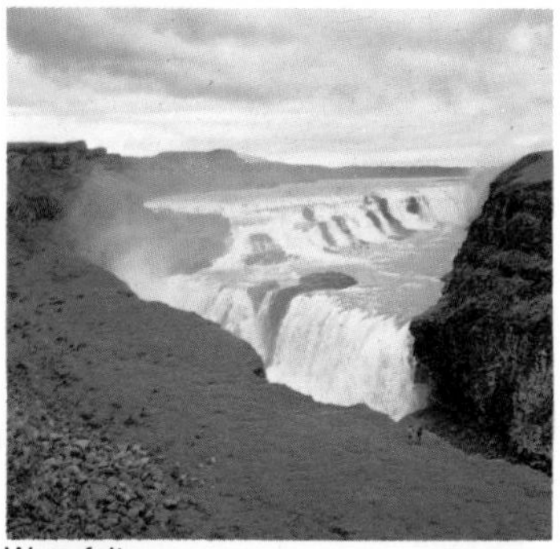

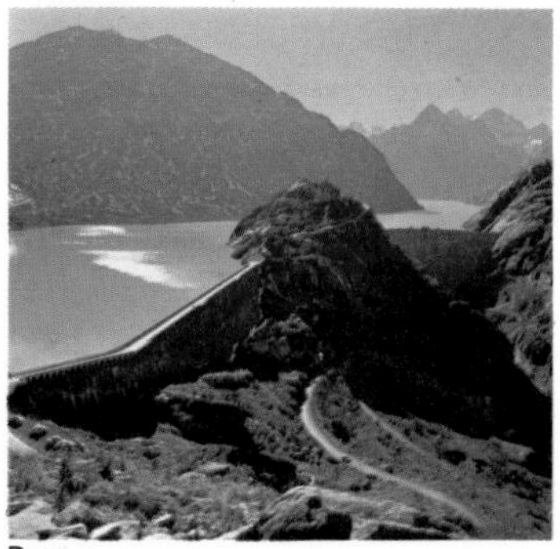

Notable Dams heights in feet

Africa

Cabora Bassa, Zambezi R.	551
Akosombo Main Dam Volta R.	462
Kariba, Zambezi R.	420
Aswan High Dam, Nile R.	360

Asia

Nurek, Vakhsh R., U.S.S.R.	1 040
Bhakra, Sutlej R., India	741
Kurobegawa, Kurobe R., Jap.	610
Charvak, Chirchik R., U.S.S.R.	551
Okutadami, Tadami R., Jap.	515
Bratsk, Angara R., U.S.S.R.	410

Oceania

Warragamba, N.S.W., Australia	449
Eucumbene, N.S.W., Australia	380

Europe

Grande Dixence, Switz.	931
Vajont, Vajont, R., Italy	856
Mauvoisin, Drance R., Switz.	777
Contra, Verzasca R., Switz.	754
Luzzone, Brenno R., Switz.	682
Tignes, Isère R., France	590
Amir Kabir, Karadj R., U.S.S.R.	590
Vidraru, Arges R., Rom.	541
Kremasta, Acheloos R., Greece	541

North America

Mica, Columbia R., Can.	794
Oroville, Feather R.,	771
Hoover, Colorado R.,	725
Glen Canyon, Colorado R.,	708
Daniel Johnson, Can.	702
New Bullards Bar, N. Yuba R.	636
Mossyrock, Cowlitz R.,	603
Shasta, Sacramento R.,	600
W.A.C. Bennett, Canada.	600
Don Pedro, Tuolumne R.,	584
Grand Coulee, Columbia R.,	551

Central and South America

Guri, Caroni R., Venezuela.	347

Metres to feet conversion table

0	500	1 000	1 500	3 000	4 500	6 000	7 500	9 000	10 500	12 000 metres
0	1 500	3 000	5 000	10 000	15 000	20 000	25 000	30 000	35 000	40 000 feet

The metric measurements shown in the mountain heights/ocean depths illustrations correspond to those used in the maps section.

Distances

	Berlin	Bombay	Buenos Aires	Cairo	Calcutta	Caracas	Chicago	Copenhagen	Darwin	Hong Kong	Honolulu	Johannesburg	Lagos	Lisbon
Berlin	Berlin	3907	7400	1795	4370	5241	4402	222	8044	5440	7310	5511	3230	1436
Bombay	6288	Bombay	9275	2706	1034	9024	8048	3990	4510	2683	8024	4334	4730	4982
Buenos Aires	11909	14925	Buenos Aires	7341	10268	3167	5599	7498	9130	11481	7558	5025	4919	5964
Cairo	2890	4355	11814	Cairo	3541	6340	6127	1992	7216	5064	8838	3894	2432	2358
Calcutta	7033	1664	16524	5699	Calcutta	9609	7978	4395	3758	1653	7048	5256	5727	5639
Caracas	8435	14522	5096	10203	15464	Caracas	2502	5215	11221	10166	6009	6847	4810	4044
Chicago	7084	12953	9011	3206	12839	4027	Chicago	4250	9361	7783	4247	8689	5973	3992
Copenhagen	357	6422	12067	9860	7072	8392	6840	Copenhagen	8017	5388	7088	5732	3436	1540
Darwin	12946	7257	14693	11612	6047	18059	15065	12903	Darwin	2654	5369	6611	8837	9391
Hong Kong	8754	4317	18478	8150	2659	16360	12526	8671	4271	Hong Kong	5543	6669	7360	6853
Honolulu	11764	12914	12164	14223	11343	9670	6836	11407	8640	8921	Honolulu	11934	10133	7821
Johannesburg	8870	6974	8088	6267	8459	11019	13984	9225	10639	10732	19206	Johannesburg	2799	5089
Lagos	5198	7612	7916	3915	9216	7741	9612	5530	14222	11845	16308	4505	Lagos	2360
Lisbon	2311	8018	9600	3794	9075	6501	6424	2478	15114	11028	12587	8191	3799	Lisbon
London	928	7190	11131	3508	7961	7507	6356	952	13848	9623	11632	9071	5017	1588
Los Angeles	9311	14000	9852	12200	13120	5812	2804	9003	12695	11639	4117	16676	12414	9122
Mexico City	9732	15656	7389	12372	15280	3586	2726	9514	14631	14122	6085	14585	11071	8676
Moscow	1610	5031	13477	2902	5534	9938	8000	1561	11350	7144	11323	9161	6254	3906
Nairobi	6370	4532	10402	3536	6179	11544	12883	6706	10415	8776	17282	2927	3807	6461
New York	6385	12541	8526	9020	12747	3430	1145	6188	16047	12950	7980	12841	8477	5422
Paris	876	7010	11051	3210	7858	7625	6650	1026	13812	9630	11968	8732	4714	1454
Peking	7822	4757	19268	7544	3269	14399	10603	7202	6011	1963	8160	11710	11457	9668
Reykjavik	2385	8335	11437	5266	8687	6915	4757	2103	13892	9681	9787	10938	6718	2948
Rio de Janeiro	10025	13409	1953	9896	15073	4546	8547	10211	16011	17704	13342	7113	6035	7734
Rome	1180	6175	11151	2133	7219	8363	7739	1531	13265	9284	12916	7743	4039	1861
Singapore	9944	3914	15879	8267	2897	18359	15078	9969	3349	2599	10816	8660	11145	11886
Sydney	16096	10160	11800	14418	9138	15343	14875	16042	3150	7374	8168	11040	15519	18178
Tokyo	8924	6742	18362	9571	5141	14164	10137	8696	5431	2874	6202	13547	13480	11149
Toronto	6497	12488	9093	9233	12561	3873	700	6265	15498	12569	7465	13374	8948	5737
Wellington	18140	12370	9981	16524	11354	13122	13451	17961	5325	9427	7513	11761	16050	19575

	Mexico City	Moscow	Nairobi	New York	Paris	Peking	Reykjavik	Rio de Janeiro	Rome	Singapore	Sydney	Tokyo	Toronto	Wellington	
5	6047	1000	3958	3967	545	4860	1482	6230	734	6179	10002	5545	4037	11272	Berlin
0	9728	3126	2816	7793	4356	2956	5179	8332	3837	2432	6313	4189	7760	7686	Bombay
2	4591	8374	6463	5298	6867	11972	7106	1214	6929	9867	7332	11410	5650	6202	Buenos Aires
0	7687	1803	2197	5605	1994	4688	3272	6149	1325	5137	8959	5947	5737	10268	Cairo
2	9494	3438	3839	7921	4883	2031	5398	9366	4486	1800	5678	3195	7805	7055	Calcutta
2	2228	6175	7173	2131	4738	8947	4297	2825	5196	11407	9534	8801	2406	8154	Caracas
2	1694	4971	8005	711	4132	6588	2956	5311	4809	9369	9243	6299	435	8358	Chicago
4	5912	970	4167	3845	638	4475	1306	6345	951	6195	9968	5403	3892	11160	Copenhagen
8	9091	7053	6472	9971	8582	3735	8632	9948	8243	2081	1957	3375	9630	3309	Darwin
2	8775	4439	5453	8047	5984	1220	6015	11001	5769	1615	4582	1786	7810	5857	Hong Kong
8	3781	7036	10739	4958	7437	5070	6081	8290	8026	6721	5075	3854	4638	4669	Honolulu
2	9063	5692	1818	7979	5426	7276	6797	4420	4811	5381	6860	8418	8310	7308	Johannesburg
3	6879	3886	2366	5268	2929	7119	4175	3750	2510	6925	9643	8376	5560	9973	Lagos
8	5391	2427	4015	3369	903	6007	1832	4805	1157	7385	11295	6928	3565	12163	Lisbon
2	5552	1552	4237	3463	212	5057	1172	5778	889	6743	10558	5942	3545	11691	London
	1549	6070	9659	2446	5645	6251	4310	6310	6331	8776	7502	5475	2170	6719	Los Angeles
		6664	9207	2090	5717	7742	4635	4780	6365	10321	8058	7024	2018	6897	Mexico City
			3942	4666	1545	3600	2053	7184	1477	5237	9008	4651	4637	10283	Moscow
				7358	4029	5727	5395	5548	3350	4635	7552	6996	7570	8490	Nairobi
					3626	6828	2613	4832	4280	9531	9935	6741	356	8951	New York
3						5106	1384	5708	687	6671	10539	6038	3738	11798	Paris
9	10724						4897	10773	5049	2783	5561	1304	6557	6700	Peking
4	14818	6344						6135	2048	7155	10325	5469	2600	10725	Reykjavik
6	3364	7510	11842						5725	9763	8389	11551	5180	7367	Rio de Janeiro
5	9200	2486	6485	5836						6229	10143	6127	4399	11523	Rome
0	12460	5794	9216	10988	8217						3915	3306	9350	5298	Singapore
6	7460	3304	8683	4206	2228	7882						4861	9800	1383	Sydney
5	7693	11562	8928	7777	9187	17338	9874						6410	5762	Tokyo
8	10243	2376	5391	6888	1105	8126	3297	9214						8820	Toronto
3	16610	8428	7460	15339	10737	4478	11514	15712	10025						Wellington
3	12969	14497	12153	15989	16962	8949	16617	13501	16324	6300					Miles
1	11304	7485	11260	10849	9718	2099	8802	18589	9861	5321	7823				
2	3247	7462	12183	574	6015	10552	4184	8336	7080	15047	15772	10316			
4	11100	16549	13664	14405	18987	10782	17260	11855	18545	8526	2226	9273	14194		

Water Resources and Vegetation

Water resources and vegetation

Fresh water is essential for life on earth and in some parts of the world it is a most precious commodity. On the other hand it is very easy for industrialised temperate states to take its existence for granted, and man's increasing demand may only be met finally by the desalination of earth's 775 million cubic miles of salt water. 70% of the earth's fresh water exists as ice.

The hydrological cycle

Water is continually being absorbed into the atmosphere as vapour from oceans, lakes, rivers and vegetation transpiration. On cooling the vapour either condenses or freezes and falls as rain, hail or snow. Most precipitation falls over the sea but one quarter falls over the land of which half evaporates again soon after falling while the rest flows back into the oceans.

Distribution of water

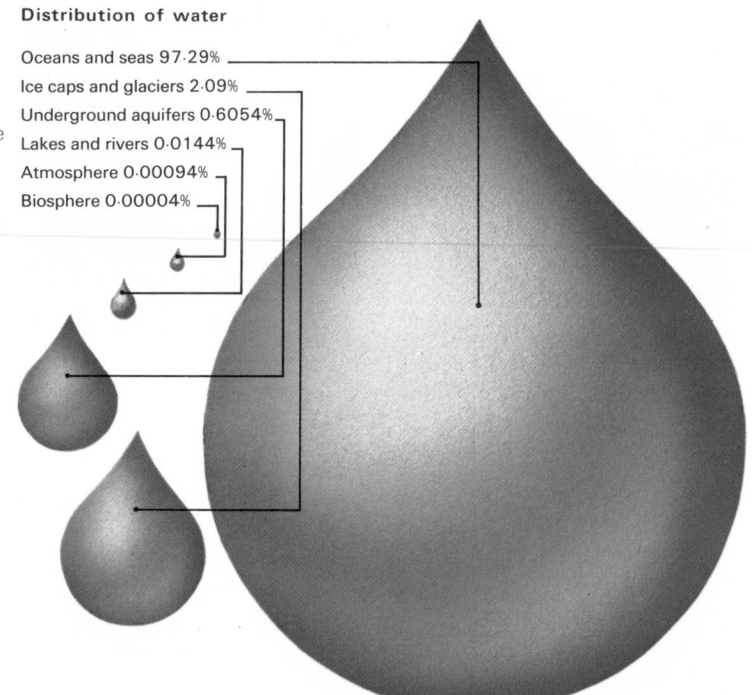

Oceans and seas 97·29%
Ice caps and glaciers 2·09%
Underground aquifers 0·6054%
Lakes and rivers 0·0144%
Atmosphere 0·00094%
Biosphere 0·00004%

Tundra

Mediterranean scrub

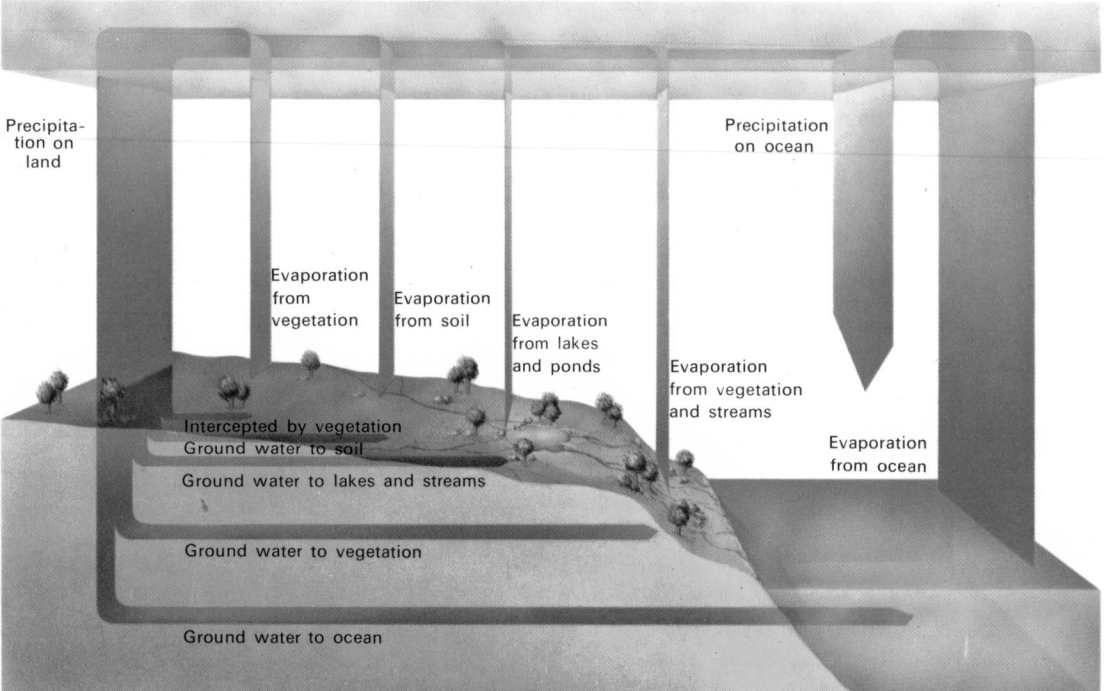

Precipitation on land

Precipitation on ocean

Evaporation from vegetation

Evaporation from soil

Evaporation from lakes and ponds

Evaporation from vegetation and streams

Evaporation from ocean

Intercepted by vegetation
Ground water to soil
Ground water to lakes and streams
Ground water to vegetation
Ground water to ocean

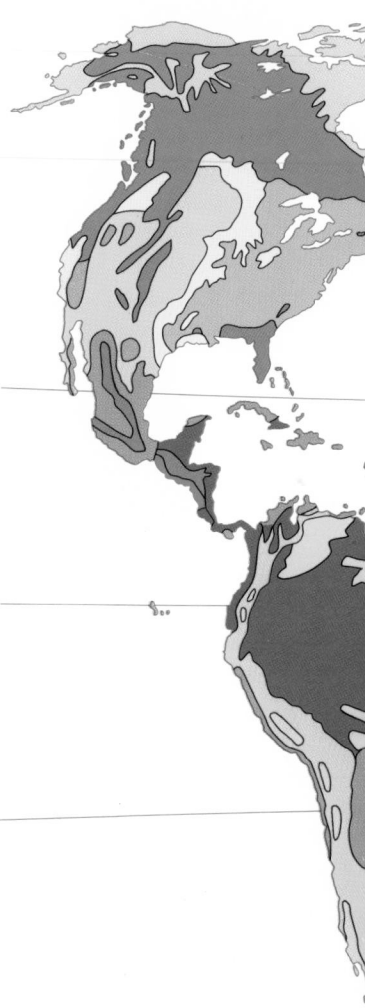

Domestic consumption of water

An area's level of industrialisation, climate and standard of living are all major influences in the consumption of water. On average Europe consumes 168 gallons per head each day of which 48 gallons is used domestically. In the U.S.A. domestic consumption is slightly higher at 71 gallons per day. The graph (right) represents domestic consumption in the U.K.

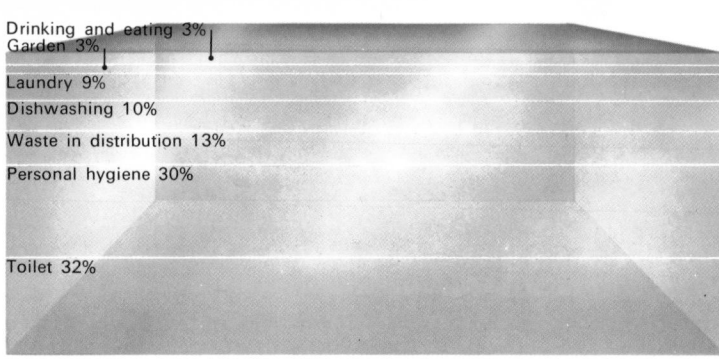

Drinking and eating 3%
Garden 3%
Laundry 9%
Dishwashing 10%
Waste in distribution 13%
Personal hygiene 30%
Toilet 32%

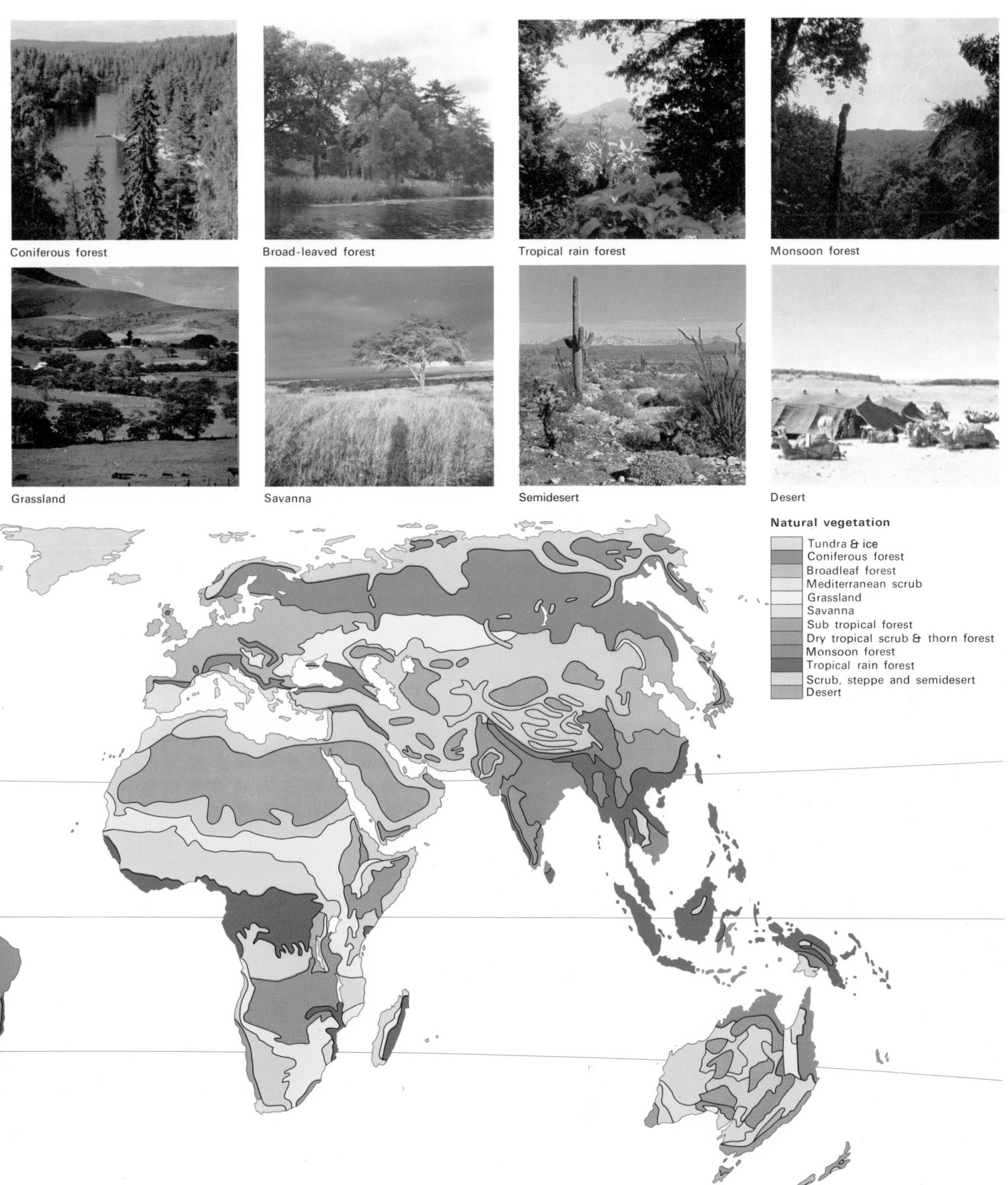

Coniferous forest

Broad-leaved forest

Tropical rain forest

Monsoon forest

Grassland

Savanna

Semidesert

Desert

Natural vegetation

Tundra & ice
Coniferous forest
Broadleaf forest
Mediterranean scrub
Grassland
Savanna
Sub tropical forest
Dry tropical scrub & thorn forest
Monsoon forest
Tropical rain forest
Scrub, steppe and semidesert
Desert

Population

Population distribution
(right and lower right)
People have always been unevenly distributed in the world. Europe has for centuries contained nearly 20% of the world's population but after the 16-19th century explorations and consequent migrations this proportion has rapidly reduced. In 1750 the Americas had 2% of the world's total: in 2000 AD they are expected to contain 16%.

The most densely populated regions are in India, China and Europe where the average density is between 60 and 120 per square mile although there are pockets of extremely high density elsewhere. In contrast Australia has only 0·9 people per square mile. The countries in the lower map have been redrawn to make their areas proportional to their populations.

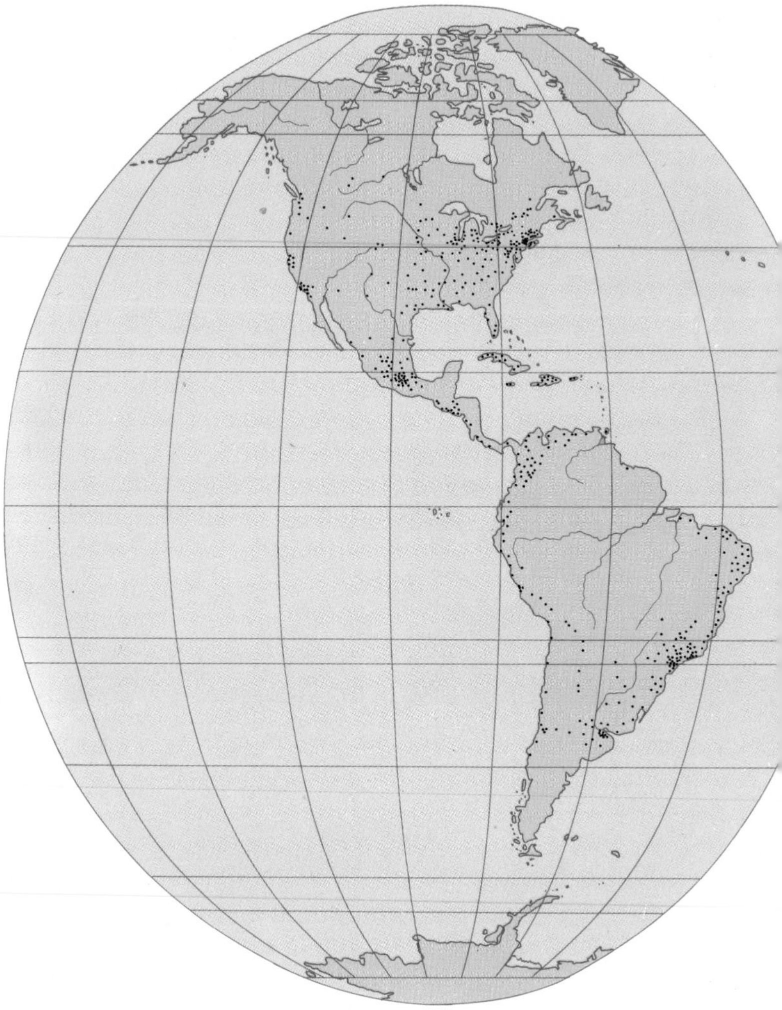

U.S.A.

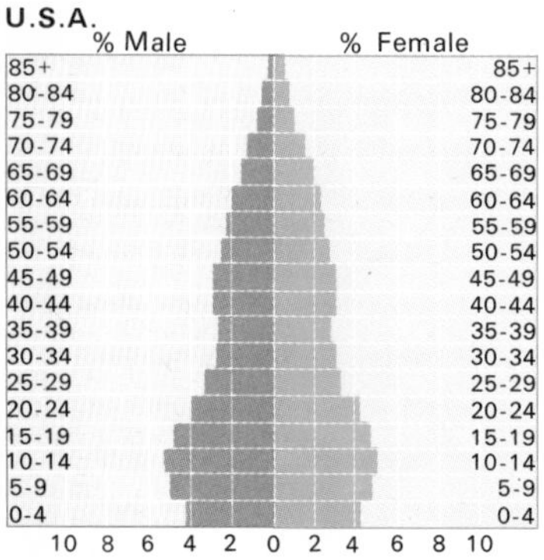

Brazil

Ghana

France

U.S.S.R.

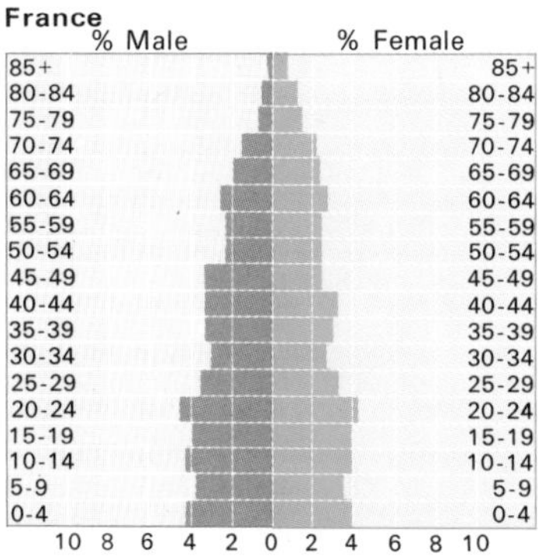

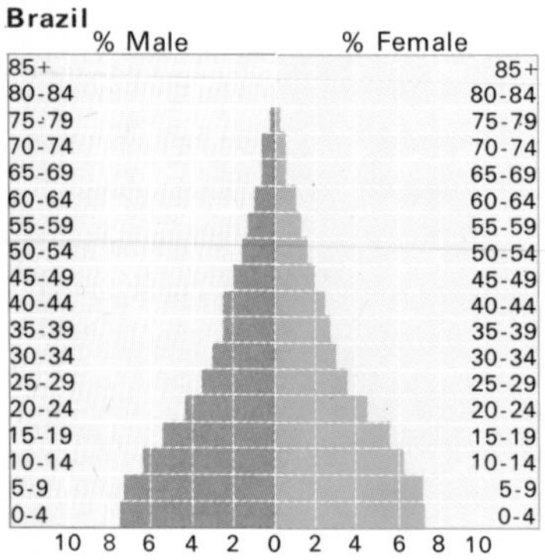

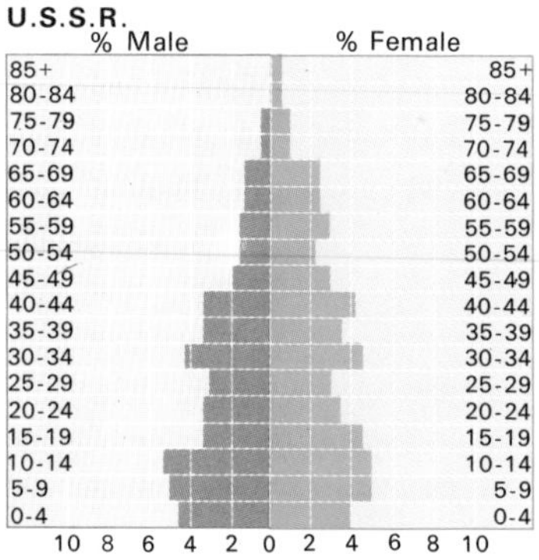

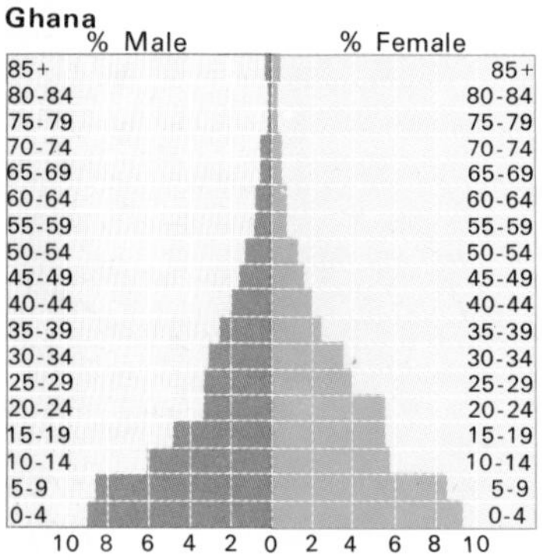

India

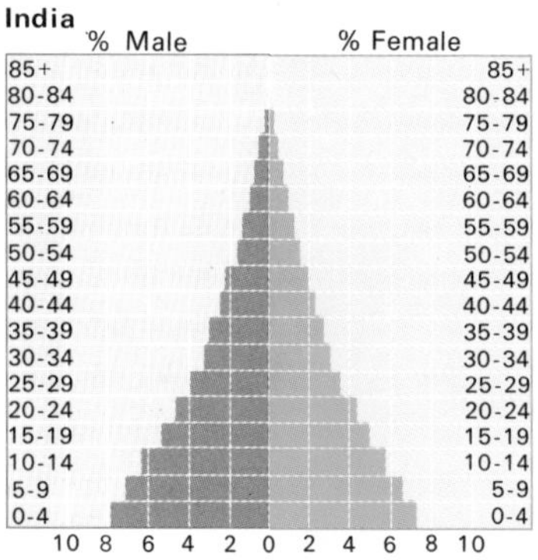

Age distribution
France shows many demographic features characteristic of European countries. Birth and death rates have declined with a moderate population growth - there are nearly as many old as young. In contrast, India and several other countries have few old and many young because of the high death rates and even higher birth rates. It is this excess that is responsible for the world's population explosion.

World population increase
Until comparatively recently there was little increase in the population of the world. About 6000 BC it is thought that there were about 200 million people and in the following 7000 years an increase of just over 100 million. In the 1800's there were about 1000 million; at present there are over 3500 million and by the year 2000 if present trends continue there would be at least 7000 million.

1650   1700   1750   1800

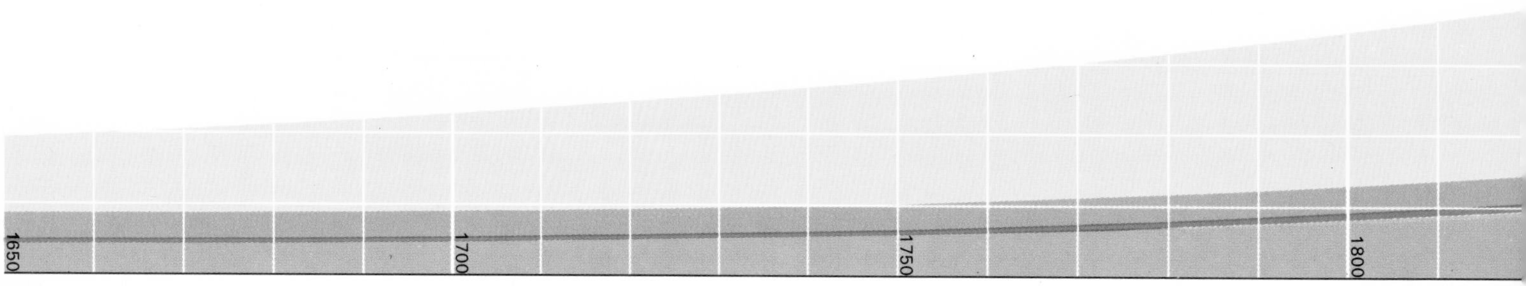

World population distribution

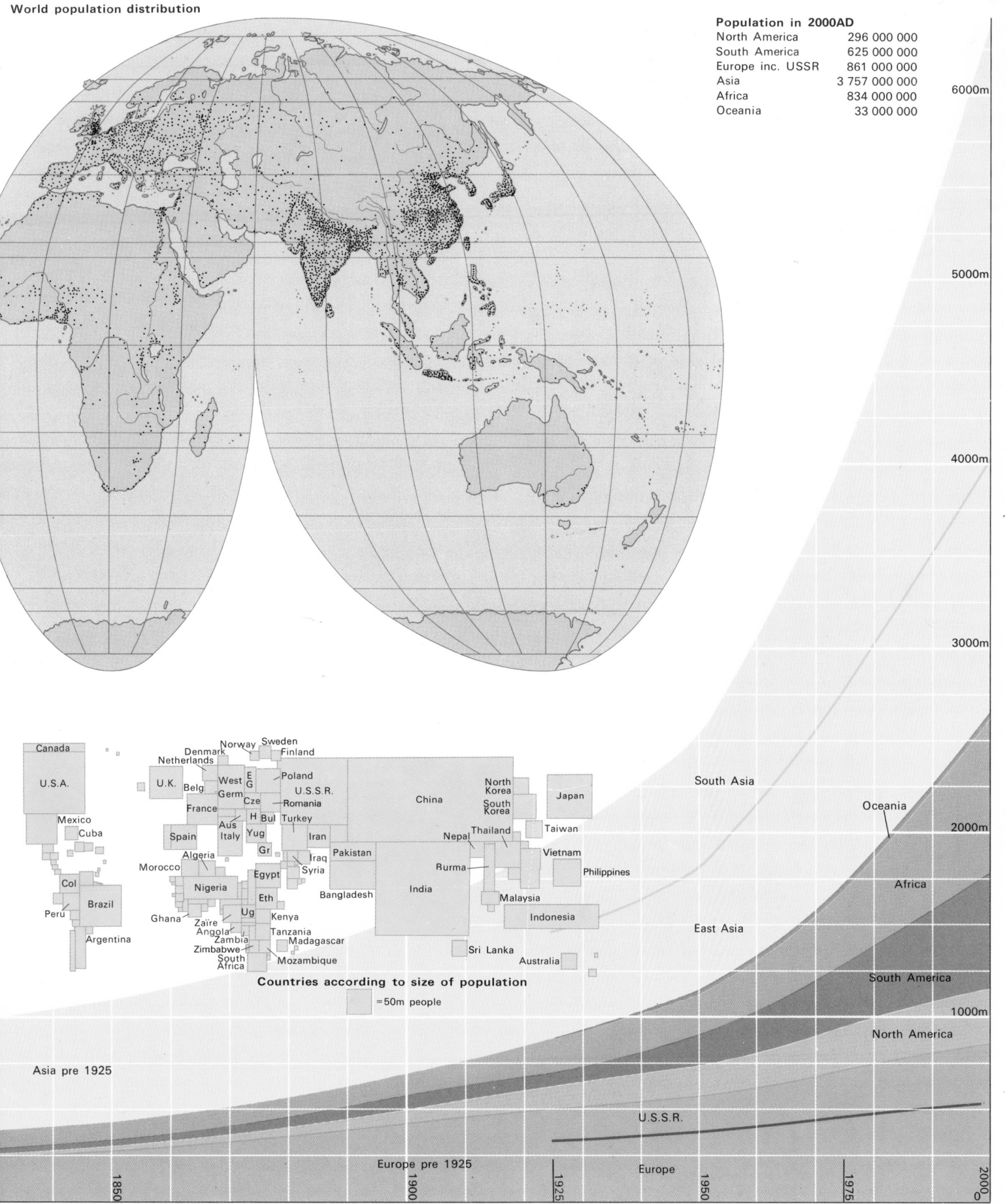

World population distribution

Population in 2000AD

North America	296 000 000
South America	625 000 000
Europe inc. USSR	861 000 000
Asia	3 757 000 000
Africa	834 000 000
Oceania	33 000 000

6000m

5000m

4000m

3000m

South Asia

Oceania

2000m

East Asia

Africa

South America

1000m

North America

Asia pre 1925

U.S.S.R.

Europe pre 1925

Europe

Countries according to size of population

= 50m people

Canada

U.S.A.

Mexico

Cuba

Col

Peru

Brazil

Argentina

Norway Sweden

Denmark Finland

Netherlands

U.K. Belg West E Poland

France Germ G U.S.S.R.

Cze Romania

Spain Aus H Bul Turkey

Italy Yug

Algeria Gr Iran

Morocco Egypt Iraq Pakistan

Syria

Nigeria Eth Bangladesh

Ghana Ug Kenya India

Zaïre Angola Tanzania

Zambia Madagascar

Zimbabwe

South Africa Mozambique

China North Korea South Korea Japan

Taiwan

Nepal Thailand Vietnam

Burma Philippines

Malaysia Indonesia

Sri Lanka

Australia

1850   1900   1925   1950   1975   2000

27

Language

Languages may be blamed partly for the division and lack of understanding between nations. While a common language binds countries together it in turn isolates them from other countries and groups. Thus beliefs, ideas and inventions remain exclusive to these groups and different cultures develop.

There are thousands of different languages and dialects spoken today. This can cause strife even within the one country, such as India, where different dialects are enough to break down the country into distinct groups.

As a result of colonization and the spread of internationally accepted languages, many countries have superimposed a completely unrelated language in order to combine isolated national groups and to facilitate international understanding, for example Spanish in South America, English in India.

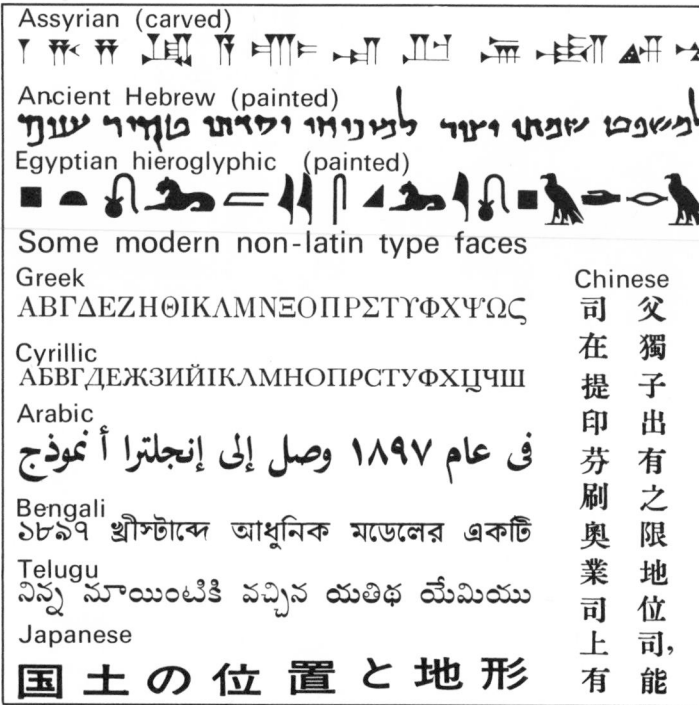

Assyrian (carved)

Ancient Hebrew (painted)

Egyptian hieroglyphic (painted)

Some modern non-latin type faces

Greek
ΑΒΓΔΕΖΗΘΙΚΛΜΝΞΟΠΡΣΤΥΦΧΨΩΣ

Cyrillic
АБВГДЕЖЗИЙІКЛМНОПРСТУФХЦЧШ

Arabic
فى عام ١٨٩٧ وصل إلى إنجلترا أ نموذج

Bengali
১৮৯৭ খ্রীস্টাব্দে আধুনিক মডেলের একটি

Telugu
నిన్న న్యూయింంటక్ వచ్చిన యతిథ యేమియు

Japanese
国土の位置と地形

Chinese
司在提印芬刷奥業司上有
父獨子出有之限地位司,能

Related languages

Certain languages showing marked similarities are thought to have developed from common parent languages for example Latin. After the retreat of the Roman Empire wherever Latin had been firmly established it remained as the new nation's language. With no unifying centre divergent development took place and Latin evolved into new languages.

Calligraphy

Writing was originally by a series of pictures, and these gradually developed in styles which were influenced by the tools generally used. Carved alphabets, such as that used by the Sumerians, tended to be angular, while those painted or written tended to be curved, as in Egyptian hieroglyphics development of which can be followed through the West Semitic, Greek and Latin alphabets to our own.

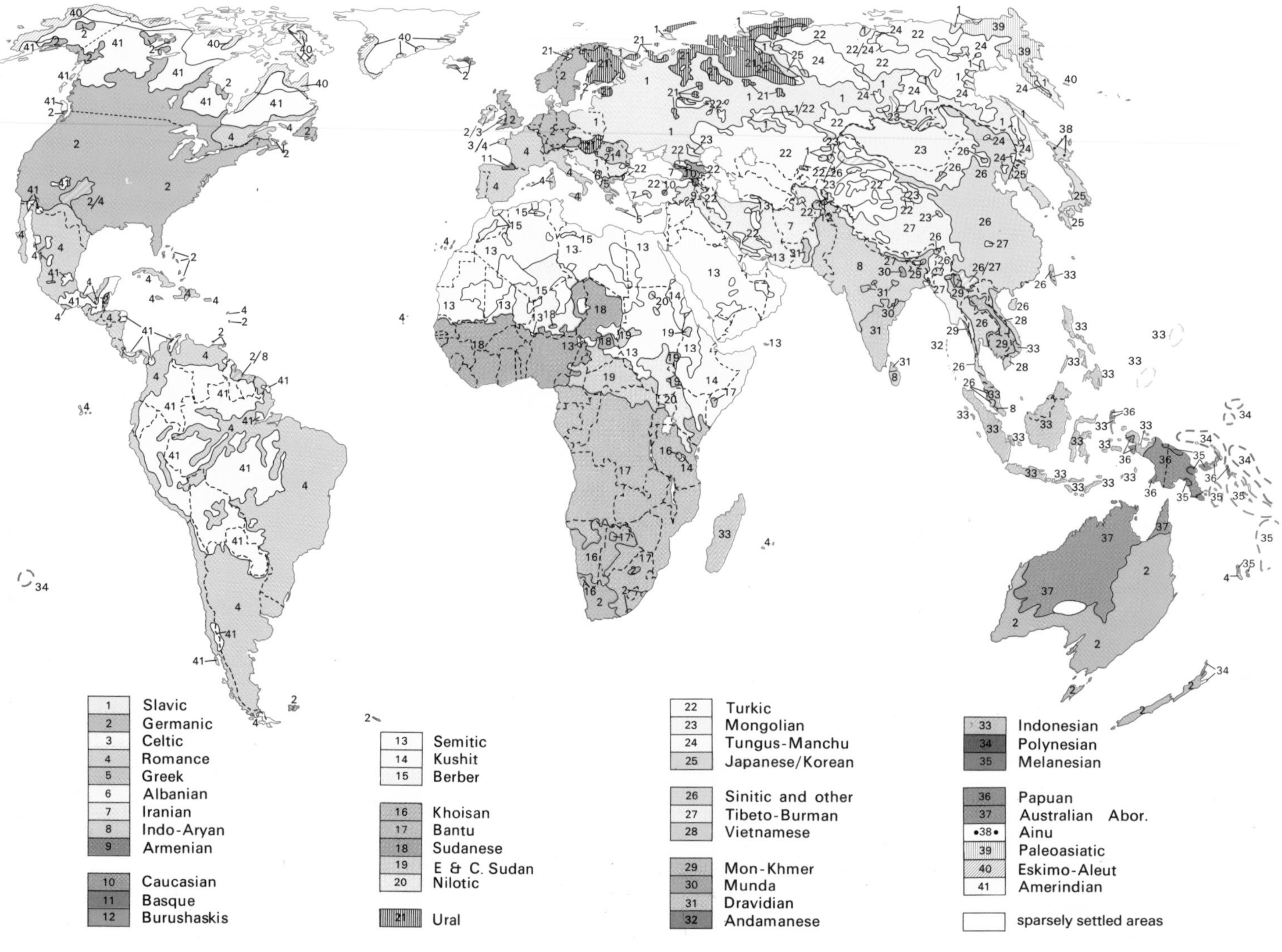

1	Slavic	
2	Germanic	
3	Celtic	
4	Romance	
5	Greek	
6	Albanian	
7	Iranian	
8	Indo-Aryan	
9	Armenian	
10	Caucasian	
11	Basque	
12	Burushaskis	

13	Semitic
14	Kushit
15	Berber
16	Khoisan
17	Bantu
18	Sudanese
19	E & C. Sudan
20	Nilotic
21	Ural

22	Turkic
23	Mongolian
24	Tungus-Manchu
25	Japanese/Korean
26	Sinitic and other
27	Tibeto-Burman
28	Vietnamese
29	Mon-Khmer
30	Munda
31	Dravidian
32	Andamanese

33	Indonesian
34	Polynesian
35	Melanesian
36	Papuan
37	Australian Abor.
•38•	Ainu
39	Paleoasiatic
40	Eskimo-Aleut
41	Amerindian
	sparsely settled areas

Religion

Throughout history man has had beliefs in supernatural powers based on the forces of nature which have developed into worship of a god and some cases gods.

Hinduism honours many gods and goddesses which are all manifestations of the one divine spirit, Brahma, and incorporates beliefs such as reincarnation, worship of cattle and the caste system.

Buddhism, an offshoot of Hinduism, was founded in north east India by Gautama Buddha (563-483 BC) who taught that spiritual and moral discipline were essential to achieve supreme peace.

Confucianism is a mixture of Buddhism and Confucius' teachings which were elaborated to provide a moral basis for the political structure of Imperial China and to cover the already existing forms of ancestor worship.

Judaism dates back to c. 13th century B.C. The Jews were expelled from the Holy Land in AD70 and only reinstated in Palestine in 1948.

Christian monastery

Jewish holy place

Hindu temple

Islam, founded in Mecca by Muhammad (570-632 AD) spread across Asia and Africa and in its retreat left isolated pockets of adherent communities.

Christianity was founded by Jesus of Nazareth in the 1st century AD The Papal authority, established in the 4th century, was rejected by Eastern churches in the 11th century. Later several other divisions developed eg. Roman Catholicism, Protestantism.

Mohammedan mosque

Buddhist temple

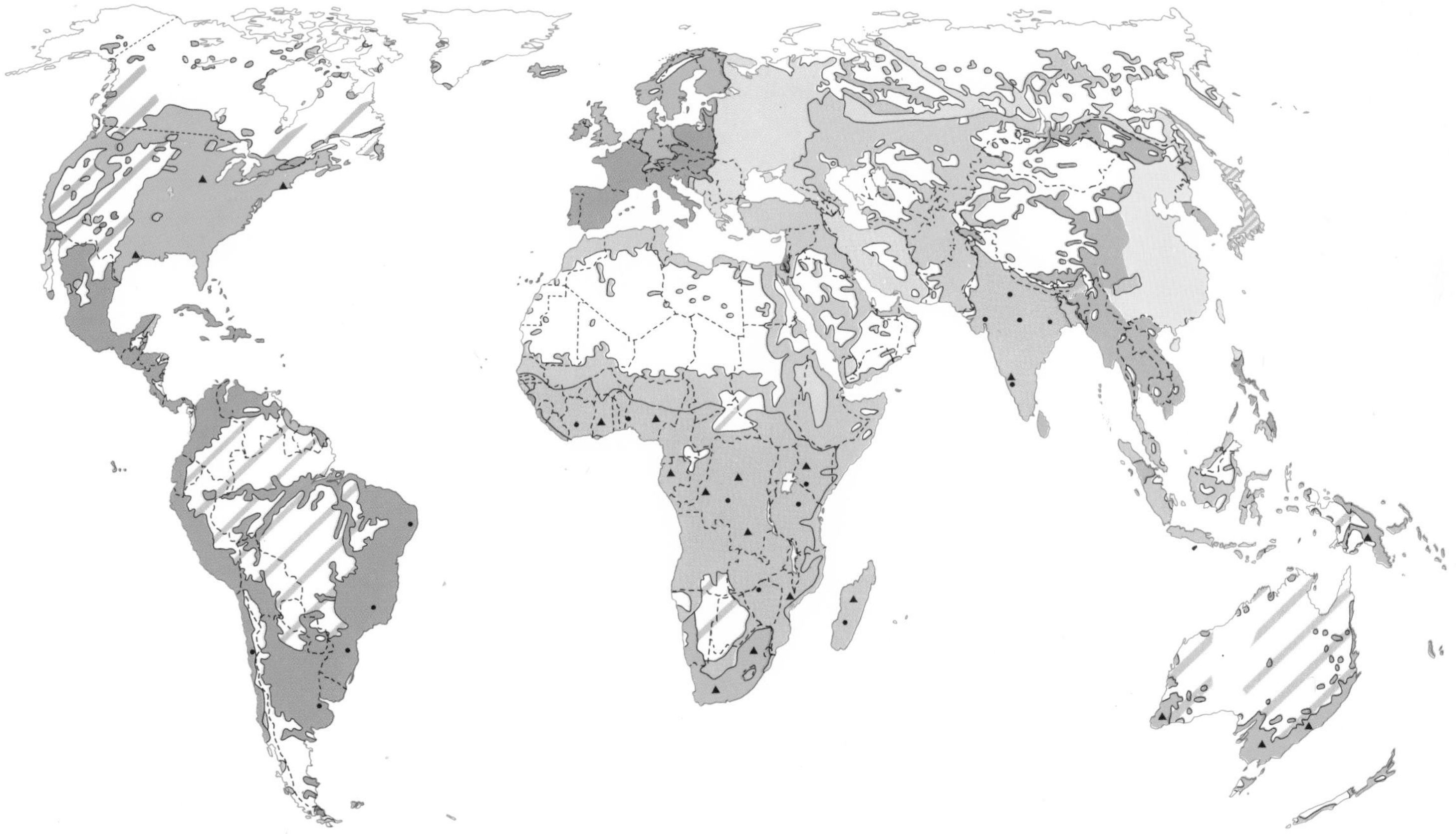

▲ Roman Catholicism	Shiah Islam	Judaism
Orthodox and other Eastern Churches	Buddhism	Shintoism
• Protestantism	Hinduism	Primitive religions
Sunni Islam	Confucianism	Uninhabited

The Growth of Cities

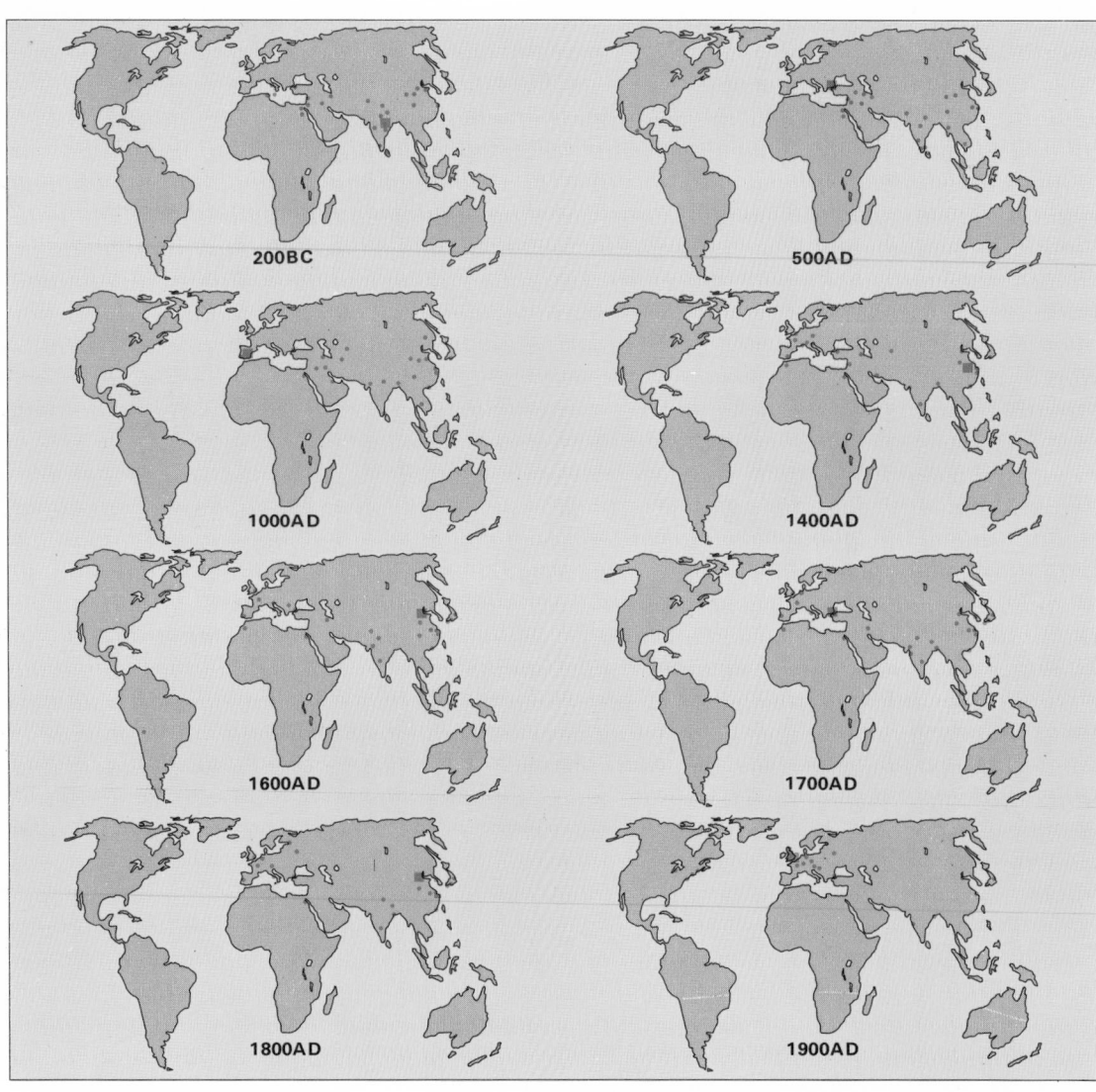

200BC

500AD

1000AD

1400AD

1600AD

1700AD

1800AD

1900AD

Cities through history
The evolution of the semi-perm anent Neolithic settlements into a city took from 5000 until 3500 BC. Efficient communications and exchange systems were developed as population densities increased as high as 15 000 to 30 000 per square mile in 2000BC in Egypt and Babylonia, compared with New York City today at 6 000.

■ The largest city in the world

· The twenty five largest cities in the world

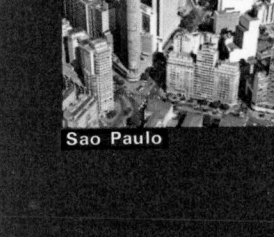

Sao Paulo

Increase in urbanisation
The increase in urbanisation is a result primarily of better sanitation and health resulting in the growth of population and secondarily to the movement of man off the land into industry and service occupations in the cities. Generally the most highly developed industrial nations are the most intensely urbanised although exceptions such as Norway and Switzerland show that rural industrialisation can exist.

Increase in urbanisation
The figures on the vertical columns show the urban population as a percentage of the total population for each country in the year shown.

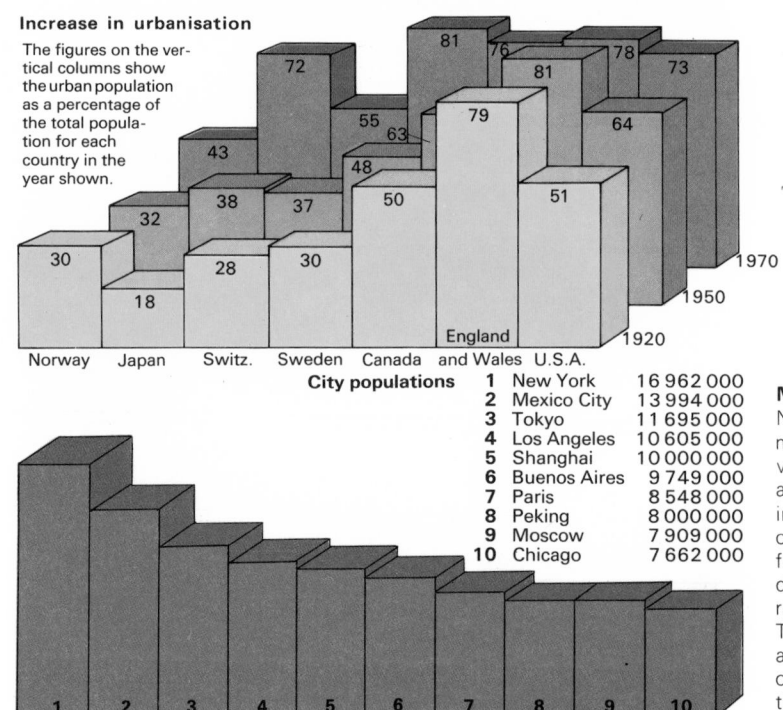

Norway   Japan   Switz.   Sweden   Canada   England and Wales   U.S.A.

1970
1950
1920

Metropolitan areas
A metropolitan area can be defined as a central city linked with surrounding communities by continuous built-up areas controlled by one municipal government. With improved communications the neighbouring communities generally continue to provide the city's work-force. The graph (right) compares the total populations of the world's ten largest cities.

City populations

1	New York	16 962 000
2	Mexico City	13 994 000
3	Tokyo	11 695 000
4	Los Angeles	10 605 000
5	Shanghai	10 000 000
6	Buenos Aires	9 749 000
7	Paris	8 548 000
8	Peking	8 000 000
9	Moscow	7 909 000
10	Chicago	7 662 000

Major cities
Normally these are not only major centres of population and wealth but also of political power and trade. They are the sites of international airports and characteristically are great ports from which imported goods are distributed using the roads and railways which focus on the city. Their staple trades and industries are varied and flexible and depend on design and fashion rather than raw material production.

New York

Sydney

Moscow

Tokyo

Hong Kong

Bombay

London

Cairo

Rio de Janeiro

Rome

Cities over 5 000 000 inhabitants

2 000 000 - 5 000 000 inhabitants

1 000 000 - 2 000 000 inhabitants

250 000 - 1 000 000 inhabitants

Food Resources: Vegetable

Cocoa, tea , coffee
These tropical or sub-tropical crops are grown mainly for export to the economically advanced countries. Tea and coffee are the world's principal beverages. Cocoa is used more in the manufacture of chocolate.

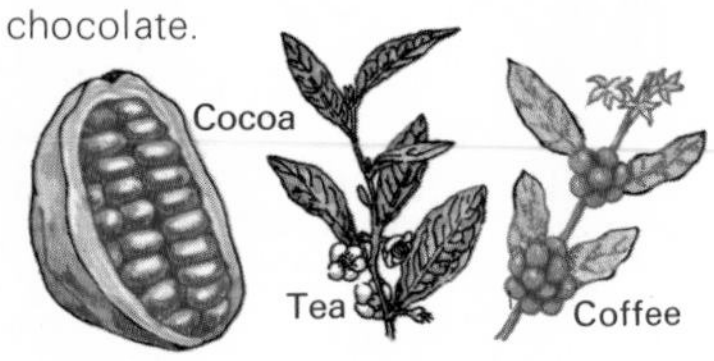

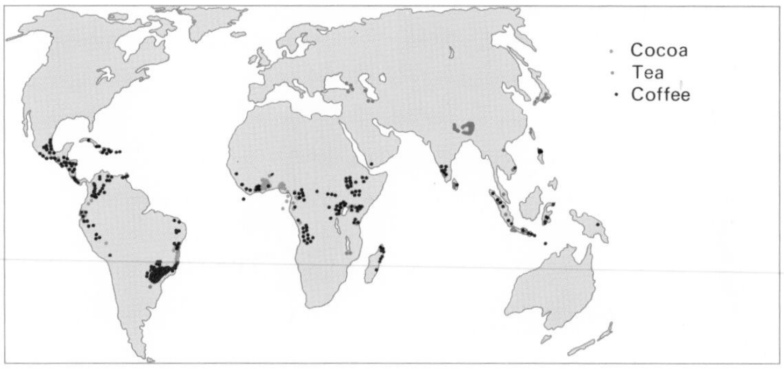

Cocoa
Tea
Coffee

Sugar beet, sugar cane
Cane Sugar - a tropical crop accounts for the bulk of the sugar entering into international trade. Beet Sugar, on the other hand, demands a temperate climate and is produced primarily for domestic consumption.

Sugar beet
Sugar cane

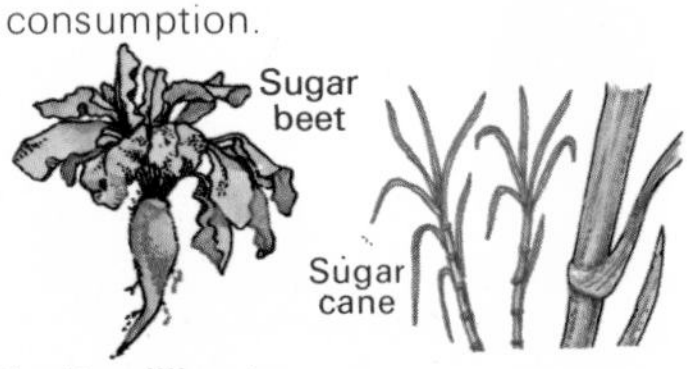

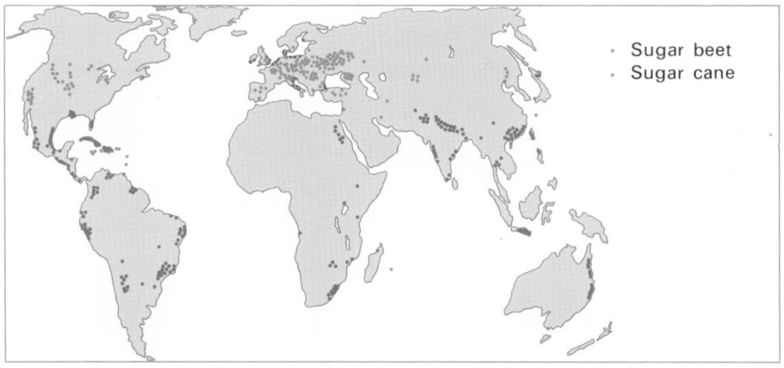

Fruit million tonnes

Italy	France	U.S.S.R	Spain	Others	Grapes 61·7
U.S.A.	Brazil	Italy Spain	Others	Citrus 49·9
Brazil	India	Philippines	Others	Bananas 39·3
China	Turkey	U.S.S.R	Others	Melons 24·1
U.S.S.R	U.S.A.	Others	Apples 31·9

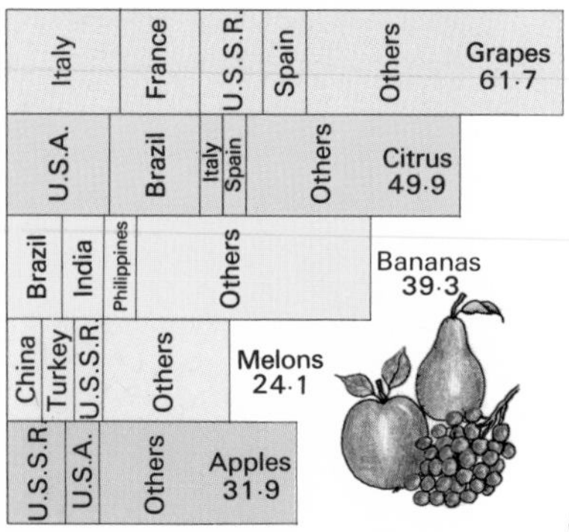

Vegetable oilseeds and oils
Despite the increasing use of synthetic chemical products and animal and marine fats, vegetable oils extracted from these crops grow in quantity, value and importance. Food is the major use- in margarine and cooking fats.

Groundnut
Soya bean

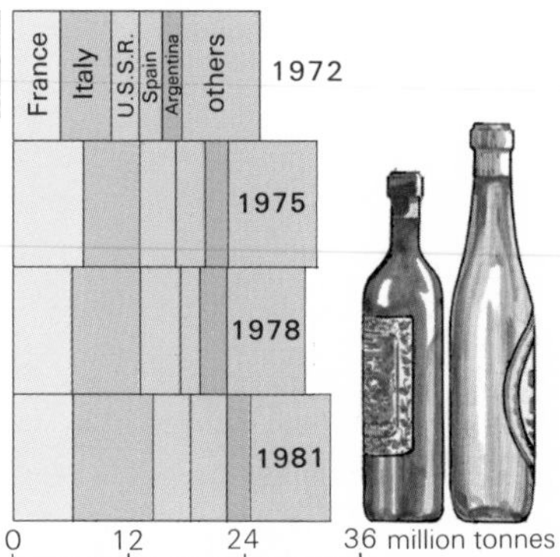

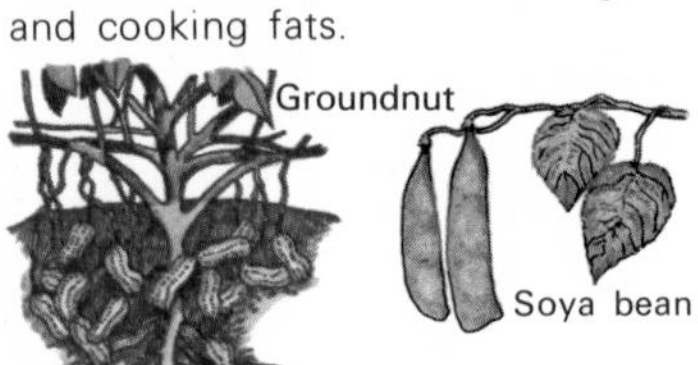

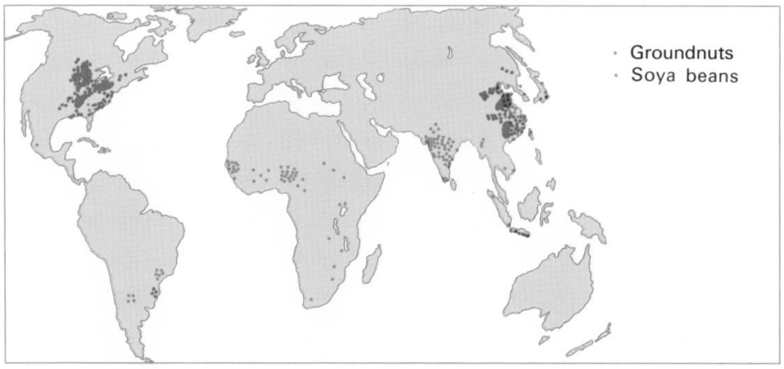

Groundnuts are also a valuable subsistence crop and the meal is used as animal feed. Soya-bean meal is a growing source of protein for humans and animals. The Mediterranean lands are the prime source of olive oil.

Rape (oil seed)
Sunflower

· Cocoa
· Tea
· Coffee

Sugar beet
Sugar cane

Wine

1972
1975
1978
1981

France | Italy | U.S.S.R. | Spain | Argentina | others

0   12   24   36 million tonnes

Fruit, wine
With the improvements in canning, drying and freezing, and in transport and marketing, the international trade and consumption of deciduous and soft fruits, citrus fruits and tropical fruits has greatly increased. Recent developments in the use of the peel will give added value to some of the fruit crops.

Over 80% of grapes are grown for wine and over a half in countries bordering the Mediterranean.

· Groundnuts
· Soya beans

· Rape seed
· Sunflower seed

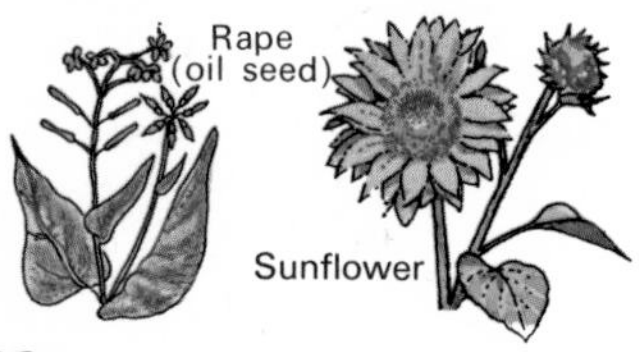

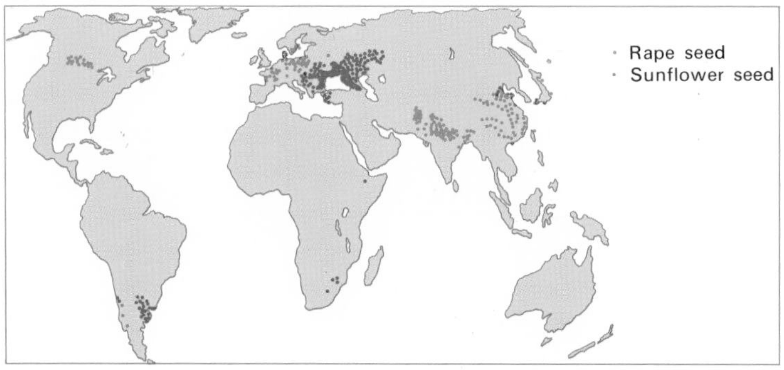

Cereals
Cereals include those members of the grain family with starchy edible seeds - wheat, maize, barley, oats, rye, rice, millets and sorghums.

Cereals and potatoes (not a cereal but starch-producing) are the principal source of food for our modern civilisations because of their high yield in bulk and food value per unit of land and labour required. They are also easy to store and transport, and provide food also for animals producing meat, fat, milk and eggs. Wheat is the principal bread grain of the temperate regions in which potatoes are the next most important food source. Rice is the principal cereal in the hotter. humid regions. especially in Asia. Oats, barley and maize are grown mainly for animal feed; millets and sorghums as main subsistence crops in Africa and India.

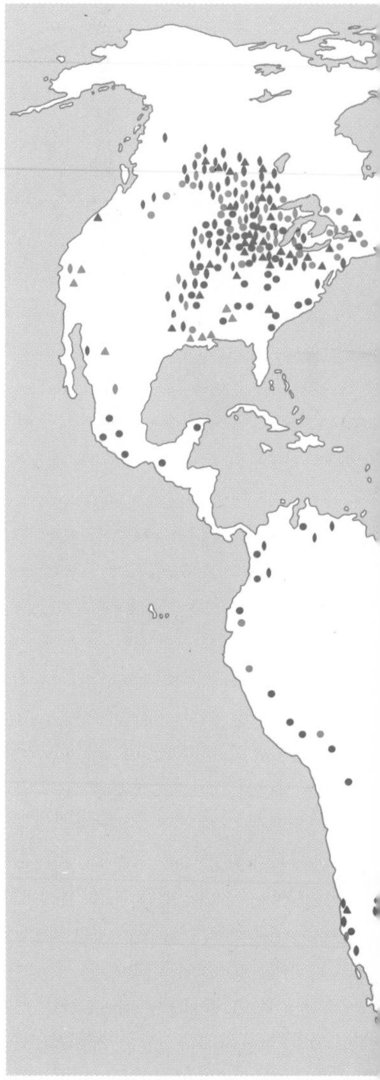

Maize (or Corn)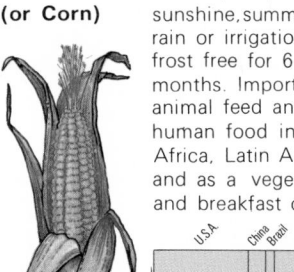
Needs plenty of sunshine, summer rain or irrigation and frost free for 6 months. Important as animal feed and for human food in Africa, Latin America and as a vegetable and breakfast cereal.

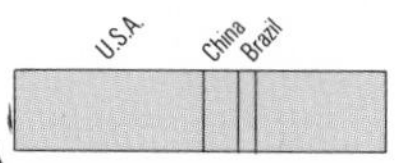

World production 451·2 million tonnes

Barley
Has the widest range of cultivation requiring only 8 weeks between seed time and harvest. Used mainly as animal-feed and by the malting industry.

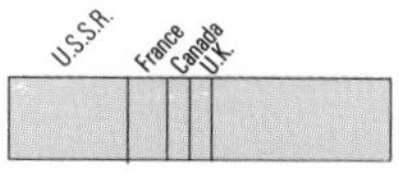

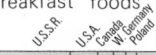
World production 158·7 million tonnes

Oats
Widely grown in temperate regions with the limit fixed by early autumn frosts. Mainly fed to cattle. The best quality oats are used for oatmeal, porridge and breakfast foods

World production 43·0 million tonnes

Rice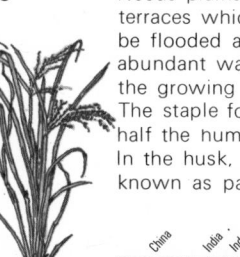
Needs plains or terraces which can be flooded and abundant water in the growing season. The staple food of half the human race. In the husk, it is known as paddy.

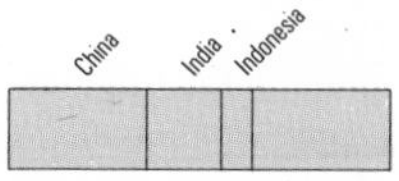

World production 403·2 million tonnes

Wheat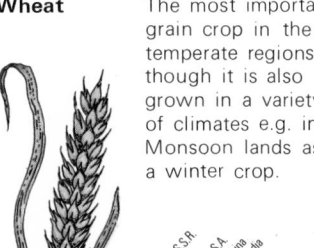
The most important grain crop in the temperate regions though it is also grown in a variety of climates e.g. in Monsoon lands as a winter crop.

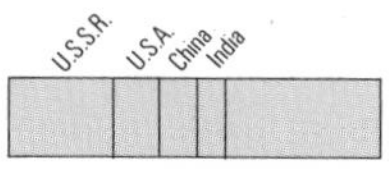

World production 458·6 million tonnes

Rye
The hardiest of cereals and more resistant to cold, pests and disease than wheat. An important foodstuff in Central and E. Europe and the U.S.S.R.

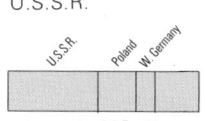
World production 24·5 million tonnes

Millets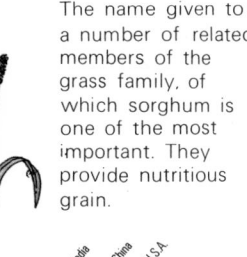
The name given to a number of related members of the grass family, of which sorghum is one of the most important. They provide nutritious grain.

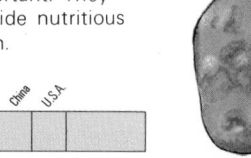
World production 100·7 million tonnes

Potato
An important food crop though less nutritious weight for weight than grain crops.

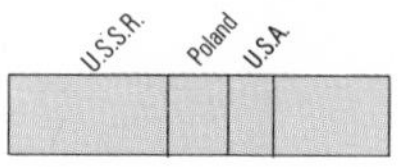

World production 227·3 million tonnes

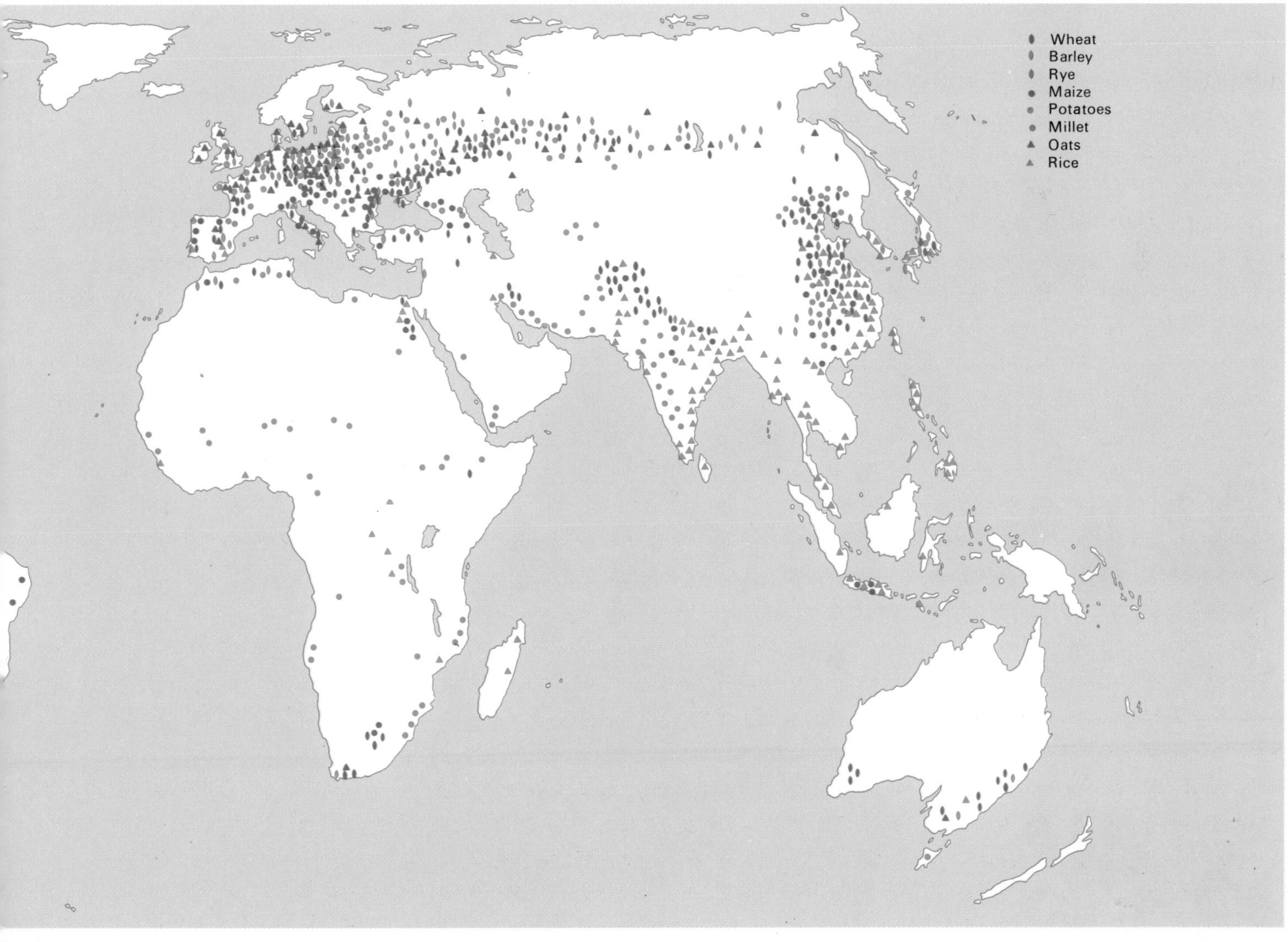

Wheat
Barley
Rye
Maize
Potatoes
Millet
Oats
Rice

Food Resources: Animal

Food resources: Animal
Meat, milk and allied foods are prime protein-providers and are also sources of essential vitamins. Meat is mainly a product of continental and savannah grasslands and the cool west coasts, particularly in Europe. Milk and cheese, eggs and fish - though found in some quantity throughout the world - are primarily a product of the temperate zones.

Beef cattle Australia, New Zealand and Argentina provide the major part of international beef exports. Western U.S.A. and Europe have considerable production of beef for their local high demand.

World production 994·0 million head

Dairy Cattle The need of herds for a rich diet and for nearby markets result in dairying being characteristic of densely-populated areas of the temperate zones - U.S.A., N.W. Europe, N. Zealand and S.E. Australia.

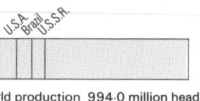
World production 222·1 million head

Cheese The principal producers are the U.S.A., W. Europe, U.S.S.R., and New Zealand and principal exporters Netherlands, New Zealand, Denmark and France.

World production 11·6 million tonne

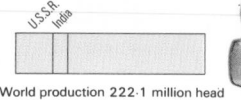

Sheep Raised mostly for wool and meat, the skins and cheese from their milk are important products in some countries. The merino yields a fine wool and crossbreds are best for meat.

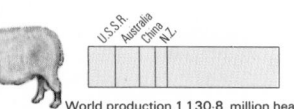
World production 1 130·8 million head

Pigs Can be reared in most climates from monsoon to cool temperate. They are abundant in China, the corn belt of the U.S.A. N.W. and C. Europe, Brazil and U.S.S.R.

World production 779·3 million head

Fish Commercial fishing requires large shoals of fish of one species within reach of markets. Freshwater fishing is also important. A rich source of protein, fish will become an increasingly valuable food source.

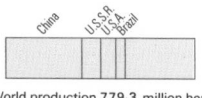
World production 72·4 million tonnes

Butter (includes Ghee) The biggest producers are U.S.S.R., India, France and West Germany.

World production 6·87 million tonnes

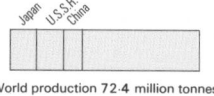

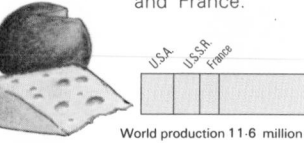

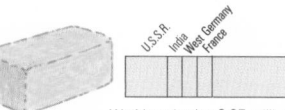

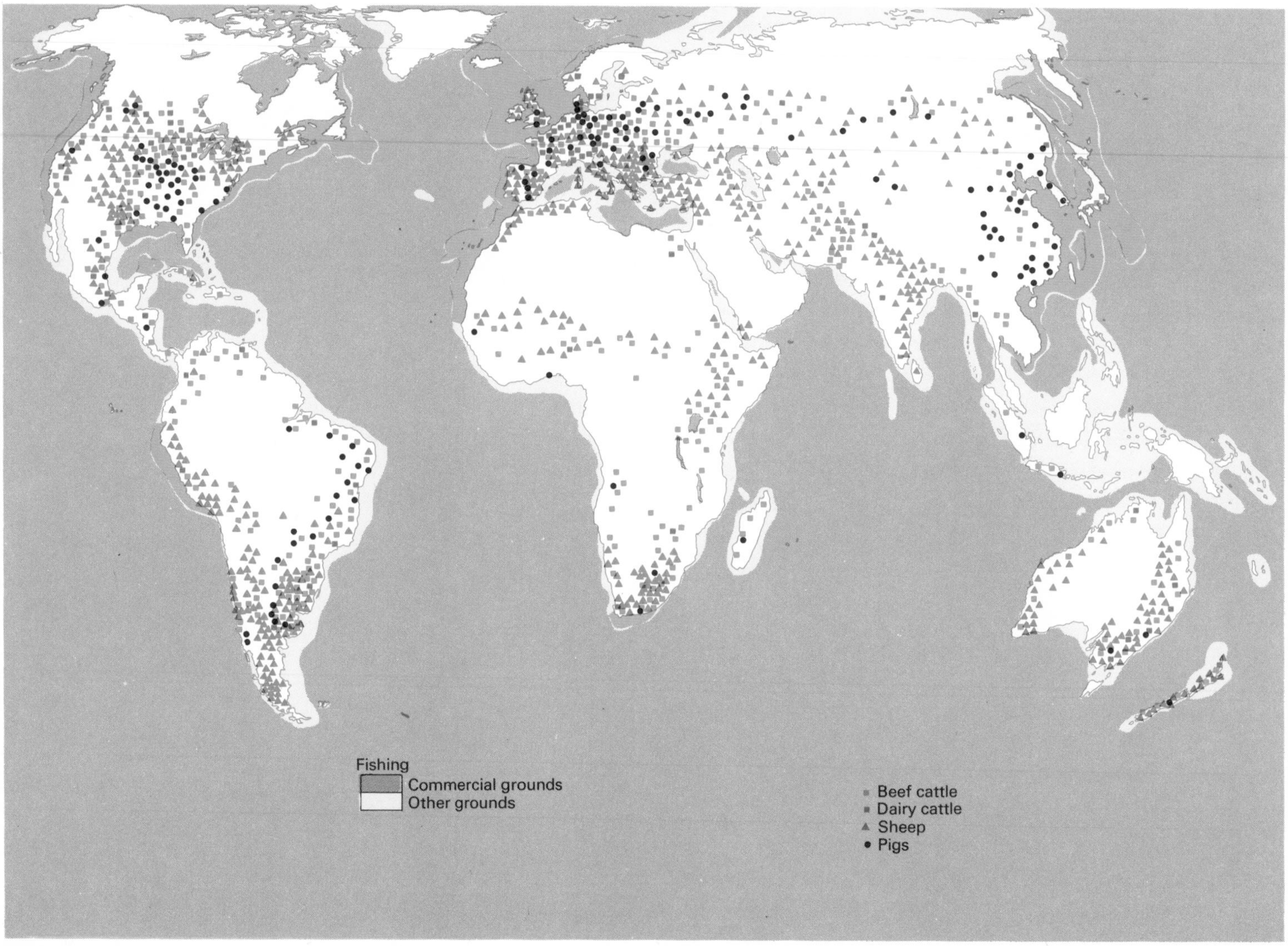

Fishing
Commercial grounds
Other grounds

- Beef cattle
- Dairy cattle
- Sheep
- Pigs

34

Nutrition

Foodstuffs fall, nutritionally, into three groups - providers of energy, protein and vitamins. Cereals and oil-seeds provide energy and second-class protein, milk, meat and allied foods provide protein and vitamins, fruit and vegetables provide vitamins, especially Vitamin C, and some energy. To avoid malnutrition, a minimum level of these three groups of foodstuffs is required: the maps and diagrams show how unfortunately widespread are low standards of nutrition and even malnutrition.

Comparison of daily diets

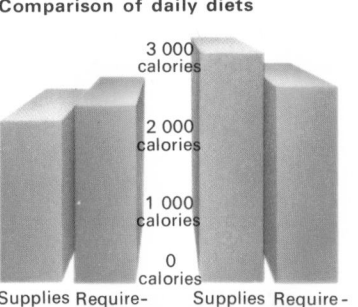

Supplies Requirements   Supplies Requirements

Far East, Near East, Africa & Latin America   Europe, Oceania & North America

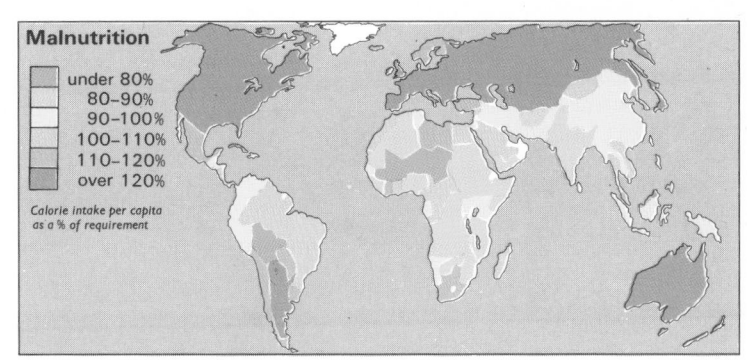

Malnutrition

- under 80%
- 80–90%
- 90–100%
- 100–110%
- 110–120%
- over 120%

Calorie intake per capita as a % of requirement

Proportions of calories

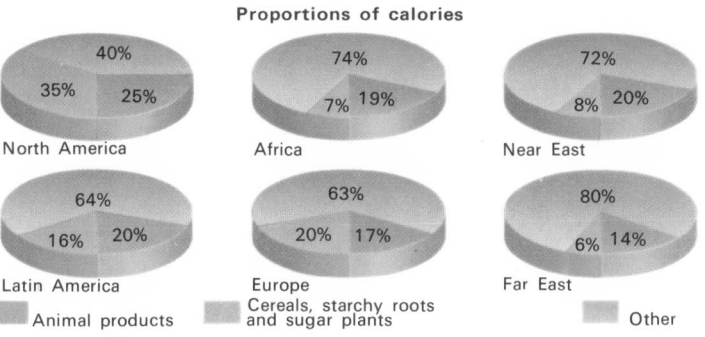

North America 40% 35% 25%
Africa 74% 7% 19%
Near East 72% 8% 20%
Latin America 64% 16% 20%
Europe 63% 20% 17%
Far East 80% 6% 14%

■ Animal products   ■ Cereals, starchy roots and sugar plants   ■ Other

People and tractors engaged in agriculture

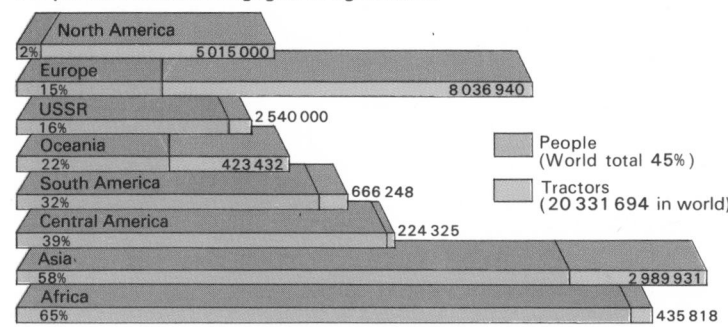

North America 2% 5 015 000
Europe 15% 8 036 940
USSR 16% 2 540 000
Oceania 22% 423 432
South America 32% 666 248
Central America 39% 224 325
Asia 58% 2 989 931
Africa 65% 435 818

People (World total 45%)
Tractors (20 331 694 in world)

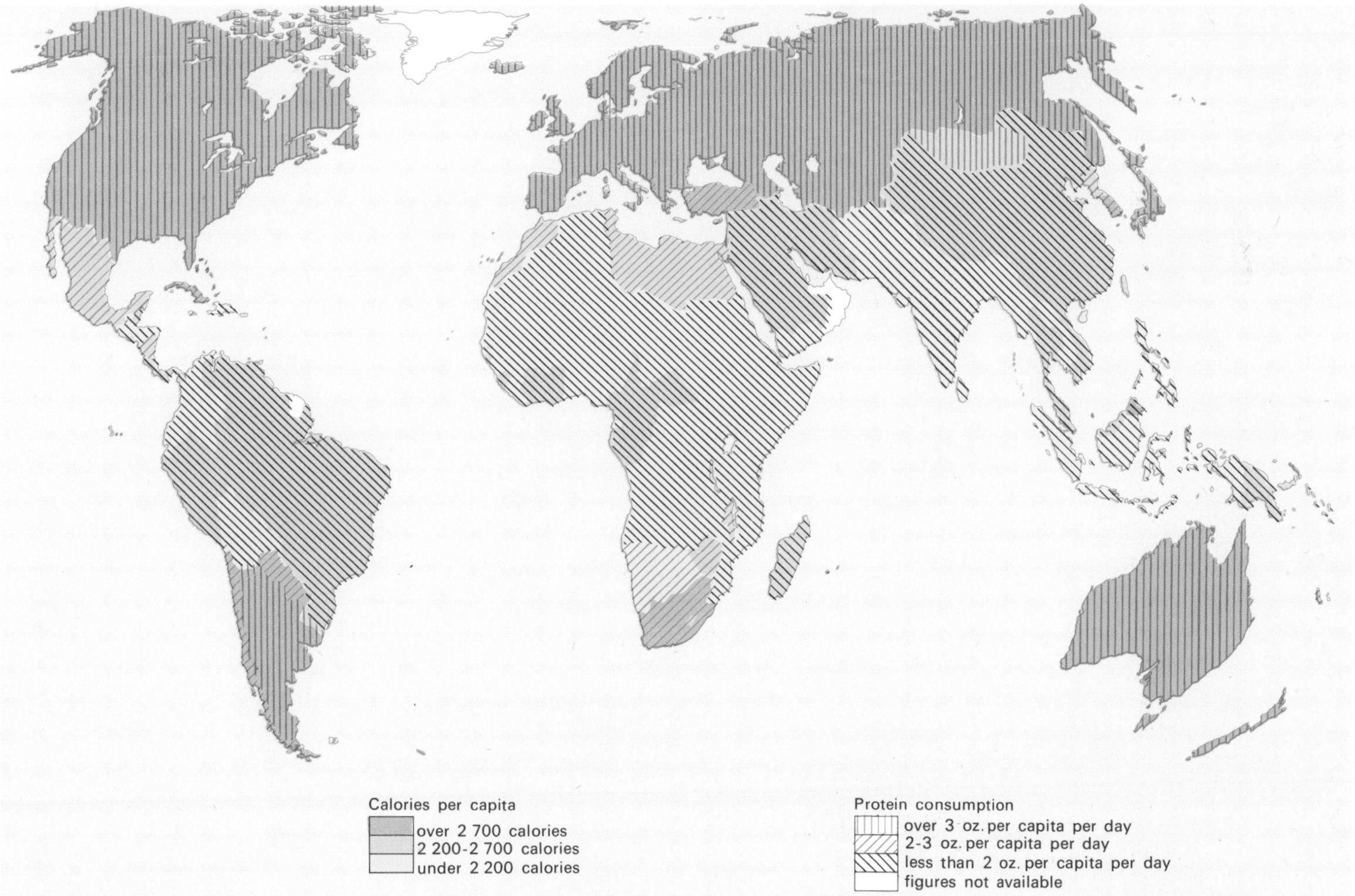

Calories per capita
- over 2 700 calories
- 2 200-2 700 calories
- under 2 200 calories

Protein consumption
- over 3 oz. per capita per day
- 2-3 oz. per capita per day
- less than 2 oz. per capita per day
- figures not available

Mineral Resources I

Primitive man used iron for tools and vessels and its use extended gradually until iron, and later steel, became the backbone of the Modern World with the Industrial Revolution in the late 18th Century. At first, local ores were used, whereas today richer iron ores in huge deposits have been discovered and are mined on a large scale, often far away from the areas where they are used; for example, in Western Australia, Northern Sweden, Venezuela and Liberia. Iron smelting plants are today increasingly located at coastal sites, where the large ore carriers can easily discharge their cargo.

Steel is refined iron with the addition of other minerals, ferro-alloys, giving to the steel their own special properties; for example, resistance to corrosion (chromium, nickel, cobalt), hardness (tungsten, vanadium), elasticity (molybdenum), magnetic properties (cobalt), high tensile strength (manganese) and high ductility (molybdenum).

Production of Ferro-alloy metals

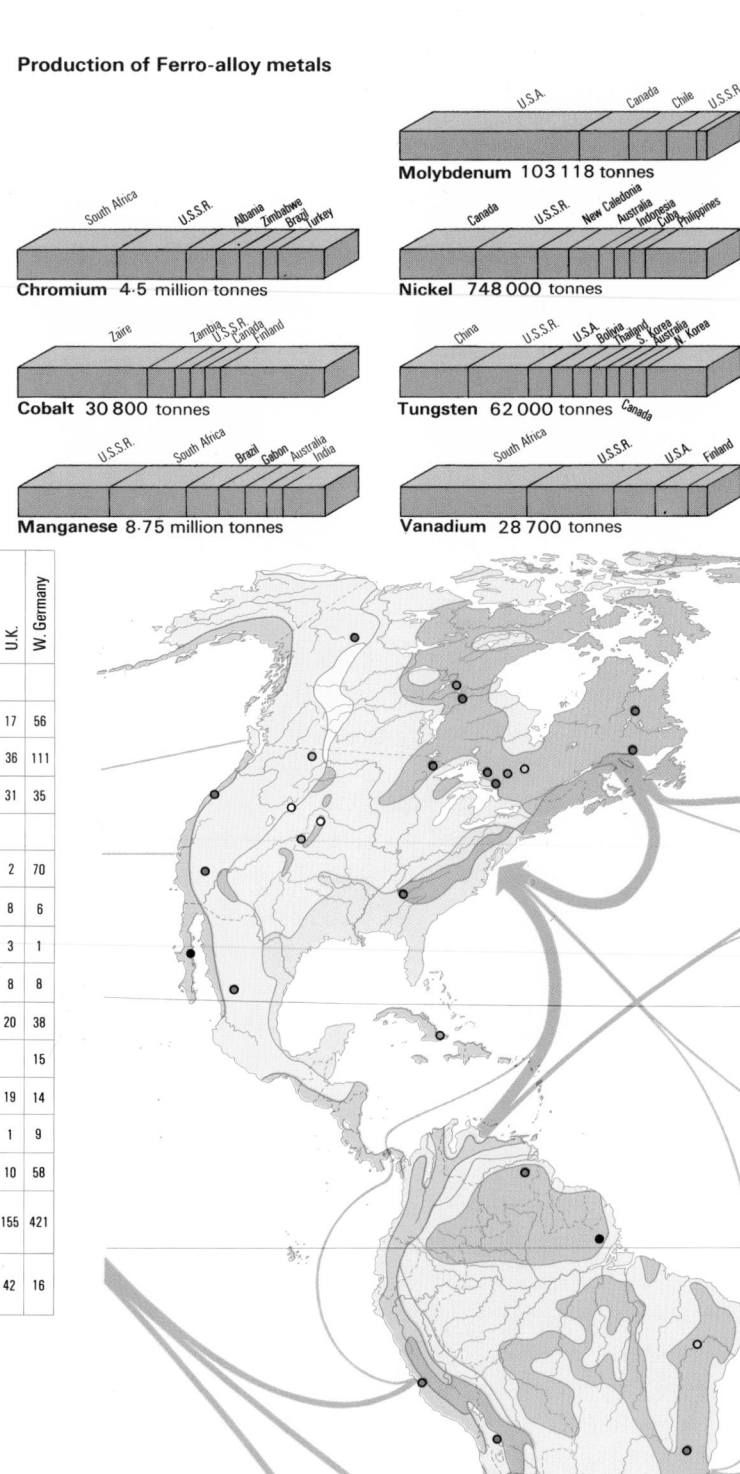

Molybdenum 103 118 tonnes

Chromium 4·5 million tonnes

Nickel 748 000 tonnes

Cobalt 30 800 tonnes

Tungsten 62 000 tonnes

Manganese 8·75 million tonnes

Vanadium 28 700 tonnes

Iron and Steel Industry of Western Europe

Major Centre / Other Important Centre

- ● / ● Iron ore
- ▲ / ▲ Iron and steel plant
- ▬ Coalfields

Kiruna
Gällivare
Teesside
Sheffield
Scunthorpe
IJmuiden
Dunkerque
South Wales
Valenciennes
Esch
The Ruhr
Salzgitter
Krakow
Ostrava
Genova
Taranto

Sources of Iron ore imported into Western Europe
hundred thousand tonnes

Imports from ▼	Austria	Belgium-Lux	France	Italy	Netherlands	Spain	U.K.	W. Germany
Algeria		7		2				
Australia		10	22	15	5	8	17	56
Brazil	13	24	43	38	18	14	36	111
Canada	2	7	4	15	8		31	35
India				6				
Liberia	3	13	19	33	9	12	2	70
Mauritania		6	21	13		3	8	6
U.S.S.R.	4			7	1		3	1
Venezuela		1	4	17		9	8	8
Others (World)	4	14	14	17			20	38
France		93						15
Norway		8					19	14
Spain		1			25		1	9
Sweden		58	19		7		10	58
Total Imports	26	242	146	163	73	46	155	421
Home produced ore	28	9	335	4		86	42	16

Iron and Steel Industry of Eastern North America

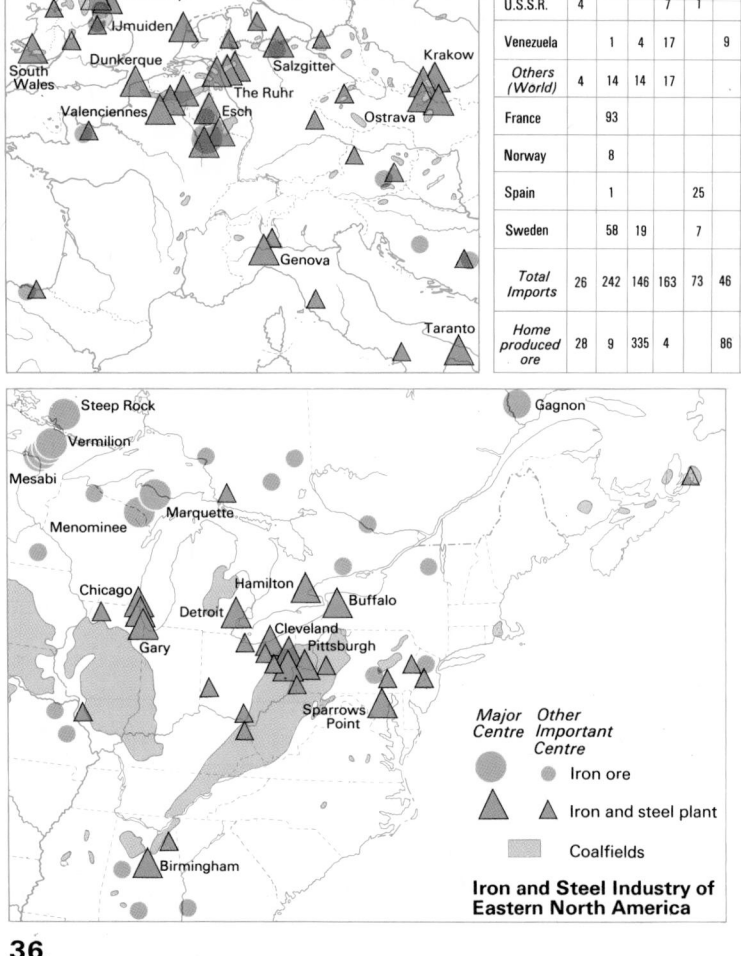

Steep Rock
Vermilion
Mesabi
Menominee
Marquette
Gagnon
Chicago
Hamilton
Detroit
Buffalo
Cleveland
Gary
Pittsburgh
Sparrows Point
Birmingham

Major Centre / Other Important Centre

- ● / ● Iron ore
- ▲ / ▲ Iron and steel plant
- ▬ Coalfields

Structural Regions

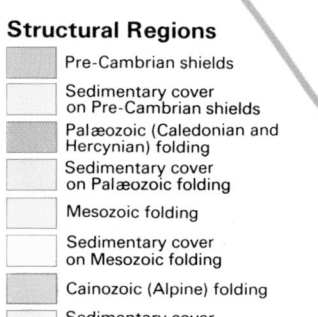

- Pre-Cambrian shields
- Sedimentary cover on Pre-Cambrian shields
- Palæozoic (Caledonian and Hercynian) folding
- Sedimentary cover on Palæozoic folding
- Mesozoic folding
- Sedimentary cover on Mesozoic folding
- Cainozoic (Alpine) folding
- Sedimentary cover on Cainozoic folding

World production of Pig iron and Ferro-alloys
Total World production 531 million tonnes

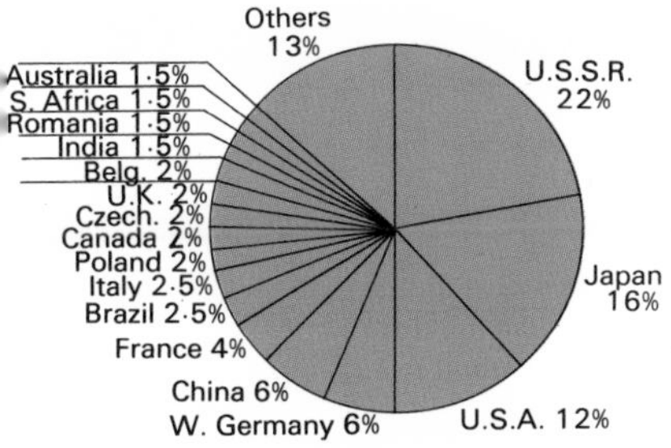

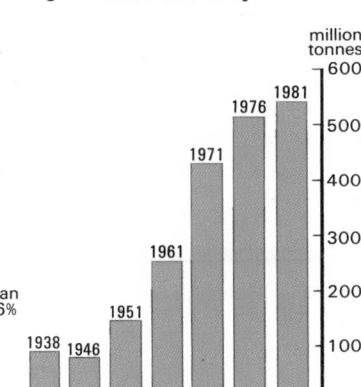

Others 13%
Australia 1·5%
S. Africa 1·5%
Romania 1·5%
India 1·5%
Belg. 2%
U.K. 2%
Czech. 2%
Canada 2%
Poland 2%
Italy 2·5%
Brazil 2·5%
France 4%
China 6%
W. Germany 6%
U.S.S.R. 22%
Japan 16%
U.S.A. 12%

Growth of World production of Pig iron and Ferro-alloys

million tonnes
600
500
400
300
200
100
0

1938 1946 1951 1961 1971 1976 1981

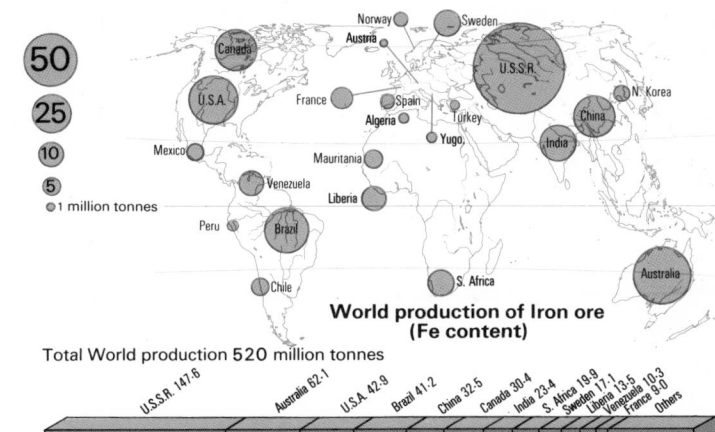

50
25
10
5
1 million tonnes

Norway Sweden Canada Austria U.S.S.R. N. Korea
U.S.A. France Spain Algeria Turkey China India
Mexico Yugo. Mauritania
Venezuela Liberia
Peru Brazil
Chile S. Africa Australia

World production of Iron ore (Fe content)
Total World production 520 million tonnes

U.S.S.R. 147·6 Australia 62·1 U.S.A. 42·9 Brazil 41·2 China 32·5 Canada 30·4 India 23·4 S. Africa 19·9 Sweden 17·1 Liberia 13·5 Venezuela 10·3 France 9·0 Others

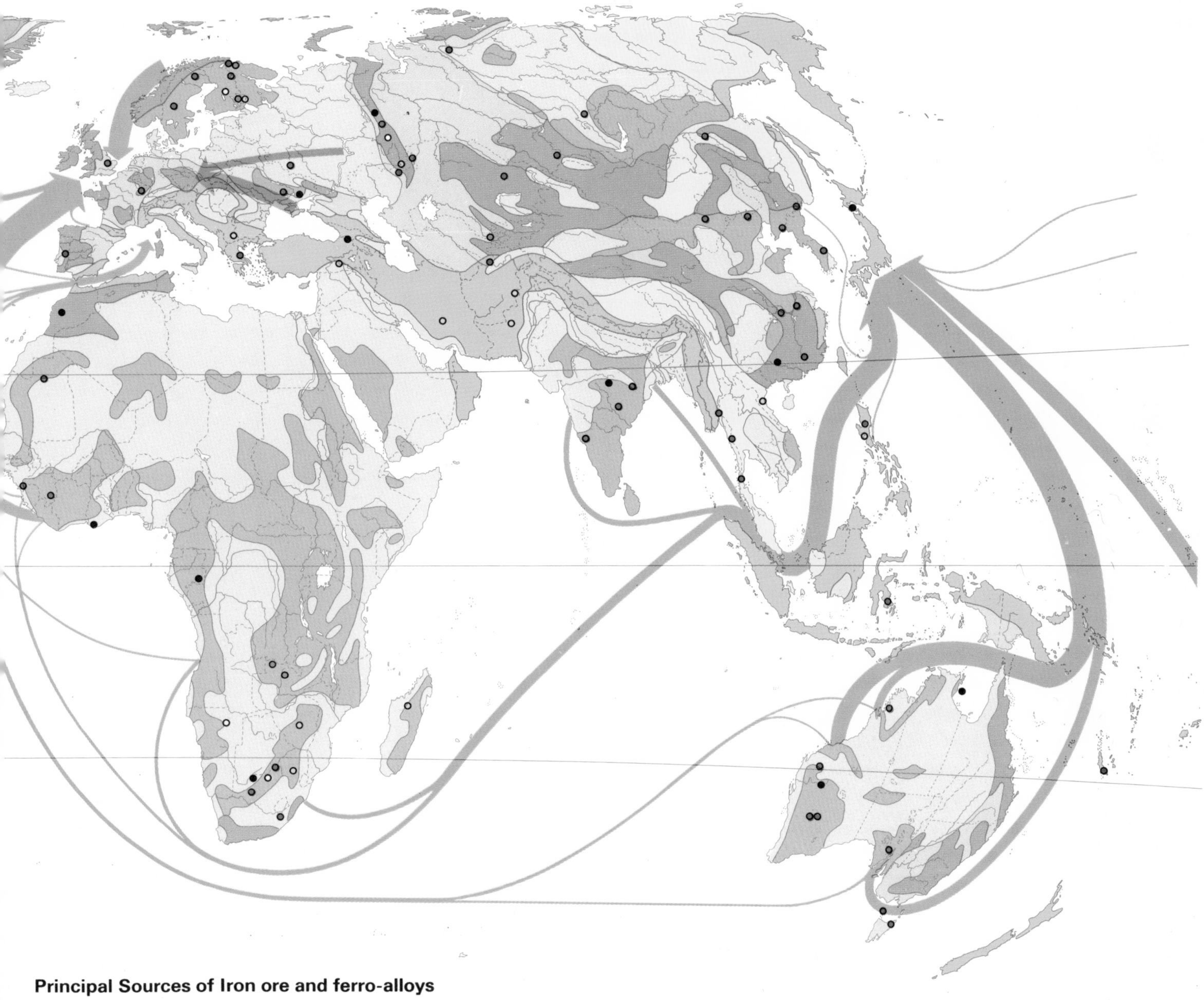

Principal Sources of Iron ore and ferro-alloys

- Iron
- Chrome
- Cobalt
- Manganese
- Molybdenum
- Nickel
- Tungsten
- Vanadium
- Iron ore trade flow

Mineral Resources II

Antimony – imparts hardness when alloyed to other metals, especially lead.
Uses: type metal, pigments to paints, glass and enamels, fireproofing of textiles

World production 64 635 tonnes

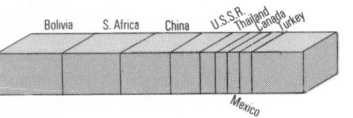

Lead – heavy, soft, malleable, acid resistant.
Uses: storage batteries, sheeting and piping, cable covering, ammunition, type metal, weights, additive to petrol.

World production 3·61 million tonnes

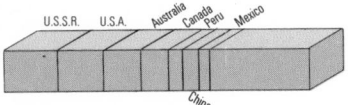

Tin – resistant to attacks by organic acids, malleable.
Uses: canning, foils, as an alloy to other metals (brass and bronze).

World production 235 200 tonnes

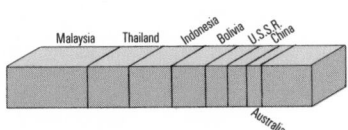

Aluminum – light, resists corrosion, good conductor.
Uses: aircraft, road and rail vehicles, domestic utensils, cables, makes highly tensile and light alloys.

World production 92·6 million tonnes (of Bauxite)

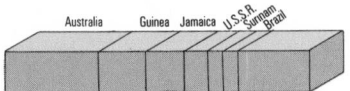

Gold – untarnishable and resistant to corrosion, highly ductile and malleable, good conductor. The pure metal is soft and it is alloyed to give it hardness.
Uses: bullion, coins, jewellery, gold-leaf, electronics.

World production 1 200 tonnes

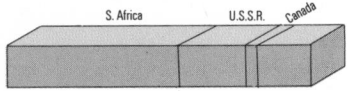

Copper – excellent conductor of electricity and heat, durable, resistant to corrosion, strong and ductile.
Uses: wire, tubing, brass (with zinc and tin), bronze (with tin), (compounds) – dyeing.

World production 7·8 million tonnes

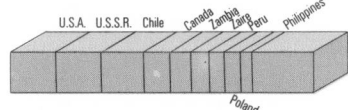

Mercury – the only liquid metal, excellent conductor of electricity
Uses: thermometers, electrical industry, gold and silver ore extraction, (compounds) – drugs, pigments, chemicals, dentistry.

World production 6 622 tonnes

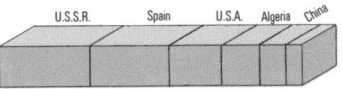

Zinc – hard metal, low corrosion factor.
Uses: brass (with copper and tin), galvanising, diecasting, medicines, paints and dyes.

World production 6·25 million tonnes

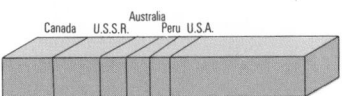

Diamonds – very hard and resistant to chemical attack, high lustre, very rare.
Uses: jewellery, cutting and abrading other materials.

World production 37·7 million carats

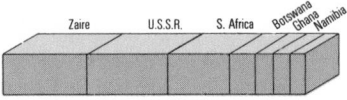

Silver – ductile and malleable, a soft metal and must be alloyed for use in coinage.
Uses: coins, jewellery, photography, electronics, medicines.

World production 10 422 tonnes

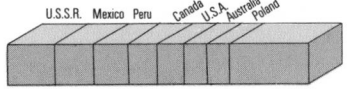

World consumption of non-ferrous metals

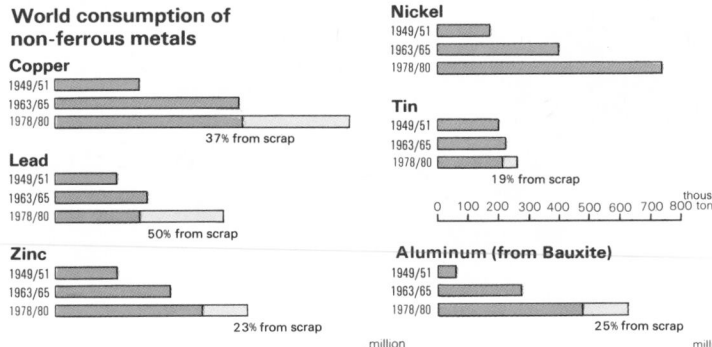

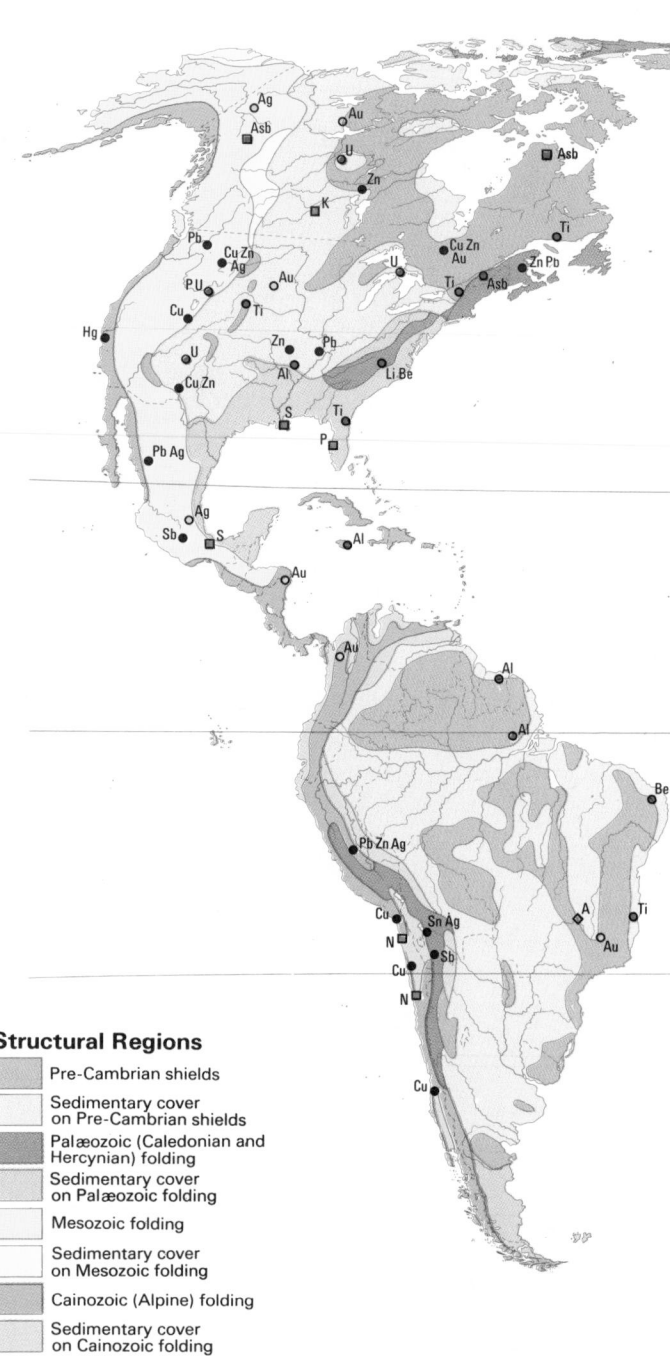

Structural Regions

- Pre-Cambrian shields
- Sedimentary cover on Pre-Cambrian shields
- Palæozoic (Caledonian and Hercynian) folding
- Sedimentary cover on Palæozoic folding
- Mesozoic folding
- Sedimentary cover on Mesozoic folding
- Cainozoic (Alpine) folding
- Sedimentary cover on Cainozoic folding

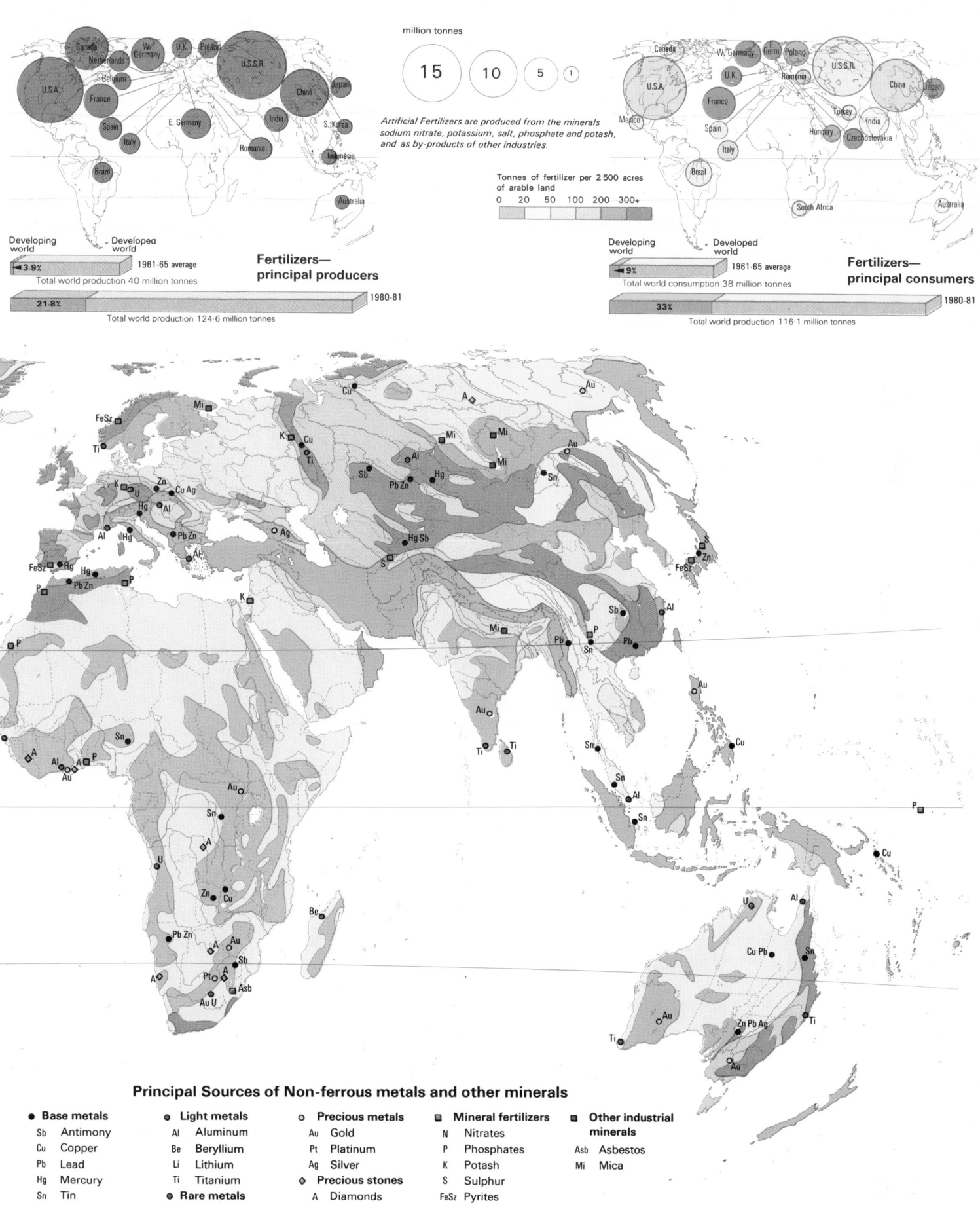

million tonnes

15   10   5   1

Artificial Fertilizers are produced from the minerals sodium nitrate, potassium, salt, phosphate and potash, and as by-products of other industries.

Tonnes of fertilizer per 2 500 acres of arable land

0   20   50   100   200   300+

Developing world — Developed world

◄ 3·9%   1961-65 average

Total world production 40 million tonnes

21·8%   1980-81

Total world production 124·6 million tonnes

Fertilizers— principal producers

Developing world — Developed world

◄ 9%   1961-65 average

Total world consumption 38 million tonnes

33%   1980-81

Total world production 116·1 million tonnes

Fertilizers— principal consumers

Principal Sources of Non-ferrous metals and other minerals

- **Base metals**

Sb	Antimony
Cu	Copper
Pb	Lead
Hg	Mercury
Sn	Tin
Zn	Zinc

- **Light metals**

Al	Aluminum
Be	Beryllium
Li	Lithium
Ti	Titanium

- **Rare metals**

U	Uranium

- ○ **Precious metals**

Au	Gold
Pt	Platinum
Ag	Silver

- ◇ **Precious stones**

A	Diamonds

Mineral fertilizers

N	Nitrates
P	Phosphates
K	Potash
S	Sulphur
FeSz	Pyrites

Other industrial minerals

Asb	Asbestos
Mi	Mica

39

Fuel and Energy

Coal

Coal is the result of the accumulation of vegetation over millions of years. Later under pressure from overlying sediments, it is hardened through four stages: peat, lignite, bituminous coal, and finally anthracite. Once the most important source of power, coal's importance now lies in the production of electricity and as a raw material in the production of plastics, heavy chemicals and disinfectants.

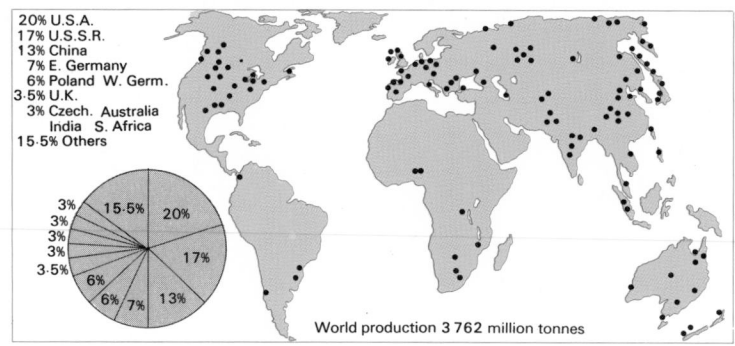

20% U.S.A.
17% U.S.S.R.
13% China
7% E. Germany
6% Poland W. Germ.
3·5% U.K.
3% Czech. Australia
India S. Africa
15·5% Others

World production 3 762 million tonnes

Coal mine

Oil

Oil is derived from the remains of marine animals and plants, probably as a result of pressure, heat and chemical action. It is a complex mixture of hydrocarbons which are refined to extract the various constituents. These include products such as gasolene, kerosene and heavy fuel oils. Oil is rapidly replacing coal because of easier handling and reduced pollution.

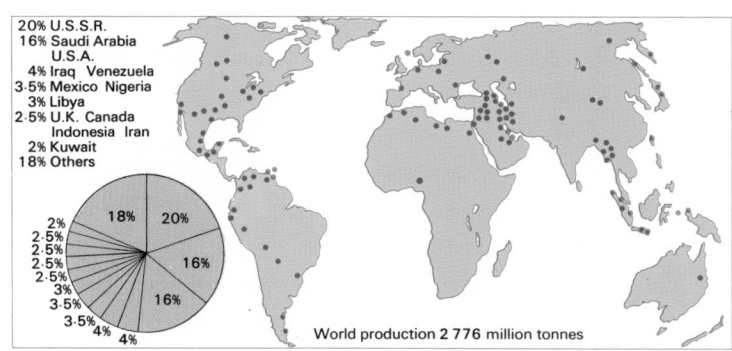
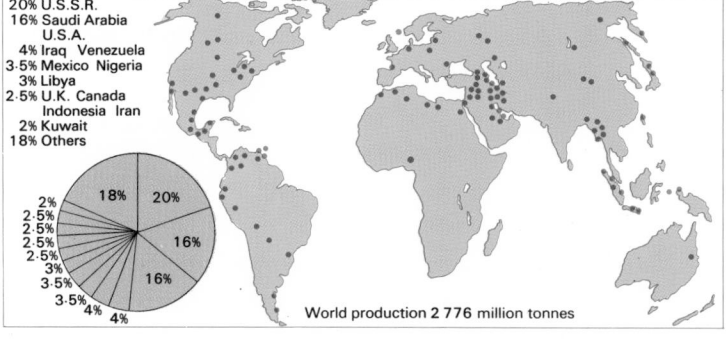

20% U.S.S.R.
16% Saudi Arabia
U.S.A.
4% Iraq Venezuela
3·5% Mexico Nigeria
3% Libya
2·5% U.K. Canada
Indonesia Iran
2% Kuwait
18% Others

World production 2 776 million tonnes

Oil derrick

Natural gas

Since the early 1960's natural gas (methane) has become one of the largest single sources of energy. By liquefaction its volume can be reduced to 1/600 of that of gas and hence is easily transported. It is often found directly above oil reserves and because it is both cheaper than coal gas and less polluting it has great potential.

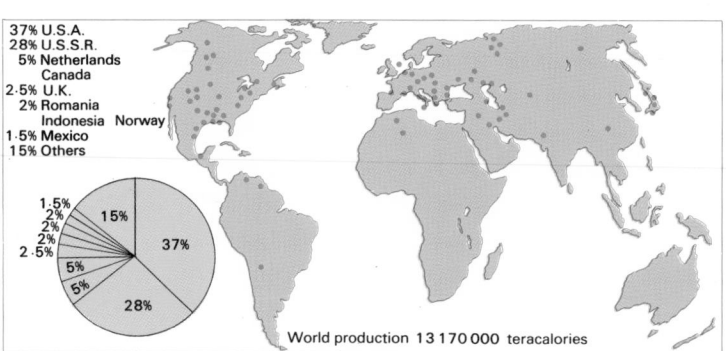

37% U.S.A.
28% U.S.S.R.
5% Netherlands
Canada
2·5% U.K.
2% Romania
Indonesia Norway
1·5% Mexico
15% Others

World production 13 170 000 teracalories

North sea gas rig

Water

Hydro-electric power stations use water to drive turbines which in turn generate electricity. The ideal site is one in which a consistently large volume of water falls a considerable height, hence sources of H.E.P. are found mainly in mountainous areas. Potential sources of hydro-electricity using waves or tides are yet to be exploited widely.

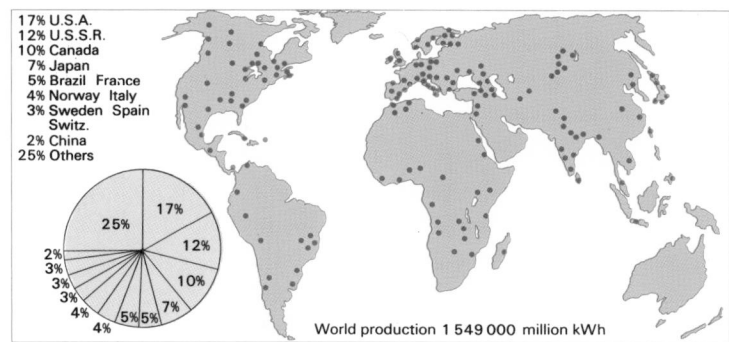

17% U.S.A.
12% U.S.S.R.
10% Canada
7% Japan
5% Brazil France
4% Norway Italy
3% Sweden Spain
Switz.
2% China
25% Others

World production 1 549 000 million kWh

Water power

Nuclear energy

The first source of nuclear power was developed in Britain in 1956. Energy is obtained from heat generated by the reaction from splitting atoms of certain elements, of which uranium and plutonium are the most important. Although the initial installation costs are very high the actual running costs are low because of the slow consumption of fuel.

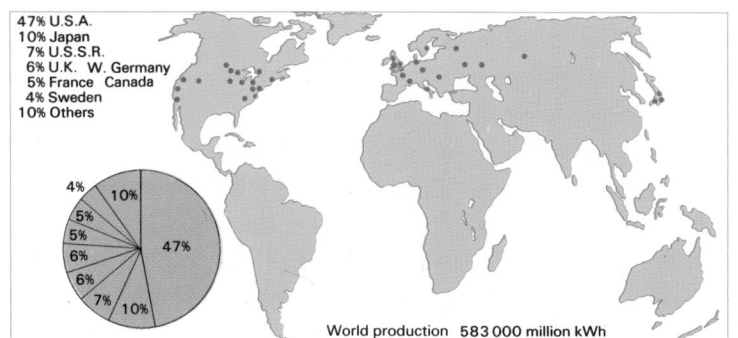

47% U.S.A.
10% Japan
7% U.S.S.R.
6% U.K. W. Germany
5% France Canada
4% Sweden
10% Others

World production 583 000 million kWh

Nuclear power station

In a short space of time these two diagrams can change markedly; there can be a cut-back in supply owing to internal political change (Iran), or in consumption by vigorous government action (U.S.A.). The production of North Sea oil has changed the balance of oil trade in the U.K. and Norway but it is very costly to extract, relatively short-lived and is small on a world scale.

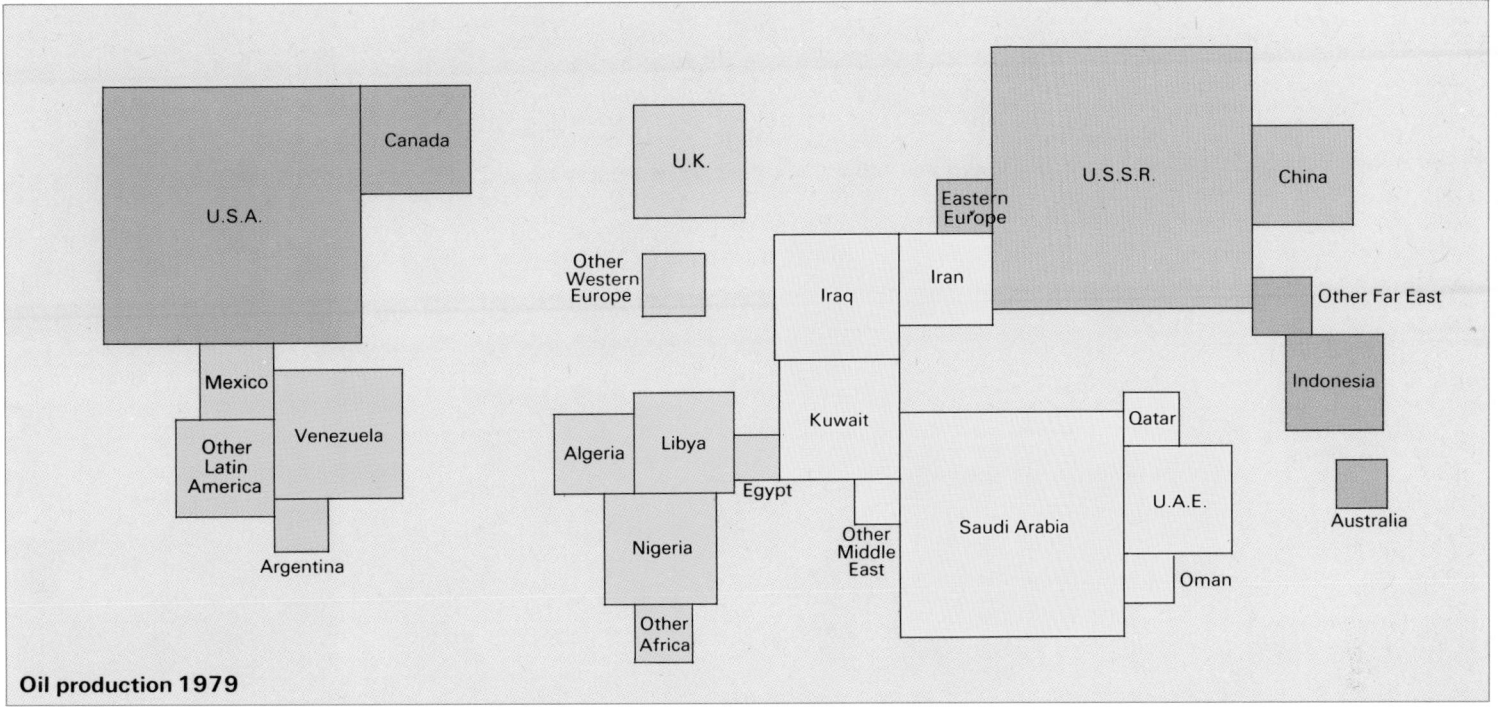

Oil production 1979

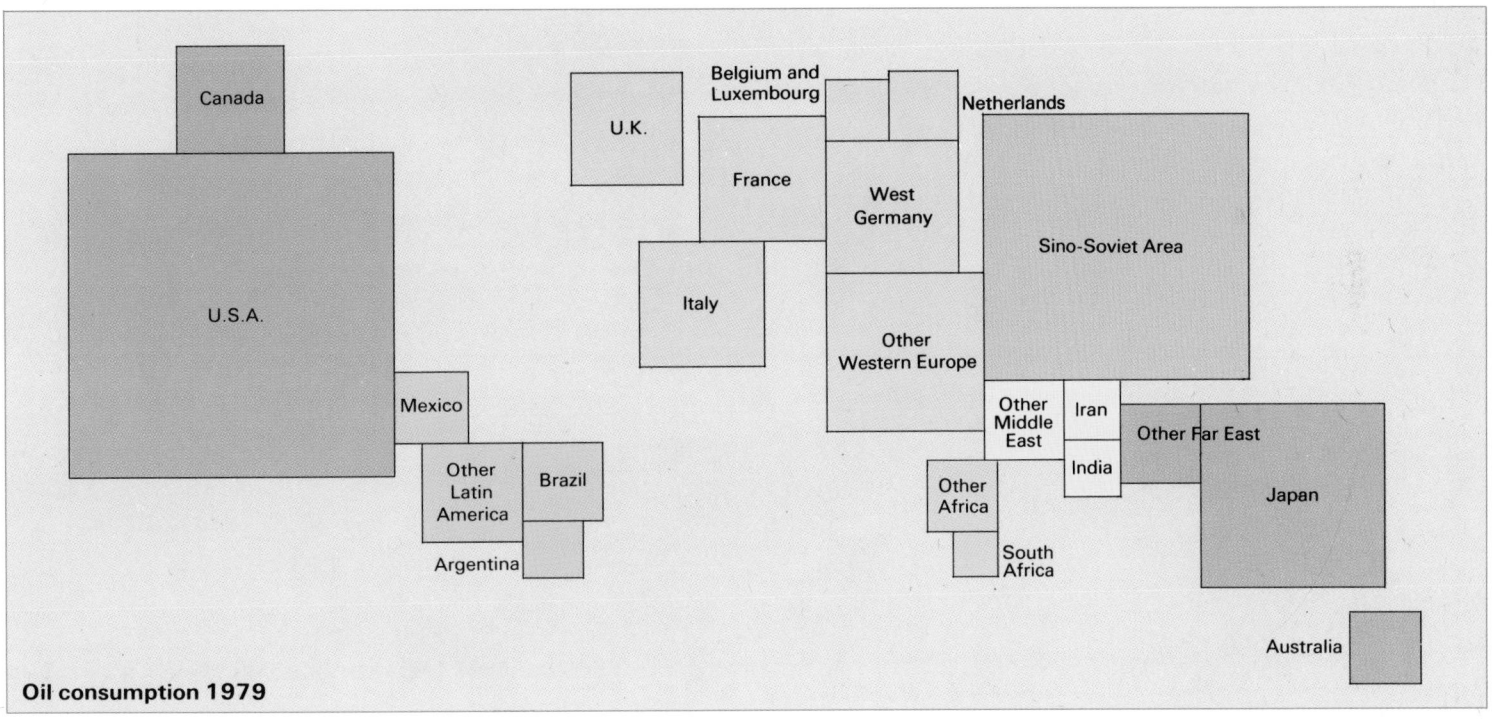

Oil consumption 1979

Oil's new super-powers *above* When countries are scaled according to their production and consumption of oil they take on new dimensions. At present, large supplies of oil are concentrated in a few countries of the Caribbean, the Middle East and North Africa, except for the vast indigenous supplies of the U.S.A. and U.S.S.R. The Middle East, with 58% of the world's reserves, produces 35% of the world's supply and yet consumes less than 3%. The U.S.A.,

despite its great production, has a deficiency of nearly 415 million tons a year, consuming 30% of the world's total. The U.S.S.R., with 11% of world reserves, produces 19% of world output and consumes 13%. Soviet production continues to grow annually although at a decreased rate since the mid-1970's. Japan, one of the largest oil importers, increased its consumption by 440% during the period 1963-73. Since then, total imports have decreased slightly.

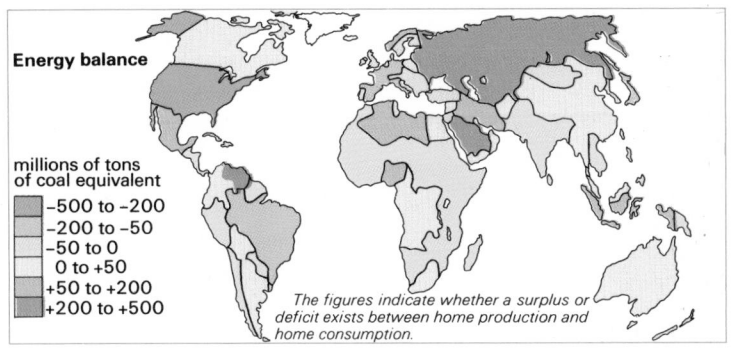

Energy balance

millions of tons of coal equivalent
- −500 to −200
- −200 to −50
- −50 to 0
- 0 to +50
- +50 to +200
- +200 to +500

The figures indicate whether a surplus or deficit exists between home production and home consumption.

Occupations

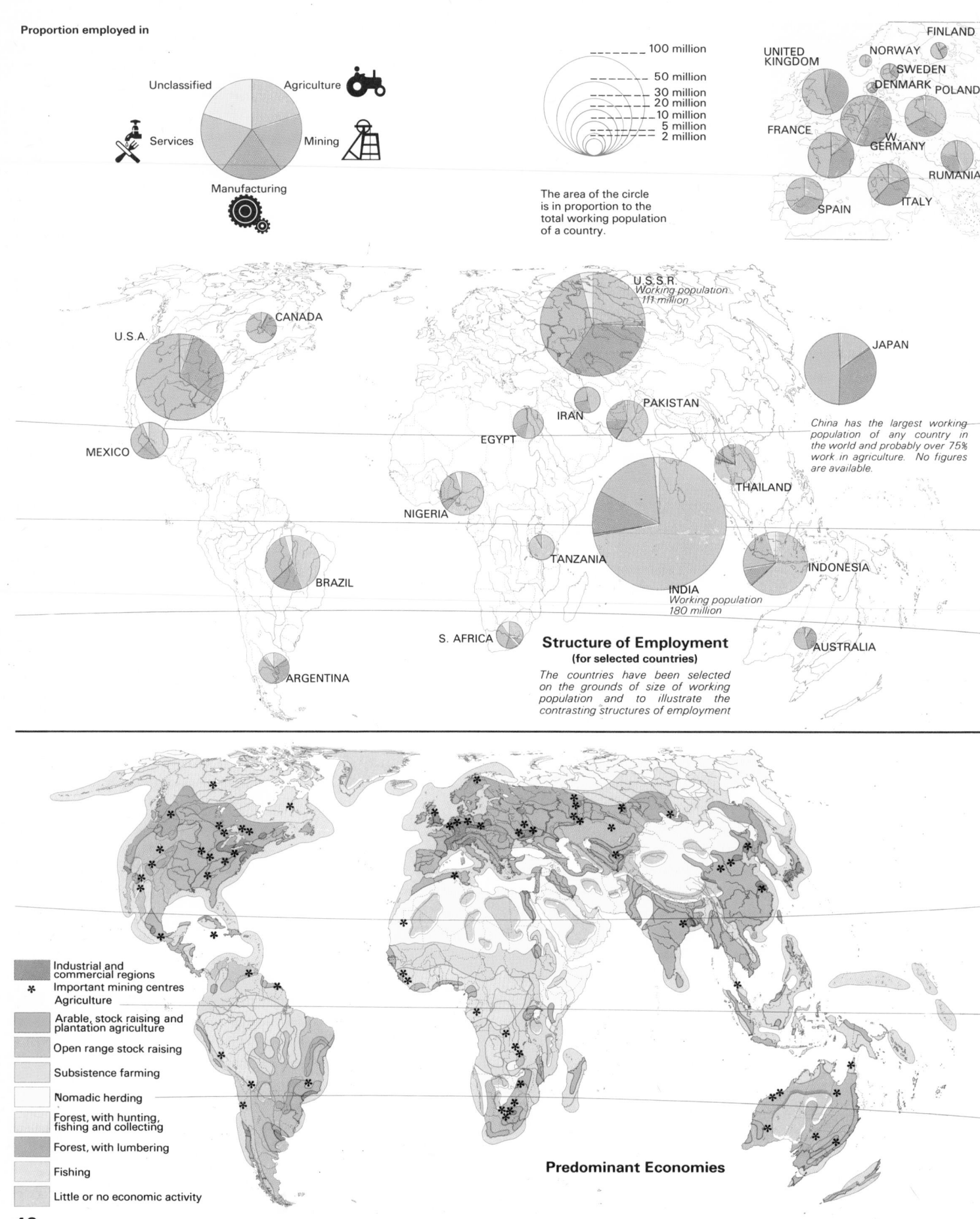

Proportion employed in

- Unclassified
- Agriculture
- Services
- Mining
- Manufacturing

- 100 million
- 50 million
- 30 million
- 20 million
- 10 million
- 5 million
- 2 million

The area of the circle is in proportion to the total working population of a country.

FINLAND
UNITED KINGDOM
NORWAY
SWEDEN
DENMARK
POLAND
FRANCE
W. GERMANY
RUMANIA
SPAIN
ITALY

CANADA
U.S.A.
MEXICO
BRAZIL
ARGENTINA
S. AFRICA
TANZANIA
NIGERIA
EGYPT
IRAN
PAKISTAN

U.S.S.R.
Working population 111 million

JAPAN

China has the largest working population of any country in the world and probably over 75% work in agriculture. No figures are available.

THAILAND
INDIA
Working population 180 million
INDONESIA
AUSTRALIA

Structure of Employment
(for selected countries)

The countries have been selected on the grounds of size of working population and to illustrate the contrasting structures of employment

- Industrial and commercial regions
- * Important mining centres

Agriculture
- Arable, stock raising and plantation agriculture
- Open range stock raising
- Subsistence farming
- Nomadic herding
- Forest, with hunting, fishing and collecting
- Forest, with lumbering
- Fishing
- Little or no economic activity

Predominant Economies

Industry

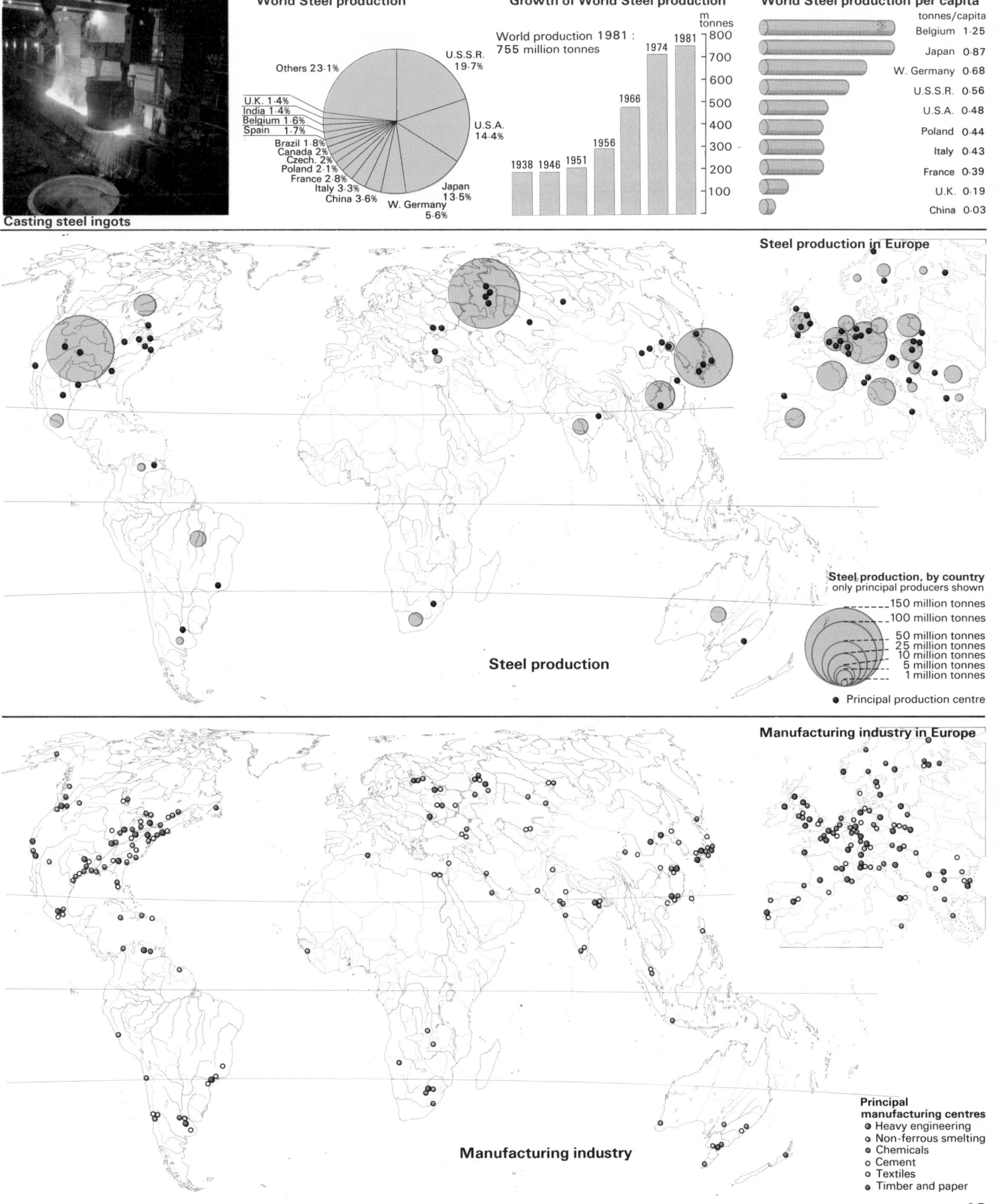

Casting steel ingots

World Steel production

Others 23·1%

U.S.S.R. 19·7%

U.K. 1·4%
India 1·4%
Belgium 1·6%
Spain 1·7%
Brazil 1·8%
Canada 2%
Czech. 2%
Poland 2·1%
France 2·8%
Italy 3·3%
China 3·6%
W. Germany 5·6%
Japan 13·5%
U.S.A. 14·4%

Growth of World Steel production

World production 1981 : 755 million tonnes

m tonnes

800
700
600
500
400
300
200
100

1938 1946 1951 1956 1966 1974 1981

World Steel production per capita

tonnes/capita

Belgium	1·25
Japan	0·87
W. Germany	0·68
U.S.S.R.	0·56
U.S.A.	0·48
Poland	0·44
Italy	0·43
France	0·39
U.K.	0·19
China	0·03

Steel production in Europe

Steel production

Steel production, by country
only principal producers shown

- 150 million tonnes
- 100 million tonnes
- 50 million tonnes
- 25 million tonnes
- 10 million tonnes
- 5 million tonnes
- 1 million tonnes

● Principal production centre

Manufacturing industry in Europe

Manufacturing industry

Principal manufacturing centres
- Heavy engineering
- Non-ferrous smelting
- Chemicals
- Cement
- Textiles
- Timber and paper

43

Transport

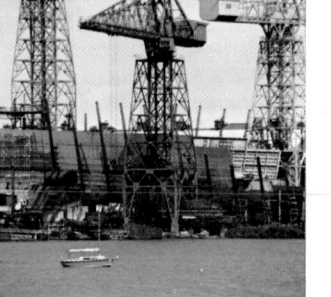

Shipyards

Country	Tonnage
Japan	9 140
S. Korea	1 207
W. Germany	665
Spain	605
Brazil	453
Sweden	363
Poland	350
U.K.	342
Finland	311
Denmark	306
U.S.A.	298
Yugoslavia	284

Shipbuilding
tonnage launched
in thousand gross
registered tons

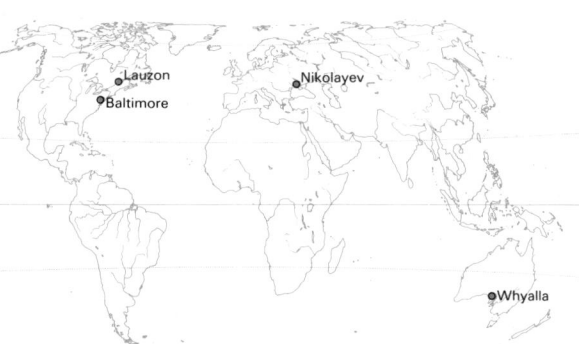

● Principal shipbuilding centres

Europe

Japan

Aircraft Industry

In 1978 there were approximately 10 000 civil passenger airliners in service. This diagram shows where they were built.

U.S.A. 53%	U.S.S.R. 33%	U.K. 6% Netherlands 3% France 2%

Trade in Aircraft and Aircraft Engines

	Exports *million U.S. $*			Imports	
	Aircraft	Engines		Aircraft	Engines
U.S.A.	5893	789	W. Germ.	1218	136
France	995	262	U.K.	651	543
W. Germ.	915	227	U.S.A.	604	132
U.K.	861	721	France	472	278
Canada	303		Canada	264	149
Neth.	288	836	Neth.	210	132
Italy	279	88	Japan	201	151

Concorde and Boeing 747

● Principal aircraft manufacturing centres

Motor vehicles

Production *thousand units*	Exports *million U.S. $*	Imports *million U.S. $*
Japan 11 184	21 601	737
U.S.A. 7 927	15 034	25 008
W. Germany 3 902	24 539	8 000
France 3 426	11 824	5 820
U.S.S.R. 2 197	1 831	1 164
Italy 1 612	5 582	4 645
Canada 1 303	9 593	11 598
U.K. 1 184	6 329	8 182
Spain 989	1 771	695

Locomotive works

Railway vehicles

Exports *million U.S. $*		Imports *million U.S. $.*	
Japan	496·9	Brazil	151·8
France	353·9	Mexico	95·3
W. Germany	329·3	U.S.A.	81·7
U.S.A.	306·0	S. Korea	69·6
U.K.	78·6	S. Africa	67·5
Italy	62·6	Egypt	53·0
Yugoslavia	57·5	W. Germany	52·7
Canada	48·5	Yugoslavia	52·2
S. Korea	41·7	Netherlands	48·1
Sweden	37·7	Sweden	44·4
Belg.-Lux.	27·8	U.K.	40·5
Switzerland	37·5	Belg.-Lux.	33·6
Spain	18·5	France	30·3
		Italy	30·0

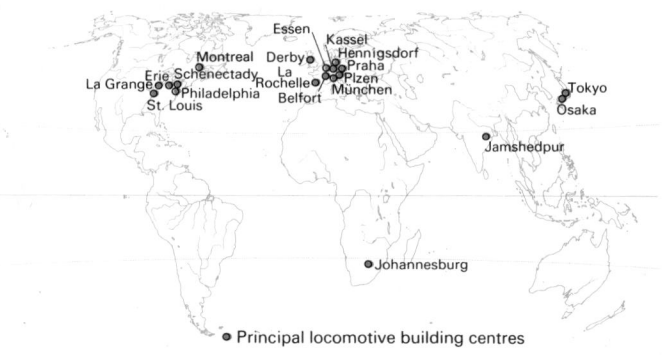

● Principal locomotive building centres

Car assembly line

Europe

● Principal motor vehicle plants

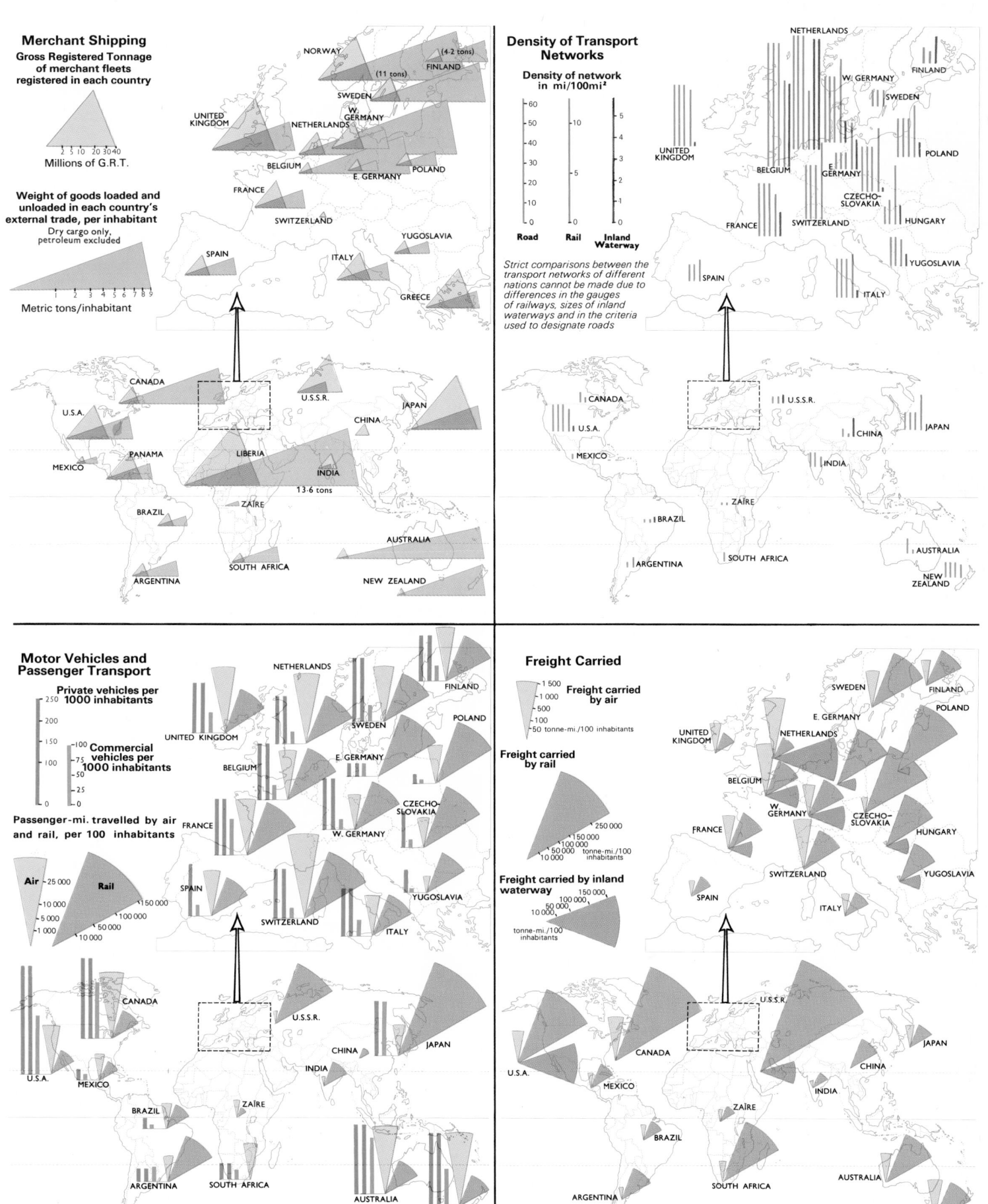

Merchant Shipping

Gross Registered Tonnage of merchant fleets registered in each country

2 5 10 20 30 40
Millions of G.R.T.

Weight of goods loaded and unloaded in each country's external trade, per inhabitant

Dry cargo only, petroleum excluded

1 2 3 4 5 6 7 8 9
Metric tons/inhabitant

NORWAY
(11 tons)
(4·2 tons)
FINLAND
SWEDEN
W. GERMANY
UNITED KINGDOM
NETHERLANDS
BELGIUM
E. GERMANY
POLAND
FRANCE
SWITZERLAND
SPAIN
YUGOSLAVIA
ITALY
GREECE

CANADA
U.S.A.
U.S.S.R.
JAPAN
CHINA
PANAMA
MEXICO
LIBERIA
INDIA
13·6 tons
BRAZIL
ZAÏRE
SOUTH AFRICA
ARGENTINA
AUSTRALIA
NEW ZEALAND

Density of Transport Networks

Density of network in mi/100mi²

Road	Rail	Inland Waterway
60		5
50	10	4
40		3
30		2
20	5	1
10		
0	0	0

Strict comparisons between the transport networks of different nations cannot be made due to differences in the gauges of railways, sizes of inland waterways and in the criteria used to designate roads

NETHERLANDS
FINLAND
W. GERMANY
SWEDEN
UNITED KINGDOM
BELGIUM
E. GERMANY
POLAND
FRANCE
SWITZERLAND
CZECHO-SLOVAKIA
HUNGARY
SPAIN
YUGOSLAVIA
ITALY

CANADA
U.S.S.R.
U.S.A.
JAPAN
MEXICO
CHINA
INDIA
BRAZIL
ZAÏRE
ARGENTINA
SOUTH AFRICA
AUSTRALIA
NEW ZEALAND

Motor Vehicles and Passenger Transport

Private vehicles per 1000 inhabitants
250
200
150
100
50
0

Commercial vehicles per 1000 inhabitants
100
75
50
25
0

Passenger-mi. travelled by air and rail, per 100 inhabitants

Air
25 000
10 000
5 000
1 000

Rail
150 000
100 000
50 000
10 000

NETHERLANDS
FINLAND
SWEDEN
POLAND
UNITED KINGDOM
BELGIUM
E. GERMANY
CZECHO-SLOVAKIA
FRANCE
W. GERMANY
SPAIN
SWITZERLAND
YUGOSLAVIA
ITALY

CANADA
U.S.A.
U.S.S.R.
JAPAN
CHINA
INDIA
MEXICO
BRAZIL
ZAÏRE
ARGENTINA
SOUTH AFRICA
AUSTRALIA
NEW ZEALAND

Freight Carried

1 500
1 000
500
100
50 tonne-mi./100 inhabitants
Freight carried by air

Freight carried by rail
250 000
150 000
100 000
50 000 tonne-mi./100 inhabitants
10 000

Freight carried by inland waterway
150 000
100 000
50 000
10 000
tonne-mi./100 inhabitants

SWEDEN
FINLAND
E. GERMANY
POLAND
UNITED KINGDOM
NETHERLANDS
BELGIUM
W. GERMANY
CZECHO-SLOVAKIA
HUNGARY
FRANCE
SWITZERLAND
YUGOSLAVIA
SPAIN
ITALY

U.S.S.R.
CANADA
JAPAN
U.S.A.
CHINA
MEXICO
INDIA
ZAÏRE
BRAZIL
ARGENTINA
SOUTH AFRICA
AUSTRALIA
NEW ZEALAND

45

Trade

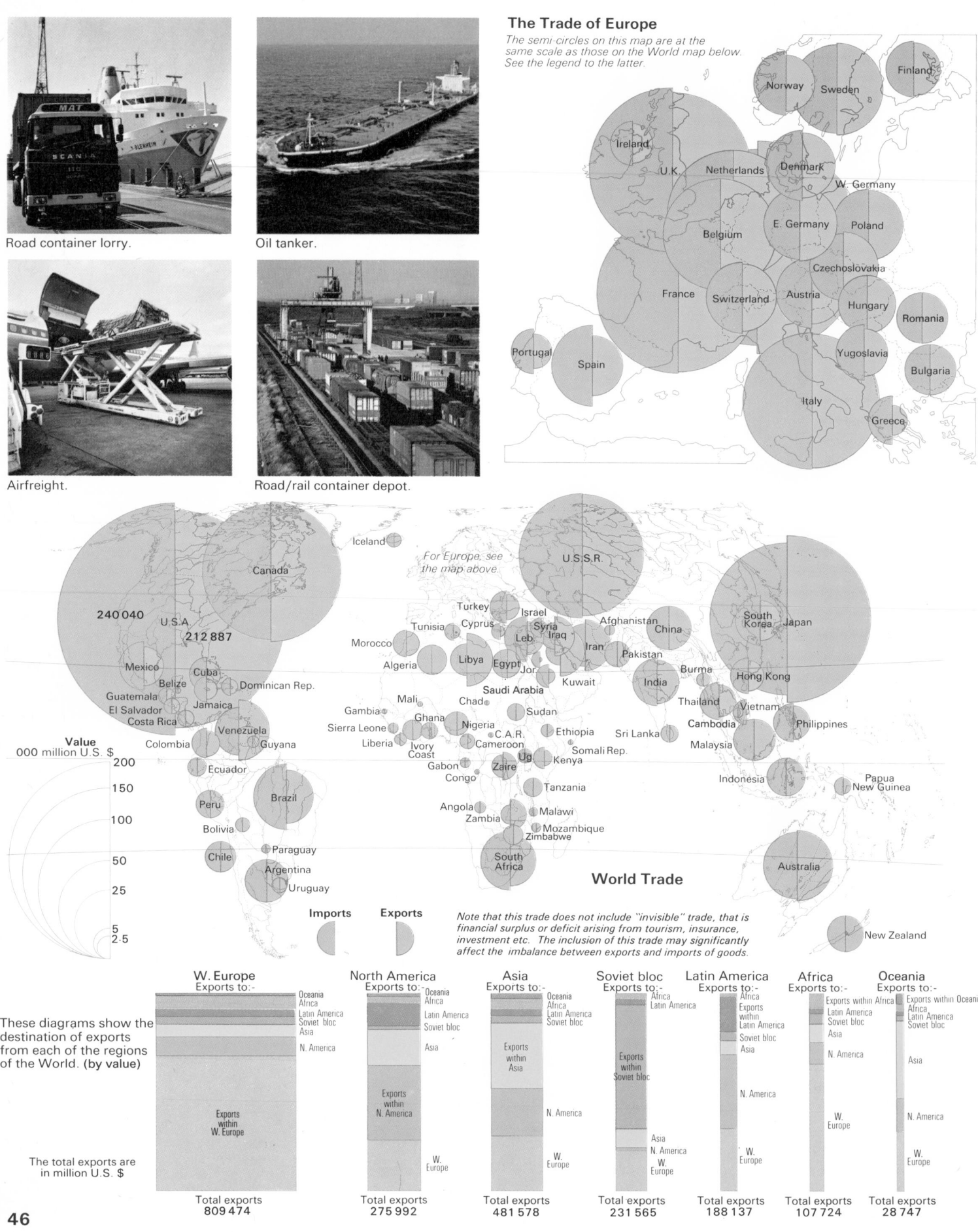

Road container lorry.

Oil tanker.

Airfreight.

Road/rail container depot.

The Trade of Europe

The semi-circles on this map are at the same scale as those on the World map below. See the legend to the latter.

Norway Sweden Finland
Ireland U.K. Netherlands Denmark W. Germany
Belgium E. Germany Poland
France Switzerland Austria Czechoslovakia Hungary Romania
Portugal Spain Yugoslavia Bulgaria
Italy Greece

Iceland Canada U.S.S.R.

For Europe, see the map above.

240 040 U.S.A 212 887

Turkey Israel Afghanistan China South Korea Japan
Tunisia Cyprus Syria Iraq Iran Pakistan
Morocco Leb. Jor.
Algeria Libya Egypt Kuwait India Burma Hong Kong
Mexico Cuba Dominican Rep. Saudi Arabia Thailand Vietnam
Guatemala Jamaica Mali Chad Sudan Sri Lanka Cambodia Philippines
El Salvador Costa Rica Gambia Ghana Nigeria C.A.R. Ethiopia Malaysia
Belize Sierra Leone Liberia Ivory Coast Cameroon Somali Rep.
Venezuela Gabon Zaire Ug. Kenya
Colombia Guyana Congo Indonesia Papua New Guinea
Ecuador Tanzania
Peru Brazil Angola Malawi
Bolivia Zambia Mozambique Zimbabwe
Paraguay South Africa Australia
Chile Argentina Uruguay

Value
000 million U.S. $
200
150
100
50
25
5
2.5

Imports Exports

World Trade

Note that this trade does not include "invisible" trade, that is financial surplus or deficit arising from tourism, insurance, investment etc. The inclusion of this trade may significantly affect the imbalance between exports and imports of goods.

New Zealand

These diagrams show the destination of exports from each of the regions of the World. (by value)

The total exports are in million U.S. $

W. Europe Exports to:-	North America Exports to:-	Asia Exports to:-	Soviet bloc Exports to:-	Latin America Exports to:-	Africa Exports to:-	Oceania Exports to:-
Oceania	Oceania	Oceania	Africa	Africa	Exports within Africa	Exports within Oceania
Africa	Africa	Africa	Latin America	Exports within Latin America	Latin America	Africa
Latin America	Latin America	Latin America			Soviet bloc	Latin America
Soviet bloc	Soviet bloc	Soviet bloc		Soviet bloc	Asia	Soviet bloc
Asia	Asia	Asia	Exports within Soviet bloc	Asia	N. America	
N. America	N. America	Exports within Asia		N. America		Asia
	Exports within N. America		N. America			N. America
Exports within W. Europe		N. America	Asia	W. Europe	W. Europe	W. Europe
	W. Europe	W. Europe	N. America			
			W. Europe			

| Total exports | Total exports | Total exports | Total exports | Total exports | Total exports | Total exports |
| 809 474 | 275 992 | 481 578 | 231 565 | 188 137 | 107 724 | 28 747 |

46

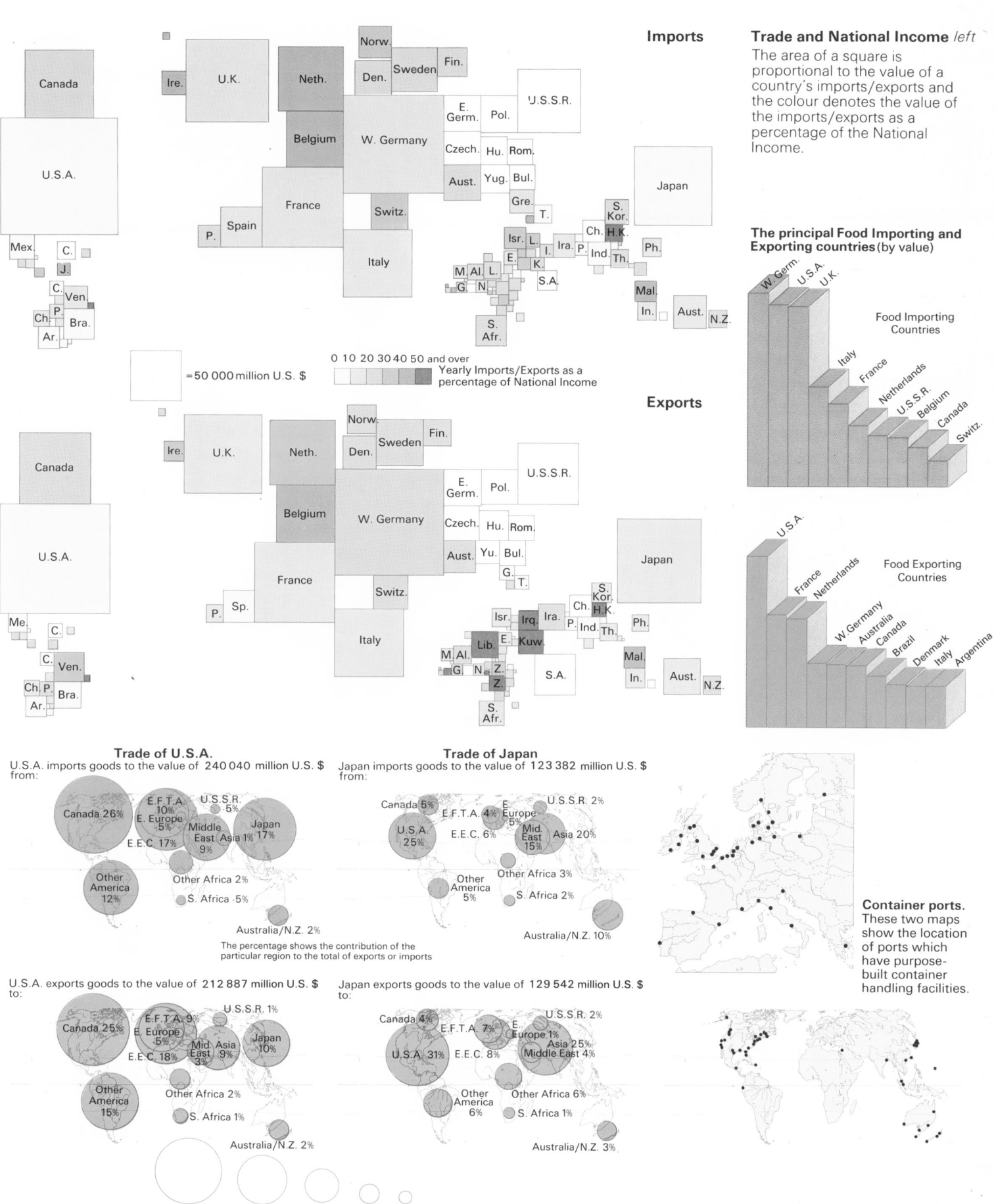

Imports

Exports

Trade and National Income *left*
The area of a square is proportional to the value of a country's imports/exports and the colour denotes the value of the imports/exports as a percentage of the National Income.

The principal Food Importing and Exporting countries (by value)

0 10 20 30 40 50 and over
Yearly Imports/Exports as a percentage of National Income

=50 000 million U.S. $

Food Importing Countries
W. Germ. U.S.A. U.K. Italy France Netherlands U.S.S.R. Belgium Canada Switz.

Food Exporting Countries
U.S.A. France Netherlands W. Germany Australia Canada Brazil Denmark Italy Argentina

Trade of U.S.A.
U.S.A. imports goods to the value of 240 040 million U.S. $ from:
Canada 26%
E.F.T.A. 10%
E. Europe 5%
E.E.C. 17%
U.S.S.R. 5%
Middle East 9%
Asia 1%
Japan 17%
Other America 12%
Other Africa 2%
S. Africa 5%
Australia/N.Z. 2%

The percentage shows the contribution of the particular region to the total of exports or imports

U.S.A. exports goods to the value of 212 887 million U.S. $ to:
Canada 25%
E.F.T.A. 9%
E. Europe 5%
E.E.C. 18%
U.S.S.R. 1%
Mid. East 3%
Asia 9%
Japan 10%
Other America 15%
Other Africa 2%
S. Africa 1%
Australia/N.Z. 2%

Trade of Japan
Japan imports goods to the value of 123 382 million U.S. $ from:
Canada 5%
E.F.T.A. 4%
E. Europe 5%
E.E.C. 6%
U.S.S.R. 2%
Mid. East 15%
Asia 20%
U.S.A. 25%
Other America 5%
Other Africa 3%
S. Africa 2%
Australia/N.Z. 10%

Japan exports goods to the value of 129 542 million U.S. $ to:
Canada 4%
E.F.T.A. 7%
E. Europe 1%
E.E.C. 8%
U.S.S.R. 2%
Asia 25%
Middle East 4%
U.S.A. 31%
Other America 6%
Other Africa 6%
S. Africa 1%
Australia/N.Z. 3%

40 000 20 000 8 000 4 000 2 000 million U.S. $

Container ports.
These two maps show the location of ports which have purpose-built container handling facilities.

47

Wealth

The living standard of a few highly developed, urbanised, industrialised countries is a complete contrast to the conditions of the vast majority of economically undeveloped, agrarian states. It is this contrast which divides mankind into rich and poor, well fed and hungry. The developing world is still an overwhelmingly agricultural world: over 70% of all its people live off the land and yet the output from that land remains pitifully low. Many Africans, South Americans and Asians struggle with the soil but the bad years occur only too frequently and they seldom have anything left over to save. The need for foreign capital then arises.

National Income

The gap between developing and developed worlds is in fact widening eg. in 1938 the incomes for the United States and India were in the proportions of 1:15; now they are 1:53.

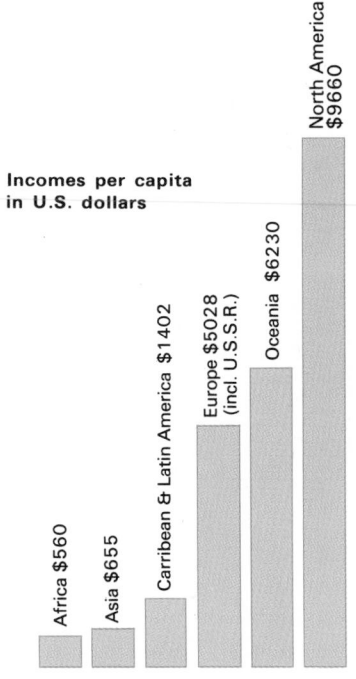

Incomes per capita in U.S. dollars

Africa $560
Asia $655
Carribean & Latin America $1402
Europe $5028 (incl. U.S.S.R.)
Oceania $6230
North America $9660

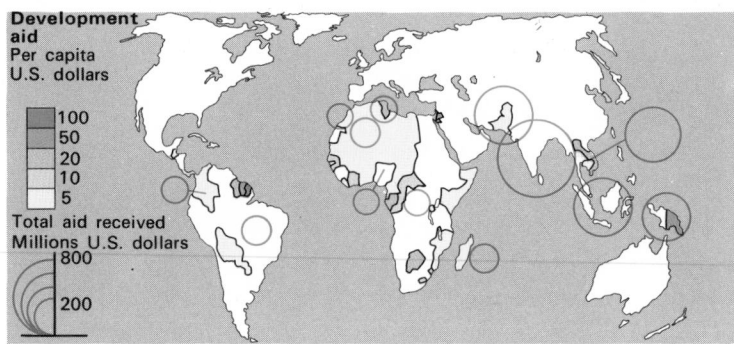

Development aid
Per capita
U.S. dollars

100
50
20
10
5

Total aid received
Millions U.S. dollars
800
200

Development aid

The provision of foreign aid, defined as assistance on concessional terms for promoting development, is today an accepted, though controversial aspect of the economic policies of most advanced countries towards less developed countries. Aid for development is based not merely on economic considerations but also on social, political and historical factors. The most important international committee set up after the war was that of the U.N.; practically all aid however has been given bi-laterally direct from an industrialised country to an under-developed country. Although aid increased during the 1950's the donated proportion of industrialised countries GNP has diminished from 0·5 to 0·4%. Less developed countries share of world trade also decreased and increased population invalidated any progress made.

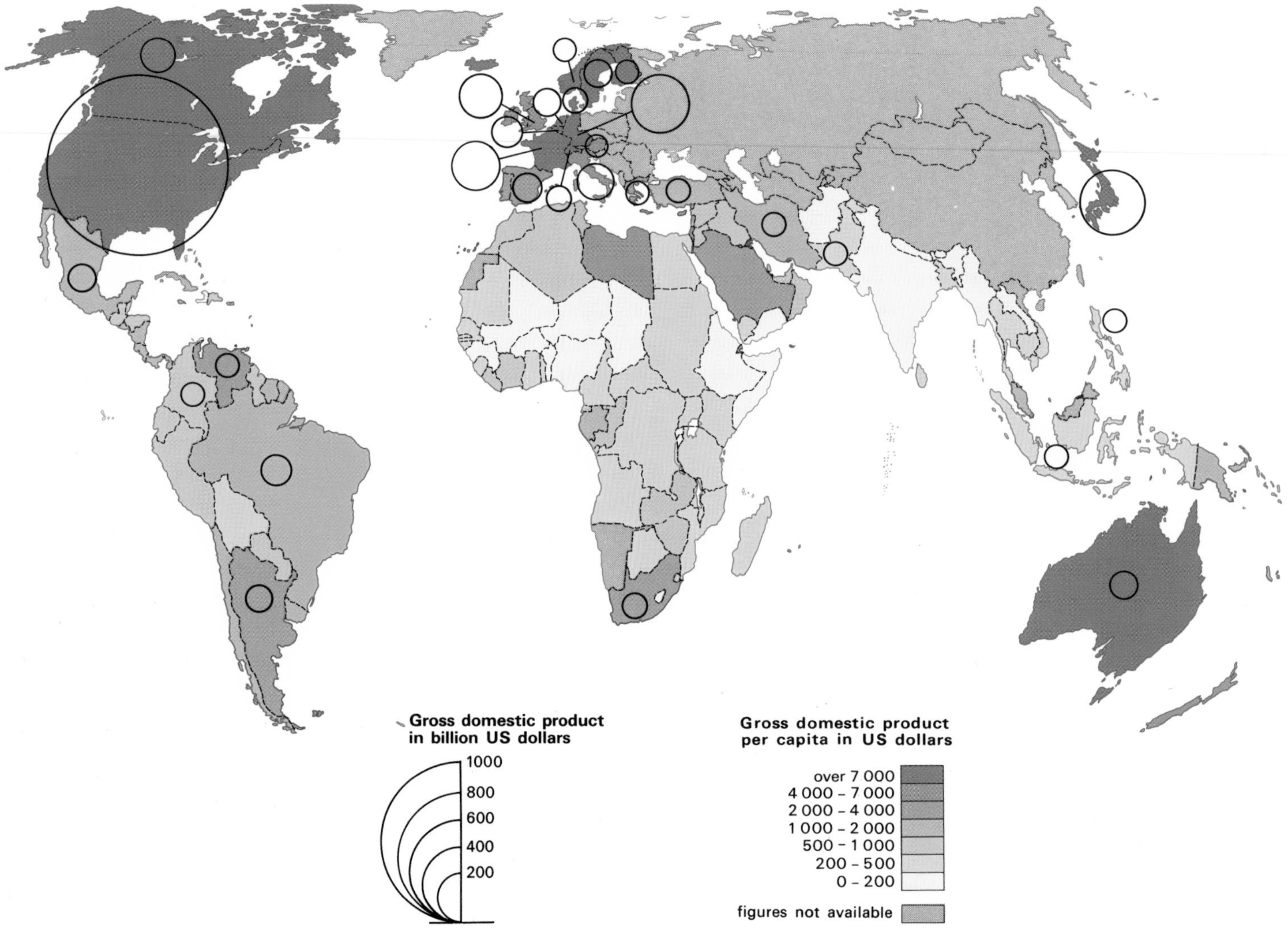

Gross domestic product in billion US dollars

1000
800
600
400
200

Gross domestic product per capita in US dollars

over 7 000
4 000 – 7 000
2 000 – 4 000
1 000 – 2 000
500 – 1 000
200 – 500
0 – 200

figures not available

SETTLEMENTS

Settlement symbols in order of size

◌ LONDON   ▣ Stuttgart   ◉ Sevilla   ◎ Bergen   ⊙ Bath   ○ Biarritz   ○ Srikolayatji

Settlement symbols and type styles vary according to
the scale of each map and indicate the importance of
towns on the map rather than specific population figures

∴ Sites of Archæological or
Historical importance

BOUNDARIES

────── International Boundaries

‒‒‒ ‒‒‒ ‒‒ International Boundaries
(Undemarcated or Undefined)

········· Internal Boundaries

International boundaries show the *de facto* situation
where there are rival claims to territory

National and
Provincial Parks

COMMUNICATIONS

═════ Motorways

━━━ Principal Railways

············ Principal Canals

·········· Motorways under construction

━━━ Other Railways

┝━━━┥ Principal Oil Pipelines

────── Principal Roads

‒‒·‒‒‒` Railways under construction

_ 3386 _ Principal Shipping Routes
(Distances in Nautical Miles)

⌒⌒ Other Roads

┤‒‒‒├ Railway Tunnels

‒‒‒‒‒ Tracks and Seasonal Roads

┤‒‒‒├ Road Tunnels

⊠ Passes

☼ Airports

PHYSICAL FEATURES

⌒⌒ Perennial Streams

⬭ Seasonal Lakes, Salt Flats

▱ Permanent Ice

‒‒‒‒·` Seasonal Streams

⬭ Swamps, Marshes

∪ Wells in Desert

▲ 8848 Spot Height
in metres

▼ 8050 Sea Depths.
in metres

1134 Height of Lake Surface
Above Sea Level, in metres

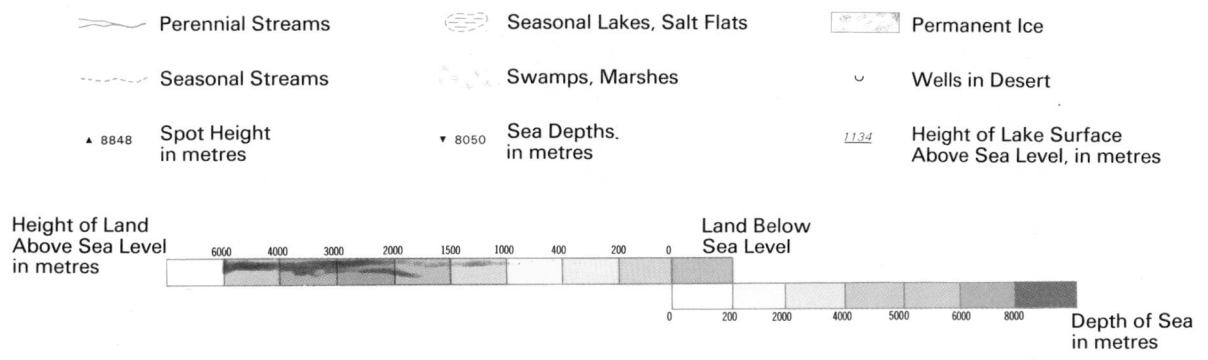

Height of Land
Above Sea Level
in metres

6060 4000 3000 2000 1500 1000 400 200 0

Land Below
Sea Level

0   200   2000   4000   5000   6000   8000

Depth of Sea
in metres

Some of the maps have different contours to
highlight and clarify the principal relief features

Abbreviations of measures used   mm Millimetres   m Metres   km Kilometres   °C Degrees Celsius   mb Millibars

STRUCTURE

1 : 95 000 000

Structural Regions of the Land

- Pre-Cambrian shields
- Sedimentary cover on Pre-Cambrian shields
- Palæozoic (Caledonian and Hercynian) folding
- Sedimentary cover on Palæozoic folding
- Mesozoic folding
- Sedimentary cover on Mesozoic folding
- Cainozoic folding
- Sedimentary cover on Cainozoic folding
- Intensive Mesozoic and Cainozoic vulcanism
- Oceanic-type crust raised above sea level

Structural Regions of the Oceans

- Regions of continental-type crust
- ⎯⎯ Limit of continental shelf
- ▬▬ Oceanic marginal troughs
- Mid-oceanic volcanic ridges
- ⎯⎯ Rift valleys in mid-oceanic ridges
- ⎯⎯ Principal faults
- +++ Frontal line of overthrust folds

GEOLOGICAL TIME SCALE

Era	System	Orogeny	Millions of years before present
Cainozoic (Tertiary, Quaternary)	Quaternary	ALPINE FOLDING	
	Pliocene		
	Miocene		
	Oligocene		
	Eocene		50
	Paleocene	LARAMIDE FOLDING	
Mesozoic (Secondary)	Cretaceous		100
	Jurassic		150
	Triassic		200
Palæozoic (Primary) — Upper	Permian		250
	Carboniferous	HERCYNIAN FOLDING	300
	Devonian		350
Palæozoic (Primary) — Lower	Silurian	CALEDONIAN FOLDING	400
	Ordovician		450
	Cambrian		500
			550
			600
Pre-Cambrian	Pre-Cambrian		

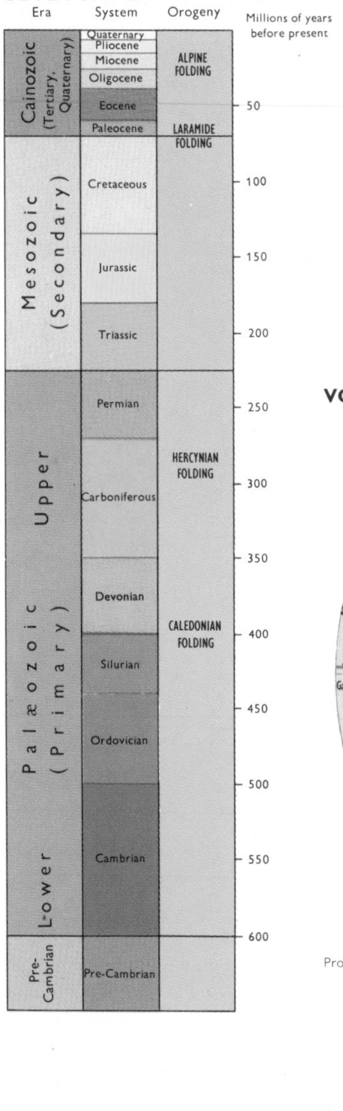

VOLCANOES

Equatorial Scale 1 : 280 000

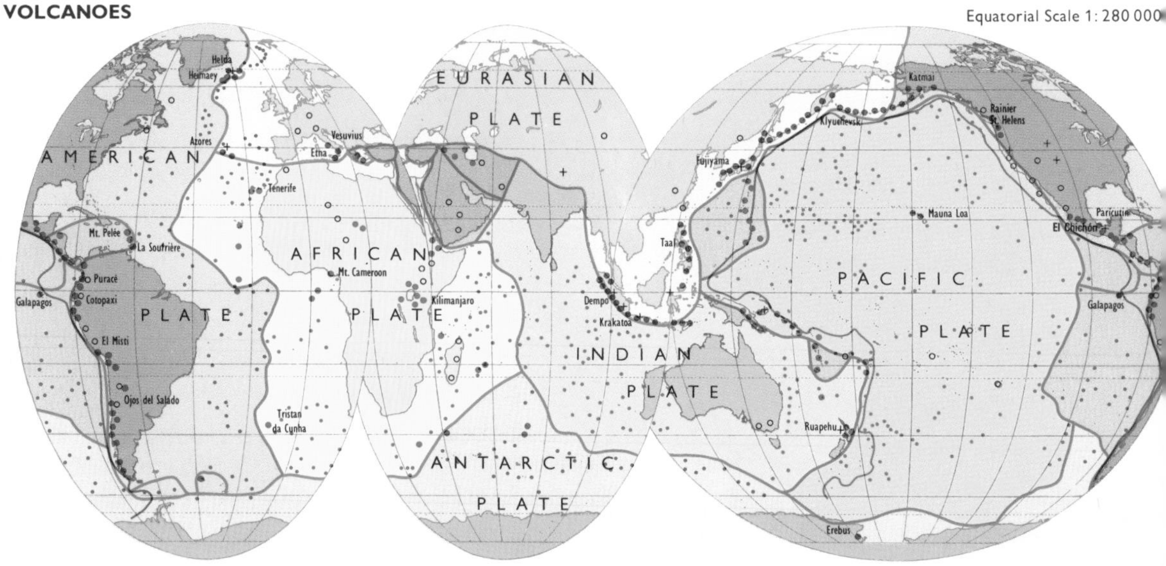

Projection: *Interrupted Mollweide's Homolographic*

- ● Land volcanoes active since 1700
- ○ Land volcanoes inactive since 1700
- · Submarine volcanoes
- + Geysers
- ⎯⎯ Plate boundaries
- ⎯⎯ Andesite line (boundary between sial continental crust and oceanic crust in the Pacific)

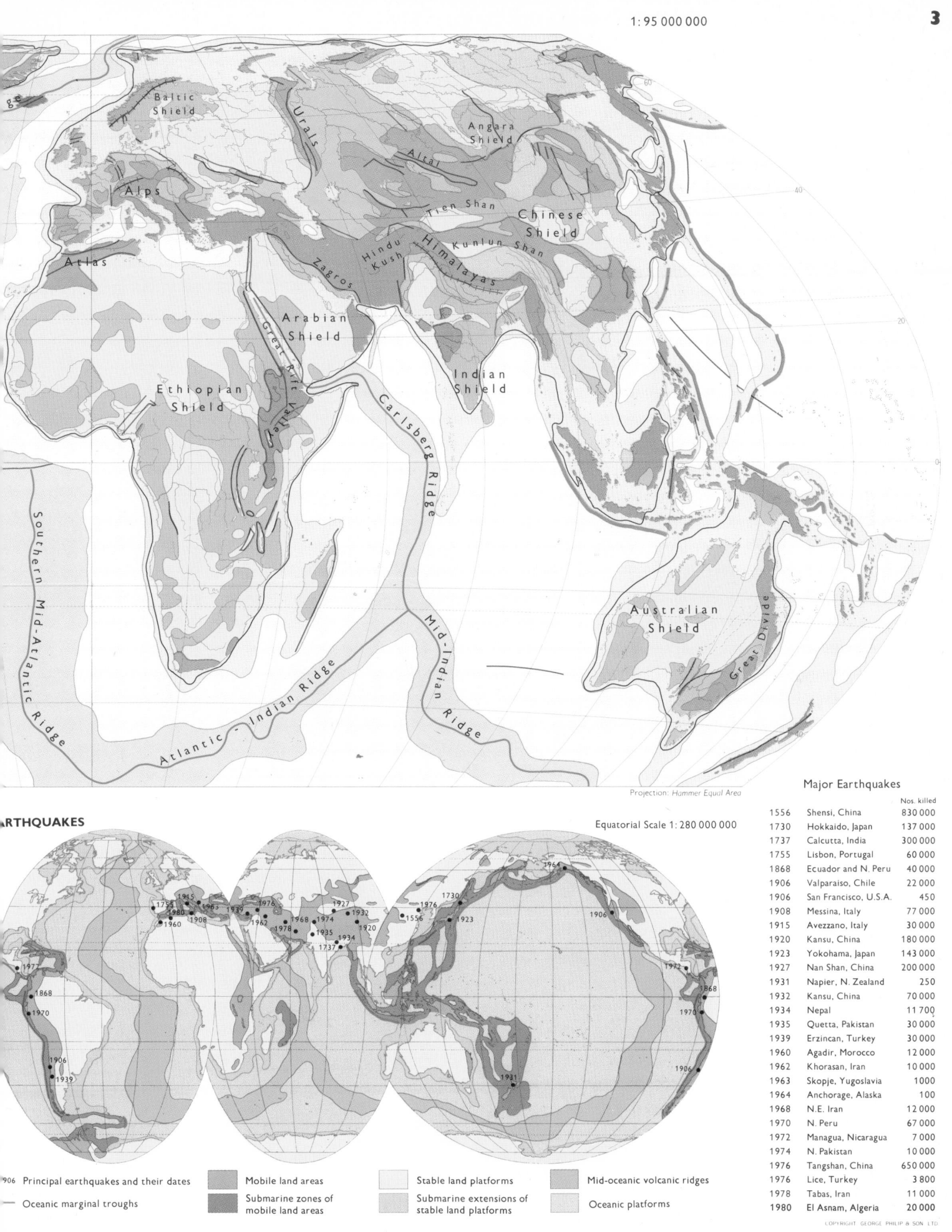

1: 95 000 000

Baltic
Shield

Urals

Angara
Shield

Altai

Alps

Tien Shan

Chinese
Shield

Atlas

Zagros

Hindu
Kush

Kunlun Shan

Himalayas

Arabian
Shield

Great Rift Valley

Indian
Shield

Ethiopian
Shield

Carlsberg Ridge

Australian
Shield

Great Dividing

Southern Mid-Atlantic Ridge

Mid-Indian Ridge

Atlantic - Indian Ridge

Projection: Hammer Equal Area

Major Earthquakes

		Nos. killed
1556	Shensi, China	830 000
1730	Hokkaido, Japan	137 000
1737	Calcutta, India	300 000
1755	Lisbon, Portugal	60 000
1868	Ecuador and N. Peru	40 000
1906	Valparaiso, Chile	22 000
1906	San Francisco, U.S.A.	450
1908	Messina, Italy	77 000
1915	Avezzano, Italy	30 000
1920	Kansu, China	180 000
1923	Yokohama, Japan	143 000
1927	Nan Shan, China	200 000
1931	Napier, N. Zealand	250
1932	Kansu, China	70 000
1934	Nepal	11 700
1935	Quetta, Pakistan	30 000
1939	Erzincan, Turkey	30 000
1960	Agadir, Morocco	12 000
1962	Khorasan, Iran	10 000
1963	Skopje, Yugoslavia	1 000
1964	Anchorage, Alaska	100
1968	N.E. Iran	12 000
1970	N. Peru	67 000
1972	Managua, Nicaragua	7 000
1974	N. Pakistan	10 000
1976	Tangshan, China	650 000
1976	Lice, Turkey	3 800
1978	Tabas, Iran	11 000
1980	El Asnam, Algeria	20 000

ARTHQUAKES

Equatorial Scale 1: 280 000 000

1906 — Principal earthquakes and their dates

— Oceanic marginal troughs

Mobile land areas

Submarine zones of mobile land areas

Stable land platforms

Submarine extensions of stable land platforms

Mid-oceanic volcanic ridges

Oceanic platforms

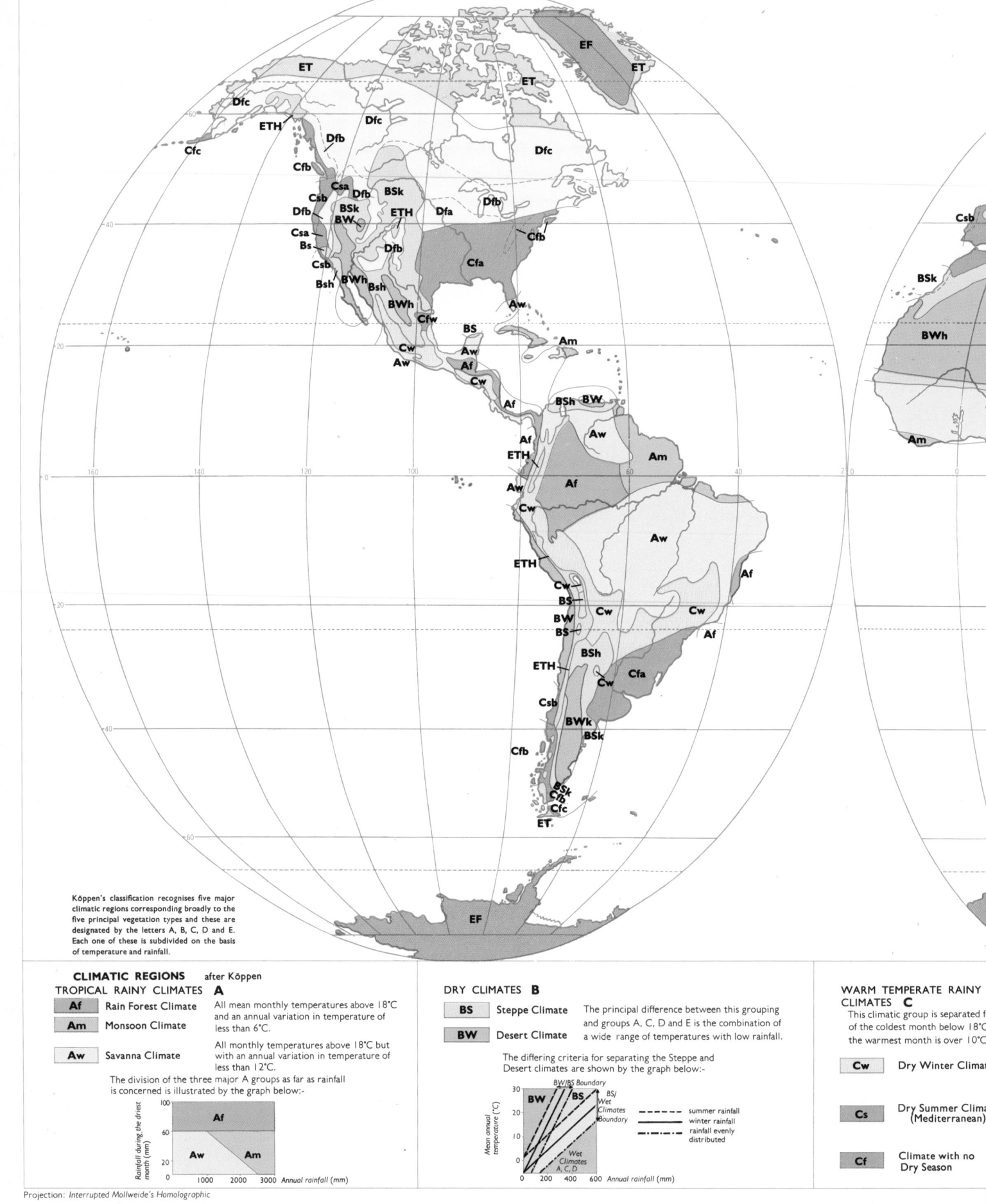

Köppen's classification recognises five major climatic regions corresponding broadly to the five principal vegetation types and these are designated by the letters A, B, C, D and E. Each one of these is subdivided on the basis of temperature and rainfall.

CLIMATIC REGIONS   after Köppen

TROPICAL RAINY CLIMATES   A

Af	Rain Forest Climate	All mean monthly temperatures above 18°C and an annual variation in temperature of less than 6°C.
Am	Monsoon Climate	All monthly temperatures above 18°C but with an annual variation in temperature of less than 12°C.
Aw	Savanna Climate	

The division of the three major A groups as far as rainfall is concerned is illustrated by the graph below:-

DRY CLIMATES   B

BS	Steppe Climate	The principal difference between this grouping and groups A, C, D and E is the combination of a wide range of temperatures with low rainfall.
BW	Desert Climate	

The differing criteria for separating the Steppe and Desert climates are shown by the graph below:-

WARM TEMPERATE RAINY CLIMATES   C

This climatic group is separated fr of the coldest month below 18°C the warmest month is over 10°C.

Cw	Dry Winter Climate
Cs	Dry Summer Clima (Mediterranean)
Cf	Climate with no Dry Season

Projection: *Interrupted Mollweide's Homolographic*

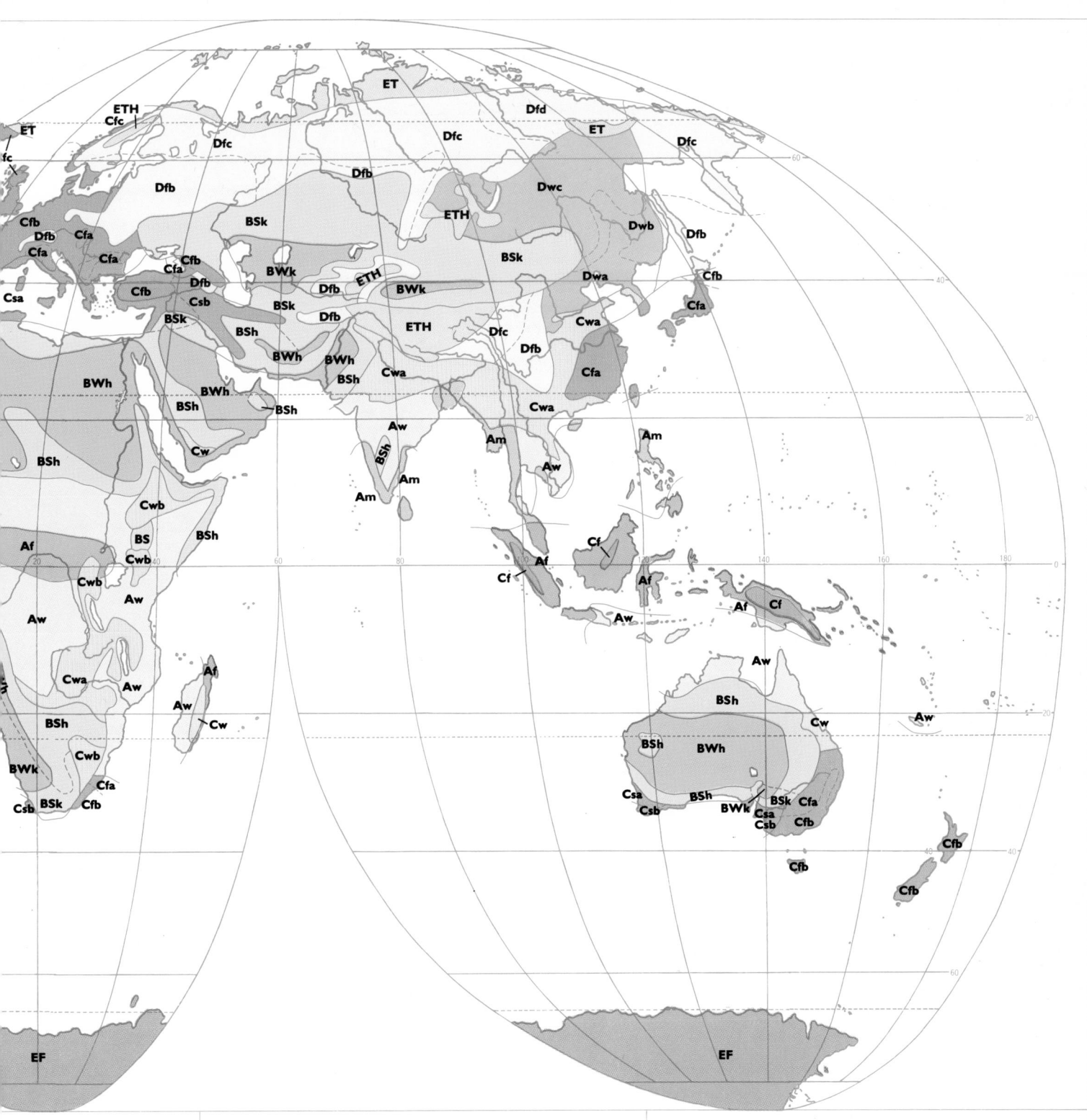

up A by having the mean temperature
ve –3°C. The mean temperature of

wettest month of summer has at least
times as much rain as the driest
ter month.

wettest month of winter has at least
ee times as much rain as the driest
nth of summer. The driest summer
nth itself has less than 30mm rainfall.

n rainfall throughout the year.

COLD TEMPERATE RAINY CLIMATES D

Dw	Dry Winter Climate	The mean temperature of the coldest month is below –3°C but the mean temperature of the warmest month is still over 10°C.
Df	Dry Summer Climate	

POLAR CLIMATES E

ET	Tundra Climate	The mean temperature of the warmest month is below 10°C giving permanently frozen subsoil.
EF	Polar Climate	The mean temperature of the warmest month is below 0°C giving permanent ice and snow.

The classification is in some cases subdivided by the addition of the following letters after the major types:-

Used with groups C and D	**a**	Hot summer—mean temperature of the hottest month above 22°C and with more than four months of over 10°C.
	b	Warm summer—mean temperature of the hottest month below 22°C but still with more than four months of over 10°C.
	c	Cool short summer—mean temperature of the hottest month below 22°C but with less than four months of over 10°C.
Used with group D	**d**	Cool short summer and cold winter—mean temperature of the hottest month below 22°C, and of the coldest month below –38°C.
Used with group B	**h**	Hot dry climate—mean annual temperature above 18°C.
	k	Cool dry climate—mean annual temperature below 18°C.
Used with group E	**H**	Polar climate due to elevation being over 1500m

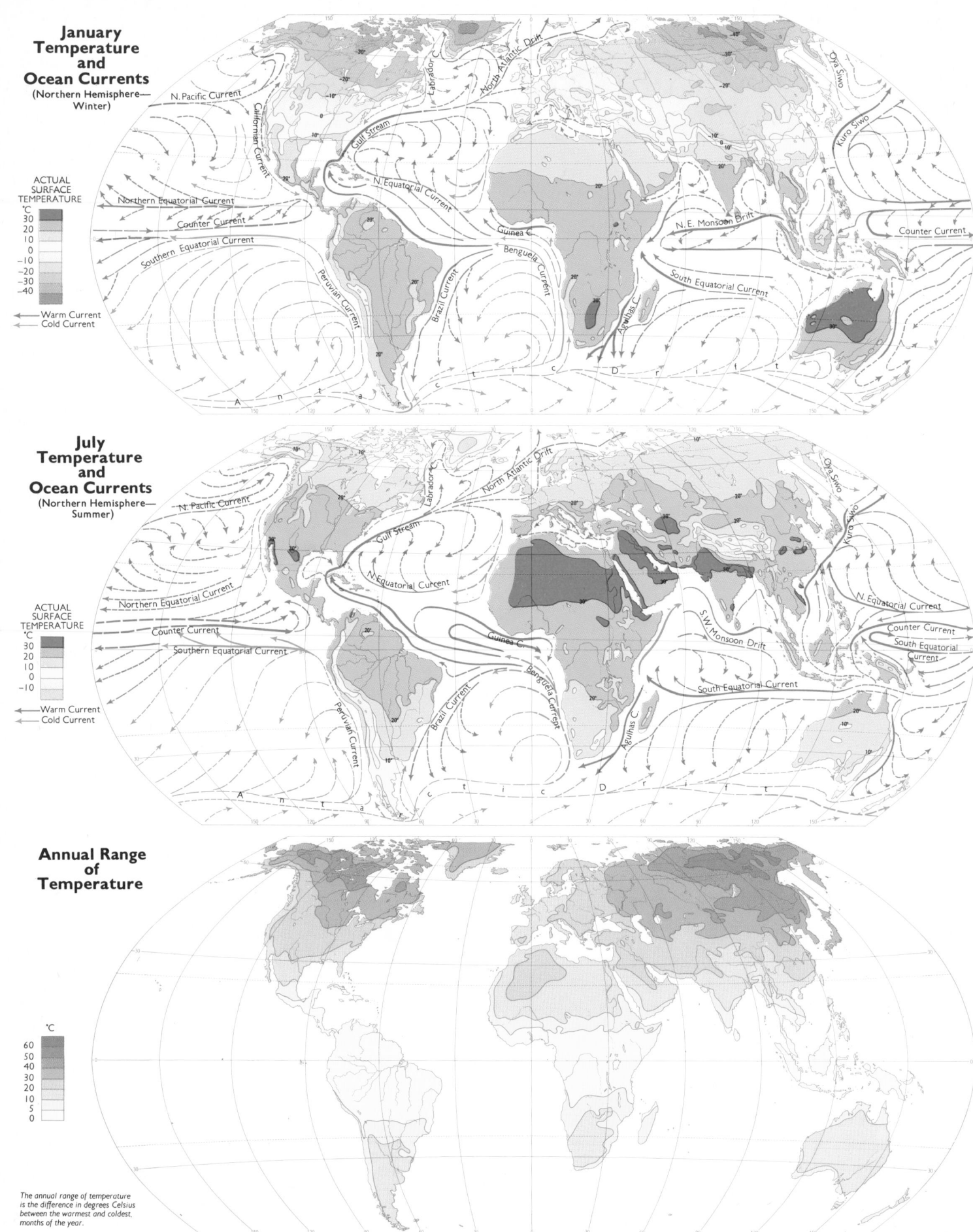

January Temperature and Ocean Currents
(Northern Hemisphere—Winter)

ACTUAL SURFACE TEMPERATURE
°C
30
20
10
0
−10
−20
−30
−40

← Warm Current
← Cold Current

July Temperature and Ocean Currents
(Northern Hemisphere—Summer)

ACTUAL SURFACE TEMPERATURE
°C
30
20
10
0
−10

← Warm Current
← Cold Current

Annual Range of Temperature

°C
60
50
40
30
20
10
5
0

The annual range of temperature
is the difference in degrees Celsius
between the warmest and coldest
months of the year.

Projection: Hammer Equal Area

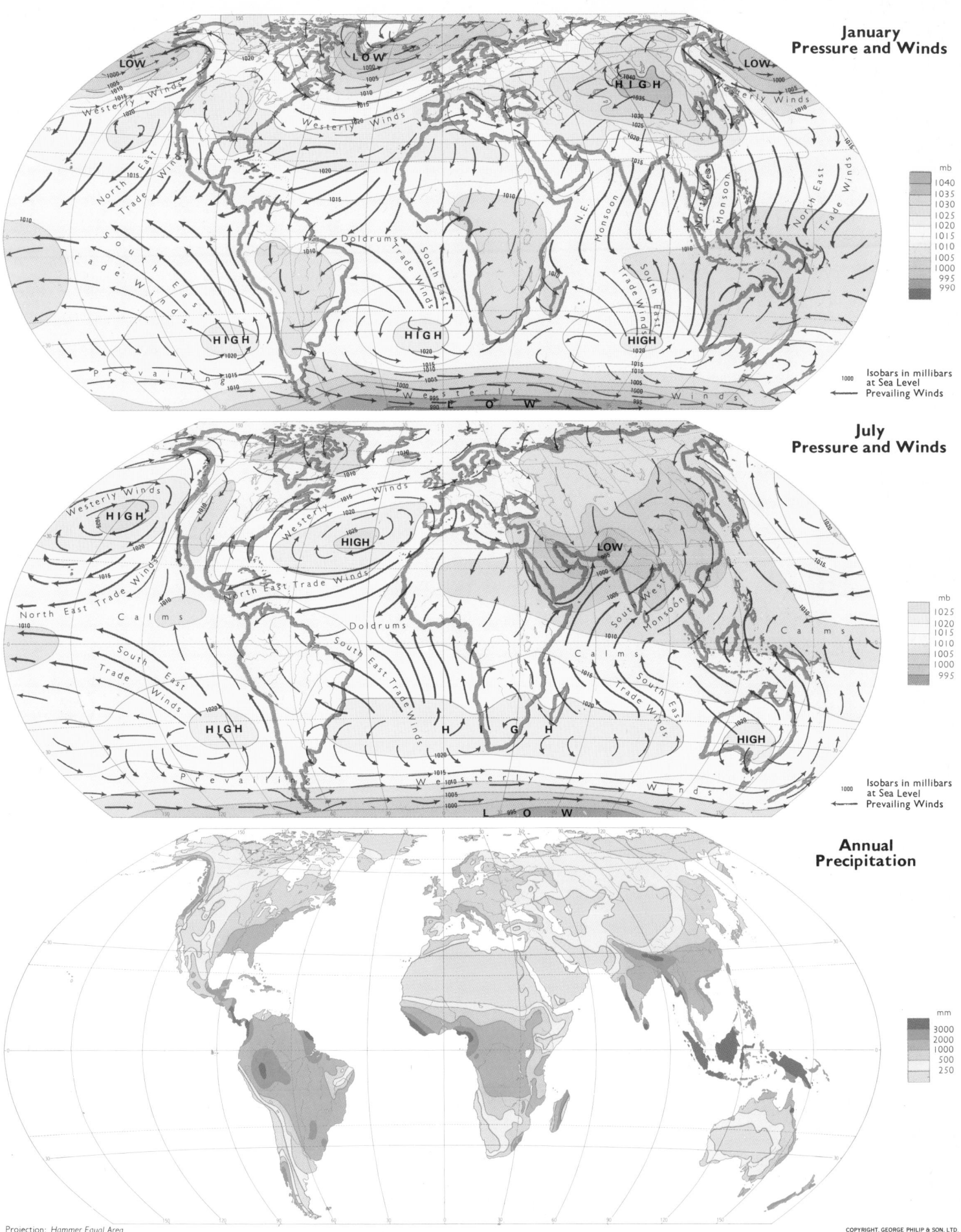

January
Pressure and Winds

July
Pressure and Winds

Annual
Precipitation

mb
1040
1035
1030
1025
1020
1015
1010
1005
1000
995
990

1000   Isobars in millibars
at Sea Level
Prevailing Winds

mb
1025
1020
1015
1010
1005
1000
995

1000   Isobars in millibars
at Sea Level
Prevailing Winds

mm
3000
2000
1000
500
250

Projection: *Hammer Equal Area*

COPYRIGHT. GEORGE PHILIP & SON. LTD.

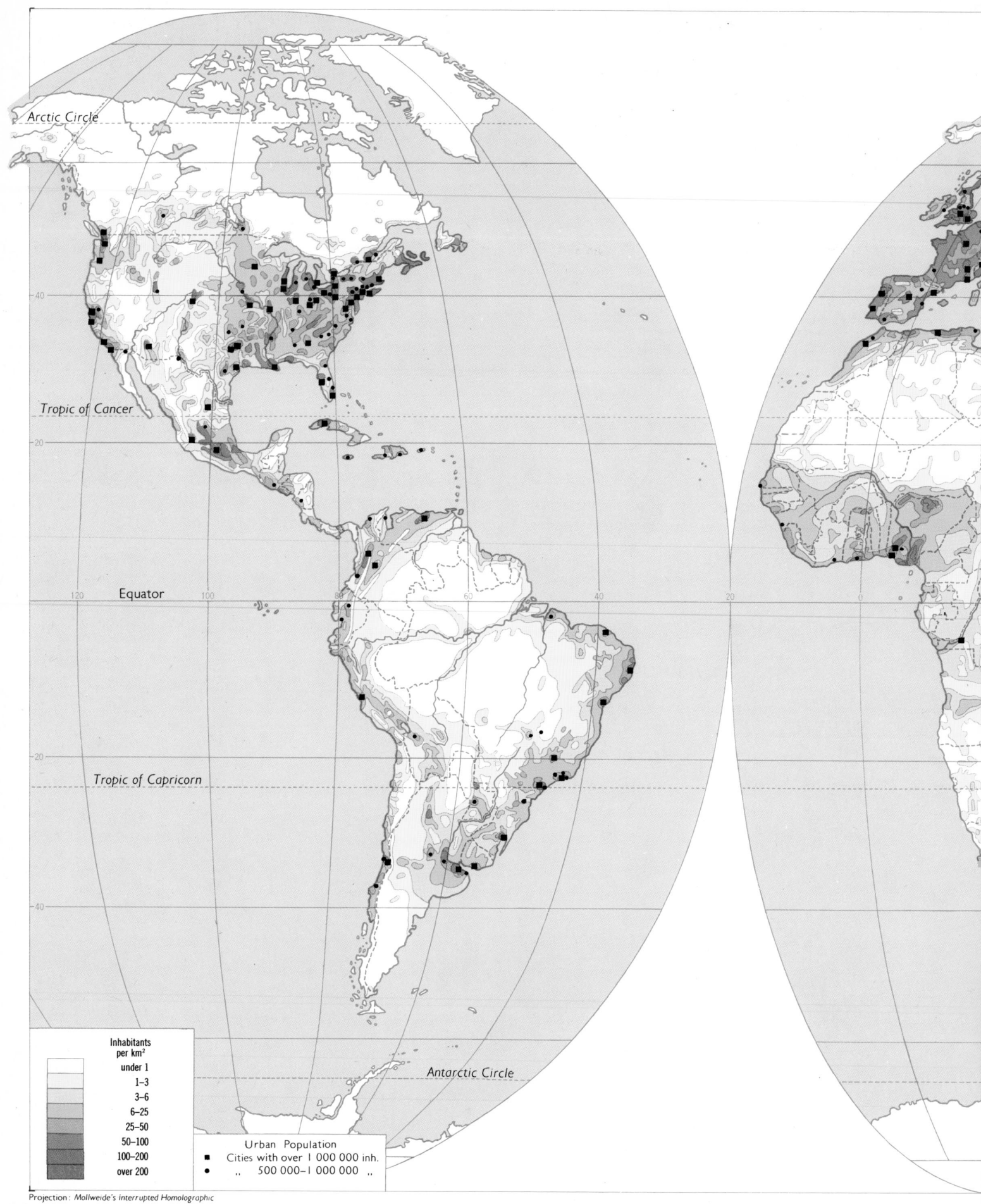

Arctic Circle

Tropic of Cancer

Equator

Tropic of Capricorn

Antarctic Circle

Inhabitants
per km²

	under 1
	1–3
	3–6
	6–25
	25–50
	50–100
	100–200
	over 200

Urban Population
■ Cities with over 1 000 000 inh.
•   ,,   500 000–1 000 000   ,,

Projection: *Mollweide's Interrupted Homolographic*

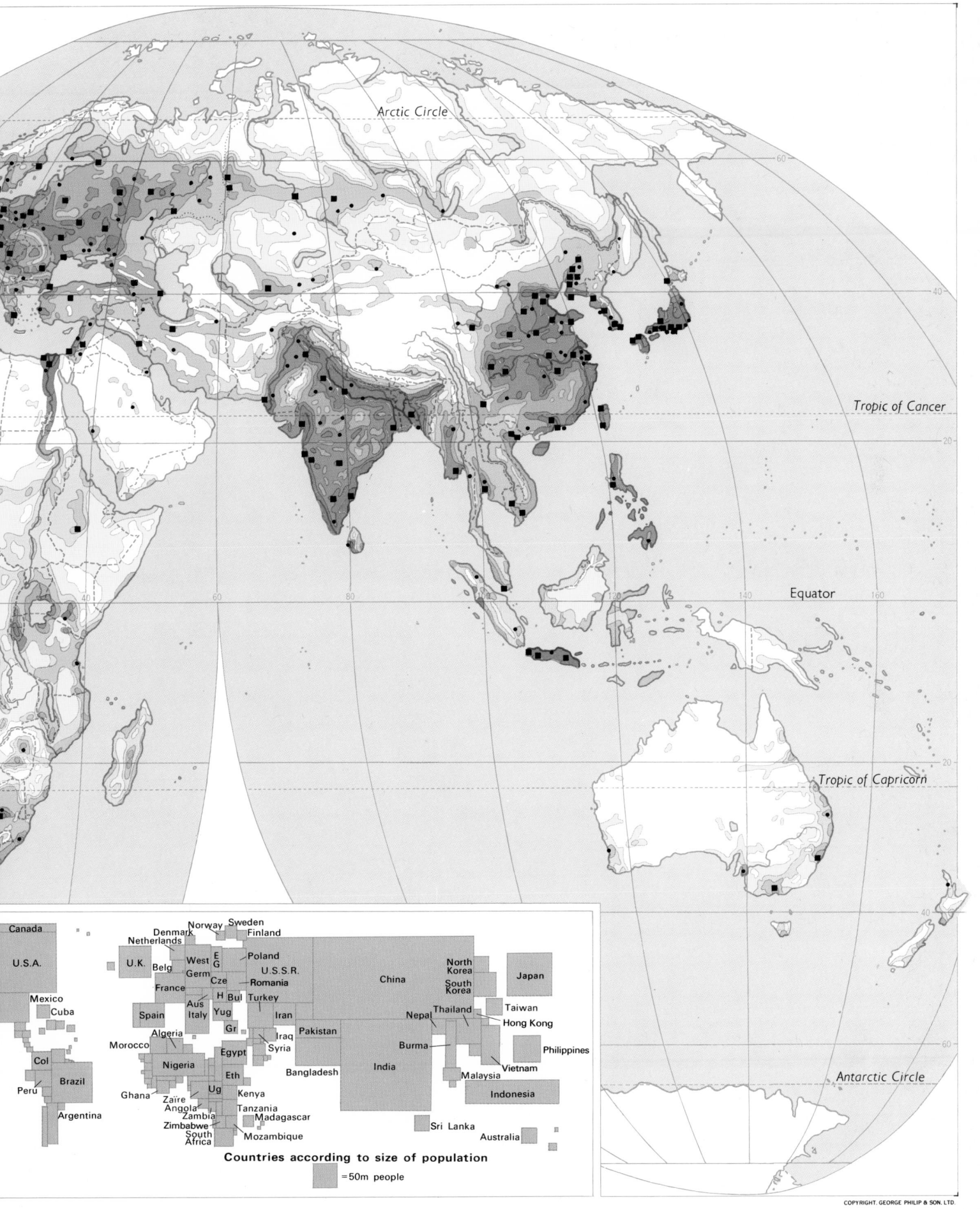

Arctic Circle

Tropic of Cancer

Equator

Tropic of Capricorn

Antarctic Circle

Canada		Norway	Sweden				
U.S.A.	Denmark		Finland			North Korea	Japan
	Netherlands		Poland	U.S.S.R.	China	South Korea	
U.K.	E G						
West Germ							
Mexico	Belg	Cze	Romania				
Cuba	France	H Bul	Turkey	Iran		Nepal	Taiwan
	Aus					Thailand	Hong Kong
Spain	Italy	Yug		Iraq	Pakistan		
Algeria	Gr		Syria			Burma	Philippines
Col	Morocco	Egypt		Bangladesh	India		Vietnam
Peru	Brazil	Nigeria	Eth			Malaysia	
	Ghana	Ug	Kenya			Indonesia	
Argentina	Zaïre	Tanzania					
	Angola	Zambia	Madagascar			Sri Lanka	
	Zimbabwe						Australia
	South Africa	Mozambique					

Countries according to size of population

☐ = 50m people

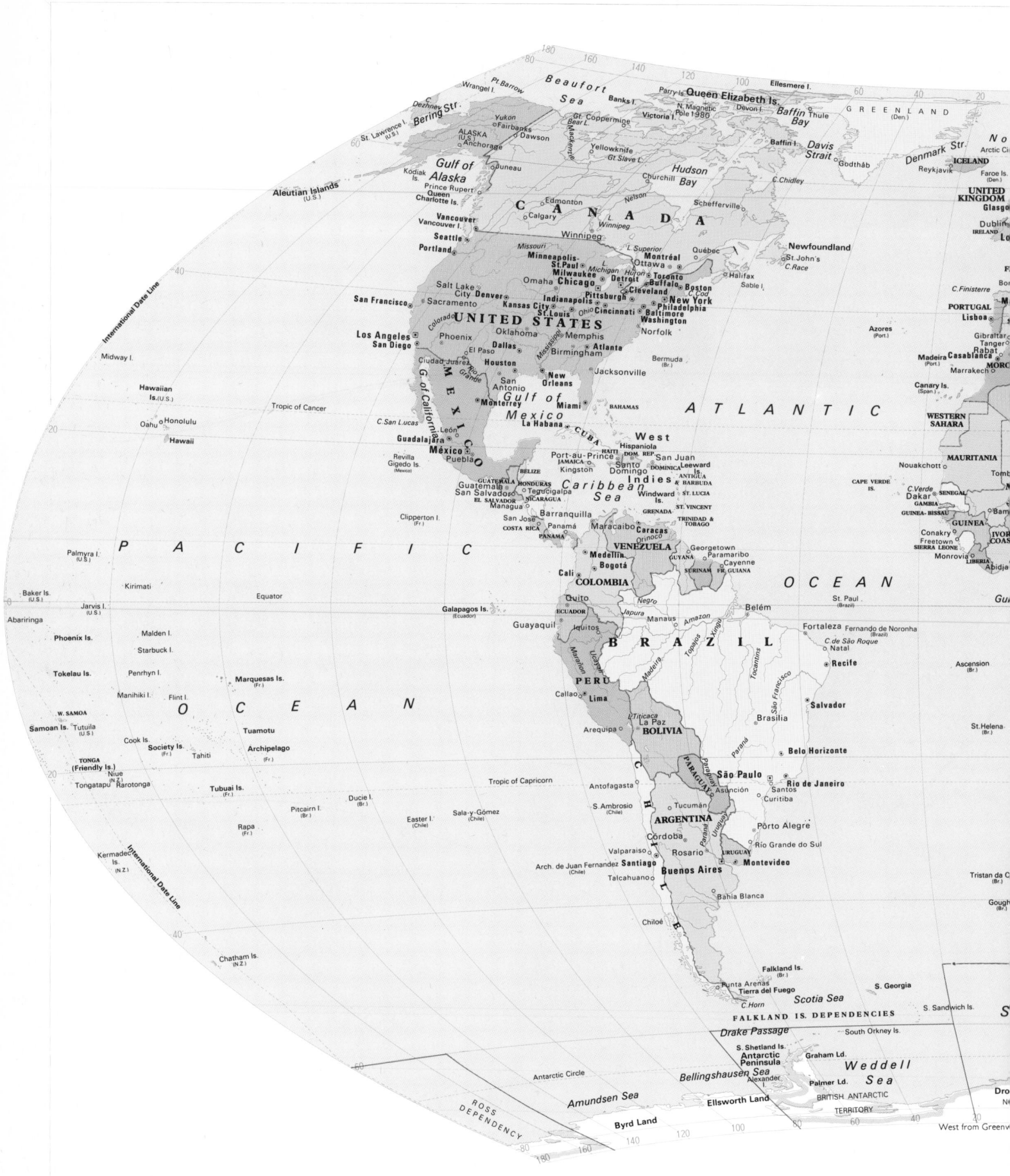

Projection: *Hammer Equal Area*

ARCTIC OCEAN

Zemlya Frantsa Iosifa
Novaya Zemlya
Barents Sea
Nord Kapp
Murmansk
Kara Sea
Severnaya Zemlya
Laptev Sea
New Siberian Is.
East Siberian Sea

Narvik
Arkhangelsk
Ust Port
Yenisey
Tiksi
Verkhoyansk
Nizhne-Kolymsk
Anadyr
Arctic Circle

NORWAY
SWEDEN
FINLAND
Helsinki
UNION OF SOVIET
Salekhard
Vilyuysk
Lena
Yakutsk
SOCIALIST REPUBLIC
Okhotsk
Bering Sea

Oslo
Stockholm
Leningrad
RUSSIAN
SOVIET FEDERATIVE
SOCIALIST
Kamchatka
Petropavlovsk-Kamchatskiy

Yaroslavl
Perm
Sverdlovsk
Ob
Novosibirsk
Tomsk
Krasnoyarsk
L.Baykal
Sea of Okhotsk
C.Lopatka

Kazan
Kuybyshev
Ufa
Chelyabinsk
Omsk
Novokuznetsk
Ulan Ude
Sakhalin
Komsomolsk

Berlin
POLAND
Warszawa
Minsk
RUSSIA
Voronezh
Saratov
Orenburg
Irtysh
Barnaul
Irkutsk
Khabarovsk
Kuril Is.

Praha
Lvov
Kharkov
Volga
Volgograd
KAZAKHSTAN
Karaganda
Ulaanbaatar
Amur
Vladivostok
Sapporo
Hakodate

Wien
Budapest
ROMANIA
Rostov
Astrakhan
Aral Sea
L.Balkhash
MONGOLIA
Haerhpin
KOREA
Japan
Tōkyō

Milano
Beograd
Bucuresti
Black Sea
Groznyy
Tbilisi
UZBEKISTAN
Alma Ata
Ch'angch'un
Shenyang
Sea of Japan
Yokohama
Nagoya

Roma
Sofiya
BULGARIA
Istanbul
Ankara
Yerevan
Baku
Samarkand
KIRGIZIA
Tashkent
CHINA
Peip'ing
T'ienching
Lüta
P'yŏngyang
Kyōto
Kōbe
Ōsaka

Napoli
Athinai
TURKEY
Izmir
Tabriz
Ashkhabad
TURKMENISTAN
Dushanbe
Lanchou
T'aiyüan
Chinan
Ch'ingtao
Pusan
Kitakyūshū

Mediterranean Sea
Crete
CYPRUS
Halab
SYRIA
Dimashq
Baghdad
Tehrān
AFGHANISTAN
Kabul
Srinagar
Hsian
Huang
Nanching
Shanghai
East China Sea

Tarābulus
Banghāzi
Iskandariya
El Qâhira
IRAQ
IRAN (PERSIA)
Eşfahān
Rawalpindi
Lahore
TIBET
Ch'engtu
Ch'ungch'ing
Wuhan
Fuchou
Ch'angsha

LIBYA
EGYPT
Nile
KUWAIT
Abadan
Shiraz
PAKISTAN
Delhi
Agra
Kanpur
NEPAL
Katmandu
BHU.
K'unming
Kwangchou
Taipei
TAIWAN (FORMOSA)

Ar Riyād
BAHRAIN
QATAR
Karachi
INDIA
Lucknow
Ganga
Dacca
BANGLA DESH
BURMA
Hanoi
Hong Kong (Br.)
Ryukyu Is.

SAUDI ARABIA.
U.A.E.
OMAN
Ahmadabad
Nagpur
Calcutta
Mandalay
Hainan
South China Sea

Makkah
Red Sea
Arabian Sea
Bombay
Pune
Bay of Bengal
Rangoon
Vientiane
VIET-NAM

Aswân
El Khartûm
YEMEN
SOUTH YEMEN
Hyderabad
Bangalore
Madras
Andaman Is.
THAILAND
Bangkok
CAMBODIA

NIGER
CHAD
SUDAN
Omdurmân
Asmera
Aden
Gulf of Aden
Socotra (S.Yemen)
Lakshadweep Is.
Nicobar Is. (India)
Phnom Penh
Phan Bho Ho Chi Minh

Karo
L.Chad
Ndjamena
Blue Nile
DJIBOUTI
SRI LANKA (CEYLON)
MALAYSIA
BRUNEI
SABAH
Cebu
PHILIPPINES
Manila

NIGERIA
CENTRAL AFRICAN REPUBLIC
Addis Abeba
ETHIOPIA
SOMALI REP.
Colombo
Dondra Hd.
Kuala Lumpur
PEN. MALAYSIA
SARAWAK
Kuching

Yaoundé
Bangui
Mogadishu
MALDIVES
Medan
Singapore
Borneo

GABON
ZAÏRE (CONGO)
Kisangani
UGANDA
KENYA
Kampala
Equator
Sumatera
Banjarmasin
Sulawesi

Libreville
Congo
Kinshasa
Victoria
Nairobi
SEYCHELLES
INDONESIA
Palembang
Ujung Pandang
Irian Jaya
PAPUA NEW GUINEA

Brazzaville
CABINDA
Kananga
Mombasa
Zanzibar
Amirante Is.
Chagos Arch. (Br.)
Jakarta
Jawa
Surabaya
Bandung
NEW GUINEA
Port Moresby

Luanda
TANZANIA
Dar es Salaam
Aldabra
Diego Garcia (Br.)
INDIAN OCEAN
Timor
Timor Sea
C.York

ANGOLA
L.Tanganyika
COMORO IS.
Cocos (Keeling Is.) (Australia)
Christmas I. (Australia)
Darwin

Benguela
ZAMBIA
Lusaka
Malawi
MADAGASCAR
Antananarivo
MAURITIUS
Rodriguez
NORTHERN TERRITORY
Cairns

ZIMBABWE
MOZAMBIQUE
Harare
Réunion (Fr.)
Tropic of Capricorn
WESTERN
QUEENSLAND
Rockhampton

NAMIBIA
BOTSWANA
Windhoek
Gaborone
Pretoria
Johannesburg
SWAZ.
Maputo
North West C.
Alice Springs
AUSTRALIA

SOUTH AFRICA
LES.
Durban
Amsterdam (Fr.)
St.Paul
AUSTRALIA
SOUTH AUSTRALIA
Brisbane

Cape Town
C.of Good Hope
Port Elizabeth
Perth
Fremantle
Kalgoorlie
NEW SOUTH WALES
Newcastle
Norfolk I. (Australia)

Pr.Edward Is. (South Africa)
Crozet Is. (Fr.)
Great Australian Bight
Adelaide
Sydney
Canberra
Lord Howe (Australia)
North C.

Kerguelen (Fr.)
VICTORIA
Melbourne
Tasman Sea
Auckland
North I.
NEW ZEALAND

McDonald I. (Australia)
Heard I. (Australia)
TASMANIA
Hobart
Wellington
C.Farewell
Christchurch
South I.

SOUTHERN OCEAN
Stewart I.
Bounty Is.
Antipodes Is.
Auckland I. (N.Z.)

Enderby Land
Antarctic Circle
Wilkes Land
S.Magnetic Pole 1980
Balleny Is.
Macquarie I. (Australia)
Campbell I. (N.Z.)

AUSTRALIAN DEPENDENCY
TERRE ADÉLIE
Ross Sea
ast from Greenwich

PACIFIC OCEAN
Tropic of Cancer
Wake I. (U.S.)
Northern Marianas (U.S.)
Guam (U.S.)
Marshall Is.
TRUST TERRITORY OF
Yap
Truk
Ponape
Caroline Is.
THE PACIFIC ISLANDS (U.S.)
KIRIBATI
NAURU
New Ireland
Rabaul
New Britain
SOLOMON IS.
TUVALU
Louisiade Arch.
Santa Cruz Is.
VANUATU
Vanua Levu
Viti Levu
FIJI
Suva
New Caledonia
Townsville

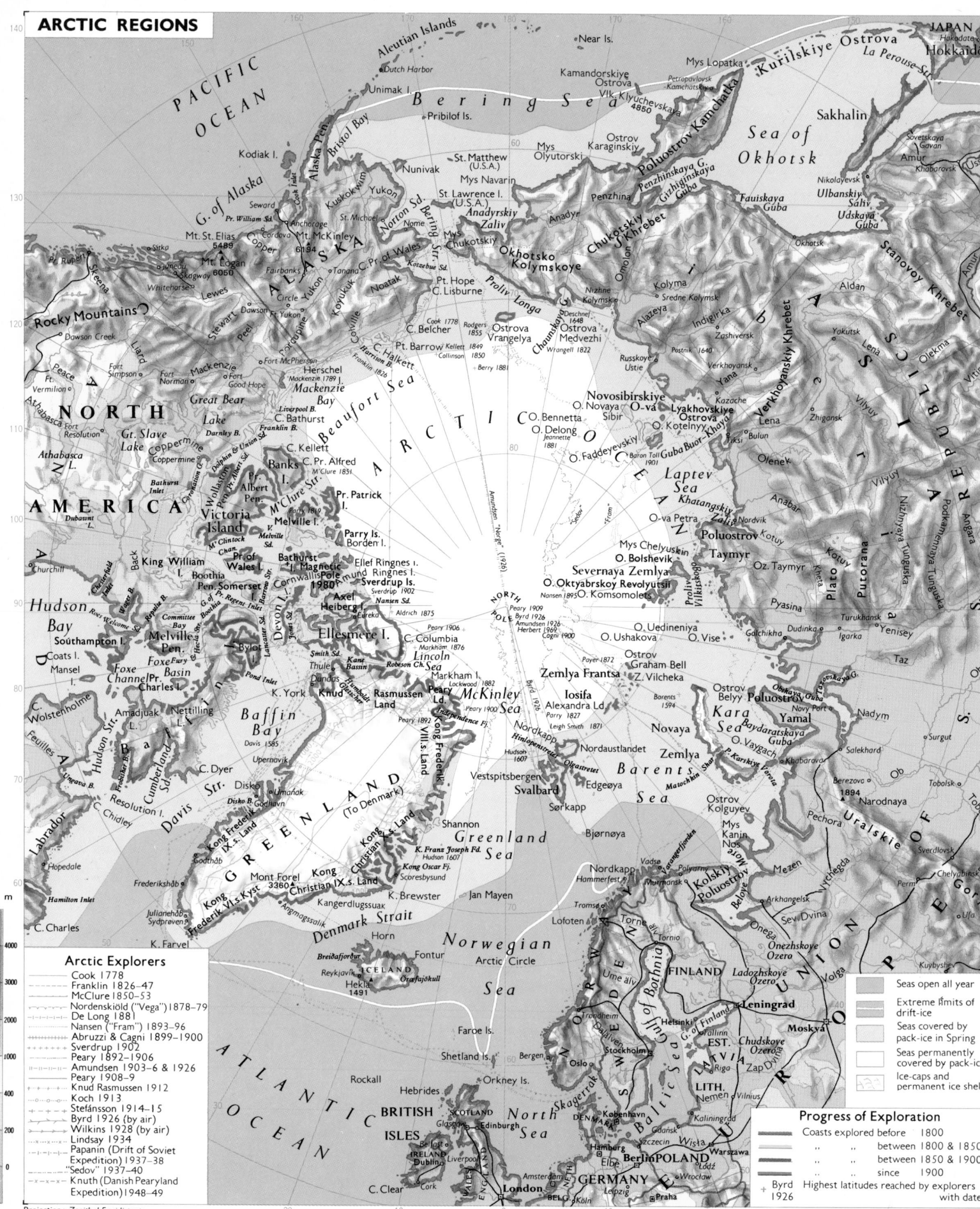

ARCTIC REGIONS

Arctic Explorers
Cook 1778
Franklin 1826–47
McClure 1850–53
Nordenskiöld ("Vega") 1878–79
De Long 1881
Nansen ("Fram") 1893–96
Abruzzi & Cagni 1899–1900
Sverdrup 1902
Peary 1892–1906
Amundsen 1903–6 & 1926
Peary 1908–9
Knud Rasmussen 1912
Koch 1913
Stefánsson 1914–15
Byrd 1926 (by air)
Wilkins 1928 (by air)
Lindsay 1934
Papanin (Drift of Soviet
Expedition) 1937–38
"Sedov" 1937–40
Knuth (Danish Pearyland
Expedition) 1948–49

Projection: *Zenithal Equidistant*

Seas open all year
Extreme limits of
drift-ice
Seas covered by
pack-ice in Spring
Seas permanently
covered by pack-ice
Ice-caps and
permanent ice shelf

Progress of Exploration
Coasts explored before   1800
     ,,   ,,   between 1800 & 1850
     ,,   ,,   between 1850 & 1900
     ,,   ,,   since   1900
+ Byrd   Highest latitudes reached by explorers
  1926   with date

ANTARCTIC REGIONS

1 : 35 000 000

400   0   400   800   1200 km

⎯ ⎯ Sub-Glacial Limits (at Sea Level) of Polar Basins

Meridian of Greenwich

SOUTHERN

NORWEGIAN DEPENDENCY

Antarctic Circle

Bouvetøya (Nor.)

South Georgia Grytviken

Zavodoski I.
Visokoi I.
Leskov I.
Candlemas I.
Saunders I. S. Sandwich Is.
Montagu I. Bristol I.

Scotia Sea
FALKLAND IS. DEPENDENCIES

Stanley
Falkland Is.

Orcadas (Argentina)
Signy I. (U.K.)
Coronation I. South Orkney Is.
Powell 1821

BRITISH ANTARCTIC TERRITORY

Weddell Sea

Bellingshausen 1820
Biscoe 1831
Sanae (S. Afr.)
Maudheim
Prinsesse Astrid Kyst Prinsesse Ragnhild Kyst
Riiser-Larsen-halvøya
Cook 1773
Lützow Holmbukta
Moore 1845

Dronning Maud Land
Sør-Rondane
Kronprins Olav Kyst
Molodezhnaya (U.S.S.R.)

Elephant I.
South Shetland Is.
Kg. George I.
Clarence I.
Joinville I.
Esperanza (Arg.)
James Ross I.
Robertson I.

Enderby Ld.
C. Borley
Kemp Land
Kemp 1833
Stefansson B.

Graham Land
Anvers I.
Antarctic Peninsula
Larsen Ice Shelf
Larsen 1893

Mac-Robertson Land
Mawson (Austr.)
C. Darnley

Biscoe Is.
Palmer Land
Vahsel Bay
General Belgrano (Argentina)
Halley Bay (U.K.)

Prince Charles Mts.
Lambert Glacier
Amery Ice Shelf
Prydz Bay
Davis "Challenger" 1874

Adelaide I. (U.K.)
Alexander I.
Charcot I.
C. Byrd

Ronne Ice Shelf
Berkner I.

American Highland

West Ice Shelf

Pensacola Mountains
3657

4267

Amundsen-Scott (U.S.)
SOUTH POLE

Wilhelm II Coast

Ellsworth Mts.
Vinson Massif 5139

ANTARCTICA

Amundsen, 14.12.1911
Byrd, 29.11.1929
2800 POLAR

Queen Mary Land
Mirnyy (U.S.S.R.)
Drygalski I.
Drygalski 1902
Davis Sea
Masson I.

Peter I's Øy (Nor.)

BYRD
Hollick Kenyon Plateau
SUB-GLACIAL

SUB-GLACIAL BASIN
Vostok (U.S.S.R.)

Scott Gl.
Knox Coast
Bowman I.

Thurston I.
C. Flying Fish
Cook 1774

Marie Byrd Land
BASIN
Mt. Sidley 4181
Rockefeller Plateau

Queen Maud Mts.
Queen Alexandra Ra.
Mt. Markham 4349

WILKES SUB-GLACIAL BASIN

Casey (Austral.)
Budd Coast
C. Poinsett
Sabrina Coast
Totten Glacier

Amundsen Sea

Getz Ice Shelf
3496

Roosevelt I.
Ross Ice Shelf
Ice Barrier
Bay of Whales

Mt. Lister
Mt. Erebus 4023
McMurdo (U.S.)
3743

Banzare Coast
Dalton Iceberg Tongue

C. Colbeck
Scott 1902

Victoria Land
Franklin I.
Terra Nova B.
Mt. Murchison 3502

Magnetic Pole (Shackleton) 1909
Clarie Coast
Porpoise Bay
Blodgett Iceberg Tongue

Ross Sea

Coulman I.
Possession I.
C. Adare
Leningradskaya (U.S.S.R.)

George V Land
Terre Adélie (Fr.)
Dumont d'Urville
Magnetic Pole (Byrd)
Magnetic Pole 1980
Dibble Glacier Tongue

ROSS DEPENDENCY

Oates Land
Wilkes 1840
C. Freshfield

Antarctic Circle

Scott I.

Balleny Is.

DRAKE PASSAGE

SOUTH PACIFIC OCEAN

Tierra del Fuego
C. de Hornos
Hoste I.
Estrecho de le Maire

Bellingshausen Sea

AUSTRALIAN DEPENDENCY

Key / Legend:

⎯ ⎯ Territory claimed by Argentina
⎯ · ⎯ Territory claimed by Chile

Seas open all year
Extreme limits of drift-ice
Seas covered by pack-ice in Spring
Ice caps and permanent ice shelf

Antarctic Explorers

⎯⎯ Cook 1772–75
········ Bellingshausen 1819–21
⎯·⎯ Weddell 1820–24
⎯··⎯ Biscoe 1831–32
⎯·⎯ D'Urville 1839–40
Byrd (U.S. Antarctic Service) 1939–41, 1946–47 (bases, Stonington I. & Little America)
····· Trans-Antarctic Route 1958

⎯×⎯ Wilkes 1839–40
⎯·⎯ Ross 1840–43
Gerlache 1898–99

⎯○⎯ Shackleton 1907–9
⎯⎯ Scott 1910–12
Amundsen 1911–12
Mawson 1911–14
Byrd 1928–30 (by air)
⎯ ⎯ ⎯ Soviet Expedition 1959

Scott (N.Z.)   Permanent Bases

Progress of Exploration

⎯⎯ Coasts explored between 1800 and 1850
⎯⎯ Coasts explored since 1900
+ Byrd 1926   Highest latitudes reached by explorers with date

Macquarie Is. (Austral.)
Campbell I. (N.Z.)
Auckland Is. (N.Z.)

on: Zenithal Equidistant

COPYRIGHT GEORGE PHILIP & SON. LTD.

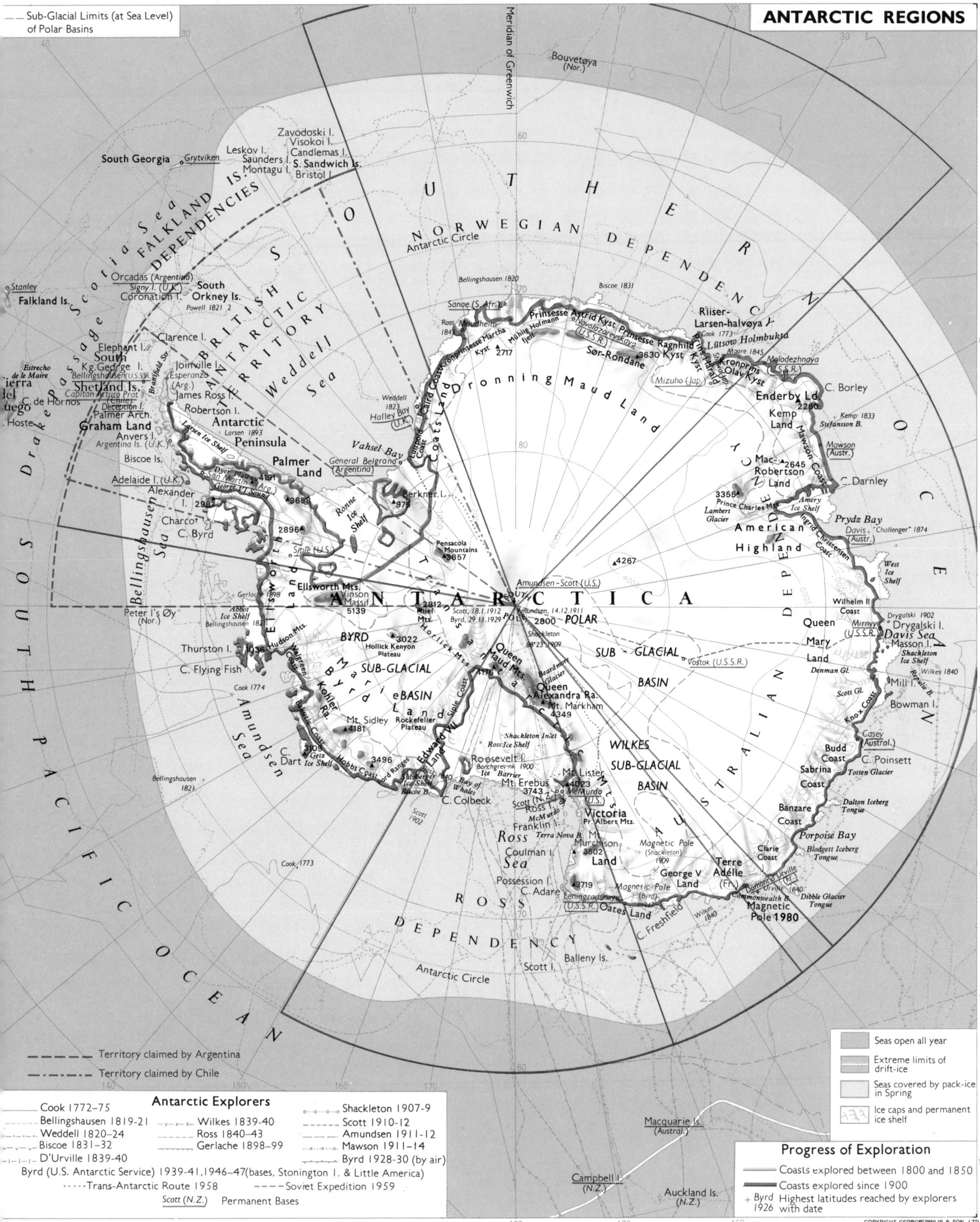

ARCTIC OCEAN
Greenland Sea
Norwegian Sea
Svalbard
ICELAND
GREENLAND
Baffin Bay
Davis Strait
Labrador Sea
Hudson Bay
CANADA
UNITED STATES
Newfoundland
NORTH ATLANTIC OCEAN
North American Basin
Sargasso Sea
Northern Mid-Atlantic Ridge
Canary Basin
Cape Verde Basin
Azores
Madeira
Islas Canarias
West Indies
Caribbean Sea
Gulf of Mexico
MEXICO
VENEZUELA
COLOMBIA
UNITED KINGDOM
IRELAND
FRANCE
SPAIN
PORTUGAL
MOROCCO
ALGERIA
TUNISIA
LIBYA
Sahara
MAURITANIA
SENEGAL
NIGERIA
G. of Guinea
Mediterranean Sea
U.S.S.R.
FINLAND
SWEDEN
POLAND
ROMANIA
Tropic of Cancer
Arctic Circle

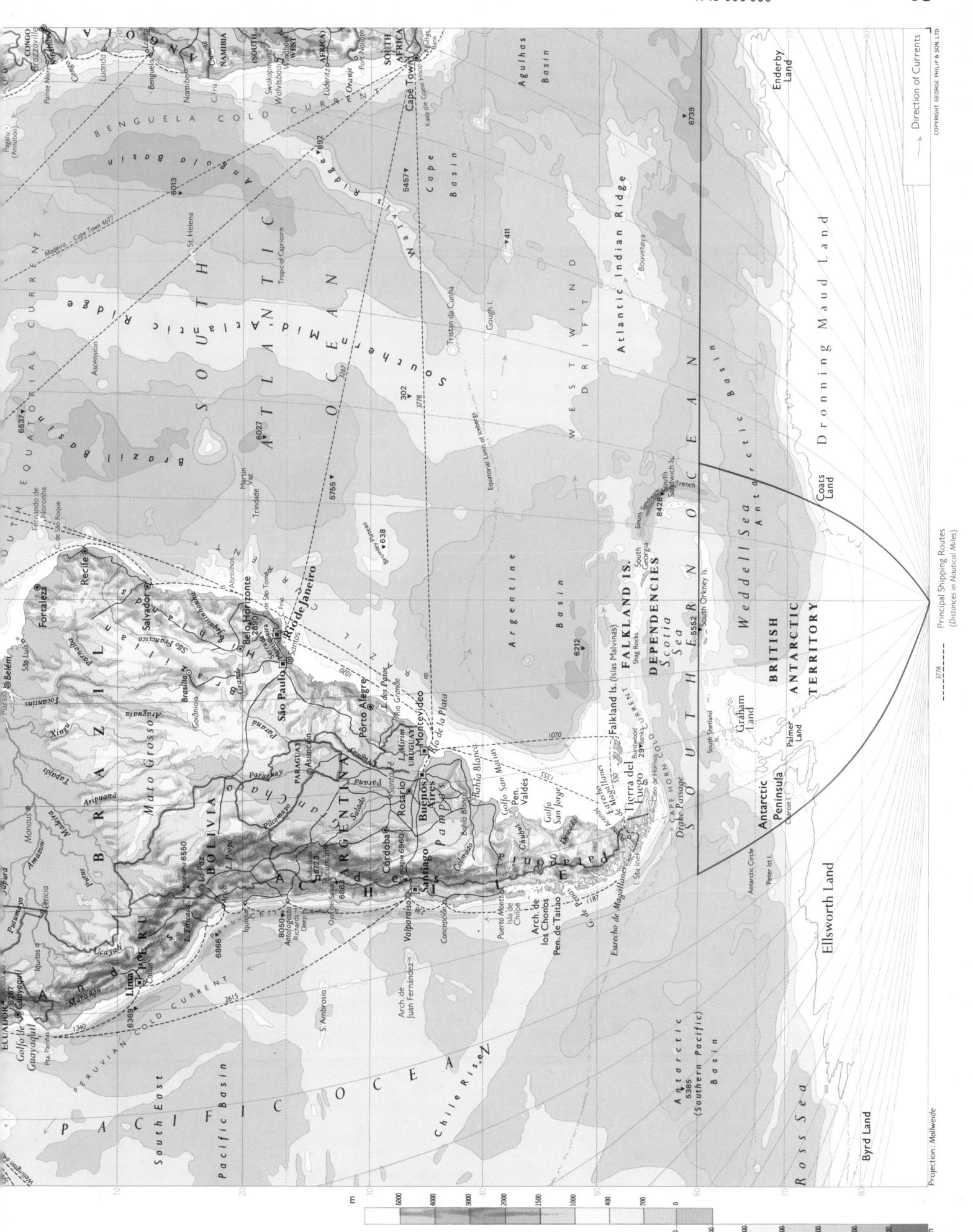

COPYRIGHT GEORGE PHILIP & SON LTD

→ Direction of Currents

──── Principal Shipping Routes
(Distances in Nautical Miles)

------ 3778

Projection: Mollweide

CONGO
BRAZZAVILLE
ANGOLA
Pagalu (Annobón)
Luanda
Pointe Noire
Congo
Cabinda
Benguela
Namibe
NAMIBIA (SOUTH WEST AFRICA)
Swakopmund
Windhoek
Lüderitz
Walvis Bay
Port Nolloth
SOUTH AFRICA
Cape Town
C. Fria
Orange
Kaap die Goeie Hoop
Agulhas
Cape Agulhas
Agulhas Bank

BENGUELA COLD CURRENT

6013
6537
Madeira – Cape Town 4677

St. Helena
Ascension
Walvis Ridge

BRAZIL
Fernando de Noronha
Natal
Recife
Fortaleza
Belém
São Luís
C. de São Roque
Salvador
Belo Horizonte
Rio de Janeiro
São Paulo
Pôrto Alegre

BENGUELA BASIN
ANGOLA BASIN
SOUTH ATLANTIC OCEAN
Mid-Atlantic Ridge
South Atlantic Ridge
Southern Mid-Atlantic Ridge
BRAZIL BASIN
SOUTH EQUATORIAL CURRENT

6027
5755
892
5457
302
3778
638
411
Tristan da Cunha
Gough I.
Martin Vaz
Trindade
Abrolhos

Tropic of Capricorn

Cape Basin
Agulhas Basin
Atlantic Indian Ridge
Bouvetøya

WEST WIND DRIFT

Equatorial Limit of Icebergs

6739

Dronning Maud Land
Enderby Land
Coats Land

Antarctic Basin
Weddell Sea
Scotia Sea
South Sandwich Is.
South Sandwich Trench
South Georgia
South Orkney Is.
8428
5552
6212
Shag Rocks
South Sandwich Is.
FALKLAND IS. DEPENDENCIES
Falkland Is. (Islas Malvinas)

BRITISH ANTARCTIC TERRITORY

Argentine Basin

1070

BOLIVIA
La Paz
PARAGUAY
Asunción
ARGENTINA
URUGUAY
Montevideo
Buenos Aires
Rosario
Santa Fé
Córdoba
Santiago
Valparaíso
Concepción
CHILE
PERU
Lima
Callao
Iquitos
Paraná
Paraguay
Pilcomayo
Salado
Colorado
L. Mirim
L. dos Patos
Río Grande
Río de la Plata
Bahía Blanca
Pen. Valdés
Golfo San Matías
Golfo San Jorge
Chubut
Desado
Pampas
Andes
Gran Chaco
Mato Grosso
Araguaia
Xingu
Tapajós
Madeira
Aripuanã
Purus
Amazon
Iça
Japurá
Putumayo
Ucayali
Marañón
ECUADOR
Guayaquil
Golfo de Guayaquil

6550
6960
8055
6861
6866
6369
1340
2815
1187
1355
550
530

PERUVIAN COLD CURRENT

FALKLAND CURRENT

Arch. de Juan Fernández
Isla de Chiloé
Arch. de los Chonos
Pen. de Taitao
S. Ambrosio
Estrecho de Magallanes
Tierra del Fuego
CAPE HORN
Cabo de Hornos
Drake Passage
Antarctic Circle
Peter I I.
Graham Land
Palmer Land
Charcot I.
South Shetland Is.
Antarctic Peninsula
Ellsworth Land
Byrd Land
Ross Sea

CAPE HORN COLD CURRENT

PACIFIC OCEAN
South East Pacific Basin
Pacific Basin
Chile Rise
Antarctic (Southern Pacific) Basin
5385

SOUTHERN OCEAN

m
6000 4000 3000 2000 1500 1000 400 200 0

m
0 200 2000 4000 5000 6000 8000

1:20 000 000

200   0   200   400   600   800 km

COPYRIGHT. GEORGE PHILIP & SON. LTD.

Ob

Ural

CASPIAN SEA
-28

Ural Mountains

Obshchi Syrt

Narodnaya 1894
Pechora 1617

Kama

Volga

Volga Uplands

Mezen

N. Dvina

Terek

Kuban

Manych

Don

Tsimlyansk Res.

Caucasus
Elbrus 5633

Rion

Kizil Irmak

Kura

Ararat 5165

L. Urmia

Kurdistan

Euphrates

Kanin Peninsula

White Sea

Kola Peninsula

Onega

L. Onega

L. Ladoga

Neva

Svir

Rybinsk Res.

Oka

Volga

Central Russian Uplands

Sea of Azov

Crimea

Str. of Kerch

BLACK SEA

Bosporus

Sea of Marmara

Anatolia

Taurus

Cyprus 1951

Nordkinn

North Cape

Lapland

L. Inari

Finland

G. of Finland

Chudskoye

L. Onega

Onega

Dvina

Low Dvina

Pripyat (Pripet) Marshes

Dnepr (Dnieper)

Bug

Ukraine

Danube

Dnestr (Dniester)

Prut

Carpathians

Transylvanian Alps

Mureş

Danube

Wallachia

Moldava

Balkans

Rhodope

Balkan Peninsula

Aegean Sea

Crete

Vesterålen

Lofoten

Scandinavia

Kjølen

Ume

Indals

Torne

Kebnekaise 2123

G. of Bothnia

Gotland

L. Riga

Niemen

BALTIC SEA

Wisła (Vistula)

Odra (Oder)

North European Plain

Plain of Hungary

Tisza

Tatra 2655

Sudetes

Moravia

Moravian Heights

Bohemian For.

Danube

Dinaric Alps

Morava

Pindus 2911

Gran Sasso 2914

ADRIATIC SEA

Str. of Otranto

Ionian Is.

Morea

C. Matapan 5121

Ionian Sea

Galdhøpiggen 2469

Vänern

Vättern

Kattegat

Skagerrak

Jutland

Elbe

Harz 1142

Erz Geb.

Weser

Rhine

Heligoland

Netherlands

Ardennes

Eifel

Taunus

Westerwald

Vosges

Black For.

Alps

Mt. Blanc 4807

Jura

Po

Apennines

Tiber

Ligurian Sea

Corsica

Sardinia

Tyrrhenian Sea

C. Blanco

Vesuvius 1277

Etna 3263

Sicily

Str. of Messina

Str. of Bonifacio

Malta

3734

NORWEGIAN SEA

Iceland
Hekla 1447
Vatnajökull 2119

Arctic Circle

Faroe Is.

Shetland Is.

Orkney Is.

Fisher Bank

Rockall

Hebrides

Ben Nevis 1343

Great Britain

Snowdon 1085

British Isles

Ireland

Irish Sea

Dogger Bank

NORTH SEA

Weser

Rhine

Seine

Loire

Gironde

Garonne

Brittany

Central Massif
Mt. Dore 1886

Rhône

Cévennes

Pyrenees
Pico de Nethou 3404

ATLANTIC OCEAN

Valentia I.

C. Clear

Land's End

English Channel

Bay of Biscay

4861

C. Finisterre

Douro

Cantabrian Mts.

Old Castile

New Castile

Iberian Peninsula

Sierra Morena

Guadalquivir

Andalusia

Sierra Nevada 3478

C. da Roca

Tagus

C. St. Vincent

C. Trafalgar

C. Spartel

Str. of Gibraltar

Maritime Atlas

Plateau of the Shotts

Er Rif

MEDITERRANEAN SEA

Balearic Is.

m 4000 2000 1000 400 200 0

0 200 2000 4000

West from Greenwich 0 East from Greenwich

Projection: Bonne

1 : 40 000 000

400   0   400   800   1200   1600 km

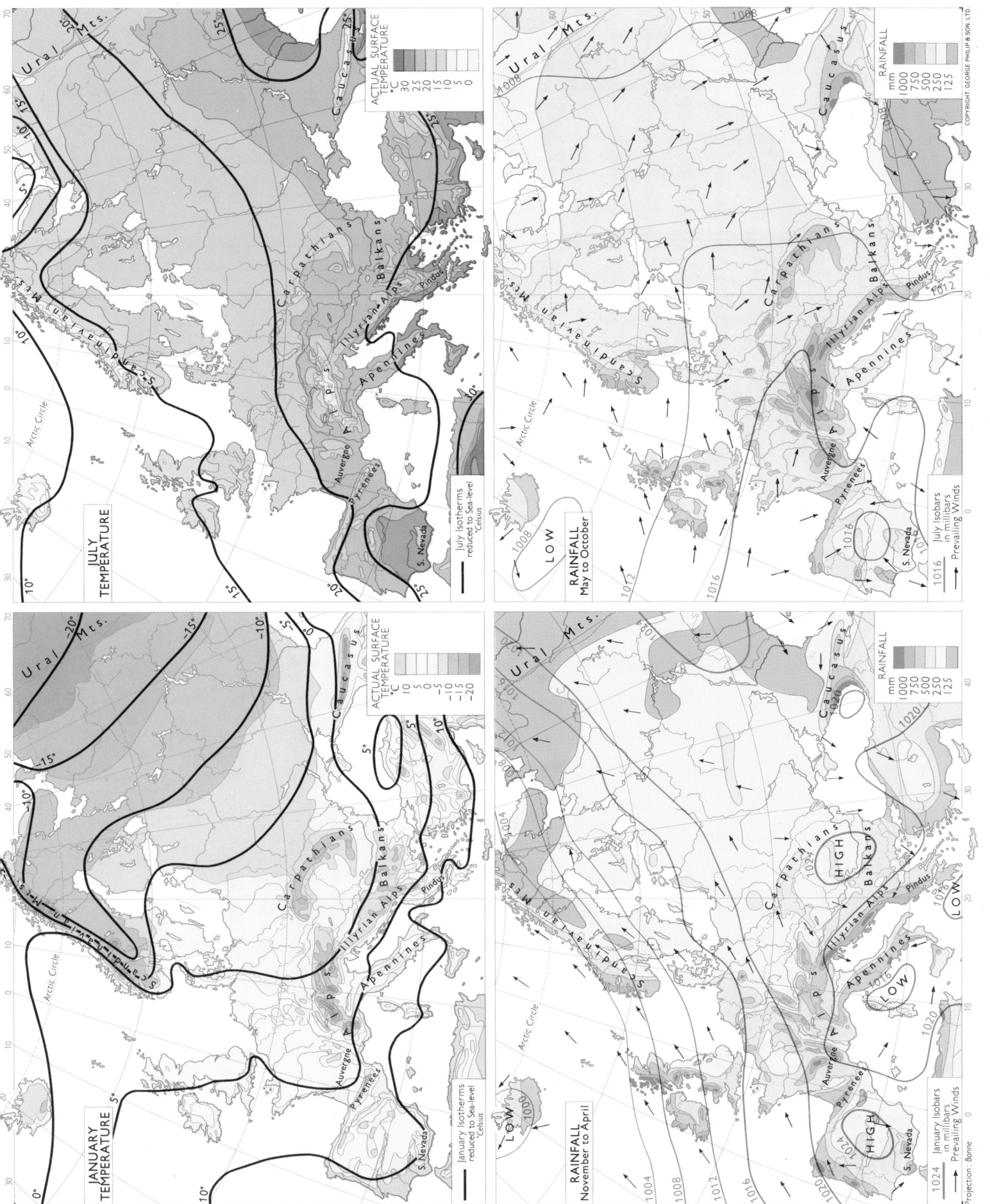

ACTUAL SURFACE TEMPERATURE
°C
30
25
20
15
10
5
0

JULY TEMPERATURE

July Isotherms reduced to Sea-level °Celsius

RAINFALL
mm
1000
750
500
250
125

RAINFALL May to October

LOW

July Isobars in millibars
Prevailing Winds

ACTUAL SURFACE TEMPERATURE
°C
10
5
0
-5
-10
-15
-20

JANUARY TEMPERATURE

January Isotherms reduced to Sea-level °Celsius

RAINFALL
mm
1000
750
500
250
125

RAINFALL November to April

HIGH
LOW

January Isobars in millibars
Prevailing Winds

Projection : Bonne

Ural Mts.
Caucasus
Carpathians
Balkans
Illyrian Alps
Pindus
Apennines
Alps
Auvergne
Pyrenees
S. Nevada
Scandinavian Mts.
Arctic Circle

1:35 000 000

400   0   400   800   1200 km

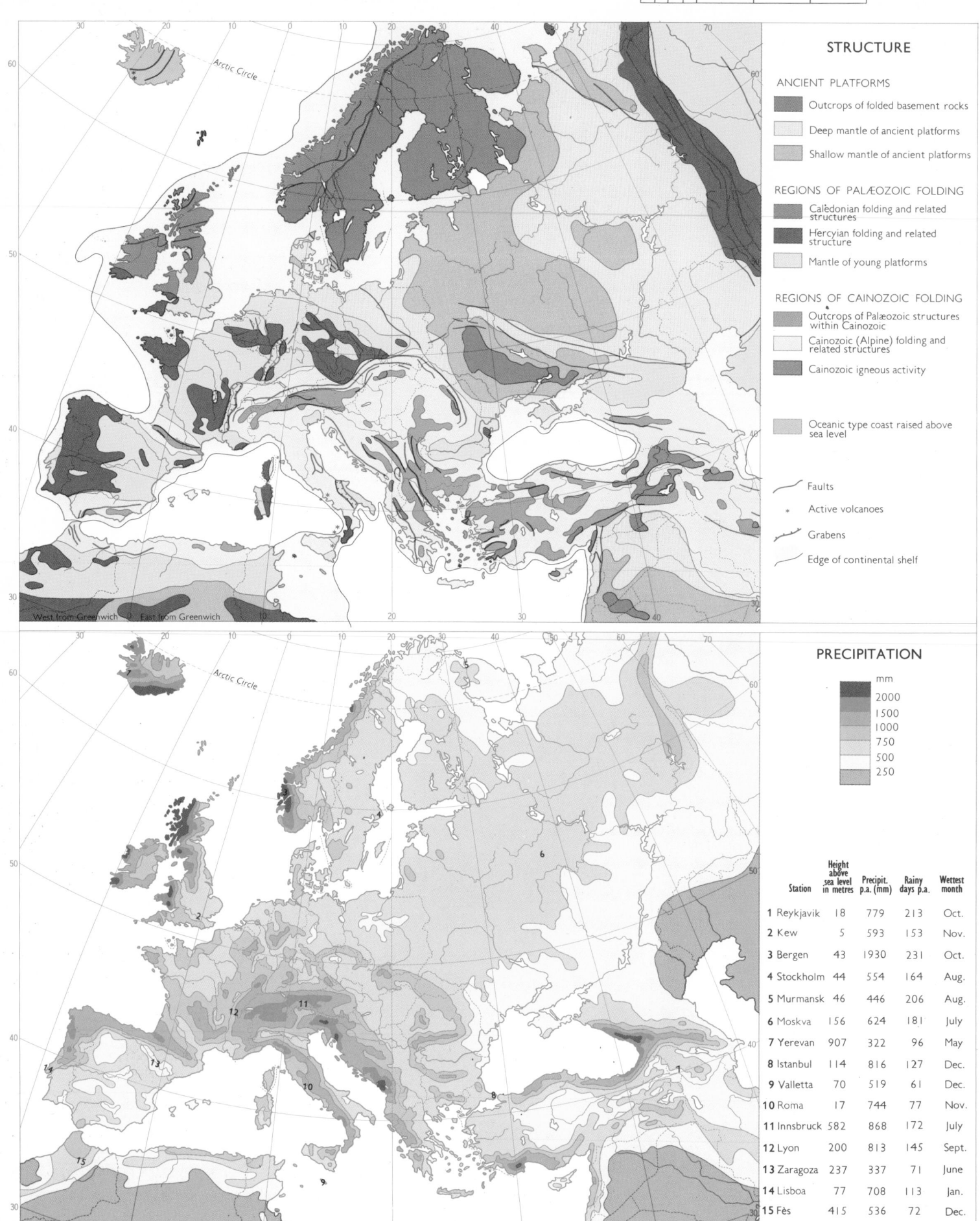

STRUCTURE

ANCIENT PLATFORMS

Outcrops of folded basement rocks

Deep mantle of ancient platforms

Shallow mantle of ancient platforms

REGIONS OF PALÆOZOIC FOLDING

Calèdonian folding and related structures

Hercyian folding and related structure

Mantle of young platforms

REGIONS OF CAINOZOIC FOLDING

Outcrops of Palæozoic structures within Cainozoic

Cainozoic (Alpine) folding and related structures

Cainozoic igneous activity

Oceanic type coast raised above sea level

Faults

＊ Active volcanoes

Grabens

Edge of continental shelf

Arctic Circle

West from Greenwich   East from Greenwich

PRECIPITATION

mm
2000
1500
1000
750
500
250

Arctic Circle

West from Greenwich   East from Greenwich

Projection: Bonne

Station	Height above sea level in metres	Precipit. p.a. (mm)	Rainy days p.a.	Wettest month
1 Reykjavik	18	779	213	Oct.
2 Kew	5	593	153	Nov.
3 Bergen	43	1930	231	Oct.
4 Stockholm	44	554	164	Aug.
5 Murmansk	46	446	206	Aug.
6 Moskva	156	624	181	July
7 Yerevan	907	322	96	May
8 Istanbul	114	816	127	Dec.
9 Valletta	70	519	61	Dec.
10 Roma	17	744	77	Nov.
11 Innsbruck	582	868	172	July
12 Lyon	200	813	145	Sept.
13 Zaragoza	237	337	71	June
14 Lisboa	77	708	113	Jan.
15 Fès	415	536	72	Dec.

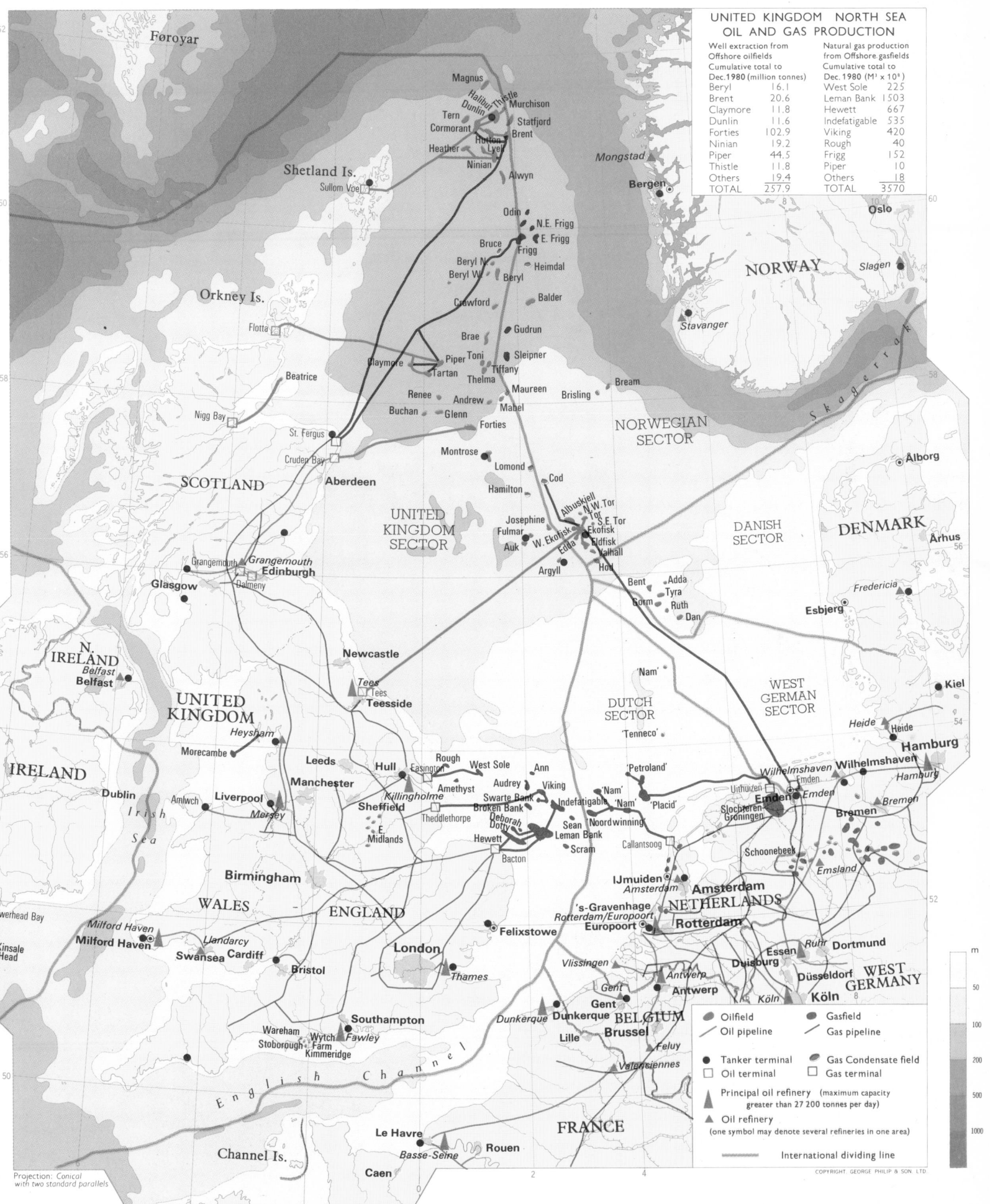

1:6 000 000

50 0 50 100 150 200 250 km

UNITED KINGDOM NORTH SEA OIL AND GAS PRODUCTION	
Well extraction from Offshore oilfields Cumulative total to Dec.1980 (million tonnes)	Natural gas production from Offshore gasfields Cumulative total to Dec.1980 ($M^3 \times 10^8$)
Beryl 16.1	West Sole 225
Brent 20.6	Leman Bank 1503
Claymore 11.8	Hewett 667
Dunlin 11.6	Indefatigable 535
Forties 102.9	Viking 420
Ninian 19.2	Rough 40
Piper 44.5	Frigg 152
Thistle 11.8	Piper 10
Others 19.4	Others 18
TOTAL 257.9	TOTAL 3570

Føroyar

Magnus
Halibut Thistle Murchison
Dunlin
Tern
Cormorant Statfjord
Heather Hutton Brent
Lyell
Ninian
Alwyn

Shetland Is.
Sullom Voe

Mongstad
Bergen
Oslo

Odin
N.E. Frigg
E. Frigg
Bruce
Frigg
Beryl N. Heimdal
Beryl W. Beryl
Balder
Crawford

Orkney Is.
Flotta

NORWAY
Slagen

Gudrun
Brae
Sleipner
Piper Toni
Claymore Tiffany
Tartan Thelma
Thelma Maureen
Renee Andrew Brisling
Buchan Mabel Bream
Glenn
Forties

Beatrice

Nigg Bay
St. Fergus
Cruden Bay
SCOTLAND
Aberdeen

Montrose
Lomond
Hamilton Cod
Albuskjell
N.W.Tor
Tor
Josephine S.E.Tor
Fulmar Ekofisk
W.Ekofisk Eldfisk
Auk Edda Valhall
Argyll Hod

NORWEGIAN
SECTOR

Skagerrak

Ålborg

UNITED
KINGDOM
SECTOR

DANISH
SECTOR
DENMARK
Århus

Grangemouth Grangemouth
Edinburgh
Glasgow Dalmeny

Bent Adda
Tyra
Gorm Ruth
Dan

Frederica

Esbjerg

N.
IRELAND
Belfast
Belfast

Newcastle

WEST
GERMAN
SECTOR

Kiel

Tees
Tees
Teesside

'Nam'

Heide
Heide

UNITED
KINGDOM

DUTCH
SECTOR

Hamburg
Hamburg

IRELAND

Heysham

'Tenneco'

Morecambe

Leeds

Rough

Dublin
Amlwch
Liverpool
Mersey

Manchester

Hull
Easington
West Sole
Amethyst
Killingholme Audrey Ann
Swarte Bank Viking
Theddlethorpe Broken Bank
Deborah
Sheffield Dotty
E. Hewett
Midlands Bacton

'Petroland'

Wilhelmshaven Wilhelmshaven
Emden
Uithuizen Emden Emden
'Nam' Slochteren
'Nam' 'Placid' Groningen Bremen Bremen
Sean Noordwinning
Leman Bank
Scram
Callantsoog Schoonebeek

Emsland

Powerhead Bay

Birmingham

WALES ENGLAND

Felixstowe

IJmuiden
Amsterdam
Amsterdam
's-Gravenhage NETHERLANDS
Rotterdam/Europoort
Europoort Rotterdam

Essen Ruhr Dortmund
Duisburg
Düsseldorf WEST
GERMANY
Köln

Kinsale
Head

Milford Haven
Milford Haven
Llandarcy
Swansea Cardiff

Bristol

London

Thames

Vlissingen

Antwerp
Gent Antwerp
Gent
Köln

Southampton
Wareham Fawley
Stoborough Wytch
Farm
Kimmeridge

Dunkerque Dunkerque
Lille

BELGIUM
Brussel
Brussel

Feluy

Valenciennes

English Channel

Le Havre
Basse-Seine Rouen

FRANCE

Channel Is.
Caen

m
50
100
200
500
1000

⬮ Oilfield		⬮ Gasfield
╱ Oil pipeline		╱ Gas pipeline
● Tanker terminal		⬮ Gas Condensate field
▢ Oil terminal		▢ Gas terminal
▲ Principal oil refinery (maximum capacity greater than 27 200 tonnes per day)		
▲ Oil refinery (one symbol may denote several refineries in one area)		
═══ International dividing line		

Projection: Conical
with two standard parallels

COPYRIGHT. GEORGE PHILIP & SON. LTD.

1:20 000 000

200   0   200   400   600   800 km

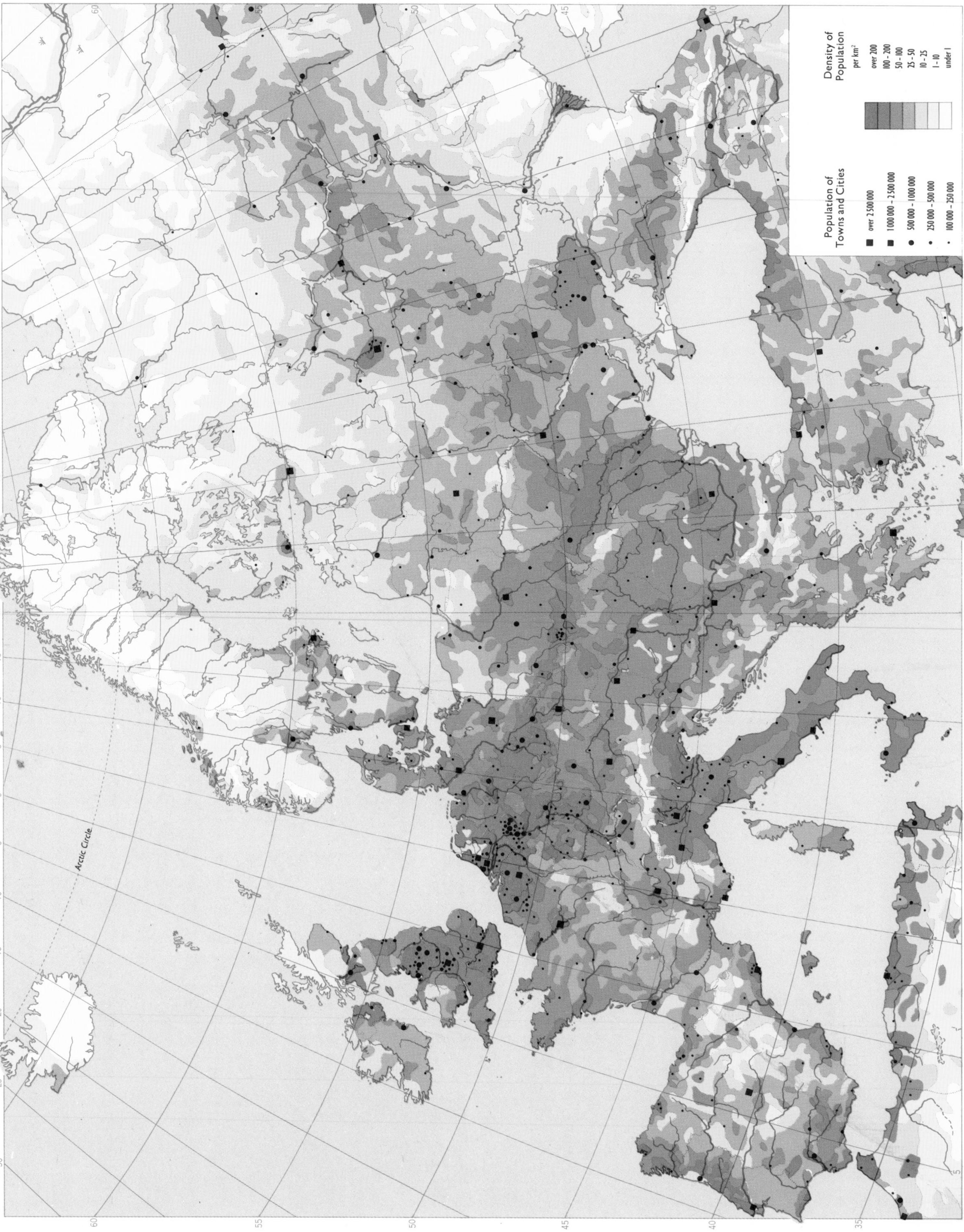

Density of
Population
per km²
over 200
100 - 200
50 - 100
25 - 50
10 - 25
1 - 10
under 1

Population of
Towns and Cities
over 2 500 000
1 000 000 - 2 500 000
500 000 - 1 000 000
250 000 - 500 000
100 000 - 250 000

Arctic Circle

COPYRIGHT GEORGE PHILIP & SON LTD

Projection: Bonne   West from Greenwich   East from Greenwich

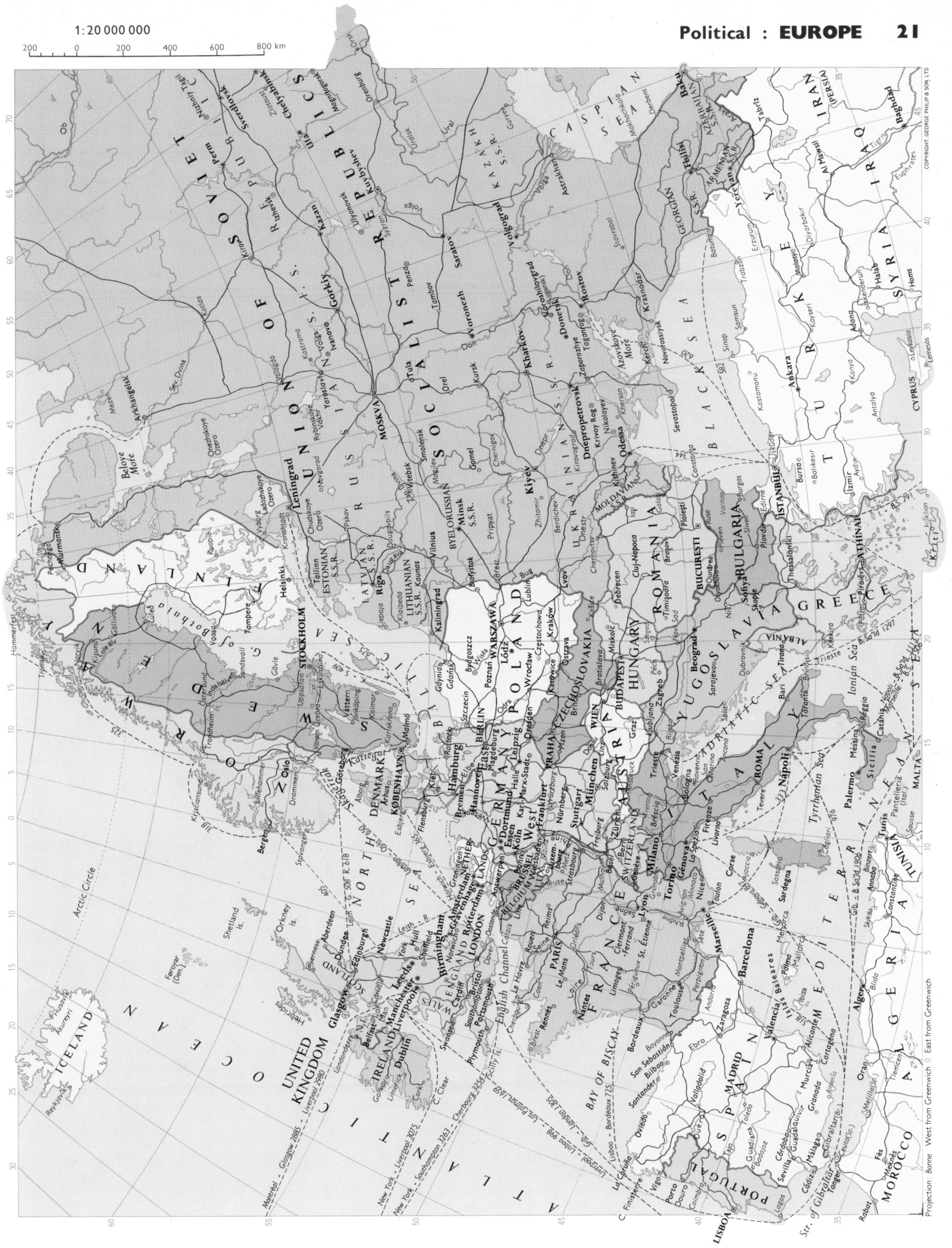

1:20 000 000

200 0 200 400 600 800 km

COPYRIGHT GEORGE PHILIP & SON LTD

ICELAND

UNITED KINGDOM

IRELAND

NORWAY

SWEDEN

FINLAND

DENMARK

GERMANY West · East

NETHERLANDS

BELGIUM

FRANCE

SWITZERLAND

AUSTRIA

ITALY

SPAIN

PORTUGAL

POLAND

CZECHOSLOVAKIA

HUNGARY

YUGOSLAVIA

ROMANIA

BULGARIA

ALBANIA

GREECE

TURKEY

CYPRUS

MALTA

MOROCCO

ALGERIA

TUNISIA

SYRIA IRAQ

IRAN (PERSIA)

UNION OF SOVIET SOCIALIST REPUBLICS

RUSSIA S.F.S.R.

ESTONIAN S.S.R.

LATVIAN S.S.R.

LITHUANIAN S.S.R.

BYELORUSSIAN S.S.R.

UKRAINIAN S.S.R.

MOLDAVIAN S.S.R.

GEORGIAN S.S.R.

ARMENIAN S.S.R.

AZERBAIJAN S.S.R.

KAZAKH S.S.R.

CASPIAN SEA

BLACK SEA

MEDITERRANEAN SEA

NORTH SEA

ATLANTIC OCEAN

Arctic Circle

Projection : Bonne   West from Greenwich 0 East from Greenwich

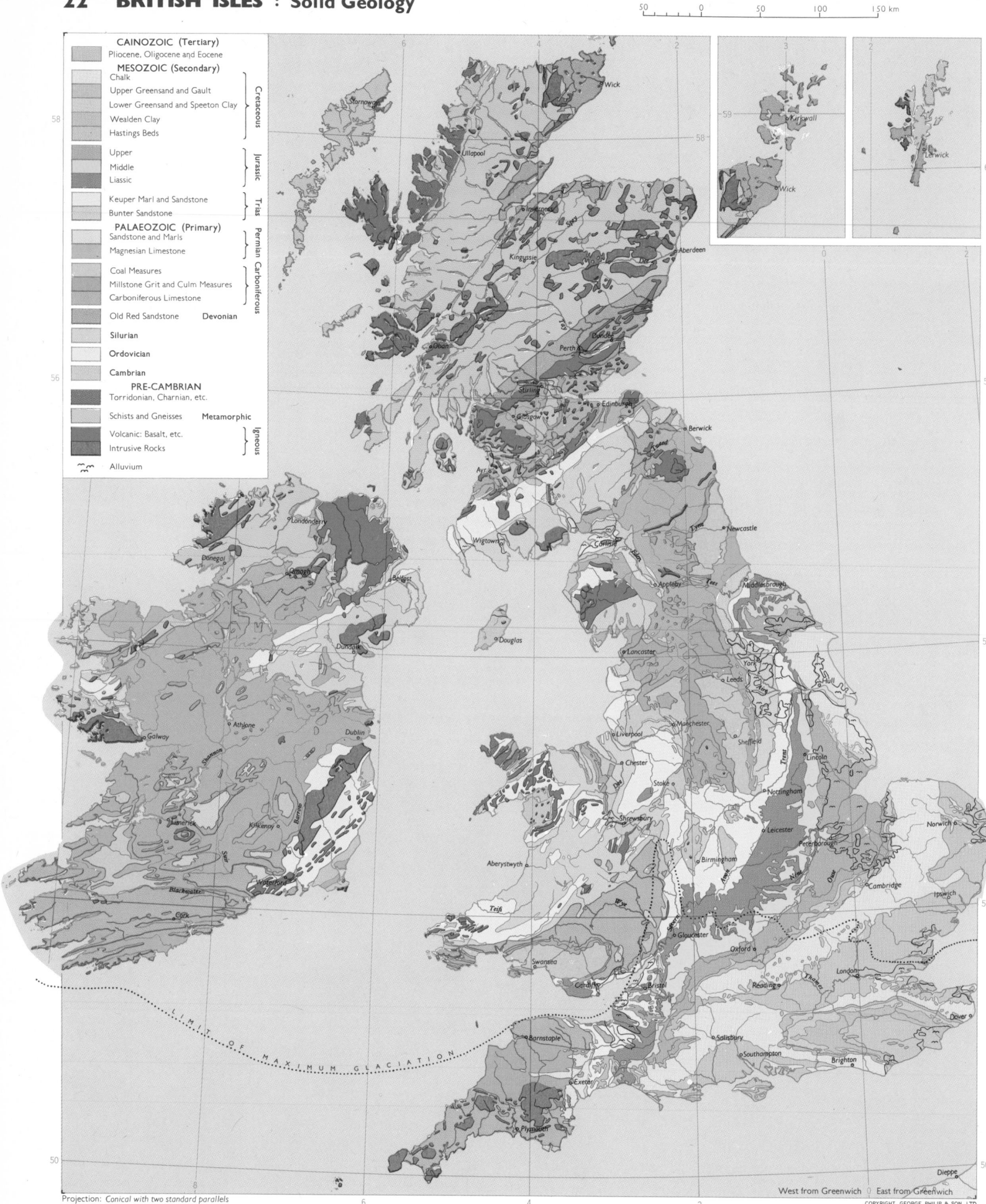

1 : 4 000 000

50   0   50   100   150 km

CAINOZOIC (Tertiary)
Pliocene, Oligocene and Eocene

MESOZOIC (Secondary)
Chalk

Cretaceous
Upper Greensand and Gault
Lower Greensand and Speeton Clay
Wealden Clay
Hastings Beds

Jurassic
Upper
Middle
Liassic

Trias
Keuper Marl and Sandstone
Bunter Sandstone

PALAEOZOIC (Primary)

Permian
Sandstone and Marls
Magnesian Limestone

Carboniferous
Coal Measures
Millstone Grit and Culm Measures
Carboniferous Limestone

Devonian
Old Red Sandstone

Silurian

Ordovician

Cambrian

PRE-CAMBRIAN
Torridonian, Charnian, etc.

Metamorphic
Schists and Gneisses

Igneous
Volcanic: Basalt, etc.
Intrusive Rocks

Alluvium

LIMIT OF MAXIMUM GLACIATION

Projection: Conical with two standard parallels

West from Greenwich 0 East from Greenwich

1 : 4 000 000

50   0   50   100   150 km

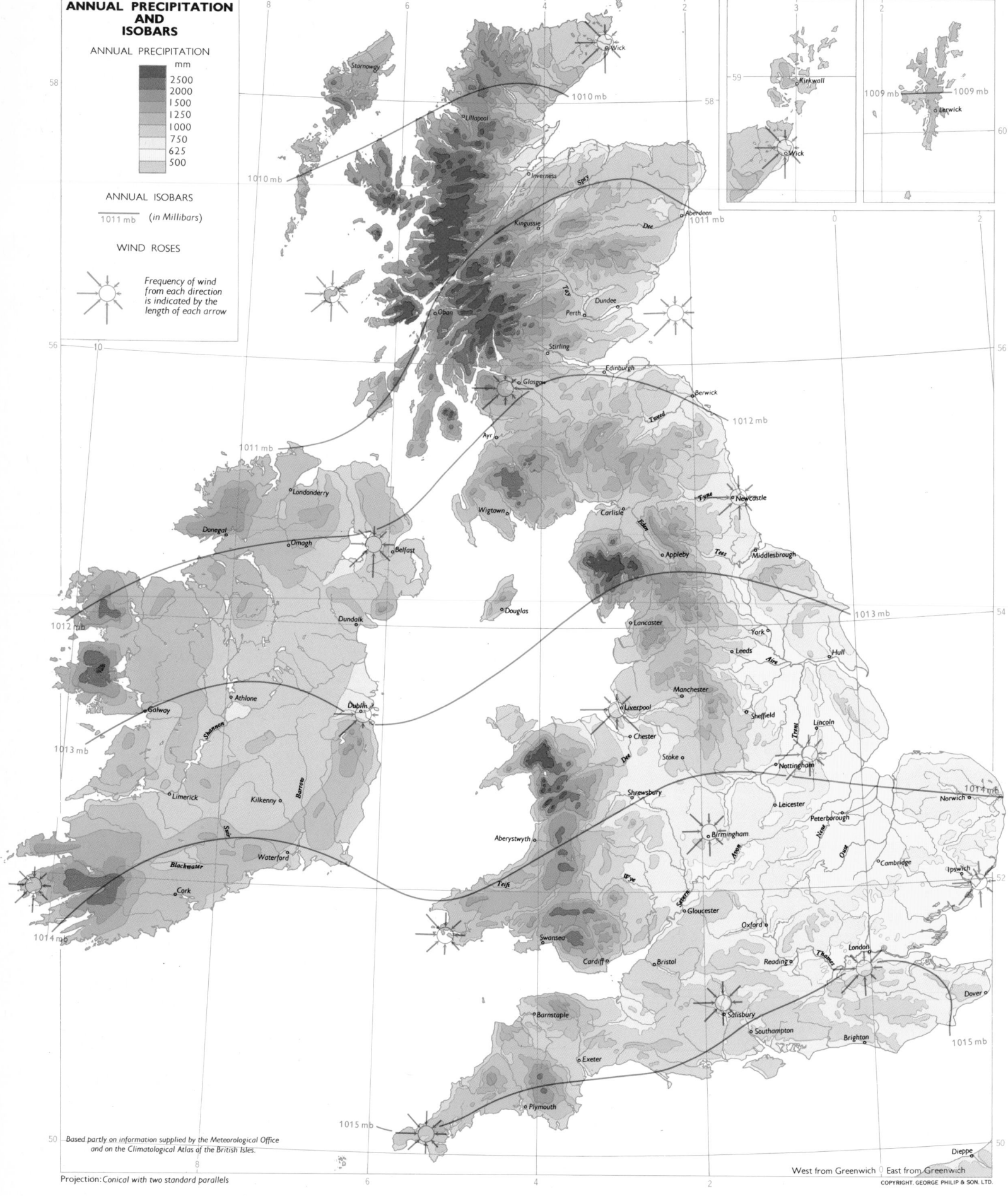

ANNUAL PRECIPITATION
AND
ISOBARS

ANNUAL PRECIPITATION

mm
2500
2000
1500
1250
1000
750
625
500

ANNUAL ISOBARS

1011 mb   (in Millibars)

WIND ROSES

Frequency of wind
from each direction
is indicated by the
length of each arrow

Based partly on information supplied by the Meteorological Office
and on the Climatological Atlas of the British Isles.

Projection: Conical with two standard parallels

West from Greenwich   East from Greenwich

COPYRIGHT. GEORGE PHILIP & SON, LTD.

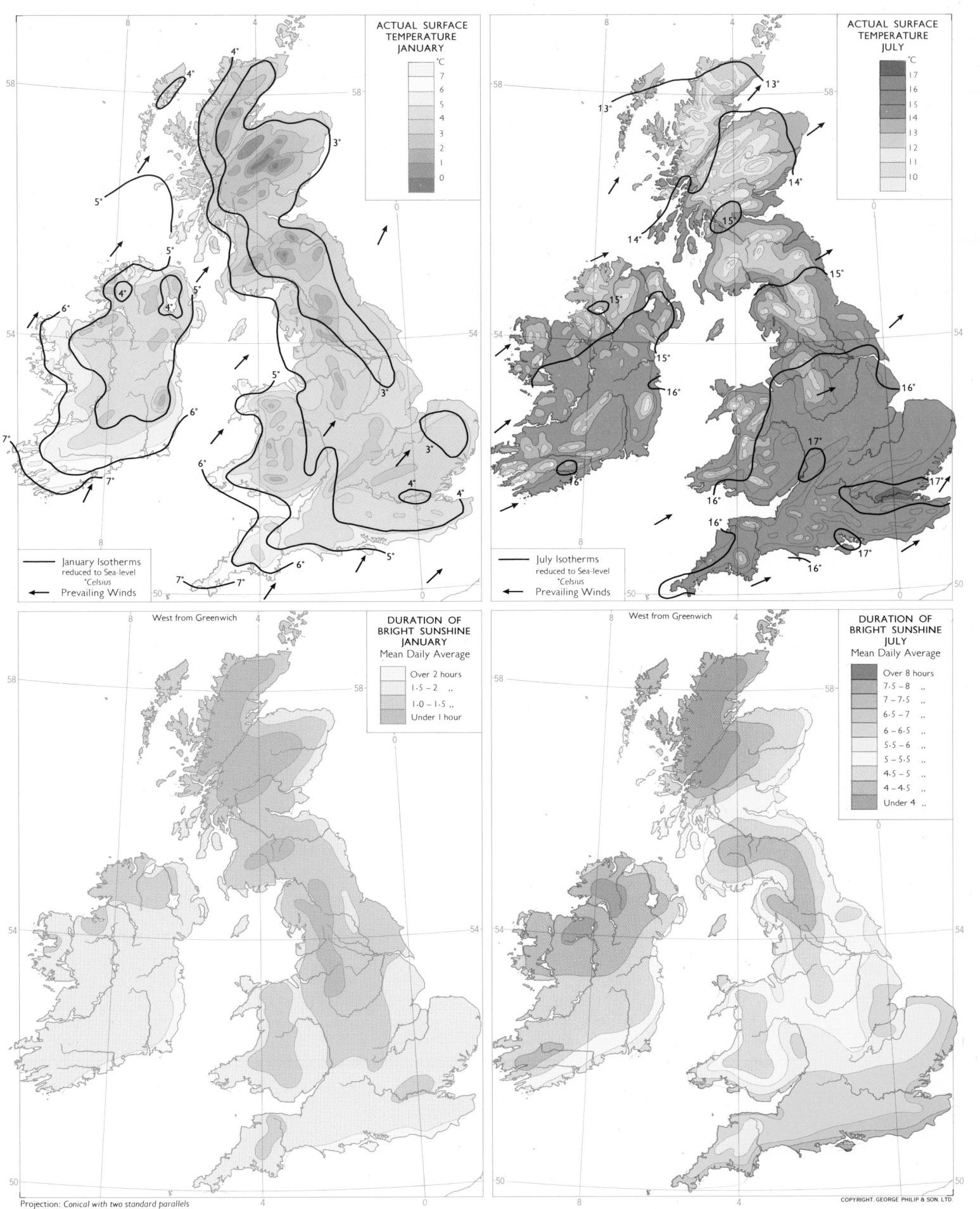

1:8 500 000

50 0 50 100 150 200 250 300 km

ACTUAL SURFACE
TEMPERATURE
JANUARY

°C
7
6
5
4
3
2
1
0

— January Isotherms
reduced to Sea-level
°Celsius
← Prevailing Winds

ACTUAL SURFACE
TEMPERATURE
JULY

°C
17
16
15
14
13
12
11
10

— July Isotherms
reduced to Sea-level
°Celsius
← Prevailing Winds

West from Greenwich

DURATION OF
BRIGHT SUNSHINE
JANUARY
Mean Daily Average

Over 2 hours
1·5 – 2 „
1·0 – 1·5 „
Under 1 hour

West from Greenwich

DURATION OF
BRIGHT SUNSHINE
JULY
Mean Daily Average

Over 8 hours
7·5 – 8 „
7 – 7·5 „
6·5 – 7 „
6 – 6·5 „
5·5 – 6 „
5 – 5·5 „
4·5 – 5 „
4 – 4·5 „
Under 4 „

Projection: *Conical with two standard parallels*

COPYRIGHT. GEORGE PHILIP & SON. LTD.

1 : 4 000 000

50   0   50   100   150 km

Projection : Conical with two standard parallels

West from Greenwich   East from Greenwich

COPYRIGHT. GEORGE PHILIP & SON. LTD.

ATLANTIC OCEAN

SCOTLAND

SUTHERLAND

CAITHNESS

Thurso

Wick

Lairg

Golspie

ROSS AND CROMARTY

Ullapool

Invergordon

Dingwall

NAIRN

Inverness

MORAY

Elgin

Lossiemouth

Fraserburgh

Banff

BANFF

Peterhead

ABERDEEN

Aberdeen

Kingussie

Ballater

Balmoral

Stonehaven

KINCARDINE

INVERNESS

Fort William

Blair Atholl

ANGUS

Forfar

Montrose

Arbroath

PERTH

Crieff

Perth

Dundee

FIFE

St. Andrews

Stirling

Kinross

Cupar

CL.-Clackmannan

KIN.-Kinross

W. Loth-West Lothian

STIRLING

Falkirk

Alloa

Kirkcaldy

Leven

Dunfermline

Forth

Dunbar

Helensburgh

Dumbarton

Edinburgh

Leith

E. LOTHIAN

Haddington

Berwick-on-Tweed

Greenock

Renfrew

Paisley

Glasgow

MIDLOTHIAN

Duns

BERWICK

Galashiels

Rothesay

Kilmarnock

Hamilton

Motherwell

PEEBLES

Kelso

Jedburgh

Alnwick

Saltcoats

Irvine

Prestwick

LANARK

Peebles

SELKIRK

Moffat

Hawick

ROXBURGH

NORTHUMBERLAND

Arran

Ayr

AYR

Sanquhar

DUMFRIES

Dumfries

Newcastle

Tynemouth

South Shields

Campbeltown

Malin Hd.

Portrush

Coleraine

Londonderry

LONDONDERRY

ANTRIM

Ballymena

Larne

WIGTOWN

Wigtown

KIRKCUDBRIGHT

Kirkcudbright

Carlisle

Gateshead

Sunderland

Durham

DURHAM

Hartlepool

Stockton

TEESSIDE

Middlesbrough

Whitby

DONEGAL

Letterkenny

Lifford

NORTHERN IRELAND

TYRONE

Omagh

ULSTER

Antrim

L. Neagh

Belfast

Bangor

Stranraer

Mull of Galloway

St. Bee's Hd.

CUMBERLAND

Whitehaven

Appleby

WESTMORLAND

Kendal

Darlington

NORTH RIDING

Northallerton

Scarborough

Donegal

Donegal Bay

Ballyshannon

SLIGO

Sligo

FERMANAGH

Enniskillen

Clones

LEITRIM

Lisburn

DOWN

Armagh

ARMAGH

Downpatrick

Newry

Dundrum

Windermere

ISLE OF MAN

Douglas

Barrow

Lancaster

YORKSHIRE

Ripon

York

Flamborough Hd.

Erris Hd.

Killala Bay

Ballina

Leitrim

MONAGHAN

Monaghan

CAVAN

Cavan

Dundalk

Greenore

Carlingford

Morecambe Bay

Blackpool

LANCASHIRE

Preston

Burnley

Keighley

WEST RIDING

Leeds

Bradford

Beverley

Hull

EAST RIDING

MAYO

Castlebar

Westport

Clare

Achill

ROSCOMMON

Roscommon

Longford

LONGFORD

WESTMEATH

Mullingar

MEATH

Drogheda

Balbriggan

IRISH SEA

Blackburn

Bolton

St. Helens

Salford

Halifax

Huddersfield

Wakefield

Barnsley

Doncaster

Rotherham

Sheffield

LINDSEY

Grimsby

Spurn Hd.

CONNACHT

Connemara

GALWAY

Galway

Athenry

Corrib

Ceannanus Mor

Tullamore

IRELAND

OFFALY

Birr

LEINSTER

Slane

Navan

Dublin

DUBLIN

(BAILE ATHA CLIATH)

Dún Laoghaire

Bray

Holyhead

ANGLESEY

Liverpool

Birkenhead

Manchester

Stockport

Macclesfield

DERBY

Chesterfield

Lincoln

LINCOLN

Boston

The Wash

Galway Bay

Liscannor

CLARE

Ennis

Nenagh

Thurles

KILDARE

LAOIS

Kilkenny

Carlow

CARLOW

Arklow

WICKLOW

Wicklow

Rhyl

Flint

Chester

Crewe

CHESHIRE

Stoke-on-Trent

Matlock

Mansfield

NOTTS

Nottingham

KESTEVEN

Grantham

Kings Lynn

NORFOLK

Norwich

Gt. Yarmouth

Lowestoft

Loop Hd.

Kilrush

Listowel

LIMERICK

Limerick

TIPPERARY

Tipperary

Carrick-on-Suir

Clonmel

KILKENNY

Enniscorthy

New Ross

WEXFORD

Wexford

Rosslare

Caernarvon Bay

Caernarvon

DENBIGH

Denbigh

Wrexham

Shrewsbury

STAFFORD

Stafford

Wolverhampton

Walsall

Burton-on-Trent

DERBY

Derby

LEICESTER

Leicester

Oakham

RUTLAND

Peterborough

HUNTS

Huntingdon

CAMBS

Cambridge

SUFFOLK

Bury St. Edmunds

EAST

Ipswich

Shannon

Rath Luire

Tralee

KERRY

Killarney

Mallow

Fermoy

CORK

Cork

Cobh

Cork Harbour

MERIONETH

Dolgelley

MONTGOMERY

Welshpool

Montgomery

Kidderminster

WORCESTER

Worcester

WARWICK

Warwick

Coventry

Rugby

Leamington

Stratford-on-Avon

NORTHAMPTON

Northampton

Wellingborough

BEDFORD

Bedford

ISLE OF ELY

WEST

MUNSTER

Cardigan Bay

Aberystwyth

CARDIGAN

Cardigan

RADNOR

Presteign

Llandrindod Wells

HEREFORD

Hereford

Buckingham

BUCKS

Luton

HERTFORD

St. Albans

Watford

ESSEX

Colchester

Harwich

The Naze

Cahirciveen

Bandon

Kinsale

Youghal

Dungarvan

WATERFORD

Waterford

Carnsore Pt.

St. George's Channel

Fishguard

St. David's Hd.

PEMBROKE

Pembroke

Haverfordwest

CARMARTHEN

Carmarthen

Llanelly

Swansea

Port Talbot

GLAMORGAN

Rhondda

Merthyr Tydfil

BRECKNOCK

Brecon

MONMOUTH

Monmouth

Newport

GLOUCESTER

Cheltenham

Gloucester

OXFORD

Oxford

Aylesbury

Slough

Windsor

Reading

LONDON

SURREY

Kingston

Chatham

Gillingham

Maidstone

Margate

Canterbury

KENT

Castletown Bere

C. Clear

Blarney

Milford Haven

Bristol Channel

Lundy

Ilfracombe

Hartland Point

Barnstaple

Bude

Weston-super-Mare

Wells

SOMERSET

Taunton

Yeovil

DEVON

Exeter

Dorchester

Bristol

Bath

Trowbridge

WILTS

Swindon

BERKS

Aldershot

Guildford

Reigate

Ashford

Dover

Folkestone

Salisbury

Winchester

HANTS

Southampton

Chichester

SUSSEX

WEST

EAST

Lewes

Hastings

Eastbourne

Brighton

Worthing

Newhaven

CORNWALL

St. Austell

Devonport

Plymouth

Truro

Camborne

Penzance

Falmouth

Land's End

Lizard

Isles of Scilly

Torquay

Start Pt.

DORSET

Poole

Bournemouth

Weymouth

Newport

Isle of Wight

Portsmouth

Axminster

ENGLISH CHANNEL

NORTH SEA

Dieppe

OUTER HEBRIDES

Lewis

Stornoway

Harris

North Uist

Benbecula

South Uist

Barra

North Minch

INNER HEBRIDES

Skye

Portree

Rhum

Eigg

Kyle of Lochalsh

Mallaig

Coll

Tiree

Staffa

Iona

Mull

Oban

ARGYLL

Colonsay

Lochgilphead

Firth of Lorn

Ballachulish

Jura

BUTE

Islay

KINTYRE

North Channel

Firth of Clyde

Pentland Firth

Moray Firth

Solway Firth

Tory I.

Aran I.

Bundoran

Boyle

Athlone

Tory I.

Orkney Is. inset:

ORKNEY

Westray

N. Ronaldsay

Sanday

Stronsay

Mainland

Kirkwall

Hoy

South Ronaldsay

Thurso

Wick

CAITHNESS

Shetland Is. inset:

Shetland Is.

Unst

Yell

Mainland

ZETLAND

Lerwick

Foula

Fair I.

1 : 4 000 000

50   0   50   100   150 km

The DISTRICTS of Northern Ireland have been numbered and can be identified by reference to this table.

1	Londonderry	14	Craigavon
2	Limavady	15	Armagh
3	Coleraine	16	Newry & Mourne
4	Ballymoney	17	Banbridge
5	Moyle	18	Down
6	Larne	19	Lisburn
7	Ballymena	20	Antrim
8	Magherafelt	21	Newtownabbey
9	Cookstown	22	Carrickfergus
10	Strabane	23	North Down
11	Omagh	24	Ards
12	Fermanagh	25	Castlereagh
13	Dungannon	26	Belfast

Orkney Is.

Shetland Is.

1 Merseyside
2 Greater Manchester
3 West Yorkshire
4 South Yorkshire
5 West Glamorgan
6 Mid Glamorgan
7 South Glamorgan

Projection: Conical with two standard parallels

West from Greenwich   0   East from Greenwich

COPYRIGHT. GEORGE PHILIP & SON. LTD.

1:1 000 000

10   0   10   20   30   40 km

West from Greenwich   East from Greenwich

Based upon the Ordnance Survey Map with the permission
of the Controller of Her Majesty's Stationery Office.
Crown Copyright Reserved.

Motorways
Motorways under construction

COPYRIGHT. GEORGE PHILIP & SON. LTD.

1:1 000 000

10   0   10   20   30   40 km

SCILLY ISLES
on same scale

Isles of Scilly

Based upon the Ordnance Survey Map with the permission of the Controller of Her Majesty's Stationery Office. Crown Copyright Reserved.

West from Greenwich

Projection : Conical with two standard parallels

m   600   400   200   100   0

m   50   m

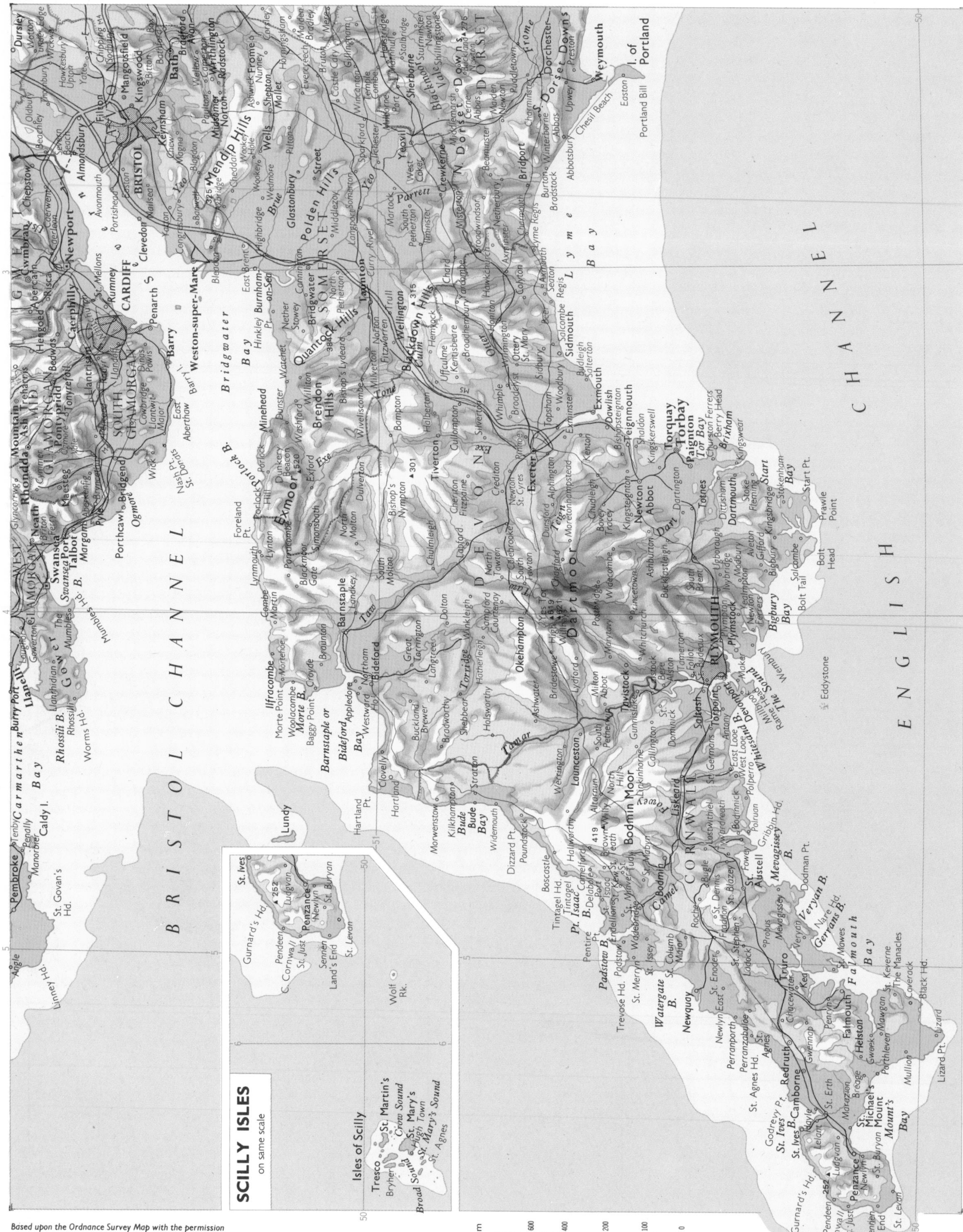

1:1 000 000

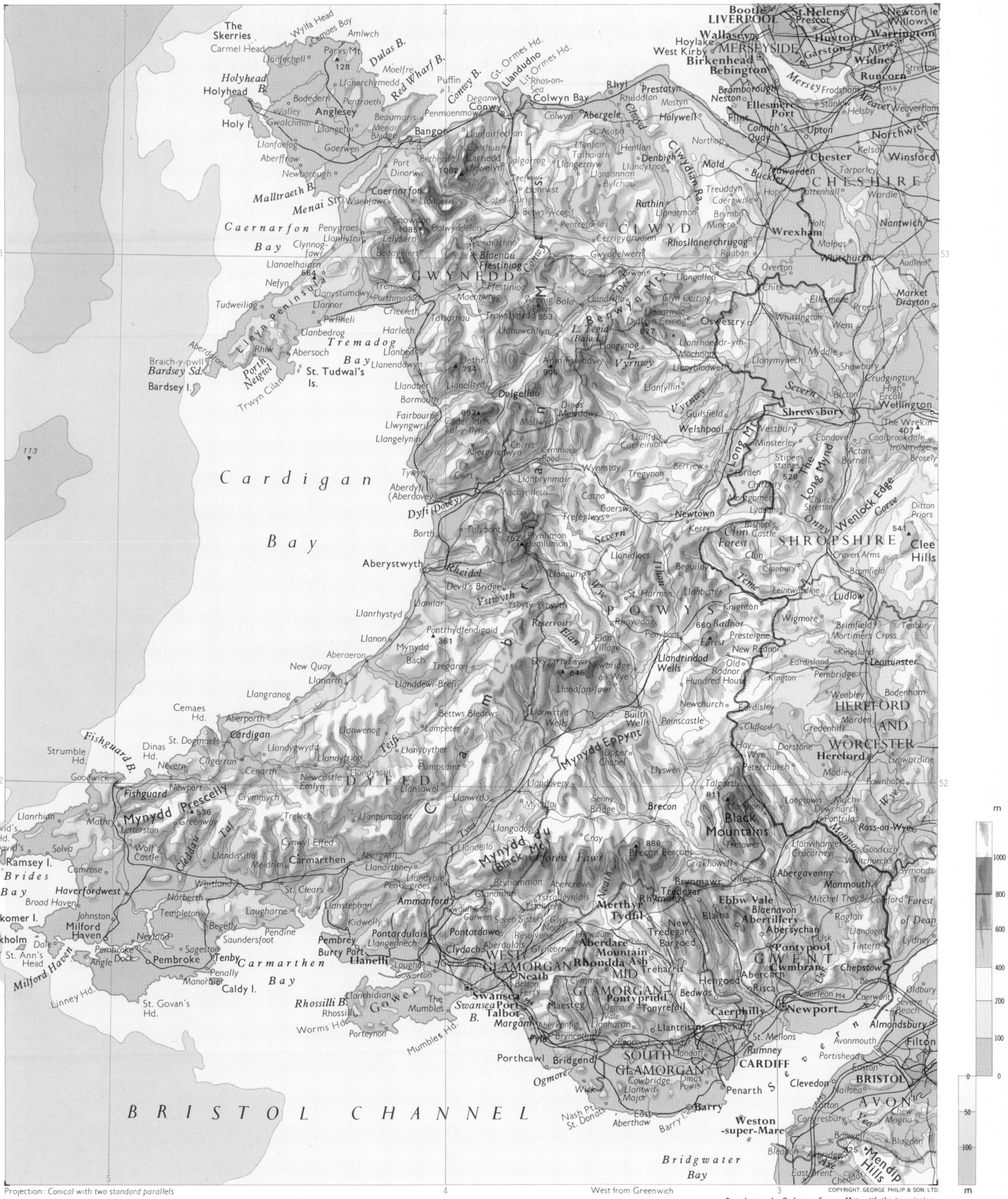

Projection: Conical with two standard parallels

West from Greenwich

Motorways
Motorways under construction

1:1 000 000

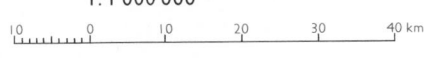

10 0 10 20 30 40 km

Continuation Northwards on same scale

N O R T H

S E A

TYNE AND WEAR

CLEVELAND

NORTH YORK MOORS

BORDERS

NORTHUMBERLAND

HADRIAN'S WALL

HUMBERSIDE

SOUTH YORKSHIRE

WEST YORKSHIRE

LINCOLNSHIRE

The Wash

NORFOLK

West from Greenwich

East from Greenwich

1:1 000 000

10   0   10   20   30   40 km

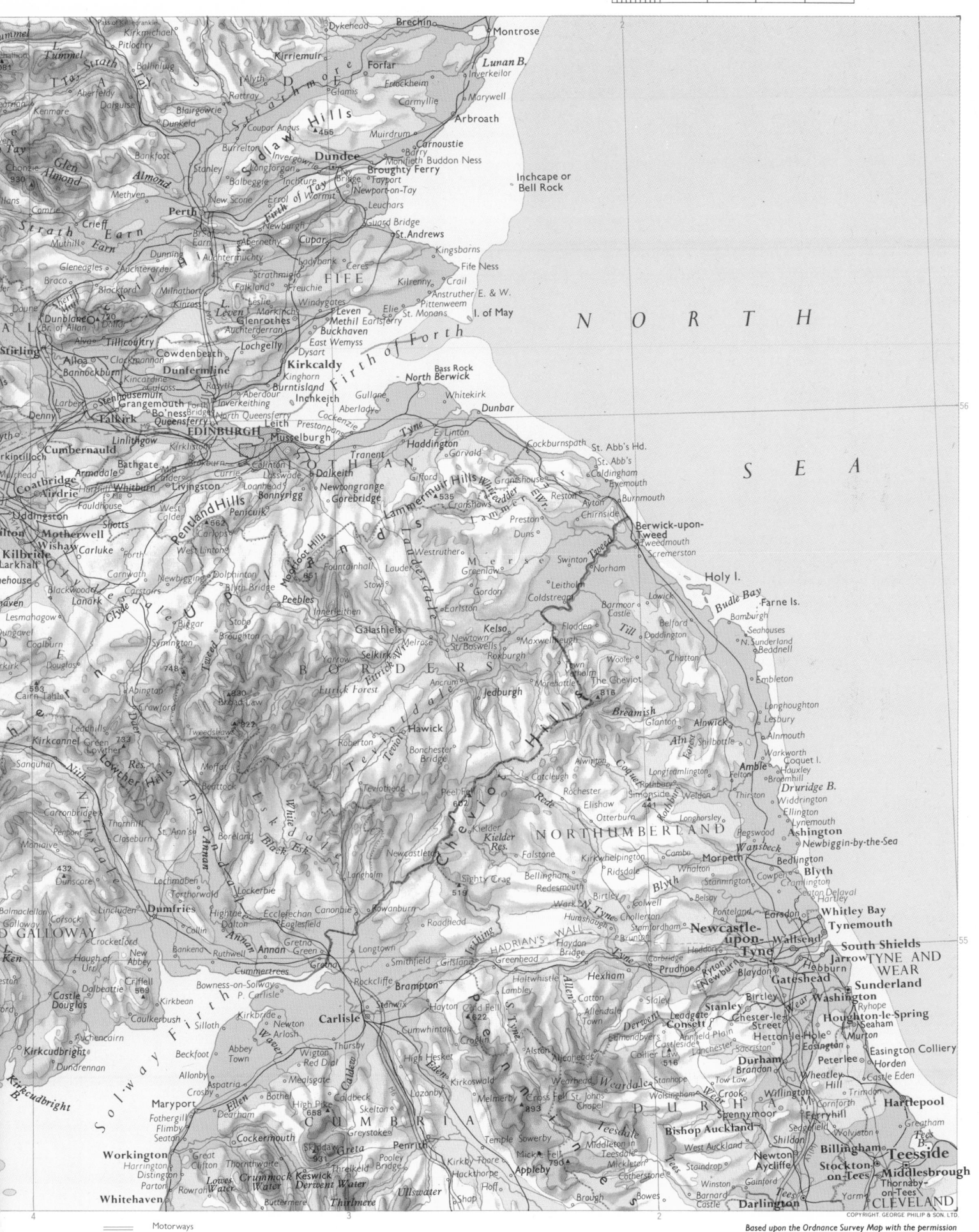

N O R T H

S E A

56

55

Motorways

Motorways under construction

COPYRIGHT GEORGE PHILIP & SON. LTD.

SHETLAND ISLANDS
on same scale

Projection : Conical with two standard parallels

37

1:1 000 000

10 0 10 20 30 40 km

ORKNEY ISLANDS on same scale

Pentland Firth

Faraid Hd.
Whiten Hd.
Durness
Heilam
Kyle of Tongue
Tongue
Loch Hope
Ben Hope 927
Borgie
Strathy Pt.
Strathy
Melvich
Portskerra
Bettyhill
Strath Halladale
Reay
Dounreay
Strathy
Dalhalvaig
Forsinain
Forsinard
Kinbrace
Strath of Kildonan
Kildonan

Holborn Hd.
Scrabster
Dunnet B.
Stroma
Dunnet Hd.
Mey
John o' Groats
Duncansby Hd.
Thurso
Dunnet
Canisbay
Duncansby
Castletown
Freswick
Sordale
Nybster
Halkirk
Keiss
Olgrinmore
Reiss
Noss Head
Watten
Wick
Staxigoe
Mybster
Wick
Achavanich
Thrumster
Braemore
Ulbster
Lybster
Latheron
Dunbeath
Berriedale
Ousdale
Ord of Caithness
Helmsdale

Sinclair's B.

Strathmore
B. Loyal 763
Loch Loyal
L.Naver
Altnaharra
B. Klibreck 961
L. nan Clar
705 Morven 628 B. Dhorain

Kinloch
More
Loch Shin
Strath Naver

Mull Hd. Papa Westray
Noup Hd.
Pierowall
Westray
Berst Ness
Rapness
Sacquoy Hd.
Wasbister
Brough Hd.
Twatt
Redland
Dounby
L. of Harray
Voy
L. of Stenness
Stromness
Graemsay
Hoy
Old Man of Hoy
Rora Hd.
Rackwick
Hoy
Hurtliness
Tor Ness
Dunnet Hd.
Mey
Canisbay

Hollandstoun
N. Ronaldsay
Dennis Hd.
N. Ronaldsay Firth
Overbister
Sanday
Start Pt.
Sanday Sound
Eday
Papa Stronsay
Rousay
Egilsay
Whitehall
Brinyan
Wyre
Stronsay
Gairsay
Lamb Hd.
Balfour
Shapinsay
Stronsay
Wide Firth
Shapinsay Sd.
Auskerry
Kirkwall
Mainland
Deer Sd.
Deerness
Orphir
Pt. of Ayre
St. Mary's
Copinsay
Scapa Flow
Rose Ness
Burray
Flotta
St. Margaret's Hope
South Ronaldsay
S. Walls
Swona
Cleat
Lyness

Pentland Firth Pentland Skerries

The North Sound
Westray Firth
Eynhallow Sd.
ORKNEY
Ward Hill 477

Lairg
Rosehall
Auchness
Oykel
Oykel Br.
Invershin
Shin
Bonar bridge
Culrain
Clashmore
Torroboll
Fleet
L. Fleet
Golspie
Embo
Dornoch
Tarbat Ness
Portmahomack

L. Brora
Brora
Brora

Dornoch Firth
Kincardine
Edderton
Kilmuir
Balintore
Fearn
B. Tharsuinn 692
Alness
Easter Ross
Kildermorie
Black Isle
Nigg
Balnapaling
Cromarty
Cromarty Firth
Balblair
Cononbridge
Dingwall
Rosemarkie
Fortrose
Nth. Kessock
Avoch
Invergordon
Evanton
Campbeltown
Alness
B. Wyvis 1045
Strathpeffer
Contin
Muir of Ord

Moray Firth

Branderburgh
Lossiemouth
Spey B.
Findochty
Portknockie
Cullen
Portsoy
Banff
Macduff
Gardenstown
Rosehearty
Troup Hd.
Kinnairds Hd.
Fraserburgh
Inverallochy
St. Combs
Rathen
Rattray Hd.
Crimond
St. Fergus
Peterhead
Boddam
Buchan Ness
Cruden Bay

Burghead
Burghead B.
Hopeman
Findhorn
Garmouth
Buckie
Spey Bay
Portgordon
Fochabers
Lhanbryde
Elgin
Kinloss
Forres
Nairn
Auldearn
Dallas
Kellas
Rothes
Keith
Craigellachie
Newmill
Aberchirder
New Pitsligo
Cuminestown
New Aberdour
Newbyth
Turriff
Buchan
Mintlaw
Longside
New Deer
Maud
Old Deer
Hatton
Fyvie
Methlick
Ellon
Newburgh

Auldearn
Littlemill
Cawdor
Ferness
Archiestown
Charlestown of Aberlour
Dufftown
Strathbogie
Huntly
Colpy
Rathienorman
Rhynie
Insch
Oldmeldrum
Formartine
Tarves
Ythan
Deveron
Fortrie
Badenscoth

Inverness
Culloden Moor
Beauly F.
Beauly
The Aird
Caledonian Canal
Dores
Craggie
Moy
Tomatin
Carrbridge
Boat of Garten
Nethy Bridge
Grantown-on-Spey
Dulnain Bridge
Aviemore
Alvie
Kincraig
Kingussie
Newtonmore
Ruthven

Glen Orrin
Muir of Ord
L. Ruthven
L. Duntelchaig
Farr
L. Ness
Dalwhinnie
Errochty
Tummel
Kinloch Rannoch
Rannoch Sta.
Loch Rannoch

Struy
Strath Glass
Milton
Lewiston
Mealfuarvonie 696
Meallfourvonie
Invermoriston
Foyers
Carn na Saobhaidhe 810
White Bridge
Monadhliath Mts.
Carn Ban 941
Carn Mor 803
Tomintoul
Carn Gorm
Carrbridge
Ladder Hills
Strathdon
Carn Mor
Don
Morven 872
Tarland
Lumphanan
Torphins
Echt
Peterculter
Cults
Aberdeen
Girdle Ness
Cove Bay

Spey
Hills of Cromdale
Strath Avon
Avon
Tomnavoulin
Delnashaug
Laggan
Cabrach
The Buck 722
Lumsden
Alford
Kemnay
Monymusk
Kintore
Ordhead
Buckieburn
Bridge of Don
Dyce
Bankhead
Balmedie
Newmachar

GRAMPIAN
Mar
Tarland
Aboyne
Banchory
Strachan
Newtonhill
Muchalls
Stonehaven

B. Avon 1171
B. MacDhui
Braemar
Braemar
Balmoral Castle
Balmoral Forest
Lochnagar 1154
Glen Muick
Ballater
Dee
Crathie
Mt. Keen 938
Glen Esk
North Esk
Clova
Rottal
Edzell
Howe of the Mearns
Fettercairn
Laurencekirk
Auchenblae
Inverbervie
Gourdon
Johnshaven
St. Cyrus

Cairngorm Mts.
Cairn Gorm 1245
1311
1295
Braemar
Braes of Angus
Glas Maol 1067
Isla
South Esk
Kirriemuir
Forfar
Glamis
Glen Shee
Kirkmichael
Pitlochry
Blair Atholl
Pass of Killiecrankie
Ballinluig
Aberfeldy
Dalguise
Dunkeld
Blairgowrie
Coupar Angus
Rattray
Alyth
Marykirk
St. Cyrus
Brechin
Montrose
Lunan B.
Inverkeilor
Friockheim
Marywell
Carmyllie
Muirdrum
Arbroath
Carnoustie
Barry
Buddon Ness
Monifieth
Broughty Ferry

Forest of Atholl
Beinn a' Ghlo 1121
Glen Tilt
Glen Garry
Garry
B. Dearg 1008
Dalnaspidal
Loch Garry
Schichallion 1081
L. Tummel
Tummel
Strath Tay
Tay
Kenmore
Loch Tay
Fortingall
B. Lawers 1214
Glen Lyon
Fearnan
Killin
Breadalbane

GRAMPIAN
HIGHLAND
MOUNTAINS
Braemar

L. Laggan
Laggan
Lochlaggan Hotel
Dalwhinnie
Creag Meagaidh 1128
Spean
Roybridge
Glen Spean
B. Alder 1148
L. Ericht
L. Treig
Glen Garry
Errochty
Blackwater Res.
Rannoch Moor
L. Laidon 98
L. Tulla 1029
B. Dorain 1074
Orchy
Breadalbane

Bankfoot

West from Greenwich

Burrelton
Sidlaw Hills 455
Dundee
Broughty Ferry

NORTH SEA

COPYRIGHT. GEORGE PHILIP & SON LTD.

Based upon the Ordnance Survey Map with the permission of the Controller of Her Majesty's Stationery Office. Crown Copyright Reserved.

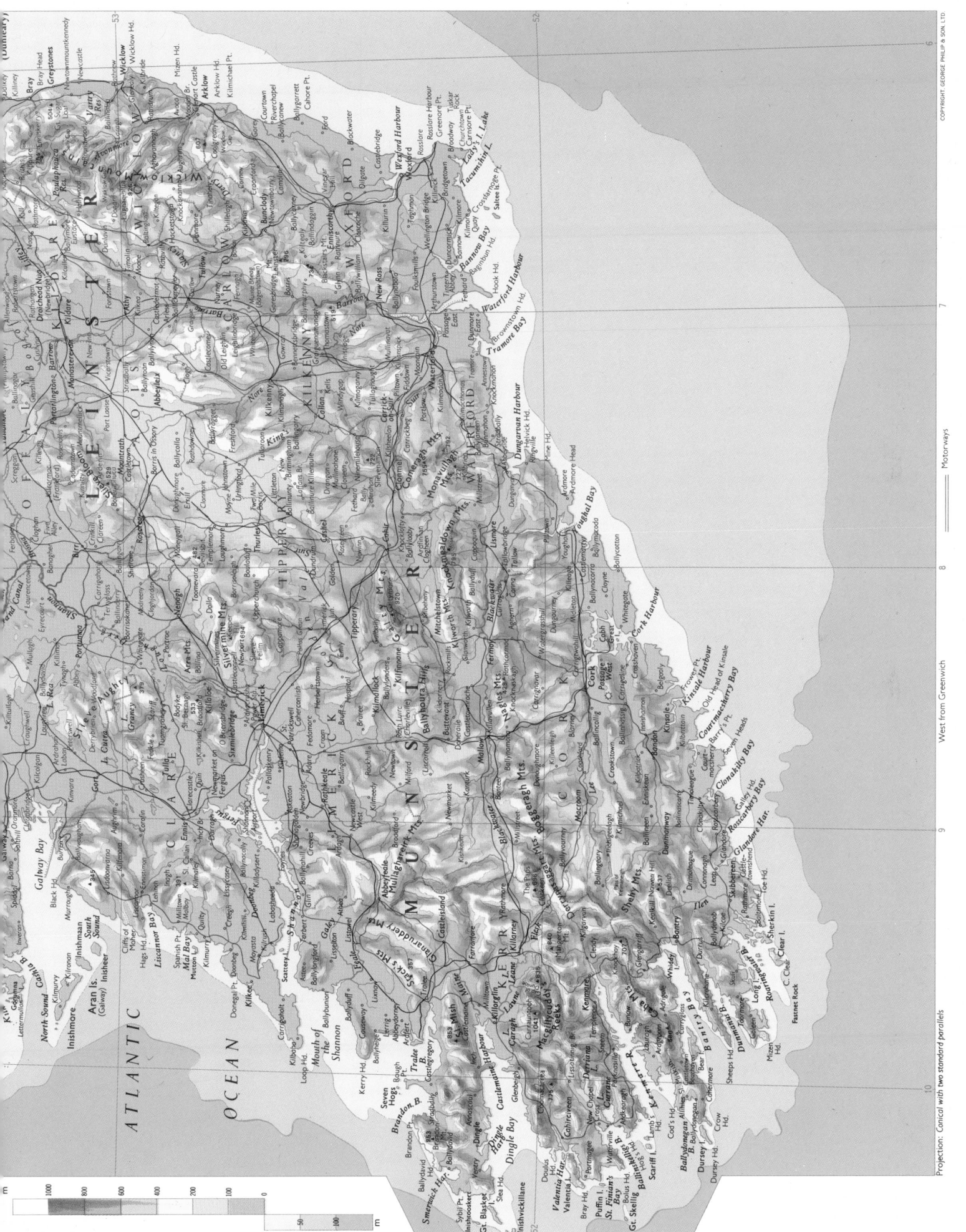

1:1 250 000

10   0   10   20   30   40   50 km

39

COPYRIGHT GEORGE PHILIP & SON LTD.

Projection: Conical with two standard parallels

West from Greenwich   Motorways

1 : 4 000 000

50   0   50   100   150 km

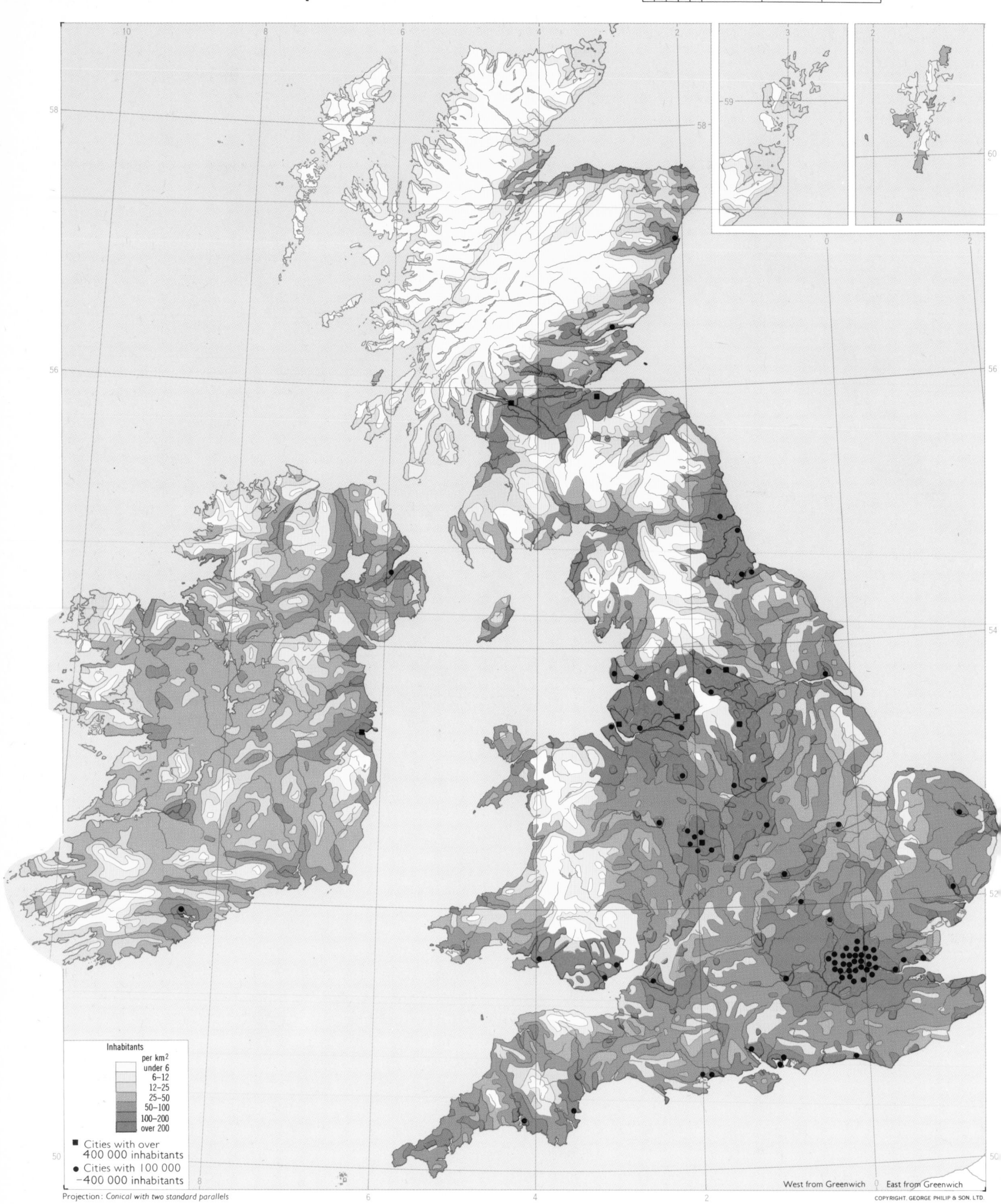

Inhabitants
per km²
under 6
6–12
12–25
25–50
50–100
100–200
over 200

■ Cities with over
   400 000 inhabitants

● Cities with 100 000
   –400 000 inhabitants

West from Greenwich   East from Greenwich

Projection: *Conical with two standard parallels*

COPYRIGHT. GEORGE. PHILIP & SON. LTD.

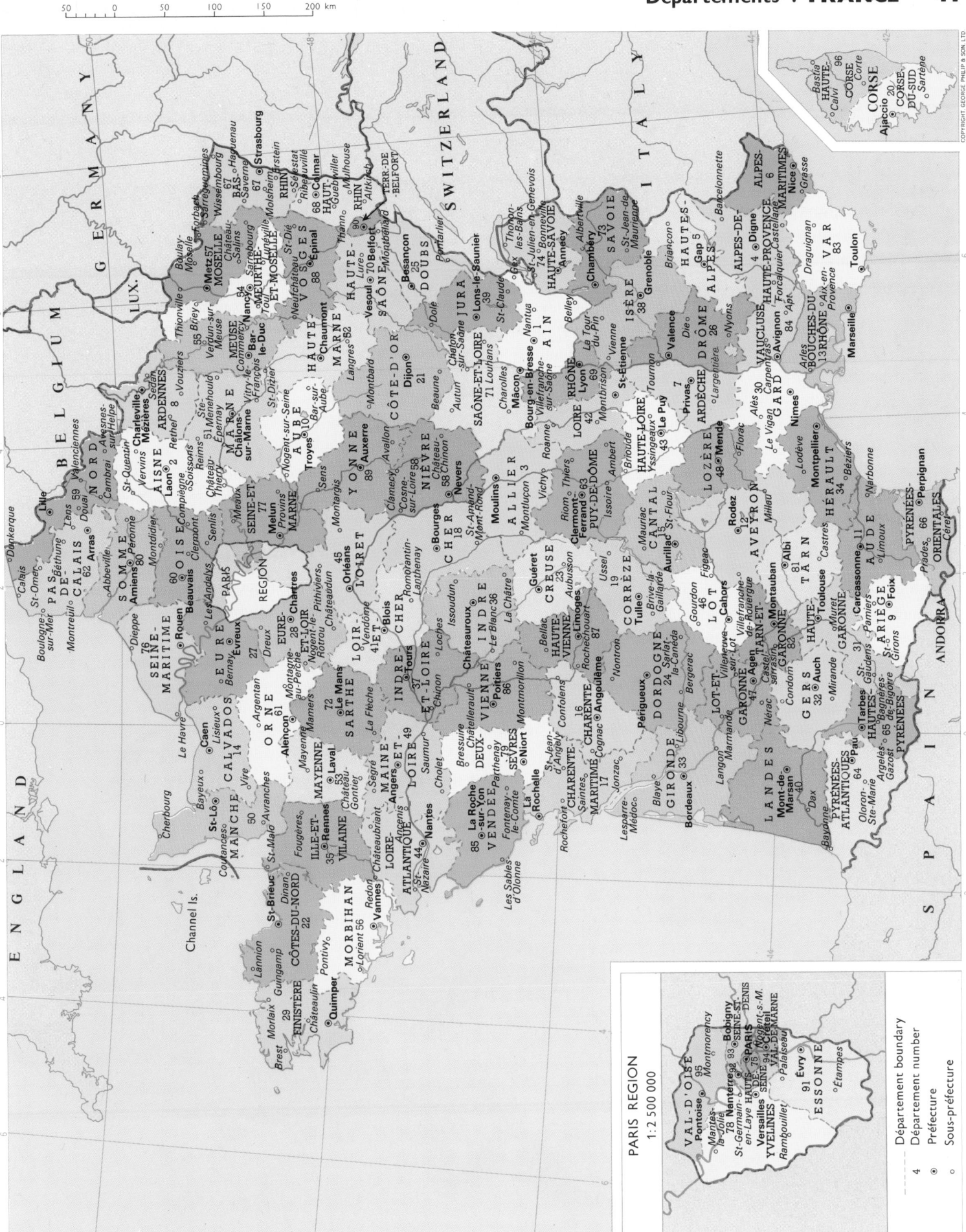

1:5 000 000

50 0 50 100 150 200 km

PARIS REGION
1:2 500 000

----- Département boundary
4 Département number
⊙ Préfecture
○ Sous-préfecture

COPYRIGHT GEORGE PHILIP & SON LTD

ENGLAND

English Channel

CHANNEL
Guernsey
St. Peter Port
ISLANDS
Jersey
St. Helier

Mer d'Iroise

Ile d'Ouessant
Brest

Baie de Bourgneuf
Ile de Noirmoutier

Ile d'Yeu

BRETAGNE

Rennes
Nantes
Angers
Le Mans

NORMANDIE
Le Havre
Caen
Rouen

Pertuis Breton
Ile de Ré
La Rochelle
Pertuis d'Antioche
Rochefort
Ile d'Oléron

Pointe de Grave

ANGOUMOIS
Angoulême

DÉPARTEMENTS IN THE PARIS AREA

1 Ville de Paris   3 Val-de-Marne
2 Seine-St.-Denis   4 Hauts-de-Seine

Projection: *Conical with two standard parallels*

West from Greenwich   East from Greenwich

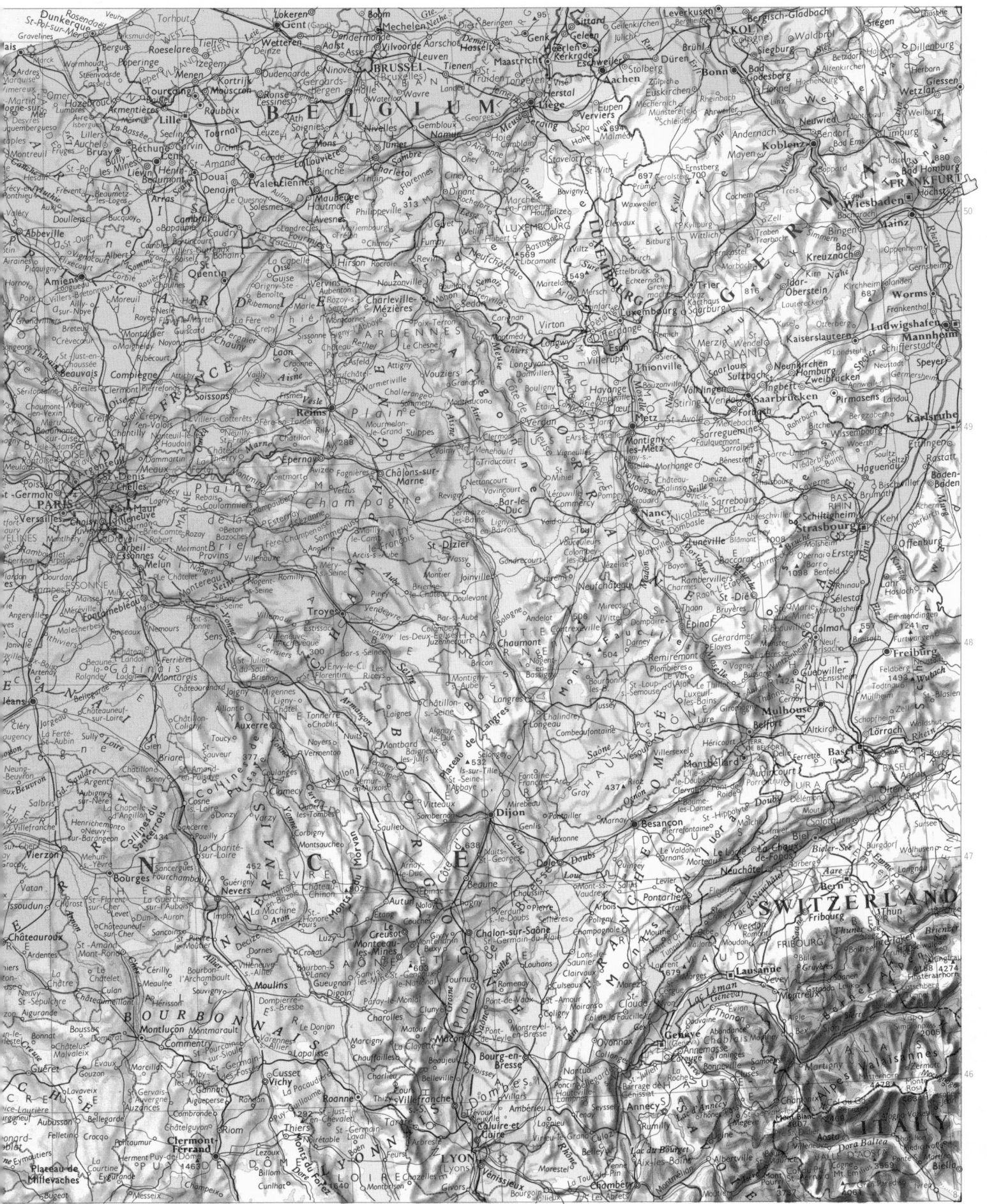

1 : 2 500 000

10 0 10 20 30 40 50 60 70 80 90 100 km

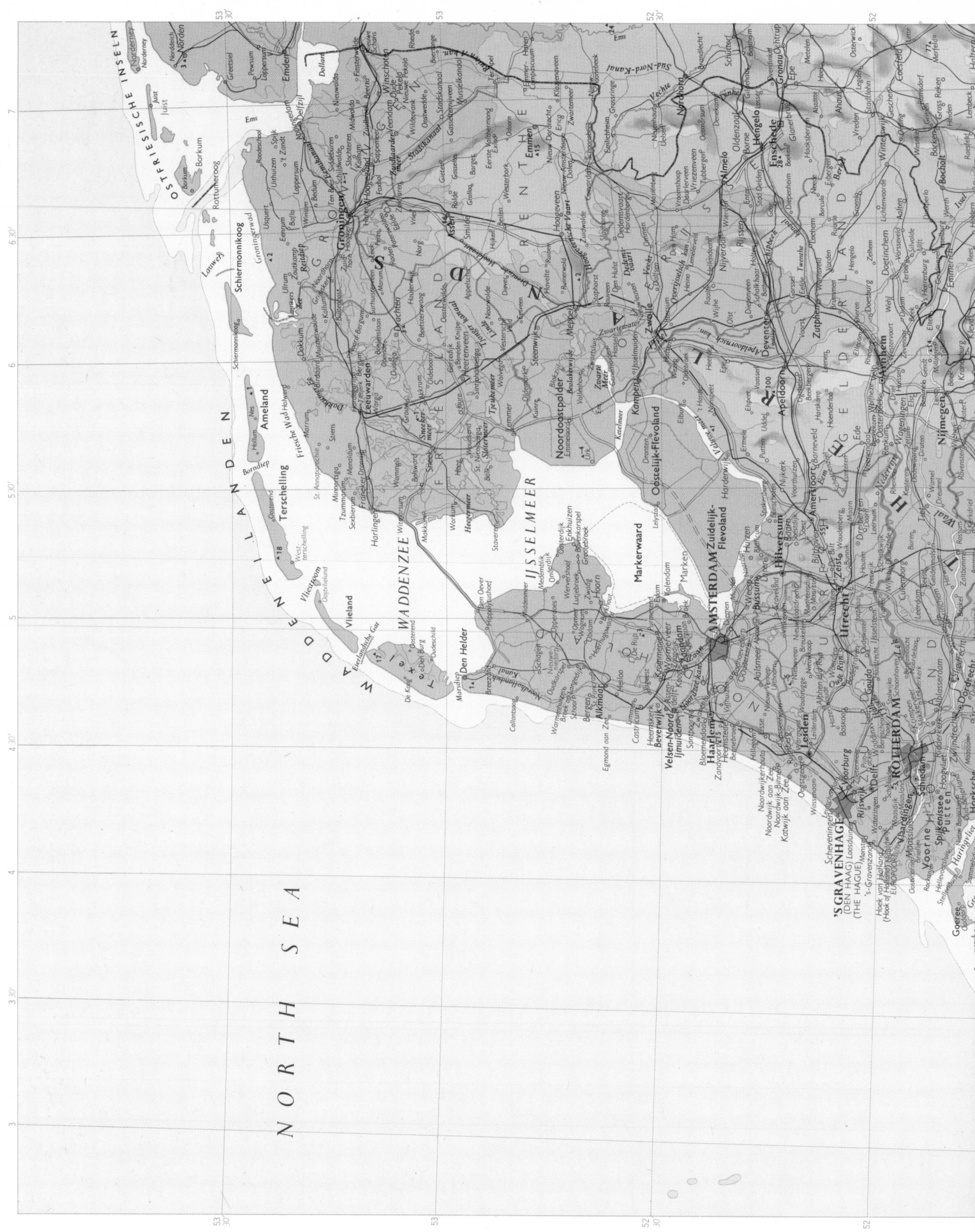
NORTH SEA
WADDENZEE
IJSSELMEER
WADDENEILANDEN
OSTFRIESISCHE INSELN
Markerwaard
Noordoostpolder
Oostelijk-Flevoland
Zuidelijk-Flevoland
Texel
Vlieland
Terschelling
Ameland
Schiermonnikoog
Borkum
Den Helder
Harlingen
Leeuwarden
Groningen
Assen
Emmen
Zwolle
Kampen
Deventer
Apeldoorn
Arnhem
Nijmegen
Almelo
Hengelo
Enschede
Amersfoort
Utrecht
Hilversum
AMSTERDAM
Haarlem
Leiden
'S GRAVENHAGE
(DEN HAAG)
(THE HAGUE)
ROTTERDAM
Schiedam
Dordrecht
Gouda
Emden
Norden

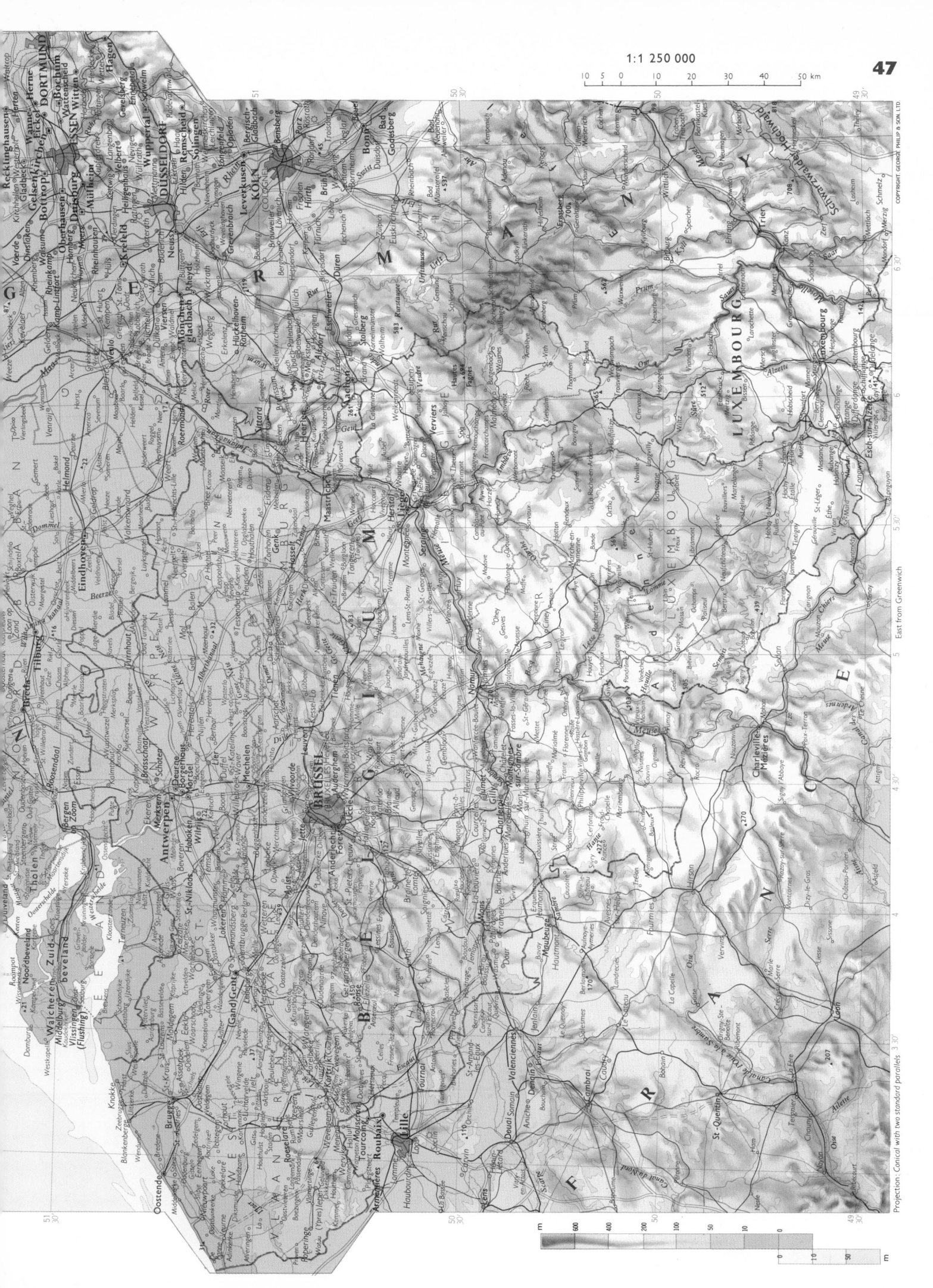

1:1 250 000

10 5 0 10 20 30 40 50 km

East from Greenwich

Projection: Conical with two standard parallels

m 600 400 200 100 50 10 0

0 10 50 m

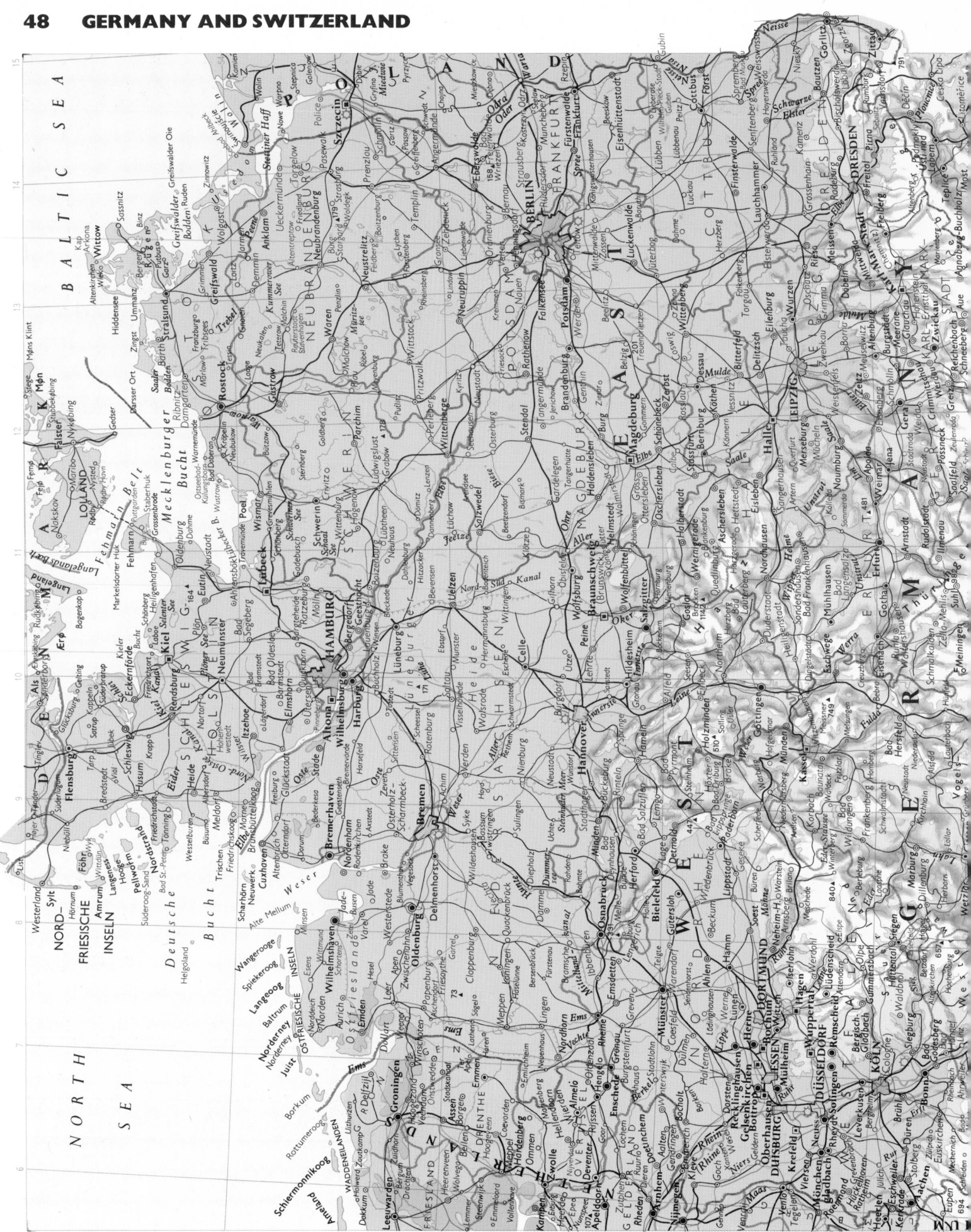
BALTIC SEA
NORTH SEA
DENMARK
POLAND
NORD-FRIESISCHE INSELN
Deutsche Bucht
Mecklenburger Bucht
BERLIN
HAMBURG
DRESDEN
LEIPZIG

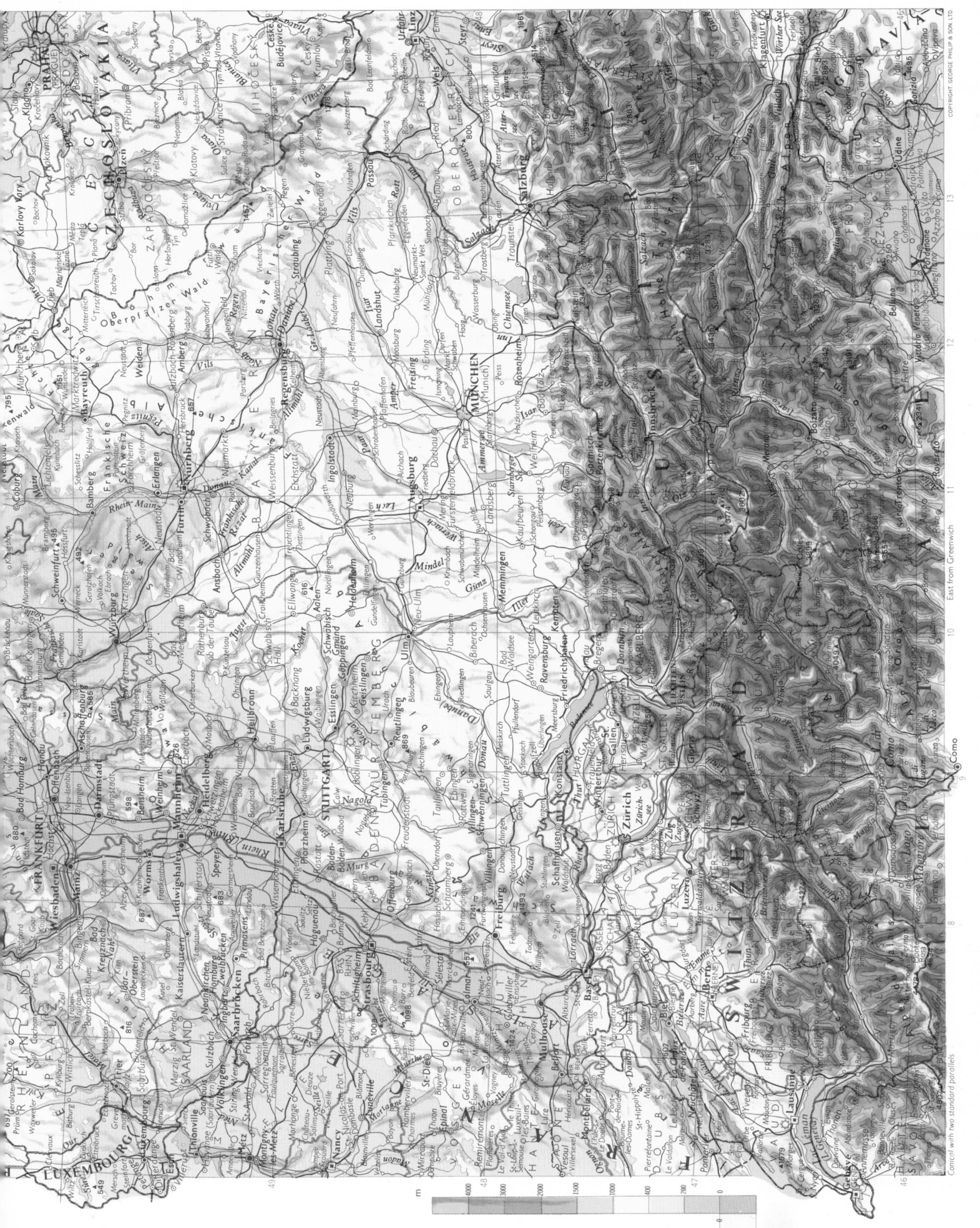

1 : 2 500 000

10 0 10 20 30 40 50 60 70 80 90 100 km

49

East from Greenwich

Conical with two standard parallels

COPYRIGHT GEORGE PHILIP & SON LTD

m 4000 3000 2000 1500 1000 400 200 0

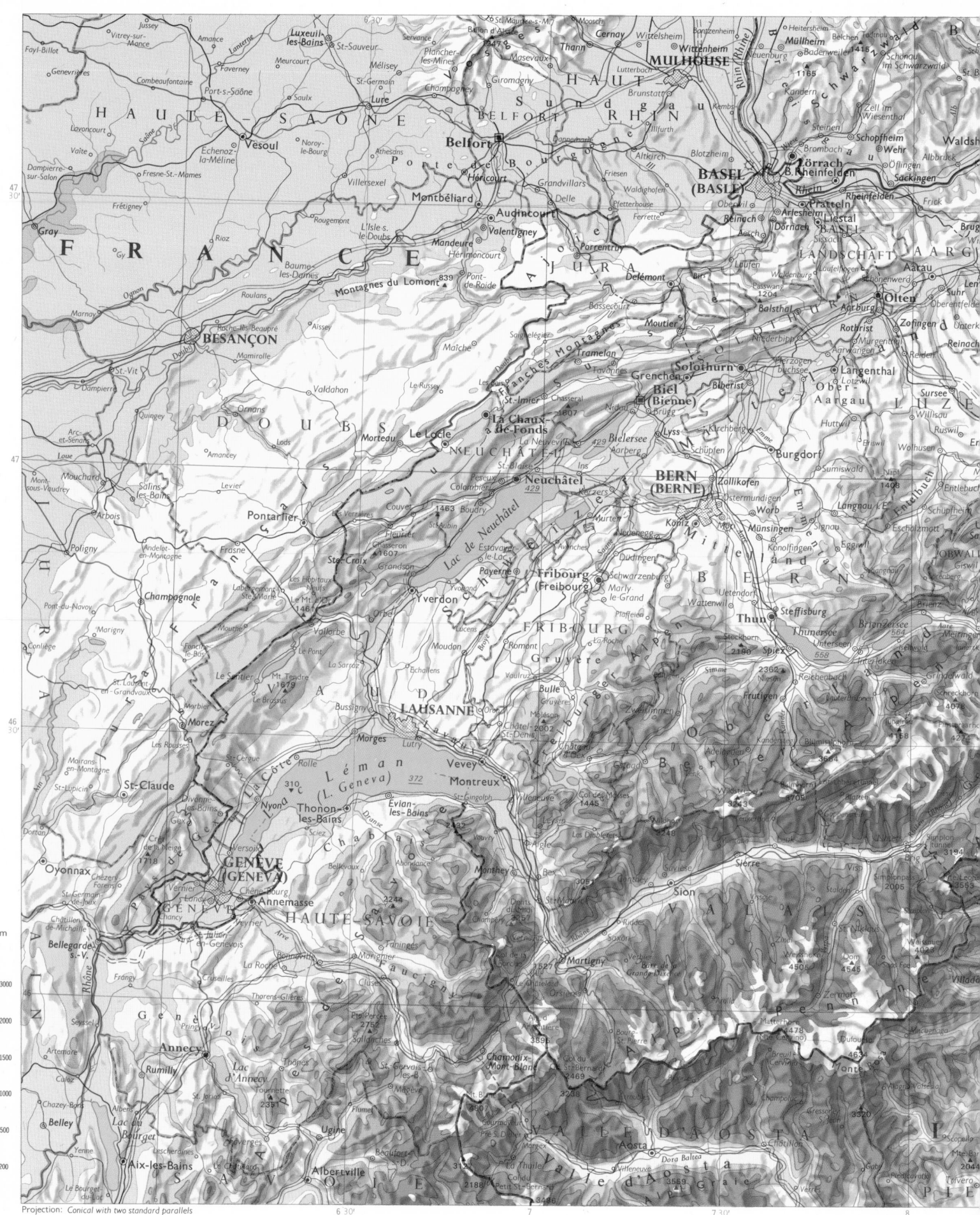

FRANCE
HAUTE-SAÔNE
DOUBS
JURA
HAUT-RHIN
BELFORT
Sundgau
Porte de Bourgogne
Franches Montagnes
NEUCHÂTEL
SOLOTHURN
BERN
FRIBOURG
VAUD
VALAIS
GENÈVE
HAUTE-SAVOIE
SAVOIE
VALLE D'AOSTA
Chablais
Faucigny
Genevois
Gruyère
Mittelland
Berner Alpen
Freiburger Alpen
Pennine Alpi
Schwarzwald
Léman (L. Geneva)
Lac de Neuchâtel
Bielersee
Thunersee
Brienzersee
Lac d'Annecy
Lac du Bourget
Rhône
Rhein
Vesoul
Lure
Luxeuil-les-Bains
Belfort
Montbéliard
Héricourt
Audincourt
Valentigney
Mandeure
L'Isle-s.-le Doubs
Baume-les-Dames
Gray
Besançon
Pontarlier
Morteau
Le Locle
La Chaux-de-Fonds
Neuchâtel
Biel (Bienne)
Grenchen
Solothurn
Delémont
Porrentruy
Moutier
Tramelan
St.-Imier
Mulhouse
Thann
Cernay
Wittenheim
Müllheim
Lörrach
Basel (Basle)
B. Rheinfelden
Pratteln
Liestal
Reinach
Dornach
Arlesheim
Olten
Aarau
Zofingen
Langenthal
Burgdorf
Bern (Berne)
Zollikofen
Worb
Münsingen
Köniz
Thun
Steffisburg
Spiez
Interlaken
Fribourg (Freiburg)
Bulle
Yverdon
Ste-Croix
Lausanne
Morges
Vevey
Montreux
Nyon
Thonon-les-Bains
Évian-les-Bains
Genève (Geneva)
Annemasse
Oyonnax
St.-Claude
Morez
Bellegarde-s.-V.
Annecy
Rumilly
Belley
Aix-les-Bains
Albertville
Chamonix-Mont-Blanc
Monthey
Martigny
Sion
Sierre
Aosta
Champagnole
Poligny
Arbois
Salins-les-Bains
Montagnes du Lomont
Projection: Conical with two standard parallels

1:1 000 000

10   0   10   20   30   40 km

Projection: Conical with two standard parallels

1 : 2 500 000

10 0 10 20 30 40 50 60 70 80 90 100 km

East from Greenwich

1:3 000 000

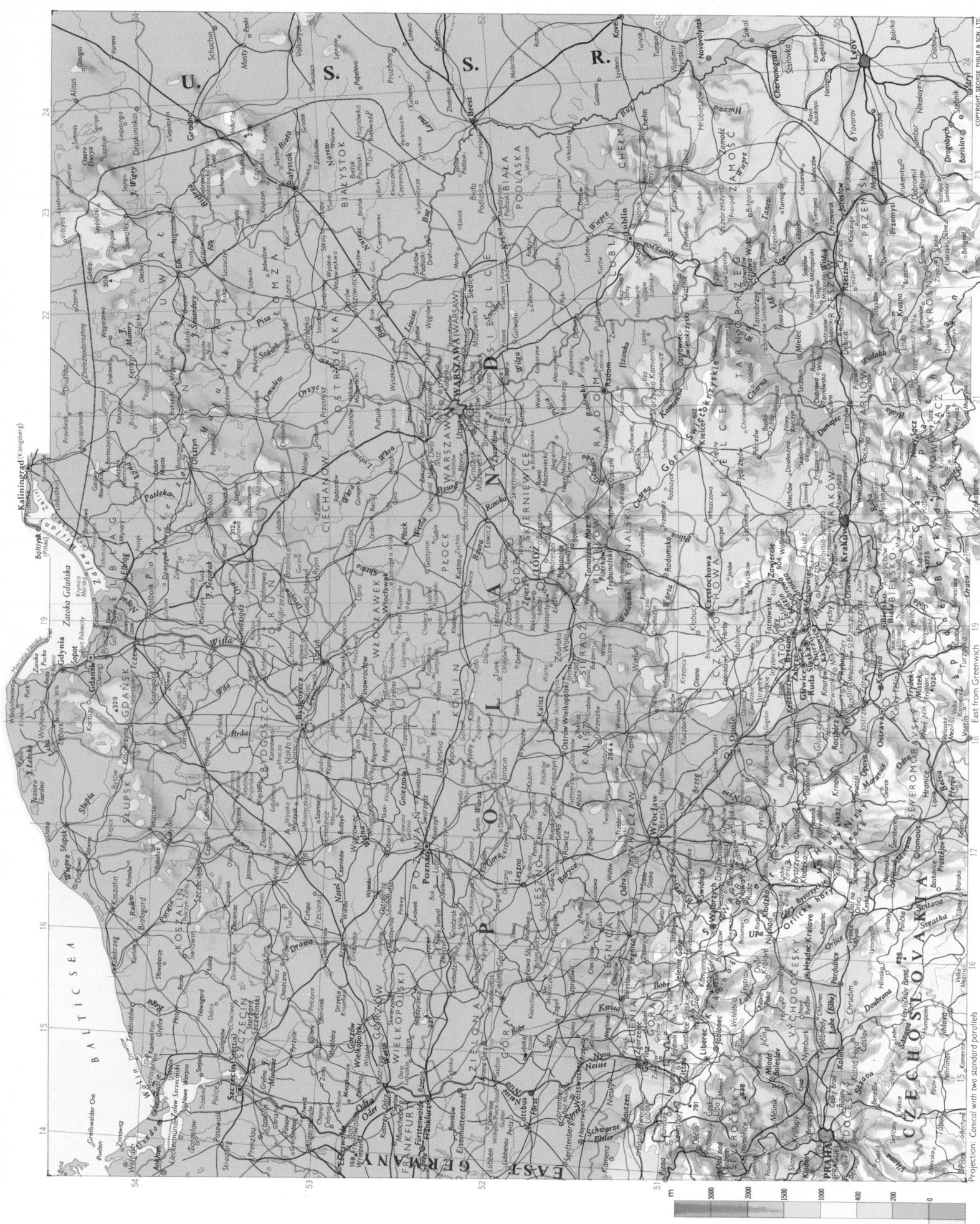

1:5 000 000

50   0   50   100   150   200 km

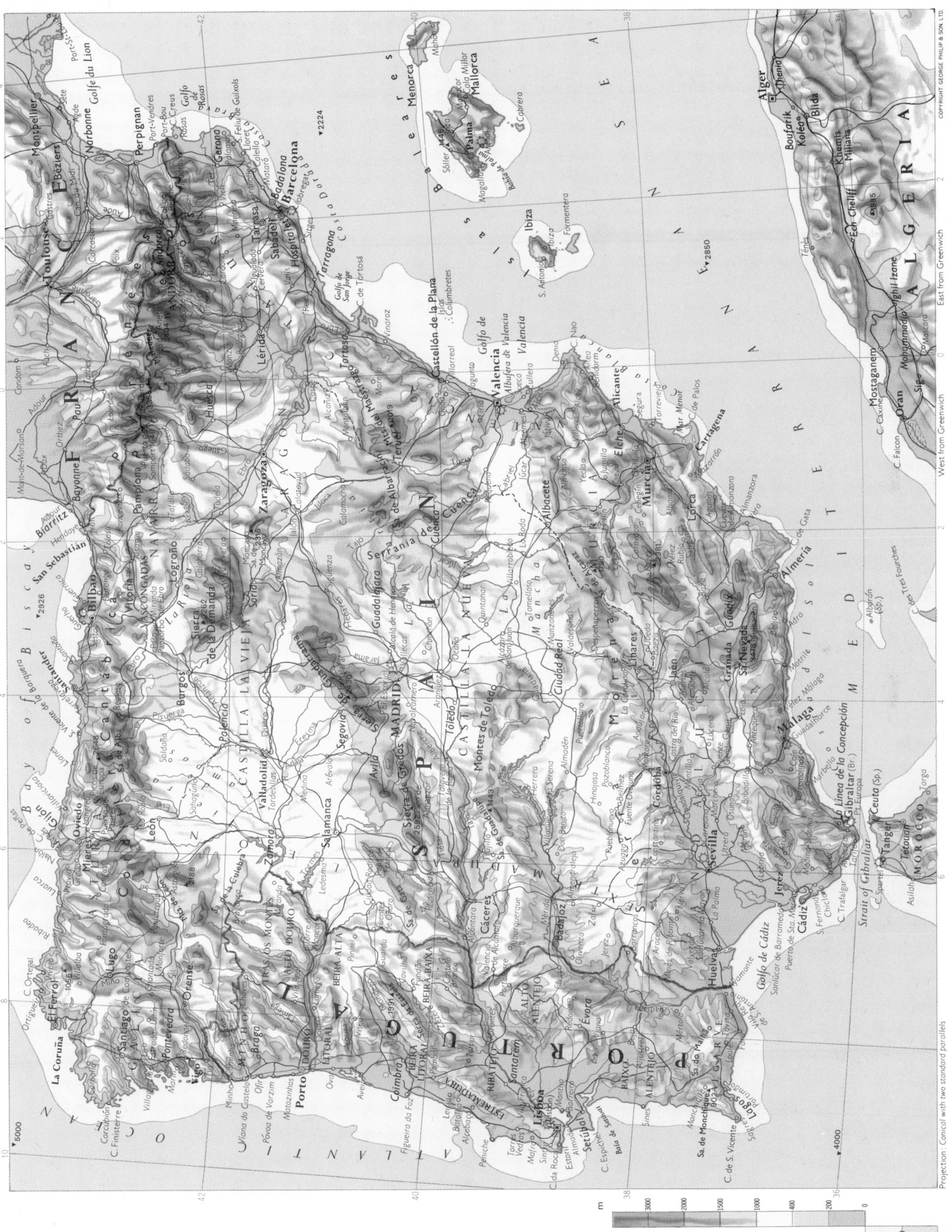

Projection : Conical with two standard parallels

West from Greenwich   East from Greenwich

COPYRIGHT: GEORGE PHILIP & SON, LTD.

m   3000   2000   1500   1000   400   200   0

0   200   m

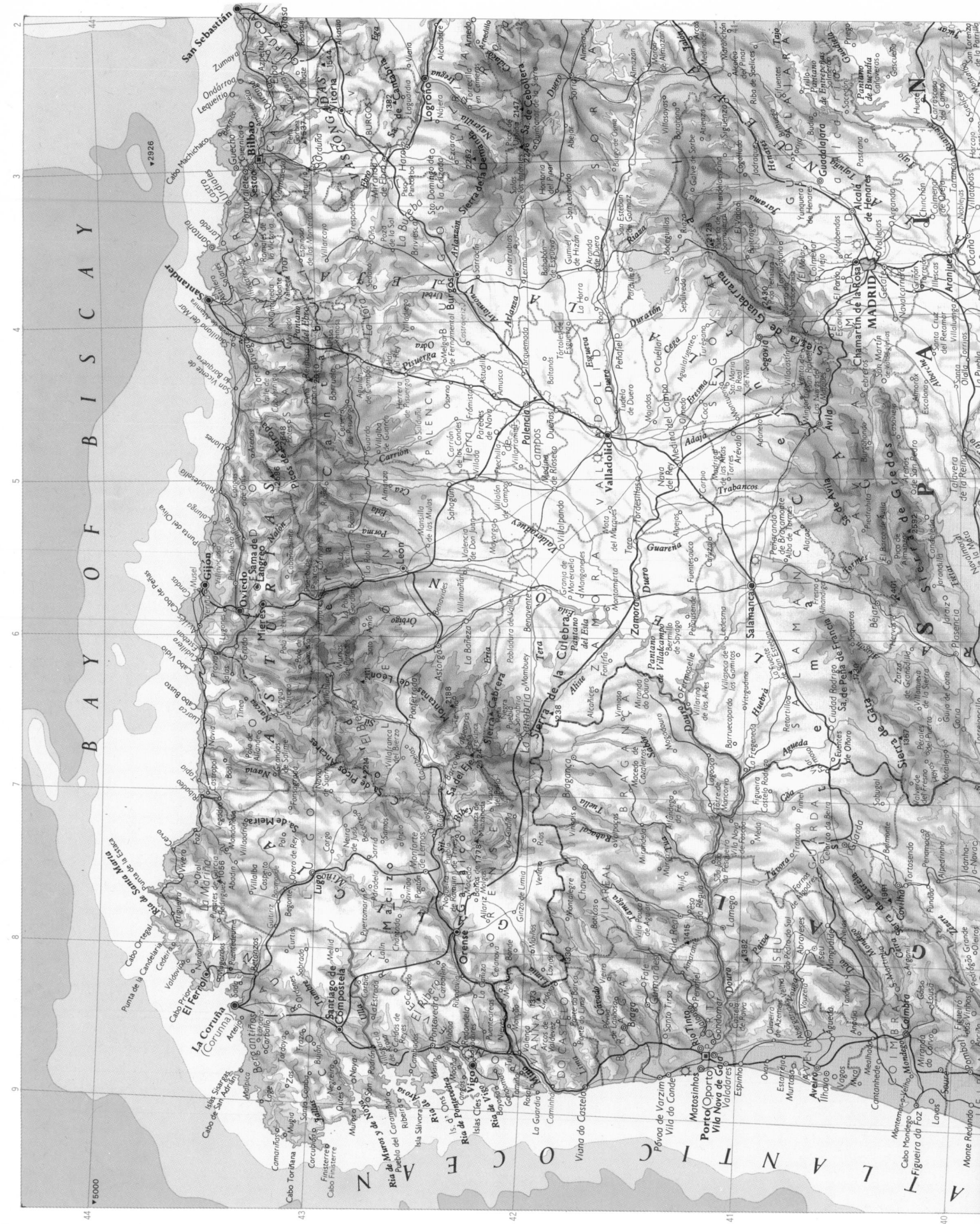
BAY OF BISCAY
ATLANTIC OCEAN
San Sebastián
Bilbao
Santander
Gijón
Oviedo
La Coruña (Corunna)
El Ferrol
Santiago de Compostela
Lugo
Orense
Vigo
León
Burgos
Logroño
Valladolid
Palencia
Zamora
Salamanca
Segovia
Avila
MADRID
Guadalajara
Alcalá de Henares
Aranjuez
Porto (Oporto)
Vila Nova de Gaia
Braga
Coimbra
Aveiro
Bragança
Vitoria
Soria
Plasencia
Sierra de Gredos
Sierra de Guadarrama
Sierra de Gata
Picos de Europa
Duero
Douro
Tajo
Pisuerga
Esla

1:2 500 000

10 0 10 20 30 40 50 60 70 80 90 100 km

MEDITERRANEAN

SEA

MOROCCO

Melilla (Sp.)

C. des Trois Fourches

Alborán (Sp.)

Al Hoceima

Tétouan

Ceuta (Sp.)

Tanger
(Tangier)

Strait of Gibraltar

Asilah

Larache

Golfo de
Almería

Golfo de
Cádiz

West from Greenwich

Projection: Conical with two standard parallels

COPYRIGHT GEORGE PHILIP & SON LTD.

MÁLAGA

Gibraltar (Br.)

La Línea de la Concepción

Algeciras

Cádiz

Sevilla

Córdoba

Granada

Jaén

Huelva

Badajoz

Cáceres

Mérida

Évora

LISBOA
(LISBON)

Setúbal

PORTUGAL

ALGARVE

Faro

Cabo de Sâo Vicente

4000

3000
2000
1500
1000
400
200
0

m

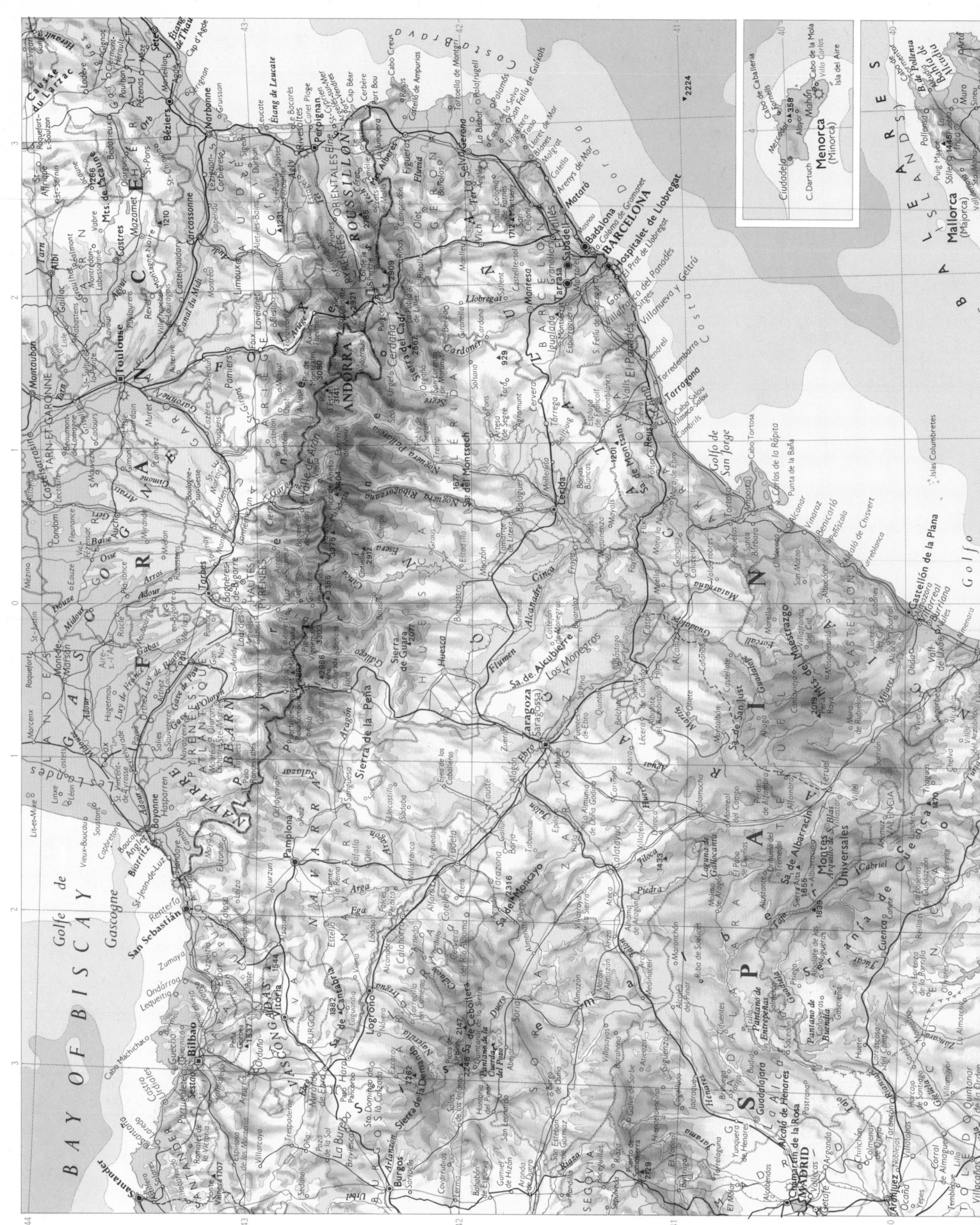
BAY OF BISCAY
Golfe de Gascogne
San Sebastián
Bilbao
Santander
Pamplona
Logroño
Burgos
Zaragoza (Saragossa)
Huesca
Lérida
Tarragona
BARCELONA
Badalona
Sabadell
Tarrasa
Gerona
Perpignan
Narbonne
Béziers
Toulouse
Carcassonne
ANDORRA
ROUSSILLON
Guadalajara
MADRID
Alcalá de Henares
Aranjuez
Cuenca
Teruel
Castellón de la Plana
Golfo de San Jorge
Menorca (Minorca)
Mahón
Ciudadela
Mallorca (Majorca)
Sierra de la Peña
Sierra de Guara
Montes Universales
Sa. de Alcubierre
Los Monegros

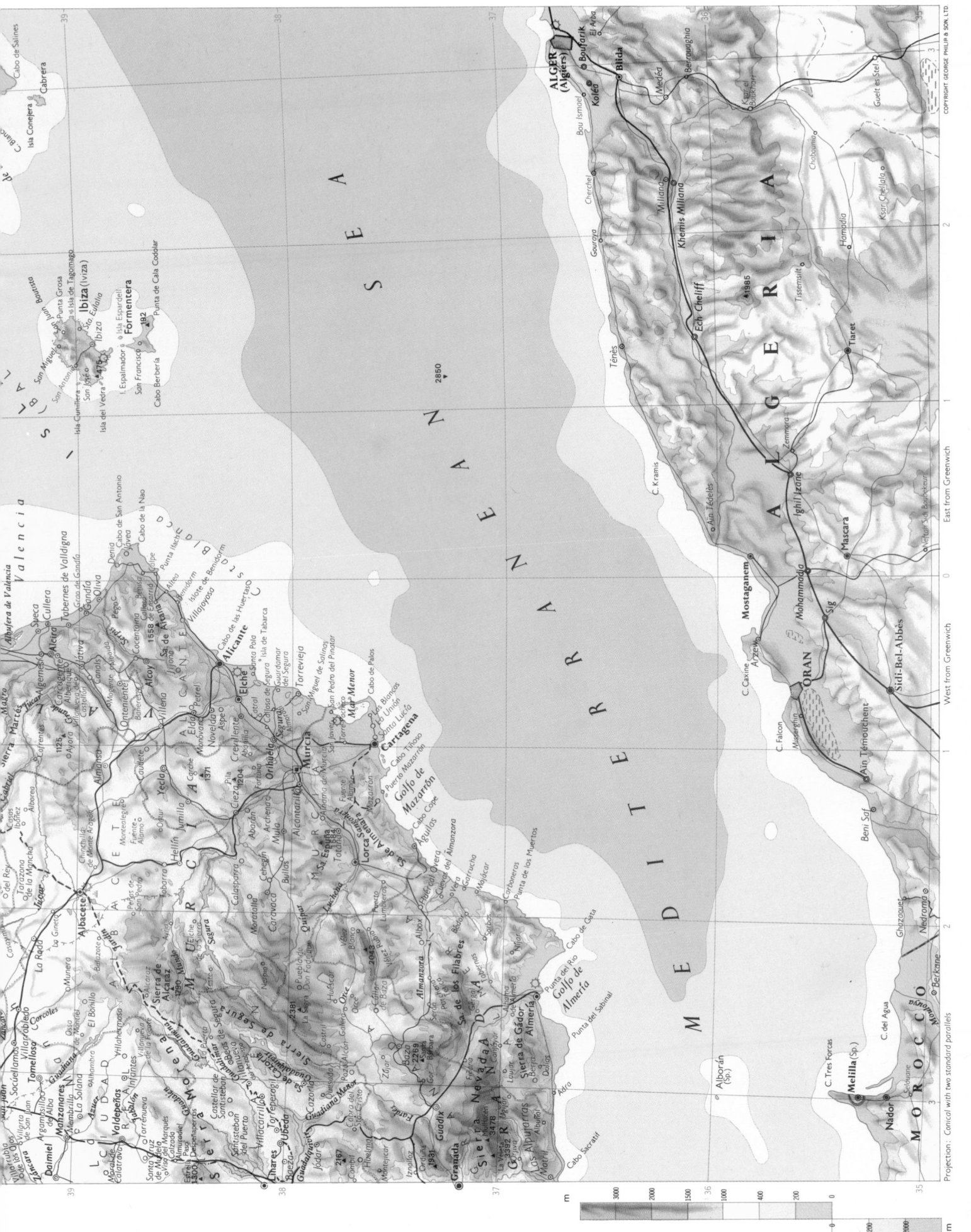

1:2 500 000

10 0 10 20 30 40 50 60 70 80 90 100 km

COPYRIGHT GEORGE PHILIP & SON LTD.

Projection: Conical with two standard parallels

East from Greenwich

West from Greenwich

M E D I T E R R A N E A N   S E A

A L G E R I A

MOROCCO

Valencia

Albufera de Valencia

BALEARIC ISLANDS

Ibiza (Iviza)

Formentera

**ALGER
(Algiers)**

Blida

Koléa

Medéa

Bou Ismael

Cherchel

Gouraya

Ténès

Ech Cheliff

Khemis Miliana

Miliana

Mostaganem

ORAN

Sidi-Bel-Abbès

Mohammadia

Sig

Arzew

C. Ferrat

C. Falcon

Mascara

Ighil Izane

Zemmora

Tiaret

Melilla

Nador

C. Tres Forcas

Alborán
(Sp.)

Albacete

Alicante

Murcia

Elche

Orihuela

Cartagena

Mar Menor

Cabo de Palos

Golfo de
Mazarrón

Golfo de
Almería

Granada

Sierra Nevada

Sierra de Gador

Almería

Lorca

m 3000 2000 1500 1000 400 200 0

m 200 2000

LONDON
Bristol
Southampton
Plymouth
Portsmouth
Brighton
English Channel
Channel Is.
Str. of Dover
's-Gravenhage
Rotterdam
NETH.
BELGIUM
Brussel
Lille
Amiens
Le Havre
Rouen
Brest
Rennes
Le Mans
Nantes
Angers
Tours
Orléans
PARIS
Versailles
Reims
Metz
Nancy
Strasbourg
Dijon
Lyon
Grenoble
St-Étienne
Clermont-Ferrand
Limoges
Bordeaux
Toulouse
Montpellier
Nîmes
Avignon
Marseille
Toulon
Nice
MONACO
Perpignan
Golfe du Lion
FRANCE
Bay of Biscay
GERMANY
Frankfurt
Köln
Düsseldorf
Essen
Dortmund
Hannover
BERLIN
Leipzig
Dresden
Stuttgart
München
Nürnberg
Augsburg
LUX.
SWITZERLAND
Bern
Zürich
Genève
Basel
Innsbruck
Salzburg
Linz
Milano
Torino
Genova
Venezia
Verona
Bologna
Firenze
Livorno
Roma
Nápoli
SAN MARINO
Ancona
Ligurian Sea
Corse
Sardegna
Cagliari
Tyrrhenian Sea
Palermo
Isole Eólie
MALTA
Valletta
SPAIN
PORTUGAL
Lisboa
Porto
MADRID
Barcelona
Zaragoza
Valencia
Sevilla
Córdoba
Granada
Málaga
Cádiz
Alicante
Murcia
Cartagena
Bilbao
Santander
Oviedo
Gijón
La Coruña
Vigo
Valladolid
Salamanca
Cordillera Cantábrica
Pyrenees
Sierra Morena
Sa. Nevada 3478
Islas Baleares
Mallorca (Majorca)
Menorca (Minorca)
Ibiza
Gibraltar (Br.)
Str. of Gibraltar
Tanger
Ceuta (Sp.)
Melilla (Sp.)
Rabat
Meknès
Fès
Oujda
MOROCCO
Haut Atlas
Alger
Oran
Constantine
Annaba
Sidi Bel Abbès
Tlemcen
Béchar
Ghardaïa
Touggourt
Ouargla
Biskra
Hassi Messaoud
Ft. Lallemand
El Goléa
Beni Abbès
ALGERIA
Tunis
Sousse
Sfax
Gabès
Djerba
TUNISIA
Chott Djerid
Chott Melrhir
Tarābulus
MEDITERRANEAN
Projection: Conical with two standard parallels.
West from Greenwich 0 East from Greenwich

1:10 000 000

100   0   100   200   300   400 km

POLAND
Poznań
Płock
Wisła (Vistula)
Warszawa
Brest
Pinsk
Polesye
Chernigov
Konotop
Desna
Sumy
Belgorod
Kharkov
Volgograd
Łódź
Radom
Lublin
Lutsk
Pripyat
Pripyat
Nezhin
Kazanskaya
Chorzów
Kielce
Bug
Styr
Gora
Zhitomir
Dnepr
Kiyev
Pereyaslav-Khmelnitskiy
Poltava
S. S. R.
Slavyansk
Voroshilovgrad
(Lugansk)
Kamensk-Shakhtinskiy
Tsimlyanskoye
Vdkhr.
Kraków
Tarnów
Przemyśl
Lvov
Rovno
Berdichev
U. Vinnitsa
Belaya Tserkov
S. S. R.
Dnepr
(Dnieper)
Pavlograd
Artemovsk
Gorlovka
Makeyevka
Shakhty
Don
Novocherkassk
Ostrava
Jablunkovský Pr.
Tešin
KRAVOY
Kamenets-Podol'skiy
Mogilev-Podolskiy
U. K. R. A.
Kirovograd
Dneprodzerzhinsk
Dnepropetrovsk
Zaporozhye
Donetsk
Rostov
Manych
Slavkov
Kolomyya
Chernovtsy
Dnestr
Balta
Voznesensk
Pervomaysk
Krivoy Rog
Zhdanov
(Mariupol)
Taganrog
Oz. Manych Gudilo
CHOSLOVAKIA
Tatry
Banská Štiavnica
MOLDAVIAN
S.S.R.
Nikolayev
Melitopol
Berdyansk
Yeisk
Tikhoretsk
Stavropol
Bratislava
Miskolc
Košice
Botoşani
Iaşi
Kishinev
Bendery
S. S. R.
Kherson
Perekop
Sea of Azov
Kerch
Krasnodar
Armavir
Debrecen
Budapest
Kecskemét
HUNGARY
Oradea
Cluj-Napoca
Pietrosul
2305
ROMANIA
Tiraspol
Ismail
Odessa
Karkinitskiy Zaliv
M. Tarkhankut
Yevpatoriya
Krymskaya
(Crimea)
Feodosiya
Novorossiysk
Tuapse
Kuban
Maykop
Hódmezővásárhely
Szeged
Pécs
Balaton
Körös
Pietrosul
2102
Belgorod
Dnestrovskiy
Sulina
Simferopol
1545
Yalta
Sukhumi
Zagreb
Subotica
Arad
Timişoara
Mureş
Sibiu
Negoiu
2535
Braşov
(Oraşul Stalin)
Galaţi
Brăila
Sevastopol
Balaklava
Poti
Novi Sad
Petrovaradin
Craiova
Piteşti
Ploieşti
Bucureşti
Constanţa
B L A C K   S E A
Batumi
Brod
Banja Luka
Sava
Smederevo
Moravа
Dunărea
(Danube)
Silistra
Tolbukhin
2211
Ince Burnu
Trabzon
Rize
BOSNA S
Sarajevo
Bosna
Niš
Pleven
Ruse
Varna
Giresun
Tirebolu
Karahisar
Durmitor
2522
Novi Pazar
Stipchenski P.
Târnovo
Stara Planina
Sliven
Burgas
Inebolu
Sinop
Samsun
Ordu
Kuzey Anadolu Dağlari
Mostar
CRNAGORA
Kotor
Cetinje
Sofiya
Musala
2925
BULGARIA
Maritsa
2566
Kastamonu
Amasya
Çorum
Tokat
Sivas
Erzincan
Lastovo
Dubrovnik
(Ragusa)
Shkodër
2764
Skopje
Vardar
Plovdiv
Rhodopi Planina
Edirne
Karadeniz Boğazı
Zanguldak
Ereğli
Bolu
Çankırı
Kral Irmak
Yozgat
Ankara
Kırşehir
Malatya
Keban
SEA
Tirana
Durrës
Elbasan
Bitola
Sérrai
Kavalla
Alexandroúpolis
Gelibolu
Tekirdağ
İstanbul
Üsküdar
İzmit
Marmara Denizi
Bilecik
Sakarya
Beypazarı
Sivrihisar
TURKEY
Gürün
Bari
Barletta
ALBANIA
Gökçeada
Çanakkale
Bandırma
Bursa
İznik Gölü
Eskişehir
Kütahya
Afyon Karahisar
Bolvadin
Tuz Gölü
Aksaray
Niğde
Kayseri
Ercyas Dağı
3770
Gaziantep
Brindisi
Táranto
GREECE
Vórioi Sporádhes
Limnos
2917
Troy
Balıkesir
Ayvalık
Maniso
Turgutlu
Küçük Menderes
Büyük Menderes
Eğridir Gölü
Beyşehir Gölü
Konya
Karaman
Tarsus
Adana
Osmaniye
İskenderun
İskenderun Körfezi
Halab
Golfo di Táranto
C. Sta. Maria di Leuca
La Sila
1929
Kérkira
Ionian Islands
Levkás
Návpaktos
Thivai
Athínai
Piraiévs
Évvoia
Khíos
Lésvos
Ikaría
Sámos
Aydın
Denizli
Muğla
Egridir
Isparta
Burdur
Elmali
Antalya
Antalya Körfezi
Mersin
Silifke
Antakya
SYRIA
Hamā'
Str. of Otranto
C. Spartivento
C. di Messina
Reggio
Kefallinía
Zákinthos
Korinthiakós Kólpos
Kórinthos
Návplion
Olympia
Kalamata
Spárti
Peloponnisos
Pátrai
Síros
Ándros
Kikládhes
Náxos
Íos
Milos
Thíra
Ródhos
4486
Dhodhekánisos
Kárpathos
Megiste
(Kastellórizon)
CYPRUS
Levkosia
(Nicosia)
Morfou
Ammókhostos
(Famagusta)
Lárnax
Tarabulus
Tripoli
Al Ladhiqiyah
Baniyas
Homs
Hamā
Bayrūt
(Beirut)
Dimashq
(Damascus)
LEBANON
ash Sheikh
2814
5121
Ákra Taínaron
Kíthira
Andikíthira
Khaniá
Idhi Óros
2456
Iráklion
Kríti
Troodhos
1951
Lemesos
Jabal ad Durūz
Bosra
4135
A
N
E
A
N
S
E
A
'Akka
Haifa
Jordan
Tel Aviv-Yafo
Jerusalem
Gaza
'Ammān
JORDAN
Bahr el Miyet
3174
Cyréne
Derna
Khalij Bómba
Tobruq
Khalij el Salūm
El 'Alamein
Matrūh
El Iskandariya
Rashid
Bahra el Burullus
Dumyāt
Bür Said
El Qantara
Ismā 'iliya
Buheirat Murrat-el-Kubra
El Arish
Ma'ān
Petra
Al Marj
(Barce)
Banghāzi
Khalij Surt
Salūm
El Mahalla el Kubra
Tanta
Gebel el Tih
Es Sinā
26374
Khaliq el 'Aqaba
El Aqaba
Barqa
EGYPT
El Qāhira
El Suweis
Khaliq es Suweis
Nile
LI BYA
El Faiyūm
Beni Suēf

- - - - - - Division between Greeks and Turks in Cyprus; Turks to the north.

LIGURIAN   SEA

C O R S E

(C O R S I C A)

Projection: Conical with two standard parallels

East from Greenwich

m

HUNGARY

SOMOGY

VENETO

FRIULI

VENEZIA GIULIA

Golfo di Venézia (Venice)

Laguna Veneta

Trieste

ISTRA

Kvarner

Kvarnerič

A D R I A T I C

S E A

MARCHE

UMBRIA

ABRUZZI

LAZIO

MOLISE

ROMA (ROME)

Vatican City

SAN MARINO

Innsbruck

Klagenfurt

Maribor

Zagreb

Ljubljana

Rijeka (Fume)

Pula

Zadar

Šibenik

Split

Pescara

Ancona

Rímini

Ravenna

Ferrara

Pádova (Padua)

Venézia

Graz

BOSNA

HERCEGOVINA

DALMACIJA

Mljet

Lastovo

FOR CONTINUATION SEE PAGE 66

CORSE

CORSICA

Iles Sanguinaires
G. d'Ajaccio
Taravo
Incudine
Solenzara
C. di Muro
2136 Zonza
Levie
Favone
G. de Valinco
Propriano
Sartène
Porto-Vecchio
Iles Cerbicales
CORSE-DU-SUD
Iles Cerbicales

Bonifacio
I. de
Cavallo
Bouches de Bonifacio
Maddalena
Santa Teresa Gallura
Caprera
La Maddalena
Costa
Punta dello Scorno
Pto Cervo
Smeralda
Arzachena

Asinara
Golfo dell'
Asinara
Coghinas
Aggius
Calangiánus
Golfo Aranci
Témpio Pausania
G. di Ólbia
Porto Tórres
1362
M. Limbara
Ólbia
Tavolara
Sorso
Sássari
Sennori
Osilo
L. di Coghinas
Tanaunella
C. dell'Argentiera
Ózieri
Posada
Fertília
Itturi
Buddusò
Siniscola
Alghero
Pattada
Bosa
1259
Bitti
Villanova
Bonárva
Oruné
C. Comino
Monteleone
1760
Nuoro
Temo
Bosa
Macomer
Dargali
Ghilarza
Sórgono
Orani
Oliena
Golfo di
SARDEGNA
Gavoi
Fonni
Orosei
C. Mannu
L. del Tirso
1834
Baunei
C. di Monte Santu
Cábras
Monti dei
Oristano
SARDEGNA
Gennargentu
Golfo di
Laconi
Arbatax
Oristano
M. Arci
Tortolì
Arborea
812
Seúlo
Lanusei
SARDINIA
Gúspini
S. Gavino
Mandas
Monreale
Villacidro
Sanluri
C. Pécora
1236
Serramanna
Dolianova
Flúminimaggiore
M. Línas
Senorbì
Villaputzu
Iglésias
Siliqua
Sestu
S. Serpedìd
Muravera
Gonnesa
1069
Sinnai
C. Ferrato
Portoscuso
Carloforte
Assemini
Selárgius
Serpentara
San Pietro
Carbónia
1116
Cagliari
Sant'Antíoco
Santadi
Golfo di
C. Carbonara
Sant'
Porto Botte
Teulada
Cágliari
Antíoco
Pula
G. di Palmas
C. Spartivento

ROMA
(Rome)
Vatican City
Tívoli
Subiaco
Arsoli
del Fuci
Fregene
Tevere
Palestrina
Tiber
Monteflavio
Lido di Óstia
Albano Lazio
Velletri
Anagni
Ísola del
(Lido di Roma)
Aprília
Cisterna di Latina
Ferentino
Monte S.
Prática
Ceccano
Alatri
di Mare
Ánzio
Latina
Ceprano
Veroli
Nettuno
Sonnino
Frosinone
Pontínia
Priverno
Sabáudia
541
Fondi
1533
Terracina
Gaeta
Fórmia
Golfo di
Zannone
Minturno
Mondrag
Palmarola
Ponza
Gaeta
Vol
Ísole
283
Ponziane
Ventotene
Ischi
7

T Y R R H E N I A N

S E A

3719

3589

Ustica

m
3000
2000
1500
1000
400
200
0
200
2000
4000
m

Iles de la
Galite

Iles de la

C. San Vito
Castellammare
del Golfo
Favarotta
Terrasini
PALERMO
Levanzo
Trápani
1110
Monreale
Bagheria
Ísole Égadi
Érice
Alcamo
S. Giuseppe
Maréttimo
Paceco
Partinico
Favignana
Calatafimi
Campòreale
Marineo
Favignana
Salemi
Córleone
1613
Lercara
Stagnone
Gibellina
Bisacquino
Friddi
Ali
Marsala
Partanna
Palazzo
Castelvetrano
Samuca
SIC
Mázara
Menfi
Bárgia
Mussomeli
del Vallo
Campobello di
Belíce
Castel
Platani
Sciacca
Ribera
Raccalmuto
San C
Cattólica Eraclea
Siculiana
Raffadali
Porto Empédocle
Agrigento
Favara
Palma di Montech
Campobell

Bizerte
(Binzert)
C. Blanc
Cani
C. Serrat
Menzel-Bourguiba
Plane
Zembra
El Kala
Mateur
C. Bon
ALGERIA
Tabarka
Tébourba
TUNIS
Halq el Oued
Béja
Medjerda
Kelibia
Bou Salem
Béja
Menzel-
Temime
Mejerda
Teboursouk
Nabeul
Golfe de Tunis
Soliman
T U N I S I A
Zaghouan
Hammamet

Pantelleria
836
Pantelleria
(It.)

M E D I T E

1319

Sicilian Channel

1:2 500 000

10 0 10 20 30 40 50 60 70 80 90 100 km

A D R I A T I C

S E A

I O N I A N

S E A

M E D I T E R R A N E A N   S E A

Golfo di Táranto

Golfo di Squillace

Golfo di Sant'Eufémia

G. di Salerno

G. di Manfredónia

G. di Policastro

G. di Gióia

Strait of Otranto

Isole Eólie o Lípari (Æolian Is.)

BASILICATA

CALABRIA

A L B A N I A

Bari

Táranto

Brindisi

Lecce

Messina

Réggio

Catánia

Siracusa

Cosenza

Catanzaro

Crotone

Cérkira (Corfu)

Projection: Conical with two standard parallels

East from Greenwich

1 : 2 500 000

10 0 10 20 30 40 50 60 70 80 90 100 km

Sofiya
Skopje
Tirana
Thessaloníki
Plovdiv
Stara Zagora
Edirne
Thásos
Samothráki
Límnos
Kérkira
Durrës
Vlorë
Berat
Elbasan
Korça
Bitola
Prilep
Pristina
Niš
Pleven
Yambol
Sliven
Kavála
Xánthi
Komotini
Sérrai
Drama
Lárisa
Vólos
Kateríni
Ioánnina
Gökçeada
Çanakkale
Sáros Körfezi
Thermaïkós Kólpos
Strimonikós Kólpos
Ayios Evstrátios
Ágion Óros

1:2 500 000

10 0 10 20 30 40 50 60 70 80 90 100 km

SEA OF CRETE (Sea of Candia)

ARKHIPÉLAGOS

KIKLÁDHES (CYCLADES)

AEGEAN

IONIAN SEA

Khíos (Chios)
Psará
Skíros
Skópelos
Ándros
Tínos
Míkonos
Náxos
Páros
Sífnos
Kíthnos
Kéa
Sérifos
Mílos
Amorgós
Ikaría
Astipálaia
Anáfi

ATTIKÍ
ATHÍNAI (ATHENS)
Piraiévs (Piræus)
Khalkís (Chalcis)
Lamía
Thívai (Thebes)
Levádhia

STEREÁ ELLÁS

PELOPÓNNISOS

Kórinthos (Corinth)
Corinth Canal
Spárti (Sparta)
Kalámai
Trípolis
Pátrai
Agrínion

Párnon Óros
Taïyetos Óros

LAKONÍA
MESSINÍA
ARKADÍA
AKHAÏA

Kefallinía (Cephalonia)
Levkás (Santa Maura)
Itháki (Ithaca)
Zákinthos (Zante)

IRÁKLION
Iráklion (Candia)
Khaniá (Canea)
Kólpos Khaniόn
Akrotíri
Khersónisos
Kólpos Soúdhas
RÉTHIMNON

Ródhos (Rhodes)
Kos
Sámos
Kárpathos
DHODHEKÁNISOS (DODECANESE)
Stenón Karpáthos
Stenón Kasos

Kythira (Cerigo)

Ephesus
Kusadasi
Samsun Dağı
Besparmak Dağı

East from Greenwich

Continuation Eastwards on same scale

Projection: Conical with two standard parallels

COPYRIGHT. GEORGE PHILIP & SON, LTD.

m
3000
2000
1500
1000
400
200
0

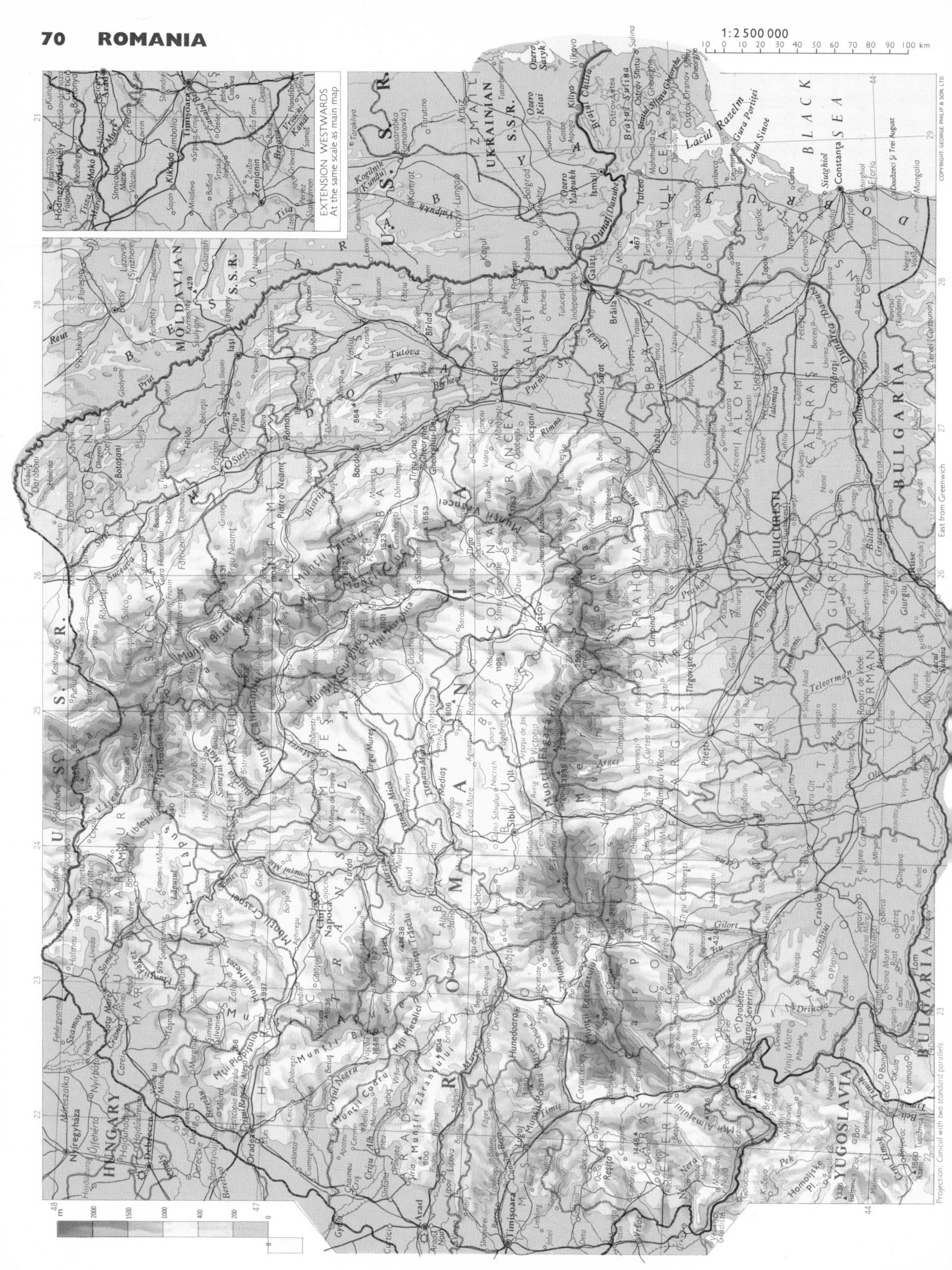

1:2 500 000

EXTENSION WESTWARDS
At the same scale as main map

1:2 500 000

10 0 10 20 30 40 50 60 70 80 90 100 km

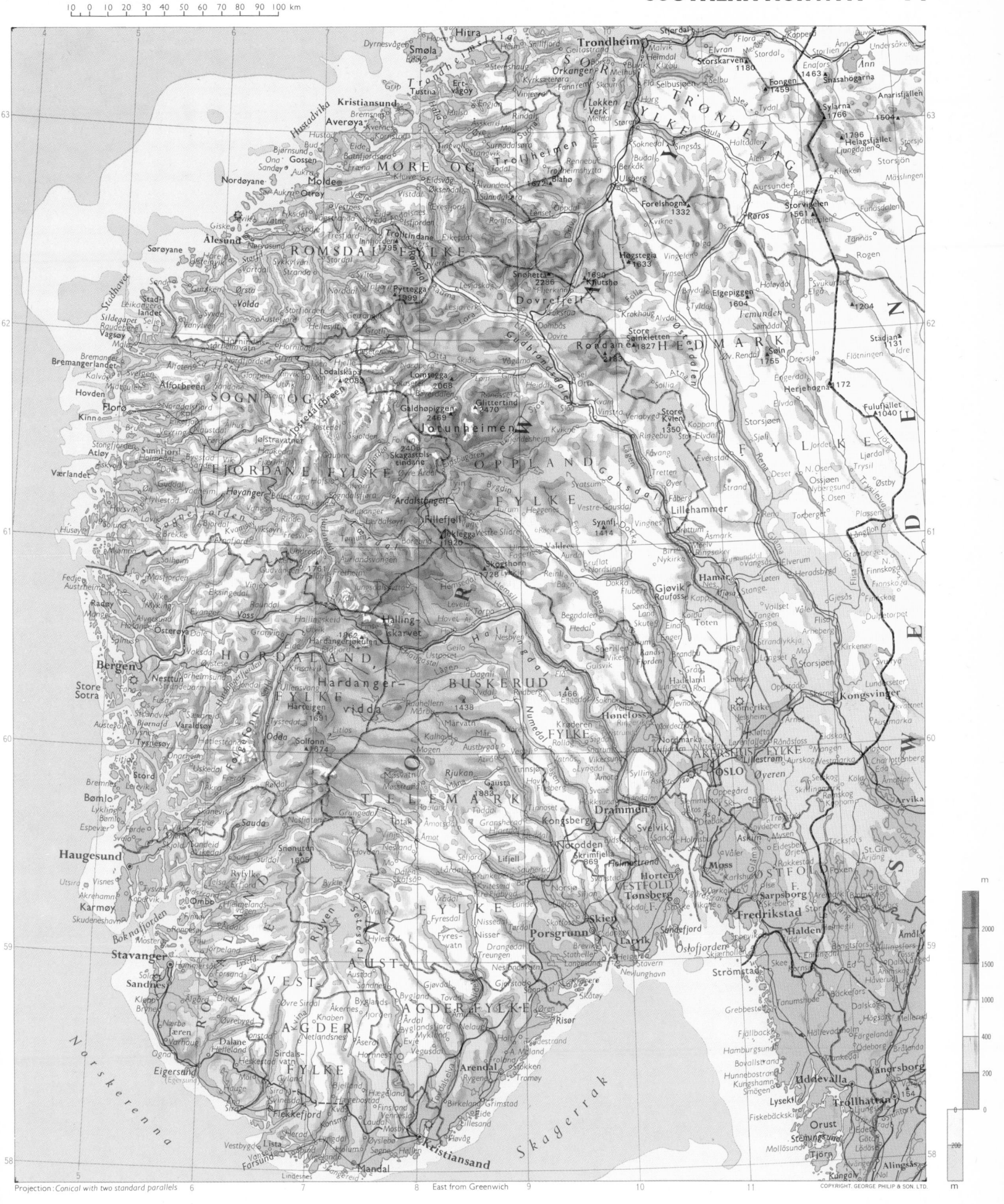

Projection: Conical with two standard parallels
East from Greenwich
COPYRIGHT. GEORGE PHILIP & SON. LTD.

Gulf of Bothnia
VÄSTERNORRLANDS LÄN
JÄMTLANDS LÄN
GÄVLEBORGS LÄN
KOPPARBERGS LÄN
VÄRMLANDS LÄN
UPPSALA LÄN
STOCKHOLMS LÄN
VÄSTMANLANDS LÄN
ÖREBRO LÄN
SÖDERMANLANDS LÄN
SØR-TRØNDELAG FYLKE
MØRE OG ROMSDAL FYLKE
HEDMARK FYLKE
OPPLAND FYLKE
BUSKERUD
TELEMARK FYLKE
AKERSHUS FYLKE
VESTFOLD
ØSTFOLD
Örnsköldsvik
Härnösand
Sundsvall
Hudiksvall
Gävle
Uppsala
STOCKHOLM
Västerås
Örebro
Karlstad
Falun
Borlänge
Mora
Östersund
Trondheim
Lillehammer
Hamar
OSLO
Drammen
Jotunheimen
Dovrefjell

1 : 2 500 000

10 0 10 20 30 40 50 60 70 80 90 100 km

73

COPYRIGHT GEORGE PHILIP & SON, LTD.

Projection: Conical with two standard parallels

East from Greenwich

m 2000 1500 1000 400 200 0

200 m

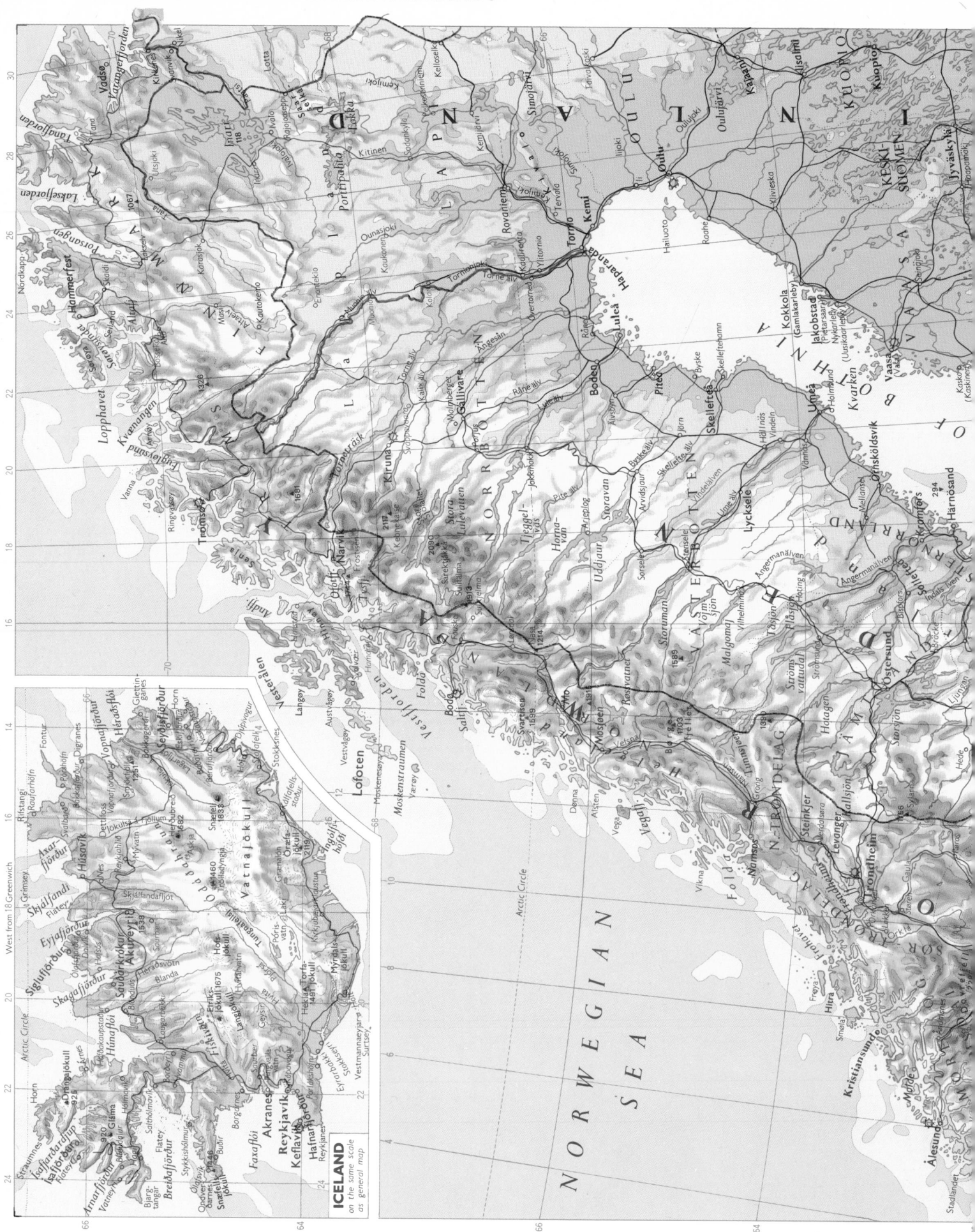

NORWEGIAN SEA
ICELAND
on the same scale as general map
Reykjavík
Keflavík
Akranes
Hafnarfjördur
Akureyri
Húsavík
Siglufjördur
Saudárkrókur
Ísafjördur
Vatnajökull
Faxaflói
Húnaflói
Skagafjördur
Eyjafjördur
Arctic Circle
West from 18 Greenwich
Lofoten
Vesterålen
Vestfjorden
Moskenstraumen
Narvik
Tromsø
Hammerfest
Vadsø
Kirkenes
Nordkapp
Porsangen
Laksefjorden
Tanafjorden
Varangerfjorden
Loppahavet
Kvænangen
Lyngen
Bodø
Mosjøen
Namsos
Steinkjer
Levanger
Trondheim
Kristiansund
Ålesund
Molde
Hitra
Frøya
Smøla
Vega
Vikna
Folda
Kiruna
Gällivare
Luleå
Boden
Piteå
Skellefteå
Umeå
Örnsköldsvik
Härnösand
Östersund
Lycksele
Storuman
Haparanda
Torneå
Kemi
Oulu
Rovaniemi
Kajaani
Kokkola
Jakobstad
Vaasa
Kuopio
Jyväskylä
Raahe
Hailuoto
Inari
Storsjön
Kvarken
NORRBOTTEN
VÄSTERBOTTEN
JÄMTLAND
N.-TRØNDELAG
OULU
LAPPI
KUOPIO
VAASA
KESKI-SUOMEN

1:5 000 000

50 0 50 100 150 200 km

FINLAND
HELSINKI (Helsingfors)
Tampere
Turku (Åbo)
Tallinn
ESTONIAN S.S.R.
Rakvere
Pärnu
Haapsalu
Viljandi
Valga
Valmiera
Riga
Rīgas Jūras Līcis (Gulf of Riga)
LATVIAN S.S.R.
Jelgava
Bauska
Ventspils
Liepaja
Klaipeda
LITHUANIAN S.S.R.
Vilnius
Kaunas
Grodno
Kaliningrad
Chernyakhovsk
Elbląg
R.S.F.S.R.
Białystok

BALTIC SEA

Saaremaa (Ösel)
Hiiumaa (Dagö)
Kingisepp
Ruhnu
Gotland
Visby
Gotska Sandön
Fårö
Öland
Bornholm
Rønne
Gdynia
Zatoka Gdańska
Gdańsk
Grudziądz
Toruń
Bydgoszcz
Szczecin (Stettin)

POLAND

GULF OF BOTHNIA

Aland (Ahvenanmaa)
Mariehamn (Maarianhamina)
STOCKHOLM
Uppsala
Eskilstuna
Västerås
Örebro
Norrköping
Nyköping
Linköping
Oxelösund
Nynäshamn
Västervik
Oskarshamn
Kalmar
Karlskrona
Karlshamn
Kristianstad
Karlstad
Vänern
Vättern
Jönköping
Växjö
Nässjö
Värnamo
Halmstad
Falkenberg
Varberg
GÖTEBORG
Göteborg
Borås
Trollhättan
Vänersborg
Uddevalla
Lidköping
Skövde
Mariestad

SWEDEN

NORWAY
OSLO
Drammen
Bergen
Stavanger
Haugesund
Kristiansand
Arendal
Grimstad
Lillesand
Kragerø
Risør
Larvik
Sandefjord
Tønsberg
Moss
Fredrikstad
Halden
Hamar
Lillehammer
Kongsberg
Skien
Porsgrunn
Notodden
TELEMARK
AUST-AGDER
VEST-AGDER
ROGALAND
Mandal
Farsund
Flekkefjord
Egersund (Eigersund)
Sandnes

Hudiksvall
Söderhamn
Gävle
Sandviken
Falun
Borlänge
Hedemora
Mora
Rättvik
Leksand
Ludvika
Avesta
Fagersta
Sala

KOPPARBERG
GÄVLEBORG
VÄRMLAND
ÖREBRO
VÄSTMANLAND
UPPSALA
SÖDERMANLAND
ÖSTERGÖTLAND
JÖNKÖPING
KRONOBERG
BLEKINGE
KALMAR
HALLAND
GÖTEBORG OCH BOHUS
ÄLVSBORG
SKARABORG

DENMARK
Skagerrak
Kattegat
The Sound
Store Bælt
Lille Bælt
Ålborg
Århus
Esbjerg
Odense
Randers
Horsens
Vejle
Kolding
Fredericia
Silkeborg
Herning
Viborg
Holstebro
Thisted
Hjørring
Frederikshavn
Roskilde
Helsingør
Malmö
Helsingborg
Landskrona
Trelleborg
Ystad
Svendborg
Nakskov
Nykøbing
Korsør
Slagelse
Næstved
Sjælland
Fyn
Lolland
Falster
Møn

Limfjorden
Læsø
Anholt
Samsø
Grenå

GERMANY
EAST GERMANY
WEST GERMANY
Hamburg
Lübeck
Kiel
Flensburg
Rostock
Schwerin
Wismar
Stralsund
Greifswald
Rügen
Usedom
Bremen
Bremerhaven
Wilhelmshaven
Oldenburg
Groningen
NETHERLANDS
Nordfriesische Inseln
Ostfriesische Inseln
Sylt
Helgoland
Weser
Elbe

East from Greenwich

Projection Conical with two standard parallels

COPYRIGHT GEORGE PHILIP & SON, LTD.

m 3000 1500 1000 600 400 200 0 200 m

R.S.F.S.R.
1. Daghestan A.S.S.R.
2. Kabardino–Balkar A.S.S.R.
3. Mari A.S.S.R.
4. Mordovian A.S.S.R.
5. North Ossetian A.S.S.R.
6. Tatar A.S.S.R.
7. Udmurt A.S.S.R.
8. Chuvash A.S.S.R.
9. Checheno–Ingush A.S.S.R.
AZERBAIJAN
10. Nakhichevan A.S.S.R.
GEORGIA
11. Abkhaz A.S.S.R.
12. Adzhar A.S.S.R.

Projection: Conical Orthomorphic with two standard parallels

East from Greenwich

1:20 000 000

200   0   200   400   600   800 km

——— Boundaries of U.S.S.R.
——— Boundaries of S.S.R.
——— Boundaries of A.S.S.R.

OCEAN

Severnaya Zemlya
Ostrov Komsomolets
Ostrov Oktyabrskoy Revolyutsii
Ostrov Bolshevik
Ostrov Pioner
Mys Arkticheskiy
Ostrov Shmidt
965

Laptev Sea
East Siberian Sea

Ostrov Henrietta
Ostrov Jeannette
Ostrova Delong
Ostrov Bennett
Novosibirskiye Ostrova
Ostrov Faddeyevskiy
Ostrov Novaya Sibir
Ostrova Lyakhovskiye
Lyakhovskiye Ostrova
Ostrov Zhokhova
3800
374

Ostrov Vrangelya
Ostrov Medvezhi

Chukotskoye More
Mys Dezhneva (East C.)
St. Lawrence I. (U.S.A.)

Poluostrov Gory Byrranga Taymyr
746
Oz Taymyr
Nordvik
Ust Olenek
Uryung-Khaya
Saskylakh
Olenek
Novorybnoye
Papigay
Khatanga
Kheta
Volochanka
Prasina

Tiksi
Bulun
Kyusyur
Mys Buorkhaya
Nizhneyansk
Kazachye
Chukochdog
Ercha
Indigirka
Srednekolymsk
Nizhne Kolymsk
Pobeda

Koryakskiy Khrebet
Sredinnyy Khrebet
Chukotskiy Khrebet
Bering Sea
Anadyrskiy Zaliv
Providenya
1843
1552

Gory Putorana
1701
Yessey
962
Kotuy
Moyero
Arctic Circle

Verkhoyansk
Khrebet Cherskogo
2399
Gora Chen
2882
3147

Magadan
Gizhiginskaya Guba
Penzhinskaya Guba
Gizhiga
Zaliv Shelikhova

Poluostrov Kamchatka
Petropavlovsk-Kamchatskiy
Ostrov Paramushir
Kamandorskiye Ostrova

Norilsk
Vilyuy
Vilyuysk
Verkhnevilyuysk
Srednevilyuysk
Nyurba
Suntar

Yakutsk
A.S.S.R.

Olekminsk
Aldan R.
Maya
Ust Maya

Okhotsk
Ayan
Sea of Okhotsk
Ostrov Bolshoy Shantar
Sakhalinskiy Zaliv
1790

Sakhalin
Nikolayevsk na-Amure
Yuzhno-Sakhalinsk
Kholmsk
Sovetskaya Gavan

Ostrov Iturup
Ostrov Kunashir
Kurilskiye Ostrova

Krasnoyarsk
Kansk
Ilanskiy
Nizhneudinsk
Bratsk
Kirensk
Ust-Ilimsk
2999
Bodaybo

Khrebet Stanovoy
Komsomolsk
2840
2078
Khabarovsk
Birobidzhan
Blagoveshchensk

Khrebet Sikhote Alin
3669
Ussuriysk
Vladivostok
Nakhodka

Hokkaido
Sapporo
Muroran
Hakodate

Irkutsk
Ulan Ude
Angarsk
1620
Cheremkhovo
Chita
Shilka
Nerchinsk
Sretensk
Nerchinskiy Zavod

Honshū
Sea of Japan
JAPAN
Niigata
To-yama
Kanazawa
Akita

MONGOLIA
Ulaanbaatar (Ulan Bator)
2800
1949
Choybalsan
Tamsagbulag

Harbin
Peh
Ch'angch'un
Chilin (Kirin)
Chongjin
Tung (Manchuria)
Fushun
Shenyang (Mukden)
Anshan
Antung

North KOREA
P'yongyang
Wŏnsan
Sŏul
Inch'on
South KOREA
Taejŏn
Pusan

Peip'ing
Changchiak'ou (Kalgan)
Paot'ou
2400
Inner Mongolia REPUBLIC

Edrengiyn Nuruu
3957
1925
Ham
GOBI
Hangayn Nuruu
Har Nuur
Hyargas Nuur
SEREPUBLIC

Kolguyev
Cheshskaya Guba
P-ov. Kanin
Timanskiy Kryazh
Bolshezemelskaya Tundra
Pechora
Arctic Circle
Kolskiy Poluostrov
Murmansk
Beloye More (White Sea)
Arkhangelsk
Onezhskaya Guba
Dvinskaya Guba
KARELIAN A.S.S.R.
Petrozavodsk
Ladozhskoye Ozero
Onezhskoye Ozero
LENINGRAD
Kronshtadt
Syktyvkar
Kotlas
Vologda
Kirov
Severnyye Uvaly
Perm
SVERDLOVSK
Nizhniy Tagil
Zlatoust
Ufa
Orenburg
KUYBYSHEV
Kazan
GORKIY
Yaroslavl
Rybinsk
Kostroma
Ivanovo
Vladimir
MOSKVA (Moscow)
Kalinin
Ryazan
Tula
Penza
Saratov
Tambov
Orel
Bryansk
Smolensk
Vitebsk
Mogilev
Minsk
Gomel
Vilnius
Kaunas
Riga
Tallinn
Pskov
Novgorod
Helsinki
Turku
Tampere
Oulu
Stockholm
Gulf of Bothnia
G. of Finland
FINLAND
SWEDEN
NORWAY
LAPPLAND
ESTONIAN S.S.R.
LATVIAN S.S.R.
LITHUANIAN S.S.R.
BYELORUSSIAN S.S.R. (WHITE RUSSIA)
RUSSIAN SOVIET FEDERATIVE SOCIALIST REPUBLIC
URAL MTS.
UDMURT A.S.S.R.
TATAR A.S.S.R.
BASHKIR A.S.S.R.
MARI A.S.S.R.
CHUVASH A.S.S.R.
MORDOVIAN A.S.S.R.
POLAND
WARSZAWA (Warsaw)
Kaliningrad
Białystok
Brest
Hiiumaa
Saaremaa
Rigas Jūras Līcis

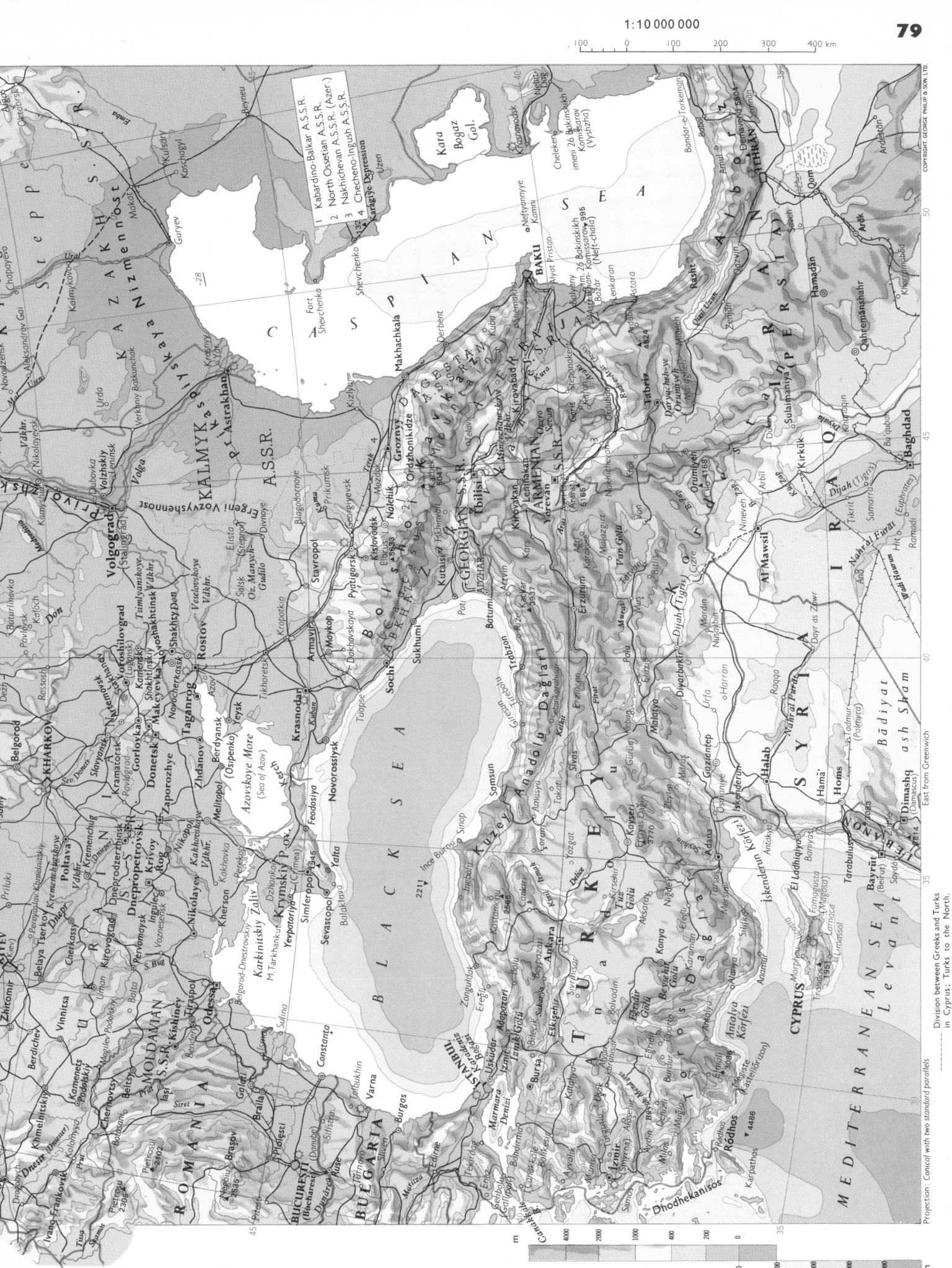

1 : 10 000 000

100   0   100   200   300   400 km

79

COPYRIGHT GEORGE PHILIP & SON, LTD.

Projection : Conical with two standard parallels

East from Greenwich

Division between Greeks and Turks
in Cyprus; Turks to the North.

Projection: Conical with two standard parallels

East from Greenwich

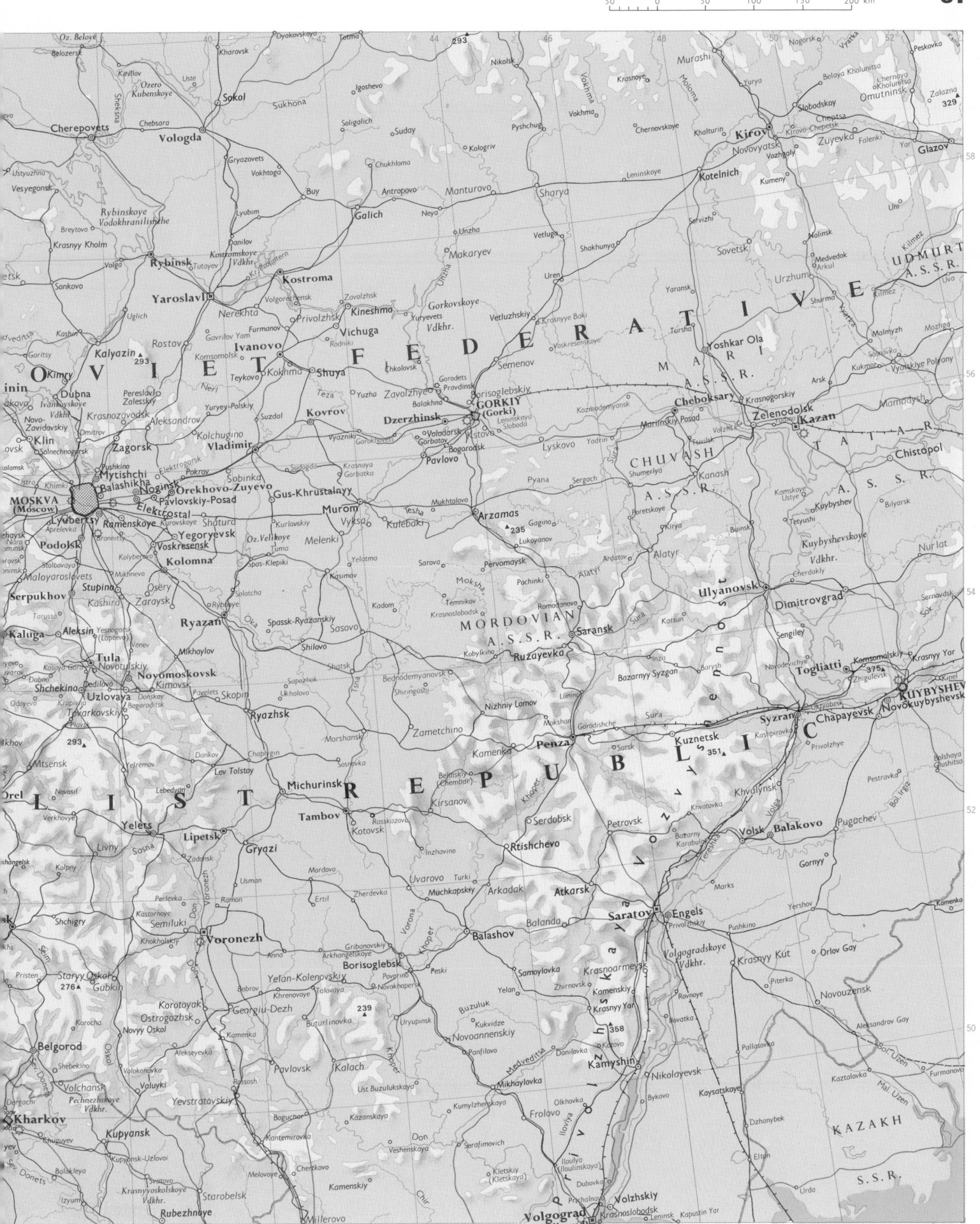

1:5 000 000

50   0   50   100   150   200 km

Oz. Beloye
Belozersk
Cherepovets
Ustyuzhna
Vesyegonsk
Vologda
Sokol
Kirillov
Uste
Ozero
Kubenskoye
Sheksna
Chebsara
Gryazovets
Sukhona
Soligalich
Suday
Pyshchug
Chernovskoye
Khalturin
Kirov
Kirovo-Chepetsk
Novovyatsk
Dyakovskoye
Tetma
Nikolsk
Murashi
Vyatka
Nagorsk
Slobodskoy
Omutninsk
Zalazna
329
Glazov
58

Rybinskoye
Vodokhranilishche
Krasnyy Kholm
Rybinsk
Tutayev
Kostroma
Yaroslavl
Galich
Neya
Manturovo
Sharya
Leninskoye
Kotelnich
Kumeny
Uni
Glazov

SOVIET FEDERATIVE

MARI A.S.S.R.
UDMURT A.S.S.R.

Kalyazin
293
Ivanovo
Shuya
Kostroma
Nerekhta
Kineshma
Vichuga
Yuryevets
Vetluzhskiy
Krasnyye Baki
Uren
Yoshkar Ola
Arsk
Kazan
56

Klin
Zagorsk
Vladimir
Kovrov
Dzerzhinsk
GORKIY (Gorki)
Cheboksary
Zelenodolsk
Chistopol
CHUVASH A.S.S.R.
TATAR A.S.S.R.

MOSKVA (Moscow)
Balashikha
Noginsk
Orekhovo-Zuyevo
Gus-Khrustalnyy
Murom
Arzamas
235
Ulyanovsk
Dimitrovgrad
54

Podolsk
Kolomna
Ryazan
Sasovo
Saransk
MORDOVIAN A.S.S.R.
Togliatti
375
KUYBYSHEV
Novokuybyshevsk

Serpukhov
Kaluga
Tula
Novomoskovsk
Ryazhsk
Penza
Kuznetsk
351
Syzran
Chapayevsk

Orel
LIST REPUBLIC
Michurinsk
Tambov
Volsk
Balakovo
52

Yelets
Lipetsk
Gryazi
Rtishchevo
Saratov
Engels
50

Voronezh
Borisoglebsk
239
358
Kamyshin
Nikolayevsk

Belgorod
Kharkov
KAZAKH S.S.R.
276
Georgiu-Dezh
Novoannenskiy
Mikhaylovka
Frolovo
Volzhskiy
Volgograd (Stalingrad)
Krasnoslobodsk

48   COPYRIGHT, GEORGE PHILIP & SON, LTD.

Projection: Conical with two standard parallels

1:5 000 000

50   0   50   100   150   200 km

40 Yelan-Kolenovskiy
Povorino
Peski
Bobrov
Khrenovoye
Talovaya
Samoylovka
Krasnoarmeysk
Zhirnovsk
Krasnyy Kut
48
Orlov Gay
50
Dzhambeyty
Georgiu-Dezh
Novokhoperskiy
Yelan
Krasnyy Yar
Rovnoye
Piterka
Novouzensk
Ostrogozhsk
Kamenka
Buturlinovka
239
Uryupinsk
Kukvidze
Buzuluk
Krasnoarmeysk
Vozyshennost
358
Vdkhr.
Ivovatka
Aleksandrov Gay
Oz. Chalkar
Chalkar
Chapayevo
Karsa
52
Pavlovsk
Rossosh
Kalach
Novoannenskiy
Panfilovo
Volgogradskoye
Kaztalovka
Mergenevskiy
Kushum
Ural
Inderborskiy
veyka
Kantemirovka
Boguchar
Ust Buzulukskaya
Medveditsa
Mikhaylovka
Kamyshin
Nikolayevsk
Yelan
Kaytalovka
Mar-Uzen
Furmanovo
Antonovo
Bazartobe
atovskiy
Meloye
Kazanskaya
Khoper
Frolovo
Ilovlya
Olkhovka
Bykovo
Dzhanybek
Verkhnii Baskunchak
Novobogatinskoye
Kalmykovo
50
Starobelsk
Chertkovo
Kletskiy
(Kletskaya)
Ilovlya
(Iloulinskaya)
Don
Veshenskaya
Serafimovich
Dubovka
Elton
Oz.Chalkar
odonetsk
Millerovo
Chir
Sovetskaya
Privolzhskaya
Pallasovka
Urda
Topol
Kamensk-Shakhtinskiy
Glubokiy
Morozovsk
Kalach na Donu
Prichalnaya
Volzhskiy
Kapustin Yar
Shungay
48
nov
Voroshilovgrad
(Lugansk)
Lenin
Volgograd
(Stalingrad)
Volga
Urda
nka
munarsk
Krasnyy Luch
edlovsk
Belaya Kalitva
Krasnoarmeysk
Akhtubinsk
(Petropavlovskiy)
Makhambet
(Yamankhalinka)
Krasnyy Luch
Krasnodon
Krasnodonetskaya
Tsimlyanskoye
Vladimirovka
Rovenki
ezhnoye
Krasny Sulin
Shakhty
Vdkhr.
voshakhtinsk
Dony
Kamenolomni
Tsimlyansk
Volgodonsk
Dubovskoye
Obilnoye
Kapaovka
Yenotayevka
Guryev
nrog
Tuzlov
Novocherkassk
Konstantinovskiy
Zvetnoye
28
Azov
Matveyev Kurgan
Bataysk
Rostov
Sh
Bolshaya Martynovka
Zimovniki
K A L M Y K
rt Katon
aya Yeya
Staro-
minskaya
Zernograd
Veselovskoye
Vdkhr.
Mechetinskaya
Manych
Kuberle
A. S. S. R.
Krasnyy Yar
Kanevskaya
Proletarskaya
Yegorlykskaya
Gigant
Oz. Manych-
Gudilo
Remontnoye
Krasnoye
Astrakhan
46
Pavlovskaya
Belaya
Glina
Salsk
Leninsk
Elista
(Stepnoi)
Priyutnoye
Mumra
Liman
Kultay
Tikhoretsk
Novoaleksandrovskaya
Ipatovo
Divnoye
Kalaus
Arzgir
Beloye Ozero
Kaspiyskiy
Korenovsk
Kropotkin
Izobil'nyy
Svetlograd
(Petrovskoye)
Starry Biryuzyak
Ust-Labinsk
Kuban
Stavropol
Blagodarnoye
Prikumsk
Kuma
C A S P I A N
Krasnodar
Armavir
831
Kurgannaya
(Kurgannaya)
Vladimirovka
Zelenokumsk
(Vorontsovo-Aleksandrovskoye)
Tyuleniy
O. Kulaly
Mangyshlakskiy
Zaliv
Maykop
Labinsk
Nevinnomyssk
Kursavka
Bryanskoye
M. Tyub Karagan
Fort Shevchenko
P.-ov.
Mangyshlak
Khadyzhensk
Apsheronsk
Urup
Cherkessk
Mineralnyye Vody
44
elagorsk
Dakhovskaya
Georgievsk
O. Chechen
Aleksandriyskaya
Shevchenko
Sochi
Krasnaya Polyana
Karachayevsk
Yessentuki
Pyatigorsk
Prokhladnyy
Mozdok
CHECHENO-
Lopatin
se
Bolsh
Teberda
Kislovodsk
Mayskiy
Nartkala
Malgobek
INGUSH
Groznyy
Gudermes
Sulak
Kizlyar
Adler
Gudauta
Nalchik
KABARDINO-
BALKAR
A.S.S.R.
Elbhenzi
Beslan
A.S.S.R.
Khasavyurt
Terek
Novyy Afon
Gagra
ABKHAZ
A.S.S.R.
5042
Tyrnyauz
5203
Kumtorkala
Makhachkala
Sukhumi
Kodori
Tkvarcheli
Sadon
Ordzhonikidze
Sogratl
Kaspiysk
Izberbash
Ochamchire
Gali
Dzhvari
Tsogeri
Kazbek
5047
Tebulos
4492
Agvali
Khunzakh
Akusha
Novokayakent
Rioni
Oni
Kakhib
Tlyarota
Dagestanskiye Ogni
Anaklia
Mikha-Tskhakaya
Sachkhere
Tskhinvali
(Staliniri)
Telavi
Madzhalis
Derbent
Kutaisi
Chiatura
Zestafoni
Khashuri
Gori
Kvareli
Logodekhi
800
Poti
Samtredia
Mtskheta
S.S.R.
Kaspi
Gurdzhaani
Mikhaylovka
Kobuleti
Makharadze
Borzhomi
Tbilisi
Signakhi
42
Batumi
ADZHAR
A.S.S.R.
Akhaltsikhe
Vale
Khrami
Shaumyani
Mirzaani
Iori
Alazan
Zakataly
(Nukha)
4466
Kutkashen
Mingechaurskoye
Vdkhr.
3629
Divichi
Hopa
Borçka
Akhalkalaki
Rustavi
Kura
Mingechaur
Agdash
Shemakha
Sumgait
Göreli
Akçaabat
Pazar
Ardanuç
Çildir
Kisir
3192
Tabz
Akstafa
Yevlakh
Geokchay
Surakhany
BAKU
Trabzon
Rize
Kaçkar
3937
Ardvuc
Kirovakan
Leninakan
Kirovabad
AZERBAIJAN
S.S.R.
Kazi Magomed
Sürmene
Olur
Sarikamis
Kars
Artik
Aragats
4090
Sevan
Ozero
Sevan
Kyurdamir
Ali-Bayramly
M.Byandovan
Çakirgöl
3063
ARMENIAN
Narman
Tortum
Araz
Kagizman
Digor
Echmiadzin
Yerevan
Mozuri
Kamo
Terter
Sabirabad
Imishly
Karachala
50
Gümüsane
cura
Bayburt
İspir
E g r i
D a
Sarikamis
İğdir
S.S.R.

ast from Greenwich
40
42
44
46
48
COPYRIGHT. GEORGE PHILIP & SON. LTD.

P r i k a s p i y s k a y a   N i z m e n n o s t
K A Z A K H   S. S. R.
D a g e s t a n   A. S. S. R.
B o l s h o i   K a v k a z
G E O R G I A N   S. S. R.
C a u c a s u s
M o u n t a i n s
Ergeni Vozyshennost

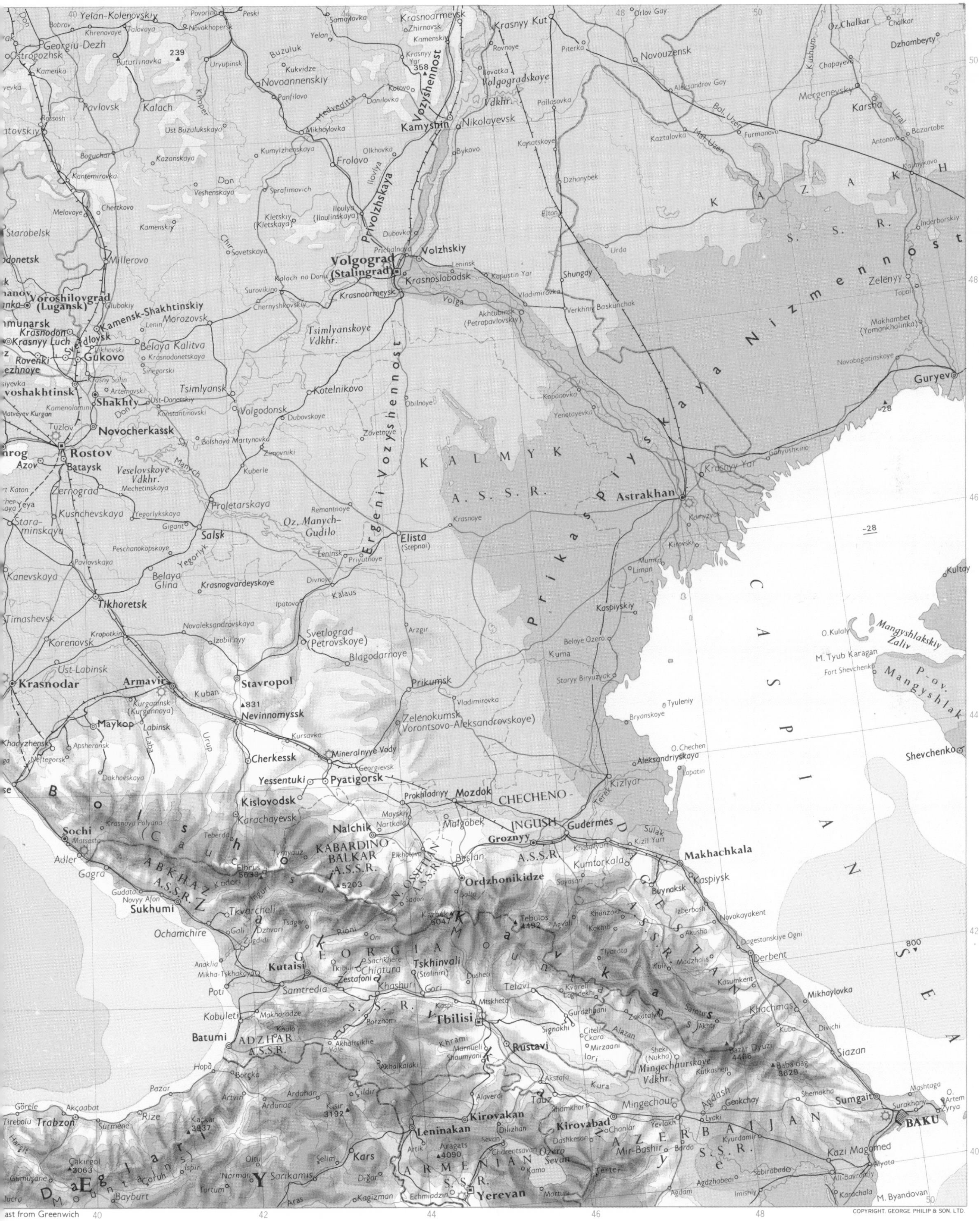

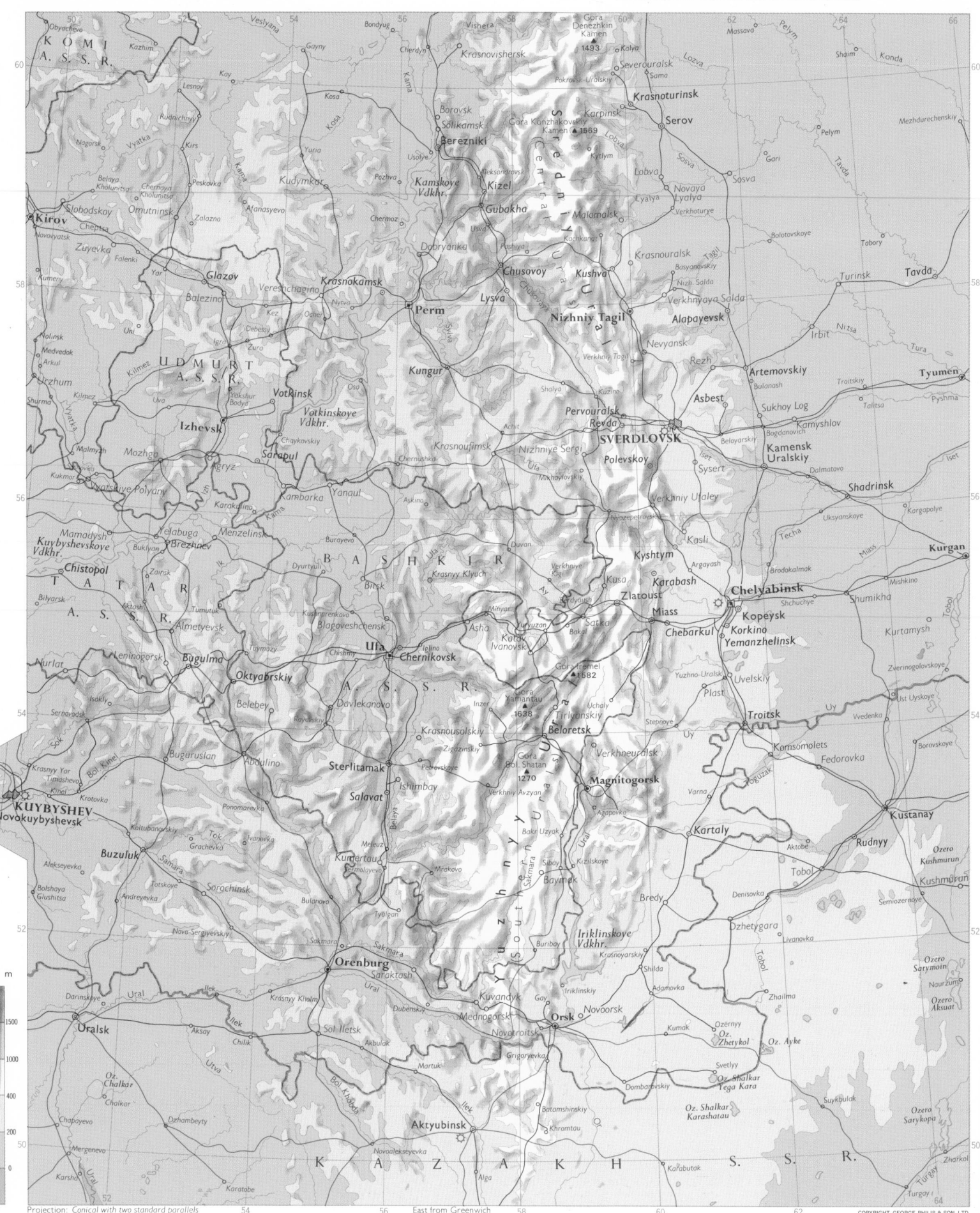

1:5 000 000

50   0   50   100   150   200 km

m
1500
1000
400
200
50
0

Projection: Conical with two standard parallels   East from Greenwich   COPYRIGHT. GEORGE PHILIP & SON. LTD.

1:5 000 000

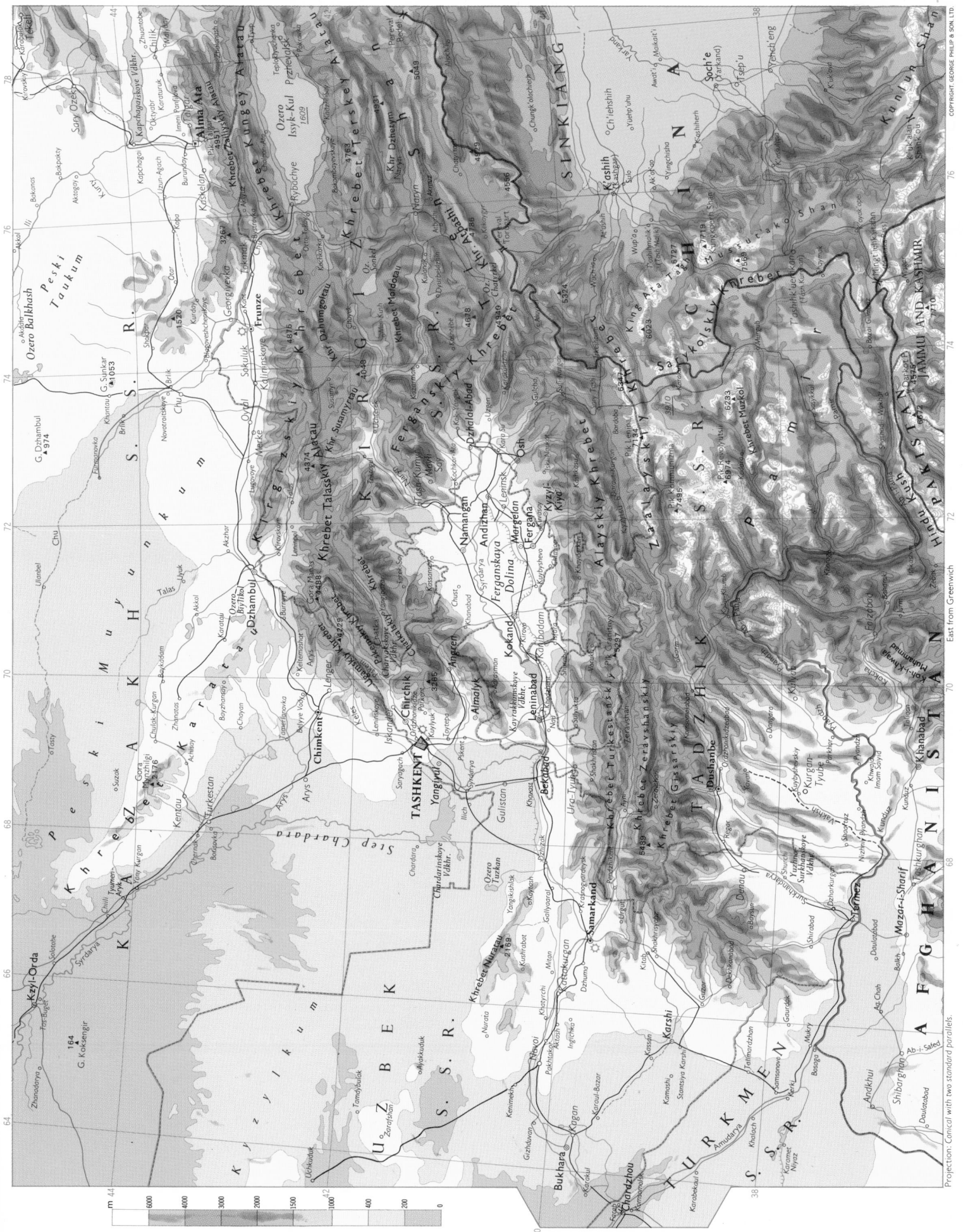

50   0   50   100   150   200 km

COPYRIGHT GEORGE PHILIP & SON LTD.

East from Greenwich

Projection: Conical with two standard parallels.

m 6000 4000 3000 2000 1500 1000 400 200 0

1:50 000 000

500   0   500   1000   1500   2000 km

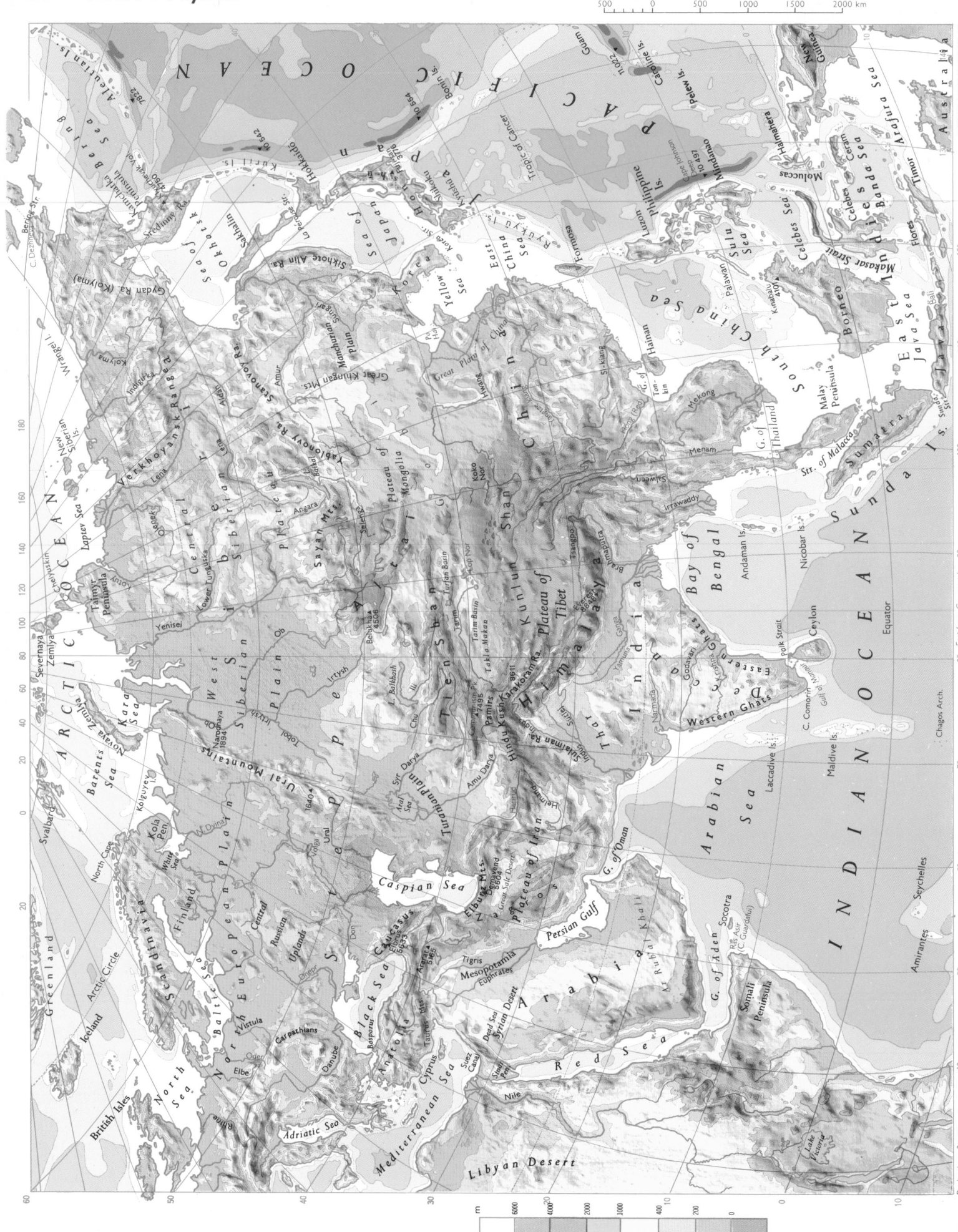

PACIFIC OCEAN

ARCTIC OCEAN

INDIAN OCEAN

Caspian Sea

Black Sea

Red Sea

Mediterranean Sea

Persian Gulf

Arabian Sea

Bay of Bengal

South China Sea

Himalaya

Plateau of Tibet

Kunlun Shan

Tien Shan

Plateau of Iran

Arabia

Rub' al Khali

Libyan Desert

Scandinavia

North European Plain

Ural Mountains

West Siberian Plain

Central Siberian Plateau

Verkhoyansk Range

m   6000   4000   2000   1000   400   200   0

0   200   2000   4000   6000   8000   m

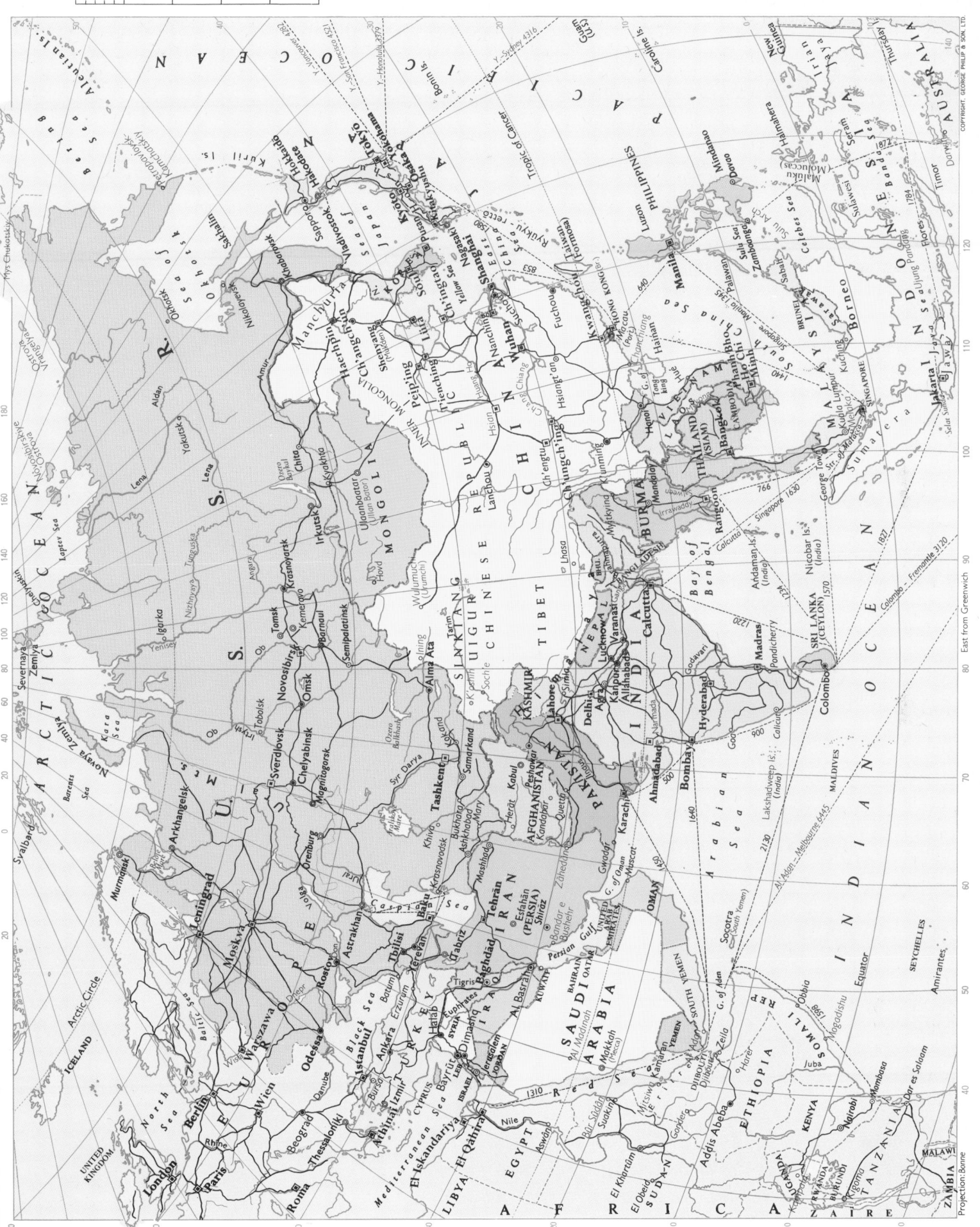

1:50 000 000

500   0   500   1000   1500   2000 km

Projection: Bonne

East from Greenwich

1:100 000 000

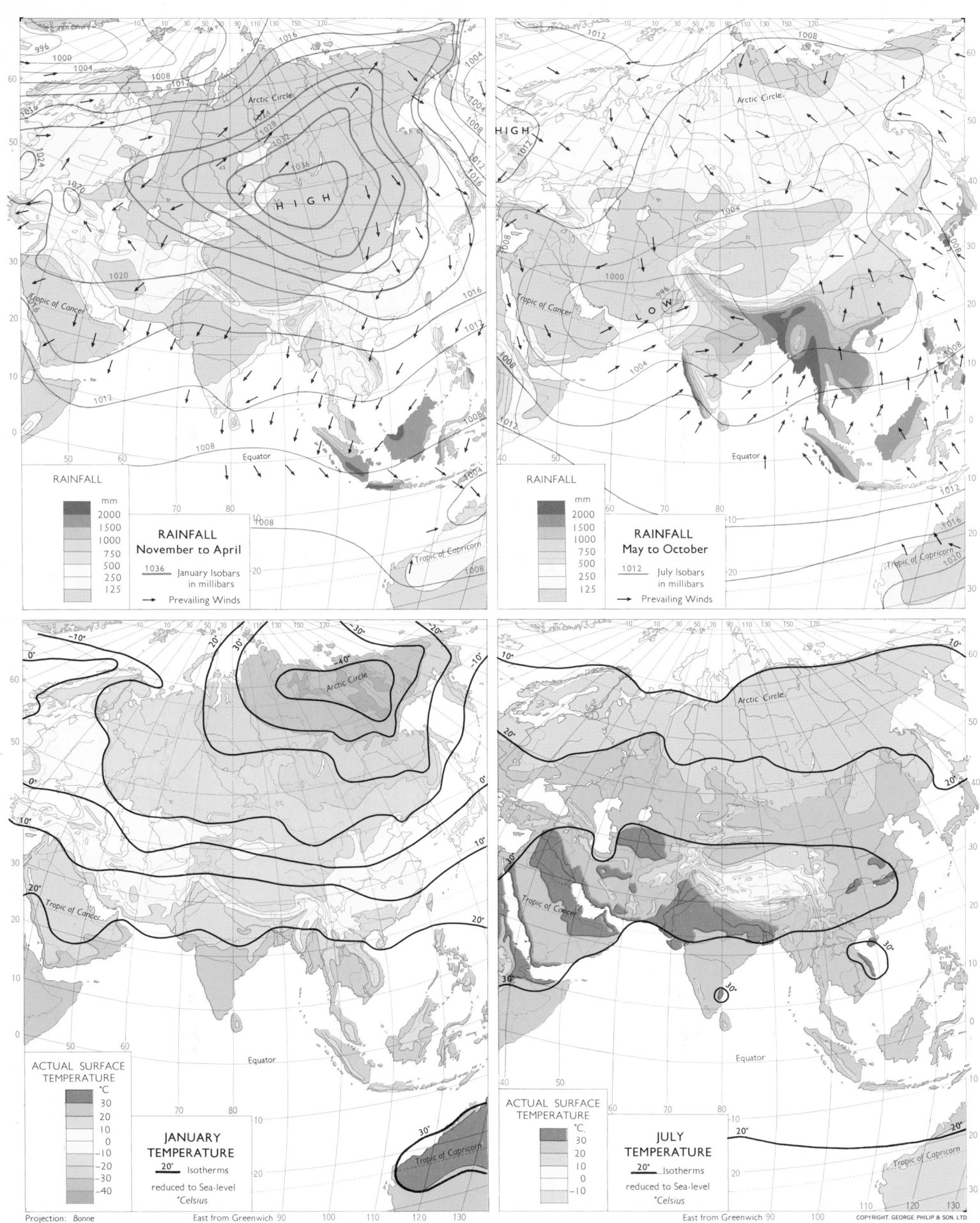

RAINFALL

mm	
2000	
1500	
1000	
750	
500	
250	
125	

RAINFALL
November to April

1036 ─── January Isobars
in millibars

→ Prevailing Winds

RAINFALL

mm	
2000	
1500	
1000	
750	
500	
250	
125	

RAINFALL
May to October

1012 ─── July Isobars
in millibars

→ Prevailing Winds

ACTUAL SURFACE
TEMPERATURE

°C	
30	
20	
10	
0	
-10	
-20	
-30	
-40	

**JANUARY
TEMPERATURE**

20° ─── Isotherms
reduced to Sea-level
°Celsius

ACTUAL SURFACE
TEMPERATURE

°C	
30	
20	
10	
0	
-10	

**JULY
TEMPERATURE**

20° ─── Isotherms
reduced to Sea-level
°Celsius

Projection: *Bonne*

East from Greenwich 90

East from Greenwich 90

COPYRIGHT GEORGE PHILIP & SON. LTD.

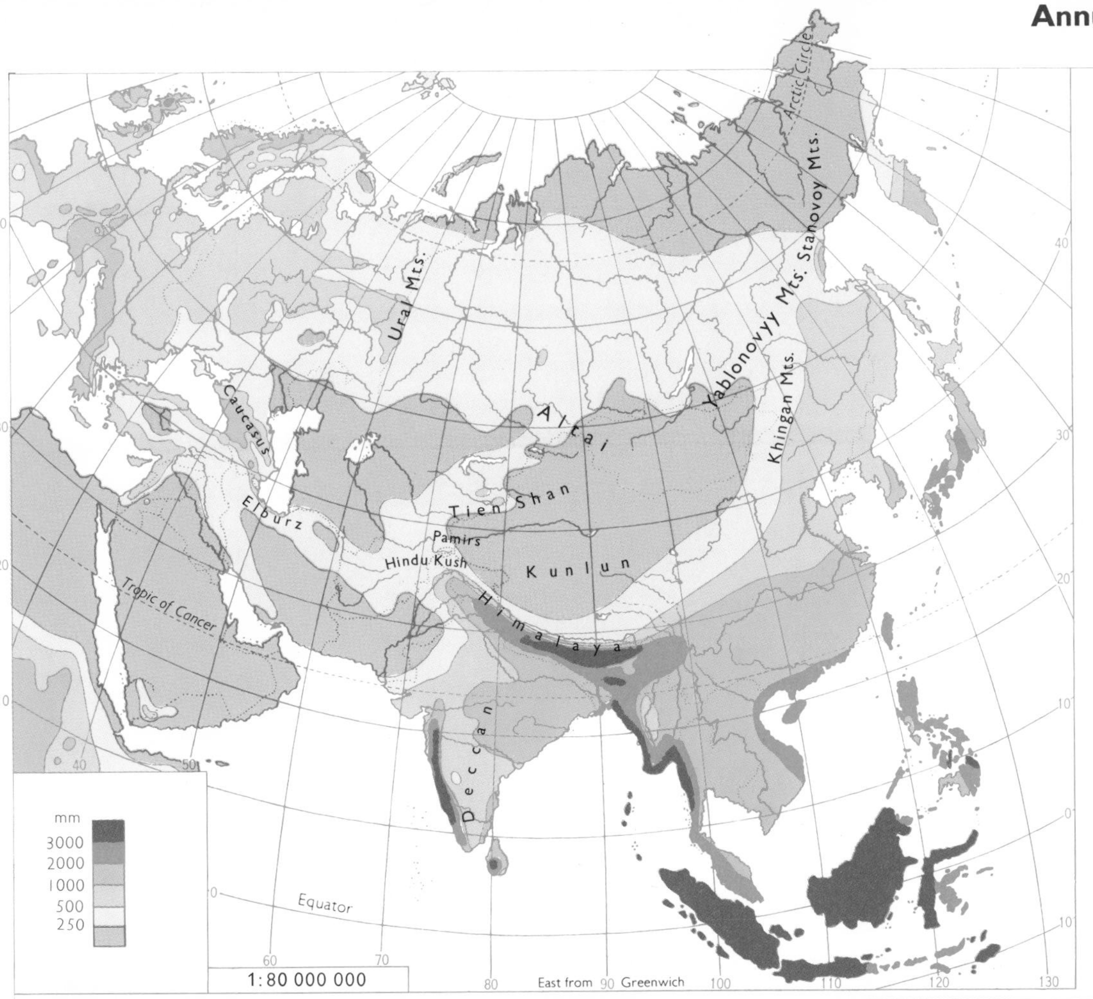

INDIA:
MONSOONS

THEIR EVOLUTION
IS SHOWN BY
MONTHLY
CLIMATE
MAPS

RAINFALL
mm per month

mm
25
50
100
200
400

—— ISOTHERMS
*Temperature in
degrees Celsius*

—— ISOBARS
(Pressure in millibars)

←—— WINDS

mm
3000
2000
1000
500
250

1:80 000 000

East from Greenwich

Equator

Tropic of Cancer

Arctic Circle

Ural Mts.
Caucasus
Elburz
Pamirs
Hindu Kush
Tien Shan
Kunlun
Altai
Yablonovyy Mts.
Stanovoy Mts.
Khingan Mts.
Himalaya
Deccan

JANUARY
FEBRUARY
MARCH
APRIL
MAY
JUNE
JULY
AUGUST
SEPTEMBER
OCTOBER
NOVEMBER
DECEMBER

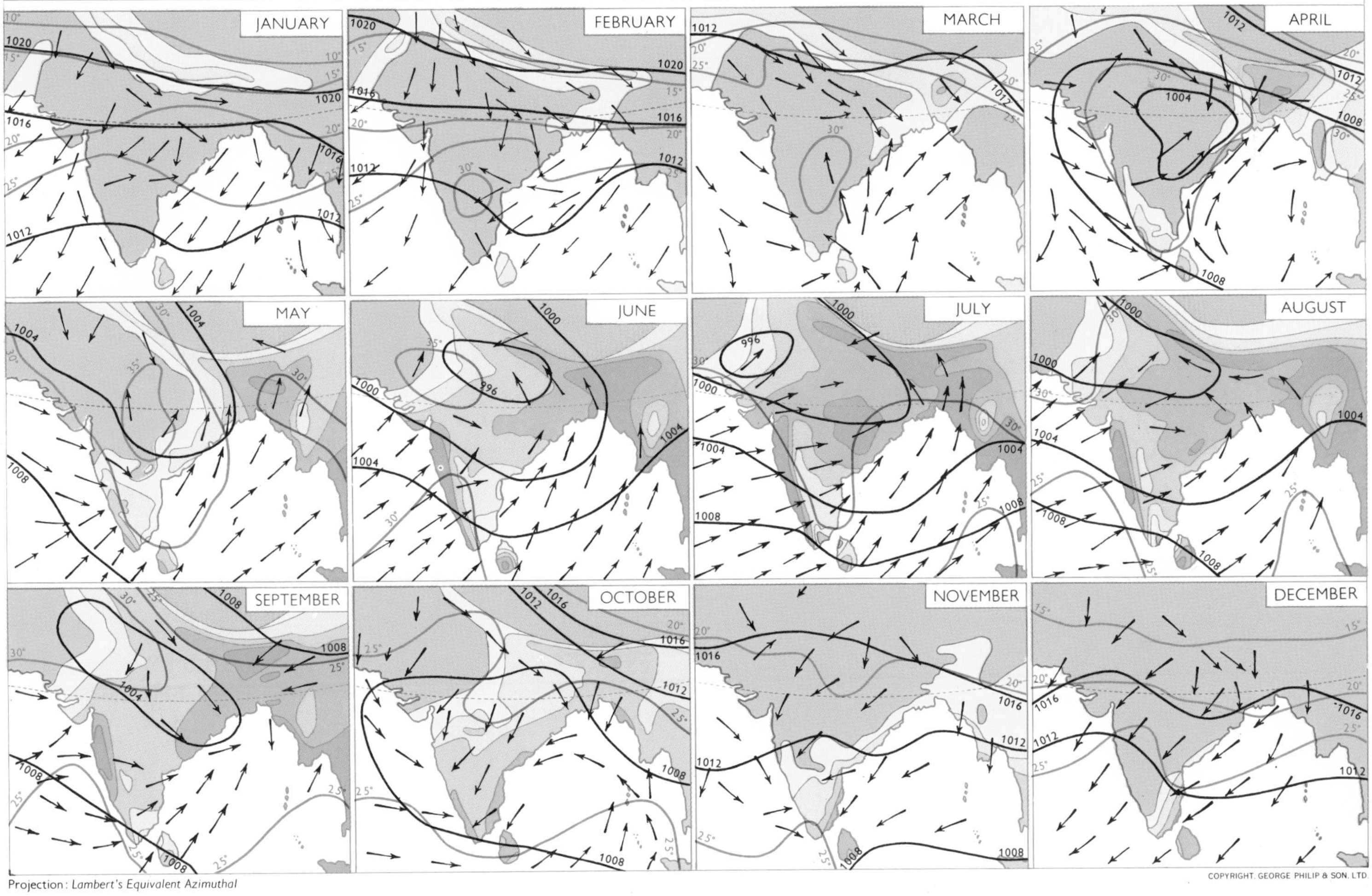

Projection: Lambert's Equivalent Azimuthal

1:1 000 000

10   10   20   30   40 km

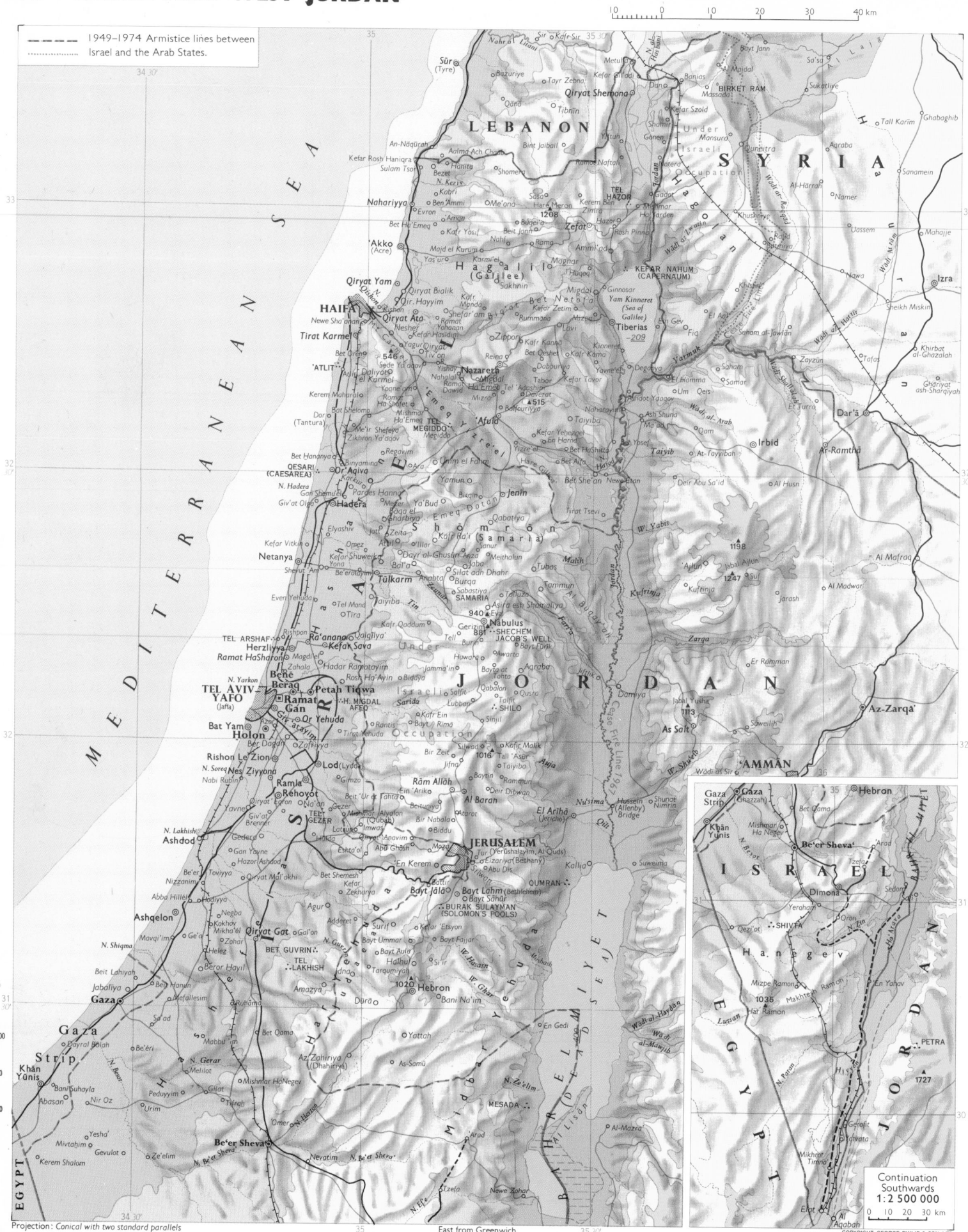

MEDITERRANEAN SEA

LEBANON

SYRIA

JORDAN

EGYPT

ISRAEL

Sūr
(Tyre)

Qiryat Shemona

BIRKET RAM

TEL HAZOR

Nahariyya

Akko
(Acre)

Qiryat Yam

HAIFA
Newe Sha'anan
Qiryat Ata
Tirat Karmel

'ATLIT

Ha Galil
(Galilee)

KEFAR NAHUM
(CAPERNAUM)

Tiberias

Yam Kinneret
(Sea of Galilee)

Nazareth

MEGIDDO
Megiddo

Afula

Irbid

Ar-Ramtha

Dar'ā

Netanya

Tūlkarm

SAMARIA

Nablus
SHECHEM
JACOB'S WELL

AMMAN

Az-Zarqa'

TEL AVIV
YAFO
(Jaffa)
Ramat
Gan
Bene
Beraq
Petah Tiqwa

Bat Yam
Holon

Rishon Le Zion
Nes Ziyyona

Ramla
Rehovot

Lod
(Lydda)

Rām Allāh

JERUSALEM
(Yerūshalayim, Al Quds)

El Arīḥā
(Jericho)

As Salt

Ashdod

GEZER

Bayt Lahm
(Bethlehem)
Bayt Jālā

QUMRAN

Ashqelon

Qiryat Gat

BET GUVRIN
TEL
LAKHISH

Hebron

Gaza

Gaza
Strip

Khān Yūnis

Be'er Sheva'

MESADA

Continuation Southwards
1:2 500 000
0   10   20   30 km

Gaza
Strip

Gaza
Ghazzah

Hebron

Khān
Yūnis

Be'er Sheva'

ISRAEL

Dimona

SHIVTA

Ha Negev

Mizpe Ramon

Makhtesh
Ramon

PETRA

JORDAN

EGYPT

1727

Elat
Al
'Aqabah

1:15 000 000

100 0 100 200 300 400 500 600 km

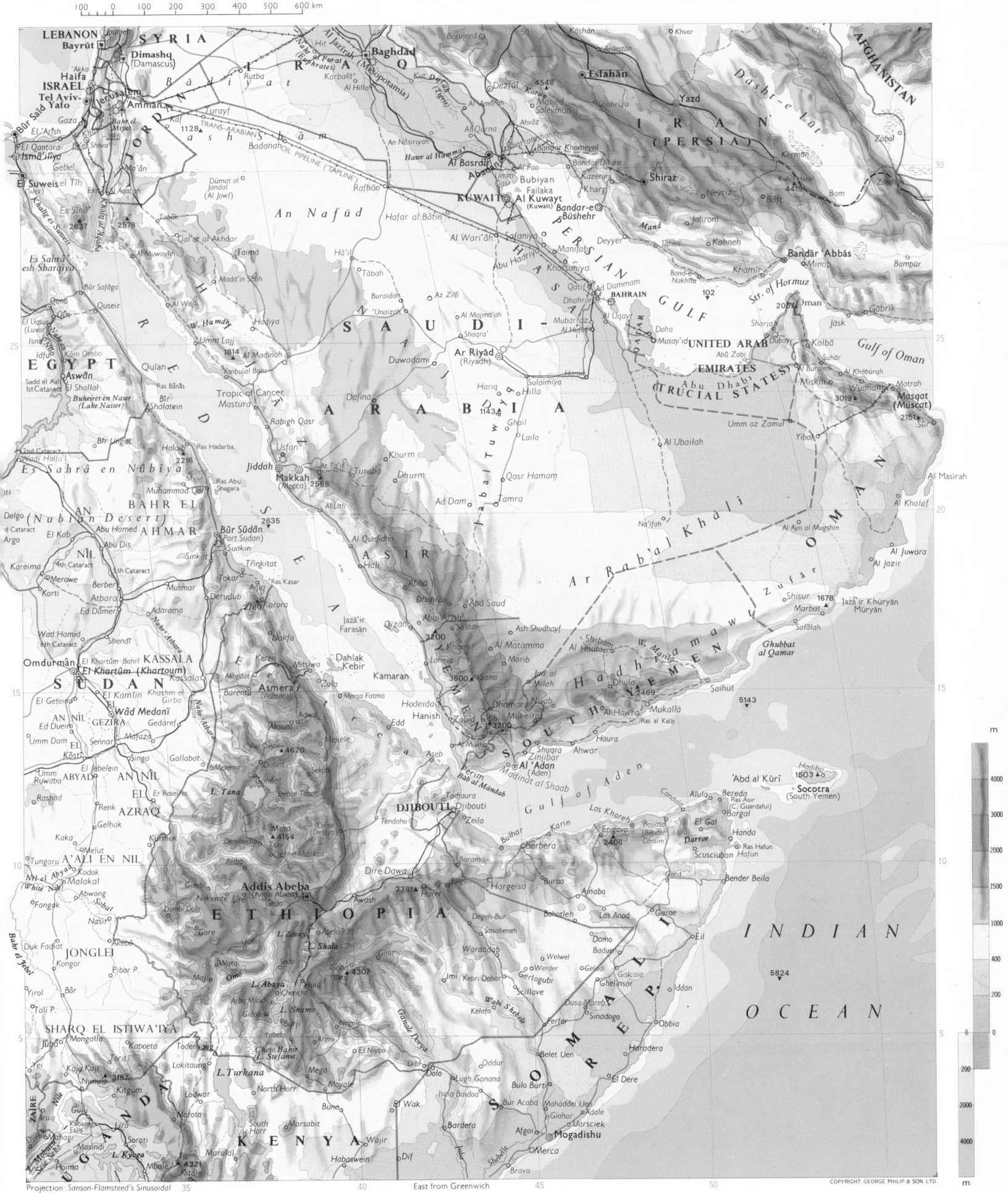

LEBANON
Bayrût
SYRIA
Dimashq
(Damascus)
Haifa
ISRAEL
Tel Aviv-
Yafo
Jerusalem
Gaza
El 'Arîsh
El Qantara
Ismâ'îliya
El Suweis
(Suez)
El Qusur
(Luxor)
Gebel
Bûr Sa'îd
Akko
Amman
Ma'ān
El 'Aqaba
Tabûk
JORDAN
Rutba
Badanah
Jûrayf
TRANS-ARABIAN
as h
Nafûd al Furât
(Euphrates)
Baghdad
IRAQ
Karbalā'
Al Hillah
An Nāsiriyah
Rafhā
OIL PIPELINE ('TAPLINE')
Dûmat al
Jandal (Al Jawf)
Qal'at al Akhdar
An Nafûd
Hā'il
Taima
'Unaizah
Buraidah
Mâdâ'in Sâlih
Tābah
Az Zilfi
Al Majma'ah
Shaqra
AFGHANISTAN
Kāshān
Khvor
Khor
Borujerd
Boroujerd
Ardestān
4548
Dezfúl
Esfahān
Masjed-e
Soleyman
Shahriza
Yazd
Al 'Amārah
Ahvāz
Ali Qurna
Hawr al Hammār
Al Basrah
Al Fao
Bandar-e Khomeyni
Umm Qasr
Bubiyan
Failaka
Bandar Dilam
Kāzerūn
Kharg
Bandar 'Abbas
Minab
Khamir
Bander
Nakhila
Band-e
Kermān
Bam
Böft
Kuh-e Hazar
4419
Zābol
IRAN
(PERSIA)
Shīrāz
Neyrīz
Jahrom
Deyyer
Taheri
Kahneh
KUWAIT
Al Kuwayt
(Kuwait)
Bandar-e
Büshehr
Hafar al Bātin
Safaniya
Al Wari'āh
Abu Hadriya
Al Khobar
Manifah
Qatif
Ad Dammam
BAHRAIN
Dhahrān
Mubarraz
Al Uqayr
Doha
Musay'id
QATAR
Abū Zabī
UNITED ARAB
EMIRATES
Abu Dhabi
(TRUCIAL STATES)
102
Str. of Hormuz
Oman
Sharjah
Dubayy
Al Buraimi
Miskin
Kalba
Suhār
Al Khābūrah
3019
Gulf of Oman
Jask
Gābrik
Bāmpūr
2057
Matrah
Masqat
(Muscat)
2151
Sûr
Al Masirah

Es Sahrâ
esh Sharqiya
2637
2578
Bûr Safâga
Quseir
Qena
W. Hamdh
Umm Lajj
1814 Al Madinah
Yanbu'al Bahr
Rabigh Qasr
Dafina
Mastura
Hariq
Duwadimi
Ar Riyâd
(Riyadh)
Hilla
Sulaimiya
1143
Jabal Tuwayq
Ghail
Laila
Al Ubailah
Umm az Zamul
Yibal
Na'ifah
Ar Rab'al Khâli
Al Ayn al Mugshin
Shisur 1678
Marbat
Salālah
Zufâr
OMAN
3019
Al Khālaf
Al Juwara
Al Jazir

EGYPT
El Uqsur
(Luxor)
Idfu
Kôm Ombo
Aswân
Sadd el Aâli
1st Cataract
El Shallal
Buheiret en Naser
(Lake Nasser)
Ras Bânâs
Bîr Shalatein
Hodiya
Qulan
Ras Hadarba
2216
Halaib
Jiddah
Makkah
(Mecca) 2565
At Tâ'if
Turaba
Khurm
Dhurm
Qasr Hamam
SAUDI-
ARABIA
Tropic of Cancer
25
Usfan

Bîr Ungat
Muhammad Qol
2635
Abu Dis
BAHR EL
AHMAR
El Kab
Abu Homed
Bûr Sûdân
(Port Sudan)
Sinkat
Suakin
Trinkitat
Tokar
Derudeb
Karora
2780
Ras Abu
Shagara
Jabal
Gerf
S E A
R E D
Al Qunfidha
Hali
Abha
Dhahran
Abu 'Arish
Aba Saud
3200
Ash Shudhayf
Al Shibam
Al Hautan
Ghail
Tamra
Ad Dam
Ad Dam
Sa'dah
Al Matmma
Mārib
Shabwah
Al Hawta
W. Masīla
Saihut
5143
Ras al Kalb
HADHRAMAWT
Ghubbat al Qamar
NUBIAN
(Nubian Desert)
AN
2nd Cataract
Wadi Halfa
Es Sahrâ en Nûbiya
Delgo
3rd Cataract
Argo
El Kab
Kareima
Merowe
Korti
Atbara
Ed Dâmer
Berber
Wâd Hamid
5th Cataract
Shendi
Musmar
Adarama
Khashm el Girba
Kassala
KASSALA
Omdurmân
El Khartûm Bahrî
El Khartûm (Khartoum)
Kamlin
Wâd Medanî
EL GEZIRA
SUDAN
El Geteina
AN NIL
Mafaza
Gedaref
Aksum
Keren
Mitsiwa
Asmera
(Asmara)
Zula
Barentu
Adwa
Mersa Fatma
Dahlak
Kebir
Kamaran
Hanish
Aksum
Mekele
Ras Dashan
4620
Dunhet
Metema
Sekota
Edd
Al Mukha
Perim
Bâb el Mandeb
Lahoja
Sana
3600
Dhamar
Zabid
3200
Hodeida
Jizân
Jazâ'ir
Farasan
Khamir
2469
Dhula
YEMEN
Ta'izz
SOUTH
YEMEN
Ibb
Ba'dan
Qataba
Dhala
Lawdar
Mukeiras
Haura
Ahwar
Shuqra
Zinjibar
Al 'Adan
Madinat al Shaab
(Aden)
Gulf of Aden
Al Hawra
Mukallā
Ras al Kalb
Saihut
5143
'Abd al Kûrî
1503
Socotra
(South Yemen)
Hadibu
Abyssinia

El Kôstî
Sennar
Singa
Gallabat
Debre Tabor
L. Tana
4154
Dembecha
Debre Markos
ETHIOPIA
Addis Abeba
(Addis Ababa)
Nakemte
Sire
Gore
Jimma
Lekemti
Metu
L. Zimay
Asela
L. Shala
Goba
4307
Gore
L. Abaya
Ari Moch
L. Shamo
Chencha
Giddle
Burji
Arero
El Niybo
Dila
Dolo
Bulo Burti
Obbia
Awash
Dire Dawa
3381
Harer
Hargeisa
Degeh-Bur
Sasabeneh
Warandab
Imi
Kebri Dehar
Gunit
Ginir
Welwel
Domo
Baduen
Werder
Gerlogubi
Ghelinsor
5824
Gakan
Iddan
DJIBOUTI
Djibouti
Zeila
Bulhar
Karin
Berbera
Las Khareh
Erigavo
2408
Bosaso
(Bender
Cassim)
El Gal
Handa
Darror
Ras Hafun
Scusciuban
Hafun
Bender Beila
Garoe
Eil
S O M A L I
INDIAN
OCEAN

SHARQ EL ISTIWA'IYA
Mongalla
Jûba
Torit
Kapoeta
ZAIRE
Guli
Lira
Kabalega
Falls
Masindi
Mbale
L. Kyoga
UGANDA
3187
Kitgum
Lokitaung
Todenyang
North Horr
L. Turkana
L. Stefanie
Cheto Bahir
Mega
Moyale
Buna
El Wak
Isla Baidoa
El Dere
Dif
Wajir
Habaswein
Marsabit
South
Horr
4321
Kadtu
Eigon
4321
KENYA
Garba Harre
Bur Acaba
Mahaddei Uen
Giohar
Afgoi
Mogadishu
Merca
Brava
Belet Uen
Haradera
Adale
Oddur
Lugh Ganana
Bardera
Uarsciek
A'ALI EN NIL
Malakal
Kodok
Abwong
Nasir
Fangak
JONGLEI
Kongor
Pibor P.
Bôr
Yirol
Tali P.
Bahr el Jebel
Duk Fadiat
Kaka
Melut
Renk
EL AZRAQ
Er Roseires
Gelhak
Kurmuk
Alibo
Gimbi
Nakemte
Omo
Sodo
 Buga
Arba Minch
Yabelo

m
4000
3000
2000
1500
1000
400
200
0
200
2000
4000
m

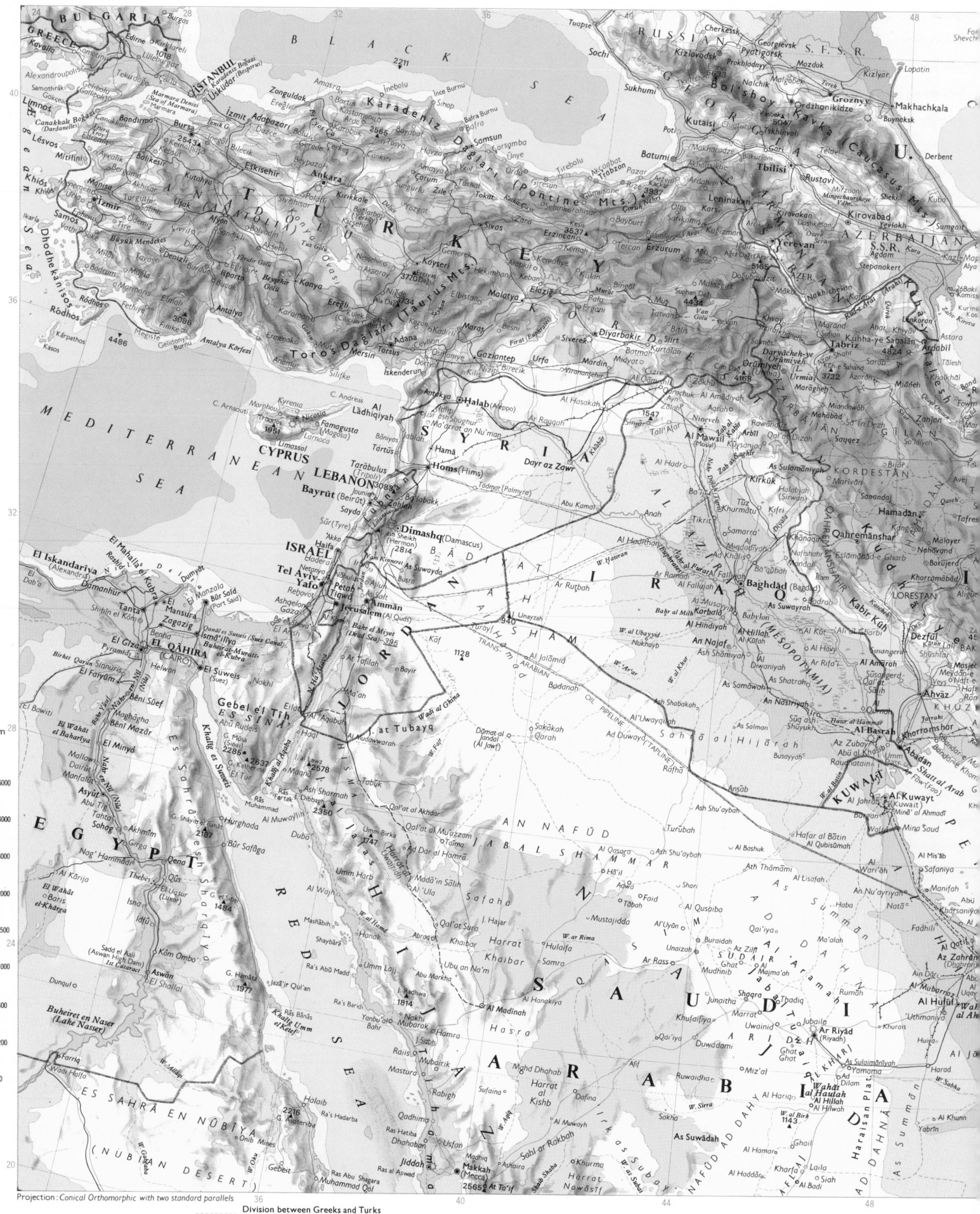

Projection: Conical Orthomorphic with two standard parallels

- - - - - Division between Greeks and Turks
in Cyprus; Turks to the North.

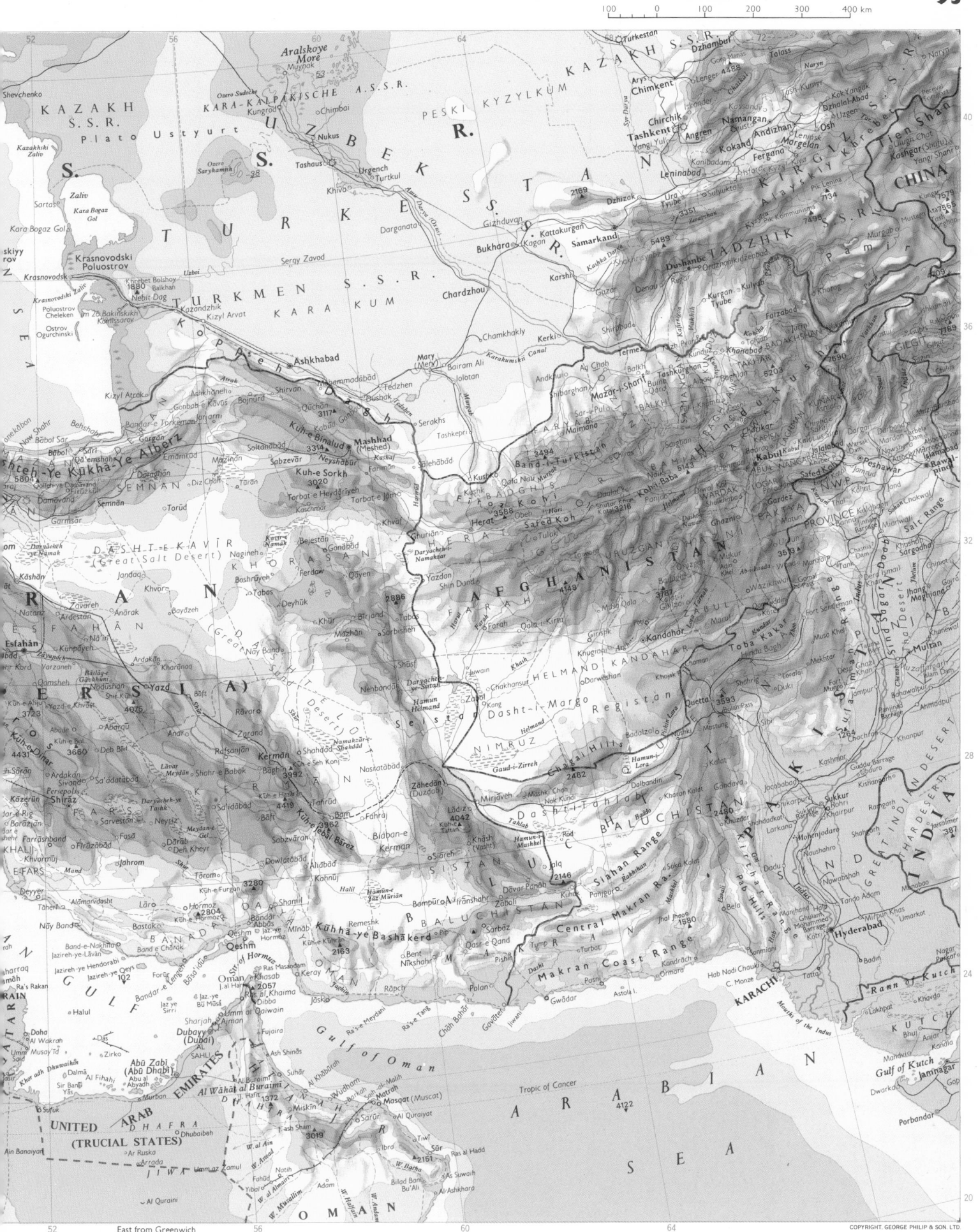

1 : 10 000 000

100   0   100   200   300   400 km

93

East from Greenwich

COPYRIGHT. GEORGE PHILIP & SON. LTD.

Projection: Conical with two standard parallels

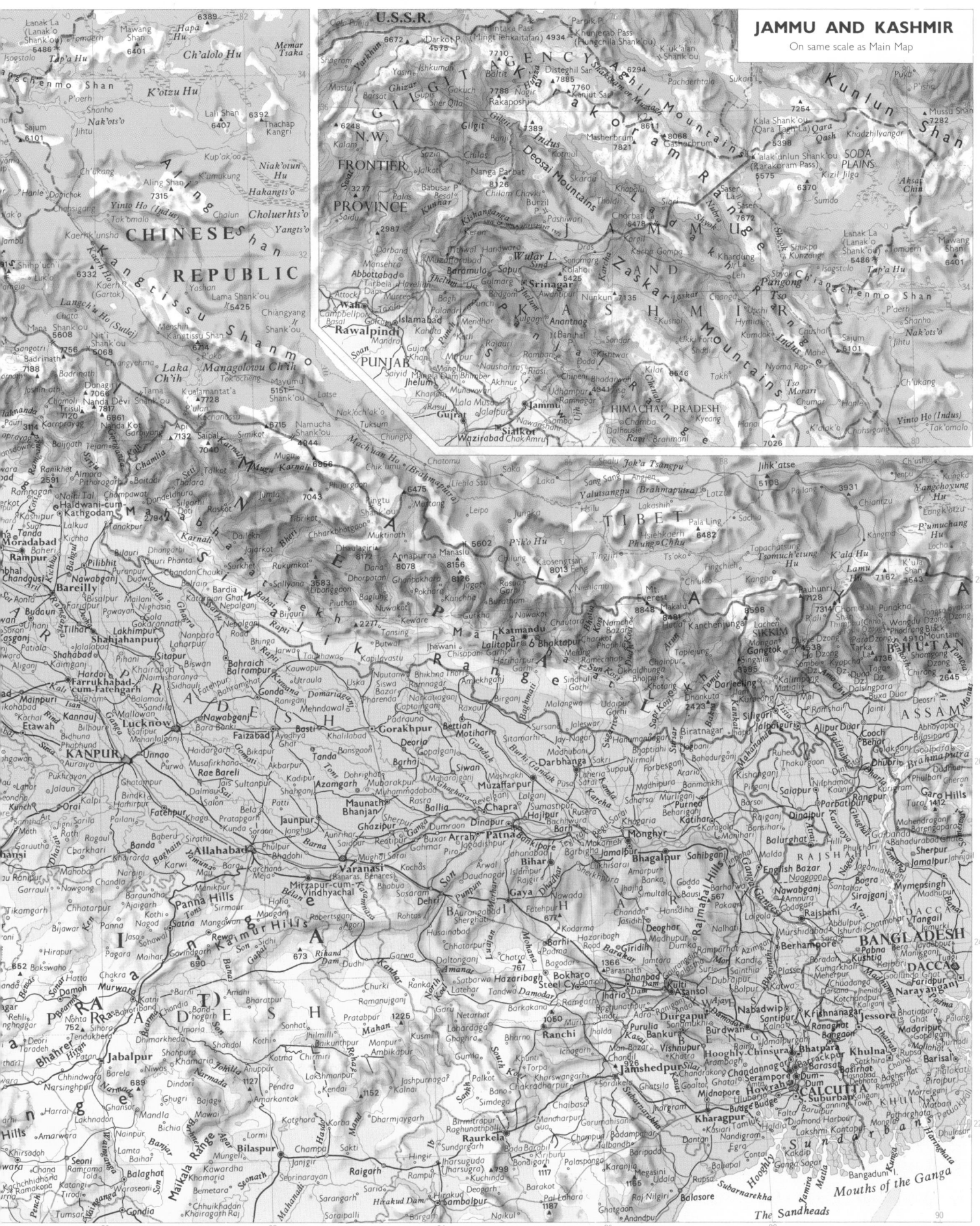

1:6 000 000

50   0   50   100   150   200   250 km

East from Greenwich

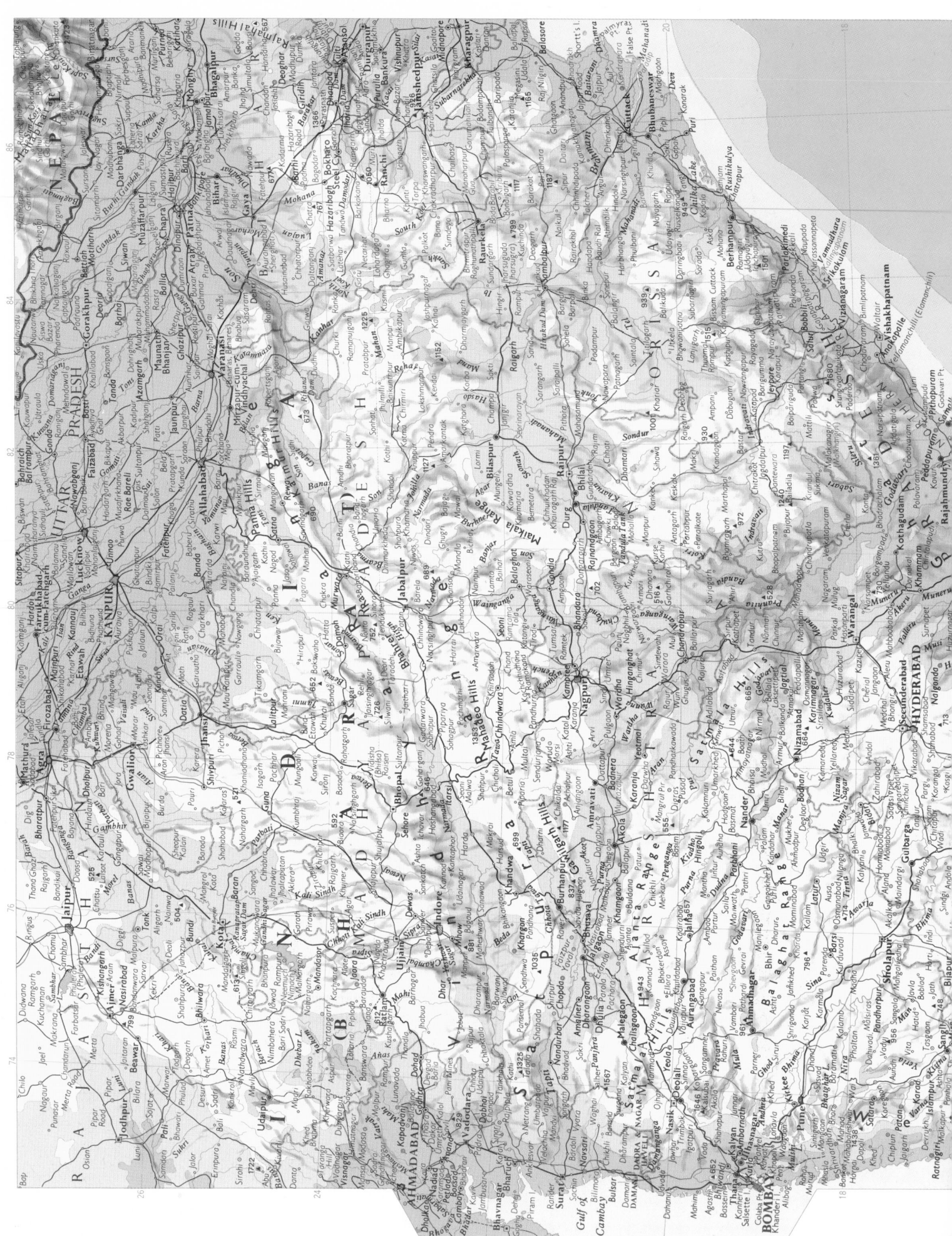
NEPAL
UTTAR PRADESH
RAJASTHAN
MADHYA PRADESH
ORISSA
BIHAR
BOMBAY
HYDERABAD
AHMADABAD
KANPUR
Agra
Jaipur
Lucknow
Allahabad
Varanasi
Patna
Jabalpur
Nagpur
Bhopal
Indore
Raipur
Cuttack
Bhubaneswar
Gulf of Cambay
Vindhya Range
Satpura Range
Mahadeo Hills
Maikala Range
Ajanta Range
Balaghat Range

1 : 6 000 000

50   0   50   100   150   200   250 km

B A Y   O F   B E N G A L

A R A B I A N   S E A

Coromandel Coast

Malabar Coast

MADRAS

BANGALORE

KARNATAKA

TAMIL NADU

KERALA

GOA

SRI LANKA (CEYLON)

Gulf of Mannar (Mannar)

Palk Strait

Colombo

Mysore

Salem

Coimbatore

Madurai

Trivandrum

Cochin

Mangalore

Calicut

Nellore

Cuddapah

Bellary

Kurnool

Kandy

C. Comorin

Dondra Head

m 3000 2000 1500 1000 400 200 0

0 200 2000 4000 m

East from 80 Greenwich

Projection: Conical with two standard parallels

1:6 000 000

50   0   50   100   150   200   250 km

CHINESE REPUBLIC

TIBET

HIMALAYA

SIKKIM

BHUTAN

ARUNACHAL PRADESH

INDIA

Mishmi Hills

Abor Hills

ASSAM

NAGALAND

KACHIN

MEGHALAYA

Garo Hills

Khasi Hills

Barail Range

MANIPUR

BANGLADESH

TRIPURA

MIZORAM

SAGAING

CHIN

DACCA

Tropic of Cancer

CALCUTTA

Howrah

KHULNA

Sundarbans

Chittagong

Cox's Bazar

The Sandheads

Mouths of the Ganga

BAY OF BENGAL

Sittwe (Akyab)

Boronga Is.

Combermere Bay

Kyaukpyu

Ramree I.

Cheduba I.

ARAKAN

BURMA

Mandalay

Monywa

Myingyan

Pakokku

Mt. Victoria
3053

SHAN

CHINA

MAGWE

KAYAH

THAILAND

Chiang Mai

Toungoo

PEGU

Pyè (Prome)

Henzada

IRRAWADDY

Bassein

Rangoon

TENASSERIM

Moulmein

G. of Martaban

Mouths of the Irrawaddy

C. Negrais

m
6000
4000
3000
2000
1500
1000
400
200
0
200
2000
m

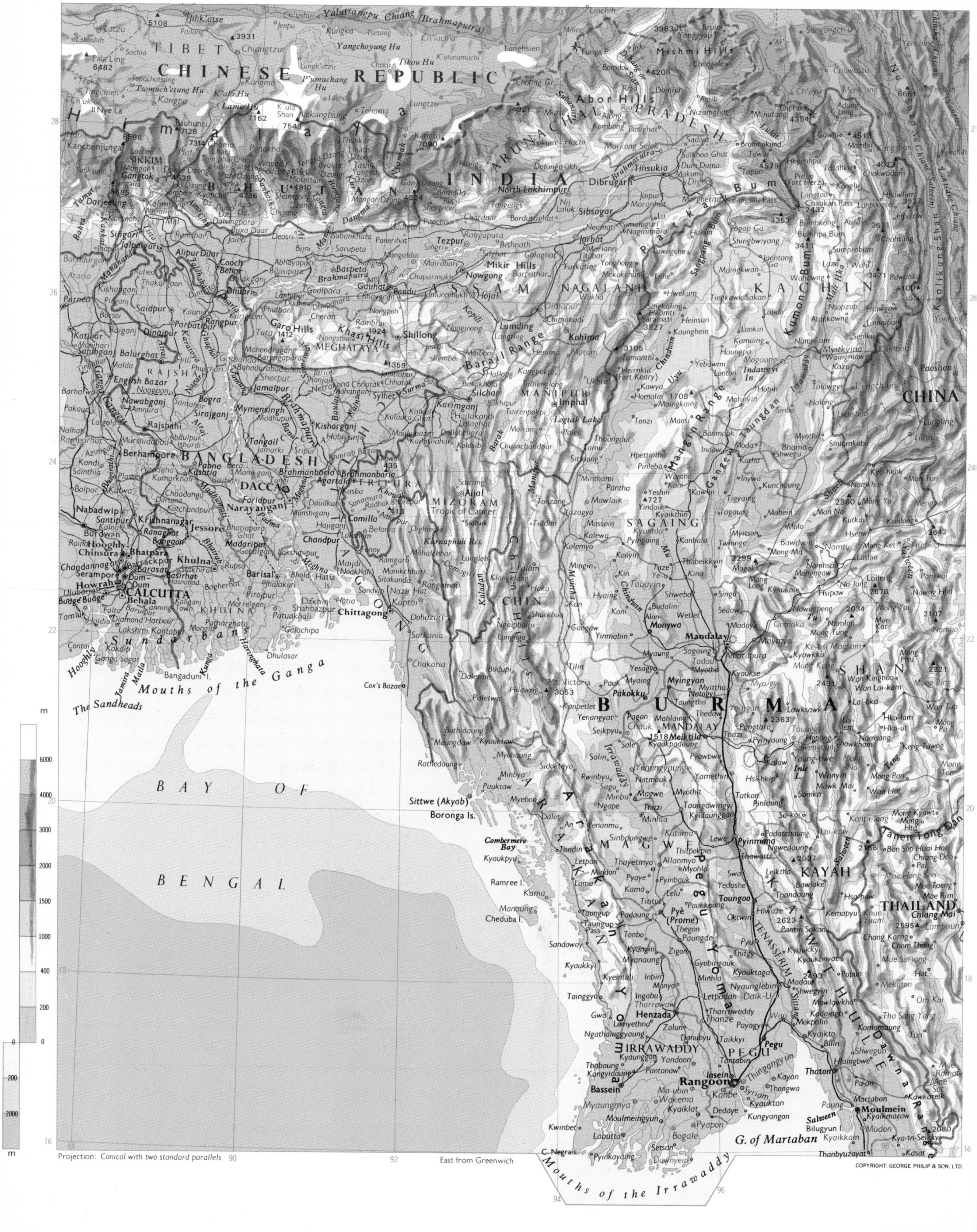

Projection: Conical with two standard parallels   East from Greenwich

COPYRIGHT. GEORGE PHILIP & SON. LTD.

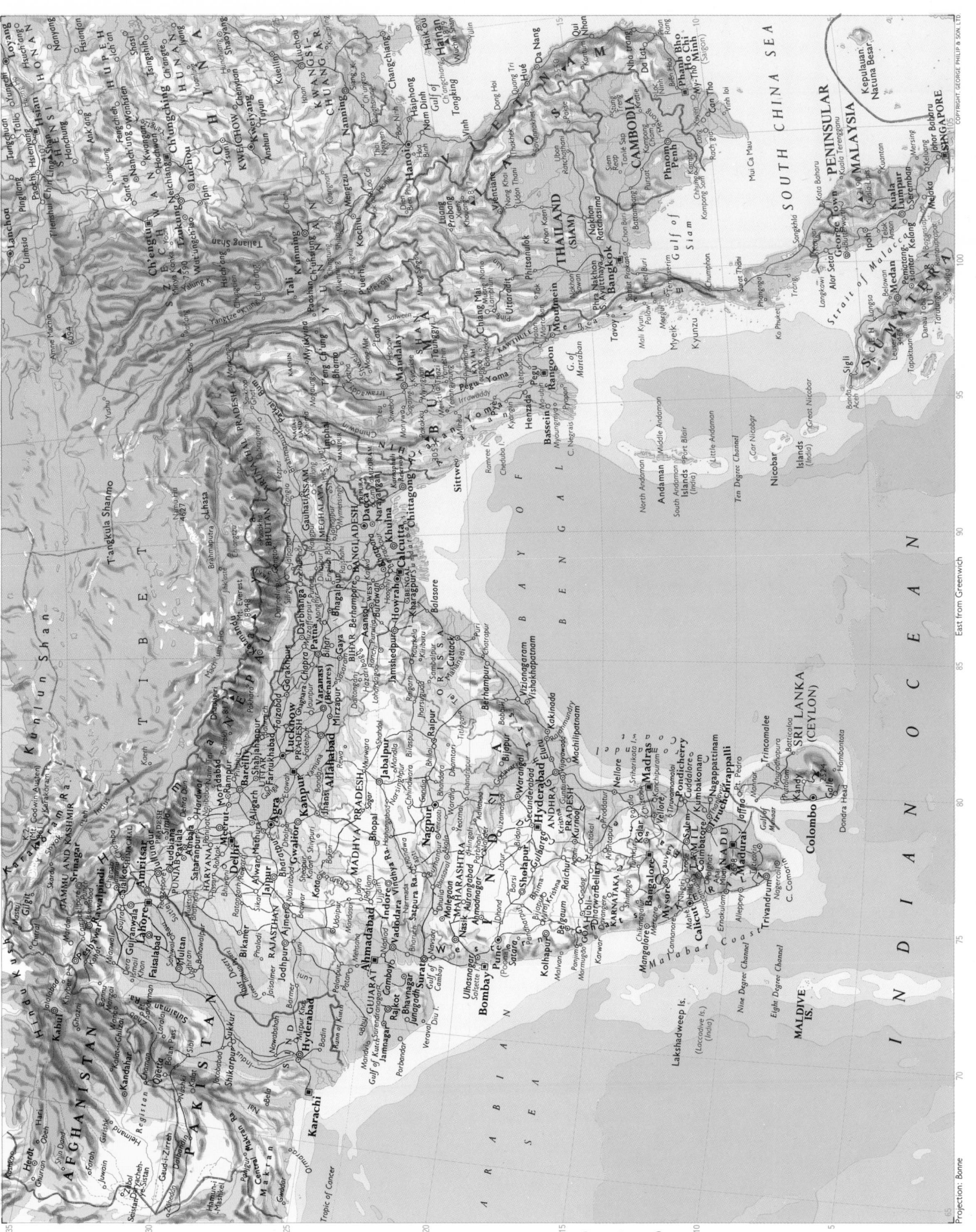

1:20 000 000

200   0   200   400   600   800 km

SOUTH CHINA SEA

COPYRIGHT GEORGE PHILIP & SON LTD.

East from Greenwich

Projection: Bonne

m
6000 4000 2000 1000/10   400   200   0

0
200
2000
4000
m

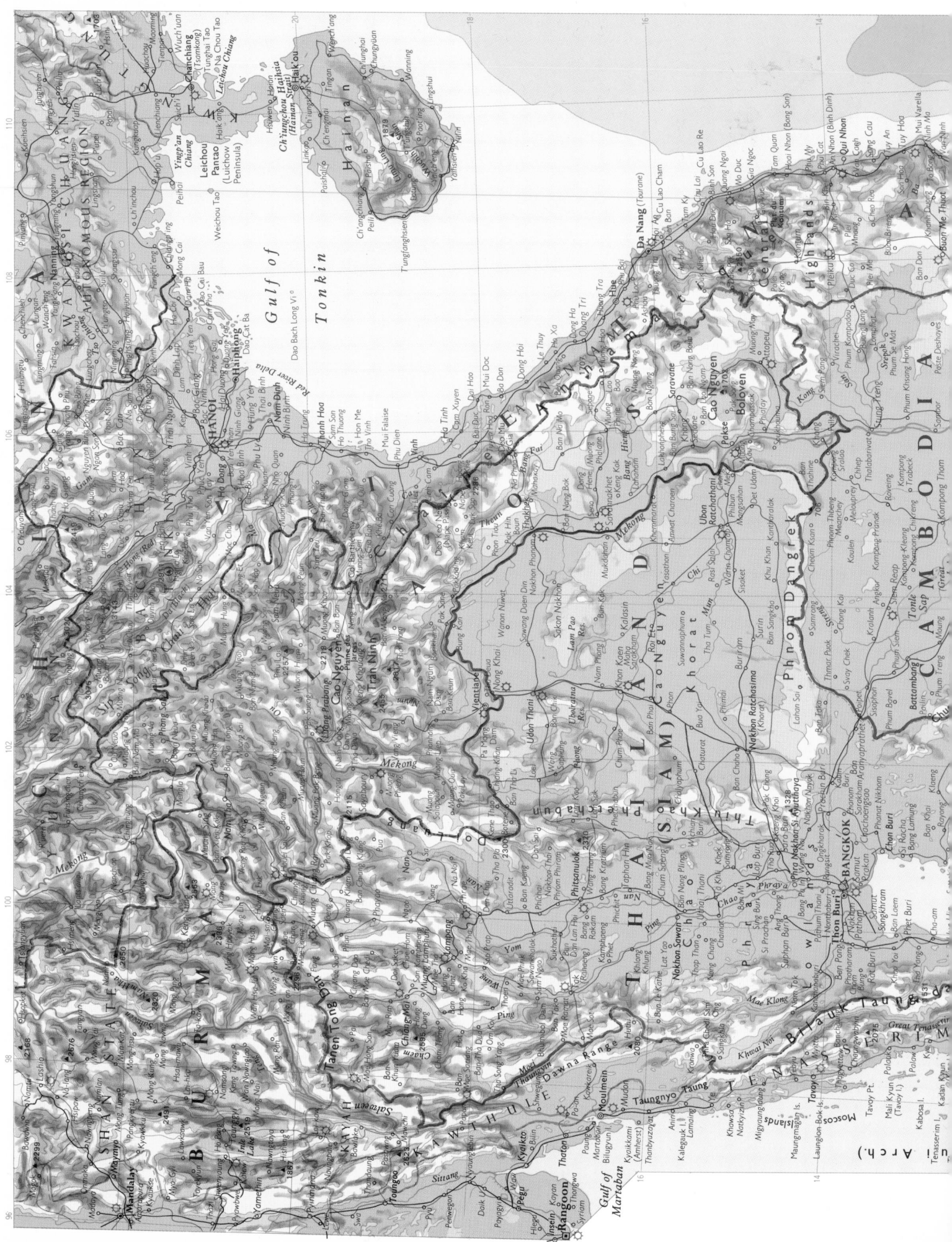

Gulf of Tonkin
Hainan
Gulf of Martaban
HANOI
Haiphong
Vientiane
BANGKOK
Thon Buri
Rangoon
Mandalay
Moulmein
Da Nang
Hue
Vinh
Luang Prabang
Chiang Mai
Battambang
Ubon Ratchathani
Nakhon Ratchasima
Udon Thani
Phitsanulok
Nakhon Sawan
Mekong
Salween
Khorat
Phnom Dangrek
Dawna Range
Bilauktaung
Tenasserim
Pegu
Toungoo
Lashio
Maymyo
Pakse
Saravane
Qui Nhon
Kontum
Pleiku

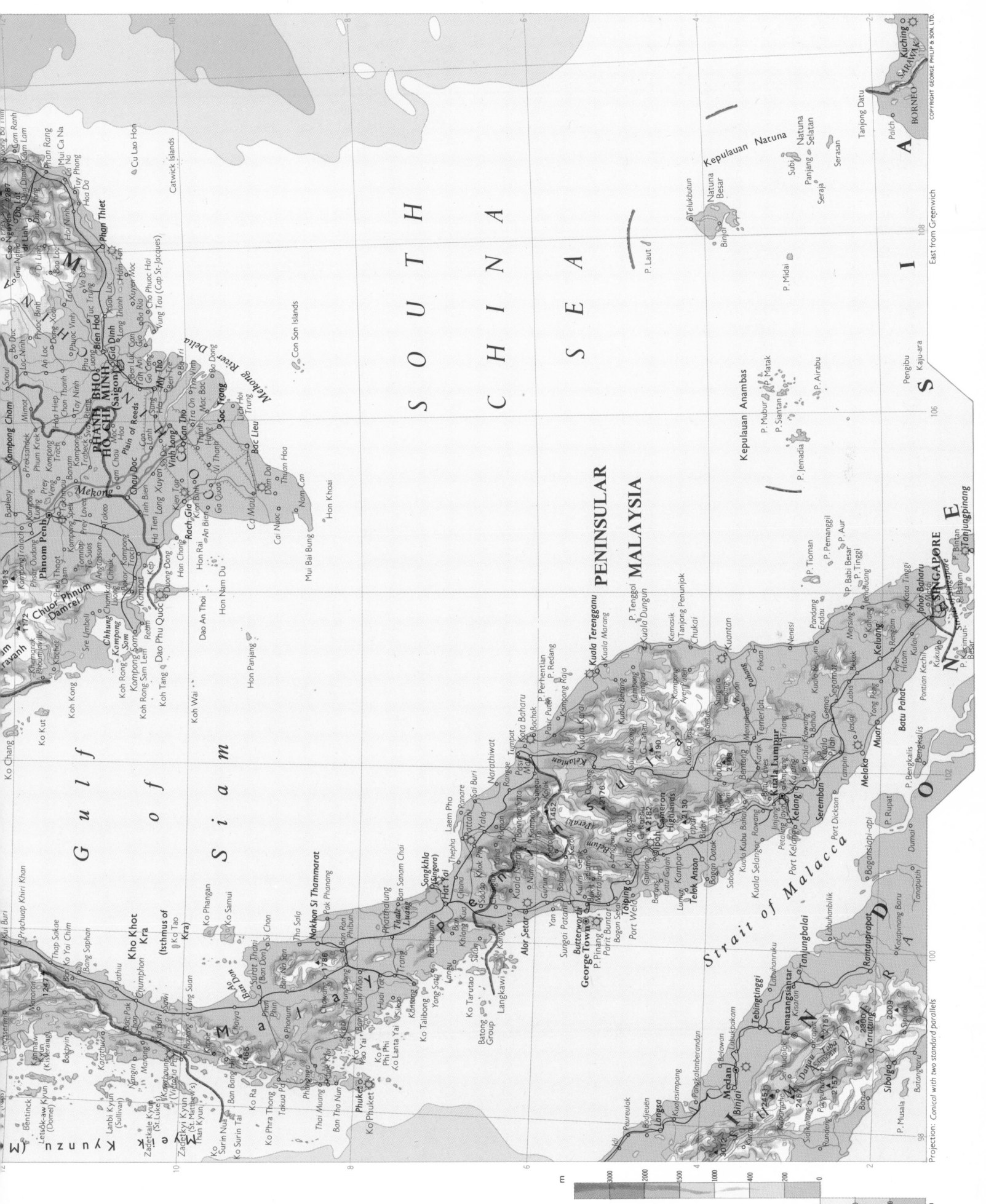

1 : 6 000 000

50   0   50   100   150   200   250 km

East from Greenwich

Projection: Conical with two standard parallels

S O U T H

C H I N A

S E A

Kepulauan Natuna

Natuna
Selatan

Tanjong Datu

BORNEO

SARAWAK

Kuching

Polch

Kepulauan Anambas

P. Laut

P. Mubur Matak
P. Siantan
P. Airabu

P. Jemadja

Pengibu

Kaju-ara

PENINSULAR

MALAYSIA

Kuala Terengganu

Kota Baharu

Kuala Krai

P. Perhentian
P. Redang

Kuala Dungun

Chukai

Kuantan

Pekan

P. Tioman

P. Pemanggil

P. Aur

P. Babi Besar
P. Tinggi

Kluang

Kota Tinggi

SINGAPORE

Johor Baharu

Batam
Bintan

Tanjungpinang

Cameron
Highlands

Kuala Lumpur

Kelang

Seremban

Melaka

Port Dickson

Batu Pahat

Bengkalis

P. Rupat

Dumai

Strait of Malacca

George Town
P. Pinang
Butterworth

Taiping

Alor Setar

Telok Anson

Bagansiapi-api

Rantauprapat

Songkhla
(Singora)

Hat Yai

Nakhon Si Thammarat

Phatthalung

Yala

Narathiwat

Pematangsiantar

Tebingtinggi

Siantar

Medan

Binjai

Sibolga

S U M A T E R A

Isthmus of
Kra

Kho Khot
Kra

Ko Samui

Ko Pha Ngan

Surat Thani

Chumphon

Phuket
Ko Phuket

Ko Lanta Yai

Ko Tarutao
Group

Langkawi

M a l a y

G u l f

o f

S i a m

Ko Chang

Ko Kut

Koh Kong

Koh Rong

Koh Tang

Koh Wai

Hon Panjang

Ca Mau

Mui Bai Bung

Con Son Islands

Mekong River Delta

HO CHI MINH
(Saigon)

PHANH BHO

Phnom Penh

Bien Hoa

My Tho

Soc Trang

Vinh Long

Rach Gia

Bac Lieu

Chau Doc

Vung Tau (Cap St-Jacques)

Phan Thiet

Phan Rang

Dao Phu Quoc

Chuor Phnum
Damrei

Catwick Islands

Cu Lao Hon

Hon Khoai

Kompong
Som

Kompong Cham

Kampot

K A M P U C H E A

V I E T N A M

m

3000 2000 1500 1000 400 200 0

m   200   2000

BURMA
THAILAND
(SIAM)
LAOS
VIET-NAM
CAMBODIA
MALAYSIA
PENINSULAR MALAYSIA
SARAWAK
SABAH
BORNEO
INDONESIA
SUMATERA
JAWA
(JAVA)
KALIMANTAN
ANDAMAN SEA
Gulf of Siam
SOUTH CHINA SEA
Strait of Malacca
INDIAN OCEAN
Java Trench
JAVA SEA
Greater Sunda Islands
G. of Martaban
Rangoon
Moulmein
Bangkok
Phra Nakhon Si Ayutthaya
Nakhon Ratchasima (Khorat)
Udon Thani
Ubon Ratchathani
Phnom Penh
PHANH BHO HO CHI MINH (Saigon)
Da Nang (Tourane)
Hue
Nha Trang
Phan Rang
Hsisha Chuntao
Spratly I.
Palawan
Phu Quoc
Ca Mau
Con Son
Ko Samui
Surat Thani
Phuket
Songkhla (Singora)
Pattani
Kota Baharu
George Town
Ipoh
Kuala Lumpur
Melaka
SINGAPORE
Johor Baharu
Kepulauan Riau
Kepulauan Lingga
Kepulauan Natuna Besar
Kepulauan Anambas
Medan
Padang
Pakanbaru
Jambi
Palembang
Bengkulu
Tanjungkarang Telukbetung
JAKARTA
Bogor
Bandung
Cirebon
Semarang
Yogyakarta
Surakarta
Surabaya
Madura
Bali
Lombok
Bangka
Belitung (Billiton)
Singkawang
Pontianak
Kuching
Sibu
Bintulu
Brunei
Kota Kinabalu (Jesselton)
Banjarmasin
Simeulue
Nias
Siberut
Enggano
Kepulauan Mentawai
Selat Karimata
Selat Sunda
Pulau Rakata (Krakatau)
NUSA TENGGARA
6073
6650
4424
3800
3466
3159
3428
3265
2563
3676
3142
3726
4101
2988
2240
2278
1768
1892
Projection: Mercator
East from Greenwich
m
4000
3000
2000
1500
1000
400
200
0
200
2000
4000
6000
8000
m

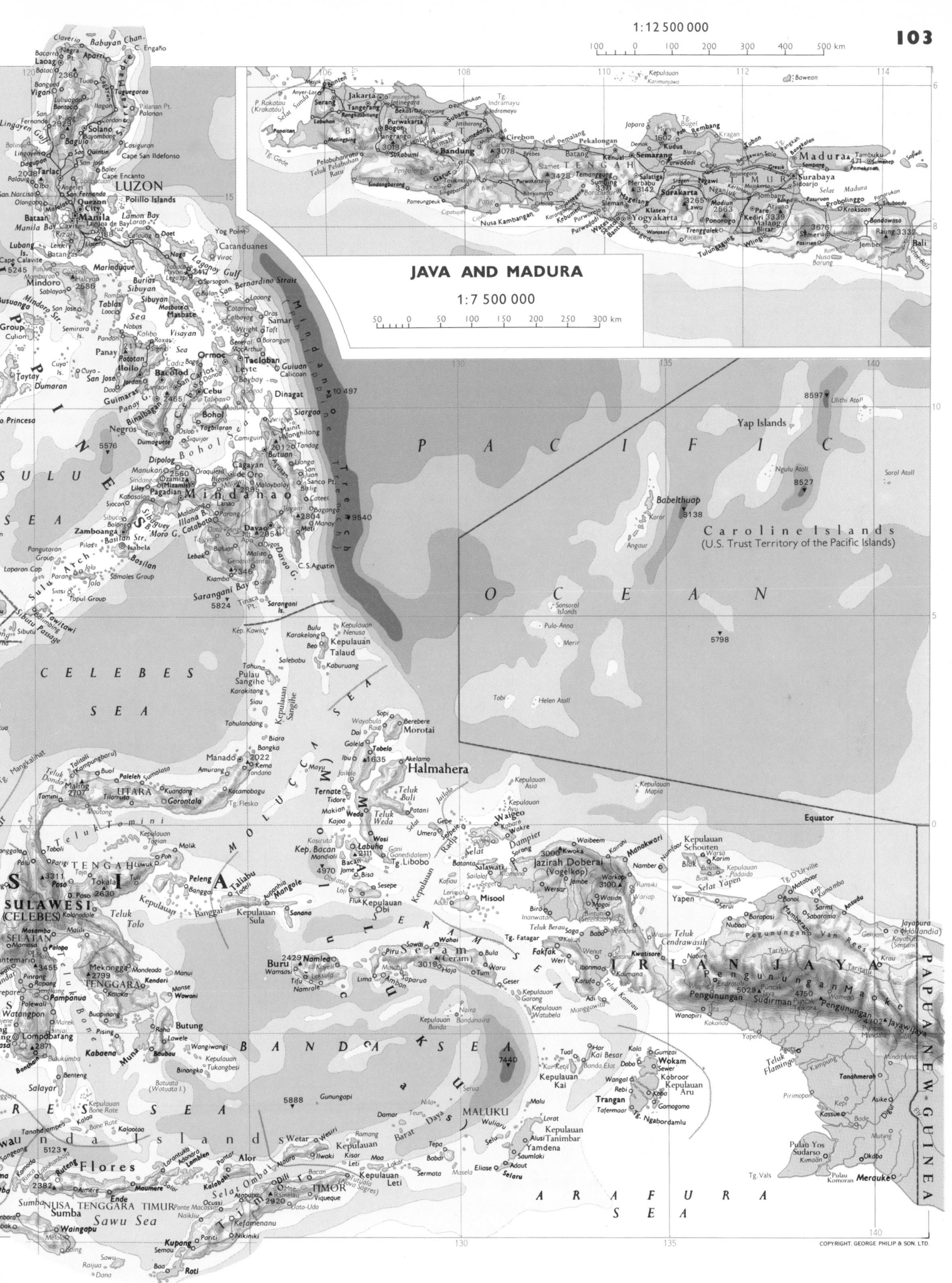

1:12 500 000

100   0   100   200   300   400   500 km

JAVA AND MADURA

1:7 500 000

50   0   50   100   150   200   250   300 km

P A C I F I C

O C E A N

Caroline Islands
(U.S. Trust Territory of the Pacific Islands)

Yap Islands

Equator

CELEBES
SEA

SULU
SEA

MINDANAO

LUZON

Manila

MOLUCCA SEA

Halmahera

SULAWESI
(CELEBES)

IRIAN JAYA

PAPUA NEW GUINEA

BANDA SEA

SERAM SEA

MALUKU

TIMOR

FLORES SEA

SAWU SEA

A R A F U R A
S E A

NUSA TENGGARA TIMUR

1 : 30 000 000

200　0　200　400　600　800　1000 km

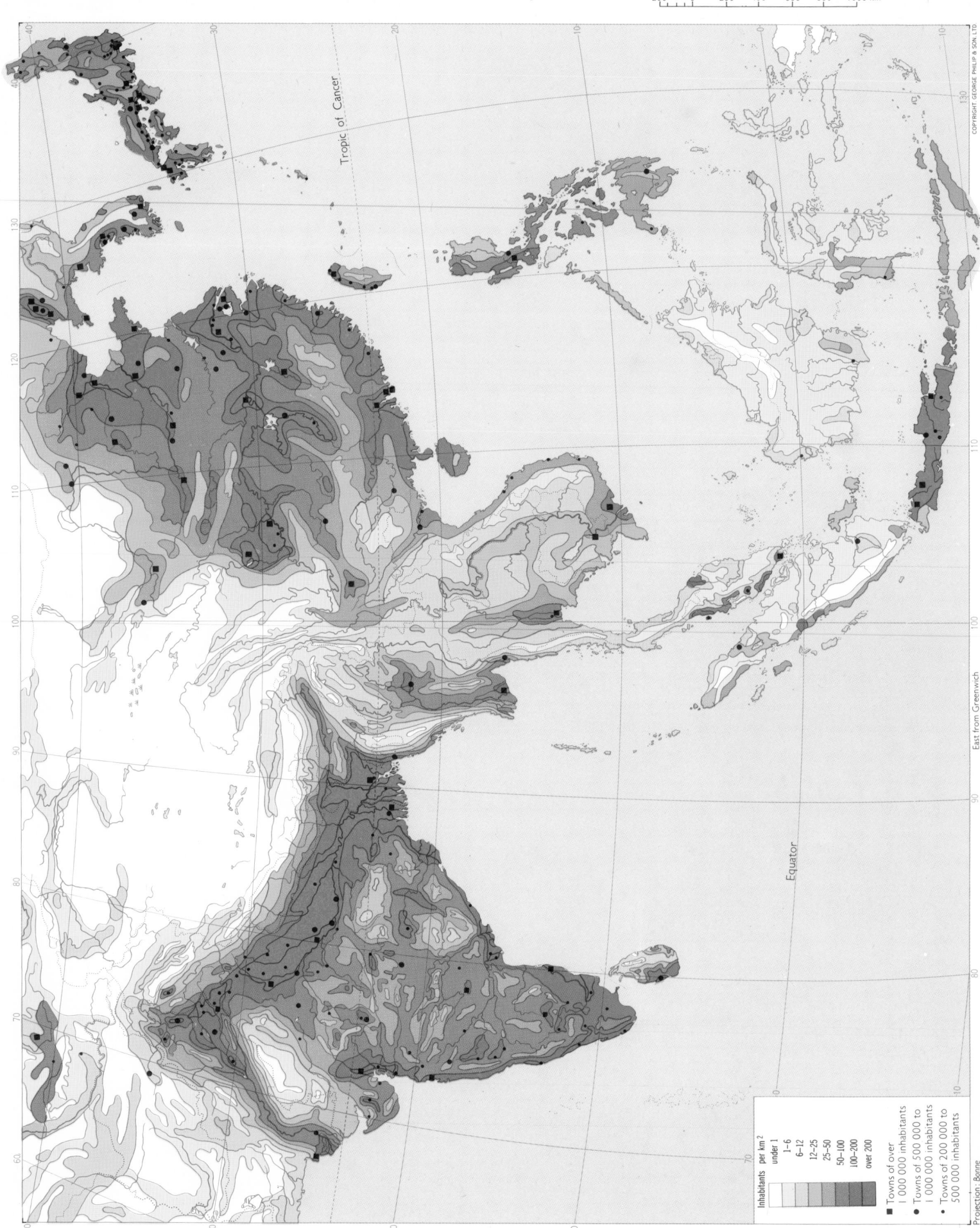

Tropic of Cancer

Equator

East from Greenwich

COPYRIGHT GEORGE PHILIP & SON LTD.

Inhabitants	per km²
	under 1
	1–6
	6–12
	12–25
	25–50
	50–100
	100–200
	over 200

■ Towns of over 1 000 000 inhabitants
● Towns of 500 000 to 1 000 000 inhabitants
● Towns of 200 000 to 500 000 inhabitants

Projection: Bonne

1:20 000 000

200   0   200   400   600   800 km

East from Greenwich

Projection: Bonne

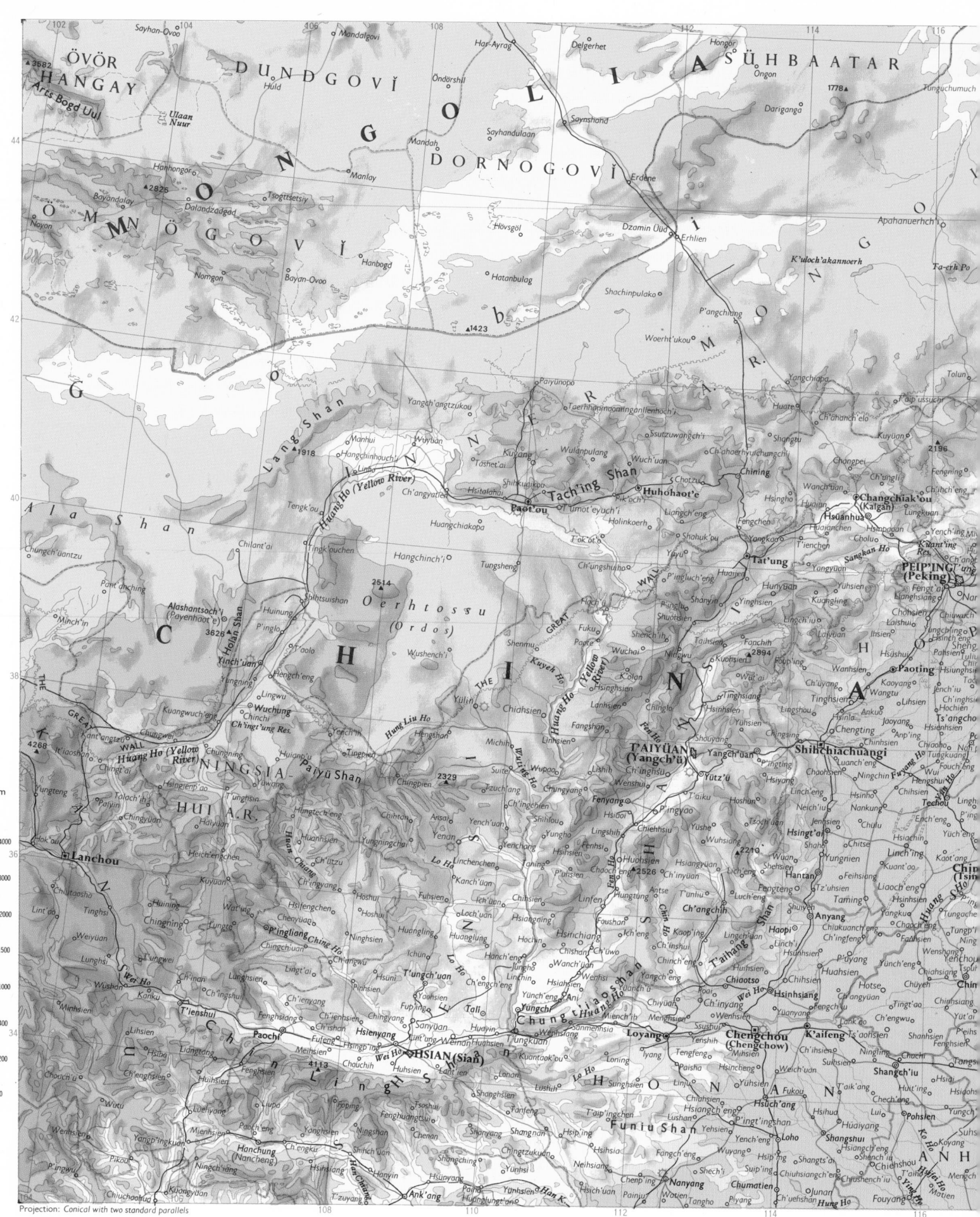

Projection: Conical with two standard parallels

1:6 000 000

50   0   50   100   150   200   250 km

East from Greenwich

COPYRIGHT. GEORGE PHILIP & SON. LTD.

m

4000
3000
2000
1500
1000
400
200
0
0
200
2000

m

Shangnan Hsiping Hsiangch'eng Shench'iu Chiehshou Ko Ho Kuchen Hungtse Hu
Yünhsi Hsihsia Fangch'eng Wuyang Hsip'ing Chiushiangch'iu Hsüeh Mengch'eng Huaiyüan Kaopao Hsinghua
Neihsiang Chenp'ing Nanyang Chumatien Junan Fouyang Fengt'ai T'iench'eng Kaoyu Tungt'ai
Chünhsien Paimu T'angho Piyang Chengyang Hsihsien Wafou Hu Shouhsien Tingyuan Laian Liuho Yangchou Kuochiao T'aihsien Jukao Jutung

HONAN **Pangfou** **KIANGSU** **Haian** Ch'itung

Kuanghua Hsiang-fou Hsinyang Tsaoyang Mingchiang Loshan Kushih Ch'engti Ch'engtung Hu P'uk'ou T'iench'ang Tanyang Haimen
Hushan Hsiangyang Suihsien Hsinyeh Chengyang Hsishien Huangch'uan Hu Hofei Chaohu Ch'angfeng **NANCHING** Chüjung Ch'angchou **(Nanking)** Chiangyin Ch'ang Chiang(Yangtze)

HUPEH Anlu Yünmeng Map'ing Kuangshui Liuan Hoshan Shuch'eng Tangt'u Maanshan Shihchiu Hu Liyang **Wuhsi** Ch'angshu Ch'ungming Tao

Ich'ang Chihchiang Tangyang T'ienmen Hanch'uan **WUHAN** Wuch'ang Hsishui Luchiang Wuwei Nan Hu Wuhu Hu Liyang Ishing **Suchou** Chiating **SHANGHAI**

ANHWEI **(Soochow)** Wuchiang
Ch'angyang Hanyang **Huangshih** Tayen Yanghsin Kuangchi P'engtse Ch'ingyang Tsingsi Hangchou Nanhui

Sungtzu Kungan Hohsien Mienyang Melchuan Hsienning Juichang Tungliu Wan Chianghsing **Hangchou** **Ningpo**

SEA OF JAPAN
SOUTH KOREA
HONSHU
Oki-Shotō
Dōgo
Daimanji-San 608
Saigō
CHŪGOKU - DISTRICT
Shimane-Hantō
Jizō-Zaki
Matsue
Sakaiminato
Hirata
Shinji-Ko
Yonago
Hi-no-Misaki
Taisha
Izumo
Yasugi
Kurayoshi
Tottori
TOTTORI
Iwami
Toyooka
Hidaka
Ōda
Sanbe-San 1126
Gōtsu
Hamada
SHIMANE
Chūgoku-Sanchi
Niimi
Tsuyama
Shōbara
Miyoshi
OKAYAMA
Takahashi
HIROSHIMA
Masuda
Okayama
Himeji
Takasago
Kakogawa
Akō
Bizen
Saidaiji
Sōja
Fuchū
Ibara
Kurashiki
Tamano
Fukuyama
Mihara
Onomichi
Kasaoka
Hagi
Ōmi-Shima
Mi-Shima
Tsuno-Shima
Nagato
Hiroshima
YAMAGUCHI
Yamaguchi
Mine
Hōfu
Iwakuni
Ōtake
Tokuyama
Kudamatsu
Yanai
Hikari
Ube
Onoda
Shimonoseki
KITAKYŪSHŪ
Hibiki-Nada
Genkai-Nada
Suō-Nada
Iyo-Nada
Hiroshima-Wan
Kure
Takehara
Aki-Nada
Hiuchi-Nada
SETO-NAIKAI
Imabari
Niihama
Saijō
Matsuyama
Iyo-mishima
Kan'onji
Marugame
Sakaide
Takamatsu
KAGAWA
Shōdo-Shima
Harima-Nada
Awaji-Shima
Sumoto
Naruto
Tokushima
TOKUSHIMA
Komatsujima
Anan
Shikoku-Sanchi
Ishizuchi-Yama 1981
Tsurugi-San 1955
EHIME
KŌCHI
Kōchi
Nankoku
Aki
Muroto
Muroto-Misaki
Tosa-Wan
Ōzu
Yawatahama
Uwajima
Sada-Misaki-Hantō
Hōyo-Kaikyō
Bungo-Suidō
Nakamura
Sukumo
Tosa-shimizu
Ashizuri-Zaki
Oki-no-Shima
Tsurumi-Saki
SHIKOKU
SHIKOKU - DISTRICT
Tsushima
Izuhara
Kara-Saki
Kō-Saki
Higasi-Suidō
Iki
Iki-Kaikyō
FUKUOKA
Nōgata
Iizuka
Yukuhashi
Nakatsu
Kunisaki
Bungotakada
Usa
Karatsu
Imari
Matsuura
Hirado
Hirado-Shima
Ikitsuki-Shima
Sasebo
Takeo
Saga
Kurume
Tosu
Amagi
Hita
Beppu
Beppu-Wan
Ōita
Usuki
Saganoseki
Kitsuki
Tsukumi
Saiki
ŌITA
Kuju-San 1787
Yame
Ōkawa
Yanagawa
Ōmuta
Arao
Kumamoto
Tamana
Kikuchi
Aso
Taketa
Ōmura
Isahaya
Nagasaki
Shimabara
Unzen-Dake 1360
NAGASAKI
Tachibana-Wan
Nomo-Zaki
KUMAMOTO
Uto
Takachiho
Nobeoka
Amakusa-Nada
Amakusa-Shotō
Hondo
Shimo-Jima
Kami-Jima
Yatsushiro
Yatsushiro-Kai
Hyūga
Ushibuka
Naga-Shima
Minamata
Hitoyoshi
MIYAZAKI
Kyūshū-Sanchi
Akune
Izumi
Ōkuchi
Saito
KYŪSHŪ
KYŪSHŪ - DISTRICT
Kami-koshiki-Jima
Koshiki-Rettō
Shimo-koshiki-Jima
Sendai
Kobayashi
Kirishima-Yama 1700
Miyazaki
Kushikino
Kagoshima
Kokubu
Miyakonojō
Nichinan
KAGOSHIMA
Kagoshima-Wan
Sakurajima
Taniyama
Kaseda
Noma-Saki
Tarumizu
Kanoya
Kushima
Shibushi-Wan
Satsuma-Hantō
Makurazaki
Ibusuki
Bō-no-Misaki
Kaimon-Dake 924
Ōsumi-Hantō
Sata-Misaki
Projection: Lambert's Conformal Conic

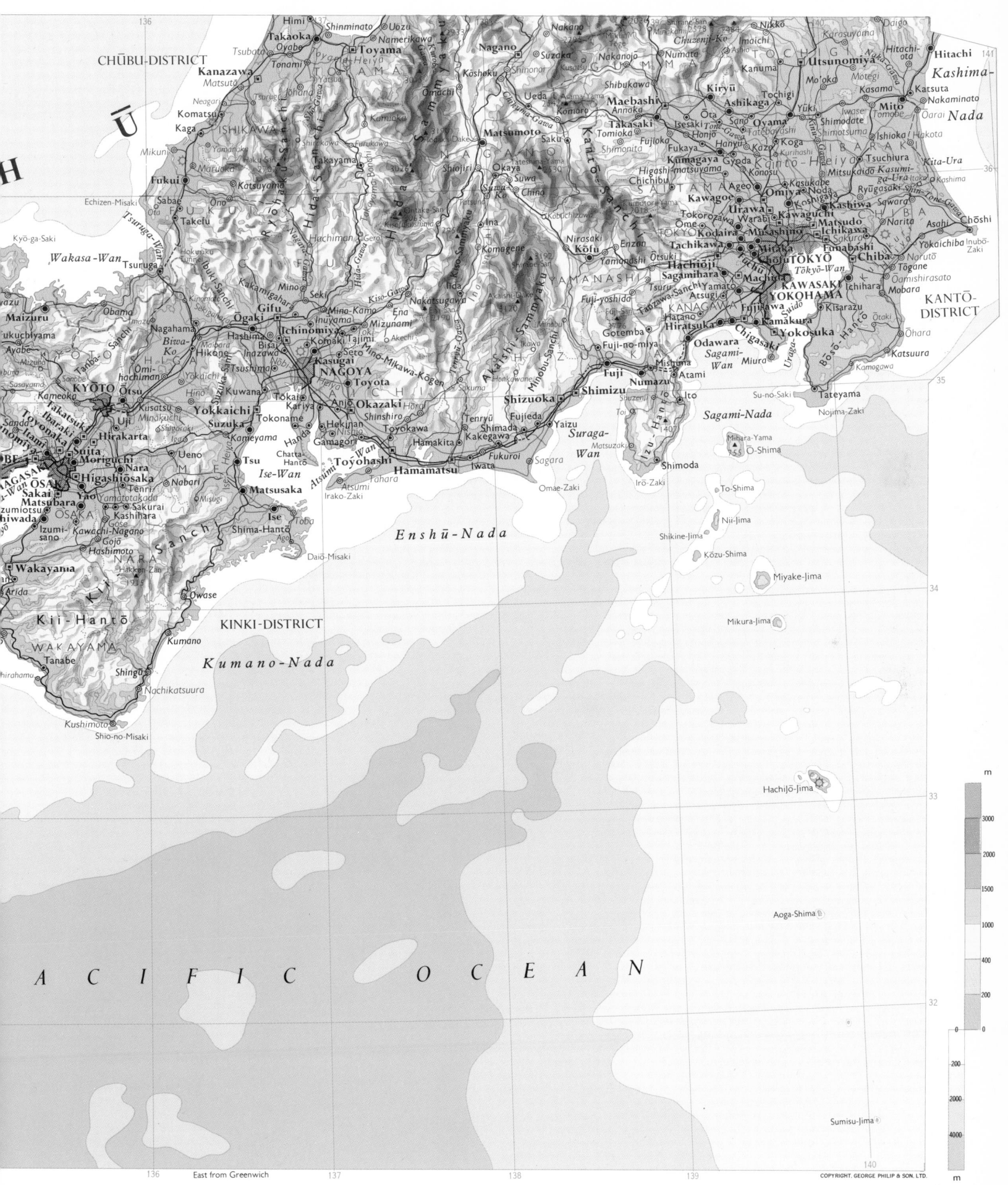

1:2 500 000

10 0 10 20 30 40 50 60 70 80 90 100 km

III

CHŪBU-DISTRICT

Himi Shinminato Uozu Nakano Nikko Daigo Hitachi-ota Hitachi
Takaoka Oyabe Namerikawa Nagano Suzaka Nakanojo Numata Chuzenji-Ko Imaichi Karasuyama Kashima-
Kanazawa Tonami Toyama Heiya Koshoku Suzaka Shibukawa Kiryū Kanuma Utsunomiya Mo'oka Kasama Mito Nakaminato Nada
Matsutō ISHIKAWA Omachi Ueda Komoro Annaka Maebashi Takasaki Ashikaga Oyama Tochigi Yūki Shimodate Motegi Tsuchiura Katsuta
Komatsu Kamioka Matsumoto Tomioka Isesaki Honjo Ota Sano Tatebayashi Gyoda Shimotsuma Ishioka Hakota
Kaga Neagari Takayama Shojiri Okaya Suwa Fukaya Kumagaya Konosu Kasukabe Ryūgasaki Kashima
Fukui Katsuyama Furukawa Nirasaki Chichibu Higashi-matsuyama Ageo Omiya Koshigaya Kashiwa Itako
Echizen-Misaki Sabae Ono Ina Kōfu Enzan Kawagoe Urawa Warabi Kawaguchi Matsudo Narita
Kyō-ga-Saki Maruoka Katsuyama Komagane Yamanashi Ome Kodaira Musashino Ichikawa Sakura Asahi
Wakasa-Wan Tsuruga-Wan Hachiman Gero Komoro Tsuru Hachioji TOKYO Mitaka Funabashi Yokaichiba Inubō-Zaki
Tsuruga Hokuriku Seki Fuji-yoshida Otsuki Tachikawa Chōfu Chiba Naruto Chōshi
Mino Nakatsugawa Gotemba Sagamihara Yamato Machida Tōgane
Maizuru Gifu Mino-Kama Ena Fuji-no-miya Hiratsuka Fujisawa Kamakura Mobara KANTŌ-DISTRICT
Obama Ogaki Hashima Inuyama Komaki Tajimi Mizunami Numazu Odawara Chigasaki Yokosuka Katsuura
Nagahama Bisai Inazawa Seto Mishima Atami Sagami-Wan Miura Kamogawa
KYŌTO Otsu Hikone Kasugai Fuji Shimizu Ito Su-no-Saki
Yokkaichi Kuwana NAGOYA Toyota Shizuoka Tateyama
Ōtsu Kusatsu Tokai Kariya Shinshiro Yaizu Suruga-Wan Sagami-Nada Nojima-Zaki
Suzuka Tsushima Anjo Okazaki Toyokawa Shimada Kakegawa Fukuroi Sagara
Kameyama Hekinan Toyohashi Hamakita Iwata Omae-Zaki Irō-Zaki Shimoda
Tsu Chatta-Hantō Gamagori Hamamatsu Fukuroi Shimoda
Nabari Ise-Wan Atsumi Tahara O-Shima
Nara Ueno Atsumi-Wan Atsuim To-Shima
Higashiōsaka Matsusaka Irako-Zaki Nii-Jima
ŌSAKA Ise Enshū-Nada Shikine-Jima Kōzu-Shima Miyake-Jima
Sakai Shima-Hantō Toba
Matsubara Sakurai Daiō-Misaki
OSAKA Kashihara Owase Mikura-Jima
Izumi-sano KINKI-DISTRICT
Wakayama NARA Kumano Kumano-Nada
WAKAYAMA Shingū
Tanabe Nachikatsuura Aoga-Shima
Kushimoto Shio-no-Misaki Hachijō-Jima

PACIFIC OCEAN

East from Greenwich COPYRIGHT. GEORGE PHILIP & SON. LTD.

Sumisu-Jima

m
3000
2000
1500
1000
400
200
0
200
2000
4000
m

1 : 7 500 000

50   0   50   100 150 200 250 300 km

CHINA

U.S.S.R.

Sikhote Alin

Turii Rog
Ozero
Khanka
Motoshih
Spassk-Dalni
Varfolomeyevka
Verkhove
Tetyukhe

Mutankiang
Ningan
Ussurysk
(Voroshilov)
Uglovaya
Suchan
Nakhodka

Vladivostok

Yenki
Hunchun

Najin

Zaliv Petra Velikogo

NORTH KOREA

Chongjin

Songjin

Tanchon

SOUTH KOREA

Kosŏng

Samchok

Ullung Do

Pusan

KOREA STRAIT

Tsushima

Tsushima-Kaikyō

Iki

Nakadori-Jima

Fukue-Jima

Sea of Okhotsk

Rebun-Tō
Rishiri-Tō
Teshio
Otoineppu
Enbetsu
Monbetsu
Yubetsu
HOKKAIDŌ
Rumoi
Shibatsu
Kitami
Abashiri
Asahigawa
Daisetsu-Zan
2290
Atsuta
Nemuro-Kaikyō

HOKKAIDŌ

Ishikari-Wan (Otaru-Wan)
Kamui-Misaki
Iwamisawa
Yūbari
Obihiro
Yoroshini Dake
2052
Nemuro
Otaru
Sapporo
Tomakomai
Kushiro
Iwanai
Setana
Shiraoi
Mombetsu
Ushiura-Wan
Muroran
Urakawa
Somani
Okushiri-Tō
Esashi
Esan-Misaki
Hakodate
Erimo-Misaki
Matsumae
Tsugaru Kaikyō
Shiriya-Zaki
Mutsu
Mutsu-Wan
Aomori
Hirosaki
Noshiro
Odate
Hachinohe
Kuji
Towada
Iwate-San
2041
Oga-Hantō
Akita
Morioka
Miyako
Honjō
Hanamaki
Kamaishi
Yokote
Kitakami
Sakata
Shinjō
Ichinoseki
Tsuruoka
Mogami
Kogota
Ishinomaki
TŌHOKU
Yamagata
Shiogama
Sendai
Iwanuma
Yonezawa
Fukushima

SEA OF JAPAN

Sado
Niigata
Shibata
Agano
Nagaoka
Bandai-San
1819
Wajima
Suzu-Misaki
Koriyama
Nanao
Kashiwazaki
Azuwakamatsu
Naoetsu
Iwaki
Himi
Takada
Kanazawa
Takaoka
Toyama-Wan
Nagano
Toyama
H
Nikkō
Hitachi
CHŪBU
Matsumoto
Ueda
Maebashi Kiryū
Utsunomiya
Fukui
Takefu
Takayama
Takasaki
Tōchigi
Tsuchiura
Mito
Chichibu
Ōmiya
Gyōdai
Suwa
Kawagoe
Shin-Tokyo
Tsuruga
Hikone
3653 San
Kōfu
Ichikawa
Chōshi
KANTŌ
Ayabe
Ōtsu
Kuwana
Fuji-San
3776
TOKYO
Maizuru
Gifu
Kawasaki
Yokosuka
Wakasa-Wan
Ichinomiya
Yokohama
Kyō-ga-Saki
Toyooka
Nagoya
Fujisawa
Hi-no-Misaki
Tottori
Toyooka
Okazaki
Shizuoka
Numazu
Atami
Izumo
Yonago
Tsuyama
Kyōto
Yokkaichi
Shimada
Tateyama
Matsue
Hokū
Kobe
Tsu
Hamamatsu
Katsuura
Hamada
Kurashiki
Himeji
Akashi
Nara
Matsusaka
Toyohashi
Ō-Shima
Masuda
Fukuyama
Osaka
Se-Wan
CHŪGOKU
Onomichi
Sakai
Toba
Nii-Jima
Hiroshima
Miihara
Kishiwada
Daiō-Misaki
Hagi
Takamatsu
Wakayama
Miyake-Jima
Yamaguchi
Marugame
KINKI
Tokuyama
Kure
Niihama
Owase
Shimonoseki
Ube
Suō-Nada
Matsuyama
Mikura-Jima
Inland Sea
Shingū
Shio-no-Misaki
Kōchi
Fukuoka
Nakatsu
Yawatahama
Karatsu
Kitakyūshū
Beppu
Toei-Wan
Muroto-Misaki
Saga
Kurume
Uwajima
SHIKOKU
Sasebo
Ōmuta
Ōita
1592
Usuki
Nakamura
Kashima
Kumamoto
Shimabara
Ashizuri-zaki
Isahaya
Yatsushiro
SHIKOKU
Nagasaki
Shimō-Jima
Minamata
Nobeoka
Hachijō-Jima
Sendai
Miyazaki
Kobayashi
Aoga-Shima
Kagoshima
Kanoya
Miyakonojō
KYŪSHŪ
Makurazaki
Kagoshima-Wan
Shibushi-Wan

PACIFIC OCEAN

Ōsumi-Shotō
Nishinoomote
Kuchinoerabu-Jima
Tane-ga-Shima
Tokara-Kaikyō
Naka-no-Shima
Yaku-Jima
Suwanose-Jima

Projection : Bonne   135   East from Greenwich   125

m
1500
1000
400
200 30
0   0
–200
m

RYŪKYŪ ISLANDS
Continuation southwards
in same scale

Ōsumi-Shotō
Kuchinoerabu-Jima
Tokara-Kaikyō
Yaku-Jima
Naka-no-Shima
Suwanose-Jima

Ryūkyū Islands (Nansei-Shotō)
Ōsumi-Shotō
Tokara-Kaikyō
Satsuna-Shotō

NAze
Kikai-Jima
Amami Ō Shima
Setouchi
Tokunoshima
Okinoerabu-Jima

Ryūkyū Islands (Nansei-Shotō)
Okinawa-Shotō

Okinawa-Jima
Ishikawa
Ginowan
Koza
Kerama-Shotō
Naha

Nansei-Shotō Trench

7507

PACIFIC OCEAN

Miyako-Jima
Hirara
Yaeyama-Shotō
Yonaguni-Jima
Iriomote-Jima
Ishigaki-Jima
Ishigaki

130

25

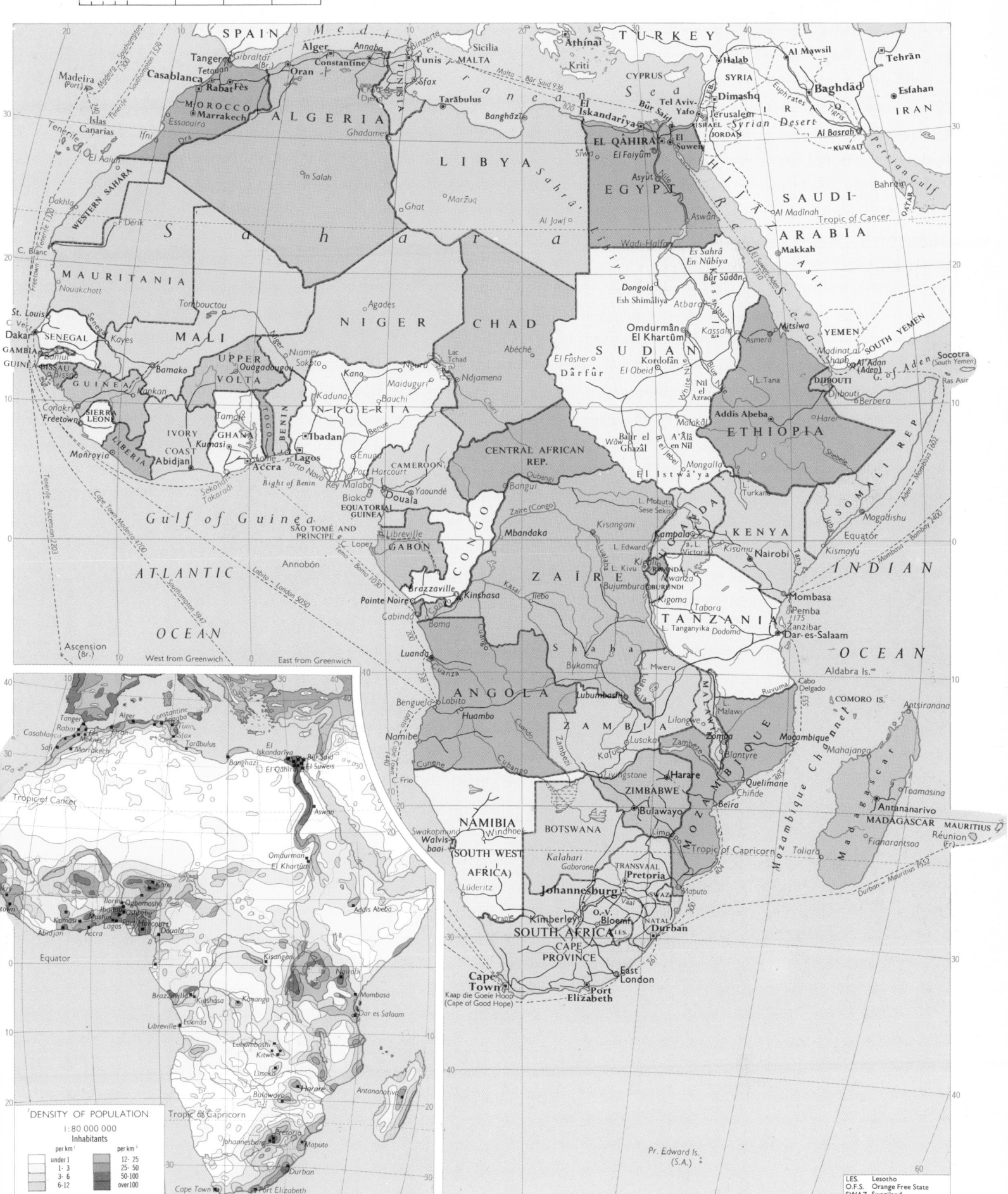

1 : 40 000 000

400   0   400   800   1200   1600 km

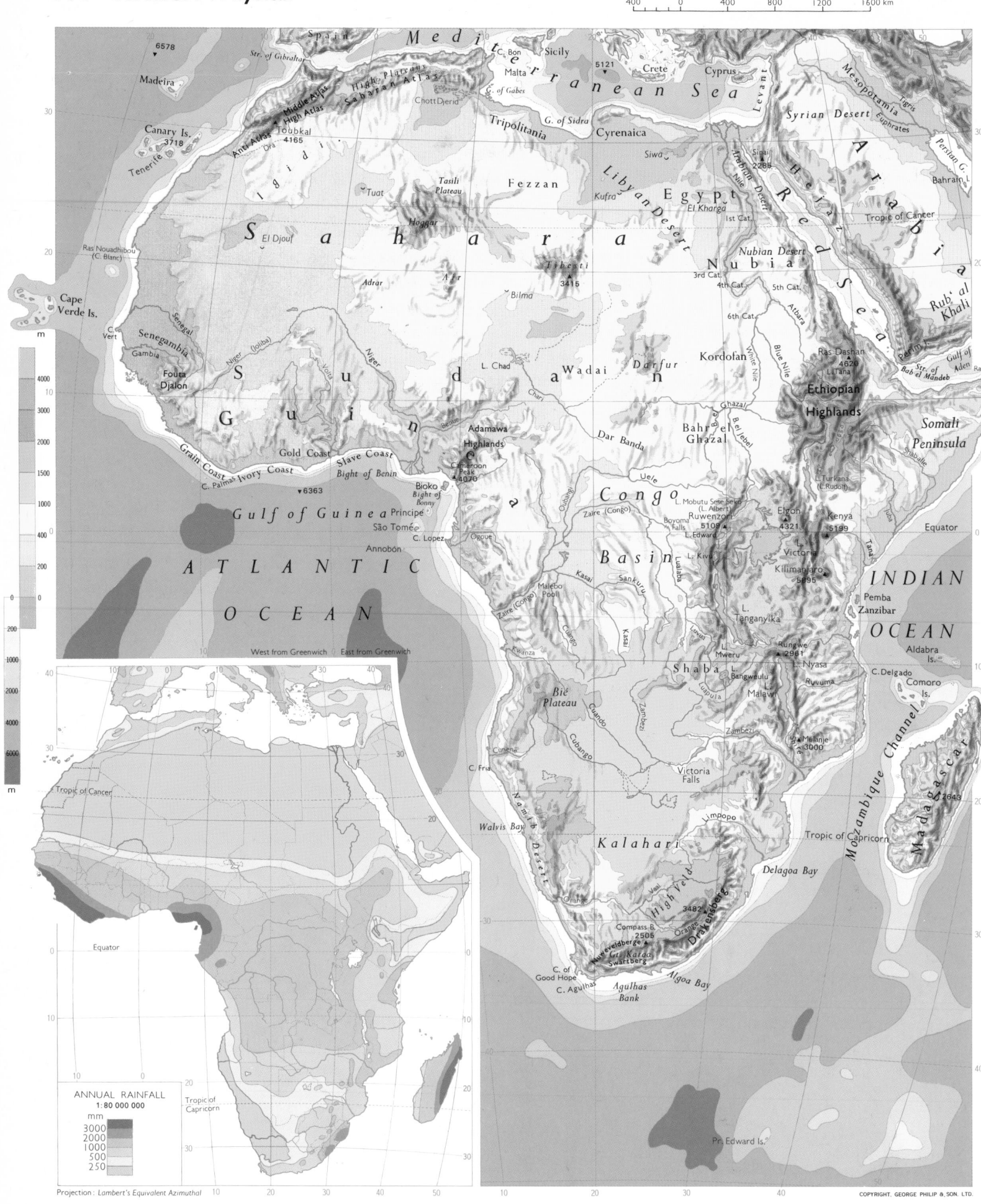

m

4000
3000
2000
1500
1000
400
200
0

0
200
1000
2000
4000
6000

m

Madeira

6578

Str. of Gibraltar

Spain

Mediterranean Sea

C. Bon   Sicily
Malta   Crete   Cyprus
Levant

Canary Is.
3718

Tenerife

High Atlas
Sabaran Atlas
Middle Atlas
Anti Atlas   Toubkal
4165

High Plateau

Chott Djerid

G. of Gabes

G. of Sidra

Tripolitania   Cyrenaica

Siwa

Syrian Desert   Euphrates   Tigris

Mesopotamia

Persian G.

Bahrain

Ras Nouadhibou
(C. Blanc)

Cape
Verde Is.

C. Vert

Senegambia

Gambia

Fouta
Djalon

Senegal

Niger (Joliba)

Igidi

El Djouf

Sahara

Adrar

Tuat

Hoggar

Tasili
Plateau

Fezzan

Aïr

Tibesti
3415

Bilma

Libyan Desert

Egypt

Kufra

El Kharga

1st Cat.

Arabian Desert

Sinai
2285

Nubian Desert

3rd Cat.   4th Cat.   5th Cat.

6th Cat.

Red Sea

Hejaz

Arabia

Rub' al
Khali

Gulf of
Aden

Bab el Mandeb

Str. of

Ras Dashan
4620
L. Tana

Tropic of Cancer

Nile

White Nile

Blue Nile

Atbara

Nubia

L. Chad

Wadai

Darfur

Kordofan

Ethiopian
Highlands

Somali
Peninsula

Jubaland

Sudan

Guinea

Niger

Volta

Benue

Grain Coast
Ivory Coast
C. Palmas
Gold Coast
Slave Coast
Bight of Benin

6363

Adamawa
Highlands
C. Cameroon
Peak
4070

Bight of
Bonny

Bioko

Gulf of Guinea

Príncipe
São Tomé

C. Lopez

Annobón

ATLANTIC

OCEAN

West from Greenwich   East from Greenwich

Chari

Dar Banda

Bahr el
Ghazal

B. el Jebel

Ghazal

Uele

Ubangi

Congo

Basin

Zaire (Congo)

Oguoé

Kasai

Malebo
Pool

Zaire (Congo)

Sankuru

Lualaba

Kasai

L. Mobutu Sese Seko
(L. Albert)

Boyoma
Falls

Ruwenzori
5109

L. Edward

L. Kivu

Elgon
4321

Kenya
5199

L.
Victoria

Kilimanjaro
5895

L.
Tanganyika

Equator

INDIAN

OCEAN

Pemba

Zanzibar

Aldabra
Is.

Shaba

Luapula

L.
Mweru

L.
Bangweulu

Rungwe
2961

L. Nyasa

Malawi

Ruvuma

C. Delgado

Comoro
Is.

Madagascar

2643

Bié
Plateau

Cuango

Cunene

C. Frio

Cuanza

Cubango

Cuando

Zambezi

Victoria
Falls

Zambezi

Limpopo

Melanje
3000

Tropic of Capricorn

Mozambique Channel

Walvis Bay

Namib Desert

Kalahari

Orange

Vaal

High Veld

Delagoa Bay

Algoa Bay

C. Fria

C. of
Good Hope
C. Agulhas

Agulhas
Bank

Nieuweldberge
Gt. Karoo
Swartberg

Compass B.
2505

Drakensberg
3482

Pr. Edward Is.

Tropic of Cancer

Equator

Tropic of
Capricorn

ANNUAL RAINFALL
1 : 80 000 000
mm
3000
2000
1000
500
250

Projection: Lambert's Equivalent Azimuthal

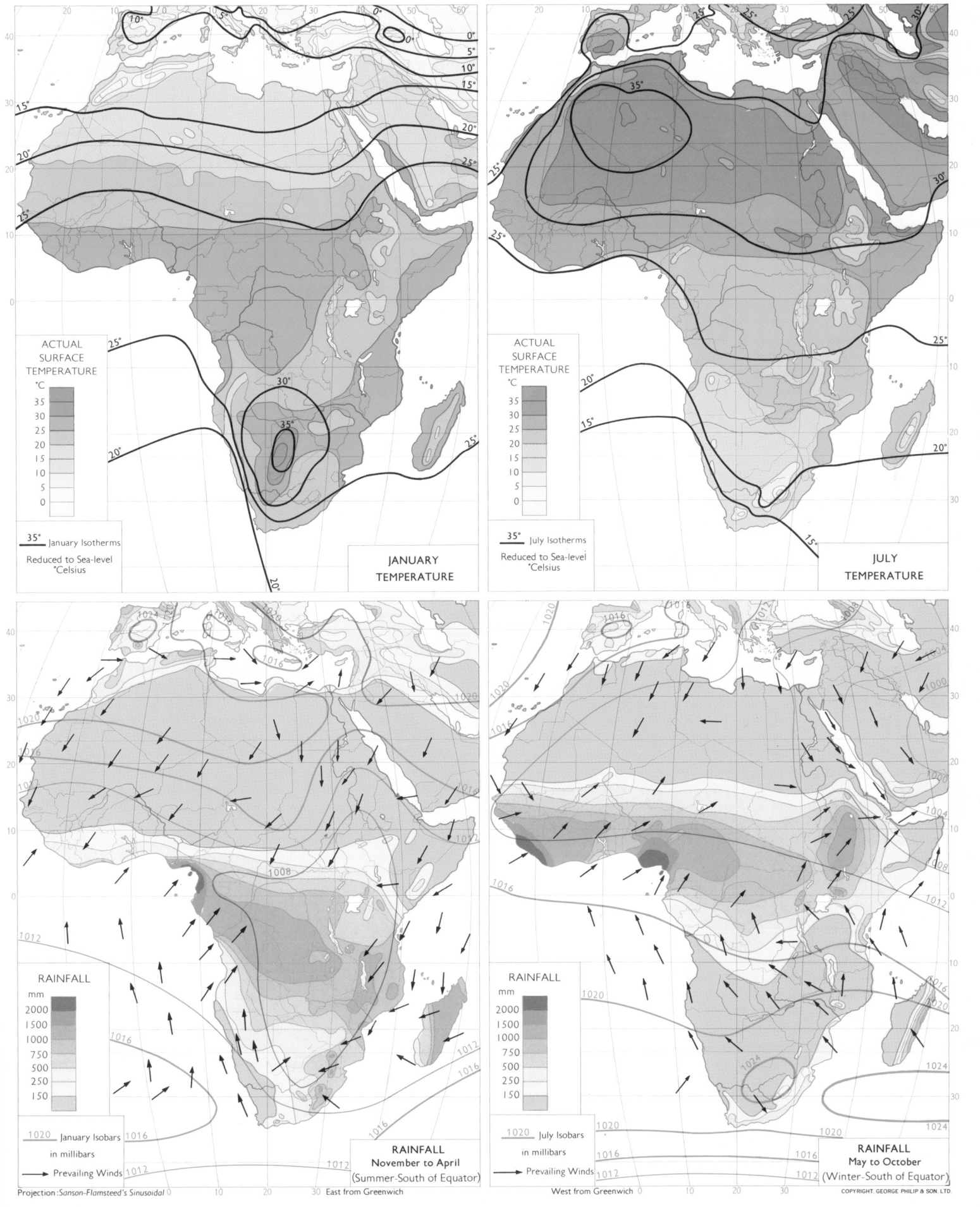

ACTUAL
SURFACE
TEMPERATURE
°C
35
30
25
20
15
10
5
0

35° January Isotherms
Reduced to Sea-level
°Celsius

JANUARY
TEMPERATURE

ACTUAL
SURFACE
TEMPERATURE
°C
35
30
25
20
15
10
5
0

35° July Isotherms
Reduced to Sea-level
°Celsius

JULY
TEMPERATURE

RAINFALL

mm
2000
1500
1000
750
500
250
150

1020 January Isobars
in millibars

Prevailing Winds

RAINFALL
November to April
(Summer-South of Equator)

RAINFALL

mm
2000
1500
1000
750
500
250
150

1020 July Isobars
in millibars

Prevailing Winds

RAINFALL
May to October
(Winter-South of Equator)

Projection: Sanson-Flamsteed's Sinusoidal   0   10   20   30   East from Greenwich

West from Greenwich   0   10   20   30   COPYRIGHT. GEORGE PHILIP & SON, LTD.

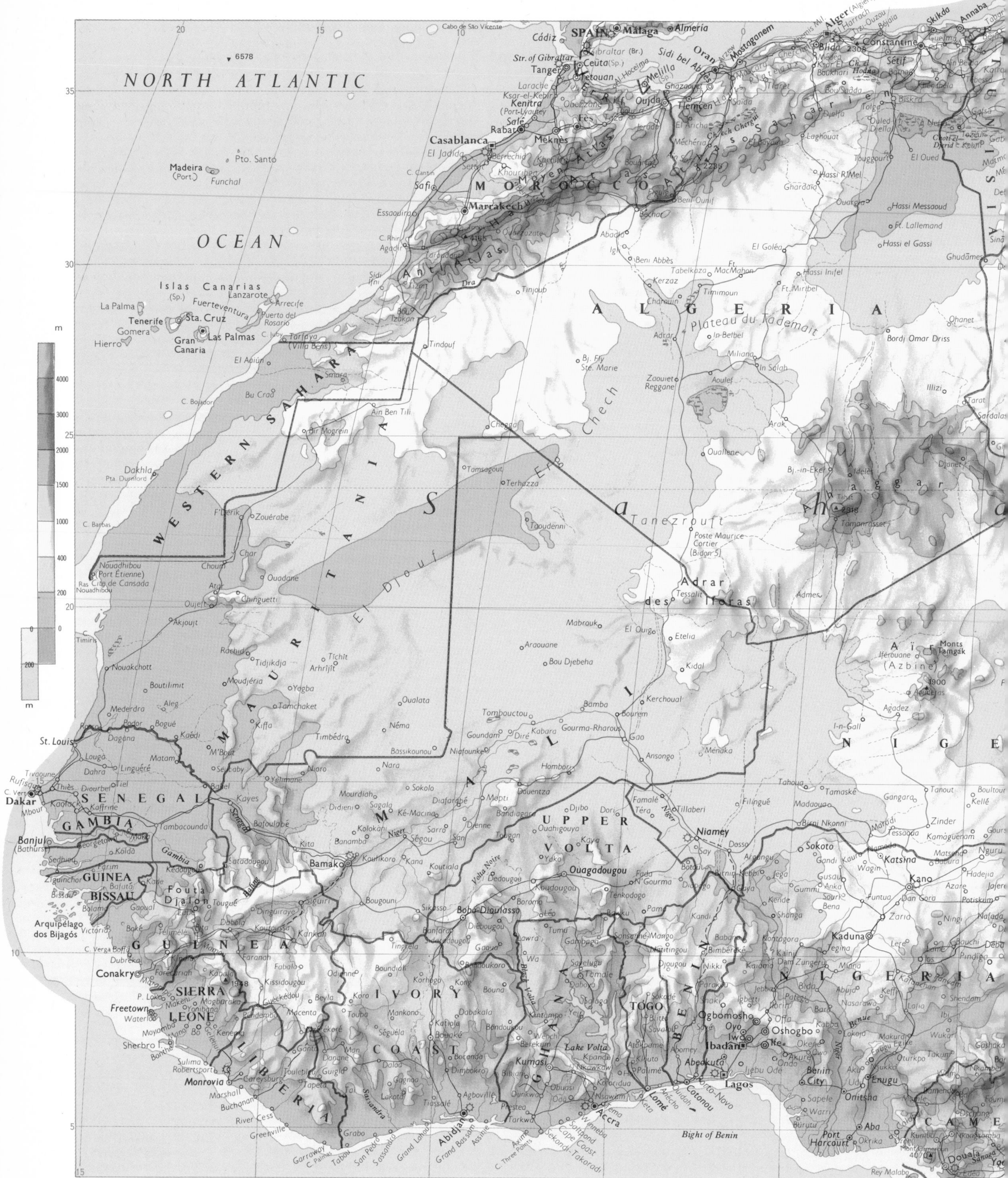

NORTH ATLANTIC

OCEAN

6578

20 15 10

SPAIN
Málaga • Almería
Cádiz • Mostaganem
Alger (Algiers) • El Harrach • Dellys • Azeffoun • Béjaïa • Skikda • Annaba
Constantine • Sétif
Str. of Gibraltar • Gibraltar (Br.) • Ceuta (Sp.) • Melilla
Tanger • Tétouan • Al Hoceima
Oujda • Tlemcen
Oran • Sidi bel Abbès
Blida
Larache • Ksar-el-Kebir
Kenitra (Port-Lyautey) • Fès • Meknès
Rabat • Salé • Casablanca
El Jadida • Berrechid
Safi
Marrakech
Essaouira
Agadir
Sidi Ifni

MOROCCO
Anti Atlas
2465
Ouarzazate
Tarfaya (Villa Bens)
Bou Izakan

ALGERIA
Plateau du Tademaït
Béchar
Beni Ounif
Abadla
Tindouf
In Salah
Reggane
Zaouiet Reggane
El Goléa
Hassi Messaoud
Ft. Lallemand
Hassi el Gassi
Ghudames
Ouargla
Touggourt
El Oued
Laghouat
Ghardaïa
Hassi R'Mel
Bordj Omar Driss
Ghat
Djanet
Illizi
Tarat
Ahaggar
Tamanrasset
Bj.-in-Eker
Adrar des Iforas
Poste Maurice Cortier (Bidon 5)

WESTERN SAHARA
El Aaiún
Smara
Bu Craa
C. Bojador
Dakhla
Pta. Durnford

MAURITANIA
Nouadhibou (Port Étienne)
Ras Cabo de Cansado
Nouadhibou
F'Derik
Zouérate
Char
Choum
Ouadane
Chinguetti
Atar
Akjoujt
Nouakchott
Boutilimit
Moudjéria
Rachid
Tidjikja
Tîchît
Arhrijît
Yagba
Tamchaket
Néma
Oualata
Kiffa
Timbédra
Bassikounou
Nara
Nioro
Kayes

Tanezrouft
Taoudenni
Terhazza
Tamsagout
El Djouf
Araouane
Mabrouk
El Ouig
Etelia
Tombouctou
Kidal
Bou Djebeha
Bamba
Gourma-Rharous
Gao
Bourem
Kerchoual
Menaka
Gourma-Rharous
Diré
Kabara
Gossi
Hombori
Bandiagara

MALI
Mopti
Douentza
Djibo
Dori
Sokolo
Ké-Macina
Ségou
Banamba
Koutiala
San
Djenné
Mourdiah
Didieni
Diafarabé
Koulikoro
Bamako
Sikasso
Bobo-Dioulasso

NIGER
Agadez
In-Gall
Tahoua
Iferouane
Monts Tamgak
Aïr (Azbine)
1900
Madaoua
Filingué
Tillabéri
Niamey
Dosso
Birni Nkonni
Tessaoua
Zinder
Maradi
Gouré
Kéllé
Tanout
Gangara

SENEGAL
St. Louis
Dakar
C. Vert
Rufisque
Thiès
Diourbel
Kaolack
Louga
Dahra
Linguère
Matam
Bakel
Podor
Kaffrine
Mbour

GAMBIA
Banjul (Bathurst)
Georgetown

GUINEA BISSAU
Bissau
Bafatá
Arquipélago dos Bijagós

GUINEA
Conakry
Fouta Djalon
Labé
Kindia
Boké
Kankan
Siguiri

SIERRA LEONE
Freetown
Waterloo
Makeni
Bo
Kenema

LIBERIA
Monrovia
Buchanan
Greenville
River Cess

IVORY COAST
Abidjan
Man
Daloa
Bouaké
Korhogo
Odienné
Dimbokro
Agboville
Grand Bassam

UPPER VOLTA
Ouagadougou
Bobo-Dioulasso
Koudougou
Dédougou
Kaya
Fada N'Gourma
Tenkodogo
Banfora

GHANA
Accra
Kumasi
Tamale
Wa
Bolgatanga
Lake Volta
Cape Coast
Sekondi-Takoradi

TOGO
Lomé
Sokodé

BENIN
Porto-Novo
Cotonou
Parakou
Kandi

NIGERIA
Lagos
Ibadan
Abeokuta
Oshogbo
Ogbomosho
Oyo
Ife
Ilorin
Kaduna
Kano
Katsina
Sokoto
Zaria
Gusau
Enugu
Onitsha
Benin City
Warri
Port Harcourt
Aba

CAMEROON
Douala
Bioko

Bight of Benin

Islas Canarias (Sp.)
Lanzarote
Arrecife
Fuerteventura
Puerto del Rosario
La Palma
Tenerife
Gomera
Hierro
Gran Canaria
Las Palmas
Sta. Cruz

Madeira (Port.)
Funchal
Pto. Santo

m
4000
3000
2000
1500
1000
400
200
0
0
200
m

35

30

25

20

15

10

5

Projection: Sanson Flamsteed's Sinusoidal

West from Greenwich 0 East from Greenwich

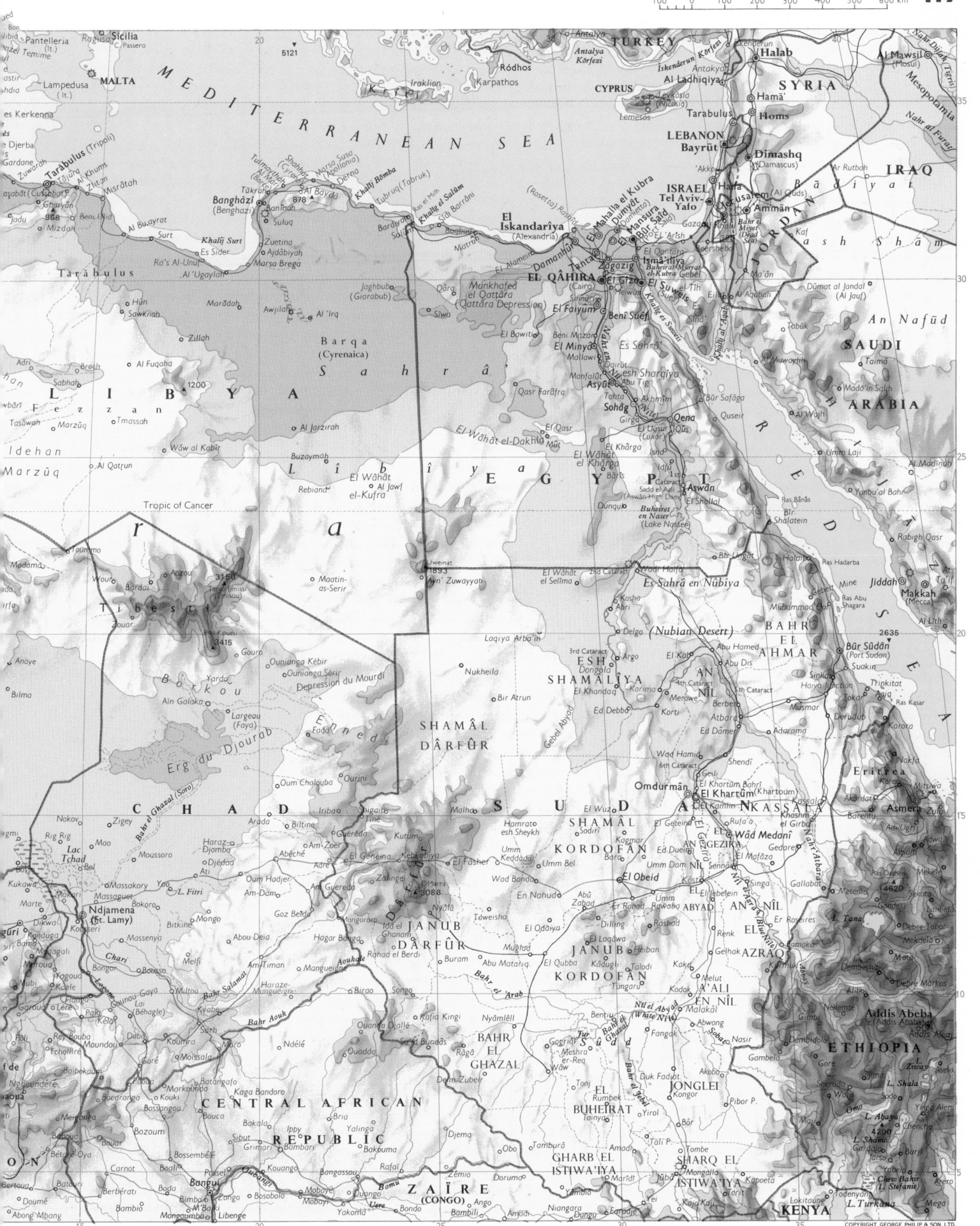

1:15 000 000

100 0 100 200 300 400 500 600 km

117

1:8 000 000

COPYRIGHT. GEORGE PHILIP & SON. LTD.

Gambia and Senegal have agreed to the
amalgamation of their economies and armies.
This new confederation is known as Senegambia.

West from Green

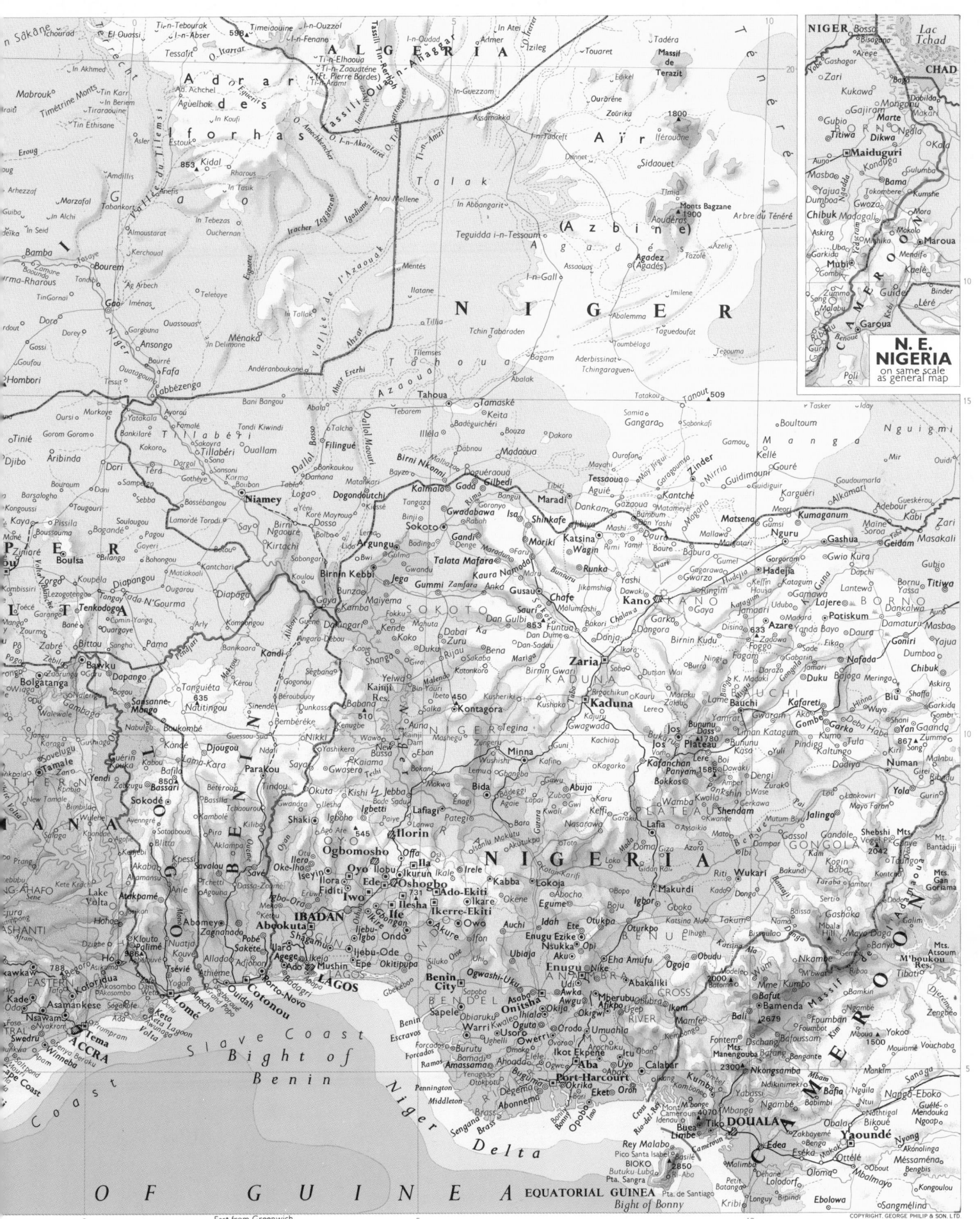

1:8 000 000

50 0 50 100 150 200 250 300 km

121

THE NILE DELTA
1:4 000 000
MEDITERRANEAN SEA
East from Greenwich
Tropic of Cancer
EGYPT
SAUDI ARABIA
JORDAN
ISRAEL
Buheiret en Naser (Lake Nasser)
Khalig es Suweis
Khalig el 'Aqaba
Es Sahrâ' el Gharbîya (Western Desert)
Sahrâ en Nûbîya (Nubian Desert)
EL BAHR EL AHMAR

1 : 8 000 000

50   0   50   100   150   200   250   300 km

East from Greenwich

Projection: Lambert's Equivalent Azimuthal

m   4000   3000   2000   1500   1000   400   200   0   200

m

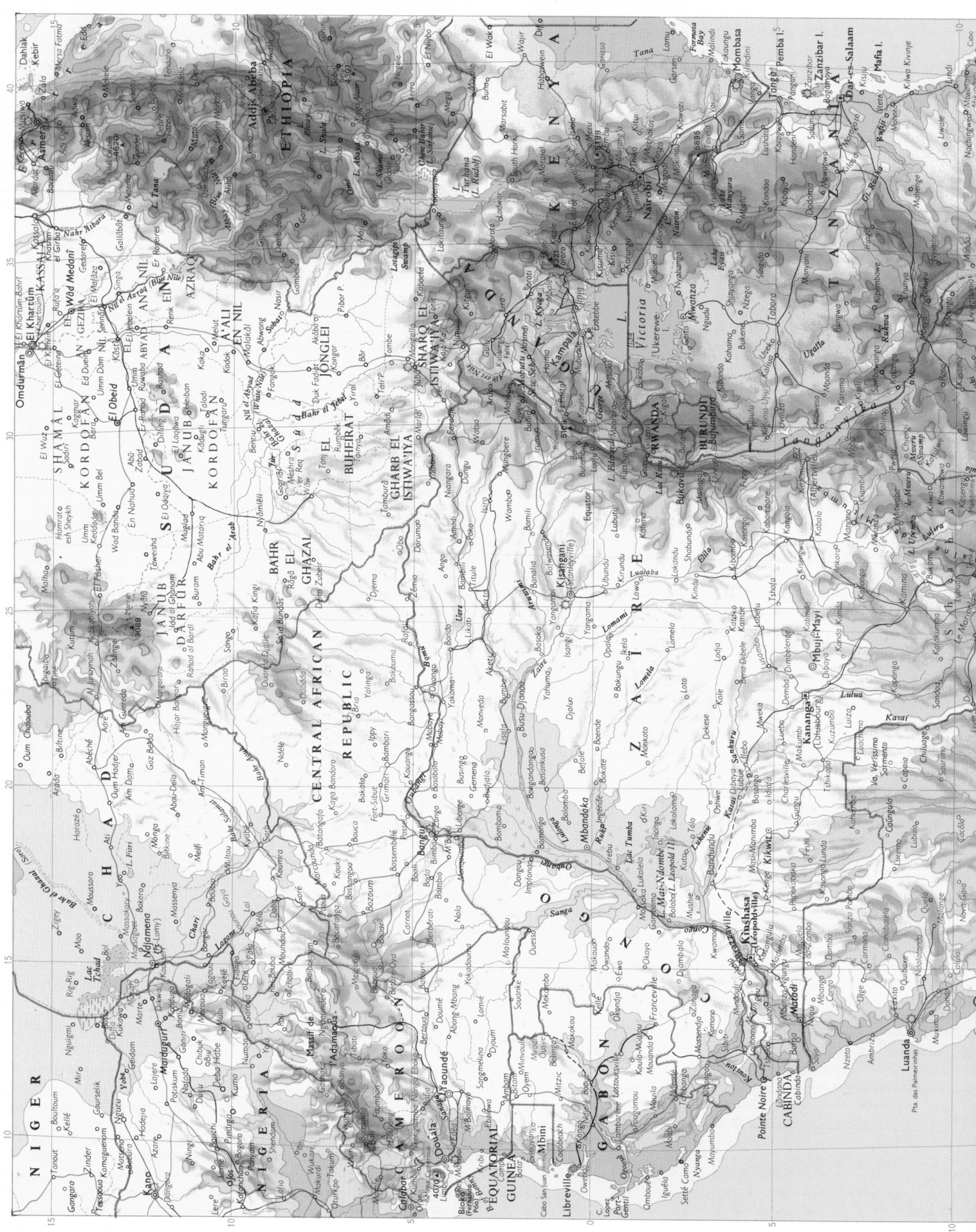
NIGER
CHAD
NIGERIA
CAMEROON
CENTRAL AFRICAN REPUBLIC
SUDAN
ETHIOPIA
UGANDA
KENYA
TANZANIA
RWANDA
BURUNDI
ZAÏRE
CONGO
GABON
EQUATORIAL GUINEA
CABINDA
Kano
Ndjamena
Maiduguri
Douala
Yaoundé
Libreville
Pointe Noire
Kinshasa
Brazzaville
Luanda
Bangui
Omdurman
El Khartûm
Addis Abeba
Asmera
Kampala
Nairobi
Mombasa
Dar-es-Salaam
Zanzibar I.
Pemba I.
Mafia I.
Kisangani
Bukavu
Kananga
Mbuji-Mayi
L. Victoria
Lac Tchad
L. Tana
L. Turkana (L. Rudolf)
Tanganyika
Massif de l'Adamaoua
Mbini
Bioko (Fernando Póo)

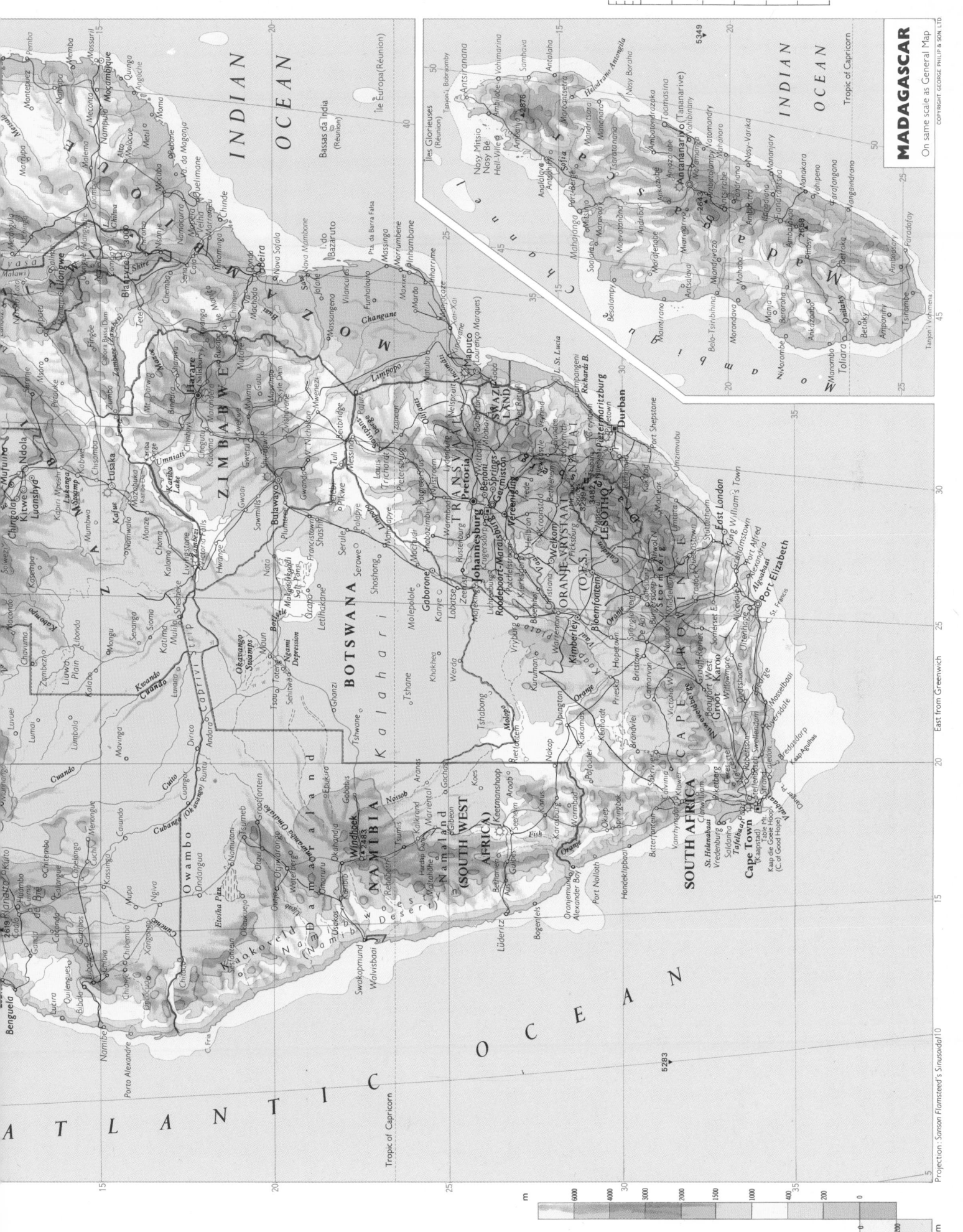

SOMALI REP.

ETHIOPIA

KENYA

UGANDA

SUDAN

TANZANIA

CENTRAL AFRICAN REPUBLIC

RWANDA

BURUNDI

CONGO

MOMBASA

Zanzibar

DAR ES SALAAM

NAIROBI

Kampala

Entebbe

Kisangani

Lake Victoria

L. Tanganyika

L. Turkana (L. Rudolf)

L. Kyoga

L. Mobutu

L. Kivu

Pemba I.

MANDERA

MARSABIT

TANA RIVER

COAST

NYANZA

CENTRAL

RIFT VALLEY

NORTHERN

EQUATOR

Nakuru

Eldoret

Kitui

Machakos

Meru

Nyeri

Thika

Arusha

Moshi

Tanga

Pangani

Dodoma

Tabora

Kigoma

Bukavu

Kindu

Buta

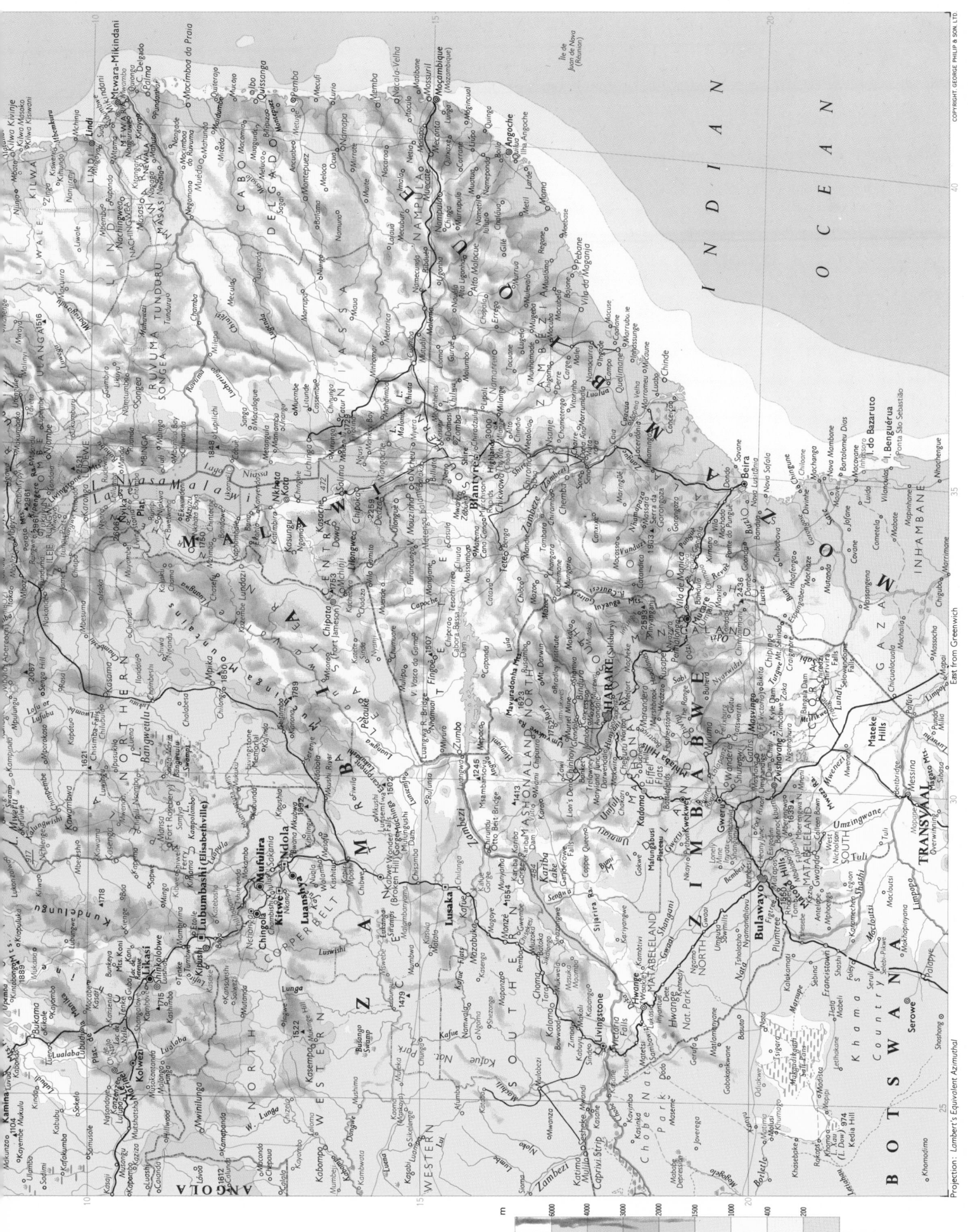

1:8 000 000

50   0   50   100   150   200   250   300 km

East from Greenwich

Projection: Lambert's Equivalent Azimuthal

I N D I A N   O C E A N

M O Z A M B I Q U E

M A L A W I

Z A M B I A

Z I M B A B W E

B O T S W A N A

A N G O L A

TRANSVAAL

CABO DELGADO

NAMPULA

ZAMBEZIA

NORTHERN

WESTERN

SOUTHERN

COPPER BELT

MASHONALAND
NORTH

MATABELELAND
NORTH

MATABELELAND
SOUTH

Lake Nyasa / Lake Malawi

Livingstone

Lusaka

Ndola
Kitwe
Mufulira
Luanshya
Chingola
Lubumbashi (Elisabethville)
Likasi
Kolwezi

Harare

Bulawayo

Gweru

Kadoma

Mutare

Blantyre

Beira

Mozambique

Angoche

Lindi

Mtwara-Mikindani

Kariba Lake

Victoria Falls

Serowe

m   6000   4000   3000   2000   1500   1000   400   200

m   200   2000

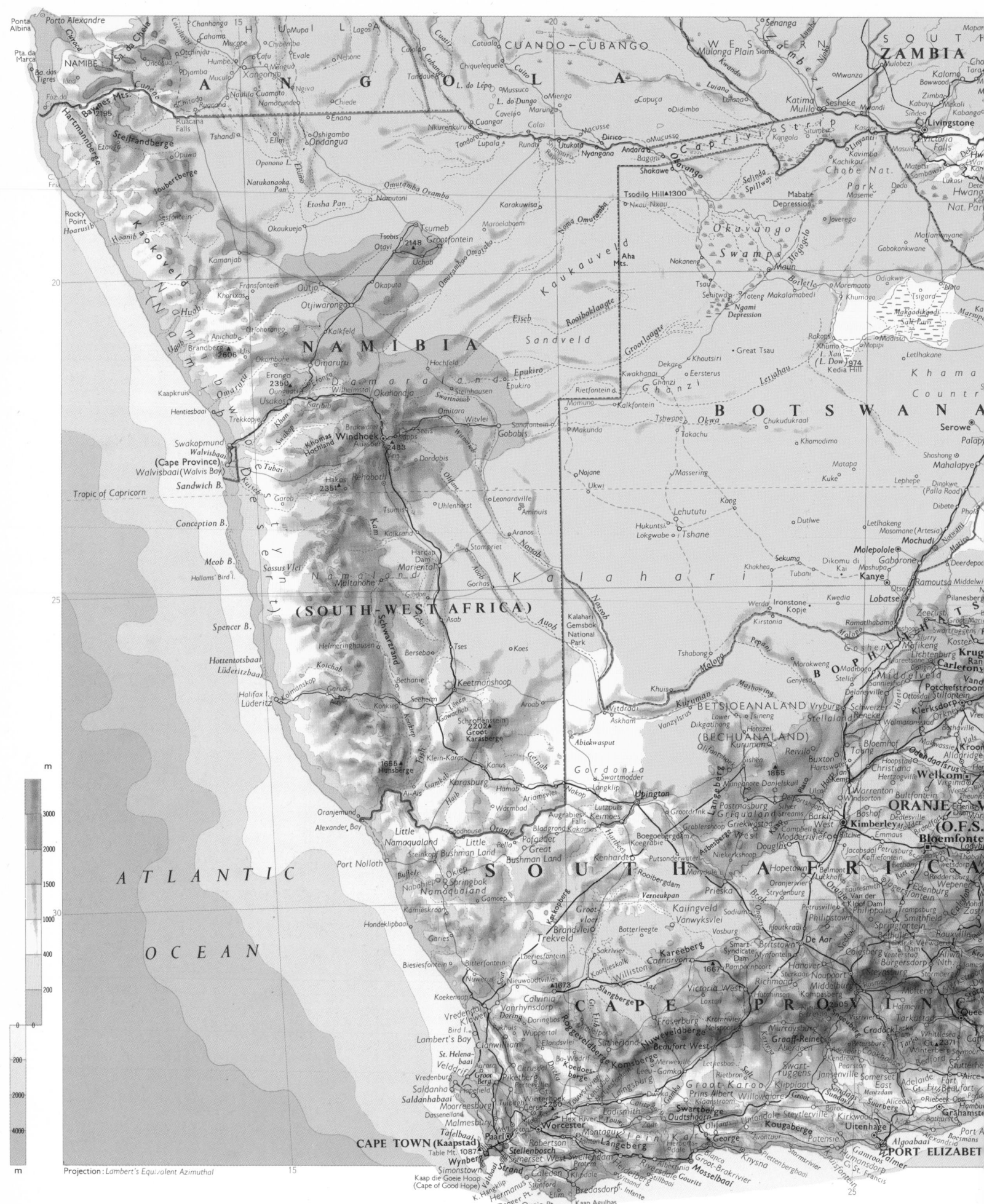

ATLANTIC

OCEAN

Projection: Lambert's Equivalent Azimuthal

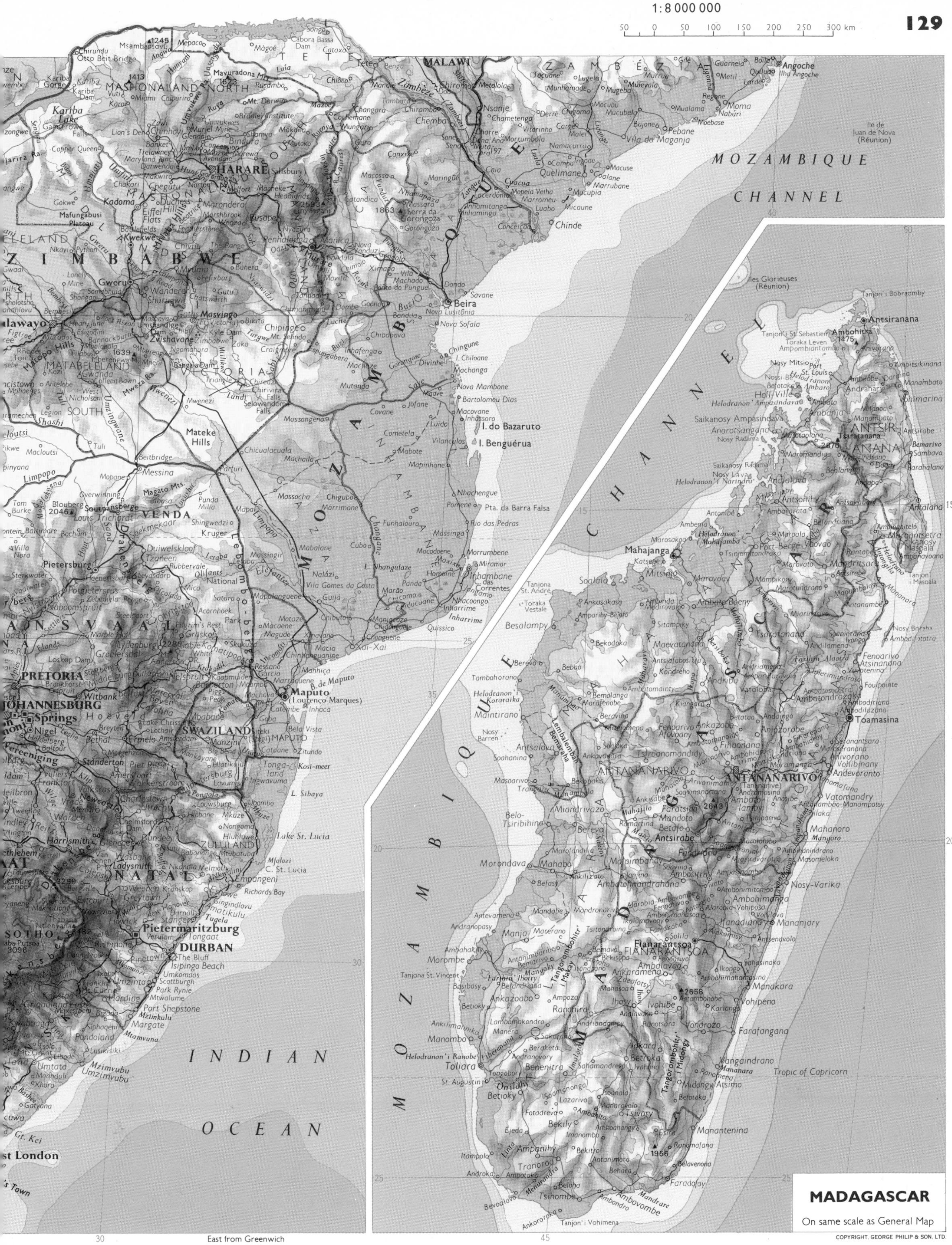

1:8 000 000
50 0 50 100 150 200 250 300 km
ZIMBABWE
MOZAMBIQUE
MOZAMBIQUE CHANNEL
INDIAN OCEAN
HARARE
Beira
Maputo (Lourenço Marques)
PRETORIA
JOHANNESBURG
SWAZILAND
Pietermaritzburg
DURBAN
NATAL
ZULULAND
VENDA
MALAWI
ZAMBÉZIA
TETE
MASHONALAND NORTH
MATABELELAND
Bulawayo
Gweru
Masvingo
Quelimane
Chinde
Angoche
Inhambane
Xai-Xai
I. do Bazaruto
I. Benguérua
Ile de Juan de Nova (Réunion)
Iles Glorieuses (Réunion)
Tropic of Capricorn
East from Greenwich
MADAGASCAR
ANTANANARIVO
FIANARANTSOA
Antsiranana
Mahajanga
Toamasina
Toliara
Antsirabe
Fianarantsoa
MADAGASCAR
On same scale as General Map

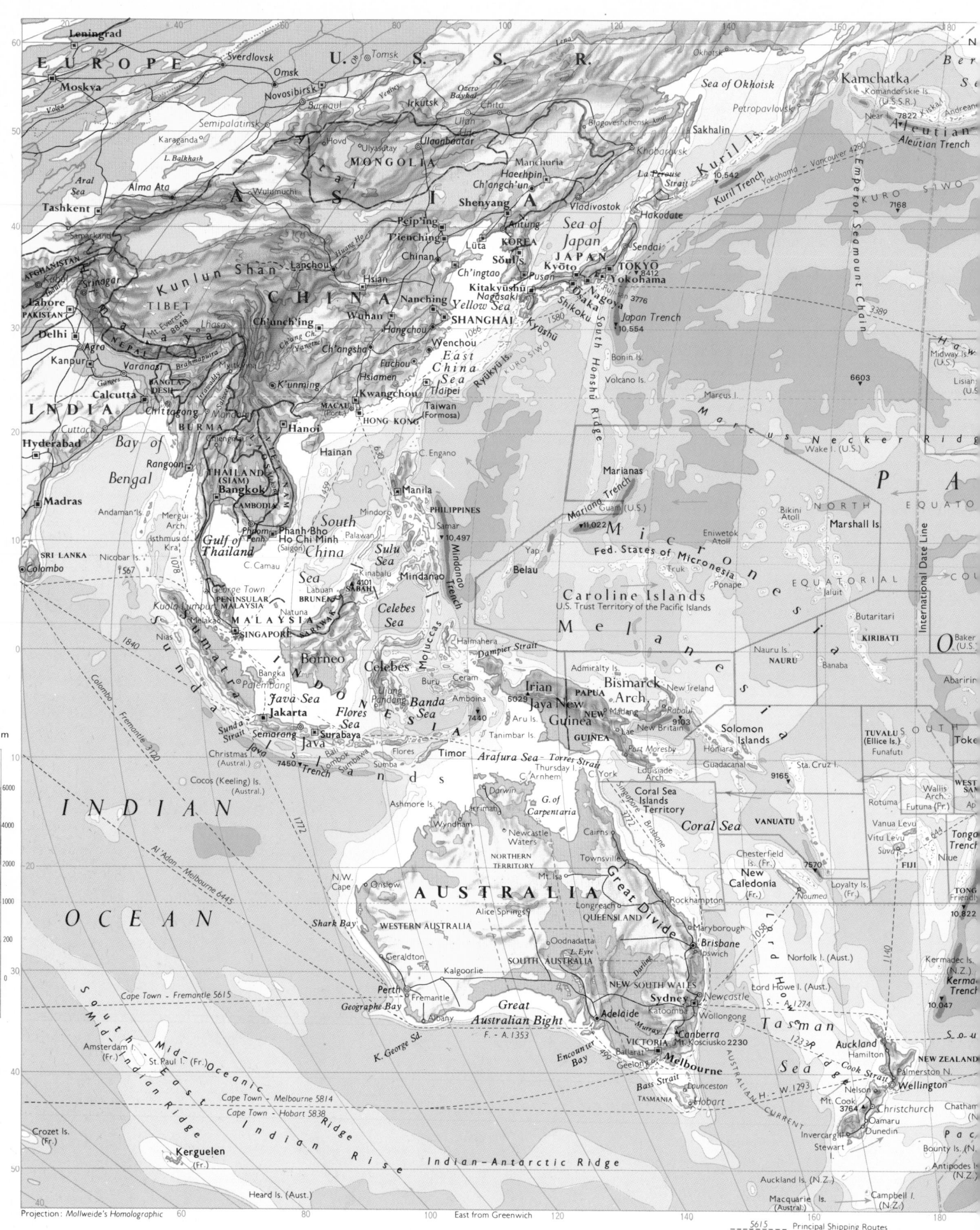

East from Greenwich

5615 Principal Shipping Routes
(Distances in Nautical Miles)

ALASKA
Bristol Bay
Gulf of Alaska
6050
Juneau
Sitka
Prince of Wales I.
Queen Charlotte Is.
Prince Rupert
Kitimat
Vancouver I.
Vancouver
Victoria
Seattle
Tacoma
Portland
C. Blanco
Mendocino Seascarp
6741
C. Mendocino
Sacramento
Oakland
San Francisco
4418
2091
Murray Seascarp
Los Angeles
San Diego
CALIFORNIAN CURRENT
Hawaiian Is.
(U.S.A.)
Ridge
Oahu
Honolulu
Hawaii
Tropic of Cancer
Clarion Fracture Zone
I. (U.S.)
FIC
CURRENT
4711
Christmas Island Ridge
CURRENT
Palmyra Is. (U.S.)
Teraina
Tabuaeran
Kirimati
EAN
Jarvis I. (U.S.)
EQUATORIAL
CURRENT
Malden I.
Starbuck I.
Equator
ry I.
ix Is.
Tongareva
Penrhyn Is.
Manihiki
Suwarrow Is.
(Suvorov)
Vostok I.
Flint I.
Cook
Islands
1302
Society Is. (Fr.)
Windward
Is.
Tahiti (Fr.)
French Polynesia
Manuae
Rarotonga
Tubuai Is.
(Austral Is.)
(Fr.)
Rapa Iti
(Fr.)
Seamount Chain
Marquesas Is.
(Fr.)
Caroline I.
Leeward Is.
Tuamotu Archipelago
(Fr.)
Tuamotu Ridge
Pitcairn I. (U.K.)
Ducie I. (U.K.)
East Pacific Ridge
Auckland - Panamá 6510
Tahiti - Panamá 4570
3666
Clipperton Fracture Zone
Clipperton I. (Fr.)
CANADA
NORTH AMERICA
GREENLAND
C. Farewell
Churchill
L. Athabasca
Dawson Creek
Hudson
Bay
Belcher Is.
James
Bay
Labrador
Scheffervile
Hamilton Inlet
Strait of Belle Isle
NORTH
BRITISH
ISLES
60
Edmonton
Lynn Lake
Rockies
Saskatoon
Prince Albert
L. Winnipeg
Regina
Calgary
Medicine Hat
Winnipeg
Mountains
Spokane
Helena
Butte
Boise
Bismarck
Missouri
Duluth
L. Superior
Sault Ste. Marie
St. Lawrence
Anticosti
G. of St. Lawrence
Newfoundland
Pr. Edward I.
C. Breton I.
C. Race
Sable I.
Southampton 3091
NORTH
Cheyenne
Snake
Salt Lake City
Des Moines
Denver
Kansas
St. Louis
Santa Fe
Oklahoma
Little Rock
El Paso
Dallas
Austin
Ciudad
Juárez
Guadalupe
6225
Pto. Eugenia
C. S. Lucas
Revilla Gigedo Is.
(Mexico)
Guadalajara
3277
Acapulco
Minneapolis
Milwaukee
CHICAGO
St. Paul
L. Michigan
Montréal
Québec
Fredericton
Saint John
Ottawa
Toronto
L. Huron
L. Ontario
Buffalo
Detroit
Pittsburgh
Cincinnati
Indianapolis
Memphis
NEW YORK
Philadelphia
Baltimore
Washington
Richmond
Norfolk
C. Hatteras
ATLANTIC
OCEAN
40
New
Orleans
Houston
San Antonio
Galveston
Mobile
Atlanta
Savannah
Jacksonville
Tampa
Miami
New York - Recife 3078
Bermuda (U.K.)
NY - C. 1972
New York - Liverpool 4550
UNITED STATES
Mississippi
Appalachian Mts.
Gulf of Mexico
Torreón
Monterrey
Tampico
San Luis Potosí
Aguascalientes
México
Veracruz
Puebla 5700
MEXICO
Sierra Madre
Gulf of California
La Habana
Yucatán Channel
Mérida
BELIZE
CUBA
Florida
Strait
BAHAMAS
West Indies
Hispaniola 9200
DOM.
REP.
HAITI
7680
JAMAICA
Kingston
Santo
Domingo
PUERTO
RICO
St. Thomas (U.S.)
Virgin Is.
Leeward
Is.
Guadeloupe
(Fr.)
Martinique
(Fr.)
BARBADOS
Windward
Is.
TRINIDAD &
TOBAGO
Panamá - Liverpool
Tropic of Cancer
20
GUATEMALA
Guatemala
HONDURAS
Tegucigalpa
EL SALVADOR
S.E. Monsoon Drift
San Salvador
NICARAGUA
Managua
CENTRAL
AMERICA
COSTA RICA
San José
PANAMA
Canal
Barranquilla
Caribbean Sea
Curaçao (Ne.)
Maracaibo
Caracas
Orinoco
VENEZUELA
10
Cocos I.
Medellín
Bogotá
Cali
COLOMBIA
C. S. Francisco
835
Galápagos
(Ecuador)
Quito
ECUADOR
Chimborazo 6287
Guayaquil
Cuenca
Manaus
Iquitos
Amazon
BRAZIL
SOUTH
C. Pariñas
C. S. Francisco
Chiclayo
Lobos I.
Trujillo
700
PERU
PERUVIAN
CURRENT
6369
Lima
Callao
AMERICA
10
Southeast
Pacific Basin
Cuzco
Arequipa
L. Titicaca
Illampu & Ancohuma
6550
Iquique
La Paz
6866
BOLIVIA
Peru
Chile
20
Tropic of Capricorn
San Félix (Chile)
San Ambrosio (Chile)
Sala-y-Gomez
(Chile)
Easter I.
(Chile)
8050
Antofagasta
Trench
755
Salta
Tucumán
Asunción
Corrientes
PARAGUAY
Pto. Alegre
30
Arch. de Juan Fernández
(Chile)
Alejandro Selkirk
Robinson Crusoe
Aconcagua
6960
Valparaíso
Santiago
Concepción
Córdoba
Rosario
Santa Fe
Paysandú
URUGUAY
Buenos Aires
La Plata
Montevideo
Río de la Plata
Mar del Plata
SOUTH
ATLANTIC
OCEAN
Andes
Neuquén
ARGENTINA
Paraná
Buenos Aires - Montevideo
1355
1795
G. of San Matías
40
Pacific-
Antarctic
Basin
Pacific - Antarctic Ridge
WEST WIND DRIFT
Chile Rise
Chonos Arch.
G. of Penas
P.A.
Valparaíso
1414
Patagonia
P.A.
P. Deseado
G. of San Jorge
Argentine
Basin
6212
Wellington
Sta. Cruz
Punta
Arenas
CAPE HORN CURRENT
Str. of Magellan
Tierra del Fuego
C. Horn
Falkland Is. (U.K.)
Stanley
South Georgia
50

160   140   120   100   West from Greenwich   80   60   40   20

COPYRIGHT. GEORGE PHILIP & SON. LTD.

Java Trench
TIMOR SEA
INDIAN OCEAN
WESTERN AUSTRALIA
NORTHERN TERRITORY
SOUTH AUSTRALIA
Ashmore Reef
Cartier I.
Scott Reef
Rowley Shoals
Bonaparte Archipelago
C. Londonderry
C. Talbot
C. Bougainville
Vansittart B.
Admiralty G.
Montague Sd.
York Sd.
Brunswick B.
Jos. Bonaparte Gulf
Cambridge G.
Queens Chan.
Drysdale
Wyndham
Kununurra
Mt. Hann 776
Kimberley
Collier B.
King Sd.
C. Levêque
Lacepede Is.
Yampi Sound
King Leopold Ras.
Mt. Ord 1007
Meda
Durack Range
Ord
Derby
C. Baskerville
Carnot B.
C. Boileau
Broome
Fitzroy
Fitzroy Crossing
Hall's Creek
Roebuck B.
C. Latouche Treville
Dampier Downs
Gordon Downs
C. Bossut
La Grange
Eighty Mile Beach
Canning Basin
Sturt
Gregory Lake
Great Sandy Desert
Dampier Archipelago
P. Hedland
Goldsworthy
De Grey
Hampton Har.
Port Samson
Roebourne
Dampier
Monte Bello Is.
Barrow I.
Preston
Pilbara
Yule
Shaw
Marble Bar
Nullagine
Throssell Ra.
L. Dora
L. Blanche
L. Mackay
Onslow
Exmouth G.
N.W. Cape
Exmouth
Learmonth
Pt. Cloates
Fortescue
Hamersley Ra.
Wittenoom
Mt. Enid
Mt. Bruce
Ophthalmia Range
Mt. Newman 1053
Newman
Robertson Ra.
Ashburton
L. Disappointment
Gibson Desert
Rawlinson Ra.
C. Farquhar
Barlee Ra.
Mt. Augustus 1105
Mt. Egerton 994
L. McLeod
Lyons
C. Cuvier
Geographe Chan.
Carnarvon
Bernier I.
Dorre I.
Gascoyne
Wooramel
Peak Hill
Robinson Ra.
L. Buchanan
Barrow Ra.
L. Carnegie
L. Wells 712
Naturaliste Chan.
Dirk Hartog I.
Shark B.
Denham
S. Passage
Steep Pt.
Wiluna
Meekatharra
Murchison
Nannine
Sanford
Cue
L. Austin
L. Yeo
Great Victoria Desert
Gantheaume B.
Tallering Peak 453
Mt. Magnet
Sandstone
Laverton
L. Rason
P. Gregory
Houtman Abrolhos
Northampton
Champion B.
Geraldton
Yalgoo
Mullewa
Mongers Lake
L. Barlee
Leonora
Malcolm
L. Carey
L. Minigwal
L. Raeside
L. Ballard
Menzies
L. Maurice
Maralinga
Ooldea
Dongara
L. Moore
Kanowna
Premier Downs
Coastal Plains
Darling Range
Bonnie Rock
Bencubbin
Kalgoorlie
Coolgardie
Boulder
Zanthus
Rawlinna
Forrest
Deakin
Nullarbor Plain
Hampton Tableland
Eucla Motel
Eyre
Head of Bight
Wedge I.
Basin
Bullfinch
Southern Cross
L. Lefroy
L. Cowan
Norseman
L. Dundas
Northam
Merredin
Kellerberrin
The Johnston Lakes
Midland Junction
Perth
Fremantle
Kwinana
York
Beverley
Brookton
Narrogin
Pt. Dover
Pt. Culver
Great Australian Bight
Newdegate
Pinjarra
Ravensthorpe
Hopetoun
Esperance
Rocky Pt.
Bunbury
Geographe B.
Collie
Wagin
Katanning
Nyabing
Gnowangerup
C. Pasley
C. Arid
Archipelago of the Recherche
C. Naturaliste
Busselton
Bridgetown
Stirling Ra.
Doubtful B.
Esperance B.
C. le Grand
Augusta
C. Leeuwin
Manjimup
Pemberton
Mt. Barker
Albany
Pt. Hood
C. Knob
Flinders B.
Pt. d'Entrecasteaux
Pt. Nuyts
Denmark
Tor B.
King George Sound
Croker I.
Cobourg Pen.
Dundas Str.
Melville I.
Bathurst I.
Van Diemen Gulf
Clarence Str.
P. Darwin
Darwin
Jabiru
Arnhem L.
Pt. Blaze
Anson B.
C. Ford
Rum Jungle
Batchelor
Pine Creek
Daly
Katherine
Roper
Mataranka
Larrimah
Victoria
Birdum
Victoria River Downs
Daly Waters
Wave Hill
Newcastle Waters
L. Woods
Powell Creek
Renner Springs
Tanami Desert
Tennant
Hordern Hills
The Granites
Reynolds Ra.
Mt. Ziel 1510
L. Macdonald
Macdonnell Ras.
James Ra.
Palmer
Finke
Hugh
L. Amadeus
Mt. Olga 1151
Ayers Rock 933
Musgrave Ranges
Mt. Woodroffe 1549
Charlotte W.
Everard Ras.
Penong
C. Adieu
Fowlers B.
Nuyts Archipelago
Streaky B.
C. Radstock
Investigator Gro.
Coffin B.
GREAT NORTHERN
N.W. COASTAL
EASTERN
GREAT EASTERN
GERALDTON
ALBANY
EYRE
DUNCAN
STUART
m
0
200
400
1000
1500
2000
2000
4000
6000
10
15
20
25
30
35
110
115
120
125
105
130
Projection: Bonne
East from Greenwich

1:14 000 000

100   0   100   200   300   400   500   600 km

CORAL

SEA

CORAL   SEA   ISLANDS

TERRITORY

PACIFIC

OCEAN

Tropic of Capricorn

QUEENSLAND

Gulf of Carpentaria

Great Barrier Reef

Great Dividing Range

Cape York Peninsula

NEW SOUTH WALES

TRALIA

VICTORIA

Australian Alps

SYDNEY

Canberra

MELBOURNE

Spencer Gulf

Bass Strait

TASMAN

SEA

TASMANIA

Hobart

1:60 000 000

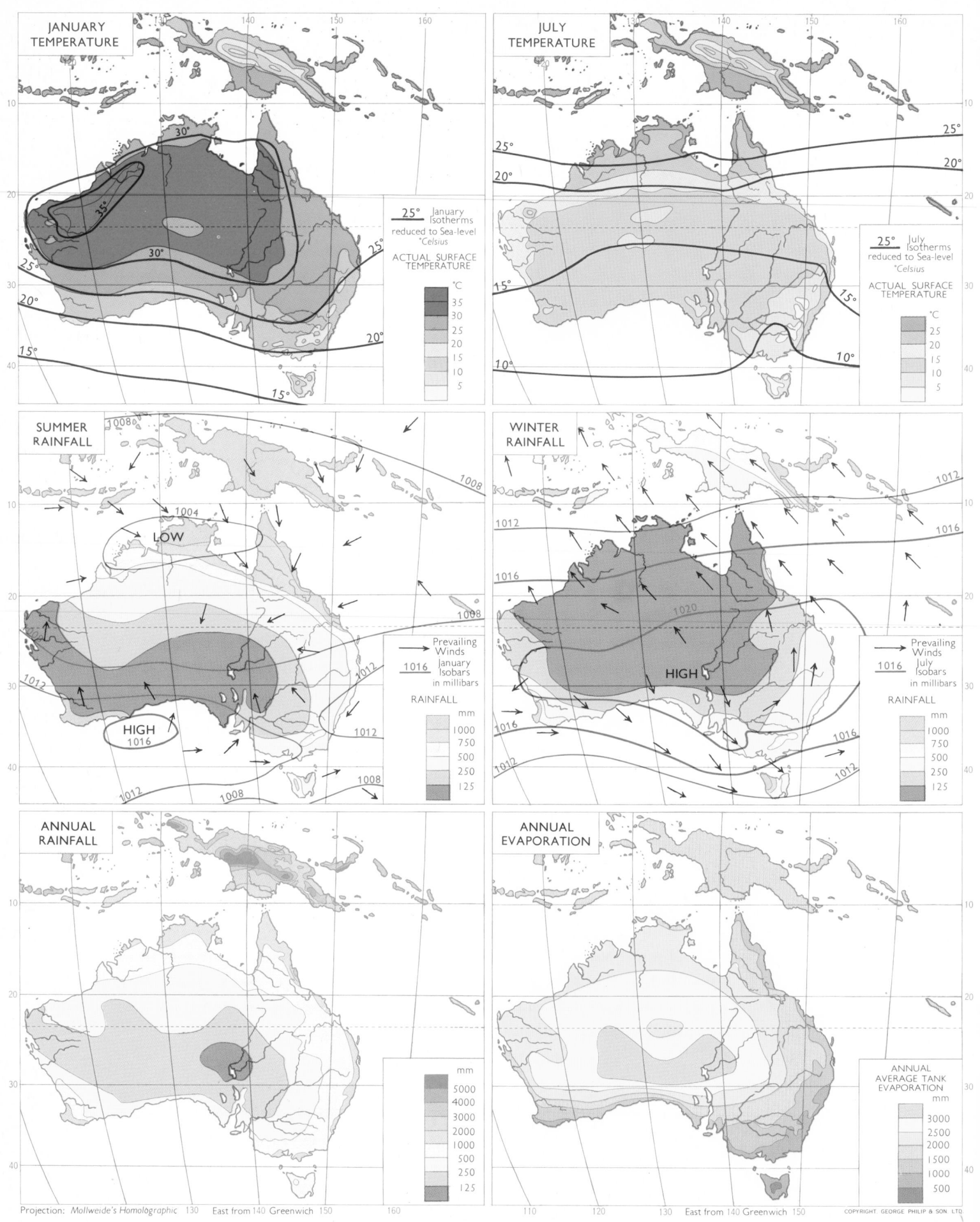

JANUARY TEMPERATURE

25° January Isotherms reduced to Sea-level °Celsius

ACTUAL SURFACE TEMPERATURE

°C
35
30
25
20
15
10
5

JULY TEMPERATURE

25° July Isotherms reduced to Sea-level °Celsius

ACTUAL SURFACE TEMPERATURE

°C
25
20
15
10
5

SUMMER RAINFALL

LOW

HIGH
1016

→ Prevailing Winds
1016 January Isobars in millibars

RAINFALL
mm
1000
750
500
250
125

WINTER RAINFALL

HIGH

→ Prevailing Winds
1016 July Isobars in millibars

RAINFALL
mm
1000
750
500
250
125

ANNUAL RAINFALL

mm
5000
4000
3000
2000
1000
500
250
125

ANNUAL EVAPORATION

ANNUAL AVERAGE TANK EVAPORATION
mm
3000
2500
2000
1500
1000
500

Projection: *Mollweide's Homolographic*   East from Greenwich   COPYRIGHT GEORGE PHILIP & SON LTD

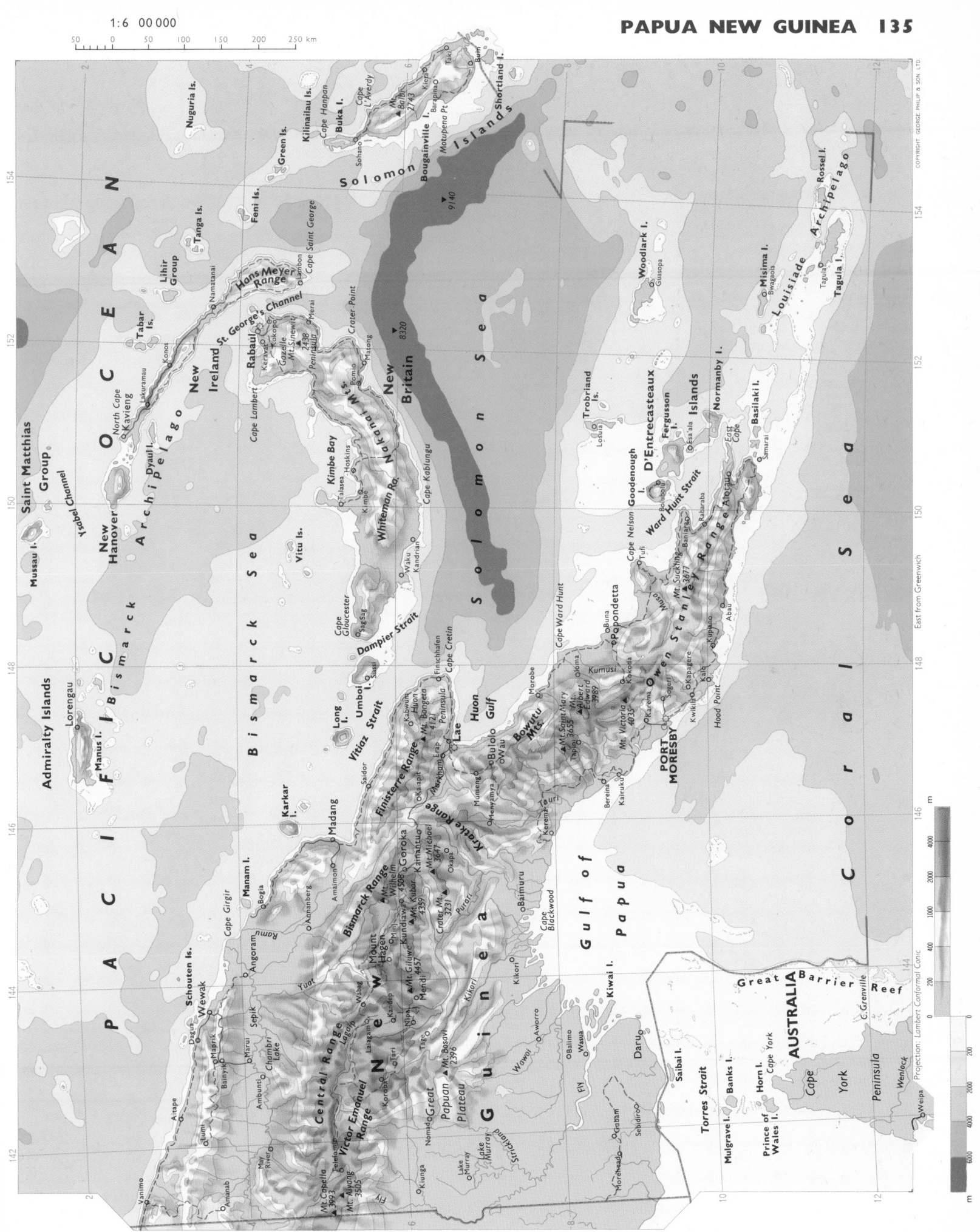

1:6 00 000

50   0   50   100   150   200   250 km

COPYRIGHT GEORGE PHILIP & SON LTD.

PACIFIC OCEAN

Nuguria Is.

Kilinailau Is.
Cape Hanpan
Buka I.
Cape L'Averdy
▲ Balbi
2743
Sohano
Bougainville I.
Motupena Pt
Bareimo
Shortland I.
Solomon Islands

Green Is.
Green I.

Tanga Is.
Feni Is.

Lihir
Group

Tabar
Is.

Hans Meyer
Range
Namatanai
Konos
Cape Lambon
Meral
Crater Point

St. George's Channel
Cape Saint George

▲ 9740

8320 ▲

Solomon Sea

Woodlark I.
Guasopa

Misima I.
Louisiade Archipelago
Rossel I.
Bwagaola
Tagula I.

Saint Matthias
Group
Mussau I.

New Hanover
North Cape
Kavieng
Lakuramau

New Ireland
Archipelago

Dyaull.
Kokopo
Kerewat
Gazelle
Peninsula
Mt. Sinewit
2438

Rabaul
Matong

Nakanai Mts.
New Britain
Whiteman Ra.
Kimbe Bay
Kimbe
Talasea Hoskins
Waku
Kandrian
Cape Kablungu

Trobriand
Is.
Losuia
Kiriwina

D'Entrecasteaux
Islands
Cape Nelson
Goodenough I.
Bolubolu
Fergusson
I.
Esa'ala
Normanby I.
East
Cape
Samarai
Basilaki I.

Ysabel Channel

Bismarck
Sea

Admiralty Islands
Lorengau
Manus I.

Cape Girgir

Schouten Is.
Wewak
Dagua
Maprik

Manam I.
Bogia

Karkar
I.
Madang

Long
I.
Umboi
I.
Vitu Is.
Cape
Gloucester
Sag Sag
Dampier Strait
Vitiaz Strait
Saidor
Saul

Finisterre Range
Amaimon
Annanberg

Huon
Peninsula
Kabwum
Finschhafen
Cape Cretin

Huon
Gulf
Lae
Markham
Erap

Morobe

Cape Ward Hunt

Popondetta
Buna
Kokoda
Kumusi

Owen Stanley Range
Mt. Suckling 3677

Tufi
Mt. Dayman

Alotau

Coral Sea

East from Greenwich
Projection: Lambert Conformal Conic

Sepik
Marui
Ambunti
Bainyik
Chambri
Lake

Angoram
Ramu

Bismarck Range
Mount
Hagen
Mt. Giluwe
4368
Kundiawa
4439
Goroka
Karimui
Mt. Michael
3647
Okapa
Crater Mt.
3231
Purari

Kratke Range
Kainantu

Bulolo
Wau
Mumeng
Menyamya
Okenamamya

Bowutu
Mts.
Morobe

Tauri

Mt. Saint Mary
3655
Mt.
Albert Edward
3989
Mt. Victoria
4035

Kwikila
Hood Point
Abau
Kupiano

PORT
MORESBY

Yanimo
Amanab
Aitape

May
River
Telefomin
Mt. Capella
3993
Mt. Aiyang
3505
Victor Emanuel
Range

Central Range

New

Guinea

Great
Papuan
Plateau

Nomad
Kikori

Gulf of
Papua

Kairuku
Bereina

Lake Murray
Lake
Murray
Balimo
Wasua
Daru
Fly
Wawoi
Kiwai I.
Cape
Blackwood
Baimuru

AUSTRALIA
Great Barrier Reef
C. Grenville

Torres Strait
Saibai I.
Mulgrave I.
Banks I.
Prince of
Wales I.
Horn I.
Cape York
Cape
York
Peninsula
Wenlock
Weipa

m
6000
4000
2000
1000
400
200
0
200
4000
6000
m

TIMOR SEA
INDIAN OCEAN
INDONESIA
NORTHERN TERRITORY
Tanami Desert
Great Sandy Desert
Gibson Desert
Timor
Sumba
Sumbawa
Roti
Sawa
Melville I.
Bathurst I.
Darwin
Katherine
Joseph Bonaparte Gulf
Cambridge Gulf
Wyndham
Kununurra
King Leopold Ranges
Durack Range
Bonaparte Archipelago
King Sound
Derby
Broome
Roebuck B.
Eighty Mile Beach
Port Hedland
Dampier Archipelago
Dampier
Roebourne
Hamersley Range
Mt. Bruce 1236
Ashburton
Exmouth Gulf
Exmouth
Onslow
Rowley Shoals
Scott Reef
Seringapatam Reef
Ashmore Reef
Hibernia Reef
Cartier I.
Lake Mackay
Lake Disappointment
Macdonnell Ranges
Tropic of Capricorn
Mt. Ord 1007
Mt. Hann 776
Fitzroy
Halls Creek
Turkey Creek P.O.
Ord
Victoria
Goldsworthy
Marble Bar
Nullagine
Mt. Newman 1053
Tom Price
Pilbara

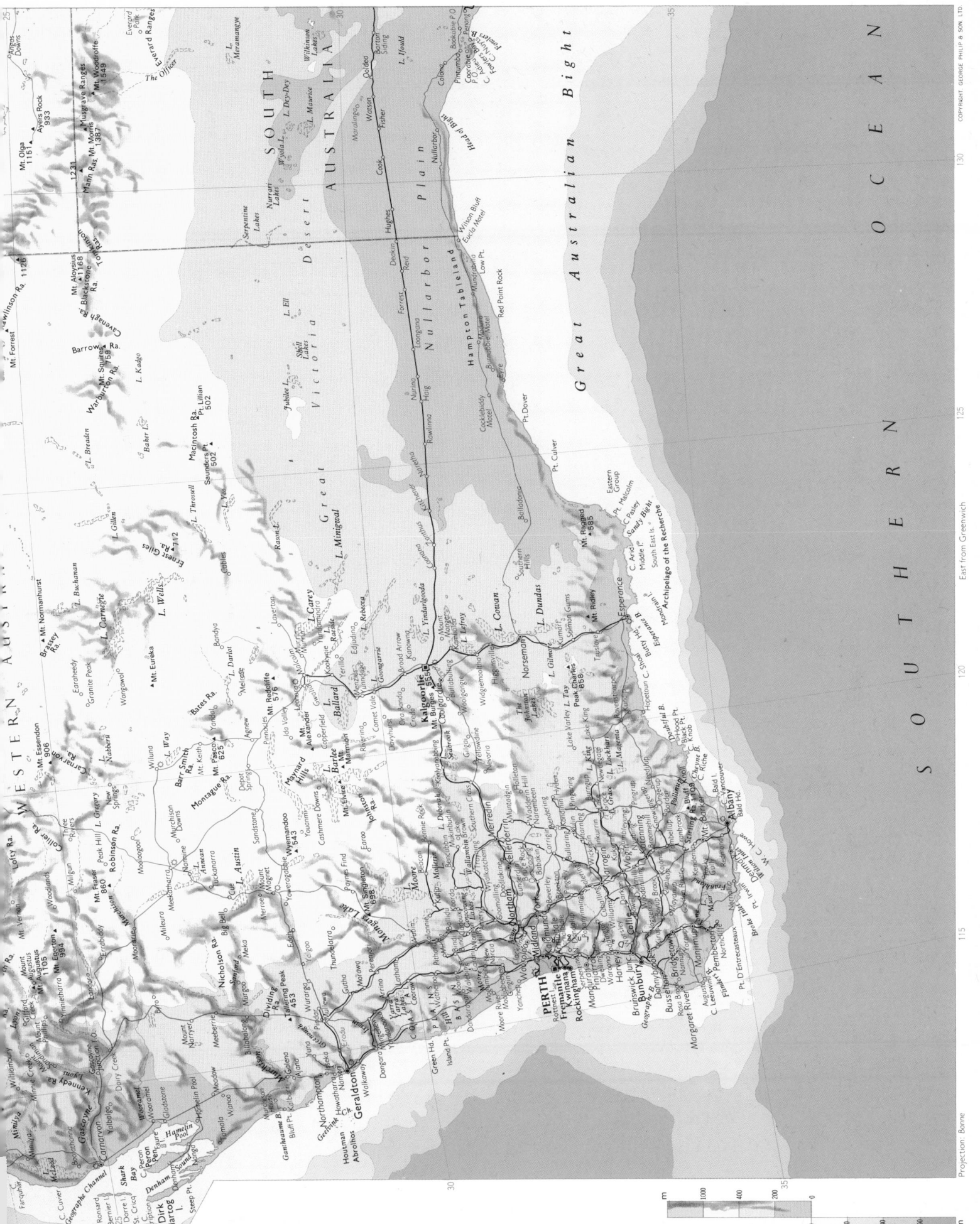

1:8 000 000

50 0 50 100 150 200 250 300 km

137

COPYRIGHT GEORGE PHILIP & SON LTD.

S O U T H E R N   O C E A N

Great Australian Bight

S O U T H   A U S T R A L I A

W E S T E R N   A U S T R A L I A

Great Victoria Desert

Nullarbor Plain

Hampton Tableland

PERTH
Fremantle
Kwinana
Rockingham

Kalgoorlie

Geraldton

Bunbury

Albany

Esperance

Norseman

East from Greenwich

Projection: Bonne

m
1000
400
200
0

m
0
200
2000
4000

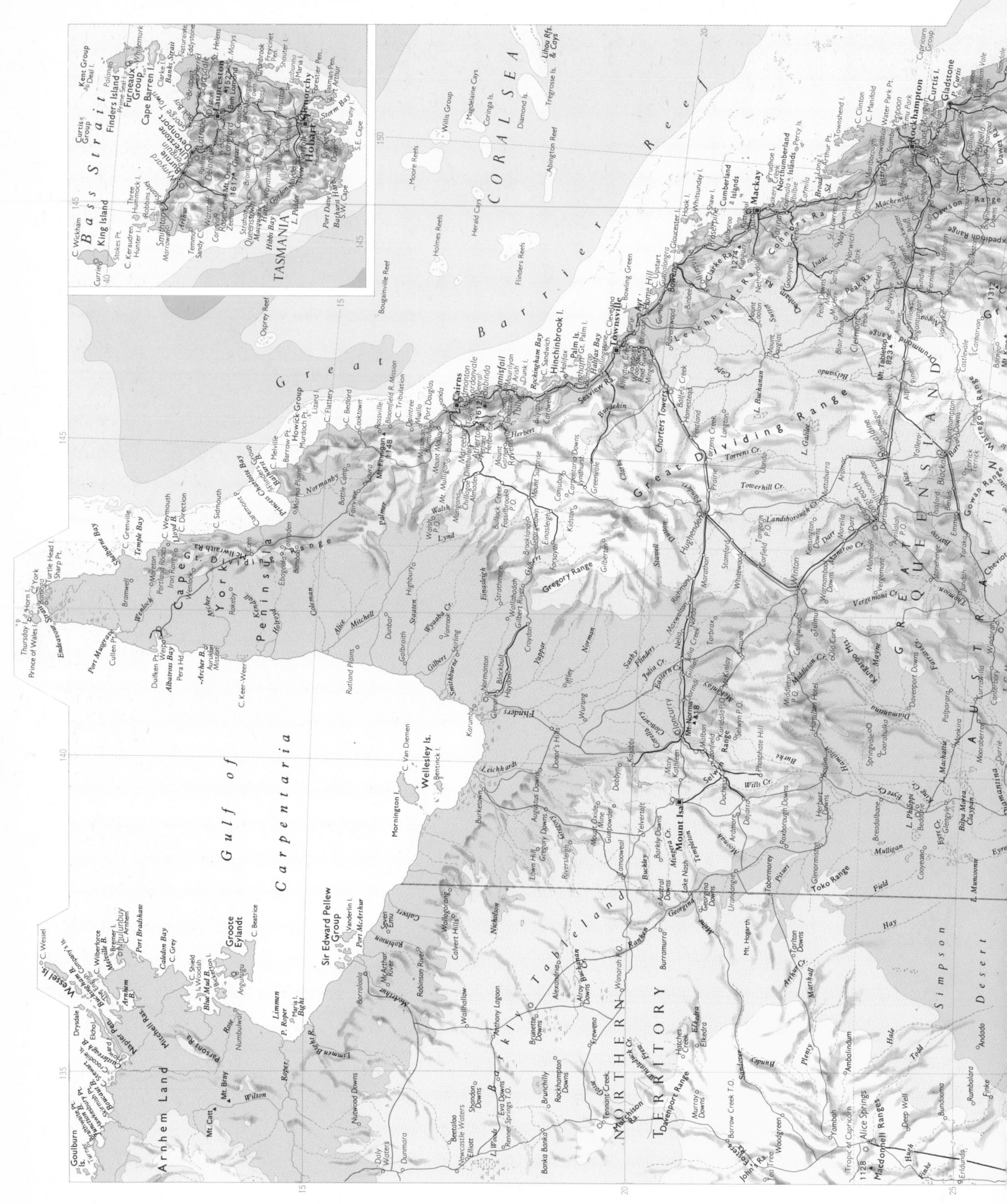
TASMANIA
Bass Strait
King Island
Finders Island
Furneaux Group
Launceston
Hobart
CORAL SEA
Great Barrier Reef
Gulf of Carpentaria
Cape York Peninsula
Great Dividing Range
QUEENSLAND
NORTHERN TERRITORY
Barkly Tableland
Arnhem Land
Simpson Desert
Groote Eylandt
Wellesley Is.
Cairns
Townsville
Mackay
Rockhampton
Gladstone
Mount Isa
Alice Springs
Macdonnell Ranges

1:8 000 000

50 0 50 100 150 200 250 300 km

T A S M A N

S E A

B a s s S t r a i t

Flinders Island

Furneaux Group

Cape Barren I.

King Island

SOUTH AUSTRALIA

NEW SOUTH WALES

BRISBANE

SYDNEY

CANBERRA

MELBOURNE

ADELAIDE

Newcastle

Wollongong

Broken Hill

Lake Eyre (North)

Lake Torrens

Lake Gairdner

Lake Frome

Spencer Gulf

Kangaroo I.

Mount Gambier

Warrnambool

Geelong

Ballarat

Bendigo

Mildura

Wagga

Whyalla

Port Pirie

Port Augusta

Murray Bridge

Projection. Bonne

East from Greenwich

135 140 145 150

30 35 40

m 1500 1000 400 200 0

200 3000 4000 m

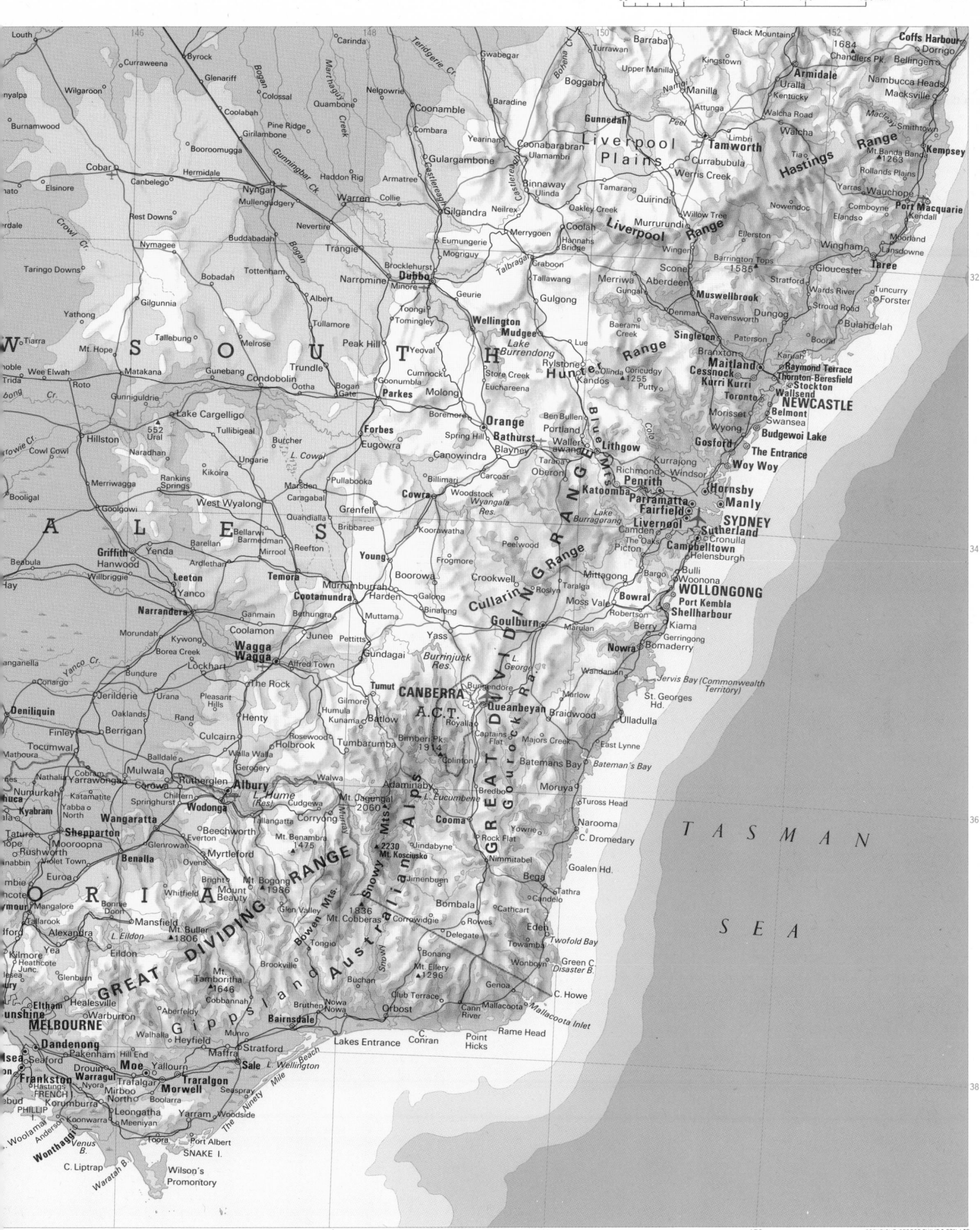

Louth 146 Curraweena Byrock 148 Carinda Gwabegar 150 Barraba Black Mountain 152 1684 Coffs Harbour
ynalpa Wilgaroon Glenariff Colossal Nelgowrie Teridgerie Ck. Turrawan Kingstown Chandlers Pk. Dorrigo
Burnamwood Coolabah Quambone Coonamble Baradine Boggabri Namoi Manilla Uralla Armidale Bellingen
nato Elsinore Pine Ridge Combara Ulamambri Gunnedah Attunga Walcha Road Nambucca Heads Macksville
rdale Cobar Hermidale Haddon Rig Gilgandra Coonabarabran Yearinan Liverpool Peel Tamworth Tia Walcha Kempsey
  Canbelego Nyngan Mullengudgery Warren Collie Neilrex Plains Currabubula Werris Creek Limbri Hastings Range Mt.Banda Banda 1263 Rollands Plains
  Rest Downs Nevertire Tamarang Quirindi Willow Tree Winger Barrington Tops 1585 Ellerston Wingham Moorland Port Macquarie Kendall
Taringo Downs Nymagee Buddabadah Bobadah Tottenham Brocklehurst Dubbo Geurie Talbragar Craboon Merriwa Aberdeen Muswellbrook Denman Scone Stratford Gloucester Taree Lansdowne
  Minore Tallawang Gulgong Gungal Ravensworth Wards River Tuncurry Forster
WSOUTH Tiarra Mt. Hope Wee Elwah Melrose Peak Hill Yeoval Wellington Mudgee Lake Burrendong Lue Baerami Creek Singleton Paterson Dungog Stroud Road Bulahdelah
Trida Roto Gunniguldrie Trundle Cumnock Rylstone Kandos Hunter Range Putty Branxton Maitland Raymond Terrace Booral
bong Cr. Gilgunnia Tullamore Goonumbla Store Creek Eucharena Olinda Concudgy 1255 Cessnock Kurri Kurri Thornton-Beresfield Stockton
  Matakana Gunebang Condobolin Ootha Parkes Molong Ben Bullen Portland Wallerawang Lithgow Kurrajong Wallsend Toronto Belmont NEWCASTLE
noble 552 Ural Lake Cargelligo Tullibigeal Bogan Gate Boremore Orange Spring Hill Bathurst Blayney Oberon Richmond Penrith Windsor Morisset Swansea Budgewoi Lake
fowie Hillston Naradhan Burcher Forbes Eugowra Canowindra Tarana Blue Mtns Katoomba Parramatta Fairfield Gosford Wyong The Entrance
Cowl Cowl Merriwagga Rankins Springs Kikoira L. Cowal Pullabooka Billimari Carcoar Woodstock Wyangala Res. Lake Burragorang Liverpool SYDNEY Manly Woy Woy Hornsby
Booligal Goolgowi West Wyalong Caragabal Grenfell Cowra Koorawatha Peelwood The Oaks Camden Cronulla Sutherland
ALES Quandialla Bribbaree Young Frogmore Crookwell Picton Campbelltown Helensburgh
  Bellarwi Barmedman Reefton Boorowa Taralga Mittagong Bargo Bulli Woonona
Beabula Griffith Hanwood Yenda Barellan Ardlethan Mirrool Murrumburrah Galong Binalong Roslyn Moss Vale Bowral Robertson Port Kembla WOLLONGONG
Hay Willbriggie Leeton Yanco Temora Harden Muttama Cullarin Goulburn Marulan Berry Shellharbour Kiama
anganella Narrandera Morundah Kywong Ganmain Coolamon Junee Pettitts Yass Gundagai Burrinjuck Res. L. George Wandanian Gerringong Bomaderry Nowra
  Borea Creek Lockhart Alfred Town Wagga Wagga Tumut CANBERRA Burrendong Jervis Bay (Commonwealth Territory) St. Georges Hd.
Deniliquin Yanco Cr. Jerilderie Urana Pleasant Hills The Rock Gilmore A.C.T. Queanbeyan Braidwood Ulladulla
  Conargo Oaklands Rand Henty Humula Kunama Batlow Royalla Marlow
Finley Berrigan Culcairn Holbrook Rosewood Tumbarumba Bimberi Pks. 1914 Captains Flat Majors Creek East Lynne
Tocumwal Mulwala Balldale Walla Walla Colinton Batemans Bay Bateman's Bay
Mathoura Cobram Yarrawonga Corowa Rutherglen Gerogery Walwa Adaminaby L. Eucumbene Bredbo Moruya
ala Numurkah Katamatite Chiltern Albury Hume (Res) Cudgewa Mt. Jagungal 2060 Cooma Wyrie Tuross Head
huca Kyabram Yabba North Springhurst Wodonga Tallangatta Corryong Murray Nimmitabel Narooma
Tatura Shepparton Mooroopna Wangaratta Beechworth Everton Mt. Benambra 1475 Jindabyne Rock Flat C. Dromedary
ope Rushworth Glenrowan Myrtleford Ovens Brights Mt. Bogong 1986 Mt. Kosciusko 2230 Bega Goalen Hd.
nabbin Euroa Benalla Whitfield Mount Beauty Bowen Mts Jimenbuen Bombala Cathcart Candelo
mbie Violet Town Bonnie Doon Mt. Buller 1806 Glen Valley 1336 Mt. Cobberas Corrowidgie Rowes Eden Twofold Bay
mour Mangalore Alexandra L. Eildon Mansfield Tongio Bonang Wonboyn Green C. Disaster B.
ury Kilmore Yea Eildon Mt. Tamboritha 1646 Brookville Buchan Delegate Towamba
lees Heathcote Junc. Glenburn Cobbannah Nowa Nowa Club Terrace Genoa C. Howe
  GREAT DIVIDING RANGE Healesville Aberfeldy Bruthen Orbost Cann River Mallacoota Inlet
nshine MELBOURNE Warburton Gippsland Walhalla Heyfield Munro Stratford Nowa Mallacoota
  Dandenong Pakenham Hill End Maffra Lakes Entrance C. Conran Point Hicks Rame Head
lsea Seaford Drouin Moe Yallourn Sale L. Wellington
on Frankston Warragul Traralgon L. Wellington
  Hastings Nyora Morwell The Ninety Mile Beach
FRENCH Korumburra Mirboo Trafalgar Seaspray
  Leongatha Northo Yarram Woodside
  Woolama Anderson Koonwarra Meeniyan Toora Port Albert
Wonthaggi Venus B. SNAKE I.
  C. Liptrap Waratah B. Wilson's Promontory

TASMAN SEA

OR IA

VICTORIA

GREAT DIVIDING RANGE

Snowy Mts

Australian Alps

Gourock Ra.

Cullarin Range

Liverpool Range

Hastings Range

Hunter Range

Blue Mts

32

34

36

38

1:3 500 000

20   0   20   40   60   80   100 km

JANUARY TEMPERATURE
1:25 000 000

ACTUAL SURFACE TEMPERATURE
°C
20
15
10
5
0

20° Isotherms
reduced to Sea-level
°Celsius

JULY TEMPERATURE
1:25 000 000

TASMAN SEA

Bay of Islands
Whangarei
Hokianga Harb.
Dargaville
Hauraki Gulf
Takapuna
Devonport
Birkenhead
AUCKLAND
Mt. Roskill
Onehunga
Manukau
Papakura
Pukekohe
Manukau Harb.
Coromandel Peninsula
Thames
Great Barrier I.
Lit. Barrier I.
Kawau I.
Hen & Chickens Islands
Bream Bay
Waikato
Huntly
Hamilton
Cambridge
Morrinsville
Te Aroha
Waihi
Tauranga
Bay of Plenty
Whakatane
Opotiki
Matamata
Te Puke
Rotorua
Rotoma
White I.
Raglan Harb.
Aotea Harb.
Kawhia Harb.
Te Awamutu
Tokoroa
Mangakino
Taupo
Lake Taupo
Gisborne
Poverty Bay
Mahia Peninsula
North Taranaki Bight
New Plymouth
Inglewood
Mt. Egmont
Stratford
Hawera
South Taranaki Bight
Wanganui
Napier
Hastings
Havelock North
Hawke Bay
HAWKE'S BAY
Taumarunui
Ngauruhoe
NAT. PARK
Ruapehu
Marton
Feilding
Dannevirke
Palmerston North
Woodville
Levin
Foxton
Shannon
Otaki
Masterton
Carterton
Greytown
Featherston
Golden Bay
Farewell Spit
C. Farewell
D'Urville Island
Tasman Bay
Nelson
Motueka
Stoke
Richmond
Picton
Blenheim
WELLINGTON
Lr. Hutt
Up. Hutt
Petone
Wainuiomata
Cook Strait
MARLBOROUGH
Kaikoura Ra.
Seaward Kaikoura

SUMMER AND WINTER RAINFALL
mm
1000
750
500
250

1012 Isobars in millibars
Prevailing Winds

SUMMER RAINFALL
November to April
1:25 000 000

WINTER RAINFALL
May to October
1:25 000 000

m
3000
2000
1000
400
200
0
200
2000
m

Projection: Conical with two standard parallels

East from Greenwich

COPYRIGHT. GEORGE PHILIP & SON. LTD.

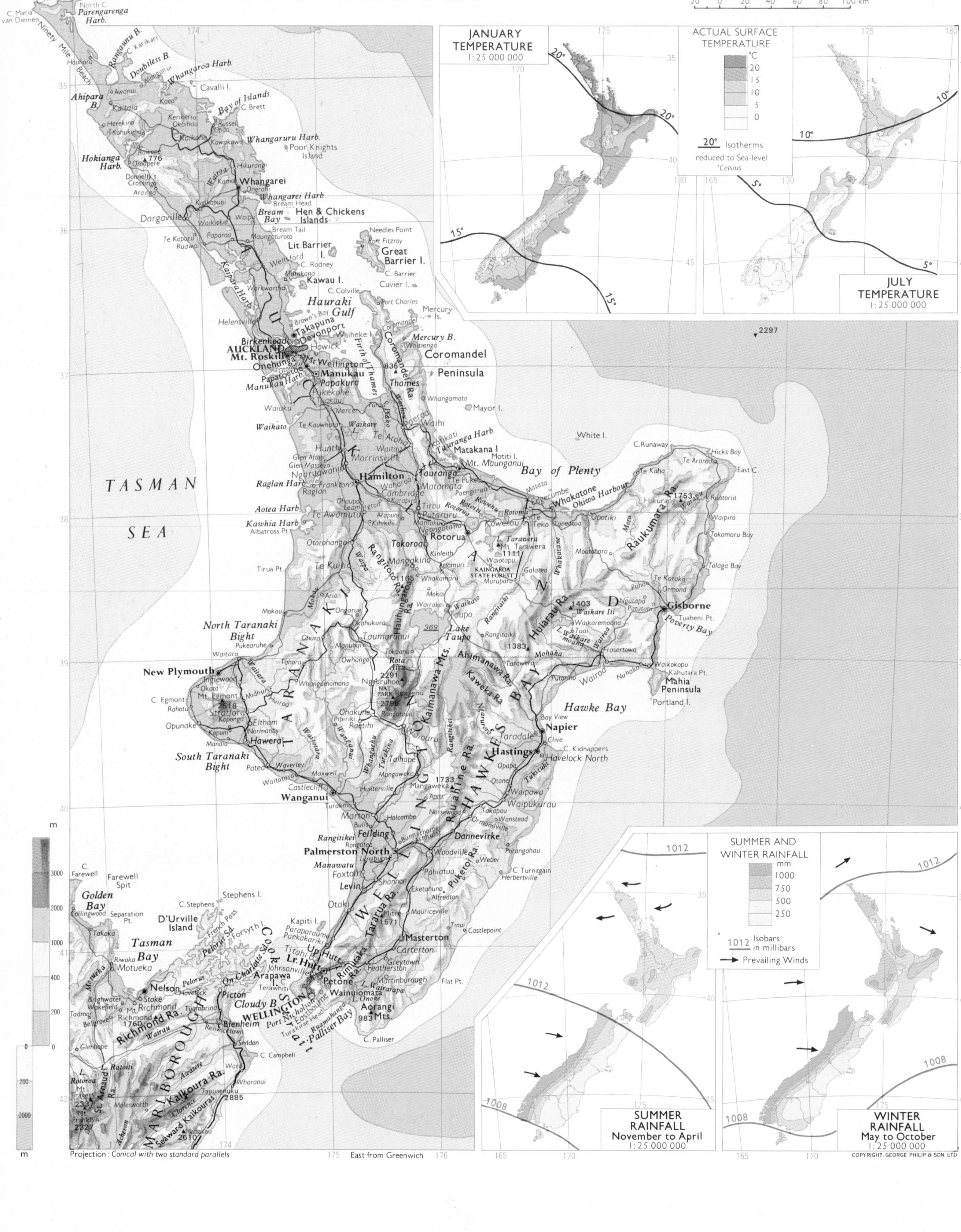

1:3 500 000

20 0 20 40 60 80 100 km

POPULATION
1:15 000 000
Inhabitants

	per km²
	under 1
	1–3
	3–6
	6–12
	12–25
	25–50
	50–100
	over 100

○ Towns of 50–100 000 inhabitants

■ Towns of over 100 000 inhabitants

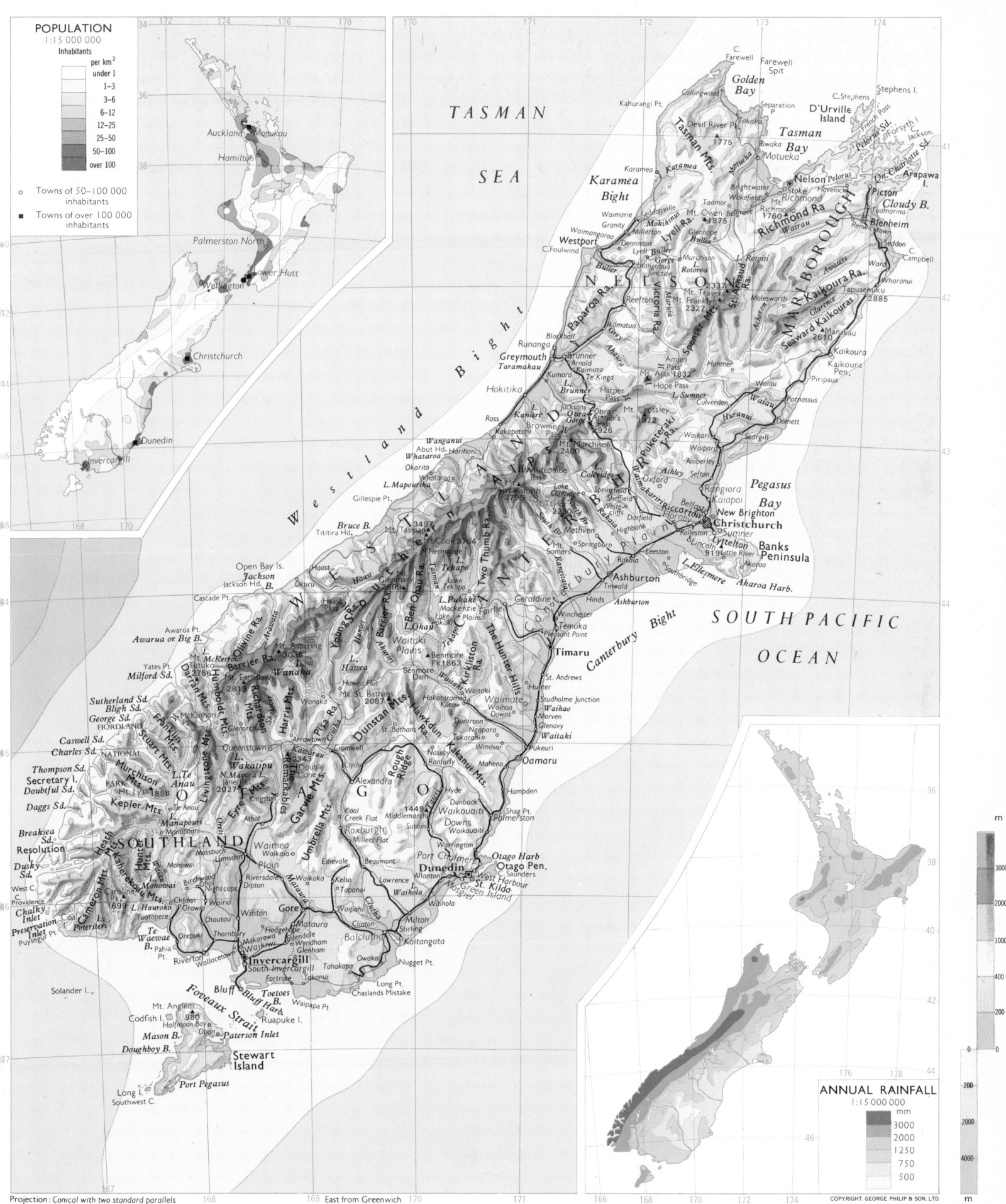

TASMAN SEA

SOUTH PACIFIC OCEAN

ANNUAL RAINFALL
1:15 000 000
mm
3000
2000
1250
750
500

m
3000
2000
1000
400
0
200
2000
4000

m

Projection: Conical with two standard parallels

East from Greenwich

COPYRIGHT. GEORGE PHILIP & SON. LTD.

Iceland
Denmark Strait
Greenland Sea
Greenland
Davis Strait
Baffin Bay
Baffin Island
Cumberland Sound
Frobisher Bay
Hudson Strait
Ungava Peninsula
Labrador
Laurentian Plateau
Newfoundland
Belle Isle Strait
Gulf of St. Lawrence
Nova Scotia
Bay of Fundy
Halifax
Montreal
Quebec
Ottawa
Toronto
Hamilton
Niagara Falls
Detroit
Chicago
New York
Philadelphia
Washington
Chesapeake Bay
Appalachian Mts
Allegheny Mts
Blue Ridge
Atlanta
Memphis
St. Louis
Kansas City
Ozark Plateau
Minneapolis
Dallas
Hudson Bay
James Bay
Belcher Is.
Southampton I.
Foxe Basin
Foxe Channel
Melville Pen.
Boothia Pen.
Gulf of Boothia
Chesterfield Inlet
Devon I.
Ellesmere I.
Axel Heiberg
Sverdrup Is.
Queen Elizabeth Islands
Lancaster Sound
Prince of Wales I.
Melville Sound
M'Clure Strait
Victoria I.
Banks I.
ARCTIC OCEAN
Beaufort Sea
Great Bear L.
Great Slave L.
L. Athabasca
Reindeer L.
Lake Winnipeg
Winnipeg
Regina
Edmonton
Calgary
Great Plains
Denver
Llano Estacado
Rocky Mountains
Mackenzie Mts
Selkirk Mts
Coast Mountains
Wasatch Mountains
Colorado Plateau
Great Basin
Death Valley
Sierra Nevada
Cascade Range
Coast Range
Los Angeles
San Francisco
Portland
Seattle
Vancouver
Vancouver I.
Juan de Fuca Strait
Queen Charlotte Sound
Queen Charlotte Islands
Alexander Archipelago
Gulf of Alaska
Alaska
Alaska Range
Mt. McKinley 6194
Brooks Range
Yukon
Alaska Pen.
Kodiak I.
Bering Strait
St. Lawrence I.
Nunivak I.
Wrangel I.
Bering Sea
Aleutian Islands
Asia
PACIFIC
ATLANTIC
Bermuda
Mendocino Seascarp
Murray Seascarp

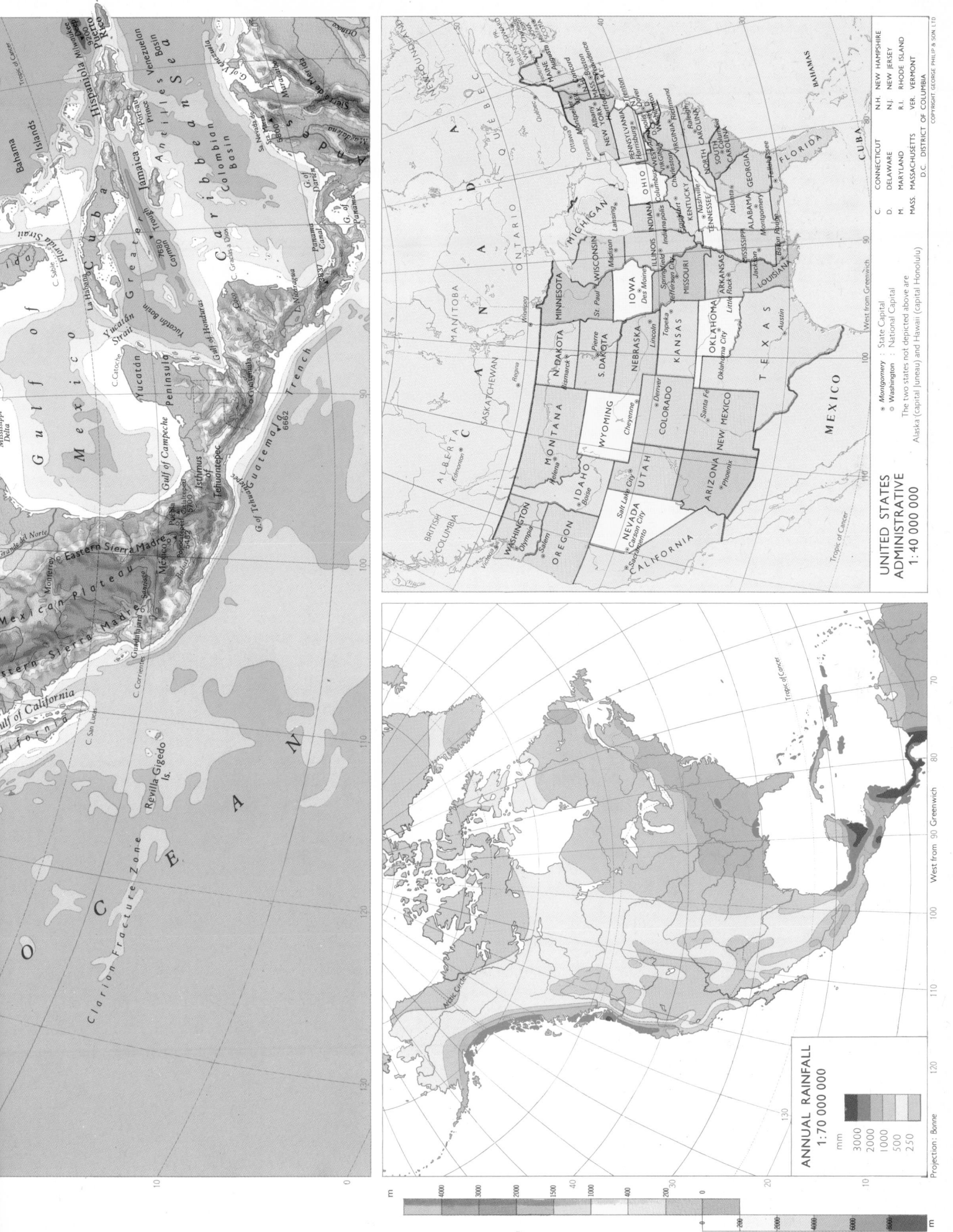

1:30 000 000

200 0 200 400 600 800 1000 km

UNITED STATES
ADMINISTRATIVE
1:40 000 000

ANNUAL RAINFALL
1:70 000 000

Projection: Bonne

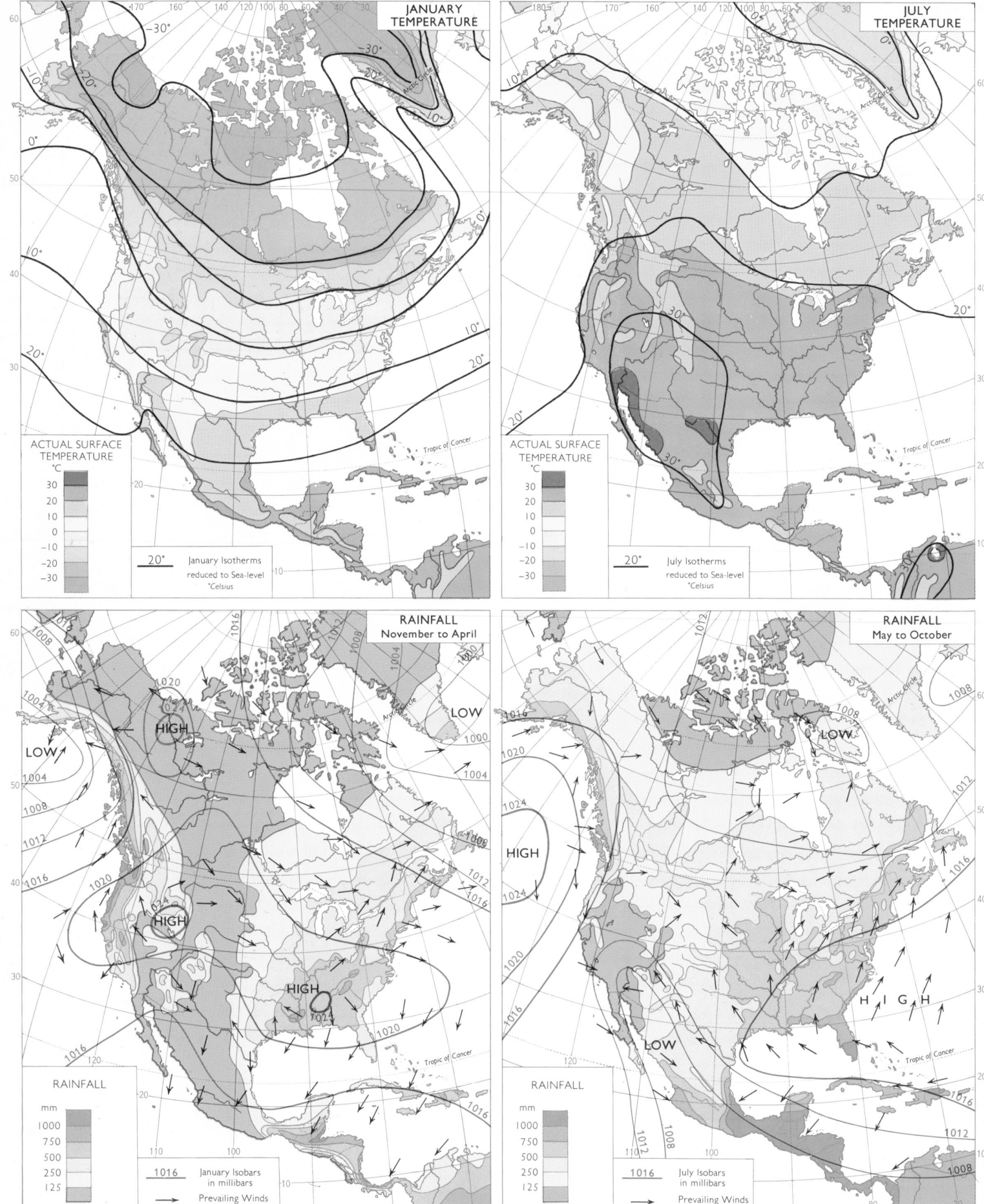

1 : 70 000 000

500   0   500   1000   1500   2000   2500 km

JANUARY TEMPERATURE

ACTUAL SURFACE
TEMPERATURE
°C
30
20
10
0
−10
−20
−30

20°   January Isotherms
reduced to Sea-level
°Celsius

JULY TEMPERATURE

ACTUAL SURFACE
TEMPERATURE
°C
30
20
10
0
−10
−20
−30

20°   July Isotherms
reduced to Sea-level
°Celsius

RAINFALL
November to April

LOW

HIGH

HIGH

HIGH

LOW

RAINFALL

mm
1000
750
500
250
125

1016   January Isobars
in millibars
→   Prevailing Winds

RAINFALL
May to October

LOW

HIGH

HIGH

LOW

H I G H

RAINFALL

mm
1000
750
500
250
125

1016   July Isobars
in millibars
→   Prevailing Winds

Projection: *Lambert's Equivalent Azimuthal*

West from 70 Greenwich

COPYRIGHT. GEORGE PHILIP & SON. LTD.

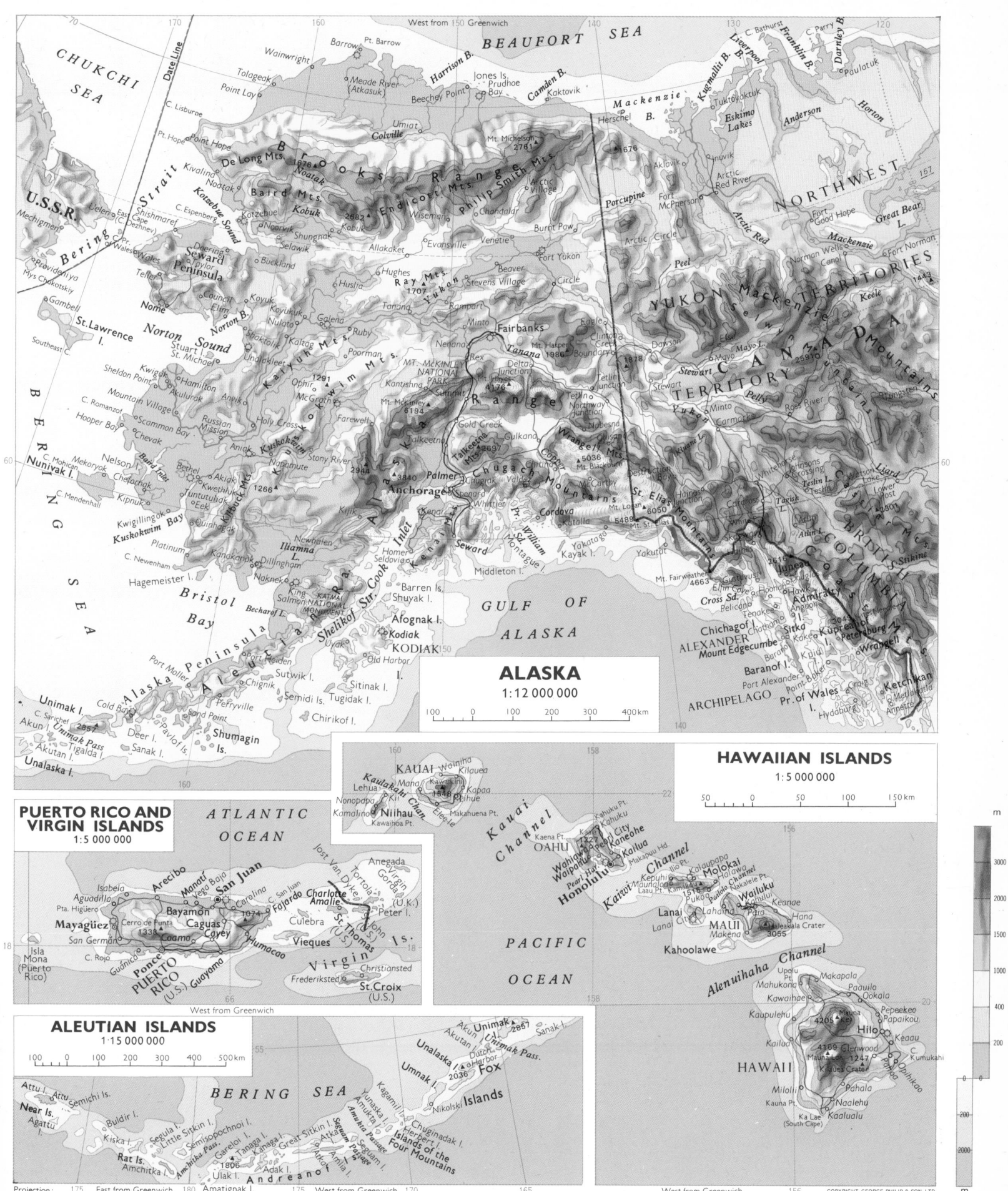
ALASKA
1:12 000 000
100 0 100 200 300 400 km
HAWAIIAN ISLANDS
1:5 000 000
50 0 50 100 150 km
PUERTO RICO AND VIRGIN ISLANDS
1:5 000 000
ALEUTIAN ISLANDS
1:15 000 000
100 0 100 200 300 400 500 km
West from 150 Greenwich
BEAUFORT SEA
CHUKCHI SEA
BERING SEA
GULF OF ALASKA
ATLANTIC OCEAN
PACIFIC OCEAN
U.S.S.R.
Bering Strait
Date Line
Brooks Range
Alaska Range
Chugach Mountains
St. Elias Mountains
Wrangell Mts.
Alaska Peninsula
Aleutian Ra.
Kenai Mts.
YUKON TERRITORY
NORTHWEST TERRITORIES
CANADA
BRITISH COLUMBIA
Mackenzie Mountains
Coast Mts.
Barrow
Pt. Barrow
Wainwright
Point Lay
Point Hope
Kotzebue
Nome
Seward Peninsula
Norton Sound
St. Lawrence I.
Nunivak I.
Fairbanks
Anchorage
Palmer
Seward
Cordova
Valdez
Kodiak
KODIAK I.
Afognak I.
Cook Inlet
Shelikof Str.
Bristol Bay
Kuskokwim Bay
Unimak I.
Unalaska I.
Shumagin Is.
Juneau
Sitka
Ketchikan
Wrangell
Petersburg
ALEXANDER ARCHIPELAGO
Mt. McKinley 6194
Mt. Logan 6050
Mt. Fairweather 4663
Yakutat
Dawson
Whitehorse
Inuvik
Aklavik
Fort Yukon
Colville
Yukon
Tanana
Mackenzie
Porcupine
Peel
Great Bear L.
Projection: Conical with two standard parallels
East from Greenwich
West from Greenwich
KAUAI
Niihau
OAHU
Honolulu
Pearl Har.
Kaneohe
Molokai
Lanai
MAUI
Kahoolawe
HAWAII
Hilo
Mauna Kea 4205
Mauna Loa 4169
Kilauea Crater
Haleakala Crater 3055
Kauai Channel
Kaiwi Channel
Alenuihaha Channel
Ka Lae (South Cape)
San Juan
Mayagüez
Ponce
Arecibo
Bayamon
Caguas
Cayey
Coamo
Humacao
Guayama
PUERTO RICO (U.S.)
Culebra
Vieques
St. Thomas (U.S.)
St. John
Charlotte Amalie
Tortola
Anegada
Virgin Is.
St. Croix (U.S.)
Christiansted
Frederiksted
Isla Mona (Puerto Rico)
Attu I.
Near Is.
Rat Is.
Amchitka I.
Kiska I.
Andreanof Is.
Adak I.
Atka I.
Umnak I.
Unalaska I.
Unimak I.
Fox Islands
Islands of the Four Mountains
Amukta Passage
Nikolski
Dutch Harbor
m
3000
2000
1500
1000
400
200
0
200
2000
COPYRIGHT GEORGE PHILIP & SON, LTD.

m

3000
2000
1500
1000
400
200
0

0
200
2000

m

Projection: Bonne

Lancaster Sound
evon Island
Arctic B.
deur
Milne
Inlet
ula
Bylot I.
1890
Pond Inlet
Pond Inlet
Scott I.
C. Hewett
2136
Baffin Bay
Svartenhuk
Halvø
Disko
Disko B.
Egedesminde
Christianshåb
Holsteinsborg
Sukkertoppen
Andre Strømfjord
2950
Kong Frederik VI's Kyst
G R E E N L A N D
Angmagssalik
60

Iglootik
Island
Hall
Lake
Melville
Prince
Charles
Fury and Hecla Str.
Foxe
C. Dyer
Cumberland
Peninsula
2591
Penny Ice Cap
Pangnirtung
Broughton
Island
Padloping Island
C. Dyer
Cape Dyer
Davis Strait
Sukkertoppen
Godthåb
Frederikshåb
Ivigtut
Julianehåb
Nanortalik
Kap Farvel
A T L A N T I C

Committee B.
Peninsula
Repulse
Bay
Rae Isthmus
T O R I E
Foxe
Basin
Nettilling L.
B A F F I N
Cumberland Sd.
C. Mercy
C. Dorchester
Hoare B.
Amadjuak
Foxe Penin.
Amadjuak
Lake
Frobisher
Bay
Frobisher Bay
Resolution I.
3809
50

N
Southampton
Coral Harbour
Coats
I.
Bell
Pen.
Digges Is.
Mansel I.
Hudson   Strait
C. Chidley
Akpatok
Ungava Bay
Port Burwell
Hebron
C. Harrison
Indian Harbour
N E W
Roe's Welcome Sd.
Wager
B.
Corbett Inlet
Inoucdjouac (Sukuk)
Maricourt
(Wakeham)
Notre Dame
de Koartac
Koartac (Notre Dame de Koartac)
Payne Bay
Arnaud (Payne)
1676
Quebec
Nutak
F O U N D
Hopedale
257
Inoucdjouac
(Port Harrison)
Payne L.
Ungava Peninsula
Koksoak
Ft. Chimo
George
Whale
Rigolet
Cartwright
Belle Isle
L A N D
Sleeper Is.
King George Is.
Baker's
Dozen
Is.
King
George I.
L. Minto
Mélèzes
Feuilles
Kaniapiskau
N
Smallwood
Reservoir
North West
River
Battle Harbr.
COAST OF LABRADOR
Belcher
Is.
C. Henrietta
Maria
Pte.
Louis-XIV
L'Eau Claire
Scheffereville
Petitsikapau
L.
Lobstick
Ashuanipi
Churchill
Falls
Churchill
Goose Bay
L. Melville
Cartwright
Bay
D
Win'sk
Grand Baleine
Poste-de-
la-Baleine
(Great Whale River)
Kanaaupscow
Ft. George
La Grande
Caniapiscau
L A B R A D O R
Notashquan
St. Augustin
Saguenay
Twillingate
Bonavista
Bonavista B.
St. John's
Big
Trout L.
Attawapiskat
Akimiski
I.
James Bay
Nouveau Comptoir
(Paint Hills)
Eastmain
1128
Ashuanipi
L.
Gagnon
Q U E B E C
Moisie
Mingan
Romaine
Notashquan
Natashquan
Harrington
Gander
Grand
Falls
Carbonear
NEWFOUNDLAND
Harbour Grace
Placentia
Trepassey
C. Race
A R I O
Joseph
Nakina
Nakina
Kenogami
Ft. Albany
Charlton
Eastmain
Fort Rupert
Rupert
House
Mistassini
L. Albanel
Chibougamau
Bétsiamites
Baie-Comeau
Pte.-des-
Monts
Sept Iles
Port-Cartier
Moisie
I. d'Anticosti
Gulf of
St. Lawrence
Îs. de la Madeleine
Cabot
Strait
C. North
Cape Breton I.
ST-PIERRE
et MIQUELON
(Fr.)
Pt. aux
Basques
6309
40
Thunder Bay
Michipicoten
Longlac
Heron Bay
Oba
Hearst
Cochrane
L. Abitibi
Tascherau
Senneterre
Rés. de Gouin
Roberval
L. St-Jean
Jonquière
Chicoutimi
Saguenay
R. St. Lawrence
Rimouski
Matane
Pén. de Gaspé
Gaspé
C. de Gaspé
Gaspé
St. Lawrence
Newcastle
Bathurst
Chatham
New Glasgow
Port Hawkesbury
Mulgrave
Sable I.
(Nova Scotia)
Superior
Franz
Timmins
Noranda
Rouyn
Kirkland Lake
Cobalt
Haileybury
Témiscaming
Val d'Or
La Tuque
Shawinigan
Trois-Rivières
Québec
1150
Lévis
Thetford Mines
Drummondville
St-Jean
Sherbrooke
St. Hyacinthe
M A I N E
Woodstock
Fredericton
N E W
B R U N S W I C K
Moncton
Amherst
Springhill
Truro
Windsor
Dartmouth
Halifax
Bridgewater
Liverpool
Shelburne
Yarmouth
C. Sable
N O V A
S C O T I A
PR. EDWARD I.
Charlottetown
Summerside
Sydney
Glace Bay
Sault Ste. Marie
Sudbury
Copper Cliff
Sault Ste. Marie
North
Bay
Parry
Sound
Pembroke
Ottawa
Hull
Lachine
MONTRÉAL
Cornwall
St. Leonard
L. Champlain
Burlington
VERMONT
Augusta
Saint
John
B. of Fundy
Digby
Bangor
Portland
Georgian
Bay
Owen Sound
Orillia
Peterboro'
Belleville
Kingston
Watertown
Utica
NEW
HAMPSHIRE
Concord
Manchester
Lowell
Lawrence
C. Cod
Boston
Providence
CONN.
New Haven
L. Huron
Cheboygan
Petoskey
Traverse
City
Ludington
TORONTO
Guelph
Hamilton
Niagara
Falls
Oshawa
Cobourg
Rochester
Syracuse
Binghamton
N E W   Y O R K
Elmira
Williamsport
Albany
Springfield
Worcester
MASS.
New York
NEW YORK
Bridgeport
Iron Mt.
Green Bay
Wausau
Antigo
Menominee
Marinette
Manitowoc
Sheboygan
Grand
Rapids
Kalamazoo
London
Stratford
Kitchener
Brantford
Brandon
St. Catharines
Woodstock
Buffalo
Jamestown
Scranton
Reading
Allentown
Wilkes Barre
P E N N S Y L V A N I A
Harrisburg
Trenton
NEW JERSEY
Milwaukee
Racine
Kenosha
Evanston
S I N
DETROIT
Windsor
South Bend
Toledo
Sandusky
Erie
Cleveland
Youngstown
Akron
CAGO
OIS
Gary
INDIANA
O H I O

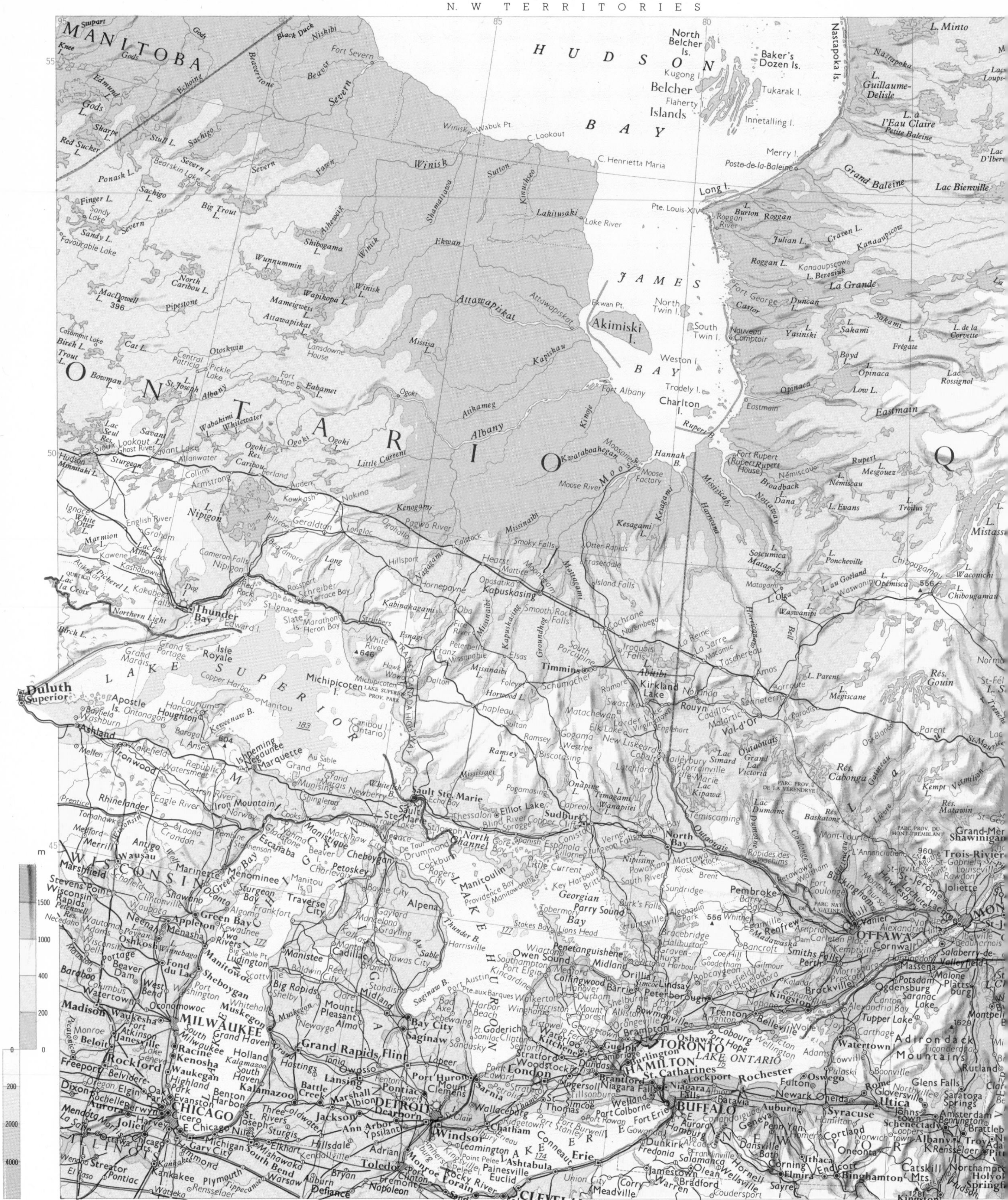

N.W TERRITORIES

MANITOBA

HUDSON BAY

JAMES BAY

ONTARIO

QUEBEC

LAKE SUPERIOR

WISCONSIN

MICHIGAN

LAKE MICHIGAN

LAKE HURON

LAKE ERIE

LAKE ONTARIO

INDIANA   OHIO   PENNSYLVANIA

NEW YORK

Belcher Islands

Akimiski I.

Duluth · Superior

Thunder Bay

Sault Ste. Marie

Sudbury

North Bay

Timmins

Kirkland Lake

Rouyn

Val-d'Or

OTTAWA

Trois-Rivières

MONTREAL

TORONTO

HAMILTON

St. Catharines

BUFFALO

Rochester

Syracuse

Utica

Albany

MILWAUKEE

CHICAGO

Grand Rapids

Flint

DETROIT

Dearborn

Windsor

London

Kitchener

CLEVELAND

Toledo

Madison

Rockford

Green Bay

Georgian Bay

Manitoulin

Lambert's Equivalent Azimuthal

1:7 000 000

50   0   50   100   150   200   250   300 km

West from Greenwich

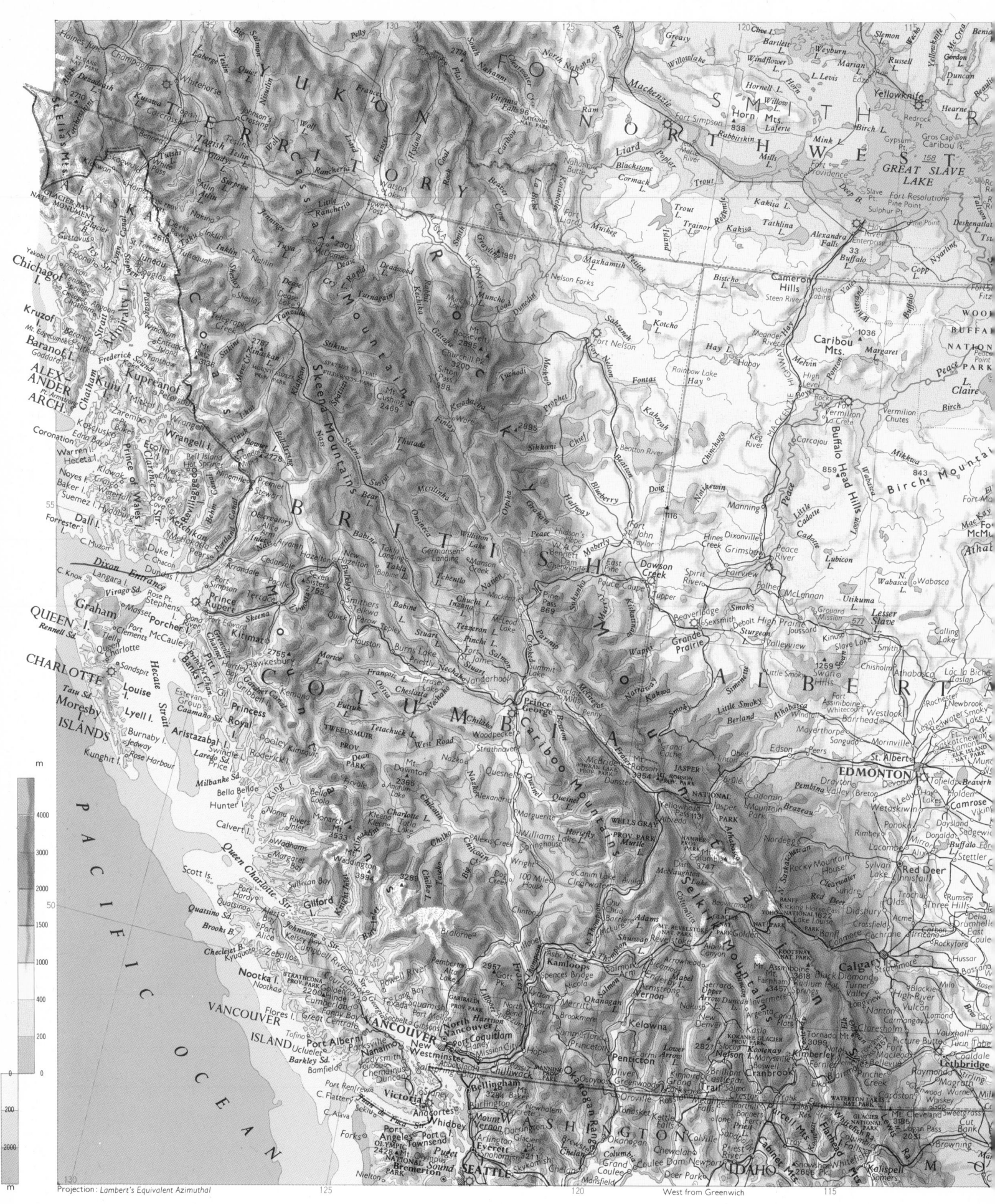

Projection: Lambert's Equivalent Azimuthal   West from Greenwich

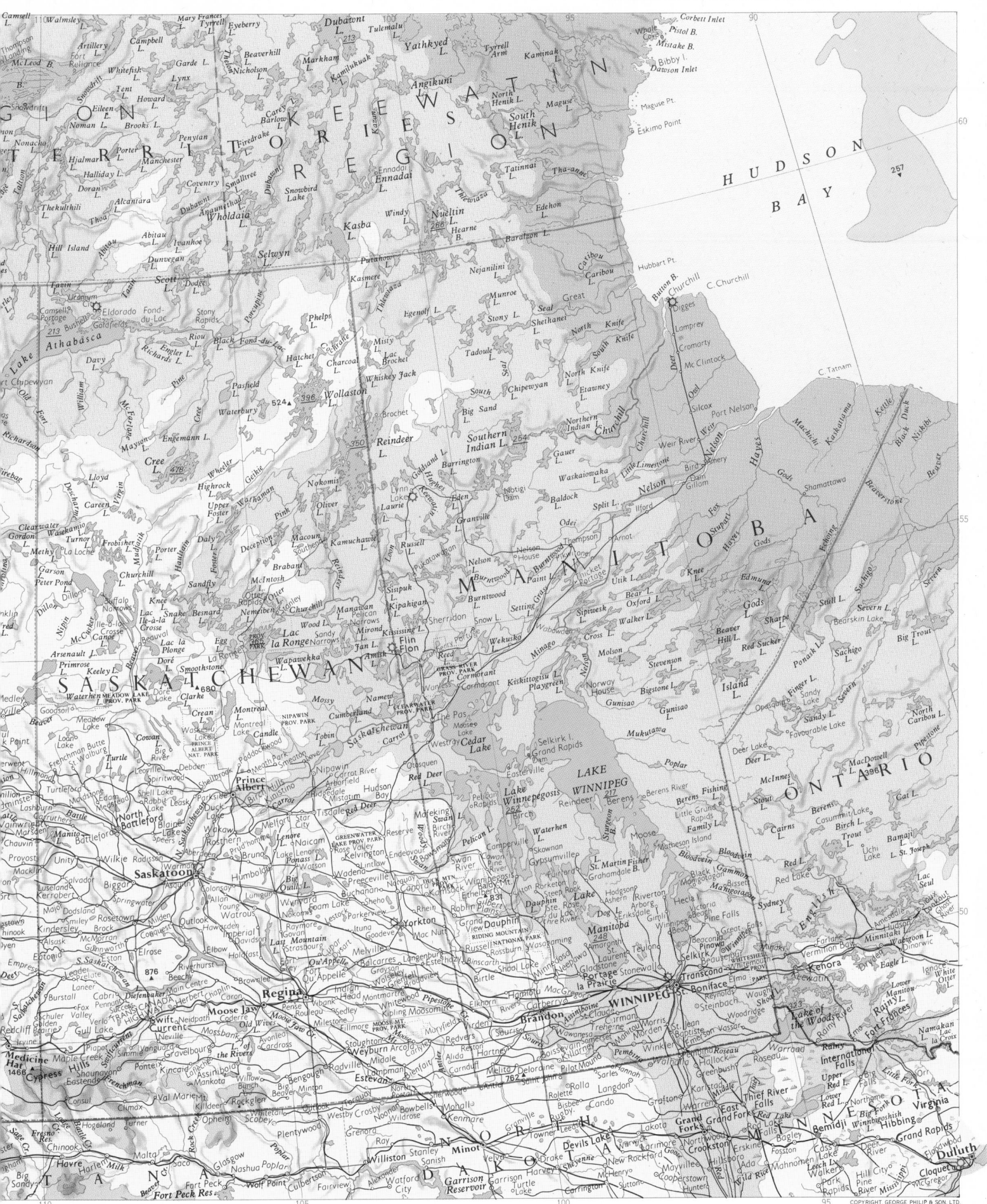

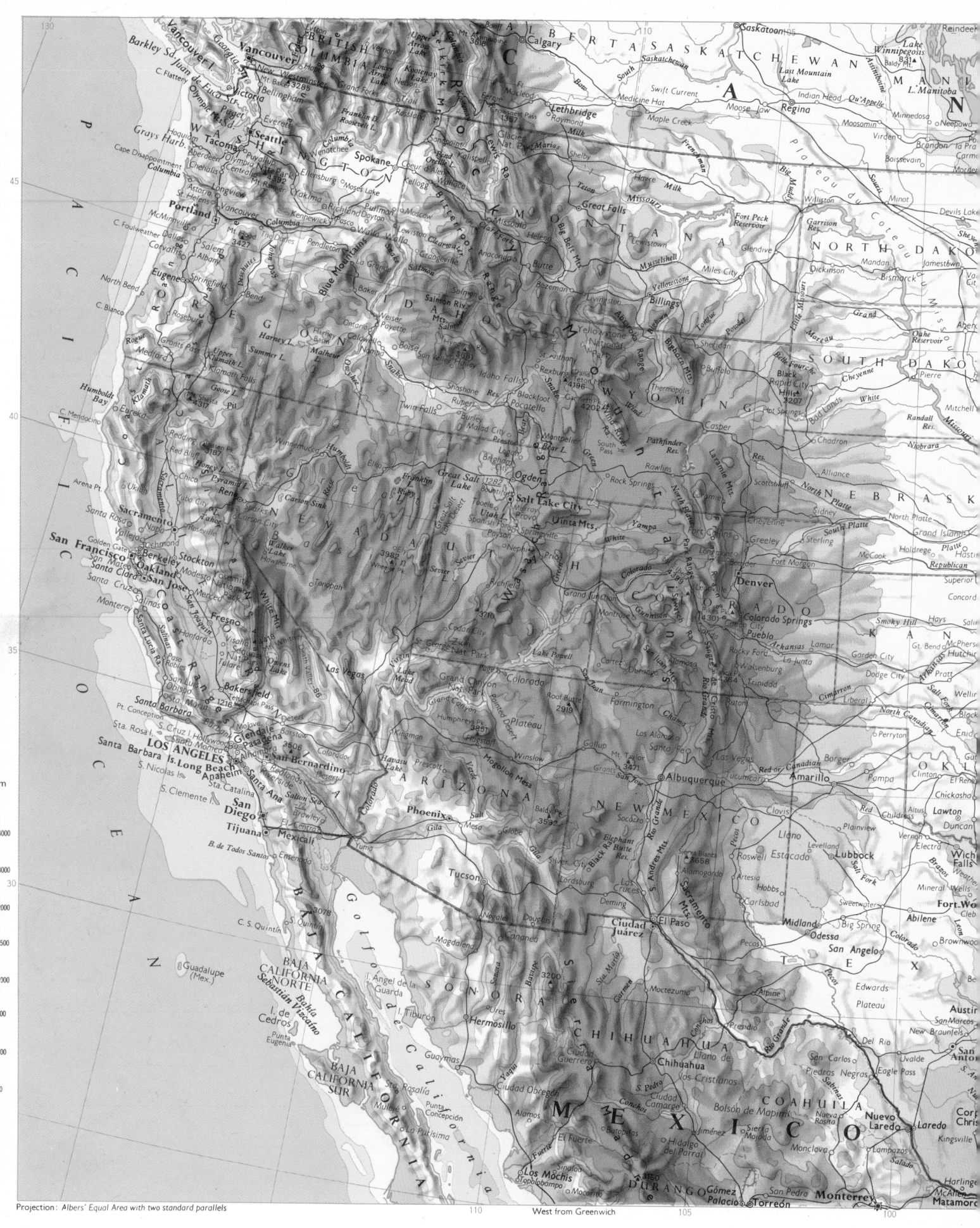

Projection: Albers' Equal Area with two standard parallels   West from Greenwich

1:12 000 000

100   0   100   200   300   400   500 km

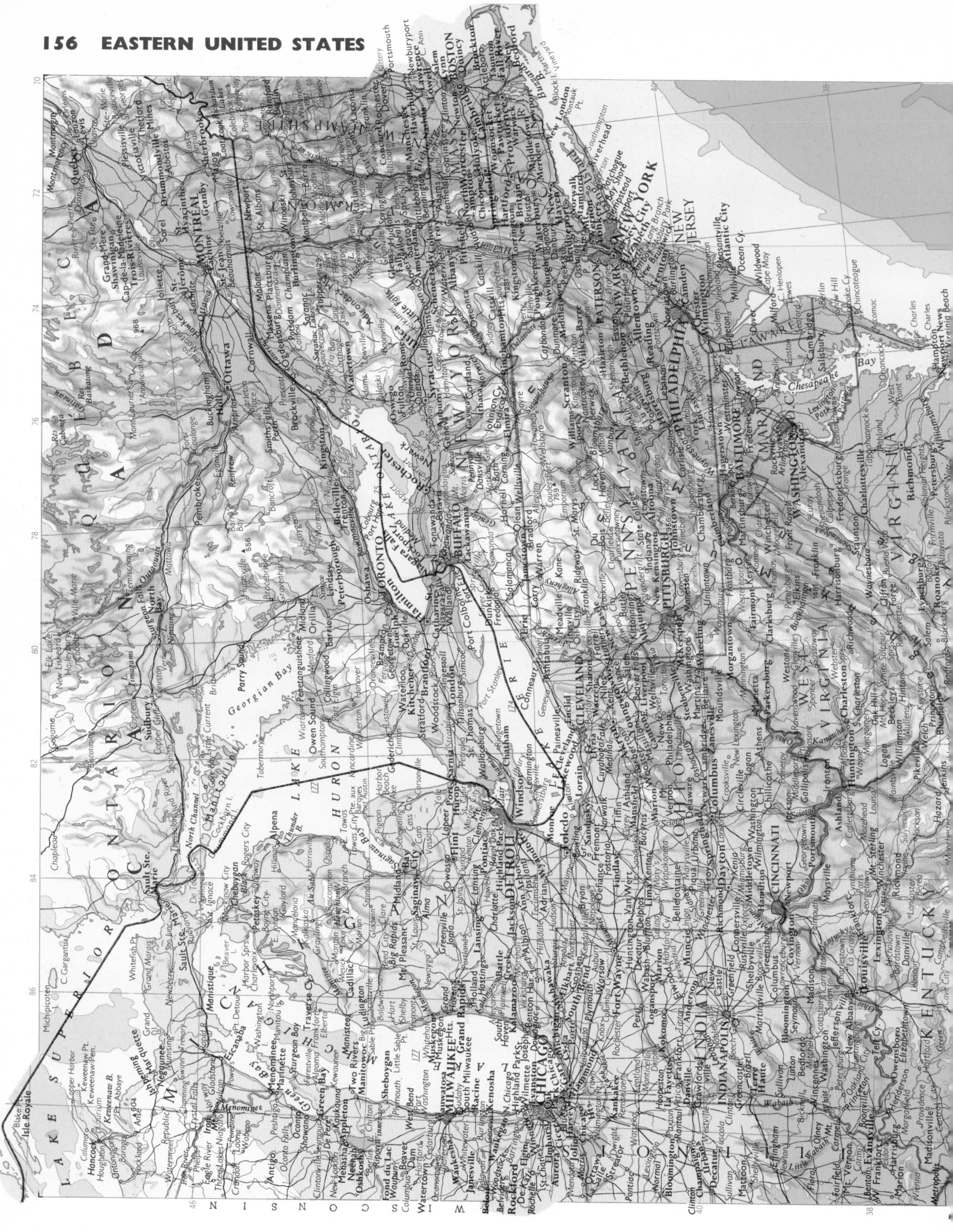
LAKE SUPERIOR
LAKE HURON
LAKE ONTARIO
Georgian Bay
CHICAGO
MILWAUKEE
DETROIT
TORONTO
BUFFALO
CLEVELAND
PITTSBURGH
PHILADELPHIA
BALTIMORE
WASHINGTON
NEW YORK
BOSTON
MONTREAL
CINCINNATI
INDIANAPOLIS

1:6 000 000

50 0 50 100 150 200 250 km

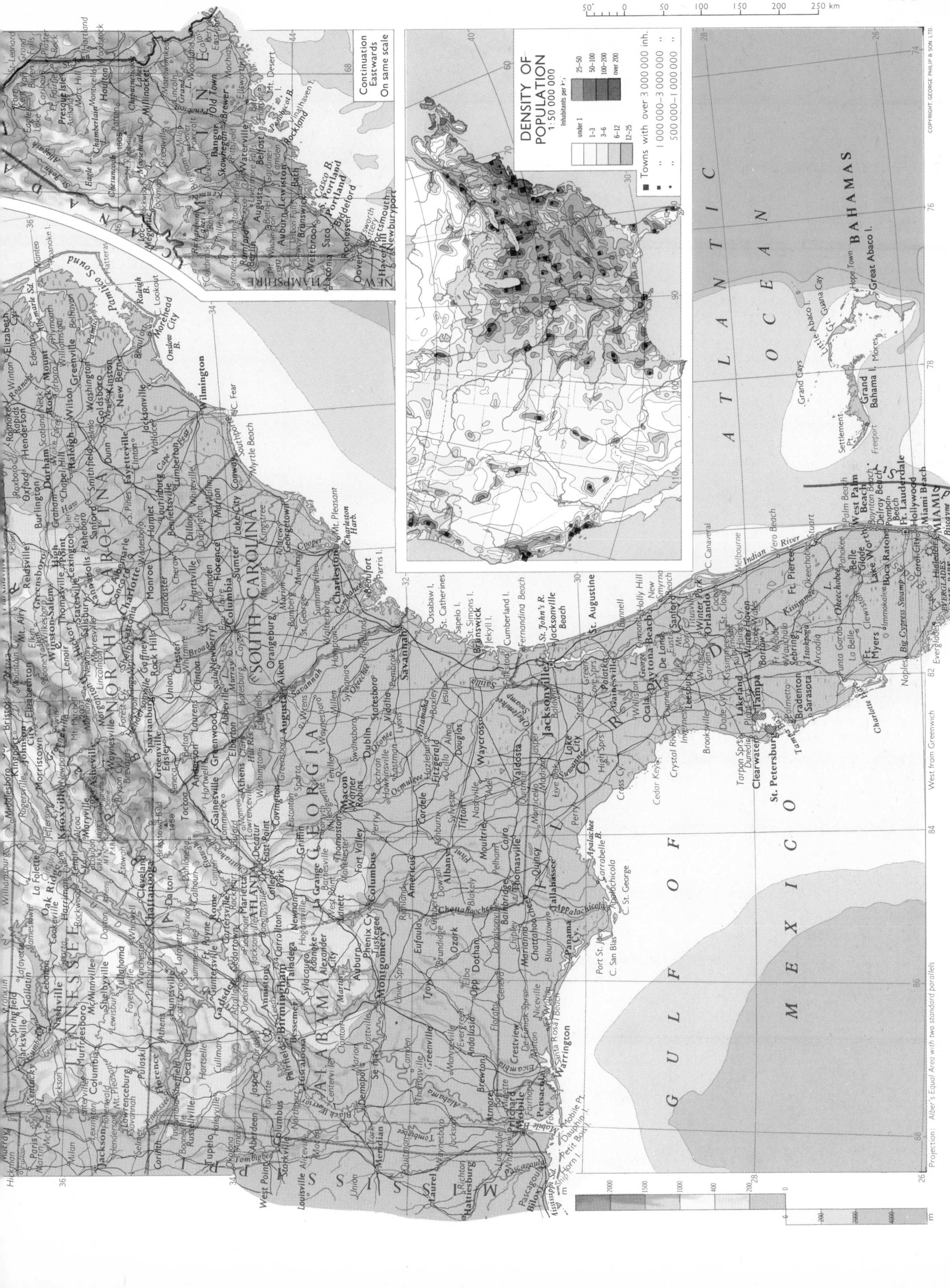

Continuation Eastwards On same scale

DENSITY OF POPULATION
1:50 000 000

Inhabitants per k²

under 1
1-3
3-6
6-12
12-25
25-50
50-100
100-200
over 200

Towns with over 3 000 000 inh. ■
1 000 000-3 000 000 ●
500 000-1 000 000 ●

COPYRIGHT GEORGE PHILIP & SON LTD.

MAINE

NEW HAMPSHIRE

NORTH CAROLINA

SOUTH CAROLINA

GEORGIA

ALABAMA

TENNESSEE

MISSISSIPPI

FLORIDA

ATLANTIC OCEAN

GULF OF MEXICO

BAHAMAS

Grand Bahama I.
Great Abaco I.
Little Abaco I.
Freeport
Settlement
Hope Town
Nassau

West from Greenwich

Projection: Alber's Equal Area with two standard parallels

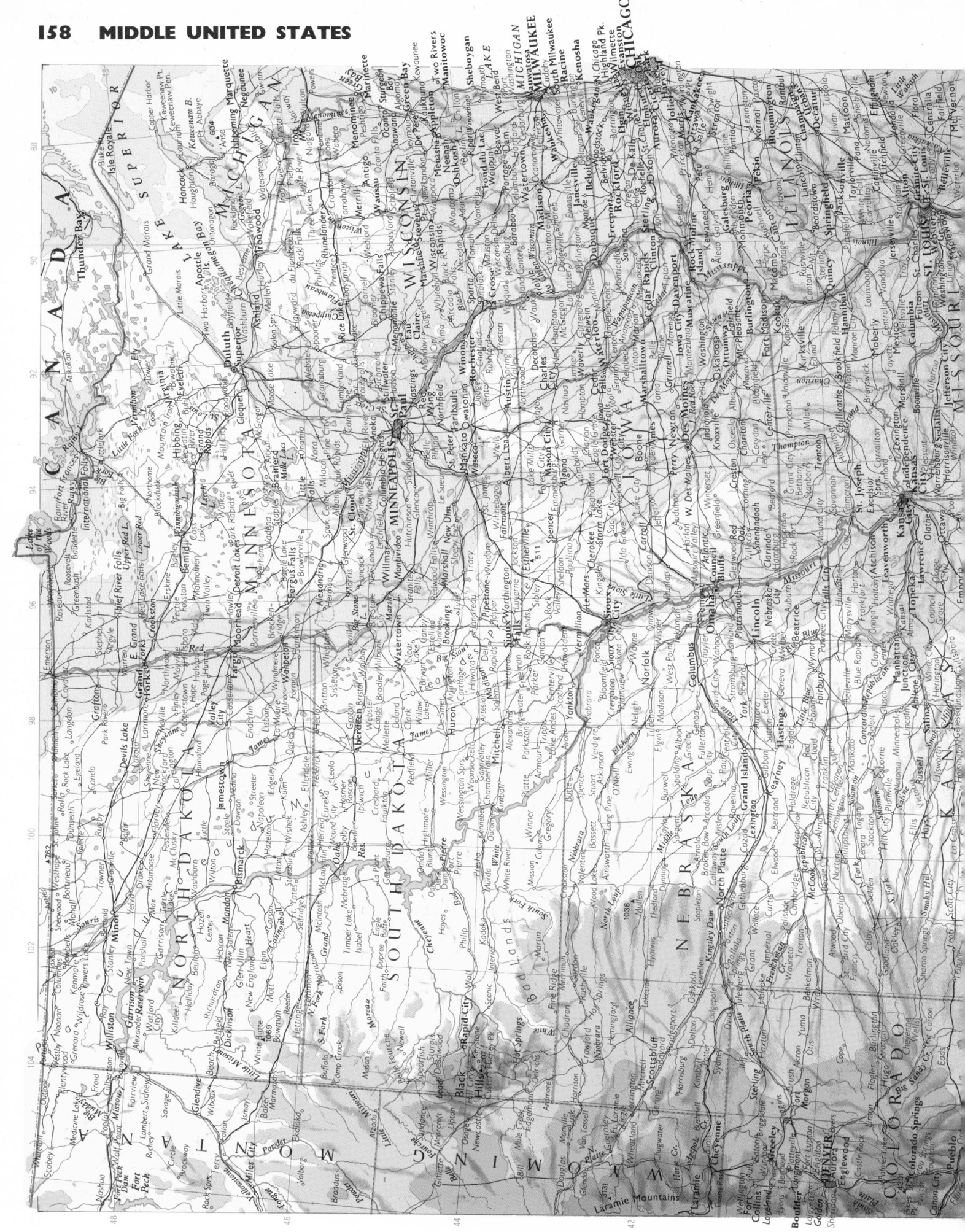
CANADA
LAKE SUPERIOR
LAKE MICHIGAN
MICHIGAN
WISCONSIN
MINNESOTA
NORTH DAKOTA
SOUTH DAKOTA
IOWA
ILLINOIS
MISSOURI
NEBRASKA
KANSAS
WYOMING
MONTANA
COLORADO
CHICAGO
MILWAUKEE
MINNEAPOLIS
St. Paul
Duluth
Superior
Thunder Bay
Des Moines
Omaha
Kansas City
ST. LOUIS
DENVER
Cheyenne
Lincoln
Sioux Falls
Fargo
Bismarck
Madison
Green Bay
Rapid City
Black Hills
Bad Lands
Laramie Mountains
Lake of the Woods
Missouri
Mississippi
48
46
44
42
104
102
100
98
96
94
92
90
88

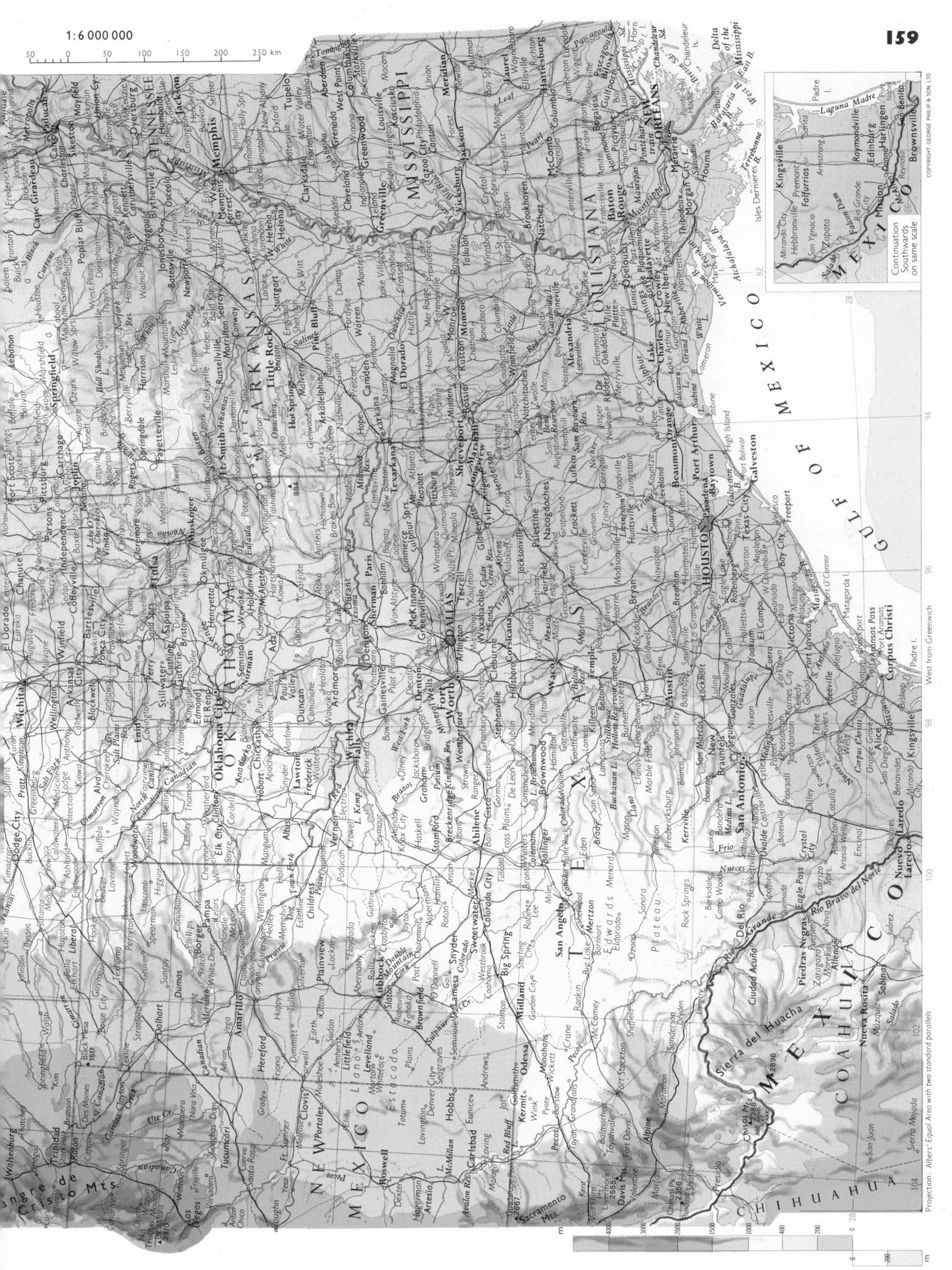

1:6 000 000

50   0   50   100   150   200   250 km

GULF OF MEXICO

MISSISSIPPI

TENNESSEE

ARKANSAS

LOUISIANA

OKLAHOMA

T E X A S

N E W   M E X I C O

NEW ORLEANS

Little Rock

Memphis

Baton Rouge

HOUSTON

DALLAS

Fort Worth

San Antonio

Austin

Corpus Christi

Galveston

Wichita

Tulsa

Oklahoma City

Amarillo

San Angelo

Laredo

Nuevo Laredo

M E X I C O

C O A H U I L A

CHIHUAHUA

Sierra del Huacha

West from Greenwich

Laguna Madre

Padre I.

Kingsville

Brownsville

Matamoros

Continuation
Southwards
on same scale

COPYRIGHT GEORGE PHILIP & SON LTD.

Projection: Albers' Equal Area with two standard parallels

1 : 6 000 000

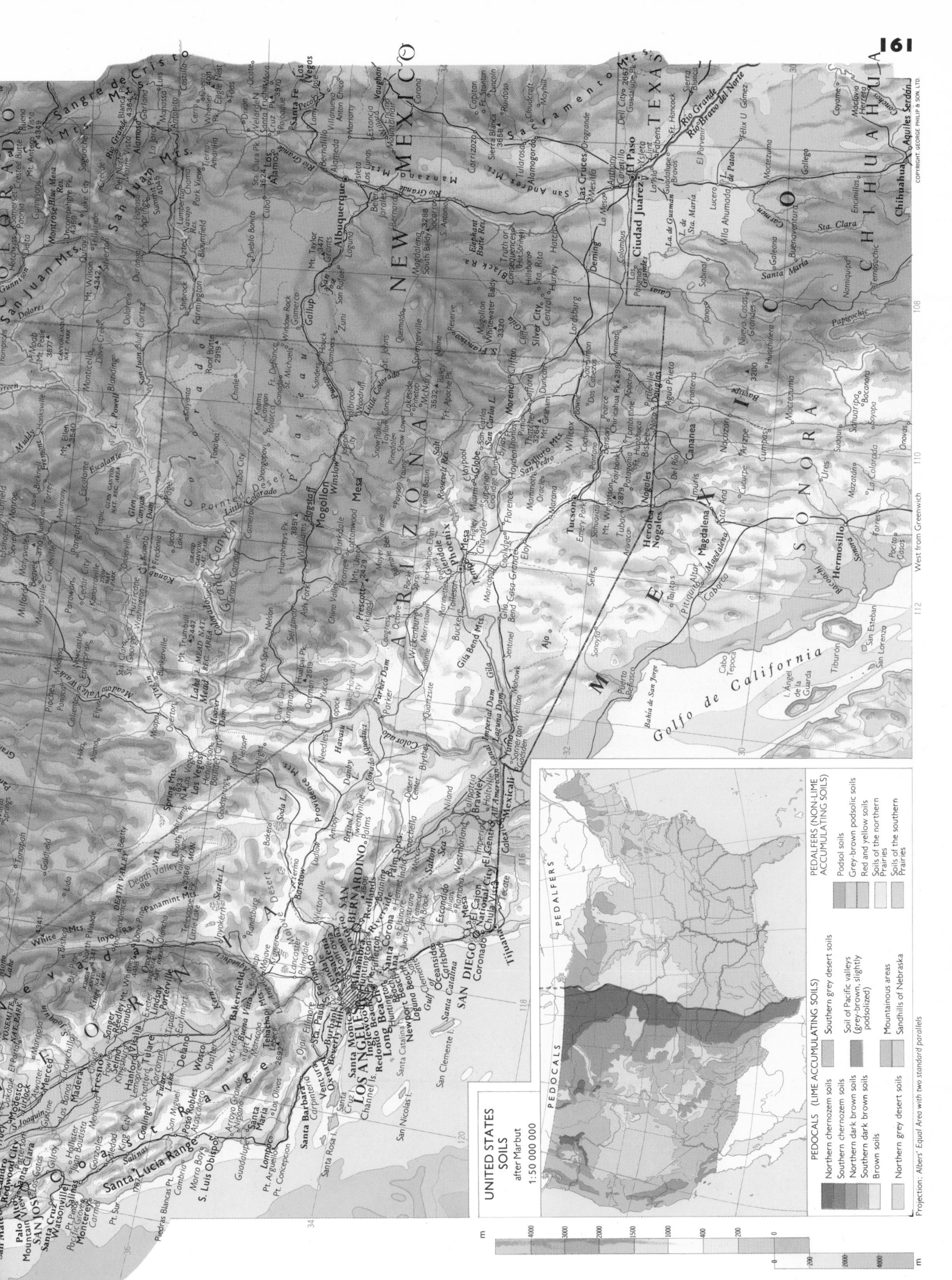

COLORADO

Sangre de Cristo Mts.

San Juan Mts.

NEW MEXICO

TEXAS

CHIHUAHUA

ARIZONA

Grand Canyon

Colorado Plateau

Mogollon Mesa

Phoenix

Tucson

SONORA

MEXICO

Golfo de California

NEVADA

CALIFORNIA

Death Valley

Mojave Desert

LOS ANGELES

SAN DIEGO

Santa Lucia Range

Coast Range

West from Greenwich

COPYRIGHT GEORGE PHILIP & SON, LTD.

Chihuahua
Aquiles Serdán

**UNITED STATES
SOILS**

after Marbut

1:50 000 000

PEDOCALS (LIME ACCUMULATING SOILS)

Northern chernozem soils
Southern chernozem soils
Northern dark brown soils
Southern dark brown soils
Brown soils
Northern grey desert soils

Southern grey desert soils
Soil of Pacific valleys (grey-brown, slightly podsolized)
Mountainous areas
Sandhills of Nebraska

PEDALFERS (NON-LIME ACCUMULATING SOILS)

Podsol soils
Grey-brown podsolic soils
Red and yellow soils
Soils of the northern Prairies
Soils of the southern Prairies

PEDALFERS

PEDOCALS

Projection: Albers' Equal Area with two standard parallels

m
4000
3000
2000
1500
1000
400
200
0

m
0
200
2000
4000

1 : 3 000 000

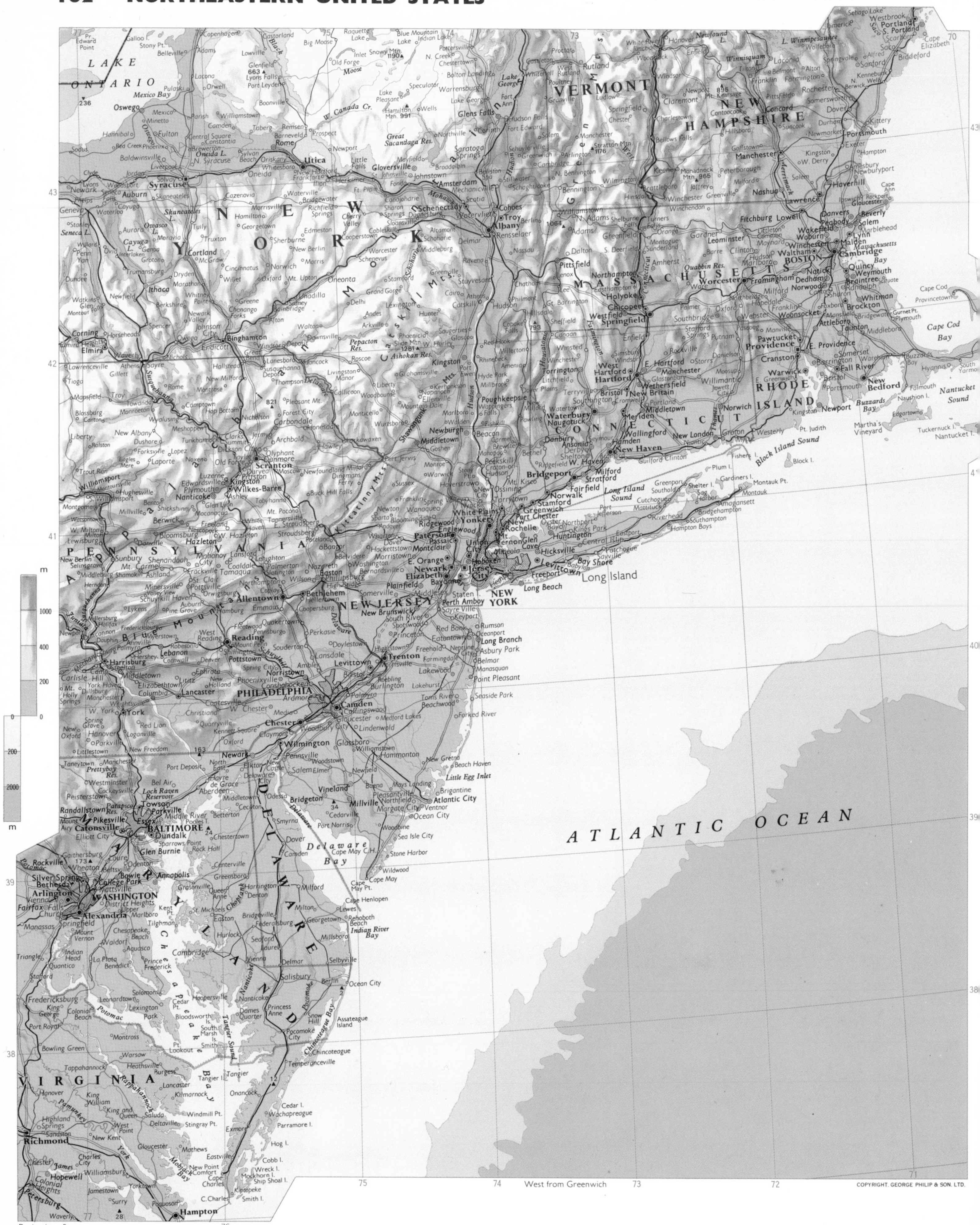

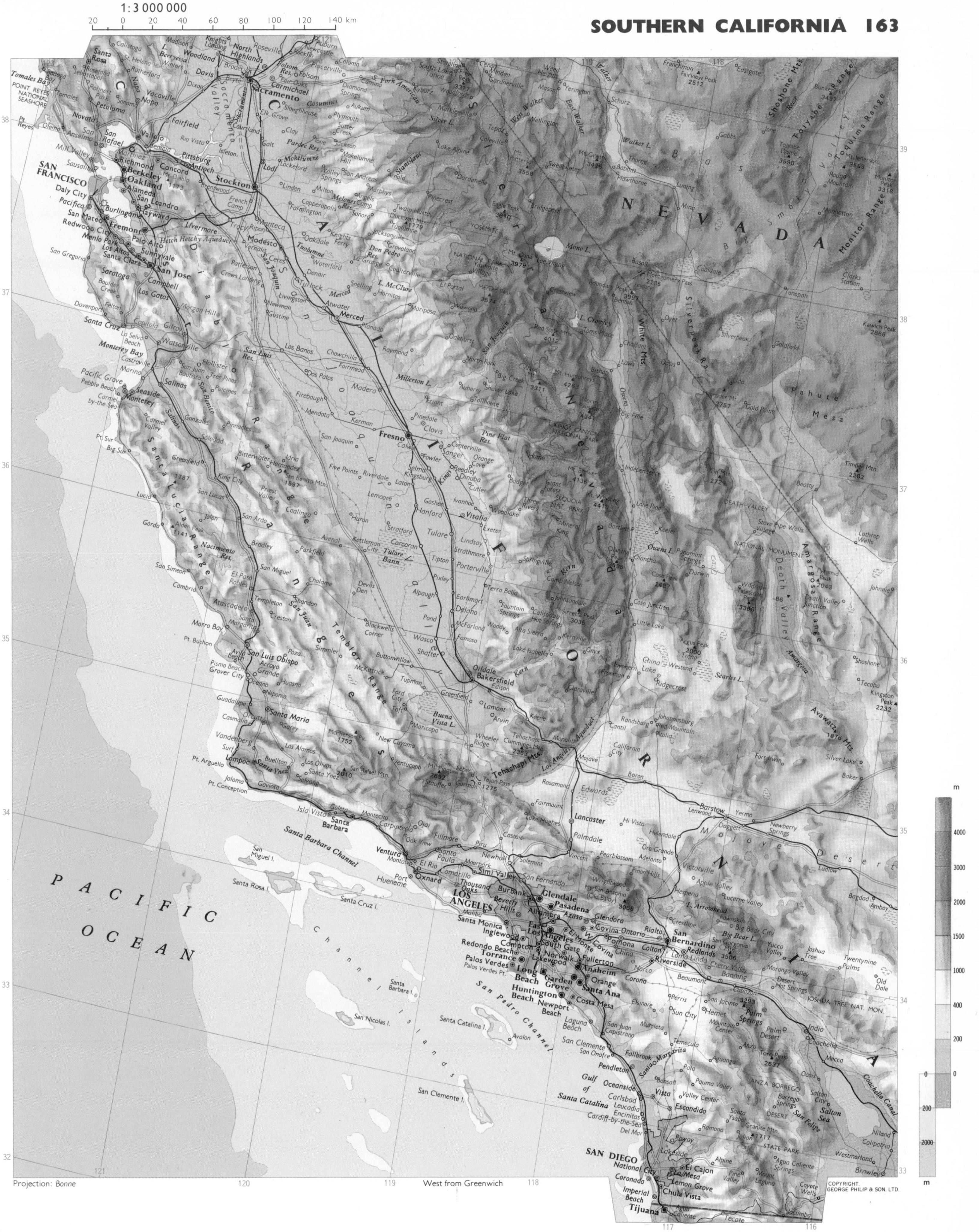

1 : 3 000 000

20 0 20 40 60 80 100 120 140 km

NEVADA

CALIFORNIA

PACIFIC OCEAN

SAN FRANCISCO
Daly City
Pacifica
San Mateo
Redwood City
Menlo Park
Palo Alto
Sunnyvale
Santa Clara
SAN JOSE
Oakland
Berkeley
Richmond
Concord
San Leandro
Hayward
Fremont
Campbell
Los Gatos
Saratoga

San Rafael
Mill Valley
Sausalito
Novato
San Anselmo
Petaluma
Santa Rosa
Vallejo
Fairfield
Napa
Vacaville
Dixon
Davis
Woodland
SACRAMENTO
Carmichael
Stockton
Lodi
Modesto
Turlock
Merced
Los Banos
Madera
Fresno
Clovis
Hanford
Visalia
Tulare
Corcoran
Porterville
Delano
Wasco
Shafter
Oildale
Bakersfield

Santa Cruz
Watsonville
Monterey Bay
Pacific Grove
Pebble Beach
Seaside
Monterey
Carmel-by-the-Sea
Salinas
Hollister
Gilroy
Gonzales
Soledad
Greenfield
King City
San Lucas
Bradley
San Miguel
Paso Robles
Atascadero
Templeton
Morro Bay
San Luis Obispo
Pismo Beach
Grover City
Arroyo Grande
Nipomo
Guadalupe
Santa Maria
Lompoc
Vandenberg
Buellton
Los Alamos
Los Olivos
Santa Ynez
Pt. Arguello
Pt. Conception

Santa Barbara
Montecito
Carpinteria
Ventura
Oxnard
Port Hueneme
Ojai
Fillmore
Santa Paula
Simi Valley
Thousand Oaks
Malibu
Santa Monica

LOS ANGELES
Burbank
Glendale
Pasadena
Beverly Hills
Inglewood
Redondo Beach
Torrance
Palos Verdes
Long Beach
Compton
South Gate
Lakewood
Norwalk
Garden Grove
Huntington Beach
Newport Beach
Costa Mesa
Anaheim
Santa Ana
Orange
Fullerton
Azusa
Glendora
Covina
W. Covina
Pomona
Ontario
Chino
Rialto
San Bernardino
Redlands
Riverside
Corona
Colton
Laguna Beach
San Juan Capistrano
San Clemente
San Onofre
Fallbrook
Oceanside
Carlsbad
Leucadia
Encinitas
Cardiff-by-the-Sea
Del Mar
Escondido
Ramona
SAN DIEGO
National City
Coronado
La Mesa
El Cajon
Lemon Grove
Chula Vista
Imperial Beach
Tijuana

Lancaster
Palmdale
Mojave
Edwards
Barstow
Yermo
Victorville
Hesperia
Apple Valley
Lucerne Valley
Big Bear City
Big Bear L.
Palm Springs
Indio
Coachella
Mecca
Salton Sea
Brawley
Calipatria
Niland
Westmorland

Santa Barbara Channel
Channel Islands
San Miguel I.
Santa Rosa I.
Santa Cruz I.
Anacapa I.
Santa Catalina I.
Avalon
San Pedro Channel
San Nicolas I.
Santa Barbara I.
San Clemente I.

DEATH VALLEY NATIONAL MONUMENT
Stove Pipe Wells
Furnace Creek
SEQUOIA NAT. PARK
YOSEMITE NATIONAL PARK
KINGS CANYON NATIONAL PARK
JOSHUA TREE NAT. MON.
ANZA-BORREGO STATE PARK

Santa Lucia Range
Temblor Range
Diablo Range
San Joaquin Valley
Tehachapi Mts.
Mojave Desert
Amargosa Range
Panamint Range
Monitor Range
Shoshone Mts.
Toquima Range
White Mts.
Mono L.
Tulare Basin
Buena Vista L.
Owens L.
Searles L.

Projection: Bonne

West from Greenwich

COPYRIGHT.
GEORGE PHILIP & SON. LTD.

m
4000
3000
2000
1500
1000
400
200
0
200
2000
m

REFERENCE TO NUMBERS

1	Federal District	5	México
2	Aguascalientes	6	Morelos
3	Guanajuato	7	Querétaro
4	Hidalgo	8	Tlaxcala

Projection: Bi-polar oblique Conical Orthomorphic

West from Greenwich

50 0 50 100 150 200 250 300 km

GULF OF MEXICO

Golfo de Campeche

STATES

ARKANSAS
MISSISSIPPI
ALABAMA
GEORGIA
FLORIDA
LOUISIANA
TEXAS

FORT WORTH · DALLAS · Denton · Denison · Sherman · Paris · Texarkana · Hope · Camden · Greenville · Tuscaloosa · Opelika · Columbus · McRae · Ocmulgee
Wichita Falls · Brownwood · Cleburne · Hillsboro · Corsicana · Tyler · Longview · Marshall · Monroe · El Dorado · Meridian · Selma · Montgomery · Phenix City · Americus · Cordele · Tifton
Waco · Palestine · Nacogdoches · Shreveport · Vicksburg · Jackson · Troy · Dothan · Albany · Waycross · Valdosta
Temple · Huntsville · Bryan · Lufkin · Alexandria · Natchez · Laurel · Hattiesburg · Flomaton · Tallahassee
Austin · Jewett · Beaumont · Lake Charles · Lafayette · Baton Rouge · Hammond · McComb · Bogalusa · MOBILE · Pensacola · Panama City · Lake City
SAN ANTONIO · HOUSTON · Port Arthur · NEW ORLEANS · Biloxi · Gulfport · C. San Blas · Apalachee Bay
Rosenberg · Galveston · Breton Sound · Mississippi Delta · Suwannee · Clearwater
Victoria · Dilley · Alice · Corpus Christi · Terrebonne B. · Atchafalaya Bay
Laredo · Kingsville · Nuevo Laredo · Zapata · Laguna Madre
Camargo · Mc Allen · Harlingen · Brownsville · Reynosa · Matamoros · Valle Hermoso
Montemorelos · Méndez · San Fernando · Laguna Madre
Linares · Villagrán · Santander-Jiménez
Ciudad Victoria · La Pesca · Soto la Marina
Ciudad Mante · Aldama · Pta. Jerez
Ciudad Madero · Tampico · Ciudad Valles · Pánuco · Tuxpan · Laguna de Tamiahua
Temapache · C. Rojo · Poza Rica · Papantla · Nautla
Pachuca · Huejutla · Tulancingo · Huauchinango · Teziutlán · Misantla
MÉXICO · Tlaxcala · Jalapa · Coatepec · Veracruz · Zempoala
PUEBLA · Amecameca · Orizaba · Córdoba · Alvarado · San Andrés Tuxtla
Cuernavaca · Tehuacán · Cosamaloapan · Coatzacoalcos · Frontera · Ciudad del Carmen
Iguala · Acayucan · Minatitlán · Villahermosa · Cárdenas · TABASCO · Paraíso · Palizada · Champotón
Chilpancingo · Oaxaca · Tuxtla Gutiérrez · San Cristóbal de las Casas · CHIAPAS · Comitán
Acapulco · Miahuatlán · Salina Cruz · Tehuantepec · Golfo de Tehuantepec · Tapachula · Tonalá · Pijijiapan · Huixtla
Puerto Escondido · Puerto Ángel · Mar Muerto · Coatepeque

Isla Desterrada · Isla Pérez
Progreso · Dzilam de Bravo · Mérida · Motul · Izamal · Temax · Tizimín · Río Lagartos · El Cuyo · C. Catoche · Pto. Juárez · El Díaz · Puerto Morelos
YUCATÁN · Valladolid · Chichén Itzá · Cozumel · Isla Cozumel · Maxcanú · Calkini · Tekax · Peto · Vigía Chico · B. de la Ascensión
Campeche · Hopelchén · QUINTANA ROO · Felipe Carrillo Puerto · B. del Espíritu Santo · Banco Chinchorro
San José Carpizo · Juárez · Bacalar · B. de Chetumal · Chetumal · Corozal
CAMPECHE · Matamoros · Orange Walk · Ambergris Cay · Turneffe Is.
Belize City · BELIZE · Belmopan · Golfo de Honduras · Roatán · Islas de la Bahía
Uaxactún · Tikal · San Ignacio · Benque Viejo · Dangriga · Puerto Cortés · Tela · La Ceiba
GUATEMALA · L. Petén Itzá · Flores · Punta Gorda · San Antonio · Livingston · Puerto Barrios · San Pedro Sula
HONDURAS · Cobán · Sa. de las Minas · Zacapa · Santa Rosa · Tegucigalpa

CUBA · Guane · La Fé · Corrientes · C. San Antonio · Canal de Yucatán · La Esperanza

COPYRIGHT GEORGE PHILIP & SON. LTD.

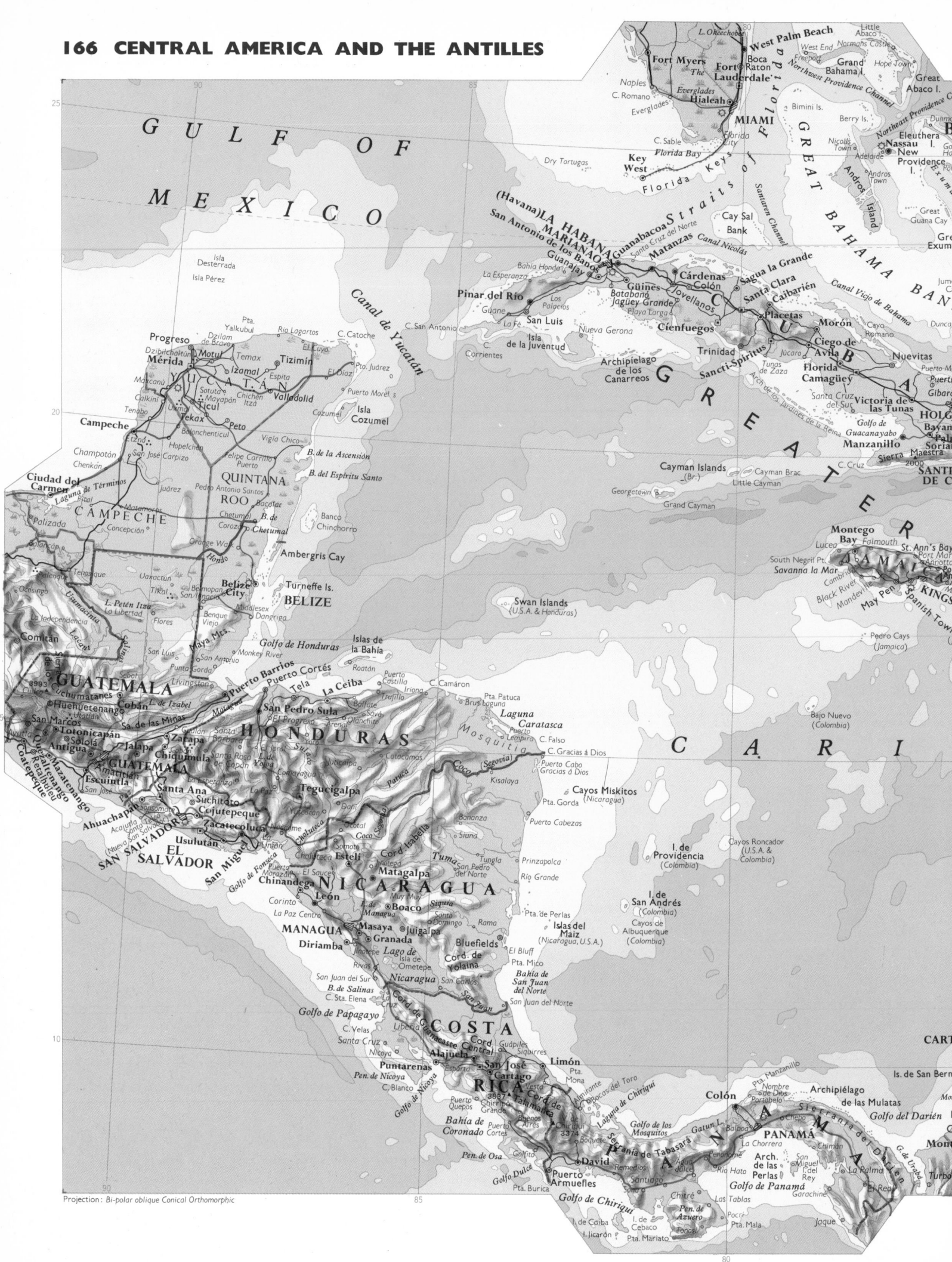

Projection: Bi-polar oblique Conical Orthomorphic

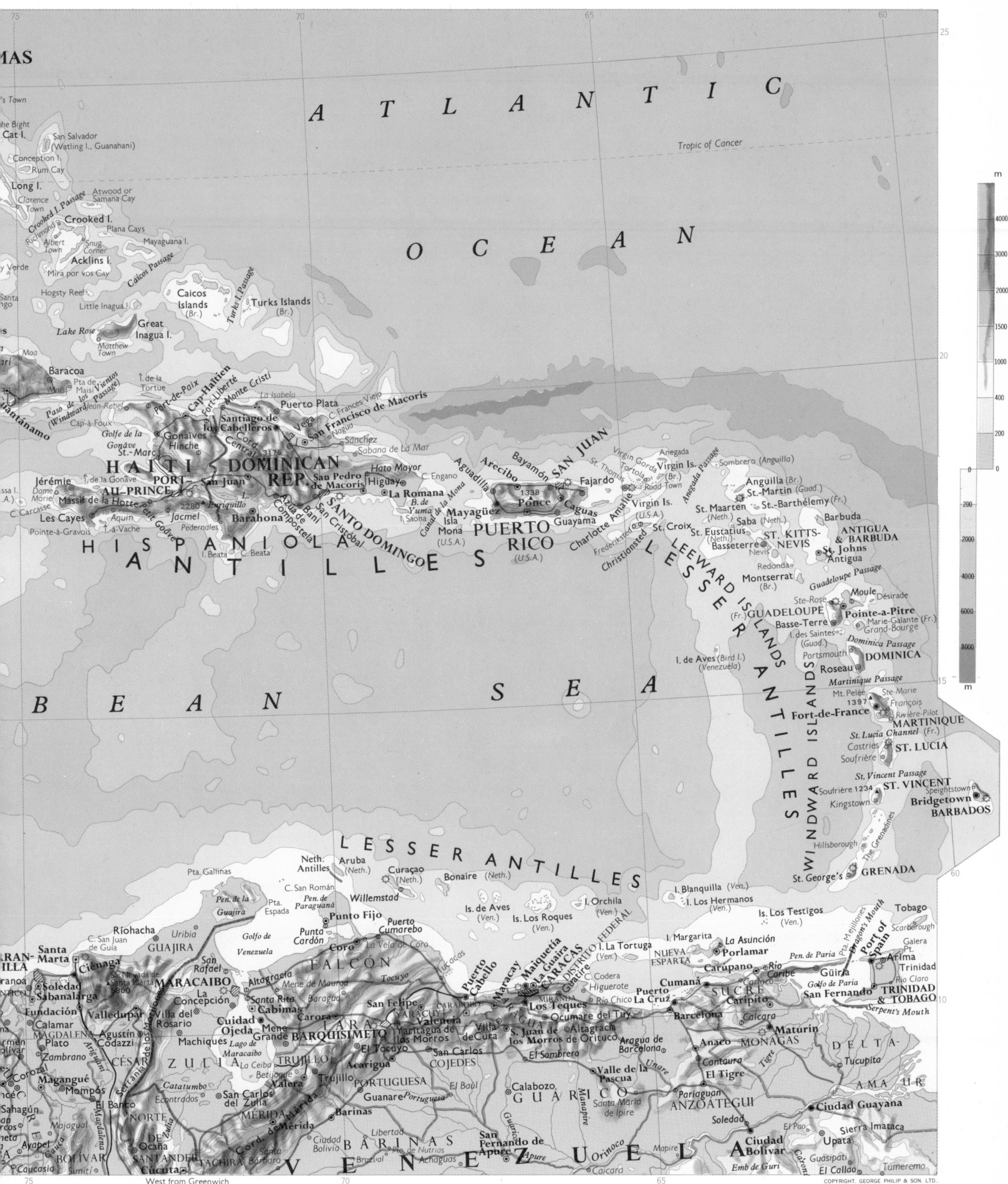

1 : 8 000 000

50   0   50   100   150   200   250   300 km

ATLANTIC

OCEAN

Tropic of Cancer

m

4000
3000
2000
1500
1000
400
200
0
200
2000
4000
6000
8000
m

MAS

's Town
he Bight
Cat I.
San Salvador
(Watling I., Guanahani)
Conception I.
Rum Cay
Long I.
Clarence
Town
Atwood or
Samana Cay
Richmond
Crooked I. Passage
Crooked I.
Plana Cays
Albert
Town
Snug
Corner
Mayaguana I.
Mira por vos Cay
Acklins I.
Caicos Passage
Hogsty Reefs
Little Inagua I.
Caicos
Islands
(Br.)
Turks Islands
(Br.)
Turks I. Passage
Santa
ngo
y Verde
Lake Rose
**Great
Inagua I.**
Matthew
Town

Moa
ari
Baracoa
Pta. de
Maisi
I. de la
Tortue
Port-Liberté
Cap-Haitien
Fort-Liberté
Monte Cristi
La Isabela
Puerto Plata
C. Frances Viejo
antánamo
Paso de los Vientos
(Windward Jean-Rabel
Passage)
Cap-à-Foux
Santiago de
los Cabelleros
San Francisco de Macoris
La
Vega
Nagua
Golfe de la
Gonâve
Gonaives
Hinche
Central
3175
Sánchez
Sabana de La Mar
Samaná
Aguadilla
Arecibo
Bayamón
SAN JUAN
St. Thomas
Virgin Gorda
Tortola
Virgin Is.
(Br.)
Anegada
Sombrero (Anguilla)
HAITI
**DOMINICAN
REP.**
San Juan
San Pedro
Higuey
C. Engano
PUERTO
1338
Ponce
Caguas
Fajardo
Virgin Is.
(U.S.A.)
Road Town
Anegada Passage
Anguilla (Br.)
St-Martin (Guad.)
St-Barthélemy (Fr.)
Jérémie
I. de la Gonâve
**PORT-
AU-PRINCE**
de Macoris
Azua de
Compostela
**SANTO
DOMINGO**
B. de
Yuma
Isla
Mona
(U.S.A.)
Mayagüez
Guayama
RICO
Charlotte Amalie
St. Croix
Frederiksted
St. Maarten
(Neth.)
Saba (Neth.)
St. Eustatius
(Neth.)
Basseterre
**ST. KITTS-
NEVIS**
Barbuda
**ANTIGUA
& BARBUDA**
St. Johns
Antigua
Damé
ssa I.
.A.)
Carcasse
Les Cayes
2280
Massif de la Hotte
Aquin
Jacmel
Pedernales
Jaragua
Barriquillo
Barahona
San Cristobal
Bani
I. Saona
Canal de la Mona
(U.S.A.)
Christiansted
Redonda
Montserrat
(Br.)
Nevis
Guadeloupe Passage
Pointe-à-Gravois
I.-à-Vache
I. Beata
C. Beata
HISPANIOLA
ANTILLES
LESSER
Ste-Rose
Moule
Désirade
GUADELOUPE
Basse-Terre
(Fr.)
Pointe-à-Pitre
Marie-Galante (Fr.)
Grand-Bourge
I. des Saintes
(Guad.)
Dominica Passage
I. de Aves (Bird I.)
(Venezuela)
Portsmouth
DOMINICA
Roseau
LEEWARD ISLANDS

B E A N   **S E A**

Martinique Passage
Ste-Marie
Mt. Pelée
1397
François
Rivière-Pilot
Fort-de-France
MARTINIQUE
St. Lucia Channel (Fr.)
Ste-Marie
Castries
Soufrière
ST. LUCIA
St. Vincent Passage
Soufrière 1234
ST. VINCENT
Kingstown
Speightstown
Bridgetown
BARBADOS
Hillsborough
The Grenadines
WINDWARD ISLANDS
ANTILLES

LESSER   ANTILLES

Neth.
Antilles
Aruba
(Neth.)
Curaçao
(Neth.)
Bonaire (Neth.)
Pta. Gallinas
C. San Román
Pen. de
Paraguaná
Willemstad
Is. de Aves
(Ven.)
Is. Los Roques
(Ven.)
I. Orchila
(Ven.)
I. Blanquilla (Ven.)
I. Los Hermanos
(Ven.)
Is. Los Testigos
(Ven.)
Tobago
Scarborough
Pen. de la
Guajira
Pta.
Espada
Pen. de
Guajira
Punto Fijo
Puerto
Cumarebo
La Vela de Coro
I. Margarita
La Asunción
NUEVA
ESPARTA
Porlamar
Pen. de Paria
Pta. Mejillones
Dragon's Mouth
**Port of
Spain**
Galera
Pt.
Arima
Trinidad
Ríohacha
Uribia
Punta
Cardón
Golfo de
Venezuela
Coro
FALCON
Tocuyo
Yaracuy
Puerto
Cabello
Maiquetía
La Guaira
CARACAS
DISTRITO
FEDERAL
I. La Tortuga
(Ven.)
Río
Caribe
Carúpano
Golfo de Paria
Güiria
Caribe
**TRINIDAD
& TOBAGO**
San Fernando
Serpent's Mouth
**Santa
Marta**
GUAJIRA
Cienaga
San
Rafael
3800
Altagracia
Mene de Mauroa
Barauta
MIRANDA
Higuerote
Río Chico
Ocumare del Tuy
Cumana
Puerto
La Cruz
SUCRE
Carúpano
Caripito
Maturin
DELTA-
ILLA
an
ranoa
Soledad
Sabanalarga
Fundación
Calamar
CESAR
Agustin
Codazzi
Valledupar
Villa del
Rosario
MARACAIBO
La
Concepción
Cabimas
Santa Rita
San Felipe
CARABOBO
Valencia
los Morros
Villa
de Cura
S. Juan de
los Morros
Maracay
Aragua de
Barcelona
Barcelona
Anaco
MONAGAS
Cantaura
Tucupita
Magangué
Mompós
Plato
Zambrano
C
MAGDALENA
Codazzi
**Cuidad
Ojeda**
Mene
Grande
BARQUISIMETO
Lago de
Maracaibo
TARA-
CARACUY
Maritagua
El Sombrero
GUARICO
Valle de la
Pascua
San
Sebastián
El Tigre
Pariaguan
Ciudad Guayana
Sierra Imataca
ACé
El Banco
Majagual
Magiual
ZULIA
La Ceiba
TRUJILLO
Betijoque
COJEDES
El Baúl
Santa María
de Ipire
Unare
ANZOATEGUI
Soledad
El Pao
Upata
Corozal
Simití
Mompós
NORTE
Machiques
Acarigua
PORTUGUESA
Calabozo
Guárico
Caroni
Sahagún
dos
an
BOLIVAR
SANTANDER
Ocaña
DE
SANTANDER
Cúcuta
TACHIRA
MERIDA
Mérida
Trujillo
Valera
Guanare
Portuguesa
Barinas
Ciudad
Bolivia
BARINAS
Libertad
Nutrias
**San
Fernando de
Apure**
Apure
Achaguas
Mantecal
Mapire
Embalse
de Guri
Caño
**Ciudad
Bolívar**
El Pao
Sierra Imataca
El Callao
Tumeremo
Ayapel
Caucasia
V E N E Z U E L A
Orinoco
Caicara
Bruzual

1:30 000 000

200 0 200 400 600 800 1000 km

Sa. Nevada de Santa Marta
Barranquilla ▲5800
Maracaibo
G. of Darien
Panama Canal
Margarita
Tobago I.
Caracas
Trinidad
5994▼

ATLANTIC

OCEAN

Cord. de Mérida
L. Maracaibo
Llanos
Orinoco
Georgetown
Guiana Highlands
2810 ▲Roraima
Sierra Pacaraima
Serra de Tumucumaque
C. Orange

Medellín
Bogotá
Cali
Cordillera Oriental
Cordillera Central
Cordillera Occidental
Magdalena
Meta
Guaviare

C. de San Francisco
Quito Cotopaxi 5897
Chimborazo 6267
Guayaquil
G. of Guayaquil
Pta. Pariñas
Pta. Aguja
Lobos Is.

Napo
Putumayo
Japurá
Caquetá
Negro
Amazon
Marañón
Ucayali
Juruá
Purus
Madeira
Manaus
Belém
Marajó I.
Pará
Equator
Tocantins
Fortaleza
Paraíba
C. São Roque
C. Branco

Huascarán 6768
Lima
Chincha Is.

Madre de Dios
Roosevelt
Guaporé
Tapajós
Xingu
Araguaia
Tocantins
Plateau of Borborema
Recife

S   e   l   v   a   s

PACIFIC

L. Titicaca
Ancohuma & Illampu 6550
La Paz
Bolivian Plateau
L. Poopó

Plateau of Mato Grosso
São Francisco
Brasília

Belo Horizonte
2890 Pico da Bandeira
Brazilian Highlands
Serra da Mantiqueira
Abrolhos Bank
Salvador

Tropic of Capricorn
8050
Atacama Desert
Peru Trench
S. Félix
S. Ambroso

Ojos del Salado 6863
Gran Chaco
Salado
Pilcomayo
Asunción
Iguaçu Falls
Paraná
Uruguay
São Paulo
Rio de Janeiro
C. Frio
Serra do Mar

OCEAN

Salinas Grandes
Córdoba
Aconcagua 6990
Uspallata Pass
Valparaíso
Santiago
Arch. de Juan Fernández
Sierra de Córdoba
L. Mar Chiquita
Rosario
Entre Ríos
Paraná
Pôrto Alegre
Lagoa dos Patos

Buenos Aires
La Plata
Montevideo
Río de la Plata
Pta. Mogotes

SOUTH

Colorado
Negro
Bahía Blanca

Pampas

ATLANTIC

G. of San Matías
Valdés Peninsula

Argentine Basin

OCEAN

Chile Rise
Chiloé I.
Chonos Archipelago
Taitao Peninsula
G. of Peñas
Wellington
Madre de Dios

Chubut
4058 S. Valentín
Patagonia
G. of San Jorge

6212

Magellan's Strait
Santa Inés
Cockburn Chan.
Beagle Chan.
C. Horn
Tierra del Fuego
Staten I.
Magellan's Strait
Falkland Islands
West Falkland
East Falkland

m
6000
4000
3000
2000
1000
400
200
0
0
200
2000
4000
6000
8000
m

West from Greenwich

1:80 000 000

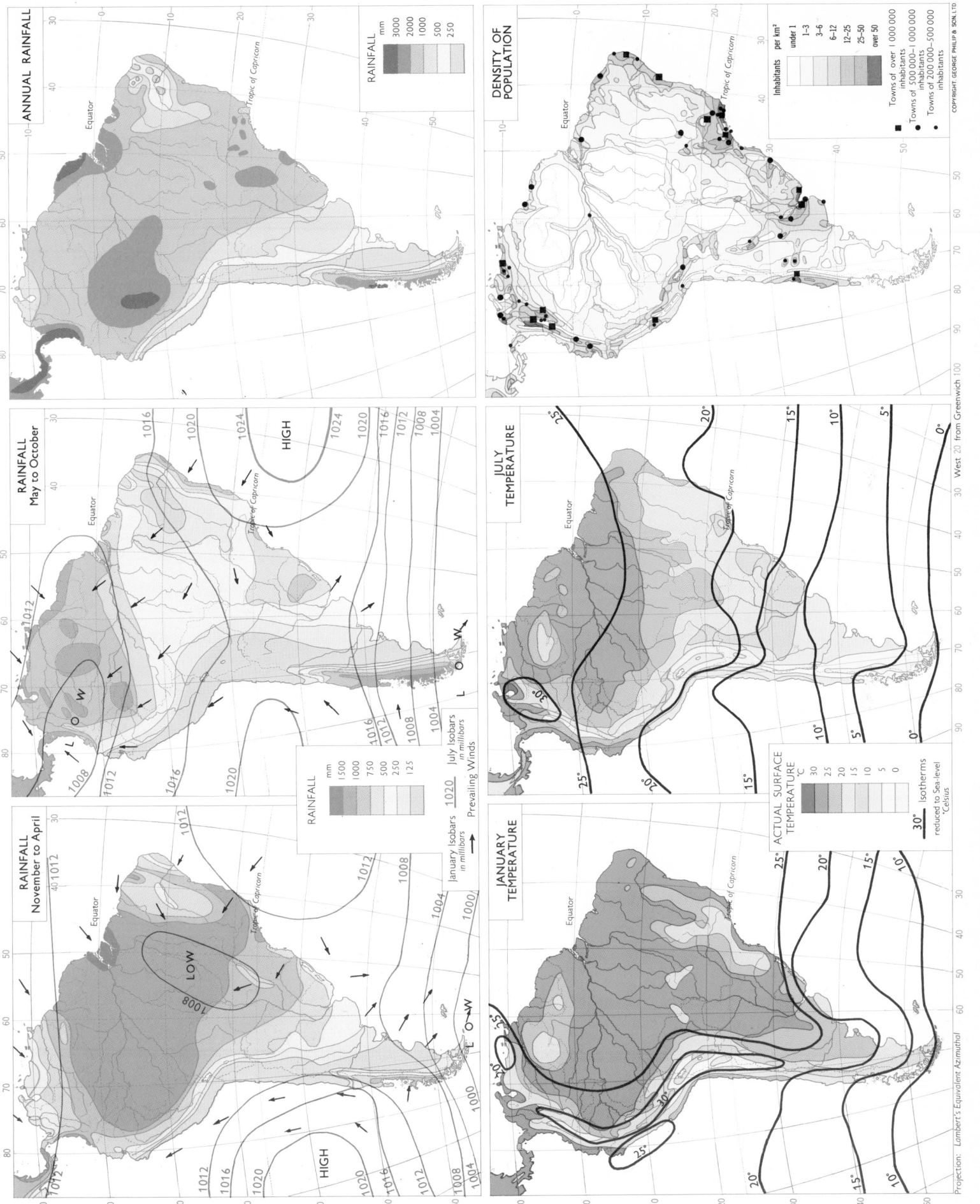

ANNUAL RAINFALL

RAINFALL
mm
3000
2000
1000
500
250

DENSITY OF POPULATION

per km²
under 1
1–3
3–6
6–12
12–25
25–50
over 50

Inhabitants

Towns of over 1 000 000 inhabitants
Towns of 500 000–1 000 000 inhabitants
Towns of 200 000–500 000 inhabitants

COPYRIGHT GEORGE PHILIP & SON, LTD.

RAINFALL
May to October

HIGH

1016
1020
1024
1020
1016
1012
1008
1004

1012
1008
1012
1016
1020

LOW
LOW

JULY TEMPERATURE

25°
20°
15°
10°
5°
0°

30°

25°
20°
15°
10°
5°
0°

RAINFALL
mm
1500
1000
750
500
250
125

1020 January Isobars in millibars
July Isobars in millibars

Prevailing Winds

RAINFALL
November to April

1012
1012
1012
1008

1004

1000

LOW
1008

HIGH

1012
1016
1020
1016
1012
1008

1012

LOW

JANUARY TEMPERATURE

25°
20°
15°
10°

25°
30°
30°

25°

20°
15°
10°

ACTUAL SURFACE TEMPERATURE
°C
30
25
20
15
10
5
0

30° Isotherms reduced to Sea-level Celsius

West 20 from Greenwich 100

Projection: Lambert's Equivalent Azimuthal

ATLANTIC OCEAN

FORTALEZA (Ceará)

NATAL

RIO GRANDE DO NORTE

RECIFE (Pernambuco)

MACEIÓ

João Pessoa (Paraíba)

C E A R Á

P I A U Í

M A R A N H Ã O

P A R Á

A M A P Á

P E R N A M B U C O

A L A G Ô A S

BELÉM (Pará)

SÃO LUIS

Teresina

Sobral

Parnaíba

Caxias

Bacabal

Pindaré Mirim

Imperatriz

Carolina

Ilha de Marajó

Macapá

Bragança

Castanhal

Capanema

Ourém

Olinda

Campina Grande

Mossoró

Aracati

Crateús

Floriano

Tocantins

Xingu

Chapada das Mangabeiras

Serra dos Carajás

Serra do Estrondo

Serra do Gurupi

Serra do Tiracambu

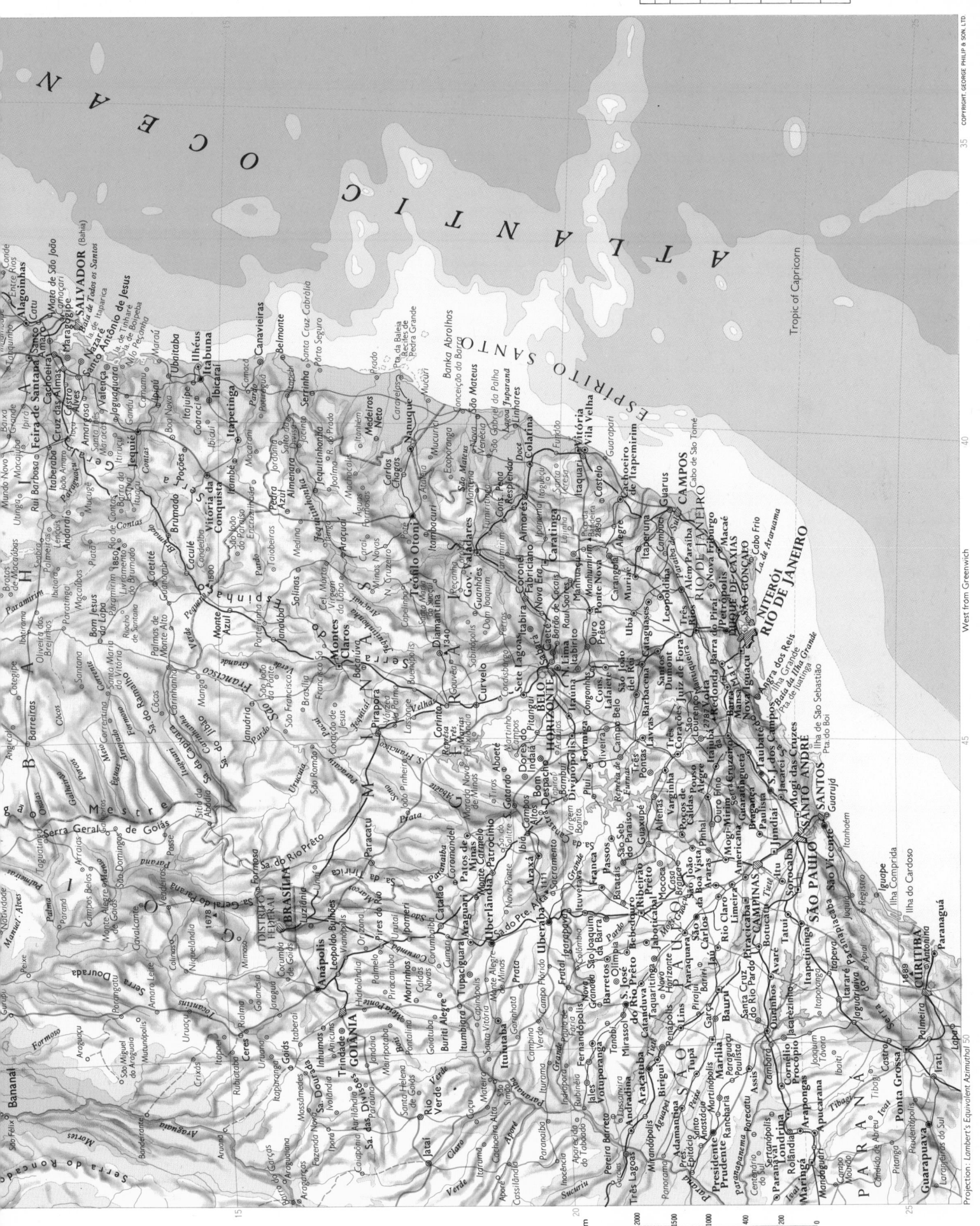

1 : 8 000 000

50   0   50   100 150 200 250 300 km

171

ATLANTIC OCEAN

Tropic of Capricorn

COPYRIGHT GEORGE PHILIP & SON, LTD.

West from Greenwich

Projection: Lambert's Equivalent Azimuthal 50

SALVADOR (Bahia)

ESPÍRITO SANTO

MINAS GERAIS

RIO DE JANEIRO

NITERÓI
RIO DE JANEIRO

SÃO PAULO

SANTO ANDRÉ
SANTOS

CURITIBA

PARANÁ

BRASÍLIA
DISTRITO FEDERAL

GOIÂNIA

m 2000 1500 1000 400 200 0

m 200 2000 4000

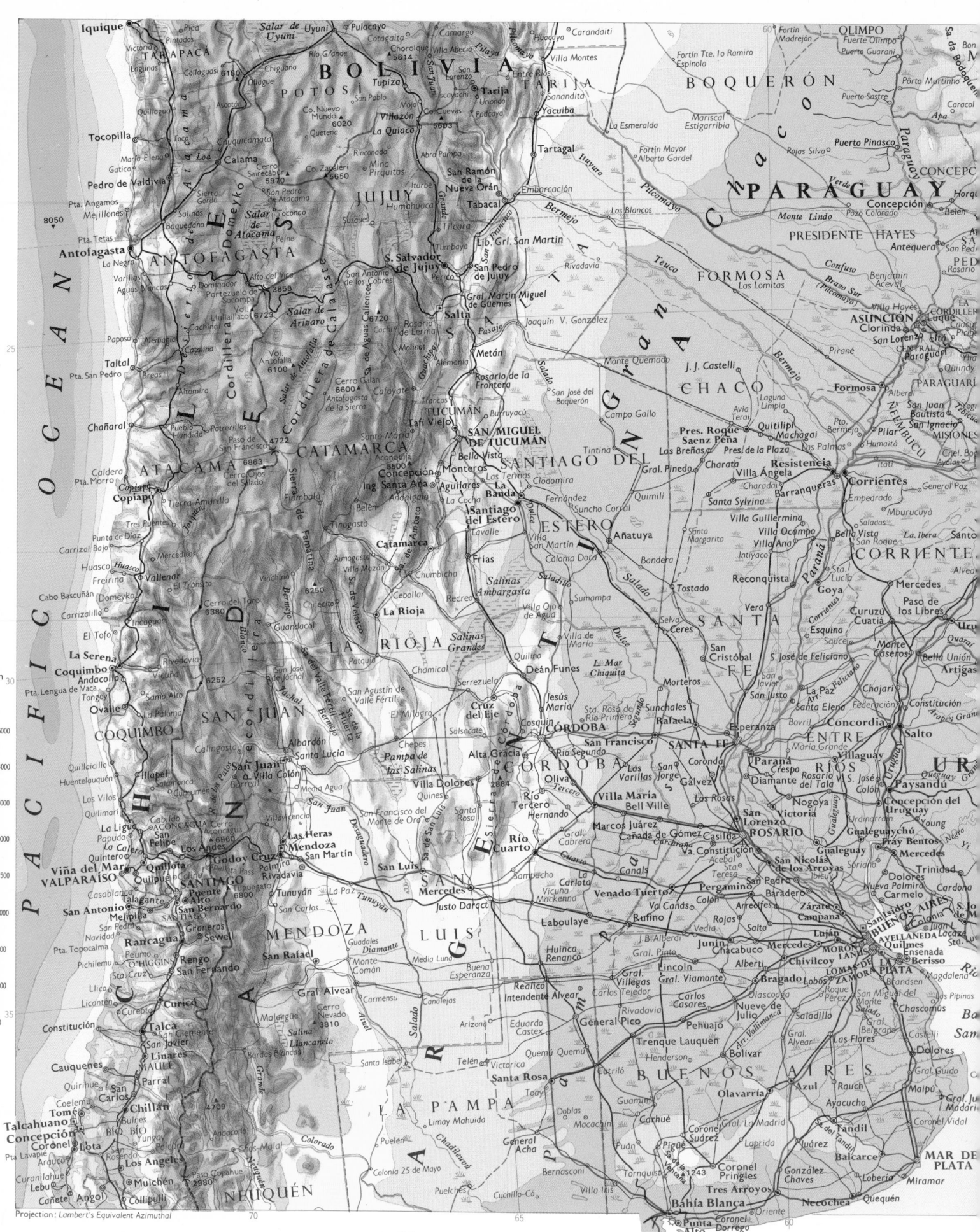
BOLIVIA
PARAGUAY
PACIFIC OCEAN
ARGENTINA
CHILE
ANDES
Gran Chaco
Desierto de Atacama
Cordillera Domeyko
Cordillera de Calalaste
Cordillera de Famatina
Pampa
TARAPACÁ
ANTOFAGASTA
ATACAMA
COQUIMBO
SANTIAGO
O'HIGGINS
MAULE
BÍO BÍO
POTOSÍ
TARIJA
BOQUERÓN
PRESIDENTE HAYES
FORMOSA
CHACO
JUJUY
SALTA
CATAMARCA
TUCUMÁN
SANTIAGO DEL ESTERO
LA RIOJA
SAN JUAN
CÓRDOBA
SANTA FE
CORRIENTES
ENTRE RÍOS
MENDOZA
SAN LUIS
LA PAMPA
BUENOS AIRES
NEUQUÉN
Iquique
Tocopilla
Pedro de Valdivia
Calama
Antofagasta
Taltal
Chañaral
Copiapó
Vallenar
La Serena
Coquimbo
Ovalle
Illapel
Viña del Mar
VALPARAÍSO
SANTIAGO
San Antonio
Rancagua
San Fernando
Curicó
Talca
Linares
Chillán
Concepción
Talcahuano
Los Angeles
Salar de Uyuni
Tupiza
Tarija
Villazón
Yacuiba
Tartagal
S. Salvador de Jujuy
Salta
San Miguel de Tucumán
Catamarca
La Rioja
Santiago del Estero
San Juan
Mendoza
San Luis
San Rafael
CÓRDOBA
Río Cuarto
Villa María
Santa Fe
Paraná
ROSARIO
Resistencia
Corrientes
Formosa
ASUNCIÓN
Concepción
Salto
Paysandú
Concordia
BUENOS AIRES
La Plata
Mar del Plata
Bahía Blanca
Santa Rosa
General Pico
Tandil
Olavarría
Necochea
Junín
Pergamino
Aconcagua
6960
Ojos del Salado
6863
Llullaillaco
6723
Projection: Lambert's Equivalent Azimuthal
70
65
60
25
30
35
m
6000
4000
3000
2000
1500
1000
400
200
0

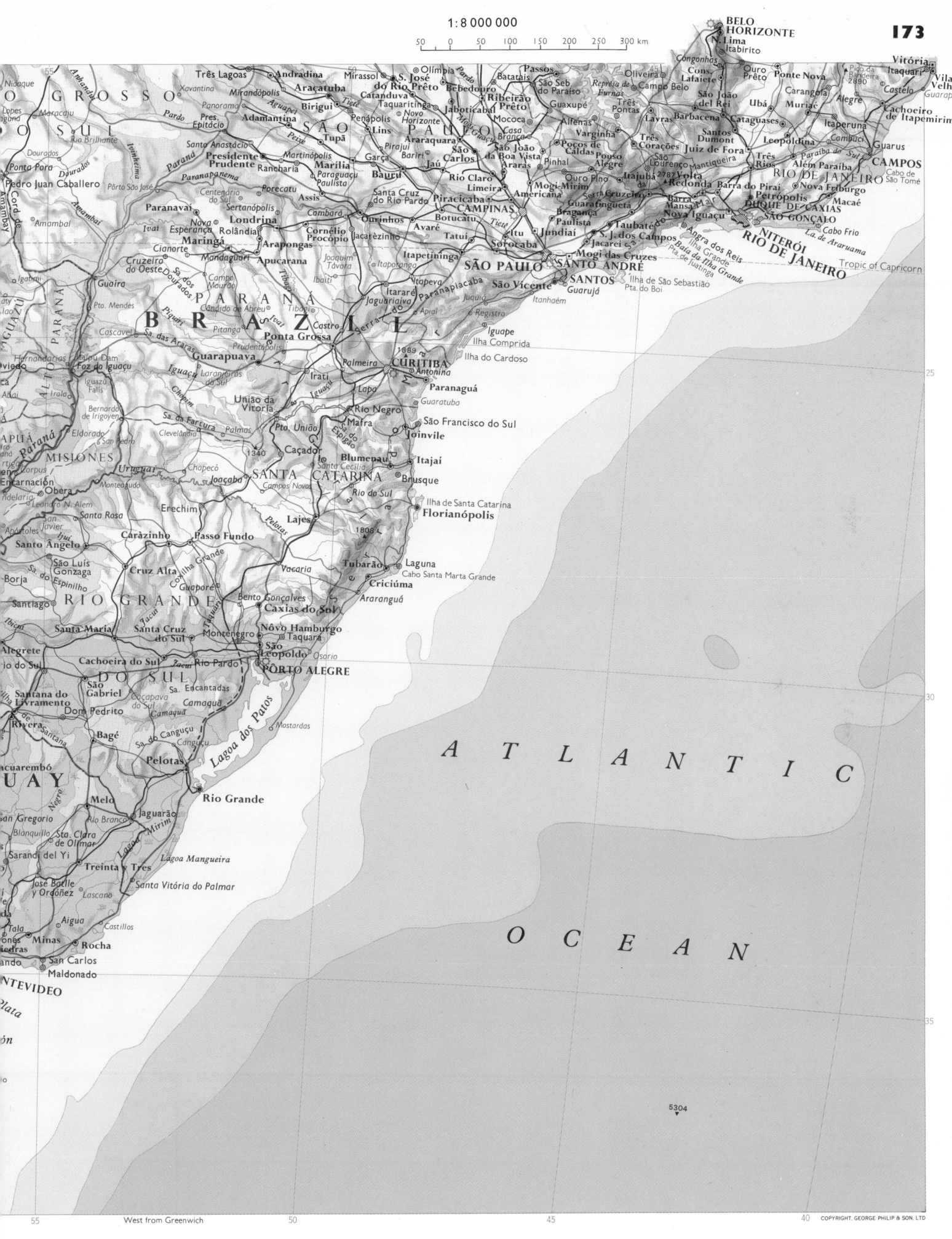

1:8 000 000

50 0 50 100 150 200 250 300 km

BELO HORIZONTE

173

ATLANTIC

OCEAN

BRAZIL

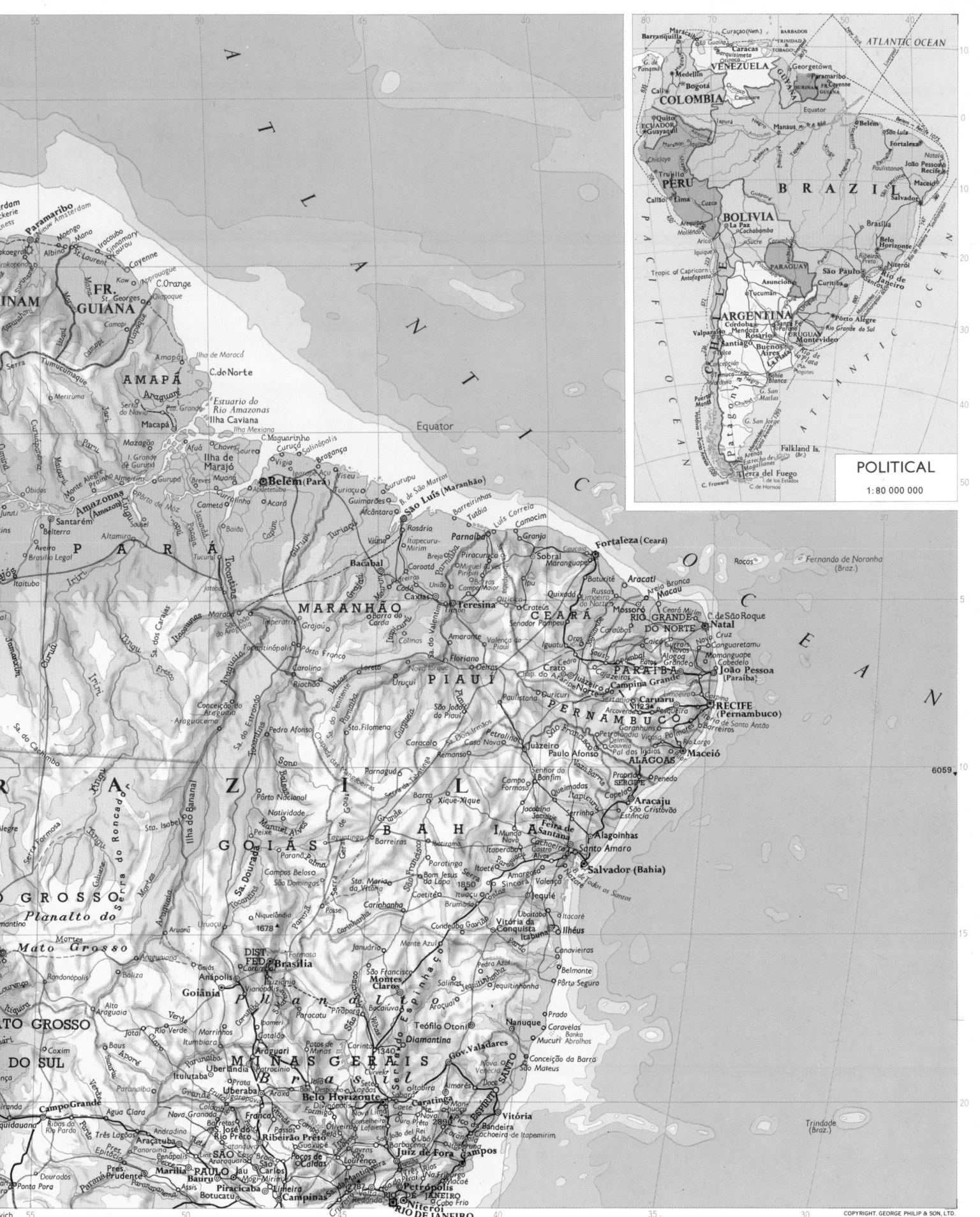

1:16 000 000

200 100 0 200 400 600 km

POLITICAL
1:80 000 000

COPYRIGHT. GEORGE PHILIP & SON, LTD.

1:16 000 000

200 100 0   200   400   600 km

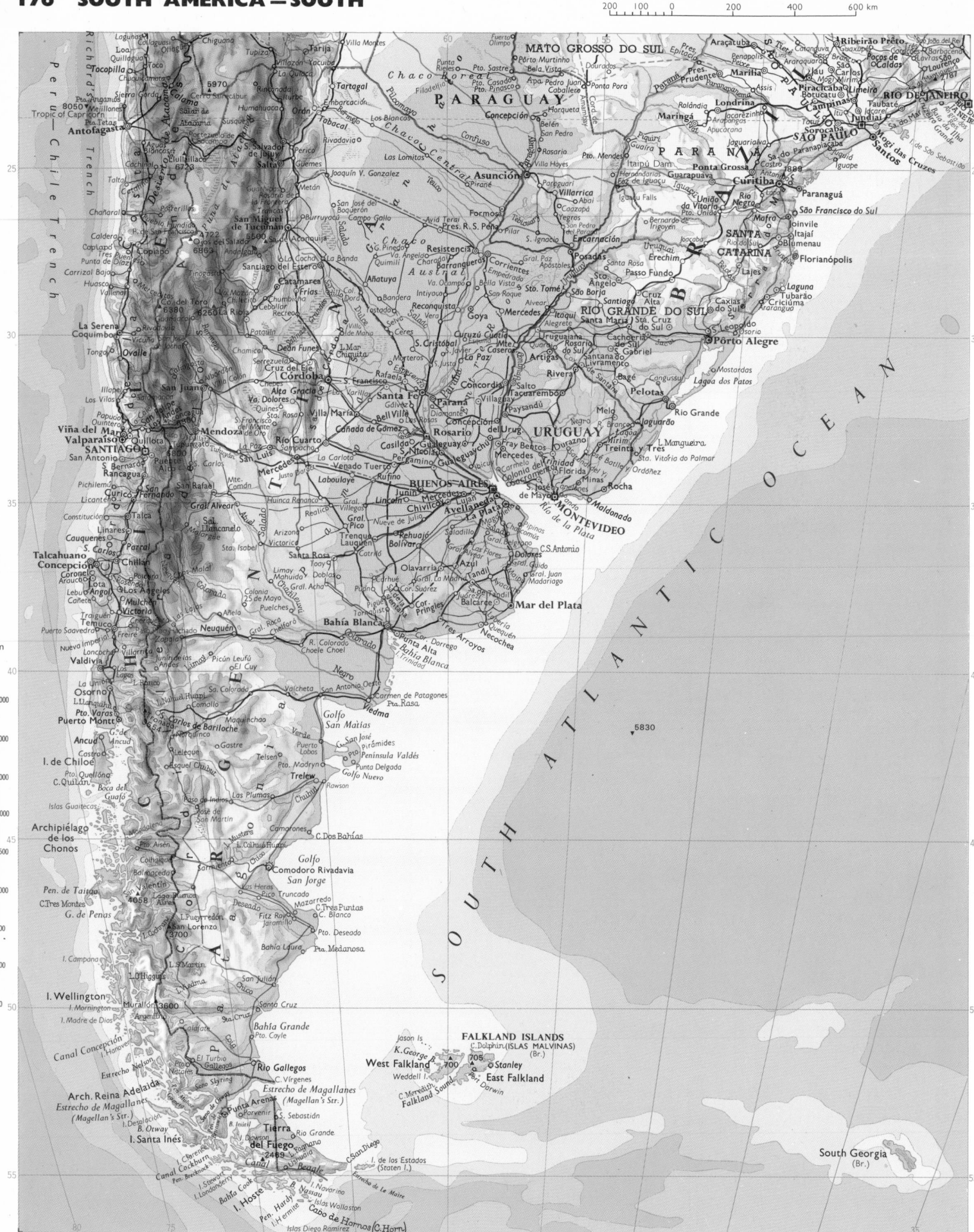

Projection: Sanson-Flamsteed's Sinusoidal

60 West from Greenwich 55

COPYRIGHT GEORGE PHILIP & SON. LTD.

INDEX

The number printed in bold type against each index entry indicates the map page where the feature will be found. The geographical coordinates which follow the name are sometimes only approximate but are close enough for the place name to be located.
An open square □ signifies that the name refers to an administrative subdivision of a country while a solid square ■ follows the name of a country. (□) follows the old county names of the U.K.
The alphabetical order of names composed of two or more words is governed primarily by the first word and then by the second. This rule applies even if the second word is a description or its abbreviation, R.,L.,I. for example. Names composed of a proper name (Gibraltar) and a description (Strait of) are positioned alphabetically by the proper name. If the same place name occurs twice or more times in the index and all are in the same country, each is followed by the name of the administrative subdivision in which it is located. The names are placed in the alphabetical order of the subdivisions. If the same place name occurs twice or more in the index and the places are in different countries they will be followed by their country names, the latter governing the alphabetical order. In a mixture of these situations the primary order is fixed by the alphabetical sequence of the countries and the secondary order by that of the country subdivisions.

A. C. T. – Australian Capital Territory
A. R. – Autonomous Region
A. S. S. R. – Autonomous Soviet Socialist Republic
Afghan. – Afghanistan
Afr. – Africa
Ala. – Alabama
Alas. – Alaska
Alg. – Algeria
Alta. – Alberta
Amer. – America
And. P. – Andhra Pradesh
Ang. – Angola
Arch. – Archipelago
Arg. – Argentina
Ariz. – Arizona
Ark. – Arkansas
Atl. Oc. – Atlantic Ocean
Austral. – Australia
B. – Baie, Bahía, Bay, Bucht, Bugt
B.A. – Buenos Aires
B.C. – British Columbia
Bangla. – Bangladesh
Barr. – Barrage
Bay. – Bayern
Belg. – Belgium
Berks. – Berkshire
Bol. – Bolshoi
Bots. – Botswana
Br. – British
Bri. – Bridge
Bt. – Bight
Bucks. – Buckinghamshire
Bulg. – Bulgaria
C. – Cabo, Cap, Cape
C. Prov. – Cape Province
Calif. – California
Camb. – Cambodia
Cambs. – Cambridgeshire
Can. – Canada
Cat. – Cataract, Cataracta
Cent. – Central
Chan. – Channel
Co. – Country
Colomb. – Colombia
Colo. – Colorado
Conn. – Connecticut
Cord. – Cordillera
Cr.. – Creek
Cumb. – Cumbria
Czech. – Czechoslovakia
D.C. – District of Columbia
Del. – Delaware
Dep. – Dependency
Derby. – Derbyshire
Des. – Desert
Dist. – District
Dj. – Djebel
Dumf. & Gall. – Dumfries and Galloway
E. – East
Eng. – England
Fed. – Federal, Federation
Fla. – Florida
For. – Forest
Fr. – France, French
Fs. – Falls
Ft. – Fort
G. – Golf, Golfo, Gulf, Guba
Ga. – Georgia
Germ. – Germany
Glam. – Glamorgan
Glos. – Gloucestershire
Gr. – Grande, Great, Greater, Group
H.K. – Hong Kong
H.P. – Himachal Pradesh
Hants. – Hampshire
Harb. – Harbor, Harbour
Hd. – Head
Here. & Worcs. – Hereford and Worcester
Herts. – Hertfordshire
Holl. – Holland
Hung. – Hungary
I.o.M. – Isle of Man
I. of W. – Isle of Wight
I.(s). – Île, Ilha, Insel, Isla, Island
Id. – Idaho
Ill. – Illinois
Ind. – Indiana
Ind. Oc. – Indian Ocean
J. – Jabal, Jabel, Jazira
Junc. – Junction
K. – Kap, Kapp
K. – Kuala
Kal. – Kalmyk A.S.S.R.
Kans. – Kansas
Kpl. – Kapell
Ky. – Kentucky
L. – Lac, Lacul, Lago, Lagoa, Lake, Limni, Loch, Lough
La. – Lousiana
Lancs. – Lancashire
Leb. – Lebanon
Leics. – Leicestershire
Lim. – Limerick
Lincs. – Lincolnshire
Lit. – Little
Lr. – Lower
Lt. Ho. – Light House
Mad. P. – Madhya Pradesh
Madag. – Madagascar
Malay. – Malaysia
Man. – Manitoba
Manch. – Manchester
Maran. – Maranhão
Mass. – Massachusetts
Md. – Maryland
Me. – Maine
Mend. – Mendoza
Mer. – Méridionale
Mich. – Michigan
Mid. – Middle
Minn. – Minnesota
Miss. – Mississippi
Mo. – Missouri
Mong. – Mongolia
Mont. – Montana
Moroc. – Morocco
Mozam. – Mozambique
Mt.(e). – Mont, Monte, Monti, Montaña, Mountain
Mys. – Mysore
N. – North, Northern, Nouveau
N.B. – New Brunswick
N.C. – North Carolina
N.D. – North Dakota
N.H. – New Hampshire
N.I. – North Island
N.J. – New Jersey
N. Mex. – New Mexico
N.S. – Nova Scotia
N.S.W. – New South Wales
N.T. – Northern Territory
N.W.T. – North West Territory
N.Y. – New York
N.Z. – New Zealand
Nat. – National
Nat Park. – National Park
Nebr. – Nebraska
Neth. – Netherlands
Nev. – Nevada
Newf. – Newfoundland
Nic. – Nicaragua
Northants. – Northamptonshire
Northumb. – Northumberland
Notts. – Nottinghamshire
O. – Oued, ouadi
O.F.S. – Orange Free State
Okla. – Oklahoma
Ont. – Ontario
Or. – Orientale
Oreg. – Oregon
Os. – Ostrov
Oxon. – Oxfordshire
Oz. – Ozero
P. – Pass, Passo, Pasul, Pulau
P.E.I. – Prince Edward Island
P.N.G. – Papua New Guinea
P.O. – Post Office
P. Rico. – Puerto Rico
Pa. – Pennsylvania
Pac. Oc. – Pacific Ocean
Pak. – Pakistan
Pass. – Passage
Pen. – Peninsula, Peninsule
Phil. – Philippines
Pk. – Park, Peak
Plat. – Plateau
P-ov. – Poluostrov
Port. – Portugal, Portuguese
Prom. – Promontory
Prov. – Province, Provincial
Pt. – Point
Pta. – Ponta, Punta
Pte. – Pointe
Qué. – Québec
Queens. – Queensland
R. – Rio, River
R.I. – Rhode Island
R.S.F.S.R. – Russian Soviet Federal Socialist Republic
Ra.(s). – Range(s)
Raj. – Rajasthan
Reg. – Region
Rep. – Republic
Res. – Reserve, Reservoir
Rhld. – Pfz. – Rheinland – Pfalz
S. – San, South
S. Afr. – South Africa
S. Austral. – South Australia
S.D. – South Dakota
S.-Holst. – Schleswig-Holstein
S.I. – South Island
S. Leone – Sierra Leone
S.S.R. – Soviet Socialist Republic
S.-U. – Sinkiang-Uighur
Sa. – Serra, Sierra
Sard. – Sardinia
Sask. – Saskatchewan
Scot. – Scotland
Sd. – Sound
Sept. – Septentrionale
Sib. – Siberia
Som. – Somerset
Span. – Spanish
Sprs. – Springs
St. – Saint
Sta. – Santa, Station
Staffs. – Staffordshire
Ste. – Sainte
Sto. – Santo
Str. – Strait, Stretto
Switz. – Switzerland
T.O. – Telegraph Office
Tas. – Tasmania
Tenn. – Tennessee
Terr. – Territory
Tex. – Texas
Tg. – Tanjung
Thai. – Thailand
Tipp. – Tipperary
Trans. – Transvaal
U.K. – United Kingdom
U.S.A. – United States of America
U.S.S.R. – Union of Soviet Socialist Republics
Ukr. – Ukraine
Ut.P. – Uttar Pradesh
Utd. – United
Va. – Virginia
Vdkhr. – Vodokhranilishche
Venez. – Venezuela
Vic. – Victoria
Viet. – Vietnam
Vol. – Volcano
Vt. – Vermont
W. – Wadi, West
W.A. – Western Australia
W. Isles – Western Isles
Wash. – Washington
Wilts. – Wiltshire
Wis. – Wisconsin
Wlkp. – Wielkopolski
Wyo. – Wyoming
Yorks. – Yorkshire
Yug. – Yugoslavia
Zimb. – Zimbabwe

Please refer to the table at the end of the index for recent placename changes in Angola, Iran, Madagascar, Mozambique, Vietnam and Zimbabwe. There is also a table giving the Pin Yin equivalents of the modified Wade-Giles nameforms for the principal Chinese placenames which appear in this Atlas.

Aabenraa-Sønderborg Amt □ Afognak I

Aabenraa-Sønderborg Amt □ **73** 55 0N 9 30 E
Aachen **48** 50 47N 6 4 E
Aadorf **15** 47 30N 8 55 E
Aaiun **116** 27 9N 13 12W
Aal **73** 55 39N 8 18 E
Aâlâ en Nîl □ **123** 8 50N 29 55 E
Aalen **49** 48 49N 10 6 E
Aalma ech Chaab **90** 33 7N 35 9 E
Aalsmeer **46** 52 17N 4 43 E
Aalsö **73** 56 23N 10 52 E
Aalst, Belg. **47** 50 56N 4 2 E
Aalst, Neth. **152** 50 57N 4 20 E
Aalten **46** 51 56N 6 35 E
Aalter **47** 51 5N 3 28 E
Aarau **50** 47 23N 8 4 E
Aarburg **50** 47 2N 7 16 E
Aardenburg **47** 51 16N 3 28 E
Aare, R. **50** 47 33N 8 14 E
Aareavaara **74** 67 27N 23 29 E
Aargau □ **50** 47 26N 8 10 E
Aarhus Amt □ **73** 56 15N 10 15 E
Aarle **47** 51 30N 5 38 E
Aarschot **47** 50 59N 4 49 E
Aarsele **47** 51 0N 3 26 E
Aartrijke **47** 51 7N 3 6 E
Aarwangen **50** 47 15N 7 46 E
Aasleagh **38** 53 37N 9 40W
Aastrup **73** 55 34N 8 49 E
Aba, Congo **126** 3 58N 30 17 E
Aba, Nigeria **121** 5 10N 7 19 E
Âbâ, Jazîrat **123** 13 30N 32 31 E
Abadan **92** 30 22N 48 20 E
Abade, Ethiopia **123** 9 22N 38 3 E
Abade, Iran **93** 31 8N 52 40 E
Abadin **56** 43 21N 7 29W
Abadla **118** 31 2N 2 45W
Abaeté **171** 19 9 S 45 27W
Abaeté, R. **171** 18 2 S 45 12W
Abaetetuba **170** 1 40 S 48 50W
Abai **173** 25 58 S 55 54W
Abak **121** 4 58N 7 50 E
Abakaliki **121** 6 22N 8 2 E
Abakan **77** 53 40N 91 10 E
Abal Nam **122** 25 20N 38 37 E
Abalemma **121** 16 12N 7 50 E
Aballetuba **170** 1 40 S 51 15W
Abanilla **59** 38 12N 1 3W
Abano Terme **63** 45 22N 11 46 E
Abarán **59** 38 12N 1 23W
Abarqu **93** 31 10N 53 20 E
Abasan **90** 31 19N 34 21 E
Abasberes **123** 11 33N 35 23 E
Abashiri **112** 44 0N 144 15 E
Abashiri-Wan **112** 44 0N 144 30 E
Abau **135** 10 11 S 148 46 E
Abaújszántó **53** 48 16N 21 12 E
Abaya L. **123** 6 30N 37 50 E
Abbadia San Salvatore **63** 42 53N 11 40 E
Abbay, R., (Nîl el Azraq) **123** 10 17N 35 22 E
Abbaye, Pt. **156** 46 58N 88 4W
Abbetorp **73** 56 57N 16 8 E
Abbeville, France **43** 50 6N 1 49 E
Abbeville, La., U.S.A. **159** 30 0N 92 7W
Abbeville, S.C., U.S.A. **157** 34 12N 82 21W
Abbey **39** 53 7N 8 25W
Abbey Town **32** 54 50N 3 18W
Abbeydorney **39** 52 21N 9 40W
Abbeyfeale **39** 52 23N 9 20W
Abbeyleix **39** 52 55N 7 20W
Abbeyside **39** 52 5N 7 36W
Abbiategrasso **62** 45 23N 8 55 E
Abbieglassie **139** 27 15 S 147 28 E
Abbotabad **94** 34 10N 73 15 E
Abbots Bromley **28** 52 50N 1 52W
Abbots Langley **29** 51 43N 0 25W
Abbotsbury **28** 50 40N 2 36W
Abbotsford, Can. **152** 49 0N 122 10W
Abbotsford, U.S.A. **158** 44 55N 90 20W
Abcoude **46** 52 17N 4 59 E
'Abd al Kuri **91** 12 5N 52 20 E
Abdulino **84** 53 42N 53 40 E
Abe, L. **123** 11 8N 41 47 E
Abéché **117** 13 50N 20 35 E
Abejar **58** 41 48N 2 47W
Abekr **123** 12 45N 28 50 E
Abêlessa **118** 22 58N 4 47 E
Abelti **123** 8 10N 37 30 E
Abengourou **120** 6 42N 3 27W
Åbenrå **73** 55 3N 9 25 E
Abeokuta **121** 7 3N 3 19 E
Aber **126** 2 12N 32 25 E
Aber-soch **31** 52 50N 4 31W
Aberaeron **31** 52 15N 4 16W
Aberayron = Aberaeron **31** 52 15N 4 16W
Abercarn **31** 51 39N 3 9W
Aberchirder **37** 57 34N 2 40W
Abercorn **139** 25 12 S 151 5 E
Abercorn = Mbala **127** 8 46 S 31 17 E
Abercrave **31** 51 48N 3 42W
Aberdare **31** 51 43N 3 27W
Aberdare Ra. **126** 0 15 S 36 50 E
Aberdaron **31** 52 48N 4 41W
Aberdeen, Austral. **141** 32 9 S 150 56 E
Aberdeen, Can. **153** 52 20N 106 8W
Aberdeen, S. Afr. **128** 32 28 S 24 2 E
Aberdeen, U.K. **37** 57 9N 2 6W
Aberdeen, Md., U.S.A. **162** 39 30N 76 14W
Aberdeen, S.D., U.S.A. **158** 45 30N 98 30W
Aberdeen, Wash., U.S.A. **160** 47 0N 123 50W
Aberdeen (□) **26** 57 18N 2 30W
Aberdour **35** 56 2N 3 18W
Aberdovey **31** 52 33N 4 3W
Aberdulais **31** 51 41N 3 46W
Aberfeldy, Austral. **141** 37 42 S 146 22 E
Aberfeldy, U.K. **37** 56 37N 3 50W
Aberffraw **31** 53 11N 4 28W
Aberfoyle **34** 56 10N 4 23W
Abergaria-a-Velha **56** 40 41N 8 32W
Abergavenny **31** 51 49N 3 1W
Abergele **31** 53 17N 3 35W
Abergwili **31** 51 52N 4 18W
Abergynolwyn **31** 52 39N 3 58W
Aberkenfig **31** 51 33N 3 36W
Aberlady **35** 56 0N 2 51W
Abernathy **159** 33 49N 101 49W
Abernethy **35** 56 19N 3 18W
Aberporth **31** 52 8N 4 32W
Abersychan **31** 51 44N 3 3W
Abertillery **31** 51 44N 3 9W
Aberystwyth **31** 52 25N 4 6W
Abha **122** 18 0N 42 34 E
Abhayapuri **98** 26 24N 90 38 E
Abidiya **122** 18 18N 34 3 E
Abidjan **120** 5 26N 3 58W
Abilene, Kans., U.S.A. **158** 39 0N 97 16W
Abilene, Texas, U.S.A. **159** 32 22N 99 40W
Abingdon, U.K. **28** 51 40N 1 17W
Abingdon, Ill., U.S.A. **158** 40 53N 90 23W
Abingdon, Va., U.S.A. **157** 36 46N 81 56W
Abington **35** 55 30N 3 42W
Abington Reef **138** 18 0 S 149 35 E
Abitan L. **153** 60 27N 107 15W
Abitan, R. **153** 59 53N 109 3W
Abitibi L. **150** 48 40N 79 40W
Abiy Adi **123** 13 39N 39 3 E
Abkhaz A.S.S.R. □ **83** 43 0N 41 0 E
Abkit **77** 64 10N 157 10 E
Abnûb **122** 27 18N 31 4 E
Åbo = Turku **75** 60 27N 22 14 E
Abo, Massif d' **119** 21 41N 16 8 E
Abocho **121** 7 35N 6 56 E
Abohar **94** 30 10N 74 10 E
Aboisso **120** 5 30N 3 5W
Aboméy **121** 7 10N 2 5 E
Abondance **45** 46 18N 6 42 E
Abong Mbang **124** 4 0N 13 8 E
Abonnema **121** 4 41N 6 49 E
Abony **53** 47 12N 20 3 E
Aboso **120** 5 23N 1 57W
Abou Deïa **117** 11 20N 19 20 E
Aboyne **37** 57 4N 2 48W
Abqaiq **92** 26 0N 49 45 E
Abra Pampa **172** 22 43 S 65 42W
Abrantes **57** 39 24N 8 7W
Abraveses **56** 40 41N 7 55 E
Abreojos, Pta. **164** 26 50N 113 40W
Abreschviller **43** 48 39N 7 6 E
Abrets, Les **45** 45 32N 5 35 E
Abri, Esh Shimâliya, Sudan **123** 20 50N 30 27 E
Abri, Kordofân, Sudan **123** 11 40N 30 21 E
Abrolhos, Arquipélago dos **171** 18 0 S 38 30W
Abrolhos, banka **171** 18 0 S 38 0W
Abrud **70** 46 19N 23 5 E
Abruzzi □ **63** 42 15N 14 0 E
Absaroka Ra. **160** 44 40N 110 0W
Abū al Khasib **92** 30 25N 48 0 E
Abū 'Ali **92** 27 20N 49 27 E
Abu Arish **91** 16 53N 42 48 E
Abû Ballas **122** 24 26N 27 36 E
Abu Deleiq **123** 15 57N 33 48 E
Abū Dhabī **93** 24 28N 54 36 E
Abû Dis **90** 31 47N 35 16 E
Abu Dis **122** 19 12N 33 38 E
Abu Dom **123** 16 18N 32 25 E
Abû Gabra **123** 11 2N 26 50 E
Abū Ghōsh **90** 31 48N 35 6 E
Abû Gubeiha **123** 11 30N 31 15 E
Abu Habl, W. **123** 12 37N 31 0 E
Abu Hamed **122** 19 32N 33 13 E
Abû Haraz, Esh Shimâliya, Sudan **122** 19 8N 32 18 E
Abû Haraz, Nîl el Azraq, Sudan **123** 14 35N 34 30 E
Abû Higar **123** 12 50N 33 59 E
Abu Kamal **92** 34 30N 41 0 E
Abu Markha **92** 25 4N 38 22 E
Abu Qîr **122** 31 18N 30 0 E
Abu Qireiya **122** 24 5N 35 28 E
Abu Qurqâs **122** 28 1N 30 44 E
Abu Salama **122** 27 10N 35 51 E
Abû Simbel **122** 22 18N 31 40 E
Abu Tig **122** 27 4N 31 15 E
Abu Tiga **123** 12 47N 34 12 E
Abû Zabad **123** 12 25N 29 10 E
Abu Zenîma **122** 29 0N 33 15 E
Abuja **121** 9 16N 7 2 E
Abunã **174** 9 40 S 65 20W
Abunã, R. **174** 9 41 S 65 20W
Aburatsu **110** 31 34N 131 24 E
Aburo, Mt. **126** 2 4N 30 53 E
Abut Hd. **143** 43 7 S 170 15 E
Abwong **123** 9 2N 32 14 E
Åby **73** 58 40N 16 10 E
Aby, Lagune **120** 5 15N 3 14W
Acacías **174** 3 59N 73 46W
Acajutla **166** 13 36N 89 50W
Açallândia **170** 5 0 S 47 50W
Acámbaro **164** 20 0N 100 40W
Acaponeta **164** 22 30N 105 20W
Acapulco de Juárez **165** 16 51N 99 56W
Acarai, Serra **175** 1 50N 57 50W
Acaraú **170** 2 53 S 40 7W
Acari **170** 6 31 S 36 38W
Acarigua **174** 9 33N 69 12W
Acatlan **165** 18 10N 98 3W
Acayucán **165** 17 59N 94 58W
Accéglio **62** 44 28N 6 59 E
Accomac **156** 37 43N 75 40W
Accra **121** 5 35N 0 6W
Accrington **32** 53 46N 2 22W
Acebal **172** 33 20 S 60 50W
Aceh □ **102** 4 0N 97 30 E
Acerenza **65** 40 50N 15 58 E
Acerra **65** 40 57N 14 22 E
Aceuchal **57** 38 39N 6 30W
Achaguas **174** 7 46N 68 14W
Achak Gomba **99** 33 30N 96 25 E
Achalpur **96** 21 22N 77 32 E
Achavanich **37** 58 22N 3 25W
Achel **47** 51 15N 5 29 E
A'ch'eng **107** 45 33N 127 0 E
Achenkirch **52** 47 32N 11 45 E
Achensee **52** 47 26N 11 45 E
Acher **94** 23 10N 72 32 E
Achern **49** 48 37N 8 5 E
Acheron, R. **143** 42 16 S 173 4 E
Achill **38** 53 56N 9 55W
Achill Hd. **38** 53 59N 10 15W
Achill I. **38** 53 58N 10 5W
Achill Sd. **38** 53 53N 9 55W
Achillbeg I. **38** 53 51N 9 58W
Achim **48** 53 1N 9 2 E
Achimota **121** 5 35N 0 15W
Achinsk **77** 56 20N 90 20 E
Achisay **85** 43 35N 68 53 E
Achit **84** 56 48N 57 54 E
Achnasheen **36** 57 35N 5 5W
Achnashellach **36** 57 28N 5 20W
Achol **123** 6 35N 31 32 E
A'Chralaig, Mt. **36** 57 11N 5 10W
Acireale **65** 37 37N 15 9 E
Ackerman **159** 33 20N 89 8W
Acklin's I. **167** 22 30N 74 0W
Acland, Mt. **133** 24 50 S 148 20 E
Aclare **38** 54 4N 8 54W
Acle **29** 52 38N 1 32 E
Acme **152** 51 33N 113 30W
Aconcagua **172** 32 50 S 70 0W
Aconcagua □ **172** 32 15 S 70 30W
Aconcagua, Cerro **172** 32 39 S 70 0W
Aconquija, Mt. **172** 27 0 S 66 0W
Acopiara **170** 6 6 S 39 27W
Açores, Is. dos **14** 38 44N 29 0W
Acquapendente **63** 42 45N 11 50 E
Acquasanta **63** 42 46N 13 24 E
Acquaviva delle Fonti **65** 40 53N 16 50 E
Acqui **62** 44 40N 8 28 E
Acre = 'Akko **90** 32 35N 35 4 E
Acre □ **174** 9 1 S 71 0W
Acre, R. **174** 10 45 S 68 25W
Acri **65** 39 29N 16 23 E
Acs **53** 47 42N 18 0 E
Acton Burnell **28** 52 37N 2 41W
Açu **170** 5 34 S 36 54W
Ad Dam **91** 20 33N 44 45 E
Ad Dammam **92** 26 20N 50 5 E
Ad Dar al Hamra **92** 27 20N 37 45 E
Ad Dawhah **93** 25 15N 51 35 E
Ad Dilam **92** 23 55N 47 10 E
Ada, Ethiopia **123** 8 48N 38 51 E
Ada, Ghana **121** 5 44N 0 40 E
Ada, Minn., U.S.A. **158** 47 20N 96 30W
Ada, Okla., U.S.A. **159** 34 50N 96 45W
Ada, Yugo. **66** 45 49N 20 9 E
Adair C. **12** 71 50N 71 0W
Adaja, R. **56** 41 15N 4 50W
Adale **91** 2 58N 46 27 E
Ådalslinden **72** 63 27N 16 55 E
Adam **93** 22 15N 57 28 E
Adamantina **171** 21 42 S 51 4W
Adamaoua, Massif de l' **121** 7 20N 12 20 E
Adamawa Highlands = Adamaoua **121** 7 20N 12 20 E
Adamello, Mt. **62** 46 10N 10 34 E
Adami Tulu **123** 7 53N 38 41 E
Adaminaby **141** 36 0 S 148 45 E
Adamovka **84** 51 32N 59 56 E
Adams, Mass., U.S.A. **162** 42 38N 73 8W
Adams, N.Y., U.S.A. **162** 43 50N 76 3W
Adams, Wis., U.S.A. **158** 43 59N 89 50W
Adam's Bridge **97** 9 15N 79 40 E
Adams L. **152** 51 10N 119 40W
Adams Mt. **160** 46 10N 121 28W
Adam's Peak **97** 6 55N 80 45 E
Adamuz **57** 38 2N 4 32W
Adana **92** 37 0N 35 16 E
Adanero **56** 40 56N 4 36W
Adapazari **92** 40 48N 30 25 E
Adarama **123** 17 10N 34 52 E
Adare **39** 52 34N 8 48W
Adare, C. **13** 71 0 S 171 0 E
Adavale **139** 25 52 S 144 32 E
Adayio **123** 14 29N 40 50 E
Adda, R. **62** 45 25N 9 30 E
Addis Ababa = Addis Abeba **123** 9 2N 38 42 E
Addis Abeba **123** 9 2N 38 42 E
Addis Alem **123** 9 0N 38 17 E
Addlestone **29** 51 22N 0 30W
Addo **29** 33 32 S 25 44 E
Addu Atoll **87** 0 30 S 73 0 E
Adebour **121** 13 17N 11 50 E
Adel **157** 31 10N 83 28W
Adelaide, Austral. **140** 34 52 S 138 30 E
Adelaide, Bahamas **166** 25 0N 77 31W
Adelaide I. **13** 67 15 S 68 30W
Adelaide Pen. **148** 68 15N 97 30W
Adelaide River **136** 13 15 S 131 7 E
Adelanto **163** 34 35N 117 22W
Adelboden **50** 46 29N 7 33 E
Adele, I. **136** 15 32 S 123 9 E
Adélie, Terre **13** 67 0 S 140 0 E
Ademuz **58** 40 5N 1 13W
Aden **91** 12 50N 45 0 E
Aden, G. of **91** 13 0N 50 0 E
Adendorp **128** 33 25 S 24 30 E
Adhoi **94** 23 26N 70 32 E
Adi **103** 4 15 S 133 30 E
Adi Daro **123** 14 20N 38 14 E
Adi Keyih **123** 14 51N 39 22 E
Adi Kwala **123** 14 38N 38 48 E
Adi Ugri **123** 14 58N 38 48 E
Adieu, C. **137** 32 0 S 132 10 E
Adieu Pt. **136** 15 14 S 124 35 E
Adigala **123** 10 24N 42 15 E
Adige, R. **63** 45 9N 11 25 E
Adigrat **123** 14 20N 39 26 E
Adilabad **96** 19 33N 78 35 E
Adin **160** 41 10N 121 0W
Adin Khel **93** 32 45N 68 5 E
Adinkerke **47** 51 5N 2 36 E
Adirampattinam **97** 10 28N 79 20 E
Adirondack Mts. **156** 44 0N 74 15W
Adis Dera **123** 10 12N 38 46 E
Adjohon **121** 6 41N 2 32 E
Adjud **70** 46 7N 27 10 E
Adjumani **126** 3 20N 31 50 E
Adlavik Is. **151** 55 2N 58 45W
Adler **83** 43 28N 39 52 E
Adliswil **51** 47 19N 8 32 E
Admer **119** 20 21N 5 27 E
Admer, Erg d' **119** 24 0N 9 5 E
Admiralty B. **13** 62 0 S 59 0W
Admiralty G. **136** 14 20 S 125 55 E
Admiralty I. **147** 57 40N 134 35W
Admiralty Inlet **160** 48 0N 122 40W
Admiralty Is. **135** 2 0 S 147 0 E
Admiralty Ra. **13** 72 0 S 164 0 E
Ado **121** 6 36N 2 56 E
Ado Ekiti **121** 7 38N 5 12 E
Adok **123** 8 10N 30 20 E
Adola **123** 11 14N 41 44 E
Adonara **103** 8 15 S 123 5 E
Adoni **97** 15 33N 77 18W
Adony **53** 47 6N 18 52 E
Adour, R. **44** 43 32N 1 32W
Adra, India **95** 23 30N 86 42 E
Adra, Spain **59** 36 43N 3 3W
Adraj **91** 20 1N 51 0 E
Adrano **65** 37 40N 14 49 E
Adrar **118** 27 51N 0 11W
Adrar des Iforhas **121** 19 40N 1 40 E
Adrasman **85** 40 38N 69 58 E
Adré **117** 13 40N 22 20 E
Adri **119** 27 32N 13 2 E
Ádria **63** 45 4N 12 3 E
Adrian, Mich., U.S.A. **156** 41 55N 84 0W
Adrian, Tex., U.S.A. **159** 35 19N 102 37W
Adriatic Sea **60** 43 0N 16 0 E
Adrigole **39** 51 44N 9 42W
Adua **103** 1 45 S 129 50 E
Aduku **126** 2 03N 32 45 E
Adula **51** 46 30N 9 3 E
Adung Long **98** 28 7N 97 42 E
Adur **97** 9 8N 76 40 E
Adwa, Ethiopia **123** 14 15N 38 52 E
Adwa, Si Arab. **92** 27 15N 42 35 E
Adwick le Street **33** 53 35N 1 12W
Adzhar A.S.S.R. □ **83** 42 0N 42 0 E
Adzopé **120** 6 7N 3 49W
Æbelø I. **73** 55 39N 10 10 E
Æbeltoft **73** 56 12N 10 41 E
Æbeltoft Vig. B. **73** 56 9N 10 35 E
Ægean Is. **61** 38 0N 25 0 E
Ægean Sea **61** 37 0N 25 0 E
Aenemuiden **47** 51 30N 3 40 E
Ænes **71** 60 5N 6 8 E
Æolian Is. = Eólie, I. **65** 38 40N 15 7 E
Aerhchin Shanmo **105** 38 0N 88 0 E
Aerhshan **105** 47 93N 119 59 E
Aerht'ai Shan **105** 48 0N 90 0 E
Æro **73** 54 53N 10 20 E
Ærø **73** 54 52N 10 25 E
Ærøskøbing **73** 54 53N 10 24 E
Aesch **50** 47 28N 7 36 E
Aëtós **69** 37 15N 21 50 E
Afafi, Massif d' **119** 22 11N 14 48 E
Afanasyevo **84** 58 52N 53 15 E
Afándou **69** 36 18N 28 12 E
Afarag, Erg **118** 23 50N 2 47 E
Afdera, Mt. **123** 13 16N 41 5 E
Affreville = Khemis Miliania **118** 36 11N 2 14 E
Affric, L. **36** 57 15N 5 5W
Affric, R. **37** 57 15N 4 50W
Afghanistan ■ **93** 33 0N 65 0 E
Afgoi **91** 2 7N 44 59 E
Afif **92** 23 53N 42 56 E
Afikpo **121** 5 53N 7 54 E
Aflisses, O. **118** 28 30N 0 50 E
Aflou **118** 34 7N 2 3 E
Afodo **123** 10 18N 34 49 E
Afogados da Ingàzeira **170** 7 45 S 37 39W
Afognak I. **147** 58 10N 152 50W

Afragola Al Wakrah

Afragola **65** 40 54N 14 15 E
Africa **114** 10 0N 20 0 E
Afton **162** 42 14N 75 31W
Aftout **118** 26 50N 3 45W
Afuá **170** 0 15 S 50 10W
Afula **90** 32 37N 35 17 E
Afyon Karahisar **92** 38 20N 30 15 E
Agadès **121** 16 58N 7 59 E
Agadir **118** 30 28N 9 35W
Agadir Tissint **118** 29 57N 7 16W
Agano, R. **112** 37 50N 139 30 E
Agapa **77** 71 27N 89 15 E
Agapovka **84** 53 18N 59 8 E
Agar **94** 23 40N 76 2 E
Agaro **123** 7 50N 36 38 E
Agartala **98** 23 50N 91 23 E
Agassiz **152** 49 14N 121 46W
Agat **123** 15 38N 38 16 E
Agattu I. **147** 52 25N 172 30 E
Agbelouvé **121** 6 35N 1 14 E
Agboville **120** 5 55N 4 15W
Agdam **83** 40 0N 46 58 E
Agdash **83** 40 44N 47 22 E
Agde **44** 43 19N 3 28 E
Agde, C. d' **44** 43 16N 3 28 E
Agdz **118** 30 47N 6 30W
Agen **44** 44 12N 0 38 E
Ageo **111** 35 58N 139 36 E
Ager Tay **119** 20 0N 17 41 E
Agersø **73** 55 13N 11 12 E
Agger **73** 56 47N 8 13 E
Aggersborg **73** 57 0N 9 16 E
Aggius **64** 40 56N 9 4 E
Aghalee **38** 54 32N 6 17W
Aghavannagh **39** 52 55N 6 25W
Aghern **39** 52 5N 8 10W
Aghil Mts. **93** 36 0N 77 0 E
Aghil Pass **93** 36 15N 76 35 E
Aginskoye **77** 51 6N 114 32 E
Agira **65** 37 40N 14 30 E
Aglou **118** 29 50N 9 50W
Agly, R. **44** 42 46N 3 3 E
Agna Branca **170** 7 57 S 47 19W
Agnes **137** 28 0 S 120 30 E
Agnew **137** 28 1 S 120 30 E
Agnews Hill **38** 54 51N 5 55W
Agnibilékrou **120** 7 10N 3 11W
Agnita **70** 45 59N 24 40 E
Agnone **65** 41 49N 14 20 E
Ago **111** 33 36N 135 29 E
Agofie **121** 8 27N 0 15 E
Agogna, R. **62** 45 8N 8 42 E
Agogo, Ghana **121** 6 50N 1 1W
Agogo, Sudan **123** 7 50N 28 45 E
Agon **42** 49 2N 1 34W
Agön **72** 61 33N 17 25 E
Agon I. **72** 61 34N 17 23 E
Agordo **63** 46 18N 12 2 E
Agout, R. **44** 43 47N 1 41 E
Agra **94** 27 17N 77 58 E
Agrado **174** 2 15N 75 46W
Agramunt **58** 41 48N 1 6 E
Agreda **58** 41 51N 1 55W
Agri **73** 56 14N 10 32 E
Ağri Daği **92** 39 50N 44 15 E
Agri, R. **65** 40 17N 16 15 E
Agrigento **64** 37 19N 13 33 E
Agrinion **69** 38 37N 21 27 E
Agrøpoli **65** 40 23N 14 59 E
Agryz **84** 56 33N 53 2 E
Agua Caliente, Mexico **164** 26 30N 108 20W
Agua Caliente, U.S.A. **163** 32 29N 116 59W
Agua Caliente Springs **163** 32 56N 116 19W
Agua Clara **175** 20 25 S 52 45W
Agua Prieta **164** 31 20N 109 32W
Aguadas **174** 5 40N 75 38W
Aguadilla **147** 18 27N 67 10W
Aguadulce **166** 8 15N 80 32W
Aguanaval, R. **164** 23 45N 103 10W
Aguanga **163** 33 27N 116 51W
Aguanus, R. **151** 50 13N 62 5W
Aguapeí, R. **171** 21 0 S 51 0W
Aguapey, R. **172** 29 7 S 56 36W
Aguaray Guazú, R. **172** 24 47 S 57 19W
Aguarico, R. **174** 0 0 77 30W
Aguas Blancas **172** 24 15 S 69 55W
Aguas Calientes, Sierra de **172** 25 26 S 67 27W
Águas Formosas **171** 17 5 S 40 57W
Aguas, R. **58** 41 20N 0 30W
Aguascalientes **164** 22 0N 102 12W
Aguascalientes □ **164** 22 0N 102 20W
Agudo **57** 38 59N 4 52W
Agueda **56** 40 34N 8 27W
Agueda, R. **56** 40 45N 6 37W
Aguelt el Kadra **118** 25 3N 7 6W
Agueni N'Ikko **118** 32 29N 5 47W
Aguié **121** 13 31N 7 46 E
Aguilafuente **56** 41 13N 4 7W
Aguilar **57** 37 31N 4 40W
Aguilar de Campóo **56** 42 47N 4 15W
Aguilares **172** 27 26 S 65 35W
Aguilas **59** 37 23N 1 35W
Aguja, C. de la **174** 11 18N 74 12W
Aguja, Pta. **174** 6 0 S 81 0W
Agulaa **123** 13 40N 39 40 E
Agulhas, Kaap **128** 34 52 S 20 0 E
Agung **102** 8 20 S 115 28 E
Agur, Israel **90** 31 42N 34 55 E
Agur, Uganda **126** 2 28N 32 55 E
Agůš **70** 46 28N 26 15 E
Agusan, R. **103** 9 20N 125 50 E
Agvali **83** 42 36N 46 8 E
Aha Mts. **128** 19 45 S 21 0 E
Ahaggar **119** 23 0N 6 30 E
Ahamansu **121** 7 38N 0 35 E
Ahar **92** 38 35N 47 0 E
Ahascragh **38** 53 24N 8 20W
Ahaura **143** 42 20 S 171 32 E
Ahaura, R. **143** 42 21 S 171 34 E
Ahaus **48** 52 4N 7 1 E
Ahelledjem **119** 26 37N 6 58 E
Ahimanawa Ra. **130** 39 5 S 176 30 E
Ahipara B. **142** 35 5 S 173 5 E
Ahiri **96** 19 30N 80 0 E
Ahlen **48** 51 45N 7 52 E
Ahmad Wal **94** 29 18N 65 58 E
Ahmadabad (Ahmedabad) **94** 23 0N 72 40 E
Ahmadnagar (Ahmednagar) **96** 19 7N 74 46 E
Ahmadpur **94** 29 12N 71 10 E
Ahmar Mts. **123** 9 20N 41 15 E
Ahoada **121** 5 8N 6 36 E
Ahoghill **38** 54 52N 6 23W
Ahome **164** 25 55N 109 11W
Ahr, R. **48** 50 25N 6 52 E
Ahrensbök **48** 54 0N 10 34 E
Ahrweiler **48** 50 31N 7 3 E
Ahsā, Wahatāal **92** 25 50N 49 0 E
Ahuachapán **166** 13 54N 89 52W
Ahuriri, R. **143** 44 31 S 170 12 E
Åhus **73** 55 56N 14 18 E
Ahvāz **92** 31 20N 48 40 E
Ahvenanmaa **75** 60 15N 20 0 E
Ahzar **121** 15 30N 3 20 E
Aibaq **93** 36 15N 68 5 E
Aichach **49** 48 28N 11 9 E
Aichi-ken □ **111** 35 0N 137 15 E
Aidone **65** 37 26N 14 26 E
Aiello Cálabro **65** 39 6N 16 12 E
Aigle **50** 46 18N 6 58 E
Aignay-le-Duc **43** 47 40N 4 43 E
Aigre **44** 45 54N 0 1 E
Aigua **173** 34 13 S 54 46W
Aigueperse **44** 46 3N 3 13 E
Aigues-Mortes **45** 43 35N 4 12 E
Aiguilles **45** 44 47N 6 51 E
Aiguillon **44** 44 18N 0 21 E
Aiguillon, L' **44** 46 20N 1 16W
Aigurande **44** 46 27N 1 49 E
Aihui **105** 50 16N 127 28 E
Aija **174** 9 50 S 77 45W
Aijal **98** 23 40N 92 44 E
Aiken **157** 33 34N 81 50W
Ailao Shan **108** 24 0N 101 30 E
Aillant-sur-Tholon **43** 47 52N 3 20 E
Aillik **151** 55 11N 59 18W
Ailly-sur-Noye **43** 49 45N 2 20 E
Ailsa Craig, I. **34** 55 15N 5 7W
Aim **77** 59 0N 133 55 E
Aimere **103** 8 45 S 121 3 E
Aimogasta **172** 28 33 S 66 50W
Aimorés **171** 19 30 S 41 4W
Aimorés, Serra dos **171** 17 50 S 40 30W
Ain □ **45** 46 5N 5 20 E
Ain Banaiyah **93** 23 0N 51 0 E
Aïn-Beïda **119** 35 50N 7 35 E
Ain ben Khellil **118** 33 15N 0 49W
Ain Ben Tili **118** 25 59N 9 27W
Aïn Benian **118** 36 48N 2 55 E
'Ain Dalla **122** 27 20N 27 23 E
Ain Dar **92** 25 55N 49 10 E
Ain el Mafki **122** 27 30N 28 15 E
Ain Girba **122** 29 20N 25 14 E
Aïn M'lila **119** 36 2N 6 35 E
Ain Qeiqab **122** 29 42N 24 55 E
Ain, R. **45** 45 52N 5 11 E
Aïn Rich **118** 34 38N 24 55 E
Aïn-Sefra **118** 32 47N 0 37W
Ain Sheikh Murzûk **122** 26 47N 27 45 E
Ain Sukhna **122** 29 32N 32 20 E
Aïn Tédelès **118** 36 0N 0 21 E
Aïn-Témouchent **118** 35 16N 1 8W
Aïn Touta **119** 35 26N 5 54 E
Ain Zeitûn **122** 29 10N 25 48 E
Aïn Zorah **118** 34 37N 3 32W
Ainabo **91** 9 0N 46 25 E
Ainazi **80** 57 50N 24 24 E
Aine Galakka **117** 18 10N 18 30 E
Ainos Óros **69** 38 10N 20 35 E
Ainsdale **32** 53 37N 3 2W
Ainsworth **158** 42 33N 99 52W
Aioi **110** 34 48N 134 28 E
Aion **77** 69 50N 169 0 E
Aipe **174** 3 13N 75 15W
Aïr **121** 18 30N 8 0 E
Airaines **43** 49 58N 1 55 E
Aird Brenish, C. **36** 58 8N 7 8W
Aird, The, dist. **37** 57 26N 4 30W
Airdrie **35** 55 53N 3 57W
Aire **43** 50 37N 2 22 E
Aire, Isla del **58** 39 48N 4 16 E
Aire, R. **43** 49 18N 5 0 E
Aire-sur-l'Adour **44** 43 42N 0 15W
Aireys Inlet **140** 38 29 S 144 5 E
Airolo **51** 46 32N 8 37 E
Airvault **42** 46 50N 0 8W
Aisgill **32** 54 23N 2 21W
Aishihik **147** 61 40N 137 46W
Aisne □ **43** 49 42N 3 40 E
Aisne, R. **43** 49 26N 2 50 E
Aït Melloul **118** 30 25N 9 29W
Aitana, Sierra de **59** 38 35N 0 24W
Aitape **135** 3 11 S 142 22 E
Aith **37** 59 8N 2 38W
Aitkin **158** 46 32N 93 43W
Aitolía Kai Akarnanía □ **69** 38 45N 21 18 E
Aitolikón **69** 38 26N 21 21 E
Aitoska Planina **67** 42 45N 27 30 E
Aiuaba **170** 6 38 S 40 7W
Aiud **70** 46 19N 23 44 E
Aix-en-Provence **45** 43 32N 5 27 E
Aix-la-Chapelle = Aachen **48** 50 47N 6 4 E
Aix-les-Bains **45** 45 41N 5 53 E
Aix-les-Thermes **44** 42 43N 1 51 E
Aix-sur-Vienne **44** 45 48N 1 8 E
Aiyang, Mt. **135** 5 10 S 141 20 E
Aiyangpienmen **107** 40 55N 124 30 E
Aiyansh **152** 55 17N 129 2W
Aiyina **69** 37 45N 23 26 E
Aiyínion **68** 40 28N 22 28 E
Aiyion **69** 38 15N 22 5 E
Aizenay **42** 46 44N 1 38W
Aizpute **80** 56 43N 21 40 E
Aizuwakamatsu **112** 37 30N 139 56 E
Ajaccio **45** 41 55N 8 40 E
Ajaccio, G. d' **45** 41 52N 8 40 E
Ajalpán **165** 18 22N 97 15W
Ajana **137** 27 56 S 114 35 E
Ajanta Ra. **96** 20 28N 75 50 E
Ajax, Mt. **143** 42 35 S 172 5 E
Ajdabiyah **119** 30 54N 20 4 E
Ajdīr, Raîs **119** 33 4N 11 44 E
Ajdovščina **63** 45 54N 13 54 E
Ajibar **123** 10 35N 38 36 E
'Ajlun **90** 32 18N 35 47 E
Ajman **93** 25 25N 55 30 E
Ajmer **94** 26 28N 74 37 E
Ajo **161** 32 18N 112 54W
Ajoie **50** 47 22N 7 0 E
Ajok **123** 9 15N 28 28 E
Ajua **120** 4 50N 1 55W
Ak Dağ **92** 36 30N 30 0 E
Akaba **121** 8 10N 1 2 E
Akabli **118** 26 49N 1 31 E
Akaishi-Dake **111** 35 27N 138 9 E
Akaishi-Sammyaku **111** 35 25N 138 10 E
Akaki Beseka **123** 8 55N 38 45 E
Akala **123** 15 39N 36 13 E
Akaroa **143** 43 49 S 172 59 E
Akaroa Harb. **131** 43 54 S 172 59 E
Akasha **122** 21 10N 30 32 E
Akashi **110** 34 45N 135 0 E
Akbou **119** 36 31N 4 31 E
Akbulak **84** 51 1N 55 37 E
Akdala **85** 45 2N 74 35 E
Akechi **111** 35 18N 137 23 E
Akegbe **121** 6 17N 7 28 E
Akelamo **103** 1 35N 129 40 E
Akershus Fylke □ **71** 60 10N 11 15 E
Akeru, R. **96** 17 25N 80 0 E
Aketi **124** 2 38N 23 47 E
Akhaïa □ **69** 38 5N 21 45 E
Akhalkalaki **83** 41 27N 43 25 E
Akhaltsikhe **83** 41 40N 43 0 E
Akharnaí **69** 38 5N 23 44 E
Akhelóös, R. **69** 39 5N 21 25 E
Akhendriá **69** 34 58N 25 16 E
Akhéron, R. **68** 39 31N 20 29 E
Akhisar **92** 38 56N 27 48 E
Akhladhókambos **69** 37 31N 22 35 E
Akhmîm **122** 26 31N 31 47 E
Akhnur **95** 32 52N 74 45 E
Akhtopol **67** 42 6N 27 56 E
Akhtubinsk (Petropavlovskiy) **83** 48 27N 46 7 E
Akhty **83** 41 30N 47 45 E
Akhtyrka **80** 50 25N 35 0 E
Aki **110** 33 30N 133 54 E
Aki-Nada **110** 34 5N 132 40 E
Akiak **147** 60 50N 161 12W
Akimiski I. **150** 52 50N 81 30W
Akimovka **82** 46 44N 35 0 E
Akincilar **69** 37 57N 27 25 E
Akinum **138** 6 15 S 149 30 E
Åkirkeby **73** 55 4N 14 55 E
Akita **112** 39 45N 140 0 E
Akita-ken □ **112** 39 40N 140 30 E
Akjoujt **120** 19 45N 14 15W
Akka **118** 29 28N 8 9W
'Akko **90** 32 35N 35 4 E
Akkol, Kazakh, U.S.S.R. **85** 45 0N 75 39 E
Akkol, Kazakh, U.S.S.R. **85** 43 36N 70 45 E
Akköy **69** 37 30N 27 18 E
Akkrum **46** 53 3N 5 50 E
Aklampa **121** 8 15N 2 10 E
Aklavik, Can. **147** 68 12N 135 0W
Aklavik, N.W.T., Can. **147** 68 12N 135 0W
Akmuz **85** 41 15N 76 10 E
Aknoul **118** 34 40N 3 55W
Akō **110** 34 45N 134 24 E
Ako **121** 10 19N 10 48 E
Akobo, R. **123** 7 10N 34 25 E
Akola **96** 20 42N 77 2 E
Akonolinga **121** 3 50N 12 18 E
Akordat **123** 15 30N 37 40 E
Akosombo Dam **121** 6 20N 0 5 E
Ak'osu **105** 41 15N 80 14 E
Akot, India **96** 21 10N 77 10 E
Akot, Sudan **123** 6 31N 30 9 E
Akpatok I. **149** 60 25N 68 8W
Akranes **74** 64 19N 22 6W
Åkrehamn **71** 59 15N 5 10 E
Akreïjit **120** 18 19N 9 11W
Akrítas Venétiko, Ákra **69** 36 43N 21 54 E
Akron, Colo., U.S.A. **158** 40 13N 103 15W
Akron, Ohio, U.S.A. **156** 41 7N 81 31W
Akrotiri, Ákra **68** 40 26N 25 27W
Aksai Chih, L. **95** 35 15N 79 55 E
Aksaray **92** 38 25N 34 2 E
Aksarka **76** 66 31N 67 50 E
Aksehir **92** 38 18N 31 30 E
Aksenovo Zilovskoye **77** 53 20N 117 40 E
Aksuat, Ozero **84** 51 32N 64 34 E
Aksum **123** 14 5N 38 40 E
Aktash, R.S.F.S.R., U.S.S.R. **84** 52 2N 52 7 E
Aktash, Uzbek S.S.R., U.S.S.R. **85** 39 55N 65 55 E
Aktobe **84** 52 55N 62 22 E
Aktogay **85** 44 25N 76 44 E
Aktyubinsk **79** 50 17N 57 10 E
Aktyuz **85** 42 54N 76 7 E
Aku **121** 6 40N 7 18 E
Akulurak **147** 62 40N 164 35W
Akun I. **147** 54 15N 165 30W
Akune **110** 32 1N 130 12 E
Akure **121** 7 15N 5 5 E
Akureyri **74** 65 40N 18 6W
Akusha **83** 42 18N 47 30 E
Akutan I. **147** 53 30N 166 0W
Akzhar **85** 43 8N 71 37 E
Al Abyār **119** 32 9N 20 29 E
Al Amadiyah **92** 37 5N 43 30 E
Al Amārah **92** 31 55N 47 15 E
Al Aqabah **92** 29 37N 35 0 E
Al Ashkhara **93** 21 50N 59 30 E
Al Ayn al Mugshin **91** 19 35N 54 40 E
Al 'Azīzīyah **119** 32 30N 13 1 E
Al Badi **92** 22 0N 46 35 E
Al Barah **90** 31 55N 35 12 E
Al Barkât **119** 24 56N 10 14 E
Al Basrah **92** 30 30N 47 50 E
Al Baydā **117** 32 30N 21 40 E
Al Bu'ayrât **119** 31 24N 15 44 E
Al Buqay'ah **90** 32 15N 35 30 E
Al Dīwaniyah **92** 32 0N 45 0 E
Al Fallujah **92** 33 20N 43 55 E
Al Fāw **92** 30 0N 48 30 E
Al Hadithan **92** 34 0N 41 13 E
Al Hamad **92** 31 30N 39 30 E
Al Hamar **92** 22 23N 46 6 E
Al Hariq **92** 23 29N 46 27 E
Al Hasakah **92** 36 35N 40 45 E
Al Hauta **91** 16 5N 48 20 E
Al Havy **92** 32 5N 46 5 E
Al Hillah, Iraq **92** 32 30N 44 25 E
Al Hillah, Si Arab. **92** 23 35N 46 50 E
Al Hilwah **92** 23 24N 46 48 E
Al Hindiya **92** 32 30N 44 10 E
Al Hoceïma **118** 35 8N 3 58W
Al Hufrah, Awbārī, Libya **119** 25 32N 14 1 E
Al Hufrah, Misrātah, Libya **119** 29 5N 18 3 E
Al Hufuf **92** 25 25N 49 45 E
Al Husayyāt **119** 30 24N 20 37 E
Al Husn **90** 32 29N 35 52 E
Al Irq **117** 29 5N 21 35 E
Al Ittihad = Madinat al Shaab **91** 12 50N 45 0 E
Al Jahrah **92** 29 25N 47 40 E
Al Jalāmid **92** 31 20N 39 45 E
Al Jarzirah **117** 26 10N 21 20 E
Al Jawf **117** 24 10N 23 24 E
Al Jazir **91** 18 30N 56 31 E
Al Jubail **92** 27 0N 49 50 E
Al Juwara **91** 19 0N 57 13 E
Al Khābūrah **93** 23 57N 57 5 E
Al Khalih **90** 31 32N 35 6 E
Al Khums (Homs) **119** 32 40N 14 17 E
Al Kut **92** 32 30N 46 0 E
Al Kuwayt **92** 29 20N 48 0 E
Al Ladhiqiyah **92** 35 30N 35 45 E
Al Līth **122** 20 9N 40 15 E
Al Madīnah **92** 24 35N 39 52 E
Al-Mafraq **90** 32 17N 36 14 E
Al Majma'ah **92** 25 57N 45 22 E
Al Manamah **93** 26 10N 50 30 E
Al Marj **117** 32 25N 20 30 E
Al Masīrah **91** 20 25N 58 50 E
Al Mawsil **92** 36 15N 43 5 E
Al Miqdadīyah **92** 34 0N 45 0 E
Al Mubarraz **92** 25 30N 49 40 E
Al Muharraq **93** 26 15N 50 40 E
Al Mukha **91** 13 18N 43 15 E
Al Musayyib **92** 32 40N 44 25 E
Al Muwaylih **92** 27 40N 35 30 E
Al Qaddāhīyah **119** 31 15N 15 9 E
Al Qamishli **92** 37 10N 41 10 E
Al Qaryah ash Sharqīyah **119** 30 28N 13 40 E
Al Qaṣabāt **119** 32 39N 14 1 E
Al Qatif **92** 26 35N 50 0 E
Al Qaṭrun **119** 24 56N 15 3 E
Al Quaisūmah **92** 28 10N 46 20 E
Al Quds **90** 31 47N 35 10 E
Al Qunfidha **122** 19 3N 41 4 E
Al Quraiyat **93** 23 17N 58 53 E
Al Qurnah **92** 31 1N 47 25 E
Al 'Ula **92** 26 35N 38 0 E
Al Uqaylah **119** 30 12N 19 10 E
Al Uqayr **92** 25 40N 50 15 E
Al' Uwayqilah **92** 30 30N 42 10 E
Al 'Uyūn **92** 26 30N 43 50 E
Al Wajh **122** 26 10N 36 30 E
Al Wakrah **93** 25 10N 51 40 E

Al Warīah

Almaden

Al Warīah 92 27 50N 47 30 E
Al Wātīyah 119 32 28N 11 57 E
Ala, Italy 62 45 46N 11 0 E
Ala, Sweden 72 61 13N 17 9 E
Ala Shan 105 40 0N 104 0 E
Alabama □ 157 31 0N 87 0W
Alabama, R. 157 31 30N 87 35W
Alaçati 69 38 16N 26 23 E
Alaejos 56 41 18N 5 13W
Alagna Valsésia 62 45 51N 7 56 E
Alagôa Grande 170 7 3 S 35 35W
Alagôas □ 170 9 0 S 36 0W
Alagoinhas 171 12 0 S 38 20W
Alagón 58 41 46N 1 12W
Alagón, R. 56 39 50N 6 50W
Alajuela 166 10 2N 84 8W
Alakamisy 129 21 19 S 47 14 E
Alakurtti 78 67 0N 30 30 E
Alam Ajaib 122 25 55N 27 14 E
Alameda, Spain 57 37 12N 4 39W
Alameda, Calif., U.S.A. 163 37 46N 122 15W
Alameda, N. Mex., U.S.A. 161 35 10N 106 43W
Alameda, S.D., U.S.A. 160 43 2N 112 30W
Alamitos, Sierra de los 164 26 30N 102 20W
Alamo 161 37 21N 115 10W
Alamogordo 161 32 59N 106 0W
Alamos 164 27 0N 109 0W
Alamosa 161 37 30N 106 0W
Åland 75 60 15N 20 0 E
Aland 96 17 36N 76 35 E
Alandroal 57 38 41N 7 24W
Ålands-hav 75 60 10N 19 30 E
Alange, Presa de 57 38 45N 6 18W
Alangouassou 120 7 30N 4 34W
Alanis 57 38 3N 5 43W
Alanya 92 36 38N 32 0 E
Alaotra, L. 129 17 30 S 48 30 E
Alapayevsk 84 57 52N 61 42 E
Alar del Rey 56 42 38N 4 20W
Alaraz 56 40 45N 5 17W
Alaşehir 79 38 23N 28 30 E
Alashantsoch'i 106 38 59N 105 45 E
Alaska □ 147 65 0N 150 0W
Alaska, G. of 147 58 0N 145 0W
Alaska Highway 152 60 0N 130 0W
Alaska Pen. 147 56 0N 160 0W
Alaska Range 147 62 50N 151 0W
Alássio 62 44 1N 8 10 E
Alatri 64 41 44N 13 21 E
Alatyr 81 54 45N 46 35 E
Alatyr, R. 81 54 45N 45 30 E
Alausí 174 2 0 S 78 50W
Álava □ 58 42 48N 2 28W
Alava, C. 160 48 10N 124 40W
Alaverdi 83 41 2N 44 37 E
Alawoona 140 34 45 S 140 30 E
Alaykel 85 40 15N 74 25 E
Alayor 58 39 57N 4 8 E
Alayskiy Khrebet 85 39 45N 72 0 E
Alazan, R. 83 41 25N 46 35 E
Alba 62 44 41N 8 1 E
Alba □ 70 46 10N 23 30 E
Alba de Tormes 56 40 50N 5 30W
Alba-Iulia 70 46 8N 23 39 E
Albac 70 46 28N 23 1 E
Albacete 59 39 0N 1 50W
Albacete □ 59 38 50N 2 0W
Albacutya, L. 140 35 45 S 141 58 E
Ålbæk 73 57 36N 10 25 E
Ålbæk Bugt 73 57 35N 10 40 E
Albaida 59 38 51N 0 31W
Albalate de las Nogueras 58 40 22N 2 18W
Albalate del Arzobispo 58 41 6N 0 31W
Albania ■ 68 41 0N 20 0 E
Albano Laziale 64 41 44N 12 40 E
Albany, Austral. 137 35 1 S 117 58 E
Albany, Ga., U.S.A. 157 31 40N 84 10W
Albany, Minn., U.S.A. 158 45 37N 94 38W
Albany, N.Y., U.S.A. 162 42 29N 73 47W
Albany, Oreg., U.S.A. 160 44 41N 123 0W
Albany, Tex., U.S.A. 159 32 45N 99 20W
Albany, R. 150 52 17N 81 31W
Albardón 172 31 20 S 68 30W
Albarracín 58 40 25N 1 26W
Albarracín, Sierra de 58 40 30N 1 30W
Albatross B. 138 12 45 S 141 30 E
Albatross Pt. 142 38 7 S 174 44 E
Albegna, R. 63 42 40N 11 28 E
Albemarle 157 35 27N 80 15W
Albemarle Sd. 157 36 0N 76 30W
Albenga 62 44 3N 8 12 E
Alberche, R. 56 40 10N 4 30W
Alberdi 172 26 14 S 58 20W
Alberes, Mts. 58 42 28N 2 56W
Alberga 139 27 12 S 135 28 E
Alberga, R. 136 26 50 S 133 40 E
Alberique 59 39 7N 0 31W
Alberni 152 49 20N 124 50W
Albersdorf 48 54 8N 9 19 E
Albert, Austral. 141 32 22 S 147 30 E
Albert, Can. 151 45 51N 64 38W
Albert, France 43 50 0N 2 38 E
Albert Canyon 152 51 8N 117 41W
Albert Edward, Mt. 135 8 20 S 147 24 E
Albert Edward Ra. 136 18 17 S 127 57 E
Albert L., Austral. 140 35 30 S 139 10 E
Albert L., U.S.A. 160 42 40N 120 8W
Albert Lea 158 43 32N 93 20W
Albert, L. = Mobutu Sese Seko, L. 126 1 30N 31 0 E
Albert Nile, R. 126 3 16N 31 38 E
Albert Town 167 22 37N 74 33 E
Alberta □ 152 54 40N 115 0W
Alberti 172 35 1 S 60 16W
Albertinia 128 34 11 S 21 34 E
Albertirsa 53 47 14N 19 37 E
Albertkanaal 47 51 14N 4 26 E
Alberton 151 46 50N 64 0W
Albertville 45 45 40N 6 22 E
Albertville = Kalemie 126 5 55 S 29 9 E
Albi 44 43 56N 2 9 E
Albia 158 41 0N 92 50W
Albina 175 5 37N 54 15W
Albina, Pta. 128 15 52 S 11 44 E
Albino 62 45 47N 9 48 E
Albion, Idaho, U.S.A. 160 42 21N 113 37W
Albion, Mich., U.S.A. 156 42 15N 84 45W
Albion, Nebr., U.S.A. 158 41 47N 98 0W
Alblasserdam 46 51 52N 4 40 E
Albocácer 58 40 21N 0 1 E
Alböke 73 56 57N 16 47 E
Alborán, I. 57 35 57N 3 0W
Alborea 59 39 17N 1 24W
Ålborg 73 57 2N 9 54 E
Ålborg Bugt 73 56 50N 10 35 E
Alborz, Reshteh-Ye Kūkhā-Ye 93 36 0N 52 0 E
Albox 59 37 23N 2 8W
Albreda 152 52 35N 119 10W
Albrighton 28 52 38N 2 17W
Albuera, La 57 38 45N 6 49W
Albufeira 57 37 5N 8 15W
Albula, R. 51 46 38N 9 30 E
Albuñol 59 36 48N 3 11W
Albuquerque 161 35 5N 106 47W
Albuquerque, Cayos de 166 12 10N 81 50W
Alburno, Mte. 65 40 32N 15 20 E
Alburquerque 57 39 15N 6 59W
Albury 141 36 3 S 146 56 E
Albuskjell, oilfield 19 56 40N 3 0 E
Alby 72 62 30N 15 28 E
Alcácer do Sal 57 38 22N 8 33W
Alcalá de Chisvert 58 40 19N 0 13 E
Alcalá de Guadaira 57 37 20N 5 50W
Alcalá de Henares 58 40 28N 3 22W
Alcalá de los Gazules 57 36 29N 5 43W
Alcalá la Real 57 37 27N 3 57W
Alcamo 64 37 59N 12 55 E
Alcanadre 58 42 24N 2 7W
Alcanadre, R. 58 41 43N 0 12W
Alcanar 58 40 33N 0 28 E
Alcanede 57 39 25N 8 49W
Alcanena 57 39 27N 8 40W
Alcañices 57 41 41N 6 21W
Alcaníz 58 41 2N 0 8W
Alcântara 170 2 20 S 44 30W
Alcántara 57 39 41N 6 57W
Alcantara L. 153 60 57N 108 9W
Alcantarilla 59 37 59N 1 12W
Alcaracejos 57 38 24N 4 58W
Alcaraz 59 38 40N 2 29W
Alcaraz, Sierra de 59 38 40N 2 20W
AlcáRovas 57 38 23N 8 9W
Alcarria, La 58 40 31N 2 45W
Alcaudete 57 37 35N 4 5W
Alcázar de San Juan 59 39 24N 3 12W
Alcester 28 52 13N 1 52W
Alcira 59 39 9N 0 30W
Alcoa 157 35 50N 84 0W
Alcobaça, Brazil 171 17 30 S 39 13W
Alcobaça, Port. 57 39 32N 9 0W
Alcobendas 58 40 32N 3 38W
Alcolea del Pinar 58 41 2N 2 28W
Alcora 58 40 5N 0 14W
Alcoutim 57 37 25N 7 28W
Alcova 160 42 37N 106 52W
Alcoy 59 38 43N 0 30W
Alcubierre, Sierra de 58 41 45N 0 22W
Alcublas 58 39 48N 0 43W
Alcudia 58 39 51N 3 9 E
Alcudia, Bahía de 58 39 45N 3 14 E
Alcudia, Sierra de la 57 38 34N 4 30W
Aldabra Is. 11 9 22 S 46 28 E
Aldama 165 22 25N 98 4W
Aldan 77 58 40N 125 30 E
Aldan, R. 77 62 30N 135 10 E
Aldborough 33 54 6N 1 21W
Aldbourne 28 51 28N 1 38W
Aldbrough 33 53 50N 0 7W
Aldeburgh 29 52 9N 1 35 E
Aldeia Nova 57 37 55N 7 24W
Alden I. 71 61 19N 4 45 E
Alder 160 45 27N 112 3W
Alder Pk. 163 35 53N 12 22W
Alderbury 28 51 4N 1 45W
Alderley Edge 32 53 18N 2 15W
Aldermaston 28 51 23N 1 9W
Alderney, I. 42 49 42N 2 12W
Aldershot 29 51 15N 0 43W
Aldersyde 152 50 40N 113 53W
Aldingham 32 54 8N 3 3W
Aledo 158 41 10N 90 50W
Alefa 123 11 55N 36 55 E
Aleg 120 17 3N 13 55W
Alegre 173 20 50 S 41 30W
Alegrete 173 29 40 S 56 0W
Aleisk 76 52 40N 83 0 E
Alejandro Selkirk, I. 131 33 50 S 80 15W
Aleksandriya, U.S.S.R. 79 50 45N 26 22 E
Aleksandriya, U.S.S.R. 82 48 42N 33 3 E
Aleksandriyskaya 83 43 59N 47 0 E
Aleksandrov 81 56 23N 38 44 E
Aleksandrov Gay. 81 50 15N 48 35 E
Aleksandrovac 66 44 28N 21 13 E
Aleksandrovka 82 48 55N 32 20 E
Aleksandrovo 67 43 14N 24 51 E
Aleksandrovsk 84 59 9N 57 33 E
Aleksandrovsk-Sakhaliniskiy 77 50 50N 142 20 E
Aleksandrovskiy Zavod 77 50 40N 117 50 E
Aleksandrovskoye 76 60 35N 77 50 E
Aleksandrów Kujawski 54 52 53N 18 43 E
Aleksandrów Łódzki 54 51 49N 19 17 E
Alekseyevka, R.S.F.S.R., U.S.S.R. 81 50 43N 38 40 E
Alekseyevka, R.S.F.S.R., U.S.S.R. 84 52 35N 51 17 E
Aleksin 81 54 31N 37 9 E
Aleksinac 66 43 31N 21 42 E
Além Paraíba 173 21 52 S 42 41W
Alemania, Argent. 172 25 40 S 65 30W
Alemania, Chile 172 25 10 S 69 55W
Ålen 71 62 51N 11 17 E
Alençon 42 48 27N 0 4 E
Alentejo, Alto- 55 39 0N 7 40W
Alentejo, Baixo- 55 38 0N 8 30W
Alenuihaha Chan. 147 20 25N 156 0W
Aleppo 92 36 10N 37 15 E
Aléria 45 42 5N 9 26 E
Alert B. 152 50 30N 127 35W
Alès 45 44 9N 4 5 E
Aleşd 70 47 3N 22 22 E
Alessándria 62 44 54N 8 37 E
Ålestrup 73 56 42N 9 29 E
Ålesund 71 62 28N 6 12 E
Alet 123 8 14N 29 2 E
Alet-les-Bains 44 43 0N 2 14 E
Aletschgletscher 50 46 28N 8 2 E
Aletschhorn 50 46 28N 8 0 E
Aleutian Is. 147 52 0N 175 0W
Aleutian Ra. 147 55 0N 155 0W
Alexander 158 47 51N 103 40W
Alexander Arch. 147 57 0N 135 0W
Alexander B. 128 28 36 S 16 33 E
Alexander City 157 32 58N 85 57W
Alexander I. 13 69 0 S 70 0W
Alexander, Mt. 137 28 58 S 120 16 E
Alexandra, Austral. 141 37 8 S 145 40 E
Alexandra, N.Z. 143 45 14 S 169 25 E
Alexandra Falls 152 60 29N 116 18W
Alexandria, Austral. 138 19 5 S 136 40 E
Alexandria, Brazil 171 6 25 S 38 1W
Alexandria, B.C., Can. 152 52 35N 122 27W
Alexandria, Ont., Can. 150 45 19N 74 38W
Alexandria, Rumania 70 43 57N 25 24 E
Alexandria, S. Afr. 128 33 38 S 26 28 E
Alexandria, U.K. 34 55 59N 4 40W
Alexandria, Ind., U.S.A. 156 40 18N 85 40W
Alexandria, La., U.S.A. 159 31 20N 92 30W
Alexandria, Minn., U.S.A. 158 45 50N 95 20W
Alexandria, S.D., U.S.A. 158 43 40N 97 45W
Alexandria, Va., U.S.A. 162 38 47N 77 1W
Alexandria = El Iskandarîya 122 31 0N 30 0 E
Alexandria Bay 156 44 20N 75 52W
Alexandrina, L. 140 35 25 S 139 10 E
Alexandroúpolis 68 40 50N 25 54 E
Alexis Creek 152 52 0N 123 20W
Alexis, R. 151 52 33N 56 8W
Alfambra 58 40 33N 1 5W
Alfândega da Fé 56 41 20N 6 59W
Alfaro 58 42 10N 1 50W
Alfatar 67 43 59N 27 13 E
Alfeld 48 52 0N 9 49 E
Alfenas 173 21 40 S 44 0W
Alfiós, R. 69 37 36N 21 54 E
Alfonsine 63 44 30N 12 1 E
Alford, Grampian, U.K. 37 57 13N 2 42W
Alford, Lincs., U.K. 33 53 16N 0 10 E
Alfred 162 43 28N 70 40W
Alfred Town 141 35 8 S 147 30 E
Alfredton 142 40 41 S 175 54 E
Alfreton 33 53 6N 1 22W
Alfriston 29 50 48N 0 10 E
Alfta 72 61 21N 16 4 E
Alftanes 74 64 29N 22 10W
Alga 84 49 53N 57 20 E
Algaba, La 57 37 27N 6 1W
Algar 57 36 40N 5 39W
Ålgård 71 58 46N 5 53 E
Ålgård 71 58 46N 5 53 E
Algarinejo 57 37 19N 4 9W
Algarve 57 37 15N 8 10W
Algeciras 57 36 9N 5 28W
Algemesí 59 39 11N 0 27W
Alger 118 36 42N 3 8 E
Algeria ■ 118 35 10N 3 11 E
Alghero 64 40 34N 8 20 E
Algiers = Alger 118 36 42N 3 8 E
Algoabaai 128 33 50 S 25 45 E
Algodonales 57 36 54N 5 24W
Algodor, R. 56 39 51N 3 48W
Algoma, Mich., U.S.A. 156 44 35N 87 27W
Algoma, Oreg., U.S.A. 160 42 25N 121 54W
Algonquin Prov. Pk. 150 45 50N 78 30W
Alhama de Almería 59 36 57N 2 34W
Alhama de Aragón 58 41 18N 1 54W
Alhama de Granada 57 37 0N 3 59W
Alhama de Murcia 59 37 51N 1 25W
Alhambra, Spain 59 38 54N 3 4W
Alhambra, U.S.A. 163 34 8N 118 10W
Alhaurín el Grande 57 36 39N 4 41W
Alhucemas = Al-Hoceïma 118 35 8N 3 58W
Ali al Gharbi 92 32 30N 46 45 E
Ali Bayramly 83 39 43N 48 52 E
Ali Khel 94 33 56N 69 35 E
Ali Sabieh 123 11 10N 42 44 E
Ália 64 37 47N 13 42 E
Aliabad 93 28 10N 57 35 E
Aliaga 58 40 40N 0 42W
Aliakmon, R. 68 40 10N 22 0 E
Alibag 96 18 38N 72 56 E
Alibo 123 9 52N 37 5 E
Alibunar 66 45 5N 20 57 E
Alicante 59 38 23N 0 30W
Alicante □ 59 38 30N 0 37W
Alice, S. Afr. 128 32 48 S 26 55 E
Alice, U.S.A. 159 27 47N 98 1W
Alice Arm 152 55 29N 129 31W
Alice Downs 136 17 45 S 127 56 E
Alice, Punta dell' 65 39 23N 17 10 E
Alice, R., Queens., Austral. 138 15 35 S 142 20 E
Alice, R., Queens., Austral. 138 24 2 S 144 50 E
Alice Springs 138 23 40 S 135 50 E
Alicedale 128 33 15 S 26 4 E
Aliceville 157 33 9N 88 10W
Alick Cr. 138 20 35 S 142 10 E
Alicudi, I. 65 38 33N 14 20 E
Alida 153 49 25N 101 55W
Aligarh, India 93 27 55N 78 10 E
Aligarh, Raj., India 94 25 55N 76 15 E
Aligarh, Ut. P., India 94 27 55N 78 10 E
Aligudarz 92 33 25N 49 45 E
Alijó 56 41 16N 7 27W
Alimena 65 37 42N 14 4 E
Alimnía 69 36 16N 27 43 E
Aling Kangri 99 31 45N 84 45 E
Alingaabro 73 56 56N 10 32 E
Alingsås 73 57 56N 12 31 E
Alipore 95 22 32N 88 24 E
Alipur 94 29 25N 70 55 E
Alipur Duar 98 26 30N 89 35 E
Aliquippa 156 40 38N 80 18W
Aliste, R. 56 41 48N 6 14W
Alivérion 69 38 24N 24 2 E
Aliwal North 128 30 45 S 26 45 E
Alix 152 52 24N 113 11W
Aljezur 57 37 18N 8 49W
Aljustrel 57 37 55N 8 10W
Alkamari 121 13 27N 11 10 E
Alken 47 50 53N 5 18 E
Alkhalaf 91 20 30N 58 13 E
Alkmaar 46 52 37N 4 45 E
All American Canal 161 32 45N 115 0W
Allada 121 6 41N 2 9 E
Allah Dad 94 25 38N 67 34 E
Allahabad 95 25 25N 81 58 E
Allakaket 147 66 30N 152 45W
Allakh Yun 77 60 50N 137 5 E
Allal Razi 118 34 30N 6 39W
Allan 153 51 53N 106 4W
Allanche 44 45 14N 2 57 E
Allanmyo 98 19 16N 95 17 E
Allanridge 128 27 45 S 26 40 E
Allansford 140 38 26 S 142 39 E
Allanton 143 45 55 S 170 15 E
Allanwater 150 50 14N 90 10W
Allaqi, Wadi 122 22 15N 34 55 E
Allard Lake 151 50 40N 63 10W
Allariz 56 42 11N 7 50W
Allassac 44 45 15N 1 29 E
Alle 47 49 51N 4 58 E
Allegan 156 42 32N 85 52W
Allegheny Mts. 156 38 0N 80 0W
Allegheny, R. 156 41 14N 79 50W
Allègre 44 45 12N 3 41 E
Allen, Bog of 39 53 15N 7 0W
Allen, L. 38 54 30N 8 5W
Allen R. 35 54 53N 2 13W
Allenby (Hussein) Bridge 90 31 53N 35 33 E
Allendale 35 54 55N 2 15W
Allende 164 28 20N 100 50W
Allenheads 35 54 49N 2 12W
Allentown 162 40 36N 75 30W
Allentsteig 52 48 41N 15 20 E
Allenwood 39 53 16N 6 53W
Alleppey 97 9 30N 76 28 E
Alleröd 73 55 54N 12 19 E
Alleur 47 50 39N 5 31 E
Allevard 45 45 24N 6 5 E
Alliance, Nebr., U.S.A. 158 42 10N 102 50W
Alliance, Ohio, U.S.A. 156 40 53N 81 7W
Allier □ 44 46 25N 3 0 E
Allier, R. 43 46 57N 3 4 E
Alligator Cr., Queens., Austral. 138 21 20 S 149 12 E
Alligator Cr., Queens., Austral. 138 19 23 S 146 58 E
Allihies 39 51 39N 10 4W
Allingåbrl 73 56 28N 10 20 E
Allingåbro 73 56 28N 10 20 E
Allinge 73 55 17N 14 50 E
Alliston 150 44 9N 79 52W
Alloa 35 56 7N 3 49W
Allonby 32 54 45N 3 27W
Allos 45 44 15N 6 38 E
Alma, Can. 151 48 35N 71 40W
Alma, Kans., U.S.A. 158 39 1N 96 22W
Alma, Mich., U.S.A. 156 43 25N 84 40W
Alma, Nebr., U.S.A. 158 40 10N 99 25W
Alma, Wis., U.S.A. 158 44 19N 91 54W
Alma Ata 85 43 15N 76 57 E
Almada 57 38 40N 9 9W
Almaden 138 17 [illegible] S 144 40 E

Almadén Amungen

Almadén	57	38 49N	4 52W
Almagro	57	38 50N	3 45W
Almalyk	85	40 50N	69 35 E
Almanor, L.	160	40 15N	121 11W
Almansa	59	38 51N	1 5W
Almanza	56	42 39N	5 3W
Almanzor, Pico de	56	40 15N	5 18W
Almanzora, R.	59	37 22N	2 21W
Almarcha, La	58	39 41N	2 24W
Almas	171	11 33 S	47 9W
Almaş, Mţii	70	44 49N	22 12 E
Almazán	58	41 30N	2 30W
Almazora	58	39 57N	0 3W
Almeirim, Brazil	175	1 30 S	52 0W
Almeirim, Port.	57	39 12N	8 37W
Almelo	46	52 22N	6 42 E
Almenar	58	41 43N	2 12W
Almenara, Brazil	171	16 11 S	40 42W
Almenara, Spain	58	39 46N	0 14W
Almenara, Sierra de	59	37 34N	1 32W
Almendralejó	57	38 41N	6 26W
Almería	59	36 52N	2 32W
Almería □	59	37 20N	2 20W
Almería, G. de	59	36 41N	2 28W
Almetyevsk	84	54 53N	52 20 E
Älmhult	73	56 32N	14 10 E
Almirante	166	9 10N	82 30W
Almiropótamos	69	38 16N	24 11 E
Almirós	69	39 11N	22 45 E
Almodôvar	57	37 31N	8 2W
Almodóvar del Campo	57	38 43N	4 10W
Almogia	57	36 50N	4 32W
Almonaster la Real	57	37 52N	6 48W
Almond R.	35	56 27N	3 27W
Almondsbury	28	51 33N	2 34W
Almonte, R.	57	39 41N	6 12W
Almora	95	29 38N	79 4 E
Almoradi	59	38 7N	0 46W
Almorox	56	40 14N	4 24W
Almoustarat	121	17 35N	0 8 E
Älmult	73	56 33N	14 8 E
Almuñécar	57	36 43N	3 41W
Almunia, La de Doña Godina	58	41 29N	1 23W
Almvik	73	57 49N	16 30 E
Aln, R.	35	55 24N	1 35W
Alness	37	57 41N	4 15W
Alness R.	37	57 45N	4 20W
Alnif	118	31 10N	5 8W
Alnmouth	35	55 24N	1 37W
Alnön I.	72	62 26N	17 33 E
Alnwick	35	55 25N	1 42W
Aloi	126	2 16N	33 10 E
Alon	98	22 12N	95 5 E
Alonsa	153	50 50N	99 0W
Alor, I.	103	8 15 S	124 30 E
Alor Setar	101	6 7N	100 22 E
Alora	57	36 49N	4 46W
Alosno	57	37 33N	7 7W
Alot'ai	105	47 52N	88 7 E
Alotau	135	10 16 S	150 30 E
Alougoum	118	30 17N	6 56W
Aloysius Mt.	137	26 0 S	128 38 E
Alpaugh	163	35 53N	119 29W
Alpedrinha	56	40 6N	7 27W
Alpena	156	45 6N	83 24W
Alpercatas, R.	170	6 2 S	44 19W
Alpes-de-Haute-Provence □	45	44 8N	6 10 E
Alpes-Maritimes □	45	43 55N	7 10 E
Alpes Valaisannes	50	46 4N	7 30 E
Alpha	138	23 39 S	146 37 E
Alphen	47	51 29N	4 58 E
Alphen aan den Rijn	46	52 7N	4 40 E
Alphington	30	50 41N	3 32W
Alpi Apuan	62	44 7N	10 14 E
Alpi Craie	43	45 40N	7 0 E
Alpi Lepontine	51	46 22N	8 27 E
Alpi Orobie	62	46 7N	10 0 E
Alpi Retiche	51	46 45N	10 0 E
Alpiarça	57	39 15N	8 35W
Alpine, Ariz., U.S.A.	161	33 57N	109 4W
Alpine, Calif., U.S.A.	163	32 50N	116 46W
Alpine, Tex., U.S.A.	159	30 35N	103 35W
Alpnach	51	46 57N	8 17 E
Alrewas	28	52 43N	1 44W
Alrø	73	55 52N	10 5 E
Alroy Downs	138	19 20 S	136 5 E
Als	73	56 46N	10 18 E
Alsace	43	48 15N	7 25 E
Alsager	32	53 7N	2 20W
Alsask	153	51 21N	109 59W
Alsásua	58	42 54N	2 10W
Alseda	73	57 27N	15 20 E
Alsen	72	63 23N	13 56 E
Alsfeld	48	50 44N	9 19 E
Alsh, L.	36	57 15N	5 39W
Alsónémedi	53	47 34N	19 15 E
Alsten	74	65 58N	12 40 E
Alston	32	54 48N	2 26W
Alta	74	69 57N	23 10 E
Alta Gracia	172	31 40 S	64 30W
Alta Lake	152	50 10N	123 0W
Alta, Sierra	58	40 31N	1 30W
Alta Sierra	163	35 42N	118 33W
Altaelva	74	69 46N	23 45 E
Altafjorden	74	70 5N	23 5 E
Altagracia	174	10 45N	71 30W
Altai = Aerht'ai Shan	105	48 0N	90 0 E
Altamaha, R.	157	31 50N	82 0W
Altamira, Brazil	175	3 0 S	52 10W
Altamira, Chile	172	25 47 S	69 51W
Altamira, Colomb.	174	2 3N	75 47W
Altamira, Mexico	165	22 24N	97 55W
Altamira, Cuevas de	56	43 20N	4 5W
Altamont	162	42 43N	74 3W
Altamura	65	40 50N	16 33 E
Altanbulag	54	50 19N	106 30 E
Altar	164	30 40N	111 50W
Altarnun	30	50 35N	4 30W
Altata	164	24 30N	108 0W
Altavista	156	37 9N	79 22W
Altdorf	51	46 52N	8 36 E
Altea	59	38 38N	0 2W
Altenberg	48	50 46N	13 47 E
Altenbruch	48	53 48N	8 44 E
Altenburg	48	50 59N	12 28 E
Altenkirchen	48	50 41N	7 38 E
Altenmarkt	52	47 43N	14 39 E
Alter do Chão	57	39 12N	7 40W
Altkirch	43	47 37N	7 15 E
Altnaharra	37	58 17N	4 27W
Alto Adige = Trentino-Alto Adige	62	46 5N	11 0 E
Alto Araguaia	175	17 15 S	53 20W
Alto Chindio	127	16 19 S	35 25 E
Alto Cuchumatanes	164	15 30N	91 10W
Alto del Inca	172	24 10 S	68 10W
Alto Ligonha	127	15 30 S	38 11 E
Alto Molocue	127	15 50 S	37 35 E
Alto Paraná □	173	25 0 S	54 50W
Alto Parnaíba	170	9 6 S	45 57W
Alto Santo	170	5 31 S	38 15W
Alto Turi	170	2 54 S	45 38W
Alto Uruguay, R.	173	27 0 S	53 30W
Alton, U.K.	29	51 8N	0 59W
Alton, Ill., U.S.A.	158	38 55N	90 5W
Alton, N.H., U.S.A.	162	43 27N	71 13W
Alton Downs	139	26 7 S	138 57 E
Altona	48	53 32N	9 56 E
Altoona	156	40 32N	78 24W
Altopáscio	62	43 50N	10 40 E
Altos	170	5 3 S	42 28W
Altrincham	32	53 25N	2 21W
Altstätten	51	47 22N	9 33 E
Alturas	160	41 36N	120 37W
Altus	159	34 30N	99 25W
Alucra	83	40 22N	38 47 E
Aluksône	80	57 24N	27 3 E
Alula	91	11 50N	50 45 E
Alupka	82	44 23N	34 2 E
Alushta	82	44 40N	34 25 E
Alusi	103	7 35 S	131 40 E
Alustante	58	40 36N	1 40W
Alva, U.K.	35	56 9N	3 49W
Alva, U.S.A.	159	36 50N	98 50W
Alvaiázere	56	39 49N	8 23W
Alvangen	73	58 0N	12 7 E
Älvängen	73	57 58N	12 8 E
Alvarado, Mexico	165	18 40N	95 50W
Alvarado, U.S.A.	159	32 25N	97 15W
Alvaro Obregón, Presa	164	27 55N	109 52W
Alvastra	73	58 20N	14 44 E
Alvdal	71	62 6N	10 37 E
Alvear	172	29 5 S	56 30W
Alvechurch	28	52 22N	1 58W
Alverca	57	38 56N	9 1W
Alveringen	47	51 1N	2 43 E
Älvesta	73	56 54N	14 35 E
Älvho	72	61 30N	14 45 E
Alvie, Austral.	140	38 14 S	143 30 E
Alvie, U.K.	37	57 10N	3 50W
Alvin	159	29 23N	95 12W
Alvito	57	38 15N	8 0W
Älvkarleby	75	60 32N	17 40 E
Alvra, Pic d'	51	46 35N	9 50 E
Älvros	72	62 3N	14 38 E
Älvsborgs län □	73	58 30N	12 30 E
Älvsby	74	65 42N	20 52 E
Älvsbyn	74	65 40N	20 0 E
Alvsered	73	57 14N	12 51 E
Alwar	94	27 38N	76 34 E
Alwaye	97	10 8N	76 24 E
Alwinton	35	55 20N	2 7W
Alwyn, oilfield	19	60 30N	1 45 E
Alyangula	133	13 55 S	136 30 E
Alyaskitovyy	77	64 45N	141 30 E
Alyata	83	39 58N	49 25 E
Alyth	37	56 38N	3 15W
Alzada	158	45 3N	104 22W
Alzano Lombardo	62	45 44N	9 43 E
Alzette, R.	47	49 45N	6 6 E
Alzey	49	49 48N	8 4 E
Am-Dam	117	12 40N	20 35 E
Am Djeress	117	16 15N	22 50 E
Am Guereda	117	12 53N	21 14 E
Am Timan	117	11 0N	20 10 E
Am-Zoer	124	14 13N	21 23 E
Amadeus, L.	137	24 54 S	131 0 E
Amadi, Congo	126	3 40N	26 40 E
Amadi, Sudan	123	5 29N	30 25 E
Amadi, Zaïre	126	3 40N	26 40 E
Amadia	92	37 6N	43 30 E
Amadjuak	149	64 0N	72 39W
Amadjuak L.	149	65 0N	71 8W
Amadora	57	38 45N	9 13W
Amaga	174	6 3N	75 42W
Amagansett	162	40 58N	72 8W
Amagasaki	111	34 42N	135 20 E
Amager	73	55 37N	12 35 E
Amagi	110	33 25N	130 39 E
Amagunze	121	6 20N	7 40 E
Amaimon	135	5 12 S	145 30 E
Amakusa-Nada	110	32 35N	130 5 E
Amakusa-Shotō	110	32 15N	130 10 E
Åmål	72	59 2N	12 40 E
Åmål	72	59 3N	12 42 E
Amalapuram	96	16 35N	81 55 E
Amalfi, Colomb.	174	6 55N	75 4W
Amalfi, Italy	65	40 39N	14 34 E
Amaliás	69	37 47N	21 22 E
Amalner	96	21 5N	75 5 E
Amambaí	173	23 5 S	55 13W
Amambaí, R.	173	23 22 S	53 56W
Amambay □	173	23 0 S	56 0W
Amambay, Cordillera de	173	20 30 S	56 0W
Amami-O-Shima	112	28 0N	129 0 E
Amanab	135	3 40 S	141 14 E
Amandola	63	42 59N	13 21 E
Amanfrom	121	7 20N	0 25 E
Amangeldy	76	50 10N	65 10 E
Amantea	65	39 8N	16 3 E
Amapá	170	2 5N	50 50W
Amapá □	170	1 40N	52 0W
Amar Gedid	123	14 27N	25 13 E
Amara, Iraq	92	31 57N	47 12 E
Amara, Sudan	123	10 25N	34 10 E
Amarante, Brazil	170	6 14 S	42 50W
Amarante, Port.	56	41 16N	8 5W
Amarante do Maranhão	170	5 36 S	46 45W
Amaranth	153	50 36N	98 43W
Amarapura	98	21 54N	96 3 E
Amaravati, R.	97	10 50N	77 42 E
Amaravati = Amraoti	96	20 55N	77 45 E
Amareleja	57	38 12N	7 13W
Amargosa	171	13 2 S	39 36W
Amargosa, R.	163	36 14N	116 51W
Amargosa Ra., mts	163	36 25N	116 40W
Amarillo	159	35 14N	101 46W
Amaro Leite	171	13 58 S	49 9W
Amaro, Mt.	63	42 5N	14 6 E
Amarpur, India	99	23 30N	91 45 E
Amarpur, Bihar, India	95	25 5N	87 0 E
Amarpur, Tripura, India	99	23 30N	91 45 E
Amasra	92	41 45N	32 30 E
Amassama	121	5 1N	6 2 E
Amasya	92	40 40N	35 50 E
Amatignak I.	147	51 19N	179 10W
Amatikulu	129	29 3 S	31 33 E
Amatitlán	166	14 29N	90 38W
Amatrice	63	42 38N	13 16 E
Amay	47	50 33N	5 19 E
Amazon, R.	175	2 0 S	53 30W
Amazonas □, Brazil	174	4 20 S	64 0W
Amazonas □, Colomb.	174	1 0 S	72 0W
Amazonas □, Venez.	174	3 30N	66 0W
Amazonas, R.	175	2 0 S	53 30W
Ambad	96	19 38N	75 50 E
Ambahakily	129	21 36 S	43 41 E
Ambala	94	30 23N	76 56 E
Ambalangoda	97	6 15N	80 5 E
Ambalapuzha	97	9 25N	76 25 E
Ambalavao	129	21 50 S	46 56 E
Ambalindum	138	23 23 S	134 40 E
Ambam	124	2 20N	11 15 E
Ambanifilao	129	12 48 S	49 47 E
Ambanja	129	13 40 S	48 27 E
Ambararata	129	13 41 S	48 27 E
Ambarchik	77	69 40N	162 20 E
Ambarijeby	129	14 56 S	47 41 E
Ambarnath	96	19 12N	73 22 E
Ambaro, B. d'	129	13 23 S	48 38 E
Ambasamudram	97	8 43N	77 25 E
Ambato	174	1 5 S	78 42W
Ambato-Boéni	129	16 28 S	46 43 E
Ambato, Sierra de	172	28 25N	66 10W
Ambatolampy	129	19 20 S	47 35 E
Ambatondrazaka	129	17 55 S	48 28 E
Ambatosoratra	129	17 37 S	48 31 E
Ambenja	129	15 17 S	46 58 E
Ambeno	103	9 20 S	124 30 E
Amberg	49	49 25N	11 52 E
Ambergris Cay	165	18 0N	88 0W
Ambérieu-en-Bugey	45	45 57N	5 20 E
Amberley	143	43 9 S	172 44 E
Ambert	44	45 33N	3 44 E
Ambevongo	129	15 25 S	42 26 E
Ambia	129	16 11 S	45 33 E
Ambidédi	120	14 35N	11 47W
Ambikapur	95	23 15N	83 15 E
Ambikol	122	21 20N	30 50 E
Ambilobé	125	13 10 S	49 3 E
Ambinanindrano	129	20 5 S	48 23 E
Ambjörnarp	73	57 25N	13 17 E
Amble	35	55 20N	1 36W
Ambler	162	40 9N	75 13W
Ambleside	32	54 26N	2 58W
Amblève	47	50 21N	6 10 E
Amblève, R.	47	50 25N	5 45 E
Ambo, Begemdir & Simen, Ethiopia	123	12 20N	37 30 E
Ambo, Shewa, Ethiopia	123	9 0N	37 48 E
Ambo, Peru	174	10 5 S	76 10W
Ambodifototra	129	16 59 S	49 52 E
Ambodilazana	129	18 6 S	49 10 E
Ambohimahasoa	129	21 7 S	47 13 E
Ambohimanga du Sud	129	20 52 S	47 36 E
Ambon	103	3 35 S	128 20 E
Ambongao, Cones d'	129	17 0 S	45 0 E
Amboseli L.	126	2 40 S	37 10 E
Ambositra	129	20 31 S	47 25 E
Amboy	163	34 33N	115 51W
Ambre, C. d'	129	12 40 S	49 10 E
Ambre, Mt. d'	125	12 30 S	49 10 E
Ambriz	124	7 48 S	13 8 E
Ambrizete	124	7 10 S	12 52 E
Ambunti	135	4 13 S	142 52 E
Ambut	97	12 48N	78 43 E
Amby	139	26 30 S	148 11 E
Amchitka I.	147	51 30N	179 0W
Amchitka P.	147	51 30N	179 0W
Amderma	76	69 45N	61 30 E
Ameca	164	20 30N	104 0W
Ameca, R.	164	20 40N	105 15W
Amecameca	165	19 10N	98 57W
Ameland	46	53 27N	5 45 E
Amélia	63	42 34N	12 25 E
Amèlie-les-Bains-Palalda	44	42 29N	2 41 E
Amen	77	68 45N	180 0 E
Amendolaro	65	39 58N	16 34 E
Amenia	162	41 51N	73 33W
America	47	51 27N	5 59 E
American Falls	160	42 46N	112 56W
American Falls Res.	160	43 0N	112 50W
American Highland	13	73 0 S	75 0 E
Americana	173	22 45 S	47 20W
Americus	157	32 0N	84 10W
Amersfoort, Neth.	46	52 9N	5 23 E
Amersfoort, S. Afr.	129	26 59 S	29 53 E
Amersham	29	51 40N	0 38W
Amery, Austral.	137	31 9 S	117 5 E
Amery, Can.	153	56 34N	94 3W
Ames	158	42 0N	93 40W
Amesbury, U.K.	28	51 10N	1 46W
Amesbury, U.S.A.	162	42 50N	70 52W
Amesdale	153	50 2N	92 55W
Ameson	150	49 50N	84 35W
Amethyst, gasfield	19	53 38N	0 40 E
Amfiklia	69	38 38N	22 35 E
Amfilokhia	69	38 52N	21 9 E
Amfipolis	68	40 48N	23 52 E
Amfissa	69	38 32N	22 22 E
Amga, R.	77	61 0N	132 0 E
Amgu	77	45 45N	137 15 E
Amherst, Burma	99	16 2N	97 20 E
Amherst, Can.	151	45 48N	64 8W
Amherst, Mass., U.S.A.	162	42 21N	72 30W
Amherst, Tex., U.S.A.	159	34 0N	102 24W
Amherst, Mt.	136	18 11 S	126 59 E
Amherstburg	150	42 6N	83 6W
Amiata Mte.	63	42 54N	11 40 E
Amiens	43	49 54N	2 16 E
Amigdhalokefáli	69	35 23N	23 30 E
Amili	98	28 25N	95 52 E
Amíndaion	68	40 42N	21 42 E
Amirante Is.	11	6 0 S	53 0 E
Amisk L.	153	54 35N	102 15W
Amistati, Presa	164	29 24N	101 0W
Amite	159	30 47N	90 31W
Åmli	71	58 45N	8 32 E
Amlia I.	147	52 5N	173 30W
Amlwch	31	53 24N	4 21W
Amm Adam	123	16 20N	36 1 E
'Ammān	90	32 0N	35 52 E
Ammanford	31	51 48N	4 0W
Ammerån	72	63 9N	16 13 E
Ammerån	72	63 0N	16 13 E
Ammersee	49	48 0N	11 7 E
Ammerzoden	46	51 45N	5 13 E
Ammi'ad	90	32 55N	35 32 E
Amnat Charoen	100	15 51N	104 38 E
Amne Machin	105	34 30N	100 0 E
Amnéville	43	49 16N	6 9 E
Amo Chiang, R.	108	22 56N	101 47 E
Amorebieta	58	43 13N	2 44W
Amorgós	69	36 50N	25 57 E
Amory	57	33 59N	88 30W
Amos	150	48 35N	78 5W
Åmot	71	59 54N	9 54 E
Åmot	71	59 34N	8 0 E
Åmotsdal	71	59 37N	8 26 E
Amour, Djebel	118	33 42N	1 37 E
Amoy = Hsiamen	109	24 25N	118 4 E
Amozoc	165	19 2N	98 3W
Ampang	101	3 8N	101 45 E
Ampanihy	129	24 40 S	44 45 E
Amparihy Est.	129	23 57 S	47 20 E
Ampasindava, B. d'	129	13 40 S	48 15 E
Ampasindava, Presqu'île d'	129	13 42 S	47 55W
Amper	121	9 25N	9 40 E
Ampère	119	35 44N	5 27 E
Ampleforth	33	54 13N	1 8W
Ampombiantambo	129	12 42 S	48 57 E
Amposta	58	40 43N	0 34 E
Ampotaka	129	25 3 S	44 41 E
Ampoza	129	22 20 S	44 44 E
Ampthill	29	52 3N	0 30W
Amqa	90	32 59N	35 10 E
Amqui	151	48 28N	67 27W
Amraoti	96	20 55N	77 45 E
Amreli	94	21 35N	71 17 E
Amrenene el Kasba	118	22 10N	0 30 E
Amriswil	51	47 33N	9 18 E
Amritsar	94	31 35N	74 57 E
Amroha	95	28 53N	78 30 E
Amrum	48	54 37N	8 21 E
Amsel	119	22 47N	5 29 E
Amsterdam, Neth.	46	52 23N	4 54 E
Amsterdam, U.S.A.	162	42 58N	74 10W
Amsterdam, I.	11	37 30 S	77 30 E
Amstetten	52	48 7N	14 51 E
Amu Darya, R.	76	37 50N	65 0 E
Amuay	174	11 50N	70 10W
Amukta I.	147	52 29N	171 20W
Amund Ringnes I.	12	78 20N	96 25W
Amundsen Gulf	148	71 0N	124 0W
Amundsen Sea	13	72 0 S	115 0W
Amungen	72	61 10N	15 40 E

Amuntai **Anza**

Amuntai **102** 2 28 S 115 25 E
Amur, R. **77** 53 30N 122 30 E
Amurang **103** 1 5N 124 40 E
Amuri Pass **143** 42 31 S 172 11 E
Amurrio **58** 43 3N 3 0W
Amurzet **77** 47 50N 131 5 E
Amusco **56** 42 10N 4 28W
Amvrakikós Kólpos **69** 39 0N 20 55 E
Amvrosiyvka **83** 47 43N 38 30 E
Amzeglouf **118** 26 50N 0 1 E
An **98** 22 29N 96 54 E
An Bien **101** 9 45N 105 0 E
An Geata Mór, (Binghamstown) **38** 54 13N 10 0W
An Hoa **100** 15 30N 108 20 E
An Loc **101** 11 40N 106 50 E
An Nafud **92** 28 15N 41 0 E
An Najaf **92** 32 3N 44 15 E
An-Nāqūrah **90** 33 7N 35 8 E
An Nasiriyah **92** 31 0N 46 15 E
An Nawfaliyah **119** 30 54N 17 58 E
An Nhon (Binh Dinh) **100** 13 55N 109 7 E
An Nîl □ **123** 17 30N 33 0 E
An Nîl el Abyad □ **123** 14 0N 32 15 E
An Nu'ayriyah **92** 27 30N 48 30 E
An Teallach, Mt. **36** 57 49N 5 18W
An Thoi, Dao **101** 9 58N 104 0 E
An Tuc **100** 13 57N 108 39 E
An Uaimh **38** 53 39N 6 40W
Ana-Sira **71** 58 17N 6 25 E
Anabta **90** 32 19N 35 7 E
Anabuki **110** 34 2N 134 11 E
Anaco **174** 9 27N 64 28W
Anaconda **160** 46 7N 113 0W
Anacortes **160** 48 30N 122 40W
Anadarko **159** 35 4N 98 15W
Anadia, Brazil **170** 9 42 S 36 18W
Anadia, Port. **56** 40 26N 8 27W
Anadolu **92** 38 0N 29 0 E
Anadyr **77** 64 35N 177 20 E
Anadyr, R. **77** 66 50N 171 0 E
Anadyrskiy Zaliv **77** 64 0N 180 0 E
Anáfi **69** 36 22N 25 48 E
Anafópoulo **69** 36 17N 25 50 E
Anagni **64** 41 44N 13 8 E
Anah **92** 34 25N 42 0 E
Anaheim **163** 33 50N 118 0W
Anahim Lake **152** 52 28N 125 18W
Anáhuac **164** 27 14N 100 9W
Anai Mudi, Mt. **97** 10 12N 77 20 E
Anaimalai Hills **97** 10 20N 76 40 E
Anajás **170** 0 59 S 49 57W
Anajatuba **170** 3 16 S 44 37W
Anakapalle **96** 17 42N 83 06 E
Anakie **138** 23 32 S 147 45 E
Anaklia **83** 42 22N 41 35 E
Analalava **129** 14 35 S 48 0 E
Analapasy **129** 25 11 S 46 40 E
Anam **121** 6 19N 6 41 E
Anambar, R. **94** 30 10N 68 50 E
Anambas, Kepulauan **102** 3 20N 106 30 E
Anamoose **158** 47 55N 100 7W
Anamosa **158** 42 7N 91 17W
Anamur **92** 36 8N 32 58 E
Anan **110** 33 54N 134 40 E
Anand **94** 22 32N 72 59 E
Anandpur **96** 21 16N 86 13 E
Anánes **69** 36 33N 24 9 E
Anantapur **97** 14 39N 77 42 E
Anantnag **95** 33 45N 75 10 E
Ananyev **82** 47 44N 29 57 E
Anapa **82** 44 55N 37 25 E
Anápolis **171** 16 15 S 48 50W
Anar **93** 30 55N 55 13 E
Anarak **93** 33 25N 53 40 E
Anatolia = Anadolu **92** 38 0N 29 0 E
Anatone **160** 46 9N 117 4W
Añatuya **172** 28 20 S 62 50W
Anaunethad L. **153** 60 55N 104 25W
Anaye **117** 19 15N 12 50 E
Anbyŏn **107** 39 1N 127 35 E
Ancaster **33** 52 59N 0 32W
Ancenis **42** 47 21N 1 10W
Anch'i **109** 25 3N 118 13 E
Anch'ing **109** 30 37N 117 0 E
Anch'iu **107** 36 25N 119 10 E
Ancholme, R. **33** 53 42N 0 32W
Anchorage **147** 61 10N 149 50W
Ancião **56** 39 56N 8 27W
Ancohuma, Nevada **174** 16 0 S 68 50W
Ancon **164** 8 57N 79 33W
Ancón **174** 11 50 S 77 10W
Ancona **63** 43 37N 13 30 E
Ancrum **35** 55 31N 2 35W
Ancud **176** 42 0 S 73 50W
Ancud, G. de **176** 42 0 S 73 0W
Andacollo, Argent. **172** 37 10 S 70 42W
Andacollo, Chile **172** 30 15 S 71 10W
Andado **138** 25 25 S 135 15 E
Andalgalá **172** 27 40 S 66 30W
Åndalsnes **71** 62 35N 7 43 E
Andalucía **57** 37 35N 5 0W
Andalusia **157** 31 51N 86 30W
Andalusia = Andalucía **57** 37 35N 5 0W
Andaman Is. **101** 12 30N 92 30 E
Andaman Sea **101** 13 0N 96 0 E
Andaman Str. **101** 12 15N 92 20 E
Andara **128** 18 2 S 21 9 E
Andaraí **171** 12 48 S 41 20W
Andeer **51** 46 36N 9 26 E
Andelfingen **51** 47 36N 8 41 E
Andelot **43** 46 51N 5 56 E
Andelys, Les **42** 49 15N 1 25 E
Andenne **47** 50 30N 5 5 E
Andéranboukane **121** 15 26N 3 2 E
Anderlecht **47** 50 50N 4 19 E
Anderlues **47** 50 25N 4 16 E
Andermatt **51** 46 38N 8 35 E
Andernach **48** 50 24N 7 25 E
Andernos **44** 44 44N 1 6W
Anderslöv **73** 55 26N 13 19 E
Anderson, Austral. **141** 38 32 S 145 27 E
Anderson, Calif., U.S.A. **160** 40 30N 122 19W
Anderson, Ind., U.S.A. **156** 40 5N 85 40W
Anderson, Mo., U.S.A. **159** 36 43N 94 29W
Anderson, S.C., U.S.A. **157** 34 32N 82 40W
Anderson, Mt. **129** 25 5 S 30 42 E
Anderson, R. **147** 69 42N 129 0W
Anderstorp **73** 57 19N 13 39 E
Andes **162** 42 12N 74 47W
Andes, mts. **174** 20 0 S 68 0W
Andfjorden **74** 69 10N 16 20 E
Andhra, L. **96** 18 30N 73 32 E
Andhra Pradesh □ **97** 15 0N 80 0 E
Andikíthira **69** 35 52N 23 15 E
Andimilos **69** 36 47N 24 12 E
Andíparos **69** 37 0N 25 3 E
Andípaxoi **69** 39 9N 20 13 E
Andípsara **69** 38 30N 25 29 E
Andizhan **76** 41 10N 72 0 E
Andkhui **93** 36 52N 65 8 E
Andoharano **129** 22 58 S 43 45 E
Andol **96** 17 51N 78 4 E
Andong **107** 36 40N 128 43 E
Andorra ■ **58** 42 30N 1 30 E
Andorra La Vella **58** 42 31N 1 32 E
Andover, U.K. **28** 51 13N 1 29W
Andover, U.S.A. **162** 40 59N 74 44W
Andradina **171** 20 54 S 51 23W
Andrahary, Mt. **129** 13 37 S 49 17 E
Andraitx **58** 39 35N 2 25 E
Andramasina **129** 19 11 S 47 35 E
Andrano-Velona **129** 18 10 S 46 52 E
Andranopasy **129** 21 17 S 43 44 E
Andreanof Is. **147** 51 0N 178 0W
Andreapol **80** 56 40N 32 17 E
Andreas **32** 54 23N 4 25W
Andrespol **54** 51 45N 19 34 E
Andrew, oilfield **19** 58 4N 1 24 E
Andrews, S.C., U.S.A. **157** 33 29N 79 30W
Andrews, Tex., U.S.A. **159** 32 18N 102 33W
Andreyevka **84** 52 19N 51 55 E
Ándria **65** 41 13N 16 17 E
Andrian **65** 46 30N 11 13 E
Andriba **129** 17 30 S 46 58 E
Andrijevica **66** 42 45N 19 48 E
Andrítsaina **69** 37 29N 21 52 E
Androka **129** 24 58 S 44 2 E
Ándros **69** 37 50N 24 50 E
Andros I. **166** 24 30N 78 0W
Andros Town **166** 24 43N 77 47W
Andrychów **54** 49 51N 19 18 E
Andújar **57** 38 3N 4 5W
Aneby **73** 57 48N 14 49 E
Anécho **121** 6 12N 1 34 E
Anegada I. **147** 18 45N 64 20W
Anergane **118** 31 4N 7 14W
Aneto, Pico de **58** 42 37N 0 40 E
Anfeg **119** 22 29N 5 58 E
Anfu **109** 27 23N 114 37 E
Ang Thong **100** 14 35N 100 31 E
Anga **77** 60 35N 132 0 E
Angamos, Punta **172** 23 1 S 70 32W
Anganch'i **98** 47 9N 123 48 E
Angara, R. **77** 58 30N 97 0 E
Angarsk **77** 52 30N 104 0 E
Angas Downs **137** 24 49 S 132 14 E
Angas Ra. **137** 23 0 S 127 50 E
Angaston **140** 34 30 S 139 8 E
Ånge **72** 62 31N 15 35 E
Angebo **72** 61 58N 16 22 E
Angel de la Guarda, I. **164** 29 30N 113 30W
Ängelholm **73** 56 15N 12 58 E
Angellala **139** 26 24 S 146 54 E
Angels Camp **163** 38 8N 120 30W
Ängelsberg **72** 59 58N 16 0 E
Angenong **99** 31 57N 94 10 E
Anger, R. **123** 9 30N 36 35 E
Angereb **123** 13 11N 37 7 E
Ångereb, R. **123** 14 0N 36 0 E
Ångermanälven **72** 62 40N 18 0 E
Angermünde **48** 53 1N 14 0 E
Angers **42** 47 30N 0 35W
Angerville **43** 48 19N 2 0 E
Ängesån **74** 66 50N 22 15 E
Anghiari **63** 43 32N 12 3 E
Angical **171** 12 0 S 44 42W
Angical do Piauí **171** 6 5 S 42 44W
Angikuni L. **153** 62 0N 100 0W
Angkor **100** 13 22N 103 50 E
Angle **31** 51 40N 5 3W
Anglem Mt. **143** 46 45 S 167 53 E
Anglés **58** 41 57N 2 38 E
Anglesey (□) **26** 53 17N 4 20W
Anglesey, I. **31** 53 17N 4 20W
Anglet **44** 43 29N 1 31W
Angleton **159** 29 12N 95 23W
Angleur **47** 50 36N 5 35 E
Anglure **43** 48 35N 3 50 E
Angmagssalik **12** 65 40N 37 20W
Angmering **29** 50 48N 0 28W
Ango **126** 4 10N 26 5 E
Angoche **127** 16 8 S 40 0 E
Angoche, I. **127** 16 20 S 39 50 E
Angol **172** 37 56 S 72 45W
Angola **156** 41 40N 85 0W
Angola ■ **125** 12 0 S 18 0 E
Angoon **147** 57 40N 134 40W
Angoram **135** 4 4 S 144 4 E
Angoulême **44** 45 39N 0 10 E
Angoumois **44** 45 30N 0 25 E
Angra dos Reis **173** 23 0 S 44 10W
Angra-Juntas **128** 27 39 S 15 31 E
Angran **76** 80 59N 69 3 E
Angren **85** 41 1N 70 12 E
Angtassom **101** 11 1N 104 41 E
Angu **126** 3 25N 24 28 E
Anguilla ■ **167** 18 14N 63 5W
Angurugu **138** 14 0 S 136 25 E
Angus (□) **26** 56 45N 2 55W
Angus, Braes of **37** 56 51N 3 0W
Anhanduí, R. **173** 21 46 S 52 9W
Anhée **47** 50 18N 4 53 E
Anholt **73** 56 42N 11 33 E
Anhsi **105** 40 30N 96 0 E
Anhsiang **109** 29 24N 112 9 E
Anhua, Hunan, China **109** 28 22N 111 10 E
Anhua, Kwangsi-Chuang, China **108** 25 10N 108 21 E
Anhwei □ **109** 33 15N 116 50 E
Ani, Kiangsi, China **109** 28 50N 115 32 E
Ani, Shansi, China **106** 35 3N 111 2 E
Aniak **147** 61 58N 159 50W
Anicuns **171** 16 28 S 49 58W
Anidhros **69** 36 38N 25 43 E
Anié **121** 7 42N 1 8 E
Animas **161** 31 58N 108 58W
Ånimskog **73** 58 53N 12 35 E
Anin **101** 15 36N 97 50 E
Anivorano **129** 18 44 S 48 58 E
Anjangaon **96** 21 10N 77 20 E
Anjar **94** 23 6N 70 10 E
Anjen **109** 26 42N 113 19 E
Anjiabé **129** 12 7 S 49 20 E
Anjidiv I. **97** 14 40N 74 10 E
Anjō **111** 34 57N 137 5 E
Anjou **42** 47 20N 0 15W
Anjozorobe **129** 18 22 S 47 52 E
Anju **107** 39 36N 125 40 E
Anka **121** 12 13N 5 58 E
Ank'ang **108** 32 38N 109 5 E
Ankara **92** 40 0N 32 54 E
Ankaramena **129** 21 57 S 46 39 E
Ankazoabo **129** 22 18 S 44 31 E
Ankazobé **129** 18 20 S 47 10 E
Ankazotokana **129** 21 20 S 48 9 E
Ankisabé **129** 19 17 S 46 29 E
Anklesvar **96** 21 38N 73 3 E
Ankober **123** 9 35N 39 40 E
Ankoro **126** 6 45 S 26 55 E
Ankuang **107** 45 19N 123 40 E
Ankuo **106** 38 25N 115 19 E
Anlu **109** 31 12N 113 38 E
Anlung **108** 25 6N 106 31 E
Anmyŏn Do **107** 36 25N 126 25 E
Ånn **72** 63 19N 12 34 E
Ann Arbor **156** 42 17N 83 45W
Ann C., Antarct. **13** 66 30 S 50 30 E
Ann C., U.S.A. **162** 42 39N 70 37W
Ann, gasfield **19** 53 40N 2 5 E
Ånn L. **72** 63 15N 12 35 E
Anna, U.S.A. **159** 37 28N 89 10W
Anna, U.S.S.R. **81** 51 38N 40 23 E
Anna Branch, R. **139** 34 2 S 141 50 E
Anna Plains **136** 19 17 S 121 37 E
Annaba **119** 36 50N 7 46 E
Annaberg-Buchholz **48** 50 34N 12 58 E
Annagassan **38** 53 53N 6 20W
Annagh Hd. **38** 54 15N 10 5W
Annaka **111** 36 19N 138 54 E
Annalee, R. **38** 54 3N 7 15W
Annalong **38** 54 7N 5 55W
Annam = Trung-Phan **101** 16 30N 107 30 E
Annamitique, Chaîne **100** 17 0N 106 0 E
Annan **35** 55 0N 3 17W
Annan, R. **35** 54 58N 3 18W
Annanberg **135** 4 52 S 144 42 E
Annandale **35** 55 10N 3 25W
Annapolis **162** 39 0N 76 30W
Annapolis Royal **151** 44 44N 65 32W
Annapurna **95** 28 34N 83 50 E
Annascaul **39** 52 10N 10 3W
Anne, oilfield **19** 55 24N 5 7 E
Annean, L. **137** 26 54 S 118 14 E
Anneberg **73** 57 32N 12 6 E
Annecy **45** 45 55N 6 8 E
Annecy, L. d' **45** 45 52N 6 10 E
Annemasse **45** 46 12N 6 16 E
Annestown **39** 52 8N 7 18W
Annette **147** 55 2N 131 35W
Annfield Plain **33** 54 52N 1 45W
Annie Peak **137** 33 53 S 119 59 E
Anning **108** 24 58N 102 30 E
Anningle **136** 21 50 S 133 7 E
Anniston **157** 33 45N 85 50W
Annobón **114** 1 35 S 3 35 E
Annonay **45** 45 15N 4 40 E
Annonciation, L' **150** 46 25N 74 55W
Annot **45** 43 58N 6 38 E
Annotto Bay **166** 18 17N 77 3W
Annuello **140** 34 53 S 142 55 E
Annville **162** 40 18N 76 32W
Áno Arkhánai **69** 35 16N 25 11 E
Áno Porróia **68** 41 17N 23 2 E
Áno Viánnos **69** 35 2N 25 21 E
Anoka **158** 45 10N 93 26W
Anorotsangana **129** 13 56 S 47 55 E
Anp'ing, Hopei, China **106** 38 13N 115 31 E
Anp'ing, Liaoning, China **107** 41 10N 123 30 E
Ans **47** 50 39N 5 32 E
Ansai **106** 36 54N 109 10 E
Ansbach **49** 49 17N 10 34 E
Anse au Loup, L' **151** 51 32N 56 50W
Anse, L' **150** 46 47N 88 28W
Anseba, R. **123** 16 15N 37 45 E
Anserma **174** 5 13N 75 48W
Anseroeul **47** 50 43N 3 32 E
Anshan **107** 41 3N 122 58 E
Anshun **105** 26 2N 105 57 E
Ansley **158** 41 19N 99 24W
Ansó **58** 42 51N 0 48W
Anson **159** 32 46N 99 54W
Anson B. **136** 13 20 S 130 6 E
Ansongo **121** 15 25N 0 35 E
Ansonia **162** 41 21N 73 6W
Ansonville **150** 48 46N 80 43W
Anstey **28** 52 41N 1 14W
Anstey Hill **109** 34 51 S 138 44 E
Anstruther **35** 56 14N 2 40W
Ansudu **103** 2 11 S 139 22 E
Antabamba **174** 14 40 S 73 0W
Antakya **92** 36 14N 36 10 E
Antalaha **129** 14 57 S 50 20 E
Antalya **92** 36 52N 30 45 E
Antalya Körfezi **92** 36 15N 31 30 E
Antananrivo **125** 18 55 S 47 35 E
Antanimbaribé **129** 21 30 S 44 48 E
Antarctic Pen. **13** 67 0 S 60 0W
Antarctica **125** 90 0 S 0 0
Antela, Laguna **56** 42 7N 7 40W
Antelope **127** 21 2 S 28 31 E
Anten **73** 58 5N 12 22 E
Antenor Navarro **170** 6 44 S 38 27W
Antequera, Parag. **172** 24 8 S 57 7W
Antequera, Spain **57** 37 5N 4 33W
Antero Mt. **161** 38 45N 106 43W
Anthemoús **68** 40 31N 23 15 E
Anthony, Kans., U.S.A. **159** 37 8N 98 2W
Anthony, N. Mex., U.S.A. **161** 32 1N 106 37W
Anthony Lagoon **138** 18 0 S 135 30 E
Anti Atlas, Mts. **118** 30 30N 6 30W
Antibes **45** 43 34N 7 6 E
Antibes, C. d' **45** 43 31N 7 7 E
Anticosti, Î. de **151** 49 30N 63 0W
Antifer, C. d' **42** 49 41N 0 10 E
Antigo **158** 45 8N 89 5W
Antigonish **151** 45 38N 61 58W
Antigua **166** 14 34N 90 41W
Antigua Bahama, Canal de la **166** 22 10N 77 30W
Antigua, I. **167** 17 0N 61 50W
Antilla **166** 20 40N 75 50W
Antimony **161** 38 7N 112 0W
Antioch **163** 38 7N 121 45W
Antioquia **174** 6 40N 75 55W
Antioquia □ **174** 7 0N 75 30W
Antipodes Is. **130** 49 45 S 178 40 E
Antler **158** 48 58N 101 18W
Antler, R. **153** 49 8N 101 0W
Antlers **159** 34 15N 95 35W
Antofagasta **172** 23 50 S 70 30W
Antofagasta □ **172** 24 0 S 69 0W
Antofagasta de la Sierra **172** 26 5 S 67 20W
Antofallá **172** 25 30 S 68 5W
Antofalla, Salar de **172** 25 40 S 67 45W
Antoing **47** 50 34N 3 27 E
Anton **159** 33 49N 102 5W
Anton Chico **161** 35 12N 105 5W
Antongil, B. d' **129** 15 30 S 49 50 E
Antonibe **129** 15 7 S 47 24 E
Antonibe, Presqu'île d' **129** 15 30 S 49 50 E
Antonina **173** 25 26 S 48 42W
Antonito **161** 37 4N 106 1W
Antonovo **83** 49 25N 51 42 E
Antony **30** 50 22N 4 13W
Antrain **42** 48 28N 1 30W
Antrim **38** 54 43N 6 13W
Antrim □ **38** 54 42N 6 20W
Antrim Co. **38** 54 58N 6 20W
Antrim, Mts. of **38** 54 57N 6 8W
Antrim Plateau **136** 18 8 S 128 20 E
Antrodoco **63** 42 25N 13 4 E
Antropovo **81** 58 26N 42 51 E
Antsalova **129** 18 40 S 44 37 E
Antse **106** 36 15N 112 15 E
Antsirabé **129** 19 55 S 47 2 E
Antsohihy **129** 14 50 S 47 50 E
Ant'u **107** 43 6N 128 54 E
Antung **107** 40 10N 124 18 E
Antungwei **107** 35 10N 119 20 E
Antwerp **140** 36 17 S 142 4 E
Antwerp = Antwerpen **47** 51 13N 4 25 E
Antwerpen **47** 51 13N 4 25 E
Antwerpen □ **47** 51 15N 4 40 E
Antz'u **106** 39 31N 116 41 E
Anupgarh **94** 29 10N 73 10 E
Anuradhapura **97** 8 22N 80 28 E
Anvaing **47** 50 41N 3 34 E
Anvers = Antwerp(en) **47** 51 13N 4 25 E
Anvers I. **13** 64 30 S 63 40W
Anvik **147** 62 37N 160 20W
Anxious B. **139** 33 24 S 134 45 E
Anyama **120** 5 30N 4 3W
Anyang **106** 36 7N 114 26 E
Anyer-Lor **103** 6 6 S 105 56 E
Anyüan **109** 25 9N 115 21 E
Anza, Jordan **90** 32 22N 35 12 E
Anza, U.S.A. **163** 33 35N 116 39W

Anza Borrego Desert State Park Arizpe

Anza Borrego Desert State Park 163 33 0N 116 26W
Anzhero-Sudzhensk 76 56 10N 83 40E
Anzio 64 41 28N 12 37E
Aoga-Shima 111 32 28N 139 46E
Aoiz 58 42 46N 1 22W
Aomori 112 40 45N 140 45E
Aomori-ken □ 112 40 45N 140 40E
Aonla 95 28 16N 79 11E
Aono-Yama 110 34 28N 131 48E
Aorangi Mts. 142 41 49S 175 22E
Aoreora 118 28 51N 10 53W
Aosta 62 45 43N 7 20E
Aoudéras 121 17 45N 8 20E
Aouinet Torkoz 118 28 31N 9 46W
Aoukar □ 118 23 50N 2 45W
Aouker 120 23 48N 4 0W
Aoulef el Arab 118 26 55N 1 2E
Aoullouz 118 30 44N 8 1W
Apa 108 32 55N 101 40E
Apa, R. 172 22 6S 58 2W
Apache, Ariz., U.S.A. 161 31 46N 109 6W
Apache, Okla., U.S.A. 159 34 53N 98 22W
Apahanuerhch'i 106 43 58N 116 2E
Apalachee B. 157 30 0N 84 0W
Apalachicola 157 29 40N 85 0W
Apalachicola, R. 157 30 0N 85 0W
Apapa 121 6 25N 3 25E
Apaporis, R. 174 0 30S 70 30W
Aparecida do Taboado 171 20 5S 51 5W
Aparri 103 18 22N 121 38E
Aparurén 174 5 6N 62 8W
Apateu 70 46 36N 21 47E
Apatin 66 45 40N 19 0E
Apatzingán 164 19 0N 102 20W
Apeldoorn 46 52 13N 5 57E
Apeldoornsch Kanal 46 52 29N 6 5E
Apen 48 53 12N 7 47E
Apenam 102 8 35S 116 13E
Apennines 16 44 20N 10 20E
Apia 174 5 5N 75 58W
Apiacás, Serra dos 174 9 50S 57 0W
Apiaí 174 24 31S 48 50W
Apinajé 171 11 31S 48 18W
Apiti 142 39 58S 175 54E
Apizaco 165 19 26N 98 9W
Aplahové 121 6 56N 1 41E
Aplao 174 16 0S 72 40W
Apo, Mt. 103 6 53N 125 14E
Apodi 170 5 39S 37 48W
Apolda 48 51 1N 11 30E
Apollo Bay 140 38 45S 143 40E
Apollonia, Greece 69 36 58N 24 43E
Apollonia, Libya 117 32 52N 21 59E
Apolo 174 14 30S 68 30W
Aporé, R. 171 19 27S 50 57W
Aporema 170 1 14N 50 49W
Apostle Is. 158 46 50N 90 30W
Apóstoles 173 28 0S 56 0W
Apostolovo 82 47 39N 33 39E
Apoteri 174 4 2N 58 32W
Appalachian Mts. 156 38 0N 80 0W
Appelscha 46 52 57N 6 21E
Appeninni 65 41 0N 15 0E
Appeninno Ligure 62 44 30N 9 0E
Appenzell 51 47 20N 9 25E
Appenzell-Ausser Rhoden □ 51 47 23N 9 23E
Appenzell-Inner Rhoden □ 51 47 20N 9 25E
Appiano 63 46 27N 11 17E
Appingedam 46 53 19N 6 51E
Apple Valley 163 34 30N 117 11W
Appleby 32 54 35N 2 29W
Applecross 36 57 26N 5 50W
Applecross For. 36 57 27N 5 40W
Appledore, Devon, U.K. 30 51 3N 4 12W
Appledore, Kent, U.K. 29 51 2N 0 47E
Appleton 156 44 17N 88 25W
Approuague 170 4 20N 52 0W
Apreivka 81 55 33N 37 4E
Apricena 65 41 47N 15 25E
Aprigliano 65 39 17N 16 19E
Aprília 64 41 38N 12 38E
Apsheronsk 83 44 28N 39 42E
Apsley Str. 136 11 35S 130 28E
Apt 45 43 53N 5 24E
Apucarana 173 23 55S 51 33W
Apulia = Puglia 65 41 0N 16 30E
Apure □ 174 7 10N 68 50W
Apure, R. 174 8 0N 69 20W
Apurímac, R. 174 12 10S 73 30W
Apurito, R. 174 7 50N 67 0W
Apuseni, Munţii 70 46 30N 22 45E
Aq Chah 93 37 0N 66 5E
'Aqaba 122 29 31N 35 0E
'Aqaba, Khalīj al 92 28 15N 33 20E
Aqiq 122 18 14N 38 12E
Aqiq, Khalîg 122 18 20N 38 10E
'Aqraba 90 32 9N 35 20E
'Aqrah 92 36 46N 43 45E
Aquanish 151 50 14N 62 2W
Aquasco 162 38 35N 76 43W
Aquidaba 171 10 17S 37 2W
Aquidauana 175 20 30S 55 50W
Aquila, L' 63 42 21N 13 24E
Aquiles Serdán 164 28 37N 105 54W
Aquin 167 18 16N 73 24W
Ar Ramadi 92 33 25N 43 20E
Ar-Ramthā 90 32 34N 36 0E
Ar Rass 92 25 50N 43 40E
Ar Rifai 92 31 50N 46 10E
Ar Riyād 92 24 41N 46 42E
Ar Rub 'al Khālī 91 21 0N 51 0E
Ar Rutbah 92 33 0N 40 15E
Arab, Khalîg el 122 30 55N 29 0E
Arab, Shott al 92 30 0N 48 31E
Araba 121 13 7N 5 0E
Arabatskaya Strelka 82 45 40N 35 0E
Arabba 63 46 30N 11 51E
Arabelo 174 4 55N 64 13W
Arabia 86 25 0N 45 0E
Arabian Desert 122 28 0N 32 20E
Arabian Sea 86 16 0N 65 0E
Aracajú 170 10 55S 37 4W
Aracataca 174 10 38N 74 9W
Aracati 170 4 30S 37 44W
Araçatuba 173 21 10S 50 30W
Aracena 57 37 53N 6 38W
Aracruz 171 19 49S 40 16W
Araçuaí 171 16 52S 42 4W
Araçuaí, R. 171 16 46S 42 2W
Arad 66 46 10N 21 20E
Arada 117 15 0N 20 20E
Aradu Nou 66 46 8N 21 20E
Arafura Sea 103 10 0S 135 0E
Aragats 83 40 30N 44 15E
Aragón 58 41 25N 1 0W
Aragón, R. 58 42 35N 0 50W
Aragona 64 37 24N 13 36E
Aragua □ 174 10 0N 67 10W
Aragua de Barcelona 174 9 28N 64 49W
Araguacema 170 8 50S 49 20W
Araguaçu 171 12 49S 49 51W
Araguaia, R. 170 7 0S 49 15W
Araguaína 170 7 12S 48 12W
Araguari 171 18 38S 48 11W
Araguari, R. 170 1 0N 51 40W
Araguatins 170 5 38S 48 7W
Araioses 170 2 53S 41 55W
Arak 118 25 20N 3 45E
Arāk 92 34 0N 49 40E
Arakan □ 98 19 0N 94 15E
Arakan Coast 99 19 0N 94 0E
Arakan Yoma 98 20 0N 94 30E
Arákhova 69 38 28N 22 35E
Araks, R. = Aras, Rud-e 92 39 10N 47 10E
Aral Sea = Aralskoye More 76 44 30N 60 0E
Aralsk 76 46 50N 61 20E
Aralskoye More 76 44 30N 60 0E
Aramac 138 22 58S 145 14E
Arambagh 95 22 53N 87 48E
Aramŭ, Mţii de 70 47 10N 22 30E
Aran Fawddwy, Mt. 31 52 48N 3 40W
Aran, I. 38 55 0N 8 30W
Aran Is. 39 53 5N 9 42W
Aranci 64 41 5N 3 40W
Aranci, Golfo 64 41 0N 9 35E
Aranda de Duero 58 41 39N 3 42W
Arandelovac 66 44 18N 20 37E
Aranga 142 35 44S 173 40E
Aranjuez 56 40 1N 3 40W
Aranos 125 24 9S 19 7E
Aransas Pass 159 28 0N 97 9W
Aranyaprathet 101 13 41N 102 30E
Aranzazu 174 5 16N 75 30W
Arao 110 32 59N 130 25E
Araouane 120 18 55N 3 30W
Arapahoe 158 40 22N 99 53W
Arapari 170 5 34S 49 15W
Arapawa I. 131 41 13S 174 20E
Arapey Grande, R. 172 30 55S 57 49W
Arapiraca 170 9 45S 36 39W
Arapkir 92 39 5N 38 30E
Arapongas 173 23 29S 51 28W
Arapuni 130 38 3S 175 37E
Araranguá 173 29 0S 49 30W
Araraquara 171 21 50S 48 0W
Araras 173 5 15S 60 35W
Ararás, Serra dos 173 25 0S 53 10W
Ararat, Austral. 140 37 16S 143 0E
Ararat, Turkey 92 39 50N 44 15E
Ararat, Mt. = Ağri Daği 92 39 50N 44 15E
Arari 170 3 28S 44 47W
Araria 95 26 9N 87 33E
Araripe 171 7 12S 40 8W
Araripe, Chapada do 170 7 20S 40 0W
Araripina 170 7 33S 40 34W
Araro 123 4 41N 38 50E
Araruama, Lagoa de 173 22 53S 42 12W
Araruna 170 6 52S 35 44W
Åras 71 59 42N 10 31E
Aras, Rud-e 92 39 10N 47 10E
Araticu 170 1 58S 49 51W
Arauca 174 7 0N 70 40W
Arauca □ 174 6 40N 71 0W
Arauca, R. 174 7 30N 69 0W
Arauco 172 37 16S 73 25W
Arauco □ 172 37 40S 73 25W
Araújos 171 19 56S 45 14W
Arauquita 174 7 2N 71 25W
Araure 174 9 34N 69 13W
Arawa 123 9 57N 41 58E
Arawhata 143 43 59S 168 38E
Arawhata, R. 143 44 0S 168 40E
Araxá 171 19 35S 46 55W
Araya, Pen. de 174 10 40N 64 0W
Arba 123 9 0N 40 20E
Arba Jahan 126 2 5N 39 2E
Arba, L' 118 36 40N 3 9E
Arba Minch 123 6 0N 37 30E
Arbah, Wadi al 90 30 30N 35 5E
Arbatax 64 39 57N 9 42E
Arbedo 51 46 12N 9 3E
Arbeláez 174 4 17N 74 26W
Arbīl 92 36 15N 44 5E
Arboga 72 59 24N 15 52E
Arbois 43 46 55N 5 46E
Arbon 51 47 31N 9 26E
Arbore 123 5 3N 36 50E
Arborea 64 39 46N 8 34E
Arborfield 153 53 6N 103 39W
Arborg 153 50 54N 97 13W
Arbrå 72 61 28N 16 22E
Arbresle, L 45 45 50N 4 26E
Arbroath 37 56 34N 2 35W
Arbuckle 160 39 3N 122 2W
Arbus 64 39 30N 8 33E
Arbuzinka 82 47 52N 31 25E
Arc 43 47 28N 5 34E
Arcachon 44 44 40N 1 10W
Arcachon, Bassin d' 44 44 42N 1 10W
Arcadia, Fla., U.S.A. 157 27 20N 81 50W
Arcadia, La., U.S.A. 159 32 34N 92 53W
Arcadia, Nebr., U.S.A. 158 41 29N 99 4W
Arcadia, Wis., U.S.A. 158 44 13N 91 29W
Arcata 160 40 55N 124 4W
Arcévia 63 43 29N 12 58E
Archangel = Arkhangelsk 78 64 40N 41 0E
Archar 66 43 50N 22 54E
Archbald 162 41 30N 75 31W
Archena 59 38 9N 1 16W
Archer B. 138 13 20S 141 30E
Archer, R. 138 13 25S 142 50E
Archers Post 126 0 35N 37 35E
Archidona 57 37 6N 4 22W
Archiestown 37 57 28N 3 20W
Arci, Monte 64 39 47N 8 44E
Arcidosso 63 42 51N 11 30E
Arcila = Asilah 118 35 29N 6 0W
Arcis-sur-Aube 43 48 32N 4 10E
Arckaringa 139 27 56S 134 45E
Arckaringa Cr. 139 28 10S 135 22E
Arco, Italy 62 45 55N 10 54E
Arco, U.S.A. 160 43 45N 113 16W
Arcola 153 49 40N 102 30W
Arcoona 140 31 2S 137 1E
Arcos, Brazil 171 20 17S 45 32W
Arcos, Spain 58 41 12N 2 16W
Arcos de los Frontera 57 36 45N 5 49W
Arcot 97 12 53N 79 20E
Arcoverde 170 8 25S 37 4W
Arctic Ocean 12 78 0N 160 0W
Arctic Red, R. 147 66 0N 132 0W
Arctic Red River 147 67 15N 134 0W
Arctic Village 147 68 5N 145 45W
Arda, R., Bulg. 67 41 40N 25 40E
Arda, R., Italy 62 44 53N 9 52E
Ardabil 92 38 15N 48 18E
Ardagh 39 52 30N 9 5W
Ardakan 93 30 20N 52 5E
Årdal 71 59 9N 6 13E
Ardales 57 36 53N 4 51W
Årdalstangen 71 61 14N 7 43E
Ardara 38 54 47N 8 25W
Ardatov 81 54 51N 46 15E
Ardavasar 36 57 3N 5 54E
Ardbeg 34 55 38N 6 6W
Ardcath 38 53 36N 6 21W
Ardcharnich 36 57 52N 5 5W
Ardchyle 34 56 26N 4 24W
Ardèche □ 45 44 42N 4 16E
Ardee 38 53 51N 6 32W
Arden Stby. 73 56 46N 9 52E
Ardennes 47 49 30N 5 10E
Ardennes □ 43 49 35N 4 40E
Ardentes 43 46 45N 1 50E
Ardentinny 34 56 3N 4 56E
Arderin, Mt. 39 53 3N 7 40W
Ardestan 93 33 20N 52 25E
Ardfert 39 52 20N 9 49W
Ardfinnan 39 52 20N 7 53W
Ardglass 38 54 16N 5 38W
Ardgour 36 56 45N 5 25W
Ardgroom 39 51 44N 9 53W
Ardhas, R. 68 41 36N 26 25E
Ardhasig 36 57 55N 6 51W
Ardhéa 68 40 58N 22 3E
Ardila, R. 57 38 10N 7 20W
Ardingly 29 51 3N 0 3W
Ardino 67 41 34N 25 9E
Ardivachar Pt. 36 57 23N 7 25W
Ardkearagh 39 51 48N 10 11W
Ardkeen 38 54 27N 5 31W
Ardlethan 141 34 22S 146 53E
Ardlui 34 56 19N 4 43W
Ardmore, Austral. 138 21 39S 139 11E
Ardmore, Okla., U.S.A. 159 34 10N 97 5W
Ardmore, Pa., U.S.A. 162 39 58N 75 18W
Ardmore, S.D., U.S.A. 158 43 0N 103 40W
Ardmore Hd. 39 51 58N 7 43W
Ardmore Pt. 34 55 40N 6 0W
Ardnacrusha 39 52 43N 8 38W
Ardnamurchan, Pen. 36 56 43N 6 0W
Ardnamurchan Pt. 36 56 44N 6 14W
Ardnaree 38 54 6N 9 8W
Ardnave Pt. 34 55 54N 6 20W
Ardooie 47 50 59N 3 13E
Ardore Marina 65 38 11N 16 10E
Ardrahan 39 53 10N 8 48W
Ardres 43 50 50N 2 0E
Ardrishaig 34 56 0N 5 27W
Ardrossan, Austral. 140 34 26S 137 53E
Ardrossan, U.K. 34 55 39N 4 50W
Ards □ 38 54 35N 5 30W
Ards Pen. 38 54 30N 5 25W
Ardud 70 47 37N 22 52E
Ardunac 83 41 8N 42 5E
Ardvoulie Castle 36 58 0N 6 45W
Ardwell 37 57 20N 3 5W
Åre 72 63 22N 13 15E
Arecibo 147 18 29N 66 42W
Areia Branca 170 5 0S 37 0W
Aremark 71 59 15N 11 42E
Arena de la Ventana, Punta 164 24 4N 109 52W
Arenales, Cerro 176 47 5S 73 40W
Arenas 56 43 17N 4 50W
Arenas de San Pedro 56 40 12N 5 5W
Arenas, Pta. 174 10 20N 62 39W
Arendal 71 58 28N 8 46E
Arendonk 47 51 19N 5 5E
Arendsee 48 52 52N 11 27E
Arenig Fach, Mt. 31 52 55N 3 45E
Arenig Fawr, Mt. 31 52 56N 3 45W
Arenys de Mar 58 41 35N 2 33E
Arenzano 62 44 24N 8 40E
Areópolis 69 36 40N 22 22E
Arequipa 174 16 20S 71 30W
Arero 123 4 41N 38 50E
Arês 171 6 11S 35 9W
Arès 44 44 47N 1 8W
Arévalo 56 41 3N 4 43W
Arezzo 63 43 28N 11 50E
Arga, R. 58 42 30N 1 50W
Argalasti 68 39 13N 23 13E
Argamasilla de Alba 59 39 8N 3 5W
Arganda 58 40 19N 3 26W
Arganil 56 40 13N 8 3W
Argayash 84 55 29N 60 52E
Argelès-Gazost 44 43 0N 0 6W
Argelès-sur-Mer 44 42 34N 3 1E
Argent-sur-Sauldre 43 47 33N 2 25E
Argenta, Can. 152 50 20N 116 55W
Argenta, Italy 63 44 37N 11 50E
Argentan 42 48 45N 0 1W
Argentário, Mte. 63 42 23N 11 11E
Argentat 44 45 6N 1 56E
Argentera 62 44 23N 6 58E
Argenteuil 43 48 57N 2 14E
Argentia 151 47 18N 53 58W
Argentiera, C. dell' 64 40 44N 8 8E
Argentière, Aiguilles d' 50 45 58N 7 2E
Argentina 174 0 34N 74 17W
Argentina ■ 176 35 0S 66 0W
Argentino, L. 176 50 10S 73 0W
Argenton-sur-Creuse 44 46 36N 1 30E
Argentré 42 48 5N 0 40W
Argeş □ 70 45 0N 24 45E
Argeş, R. 70 44 30N 25 50E
Arghandab, R. 94 32 15N 66 23E
Argo 122 19 28N 30 30E
Argo, I. 122 19 28N 30 30E
Argolikós Kólpos 69 37 20N 22 52E
Argolís □ 69 37 38N 22 50E
Argonne 43 49 0N 5 20E
Árgos 69 37 40N 22 43E
Árgos Orestikón 68 40 27N 21 26E
Argostólion 69 38 12N 20 33E
Arguedas 58 42 11N 1 36W
Arguello, Pt. 163 34 34N 120 40W
Argun, R. 77 53 20N 121 28E
Argungu 121 12 40N 4 31E
Argus Pk. 163 35 52N 117 26W
Argyle 158 48 23N 96 49W
Argyle Downs 136 16 17S 128 47E
Argyle, L. 136 16 20S 128 40E
Argyll (□) 26 56 18N 5 15W
Argyll, Dist. 34 56 14N 5 10W
Argyll, oilfield 19 56 8N 3 5E
Argyrádhes 68 39 27N 19 58E
Århus 73 56 8N 10 11E
Aria 142 38 33S 175 0E
Ariamsvlei 128 28 9S 19 51E
Ariana 119 36 52N 10 12E
Ariano Irpino 65 41 10N 15 4E
Ariano nel Polèsine 63 44 56N 12 5E
Aribinda 121 14 17N 0 52W
Arica, Chile 174 18 32S 70 20W
Arica, Colomb. 174 2 0S 71 50W
Arica, Peru 174 1 30S 75 30W
Arid, C. 137 34 1S 123 10E
Arida 111 33 29N 135 44E
Ariège □ 44 42 56N 1 30E
Ariège, R. 44 42 56N 1 25E
Arieş, R. 70 46 24N 23 20E
Arilje 66 43 44N 20 7E
Arima 167 10 38N 61 17W
Arinagour 34 56 38N 6 31W
Arinos, R. 174 11 15S 57 0W
Ario de Rosales 164 19 12N 101 42W
Aripuanã 174 9 25S 60 30W
Aripuanã, R. 174 7 30S 60 25W
Ariquemes 174 9 55S 63 6W
Arisaig 36 56 55N 5 50W
Arisaig, Sd. of 36 56 50N 5 50W
Arîsh, W. el 122 30 25N 34 52E
Arismendi 174 8 29N 68 22W
Arissa 123 11 10N 41 35E
Aristazabal, I. 152 52 40N 129 10W
Arita 110 33 11N 129 54E
Arivaca 161 31 37N 111 25W
Arivonimamo 129 19 1S 47 11E
Ariyalur 97 11 8N 79 8E
Ariza 58 41 19N 2 3W
Arizaro, Salar de 172 24 40S 67 50W
Arizona 172 35 45S 65 25W
Arizona □ 161 34 20N 111 30W
Arizpe 164 30 20N 110 11W

Arjang Atalaia

Arjang	72	59 24N	12 9 E
Arjäng	72	59 24N	12 8 E
Arjeplog	74	66 3N	18 2 E
Arjona, Colomb.	174	10 14N	75 22W
Arjona, Spain	57	37 56N	4 4W
Arjuno	103	7 49 S	112 19 E
Arka	77	60 15N	142 0 E
Arkadak	81	51 58N	43 19 E
Arkadelphia	159	34 5N	93 0W
Arkadhia □	69	37 30N	22 20 E
Arkaig, L.	36	56 58N	5 10W
Arkansas □	159	35 0N	92 30W
Arkansas City	159	37 4N	97 3W
Arkansas, R.	159	35 20N	93 30W
Arkathos, R.	68	39 20N	21 4 E
Arkhángelos	69	36 13N	28 7 E
Arkhangelsk	78	64 40N	41 0 E
Arkhangelskoye	81	51 32N	40 58 E
Arkiko	123	15 33N	39 30 E
Arkle R.	32	54 25N	2 0W
Arklow	39	52 48N	6 10W
Arklow Hd.	39	52 46N	6 10W
Arkoi	69	37 24N	26 44 E
Arkona, Kap	48	54 41N	13 26 E
Arkonam	97	13 7N	79 43 E
Arkösund	73	58 29N	16 56 E
Arkoúdhi	69	38 33N	20 43 E
Arkticheskiy, Mys	77	81 10N	95 0 E
Arkul	84	57 17N	50 3 E
Arkville	162	42 9N	74 37W
Arlanc	44	45 25N	3 42 E
Arlanza, R.	56	42 6N	4 0W
Arlanzón, R.	56	42 12N	4 0W
Arlberg Pass	49	49 9N	10 12 E
Arlee	160	47 10N	114 4W
Arles	45	43 41N	4 40 E
Arlesheim	50	47 30N	7 37 E
Arless	39	52 53N	7 1W
Arlington, S. Afr.	129	28 1 S	27 53 E
Arlington, Oreg., U.S.A.	160	45 48N	120 6W
Arlington, S.D., U.S.A.	158	44 25N	97 4W
Arlington, Va., U.S.A.	162	38 52N	77 5W
Arlington, Vt., U.S.A.	162	43 5N	73 9W
Arlington, Wash., U.S.A.	160	48 11N	122 4W
Arlon	47	49 42N	5 49 E
Arlöv	73	55 38N	13 5 E
Arly	121	11 35N	1 28 E
Armadale, Austral.	137	32 12 S	116 0 E
Armadale, Lothian, U.K.	35	55 54N	3 42W
Armadale, Skye, U.K.	36	57 24N	5 54W
Armagh, Can.	137	46 41N	70 32W
Armagh, U.K.	38	54 22N	6 40W
Armagh □	38	54 18N	6 37W
Armagh Co.	38	54 16N	6 35W
Armagnac	44	43 44N	0 10 E
Armançon, R.	43	47 51N	4 7 E
Armavir	83	45 2N	41 7 E
Armenia	174	4 35N	75 45W
Armenian S.S.R. □	83	40 0N	41 0 E
Armeniş	70	45 13N	22 17 E
Armentières	43	50 40N	2 50 E
Armero	174	4 58N	74 54W
Armidale	141	30 30 S	151 40 E
Armour	158	43 20N	98 25W
Armoy	38	55 8N	6 20W
Arms	150	49 34N	86 3W
Armstead	160	45 0N	112 56W
Armstrong, B.C., Can.	152	50 25N	119 10W
Armstrong, Ont., Can.	150	50 18N	89 4W
Armstrong, U.S.A.	159	26 59N	90 48W
Armstrong Cr.	136	16 35 S	131 40 E
Armur	96	18 48N	78 16 E
Arnaia	68	40 30N	23 40 E
Arnarfjörður	74	65 48N	23 40W
Arnay-le-Duc	43	47 10N	4 27 E
Arnedillo	58	42 13N	2 14W
Arnedo	58	42 12N	2 5W
Árnes	74	66 1N	21 31W
Årnes	71	60 7N	11 28 E
Arnett	159	36 9N	99 44W
Arney	38	54 17N	7 41W
Arnhem	46	51 58N	5 55 E
Arnhem B.	138	12 20 S	136 10 E
Arnhem, C.	138	12 20 S	137 0 E
Arnhem Ld.	138	13 10 S	135 0 E
Arni	97	12 43N	79 19 E
Arnissa	68	40 47N	21 49 E
Arno Bay	140	33 54 S	136 34 E
Arno, R.	62	43 44N	10 20 E
Arnold, N.Z.	143	42 29 S	171 25 E
Arnold, U.K.	33	53 0N	1 8W
Arnold, Calif., U.S.A.	163	38 15N	120 20W
Arnold, Nebr., U.S.A.	158	41 29N	100 10W
Arnoldstein	52	46 33N	13 43 E
Arnot	153	55 46N	96 41W
Arnøy	74	70 9N	20 40 E
Arnprior	150	45 26N	76 21W
Arnsberg	48	51 25N	8 10 E
Arnside	32	54 12N	2 49W
Arnstadt	48	50 50N	10 56 E
Aroa	174	10 26N	68 54W
Aroab	125	26 41 S	19 39 E
Aroánia Óri	69	37 56N	22 12 E
Aroche	57	37 56N	6 57W
Aroeiras	170	7 31 S	35 41W
Arolla	50	46 2N	7 29 E
Arolsen	48	51 23N	9 1 E
Arona	62	45 45N	8 32 E
Arosa	51	46 47N	9 41 E
Arosa, Ría de	56	42 28N	8 57W
Arpajon, Cantal, France	44	44 54N	2 28 E
Arpajon, Seine et Oise, France	43	48 37N	2 12 E
Arpino	64	41 40N	13 35 E
Arra Mts.	39	52 50N	8 22W
Arrabury	139	26 45 S	141 0 E
Arrah	95	25 35N	84 32 E
Arraias	171	12 56 S	46 57W
Arraias, R.	170	7 30 S	49 20W
Arraiolos	57	38 44N	7 59W
Arran, I.	34	55 34N	5 12W
Arrandale	152	54 57N	130 0W
Arras	43	50 17N	2 46 E
Arreau	44	42 54N	0 22 E
Arrecife	116	28 59N	13 40W
Arrecifes	172	34 06 S	60 9W
Arrée, Mts. d'	42	48 26N	3 55W
Arriaga, Chiapas, Mexico	165	16 15N	93 52W
Arriaga, San Luís de Potosí, Mexico	164	21 55N	101 23W
Arrild	73	55 8N	8 58 E
Arrililah P.O.	138	23 43 S	143 54 E
Arrino	137	29 30 S	115 40 E
Arrochar	34	56 12N	4 45W
Arrojado, R.	171	13 24 S	44 20W
Arromanches-les-Bains	42	49 20N	0 38W
Arronches	57	39 8N	7 16W
Arrou	42	48 6N	1 8 E
Arrow L.	38	54 3N	8 20W
Arrow Rock Res.	160	43 45N	115 50W
Arrowhead	152	50 40N	117 55W
Arrowhead, L.	163	34 16N	117 10W
Arrowsmith, Mt.	143	30 7N	141 38 E
Arrowtown	143	44 57 S	168 50 E
Arroyo de la Luz	57	39 30N	6 38W
Arroyo Grande	163	35 9N	120 32W
Års	73	56 48N	9 30 E
Ars	44	46 13N	1 30W
Ars-sur-Moselle	43	49 5N	6 4 E
Arsenault L.	153	53 6N	108 32W
Arsiero	63	45 49N	11 22 E
Arsikere	97	13 15N	76 15 E
Arsk	81	56 10N	49 50 E
Årskogen	72	62 8N	17 20 E
Árta	69	39 8N	21 2 E
Artá	58	39 40N	3 20 E
Árta □	68	39 15N	26 0 E
Arteaga	164	18 50N	102 20W
Arteijo	56	43 19N	8 29W
Artem,Os.	83	40 28N	50 20 E
Artémou	120	15 38N	12 16W
Artemovsk	82	48 35N	37 55 E
Artemovsk	83	54 45N	93 35 E
Artemovskiy	84	57 21N	61 54 E
Artenay	43	48 5N	1 50 E
Artern	48	51 22N	11 18 E
Artesa de Segre	58	41 54N	1 3 E
Artesia	159	32 55N	104 25W
Artesia Wells	159	28 17N	99 18W
Artesian	158	44 2N	97 54W
Arth	51	47 4N	8 31 E
Arthez-de-Béarn	44	43 29N	0 38W
Arthington	120	6 35N	10 45W
Arthur Cr.	138	22 30 S	136 25 E
Arthur Pt.	138	22 7 S	150 3 E
Arthur, R.	138	41 2 S	144 40 E
Arthur's Pass	143	42 54 S	171 35 E
Arthur's Town	167	24 38N	75 42W
Arthurstown	39	52 15N	6 58W
Artigas	172	30 20 S	56 30W
Artigavan	38	54 51N	7 24W
Artik	83	40 38N	44 50 E
Artillery L.	153	63 9N	107 52W
Artois	43	50 20N	2 30 E
Artotina	69	38 42N	22 2 E
Artvin	92	41 14N	41 44 E
Aru, Kepulauan	103	6 0 S	134 30 E
Arua	126	3 1N	30 58 E
Aruanã	171	15 0 S	51 10W
Aruba I.	167	12 30N	70 0W
Arudy	44	43 7N	0 28W
Arumpo	140	33 48 S	142 55 E
Arun, R.	95	27 30N	87 15 E
Arun R.	29	50 48N	0 33W
Arunachal Pradesh □	98	28 0N	95 0 E
Arundel	29	50 52N	0 32W
Aruppukottai	97	9 31N	78 8 E
Arusha	126	3 20 S	36 40 E
Arusha □	126	4 0 S	36 30 E
Arusha Chini	126	3 32 S	37 20 E
Arusi □	123	7 45N	39 00 E
Aruvi	97	8 48N	79 53 E
Aruwimi, R.	126	1 30N	25 0 E
Arva	38	53 57N	7 35W
Arvada	160	44 43N	106 6W
Arvaklu	97	8 20N	79 58 E
Arvayheer	105	46 15N	102 48 E
Arve, R.	45	46 11N	6 8 E
Arvi	96	20 59N	78 16 E
Arvida	151	48 25N	71 14W
Arvidsjaur	74	65 35N	19 10 E
Arvika	72	59 40N	12 36 E
Arvin	163	35 12N	118 50W
Arys	85	42 26N	68 48 E
Arys, R.	85	42 45N	68 15 E
Arzachena	64	41 5N	9 27 E
Arzamas	81	55 27N	43 55 E
Arzew	118	35 50N	0 23W
Arzgir	83	45 18N	44 23 E
Arzignano	63	45 30N	11 20 E
As	47	51 1N	5 35 E
Aš	52	50 13N	12 12 E
As Salt	90	32 2N	35 43 E
As Samawah	92	31 15N	45 15 E
As-Samū	90	31 24N	35 4 E
As Sulaimānīyah	92	35 35N	45 29 E
As Sulṭon	119	31 4N	17 8 E
As Suwaih	93	22 10N	59 33 E
As Suwayda	92	32 40N	36 30 E
As Suwayrah	92	32 55N	45 0 E
Asab	128	25 30 S	18 0 E
Asaba	121	6 12N	6 38 E
Asadabad	92	34 50N	48 10 E
Asafo	120	6 20N	2 40W
Asahi	111	35 43N	140 39 E
Asahi-Gawa, R.	110	34 36N	133 58 E
Asahikawa	112	43 45N	142 30 E
Asale, L.	123	14 0N	40 20 E
Asama-Yama	111	36 24N	138 31 E
Asamankese	121	5 50N	0 40W
Asankrangwa	120	5 45N	2 30W
Asansol	95	23 40N	87 1 E
Åsarna	72	62 40N	14 20 E
Åsarna	72	62 39N	14 22 E
Asbe Teferi	123	9 4N	40 49 E
Asbesberge	128	29 0 S	23 0 E
Asbest	84	57 0N	61 30 E
Asbestos	151	45 47N	71 58W
Asbury Park	162	40 15N	74 1W
Ascensión	164	31 6N	107 59W
Ascensión, B. de la	165	19 50N	87 20W
Ascension, I.	15	8 0 S	14 15W
Aschach	49	48 23N	14 0 E
Aschaffenburg	49	49 58N	9 8 E
Aschendorf	48	53 2N	7 22 E
Aschersleben	48	51 45N	11 28 E
Asciano	63	43 14N	11 32 E
Áscoli Piceno	63	42 51N	13 34 E
Áscoli Satriano	65	41 11N	15 32 E
Ascona	51	46 9N	8 46 E
Ascope	174	7 46 S	79 8W
Ascot	29	51 24N	0 41W
Ascotán	172	21 45 S	68 17W
Aseb	123	13 0N	42 40 E
Åseda	73	57 10N	15 20 E
Åseda	73	57 10N	15 20 E
Asedjrad	118	24 51N	1 29 E
Asela	123	8 0N	39 0 E
Asenovgrad	67	42 1N	24 51 E
Åseral	71	58 37N	7 25 E
Åseral	71	58 38N	7 26 E
Asfeld	43	49 27N	4 5 E
Asfordby	29	52 45N	0 57W
Asfûn el Matâ'na	122	25 26N	32 30 E
Åsgårdstrand	71	59 22N	10 27 E
Ash	29	51 17N	1 16 E
Ash Fork	161	35 14N	112 32W
Ash Grove	159	37 21N	93 36W
Ash Shâm,Bâdiyat	92	31 30N	40 0 E
Ash Shāmīyah	92	31 55N	44 35 E
Ash Shatrah	92	31 30N	46 10 E
Ash Shuna	90	32 32N	35 34 E
Asha	84	55 0N	57 16 E
Ashaira	122	21 40N	40 40 E
Ashanti	121	7 30N	2 0W
Ashau	100	16 6N	107 22 E
Ashbourne, Ireland	38	53 31N	6 24W
Ashbourne, U.K.	33	53 2N	1 44W
Ashburn	157	31 42N	83 40W
Ashburton, N.Z.	143	43 53 S	171 48 E
Ashburton, U.K.	30	50 31N	3 45W
Ashburton Downs	136	23 25 S	117 4 E
Ashburton, R., Austral.	136	21 40 S	114 56 E
Ashburton, R., N.Z.	131	44 2 S	171 50 E
Ashby-de-la-Zouch	28	52 45N	1 29W
Ashchurch	28	52 0N	2 7W
Ashcroft	152	50 40N	121 20W
Ashdod	90	31 49N	34 35 E
Ashdot Ya'aqov	90	32 39N	35 35 E
Ashdown Forest	29	51 4N	0 2 E
Asheboro	157	35 43N	79 46W
Asherton	159	28 25N	99 43W
Asheville	157	35 39N	82 30W
Asheweig, R.	150	54 17N	87 12W
Ashford, Austral.	139	29 15 S	151 3 E
Ashford, Derby., U.K.	33	53 13N	1 43W
Ashford, Kent, U.K.	29	51 8N	0 53 E
Ashford, U.S.A.	160	46 45N	122 2W
Ashikaga	111	36 28N	139 29 E
Ashington	35	55 12N	1 35W
Ashio	111	36 38N	139 27 E
Ashizuri-Zaki	110	32 35N	132 50 E
Ashkarkot	94	33 3N	67 58 E
Ashkhabad	76	38 0N	57 50 E
Ashland, Kans., U.S.A.	159	37 13N	99 43W
Ashland, Ky., U.S.A.	156	38 25N	82 40W
Ashland, Me., U.S.A.	151	46 34N	68 26W
Ashland, Mont., U.S.A.	160	45 41N	106 12W
Ashland, Nebr., U.S.A.	158	41 5N	96 27W
Ashland, Ohio, U.S.A.	156	40 52N	82 20W
Ashland, Oreg., U.S.A.	160	42 10N	122 38W
Ashland, Pa., U.S.A.	162	40 45N	76 22W
Ashland, Va., U.S.A.	156	37 46N	77 30W
Ashland, Wis., U.S.A.	158	46 40N	90 52W
Ashley, N.D., U.S.A.	158	46 3N	99 23W
Ashley, Pa., U.S.A.	162	41 14N	75 53W
Ashmont	152	54 7N	111 29W
Ashmore Is.	136	12 14 S	123 50 E
Ashmore Reef	136	12 14 S	123 5 E
Ashmûn	122	30 18N	30 55 E
Ashokan Res.	162	41 56N	74 13W
Ashquelon	90	31 42N	34 55 E
Ashtabula	156	41 52N	80 50W
Ashti	96	18 50N	75 15 E
Ashton, S. Afr.	128	33 50 S	20 5 E
Ashton, U.S.A.	160	44 6N	111 30W
Ashton-in-Makerfield	32	53 29N	2 39W
Ashton-u.-Lyne	32	53 30N	2 8 E
Ashuanipi, L.	151	52 45N	66 15W
Ashurst	142	40 16 S	175 45 E
Ashurstwood	29	51 6N	0 2 E
Ashwater	30	50 43N	4 18W
Ashwick	28	51 13N	2 31W
Asia	86	45 0N	75 0 E
Asia, Kepulauan	103	1 0N	131 13 E
Asiago	63	45 52N	11 30 E
Asifabad	96	19 30N	79 24 E
Asilah	118	35 29N	6 0W
Asinara	64	41 5N	8 15 E
Asinara, G. dell'	64	41 0N	8 30 E
Asinara I.	64	41 5N	8 15 E
Asino	76	57 0N	86 0 E
Asir	91	18 40N	42 30 E
Asir, Ras	91	11 55N	51 10 E
Aska	96	19 37N	84 42 E
Askeaton	39	52 37N	8 58W
Asker	71	59 50N	10 26 E
Askersund	73	58 53N	14 55 E
Askim	71	59 35N	11 10 E
Askino	84	56 5N	56 34 E
Askja	74	65 3N	16 48W
Åskloster	73	57 13N	12 11 E
Askrigg	32	54 19N	2 6W
Asl	122	29 33N	32 44 E
Aslackby	33	52 53N	0 23W
Asmar	93	35 10N	71 27 E
Asmera (Asmara)	123	15 19N	38 55 E
Asnæs	73	55 40N	11 0 E
Åsnen	73	56 35N	15 45 E
Åsnes	71	60 37N	11 59 E
Asni	118	31 17N	7 58W
Aso	110	33 0N	130 42 E
Aso-Zan	110	32 53N	131 6 E
Asoa	126	4 35N	25 48 E
Asola	62	45 12N	10 25 E
Asotin	60	46 14N	117 2W
Aspatria	32	54 45N	3 20W
Aspe	59	38 20N	0 40W
Aspen	161	39 12N	106 56W
Aspermont	159	33 11N	100 15W
Aspiring, Mt.	143	44 23 S	168 46 E
Aspres	45	44 32N	5 44 E
Aspur	94	23 58N	74 7 E
Asquith	153	52 8N	107 13W
Assa	118	28 35N	9 6W
Assaba, Massif de l'	120	16 10N	11 45W
Assam □	98	25 45N	92 30 E
Assamakka	121	19 21N	5 38 E
Assateague I.	162	38 5N	75 6W
Asse	47	50 54N	4 6 E
Assebroek	47	51 11N	3 17 E
Assekrem	119	23 16N	5 49 E
Assémini	64	39 18N	9 0 E
Assen	46	53 0N	6 35 E
Assendelft	46	52 29N	4 45 E
Assenede	47	51 14N	3 46 E
Assens, Odense, Denmark	73	56 41N	10 3 E
Assens, Randers, Denmark	73	55 16N	9 55 E
Assesse	47	50 22N	5 2 E
Assiniboia	153	49 40N	105 59W
Assiniboine, R.	153	49 53N	97 8W
Assinica L.	150	50 30N	75 20W
Assinie	120	5 9N	3 17W
Assis	173	22 40 S	50 20W
Assisi	63	43 4N	12 36 E
Ássos	69	38 22N	20 33 E
Assynt	36	58 25N	5 10W
Assynt, L.	36	58 25N	5 15W
Astakidha	69	35 53N	26 50 E
Astalfort	44	44 4N	0 40 E
Astara	79	38 30N	48 50 E
Astee	39	52 33N	9 36W
Asten	47	51 24N	5 45 E
Asti	62	44 54N	8 11 E
Astillero	56	43 24N	3 49W
Astipálaia	69	36 32N	26 22 E
Aston, C.	149	70 10N	67 40W
Aston Clinton	29	51 48N	0 44W
Astorga	56	42 29N	6 8W
Astoria	160	46 16N	123 50W
Åstorp	73	56 6N	12 55 E
Astrakhan	83	46 25N	48 5 E
Astudillo	56	42 12N	4 22W
Asturias	56	43 15N	6 0W
Astwood Bank	28	52 15N	1 55W
Asunción	172	25 21 S	57 30W
Asunción, La	174	11 2N	63 53W
Åsunden	73	57 47N	13 18 E
Asutri	123	15 25N	35 45 E
Aswa, R.	126	2 30N	33 5 E
Aswad,Rasal	122	21 20N	39 0 E
Aswân	122	24 4N	32 57 E
Aswân High Dam = Sadd el Aali	122	24 5N	32 54 E
Asyût	122	27 11N	31 4 E
Asyûti, Wadi	122	27 18N	31 20 E
Aszód	53	47 39N	19 28 E
At Tafilah	92	30 45N	35 30 E
At Ta'if	122	21 5N	40 27 E
Atacama	172	25 40 S	67 40W
Atacama □	172	27 30 S	70 0W
Atacama, Desierto de	176	24 0 S	69 20W
Atacama, Salar de	172	24 0 S	68 20W
Ataco	174	3 35N	75 23W
Atakor	119	23 27N	5 31 E
Atakpamé	121	7 31N	1 13 E
Atalaia	114	9 25 S	36 0W

Atalándi Ayutla

Atalándi 69 38 39N 22 58 E
Atalaya 174 10 45 S 73 50W
Ataléia 171 18 3 S 41 6W
Atami 111 35 0N 139 55 E
Atankawng 98 25 50N 97 47 E
Atar 116 20 30N 13 5W
Atara 77 63 10N 129 10 E
Ataram, Erg d' 118 23 57N 2 0 E
Atarfe 57 37 13N 3 40W
Atascadero 163 35 32N 120 44W
Atasu 76 48 30N 71 0 E
Atauro 103 8 10 S 125 30 E
Atbara 122 17 42N 33 59 E
Atbara, R. 122 17 40N 33 56 E
Atbashi 85 41 10N 75 48 E
Atbashi, Khrebet 85 40 50N 75 30 E
Atchafalaya B. 159 29 30N 91 20W
Atchison 158 39 40N 95 0W
Atebubu 121 7 47N 1 0W
Ateca 58 41 20N 1 49W
Aterno, R. 63 42 18N 13 45 E
Atesine, Alpi 62 46 55N 11 30 E
Atessa 63 42 5N 14 27 E
Ath 47 50 38N 3 47 E
Ath Thamami 92 27 45N 35 30 E
Athabasca 152 54 45N 113 20W
Athabasca, L. 153 59 15N 109 15W
Athabasca, R. 153 58 40N 110 50W
Athboy 38 53 37N 6 55W
Athea 39 52 27N 9 18W
Athenry 39 53 18N 8 45W
Athens, Ala., U.S.A. 157 34 49N 86 58W
Athens, Ga., U.S.A. 157 33 56N 83 24W
Athens, N.Y., U.S.A. 162 42 15N 73 48W
Athens, Ohio, U.S.A. 156 39 52N 82 6W
Athens, Pa., U.S.A. 162 41 57N 76 36W
Athens, Tex., U.S.A. 159 32 11N 95 48W
Athens = Athínai 69 37 58N 23 46 E
Atherstone 28 52 35N 1 32W
Atherton, Austral. 138 17 17 S 145 30 E
Atherton, U.K. 32 53 32N 2 30W
Athiéme 121 6 37N 1 40 E
Athínai 69 37 58N 23 46 E
Athleague 38 53 34N 8 17W
Athlone 38 53 26N 7 57W
Athni 96 16 44N 75 6 E
Athol 143 45 30 S 168 35 E
Atholl, Forest of 37 56 51N 3 50W
Atholville 151 47 59N 66 43W
Áthos, Mt. 68 40 9N 24 22 E
Athus 47 49 34N 5 50 E
Athy 39 53 0N 7 0W
Ati 123 13 5N 29 2 E
Atiak 126 3 12N 32 2 E
Atiamuri 142 38 24 S 176 5 E
Atico 174 16 14 S 73 40W
Atienza 58 41 12N 2 52W
Atikokan 150 48 45N 91 37W
Atikonak L. 151 52 40N 64 32W
Atka, U.S.A. 147 52 5N 174 40W
Atka, U.S.S.R. 77 60 50N 151 48 E
Atkarsk 81 51 55N 45 2 E
Atkasuk (Meade River) 147 70 30N 157 20W
Atkinson 158 42 35N 98 59W
Atlanta, Ga., U.S.A. 157 33 50N 84 24W
Atlanta, Tex., U.S.A. 159 33 7N 94 8W
Atlantic 158 41 25N 95 0W
Atlantic City 162 39 25N 74 25W
Atlantic Ocean 14 0 0 20 0W
Atlántico □ 174 10 45N 75 0W
Atlas, Great, Mts. 114 33 0N 5 0W
Atlin 147 59 31N 133 41W
Atlin Lake 147 59 26N 133 45W
'Atlit 90 32 42N 34 56 E
Atløy 71 61 21N 4 58 E
Atmakur 97 14 37N 79 40 E
Atmore 157 31 2N 87 30W
Atnarko 152 52 25N 126 0W
Atō 110 34 25N 131 40 E
Atoka 159 34 22N 96 10W
Átokos 69 38 28N 20 49 E
Atolia 163 35 19N 117 37W
Atotonilco el Alto 164 20 20N 98 40W
Atouguia 57 39 20N 9 20W
Atoyac, R. 165 16 30N 97 31W
Åtrafors 73 57 02N 12 40 E
Atrak, R. 93 37 50N 57 0 E
Ätran 73 57 7N 12 57 E
Atrato, R. 174 6 40N 77 0W
Atrauli 94 28 2N 78 20 E
Atri 63 42 35N 14 0 E
Atsbi 122 13 52N 39 50 E
Atsumi 111 34 35N 137 4 E
Atsumi-Wan 111 34 44N 137 13 E
Atsuta 112 43 24N 141 26 E
Attalla 157 34 2N 86 5W
Attawapiskat 150 52 56N 82 24W
Attawapiskat, L. 150 52 18N 87 54W
Attawapiskat, R. 150 52 57N 82 18W
Attendorn 48 51 8N 7 54 E
Attersee 52 47 55N 13 31 E
Attert 47 49 45N 5 47 E
Attica 156 40 20N 87 15W
Attichy 43 49 25N 3 3 E
Attigny 43 49 28N 4 35 E
Attikamagen L. 151 55 0N 66 30W
Attiki Kai Arkhipélagos □ 69 38 10N 23 40 E
Attil 90 32 23N 35 4 E
Attleboro 162 41 56N 71 18W
Attleborough 29 52 32N 1 1 E
Attock 94 33 52N 72 20 E
Attopeu 100 14 48N 106 50 E
Attu 147 52 55N 173 10W
Attunga 141 30 55 S 150 50 E
Attur 97 11 35N 78 30 E
Attymon 39 53 20N 8 37W
Atuel, R. 172 36 17 S 66 50W
Atvidaberg 73 58 12N 16 0 E
Atwater 163 37 21N 120 37W
Atwood 158 39 52N 101 3W
Au Sable Pt. 150 46 0N 86 0W
Au Sable, R. 156 44 25N 83 20W
Aubagne 45 43 17N 5 37 E
Aubange 47 49 34N 5 48 E
Aubarede Pt. 103 17 15N 122 20 E
Aube □ 43 48 15N 4 0 E
Aubel 47 50 42N 5 51 E
Aubenas 45 44 37N 4 24 E
Aubenton 43 49 50N 4 12 E
Auberry 163 37 7N 119 29W
Aubigny-sur-Nère 43 47 30N 2 24 E
Aubin 44 44 33N 2 15 E
Aubrac, Mts. d' 44 44 38N 2 58 E
Auburn, Ala., U.S.A. 157 32 37N 85 30W
Auburn, Calif., U.S.A. 160 38 50N 121 4W
Auburn, Ind., U.S.A. 156 41 20N 85 0W
Auburn, Nebr., U.S.A. 158 40 25N 95 50W
Auburn, N.Y., U.S.A. 162 42 57N 76 39W
Auburn, Penn., U.S.A. 162 40 36N 76 6W
Auburn Range 139 25 15 S 150 30 E
Auburndale 157 28 5N 81 45W
Aubusson 44 45 57N 2 11 E
Auch 44 43 39N 0 36 E
Auchel 43 50 30N 2 29 E
Auchenblae 37 56 54N 2 26W
Auchencairn 35 54 51N 3 52W
Auchi 121 7 6N 6 13 E
Auchinleck 34 55 28N 4 18W
Auchness 37 58 0N 4 36W
Auchterarder 35 56 18N 3 43W
Auchterderran 35 56 8N 3 16W
Auchtermuchty 35 56 18N 3 15W
Auchtertyre 36 57 17N 5 35W
Auckland 142 36 52 S 174 46 E
Auckland □ 142 38 35 S 177 0 E
Auckland Is. 142 51 0 S 166 0 E
Aude □ 44 43 8N 2 28 E
Aude, R. 44 44 13N 3 15 E
Auden 150 50 14N 87 53W
Auderghem 47 50 49N 4 26 E
Auderville 42 49 43N 1 57W
Audierne 42 48 1N 4 34W
Audincourt 43 47 30N 6 50 E
Audlem 32 52 59N 2 31W
Audo Ra. 123 6 20N 41 50 E
Audrey, gasfield 19 53 35N 2 0 E
Audubon 158 41 43N 94 56W
Aue 48 50 34N 12 43 E
Auerbach 48 50 30N 12 25 E
Auffay 42 49 43N 1 07 E
Augathella 139 25 48 S 146 35 E
Augher 38 54 25N 7 10W
Aughnacloy 38 54 25N 6 58W
Aughrim, Clare, Ireland 39 53 0N 8 57W
Aughrim, Galway, Ireland 39 53 18N 8 19W
Aughrim, Wicklow, Ireland 39 52 52N 6 20W
Aughrus More 38 53 34N 10 10W
Augrabies Falls 128 28 35 S 20 20 E
Augsburg 49 48 22N 10 54 E
Augusta, Italy 65 37 14N 15 12 E
Augusta, Ark., U.S.A. 159 35 17N 91 25W
Augusta, Ga., U.S.A. 157 33 29N 81 59W
Augusta, Kans., U.S.A. 159 37 40N 97 0W
Augusta, Me., U.S.A. 151 44 20N 69 46 E
Augusta, Mont., U.S.A. 160 47 30N 112 29W
Augusta, Wis., U.S.A. 158 44 41N 91 8W
Augustenborg 73 54 57N 9 53 E
Augustine 159 31 30N 94 37W
Augusto Cardosa 127 12 40 S 34 50 E
Augustów 54 53 51N 23 00 E
Augustus Downs 138 18 35 S 139 55 E
Augustus I. 136 15 20 S 124 30 E
Augustus, Mt. 137 24 20 S 116 50 E
Auk, oilfield 19 56 25N 2 15 E
Aukan 123 15 29N 40 50 E
Aukum 163 38 34N 120 43W
Auld, L. 136 22 32 S 123 44 E
Auldearn 37 57 34N 3 50W
Aulla 62 44 12N 9 57 E
Aulnay 44 46 2N 0 22W
Aulne, R. 42 48 17N 4 16W
Ault 158 40 40N 104 42W
Ault-Onival 42 50 5N 1 29 E
Aultbea 36 57 50N 5 36W
Aulus-les-Bains 44 42 49N 1 19 E
Aumale 43 49 46N 1 46 E
Aumont-Aubrac 44 44 43N 3 17 E
Auna 121 10 9N 4 42 E
Aundh 96 17 33N 74 23 E
Aunis 44 46 0N 0 50W
Auponhia 103 1 58 S 125 27 E
Aups 45 43 37N 6 15 E
Aur, P. 101 2 35N 104 10 E
Aura 98 26 59N 97 57 E
Aurahorten, Mt. 71 59 15N 6 53 E
Auraiya 95 26 28N 79 33 E
Aurangabad, Bihar, India 95 24 45N 84 18 E
Aurangabad, Maharashtra, India 96 19 50N 75 23 E
Auray 42 47 40N 3 0W
Aurès 119 35 8N 6 30 E
Aurich 48 53 28N 7 30 E
Aurilândia 171 16 44 S 50 28W
Aurillac 44 44 55N 2 26 E
Aurlandsvangen 71 60 55N 7 12 E
Auronza 63 46 33N 12 27 E
Aurora, Brazil 171 6 57 S 38 58W
Aurora, S. Afr. 128 32 40 S 18 29 E
Aurora, Colo., U.S.A. 158 39 44N 104 55W
Aurora, Ill., U.S.A. 156 41 42N 88 12W
Aurora, Mo., U.S.A. 159 36 58N 93 42W
Aurora, Nebr., U.S.A. 158 40 55N 98 0W
Aurora, N.Y., U.S.A. 162 42 45N 76 42W
Aurskog 71 59 55N 11 26 E
Aurukun Mission 138 13 20 S 141 45 E
Aus 128 26 35 S 16 12 E
Auskerry I. 37 59 2N 2 35W
Aust-Agder fylke □ 75 58 55N 7 40 E
Austad 71 58 58N 7 37 E
Austerlitz = Slavikov 53 49 10N 16 52 E
Austevoll 71 60 5N 5 13 E
Austin, Austral. 137 27 40 S 117 50 E
Austin, Minn., U.S.A. 158 43 37N 92 59W
Austin, Nev., U.S.A. 160 39 30N 117 1W
Austin, Tex., U.S.A. 159 30 20N 97 45W
Austin, L. 137 27 40 S 118 0 E
Austral Downs 138 20 30 S 137 45 E
Austral Is. = Tubuai, Îles 143 25 0 S 150 0 E
Australia ■ 133 23 0 S 135 0 E
Australian Alps 141 36 30 S 148 8 E
Australian Cap. Terr. 139 35 15 S 149 8 E
Australian Dependency 13 73 0 S 90 0 E
Austria ■ 52 47 0N 14 0 E
Austvågøy 74 68 20N 14 40 E
Autelbas 47 49 39N 5 52 E
Auterive 44 43 21N 1 29 E
Authie, R. 43 50 22N 1 38 E
Autlan 164 19 40N 104 30W
Autun 43 46 58N 4 17 E
Auvelais 47 50 27N 4 38 E
Auvergne, Austral. 136 15 39 S 130 1 E
Auvergne, France 44 45 20N 3 0 E
Auxerre 43 47 48N 3 32 E
Auxi-le-Château 43 50 15N 2 8 E
Auxonne 43 47 10N 5 20 E
Auzances 44 46 2N 2 30 E
Avaldsnes 71 59 21N 5 20 E
Avallon 43 47 30N 3 53 E
Avalon 163 33 21N 118 20W
Avalon Pen. 151 47 30N 53 20W
Avalon Res. 159 32 30N 104 30W
Avanigadda 97 16 0N 80 56 E
Avaré 173 23 4 S 48 58W
Ávas 68 40 57N 25 56 E
Avawata Mts. 163 35 30N 116 20W
Avebury 28 51 25N 1 52W
Aveh 92 35 40N 49 15 E
Aveiro, Brazil 175 3 10 S 55 5W
Aveiro, Port. 56 40 37N 8 38W
Aveiro □ 56 40 40N 8 35W
Avelgem 47 50 47N 3 27 E
Avellaneda 172 34 50 S 58 10W
Avellino 65 40 54N 14 46 E
Avenal 163 36 0N 120 8W
Avenchen 50 46 53N 7 2 E
Averøya 71 63 0N 7 35 E
Aversa 65 40 58N 14 11 E
Avery 160 47 22N 115 56W
Aves, Islas de 174 12 0N 67 40W
Avesnes-sur-Helpe 43 50 8N 3 55 E
Avesta 72 60 9N 16 10 E
Aveton Gifford 30 50 17N 3 51W
Aveyron □ 44 44 22N 2 45 E
Avezzano 63 42 2N 13 24 E
Avgó 69 35 33N 25 37 E
Aviá Terai 172 26 45 S 60 50W
Aviano 63 46 3N 12 35 E
Avich, L. 34 56 17N 5 25W
Aviemore 37 57 11N 3 50W
Avigliana 62 45 7N 7 13 E
Avigliano 65 40 44N 15 41 E
Avignon 45 43 57N 4 50 E
Ávila 56 40 39N 4 43W
Ávila □ 56 40 30N 5 0W
Avila Beach 163 35 11N 120 44W
Ávila, Sierra de 56 40 40N 5 0W
Avilés 56 43 35N 5 57W
Avionárion 69 38 31N 24 8 E
Avisio, R. 63 46 14N 11 18 E
Aviz 57 39 4N 7 53W
Avize 43 48 59N 4 0 E
Avoca, Austral. 139 37 5 S 143 26 E
Avoca, Ireland 39 52 52N 6 13W
Avoca, R., Austral. 140 35 40 S 143 43 E
Avoca, R., Ireland 39 52 48N 6 10W
Avoch 37 57 34N 4 10W
Avola, Can. 152 51 45N 119 19W
Avola, Italy 65 36 56N 15 7 E
Avon 158 43 0N 98 3W
Avon □ 28 51 30N 2 40W
Avon Downs 133 19 58 S 137 25 E
Avon Is. 133 19 37 S 158 17 E
Avon, R., Austral. 137 31 40 S 116 7 E
Avon, R., Avon, U.K. 28 51 30N 2 43W
Avon, R., Grampian, U.K. 37 57 25N 3 25W
Avon, R., Hants., U.K. 28 50 44N 1 45W
Avon, R., Warwick, U.K. 28 52 0N 2 9W
Avondale, N.Z. 142 36 54 S 174 42 E
Avondale, Rhod. 127 17 43 S 30 58 E
Avonlea 153 50 0N 105 0W
Avonmouth 28 51 30N 2 42W
Avranches 42 48 40N 1 20W
Avrig 70 45 43N 24 21 E
Avrillé 44 46 28N 1 28W
Avtovac 66 43 9N 18 35 E
Avu Meru □ 126 3 20 S 36 50 E
Awag el Baqar 123 10 10N 33 10 E
Awaji 111 34 32N 135 1 E
Awaji-Shima 110 34 30N 134 50 E
Awali 93 26 0N 50 30 E
Awantipur 95 33 55N 75 3 E
Awanui 142 35 4 S 173 17 E
Awarja, R. 96 18 0N 76 15 E
Awarta 90 32 10N 35 17 E
Awarua Pt. 143 44 15 S 168 5 E
Awasa, L. 123 7 0N 38 30 E
Awash 123 9 1N 40 10 E
Awash, R. 123 11 30N 42 0 E
Awaso 120 6 15N 2 22W
Awatere, R. 143 41 37 S 174 10 E
Awbarī 119 26 46N 12 57 E
Awe, L. 34 56 15N 5 15W
Aweil 123 8 42N 27 20 E
Awgu 121 6 4N 7 24 E
Awjilah 117 29 8N 21 7 E
Aworro 135 7 43 S 143 11 E
Ax-les-Thermes 44 42 44N 1 50 E
Axarfjörður 74 66 15N 16 45W
Axbridge 28 51 17N 2 50W
Axe Edge 32 53 14N 2 2W
Axe R. 28 51 17N 2 52W
Axel 47 51 16N 3 55 E
Axel Heiberg I. 12 80 0N 90 0W
Axelfors 73 57 26N 13 7 E
Axholme, Isle of 33 53 30N 1 10 E
Axim 120 4 51N 2 15W
Axintele 70 44 37N 26 47 E
Axiós, R. 68 40 57N 22 35 E
Axmarsbruk 72 61 3N 17 10 E
Axminster 30 50 47N 3 1W
Axmouth 30 50 43N 3 2W
Axstedt 48 53 26N 8 43 E
Axvall 73 58 23N 13 34 E
Ay 43 49 3N 4 0 E
Ay, R. 84 56 8N 57 40 E
Ayabaca 174 4 40 S 79 53W
Ayabe 111 35 20N 135 20 E
Ayacucho, Argent. 172 37 5 S 58 20W
Ayacucho, Peru 174 13 0 S 74 0W
Ayaguz 76 48 10N 80 0 E
Ayakkuduk 85 41 12N 65 12 E
Ayakok'umu Hu 105 37 30N 89 20 E
Ayakudi 97 10 57N 77 6 E
Ayamonte 57 37 12N 7 24W
Ayan 77 56 30N 138 16 E
Ayancık 82 41 57N 34 18 E
Ayapel 174 8 19N 75 9W
Ayapel, Sa. de 174 7 45N 75 30W
Ayaş 82 40 10N 32 14 E
Ayaviri 174 14 50 S 70 35W
Aydın □ 92 37 40N 27 40 E
Aye 47 50 14N 5 18 E
Ayenngré 121 8 40N 1 1 E
Ayer Hitam 101 1 55N 103 11 E
Ayeritam 101 5 24N 100 15 E
Ayers Rock 136 25 23 S 131 5 E
Ayiá 68 39 43N 22 45 E
Ayía Anna 69 38 52N 23 24 E
Ayía Marína, Kásos, Greece 69 35 27N 26 53 E
Ayía Marína, Leros, Greece 69 37 11N 26 48 E
Ayía Paraskeví 68 39 14N 26 16 E
Ayía Rouméli 69 35 14N 23 58 E
Ayiássos 69 39 5N 26 23 E
Áyios Andréas 69 37 21N 22 45 E
Áyios Evstrátios 68 39 34N 24 58 E
Áyios Ioánnis, Ákra 69 35 20N 25 40 E
Áyios Kírikos 69 37 34N 26 17 E
Áyios Matthaíos 68 39 30N 19 47 E
Áyios Míron 69 35 15N 25 1 E
Áyios Nikólaos 69 35 11N 25 41 E
Áyios Pétros 69 38 38N 20 33 E
Áyios Yeóryios 69 37 28N 23 57 E
Aykathonisi 69 37 28N 27 0 E
Ayke, Ozero 84 51 57N 61 36 E
Aylesbury 29 51 48N 0 49W
Aylesford 29 51 18N 0 29 E
Aylmer L. 148 64 0N 108 30W
Aylsham 29 52 48N 1 16 E
Ayn Zālah 92 36 45N 42 35 E
'Ayn Zaqqūt 119 29 0N 19 30 E
Ayna 59 38 34N 2 3W
Aynho 28 51 59N 1 15W
Ayni 85 39 23N 68 32 E
Ayolas 172 27 10 S 56 59W
Ayom 123 7 49N 28 23 E
Ayon, Ostrov 77 69 50N 169 0 E
Ayora 59 39 3N 1 3W
Ayr, Austral. 138 19 35 S 147 25 E
Ayr, U.K. 34 55 28N 4 37W
Ayr (□) 26 55 25N 4 25W
Ayr, Heads of 34 55 25N 4 43W
Ayr, R. 34 55 29N 4 40W
Ayre, Pt. of 37 58 55N 2 43W
Ayre, Pt. of I.o.M. 32 54 27N 4 21W
Aysgarth 32 54 18N 2 0W
Aysha 123 10 50N 42 23 E
Ayton 138 15 45 S 145 25 E
Ayton, Borders, U.K. 35 55 51N 2 6W
Ayton, N. Yorks., U.K. 33 54 15N 0 29W
Aytos 67 42 47N 27 16 E
Aytoska Planina 67 42 45N 27 30 E
Ayu, Kepulauan 103 0 35N 131 5 E
Ayutla, Guat. 166 14 40N 92 10W

Ayutla Balasore

Ayutla, Mexico 165 16 58N 99 17W
Ayutthaya = Phra Nakhon Si A. 101 14 25N 100 30 E
Ayvalık 92 39 20N 26 46 E
Aywaille 47 50 28N 5 40 E
Az Zahiriya 90 31 25N 34 58 E
Az Zahran 92 26 10N 50 7 E
Az-Zarqā 90 32 5N 36 4 E
Az Zāwiyah 119 32 52N 12 56 E
Az-Zilfī 92 26 12N 44 52 E
Az Zintān 119 31 59N 12 9 E
Az Zubayr 92 30 20N 47 50 E
Azambuja 57 39 4N 8 51W
Azamgarh 95 26 35N 83 13 E
Azaouak, Vallée de l' 121 15 50N 3 20 E
Azārbāijān □ 92 37 0N 44 30 E
Azare 121 11 55N 10 10 E
Azay-le-Rideau 42 47 16N 0 30 E
Azazga 119 36 48N 4 22 E
Azbine = Aïr 121 18 0N 8 0 E
Azeffoun 119 36 51N 4 26 E
Azemmour 118 33 14N 9 20W
Azerbaijan S.S.R. □ 83 40 20N 48 0 E
Azezo 123 12 28N 37 15 E
Azilal,Beni Mallal 118 32 0N 6 30W
Azimganj 95 24 14N 84 16 E
Aznalcóllar 57 37 32N 6 17W
Azogues 174 2 35 S 78 0W
Azor 90 32 2N 34 48 E
Azores, Is. 14 38 44N 29 0W
Azov 83 47 3N 39 25 E
Azov Sea = Azovskoye More 82 46 0N 36 30 E
Azovskoye More 82 46 0N 36 30 E
Azovy 76 64 55N 64 35 E
Azpeitia 58 43 12N 2 19W
Azrou 118 33 28N 5 19W
Aztec 161 36 54N 108 0W
Azúa de Compostela 167 18 25N 70 44W
Azuaga 57 38 16N 5 39W
Azuara 58 41 15N 0 53W
Azuara, R. 58 41 12N 0 55W
Azúcar, Presa del 165 26 0N 99 5W
Azuer, R. 57 38 50N 3 15W
Azuero, Pen. de 166 7 30N 80 30W
Azul 172 36 42 S 59 43W
Azusa 163 34 8N 117 52W
Azzaba 119 36 48N 7 6 E
Azzano Décimo 63 45 53N 12 46 E

B

B. Curri 68 42 22N 20 5 E
Ba Don 100 17 45N 106 26 E
Ba Dong 101 9 40N 106 33 E
Ba Ngoi = Cam Lam 101 11 50N 109 10 E
Ba, R. 56 13 5N 109 0 E
Ba Tri 101 10 2N 106 36 E
Baa 103 10 50 S 123 0 E
Baamonde 56 43 7N 7 44W
Baar 51 47 12N 8 32 E
Baarle Nassau 47 51 27N 4 56 E
Baarlo 47 51 20N 6 6 E
Baarn 46 52 12N 5 17 E
Bāb el Māndeb 91 12 35N 43 25 E
Baba Burnu 68 39 29N 26 2 E
Baba dag 83 41 0N 48 55 E
Baba, Mt. 67 42 44N 23 59 E
Babaçulândia 170 7 13 S 47 46W
Babadag 70 44 53N 28 44 E
Babaeski 67 41 26N 27 6 E
Babahoyo 174 1 40 S 79 30W
Babakin 137 32 7 S 118 1 E
Babana 121 10 31N 3 46 E
Babar, Alg. 119 35 10N 7 6 E
Babar, Pak. 94 31 7N 69 32 E
Babar, I. 103 8 0 S 129 30 E
Babarkach 94 29 45N 68 0 E
Babayevo 81 59 24N 35 55 E
Babb 160 48 56N 113 27W
Babbitt 163 38 32N 118 39W
Babenhausen 49 49 57N 8 56 E
Babi Besar, P. 101 2 25N 103 59 E
Babia Gora 54 49 38N 19 38 E
Babile 123 9 16N 42 11 E
Babinda 138 17 20 S 145 56 E
Babine 152 55 20N 126 35W
Babine L. 152 54 48N 126 0W
Babine, R. 152 55 45N 127 44W
Babo 103 2 30 S 133 30 E
Babócsa 53 46 2N 17 21 E
Babol 93 36 40N 52 50 E
Babol Sar 93 36 45N 52 45 E
Baboma 126 2 30N 28 10 E
Baborówo Kietrz 53 50 7N 18 1 E
Baboua 124 5 49N 14 58 E
Babuna, mts. 66 41 30N 21 40 E
Babura 121 12 51N 8 59 E
Babusar Pass 95 35 12N 73 59 E
Babushkin 81 55 45N 37 40 E
Babušnica 66 43 7N 22 27 E
Babylon, Iraq 92 32 40N 44 30 E
Babylon, U.S.A. 162 40 42N 73 20W
Bač 66 45 29N 19 17 E
Bac Can 100 22 08N 105 49 E
Bac Giang 100 21 16N 106 11 E
Bac Kan 101 22 5N 105 50 E
Bac Lieu = Vinh Loi 101 9 17N 105 43 E
Bac Ninh 100 21 13N 106 4 E
Bac Phan 100 22 0N 105 0 E
Bac Quang 100 22 30N 104 48 E
Bacabal 170 4 15N 44 45W
Bacalar 165 18 12N 87 53W
Bacan,Pulau 103 0 50 S 127 30 E
Bacarès, Le 44 42 47N 3 3 E
Bacarra 103 18 15N 120 37 E
Baccarat 43 48 28N 6 42 E
Bacchus Marsh 140 37 43 S 144 27 E
Bacerac 164 30 18N 108 50W
Bach Long Vi,Dao 100 20 10N 107 40 E
Bachaquero 174 9 56N 71 8W
Bacharach 49 50 3N 7 46 E
Bachclina 76 57 45N 67 20 E
Bachok 101 6 4N 102 25 E
Bachuma 123 6 31N 36 1 E
Bačina 66 43 42N 21 23 E
Back 36 58 17N 6 20W
Back, R. 148 65 10N 104 0W
Bačka Palanka 66 45 17N 19 27 E
Bačka Topola 66 45 49N 19 39 E
Bäckefors 73 58 48N 12 9 E
Bački Petrovac 66 45 29N 19 32 E
Backnang 49 48 57N 9 26 E
Backstairs Passage 133 35 40 S 138 5 E
Bacolod 103 10 40N 122 57 E
Bacqueville 42 49 47N 1 0 E
Bacs-Kiskun □ 53 46 43N 19 30 E
Bácsalmás 53 46 8N 19 17 E
Bacton 29 52 50N 1 29 E
Bacuit 103 11 20N 119 20 E
Bacup 32 53 42N 2 12W
Bacŭu 70 46 35N 26 55 E
Bacŭu □ 70 46 30N 26 45 E
Bad Aussee 52 47 43N 13 45 E
Bad Axe 150 43 48N 82 59W
Bad Bergzabem 49 49 6N 8 0 E
Bad Bramstedt 48 53 56N 9 53 E
Bad Doberan 48 54 6N 11 55 E
Bad Driburg 48 51 44N 9 0 E
Bad Ems 49 50 22N 7 44 E
Bad Frankenhausen 48 51 21N 11 3 E
Bad Freienwalde 52 52 46N 14 2 E
Bad Godesberg 48 50 41N 7 4 E
Bad Hersfeld 48 50 52N 9 42 E
Bad Hofgastein 52 47 17N 13 6 E
Bad Homburg 49 50 17N 8 33 E
Bad Honnef 48 50 39N 7 13 E
Bad Ischl 52 47 44N 13 38 E
Bad Kissingen 49 50 11N 10 5 E
Bad Kreuznach 49 49 47N 7 47 E
Bad Lands 158 43 40N 102 10W
Bad Lauterberg 48 51 38N 10 29 E
Bad Leonfelden 52 48 31N 14 18 E
Bad Lippspringe 48 51 47N 8 46 E
Bad Mergentheim 49 49 29N 9 47 E
Bad Münstereifel 48 50 33N 6 46 E
Bad Nauheim 49 50 24N 8 45 E
Bad Oeynhausen 48 52 16N 8 45 E
Bad Oldesloe 48 53 56N 10 17 E
Bad Orb 49 50 16N 9 21 E
Bad Pyrmont 48 51 59N 9 5 E
Bad, R. 158 44 10N 100 50W
Bad Ragaz 51 47 0N 9 30 E
Bad St. Peter 48 54 23N 8 32 E
Bad Salzuflen 48 52 8N 8 44 E
Bad Segeberg 48 53 58N 10 16 E
Bad Tölz 49 47 43N 11 34 E
Bad Waldsee 49 47 56N 9 46 E
Bad Wildungen 48 51 7N 9 10 E
Bad Wimpfen 49 49 12N 9 10 E
Bad Windsheim 49 49 29N 10 25 E
Badagara 97 11 35N 75 40 E
Badagri 121 6 25N 2 55 E
Badajoz 57 38 50N 6 59W
Badajoz □ 57 38 40N 6 30W
Badakhshan □ 93 36 30N 71 0 E
Badalona 58 41 26N 2 15 E
Badalzai 94 29 50N 65 35 E
Badampahar 96 22 10N 86 10 E
Badanah 92 30 58N 41 30 E
Badas 102 4 33N 114 25 E
Badas, Kepulauan 102 0 45N 107 5 E
Baddo, R. 93 28 15N 65 0 E
Bade 103 7 10 S 139 35 E
Baden, Austria 53 48 1N 16 13 E
Baden, Switz. 51 47 28N 8 18 E
Baden-Baden 49 48 45N 8 15 E
Baden Park 140 32 8 S 144 12 E
Baden-Württemberg □ 49 48 40N 9 0 E
Badenoch 37 58 16N 4 5W
Badenscoth 37 57 27N 2 30W
Badeso 123 9 58N 40 52 E
Badgastein 52 47 7N 13 9 E
Badger, Can. 151 49 0N 56 4W
Badger, U.S.A. 163 36 38N 119 1W
Badghis □ 93 35 0N 63 0 E
Badgom 95 34 1N 74 45 E
Badhoevedorp 46 52 20N 4 47 E
Badia Polesine 63 45 6N 11 30 E
Badin 94 24 38N 68 54 E
Badnera 96 20 48N 77 44 E
Badogo 120 11 2N 8 13W
Badrinath 95 30 45N 79 30 E
Baduen 91 7 15N 47 40 E
Badulla 97 7 1N 81 7 E
Badupi 98 21 36N 93 27 E
Bække 73 55 35N 9 6 E
Baena 57 37 37N 4 20W
Baerami Creek 141 32 27 S 150 27 E
Baetas 174 6 5 S 62 15W
Baexem 47 51 13N 5 53 E
Baeza, Ecuador 174 0 25 S 77 45W
Baeza, Spain 59 37 57N 3 25W
Bafa 93 31 40N 55 25 E
Bafa Gölü 69 37 30N 27 29 E
Bafatá 120 12 8N 15 20W
Baffin Bay 12 72 0N 64 0W
Baffin I. 149 68 0N 75 0W
Bafia 121 4 40N 11 10 E
Bafilo 121 9 22N 1 22 E
Bafing, R. 120 11 40N 10 45W
Baflo 46 53 22N 6 31 E
Bafoulabé 120 13 50N 10 55W
Bafq 93 31 40N 55 20 E
Bafra 82 41 34N 35 54 E
Baft 93 29 15N 56 38 E
Bafut 121 6 6N 10 2 E
Bafwakwandji 126 1 12N 26 52 E
Bafwasende 126 1 3N 27 5 E
Bagalkot 96 16 10N 75 40 E
Bagamoyo 126 6 28 S 38 55 E
Bagamoyo □ 126 6 20 S 38 30 E
Bagan Datok 101 3 59N 100 47 E
Bagan Serai 101 5 1N 100 32 E
Bagan Siapiapi 102 2 12N 100 50 E
Baganga 103 7 34N 126 33 E
Bagasra 94 21 59N 71 77 E
Bagawi 123 12 20N 34 18 E
Bagdad 163 34 35N 115 53W
Bagdarin 77 54 26N 113 36 E
Bagé 173 31 20 S 54 15W
Bagenalstown = Muine Bheag 39 52 42N 6 57W
Baggs 160 41 8N 107 46W
Baggy Pt. 30 51 11N 4 12W
Bagh 95 33 59N 73 45 E
Bagh nam Faoileann, B. 36 57 22N 7 13W
Baghdād 92 33 20N 44 30 E
Bagherhat 98 22 40N 89 47 E
Bagheria 64 38 5N 13 30 E
Baghin 93 30 12N 56 45 E
Baghlan 93 36 12N 69 0 E
Baghlan □ 93 36 0N 68 30 E
Baginbun Hd. 39 52 10N 6 50W
Bagley 158 47 30N 95 22W
Bagnacavallo 63 44 25N 11 58 E
Bagnara Cálabra 65 38 16N 15 49 E
Bagnères-de-Bigorre 44 43 5N 0 9 E
Bagnères-de-Luchon 44 42 47N 0 38 E
Bagni di Lucca 62 44 1N 10 37 E
Bagno di Romagna 63 43 50N 11 59 E
Bagnoles-de-l'Orne 42 48 32N 0 25W
Bagnolo Mella 62 45 27N 10 14 E
Bagnols-les-Bains 44 44 30N 3 40 E
Bagnols-sur-Cèze 45 44 10N 4 36 E
Bagnorégio 63 42 38N 12 7 E
Bagolino 62 45 49N 10 28 E
Bagotville 151 48 22N 70 54W
Bagrdan 66 44 5N 21 11 E
Bagshot 29 51 22N 0 41W
Baguio 103 16 26N 120 34 E
Bahabón de Esgueva 58 41 52N 3 43W
Bahadurabad 98 25 11N 89 44 E
Bahadurgarh 94 28 40N 76 57 E
Bahama, Canal Viejo de 166 22 10N 77 30W
Bahama Is. 167 24 40N 74 0W
Bahamas ■ 167 24 0N 74 0W
Baharîya,El Wâhât el 122 28 0N 28 50 E
Bahau 101 2 48N 102 26 E
Bahawalnagar 94 30 0N 73 15 E
Bahawalpur 94 29 37N 71 40 E
Bahawalpur □ 94 29 5N 71 3 E
Baheri 95 28 45N 79 34 E
Baheta 123 13 27N 42 10 E
Bahi 126 5 58 S 35 21 E
Bahi Swamp 126 6 10 S 35 0 E
Bahia = Salvador 171 13 0 S 38 30W
Bahia □ 171 12 0N 42 0W
Bahía Blanca 172 38 35 S 62 13W
Bahía de Caráquez 174 0 40 S 80 27W
Bahía Honda 166 22 54N 83 10W
Bahía, Islas de la 166 16 45N 86 15W
Bahia Laura 176 48 10 S 66 30W
Bahia Negra 174 20 5 S 58 5W
Bahir Dar Giyorgis 123 11 33N 37 25 E
Bahmer 118 27 32N 0 10W
Bahönye 53 46 25N 17 28 E
Bahr Aouk 124 9 20N 20 40 E
Bahr Dar 123 11 37N 37 10 E
Bahr el Abiad 123 9 30N 31 40 E
Bahr el Ahmer □ 122 20 0N 35 0 E
Bahr el Arab 123 9 50N 27 10 E
Bahr el Azraq 123 10 30N 35 0 E
Bahr el Ghazâl □ 123 7 0N 28 0 E
Bahr el Ghazâl, R. 123 9 0N 30 0 E
Bahr el Jebel 123 7 30N 30 30 E
Bahr Salamat 124 10 0N 19 0 E
Bahr Yûsef 122 28 25N 30 35 E
Bahra 92 21 25N 39 32 E
Bahra el Burullus 122 31 28N 30 48 E
Bahra el Manzala 122 31 28N 32 01 E
Bahraich 95 27 38N 81 50 E
Bahrain ■ 93 26 0N 50 35 E
Bahramabad 93 30 28N 56 2 E
Bahu Kalat 93 25 50N 61 20 E
Bai 120 13 35N 3 28W
Bai Bung, Mui 101 8 38N 104 44 E
Bai Duc 100 18 3N 105 49 E
Bai Thuong 100 19 54N 105 23 E
Baia-Mare 70 47 40N 23 17 E
Baia-Sprie 70 47 41N 23 43W
Baião 170 2 40 S 49 40W
Baïbokoum 117 7 40N 14 45 E
Baidoa 91 3 8N 43 30 E
Baie Comeau 151 49 12N 68 10W
Baie de l'Abri 151 50 3N 67 0W
Baie Johan Beetz 151 50 18N 62 50W
Baie St. Paul 151 47 28N 70 32W
Baie Trinité 151 49 25N 67 20W
Baie Verte 151 49 55N 56 12W
Baignes 44 45 28N 0 25W
Baigneux-les-Juifs 43 47 31N 4 39 E
Ba'ījī 92 35 0N 43 30 E
Baikal, L. 77 53 0N 108 0 E
Bailadila, Mt. 96 18 43N 81 15 E
Baildon 33 53 52N 1 46W
Baile Atha Cliath = Dublin 39 53 20N 6 18W
Bailei 123 6 44N 40 18 E
Bailén 57 38 8N 3 48W
Baileux 47 50 2N 4 23 E
Bailhongal 97 15 55N 74 53 E
Bailique, Ilha 170 1 2N 49 58W
Bailleul 43 50 44N 2 41 E
Baillieborough 38 53 55N 7 0W
Baimuru 135 7 35 S 144 51 E
Bain-de-Bretagne 42 47 50N 1 40W
Bainbridge, U.K. 32 54 18N 2 7W
Bainbridge, Ga., U.S.A. 157 30 53N 84 34W
Bainbridge, N.Y., U.S.A. 162 42 17N 75 29W
Baing 103 10 14 S 120 34 E
Bainville 158 48 8N 104 10W
Bainyik 135 3 40 S 143 4 E
Baird 159 32 25N 99 25W
Baird Inlet 147 64 49N 164 18W
Baird Mts. 147 67 10N 160 15W
Bairnsdale 141 37 48 S 147 36 E
Baissa 121 7 14N 10 38 E
Baitadi 95 29 35N 80 25 E
Baixa Grande 171 11 57 S 40 11W
Baiyuda 122 17 35N 32 07 E
Baja 53 46 12N 18 59 E
Baja California 164 32 10N 115 12W
Baja, Pta. 164 29 50N 116 0W
Bajah, Wadi 122 23 14N 39 20 E
Bajana 94 23 7N 71 49 E
Bajimba 139 29 22 S 152 0 E
Bajimba, Mt. 139 29 17 S 152 6 E
Bajina Bašta 66 43 58N 19 35 E
Bajitpur 95 24 13N 91 0 E
Bajmok 66 45 57N 19 24 E
Bajo Boquete 167 8 49N 82 27W
Bajoga 121 10 57N 11 20 E
Bajool 138 23 40 S 150 35 E
Bak 53 46 43N 16 51 E
Bakal 84 54 56N 58 48 E
Bakala 117 6 15N 20 20 E
Bakanas 85 44 50N 76 15 E
Bakar 63 45 18N 14 32 E
Bakel, Neth. 47 51 30N 5 45 E
Bakel, Senegal 120 14 56N 12 20W
Baker, Calif., U.S.A. 163 35 16N 116 8W
Baker, Mont., U.S.A. 158 46 22N 104 12W
Baker, Nev., U.S.A. 160 38 59N 114 7W
Baker, Oreg., U.S.A. 160 44 50N 117 55W
Baker Is. 130 0 10N 176 35 E
Baker, L., Austral. 137 26 54 S 126 5 E
Baker, L., Can. 148 64 0N 96 0W
Baker Lake 148 64 20N 96 3W
Baker Mt. 160 48 50N 121 49W
Baker's Dozen Is. 150 56 45N 78 45W
Bakersfield 163 35 25N 119 0W
Bakewell 33 53 13N 1 40W
Bakhchisaray 82 44 40N 33 45 E
Bakhmach 80 51 10N 32 45 E
Bakhtiari □ 92 32 0N 49 0 E
Bakia 123 5 18N 25 45 E
Bakinskikh Komissarov 92 39 20N 49 15 E
Bakırköy 67 40 59N 28 53 E
Bakkafjörðr 74 66 2N 14 48W
Bakkagerði 74 65 31N 13 49W
Bakke 71 58 25N 6 39 E
Bakony Forest = Bakony Hegység 53 47 10N 17 30 E
Bakony Hegység 53 47 10N 17 30 E
Bakony, R. 53 47 35N 17 54 E
Bakori 121 11 34N 7 25 E
Bakouma 117 5 40N 22 56 E
Bakov 52 50 27N 14 55 E
Bakpakty 85 44 35N 76 40 E
Bakr Uzyak 84 52 59N 58 38 E
Baku 83 40 25N 49 45 E
Bakwanga = Mbuji Mayi 124 6 9 S 23 40 E
Bal'a 90 32 20N 35 6 E
Bala, L. = Tegid, L. 31 52 53N 3 38W
Balabac I. 102 8 0N 117 0 E
Balabac, Selat 102 7 53N 117 5 E
Balabagh 94 34 25N 70 12 E
Balabakk 92 34 0N 36 10 E
Balabalangan, Kepulauan 102 2 20 S 117 30 E
Balaghat 96 21 49N 80 12 E
Balaghat Ra. 96 18 50N 76 30 E
Balaguer 58 41 50N 0 50 E
Balakhna 81 56 35N 43 32 E
Balaklava, Austral. 140 34 7 S 138 22 E
Balaklava, U.S.S.R. 82 44 30N 33 30 E
Balakleya 82 49 28N 36 55 E
Balakovo 81 52 4N 47 55 E
Balallan 36 58 5N 6 35W
Balancán 165 17 48N 91 32W
Balanda 81 51 30N 44 40 E
Balangir 96 20 43N 83 35 E
Balapur 96 21 22N 76 45 E
Balashikha 81 55 49N 37 59 E
Balashov 81 51 30N 43 10 E
Balasinor 94 22 57N 73 23 E
Balasore 96 21 35N 87 3 E

Balassagyarmat	53	48 4N	19 15 E
Balât	122	25 36N	29 19 E
Balaton	53	46 50N	17 40 E
Balatonfüred	53	46 58N	17 54 E
Balatonszentgyörgy	53	46 41N	17 19 E
Balazote	59	38 54N	2 09W
Balbeggie	35	56 26N	3 19W
Balbi, Mt.	135	5 55S	154 58 E
Balblair	37	57 39N	4 11W
Balboa	166	9 0N	79 30W
Balbriggan	38	53 35N	6 10W
Balcarce	172	38 0S	58 10W
Balcarres	153	50 50N	103 35W
Balchik	67	43 28N	28 11 E
Balclutha	143	46 15S	169 45 E
Bald Hd.	137	35 6S	118 1 E
Bald Hill, W. Australia, Austral.	137	31 36S	116 13 E
Bald Hill, W. Australia, Austral.	137	24 55S	119 57 E
Bald I.	137	34 57S	118 27 E
Bald Knob	159	35 20N	91 35W
Baldegger-See	51	47 12N	8 17 E
Balder, oilfield	19	59 10N	2 20 E
Balderton	33	53 3N	0 46W
Baldock	29	51 59N	0 11W
Baldock L.	153	56 33N	97 57W
Baldoyle	38	53 24N	6 10W
Baldwin, Fla., U.S.A.	156	30 15N	82 10W
Baldwin, Mich., U.S.A.	156	43 54N	85 53W
Baldwinsville	162	43 10N	76 19W
Bale	63	45 4N	13 46 E
Baleares □	58	39 30N	3 0 E
Baleares, Islas	58	39 30N	3 0 E
Balearic Is. = Baleares, Islas	58	39 30N	3 0 E
Baleia, Ponta da	171	17 40S	39 7W
Balen	47	51 10N	5 10 E
Baler	103	15 46N	121 34 E
Balerna	51	45 52N	9 0 E
Baleshare I.	36	57 30N	7 21W
Balezino	84	58 2N	53 6 E
Balfate	166	15 48N	86 25W
Balfe's Creek	138	20 12S	145 55 E
Balfour, S. Afr.	129	26 38S	28 35 E
Balfour, U.K.	37	59 2N	2 54W
Balfour Downs	137	22 45S	120 50 E
Balfouriyya	90	32 38N	35 18 E
Balfron	34	56 4N	4 20W
Bali	121	5 54N	10 0 E
Bali □	102	8 20S	115 0 E
Bali, I.	102	8 20S	115 0 E
Bali, Selat	103	8 30S	114 35 E
Baligród	54	49 20N	22 17 E
Balikesir	92	39 35N	27 58 E
Balikpapan	102	1 10S	116 55 E
Balimbing	103	5 10N	120 3 E
Balimo	135	8 6S	142 57 E
Baling	101	5 41N	100 55 E
Balintore	37	57 45N	3 55W
Balipara	99	26 50N	92 45 E
Balit	95	36 15N	74 40 E
Baliza	175	16 0S	52 20W
Balk	46	52 54N	5 35 E
Balkan Mts. = Stara Planina	67	43 15N	23 0 E
Balkan Pen.	16	42 0N	22 0 E
Balkh = Wazirabad	93	36 44N	66 47 E
Balkh □	93	36 30N	67 0 E
Balkhash	76	46 50N	74 50 E
Balkhash, Ozero	76	40 0N	74 50 E
Balla, Ireland	38	53 48N	9 7W
Balla, Pak.	99	24 10N	91 35 E
Ballachulish	36	56 40N	5 10W
Balladonia	137	32 27S	123 51 E
Ballagan Pt.	38	54 0N	6 6W
Ballaghaderreen	38	53 55N	8 35W
Ballantrae	34	55 6N	5 0W
Ballara	140	32 19S	140 45 E
Ballarat	139	37 33S	143 50 E
Ballard, L.	137	29 20S	120 10 E
Ballarpur	96	19 50N	79 23 E
Ballater	37	57 2N	3 2W
Ballaugh	32	54 20N	4 32W
Balldale	141	36 20N	146 33 E
Ballenas, Canal de las	164	29 10N	113 45W
Balleni	70	45 48N	27 51 E
Balleny Is.	13	66 30S	163 0 E
Ballia	95	25 46N	84 12 E
Ballickmoyler	39	52 54N	7 2W
Ballidu	137	30 35S	116 45 E
Ballina, Austral.	139	28 50S	153 31 E
Ballina, Mayo, Ireland	38	54 7N	9 10W
Ballina, Tipp., Ireland	39	52 49N	8 27W
Ballinagar	39	53 15N	7 21W
Ballinagh = Bellananagh	38	53 55N	7 25W
Ballinalack	38	53 38N	7 28W
Ballinalea	39	53 0N	6 8W
Ballinalee	38	53 46N	7 40W
Ballinamallard	38	54 30N	7 36W
Ballinameen	38	53 54N	8 19W
Ballinamore	38	54 3N	7 48W
Ballinamore Bridge	38	53 30N	8 24W
Ballinascarty	39	51 40N	8 52W
Ballinasloe	39	53 20N	8 12W
Ballincollig	39	51 52N	8 35W
Ballindaggin	39	52 33N	6 43W
Ballinderry	38	53 2N	8 13W
Ballinderry R.	38	54 40N	6 32W
Ballindine	38	53 40N	8 57W
Ballineen	39	51 43N	8 57W
Balling	73	56 38N	8 51 E
Ballingarry, Lim., Ireland	39	53 1N	8 3W
Ballingarry, Tipp., Ireland	39	52 29N	8 50W
Ballingarry, Tipp., Ireland	39	52 35N	7 32W
Ballingeary	39	51 51N	9 13W
Ballinger	159	31 45N	99 58W
Ballinhassig	39	51 48N	8 33W
Ballinlough	38	53 45N	8 39W
Ballinluig	37	56 40N	3 40W
Ballinrobe	38	53 36N	9 13W
Ballinskelligs	39	51 50N	10 17W
Ballinskelligs B.	39	51 46N	10 11W
Ballintober	38	53 43N	8 25W
Ballintoy	38	55 13N	6 20W
Ballintra	38	54 35N	8 9W
Ballinunty	39	52 36N	7 40W
Ballinure	39	52 34N	7 46W
Ballivian	172	22 41S	62 10W
Ballivor	38	53 32N	6 50W
Ballo Pt.	79	8 55N	13 18W
Balloch	34	56 0N	4 35W
Ballon	39	48 10N	0 16 E
Ballston Spa	162	43 0N	73 51W
Ballybay	38	54 8N	6 52W
Ballybofey	38	54 48N	7 47W
Ballyboghil	38	53 32N	6 16W
Ballybogy	38	55 8N	6 33W
Ballybunion	39	52 30N	9 40W
Ballycanew	39	52 37N	6 18W
Ballycarney	39	52 35N	6 44W
Ballycastle	38	55 12N	6 15W
Ballycastle B.	38	55 12N	6 15W
Ballyclare, Ireland	38	53 40N	8 0W
Ballyclare, U.K.	38	54 46N	6 0W
Ballyclerahan	39	52 25N	7 48W
Ballycolla	39	52 53N	7 27W
Ballyconneely	38	53 27N	10 5W
Ballyconneely B.	38	53 23N	10 8W
Ballyconnell	38	54 7N	7 35W
Ballycotton	39	51 50N	8 0W
Ballycroy	38	54 2N	9 49W
Ballydavid	39	53 12N	8 28W
Ballydavid Hd.	39	52 15N	10 20W
Ballydehob	39	51 34N	9 28W
Ballydonegan	39	51 37N	10 12W
Ballydonegan B.	39	51 38N	10 6W
Ballyduff, Kerry, Ireland	39	52 27N	9 40W
Ballyduff, Waterford, Ireland	39	52 9N	8 2W
Ballyforan	38	53 29N	8 18W
Ballygar	38	53 33N	8 20W
Ballygarrett	39	52 34N	6 15W
Ballygawley	38	54 27N	7 2W
Ballyglass	38	53 45N	9 9W
Ballygorman	38	55 23N	7 20W
Ballyhahill	39	52 33N	9 13W
Ballyhaise	38	54 3N	7 20W
Ballyhalbert	38	54 30N	5 28W
Ballyhaunis	38	53 47N	8 47W
Ballyheige I.	39	52 22N	9 51W
Ballyhoura Hills	39	52 18N	8 33W
Ballyjamesduff	38	53 52N	7 11W
Ballylanders	39	52 25N	8 21W
Ballylaneen	39	52 10N	7 25W
Ballylongford	39	52 34N	9 30W
Ballylooby	39	52 20N	7 59W
Ballylynan	39	52 57N	7 02W
Ballymacoda	39	51 53N	7 56W
Ballymagorry	38	54 52N	7 26W
Ballymahon	39	53 35N	7 45W
Ballymena	38	54 53N	6 18W
Ballymena □	38	54 53N	6 18W
Ballymoe	38	53 41N	8 28W
Ballymoney	38	55 5N	6 30W
Ballymoney □	38	55 5N	6 23W
Ballymore	39	53 30N	7 40W
Ballymore Eustace	39	53 8N	6 38W
Ballymote	38	54 5N	8 30W
Ballymurphy	39	52 33N	6 52W
Ballymurray	38	53 36N	8 8W
Ballynabola	39	52 21N	6 50W
Ballynacally	39	52 42N	9 7W
Ballynacargy	38	53 35N	7 32W
Ballynacorra	39	51 53N	8 10W
Ballynagore	38	53 24N	7 29W
Ballynahinch	38	54 24N	5 55W
Ballynahown	38	53 21N	7 52W
Ballynameen	38	54 58N	6 41W
Ballynamona	39	52 5N	8 39W
Ballynure	38	54 47N	5 59W
Ballyquintin, Pt.	38	54 20N	5 30W
Ballyragget	39	52 47N	7 20W
Ballyroan	39	52 57N	7 20W
Ballyronan	38	54 43N	6 32W
Ballyroney	38	54 17N	6 8W
Ballysadare	38	54 12N	8 30W
Ballyshannon	38	54 30N	8 10W
Ballyvaughan	39	53 7N	9 10W
Ballyvourney	39	51 57N	9 10W
Ballyvoy	38	55 11N	6 11W
Ballywalter	38	54 33N	5 30W
Ballywilliam	39	52 27N	6 52W
Balmaceda	176	46 0S	71 50W
Balmaclellan	35	55 6N	4 5W
Balmazújváros	53	47 37N	21 21 E
Balmedie	37	57 14N	2 4W
Balmhorn	50	46 26N	7 42 E
Balmoral	140	37 15S	141 48 E
Balmoral For.	37	57 0N	3 15W
Balmorhea	159	31 2N	103 41W
Balnapaling	37	57 42N	4 2W
Balonne, R.	139	28 47S	147 56 E
Balovale	125	13 30S	23 15 E
Balquhidder	34	56 22N	4 22W
Balrampur	95	27 30N	82 20 E
Balranald	140	34 38S	143 33 E
Balş	70	44 22N	24 5 E
Balsas	165	18 0N	99 40W
Balsas, R., Goias, Brazil	170	9 0S	48 0W
Balsas, R., Maranhão, Brazil	170	7 15S	44 35W
Balsas, R., Mexico	164	18 30N	101 20W
Bålsta	72	59 35N	17 30 E
Balsthal	50	47 19N	7 41 E
Balta, Rumania	70	44 54N	22 38 E
Balta, U.S.A.	158	48 12N	100 7W
Balta, U.S.S.R.	82	48 2N	29 45 E
Balta, I.	36	60 44N	0 49W
Baltanás	56	41 56N	4 15W
Baltasound	36	60 47N	0 53W
Baltic Sea	75	56 0N	20 0 E
Baltiisk	75	54 38N	19 55 E
Baltim	122	31 35N	31 10 E
Baltimore, Ireland	39	51 29N	9 22W
Baltimore, U.S.A.	162	39 18N	76 37W
Baltinglass	39	52 57N	6 42W
Baltrum	48	53 43N	7 25 E
Baluchistan □	93	27 30N	65 0 E
Balurghat	95	25 15N	88 44 E
Balvicar	34	56 17N	5 38W
Balygychan	77	63 56N	154 12 E
Bam	93	29 7N	58 14 E
Bam La	99	29 25N	98 35 E
Bama	121	11 33N	13 33 E
Bamako	120	12 34N	7 55W
Bamba	121	17 5N	1 0W
Bambari	117	5 40N	20 35 E
Bambaroo	107	18 50S	146 11 E
Bamberg, Ger.	49	49 54N	10 53 E
Bamberg, U.S.A.	157	33 19N	81 1W
Bambesi	123	9 45N	34 40 E
Bambey	120	14 42N	16 28W
Bambili	126	3 40N	26 0 E
Bamboo	138	14 34S	143 20 E
Bambouti	126	5 25N	27 12 E
Bambuí	171	20 1S	45 58W
Bamburgh	35	55 36N	1 42W
Bamenda	121	5 57N	10 11 E
Bamfield	152	48 45N	125 10W
Bamford	33	53 21N	1 41W
Bamian □	93	35 0N	67 0 E
Bamkin	121	6 3N	11 27 E
Bampton, Devon, U.K.	30	50 59N	3 29W
Bampton, Oxon., U.K.	28	51 44N	1 33W
Bampur	93	27 15N	60 21 E
Bampur, R.	93	27 20N	59 30 E
Ban Aranyaprathet	100	13 41N	102 30 E
Ban Ban	100	19 31N	103 15 E
Ban Bang Hin	101	9 32N	98 35 E
Ban Bua Chum	101	15 11N	101 12 E
Ban Bua Yai	100	15 33N	102 26 E
Ban Chiang Klang	100	19 15N	100 55 E
Ban Chik	100	17 15N	102 22 E
Ban Choho	100	15 2N	102 9 E
Ban Dan Lan Hoi	100	17 0N	99 35 E
Ban Don	100	12 53N	107 48 E
Ban Don = Surat Thani	101	9 8N	99 20 E
Ban Don, Go	101	9 20N	99 25 E
Ban Dong	100	19 14N	100 3 E
Ban Hong	100	18 18N	98 50 E
Ban Houei Sai	101	20 22N	100 32 E
Ban Kaeng	100	17 29N	100 7 E
Ban Kantang	101	7 25N	99 31 E
Ban Keun	100	18 22N	102 35 E
Ban Khai	100	12 46N	101 18 E
Ban Khe Bo	101	19 10N	104 39 E
Ban Kheun	100	20 13N	101 7 E
Ban Khlong Kua	101	6 57N	100 8 E
Ban Khuan Mao	101	7 50N	99 37 E
Ban Khun Yuam	100	18 49N	97 57 E
Ban Ko Yai Chim	101	11 17N	99 26 E
Ban Kok	100	16 40N	103 40 E
Ban Laem	100	13 13N	99 59 E
Ban Lao Ngam	100	15 28N	106 10 E
Ban Le Kathe	100	15 49N	98 53 E
Ban Mae Chedi	100	19 11N	99 31 E
Ban Mae Laeng	100	20 1N	99 17 E
Ban Mae Sariang	100	18 0N	97 56 E
Ban Me Thuot	100	12 40N	108 3 E
Ban Mi	100	15 3N	100 32 E
Ban Muong Mo	100	19 4N	103 58 E
Ban Na Mo	100	17 7N	105 40 E
Ban Na San	101	8 33N	99 52 E
Ban Na Tong	100	20 56N	101 47 E
Ban Nam Bac	100	20 38N	102 20 E
Ban Nam Ma	100	22 2N	101 37 E
Ban Ngang	100	15 59N	106 11 E
Ban Nong Bok	100	17 5N	104 48 E
Ban Nong Boua	100	15 40N	106 33 E
Ban Nong Pling	100	15 40N	100 10 E
Ban Pak Chan	101	10 32N	98 51 E
Ban Phai	100	16 4N	102 44 E
Ban Pong	100	13 50N	99 55 E
Ban Ron Phibun	101	8 9N	99 51 E
Ban Sanam Chai	101	7 33N	100 25 E
Ban Sangkha	100	14 37N	103 52 E
Ban Tak	100	17 2N	99 4 E
Ban Tako	100	14 5N	102 40 E
Ban Takua Pa	101	8 55N	98 25 E
Ban Tha Dua	100	17 59N	98 39 E
Ban Tha Li	100	17 37N	101 25 E
Ban Tha Nun	101	8 12N	98 18 E
Ban Thahine	100	14 12N	105 33 E
Ban Thateng	101	15 25N	106 27 E
Ban Xien Kok	100	20 54N	100 39 E
Ban Yen Nhan	100	20 57N	106 2 E
Baña, La, Punta de	58	40 33N	0 40 E
Banadar Daryay Oman □	93	25 30N	56 0 E
Banadia	174	6 54N	71 49W
Banagher	39	53 12N	8 0W
Banalia	126	1 32N	25 5 E
Banam	101	11 20N	105 17 E
Banamba	120	13 29N	7 22W
Banana	138	24 28S	150 8 E
Bananal, I. do	171	11 30S	50 30W
Banaras = Varanasi	95	25 22N	83 8 E
Banas, R., Gujarat, India	94	24 25N	72 30 E
Banas, R., Madhya Pradesh, India	95	24 15N	81 30 E
Bânâs, Ras.	122	23 57N	35 50 E
Banat □	66	45 45N	21 15 E
Banbridge	38	54 21N	6 17W
Banbridge □	38	54 21N	6 16W
Banbury	28	52 4N	1 21W
Banchory	37	57 3N	2 30W
Bancroft	150	45 3N	77 51W
Bancroft = Chililabombwe	127	12 18S	27 43 E
Band	67	46 30N	24 25 E
Band-i-Turkistan, Ra.	93	35 2N	64 0 E
Banda	95	25 30N	80 26 E
Banda Aceh	102	5 35N	95 20 E
Banda Banda, Mt.	141	31 10S	152 28 E
Banda Flat	103	5 40S	133 5 E
Banda, Kepulauan	103	4 37S	129 50 E
Banda, La	172	27 45S	64 10W
Banda, Punta	164	31 47N	116 50W
Banda Sea	103	6 0S	130 0 E
Bandama, R.	120	6 32N	5 30W
Bandanwara	94	26 9N	74 38 E
Bandar = Masulipatnam	97	16 12N	81 12 E
Bandar 'Abbās	93	27 15N	56 15 E
Bandar-e Būshehr	93	28 55N	50 55 E
Bandar-e Chārak	93	26 45N	54 20 E
Bandar-e Deylam	92	30 5N	50 10 E
Bandar-e Lengeh	93	26 35N	54 58 E
Bandar-e Ma'shur	92	30 35N	49 10 E
Bandar-e-Nakhīlu	93	26 58N	53 30 E
Bandar-e-Pahlavi	92	37 30N	49 30 E
Bandar-e Rīg	93	29 30N	50 45 E
Bandar-e Shah	93	37 0N	54 10 E
Bandar-e-Shahpur	92	30 30N	49 5 E
Bandar Maharani = Muar	101	2 3N	102 34 E
Bandar Penggaram = Batu Pahat	101	1 50N	102 56 E
Bandar Seri Begawan	102	4 52N	115 0 E
Bandawe	127	11 58S	34 5 E
Bande, Belg.	47	50 10N	5 25 E
Bande, Spain	56	42 3N	7 58W
Bandeira, Pico da	173	20 26S	41 47W
Bandeirante	171	13 41S	50 48W
Bandera, Argent.	172	28 55S	62 20W
Bandera, U.S.A.	159	29 45N	99 3W
Banderas, Bahía de	164	20 40N	105 30W
Bandi-San	112	37 36N	140 4 E
Bandia, R.	96	19 30N	80 25 E
Bandiagara	120	14 12N	3 29W
Bandirma	92	40 20N	28 0 E
Bandon	39	51 44N	8 45W
Bandon, R.	39	51 40N	8 11W
Bandula	127	19 0S	33 7 E
Bandundu	124	3 15S	17 22 E
Bandung	103	6 36S	107 48 E
Bandya	137	27 40S	122 5 E
Bañeres	59	38 44N	0 38W
Banes	167	21 0N	75 42W
Bañeza, La	56	42 17N	5 54W
Banff, Can.	152	51 10N	115 34W
Banff, U.K.	37	57 40N	2 32W
Banff Nat. Park	152	51 30N	116 15W
Banfora	120	10 40N	4 40W
Bang Fai, R.	100	16 57N	104 45 E
Bang Hieng, R.	100	16 24N	105 40 E
Bang Krathum	100	16 34N	100 18 E
Bang Lamung	100	13 3N	100 56 E
Bang Mun Nak	100	16 2N	100 23 E
Bang Pa In	100	14 14N	100 35 E
Bang Rakam	100	16 45N	100 7 E
Bang Saphan	101	11 14N	99 28 E
Bangala Dam	127	21 7S	31 25 E
Bangalore	97	12 59N	77 40 E
Bangangte	121	5 8N	10 32 E
Bangaon	95	23 0N	88 47 E
Bangassou	124	4 55N	23 55 E
Bangeta, Mt.	135	6 21S	147 3 E
Banggai	103	1 40S	123 30 E
Banggi, P.	102	7 50N	117 0 E
Banghāzī	119	32 11N	20 3 E
Bangil	103	7 36S	112 50 E
Bangjang	123	11 23N	32 41 E
Bangka, Pulau, Celebes, Indon.	103	1 50N	125 5 E
Bangka, Pulau, Sumatera, Indon.	102	2 0S	105 50 E
Bangka, Selat	102	3 30S	105 30 E
Bangkalan	103	7 2S	112 46 E
Bangkinang	102	0 18N	100 5 E
Bangko	102	2 5S	102 9 E
Bangkok	100	13 45N	100 31 E
Bangladesh ■	98	24 0N	90 0 E
Bangolo	120	7 1N	7 29W
Bangor, Me., U.S.A.	151	44 48N	68 42W

Bangor **Bassevelde**

Bangor, Pa., U.S.A. **162** 40 51N 75 13W
Bangor, N.I., U.K. **38** 54 40N 5 40W
Bangor, Wales, U.K. **31** 53 13N 4 9W
Bangued **103** 17 40N 120 37 E
Bangui **124** 4 23N 18 35 E
Banguru **126** 0 30N 27 10 E
Bangweulu, L. **127** 11 0 S 30 0 E
Bangweulu Swamp **127** 11 20 S 30 15 E
Banham **29** 52 27N 1 3 E
Bani **167** 18 16N 70 22W
Bani Bangou **121** 15 3N 2 42 E
Bani, Djebel **118** 29 16N 8 0W
Bani Na'im **90** 31 31N 35 10 E
Bani, R. **120** 12 40N 6 30W
Bani Suhayla **90** 31 21N 34 19 E
Bania **120** 9 4N 3 6W
Baniara **135** 9 44 S 149 54 E
Banihal Pass **95** 33 30N 75 12 E
Banīnah **119** 32 0N 20 12 E
Baniyas **92** 35 10N 36 0 E
Banja Luka **66** 44 49N 17 26 E
Banjak, Kepulauan **102** 2 10N 97 10 E
Banjar **103** 7 24 S 108 30 E
Banjarmasin **102** 3 20 S 114 35 E
Banjarnegara **103** 7 24 S 109 42 E
Banjul **120** 13 28N 16 40W
Banka Banka **138** 18 50 S 134 0 E
Bankend **35** 55 2N 3 31W
Bankeryd **73** 57 53N 14 6 E
Banket **127** 17 27 S 30 19 E
Bankfoot **35** 56 30N 3 31W
Bankhead **37** 57 11N 2 10W
Bankilaré **121** 14 35N 0 44 E
Bankipore **95** 25 35N 85 10 E
Banks I., B.C., Can. **152** 53 20N 130 0W
Banks I., N. W. Terr., Can. **12** 73 15N 121 30W
Banks I., P.N.G. **135** 10 10 S 142 15 E
Banks Peninsula **143** 43 45 S 173 15 E
Banks Str. **138** 40 40 S 148 10 E
Bankura **95** 23 11N 87 18 E
Bankya **66** 42 43N 23 8 E
Bann R., Down, U.K. **38** 54 30N 6 31W
Bann R., Londonderry, U.K. **38** 55 10N 6 34W
Bannalec **42** 47 57N 3 42W
Bannang Sata **101** 6 16N 101 16 E
Bannerton **140** 34 42 S 142 47 E
Banning, Can. **150** 48 44N 91 56W
Banning, U.S.A. **163** 33 58N 116 58W
Banningville = Bandundu **124** 3 15 S 17 22 E
Bannockburn, Zimb. **127** 20 17 S 29 48 E
Bannockburn, U.K. **35** 56 5N 3 55W
Bannow **39** 52 12N 6 50W
Bannow B. **39** 52 13N 6 48W
Bannu **93** 33 0N 70 18 E
Bañolas **58** 42 16N 2 44 E
Banon **45** 44 2N 5 38 E
Baños de la Encina **57** 38 10N 3 46W
Baños de Molgas **56** 42 15N 7 40W
Bánovce **53** 48 44N 18 16 E
Banská Bystrica **53** 48 46N 19 14 E
Banská Stiavnica **53** 48 25N 18 55 E
Bansko **67** 41 52N 23 28 E
Banswara **94** 23 32N 74 24 E
Bantama **121** 7 48N 0 42W
Bante **121** 8 25N 1 53 E
Banteer **39** 52 8N 8 53W
Banten **103** 6 5 S 106 8 E
Bantry **39** 51 40N 9 28W
Bantry, B. **39** 51 35N 9 50W
Bantul **103** 7 55 S 110 19 E
Bantva **94** 21 29N 70 12 E
Bantval **97** 12 55N 75 0 E
Banu **93** 35 35N 69 5 E
Banwell **28** 51 19N 2 51W
Banya **67** 42 33N 24 50 E
Banyo **121** 6 52N 11 45 E
Banyuls **44** 42 29N 3 8 E
Banyumas **103** 7 32 S 109 18 E
Banyuwangi **103** 8 13 S 114 21 E
Banzare Coast **13** 66 30 S 125 0 E
Banzyville = Mobayi **124** 4 15N 21 8 E
Bao Ha **100** 22 11N 104 21 E
Bao Lac **100** 22 57N 105 40 E
Bao Loc **101** 11 32N 107 48 E
Bap **94** 27 23N 72 18 E
Bapatla **97** 15 55N 80 30 E
Bapaume **43** 50 7N 2 50 E
Bâqa el Gharbiya **90** 32 25N 35 2 E
Baqūbah **92** 33 45N 44 50 E
Baquedano **172** 23 20 S 69 52W
Bar, U.S.S.R. **82** 49 4N 27 40 E
Bar, Yugo. **66** 42 8N 19 8 E
Bar Harbor **151** 44 15N 68 20W
Bar-le-Duc **43** 48 47N 5 10 E
Bar-sur-Aube **43** 48 14N 4 40 E
Bar-sur-Seine **43** 48 7N 4 20 E
Barabai **102** 2 32 S 115 34 E
Barabinsk **76** 55 20N 78 20 E
Baraboo **158** 43 28N 89 46W
Baracoa **167** 20 20N 74 30W
Baradero **172** 33 52 S 59 29W
Baradine **141** 30 56 S 149 4 E
Baraga **158** 46 49N 88 29W
Barahona, Dom. Rep. **167** 18 13N 71 7W
Barahona, Spain **58** 41 17N 2 39W
Barail Range **99** 25 15N 93 20 E
Barakhola **99** 25 0N 92 45 E
Barakot **95** 21 33N 84 59 E
Barakula **139** 26 30 S 150 33 E
Baralaba **138** 24 13 S 149 50 E
Baralzon L. **153** 60 0N 98 3W
Baramati **96** 18 11N 74 33 E
Baramba **96** 20 25N 85 23 E
Barameiya **122** 18 32N 36 38 E
Baramula **95** 34 15N 74 20 E
Baran **94** 25 9N 76 40 E
Baranoa **174** 10 48N 74 55W
Baranof I. **147** 57 0N 135 10W
Baranovichi **80** 53 10N 26 0 E
Baranów Sandomierski **54** 50 29N 21 30 E
Baranya □ **53** 46 0N 18 15 E
Barão de Cocais **171** 19 56 S 43 28W
Barão de Grajaú **170** 6 45 S 43 1W
Barão de Melgaço **174** 11 50 S 60 45W
Baraolt **70** 46 5N 25 34 E
Barapasi **103** 2 15 S 137 5 E
Barapina **135** 6 21 S 155 25 E
Barasat **95** 22 46N 88 31 E
Barasoli **123** 13 38N 42 0W
Barat Daya, Kepuluan **103** 7 30 S 128 0 E
Barataria B. **159** 29 15N 89 45W
Baraut **94** 29 13N 77 7 E
Baraya **174** 3 10N 75 4W
Barbacena **173** 21 15 S 43 56W
Barbacoas, Colomb. **174** 1 45N 78 0W
Barbacoas, Venez. **174** 9 29N 66 58W
Barbados ■ **167** 13 0N 59 30W
Barbalha **170** 7 19 S 39 17W
Barban **63** 45 0N 14 4 E
Barbastro **58** 42 2N 0 5 E
Barbate **57** 36 13N 5 56W
Barberton, S. Afr. **129** 25 42 S 31 2 E
Barberton, U.S.A. **156** 41 0N 81 40W
Barbigha **95** 25 21N 85 47 E
Barbourville **157** 36 57N 83 52W
Barbuda I. **167** 17 30N 61 40W
Barca d'Alva **56** 41 0N 7 0W
Barca, La **164** 20 20N 102 40W
Barcaldine **138** 23 33 S 145 13 E
Barcarrota **57** 38 31N 6 51W
Barce = Al Marj **117** 32 25N 20 40 E
Barcellona Pozzo di Gotto **65** 38 8N 15 15 E
Barcelona, Spain **58** 41 21N 2 10 E
Barcelona, Venez. **174** 10 10N 64 40W
Barcelona □ **58** 41 30N 2 0 E
Barcelonette **45** 44 23N 6 40 E
Barcelos **174** 1 0 S 63 0W
Barcin **54** 52 52N 17 55 E
Barcoo, R. **138** 28 29 S 137 46 E
Barcs **53** 45 58N 17 28 E
Barczewo **54** 53 50N 20 42 E
Bard, Hd. **36** 60 6N 1 5W
Barda **83** 40 25N 47 10 E
Bardai **119** 21 25N 17 0 E
Bardas Blancas **172** 35 49 S 69 45W
Bardejov **53** 49 18N 21 15 E
Bardera **91** 2 20N 42 27 E
Bardi **62** 44 38N 9 43 E
Bardiyah **117** 31 45N 25 0 E
Bardney **33** 53 13N 0 19W
Bardo **54** 50 31N 16 42 E
Bardoc **137** 30 18 S 121 12 E
Bardoli **96** 21 12N 73 5 E
Bardsey, I. **31** 52 46N 4 47W
Bardsey Sound **31** 52 47N 4 46W
Bardstown **156** 37 50N 85 29W
Bareilly **95** 28 22N 79 27 E
Barellan **141** 34 16 S 146 24 E
Barengapara **98** 25 14N 90 14 E
Barentin **42** 49 33N 0 58 E
Barenton **42** 48 38N 0 50W
Barents Sea **12** 73 0N 39 0 E
Barentu **123** 15 2N 37 35 E
Barfleur **42** 49 40N 1 17W
Barford **28** 52 15N 1 35W
Barga **62** 44 5N 10 30 E
Bargal **91** 11 25N 51 0 E
Bargara **138** 24 50 S 152 25 E
Barge **62** 44 43N 7 19 E
Barge, La **160** 41 12N 110 4W
Bargnop **123** 9 32N 28 25 E
Bargo **141** 34 18 S 150 35 E
Bargoed **31** 51 42N 3 22W
Bargteheide **48** 53 42N 10 13 E
Barguzin **77** 53 37N 109 37 E
Barh **95** 25 29N 85 46 E
Barhaj **95** 26 18N 83 44 E
Barham **29** 51 12N 1 10 E
Barhi **95** 24 15N 85 25 E
Bari, India **94** 26 39N 77 39 E
Bari, Italy **65** 41 6N 16 52 E
Bari Doab **94** 30 20N 73 0 E
Baria = Phuoc Le **101** 10 39N 107 19 E
Bariadi □ **126** 2 45 S 34 40 E
Barika **118** 35 23N 5 22 E
Barinas **174** 8 36N 70 15W
Barinas □ **174** 8 10N 69 50W
Baring C. **148** 70 0N 117 30W
Baringo **126** 0 47N 36 16 E
Baringo □ **126** 0 55N 36 0 E
Baringo, L. **126** 0 47N 36 16 E
Barinitas **174** 8 45N 70 25W
Baripada **96** 21 57N 86 45 E
Bariri **171** 22 4 S 48 44W
Bârîs **122** 24 42N 30 31 E
Barisal **98** 22 30N 90 20 E
Barisan, Bukit **102** 3 30 S 102 15 E
Barito, R. **102** 2 50 S 114 50 E
Barjac **45** 44 20N 4 22 E
Barjols **45** 43 34N 6 2 E
Barjūji, W. **119** 25 26N 12 12 E
Bark L. **150** 46 58N 82 25W
Barka **122** 17 30N 37 34 E
Barkah **93** 23 40N 58 0 E
Barker, Mt. **139** 35 4 S 138 55 E
Barking **29** 51 31N 0 10 E
Barkley Sound **152** 48 50N 125 10W
Barkly Downs **138** 20 30 S 138 30 E
Barkly East **129** 30 58 S 27 33 E
Barkly Tableland **138** 19 50 S 138 40 E
Barkly West **128** 28 5 S 24 31 E
Barkol, Wadi **122** 17 40N 32 0 E
Barksdale **159** 29 47N 100 2W
Barlborough **33** 53 17N 1 17W
Barlby **33** 53 48N 1 3W
Barlee, L. **137** 29 15 S 119 30 E
Barlee, Mt. **137** 24 35 S 128 10 E
Barlee Ra. **137** 23 30 S 116 0 E
Barlett **163** 36 29N 118 2W
Barletta **65** 41 20N 16 17 E
Barlinek **54** 53 0N 15 15 E
Barlingbo **73** 57 35N 18 27 E
Barlow L. **153** 62 00N 103 0W
Barmby Moor **33** 53 55N 0 47W
Barmedman **141** 34 9 S 147 21 E
Barmer **94** 25 45N 71 20 E
Barmera **140** 34 15 S 140 28 E
Barmoor **35** 55 38N 2 0W
Barmouth **31** 52 44N 4 3W
Barmstedt **48** 53 47N 9 46 E
Barna **39** 53 14N 9 10W
Barnaderg **38** 53 29N 8 43W
Barnagar **94** 23 7N 75 19 E
Barnard Castle **32** 54 33N 1 55W
Barnato **141** 31 38 S 145 0 E
Barnaul **76** 53 20N 83 40 E
Barnby Moor **33** 53 21N 1 0W
Barne Inlet **13** 80 15 S 160 0 E
Barnes **141** 36 2 S 144 47 E
Barnesville **157** 33 6N 84 9W
Barnet **29** 51 37N 0 15W
Barnetby le Wold **33** 53 34N 0 24W
Barneveld, Neth. **96** 52 7N 5 36 E
Barneveld, U.S.A. **162** 43 16N 75 14W
Barneville **42** 49 23N 1 46W
Barney, Mt. **133** 28 17 S 152 44 E
Barngo **138** 25 3 S 147 20 E
Barnhart **159** 31 10N 101 8W
Barnoldswick **32** 53 55N 2 11W
Barnsley **33** 53 33N 1 29W
Barnstaple **30** 51 5N 4 3W
Barnstaple B. **30** 51 5N 4 25W
Barnsville **158** 46 43N 96 28W
Baro **121** 8 35N 6 18 E
Baro, R. **123** 8 25N 33 40 E
Baroda **94** 25 29N 76 35 E
Baroda = Vadodara, India **93** 22 20N 73 10 E
Baroda = Vadodara, Gujarat, India **94** 22 20N 73 10 E
Baron Ra. **136** 23 30 S 127 45 E
Barpali **96** 21 11N 83 35 E
Barpathar **98** 26 17N 93 53 E
Barpeta **95** 26 20N 91 10 E
Barqa **117** 27 0N 20 0 E
Barqin **119** 27 33N 13 34 E
Barques, Pte. aux **156** 44 5N 82 55W
Barquinha **57** 39 28N 8 25W
Barquisimeto **174** 9 58N 69 13W
Barr, France **43** 48 25N 7 28 E
Barr, U.K. **34** 55 13N 4 44W
Barr Smith Ra. **137** 27 10 S 120 15 E
Barra, Brazil **170** 11 5 S 43 10W
Barra, Gambia **120** 13 21N 16 36W
Barra da Estiva **171** 13 38 S 41 19W
Barra de Navidad **164** 19 12N 104 41W
Barra do Corda **170** 5 30 S 45 10W
Barra do Mendes **171** 11 43 S 42 4W
Barra do Piraí **173** 22 30 S 43 50W
Barra Falsa, Pta. da **129** 22 58 S 35 37 E
Barra Hd. **36** 56 47N 7 40W
Barra, I. **36** 57 0N 7 30W
Barra Mansa **173** 22 35 S 44 12W
Barra, Sd. of **36** 57 4N 7 25W
Barraba **141** 30 21 S 150 35 E
Barrackpur **95** 22 44N 88 30 E
Barrafranca **65** 37 22N 14 10 E
Barranca, Lima, Peru **174** 10 45 S 77 50W
Barranca, Loreto, Peru **174** 4 50 S 76 50W
Barrancabermeja **174** 7 0N 73 50W
Barrancas, Colomb. **174** 10 57N 72 50W
Barrancas, Venez. **174** 8 55N 62 5W
Barrancos **57** 38 10N 6 58W
Barranqueras **172** 27 30 S 59 0W
Barranquilla, Atlántico, Colomb. **174** 11 0N 74 50W
Barranquilla, Vaupés, Colomb. **174** 1 39N 72 19W
Barras, Brazil **170** 4 15 S 42 18W
Barras, Colomb. **174** 1 45 S 73 13W
Barraute **150** 48 26N 77 38W
Barre, U.S.A. **156** 44 15N 72 30W
Barre, U.S.A. **162** 42 26N 72 6W
Barreal **172** 31 33 S 69 28W
Barreiras **171** 12 8 S 45 0W
Barreirinhas **170** 2 30 S 42 50W
Barreiro **57** 38 40N 9 6W
Barreiros **170** 8 49 S 35 12W
Barrême **45** 43 57N 6 23 E
Barren I. **101** 12 17N 95 50 E
Barren Is., Madag. **129** 18 25 S 43 40 E
Barren Is., U.S.A. **147** 58 45N 152 0W
Barren Junc. **139** 30 5 S 149 0 E
Barretos **171** 20 30 S 48 35W
Barrhead, Can. **152** 54 10N 114 24W
Barrhead, U.K. **34** 55 48N 4 23W
Barrhill **34** 55 7N 4 46W
Barrie **150** 44 24N 79 40W
Barrier, C. **142** 36 25 S 175 32 E
Barrier Ra., Austral. **140** 31 0 S 141 30 E
Barrier Ra., N.Z. **143** 44 5 S 169 42 E
Barrier Rf., Gt. **138** 19 0 S 149 0 E
Barrière **152** 51 12N 120 7W
Barrington, Austral. **133** 31 58 S 151 55 E
Barrington, Ill., U.S.A. **156** 42 8N 88 5W
Barrington, R.I., U.S.A. **162** 41 43N 71 20W
Barrington L. **153** 56 55N 100 15W
Barrington Tops. **141** 32 6 S 151 28 E
Barringun **139** 29 1 S 145 41 E
Barrow **147** 71 16N 156 50W
Barrow Creek T.O. **138** 21 30 S 133 55 E
Barrow I. **136** 20 45 S 115 20 E
Barrow-in-Furness **32** 54 8N 3 15W
Barrow Pt. **138** 14 20 S 144 40 E
Barrow, Pt. **147** 71 22N 156 30W
Barrow, R. **39** 52 10N 6 57W
Barrow Ra. **137** 26 0 S 127 40 E
Barrow Strait **12** 74 20N 95 0W
Barrow upon Humber **33** 53 41N 0 22W
Barrowford **32** 53 51N 2 14W
Barruecopardo **56** 41 4N 6 40W
Barruelo **56** 42 54N 4 17W
Barry, S. Glam., U.K. **31** 51 23N 3 19W
Barry, Tayside, U.K. **35** 56 29N 2 45W
Barry I. **31** 51 23N 3 17W
Barry's Bay **150** 45 29N 77 41W
Barry's Pt. **39** 51 36N 8 40W
Barsalogho **121** 13 25N 1 3W
Barsat **95** 36 10N 72 45 E
Barsi **96** 18 10N 75 50 E
Barsø **73** 55 7N 9 33 E
Barsoi **99** 25 48N 87 57 E
Barstow, Calif., U.S.A. **163** 34 58N 117 2W
Barstow, Tex., U.S.A. **170** 31 30N 103 25W
Barthélemy, Col **100** 19 26N 104 6 E
Bartica **174** 6 25N 58 40W
Bartle Frere, Mt. **138** 17 27 S 145 50 E
Bartlesville **159** 36 50N 95 58W
Bartlett **159** 30 46N 97 30W
Bartlett, L. **152** 63 5N 118 20W
Bartolomeu Dias **127** 21 10 S 35 8 E
Barton **33** 54 28N 1 38W
Barton Siding **137** 30 31 S 132 39 E
Barton-upon-Humber **33** 53 41N 0 27W
Bartoszyce **54** 54 15N 20 55 E
Bartow **157** 27 53N 81 49W
Barú, I. de **174** 10 15N 75 35W
Baruth **48** 52 3N 13 31 E
Barvas **36** 58 21N 6 31W
Barvaux **47** 50 21N 5 29 E
Barvenkovo **82** 48 57N 37 0 E
Barwani **94** 22 2N 74 57 E
Barwell **28** 52 35N 1 22W
Barysh **81** 49 2N 25 18 E
Bas-Rhin □ **43** 48 40N 7 30 E
Bašaid **66** 45 38N 20 25 E
Basa'idu **93** 26 35N 55 20 E
Basal **94** 33 33N 72 13 E
Basalt **163** 38 0N 118 15W
Basankusa **124** 1 5N 19 50 E
Basawa **94** 34 15N 70 50 E
Bascharage **47** 49 34N 5 55 E
Bascuñán, Cabo **172** 28 52 S 71 35W
Basècles **47** 50 32N 3 39 E
Basel (Basle) **50** 47 35N 7 35 E
Basel Landschaft □ **50** 47 26N 7 45 E
Basel-Stadt □ **50** 47 35N 7 35 E
Basento, R. **65** 40 35N 16 10 E
Bashi Channel **105** 21 15N 122 0 E
Bashkir A.S.S.R. □ **84** 54 0N 57 0 E
Basilaki, I. **135** 10 35 S 151 0 E
Basilan, Selat **103** 6 50N 122 0 E
Basilanl, I. **103** 6 35N 122 0 E
Basildon **29** 51 34N 0 29 E
Basilicata □ **65** 40 30N 16 0 E
Basim **96** 20 3N 77 0 E
Basin **160** 44 22N 108 2W
Basing **28** 51 16N 1 3W
Basingstoke **28** 51 15N 1 5W
Basirhat **98** 22 40N 88 54 E
Baskatong Res. **150** 46 46N 75 50W
Baskerville C. **136** 17 10 S 122 15 E
Basle = Basel **50** 47 35N 7 35 E
Basmat **96** 19 15N 77 12 E
Basoda **94** 23 52N 77 54 E
Basodino **51** 46 25N 8 28 E
Basoka **126** 1 16N 23 40 E
Basongo **124** 4 15 S 20 20 E
Basque Provinces = Vascongadas **58** 42 50N 2 45W
Basra = Al Basrah **92** 30 30N 47 50 E
Bass Rock **35** 56 5N 2 40W
Bass Strait **138** 39 15 S 146 30 E
Bassano, del Grappa **63** 45 45N 11 45 E
Bassari **121** 9 19N 0 57 E
Bassas da India **125** 22 0 S 39 0 E
Basse **120** 13 13N 14 15W
Basse-Terre, I. **167** 16 0N 61 40W
Bassecourt **50** 47 20N 7 15 E
Bassée, La **43** 50 31N 2 49 E
Bassein, Burma **98** 16 30N 94 30 E
Bassein, India **96** 19 26N 72 48 E
Bassein Myit **99** 16 45N 94 30 E
Bassenthwaite, L. **32** 54 40N 3 14W
Basseterre **167** 17 17N 62 43W
Bassett, Nebr., U.S.A. **158** 42 37N 99 30W
Bassett, Va., U.S.A. **157** 36 48N 79 59W
Bassevelde **47** 51 15N 3 41 E

Bassi **Bekkjarvik**

Bassi **94** 30 44N 76 21 E
Bassigny **43** 48 0N 5 10 E
Bassikounou **120** 15 55N 6 1W
Bassilly **47** 50 40N 3 56 E
Bassum **48** 52 50N 8 42 E
Båstad **73** 56 25N 12 51 E
Båstad **73** 56 25N 12 51 E
Bastak **93** 27 15N 54 25 E
Bastar **96** 19 25N 81 40 E
Basti **95** 26 52N 82 55 E
Bastia **45** 42 40N 9 30 E
Bastia Umbra **63** 43 4N 12 34 E
Bastide, La **44** 44 35N 3 55 E
Bastogne **47** 50 1N 5 43 E
Baston **29** 52 43N 0 19W
Bastrop **159** 30 5N 97 22W
Basuto **128** 19 50 S 26 25 E
Basutoland = Lesotho **129** 29 0 S 28 0 E
Basyanovskiy **84** 58 19N 60 44 E
Bat Yam **90** 32 2N 34 44 E
Bata, Eq. Guin. **124** 1 57N 9 50 E
Bata, Rumania **70** 46 1N 22 4 E
Bataan **103** 14 40N 120 25 E
Bataan Pen. **103** 14 38N 120 30 E
Batabanó **166** 22 40N 82 20W
Batabanó, G. de **167** 22 30N 82 30W
Batac **103** 18 3N 120 34 E
Batagoy **77** 67 38N 134 38 E
Batak **67** 41 57N 24 12 E
Batalha **57** 39 40N 8 50W
Batama **126** 0 58N 26 33 E
Batamay **77** 63 30N 129 15 E
Batamshinskiy **84** 50 36N 58 16 E
Batang **103** 6 55 S 109 40 E
Batangafo **117** 7 25N 18 20 E
Batangas **103** 13 35N 121 10 E
Batanta, I. **103** 0 55N 130 40 E
Bataszék **66** 46 10N 18 44 E
Batatais **173** 20 54 S 47 37W
Batavia **156** 43 0N 78 10W
Bataysk **83** 47 3N 39 45 E
Batchelor **136** 13 4 S 131 1 E
Bateman's B. **141** 35 40 S 150 12 E
Batemans Bay **141** 35 44 S 150 11 E
Bates Ra. **137** 27 25 S 121 0 E
Batesburg **157** 33 54N 81 32W
Batesville, Ark., U.S.A. **159** 35 48N 91 40W
Batesville, Miss., U.S.A. **159** 34 17N 89 58W
Batesville, Tex., U.S.A. **159** 28 59N 99 38W
Batetski **80** 58 47N 30 16 E
Bath, U.K. **28** 51 22N 2 22W
Bath, Maine, U.S.A. **151** 43 50N 69 49W
Bath, N.Y., U.S.A. **156** 42 20N 77 17W
Batheay **101** 11 59N 104 57 E
Bathford **28** 51 23N 2 18W
Bathgate **35** 55 54N 3 38W
Bâthie, La **46** 45 37N 6 28 E
Bathmen **46** 52 15N 6 29 E
Bathurst, Austral. **141** 33 25 S 149 31 E
Bathurst, Can. **151** 47 37N 65 43W
Bathurst B. **138** 14 16 S 144 25 E
Bathurst C. **147** 70 30N 128 30W
Bathurst, C. **147** 70 34N 128 0W
Bathurst, Gambia = Banjul **120** 13 28N 16 40W
Bathurst Harb. **138** 43 15 S 146 10 E
Bathurst I., Austral. **136** 11 30 S 130 10 E
Bathurst I., Can. **12** 76 30N 130 10W
Bathurst Inlet **148** 66 50N 108 1W
Batie **120** 9 53N 2 53W
Batley **33** 53 43N 1 38W
Batlow **141** 35 31 S 148 9 E
Batman **92** 37 55N 41 5 E
Batna **119** 35 34N 6 15 E
Batoka **127** 16 45 S 27 15 E
Baton Rouge **159** 30 30N 91 5W
Batong, Ko **101** 6 32N 99 12 E
Batopilas **164** 27 45N 107 45W
Batouri **124** 4 30N 14 25 E
Battambang **100** 13 7N 103 12 E
Batticaloa **97** 7 43N 81 45 E
Battice **47** 50 39N 5 50 E
Battipáglia **65** 40 38N 15 0 E
Battir **90** 31 44N 35 8 E
Battle, Can. **153** 52 58N 110 52W
Battle, U.K. **29** 50 55N 0 30 E
Battle Camp **138** 15 20 S 144 40 E
Battle Creek **156** 42 20N 85 36W
Battle Harbour **151** 52 16N 55 35W
Battle Lake **158** 46 20N 95 43W
Battle Mountain **160** 40 45N 117 0W
Battle, R. **153** 52 43N 108 15W
Battlefields **127** 18 37 S 29 47 E
Battleford **153** 52 45N 108 15W
Battonya **53** 46 16N 21 3 E
Batu Caves **101** 3 15N 101 40 E
Batu Gajah **101** 4 28N 101 3 E
Batu, Kepulauan **102** 0 30 S 98 25 E
Batu, Mt. **123** 6 55N 39 45 E
Batu Pahat **101** 1 50N 102 56 E
Batuata, P. **103** 6 30 S 122 20 E
Batulaki **103** 5 40N 125 30 E
Batumi **83** 41 30N 41 30 E
Baturadja **102** 4 11 S 104 15 E
Baturité **170** 4 28 S 38 45W
Baturité, Serra de **170** 4 25 S 39 0W
Baubau **103** 5 25 S 123 50 E
Bauchi **121** 10 22N 9 48 E
Bauchi □ **121** 10 0N 10 0 E
Baud **42** 47 52N 3 1W
Baudette **158** 48 46N 94 35W
Baudouinville = Moba **126** 7 0 S 29 48 E
Baudour **47** 50 29N 3 50 E
Bauer, C. **139** 32 44 S 134 4 E
Baugé **42** 47 31N 0 8W
Bauhinia Downs **138** 24 35 S 149 18 E
Baule, La **42** 47 18N 2 23W
Bauma **51** 47 3N 8 53 E
Baume les Dames **43** 47 22N 6 22 E
Baunei **64** 40 2N 9 41 E
Bauru **173** 22 10 S 49 0W
Baús **175** 18 22 S 52 47W
Bauska **80** 56 25N 25 15 E
Bautzen **48** 51 11N 14 25 E
Baux, Les **45** 43 45N 4 51 E
BavaniŠte **66** 44 49N 20 53 E
Bavaria = Bayern **49** 49 7N 11 30 E
Båven **72** 59 35N 17 30 E
Bavispe, R. **164** 29 30N 109 11W
Bawdsey **29** 52 1N 1 27 E
Bawdwin **98** 23 5N 97 50 E
Bawean **102** 5 46 S 112 35 E
Bawku **121** 11 3N 0 19W
Bawlake **98** 19 11N 97 21 E
Bawnboy **38** 54 8N 7 40W
Bawtry **33** 53 25N 1 1W
Baxley **157** 31 43N 82 23W
Baxter Springs **159** 37 3N 94 45W
Bay Bulls **151** 47 19N 52 50W
Bay City, Mich., U.S.A. **156** 43 35N 83 51W
Bay City, Oreg., U.S.A. **160** 45 45N 123 58W
Bay City, Tex., U.S.A. **159** 28 59N 95 55W
Bay de Verde **151** 48 5N 52 54W
Bay, Laguna de **103** 14 20N 121 11 E
Bay of Islands **142** 35 15 S 174 6 E
Bay St. Louis **159** 30 18N 89 22W
Bay Shore **162** 40 44N 73 15W
Bay Springs **159** 31 58N 89 18W
Bay View **142** 39 25 S 176 50 E
Baya **127** 11 53 S 27 25 E
Bayamo **166** 20 20N 76 40W
Bayamón **147** 18 24N 66 10W
Bayan Kara Shan **99** 34 0N 98 0 E
Bayan-Ovoo **106** 47 47N 112 5 E
Bayana **94** 26 55N 77 18 E
Bayanaul **76** 50 45N 75 45 E
Bayandalay **106** 43 30N 103 29 E
Bayanga **124** 2 53N 16 19 E
Bayanhongor **105** 46 8N 100 43 E
Bayard **158** 41 48N 103 17W
Baybay **103** 10 40N 124 55 E
Bayble **36** 58 12N 6 13W
Bayburt **92** 40 15N 40 20 E
Bayerischer Wald **49** 49 0N 13 0 E
Bayern □ **49** 49 7N 11 30 E
Bayeux **42** 49 17N 0 42W
Bayfield **158** 46 50N 90 48W
Bayir **92** 30 45N 36 55 E
Baykadam **85** 43 48N 69 58 E
Baykal, Oz. **77** 53 0N 108 0 E
Baykit **77** 61 50N 95 50 E
Baykonur **76** 47 48N 65 50 E
Baymak **84** 52 36N 58 19 E
Baynes Mts. **128** 17 15 S 13 0 E
Bayombong **103** 16 30N 121 10 E
Bayon **43** 48 30N 6 20 E
Bayona **56** 42 6N 8 52W
Bayonne, France **44** 43 30N 1 28W
Bayonne, U.S.A. **162** 40 41N 74 7W
Bayovar **174** 5 50 S 81 0W
Baypore, R. **97** 11 10N 75 47 E
Bayram-Ali **76** 37 37N 62 10 E
Bayreuth **49** 49 56N 11 35 E
Bayrischzell **49** 47 39N 12 1 E
Bayrūt **92** 33 53N 35 31 E
Baysun **85** 38 12N 67 12 E
Bayt Aula **90** 31 37N 35 2 E
Bayt Fajjar **90** 31 38N 35 9 E
Bayt Fūrīk **90** 32 11N 35 20 E
Bayt Jala **90** 31 43N 35 11 E
Bayt Lahm **90** 31 43N 35 12 E
Bayt Rīma **90** 32 2N 35 6 E
Bayt Sāhūr **90** 31 42N 35 13 E
Bayt Ummar **90** 31 38N 35 7 E
Bayta at Tahtā **90** 32 9N 35 18 E
Baytin **90** 31 56N 35 14 E
Baytown **159** 29 42N 94 57W
Bayzhansay **85** 43 14N 69 54 E
Bayzo **121** 13 52N 4 35 E
Baza **59** 37 30N 2 47W
Bazar Dyuzi **83** 41 12N 48 10 E
Bazarny Karabulak **81** 52 30N 46 20 E
Bazarnyy Syzgan **81** 53 45N 46 40 E
Bazartobe **83** 49 26N 51 45 E
Bazaruto, I. do **129** 21 40 S 35 28 E
Bazas **44** 44 27N 0 13W
Bazuriye **90** 33 15N 35 16 E
Beabula **141** 34 26 S 145 9 E
Beach **158** 46 57N 104 0W
Beach Haven **162** 39 34N 74 14W
Beachley **28** 51 37N 2 39W
Beachport **140** 37 29 S 140 0 E
Beachwood **162** 39 55N 74 8W
Beachy Head **29** 50 44N 0 16 E
Beacon, Austral. **137** 30 26 S 117 52 E
Beacon, U.S.A. **162** 41 32N 73 58W
Beaconia **153** 50 25N 96 31W
Beaconsfield, Austral. **133** 41 11 S 146 48 E
Beaconsfield, U.K. **29** 51 36N 0 39W
Beadnell **35** 55 33N 1 38W
Beagle Bay **136** 16 32 S 122 54 E
Beagle, Canal **176** 55 0 S 68 30W
Bealanana **129** 14 33N 48 44 E
Bealey **143** 43 2 S 171 36 E
Beaminster **28** 50 48N 2 44W
Bear I. **39** 51 38N 9 50W
Bear I. Nor. **12** 74 30N 19 0 E
Bear L., B.C., Can. **152** 56 10N 126 52W
Bear L., Man., Can. **153** 55 8N 96 0W
Bear L., U.S.A. **160** 42 0N 111 20W
Bearcreek **160** 45 11N 109 6W
Beardmore **150** 49 36N 87 57W
Beardmore Glacier **13** 84 30 S 170 0 E
Beardstown **158** 40 0N 90 25W
Bearn **44** 43 28N 0 36W
Bearpaw Mt. **160** 48 15N 109 55W
Bearsden **34** 55 55N 4 21W
Bearskin Lake **150** 53 58N 91 2W
Bearsted **29** 51 15N 0 35 E
Beas de Segura **59** 38 15N 2 53W
Beasain **58** 43 3N 2 11W
Beata, C. **167** 17 40N 71 30W
Beata, I. **167** 17 34N 71 31W
Beatrice, Zimb. **127** 18 15 S 30 55 E
Beatrice, U.S.A. **158** 40 20N 96 40W
Beatrice, C. **138** 14 20 S 136 55 E
Beatrice, oilfield **19** 58 7N 3 6W
Beattock **35** 55 19N 3 27W
Beatton, R. **152** 56 15N 120 45W
Beatton River **152** 57 26N 121 20W
Beatty **163** 36 58N 116 46W
Beaucaire **45** 43 48N 4 39 E
Beauce, Plaines de **43** 48 10N 2 0 E
Beauceville **151** 46 13N 70 46W
Beaudesert **139** 27 59 S 153 0 E
Beaufort, Austral. **140** 37 25 S 143 25 E
Beaufort, Malay. **102** 5 30N 115 40 E
Beaufort, N.C., U.S.A. **157** 34 45N 76 40W
Beaufort, S.C., U.S.A. **157** 32 25N 80 40W
Beaufort Sea **12** 72 0N 140 0W
Beaufort-West **128** 32 18 S 22 36 E
Beaugency **43** 47 47N 1 38 E
Beauharnois **150** 45 20N 73 52W
Beaujeu **45** 46 10N 4 35 E
Beaujolais **45** 46 0N 4 25 E
Beaulieu, Loiret, France **44** 47 31N 2 49 E
Beaulieu, Vendée, France **45** 46 41N 1 37W
Beaulieu, U.K. **28** 50 49N 1 27W
Beaulieu, R. **152** 62 3N 113 11W
Beauly **37** 57 29N 4 27W
Beauly Firth **37** 57 30N 4 20W
Beauly, R. **37** 57 26N 4 28W
Beaumaris **31** 53 16N 4 7W
Beaumetz-les-Loges **43** 50 15N 2 40 E
Beaumont, Belg. **47** 50 15N 4 14 E
Beaumont, France **44** 44 45N 0 46 E
Beaumont, N.Z. **143** 45 50 S 169 33 E
Beaumont, Calif., U.S.A. **163** 33 56N 116 58W
Beaumont, Tex., U.S.A. **159** 30 5N 94 8W
Beaumont-le-Roger **42** 49 4N 0 47 E
Beaumont-sur-Oise **43** 49 9N 2 17 E
Beaune **43** 47 2N 4 50 E
Beaune-la-Rolande **43** 48 4N 2 25 E
Beauraing **47** 50 7N 4 57 E
Beausejour **153** 50 5N 96 35 E
Beausset, Le **45** 43 10N 5 46 E
Beauvais **43** 49 25N 2 8 E
Beauval **153** 55 9N 107 37W
Beauvoir, Deux Sèvres, France **44** 46 12N 0 30W
Beauvoir, Vendée, France **42** 46 55N 2 1W
Beaver, Alaska, U.S.A. **147** 66 20N 147 30W
Beaver, Okla., U.S.A. **159** 36 52N 100 31W
Beaver, Utah, U.S.A. **161** 38 20N 112 45W
Beaver City **158** 40 13N 99 50W
Beaver Dam **158** 43 28N 88 50W
Beaver Falls **156** 40 44N 80 20W
Beaver Hill L. **153** 54 16N 94 59W
Beaver I. **150** 45 40N 85 31W
Beaver, R. **152** 59 52N 124 20W
Beaver, R **150** 55 55N 87 48W
Beaver, R. **153** 55 26N 107 45W
Beaverhill L., Man., Can. **153** 54 5N 94 50W
Beaverhill L., N.W.T., Can. **153** 63 2N 111 22W
Beaverhill L., Alb. **152** 53 27N 112 32W
Beaverlodge **152** 55 11N 119 29W
Beavermouth **152** 51 32N 117 23W
Beaverstone, R. **150** 54 59N 89 25W
Beawar **94** 26 3N 74 18 E
Bebedouro **173** 21 0 S 48 25W
Bebington **32** 53 23N 3 1W
Beboa **129** 17 22 S 44 33 E
Bebra **48** 50 59N 9 48 E
Beccles **29** 52 27N 1 33 E
Bečej **66** 45 36N 20 3 E
Beceni **70** 45 23N 26 48 E
Becerreá **56** 42 51N 7 10W
Béchar **118** 31 38N 2 18 E
Becharof L. **147** 58 0N 156 30W
Bechuanaland = Botswana **125** 23 0 S 24 0 E
Bechyně **52** 49 17N 14 29 E
Beckermet **32** 54 26N 3 31W
Beckfoot **32** 54 50N 3 25W
Beckingham **33** 53 24N 0 49W
Beckley **156** 37 50N 81 8W
Bécon **42** 47 30N 0 50W
Bečva, R. **53** 49 31N 17 40 E
Bedale **33** 54 18N 1 35W
Bédar **59** 37 11N 1 59W
Bédarieux **44** 43 37N 3 10 E
Bédarrides **45** 44 2N 4 54 E
Beddone, Mt. **138** 25 50 S 134 20 E
Bedele **123** 8 31N 35 44 E
Bedel, Pereval **85** 41 26N 78 26 E
Bederkesa **48** 53 37N 8 50 E
Bedford, Can. **150** 45 7N 72 59W
Bedford, S. Afr. **128** 32 40 S 26 10 E
Bedford, U.K. **29** 52 8N 0 29W
Bedford, Ind., U.S.A. **156** 38 50N 86 30W
Bedford, Iowa, U.S.A. **158** 40 40N 94 41W
Bedford, Ohio, U.S.A. **156** 41 23N 81 32W
Bedford, Va., U.S.A. **156** 37 25N 79 30W
Bedford □ **29** 52 4N 0 28W
Bedford, C. **138** 15 14 S 145 21 E
Bedford Downs **136** 17 19 S 127 20 E
Bedford Level **29** 52 25N 0 5 E
Bedków **54** 51 36N 19 44 E
Bedlington **35** 55 8N 1 35W
Bednesti **152** 53 50N 123 10W
Bednja, R. **63** 46 12N 16 25 E
Bednodemyanovsk **81** 53 55N 43 15 E
Bedourie **138** 24 30 S 139 30 E
Bedretto **51** 46 31N 8 31 E
Bedum **47** 53 18N 6 36 E
Bedwas **31** 51 36N 3 10W
Bedworth **28** 52 28N 1 29W
Bedzin **54** 50 19N 19 7 E
Bee L. **36** 57 22N 7 21W
Beebyn **137** 27 0 S 117 48 E
Beech Grove **156** 39 40N 86 2W
Beechey Point **147** 70 27N 149 18W
Beechworth **141** 36 22 S 146 43 E
Beechy **153** 50 53N 107 24W
Beeford **33** 53 58N 0 18W
Beek, Gelderland, Neth. **46** 51 55N 6 11 E
Beek, Limburg, Neth. **47** 50 57N 5 48 E
Beek, Noord Brabant, Neth. **47** 51 32N 5 38 E
Beekbergen **46** 52 10N 5 58 E
Beelitz **48** 52 14N 12 58 E
Beemem **47** 51 9N 3 21 E
Beenleigh **139** 27 43 S 153 10 E
Beer **30** 50 41N 3 5W
Be'er Sheva' **90** 31 15N 34 48 E
Be'er Sheva', N. **90** 31 12N 34 40 E
Be'er Toviyyao **90** 31 44N 34 42 E
Be'eri **90** 31 25N 34 30 E
Be'erotayim **90** 32 19N 34 59 E
Beersheba = Be'er Sheva' **90** 31 15N 34 48 E
Beerta **46** 53 11N 7 6 E
Beerze, R. **46** 51 39N 5 20 E
Beesd **46** 51 53N 5 11 E
Beesel **47** 51 16N 6 2 E
Beeskow **48** 52 9N 14 14 E
Beeston **33** 52 55N 1 11W
Beetaloo **138** 17 15 S 133 50 E
Beetsterzwaag **46** 53 4N 6 5 E
Beetzendorf **48** 52 42N 11 6 E
Beeville **159** 28 27N 97 44W
Befale **124** 0 25N 20 45 E
Befandriana **125** 21 55 S 44 0 E
Befotaka, Diégo-Suarez, Madag. **129** 14 30 S 48 0 E
Befotaka, Fianarantsoa, Madag. **129** 23 49 S 47 0 E
Beg, L. **38** 54 48N 6 28W
Bega **141** 36 41 S 149 51 E
Bega, Canalul **66** 45 37N 20 46 E
Begelly **31** 51 45N 4 44W
* Begemdir & Simen □ **123** 13 55N 37 30 E
Begna **71** 60 41N 9 42 E
Begonte **56** 43 10N 7 40W
Begu-Sarai **95** 25 24N 86 9 E
Beguildy **31** 52 25N 3 11W
Béhagle = Lai **117** 9 25N 16 30 E
Behara **125** 24 55 S 46 20 E
Behbehan **92** 30 30N 50 15 E
Behror **94** 27 51N 76 20 E
Behshahr **93** 36 45N 53 35 E
Beida (Al Bayda) **117** 32 30N 21 40 E
Beighton **33** 53 21N 1 21W
Beilen **46** 52 52N 6 27 E
Beilngries **49** 49 1N 11 27 E
Beilpajah **140** 32 54 S 143 52 E
Beilul **123** 13 2N 42 20 E
Beinn a' Ghlo, Mt. **37** 56 51N 3 42W
Beinn Mhor, Mt. **36** 57 59N 6 39W
Beira **127** 19 50 S 34 52 E
Beira-Alta **55** 40 35N 7 35W
Beira-Baixa **55** 40 2N 7 30W
Beira-Litoral **55** 40 5N 8 30W
Beirut = Bayrūt **92** 33 53N 35 31 E
Beit Bridge **127** 14 58 S 30 15 E
Beit Hanum **90** 31 32N 34 32 E
Beit Lahiya **90** 31 32N 34 30 E
Beit 'Ur et Tahta **90** 31 54N 35 5 E
Beit Yosef **90** 32 34N 35 33 E
Beitbridge **127** 22 12 S 30 0 E
Beith **34** 55 45N 4 38W
Beituniya **90** 31 54N 35 10 E
Beiuş **70** 46 40N 22 21 E
Beja **57** 38 2N 7 53W
Béja **119** 36 43N 9 12 E
Beja □ **57** 37 55N 7 55W
Béjaïa **119** 36 42N 5 2 E
Béjar **56** 40 23N 5 46W
Bejestan **93** 34 30N 58 5 E
Bekabad **85** 40 13N 69 14 E
Bekasi **103** 6 20 S 107 0 E
Békés **53** 46 47N 21 9 E
Békés □ **53** 46 45N 21 0 E
Békéscsaba **53** 46 40N 21 10 E
Bekily **129** 24 13 S 45 19 E
Bekkevoort **47** 50 57N 4 58 E
Bekkjarvik **71** 60 1N 5 13 E

*Renamed Gonder

Bekoji **Berghem**

Bekoji 123 7 40N 38 20E
Bekok 101 2 20N 103 7E
Bekopaka 129 19 9S 44 45E
Bekwai 121 6 30N 1 34W
Bel Air 162 39 32N 76 21W
Bela, India 95 25 50N 82 0E
Bela, Pak. 94 26 12N 66 20E
Bela Crkva 66 44 55N 21 27E
Bela Palanka 66 43 13N 22 17E
Bela Vista, Brazil 173 22 12S 56 20W
Bela Vista, Mozam. 129 26 10S 32 44E
Bélâbre 44 46 34N 1 8E
Belaia, Mt. 123 11 25N 36 8E
Belalcázar 57 38 35N 5 10W
Belanovica 66 44 15N 20 23E
Belavenona 129 24 50S 47 4E
Belawan 102 3 33N 98 32E
Belaya Glina 83 46 5N 40 48E
Belaya Kalitva 83 48 13N 40 50E
Belaya Kholunitsa 84 58 41N 50 13E
Belaya, R. 84 55 54N 53 33E
Belaya Tserkov 80 49 45N 30 10E
Belbroughton 28 52 23N 2 5W
Belceşti 70 47 19N 27 7E
Belchatów 54 51 21N 19 22E
Belcher, C. 12 75 0N 160 0W
Belcher Is. 150 56 15N 78 45W
Belchite 58 41 18N 0 43W
Belclare 38 53 29N 8 55W
Belcoo 38 54 18N 7 52W
Belderg 38 54 18N 9 33W
Beldringe 73 55 28N 10 21E
Belebey 84 54 7N 54 7E
Belém de São Francisco 170 8 46S 38 58W
Belém (Pará) 170 1 20S 48 30W
Belén, Argent. 172 27 40S 67 5W
Belén, Colomb. 174 1 26N 75 56W
Belén, Parag. 172 23 30S 57 6W
Belen 161 34 40N 106 50W
Belene 67 43 39N 25 10E
Bélesta 44 42 55N 1 56E
Belet Uen 91 4 30N 45 5E
Belev 81 53 50N 36 5E
Belfast, N.Z. 143 43 27S 172 39E
Belfast, S. Afr. 129 25 42S 30 2E
Belfast, U.K. 38 54 35N 5 56W
Belfast, U.S.A. 151 44 30N 69 0W
Belfast □ 38 54 35N 5 56W
Belfast, L. 38 54 40N 5 50W
Belfeld 47 51 18N 6 6E
Belfeoram 151 47 32N 55 30W
Belfield 158 46 54N 103 11W
Belford 35 55 36N 1 50W
Belfort 43 47 38N 6 50E
Belfort □ 43 47 38N 6 52E
Belfry 160 45 10N 109 2W
Belgaum 97 15 55N 74 35E
Belgioioso 62 45 9N 9 21E
Belgium ■ 47 51 30N 5 0E
Belgooly 138 51 44N 8 30W
Belgorod 82 50 35N 36 35E
Belgorod Dnestrovskiy 82 46 11N 30 23E
Belgrade 160 45 50N 111 10W
Belgrade = Beograd 66 44 50N 20 37E
Belgrove 143 41 27S 172 59E
Belhaven 157 35 34N 76 35W
Beli 121 7 52N 10 58E
Beli Drim, R. 66 42 25N 20 34E
Beli Manastir 66 45 45N 18 36E
Beli Timok, R. 66 43 39N 22 14E
Belice, R. 64 37 44N 12 58E
Belinga 124 1 10N 13 2E
Belingwe 127 20 29S 29 57E
Belingwe, N., mt. 127 20 37S 29 55E
Belinsky (Chembar) 81 53 0N 43 25E
Belinţ 66 45 48N 21 54E
Belinyu 102 1 35S 105 50E
Beliton, Is. 102 3 10S 107 50E
Belitung, I. 102 3 10S 107 50E
Beliu 70 46 30N 22 0E
Belize ■ 165 17 0N 88 30W
Belize City 165 17 25N 88 0W
Beljanica 66 44 08N 21 43E
Bell 151 53 50N 53 10E
Bell Bay 138 41 6S 146 53E
Bell I. 151 50 46N 55 35W
Bell Irving, R. 152 56 12N 129 5W
Bell Peninsula 149 63 50N 82 0W
Bell, R. 150 49 48N 77 38W
Bell Rock = Inchcape Rock 35 56 26N 2 24W
Bell Ville 172 32 40S 62 40W
Bella Bella 152 52 10N 128 10W
Bella Coola 152 52 25N 126 40W
Bella Unión 172 30 15S 57 40W
Bella Vista, Corrientes, Argent. 172 28 33S 59 0W
Bella Vista, Tucuman, Argent. 172 27 10S 65 25W
Bella Yella 120 7 24N 10 9W
Bellacorick 38 54 8N 9 35W
Bellaghy 38 54 50N 6 31W
Bellágio 62 45 59N 9 15E
Bellaire 156 40 1N 80 46W
Bellananagh 38 53 55N 7 25W
Bellarena 38 55 7N 6 57W
Bellarwi 141 34 6S 147 13E
Bellary 97 15 10N 76 56E
Bellata 139 29 53S 149 46E
Bellavary 38 53 54N 9 9W
Belle Fourche 158 44 43N 103 52W
Belle Fourche, R. 158 44 25N 105 0W
Belle Glade 157 26 43N 80 38W
Belle Ile 42 47 20N 3 10W
Belle Isle 151 51 57N 55 25W
Belle-Isle-en-Terre 42 48 33N 3 23W
Belle Isle, Str. of 151 51 30N 56 30W
Belle, La 157 26 45N 81 22W
Belle Plaine, Iowa, U.S.A. 158 41 51N 92 18W
Belle Plaine, Minn., U.S.A. 158 44 35N 93 48W
Belledonne 45 45 11N 6 0E
Belledune 151 47 55N 65 50W
Belleek 38 54 30N 8 6W
Bellefontaine 156 40 20N 83 45W
Bellefonte 156 40 56N 77 45W
Bellegarde, Ain, France 45 46 4N 5 49E
Bellegarde, Creuse, France 43 45 59N 2 19E
Bellegarde, Loiret, France 43 48 0N 2 26E
Belleoram 151 47 31N 55 25W
Belleville, Can. 150 44 10N 77 23W
Belleville, Rhône, France 45 46 7N 4 45E
Belleville, Vendée, France 42 46 48N 1 28W
Belleville, Ill., U.S.A. 158 38 30N 90 0W
Belleville, Kans., U.S.A. 158 39 51N 97 38W
Belleville, N.Y., U.S.A. 162 43 46N 76 10W
Bellevue, Can. 152 49 35N 114 22W
Bellevue, U.S.A. 160 43 25N 144 23W
Belley 45 45 46N 5 41E
Bellin (Payne Bay) 149 60 0N 70 0W
Bellingen 141 30 25S 152 50E
Bellingham, U.K. 35 55 09N 2 16W
Bellingham, U.S.A. 160 48 45N 122 27W
Bellingshausen Sea 13 66 0S 80 0W
Bellinzona 51 46 11N 9 1E
Bello 174 6 20N 75 33W
Bellona Reefs 133 21 26S 159 0E
Bellows Falls 162 43 10N 72 30W
Bellpat 94 29 0N 68 5E
Bellpuig 58 41 37N 1 1E
Belluno 63 46 8N 12 6E
Bellville 159 29 58N 96 18W
Belmar 162 40 10N 74 2W
Bélmez 57 38 17N 5 17W
Belmont, Austral. 141 33 4S 151 42E
Belmont, U.S.A. 162 43 27N 71 29W
Belmonte, Brazil 171 16 0S 39 0W
Belmonte, Port. 56 40 21N 7 20W
Belmonte, Spain 58 39 34N 2 43W
Belmopan 165 17 18N 88 30W
Belmore 140 33 34S 141 13E
Belmullet 38 54 13N 9 58W
Belo Horizonte 171 19 55S 43 56W
Belo Jardim 170 8 20S 36 26W
Belo-sur-Mer 129 20 42S 44 33E
Belo-sur-Tsiribihana 129 19 40S 43 30E
Belogorsk, R.S.F.S.R., U.S.S.R. 77 51 0N 128 20E
Belogorsk, Ukraine, U.S.S.R. 82 45 3N 34 35E
Belogradchik 66 43 37N 22 40E
Belogradets 67 43 22N 27 18E
Beloha 129 25 10S 45 3E
Beloit, Kans., U.S.A. 158 39 32N 98 9W
Beloit, Wis., U.S.A. 158 42 35N 89 0W
Belokholunitskiy 81 58 55N 50 43E
Belomorsk 78 64 35N 34 30E
Belonia 98 23 15N 91 30E
Belopolye 80 51 14N 34 20E
Beloretsk 84 53 58N 58 24E
Belovo 76 54 30N 86 0E
Beloyarskiy 84 56 45N 61 24E
Beloye More 78 66 0N 38 0E
Beloye, Oz. 78 60 10N 37 35E
Beloye Ozero 83 45 15N 46 50E
Belozersk 81 60 0N 37 30E
Belpasso 65 37 37N 15 0E
Belper 33 53 2N 1 29W
Belsay 35 55 6N 1 53W
Belsele 47 51 9N 4 6E
Belsito 64 37 50N 13 47E
Beltana 140 30 48S 138 25E
Belterra 175 2 45S 55 0W
Beltinci 63 46 37N 16 20E
Belton, Humberside, U.K. 33 53 33N 0 49W
Belton, Norfolk, U.K. 29 52 35N 1 39E
Belton, S.C., U.S.A. 157 34 31N 82 39W
Belton, Tex., U.S.A. 159 31 4N 97 30W
Beltra, Mayo, Ireland 38 53 57N 9 24W
Beltra, Sligo, Ireland 38 54 12N 8 36W
Beltra L. 38 53 56N 9 28W
Beltsy 82 47 48N 28 0E
Belturbet 38 54 6N 7 28W
Belukha 76 49 50N 86 50E
Beluran 102 5 48N 117 35E
Beluša 53 49 5N 18 27E
Belušió 66 43 50N 21 10E
Belvedere Maríttimo 65 39 37N 15 52E
Belvès 44 44 46N 1 0E
Belvidere, Ill., U.S.A. 158 42 15N 88 55W
Belvidere, N.J., U.S.A. 162 40 48N 75 5W
Belville 38 54 40N 9 22W
Belvis de la Jara 57 39 45N 4 57W
Belyando, R. 138 21 38S 146 50E
Belyj Jar 76 58 26N 84 39E
Belyy 80 55 48N 32 51E
Belyy, Ostrov 76 73 30N 71 0E
Belyye Vody 85 42 25N 69 50E
Belz 80 50 23N 24 1E
Belzig 48 52 8N 12 36E
Belzoni 159 33 12N 90 30W
Bemaraha, Plat. du 129 18 40S 44 45E
Bemarivo, Majunga, Madag. 129 17 6S 44 31E
Bemarivo, Tuléar, Madag. 129 21 45S 44 45E
Bemarivo, R. 129 21 45S 44 45E
Bemavo 129 21 33S 45 25E
Bembéréke 121 10 11N 2 43E
Bembesi 127 20 0S 28 58E
Bembesi, R. 127 20 0S 28 58E
Bembézar, R. 57 38 0N 5 20W
Bembridge 28 50 41N 1 4W
Bemidji 158 47 30N 94 50W
Bemmel 46 51 54N 5 54E
Ben Alder 37 55 59N 4 30W
Ben Avon 37 57 6N 3 28W
Ben Bheigeir, Mt. 34 55 43N 6 6W
Ben Bullen 141 33 12S 150 2E
Ben Chonzine 35 56 27N 4 0W
Ben Cruachan, Mt. 34 56 26N 5 8W
Ben Dearg 37 57 47N 4 58W
Ben Dearg, mt. 37 56 54N 3 49W
Ben Dhorain 37 58 7N 3 50W
Ben Dorian 34 56 30N 4 42W
Ben Gardane 119 33 11N 11 11E
Ben Hee 37 58 16N 4 43W
Ben Hope, mt. 37 58 24N 4 36W
Ben Klibreck 37 58 14N 4 25W
Ben Lawers, mt. 37 56 33N 4 13W
Ben Lomond, mt. 139 30 1S 151 43E
Ben Lomond mt. 138 41 38S 147 42E
Ben Lomond, mt. 34 56 12N 4 39W
Ben Loyal 37 58 25N 4 25W
Ben Luc 101 10 39N 106 29E
Ben Lui, mt. 34 56 24N 4 50W
Ben Macdhui 37 57 4N 3 40W
Ben Mhor 36 57 16N 7 21W
Ben More, Mull, U.K. 34 56 26N 6 2W
Ben More, Perth, U.K. 34 56 23N 4 31W
Ben More Assynt 37 58 7N 4 51W
Ben Nevis, mt., N.Z. 143 45 15S 169 0E
Ben Nevis, mt., U.K. 36 56 48N 5 0W
Ben Ohau Ra. 143 44 1S 170 4E
Ben Quang 100 17 3N 106 55E
Ben Stack 36 58 20N 4 58W
Ben Tharsiunn 37 57 47N 4 20W
Ben Venue 34 56 13N 4 28W
Ben Vorlich 34 56 22N 4 15W
Ben Wyvis, mt. 37 57 40N 4 35W
Bena 121 11 20N 5 50E
Bena Dibele 124 4 4S 22 50E
Benagalbón 57 36 45N 4 15W
Benagerie 140 31 25S 140 22E
Benahmed 118 33 4N 7 9W
Benalla 141 36 30S 146 0E
Benambra, Mt. 141 36 31S 147 34E
Benamejí 57 37 16N 4 33W
Benanee 140 34 31S 142 52E
Benares = Varanasi 95 25 22N 83 8E
Benavente, Port. 57 38 59N 8 49W
Benavente, Spain 56 42 2N 5 43W
Benavides, Spain 56 42 30N 5 54W
Benavides, U.S.A. 159 27 35N 98 28W
Benbane Hd. 38 55 15N 6 30W
Benbaun, Mt. 38 53 30N 9 50W
Benbecula, I. 36 57 26N 7 21W
Benbonyathe, Mt. 140 30 25S 139 11E
Benburb 38 54 25N 6 42W
Bencubbin 137 30 48S 117 52E
Bend 160 44 2N 121 15W
Bendel □ 121 6 0N 6 0E
Bender Beila 91 9 30N 50 48E
Bender Cassim 91 11 12N 49 18E
Bendering 137 32 23S 118 18E
Bendery 82 46 50N 29 50E
Bendigo 140 36 40S 144 15E
Beneden Knijpe 46 52 58N 5 59E
Benedick 162 38 31N 76 41W
Beneditinos 170 5 27S 42 22W
Benedito Leite 170 7 13S 44 34W
Benei Beraq 129 32 5N 34 50E
Bénéna 120 13 9N 4 17W
Beneraird, Mt. 34 55 4N 4 57W
Benešóv 52 49 46N 14 41E
Bénestroff 43 48 54N 6 45E
Benet 44 46 22N 0 35W
Benevento 65 41 7N 14 45E
Benfeld 43 48 22N 7 34E
Beng Lovea 100 12 36N 105 34E
Benga 127 16 11S 33 40E
Bengal, Bay of 99 15 0N 90 0E
Bengawan Solo 103 7 5S 112 25E
Benghazi = Banghāzī 119 32 11N 20 3E
Bengkalis 102 1 30N 102 10E
Bengkulu 102 3 50S 102 12E
Bengkulu □ 102 3 48S 102 16E
Bengough 153 49 25N 105 10W
Benguela 125 12 37S 13 25E
Benguerir 118 32 16N 7 56W
Benguérua, Î. 129 21 58S 35 28E
Benha 122 30 26N 31 8E
Beni 126 0 30N 29 27E
Beni Abbès 118 30 5N 2 5W
Beni Haoua 118 36 30N 1 30E
Benî Mazâr 122 28 32N 30 44E
Beni Mellal 118 32 21N 6 21W
Beni Ounif 118 32 0N 1 10W
Beni, R. 174 10 30S 66 0W
Beni Saf 118 35 17N 1 15W
Benî Suêf 122 29 5N 31 6E
Beniah L. 152 63 23N 112 17W
Benicarló 58 40 23N 0 23E
Benicia 163 38 3N 122 9W
Benidorm 59 38 33N 0 9W
Benidorm, Islote de 59 38 31N 0 9W
Benin ■ 121 10 0N 2 0E
Benin, Bight of 121 5 0N 3 0E
Benin City 121 6 20N 5 31E
Benington 33 52 59N 0 5E
Benisa 59 38 43N 0 03E
Benjamin Aceval 172 24 58S 57 34W
Benjamin Constant 174 4 40S 70 15W
Benjamin Hill 164 30 10N 111 10W
Benkelman 158 40 7N 101 32W
Benlidi 138 24 35S 144 50E
Benmore Pk. 143 44 25S 170 8E
Bennane Hd. 34 55 9N 5 2W
Bennebroek 46 52 19N 4 36E
Bennekom 46 52 0N 5 41E
Bennett 147 59 56N 134 53W
Bennettsbridge 39 52 36N 7 12W
Bennettsville 157 34 38N 79 39W
Bennington 162 42 52N 73 12W
Benoa 102 8 50S 115 20E
Bénodet 42 47 53N 4 7W
Benoni 129 26 11S 28 18E
Benoud 118 32 20N 0 16E
Benque Viejo 165 17 5N 89 8W
Bensheim 49 49 40N 8 38E
Benson, U.K. 28 51 37N 1 6W
Benson, U.S.A. 161 31 59N 110 19W
Bent 93 26 20N 59 25E
Benteng 103 6 10S 120 30E
Bentinck I. 138 17 3S 139 35E
Bentiu 123 9 10N 29 55E
Bentley, Hants., U.K. 29 51 12N 0 52W
Bentley, S. Yorks, U.K. 33 53 33N 1 9W
Bento Gonçalves 173 29 10S 51 31W
Benton, Ark., U.S.A. 159 34 30N 92 35W
Benton, Calif., U.S.A. 163 37 48N 118 32W
Benton, Ill., U.S.A. 158 38 0N 88 55W
Benton, Pa., U.S.A. 162 41 12N 76 23W
Benton Harbor 156 42 10N 86 28W
Bentong 101 3 31N 101 55E
Bentu Liben 123 8 32N 38 21E
Benue □ 121 7 30N 7 30E
Benue Plateau □ 121 8 0N 8 30E
Benue, R. 121 7 50N 6 30E
Benwee Hd. 38 54 20N 9 50W
Beo 103 4 25N 126 50E
Beograd 66 44 50N 20 37E
Beowawe 160 40 45N 117 0W
Beppu 110 33 15N 131 30E
Beppu-Wan 110 33 18N 131 34E
Ber Dagan 90 32 1N 34 49E
Bera 98 24 5N 89 37E
Beragh 38 54 34N 7 10W
Berakit 123 14 38N 39 29E
Berati 68 40 43N 19 59E
Berber 122 18 0N 34 0E
Berbéra 117 10 33N 16 35E
Berbera 91 10 30N 45 2E
Berbérati 124 4 15N 15 40E
Berberia, Cabo 59 38 39N 1 24E
Berbice, R. 174 5 20N 58 10W
Berceto 62 44 30N 10 0E
Berchtesgaden 49 47 37N 13 1E
Berck-sur-Mer 43 50 25N 1 36E
Berdichev 82 49 57N 28 30E
Berdsk 76 54 47N 83 2E
Berdyansk 82 46 45N 36 50E
Berdyaush 84 55 9N 59 9E
Bere Alston 30 50 29N 4 11W
Bere Regis 28 50 45N 2 13W
Berea 156 37 35N 84 18W
Berebere 103 2 25N 128 45E
Bereda 91 11 45N 51 0E
Bereina 135 8 39S 146 30E
Berekum 120 7 29N 2 34W
Berenice 122 24 2N 35 25E
Berens I. 153 52 18N 97 18W
Berens, R. 153 51 21N 97 0W
Berens River 153 52 25N 97 0W
Berestechko 80 50 22N 25 5E
Bereşti 70 46 6N 27 50E
Berettyo, R. 53 47 32N 21 47E
BerettyóIjfalu 53 47 13N 21 33E
Beretŭu, R. 70 47 30N 22 7E
Berevo 129 19 44S 44 58E
Berevo-sur-Ranobe 129 17 14S 44 17E
Bereza 80 52 31N 24 51E
Berezhany 80 49 26N 24 58E
Berezina, R. 80 54 10N 28 10E
Berezna 80 51 35N 30 46E
Berezniki 84 59 24N 56 46E
Berezovka 82 47 25N 30 55E
Berezovo 76 64 0N 65 0E
Berg 71 59 10N 11 18E
Berga, Spain 58 42 6N 1 48E
Berga, Kalmar, Sweden 73 57 14N 16 3E
Berga, Kronoberg, Sweden 73 56 55N 14 0E
Bergama 92 39 8N 27 15E
Bergambacht 46 51 56N 4 48E
Bérgamo 62 45 42N 9 40E
Bergantiños 56 43 20N 8 40W
Bergedorf 48 53 28N 10 12E
Bergeijk 47 51 19N 5 21E
Bergen, Ger. 48 54 24N 13 26E
Bergen, Norway 71 60 23N 5 20E
Bergen-Binnen 46 52 40N 4 43E
Bergen-op-Zoom 47 51 30N 4 18E
Bergerac 44 44 51N 0 30E
Bergheim 48 50 57N 6 38E
Berghem 46 51 46N 5 33E

Bergisch-Gladbach Billesdon

Bergisch-Gladbach	48	50 59N	7 9E
Bergkvara	73	56 23N	16 5E
Bergschenhoek	46	51 59N	4 30E
Bergsjö	72	61 59N	17 3E
Berguent	118	34 1N	2 0W
Bergues	43	50 58N	2 24E
Bergum	46	53 13N	5 59E
Bergvik	72	61 16N	16 50E
Berhala, Selat	102	1 0S	104 15E
Berhampore	95	24 2N	88 27E
Berhampur	96	19 15N	84 54E
Berheci, R.	70	46 7N	27 19E
Berhungra	139	34 46S	147 52E
Bering Sea	130	58 0N	167 0E
Bering Str.	147	66 0N	170 0W
Beringarra	137	26 0S	116 55E
Beringen, Belg.	47	51 3N	5 14E
Beringen, Switz.	51	47 38N	8 34E
Beringovskiy	77	63 3N	179 19E
Berislav	82	46 50N	33 30E
Berisso	172	34 40S	58 0W
Berja	59	36 50N	2 56W
Berkane	118	34 52N	2 20W
Berkel, R.	46	52 8N	6 12E
Berkeley	163	37 52N	122 20W
Berkeley Springs	156	39 38N	78 12W
Berkhamsted	29	51 45N	0 33W
Berkhout	46	52 38N	4 59E
Berkner I.	13	79 30S	50 0W
Berkovitsa	67	43 16N	23 8E
Berkshire	162	42 19N	76 11W
Berkshire □	28	51 30N	1 20W
Berkshire Downs	28	51 30N	1 30W
Berkyk	71	62 50N	9 59E
Berlaar	47	51 7N	4 39E
Berland, R.	152	54 0N	116 50W
Berlanga	57	38 17N	5 50W
Berlave	47	51 2N	4 0E
Berleburg	48	51 3N	8 22E
Berlenga, I.	75	39 25N	9 30W
Berlick	47	51 22N	6 9E
Berlin, Ger.	48	52 32N	13 24E
Berlin, Md., U.S.A.	162	38 19N	75 12W
Berlin, N.H., U.S.A.	156	44 29N	71 10W
Berlin, N.Y., U.S.A.	162	42 42N	73 23W
Berlin, E. □	48	52 30N	13 30E
Berlin, W. □	48	52 30N	13 20E
Bermeja, Sierra	57	36 45N	5 11W
Bermejo, R., Formosa, Argent.	172	26 30S	58 50W
Bermejo, R., San Juan, Argent.	172	30 0S	68 0W
Bermeo	58	43 25N	2 47W
Bermillo de Sayago	56	41 22N	6 8W
Bermuda, I.	10	32 45N	65 0W
Bern (Berne)	50	46 57N	7 28E
Bern (Berne) □	50	46 45N	7 40E
Bernalda	65	40 24N	16 44E
Bernalillo	161	35 17N	106 37W
Bernam, R.	101	3 45N	101 5E
Bernardo de Irigoyen	173	26 15S	53 40W
Bernardsville	162	40 43N	74 34W
Bernasconi	172	37 55S	63 44W
Bernau	49	47 53N	12 20E
Bernay	42	49 5N	0 35E
Berndorf	52	47 59N	16 1E
Berne = Bern	50	46 57N	7 28E
Berner Alpen	50	46 27N	7 35E
Berneray, I.	36	56 47N	7 38W
Bernese Oberland = Oberland	50	46 27N	7 35E
Bernier I.	137	24 50S	113 12E
Bernina Pass	51	46 22N	9 54E
Bernina, Piz	51	46 20N	9 54E
Bernissart	47	50 28N	3 39E
Beroroha	125	21 40S	45 10E
Béroubouey	121	10 34N	2 46E
Beroun	52	49 57N	14 5E
Berounka, R.	52	50 0N	13 47E
Berovo	66	41 42N	22 51E
Berrahal	119	36 54N	7 33E
Berre	45	43 28N	5 11E
Berre, Étang de	45	43 27N	5 5E
Berrechid	118	33 18N	7 36W
Berri	140	34 14S	140 35E
Berriedale	37	58 12N	3 30W
Berriew	31	52 36N	3 12W
Berrigan	141	35 38S	145 49E
Berrouaghia	118	36 10N	2 53E
Berrwillock	140	35 36S	142 59E
Berry, Austral.	141	34 46S	150 43E
Berry, France	43	47 0N	2 0E
Berry Hd.	30	50 24N	3 29W
Berry Is.	166	25 40N	77 50W
Berryville	159	36 23N	93 35W
Bersenbrück	48	52 33N	7 56E
Berst Ness	37	59 16N	3 0W
Berthaund	158	40 21N	105 5W
Berthier Is.	136	14 29S	124 59E
Berthold	158	48 19N	101 45W
Bertincourt	43	50 5N	2 58E
Bertoua	124	4 30N	13 45E
Bertraghboy, B.	38	53 22N	9 54W
Bertrand	158	40 35N	99 38W
Bertrange	47	49 37N	6 3E
Bertrix	47	49 51N	5 15E
Beruas	101	4 30N	100 47E
Berufjörður	74	64 48N	14 29W
Berur Hayil	90	31 34N	34 38E
Berwick	162	41 4N	76 17W
Berwick (□)	26	55 46N	2 30W
Berwick-upon-Tweed	35	55 47N	2 0W
Berwyn Mts.	31	52 54N	3 26W
Beryl N., oilfield	19	59 37N	1 30E
Beryl, oilfield	19	59 28N	1 30E
Beryl W., oilfield	19	59 32N	1 20E
Berzasca	66	44 39N	21 58E
Berzence	53	46 12N	17 11E
Besal	95	35 4N	73 56E
Besalampy	129	16 43S	44 29E
Besançon	43	47 9N	6 0E
Besar	102	2 40S	116 0E
Beserah	101	3 50N	103 21E
Beshenkovichi	80	55 2N	29 29E
Beška	66	45 8N	20 6E
Beskids, Mts.	53	49 35N	18 40E
Beslan	83	43 22N	44 28E
Besna Kobila	66	42 31N	22 10E
Besnard L.	153	55 25N	106 0W
Beşparmak Daği	69	37 32N	27 30E
Bessarabiya	70	46 20N	29 0E
Bessarabka	82	46 21N	28 51E
Bessbrook	38	54 12N	6 25W
Bessèges	45	44 18N	4 8E
Bessemer	158	46 27N	90 0W
Bessin	42	49 21N	1 0W
Bessines-sur-Gartempe	42	46 6N	1 22E
Best	47	51 31N	5 23E
Bet Alfa	90	32 31N	35 25E
Bet Guvrin	90	31 37N	34 54E
Bet Hashitta	90	32 31N	35 27E
Bet Ha'tmeq	90	32 58N	35 8E
Bet Qeshet	90	32 41N	35 21E
Bet She'an	90	32 30N	35 30E
Bet Tadjine, Djebel	118	29 0N	3 30W
Bet Yosef	90	32 34N	35 33E
Betafo	129	19 50S	46 51E
Betanzos	56	43 15N	8 12W
Bétaré-Oya	124	5 40N	14 5E
Betekom	47	50 59N	4 47E
Bétera	58	39 35N	0 28W
Bethal	129	26 27S	29 28E
Bethanien	125	26 31S	17 8E
Bethany, S. Afr.	128	29 34S	25 59E
Bethany, U.S.A.	158	40 18N	94 0W
Bethany = Eizariya	90	31 47N	35 15E
Bethel, U.S.A.	147	60 50N	161 50W
Bethel, Conn., U.S.A.	162	41 22N	73 25W
Bethesda, U.K.	31	53 11N	4 3W
Bethesda, U.S.A.	162	38 59N	77 6W
Bethlehem, S. Afr.	129	28 14S	28 18E
Bethlehem, U.S.A.	162	40 39N	75 24W
Bethlehem = Bayt Lahm	90	31 43N	35 12E
Bethulie	128	30 30S	25 59E
Béthune	43	50 30N	2 38E
Béthune, R.	42	49 56N	1 5E
Bethungra	141	34 45S	147 51E
Betijoque	174	9 23N	70 44W
Betim	171	19 58S	44 13W
Betioky	129	23 48S	44 20E
Beton Bazoches	43	48 42N	3 15E
Betong	101	5 45N	101 5E
Betoota	138	25 40S	140 42E
Betroka	129	23 16S	46 0E
Betsiamites	151	48 56N	68 40W
Betsiamites, R.	151	48 56N	68 40W
Betsiboka, R.	129	17 0S	47 0E
Betsjoeanaland	128	26 30S	22 30E
Bettembourg	47	49 31N	6 6E
Betterton	162	39 52N	76 4W
Betteshanger	29	51 14N	1 20E
Bettiah	95	26 48N	84 33E
Bettles	147	66 54N	150 50W
Bèttola	62	44 46N	9 35E
Bettws Bledrws	31	52 9N	4 2W
Bettyhill	37	58 31N	4 12W
Betul	96	21 48N	77 59E
Betung	102	2 0S	103 10E
Betws-y-Coed	31	53 4N	3 49W
Beuca	70	44 14N	24 56E
Beuil	45	44 6N	7 0E
Beulah, Can.	153	50 16N	101 02W
Beulah, U.S.A.	158	47 18N	101 47W
Beuvronne, La	46	48 59N	2 41E
Bevensen	48	53 5N	10 34E
Beveren	47	51 12N	4 16E
Beverley, Austral.	137	32 9S	116 56E
Beverley, U.K.	33	53 52N	0 26W
Beverlo	47	51 7N	5 13E
Beverly, Can.	152	53 36N	113 21W
Beverly, Mass., U.S.A.	162	42 32N	70 50W
Beverly, Wash., U.S.A.	160	46 55N	119 59W
Beverly Hills	163	34 4N	118 29W
Beverwijk	46	52 28N	4 38E
Bewdley	28	52 23N	2 19W
Bex	50	46 15N	7 0E
Bexhill	29	50 51N	0 29E
Bexley	29	51 26N	0 10E
Beyin	120	5 1N	2 41W
Beykoz	67	41 8N	29 7E
Beyla	120	8 30N	8 38W
Beynat	44	45 8N	1 44E
Beyneu	76	45 10N	55 3E
Beypazaı	92	40 10N	31 48E
Beyşehir Gölü	92	37 40N	31 45E
Bezdan	66	45 28N	18 57E
Bezerros	171	8 14S	35 45W
Bezet	90	33 4N	35 8E
Bezhitsa	80	53 19N	34 17E
Béziers	44	43 20N	3 12E
Bezwada = Vijayawada	97	16 31N	80 39E
Bhachau	93	23 20N	70 16E
Bhadarwah	95	32 58N	75 46E
Bhadra, R.	97	13 0N	76 0E
Bhadrakh	96	21 10N	86 30E
Bhadravati	97	13 49N	76 15E
Bhagalpur	95	25 10N	87 0E
Bhairab	98	22 51N	89 34E
Bhairab Bazar	98	24 4N	90 58E
Bhaisa	96	19 10N	77 58E
Bhakkar	94	31 40N	71 5E
Bhakra Dam	95	31 30N	76 45E
Bhamo	98	24 15N	97 15E
Bhamragarh	96	19 30N	80 40E
Bhandara	96	21 5N	79 42E
Bhanrer Ra.	94	23 40N	79 45E
Bharat = India	93	24 0N	78 0E
Bharatpur	94	27 15N	77 30E
Bharuch	96	21 47N	73 0E
Bhatghar L.	96	18 10N	73 48E
Bhatiapara Ghat	98	23 13N	89 42E
Bhatkal	97	13 58N	74 35E
Bhatpara	95	22 50N	88 25E
Bhattiprolu	97	16 7N	80 45E
Bhaun	94	32 55N	72 40E
Bhaunagar = Bhavnagar	94	21 45N	72 10E
Bhavani	97	11 27N	77 43E
Bhavani, R.	97	11 30N	77 15E
Bhavnagar	94	21 45N	72 10E
Bhawanipatna	96	19 55N	83 30E
Bhera	94	32 29N	72 57E
Bhilsa = Vidisha	94	23 28N	77 53E
Bhilwara	94	25 25N	74 38E
Bhima, R.	96	17 20N	76 30E
Bhimber	95	32 59N	74 3E
Bhimvaram	96	16 30N	81 30E
Bhind	95	26 30N	78 46E
Bhir	96	19 4N	75 58E
Bhiwandi	96	19 15N	73 0E
Bhiwani	94	28 50N	76 9E
Bhola	98	22 45N	90 35E
Bhongir	96	17 30N	78 56E
Bhopal	94	23 20N	77 53E
Bhor	96	18 12N	73 53E
Bhubaneswar	96	20 15N	85 50E
Bhuj	94	23 15N	69 49E
Bhumibol Dam	100	17 15N	98 58E
Bhusaval	96	21 15N	69 49E
Bhutan ■	98	27 25N	89 50E
Biafra, B. of = Bonny, Bight of	121	3 30N	9 20E
Biak	103	1 0S	136 0E
Biała	54	50 24N	17 40E
Biała Piska	54	53 37N	22 5E
Biała Podlaska	54	52 4N	23 6E
Biała Podlaska □	54	52 0N	23 0E
Biała, R.	54	49 46N	20 53E
Białogard	54	54 2N	15 58E
Biały Bór	54	53 53N	16 51E
Białystok	54	53 10N	23 10E
Białystok □	54	53 9N	23 10E
Biancavilla	65	37 39N	14 50E
Biano Plateau = Manika Plateau	127	9 55S	26 24E
Biaro	103	2 5N	125 26E
Biarritz	44	43 29N	1 33W
Biasca	51	46 22N	8 58E
Biba	122	28 55N	31 0E
Bibaī	112	43 19N	141 52E
Bibby I.	153	61 55N	93 0W
Biberach	49	48 5N	9 49E
Biberist	50	47 11N	7 34E
Bibey, R.	56	42 24N	7 13W
Bibiani	120	6 30N	2 8W
Bibile	97	7 10N	81 25E
Biboohra	138	16 56S	145 25E
Bibungwa	126	2 40S	28 15E
Bibury	28	51 46N	1 50W
Bic	151	48 20N	68 41W
Bicaj	68	42 0N	20 25E
Bicaz	70	46 53N	26 5E
Biccari	65	41 23N	15 12E
Bicester	28	51 53N	1 9W
Biche, La, R.	152	59 57N	123 50W
Bichena	123	10 28N	38 10E
Bickerton I.	138	13 45S	136 10E
Bicknell, Ind., U.S.A.	156	38 50N	87 20W
Bicknell, Utah, U.S.A.	161	38 16N	111 35W
Bicsad	70	47 56N	23 28E
Bicton	28	52 43N	2 47W
Bida	121	9 3N	5 58E
Bidar	96	17 55N	77 35E
Biddeford	151	43 30N	70 28W
Biddenden	29	51 7N	0 40E
Biddu	90	31 50N	35 8E
Biddulph	32	53 8N	2 11W
Biddwara	123	5 11N	38 34E
Biddya	90	32 7N	35 4E
Bideford	30	51 1N	4 13W
Bideford Bay	30	51 5N	4 20W
Bidford on Avon	28	52 9N	1 53W
Bidor	101	4 6N	101 15E
Bidura	140	34 10S	143 21E
Bié	125	12 22S	16 55E
Bié Plateau	125	12 0S	16 0E
Bieber	160	41 4N	121 6W
Biel (Bienne)	50	47 8N	7 14E
Bielawa	54	50 43N	16 37E
Bielé Karpaty	53	49 5N	18 0E
Bielefeld	48	52 2N	8 31E
Bielersee	50	47 6N	7 5E
Biella	62	45 33N	8 3E
Bielsk Podlaski	54	52 47N	23 12E
Bielsko-Biała	54	49 50N	19 8E
Bielsko-Biała □	54	49 45N	19 15E
Bien Hoa	101	10 57N	106 49E
Bienfait	153	49 10N	102 50W
Bienne = Biel	50	47 8N	7 14E
Bienvenida	57	38 18N	6 12W
Bienville, L.	150	55 5N	72 40W
Biescas	58	42 37N	0 20W
Biesiesfontein	128	30 57S	17 58E
Bietigheim	49	48 57N	9 8E
Bievre	47	49 57N	5 1E
Biferno, R.	65	41 40N	14 38E
Big B.	151	55 43N	60 35W
Big Bear City	163	34 16N	116 51W
Big Bear L.	163	34 15N	116 56W
Big Beaver	153	49 10N	105 10W
Big Beaver House	150	52 59N	89 50W
Big Bell	137	27 21S	117 40E
Big Belt Mts.	160	46 50N	111 30W
Big Bend	129	26 50S	32 2E
Big Bend Nat. Park	159	29 15N	103 15W
Big Black, R.	159	32 35N	90 30W
Big Blue, R.	158	40 20N	96 40W
Big Cr.	152	51 42N	122 41W
Big Creek	163	37 11N	119 14W
Big Cypress Swamp	157	26 12N	81 10W
Big Delta	147	64 15N	145 0W
Big Falls	158	48 11N	93 48W
Big Horn	160	46 11N	107 25W
Big Horn Mts. = Bighorn Mts.	160	44 30N	107 30W
Big Horn R.	160	45 30N	108 10W
Big Lake	159	31 12N	101 25W
Big Moose	162	43 49N	74 58W
Big Muddy, R.	158	48 25N	104 45W
Big Pine	163	37 12N	118 17W
Big Piney	160	42 32N	110 3W
Big Quill L.	153	51 55N	105 22W
Big, R.	151	54 50N	58 55W
Big Rapids	156	43 42N	85 27W
Big River	153	53 50N	107 0W
Big Sable Pt.	156	44 5N	86 30W
Big Salmon	147	61 50N	136 0W
Big Sand L.	153	57 45N	99 45W
Big Sandy	160	48 12N	110 9W
Big Sandy Cr.	158	38 52N	103 11W
Big Sioux, R.	158	44 20N	96 53W
Big Smoky Valley	163	38 30N	117 15W
Big Snowy Mt.	160	46 50N	109 15W
Big Spring	159	32 10N	101 25W
Big Springs	158	41 4N	102 3W
Big Stone City	158	45 20N	96 30W
Big Stone Gap	157	36 52N	82 45W
Big Stone L.	158	44 25N	96 35W
Big Sur	163	36 15N	121 48W
Big Trout L.	150	53 40N	90 0W
Biganos	44	44 39N	0 59W
Bigbury	30	50 17N	3 52W
Bigbury B.	30	50 18N	3 58W
Bigerymunal, Mt.	137	27 25S	120 40E
Bigfork	160	48 3N	114 2W
Biggar	153	52 4N	108 0W
Bigge I.	136	14 35S	125 10E
Biggenden	139	25 31S	152 4E
Biggleswade	29	52 6N	0 16W
Bighorn Mts.	160	44 30N	107 30W
Bignona	120	12 52N	16 23W
Bigorre	44	43 5N	0 2E
Bigstone L.	153	53 42N	95 44W
Bigtimber	160	45 53N	110 0W
Bigwa	126	7 10S	39 10E
Bihaó	63	44 49N	15 57E
Bihar	95	25 5N	85 40E
Bihar □	95	25 0N	86 0E
Biharamulo	126	2 25S	31 25E
Biharamulo □	126	2 30S	31 20E
Biharkeresztes	53	47 8N	21 44E
Bihé Plateau	125	12 0S	16 0E
Bihor □	70	47 0N	22 10E
Bihor, Munţii	70	46 29N	22 47E
Bijagós, Arquipélago dos	120	11 15N	16 10W
Bijaipur	94	26 2N	77 36E
Bijapur, Mad. P., India	96	18 50N	80 50E
Bijapur, Mysore, India	96	16 50N	75 55E
Bijar	92	35 52N	47 35E
Bijeljina	66	44 46N	19 17E
Bijni	98	26 30N	90 40E
Bijnor	94	29 27N	78 11E
Bikaner	94	28 2N	73 18E
Bikapur	95	26 30N	82 7E
Bikin	77	46 50N	134 20E
Bikini, atoll	130	12 0N	167 30E
Bikoro	124	0 48S	18 15E
Bikoué	121	5 55S	11 50E
Bilād Banī Bū 'Ali	93	22 0N	59 20E
Bilara	94	26 14N	73 53E
Bilaspara	98	26 13N	90 14E
Bilaspur, India	99	22 2N	82 15E
Bilaspur, Mad. P., India	95	22 2N	82 15E
Bilaspur, Punjab, India	94	31 19N	76 50E
Bilauk Taungdan	100	13 0N	99 0E
Bilbao	58	43 16N	2 56W
Bilbor	70	47 18N	25 30E
Bildudalur	74	65 41N	23 36W
Bilecik	92	40 5N	30 5E
Bileóa	66	42 53N	18 27E
Bilibino	77	68 3N	166 20E
Bilibiza	127	12 30S	40 20E
Bilin	98	17 14N	97 15E
Bilir	77	65 40N	131 20E
Bilishti	68	40 37N	20 59E
Bill	158	43 18N	105 18W
Billa	121	8 55N	12 15E
Billabalong	137	27 25S	115 49E
Billericay	29	51 38N	0 25E
Billesdon	29	52 38N	0 56W

Billiluna Blenheim

Billiluna 136 19 37S 127 41E
Billimari 71 33 41S 148 37E
Billingham 33 54 36N 1 18W
Billinghay 33 53 5N 0 17W
Billings 160 45 43N 108 29W
Billingsfors 72 58 59N 12 15E
Billingshurst 29 51 2N 0 28W
Billom 44 45 43N 3 20E
Bilma 117 18 50N 13 30E
Bilo Gora 66 45 53N 17 15E
Biloela 138 24 24S 150 31E
Biloxi 159 30 30N 89 0W
Bilpa Morea Claypan 138 25 0S 140 0E
Bilston 28 52 34N 2 5W
Bilthoven 46 52 8N 5 12E
Biltine 117 14 40N 20 50E
Bilugyun 98 16 24N 97 32E
Bilyana 138 18 5S 145 50E
Bilyarsk 84 54 58N 50 22E
Bilzen 47 50 52N 5 31E
Bima 103 8 22S 118 49E
Bimban 122 24 24N 32 54E
Bimberi Peak, mt. 141 35 44S 148 51E
Bimbila 121 8 54N 0 5E
Bimbo 124 4 15N 18 33E
Bina-Etawah 94 24 13N 78 14E
Binačka Morava, R. 66 42 30N 19 35E
Binalbagan 103 10 12N 122 50E
Binalong 141 34 40S 148 39E
Binatang 102 2 10N 111 40E
Binbrook 33 53 26N 0 9W
Binche 47 50 26N 4 10E
Binda 139 27 52S 147 21E
Bindi Bindi 137 30 37S 116 22E
Bindle 139 27 40S 148 45E
Bindura 127 17 18S 31 18E
Bingara, N.S.W., Austral. 139 29 52S 150 36E
Bingara, Queens., Austral. 139 28 10S 144 37E
Bingen 49 49 57N 7 53E
Bingerville 120 5 18N 3 49W
Bingham, U.K. 33 52 57N 0 55W
Bingham, U.S.A. 151 45 5N 69 50W
Bingham Canyon 160 40 31N 112 10W
Binghamton 38 42 9N 75 54W
Bingley 32 53 51N 1 50W
Bingöl 92 39 20N 41 0E
Binh Dinh = An Nhon 100 13 55N 109 7E
Binh Khe 100 13 57N 108 51E
Binh Son 100 15 20N 108 40E
Binjai 102 3 50N 98 30E
Binnaway 141 31 28S 149 24E
Binongko 103 5 55S 123 55E
Binscarth 153 50 37N 101 17W
Bint 93 26 22N 59 25E
Bint Jaibail 90 33 8N 35 25E
Bintan 102 1 0N 104 0E
Bintulu 102 3 10N 113 0E
Binyamina 90 32 32N 34 56E
Binza 123 5 25N 28 40E
Binzert = Bizerte 119 37 15N 9 50E
Bío-Bío □ 172 37 35S 72 0W
Bio Culma 123 7 20N 42 15E
Biograd 63 43 56N 15 29E
Biokovo 66 43 23N 17 0E
Biougra 118 30 15N 9 14W
Biq'at Bet Netofa 90 32 49N 35 22E
Bir 93 19 0N 75 54E
Bîr Abû Hashim 122 23 42N 34 6E
Bîr Abû M'nqar 122 26 33N 27 33E
Bir Adal Deib 122 22 35N 36 10E
Bir al Malfa 119 31 58N 15 18E
Bir 'Asal 122 25 55N 34 20E
Bir Autrun 117 18 15N 26 40E
Bir Dhu'fân 119 31 59N 14 32E
Bîr Diqnash 122 31 3N 25 23E
Bir el Abbes 118 26 7N 6 9W
Bir-el-Ater 119 34 46N 8 3E
Bîr el Basur 122 29 51N 25 49E
Bîr el Gellaz 122 30 50N 26 40E
Bîr el Shaqqa 122 30 54N 25 1E
Bir Fuad 122 30 35N 26 28E
Bir Haimur 122 22 45N 33 40E
Bîr Kanayis 122 24 59N 33 15E
Bîr Kerawein 122 27 10N 28 25E
Bir Lemouissat 118 25 0N 10 32W
Bîr Maql 122 23 7N 33 40E
Bîr Misaha 122 22 13N 27 59E
Bir Mogreïn, (Fort Trinquet) 116 25 10N 11 25W
Bîr Murr 122 23 28N 30 10E
Bir Nabala 90 31 52N 35 12E
Bîr Nakheila 122 24 1N 30 50E
Bîr Qâtrani 122 30 55N 26 10E
Bîr Ranga 122 24 25N 35 15E
Bir Ras 123 12 0N 44 0E
Bîr Sahara 122 22 54N 28 40E
Bîr Seiyâla 122 25 10N 34 50E
Bir Semguine 118 30 1N 5 39W
Bîr Shalatein 122 23 5N 35 25E
Bîr Shebb 122 22 25N 29 40E
Bîr Shût 122 23 50N 35 15E
Bîr Terfawi 122 22 57N 28 55E
Bîr Umm Qubûr 122 24 35N 34 2E
Bîr Ungât 122 22 8N 33 48E
Bîr Za'farâna 122 29 10N 32 40E
Bîr Zāmus 119 24 16N 15 6E
Bîr Zeidûn 122 25 45N 34 40E
Bir Zeit 90 31 59N 35 11E
Bira 103 2 3S 132 2E
Bîra 70 47 2N 27 3E
Biramfero 120 11 40N 9 10W
Birao 117 10 20N 22 40E
Birawa 126 2 20S 28 48E
Bîrca 70 43 59N 23 36E
Birch 29 51 50N 0 54E
Birch Hills 153 52 59N 105 25W
Birch I. 153 52 26N 99 54W
Birch L., N.W.T., Can. 152 62 4N 116 33W
Birch L., Ont., Can. 150 51 23N 92 18W
Birch L., U.S.A. 150 47 48N 91 43W
Birch Mts. 152 57 30N 113 10W
Birch River 153 52 24N 101 6W
Birchington 29 51 22N 1 18E
Birchip 140 35 56S 142 55E
Birchiş 70 45 58N 22 0E
Birchwood 143 45 55S 167 53E
Bird 153 56 30N 94 13W
Bird City 158 39 48N 101 33W
Bird I., Austral. 133 22 10S 155 28E
Bird I., S. Afr. 128 32 3S 18 17E
Birdaard 46 53 18N 5 53E
Birdhip 139 35 52S 142 50E
Birdlip 28 51 50N 2 7W
Birdsville 138 25 51S 139 20E
Birdum 136 15 39S 133 13E
Birecik 92 37 0N 38 0E
Bireuen 102 5 14N 96 39E
Birhan 123 10 45N 37 55E
Birifo 120 13 30N 14 0E
Birigui 173 21 18S 50 16W
Birimgan 138 22 41S 147 25E
Birjand 93 32 57N 59 10E
Birk 122 18 8N 41 30E
Birka 122 22 11N 40 38E
Birkdale 32 53 38N 3 2W
Birkenhead, N.Z. 142 36 49S 174 46E
Birkenhead, U.K. 32 53 24N 3 1W
Birket Qârûn 122 29 30N 30 40E
Birkfeld 52 47 21N 15 45E
Birkhadem 118 36 43N 3 3E
Bîrlad 70 46 15N 27 38E
Birmingham, U.K. 28 52 30N 1 55W
Birmingham, U.S.A. 157 33 31N 86 50W
Birmitrapur 96 22 30N 84 10E
Birni Ngaouré 121 13 5N 2 51E
Birni Nkonni 121 13 55N 5 15E
Birnin Gwari 121 11 0N 6 45E
Birnin Kebbi 121 12 32N 4 12E
Birnin Kudu 121 11 30N 9 29E
Birobidzhan 77 48 50N 132 50E
Birqin 90 32 23N 35 15E
Birr 39 53 7N 7 55W
Birrie, R. 139 29 43S 146 37E
Birs, R. 50 47 24N 7 32E
Birsilpur 94 28 11N 72 58E
Birsk 84 55 25N 55 30E
Birtin 70 46 59N 22 31E
Birtle 153 50 30N 101 5W
Birtley, Northumberland, U.K. 35 55 5N 2 12W
Birtley, Tyne & Wear, U.K. 35 54 53N 1 34W
Birur 93 13 30N 75 55E
Biryuchiy, Ostrov 82 46 10N 35 0E
Birzai 80 56 11N 24 45E
Bîrzava 70 46 7N 21 59E
Bisa 103 1 10S 127 40E
Bisáccia 65 41 0N 15 20E
Bisacquino 64 37 42N 13 13E
Bisai 111 35 16N 136 44E
Bisalpur 95 28 14N 79 48E
Bisbal, La 58 41 58N 3 2E
Bisbee 161 31 30N 110 0W
Biscay, B. of 14 45 0N 2 0W
Biscayne B. 157 25 40N 80 12W
Biscéglie 65 41 14N 16 30E
Bischofshofen 52 47 26N 13 14E
Bischofswerda 48 51 8N 14 11E
Bischofszell 51 47 29N 9 15E
Bischwiller 43 48 41N 7 50E
Biscoe I. 13 66 0S 67 0W
Biscostasing 150 47 18N 82 9W
Biscucuy 174 9 22N 69 59W
Biševo, I. 63 42 57N 16 3E
Bisha 123 15 30N 37 31E
Bisha, Wadi 122 20 30N 43 0E
Bishop, Calif., U.S.A. 163 37 20N 118 26W
Bishop, Tex., U.S.A. 159 27 35N 97 49W
Bishop Auckland 33 54 40N 1 40W
Bishop's Castle 28 52 29N 3 0W
Bishop's Cleeve 28 51 56N 2 3W
Bishop's Falls 151 49 2N 55 30W
Bishop's Frome 28 52 8N 2 29W
Bishops Lydeard 28 51 4N 3 12W
Bishop's Nympton 30 50 58N 3 44W
Bishop's Stortford 29 51 52N 0 11E
Bishop's Waltham 28 50 57N 1 13W
Bishopsteignton 30 50 32N 3 32W
Bishopstoke 28 50 58N 1 19W
Bisignano 65 30 30N 16 17E
Bisina, L. 126 1 38N 33 56E
Biskra 119 34 50N 5 44E
Biskupiec 54 53 53N 20 58E
Bislig 103 8 15N 126 27E
Bismarck 158 46 49N 100 49W
Bismarck Arch. 135 2 30S 150 0E
Bismarck Ra. 135 5 35S 145 0E
Bismarck Sea 135 4 10S 146 50E
Bismark 48 52 39N 11 31E
Biso 126 1 44N 31 26E
Bison 158 45 34N 102 28W
Bispfors 74 63 1N 16 39E
Bispgarden 72 63 2N 16 40E
Bissagos = Bijagós 120 11 15N 16 10W
Bissau 120 11 45N 15 45W
Bissett 153 51 2N 95 41W
Bissikrima 120 10 50N 10 58W
Bistcho L. 152 59 45N 118 50W
Bistreţu 70 43 54N 23 23E
Bistrica = Ilirska Bistrica 63 45 34N 14 14E
Bistriţa 70 47 9N 24 35E
Bistriţa Năsăud □ 70 47 15N 24 30E
Bistriţa, R. 70 47 10N 24 30E
Bistriţei, Munţii 70 47 15N 25 40E
Biswan 95 27 29N 81 2E
Bisztynek 54 54 8N 20 53E
Bitam 124 2 5N 11 25E
Bitche 43 48 58N 7 25E
Bitkine 124 11 59N 18 13E
Bitlis 92 38 20N 42 3E
Bitola (Bitolj) 66 41 5N 21 21E
Bitonto 65 41 7N 16 40E
Bitter Creek 160 41 39N 108 36W
Bitter L., Gt. 122 30 15N 32 40E
Bitter L. = Buheirat-Murrat el Kubra 122 30 15N 32 40E
Bitterfeld 48 51 36N 12 20E
Bitterfontein 128 31 0S 18 32E
Bitteroot, R. 160 46 30N 114 20W
Bitterroot Range 160 46 0N 114 20W
Bitterwater 163 36 23N 121 0W
Bitti 64 40 29N 9 20E
Bitton 28 51 25N 2 27W
Bittou 121 11 17N 0 18W
Bitumount 152 57 26N 112 40W
Biu 121 10 40N 12 3E
Bivolari 70 47 31N 27 27E
Bivolu 70 47 16N 25 58E
Biwa-Ko 111 35 15N 135 45E
Biwabik 158 47 33N 92 19W
Biylikol, Ozero 85 43 5N 70 45E
Biysk 76 52 40N 85 0E
Bizana 129 30 50S 29 52E
Bizen 110 34 43N 134 8E
Bizerte (Binzert) 119 37 15N 9 50E
Bjandovan, Mys 83 39 45N 49 28E
Bjargtangar 74 65 30N 24 30W
Bjärka-Säby 73 58 16N 15 44E
Bjarnanes 74 64 20N 15 6W
Bjelasica 66 42 50N 19 40E
Bjelo Polje 66 43 1N 19 45E
Bjelovar 66 45 56N 16 49E
Bjerringbro 73 56 23N 9 39E
Björbo 72 60 27N 14 44E
Björkhamre 72 61 24N 16 25E
Björkhult 73 57 50N 15 40E
Björneborg 72 59 14N 14 16E
Bjuv 73 56 5N 12 55E
Bla Bheinn 36 57 14N 6 7W
Blaby 28 52 34N 1 10W
Blace 66 43 18N 21 17E
Blachownia 54 50 49N 18 56E
Black Combe, mt. 32 54 16N 3 20W
Black Diamond 152 50 45N 114 14W
Black Esk R. 35 55 14N 3 13W
Black Forest = Schwarzwald 49 48 0N 8 0E
Black Hd., Ireland 39 53 9N 9 18W
Black Hd., Antrim, U.K. 38 54 56N 5 42W
Black Hd., Cornwall, U.K. 30 50 1N 5 6W
Black Hills 158 44 0N 103 50W
Black I. 153 51 12N 96 30W
Black Island Sd. 162 41 10N 71 45W
Black Isle, Reg. 37 57 35N 4 15W
Black L., Can. 153 59 12N 105 15W
Black L., U.S.A. 156 45 28N 84 15W
Black Mesa, Mt. 159 36 57N 102 55W
Black Mt. = Mynydd Du 31 51 45N 3 45W
Black Mountain 141 30 18S 151 39E
Black Mts. 31 51 52N 3 5W
Black Pt. 137 34 30S 119 25E
Black R. 38 53 54N 7 42W
Black, R., Ark., U.S.A. 159 36 15N 90 45W
Black, R., N.Y., U.S.A. 162 43 59N 76 40W
Black, R., Wis., U.S.A. 158 44 18N 90 52W
Black, R., Vietnam = Da, R. 100 21 15N 105 20E
Black Range, Mts. 161 33 30N 107 55W
Black River 166 18 0N 77 50W
Black Rock 140 32 50S 138 44E
Black Sea 21 43 30N 35 0E
Black Volta, R. 120 9 0N 2 40W
Black Warrior, R. 157 33 0N 87 45W
Blackall 138 24 25S 145 45E
Blackball 143 42 22S 171 26E
Blackbull 138 17 55S 141 45E
Blackburn 32 53 44N 2 30W
Blackburn, Mt. 147 61 5N 142 3W
Blackbutt 139 26 51S 152 6E
Blackdown Hills 28 50 57N 3 15W
Blackduck 158 47 43N 94 32W
Blackfoot 160 43 13N 112 12W
Blackfoot, R. 160 47 0N 113 35W
Blackford 35 56 15N 3 48W
Blackie 152 50 36N 113 37W
Blackmoor Gate 30 51 9N 3 55W
Blackmoor Vale 28 50 54N 2 28W
Blackpool 32 53 48N 3 3W
Blackridge 138 22 35S 147 35E
Blackrock 39 53 18N 6 11W
Blacks Harbour 151 45 3N 66 49W
Blacksburg 156 37 17N 80 23W
Blacksod B. 38 54 6N 10 0W
Blacksod Pt. 38 54 7N 10 5W
Blackstairs Mt. 39 52 33N 6 50W
Blackstone 156 37 6N 78 0W
Blackstone, R. 152 61 5N 122 55W
Blackstone Ra. 137 26 00S 129 00E
Blackville 151 46 44N 65 50W
Blackwater, Austral. 138 23 35S 148 53E
Blackwater, Can. 152 53 20N 123 0W
Blackwater, Ireland 39 52 26N 6 20W
Blackwater Cr. 139 25 56S 144 30E
Blackwater, R., Limerick, Ireland 39 51 55N 7 50W
Blackwater, R., Meath, Ireland 38 53 40N 6 40W
Blackwater, R., Essex, U.K. 29 51 44N 0 53E
Blackwater, R., Ulster, U.K. 38 54 31N 6 35W
Blackwater Res. 37 56 42N 4 45W
Blackwell 159 36 55N 97 20W
Blackwells Corner 163 35 37N 119 47W
Blackwood 35 55 40N 3 56W
Blackwood, C. 135 7 49S 144 31E
Bladel 47 51 22N 5 13E
Bladinge 73 56 52N 14 29E
Blädinge 73 56 52N 14 29E
Blaenau Ffestiniog 31 53 0N 3 57W
Blaenavon 31 51 46N 3 5W
Blagaj 66 43 16N 17 55E
Blagdon 28 51 19N 2 42W
Blagnac 44 43 38N 1 24E
Blagodarnoye 83 45 7N 43 37E
Blagoevgrad (Gorna Dzhumayo) 66 42 2N 23 5E
Blagoveshchensk, Amur, U.S.S.R. 77 50 20N 127 30E
Blagoveshchensk, Urals, U.S.S.R. 84 55 1N 55 59E
Blagoveshchenskoye 85 43 18N 74 12E
Blaina 31 51 46N 3 10W
Blaine 160 48 59N 122 43W
Blaine Lake 153 52 51N 106 52W
Blainville 43 48 33N 6 23E
Blair 158 41 38N 96 10W
Blair Athol 138 22 42S 147 31E
Blair Atholl 37 56 46N 3 50W
Blairgowrie 37 56 36N 3 20W
Blairmore 152 49 40N 114 25W
Blaj 70 46 10N 23 57E
Blake Pt. 158 48 12N 88 27W
Blakely 157 31 22N 85 0W
Blakeney, Glos., U.K. 28 51 45N 2 29W
Blakeney, Norfolk, U.K. 29 52 57N 1 1E
Blâmont 43 48 35N 6 50E
Blanc, C., Maurit. 116 20 50N 17 0W
Blanc, C., Tunisia 119 37 15N 9 56E
Blanc, Le 44 46 37N 1 3E
Blanc, Mont 45 45 48N 6 50E
Blanc Sablon 151 51 24N 57 8W
Blanca, Bahía 176 39 10S 61 30W
Blanca Peak 161 37 35N 105 29W
Blanchard 159 35 8N 97 40W
Blanche, C. 139 33 1S 134 9E
Blanche L., S. Austral., Austral. 139 29 15S 139 40E
Blanche L., W. Austral., Austral. 136 22 25S 123 17E
Blanco, S. Afr. 128 33 55S 22 23E
Blanco, U.S.A. 159 30 7N 98 30W
Blanco, C., C. Rica 166 9 34N 85 8W
Blanco, C., Peru 174 4 10S 81 10W
Blanco, C., Spain 59 39 21N 2 51E
Blanco, C., U.S.A. 160 42 50N 124 40W
Blanco, R. 172 31 54S 69 42W
Blanda 74 65 20N 19 40W
Blandford Forum 28 50 52N 2 10W
Blanding 161 37 35N 109 30W
Blanes 58 41 40N 2 48E
Blangy 43 49 14N 0 17E
Blanice, R. 52 49 10N 14 5E
Blankenberge 47 51 20N 3 9E
Blankenburg 48 51 46N 10 56E
Blanquefort 44 44 55N 0 38W
Blanquilla, La 174 11 51N 64 37W
Blanquillo 173 32 53S 55 37W
Blansko 53 49 22N 16 40E
Blantyre 127 15 45S 35 0E
Blaricum 46 52 16N 5 14E
Blarney 39 51 57N 8 35W
Błaski 54 51 38N 18 30E
Blatná 52 49 25N 13 52E
Blatnitsa 67 43 41N 28 32E
Blatten 50 46 16N 8 0E
Blåvands Huk 75 55 33N 8 4E
Blaydon 35 54 56N 1 47W
Blaye 44 45 8N 0 40W
Blaye-les-Mines 44 44 1N 2 8E
Blayney 141 33 32S 149 14E
Blaze, Pt. 136 12 56S 130 11E
Błazowa 54 49 53N 22 7E
Bleadon 28 51 18N 2 57W
Blean 29 51 18N 1 3E
Bleasdale Moors 32 53 57N 2 40W
Bleckede 48 53 18N 10 43E
Bled 63 46 27N 14 7E
Blednaya, Gora 76 65 50N 65 30E
Bléharis 47 50 31N 3 25E
Bleiburg 52 46 35N 14 49E
Blejeşti 70 44 19N 25 27E
Blekinge län □ 73 56 20N 15 20E
Blenheim 143 41 38S 174 5E

Bléone, R. **45** 44 5N 6 0E
Bletchingdon **28** 51 51N 1 16W
Bletchley **29** 51 59N 0 44W
Bleymard, Le **44** 44 30N 3 42E
Blidet Amor **119** 32 59N 5 58E
Blidö **72** 59 37N 18 53E
Blidsberg **73** 57 56N 13 30E
Bligh Sound **143** 44 47S 167 32E
Blind River **150** 46 10N 82 58W
Blinishti **68** 41 52N 19 58E
Blinnenhorn **51** 46 26N 8 19E
Blisworth **29** 52 11N 0 56W
Blitar **103** 8 5S 112 11E
Blitta **121** 8 23N 1 6E
Block I. **162** 41 11N 71 35W
Blockley **28** 52 1N 1 45W
Bloemendaal **46** 52 24N 4 39E
Bloemfontein **128** 29 6S 26 14E
Bloemhof **128** 27 38S 25 32E
Blofield **29** 52 38N 1 25E
Blois **42** 47 35N 1 20E
Blokziji **46** 52 43N 5 58E
Blomskog **72** 59 16N 12 2E
Blonduös **74** 65 40N 20 12W
Bloodsworth Is. **162** 38 9N 76 3W
Bloodvein, R. **153** 51 47N 96 43W
Bloody Foreland **38** 55 10N 8 18W
Bloomer **158** 45 8N 91 30W
Bloomfield, Iowa, U.S.A. **158** 40 44N 92 26W
Bloomfield, N. Mexico, U.S.A. **161** 36 46N 107 59W
Bloomfield, Nebr., U.S.A. **158** 42 38N 97 15W
Bloomfield R. **138** 15 56S 145 22E
Bloomingdale **162** 41 33N 74 26W
Bloomington, Ill., U.S.A. **158** 40 49N 89 0W
Bloomington, Ind., U.S.A. **156** 39 10N 86 30W
Bloomsburg **162** 41 0N 76 30W
Blora **103** 6 57S 111 25E
Blossburg **162** 41 40N 77 4W
Blouberg **129** 23 8S 29 0E
Blountstown **157** 30 28N 85 5W
Bloxham **28** 52 1N 1 22W
Bludenz **52** 47 10N 9 50E
Blue I. **156** 41 40N 87 40W
Blue Lake **160** 40 53N 124 0W
Blue Mesa Res. **161** 38 30N 107 15W
Blue Mountain Lake **162** 43 52N 74 30W
Blue Mountain Peak **167** 18 0N 76 40W
Blue Mts., Austral. **133** 33 40S 150 0E
Blue Mts., Jamaica **167** 18 0N 76 40W
Blue Mts., Ore., U.S.A. **160** 45 15N 119 0W
Blue Mts., Pa., U.S.A. **156** 40 30N 76 0W
Blue Mud B. **138** 13 30S 136 0E
Blue Nile = Nîl el Azraq **123** 12 30N 34 30E
Blue Nile □ = An Nîl el Azraq □ **123** 12 30N 34 30E
Blue Nile, R. = Nîl el Azraq **123** 10 30N 35 0E
Blue Ridge, Mts. **157** 36 30N 80 15W
Blue Stack Mts. **38** 54 46N 8 5W
Blueberry, R. **152** 56 45N 120 49W
Bluefield **156** 37 18N 81 14W
Bluefields **166** 12 0N 83 50W
Bluemull Sd. **36** 60 45N 1 0W
Blueskin B. **143** 45 44S 170 38E
Bluff, Austral. **138** 23 35S 149 4E
Bluff, N.Z. **143** 46 37S 168 20E
Bluff, U.S.A. **147** 64 50N 147 15W
Bluff Downs **138** 19 37S 145 30E
Bluff Harbour **143** 46 36S 168 21E
Bluff Knoll, Mt. **137** 34 24S 118 15E
Bluff Pt. **137** 27 50S 114 5E
Bluffton **156** 40 43N 85 9W
Blumenau **173** 27 0S 49 0W
Blumenthal **48** 53 5N 12 20E
Blümisalphorn **50** 46 30N 7 47E
Blundeston **29** 52 33N 1 42E
Blunt **158** 44 32N 100 0W
Bly **160** 42 23N 121 0W
Blyberg **72** 61 9N 14 11E
Blyth, Austral. **140** 33 49S 138 28E
Blyth, Northumberland, U.K. **35** 55 8N 1 32W
Blyth, Notts., U.K. **33** 53 22N 1 2W
Blyth Bridge **35** 55 41N 3 22W
Blyth, R. **35** 55 8N 1 30W
Blythburgh **29** 52 19N 1 36E
Blythe **161** 33 40N 114 33W
Blyton **33** 53 25N 0 42W
Bo, Norway **71** 59 25N 9 3E
Bo, S. Leone **120** 7 55N 11 50W
Bo Duc **101** 11 58N 106 50E
Bō-no-Misaki **110** 31 15N 130 13E
Boa I. **38** 54 30N 7 50W
Boa Nova **171** 14 22S 40 10W
Boa Viagem **170** 5 7S 39 44W
Boa Vista **174** 2 48N 60 30W
Boaco **166** 12 29N 85 35W
Boal **56** 43 25N 6 49W
Boat of Garten **37** 57 15N 3 45W
Boatman **139** 27 16S 146 55E
Bobadah **141** 32 19S 146 41E
Bobbili **96** 18 35N 83 30E
Bóbbio **62** 44 47N 9 22E
Bobcaygeon **150** 44 33N 78 33W
Böblingen **57** 48 41N 9 1E
Bobo-Dioulasso **120** 11 8N 4 13W
Boboc **67** 45 13N 26 59E

Bobolice **54** 53 58N 16 37E
Boboshevo **66** 42 9N 23 0E
Bobov Dol **66** 42 20N 23 0E
Bóbr, R. **54** 51 50N 15 15E
Bobrinets **82** 48 4N 32 5E
Bobrov **81** 51 5N 40 2E
Bobruysk **80** 53 10N 29 15E
Bobures **174** 9 15N 71 11W
Boca de Uracoa **174** 9 8N 62 20W
Bôca do Acre **174** 8 50S 67 27W
Bocage **41** 49 0N 1 0W
Bocaiúva **171** 17 7S 43 49W
Bocanda **120** 7 5N 4 31W
Bocaranga **117** 7 0N 15 35E
Bocas del Dragon **174** 11 0N 61 50W
Bocas del Toro **166** 9 15N 82 20W
Bocdam **36** 59 55N 1 16W
Boceguillas **58** 41 20N 3 39W
Bochnia **54** 49 58N 20 27E
Bocholt, Belg. **47** 51 10N 5 35E
Bocholt, Ger. **48** 51 50N 6 35E
Bochov **52** 50 9N 13 3E
Bochum **48** 51 28N 7 12E
Bockenem **48** 52 1N 10 8E
Bocoyna **164** 27 52N 107 35W
Bocq, R. **47** 50 20N 4 55E
Boçsa Montanŭ **66** 45 21N 21 47E
Boda **124** 4 19N 17 26E
Böda **73** 57 15N 17 3E
Boda **74** 57 15N 17 0E
Bodaybo **77** 57 50N 114 0E
Boddam **37** 57 28N 1 46W
Boddington **137** 32 50S 116 30E
Bodedern **31** 53 17N 4 29W
Bodegraven **46** 52 5N 4 46E
Boden **74** 65 50N 21 42E
Bodenham **28** 52 9N 2 41W
Bodensee **51** 47 35N 9 25E
Bodenteich **48** 52 49N 10 41E
Boderg, L. **38** 53 52N 8 0W
Bodhan **96** 18 40N 77 55E
Bodiam **29** 51 1N 0 33E
Bodinayakkanur **97** 10 2N 77 10E
Bodinga **121** 12 58N 5 10E
Bodinnick **30** 50 20N 4 37W
Bodio **51** 46 23N 8 55E
Bodmin **30** 50 28N 4 44W
Bodmin Moor **30** 50 33N 4 36W
Bodø **74** 67 17N 14 24E
Bodrog, R. **53** 48 15N 21 35E
Bodrum **92** 37 5N 27 30E
Bódva, R. **53** 48 19N 20 45E
Bodyke **39** 52 53N 8 38W
Boechout **47** 51 10N 4 30E
Boegoebergdam **128** 29 7S 22 9E
Boekelo **46** 52 12N 6 49E
Boelenslaan **46** 53 10N 6 10E
Boën **45** 45 44N 4 0E
Boende **124** 0 24S 21 12E
Boerne **159** 29 48N 98 41W
Boertange **46** 53 1N 7 12E
Boezinge **47** 50 54N 2 52E
Boffa **120** 10 16N 14 3W
Bofin L. **38** 53 51N 7 55W
Bofors **72** 59 19N 14 34E
Bogale **98** 21 16N 92 24E
Bogalusa **159** 30 50N 89 55W
Bogan Gate **141** 33 7S 147 49E
Bogan, R. **141** 32 45S 148 8E
Bogantungan **138** 23 41S 147 17E
Bogata **159** 33 26N 95 10W
Bogatió **66** 44 51N 19 30E
Bogdan, Mt. **67** 42 37N 24 20E
Bogdanovitch **84** 56 47N 62 1E
Bogenfels **125** 27 25S 15 25E
Bogense **73** 55 34N 10 5E
Boggabilla **139** 28 36S 150 24E
Boggabri **141** 30 45S 150 0E
Boggeragh Mts. **39** 52 2N 8 55W
Boghari = Ksar el Boukhari **118** 35 51N 2 52E
Bogia **135** 4 9S 145 0E
Bognor Regis **29** 50 47N 0 40W
Bogø **73** 54 55N 12 2E
Bogo **103** 11 3N 124 0E
Bogodukhov **80** 50 9N 35 33E
Bogong, Mt. **141** 36 47S 147 17E
Bogor **103** 6 36S 106 48E
Bogoro **121** 9 37N 9 29E
Bogoroditsk **81** 53 47N 38 8E
Bogorodsk **81** 56 4N 43 30E
Bogorodskoye **77** 52 22N 140 30E
Bogoso **120** 5 38N 2 3W
Bogotá **174** 4 34N 74 0W
Bogotol **76** 56 15N 89 50E
Bogra **98** 24 51N 89 22E
Boguchany **77** 58 40N 97 30E
Boguchar **83** 49 55N 40 32E
Bogué **120** 16 45N 14 10W
Boguslav **82** 49 47N 30 53E
Boguszów Lubawka **54** 50 43N 15 56E
Bohain **43** 49 59N 3 28E
Bohemia **52** 50 0N 14 0E
Bohemia Downs **136** 18 53S 126 14E
Bohemian Forest = Böhmerwald **49** 49 30N 12 40E
Bohena Cr. **139** 30 17S 149 42E
Boheraphuca **39** 53 1N 7 45W
Bohinjska Bistrica **63** 46 17N 14 1E
Böhmerwald **49** 49 30N 12 40E
Bohmte **48** 52 24N 8 20E
Bohola **38** 53 54N 9 4W
Boholl, I. **103** 9 50N 124 10E

Bohotleh **91** 8 20N 46 25E
Boi **121** 9 35N 9 27E
Boi, Pta. de **173** 23 55S 45 15W
Boiano **65** 41 28N 14 29E
Boiestown **151** 46 27N 66 26W
Boigu I. **138** 9 15S 143 30E
Boileau, C. **136** 17 40S 122 7E
Boipeba, I. de **171** 13 39S 38 55W
Bois, Les **50** 47 11N 6 50E
Bois, R. **171** 18 35S 50 2W
Boischot **47** 51 3N 4 47E
Boisdale L. **36** 57 9N 7 19W
Boise **160** 43 43N 116 9W
Boise City **159** 36 45N 102 30W
Boissevain **153** 49 15N 100 0W
Boite, R. **63** 46 24N 12 13E
Boitzenburg **48** 55 16N 13 36E
Boizenburg **48** 53 22N 10 42E
Bojador C. **116** 26 0N 14 30W
Bojanow **54** 51 43N 16 42E
Bøjden **73** 55 6N 10 7E
Bojnurd **93** 37 30N 57 20E
Bojonegoro **103** 7 11S 111 54E
Boju **121** 7 22N 7 55E
Boka **66** 45 22N 20 52E
Boka Kotorska **66** 42 23N 18 32E
Bokala **120** 8 31N 4 33W
Boké **120** 10 56N 14 17W
Bokhara, R. **139** 29 55S 146 42E
Bokkos **121** 9 17N 9 1E
Boknafjorden **71** 59 14N 5 40E
Bokombayevskoye **85** 47 7N 77 0E
Bokoro **117** 12 25N 17 14E
Bokote **124** 0 12S 21 8E
Bokpyin **101** 11 18N 98 42E
Boksitogorsk **80** 59 32N 33 56E
Bokungu **124** 0 35S 22 50E
Bol, Chad **124** 13 30N 15 0E
Bol, Yugo. **63** 43 18N 16 38E
Bolama **120** 11 30N 15 30W
Bolan Pass **93** 29 50N 67 20E
Bolangum **140** 36 42S 142 54E
Bolaños, R. **164** 22 0N 104 10W
Bolbec **42** 49 30N 0 30E
Bolchereche **76** 56 4N 74 45E
Boldeşti **70** 45 3N 26 2E
Bole **123** 6 36N 37 20E
Bolekhov **80** 49 0N 24 0E
Bolesławiec **54** 51 17N 15 37E
Bolgary **78** 55 3N 48 50E
Bolgatanga **121** 10 44N 0 53W
Bolgrad **82** 45 40N 28 32E
Boli **123** 6 2N 28 48E
Bolinao C. **103** 16 30N 119 55E
Bolívar, Argent. **172** 36 15S 60 53W
Bolívar, Antioquía, Colomb. **174** 5 50N 76 1W
Bolívar, Cauca, Colomb. **174** 2 0N 77 0W
Bolivar, Mo., U.S.A. **159** 37 38N 93 22W
Bolivar, Tenn., U.S.A. **159** 35 14N 89 0W
Bolívar □ **174** 9 0N 74 40W
Bolivia ■ **174** 17 6S 64 0W
Boljevac **66** 43 51N 21 58E
Bolkhov **81** 53 25N 36 0E
Bollène **45** 44 18N 4 45E
Bollington **32** 53 18N 2 8W
Bollnäs **72** 61 21N 16 24E
Bollon **139** 28 2S 147 29E
Bollstabruk **72** 63 1N 17 40E
Bollullos **57** 37 19N 6 32W
Bolmen **73** 56 55N 13 40E
Bolney **29** 50 59N 0 11W
Bolo Silase **123** 8 51N 39 27E
Bolobo **124** 2 6S 16 20E
Bologna **63** 44 30N 11 20E
Bologne **43** 48 10N 5 8E
Bologoye **80** 57 55N 34 0E
Bolomba **124** 0 35N 19 0E
Bolonchenticul **165** 20 0N 89 49W
Bolong **103** 6 6N 122 16E
Bolotovskoye **84** 58 31N 62 28E
Boloven, Cao Nguyen **100** 15 10N 106 30E
Bolpur **95** 23 40N 87 45E
Bolsena **63** 42 40N 11 58E
Bolsena, L. di **63** 42 35N 11 55E
Bolshaya Glushitsa **81** 52 24N 50 29E
Bolshaya Khobda, R. **84** 50 50N 54 53E
Bolshaya Kinel, R. **84** 53 14N 50 30E
Bolshaya Lepetrikha **82** 47 11N 33 57E
Bolshaya Martynovka **83** 47 12N 41 46E
Bolshaya Shatan, Gora **84** 53 37N 58 3E
Bolshevik, Ostrov **77** 78 30N 102 0E
Bolshezemelskaya Tundra **78** 67 0N 56 0E
Bolshoi Kavkas **83** 42 50N 44 0E
Bolshoi Tuters, O. **80** 59 44N 26 57E
Bolshoy Atlym **76** 62 25N 66 50E
Bolshoy Tokmak **82** 47 16N 35 42E
Bol'soj T'uters, O. **80** 59 44N 26 57E
Bolsover **33** 53 14N 1 18W
Bolsward **46** 53 3N 5 32E
Bolt Head **30** 50 13N 3 48W
Bolt Tail **30** 50 13N 3 55W
Boltaña **58** 42 28N 0 4E
Boltigen **50** 46 38N 7 24E
Bolton **32** 53 35N 2 26W
Bolton Abbey **32** 53 59N 1 53W
Bolton by Bowland **32** 53 56N 2 21W
Bolton Landing **162** 43 32N 73 35W
Bolton le Sands **32** 54 7N 2 49W
Bolton-on-Dearne **33** 53 31N 1 19W
Bolu **92** 40 45N 31 35E

Bolubolu **135** 9 21S 150 20E
Bolus Hd. **39** 51 48N 10 20W
Bolvadin **92** 38 45N 31 57E
Bolzano (Bozen) **63** 46 30N 11 20E
Bom Conselho **170** 9 42S 37 26W
Bom Despacho **171** 19 43S 45 15W
Bom Jardim **171** 7 47S 35 35W
Bom Jesus **170** 9 4S 44 22W
Bom Jesus da Gurguéia, Serra **170** 9 0S 43 0W
Bom Jesus da Lapa **171** 13 15S 43 25W
Boma **124** 5 50S 13 4E
Bomaderry **141** 34 52S 150 37E
Bōmba, Khalīj **117** 32 20N 23 15E
Bomba, La **164** 31 53N 115 2W
Bombala **141** 36 56S 149 15E
Bombarral **57** 39 15N 9 9W
Bombay **96** 18 55N 72 50E
Bomboma **124** 2 25N 18 55E
Bombombwa **126** 2 18N 19 3E
Bomi Hills **120** 7 1N 10 38E
Bomili **126** 1 45N 27 5E
Bomokandi, R. **126** 3 10N 28 15E
Bomongo **124** 1 27N 18 21E
Bomu, R. **124** 4 40N 23 30E
Bon C. **119** 37 1N 11 2E
Bon Sar Pa **100** 12 24N 107 35E
Bonaduz **15** 46 49N 9 25E
Bonaire, I. **167** 12 10N 68 15W
Bonang **141** 37 11S 148 41E
Bonanza **166** 13 54N 84 35W
Bonaparte Archipelago **136** 14 0S 124 30E
Boñar **56** 42 52N 5 19W
Bonarbridge **37** 57 53N 4 20W
Bonäset **72** 63 16N 18 45E
Bonaventure **151** 48 5N 65 32W
Bonavista **151** 48 40N 53 5W
Bonavista, C. **151** 48 42N 53 5W
Bonchester Bri. **35** 55 23N 2 36W
Bonchurch **28** 50 36N 1 11W
Bondeno **63** 44 53N 11 22E
Bondo **124** 3 55N 23 53E
Bondoukoro **120** 9 51N 4 25W
Bondoukou **120** 8 2N 2 47W
Bondowoso **120** 7 56S 113 49E
Bondyug **84** 60 29N 55 56E
Bone Rate, I. **103** 7 25S 121 5E
Bone Rate, Kepulauan **103** 6 30S 121 10E
Bone, Teluk **103** 4 10S 120 50E
Bonefro **65** 41 42N 14 55E
Bo'ness **35** 56 0N 3 38W
Bong Son = Hoai Nhon **100** 14 26N 109 1E
Bongandanga **124** 1 24N 21 3E
Bonge **123** 6 5N 37 16E
Bongor **117** 10 35N 15 20E
Bongouanou **120** 6 42N 4 15W
Bonham **159** 33 30N 96 10W
Bonherden **47** 51 1N 4 32E
Bonifacio **45** 41 24N 9 10E
Bonifacio, Bouches de **64** 41 12N 9 15E
Bonin Is. **130** 27 0N 142 0E
Bonito de Santa Fé **171** 7 19S 38 31W
Bonn **48** 50 43N 7 6E
Bonnat **44** 46 20N 1 53E
Bonne B. **151** 40 31N 58 0W
Bonne Espérance, I. **151** 51 24N 57 40W
Bonne Terre **159** 37 55N 90 38W
Bonners Ferry **160** 48 38N 116 21W
Bonnert **47** 49 43N 5 49E
Bonnétable **42** 48 11N 0 25E
Bonneuil Matours **42** 46 41N 0 34E
Bonneville **45** 46 5N 6 24E
Bonney, L. **140** 37 50S 140 20E
Bonnie Doon **141** 37 2S 145 53E
Bonnie Rock **137** 30 29S 118 22E
Bonny, France **43** 47 34N 2 50E
Bonny, Nigeria **121** 4 25N 7 13E
Bonny, Bight of **121** 3 30N 9 20E
Bonny, R. **121** 4 20N 7 14E
Bonnyrigg **35** 55 52N 3 8W
Bonnyville **153** 54 20N 110 45W
Bonoi **103** 1 45S 137 41E
Bonorva **64** 40 25N 8 47E
Bonsall **163** 33 16N 117 14W
Bontang **102** 0 10N 117 30E
Bonthain **103** 5 34S 119 56E
Bonthe **120** 7 30N 12 33W
Bonyeri **120** 5 1N 2 46W
Bonyhád **53** 46 18N 18 32E
Bonython Ra. **136** 23 40S 128 45E
Boogardie **137** 28 2S 117 45E
Bookabie P.O. **137** 31 50S 132 41E
Booker **159** 36 29N 100 30W
Boolaboolka, L. **140** 32 38S 143 10E
Boolarra **141** 38 20S 146 20E
Boolathanna **137** 21 40S 113 41E
Boolcoomata **140** 31 57S 140 33E
Booleroo Centre **140** 32 53S 138 21E
Booligal **141** 33 58S 144 53E
Booloo Downs **137** 23 52S 119 33E
Boom **47** 51 6N 4 20E
Boonah **139** 27 58S 152 41E
Boondall **108** 27 20S 153 4E
Boone, Iowa, U.S.A. **158** 42 5N 93 53W
Boone, N.C., U.S.A. **157** 36 14N 81 43W
Booneville, Ark., U.S.A. **159** 35 10N 93 54W
Booneville, Miss., U.S.A. **157** 34 39N 88 34W
Boongoondoo **138** 22 55S 145 55E
Boonville, Ind., U.S.A. **156** 38 3N 87 13W
Boonville, Mo., U.S.A. **158** 38 57N 92 45W
Boonville, N.Y., U.S.A. **162** 43 31N 75 20W
Booral **141** 32 30S 151 56E

Boorindal **Bramminge**

Boorindal **139** 30 22 S 146 11 E
Booroomugga **141** 31 17 S 146 27 E
Boorowa **141** 34 28 S 148 44 E
Boot **32** 54 24N 3 18W
Boothia, Gulf of **149** 71 0N 91 0W
Boothia Pen. **148** 71 0N 94 0W
Bootle, Cumb., U.K. **32** 54 17N 3 24W
Bootle, Merseysude, U.K. **32** 53 28N 3 1W
Booué **124** 0 5 S 11 55 E
Bopeechee **139** 29 36 S 137 22 E
Bophuthatswana □ **126** 26 0 S 26 0 E
Bopo **79** 7 33N 7 50 E
Boppard **49** 50 13N 7 36 E
Boquete **166** 8 46N 82 27W
Boquillas **164** 29 17N 102 53W
Bor **52** 49 41N 12 45 E
Bôr **123** 6 10N 31 40 E
Bor, Sweden **73** 57 9N 14 10 E
Bor, Yugo. **66** 44 8N 22 7 E
Borah, Mt. **160** 44 19N 113 46W
Borang **123** 4 50N 30 59 E
Borås **73** 57 43N 12 56 E
Borås **73** 57 43N 12 56 E
Borazjan **93** 29 22N 51 10 E
Borba, Brazil **174** 4 12 S 59 34W
Borba, Port. **57** 38 50N 7 26W
Borborema, Planalto da **170** 7 0 S 37 0W
Borçka **83** 41 25N 41 41 E
Borculo **46** 52 7N 6 31 E
Borda, C. **140** 35 45 S 136 34 E
Bordeaux **44** 44 50N 0 36W
Borden, Austral. **137** 34 3 S 118 12 E
Borden, Can. **151** 46 18N 63 47W
Borden I. **12** 78 30N 111 30W
Borders □ **35** 55 45N 2 50W
Bordertown **140** 36 19 S 140 45 E
Borðeyri **74** 65 12N 21 6W
Bordighera **62** 43 47N 7 40 E
Bordj bou Arridj **119** 36 4N 4 45 E
Bordj Djeneiene **119** 31 47N 10 3 E
Bordj el Hobra **119** 32 9N 4 51 E
Bordj Fly Ste. Marie **118** 27 19N 2 32W
Bordj-in-Eker **119** 24 9N 5 3 E
Bordj Ménaiel **119** 36 46N 3 43 E
Bordj Nili **118** 33 28N 3 2 E
Bordj Zelfana **119** 32 27N 4 15 E
Bordoba **85** 39 31N 73 16 E
Bordon Camp **29** 51 6N 0 52W
Borea Creek **141** 35 5 S 146 35 E
Borehamwood **29** 51 40N 0 15W
Borek Wlkp. **54** 51 54N 17 11 E
Boreland **35** 55 12N 3 16W
Boremore **141** 33 15 S 149 0 E
Borensberg **73** 58 34N 15 17 E
Borgarnes **74** 64 32N 21 55W
Borgefjellet **74** 65 20N 13 45 E
Borger, Neth. **46** 52 54N 6 33 E
Borger, U.S.A. **159** 35 40N 101 20W
Borgerhout **47** 51 12N 4 28 E
Borghamn **73** 58 23N 14 41 E
Borgholm **73** 56 52N 16 39 E
Bórgia **65** 38 50N 16 30 E
Borgie R. **37** 58 28N 4 20W
Borgo San Dalmazzo **62** 44 19N 7 29 E
Borgo San Lorenzo **63** 43 57N 11 21 E
Borgo Val di Taro **62** 44 29N 9 47 E
Borgomanero **62** 45 41N 8 28 E
Borgonovo Val Tidone **62** 45 1N 9 28 E
Borgorose **63** 42 12N 13 14 E
Borgosésia **62** 45 43N 8 17 E
Borgvattnet **72** 63 26N 15 48 E
Borhaug **71** 58 6N 6 33 E
Borikhane **100** 18 33N 103 43 E
Borisoglebsk **81** 51 27N 42 5 E
Borisoglebskiy **81** 56 28N 43 59 E
Borisov **80** 54 17N 28 28 E
Borisovka **85** 43 15N 68 10 E
Borisovo-Sudskoye **81** 59 58N 35 57 E
Borispol **80** 50 21N 30 59 E
Borja, Peru **174** 4 20 S 77 40W
Borja, Spain **58** 41 48N 1 34W
Borjas Blancas **58** 41 31N 0 52 E
Borkou **117** 18 15N 18 50 E
Borlänge **72** 60 29N 15 26 E
Borley, C. **13** 66 15 S 52 30 E
Bormida, R. **62** 44 35N 8 10 E
Bórmio **62** 46 28N 10 22 E
Born **47** 51 2N 5 49 E
Borna **48** 51 8N 12 31 E
Borndiep, Str. **46** 53 27N 5 35 E
Borne **46** 52 18N 6 46 E
Bornem **47** 51 6N 4 14 E
Borneo, I. **102** 1 0N 115 0 E
Bornholm, I. **73** 55 10N 15 0 E
Bornholmsgattet **73** 55 15N 14 20 E
Borno □ **121** 12 30N 12 30 E
Bornos **57** 36 48N 5 42W
Bornu Yassa **121** 12 14N 12 25 E
Borodino **80** 55 31N 35 40 E
Borogontsy **77** 62 42N 131 8 E
Boromo **120** 11 45N 2 58W
Boron **163** 35 0N 117 39W
Boronga Is. **98** 19 58N 93 6 E
Borongan **103** 11 37N 125 26 E
Bororen **138** 24 13 S 151 33 E
Borotangba Mts. **123** 6 30N 25 0 E
Boroughbridge **33** 54 6N 1 23W
Borovan **67** 43 27N 23 45 E
Borovichi **80** 58 25N 33 55 E
Borovsk, Moscow, U.S.S.R. **81** 55 12N 36 24 E
Borovsk, Urals, U.S.S.R. **84** 59 43N 56 40 E
Borovskoye **84** 53 48N 64 12 E
Borradaile, Mt. **136** 12 5 S 132 51 E
Borrby **73** 55 27N 14 10 E
Borrego Springs **163** 33 15N 116 23W
Borriol **58** 40 4N 0 4W
Borris **39** 32 36N 6 57W
Borris-in-Ossory **39** 52 57N 7 40W
Borrisokane **39** 53 0N 8 8W
Borrisoleigh **39** 52 48N 7 58W
Borroloola **138** 16 4 S 136 17 E
Borrowdale **32** 54 31N 3 10W
Borsa **70** 47 41N 24 50 E
Borsod-Abaúj-Zemplén □ **53** 48 20N 21 0 E
Borssele **47** 51 26N 3 45 E
Bort-les-Orgues **44** 45 24N 2 29 E
Borth **31** 52 29N 4 3W
Borujerd **92** 33 55N 48 50 E
Borve **36** 58 25N 6 28W
Borzhomi **83** 41 48N 43 28 E
Borzna **80** 51 18N 32 26 E
Borzya **77** 50 24N 116 31 E
Bos. Dubica **63** 45 10N 16 50 E
Bos. Gradiška **66** 45 10N 17 15 E
Bos. Grahovo **63** 44 12N 16 26 E
Bos. Kostajnica **63** 45 11N 16 33 E
Bos. Krupa **63** 44 53N 16 10 E
Bos. Novi **63** 45 2N 16 22 E
Bos. Petrovac **63** 44 35N 16 21 E
Bos. Samac **66** 45 3N 18 29 E
Bosa **64** 40 17N 8 32 E
Bosaga **85** 37 33N 65 41 E
Bosanska Brod **66** 45 10N 18 0 E
Bosanski Novi **63** 45 2N 16 22 E
Bosavi, Mt. **135** 6 30 S 142 49 E
Bosbury **28** 52 5N 2 27W
Boscastle **30** 50 42N 4 42W
Boscotrecase **65** 40 46N 14 28 E
Bosham **29** 50 50N 0 51W
Boshoek **128** 25 30 S 27 9 E
Boshof **128** 28 31 S 25 13 E
Boshrūyeh **93** 33 50N 57 30 E
Bosilegrad **66** 42 30N 22 27 E
Boskoop **46** 52 4N 4 40 E
Boskovice **53** 49 29N 16 40 E
Bosna i Hercegovina □ **66** 44 0N 18 0 E
Bosna, R. **66** 44 50N 18 10 E
Bosnia = Bosna **66** 44 0N 18 0 E
Bosnik **103** 1 5 S 136 10 E
Bōsō-Hantō **111** 35 20N 140 20 E
Bosobolo **124** 4 15N 19 50 E
Bosporus = Karadeniz Boğazı **92** 41 10N 29 10 E
Bossangoa **117** 6 35N 17 30 E
Bossekop **74** 69 57N 23 15 E
Bossembélé **117** 5 25N 17 40 E
Bossier City **159** 32 28N 93 38W
Bosso **121** 13 43N 13 19 E
Bossut C. **136** 18 42 S 121 35 E
Boston, U.K. **33** 52 59N 0 2W
Boston, U.S.A. **162** 42 20N 71 0W
Boston Bar **152** 49 52N 121 22W
Bosut, R. **66** 45 5N 19 2 E
Boswell, Can. **152** 49 28N 116 45W
Boswell, U.S.A. **159** 34 1N 95 30W
Botad **94** 22 15N 71 40 E
Botany Bay **139** 34 0 S 151 14 E
Botene **100** 17 35N 101 12 E
Botevgrad **67** 42 55N 23 47 E
Bothaville **128** 27 23 S 26 34 E
Bothel **32** 54 43N 3 16W
Bothnia, G. of **74** 63 0N 21 0 E
Bothwell **138** 42 20 S 147 1 E
Boticas **56** 41 41N 7 40W
Botletle R. **128** 20 10 S 24 10 E
Botoroaga **70** 44 8N 25 32 E
Botoşani **70** 47 42N 26 41 E
Botoşani □ **70** 47 50N 26 50 E
Botro **120** 7 51N 5 19W
Botswana ■ **125** 22 0 S 24 0 E
Bottesford **33** 52 57N 0 48W
Bottineau **158** 48 49N 100 25W
Bottrop **48** 51 34N 6 59 E
Botucatu **173** 22 55 S 48 30W
Botwood **151** 49 6N 55 23W
Bou Alam **118** 33 50N 1 26 E
Bou Ali **118** 27 11N 0 4W
Bou Djébéha **120** 18 25N 2 45W
Bou Garfa **118** 27 4N 7 59W
Bou Guema **118** 28 49N 0 19 E
Bou Iblane, Djebel **118** 33 50N 4 0W
Bou Ismail **118** 36 38N 2 42 E
Bou Izakarn **118** 29 12N 6 46W
Bou Kahil, Djebel **118** 34 22N 9 23 E
Bou Saâda **119** 35 11N 4 9 E
Bou Salem **119** 36 45N 9 2 E
Bouaké **120** 7 40N 5 2W
Bouar **124** 6 0N 15 40 E
Bouârfa **118** 32 32N 1 58 E
Bouca **117** 6 45N 18 25 E
Boucau **44** 43 32N 1 29W
Boucaut B. **138** 12 0 S 134 25 E
Bouches-du-Rhône □ **45** 43 37N 5 2 E
Bouda **118** 27 50N 0 27W
Boudenib **118** 31 59N 3 31W
Boudry **50** 46 57N 6 50 E
Boufarik **118** 36 34N 2 58 E
Bougainville C. **136** 13 57 S 126 4 E
Bougainville I. **135** 6 0 S 155 0 E
Bougainville Reef **138** 15 30 S 147 5 E
Bougaroun, C. **119** 37 6N 6 30 E
Bougie = Béjaïa **119** 36 42N 5 2 E
Bougouni **120** 11 30N 7 20W
Bouillon **47** 49 44N 5 3 E
Bouïra **119** 36 20N 3 59 E
Boujad **118** 32 46N 6 24W
Bouladuff **39** 52 42N 7 55W
Boulder, Austral. **132** 30 46 S 121 30 E
Boulder, Colo., U.S.A. **158** 40 3N 105 10W
Boulder, Mont., U.S.A. **160** 46 14N 112 4W
Boulder City **161** 36 0N 114 50W
Boulder Creek **163** 37 7N 122 7W
Boulder Dam = Hoover Dam **161** 36 0N 114 45W
Bouleau, Lac au **150** 47 40N 77 35W
Boulhaut **118** 33 30N 7 1W
Boulia **138** 22 52 S 139 51 E
Bouligny **43** 49 17N 5 45 E
Boulogne, R. **42** 46 50N 1 25W
Boulogne-sur-Gesse **44** 43 18N 0 38 E
Boulogne-sur-Mer **43** 50 42N 1 36 E
Boulsa **121** 12 39N 0 34W
Boultoum **121** 14 45N 10 25 E
Boumalne **118** 31 25N 6 0W
Boun Neua **100** 21 38N 101 54 E
Boun Tai **100** 21 23N 101 58 E
Bouna **120** 9 10N 3 0W
Boundary **147** 64 11N 141 2W
Boundary Pk. **163** 37 51N 118 21W
Boundiali **120** 9 30N 6 20W
Bountiful **160** 40 57N 111 58W
Bounty I. **130** 46 0 S 180 0 E
Bour Khaya **77** 71 50N 133 10 E
Bourbon-l'Archambault **44** 46 36N 3 4 E
Bourbon-Lancy **44** 46 37N 3 45 E
Bourbonnais **44** 46 28N 3 0 E
Bourbonne **43** 47 59N 5 45 E
Bourem **121** 17 0N 0 24W
Bourg **44** 45 3N 0 34W
Bourg-Argental **45** 45 18N 4 32 E
Bourg-de-Péage **45** 45 2N 5 3 E
Bourg-en-Bresse **45** 46 13N 5 12 E
Bourg-St.-Andéol **45** 44 23N 4 39 E
Bourg-St.-Maurice **45** 45 35N 6 46 E
Bourg-St.-Pierre **50** 45 57N 7 12 E
Bourganeuf **44** 45 57N 1 45 E
Bourges **43** 47 9N 2 25 E
Bourget, L. du **45** 45 44N 5 52 E
Bourgneuf **42** 47 2N 1 58W
Bourgneuf, B. de **42** 47 3N 2 10W
Bourgneuf, Le **42** 48 10N 0 59W
Bourgogne **43** 47 0N 4 30 E
Bourgoin-Jallieu **45** 45 36N 5 17 E
Bourke **139** 30 8 S 145 55 E
Bourlamaque **150** 48 5N 77 56W
Bourne **29** 52 46N 0 22W
Bournemouth **28** 50 43N 1 53W
Bourriot-Bergonce **44** 44 7N 0 14W
Bourton-on-the-Water **28** 51 53N 1 45W
Bouscat, Le **44** 44 53N 0 32W
Boussac **44** 46 22N 2 13 E
Boussens **44** 43 12N 0 58 E
Bousso **117** 10 34N 16 52 E
Boussu **47** 50 26N 3 48 E
Bouthillier, Le **151** 47 47N 64 55W
Boutilimit **120** 17 45N 14 40W
Bouvet I. **15** 55 0 S 3 30 E
Bouznika **118** 33 46N 7 6W
Bouzonville **43** 49 17N 6 32 E
Bova Marina **65** 37 59N 15 56 E
Bovalino Marina **65** 38 9N 16 10 E
Bovec **63** 46 20N 13 33 E
Bovenkarspel **46** 52 41N 5 14 E
Bóves **62** 44 19N 7 29 E
Boves **62** 44 19N 7 33 E
Bovey Tracey **30** 50 36N 3 40W
Bovigny **47** 50 12N 5 55 E
Bovill **160** 46 58N 116 27W
Bovino **65** 41 15N 15 20 E
Bow Island **152** 49 50N 111 23W
Bow, R. **152** 51 10N 115 0W
Bowbells **158** 48 47N 102 19W
Bowdle **158** 45 30N 100 2W
Bowelling **137** 33 25 S 116 30 E
Bowen **138** 20 0 S 148 16 E
Bowen Mts. **141** 37 0 S 148 0 E
Bowen, R. **138** 20 24 S 147 20 E
Bowes **32** 54 31N 1 59W
Bowie, U.S.A. **162** 39 0N 76 47W
Bowie, Ariz., U.S.A. **161** 32 15N 109 30W
Bowie, Tex., U.S.A. **159** 33 33N 97 50W
Bowland, Forest of **32** 54 0N 2 30W
Bowling Green, Ky., U.S.A. **156** 37 0N 86 25W
Bowling Green, Ohio, U.S.A. **156** 41 22N 83 40W
Bowling Green, Va., U.S.A. **162** 38 3N 77 21W
Bowling Green, C. **138** 19 19 S 147 25 E
Bowman **158** 46 12N 103 21W
Bowman, I. **13** 65 0 S 104 0 E
Bowmans **140** 34 10 S 138 17 E
Bowmanville **150** 43 55N 78 41W
Bowmore **34** 55 45N 6 18W
Bowness, Can. **152** 50 55N 114 25W
Bowness, Solway, U.K. **32** 54 57N 3 13W
Bowness, Windermere, U.K. **32** 54 22N 2 56W
Bowral **141** 34 26 S 150 27 E
Bowraville **139** 30 37 S 152 52 E
Bowron, R. **152** 54 3N 121 50W
Bowser L. **152** 56 30N 129 30W
Bowsman **153** 52 14N 101 12W
Bowutu Mts. **135** 7 45 S 147 10 E
Bowwood **127** 17 5 S 26 20 E
Box **28** 51 24N 2 16W
Box Hill **29** 51 16N 0 16W
Boxelder Creek **160** 47 20N 108 30W
Boxholm **73** 58 12N 15 3 E
Boxley **29** 51 17N 0 34 E
Boxmeer **47** 51 38N 5 56 E
Boxtel **47** 51 36N 5 9 E
Boyabat **82** 41 28N 34 42 E
Boyacá □ **174** 5 30N 72 30W
Boyanup **137** 33 30 S 115 40 E
Boyce **159** 31 25N 92 39W
Boyd L. **150** 61 30N 103 20W
Boyer, R. **152** 58 27N 115 57W
Boyle **38** 53 58N 8 19W
Boyne City **156** 45 13N 85 1W
Boyne, R. **38** 53 40N 6 34W
Boynton Beach **157** 26 31N 80 3W
Boyoma, Chutes **124** 0 12N 25 25 E
Boyup Brook **137** 33 50 S 116 23 E
Bozburun **69** 36 43N 28 8 E
Bozcaada **68** 39 49N 26 3 E
Bozeat **29** 52 14N 0 41W
Bozeman **160** 45 40N 111 0W
Bozepole Wlk. **54** 54 33N 17 56 E
Bozevac **66** 44 32N 21 24 E
Bozouls **44** 44 28N 2 43 E
Bozoum **117** 6 25N 16 35 E
Bozovici **70** 44 56N 22 1 E
Bra **62** 44 41N 7 50 E
Brabant □ **47** 50 46N 4 30 E
Brabant L. **153** 54 18N 108 5W
Brabrand **73** 56 9N 10 7 E
BraC **63** 43 20N 16 40 E
Bracadale **36** 57 22N 6 24W
Bracadale, L. **36** 57 20N 6 30W
Bracciano **63** 42 6N 12 10 E
Bracciano, L. di **63** 42 8N 12 11 E
Bracebridge **150** 45 2N 79 19W
Bracebridge Heath **33** 53 13N 0 32W
Brach **119** 27 31N 14 20 E
Bracieux **43** 47 30N 1 30 E
Bräcke **72** 62 45N 15 26 E
Brackettville **159** 29 21N 100 20W
Brackley **28** 52 3N 1 9W
Bracknell **29** 51 24N 0 45W
Braco **35** 56 16N 3 55W
Brad **70** 46 10N 22 50 E
Brădano, R. **65** 40 41N 16 20 E
Bradda Hd. **32** 54 6N 4 46W
Bradenton **157** 27 25N 82 35W
Bradford, U.K. **33** 53 47N 1 45W
Bradford, Pa., U.S.A. **156** 41 54N 78 41W
Bradford, Vt., U.S.A. **162** 43 59N 72 9W
Bradford-on-Avon **28** 51 20N 2 15W
Brading **28** 50 41N 1 9W
Bradley, Ark., U.S.A. **159** 33 7N 93 39W
Bradley, Calif., U.S.A. **163** 35 52N 120 48W
Bradley, S.D., U.S.A. **158** 45 10N 97 40W
Bradley Institute **127** 17 7 S 31 25 E
Bradore Bay **151** 51 27N 57 18W
Bradshaw **136** 15 21 S 130 16 E
Bradwell-on-Sea **29** 51 44N 0 55 E
Bradworthy **30** 50 54N 4 22W
Brady **159** 31 8N 99 25W
Brae **36** 60 23N 1 20W
Brae, oilfield **19** 58 45N 1 18 E
Brædstrup **73** 55 58N 9 37 E
Braemar, Queens., Austral. **139** 25 35 S 152 20 E
Braemar, S. Austral., Austral. **140** 33 12 S 139 35 E
Braemar, U.K. **37** 57 2N 3 20W
Braemar, dist. **37** 57 2N 3 20W
Braemore, Grampian, U.K. **37** 58 16N 3 33W
Braemore, Highland, U.K. **36** 57 45N 5 2W
Braeriach Mt. **37** 57 4N 3 44W
Braga **56** 41 35N 8 25W
Braga □ **56** 41 30N 8 30W
Bragado **172** 35 2 S 60 27W
Bragança, Brazil **170** 1 0 S 47 2W
Bragança, Port. **56** 41 48N 6 50W
Bragança □ **56** 41 30N 6 45W
Bragança Paulista **173** 22 55 S 46 32W
Brahmanbaria **98** 23 50N 91 15 E
Brahmani, R. **96** 21 0N 85 15 E
Brahmaputra, R. **98** 26 30N 93 30 E
Brahmaur **93** 32 28N 76 32 E
Braich-y-Pwll **31** 52 47N 4 46W
Braidwood **141** 35 27 S 149 49 E
Brailsford **33** 52 58N 1 35W
Braine-l'Alleud **47** 50 42N 4 23 E
Braine-le-Comte **47** 50 37N 4 8 E
Brainerd **158** 46 20N 94 10W
Braintree, U.K. **29** 51 53N 0 34 E
Braintree, U.S.A. **162** 42 11N 71 0W
Braithwaite Pt. **138** 12 5 S 133 50 E
Brak, R. **128** 29 50 S 23 10 E
Brake **48** 53 19N 8 30 E
Brakel **46** 51 49N 5 5 E
Brakne-Hoby **73** 56 12N 15 8 E
Bräkne-Hoby **73** 56 14N 15 6 E
Brakpan **129** 26 13 S 28 20 E
Brakwater **128** 22 28 S 17 3 E
Brålanda **73** 58 34N 12 21 E
Brålanda **73** 58 34N 12 21 E
Bralila **70** 45 19N 27 59 E
Bralila □ **70** 45 5N 27 30 E
Bralorne **152** 50 50N 123 15W
Bramford **29** 52 5N 1 6 E
Bramminge **73** 55 28N 8 42 E

Bramon Brøttum

Bramon 72 62 14N 17 40E
Brampton, Can. 150 43 45N 79 45W
Brampton, Cambs., U.K. 29 52 19N 0 13W
Brampton, Cumb., U.K. 32 54 56N 2 43W
Bramsche 48 52 25N 7 58E
Bramshott 29 51 5N 0 47W
Bramwell 138 12 8S 142 37E
Brancaster 29 52 58N 0 40E
Branco, Cabo 170 7 9S 34 47W
Branco, R. 174 0 0 61 15W
Brande 73 55 57N 9 8E
Brandenburg 48 52 24N 12 33E
Brander, Pass of 34 56 25N 5 10W
Branderburgh 37 57 43N 3 17W
Brandfort 128 28 40S 26 30E
Brandon, Can. 153 49 50N 99 57W
Brandon, Durham, U.K. 33 54 46N 1 37W
Brandon, Suffolk, U.K. 29 52 27N 0 37E
Brandon, U.S.A. 156 43 48N 73 4W
Brandon, U.S.A. 162 44 2N 73 5W
Brandon B. 39 52 17N 10 8W
Brandon, Mt. 39 52 15N 10 15W
Brandon Pt. 39 52 18N 10 10W
Brandsen 172 35 10S 58 15W
Brandval 71 60 19N 12 1E
Brandvlei 128 30 25S 20 30E
Brandýs 52 50 10N 14 40E
Branford 162 41 15N 72 48W
Braniewo 54 54 25N 19 50E
Brännarp 73 56 46N 12 38E
Bransby 139 28 10S 142 0E
Bransfield Str. 13 63 0S 59 0W
Branson, Colo., U.S.A. 159 37 4N 103 53W
Branson, Mo., U.S.A. 159 36 40N 93 18W
Branston 33 53 13N 0 28W
Brantford 150 43 15N 80 15W
Brantôme 44 45 22N 0 39E
Branxholme 140 37 52S 141 49E
Branxton 141 32 38S 151 21E
Branzi 62 46 0N 9 46E
Bras d'or, L. 151 45 50N 60 50W
Brasiléia 174 11 0S 68 45W
Brasília 171 15 47S 47 55E
Braslav 80 55 38N 27 0E
Braslovče 63 46 21N 15 3E
Braşov 70 45 38N 25 35E
Braşov □ 70 45 45N 25 15E
Brass 121 4 35N 6 14E
Brass, R. 121 4 15N 6 13E
Brasschaat 47 51 19N 4 27E
Brassey, Barisan 102 5 0N 117 15E
Brassey Ra. 137 25 8S 122 15E
Brasstown Bald, Mt. 157 34 54N 83 45W
Brassus, Le 50 46 35N 6 13E
Brasted 29 51 16N 0 8E
Bratislava 53 48 10N 17 7E
Bratsk 77 56 10N 101 30E
Bratteborg 73 57 37N 14 4E
Brattleboro 162 42 53N 72 37W
Brattvær 71 63 25N 7 48E
Braţul Chilia, R. 70 45 25N 29 20E
Braţul Sfîntu Gheorghe, R. 70 45 0N 29 20E
Braţul Sulina, R. 70 45 10N 29 20E
Bratunac 66 44 13N 19 21E
Braunau 52 48 15N 13 3E
Braunschweig 48 52 17N 10 28E
Braunton 30 51 6N 4 9W
Brava 91 1 20N 44 8E
Bråvikeh 72 58 38N 16 32E
Bravo del Norte, R. 164 30 30N 105 0W
Brawley 163 32 58N 115 30W
Bray, France 43 49 15N 1 40E
Bray, Ireland 39 53 12N 6 6W
Bray, U.K. 29 51 30N 0 42W
Bray Hd. 39 51 52N 10 26W
Bray, Mt. 138 14 0N 134 30E
Bray-sur-Seine 43 48 25N 3 14E
Brazeau, R. 152 52 55N 115 14W
Brazil 156 39 30N 87 8W
Brazil ■ 174 5 0N 20 0W
Brazilian Highlands 170 18 0S 46 30W
Brazo Sur, R. 172 25 30S 58 0W
Brazos, R. 159 30 30N 96 20W
Brazzaville 124 4 9S 15 12E
Brčko 66 44 54N 18 46E
Breadalbane, Austral. 138 23 50S 139 35E
Breadalbane, U.K. 34 56 30N 4 15W
Breaden, L. 137 25 51S 125 28E
Breage 30 50 6N 5 17W
Breaksea Sd. 143 45 35S 166 35E
Bream Bay 142 35 56S 174 28E
Bream Head 142 35 51S 174 36E
Bream Tail 142 36 3S 174 36E
Breamish, R. 35 55 30N 1 55W
Breas 172 25 29S 70 24W
Brebes 103 6 52S 109 3E
Brechin 37 56 44N 2 40W
Brecht 47 51 21N 4 38E
Breckenridge, Colo., U.S.A. 160 39 30N 106 2W
Breckenridge, Minn., U.S.A. 158 46 20N 96 36W
Breckenridge, Tex., U.S.A. 159 32 48N 98 55W
Breckland 23 52 30N 0 40E
Brecknock (□) 26 51 58N 3 25W
Břeclav 53 48 46N 16 53E
Brecon 31 51 57N 3 23W
Brecon Beacons 31 51 53N 3 27W
Breda 47 51 35N 4 45E
Bredaryd 73 57 10N 13 45E
Bredasdorp 128 34 33S 20 2E
Bredbo 141 35 58S 149 10E
Brede 29 50 56N 0 37E
Bredene 47 51 14N 2 59E
Bredon Hill 28 52 3N 2 2W
Bredy 84 52 26N 60 21E
Bree 47 51 8N 5 35E
Breezand 46 52 53N 4 49E
Bregalnica, R. 66 41 50N 22 20E
Bregenz 52 47 30N 9 45E
Bregning 73 56 8N 8 30E
Bréhal 42 48 53N 1 30W
Bréhat, I. de 42 48 51N 3 0W
Breiðafjörður 74 65 15N 23 15W
Breil 45 43 56N 7 31E
Breisach 49 48 2N 7 37E
Brejinho de Nazaré 170 11 1S 48 34W
Brejo 170 3 41S 42 47W
Brekke 71 61 1N 5 26E
Bremangerlandet 71 61 51N 5 0E
Bremangerpollen 71 61 51N 5 0E
Bremen 48 53 4N 8 47E
Bremen □ 48 53 6N 8 46E
Bremer I. 138 12 5S 136 45E
Bremerhaven 48 53 34N 8 35E
Bremerton 160 47 30N 122 38W
Bremervörde 48 53 28N 9 10E
Bremgarten 51 47 21N 8 21E
Bremnes 71 59 47N 5 8E
Bremsnes 71 63 6N 7 40E
Brendon Hills 28 51 6N 3 25W
Brenes 57 37 32N 5 54W
Brenham 159 30 5N 96 27W
Brenner Pass 52 47 0N 11 30E
Breno 62 45 57N 10 20E
Brent, Can. 150 46 2N 78 29W
Brent, U.K. 29 51 33N 0 18W
Brent, oil and gasfield 19 61 0N 1 45E
Brenta, R. 63 45 11N 12 18E
Brentwood, U.K. 29 51 37N 0 19W
Brentwood, U.S.A. 163 37 55N 121 42W
Bréscia 62 45 33N 10 13E
Breskens 47 51 23N 3 33E
Breslau = Wrocław. 54 51 5N 17 5E
Bresle, R. 43 50 4N 1 21E
Bresles 43 49 25N 2 13E
Bressanone 63 46 43N 11 40E
Bressay 36 60 10N 1 6W
Bressay I. 36 60 10N 1 5W
Bressay Sd. 36 60 8N 1 10W
Bresse, La 43 48 0N 6 53E
Bresse, Plaine de 43 46 20N 5 10E
Bressuire 42 46 51N 0 30W
Brest, France 42 48 24N 4 31W
Brest, U.S.S.R. 80 52 10N 23 40E
Bretagne 42 48 0N 3 0W
Bretçu 70 46 7N 26 18E
Breteuil 43 49 38N 2 18E
Breton 152 53 7N 114 28W
Breton Sd. 159 29 40N 89 12W
Brett, C. 142 35 10S 174 20E
Bretten 49 49 2N 8 43E
Bretuil 42 48 50N 0 53E
Breukelen 46 52 10N 5 0E
Brevard 157 35 19N 82 42W
Breves 170 1 40S 50 29W
Brevik 71 59 4N 9 42E
Brewarrina 139 30 0S 146 51E
Brewer 151 44 43N 68 50W
Brewer, Mt. 163 36 44N 118 28W
Brewerton 162 43 14N 76 9W
Brewood 28 52 41N 2 10W
Brewster, N.Y., U.S.A. 162 41 23N 73 37W
Brewster, Wash., U.S.A. 160 48 10N 119 51W
Brewster, Kap 12 70 7N 22 0W
Brewton 157 31 9N 87 2W
Breyten 129 26 16S 30 0E
Breytovo 81 58 18N 37 50E
Brézina 118 33 4N 1 14E
Březnice 52 49 32N 13 57E
Breznik 66 42 44N 22 50E
Brezno 53 48 50N 19 40E
Bria 117 6 30N 21 58E
Briançon 45 44 54N 6 39E
Briare 43 47 38N 2 45E
Bribbaree 141 34 10S 147 51E
Bribie I. 139 27 0S 152 58E
Brickaville 129 18 49S 49 4E
Bricon 43 48 5N 5 0E
Bricquebec 42 49 29N 1 39W
Bride 32 54 24N 4 23W
Bridestowe 30 50 41N 4 7W
Bridge 29 51 14N 1 8E
Bridge of Allan 35 56 9N 3 57W
Bridge of Don 37 57 10N 2 8W
Bridge of Earn 35 56 20N 3 25W
Bridge of Orchy 34 56 29N 4 48W
Bridge of Weir 34 55 51N 4 35W
Bridge, R. 152 50 50N 122 40W
Bridgehampton 162 40 56N 72 18W
Bridgend, Islay, U.K. 34 55 46N 6 15W
Bridgend, Mid Glam., U.K. 31 51 30N 3 35W
Bridgeport, Calif., U.S.A. 163 38 14N 119 15W
Bridgeport, Conn., U.S.A. 162 41 12N 73 12W
Bridgeport, Nebr., U.S.A. 158 41 42N 103 10W
Bridgeport, Tex., U.S.A. 159 33 15N 97 45W
Bridger 160 45 20N 108 58W
Bridgeton 162 39 29N 75 10W
Bridgetown, Austral. 137 33 58S 116 7E
Bridgetown, Barbados 167 13 0N 59 30W
Bridgetown, Can. 151 44 55N 65 18W
Bridgetown, Ireland 39 52 13N 6 33W
Bridgeville 162 38 45N 75 36W
Bridgewater, Austral. 140 36 36S 143 59E
Bridgewater, Can. 151 44 25N 64 31W
Bridgewater, Mass., U.S.A. 162 41 59N 70 56W
Bridgewater, N.Y., U.S.A. 162 42 58N 75 15W
Bridgewater, S.D., U.S.A. 158 43 34N 97 29W
Bridgewater, C. 140 38 23S 141 23E
Bridgnorth 28 52 33N 2 25W
Bridgwater 28 51 7N 3 0W
Bridgwater B. 28 51 15N 3 15W
Bridlington 33 54 6N 0 11W
Bridlington B. 33 54 4N 0 10W
Bridport, Austral. 138 40 59S 147 23E
Bridport, U.K. 28 50 43N 2 45W
Brie-Comte-Robert 43 48 40N 2 35E
Brie, Plaine de 43 48 35N 3 10E
Briec 42 48 6N 4 0W
Brielle 46 51 54N 4 10E
Brienne-le-Château 43 48 24N 4 30E
Brienon 43 48 0N 3 35E
Brienz 50 46 46N 8 2E
Brienzersee 50 46 44N 7 53E
Brierfield 32 53 49N 2 15W
Brierley Hill 28 52 29N 2 7W
Briey 43 49 14N 5 57E
Brig 50 46 18N 7 59E
Brigantine 162 39 24N 74 22W
Brigg 33 53 33N 0 30W
Briggsdale 158 40 40N 104 20W
Brigham City 160 41 30N 112 1W
Brighouse 33 53 42N 1 47W
Brighstone 29 50 38N 1 36W
Bright 141 36 42S 146 56E
Brightlingsea 29 51 49N 1 1E
Brighton, Austral. 140 35 5S 138 30E
Brighton, Can. 150 44 2N 77 44W
Brighton, U.K. 29 50 50N 0 9W
Brighton, U.S.A. 158 39 59N 104 50W
Brightstone 28 50 38N 1 23W
Brightwater 143 41 22S 173 9E
Brignogan-Plage 42 48 40N 4 20W
Brignoles 45 43 25N 6 5E
Brigstock 29 52 27N 0 38W
Brihuega 58 40 45N 2 52W
Brikama 120 13 15N 16 45W
Brill 28 51 49N 1 3W
Brilliant 152 49 19N 117 38W
Brilon 48 51 23N 8 32E
Brim 140 36 3S 142 27E
Brimfield 28 52 18N 2 42W
Bríndisi 65 40 39N 17 55E
Brinkley 159 34 55N 91 15W
Brinklow 28 52 25N 1 22W
Brinkworth, Austral. 140 33 42S 138 26E
Brinkworth, U.K. 28 51 33N 1 59W
Brinyan 37 59 8N 3 0W
Brion I. 151 47 46N 61 26W
Brionne 42 49 11N 0 43E
Brionski, I. 63 44 55N 13 45E
Brioude 44 45 18N 3 23E
Briouze 42 48 42N 0 23W
Brisbane 139 27 25S 153 2E
Brisbane, R. 139 27 24S 153 9E
Brisignella 63 44 14N 11 46E
Bristol, U.K. 28 51 26N 2 35W
Bristol, Conn., U.S.A. 162 41 44N 72 57W
Bristol, Pa., U.S.A. 162 40 6N 74 52W
Bristol, R.I., U.S.A. 162 41 40N 71 15W
Bristol, S.D., U.S.A. 158 45 25N 97 43W
Bristol B. 147 58 0N 160 0W
Bristol Channel 30 51 18N 4 30W
Bristol I. 13 58 45S 28 0W
Bristol L. 161 34 23N 116 0W
Briston 29 52 52N 1 4E
Bristow 159 35 5N 96 28W
British Antarctic Territory 13 66 0S 45 0W
British Columbia □ 152 55 0N 125 15W
British Guiana = Guyana 174 5 0N 59 0W
British Honduras = Belize 165 17 0N 88 30W
British Isles 16 55 0N 4 0W
Briton Ferry 31 51 37N 3 50W
Brits 129 25 37S 27 48E
Britstown 128 30 37S 23 30E
Britt 150 45 46N 80 34W
Brittany = Bretagne 42 48 0N 3 0W
Brittas 39 53 14N 6 29W
Brittatorp 73 57 3N 14 58E
Britton 158 45 50N 97 47W
Brive-la-Gaillarde 44 45 10N 1 32E
Briviesca 58 42 32N 3 19W
Brixham 30 50 24N 3 31W
Brixton 138 23 32S 144 57E
Brixworth 29 52 20N 0 54W
Brize Norton 28 51 46N 1 35W
Brlik, U.S.S.R. 76 44 0N 74 5E
Brlik, Kazakh S.S.R., U.S.S.R. 85 44 5N 73 31E
Brlik, Kazakh S.S.R., U.S.S.R. 85 43 40N 73 49E
Brno 53 49 10N 16 35E
Bro 72 59 13N 13 2E
Broach = Bharuch 96 21 47N 73 0E
Broad Arrow 137 30 23S 121 15E
Broad B. 36 58 14N 6 16W
Broad Chalke 28 51 2N 1 54W
Broad Clyst 30 50 46N 3 27W
Broad Haven, Ireland 38 54 20N 9 55W
Broad Haven, U.K. 31 51 46N 5 6W
Broad Law, Mt. 35 55 30N 3 22W
Broad, R. 157 34 30N 81 26W
Broad Sd., Austral. 138 22 0S 149 45E
Broad Sd., U.K. 30 49 56N 6 19W
Broadalbin 162 43 3N 74 12W
Broadford, Austral. 141 37 14S 145 4E
Broadford, Clare, Ireland 39 52 48N 8 38W
Broadford, Limerick, Ireland 39 52 21N 8 59W
Broadford, U.K. 36 57 14N 5 55W
Broadhembury 30 50 49N 3 16W
Broadhurst Ra. 136 22 30S 122 30E
Broads, The 29 52 45N 1 30E
Broadsound Ra. 133 22 50S 149 30E
Broadstairs 29 51 21N 1 28E
Broadus 158 45 28N 105 27W
Broadview 153 50 22N 102 35W
Broadway, Ireland 39 52 13N 6 23W
Broadway, U.K. 28 52 2N 1 51W
Broadwindsor 28 50 49N 2 49W
Broager 73 54 53N 9 40E
Broaryd 73 57 7N 13 15E
Brochet, Man., Can. 153 57 53N 101 40W
Brochet, Manitoba, Can. 153 57 55N 101 40W
Brochet, Québec, Can. 150 47 12N 72 42W
Brochet, L. 153 58 36N 101 35W
Brock 153 51 26N 108 43W
Brocken 48 51 48N 10 40E
Brockenhurst 28 50 49N 1 34W
Brocklehurst 141 32 9S 148 38E
Brockman Mt. 137 22 25S 117 15E
Brockville 150 44 35N 75 41W
Brockway 158 47 18N 105 46W
Brockworth 28 51 51N 2 9W
Brod 66 41 35N 21 17E
Brodarevo 66 43 14N 19 44E
Brodeur Pen. 149 72 30N 88 10W
Brodick 34 55 34N 5 9W
Brodnica 54 53 15N 19 25E
Brodokalmak 84 55 35N 62 6E
Brody 80 50 5N 25 10E
Broechem 47 51 11N 4 38E
Broek 46 52 26N 5 0E
Broek op Langedijk 46 52 41N 4 49E
Brogan 160 44 14N 117 32W
Broglie 42 49 0N 0 30E
Brok 54 52 43N 21 52E
Broke Inlet 137 34 55S 116 25E
Broken Bank, gasfield 19 53 20N 2 4E
Broken Bow, Nebr., U.S.A. 158 41 25N 99 35W
Broken Bow, Okla., U.S.A. 159 34 2N 94 43W
Broken Hill 140 31 58S 141 29E
Broken Hill = Kabwe 127 14 27S 28 28E
Brokind 73 58 13N 15 42E
Bromborough 32 53 20N 3 0W
Bromham 28 51 23N 2 3W
Bromhead 153 49 18N 103 40W
Bromley 29 51 20N 0 5E
Bromölla 73 56 5N 14 28E
Brompton 33 54 22N 1 25W
Bromsgrove 28 52 20N 2 3W
Bromyard 28 52 12N 2 30W
Brønderslev 73 57 16N 9 57E
Brong Ahafo 120 7 50N 2 0E
Bronkhorstspruit 129 25 46S 28 45E
Bronnitsy 81 55 27N 38 10E
Bronte, Italy 65 37 48N 14 49E
Bronte, U.S.A. 159 31 54N 100 18W
Bronte Park 138 42 8S 146 30E
Brookeborough 38 54 19N 7 23W
Brookfield 158 39 50N 93 4W
Brookhaven 159 31 40N 90 25W
Brookings, Oreg., U.S.A. 160 42 4N 124 10W
Brookings, S.D., U.S.A. 158 44 20N 96 45W
Brooklands 138 18 5S 144 0E
Brookmere 152 49 52N 120 53W
Brooks 152 50 35N 111 55W
Brooks B. 152 50 15N 127 55W
Brooks L. 153 61 55N 106 35W
Brooks Ra. 147 68 40N 147 0W
Brooksville 157 28 32N 82 21W
Brookton 137 32 22S 116 57E
Brookville 156 39 25N 85 0W
Brooloo 139 26 30S 152 43E
Broom, L. 36 57 55N 5 15W
Broome 136 18 0S 122 15E
Broomehill 137 31 51S 117 39E
Broomfield 28 51 46N 0 28E
Broomhill 35 55 19N 1 36W
Broons 42 48 20N 2 16W
Brora 37 58 0N 3 50W
Brora L. 37 58 3N 3 58W
Brora, R. 37 58 4N 3 52W
Brosarp 73 55 44N 14 8E
Brösarp 73 55 43N 14 6E
Broseley 28 52 36N 2 30W
Brosna, R. 39 53 8N 8 0W
Broşteni 70 47 14N 25 43E
Brotas de Macaúbas 171 12 0S 42 38W
Brothers 160 43 56N 120 39W
Brothertoft 33 53 0N 0 5W
Brotton 33 54 34N 0 55W
Brøttum 71 61 2N 10 34E

Brough **Bura**

Brough, Cumbria, U.K. **32** 54 32N 2 19W
Brough, Humberside, U.K. **33** 53 44N 0 35W
Brough Hd. **37** 59 8N 3 20W
Broughams Gate **140** 30 51S 140 59E
Broughshane **38** 54 54N 6 12W
Broughton, Austral. **138** 20 10S 146 20E
Broughton, Borders, U.K. **35** 55 37N 3 25W
Broughton, Humberside, U.K. **33** 53 33N 0 36W
Broughton, Northampton, U.K. **29** 52 22N 0 45W
Broughton, Yorkshire, U.K. **33** 54 26N 1 8W
Broughton-in-Furness **32** 54 17N 3 12W
Broughty Ferry **35** 56 29N 2 50W
Broumov **53** 50 35N 16 20E
Brouwershaven **46** 51 45N 3 55E
Brouwershavensche Gat **46** 51 46N 3 50E
Brovary **80** 50 34N 30 48E
Brovst **73** 57 6N 9 31E
Browerville **158** 46 3N 94 50W
Brown, Mt. **140** 32 30S 138 0E
Brown, Pt. **139** 32 32S 133 50E
Brown Willy, Mt. **30** 50 35N 4 34W
Brownfield **159** 33 10N 102 15W
Browngrove **38** 53 33N 8 49W
Brownhills **28** 52 38N 1 57W
Browning **160** 48 35N 113 10W
Brownlee **153** 50 43N 106 1W
Browns Bay **142** 36 40S 174 40E
Brownstown Hd. **39** 52 8N 7 8W
Brownsville, Oreg., U.S.A. **160** 44 29N 123 0W
Brownsville, Tenn., U.S.A. **159** 35 35N 89 15W
Brownsville, Tex., U.S.A. **159** 25 56N 97 25W
Brownwood **159** 31 45N 99 0W
Brownwood, L. **159** 31 51N 98 35W
Browse I. **136** 14 7S 123 33E
Broxburn **35** 55 56N 3 23W
Broye, R. **50** 46 52N 6 58E
Brozas **57** 39 37N 6 47W
Bruas **101** 4 31N 100 46E
Bruay-en-Artois **43** 50 29N 2 33E
Bruce Bay **143** 43 35S 169 42E
Bruce, gasfield **19** 59 45N 1 32E
Bruce Mines **150** 46 20N 83 45W
Bruce, Mt. **136** 22 37S 118 8E
Bruce Rock **137** 31 52S 118 8E
Bruchsal **49** 49 9N 8 39E
Bruck a.d. Leitha **53** 48 1N 16 47E
Bruck a.d. Mur **52** 47 24N 15 16E
Brückenau **49** 50 17N 9 48E
Brŭdiceni **70** 45 3N 23 4E
Brue, R. **28** 51 10N 2 59W
Bruernish Pt. **36** 57 0N 7 22W
Bruff **39** 52 29N 8 35W
Brugelette **47** 50 35N 3 52E
Bruges = Brugge **47** 51 13N 3 13E
Brugg **50** 47 29N 8 11E
Brugge **47** 51 13N 3 13E
Brühl **48** 50 49N 6 51E
Bruinisse **47** 51 40N 4 5E
Brûlé **152** 53 15N 117 58W
Brûlon **42** 47 58N 0 15W
Brûly **47** 49 58N 4 32E
Brumado **171** 14 14S 41 40W
Brumado, R. **171** 14 13S 41 40W
Brumath **43** 48 43N 7 40E
Brummen **46** 52 5N 6 10E
Brumunddal **71** 60 53N 10 56E
Brunchilly **138** 18 50S 134 30E
Brundidge **157** 31 43N 85 45W
Bruneau **160** 42 57N 115 55W
Bruneau, R. **160** 42 45N 115 50W
Brunei = Bandar Seri Begawan **102** 4 52N 115 0E
Brunei ■ **102** 4 50N 115 0E
Brunette Downs **138** 18 40S 135 55E
Brunflo **72** 63 5N 14 50E
Brunico **63** 46 50N 11 55E
Brünig, Col de **50** 46 46N 8 8E
Brunkeberg **71** 59 26N 8 28E
Brunna **72** 59 52N 17 25E
Brunnen **51** 46 59N 8 37E
Brunner **143** 42 27S 171 20E
Brunner, L. **143** 42 27S 171 20E
Brunnsvik **72** 60 12N 15 8E
Bruno **153** 52 20N 105 30W
Brunsberg **72** 59 38N 12 52E
Brunsbüttelkoog **48** 53 52N 9 13E
Brunssum **47** 50 57N 5 59E
Brunswick, Ga., U.S.A. **157** 31 10N 81 30W
Brunswick, Md., U.S.A. **156** 39 20N 77 38W
Brunswick, Me., U.S.A. **151** 43 53N 69 50W
Brunswick, Mo., U.S.A. **158** 39 26N 93 10W
Brunswick = Braunschweig **48** 52 17N 10 28E
Brunswick B. **136** 15 15S 124 50E
Brunswick Junction **137** 33 15S 115 50E
Brunswick, Pen. de **176** 53 30S 71 30W
Bruntál **53** 50 0N 17 27E
Brunton **35** 55 2N 2 6W
Bruny I. **138** 43 20S 147 15E
Bruree **39** 52 25N 8 40W
Brus Laguna **166** 15 47N 84 35W
Brusartsi **66** 43 40N 23 5E
Brush **158** 40 17N 103 33W
Brusio **51** 46 14N 10 8E
Brusque **173** 27 5S 49 0W
Brussel **47** 50 51N 4 21E
Brussels = Bruxelles **47** 50 51N 4 21E
Brustem **47** 50 48N 5 14E
Bruthen **141** 37 42S 147 50E
Bruton **28** 51 6N 2 28W
Bruvik **71** 60 29N 5 40E
Bruxelles **47** 50 51N 4 21E
Bruyères **43** 48 10N 6 40E
Brwinow **54** 52 9N 20 40E
Bryagovo **67** 41 58N 25 8E
Bryan, Ohio, U.S.A. **156** 41 30N 84 30W
Bryan, Texas, U.S.A. **159** 30 40N 96 27W
Bryan, Mt. **140** 33 30S 139 0E
Bryansk **80** 53 13N 34 25E
Bryanskoye **83** 44 9N 47 10E
Bryant **58** 44 39N 97 26W
Bryggja **71** 61 56N 5 27E
Bryher I. **30** 49 57N 6 21W
Brymbo **31** 53 4N 3 5W
Brynamman **31** 51 49N 3 52W
Bryncethin **31** 51 33N 3 34W
Bryne **71** 58 44N 5 38E
Brynmawr **31** 51 48N 3 11W
Bryrup **73** 56 2N 9 30E
Bryson City **157** 35 28N 83 25W
Bryte **163** 38 35N 121 33W
Brza Palanka **66** 44 28N 22 37E
Brzava, R. **66** 45 21N 20 45E
Brzeg **54** 50 52N 17 30E
Brzeg Dln **54** 51 16N 16 41E
Brzesko **54** 49 59N 20 34E
Brzesść Kujawski **54** 52 36N 18 55E
Brzeszcze **54** 49 59N 19 10E
Brzeziny **54** 51 49N 19 42E
Brzozów **54** 49 41N 22 3E
Bu Athiah **119** 30 1N 15 30E
Bu Craa **116** 26 45N 17 2E
Buapinang **103** 4 40S 121 30E
Buayan **103** 5 3N 125 28E
Buba **120** 11 40N 14 59W
Bubanza **126** 3 6S 29 23E
Bucaramanga **174** 7 0N 73 0W
Buccaneer Arch. **136** 16 7S 123 20E
Bucchiánico **63** 42 20N 14 10E
Bucecea **70** 47 47N 26 28E
Bŭceşti **70** 46 50N 27 11E
Buchach **80** 49 5N 25 25E
Buchan, Austral. **141** 37 30S 148 12E
Buchan, U.K. **37** 57 32N 2 8W
Buchan Ness **37** 57 29N 1 48W
Buchan, oilfield **19** 57 55N 0 0
Buchanan, Can. **153** 51 40N 102 45W
Buchanan, Liberia **120** 5 57N 10 2W
Buchanan Cr. **138** 17 10S 138 6E
Buchanan, L., Queens., Austral. **138** 21 35S 145 52E
Buchanan, L., W. Australia, Austral. **137** 25 33S 123 2E
Buchanan, L., U.S.A. **159** 30 50N 98 25W
Buchans **151** 49 50N 56 52W
Bucharest = Bucureşti **70** 44 27N 26 10E
Buchholz **48** 53 19N 9 51E
Buchloe **49** 48 3N 10 45E
Buchlyvie **34** 56 7N 4 20W
Buchon, Pt. **163** 35 15N 120 54W
Buchs **51** 47 10N 9 28E
Buck Hill Falls **162** 41 11N 75 16W
Buck, The, mt. **37** 57 19N 3 0W
Buckden **29** 52 17N 0 16W
Bückeburg **48** 52 16N 9 2E
Buckeye **161** 33 28N 112 40W
Buckfastleigh **30** 50 28N 3 47W
Buckhannon **156** 39 2N 80 10W
Buckhaven **35** 56 10N 3 2W
Buckie **37** 57 40N 2 58W
Buckingham, Can. **150** 45 37N 75 24W
Buckingham, U.K. **29** 52 0N 0 59W
Buckingham □ **29** 51 50N 0 55W
Buckingham B. **138** 12 10S 135 40E
Buckingham Can. **97** 14 0N 80 5E
Buckinguy **139** 31 3S 147 30E
Buckland **147** 66 0N 161 5W
Buckland Brewer **30** 50 56N 4 14W
Buckle Hd. **136** 14 26S 127 52E
Buckleboo **140** 32 54S 136 12E
Buckley, U.K. **31** 53 10N 3 5W
Buckley, U.S.A. **160** 47 10N 122 2W
Bucklin **159** 37 37N 99 40W
Bucksburn **37** 57 10N 2 10W
Bucquoy **43** 50 9N 2 43E
Buctouche **151** 46 30N 64 45W
Bucureşti **70** 44 27N 26 10E
Bucyrus **156** 40 48N 83 0W
Budacul, Munte **41** 47 5N 25 40E
Budafok **53** 47 26N 19 2E
Budalin **98** 22 20N 95 10E
Budapest **53** 47 29N 19 5E
Budaun **95** 28 5N 79 10E
Budd Coast **13** 67 0S 112 0E
Buddabadah **141** 31 56S 147 14E
Buddon Ness **35** 56 29N 2 42W
Buddusò **64** 40 35N 9 18E
Bude **30** 50 49N 4 33W
Bude Bay **30** 50 50N 4 40W
Budel **47** 51 17N 5 34E
Budeşti **70** 44 13N 26 30E
Budge Budge **95** 22 30N 88 25E
Budgewoi Lake **141** 33 13S 151 34E
Budia **58** 40 38N 2 46W
Bŭdir **74** 64 49N 23 23W
Budjala **124** 2 50N 19 40E
Budle B. **35** 55 37N 1 45W
Budleigh Salterton **30** 50 37N 3 19W
Búdrio **63** 44 31N 11 31E
Budva **66** 42 17N 18 50E
Budzyn **54** 52 54N 16 59E
Buea **121** 4 10N 9 9E
Buellton **163** 34 37N 120 12W
Buena **162** 39 31N 74 56W
Buena Vista, Colo., U.S.A. **161** 38 56N 106 6W
Buena Vista, Va., U.S.A. **156** 37 47N 79 23W
Buena Vista L. **163** 35 15N 119 21W
Buenaventura **164** 29 50N 107 30W
Buenaventura, B. de **174** 3 48N 77 17W
Buendía, Pantano de **58** 40 25N 2 43W
Buenópolis **171** 17 54S 44 11W
Buenos Aires, Argent. **172** 34 30S 58 20W
Buenos Aires, Colomb. **174** 1 36N 73 18W
Buenos Aires, C. Rica **166** 9 10N 83 20W
Buenos Aires □ **172** 36 30S 60 0W
Buenos Aires, Lago **176** 46 35S 72 30W
Buesaco **174** 1 23N 77 9W
Buffalo, Can. **153** 50 49N 110 42W
Buffalo, Mo., U.S.A. **159** 37 40N 93 5W
Buffalo, Okla., U.S.A. **159** 36 55N 99 42W
Buffalo, S.D., U.S.A. **159** 45 39N 103 31W
Buffalo, Wyo., U.S.A. **160** 44 25N 106 50W
Buffalo Center **147** 64 2N 145 50W
Buffalo Head Hills **152** 57 25N 115 55W
Buffalo L. **152** 52 27N 112 54W
Buffalo Narrows **153** 55 51N 108 29W
Buffalo, R. **152** 57 50N 117 1W
Buffels, R. **129** 29 36S 17 15E
Buford **157** 34 5N 84 0W
Bug, R., Poland **54** 51 20N 23 40E
Bug, R., U.S.S.R. **82** 48 0N 31 0E
Buga **174** 4 0N 77 0W
Buganda □ **126** 0 0N 31 30E
Buganga **126** 0 25N 32 0E
Bugeat **44** 45 36N 1 55E
Buggenhout **47** 51 1N 4 12E
Buggs I. L. **157** 36 20N 78 30W
Buglawton **32** 53 12N 2 11W
Bugle **30** 50 23N 4 46W
Bugojno **66** 44 2N 17 25E
Bugsuk, I. **102** 8 15N 117 15E
Bugue, Le **44** 44 55N 0 56E
Bugulma **84** 54 33N 52 48E
Buguma **121** 4 42N 6 55E
Bugun Shara **105** 49 0N 104 0E
Buguruslan **84** 53 39N 52 26E
Buheirat-Murrat-el-Kubra **122** 30 15N 32 40E
Buhl, Idaho, U.S.A. **160** 42 35N 114 54W
Buhl, Minn., U.S.A. **158** 47 30N 92 46W
Buhŭeşti **70** 46 47N 27 32E
Buhuşi **70** 46 41N 26 45E
Buick **159** 37 8N 91 2W
Bŭicoi **70** 45 3N 25 52E
Buie L. **34** 56 20N 5 55W
Bŭileşti **70** 44 01N 23 20E
Builth Wells **31** 52 10N 3 26W
Buina Qara **93** 36 20N 67 0E
Buinsk **81** 55 0N 48 18E
Buíque **170** 8 37S 37 9W
Buis-les-Baronnies **45** 44 17N 5 16E
Buit, L. **151** 50 59N 63 13W
Buitenpost **46** 53 15N 6 9E
Buitrago **56** 41 0N 3 38W
Bujalance **57** 37 54N 4 23W
Buján **56** 42 59N 8 36W
Bujaraloz **58** 41 29N 0 10W
Buje **63** 45 24N 13 39E
Buji **135** 9 8S 142 11E
Bujnurd **93** 37 35N 57 15E
Bujumbura (Usumbura) **126** 3 16S 29 18E
Bük **53** 47 22N 16 45E
Buk **54** 52 21N 16 17E
Buka I. **135** 5 10S 154 35E
Bukachacha **77** 52 55N 116 50E
Bukama **127** 9 10S 25 50E
Bukandula **126** 0 13N 31 50E
Bukavu **126** 2 20S 28 52E
Bukene **126** 4 15S 32 48E
Bukhara **85** 39 48N 64 25E
Bukima **126** 1 50S 33 25E
Bukit Mertajam **101** 5 22N 100 28E
Bukittinggi **102** 0 20S 100 20E
Bukkapatnam **97** 14 14N 77 46E
Buklyan **84** 55 42N 52 10E
Bukoba **126** 1 20S 31 49E
Bukoba □ **126** 1 30S 32 0E
Bukowno **54** 50 17N 19 35E
Bukrale **123** 4 32N 42 0E
Bukuru **121** 9 42N 8 48E
Bukuya **126** 0 40N 31 52E
Bula **120** 12 7N 15 43W
Bülach **51** 47 31N 8 32E
Bulahdelah **141** 32 23S 152 13E
Bulan **103** 12 40N 123 52E
Bulanash **84** 57 16N 62 0E
Bulandshahr **94** 28 28N 77 58E
Bulanovo **84** 52 27N 55 10E
Bulantai **99** 36 33N 92 18E
Bŭlâq **122** 25 10N 30 38E
Bulawayo **127** 20 7S 28 32E
Buldana **96** 20 30N 76 18E
Buldir I. **147** 52 20N 175 55E
Bulford **28** 51 11N 1 45W
Bulgan **105** 48 45N 103 34E
Bulgaria ■ **67** 42 35N 25 30E
Bulgroo **138** 25 47S 143 58E
Bulgunnia **139** 30 10S 134 53E
Bulhar **91** 10 25N 44 30E
Buli, Teluk **103** 1 5N 128 25E
Buliluyan, C. **102** 8 20N 117 15E
Bulki **123** 6 11N 36 31E
Bulkington **163** 52 29N 1 25W
Bulkley, R. **152** 55 15N 127 40W
Bulkur **77** 71 50N 126 30E
Bull Shoals L. **159** 36 40N 93 5W
Bullabulling **137** 31 1S 120 32E
Bullange **47** 50 24N 6 15E
Bullaque, R. **57** 39 20N 4 13W
Bullara **136** 22 40S 114 3E
Bullaring **137** 32 30S 117 45E
Bullas **59** 38 2N 1 40W
Bulle **50** 46 37N 7 3E
Buller Gorge **143** 41 40S 172 10E
Buller, Mt. **141** 37 10S 146 28E
Buller, R. **143** 41 44S 171 36E
Bullfinch **137** 30 58S 119 3E
Bulli **141** 34 15S 150 57E
Bullock Cr. **138** 17 51S 143 45E
Bulloo Downs, Queens., Austral. **139** 28 31S 142 57E
Bulloo Downs, W.A., Austral. **137** 24 0S 119 32E
Bulloo L. **139** 28 43S 142 25E
Bulloo, R. **139** 28 43S 142 30E
Bulls **142** 40 10S 175 24E
Bully-les-Mines **43** 50 27N 2 44E
Bulnes **172** 36 42S 72 19W
Bulo Burti **91** 3 50N 45 33E
Bulolo **135** 7 10S 146 40E
Bulpunga **140** 33 47S 141 45E
Bulqiza **68** 40 30N 20 21E
Bulsar **96** 20 40N 72 58E
Bultfontein **128** 28 18S 26 10E
Bulu Karakelong **103** 4 35N 126 50E
Buluan **103** 9 0N 125 30E
Bŭlŭciţa **70** 44 23N 23 8E
Bulukumba **103** 5 33S 120 11E
Bulun **77** 70 37N 127 30E
Bulwell **33** 53 1N 1 12W
Bumba **124** 2 13N 22 30E
Bumbiri I. **126** 1 40S 31 55E
Bumble Bee **161** 34 8N 112 18W
Bumbum **121** 14 10N 8 10E
Bumhkang **98** 26 51N 97 40E
Bumhpa Bum **98** 26 51N 97 14E
Bumi, R. **127** 17 30S 28 30E
Bumtang, R. **98** 26 56N 90 53E
Buna, Kenya **124** 2 58N 39 30E
Buna, P.N.G. **135** 8 42S 148 27E
Bunaiyin **92** 23 10N 51 8E
Bunaw **39** 51 47N 9 50W
Bunazi **126** 1 3S 31 23E
Bunbeg **38** 55 4N 8 18W
Bunbury **132** 33 20S 115 35E
Bunclody **39** 52 40N 6 40W
Buncrana **38** 55 8N 7 28W
Bundaberg **139** 24 54S 152 22E
Bünde **48** 52 11N 8 33E
Bundey, R. **138** 21 46S 135 37E
Bundi **94** 25 30N 75 35E
Bundooma **138** 24 54S 134 16E
Bundoran **38** 54 24N 8 17W
Bundukia **123** 5 14N 30 55E
Bundure **141** 35 10S 146 1E
Bŭneasa **70** 45 56N 27 55E
Bunessan **34** 56 18N 6 15W
Bung Kan **100** 18 23N 103 37E
Bungay **29** 52 27N 1 26E
Bungendore **141** 35 14S 149 30E
Bungil Cr. **138** 27 5S 149 5E
Bungō-Suidō **110** 33 0N 132 15E
Bungoma **126** 0 34N 34 34E
Bungotakada **110** 33 35N 131 25E
Bungu **126** 7 35S 39 0E
Bunguran N. Is. **102** 4 45N 108 0E
Bunia **126** 1 35N 30 20E
Bunji **95** 35 45N 74 40E
Bunju **102** 3 35N 117 50E
Bunker Hill **163** 39 15N 117 8W
Bunkerville **161** 36 47N 114 6W
Bunkie **159** 31 1N 92 12W
Bunmahon **39** 52 8N 7 22W
Bunnanaddan **38** 54 3N 8 35W
Bunnell **157** 29 28N 81 12W
Bunnik **46** 52 4N 5 12E
Bunnyconnellan **38** 54 7N 9 1W
Bunnythorpe **142** 40 16S 175 39E
Buñol **59** 39 25N 0 47W
Bunsbeek **47** 50 50N 4 56E
Bunschoten **46** 52 14N 5 22E
Buntingford **29** 51 57N 0 1W
Buntok **102** 1 40S 114 58E
Bununu **121** 9 51N 9 32E
Bununu Doss **121** 10 6N 9 25E
Bunwell **29** 52 30N 1 9E
Bunyoro □ = Western □ **126** 1 45N 31 30E
Bunza **121** 12 8N 4 0E
Búoareyri **74** 65 2N 14 13W
Buol **103** 1 15N 121 32E
Buon Brieng **100** 13 9N 108 12E
Buong Long **100** 13 44N 106 59E
Buorkhaya, Mys **77** 71 50N 133 10E
Buqbuq **122** 31 29N 25 29E
Buqei'a **90** 32 58N 35 20E
Bur Acaba **91** 3 12N 44 20E
Bûr Fuad **122** 31 15N 32 20E
Bûr Safâga **122** 26 43N 33 57E
Bûr Sa'îd **122** 31 16N 32 18E
Bûr Sûdân **122** 19 32N 37 9E
Bûr Taufiq **122** 29 54N 32 32E
Bura **126** 1 4S 39 58E

Buraidah Caithness, Ord of, C

Buraidah	92	26 20N	44 8 E
Buraimī, Al Wāhāt al	93	24 15N	55 43 E
Burak Sulayman	90	31 42N	35 7 E
Burama	91	9 55N	43 7 E
Burao	91	9 32N	45 32 E
Buras	159	29 20N	89 33W
Burayevo	84	55 50N	55 24 E
Burbage, Derby, U.K.	32	53 15N	1 55W
Burbage, Leics., U.K.	28	52 31N	1 20W
Burbage, Wilts., U.K.	28	51 21N	1 40W
Burbank	163	34 9N	118 23W
Burcher	141	33 30S	147 16 E
Burdekin, R.	138	19 38S	147 25 E
Burdett	152	49 50N	111 32W
Burdur	92	37 45N	30 22 E
Burdwan	95	23 16N	87 54 E
Bure	123	10 40N	37 4 E
Bure, R.	29	52 38N	1 45 E
Bureba, La	58	42 36N	3 24W
Buren	46	51 55N	5 20 E
Burfell	74	64 5N	20 56W
Burford	28	51 48N	1 38W
Burg, Magdeburg, Ger.	48	52 16N	11 50 E
Burg, Schleswig-Holstein, Ger.	48	54 25N	11 10 E
Burg el Arab	122	30 54N	29 32 E
Burg et Tuyur	122	20 55N	27 56 E
Burgan	92	29 0N	47 57 E
Burgas	67	42 33N	27 29 E
Burgaski Zaliv	67	42 30N	27 39 E
Burgdorf, Ger.	48	52 27N	10 0 E
Burgdorf, Switz.	50	47 3N	7 37 E
Burgenland □	53	47 20N	16 20 E
Burgeo	151	47 37N	57 38W
Burgersdorp	128	31 0S	26 20 E
Burges, Mt.	137	30 50S	121 5 E
Burgess	162	37 53N	76 21W
Burgess Hill	29	50 57N	0 7W
Burgh-le-Marsh	33	53 10N	0 15 E
Burghclere	28	51 19N	1 20W
Burghead	37	57 42N	3 30W
Burghead B.	37	57 40N	3 33W
Búrgio	64	37 35N	13 18 E
Bürglen	51	46 53N	8 40 E
Burglengenfeld	49	49 11N	12 2 E
Burgo de Osma	58	41 35N	3 4W
Burgohondo	56	40 26N	4 47W
Burgos	58	42 21N	3 41W
Burgos □	58	42 21N	3 42W
Burgstädt	48	50 55N	12 49 E
Burgsteinfurt	48	52 9N	7 23 E
Burgsvik	73	57 3N	18 19 E
Burguillos del Cerro	57	38 23N	6 35W
Burgundy = Bourgogne	43	47 0N	4 30 E
Burhanpur	96	21 18N	76 20 E
Burhou Rocks	42	49 45N	2 15W
Buri Pen.	123	15 25N	39 55 E
Burias, I.	103	12 55N	123 5 E
Buribay	84	51 57N	58 10 E
Burica, Punta	166	8 3N	82 51W
Burigi, L.	126	2 2S	31 22 E
Burin, Can.	151	47 1N	55 14W
Burin, Jordan	90	32 11N	35 15 E
Buriram	100	15 0N	103 0 E
Buriti Alegre	171	18 9S	49 3W
Buriti Bravo	170	5 50S	43 50W
Buriti dos Lopes	170	3 10S	41 52W
Burji	123	5 29N	37 51 E
Burkburnett	159	34 7N	98 35W
Burke	160	47 31N	115 56W
Burke, R.	138	23 12S	139 33 E
Burketown	138	17 45S	139 33 E
Burk's Falls	150	45 37N	79 24W
Burley, Hants, U.K.	28	50 49N	1 41W
Burley, N. Yorks., U.K.	33	53 55N	1 46W
Burley, U.S.A.	160	42 37N	113 55W
Burlingame	163	37 35N	122 21W
Burlington, Colo., U.S.A.	158	39 21N	102 18W
Burlington, Iowa, U.S.A.	158	40 50N	91 5W
Burlington, Kans., U.S.A.	158	38 15N	95 47W
Burlington, N.C., U.S.A.	157	36 7N	79 27W
Burlington, N.J., U.S.A.	162	40 5N	74 50W
Burlington, Wash., U.S.A.	160	48 29N	122 19W
Burlington, Wis., U.S.A.	156	42 41N	88 18W
Burlyu-Tyube	76	46 30N	79 10 E
Burma ■	98	21 0N	96 30 E
Burnabbie	137	32 7S	126 21 E
Burnaby I.	152	52 25N	131 19W
Burnamwood	141	31 7S	144 53 E
Burnet	159	30 45N	98 11W
Burnett, R.	133	24 45S	152 23 E
Burney	160	40 56N	121 41W
Burnfoot	38	55 4N	7 15W
Burngup	137	33 2S	118 42 E
Burnham, Essex, U.K.	29	51 37N	0 50 E
Burnham, Somerset, U.K.	28	51 14N	3 0W
Burnham Market	29	52 57N	0 43 E
Burnie	138	41 4S	145 56 E
Burnley	32	53 47N	2 15W
Burnmouth	35	55 50N	2 4W
Burnoye	85	42 36N	70 47 E
Burns, Oreg., U.S.A.	160	43 40N	119 4W
Burns, Wyo., U.S.A.	158	41 13N	104 18W
Burns Lake	152	54 20N	125 45W
Burnside, L.	137	25 25S	123 0 E
Burnt Paw	147	67 2N	142 43W
Burntisland	35	56 4N	3 14W
Burntwood L.	153	55 22N	100 26W
Burntwood, R.	153	56 8N	96 34W
Burqa	90	32 18N	35 11 E
Burra	140	33 40S	138 55 E
Burragorang, L.	141	33 52S	150 37 E
Burramurra	138	20 25N	137 15 E
Burravoe	36	60 30N	1 3W
Burray I.	37	58 50N	2 54W
Burreli	68	41 36N	20 1 E
Burrelton	35	56 30N	3 16W
Burren	39	53 9N	9 5W
Burren Junction	139	30 7S	148 59 E
Burrendong Dam	139	32 39S	149 6 E
Burrendong Res.	141	32 45S	149 10 E
Burriana	58	39 50N	0 4W
Burrinjuck Res.	141	35 0S	148 36 E
Burro, Serranías del	164	29 0N	102 0W
Burrow Hd.	34	54 40N	4 23W
Burrundie	136	13 32S	131 42 E
Burruyacú	172	26 30S	64 40W
Burry Port	31	51 41N	4 17W
Bursa	92	40 15N	29 5 E
Burseryd	73	57 12N	13 17 E
Burstall	153	50 39N	109 54W
Burstwick	33	53 43N	0 6W
Burton	32	54 10N	2 43W
Burton Agnes	33	54 4N	0 18W
Burton Bradstock	28	50 41N	2 43W
Burton Fleming	33	54 8N	0 20W
Burton L.	150	54 45N	78 20W
Burton Latimer	29	52 23N	0 41W
Burton upon Stather	33	53 39N	0 41W
Burton-upon-Trent	28	52 48N	1 39W
Burtonport	38	54 59N	8 26W
Burtundy	140	33 45S	142 15 E
Burtville	137	28 42S	122 33 E
Buru, I.	103	3 30S	126 30 E
Burufu	120	10 25N	2 50W
Burujird	92	33 58N	48 41 E
Burullus, Bahra el	122	31 25N	31 0 E
Burunday	85	43 20N	76 51 E
Burundi ■	126	3 15S	30 0 E
Burung	102	0 21N	108 25 E
Bururi	126	3 57S	29 37 E
Burutu	121	5 20N	5 29 E
Burwash	29	50 59N	0 24 E
Burwash Landing	147	61 21N	139 0W
Burwell, U.K.	29	52 17N	0 20 E
Burwell, U.S.A.	158	41 49N	99 8W
Bury	32	53 36N	2 19W
Bury St. Edmunds	29	52 15N	0 42 E
Buryat A.S.S.R. □	77	53 0N	110 0 E
Burzenin	54	51 28N	18 47 E
Busalla	62	44 34N	8 58 E
Busango Swamp	127	14 15S	25 45 E
Busayyah	92	30 0N	46 10 E
Busby	152	53 55N	114 0W
Bushati	68	41 58N	19 34 E
Bushell	153	59 31N	108 45W
Bushenyi	126	0 35S	30 10 E
Bushey	29	51 38N	0 20W
Bushman Land	128	29 30S	19 30 E
Bushmills	38	55 14N	6 32W
Bushnell, Ill., U.S.A.	158	40 32N	90 30W
Bushnell, Nebr., U.S.A.	158	41 18N	103 50W
Busia □	126	0 25N	34 6 E
Busie	120	10 29N	2 22W
Businga	124	3 16N	20 59 E
Buskerud fylke □	75	60 13N	9 0 E
Busko Zdrój	54	50 28N	20 42 E
Busovača	66	44 6N	17 53 E
Busra	92	32 30N	36 25 E
Bussa	121	10 11N	4 32 E
Bussang	43	47 50N	6 50 E
Busselton	137	33 42S	115 15 E
Bussigny	50	46 33N	6 33 E
Bussum	46	52 16N	5 10 E
Bustard Hd.	133	24 0S	151 48 E
Busto Arsizio	62	45 40N	8 50 E
Busto, C.	56	43 34N	6 28W
Busu-Djanoa	124	1 50N	21 5 E
Busuangal, I.	103	12 10N	120 0 E
Büsum	48	54 7N	8 50 E
Buta	126	2 50N	24 53 E
Butare	126	2 31S	29 52 E
Bute	140	33 51S	138 2 E
Bute (□)	26	55 40N	5 10W
Bute, I.	34	55 48N	5 2W
Bute Inlet	152	50 40N	124 53W
Bute, Kyles of	34	55 55N	5 10W
Bute, Sd. of	34	55 43N	5 8W
Butemba	126	1 9N	31 37 E
Butembo	126	0 9N	29 18 E
Butera	65	37 10N	14 10 E
Bütgenbach	47	50 26N	6 12 E
Buthidaung	98	20 52N	92 32 E
Butiaba	126	1 50N	31 20 E
Butler	158	38 17N	94 18W
Bütschwil	51	47 23N	9 5 E
Butte, Mont., U.S.A.	160	46 0N	112 31W
Butte, Nebr., U.S.A.	158	42 56N	98 54W
Butterfield, Mt.	137	24 45S	128 7 E
Buttermere	32	54 32N	3 17W
Butterworth	101	5 24N	100 23 E
Buttevant	39	52 14N	8 40 E
Buttfield, Mt.	137	24 45S	128 9 E
Button B.	153	58 45N	94 23W
Buttonwillow	163	35 24N	119 28W
Butty Hd.	137	33 54S	121 39 E
Butuan	103	8 57N	125 33 E
Butuku-Luba	121	3 29N	8 33 E
Butung, I.	103	5 0S	122 45 E
Buturlinovka	81	50 50N	40 35 E
Butzbach	48	50 24N	8 40 E
Buxar	95	25 34N	83 58 E
Buxton, S. Afr.	128	27 38S	24 42 E
Buxton, U.K.	32	53 16N	1 54W
Buxy	43	46 44N	4 40 E
Buyaga	77	59 50N	127 0 E
Buynaksk	83	42 36N	47 42 E
Buyr Nuur	105	47 50N	117 42 E
Büyük çekmece	67	41 2N	28 35 E
Büyük Kemikli Burun	68	40 20N	26 15 E
Büyük Menderes, R.	79	37 45N	27 40 E
Buzançais	42	46 54N	1 25 E
Buzau, Pasul	70	45 35N	26 12 E
Buzaymah	117	24 35N	22 0 E
Buzen	110	33 35N	131 5 E
Buzet	63	45 24N	13 58 E
Buzi, R.	127	19 52S	34 30 E
Buziaş	66	45 38N	21 36 E
Buzuluk	84	52 48N	52 12 E
Buzuluk, R.	81	50 50N	52 12 E
Buzău	70	45 10N	26 50 E
Buzău □	70	45 20N	26 30 E
Buzău, R.	70	45 10N	27 20 E
Buzzards Bay	162	41 45N	70 38W
Bwagaoia	135	10 40S	152 52 E
Bwana Mkubwe	127	13 8S	28 38 E
Byala, Ruse, Bulg.	67	43 28N	25 44 E
Byala, Varna, Bulg.	67	42 53N	27 55 E
Byala Slatina	67	43 26N	23 55 E
Byandovan, Mys	83	39 45N	49 28 E
Bychawa	54	51 1N	22 36 E
Byczyha	54	51 7N	18 12 E
Bydgoszcz	54	53 10N	18 0 E
Bydgoszcz □	54	53 16N	17 33 E
Byelorussian S.S.R. □	80	53 30N	27 0 E
Byers	158	39 46N	104 13W
Byfield	28	52 10N	1 15W
Bygland	71	58 50N	7 48 E
Byglandsfjord	71	58 40N	7 50 E
Byglandsfjorden	71	58 44N	7 50 E
Byhalia	159	34 53N	89 41W
Bykhov	80	53 31N	30 14 E
Bykle	71	59 20N	7 22 E
Bykovo	83	49 50N	45 25 E
Bylas	161	33 11N	110 9W
Bylchau	31	53 9N	3 32W
Bylderup	73	54 57N	9 6 E
Bylot I.	149	73 13N	78 34W
Byrd Land = Marie Byrd Land	13	79 30S	125 0W
Byrd Sub-Glacial Basin	13	82 0S	120 0W
Byro	137	26 5S	116 11 E
Byrock	141	30 40S	146 27 E
Byron B.	151	54 42N	57 40W
Byron, C.	133	28 38S	153 40W
Byrranga, Gory	77	75 0N	100 0 E
Byrum	73	57 16N	11 0 E
Byske	74	64 57N	21 11 E
Byske, R.	74	65 20N	20 0 E
Bystrovka	85	42 47N	75 42 E
Bystrzyca Kłodzka	54	50 19N	16 39 E
Byten	80	52 50N	25 27 E
Bytom	54	50 25N	19 0 E
Bytom Ordz.	54	51 44N	15 48 E
Bytów	54	54 10N	17 30 E
Byumba	126	1 35S	30 4 E
Byvalla	72	61 22N	16 27 E
Bzéma	117	24 50N	22 20 E
Bzenec	53	48 58N	17 18 E

C

Ca Mau = Quan Long	101	9 7N	105 8 E
Ca Mau, Mui = Bai Bung	101	8 35N	104 42 E
Ca Na	101	11 20N	108 54 E
Ca, R.	100	18 45N	105 45 E
Caacupé	172	25 23N	57 5W
Caamano Sd.	152	52 55N	129 25W
Caatingas	170	7 0S	52 30W
Caazapá	172	26 8S	56 19W
Caazapá □	173	26 10S	56 0W
Caballería, Cabo de	58	40 5N	4 5 E
Cabañaquinta	56	43 10N	5 38W
Cabanatuan	103	15 30N	121 5 E
Cabanes	58	40 9N	0 2 E
Cabano	151	47 40N	68 56 E
Cabazon	163	33 55N	116 47W
Cabbage Tree Hd.	108	27 20S	153 5 E
Cabedelo	170	7 0S	34 50W
Cabeza del Buey	57	38 44N	5 13W
Cabildo	172	32 30S	71 5W
Cabimas	174	10 30N	71 25W
Cabinda	124	5 40S	12 11 E
Cabinda □	124	5 0S	12 30 E
Cabinet Mts.	160	48 0N	115 30W
Cables	137	27 55S	123 25 E
Cableskill	162	42 39N	74 30W
Cabo Blanco	176	47 56S	65 47W
Cabo Delgado □	127	10 35S	40 35 E
Cabo Frio	173	22 51S	42 3W
Cabo Pantoja	174	1 0S	75 10W
Cabonga Reservoir	150	47 20N	76 40W
Cabool	159	37 10N	92 8W
Caboolture	139	27 5S	152 58 E
Cabora Bassa Dam	127	15 20S	32 50 E
Caborca (Heroica)	164	30 40N	112 10W
Cabot Strait	151	47 15N	59 40W
Cabra	57	37 30N	4 28W
Cabra del Santo Cristo	59	37 42N	3 16W
Cabrach	37	57 20N	3 0W
Cabras	64	39 57N	8 30 E
Cabrera, I.	59	39 6N	2 59 E
Cabrera, Sierra	56	42 12N	6 40W
Cabri	153	50 35N	108 25W
Cabriel, R.	59	39 20N	1 20W
Cabruta	174	7 50N	66 10W
Caburan	103	6 3N	125 45 E
Cabuyaro	174	4 18N	72 49W
Cacabelos	56	42 36N	6 44W
Čačak	66	43 54N	20 20 E
Cáceres, Brazil	174	16 5S	57 40W
Cáceres, Colomb.	174	7 35N	75 20W
Cáceres, Spain	57	39 26N	6 23W
Cáceres □	57	39 45N	6 0W
Cache B.	150	46 26N	80 1W
Cache Bay	150	46 22N	80 0W
Cachepo	57	37 20N	7 49W
Cacheu	120	12 14N	16 8W
Cachi	172	25 5S	66 10W
Cachimbo, Serra do	175	9 30S	55 0W
Cáchira	174	7 21N	73 17W
Cachoeira	171	12 30S	39 0W
Cachoeira Alta	171	18 48S	50 58W
Cachoeira de Itapemirim	173	20 51S	41 7W
Cachoeira do Sul	173	30 3S	52 53W
Cachoeiro do Arari	170	1 1S	48 58W
Cachopo	57	37 20N	7 49W
Cacolo	124	10 9S	19 21 E
Caconda	125	13 48S	15 8 E
Caçu	171	18 37S	51 4W
Caculé	171	14 30S	42 13W
Cadamstown	39	53 7N	7 39W
Cadarga	139	26 8S	150 58 E
Cadaux	137	30 48S	117 15 E
Čadca	53	49 26N	18 45 E
Caddo	159	34 8N	96 18W
Cadenazzo	51	46 9N	8 57 E
Cader Idris	31	52 43N	3 56W
Cadereyta Jiménez	165	25 40N	100 0W
Cadí, Sierra del	58	42 17N	1 42 E
Cadibarrawirracanna, L.	139	28 52S	135 27 E
Cadillac, Can.	150	48 14N	78 23W
Cadillac, France	44	44 38N	0 20W
Cadillac, U.S.A.	156	44 16N	85 25W
Cadiz	103	11 30N	123 15 E
Cádiz	57	36 30N	6 20W
Cádiz □	57	36 36N	5 45W
Cádiz, G. de	57	36 40N	7 0W
Cadomin	152	53 2N	117 20W
Cadotte, R.	152	56 43N	117 10W
Cadours	44	43 44N	1 2 E
Cadoux	137	30 46S	117 7 E
Caen	42	49 10N	0 22W
Caenby Corner	33	53 23N	0 32W
Caergwrle	29	53 6N	3 3W
Caerhun	31	53 14N	3 50W
Caerleon	31	51 37N	2 57W
Caernarfon	31	53 8N	4 17W
Caernarfon B.	31	53 4N	4 40W
Caernarvon = Caernarfon	31	53 8N	4 17W
Caernarvon (□)	26	53 8N	4 17W
Caerphilly	31	51 34N	3 13W
Caersws	31	52 32N	3 27W
Caerwent	31	51 37N	2 47W
Cæsarea = Qesari	90	32 30N	34 53 E
Caeté	171	20 0S	43 40W
Caetité	171	13 50S	42 50W
Cafayate	172	26 2S	66 0W
Cafu	128	16 30S	15 8 E
Cagayan de Oro	103	8 30N	124 40 E
Cagayan, R.	103	18 25N	121 42 E
Cagli	63	43 32N	12 38 E
Cágliari	64	39 15N	9 6 E
Cágliari, G. di	64	39 8N	9 10 E
Cagnano Varano	65	41 49N	15 47 E
Cagnes-sur-Mer	45	43 40N	7 9 E
Caguas	147	18 14N	66 4W
Caha Mts.	39	51 45N	9 40W
Caher I.	38	53 44N	10 1W
Caherconlish	39	52 36N	8 30W
Cahermore	39	51 35N	10 2W
Cahir	39	52 23N	7 56W
Cahirciveen	39	51 57N	10 13W
Cahore Pt.	39	52 34N	6 11W
Cahors	44	44 27N	1 27 E
Cahuapanas	174	5 15S	77 0W
Cai Ban, Dao	100	21 10N	107 27 E
Cai Nuoc	101	8 56N	105 1 E
Caianda	127	11 29S	23 31 E
Caibarién	166	22 30N	79 30W
Caicara	174	7 38N	66 10W
Caicó	170	6 20S	37 0W
Caicos Is.	167	21 40N	71 40W
Caicos Passage	167	22 45N	72 45W
Caihaique	176	45 30S	71 45W
Caird Coast	13	75 0S	25 0W
Cairn Gorm	37	57 7N	3 40W
Cairn Table	35	55 30N	4 0W
Cairngorm Mts.	37	57 6N	3 42W
Cairnryan	34	54 59N	5 0W
Cairns	138	16 57S	145 45 E
Cairo, Ga., U.S.A.	157	30 52N	84 12W
Cairo, Illinois, U.S.A.	159	37 0N	89 10W
Cairo, N.Y., U.S.A.	162	42 18N	74 0W
Cairo = El Qâhira	122	30 1N	31 14 E
Cairo Montenotte	62	44 23N	8 16 E
Caister-on-Sea	29	52 38N	1 43 E
Caistor	33	53 29N	0 20W
Caithness (□)	26	58 25N	3 25W
Caithness, Ord of, C.	37	58 35N	3 37W

Caiundo Canton

Caiundo	**125**	15 50 S	17 52 E
Caiza	**174**	20 2 S	65 40 W
Cajamarca	**174**	7 5 S	78 28 W
Cajapió	**170**	2 58 S	44 48 W
Cajarc	**44**	44 29 N	1 50 E
Çajàzeiros	**170**	7 0 S	38 30 W
Çajetina	**66**	43 47 N	19 42 E
Čajniče	**66**	43 34 N	19 5 E
Çakirgöl	**83**	40 33 N	39 40 E
Cala	**57**	37 59 N	6 21 W
Cala Cadolar	**59**	38 38 N	1 35 E
Cala, R.	**57**	37 50 N	6 8 W
Calabar	**121**	4 57 N	8 20 E
Calabozo	**174**	9 0 N	67 20 W
Calábria □	**65**	39 24 N	16 30 E
Calaburras, Pta. de	**57**	36 30 N	4 38 W
Calaceite	**58**	41 1 N	0 11 E
Calafat	**70**	43 58 N	22 59 E
Calafate	**176**	50 25 S	72 25 W
Calahorra	**58**	42 18 N	1 59 W
Calais, France	**43**	50 57 N	1 56 E
Calais, U.S.A.	**151**	45 5 N	67 20 W
Calais, Pas de	**160**	50 57 N	1 20 E
Calalaste, Sierra de	**172**	25 0 S	67 0 W
Calama, Brazil	**174**	8 0 S	62 50 W
Calama, Chile	**172**	22 30 S	68 55 W
Calamar, Bolívar, Colomb.	**174**	10 15 N	74 55 W
Calamar, Vaupés, Colomb.	**174**	1 58 N	72 32 W
Calamian Group	**103**	11 50 N	119 55 E
Calamocha	**58**	40 50 N	1 17 W
Calanaque	**174**	0 5 S	64 0 W
Calañas	**57**	37 40 N	6 53 W
Calanda	**58**	40 56 N	0 15 W
Calang	**102**	4 30 N	95 43 E
Calangiánus	**64**	40 56 N	9 12 E
Calapan	**103**	13 25 N	121 7 E
Calasparra	**59**	38 14 N	1 41 W
Calatafimi	**64**	37 56 N	12 50 E
Calatayud	**58**	41 20 N	1 40 W
Calauag	**103**	13 55 N	122 15 E
Calavà, C.	**65**	38 11 N	14 55 E
Calavite, Cape	**103**	13 26 N	120 10 E
Calbe	**48**	51 57 N	11 47 E
Calca	**174**	13 10 S	72 0 W
Calci	**62**	43 44 N	10 31 E
Calcidica = Khalkidhikí □	**170**	40 25 N	23 40 E
Calcutta	**95**	22 36 N	88 24 E
Caldaro	**63**	46 23 N	11 15 E
Caldas □	**174**	5 15 N	75 30 W
Caldas da Rainha	**57**	39 24 N	9 8 W
Caldas de Reyes	**56**	42 36 N	8 39 W
Caldas Novas	**171**	17 45 S	48 38 W
Caldbeck	**32**	54 45 N	3 3 W
Calder Bridge	**32**	54 27 N	3 31 W
Calder Hall	**32**	54 26 N	3 31 W
Calder, R.	**33**	53 44 N	1 21 W
Caldera	**172**	27 5 S	70 55 W
Caldew R.	**32**	54 54 N	2 59 W
Caldiran	**92**	39 7 N	44 0 E
Caldwell, Idaho, U.S.A.	**160**	43 45 N	116 42 W
Caldwell, Kans., U.S.A.	**159**	37 5 N	97 37 W
Caldwell, Texas, U.S.A.	**159**	30 30 N	96 42 W
Caldy I.	**31**	51 38 N	4 42 W
Caledon, S. Afr.	**128**	34 14 S	19 26 E
Caledon, U.K.	**38**	54 22 N	6 50 W
Caledon B.	**138**	12 45 S	137 0 E
Caledon, R.	**128**	30 0 S	26 46 E
Caledonian Can.	**37**	56 50 N	5 6 W
Calella	**58**	41 37 N	2 40 E
Calemba	**128**	16 0 S	15 38 E
Calera, La	**172**	32 50 S	71 10 W
Calexico	**161**	32 40 N	115 33 W
Calf of Man	**32**	54 4 N	4 48 W
Calgary, Can.	**152**	51 0 N	114 10 W
Calgary, U.K.	**34**	56 34 N	6 17 W
Calhoun	**157**	34 30 N	84 55 W
Cali	**174**	3 25 N	76 35 W
Caliach Pt.	**34**	56 37 N	6 20 W
Calicoan, I.	**103**	10 59 N	125 50 E
Calicut	**93**	11 15 N	75 43 E
Calicut, (Kozhikode)	**97**	11 15 N	75 43 E
Caliente	**161**	37 43 N	114 34 W
California	**158**	38 37 N	92 30 W
California □	**160**	37 25 N	120 0 W
California, Baja	**164**	32 10 N	115 12 W
California, Baja, T.N. □	**164**	30 0 N	115 0 W
California, Baja, T.S. □	**164**	25 50 N	111 50 W
California City	**163**	35 7 N	117 57 W
California, Golfo de	**164**	27 0 N	111 0 W
California Hot Springs	**163**	35 51 N	118 41 W
California, Lr. = California, Baja	**164**	25 50 N	111 50 W
Calilegua	**172**	23 45 S	64 42 W
Călimănești	**70**	45 14 N	24 20 E
Calingasta	**172**	31 15 S	69 30 W
Calipatria	**161**	33 8 N	115 30 W
Calistoga	**160**	38 36 N	122 32 W
Calitri	**65**	40 54 N	15 25 E
Calkiní	**165**	20 21 N	90 3 W
Callabonna, L.	**139**	29 40 S	140 5 E
Callac	**42**	48 25 N	3 27 W
Callafo	**91**	6 48 N	43 47 E
Callan	**39**	52 33 N	7 25 W
Callanish	**36**	58 12 N	6 43 W
Callantsoog	**46**	52 50 N	4 42 E
Callao	**174**	12 0 S	77 0 W
Callaway	**158**	41 20 N	99 56 W
Calles	**165**	23 2 N	98 42 W
Callicoon	**162**	41 46 N	75 3 W
Callide	**138**	24 18 S	150 28 E
Calling Lake	**152**	55 15 N	113 12 W
Callington	**30**	50 30 N	4 19 W
Calliope	**138**	24 0 S	151 16 E
Callosa de Ensarriá.	**59**	38 40 N	0 8 W
Callosa de Segura	**59**	38 1 N	0 53 W
Callow	**38**	53 58 N	9 2 W
Calne	**28**	51 26 N	2 0 W
Calola	**128**	16 25 S	17 48 E
Calore, R.	**65**	41 8 N	14 45 E
Caloundra	**139**	26 45 S	153 10 E
Calpe	**59**	38 39 N	0 3 E
Calshot	**28**	50 49 N	1 18 W
Calstock, Can.	**150**	49 47 N	84 9 W
Calstock, U.K.	**30**	50 30 N	4 13 W
Caltabellotta	**64**	37 36 N	13 11 E
Caltagirone	**65**	37 13 N	14 30 E
Caltanissetta	**65**	37 30 N	14 3 E
Caluire-et-Cuire	**45**	45 49 N	4 51 E
Calulo	**124**	10 1 S	14 56 E
Calumbo	**124**	9 0 S	13 20 E
Caluso	**62**	45 18 N	7 52 E
Calvados □	**42**	49 5 N	0 15 W
Calvert	**159**	30 59 N	96 50 W
Calvert Hills	**138**	17 15 S	137 20 E
Calvert I.	**152**	51 30 N	128 0 W
Calvert, R.	**138**	16 17 S	137 44 E
Calvert Ra.	**136**	24 0 S	122 30 E
Calvillo	**164**	21 51 N	102 43 W
Calvinia	**128**	31 28 S	19 45 E
Calwa	**163**	36 42 N	119 46 W
Calzada Almuradiel	**59**	38 32 N	3 28 W
Calzada de Calatrava	**57**	38 42 N	3 46 W
Cam Lam	**101**	11 54 N	109 10 E
Cam Pha	**100**	21 1 N	107 18 E
Cam, R.	**29**	52 21 N	0 16 E
Cam Ranh	**101**	11 54 N	109 12 E
Cam Xuyen	**100**	18 15 N	106 0 E
Camabatela	**124**	8 20 S	15 26 E
Camacã	**171**	15 24 S	39 30 W
Camaçari	**171**	12 41 S	38 18 W
Camacho	**164**	24 25 N	102 18 W
Camaguán	**174**	8 6 N	67 36 W
Camagüey	**166**	21 20 N	78 0 W
Camaiore	**62**	43 57 N	10 18 E
Camamu	**171**	13 57 S	39 7 W
Camaná	**174**	16 30 S	72 50 W
Camaquã, R.	**173**	30 50 S	52 50 W
Camaret	**42**	48 16 N	4 37 W
Camargo	**174**	20 38 S	65 15 E
Camargue	**45**	43 34 N	4 34 E
Camarillo	**163**	34 13 N	119 2 W
Camariñas	**56**	43 8 N	9 12 W
Camarón, C.	**166**	16 0 N	85 0 W
Camarones, Argent.	**176**	44 50 S	65 40 W
Camarones, Chile	**174**	19 0 S	69 58 W
Camas	**160**	45 35 N	122 24 W
Camas Valley	**160**	43 0 N	123 46 W
Cambados	**56**	42 31 N	8 49 W
Cambará	**173**	23 2 S	50 5 W
Cambay	**94**	22 23 N	72 33 E
Cambay, G. of	**94**	20 45 N	72 30 E
Camberley	**29**	51 20 N	0 44 W
Cambil	**59**	37 40 N	3 33 W
Cambo	**35**	55 9 N	1 57 W
Cambo-les-Bains	**44**	43 22 N	1 23 W
Cambodia ■	**100**	12 15 N	105 0 E
Camborne	**30**	50 13 N	5 18 W
Cambrai	**43**	50 11 N	3 14 E
Cambria	**163**	35 44 N	121 6 W
Cambrian Mts.	**31**	52 25 N	3 52 W
Cambridge, Can.	**150**	43 23 N	80 15 W
Cambridge, Jamaica	**166**	18 18 N	77 54 W
Cambridge, N.Z.	**142**	37 54 S	175 29 E
Cambridge, U.K.	**29**	52 13 N	0 8 E
Cambridge, Idaho, U.S.A.	**160**	44 36 N	116 52 W
Cambridge, Mass., U.S.A.	**162**	42 20 N	71 8 W
Cambridge, Md., U.S.A.	**162**	38 33 N	76 2 W
Cambridge, Minn., U.S.A.	**158**	45 34 N	93 15 W
Cambridge, Nebr., U.S.A.	**158**	40 20 N	100 12 W
Cambridge, N.Y., U.S.A.	**162**	43 2 N	73 22 W
Cambridge, Ohio, U.S.A.	**156**	40 1 N	81 22 W
Cambridge Bay	**148**	69 10 N	105 0 W
Cambridge Gulf	**136**	14 45 S	128 0 E
Cambridgeshire □	**29**	52 12 N	0 7 E
Cambrils	**58**	41 8 N	1 3 E
Cambuci	**173**	21 35 S	41 55 W
Camden, Austral.	**141**	34 1 S	150 43 E
Camden, U.K.	**29**	51 33 N	0 10 W
Camden, Ala., U.S.A.	**157**	31 59 N	87 15 W
Camden, Ark., U.S.A.	**159**	33 30 N	92 50 W
Camden, Del., U.S.A.	**162**	39 7 N	75 33 W
Camden, Me., U.S.A.	**151**	44 14 N	69 6 W
Camden, N.J., U.S.A.	**162**	39 57 N	75 1 W
Camden, N.Y., U.S.A.	**162**	43 20 N	75 45 W
Camden, S.C., U.S.A.	**157**	34 17 N	80 34 W
Camden, B.	**147**	71 0 N	145 0 W
Camden Sound	**136**	15 27 S	124 25 E
Camel R.	**30**	50 28 N	4 49 W
Camelford	**30**	50 37 N	4 41 W
Camembert	**42**	48 53 N	0 10 E
Cámeri	**62**	45 30 N	8 40 E
Camerino	**63**	43 10 N	13 4 E
Cameron, Ariz., U.S.A.	**161**	35 55 N	111 31 W
Cameron, La., U.S.A.	**159**	29 50 N	93 18 W
Cameron, Mo., U.S.A.	**158**	39 42 N	94 14 W
Cameron, Tex., U.S.A.	**159**	30 53 N	97 0 W
Cameron Falls	**150**	49 8 N	88 19 W
Cameron Highlands	**101**	4 27 N	101 22 E
Cameron Hills	**152**	59 48 N	118 0 W
Cameron Mts.	**143**	46 1 S	167 0 E
Cameroon ■	**124**	3 30 N	12 30 E
Camerota	**65**	40 2 N	15 21 E
Cameroun, Mt.	**121**	4 45 N	8 55 E
Cameroun, R.	**121**	4 0 N	9 35 E
Camerton	**28**	51 18 N	2 27 W
Cametá	**170**	2 0 S	49 30 W
Caminha	**56**	41 50 N	8 50 W
Camino	**163**	38 47 N	120 40 W
Camira Creek	**139**	29 15 S	152 58 E
Camiranga	**170**	1 48 S	46 17 W
Cammachmore	**37**	57 2 N	2 9 W
Camocim	**170**	2 55 S	40 50 W
Camogli	**62**	44 21 N	9 9 E
Camolin	**39**	52 37 N	6 26 W
Camooweal	**138**	19 56 S	138 7 E
Camopi, R.	**175**	3 12 N	52 17 W
Camp Crook	**158**	45 36 N	103 59 W
Camp Hill	**162**	40 15 N	76 56 W
Camp Nelson	**163**	36 8 N	118 39 W
Camp Wood	**159**	29 47 N	100 0 W
Campagna	**65**	40 40 N	15 5 E
Campana	**172**	34 10 S	58 55 W
Campana, I.	**176**	48 20 S	75 10 W
Campanario	**57**	38 52 N	5 36 W
Campania □	**65**	40 50 N	14 45 E
Campbell	**163**	37 17 N	121 57 W
Campbell, C.	**143**	41 47 S	174 18 E
Campbell I.	**142**	52 30 S	169 0 E
Campbell L.	**153**	63 14 N	106 55 W
Campbell River	**152**	50 5 N	125 20 W
Campbell Town	**138**	41 52 S	147 30 E
Campbellpur	**94**	33 46 N	72 20 E
Campbellsville	**156**	37 23 N	85 12 W
Campbellton, Alta., Can.	**152**	53 32 N	113 15 W
Campbellton, N.B., Can.	**151**	47 57 N	66 43 W
Campbelltown, Austral.	**141**	34 4 S	150 49 E
Campbelltown, U.K.	**37**	57 34 N	4 2 W
Campbeltown	**34**	55 25 N	5 36 W
Campeche	**165**	19 50 N	90 32 W
Campeche □	**165**	19 50 N	90 32 W
Campeche, Golfo de	**165**	19 30 N	93 0 W
Camperdown	**140**	38 14 S	143 9 E
Camperville	**153**	51 59 N	100 9 W
Campi Salentina	**65**	40 22 N	18 2 E
Campidano	**64**	39 30 N	8 40 E
Campillo de Altobuey	**58**	39 36 N	1 49 W
Campillo de Llerena	**57**	38 30 N	5 50 W
Campillos	**57**	37 4 N	4 51 W
Campina Grande	**170**	7 20 S	35 47 W
Campiña, La	**57**	37 45 N	4 45 W
Campina Verde	**171**	19 31 S	49 28 W
Campinas	**173**	22 50 S	47 0 W
Campine	**47**	51 8 N	5 20 E
Campinho	**170**	14 30 S	39 10 W
Campli	**63**	42 44 N	13 40 E
Campo	**124**	2 15 N	9 58 E
Campo Beló	**171**	21 0 S	45 30 W
Campo de Criptana	**59**	39 25 N	3 7 W
Campo de Gibraltar	**57**	36 15 N	5 25 W
Campo Flórido	**171**	19 47 S	48 35 W
Campo Formoso	**170**	10 30 S	40 20 W
Campo Grande	**175**	20 25 S	54 40 W
Campo Maior, Brazil	**170**	4 50 S	42 12 W
Campo Maior, Port.	**57**	38 59 N	7 7 W
Campo Mourão	**171**	24 3 S	52 22 W
Campo Tencia	**51**	46 26 N	8 43 E
Campo Túres	**63**	46 53 N	11 55 E
Campoalegre	**174**	2 41 N	75 20 W
Campobasso	**65**	41 34 N	14 40 E
Campobello di Licata	**64**	37 16 N	13 55 E
Campobello di Mazara	**64**	37 38 N	12 45 E
Campofelice	**64**	37 54 N	13 53 E
Camporeale	**64**	37 53 N	13 3 E
Campos	**173**	21 50 S	41 20 W
Campos Altos	**171**	19 41 S	46 10 W
Campos Belos	**171**	13 10 S	46 45 W
Campos del Puerto	**59**	39 26 N	3 1 E
Campos Novos	**173**	27 21 S	51 20 W
Campos Sales	**170**	7 4 S	40 23 W
Camprodón	**58**	42 19 N	2 23 E
Campsie Fells	**23**	56 2 N	4 20 W
Camptown	**162**	41 44 N	76 14 W
Campuya, R.	**174**	1 10 S	74 0 W
Camrose, Can.	**152**	53 0 N	112 50 W
Camrose, U.K.	**31**	51 50 N	5 2 W
Camsall L.	**153**	72 32 N	106 47 W
Camsell Portage	**153**	59 37 N	109 15 W
Camurra	**139**	29 21 S	149 52 E
Can Gio	**101**	10 25 N	106 58 E
Can Tho	**101**	10 2 N	105 46 E
Canada ■	**148**	60 0 N	100 0 W
Cañada de Gómez	**73**	32 55 S	61 30 W
Canadian	**159**	35 56 N	100 25 W
Canadian, R.	**159**	36 0 N	98 45 W
Canairiktok, R.	**151**	54 30 N	62 30 W
Canajoharie	**162**	42 54 N	74 35 W
Çanakkale	**68**	40 8 N	26 30 E
Çanakkale Boğazi	**68**	40 0 N	26 0 E
Canal de l'Est	**43**	48 45 N	5 35 E
Canal Flats	**152**	50 10 N	115 48 W
Canal latéral à la Garonne	**44**	44 25 N	0 15 E
Canalejas	**172**	35 15 S	66 34 W
Canals	**172**	33 35 S	62 40 W
Canáls	**59**	38 58 N	0 35 W
Canandaigua	**156**	42 55 N	77 18 W
Cananea	**164**	31 0 N	110 20 W
Canarias, Islas	**116**	29 30 N	17 0 W
Canarreos, Arch. de los	**166**	21 35 N	81 40 W
Canary Is. = Canarias, Islas	**116**	29 30 N	17 0 W
Canastra, Serra da	**171**	20 0 S	46 20 W
Canatlán	**164**	24 31 N	104 47 W
Canaveral, C.	**157**	28 28 N	80 31 W
Cañaveras	**58**	40 27 N	2 14 W
Canavieiras	**171**	15 39 S	39 0 W
Canbelego	**141**	31 32 S	146 18 E
Canberra	**141**	35 15 S	149 8 E
Canby, Calif., U.S.A.	**160**	41 26 N	120 58 W
Canby, Minn., U.S.A.	**158**	44 44 N	96 15 W
Canby, Oregon, U.S.A.	**160**	45 24 N	122 45 W
Cancale	**42**	48 40 N	1 50 W
Candala	**91**	11 30 N	49 58 E
Candas	**56**	43 35 N	5 45 W
Candé	**42**	47 34 N	1 0 W
Candea = Iráklion	**69**	35 20 N	25 12 E
Candela	**65**	41 8 N	15 31 E
Candelaria	**173**	27 29 S	55 44 W
Candelaria, Pta. de la	**56**	43 45 N	8 0 W
Candeleda	**56**	40 10 N	5 14 W
Candelo	**141**	36 47 S	149 43 E
Candia = Iráklion	**69**	35 20 N	25 12 E
Cândido de Abreu	**171**	24 35 S	51 20 W
Cândido Mendes	**170**	1 27 S	45 43 W
Candle L.	**153**	53 50 N	105 18 W
Cando	**158**	48 30 N	99 14 W
Canea = Khaniá	**69**	35 30 N	24 4 E
Canela	**170**	10 15 S	48 25 W
Canelli	**62**	44 44 N	8 18 E
Canelones	**172**	34 32 S	56 10 W
Canet-Plage	**44**	42 41 N	3 2 E
Cañete, Chile	**172**	37 50 S	73 30 W
Cañete, Cuba	**167**	20 36 N	74 43 W
Cañete, Peru	**174**	13 0 S	76 30 W
Cañete, Spain	**58**	40 3 N	1 54 W
Cañete de las Torres	**57**	37 53 N	4 19 W
Canfranc	**58**	42 42 N	0 31 W
Cangamba	**125**	13 40 S	19 54 E
Cangas	**56**	42 16 N	8 47 W
Cangas de Narcea	**56**	43 10 N	6 32 W
Cangas de Onís	**56**	43 21 N	5 8 W
Canguaretama	**170**	6 20 S	35 5 W
Canguçu	**173**	31 22 S	52 43 W
Canhotinho	**171**	8 53 S	36 12 W
Cani, Is.	**119**	36 21 N	10 5 E
Canicado	**125**	24 2 S	33 2 E
Canicatti	**64**	37 21 N	13 50 E
Canicattini	**65**	37 1 N	15 3 E
Canim, L.	**152**	51 45 N	120 50 W
Canim Lake	**152**	51 17 N	120 54 W
Canindé	**170**	4 22 S	39 19 W
Canindé, R.	**170**	6 15 S	42 52 W
Canipaan	**102**	8 33 N	117 15 E
Canisbay	**37**	58 38 N	3 6 W
Canisp Mt.	**36**	58 8 N	5 5 W
Cañitas	**164**	23 36 N	102 43 W
Cañiza, La	**56**	42 13 N	8 16 W
Cañizal	**56**	41 20 N	5 22 W
Canjáyar	**59**	37 1 N	2 44 W
Cankırı	**92**	40 40 N	33 30 E
Cankuzo	**126**	3 10 S	30 31 E
Canlaon, Mt.	**103**	9 27 N	118 25 E
Canmore	**152**	51 7 N	115 18 W
Cann River	**141**	37 35 S	149 7 E
Canna I.	**36**	57 3 N	6 33 W
Canna, Sd. of	**36**	57 1 N	6 30 W
Cannanore	**97**	11 53 N	75 27 E
Cannes	**45**	43 32 N	7 0 E
Cannich	**37**	57 20 N	4 48 W
Canning Basin	**136**	19 50 S	124 0 E
Canning Town	**95**	22 23 N	88 40 E
Cannington	**28**	51 8 N	3 4 W
Cannock	**28**	52 42 N	2 2 W
Cannock Chase, hills	**23**	52 43 N	2 0 W
Cannon Ball, R.	**158**	46 20 N	101 20 W
Cannondale, Mt.	**138**	25 13 S	148 57 E
Caño Colorado	**174**	2 18 N	68 22 W
Canoe L.	**153**	55 10 N	108 15 W
Canol	**147**	65 15 N	126 50 W
Canon City	**158**	39 30 N	105 20 W
Canonbie	**35**	55 4 N	2 58 W
Canopus	**140**	33 29 S	140 42 E
Canora	**153**	51 40 N	102 30 W
Canosa di Púglia	**65**	41 13 N	16 4 E
Canourgue, Le	**44**	44 26 N	3 13 E
Canowindra	**141**	33 35 S	148 38 E
Canso	**151**	45 20 N	61 0 W
Cantabria, Sierra de	**58**	42 40 N	2 30 W
Cantabrian Mts. = Cantábrica	**56**	43 0 N	5 10 W
Cantábrica, Cordillera	**56**	43 0 N	5 10 W
Cantal □	**44**	45 4 N	2 45 E
Cantanhede	**56**	40 20 N	8 36 W
Cantaura	**174**	9 19 N	64 21 W
Çantavieja	**58**	40 31 N	0 25 W
Čantavir	**66**	45 55 N	19 46 E
Canterbury, Austral.	**138**	25 23 S	141 53 E
Canterbury, U.K.	**29**	51 17 N	1 5 E
Canterbury □	**143**	43 45 S	171 19 E
Canterbury Bight	**143**	44 16 S	171 55 E
Canterbury Plains	**143**	43 55 S	171 22 E
Cantil	**163**	35 18 N	117 58 W
Cantillana	**57**	37 36 N	5 50 W
Canto do Buriti	**170**	8 7 S	42 58 W
Canton, Ga., U.S.A.	**157**	34 13 N	84 29 W
Canton, Ill., U.S.A.	**158**	40 32 N	90 0 W
Canton, Mass., U.S.A.	**162**	42 9 N	71 9 W
Canton, Miss., U.S.A.	**159**	32 40 N	90 1 W
Canton, Mo., U.S.A.	**158**	40 10 N	91 33 W
Canton, Ohio, U.S.A.	**156**	40 47 N	81 22 W
Canton, Okla., U.S.A.	**159**	36 5 N	98 36 W

Canton Cascade

Canton, Pa., U.S.A. 162 41 39N 76 51W
Canton, S.D., U.S.A. 158 43 20N 96 35W
Canton = Kuangchou 109 23 10N 113 10E
Canton I. 130 2 30S 172 0W
Canton L. 159 36 12N 98 40W
Cantù 62 45 44N 9 8E
Canudos 174 7 13S 58 5W
Canulloit 161 31 58N 106 36W
Canutama 174 6 30S 64 20W
Canvey 29 51 32N 0 35E
Canyon, Can. 147 47 25N 84 36W
Canyon, Texas, U.S.A. 159 35 0N 101 57W
Canyon, Wyo., U.S.A. 160 44 43N 110 36W
Canyonlands Nat. Park 161 38 25N 109 30W
Canyonville 160 42 55N 123 14W
Canzo 62 45 54N 9 18E
Cao Bang 100 22 40N 106 15E
Cao Lanh 101 10 27N 105 38E
Caoles 34 56 32N 6 43W
Caolisport, Loch 34 55 54N 5 40W
Cáorle 63 45 36N 12 51E
Cap-aux-Meules 151 47 23N 61 52W
Cap Chat 151 49 6N 66 40W
Cap-de-la-Madeleine 150 46 22N 72 31W
Cap Haïtien 167 19 40N 72 20W
Cap St.-Jacques = Vung Tau 101 10 21N 107 4E
Capa Stilo 65 38 25N 16 25E
Capáccio 65 40 26N 15 4E
Capaia 124 8 27S 20 13E
Capanaparo, R. 174 7 0N 67 30W
Capanema 170 1 12S 47 11W
Caparo, R. 174 7 30N 70 30W
Capatárida 174 11 11N 70 37W
Capbreton 44 43 39N 1 26W
Capdenac 44 44 34N 2 5E
Cape Barren I. 138 40 25S 148 15E
Cape Breton Highlands Nat. Park 151 46 50N 60 40W
Cape Breton I. 151 46 0N 60 30W
Cape Charles 162 37 15N 75 59W
Cape Coast 121 5 5N 1 15W
Cape Cod B. 162 41 50N 70 18W
Cape Dorset 149 64 14N 76 32W
Cape Dyer 149 66 40N 61 22W
Cape Fear, R. 157 34 30N 78 25W
Cape Girardeau 159 37 20N 89 30W
Cape Jervis 140 35 40S 138 5E
Cape May 162 39 1N 74 53W
Cape May C.H. 162 39 5N 74 50W
Cape May Pt. 162 38 56N 74 56W
Cape Montague 151 46 5N 62 25W
Cape Palmas 120 4 25N 7 49W
Cape Preston 136 20 51S 116 12E
Cape Province □ 128 32 0S 23 0E
Cape, R. 138 20 37S 147 1E
Cape Tormentine 151 46 8N 63 47W
Cape Town (Kaapstad) 128 33 55S 18 22E
Cape Verde Is. 14 17 10N 25 20W
Cape York Peninsula 138 33 34S 115 33E
Capel 29 51 8N 0 18W
Capel Curig 31 53 6N 3 55W
Capela 170 10 30S 37 0W
Capela de Campo 170 4 40S 41 55W
Capelinha 171 17 42S 42 31W
Capella 138 23 2S 148 1E
Capella, G. 138 4 45S 140 50E
Capella, Mt. 135 5 4S 141 8E
Capelle, La 43 49 59N 3 50E
Capendu 44 43 11N 2 31E
Capernaum = Kefar Nahum 90 32 54N 35 32E
Capestang 44 43 20N 3 2E
Capim 170 1 41S 47 47W
Capim, R. 170 3 0S 48 0W
Capinópolis 171 18 41S 49 35W
Capitan 161 33 40N 105 41W
Capitola 163 36 59N 121 57W
Capivara, Serra da 171 14 35S 45 0W
Capizzi 65 37 50N 14 26E
Čapljina 66 43 35N 17 43E
Capoche, R. 127 15 0S 32 45E
Cappamore 39 52 38N 8 20W
Cappoquin 39 52 9N 7 46W
Capraia, I. 62 43 2N 9 50E
Caprarola 63 42 21N 12 11E
Capreol 150 46 43N 80 56W
Caprera, I. 64 41 12N 9 28E
Capri, I. 65 40 34N 14 15E
Capricorn, C. 133 23 30S 151 13E
Capricorn Group 138 23 30S 151 55E
Capricorn Ra. 136 23 20S 117 0E
Caprino Veronese 62 45 37N 10 47E
Caprivi Strip 128 18 0S 23 0E
Captainganj 95 26 55N 83 45E
Captain's Flat 141 35 35S 149 27E
Captieux 44 44 18N 0 16W
Cápua 65 41 7N 14 15E
Capulin 159 36 48N 103 59W
Caquetá □ 174 1 0N 74 0W
Caquetá, R. 174 1 0N 76 20W
Cáqueza 174 4 25N 73 57W
Carabobo 174 10 10N 68 5W
Caracal 70 44 8N 24 22E
Caracaraí 174 1 50N 61 8W
Caracas 174 10 30N 66 55W
Caracol, Piauí, Brazil 170 9 15S 43 45W
Caracol, Rondonia, Brazil 174 9 15S 64 20W
Caradoc 140 30 35S 143 5E
Caragabal 141 33 49S 147 45E
Caragh L. 39 52 3N 9 50W
Caráglio 62 44 25N 7 25E
*Renamed Abariringa

Caraí 171 17 12S 41 42W
Carajás, Serra dos 170 6 0S 51 30W
Caramanta 174 5 33N 75 38W
Carangola 173 20 50S 42 5W
Carani 137 30 57S 116 28E
Caransebeş 70 45 28N 22 18E
Carapelle, R. 65 41 20N 15 35E
Caraş Severin □ 66 45 10N 22 10E
Caraşova 66 45 11N 21 51E
Caratasca, Laguna 166 15 30N 83 40W
Caratec 42 48 40N 3 55W
Caratinga 171 19 50S 42 10W
Caratunk 151 45 13N 69 55W
Caraúbas 170 7 43S 36 31W
Caravaca 59 38 8N 1 52W
Caravággio 62 45 30N 9 39E
Caravelas 171 17 45S 39 15W
Caraveli 174 15 45S 73 25W
Caràzinho 173 28 0S 53 0W
Carballino 56 42 26N 8 5W
Carballo 56 43 13N 8 41W
Carberry 153 49 50N 99 25W
Carbia 56 42 48N 8 14W
Carbó 164 29 42N 110 58W
Carbon 152 51 30N 113 9W
Carbonara, C. 64 39 8N 9 30E
Carbondale, Colo, U.S.A. 160 39 30N 107 10W
Carbondale, Ill., U.S.A. 159 37 45N 89 10W
Carbondale, Pa., U.S.A. 162 41 37N 75 30W
Carbonear 151 47 42N 53 13W
Carboneras 59 37 0N 1 53W
Carboneras de Guadazaón 58 39 54N 1 50W
Carbonia 64 39 10N 8 30E
Carbost 36 57 19N 6 21W
Carbury 38 53 22N 6 58W
Carcabuey 57 37 27N 4 17W
Carcagente 59 39 8N 0 28W
Carcajou 152 57 47N 117 6W
Carcasse, C. 167 18 30N 74 28W
Carcassonne 44 43 13N 2 20E
Carche 59 38 26N 1 9W
Carcoar 141 33 36S 149 8E
Carcross 147 60 13N 134 45W
Cardabia 136 23 2S 113 55E
Cardamom Hills 97 9 30N 77 15E
Cárdenas, Cuba 166 23 0N 81 30W
Cárdenas, San Luis Potosí, Mexico 166 22 0N 99 41W
Cárdenas, Tabasco, Mexico 165 17 59N 93 21W
Cardenete 58 39 46N 1 41W
Cardiff 31 51 28N 3 11W
Cardiff-by-the-Sea 163 33 1N 117 17W
Cardigan 31 52 6N 4 41W
Cardigan (□) 26 52 6N 4 41W
Cardigan B. 31 52 30N 4 30W
Cardington 29 52 7N 0 23W
Cardón 174 11 37N 70 14W
Cardona, Spain 58 41 56N 1 40E
Cardona, Uruguay 172 33 53S 57 18W
Cardoner, R. 58 42 0N 1 33E
Cardross 153 49 50N 105 40W
Cardston 152 49 15N 113 20W
Cardwell 138 18 14S 146 2E
Careen L. 153 57 0N 108 11W
Carei 70 47 40N 22 29E
Carentan 42 49 19N 1 15W
Carey, Idaho, U.S.A. 160 43 19N 113 58W
Carey, Ohio, U.S.A. 156 40 58N 83 22W
Carey, L. 137 29 0S 122 15E
Carey L. 153 62 12N 102 55W
Careysburg 120 6 34N 10 30W
Cargados Garajos, Is. 11 17 0S 59 0E
Cargelligo, L. 139 33 17S 146 24E
Cargèse 45 42 7N 8 35E
Carhaix-Plouguer 42 48 18N 3 36W
Carhué 172 37 10S 62 50W
Cariacica 171 20 16S 40 25W
Cariaco 174 10 29N 63 33W
Caribaná, Pta. 174 8 37N 76 52W
Caribbean Sea 167 15 0N 75 0W
Cariboo Mts. 152 53 0N 121 0W
Caribou, Can. 153 53 15N 121 55W
Caribou, U.S.A. 151 46 55N 68 0W
Caribou I. 150 47 22N 85 49W
Caribou Is. 152 61 55N 113 15W
Caribou L., Man., Can. 153 59 21N 96 10W
Caribou L., Ont., Can. 150 50 25N 89 5W
Caribou Mts. 152 59 12N 115 40W
Caribou, R., Man., Can. 153 59 20N 94 44W
Caribou, R., N.W.T., Can. 152 61 27N 125 45W
Carichic 164 27 56N 107 3W
Carignan 43 49 38N 5 10E
Carignano 62 44 55N 7 40E
Carillo 164 26 50N 103 55W
Carinda 141 30 28S 147 41E
Cariñena 58 41 20N 1 13W
Carinhanha 171 14 15S 44 0W
Carinhanha, R. 171 14 20S 43 47W
Carini 64 38 9N 13 10E
Carinish 36 57 31N 7 20W
Carinola 64 41 11N 13 58E
Carinthia □ = Kärnten 52 46 52N 13 30E
Caripito 174 10 8N 63 6W
Caririacu 171 7 2S 39 17W
Carisbrooke 28 50 42N 1 19W
Caritianas 174 9 20S 63 0W
Cark 32 54 11N 2 59W
Carlentini 65 37 15N 15 2E
Carleton Place 150 45 8N 76 9W

Carleton Rode 29 52 30N 1 6E
Carletonville 128 26 23S 27 22E
Carlin 160 40 50N 116 5W
Carlingford 38 54 3N 6 10W
Carlingford, L. 38 54 0N 6 5W
Carlinville 158 39 20N 89 55W
Carlisle, U.K. 32 54 54N 2 55W
Carlisle, U.S.A. 162 40 12N 77 10W
Carlitte, Pic 44 42 35N 1 43E
Carloforte 64 39 10N 8 18E
Carlops 35 55 47N 3 20W
Carlos Casares 172 35 53S 61 20W
Carlos Chagas 171 17 43S 40 45W
Carlos Tejedor 172 35 25S 62 25W
Carlota, La 172 33 30S 63 20W
Carlow 39 52 50N 6 58W
Carlow □ 39 52 43N 6 50W
Carloway 36 58 17N 6 48W
Carlsbad, Calif., U.S.A. 163 33 11N 117 25W
Carlsbad, N. Mex., U.S.A. 159 32 20N 104 7W
Carlton 33 52 58N 1 6W
Carlton Colville 29 52 27N 1 41E
Carlton Miniott 33 54 13N 1 22W
Carluke 35 55 44N 3 50W
Carlyle, Can. 153 49 40N 102 20W
Carlyle, U.S.A. 158 38 38N 89 23W
Carmacks 147 62 5N 136 16W
Carmagnola 62 44 50N 7 42E
Carman 153 49 30N 98 0W
Carmangay 152 50 10N 113 10W
Carmanville 151 49 23N 54 19W
Carmarthen 31 51 52N 4 20W
Carmarthen (□) 26 53 40N 4 18W
Carmarthen B. 31 51 40N 4 30W
Carmaux 44 44 3N 2 10E
Carmel, Calif., U.S.A. 163 36 38N 121 55W
Carmel, N.Y., U.S.A. 162 41 25N 73 38W
Carmel Hd. 31 53 24N 4 34W
Carmel Mt. 90 32 45N 35 3E
Carmel Valley 163 36 29N 121 43W
Carmelo 172 34 0S 58 10W
Carmen, Colomb. 174 9 43N 75 8W
Carmen, Parag. 173 27 13S 56 12W
Carmen de Patagones 176 40 50S 63 0W
Carmen, I. 164 26 0N 111 20W
Carmen, R. 164 30 42N 106 29W
Cármenes 56 42 58N 5 34W
Carmensa 172 35 15S 67 40W
Carmi 156 38 6N 88 10W
Carmichael 163 38 38N 121 19W
Carmila 138 21 55S 149 24E
Carmo do Paranaiba 171 18 59S 46 21W
Carmona 57 37 28N 5 42W
Carmyllie 37 56 36N 2 41W
Carn Ban 37 57 6N 4 15W
Carn Eige 36 57 17N 5 9W
Carn Glas Chorie 37 57 20N 3 50W
Carn Mor 37 57 14N 3 13W
Carn na Saobhaidh 37 57 12N 4 20W
Carna 39 53 20N 9 50W
Carnarvon, Queens., Austral. 138 24 48S 147 45E
Carnarvon, W. Austral., Austral. 137 24 51S 113 42E
Carnarvon, S. Afr. 128 30 56S 22 8E
Carnarvon Ra., Queensland, Austral. 138 25 15S 148 30E
Carnarvon Ra., W.A., Austral. 137 25 0S 120 45E
Carnaxide 57 38 43N 9 14W
Carncastle 38 54 55N 5 52W
Carndonagh 38 55 15N 7 16W
Carnduff 153 49 10N 101 50W
Carnedd Llewelyn, Mt. 31 53 9N 3 58W
Carnegie, L. 137 26 5S 122 30E
Carnew 39 52 43N 6 30W
Carney 38 54 20N 8 30W
Carnforth 32 54 8N 2 47W
Carnic Alps = Karnische Alpen 63 46 34N 12 50E
Carnlough 38 55 0N 6 0W
Carno 31 52 34N 3 31W
Carnon 44 43 32N 3 59E
Carnot 124 4 59N 15 56E
Carnot B. 136 17 20S 121 30E
Carnoustie 35 56 30N 2 41W
Carnsore Pt. 39 52 10N 6 20W
Carnwath 35 55 42N 3 38W
Caro 156 43 29N 83 27W
Carolina, Brazil 170 7 10S 47 30W
Carolina, S. Afr. 129 26 5S 30 6E
Carolina, La 57 38 17N 3 38W
Caroline I. 131 9 15S 150 3W
Caroline Is. 130 8 0N 150 0E
Caroline Pk. 143 45 57S 167 15E
Carolside 152 51 20N 111 40W
Caron 153 50 30N 105 50W
Caroni, R. 174 6 0N 62 40W
Carora 174 10 11N 70 5W
Carovigno 65 40 42N 17 40E
Carpathians, Mts. 53 49 40N 19 30E
Carpaţii Meridionali 70 45 30N 25 0E
Carpenédolo 62 45 22N 10 25E
Carpentaria Downs 138 18 44S 144 20E
Carpentaria, G. of 133 14 0S 139 0E
Carpentras 45 44 3N 5 2E
Carpi 62 44 47N 10 52E
Carpina 170 7 51S 35 15W
Carpino 65 41 50N 15 51E
Carpinteria 163 34 25N 119 31W
Carpio 56 41 13N 5 7W
Carpolac = Morea 140 36 45S 141 18E

Carr Boyd Ra. 136 16 15S 128 35E
Carra L. 38 53 41N 9 12W
Carrabelle 157 29 52N 84 40W
Carracastle 38 53 57N 8 42W
Carradale 34 55 35N 5 30W
Carraipia 174 11 16N 72 22W
Carrara 62 44 5N 10 7E
Carrascosa del Campo 58 40 2N 2 45W
Carrauntohill, Mt. 39 52 0N 9 49W
Carraweena 139 29 10S 140 0E
Carrbridge 37 57 17N 3 50W
Carriacou, I. 167 12 30N 61 28W
Carribee 140 35 7S 136 57E
Carrick 38 54 40N 8 39W
Carrick, dist. 34 55 12N 4 38W
Carrick-on-Shannon 38 53 57N 8 7W
Carrick-on-Suir 39 52 22N 7 30W
Carrick Ra. 143 45 15S 169 8E
Carrickart 38 55 10N 7 47W
Carrickbeg 39 52 20N 7 25W
Carrickboy 38 53 36N 7 40W
Carrickfergus 36 54 43N 5 50W
Carrickfergus □ 38 54 43N 5 49W
Carrickmacross 38 54 0N 6 43W
Carrieton 140 32 25S 138 31E
Carrigaholt 39 52 37N 9 42W
Carrigahorig 39 53 4N 8 10W
Carrigaline 39 51 49N 8 22W
Carrigallen 38 53 59N 7 40W
Carrigan Hd. 38 54 38N 8 40W
Carrignavar 39 52 0N 8 29W
Carrigtwohill 39 51 55N 8 15W
Carrington 158 47 30N 99 7W
Carrión de los Condes 56 42 20N 4 37W
Carrión, R. 56 42 42N 4 47W
Carrizal 174 12 1N 72 11W
Carrizal Bajo 172 28 5S 71 20W
Carrizalillo 172 29 0S 71 30W
Carrizo Cr. 159 36 30N 103 40W
Carrizo Springs 159 28 28N 99 50W
Carrizozo 161 33 40N 105 57W
Carroll 158 42 2N 94 55W
Carrollton, Ga., U.S.A. 157 33 36N 85 5W
Carrollton, Ill., U.S.A. 158 39 20N 90 25W
Carrollton, Ky., U.S.A. 156 38 40N 85 10W
Carrollton, Mo., U.S.A. 158 39 19N 93 24W
Carron L. 36 57 22N 5 35W
Carron R., U.K. 36 57 30N 5 30W
Carron R., U.K. 37 57 51N 4 21W
Carrot, R. 153 53 50N 101 17W
Carrot River 153 53 17N 103 35W
Carrouges 42 48 34N 0 10W
Carrowkeel 38 55 7N 7 12W
Carrowmore L. 38 54 12N 9 48W
Carruthers 153 52 52N 109 16W
Carryduff 38 54 34N 5 52W
Çarşamba 92 41 15N 36 45E
Carsoli 63 42 7N 13 3E
Carson 158 46 27N 101 29W
Carson City 160 39 12N 119 46W
Carson Sink 160 39 50N 118 40W
Carsonville 156 43 25N 82 39W
Carsphairn 34 55 13N 4 15W
Carstairs 35 55 42N 3 41W
Cartagena, Colomb. 174 10 25N 75 33W
Cartagena, Spain 59 37 38N 0 59W
Cartago, Colomb. 174 4 45N 75 55W
Cartago, C. Rica 166 9 50N 84 0W
Cartaret 42 49 23N 1 47W
Cartaxo 57 39 10N 8 47W
Cartaya 57 37 16N 7 9W
Cartersville 157 34 11N 84 48W
Carterton 142 41 2S 175 31E
Carthage, Ark., U.S.A. 159 34 4N 92 32W
Carthage, Ill., U.S.A. 158 40 25N 91 10W
Carthage, Mo., U.S.A. 159 37 10N 94 20W
Carthage, N.Y., U.S.A. 156 43 59N 75 37W
Carthage, S.D., U.S.A. 158 44 14N 97 38W
Carthage, Texas, U.S.A. 159 32 8N 94 20W
Cartier I. 136 12 31S 123 29E
Cartmel 32 54 13N 2 57W
Cartwright 151 53 41N 56 58W
Caruaru 170 8 15S 35 55W
Carúpano 174 10 45N 63 15W
Carutapera 170 1 13S 46 1W
Caruthersville 159 36 10N 89 40W
Carvarzere 63 45 8N 12 7E
Carvin 43 50 30N 2 57E
Carvoeiro 174 1 30S 61 59W
Carvoeiro, Cabo 57 39 21N 9 24W
Casa Agapito 174 2 3N 73 58W
Casa Branca, Brazil 171 21 46S 47 4W
Casa Branca, Port. 57 38 29N 8 12W
Casa Grande 161 32 53N 111 51W
Casa Nova 170 9 10S 41 5W
Casablanca, Chile 172 33 20S 71 25W
Casablanca, Moroc. 118 33 36N 7 36W
Casacalenda 65 41 45N 14 50E
Casalbordino 63 42 10N 14 34E
Casale Monferrato 62 45 8N 8 28E
Casalmaggiore 62 44 59N 10 25E
Casalpusterlengo 62 45 10N 9 40E
Casamance, R. 120 12 54N 15 0W
Casamássima 65 40 58N 16 55E
Casanare, R. 174 6 30N 71 20W
Casarano 65 40 0N 18 10E
Casares 57 36 27N 5 16W
Casas Grandes 164 30 22N 108 0W
Casas IbáPez 59 39 17N 1 30W
Casasimarro 59 39 22N 2 3W
Casatejada 56 39 54N 5 40W
Casavieja 56 40 17N 4 46W
Cascade, Idaho, U.S.A. 160 44 30N 116 2W

Cascade Cepin

Cascade, Mont., U.S.A. 160 47 16N 111 46W
Cascade Locks 160 45 44N 121 54W
Cascade Pt. 143 44 1S 168 20E
Cascade Ra. 160 45 0N 121 30W
Cascais 57 38 41N 9 25W
Cascina 62 43 40N 10 32E
Caselle Torinese 62 45 12N 7 39E
Caserta 65 41 5N 14 20E
Cashel 39 52 31N 7 53W
Cashla B. 39 53 12N 9 37W
Cashmere 160 47 31N 120 30W
Cashmere Downs 137 28 57S 119 35E
Casigua 174 11 2N 71 1W
Casiguran 103 16 15N 122 15E
Casilda 172 33 10S 61 10W
Casimcea 70 44 45N 28 23E
Casino 139 28 52S 153 3E
Casiquiare, R. 174 2 45N 66 20W
Caslan 152 54 38N 112 31W
Casma 174 9 30S 78 20W
Casmalia 163 34 50N 120 32W
Casola Valsenio 63 44 12N 11 40E
Cásoli 63 42 7N 14 18E
Caspe 58 41 14N 0 1W
Casper 160 42 52N 106 27W
Caspian Sea 79 43 0N 50 0E
Casquets 42 49 46N 2 15W
Cass City 156 43 34N 83 15W
Cass Lake 158 47 23N 94 38W
Cassá de la Selva 58 41 53N 2 52E
Cassano Iónio 65 39 47N 16 20E
Cassel 43 50 48N 2 30E
Casselton 158 47 0N 97 15W
Cássia 171 20 36S 46 56W
Cassiar 152 59 16N 129 40W
Cassiar Mts. 152 59 30N 130 30W
Cassils 152 50 29N 112 15W
Cassinga 125 15 5S 16 23E
Cassino 64 41 30N 13 50E
Cassiporé, C. 170 3 50N 51 5W
Cassis 45 43 14N 5 32E
Cassville 159 36 45N 93 59W
Càstagneto Carducci 62 43 9N 10 36E
Castaic 163 34 30N 118 38W
Castanhal 170 1 18S 47 55W
Castanheiro 174 0 17S 65 38W
Casteau 47 50 32N 4 2E
Castéggio 62 45 1N 9 8E
Castejón de Monegros 58 41 37N 0 15W
Castel di Sangro 65 41 41N 14 5E
Castel San Giovanni 62 45 4N 9 25E
Castel San Pietro 63 44 23N 11 30E
Castelbuono 65 37 56N 14 4E
Casteldelfino 62 44 35N 7 4E
Castelfiorentino 62 43 36N 10 58E
Castelfranco Emília 62 44 37N 11 2E
Castelfranco Veneto 63 45 40N 11 56E
Casteljaloux 44 44 19N 0 6E
Castellabate 65 40 18N 14 55E
Castellammare del Golfo 64 38 2N 12 53E
Castellammare di Stábia 65 40 47N 14 29E
Castellammare, G. di 64 38 5N 12 55E
Castellamonte 62 45 23N 7 42E
Castellana Grotte 65 40 53N 17 10E
Castellane 45 43 50N 6 31E
Castellaneta 65 40 40N 16 57E
Castellar de Santisteban 59 38 16N 3 8W
Castelleone 62 45 19N 9 47E
Castelli 172 36 7S 57 47W
Castelló de Ampurias 58 42 15N 3 4E
Castellón □ 58 40 15N 0 5W
Castellón de la Plana 58 39 58N 0 3W
Castellote 58 40 48N 0 15W
Castelltersol 58 41 45N 2 8E
Castelmáuro 65 41 50N 14 40E
Castelnau-de-Médoc 44 45 2N 0 48W
Castelnaudary 44 43 20N 1 58E
Castelnovo ne' Monti 62 44 27N 10 26E
Castelnuovo di Val di Cécina 62 43 12N 10 54E
Castelo 173 20 53S 41 42E
Castelo Branco 56 39 50N 7 31W
Castelo Branco □ 56 39 52N 7 45W
Castelo de Paiva 56 41 2N 8 16W
Castelo de Vide 57 39 25N 7 27W
Castelo do Piaúi 170 5 20S 41 33W
Castelsarrasin 44 44 2N 1 7E
Casteltérmini 64 37 32N 13 38E
Castelvetrano 64 37 40N 12 46E
Casterton 140 37 30S 141 30E
Castets 44 43 52N 1 6W
Castiglione del Lago 63 43 7N 12 3E
Castiglione della Pescáia 62 42 46N 10 53E
Castiglione della Stiviere 62 45 23N 10 30E
Castiglione Fiorentino 63 43 20N 11 55E
Castilblanco 57 39 17N 5 5W
Castilla La Nueva 57 39 45N 3 20W
Castilla La Vieja 56 41 55N 4 0W
Castilla, Playa de 57 37 0N 6 33W
Castille = Castilla 56 40 0N 3 30W
Castilletes 174 11 51N 71 19W
Castillón 164 28 20N 103 38W
Castillon-en-Couserans 44 42 56N 1 1E
Castillon-la-Bataille 44 44 51N 0 2W
Castillonès 44 44 39N 0 37E
Castillos 173 34 12S 53 52W
Castle Acre 29 52 42N 0 42W
Castle Cary 28 51 5N 2 32W
Castle Dale 160 39 11N 111 1W
Castle Donington 28 52 50N 1 20W
Castle Douglas 35 54 57N 3 57W
Castle Eden 54 54 45N 1 20W
Castle Point 142 40 54N 176 15E
Castle Rock, Colo., U.S.A. 158 39 26N 104 50W
Castle Rock, Wash., U.S.A. 160 46 20N 122 58W
Castlebar 38 53 52N 9 17W
Castlebay 36 56 57N 7 30W
Castlebellingham 38 53 53N 6 22W
Castleblakeney 38 53 26N 8 28W
Castleblayney 38 54 7N 6 44W
Castlebridge 39 52 23N 6 28W
Castlecliff 142 39 57S 174 59E
Castlecomer 39 52 49N 7 13W
Castleconnell 39 52 44N 8 30W
Castledawson 38 54 47N 6 35W
Castlederg 38 54 43N 7 35W
Castledermot 39 52 55N 6 50W
Castlefinn 38 54 47N 7 35W
Castleford 33 53 43N 1 21W
Castlegar 152 49 20N 117 40W
Castlegate 160 39 45N 110 57W
Castlegregory 39 52 16N 10 0W
Castlehill 38 51 1N 9 49W
Castleisland 39 52 14N 9 28W
Castlemaine, Austral. 140 37 2S 144 12E
Castlemaine, Ireland 39 52 10N 9 42W
Castlemaine Harb. 39 52 8N 9 50W
Castlemartyr 39 51 54N 8 3W
Castlepollard 38 53 40N 7 20W
Castlereagh 38 53 47N 8 30W
Castlereagh □ 38 54 33N 5 33W
Castlereagh B. 138 12 10S 135 10E
Castlereagh, R. 141 30 12S 147 32E
Castleside 32 54 50N 1 52W
Castleton, Derby., U.K. 33 53 20N 1 47W
Castleton, N. Yorks., U.K. 33 54 27N 0 57W
Castleton, U.S.A. 162 43 37N 73 11W
Castletown, Geoghegan, Ireland 38 53 27N 7 30W
Castletown, Laois, Ireland 38 52 58N 7 31W
Castletown, Meath, Ireland 39 53 47N 6 41W
Castletown, I. of Man 32 54 4N 4 40W
Castletown, U.K. 37 58 35N 3 22W
Castletown Bearhaven 39 51 40N 9 54W
Castletownroche 39 52 10N 8 28W
Castletownshend 39 51 31N 9 11W
Castlevale 138 24 30S 146 48E
Castlewellan 38 54 16N 5 57W
Castor 152 52 15N 111 50W
Castorland 162 43 53N 75 31W
Castres 44 43 37N 2 13E
Castricum 46 52 33N 4 40E
Castries 167 14 0N 60 50W
Castril 59 37 48N 2 46W
Castro, Brazil 173 24 45S 50 0W
Castro, Chile 176 42 30S 73 50W
Castro Alves 171 12 46S 39 26W
Castro del Río 57 37 41N 4 29W
Castro Marim 57 37 13N 7 26W
Castro Urdiales 58 43 23N 3 19W
Castro Verde 57 37 41N 8 4W
Castrojeriz 56 42 17N 4 9W
Castropol 56 43 32N 7 0W
Castroreale 65 38 5N 15 15E
Castrovíllari 65 39 49N 16 11E
Castroville, Calif., U.S.A. 163 36 46N 121 45W
Castroville, Tex, U.S.A. 159 29 20N 98 53W
Castuera 57 38 43N 5 37W
Casummit L. 150 51 29N 92 22W
Cat Ba 100 20 50N 107 0E
Cat I., Bahamas 167 24 30N 75 30W
Cat I., U.S.A. 159 30 15N 89 7W
Cat L. 150 51 40N 91 50W
Çata 53 47 58N 18 38E
Catacamas 166 14 54N 85 56W
Catacaos 174 5 20S 80 45W
Cataguases 173 21 23S 42 39W
Catahoula L. 159 31 30N 92 5W
Catalão 171 18 10S 47 57W
Çatalca 92 41 9N 28 28E
Catalina 151 48 31N 53 4W
Catalonia = Cataluña 58 41 40N 1 15E
Cataluña 58 41 40N 1 15E
Catamarca 172 28 30S 65 50W
Catamarca □ 172 28 30S 65 50W
Catanduanas, Is. 103 13 50N 124 20E
Catanduva 173 21 5S 48 58W
Catánia 65 37 31N 15 4E
Catánia, G. di 65 37 25N 15 8E
Catanzaro 65 38 54N 16 38E
Catarman 103 12 28N 124 1E
Catastrophe C. 136 34 59S 136 0E
Catcleugh 35 55 19N 2 22W
Cateau, Le 43 50 6N 3 30E
Cateel 103 7 47N 126 24E
Catende 170 8 40S 35 43W
Caterham 29 51 16N 0 4W
Cathcart, Austral. 141 36 2S 149 24E
Cathcart, S. Afr. 128 32 18S 27 10E
Catine 41 46 30N 0 15W
Catio 120 11 17N 15 15W
Catismiña 174 4 5N 63 52W
Catita 170 9 31S 43 1W
Catlettsburg 156 38 23N 82 38W
Cato I. 133 23 15S 155 32E
Catoche, C. 165 21 40N 87 0W
Catolé 171 7 19S 36 1W
Catolé do Rocha 170 6 21S 37 45W
Caton 32 54 5N 2 41W
Catonsville 162 39 16N 76 44W
Catral 59 38 10N 0 47W
Catria, Mt. 63 43 28N 12 42E
Catrimani 174 0 27N 61 41W
Catrine 34 55 30N 4 20W
Catsfield 29 50 53N 0 28E
Catskill 162 42 14N 73 52W
Catskill Mts. 162 42 15N 74 15W
Catt, Mt. 138 13 49S 134 23E
Catterick 33 54 23N 1 38W
Cattólica 63 43 58N 12 43E
Cattólica Eraclea 64 37 27N 13 24E
Catton 35 54 56N 2 16W
Catu 171 12 21S 38 23W
Catuala 128 16 25S 19 2E
Catur 127 13 45S 35 30E
Catwick Is. 101 10 0N 109 0E
Cauca □ 174 2 30N 76 50W
Cauca, R. 174 7 25N 75 30W
Caucasia 174 8 0N 75 12W
Caucasus Mts. = Bolshoi Kavkas 83 42 50N 44 0E
Caucaia 170 3 40S 38 35W
Caudebec-en-Caux 42 49 30N 0 42E
Caudete 59 38 42N 1 2W
Caudry 43 50 7N 3 22E
Caulkerbush 35 54 54N 3 40W
Caulnes 42 48 18N 2 10W
Caulónia 65 38 23N 16 25E
Caungula 124 8 15S 18 50E
Cáuquenes 172 36 0S 72 30W
Caura, R. 174 6 20N 64 30W
Cauresi, R. 127 17 40S 33 10E
Causapscal 151 48 19N 67 12W
Causeway 39 52 25N 9 45W
Caussade 44 44 10N 1 33E
Cauterets 44 42 52N 0 8W
Cauvery, R. 93 12 0N 77 45E
Caux 42 49 38N 0 35E
Cava dei Tirreni 65 40 42N 14 42E
Cávado, R. 56 41 37N 8 15W
Cavaillon 45 43 50N 5 2E
Cavalaire-sur-Mer 45 43 10N 6 33E
Cavalcante 171 13 48S 47 30W
Cavalerie, La 44 44 0N 3 10E
Cavalese 63 46 17N 11 29E
Cavalier 158 48 50N 97 39W
Cavalli Is. 142 35 0S 173 58E
Cavallo, I. 45 41 22N 9 16E
Cavally, R. 120 5 0N 7 40W
Cavan 38 54 0N 7 22W
Cavan □ 38 53 58N 7 10W
Cavanagh Ra. 137 26 10S 122 50E
Cavárzere 63 45 8N 12 6E
Cave City 156 37 13N 85 57W
Cavenagh Range 137 26 12S 127 55E
Cavendish 140 37 31S 142 2E
Cavers 150 48 55N 87 41W
Caviana, Ilha 170 0 15N 50 0W
Cavite 103 14 20N 120 55E
Cavour 62 44 47N 7 22E
Cavtat 66 42 35N 18 13E
Cawdor 37 57 31N 3 56W
Cawkers Well 140 31 41S 142 57E
Cawndilla, L. 140 32 30S 142 15E
Cawnpore = Kanpur 95 26 35N 80 20E
Cawood 33 53 50N 1 7W
Cawston 29 52 47N 1 10E
Caxias 174 5 0S 43 27W
Caxias do Sul 173 29 10S 51 10W
Caxine, C. 118 35 56N 0 27W
Caxito 124 8 30S 13 30E
Cay Sal Bank 166 23 45N 80 0W
Cayambe 174 0 3N 78 22W
Cayce 157 33 59N 81 2W
Cayenne 175 5 0N 52 18W
Cayes, Les 167 18 15N 73 46W
Cayeux-sur-Mer. 43 50 10N 1 30E
Cayey 147 18 7N 66 10W
Caylus 44 44 15N 1 47E
Cayman Brac, I. 166 19 43N 79 49W
Cayman Is. 166 19 40N 79 50W
Cayo 165 17 10N 89 0W
Cayo Romano, I. 167 22 0N 73 30W
Cayuga 162 42 28N 76 30W
Cayuga L. 162 42 45N 76 45W
Cazalla de la Sierra 57 37 56N 5 45W
Cazaux et de Sanguinet, Étang de 44 44 29N 1 10W
Cazenovia 162 42 56N 75 51W
Cazères 44 43 13N 1 5E
Čazin 63 44 57N 15 57E
Čazma 63 45 45N 16 39E
Cazombo 125 12 0S 22 48E
Cazorla, Spain 59 37 55N 3 2W
Cazorla, Venez. 174 8 1N 67 0W
Cazorla, Sierra de 59 38 5N 2 55W
Cea, R. 56 42 40N 5 5W
Ceamurlia de Jos 67 44 43N 28 47E
Ceanannas Mor 38 53 42N 6 53W
Ceará = Fortaleza 170 3 35S 38 35W
Ceará □ 170 5 0S 40 0W
Ceará Mirim 170 5 38S 35 25W
Ceauru, L. 70 44 58N 23 11E
Cebaco, I. 166 7 33N 81 9W
Cebollar 172 29 10S 66 35W
Cebollera, Sierra de 58 42 0N 2 30W
Cebreros 56 40 27N 4 28W
Cebú 103 10 18N 123 54E
Cebú, I. 103 10 15N 123 40E
Ceccano 64 41 34N 13 18E
Cece 53 46 46N 18 39E
Cechi 120 6 15N 4 25W
Cecil Plains 139 27 30S 151 11E
Cecilton 162 39 24N 75 52W
Cécina 62 43 19N 10 33E
Cécina, R. 62 43 19N 10 40E
Ceclavin 56 39 50N 6 45W
Cedar City 161 37 41N 113 3W
Cedar Creek Res. 159 32 15N 96 0W
Cedar Falls 158 42 39N 92 29W
Cedar I. 162 37 35N 75 32W
Cedar Key 157 29 9N 83 5W
Cedar L. 153 53 20N 100 10W
Cedar Pt. 162 38 18N 76 25W
Cedar, R. 158 41 50N 91 20W
Cedar Rapids 158 42 0N 91 38W
Cedarburg 156 43 18N 87 55W
Cedartown 157 34 1N 85 15W
Cedarvale 152 55 1N 128 22W
Cedarville 160 41 37N 120 13W
Cedeira 56 43 39N 8 2W
Cedral 164 23 50N 100 42W
Cedrino, R. 64 40 8N 9 25E
Cedro 170 6 34S 39 3W
Cedros, I. de 164 28 10N 115 20W
Ceduna 139 32 7S 133 46E
Cedynia 54 52 53N 14 12E
Ceepeecee 152 49 52N 126 42W
Cefalù 65 38 3N 14 1E
Cega, R. 56 41 17N 4 10W
Cegléd 53 47 11N 19 47E
Céglie Messápico 65 40 39N 17 31E
Cehegín 59 38 6N 1 48W
Cehu-Silvaniei 70 47 24N 23 9E
Ceiba, La 166 15 40N 86 50W
Ceica 70 46 53N 22 10E
Ceira, R. 56 40 15N 7 55W
Cekhira 119 34 20N 10 5E
Celano 63 42 6N 13 30E
Celanova 56 42 9N 7 58W
Celaya 164 20 31N 100 37W
Celbridge 39 53 20N 6 33W
Celebes I. = Sulawesi 103 2 0S 120 0E
Celebes Sea 103 3 0N 123 0E
Celga 123 12 38N 37 3E
Celina 156 40 32N 84 31W
Čelió 66 44 43N 18 47E
Celje 63 46 16N 15 18E
Cellar Hd. 36 58 25N 6 10W
Celldömölk 53 47 16N 17 10E
Celle 48 52 37N 10 4E
Celles 47 50 42N 3 28E
Celorica da Beira 56 40 38N 7 24W
Cemaes Bay 31 53 24N 4 27W
Cemaes Hd. 31 52 7N 4 44W
Cement 159 34 56N 98 8W
Čemerno 66 43 26N 20 26E
Cemmaes Road 31 52 39N 3 41W
Cenarth 31 52 3N 4 32W
Cenis, Col du Mt. 45 45 15N 6 55E
Ceno, R. 62 44 40N 9 52E
Cenon 44 44 50N 0 33W
Centallo 62 44 30N 7 35E
Centenário do Sul 171 22 48S 51 57W
Center, N.D., U.S.A. 158 47 9N 101 17W
Center, Texas, U.S.A. 159 31 50N 94 10W
Centerfield 160 39 9N 111 56W
Centerville, Ala., U.S.A. 157 32 55N 87 7W
Centerville, Calif., U.S.A. 163 36 44N 119 30W
Centerville, Iowa, U.S.A. 158 40 45N 92 57W
Centerville, Miss., U.S.A. 159 31 10N 91 3W
Centerville, S.D., U.S.A. 158 43 10N 96 58W
Centerville, Tenn., U.S.A. 157 35 46N 87 29W
Centerville, Tex., U.S.A. 159 31 15N 95 56W
Cento 63 44 43N 11 16E
Central 170 11 8S 42 8W
Central □, Kenya 126 0 30S 33 30E
Central □, Malawi 126 13 30S 33 30E
Central □, U.K. 34 56 0N 4 30W
Central □, Zambia 127 14 25S 28 50E
Central African Republic ■ 124 7 0N 20 0E
Central Auckland □ 142 37 30S 175 30E
Central City, Ky., U.S.A. 156 37 20N 87 7W
Central City, Nebr., U.S.A. 158 41 8N 98 0W
Central, Cordillera, C. Rica 166 10 10N 84 5W
Central, Cordillera, Dom. Rep. 167 19 15N 71 0W
Central I., L. Turkana 126 3 30N 36 0E
Central Islip 162 40 49N 73 13W
Central Makran Range 93 26 30N 64 15E
Central Patricia 150 51 30N 90 9W
Central Ra. 135 5 0S 143 0E
Central Russian Uplands 16 54 0N 36 0E
Central Siberian Plateau 77 65 0N 105 0E
Central Square 162 43 17N 76 9W
Centralia, Ill., U.S.A. 158 38 32N 89 5W
Centralia, Mo., U.S.A. 158 39 12N 92 6W
Centralia, Wash., U.S.A. 160 46 46N 122 59W
Centúripe 65 37 37N 14 41E
Cephalonia = Kefallinia 69 38 28N 20 30E
Cepin 66 45 32N 18 34E

Ceprano Château d'Oex

Ceprano 64 41 33N 13 30 E
Ceptura 70 45 1N 26 21 E
Ceram I. = Seram I. 103 3 10S 129 0 E
Ceram Sea 103 2 30S 128 30 E
Cerbère 44 42 26N 3 10 E
Cerbicales, Îles 45 41 33N 9 22 E
Cerbu 70 44 46N 24 46 E
Cercal 57 37 48N 8 40W
Cercemaggiore 65 41 27N 14 43 E
Cerdaña 58 42 22N 1 35 E
Cerdedo 56 42 33N 8 23W
Cerea 63 45 12N 11 13 E
Ceres, Argent. 172 29 55S 61 55W
Ceres, Brazil 171 15 17S 49 35W
Ceres, Italy 62 45 19N 7 22 E
Ceres, S. Afr. 128 33 21S 19 18 E
Ceres, U.K. 35 56 18N 2 57W
Ceres, U.S.A. 163 37 35N 120 57W
Céret 44 42 30N 2 42 E
Ceretè 174 8 53N 75 48W
Cerfontaine 47 50 11N 4 26 E
Cerignola 65 41 17N 15 53 E
Cerigo = Kíthira 69 36 9N 23 0 E
Cérilly 44 46 37N 2 50 E
Cerisiers 43 48 8N 3 30 E
Cerizay 42 46 50N 0 40W
Çerkeş 92 40 40N 32 58 E
Cerknica 63 45 48N 14 21 E
Çermerno 66 43 35N 20 25 E
Cerna 70 44 4N 28 17 E
Cerna, R. 70 44 45N 24 0 E
Cernavodů 70 44 22N 28 3 E
Cernay 43 47 44N 7 10 E
Cerne Abbas 28 50 49N 2 29W
Cernik 66 45 17N 17 22 E
Cerralvo, I. 164 24 20N 109 45 E
Cerreto Sannita 65 41 17N 14 34 E
Cerrig-y-druidion 31 53 2N 3 34W
Cerritos 164 22 20N 100 20W
Cerro 161 36 47N 105 36W
Cêrro Corá 171 6 3S 36 21W
Cerro de Punta, Mt. 147 18 10N 67 0W
Certaldo 62 43 32N 11 2 E
Cervaro, R. 65 41 21N 15 30 E
Cervera 58 41 40N 1 16 E
Cervera de Pisuerga 56 42 51N 4 30W
Cervera del Río Alhama 58 42 2N 1 58W
Cérvia 63 44 15N 12 20 E
Cervignano del Friuli 63 45 49N 13 20 E
Cervinara 65 41 2N 14 36 E
Cervo 56 43 40N 7 24W
Cervoine 45 42 20N 9 29 E
Cesanàtico 63 44 12N 12 22 E
César □ 174 9 0N 73 30W
Cesaro 65 37 50N 14 38 E
Cesena 63 44 9N 12 14 E
Cesenàtico 63 44 12N 12 22 E
Cësis 80 57 17N 25 28 E
Česká Třebová 53 49 54N 16 27 E
Ceske Budějovice 52 48 55N 14 25 E
České Velenice 52 48 45N 15 1 E
Českézemě 52 50 0N 14 0 E
Ceskomoravská Vrchovina 52 49 20N 15 45 E
Český Brod 52 50 4N 14 52 E
Český Krumlov 52 48 43N 14 21 E
Český Těšin 53 49 45N 18 39 E
Çeşme 69 38 20N 26 23 E
Cess, R. 120 5 25N 9 35W
Cessnock 141 32 50S 151 21 E
Cestos, R. 120 5 30N 9 30W
Cetate 70 44 7N 23 2 E
Cetina, R. 63 43 50N 16 30 E
Cetinje 66 42 23N 18 59 E
Cetraro 65 39 30N 15 56 E
Ceuta 118 35 52N 5 18W
Ceva 62 44 23N 8 0 E
Cévennes, mts. 44 44 10N 3 50 E
Ceylon = Sri Lanka ■ 97 7 30N 80 50 E
Cha-am 100 12 48N 99 58 E
Cha Pa 100 22 21N 103 50 E
Chaam 47 51 30N 4 52 E
Chabeuil 45 44 54N 5 1 E
Chabjuwardoo B. 137 23 0S 113 30 E
Chablais 45 46 20N 6 36 E
Chablis 43 47 47N 3 48 E
Chabounia 118 35 30N 2 38 E
Chacabuco 172 34 40S 60 27W
Chacewater 30 50 15N 5 8W
Chachapoyas 174 6 15S 77 50W
Chachoengsao 100 13 42N 101 5 E
Chachran 93 28 55N 70 30 E
Chachro 94 25 5N 70 15 E
Chaco □ 172 25 0S 61 0W
Chaco Austral 176 27 30S 61 40W
Chaco Boreal 172 22 30S 60 10W
Chaco Central 176 24 0S 61 0W
Chad ■ 117 12 30N 17 15 E
Chadan 77 51 17N 91 35 E
Chadileuvú, R. 172 37 0S 65 55W
Chadiza 127 14 10S 33 34 E
Chadron 158 42 50N 103 0W
Chadyr-Lunga 82 46 3N 28 51 E
Chae Hom 100 18 43N 99 35 E
Chaem, R. 100 18 11N 98 38 E
Chaeryŏng 107 38 24N 125 36 E
Chafurray 174 3 10N 73 14W
Chagai 93 29 30N 63 0 E
Chagai Hills 93 29 30N 63 0 E
Chagda 77 58 45N 130 30 E
Chagford 30 50 40N 3 50W
Chagny 43 46 57N 4 45 E
Chagoda 80 59 10N 35 25 E
Chagos Arch. 86 6 0S 72 0 E
Chāh Bahār 93 25 20N 60 40 E
Ch'ahaerhyuichungch'i 106 41 18N 112 48 E
Ch'ahanch'elo 106 41 41N 114 15 E
Chahar Buriak 93 30 15N 62 0 E
Chāhr-e Babak 93 30 10N 55 20 E
Chahsikiang 105 32 32N 79 41 E
Chahtung 98 26 41N 98 10 E
Chai-nat 100 15 11N 100 8 E
Chaibasa 99 22 42N 85 49 E
Chaillé-les-Marais 44 46 25N 1 2W
Chaise Dieu, La 44 45 20N 3 40 E
Chaiya 101 9 23N 99 14 E
Chaiyaphum 100 15 48N 102 2 E
Chaize-le-Vicomté, La 42 46 40N 1 18W
Chaj Doab 94 32 0N 73 0 E
Chajari 172 30 42N 58 0W
Chakaria 98 21 45N 92 5 E
Chake Chake 126 5 15S 39 45 E
Chakhansur 93 31 10N 62 0 E
Chaklashi 94 22 40N 72 52 E
Chakonipau, L. 151 56 18N 68 30W
Chakradharpur 95 22 45N 85 40 E
Chakwadam 98 27 29N 98 31 E
Chakwal 94 32 50N 72 45 E
Chala 174 15 48S 74 20W
Chalais 44 45 16N 0 3 E
Chalakudi 97 10 18N 76 20 E
Chalcatongo 165 17 4N 97 34W
Chalchihuites 164 23 29N 103 53W
Chalcis = Khalkís 69 38 27N 23 42 E
Chale 28 50 35N 1 19W
Chaleur B. 151 47 55N 65 30W
Chalfant 163 37 32N 118 21W
Chalfont St. Peter 29 51 36N 0 33W
Chalhuanca 174 14 15S 73 5W
Ch'aling 109 26 47N 113 45 E
Chaling Hu 105 34 55N 98 0 E
Chalisgaon 96 20 30N 75 10 E
Chalkar 83 50 35N 51 52 E
Chalkar Oz. 83 50 33N 51 45 E
Chalky Inlet 143 46 3S 166 31 E
Challans 42 46 50N 1 52W
Challapata 174 19 0S 66 50W
Challerange 43 49 18N 4 46 E
Challis 160 44 32N 114 25W
Chalna 95 22 36N 89 35 E
Chalon-sur-Saône 43 46 48N 4 50 E
Chalonnes 42 47 20N 0 45W
Châlons-sur-Marne 43 48 58N 4 20 E
Châlus 44 45 39N 0 58 E
Cham, Ger. 49 49 12N 12 40 E
Cham, Switz. 51 47 11N 8 28 E
Cham, Cu Lao 100 15 57N 108 30 E
Chama, R. 127 36 57N 106 37W
Chaman 93 30 58N 66 25 E
Chamarajanagar-Ramasamudram 97 11 52N 76 52 E
Chamartín de la Rosa 58 40 28N 3 40W
Chamba, India 94 32 35N 76 10 E
Chamba, Tanz. 125 11 37S 37 0 E
Chambal, R. 94 26 0N 76 55 E
Chamberlain, Austral. 136 15 58S 127 54 E
Chamberlain, U.S.A. 158 43 50N 99 21W
Chambers 161 35 13N 109 30W
Chambersburg 156 39 53N 77 41W
Chambéry 45 45 34N 5 55 E
Chambeshi 127 12 39S 28 1 E
Chambeshi, R. 124 10 20S 31 58 E
Chambois 42 48 48N 0 6 E
Chambon-Feugerolles, Le 45 45 24N 4 18 E
Chambon, Le 45 45 35N 4 26 E
Chambord 151 48 25N 72 6W
Chamboulive 44 45 26N 1 42 E
Chambri L. 135 4 15S 143 10 E
Chamela 164 19 32N 105 5W
Chamical 172 30 22S 66 27W
Chamkar Luong 101 11 0N 103 45 E
Chamonix 45 45 55N 6 51 E
Champa 95 22 2N 82 43 E
Champagne, Can. 152 60 49N 136 30W
Champagne, France 43 49 0N 4 40 E
Champagnole 43 46 45N 5 55 E
Champaign 156 40 8N 88 14W
Champassak 100 14 53N 105 52 E
Champaubert 43 48 50N 3 45 E
Champdeniers 44 46 29N 0 25W
Champeix 44 45 37N 3 8 E
Champerico 166 14 18N 91 55W
Champier 50 45 27N 5 17 E
Champion B. 137 28 44S 114 36 E
Champlain 151 46 27N 72 24W
Champotón 165 19 20N 90 50W
Chamusca 57 39 21N 8 29W
Chana 101 6 55N 100 44 E
Chañaral 172 26 15S 70 50W
Chanasma 94 23 44N 72 5 E
Chanca, R. 57 37 49N 7 15W
Chanchiang 109 21 15N 110 20 E
Chancy 50 46 8N 6 0 E
Chanda 96 19 57N 79 25 E
Chandalar 147 67 30N 148 35W
Chandausi 95 28 27N 78 49 E
Chandeleur Is. 59 29 45N 88 53W
Chandeleur Sd. 159 29 58N 88 40W
Chandernagore 95 22 52N 88 24 E
Chandigarh 94 30 30N 76 58 E
Chandler, Can. 151 48 18N 64 46W
Chandler, Ariz., U.S.A. 161 33 20N 111 56W
Chandler, Okla., U.S.A. 159 35 43N 97 20W
Chandler's Ford 28 50 59N 1 23W
Chandlers Peak 141 30 24S 152 10 E
Chandmani 105 45 20N 97 59 E
Chandpur, Bangla. 98 22 8N 90 55 E
Chandpur, India 94 29 8N 78 19 E
Chang 94 26 59N 68 30 E
Ch'ang Chiang, R. 109 31 40N 121 50 E
Chang, Ko 101 12 0N 102 23 E
Changa 95 33 53N 77 35 E
Changanacheri 97 9 25N 76 31 E
Changane, R. 125 23 30S 33 50 E
Ch'anganpao 108 26 9N 109 42 E
Changchiak'ou 106 40 50N 114 53 E
Ch'angchiang 100 19 19N 108 43 E
Ch'angchih 106 36 11N 113 6 E
Ch'angchou 109 31 47N 119 58 E
Changchou 109 24 31N 117 40 E
Ch'angch'un 107 43 58N 125 19 E
Ch'angch'unling 107 45 22N 125 28 E
Changdori 107 38 30N 127 40 E
Ch'angfeng 109 32 27N 117 9 E
Changhsing 109 31 0N 119 56 E
Ch'anghua 109 30 10N 119 15 E
Changhua 109 24 2N 120 30 E
Changhŭng 107 34 41N 126 52 E
Changhŭngni 107 40 24N 128 19 E
Ch'angi 107 36 51N 119 23 E
Changjin 107 40 23N 127 15 E
Changjin-chŏsuji 107 40 30N 127 15 E
Changkuangts'ai Ling 107 45 50N 128 50 E
Changli 107 39 40N 119 19 E
Ch'angling 107 44 16N 123 57 E
Ch'anglo, Fukien, China 109 25 58N 119 31 E
Ch'anglo, Fukien, China 109 26 40N 117 20 E
Ch'anglo, Kwangtung, China 109 24 4N 115 37 E
Changlun 101 6 25N 100 26 E
Changming 108 31 44N 104 44 E
Ch'angning, Hunan, China 109 26 25N 112 15 E
Ch'angning, Szechwan, China 108 28 38N 104 57 E
Ch'angning, Yunnan, China 108 24 50N 99 36 E
Ch'angpai 107 41 26N 128 0 E
Ch'angpai Shan 107 42 25N 129 0 E
Changpei 106 41 7N 114 51 E
Ch'angp'ing 106 40 12N 116 12 E
Changp'ing 109 25 18N 117 24 E
Changpu 109 24 2N 117 31 E
Ch'angsha 109 28 15N 113 0 E
Ch'angshan 109 28 57N 118 31 E
Ch'angshou 108 29 50N 107 2 E
Ch'angshu 109 31 33N 120 45 E
Ch'angshun 108 25 59N 106 25 E
Ch'angt'ai 109 24 34N 117 50 E
Ch'angte 109 29 5N 111 42 E
Ch'angt'ing 109 25 52N 116 20 E
Ch'angt'u 107 42 47N 124 0 E
Ch'angtu 108 31 10N 97 14 E
Ch'angt'u Shan 109 30 15N 122 20 E
Ch'angwu 106 35 9N 107 42 E
Changwu 107 42 24N 122 30 E
Ch'angyang 109 30 28N 111 9 E
Ch'angyatien 106 40 40N 108 46 E
Changyeh 105 38 56N 100 37 E
Changyŏn 107 38 15N 125 6 E
Ch'angyüan 106 35 17N 114 50 E
Chanhanga 128 16 0S 14 8 E
Chanhua 107 37 42N 118 8 E
Chani 108 25 36N 103 49 E
Channapatna 97 12 40N 77 15 E
Channel Is. 42 49 30N 2 40W
Channel Islands 163 33 30N 119 0W
Channing, Mich., U.S.A. 156 46 9N 88 1W
Channing, Tex., U.S.A. 159 35 45N 102 20W
Chantada 56 42 36N 7 46W
Chanthaburi 100 12 38N 102 12 E
Chantilly 43 49 12N 2 29 E
Chantonnay 42 46 40N 1 3W
Chantrey Inlet 148 67 48N 96 20W
Chanute 159 37 45N 85 25W
Chanyü 107 44 39N 122 45 E
Chanza, R. 57 37 49N 7 15W
Ch'ao Hu 109 31 40N 117 30 E
Chao Phraya Lowlands 100 15 30N 100 0 E
Chao Phraya, R. 100 13 32N 100 36 E
Ch'aoan 109 23 41N 116 33 E
Chaoan 109 23 47N 117 5 E
Chaoch'eng, Shansi, China 106 36 26N 111 43 E
Chaoch'eng, Shantung, China 106 36 3N 115 35 E
Chaochiao 108 28 1N 102 49 E
Chaoch'ing 109 23 7N 112 24 E
Chaohsien 106 37 45N 114 46 E
Ch'aohsien 109 31 41N 117 49 E
Chaop'ing 109 24 1N 110 59 E
Chaot'ung 108 27 19N 103 42 E
Ch'aoyang, Kwangtung, China 109 23 10N 116 30 E
Ch'aoyang, Liaoning, China 107 41 46N 120 16 E
Chaoyüan, Heilungkiang, China 107 45 30N 125 8 E
Chaoyüan, Shantung, China 107 37 22N 120 24 E
Chap Kuduk 76 48 45N 55 5 E
Chapala 127 15 50S 37 35 E
Chapala, Lago de 164 20 10N 103 20W
Chaparmukh 98 26 12N 92 31 E
Chapayevo 83 50 25N 51 10 E
Chapayevsk 81 53 0N 49 40 E
Chapecó 173 27 14S 52 41W
Chapel-en-le-Frith 32 53 19N 1 54W
Chapel Hill 157 35 53N 79 3W
Chapelle-d'Angillon, La 43 47 21N 2 25 E
Chapelle Glain, La 42 47 38N 1 11W
Chapeyevo 84 50 12N 51 10 E
Chapleau 150 47 50N 83 24W
Chaplin 153 50 28N 106 40W
Chaplino 82 48 8N 36 15 E
Chaplygin 81 53 15N 39 55 E
Chapra 95 25 48N 84 50 E
Char 116 21 40N 12 45W
Chara 77 56 54N 118 12 E
Charadai 172 27 35S 60 0W
Charagua 174 19 45S 63 10W
Charak 93 26 46N 54 18 E
Charalá 174 6 17N 73 10W
Charaña 174 17 30S 69 35W
Charapita 174 0 37S 74 21W
Charata 172 27 13S 61 14W
Charcas 164 23 10N 101 20W
Charcoal L. 153 58 49N 102 22W
Charcot I. 13 70 0S 75 0W
Chard, Can. 153 55 55N 111 10W
Chard, U.K. 28 50 52N 2 59W
Chardara 76 41 16N 67 59 E
Chardara, Step 85 42 20N 68 0 E
Charduar 98 26 51N 92 46 E
Chardzhou 85 39 6N 63 34 E
Charente-Maritime □ 44 45 50N 0 35W
Charente □ 44 45 50N 0 16W
Charente, R. 44 45 41N 0 30W
Charentsavan 83 40 35N 44 41 E
Chârib, G. 122 28 6N 32 54 E
Charikar 93 35 0N 69 10 E
Charing 29 51 12N 0 49 E
Charité, La 43 47 10N 3 0 E
Chariton R. 158 39 19N 92 58W
Charkhari 95 25 24N 79 45 E
Charkhi Dadri 94 28 37N 76 17 E
Charlbury 28 51 52N 1 29W
Charlemont 38 54 26N 6 40W
Charleroi 47 50 24N 4 27 E
Charles, C. 162 37 10N 75 52W
Charles City, Iowa, U.S.A. 158 43 2N 92 41W
Charles City, Va., U.S.A. 162 37 20N 77 4W
Charles L. 153 59 50N 110 33W
Charles, Pk. 137 32 53S 121 8 E
Charles Town 156 39 20N 77 50W
Charleston, Miss., U.S.A. 159 34 2N 90 3W
Charleston, Mo., U.S.A. 159 36 52N 89 20W
Charleston, S.C., U.S.A. 157 32 47N 79 56W
Charleston, W. Va., U.S.A. 157 38 24N 81 36W
Charlestown, Ireland 38 53 58N 8 48W
Charlestown, S. Afr. 129 27 26S 29 53 E
Charlestown, Ind., U.S.A. 156 38 29N 85 40W
Charlestown, N.H., U.S.A. 162 43 14N 72 24W
Charlestown of Aberlour 37 57 27N 3 13W
Charlesville 124 5 27S 20 59 E
Charleville 139 26 24S 146 15 E
Charleville-Mézières 43 49 44N 4 40 E
Charleville = Rath Luirc 39 52 21N 8 40W
Charlevoix 156 45 19N 85 14W
Charlieu 45 46 10N 4 10 E
Charlotte, Mich., U.S.A. 156 42 36N 84 48W
Charlotte, N.C., U.S.A. 157 35 16N 80 46W
Charlotte Amalie 147 18 22N 64 56W
Charlotte Harb. 157 26 45N 82 10W
Charlotte Waters 136 25 56N 134 54 E
Charlottenberg 72 59 54N 12 17 E
Charlottesville 156 38 1N 78 30W
Charlottetown 151 46 14N 63 8W
Charlton, Austral. 140 36 16S 143 24 E
Charlton, U.S.A. 158 40 59N 93 20W
Charlton I. 150 52 0N 79 20W
Charlton Kings 28 51 52N 2 3W
Charlwood 29 51 8N 0 12W
Charmes 43 48 22N 6 17 E
Charminster 28 50 43N 2 28W
Charmouth 28 50 45N 2 54W
Charnwood Forest 23 52 43N 1 18W
Charny 151 46 43N 71 15W
Charolles 45 46 27N 4 16 E
Charost 43 47 0N 2 7 E
Charouïne 118 29 0N 0 15W
Charre 127 17 19S 35 10 E
Charroux 44 46 9N 0 25 E
Charsadda 94 34 7N 71 45 E
Charters Towers 138 20 5S 146 13 E
Chartham 29 51 14N 1 1 E
Chartre, La 42 47 42N 0 34 E
Chartres 42 48 29N 1 30 E
Chascomús 172 35 30S 58 0W
Chasefu 127 11 55N 32 58 E
Chaslands Mistake 143 46 38S 169 22 E
Chasseneuil-sur-Bonnieure 44 45 52N 0 29 E
Chata 94 27 42N 77 30 E
Châtaigneraie, La 42 46 38N 0 45W
Chatal Balkan = Udvoy Balkan 67 42 50N 26 50 E
Château-Chinon 43 47 4N 3 56 E
Château d'Oex 50 46 28N 7 8 E

Château-du-Loir 42 47 40N 0 25 E
Château Gontier 42 47 50N 0 42W
Château-la-Vallière 42 47 30N 0 20 E
Château-Landon 43 48 8N 2 40 E
Château, Le 44 45 52N 1 12W
Château Porcien 43 49 31N 4 13 E
Château Renault 42 47 36N 0 56 E
Château-Salins 43 48 50N 6 30 E
Château-Thierry 43 49 3N 3 20 E
Châteaubourg 43 48 7N 1 25W
Châteaubriant 42 47 43N 1 23W
Châteaudun 42 48 3N 1 20 E
Châteaugiron 42 48 3N 1 30W
Châteaulin 42 48 11N 4 8W
Châteaumeillant 44 46 35N 2 12 E
Châteauneuf 42 48 35N 1 15 E
Châteauneuf-du-Faou 42 48 11N 3 50W
Châteauneuf-sur-Charente 44 45 36N 0 3W
Châteauneuf-sur-Cher 43 46 52N 2 18 E
Châteauneuf-sur-Loire 43 47 52N 2 13 E
Châteaurenard 45 43 53N 4 51 E
Châteauroux 43 46 50N 1 40 E
Châtel-Guyon 44 45 55N 3 4 E
Châtel St. Denis 50 46 32N 6 54 E
Châtelaillon-Plage 44 46 5N 1 5W
Châtelard, Le 50 46 4N 6 57 E
Châtelaudren 42 48 33N 2 59W
Chatelet 47 50 24N 4 32 E
Châtelet, Le, Cher, France 44 46 40N 2 20 E
Châtelet, Le, Seine et Marne, France 43 48 30N 2 47 E
Châtellerault 42 46 50N 0 30 E
Châtelus-Malvaleix 44 46 18N 2 1 E
Chatham, N.B., Can. 151 47 2N 65 28W
Chatham, Ont., Can. 150 42 24N 82 11W
Chatham, U.K. 29 51 22N 0 32 E
Chatham, Alaska, U.S.A. 147 57 30N 135 0W
Chatham, La., U.S.A. 159 32 22N 92 26W
Chatham, N.Y., U.S.A. 162 42 21N 73 32W
Chatham Is. 130 44 0 S 176 40W
Chatham Str. 152 57 0N 134 40W
Châtillon, Loiret, France 43 47 36N 2 44 E
Châtillon, Marne, France 43 49 5N 3 43 E
Chatillon 62 45 45N 7 40 E
Châtillon-Coligny 43 47 50N 2 51 E
Châtillon-en-Bazois 43 47 3N 3 39 E
Châtillon-en-Diois 45 44 41N 5 29 E
Châtillon-sur-Seine 43 47 50N 4 33 E
Châtillon-sur-Sèvre 42 46 56N 0 45W
Chatkal, R. 85 41 38N 70 1 E
Chatkalskiy Khrebet 85 41 30N 70 45 E
Chatmohar 95 24 15N 89 26 E
Chatra 95 24 12N 84 56 E
Chatrapur 96 19 22N 85 2 E
Châtre, La 44 46 35N 1 59 E
Chatsworth 127 19 32 S 30 46 E
Chatta-Hantō 111 34 45N 136 55 E
Chattahoochee 157 30 43N 84 51W
Chattanooga 157 35 2N 85 17W
Chatteris 29 52 27N 0 3 E
Chatton 35 55 34N 1 55W
Chaturat 100 15 34N 101 51 E
Chatyrkel, Ozero 85 40 40N 75 18 E
Chatyrtash 85 40 55N 76 25 E
Chau Phu 101 10 42N 105 7 E
Chaudes-Aigues 44 44 51N 3 1 E
Chauffailes 44 46 13N 4 20 E
Chauk 98 20 53N 94 49 E
Chaukan La 99 27 0N 97 15 E
Chaukan Pass 98 27 8N 97 10 E
Chaulnes 43 49 48N 2 47 E
Chaumont 43 48 7N 5 8 E
Chaumont-en-Vexin 43 49 16N 1 53 E
Chaumont-sur-Loire 42 47 29N 1 11 E
Chaunay 44 46 13N 0 9 E
Chauny 43 49 37N 3 12 E
Chausey, Îs. 42 48 52N 1 49W
Chaussin 43 46 59N 5 22 E
Chauvin 153 52 45N 110 10W
Chaux de Fonds, La 50 47 7N 6 50 E
Chaves, Brazil 170 0 15 S 49 55W
Chaves, Port. 56 41 45N 7 32W
Chavuma 125 13 10 S 22 55 E
Chawang 101 8 25N 99 30 E
Ch'aya 108 30 35N 98 3 E
Chayan 85 43 5N 69 25 E
Chayek 85 41 55N 74 30 E
Chaykovskiy 84 56 47N 54 9 E
Chazelles-sur-Lyon 45 45 39N 4 22 E
Cheadle, Gr. Manchester, U.K. 32 53 23N 2 14W
Cheadle, Staffs., U.K. 32 52 59N 1 59W
Cheadle Hulme 32 53 22N 2 12W
Cheb (Eger) 52 50 9N 12 20 E
Chebarkul 84 55 0N 60 25 E
Cheboksary 81 56 8N 47 30 E
Cheboygan 156 45 38N 84 29W
Chebsara 81 59 10N 38 45 E
Chech, Erg 118 25 0N 2 15W
Chechaouen 118 35 9N 5 15W
Chechen 83 43 59N 47 40 E
Chech'eng 106 34 4N 115 13 E
Checheno-Ingush, A.S.S.R. □ 83 43 30N 45 29 E
Chechon 107 37 8N 128 12 E
Checiny 54 50 46N 20 37 E
Checleset B. 152 50 5N 127 35W
Checotah 159 35 31N 95 30W
Chedabucto B. 151 45 25N 61 8W
Cheddar 28 51 16N 2 47W
Cheddleton 32 53 5N 2 2W
Cheduba I. 98 18 45N 93 40 E
Cheepie 139 26 43 S 144 59 E
Ch'eerhch'en Ho, R. 105 39 30N 88 15 E
Chef-Boutonne 44 46 7N 0 4W
Chefoo = Yent'ai 107 37 30N 121 12 E
Chefornak 147 60 10N 164 15W
Chegdomyn 77 51 7N 132 52 E
Chegga 118 25 15N 5 40W
Chehalis 160 46 44N 122 59W
Cheju 107 33 28N 126 30 E
Cheju Do 107 33 29N 126 34 E
Chejung 109 27 13N 119 52 E
Chekalin 81 54 10N 36 10 E
Chekao 109 31 46N 117 45 E
Chekiang □ 109 29 30N 120 0 E
Chela, Sa. da 128 16 20 S 13 20 E
Chelan, Can. 153 52 38N 103 22 E
Chelan, U.S.A. 160 47 49N 120 0W
Chelan, L. 152 48 5N 120 30W
Cheleken 76 39 26N 53 7 E
Chelforó 176 39 0 S 66 40W
Chéliff, O. 118 36 0N 0 8 E
Chelkar 76 47 40N 59 32 E
Chelkar Tengiz, Solonchak 76 48 0N 62 30 E
Chellala Dahrania 118 33 2N 0 1 E
Chelles 43 48 52N 2 33 E
Chełm 54 51 8N 23 30 E
Chełm □ 54 51 15N 23 30 E
Chelmarsh 28 52 29N 2 25W
Chełmek 54 50 6N 19 16 E
Chelmer, R. 29 51 45N 0 42 E
Chełmno 54 53 20N 18 30 E
Chelmsford 29 51 44N 0 29 E
Chełmza 54 53 10N 18 39 E
Chelsea, Austral. 141 38 5 S 145 8 E
Chelsea, Okla., U.S.A. 159 36 35N 95 25W
Chelsea, Vermont, U.S.A. 162 43 59N 72 27W
Cheltenham 28 51 55N 2 5W
Chelva 58 39 45N 1 0W
Chelyabinsk 84 55 10N 61 24 E
Chelyuskin, C. 86 77 30N 103 0 E
Chemainus 152 48 55N 123 48W
Chemikovsk 78 56 31N 58 11 E
Chemillé 42 47 14N 0 45W
Chemnitz = Karl-Marx-Stadt 48 50 50N 12 55 E
Chemor 101 4 44N 101 6 E
Chemult 160 43 14N 121 54W
Chen, Gora 77 65 10N 141 20 E
Chenab, R. 94 30 40N 73 30 E
Chenachane, O. 118 25 30N 3 30W
Chenan 106 33 16N 109 1 E
Chenango Forks 162 42 15N 75 51W
Chencha 123 6 15N 37 32 E
Ch'ench'i 109 28 1N 110 13 E
Ch'enchiachiang 107 34 25N 119 50 E
Chenchiang 109 32 12N 119 27 E
Chenchieh 108 23 15N 107 9 E
Chênée 47 50 37N 5 37 E
Cheney 160 47 38N 117 34W
Chenfeng 108 25 25N 105 51 E
Chengan 108 28 30N 107 30 E
Ch'engch'eng 106 35 6N 109 52 E
Ch'engchiang 108 24 40N 102 55 E
Chengchou 106 34 38N 113 43 E
Chengchow = Chengchou 106 34 38N 113 43 E
Chengelee 98 28 47N 96 16 E
Chengho 109 27 25N 118 46 E
Ch'enghsi Hu 109 32 22N 116 12 E
Ch'enghsien, Chekiang, China 109 29 30N 120 48 E
Ch'enghsien, Kansu, China 106 33 42N 105 36 E
Ch'engk'ou 108 31 58N 108 48 E
Ch'engku 106 33 9N 107 22 E
Ch'engkung 108 24 53N 102 45 E
Ch'engmai 100 19 44N 109 59 E
Ch'engpu 109 26 12N 110 5 E
Ch'engte 107 41 0N 117 58 E
Chengting 106 38 8N 114 37 E
Ch'engtu 108 30 45N 104 0 E
Ch'engtung Hu 109 32 17N 116 23 E
Ch'engtzut'uan 107 39 30N 122 30 E
Ch'engwu 106 35 0N 115 56 E
Ch'engyang 107 36 20N 120 16 E
Chengyang 109 32 36N 114 23 E
Chengyangkuan 109 32 29N 116 37 E
Chenhai 109 29 57N 121 42 E
Ch'enhsien 109 25 48N 113 2 E
Chenhsiung 108 27 27N 104 50 E
Chenhsü 109 27 6N 120 16 E
Chenkán 165 19 8N 90 58W
Chenk'ang 108 24 4N 99 18 E
Chenlai 107 45 52N 123 12 E
Chenning 108 25 57N 105 51 E
Chenp'ing 106 33 2N 112 14 E
Ch'enp'ing 108 31 52N 109 31 E
Chenyüan, Kansu, China 106 35 59N 107 2 E
Chenyüan, Kweichow, China 108 27 0N 108 20 E
Cheo Reo = Hau Bon 101 13 25N 108 28 E
Cheom Ksan 100 14 13N 104 56 E
Chepelare 67 41 44N 24 40 E
Chepén 174 7 10 S 79 15W
Chepes 172 31 20 S 66 35W
Chepo 166 9 10N 79 6W
Chepstow 31 51 38N 2 40W
Cheptsa, R. 81 58 36N 50 4 E
Cheptulil, Mt. 126 1 25N 35 35 E
Chequamegon B. 158 46 40N 90 30W
Chequeche 127 14 13 S 38 30 E
Cher □ 43 47 10N 2 30 E
Chér, R. 43 47 10N 2 10 E
Cheran 98 25 45N 90 44 E
Cherasco 62 44 39N 7 50 E
Cheratte 47 50 40N 5 41 E
Cheraw 157 34 42N 79 54W
Cherbourg 42 49 39N 1 40W
Cherchell 118 36 35N 2 12 E
Cherdakly 81 54 25N 48 50 E
Cherdyn 84 60 24N 56 29 E
Cheremkhovo 77 53 32N 102 40 E
Cherepanovo 76 54 15N 83 30 E
Cherepovets 81 59 5N 37 55 E
Chergui, Chott Ech 118 34 10N 0 25 E
Cheri 121 13 26N 11 21 E
Cherikov 80 53 32N 31 20 E
Cheriton 28 51 3N 1 9W
Cheriton Fitzpaine 30 50 51N 3 38W
Cherkessk 83 44 25N 42 10 E
Cherlak 76 54 15N 74 55 E
Chermoz 84 58 46N 56 10 E
Chernak 85 43 24N 68 2 E
Chernaya Kholunitsa 84 58 51N 51 52 E
Cherni, Mt. 67 42 35N 23 18 E
Chernigov 80 51 28N 31 20 E
Chernikovsk 84 54 48N 56 8 E
Chernobyl 80 51 13N 30 15 E
Chernogorsk 77 54 5N 91 10 E
Chernomorskoye 82 45 31N 32 46 E
Chernovskoye 81 58 48N 47 20 E
Chernovtsy 82 48 0N 26 0 E
Chernoye 77 70 30N 89 10 E
Chernushka 84 56 29N 56 3 E
Chernyakhovsk 80 54 29N 21 48 E
Chernyshevskiy 77 62 40N 112 30 E
Chernyshkovskiy 83 48 30N 42 28 E
Cherokee, Iowa, U.S.A. 158 42 40N 95 30W
Cherokee, Okla., U.S.A. 159 36 45N 98 25W
Cherokees, L. of the 159 36 50N 95 12W
Cherquenco 176 38 35 S 72 0W
Cherrapunji 99 25 17N 91 47 E
Cherry Creek 160 39 50N 114 58W
Cherry Valley, U.S.A. 162 42 48N 74 45W
Cherry Valley, U.S.A. 163 33 59N 116 57W
Cherryvale 159 37 20N 95 33W
Cherskiy 77 68 45N 161 18 E
Cherskogo Khrebet 77 65 0N 143 0 E
Chertkovo 83 49 25N 40 19 E
Chertsey 29 51 23N 0 30W
Cherven 80 53 45N 28 13 E
Cherven-Bryag 67 43 17N 24 7 E
Cherwell, R. 28 51 46N 1 18W
Chesapeake Bay 162 38 0N 76 12W
Chesapeake Beach 162 38 41N 76 32W
Chesha B. = Cheshskaya G. 78 67 20N 47 0 E
Chesham 29 51 42N 0 36W
Cheshire □ 32 53 14N 2 30W
Cheshunt 29 51 42N 0 1W
Chesil Beach 23 50 37N 2 33W
Cheslatta L. 152 53 49N 125 20W
Chesne, Le 43 49 30N 4 45 E
Cheste 59 39 30N 0 41W
Chester, U.K. 32 53 12N 2 53W
Chester, Calif., U.S.A. 160 40 22N 121 22W
Chester, Ill., U.S.A. 158 37 58N 89 50W
Chester, Mont., U.S.A. 160 48 31N 111 0W
Chester, Pa., U.S.A. 162 39 54N 75 20W
Chester, S.C., U.S.A. 157 34 44N 81 13W
Chester, Va., U.S.A. 162 37 21N 77 27W
Chester, Vt., U.S.A. 162 43 16N 72 36W
Chester-le-Street 33 54 53N 1 34W
Chesterfield, Can. 148 63 0N 91 0W
Chesterfield, U.K. 33 53 14N 1 26W
Chesterfield, U.S.A. 162 37 23N 77 31W
Chesterfield I. 129 16 20 S 43 58 E
Chesterfield, Îles 133 19 52 S 158 15 E
Chesterfield Inlet 148 63 30N 90 45W
Chesterton Range 138 25 30 S 147 27 E
Chestertown 162 39 13N 76 4W
Chesuncook L. 151 46 0N 69 10W
Chetaibi 119 37 1N 7 20 E
Cheticamp 151 46 37N 60 59W
Chetumal 165 18 30N 88 20W
Chetumal, Bahía de 165 18 40N 88 10W
Chetwynd 152 55 45N 121 45W
Chevanceaux 44 45 18N 0 14W
Cheviot Hills 35 55 20N 2 30W
Cheviot Ra. 138 25 20 S 143 45 E
Cheviot, The 35 55 29N 2 8W
Chew Bahir 123 4 40N 30 50 E
Chew Magna 28 51 21N 2 37W
Chewelah 160 48 17N 117 43W
Cheyenne, Okla., U.S.A. 159 35 40N 99 40W
Cheyenne, Wyo., U.S.A. 158 41 9N 104 49W
Cheyenne, R. 158 44 50N 101 0W
Cheyenne Wells 158 38 51N 102 23W
Cheylard, Le 45 44 55N 4 25 E
Cheyne B. 137 34 35 S 118 50 E
Chhabra 94 24 40N 76 54 E
Chhang 102 12 15N 104 14 E
Chhatak 95 25 5N 91 37 E
Chhatarpur 95 24 55N 79 43 E
Chhep 100 13 45N 105 24 E
Chhindwara 95 22 2N 78 59 E
Chhlong 101 12 15N 105 58 E
Chhuk 101 10 46N 104 8 E
Chi, R. 100 15 11N 104 43 E
Chiaho 109 25 33N 112 15 E
Chiahsiang 106 35 25N 116 21 E
Chiahsien, Hensi, China 106 38 6N 110 28 E
Chiahsien, Honan, China 106 33 58N 113 13 E
Chiahsing 109 30 45N 120 43 E
Chiai 109 23 29N 120 25 E
Chiali 109 23 10N 120 11 E
Chialing Chiang, R. 108 30 2N 106 19 E
Chiamussu 105 46 50N 130 21 E
Chian, Kiangsi, China 109 27 8N 115 0 E
Chian, Kirin, China 107 41 6N 126 10 E
Chiang Dao 100 19 22N 98 58 E
Chiang Kham 100 19 32N 100 18 E
Chiang Khan 100 17 52N 101 36 E
Chiang Khong 100 20 17N 100 24 E
Chiang Mai 100 18 47N 98 59 E
Chiang Saen 100 20 16N 100 5 E
Chiangch'eng 108 22 36N 101 50 E
Chiangchiat'un 107 40 54N 120 36 E
Chiangching 108 29 13N 106 15 E
Chiangchun 109 23 5N 120 5 E
Chianghua 109 25 2N 111 45 E
Chiangk'ou 108 27 42N 108 50 E
Chiangling 109 30 21N 112 5 E
Chiangmen 109 22 37N 113 3 E
Chiangpei 108 29 47N 106 29 E
Chiangp'ing 108 21 36N 108 8 E
Chiangshan 109 28 45N 118 37 E
Chiangta 108 31 28N 99 12 E
Chiangti 108 27 1N 103 37 E
Chiangyin 109 31 50N 120 18 E
Chiangyü 108 31 47N 104 45 E
Chiangyung 109 25 16N 111 20 E
Chianie 125 15 35 S 13 40 E
Ch'iaochia 108 26 57N 103 3 E
Chiaochou Wan 107 36 10N 120 15 E
Chiaoho, Hopei, China 106 38 1N 116 17 E
Chiaoho, Kirin, China 107 43 42N 127 19 E
Chiaohsien 107 36 20N 120 0 E
Chiaoling 109 24 40N 117 10 E
Chiaotso 106 35 17N 113 18 E
Chiapa de Corzo 165 16 42N 93 0W
Chiapa, R. 165 16 42N 93 0W
Chiapas □ 165 17 0N 92 45W
Chiaramonte Gulfi 65 37 1N 14 41 E
Chiaravalle 63 38 41N 16 24 E
Chiaravalle Centrale 65 38 41N 16 25 E
Chiari 62 45 31N 9 55 E
Chiashan 109 32 37N 118 8 E
Chiasso 51 45 50N 9 0 E
Chiating 109 31 21N 121 15 E
Chiautla 165 18 18N 98 34W
Chiávari 62 44 20N 9 20 E
Chiavenna 62 46 18N 9 23 E
Chiawang 107 34 30N 117 22 E
Chiayü 109 29 59N 113 54 E
Chiba 111 35 30N 140 7 E
Chiba-ken □ 111 35 30N 140 20 E
Chibabava 129 20 25 S 33 35 E
Chibemba 125 15 48 S 14 8 E
Chibougamau 150 49 56N 74 24W
Chibougamau L. 150 49 50N 74 20W
Chibougamau, R. 150 49 50N 75 40W
Chibuk 121 10 52N 12 50 E
Chibuto 129 24 40 S 33 33 E
Chic-Chocs, Mts. 151 48 55N 66 0W
Chic-Chocs, Parc Prov. des 151 48 55N 66 20W
Chicacole = Srikakulam 97 18 14N 84 4 E
Chicago 156 41 53N 87 40W
Chicago Heights 156 41 29N 87 37W
Chicago North 156 42 20N 87 50W
Chichagof I. 152 58 0N 136 0W
Chichaoua 118 31 32N 8 44W
Chichén Itzá 165 20 40N 88 32W
Chichester 29 50 50N 0 47W
Chichester Ra. 136 21 35 S 117 45 E
Chich'i 109 30 4N 118 34 E
Ch'ichiang 108 29 0N 106 40 E
Chichibu 111 36 5N 139 10 E
Ch'ich'ihaerh 105 47 22N 123 57 E
Chichiriviche 174 10 56N 68 16W
Ch'ich'un 109 30 14N 115 25 E
Chickasha 159 35 0N 98 0W
Chicken Hd. 31 58 10N 6 15W
Chiclana de la Frontera 57 36 26N 6 9W
Chiclayo 174 6 42 S 79 50W
Chico 160 39 45N 121 54W
Chico, R., Chubut, Argent. 160 44 0 S 67 0W
Chico, R., Santa Cruz, Argent. 176 49 30 S 69 30W
Chicoa 125 15 35 S 32 20 E
Chicomo 129 24 31 S 34 6 E
Chicontepec 165 20 58N 98 10W
Chicopee 162 42 6N 72 37W
Chicoutimi 151 48 28N 71 5W
Chidambaram 97 11 20N 79 45 E
Chiddingfold 29 51 6N 0 37W
Chidenguele 129 24 55 S 34 2 E
Chidley C. 149 60 23N 64 26W
Chiehhsiu 106 37 0N 111 55 E
Ch'iehmo 105 38 8N 85 32 E
Chiehshou 106 33 20N 115 24 E
Chiehyang 109 23 37N 116 19 E
Chiem Hoa 100 22 12N 105 17 E
Chiemsee 49 47 53N 12 27 E
Chiench'ang 107 41 16N 124 28 E
Chiench'angying 107 40 8N 118 50 E
Ch'iench'engchen 108 27 12N 109 50 E

Ch'ienchiang, Hupeh, China	109	30 25N	112 51 E
Ch'ienchiang, Kwangsi-Chuang, China	108	23 40N	108 58 E
Ch'ienchiang, Szechwan, China	108	29 31N	108 46 E
Chiench'uan	108	26 28N	99 52 E
Chiengi	124	8 45 S	29 10 E
Chienho	108	26 39N	108 35 E
Ch'ienhsi	108	27 3N	106 0 E
Ch'ienhsien	106	34 30N	108 10 E
Chienko	108	32 0N	105 23 E
Chienli	109	29 49N	112 53 E
Chienou	109	27 5N	118 20 E
Ch'ienshan, Anhwei, China	109	30 41N	116 35 E
Ch'ienshan, Kiangsi, China	109	28 18N	117 40 E
Chienshih	108	30 40N	109 43 E
Chienshui	108	23 37N	102 49 E
Chiente	109	29 29N	119 16 E
Chienti, R.	63	43 15N	13 30 E
Chienwei	108	29 13N	103 56 E
Chienyang	109	27 21N	118 5 E
Ch'ienyang, Hunan, China	109	27 18N	110 10 E
Ch'ienyang, Kansu, China	106	34 35N	107 2 E
Chienyang	108	30 24N	104 33 E
Chierhkalang	107	43 6N	122 54 E
Chieri	62	45 0N	7 50 E
Chiese, R.	62	45 45N	10 35 E
Chieti	63	42 22N	14 10 E
Chièvres	47	50 35N	3 48 E
Chigasaki	111	35 19N	139 24 E
Chignecto B.	151	45 48N	64 40W
Chignik	147	56 15N	158 27W
Chigorodó	174	7 41N	76 42W
Chiguana	172	21 0 S	67 50W
Chihari	107	38 40N	126 30 E
Ch'ihch'i	109	21 59N	112 58 E
Chihchiang, Hunan, China	108	27 27N	109 41 E
Chihchiang, Hupei, China	109	30 19N	111 30 E
Chihchin	108	26 42N	105 45 E
Ch'ihfeng	107	42 18N	118 57 E
Chihkou	107	35 55N	119 13 E
Chihli, G. of = Po Hai	107	38 40N	119 0 E
Ch'ihshui	108	29 29N	105 38 E
Ch'ihshui Ho, R.	108	28 53N	105 48 E
Chihsi	107	45 20N	130 55 E
Ch'ihsien	106	34 33N	114 47 E
Chihsien, Honan, China	106	35 25N	114 5 E
Chihsien, Hopei, China	106	37 34N	115 34 E
Chihsien, Shansi, China	106	36 8N	110 39 E
Chihtan	106	36 56N	108 47 E
Chihte	109	30 9N	117 0 E
Chihuahua	164	28 40N	106 3W
Chihuahua □	164	28 40N	106 3W
Chihuatlán	164	19 14N	104 35W
Chiili	85	44 20N	66 15 E
Chik Ballapur	97	13 25N	77 45 E
Chikawawa	127	16 2 S	34 50 E
Chikhli	96	20 20N	76 18 E
Chikmagalur	97	13 15N	75 45 E
Chikodi	96	16 26N	74 38 E
Chikonde	127	12 16 S	31 38 E
Ch'ik'ou	107	38 37N	117 35 E
Chikugo	110	33 14N	130 28 E
Chikuma-Gawa, R.	111	36 59N	138 35 E
Chilac	165	18 20N	97 24W
Chilako, R.	152	53 53N	122 57W
Chilam Chavki	95	35 5N	75 5 E
Chilanga	127	15 33 S	28 16 E
Chilant'ai	106	39 45N	105 45 E
Chilapa	165	17 40N	99 20W
Chilas	95	35 25N	74 5 E
Chilaw	93	7 30N	79 50 E
Chilcotin, R.	152	51 44N	122 23W
Childers	139	25 15 S	152 17 E
Childress	159	34 30N	100 50W
Chile ■	176	35 0 S	71 15W
Chilecito	172	29 0 S	67 40W
Chilete	174	7 10 S	78 50W
Chilham	29	51 15N	0 59 E
Chilik, Kazakh S.S.R., U.S.S.R.	84	51 7N	53 55 E
Chilik, Kirgiz S.S.R., U.S.S.R.	85	43 33N	78 17 E
Chililabombwe (Bancroft)	125	12 18 S	27 43 E
Chilin	105	43 53N	126 38 E
Ch'ilin Hu	105	31 50N	89 0 E
Chilka L.	96	19 40N	85 25 E
Chilko, L.	152	52 60N	124 10W
Chilko, R.	152	52 6N	124 9W
Chillagoe	138	17 14 S	144 33 E
Chillán	172	36 40 S	72 10W
Chillicothe, Ill., U.S.A.	158	40 55N	89 32W
Chillicothe, Mo., U.S.A.	158	39 45N	93 30W
Chillicothe, Ohio, U.S.A.	156	39 53N	82 58W
Chilliwack	152	49 10N	122 0W
Chilo	94	27 12N	73 32 E
Chiloane, Î.	129	20 40 S	34 55 E
Chiloé, I. de	176	42 50 S	73 45W
Chilpancingo	165	17 30N	99 40W
Chiltern	141	36 10 S	146 36 E
Chiltern Hills	29	51 44N	0 42W
Chilton	156	44 1N	88 12W
Chiluage	124	9 15 S	21 42 E
Chilubula	127	10 14 S	30 51 E
Chilumba	127	10 28 S	34 12 E
Chilung	109	25 3N	121 45 E
Chilwa, L. (Shirwa)	127	15 15 S	35 40 E
Chimacum	160	48 1N	122 53W
Chimaltitán	164	21 46N	103 50W
Chimán	166	8 45N	78 40W
Chimay	47	50 3N	4 20 E
Chimbay	76	42 57N	59 47 E
Chimborazo	174	1 20 S	78 55W
Chimbote	174	9 0 S	78 35W
Ch'imen	109	29 56N	117 47 E
Chimion	85	40 15N	71 32 E
Chimishliya	70	46 34N	28 44 E
Chimkent	85	42 18N	69 36 E
Chimo	107	36 23N	120 27 E
Chimpembe	127	9 31 S	29 33 E
Chin □	98	22 0N	93 0 E
Chin Chiang, R.	109	28 23N	115 48 E
Chin Hills	98	22 30N	93 30 E
Chin Ho, R.	106	35 2N	113 25 E
Chin Ling Shan	106	34 0N	107 0 E
Ch'in Shui, R.	109	26 13N	115 15 E
China	164	25 40N	99 20W
China ■	105	30 0N	110 0 E
China Lake	163	35 44N	117 37W
Chinacates	164	25 0N	105 14W
Chinacota	174	7 37N	72 36W
Ch'inan	106	34 50N	105 35 E
Chinan	106	36 32N	117 0 E
Chinandega	166	12 30N	87 0W
Chinati Pk.	159	30 0N	104 25W
Chincha Alta	174	13 20 S	76 0W
Chinch'eng	106	35 30N	112 50 E
Chinchi	106	37 57N	106 6 E
Chinch'i	109	27 54N	116 44 E
Chinchiang, Fukien, China	109	24 54N	118 35 E
Chinchiang, Kiangsi, China	109	29 44N	115 59 E
Chinchiang, Yunnan, China	108	26 14N	100 34 E
Chinchilla	139	26 45 S	150 38 E
Chinchilla de Monte Aragón	59	38 53N	1 40W
Chinchón	58	40 9N	3 26W
Chinchorro, Banco	165	18 35N	87 20W
Ch'inchou	108	21 58N	108 35 E
Chinchou	107	41 8N	121 6 E
Chinch'uan	108	31 30N	101 55 E
Chincoteague	162	37 58N	75 21W
Chincoteague B.	162	38 5N	75 8W
Chinde	127	18 45 S	36 30 E
Chindo	107	34 28N	126 15 E
Chindwin, R.	98	21 26N	95 15 E
Chineni	95	33 2N	75 15 E
Ch'ing Chiang, R.	109	29 51N	112 22 E
Ch'ing Hai	105	37 0N	100 20 E
Ching Ho, R.	106	34 29N	109 5 E
Ching Shan	109	31 40N	111 30 E
Chinga	127	15 13 S	38 35 E
Chingan	109	28 52N	115 22 E
Ch'ingchen	108	26 32N	106 30 E
Ch'ingch'eng	107	37 11N	117 42 E
Chingchiang	109	32 2N	120 16 E
Ch'ingchiang, Kiangsi, China	109	28 5N	115 30 E
Ch'ingchiang, Kiangsu, China	107	33 33N	119 4 E
Ch'ingchien	106	37 12N	110 6 E
Chingch'uan	106	35 15N	107 22 E
Ch'ingfeng	106	35 54N	115 7 E
Chinghai	106	38 56N	116 55 E
Ch'inghomen	107	41 45N	121 25 E
Chinghsi	108	23 8N	106 25 E
Ch'inghsien	106	38 35N	116 48 E
Chinghsien	109	30 42N	118 23 E
Ch'inghsü	106	37 40N	112 20 E
Chinghung	108	22 0N	100 49 E
Chingi Chiang, R.	108	29 32N	103 44 E
Chingku	108	23 28N	100 42 E
Chingleput	97	12 42N	79 58 E
Ch'ingliu	109	26 12N	116 48 E
Chinglo	106	38 24N	111 54 E
Ch'inglung	108	25 48N	105 14 E
Chingmen	109	30 58N	112 6 E
Chingning, Chekiang, China	109	27 58N	119 38 E
Chingning, Kansu, China	106	35 30N	105 45 E
Chingola	127	12 31 S	27 53 E
Chingole	127	13 4 S	34 17 E
Chingpien	106	37 24N	108 36 E
Chingpo Hu	107	43 50N	128 50 E
Ch'ingp'u	109	31 9N	121 6 E
Chingshan	109	31 2N	113 3 E
Chingshih	109	29 40N	111 50 E
Ch'ingshui	106	34 44N	106 2 E
Chingsing	106	38 5N	114 8 E
Chingt'ai	106	37 10N	104 8 E
Ch'ingtao	107	36 5N	120 25 E
Chingte	109	30 19N	118 31 E
Chingtechen	109	29 19N	117 15 E
Ch'ingt'ien	109	28 9N	120 17 E
Chingtung	108	24 22N	100 50 E
Chingtzukuan	106	33 13N	111 2 E
Chinguar	125	12 18 S	16 45 E
Chinguetti	116	20 25N	12 15W
Chingune	129	20 33 S	35 0 E
Ch'ingyang	105	36 5N	107 40 E
Chingyang	106	34 32N	108 52 E
Ch'ingyang, Anhwei, China	109	30 38N	117 50 E
Ch'ingyang, Ningsia Hui, China	106	36 5N	107 40 E
Chingyü	107	42 22N	126 45 E
Chingyüan	106	36 35N	104 40 E
Ch'ingyüan, Chekiang, China	109	27 37N	119 3 E
Ch'ingyüan, Kwangtung, China	109	23 42N	112 58 E
Ch'ingyüan, Liaoning, China	107	42 6N	124 55 E
Ch'ingyün	107	37 53N	117 23 E
Chinhae	107	35 9N	128 40 E
Chinhanguanine	129	25 21 S	32 30 E
Chinhsi	107	40 49N	120 55 E
Chinhsiang	106	35 5N	116 18 E
Chinhsien, Hopei, China	106	38 2N	115 2 E
Chinhsien, Kiangsi, China	109	28 22N	116 14 E
Chinhsien, Liaoning, China	107	39 6N	121 3 E
Chinhua	109	29 9N	119 41 E
Ch'inhuangtao	107	39 57N	119 40 E
Chining, Inner Mongolia, China	106	41 2N	113 8 E
Chining, Shantung, China	106	35 19N	116 36 E
Chiniot	94	31 45N	73 0 E
Chinipas	164	27 22N	108 32W
Chinju	107	35 12N	128 2 E
Chink'ou	109	30 20N	114 7 E
Chinle	161	36 14N	109 38W
Chinmen	109	24 27N	118 21 E
Chinmen Tao, I.	109	24 25N	118 25 E
Chinnamanur	97	9 50N	77 16 E
Chinnampo	107	38 52N	125 28 E
Chinning	108	24 40N	102 35 E
Chinnur	96	18 57N	79 43 E
Chino, Japan	111	35 59N	138 9 E
Chino, U.S.A.	163	34 1N	117 41W
Chino Valley	161	34 54N	112 28W
Chinon	42	47 10N	0 15 E
Chinook, Can.	153	51 28N	110 59W
Chinook, U.S.A.	160	48 35N	109 19W
Chinp'ing, Kweichow, China	108	26 40N	109 7 E
Chinp'ing, Yunnan, China	108	22 46N	103 15 E
Chinsali	124	10 30 S	32 2 E
Chinsha	108	27 29N	106 15 E
Chinsha Chiang, R. = Yangtze Chiang, R.	108	27 30N	99 30 E
Chinshan	109	30 3N	121 13 E
Ch'inshui	106	35 41N	112 11 E
Chintamani	97	13 26N	78 3 E
Chint'an	109	31 45N	119 35 E
Chint'ang	108	30 51N	104 27 E
Chinwangtao = Ch'inhuangtao	107	39 57N	119 40 E
Ch'inyang	106	35 5N	112 55 E
Ch'inyüan	106	36 31N	112 15 E
Chióggia	63	45 13N	12 15 E
Chíos = Khíos	69	38 27N	26 9 E
Chip Lake	152	53 35N	115 35W
Chipai L.	150	52 56N	87 53W
Chipata (Ft. Jameson)	127	13 38 S	32 28 E
Chipewyan L.	153	58 0N	98 27W
Chipinga	127	20 13 S	32 36 E
Chipiona	57	36 44N	6 26W
Chipley	157	30 45N	85 32W
Chiplun	96	17 31N	73 34 E
Chipman	151	46 6N	65 53W
Chipoka	127	13 57 S	34 28 E
Chiporovtsi	66	43 24N	22 52 E
Chippenham	28	51 27N	2 7W
Chippewa Falls	158	44 55N	91 22W
Chippewa, R.	158	44 45N	91 55W
Chipping Campden	28	52 4N	1 48W
Chipping Norton	28	51 56N	1 32W
Chipping Ongar	29	51 43N	0 15 E
Chipping Sodbury	28	51 31N	2 23W
Chiquian	174	10 10 S	77 0W
Chiquimula	166	14 51N	89 37W
Chiquinquirá	174	5 37N	73 50W
Chir, R.	83	48 45N	42 10 E
Chirala	97	15 50N	80 20 E
Chiramba	127	16 55 S	34 39 E
Chiran	110	31 22N	130 27 E
Chiras	93	35 14N	65 40 E
Chirawa	94	28 14N	75 42 E
Chirayinkil	97	8 41N	76 49 E
Chirbury	28	52 35N	3 6W
Chirchik	85	41 29N	69 35 E
Chirfa	117	20 55N	12 14 E
Chiricahua Pk.	161	31 53N	109 14W
Chirikof I.	147	55 50N	155 40W
Chiriquí, Golfo de	166	8 0N	82 10W
Chiriquí, Lago de	166	9 10N	82 0W
Chiriquí, Vol.	166	8 55N	82 35W
Chirivira Falls	127	21 10 S	32 12 E
Chirk	31	52 57N	3 4W
Chirmiri	99	23 15N	82 20 E
Chirnogi	70	44 7N	26 32 E
Chirnside	35	55 47N	2 11W
Chiromo	125	16 30 S	35 7 E
Chirpan	67	42 10N	25 19 E
Chirripó Grande, cerro	166	9 29N	83 29W
Chisamba	127	14 55 S	28 20 E
Chisapani Garhi	99	27 30N	84 2 E
Ch'ishan	106	34 28N	107 35 E
Chishan	106	35 36N	110 59 E
Ch'ishan	109	22 44N	120 31 E
Chishmy	84	54 35N	55 23 E
Chisholm	152	54 55N	114 10W
Chishou	108	28 12N	109 43 E
Chishui	109	27 14N	115 10 E
Chisimba Falls	127	10 12 S	30 56 E
Chisineu Criş	66	46 32N	21 37 E
Chisledon	28	51 30N	1 44W
Chisone, R.	62	45 0N	7 5 E
Chisos Mts.	159	29 20N	103 15W
Chistian Mandi	94	29 50N	72 55 E
Chistopol	81	55 25N	50 38 E
Chita, Colomb.	174	6 11N	72 28W
Chita, U.S.S.R.	77	52 0N	113 25 E
Chitado	125	17 10 S	14 8 E
Ch'it'ai	105	44 1N	89 28 E
Chitapur	96	17 10N	76 50 E
Chitembo	125	13 30 S	16 50 E
Chitina	147	61 30N	144 30W
Chitinghsilin	105	32 51N	92 28 E
Chitipa	127	9 41 S	33 19 E
Chitokoloki	125	13 43 S	23 4 E
Chitorgarh	94	24 52N	74 43 E
Chitrakot	96	19 20N	81 40 E
Chitral	93	35 50N	71 56 E
Chitravati, R.	97	14 30N	78 0 E
Chitré	167	7 59N	80 27W
Chitse	106	36 54N	114 52 E
Chittagong	98	22 19N	91 55 E
Chittagong □	98	24 5N	91 25 E
Chittoor	97	13 15N	79 5 E
Chittur	97	10 40N	76 45 E
Chitu	123	8 38N	37 58 E
Ch'itung, Hunan, China	109	26 47N	112 7 E
Ch'itung, Kiangsu, China	109	31 49N	121 40 E
Chiuant'u	107	42 33N	128 19 E
Chiuchaohua	108	32 20N	105 45 E
Chiuch'engch'i	108	27 10N	108 42 E
Chiuchiang, Kiangsi, China	109	29 43N	115 55 E
Chiuchiang, Kwangtung, China	109	22 50N	112 50 E
Chiuch'üan	105	39 46N	98 34 E
Chiuhsiangch'eng	109	33 13N	114 50 E
Chiukuanch'eng	106	35 50N	115 22 E
Chiuling Shan	109	28 50N	114 20 E
Chiuliuch'eng	108	24 32N	109 15 E
Chiulung	108	28 59N	101 32 E
Ch'iungchou Haihsia	100	20 10N	110 15 E
Ch'iunghai	100	19 15N	110 26 E
Chiunglai	108	30 25N	103 30 E
Chiunglai Shan	108	31 20N	102 50 E
Ch'iungshan	100	19 51N	110 26 E
Chiuningkang	109	26 48N	114 6 E
Ch'iupei	108	24 3N	104 12 E
Chiushench'iu	106	33 10N	115 8 E
Chiushengch'i	108	27 31N	109 12 E
Chiusi	63	43 1N	11 58 E
Chiut'ai	107	44 10N	125 49 E
Chiutaosha	106	35 39N	103 45 E
Chiuwuch'ing	106	39 23N	116 53 E
Chiva	59	39 27N	0 41W
Chivasso	62	45 10N	7 52 E
Chivilcoy	172	35 0 S	60 0W
Chiwanda	127	11 23 S	34 55 E
Chiwefwe	127	13 37 S	29 31 E
Chiyang	107	37 0N	117 13 E
Ch'iyang	109	20 35N	111 52 E
Chiyüan	106	35 5N	112 39 E
Chiyün	109	28 35N	120 2 E
Chizera	127	13 10 S	25 0 E
Chkalov = Orenburg	78	52 0N	55 5 E
Chkolovsk	81	56 50N	43 10 E
Chlumec	52	50 9N	15 29 E
Chmielnik	54	50 37N	20 43 E
Cho Bo	100	20 46N	105 10 E
Cho Do	107	38 30N	124 40 E
Cho Phuoc	101	10 26N	107 18 E
Choba	126	2 30N	38 5 E
Chobe National Park	128	21 30 S	25 0 E
Chobe, R.	128	18 10 S	24 10 E
Chobol	121	11 53N	13 1 E
Chochiwŏn	107	36 37N	127 18 E
Chocianów	54	51 35N	15 33 E
Chociwel	54	53 29N	15 21 E
Chocó □	174	6 0N	77 0W
Chocontá	174	5 9N	73 41W
Chodaków	54	52 16N	20 18 E
Chodavaram	96	17 40N	82 50 E
Chodecz	54	52 56N	19 2 E
Chodziez	54	52 58N	17 0 E
Choele Choel	176	39 11 S	65 40W
Chōfu	111	35 39N	139 33 E
Chohsien	106	39 30N	116 0 E
Choiseul I.	130	7 0 S	156 40 E
Choisy-le-Roi	43	48 45N	2 24 E
Choix	164	26 40N	108 10W
Chojna	54	52 58N	14 25 E
Chojnice	54	53 42N	17 40 E
Chojnów	54	51 25N	15 58 E
Choke Mts.	123	11 18N	37 15 E
Chokurdakh	77	70 38N	147 55 E
Cholame	163	35 44N	120 18W
Cholet	42	47 4N	0 52W
Chollerton	35	55 4N	2 7W
Cholpon-Ata	85	42 40N	77 6 E
Cholsey	28	51 34N	1 10W
Cholu	106	40 19N	115 5 E
Choluteca	166	13 20N	87 14W
Choluteca, R.	166	13 5N	87 20W
Chom Bung	100	13 37N	99 36 E
Chom Thong	100	18 25N	98 41 E
Choma	127	16 48 S	26 59 E
Chomen Swamp	123	9 20N	37 10 E

Chomu **Clee Hills**

Chomu 94 27 15N 75 40 E
Chomutov 52 50 28N 13 23 E
Chon Buri 100 13 22N 100 59 E
Chon Thanh 101 11 24N 106 36 E
Chŏnan 107 36 48N 127 9 E
Chonburi 101 13 21N 101 1 E
Chone 174 0 40 S 80 0W
Chong Kai 100 13 57N 103 35 E
Chong Mek 100 15 10N 105 27 E
Chŏngdo 107 35 38N 128 42 E
Chŏngha 107 36 12N 129 21 E
Chŏngjin 107 41 47N 129 50 E
Chŏngju 107 39 40N 125 5 E
Chŏngŭp 107 35 35N 126 50 E
Chŏnju 107 35 50N 127 4 E
Chonos, Arch. de los 176 45 0 S 75 0W
Chopda 96 21 20N 75 15 E
Chopim, R. 173 25 35 S 53 5W
Choptank, R. 162 38 41N 76 0W
Chorbat La 95 34 42N 76 37 E
Chorley 32 53 39N 2 39W
Chormet el Melah 119 30 11N 16 29 E
Chorolque, Cerro 172 20 59 S 66 5W
Choroszcz 54 53 10N 22 59 E
Chortkov 80 49 2N 25 46 E
Chorul Tso 95 32 30N 82 30 E
Chŏrwŏn 107 38 15N 127 10 E
Chorzele 54 53 15N 21 2 E
Chorzów 54 50 18N 19 0 E
Chos-Malal 172 37 15 S 70 5W
Chosan 107 40 50N 125 47 E
Choshi 111 35 45N 140 45 E
Choszczno 54 53 7N 15 25 E
Choteau 160 47 50N 112 10W
Chotila 94 22 30N 71 15 E
Chotzu 106 40 52N 112 33 E
Chou Shan 109 30 2N 122 6 E
Chouchih 106 34 8N 108 14 E
Chouch'ü 106 33 46N 104 18 E
Chouning 109 27 15N 119 13 E
Chouts'un 107 36 48N 117 52 E
Ch'ouyang 108 23 14N 104 35 E
Chowchilla 163 37 11N 120 12W
Chowkham 98 20 52N 97 28 E
Choybalsan 105 48 4N 114 30 E
Christchurch, N.Z. 143 43 33 S 172 47 E
Christchurch, U.K. 28 50 44N 1 47W
Christiana, S. Afr. 128 27 52 S 25 8 E
Christiana, U.S.A. 162 39 40N 75 40W
Christiansfeld 73 55 21N 9 29 E
Christiansö, I. 73 55 19N 15 12 E
Christiansted 147 17 45N 64 42W
Christie B. 153 62 32N 111 10W
Christina, R. 153 56 40N 111 3W
Christmas Cr. 136 18 53 S 125 55 E
Christmas Creek 136 18 29 S 125 23 E
Christmas I., Ind. Oc. 142 10 0 S 105 40 E
Christmas I., Pac. Oc. 131 1 58N 157 27W
Christopher L. 137 24 49 S 127 42 E
Chrudim 52 49 58N 15 43 E
Chrzanów 54 50 10N 19 21 E
Chtimba 127 10 35 S 34 13 E
Chu 85 43 36N 73 42 E
Ch'u Chiang, R. 108 30 2N 106 19 E
Chu Chua 152 51 22N 120 10W
Chu Lai 100 15 28N 108 45 E
Chu, R., U.S.S.R. 85 45 0N 67 44 E
Chu, R., Viet. 100 19 53N 105 45 E
Chuadanga 98 23 38N 88 51 E
Ch'üanchou, Fukien, China 109 24 56N 118 35 E
Ch'üanchou, Kwangsi-Chuang, China 109 25 59N 111 4 E
Chuangho 107 39 42N 123 0 E
Chüannan 109 24 50N 114 40 E
Chūbu □ 112 36 45N 137 30 E
Chubut, R. 176 43 0 S 70 0W
Chuch'eng 107 36 0N 119 16 E
Chuch'i 108 32 19N 109 52 E
Chuchi, Chekiang, China 109 29 43N 120 14 E
Chuchi, Honan, China 106 34 27N 115 39 E
Chuchi L. 152 55 12N 124 30W
Ch'uching 108 25 34N 103 45 E
Chuchou 109 27 50N 113 10 E
Chudleigh 30 50 35N 3 36W
Chudovo 80 59 10N 31 30 E
Chudskoye, Oz. 80 58 13N 27 30 E
Ch'üehshan 109 32 48N 114 1 E
Chugach Mts. 147 62 0N 146 0W
Chugiak 147 61 7N 149 10W
Chuginadak I. 147 52 50N 169 45W
Chūgoku □ 110 35 0N 133 0 E
Chūgoku-Sanchi 110 35 0N 133 0 E
Chuguyev 82 49 55N 36 45 E
Chugwater 158 41 48N 104 47W
Chuhai 109 22 17N 113 34 E
Chühsien 107 35 35N 118 49 E
Ch'uhsien, China 109 28 57N 118 58 E
Ch'uhsien, China 109 32 18N 118 18 E
Chuhsien 105 28 57N 118 58 E
Ch'ühsien 108 30 51N 107 1 E
Ch'uhsiung 108 25 2N 101 32 E
Chüjung 109 31 56N 119 10 E
Chukai 101 4 13N 103 25 E
Chukhloma 81 58 45N 42 40 E
Chūko 111 36 44N 139 27 E
Chukotskiy Khrebet 77 68 0N 175 0 E
Chukotskiy, Mys 77 66 10N 169 3 E
Chukotskoye More 77 68 0N 175 0W
Chula Vista 163 32 39N 117 8W
Chulak-Kurgan 85 43 46N 69 9 E
Chülu 106 37 13N 115 1 E
Renamed Teraina

Chulucanas 174 5 0 S 80 0W
Chum Phae 100 16 32N 102 6 E
Chum Saeng 100 15 55N 100 15 E
Chumar 95 32 40N 78 35 E
Chumatien 109 33 0N 114 4 E
Chumbicha 172 29 0 S 66 10W
Chumerna 67 42 45N 25 55 E
Chumikan 77 54 40N 135 10 E
Chumphon 101 10 35N 99 14 E
Chumuare 127 14 31 S 31 50 E
Chumunjin 107 37 55N 127 44 E
Chunchŏn 107 37 58N 127 44 E
Chunga 127 15 0 S 26 2 E
Ch'ungan 109 27 45N 118 0 E
Ch'ungch'ing, Szechwan, China 108 29 30N 106 30 E
Ch'ungch'ing, Szechwan, China 108 30 27N 103 43 E
Chungch'üantzu 106 39 22N 102 42 E
Chunggang ŭp 107 41 48N 126 48 E
Chunghsiang 109 31 10N 112 35 E
Chunghsien 108 30 17N 108 4 E
Chunghwa 107 38 52N 125 47 E
Ch'ungi 109 25 42N 114 19 E
Ch'ungjen 109 27 44N 116 2 E
Chungju 107 36 58N 127 58 E
Chungkang 107 43 42N 127 37 E
Chungking = Ch'ungch'ing 108 29 30N 106 30 E
Ch'ungli 106 40 5N 115 12 E
Chungli 109 24 57N 121 13 E
Ch'ungming 109 31 27N 121 24 E
Ch'ungming Tao, I. 109 31 35N 121 40 E
Chungmu 107 34 50N 128 20 E
Chungning 106 35 22N 105 40 E
Chungshan, Kwangsi-Chuang, China 109 24 30N 111 17 E
Chungshan, Kwangtung, China 109 22 31N 113 20 E
Ch'ungshuiho 106 39 54N 111 34 E
Ch'ungte 109 30 32N 120 26 E
Chungt'iaoshan 106 35 0N 111 30 E
Chungtien 108 27 51N 99 42 E
Ch'ungtso 108 22 20N 107 20 E
Chungtu 108 24 41N 109 42 E
Chungwei 106 37 35N 105 10 E
Chungyang 106 37 24N 111 10 E
Chungyang Shanmo 109 23 10N 121 0 E
Chungyüan 100 19 9N 110 28 E
Chünhsien 109 32 40N 111 15 E
Chunian 94 31 10N 74 0 E
Chunya 127 8 30 S 33 27 E
Chunya □ 126 7 48 S 33 0 E
Ch'unyang 107 43 42N 129 26 E
Chuquibamba 174 15 47N 72 44W
Chuquicamata 172 22 15 S 69 0W
Chuquisaca □ 172 23 30 S 63 30W
Chur 51 46 52N 9 32 E
Churachandpur 98 24 20N 93 40 E
Church Hill 38 55 0N 7 53W
Church House 152 50 20N 125 10W
Church Stretton 28 52 32N 2 49W
Churchdown 28 51 53N 2 9W
Churchill 153 58 47N 94 11W
Churchill, C. 153 58 46N 93 12W
Churchill Falls 151 53 36N 64 19W
Churchill L. 153 55 55N 108 20W
Churchill Pk. 152 58 10N 125 10W
Churchill, R., Man., Can. 153 58 47N 94 12W
Churchill, R., Newf., Can. 151 53 19N 60 10W
Churchill, R., Sask., Can. 153 58 47N 94 12W
Churchtown 39 52 12N 6 20W
Churfisten 51 47 8N 9 17 E
Churston Ferrers 30 50 23N 3 32W
Churu 94 28 20N 75 0 E
Churuguaro 174 10 49N 69 32W
Churwalden 51 46 47N 9 33 E
Chusan 109 32 13N 110 24 E
Chushul 95 33 40N 78 40 E
Chusovaya, R. 84 58 18N 56 22 E
Chusovoy 84 58 15N 57 40 E
Chust 85 41 0N 71 13 E
Ch'ützu 106 36 24N 107 27 E
Chuuronjang 107 41 35N 129 40 E
Chuvash A.S.S.R. □ 81 55 30N 48 0 E
Chuwassu 108 28 48N 97 27 E
Ch'üwu 106 35 35N 111 23 E
Ch'üyang 106 38 37N 114 41 E
Chüyeh 106 35 23N 116 6 E
Ciacova 66 45 35N 21 10 E
Cicero 156 41 48N 87 48W
Cicero Dantas 170 10 36 S 38 23W
Cidacos, R. 58 42 15N 2 10W
Cide 82 41 40N 32 50 E
Ciechanów 54 52 52N 20 38 E
Ciechanów □ 54 53 0N 20 30 E
Ciechocinek 54 52 53N 18 45 E
Ciego de Avila 166 21 50N 78 50W
Ciénaga 174 11 1N 74 15W
Ciénaga de Oro 174 8 53N 75 37W
Cienfuegos 166 22 10N 80 30W
Cieplice Ślaskie Zdrój 54 50 50N 15 40 E
Cierp 44 42 55N 0 40 E
Cies, Islas 56 42 12N 8 55W
Cieszyn 54 49 45N 18 35 E
Cieza 59 38 17N 1 23W
Cifuentes 58 40 47N 2 37W
Ciha Pa. 101 22 20N 103 47 E
Cijara, Pantano de 57 39 18N 4 52W
Cijulang 103 7 42 S 108 27 E

Cikampek 103 6 23 S 107 28 E
Cilacap 103 7 43 S 109 0 E
Cıldır 83 41 10N 43 20 E
Cilgerran 31 52 4N 4 39W
Cilician Gates P. 92 37 20N 34 52 E
Cilician Taurus 92 36 40N 34 0 E
Cîlnicu 70 44 54N 23 4 E
Cimarron, Kans., U.S.A. 159 37 50N 100 20W
Cimarron, N. Mex., U.S.A. 159 36 30N 104 52W
Cimarron, R. 159 37 10N 102 10W
Cîmpia Turzii 70 46 34N 23 53 E
Cîmpina 70 45 10N 25 45 E
Cîmpulung, Argeş, Rumania 70 45 17N 25 3 E
Cîmpulung, Suceava, Rumania 70 47 32N 25 30 E
Cîmpuri 67 46 0N 26 50 E
Cinca, R. 58 42 20N 0 9 E
Cincer 66 43 55N 17 5 E
Cinch, R. 157 36 0N 84 15W
Cincinnati 156 39 10N 84 26W
Cincinnatus 162 42 33N 75 54W
Cinderford 28 51 49N 2 30W
Cîndeşti 70 45 15N 26 42 E
Ciney 47 50 18N 5 5 E
Cinigiano 63 42 53N 11 23 E
Cinogli 63 43 23N 13 10 E
Cinto, Mt. 45 42 24N 8 54 E
Cioranii 70 44 45N 26 25 E
Çiotat, La 45 43 12N 5 36 E
Čiovo 63 43 30N 16 17 E
Cipó 171 11 6 S 38 31W
Circle, Alaska, U.S.A. 147 65 50N 144 10W
Circle, Montana, U.S.A. 158 47 26N 105 35W
Circleville, Ohio, U.S.A. 156 39 35N 82 57W
Circleville, Utah, U.S.A. 161 38 12N 112 24W
Cirebon 103 6 45 S 108 32 E
Cirencester 28 51 43N 1 59W
Cireşu 70 44 47N 22 31 E
Cirey-sur-Vezouze 43 48 35N 6 57 E
Ciriè 62 45 14N 7 35 E
Cirò 65 39 23N 17 3 E
Cisco 159 32 25N 99 0W
Cislău 70 45 14N 26 33 E
Cisna 54 49 12N 22 20 E
Cisneros 174 6 33N 75 4W
Cisnădie 70 45 42N 24 9 E
Cisterna di Latina 64 41 35N 12 50 E
Cisternino 65 40 45N 17 26 E
Cité de Cansado 116 20 51N 17 0W
Citega (Kitega) 126 3 30 S 29 58 E
Citeli-Ckaro 83 41 33N 46 0 E
Citlaltépetl, mt. 165 19 0N 97 20W
Citrusdal 128 32 35 S 19 0 E
Città della Pieve 63 42 57N 12 0 E
Città di Castello 63 43 27N 12 14 E
Città Sant' Angelo 63 42 32N 14 5 E
Cittadella 63 45 39N 11 48 E
Cittaducale 63 42 24N 12 58 E
Cittanova 65 38 22N 16 0 E
Ciucaş, mt. 70 45 31N 25 56 E
Ciudad Acuña 164 29 20N 101 10W
Ciudad Altamirano 164 18 20N 100 40W
Ciudad Bolívar 174 8 5N 63 30W
Ciudad Camargo 164 27 41N 105 10W
Ciudad de Valles 165 22 0N 98 30W
Ciudad del Carmen 165 18 20N 97 50W
Ciudad Delicias = Delicias 164 28 10N 105 30W
Ciudad Guerrero 164 28 33N 107 28W
Ciudad Guzmán 164 19 40N 103 30W
Ciudad Juárez 164 31 40N 106 28W
Ciudad Madero 165 22 19N 97 50W
Ciudad Mante 165 22 50N 99 0W
Ciudad Obregón 164 27 28N 109 59W
Ciudad Piar 174 7 27N 63 19W
Ciudad Real 57 38 59N 3 55W
Ciudad Real □ 57 38 50N 4 0W
Ciudad Rodrigo 56 40 35N 6 32W
Ciudad Trujillo = Sto. Domingo 167 18 30N 70 0W
Ciudad Victoria 165 23 41N 99 9W
Ciudadela 58 40 0N 3 50 E
Ciulnița 70 44 26N 27 22 E
Civa, B. 82 41 20N 36 40 E
Cividale del Friuli 63 46 6N 13 25 E
Civita Castellana 63 42 18N 12 24 E
Civitanova Marche 63 43 18N 13 41 E
Civitavécchia 63 42 6N 11 46 E
Civitella del Tronto 63 42 48N 13 40 E
Civray 44 46 10N 0 17 E
Çivril 92 38 20N 29 55 E
Cixerri, R. 64 39 45N 8 40 E
Cizre 92 37 19N 42 10 E
Clabach 34 56 38N 6 36W
Clabby 38 54 24N 7 22W
Clach Leathad 34 56 36N 7 52W
Clachan, N. Uist., U.K. 36 57 33N 7 20W
Clachan, Strathclyde, U.K. 34 55 45N 5 35W
Clackline 137 31 40 S 116 32 E
Clackmannan 35 56 10N 3 50W
Clackmannan (□) 26 56 10N 3 47W
Clacton-on-Sea 29 51 47N 1 10 E
Cladich 34 56 21N 5 5W
Claire, L. 152 58 35N 112 5W
Clairemont 159 33 9N 100 44W
Clairvaux-les-Laes 45 46 35N 5 45 E
Clamecy 43 47 28N 3 30 E

Clane 39 53 18N 6 40W
Clanfield 29 50 56N 1 0W
Clanton 157 32 48N 86 36W
Clanwilliam 128 32 11 S 18 52 E
Clar, L. nan 37 58 17N 4 8W
Clara 39 53 20N 7 38W
Clara, R. 138 19 8 S 142 30 E
Claraville 163 35 24N 118 20W
Clare, N.S.W., Austral. 140 33 24 S 143 54 E
Clare, S. Austral., Austral. 140 33 50 S 138 37 E
Clare, N. Ireland, U.K. 38 54 25N 6 19W
Clare, Suffolk, U.K. 29 52 5N 0 36 E
Clare, U.S.A. 156 43 47N 84 45W
Clare □ 39 52 20N 7 38W
Clare I. 38 53 48N 10 0W
Clare, R. 38 53 20N 9 0W
Clarecastle 39 52 50N 8 58W
Clareen 39 53 4N 7 49W
Claregalaway 39 53 20N 8 57W
Claremont 162 43 23N 72 20W
Claremont Pt. 138 14 1 S 143 41 E
Claremore 159 36 20N 95 20W
Claremorris 38 53 45N 9 0W
Clarence I. 13 61 30 S 53 50W
Clarence, I. 176 54 0 S 72 0W
Clarence, R., Austral. 139 29 25 S 153 22 E
Clarence, R., N.Z. 143 42 10 S 173 56 E
Clarence Str., Austral. 136 12 0 S 131 0 E
Clarence Str., U.S.A. 152 55 40N 132 10W
Clarence Town 167 23 6N 74 59W
Clarendon, Ark., U.S.A. 159 34 41N 91 20W
Clarendon, Tex., U.S.A. 159 34 58N 100 54W
Clarenville 151 48 10N 54 1W
Claresholm 152 50 0N 113 45W
Clarie Coast 13 67 0 S 135 0 E
Clarinbridge 39 53 13N 8 55W
Clarinda 158 40 45N 95 0W
Clarion 158 42 41N 93 46W
Clark 158 44 55N 97 45W
Clark Fork 160 48 9N 116 9W
Clark Fork, R. 160 48 0N 115 40W
Clark Hill Res. 157 33 45N 82 20W
Clarkdale 161 34 53N 112 3W
Clarke City 151 50 12N 66 38W
Clarke, I. 138 40 32 S 148 10 E
Clarke L. 153 54 24N 106 54W
Clarke Ra. 138 20 45 S 148 20 E
Clarks Fork, R. 160 45 0N 109 30W
Clark's Harbour 151 43 25N 65 38W
Clarks Station 163 38 8N 116 42W
Clarks Summit 162 41 31N 75 44W
Clarksburg 156 39 18N 80 21W
Clarksdale 159 34 12N 90 33W
Clarkston 160 46 28N 117 2W
Clarksville, Ark., U.S.A. 159 35 29N 93 27W
Clarksville, Tenn., U.S.A. 157 36 32N 87 20W
Clarksville, Tex., U.S.A. 159 33 37N 94 59W
Claro, R. 171 19 8 S 50 40W
Clashmore 37 57 53N 4 8W
Clatskanie 160 46 9N 123 12W
Clatteringshaws L. 34 55 3N 4 17W
Claude 159 35 8N 101 22W
Claudio 171 20 26 S 44 46W
Claudy 38 54 55N 7 10W
Claunie L. 36 57 8N 5 6W
Claveria 103 18 37N 121 15 E
Claverley 28 52 32N 2 19W
Clay 163 38 17N 121 10W
Clay Center 158 39 27N 97 9W
Clay Cross 33 53 11N 1 26W
Clay Hd. 32 54 13N 4 23W
Claydon 29 52 6N 1 7 E
Clayette, La 45 46 17N 4 19 E
Claymont 162 39 48N 75 28W
Claymore, oilfield 19 58 30N 0 15W
Claypool 161 33 27N 110 55W
Clayton, Idaho, U.S.A. 160 44 12N 114 31W
Clayton, N. Mex., U.S.A. 159 36 30N 103 10W
Cle Elum 160 47 15N 120 57W
Cleady 39 51 53N 9 32W
Clear C. 39 51 26N 9 30W
Clear I. 39 51 26N 9 30W
Clear Lake, Calif., U.S.A. 160 39 5N 122 47W
Clear Lake, S.D., U.S.A. 158 44 48N 96 41W
Clear Lake, Wash., U.S.A. 160 48 27N 122 15W
Clear Lake Res. 160 41 55N 121 10W
Clearfield, Pa., U.S.A. 156 41 0N 78 27W
Clearfield, Utah, U.S.A. 160 41 10N 112 0W
Clearmont 160 44 43N 106 29W
Clearwater, Can. 152 51 38N 120 2W
Clearwater, U.S.A. 157 27 58N 82 45W
Clearwater Cr. 152 61 36N 125 30W
Clearwater L. 150 56 10N 75 0W
Clearwater, Mts. 160 46 20N 115 30W
Clearwater Prov. Park 153 54 0N 101 0W
Clearwater, R., Alta., Can. 152 52 22N 114 57W
Clearwater, R., Alta., Can. 153 56 44N 111 23W
Clearwater, R., B.C., Can. 152 51 38N 120 3W
Cleat 37 58 45N 2 56W
Cleator Moor 32 54 30N 3 32W
Cleburne 159 32 18N 97 25W
Cleddau R. 31 51 46N 4 44W
Clee Hills 23 52 26N 2 35W

Cleethorpes Columbia

Cleethorpes 33 53 33N 0 2W
Cleeve Cloud 28 51 56N 2 0W
Cleggan 38 53 33N 10 7W
Clelles 45 44 50N 5 38E
Clemency 47 49 35N 5 53E
Clent 28 52 25N 2 6W
Cleobury Mortimer 28 52 23N 2 28W
Clerke Reef 136 17 22S 119 20E
Clerks Rocks 13 56 0S 36 30W
Clermont 133 22 49S 147 39E
Clermont-en-Argonne 43 49 5N 5 4E
Clermont-Ferrand 44 45 46N 3 4E
Clermont-l'Hérault 44 43 38N 3 26E
Clerval 43 47 25N 6 30E
Cléry-Saint-André 43 47 50N 1 46E
Cles 62 46 21N 11 4E
Clevedon 28 51 26N 2 52W
Cleveland, Austral. 139 27 30S 153 15E
Cleveland, Miss., U.S.A. 159 33 43N 90 43W
Cleveland, Ohio, U.S.A. 156 41 28N 81 43W
Cleveland, Okla., U.S.A. 159 36 21N 96 33W
Cleveland, Tenn., U.S.A. 157 35 9N 84 52W
Cleveland, Tex., U.S.A. 159 30 18N 95 0W
Cleveland □ 33 54 35N 1 8E
Cleveland, C. 138 19 11S 147 1E
Cleveland Hills 33 54 25N 1 11W
Clevelândia 173 26 24S 52 23W
Clevvaux 47 50 4N 6 2E
Clew Bay 38 53 54N 9 50W
Clewiston 157 26 44N 80 50W
Cley 29 52 57N 1 3E
Clifden, Ireland 38 53 30N 10 2W
Clifden, N.Z. 143 46 1S 167 42E
Clifden B. 38 53 29N 10 5W
Cliff 161 33 0N 108 44W
Cliffe 29 51 27N 0 31E
Cliffony 38 54 25N 8 28W
Clifford 28 52 6N 3 6W
Clift Sound 36 60 4N 1 17W
Clifton, Austral. 139 27 59S 151 53E
Clifton, Ariz., U.S.A. 161 33 8N 109 23W
Clifton, Tex., U.S.A. 159 31 46N 97 35W
Clifton Forge 156 37 49N 79 51W
Climax 153 49 10N 108 20W
Clingmans Dome 157 35 35N 83 30W
Clint 161 31 37N 106 11W
Clinton, B.C., Can. 152 51 6N 121 35W
Clinton, Ont., Can. 150 43 37N 81 32W
Clinton, N.Z. 143 46 12S 169 23E
Clinton, Ark., U.S.A. 159 35 37N 92 30W
Clinton, Conn., U.S.A. 162 41 17N 72 32W
Clinton, Ill., U.S.A. 158 40 8N 89 0W
Clinton, Ind., U.S.A. 156 39 40N 87 22W
Clinton, Iowa, U.S.A. 158 41 50N 90 12W
Clinton, Mass., U.S.A. 162 42 26N 71 40W
Clinton, Mo., U.S.A. 158 38 20N 93 46W
Clinton, N.C., U.S.A. 157 35 5N 78 15W
Clinton, Okla., U.S.A. 159 35 30N 99 0W
Clinton, S.C., U.S.A. 157 34 30N 81 54W
Clinton, Tenn., U.S.A. 157 36 6N 84 10W
Clinton C. 138 22 30S 150 45E
Clinton Colden L. 148 64 58N 107 27W
Clintonville 158 44 35N 88 46W
Clipperton, I. 143 10 18N 109 13W
Clipston 29 52 26N 0 58W
Clisson 42 47 5N 1 16W
Clitheroe 32 53 52N 2 23W
Clive 142 39 36S 176 58E
Clive L. 152 63 13N 118 54W
Cloates, Pt. 136 22 43S 113 40E
Clocolan 129 28 55S 27 34E
Clodomira 172 27 35S 64 14W
Clogh 39 52 51N 7 11W
Cloghan, Donegal, Ireland 38 54 50N 7 56W
Cloghan, Offaly, Ireland 39 53 13N 7 53W
Cloghan, W'meath, Ireland 38 53 33N 7 15W
Clogheen 39 52 17N 8 0W
Clogher 38 54 25N 7 10W
Clogher Hd. 38 53 48N 6 15W
Cloghjordan 39 52 57N 8 2W
Cloghran 38 53 26N 6 14W
Clonakilty 39 51 37N 8 53W
Clonakilty B. 39 51 33N 8 50W
Clonbur 38 53 32N 9 21W
Cloncurry, Austral. 138 20 40S 140 28E
Cloncurry, Ireland 38 53 26N 6 47W
Cloncurry, R. 138 18 37S 140 40E
Clondalkin 39 53 20N 6 25W
Clonee 38 53 25N 6 28W
Cloneen 39 52 28N 7 36W
Clones 38 54 10N 7 13W
Clonkeen 39 51 59N 9 20W
Clonmany 38 55 16N 7 24W
Clonmel 39 52 22N 7 42W
Clonmore 39 52 49N 6 35W
Clonroche 39 52 27N 6 42W
Clontarf 38 53 22N 6 10W
Cloonakool 38 54 6N 8 47W
Cloone 38 53 57N 7 47W
Cloonfad 38 53 41N 8 45W
Cloppenburg 48 52 50N 8 3E
Cloquet 158 46 40N 92 30W
Clorinda 172 25 16S 57 45W
Closeburn 35 55 13N 3 45W
Cloud Peak 160 44 30N 107 10W
Cloudcroft 161 33 0N 105 48W
Cloudy B. 143 41 25S 174 10E
Clough, Ballymena, U.K. 38 54 58N 6 16W
Clough, Down, U.K. 38 54 18N 5 50W
Cloughton 33 54 20N 0 27W
Clova 37 56 50N 3 4W
Clovelly 30 51 0N 4 25W
Cloverdale 160 38 49N 123 0W
Clovis, Calif., U.S.A. 163 36 54N 119 45W
Clovis, N. Mex., U.S.A. 159 34 20N 103 10W
Clowne 33 53 18N 1 16W
Cloyne 39 51 52N 8 7W
Club Terrace 141 37 35S 148 58E
Cluj-Napoca 70 46 47N 23 38E
Cluj □ 70 46 45N 23 30E
Clun 28 52 26N 3 2W
Clun Forest 28 52 27N 3 7W
Clunbury 28 52 25N 2 55W
Clunes, Austral. 140 37 20S 143 45E
Clunes, U.K. 36 56 57N 4 58W
Cluny 45 46 26N 4 38E
Cluses 45 46 5N 6 35E
Clusone 62 45 54N 9 58E
Clutha, R. 143 46 20S 169 49E
Clwyd □ 31 53 5N 3 20W
Clwyd, R. 31 53 12N 3 30W
Clwydian Ra. 31 53 10N 3 15W
Clydach 31 51 42N 3 54W
Clyde, Austral. 139 28 48S 143 40E
Clyde, Can. 149 70 30N 68 30W
Clyde, N.Z. 143 45 12S 169 20E
Clyde, Firth of 34 55 20N 5 0W
Clyde, R. 34 55 46N 4 58W
Clydebank 34 55 54N 4 25W
Clydesdale 35 55 42N 3 50W
Clynnog-fawr 31 53 2N 4 22W
Côa, R. 56 40 45N 7 0W
Coachella 163 33 44N 116 13W
Coachella Canal 163 32 43N 114 57W
Coachford 39 51 54N 8 48W
Coachman's Cove 151 50 6N 56 20W
Coagh 38 54 39N 6 37W
Coahoma 159 32 17N 101 20W
Coahuayana, R. 164 18 41N 103 45W
Coahuayutla 164 18 19N 101 42W
Coahuila □ 164 27 0N 112 30W
Coal Creek Flat 143 45 27S 169 19E
Coal I. 143 46 8S 166 40E
Coal, R. 152 59 39N 126 57W
Coalane 127 17 48S 37 2E
Coalbrookdale 28 52 38N 2 30W
Coalburn 35 55 35N 3 55W
Coalcomán 164 18 40N 103 10W
Coaldale, Can. 152 49 45N 112 35W
Coaldale, U.S.A. 163 38 2N 117 55W
Coaldale, Pa., U.S.A. 162 40 50N 75 54W
Coalgate 159 34 35N 96 13W
Coalinga 163 36 10N 120 21W
Coalisland 38 54 33N 6 42W
Coalspur 152 53 15N 117 0W
Coalville, U.K. 28 52 43N 1 21W
Coalville, U.S.A. 160 40 58N 111 24W
Coamo 147 18 5N 66 22W
Coaraci 171 14 38S 39 32W
Coari 174 4 8S 63 7W
Coast □ 126 2 40S 39 45E
Coast Mts. 152 52 0N 126 0W
Coast Range 163 40 0N 124 0W
Coastal Plains Basin 137 30 10S 115 30E
Coatbridge 35 55 52N 4 2W
Coatepec 165 19 27N 96 58W
Coatepeque 166 14 46N 91 55W
Coatesville 162 39 59N 75 30W
Coaticook 151 45 10N 71 46W
Coats I. 149 62 30N 83 0W
Coats Land 13 77 0S 25 0W
Coatzacoalcos 165 18 7N 94 35W
Cobadin 70 44 5N 28 13E
Cobalt 150 47 25N 79 42W
Cobán 166 15 30N 90 21W
Cobar 141 31 27S 145 48E
Cobb I. 162 37 17N 75 42W
Cobbannah 141 37 37S 147 12E
Cobberas, Mt. 141 36 53S 148 12E
Cobden 140 38 20S 143 3E
Cóbh 39 51 50N 8 18W
Cobija 174 11 0S 68 50W
Cobourg 150 43 58N 78 10W
Cobourg Pen. 136 11 20S 132 15E
Cobram 141 35 54S 145 40E
Cobre 160 41 6N 114 25W
Cóbué 125 12 0S 34 58E
Coburg 49 50 15N 10 58E
Coca 56 41 13N 4 32W
Coca, R. 174 0 5S 77 5W
Cocal 170 3 28S 41 34W
Cocanada = Kakinada 96 16 55N 82 20E
Cocentaina 59 38 45N 0 27W
Cocha, La 172 27 50S 65 40W
Cochabamba 174 17 15S 66 20W
Coche, I. 174 10 47N 63 56W
Cochem 49 50 8N 7 7E
Cochemane 127 17 0S 32 54E
Cochilha Grande de Albardão 173 28 30S 51 30W
Cochin 97 9 55N 76 22E
Cochin China 101 10 30N 106 0E
Cochin China = Nam-Phan 101 10 30N 106 0E
Cochise 161 32 6N 109 58W
Cochran 157 32 25N 83 23W
Cochrane, Alta., Can. 152 51 11N 114 30W
Cochrane, Ont., Can. 150 49 0N 81 0W
Cochrane, L. 176 47 10S 72 0W
Cochrane, R. 153 57 53N 101 34W
Cockatoo I. 136 16 6S 123 37E
Cockburn 140 32 5S 141 0E
Cockburn, Canal 176 54 30S 72 0W
Cockburn, C. 136 11 20S 132 52E
Cockburn I. 150 45 55N 83 22W
Cockburn Ra. 136 15 46S 128 0E
Cockburnspath 35 55 56N 2 23W
Cockenzie 35 55 58N 2 59W
Cockerham 32 53 58N 2 49W
Cockermouth 32 54 40N 3 22W
Cockeysville 162 39 29N 76 39W
Cockfield 29 52 8N 0 47E
Cocklebiddy 137 32 0S 126 3E
Coco Chan. 101 13 50N 93 25E
Coco Is. 101 14 0N 93 12E
Coco, Pta. 174 2 58N 77 43W
Coco, R. (Wanks) 166 14 10N 85 0W
Cocoa 157 28 22N 80 40W
Cocobeach 124 0 59N 9 34E
Cocoli, R. 120 12 0N 14 0W
Cocora 70 44 45N 27 3E
Côcos 171 14 10S 44 33W
Cocos (Keeling) Is. 11 12 12S 96 54E
Côcos, R. 171 12 44S 44 48W
Cod, C. 162 42 8N 70 10W
Cod, gasfield 19 57 8N 2 35E
Codajás 174 3 40S 62 0W
Coddenham 29 52 8N 1 8E
Codera, C. 174 10 35N 66 4W
Coderre 153 50 11N 106 31W
Codigoro 63 44 50N 12 5E
Codó 170 4 30S 43 55W
Codogno 62 45 10N 9 42E
Codróipo 63 45 57N 13 0E
Codru, Munţii 70 46 30N 22 15E
Cods Hd. 39 51 40N 10 7W
Cody 160 44 35N 109 0W
Coe Hill 150 44 52N 77 50W
Coelemu 172 36 30S 72 48W
Coelho Neto 170 4 15S 43 0W
Coen 138 13 52S 143 12E
Coesfeld 48 51 56N 7 10E
Coeur d'Alene 160 47 45N 116 51W
Coevorden 46 52 40N 6 44E
Coffeyville 159 37 0N 95 40W
Coffin B. Pen. 136 34 20S 135 10E
Coffs Harbour 141 30 16S 153 5E
Cofre de Perote, Cerro 165 19 30N 97 10W
Cofrentes 59 39 13N 1 5W
Cogealac 70 44 36N 28 36E
Coggeshall 29 51 53N 0 41E
Coghinas, R. 64 40 55N 8 48E
Cognac 44 45 41N 0 20W
Cogne 62 45 37N 7 21E
Cogolludo 58 40 59N 3 10W
Cohagen 160 47 2N 106 45W
Cohoes 162 42 47N 73 42W
Cohuna 140 35 45S 144 15E
Coiba I. 166 7 30N 81 40W
Coig, R. 176 51 0S 70 20W
Coigach, dist. 36 58 0N 5 10W
Coillore 36 57 21N 6 23W
Coimbatore 97 11 2N 76 59E
Coimbra 56 40 15N 8 27W
Coimbra □ 56 40 12N 8 25W
Coín 57 36 40N 4 48W
Cojedes □ 174 9 20N 68 20W
Cojimies 174 0 20N 80 0W
Cojocna 70 46 45N 23 50E
Cojutepequé 166 13 41N 88 54W
Čoka 66 45 57N 20 12E
Cokeville 160 42 4N 111 0W
Col di Tenda 62 44 7N 7 36E
Colaba Pt. 96 18 54N 72 47E
Colac 140 38 21S 143 35E
Colachel 97 8 10N 77 15E
Colares 57 38 48N 9 30W
Colatina 171 19 32S 40 37W
Colbinabbin 141 36 38S 144 48E
Colby, U.K. 32 54 6N 4 42W
Colby, U.S.A. 158 39 27N 101 2W
Colchagua □ 172 34 30S 71 0W
Colchester 29 51 54N 0 55E
Cold Fell 32 54 54N 2 40W
Coldingham 35 55 53N 2 10W
Coldstream 35 55 39N 2 14W
Coldwater 159 37 18N 99 24W
Coldwell 150 48 45N 86 30W
Colebrook 138 42 31S 147 12E
Colebrooke 30 50 45N 3 44W
Coleford 28 51 46N 2 38W
Coleman, Can. 152 49 40N 114 30W
Coleman, U.S.A. 159 31 52N 99 30W
Coleman, R. 138 15 6S 141 38E
Colenso 129 28 44S 29 50E
Coleraine, Austral. 140 37 36S 141 40E
Coleraine, U.K. 38 55 8N 6 40E
Coleraine □ 38 55 8N 6 40E
Coleridge, L. 143 43 17S 171 30E
Coleroon, R. 97 11 0N 79 0E
Colesberg 128 30 45S 25 5E
Coleshill 28 52 30N 1 42W
Coleville 163 38 44N 119 30W
Colfax, La., U.S.A. 159 31 35N 92 39W
Colfax, Wash., U.S.A. 160 46 57N 117 28W
Colgrave Sd. 36 60 35N 1 0W
Colhué Huapi, L. 176 45 30S 69 0W
Cólico 62 46 8N 9 22E
Coligny 128 26 24N 5 21E
Colima 164 19 10N 103 40W
Colima □ 164 19 10N 103 40W
Colima, Nevado de 164 19 30N 103 40W
Colina 172 33 13S 70 45W
Colina do Norte 120 12 28N 15 0W
Colinas, Goiás, Brazil 171 14 15S 48 2W
Colinas, Maranhão, Brazil 170 6 0S 44 10W
Colinton, Austral. 141 35 50S 149 10E
Colinton, U.K. 35 55 54N 3 17W
Coll, I. 34 56 40N 6 35W
Collaguasi 172 21 5S 68 45W
Collarada, Peña 58 42 43N 0 29W
Collarenebri 139 29 33S 148 36E
Collbran 161 39 16N 107 58W
Colle Salvetti 62 43 34N 10 27E
Colle Sannita 65 41 22N 14 48E
Colléchio 62 44 23N 10 10E
Colleen Bawn 127 21 0S 29 12E
College Park, Ga., U.S.A. 157 33 42N 84 27W
College Park, Md., U.S.A. 162 39 0N 76 55W
Collette 151 46 40N 65 30W
Collie, N.S.W., Austral. 141 31 41S 148 18E
Collie, W. Austral., Austral. 137 33 22S 116 8E
Collier B. 136 16 10S 124 15E
Collier Law Pk. 32 54 47N 1 59W
Collier Ra. 137 24 45S 119 10E
Collin 35 55 4N 3 30W
Colline Metallifere 62 43 10N 11 0E
Collingbourne 28 51 16N 1 39W
Collingswood 162 39 55N 75 4W
Collingwood, Austral. 138 22 20S 142 31E
Collingwood, Can. 150 44 29N 80 13W
Collingwood, N.Z. 143 40 25S 172 40E
Collingwood B. 138 9 30S 149 30E
Collins 150 50 17N 89 27W
Collinsville 138 20 30S 147 56E
Collipulli 172 37 55S 72 30W
Collison Ra. 136 14 49S 127 25E
Collo 119 36 58N 6 37E
Collon 38 53 46N 6 29W
Collonges 45 46 9N 5 52E
Collooney 38 54 11N 8 28W
Colmar 43 48 5N 7 20E
Colmars 45 44 11N 6 39E
Colmenar 57 36 54N 4 20W
Colmenar de Oreja 58 40 6N 3 25W
Colmenar Viejo 56 40 39N 3 47W
Colmor 159 36 18N 104 36W
Colne 32 53 51N 2 11W
Colne, R., Essex, U.K. 29 51 55N 0 50E
Colne, R., Herts., U.K. 29 51 36N 0 30W
Colnett, Cabo 164 31 0N 116 20W
Colo, R. 141 33 25S 150 52E
Cologna Véneta 63 45 19N 11 21E
Colomb-Béchar = Béchar 118 31 38N 2 18E
Colombey-les-Belles 43 48 32N 5 54E
Colombey-les-deux Églises 43 48 20N 4 50E
Colômbia 171 20 10S 48 40W
Colombia 174 3 24N 79 49W
Colombia ■ 174 3 45N 73 0W
Colombier 50 46 58N 6 53E
Colombo 97 6 56N 79 58E
Colombus, Kans., U.S.A. 159 37 15N 94 30W
Colombus, Nebr., U.S.A. 158 41 30N 97 25W
Colombus, N.Mex., U.S.A. 161 31 54N 107 43W
Colome 158 43 20N 99 44W
Colón, Argent. 172 32 12S 58 30W
Colón, Cuba 166 22 42N 80 54W
Colón, Panama 166 9 20N 80 0W
Colonel Hill 167 22 50N 74 21W
Colonella 63 42 52N 13 50E
Colonia del Sacramento 173 34 25S 57 50W
Colonia Dora 172 28 34S 62 59W
Colonia Las Heras 176 46 30S 69 0W
Colonia Sarmiento 176 45 30S 68 15W
Colonial Hts. 162 37 15N 77 25W
Colonne, C. delle 65 39 2N 17 11E
Colonsay 153 51 59N 105 52W
Colonsay, I. 34 56 4N 6 12W
Colorado □ 154 37 40N 106 0W
Colorado Aqueduct 161 34 17N 114 10W
Colorado City 159 32 25N 100 50W
Colorado Desert 154 34 20N 116 0W
Colorado Plateau 161 36 40N 110 30W
Colorado, R., Argent. 172 37 30S 69 0W
Colorado, R., Ariz., U.S.A. 161 33 30N 114 30W
Colorado, R., Calif., U.S.A. 161 34 0N 114 33W
Colorado, R., Tex., U.S.A. 159 29 40N 96 30W
Colorado Springs 158 38 55N 104 50W
Colorno 62 44 55N 10 21E
Colossal 141 30 52S 147 3E
Colotepec 165 15 47N 97 3W
Colotlán 164 22 6N 103 16W
Colpy 37 57 23N 2 35W
Colsterworth 29 52 48N 0 37W
Coltishall 29 52 44N 1 21E
Colton, Calif., U.S.A. 163 34 4N 117 20W
Colton, Wash., U.S.A. 160 46 41N 117 6W
Columbia, La., U.S.A. 159 32 7N 92 5W
Columbia, Miss., U.S.A. 159 31 16N 89 50W
Columbia, Mo., U.S.A. 158 38 58N 92 20W
Columbia, Pa., U.S.A. 162 40 2N 76 30W
Columbia, S.C., U.S.A. 157 34 0N 81 0W

Columbia Coroaci

Columbia, Tenn., U.S.A.	157	35 40N	87 0W
Columbia, C.	12	83 0N	70 0W
Columbia City	156	41 8N	85 30W
Columbia, District of □	156	38 55N	77 0W
Columbia Falls	160	48 25N	114 16W
Columbia Heights	158	45 5N	93 10W
Columbia, Mt.	152	52 8N	117 20W
Columbia Basin	160	47 30N	118 30W
Columbia, R.	160	45 49N	120 0W
Columbretes, Is.	58	39 50N	0 50 E
Columbus, Ga., U.S.A.	157	32 30N	84 58W
Columbus, Ind., U.S.A.	156	39 14N	85 55W
Columbus, Miss., U.S.A.	157	33 30N	88 26W
Columbus, Mont., U.S.A.	160	45 45N	109 14W
Columbus, N.D., U.S.A.	158	48 52N	102 48W
Columbus, Ohio, U.S.A.	156	39 57N	83 1W
Columbus, Tex., U.S.A.	159	29 42N	96 33W
Columbus, Wis., U.S.A.	158	43 20N	89 2W
Colunda	125	12 7 S	23 36 E
Colunga	56	43 29N	5 16W
Colusa	160	39 15N	122 1W
Colville	160	48 33N	117 54W
Colville, C.	142	36 29 S	175 21 E
Colville, R.	147	69 15N	152 0W
Colwell	35	55 4N	2 4W
Colwich	28	52 48N	1 58W
Colwyn	31	53 17N	3 43W
Colwyn Bay	31	53 17N	3 44W
Colyton	30	50 44N	3 4W
Comácchio	63	44 41N	12 10 E
Comalcalco	165	18 16N	93 13W
Comallo	176	41 0 S	70 5W
Comana	70	44 10N	26 10 E
Comanche, Okla., U.S.A.	159	34 27N	97 58W
Comanche, Tex., U.S.A.	159	31 55N	98 35W
Comănești	70	46 25N	26 26 E
Comayagua	166	14 25N	87 37W
Combahee, R.	157	32 45N	80 50W
Combara	141	31 10 S	148 22 E
Combe Martin	30	51 12N	4 2W
Combeaufontaine	43	47 38N	5 54 E
Comber	38	54 33N	5 45W
Combermere Bay	98	19 37N	93 34 E
Comblain	47	50 29N	5 35 E
Combles	43	50 0N	2 50 E
Combourg	42	48 25N	1 46W
Comboyne	141	31 34 S	152 34 E
Combronde	44	45 58N	3 5 E
Comeragh Mts.	39	52 17N	7 35W
Comercinho	171	16 19 S	41 47W
Comet	138	23 36 S	148 38 E
Comet Vale	137	29 55 S	121 4 E
Comilla	98	23 28N	91 10 E
Comines	47	50 46N	3 0 E
Comino, C.	64	40 28N	9 47 E
Cómiso	65	36 57N	14 35 E
Comitán	165	16 18N	92 9W
Commentry	44	46 20N	2 46 E
Commerce, Ga., U.S.A.	157	34 10N	83 25W
Commerce, Tex., U.S.A.	159	33 15N	95 50W
Commercy	43	48 40N	5 34 E
Committee B.	149	68 30N	86 30W
Commonwealth B.	13	67 0 S	144 0 E
Commoron Cr., R.	139	28 22 S	150 8 E
Communism Pk. = Kommunizma, Pk.	93	38 40N	72 20 E
Como	62	45 48N	9 5 E
Como, L. di	62	46 5N	9 17 E
Comodoro Rivadavia	176	45 50 S	67 40W
Comores, Arch. des	11	10 0 S	50 0 E
Comores, Is.	11	12 10 S	44 15 E
Comorin, C.	97	8 3N	77 40 E
Comorişte	70	45 10N	21 35 E
Comoro Is.	11	12 10 S	44 15 E
Comox	152	49 42N	124 55W
Compiègne	43	49 24N	2 50 E
Compíglia Maríttima	62	43 4N	10 37 E
Comporta	57	38 22N	8 46W
Compostela	164	21 15N	104 53W
Comprida, I.	173	24 50 S	47 42W
Compton, U.K.	28	51 2N	1 19W
Compton, U.S.A.	163	33 54N	118 13W
Compton Downs	139	30 28 S	146 30 E
Comrie	35	56 22N	4 0W
Con Cuong	100	19 2N	104 54 E
Côn Dao	101	8 45N	106 45 E
Con Son, Is.	101	8 41N	106 37 E
Conakry	120	9 29N	13 49W
Conara Junction	138	41 50 S	147 26 E
Conargo	141	35 16 S	145 10 E
Conatlán	164	24 30N	104 42W
Concarneau	42	47 52N	3 56W
Conceição, Brazil	170	7 33 S	38 31W
Conceição, Mozam.	127	18 47 S	36 7 E
Conceição da Barra	171	18 35 S	39 45W
Conceição do Araguaia	170	8 0 S	49 2W
Conceição do Canindé	170	7 54 S	41 34W
Conceição do Mato Dentro	171	19 1 S	43 25W
Concepcián	165	18 15N	90 5W
Concepción, Argent.	172	27 20 S	65 35W
Concepción, Boliv.	174	15 50 S	61 40W
Concepción, Chile	172	36 50 S	73 0W
Concepción, Colomb.	174	0 5N	75 37W
Concepción, Parag.	172	23 30 S	57 20W
Concepción, Venez.	174	10 48N	71 46W
Concepción □	172	37 0 S	72 30W
Concepcion, C.	154	34 30N	120 34W
Concepción del Oro	164	24 40N	101 30W
Concepción del Uruguay	172	32 35 S	58 20W
Concepción, L.	174	17 20 S	61 10W
Concepción, La = Ri-Aba	121	3 28N	84 0 E
Concepción, Punta	164	26 55N	111 50W
Concepción, R.	164	30 32N	113 2W
Conception B.	128	23 55 S	14 22 E
Conception I.	167	23 52N	75 9W
Conception, Pt.	163	34 27N	120 28W
Concession	127	17 27 S	30 56 E
Conchas Dam	159	35 25N	104 10W
Conche	151	50 48N	55 58W
Conches-en-Ouche	50	48 58N	0 58 E
Concho	161	34 32N	109 43W
Concho, R.	159	31 30N	100 8W
Conchos, R., Chihnahua, Mexico	164	29 20N	105 0W
Conchos, R., Tamaulipas, Mexico	165	25 0N	97 32W
Concon	172	32 56 S	71 33W
Concord, Calif., U.S.A.	163	37 59N	122 2W
Concord, N.C., U.S.A.	157	35 28N	80 35W
Concord, N.H., U.S.A.	162	43 12N	71 30W
Concórdia, Argent.	172	31 20 S	58 2W
Concórdia, Brazil	174	4 36 S	66 36W
Concordia, Colomb.	174	2 39N	72 47W
Concordia, Mexico	164	23 18N	106 2W
Concordia, U.S.A.	158	39 35N	97 40W
Concordia, La	165	16 8N	92 38W
Concots	44	44 26N	1 40 E
Concrete	160	48 35N	121 49W
Condah	140	37 57 S	141 44 E
Condamine, R.	133	27 7 S	149 48 E
Condat	44	45 21N	2 46 E
Conde	171	11 49 S	37 37W
Condé	43	50 26N	3 34 E
Conde	158	45 13N	98 5W
Condé-sur-Noireau	42	48 51N	0 33W
Condeúba	171	15 0 S	42 0W
Condobolin	141	33 4 S	147 6 E
Condom	44	43 57N	0 22 E
Condon	160	45 15N	120 8W
Condove	62	45 8N	7 19 E
Condover	28	52 39N	2 46W
Conegliano	63	45 53N	12 18 E
Conejera, I.	59	39 11N	2 58 E
Conejos	164	26 14N	103 53W
Conflans-en-Jarnisy	43	49 10N	5 52 E
Confolens	44	46 2N	0 40 E
Confuso, R.	172	24 10 S	59 0W
Congleton	32	53 10N	2 12W
Congo	170	7 48 S	36 40W
Congo ■	124	1 0 S	16 0 E
Congo Basin	114	0 10 S	24 30 E
Congo, Democratic Rep. of = Zaïre ■	124	3 0 S	22 0 E
Congo (Kinshasa) ■ = Zaïre ■	124	1 0 S	16 0 E
Congo, R. = Zaïre, R.	124	1 30N	28 0 E
Congonhas	173	20 30 S	43 52W
Congresbury	28	51 20N	2 49W
Congress	161	34 11N	112 56W
Conguco	113	31 25 S	52 30W
Conil	57	36 17N	6 10W
Coningsby	33	53 7N	0 9W
Conisbrough	33	53 29N	1 12W
Coniston, Can.	150	46 29N	80 51W
Coniston, U.K.	32	54 22N	3 6W
Coniston Water	32	54 20N	3 5W
Conjeevaram = Kancheepuram	97	12 52N	79 45 E
Conjuboy	138	18 35 S	144 45 E
Conklin	153	55 38N	111 5W
Conlea	139	30 7 S	144 35 E
Conn, L.	38	54 3N	9 15W
Conna	39	52 5N	8 8W
Connacht	38	53 23N	8 40W
Connah's Quay	31	53 13N	3 6W
Conneaut	156	41 55N	80 32W
Connecticut □	162	41 40N	72 40W
Connecticut, R.	162	41 17N	72 21W
Connel	34	56 27N	5 24W
Connel Park	34	55 22N	4 15W
Connell	160	46 45N	118 58W
Connemara	38	53 29N	9 45W
Conner, La	160	48 22N	122 27W
Connersville	156	39 40N	85 10W
Connonagh	39	51 35N	9 8W
Connor, Mt.	136	14 34 S	126 4 E
Connors Ra.	138	21 40 S	149 10 E
Conoble	141	32 55 S	144 42 E
Cononaco, R.	174	1 20 S	76 30W
Conquest	153	51 32N	107 14W
Conquet, Le	42	48 21N	4 46W
Conrad	160	48 11N	112 0W
Conran, C.	141	37 49 S	148 44 E
Conroe	159	30 15N	95 28W
Conselheiro Lafaiete	173	20 40 S	43 48W
Conselheiro Pena	171	19 10 S	41 30W
Consett	32	54 52N	1 50W
Conshohocken	162	40 5N	75 18W
Consort	153	52 1N	110 46W
Constance = Konstanz	49	47 39N	9 10 E
Constance, L. = Bodensee	51	47 35N	9 25 E
Constanţa	70	44 14N	28 38 E
Constanţa □	70	44 15N	28 15 E
Constantia	162	43 15N	76 1W
Constantina	57	37 51N	5 40W
Constantine	119	36 25N	6 42 E
Constitución, Chile	172	35 20 S	72 30W
Constitución, Uruguay	172	31 0 S	58 10W
Consuegra	57	39 28N	3 43W
Consul	153	49 20N	109 30W
Contact	160	41 50N	114 56W
Contai	95	21 54N	87 55 E
Contamana	174	7 10 S	74 55W
Contarina	63	45 2N	12 13 E
Contas, R.	171	13 5 S	41 53W
Contes	45	43 49N	7 19 E
Conthey	50	46 14N	7 28 E
Contin	37	57 34N	4 35W
Contoocook	162	43 13N	71 45W
Contra Costa	129	25 9 S	33 30 E
Contres	43	47 24N	1 26 E
Contrexéville	43	48 6N	5 53 E
Convención	174	8 28N	73 21W
Conversano	65	40 57N	17 8 E
Convoy	38	54 52N	7 40W
Conway, Ark., U.S.A.	159	35 5N	92 30W
Conway, N.H., U.S.A.	162	43 58N	71 8W
Conway, S.C., U.S.A.	157	33 49N	79 2W
Conway = Conwy	31	53 17N	3 50W
Conway, L.	139	28 17 S	135 35 E
Conwy	31	53 17N	3 50W
Conwy Bay	31	53 17N	3 57W
Conwy, R.	31	53 18N	3 50W
Coober Pedy	136	29 1 S	134 43 E
Coobina	137	23 22 S	120 10 E
Cooch Behar	98	26 22N	89 29 E
Cook, Austral.	137	30 37 S	130 25 E
Cook, U.S.A.	158	47 49N	92 39W
Cook, Bahía	176	55 10 S	70 0W
Cook Inlet	147	59 0N	151 0W
Cook Is.	131	20 0 S	160 0W
Cook, Mount	143	43 36 S	170 9 E
Cook Strait	143	41 15 S	174 29 E
Cooke Plains	140	35 23 S	139 34 E
Cookeville	157	36 12N	85 30W
Cookham	29	51 33N	0 42W
Cookhouse	128	32 44 S	25 47 E
Cookstown	38	54 40N	6 43W
Cookstown □	38	54 40N	6 43W
Cooktown	138	15 30 S	145 16 E
Coolabah	141	31 1 S	146 43 E
Cooladdi	139	26 37 S	145 23 E
Coolah	141	31 48 S	149 41 E
Coolamon	141	34 46 S	147 8 E
Coolaney	38	54 10N	8 36W
Coolangatta	139	28 11 S	153 29 E
Coole	38	53 42N	7 23W
Coolgardie	137	30 55 S	121 8 E
Coolgreany	39	52 46N	6 14W
Coolibah	136	15 33 S	130 56 E
Coolidge	161	33 1N	111 35W
Coolidge Dam	161	33 10N	110 30W
Coolmore	38	54 33N	8 12W
Cooma	141	36 12 S	149 8 E
Coomacarrea Mts.	39	51 59N	10 0W
Coonabarabran	141	31 14 S	149 18 E
Coonalpyn	140	35 43 S	139 52 E
Coonamble	141	30 56 S	148 27 E
Coonana	137	31 0 S	123 0 E
Coondapoor	97	13 42N	74 40 E
Coongie	139	27 9 S	140 8 E
Coongoola	139	27 43 S	145 47 E
Cooninie, L.	139	26 4 S	139 59 E
Coonoor	97	11 10N	76 45 E
Cooper	159	33 20N	95 40W
Cooper Cr.	139	28 29 S	137 46 E
Cooper, R.	157	33 0N	79 55W
Coopersburg	162	40 31N	75 23W
Cooperstown, N.D., U.S.A.	158	47 30N	98 14W
Cooperstown, New York, U.S.A.	162	42 42N	74 57W
Coorabie P.O.	137	31 54 S	132 18 E
Coorabulka	138	23 41 S	140 20 E
Coorong, The	133	35 50 S	139 20 E
Coorow	137	29 53 S	116 2 E
Cooroy	139	26 22 S	152 54 E
Coos Bay	160	43 26N	124 7W
Cootamundra	141	34 36 S	148 1 E
Cootehill	38	54 5N	7 5W
Cooyar	139	26 59 S	151 51 E
Cooyeana	138	24 29 S	138 45 E
Copahué, Paso	172	37 49 S	71 8W
Copainalá	165	17 8N	93 11W
Copake Falls	162	42 7N	73 31W
Copán	166	14 50N	89 9W
Cope	158	39 44N	102 50W
Cope, Cabo	59	37 26N	1 28W
Cope Cope	140	36 27 S	143 5 E
Copeland I.	38	54 38N	5 33W
Copenhagen	162	43 54N	75 41W
Copenhagen = København	73	55 41N	12 34 E
Copertino	65	40 17N	18 2W
Copeville	140	34 47 S	139 51 E
Copiapó	172	27 15 S	70 20 E
Copiapó, R.	172	27 19 S	70 56W
Copinsay I.	37	58 54N	2 40W
Coplay	162	40 44N	75 29W
Copley	140	30 24 S	138 26 E
Copp L.	152	60 14N	114 40W
Copparo	63	44 52N	11 49 E
Copper Center	147	62 10N	145 25W
Copper Cliff	150	46 28N	81 4W
Copper Harbor	156	47 31N	87 55W
Copper Mountain	152	49 20N	120 30W
Copper Queen	127	17 29 S	29 18 E
Copper R.	147	61 30N	144 30W
Copperbelt □	127	13 15N	27 30 E
Copperfield	137	29 1 S	120 26 E
Coppermine	148	67 50N	115 5W
Coppermine, R.	148	67 49N	115 4W
Copperopolis	163	37 58N	120 38W
Cöppingen	49	48 42N	9 40 E
Copythorne	28	50 56N	1 34W
Coquet, I.	35	55 21N	1 30W
Coquet, R.	35	55 18N	1 45W
Coquilhatville = Mbandaka	124	0 1N	18 18 E
Coquille	160	43 15N	124 6W
Coquimbo	172	30 0 S	71 20W
Coquimbo □	172	31 0 S	71 0W
Cora, oilfield	19	55 45N	4 45 E
Corabia	70	43 48N	24 30 E
Coraçáo de Jesus	171	11 39 S	39 56W
Coracora	174	15 5 S	73 45W
Coradi, Is.	65	40 27N	71 10 E
Coral Harbour	149	64 8N	83 10W
Coral Rapids	150	50 20N	81 40W
Coral Sea	142	15 0 S	150 0 E
Coral Sea Islands Terr.	133	20 0 S	155 0 E
Corato	65	41 12N	16 22 E
Corbeil-Essonnes	43	48 36N	2 26 E
Corbie	43	49 54N	2 30 E
Corbières, mts.	44	42 55N	2 35 E
Corbigny	43	47 16N	3 40 E
Corbin	156	37 0N	84 3W
Corbion	47	49 48N	5 0 E
Corbones, R.	57	37 25N	5 35W
Corbridge	35	54 58N	2 0W
Corby, Lincs., U.K.	29	52 49N	0 31W
Corby, Northants., U.K.	29	52 29N	0 41W
Corcoles, R.	59	39 12N	2 40W
Corcoran	163	36 6N	119 35W
Corcubión	56	42 56N	9 12W
Cord. de Caravaya	174	14 0 S	70 30W
Cordele	157	31 55N	83 49W
Cordell	159	35 18N	99 0W
Cordenons	63	45 59N	12 42 E
Cordes	44	44 5N	1 57 E
Cordillera Oriental	174	5 0N	74 0W
Cordisburgo	171	19 7 S	44 21W
Córdoba	172	31 20 S	64 10W
Cordoba	164	26 20N	103 20W
Córdoba, Mexico	165	18 50N	97 0W
Córdoba, Spain	57	37 50N	4 50W
Córdoba □, Argent.	172	31 22 S	64 15W
Córdoba □, Colomb.	174	8 20N	75 40W
Córdoba □, Spain	57	38 5N	5 0W
Córdoba, Sierra de	172	31 10 S	64 25W
Cordon	103	16 42N	121 32 E
Cordova, Ala., U.S.A.	157	33 45N	87 12W
Cordova, Alaska, U.S.A.	147	60 36N	145 45W
Corella	58	42 7N	1 48W
Corella, R.	138	19 34 S	140 47 E
Coremas	170	7 1 S	37 58W
Corfe Castle	28	50 58N	2 3W
Corfe Mullen	28	50 45N	2 0W
Corfield	138	21 40 S	143 21 E
Corfu = Kerkira	68	39 38N	19 50 E
Corgo	56	42 56N	7 25W
Cori	64	41 39N	12 53 E
Coria	56	40 0N	6 33W
Coricudgy, Mt.	141	32 51 S	150 24 E
Corigliano Cálabro	65	39 36N	16 31 E
Coringa Is.	138	16 58 S	149 58 E
Corinna	138	41 35 S	145 10 E
Corinth, Miss., U.S.A.	157	34 54N	88 30W
Corinth, N.Y., U.S.A.	162	43 15N	73 50W
Corinth = Korinthos	69	37 56N	22 55 E
Corinth Canal	69	37 48N	23 0 E
Corinth, G. of = Korinthiakós	69	38 16N	22 30 E
Corinto, Brazil	171	18 20 S	44 30W
Corinto, Nic.	166	12 30N	87 10W
Corj □	70	45 5N	23 25 E
Cork	39	51 54N	8 30W
Cork □	39	51 50N	8 50W
Cork Harbour	39	51 46N	8 16W
Corlay	42	48 20N	3 5W
Corleone	64	37 48N	13 16 E
Corleto Perticara	65	40 23N	16 2 E
Çorlu	67	41 11N	27 49 E
Cormack L.	152	60 56N	121 37W
Cormóns	63	45 58N	13 29 E
Cormorant	153	54 14N	100 35W
Cormorant L.	153	54 15N	100 50W
Cormorant, oilfield	19	61 0N	1 10 E
Corn Hill, Mt.	38	53 48N	7 43W
Corn Is.	167	12 0N	83 0W
Cornelio	164	29 55N	111 8W
Cornélio Procópio	173	23 7 S	50 40W
Cornell	158	45 10N	91 8W
Corner Brook	151	48 57N	57 58W
Corner Inlet	133	38 45 S	146 20 E
Cornforth	33	54 42N	1 28W
Corniglio	62	44 29N	10 5 E
Corning, Ark., U.S.A.	159	36 27N	90 34W
Corning, Calif., U.S.A.	160	39 56N	122 9W
Corning, Iowa, U.S.A.	158	40 57N	94 40W
Corning, N.Y., U.S.A.	162	42 10N	77 3W
Cornwall, Austral.	138	41 33 S	148 7 E
Cornwall, Can.	150	45 2N	74 44W
Cornwall, U.S.A.	162	40 17N	76 25W
Cornwall □	30	50 26N	4 40W
Cornwall, C.	30	50 8N	5 42W
Cornwallis I.	12	75 8N	95 0W
Corny Pt.	140	34 55 S	137 0 E
Coro	174	11 25N	69 41W
Coroaci	171	18 35 S	42 17W

Coroatá Crooksville

Coroatá 170 4 20 S 44 0W
Corocoro 174 17 15 S 69 19W
Corofin 39 53 27N 8 50W
Coroico 174 16 0 S 67 50W
Coromandel, Brazil 171 18 28 S 47 13W
Coromandel, N.Z. 142 36 45 S 175 31 E
Coromandel Coast 97 12 30N 81 0 E
Coromandel Pen. 142 37 0 S 175 45 E
Coromandel Ra. 142 37 0 S 175 40 E
Coromorant, L. 153 54 20N 100 50W
Corona, Austral. 139 31 16 S 141 24 E
Corona, Calif., U.S.A. 163 33 49N 117 36W
Corona, N. Mex., U.S.A. 161 34 15N 105 32W
Coronada B. 166 9 0N 83 40W
Coronado 163 32 45N 117 9W
Coronado, Bahía de 166 9 0N 83 40W
Coronation 152 52 5N 111 27W
Coronation Gulf 148 68 25N 112 0W
Coronation I., Antarct. 13 60 45 S 46 0W
Coronation I., U.S.A. 152 55 52N 134 20W
Coronation Is. 136 14 57 S 124 55 E
Coronda 172 31 58 S 60 56W
Coronel 172 37 0 S 73 10W
Coronel Bogado 172 27 11 S 56 18W
Coronel Dorrego 172 38 40 S 61 10W
Coronel Fabriciano 171 19 31 S 42 38W
Coronel Murta 171 16 37 S 42 11W
Coronel Oviedo 172 25 24 S 56 30W
Coronel Pringles 172 38 0 S 61 30W
Coronel Suárez 172 37 30 S 62 0W
Coronel Vidal 172 37 28 S 57 45W
Coronie 170 5 55N 56 25W
Corovoda 68 40 31N 20 14 E
Corowa 141 35 58 S 146 21 E
Corozal, Belize 165 18 30N 88 30W
Corozal, Colomb. 174 9 19N 75 18W
Corpach 36 56 50N 5 9W
Corps 45 44 50N 5 56 E
Corpus 173 27 10 S 55 30W
Corpus Christi 159 27 50N 97 28W
Corpus Christi L. 159 28 5N 97 54W
Corque 174 18 10 S 67 50W
Corral de Almaguer 58 39 45N 3 10W
Corran 36 56 44N 5 14W
Corrandibby Ra. 137 26 0 S 115 20 E
Corraun Pen. 38 53 58N 10 15W
Corrégio 62 44 46N 10 47 E
Corrente 170 10 27 S 45 10W
Corrente, R. 170 13 8 S 43 28W
Correntes, C. das 129 24 6 S 35 34 E
Correntina 171 13 20 S 44 39W
Corrèze □ 44 45 20N 1 45 E
Corrib, L. 38 53 25N 9 10W
Corrie 34 55 39N 5 10W
Corrientes 172 27 30 S 58 45W
Corrientes □ 172 28 0 S 57 0W
Corrientes, C., Colomb. 174 5 30N 77 34W
Corrientes, C., Cuba 166 21 43N 84 30W
Corrientes, C., Mexico 164 20 25N 105 42W
Corrientes, R., Argent. 172 30 21 S 59 33W
Corrientes, R., Colomb. 174 3 15 S 75 58W
Corrigan 159 31 0N 94 48W
Corrigin 137 32 20 S 117 53 E
Corringham 33 53 25N 0 42W
Corris 31 52 41N 3 49W
Corrowidgie 141 36 56 S 148 50 E
Corry 156 41 55N 79 39W
Corryong 141 36 12 S 147 53 E
Corryvrecken, G. of 34 56 10N 5 44W
Corse, C. 45 43 1N 9 25 E
Corse-du-Sud □ 45 41 45N 9 0 E
Corse, Î 45 42 0N 9 0 E
Corsewall Pt. 34 55 0N 5 10W
Corsham 28 51 25N 2 11W
Corsica = Corse 45 42 0N 9 0 E
Corsicana 159 32 5N 96 30W
Corsley 28 51 12N 2 14W
Corsock 35 55 54N 3 56W
Corté 45 42 19N 9 11 E
Corte do Pinto 57 37 42N 7 29W
Cortegana 57 37 52N 6 49W
Cortez 161 37 24N 108 35W
Cortina d'Ampezzo 63 46 32N 12 9 E
Cortland 162 42 35N 76 11W
Corton 29 52 31N 1 46 E
Cortona 63 43 16N 12 0 E
Coruche 57 38 57N 8 30W
Çorum 92 40 30N 35 5 E
Corumbá, Goias, Brazil 171 16 0 S 48 50W
Corumbá, Mato Grosso, Brazil 174 19 0 S 57 30W
Corumbá R. 171 17 25 S 48 30W
Corumbaiba 171 18 9 S 48 34W
Coruña □ 56 43 0N 8 37 E
Coruña, La 56 43 20N 8 25W
Coruña, La □ 56 43 10N 8 30W
Corund 70 46 30N 25 13 E
Corunna = La Coruña 56 43 20N 8 25W
Coruripe 171 10 5 S 36 10W
Corvallis 160 44 36N 123 15W
Corve, R. 28 52 22N 2 43W
Corvette, L. de la 150 53 25N 73 55W
Corwen 31 52 59N 3 23W
Corydon 158 40 42N 93 22W
Cosalá 164 24 28N 106 40W
Cosamaloapán 165 18 23N 95 50W
Coseley 28 52 33N 2 6W
Cosenza 65 39 17N 16 14 E
Coşereni 70 44 38N 26 35 E
Cosham 28 50 51N 1 3W
Coshocton 156 40 17N 81 51W
Cosne-s.-Loire 43 47 24N 2 54 E
Coso Junction 163 36 3N 117 57W
Coso Pk. 163 36 13N 117 44W
Cospeito 56 43 12N 7 34W
Cosquín 172 31 15 S 64 30W
Cossato 62 45 34N 8 10 E
Cossé-le-Vivien 42 47 57N 0 54W
Costa Azul 50 43 25N 6 50 E
Costa Blanca 59 38 25N 0 10W
Costa Brava 58 41 30N 3 0 E
Costa del Sol 57 36 30N 4 30W
Costa Dorada 58 40 45N 1 15 E
Costa Mesa 163 33 39N 117 55W
Costa Rica 164 31 20N 112 40W
Costa Rica ■ 166 10 0N 84 0W
Costa Smeralda 64 41 5N 9 35 E
Costelloe 39 53 20N 9 33W
Costessey 29 52 40N 1 11 E
Costigliole d'Asti 62 44 48N 8 11 E
Costilla 161 37 0N 105 30W
Coştiui 70 47 53N 24 2 E
Cosumnes, R. 163 38 14N 121 25W
Coswig 48 51 52N 12 31 E
Cotabato 103 7 14N 124 15 E
Cotabena 140 31 42 S 138 11 E
Cotagaita 172 20 45 S 65 30W
Côte d'Azur 45 43 25N 6 50 E
Côte d'Or 43 47 10N 4 50 E
Côte d'Or □ 43 47 30N 4 50 E
Côte, La 50 46 25N 6 15 E
Côte-St. André, La 45 45 24N 5 15 E
Coteau des Prairies 158 44 30N 97 0W
Coteau du Missouri, Plat. du 154 47 0N 101 0W
Cotegipe 171 12 2 S 44 15W
Cotentin 42 49 30N 1 30W
Côtes de Meuse 43 49 15N 5 22 E
Côtes-du-Nord □ 42 48 25N 2 40W
Cotherstone 32 54 34N 1 59W
Cotiella 58 42 31N 0 19 E
Cotina, R. 66 43 36N 19 9 E
Cotonou 121 6 20N 2 25 E
Cotopaxi, Vol. 174 0 30 S 78 30W
Cotronei 65 39 9N 16 27 E
Cotswold Hills 28 51 42N 2 10W
Cottage Grove 160 43 48N 123 2W
Cottbus 48 51 44N 14 20 E
Cottbus □ 48 51 43N 13 30 E
Cottenham 29 52 18N 0 8 E
Cottingham 36 53 47N 0 23W
Cottonwood, Can. 152 53 5N 121 50W
Cottonwood, U.S.A. 161 34 48N 112 1W
Coubre, Pte. de la 44 45 42N 1 15W
Couches 43 46 53N 4 30 E
Couço 57 38 59N 8 17W
Coudersport 156 41 45N 78 1W
Couedic, C. du 140 36 5 S 136 40 E
Couëron 42 47 13N 1 44W
Coueson, R. 42 48 20N 1 15W
Couhé-Vérac 44 46 18N 0 12 E
Couillet 47 50 23N 4 28 E
Coulags 36 57 26N 5 24W
Coulanges, Deux Sèvres, France 44 46 58N 0 35W
Coulanges, Yonne, France 43 47 30N 3 30 E
Coulee City 160 47 44N 119 12W
Coulman I. 13 73 35 S 170 0 E
Coulommiers 43 48 50N 3 3 E
Coulonge, R. 150 45 52N 76 46W
Coulport 34 56 3N 4 53W
Coulterville 163 37 42N 120 12W
Council 147 64 55N 163 45W
Council Bluffs 158 41 20N 95 50W
Council Grove 158 38 41N 96 30W
Coupar Angus 35 56 33N 3 17W
Courantyne, R. 174 5 0N 57 45W
Courçon 44 46 15N 0 50W
Cours 45 46 7N 4 19 E
Courseulles 42 49 20N 0 29W
Court-St.-Etienne 47 50 38N 4 34 E
Courtenay 152 49 45N 125 0W
Courtine, La 44 45 43N 2 16 E
Courtland 163 38 20N 121 34W
Courtmacsherry 39 51 38N 8 43W
Courtmacsherry B. 39 51 37N 8 37W
Courtown 39 52 39N 6 14W
Courtrai = Kortrijk 47 50 50N 3 17 E
Courville 42 48 28N 1 15 E
Coutances 42 49 3N 1 28W
Couterne 42 48 30N 0 25W
Coutras 44 45 3N 0 8W
Coutts 152 49 0N 111 57W
Couvet 50 46 57N 6 38 E
Couvin 47 50 3N 4 29 E
Covarrubias 58 42 4N 3 31W
Covasna 70 45 50N 26 10 E
Covasna □ 70 45 50N 26 0 E
Cove Bay 37 57 5N 2 5W
Coventry 28 52 25N 1 31W
Coventry L. 153 61 15N 106 15W
Cover R. 32 54 14N 1 45W
Coverack 30 50 2N 5 6W
Covilhã 56 40 17N 7 31W
Covina 163 34 5N 117 52W
Covington, Ga., U.S.A. 157 33 36N 83 50W
Covington, Ky., U.S.A. 156 39 5N 84 30W
Covington, Okla., U.S.A. 159 36 21N 97 36W
Covington, Tenn., U.S.A. 159 35 34N 89 39W
Cowal Creek Settlement 138 10 54 S 142 20 E
Cowal, dist. 34 56 5N 5 8W
Cowal, L. 141 33 40 S 147 25 E
Cowan 153 52 5N 100 45W
Cowan, L. 137 31 45 S 121 45 E
Cowan L. 153 54 0N 107 15W
Cowangie 140 35 12 S 141 26 E
Coward Springs 139 29 24 S 136 48 E
Cowarie 139 27 45 S 138 15 E
Cowarna 137 30 55 S 122 40 E
Cowbridge 31 51 28N 3 28W
Cowcowing Lakes 137 30 55 S 117 20 E
Cowdenbeath 35 56 7N 3 20W
Cowell 140 33 39 S 136 56 E
Cowes 28 50 45N 1 18W
Cowfold 29 50 58N 0 16W
Cowl Cowl 141 33 36 S 145 18 E
Cowley 28 51 43N 1 12W
Cowpen 35 55 8N 1 34W
Cowra 141 33 49 S 148 42 E
Coxim 175 18 30 S 54 55W
Cox's Bazar 98 21 26N 91 59 E
Cox's Cove 151 49 7N 58 5W
Coyame 164 29 28N 105 6W
Coylton 34 55 26N 4 31W
Coyuca de Benítez 165 17 1N 100 8W
Coyuca de Catalán 164 18 58N 100 41W
Cozad 158 40 55N 99 57W
Cozie, Alpi 62 44 50N 6 59 E
Cozumel 165 20 31N 86 55W
Cozumel, Isla de 165 20 30N 86 40W
Craanford 39 52 40N 6 23W
Craboon 141 32 3 S 149 30 E
Cracow 139 25 17 S 150 17 E
Cradock 128 32 8 S 25 36 E
Craggie 37 57 25N 4 6W
Craig, Alaska, U.S.A. 147 55 30N 133 5W
Craig, Colo., U.S.A. 160 40 32N 107 44W
Craigavon = Portadown 38 54 27N 6 26W
Craigavon = Lurgan 38 54 28N 6 20W
Craigellachie 37 57 29N 3 9W
Craighouse 34 55 50N 5 58W
Craigmore 127 20 28 S 32 30 E
Craignish, L. 34 56 11N 5 32W
Craigtown 37 58 30N 3 53W
Crail 35 56 16N 2 38W
Crailsheim 49 49 7N 10 5 E
Craiova 70 44 21N 23 48 E
Cramlington 35 55 5N 1 36W
Crampel 117 7 8N 19 81 E
Cramsie 138 23 20 S 144 15 E
Cranberry Portage 153 54 35N 101 23W
Cranborne 28 50 55N 1 55W
Cranborne Chase 29 50 56N 2 6W
Cranbrook, Tas., Austral. 138 42 0 S 148 5 E
Cranbrook, W. Austral., Austral. 137 34 18 S 117 33 E
Cranbrook, Can. 152 49 30N 115 46W
Cranbrook, U.K. 29 51 6N 0 33 E
Crandon 158 45 32N 88 52W
Crane, Oregon, U.S.A. 160 43 21N 118 39W
Crane, Texas, U.S.A. 159 31 26N 102 27W
Cranfield Pt. 38 54 1N 6 3W
Cranleigh 29 51 8N 0 29W
Cranshaws 35 55 51N 2 30W
Cranston 162 41 47N 71 27W
Cranwell 33 53 4N 0 29W
Craon 42 47 50N 0 58W
Craonne 43 49 27N 3 46 E
Crasna 70 46 32N 27 51 E
Crasna, R. 70 47 44N 27 35 E
Crater Lake 160 42 55N 122 3W
Crater Mt. 135 6 37 S 145 7 E
Crater Pt. 135 5 25 S 152 9 E
Crateús 170 5 10 S 40 50W
Crathie 37 57 3N 3 12W
Crati, R. 65 39 41N 16 30 E
Crato, Brazil 171 7 10 S 39 25W
Crato, Port. 57 39 16N 7 39W
Crau 45 43 32N 4 40 E
Craughwell 39 53 15N 8 44W
Craven Arms 28 52 27N 2 49W
Crawford, U.K. 35 55 28N 3 40W
Crawford, U.S.A. 158 42 40N 103 25W
Crawford, oilfield 19 59 7N 1 30 E
Crawfordsville 156 40 2N 86 51W
Crawley 29 51 7N 0 10W
Cray 31 51 55N 3 38W
Crazy Mts. 160 46 14N 110 30W
Creag Meagaidh, mt. 37 56 57N 4 38W
Crean L. 153 54 5N 106 9W
Crèche, La 44 46 23N 0 19W
Crécy-en-Brie 43 48 50N 2 53 E
Crécy-en-Ponthieu 43 50 15N 1 53 E
Crécy-sur-Serre 43 49 40N 3 32 E
Credenhill 28 52 6N 2 49W
Crediton 30 50 47N 3 39W
Credo 137 30 28 S 120 45 E
Cree L. 153 57 30N 106 30W
Cree, R., Can. 153 58 57N 105 47W
Cree, R., U.K. 34 54 51N 4 24W
Creede 161 37 56N 106 59W
Creegh 39 52 45N 9 25W
Creel 164 27 45N 107 38W
Creeside 34 55 4N 4 41W
Creeslough 38 55 8N 7 55W
Creetown 34 54 54N 4 23W
Creeves 39 52 33N 9 3W
Creggan 38 54 39N 7 0W
Cregganbaun 38 53 42N 9 48W
Creighton 158 42 30N 97 52W
Creil 43 49 15N 2 34 E
Crema 62 45 21N 9 40 E
Cremona 62 45 8N 10 2 E
Crepaja 66 45 1N 20 38 E
Crépy 43 49 37N 3 32 E
Crépy-en-Valois 43 49 14N 2 54 E
Cres 63 44 58N 14 25 E
Cresbard 158 45 13N 98 57W
Crescent, Okla., U.S.A. 159 35 38N 97 36W
Crescent, Oreg., U.S.A. 160 43 30N 121 37W
Crescent City 160 41 45N 124 12W
Crescentino 62 45 11N 8 7 E
Crespino 63 44 59N 11 51 E
Crespo 172 32 2 S 60 19W
Cressman 150 47 40N 72 55W
Cressy 140 38 2 S 143 40 E
Crest 45 44 44N 5 2 E
Crested Butte 161 38 57N 107 0W
Crestline 163 34 14N 117 18W
Creston, Can. 152 49 10N 116 31W
Creston, Calif., U.S.A. 163 35 32N 120 33W
Creston, Iowa, U.S.A. 158 41 0N 94 20W
Creston, Wash., U.S.A. 160 47 47N 118 36W
Creston, Wyo., U.S.A. 160 41 46N 107 50W
Crestone 161 35 2N 106 0W
Crestview, Calif., U.S.A. 163 37 46N 118 58W
Crestview, Fla., U.S.A. 157 30 45N 86 35W
Creswick 140 37 25 S 143 51 E
Crete 158 40 38N 96 58W
Crete = Kriti 69 35 15N 25 0 E
Crete, La, Can. 152 58 10N 116 29W
Crete, La, Alta., Can. 152 58 11N 116 24W
Crete, Sea of 69 26 0N 25 0 E
Cretin, C. 135 6 40 S 147 53 E
Creus, C. 58 42 20N 3 19 E
Creuse □ 44 46 0N 2 0 E
Creuse, R. 44 47 0N 0 34 E
Creusot, Le 43 46 50N 4 24 E
Creuzburg 48 51 3N 10 15 E
Crevalcore 63 44 41N 11 10 E
Crèvecœur-le-Grand 43 49 37N 2 5 E
Crevillente 59 38 12N 0 48W
Crewe 32 53 6N 2 28W
Crewkerne 28 50 53N 2 48W
Crianlarich 34 56 24N 4 37W
Crib Point 139 38 22 S 145 13 E
Criccieth 31 52 55N 4 15W
Criciúma 173 28 40 S 49 23W
Crick 28 52 22N 1 9W
Crickhowell 31 51 52N 3 8W
Cricklade 28 51 38N 1 50W
Crieff 35 56 22N 3 50W
Criffell Mt. 35 54 56N 3 38W
Crikvenica 63 45 11N 14 40 E
Crillon, Mt. 152 58 39N 137 14W
Crimea = Krymskaya 82 45 0N 34 0 E
Crimmitschau 48 50 48N 12 23 E
Crimond 37 57 35N 1 53W
Crinan Canal 34 56 4N 5 30W
Crinkill 39 53 5N 7 55 E
Cristalândia 170 10 36 S 49 11W
Cristeşti 70 47 15N 26 33 E
Cristino Castro 170 8 49 S 44 13W
Crişul Alb, R. 66 46 25N 21 40 E
Crişul Negru, R. 70 46 38N 22 26 E
Crişul Repede, R. 70 47 20N 22 25 E
Crivitz 48 53 35N 11 39 E
Crixás 171 14 27 S 49 58W
Crna Gora □ 66 42 40N 19 20 E
Crna Trava 66 42 49N 22 19 E
Crni Drim, R. 66 41 17N 20 40 E
Crni Timok, R. 66 43 53N 22 0 E
Črnoljeva Planina 66 42 20N 21 0 E
Črnomelj 63 45 33N 15 10 E
Croagh Patrick, mt. 38 53 46N 9 40W
Croatia = Hrvatska 63 45 20N 16 0 E
Crocker, Barisan 102 5 0N 116 30 E
Crocketford 35 55 3N 3 49W
Crockets Town 38 54 8N 9 7W
Crockett 159 31 20N 95 30W
Crocodile Is. 138 11 43 S 135 8 E
Crocodile, R. 129 25 30 S 31 15 E
Crocq 44 45 52N 2 21 E
Croghan 38 53 55N 8 13W
Croglin 32 54 50N 2 37W
Crohy Hd. 38 54 55N 8 28W
Croisic, Le 42 47 18N 2 30W
Croisic, Pte. du. 42 47 19N 2 31W
Croix, La, L. 150 48 20N 92 15W
Croker, C. 136 10 58 S 132 35 E
Croker, I. 136 11 12N 132 32 E
Crolly 38 55 2N 8 16W
Cromalt Hills 36 58 0N 5 2W
Cromarty, Can. 153 58 3N 94 9W
Cromarty, U.K. 37 57 40N 4 2W
Cromarty Firth 37 57 40N 4 15W
Cromdale, Hills of 37 57 20N 3 28W
Cromer 29 52 56N 1 18 E
Cromore 36 58 6N 6 23W
Cromwell, N.Z. 143 45 3 S 169 14 E
Cromwell, U.S.A. 162 41 36N 72 39W
Cronat 43 46 43N 3 40 E
Crondall 29 51 13N 0 51W
Cronulla 141 34 3 S 151 8 E
Crook 33 54 43N 1 45W
Crooked I. 167 22 50N 74 10W
Crooked Island Passage 167 23 0N 74 30W
Crooked, R., Can. 152 54 10N 122 35W
Crooked, R., U.S.A. 160 44 30N 121 0W
Crooklands 32 54 16N 2 43W
Crookston, Minn., U.S.A. 158 47 50N 96 40W
Crookston, Nebr., U.S.A. 158 42 56N 100 45W
Crookstown 39 51 50N 8 50W
Crooksville 156 39 45N 82 8W

Crookwell Dalandzadgad

Crookwell 141 34 28S 149 24E
Croom 39 52 32N 8 43W
Crosby, Cumb., U.K. 32 54 45N 3 25W
Crosby, Merseyside, U.K. 32 53 30N 3 2W
Crosby, Minn., U.S.A. 158 46 28N 93 57W
Crosby, N.D., U.S.A. 153 48 55N 103 18W
Crosby Ravensworth 32 54 34N 2 35W
Crosbyton 159 33 37N 101 12W
Cross City 157 29 35N 83 5W
Cross Fell 32 54 44N 2 29W
Cross L. 153 54 45N 97 30W
Cross Plains 159 32 8N 99 7W
Cross, R. 121 4 46N 8 20E
Cross River □ 121 6 0N 8 0E
Cross Sound 147 58 20N 136 30W
Crossakiel 38 53 43N 7 2W
Crossbost 36 58 8N 6 27W
Crossdoney 38 53 57N 7 27W
Crosse, La, Kans., U.S.A. 158 38 33N 99 20W
Crosse, La, Wis., U.S.A. 158 43 48N 91 13W
Crossett 159 33 10N 91 57W
Crossfarnoge Pt. 39 52 10N 6 37W
Crossfield 152 51 25N 114 0W
Crossgar 38 54 22N 5 46W
Crosshaven 39 51 48N 8 19W
Crosshill 34 55 19N 4 39W
Crossley, Mt. 143 42 50S 172 5E
Crossmaglen 38 54 5N 6 37W
Crossmolina 38 54 6N 9 21W
Croton-on-Hudson 162 41 12N 73 55W
Crotone 65 39 5N 17 6E
Crouch, R. 29 51 37N 0 53E
Crow Agency 160 45 40N 107 30W
Crow Hd. 39 51 34N 10 9W
Crow, R. 152 59 41N 124 20W
Crow Sound 30 49 56N 6 16W
Crowborough 29 51 3N 0 9E
Crowell 159 33 59N 99 45W
Crowl Creek 141 32 0S 145 30E
Crowland 29 52 41N 0 10W
Crowle 33 53 36N 0 49W
Crowley 159 30 15N 92 20W
Crowley, L. 163 37 53N 118 42W
Crowlin Is. 36 57 20N 5 50W
Crown Point 156 41 24N 87 23W
Crows Landing 163 37 23N 121 6W
Crows Nest 139 27 16S 152 4E
Crowsnest Pass 152 49 40N 114 40W
Croyde 30 51 7N 4 13W
Croydon, Austral. 138 18 13S 142 14E
Croydon, U.K. 29 51 18N 0 5W
Crozet, Île 11 46 27S 52 0E
Crozon 42 48 15N 4 30W
Cruces, Pta. 174 6 39N 77 32W
Cruden Bay 37 57 25N 1 50W
Crudgington 28 52 46N 2 33W
Crumlin 38 54 38N 6 12W
Crummer Peaks 138 6 40S 144 0E
Crummock Water L. 32 54 33N 3 18W
Crusheen 39 52 57N 8 54W
Cruz, C. 166 19 50N 77 50W
Cruz das Almas 171 12 40S 39 6W
Cruz de Malta 170 8 15S 40 20W
Cruz del Eje 172 30 45S 64 50W
Cruz, La, Colomb. 174 1 35N 76 58W
Cruz, La, C. Rica 166 11 4N 85 39W
Cruz, La, Mexico 164 23 55N 106 54W
Cruzeiro 173 22 50S 45 0W
Cruzeiro do Oeste 173 23 46S 53 4W
Cruzeiro do Sul 174 7 35S 72 35W
Cry L. 152 58 45N 128 5W
Cryfow Sl. 54 51 2N 15 24E
Crymmych 31 51 59N 4 40W
Crystal Brook 140 33 21S 138 12E
Crystal City, Mo., U.S.A. 158 38 15N 90 23W
Crystal City, Tex., U.S.A. 159 28 40N 99 50W
Crystal Falls 156 46 9N 88 11W
Crystal River 157 28 54N 82 35W
Crystal Springs 159 31 59N 90 25W
Čáslav 52 49 54N 15 22E
Csongrád 53 46 43N 20 12E
Csongrád □ 53 46 32N 20 15E
Csorna 53 47 38N 17 18E
Csurgo 53 46 16N 17 9E
Ctesiphon 92 33 9N 44 35E
Cu Lao Hon 101 10 54N 108 18E
Cua Rao 100 19 16N 104 27E
Cuácua, R. 127 18 0S 36 0E
Cuamato 128 17 2S 15 7E
Cuamba = Nova Preixo 127 14 45S 36 22E
Cuando 128 16 25S 22 2E
Cuando Cubango □ 128 16 25S 20 0E
Cuando, R. 125 14 0S 19 30E
Cuangar 128 17 28S 14 40E
Cuango 124 6 15S 16 35E
Cuarto, R. 172 33 25S 63 2W
Cuatrociénegas de Carranza 164 26 59N 102 5W
Cuauhtémoc 164 28 25N 106 52W
Cuba, Port. 57 38 10N 7 54W
Cuba, U.S.A. 161 36 0N 107 0W
Cuba ■ 166 22 0N 79 0W
Cuballing 137 32 50S 117 10E
Cubango, R. 128 16 15S 17 45E
Cuchi 125 14 37S 17 10E
Cuchumatanes, Sierra de los 166 15 35N 91 25W
Cuckfield 29 51 0N 0 8W
Cucurpe 164 30 20N 110 43W
Cucurrupí 174 4 23N 76 56W
Cúcuta 174 7 54N 72 31W
Cudahy 156 42 54N 87 50W
Cudalbi 70 45 46N 27 41E
Cuddalore 97 11 46N 79 45E
Cuddapah 97 14 30N 78 47E
Cuddapan, L. 138 25 45S 141 26E
Cudgewa 141 36 10S 147 42E
Cudillero 56 43 33N 6 9W
Cudworth 33 53 35N 1 25W
Cue 137 27 25S 117 54E
Cuéllar 56 41 23N 4 21W
Cuenca, Ecuador 174 2 50S 79 9W
Cuenca, Spain 58 40 5N 2 10W
Cuenca □ 58 40 0N 2 0W
Cuenca, Serranía de 58 39 55N 1 50W
Cuencamé 164 24 53N 103 41W
Cuerda del Pozo, Pantano de la 58 41 51N 2 44W
Cuernavaca 165 18 50N 99 20W
Cuero 159 29 5N 97 17W
Cuers 45 43 14N 6 5E
Cuervo 159 35 5N 104 25W
Cuesmes 47 50 26N 3 56E
Cuevas de Altamira 56 43 20N 4 5W
Cuevas del Almanzora 59 37 18N 1 58W
Cuevo 174 20 25N 63 30W
Cugir 70 43 48N 23 25E
Cugno 123 6 14N 42 31E
Cuhimbre 174 0 10S 75 23W
Cuiabá 175 15 30S 56 0W
Cuiabá, R. 175 16 50S 56 30W
Cuidad Bolivar 174 8 21N 70 34W
Cuilcagh, Mt. 38 54 12N 7 50W
Cuilco 166 15 24N 91 58W
Cuillin Hills 36 57 14N 6 15W
Cuillin Sd. 36 57 4N 6 20W
Cuima 125 13 0S 15 45E
Cuiseaux 45 46 30N 5 22E
Cuité 170 6 29S 36 9W
Cuito, R. 128 16 50S 19 30E
Cuitzeo, L. 164 19 55N 101 5W
Cujmir 70 44 13N 22 57E
Culan 44 46 34N 2 20E
Cŭlaraşi 43 44 14N 27 23E
Culbertson 158 48 9N 104 30W
Culburra 140 35 50S 139 58E
Culcairn 141 35 41S 147 3E
Culdaff 38 55 17N 7 10W
Culebra, I. 147 18 19N 65 17W
Culebra, Sierra de la 56 41 55N 6 20W
Culemborg 46 51 58N 5 14E
Culgoa 140 35 44S 143 6E
Culgoa, R. 139 29 56S 146 20E
Culiacán 164 24 50N 107 40W
Culiacán, R. 164 24 30N 107 42W
Cŭlimani, Munţii 70 47 12N 25 0E
Cŭlineşti 70 45 21N 24 18E
Culion, I. 103 11 54N 120 1E
Cúllar de Baza 59 37 35N 2 34W
Cullarin Range 141 34 30S 149 30E
Cullaville 38 54 4N 6 40W
Cullen, Austral. 136 13 58S 131 54E
Cullen, U.K. 37 57 45N 2 50W
Cullen Pt. 138 11 57S 141 54E
Cullera 59 39 9N 0 17W
Cullin L. 38 53 58N 9 12W
Cullivoe 36 60 43N 1 0W
Cullman 157 34 13N 86 50W
Culloden Moor 37 57 29N 4 7W
Cullompton 30 50 52N 3 23W
Cullyhanna 38 54 8N 6 35W
Culm, R. 30 50 46N 3 31W
Culoz 45 45 47N 5 46E
Culpataro 140 33 40S 144 22E
Culpeper 156 38 29N 77 59W
Culrain 37 57 55N 4 25W
Culross 35 56 4N 3 38W
Cults 37 57 8N 2 10W
Culuene, R. 175 12 15S 53 10W
Culvain Mt. 36 56 55N 5 19W
Culver, Pt. 137 32 54S 124 43E
Culverden 143 42 47S 172 49E
Cumali 69 36 42N 27 28E
Cumaná 174 10 30N 64 5W
Cumari 171 18 16S 48 11W
Cumberland, Can. 152 49 40N 125 0W
Cumberland, Md., U.S.A. 156 39 40N 78 43W
Cumberland, Wis., U.S.A. 158 45 32N 92 3W
Cumberland (□) 26 54 44N 2 55W
Cumberland I. 157 30 52N 81 30W
Cumberland Is. 138 20 35S 149 10E
Cumberland L. 153 54 3N 102 18W
Cumberland Pen. 149 67 0N 64 0W
Cumberland Plat. 157 36 0N 84 30W
Cumberland, R. 157 36 15N 87 0W
Cumberland Sd. 149 65 30N 66 0W
Cumborah 139 29 40S 147 45E
Cumbrae Is. 34 55 46N 4 54W
Cumbres Mayores 57 38 4N 6 39W
Cumbria □ 32 54 35N 2 55W
Cumbrian Mts. 32 54 30N 3 0W
Cumbum 97 15 40N 79 10E
Cuminestown 37 57 32N 2 17W
Cummerower See 48 53 47N 12 52E
Cummertrees 35 55 0N 3 20W
Cummings Mtn. 163 35 2N 118 34W
Cummins 139 34 16S 135 43E
Cumnock, Austral. 141 32 59S 148 46E
Cumnock, U.K. 34 55 27N 4 18W
Cumnor 28 51 44N 1 20W
Cumpas 164 30 0N 109 48W
Cumuruxatiba 171 17 6S 39 13W
Cumwhinton 32 54 51N 2 49W
Cuñaré 174 0 49N 72 32W
Cuncumén 172 31 53S 70 38W
Cunderdin 137 31 37S 117 12E
Cundinamarca □ 174 5 0N 74 0W
Cunene, R. 128 17 0S 15 0E
Cúneo 62 44 23N 7 31E
Cunillera, I. 59 38 59N 1 13E
Cunlhat 44 45 38N 3 32E
Cunnamulla 139 28 2S 145 38E
Cunninghame, Reg. 34 55 38N 4 35W
Cuorgnè 62 45 23N 7 39E
Cupar, Can. 153 50 57N 104 10W
Cupar, U.K. 35 56 20N 3 0W
Cupica 174 6 50N 77 30W
Çupica, Golfo de 174 6 25N 77 30W
Ćuprija 66 43 57N 21 26E
Curaçá 170 8 59S 39 54W
Curaçao, I. 167 12 10N 69 0W
Curanilahue 172 37 29S 73 28W
Curaray, R. 174 1 30S 75 30W
Curatabaca 174 6 19N 62 51W
Curbarado 174 7 3N 76 54W
Curbur 137 26 28S 115 55E
Cure, La 50 46 28N 6 4E
Curepto 172 35 8S 72 1W
Curiapo 174 8 33N 61 5W
Curicó 172 34 55S 71 20W
Curicó □ 172 34 50S 71 15W
Curimatá 170 10 2S 44 17W
Curiplaya 174 0 16N 74 52W
Curitiba 173 25 20S 49 10W
Curlew Mts. 38 54 0N 8 20W
Curoca Norte 128 16 15S 12 58E
Currabubula 141 31 16S 150 44E
Curracunya 139 28 29S 144 9E
Curraglass 39 52 5N 8 4W
Currais Novos 170 6 13S 36 30W
Curralinho 170 1 35S 49 30W
Curran, L. = Terewah, L. 139 29 50S 147 24E
Currane L. 39 51 50N 10 8W
Currant 160 38 51N 115 32W
Curranyalpa 141 30 53S 144 39E
Curraweena 141 30 47S 145 54E
Currawilla 138 25 10S 141 20E
Current, R. 159 37 15N 91 10W
Currie, Austral. 138 39 56S 143 53E
Currie, U.K. 35 55 53N 3 17W
Currie, U.S.A. 160 40 16N 114 45W
Currie, Mt. 129 30 29S 29 21E
Currituck Sd. 157 36 20N 75 50W
Curry Rivel 28 51 2N 2 52W
Curryglass 39 51 40N 9 50W
Curtea-de-Argeş 70 45 12N 24 42E
Curtis, Spain 56 43 7N 8 4W
Curtis, U.S.A. 158 40 41N 100 32W
Curtis, I. 138 23 35S 151 10E
Curtis, Pt. 138 23 53S 151 21E
Curuá, I. 170 0 48N 50 10W
Curuapanema, R. 175 7 0S 54 30W
Curuçá 170 0 35S 47 50W
Curuguaty 173 24 19S 55 49W
Curupira, Serra 174 1 25N 64 30W
Cururupu 170 1 50S 44 50W
Curuzú Cuatiá 172 29 50S 58 5W
Curvelo 171 18 45S 44 27W
Curyo 140 35 50S 142 47E
Cushendall 38 55 5N 6 3W
Cushendun 38 55 8N 6 3W
Cushina 39 53 11N 7 10W
Cushing, Mt. 152 57 35N 126 57W
Cusihuiriáchic 164 28 10N 106 50W
Cussabat 119 32 39N 14 1E
Cusset 44 46 8N 3 28E
Custer 158 43 45N 103 38W
Cut Bank 160 48 40N 112 15W
Cutchogue 162 41 1N 72 30W
Cuthbert 157 31 47N 84 47W
Cutler 163 36 31N 119 17W
Cutra L. 39 53 2N 8 48W
Cutro 65 39 1N 16 58E
Cuttaburra, R. 139 29 43S 144 22E
Cuttack 96 20 25N 85 57E
Cuvier, C. 137 23 14S 113 22E
Cuvier I. 142 36 27S 175 50E
Cuxhaven 48 53 51N 8 41E
Cuyabeno 174 0 16S 75 53W
Cuyahoga Falls 156 41 8N 81 30W
Cuyo 103 10 50N 121 5E
Cuyuni, R. 175 7 0N 59 30W
Cuzco 174 13 32S 72 0W
Cuzco, Mt. 174 20 0S 66 50W
Čŭzŭneşti 70 44 36N 27 3E
Čvrsnica, Mt. 66 43 36N 17 35E
Cwmbran 31 51 39N 3 0W
Cwrt 31 52 35N 3 55W
Cyangugu 126 2 29S 28 54E
Cybinka 54 52 12N 14 46E
Cyclades = Kikladhes 69 37 20N 24 30E
Cygnet 138 43 8S 147 1E
Cymmer 31 51 37N 3 38W
Cynthiana 156 38 23N 84 10W
Cynwyl Elfed 31 51 55N 4 22W
Cypress Hills 153 49 40N 109 30W
Cyprus ■ 92 35 0N 33 0E
Cyrenaica □ 117 27 0N 20 0E
Cyrene 117 32 39N 21 18E
Czaplinek 54 53 34N 16 14E
Czar 153 52 27N 110 50W
Czarne 54 53 42N 16 58E
Czarnków 54 52 55N 16 38E
Czechoslovakia ■ 53 49 0N 17 0E
Czechowice-Dziedzice 54 49 54N 18 59E
Czeladz 54 50 16N 19 2E
Czempin 54 52 9N 16 33E
Czersk 54 53 46N 17 58E
Czerwiensk 54 52 1N 15 13E
Czerwionka 54 50 7N 18 37E
Częstochowa 54 50 49N 19 7E
Częstochowa □ 54 50 45N 19 0E
Czlopa 54 53 6N 16 6E
Człuchów 54 53 41N 17 22E

D

Da Lat 101 11 56N 108 25E
Da Nang 100 16 4N 108 13E
Da, R. 100 21 15N 105 20E
Daarlerveen 46 52 26N 6 34E
Dab'a, Ras el 122 31 3N 28 31E
Dabai 121 11 25N 5 15E
Dabajuro 174 11 2N 70 40W
Dabakala 120 8 15N 4 20W
Dabatou 120 11 50N 9 20W
Dabburiya 90 32 42N 35 22E
Daberas 128 25 27S 18 30E
Dabhoi 94 22 10N 73 20E
Dabie 54 53 27N 14 45E
Dabola 120 10 50N 11 5W
Dabong 101 5 23N 103 1E
Dabou 120 5 20N 4 23W
Daboya 121 9 30N 1 20W
Dabra Berhan 123 9 42N 39 15E
Dabra Sina 123 9 51N 39 45E
Dabra Tabor 123 11 50N 37 58E
Dabra Zabit 123 11 48N 38 30E
Dabrowa Górnicza 54 50 15N 19 10E
Dabrowa Tarnówska 54 50 10N 20 59E
Dabrówno 54 53 27N 20 2E
Dabus, R. 123 10 12N 35 0E
Dacca 98 23 43N 90 26E
Dacca □ 98 24 0N 90 25E
Dachau 49 48 16N 11 27E
Dadanawa 174 3 0N 59 30W
Daday 82 41 28N 33 35E
Daddato 123 12 24N 42 45E
Dade City 157 28 20N 82 12W
Dadiya 121 9 35N 11 24E
Dadra and Nagar Haveli □ 96 20 5N 73 0E
Dadri = Charkhi Dadri 94 28 37N 76 17E
Dadu 94 26 45N 67 45E
Daer R. 35 55 23N 3 39W
Daet 103 14 2N 122 55E
Dagaio 123 6 8N 40 40E
Dagana 120 16 30N 15 20W
Dagash 122 19 19N 33 25E
Dagestan, A.S.S.R. □ 83 42 30N 47 0E
Daggett 163 34 43N 116 52W
Daggs Sd. 143 45 23S 166 45E
Daghfeli 122 19 18N 32 40E
Daghirie 123 11 40N 41 50E
Dagö = Hiiumaa 80 58 50N 22 45E
Dagoreti 126 1 18S 36 4E
Dagua 135 3 27S 143 20E
Dagupan 103 16 3N 120 20E
Dahab 122 28 30N 34 31E
Dahlak Kebir 123 15 50N 40 10E
Dahlenburg 48 53 11N 10 43E
Dahlonega 157 34 35N 83 59W
Dahme 48 51 51N 13 25E
Daho 121 10 28N 11 18E
Dahomey ■ = Benin ■ 121 8 0N 2 0E
Dahra 120 15 22N 15 30W
Dahra, Massif de 118 36 7N 1 21E
Dai Hao 100 18 1N 106 25E
Dai-Sen 110 35 22N 133 32E
Daigo 111 36 46N 140 21E
Dailly 34 55 16N 4 44W
Daimanji-San 110 36 14N 133 20E
Daimiel 59 39 5N 3 35W
Daintree 138 16 20S 145 20E
Daiō-Misaki 111 34 15N 136 45E
Dairen = Lüta 107 38 55N 121 40E
Dairût 122 27 34N 30 43E
Dairymple 34 55 24N 4 36W
Daisetsu-Zan 112 43 30N 142 57E
Daitari 96 21 10N 85 46E
Daitō 110 35 19N 132 58E
Dajarra 138 21 42S 139 30E
Dak Dam 100 12 20N 107 21E
Dak Nhe 100 15 28N 107 48E
Dak Pek 100 15 4N 107 44E
Dak Song 101 12 19N 107 35E
Dak Sui 100 14 55N 107 43E
Dakala 121 14 27N 2 27E
Dakar 120 14 34N 17 29W
Dakhla 116 23 50N 15 53W
Dakhla, El Wâhât el- 122 25 30N 28 50E
Dakhovskaya 83 44 13N 40 13E
Dakingari 121 11 37N 4 1E
Dakor 94 22 45N 73 11E
Dakoro 121 14 31N 6 46E
Dakota City 158 42 27N 96 28W
Dakota, North 158 47 30N 100 0W
Đakovica 66 42 22N 20 26E
Dakovo 66 45 19N 18 24E
Dakra 120 15 22N 15 30W
Dalaba 120 10 42N 12 15W
Dalälven, L. 72 61 27N 17 15E
Dalandzadgad 106 43 27N 104 30E

Dalarö Degeh-Bur

Dalarö 75 59 8N 18 24 E
Dalat 101 12 3N 108 32 E
Dalbandin 93 29 0N 4 23 E
Dalbeattie 35 54 55N 3 50W
Dalbosjön, L. 73 58 40N 12 45 E
Dalby, Austral. 139 27 10 S 151 17 E
Dalby, Sweden 73 55 42N 13 22 E
Dale, Sogn og Fjordane, Norway 71 61 27N 7 28 E
Dale, Sogn og Fjordane, Norway 71 61 22N 5 23 E
Dale, U.K. 31 51 42N 5 11W
Dalen, Neth. 46 52 42N 6 46 E
Dalen, Norway 71 59 26N 8 0 E
Dalet 98 19 59N 93 51 E
Daletme 98 21 36N 92 46 E
Dalfsen 46 52 31N 6 16 E
Dalga 122 27 39N 30 41 E
Dalgaranger, Mt. 137 27 50 S 117 5 E
Dalhalvaig 37 58 28N 3 53W
Dalhart 159 36 0N 102 30W
Dalhousie, Can. 151 48 0N 66 26W
Dalhousie, India 94 32 38N 76 0 E
Daliburgh 36 57 10N 7 23W
Dalj 174 45 28N 18 58 E
Dalkeith 35 55 54N 3 5W
Dalkey 39 53 16N 6 7W
Dall I. 152 54 59N 133 25W
Dallarnil 139 25 19 S 152 2 E
Dallas, U.K. 37 57 33N 3 32W
Dallas, Oregon, U.S.A. 160 45 0N 123 15W
Dallas, Texas, U.S.A. 159 32 50N 96 50W
Dallol 123 14 14N 40 17 E
Dalmacija 66 43 20N 17 0 E
Dalmally 34 56 25N 5 0W
Dalmatia = Dalmacija 66 43 20N 17 0 E
Dalmatovo 84 56 16N 62 56 E
Dalmellington 34 55 20N 4 25W
Dalneretchensk 77 45 50N 133 40 E
Daloa 120 7 0N 6 30W
Dalry 34 55 44N 4 42W
Dalrymple, Mt. 133 21 1 S 148 39 E
Dalsjöfors 73 57 46N 18 5 E
Dalskog 73 58 44N 12 18 E
Dalton, Can. 150 48 11N 84 1W
Dalton, Cumbria, U.K. 33 54 9N 3 11W
Dalton, Dumfries, U.K. 35 55 3N 3 22W
Dalton, N. Yorks., U.K. 33 54 28N 1 32W
Dalton, Ga., U.S.A. 103 34 45N 85 0W
Dalton, Mass., U.S.A. 162 42 28N 73 11W
Dalton, Nebr., U.S.A. 158 41 27N 103 0W
Dalton Post 152 66 42N 137 0W
Daltonganj 95 24 0N 84 4 E
Dalvík 74 65 58N 18 32W
Dalwhinnie 37 56 56N 4 14W
Daly City 163 37 42N 122 28W
Daly L. 153 56 32N 105 39W
Daly, R. 136 13 21 S 130 18 E
Daly Waters 138 16 15 S 133 24 E
Dalystown 38 53 26N 7 23W
Dam 170 4 45N 55 0W
Dam Doi 101 8 59N 105 12 E
Dam Gillan 153 56 20N 94 40W
Dam Ha 100 21 21N 107 36 E
Dama, Wadi 122 27 12N 35 50 E
Daman 96 20 25N 72 57 E
Daman □ 96 20 25N 72 58 E
Damanhûr 122 31 0N 30 30 E
Damar, I. 103 7 15 S 128 30 E
Damaraland 128 21 0 S 17 0 E
Damascus = Dimashq 92 33 30N 36 18 E
Damaturu 121 11 45N 11 55 E
Damāvand 93 36 0N 52 0 E
Damāvand, Qolleh-ye 93 35 45N 52 10 E
Damba, Angola 124 6 44 S 15 29 E
Damba, Ethiopia 123 15 10N 38 47 E
Dâmbovnic, R. 70 44 28N 25 18 E
Dame Marie 167 18 36N 74 26W
Damerham 28 50 57N 1 52W
Dames Quarter 162 38 11N 75 54W
Damghan 93 36 10N 54 17 E
Damietta = Dumyât 122 31 24N 31 48 E
Damin 93 27 30N 60 40 E
Damiya 90 32 6N 35 34 E
Damman 92 26 25N 50 2 E
Dammarie 43 48 20N 1 30 E
Dammartin 43 49 3N 2 41 E
Dammastock 51 46 38N 8 24 E
Damme 48 52 32N 8 12 E
Damodar, R. 95 23 17N 87 35 E
Damoh 95 23 50N 79 28 E
Dampier 136 20 41 S 116 42 E
Dampier Arch. 136 20 38 S 116 32 E
Dampier Downs 136 18 24 S 123 5 E
Dampier, Selat 103 0 40 S 131 0 E
Dampier Str. 135 5 50 S 148 0 E
Damrei, Chuor Phnum 101 12 30N 103 0 E
Damville 42 48 51N 1 5 E
Damvillers 43 49 20N 5 21 E
Dan Chadi 121 12 47N 5 17 E
Dan Dume 121 11 28N 7 8 E
Dan Gora 121 11 30N 8 7 E
Dan Gulbi 121 11 40N 6 15 E
Dan, oilfield 19 55 30N 5 10 E
Dan Sadau 121 11 25N 6 20 E
Dana 103 11 0 S 122 52 E
Dana, Lac 150 50 53N 77 20W
Dana, Mt 163 37 54N 119 12W
Danakil Depression 123 12 45N 41 0 E
Danao 103 10 31N 124 1 E
Danbury 162 41 23N 73 29W
Danby L. 161 34 17N 115 0W
Dand 94 31 28N 65 32 E
Dandaragan 137 30 40 S 115 40 E
Dandeldhura 95 29 20N 80 35 E
Dandeli 93 15 5N 74 30 E
Dandenong 141 38 0 S 145 15 E
Dandkandi 98 23 32N 90 43 E
Danforth 151 45 39N 67 57W
Dang Raek 101 14 40N 104 0 E
Dangara 85 38 6N 69 22 E
•Danger Is. 131 10 53 S 165 49W
Danger Pt. 128 34 40 S 19 17 E
Dangla 123 11 18N 36 56 E
Dangora 121 11 30N 8 7 E
Dangrek, Phnom 100 14 15N 105 0 E
Daniel 160 42 56N 110 2W
Daniel's Harbour 151 50 13N 57 35W
Danielskull 128 28 11 S 23 33 E
Danielson 162 41 50N 71 52W
Danilov 81 58 16N 40 13 E
Danilovgrad 66 42 38N 19 9 E
Danilovka 81 50 25N 44 12 E
Danissa 126 3 15N 40 58 E
Danja 121 11 29N 7 30 E
Dankalwa 121 11 52N 12 12 E
Dankama 121 13 20N 7 44 E
Dankhar Gompa 93 32 10N 78 10 E
Dankov 81 53 20N 39 5 E
Danlí 166 14 4N 86 35W
Dannemora 75 60 12N 17 51 E
Dannenberg 48 53 7N 11 4 E
Dannevirke 142 40 12 S 176 8 E
Dannhauser 129 28 0 S 30 3 E
Dansalan 103 8 2N 124 30 E
Dansville 156 42 32N 77 41W
Dantan 95 21 57N 87 20 E
Danube, R. 53 45 0N 28 20W
Danubyo 98 17 15N 95 35 E
Danvers 162 42 34N 70 55 E
Danville, Ill., U.S.A. 156 40 10N 87 40W
Danville, Ky., U.S.A. 156 37 40N 84 45W
Danville, Pa., U.S.A. 162 40 58N 76 37W
Danville, Va., U.S.A. 157 36 40N 79 20W
Danzig = Gdansk 54 54 22N 18 40 E
Dão 103 10 30N 122 6 E
Dão, R. 56 40 28N 8 0W
Daosa 94 26 52N 76 20 E
Daoud = Aïn Beida 119 35 50N 7 29 E
Daoulas 42 48 22N 4 17W
Dapango 121 10 55N 0 16 E
Dar al Hamra, Ad 92 27 22N 37 43 E
Dar es Salaam 126 6 50 S 39 12 E
Dar'ā 90 32 36N 36 7 E
Darab 93 28 50N 54 30 E
Darabani 70 48 10N 26 39 E
Daraj 119 30 10N 10 28 E
Daraut Kurgan 85 39 33N 72 11 E
Daravica 66 42 32N 20 8 E
Daraw 121 24 22N 32 51 E
Darazo 121 11 1N 10 24W
Darband 94 34 30N 72 50 E
Darbhanga 95 26 15N 86 8 E
Darby 160 46 2N 114 7W
D'Arcy 152 50 35N 122 30W
Darda 66 45 40N 18 41 E
Dardanelle 163 38 2N 119 50W
Dardanelles = Canakkale Bogłazi 92 40 0N 26 20 E
Dardenelle 159 35 12N 93 9W
Darent, R. 29 51 22N 0 12 E
Darfield 143 43 29 S 172 7 E
Darfo 62 45 43N 10 11 E
Dargai 94 34 25N 71 45 E
Dargan Ata 76 40 40N 62 20 E
Dargaville 142 35 57 S 173 52 E
Darharala 120 8 23N 4 20W
Dari 123 5 48N 30 26 E
Darién, G. del 174 9 0N 77 0W
Darién, Serranía del 174 8 30N 77 30W
Dariganga 106 45 5N 113 45 E
Darinskoye 84 51 20N 51 44 E
Darjeeling 95 27 3N 88 18 E
Dark Cove 151 48 47N 54 13W
Darkan 137 33 20 S 116 43 E
Darke Peak 140 33 27 S 136 12 E
Darkot Pass 95 36 45N 73 26 E
Darlaston 28 52 35N 2 1W
Darling Downs 139 28 30 S 152 0 E
Darling, R. 140 34 4 S 141 54 E
Darling Ra. 137 32 30 S 116 0 E
Darlington, U.K. 33 54 33N 1 33W
Darlington, S.C., U.S.A. 157 34 18N 79 50W
Darlington, Wis., U.S.A. 158 42 43N 90 7W
Darlot, L. 137 27 48 S 121 35 E
Darłowo 54 54 25N 16 25 E
Darmstadt 49 49 51N 8 40 E
Darnall 129 29 23 S 31 18 E
Darnétal 42 49 25N 1 10 E
Darney 43 48 5N 6 0 E
Darnick 140 32 48 S 143 38 E
Darnley B. 147 69 30N 123 30W
Darnley, C. 13 68 0 S 69 0 E
Daroca 58 41 9N 1 25W
Darr 138 23 13 S 144 7 E
Darr, R. 138 23 39 S 143 50 E
Darragh 39 52 47N 9 7W
Darran Mts. 143 44 37 S 167 59 E
Darrington 160 48 14N 121 37W
Darror, R. 91 10 30N 50 0 E
Darsana 98 23 35N 88 48 E
Darsi 97 15 46N 79 44 E
Darsser Ort 48 44 27N 12 30 E
Dart, R., N.Z. 143 44 20 S 168 20 E
Dart, R., U.K. 30 50 24N 3 36W
*Renamed Pukapuka
Dartford 29 51 26N 0 15 E
Dartington 30 50 26N 3 42W
Dartmoor, Austral. 140 37 56N 141 19 E
Dartmoor, U.K. 30 50 36N 4 0W
Dartmouth, Austral. 138 23 31 S 144 44 E
Dartmouth, Can. 151 44 40N 63 30W
Dartmouth, U.K. 30 50 21N 3 35W
Dartmouth, L. 139 26 4 S 145 18 E
Darton 33 53 36N 1 32W
Dartuch, C. 58 39 55N 3 49 E
Daru, P.N.G. 135 9 3 S 143 13 E
Daru, S. Leone 120 8 0N 10 52W
Darvel 34 55 37N 4 20W
Darvel Bay 103 4 50N 118 20 E
Darwen 32 53 42N 2 29W
Darwha 96 20 15N 77 45 E
Darwin, Austral. 136 12 25 S 130 51 E
Darwin, U.S.A. 163 36 15N 117 35W
Darwin, Mt. 127 16 45 S 31 33 E
Darwin River 136 12 50 S 130 58 E
Daryacheh-ye-Sistan 93 31 0N 61 0 E
Daryapur 96 20 55N 77 20 E
Dase 123 14 53N 37 15 E
Dashato, R. 123 7 25N 42 40 E
Dashkesan 83 40 40N 46 0 E
Dasht-e Kavīr 93 34 30N 55 0 E
Dasht-e Lut 93 31 30N 58 0 E
Dasht-i-Khash 93 32 0N 62 0 E
Dasht-i-Margo 93 30 40N 62 30 E
Dasht-i-Nawar 93 33 52N 68 0 E
Dasht, R. 93 25 40N 62 20 E
Daska 94 32 20N 74 20 E
Dassa-Zoume 121 7 46N 2 14 E
Dasseneiland 128 33 37 S 18 3 E
Datça 69 36 46N 27 40 E
Datia 95 25 39N 78 27 E
Dattapur 96 20 45N 78 15 E
Daugava 80 57 0N 24 0 E
Daugavpils 80 55 53N 26 32 E
Daulat Yar 93 34 30N 65 45 E
Daulatabad 96 19 57N 75 15 E
Daun 49 50 5N 6 53 E
Dauphin, Can. 153 51 9N 100 5W
Dauphin, U.S.A. 162 40 22N 76 56W
Dauphin I. 157 30 16N 88 10W
Dauphin L. 153 51 20N 99 45W
Dauphiné 45 45 15N 5 25 E
Dauqa 122 19 30N 41 0 E
Daura, Kano, Nigeria 121 13 2N 8 21 E
Daura, N.-E., Nigeria 121 11 31N 11 24 E
Davadi 120 14 10N 16 3W
Davangere 97 14 25N 75 50 E
Davao 103 7 0N 125 40 E
Davao, G. of 103 6 30N 125 48 E
Davar Panab 93 27 25N 62 15 E
Dave 74 52 55N 1 50W
Davenport, Calif., U.S.A. 163 37 1N 122 12W
Davenport, Iowa, U.S.A. 158 41 30N 90 40W
Davenport, Wash., U.S.A. 160 47 40N 118 5W
Davenport Downs 138 24 8 S 141 7 E
Davenport Ra. 138 20 28 S 134 0 E
Daventry 28 52 16N 1 10W
David 166 8 30N 82 30W
David City 158 41 18N 97 10W
David Gorodok 80 52 4N 27 8 E
Davidson 153 51 16N 105 59W
Davik 71 61 53N 5 33 E
Davis 163 38 33N 121 45W
Davis Dam 161 35 11N 114 35W
Davis Inlet 151 55 50N 60 45W
Davis Mts. 159 30 42N 104 15W
Davis Str. 149 65 0N 58 0W
Davlekanovo 84 54 13N 55 3 E
Davos 51 46 48N 9 49 E
Davy L. 153 58 53N 108 18W
Davyhurst 137 30 2 S 120 40 E
Dawa, R. 123 5 0N 39 5 E
Dawaki, Jos, Nigeria 121 9 25N 9 33 E
Dawaki, Kano, Nigeria 121 12 5N 8 23 E
Dawayima 90 31 33N 34 55 E
Dawes Ra. 138 24 40 S 150 40 E
Dawley 28 52 40N 2 29W
Dawlish 30 50 34N 3 28W
Dawna Range 98 16 30N 98 30 E
Dawnyein 98 15 54N 95 36 E
Dawros Hd. 38 54 48N 8 32W
Dawson, Can. 147 64 10N 139 30W
Dawson, Ga., U.S.A. 157 31 45N 84 28W
Dawson, N.D., U.S.A. 158 46 56N 99 45W
Dawson Creek 152 55 45N 120 15W
Dawson, I. 176 53 50 S 70 50W
Dawson Inlet 153 61 50N 93 25W
Dawson, R. 133 23 25 S 150 10 E
Dawson Range 138 24 30 S 149 48 E
Dawson's 127 17 0 S 30 57 E
Daylesford 140 37 21 S 144 9 E
Dayr al-Ghusūn 90 32 21N 35 4 E
Dayr az Zawr 92 35 20N 40 5 E
Daysland 152 52 50N 112 20W
Dayton, Ohio, U.S.A. 156 39 45N 84 10W
Dayton, Tenn., U.S.A. 157 35 30N 85 1W
Dayton, Wash., U.S.A. 160 46 20N 118 0W
Daytona Beach 157 29 14N 81 0W
Dayville 160 44 33N 119 37W
De Aar 128 30 39 S 24 0 E
De Bilt 46 52 6N 5 11 E
De Funiak Springs 157 30 42N 86 10W
De Grey 136 20 12 S 119 12 E
De Grey, R. 136 20 0 S 119 13 E
De Kalb 158 41 55N 88 45W
De Koog 46 53 6N 4 46 E
De Land 157 29 1N 81 19W
De Leon 159 32 9N 98 35W
De Long Mts. 147 68 10N 163 0W
De Long, Ostrova 77 76 40N 149 20 E
De Panne 47 51 6N 2 34 E
De Pere 156 44 28N 88 1W
De Queen 159 34 3N 94 24W
De Quincy 159 30 30N 93 27W
De Ridder 159 30 48N 93 15W
De Rijp 46 52 33N 4 51 E
De Smet 158 44 25N 97 35W
De Tour Village 156 45 49N 83 56W
De Witt 159 34 19N 91 20W
Dead Sea = Miyet, Bahr el 92 31 30N 35 30 E
Deadwood 58 44 25N 103 43W
Deadwood L. 152 59 10N 128 30W
Deaf Adder Cr. 136 13 0 S 132 47 E
Deakin 137 30 46 S 129 58 E
Deal 29 51 13N 1 25 E
Dealesville 128 28 41 S 25 44 E
Dean, Forest of 28 51 50N 2 35W
Deán Funes 172 30 20 S 64 20W
Dearborn 150 42 18N 83 15W
Dearham 32 54 43N 3 28W
Dease L. 152 58 40N 130 5W
Dease Lake 152 58 25N 130 6W
Dease, R. 152 59 56N 128 32W
Death Valley 163 36 27N 116 52W
Death Valley Junc. 163 36 21N 116 30W
Death Valley Nat. Monument 163 36 30N 117 0W
Deauville 42 49 23N 0 2 E
Deba Habe 121 10 14N 11 20 E
Debaltsevo 82 48 22N 38 26 E
Debar 66 41 21N 20 37 E
Debba 123 14 20N 41 18 E
Debden 153 53 30N 106 50W
Debdou 118 33 59N 3 0W
Debeeti 128 23 45 S 26 32 E
Deben, R. 29 52 4N 1 19 E
Debenham 29 52 14N 1 10 E
Debessy 84 57 39N 53 49 E
Dębica 54 50 2N 21 25 E
Deblin 54 51 34N 21 50 E
Debo, L. 120 15 14N 3 57W
Debolt 152 55 12N 118 1W
Deborah, gasfield 19 53 4N 1 50 E
Deborah, L. 137 30 45 S 119 0 E
Debrc 66 44 38N 19 53 E
Debre Birhan 123 9 41N 39 31 E
Debre Markos 123 10 20N 37 40 E
Debre May 123 11 20N 37 25 E
Debre Sina 123 9 51N 39 50 E
Debre Tabor 123 11 50N 38 26 E
Debrecen 53 47 33N 21 42 E
Dečani 66 42 30N 20 10 E
Decatur, Ala., U.S.A. 157 34 35N 87 0W
Decatur, Ga., U.S.A. 157 33 47N 84 17W
Decatur, Ill., U.S.A. 158 39 50N 89 0W
Decatur, Ind., U.S.A. 156 40 52N 85 28W
Decatur, Texas, U.S.A. 159 33 15N 97 35W
Decazeville 44 44 34N 2 15 E
Deccan 97 14 0N 77 0 E
Deception I. 13 63 0 S 60 15W
Deception L. 153 56 33N 104 13W
Deception, Mt. 140 30 42 S 138 16 E
Decize 43 46 50N 3 28 E
Decollatura 65 39 2N 16 21 E
Decorah 158 43 20N 91 50W
Deda 70 46 56N 24 50 E
Dedaye 98 16 24N 95 53 E
Deddington 28 51 58N 1 19W
Dedemsvaart 46 52 36N 6 28 E
Dedham 162 42 14N 71 10W
Dedilovo 81 53 59N 37 50 E
Dédougou 120 12 30N 3 35W
Deduru Oya 97 7 32N 81 45 E
Dedza 127 14 20 S 34 20 E
Dee, R., Eng.-Wales, U.K. 31 53 15N 3 7W
Dee, R., Scot., U.K. 37 57 4N 2 7W
Deel R. 38 53 35N 7 9W
Deelish 39 51 41N 9 18W
Deep B. 152 61 15N 116 35W
Deep Lead 140 37 0 S 142 43 E
Deep Well 138 24 20 S 134 0 E
Deepdale 136 26 22 S 114 20 E
Deeping Fen 29 52 45N 0 15W
Deeping, St. Nicholas 29 52 44N 0 11W
Deepwater 139 29 25 S 151 51 E
Deer I. 147 54 55N 162 20W
Deer Lake, Newf., Can. 151 49 11N 57 27W
Deer Lake, Ontario, Can. 153 52 36N 94 20W
Deer Lodge 160 46 25N 112 40W
Deer Park 160 47 55N 117 21W
Deer, R. 153 58 23N 94 13W
Deer River 158 47 21N 93 44W
Deer Sound 37 58 58N 2 50W
Deeral 138 17 14 S 145 55 E
Deerdepoort 128 24 37 S 26 27 E
Deering 147 66 5N 162 50W
Deerlijk 47 50 51N 3 22 E
Deerness 37 58 57N 2 44W
Deesa 94 24 18N 72 10 E
Deferiet 162 44 2N 75 41W
Defiance 156 41 20N 84 20W
Deganwy 31 53 18N 3 49W
Deganya 90 32 43N 35 34 E
Degebe, R. 57 38 21N 7 37W
Degeh-Bur 91 8 11N 43 31 E

Degema	121	4 50N	6 48 E
Degerfors	74	64 16N	19 46 E
Degersfor	73	59 20N	14 28 E
Degersheim	51	47 23N	9 12 E
Degersiö	72	63 13N	18 3 E
Deggendorf	49	48 49N	12 59 E
Degloor	96	18 34N	77 33 E
Deh Bīd	93	30 39N	53 11 E
Deh Kheyr	93	28 45N	54 40 E
Deh Titan	93	33 45N	63 50 E
Dehibat	119	32 0N	10 47 E
Dehiwala	97	6 50N	79 51 E
Dehkhvareqan	92	37 50N	45 55 E
Dehra Dun	94	30 20N	78 4 E
Dehri	95	24 50N	84 15 E
Deinze	47	50 59N	3 32 E
Deir Abu Sa'id	90	32 30N	38 42 E
Deir Dibwan	90	31 55N	35 15 E
Dej	70	47 10N	23 52 E
Deje	72	59 35N	13 29 E
Dekar	128	18 30 S	23 10 E
Dekemhare	123	15 6N	39 0 E
Dekese	124	3 24 S	21 24 E
Dekhkanabad	85	38 21N	66 30 E
Del Mar	163	32 58N	117 16W
Del Norte	161	37 47N	106 27W
Del Rey, Rio	121	4 30N	8 48 E
Del Rio, Mexico	164	29 22N	100 54W
Del Rio, U.S.A.	159	29 15N	100 50W
Delabole	30	50 37N	4 45W
Delagoa B.	129	25 50 S	32 45 E
Delagua	159	32 35N	104 40W
Delai	122	17 21N	36 6 E
Delambre I.	136	20 27 S	117 4 E
Delano	163	35 48N	119 13W
Delareyville	128	26 41 S	25 26 E
Delavan	158	42 40N	88 39W
Delaware	156	40 20N	83 0W
Delaware □	162	39 0N	75 40W
Delaware B.	162	38 50N	75 0W
Delaware City	162	39 34N	75 36W
Delaware, R.	162	39 20N	75 25W
Delčevo	66	41 58N	22 46 E
Delchirach	37	57 23N	3 20W
Delegate	141	37 4 S	148 56 E
Delémont	50	47 22N	7 20 E
Delft	46	52 1N	4 22 E
Delft I.	97	9 30N	79 40 E
Delfzijl	46	53 20N	6 55 E
Delgado, C.	127	10 45 S	40 40 E
Delgerhet	106	45 50N	110 30 E
Delgo	122	20 6N	30 40 E
Delhi, India	94	28 38N	77 17 E
Delhi, U.S.A.	162	42 17N	74 56W
Deli Jovan	66	44 13N	22 9 E
Delia	152	51 38N	112 23W
Delice, R.	92	39 45N	34 15 E
Delicias	164	28 10N	105 30W
Delicias, Laguna	164	28 7N	105 40W
Delimiro Gouveia	170	9 23 S	37 59W
Delitzsch	48	51 32N	12 22 E
Dell City	161	31 58N	105 19W
Dell Rapids	158	43 53N	96 44W
Delle	43	47 30N	7 2 E
Dellys	119	36 50N	3 57 E
Delmar, Del., U.S.A.	162	38 27N	75 34W
Delmar, N.Y., U.S.A.	162	42 5N	73 50W
Delmenhorst	48	53 3N	8 37 E
Delmiro	170	9 24 S	38 6W
Delnice	63	45 23N	14 50 E
Deloraine, Austral.	138	41 30 S	146 40 E
Deloraine, Can.	153	49 15N	100 29W
Delorme, L.	151	54 31N	69 52W
Delovo	66	44 55N	20 52 E
Delphi	156	40 37N	86 40W
Delphos	156	40 51N	84 17W
Delportshoop	128	28 22 S	24 20 E
Delray Beach	157	26 27N	80 4W
Delsbo	72	61 48N	16 32 E
Delta, Colo., U.S.A.	161	38 44N	108 5W
Delta, Utah, U.S.A.	160	39 21N	112 29W
Delta Amacuro □	174	8 30N	61 30W
Deltaville	162	37 33N	76 20W
Delungra	139	29 39 S	150 51 E
Delvin	38	53 37N	7 8W
Delvina	68	39 59N	20 4 E
Delvinákion	68	39 57N	20 32 E
Demak	103	6 50 S	110 40 E
Demanda, Sierra de la	58	42 15N	3 0W
Demba	124	5 28 S	22 15 E
Dembecha	123	10 32N	37 30 E
Dembi	123	8 5N	36 25 E
Dembia	126	3 33N	25 48 E
Dembidolo	123	8 34N	34 50 E
Demchok	93	32 40N	79 29 E
Demer, R.	47	51 0N	5 8 E
Demerais, L.	150	47 35N	77 0W
Demerara, R.	174	7 0N	58 0W
Demidov	80	55 10N	31 30 E
Deming	161	32 10N	107 50W
Demini, R.	174	0 46N	62 56W
Demmin	48	53 54N	13 2 E
Demmit	152	55 20N	119 50W
Demnate	118	31 44N	6 59W
Demonte	62	44 18N	7 18 E
Demopolis	157	32 30N	87 48W
Dempo, Mt.	102	4 10 S	103 15 E
Demyansk	80	57 30N	32 27 E
Den Bemmel	46	51 43N	4 26 E
Den Burg	46	53 3N	4 47 E
Den Chai	100	17 59N	100 4 E
Den Dungen	47	51 41N	5 22 E
Den Haag = 's Gravenhage	46	52 7N	4 17 E
Den Ham	46	52 28N	6 30 E
Den Helder	46	52 57N	4 45 E
Den Hulst	46	52 36N	6 16 E
Den Oever	46	52 56N	5 2 E
Denain	43	50 20N	3 22 E
Denair	163	37 32N	120 48W
Denau	85	38 16N	67 54 E
Denbigh	31	53 12N	3 26W
Denbigh (□)	26	53 8N	3 30W
Denby Dale	33	53 35N	1 40W
Denchin	99	31 35N	95 15 E
Dendang	102	3 7 S	107 56 E
Dender, R.	47	51 2N	4 6 E
Denderhoutem	47	50 53N	4 2 E
Denderleeuw	47	50 54N	4 5 E
Dendermonde	47	51 2N	4 5 E
Deneba	123	9 47N	39 10 E
Denekamp	46	52 22N	7 1 E
Denezhkin Kamen, Gora	84	60 25N	59 32 E
Denge	121	12 52N	5 21 E
Dengi	121	9 25N	9 55 E
Denham	137	25 56 S	113 31 E
Denham Ra.	138	21 55 S	147 46 E
Denham Sd.	137	25 45 S	113 15 E
Denholm	153	52 40N	108 0W
Denia	59	38 49N	0 8 E
Denial B.	139	32 14 S	133 32 E
Deniliquin	141	35 30 S	144 58 E
Denison, Iowa, U.S.A.	158	42 0N	95 18W
Denison, Texas, U.S.A.	159	33 50N	96 40W
Denison Plains	136	18 35 S	128 0 E
Denison Range	136	28 30 S	136 5 E
Denisovka	84	52 28N	61 46 E
Denizli	92	37 42N	29 2 E
Denkez Iyesus	123	12 27N	37 43 E
Denman	141	32 24 S	150 42 E
Denmark	137	34 59 S	117 18 E
Denmark ■	73	55 30N	9 0 E
Denmark Str.	14	66 0N	30 0W
Dennis Hd.	37	59 23N	2 26W
Denniston	143	41 45 S	171 49 E
Denny	35	56 1N	3 55W
Denpasar	102	8 45 S	115 5 E
Dent	32	54 17N	2 28W
Denton, E. Sussex, U.K.	29	50 48N	0 5 E
Denton, Gr. Manchester, U.K.	32	53 26N	2 10W
Denton, Lincs., U.K.	33	52 52N	0 42W
Denton, Md., U.S.A.	162	38 53N	75 50W
Denton, Mont., U.S.A.	160	47 25N	109 56W
Denton, Texas, U.S.A.	159	33 12N	97 10W
D'Entrecasteaux, C.	137	34 50 S	115 59 E
D'Entrecasteaux Is.	135	9 0 S	151 0 E
D'Entrecasteaux Pt.	137	34 50 S	115 57 E
Dents du Midi	50	46 10N	6 56 E
Denu	121	6 4N	1 8 E
Denver, Colo., U.S.A.	158	39 45N	105 0W
Denver, Pa., U.S.A.	162	40 14N	76 8W
Denver City	159	32 58N	102 48W
Deoband	94	29 42N	77 43 E
Deobhog	96	19 53N	82 44 E
Deogarh	96	21 32N	84 45 E
Deoghar	95	24 30N	86 59 E
Deolali	96	19 50N	73 50 E
Deoli	94	25 50N	75 50 E
Deoria	95	26 31N	83 48 E
Deosai, Mts.	95	35 40N	75 0 E
Deposit	162	42 5N	75 23W
Depot Spring	137	27 55 S	120 3 E
Depuch I.	136	20 35 S	117 44 E
Deputatskiy	77	69 18N	139 54 E
Dera Ghazi Khan	94	30 5N	70 43 E
Dera Ismail Khan	94	31 50N	70 50 E
Dera Ismail Khan □	94	32 30N	70 0 E
Derati Wells	126	3 52N	36 37 E
Derbent	74	42 5N	48 15 E
Derby, Austral.	136	17 18 S	123 38 E
Derby, U.K.	33	52 55N	1 28W
Derby, U.S.A.	162	41 20N	73 5W
Derby □	33	52 55N	1 28W
Derecske	53	47 20N	21 33 E
Derg, L.	39	53 0N	8 20W
Derg, R.	38	54 42N	7 26W
Dergachi	81	50 3N	36 3 E
Dergaon	99	26 45N	94 0 E
Dermantsi	67	43 8N	24 17 E
Derna	117	32 40N	22 35 E
Dernieres Isles	159	29 0N	90 45W
Derriana, L.	39	51 54N	10 1W
Derrinallum	140	37 57 S	143 15 E
Derry R.	39	52 43N	6 35W
Derrybrien	39	53 4N	8 38W
Derrygonnelly	38	54 25N	7 50W
Derrygrogan	39	53 19N	7 23W
Derrykeighan	38	55 8N	6 30W
Derrylin	38	54 12N	7 34W
Derry = Londonderry	38	55 0N	7 19W
Derrynasaggart Mts.	39	51 58N	9 15W
Derryrush	38	53 23N	9 40W
Derryveagh Mts.	38	55 0N	8 40W
Derudub	122	17 31N	36 7 E
Dervaig	34	56 35N	6 13W
Derval	42	47 40N	1 41W
Dervéni	69	38 8N	22 25 E
Derwent	153	53 41N	110 58W
Derwent, R., Derby, U.K.	33	52 53N	1 17W
Derwent, R., N. Yorks., U.K.	33	53 45N	0 57W
Derwent, R., Tyne & Wear, U.K.	35	54 58N	1 40W
Derwentwater, L.	32	53 34N	3 9W
Des Moines, Iowa, U.S.A.	158	41 35N	93 37W
Des Moines, N. Mex., U.S.A.	159	36 50N	103 51W
Des Moines, R.	158	40 23N	91 25W
Desaguadero, R., Argent.	172	33 28 S	67 15W
Desaguadero, R., Boliv.	174	17 30 S	68 0W
Desborough	29	52 27N	0 50W
Deschaillons	151	46 32N	72 7W
Descharme, R.	153	56 51N	109 13W
Deschutes, R.	160	45 30N	121 0W
Dese	123	11 5N	39 40 E
Deseado, R.	176	40 0 S	69 0W
Desemboque	164	30 30N	112 27W
Desenzano del Gardo	62	45 28N	10 32 E
Desert Center	161	33 45N	115 27W
Desert Hot Springs	163	33 58N	116 30W
Desertmartin	38	54 47N	6 40W
Desford	28	52 38N	1 19W
Désirade, I.	167	16 18N	61 3W
Deskenatlata L.	152	60 55N	112 3W
Desna, R.	80	52 0N	33 15 E
Desnŭtui, R.	70	44 15N	23 27 E
Desolación, I.	176	53 0 S	74 0W
Despeñaperros, Paso	59	38 24N	3 30W
Despotovac	66	44 6N	21 30 E
Dessa	121	14 44N	1 6 E
Dessau	48	51 49N	12 15 E
Dessel	47	51 15N	5 7 E
Dessye = Dese	123	11 5N	39 40 E
D'Estress B.	140	35 55 S	137 45 E
Desuri	94	25 18N	73 35 E
Desvrès	43	50 40N	1 48 E
Det Udom	100	14 54N	105 5 E
Detinjá, R.	66	43 51N	19 45 E
Detmold	48	51 55N	8 50 E
Detour Pt.	156	45 37N	86 35W
Detroit, Mich., U.S.A.	150	42 13N	83 22W
Detroit, Tex., U.S.A.	159	33 40N	95 10W
Detroit Lakes	158	46 50N	95 50W
Dett	127	18 32 S	26 57 E
Dettifoss	74	65 49N	16 24W
Děčin	52	50 47N	14 12 E
Deurne, Belg.	47	51 12N	4 24 E
Deurne, Neth.	47	51 27N	5 49 E
Deutsche Bucht	48	54 10N	7 51 E
Deutschlandsberg	52	46 49N	15 14 E
Deux-Acren, Les	47	50 44N	3 51 E
Deux-Sèvres □	42	46 35N	0 20W
Deva	70	45 53N	22 55 E
Devakottai	97	9 55N	78 45 E
Devaprayag	95	30 13N	78 35 E
Dévaványa	53	47 2N	20 59 E
Deveci Daği	82	40 10N	36 0 E
Devecser	53	47 6N	17 26 E
Deventer	46	52 15N	6 10 E
Deveron, R.	37	57 40N	2 31W
Devesel	70	44 28N	22 41 E
Devgad, I.	97	14 48N	74 5 E
Devil R., Pk.	143	40 56 S	172 37 E
Devils Bridge	31	52 23N	3 50W
Devils Den	163	35 46N	119 58W
Devils Lake	158	48 5N	98 50W
Devils Paw, mt.	152	58 47N	134 0W
Devils Pt.	97	9 26N	80 6 E
Devilsbit Mt.	39	52 50N	7 58W
Devin	67	41 44N	24 24 E
Devizes	28	51 21N	2 0W
Devnya	67	43 13N	27 33 E
Devolli, R.	68	40 57N	20 15 E
Devon	152	53 24N	113 44W
Devon I.	12	75 47N	88 0W
Devonport, Austral.	138	41 10 S	146 22 E
Devonport, N.Z.	142	36 49 S	174 49 E
Devonport, U.K.	30	50 23N	4 11W
Devonshire □	30	50 50N	3 40W
Dewas	94	22 59N	76 3 E
Dewetsdorp	128	29 33 S	26 39 E
Dewgad Baria	94	22 40N	73 55 E
Dewsbury	33	53 42N	1 38W
Dexter, Mo., U.S.A.	159	36 50N	90 0W
Dexter, N. Mex., U.S.A.	159	33 15N	104 25W
Dey-Dey, L.	137	29 12 S	131 4 E
Deyhuk	93	33 15N	104 25W
Deyyer	93	27 55N	51 55 E
Dezadeash L.	152	60 28N	136 58W
Dezfūl	92	32 20N	48 30 E
Dezh Shahpur	92	35 30N	46 25 E
Dezhneva, Mys	77	66 10N	169 3 E
Dhaba	92	27 25N	35 40 E
Dháfni	69	37 48N	22 1 E
Dhahaban	122	21 58N	39 3 E
Dhahiriya = Qz Zahiriya	90	31 25N	34 58 E
Dhahran	92	26 9N	50 10 E
Dhama Dzong	99	28 15N	91 15 E
Dhamási	68	39 43N	22 11 E
Dhampur	95	29 19N	78 33 E
Dhamtari	96	20 42N	81 35 E
Dhanbad	95	23 50N	86 30 E
Dhangarhi	99	28 55N	80 40 E
Dhankuta	95	26 55N	87 20 E
Dhanora	96	20 20N	80 22 E
Dhar	94	22 35N	75 26 E
Dharampur, Mad. P., India	94	22 13N	75 18 E
Dharampur, Maharashtra, India	96	20 32N	73 17 E
Dharapuram	97	10 45N	77 34 E
Dharmapuri	97	12 10N	78 10 E
Dharmavaram	97	14 29N	77 44 E
Dharmsala, (Dharamsala)	94	32 16N	73 23 E
Dhaulagiri Mt.	95	28 45N	83 45 E
Dhebar, L.	94	24 10N	74 0 E
Dhenkanal	96	20 45N	85 35 E
Dhenoúsa	69	37 8N	25 48 E
Dhesfina	69	38 25N	22 31 E
Dheskáti	68	39 55N	21 49 E
Dhespotikó	69	36 57N	24 58 E
Dhidhimótikhon	68	41 22N	26 29 E
Dhikti, Mt.	69	35 8N	25 29 E
Dhilianáta	69	38 15N	20 34 E
Dhílos	69	37 23N	25 15 E
Dhimitsána	69	37 36N	22 3 E
Dhirfis, Mt.	69	38 40N	23 54 E
Dhodhekánisos	69	36 35N	27 0 E
Dhofar	91	17 0N	54 10 E
Dhokós	69	37 20N	23 20 E
Dholiana	68	39 54N	20 32 E
Dholka	94	22 44N	72 29 E
Dholpur	94	26 45N	77 59 E
Dhomokós	69	39 10N	22 18 E
Dhond	96	18 26N	74 40 E
Dhoraji	94	21 45N	70 37 E
Dhoxáthon	68	41 9N	24 16 E
Dhragonisi	69	37 27N	25 29 E
Dhrangadhra	94	22 59N	71 31 E
Dhriopós	69	37 35N	24 35 E
Dhrol	94	22 40N	70 25 E
Dhubaibah	93	23 25N	54 35 E
Dhubri	98	26 2N	90 2 E
Dhulasar	98	21 52N	90 14 E
Dhulia	96	20 58N	74 50 E
Dhupdhara	98	25 58N	91 4 E
Dhurm	122	20 18N	42 53 E
Di Linh	101	11 35N	108 4 E
Di Linh, Cao Nguyen	101	11 30N	108 0 E
Día, I.	69	35 26N	25 13 E
Diable, Mt.	163	37 53N	121 56W
Diablerets, Les	50	46 22N	7 10 E
Diablo Range	163	37 0N	121 5W
Diafarabé	120	14 17N	4 57W
Diala	120	13 59N	10 0W
Dialakoro	120	12 18N	7 54W
Diallassagou	120	13 47N	3 41W
Diamante	172	32 5 S	60 40W
Diamante, R.	172	34 31 S	66 56W
Diamantina	171	18 5 S	43 40W
Diamantina, R.	138	22 25 S	142 20 E
Diamantino	175	14 30 S	56 30W
Diamond Harbour	95	22 11N	88 14 E
Diamond Is.	138	17 25 S	151 5 E
Diamond Mts.	160	40 0N	115 58W
Diamond Springs	163	38 42N	120 49W
Diamondville	160	41 51N	110 30W
Diano Marina	62	43 55N	8 3 E
Dianópolis	171	11 38 S	46 50W
Dianra	120	8 45N	6 14W
Diaole, Î. du.	170	5 15N	52 45W
Diapaga	121	12 5N	1 46 E
Diapangou	121	12 5N	0 10 E
Diapur	140	36 19 S	141 29 E
Diariguila	120	10 35N	10 2W
Dibai (Dubai)	93	25 15N	55 20 E
Dibaya	124	6 20 S	22 0 E
Dibaya Lubue	124	4 12 S	19 54 E
Dibba	93	25 45N	56 16 E
Dibbi	123	4 10N	41 52 E
Dibden	28	50 53N	1 24W
Dibega	92	35 50N	43 46 E
Dibër	68	41 38N	20 15 E
Dibete	128	23 45 S	26 32 E
Dibi	123	4 10N	41 52 E
Dibrugarh	98	27 29N	94 55 E
Dibulla	174	11 17N	73 19W
Dickinson	158	46 50N	102 40W
Dickson	157	36 5N	87 22W
Dickson City	162	41 29N	75 40W
Dicomano	63	43 53 S	11 30 E
Didam	46	51 57N	6 8 E
Didcot	28	51 36N	1 14W
Didesa, W.	123	9 40N	35 50 E
Didiéni	120	14 5N	7 50W
Didsbury	152	51 35N	114 10W
Didwana	94	27 17N	74 25 E
Die	45	44 47N	5 22 E
Diébougou	120	11 0N	3 15W
Diefenbaker L.	153	51 0N	106 55W
Diego Garcia, I.	11	9 50 S	75 0 E
Diégo Suarez	129	12 25 S	49 20 E
Diekirch	47	49 52N	6 10 E
Diélette	42	49 33N	1 52W
Diéma	120	14 32N	9 3W
Diemen	46	52 21N	4 58 E
Dieméring	120	12 29N	16 47W
Dien Ban	100	15 53N	108 16 E
Diên Biên Phu	100	21 20N	103 0 E
Dien Khanh	101	12 15N	109 6 E
Diepenheim	46	52 12N	6 33 E
Diepenveen	46	52 18N	6 9 E
Diepholz	48	52 37N	8 22 E
Diepoldsau	51	47 23N	9 40 E
Dieppe	42	49 54N	1 4 E
Dieren	46	52 3N	6 6 E
Dierks	159	34 9N	94 0W
Diessen	47	51 29N	5 10 E
Diessenhofen	51	47 42N	8 46 E
Diest	47	50 58N	5 4 E
Dietikon	51	47 24N	8 24 E
Dieulefit	45	44 32N	5 4 E
Dieuze	43	48 30N	6 40 E

Diever	46	52 51N	6 19 E
Diffa	121	13 34N	12 33 E
Differdange	47	49 81N	5 54 E
Dig	94	27 28N	77 20 E
Digba	126	4 25N	25 42 E
Digboi	98	27 23N	95 38 E
Digby	151	44 41N	65 50W
Digges	153	58 40N	94 0W
Digges Is.	149	62 40N	77 50W
Digges Lamprey	153	58 33N	94 8W
Dighinala	98	23 15N	92 5 E
Dighton	158	38 30N	100 26W
Digne	45	44 5N	6 12 E
Digoin	44	46 29N	3 58 E
Digos	103	6 45N	125 20 E
Digranes	74	66 4N	14 44 E
Digras	96	20 6N	77 45 E
Dihang, R.	99	27 30N	96 30 E
Dijlah	92	37 0N	42 30 E
Dijle, R.	47	50 58N	4 41 E
Dijon	43	47 20N	5 0 E
Dikala	123	4 45N	31 28 E
Dikhal	123	11 8N	42 20 E
Dikomu di Kai, Mt.	128	24 51 S	24 36 E
Diksmuide	47	51 2N	2 52 E
Dikson	76	73 40N	80 5 E
Dikumbiya	123	14 45N	37 30 E
Dikwa	121	12 4N	13 30 E
Dila	123	6 14N	38 22 E
Dilam	92	23 55N	47 10 E
Dilbeek	47	50 51N	4 17 E
Dili	103	8 39 S	125 34 E
Dilizhan	83	41 46N	44 57 E
Dillenburg	48	50 44N	8 17 E
Dilley	159	28 40N	99 12W
Dilling	123	12 3N	29 35 E
Dillingen	49	49 22N	6 42 E
Dillingham	147	59 5N	158 30W
Dillon, Can.	153	55 56N	108 56W
Dillon, Mont., U.S.A.	160	45 9N	112 36W
Dillon, S.C., U.S.A.	157	34 26N	79 20W
Dillon, R.	153	55 56N	108 56W
Dillsburg	162	40 7N	77 2W
Dilolo	14	10 28 S	22 18 E
Dilsen	47	51 2N	5 44 E
Dilston	138	41 22 S	147 10 E
Dima	123	6 19N	36 15 E
Dimapur	98	25 54N	93 45 E
Dimas	164	23 43N	106 47W
Dimashq	92	33 30N	36 18 E
Dimbelenge	124	4 30N	23 0 E
Dimbokro	120	6 45N	4 30W
Dimboola	140	36 28 S	142 0 E
Dîmboviţa □	70	45 0N	25 30 E
Dîmbovita, R.	70	44 40N	26 0 E
Dimbulah	138	17 2 S	145 4 E
Dimitriya Lapteva, Proliv	77	73 0N	140 0 E
Dimitrovgrad, Bulg.	67	42 5N	25 35 E
Dimitrovgrad, U.S.S.R.	81	54 25N	49 33 E
Dimitrovgrad, Yugo.	66	43 0N	22 48 E
Dimmitt	159	34 36N	102 16W
Dimo	123	5 19N	29 10 E
Dimona	90	31 2N	35 1 E
Dimovo	66	43 43N	22 50 E
Dinagat I.	103	10 10N	125 40 E
Dinajpur	98	25 33N	88 43 E
Dinan	42	48 28N	2 2W
Dinant	47	50 16N	4 55 E
Dinapore	95	25 38N	85 5 E
Dinar	92	38 5N	30 15 E
Dinard	42	48 38N	2 6W
Dinaric Alps	16	44 0N	17 30 E
Dinas Hd.	31	52 2N	4 56W
Dinas Mawddwy	31	52 44N	3 41W
Dinas Powis	31	51 25N	3 14W
Dinder, Nahr ed	123	12 32N	35 0 E
Dindi, R.	96	16 24N	78 15 E
Dindigul	97	10 25N	78 0 E
Dingelstädt	48	51 19N	10 19 E
Dingila	126	3 25N	26 25 E
Dingle	39	52 9N	10 17W
Dingle B.	39	52 3N	10 20W
Dingle Harbour	39	52 7N	10 12W
Dingmans Ferry	162	41 13N	74 55W
Dingo	138	23 38 S	149 19 E
Dingolfing	49	48 38N	12 30 E
Dinguiraye	120	11 30N	10 35W
Dingwall	37	57 36N	4 26W
Dingyadi	121	13 0N	0 53 E
Dinh Lap	100	21 33N	107 6 E
Dinh, Mui	101	11 22N	109 1 E
Dinhata	98	26 8N	89 27 E
Dinkel	46	52 30N	6 58 E
Dinokwe (Palla Road)	128	23 29 S	26 37 E
Dinosaur National Monument	160	40 30N	108 45W
Dinslaken	47	51 34N	6 41 E
Dintel, R.	47	51 39N	4 22 E
Dinuba	163	36 37N	119 22W
Dinxperlo	46	51 52N	6 30 E
Dio	73	56 37N	14 15 E
Diosgyör	53	48 7N	20 43 E
Diosig	70	47 18N	22 2 E
Dioundiou	121	12 37N	3 33 E
Diourbel	120	14 39N	16 12W
Diphu Pass	98	28 9N	97 20 E
Diplo	94	24 25N	69 35 E
Dipolog	103	8 36N	123 20 E
Dipşa	70	46 58N	24 27 E
Dipton	143	45 54 S	168 22 E
Dir	93	35 08N	71 59 E
Diré	120	15 20N	3 25W
Dire Dawa	123	9 35N	41 45 E
Direction, C.	138	12 51 S	143 32 E
Diriamba	166	11 51N	86 19W
Dirico	125	17 50 S	20 42 E
Dirk Hartog I.	137	25 50 S	113 5 E
Dirranbandi	139	28 33 S	148 17 E
Disa	123	12 5N	34 15 E
Disappointment, C.	160	46 20N	124 0W
Disappointment L.	136	23 20 S	122 40 E
Disaster B.	141	37 15 S	150 0 E
Discovery	148	63 0N	115 0W
Discovery B.	140	38 10 S	140 40 E
Disentis	51	46 42N	8 50 E
Dishna	122	26 9N	32 32 E
Disina	121	11 35N	9 50 E
Disko	12	69 45N	53 30W
Disko Bugt	12	69 10N	52 0W
Disna	80	55 32N	28 11 E
Disna, R.	80	55 20N	27 30 E
Dison	47	50 37N	5 51 E
Diss	29	52 23N	1 6 E
Disteghil Sar	95	36 20N	75 5 E
Distington	32	54 35N	3 33W
District Heights	162	38 51N	76 53W
District of Columbia □	162	38 55N	77 0W
Distrito Federal □, Brazil	171	15 45 S	47 45W
Distrito Federal □, Venez.	174	10 30N	66 55W
Disûq	122	31 8N	30 35 E
Ditchingham	29	52 28N	1 26 E
Ditchling & Beacon	29	50 59N	0 7W
Ditinn	120	10 53N	12 11W
Dittisham	30	50 22N	3 36W
Ditton Priors	28	52 30N	2 33W
Diu, I.	94	20 45N	70 58 E
Diver	150	46 44N	79 30W
Dives	42	49 18N	0 8W
Dives, R.	42	49 18N	0 7W
Divi Pt.	97	15 59N	81 9 E
Divichi	83	41 15N	48 57 E
Divide	160	45 48N	112 47W
Dividing Ra.	137	27 45 S	116 0 E
Divinopólis	171	20 10 S	44 54W
Divisões, Serra dos	171	17 0 S	51 0W
Divnoye	83	45 55N	43 27 E
Divo	120	5 48N	5 15W
Diwal Kol	94	34 23N	67 52 E
Dixie	160	45 37N	115 27W
Dixon, Calif., U.S.A.	163	38 27N	121 49W
Dixon, Ill., U.S.A.	158	41 50N	89 30W
Dixon, Mont., U.S.A.	160	47 19N	114 25W
Dixon, N. Mex., U.S.A.	161	36 15N	105 57W
Dixon Entrance	153	54 30N	132 0W
Dixonville	152	56 32N	117 40W
Diyarbakir	92	37 55N	40 18 E
Dizzard Pt.	30	50 46N	4 38W
Djabotaoure	121	8 35N	0 58 E
Djado	119	21 4N	12 14 E
Djado, Plateau du	119	21 29N	12 21 E
Djakarta = Jakarta	103	6 9 S	106 49 E
Djakovo	66	45 19N	18 24 E
Djamâa	119	33 32N	5 59 E
Djamba	128	16 45 S	13 58 E
Djambala	124	2 20 S	14 30 E
Djanet	119	24 35N	9 32 E
Djang	121	5 30N	10 5 E
Djaul I.	135	2 58 S	150 57 E
Djawa = Jawa	103	7 0 S	110 0 E
Djebiniana	119	35 1N	11 0 E
Djelfa	118	34 40N	3 15 E
Djema	126	6 9N	25 15 E
Djeneïene	119	31 45N	10 9 E
Djenné	120	14 0N	4 30W
Djenoun, Garet el	119	25 4N	5 31 E
Djerba	119	33 52N	10 51 E
Djerba, Île de	119	33 56N	11 0 E
Djerid, Chott	119	33 42N	8 30 E
Djibo	121	14 15N	1 35W
Djibouti	123	11 30N	43 5 E
Djibouti ■	123	11 30N	42 15 E
Djidjelli	119	36 52N	5 50 E
Djirlange	101	11 44N	108 15 E
Djofra	119	28 59N	15 47 E
Djolu	124	0 45N	22 5 E
Djorf el Youdi	118	32 14N	9 8W
Djougou	121	9 40N	1 45 E
Djoum	124	2 41N	12 35 E
Djourab, Erg du	117	16 40N	18 50 E
Djugu	126	1 55N	30 35 E
Djúpivogur	74	64 39N	14 17W
Djursholm	72	59 25N	18 6 E
Djursland	73	56 27N	10 45 E
Dmitriev-Lgovskiy	80	52 10N	35 0 E
Dmitriya Lapteva, Proliv	77	73 0N	140 0 E
Dmitrov	81	56 25N	37 32 E
Dmitrovsk Orlovskiy	80	52 29N	35 10 E
Dneiper, R. = Dnepr	82	52 29N	35 10 E
Dnepr, R.	82	50 0N	31 0 E
Dneprodzerzhinsk	82	48 32N	34 30 E
Dneprodzerzhinskoye Vdkhr.	77	49 0N	34 0 E
Dnepropetrovsk	82	48 30N	35 0 E
Dneprorudnoye	82	47 21N	34 58 E
Dnestr, R.	82	48 30N	26 30 E
Dnestrovski = Belgorod	82	50 35N	36 35 E
Dniester = Dnestr	82	48 30N	26 30 E
Dno	80	57 50N	29 58 E
Doan Hung	100	21 38N	105 10 E
Doba	117	8 40N	16 50 E
Dobané	126	6 20N	24 39 E
Dobbiaco	63	46 44N	12 13 E
Dobbyn	138	19 44 S	139 59 E
Dobczyce	54	49 52N	20 25 E
Döbeln	48	51 7N	13 10 E
Doberai, Jazirah	103	1 25 S	133 0 E
Dobiegniew	54	52 59N	15 45 E
Doblas	172	37 5 S	64 0W
Dobo	103	5 45 S	134 15 E
Doboj	66	44 46N	18 6 E
Dobra, Poland	54	53 34N	15 20 E
Dobra, Dîmboviţa, Rumania	67	44 52N	25 40 E
Dobra, Hunedoara, Rumania	70	45 54N	22 36 E
Dobre Miasto	54	53 58N	20 26 E
Dobrinishta	67	41 49N	23 34 E
Dobriš	52	49 46N	14 10 E
Dobrodzien	54	50 45N	18 25 E
Dobrogea	70	44 30N	28 15 E
Dobruja = Dobrogea	70	44 30N	28 15 E
Dobrush	80	52 28N	30 35 E
Dobryanka	84	58 27N	56 25 E
Dobrzyn n. Wisła	54	52 39N	19 22 E
Dobtong	123	6 25N	31 40 E
Doc, Mui	100	17 58N	106 30 E
Doce, R.	171	19 37 S	39 49W
Docking	29	52 55N	0 39 E
Doda	95	33 10N	75 34 E
Döda Fallet	72	63 4N	16 35 E
Doddington	29	52 29N	0 3 E
Dodecanese = Dhodhekánisos	69	36 35N	27 0 E
Dodewaard	46	51 55N	5 39 E
Dodge Center	158	44 1N	92 57W
Dodge City	159	37 42N	100 0W
Dodge L.	153	59 50N	105 36W
Dodgeville	158	42 55N	90 8W
Dodman Pt.	30	50 13N	4 49W
Dodo	123	5 10N	29 57 E
Dodola	123	6 59N	39 11 E
Dodoma	126	6 8 S	35 45 E
Dodoma □	126	6 0 S	36 0 E
Dodsland	153	51 50N	108 45W
Dodson	160	48 23N	108 4W
Doesburg	46	52 1N	6 9 E
Doetinchem	46	51 59N	6 18 E
Doftana	70	45 17N	25 45 E
Dog Creek	152	51 35N	122 14W
Dog L., Man., Can.	152	51 2N	98 31W
Dog L., Ont., Can.	150	48 12N	89 16W
Dog, R.	152	57 50N	94 40W
Doganbey	69	37 40N	27 10 E
Dogi	93	32 20N	62 50 E
Dogliani	62	44 35N	7 55 E
Dōgo	110	36 15N	133 16 E
Dōgo-San	110	35 2N	133 13 E
Dogondoutchi	121	13 38N	4 2 E
Dogoraoua	121	14 0N	5 31 E
Dogran	94	31 48N	73 35 E
Dohad	94	22 50N	74 15 E
Dohazari	99	22 10N	92 5 E
Doheny	150	47 4N	72 35W
Doherty	150	46 58N	79 44W
Doi, I.	103	2 21N	127 49 E
Doi Luang	101	18 20N	101 30 E
Doi Saket	100	18 52N	99 9 E
Doig, R., Alta., Can.	152	56 57N	120 0W
Doig, R., B.C., Can.	152	56 25N	120 40W
Dois Irmãos, Serra	171	8 30 S	41 5W
Dokka	71	60 49N	10 7 E
Dokka, R.	71	61 7N	10 0 E
Dokkum	46	53 20N	5 59 E
Dokkumer Ee, R.	46	53 18N	5 52 E
Dokri Mohenjodaro	94	27 25N	68 7 E
Dol	42	48 34N	1 47W
Dolak, Pulau = Kolepom, P.	103	8 0 S	138 30 E
Doland	158	44 55N	98 5W
Dolbeau	151	48 53N	72 18W
Dôle	43	47 7N	5 31 E
Doleib, W.	123	10 30N	33 15 E
Dolgarrog	31	53 11N	3 50W
Dolgellau	31	52 44N	3 53W
Dolgelly = Dolgellau	31	52 44N	3 53W
Dolginovo	80	54 39N	27 29 E
Dolianovo	64	39 23N	9 11 E
Dolinskaya	82	48 16N	32 36 E
Dolisie	124	4 0 S	13 10 E
Dolj □	70	44 10N	23 30 E
Dolla	39	52 47N	8 12W
Dollar	35	56 9N	3 41W
Dollart	46	53 20N	7 10 E
Dolna Banya	67	42 18N	23 44 E
Dolni Dubnik	67	43 24N	24 26 E
Dolo	63	45 25N	12 4 E
Dolo Bay	123	4 11N	42 3 E
Dolomites = Dolomiti	63	46 30N	11 40 E
Dolomiti	63	46 30N	11 40 E
Dolores, Argent.	172	36 20 S	57 40W
Dolores, Mexico	164	28 53N	108 27W
Dolores, Uruguay	172	33 34 S	58 15W
Dolores, Colo., U.S.A.	161	37 30N	108 30W
Dolores, Tex., U.S.A.	159	27 40N	99 38W
Dolores, R.	159	38 30N	108 55W
Đolovo	66	44 55N	20 52 E
Dolphin and Union Str.	148	69 5N	114 45W
Dolphin C.	176	51 10 S	50 0W
Dolphinton	35	55 42N	3 28W
Dolsk	54	51 59N	17 3 E
Dolton	30	50 53N	4 2W
Dolwyddelan	31	53 3N	3 53W
Dom	50	46 6N	7 50 E
Dom Joaquim	171	18 57 S	43 16W
Dom Pedrito	173	31 0 S	54 40W
Dom Pedro	170	4 29 S	44 27W
Doma	121	8 25N	8 18 E
Domasi	127	15 22 S	35 10 E
Domat Ems	51	46 50N	9 27 E
Domazlice	52	49 28N	13 0 E
Dombarovskiy	84	50 46N	59 32 E
Dombås	71	62 6N	9 4 E
Dombasle	43	49 8N	5 10 E
Dombe Grande	125	12 56 S	13 8 E
Dombes	45	46 3N	5 0 E
Dombóvár	53	46 21N	18 9 E
Dombrád	53	48 13N	21 54 E
Domburg	47	51 34N	3 30 E
Domel, I = Letsok-aw-kyun	101	11 30N	98 25 E
Domérat	44	46 21N	2 32 E
Domett	143	42 53 S	173 12 E
Domeyko	172	29 0 S	71 30W
Domeyko, Cordillera	172	24 30 S	69 0W
Domfront	42	48 37N	0 40W
Dominador	172	24 21 S	69 20W
Dominica I.	167	15 20N	61 20W
Dominica Passage	167	15 10N	61 20W
Dominican Rep. ■	167	19 0N	70 30W
Dömitz	48	53 9N	11 13 E
Domme	44	44 48N	1 12 E
Dommel, R.	47	51 30N	5 20 E
Dommerby	73	56 33N	9 5 E
Domo	91	7 50N	47 10 E
Domodossóla	62	46 6N	8 19 E
Dompaire	43	48 14N	6 14 E
Dompierre	44	46 31N	3 41 E
Dompin	120	5 10N	2 5W
Domrémy	43	48 26N	5 40 E
Domsjö	72	63 16N	18 41 E
Domville, Mt.	139	28 1 S	151 15 E
Domvraina	69	38 15N	22 59 E
Domzale	63	46 9N	3 6 E
Don Benito	57	38 53N	5 51W
Don, C.	136	11 18 S	131 46 E
Don Duong	101	11 51N	108 35 E
Don Martín, Presa de	164	27 30N	100 50W
Don Pedro Res.	163	37 43N	120 24W
Don, R., India	97	16 40N	75 55W
Don, R., Eng., U.K.	33	53 41N	0 51W
Don, R., Scot., U.K.	37	57 14N	2 5W
Don, R., U.S.S.R.	83	49 35N	41 40 E
Dona Ana	127	17 25 S	35 17 E
Donabate	38	53 30N	6 9W
Donadea	38	53 20N	6 45W
Donaghadee	38	54 38N	5 32W
Donaghmore, Ireland	39	52 54N	7 37W
Donaghmore, U.K.	38	54 33N	6 50W
Donald	140	36 23 S	143 0 E
Donalda	152	52 35N	112 34W
Donaldsonville	159	30 2N	91 50W
Donalsonville	157	31 3N	84 52W
Donard	39	53 1N	6 37W
Donau-Kanal	49	49 1N	11 27 E
Donau, R.	53	47 55N	17 20 E
Donaueschingen	49	47 57N	8 30 E
Donawitz	52	47 22N	15 4 E
Doncaster	33	53 31N	1 9W
Dondo, Angola	74	9 45 S	14 25 E
Dondo, Mozam.	127	19 33 S	34 46 E
Dondo, Teluk	103	0 29N	120 45 E
Dondra Head	97	5 55N	80 40 E
Donegal	38	54 39N	8 8W
Donegal □	38	54 53N	8 0W
Donegal B.	38	54 30N	8 35W
Donegal Har.	38	54 35N	8 15W
Donegal Pt.	39	52 44N	9 38W
Doneraile	39	52 13N	8 37W
Donets, R.	81	48 50N	38 45 E
Donetsk	82	48 0N	37 45 E
Dong	121	9 20N	12 15 E
Dong Ba Thin	101	12 8N	109 13 E
Dong Dang	100	21 4N	106 57 E
Dong Giam	100	19 15N	105 31 E
Dong Ha	100	16 49N	107 8 E
Dong Hene	100	16 16N	105 18 E
Dong Hoi	100	17 29N	106 36 E
Dong Khe	100	22 26N	106 27 E
Dong Van	100	23 16N	105 22 E
Dong Xoai	101	11 32N	106 55 E
Donga	121	7 45N	10 2 E
Dongara	137	29 14 S	114 57 E
Dongargarh	96	21 10N	80 40 E
Dongen	47	51 38N	4 56 E
Donges	42	47 18N	2 4W
Donggala	103	0 30 S	119 40 E
Dongola	122	19 9N	30 22 E
Dongou	124	2 0N	18 5 E
Donhead	28	51 1N	2 8W
Donington	33	52 54N	0 12W
Donington, C.	140	34 45 S	136 0 E
Doniphan	159	36 40N	90 50W
Donja Stubica	63	45 59N	16 0 E
Donji Dušnik	66	43 12N	22 5 E
Donji Miholjac	66	45 45N	18 10 E
Donji Milanovac	66	44 28N	22 6 E
Donji Vakuf	66	44 8N	17 24 E
Donjon, Le	44	46 22N	3 48 E
Dønna	74	66 6N	12 30 E
Donna	74	66 6N	12 30 E
Donna	159	26 12N	98 2W
Donna Nook, Pt.	33	53 29N	0 9 E
Donnaconna	151	46 41N	71 41W
Donnelly's Crossing	142	35 42 S	173 38 E
Donnybrook	137	33 34 S	115 48 E
Donor's Hills	138	18 42 S	140 33 E
Donoughmore	39	52 0N	8 42W
Donskoy	81	53 55N	38 15W

Donya Lendava Duncan Town

Donya Lendava	63	46 35N	16 25E
Donzère	45	44 28N	4 43E
Donzy	43	47 20N	3 6E
Dooagh	38	53 59N	10 7W
Doochary	38	54 54N	8 10W
Doodlakine	137	31 34S	117 51E
Dooega Hd.	38	53 54N	10 3W
Doon L.	34	55 15N	4 22W
Doon, R.	34	55 26N	4 41W
Doonbeg	39	52 44N	9 31W
Doonbeg R.	39	52 42N	9 20W
Doorn	46	52 2N	5 20E
Dor (Tantura)	90	32 37N	34 55E
Dora Báltea, R.	62	45 42N	7 25E
Dora, L.	136	22 0S	123 0E
Dora Riparia, R.	62	45 7N	7 24E
Dorada, La	174	5 30N	74 40W
Dorading	123	8 30N	33 5E
Doran L.	153	61 13N	108 6W
Dorat, Le	44	46 14N	1 5E
Dörby	73	56 20N	16 12E
Dorchester, Dorset, U.K.	28	50 42N	2 28W
Dorchester, Oxon., U.K.	28	51 38N	1 10W
Dorchester, C.	149	65 27N	77 27W
Dordogne □	44	45 5N	0 40E
Dordogne, R.	44	45 2N	0 36W
Dordrecht, Neth.	46	51 48N	4 39E
Dordrecht, S. Afr.	128	31 20S	27 3E
Doré L.	153	54 46N	107 17W
Doré Lake	153	54 38N	107 54W
Dore, Mt.	44	45 32N	2 50E
Dore, R.	44	45 59N	3 28E
Dores	37	57 22N	4 20W
Dores do Indaiá	171	19 27S	45 36W
Dorfen	49	48 16N	12 10E
Dorgali	64	40 18N	9 35E
Dori	121	14 3N	0 2W
Doring, R.	128	32 30S	19 30E
Dorion	150	45 23N	74 3W
Dorking	29	51 14N	0 20W
Dormaa-Ahenkro	120	7 15N	2 52W
Dormo, Ras	123	13 14N	42 35E
Dornach	50	47 29N	7 37E
Dornberg	63	45 45N	13 50E
Dornbirn	52	47 25N	9 45E
Dornes	43	46 48N	3 18E
Dornie	36	57 17N	5 30W
Dornoch	37	57 52N	4 0W
Dornoch, Firth of	37	57 52N	4 0W
Dornogovi □	106	44 0N	110 0E
Doro	121	16 9N	0 51W
Dorog	53	47 42N	18 45E
Dorogobuzh	80	54 50N	33 10E
Dorohoi	70	47 56N	26 30E
Döröö Nuur	105	47 40N	93 30E
Dorre I.	137	25 13S	113 12E
Dorrigo	141	30 20S	152 44E
Dorris	160	41 59N	121 58W
Dorset □	28	50 48N	2 25W
Dorsten	48	51 40N	6 55E
Dorstone	28	52 4N	3 0W
Dortmund	48	51 32N	7 28E
Dörtyol	92	36 52N	36 12E
Dorum	48	53 40N	8 33E
Doruma	126	4 42N	27 33E
Dorya, W.	123	5 15N	41 30E
Dos Bahías, C.	176	44 58S	65 32W
Dos Cabezas	161	32 1N	109 37W
Dos Hermanas	57	37 16N	5 55W
Dos Palos	163	36 59N	120 37W
Dosara	121	12 20N	6 5E
Doshi	93	35 35N	68 50E
Dosso	121	13 0N	3 13E
Döstrup	73	56 41N	9 42E
Dot	152	50 12N	121 25W
Dothan	157	31 10N	85 25W
Dottignies	47	50 44N	3 19E
Dotty, gasfield	19	53 3N	1 48E
Douai	43	50 21N	3 4E
Douala	121	4 0N	9 45E
Douarnenez	42	48 6N	4 21W
Double Island Pt.	139	25 56S	153 11E
Doubrava, R.	52	49 40N	15 30E
Doubs □	43	47 10N	6 20E
Doubs, R.	43	46 53N	5 1E
Doubtful B.	137	34 15S	119 28E
Doubtful Sd.	143	45 20S	166 49E
Doubtless B.	142	34 55S	173 26E
Doucet	150	48 15N	76 35W
Doudeville	42	49 43N	0 47E
Doué	42	47 11N	0 20W
Douentza	120	14 58N	2 48W
Douglas, S. Afr.	128	29 4S	23 46E
Douglas, U.K.	32	54 9N	4 29W
Douglas, U.K.	35	55 33N	3 50W
Douglas, Alaska, U.S.A.	147	58 23N	134 32W
Douglas, Ariz., U.S.A.	161	31 21N	109 30W
Douglas, Ga., U.S.A.	157	31 32N	82 52W
Douglas, Wyo., U.S.A.	158	42 45N	105 20W
Douglas Hd.	32	54 9N	4 28W
Douglastown	151	48 46N	64 24W
Douglasville	157	33 46N	84 43W
Douirat	118	33 2N	4 11W
Doukáton, Ákra	69	38 34N	20 30E
Doulevant	43	48 22N	4 53E
Doullens	43	50 10N	2 20E
Doulus Hd.	39	51 57N	10 19W
Doumé	124	4 15N	13 25E
Douna	120	12 40N	6 0W
Dounby	37	59 4N	3 13W
Doune	35	56 12N	4 3W
Dounreay	37	58 40N	3 28W
Dour	47	50 24N	3 46E
Dourada, Serra	171	13 10S	48 45W
Dourados	173	22 9S	54 50W
Dourados, R.	173	21 58S	54 18W
Dourdan	43	48 30N	2 0E
Douro Litoral □	55	41 10N	8 20W
Douro, R.	56	41 1N	8 16W
Douŭzeci Si Trei August	70	43 50N	28 40E
Douvaine	45	46 19N	6 16E
Douz	119	33 25N	9 0E
Dove	32	52 51N	1 36W
Dove Brook	151	53 40N	57 40W
Dove Creek	161	37 53N	108 59W
Dove Dale	33	53 10N	1 47W
Dove, R.	33	54 20N	0 55W
Dover, Austral.	138	43 18S	147 2E
Dover, U.K.	29	51 7N	1 19E
Dover, Del., U.S.A.	162	39 10N	75 31W
Dover, N.H., U.S.A.	162	43 5N	70 51W
Dover, N.J., U.S.A.	162	40 53N	74 34W
Dover, Ohio, U.S.A.	156	40 32N	81 30W
Dover-Foxcroft	151	45 14N	69 14W
Dover Plains	162	41 43N	73 35W
Dover, Pt.	137	32 32S	125 32E
Dover, Str. of	16	51 0N	1 30E
Doveridge	32	52 54N	1 49E
Dovey, R.	31	52 32N	4 0W
Dovre	71	62 0N	9 15E
Dovrefjell	71	62 15N	9 33E
Dowa	127	13 38S	33 58E
Dowagiac	156	42 0N	86 8W
Dowlatabad	93	28 20N	50 40E
Down □	38	54 20N	5 50W
Down, Co.	38	54 20N	6 0W
Downey	160	42 29N	112 3W
Downham	29	52 26N	0 15E
Downham Market	29	52 36N	0 22E
Downhill	38	55 10N	6 48W
Downieville	160	39 34N	120 50W
Downpatrick	38	54 20N	5 43W
Downpatrick Hd.	38	54 20N	9 21W
Downs Division	139	27 10S	150 44E
Downs, The	38	53 30N	7 15W
Downsville	162	42 5N	74 60W
Downton	28	51 0N	1 44W
Dowra	38	54 11N	8 2W
Doylestown	162	40 21N	75 10W
Doyung	99	33 40N	99 25E
Dra, Cap	118	28 58N	11 0W
Draa, O.	118	30 29N	6 1W
Drachten	46	53 7N	6 5E
Drăgăneşti	70	44 9N	24 32E
Drăgăneşti-Viaşca	70	44 5N	25 33E
Dragaš	66	42 5N	20 35E
Drăgăsani	70	44 39N	24 17E
Dragina	66	44 30N	19 25E
Dragocvet	66	44 0N	21 15E
Dragonera, I.	58	39 35N	2 19E
Dragon's Mouth	174	11 0N	61 50W
Dragovistica, (Berivol)	66	42 22N	22 39E
Draguignan	45	43 30N	6 27E
Drain	160	43 45N	123 17W
Drake, Austral.	139	28 55S	152 25E
Drake, U.S.A.	158	47 56N	100 31W
Drake Passage	13	58 0S	68 0W
Drakensberg	129	31 0S	25 0E
Dráma	68	41 9N	24 10E
Dráma □	68	41 10N	24 0E
Drammen	71	59 42N	10 12E
Drangajökull	74	66 9N	22 15W
Drangan	39	52 32N	7 36W
Drangedal	71	59 6N	9 3E
Dranov, Ostrov	70	44 55N	29 30E
Draperstown	38	54 48N	6 47E
Dras	95	34 25N	75 48E
Drau, R.	52	47 46N	13 33E
Drava, R.	66	45 50N	18 0W
Draveil	43	48 41N	2 25E
Dravograd	63	46 36N	15 5E
Drawa, R.	54	53 6N	15 56E
Drawno	54	53 13N	15 46E
Drawsko Pom	54	53 35N	15 50E
Drayton Valley	152	53 25N	114 58W
Dreghorn	34	55 36N	4 30W
Dreibergen	46	52 3N	5 17E
Drejö	73	54 58N	10 25E
Dren	66	43 8N	20 44E
Drenagh	38	55 3N	6 55W
Drenthe □	54	52 52N	6 40E
Drentsche Hoofdvaart	46	52 39N	6 4E
Dresden	48	51 2N	13 45E
Dresden □	48	51 12N	14 0E
Dreumel	47	51 51N	5 26E
Dreux	42	48 44N	1 23E
Drezdenko	54	52 50N	15 49E
Driel	46	51 57N	5 49E
Driffield	33	54 0N	0 25W
Driftwood	150	49 8N	81 23E
Drigana	119	20 51N	12 17E
Driggs	160	43 50N	111 8W
Drimnin	36	56 36N	6 0W
Drimoleague	39	51 40N	9 15W
Drin-i-zi, R.	68	41 37N	20 28E
Drina, R.	66	44 30N	19 10E
Drincea, R.	70	44 20N	22 55E
Drînceni	70	46 49N	28 10E
Drini, R.	68	42 20N	20 0E
Drinjača, R.	66	44 20N	19 0E
Driva	71	62 33N	9 38E
Driva, R.	71	62 34N	9 33E
Drivstua	71	62 26N	9 37E
Drniš	63	43 51N	16 10E
Drøbak	71	59 39N	10 39E
Dröbak	75	59 39N	10 48E
Drobbakk	71	59 39N	10 39E
Drobin	54	52 42N	19 58E
Drogheda	38	53 45N	6 20W
Drogichin	80	52 15N	25 8E
Drogobych	80	49 20N	23 30E
Droichead Nua	39	53 11N	6 50W
Droitwich	28	52 16N	2 10W
Dromahair	38	54 13N	8 18W
Dromara	38	54 21N	6 1W
Dromard	38	54 14N	8 40W
Drôme □	45	44 38N	5 15E
Drôme, R.	45	44 46N	4 46E
Dromedary, C.	141	36 17S	150 10E
Dromiskin	38	53 56N	6 25W
Dromod	38	53 52N	7 55W
Dromore, Down, U.K.	38	54 24N	6 10W
Dromore, Tyrone, U.K.	38	54 31N	7 28W
Dromore West	38	54 15N	8 50W
Dronero	62	44 29N	7 22E
Dronfield, Austral.	138	21 12S	140 3E
Dronfield, U.K.	33	53 18N	1 29W
Dronninglund	73	57 10N	10 19E
Dronrijp	46	53 11N	5 39E
Drosendorf	52	48 52N	15 37E
Drouin	141	38 10S	145 53E
Drouzhba	67	43 22N	28 0E
Drum	38	54 6N	7 9W
Drumbeg, N. Ire., U.K.	38	54 33N	6 0W
Drumbeg, Scot., U.K.	36	58 15N	5 12W
Drumcard	38	54 14N	7 42W
Drumcliffe	38	54 20N	8 30W
Drumcondra	38	53 50N	6 40W
Drumheller	152	51 25N	112 40W
Drumjohn	34	55 14N	4 15W
Drumkeerin	38	54 10N	8 8W
Drumlish	38	53 50N	7 47W
Drummond	160	46 46N	113 4W
Drummond I.	150	46 0N	83 40W
Drummond Pt.	139	34 9S	135 16E
Drummond Ra.	138	23 45S	147 10E
Drummondville	150	45 55N	72 25W
Drummore	34	54 41N	4 53W
Drumquin	38	54 38N	7 30W
Drumright	159	35 59N	96 38W
Drumshanbo	38	54 2N	8 4W
Drumsna	38	53 57N	8 0W
Drunen	47	51 41N	5 8E
Druridge B.	35	55 16N	1 32W
Druskinankaj	80	54 3N	23 58E
Drut, R.	80	52 32N	30 0E
Druten	46	51 53N	5 36E
Druya	80	55 45N	27 15E
Druzhina	77	68 14N	145 18E
Drvar	63	44 21N	16 2E
Drvenik	63	43 27N	16 3E
Dry Tortugas	166	24 38N	82 55W
Dryanovo	67	42 59N	25 28E
Dryden, Can.	153	49 50N	92 50W
Dryden, N.Y., U.S.A.	162	42 30N	76 18W
Dryden, Tex., U.S.A.	159	30 3N	102 3W
Drygalski I.	13	66 0S	92 0E
Drygarn Fawr	31	52 13N	3 39W
Drymen	70	56 4N	4 28W
Drynoch	36	57 17N	6 18W
Drysdale I.	138	11 41S	136 0E
Drysdale, R.	136	13 59S	126 51E
Dschang	121	5 32N	10 3E
Du	121	10 26N	1 34W
Du Bois	156	41 8N	78 46W
Du Quoin	158	38 0N	89 10W
Duanesburg	162	42 45N	74 11W
Duaringa	138	23 42S	149 42E
Duba	92	27 10N	35 40E
Dubai = Dubayy	93	25 18N	55 20E
Dubawnt, L.	153	63 4N	101 42W
Dubawnt, R.	153	64 33N	100 6W
Dubayy	93	25 18N	55 20E
Dubbeldam	46	51 47N	4 43E
Dubbo	141	32 11S	148 35E
Dubele	126	2 56N	29 35E
Dübendorf	51	47 24N	8 37E
Dubenskiy	84	51 27N	56 38E
Dubh Artach	34	56 8N	6 40W
Dubica	63	45 17N	16 48E
Dublin, Ireland	38	53 20N	6 18W
Dublin, Ga., U.S.A.	157	32 30N	83 0W
Dublin, Tex., U.S.A.	159	32 0N	98 20W
Dublin □	38	53 24N	6 20W
Dublin, B.	39	53 18N	6 20W
Dubna	81	54 8N	36 52E
Dubno	80	50 25N	25 45E
Dubois	160	44 7N	112 9W
Dubossary	82	47 15N	29 10E
Dubossay Vdkhr.	82	47 30N	29 0E
Dubovka	83	49 5N	44 50E
Dubovskoye	83	47 28N	42 40E
Dubrajpur	95	23 48N	87 25E
Dubrékah	120	9 46N	13 31W
Dubrovitsa	80	51 31N	26 35E
Dubrovnik	66	42 39N	18 6E
Dubrovskoye	77	58 55N	111 0E
Dubuque	158	42 30N	90 41W
Duchesne	160	40 14N	110 22W
Duchess	138	21 20S	139 50E
Ducie I.	131	24 47S	124 40W
Duck Cr., N.S.W., Austral.	139	31 4S	147 6E
Duck Cr., W. Australia, Austral.	136	22 37S	116 53E
Duck Lake	153	52 50N	106 16W
Duck, Mt.	153	51 27N	100 35W
Duck Mt. Prov. Parks	153	51 45N	101 0W
Duckwall Mtn.	163	37 58N	120 7W
Duddington	29	52 36N	0 32W
Duddon R.	32	54 12N	3 15W
Düdelange	47	49 29N	6 5E
Duderstadt	48	51 30N	10 15E
Dudhi	99	24 15N	83 10E
Dudhnai	98	25 59N	90 47E
Düdingen	50	46 52N	7 12E
Dudinka	77	69 30N	86 0E
Dudley	28	52 30N	2 5W
Dudna, R.	96	19 36N	76 20E
Dueñas	56	41 52N	4 33W
Düeni	47	44 51N	28 10E
Dueodde	73	54 59N	15 4E
Dueré	171	11 20S	49 17W
Duero, R.	56	41 37N	4 25W
Duff Is.	142	9 0S	167 0E
Duffel	47	51 6N	4 30E
Duffield	33	52 59N	1 30W
Dufftown	37	57 26N	3 9W
Dufourspitz	50	45 56N	7 52E
Dugi, I.	63	44 0N	15 0E
Dugo Selo	63	45 51N	16 18E
Duhak	93	33 20N	57 30E
Duifken Pt.	138	12 33S	141 38E
Duisburg	48	51 27N	6 42E
Duitama	174	5 50N	73 2W
Duiveland	47	51 38N	4 0E
Duiwelskloof	129	23 42S	30 10E
Dukana	126	3 59N	37 20E
Dukati	68	40 16N	19 32E
Duke I.	152	54 50N	131 20W
Dukhan	93	25 25N	50 50E
Dukhovshchina	80	55 15N	32 27E
Duki	93	30 14N	68 25E
Dukla	54	49 30N	21 35E
Duku, North-Eastern, Nigeria	121	10 43N	10 43E
Duku, North-Western, Nigeria	121	11 11N	4 55E
Dulas B.	31	53 22N	4 16W
Dulawan	103	7 5N	124 20E
Dulce, Golfo	166	8 40N	83 20W
Dulce, R.	172	29 30S	63 0W
Duleek	38	53 40N	6 24W
Dülgopol	67	43 3N	27 22E
Dullewala	94	31 50N	71 25E
Dülmen	48	51 49N	7 18E
Dulnain Bridge	37	57 19N	3 40W
Dulovo	67	43 48N	27 9E
Dululu	138	23 48S	150 15E
Duluth	158	46 48N	92 10W
Dulverton	28	51 2N	3 33W
Dum Dum	95	22 39N	88 26E
Dum Duma	99	27 40N	95 40E
Dumaguete	103	9 17N	123 15E
Dumai	102	1 35N	101 20E
Dumaran I.	103	10 33N	119 50E
Dumaring	103	1 46N	118 10E
Dumas, Ark., U.S.A.	159	33 52N	91 30W
Dumas, Okla., U.S.A.	159	35 50N	101 58W
Dūmat al Jandal	92	29 55N	39 40E
Dumba I.	71	61 43N	4 50E
Dumbarton	34	55 58N	4 35W
Dumbleyung	137	33 17S	117 42E
Dumbrŭveni	70	46 14N	24 34E
Dumfries	35	55 4N	3 37W
Dumfries & Galloway □	35	54 30N	4 0W
Dumfries (□)	26	55 0N	3 30W
Dŭmienesti	70	46 44N	27 1E
Dumka	95	24 20N	87 22E
Dumoine L.	150	46 55N	77 55W
Dumoine, R.	150	46 13N	77 51W
Dumraon	95	25 33N	84 8E
Dumyât	122	31 24N	31 48E
Dumyât, Masabb	122	31 28N	32 0E
Dun Laoghaire, (Dunleary)	39	53 17N	6 9W
Dun-le-Palestel	44	46 18N	1 39E
Dun-sur-Auron	43	46 53N	2 33E
Duna, R.	53	45 51N	18 48E
Dunaff Hd.	38	55 18N	7 30W
Dunaföldvár	53	46 50N	18 57E
Dunai, R.	53	47 50N	18 52E
Dunaj, R.	67	45 17N	29 32E
Dunajec, R.	54	50 12N	20 52E
Dunajska Streda	53	48 0N	17 37E
Dunamanagh	38	54 53N	7 20W
Dunans	34	56 4N	5 9W
Dunany Pt.	38	53 51N	6 15W
Dunapatai	53	46 39N	19 4E
Dunaszekcsö	53	46 22N	18 45E
Dunaújváros	53	47 0N	18 57E
Dunav, R.	66	45 0N	20 21E
Dunavtsi	66	43 57N	22 53E
Dunback	143	45 23S	170 36E
Dunbar, Austral.	138	16 0S	142 22E
Dunbar, U.K.	35	56 0N	2 32W
Dunbarton (□)	26	56 4N	4 42W
Dunbeath	37	58 15N	3 25W
Dunblane	35	56 10N	3 58W
Dunboyne	38	53 25N	6 30W
Duncan, Can.	152	48 45N	123 40W
Duncan, Ariz., U.S.A.	161	32 46N	109 6W
Duncan, Okla., U.S.A.	159	34 25N	98 0W
Duncan L.	152	62 51N	113 58W
Duncan, L., Brit. Col., Can.	150	50 20N	117 0W
Duncan, L., Qué., Can.	152	53 29N	77 58W
Duncan Pass.	101	11 0N	92 30E
Duncan Town	166	22 15N	75 45W

Duncansby Ecoporanga

Duncansby 37 58 37N 3 3W
Duncansby Head 37 58 39N 3 0W
Dunchurch 28 52 21N 1 19W
Duncormick 39 53 14N 6 40W
Dundalk, Ireland 38 53 55N 6 45W
Dundalk, U.S.A. 162 39 15N 76 31W
Dundalk, B. 38 53 55N 6 15W
Dundas 150 43 17N 79 59W
Dundas I. 152 54 30N 130 50W
Dundas, L. 137 32 35S 121 50E
Dundas Str. 136 11 15S 131 35E
Dundee, S. Afr. 129 28 11S 30 15E
Dundee, U.K. 35 56 29N 3 0W
Dundee, U.S.A. 162 42 32N 76 59W
Dundgovi □ 106 45 10N 106 0E
Dundo 124 7 23S 20 48E
Dundonald 38 54 37N 5 50W
Dundoo 139 27 40S 144 37E
Dundrennan 35 54 49N 3 56W
Dundrum, Ireland 39 53 17N 6 15W
Dundrum, U.K. 38 54 17N 5 50W
Dundwara 95 27 48N 79 9E
Dunedin, N.Z. 143 45 50S 170 33E
Dunedin, U.S.A. 157 28 1N 82 45W
Dunedin, R. 152 59 30N 124 5W
Dunfanaghy 38 55 10N 7 59W
Dunfermline 35 56 5N 3 28W
Dungannon 38 54 30N 6 47W
Dungannon □ 38 54 30N 6 55W
Dungarpur 94 23 52N 73 45E
Dungarvan 39 52 6N 7 40W
Dungarvan Harb. 39 52 5N 7 35W
Dungas 121 13 4N 9 20E
Dungavel 35 55 37N 4 7W
Dungbura La 99 34 41N 93 18E
Dungeness 29 50 54N 0 59E
Dungiven 38 54 55N 6 56W
Dunglow 38 54 57N 8 20W
Dungo, L. do 128 17 15S 19 0E
Dungog 141 32 22S 151 40E
Dungourney 39 51 58N 8 5W
Dungu 124 2 32N 28 22E
Dungunâb 122 21 10N 37 9E
Dungunâb, Khalîg 122 21 5N 37 12E
Dunhinda Falls 97 7 5N 81 6E
Dunières 45 45 13N 4 20E
Dunk I. 138 17 59S 146 14E
Dunkeld, Austral. 140 37 40S 142 22E
Dunkeld, U.K. 37 56 34N 3 36W
Dunkerque 43 51 2N 2 20E
Dunkery Beacon 28 51 15N 3 37W
Dunkineely 38 54 38N 8 22W
Dunkirk 156 42 30N 79 18W
Dunkirk = Dunkerque 43 51 2N 2 20E
Dunkuj 123 11 15N 33 0E
Dunkur 123 11 58N 35 58E
Dunkwa, Central, Ghana 120 6 0N 1 47W
Dunkwa, Central, Ghana 121 5 30N 1 0W
Dunlap 158 41 50N 95 30W
Dunlavin 39 53 3N 6 40W
Dunleary = Dun Laoghaire 39 53 17N 6 8W
Dunleer 38 53 50N 6 23W
Dunlin, oilfield 19 61 12N 1 40E
Dunloe, Gap of 39 52 2N 9 40W
Dunlop 34 55 43N 4 32W
Dunloy 38 55 1N 6 25W
Dunmanus B. 39 51 31N 9 50W
Dunmanway 39 51 43N 9 8W
Dunmara 138 16 42S 133 25E
Dunmod 105 47 45N 106 58E
Dunmore, Ireland 38 53 37N 8 44W
Dunmore, U.S.A. 162 41 27N 75 38W
Dunmore East 39 52 9N 7 0W
Dunmore Town 166 25 30N 76 39W
Dunmurry 38 54 33N 6 0W
Dunn 157 35 18N 78 36W
Dunnellon 157 29 4N 82 28W
Dunnet 37 58 37N 3 20W
Dunnet B. 37 58 37N 3 23W
Dunnet Hd. 37 58 38N 3 22W
Dunning, U.K. 35 56 18N 3 37W
Dunning, U.S.A. 158 41 52N 100 4W
Dunolly 140 36 51S 143 44E
Dunoon 34 55 57N 4 56W
Dunqul 122 23 40N 31 10E
Duns 35 55 47N 2 20W
Dunscore 35 55 8N 3 48W
Dunseith 158 48 49N 100 2W
Dunsford 30 50 41N 3 40W
Dunshaughlin 38 53 31N 6 32W
Dunsmuir 160 41 0N 122 10W
Dunstable 29 51 53N 0 31W
Dunstan Mts. 143 44 53S 169 35E
Dunster, Can. 152 53 8N 119 50W
Dunster, U.K. 28 51 11N 3 28W
Dunston 28 52 46N 2 7W
Duntelchaig, L. 37 57 20N 4 18W
Dunton Green 29 51 17N 0 11E
Duntroon 143 44 51S 170 40E
Dunûrea, R. 70 45 0N 29 40E
Dunvegan 36 57 26N 6 35W
Dunvegan Hd. 36 57 30N 6 42W
Dunvegan L. 153 60 8N 107 10W
Duong Dong 101 10 13N 103 58E
Dupree 158 45 4N 101 35W
Dupuyer 160 48 11N 112 31W
Duque de Caxias 173 22 45S 43 19W
Dura 90 31 31N 35 1E
Durack 136 15 33S 127 52E
Durack Ra. 136 16 50S 127 40E
Durance, R. 45 43 55N 4 45E
Durand 156 42 54N 83 58W
Durango, Mexico 164 24 3N 104 39W
Durango, Spain 58 43 13N 2 40W
Durango, U.S.A. 161 37 10N 107 50W
Durango □ 164 25 0N 105 0W
Duranillin 137 33 30S 116 45E
Durant 159 34 0N 96 25W
Duratón, R. 56 41 27N 4 0W
Durazno 172 33 25S 56 38W
Durazzo = Durrësi 68 41 19N 19 28E
Durban, France 44 43 0N 2 49W
Durban, S. Afr. 129 29 49S 31 1E
Dúrcal 57 37 0N 3 34W
Đurđevac 66 46 2N 17 3E
Düren 48 50 48N 6 30E
Durg 96 21 15N 81 22E
Durgapur 95 23 30N 87 9E
Durham, Can. 150 44 10N 80 49W
Durham, U.K. 33 54 47N 1 34W
Durham, N.C., U.S.A. 157 36 0N 78 55W
Durham, N.H., U.S.A. 162 43 8N 70 56W
Durham □ 32 54 42N 1 45W
Durham Downs 139 26 6S 149 3E
Durlstone Hd. 28 50 35N 1 58W
Durmitor Mt. 66 43 18N 19 0E
Dûrmûneşti 70 46 21N 26 33E
Durness 37 58 34N 4 45W
Durness, Kyle of 37 58 35N 4 55W
Durrandella 138 24 3S 146 35E
Durrësi 68 41 19N 19 28E
Durrie 138 25 40S 140 15E
Durrington 28 51 12N 1 47W
Durrow 39 53 20N 7 31W
Durrus 39 51 37N 9 32W
Dursey Hd. 39 51 34N 10 41W
Dursey I. 39 51 36N 10 12W
Dursley 28 51 41N 2 21W
Durtal 42 47 40N 0 18W
Duru 126 4 20N 28 50E
Durup 73 56 45N 8 57E
D'Urville Island 143 40 50S 173 55E
Duryea 162 41 20N 75 45W
Dusa Mareb 91 5 40N 46 33E
Dûsh 122 24 35N 30 41E
Dushak 76 37 20N 60 10E
Dushanbe 85 38 33N 68 48E
Dusheti 83 42 0N 44 55E
Dushore 162 41 31N 76 24W
Dusky Sd. 143 45 47S 166 30E
Dussejour, C. 136 14 45S 128 13E
Düsseldorf 48 51 15N 6 46E
Dussen 46 51 44N 4 59E
Duszniki Zdrój 54 51 26N 16 22E
Dutch Harbour 147 53 54N 166 35W
Dutlhe 128 23 58S 23 46E
Dutsan Wai 121 10 50N 8 10E
Dutton, R. 138 20 44S 143 10E
Duvan 84 55 42N 57 54E
Duved 72 63 24N 12 55E
Duvno 66 43 42N 17 13E
Duwadami 92 24 35N 44 15E
Duzdab = Zāhedān 93 29 30N 60 50E
Dve Mogili 67 43 47N 25 55E
Dvina, Sev. 78 56 30N 24 0E
Dvina, Zap. 80 61 40N 45 30E
Dvinsk = Daugavpils 80 55 33N 26 32E
Dvinskaya Guba 78 65 0N 39 0E
Dvor 63 45 4N 16 22E
Dvorce 53 49 50N 17 34E
Dvur Králové 52 50 27N 15 50E
Dwarka 94 22 18N 69 8E
Dwellingup 137 32 43S 116 4E
Dwight 156 41 5N 88 25W
Dyakovskoya 81 60 5N 41 12E
Dyatkovo 80 53 48N 34 27E
Dyaul, I. 138 3 0S 150 55E
Dyce 37 57 12N 2 11W
Dyer 163 37 40N 118 5W
Dyer, C. 149 67 0N 61 0W
Dyerbeldzhin 85 41 13N 74 54E
Dyersburg 159 36 2N 89 20W
Dyfed □ 31 52 0N 4 30W
Dyje, R. 53 48 50N 16 45E
Dyke Acland Bay 138 8 45S 148 45E
Dykehead 37 56 43N 3 0W
Dyle, R. 47 50 58N 4 41E
Dymchurch 29 51 2N 1 0E
Dymock 28 51 58N 2 27W
Dynevor Downs 139 28 10S 144 20E
Dynów 54 49 50N 22 11E
Dypvag 71 79 40N 9 8E
Dyrnes 71 63 25N 7 52E
Dysart, Can. 153 50 57N 104 2W
Dysart, U.K. 35 56 8N 3 8W
Dysjön 72 62 38N 15 31E
Dyulgeri 67 42 18N 27 23E
Dyurtyuli 84 55 9N 54 4E
Dzambeyty 83 50 15N 52 30E
Dzaudzhikau = Ordzhonikidze 83 43 0N 44 35E
Dzerzhinsk 80 53 40N 27 7E
Dzhailma 76 51 30N 61 50E
Dzhalal-Abad 84 40 56N 73 0E
Dzhalinda 77 53 40N 124 0E
Dzhambeyty 84 50 16N 52 35E
Dzhambul 85 42 54N 71 22E
Dzhambul, Gora 85 44 54N 73 0E
Dzhankoi 82 45 40N 34 30E
Dzhanybek 83 49 25N 46 50E
Dzhardzhan 77 68 10N 123 5E
Dzharkurgan 85 37 31N 67 25E
Dzhelinde 77 70 0N 114 20E
Dzherzhinsk 80 53 48N 27 19E
Dzhetygara 84 52 11N 61 12E
Dzhetym, Khrebet 85 41 30N 77 0E
Dzhezkazgan 76 47 10N 67 40E
Dzhizak 85 40 6N 67 50E
Dzhugdzur, Khrebet 77 57 30N 138 0E
Dzhuma 85 39 42N 66 40E
Dzhumgoltau, Khrebet 85 42 15N 74 30E
Dzhungarskiye Vorota 76 45 0N 82 0E
Dzhvari 83 42 42N 42 4E
Działdowo 54 53 15N 20 15E
Działoszyce 54 50 22N 20 20E
Działoszyn 54 51 6N 18 50E
Dzibilchaltún 165 21 5N 89 36W
Dzierzgon 54 53 58N 19 20E
Dzierzoniow 54 50 45N 16 39E
Dzilam de Bravo 165 21 24N 88 53W
Dzioua 119 33 14N 5 14E
Dziwnów 54 54 2N 14 45E
Dzungaria 105 44 10N 88 0E
Dzungarian Gates = Dzhungarskiye V. 105 45 0N 82 0E

E

Eabamet, L. 150 51 30N 87 46W
Eads 158 38 30N 102 46W
Eagle, Alaska, U.S.A. 147 64 44N 141 29W
Eagle, Colo., U.S.A. 160 39 45N 106 55W
Eagle Butt 158 45 1N 101 12W
Eagle Grove 158 42 37N 93 53W
Eagle L., Calif., U.S.A. 160 40 35N 120 50W
Eagle L., Me., U.S.A. 151 46 23N 69 22W
Eagle Lake 159 29 35N 96 21W
Eagle Nest 161 36 33N 105 13W
Eagle Pass 159 28 45N 100 35W
Eagle Pk. 163 38 10N 119 25W
Eagle Pt. 136 16 11S 124 23E
Eagle, R. 151 53 36N 57 26W
Eagle River 158 45 55N 89 17W
Eaglehawk 140 36 43S 144 16E
Eagles Mere 162 41 25N 76 33W
Eaglesfield 35 55 3N 3 12W
Eagleshan 34 55 44N 4 18W
Eakring 33 53 9N 0 59W
Ealing 29 51 30N 0 19W
Earaheedy 137 25 34S 121 29E
Earby 32 53 55N 2 8W
Eardisland 28 52 14N 2 50W
Eardisley 28 52 8N 3 0W
Earith 29 52 21N 0 1E
Earl Grey 153 50 57N 104 43W
Earl Shilton 28 52 35N 1 20W
Earl Soham 29 52 14N 1 15E
Earle 159 35 18N 90 26W
Earlimart 163 35 53N 119 16W
Earls Barton 29 52 16N 0 44W
Earl's Colne 29 51 56N 0 43E
Earlsferry 35 56 11N 2 50W
Earlston 35 55 39N 2 40W
Earn, L. 34 56 23N 4 14W
Earn, R. 35 56 20N 3 19W
Earnslaw, Mt. 143 44 32S 168 27E
Earoo 137 29 34S 118 22E
Earsdon 35 55 4N 1 30W
Earth 159 34 18N 102 30W
Easebourne 29 51 0N 0 42W
Easington, Durham, U.K. 33 54 50N 1 24W
Easington, Yorks., U.K. 33 54 40N 0 7W
Easington Colliery 33 54 49N 1 19W
Easingwold 33 54 8N 1 11W
Easky 38 54 17N 8 58W
Easley 157 34 52N 82 35W
East Aberthaw 31 51 23N 3 23W
East Anglian Hts. 29 52 10N 0 17E
East Angus 151 45 30N 71 40W
East, B. 159 29 2N 89 16W
East Barming 29 51 15N 0 29E
East Bathurst 151 47 35N 65 40W
East Bengal 99 24 0N 90 0E
East Bergholt 29 51 58N 1 2E
East Beskids, mts. 53 49 30N 18 45E
East Brent 28 51 14N 2 55W
East C., N.Z. 142 37 42S 178 35E
East C., P.N.G. 135 10 13S 150 53E
East Chicago 156 41 40N 87 30W
East China Sea 105 30 5N 126 0E
East Coulee 152 51 23N 112 27W
East Cowes 28 50 45N 1 17W
East Dereham 29 52 40N 0 57E
East Falkland 176 51 30S 58 30W
East Fen 33 53 4N 0 5E
East Florenceville 151 46 26N 67 36W
East Grand Forks 158 47 55N 97 5W
East Greenwich 162 41 40N 71 27W
East Grinstead 29 51 8N 0 1W
East Harling 29 52 26N 0 55E
East Hartford 162 41 46N 72 39W
East Helena 160 46 37N 111 58W
East Ilsley 28 51 33N 1 15W
East Indies 102 0 0 120 0E
East Jordan 156 45 10N 85 7W
East Kilbride 35 55 46N 4 10W
East Kirkby 33 53 5N 1 15W
East Lansing 156 42 44N 84 37W
East Linton 35 56 0N 2 40W
East Liverpool 156 40 39N 80 35W
East London 129 33 0S 27 55E
East Looe 30 50 22N 4 28W
East Los Angeles 163 34 1N 118 9W
East Lynne 141 35 35S 150 16E
East Main (Eastmain) 151 52 20N 78 30W
East Markham 33 53 15N 0 53W
East Midlands, oilfield 19 53 20N 0 45W
East Moor 33 53 15N 1 30W
East, Mt. 137 29 0S 122 30E
East Orange 162 40 46N 74 13W
East P. 151 46 27N 61 58W
East Pakistan = Bangladesh 99 24 0N 90 0E
East Pine 152 55 48N 120 5W
East Point 157 33 40N 84 28W
East Providence 162 41 49N 71 23W
East Retford 33 53 19N 0 55W
East St. Louis 158 38 36N 90 10W
East Schelde, R. 47 51 38N 3 40E
E. Siberian Sea 77 73 0N 160 0E
East Stroudsburg 162 41 0N 75 11W
East Sussex □ 29 50 55N 0 20E
East Tawas 156 44 17N 83 31W
East Toorale 139 30 27S 145 28E
East Walker, R. 163 38 52N 119 10W
East Wemyss 35 56 8N 3 5W
East Woodhay 28 51 21N 1 26W
Eastbourne, N.Z. 142 41 19S 174 55E
Eastbourne, U.K. 29 50 46N 0 18E
Eastchurch 29 51 23N 0 53E
Eastend 153 49 32N 108 50W
Easter Islands 143 27 0S 109 0W
Easter Ross, dist. 37 57 50N 4 35W
Easter Skeld 36 60 12N 1 27W
Eastern □ 126 0 0S 38 30E
Eastern Cr. 138 20 40S 141 35E
Eastern Ghats 97 15 0N 80 0E
Eastern Group, Is. 137 33 30S 124 30E
Eastern Province □ 120 8 15N 11 0W
Easterville 153 53 8N 99 49W
Easthampton 162 42 16N 72 40W
Eastland 159 32 26N 98 45W
Eastleigh 28 50 58N 1 21W
Eastmain (East Main) 150 52 20N 78 30W
Eastmain, R. 150 52 27N 72 26W
Eastman 157 32 13N 83 41W
Eastnor 28 52 2N 2 22W
Easton, Dorset, U.K. 28 50 32N 2 27W
Easton, Northants., U.K. 29 52 37N 0 31W
Easton, Somerset, U.K. 28 51 28N 2 42W
Easton, Md., U.S.A. 162 38 47N 76 7W
Easton, Pa., U.S.A. 162 40 41N 75 15W
Easton, Wash., U.S.A. 160 47 14N 121 8W
Eastport, Maine, U.S.A. 151 44 57N 67 0W
Eastport, N.Y., U.S.A. 162 40 50N 72 44W
Eastry 29 51 15N 1 19E
Eastview 150 45 27N 75 40W
Eastville 162 37 21N 75 57W
Eastwood 33 53 2N 1 17W
Eaton, U.K. 29 52 52N 0 46W
Eaton, U.S.A. 158 40 35N 104 42W
Eaton, L. 136 22 55S 130 57E
Eaton Socon 29 52 13N 0 18W
Eatonia 153 51 13N 109 25W
Eatonton 157 33 22N 83 24W
Eatontown 162 40 18N 74 7W
Eau Claire, S.C., U.S.A. 157 34 5N 81 2W
Eau Claire, Wis., U.S.A. 158 44 46N 91 30W
Eauze 44 43 53N 0 7E
Eaval, Mt. 36 57 33N 7 12W
Ebagoola 138 14 15S 143 12E
Eban 121 9 40N 4 50E
Ebberston 33 54 14N 0 35W
Ebbw Vale 31 51 47N 3 12W
Ebeggui 119 26 2N 6 0E
Ebeltoft 75 56 12N 10 41E
Ebensee 52 47 48N 13 46E
Eberbach 49 49 27N 8 59E
Eberswalde 48 52 49N 13 50E
Ebikon 51 47 5N 8 21E
Ebingen 49 48 13N 9 1E
Ebino 110 32 2N 130 48E
Ebnat-Kappel 51 47 16N 9 7E
Eboli 65 40 39N 15 2E
Ebolowa 121 2 55N 11 10E
Ebony 128 22 6S 15 15E
Ébrié, Lagune 120 5 12N 4 40W
Ebro, Pantano del 56 43 0N 3 58W
Ebro, R. 58 41 49N 1 5W
Ebstorf 48 53 2N 10 23E
Ecaussines-d' Enghien 47 50 35N 4 11E
Ecclefechan 35 55 3N 3 18W
Eccleshall 28 52 52N 2 14W
Eceabat 68 40 11N 26 21E
Éceuillé 42 47 10N 1 19E
Ech Chebbi 118 26 41N 0 29E
Echallens 50 46 38N 6 38E
Echaneni 77 27 33S 32 6E
Echelles, Les 45 45 27N 5 45E
Echizen-Misaki 111 35 59N 135 57E
Echmiadzin 83 40 12N 44 19E
Echo Bay, N.W.T., Can. 148 66 10N 117 40W
Echo Bay, Ont., Can. 150 46 29N 84 4W
Echoing, R. 153 55 51N 92 5W
Echt, Neth. 47 51 7N 5 52E
Echt, U.K. 37 57 8N 2 26W
Echternach 47 49 49N 6 3E
Echuca 141 36 3S 144 46E
Ecija 57 37 30N 5 10W
Eck L. 34 56 5N 5 0W
Eckernförde 48 54 26N 9 50E
Eckington 33 53 19N 1 21W
Eclipse Is. 136 13 54S 126 19E
Écommoy 42 47 50N 0 17E
Ecoporanga 171 18 23S 40 50W

Écos	43	49 9N	1 35 E
Écouché	42	48 42N	0 10W
Ecuador ■	174	2 0S	78 0W
Ed	73	58 55N	11 55 E
Ed Dabbura	122	17 40N	34 15 E
Ed Damer	122	17 27N	34 0 E
Ed Debba	122	18 0N	30 51 E
Ed-Déffa	122	30 40N	26 30 E
Ed Deim	123	10 10N	28 20 E
Ed Dueim	123	14 0N	32 10 E
Ed Dzong	99	32 11N	90 12 E
Edah	137	28 16S	117 10 E
Edam, Can.	153	53 11N	108 46W
Edam, Neth.	46	52 31N	5 3 E
Edapally	97	11 19N	78 3 E
Eday, I.	37	59 11N	2 47W
Eday Sd.	37	59 12N	2 45W
Edd	123	14 0N	41 30 E
Edda, oilfield	19	56 25N	3 15 E
Edderton	37	57 50N	4 10W
Eddrachillis B.	36	58 16N	5 10W
Eddystone	30	50 11N	4 16W
Eddystone Pt.	138	40 59S	148 20 E
Ede, Neth.	46	52 4N	5 40 E
Ede, Nigeria	121	7 45N	4 29 E
Ede, Sweden	72	62 10N	16 50 E
Édea	121	3 51N	10 9 E
Edegem	47	51 10N	4 27 E
Edehon L.	153	60 25N	97 15W
Edekel, Adrar	119	23 56N	6 47 E
Eden, Austral.	141	37 3S	149 55 E
Eden, U.K.	38	54 44N	5 47W
Eden, Tex., U.S.A.	159	31 16N	99 50W
Eden, Wyo., U.S.A.	160	42 2N	109 27W
Eden L.	153	56 38N	100 15W
Eden, R.	32	54 57N	3 2W
Edenbridge	29	51 12N	0 4 E
Edenburg	128	29 43S	25 58 E
Edendale	143	46 19S	168 48 E
Edenderry	39	53 21N	7 3W
Edenton	157	36 5N	76 36W
Edenville	129	27 37S	27 34 E
Ederny	38	54 32N	7 40W
Edgar	158	40 25N	98 0W
Edgartown	162	41 22N	70 28W
Edge Hill	28	52 7N	1 28W
Edge I.	12	77 45N	22 30 E
Edgecumbe	142	37 59S	176 47 E
Edgefield	157	33 43N	81 59W
Edgeley	158	46 27N	98 41W
Edgemont	158	43 15N	103 53W
Edgeøya	12	77 45N	22 30 E
Edgeworthstown = Mostrim	38	53 42N	7 36W
Edhessa	68	40 48N	22 5 E
Edievale	143	45 49S	169 22 E
Edina, Liberia	120	6 0N	10 19W
Edina, U.S.A.	158	40 6N	92 10W
Edinburg	159	26 22N	98 10W
Edinburgh	35	55 57N	3 12W
Edington	28	51 17N	2 6W
Edirne	67	41 40N	26 45 E
Edison	163	35 21N	118 52W
Edithburgh	140	35 5S	137 43 E
Edjeleh	119	28 25N	9 40 E
Edjudina	137	29 48S	122 23 E
Edmeston	162	42 42N	75 15W
Edmond	159	35 37N	97 30W
Edmondbyers	32	54 50N	1 59W
Edmonds	160	47 47N	122 22W
Edmonton, Austral.	138	17 2S	145 46 E
Edmonton, Can.	152	53 30N	113 30W
Edmund L.	153	54 45N	93 17W
Edmundston	151	47 23N	68 20W
Edna	159	29 0N	96 40W
Edna Bay	152	55 55N	133 40W
Edolo	62	46 10N	10 21 E
Edouard, L.	126	0 25S	29 40 E
Edremit	92	39 40N	27 0 E
Edsbyn	72	61 23N	15 49 E
Edsel Ford Ra.	13	77 0S	143 0W
Edsele	72	63 25N	16 32 E
Edson	152	53 40N	116 28W
Eduardo Castex	172	35 50S	64 25W
Edward I.	150	48 22N	88 37W
Edward, L. (Idi Amin Dada, L.)	126	0 25S	29 40 E
Edward, R.	140	35 0S	143 30 E
Edward VII Pen.	13	80 0S	160 0W
Edwards	163	34 55N	117 51W
Edwards Plat.	159	30 30N	101 5W
Edwardsville	162	41 15N	75 56W
Edzell	37	56 49N	2 40W
Edzo	152	62 49N	116 4W
Eefde	46	52 10N	6 13 E
Eek	147	60 10N	162 0W
Eekloo	47	51 11N	3 33 E
Eelde	46	53 8N	6 34 E
Eem, R.	46	52 16N	5 20 E
Eems Kanaal	46	53 18N	6 46 E
Eems, R.	46	53 26N	6 57 E
Eenrum	46	53 22N	6 28 E
Eernegem	47	51 8N	3 2 E
Eerste Valthermond	46	52 53N	6 58 E
Eersterivier	128	34 0S	18 45 E
Efate, I. (Vate)	46	17 40S	168 25 E
Eferding	52	48 18N	14 1 E
Efferi	119	24 30N	9 28 E
Effingham	156	39 8N	88 30W
Effiums	121	6 35N	8 0 E
Effretikon	51	47 25N	8 42 E
Efiduasi	121	6 45N	1 25W
Eforie Sud	70	44 1N	28 37 E
Ega, R.	58	42 32N	1 58W
Egadi, Isole	64	37 55N	12 10 E
Eganville	150	45 32N	77 5W
Egeland	158	48 42N	99 6W
Egenolf L.	153	59 3N	100 0W
Eger	53	47 53N	20 27 E
Eger, R.	53	47 43N	20 32 E
Egersund = Eigersund	75	58 26N	6 1 E
Egerton, Mt.	137	24 42S	117 44 E
Egg L.	153	55 5N	105 30W
Eggenburg	52	48 38N	15 50 E
Eggiwil	50	46 52N	7 47 E
Egham	29	51 25N	0 33W
Egilsay I.	37	59 10N	2 56W
Eginbah	136	20 53S	119 47 E
Egletons	44	45 24N	2 3 E
Eglisau	51	47 35N	8 31 E
Egmond-aan-Zee	46	52 37N	4 38 E
Egmont, C.	142	39 16S	173 45 E
Egmont, Mt.	142	39 17S	174 5 E
Egogi Bad	123	13 10N	41 30 E
Egremont	32	54 28N	3 33W
Eğridir Gölü	92	37 53N	30 50 E
Egton	33	54 27N	0 45W
Egtved	73	55 38N	9 18 E
Égua	174	5 5N	68 0W
Éguas, R.	171	13 26S	44 14W
Égume	121	7 30N	7 14 E
Éguzon	44	46 27N	1 33 E
Egvekinot	77	66 19N	179 50W
Egyek	53	47 39N	20 52 E
Egypt ■	122	28 0N	31 0 E
Eha Amufu	121	6 30N	7 40 E
Ehime-ken □	110	33 30N	132 40 E
Ehingen	49	48 16N	9 43 E
Ehrwald	52	47 24N	10 56 E
Eibar	58	43 11N	2 28W
Eibergen	46	52 6N	6 39 E
Eichstätt	49	48 53N	11 12 E
Eidanger	71	59 7N	9 43 E
Eide	71	60 31N	6 44 E
Eider, R.	48	54 15N	8 50 E
Eidsberg	71	59 32N	11 16 E
Eidsfoss	71	59 36N	10 2 E
Eidsvold	139	25 25S	151 12 E
Eidsvoll	75	60 19N	11 14 E
Eifel	49	50 10N	6 45 E
Eiffel Flats	127	18 20S	30 0 E
Eigersund	71	58 26N	6 1 E
Eigg, I.	36	56 54N	6 10W
Eigg, Sd. of	36	56 52N	6 15W
Eighty Mile Beach	136	19 30S	120 40 E
Eil	91	8 0N	49 50 E
Eil, L.	36	56 50N	5 15W
Eilat	90	29 30N	34 56 E
Eildon	141	37 14S	145 55 E
Eildon, L.	139	37 10S	146 0 E
Eileen L.	153	62 16N	107 37W
Eilenburg	48	51 28N	12 38 E
Ein 'Arik	90	31 54N	35 8 E
Ein el Luweiqa	123	14 5N	33 50 E
Einasleigh	138	18 32S	144 5 E
Einasleigh, R.	138	17 30S	142 17 E
Einbeck	48	51 48N	9 50 E
Eindhoven	47	51 26N	5 30 E
Einsiedeln	51	47 7N	8 46 E
Eiriksjökull	74	64 46N	20 24W
Eirlandsche Gat	46	53 12N	4 54 E
Eirunepé	174	6 35S	70 0W
Eisden	47	50 59N	5 42 E
Eisenach	48	50 58N	10 18 E
Eisenberg	48	50 59N	11 50 E
Eisenerz	52	47 32N	15 54 E
Eisenhüttenstadt	48	52 9N	14 41 E
Eisenkappel	52	46 29N	14 36 E
Eisenstadt	53	47 51N	16 31 E
Eiserfeld	47	50 50N	8 0 E
Eisfeld	49	50 25N	10 54 E
Eishort, L.	36	57 9N	6 0W
Eisleben	48	51 31N	11 31 E
Eizariya (Bethany)	90	31 47N	35 15 E
Ejby	73	55 25N	9 56 E
Eje, Sierra del	56	42 24N	6 54W
Ejea de los Caballeros	58	42 7N	1 9W
Ejido	174	8 33N	71 14W
Ejura	121	7 25N	1 25 E
Ejutla	165	16 34N	96 44W
Ekalaka	158	45 55N	104 30 E
Ekawasaki	110	33 13N	132 46 E
Ekeryd	73	57 37N	14 6 E
Eket	121	4 38N	7 56W
Eketahuna	142	40 38S	175 43 E
Ekhínos	68	41 16N	25 1W
Ekibastuz	76	51 40N	75 22 E
Ekimchan	77	53 0N	133 0W
Ekofisk, oilfield	19	56 35N	3 30 E
Ekofisk, W., oilfield	19	56 35N	3 5 E
Ekoli	126	0 23S	24 13 E
Ekoln, I.	72	59 45N	17 40 E
Eksjö	73	57 40N	14 58W
Ekwan Pt.	150	53 16N	82 7W
Ekwan, R.	150	53 12N	82 15W
El Abiodh	118	32 53N	0 31 E
El Aïoun	118	34 33N	2 30W
El 'Aiyat	122	29 36N	31 15 E
El Alamein	122	30 48N	28 58 E
El Aqaba	90	29 31N	35 0 E
El Arahal	57	37 15N	5 33W
El Araq	122	28 40N	26 20 E
El Arba	118	36 28N	3 12 E
El Arba du Rharb	118	34 50N	5 59W
El Aricha	118	34 13N	1 16W
El Arīhā	90	31 52N	35 27 E
El Arish	138	17 49S	146 1 E
El 'Arîsh	122	31 8N	33 50 E
El Arnaud	119	36 7N	5 49 E
El Arrouch	119	36 37N	6 53 E
* El Asnam	118	36 10N	1 20 E
El Astillero	56	43 24N	3 49W
El Badâri	122	27 4N	31 25 E
El Bahrein	122	28 30N	26 25 E
El Ballâs	122	26 2N	32 43 E
El Balyana	122	26 10N	32 3 E
El Baqeir	122	18 40N	33 40 E
El Barco de Ávila	56	40 21N	5 31W
El Barco de Valdeorras	56	42 23N	7 0W
El Bauga	122	18 18N	33 52 E
El Baúl	174	8 57N	68 17W
El Bawiti	122	28 25N	28 45 E
El Bayadh	118	33 40N	1 1 E
El Bierzo	56	42 45N	6 30W
El Biodh	118	26 0N	6 32W
El Bluff	166	11 59N	83 40W
El Bonillo	59	38 57N	2 35W
El Cajon	163	32 49N	117 0W
El Callao	174	7 25N	61 50W
El Camp	58	41 5N	1 10 E
El Campo	159	29 10N	96 20W
El Carmen	174	1 16N	66 52W
El Castillo	57	37 41N	6 19W
El Centro	161	32 50N	115 40W
El Cerro, Boliv.	174	17 30S	61 40W
El Cerro, Spain	57	37 45N	6 57W
El Cocuy	174	6 25N	72 27W
El Coronil	57	37 5N	5 38W
El Cuy	176	39 55S	68 25W
El Cuyo	165	21 30N	87 40W
El Dab'a	122	31 0N	28 27 E
El Dátil	164	30 7N	112 15W
El Deir	122	25 25N	32 20 E
El Dere	91	3 50N	47 8 E
El Diaz	165	21 1N	87 17W
El Dificul	174	9 51N	74 14W
El Díos	164	20 40N	87 20W
El Diviso	174	1 22N	78 14W
El Djouf	120	20 0N	11 30 E
El Dorado, Colomb.	174	1 11N	71 52W
El Dorado, Ark., U.S.A.	159	33 10N	92 40W
El Dorado, Kans., U.S.A.	159	37 55N	96 56W
El Dorado, Venez.	174	6 55N	61 30W
El Dorado Springs	159	37 54N	93 59W
El Eglab	118	26 20N	4 30W
El Escorial	56	40 35N	4 7W
El Faiyûm	122	29 19N	30 50 E
El Fâsher	123	13 33N	25 26 E
El Fashn	122	28 50N	30 54 E
El Ferrol	56	43 29N	3 14W
El Fifi	123	10 4N	25 0 E
El Fuerte	164	26 30N	108 40W
El Gal	91	10 58N	50 20 E
El Gebir	123	13 40N	29 40 E
El Gedida	122	25 40N	28 30 E
El Geneina	117	13 27N	22 45 E
El Geteina	123	14 50N	32 27 E
El Gezira	123	14 0N	33 0 E
El Gezira □	123	15 0N	33 0 E
El Gîza	122	30 0N	31 10 E
El Goléa	118	30 30N	2 50 E
El Guettar	119	34 5N	4 38 E
El Hadjire	119	32 36N	5 30 E
El Hagiz	123	15 15N	35 50 E
El Hajeb	118	33 41N	5 23W
El Hammâm	122	30 52N	29 25 E
El Hank, Alg.	118	25 38N	5 29W
El Hank, Maurit.	118	24 37N	7 0W
El Haql	122	29 15N	34 59 E
El Hawata	123	13 25N	34 42 E
El Heiz	122	27 50N	28 40 E
El 'Idisât	122	25 30N	32 35 E
El Iskandarîya	122	31 0N	30 0 E
El Istwâ'ya □	123	5 0N	30 0 E
El Jadida	118	33 16N	9 31W
El Jorf Lasfar, C.	118	33 5N	8 54W
El Kab	122	19 27N	32 46 E
El Kala	119	36 50N	8 30 E
El Kamlin	123	15 3N	33 11 E
El Kantara, Alg.	119	35 14N	5 45 E
El Kantara, Tunisia	119	33 45N	10 58 E
El Karaba	122	18 32N	33 41 E
El Kef	119	36 12N	8 47 E
El Kelâa des Srarhna	118	32 4N	7 27W
El Khandaq	122	18 30N	30 30 E
El Khârga	122	25 30N	30 33 E
El Khartûm	123	15 31N	32 35 E
El Khartûm Bahrî	123	15 40N	32 31 E
El-Khroubs	119	36 10N	6 55 E
El Khureiba	122	28 3N	35 10 E
El Kseur	119	36 46N	4 49 E
El Ksiba	118	32 45N	6 1W
El Kuntilla	122	30 1N	34 45 E
El Ladhiqiya	92	35 20N	35 30 E
El Laqeita	122	25 50N	33 15 E
El Leiya	123	16 15N	35 28 E
El Mafâza	123	13 38N	34 30 E
El Mahalla el Kubra	122	31 0N	31 0 E
El Mahârîq	122	25 35N	30 35 E
El Maiz	118	28 19N	0 9W
El-Maks el-Bahari	122	24 30N	30 40 E
El Manshâh	122	26 26N	31 50 E
El Mansour	118	27 47N	0 14W
El Mansûra	122	31 0N	31 19 E
El Mantico	174	7 27N	62 32W
El Manzala	122	31 10N	31 50 E
El Marâgha	122	26 35N	31 10 E
El Masid	123	15 15N	33 0 E
El Matariya	122	31 15N	32 0 E
El Meghaier	119	33 55N	5 58 E
El Melfa	119	31 58N	15 18 E
El Meraguen	118	28 0N	0 7W
El Metemma	123	16 50N	33 10 E
El Miamo	174	7 39N	61 46W
El Milagro	172	30 59S	65 59W
El Milheas	118	25 27N	6 57W
El Milia	119	36 51N	6 13 E
El Minyâ	122	28 7N	30 33 E
El Molar	58	40 42N	3 45W
El Monte	163	34 4N	118 2W
El Mreyye	120	18 0N	6 0W
El Obeid	123	13 8N	30 10 E
El Oro = Sta. María del Oro	164	25 50N	105 20W
El Oro de Hidalgo	165	19 48N	100 8W
El Oued	119	33 20N	6 58 E
El Ouig	120	19 31N	0 27 E
El Palmar	174	7 58N	61 53W
El Palmito, Presa	164	25 40N	105 3W
El Panadés	58	41 10N	1 30 E
El Pao	174	9 38N	68 8W
El Pardo	56	40 31N	3 47W
El Paso	161	31 50N	106 30W
El Paso Robles	163	35 38N	120 41W
El Pedernoso	59	39 29N	2 45W
El Pedroso	57	37 51N	5 45W
El Pilar	174	10 32N	63 9W
El Pobo de Dueñas	58	40 46N	1 39W
El Portal	163	37 44N	119 49W
El Porvenir, Mexico	164	31 15N	105 51W
El Porvenir, Venez.	174	4 42N	71 19W
El Prat de Llobregat	58	41 18N	2 3 E
El Progreso	166	15 26N	87 51W
El Provencio	59	39 23N	2 35W
El Pueblito	164	29 3N	105 4W
El Qahîra	122	30 1N	31 14 E
El Qantara	122	30 51N	32 20 E
El Qasr	122	25 44N	28 42 E
El Qubba	123	11 10N	27 5 E
El Quseima	122	30 40N	34 15 E
El Qusîya	122	27 29N	30 44 E
El Râshda	122	25 36N	28 57 E
El Reno	159	35 30N	98 0W
El Rheauya	118	25 52N	6 30W
El Ribero	56	42 30N	8 30W
El Rîdisiya	122	24 56N	32 51 E
El Rio	163	34 14N	119 10W
El Ronquillo	57	37 44N	6 10W
El Rubio	57	37 22N	5 0W
El Saff	122	29 34N	31 16 E
El Salado	174	8 56N	73 55W
El Salto	164	23 47N	105 22W
El Salvador ■	166	13 50N	89 0W
El Sancejo	57	37 4N	5 6W
El Sauce	166	13 0N	86 40W
El Shallal	122	24 0N	32 53 E
El Suweis	122	29 58N	32 31 E
El Temblador	174	8 59N	62 44W
El Thamad	122	29 40N	34 28 E
El Tigre	174	8 55N	64 15W
El Tocuyo	174	9 47N	69 48W
El Tofo	172	29 22S	71 18W
El Tránsito	172	28 52S	70 17W
El Tûr	122	28 14N	33 36 E
El Turbio	176	51 30S	72 40W
El Uqsur	122	25 41N	32 38 E
El Vado	58	41 2N	3 18W
El Vallés	58	41 35N	2 20 E
El Vigia	174	8 38N	71 39W
El Wak	124	2 49N	40 56 E
El Waqf	122	25 45N	32 15 E
El Wâsta	122	29 19N	31 12 E
El Weguet	123	5 28N	42 17 E
Ela	123	12 50N	42 20 E
Elafónisos	69	36 29N	22 56 E
Elaine	140	37 44S	144 2 E
Elamanchili = Yellamanchilli	96	17 26N	82 50 E
Elan R.	31	52 17N	3 40W
Elan Village	31	52 18N	3 34W
Elands	141	31 37S	152 20 E
Elandsvlei	128	32 19S	19 31 E
Élassa	69	35 18N	26 21 E
Elassón	68	39 53N	22 12 E
Elat	103	5 40S	133 5 E
Elateia	69	38 37N	22 46 E
Elâziğ	92	38 37N	39 22 E
Elba	157	31 27N	86 4W
Elba, I.	62	42 48N	10 15 E
Elbasani	68	41 9N	20 9 E
Elbasani-Berati	68	40 58N	20 0 E
Elbe, R.	48	53 15N	10 7 E
Elbert, Mt.	161	39 12N	106 36W
Elberta	156	44 35N	86 14W
Elberton	157	34 7N	82 51W
Elbeuf	42	49 17N	1 2 E
Elbląg □	54	54 15N	19 30 E
Elblag (Elbing)	54	54 10N	19 25 E
Elbow	153	51 7N	106 35W
Elbrus, Mt.	83	43 30N	42 30 E
Elburg	46	52 26N	5 50 E
Elburz Mts. = Alborz	93	36 0N	52 0 E
Elche	59	38 15N	0 42W
Elche de la Sierra	59	38 27N	2 3W
Elcho I.	138	11 55S	135 45 E
Elda	59	38 29N	0 47W
Eldfisk, oilfield	19	56 25N	3 30 E
Eldon, Iowa, U.S.A.	97	40 50N	92 12W
Eldon, Mo., U.S.A.	158	38 20N	92 38W
Eldora	158	42 20N	93 5W
Eldorado, Argent.	173	26 28S	54 43W

*Renamed Ech Cheliff

Eldorado Ermelo

Eldorado, Ont., Can. 97 44 40N 77 32W
Eldorado, Sask., Can. 153 59 35N 108 30W
Eldorado, Mexico 164 24 0N 107 30W
Eldorado, Ill., U.S.A. 156 37 50N 88 25W
Eldorado, Tex., U.S.A. 159 30 52N 100 35W
Eldoret 126 0 30N 35 25 E
Electra 159 34 0N 99 0W
Eleele 147 21 54N 159 35W
Elefantes, R. 129 24 0 S 32 30 E
Elektrogorsk 81 55 56N 38 50 E
Elektrostal 81 55 41N 38 32 E
Elele 121 5 5N 6 50 E
Elena 67 42 55N 25 53 E
Elephant Butte Res. 161 33 45N 107 30W
Elephant I. 13 61 0 S 55 0W
Elephant Pass 97 9 35N 80 25 E
Elesbão Veloso 170 6 13 S 42 8W
Eleshnitsa 67 41 52N 23 36 E
Eleuthera I. 166 25 0N 76 20W
Elevsis 69 38 4N 23 26 E
Elevtheroúpolis 68 40 52N 24 20 E
Elfin Cove 147 58 11N 136 20W
Elgåhogna, Mt. 72 62 7N 12 7 E
Elgepiggen 71 62 10N 11 21 E
Elgeyo-Marakwet □ 126 0 45N 35 30 E
Elgg 51 47 29N 8 52 E
Elgin, Can. 151 45 48N 65 10W
Elgin, U.K. 37 57 39N 3 20W
Elgin, Ill., U.S.A. 156 42 0N 88 20W
Elgin, N.D., U.S.A. 158 46 24N 101 46W
Elgin, Nebr., U.S.A. 158 41 58N 98 3W
Elgin, Nev., U.S.A. 161 37 27N 114 36W
Elgin, Oreg., U.S.A. 160 45 37N 118 0W
Elgin, Texas, U.S.A. 159 30 21N 97 22W
Elgol 36 57 9N 6 6W
Elgon, Mt. 126 1 10N 34 30 E
Elham 29 51 9N 1 7 E
Eliase 103 8 10 S 130 55 E
Elida 159 33 56N 103 41W
Elie 153 49 48N 97 52W
Elie de Beaumont, Mt. 143 43 30 S 170 20 E
Elikón, Mt. 69 38 18N 22 45 E
Elim 147 64 35N 162 20W
Elin Pelin 126 42 40N 23 38 E
Elisabethville = Lubumbashi 127 11 32 S 27 38 E
Eliseu Martins 170 8 13 S 43 42W
Elishaw 35 55 16N 2 14W
Elista 83 46 16N 44 14 E
Elit 123 15 10N 37 0 E
Elizabeth, Austral. 140 34 42 S 138 41 E
Elizabeth, U.S.A. 162 40 37N 74 12W
Elizabeth City 157 36 18N 76 16W
Elizabetha 126 1 3N 23 37 E
Elizabethton 157 36 20N 82 13W
Elizabethtown, Ky., U.S.A. 156 37 40N 85 54W
Elizabethtown, Pa., U.S.A. 162 40 8N 76 36W
Elizondo 58 43 12N 1 30W
Elk City 159 35 25N 99 25W
Elk Grove 163 38 25N 121 22W
Elk Island Nat. Park 152 53 47N 112 59W
Elk Lake 150 47 40N 80 25W
Elk Point 153 53 54N 110 55W
Elk River, Idaho, U.S.A. 160 46 50N 116 8W
Elk River, Minn., U.S.A. 158 45 17N 93 34W
Elkedra 138 21 9 S 135 26 E
Elkedra, R. 138 21 8 S 136 22 E
Elkhart, Ind., U.S.A. 156 41 42N 85 55W
Elkhart, Kans., U.S.A. 159 37 3N 101 54W
Elkhorn 153 49 59N 101 14W
Elkhorn, R. 158 42 0N 98 15W
Elkhotovo 83 43 19N 44 15 E
Elkhovo 67 42 10N 26 40 E
Elkin 157 36 17N 80 50W
Elkins 156 38 53N 79 53W
Elko, Can. 152 49 20N 115 10W
Elko, U.S.A. 160 40 40N 115 50W
Elkton 162 39 36N 75 50W
Ell, L. 137 29 13 S 127 46 E
Elland 33 53 41N 1 49W
Ellecom 46 52 2N 6 6 E
Ellef Ringnes I. 12 78 30N 102 2W
Ellen, Mt. 161 38 4N 110 56W
Ellen R. 32 54 44N 3 24W
Ellendale, Austral. 136 17 56 S 124 48 E
Ellendale, U.S.A. 158 46 3N 98 30W
Ellensburg 160 47 0N 120 30W
Ellenville 162 41 42N 74 23W
Eller Beck Bri. 33 54 23N 0 40W
Ellerston 141 31 49 S 151 20 E
Ellery, Mt. 141 37 28 S 148 40 E
Ellesmere 32 52 55N 2 53W
Ellesmere I. 12 79 30N 80 0W
Ellesmere, L. 131 43 46 S 172 27 E
Ellesmere Port 32 53 17N 2 55W
Ellesworth Land 13 74 0 S 85 0W
Ellezelles 47 50 44N 3 42 E
Ellice Is. 130 8 0 S 176 0 E
Ellicott City 162 39 16N 76 48W
Ellington 35 55 14N 1 34W
Ellinwood 158 38 27N 98 37W
Elliot, Austral. 138 17 33 S 133 32 E
Elliot, S. Afr. 129 31 22 S 27 48 E
Elliot Lake 150 46 35N 82 35W
Ellis 158 39 0N 99 39W
Ellisville 157 31 38N 89 12W
Ellon 37 57 21N 2 5W
Ellore = Eluru 96 16 48N 81 8 E
Ells, R. 152 57 18N 111 40W
Ellsworth 158 38 47N 98 15W
Ellsworth Land 13 76 0 S 89 0W
Ellwangen 49 48 57N 10 9 E
Ellwood City 156 40 52N 80 19W
Elm 51 46 54N 9 10 E
Elma, Can. 153 49 52N 95 55W
Elma, U.S.A. 160 47 0N 123 30 E
Elmer 162 39 36N 75 10W
Elmhurst 156 41 52N 87 58W
Elmina 121 5 5N 1 21W
Elmira, Can. 151 46 30N 61 59W
Elmira, U.S.A. 162 42 8N 76 49W
Elmira Heights 162 42 8N 76 50W
Elmore, Austral. 140 36 30 S 144 37 E
Elmore, U.S.A. 163 33 7N 115 49W
Elmshorn 48 53 44N 9 40 E
Elmswell 29 52 14N 0 53 E
Elorza 174 7 3N 69 31W
Eloy 161 32 46N 111 46W
Éloyes 43 48 6N 6 36 E
Elphin, Ireland 38 53 50N 8 11W
Elphin, U.K. 36 58 4N 5 3W
Elphinstone 138 21 30 S 148 17 E
Elrose 153 51 12N 108 0W
Elsas 150 48 32N 82 55W
Elsinore, Austral. 141 31 35 S 145 11 E
Elsinore, Cal., U.S.A. 163 33 40N 117 15W
Elsinore, Utah, U.S.A. 161 38 40N 112 2W
Elsinore = Helsingor 73 56 2N 12 35 E
Elspe 48 51 10N 8 1 E
Elspeet 46 52 17N 5 48 E
Elst 46 51 55N 5 51 E
Elsterwerda 48 51 27N 13 32 E
Elstree 29 51 38N 0 16W
Elten 46 51 52N 6 9 E
Eltham, Austral. 141 37 43 S 145 12 E
Eltham, N.Z. 142 39 26 S 174 19 E
Elton 83 49 5N 46 52 E
Eluru 96 16 48N 81 8 E
Elvas 57 38 50N 7 17W
Elven 42 47 44N 2 36W
Elverum 71 60 53N 11 34 E
Elvire, Mt. 137 21 52 S 116 50 E
Elvire, R. 136 17 51 S 128 11 E
Elvo, R. 62 45 32N 8 14 E
Elvran 71 63 24N 11 3 E
Elwood, Ind., U.S.A. 156 40 20N 85 50W
Elwood, Nebr., U.S.A. 158 40 38N 99 51W
Ely, U.K. 29 52 24N 0 16 E
Ely, Minn., U.S.A. 158 47 54N 91 52W
Ely, Nev., U.S.A. 160 39 10N 114 50W
Elyashiv 90 32 23N 34 55 E
Elyria 156 41 22N 82 8W
Emådalen 72 61 20N 14 44 E
Emaiygi, R. 80 58 30N 26 30 E
Emba 76 48 50N 58 8 E
Embarcación 172 23 10 S 64 0W
Embarras Portage 153 58 27N 111 28W
Embleton 35 55 30N 1 38W
Embo 37 57 55N 4 0W
Embóna 69 36 13N 27 51 E
Embrach 51 47 30N 8 36 E
Embrun 45 44 34N 6 30 E
Embu 126 0 32 S 37 38 E
Embu □ 126 0 30 S 37 35 E
Emden 48 53 22N 7 12 E
Emeq Hula 90 33 5N 35 8 E
'Emeq Yizre'el 90 32 35N 35 12 E
Emerald 138 23 32 S 148 10 E
Emerson 153 49 0N 97 10W
Emery 161 38 59N 111 17W
Emery Park 161 32 10N 110 59W
Emi Koussi, Mt. 117 20 0N 18 55 E
Emilia-Romagna □ 62 44 33N 10 40 E
Emilius, Mt. 62 45 41N 7 23 E
Eminabad 94 32 2N 74 8 E
Emine 67 42 40N 27 56 E
Emlichheim 48 52 37N 6 51 E
Emly 39 52 28N 8 20W
Emmaboda 73 56 37N 15 32 E
Emmaus 162 40 32N 75 30W
Emme, R. 50 47 0N 7 42 E
Emmeloord 46 52 44N 5 46 E
Emmen, Neth. 47 52 48N 6 57 E
Emmen, Switz. 51 47 4N 8 17 E
Emmendingen 49 48 7N 7 51 E
Emmental 50 47 0N 7 35 E
Emmer-Compascum 46 52 49N 7 2 E
Emmerich 48 51 50N 6 12 E
Emmet 138 24 45 S 144 30 E
Emmetsburg 158 43 3N 94 40W
Emmett 160 43 51N 116 33W
Emöd 53 47 57N 20 47 E
Emona 67 42 43N 27 53 E
Empalme 164 28 1N 110 49W
Empangeni 129 28 50 S 31 52 E
Empedrado 172 28 0 S 58 46W
Empoli 62 43 43N 10 57 E
Emporia, Kans., U.S.A. 158 38 25N 96 16W
Emporia, Va., U.S.A. 157 36 41N 77 32W
Emporium 156 41 30N 78 17W
Empress 153 50 57N 110 0W
Emptinne 47 50 19N 5 8 E
Ems, R. 48 52 37N 7 16 E
Emsdetten 48 52 11N 7 31 E
Emsworth 29 50 51N 0 56 E
Emu 140 36 44 S 143 26 E
Emu Park 138 23 13 S 150 50 E
Emu Ra. 136 23 0 S 122 0 E
Emyvale 38 54 20N 6 57W
En Gedi 90 31 28N 35 25 E
En Harod 90 32 33N 35 22 E
'En Kerem 90 31 47N 35 6 E
En Nahud 123 12 45N 28 25 E
en Namous, O. 118 31 15N 0 10W
Ena 111 35 25N 137 25 E
Ena-San 111 35 26N 137 36 E
Enafors 72 63 17N 12 20 E
Enambú 174 1 1N 70 17W
Enana 128 17 30 S 16 23 E
Enånger 72 61 30N 17 9 E
Enard B. 36 58 5N 5 20W
Enbetsu 112 44 44N 141 47 E
Encantadas, Serra 173 30 40 S 53 0W
Encanto, Cape 103 20 20N 121 40 E
Encarnación 173 27 15 S 56 0W
Encarnación de Diaz 164 21 30N 102 20W
Ench'eng 106 37 9N 116 16 E
Enchi 120 5 53N 2 48W
Encinal 159 28 3N 99 25W
Encinillas 164 33 3N 117 17W
Encinitas 163 33 3N 117 17W
Encino 161 34 46N 106 16W
Encounter B. 140 35 45 S 138 45 E
Encruzilhada 171 15 31 S 40 54W
Endau 101 2 40N 103 38 E
Endau, R. 101 2 30N 103 30 E
Ende 103 8 45 S 121 30 E
Endeavour 153 52 10N 102 39W
Endeavour Str. 138 10 45 S 142 0 E
Endelave 73 55 46N 10 18 E
Enderbury I. 131 3 8 S 171 5W
Enderby, Can. 152 50 35N 119 10W
Enderby, U.K. 28 52 35N 1 15W
Enderby I. 136 20 35 S 116 30 E
Enderby Land 13 66 0 S 53 0 E
Enderlin 158 46 45N 97 41W
Endicott, N.Y., U.S.A. 162 42 6N 76 2W
Endicott, Wash., U.S.A. 160 47 0N 117 45W
Endicott Mts. 147 68 0N 152 30W
Endröd 53 46 55N 20 47 E
Endyalgout I. 136 11 40 S 132 35 E
Enebakk 71 59 46N 11 9 E
Enez 68 40 45N 26 5 E
Enfida 119 36 6N 10 28 E
Enfield, U.K. 29 51 39N 0 4W
Enfield, U.S.A. 162 43 34N 71 57W
Engadin 51 46 45N 10 10 E
Engadine, Lower = Engiadina Bassa 51 46 51N 10 18 E
Engadine, Upper = Engiadin 'Ota 51 46 38N 10 0 E
Engano, C. 167 18 30N 68 20W
Engaño, C. 103 18 35N 122 23 E
Engeddi 90 31 28N 35 25 E
Engelberg 51 46 48N 8 26 E
Engels 81 51 28N 46 6 E
Engemann L. 153 55 55N 106 55W
Enger 71 60 35N 10 20 E
Enggano, I. 102 5 20 S 102 40 E
Enghien 47 50 37N 4 2 E
Engiadin 'Ota 51 46 38N 10 0 E
Engiadina Bassa 51 46 51N 10 18 E
Engkilili 102 1 3N 111 42 E
England 159 34 30N 91 58W
England □ 27 53 0N 2 0W
Englee 151 50 45N 56 5W
Englefield 140 37 21 S 141 48 E
Englehart 150 47 49N 79 52W
Engler L. 153 59 8N 106 52W
Englewood, Colo., U.S.A. 158 39 40N 105 0W
Englewood, Kans., U.S.A. 159 37 7N 99 59W
Englewood, N.J., U.S.A. 162 40 54N 73 59W
English Bazar 95 24 58N 88 21 E
English Channel 42 50 0N 2 0W
English Company Is. 133 12 0 S 137 0 E
English, R. 153 50 30N 93 50W
English River 150 49 20N 91 0W
Enid 159 36 26N 97 52W
Enipévs, R. 68 39 22N 22 17 E
Eniwetok 131 11 30N 152 16 E
Enjil 118 33 12N 4 32W
Enkeldoorn 127 19 2 S 30 52 E
Enkhuizen 46 52 42N 5 17 E
Enköping 72 59 37N 17 4 E
Enlo 108 24 0N 107 7 E
Enna 65 37 34N 14 15 E
Ennadai 153 61 8N 100 53W
Ennadai L. 153 61 0N 101 0W
Ennedi 117 17 15N 22 0 E
Ennell L. 38 53 29N 7 25W
Ennerdale Water 32 54 32N 3 24W
Enngonia 139 29 21 S 145 50 E
Enningdal 71 58 59N 11 33 E
Ennis, Ireland 39 52 51N 8 59W
Ennis, Mont., U.S.A. 160 45 27N 111 48W
Ennis, Texas, U.S.A. 159 32 15N 96 40W
Enniscorthy 39 52 30N 6 35W
Enniskean 39 51 44N 8 56W
Enniskerry 39 53 12N 6 10W
Enniskillen 38 54 20N 7 40W
Ennistimon 39 52 56N 9 18W
Enns 52 48 12N 14 28 E
Enns, R. 52 48 8N 14 27 E
Enoggera Range 108 27 26 S 152 56 E
Enoggera Res. 109 27 27 S 152 55 E
Enontekiö 74 68 23N 23 37 E
Enp'ing 109 22 11N 112 18 E
Enriquillo, L. 167 18 20N 72 5W
Ens 46 52 38N 5 50 E
Enschede 46 52 13N 6 53 E
Ensenada, Argent. 172 34 55 S 57 55W
Ensenada, Mexico 164 31 50N 116 50W
Enshih 108 30 18N 109 27 E
Enshū-Nada 111 34 27N 137 38 E
Ensisheim 43 47 50N 7 20 E
Enstone 28 51 55N 1 25W
Entebbe 126 0 4N 32 28 E
Enter 46 52 17N 6 35 E
Enterprise, Can. 152 60 47N 115 45W
Enterprise, Oreg., U.S.A. 160 45 30N 117 11W
Enterprise, Utah, U.S.A. 161 37 37N 113 36W
Entlebuch 50 46 59N 8 4 E
Entrance 152 53 25N 117 50W
Entre Rios, Boliv. 172 21 30 S 64 25W
Entre Rios, Mozam. 127 14 57 S 37 20 E
Entre Rios □ 172 30 30 S 58 30W
Entre Rios, Bahia 171 11 56 S 38 5W
Entrecasteaux, Pt. d' 137 34 50 S 115 56 E
Entrepeñas, Pantano de 58 40 34N 2 42W
Entwistle 152 53 30N 115 0W
Enugu 121 6 30N 7 30 E
Enugu Ezike 121 7 0N 7 29 E
Enumclaw 160 47 12N 122 0W
Envermeu 42 49 53N 1 15 E
Envigado 174 6 10N 75 35W
Enza, R. 62 44 33N 10 22 E
Enzan 111 35 42N 138 44 E
Eólie o Lipari, Is. 65 38 30N 14 50 E
Epa 138 8 28 S 146 52 E
Epanomí 68 40 25N 22 59 E
Epe, Neth. 47 52 21N 5 59 E
Epe, Nigeria 121 6 36N 3 59 E
Épernay 43 49 3N 3 56 E
Épernon 43 48 35N 1 40 E
Ephesus 92 38 0N 27 30 E
Ephraim 160 39 30N 111 37W
Ephrata, Pa., U.S.A. 162 40 11N 76 11W
Ephrata, Wash., U.S.A. 160 47 28N 119 32W
Épila 58 41 36N 1 17W
Épinac-les-Mines 43 46 59N 4 31 E
Épinal 43 48 19N 6 27 E
Episcopia Bihorului 70 47 12N 21 55 E
Epitálion 69 37 37N 21 30 E
Eport L. 36 57 33N 7 10W
Epping 29 51 42N 0 8 E
Epping Forest 29 51 40N 0 5 E
Epsom 29 51 19N 0 16W
Epukiro 125 21 30 S 19 0 E
Epworth 33 53 30N 0 50W
Equatorial Guinea ■ 124 2 0 S 78 0W
Équeurdreville-Hainneville 42 49 40N 1 40W
Er Rahad 123 12 45N 30 32 E
Er Rif 118 35 1N 4 1W
Er Roseires 123 11 55N 34 30 E
Er Rumman 90 32 9N 35 48 E
Eradu 137 28 40 S 115 2 E
Erandol 96 20 56N 75 20 E
Erap 135 6 37 S 146 51 E
Erāwadī Myit, R. = Irrawaddy, R. 98 19 30N 95 15 E
Erba, Italy 62 45 49N 9 12 E
Erba, Sudan 122 19 5N 36 40 E
Ercha 77 69 45N 147 20 E
Erciyas Daği 92 38 30N 35 30 E
Erdene 106 44 30N 111 10 E
Erding 49 48 18N 11 55 E
Erebus, Mt. 13 77 35 S 167 0 E
Erechim 173 27 35 S 52 15W
Ereğli 92 41 15N 31 30 E
Erei, Monti 65 37 20N 14 20 E
Erembodegem 47 50 56N 4 4 E
Eresma, R. 56 41 13N 4 30W
Eressós 69 39 11N 25 57 E
Erewadi Myitwanya 99 15 30N 95 0 E
Erfenis Dam 128 28 30 S 26 50 E
Erfjord 71 59 20N 6 14 E
Erfoud 118 31 30N 4 15W
Erfurt 48 50 58N 11 2 E
Erfurt □ 48 51 10N 10 30 E
Ergani 92 38 26N 39 49 E
Ergene, R. 67 41 20N 27 0 E
Ergeni Vozyshennost 83 47 0N 44 0 E
Erhlien 106 43 42N 112 2 E
Erhlin 109 23 54N 120 22 E
Erhtao Chiang, R. 107 42 35N 128 10 E
Erhyüan 108 26 7N 99 57 E
Eria, R. 56 42 10N 6 8W
Eriba 123 16 40N 36 10 E
Eriboll, L. 37 58 28N 4 41W
Érica 46 52 43N 6 56 E
Érice 64 38 4N 12 34 E
Ericht, L. 37 56 50N 4 25W
Erie 156 42 10N 80 7W
Erigavo 91 10 35N 47 35 E
Erikoúsa 68 39 55N 19 14 E
Eriksdale 153 50 52N 98 7W
Erikslund 72 62 31N 15 54 E
Erimanthos 69 37 57N 21 50 E
Erimo-misaki 112 41 50N 143 15 E
Eriskay I. 36 57 4N 7 18W
Eriskay, Sd. of 36 57 5N 7 20W
Erisort L. 36 58 5N 6 30W
Eriswil 50 47 5N 7 46 E
Erith 152 53 25N 116 46W
Erithrai 69 38 13N 23 20 E
Eritrea □ 123 14 0N 41 0 E
Erjas, R. 56 39 45N 6 52W
Erker, L. 72 59 51N 18 29 E
Erlangen 49 49 35N 11 0 E
Erldunda 138 25 14 S 133 12 E
Ermelo, Neth. 46 52 35N 5 35 E
Ermelo, S. Afr. 129 26 31 S 29 59 E

Ermenak Fairmount

Ermenak 92 36 44N 33 0 E
Ermióni 69 37 23N 23 15 E
Ermoúpolis = Siros 69 37 28N 24 57 E
Ernakulam 97 9 59N 76 19 E
Erne, Lough 38 54 26N 7 46W
Erne, R. 38 54 30N 8 16W
Ernée 42 48 18N 0 56W
Ernest Giles Ra. 137 27 0 S 123 45 E
Erode 97 11 24N 77 45 E
Eromanga 139 26 40 S 143 11 E
Erongo 128 21 39 S 15 58 E
Erongoberg 128 21 45 S 15 32 E
Erp 47 51 36N 5 37 E
Erquelinnes 47 50 19N 4 8 E
Erquy 42 48 38N 2 29W
Erquy, Cap d' 42 48 39N 2 29W
Err, Piz d' 51 46 34N 9 43 E
Errabiddy 137 25 25 S 117 5 E
Erramala Hills 97 15 30N 78 15 E
Errer, R. 123 42 35N 8 40 E
Errigal, Mt. 38 55 2N 8 8W
Errill 39 52 52N 7 40W
Erris Hd. 38 54 19N 10 0W
Errochty, L. 37 56 45N 4 10W
Errogie 37 57 16N 4 23W
Errol 35 56 24N 3 13W
Erseka 68 40 22N 20 40 E
Erskine 158 47 37N 96 0W
Erstein 43 48 25N 7 38 E
Erstfeld 51 46 50N 8 38 E
Ertil 81 51 55N 40 50 E
Ertvågøy 71 63 12N 8 25 E
Ertvelde 47 51 11N 3 45 E
Erundu 128 20 39 S 16 26 E
Eruwa 121 7 33N 3 26 E
Ervalla 72 59 28N 15 16 E
Ervy-le-Châtel 43 48 2N 3 55 E
Erwin 157 36 10N 82 28W
Erzgebirge 48 50 25N 13 0 E
Erzin 77 50 15N 95 10 E
Erzincan 92 39 46N 39 30 E
Erzurum 92 39 57N 41 15 E
Es Sahrâ' Esh Sharqîya 122 26 0N 33 30 E
Es Sider 119 30 50N 18 21 E
Es Sînâ' 122 29 0N 34 0 E
Es Souk 121 18 48N 1 2 E
Es Sûkî 123 13 20N 34 58 E
Esa'ala 135 9 45 S 150 49 E
Esambo 126 3 48 S 23 30 E
Esan-misaki 112 41 40N 141 10 E
Esbjerg 73 55 29N 8 29 E
Escada 170 8 22 S 35 14W
Escalante 161 37 47N 111 37W
Escalante, R. 161 37 45N 111 0W
Escalón 164 26 40N 104 20W
Escalona 56 40 9N 4 29W
Escambia, R. 157 30 45N 87 15W
Escanaba 156 45 44N 87 5W
Escant, R. 47 51 2N 3 45 E
Esch-sur-Alzette 47 49 32N 6 0 E
Eschallens 50 46 39N 6 38 E
Eschede 48 52 44N 10 13 E
Escholzmatt 50 46 55N 7 56 E
Eschwege 48 51 10N 10 3 E
Eschweiler 48 50 49N 6 14 E
Escondida, La 164 24 6N 99 55W
Escondido 163 33 9N 117 4W
Escrick 33 53 53N 1 3W
Escuinapa 164 22 50N 105 50W
Escuintla 166 14 20N 90 48W
Escuminac 151 48 0N 67 0W
Escutillas = Ceba 174 6 33N 70 24W
Eséka 121 3 41N 10 44 E
Esens 48 53 40N 7 35 E
Esera, R. 58 42 24N 0 22 E
Esfahan □ 93 33 0N 53 0 E
Esgueva, R. 56 41 46N 4 14W
Esh Sham = Dimashq 92 33 30N 36 18 E
Esh Shamâlîya □ 122 19 0N 31 0 E
Esha Ness 36 60 30N 1 36W
Eshowe 129 28 50 S 31 30 E
Eshta' ol 90 31 47N 35 0 E
Esiama 120 4 48N 2 25W
Esino, R. 63 43 28N 13 8 E
Esk R. 32 54 23N 3 21W
Esk, R., Dumfries, U.K. 35 54 58N 3 4W
Esk, R., N. Yorks., U.K. 33 54 27N 0 36W
Eskdale 35 55 12N 3 4W
Eskifjördur 74 65 3N 13 55W
Eskilstuna 72 59 22N 16 32 E
Eskimo Ls. 147 69 15N 132 17W
Eskimo Pt. 153 61 10N 94 3W
Eskişehir 92 39 50N 30 35 E
Esla, R. 56 41 45N 5 50W
Eslöv 73 55 50N 13 20 E
Esmeralda, La 172 22 16 S 62 33W
Esmeraldas 174 1 0N 79 40W
Esneux 47 50 32N 5 33 E
Espa 71 60 35N 11 15 E
Espada, Pta. 174 12 5N 71 7W
Espalion 44 44 32N 2 47 E
Espalmador, I. 59 38 48N 1 26 E
Espanola 150 46 15N 81 46W
Espardell, I. del 59 38 47N 1 25 E
Esparraguera 58 41 33N 1 52 E
Esparta 166 9 59N 84 40W
Espejo 57 37 40N 4 34W
Espenberg, C. 147 66 35N 163 40W
Esperança 170 7 1 S 35 51W
Esperance 137 33 45 S 121 55 E
Esperance B. 137 33 48 S 121 55 E
Esperantinópolis 170 4 53 S 44 53W
Esperanza 172 31 29 S 61 3W
Esperanza, La, Argent. 172 24 9 S 64 52W
Esperanza, La, Boliv. 174 14 20 S 62 0W
Esperanza, La, Cuba 166 22 46N 83 44W
Esperanza, La, Hond. 166 14 15N 88 10W
Espéraza 44 42 56N 2 14 E
Espevær Lt. Ho. 71 59 35N 5 7 E
Espichel, C. 57 38 22N 9 16W
Espiel 57 38 11N 5 1W
Espigão, Serra do 173 26 35 S 50 30W
Espinal 174 4 9N 74 53W
Espinazo, Sierra del = Espinhaço, Serra do 171 17 30 S 43 30W
Espinhaço, Serra do 171 17 30 S 43 30W
Espinho 56 41 1N 8 38W
Espinilho, Serra do 173 28 30 S 55 0W
Espino 174 8 34N 66 1W
Espinosa de los Monteros 56 43 5N 3 34W
Espírito Santo □ 171 20 0 S 40 45W
Espíritu Santo, B. del 165 19 15N 79 40W
Espíritu Santo, I. 164 24 30N 110 23W
Espita 165 21 1N 88 19W
Esplanada 171 11 47 S 37 57W
Espluga de Francolí 58 41 24N 1 7 E
Espuña, Sierra de 59 37 51N 1 35W
Espungabera 129 20 29 S 32 45 E
Esquel 176 42 40 S 71 20W
Esquimalt 148 48 30N 123 23W
Esquina 172 30 0 S 59 30W
Essaouira (Mogador) 118 31 32N 9 42W
Essarts, Les 42 46 47N 1 12W
Essebie 126 2 58N 30 40 E
Essen, Belg. 47 51 28N 4 28 E
Essen, Ger. 48 51 28N 6 59 E
Essendon, Mt. 137 25 0 S 120 30 E
Essequibo, R. 174 5 45N 58 50W
Essex 162 39 18N 76 29W
Essex □ 29 51 48N 0 30 E
Esslingen 49 48 43N 9 19 E
Essonne □ 43 48 30N 2 20 E
Essvik 72 62 18N 17 24 E
Estadilla 58 42 4N 0 16 E
Estados, I. de los 176 54 40 S 64 30W
Estagel 44 42 47N 2 40 E
Estância 170 11 16 S 37 26W
Estancia 161 34 50N 106 1W
Estarreja 56 40 45N 8 35W
Estats, P. d' 44 42 40N 1 40 E
Estavayer le Lac 50 46 51N 6 51 E
Estcourt 129 28 58 S 29 53 E
Este 63 45 12N 11 40 E
Esteban 56 43 33N 6 5W
Esteli 166 13 9N 86 22W
Estella 58 42 40N 2 0W
Estelline, S.D., U.S.A. 158 44 39N 96 52W
Estelline, Texas, U.S.A. 159 34 35N 100 27W
Estena, R. 57 39 23N 4 44W
Estepa 57 37 17N 4 52W
Estepona 57 36 24N 5 7W
Esterhazy 153 50 37N 102 5W
Esternay 43 48 44N 3 33 E
Esterri de Aneu 58 42 38N 1 5 E
Estevan 153 49 10N 102 59W
Estevan Group 152 53 3N 129 38W
Estherville 158 43 25N 94 50W
Estissac 43 48 16N 3 48 E
Eston, Can. 153 51 8N 108 40W
Eston, U.K. 33 54 33N 1 6W
Estonian S.S.R. □ 80 48 30N 25 30 E
Estoril 57 38 42N 9 23W
Estrada, La 56 42 43N 8 27W
Estrêla, Serra da 56 40 10N 7 45W
Estrella 59 38 25N 3 35W
Estremadura 57 39 0N 9 0W
Estremoz 57 38 51N 7 39W
Estrondo, Serra do 170 7 20 S 48 0W
Esztergom 53 47 47N 18 44 E
Et Tieta 118 29 37N 9 15W
Et Turra 90 32 39N 35 39 E
Étables-sur-Mer 42 48 38N 2 51W
Etah 95 27 35N 78 40 E
Étain 43 49 13N 5 38 E
Étalle 47 49 40N 5 36 E
Etamamu 151 50 18N 59 59W
Étampes 43 48 26N 2 10 E
Étang 43 46 52N 4 10 E
Etanga 128 17 55 S 13 00 E
Étaples 43 50 30N 1 39 E
Etawah 95 26 48N 79 6 E
Etawah, R. 157 34 20N 84 15W
Etawney L. 153 57 50N 96 50W
Etchingham 29 51 0N 0 27 E
Eteh 121 7 2N 7 28 E
Etelia 121 19 10N 0 55 E
Ethe 47 49 35N 5 35 E
Ethel Creek 136 22 55 S 120 11 E
Ethel, Oued el 118 28 31N 3 37W
Ethelbert 153 51 32N 100 25W
Ethiopia ■ 91 8 0N 40 0 E
Ethiopian Highlands 114 10 0N 37 0 E
Etive, L. 34 56 30N 5 12W
Etna, Mt. 65 37 45N 15 0 E
Etne 71 59 40N 5 56 E
Etoile 127 11 33 S 27 30 E
Etolin I. 152 56 5N 132 20W
Eton 29 51 29N 0 37W
Etoshapan 128 18 40 S 16 30 E
Etowah 157 35 20N 84 30W
Étrépagny 42 49 18N 1 36 E
Étretat 42 49 42N 0 12 E
Etroits, Les 151 47 24N 68 54W
Etropole 68 43 50N 24 0 E
Ettelbrüch 47 49 50N 6 5 E
Ettelbruck 47 49 51N 6 5 E
Etten 47 51 34N 4 38 E
Ettington 28 52 8N 1 38W
Ettlingen 49 48 58N 8 25 E
Ettrick Forest 35 55 30N 3 0W
Ettrick Water 35 55 31N 2 55W
Etuku 126 3 42 S 25 45 E
Etzatlán 164 20 48N 104 5W
Etzna 165 19 35N 90 15W
Eu 42 50 3N 1 26 E
Euboea = Évvoia 69 38 40N 23 40 E
Euchareena 141 32 57 S 149 6 E
Eucla Basin 137 31 19 S 126 9 E
Euclid 156 41 32N 81 31W
Euclides da Cunha 170 10 31 S 39 1W
Eucumbene, L. 141 36 2 S 148 40 E
Eudora 159 33 5N 91 17W
Eudunda 140 34 12 S 139 7 E
Eufaula, Ala., U.S.A. 157 31 55N 85 11W
Eufaula, Okla., U.S.A. 159 35 20N 95 33W
Eufaula, L. 159 35 15N 95 28W
Eugene 160 44 0N 123 8W
Eugenia, Punta 164 27 50N 115 5W
Eugowra 141 33 22 S 148 24 E
Eulo 139 28 10 S 145 3 E
Eumungerie 141 31 56N 148 36 E
Eunice, La., U.S.A. 159 30 35N 92 28W
Eunice, N. Mex., U.S.A. 159 32 30N 103 10W
Eupen 47 50 37N 6 3 E
Euphrates = Furat, Nahr al 92 33 30N 43 0 E
Eure □ 42 49 6N 1 0 E
Eure-et-Loir □ 42 48 22N 1 30 E
Eureka, Can. 12 80 0N 85 56W
Eureka, Calif., U.S.A. 160 40 50N 124 0W
Eureka, Kans., U.S.A. 159 37 50N 96 20W
Eureka, Mont., U.S.A. 160 48 53N 115 6W
Eureka, Nev., U.S.A. 160 39 32N 116 2W
Eureka, S.D., U.S.A. 158 45 49N 99 38W
Eureka, Utah, U.S.A. 160 40 0N 112 0W
Eureka, Mt. 137 26 35 S 121 35 E
Eurelia 140 32 33 S 138 35 E
Euroa 141 36 44 S 145 35 E
Europa, Île 125 22 20 S 40 22 E
Europa, Picos de 56 43 10N 5 0W
Europa Pt. 55 36 2N 6 32W
Europa Pt. = Europa, Pta. de 57 36 3N 5 21W
Europa, Pta. de 57 36 3N 5 21W
Europe 16 20 0N 20 0 E
Europoort 46 51 57N 4 10 E
Euskirchen 48 50 40N 6 45 E
Eustis 157 28 54N 81 36W
Eutin 48 54 7N 10 38 E
Eutsuk L. 152 53 20N 126 45W
Euxton 32 53 41N 2 42W
Eva Downs 138 18 1 S 134 52 E
Eval, Mt. 90 32 15N 35 15 E
Evanger 71 60 39N 6 7 E
Evans 158 40 25N 104 43W
Evans Head 139 29 7 S 153 27 E
Evans L. 150 50 50N 77 0W
Evans P. 158 41 0N 105 35W
Evanston, Ill., U.S.A. 156 42 0N 87 40W
Evanston, Wy., U.S.A. 160 41 10N 111 0W
Evansville, Ind., U.S.A. 156 38 0N 87 35W
Evansville, Wis., U.S.A. 158 42 47N 89 18W
Evanton 37 57 40N 4 20W
Evato 129 20 37 S 47 10 E
Évaux-les-Bains 44 46 12N 2 29 E
Eveleth 158 47 35N 92 40W
Even Yahuda 90 32 16N 34 53 E
Evensk 77 61 57N 159 14 E
Evenstad 71 61 25N 11 7 E
Everard, C. 141 37 49 S 149 17 E
Everard, L. 139 31 30 S 135 0 E
Everard Ras. 137 27 5 S 132 28 E
Evercreech 28 51 8N 2 30W
Everdale 141 31 52 S 144 46 E
Evere 47 50 52N 4 25 E
Everest, Mt. 95 28 5N 86 58 E
Everett 160 48 0N 122 10W
Evergem 47 51 7N 3 43 E
Everglades 157 26 0N 80 30W
Evergreen 157 31 28N 86 55W
Everöd 73 55 53N 14 5 E
Everson 160 48 57N 122 22W
Everton 141 36 25 S 146 33 E
Evesham 28 52 6N 1 57W
Evian-les-Bains 45 46 24N 6 35 E
Evinayong 124 1 50N 10 35 E
Évinos, R. 69 38 27N 21 40 E
Evisa 45 42 15N 8 48 E
Évora 57 38 33N 7 57W
Évora □ 57 38 33N 7 50W
Évreux 42 49 0N 1 8 E
Évritania □ 69 39 5N 21 30 E
Évron 42 48 23N 1 58W
Évros □ 68 41 10N 26 0 E
Evrótas, R. 69 36 50N 22 40 E
Évvoia 69 38 30N 24 0 E
Évvoia □ 69 38 40N 23 40 E
Ewe, L. 36 57 49N 5 38W
Ewell 29 51 20N 0 15W
Ewhurst 29 51 9N 0 25W
Ewing 158 42 18N 98 22W
Ewo 124 0 48 S 14 45 E
Exaltación 174 13 10 S 65 20W
Excelsior 139 33 6 S 149 59W
Excelsior Springs 158 39 20N 94 10W
Excideuil 44 45 20N 1 4 E
Exe, R. 30 50 38N 3 27W
Exeter, U.K. 30 50 43N 3 31W
Exeter, Calif., U.S.A. 163 36 17N 119 9W
Exeter, Nebr., U.S.A. 158 40 43N 97 30W
Exeter, N.H., U.S.A. 162 43 0N 70 58W
Exford 28 51 8N 3 39W
Exloo 46 52 53N 6 52 E
Exmes 42 48 45N 0 10 E
Exminster 30 50 40N 3 29W
Exmoor 30 51 10N 3 59W
Exmore 162 37 32N 75 50W
Exmouth, Austral. 136 22 6 S 114 0 E
Exmouth, U.K. 30 50 37N 3 26W
Exmouth G. 136 22 15 S 114 15 E
Expedition Range 138 24 30 S 149 12 E
Exton 29 52 42N 0 38W
Extremadura 57 39 30N 6 5W
Exu 171 7 31 S 39 43W
Exuma Sound 166 24 30N 76 20W
Eyam 33 53 17N 1 40W
Eyasi, L. 126 3 30 S 35 0 E
Eyawaddi Myii 98 15 50N 95 6 E
Eye, Camb., U.K. 29 52 36N 0 11W
Eye, Norfolk, U.K. 29 52 19N 1 9 E
Eye Pen. 36 58 13N 6 10W
Eyeberry L. 153 63 8N 104 43W
Eyemouth 35 55 53N 2 5W
Eygurande 44 45 40N 2 26 E
Eyhatten 47 50 43N 6 1 E
Eyisen 82 41 0N 36 50 E
Eyjafjorður 74 66 15N 18 30W
Eymet 44 44 40N 0 25 E
Eymoutiers 44 45 40N 1 45 E
Eynhallow Sd. 37 59 8N 3 7W
Eynort, L. 36 57 13N 7 18W
Eynsham 28 51 47N 1 21W
Eyrarbakki 74 63 52N 21 9W
Eyre 137 32 15 S 126 18 E
Eyre Cr. 138 26 40 S 139 0 E
Eyre, L. 133 29 30 S 137 26 E
Eyre L., (North) 139 28 30 S 137 20 E
Eyre L., (South) 139 29 18 S 137 25 E
Eyre Mts. 143 45 25 S 168 25 E
Eyre Pen. 139 33 30 S 137 17 E
Eyrecourt 39 53 12N 8 8W
Ez Zeidab 122 17 25N 33 55 E
Ez Zergoun, W. 118 32 45N 2 25 E
Ezcaray 58 42 19N 3 0W
Ezine 68 39 48N 26 12 E

F

Fabens 161 31 30N 106 8W
Fåborg 73 55 6N 10 15 E
Fabriano 63 43 20N 12 52 E
Fabrizia 65 38 29N 16 19 E
Făcăeni 70 44 32N 27 53 E
Facatativá 174 4 49N 74 22W
Facture 44 44 39N 0 58W
Fada 117 17 13N 21 34 E
Fada-n-Gourma 121 12 10N 0 30 E
Fadd 53 46 28N 18 49 E
Faddeyevski, Ostrov 77 76 0N 150 0 E
Fadhili 92 26 55N 49 10 E
Fadlab 122 17 42N 34 2 E
Faenza 63 44 17N 11 53 E
Fafa 121 15 22N 0 48 E
Fafe 56 41 27N 8 11W
Fagam 121 11 1N 10 1 E
Fågelsjö 72 61 50N 14 35 E
Fagerhult 73 57 8N 15 40 E
Fagernes 75 60 59N 9 14 E
Fagersta 72 60 1N 15 46 E
Fåglavik 73 58 6N 13 6 E
Fagnano Castello 65 39 31N 16 4 E
Fagnano, L. 176 54 30 S 68 0W
Fagnières 43 48 58N 4 20 E
Fahral 93 29 0N 59 0 E
Fahūd 93 22 18N 56 28 E
Faid 92 27 1N 42 52 E
Faido 51 46 29N 8 48 E
Fair, C. 138 12 24 S 143 16 E
Fair Hd. 38 55 14N 6 10W
Fair Isle 23 59 30N 1 40W
Fair Oaks 163 38 39N 121 16W
Fairbank 161 31 44N 110 12W
Fairbanks 147 64 59N 147 40W
Fairbourne 31 52 42N 4 3W
Fairbury 158 40 5N 97 5W
Fairfax, Okla., U.S.A. 159 36 37N 96 45W
Fairfax, Va., U.S.A. 162 38 51N 77 18W
Fairfield, Austral. 141 33 53 S 150 57 E
Fairfield, Ala., U.S.A. 157 33 30N 87 0W
Fairfield, Calif., U.S.A. 163 38 14N 122 1W
Fairfield, Conn., U.S.A. 162 41 8N 73 16W
Fairfield, Idaho, U.S.A. 160 43 27N 114 52W
Fairfield, Ill., U.S.A. 156 38 20N 88 20W
Fairfield, Iowa, U.S.A. 158 41 0N 91 58W
Fairfield, Mont., U.S.A. 160 47 40N 112 0W
Fairfield, Texas, U.S.A. 159 31 40N 96 0W
Fairford, Can. 153 51 37N 98 38W
Fairford, U.K. 28 51 42N 1 48W
Fairhope 157 30 35N 87 50W
Fairlie, N.Z. 143 44 5 S 170 49 E
Fairlie, U.K. 34 55 44N 4 52W
Fairlight 29 50 53N 0 40 E
Fairmead 163 37 5N 120 10W
Fairmont, Minn., U.S.A. 158 43 37N 94 30W
Fairmont, W. Va., U.S.A. 156 39 29N 80 10W
Fairmont Hot Springs 152 50 20N 115 56W
Fairmount 163 34 45N 118 26W

Fairplay 161 39 9N 107 0W
Fairport 156 43 8N 77 29W
Fairview, Austral. 138 15 31S 144 17E
Fairview, Can. 152 56 5N 118 25W
Fairview, N. Dak., U.S.A. 158 47 49N 104 7W
Fairview, Okla., U.S.A. 159 36 19N 98 30W
Fairview, Utah, U.S.A. 160 39 50N 111 0W
Fairweather, Mt. 147 58 55N 137 45W
Faith 158 45 2N 102 4W
Faither, The, C. 36 60 34N 1 30W
Faizabad, Afghan. 93 37 7N 70 33E
Faizabad, India 95 26 45N 82 10E
Faizpur 96 21 14N 75 49E
Fajardo 147 18 20N 65 39W
Fakenham 29 52 50N 0 51E
Fakfak 103 3 0S 132 15E
Fakiya 170 42 10N 27 4E
Fakobli 120 7 23N 7 23W
Fakse 73 55 15N 12 8E
Fakse B. 73 55 11N 12 15E
Fakse Ladeplads 73 55 16N 12 9E
Fak'u 107 42 31N 123 26E
Falaise 42 48 54N 0 12W
Falaise, Mui 100 19 6N 105 45E
Falakrón Óros 68 41 15N 23 58E
Falam 98 23 0N 93 45E
Falcarragh 38 55 8N 8 8W
Falces 58 42 24N 1 48W
Falcón □ 174 11 0N 69 50W
Falcon, C. 118 35 50N 0 50W
Falcón Dam 159 26 50N 99 20W
Falconara Marittima 63 43 37N 13 23E
Faldingworth 33 53 21N 0 22W
Faléa 120 12 16N 11 17W
Falelatai 84 13 55S 171 59W
Falenki 84 58 22N 51 35E
Faleshty 82 47 32N 27 44E
Falfurrias 159 27 8N 98 8W
Falher 152 55 44N 117 15W
Falkenberg, Ger. 48 51 34N 13 13E
Falkenberg, Sweden 73 56 54N 12 30E
Falkensee 48 52 35N 13 6E
Falkenstein 48 50 27N 12 24E
Falkirk 35 56 0N 3 47W
Falkland 35 56 15N 3 13W
Falkland Is. 176 51 30S 59 0W
Falkland Is. Dep. 13 57 0S 40 0W
Falkland Sd. 176 52 0S 60 0W
Falkonéra 69 36 50N 23 52E
Falköping 73 58 12N 13 33E
Fall Brook 161 33 25N 117 12W
Fall River 162 41 45N 71 5W
Fall River Mills 160 41 1N 121 30W
Fallbrook 163 33 23N 117 15W
Fallmore 38 54 6N 10 5W
Fallon, Mont., U.S.A. 158 46 52N 105 8W
Fallon, Nev., U.S.A. 160 39 31N 118 51W
Falls Church 162 38 53N 77 11W
Falls City, Nebr., U.S.A. 158 40 0N 95 40W
Falls City, Oreg., U.S.A. 160 44 54N 123 29W
Falmey 121 12 36N 2 51E
Falmouth, Jamaica 166 18 30N 77 40W
Falmouth, U.K. 30 50 9N 5 5W
Falmouth, Ky., U.S.A. 156 38 40N 84 20W
Falmouth, Mass., U.S.A. 162 41 34N 70 38W
Falmouth B. 30 50 7N 5 3E
False B. 128 34 15S 18 40E
False Divi Pt. 97 15 35N 80 50E
Falset 58 41 7N 0 50E
Falso, C. 166 15 12N 83 21W
Falster 73 54 45N 11 55E
Falsterbo 73 55 23N 12 50E
Falsterbokanalen 73 55 25N 12 56E
Falstone 35 55 10N 2 26W
Faluja 90 31 48N 31 37E
Falun 72 60 37N 15 37E
Famagusta 92 35 8N 33 55E
Famaka 123 11 24N 34 52E
Famatina, Sierra, de 172 29 5S 68 0W
Family L. 153 51 54N 95 27W
Famoso 163 35 37N 119 12W
Fampotabe 129 15 56S 50 8E
Fan i Madh, R. 68 41 56N 20 16E
Fana, Mali 120 13 0N 6 56W
Fana, Norway 71 60 16N 5 20E
Fanad Hd. 38 55 17N 7 40W
Fanambana 129 13 34S 50 0E
Fanárion 68 39 24N 21 47E
Fanch'ang 109 31 2N 118 13E
Fanchiat'un 107 43 42N 125 5E
Fanchih 106 39 14N 113 19E
Fandriana 129 20 14S 47 21E
Fang 100 19 55N 99 13E
Fangch'eng, Honan, China 106 33 16N 112 59E
Fangch'eng, Kwangsi-Chuang, China 108 21 46N 108 21E
Fanghsien 109 32 0N 111 0E
Fangliao 109 22 22N 130 35E
Fangshan 106 38 0N 111 16E
Fangtzu 107 36 39N 119 15E
Fannich, L. 36 57 40N 5 0W
*Fanning I. 131 3 51N 159 22W
Fanny Bay 152 49 27N 124 48W
Fanø 73 55 25N 8 25E
Fano 63 43 50N 13 0E
Fanø, I. 73 55 25N 8 25E
Fanshaw 152 57 11N 133 30W
Fao (Al Fāw) 92 30 0N 48 30E
Faqirwali 94 29 27N 73 0E
*Renamed Tubuaeran

Fara in Sabina 63 42 13N 12 44E
Farab 85 39 9N 63 36E
Faraday Seamount Group 14 50 0N 27 0W
Faradje 126 3 50N 29 45E
Farafangana 129 22 49S 47 50E
Farâfra, El Wâhât el- 122 27 15N 28 20E
Farah 93 32 20N 62 7E
Farah □ 93 32 25N 62 10E
Farahalana 129 14 26S 50 10E
Faraid, Gebel 122 23 33N 35 19E
Faraid Hd. 37 58 35N 4 48W
Faramana 120 11 56N 4 45W
Faranah 120 10 3N 10 45W
Farasān, Jazā'ir 91 16 45N 41 55E
Farasan Kebir 91 16 40N 42 0E
Faratsiho 129 19 24S 46 57E
Fardes, R. 59 37 25N 3 10W
Fareham 28 50 52N 1 11W
Farewell 147 62 30N 154 0W
Farewell, C. 143 40 29S 172 43E
Farewell C. = Farvel, K. 12 59 48N 43 55W
Farewell Spit 143 40 35S 173 0E
Farfán 174 0 16N 76 41W
Fargo 158 47 0N 97 0W
Faria, R. 90 32 12N 35 27E
Faribault 158 44 15N 93 19W
Faridkot 94 30 44N 74 45E
Faridpur, Bangla. 98 23 15N 90 0E
Faridpur, India 95 18 14N 79 34E
Farila 72 61 48N 15 50E
Färila 72 61 48N 15 50E
Farim 120 12 27N 15 17W
Farimān 93 35 40N 60 0E
Farina 139 30 3S 138 15E
Faringdon 28 51 39N 1 34W
Faringe 72 59 55N 18 7E
Farinha, R. 170 6 15S 47 30W
Färjestaden 73 56 38N 16 25E
Farmakonisi 69 37 17N 27 8E
Farmerville 159 32 48N 92 23W
Farmingdale 162 40 12N 74 10W
Farmington, Calif., U.S.A. 163 37 56N 121 0W
Farmington, N. Mex., U.S.A. 161 36 45N 108 28W
Farmington, N.H., U.S.A. 162 43 25N 71 3W
Farmington, Utah, U.S.A. 160 41 0N 111 58W
Farmington, R. 162 41 51N 72 38W
Farmville 156 37 19N 78 22W
Farnborough 29 51 17N 0 46W
Farne Is. 35 55 38N 1 37W
Farnham 29 51 13N 0 49W
Farnham, Mt. 152 45 20N 72 55W
Farnworth 32 53 33N 2 24W
Faro, Brazil 175 2 0S 56 45W
Faro, Port. 57 37 2N 7 55W
Fårö 75 58 0N 19 10E
Faro □ 57 37 12N 8 10W
Faroe Is. 16 62 0N 7 0W
Farquhar, C. 137 23 38S 113 36E
Farquhar, Mt. 136 22 18S 116 53E
Farr 37 57 21N 4 13W
Farranfore 39 52 10N 9 32W
Farrars, Cr. 138 25 35S 140 43E
Farrashband 93 28 57N 52 5E
Farrell 156 41 13N 80 29W
Farrell Flat 140 33 48S 138 48E
Farrukhabad 95 27 30N 79 32E
Fars □ 93 29 30N 55 0E
Fársala 68 39 17N 22 23E
Farsø 73 56 46N 9 19E
Farsö 73 56 48N 9 20E
Farstrup 73 56 59N 9 28E
Farsund 71 58 5N 6 55E
Fartura, Serra da 173 26 21S 52 52W
Faru 121 12 48N 6 12E
Farum 73 55 49N 12 21E
Farvel, Kap 12 59 48N 43 55W
Farwell 159 34 25N 103 0W
Faryab 93 28 7N 57 14E
Fasa 93 29 0N 53 32E
Fasag 36 57 33N 5 32W
Fasano 65 40 50N 17 20E
Fashoda 123 9 50N 32 2E
Faskari 79 11 42N 6 58E
Faslane 34 56 3N 4 49W
Fastnet Rock 39 51 22N 9 37W
Fastov 80 50 7N 29 57E
Fatehgarh 95 27 25N 79 35E
Fatehpur, Raj., India 94 28 0N 75 4E
Fatehpur, Ut. P., India 95 27 8N 81 7E
Fatick 120 14 19N 16 27W
Fatima 151 47 24N 61 53W
Fátima 57 39 37N 8 39W
Fatoya 120 11 37N 9 10W
Faucilles, Monts 43 48 5N 5 50E
Fauldhouse 35 55 50N 3 44W
Faulkton 158 45 4N 99 8W
Faulquemont 43 49 3N 6 36E
Fauquembergues 43 50 36N 2 5E
Faure I. 137 25 52S 113 50E
Fauresmith 128 29 44S 25 17E
Fauske 74 67 17N 15 25E
Fauvillers 47 49 51N 5 40E
Faux-Cap 129 25 33S 45 32E
Favara 64 37 19N 13 39E
Faversham 29 51 18N 0 54E
Favignana 64 37 56N 12 18E
Favone 45 41 47N 9 26E

Favourable Lake 150 52 50N 93 39W
Fawley 28 50 49N 1 20W
Fawn, R. 150 52 22N 88 20W
Fawnskin 163 34 16N 116 56W
Faxaflói 74 64 29N 23 0W
Faxälven 72 63 13N 17 13E
Faya = Largeau 117 17 58N 19 6E
Fayence 45 43 38N 6 42E
Fayette, Ala., U.S.A. 157 33 40N 87 50W
Fayette, La., U.S.A. 156 40 22N 86 52W
Fayette, Mo., U.S.A. 158 39 10N 92 40W
Fayetteville, Ark., U.S.A. 159 36 0N 94 5W
Fayetteville, N.C., U.S.A. 157 35 0N 78 58W
Fayetteville, Tenn., U.S.A. 157 35 0N 86 30W
Fayón 58 41 15N 0 20E
Fazeley 28 52 36N 1 42W
Fazenda Nova 171 16 11S 50 48W
Fazilka 94 30 27N 74 2E
Fazilpur 94 29 18N 70 29E
F'Derik 116 22 40N 12 45W
Fé, La 166 22 2N 84 15W
Feakle 39 52 56N 8 41W
Feale, R. 39 52 26N 9 28W
Fear, C. 157 33 45N 78 0W
Fearn 37 57 47N 4 0W
Fearnan 37 56 34N 4 6W
Feather, R. 160 39 30N 121 20W
Featherston 142 41 6S 175 20E
Featherstone 127 18 42S 30 55E
Fécamp 42 49 45N 0 22E
Fedala = Mohammeda 118 33 44N 7 21W
Fedamore 39 52 33N 8 36W
Federación 172 31 0S 57 55W
Federalsburg 162 38 42N 75 47W
Fedjadj, Chott el 119 33 52N 9 14E
Fedje 71 60 47N 4 43E
Fedorovka 84 53 38N 62 42E
Feeagh L. 38 53 56N 9 35W
Feeny 38 54 54N 7 0W
Fehérgyarmat 53 48 0N 22 30E
Fehmarn 48 54 26N 11 10E
Fehmarn Bælt 73 54 35N 11 20E
Feihsiang 106 36 32N 114 47E
Feihsien 107 35 12N 118 0E
Feilding 142 40 13S 175 35E
*Feira 65 15 35S 30 16E
Feira de Santana 171 12 15S 38 57W
Fejér □ 53 47 9N 18 30E
Fejø 73 54 55N 11 30E
Felanitx 59 39 27N 3 7E
Feldbach 52 46 57N 15 52E
Feldberg 48 53 20N 13 26E
Feldberg, mt. 49 47 51N 7 58E
Feldis 51 46 48N 9 26E
Feldkirch 52 47 15N 9 37E
Feldkirchen 52 46 44N 14 6E
Felhit 123 16 40N 38 1E
Felipe Carrillo Puerto 165 19 38N 88 3W
Felixlândia 171 18 47S 44 55W
Felixstowe 29 51 58N 1 22W
Felletin 44 45 53N 2 11E
Felpham 29 50 47N 0 38W
Felton, U.K. 35 55 18N 1 42W
Felton, U.S.A. 163 37 3N 122 4W
Feltre 63 46 1N 11 55E
Feltwell 29 52 29N 0 32E
Femø 73 54 58N 11 53E
Femunden 71 62 10N 11 53E
Fen Ho, R. 106 35 36N 110 42E
Fench'ing 108 24 35N 99 54E
Fénérive 129 17 22S 49 25E
Fenerwa 123 13 5N 39 3E
Fengári 68 40 25N 25 32E
Fengchen 106 40 30N 113 0E
Fengch'eng, Kiangsi, China 109 28 10N 115 43E
Fengch'eng, Liaoning, China 107 40 30N 124 2E
Fengchieh 108 31 3N 109 28E
Fengch'iu 106 35 2N 114 24E
Fenghsiang 106 34 26N 107 18E
Fenghsien, Kiangsu, China 106 34 42N 116 34E
Fenghsien, Shanghai, China 109 30 55N 121 27E
Fenghsien, Shensi, China 106 33 56N 106 41E
Fenghsin 109 28 42N 115 23E
Fenghua 109 29 40N 121 24E
Fenghuang 108 27 58N 109 19E
Fenghuangtsui 106 33 30N 109 27E
Fengi 108 25 35N 100 18E
Fengjun 107 39 51N 118 8E
Fengk'ai 109 23 26N 111 30E
Fengkang 108 27 58N 107 47E
Fengloho 109 31 29N 112 29E
Fengning 106 41 12N 116 32E
Fengshan, Hopei, China 107 41 13N 117 6E
Fengshan, Kwangsi-Chuang, China 108 24 32N 107 3E
Fengt'ai, Anhwei, China 109 32 44N 116 43E
Fengt'ai, Peip'ing, China 106 39 51N 116 17E
Fengteng 106 36 25N 114 14E
Fengtu 108 29 58N 107 59E
Fengyuang 109 32 52N 117 32E
Fenhsi 106 36 38N 111 31E
Feni 109 27 48N 114 41E
Feni Is. 135 4 0S 153 40E
Fenit 39 52 17N 9 51W
*Renamed Luangwa

Fennagh 39 52 42N 6 50W
Fennimore 158 42 58N 90 41W
Fenny 98 22 55N 91 32E
Fenny Bentley 33 53 4N 1 43W
Fenny Compton 28 52 9N 1 20W
Fenny Stratford 29 51 59N 0 42W
Feno, C. de 45 41 58N 8 33E
Fenoarivo 129 18 26S 46 34E
Fens, The 29 52 45N 0 2E
Fenton, Can. 153 53 0N 105 35W
Fenton, U.S.A. 156 42 47N 83 44W
Fenwick 34 55 38N 4 25W
Fenyang 106 37 19N 111 46E
Feodosiya 82 45 2N 35 28E
Fer, C. de 119 37 3N 7 10E
Ferbane 39 53 17N 7 50W
Ferdows 93 33 58N 58 2E
Fère-Champenoise 43 48 45N 4 0E
Fère-en-Tardenois 43 49 10N 3 30E
Fère, La 43 49 40N 3 20E
Ferentino 64 41 42N 13 14E
Ferfer 91 5 18N 45 20E
Fergana 85 40 23N 71 46E
Ferganskaya Dolina 85 40 50N 71 30E
Ferganskiy Khrebet 85 41 0N 73 50E
Fergus 150 43 43N 80 24W
Fergus Falls 158 46 25N 96 0W
Fergus, R. 39 52 45N 9 0W
Ferguson 150 47 50N 73 30W
Fergusson I. 135 9 30S 150 45E
Fériana 119 34 59N 8 33E
Feričanci 66 45 32N 18 0E
Ferkane 119 34 37N 7 26E
Ferkéssédougou 120 9 35N 5 6W
Ferlach 52 46 32N 14 18E
Ferland 150 50 19N 88 27W
Ferlo, Vallée du 120 15 15N 14 15W
Fermanagh (□) 38 54 21N 7 40W
Fermo 63 43 10N 13 42E
Fermoselle 56 41 19N 6 27W
Fermoy 39 52 4N 8 18W
Fernagh 38 54 2N 7 51W
Fernan Nuñ,z 57 37 40N 4 44W
Fernández 172 27 55S 63 50W
Fernandina 157 30 40N 81 30W
Fernando de Noronha, I. 170 4 0S 33 10W
Fernando do Noronho □ 170 4 0S 33 10W
Fernando Póo = Bioko 113 3 30N 8 40E
Fernandópolis 171 20 16S 50 14W
Ferndale, Calif., U.S.A. 160 40 37N 124 12W
Ferndale, Wash., U.S.A. 160 48 51N 122 41W
Ferness 37 57 28N 3 44W
Fernhurst 29 51 3N 0 43W
Fernie 152 49 30N 115 5W
Fernilea 36 57 18N 6 24W
Fernlees 138 23 51S 148 7E
Fernley 160 39 42N 119 20W
Feroke 97 11 9N 75 46E
Ferozepore 94 30 55N 74 40E
Férrai 68 40 53N 26 10E
Ferrandina 65 40 30N 16 28E
Ferrara 63 44 50N 11 36E
Ferrato, C. 64 39 18N 9 39E
Ferreira do Alentejo 57 38 4N 8 6W
Ferreñafe 174 6 35S 79 50W
Ferret, C. 44 44 38N 1 15W
Ferrette 43 47 30N 7 20E
Ferriday 159 31 35N 91 33W
Ferrières 43 48 5N 2 48E
Ferriete 62 44 40N 9 30E
Ferrol 56 43 29N 8 15W
Ferron 160 39 3N 111 3W
Ferros 171 19 14S 43 2W
Ferryhill 33 54 42N 1 32W
Ferryland 151 47 2N 52 53W
Ferté Bernard, La 42 48 10N 0 40E
Ferté, La 43 48 57N 3 6E
Ferté-Mace, La 42 48 35N 0 21W
Ferté-St. Aubin, La 43 47 42N 1 57E
Ferté-Vidame, La 42 48 37N 0 53E
Fertile 158 47 37N 96 18W
Fertília 64 40 37N 8 13E
Fertöszentmiklós 53 47 35N 16 53E
Fès 118 34 0N 5 0W
Feschaux 47 50 9N 4 54E
Feshi 124 6 0S 18 10E
Fessenden 158 47 42N 99 44W
Fet 71 59 57N 11 12E
Feteşti 70 44 22N 27 51E
Fethaland, Pt. 36 60 39N 1 20W
Fethard 39 52 29N 7 42W
Fethiye 92 36 36N 29 10E
Fetlar, I. 36 60 36N 0 52W
Fettercairn 37 56 50N 2 33W
Feuerthalen 51 47 37N 8 38E
Feurs 45 45 45N 4 13E
Fezzan 117 27 0N 15 0E
Ffestiniog 31 52 58N 3 56W
Fforest Fawr, mt. 31 51 52N 3 35W
Fiambalá 172 27 45S 67 37W
Fianarantsoa 125 21 20S 46 45E
Fianarantsoa □ 129 19 30S 47 0E
Fianga 117 9 55N 15 20E
Fibiş 66 45 57N 21 26E
Fichot, I. 151 51 12N 55 40W
Fichtelgebirge 49 50 10N 12 0E
Ficksburg 129 28 51S 27 53E
Fiddown 39 52 20N 7 20W
Fidenza 62 44 51N 10 3E
Field 150 46 31N 80 1W

Field I **Fort Garland**

Field I. 136 12 5 S 132 23 E
Field, R. 138 23 48 S 138 0 E
Fields Finds 137 29 0 S 117 10 E
Fierenana 129 18 29 S 48 24 E
Fiéri 68 40 43N 19 33 E
Fiesch 50 46 25N 8 12 E
Fife □ 35 56 13N 3 2W
Fife Ness 35 56 17N 2 35W
Fifth Cataract 123 18 15N 33 50 E
Figeac 44 44 37N 2 2 E
Figline Valdarno 63 43 37N 11 28 E
Figtree 127 20 22 S 28 20 E
Figueira da Foz 56 40 7N 8 54W
Figueiró dos Vinhos 56 39 55N 8 16W
Figueras 58 42 18N 2 58 E
Figuig 118 32 5N 1 11W
Fihaonana 129 18 36 S 47 12 E
Fiherenana, R. 129 22 50 S 44 0 E
Fiji ■ 142 17 20 S 179 0 E
Fiji Is. 130 17 20 S 179 0 E
Fik 90 32 46N 35 41 E
Fika 121 11 15N 11 13 E
Filabres, Sierra de los 59 37 13N 2 20W
Filadélfia, Brazil 170 7 21 S 47 30W
Filadélfia, Italy 65 38 47N 16 17 E
Filadelfia 172 22 25 S 60 0W
Fil'akovo 53 48 17N 19 50 E
Filby 29 52 40N 1 39 E
Filchner Ice Shelf 13 78 0 S 60 0W
Filer 160 42 30N 114 35W
Filey 33 54 13N 0 18W
Filey B. 33 54 12N 0 15W
Filiaşi 70 44 32N 23 31 E
Filiátes 68 39 38N 20 16 E
Filiatrá 69 37 9N 21 35 E
Filicudi, I. 65 38 35N 14 33 E
Filiouri, R. 68 41 15N 25 40 E
Filipstad 72 59 43N 14 9 E
Filisur 51 46 41N 9 40 E
Fillmore, Can. 153 49 50N 103 25W
Fillmore, U.S.A. 163 34 23N 118 58W
Filottrano 63 43 28N 13 20 E
Filton 28 51 29N 2 34 E
Filyos 82 41 34N 32 4 E
Filyos çayi 92 41 35N 32 10 E
Finale Ligure 62 44 10N 8 21 E
Finale nell' Emília 63 44 50N 11 18 E
Fiñana 59 37 10N 2 50W
Fincham 29 52 38N 0 30 E
Findhorn 37 57 39N 3 36W
Findhorn, R. 37 57 38N 3 38W
Findlay 156 41 0N 83 41W
Findon 29 50 53N 0 24W
Finea 38 53 46N 7 23W
Finedon 29 52 20N 0 40W
Finger L. 153 53 9N 93 30W
Fingest 29 51 35N 0 52W
Finglas 38 53 22N 6 18W
Fingõe 127 15 12 S 31 50 E
Finike 92 36 21N 30 10 E
Finistère □ 42 48 20N 4 0W
Finisterre 56 42 54N 9 16W
Finisterre, C. 56 42 50N 9 19W
Finisterre Ra. 135 6 0 S 146 30 E
Finke 138 25 34 S 134 35 E
Finke, R. 138 24 54 S 134 16 E
Finland ■ 78 70 0N 27 0 E
Finland, G. of 78 60 0N 26 0 E
Finlay, R. 152 55 50N 125 10W
Finley, Austral. 141 35 38 S 145 35 E
Finley, U.S.A. 158 47 35N 97 50W
Finn, R. 38 54 50N 7 55W
Finnart 34 56 7N 4 48W
Finnigan, Mt. 138 15 49 S 145 17 E
Finniss 140 35 24 S 138 48 E
Finniss, C. 139 33 38 S 134 51 E
Finnmark fylke □ 74 69 30N 25 0 E
Finschhafen 135 6 33 S 147 50 E
Finse 71 60 36N 7 30 E
Finspång 73 58 45N 15 43 E
Finsta 72 59 45N 18 34 E
Finsteraarhorn 50 46 31N 8 10 E
Finsterwalde 48 51 37N 13 42 E
Finsterwolde 46 53 12N 7 6 E
Finstown 37 59 0N 3 8W
Fintona 38 54 30N 7 20W
Fintown 38 54 52N 8 8W
Finucanel I. 132 20 19 S 118 30 E
Finvoy 38 55 0N 6 29W
Fionn L. 36 57 46N 5 30W
Fionnphort 34 56 19N 6 23W
Fiora, R. 63 42 25N 11 35 E
Fiordland National Park 143 45 0 S 167 50 E
Fiorenzuola d'Arda 62 44 56N 9 54 E
Fiq 90 32 46N 35 41 E
Fire River 150 48 47N 83 36W
Firebag, R. 153 57 45N 111 21W
Firebaugh 163 36 52N 120 27W
Firedrake L. 153 61 25N 104 30W
Firenze 63 43 47N 11 15 E
Firkessédougou 120 9 35N 5 6W
Firmi 44 44 32N 2 19 E
Firminy 45 45 23N 4 18 E
Firoz Kohi 93 34 45N 63 0 E
Firozabad 95 27 10N 78 25 E
First Cataract 122 24 1N 32 51 E
Fīrūzābād 93 28 52N 52 35 E
Firuzkuh 93 35 50N 52 40 E
Firvale 152 52 27N 126 13W
Fish, R. 128 27 40 S 17 30 E
Fisher 137 30 30 S 131 0 E
Fisher B. 153 51 35N 97 13W
Fishguard 31 51 59N 4 59W
Fishguard B. 31 52 2N 4 58W
Fishing L. 153 52 10N 95 24W
Fishkill 162 41 32N 73 53W
Fishtoft 33 52 27N 0 2 E
Fishtown 120 4 24N 7 45 E
Fiskivötn 74 64 50N 20 45W
Fiskum 71 59 42N 9 46 E
Fismes 43 49 20N 3 40 E
Fister 71 59 10N 6 5 E
Fitchburg 162 42 35N 71 47W
Fitero 58 42 4N 1 52W
Fitful Hd. 36 59 54N 1 20W
Fitjar 71 59 55N 5 17 E
Fitri, L. 124 12 50N 17 28 E
Fitz Roy 176 47 10 S 67 0W
Fitzgerald, Can. 152 59 51N 111 36W
Fitzgerald, U.S.A. 157 31 45N 83 10W
Fitzmaurice, R. 136 14 50 S 129 50 E
Fitzpatrick 150 47 29N 72 46W
Fitzroy Crossing 136 18 9 S 125 38 E
Fitzroy, R., Queens., Austral. 138 23 32 S 150 52 E
Fitzroy, R., W. Australia, Austral. 136 17 25 S 124 0 E
Fiume = Rijeka 63 45 20N 14 21 E
Fiumefreddo Brúzio 65 39 14N 16 4 E
Five Alley 39 53 9N 7 51W
Five Points 163 36 26N 120 6W
Fivemiletown 38 54 23N 7 20W
Fizi 126 4 17 S 28 55 E
Fjæra 71 59 52N 6 22 E
Fjaere 71 58 23N 8 36 E
Fjellerup 73 56 29N 10 34 E
Fjerritslev 73 57 5N 9 15 E
Fkih ben Salah 118 32 45N 6 45W
Fla 71 60 25N 9 26 E
Flå 71 63 13N 10 18 E
Flagler 158 39 20N 103 4W
Flagstaff 161 35 10N 111 40W
Flagstone 152 49 4N 115 10W
Flaherty, I. 150 56 15N 79 15W
Flåm 75 60 52N 7 14 E
Flambeau, R. 158 45 40N 90 50W
Flamborough 33 54 7N 0 7W
Flamborough Hd. 33 54 8N 0 4W
Flaming Gorge Dam 160 40 50N 109 25W
Flaming Gorge L. 160 41 15N 109 30W
Flamingo, Teluk 103 5 30 S 138 0 E
Flanders = Flandres 47 51 10N 3 15 E
Flandre Occidental □ 47 51 0N 3 0 E
Flandre Orientale □ 47 51 0N 4 0 E
Flandreau 158 44 5N 96 38W
Flandres, Plaines des 47 51 10N 3 15 E
Flannan Is. 23 58 9N 7 52W
Flaren L. 73 57 2N 14 5 E
Flåsjön 74 64 5N 15 50 E
Flat, R. 152 61 51N 128 0W
Flat River 159 37 50N 90 30W
Flatey, Barðastrandarsýsla, Iceland 74 66 10N 17 52W
Flatey, Suður-þingeyjarsýsla, Iceland 74 65 22N 22 56W
Flathead L. 160 47 50N 114 0W
Flattery, C., Austral. 138 14 58 S 145 21 E
Flattery, C., U.S.A. 160 48 21N 124 43W
Flavy-le-Martel 43 49 43N 3 12 E
Flawil 51 47 26N 9 11 E
Flaxton 158 48 52N 102 24W
Flèche, La 42 47 42N 0 5W
Fleeming, C. 136 11 15 S 131 21 E
Fleet 29 51 16N 0 50W
Fleetwood, U.K. 32 53 55N 3 1W
Fleetwood, U.S.A. 162 40 27N 75 49W
Flekkefjord 71 58 18N 6 39 E
Flémalle 47 50 36N 5 28 E
Flensborg Fjord 73 54 50N 9 40 E
Flensburg 48 54 46N 9 28 E
Flers 42 48 47N 0 33W
Flesberg 71 59 51N 9 22 E
Fletton 29 52 34N 0 13W
Fleurance 44 43 52N 0 40 E
Fleurier 50 46 54N 6 35 E
Fleurus 47 50 29N 4 32 E
Flickerbäcken 72 61 47N 12 34 E
Flims 51 46 50N 9 17 E
Flin Flon 153 54 46N 101 53W
Flinders B. 137 34 19 S 115 9 E
Flinders Group, Is. 138 14 11 S 144 15 E
Flinders I. 138 40 0 S 148 0 E
Flinders, R. 138 17 36 S 140 36 E
Flinders Ranges 140 31 30 S 138 30 E
Flinders Reefs 138 17 37 S 148 31 E
Flint 156 43 5N 83 19W
Flint (□) 26 53 15N 3 12W
Flint, I. 131 11 26 S 151 48W
Flint, R. 157 31 20N 84 10W
Flinton 139 27 55 S 149 32 E
Fliseryd 73 57 6N 16 15 E
Flitwick 29 51 59N 0 30W
Flix 58 41 14N 0 32 E
Flixecourt 43 50 0N 2 5 E
Flobecq 47 50 44N 3 45 E
Floda 72 60 30N 14 53 E
Flodden 35 55 37N 2 8W
Floodwood 158 46 55N 92 55W
Flora, N. Tröndelag, Norway 71 63 27N 11 22 E
Flora, Sogn & Fjordane, Norway 71 61 35N 5 1 E
Flora, U.S.A. 156 38 40N 88 30W
Florac 44 44 20N 3 37 E
Florala 157 31 0N 86 20W
Florânia 170 6 8 S 36 49W
Floreffe 47 50 26N 4 46 E
Florence, Ala., U.S.A. 157 34 50N 87 50W
Florence, Ariz., U.S.A. 161 33 0N 111 25W
Florence, Colo., U.S.A. 158 38 26N 105 0W
Florence, Oreg., U.S.A. 160 44 0N 124 3W
Florence, S.C., U.S.A. 157 34 5N 79 50W
Florence = Firenze 63 43 47N 11 15 E
Florence, L. 139 28 53 S 138 9 E
Florennes 47 50 15N 4 35 E
Florensac 44 43 23N 3 28 E
Florenville 47 49 40N 5 19 E
Flores, Azores 16 39 13N 31 13W
Flores, Brazil 170 7 51 S 37 59W
Flores, Guat. 166 16 50N 89 40W
Flores I. 152 49 20N 126 10W
Flores, I. 103 8 35 S 121 0 E
Flores Sea 102 6 30 S 124 0 E
Floresta 170 9 46 S 37 26W
Floresville 159 29 10N 98 10W
Floriano 170 6 50 S 43 0W
Florianópolis 173 27 30 S 48 30W
Florida, Cuba 166 21 32N 78 14W
Florida, Uruguay 173 34 7 S 56 10W
Florida □ 157 28 30N 82 0W
Florida B. 167 25 0N 81 20W
Florida Keys 167 25 0N 80 40W
Florida, Strait of 167 25 0N 80 0W
Florídia 65 37 6N 15 9 E
Flórina 68 40 48N 21 26 E
Flórina □ 68 40 45N 21 20 E
Florningen 72 61 50N 12 16 E
Florø 71 61 35N 5 1 E
Flosta 71 58 32N 8 56 E
Flower's Cove 151 51 14N 56 46W
Floydada 159 33 58N 101 18W
Flüela Pass 51 46 45N 9 57 E
Fluk 103 1 42 S 127 38 E
Flumen, R. 58 41 50N 0 25W
Flumendosa, R. 64 39 30N 9 25 E
Fluminimaggiore 64 39 25N 8 30 E
Flums 51 47 6N 9 21 E
Flushing = Vlissingen 47 51 26N 3 34 E
Fluviá, R. 58 42 12N 3 7 E
Fly, R. 135 8 25 S 143 0 E
Foam Lake 153 51 40N 103 32W
Foča 66 43 31N 18 47 E
Focşani 70 45 41N 27 15 E
Fofo Fofo 138 8 9 S 147 6 E
Foggaret el Arab 118 27 3N 2 59 E
Foggaret ez Zoua 118 27 20N 3 0 E
Fóggia 65 41 28N 15 31 E
Foggo 121 11 21N 9 57 E
Foglia, R. 63 43 50N 12 32 E
Fogo 151 49 43N 54 17W
Fogo I. 151 49 40N 54 5W
Fohnsdorf 52 47 12N 14 40 E
Föhr 48 54 40N 8 30 E
Foia, Cerro da 57 37 19N 8 10W
Foix 44 42 58N 1 38 E
Fojnica 66 43 59N 17 51 E
Fokang 109 23 52N 113 31 E
Fokino 80 53 30N 34 10 E
Fokis □ 69 38 30N 22 15 E
Fokstua 71 62 8N 9 16 E
Folda, Nord-Trøndelag, Norway 74 64 41N 10 50 E
Folda, Nordland, Norway 74 67 38N 14 50 E
Földeák 53 46 19N 20 30 E
Folette, La 157 36 23N 84 9W
Foley 128 30 25N 87 40W
Foleyet 150 48 15N 82 25W
Folgefonni 71 60 23N 6 34 E
Foligno 63 42 58N 12 40 E
Folkestone 29 51 5N 1 11 E
Folkston 157 30 55N 82 0W
Follett 159 36 30N 100 12W
Follónica 62 42 55N 10 45 E
Folsom 160 38 41N 121 7W
Fond-du-Lac 153 59 19N 107 12W
Fond du lac 158 43 46N 88 26W
Fond-du-Lac, R. 153 59 17N 106 0W
Fondak 118 35 34N 5 35W
Fondi 64 41 21N 13 25 E
Fonfría 56 41 37N 6 9W
Fongen 71 63 11N 11 38 E
Fonni 64 40 5N 9 16 E
Fonsagrada 56 43 8N 7 4W
Fonseca, G. de 166 13 10N 87 40W
Fontaine-Française 43 47 32N 5 21 E
Fontainebleau 43 48 24N 2 40 E
Fontas, R. 152 58 14N 121 48W
Fonte Boa 174 2 25 S 66 0W
Fontem 121 5 32N 9 52 E
Fontenay-le-Comte 44 46 28N 0 48W
Fontenelle 151 48 54N 64 33W
Fontur 74 66 23N 14 32W
Fonyód 53 46 44N 17 33 E
Foochow = Fuchou 109 26 5N 119 18 E
Foping 106 33 22N 108 19 E
Foppiano 62 46 21N 8 24 E
Föra 73 57 1N 16 51 E
Forbach 43 49 10N 6 52 E
Forbes 141 33 22 S 148 0 E
Forbesganj 95 26 17N 87 18 E
Forcados 121 5 26N 5 26 E
Forcados, R. 121 5 25N 5 20 E
Forcall, R. 58 40 40N 0 12W
Forcalquier 45 43 58N 5 47 E
Forchheim 49 49 42N 11 4 E
Forclaz, Col de la 50 46 3N 7 1 E
Ford City 163 35 9N 119 27W
Førde 71 61 27N 5 53 E
Fordingbridge 28 50 56N 1 48W
Fordongianus 44 40 0N 8 50 E
Fords Bridge 139 29 41 S 145 29 E
Fordyce 159 33 50N 92 20W
Forécariah 120 9 20N 13 10W
Forel 12 66 52N 36 55W
Foremost 152 49 26N 111 25W
Forenza 65 40 50N 15 50 E
Forest, Belg. 47 50 49N 4 20 E
Forest, U.S.A. 159 32 21N 89 27W
Forest City, Ark., U.S.A. 159 35 0N 90 50W
Forest City, Iowa, U.S.A. 158 43 12N 93 39W
Forest City, N.C., U.S.A. 157 35 23N 81 50W
Forest Grove 160 45 31N 123 4W
Forest Lawn 152 51 4N 114 0W
Forest Row 29 51 6N 0 3 E
Forestburg 152 52 35N 112 1W
Forestier Pen. 138 43 0 S 148 0 E
Forestville, Can. 151 48 48N 69 20W
Forestville, U.S.A. 156 44 41N 87 29W
Forez, Mts. du 44 45 40N 3 50 E
Forfar 37 56 40N 2 53W
Forges-les-Eaux 43 49 37N 1 30 E
Forget 150 49 40N 102 50W
Forked River 162 39 50N 74 12W
Forks 160 47 56N 124 23W
Forksville 162 41 29N 76 35W
Forlì 63 44 14N 12 2 E
Forman 158 46 9N 97 43W
Formazza 62 46 23N 8 26 E
Formby Pt. 32 53 33N 3 7W
Formentera, I. 59 38 40N 1 30 E
Formentor, C. de 58 39 58N 3 13 E
Fórmia 64 41 15N 13 34 E
Formiga 171 20 27 S 45 25W
Formigine 62 44 37N 10 51 E
Formiguères 44 42 37N 2 5 E
Formosa, Argent. 172 26 15 S 58 10W
Formosa, Brazil 171 15 32 S 47 20W
Formosa = Taiwan ■ 109 24 0N 121 0 E
Formosa □ 172 26 5 S 58 10W
Formosa Bay 126 2 40 S 40 20 E
Formosa Strait 109 24 40N 120 0 E
Formoso, R. 171 10 34 S 49 56W
Fornaes, C. 73 56 27N 10 58 E
Fornells 58 40 4N 4 4 E
Fornos de Algodres 56 40 38N 7 32W
Fornovo di Taro 62 44 42N 10 7 E
Forres 37 57 37N 3 38W
Forrest, Vic., Austral. 140 38 22 S 143 40 E
Forrest, W. Australia, Austral. 137 30 51 S 128 6 E
Forrest Lakes 137 29 12 S 128 46 E
Forrest, Mt. 137 24 48 S 127 45 E
Forrières 47 50 8N 5 17 E
Fors, Jämtland, Sweden 72 63 0N 16 40 E
Fors, Kopparberg, Sweden 72 60 14N 16 20 E
Forsa 72 61 44N 16 55 E
Forsand 71 58 54N 6 5 E
Forsayth 138 18 33 S 143 34 E
Forsbacka 72 60 39N 16 54 E
Forse 72 63 8N 17 1 E
Forserum 73 57 42N 14 30 E
Forshaga 72 59 33N 13 29 E
Forshem 73 58 38N 13 30 E
Forsmo 72 63 16N 17 11 E
Forst 48 51 43N 14 37 E
Forster 141 32 12 S 152 31 E
Forsyth, Ga., U.S.A. 157 33 4N 83 55W
Forsyth, Mont., U.S.A. 160 46 14N 106 37W
Forsyth I. 143 40 58 S 174 5 E
Fort Albany 150 52 15N 81 35W
Fort Ann 162 43 25N 73 30W
Fort Apache 161 33 50N 110 0W
Fort Archambault = Sarh 117 9 5N 18 23 E
Fort Assiniboine 152 54 20N 114 45W
Fort Augustus 37 57 9N 4 40W
Fort Babine 152 55 22N 126 37W
Fort Beaufort 128 32 46 S 26 40 E
Fort Benton 160 47 50N 110 40W
Fort Bragg 160 39 28N 123 50W
Fort Bretonnet = Bousso 117 10 34N 16 52 E
Fort Bridger 160 41 22N 110 20W
Fort Charlet = Djanet 121 24 35N 9 32 E
Fort Chimo 149 58 6N 68 25W
Fort Chipewyan 153 58 42N 111 8W
Fort Collins 158 40 30N 105 4W
Fort Coulonge 150 45 50N 76 45W
Fort Crampel = Kaga Bandoro 117 7 8N 19 18 E
Fort-Dauphin 129 25 2 S 47 0 E
Fort Davis 159 30 38N 103 53W
Fort-de-France 167 14 36N 61 2W
Fort de Polignac = Illizi 119 26 31N 8 32 E
Fort de Possel = Possel 124 5 5N 19 10 E
Fort Defiance 161 35 47N 109 4W
Fort Dodge 158 42 29N 94 10W
Fort Flatters = Bordj Omar Driss 119 27 10N 6 40 E
Fort Foureau = Kousseri 117 12 0N 14 55 E
Fort Frances 153 48 35N 93 25W
Fort Franklin 148 65 30N 123 45W
Fort Garland 161 37 28N 105 30W

Fort George Frýdek-Místek

Fort George 151 53 50N 79 0W
Fort George, R. 150 53 50N 77 0W
Fort Good-Hope 147 66 14N 128 40W
Fort Gouraud = F'Dérik 116 22 40N 12 45W
Fort Grahame 152 56 30N 124 35W
Fort Hancock 161 31 19N 105 56W
Fort Hauchuca 161 31 32N 110 30W
Fort Hertz (Putao) 99 27 28N 97 30 E
Fort Hope 150 51 30N 88 10W
Fort Irwin 163 35 16N 116 34W
Fort Jameson = Chipata 127 13 38 S 32 38 E
Fort Johnston 127 14 25 S 35 16 E
Fort Kent 151 47 12N 68 30W
Fort Klamath 160 42 45N 122 0W
Fort Lallemand 119 31 13N 6 17 E
Fort-Lamy = Ndjamena 117 12 4N 15 8 E
Fort Lapperrine = Tamanrasset 119 22 56N 5 30 E
Fort Laramie 158 42 15N 104 30W
Fort Lauderdale 157 26 10N 80 5W
Fort Liard 152 60 20N 123 30W
Fort Liberté 167 19 42N 71 51W
Fort Lupton 158 40 8N 104 48W
Fort Mackay 152 57 12N 111 41W
Fort McKenzie 151 57 20N 69 0W
Fort Macleod 152 49 45N 113 30W
Fort MacMahon 118 29 51N 1 45 E
Fort McMurray 152 56 44N 111 23W
Fort McPherson 147 67 30N 134 55W
Fort Madison 158 40 39N 91 20W
Fort Meade 157 27 45N 81 45W
Fort Miribel 118 29 31N 2 55 E
Fort Morgan 158 40 10N 103 50W
Fort Myers 157 26 30N 82 0W
Fort Nelson 152 58 50N 122 38W
Fort Nelson, R. 152 59 32N 124 0W
Fort Norman 147 64 57N 125 30W
Fort Pacot (Chirfa) 119 20 55N 12 14 E
Fort Payne 157 34 25N 85 44W
Fort Peck 160 47 1N 105 30W
Fort Peck Dam 160 48 0N 106 20W
Fort Peck Res. 160 47 40N 107 0W
Fort Pierce 158 27 29N 80 19W
Fort Pierre 158 44 25N 100 25W
Fort Pierre Bordes 118 20 0N 2 55 E
Fort Portal 126 0 40N 30 20 E
Fort Providence 152 61 21N 117 40W
Fort Qu'Appelle 153 50 45N 103 50W
Fort Randall 147 55 10N 162 48W
Fort Reliance 153 63 0N 109 20W
Fort Resolution 152 61 10N 113 40W
Fort Rixon 127 20 2 S 29 17 E
Fort Roseberry = Mansa 127 11 10 S 28 50 E
Fort Rupert (Rupert House) 150 51 30N 78 40W
Fort Saint 119 30 13N 9 31 E
Fort St. James 152 54 30N 124 10W
Fort St. John 152 56 15N 120 50W
Fort Sandeman 94 31 20N 69 25 E
Fort Saskatchewan 152 53 40N 113 15W
Fort Scott 159 38 0N 94 40W
Fort Selkirk 147 62 43N 137 22W
Fort Severn 150 56 0N 87 40W
Fort Shevchenko 83 44 30N 50 10W
Fort Sibut = Sibut 117 5 52N 19 10 E
Fort Simpson 152 61 45N 121 23W
Fort Smith, Can. 152 60 0N 111 51W
Fort Smith, U.S.A. 159 35 25N 94 25W
Fort Stanton 161 33 33N 105 36W
Fort Stockton 159 30 48N 103 2W
Fort Sumner 159 34 24N 104 8W
Fort Thomas 161 33 2N 109 59W
Fort Trinquet = Bir Mogrein 116 25 10N 11 25W
Fort Valley 157 32 33N 83 52W
Fort Vermilion 152 58 24N 116 0W
Fort Victoria 127 20 8 S 30 55 E
Ft. Walton Beach 157 30 25N 86 40W
Fort Wayne 156 41 5N 85 10W
Fort William 36 56 48N 5 8W
Fort William = Thunder Bay 150 48 20N 89 10W
Fort Worth 159 32 45N 97 25W
Fort Yates 158 46 8N 100 38W
Fort Yukon 147 66 35N 145 12W
Fortaleza 170 3 35 S 38 35W
Forte Coimbra 174 19 55 S 57 48W
Forte Rocadas 125 16 38 S 15 22 E
Forteau 151 51 28N 57 1W
Fortescue 136 21 4 S 116 4 E
Fortescue, R. 136 21 20 S 116 5 E
Forth, Firth of 35 56 5N 2 55W
Forthassa Rharbia 118 32 52N 1 11W
Forties, oilfield 19 57 40N 1 0 E
Fortín Corrales 174 22 21 S 60 35W
Fortín Guachalla 174 22 22 S 62 23W
Fortín Rojas Silva 172 22 40 S 59 3W
Fortín Siracuas 174 21 3 S 61 46W
Fortín Teniente Montania 172 22 1 S 59 45W
Fortore, R. 63 41 40N 15 0 E
Fortrose 143 46 38 S 168 45 E
Fortuna, Spain 59 38 11N 1 7W
Fortuna, Cal., U.S.A. 160 48 38N 124 8W
Fortuna, N.D., U.S.A. 158 48 55N 103 48W
Fortune Bay 151 47 30N 55 22W
Forty Mile 147 64 20N 140 30W
Forūr 93 26 20N 54 30 E
Fos 62 43 20N 4 57 E
Fos do Jordão 174 9 30 S 72 14W
Fos-sur-Mer 45 43 26N 4 56 E
Foshan 109 23 4N 113 5 E
Fossacesia 63 42 15N 14 30 E
Fossano 62 44 39N 7 40 E
Fosses-la-Ville 47 50 24N 4 41 E
Fossil 160 45 0N 120 9W
Fossilbrook 138 17 47 S 144 29 E
Fossombrone 63 43 41N 12 49 E
Fosston 158 47 33N 95 39W
Foster, R. 153 55 47N 105 49W
Fosters Ra. 138 21 35 S 133 48 E
Fostoria 156 41 8N 83 25W
Fou Chiang, R. 108 30 3N 106 21 E
Fouch'eng 106 37 52N 116 8 E
Fougamou 124 1 38 S 11 39 E
Fougères 42 48 21N 1 14W
Fouhsinshih 107 42 13N 121 51 E
Foul Pt. 97 8 35N 81 25 E
Foula, I. 23 60 10N 2 5W
Fouling 108 29 40N 107 20 E
Foulpointe 129 17 41 S 49 31 E
Foum el Alba 118 20 45N 3 0W
Foum el Kreneg 118 29 0N 0 58W
Foum Tatahouine 119 32 57N 10 29 E
Foum Zguid 118 30 2N 6 59W
Foumban 121 5 45N 10 50 E
Foundiougne 120 14 5N 16 32W
Founing 107 33 47N 119 48 E
Fountain, Colo., U.S.A. 158 38 42N 104 40W
Fountain, Utah, U.S.A. 160 39 41N 111 50W
Fountain Springs 163 35 54N 118 51W
Foup'ing 106 38 55N 114 13 E
Four Mts., Is. of the 147 52 0N 170 30W
Fourchambault 43 47 0N 3 3 E
Fourchu 151 45 43N 60 17W
Fourcroy, C. 136 11 45 S 130 2 E
Fourmies 43 50 1N 4 2 E
Fournás 69 39 3N 21 52 E
Foúrnoi 69 37 36N 26 32 E
Fours 43 46 50N 3 42 E
Foushan 106 35 58N 111 51 E
Fouta Djalon 120 11 20N 12 10W
Foux, Cap-à- 167 19 43N 73 27W
Fouyang 109 32 55N 115 52 E
Foveaux Str. 143 46 42 S 168 10 E
Fowler, Calif., U.S.A. 163 36 41N 119 41W
Fowler, Colo., U.S.A. 158 38 10N 104 0W
Fowler, Kans., U.S.A. 159 37 28N 100 7W
Fowlers B. 137 31 59 S 132 34 E
Fowlers Bay 137 32 0 S 132 29 E
Fowlerton 159 28 26N 98 50W
Fox Is. 147 52 30N 166 0W
Fox, R. 153 56 3N 93 18W
Fox Valley 153 50 30N 109 25W
Foxboro 162 42 4N 71 16W
Foxe Basin 149 68 30N 77 0W
Foxe Channel 149 66 0N 80 0W
Foxe Pen. 149 65 0N 76 0W
Foxen, L. 72 59 25N 11 55 E
Foxhol 46 53 10N 6 43 E
Foxpark 160 41 4N 106 6W
Foxton 142 40 29 S 175 18 E
Foyle, Lough 38 55 6N 7 8W
Foynes 38 52 30N 9 5W
Foz 56 43 33N 7 20W
Foz do Cunene 128 17 15 S 11 55 E
Foz do Gregório 174 6 47 S 71 0W
Foz do Iguaçu 173 25 30 S 54 30W
Frackville 162 40 46N 76 15W
Fraga 58 41 32N 0 21 E
Fraire 47 50 16N 4 31 E
Frameries 47 50 24N 3 54 E
Framlingham 29 52 14N 1 20 E
Franca 171 20 25 S 47 30W
Francavilla al Mare 63 42 25N 14 16 E
Francavilla Fontana 65 40 32N 17 35 E
France ■ 41 47 0N 3 0 E
Frances 140 36 41 S 140 55 E
Frances Creek 136 13 25 S 132 3 E
Frances L. 152 61 23N 129 30W
Frances, R. 152 60 16N 129 10W
Francés Viejo, C. 167 19 40N 70 0W
Franceville 124 1 40 S 13 32 E
Franche Comté □ 43 46 30N 5 50 E
Franches Montagnes 50 47 10N 7 0 E
Francis-Garnier 118 36 30N 1 30 E
Francis Harbour 151 52 34N 55 44W
Francisco I. Madero, Coahuila, Mexico 164 25 48N 103 18W
Francisco I. Madero, Durango, Mexico 164 24 32N 104 22W
Francisco Sá 171 16 28 S 43 30W
Francistown 125 21 7 S 27 33 E
Francofonte 65 37 13N 14 50 E
François 151 47 35N 56 45W
Francois L. 152 54 0N 125 30W
François, Le 167 14 38N 60 57W
Francorchamps 47 50 27N 5 57 E
Franeker 46 53 12N 5 33 E
Frankado 123 12 30N 43 12 E
Frankenberg 48 51 3N 8 47 E
Frankenthal 49 49 32N 8 21 E
Frankford = Kilcormac 39 53 10N 7 43W
Frankfort, Ind., U.S.A. 156 40 20N 86 33W
Frankfort, Kans., U.S.A. 158 39 42N 96 26W
Frankfort, Ky., U.S.A. 156 38 12N 84 52W
Frankfort, Mich., U.S.A. 156 44 38N 86 14W
Frankfort, N.Y., U.S.A. 162 43 2N 75 4W
Frankfurt □ 48 52 30N 14 0 E
Frankfurt am Main 49 50 7N 8 40 E
Frankfurt an der Oder 48 52 50N 14 31 E
Fränkische Alb 49 49 20N 11 30 E
Fränkische Saale 49 50 7N 9 49 E
Fränkische Saale, R. 49 50 7N 9 49 E
Fränkische Schweiz 49 49 45N 11 10 E
Frankland, R. 137 35 0 S 116 48 E
Franklin, Ky., U.S.A. 157 36 40N 86 30W
Franklin, La., U.S.A. 159 29 45N 91 30W
Franklin, Mass., U.S.A. 162 42 4N 71 23W
Franklin, Nebr., U.S.A. 158 40 9N 98 55W
Franklin, N.H., U.S.A. 162 43 28N 71 39W
Franklin, N.J., U.S.A. 162 41 9N 74 38W
Franklin, Pa., U.S.A. 156 41 22N 79 45W
Franklin, Tenn., U.S.A. 157 35 54N 86 53W
Franklin, Va., U.S.A. 157 36 40N 76 58W
Franklin, W. Va., U.S.A. 156 38 38N 79 21W
*Franklin □ 149 71 0N 99 0W
Franklin B. 147 69 45N 126 0W
Franklin D. Roosevelt L. 160 48 30N 118 16W
Franklin I. 13 76 10 S 168 30 E
Franklin, L. 160 40 20N 115 26W
Franklin Mts., Can. 148 66 0N 125 0W
Franklin Mts., N.Z. 143 44 55 S 167 45 E
Franklin Str. 148 72 0N 96 0W
Franklinton 159 30 53N 90 10W
Franklyn Mt. 143 42 4 S 172 42 E
Franks Peak 160 43 50N 109 5W
Frankston 141 38 8 S 145 8 E
Frankton Junc. 142 37 47 S 175 16 E
Fränsta 72 62 30N 16 11 E
Frant 29 51 5N 0 17 E
Frantsa Josifa, Zemlya 76 76 0N 62 0 E
Franz 150 48 25N 84 30W
Franz Josef Fd. 12 73 20N 22 0 E
Franz Josef Land = Frantsa Josifa 76 76 0N 62 0 E
Franzburg 48 54 9N 12 52 E
Frascati 64 41 48N 12 41 E
Fraser I. 139 25 15 S 153 10 E
Fraser L. 152 54 0N 124 50W
Fraser, Mt. 137 25 35 S 118 20 E
Fraser, R., B.C., Can. 152 49 7N 123 11W
Fraser, R., Newf., Can. 151 56 39N 63 10W
Fraserburg 128 31 55 S 21 30 E
Fraserburgh 37 57 41N 2 0W
Fraserdale 150 49 55N 81 37W
Frasertown 142 38 58 S 177 28 E
Frashëri 68 40 23N 20 26 E
Frasne 43 46 50N 6 10 E
Frater 150 47 20N 84 25W
Frauenfeld 51 47 34N 8 54 E
Fray Bentos 172 33 10 S 58 15W
Frazier Downs P.O. 136 18 48 S 121 42 E
Frechilla 56 42 8N 4 50W
Fredericia 73 55 34N 9 45 E
Frederick, Md., U.S.A. 162 39 25N 77 23W
Frederick, Okla., U.S.A. 159 34 22N 99 0W
Frederick, S.D., U.S.A. 158 45 55N 98 29W
Frederick Reef 133 20 58 S 154 23 E
Frederick Sd. 153 57 10N 134 0W
Fredericksburg, Tex., U.S.A. 159 30 17N 98 55W
Fredericksburg, Va., U.S.A. 162 38 16N 77 29W
Frederickstown 159 37 35N 90 15W
Fredericton 151 45 57N 66 40W
Fredericton Junc. 151 45 41N 66 40W
Frederiksberg 72 60 12N 14 25 E
Frederiksborg Amt □ 73 55 50N 12 10 E
Frederikshåb 12 62 0N 49 30W
Frederikshavn 73 57 28N 10 31 E
Frederikssund 73 55 50N 12 3 E
Frederiksted 147 17 43N 64 53W
Fredonia, Ariz., U.S.A. 161 36 59N 112 36W
Fredonia, Kans., U.S.A. 159 37 34N 95 50W
Fredonia, N.Y., U.S.A. 156 42 26N 79 20W
Fredrikstad 71 59 13N 10 57 E
Freehold 162 40 15N 74 18W
Freel Pk. 163 38 52N 119 53W
Freeland 162 41 3N 75 48W
Freeling, Mt. 136 22 35 S 133 06 E
Freels, C. 151 49 15N 53 30W
Freeman, Calif., U.S.A. 163 35 35N 117 53W
Freeman, S.D., U.S.A. 158 43 25N 97 20W
Freeport, Bahamas 167 25 45N 88 30 E
Freeport, Can. 151 44 15N 66 20W
Freeport, Ill., U.S.A. 158 42 18N 89 40W
Freeport, N.Y., U.S.A. 162 40 39N 73 35W
Freeport, Tex., U.S.A. 159 28 55N 95 22W
Freetown 120 8 30N 13 10W
Freevater Forest 37 57 51N 4 45W
Fregenal de la Sierra 57 38 10N 6 39W
Fregene 64 41 50N 12 12 E
Fregeneda, La 56 40 58N 6 54W
Fréhel C. 42 48 40N 2 20W
Freiberg 48 50 55N 13 20 E
Freibourg = Fribourg 50 46 49N 7 9 E
Freiburg, Baden, Ger. 49 48 0N 7 52 E
Freiburg, Sachsen, Ger. 48 53 49N 9 17 E
Freiburger Alpen 50 46 37N 7 10 E
Freire 176 39 0 S 72 50W
Freirina 172 28 30 S 70 27W
Freising 49 48 24N 11 47 E
Freistadt 52 48 30N 14 30 E
Freital 48 51 0N 13 40 E
Fréjus 45 43 25N 6 44 E
Fremantle 137 32 1 S 115 47 E
Fremont, Calif., U.S.A. 163 37 32N 122 57W
Fremont, Mich., U.S.A. 156 43 29N 85 59W
Fremont, Nebr., U.S.A. 158 41 30N 96 30W
Fremont, Ohio, U.S.A. 156 41 20N 83 5W
Fremont, L. 160 43 0N 109 50W

*Now part of Central Arctic and Baffin

Fremont, R. 161 38 15N 110 20W
French Camp 163 37 53N 121 16W
French Cr. 156 41 30N 80 2W
French Guiana ■ 175 4 0N 53 0W
French I. 141 38 20 S 145 22 E
French Terr. of Afars & Issas □ = Djibouti 123 11 30N 42 15 E
Frenchglen 160 42 56N 119 0W
Frenchman Butte 153 53 36N 109 36W
Frenchman Creek, R. 158 40 34N 101 35W
Frenchman, R. 160 49 25N 108 20W
Frenchpark 38 53 53N 8 25W
Frenda 118 35 2N 1 1 E
Fresco, R. 175 7 15 S 51 30W
Freshfield, C. 13 68 25 S 151 10 E
Freshford 39 52 45N 7 25W
Freshwater 28 50 42N 1 31W
Fresnillo 164 23 10N 103 0W
Fresno 163 36 47N 119 50W
Fresno Alhandiga 56 40 42N 5 37W
Fresno Res. 160 48 47N 110 0W
Freswick 37 58 35N 3 5W
Freuchie 35 56 14N 3 8W
Freudenstadt 49 48 27N 8 25 E
Freux 47 49 59N 5 27 E
Frévent 43 50 15N 2 17 E
Frew, R. 138 20 0 S 135 38 E
Frewena 138 19 50 S 135 50 E
Freycinet, C. 137 34 9 S 115 0 E
Freycinet Pen. 138 42 10 S 148 25 E
Fria 120 10 27N 13 32W
Fria, La 174 8 13N 72 15W
Friant 163 36 59N 119 43W
Frías 172 28 40 S 65 5W
Fribourg 50 46 49N 7 9 E
Fribourg □ 50 45 40N 7 0 E
Frick 50 47 31N 8 1 E
Fridafors 73 56 25N 14 39 E
Fridaythorpe 33 54 2N 0 40W
Friedberg, Bayern, Ger. 49 48 21N 10 59 E
Friedberg, Hessen, Ger. 10 50 19N 8 45 E
Friedland 49 53 40N 13 33 E
Friedrichshafen 49 47 39N 9 29 E
Friedrichskoog 48 54 1N 8 52 E
Friedrichsort 48 54 24N 10 11 E
Friedrichstadt 48 54 23N 9 6 E
Friendly (Tonga) Is. 130 19 50 S 174 30W
Friesach 52 46 57N 14 24 E
Friesack 48 52 43N 12 35 E
Friesche Wad 46 53 22N 5 44 E
Friesland □ 46 53 5N 5 50 E
Friesoythe 48 53 1N 7 51 E
Frigate, L. 150 53 15N 74 45W
Frigg E., gasfield 19 59 50N 2 20 E
Frigg, gasfield 19 59 50N 2 15 E
Frigg N.E., gasfield 19 60 0N 2 17 E
Frillesås 73 57 20N 12 12 E
Frimley 29 51 18N 0 43W
Frinnaryd 73 57 55N 14 50 E
Frinton-on-Sea 29 51 50N 1 16 E
Frio, C. 128 18 0 S 12 0 E
Frio, R. 159 29 40N 99 40W
Friockheim 37 56 39N 2 40W
Friona 159 34 40N 102 42W
Frisa, Loch 34 56 34N 6 5W
Frisian Is. 48 53 30N 6 0 E
Fristad 73 57 50N 13 0 E
Fritch 159 35 40N 101 35W
Fritsla 73 57 33N 12 47 E
Fritzlar 48 51 8N 9 19 E
Friuli-Venezia-Giulia □ 63 46 0N 13 0 E
Frizington 32 54 33N 3 30W
Frobisher B. 149 63 0N 67 0W
Frobisher L. 153 56 20N 108 15W
Frobisher Sd. 149 62 30N 66 0W
Frodsham 32 53 17N 2 45W
Frogmore 141 34 15 S 148 52 E
Frohavet 74 64 5N 9 35 E
Froid 158 48 20N 104 29W
Froid-Chapelle 47 50 9N 4 19 E
Frolovo 83 49 45N 43 30 E
Fromberg 160 45 19N 108 58W
Frombork 54 54 21N 19 41 E
Frome 28 51 16N 2 17W
Frome Downs 140 31 13 S 139 46 E
Frome, L. 140 30 45 S 139 45 E
Frome, R. 28 50 44N 2 5W
Fromentine 42 46 53N 2 9W
Frómista 56 42 16N 4 25W
Front Range 160 40 0N 105 10W
Front Royal 156 38 55N 78 10W
Fronteira 57 39 3N 7 39W
Fronteiras 170 7 5 S 40 37W
Frontera 165 18 30N 92 40W
Frontignan 44 43 27N 3 45 E
Frosinone 64 41 38N 13 20 E
Frosolone 65 41 34N 14 27 E
Frostburg 156 39 43N 78 57W
Frostisen 74 68 14N 17 10 E
Frouard 43 48 47N 6 8 E
Frövi 72 59 28N 15 24 E
Frower Pt. 39 51 40N 8 30W
Froya 71 63 43N 8 40 E
Frøya 71 63 43N 8 40 E
Fröya I. 74 63 45N 8 45 E
Fruges 43 50 30N 2 8 E
Frumoasa 70 46 28N 25 48 E
Frunze 85 42 54N 74 36 E
Fruška Gora 66 45 7N 19 30 E
Frutal 171 20 0 S 49 0W
Frutigen 50 46 35N 7 38 E
Frýdek-Místek 53 49 40N 18 20 E

Frýdlant

Garibaldi Prov. Park

Frýdlant, Severočeský, Czech. 52 50 56N 15 9 E
Frýdlant, Severomoravsky, Czech. 53 49 35N 18 20 E
Fryvaldov = Jesenik 53 50 0N 17 8 E
Fthiótis □ 69 38 50N 22 25 E
Fu 72 60 57N 14 44 E
Fuan 109 27 9N 119 38 E
Fucécchio 62 43 44N 10 51 E
Fuch'ing 109 25 43N 119 22 E
Fuchou, Fukien, China 109 26 5N 119 18 E
Fuchou, Liaoning, China 107 39 45N 121 45 E
Fuchū 110 34 34N 133 14 E
Fūchū 111 35 40N 139 29 E
Fuch'üan 108 26 42N 107 33 E
Fuch'uan 109 24 50N 111 16 E
Fucino, L. 44 42 0N 13 30 E
Fuencaliente 57 38 25N 4 18W
Fuengirola 57 36 32N 4 41W
Fuente-Alamo 59 38 44N 1 24W
Fuente de Cantos 57 38 15N 6 18W
Fuente de San Esteban, La 56 40 49N 6 15W
Fuente del Maestre 57 38 31N 6 28W
Fuente el Fresno 57 39 14N 3 46W
Fuente Ovejuna 57 38 15N 5 25W
Fuentes de Andalucía 57 37 28N 5 20W
Fuentes de Ebro 58 41 31N 0 38W
Fuentes de León 57 38 5N 6 32W
Fuentes de Oñoro 56 40 33N 6 52W
Fuentesaúco 56 41 15N 5 30W
Fuerte Olimpo 172 21 0 S 58 0W
Fuerte, R. 164 26 0N 109 0W
Fuerteventura, I. 116 28 30N 14 0W
Fuertey 38 53 37N 8 16W
Fufeng 106 34 20N 107 51 E
Fŭget 70 45 52N 22 10 E
Fŭget, Munţii 70 45 50N 22 9 E
Fugløysund 74 70 15N 20 20 E
Fŭgŭraş 70 45 48N 24 58 E
Fŭgŭraş, Munţii 70 45 40N 24 40 E
Fuhai 105 47 6N 87 23 E
Fuhsien, Liaoning, China 107 39 38N 122 0 E
Fuhsien, Shensi, China 106 36 2N 109 20 E
Fuhsingchen 108 22 47N 101 5 E
Fujaira 93 25 7N 56 18 E
Fuji 111 35 9N 138 39 E
Fuji-no-miya 111 35 20N 138 40 E
Fuji-San 111 35 22N 138 44 E
Fuji-yoshida 111 35 30N 138 46 E
Fujieda 111 34 52N 138 16 E
Fujioka 111 36 15N 139 5 E
Fujisawa 111 35 22N 139 29 E
Fukien □ 109 26 0N 117 30 E
Fukou 106 34 3N 114 27 E
Fuku 106 39 2N 111 3 E
Fukuchiyama 111 35 25N 135 9 E
Fukui 111 36 0N 136 10 E
Fukui-ken □ 111 36 0N 136 12 E
Fukuma 110 33 46N 130 28 E
Fukung 108 26 58N 98 54 E
Fukuoka 110 33 30N 130 30 E
Fukuoka-ken □ 110 33 30N 131 0 E
Fukuroi 111 34 45N 137 55 E
Fukushima 112 37 30N 140 15 E
Fukushima-ken □ 112 37 30N 140 15 E
Fukuyama 110 34 35N 133 20 E
Fŭlciu 70 46 17N 28 7 E
Fulda 48 50 32N 9 41 E
Fullerton, Calif., U.S.A. 163 33 52N 117 58W
Fullerton, Nebr., U.S.A. 158 41 25N 98 0W
Fulmar, oilfield 19 56 30N 2 8 E
Fülöpszállás 53 46 49N 19 16 E
Fŭlticeni 70 47 21N 26 20W
Fulton, Mo., U.S.A. 158 38 50N 91 55W
Fulton, N.Y., U.S.A. 162 43 20N 76 22W
Fuluälven 72 61 18N 13 4 E
Fulufjället 72 61 32N 12 41 E
Fulungch'üan 107 44 24N 124 37 E
Fülüpszállás 53 46 49N 19 16 E
Fumay 43 50 0N 4 40 E
Fumbusi 121 10 25N 1 20W
Fumel 44 44 30N 0 58 E
Fumin 108 25 14N 102 29 E
Funabashi 111 35 45N 140 0 E
Funafuti, I. 130 8 30 S 179 0 E
Funchal 116 32 45N 16 55W
Fundación 174 10 31N 74 11W
Fundão, Brazil 171 19 55 S 40 24W
Fundão, Port. 56 40 8N 7 30W
Fundu 127 14 58 S 30 14 E
Fundy, B. of 151 45 0N 56 0W
Funes 174 1 0N 77 28W
Funing, Hopei, China 107 39 54N 119 12 E
Funing, Yunnan, China 108 23 37N 105 36 E
Funiu Shan 106 33 40N 112 30 E
Funsi 120 10 21N 1 54W
Funtua 121 11 30N 7 18 E
Fupien 108 31 18N 102 27 E
Fup'ing 106 34 47N 109 7 E
Fur 73 56 50N 9 0 E
Furat, Nahr al 92 33 30N 43 0 E
Furbero 165 20 22N 97 31W
Furka Pass 51 46 34N 8 35 E
Furmanov 81 57 25N 41 3 E
Furmanovka 85 44 17N 72 57 E
Furmanovo 83 49 42N 49 25 E
Furnas, Reprêsa de 173 20 50 S 45 0W
Furneaux Group 138 40 10 S 147 50 E
Furness, Pen. 32 54 12N 3 10W
Fürstenau 48 52 32N 7 40 E
Fürstenfeld 52 47 3N 16 3 E
Fürstenfeldbruck 49 48 10N 11 15 E
Fürstenwalde 48 52 20N 14 3 E
Fürth 49 49 29N 11 0 E
Fürth i. Wald 49 49 19N 12 51 E
Furtwangen 49 48 3N 8 14 E
Furudal 72 61 10N 15 11 E
Furukawa 111 36 14N 137 11 E
Furusund 72 59 40N 18 55 E
Fury and Hecla Str. 149 69 56N 84 0W
Fusa 71 60 12N 5 37 E
Fusagasugá 174 4 21N 74 22W
Fuscaldo 65 39 25N 16 1 E
Fushan 107 37 30N 121 5 E
Fushë Arrëzi 68 42 4N 20 2 E
Fushun, Liaoning, China 107 41 50N 123 55 E
Fushun, Szechwan, China 108 29 13N 105 0 E
Fush'un Chiang, R. 109 30 5N 120 5 E
Fusio 51 46 27N 8 40 E
Füssen 49 47 35N 10 43 E
Fusui 108 22 35N 107 58 E
Fusung 107 42 15N 127 20 E
Futago-Yama 110 33 35N 131 36 E
Futing 109 27 15N 120 10 E
Futuk 121 9 45N 10 56 E
Futuna I. 130 14 25 S 178 20 E
Fŭurei 70 45 6N 27 19 E
Fuwa 122 31 12N 30 33 E
Fuyang 109 30 5N 119 56 E
Fuyang Ho, R. 106 38 14N 116 5 E
Fuyü 107 45 10N 124 50 E
Fuyüan 105 47 40N 132 30 E
Füzesgyarmat 53 47 6N 21 14 E
Fwaka 125 12 5 S 29 25 E
Fylde 32 53 50N 2 58W
Fylingdales Moor 33 54 22N 0 32W
Fyn 73 55 20N 10 30 E
Fyne, L. 34 56 0N 5 20W
Fyns Amt □ 73 55 15N 10 30 E
Fynshav 73 54 59N 9 59 E
Fyresvatn 71 59 6N 8 10 E
Fyvie 37 57 26N 2 24W

G

Gaanda 121 10 10N 12 27 E
Gaba 123 6 20N 35 7 E
Gaba Tula 82 0 20N 38 35 E
Gabah, C. 91 8 0N 50 0 E
Gabarin 121 11 8N 10 27 E
Gabbs 163 38 52N 117 55W
Gabela 124 11 0 S 14 37 E
Gaberones = Gaborone 128 24 37 S 25 57 E
Gabès 119 33 53N 10 2 E
Gabès, Golfe de 119 34 0N 10 30 E
Gabgaba, W. 122 22 10N 33 5 E
Gabin 54 52 23N 19 41 E
Gabon ■ 124 0 10 S 10 0 E
Gaborone 128 24 37 S 25 57 E
Gabrovo 67 42 52N 25 27 E
Gacé 42 48 49N 0 20 E
Gach Saran 93 30 15N 50 45 E
Gacko 66 43 10N 18 33 E
Gada 121 13 38N 5 36 E
Gadag 97 15 30N 75 45 E
Gadamai 123 17 11N 36 10 E
Gadap 94 25 5N 67 28 E
Gadarwara 95 22 50N 78 50 E
Gäddede 74 64 30N 14 15 E
Gadebusch 48 53 41N 11 6 E
Gadein 123 8 10N 28 45 E
Gadhada 94 22 0N 71 35 E
Gadmen 51 46 45N 8 16 E
Gádor, Sierra de 59 36 57N 2 45W
Gadsden, Ala., U.S.A. 157 34 1N 86 0W
Gadsden, Ariz., U.S.A. 161 32 35N 114 47W
Gadwal 96 16 10N 77 50 E
Gaerwen 31 53 13N 4 17W
Gaeta 64 41 12N 13 35 E
Gaeta, G. di 64 41 0N 13 25 E
Gaffney 157 35 10N 81 31W
Gafsa 119 34 24N 8 51 E
Gagarin (Gzhatsk) 80 55 30N 35 0 E
Gagetown 151 45 46N 66 29W
Gagino 81 55 15N 45 10 E
Gagliano del Capo 65 39 50N 18 23 E
Gagnef 72 60 36N 15 5 E
Gagnoa 120 6 4N 5 55W
Gagnon 151 51 50N 68 5W
Gagnon, L. 153 62 3N 110 27W
Gagra 83 43 20N 40 10 E
Gah 44 43 12N 0 27W
Gahini 126 1 50 S 30 30 E
Gahmar 95 25 27N 83 55 E
Gaibandha 98 25 20N 89 36 E
Gaïdhouronísi 69 34 53N 25 41 E
Gail 159 32 48N 101 25W
Gail, R. 52 46 37N 13 15 E
Gaillac 44 43 54N 1 54 E
Gaillon 42 49 10N 1 20 E
Gaima 135 8 9 S 142 59 E
Gainesville, Fla., U.S.A. 157 29 38N 82 20W
Gainesville, Ga., U.S.A. 157 34 17N 83 47W
Gainesville, Mo., U.S.A. 159 36 35N 92 26W
Gainesville, Tex., U.S.A. 159 33 40N 97 10W
Gainford 33 54 34N 1 44W
Gainsborough 33 53 23N 0 46W
Gairdner L. 140 31 30 S 136 0 E
Gairloch 36 57 42N 5 40W
Gairloch L. 36 57 43N 5 45W
Gairlochy 36 56 55N 5 0W
Gairsay, I. 37 59 4N 2 59W
Gais 51 47 22N 9 27 E
Gaithersburg 162 39 9N 77 12W
Gaj 66 45 28N 17 3 E
Gajale 121 11 25N 8 10 E
Gajiram 121 12 29N 13 9 E
Gakuch 95 36 7N 73 45 E
Gal Oya Res. 97 8 5N 80 55 E
Galachipa 98 22 8N 90 26 E
Galadi 121 13 5N 6 20 E
Galán, Cerro 172 25 55 S 66 52W
Galana, R. 126 3 0 S 39 10 E
Galangue 125 13 48 S 16 3 E
Galanta 53 48 11N 17 45 E
Galápagos, Is. 131 0 0 89 0W
Galas, R. 101 4 55N 101 57 E
Galashiels 35 55 37N 2 50W
Galatás 69 37 30N 23 26 E
Galatea 142 38 24 S 176 45 E
Galaţi 70 45 27N 28 2 E
Galaţi □ 70 45 45N 27 30 E
Galatina 65 40 10N 18 10 E
Galátone 65 40 8N 18 3 E
Galax 157 36 42N 80 57W
Galaxídhion 69 38 22N 22 23 E
Galbally 39 52 24N 8 17W
Galbraith 138 16 25 S 141 30 E
Galdhøpiggen 71 61 38N 8 18 E
Galeana 164 24 50N 100 4W
Galela 103 1 50N 127 55 E
Galena, Austral. 137 27 48 S 114 42 E
Galena, U.S.A. 147 64 42N 157 0W
Galeota Point 167 10 8N 61 0W
Galera 59 37 45N 2 33W
Galera, Pta. de la 174 10 48N 75 16W
Galesburg 158 40 57N 90 23W
Galey R. 39 52 30N 9 23W
Galgate 32 53 59N 2 47W
Galheirão, R. 171 12 23 S 45 5W
Galheiros 171 13 18 S 46 25W
Galicea Mare 70 44 4N 23 19 E
Galich, R.S.F.S.R., U.S.S.R. 81 58 23N 42 18 E
Galich, Uk., U.S.S.R. 80 49 10N 24 40 E
Galiche 67 43 34N 23 50 E
Galicia 56 42 43N 8 0W
Galijp 46 53 10N 5 58 E
Galilee = Hagalil 90 32 53N 35 18 E
Galilee, L. 138 22 20 S 145 50 E
Galite, Is. de la 119 37 30N 8 59 E
Galivro Mts. 161 32 40N 110 30W
Gallan Hd. 36 58 14N 7 0W
Gallarate 62 45 40N 8 48 E
Gallatin 157 36 24N 86 27W
Galle 97 6 5N 80 10 E
Gallego 164 29 49N 106 22W
Gállego, R. 58 42 23N 0 30W
Gallegos, R. 176 51 50 S 71 0W
Galley Hd. 39 51 32N 8 56W
Galliate 62 45 27N 8 44 E
Gallinas, Pta. 174 12 28N 71 40W
Gallipoli 65 40 8N 18 0 E
Gallipoli = Gelibolu 68 40 28N 26 43 E
Gallipolis 156 38 50N 82 10W
Gällivare 74 67 9N 20 40 E
Gällö 72 62 56N 15 15 E
Gallo, C. di 64 38 13N 13 19 E
Gallocanta, Laguna de 58 40 58N 1 30W
Galloway 34 55 0N 4 25W
Galloway, Mull of 34 54 38N 4 50W
Gallup 161 35 30N 108 54W
Gallur 58 41 52N 1 19W
Gallyaaral 85 40 2N 67 35 E
Galmi 121 13 58N 5 41 E
Gal'on 90 31 38N 34 51 E
Galong 141 34 37 S 148 34 E
Galoya 93 8 10N 80 55 E
Galston 34 55 36N 4 22W
Galt, Can. 150 43 21N 80 19W
Galt, U.S.A. 163 38 15N 121 18W
Galtström 72 62 10N 17 30 E
Galtür 52 46 58N 10 11 E
Galty Mts. 39 52 22N 8 10W
Galtymore, Mt. 39 52 22N 8 12W
Galva 158 41 10N 90 0W
Galve de Sorbe 58 41 13N 3 10W
Galveston 159 29 15N 94 48W
Galveston B. 159 29 30N 94 50W
Gálvez, Argent. 172 32 0 S 61 20W
Gálvez, Spain 57 39 42N 4 16W
Galway 39 53 16N 9 4W
Galway □ 38 53 16N 9 3W
Galway B. 39 53 10N 9 20W
Gam, R. 100 21 55N 105 12 E
Gamagōri 111 34 50N 137 14 E
Gamare, L. 123 11 32N 41 40 E
Gamarra 174 8 20N 73 45W
Gamawa 121 12 10N 10 31 E
Gambaga 121 10 30N 0 28W
Gambat 94 27 17N 68 26 E
Gambela 123 8 14N 34 38 E
Gambell 147 63 55N 171 50W
Gambia ■ 120 13 25N 16 0W
Gambia, R. 120 13 20N 15 45W
Gambier, C. 136 11 56 S 130 57 E
Gambier Is. 140 35 3 S 136 30 E
Gamboli 94 29 53N 68 24 E
Gamboma 124 1 55 S 15 52 E
Gamboola 138 16 29 S 143 43 E
Gameleira 170 7 50 S 50 0W
Gamerco 161 35 33N 108 56W
Gamleby 73 57 54N 16 20W
Gamlingay 29 52 9N 0 11W
Gammelgarn 171 57 24N 18 49 E
Gammon, R. 153 51 24N 95 44W
Gamōda-Saki 110 33 50N 134 45 E
Gan (Addu Atoll) 87 0 10 S 71 10 E
Gan Shemu'el 90 32 28N 34 56 E
Gan Yavne 90 31 48N 34 42 E
Ganado, Ariz., U.S.A. 161 35 46N 109 41W
Ganado, Tex., U.S.A. 159 29 4N 96 31W
Gananoque 150 44 20N 76 10W
Ganaveh 93 29 35N 50 35 E
Gand 47 51 2N 3 37 E
Gandak, R. 95 27 0N 84 8 E
Gandava 94 28 32N 67 32 E
Gander 151 48 18N 54 29W
Gander L. 151 48 58N 54 35W
Ganderowe Falls 127 17 20 S 29 10 E
Gandesa 58 41 3N 0 26 E
Gand = Gent 47 51 2N 3 37 E
Gandhi Sagar 94 24 40N 75 40 E
Gandi 121 12 55N 5 49 E
Gandía 59 38 58N 0 9W
Gandino 62 45 50N 9 52 E
Gandole 121 8 28N 11 35 E
Gandu 171 13 45 S 39 30W
Ganedidalem = Gani 103 0 48 S 128 14 E
Ganetti 122 18 0N 31 10 E
Ganga, Mouths of the 95 21 30N 90 0 E
Ganga, R. 95 25 0N 88 0 E
Ganganagar 94 29 56N 73 56 E
Gangapur 94 26 32N 76 37 E
Gangara 121 14 35N 8 40 E
Gangavati 97 15 30N 76 36 E
Gangaw 98 22 5N 94 15 E
Ganges 44 43 56N 3 42 E
Ganges = Ganga, R. 95 25 0N 88 0 E
Gangoh 94 29 46N 77 18 E
Gangtok 98 27 20N 88 37 E
Ganj 95 27 45N 78 47 E
Ganmain 141 34 47 S 147 1 E
Gannat 44 46 7N 3 11 E
Gannett Pk. 160 43 15N 109 47W
Gannvalley 158 44 3N 98 57W
Ganserdorf 53 48 20N 16 43 E
Ganta (Gompa) 120 7 15N 8 59W
Gantheaume B. 137 27 40 S 114 10 E
Gantheaume, C. 140 36 4 S 137 25 E
Gantsevichi 80 52 42N 26 30 E
Ganyushkino 83 46 35N 49 20 E
Ganzi 123 4 30N 31 5 E
Gao □ 121 18 0N 1 0 E
Gao Bang 101 22 37N 106 18 E
Gaoua 120 10 20N 3 8W
Gaoual 120 11 45N 13 25W
Gaouz 118 31 52N 4 20W
Gap 45 44 33N 6 5 E
Gar Dzong 93 32 20N 79 55 E
Gara, L. 38 53 57N 8 26W
Garachiné 166 8 0N 78 12W
Garanhuns 170 8 50 S 36 30W
Garawe 120 4 35N 8 0W
Garba Tula 126 0 30N 38 32 E
Garber 159 36 30N 97 36W
Garberville 160 40 11N 123 50W
Garboldisham 29 52 24N 0 57 E
Garça 171 22 14 S 49 37W
Garças, R. 170 8 43 S 39 41W
Gard □ 45 44 2N 4 10 E
Garda, L. di 62 45 40N 10 40 E
Gardanne 45 43 27N 5 27 E
Garde L. 153 62 50N 106 13W
Gardelegen 48 52 32N 11 21 E
Garden City, Kans., U.S.A. 159 38 0N 100 45W
Garden City, Tex., U.S.A. 159 31 52N 101 28W
Garden Grove 163 33 47N 117 55W
Gardenstown 37 57 40N 2 20W
Gardez 94 33 31N 68 59 E
Gardhiki 69 38 50N 21 55 E
Gardian 117 15 45N 19 40 E
Gardiner, Can. 150 49 19N 81 2W
Gardiner, Mont., U.S.A. 160 45 3N 110 53W
Gardiner, New Mexico, U.S.A. 159 36 55N 104 29W
Gardiners I. 162 41 4N 72 5W
Gardner 162 42 35N 72 0W
Gardner Canal 152 53 27N 128 8W
Gardnerville 160 38 59N 119 47W
Gardo 91 9 18N 49 20 E
Gare, L. 34 56 1N 4 50W
Garelochhead 34 56 7N 4 50W
Gareloi I. 147 51 49N 178 50W
Garešnica 66 45 36N 16 56 E
Garéssio 62 44 12N 8 1 E
Garey 163 34 53N 120 19W
Garfield, Utah, U.S.A. 160 40 45N 112 15W
Garfield, Wash., U.S.A. 160 47 3N 117 8W
Garforth 33 53 48N 1 22W
Gargaliánoi 69 37 4N 21 38 E
Gargano, Mte. 65 41 43N 15 43 E
Gargans, Mt. 44 45 37N 1 39 E
Gargantua, C. 150 47 35N 85 0W
Gargoune 121 15 56N 0 13 E
Gargrave 32 53 58N 2 7W
Garhshankar 94 31 13N 76 11 E
Gari 84 59 26N 62 21 E
Garibaldi 152 49 56N 123 15W
Garibaldi Prov. Park 152 49 50N 122 40W

Gheorghe Gheorghiu-Dej **Gobo**

Gheorghe Gheorghiu-Dej	**70**	46	17N	26	47 E
Gheorgheni	**70**	46	43N	25	41 E
Ghergani	**70**	44	37N	25	37 E
Gherla	**70**	47	0N	23	57 E
Ghilarza	**64**	40	8N	8	50 E
Ghisonaccia	**45**	42	1N	9	26 E
Ghizao	**94**	33	30N	65	59 E
Ghizar, R.	**95**	36	10N	73	4 E
Ghod, R.	**96**	18	40N	74	15 E
Ghorat □	**93**	34	0N	64	20 E
Ghost River, Can.	**150**	50	10N	91	27W
Ghost River, Ont., Can.	**150**	51	25N	83	20W
Ghot Ogrein	**122**	31	10N	25	20 E
Ghotaru	**94**	27	20N	70	1 E
Ghotki	**94**	28	5N	69	30 E
Ghudâmis	**119**	30	11N	9	29 E
Ghugri	**95**	22	39N	80	41 E
Ghugus	**96**	20	0N	79	0 E
Ghulam Mohammad Barrage	**94**	25	30N	67	0 E
Ghuriān	**93**	34	17N	61	25 E
Gia Dinh	**101**	10	49N	106	42 E
Gia Lai = Pleiku	**101**	14	3N	108	0 E
Gia Nghia	**101**	12	0N	107	42 E
Gia Ngoc	**100**	14	50N	108	58 E
Gia Vuc	**100**	14	42N	108	34 E
Giamda Dzong	**99**	30	3N	93	2 E
Giannutri, I.	**62**	42	16N	11	5 E
Giant Forest	**163**	36	36N	118	43W
Giant Mts. = Krkonose	**52**	50	50N	16	10 E
Giant's Causeway	**38**	55	15N	6	30W
Giarabub = Jaghbub	**117**	29	42N	24	38 E
Giarre	**65**	37	44N	15	10 E
Giaveno	**62**	45	3N	7	20 E
Gibara	**166**	21	0N	76	20W
Gibbon	**158**	40	49N	98	45W
Gibe, R.	**123**	6	25N	36	10 E
Gibellina	**64**	37	48N	13	0 E
Gibeon	**128**	25	7 S	17	45 E
Gibraléon	**57**	37	23N	6	58W
Gibraltar	**57**	36	7N	5	22W
Gibraltar Pt.	**33**	53	6N	0	20 E
Gibraltar, Str. of	**57**	35	55N	5	40W
Gibson Des.	**136**	24	0 S	126	0 E
Gibsons	**152**	49	24N	123	32W
Gida. G.	**12**	72	30N	77	0 E
Giddalur	**97**	15	20N	78	57 E
Gidde	**123**	5	40N	37	25 E
Giddings	**159**	30	11N	96	58W
Gide	**123**	9	52N	35	5 E
Gien	**43**	47	40N	2	36 E
Giessen	**48**	50	34N	8	40 E
Gieten	**46**	53	0N	6	46 E
Gif-sur-Yvette	**46**	48	42N	2	8 E
Gifatin, Geziret	**122**	27	10N	33	50 E
Gifford	**35**	55	54N	2	45W
Gifford Creek	**137**	24	3 S	116	16 E
Gifhorn	**48**	52	29N	10	32 E
Gifu	**111**	35	30N	136	45 E
Gifu-ken □	**111**	36	0N	137	0 E
Gigant	**83**	46	28N	41	30 E
Giganta, Sa. de la	**164**	25	30N	111	30W
Gigen	**67**	43	40N	24	28 E
Giggleswick	**32**	54	5N	2	19W
Gigha, I.	**39**	55	42N	5	45W
Giglio, I.	**62**	42	20N	10	52 E
Gignac	**44**	43	39N	3	32 E
Gigüela, R.	**58**	39	47N	3	0W
Gijón	**56**	43	32N	5	42W
Gil I.	**152**	53	12N	129	15W
Gila Bend	**161**	33	0N	112	46W
Gila Bend Mts.	**161**	33	15N	113	0W
Gila, R.	**161**	33	5N	108	40W
Gilau	**138**	5	38 S	149	3 E
Gilbedi	**121**	13	40N	5	45 E
* Gilbert Is.	**130**	1	0 S	176	0 E
Gilbert Plains	**153**	51	9N	100	28W
Gilbert, R.	**138**	16	35 S	141	15 E
Gilbert River	**138**	18	9 S	142	52 E
Gilberton	**138**	19	16 S	143	35 E
Gilbués	**170**	9	50 S	45	21W
Gilford	**38**	54	23N	6	20W
Gilford I.	**152**	50	40N	126	30W
Gilgai	**137**	31	15 S	119	56 E
Gilgandra	**141**	31	43 S	148	39 E
Gilgil	**126**	0	30 S	36	20 E
Gilgit	**95**	35	50N	74	15 E
Gilgit, R.	**95**	35	50N	74	25 E
Gilgunnia	**141**	32	26 S	146	2 E
Giligulgul	**139**	26	26 S	150	0 E
Gilima	**126**	3	53N	28	15 E
Giljeva Planina	**66**	43	9N	20	0 E
Gill L.	**38**	54	15N	8	25W
Gillam	**153**	56	20N	94	40W
Gilleleje	**73**	56	8N	12	19 E
Gillen, L.	**137**	26	11 S	124	38 E
Gilles, L.	**140**	32	50 S	136	45 E
Gillespie Pt.	**143**	43	24 S	169	49 E
Gillett	**162**	41	57N	76	48W
Gillette	**158**	44	20N	105	38W
Gilliat	**138**	20	40 S	141	28 E
Gillingham, Dorset, U.K.	**28**	51	2N	2	15W
Gillingham, Kent, U.K.	**29**	51	23N	0	34 E
Gilmer	**159**	32	44N	94	55W
Gilmore	**141**	35	14 S	148	12 E
Gilmore, L.	**137**	32	29 S	121	37 E
Gilmour	**150**	44	48N	77	37W
Gilo	**123**	7	35N	34	30 E
Gilo, R.	**161**	33	5N	108	40W
Gilort, R.	**70**	44	38N	23	32 E
Gilroy	**163**	37	1N	121	37W
Gilsland	**32**	55	0N	2	34W
Gilău	**70**	46	45N	23	23W
Giluwe, Mt.	**135**	6	8 S	143	52 E
Gilwern	**31**	51	49N	3	5W
Gilze	**47**	51	32N	4	57 E
Gimåfors	**72**	62	40N	16	25 E
Gimbi	**123**	9	3N	35	42 E
Gimigliano	**65**	38	53N	16	32 E
Gimli	**153**	50	40N	97	10W
Gimmi	**123**	9	0N	37	20 E
Gimo	**72**	60	11N	18	12 E
Gimont	**44**	43	38N	0	52 E
Gimzo	**90**	31	56N	34	56 E
Gin Ganga	**97**	6	5N	80	7 E
Gin Gin	**139**	25	0 S	151	44 E
Ginâh	**122**	25	21N	30	30 E
Gindie	**138**	23	44 S	148	8 E
Gineta, La	**59**	39	8N	2	1W
Gingin	**137**	31	22 S	115	54 E
Gîngiova	**70**	43	54N	23	50 E
Ginir	**123**	7	12N	40	40 E
Ginosa	**65**	40	35N	16	45 E
Ginowan	**112**	26	15N	127	47 E
Ginzo de Limia	**56**	42	3N	7	47W
Giohar	**91**	2	20N	45	15 E
Gióia del Colle	**65**	40	49N	16	55 E
Gióia, G. di	**65**	38	30N	15	50 E
Gióia Táuro	**65**	38	26N	15	53 E
Gioiosa Iónica	**65**	38	20N	16	19 E
Gióna, Óros	**69**	38	38N	22	14 E
Giong, Teluk	**103**	4	50N	118	20 E
Giovi, P. dei	**45**	44	30N	8	55 E
Giovinazzo	**65**	41	10N	16	40 E
Gippsland	**133**	37	45 S	147	15 E
Gir Hills	**94**	21	0N	71	0 E
Girab	**94**	26	2N	70	38 E
Giralla	**136**	22	31 S	114	15 E
Giraltovce	**53**	49	7N	21	32 E
Girard	**159**	37	30N	94	50W
Girardot	**174**	4	18N	74	48W
Girdle Ness	**37**	57	9N	2	2W
Giresun	**92**	40	45N	38	30 E
Girga	**122**	26	17N	31	55 E
Girgir, C.	**135**	3	50 S	144	35 E
Giridih	**95**	24	10N	86	21 E
Girifalco	**65**	38	49N	16	25 E
Girilambone	**141**	31	16 S	146	57 E
Girishk	**93**	31	47N	64	24 E
Giro	**121**	11	7N	4	42 E
Giromagny	**43**	47	44N	6	50 E
Gironde □	**44**	44	45N	0	30W
Gironde, R.	**44**	45	27N	0	53W
Gironella	**58**	42	2N	1	53 E
Giru	**138**	19	30 S	147	5 E
Girvan	**34**	55	15N	4	50W
Girvan R.	**34**	55	18N	4	51W
Gisborne	**142**	38	39 S	178	5 E
Gisburn	**32**	53	56N	2	16W
Gisenyi	**126**	1	41 S	29	30 E
Giske	**71**	62	30N	6	3 E
Gisla	**36**	58	7N	6	53W
Gislaved	**73**	57	19N	13	32 E
Gisors	**43**	49	15N	1	40 E
Gissarskiy, Khrebet	**85**	39	0N	69	0 E
Gistel	**47**	51	9N	2	59 E
Giswil	**50**	46	50N	8	11 E
Gitega (Kitega)	**126**	3	26 S	29	56 E
Gits	**47**	51	0N	3	6 E
Giubiasco	**51**	46	11N	9	1 E
Giugliano in Campania	**65**	40	55N	14	12 E
Giulianova	**63**	42	45N	13	58 E
Giurgeni	**70**	44	45N	27	38 E
Giurgiu	**70**	43	52N	25	57 E
Giv'at Brenner	**90**	31	52N	34	47 E
Give	**73**	55	51N	9	13 E
Givet	**43**	50	8N	4	49 E
Givors	**45**	45	35N	4	45 E
Givry, Belg.	**47**	50	23N	4	2 E
Givry, France	**43**	46	41N	4	46 E
Giza (El Giza)	**122**	30	1N	31	11 E
Gizhduvan	**85**	40	6N	64	41 E
Gizhiga	**77**	62	0N	150	27 E
Gizhiginskaya, Guba	**77**	61	0N	158	0 E
Gizycko	**54**	54	2N	21	48 E
Gizzeria	**65**	38	57N	16	10 E
Gjegjan	**68**	41	58N	20	3 E
Gjerpen	**71**	59	15N	9	33 E
Gjerstad	**71**	58	54N	9	0 E
Gjiri-i-Vlorës	**68**	40	29N	19	27 E
Gjirokastër	**68**	40	7N	20	16 E
Gjoa Haven	**148**	68	20N	96	0W
Gjovdal	**71**	58	52N	8	19 E
Gjøvik	**71**	60	47N	10	43 E
Glace Bay	**151**	46	11N	59	58W
Glacier B.	**152**	58	30N	136	10W
Glacier Nat. Park	**152**	51	15N	117	30W
Glacier National Park	**160**	48	35N	113	40W
Glacier Peak Mt.	**160**	48	7N	121	7W
Gladewater	**159**	32	30N	94	58W
Gladstone, Queens., Austral.	**74**	23	52 S	151	16 E
Gladstone, S.A., Austral.	**140**	33	15 S	138	22 E
Gladstone, W. Australia, Austral.	**137**	25	57 S	114	17 E
Gladstone, Can.	**153**	50	13N	98	57W
Gladstone, U.S.A.	**156**	45	52N	87	1W
Gladwin	**156**	43	59N	84	29W
Gladys L.	**152**	59	50N	133	0W
Glafsfjorden	**72**	59	30N	12	45 E
Głagów Małapolski	**53**	50	10N	21	56 E
Gláma	**74**	65	48N	23	0W
Glåma, R.	**71**	60	30N	12	8 E
Glamis	**37**	56	37N	3	0W
Glamorgan (□)	**26**	51	37N	3	35W
Glamorgan, Vale of	**23**	50	45N	3	15W
Glan, Phil.	**103**	5	45N	125	20 E
Glan, Sweden	**73**	58	37N	16	0 E
Glanaman	**31**	51	48N	3	56W
Glanaruddery Mts.	**39**	52	20N	9	27W
Glandore	**39**	51	33N	9	7W
Glandore Harb.	**39**	51	33N	9	8W
Glanerbrug	**46**	52	13N	6	58 E
Glanton	**35**	55	25N	1	54W
Glanworth	**39**	52	10N	8	25W
Glarner Alpen	**51**	46	50N	9	0 E
Glärnisch	**51**	47	0N	9	0 E
Glarus	**51**	47	3N	9	4 E
Glarus □	**51**	47	0N	9	5 E
Glas Maol	**37**	56	52N	3	20W
Glasco, Kans., U.S.A.	**158**	39	25N	97	50W
Glasco, N.Y., U.S.A.	**162**	42	3N	73	57W
Glasgow, U.K.	**34**	55	52N	4	14W
Glasgow, Ky., U.S.A.	**156**	37	2N	85	55W
Glasgow, Mont., U.S.A.	**160**	48	12N	106	35W
Glasnevin	**38**	53	22N	6	18W
Glassboro	**162**	39	42N	75	7W
Glasslough	**38**	54	20N	6	53W
Glastonbury, U.K.	**28**	51	9N	2	42W
Glastonbury, U.S.A.	**162**	41	42N	72	27W
Glatt, R.	**51**	47	28N	8	32 E
Glattfelden	**51**	47	33N	8	30 E
Glauchau	**48**	50	50N	12	33 E
Glazov	**81**	58	9N	52	40 E
Glbovo	**67**	42	1N	24	43 E
Gleichen	**152**	50	50N	113	0W
Gleisdorf	**52**	47	6N	15	44 E
Glemsford	**29**	52	6N	0	41 E
Glen Affric	**36**	57	15N	5	0W
Glen Afton	**142**	37	46 S	175	4 E
Glen Almond	**35**	56	28N	3	50W
Glen B.	**38**	54	43N	8	45W
Glen Burnie	**162**	39	10N	76	37W
Glen Canyon Dam	**161**	37	0N	111	25W
Glen Canyon Nat. Recreation Area	**161**	37	30N	111	0W
Glen Coe	**23**	56	40N	5	0W
Glen Cove	**162**	40	51N	73	37W
Glen Esk	**37**	56	53N	2	50W
Glen Etive	**34**	56	37N	5	0W
Glen Florrie	**136**	22	55 S	115	59 E
Glen Garry, Inv., U.K.	**36**	57	3N	5	7W
Glen Garry, Per., U.K.	**37**	56	47N	4	5W
Glen Gowrie	**140**	31	4 S	143	10 E
Glen Helen	**32**	54	14N	4	35W
Glen Innes	**139**	29	40 S	151	39 E
Glen Lyon, U.K.	**37**	56	35N	4	20W
Glen Lyon, U.S.A.	**162**	41	10N	76	7W
Glen Massey	**142**	37	38 S	175	2 E
Glen Mor	**37**	57	12N	4	37 E
Glen Moriston	**36**	57	10N	4	58W
Glen Orchy	**34**	56	27N	4	52W
Glen Orrin	**37**	57	30N	4	45W
Glen Oykel	**37**	58	5N	4	50W
Glen, R.	**29**	52	50N	0	7W
Glen Shee	**37**	56	45N	3	25W
Glen Shiel	**36**	57	8N	5	20W
Glen Spean	**37**	56	53N	4	40W
Glen Trool Lodge	**34**	55	5N	4	30W
Glen Ullin	**158**	46	48N	101	46W
Glen Valley	**141**	36	54 S	147	28 E
Glenade	**38**	54	22N	8	17W
Glenamoy	**38**	54	14N	9	40W
Glénans, Is. de	**42**	47	42N	4	0W
Glenariff	**141**	30	50 S	146	33 E
Glenarm	**38**	54	58N	5	58W
Glenart Castle	**39**	52	48N	6	12W
Glenavy, N.Z.	**143**	44	54 S	171	7 E
Glenavy, U.K.	**38**	54	36N	6	12W
Glenbarr	**34**	55	34N	5	40W
Glenbeigh	**39**	52	3N	9	57W
Glenbrittle	**36**	57	13N	6	18W
Glenbrook	**142**	33	46 S	150	37 E
Glenburn	**141**	37	37 S	145	26 E
Glencoe, S. Afr.	**129**	28	11 S	30	11 E
Glencoe, U.S.A.	**158**	44	45N	94	10W
Glencolumbkille	**38**	54	43N	8	41W
Glendale, Can.	**150**	46	45N	84	2W
Glendale, Zimb.	**127**	17	22 S	31	5 E
Glendale, Ariz., U.S.A.	**161**	33	40N	112	8W
Glendale, Calif., U.S.A.	**163**	34	7N	118	18W
Glendale, Oreg., U.S.A.	**160**	42	44N	123	29W
Glendive	**158**	47	7N	104	40W
Glendo	**158**	42	30N	105	0W
Glendora	**163**	34	8N	117	52W
Gleneagles	**35**	56	16N	3	44W
Glenealy	**39**	52	59N	6	10W
Gleneely	**38**	52	14N	7	8W
Glenelg, Austral.	**140**	34	58 S	138	31 E
Glenelg, U.K.	**36**	57	13N	5	37W
Glenelg, R.	**140**	38	4 S	140	59 E
Glenfarne	**38**	54	17N	8	0W
Glenfield	**162**	43	43N	75	24W
Glenfinnan	**36**	56	52N	5	28W
Glengad Hd.	**38**	55	19N	7	11W
Glengariff	**39**	51	45N	9	33W
Glengormley	**38**	54	41N	5	57W
Glengyle	**138**	24	48 S	139	37 E
Glenham	**143**	46	26 S	168	52 E
Glenhope	**143**	41	40 S	172	39 E
Glenisland	**38**	53	54N	9	24W
Glenkens, The	**34**	55	10N	4	15W
Glenluce	**34**	54	53N	4	50W
Glenmary, Mt.	**143**	44	0 S	169	55 E
Glenmaye	**32**	54	11N	4	42W
Glenmora	**159**	31	1N	92	34W
Glenmorgan	**139**	27	14 S	149	42 E
Glenn, oilfield	**19**	57	55N	0	15 E
Glennagevlagh	**38**	53	36N	9	41W
Glennamaddy	**38**	53	37N	8	33W
Glenn's Ferry	**160**	43	0N	115	15W
Glenoe	**38**	54	47N	5	50W
Glenorchy, S. Austral., Austral.	**140**	31	55 S	139	46 E
Glenorchy, Tas., Austral.	**138**	42	49 S	147	18 E
Glenorchy, Vic., Austral.	**140**	36	55 S	142	41 E
Glenore	**138**	17	50 S	141	12 E
Glenormiston	**138**	22	55 S	138	50 E
Glenreagh	**139**	30	2 S	153	1 E
Glenrock	**160**	42	53N	105	55W
Glenrothes	**35**	56	12N	3	11W
Glenrowan	**141**	36	29 S	146	13 E
Glenroy, S. Australia, Austral.	**140**	37	13 S	140	48 E
Glenroy, W. Australia, Austral.	**136**	17	16 S	126	14 E
Glenroy, S. Afr.	**132**	26	23 S	28	17 E
Glens Falls	**162**	43	19N	73	39W
Glentane	**38**	53	25N	8	30W
Glenties	**38**	54	48N	8	18W
Glenville	**156**	38	56N	80	50W
Glenwood, Alta., Can.	**152**	49	21N	113	31W
Glenwood, Newf., Can.	**151**	49	0N	54	47W
Glenwood, Ark., U.S.A.	**159**	34	20N	93	30W
Glenwood, Hawaii, U.S.A.	**147**	19	29N	155	10W
Glenwood, Iowa, U.S.A.	**158**	41	7N	95	41W
Glenwood, Minn., U.S.A.	**158**	45	38N	95	21W
Glenwood Sprs.	**160**	39	39N	107	15W
Gletsch	**51**	46	34N	8	22 E
Glettinganes	**51**	65	30N	13	37W
Glin	**39**	52	34N	9	17W
Glina	**63**	45	20N	16	6 E
Glinojeck	**54**	52	49N	20	21 E
Glinsk	**39**	53	23N	9	49W
Glittertind	**71**	61	40N	8	32 E
Gliwice (Gleiwitz)	**54**	50	22N	18	41 E
Globe	**161**	33	25N	110	53W
Glodeanu-Siliştea	**70**	44	50N	26	48 E
Glödnitz	**52**	46	53N	14	7 E
Glodyany	**70**	47	45N	27	31 E
Gloggnitz	**52**	47	41N	15	56 E
Głogów	**54**	51	37N	16	5 E
Głogowek	**54**	50	21N	17	53 E
Gloria, La	**174**	8	37N	73	48W
Glorieuses, Îs.	**129**	11	30 S	47	20 E
Glossop	**32**	53	27N	1	56W
Gloucester, Austral.	**141**	32	0 S	151	59 E
Gloucester, U.K.	**28**	51	52N	2	15W
Gloucester, U.S.A.	**162**	42	38N	70	39W
Gloucester, Va., U.S.A.	**162**	37	25N	76	32W
Gloucester, C.	**135**	5	26 S	148	21 E
Gloucester City	**162**	39	54N	75	8W
Gloucester, I.	**138**	20	0 S	148	30 E
Gloucestershire □	**28**	51	44N	2	10W
Gloversville	**162**	43	5N	74	18W
Glovertown	**151**	48	40N	54	03W
Głubczyce	**54**	50	13N	17	52 E
Glubokiy	**83**	48	35N	40	25 E
Glubokoye	**80**	55	10N	27	45 E
Głucholazy	**54**	50	19N	17	24 E
Glücksburg	**48**	54	48N	9	34 E
Glückstadt	**48**	53	46N	9	28 E
Gluepot	**140**	33	45 S	140	0 E
Glukhov	**80**	51	40N	33	50 E
Glussk	**80**	52	53N	28	41 E
Gł ó wno	**54**	51	59N	19	42 E
Glyn-ceiriog	**31**	52	56N	3	12W
Glyn Neath	**31**	51	45N	3	37W
Glyncorrwg	**31**	51	40N	3	39W
Glyngøre	**73**	56	46N	8	52 E
Glynn	**39**	52	29N	6	55W
Gmünd, Kärnten, Austria	**52**	46	54N	13	31 E
Gmünd, Niederösterreich, Austria	**52**	48	45N	15	0 E
Gmunden	**52**	47	55N	13	48 E
Gnarp	**72**	62	3N	17	16 E
Gnesta	**72**	59	3N	17	17 E
Gniew	**54**	53	50N	18	50 E
Gniewkowo	**54**	52	54N	18	25 E
Gniezno	**54**	52	30N	17	35 E
Gnoien	**48**	53	58N	12	41 E
Gnopp	**123**	8	47N	29	50 E
Gnosall	**28**	52	48N	2	15W
Gnosjö	**73**	57	22N	13	43 E
Gnowangerup	**137**	33	58 S	117	59 E
Go Cong	**101**	10	22N	106	40 E
Gō-no-ura	**110**	33	44N	129	40 E
Goa	**97**	15	33N	73	59 E
Goa □	**97**	15	33N	73	59 E
Goageb	**128**	26	49 S	17	15 E
Goalen Hd.	**141**	36	33 S	150	4 E
Goalpara	**98**	26	10N	90	40 E
Goalundo	**95**	23	50N	89	47 E
Goaso	**120**	6	48N	2	30W
Goat Fell	**34**	55	37N	5	11W
Goba, Ethiopia	**123**	7	1N	39	59 E
Goba, Mozam.	**125**	26	15 S	32	13 E
Gobabis	**128**	22	16 S	19	0 E
Gobi, desert	**105**	44	0N	111	0 E
Gobichettipalayam	**97**	11	31N	77	21 E
Gobō	**111**	33	53N	135	10 E
Gobo	**123**	5	40N	30	10 E

* *Renamed Kiribati*

Goch Grand Bassa

Goch 48 51 40N 6 9 E
Gochas 125 24 59 S 19 25 E
Godalming 29 51 12N 0 37W
Godavari Point 96 17 0N 82 20 E
Godavari, R. 96 19 5N 79 0 E
Godbout 151 49 20N 67 38W
Godda 95 24 50N 87 20 E
Goddua 119 26 26N 14 19 E
Godech 66 43 1N 23 4 E
Godegård 73 58 43N 15 8 E
Goderich 150 43 45N 81 41W
Goderville 42 49 38N 0 22 E
Godhavn 12 69 15N 53 38W
Godhra 94 22 49N 73 40 E
Godmanchester 29 52 19N 0 11W
Gödöllö 53 47 38N 19 25 E
Godoy Cruz 172 32 56 S 68 52W
Godrevy Pt. 30 50 15N 5 24W
Gods L. 153 54 40N 94 15W
Gods, R. 153 56 22N 92 51W
Godshill 28 50 38N 1 13W
Godstone 29 51 15N 0 3W
Godthåb 12 64 10N 51 46W
Godwin Austen (K2) 93 36 0N 77 0 E
Goeie Hoop, Kaap die 128 34 24 S 18 30 E
Goeland, L. 150 49 50N 76 48W
Goeree 46 51 50N 4 0 E
Goes 47 51 30N 3 55 E
Goffstown 162 43 1N 71 36W
Gogama 150 47 35N 81 43W
Gogango 138 23 40 S 150 2 E
Gogebic, L. 158 46 30N 89 34W
Gogha 94 21 32N 72 9 E
Gogolin 54 50 30N 18 0 E
Gogra, R. = Ghaghara 99 26 0N 84 20 E
Gogriâl 123 8 30N 28 0 E
Goiana 170 7 33 S 34 59W
Goiandira 171 11 46 S 46 40W
Goianésia 171 15 18 S 49 7W
Goiânia 171 16 35 S 49 20W
Goiás 171 15 55 S 50 10W
Goiás □ 170 12 10 S 48 0W
Goiatuba 171 18 1 S 49 23W
Goil L. 34 56 8N 4 52W
Goirle 47 51 31N 5 4 E
Góis 56 40 10N 8 6W
Goisern 52 47 38N 13 38 E
Gojam □ 123 10 55N 36 30 E
Gojeb, W. 123 7 12N 36 40 E
Gojō 111 34 21N 135 42 E
Gojra 94 31 10N 72 40 E
Gokak 97 16 11N 74 52 E
Gokarannath 95 27 57N 80 39 E
Gokarn 97 14 33N 74 17 E
Gökçeada 68 40 10N 26 0 E
Gokteik 99 22 26N 97 0 E
Gokurt 94 29 47N 67 26 E
Gøl 73 57 4N 9 42 E
Gola 95 28 3N 80 32 E
Gola I. 38 55 4N 8 20W
Golaghat 98 26 30N 94 0 E
Golakganj 95 26 8N 89 52 E
Golaya Pristen 82 46 29N 32 23 E
Golchikha 12 71 45N 84 0 E
Golconda 160 40 58N 117 32W
Gold Beach 160 42 25N 124 25W
Gold Coast, Austral. 139 28 0 S 153 25 E
Gold Coast, W. Afr. 121 4 0N 1 40W
Gold Creek 147 62 45N 149 45W
Gold Hill 160 42 28N 123 2W
Gold Point 163 37 21N 117 21W
Gold River 152 49 40N 126 10 E
Goldach 51 47 28N 9 28 E
Goldau 51 47 3N 8 33 E
Goldberg 48 53 34N 12 6 E
Golden, Can. 152 51 20N 117 0W
Golden, Ireland 39 52 30N 8 0W
Golden, U.S.A. 158 39 42N 105 30W
Golden Bay 143 40 40 S 172 50 E
Golden Gate 160 37 54N 122 30W
Golden Hinde, mt. 152 49 40N 125 44W
Golden Prairie 153 50 13N 109 37W
Golden Rock 97 10 45N 78 48 E
Golden Vale 39 52 33N 8 17W
Goldendale 160 45 53N 120 48W
Goldfield 163 37 45N 117 13W
Goldfields 153 59 28N 108 29W
Goldpines 153 50 45N 93 05W
Goldsand L. 153 57 2N 101 8W
Goldsboro 157 35 24N 77 59W
Goldsmith 159 32 0N 102 40W
Goldsworthy 136 20 21 S 119 30 E
Goldsworthy, Mt. 136 20 23 S 119 31 E
Goldthwaite 159 31 25N 98 32W
Goleen 39 51 30N 9 43W
Golegã 57 39 24N 8 29W
Goleniów 54 53 35N 14 50 E
Goleta 163 34 27N 119 50W
Golfito 166 8 41N 83 5W
Golfo degli Aranci 65 41 0N 9 38 E
Goliad 159 28 40N 97 22W
Golija 66 43 22N 20 15 E
Golija, Mts. 66 43 5N 18 45 E
Golina 54 52 15N 18 4 E
Golo, R. 45 42 31N 9 32 E
Golovanesvsk 82 48 25N 30 30 E
Gölpazari 82 40 17N 30 17 E
Golra 94 33 37N 72 56 E
Golspie 37 57 58N 3 58W
Golub Dobrzyn 54 53 7N 19 2 E
Golubac 66 44 38N 21 38 E
Golyama Kamchiya, R. 67 43 2N 27 18 E
Goma, Ethiopia 123 8 29N 36 53 E
Goma, Rwanda 126 2 11 S 29 18 E
Goma, Zaïre 126 1 37 S 29 10 E
Gomare 128 19 25 S 22 8 E
Gomati, R. 95 26 30N 81 50 E
Gombari 126 2 45N 29 3 E
Gombe 121 10 19N 11 2 E
Gombe, R. 126 4 30 S 32 50 E
Gombi 121 10 12N 12 45 E
Gomel 80 52 28N 31 0 E
Gomera, I. 116 28 10N 17 5W
Gometra I. 34 56 30N 6 18W
Gómez Palacio 164 25 40N 104 40W
Gommern 48 52 54N 11 47 E
Gomogomo 103 6 25 S 134 53 E
Gomoh 99 23 52N 86 10 E
Gomotartsi 66 44 6N 22 57 E
Goms 50 46 30N 8 15 E
Gonābād 93 34 15N 58 45 E
Gonaïves 167 19 20N 72 50W
Gonâve, G. de la 167 19 29N 72 42W
Gonâve, I. de la 167 18 45N 73 0W
Gönc 53 48 28N 21 14 E
Gonda 95 27 9N 81 58 E
Gondab-e Kāvūs 93 37 20N 55 25 E
Gondal 94 21 58N 70 52 E
Gonder 123 12 23N 37 30 E
Gondia 96 21 30N 80 10 E
Gondola 127 19 4 S 33 37 E
Gondomar, Port. 56 41 10N 8 35W
Gondomar, Spain 56 42 7N 8 45W
Gondrecourt-le-Château 43 48 26N 5 30 E
Gongola □ 121 8 0N 12 0 E
Gongola, R. 121 10 30N 10 22 E
Goniadz 54 53 30N 22 44 E
Goniri 121 11 30N 12 15 E
Gonnesa 64 39 17N 8 27 E
Gonno-Altaysk 76 51 50N 86 5 E
Gonnos 68 39 52N 22 29 E
Gonnosfanadiga 64 39 30N 8 39 E
Gonzales, Calif., U.S.A. 163 36 35N 121 30W
Gonzales, Tex., U.S.A. 159 29 30N 97 30W
González Chaves 172 38 02 S 60 05W
Good Hope, C. of = Goeie Hoop 128 34 24 S 18 30 E
Goode 139 31 58 S 133 45 E
Goodenough I. 135 9 20 S 150 15 E
Gooderham 150 44 54N 78 21W
Goodeve 153 51 4N 103 10W
Gooding 160 43 0N 114 50W
Goodland 158 39 22N 101 44W
Goodnight 159 35 4N 101 13W
Goodooga 139 29 1 S 147 28 E
Goodrich 28 51 52N 2 38W
Goodsoil 153 54 24N 109 13W
Goodsprings 161 35 51N 115 30W
Goodwick 31 52 0N 5 0W
Goodwin, Mt. 136 14 13 S 129 32 E
Goodwood 29 50 53N 0 44W
Goole 33 53 42N 0 52W
Goolgowi 141 33 58 S 145 41 E
Goolwa 140 35 30 S 138 47 E
Goomalling 137 31 15 S 116 42 E
Goombalie 139 29 59 S 145 26 E
Goonalga 140 31 45 S 143 37 E
Goonda 127 19 48 S 33 57 E
Goondiwindi 139 28 30 S 150 21 E
Goongarrie 137 30 2 S 121 8 E
Goonumbla 141 32 59 S 148 11 E
Goonyella 138 21 47 S 147 58 E
Goor 46 52 13N 6 33 E
Gooray 139 28 25 S 150 2 E
Goose Bay 151 53 15N 60 20W
Goose L. 160 42 0N 120 30W
Goose R. 151 53 20N 60 35W
Goothinga 138 17 36 S 140 50 E
Gooty 97 15 7N 77 41 E
Gop 93 22 5N 69 50 E
Gopalganj, Bangla. 98 23 1N 89 50 E
Gopalganj, India 95 26 28N 84 30 E
Goppenstein 50 46 23N 7 46 E
Göppingen 49 48 42N 9 40 E
Gor 59 37 23N 2 58W
Góra 54 51 40N 16 31 E
Gorakhpur 95 26 47N 83 32 E
Gorbatov 81 56 12N 43 2 E
Gorbea, Peña 58 43 1N 2 50W
Gorda 163 35 53N 121 26W
Gorda, Punta 166 14 10N 83 10W
Gordon, Austral. 140 32 7 S 138 20 E
Gordon, U.K. 35 55 41N 2 32W
Gordon, U.S.A. 158 42 49N 102 6W
Gordon B. 136 11 35 S 130 10 E
Gordon Downs 136 18 48 S 128 40 E
Gordon L., Alta., Can. 153 56 30N 110 25W
Gordon L., N.W.T., Can. 152 63 5N 113 11W
Gordon, R. 138 42 27 S 145 30 E
Gordon River 137 34 10 S 117 15 E
Gordonia 128 28 13 S 21 10 E
Gordonvale 138 17 5 S 145 50 E
Gore 139 28 17 S 151 30 E
Goré 117 7 59N 16 49 E
Gore, Ethiopia 123 8 12N 35 32 E
Gore, N.Z. 143 46 5 S 168 58 E
Gore B. 150 45 57N 82 28W
Gorebridge 35 55 51N 3 2W
Goresbridge 39 52 38N 7 0W
Gorey 39 52 41N 6 18W
Gorgan 93 36 55N 54 30 E
Gorge, The 138 18 27 S 145 30 E
Gorgona, I. 174 3 0N 78 10W
Gorgona I. 62 43 27N 9 52 E
Gorgora 123 12 15N 37 17 E
Gori 83 42 0N 44 7 E
Gorinchem 46 51 50N 4 59 E
Goring, Oxon, U.K. 28 51 31N 1 8W
Goring, Sussex, U.K. 29 50 49N 0 26W
Gorinhatã 171 19 15 S 49 45W
Goritsy 81 57 4N 36 43 E
Gorizia 63 45 56N 13 37 E
Gorka 54 51 39N 16 58 E
Gorki = Gorkiy 81 56 20N 44 0 E
Gorkiy 81 57 20N 44 0 E
Gorkovskoye Vdkhr. 81 57 2N 43 4 E
Gorleston 29 52 35N 1 44 E
Gorlev 73 55 30N 11 15 E
Gorlice 54 49 35N 21 11 E
Görlitz 54 51 10N 14 59 E
Gorlovka 81 48 25N 37 58 E
Gorman, Calif., U.S.A. 163 34 47N 118 51W
Gorman, Tex., U.S.A. 159 32 15N 98 43W
Gorna Oryakhovitsa 67 43 7N 25 40 E
Gorna Radgona 63 46 40N 16 2 E
Gornja Tuzla 66 44 35N 18 46 E
Gornji Grad 63 46 20N 14 52 E
Gornji Milanovac 66 44 00N 20 29 E
Gornji Vafuk 66 43 57N 17 34 E
Gorno Ablanovo 67 43 37N 25 43 E
Gorno Filinskoye 76 60 5N 70 0 E
Gornyy 81 51 50N 48 30 E
Gorodenka 82 48 41N 25 29 E
Gorodets 81 56 38N 43 28 E
Gorodische 81 53 13N 45 40 E
Gorodnitsa 80 50 46N 27 26 E
Gorodnya 80 51 55N 31 33 E
Gorodok, Byelorussia, U.S.S.R. 80 55 30N 30 3 E
Gorodok, Ukraine, U.S.S.R. 80 49 46N 23 32 E
Goroka 135 6 7 S 145 25 E
Goroke 140 36 43 S 141 29 E
Gorokhov 80 50 15N 24 45 E
Gorokhovets 81 56 13N 42 39 E
Gorom Gorom 121 14 26N 0 14W
Goromonzi 127 17 52 S 31 22 E
Gorong, Kepulauan 103 4 5 S 131 15 E
Gorongosa, Sa. da 127 18 27 S 32 2 E
Gorongose, R. 129 20 40 S 34 30 E
Gorontalo 103 0 35N 123 13 E
Goronyo 121 13 29N 5 39 E
Gorredijk 46 53 0N 6 3 E
Gorron 42 48 25N 0 50W
Gorseinon 31 51 40N 4 2W
Gorssel 46 52 12N 6 12 E
Gort 39 53 4N 8 50W
Gortin 38 54 43N 7 13W
Gorumahisani 96 22 20N 86 24 E
Gorumna I. 39 53 15N 9 44W
Gorzkowice 54 51 13N 19 36 E
Gorzno 54 53 12N 19 38 E
Gorzów Slaski 54 51 3N 18 22 E
Gorzów Wielkopolski 54 52 43N 15 15 E
Gorzów Wielkopolski □ 54 52 45N 15 30 E
Gosainthan, Mt. 99 28 20N 85 45 E
Gosberton 33 52 52N 0 10W
Göschenen 51 46 40N 8 36 E
Göse 111 34 27N 135 44 E
Gosford 141 33 23N 151 18 E
Gosforth 32 54 24N 3 27W
Goshen, S. Afr. 128 25 50 S 25 0 E
Goshen, Calif., U.S.A. 163 36 21N 119 25W
Goshen, Ind., U.S.A. 156 41 36N 85 46W
Goshen, N.Y., U.S.A. 162 41 23N 74 21W
Goslar 48 51 55N 10 23 E
Gospič 63 44 35N 15 23 E
Gosport 28 50 48N 1 8W
Gossa, I. 71 62 52N 6 50 E
Gossau 51 47 25N 9 15 E
Gosse, R. 138 19 32 S 134 37 E
Gostivar 66 41 48N 20 57 E
Gostyn 54 51 50N 17 3 E
Gostynin 54 52 26N 19 29 E
Göta 73 58 6N 12 10 E
Göta älv 73 57 42N 11 54 E
Göta Kanal 73 58 35N 14 15 E
Götaland, reg. 73 58 0N 14 0 E
Göteborg 73 57 43N 11 59 E
Göteborg & Bohus □ 75 58 20N 11 50 E
Gotemba 111 35 18N 138 56 E
Götene 73 58 32N 13 30 E
Gotha 48 50 56N 10 42 E
Gothenburg 158 40 58N 100 8W
Gothenburg = Göteborg 73 57 43N 11 59 E
Gotse Delchev (Nevrokop) 67 41 43N 23 46 E
Gotska Sandön 75 58 24N 19 15 E
Gōtsu 110 35 0N 132 14 E
Göttingen 48 51 31N 9 55 E
Gottwaldov (Zlin) 53 49 14N 17 40 E
Gouda 46 52 1N 4 42 E
Goudhurst 29 51 7N 0 28 E
Goudiry 120 14 15N 12 45 E
Gough I. 15 40 10 S 9 45W
Gouin Res. 150 48 35N 74 40W
Gouitafla 120 7 30N 5 53W
Goula Touila 118 21 50N 1 57 E
Goulburn 141 34 44 S 149 44 E
Goulburn Is. 138 11 40 S 133 20 E
Gould, mt. 137 25 46 S 117 18 E
Goulia 120 10 1N 7 11W
Goulimine 118 28 50N 10 0W
Goulmima 118 31 41N 4 57W
Gouménissa 68 40 56N 22 37 E
Goumeur 119 20 40N 18 30 E
Goundam 135 16 25N 3 45W
Gounou-Gaya 124 9 38N 15 31 E
Goúra 69 37 56N 22 20 E
Gourara 118 29 0N 0 30 E
Gouraya 118 36 31N 1 56 E
Gourdon, France 44 44 44N 1 23 E
Gourdon, U.K. 37 56 50N 2 15W
Gouré 121 14 0N 10 10 E
Gourits, R. 128 34 15 S 21 45 E
Gourma Rharous 121 16 55N 2 5W
Gournay-en-Bray 43 49 29N 1 44 E
Gouro 117 19 30N 19 30 E
Gourock 34 55 58N 4 49W
Gourock Ra. 141 36 0 S 149 25 E
Gourselik 121 13 31N 10 52 E
Goursi 120 12 42N 2 37W
Gouvêa 171 18 27 S 43 44W
Gouzon 44 46 12N 2 14 E
Govan 153 51 20N 105 0W
Gove 133 12 25 S 136 55 E
Goverla 82 48 9N 24 30 E
Governador Valadares 171 18 15 S 41 57W
Governor's Harbour 166 25 10N 76 14W
Gowan 138 25 0 S 145 0 E
Gowanda 156 42 29N 78 58W
Gower, The 31 51 35N 4 10W
Gowerton 31 51 38N 4 2W
Gowna, L. 38 53 52N 7 35W
Gowran 39 52 38N 7 5W
Goya 172 29 10 S 59 10W
Goyder's Lagoon 139 27 3 S 139 58 E
Goyllarisquizga 174 10 19 S 76 31W
Goz Beîda 117 12 20N 21 30 E
Goz Regeb 123 16 3N 35 33 E
Gozdnica 54 51 28N 15 4 E
Gozo (Ghaudex) 60 36 0N 14 13 E
Graaff-Reinet 128 32 13 S 24 32 E
Graasten 73 54 57N 9 34 E
Grabow 48 53 17N 11 31 E
Grabów 54 51 31N 18 7 E
Grabs 51 47 11N 9 27 E
Gračac 63 44 18N 15 57 E
Gračanica 66 44 43N 18 18 E
Graçay 43 47 10N 1 50 E
Grace 160 42 38N 111 46W
Grace, L., (North) 137 33 10 S 118 20 E
Grace, L., (South) 137 33 15 S 118 25 E
Graceville 158 45 36N 96 23W
Grachevka 84 52 55N 52 52 E
Gracias a Dios, C. 166 15 0N 83 20W
Gradačac 66 44 52N 18 26 E
Gradaús 170 7 43 S 51 11W
Gradaús, Serra dos 170 8 0 S 50 45W
Gradeska Planina 66 41 30N 22 15 E
Gradets 67 42 46N 26 30 E
Gradignan 66 44 47N 0 36W
Gradnitsa 67 42 57N 24 58 E
Grado, Italy 63 45 40N 13 20 E
Grado, Spain 56 43 23N 6 4W
Gradule 139 28 32 S 149 15 E
Grady 159 34 52N 103 15W
Graeca, Lacul 70 44 5N 26 10 E
Graemsay I. 37 58 56N 3 17W
Graénalon, L. 74 64 10N 17 20W
Grafham Water 29 52 18N 0 17W
Grafton, Austral. 139 29 38 S 152 58 E
Grafton, U.S.A. 158 48 30N 97 25W
Grafton, C. 133 16 51 S 146 0 E
Gragnano 65 40 42N 14 30 E
Graham, Can. 150 49 20N 90 30W
Graham, N.C., U.S.A. 157 36 5N 79 22W
Graham, Tex., U.S.A. 159 33 7N 98 38W
Graham Bell, Os. 76 80 5N 70 0 E
Graham I. 152 53 40N 132 30W
Graham Land 13 65 0 S 64 0W
Graham Mt. 161 32 46N 109 58W
Graham, R. 152 56 31N 122 17W
Grahamdale 153 51 23N 98 30W
Grahamstown 128 33 19 S 26 31 E
Grahamsville 162 41 51N 74 33W
Grahovo 66 42 40N 18 4 E
Graïba 119 34 30N 10 13 E
Graide 47 49 58N 5 4 E
Graigue 39 52 51N 6 56W
Graiguenamanagh 39 52 32N 6 58W
Grain Coast 120 4 20N 10 0W
Grainthorpe 33 53 27N 0 5 E
Graivoron 80 50 29N 35 39 E
Grajaú 170 5 50 S 46 30W
Grajaú, R. 170 3 41 S 44 48W
Grajewo 54 53 39N 22 30 E
Gramada 66 43 49N 22 39 E
Gramat 44 44 48N 1 43 E
Gramisdale 36 57 29N 7 18W
Grammichele 65 37 12N 14 37 E
Grampian □ 37 57 0N 3 0W
Grampians, Mts. 140 37 0 S 142 20 E
Gran Canaria 116 27 55N 15 35W
Gran Chaco 156 25 0 S 61 0W
Gran Paradiso 62 49 33N 7 17 E
Gran Sabana, La 174 5 30N 61 30W
Gran Sasso d'Italia, Mt. 44 42 25N 13 30 E
Granada, Nic. 166 11 58N 86 0W
Granada, Spain 59 37 10N 3 35W
Granada, U.S.A. 158 38 5N 102 13W
Granada □ 57 37 5N 4 30W
Granard 38 53 47N 7 30W
Granbo 72 61 16N 13 33 E
Granbury 159 32 28N 97 48W
Granby 150 45 25N 72 45W
Grand Bahama I. 166 26 40N 78 30W
Grand Bank 151 47 6N 55 48W
Grand Bassa 120 6 0N 10 2W

Grand Bassam Grillby

Grand Bassam 120 5 10N 3 49W
Grand Béréby 120 4 38N 6 55W
Grand-Bourg 167 15 53N 61 19W
Grand Canal 39 53 15N 8 10W
Grand Canyon National Park 161 36 15N 112 20W
Grand Cayman 166 19 20N 81 20W
Grand Cess 120 4 40N 8 12W
Grand 'Combe, La 45 44 13N 4 2E
Grand Coulee 160 47 48N 119 1W
Grand Coulee Dam 160 48 0N 118 50W
Grand Erg Occidental 118 30 20N 1 0E
Grand Erg Oriental 119 30 0N 6 30E
Grand Falls 151 47 2N 67 46W
Grand Forks, Can. 152 49 0N 118 30W
Grand Forks, U.S.A. 158 48 0N 97 3W
Grand-Fougeray 42 47 43N 1 44W
Grand Fougeray, Le 42 47 44N 1 43W
Grand Haven 156 43 3N 86 13W
Grand I. 150 46 30N 86 40W
Grand Island 158 40 59N 98 25W
Grand Isle 159 29 15N 89 58W
Grand Junction 161 39 0N 108 30W
Grand L., N.B., Can. 151 45 57N 66 7W
Grand L., Newf., Can. 151 48 45N 57 45W
Grand L., Newf., Can. 151 53 40N 60 30W
Grand L., Newf., Can. 151 49 0N 57 30W
Grand L., U.S.A. 159 29 55N 92 45W
Grand Lac 150 47 35N 77 35W
Grand Lahou 120 5 10N 5 0W
Grand Lake 160 40 20N 105 54W
Grand-Leez 47 50 35N 4 45E
Grand Lieu, Lac de 42 47 6N 1 40W
Grand Manan I. 151 44 45N 66 52W
Grand Marais, Can. 158 47 45N 90 25W
Grand Marais, U.S.A. 156 46 39N 85 59W
Grand Mère 150 46 36N 72 40W
Grand Motte, La 45 48 35N 1 4E
Grand Popo 121 6 15N 1 44E
Grand Portage 150 47 58N 89 41W
Grand Pressigny, Le 42 46 55N 0 48E
Grand, R., Mo., U.S.A. 160 39 23N 93 27W
Grand, R., S.D., U.S.A. 160 45 45N 101 30W
Grand Rapids, Can. 153 53 12N 99 19W
Grand Rapids, Mich., U.S.A. 156 42 57N 85 40W
Grand Rapids, Minn., U.S.A. 158 47 19N 93 29W
Grand St.-Bernard, Col. du 50 45 53N 7 11E
Grand Teton 160 43 45N 110 57W
Grand Valley 160 39 30N 108 2W
Grand View 153 51 11N 100 51W
Grandas de Salime 56 43 13N 6 53W
Grande 170 11 30S 44 30W
Grande, B. 176 50 30S 68 20W
Grande Baie 151 48 19N 70 52W
Grande Cache 152 53 53N 119 8W
Grande, Coxilha 173 28 18S 51 30W
Grande de Santiago, R. 164 21 20N 105 50W
Grande Dixence, Barr. de la 50 46 5N 7 23E
Grande-Entrée 151 47 30N 61 40W
Grande, I. 171 23 9S 44 14W
Grande, La 160 45 15N 118 0W
Grande Prairie 152 55 15N 118 50W
Grande, R., Jujuy, Argent. 172 23 9S 65 52W
Grande, R., Mendoza, Argent. 172 36 52S 69 45W
Grande R. 174 18 35S 63 0W
Grande, R., Brazil 171 20 0S 50 0W
Grande, R., Spain 59 39 6N 0 48W
Grande, R., U.S.A. 159 29 20N 100 40W
Grande Rivière 151 48 26N 64 30W
Grande, Serra, Goiás, Brazil 170 11 15S 46 30W
Grande, Serra, Maranhao, Brazil 170 4 30S 41 20W
Grande, Serra, Piauí, Brazil 170 8 0S 45 0W
Grande Vallée 151 49 14N 65 8W
Grandes Bergeronnes 151 48 16N 69 35W
Grandfalls 159 31 21N 102 51W
Grandglise 47 50 30N 3 42E
Grandoe Mines 152 56 29N 129 54W
Grândola 57 38 12N 8 35W
Grandpré 43 49 20N 4 50E
Grandson 50 46 49N 6 39E
Grandview, Can. 153 51 10N 100 42W
Grandview, U.S.A. 160 46 13N 119 58W
Grandvilliers 43 49 40N 1 57E
Graneros 172 34 5S 70 45W
Graney L. 39 53 0N 8 40W
Grange 38 54 24N 8 32W
Grange, La, Austral. 136 18 45S 121 43E
Grange, La, U.S.A. 163 37 42N 120 27W
Grange, La, Ga., U.S.A. 157 33 4N 85 0W
Grange, La, Ky., U.S.A. 156 38 20N 85 20W
Grange, La, Tex., U.S.A. 159 29 54N 96 52W
Grange-over-Sands 32 54 12N 2 55W
Grangemouth 35 56 1N 3 43W
Granger 160 46 25N 120 5W
Grangesberg 72 60 6N 15 1E
Grängesberg 72 60 6N 15 1E
Grangetown 33 54 36N 1 7W
Grangeville 160 45 57N 116 4W
Granite City 158 38 45N 90 3W
Granite Falls 158 44 45N 95 35W
Granite Mtn. 163 33 5N 116 28W
Granite Peak 137 25 40S 121 20E
Granite Pk., mt. 160 45 8N 109 52W
Granitnyy, Pik 85 39 32N 70 20E
Granity 143 41 39S 171 51E
Granja 170 3 17S 40 50W
Granja de Moreruela 56 41 48N 5 44W
Granja de Torrehermosa 57 38 19N 5 35W
Gränna 73 58 1N 14 28E
Granollers 58 41 39N 2 18E
Gransee 48 53 0N 13 10E
Grant, Can. 150 50 6N 86 18W
Grant, U.S.A. 158 40 53N 101 42W
Grant City 158 40 30N 94 25W
Grant, I. 136 11 10S 132 52E
Grant, Mt. 163 38 34N 118 48W
Grant Range Mts. 161 38 30N 115 30W
Grantham 33 52 55N 0 39W
Grantown-on-Spey 37 57 19N 3 36W
Grants 161 35 14N 107 57W
Grant's Pass 160 42 30N 123 22W
Grantsburg 158 45 46N 92 44W
Grantshouse 35 55 53N 2 17W
Grantsville 160 40 35N 112 32W
Granville, France 42 48 50N 1 35W
Granville, U.K. 38 54 30N 6 47W
Granville, N.D., U.S.A. 158 48 18N 100 48W
Granville, N.Y., U.S.A. 162 43 24N 73 16W
Granville L. 153 56 18N 100 30W
Grao de Gandía 59 39 0N 0 27W
Grapeland 159 31 30N 95 25W
Gras, L. de 148 64 30N 110 30W
Graskop 129 24 56S 30 49E
Gräsmark 72 59 58N 12 44E
Grasmere, Austral. 139 35 1S 117 45E
Grasmere, U.K. 32 54 28N 3 2W
Gräsö 72 60 21N 18 28E
Graso 72 60 28N 18 35E
Grasonville 162 38 57N 76 13W
Grass, R. 153 56 3N 96 33W
Grass Range 160 47 0N 109 0W
Grass River Prov. Park 153 54 40N 100 50W
Grass Valley, Calif., U.S.A. 160 39 18N 121 0W
Grass Valley, Oreg., U.S.A. 160 45 28N 120 48W
Grassano 65 40 38N 16 17E
Grasse 45 43 38N 6 56E
Grassington 32 54 5N 2 0W
Grassmere 140 31 24S 142 38E
Grate's Cove 151 48 8N 53 0W
Graubünden (Grisons) □ 51 46 45N 9 30E
Graulhet 44 43 45N 1 58E
Graus 58 42 11N 0 20E
Gravatá 170 6 59S 35 29W
Grave 46 51 46N 5 44E
Grave, Pte. de 44 45 34N 1 4W
's-Graveland 46 52 15N 5 7E
Gravelbourg 153 49 50N 106 35W
Gravelines 43 51 0N 2 10E
's-Gravendeel 46 51 47N 4 37E
's-Gravenhage 46 52 7N 4 17E
's-Gravenpolder 47 51 28N 3 54E
's-Gravensande 46 52 0N 4 9E
Graversfors 73 58 42N 16 8E
Gravesend, Austral. 139 29 35S 150 20E
Gravesend, U.K. 29 51 25N 0 22E
Gravina di Púglia 65 40 48N 16 25E
Gravir 36 58 2N 6 25W
Gravois, Pointe-à 167 16 15N 73 45W
Gravone, R. 45 42 3N 8 54E
Grävsnäs 73 58 5N 12 29E
Gray 43 47 27N 5 35E
Grayling 156 44 40N 84 42W
Grayling, R. 152 59 21N 125 0W
Grayrigg 32 54 22N 2 40W
Grays Harbor 160 46 55N 124 8W
Grays L. 160 43 8N 111 30W
Grays Thurrock 29 51 28N 0 23E
Grayson 153 50 45N 102 40W
Grayvoron 80 50 29N 35 39E
Graz 52 47 4N 15 27E
Grazalema 57 36 46N 5 23W
Grdelica 66 42 55N 22 3E
Greasy L. 152 62 55N 122 12W
Great Abaco I. 166 26 15N 77 10W
Great Australia Basin 133 26 0S 140 0E
Great Australian Bight 137 33 30S 130 0E
Great Ayton 33 54 29N 1 8W
Great Baddow 29 51 43N 0 31E
Great Bahama Bank 166 23 15N 78 0W
Great Barrier I. 142 36 11S 175 25E
Great Barrier Reef 138 19 0S 149 0E
Great Barrington 162 42 11N 73 22W
Great Basin 154 40 0N 116 30W
Great Bear L. 148 65 0N 120 0W
Great Bear, R. 148 65 0N 124 0W
Great Belt 73 55 20N 11 0E
Great Bena 162 41 57N 75 45W
Great Bend 158 38 25N 98 55W
Great Bentley 29 51 51N 1 5E
Great Bernera, I. 137 58 15N 6 50W
Great Bitter Lake 122 30 15N 32 40E
Great Blasket, I. 39 52 5N 10 30W
Great Britain 16 54 0N 2 15W
Great Bushman Land 128 29 20S 19 20E
Great Central 152 49 20N 125 10W
Great Chesterford 29 52 4N 0 11E
Great Clifton 32 54 39N 3 29W
Great Coco I. 101 14 10N 93 25E
Great Divide 141 23 0S 146 0E
Great Dunmow 29 51 52N 0 22E
Great Exuma I. 166 23 30N 75 50W
Great Falls, Can. 153 50 27N 96 1W
Great Falls, U.S.A. 160 47 27N 111 12W
Great Fish R., S. Afr. 128 33 28S 27 5E
Great Fish R., S. Afr. 128 31 30S 20 16E
Great Gonerby 33 52 56N 0 40W
Great Guana Cay 166 24 0N 76 20W
Great Hanish 123 13 40N 43 0E
Great Harbour Deep 151 50 35N 56 25W
Great Harwood 32 52 41N 2 49W
Great I., Can. 153 58 53N 96 35W
Great I., Ireland 39 51 52N 8 15W
Great Inagua I. 167 21 0N 73 20W
Gt. Indian Desert = Thar Desert 94 28 0N 72 0E
Great Jarvis 151 47 39N 57 12W
Great Karoo = Groot Karoo 128 32 30S 23 0E
Great Lake 138 41 50S 146 30E
Great Lakes 153 44 0N 82 0W
Great Malvern 28 52 7N 2 19W
Great Massingham 29 52 47N 0 41E
Great Missenden 29 51 42N 0 42W
Gt. Namaqualand = Groot Namakwaland 128 26 0S 18 0E
Great Orme's Head 31 53 20N 3 52W
Great Ouse, R. 29 52 20N 0 8E
Great Palm I. 138 18 45S 146 40E
Great Papuan Plateau 135 6 30S 142 25E
Great Plains 50 45 0N 100 0W
Great Ruaha, R. 126 7 30S 35 0E
Great Salt Lake 160 41 0N 112 30W
Great Salt Lake Desert 160 40 20N 113 50W
Great Salt Plains Res. 159 36 40N 98 15W
Great Sandy Desert 136 21 0S 124 0E
Great Sandy I. = Fraser I. 139 25 15S 153 0E
Great Scarcies, R. 120 9 30N 12 40W
Great Shefford 28 51 29N 1 27W
Great Shelford 29 52 9N 0 9E
Great Shunner Fell 32 54 22N 2 16W
Great Sitkin I. 147 52 0N 176 10W
Great Slave L. 152 61 23N 115 38W
Great Stour, R. 29 51 21N 1 15E
Gt. Sugar Loaf, mt. 39 53 10N 6 10W
Great Torrington 30 50 57N 4 9W
Gt. Victoria Des. 137 29 30S 126 30E
Great Wall 106 38 30N 109 30E
Gt. Waltham 29 51 47N 0 29E
Great Whale, R. 150 55 20N 75 30W
Great Whernside, mt. 147 54 9N 1 59W
Great Winterhoek, mt. 128 33 07S 19 10E
Great Wyrley 28 52 40N 2 1W
Great Yarmouth 29 52 40N 1 45E
Great Yeldham 29 52 1N 0 33E
Greater Antilles 167 17 40N 74 0W
Greater Manchester □ 32 53 30N 2 15W
Greatham 33 54 38N 1 14W
Grebbestad 73 58 42N 11 15E
Grebenka 80 50 9N 32 22E
Greco, Mt. 64 41 48N 14 0E
Gredos, Sierra de 56 40 20N 5 0W
Greece ■ 68 40 0N 23 0E
Greeley, Colo., U.S.A. 158 40 30N 104 40W
Greeley, Nebr., U.S.A. 158 41 36N 98 32W
Green B. 156 45 0N 87 30W
Green Bay 156 44 30N 88 0W
Green C. 141 37 13S 150 1E
Green Cove Springs 157 29 59N 81 40W
Green Hammerton 33 54 2N 1 17W
Green Hd. 137 30 5S 114 56E
Green Is. 135 4 35S 154 10E
Green Island 143 45 55S 170 26E
Green Lowther, Mt. 35 55 22N 3 44W
Green R., Ky., U.S.A. 156 37 54N 87 30W
Green R., Utah, U.S.A. 161 39 0N 110 6W
Green R., Wyo., U.S.A. 160 43 2N 110 2W
Green R., Wyo., U.S.A. 160 41 44N 109 28W
Greenbush 158 48 46N 96 10W
Greencastle, U.K. 38 54 2N 6 5W
Greencastle, U.S.A. 156 39 40N 86 48W
Greene 162 42 20N 75 45W
Greenfield, Calif., U.S.A. 163 35 15N 119 0W
Greenfield, Calif., U.S.A. 163 36 19N 121 15W
Greenfield, Ind., U.S.A. 156 39 47N 85 51W
Greenfield, Iowa, U.S.A. 158 41 18N 94 28W
Greenfield, Mass., U.S.A. 162 42 38N 72 38W
Greenfield, Miss., U.S.A. 159 37 28N 93 50W
Greenhead 35 54 58N 2 31W
Greening 150 48 10N 74 55W
Greenisland 38 54 42N 5 50W
Greenland 12 66 0N 45 0W
Greenland Sea 12 73 0N 10 0W
Greenlaw 35 55 42N 2 28W
Greenock 34 55 57N 4 46W
Greenodd 32 54 14N 3 3W
Greenore 38 54 2N 6 8W
Greenore Pt. 39 52 15N 6 20W
Greenough, R. 137 28 54S 115 36E
Greenport 162 41 5N 72 23W
Greensboro, Ga., U.S.A. 157 33 34N 83 12W
Greensboro, Md., U.S.A. 162 38 59N 75 48W
Greensboro, N.C., U.S.A. 157 36 7N 79 46W
Greensburg, Ind., U.S.A. 156 39 20N 85 30W
Greensburg, Kans., U.S.A. 159 37 38N 99 20W
Greensburg, Pa., U.S.A. 156 40 18N 79 31W
Greenstone Pt. 36 57 55N 5 38W
Greenville, Liberia 120 5 7N 9 6W
Greenville, Ala., U.S.A. 157 31 50N 86 37W
Greenville, Calif., U.S.A. 160 40 8N 121 0W
Greenville, Ill., U.S.A. 158 38 53N 89 22W
Greenville, Me., U.S.A. 151 45 30N 69 32W
Greenville, Mich., U.S.A. 156 43 12N 85 14W
Greenville, Miss., U.S.A. 159 33 25N 91 0W
Greenville, N.C., U.S.A. 157 35 37N 77 26W
Greenville, N.H., U.S.A. 162 42 46N 71 49W
Greenville, N.Y., U.S.A. 162 42 25N 74 1W
Greenville, Ohio, U.S.A. 156 40 5N 84 38W
Greenville, Pa., U.S.A. 156 41 23N 80 22W
Greenville, S.C., U.S.A. 157 34 54N 82 24W
Greenville, Tenn., U.S.A. 157 36 13N 82 51W
Greenville, Tex., U.S.A. 159 33 5N 96 5W
Greenwater Lake Prov. Park 153 52 32N 103 30W
Greenway 31 51 56N 4 49W
Greenwich, U.K. 29 51 28N 0 0
Greenwich, Conn., U.S.A. 162 41 1N 73 38W
Greenwich, N.Y., U.S.A. 162 43 2N 73 36W
Greenwood, Can. 152 49 10N 118 40W
Greenwood, Miss., U.S.A. 159 33 30N 90 4W
Greenwood, S.C., U.S.A. 157 34 13N 82 13W
Greenwood, Mt. 136 13 48S 130 4E
Gregory 158 43 14N 99 20W
Gregory Downs 138 18 35S 138 45E
Gregory, L. 139 28 55S 139 0E
Gregory L. 136 20 5S 127 0E
Gregory, L. 137 25 38S 119 58E
Gregory Lake 136 20 10S 127 30E
Gregory, R. 138 17 53S 139 17E
Gregory Ra., Queens., Austral. 138 19 30S 143 40E
Gregory Ra., W. Austral., Austral. 136 21 20S 121 12E
Greian Hd. 36 57 1N 7 30W
Greiffenberg 48 53 6N 13 57E
Greifswald 48 54 6N 13 23E
Greifswalder Bodden 48 54 12N 13 35E
Greifswalder Oie 48 54 15N 13 55E
Grein 52 48 14N 14 51E
Greiner Wald 52 48 30N 15 0E
Greiz 48 50 39N 12 12E
Gremikha 78 67 50N 39 40E
Grenå 73 56 25N 10 53E
Grenada 159 33 45N 89 50W
Grenada I. ■ 167 12 10N 61 40W
Grenade 44 43 47N 1 17E
Grenadines 167 12 40N 61 20W
Grenchen 50 47 12N 7 24E
Grenen 73 57 44N 10 40E
Grenfell, Austral. 141 33 52S 148 8E
Grenfell, Can. 153 50 30N 102 56W
Grenoble 45 45 12N 5 42E
Grenora 158 48 38N 103 54W
Grenville, C. 138 12 0S 143 13E
Grenville Chan. 152 53 40N 129 46W
Gréoux-les-Bains 45 43 55N 5 52E
Gresham 160 45 30N 122 31W
Gresik 103 9 13S 112 38E
Gressoney St. Jean 62 45 49N 7 47E
Greta 32 54 9N 2 36W
Greta R. 32 54 36N 3 5W
Gretna, U.K. 35 54 59N 3 4W
Gretna, U.S.A. 159 30 0N 90 2W
Gretna Green 35 55 0N 3 3W
Gretton 29 52 33N 0 40W
Grevelingen Krammer 46 51 44N 4 0E
Greven 48 52 7N 7 36E
Grevená 68 40 4N 21 25E
Grevená □ 68 40 2N 21 25E
Grevenbroich 48 51 6N 6 32E
Grevenmacher 47 49 41N 6 26E
Grevesmühlen 48 53 51N 11 10E
Grevie 73 56 22N 12 46E
Grevinge 73 55 48N 11 34E
Grey, C. 138 13 0S 136 35E
Grey, R. 143 42 27S 171 12E
Grey Range 133 27 0S 143 30E
Grey Res. 151 48 20N 56 30W
Greyabbey 38 54 32N 5 35W
Greybull 160 44 30N 108 3W
Greystone 32 54 39N 2 52W
Greystones 39 53 9N 6 4W
Greytown, N.Z. 142 41 5S 175 29E
Greytown, S. Afr. 129 29 1S 30 36E
Gribanovskiy 81 51 28N 41 50E
Gribbell I. 152 53 23N 129 0W
Gribbin Head 30 50 18N 4 41W
Gridley 160 39 27N 121 47W
Griekwastad 128 28 49S 23 15E
Griffin 157 33 17N 84 14W
Griffith 141 34 18S 146 2E
Griffith Mine 153 50 47N 93 25W
Grigoryevka 84 50 48N 58 18E
Grijalva, R. 164 16 20N 92 20W
Grijpskerk 46 53 16N 6 18E
Grillby 72 59 38N 17 15E

Grim, C **Gus**

Grim, C. 133 40 45S 144 45E
Grimaïlov 80 49 20N 26 5E
Grimari 117 5 43N 20 0E
Grimbergen 47 50 56N 4 22E
Grimeton 73 57 6N 12 25E
Griminish Pt. 36 57 40N 7 30W
Grimma 48 51 14N 12 44E
Grimmen 48 54 6N 13 2E
Grimsay I. 36 57 29N 7 12W
Grimsby 33 53 35N 0 5W
Grimsel Pass 51 46 34N 8 23E
Grímsey 74 66 33N 18 0W
Grimshaw 152 56 10N 117 40W
Grimstad 71 58 22N 8 35E
Grindelwald 50 46 38N 8 2E
Grindsted 73 55 46N 8 55E
Grindstone Island 151 47 25N 62 0W
Grindu 70 44 44N 26 50E
Grinduşul, Mt. 70 46 40N 26 7E
Griñón 56 40 13N 3 51W
Grinnell 158 41 45N 92 43W
Grip 71 63 16N 7 37E
Griqualand East 129 30 30S 29 0E
Griqualand West 128 28 40S 23 30E
Griquet 151 51 30N 55 35W
Grisolles 44 43 49N 1 19E
Grisons □ 49 46 40N 9 30E
Grisslehamm 72 60 5N 18 49E
Grita, La 174 8 8N 71 59W
Gritley 37 58 56N 2 45W
Grivegnée 47 50 37N 5 36E
Griz Nez 43 50 50N 1 35E
Grizebeck 32 54 16N 3 10W
Grmeč Planina 63 44 43N 16 16E
Groais I. 151 50 55N 55 35W
Groblersdal 129 25 15S 29 25E
Grobming 52 47 27N 13 54E
Grocka 66 44 40N 20 42E
Grodek 80 52 46N 23 38E
Grodkow 54 50 43N 17 40E
Grodno 80 53 42N 23 52E
Grodzisk Mazowiecki 54 52 7N 20 37E
Grodzisk Wlkp. 54 52 15N 16 22E
Grodzyanka 80 53 31N 28 42E
Groenlo 46 52 2N 6 37E
Groesbeck 159 31 32N 96 34W
Groesbeek 46 51 47N 5 58E
Groix 42 47 38N 3 29W
Groix, I. de 42 47 38N 3 28W
Grójec 54 51 50N 20 58E
Grolloo 46 52 56N 6 41E
Gronau 48 52 13N 7 2E
Grong 74 64 25N 12 8E
Groningen 46 53 15N 6 35E
Groningen □ 46 53 16N 6 40E
Groninger Wad 46 53 27N 6 30E
Grönskåra 73 57 5N 15 43E
Gronsveld 47 50 49N 5 44E
Groom 159 35 12N 100 59W
Groomsport 38 54 41N 5 37W
Groot Berg, R. 128 32 50S 18 20E
Groot-Brakrivier 128 34 2S 22 18E
Groot Karoo 128 32 35S 23 0E
Groot Namakwaland = Namaland 128 26 0S 18 0E
Groot, R. 128 33 10S 23 35E
Groote Eylandt 138 14 0S 136 50E
Grootebroek 46 52 41N 5 13E
Grootfontein 128 19 31S 18 6E
Grootlaagte, R. 128 21 10S 21 20E
Gros C. 152 61 59N 113 32W
Grosa, Punta 59 39 6N 1 36E
Grósio 62 46 18N 10 17E
Grosne, R. 45 46 30N 4 40E
Gross Glockner 52 47 5N 12 40E
Gross Ottersleben 48 52 5N 11 33E
Grossa, Pta. 170 1 20N 50 0W
Grossenbrode 48 54 21N 11 4E
Grossenhain 48 51 17N 13 32E
Grosseto 62 42 45N 11 7E
Grossgerungs 52 48 34N 14 57E
Grosswater B. 151 54 20N 57 40W
Grote Gette, R. 47 50 51N 5 6E
Grote Nete, R. 47 51 8N 4 34E
Groton, U.S.A. 162 41 22N 72 12W
Groton, U.S.A. 162 42 36N 76 22W
Grottaglie 65 40 32N 17 25E
Grottaminarda 65 41 5N 15 4E
Grouard Mission 152 55 33N 116 9W
Grouin, Pointe du 42 48 43N 1 51W
Groundhog, R. 150 48 45N 82 20W
Grouse Creek 160 41 51N 113 57W
Grouw 46 53 5N 5 51E
Groveland 163 37 50N 120 14W
Grovelsjön 72 62 6N 12 16E
Grover City 163 35 7N 120 37W
Groveton 159 31 5N 95 4W
Groznjan 63 45 22N 13 43E
Groznyy 83 43 20N 45 45E
Grubbenvorst 47 51 25N 6 9E
Grubišno Polje 66 45 44N 17 12E
Grudusk 54 53 3N 20 38E
Grudziadz 54 53 30N 18 47E
Gruinard B. 36 57 56N 5 35W
Gruissan 44 43 8N 3 7E
Grumo Appula 65 41 2N 16 43E
Grums 72 59 22N 13 5E
Grünau 125 27 45S 18 26E
Grünberg 48 50 37N 8 55E
Grundy Center 158 42 22N 92 45W
Grungedal 71 59 44N 7 43E
Gruting Voe 36 60 12N 1 32W
Gruver 159 36 19N 101 20W
Gruyères 50 46 35N 7 4E
Gruza 66 43 54N 20 46E
Gryazi 81 52 30N 39 58E
Gryazovets 81 58 50N 40 20E
Grybów 54 49 36N 20 55E
Grycksbo 72 60 40N 15 29E
Gryfice 54 53 55N 15 13E
Gryfino 54 53 16N 14 29E
Grytgöl 73 58 49N 15 33E
Grythyttan 72 59 41N 14 32E
Grytviken 13 53 50S 37 10W
Gstaad 50 46 28N 7 18E
Gua 99 22 18N 85 20E
Gua Musang 101 4 53N 101 58E
Guacanayabo, Golfo de 166 20 40N 77 20W
Guacara 174 10 14N 67 53W
Guachípas 172 25 40S 65 30W
Guachiría, R. 174 5 30N 71 30W
Guadajoz, R. 57 37 50N 4 51W
Guadalajara, Mexico 164 20 40N 103 20W
Guadalajara, Spain 58 40 37N 3 12W
Guadalajara □ 58 40 47N 3 0W
Guadalcanal 57 38 5N 5 52W
Guadalcanal, I. 130 9 32S 160 12E
Guadalén, R. 59 38 30N 3 7W
Guadales 172 34 30S 67 55W
Guadalete, R. 57 36 45N 5 47W
Guadalhorce, R. 57 36 50N 4 42W
Guadalimar, R. 59 38 10N 2 53W
Guadalmena, R. 59 38 31N 2 50W
Guadalmez, R. 57 38 33N 4 42W
Guadalope, R. 58 41 0N 0 13W
Guadalquivir, R. 57 38 0N 4 0W
Guadalupe, Brazil 170 6 44S 43 47W
Guadalupe, Spain 57 39 27N 5 17W
Guadalupe, U.S.A. 163 34 59N 120 33W
Guadalupe Bravos 164 31 20N 106 10W
Guadalupe de los Reyes 164 25 23N 104 15W
Guadalupe I. 131 29 0N 118 50W
Guadalupe Pk. 161 31 50N 105 30W
Guadalupe, R. 159 29 25N 97 30W
Guadalupe, Sierra de 55 39 28N 5 30W
Guadalupe y Calvo 164 26 6N 106 58W
Guadarrama, Sierra de 56 41 0N 4 0W
Guadeloupe, I. 167 16 20N 61 40W
Guadeloupe Passage 167 16 50N 68 15W
Guadiamar, R. 57 37 9N 6 20W
Guadiana Menor, R. 59 37 45N 3 7W
Guadiana, R. 57 37 45N 7 35W
Guadiaro, R. 57 36 39N 5 17W
Guadiato, R. 57 37 55N 4 53W
Guadiela, R. 58 40 30N 2 23W
Guadix 59 37 18N 3 11W
Guafo, Boca del 176 43 35S 74 0W
Guaina 174 5 9N 63 36W
Guainía □ 174 2 30N 69 00W
Guaíra 173 24 5S 54 10W
Guaira, La 174 10 36N 66 56W
Guaitecas, Islas 176 44 0S 74 30W
Guajará-Mirim 174 10 50S 65 20W
Guajira, La □ 174 11 30N 72 30W
Guajira, Pen. de la 167 12 0N 72 0W
Gualan 166 15 8N 89 22W
Gualdo Tadino 63 43 14N 12 46E
Gualeguay 172 33 10S 59 20W
Gualeguaychú 172 33 3S 58 31W
Guam I. 130 13 27N 144 45E
Guamá 170 1 37S 47 29W
Guama 174 10 16N 68 49W
Guamá, R. 170 1 29S 48 30W
Guamareyes 174 0 30S 73 0W
Guaminí 172 37 1S 62 28W
Guampí, Sierra de 174 6 0N 65 35W
Guamuchil 164 25 25N 108 3W
Guanabacoa 166 23 8N 82 18W
Guanabara □ 173 23 0S 43 25W
Guanacaste 166 10 40N 85 30W
Guanacaste, Cordillera del 166 10 40N 85 4W
Guanacevío 164 25 40N 106 0W
Guanajay 166 22 56N 82 42W
Guanajuato 164 21 0N 101 20W
Guanajuato □ 164 20 40N 101 20W
Guanambi 171 14 13S 42 47W
Guanare 174 8 42N 69 12W
Guanare, R. 174 8 50N 68 50W
Guandacol 172 29 30S 68 40W
Guane 166 22 10N 84 0W
Guanhães 171 18 47S 42 57W
Guanica 147 17 58N 66 55W
Guanipa, R. 174 9 20N 63 30W
Guanta 174 10 14N 64 36W
Guantánamo 167 20 10N 75 20W
Guapí 174 2 36N 77 54W
Guápiles 166 10 10N 83 46W
Guaporé 173 12 0S 64 0W
Guaporé, R. 174 13 0S 63 0W
Guaqui 174 16 41S 68 54W
Guara, Sierra de 58 42 19N 0 15W
Guarabira 170 6 51S 35 29W
Guarapari 173 20 40S 40 30W
Guarapuava 171 25 20S 51 30W
Guaratinguetá 173 22 49S 45 9W
Guaratuba 173 25 53S 48 38W
Guard Bridge 35 56 21N 2 52W
Guarda 56 40 32N 7 20W
Guarda □ 56 40 40N 7 20W
Guardafui, C. = Asir, Ras 91 11 55N 51 10E
Guardamar del Segura 59 38 5N 0 39W
Guardavalle 65 38 31N 16 30E
Guardia, La 56 41 56N 8 52W
Guardiagrele 63 42 11N 14 11E
Guardo 56 42 47N 4 50W
Guareña 57 38 51N 6 6W
Guareña, R. 56 41 25N 5 25W
Guaria □ 172 25 45N 56 30W
Guárico □ 174 8 40N 66 35W
Guarujá 173 24 2S 46 25W
Guarus 173 21 30S 41 20W
Guasave 164 25 34N 108 27W
Guasdualito 174 7 15N 70 44W
Guasipati 174 7 28N 61 54W
Guasopa 135 9 12S 152 56E
Guastalla 62 44 55N 10 40E
Guatemala 166 14 40N 90 30W
Guatemala ■ 166 15 40N 90 30W
Guatire 174 10 28N 66 32W
Guaviare, R. 174 3 30N 71 0W
Guaxupé 173 21 10S 47 5W
Guayabal 174 4 43N 71 37W
Guayama 147 17 59N 66 7W
Guayaquil 174 2 15S 79 52W
Guayaquil, Golfo de 174 3 10S 81 0W
Guaymallen 172 32 50S 68 45W
Guaymas 164 27 50N 111 0W
Guba, Ethiopia 123 4 52N 39 18E
Guba, Zaïre 127 10 38S 26 27E
Gubakha 84 58 52N 57 36E
Gubam 135 8 39S 141 53E
Gúbbio 63 43 20N 12 34E
Gubio 121 12 30N 12 42E
Gubkin 81 51 17N 37 32E
Guča 66 43 46N 20 15E
Guchil 101 5 35N 102 10E
Gudalur 97 11 30N 76 29E
Gudata 83 43 7N 40 32E
Gudbransdal 75 61 33N 10 0E
Guddu Barrage 93 28 30N 69 50E
Gudenå 73 56 27N 9 40E
Gudermes 83 43 24N 46 20E
Gudhjem 73 55 12N 14 58E
Gudiña, La 56 42 4N 7 8W
Gudivada 96 16 30N 81 15E
Gudiyatam 97 12 57N 78 55E
Gudmundra 72 62 56N 17 47E
Gudrun, gasfield 19 58 50N 1 48E
Gudur 97 14 12N 79 55E
Guebwiller 43 47 55N 7 12E
Guecho 58 43 21N 2 59W
Guéckédou 120 8 40N 10 5W
Guelma 119 36 25N 7 29E
Guelph 150 43 35N 80 20W
Guelt es Stel 118 35 12N 3 1E
Guelttara 118 29 23N 2 10W
Guemar 119 33 30N 6 57E
Guéméné-Penfao 42 47 38N 1 50W
Guéméné-sur-Scorff 42 48 4N 3 13W
Güemes 172 24 50S 65 0W
Guéné 121 11 44N 3 16E
Guer 42 47 54N 2 8W
Guérande 42 47 20N 2 26W
Guerche, La 42 47 57N 1 16W
Guerche-sur-l'Aubois, La 43 46 58N 2 56E
Guercif 118 34 14N 3 21W
Guéréda 124 14 31N 22 5E
Guéret 44 46 11N 1 51E
Guérigny 43 47 6N 3 10E
Guernica 58 43 19N 2 40W
Guernsey 158 42 19N 104 45W
Guernsey I. 42 49 30N 2 35W
Guerrara, Oasis, Alg. 119 32 51N 4 35E
Guerrara, Saoura, Alg. 118 28 5N 0 8W
Guerrero □ 165 17 30N 100 0W
Guerzim 118 29 45N 1 47W
Güeş ti 70 44 48N 25 19E
Guestling Green 29 50 53N 0 40E
Gueugnon 45 46 36N 4 3E
Gueydan 159 30 3N 92 30W
Guezendi = Ghesendor 119 21 14N 18 14E
Guglia, P. dal 51 46 28N 9 45E
Guglionesi 63 41 55N 14 54E
Guhra 93 27 36N 56 8E
Guia Lopes da Laguna 173 21 26S 56 7W
Guiana Highlands 174 5 0N 60 0W
Guibes 128 26 41S 16 49E
Guider 121 9 55N 13 59E
Guidimouni 121 13 42N 9 31E
Guiglo 120 6 45N 7 30W
Guija 125 34 35S 33 15E
Guijo de Coria 56 40 6N 6 28W
Guildford 29 51 14N 0 34W
Guilford, Conn., U.S.A. 162 41 15N 72 40W
Guilford, Me., U.S.A. 151 45 12N 69 25W
Guillaumes 45 44 5N 6 52E
Guillestre 45 44 39N 6 40E
Guilsfield 31 52 42N 3 9W
Guilvinec 42 47 48N 4 17W
Guimarães, Braz. 170 2 9S 44 35W
Guimarães, Port. 56 41 28N 8 24W
Guimaras I. 103 10 35N 122 37E
Guinea ■ 120 10 20N 10 0W
Guinea Bissau ■ 120 12 0N 15 0W
Guinea, Gulf of 121 3 0N 2 30E
Guinea, Port. = Guinea Bissau 120 12 0N 15 0W
Güines 166 22 50N 82 0W
Guingamp 42 48 34N 3 10W
Guipavas 42 48 26N 4 29W
Guipúzcoa □ 58 43 12N 2 15W
Guir, O. 118 29 29N 2 58W
Guirgo 121 11 54N 1 21W
Güiria 174 10 32N 62 18W
Guisborough 33 54 32N 1 2W
Guiscard 43 49 40N 3 0E
Guise 43 49 52N 3 35E
Guitiriz 56 43 11N 7 50W
Guivan 103 11 5N 125 55E
Gujan-Mestras 44 44 38N 1 4W
Gujar Khan 84 33 15N 73 21E
Gujarat □ 94 23 20N 71 0E
Gujranwala 94 32 10N 74 12E
Gujrat 94 32 40N 74 2E
Gukhothae 101 17 2N 99 50E
Gukovo 83 48 1N 39 58E
Gulak 121 10 50N 13 30E
Gulargambone 141 31 20S 148 30E
Gulbahar 93 35 5N 69 10E
Gulbargâ 96 17 20N 76 50E
Gulbene 80 57 8N 26 52E
Gulcha 85 40 19N 73 26E
Guldborg Sd. 73 54 39N 11 50E
Guledgud 97 16 3N 75 48E
Gulf Basin 136 15 20S 129 0E
Gulfport 159 30 28N 89 3W
Gulgong 141 32 20S 149 30E
Gulistan, Pak. 94 30 36N 66 35E
Gulistan, U.S.S.R. 85 40 29N 68 46E
Gulkana 147 62 15N 145 48W
Gull Lake 153 50 10N 108 29W
Gullane 35 56 2N 2 50W
Gullegem 47 50 51N 3 13E
Gullringen 73 57 48N 15 44E
Güllük 69 37 12N 27 36E
Gulma 121 12 40N 4 23E
Gulmarg 95 34 3N 74 25E
Gulnam 123 6 55N 29 30E
Gulnare 140 33 27S 138 27E
Gulpaigan 92 33 26N 50 20E
Gulpen 47 50 49N 5 53E
Gülpinar 68 39 32N 26 10E
Gulshad 76 46 45N 74 25E
Gulsvik 71 60 24N 9 38E
Gulu 126 2 48N 32 17E
Gulwe 126 6 30S 36 25E
Gulyaypole 82 47 45N 36 21E
Gum Lake 140 32 42S 143 9E
Gumal, R. 94 32 5N 70 5E
Gumbaz 94 30 2N 69 0E
Gumel 121 12 39N 9 22E
Gumiel de Hizán 58 41 46N 3 41W
Gumlu 138 19 53S 147 41E
Gumma-ken □ 111 36 30N 138 20E
Gummersbach 48 51 2N 7 32E
Gummi 121 12 4N 5 9E
Gümüsane 92 40 30N 39 30E
Gümüşhaciköy 82 40 50N 35 18E
Gumzai 103 5 28S 134 42E
Guna 94 24 40N 77 19E
Guna Mt. 123 11 50N 37 40E
Gundagai 141 35 3S 148 6E
Gundih 103 7 10S 110 56E
Gundlakamma, R. 97 15 30N 80 15E
Gunebang 141 33 5S 146 38E
Gungal 141 32 17S 150 32E
Gungi 123 10 20N 38 3E
Gungu 124 5 43S 19 20E
Gunisao L. 153 53 33N 96 15W
Gunisao, R. 153 53 56N 97 53W
Gunnedah 141 30 59S 150 15E
Gunniguldrie 141 33 12S 146 8E
Gunningbar Cr. 141 31 14S 147 6E
Gunnison, Colo., U.S.A. 161 38 32N 106 56W
Gunnison, Utah, U.S.A. 160 39 11N 111 48W
Gunnison, R. 161 38 50N 108 30W
Gunnworth 153 51 20N 108 9W
Guntakal 97 15 11N 77 27E
Guntersville 157 34 18N 86 16W
Guntong 101 4 36N 101 3E
Guntur 96 16 23N 80 30E
Gunungapi 103 6 45S 126 30E
Gunungsitoli 102 1 15N 97 30E
Gunungsugih 102 4 58S 105 7E
Gunupur 96 19 5N 83 50E
Gunworth 153 51 20N 108 10W
Gunza 124 10 50S 13 50E
Gunzenhausen 49 49 6N 10 45E
Gupis 95 36 15N 73 20E
Gura 94 25 12N 71 39E
Gura Humorului 70 47 35N 25 53E
Gura Teghii 70 45 30N 26 25E
Gurage, mt. 123 8 20N 38 20E
Gurchan 92 34 55N 49 25E
Gurdaspur 94 32 5N 75 25E
Gurdon 159 33 55N 93 10W
Gurdzhaani 83 41 43N 45 52E
Gurgan 93 36 51N 54 25E
Gurgaon 94 28 33N 77 10E
Gurghiu, Munţii 70 46 41N 25 15E
Gurguéia, R. 170 6 50S 43 24W
Guria 62 44 30N 9 0E
Gurk, R. 52 46 48N 14 20E
Gurkha 95 28 5N 84 40E
Gurla Mandhata 95 30 30N 81 10E
Gurley 139 29 45S 149 48E
Gurnard's Head 30 50 12N 5 37W
Gurnet Pt. 162 42 1N 70 34W
Gurrumbah 138 17 30S 144 55E
Gurun 101 5 49N 100 27E
Gürün 92 38 41N 37 22E
Gurupá 175 1 20S 51 45W
Gurupá, I. Grande de 175 1 0S 51 45W
Gurupi 171 11 43S 49 4W
Gurupi, R. 170 3 20S 47 20W
Gurupi, Serra do 170 5 0S 47 30W
Guryev 83 47 5N 52 0E
Gus 126 3 2N 36 57E

Gus-Khrsutalnyy Han Chiang, R

Gus-Khrsutalnyy 81 55 42N 40 35 E
Gusau 121 12 18N 6 31 E
Gusev 80 54 35N 22 20 E
Gushiago 121 9 55N 0 15W
Gusinje 66 42 35N 19 50 E
Gúspini 64 39 32N 8 38 E
Gusselby 72 59 38N 15 14 E
Güssing 53 47 3N 16 20 E
Gustanj 63 46 36N 14 49 E
Gustavus 147 58 25N 135 58W
Gustine 163 37 21N 121 0W
Güstrow 48 53 47N 12 12 E
Gusum 73 58 16N 16 30 E
Gŭtaia 70 45 26N 21 30 E
Gütersloh 48 51 54N 8 25 E
Gutha 137 28 58 S 115 55 E
Guthalungra 138 19 52 S 147 50 E
Guthrie 159 35 55N 97 30W
Guttannen 51 46 38N 8 18 E
Guttenberg 158 42 46N 91 10W
Guyana ■ 174 5 0N 59 0W
Guyenne 44 44 30N 0 40 E
Guyman 159 36 45N 101 30W
Guyra 139 30 15 S 151 40 E
Guzar 85 38 36N 66 15 E
Guzmán, Laguna de 164 31 25N 107 25W
Gwa 98 17 30N 94 40 E
Gwaai 127 19 15 S 27 45 E
Gwabegar 141 30 31 S 149 0 E
Gwadabawa 121 13 20N 5 15 E
Gwādar 93 25 10N 62 18 E
Gwagwada 121 10 15N 7 15 E
Gwalchmai 31 53 16N 4 23W
Gwalia 137 28 54 S 121 20 E
Gwalior 94 26 12N 78 10 E
Gwanara 121 18 55N 3 10 E
Gwanda 127 20 55 S 29 0 E
Gwandu 121 12 30N 4 41 E
Gwane 126 4 45N 25 48 E
Gwaram 121 11 15N 9 51 E
Gwarzo 121 12 20N 8 55 E
Gwasero 121 9 30N 8 30 E
Gwaun-Cae-Gurwen 31 51 46N 3 51W
Gweebarra B. 38 54 52N 8 21W
Gweedore 38 55 4N 8 15W
Gweek 30 50 6N 5 12W
Gwelo 125 19 28 S 29 45 E
Gwennap 30 50 12N 5 9W
Gwent □ 31 51 45N 2 55W
Gweta 128 20 12 S 25 17 E
Gwi 121 9 0N 7 10 E
Gwinn 156 46 15N 87 29W
Gwio Kura 121 12 40N 11 2 E
Gwolu 120 10 58N 1 59W
Gwoza 121 11 12N 13 40 E
Gwyddelwern 31 53 2N 3 23W
Gwydir, R. 139 29 27 S 149 48 E
Gwynedd □ 31 53 0N 4 0W
Gya La 95 28 45N 84 45 E
Gyangtse 99 28 50N 89 33 E
Gydanskiy P-ov. 76 70 0N 78 0 E
Gyland 71 58 24N 6 45 E
Gympie 139 26 11 S 152 38 E
Gyobingauk 98 18 13N 95 39 E
Gyoda 111 36 10N 139 30 E
Gyoma 53 46 56N 20 58 E
Gyöngyös 53 47 48N 20 15 E
Györ 53 47 41N 17 40 E
Györ-Sopron □ 53 47 40N 17 20 E
Gypsum Palace 140 32 37 S 144 9 E
Gypsum Pt. 152 61 53N 114 35W
Gypsumville 153 51 45N 98 40W
Gyttorp 72 59 31N 14 58 E
Gyula 53 46 38N 21 17 E
Gzhatsk = Gagarin 80 55 30N 35 0 E

H

Ha Coi 100 21 26N 107 46 E
Ha Dong 100 20 58N 105 46 E
Ha Giang 100 22 50N 104 59 E
Ha Nam = Phu-Ly 100 20 35N 105 50 E
Ha Tien 101 10 23N 104 29 E
Ha Tinh 100 18 20N 105 54 E
Ha Trung 100 20 0N 105 50 E
Haa, The 36 60 20N 1 0 E
Haacht 47 50 59N 4 37 E
Haag 49 48 11N 12 12 E
Haaksbergen 46 52 9N 6 45 E
Haaltert 47 50 55N 4 1 E
Haamstede 47 51 42N 3 45 E
Haapamäki 74 62 18N 24 28 E
Haapsalu 80 58 56N 23 30 E
Haarby 73 55 13N 10 8 E
Haarlem 46 52 23N 4 39 E
Haast 143 43 51 S 169 1 E
Haast P. 143 44 6 S 169 21 E
Haast, R. 143 43 50 S 169 2 E
Haastrecht 46 52 0N 4 47 E
Hab Nadi Chauki 94 25 0N 66 50 E
Hab, R. 93 25 15N 67 8 E
Haba 92 27 10N 47 0 E
Habana, La 166 23 8N 82 22W
Habaswein 126 1 2N 39 30 E
Habay 152 58 50N 118 44W
Habay-la-Neuve 47 49 44N 5 38 E
Habiganj 98 24 24N 91 30 E
Hablingbo 73 57 12N 18 16 E
Habo 73 57 55N 14 6 E
Haccourt 47 50 44N 5 40 E
Hachenburg 48 50 40N 7 49 E
Hachijō-Jima 111 33 5N 139 45 E
Hachinohe 112 40 30N 141 29 E
Hachiōji 111 35 30N 139 30 E
Hachŏn 107 40 29N 129 2 E
Hachy 47 49 42N 5 41 E
Hacketstown 39 52 52N 6 35W
Hackett 152 52 9N 112 28W
Hackettstown 162 40 51N 74 50W
Hackney 29 51 33N 0 2W
Hackthorpe 32 54 37N 2 42W
Hadali 94 32 16N 72 11 E
Hadarba, Ras 122 22 4N 36 51 E
Hadd, Ras al 93 22 35N 59 50 E
Haddenham 29 51 46N 0 56W
Haddington 35 55 57N 2 48W
Haddon Rig 141 31 27 S 147 52 E
Hadeija 121 12 30N 10 5 E
Hadeija, R. 121 12 20N 9 30W
Haden 139 27 13 S 151 54 E
Hadera 90 32 27N 34 55 E
Haderslev 73 55 15N 9 30 E
Hadhra 122 20 10N 41 5 E
Hadhramaut = Hadramawt 91 15 30N 49 30 E
Hadibu 91 12 35N 54 2 E
Hadjeb el Aïoun 119 35 21N 9 32 E
Hadleigh 29 52 3N 0 58 E
Hadley 28 52 42N 2 28W
Hadlow 29 51 12N 0 20 E
Hadong 107 35 5N 127 44 E
Hadramawt 91 15 30N 49 30 E
Hadrians Wall 35 55 0N 2 30W
Hadsten 73 56 19N 10 3 E
Hadsund 73 56 44N 10 8 E
Haeju 107 38 3N 125 45 E
Haenam 107 34 34N 126 15 E
Haerhpin 107 45 45N 126 45 E
Hafar al Batin 92 28 25N 46 50 E
Hafizabad 94 32 5N 73 40 E
Haflong 98 25 10N 93 5 E
Hafnarfjörður 74 64 4N 21 57W
Haft-Gel 92 31 30N 49 32 E
Hafun 91 10 25N 51 16 E
Hafun, Ras 91 10 29N 51 20 E
Hagalil 90 32 53N 35 18 E
Hagar Banga 117 10 40N 22 45 E
Hagari, R. 97 14 0N 76 45 E
Hagemeister I. 147 58 42N 161 0W
Hagen 48 51 21N 7 29 E
Hagenow 48 53 25N 11 10 E
Hagerman 159 33 5N 104 22W
Hagerstown 156 39 39N 77 46W
Hagetmau 44 43 39N 0 37W
Hagfors 72 60 3N 13 45 E
Häggenås 72 63 24N 14 55 E
Hagi, Iceland 74 65 28N 23 25W
Hagi, Japan 110 34 30N 131 30 E
Hagion Evstratios 68 39 30N 25 0 E
Hagion Óros 68 40 37N 24 6 E
Hags Hd. 39 52 57N 9 30W
Hague, C. de la 42 49 44N 1 56W
Hague, The = s'-Gravenhage 47 52 7N 4 17 E
Haguenau 43 48 49N 7 47 E
Hai □ 126 3 10 S 37 10 E
Hai Duong 100 20 56N 106 19 E
Haian, Kiangsu, China 109 32 37N 120 33 E
Haian, Kwangtung, China 109 20 18N 110 11 E
Haich'eng, Fukien, China 109 24 24N 117 51 E
Haich'eng, Liaoning, China 107 40 52N 122 45 E
Haichou 107 34 34N 119 6 E
Haichou Wan 107 35 0N 119 30 E
Haidar Khel 94 33 58N 68 38 E
Haifa 90 32 46N 35 0 E
Haifeng 109 22 59N 115 21 E
Haig 137 30 55 S 126 10 E
Haiger 48 50 44N 8 12 E
Haik'ang 109 20 56N 110 4 E
Haik'ou 109 20 5N 110 20 E
Hā'il 92 27 28N 42 2 E
Hailaerh 105 49 12N 119 42 E
Hailakandi 98 24 42N 92 34 E
Hailey 160 43 30N 114 15W
Haileybury 150 47 30N 79 38W
Hailin 107 44 32N 129 24 E
Hailing Tao 109 21 37N 111 65 E
Hailsham 29 50 52N 0 17 E
Hailun 105 47 27N 126 56 E
Hailung 107 42 30N 125 40 E
Hailuoto 74 65 3N 24 45 E
Haimen, Chekiang, China 109 28 39N 121 25 E
Haimen, Kwangtung, China 109 23 15N 116 35 E
Hainan 100 19 0N 110 0 E
Hainan Str. = Ch'iungcho Haihsia 100 20 10N 110 15 E
Hainaut □ 47 50 30N 4 0 E
Hainburg 53 48 9N 16 56 E
Haines, Alaska, U.S.A. 147 59 20N 135 36W
Haines, Oreg., U.S.A. 160 44 51N 117 59W
Haines City 157 28 6N 81 35W
Haines Junction 147 60 45N 137 30W
Hainfeld 52 48 3N 15 48 E
Haining 109 30 23N 120 30 E
Hainton 33 53 21N 0 13W
Haiphong 100 20 47N 106 35 E
Hait'an Tao 109 25 35N 119 45 E
Haiti ■ 167 19 0N 72 30W
Haiya Junc. 122 18 20N 36 40 E
Haiyang 107 36 45N 121 15 E
Haiyen 109 30 28N 120 57 E
Haiyüan, Kwangsi-Chuang, China 108 22 6N 107 25 E
Haiyüan, Ningsia Hui, China 106 36 32N 105 40 E
Haja 103 3 19 S 129 37 E
Hajdú-Bihar □ 53 47 30N 21 30 E
Hajdúböszörmény 53 47 40N 21 30 E
Hajdúdurog 53 47 48N 21 30 E
Hajdúhadház 53 47 40N 21 40 E
Hajdúnánás 53 47 50N 21 26 E
Hajdúsámson 53 47 37N 21 42 E
Hajdúszobaszló 53 47 27N 21 22 E
Haji Langar 93 35 50N 79 20 E
Hajiganj 98 23 15N 90 50 E
Hajipur 95 25 45N 85 20 E
Hajr 93 24 0N 56 34 E
Haka 98 22 39N 93 37 E
Hakansson, Mts. 127 8 40 S 25 45 E
Hakantorp 73 58 18N 12 55 E
Håkantorp 73 58 18N 12 55 E
Hakataramea 143 44 30 S 170 30 E
Hakataramea, R. 143 44 35 S 170 40 E
Hakken-Zan 111 34 10N 135 54 E
Hakodate 112 41 45N 140 44 E
Hakota 111 36 5N 140 30 E
Haku-San 111 36 9N 136 46 E
Hakun 98 26 46N 95 42 E
Hala 93 25 43N 68 20 E
Hala Hu 105 38 15N 97 40 E
Halab = Aleppo 92 36 10N 37 15 E
Halabjah 92 35 10N 45 58 E
Halaib 122 22 5N 36 30 E
Halanzy 47 49 33N 5 44 E
Halawa 147 21 9N 156 47W
Halbe 122 19 40N 42 15 E
Halberstadt 48 51 53N 11 2 E
Halberton 30 50 55N 3 24W
Halcombe 142 40 8 S 175 30 E
Halcyon, Mt. 103 13 0N 121 30 E
Halden 72 59 7N 11 23 E
Haldensleben 48 52 17N 11 30 E
Haldia 99 22 5N 88 3 E
Haldwani 95 29 25N 79 30 E
Hale 32 53 24N 2 21W
Hale, R. 138 24 56 S 135 53 E
Haleakala Crater 147 20 43N 156 12W
Halen 47 50 57N 5 6 E
Halesowen 28 52 27N 2 2W
Halesworth 29 52 21N 1 30 E
Haleyville 157 34 15N 87 40W
Half Assini 120 5 1N 2 50W
Halfmoon B. 143 46 50 S 168 5 E
Halfway 160 44 56N 117 8W
Halfway, R. 152 56 12N 121 32W
Halhul 90 31 35N 35 7 E
Hali 122 18 40N 41 15 E
Haliburton 150 45 3N 78 30W
Halibut, oilfield 19 61 20N 1 36 E
Halifax, Austral. 138 18 32 S 146 22 E
Halifax, Can. 151 44 38N 63 35W
Halifax, U.K. 32 53 43N 1 51W
Halifax, U.S.A. 162 40 25N 76 55W
Halifax B. 138 18 50 S 147 0 E
Halifax I. 128 26 38 S 15 4 E
Halil, R. 93 27 40N 58 30 E
Halkirk 37 58 30N 3 30W
Hall 52 47 17N 11 30 E
Hall Land 12 81 20N 60 0W
Hall Pt. 136 15 40 S 124 23 E
Hallabro 73 56 22N 15 5 E
Halland 73 56 55N 12 50 E
Hallands län □ 73 56 50N 12 50 E
Hallands Väderö 73 56 27N 12 34 E
Hallandsås 73 56 22N 13 0 E
Halle, Belg. 47 50 44N 4 13W
Halle, Nordrhein-Westfalen, Ger. 48 52 4N 8 20 E
Halle, Sachsen-Anhalt, Ger. 48 51 29N 12 0 E
Halle □ 48 51 28N 11 58 E
Hällefors 72 59 47N 14 31 E
Hallein 52 47 40N 13 5 E
Hällekis 73 58 38N 13 27 E
Hallett 140 33 25 S 138 55 E
Hallettsville 159 29 28N 96 57W
Hallevadsholm 73 58 37N 11 33 E
Hällevadsholm 73 58 35N 11 33 E
Halley Bay 13 75 31 S 26 36W
Hallia, R. 96 16 55N 79 10 E
Halliday 158 47 20N 102 25W
Halliday L. 153 61 21N 108 56W
Hallim 107 33 24N 126 15 E
Hallingdal, R. 75 60 34N 9 12 E
Hallingskeid 71 60 40N 7 17 E
Hällnäs 74 64 19N 19 36 E
Hallock 153 48 47N 97 57W
Hallow 28 52 14N 2 15W
Hall's Creek 136 18 16 S 127 46 E
Hallsberg 72 59 5N 15 7 E
Hallstahammar 72 59 38N 16 15 E
Hallstatt 52 47 33N 13 38 E
Hallstavik 72 60 5N 18 37 E
Hallstead 162 41 56N 75 45W
Hallwiler See 50 47 16N 8 12 E
Hallworthy 30 50 38N 4 34W
Halmahera, I. 103 0 40N 128 0 E
Halmeu 70 47 57N 23 2 E
Halmstad 73 56 41N 12 52 E
Halq el Oued 119 36 53N 10 10 E
Hals 73 56 59N 10 18 E
Halsa 71 63 3N 8 14 E
Halsafjorden 71 63 5N 8 10 E
Hälsingborg = Helsingborg 73 56 3N 12 42 E
Halstad 158 47 21N 96 41W
Halstead 29 51 59N 0 39 E
Haltdalen 71 62 56N 11 8 E
Haltern 48 51 44N 7 10 E
Haltwhistle 35 54 58N 2 27W
Ham 128 49 44N 3 3 E
Ham Tan 101 10 40N 107 45 E
Ham Yen 100 22 4N 105 3 E
Hamā 92 35 5N 36 40 E
Hamab 128 28 7 S 19 16 E
Hamad 123 15 20N 33 32 E
Hamada 110 34 50N 132 10 E
Hamadān 92 34 52N 48 32 E
Hamadān □ 92 35 0N 49 0 E
Hamadh 122 24 55N 39 3 E
Hamadia 118 35 28N 1 57 E
Hamakita 111 34 45N 137 47 E
Hamale 120 10 56N 2 45W
Hamamatsu 111 34 45N 137 45 E
Hamar 71 60 48N 11 7 E
Hamar Koke 123 51 5N 36 45 E
Hamarøy 74 68 5N 15 38 E
Hamâta, Gebel 122 24 17N 35 0 E
Hambantota 93 6 10N 81 10 E
Hamber Prov. Park 152 52 20N 118 0W
Hambledon 28 50 56N 1 6W
Hambleton Hills 33 54 17N 1 12W
Hamburg, Ger. 48 53 32N 9 59 E
Hamburg, Ark., U.S.A. 159 33 15N 91 47W
Hamburg, Iowa, U.S.A. 158 40 37N 95 38W
Hamburg, Pa., U.S.A. 162 40 33N 76 0W
Hamburg □ 48 53 30N 10 0 E
Hamden 162 41 21N 72 56W
Hame 75 61 30N 24 0 E
Hämeen Lääni 75 61 24N 24 10 E
Hämeenlinna 75 61 0N 24 28 E
Hamelin Pool 137 26 22 S 114 20 E
Hamelin Pool Bay 137 26 10 S 114 5 E
Hameln 48 52 7N 9 24 E
Hamersley 136 22 20 S 117 37 E
Hamersley Ra. 136 22 0 S 117 45 E
Hamhung 107 40 0N 127 30 E
Hami 105 42 47N 93 32 E
Hamilton, Austral. 140 37 45 S 142 2 E
Hamilton, Can. 150 43 20N 79 50W
Hamilton, N.Z. 142 37 47 S 175 19 E
Hamilton, U.K. 35 55 47N 4 2W
Hamilton, Alas., U.S.A. 147 62 55N 164 0W
Hamilton, Mont., U.S.A. 160 46 20N 114 6W
Hamilton, N.Y., U.S.A. 162 42 49N 75 31W
Hamilton, Ohio, U.S.A. 156 39 20N 84 35W
Hamilton, Tex., U.S.A. 159 31 40N 98 5W
Hamilton Downs 106 21 25 S 142 23 E
Hamilton, gasfield 19 56 54N 2 13 E
Hamilton Hotel 138 22 45 S 140 40 E
Hamilton Inlet 151 54 0N 57 30W
Hamilton Mt. 162 43 25N 74 22W
Hamilton, R., Queens., Austral. 138 23 30 S 139 47 E
Hamilton, R., S. Austral., Austral. 136 26 40 S 134 20 E
Hamiota 153 50 11N 100 38W
Hamlet 157 34 56N 79 40W
Hamley Bridge 140 34 17 S 138 35 E
Hamlin 159 32 58N 100 8W
Hamm 48 51 40N 7 58 E
Hammam bou Hadjar 118 35 23N 0 58W
Hammamet 119 36 24N 10 38 E
Hammamet, G. de 119 36 10N 10 48 E
Hammarö, I. 72 59 20N 13 30 E
Hammarstrand 72 63 7N 16 20 E
Hamme 47 51 6N 4 8 E
Hamme-Mille 47 50 47N 4 43 E
Hammel 73 56 16N 9 52 E
Hammelburg 49 50 7N 9 54 E
Hammenton 156 39 40N 74 47W
Hammeren 73 55 18N 14 47 E
Hammerfest 74 70 39N 23 41 E
Hammersmith 29 51 30N 0 15W
Hammond, Ind., U.S.A. 156 41 40N 87 30W
Hammond, La., U.S.A. 159 30 32N 90 30W
Hammonton 162 39 38N 74 48W
Hamnavoe 36 60 25N 1 5W
Hamneda 73 56 41N 13 51 E
Hamoir 47 50 25N 5 32 E
Hamont 47 51 15N 5 32 E
Hampden 143 45 18 S 170 50 E
Hampshire □ 28 51 3N 1 20W
Hampshire Downs 28 51 10N 1 10W
Hampton, Ark., U.S.A. 159 33 35N 92 29W
Hampton, Iowa, U.S.A. 158 42 42N 93 12W
Hampton, N.H., U.S.A. 162 42 56N 70 48W
Hampton, S.C., U.S.A. 157 32 52N 81 2W
Hampton, Va., U.S.A. 162 37 4N 76 18W
Hampton Bays 162 40 53N 72 31W
Hampton Harbour 136 20 30 S 116 30 E
Hampton in Arden 28 52 26N 1 42W
Hampton Tableland 137 32 0N 127 0 E
Hamra 92 24 2N 38 55 E
Hamrange 72 60 59N 17 5 E
Hamrat esh Sheykh 123 14 45N 27 55 E
Hamre 71 60 33N 5 20 E
Hamun Helmand 93 31 15N 61 15 E
Hamun-i-Lora, Pak. 93 29 38N 64 58 E
Hamun-i-Lora, Pak. 93 29 38N 64 58 E
Hamun-i-Mashkel 93 28 30N 63 0 E
Hamyang 107 35 32N 127 42 E
Han Chiang, R., Hupeh, China 109 30 35N 114 15 E

Han Chiang, R Hawzen

Name	Page	Lat.	Long.
Han Chiang, R., Kwangtung, China	**109**	23 30N	116 48 E
Hana	**147**	20 45N	155 59W
Hanak	**122**	25 32N	37 0 E
Hanamaki	**112**	39 23N	141 7 E
Hanang □	**126**	4 10 S	35 40 E
Hanang, mt.	**126**	4 30 S	35 25 E
Hanau	**49**	50 8N	8 56 E
Hanbogd	**106**	43 11N	107 10 E
Hanch'eng	**106**	35 30N	110 30 E
Hanchiang	**109**	25 29N	119 5 E
Hanch'uan	**109**	30 39N	113 46 E
Hanchuang	**107**	34 36N	117 22 E
Hanchung	**106**	33 10N	107 2 E
Hancock, Mich., U.S.A.	**158**	47 10N	88 35W
Hancock, Minn., U.S.A.	**158**	45 26N	95 46W
Hancock, Pa., U.S.A.	**162**	41 57N	75 19W
Handa, Japan	**111**	34 53N	137 0 E
Handa, Somalia	**91**	10 37N	51 2 E
Handa I.	**36**	58 23N	5 10W
Handen	**72**	59 12N	18 12 E
Handeni	**124**	5 25 S	38 2 E
Handeni □	**126**	5 30 S	38 0 E
Handlová	**155**	48 45N	18 35 E
Handub	**122**	19 15N	37 25 E
Handwara	**95**	34 21N	74 20 E
Handzame	**47**	51 2N	3 0 E
Hanegev	**90**	30 50N	35 0 E
Haney	**152**	49 12N	122 40W
Hanford	**163**	36 25N	119 39W
Hang Chat	**100**	18 20N	99 21 E
Hang Dong	**100**	18 41N	98 55 E
Hangang, R.	**107**	37 50N	126 30 E
Hangayn Nuruu	**105**	47 30N	100 0 E
Hangchinch'i	**106**	39 54N	108 56 E
Hangchinhouch'i	**106**	41 55N	107 15 E
Hangchou	**109**	30 15N	120 8 E
Hangchou Wan	**109**	30 30N	121 30 E
Hanger	**73**	57 6N	13 58 E
Hangklip, K.	**128**	34 26 S	18 48 E
Hangö (Hanko)	**75**	59 59N	22 57 E
Hanhongor	**106**	43 55N	104 28 E
Hanish J.	**91**	13 45N	42 46 E
Hanita	**90**	33 5N	35 10 E
Hankinson	**158**	46 9N	96 58W
Hanko = Hangö	**75**	59 59N	22 57 E
Hank'ou	**109**	30 40N	114 18 E
Hankow = Hank'ou	**109**	30 40N	114 18 E
Hanksville	**161**	38 19N	110 45W
Hanku	**107**	39 16N	117 50 E
Hanle	**95**	32 42N	79 4 E
Hanmer	**143**	42 32 S	172 50 E
Hann, Mt.	**136**	16 0 S	126 0 E
Hann, R.	**136**	17 26 S	126 17 E
Hanna	**152**	51 40N	111 54W
Hannaford	**158**	47 23N	98 18W
Hannah	**158**	48 58N	98 42W
Hannah B.	**150**	51 40N	80 0W
Hannahs Bridge	**141**	31 55 S	149 41 E
Hannibal, Mo., U.S.A.	**158**	39 42N	91 22W
Hannibal, N.Y., U.S.A.	**162**	43 19N	76 35W
Hannik	**122**	18 12N	32 20 E
Hanningfield Water	**29**	51 40N	0 30 E
Hannover	**48**	52 23N	9 43 E
Hannut	**47**	50 40N	5 4 E
Hanö	**73**	56 0N	14 50 E
Hanö, I.	**73**	56 2N	14 50 E
Hanöbukten	**73**	55 35N	14 30 E
Hanoi	**100**	21 5N	105 55 E
Hanover, S. Afr.	**128**	31 4 S	24 29 E
Hanover, N.H., U.S.A.	**162**	43 43N	72 17W
Hanover, Pa., U.S.A.	**162**	39 46N	76 59W
Hanover, Va., U.S.A.	**162**	37 46N	77 22W
Hanover = Hannover	**48**	52 23N	9 43 E
Hanover, I.	**176**	51 0 S	74 50W
Hanpan, C.	**135**	5 0 S	154 35 E
Hans Meyer Ra.	**135**	4 20 S	152 55 E
Hansholm	**73**	57 8N	8 38 E
Hanshou	**109**	28 55N	111 58 E
Hansi	**94**	29 10N	75 57 E
Hansjö	**72**	61 10N	14 40 E
Hanson, L.	**140**	31 0 S	136 15 E
Hanson Range	**136**	27 0 S	136 30 E
Hansted	**73**	57 8N	8 36 E
Hantan	**105**	36 42N	114 30 E
Hante	**47**	50 19N	4 11 E
Hanton	**106**	36 42N	114 30 E
Hanwood	**141**	34 26 S	146 3 E
Hanyang	**109**	30 35N	114 0 E
Hanyin	**108**	32 53N	108 37 E
Hanyü	**111**	36 10N	139 32 E
Hanyüan	**108**	29 21N	102 43 E
Haoch'ing	**108**	26 34N	100 12 E
Haokang	**105**	47 25N	132 8 E
Haopi	**106**	35 57N	114 13 E
Haparanda	**74**	65 52N	24 8 E
Hapert	**47**	51 22N	5 15 E
Happy	**159**	34 47N	101 50W
Happy Camp	**160**	41 52N	123 30W
Happy Valley	**151**	53 15N	60 20W
Hapsu	**107**	41 13N	128 51 E
Hapur	**94**	28 45N	77 45 E
Haql	**92**	29 10N	35 0 E
Har	**103**	5 16 S	133 14 E
Har-Ayrag	**106**	45 47N	109 16 E
Har Tuv	**90**	31 46N	35 0 E
Har Us Nuur	**105**	48 0N	92 10 E
Har Yehuda	**90**	31 35N	34 57 E
Harad	**92**	24 15N	49 0 E
Haradera	**91**	4 33N	47 38 E
Haradh	**92**	24 15N	49 0 E
Haramsøya	**71**	62 39N	6 12 E
Haran	**92**	36 48N	39 0 E
Harat	**123**	16 5N	39 26 E
Haraze	**117**	14 20N	19 12 E
Haraze-Mangueigne	**117**	7 22N	17 3 E
Harbin = Haerhpin	**107**	45 45N	126 45 E
Harboør	**73**	56 38N	8 10 E
Harbor Beach	**156**	43 50N	82 38W
Harbor Springs	**156**	45 28N	85 0W
Harbour Breton	**151**	47 29N	55 50W
Harbour Deep	**151**	50 25N	56 30W
Harbour Grace	**151**	47 40N	53 22W
Harburg	**48**	53 27N	9 58 E
Hårby	**73**	55 13N	10 7 E
Harcourt	**138**	24 17 S	149 55 E
Harda	**94**	22 27N	77 5 E
Hardangerfjorden.	**71**	60 15N	6 0 E
Hardangerjøkulen	**71**	60 30N	7 0 E
Hardangervidda	**71**	60 20N	7 20 E
Hardap Dam	**128**	24 32 S	17 50 E
Hardegarijp	**46**	53 13N	5 57 E
Harden	**141**	34 32 S	148 24 E
Hardenberg	**46**	52 34N	6 37 E
Harderwijk	**46**	52 21N	5 38 E
Hardey, R.	**136**	22 45 S	116 8 E
Hardin	**160**	45 50N	107 35W
Harding	**129**	30 22 S	29 55 E
Harding Ra.	**136**	16 17 S	124 55 E
Hardisty	**152**	52 40N	111 18W
Hardman	**160**	45 12N	119 49W
Hardoi	**95**	27 26N	80 15 E
Hardwar	**94**	29 58N	78 16 E
Hardy	**159**	36 20N	91 30W
Hardy, Pen.	**176**	55 30 S	68 20W
Hare B.	**151**	51 15N	55 45W
Hare Gilboa	**90**	32 31N	35 25 E
Hare Meron	**90**	32 59N	35 24 E
Harelbeke	**47**	50 52N	3 20 E
Haren, Ger.	**48**	52 47N	7 18 E
Haren, Neth.	**46**	53 11N	6 36 E
Harer	**123**	9 20N	42 8 E
Harer □	**123**	7 12N	42 0 E
Hareto	**123**	9 23N	37 6 E
Harfleur	**42**	49 30N	0 10 E
Hargeisa	**91**	9 30N	44 2 E
Hargshamn	**72**	60 12N	18 30 E
Hari, R., Afghan.	**93**	34 20N	64 30 E
Hari, R., Indon.	**102**	1 10 S	101 50 E
Haricha, Hamada el	**118**	22 40N	3 15W
Harihar	**97**	14 32N	75 44 E
Harim, J. al	**60**	26 0N	56 10 E
Harima-Nada	**110**	34 30N	134 35 E
Haringey	**29**	51 35N	0 7W
Haringhata, R.	**98**	22 0N	89 58 E
Haringvliet	**46**	51 48N	4 10 E
Haripad	**97**	9 14N	76 28 E
Harirúd	**93**	35 0N	61 0 E
Harkat	**122**	20 25N	39 40 E
Harlan, Iowa, U.S.A.	**158**	41 37N	95 20W
Harlan, Tenn., U.S.A.	**157**	36 58N	83 20W
Harlech	**31**	52 52N	4 7W
Harlem	**160**	48 29N	108 39W
Harleston	**29**	52 25N	1 18 E
Harlingen, Neth.	**46**	53 11N	5 25 E
Harlingen, U.S.A.	**159**	26 30N	97 50W
Harlow	**29**	51 47N	0 9 E
Harlowton	**160**	46 30N	109 54W
Harmånger	**72**	61 55N	17 20 E
Harmil	**123**	16 30N	40 10 E
Harney Basin	**160**	43 30N	119 0W
Harney L.	**160**	43 0N	119 0W
Harney Pk.	**158**	43 52N	103 33W
Härnön	**72**	62 36N	18 0 E
Härnösand	**72**	62 38N	18 5 E
Haro	**58**	42 35N	2 55W
Haro, C.	**164**	27 50N	110 55W
Haroldswick	**36**	60 48N	0 50W
Håroy	**73**	55 13N	10 8 E
Harp L.	**151**	55 5N	61 50W
Harpe, La	**158**	40 30N	91 0W
Harpenden	**29**	51 48N	0 20W
Harpenhalli	**97**	14 47N	76 2 E
Harper	**120**	4 25N	7 43 E
Harper Mt.	**147**	64 15N	143 57W
Harplinge	**73**	56 45N	12 45 E
Harport L.	**36**	57 20N	6 20W
Harput	**92**	38 48N	39 15 E
Harrand	**94**	29 28N	70 3 E
Harrat al Kishb	**92**	22 30N	40 15 E
Harrat al Umuirid	**92**	26 50N	38 0 E
Harrat Khaibar	**122**	25 45N	40 0 E
Harrat Nawāsīf	**122**	21 30N	42 0 E
Harray, L. of	**37**	59 0N	3 15W
Harricana, R.	**150**	50 30N	79 10W
Harrietsham	**29**	51 15N	0 41 E
Harriman	**157**	36 0N	84 35W
Harrington, U.K.	**32**	54 37N	3 55W
Harrington, U.S.A.	**162**	38 56N	75 35W
Harrington Harbour	**151**	50 31N	59 30W
Harris	**36**	57 50N	6 55W
Harris L.	**136**	31 10 S	135 10 E
Harris Mts.	**143**	44 49 S	168 49 E
Harris, Sd. of	**36**	57 44N	7 6W
Harrisburg, Ill., U.S.A.	**159**	37 42N	88 30W
Harrisburg, Nebr., U.S.A.	**158**	41 36N	103 46W
Harrisburg, Oreg., U.S.A.	**160**	44 25N	123 10W
Harrisburg, Pa., U.S.A.	**162**	40 18N	76 52W
Harrismith	**129**	28 15 S	29 8 E
Harrison, Ark., U.S.A.	**159**	36 10N	93 4W
Harrison, Idaho, U.S.A.	**160**	47 30N	116 51W
Harrison, Nebr., U.S.A.	**158**	42 42N	103 52W
Harrison B.	**147**	70 25N	151 0W
Harrison, C.	**151**	55 0N	58 0W
Harrison L.	**152**	49 33N	121 50W
Harrisonburg	**156**	38 28N	78 52W
Harrisonville	**158**	38 45N	93 45W
Harriston	**150**	43 57N	80 53W
Harrisville	**150**	44 40N	83 19W
Harrogate	**33**	53 59N	1 32W
Harrow	**29**	51 35N	0 15W
Harry, L.	**139**	29 23 S	138 19 E
Harsefeld	**48**	53 26N	9 31 E
Harskamp	**46**	52 8N	5 46 E
Harstad	**74**	68 48N	16 30 E
Hart	**156**	43 42N	86 21W
Hart, L.	**140**	31 10 S	136 25 E
Hartbees, R.	**128**	29 8 S	20 48 E
Hartberg	**52**	47 17N	15 58 E
Harteigen, Mt.	**71**	60 11N	7 5 E
Hartest	**29**	52 7N	0 41 E
Hartford, Conn., U.S.A.	**162**	41 47N	72 41W
Hartford, Ky., U.S.A.	**156**	37 26N	86 50W
Hartford, S.D., U.S.A.	**158**	43 40N	96 58W
Hartford, Wis., U.S.A.	**158**	43 18N	88 25W
Hartford City	**156**	40 22N	85 20W
Harthill	**35**	55 52N	3 45W
Hartland, Can.	**151**	46 20N	67 32W
Hartland, U.K.	**30**	50 59N	4 29W
Hartland Pt.	**30**	51 2N	4 32W
Hartlebury	**28**	52 20N	2 13W
Hartlepool	**33**	54 42N	1 11W
Hartley, Zimb.	**127**	18 10 S	30 7 E
Hartley, U.K.	**35**	55 5N	1 27W
Hartley Bay	**152**	53 25N	129 15W
Hartmannberge	**128**	17 0 S	13 0 E
Hartney	**153**	49 30N	100 35W
Hartpury	**28**	51 55N	2 18W
Hartselle	**157**	34 25N	86 55W
Hartshorne	**159**	34 51N	95 30W
Hartsville	**157**	34 23N	80 2W
Hartwell	**157**	34 21N	82 52W
Harunabad	**94**	29 35N	73 2 E
Harur	**97**	12 3N	78 29 E
Harvard, Mt.	**161**	39 0N	106 5W
Harvey, Austral.	**137**	33 5 S	115 54 E
Harvey, Ill., U.S.A.	**156**	41 40N	87 50W
Harvey, N.D., U.S.A.	**158**	47 50N	99 58W
Harwell	**28**	51 40N	1 17W
Harwich	**29**	51 56N	1 18 E
Harwood	**33**	53 54N	1 30W
Haryana □	**94**	29 0N	76 10 E
Harz	**48**	51 40N	10 40 E
Harzé	**47**	50 27N	5 40 E
Harzgerode	**48**	51 38N	11 8 E
Hasa	**92**	26 0N	49 0 E
Hasaheisa	**123**	14 25N	33 20 E
Hasani	**122**	25 0N	37 8 E
Hasanpur	**94**	28 51N	78 9 E
Haselünne	**48**	52 40N	7 30 E
Hasharon	**90**	32 12N	34 49 E
Hashefela	**90**	31 30N	34 43 E
Hashima	**111**	35 20N	136 40 E
Hashimoto	**111**	34 19N	135 37 E
Hasjö	**72**	63 2N	16 20 E
Håsjö	**72**	63 1N	16 5 E
Haskell, Kans., U.S.A.	**159**	35 51N	95 40W
Haskell, Tex., U.S.A.	**159**	33 10N	99 45W
Haskier Is.	**36**	57 42N	7 40W
Haslach	**49**	48 16N	8 7 E
Hasle	**73**	55 11N	14 44 E
Haslemere	**29**	51 5N	0 41W
Haslev	**73**	55 18N	11 57 E
Haslingden	**32**	53 43N	2 20W
Hasparren	**44**	43 24N	1 18W
Hassan	**92**	13 0N	76 5 E
Hasselt, Belg.	**47**	50 56N	5 21 E
Hasselt, Neth.	**46**	52 36N	6 6 E
Hassene, Ad.	**118**	21 0N	4 0 E
Hassfurt	**49**	50 2N	10 30 E
Hassi Berrekrem	**119**	33 45N	5 16 E
Hassi Daoula	**119**	33 4N	5 38 E
Hassi el Biod	**119**	28 30N	6 0 E
Hassi el Heïda	**74**	29 34N	0 14W
Hassi Inifel	**118**	29 50N	3 41 E
Hassi Marroket	**119**	30 10N	3 0 E
Hassi Messaoud	**119**	31 43N	6 8 E
Hassi Taguenza	**172**	29 8N	0 23W
Hassi Zerzour	**118**	30 51N	3 56W
Hässleby	**73**	57 37N	15 30 E
Hässleholmen	**73**	56 9N	13 45 E
Hastière-Lavaux	**47**	50 13N	4 49 E
Hastigrow	**37**	58 32N	3 15W
Hastings, Austral.	**141**	38 18 S	145 12 E
Hastings, N.Z.	**142**	39 39 S	176 52 E
Hastings, U.K.	**29**	50 51N	0 36 E
Hastings, Mich., U.S.A.	**156**	42 40N	82 20W
Hastings, Minn., U.S.A.	**158**	44 41N	92 51W
Hastings, Nebr., U.S.A.	**158**	40 34N	98 22W
Hastings Ra.	**141**	31 15 S	152 14 E
Hästveda	**73**	56 17N	13 55 E
Hat Nhao	**101**	14 46N	106 32 E
Hat Yai	**101**	7 1N	100 27 E
Hatanbulag	**106**	43 8N	109 14 E
Hatano	**111**	35 22N	139 14 E
Hatch	**161**	32 45N	107 8W
Hatches Creek	**138**	20 56 S	135 12 E
Hatchet L.	**153**	58 36N	103 40W
Haţeg	**70**	45 36N	22 55 E
Haţeg, Mţii	**70**	45 25N	23 0 E
Hatert	**46**	51 49N	5 50 E
Hatfield	**29**	51 46N	0 11W
Hatfield Broad Oak	**29**	51 48N	0 16 E
Hatfield Post Office	**140**	33 54N	143 49 E
Hatgal	**105**	50 26N	100 9 E
Hatherleigh	**30**	50 49N	4 4W
Hathersage	**33**	53 20N	1 39W
Hathras	**94**	27 36N	78 6 E
Hatia	**99**	22 30N	91 5 E
Hato de Corozal	**174**	6 11N	71 45W
Hato Mayor	**167**	18 46N	69 15W
Hattah	**140**	34 48N	142 17 E
Hattem	**46**	52 28N	6 4 E
Hatteras, C.	**157**	35 10N	75 30W
Hattiesburg	**159**	31 20N	89 20W
Hatton, Can.	**153**	50 2N	109 50W
Hatton, U.K.	**37**	57 24N	1 57W
Hatvan	**53**	47 40N	19 45 E
Hau Bon (Cheo Reo)	**100**	13 25N	108 28 E
Hau Duc	**100**	15 20N	108 13 E
Hauchinango	**164**	20 12N	97 45W
Haug	**71**	60 23N	10 26 E
Haugastøl	**71**	60 30N	7 50 E
Haugesund	**71**	59 23N	5 13 E
Haugh of Urr	**35**	55 0N	3 51W
Haughangaroa Ra.	**142**	38 42 S	175 40 E
Haughley	**29**	52 13N	0 59 E
Haukelisæter	**71**	59 51N	7 9 E
Haulerwijk	**46**	53 4N	6 20 E
Haultain, R.	**153**	55 51N	106 46W
Haungpa	**98**	25 29N	96 7 E
Haura	**91**	13 50N	47 35 E
Hauraki Gulf	**142**	36 35 S	175 5 E
Hausruck	**52**	48 6N	13 30 E
Haut Atlas	**118**	32 0N	7 0W
Haut-Rhin □	**43**	48 0N	7 15 E
Haut Zaïre □	**126**	2 20N	26 0 E
Hauta Oasis	**92**	23 40N	47 0 E
Hautah, Wahāt al	**92**	23 40N	47 0 E
Haute-Corse □	**45**	42 30N	9 30 E
Haute-Garonne □	**44**	43 28N	1 30 E
Haute-Loire □	**44**	45 5N	3 50 E
Haute-Marne □	**43**	48 10N	5 20 E
Haute-Saône □	**43**	47 45N	6 10 E
Haute-Savoie □	**45**	46 0N	6 20 E
Haute-Vienne □	**44**	45 50N	1 10 E
Hauterive	**151**	49 10N	68 16W
Hautes-Alpes □	**45**	44 42N	6 20 E
Hautes Fagnes	**47**	50 34N	6 6 E
Hautes-Pyrénées □	**44**	43 0N	0 10 E
Hauteville-Lompnes	**45**	45 59N	5 35 E
Hautmont	**43**	50 15N	3 55 E
Hautrage	**47**	50 29N	3 46 E
Hauts-de-Seine □	**43**	48 52N	2 15 E
Hauts Plateaux	**118**	34 14N	1 0 E
Hauxley	**35**	55 21N	1 35W
Havana	**158**	40 19N	90 3W
Havana = La Habana	**166**	23 8N	82 22W
Havant	**29**	50 51N	0 59W
Havasu, L.	**161**	34 18N	114 8W
Havdhem	**73**	57 10N	18 20 E
Havelange	**47**	50 23N	5 15 E
Havelian	**94**	34 2N	73 10 E
Havelock, N.B., Can.	**151**	46 2N	65 24W
Havelock, Ont., Can.	**150**	44 26N	77 53W
Havelock, N.Z.	**143**	41 17 S	173 48 E
Havelock I.	**101**	11 55N	93 2 E
Havelte	**46**	52 46N	6 14 E
Haverfordwest	**31**	51 48N	4 59W
Haverhill, U.K.	**29**	52 6N	0 27 E
Haverhill, U.S.A.	**162**	42 50N	71 2W
Haveri	**97**	14 53N	75 24 E
Haverigg	**32**	54 12N	3 16W
Havering	**29**	51 33N	0 20 E
Haverstraw	**162**	41 12N	73 58W
Håverud	**73**	58 50N	12 28 E
Havîrna	**70**	48 4N	26 43 E
Havličkuv Brod	**52**	49 36N	15 33 E
Havnby	**73**	55 5N	8 34 E
Havre	**160**	48 40N	109 34W
Havre-Aubert	**151**	47 12N	62 0W
Havre de Grace	**162**	39 33N	76 6W
Havre, Le	**42**	49 30N	0 5 E
Havre St. Pierre	**151**	50 18N	63 33W
Havza	**92**	41 0N	35 35 E
Haw, R.	**157**	37 43N	80 52W
Hawaii □	**147**	20 30N	157 0W
Hawaii I.	**147**	20 0N	155 0W
Hawaiian Is.	**147**	20 30N	156 0W
Hawarden, Can.	**153**	51 25N	106 36W
Hawarden, U.K.	**31**	53 11N	3 2W
Hawarden, U.S.A.	**158**	43 2N	96 28W
Hawea Flat	**143**	44 40 S	169 19 E
Hawea Lake	**143**	44 28 S	169 19 E
Hawera	**142**	39 35 S	174 19 E
Hawes	**32**	54 18N	2 12W
Hawes Water, L.	**32**	54 32N	2 48W
Hawick	**35**	55 25N	2 48W
Hawk Junction	**150**	48 30N	84 38W
Hawkchurch	**30**	50 47N	2 56W
Hawkdun Ra.	**143**	44 53 S	170 5 E
Hawke B.	**142**	39 25N	177 20 E
Hawker	**28**	31 59 S	138 22 E
Hawke's Bay □	**142**	39 45 S	176 35 E
Hawke's Harbour	**151**	53 2N	55 50W
Hawkesbury	**150**	45 35N	74 40W
Hawkesbury I.	**152**	53 37N	129 3W
Hawkesbury Pt.	**138**	11 55 S	134 5 E
Hawkesbury River	**133**	33 50 S	151 44W
Hawkesbury Upton	**28**	51 34N	2 19W
Hawkhurst	**29**	51 2N	0 31 E
Hawkinsville	**157**	32 17N	83 30W
Hawkshead	**32**	54 23N	3 0W
Hawkwood	**139**	25 45 S	150 50 E
Hawley, Minn., U.S.A.	**158**	46 58N	96 20W
Hawley, Pa., U.S.A.	**162**	41 28N	75 11W
Haworth	**32**	53 50N	1 57W
Hawsker	**33**	54 27N	0 34W
Hawthorne	**163**	38 31N	118 37W
Hawzen	**123**	13 58N	39 28 E

Haxby Higashiōsaka

Haxby	**33**	54 1N	1 4W
Haxtun	**158**	40 40N	102 39W
Hay, Austral.	**141**	34 30 S	144 51 E
Hay, U.K.	**31**	52 4N	3 9W
Hay, C.	**136**	14 5 S	129 29 E
Hay L.	**152**	58 50N	118 50W
Hay Lakes	**152**	53 12N	113 2W
Hay, R., Austral.	**138**	24 10 S	137 20 E
Hay, R., Can.	**152**	60 0N	116 56W
Hay River	**152**	60 51N	115 44W
Hay Springs	**158**	42 40N	102 38W
Hayange	**43**	49 20N	6 2 E
Hayato	**110**	31 40N	130 43 E
Hayburn Wyke	**33**	54 22N	0 28W
Haycock	**147**	65 10N	161 20W
Hayden, Ariz., U.S.A.	**161**	33 2N	110 54W
Hayden, Wyo., U.S.A.	**160**	40 30N	107 22W
Haydenville	**162**	42 22N	72 42W
Haydon	**138**	18 0 S	141 30 E
Haydon Bridge	**35**	54 58N	2 15W
Haye Descartes, La	**42**	46 58N	0 42 E
Haye-du-Puits, La	**42**	49 17N	1 33W
Hayes	**158**	44 22N	101 1W
Hayes Pen.	**12**	75 30N	65 0W
Hayes, R.	**153**	57 3N	92 12W
Hayle	**30**	50 12N	5 25W
Haymana	**92**	39 30N	32 35 E
Haynesville	**159**	33 0N	93 7W
Hays, Can.	**152**	50 6N	111 48W
Hays, U.S.A.	**158**	38 55N	99 25W
Hayton	**32**	54 55N	2 45W
Hayward, Calif., U.S.A.	**163**	37 40N	122 5W
Hayward, Wis., U.S.A.	**158**	46 2N	91 30W
Hayward's Heath	**29**	51 0N	0 5W
Hazard	**156**	37 18N	83 10W
Hazaribagh	**95**	23 58N	85 26 E
Hazaribagh Road	**95**	24 12N	85 57 E
Hazebrouck	**43**	50 42N	2 31 E
Hazelton, Can.	**152**	55 20N	127 42W
Hazelton, U.S.A.	**158**	46 30N	100 15W
Hazen	**160**	39 37N	119 2W
Hazerswoude	**46**	52 5N	4 36 E
Hazlehurst	**157**	31 50N	82 35W
Hazleton	**156**	40 58N	76 0W
Hazlett, L.	**136**	21 30 S	128 48 E
Hazrat Imam	**93**	37 15N	68 50 E
Heacham	**29**	52 55N	0 30 E
Head of Bight	**137**	31 30 S	131 25 E
Headcorn	**29**	51 10N	0 39 E
Headford	**38**	53 28N	9 6W
Headington	**28**	51 46N	1 13W
Headlands	**127**	18 15 S	32 2 E
Healdsburg	**160**	38 33N	122 51W
Healdton	**159**	34 16N	97 31W
Healesville	**141**	37 35 S	145 30 E
Heanor	**33**	53 1N	1 20W
Heard I.	**11**	53 0 S	74 0 E
Hearne	**159**	30 54N	96 35W
Hearne B.	**153**	60 10N	99 10W
Hearne L.	**152**	62 20N	113 10W
Hearst	**150**	49 40N	83 41W
Heart, R.	**158**	46 40N	101 30W
Heart's Content	**151**	47 54N	53 27W
Heath Mts.	**143**	45 39 S	167 9 E
Heath Pt.	**151**	49 8N	61 40W
Heath Steele	**151**	47 17N	66 5W
Heathcote	**141**	36 56 S	144 45 E
Heather, oilfield	**19**	60 55N	0 50 E
Heathfield	**29**	50 58N	0 18 E
Heathsville	**162**	37 55N	76 28W
Heavener	**159**	34 54N	94 36W
Hebbronville	**159**	27 20N	98 40W
Hebburn	**35**	54 59N	1 30W
Hebden Bridge	**32**	53 45N	2 0W
Hebel	**139**	28 58 S	147 47 E
Heber Springs	**159**	35 29N	91 39W
Hebgen, L.	**160**	44 50N	111 15W
Hebrides, U.K.	**36**	57 30N	7 0W
Hebrides, Inner Is., U.K.	**36**	57 20N	6 40W
Hebrides, Outer Is., U.K.	**36**	57 50N	7 25W
Hebron, Can.	**149**	58 12N	62 38W
Hebron, N.D., U.S.A.	**158**	46 56N	102 2W
Hebron, Nebr., U.S.A.	**158**	40 15N	97 33W
Hebron (Al Khalil)	**90**	31 32N	35 6 E
Heby	**72**	59 56N	16 53 E
Hecate Str.	**152**	53 10N	130 30W
Hechingen	**49**	48 20N	8 58 E
Hechtel	**47**	51 8N	5 22 E
Heckington	**33**	52 59N	0 17W
Hecla	**158**	45 56N	98 8W
Hecla I.	**153**	51 10N	96 43W
Hecla Mt.	**36**	57 18N	7 15W
Heddal	**71**	59 36N	9 20 E
Heddon	**35**	55 0N	1 47W
Hédé	**42**	48 18N	1 49W
Hede	**72**	62 23N	13 30 E
Hedemora	**72**	60 18N	15 58 E
Hedgehope	**143**	46 12 S	168 34 E
Hedley	**159**	34 53N	100 39W
Hedmark □	**75**	61 17N	11 40 E
Hedmark fylke □	**71**	61 17N	11 40 E
Hednesford	**28**	52 43N	2 0W
Hedon	**33**	53 44N	0 11W
Hedrum	**71**	59 7N	10 5 E
Heeg	**46**	52 58N	5 37 E
Heegermeer	**46**	52 56N	5 32 E
Heemskerk	**46**	52 31N	4 40 E
Heemstede	**46**	52 22N	4 37 E
Heer	**47**	50 50N	5 43 E
Heerde	**46**	52 24N	6 2 E
's Heerenburg	**46**	51 53N	6 16 E
's Heerenloo	**46**	52 19N	5 36 E
Heerenveen	**46**	52 57N	5 55 E
Heerhugowaard	**46**	52 40N	4 51 E
Heerlen	**47**	50 55N	6 0 E
Heerlerheide	**47**	50 54N	5 58 E
Heers	**47**	50 45N	5 18 E
Heesch	**46**	51 44N	5 32 E
Heestert	**47**	50 47N	3 25 E
Heeze	**47**	51 23N	5 35 E
Hegyalja, Mts.	**53**	48 25N	21 25 E
Heich'engchen	**106**	36 16N	106 19 E
Heide	**48**	54 10N	9 7 E
Heide, oilfield	**19**	54 5N	9 5 E
Heidelberg, Ger.	**49**	49 23N	8 41 E
Heidelberg, C. Prov., S. Afr.	**128**	34 6 S	20 59 E
Heidelberg, Trans., S. Afr.	**129**	26 30 S	28 23 E
Heidenheim	**49**	48 40N	10 10 E
Heigun-To	**110**	33 47N	132 14 E
Heikant	**47**	51 15N	4 1 E
Heilam	**37**	58 31N	4 40W
Heilbron	**129**	27 16 S	27 59 E
Heilbronn	**49**	49 8N	9 13 E
Heiligenblut	**52**	47 2N	12 51 E
Heiligenhafen	**48**	54 21N	10 58 E
Heiligenstadt	**48**	51 22N	10 9 E
Heilungkiang □	**46**	48 0N	128 0 E
Heim	**71**	63 26N	9 5 E
Heimdal, gasfield	**19**	59 35N	2 15 E
Heino	**46**	52 26N	6 14 E
Heinola	**75**	61 13N	26 24 E
Heinsburg	**153**	53 50N	110 30W
Heinsch	**47**	49 42N	5 44 E
Heinsun	**98**	25 52N	95 35 E
Heinze Is.	**101**	14 25N	97 45 E
Heirnkut	**98**	25 14N	94 44 E
Heishan	**107**	41 40N	122 3 E
Heishui, Liaoning, China	**107**	42 6N	119 22 E
Heishui, Szechwan, China	**108**	32 15N	103 0 E
Heist	**47**	51 20N	3 15 E
Heist-op-den-Berg	**47**	51 5N	4 44 E
Heistad	**71**	59 35N	9 40 E
Hejaz = Hijãz	**92**	26 0N	37 30 E
Hekelegem	**47**	50 55N	4 7 E
Hekimhan	**92**	38 50N	38 0 E
Hekinan	**111**	34 52N	137 0 E
Hekla	**74**	63 56N	19 35W
Hel	**54**	54 38N	18 50 E
Helagsfjället	**72**	62 54N	12 25 E
Helchteren	**47**	51 4N	5 22 E
Helden	**47**	51 19N	6 0 E
Helechosa	**57**	39 22N	4 53W
Helena, Ark., U.S.A.	**159**	34 30N	90 35W
Helena, Mont., U.S.A.	**160**	46 40N	112 0W
Helendale	**163**	34 45N	117 19W
Helensburgh, Austral.	**141**	34 11 S	151 1 E
Helensburgh, U.K.	**34**	56 0N	4 44W
Helensville	**142**	36 41 S	174 29 E
Helets	**90**	31 36N	34 39 E
Helgasjön	**73**	57 0N	14 50 E
Helgeland	**74**	66 20N	13 30 E
Helgeroa	**71**	59 0N	9 45 E
Helgoland, I.	**48**	54 10N	7 51 E
Helgum	**72**	63 25N	16 50 E
Heligoland = Helgoland	**48**	54 10N	7 51 E
Heliopolis	**122**	30 6N	31 17 E
Hell-Ville	**129**	13 25 S	48 16 E
Hellebæk	**73**	56 4N	12 32 E
Helleland	**71**	58 33N	6 7 E
Hellendoorn	**46**	52 24N	6 27 E
Hellertown	**162**	40 35N	75 21W
Hellevoetsluis	**46**	51 50N	4 8 E
Helli Ness	**36**	60 3N	1 10W
Hellick Kenyon Plateau	**13**	82 0 S	110 0W
Hellifield	**32**	54 0N	2 13W
Hellín	**59**	38 31N	1 40W
Hellum	**73**	57 16N	10 10 E
Helmand □	**93**	31 20N	64 0 E
Helmand, R.	**94**	34 0N	67 0 E
Helmond	**47**	51 29N	5 41 E
Helmsdale	**37**	58 7N	3 40W
Helmsley	**33**	54 15N	1 2W
Helmstedt	**48**	52 16N	11 0 E
Helnæs	**73**	55 9N	10 0 E
Helper	**160**	39 44N	110 56W
Helperby	**33**	54 8N	1 20W
Helsby	**32**	53 16N	2 47W
Helsingborg	**73**	56 3N	12 42 E
Helsinge	**73**	56 2N	12 12 E
Helsingfors = Helsinki	**75**	60 15N	25 3 E
Helsingør	**73**	56 2N	12 35 E
Helsinki (Helsingfors)	**75**	60 15N	25 3 E
Helston	**30**	50 7N	5 17W
Helvick Hd.	**39**	52 3N	7 33W
Helvoirt	**47**	51 38N	5 14 E
Helwân	**122**	29 50N	31 20 E
Hem	**71**	59 26N	10 0 E
Hemavati, R.	**97**	12 50N	67 0 E
Hemel Hempstead	**29**	51 45N	0 28W
Hemet	**163**	33 45N	116 59W
Hemingford	**158**	42 21N	103 4W
Hemphill	**159**	31 21N	93 49W
Hempstead	**159**	30 5N	96 5W
Hempton	**29**	52 50N	0 49 E
Hemse	**73**	57 15N	18 22 E
Hemsö, I.	**72**	62 43N	18 5 E
Hemsön	**72**	62 42N	18 5 E
Hemsworth	**33**	53 37N	1 21W
Hemyock	**30**	50 55N	1 13W
Hen & Chicken Is.	**142**	35 58 S	174 45 E
Henares, R.	**58**	40 55N	3 0W
Hendaye	**44**	43 23N	1 47W
Henderson, Argent.	**172**	36 18 S	61 43W
Henderson, U.K.	**36**	57 42N	5 47W
Henderson, Ky., U.S.A.	**156**	37 50N	87 38W
Henderson, Nev., U.S.A.	**161**	36 2N	115 0W
Henderson, Pa., U.S.A.	**157**	35 25N	88 40W
Henderson, Tex., U.S.A.	**159**	32 5N	94 49W
Hendersonville	**157**	35 21N	82 28W
Hendon	**139**	28 5 S	151 50 E
Hendorf	**70**	46 4N	24 5 E
Henfield	**29**	50 56N	0 17W
Hengch'eng	**106**	38 26N	106 26 E
Hengelo, Gelderland, Neth.	**46**	52 3N	6 19 E
Hengelo, Overijssel, Neth.	**46**	52 16N	6 48 E
Hengfeng	**109**	28 25N	117 35 E
Henghsien	**108**	22 36N	109 16 E
Hengoed	**31**	51 39N	3 14W
Hengshan, Hunan, China	**109**	27 15N	112 51 E
Hengshan, Shansi, China	**106**	37 56N	108 53 E
Hengshui	**106**	37 43N	115 42 E
Hengtaohotze	**107**	44 55N	129 3 E
Hengyang	**109**	26 51N	112 30 E
Hengyanghsien	**109**	26 58N	112 21 E
Hénin-Beaumont	**43**	50 25N	2 58 E
Henley	**29**	51 32N	0 53W
Henley-in-Arden	**28**	52 18N	1 47W
Henllan	**31**	53 13N	3 29W
Henlopen, C.	**162**	38 48N	75 5W
Henlow	**29**	51 2N	0 18W
Hennan, L.	**72**	62 3N	15 55 E
Henne	**73**	55 44N	8 11 E
Hennebont	**42**	47 49N	3 19W
Hennenman	**128**	27 59 S	27 1 E
Hennessy	**159**	36 8N	97 53W
Hennigsdorf	**48**	52 38N	13 13 E
Henribourg	**153**	53 25N	105 38W
Henrichemont	**43**	47 20N	2 21 E
Henrietta	**159**	33 50N	98 15W
Henrietta Maria C.	**150**	55 9N	82 20W
Henry	**158**	41 5N	89 20W
Henryetta	**159**	35 2N	96 0W
Henstridge	**28**	50 59N	2 24W
Hentiyn Nuruu	**105**	48 30N	108 30 E
Henty	**141**	35 30N	147 0 E
Henzada	**98**	17 38N	95 35 E
Heppner	**160**	45 27N	119 34W
Herad	**71**	58 8N	6 47 E
Héraðsflói	**74**	65 42N	14 12W
Héradsvötn	**74**	65 25N	19 5W
Herald Cays	**138**	16 58 S	149 9 E
Herãt	**93**	34 20N	62 7 E
Herãt □	**93**	35 0N	62 0 E
Hérault □	**44**	43 34N	3 15 E
Hérault, R.	**44**	43 20N	3 32 E
Herbert	**153**	50 30N	107 10W
Herbert Downs	**138**	23 7 S	139 9 E
Herbert I.	**147**	52 49N	170 10W
Herbert, R.	**138**	18 31 S	146 17 E
Herberton	**138**	17 28 S	145 25 E
Herbertstown	**39**	52 32N	8 29W
Herbiers, Les	**42**	46 52N	1 0W
Herbignac	**42**	47 27N	2 18W
Herborn	**48**	50 40N	8 19 E
Herby	**54**	50 45N	18 50 E
Hercegnovi	**66**	42 30N	18 33 E
Herðubreið	**74**	65 11N	16 21W
Herdla	**71**	60 34N	4 56 E
Hereford, U.K.	**28**	52 4N	2 42W
Hereford, U.S.A.	**159**	34 50N	102 28W
Hereford and Worcester □	**28**	52 10N	2 30W
Herefordshire □	**26**	52 15N	2 50W
Herefoss	**71**	58 32N	8 32 E
Herekino	**142**	35 18 S	173 11 E
Herent	**47**	50 54N	4 40 E
Herentals	**47**	51 12N	4 51 E
Herenthout	**47**	51 8N	4 45 E
Herfølge	**73**	55 26N	12 9 E
Herford	**48**	52 7N	8 40 E
Héricourt	**43**	47 32N	6 55 E
Herington	**158**	38 43N	97 0W
Herisau	**51**	47 22N	9 17 E
Hérisson	**44**	46 32N	2 42 E
Herjehogna	**75**	61 43N	12 7 E
Herk, R.	**47**	50 56N	5 12 E
Herkenbosch	**47**	51 9N	6 4 E
Herkimer	**162**	43 0N	74 59W
Herm I.	**42**	49 30N	2 28W
Herma Ness	**36**	60 50N	0 54W
Hermagor	**52**	46 38N	13 23 E
Herman	**158**	45 51N	96 8W
Hermandez	**163**	36 24N	120 46W
Hermann	**158**	38 40N	91 25W
Hermannsburg	**48**	52 49N	10 6 E
Hermannsburg Mission	**136**	23 57 S	132 45 E
Hermanus	**128**	34 27 S	19 12 E
Herment	**44**	45 45N	2 24 E
Hermidale	**141**	31 30 S	146 42 E
Hermiston	**160**	45 50N	119 16W
Hermitage	**143**	43 44 S	170 5 E
Hermitage B.	**151**	47 33N	56 10W
Hermite, Is.	**176**	55 50 S	68 0W
Hermon, Mt. = Sheikh, J. ash	**92**	33 20N	36 0 E
Hermosillo	**164**	29 10N	111 0W
Hernad, R.	**53**	48 20N	21 15 E
Hernandarias	**173**	25 20 S	54 40W
Hernando, Argent.	**172**	32 28 S	63 40W
Hernando, U.S.A.	**159**	34 50N	89 59W
Herndon	**162**	40 43N	76 51W
Herne, Belg.	**47**	50 44N	4 2 E
Herne, Ger.	**48**	51 33N	7 12 E
Herne Bay	**29**	51 22N	1 8 E
Herne Hill	**137**	31 45 S	116 5 E
Herning	**73**	56 8N	8 58 E
Heroica Nogales	**164**	31 14N	110 56W
Heron Bay	**150**	48 40N	85 25W
Heröy	**71**	62 18N	5 45 E
Herreid	**158**	45 53N	100 5W
's Herrenbroek	**46**	52 32N	6 1 E
Herrera	**57**	39 12N	4 50W
Herrera de Alcántar	**57**	39 39N	7 25W
Herrera de Pisuerga	**56**	42 35N	4 20W
Herrera del Duque	**57**	39 10N	5 3W
Herrero, Punta	**165**	19 17N	87 27W
Herrick	**138**	41 5 S	147 55 E
Herrin	**159**	37 50N	89 0W
Herrljunga	**73**	58 5N	13 1 E
Hersbruck	**49**	49 30N	11 25 E
Herschel I.	**147**	69 35N	139 5W
Herseaux	**47**	50 43N	3 15 E
Herselt	**47**	51 3N	4 53 E
Herserange	**47**	49 30N	5 48 E
Hershey	**162**	40 17N	76 39W
Herstal	**47**	50 40N	5 38 E
Herstmonceux	**29**	50 53N	0 21 E
Hersvik	**71**	61 10N	4 53 E
Hertford	**29**	51 47N	0 4W
Hertford □	**29**	51 51N	0 5W
's Hertogenbosch	**47**	51 42N	5 18 E
Hertzogville	**128**	28 9 S	25 30 E
Hervás	**56**	40 16N	5 52W
Herve	**47**	50 38N	5 48 E
Hervey B.	**133**	25 0 S	152 52 E
*Hervey Is.	**131**	19 30 S	159 0W
Hervey Junction	**150**	46 50N	72 29W
Herwijnen	**46**	51 50N	5 7 E
Herzberg, Cottbus, Ger.	**48**	51 40N	13 13 E
Herzberg, Niedersachsen, Ger.	**48**	51 38N	10 20 E
Herzele	**47**	50 53N	3 53 E
Herzliyya	**90**	32 10N	34 50 E
Herzogenbuchsee	**50**	47 11N	7 42 E
Herzogenburg	**52**	48 17N	15 41 E
Hesdin	**43**	50 21N	2 0 E
Hesel	**48**	53 18N	7 36 E
Heskestad	**71**	58 28N	6 22 E
Hesperange	**47**	49 35N	6 10 E
Hesperia	**163**	34 25N	117 18W
Hesse = Hessen	**48**	50 57N	9 20 E
Hessen □	**48**	50 57N	9 20 E
Hessle	**33**	53 44N	0 28 E
Hetch Hetchy Aqueduct	**163**	37 36N	121 25W
Heteren	**46**	51 58N	5 46 E
Hethersett	**29**	52 35N	1 10 E
Hettinger	**158**	46 8N	102 38W
Hetton-le-Hole	**35**	54 49N	1 26W
Hettstedt	**48**	51 39N	11 30 E
Heugem	**47**	50 49N	5 42 E
Heule	**47**	50 51N	3 15 E
Heusden, Belg.	**47**	51 2N	5 17 E
Heusden, Neth.	**46**	51 44N	5 8 E
Hève, C. de la	**42**	49 30N	0 5 E
Heverlee	**47**	50 52N	4 42 E
Heves □	**53**	47 50N	20 0 E
Hevron, N.	**90**	31 28N	34 52 E
Hewett, C.	**149**	70 16N	67 45W
Hewett, gasfield	**19**	53 5N	1 50 E
Hex River	**128**	33 30 S	19 35 E
Hexham	**35**	54 58N	2 7W
Heybridge	**29**	51 44N	0 42 E
Heyfield	**141**	37 59 S	146 47 E
Heysham	**32**	54 5N	2 53W
Heytesbury	**28**	51 11N	2 7W
Heythuysen	**47**	51 15N	5 55 E
Heywood, Austral.	**140**	38 8 S	141 37 E
Heywood, U.K.	**32**	53 36N	2 13W
Hi-no-Misaki	**110**	35 26N	132 38 E
Hi Vista	**163**	34 44N	117 46W
Hiamen	**109**	31 52N	121 15 E
Hiawatha, Kans., U.S.A.	**158**	39 55N	95 33W
Hiawatha, Utah, U.S.A.	**160**	39 37N	111 1W
Hibbing	**158**	47 30N	93 0W
Hibbs B.	**138**	42 35 S	145 15 E
Hibbs, Pt.	**138**	42 38 S	145 15 E
Hibernia Reef	**136**	12 0 S	123 23 E
Hibiki-Nada	**110**	34 0N	130 0 E
Hickman	**159**	36 35N	89 8W
Hickory	**157**	35 46N	81 17W
Hicks Bay	**142**	37 34 S	178 21 E
Hicksville	**162**	40 46N	73 30W
Hida-Gawa	**70**	47 10N	23 9 E
Hida-Gawa, R.	**111**	35 26N	137 3 E
Hida-Sammyaku	**111**	36 30N	137 40 E
Hida-Sanchi	**111**	36 10N	137 0 E
Hidaka	**110**	35 30N	134 44 E
Hidalgo □	**164**	20 30N	99 10W
Hidalgo del Parral	**164**	26 58N	105 40W
Hidalgo, Presa M.	**164**	26 30N	108 35W
Hiddensee	**48**	54 30N	13 6 E
Hidrolândia	**171**	17 0 S	49 15W
Hieflau	**52**	47 36N	14 46 E
Hiendelaencina	**58**	41 5N	3 0W
Hierro I.	**116**	27 57N	17 56 E
Higashi-matsuyama	**111**	36 2N	139 25 E
Higashiōsaka	**111**	34 40N	135 37 E

**Renamed Manuae*

Higasi-Suidō Hong Kong ■

Higasi-Suidō	110	34 0N	129 30 E
Higgins	159	36 9N	100 1W
Higginsville	137	31 42 S	121 38 E
Higgs I. L.	157	36 20N	78 30W
High Atlas = Haut Atlas	118	32 30N	5 0W
High Bentham	32	54 8N	2 31W
High Borrow Bri.	32	54 26N	2 43W
High Bridge	162	40 40N	74 54W
High Ercall	28	52 46N	2 37W
High Hesket	32	54 47N	2 49W
High I.	151	56 40N	61 10W
High Island	159	29 32N	94 22W
High Level	152	58 31N	117 8W
High Pike, mt.	32	54 43N	3 4W
High Point	157	35 57N	79 58W
High Prairie	152	55 30N	116 30W
High River	152	50 30N	113 50W
High Springs	157	29 50N	82 40W
High Tatra	53	49 30N	20 00 E
High Veld = Hoëveld	129	26 30 S	30 0 E
High Willhays, hill	30	50 41N	3 59W
High Wycombe	29	51 37N	0 45W
Higham Ferrers	29	52 18N	0 36W
Highbank	138	47 34 S	171 45 E
Highbridge	28	51 13N	2 59W
Highbury	138	16 25 S	143 9 E
Highclere	28	51 20N	1 22W
Highland □	36	57 30N	5 0W
Highland Pk.	156	42 10N	87 50W
Highland Springs	162	37 33N	77 20W
Highley	28	52 25N	2 23W
Highmore	158	44 35N	99 26W
Highrock L.	153	57 5N	105 32W
Hightae	35	55 5N	3 27W
Hightstown	162	40 16N	74 31W
Highworth	28	51 38N	1 42W
Higley	161	33 27N	111 46W
Higüay	167	18 37N	68 42W
Higüero, Pta.	147	18 22N	67 16W
Hiiumaa	80	58 50N	22 45 E
Híjar	58	41 10N	0 27W
Hijāz	91	26 0N	37 30 E
Hiji	110	33 22N	131 32 E
Hijken	46	52 54N	6 30 E
Hikari	110	33 58N	131 58 E
Hiketa	110	34 13N	134 24 E
Hiko	161	37 30N	115 13W
Hikone	111	35 15N	136 10 E
Hikurangi, East Court	142	37 55 S	178 4 E
Hikurangi, Mt.	142	37 55 S	178 4 E
Hilawng	98	21 23N	93 48 E
Hildburghhausen	49	50 24N	10 43 E
Hildesheim	48	52 9N	9 55 E
Hilgay	29	52 34N	0 23 E
Hill	150	45 40N	74 45W
Hill City, Idaho, U.S.A.	160	43 20N	115 2W
Hill City, Kans., U.S.A.	158	39 25N	99 51W
Hill City, Minn., U.S.A.	158	46 57N	93 35W
Hill City, S.D., U.S.A.	158	43 58N	103 35W
Hill End	141	38 1 S	146 9 E
Hill Island L.	153	60 30N	109 50W
Hill, R.	137	30 23 S	115 3 E
Hilla, Iraq	92	32 30N	44 27 E
Hilla, Si Arab.	92	23 35N	46 50 E
Hillared	73	57 37N	13 10 E
Hillegom	46	52 18N	4 35 E
Hillerød	73	55 56N	12 19 E
Hillerstorp	73	57 20N	13 52 E
Hilli	98	25 17N	89 1 E
Hillingdon	29	51 33N	0 29W
Hillman	156	45 5N	83 52W
Hillmond	153	53 26N	109 41W
Hillsboro, Kans., U.S.A.	158	38 28N	97 10W
Hillsboro, N. Mex., U.S.A.	161	33 0N	107 35W
Hillsboro, N. Mex., U.S.A.	161	33 0N	107 35W
Hillsboro, N.D., U.S.A.	158	47 23N	97 9W
Hillsboro, N.H., U.S.A.	156	43 8N	71 56W
Hillsboro, Oreg., U.S.A.	160	45 31N	123 0W
Hillsboro, Tex., U.S.A.	159	32 0N	97 10W
Hillsborough, U.K.	38	54 28N	6 6W
Hillsborough, W. Indies	167	12 28N	61 28W
Hillsdale, Mich., U.S.A.	156	41 55N	84 40W
Hillsdale, N.Y., U.S.A.	162	42 11N	73 30W
Hillside	136	21 45 S	119 23 E
Hillsport	150	49 27N	85 34W
Hillston	141	33 30 S	145 31 E
Hillswick	36	60 29N	1 28W
Hilltown	38	54 12N	6 8W
Hilo	147	19 44N	155 5W
Hilonghilong, mt.	103	9 10N	125 45 E
Hilpsford Pt.	32	54 4N	3 12W
Hilvarenbeek	47	51 29N	5 8 E
Hilversum	46	52 14N	5 10 E
Himachal Pradesh □	94	31 30N	77 0 E
Himalaya	99	29 0N	84 0 E
Himara	68	40 8N	19 43 E
Himatnagar	93	23 37N	72 57 E
Hime-Jima	110	33 43N	131 40 E
Himeji	110	34 50N	134 40 E
Himi	111	36 50N	137 0 E
Himmerland	73	56 45N	9 30 E
Hims = Homs	92	34 40N	36 45 E
Hinako, Kepulauan	102	0 50N	97 20 E
Hinche	167	19 9N	72 1W
Hinchinbrook I.	138	18 20 S	146 15 E
Hinckley, U.K.	28	52 33N	1 21W
Hinckley, U.S.A.	160	39 18N	112 41W
Hindås	73	57 42N	12 27 E
Hindaun	94	26 44N	77 5 E
Hinde Rapids (Hells Gate)	126	5 25 S	27 3 E
Hinderwell	33	54 32N	0 45W
Hindhead	29	51 6N	0 42W
Hindley	32	53 32N	2 35W
Hindmarsh L.	140	36 5 S	141 55 E
Hindol	95	20 40N	85 10 E
Hinds	143	43 59 S	171 36 E
Hindsholm	73	55 30N	10 40 E
Hindu Bagh	94	30 56N	67 57 E
Hindu Kush	93	36 0N	71 0 E
Hindubagh	93	30 56N	67 57 E
Hindupur	97	13 49N	77 32 E
Hines Creek	152	56 20N	118 40W
Hinganghat	96	20 30N	78 59 E
Hingeon	47	50 32N	4 59 E
Hingham, U.K.	29	52 35N	0 59 E
Hingham, U.S.A.	160	48 40N	110 29W
Hingol, R.	93	25 30N	65 30 E
Hingoli	96	19 41N	77 15 E
Hinkley Pt.	28	50 59N	3 32W
Hinlopenstretet	12	79 35N	18 40 E
Hinna	121	10 25N	11 28 E
Hinnøy	74	68 40N	16 28 E
Hino	111	35 0N	136 15 E
Hinojosa	55	38 30N	5 17W
Hinojosa del Duque	57	38 30N	5 17W
Hinokage	110	32 39N	131 24 E
Hinsdale	160	48 26N	107 2W
Hinstock	28	52 50N	2 28W
Hinterrhein, R.	51	46 40N	9 25 E
Hinton, Can.	152	53 26N	117 34W
Hinton, U.S.A.	156	37 40N	80 51W
Hinwil	51	47 18N	8 51 E
Hippolytushoef	46	52 54N	4 58 E
Hirado	110	33 22N	129 33 E
Hirado-Shima	110	33 20N	129 30 E
Hirakarta	111	34 48N	135 40 E
Hirakud	96	21 32N	83 51 E
Hirakud Dam	96	21 32N	83 45 E
Hirara	112	24 48N	125 17 E
Hirata	110	35 24N	132 49 E
Hiratsuka	111	35 19N	139 21 E
Hirhafok	119	23 49N	5 45 E
Hirlŭu	70	47 23N	27 0 E
Hiromi	110	33 13N	132 36 E
Hirosaki	112	40 34N	140 28 E
Hiroshima	110	34 30N	132 30 E
Hiroshima-ken □	112	34 50N	133 0 E
Hiroshima-Wan	110	34 5N	132 20 E
Hirsoholmene	73	57 30N	10 36 E
Hirson	43	49 55N	4 4 E
Hîrşova	70	44 40N	27 59 E
Hirtshals	73	57 36N	9 57 E
Hirwaun	31	51 43N	3 30W
Hisoy	71	58 26N	8 44 E
Hispaniola, I.	165	19 0N	71 0W
Hissar	94	29 12N	75 45 E
Histon	29	52 15N	0 6 E
Hita	110	33 20N	130 58 E
Hitachi	111	36 36N	140 39 E
Hitachiota	111	36 30N	140 30 E
Hitchin	29	51 57N	0 16W
Hitoyoshi	110	32 13N	130 45 E
Hitra	71	63 30N	8 45 E
Hitzacker	48	53 9N	11 1 E
Hiuchi-Nada	110	34 5N	133 20 E
Hjalmar L.	153	61 33N	109 25W
Hjälmare Kanal	72	59 20N	15 59 E
Hjälmaren	72	59 18N	15 40 E
Hjartdal	71	59 37N	8 41 E
Hjärtsäter	73	58 35N	12 3 E
Hjerkinn	71	62 13N	9 33 E
Hjerpsted	73	55 2N	8 39 E
Hjo	73	58 22N	4 17 E
Hjørring	73	57 29N	9 59 E
Hjorted	73	57 37N	16 19 E
Hjortkvarn	73	58 54N	15 26 E
Hko-ut	98	21 40N	97 46 E
Hkyenhpa	98	27 43N	97 25 E
Hlaingbwe	98	17 8N	97 50 E
Hlinsko	52	49 45N	15 54 E
Hlohovec	53	48 26N	17 49 E
Hlwaze	98	18 54N	96 37 E
Ho	121	6 37N	0 27 E
Ho Chi Minh, Phanh Bho	101	10 58N	106 40 E
Ho Thuong	100	19 32N	105 48 E
Hoa Binh	100	20 50N	105 20 E
Hoa Da (Phan Ri)	100	11 16N	108 40 E
Hoa Hiep	101	11 34N	105 51 E
Hoadley	152	52 45N	114 30W
Hoai Nhon (Bon Son)	100	14 28N	109 1 E
Hoare B.	149	65 17N	62 55W
Hobart, Austral.	138	42 50 S	147 21 E
Hobart, U.S.A.	159	35 0N	99 5W
Hobbs	159	32 40N	103 3W
Hobjærg	73	56 19N	9 32 E
Hobo	174	2 35N	75 30W
Hoboken, Belg.	47	51 11N	4 21 E
Hoboken, U.S.A.	162	40 45N	74 4W
Hobro	73	56 39N	9 46 E
Hobscheid	47	49 42N	5 57 E
Hoburg C.	73	56 54N	18 8 E
Hoburgen	73	56 55N	18 7 E
Hochang	108	27 8N	104 45 E
Hochatown	159	34 11N	94 39W
Hochdorf	51	47 10N	8 17 E
Hochiang	108	28 48N	105 48 E
Hochien	106	38 26N	116 5 E
Hoch'ih	108	24 43N	108 2 E
Hoching	106	35 37N	110 43 E
Hoch'iu	109	32 21N	116 13 E
Höchst	49	50 6N	8 33 E
Hoch'ü	106	39 26N	111 8 E
Hoch'uan	108	30 2N	106 18 E
Hockenheim	49	49 18N	8 33 E
Hod, oilfield	19	56 10N	3 25 E
Hodaka-Dake	111	36 17N	137 39 E
Hodde	73	55 42N	8 39 E
Hodder R.	32	53 57N	2 27W
Hoddesdon	29	51 45N	0 1W
Hodeïda	91	14 50N	43 0 E
Hodge, R.	33	54 14N	0 55W
Hodgson	153	51 13N	97 36W
Hódmezóvásárhely	53	46 28N	20 22 E
Hodna, Chott el	119	35 30N	5 0 E
Hodonín	53	48 50N	17 0 E
Hodsager	73	56 19N	8 51 E
Hoeamdong	107	42 30N	130 16 E
Hoëdic, I.	42	47 21N	2 52W
Hoegaarden	47	50 47N	4 53 E
Hoek van Holland	46	52 0N	4 7 E
Hoeksche Waard	46	51 46N	4 25 E
Hoenderloo	46	52 7N	5 52 E
Hoengsŏng	107	37 29N	127 59 E
Hoensbroek	47	50 55N	5 55 E
Hoeryong	107	42 30N	129 58 E
Hoeselt	47	50 51N	5 29 E
Hoëveld	129	26 30 S	30 0 E
Hoeven	47	51 35N	4 35 E
Hoeyang	107	38 43N	127 36 E
Hof, Ger.	49	50 18N	11 55 E
Hof, Iceland	74	64 33N	14 40W
Höfðakaupstaður	74	65 50N	20 19W
Hofei	109	31 52N	117 15 E
Hoff	32	54 34N	2 31W
Hofgeismar	48	51 29N	9 23 E
Hofors	72	60 35N	16 15 E
Hofsjökull	74	64 49N	18 48W
Hofsós	74	65 53N	19 26W
Hōfu	110	34 3N	131 34 E
Hofuf	92	25 20N	49 40 E
Hög-Gia, Mt.	71	62 23N	10 7 E
Hog I.	162	37 26N	75 42W
Hogan Group	139	39 13 S	147 1 E
Höganäs	73	56 13N	12 34 E
Hogansville	157	33 14N	84 50W
Hogarth, Mt.	138	21 50 S	137 0 E
Hogeland	160	48 51N	108 40W
Högen	72	61 47N	14 11 E
Hogenaki Falls	97	12 6N	77 50 E
Högfors, Örebro, Sweden	72	59 58N	15 3 E
Högfors, Västmanlands, Sweden	72	60 2N	16 3 E
Hoggar = Ahaggar	119	23 0N	6 30 E
Hōgo-Kaikyo	110	33 20N	131 58 E
Hog's Back, hill	29	51 13N	0 40W
Hogs Hd.	39	51 46N	10 13W
Högsäter	73	58 38N	12 5 E
Högsby	73	57 10N	16 1 E
Högsjo	72	59 4N	15 44 E
Hogsthorpe	33	53 13N	0 19 E
Hogsty Reef	167	21 41N	73 48W
Hohe Rhön	49	50 24N	9 58 E
Hohe Tauern	52	47 11N	12 40 E
Hohenau	53	48 36N	16 55 E
Hohenems	52	47 22N	9 42 E
Hohenstein Ernstthal	52	50 48N	12 43 E
Hohenwald	157	35 35N	87 30W
Hohenwestedt	48	54 6N	9 40 E
Hohoe	121	7 8N	0 32 E
Hohsi	108	24 9N	102 38 E
Hohsien, Anhwei, China	109	31 43N	118 22 E
Hohsien, Kwangsi-Chuang, China	109	24 25N	111 31 E
Hohsüeh	109	30 2N	112 25 E
Hôi An	100	15 30N	108 19 E
Hoi Xuan	100	20 25N	105 9 E
Hoisington	158	38 33N	98 50W
Højer	73	54 58N	8 42 E
Hōjō	110	33 58N	132 46 E
Hok	73	57 31N	14 16 E
Hokensås	73	58 0N	14 5 E
Hökensås	73	58 0N	14 5 E
Hökerum	73	57 51N	13 16 E
Hokianga Harbour	142	35 31 S	173 22 E
Hokitika	143	42 42 S	171 0 E
Hokkaidō	112	43 30N	143 0 E
Hokkaidō □	112	43 30N	143 0 E
Hokksund	71	59 44N	9 59 E
Hok'ou, Kansu, China	106	36 9N	103 29 E
Hok'ou, Kwantang, China	109	23 13N	112 45 E
Hok'ou, Yunnan, China	108	22 39N	103 57 E
Hokow	101	22 39N	103 57 E
Hol-Hol.	123	11 20N	42 50 E
Holan Shan	106	38 50N	105 50 E
Holbæk	73	55 43N	11 43 E
Holbeach	29	52 48N	0 1 E
Holbeach Marsh	29	52 52N	0 5 E
Holborn Hd.	37	58 37N	3 30W
Holbrook, Austral.	141	35 42 S	147 18 E
Holbrook, U.S.A.	161	35 0N	110 0W
Holden	152	53 13N	112 11W
Holden Fillmore	160	39 0N	112 26W
Holdenville	159	35 5N	96 25W
Holder	140	34 21 S	140 0 E
Holderness	33	53 45N	0 5W
Holdfast	153	50 58N	105 25W
Holdrege	153	40 25N	99 30W
Hole	71	60 6N	10 12 E
Hole-Narsipur	97	12 48N	76 16 E
Holešov	53	49 20N	17 35 E
Holguín	166	20 50N	76 20W
Holinkoerh	106	40 23N	111 53 E
Holíč	53	48 49N	17 10 E
Holkham	29	52 57N	0 48 E
Holla, Mt.	123	7 5N	36 35 E
Hollabrunn	52	48 34N	16 5 E
Hollams Bird I.	128	24 40 S	14 30 E
Holland	156	42 47N	86 7W
Holland Fen	33	53 0N	0 8W
Holland-on-Sea	29	51 48N	1 12 E
Hollandia = Jajapura	103	2 28 S	140 38 E
Hollands Bird I.	128	24 40 S	14 30 E
Hollandsch Diep	47	51 41N	4 30 E
Hollandsch IJssel, R.	46	51 55N	4 34 E
Hollandstoun	37	59 22N	2 25W
Höllen	71	58 6N	7 49 E
Holleton	137	31 55 S	119 0 E
Hollidaysburg	156	40 26N	78 25W
Hollis	159	34 45N	99 55W
Hollister	161	36 51N	121 24W
Hollum	46	53 26N	5 38 E
Holly	158	38 7N	102 7W
Holly Hill	157	29 15N	81 3W
Holly Springs	159	34 45N	89 25W
Hollymount	38	53 40N	9 7W
Hollywood, Ireland	39	53 6N	6 35W
Hollywood, Calif., U.S.A.	154	34 7N	118 25W
Hollywood, Fla., U.S.A.	157	26 0N	80 9W
Holm	72	62 40N	16 40 E
Holman Island	148	71 0N	118 0W
Hólmavík	74	65 42N	21 40W
Holme, Humberside,, U.K.	33	53 50N	0 48W
Holme, N. Yorks., U.K.	32	53 34N	1 50W
Holmedal	71	59 46N	5 50 E
Holmedal, Fjordane	71	61 22N	5 11 E
Holmegil	72	59 10N	11 44 E
Holmes Chapel	32	53 13N	2 21W
Holmes Reefs	138	16 27 S	148 0 E
Holmestrand	71	59 31N	10 14 E
Holmfirth	33	53 34N	1 48W
Holmsbu	71	59 32N	10 27 E
Holmsjön	72	62 26N	15 20 E
Holmsland Klit	73	56 0N	8 5 E
Holmsund	74	63 41N	20 20 E
Holmwood	29	51 12N	0 19W
Hölö	72	59 3N	17 36 E
Holo Ho, R.	107	44 54N	122 22 E
Holod	70	46 49N	22 8 E
Holon	90	32 2N	34 47 E
Holroyd, R.	138	14 10 S	141 36 E
Holsen	71	61 25N	6 8 E
Holstebro	73	56 22N	8 37 E
Holsworthy	30	50 48N	4 21W
Holt, Iceland	74	63 33N	19 48W
Holt, Clwyd, U.K.	31	53 4N	2 52W
Holt, Norfolk, U.K.	29	52 55N	1 4 E
Holte	73	55 50N	12 29 E
Holten	46	52 17N	6 26 E
Holton Harbour	151	54 31N	57 12W
Holton le Clay	33	53 29N	0 3W
Holtville	161	32 50N	115 27W
Holum	71	58 6N	7 32 E
Holwerd	46	53 22N	5 54 E
Holy Cross	147	62 10N	159 52W
Holy I., England, U.K.	35	55 42N	1 48W
Holy I., Scotland, U.K.	34	55 31N	5 4W
Holy I., Wales, U.K.	31	53 17N	4 37W
Holyhead	31	53 18N	4 38W
Holyhead B.	31	53 20N	4 35W
Holyoke, Mass., U.S.A.	162	42 14N	72 37W
Holyoke, Nebr., U.S.A.	158	40 39N	102 18W
Holyrood	151	47 27N	53 8W
Holywell	31	53 16N	3 14W
Holywood	38	54 38N	5 50W
Holzminden	48	51 49N	9 31 E
Homa Bay	126	0 36 S	34 22 E
Homa Bay □	126	0 50 S	34 30 E
Homalin	98	24 55N	95 0 E
Homberg	48	51 2N	9 20 E
Hombori	121	15 20N	1 38W
Homburg	49	49 19N	7 21 E
Home B.	149	68 40N	67 10W
Home Hill	138	19 43 S	147 25 E
Homedale	160	43 42N	116 59W
Homer, Alaska, U.S.A.	147	59 40N	151 35W
Homer, La., U.S.A.	159	32 50N	93 4W
Homestead, Austral.	138	20 20 S	145 40 E
Homestead, U.S.A.	157	25 29N	80 27W
Hominy	159	36 26N	96 24W
Homnabad	96	17 45N	77 5 E
Homoine	129	23 55 S	35 8 E
Homorod	70	46 5N	25 15 E
Homs = Al Khums	119	32 40N	14 17 E
Homs (Hims)	92	34 40N	36 45 E
Hon Chong	101	10 16N	104 38 E
Hon Me	100	19 23N	105 56 E
Honan □	106	34 10N	113 10 E
Honbetsu	112	43 7N	143 37 E
Honda	174	5 12N	74 45W
Hondeklipbaai	125	30 19 S	17 17 E
Hondo, Japan	110	32 27N	130 12 E
Hondo, U.S.A.	159	29 22N	99 6W
Hondo, R.	165	18 25N	88 21W
Honduras ■	166	14 40N	86 30W
Honduras, Golfo de	166	16 50N	87 0W
Hönefoss	71	60 10N	10 12 E
Honey L.	160	40 13N	120 14W
Honfleur	42	49 25N	0 13 E
Höng	73	55 30N	11 14 E
Hong Gai	100	20 57N	107 5 E
Hong Kong ■	109	22 11N	114 14 E

Hong, R Hsiushui

Hong, R. 100 20 17N 106 34 E
Hongchŏn 107 37 44N 127 53 E
Hongha, R. 101 22 0N 104 0 E
Hongor 106 45 56N 112 50 E
Hongsa 100 19 43N 101 20 E
Hongsŏng 107 36 37N 126 38 E
Honguedo, Détroit d' 151 49 15N 64 0W
Hongwon 107 40 0N 127 56 E
Honiara 142 9 30 S 160 0 E
Honington 33 52 58N 0 35W
Honiton 30 50 48N 3 11W
Honjo, Akita, Japan 112 39 23N 140 3 E
Honjo, Gumma, Japan 111 36 14N 139 11 E
Honkawane 111 35 5N 138 5 E
Honkorâb, Ras 122 24 35N 35 10 E
Honolulu 147 21 19N 157 52W
Honshū 112 36 0N 138 0 E
Hontoria del Pinar 58 41 50N 3 10W
Hoo 29 51 25N 0 33 E
Hood Mt. 160 45 15N 122 0W
Hood, Pt. 137 34 23 S 119 34 E
Hood Pt. 135 10 4 S 147 45 E
Hood River 160 45 45N 121 37W
Hoodsport 160 47 24N 123 7W
Hooge 48 54 31N 8 36 E
Hoogerheide 47 51 26N 4 20 E
Hoogeveen 46 52 44N 6 30 E
Hoogeveensche Vaart 46 52 42N 6 12 E
Hoogezand 46 53 11N 6 45 E
Hooghly-Chinsura 95 22 53N 88 27 E
Hooghly, R. 95 21 59N 88 10 E
Hoogkerk 46 53 13N 6 30 E
Hooglede 47 50 59N 3 5 E
Hoogstraten 47 51 24N 4 46 E
Hoogvliet 46 51 52N 4 21 E
Hook 29 51 17N 0 55W
Hook Hd. 39 52 8N 6 57W
Hook I. 138 20 4 S 149 0 E
Hook of Holland = Hoek v. Holland 47 52 0N 4 7 E
Hooker 159 36 55N 101 10W
Hooker Cr. 136 18 23 S 130 50 E
Hoonah 147 58 15N 135 30W
Hooper Bay 147 61 30N 166 10W
Hoopersville 162 38 16N 76 11W
Hoopeston 156 40 30N 87 40W
Hoopstad 128 27 50 S 25 55 E
Höör 73 55 55N 13 33 E
Hoorn 46 52 38N 5 4 E
Hoover Dam 161 36 0N 114 45W
Hop Bottom 162 41 41N 75 47W
Hopà 83 41 28N 41 30 E
Hope, Can. 152 49 25N 121 25 E
Hope, U.K. 31 53 7N 3 2W
Hope, Ark., U.S.A. 159 33 40N 93 30W
Hope, N.D., U.S.A. 158 47 21N 97 42W
Hope Bay 13 65 0 S 55 0W
Hope, L. 139 28 24 S 139 18 E
Hope L. 37 58 24N 4 38W
Hope Pt. 147 68 20N 166 50W
Hope Town 157 26 30N 76 30W
Hopedale, Can. 151 55 28N 60 13W
Hopedale, U.S.A. 162 42 8N 71 33W
Hopefield 128 33 3 S 18 22 E
Hopei □ 107 39 25N 116 45 E
Hopelchén 165 19 46N 89 50W
Hopeman 37 57 42N 3 26W
Hopen 71 63 27N 8 2 E
Hopetoun 137 33 57 S 120 7 E
Hopetown, Austral. 140 35 42 S 142 22 E
Hopetown, S. Afr. 128 29 34 S 24 3 E
Hopewell 162 37 18N 77 17W
Hopien-Ts'un 108 27 40N 101 55 E
Hopin 98 21 14N 96 53 E
Hop'ing 109 24 26N 114 56 E
Hopkins 158 40 31N 94 45W
Hopkins, L. 136 24 15 S 128 35 E
Hopkinsville 157 36 52N 87 26W
Hopland 160 39 0N 123 7W
Hopo 108 31 24N 99 0 E
Hoptrup 73 55 11N 9 28 E
Hop'u 108 21 41N 109 10 E
Hoquiam 160 46 50N 123 55W
Hōrai 111 34 58N 137 32 E
Horazdovice 52 49 19N 13 42 E
Hörby 73 55 50N 13 44 E
Horcajo de Santiago 58 39 50N 3 1W
Hordaland fylke □ 71 60 25N 6 15 E
Horden 33 54 45N 1 17W
Hordern Hills 136 20 40 S 130 20 E
Hordio 91 10 36N 51 8 E
Horezu 70 45 6N 24 0 E
Horgen 51 47 15N 8 35 E
Horgoš 66 46 10N 20 0 E
Horice 52 50 21N 15 39 E
Horley 29 51 10N 0 10W
Horlick Mts. 13 84 0 S 102 0W
Hormoz 93 27 35N 55 0 E
Hormuz, I. 93 27 8N 56 28 E
Hormuz Str. 93 26 30N 56 30 E
Horn, Austria 52 48 39N 15 40 E
Horn, Isafjarðarsýsla, Iceland 74 66 28N 22 28W
Horn, Suður-Múlasýsla, Iceland 74 65 10N 13 31W
Horn, Neth. 47 51 12N 5 57 E
Horn, Cape = Hornos, C. de 176 55 50 S 67 30W
Horn Head 38 55 13N 8 0W
Horn I., Austral. 138 10 37 S 142 17 E
Horn I., P.N.G. 135 10 35 S 142 20 E
Horn, I. 157 30 17N 88 40W
Horn Mts. 152 62 15N 119 15W
Horn, R. 152 61 30N 118 1W
Hornachuelos 57 37 50N 5 14W
Hornavan 74 66 15N 17 30 E
Hornbæk, Frederiksborg, Denmark 73 56 5N 12 26 E
Hornbæk, Viborg, Denmark 73 56 28N 9 58 E
Hornbeck 159 31 22N 93 20W
Hornbrook 160 41 58N 122 37W
Hornburg 48 52 2N 10 36 E
Hornby 143 43 33 S 172 33 E
Horncastle 33 53 13N 0 8W
Horndal 72 60 18N 16 23 E
Horndean 29 50 56N 1 5W
Hornell 156 42 23N 77 41W
Hornell L. 152 62 20N 119 25W
Hornepayne 150 49 14N 84 48W
Hornindal 71 61 58N 6 30 E
Horningsham 28 51 11N 2 16W
Hornitos 163 37 30N 120 14W
Hornnes 71 58 34N 7 45 E
Hornos, Cabo de 176 55 50 S 67 30 E
Hornoy 43 49 50N 1 54 E
Hornsberg, Jamtland, Sweden 72 63 14N 14 40 E
Hornsberg, Kronobergs, Sweden 72 56 37N 13 47 E
Hornsby 141 33 42 S 151 2 E
Hornsea 33 53 55N 0 10W
Hornslandet Pen. 72 61 35N 17 37 E
Hornslet 73 56 18N 10 19 E
Hornu 47 50 26N 3 50 E
Hörnum 73 54 44N 8 18 E
Horovice 52 49 48N 13 53 E
Horqueta 172 23 15 S 56 55W
Horra, La 56 41 44N 3 53W
Horred 73 57 22N 12 28 E
Horse Cr. 158 41 33N 104 45W
Horse Is. 151 50 15N 55 50W
Horsefly L. 152 52 25N 121 0W
Horseheads 162 42 10N 76 49W
Horseleap 38 53 25N 7 34W
Horsens 73 55 52N 9 51 E
Horsens Fjord 73 55 50N 10 0 E
Horseshoe 137 25 27 S 118 31 E
Horseshoe Dam 161 33 45N 111 35W
Horsforth 33 53 50N 1 39W
Horsham, Austral. 140 36 44 S 142 13 E
Horsham, U.K. 29 51 4N 0 20W
Horsham St. Faith 29 52 41N 1 15 E
Horsovsky Tyn 52 49 31N 12 58 E
Horst 47 51 27N 6 3 E
Horsted Keynes 29 51 2N 0 1W
Horten 71 59 25N 10 32 E
Hortobágy, R. 53 47 30N 21 6 E
Horton 158 39 42N 95 30W
Horton-in-Ribblesdale 32 54 9N 2 19W
Horton, R. 147 69 56N 126 52W
Hörvik 73 56 2N 14 45 E
Horw 51 47 1N 8 19 E
Horwich 32 53 37N 2 33W
Horwood, L. 150 48 10N 82 20W
Hosaina 123 7 30N 37 47 E
Hosdurga 97 13 40N 76 17 E
Hose, Pegunungan 102 2 5N 114 6 E
Hoshan 109 31 24N 116 20 E
Hoshangabad 94 22 45N 77 45 E
Hoshiarpur 94 31 30N 75 58 E
Hoshui 106 36 0N 107 59 E
Hoshun 106 37 19N 113 34 E
Hosingen 47 50 1N 6 6 E
Hoskins 135 5 29 S 150 27 E
Hosmer 158 45 36N 99 29W
Hososhima 110 32 26N 131 40 E
Hospental 51 46 37N 8 34 E
Hospet 97 15 15N 76 20 E
Hospital 39 52 30N 8 28W
Hospitalet de Llobregat 58 41 21N 2 6 E
Hospitalet, L' 44 42 36N 1 47 E
Hoste, I. 176 55 0 S 69 0W
Hostens 44 44 30N 0 40W
Hoswick 36 60 0N 1 15W
Hot 100 18 8N 98 29 E
Hot Creek Ra. 160 39 0N 116 0W
Hot Springs, Ark, U.S.A. 159 34 30N 93 0W
Hot Springs, S.D., U.S.A. 158 43 25N 103 30W
Hotagen, L. 74 63 50N 14 30 E
Hotazel 128 27 17 S 23 00 E
Hotchkiss 161 38 55N 107 47W
Hotham, C. 136 12 2 S 131 18 E
Hot'ien 105 37 7N 79 55 E
Hoting 74 64 8N 16 15 E
Hotolishti 68 41 10N 20 25 E
Hotse 106 35 14N 115 27 E
Hotte, Massif de la 167 18 30N 73 45W
Hottentotsbaai 128 26 8 S 14 59 E
Hotton 47 50 16N 5 26 E
Houat, I. 42 47 24N 2 58W
Houck 161 35 15N 109 15W
Houdan 43 48 48N 1 35 E
Houdeng-Goegnies 47 50 29N 4 10 E
Houei Sai 100 20 18N 100 26 E
Houffalize 47 50 8N 5 48 E
Houghton 158 47 9N 88 39W
Houghton L. 156 44 20N 84 40W
Houghton-le-Spring 35 54 51N 1 28W
Houghton Regis 29 51 54N 0 32W
Houhora 142 34 49 S 173 9 E
Houille, R. 47 50 8N 4 50 E
Houlton 151 46 5N 68 0W
Houma 159 29 35N 90 50W
Houmt Souk = Djerba 119 33 53N 10 37 E
Houndé 120 11 34N 3 31W
Hounslow 29 51 29N 0 20W
Hourn L. 36 57 7N 5 35W
Hourtin 44 45 11N 1 4W
Housatonic, R. 162 41 10N 73 7W
Houston, Can. 152 54 25N 126 30W
Houston, Mo., U.S.A. 159 37 20N 92 0W
Houston, Tex., U.S.A. 159 29 50N 95 20W
Houten 46 52 2N 5 10 E
Houthalen 47 51 2N 5 23 E
Houthem 47 50 48N 2 57 E
Houthulst 47 50 59N 2 57 E
Houtman Abrolhos 137 28 43 S 113 48 E
Houyet 47 50 11N 5 1 E
Hova 73 58 53N 14 14 E
Høvag 71 58 10N 8 15 E
Hövåg 71 58 10N 8 16 E
Hovd 105 48 1N 91 39 E
Hovden 71 59 33N 7 22 E
Hove 29 50 50N 0 10W
Hoveton 29 52 45N 1 23 E
Hovingham 33 54 10N 0 59W
Hovmantorp 73 56 47N 15 7 E
Hövsgöl 106 43 37N 109 39 E
Hovsta 72 59 22N 15 15 E
Howakil 123 15 10N 40 16 E
Howar, W., (Shau) 123 17 0N 25 30 E
Howard, Austral. 139 25 16 S 152 32 E
Howard, Kans., U.S.A. 159 37 30N 96 16W
Howard, S.D., U.S.A. 158 44 2N 97 30W
Howard I. 138 12 10 S 135 24 E
Howard L. 153 62 15N 105 57W
Howatharra 137 28 29 S 114 33 E
Howden 33 53 45N 0 52W
Howe 160 43 48N 113 0W
Howe, C. 141 37 30 S 150 0 E
Howell 156 42 38N 84 0W
Howick, N.Z. 142 36 54 S 174 48 E
Howick, S. Afr. 129 29 28 S 30 14 E
Howick Group 138 14 20 S 145 30 E
Howitt, L. 139 27 40 S 138 40 E
Howley 151 49 12N 57 2W
Howmore 36 57 18N 7 23W
Howrah 95 22 37N 88 27 E
Howth 38 53 23N 6 3W
Howth Hd. 38 53 21N 6 0W
Hoxne 29 52 22N 1 11 E
Höxter 48 51 45N 9 26 E
Hoy I. 37 58 50N 3 15W
Hoy Sd. 37 58 57N 3 20W
Hoya 48 52 47N 9 10 E
Høyanger 71 61 25N 6 50 E
Höydalsmo 71 59 30N 8 15 E
Hoyerswerda 48 51 26N 14 14 E
Hoylake 32 53 24N 3 11W
Höyland 71 58 50N 5 43 E
Hoyleton 140 34 2 S 138 34 E
Hoyos 56 40 9N 6 45W
Hoyüan 109 23 50N 114 40 E
Hpawlum 98 27 12N 98 12 E
Hpettintha 98 24 14N 95 23 E
Hpizow 98 26 57N 98 24 E
Hpungan Pass 99 27 30N 96 55 E
Hrádec Králové 52 50 15N 15 50 E
Hrádek 53 48 46N 16 16 E
Hranice 53 49 34N 17 45 E
Hron, R. 53 48 0N 18 4 E
Hrubieszów 54 50 49N 23 51 E
Hrubý Nizký Jeseník 53 50 7N 17 10 E
Hrvatska 63 45 20N 16 0 E
Hsenwi 98 23 22N 97 55 E
Hsi Chiang, R. 109 22 20N 113 20 E
Hsiach'engtzu, Heilungkiang, China 107 44 41N 130 27 E
Hsiach'engtzu, Schechwan, China 108 29 24N 101 46 E
Hsiachiang 109 27 33N 115 10 E
Hsiaching 106 36 57N 115 59 E
Hsiach'uan Shan 109 21 40N 112 37 E
Hsiahsien 106 35 12N 111 11 E
Hsiai 106 34 17N 116 11 E
Hsiakuan 108 25 39N 100 9 E
Hsiamen 109 24 30N 118 7 E
Hsian 106 34 17N 109 0 E
Hsiang Chiang, R. 109 29 30N 113 10 E
Hsiangch'eng, Honan, China 106 33 50N 113 29 E
Hsiangch'eng, Honan, China 106 33 13N 114 50 E
Hsiangch'eng, Szechwan, China 108 29 0N 99 46 E
Hsiangchou 108 23 58N 109 41 E
Hsiangfan 109 32 7N 112 9 E
Hsianghsiang 109 27 46N 112 30 E
Hsiangning 106 36 1N 110 47 E
Hsiangshan 109 29 18N 121 37 E
Hsiangshuik'ou 107 34 12N 119 34 E
Hsiangt'an 109 27 55N 112 52 E
Hsiangtu 108 23 14N 106 57 E
Hsiangyang 109 32 2N 112 6 E
Hsiangyin 109 28 40N 112 53 E
Hsiangyüan 106 36 32N 113 2 E
Hsiangyün 108 25 29N 100 35 E
Hsiaochin 108 31 1N 102 23 E
Hsiaofeng 109 30 36N 119 33 E
Hsiaohsien 106 34 2N 116 56 E
Hsiaohsinganling Shan 105 48 45N 127 0 E
Hsiaoi 106 37 7N 111 46 E
Hsiaokan 109 30 57N 113 53 E
Hsiaoshan 109 30 10N 120 15 E
Hsiaot'ai Shan 107 36 18N 116 38 E
Hsiap'u 109 26 58N 119 57 E
Hsiawa 107 42 38N 120 31 E
Hsich'ang 108 27 50N 102 18 E
Hsichieht'o 108 30 24N 108 13 E
Hsich'uan 109 33 0N 111 24 E
Hsich'ung 108 31 0N 105 48 E
Hsiehch'eng 107 34 48N 117 15 E
Hsiehmaho 109 31 38N 111 12 E
Hsienchü 109 28 51N 120 44 E
Hsienfeng 108 29 40N 109 7 E
Hsienhsien 106 38 2N 116 12 E
Hsienning 109 29 51N 114 15 E
Hsienshui Ho, R. 108 30 5N 101 5 E
Hsienyang 106 34 22N 108 48 E
Hsienyu 109 25 24N 118 40 E
Hsifei Ho, R. 109 32 38N 116 39 E
Hsifeng, Kweichow, China 108 27 5N 106 42 E
Hsifeng, Liaoning, China 107 42 44N 124 42 E
Hsifengchen 106 35 40N 107 42 E
Hsifengk'ou 107 40 24N 118 19 E
Hsiho 106 34 2N 105 12 E
Hsihsia, Honan, China 106 33 30N 111 30 E
Hsihsia, Shantung, China 107 37 25N 120 48 E
Hsihsiang 108 33 1N 107 40 E
Hsihsien, Honan, China 109 32 24N 114 52 E
Hsihsien, Shensi, China 106 36 41N 110 56 E
Hsihua 106 33 47N 114 31 E
Hsilamunlun Ho, R. 107 43 24N 123 42 E
Hsiliao Ho, R. 107 43 24N 123 42 E
Hsilin 108 24 30N 105 3 E
Hsin Chiang, R. 109 28 50N 116 40 E
Hsin Ho, R. 107 43 33N 123 31 E
Hsinchan 107 43 52N 127 20 E
Hsinch'ang 109 29 30N 120 54 E
Hsincheng 106 34 25N 113 46 E
Hsinch'eng, Hopei, China 106 39 15N 115 59 E
Hsinch'eng, Kwangsi-Chuang, China 108 24 4N 108 40 E
Hsinchiang 106 35 40N 111 15 E
Hsinchien 108 23 58N 102 47 E
Hsinchin 107 39 25N 121 59 E
Hsinching 108 30 25N 103 49 E
Hsinchi'u 107 41 53N 119 40 E
Hsinchou 109 30 52N 114 48 E
Hsinchu 109 24 48N 120 58 E
Hsinfeng, Kiangsi, China 109 25 27N 114 58 E
Hsinfeng, Kiangsi, China 109 26 7N 116 11 E
Hsinfeng, Kwangtung, China 109 24 4N 114 12 E
Hsingan 109 25 39N 110 39 E
Hsingch'eng 107 40 40N 120 48 E
Hsingho 106 40 52N 113 58 E
Hsinghsien 106 38 31N 111 4 E
Hsinghua 107 32 55N 119 52 E
Hsinghua Wan 109 25 20N 119 20 E
Hsingi 108 25 5N 104 55 E
Hsinging 109 26 25N 110 44 E
Hsingjen 108 25 25N 105 13 E
Hsingjenp'ao 106 37 0N 105 0 E
Hsingkuo 109 26 26N 115 16 E
Hsinglung 107 40 29N 117 32 E
Hsingning 109 24 8N 115 43 E
Hsingp'ing 106 34 18N 108 26 E
Hsingshan 109 31 10N 110 51 E
Hsingt'ai 106 37 5N 114 38 E
Hsingyeh 108 22 45N 109 52 E
Hsinhailien = Lienyünchiangshih 107 34 37N 119 13 E
Hsinhsiang 106 35 15N 113 54 E
Hsinhsien, Shansi, China 106 38 24N 112 47 E
Hsinhsien, Shantung, China 106 36 15N 115 40 E
Hsinhsing 109 22 45N 112 11 E
Hsinhua 109 27 43N 111 18 E
Hsinhui 109 22 32N 113 0 E
Hsini 109 22 12N 110 53 E
Hsining 105 36 37N 101 46 E
Hsink'ai Ho, R. 107 41 10N 122 5 E
Hsinkan 109 27 45N 115 21 E
Hsinkao Shan 109 23 25N 120 52 E
Hsinlit'un 107 42 2N 122 19 E
Hsinlo 106 38 15N 114 40 E
Hsinmin 107 42 0N 122 52 E
Hsinpaoan 106 40 27N 115 23 E
Hsinpin 107 41 43N 125 2 E
Hsinp'ing 108 24 6N 101 58 E
Hsinshao 109 27 20N 111 26 E
Hsint'ai 107 35 54N 117 44 E
Hsint'ien 109 25 56N 112 13 E
Hsints'ai 109 32 44N 114 59 E
Hsinyang 109 32 10N 114 6 E
Hsinyeh 109 37 31N 112 21 E
Hsinyü 109 27 48N 114 56 E
Hsipaw 98 22 37N 97 18 E
Hsip'ing, Honan, China 106 33 34N 110 45 E
Hsip'ing, Honan, China 106 33 23N 114 2 E
Hsishni 109 30 27N 115 13 E
Hsitalahai 106 40 38N 109 38 E
Hsiu Shui, R. 109 29 13N 116 0 E
Hsiujen 109 24 26N 110 14 E
Hsiunghsien 106 38 50N 116 11 E
Hsiungyüeh 107 40 12N 122 12 E
Hsiuning 109 29 51N 118 15 E
Hsiushan 108 28 27N 108 59 E
Hsiushui 109 29 2N 114 34 E

Hsiuwen Ibara

Hsiuwen 108 26 52N 106 35 E
Hsiuyen 107 40 19N 123 15 E
Hsiyang 106 37 27N 113 46 E
Hsüanch'eng 109 30 54N 118 41 E
Hsüanen 108 29 59N 109 24 E
Hsüanhan 108 31 25N 107 38 E
Hsüanhua 106 40 38N 115 5 E
Hsüanwei 108 26 13N 104 5 E
Hsüch'ang 106 34 1N 113 53 E
Hsüchou 107 34 15N 117 10 E
Hsüehfeng Shan 109 27 0N 110 30 E
Hsüehweng Shan 109 24 24N 121 12 E
Hsun Chiang, R. 109 23 30N 111 30 E
Hsünhsien 106 35 40N 114 32 E
Hsüni 106 35 6N 108 20 E
Hsüntien 108 25 33N 103 15 E
Hsünwu 109 24 57N 115 28 E
Hsünyang 108 32 48N 109 27 E
Hsüp'u 109 27 56N 110 36 E
Hsüshui 106 39 1N 115 39 E
Hsüwen 109 20 20N 110 9 E
Hsüyung 108 28 6N 105 21 E
Htawgaw 98 25 57N 98 23 E
Hua Hin 100 12 34N 99 58 E
Huaan 109 25 1N 117 33 E
Huachacalla 164 18 45 S 68 17W
Huachinera 164 30 9N 108 55W
Huachipato 172 36 45 S 73 09W
Huacho 174 11 10 S 77 35W
Huachón 174 10 35 S 76 0W
Huachou 109 21 38N 110 35 E
Huacrachuco 174 8 35 S 76 50W
Huahsien, Honan, China 106 35 33N 114 34 E
Huahsien, Shensi, China 106 34 31N 109 46 E
Huai Yot 101 7 45N 99 37 E
Huaiachen 106 40 33N 114 30 E
Huaian, Hopei, China 106 40 33N 114 30 E
Huaian, Kiangsu, China 107 33 31N 119 8 E
Huaichi 109 24 0N 112 8 E
Huaihua 109 27 34N 109 56 E
Huaijen 106 39 50N 113 7 E
Huaijou 106 40 20N 116 37 E
Huainan 109 32 39N 117 2 E
Huaining 109 30 21N 116 42 E
Huaite 107 43 30N 124 50 E
Huaitechen 107 43 52N 124 45 E
Huaiyang 106 33 50N 115 2 E
Huaiyüan, Anhwei, China 109 32 58N 117 13 E
Huaiyüan, Kwangsi-Chuang, China 108 24 36N 108 27 E
Huajuapan 165 17 50N 98 0W
Huajung 109 29 34N 112 34 E
Hualien 109 24 0N 121 30 E
Huallaga, R. 174 5 30 S 76 10W
Hualpai Pk. 161 35 8N 113 58W
Huan Chiang, R. 106 36 4N 107 40 E
Huancabamba 174 5 10 S 79 15W
Huancané 174 15 10 S 69 50W
Huancapi 174 13 25 S 74 0W
Huancavelica 174 12 50 S 75 5W
Huancayo 174 12 5 S 75 0W
Huanchiang 108 24 50N 108 15 E
Huang Ho, R. 107 36 50N 118 20 E
Huangchiakopa 106 40 20N 109 18 E
Huangch'uan 109 32 8N 115 4 E
Huanghsien, Hunen, China 108 27 22N 109 10 E
Huanghsien, Shantung, China 107 37 38N 120 30 E
Huangkang 109 30 27N 114 50 E
Huanglienp'u 108 25 32N 99 44 E
Huangling 106 35 36N 109 17 E
Huangliu 105 18 20N 108 50 E
Huanglung 106 35 37N 109 58 E
Huanglungt'an 109 32 38N 110 33 E
Huangmei 109 30 4N 115 56 E
Huangshih 109 30 10N 115 2 E
Huangt'uan 107 36 55N 121 41 E
Huangyang 109 26 37N 111 42 E
Huangyen 109 28 37N 121 12 E
Huanhsien 106 36 32N 107 10 E
Huaning 108 24 12N 102 55 E
Huanjen 107 41 16N 125 21 E
Huanp'ing 108 26 54N 107 55 E
Huant'ai 107 36 57N 118 5 E
Huánuco 174 9 55 S 76 15W
Huap'ing 108 26 37N 101 13 E
Huap'itientzu 107 43 30N 130 2 E
Huaraz 174 9 30 S 77 32W
Huarmey 174 10 5 S 78 5W
Huasamota 164 22 30N 104 30W
Huascarán 174 9 0 S 77 30W
Huasco 172 28 24 S 71 15W
Huasco, R. 172 28 27 S 71 13W
Huasna 163 35 6N 120 24W
Huatabampo 164 26 50N 109 50W
Huate 106 41 57N 114 4 E
Huatien 107 42 58N 126 50 E
Huauchinango 165 20 11N 98 3W
Huautla 164 18 20N 96 50W
Huautla de Jiménez 165 18 8N 96 51W
Huay Namota 164 21 56N 104 30W
Huayin 106 34 36N 110 2 E
Huayllay 174 11 03 S 76 21W
Huayüan 108 28 30N 109 25 E
Hubbard 159 31 50N 96 50W
Hubbart Pt. 153 59 21N 94 41W
Hubli-Dharwar 97 15 22N 75 15 E
Huchang 107 41 25N 127 2 E
Huchuetenango 164 15 25N 91 30W
Hückelhoven-Ratheim 48 51 6N 6 3 E
Hucknall 33 53 3N 1 12W
Huddersfield 33 53 38N 1 49W
Hudi 122 17 43N 34 28 E
Hudiksvall 72 61 43N 17 10 E
Hudson, Can. 153 50 6N 92 09W
Hudson, Mich., U.S.A. 156 41 50N 84 20W
Hudson, N.H., U.S.A. 162 42 46N 71 26W
Hudson, N.Y., U.S.A. 162 42 15N 73 46W
Hudson, Wis., U.S.A. 158 44 57N 92 45W
Hudson, Wyo., U.S.A. 160 42 54N 108 37W
Hudson B. 153 59 0N 91 0W
Hudson Bay, Can. 149 60 0N 86 0W
Hudson Bay, Sask., Can. 153 52 51N 102 23W
Hudson Falls 162 43 18N 73 34W
Hudson, R. 162 40 42N 74 2W
Hudson Str. 148 62 0N 70 0W
Hudson's Hope 152 56 0N 121 54W
Hué 100 16 30N 107 35 E
Huebra, R. 56 40 54N 6 28W
Huedin 70 46 52N 23 2 E
Huehuetenango 166 15 20N 91 28W
Huejúcar 164 22 21N 103 13W
Huelgoat 42 48 22N 3 46W
Huelma 59 37 39N 3 28W
Huelva 57 37 18N 6 57W
Huelva □ 57 37 40N 7 0W
Huelva, R. 57 37 46N 6 15W
Huentelauquén 172 31 38 S 71 33W
Huércal Overa 59 37 23N 1 57W
Huerta, Sa. de la 172 31 10 S 67 30W
Huertas, C. de las 59 38 21N 0 24W
Huerva, R. 58 41 13N 1 15W
Huesca 58 42 8N 0 25W
Huesca □ 58 42 20N 0 1 E
Huéscar 59 37 44N 2 35W
Huétamo 164 18 36N 100 54W
Huete 58 40 10N 2 43W
Hugh, R. 138 25 1 S 134 10 E
Hugh Town 30 49 55N 6 19W
Hughenden 138 20 52 S 144 10 E
Hughes, Austral. 137 30 42 S 129 31 E
Hughes, U.S.A. 147 66 0N 154 20W
Hughesville 162 41 14N 76 44W
Hugo, Colo., U.S.A. 158 39 12N 103 27W
Hugo, Okla., U.S.A. 159 34 0N 95 30W
Hugoton 159 37 18N 101 22W
Huhehot = Huhohaot'e 106 40 50N 110 39 E
Huhohaot'e 106 40 50N 110 39 E
Huhsien 106 34 8N 108 34 E
Huian 109 25 4N 118 47 E
Huianp'u 106 37 30N 106 40 E
Huiarau Ra. 142 38 45 S 176 55 E
Huich'ang 109 25 32N 115 45 E
Huichapán 165 20 24N 99 40W
Huichou 109 23 5N 114 24 E
Huifa Ho, R. 107 43 6N 126 53 E
Huihsien, Honan, China 106 35 32N 113 54 E
Huihsien, Kansu, China 106 33 46N 106 6 E
Huila 128 15 30 S 15 0 E
Huila □ 174 2 30N 75 45W
Huila, Nevado del 174 3 0N 76 0W
Huilai 109 23 4N 116 18 E
Huili 108 26 39N 102 11 E
Huimin 107 37 29N 117 29 E
Huinan 107 42 40N 126 5 E
Huinca Renancó 172 34 51 S 64 22W
Huining 106 35 41N 105 8 E
Huinung 106 39 0N 106 45 E
Huiroa 142 39 15 S 174 30 E
Huise 47 50 54N 3 36 E
Huishui 108 26 8N 106 35 E
Huissen 46 51 57N 5 57 E
Huiting 106 34 6N 116 4 E
Huitse 108 26 22N 103 15 E
Huit'ung 108 26 56N 109 36 E
Huixtla 165 15 9N 92 28W
Huiya 92 24 40N 49 15 E
Huizen 46 52 18N 5 14 E
Hukawng Valley 99 26 30N 96 30 E
Hukou 109 29 45N 116 13 E
Hukuma 123 14 55N 36 2 E
Hukuntsi 128 23 58 S 21 45 E
Hula 123 6 33N 38 30 E
Hulaifa 92 25 58N 41 0 E
Hulan 105 46 0N 126 44 E
Huld 106 45 5N 105 30 E
Hülda 90 31 50N 34 51 E
Hull, Can. 150 45 20N 75 40W
Hull, U.K. 33 53 45N 0 20W
Hullavington 28 51 31N 2 9W
Hulme End 32 53 8N 1 51W
Hulst 47 51 17N 4 2 E
Hultsfred 73 57 30N 15 52 E
Hulun Ch'ih 105 49 1N 117 32 E
Humacao 147 18 9N 65 50W
Humahuaca 172 23 10 S 65 25W
Humaitá 174 7 35 S 62 40W
Humaita 172 27 2 S 58 31W
Humansdorp 128 34 2 S 24 46 E
Humber, Mouth of 33 53 32N 0 8 E
Humber, R. 33 53 40N 0 10W
Humberside □ 33 53 50N 0 30W
Humbert River 136 16 30 S 130 45 E
Humble 159 29 59N 95 10W
Humboldt, Can. 153 52 15N 105 9W
Humboldt, Iowa, U.S.A. 158 42 42N 94 15W
Humboldt, Tenn., U.S.A. 157 35 50N 88 55W
Humboldt Gletscher 12 79 30N 62 0W
Humboldt, R. 160 40 55N 116 0W
Humbolt Mts. 143 44 30 S 168 15 E
Hume 163 36 48N 118 54W
Hume, L. 141 36 0 S 147 0 E
Humenné 53 48 55N 21 50 E
Humphreys, Mt. 163 37 17N 118 40W
Humphreys Pk. 161 35 24N 111 38W
Humpolec 52 49 31N 15 20 E
Humshaugh 35 55 3N 2 8W
Humula 141 35 30 S 147 46 E
Hün 119 29 2N 16 0 E
Hun Chiang, R. 107 40 52N 125 42 E
Huna Floi 74 65 50N 20 50W
Hunan □ 109 27 30N 111 30 E
Hunch'un 107 42 52N 130 21 E
Hundested 73 55 58N 11 52 E
Hundred House 31 52 11N 3 17W
Hundred Mile House 152 51 38N 121 18W
Hundshögen, mt. 72 62 57N 13 46 E
Hunedoara 70 45 40N 22 50 E
Hunedoara □ 70 45 45N 22 54 E
Hünfeld 48 50 40N 9 47 E
Hung Chiang, R. 108 27 7N 109 57 E
Hung Ho, R. 109 32 24N 115 32 E
Hung Liu Ho, R. 106 38 3N 109 10 E
Hung Yen 100 20 39N 106 4 E
Hungan 109 31 18N 114 33 E
Hungary ■ 53 47 20N 19 20 E
Hungary, Plain of 16 47 0N 20 0 E
Hungchiang 109 27 6N 110 0 E
Hungerford, Austral. 139 28 58 S 144 24 E
Hungerford, U.K. 28 51 25N 1 30W
Hunghai Wan 109 22 45N 115 15 E
Hunghu 109 29 49N 113 30 E
Hüngnam 107 39 55N 127 45 E
Hungshui Ho, R. 108 23 24N 110 12 E
Hungtech'eng 106 36 48N 107 6 E
Hungt'ou Hsü 109 22 4N 121 25 E
Hungt'se Hu 107 33 15N 118 45 E
Hungtung 106 36 15N 111 37 E
Hungya 108 29 56N 103 25 E
Hungyüan 108 32 46N 102 42 E
Huni Valley 120 5 33N 1 56W
Hunmanby 33 54 12N 0 19W
Hunsberge 128 27 58 S 17 5 E
Hunsrück, mts. 49 50 0N 7 30 E
Hunstanton 29 52 57N 0 30 E
Hunsur 97 12 16N 76 16 E
Hunte, R. 48 52 47N 8 28 E
Hunter, N.Z. 143 44 36 S 171 2 E
Hunter, N.D., U.S.A. 158 47 12N 97 17W
Hunter, N.Y., U.S.A. 162 42 13N 74 13W
Hunter Hills, The 143 44 26 S 170 46 E
Hunter, I. 138 40 30 S 144 54 E
Hunter I. 152 51 55N 128 0W
Hunter Mts. 143 45 43 S 167 25 E
Hunter, R. 143 44 21 S 169 27 E
Hunter Ra. 141 32 45 S 150 15 E
Hunters Road 127 19 9 S 29 49 E
Hunterston 34 55 43N 4 55W
Hunterton 139 26 12 S 148 30 E
Hunterville 142 39 56 S 175 35 E
Huntingburg 156 38 20N 86 58W
Huntingdon, Can. 150 45 10N 74 10W
Huntingdon, U.K. 29 52 20N 0 11W
Huntingdon, N.Y., U.S.A. 162 40 52N 73 25W
Huntingdon, Pa., U.S.A. 156 40 28N 78 1W
Huntingdon & Peterborough (□) 26 52 23N 0 10W
Huntingdon I. 151 53 48N 56 45W
Huntington, U.K. 33 54 0N 1 4W
Huntington, Id., U.S.A. 160 44 22N 117 21W
Huntington, Ind., U.S.A. 156 40 52N 85 30W
Huntington, Ut., U.S.A. 160 39 24N 111 1W
Huntington, W. Va., U.S.A. 156 38 20N 82 30W
Huntington Beach 163 33 40N 118 0W
Huntington Park 161 34 58N 118 15W
Huntly, N.Z. 142 37 34 S 175 11 E
Huntly, U.K. 37 57 27N 2 48W
Huntsville, Can. 150 45 20N 79 14W
Huntsville, Ala., U.S.A. 157 34 45N 86 35W
Huntsville, Tex., U.S.A. 159 30 50N 95 35W
Hunyani Dams. 127 18 0 S 31 10 E
Hunyani, R. 127 18 0 S 31 10 E
Hunyüan 106 39 44N 113 42 E
Hunza, R. 95 36 24N 75 50 E
Huohsien 106 36 38N 111 43 E
Huon, G. 135 7 0 S 147 30 E
Huon Pen. 135 6 20 S 147 30 E
Huong Hoa 100 16 37N 106 45 E
Huong Khe 100 18 13N 105 41 E
Huonville 138 43 0 S 147 5 E
Huoshaop'u 107 43 23N 130 26 E
Hupei □ 109 31 5N 113 5 E
Hurbanovo 53 47 51N 18 11 E
Hurezani 70 44 49N 23 40 E
Hurghada 122 27 15N 33 50 E
Hŭrghita □ 70 46 30N 25 30 E
Hŭrghita Mţii 70 46 25N 25 35 E
Hurley, N. Mex., U.S.A. 161 32 45N 108 7W
Hurley, Wis., U.S.A. 158 46 26N 90 10W
Hurlford 34 55 35N 4 29W
Hurliness 37 58 47N 3 15W
Hurlock 162 38 38N 75 52W
Huron, Calif., U.S.A. 163 36 12N 120 6W
Huron, S.D., U.S.A. 158 44 30N 98 20W
Hurricane 161 37 10N 113 12W
Hursley 28 51 1N 1 23W
Hurso 123 9 35N 41 33 E
Hurstbourne Tarrant 28 51 17N 1 27W
Hurstpierpoint 29 50 56N 0 11W
Hurum, Buskerud, Norway 71 59 36N 10 23 E
Hurum, Oppland, Norway 71 61 9N 8 46 E
Hurunui, R. 143 42 54 S 173 18 E
Hurup 73 56 46N 8 25 E
Husaby 73 58 35N 13 25 E
Húsavík 74 66 3N 17 21W
Husband's Bosworth 28 52 27N 1 3W
Husi 70 46 41N 28 7 E
Husinish Pt. 36 57 59N 7 6W
Huskvarna 73 57 47N 14 15 E
Huslia 147 65 40N 156 30W
Husøy 71 61 3N 4 44 E
Hussar 152 51 3N 112 41W
Hussein (Allenby) Br. 90 31 53N 35 33 E
Hustopéce 53 48 57N 16 43 E
Husum, Ger. 48 54 27N 9 3 E
Husum, Sweden 72 63 21N 19 12 E
Hutchinson, Kans., U.S.A. 159 38 3N 97 59W
Hutchinson, Minn, U.S.A. 158 44 50N 94 22W
Huttenberg 52 46 56N 14 33 E
Hüttental 47 50 53N 8 1 E
Huttig 159 33 5N 92 10W
Hutton, Mt. 139 25 51 S 148 20 E
Hutton, oilfield 19 61 0N 1 30 E
Hutton Ra. 137 24 45 S 124 30 E
Huttwil 50 47 7N 7 50 E
Huwarā 90 32 9N 35 15 E
Huwun 123 4 23N 40 6 E
Huy 47 50 31N 5 15 E
Huyton 32 53 25N 2 52W
Hvaler 71 59 4N 11 1 E
Hvammsfjörður 74 65 4N 22 5W
Hvammur 74 65 13N 21 49W
Hvar 63 43 10N 16 45 E
Hvar, I. 63 43 11N 16 28 E
Hvarski Kanal 63 43 15N 16 35 E
Hvítá, Arnessýsla, Iceland 74 64 0N 20 58W
Hvítá, Mýrasýsla, Iceland 74 64 40N 21 5W
Hvítárvatn 74 63 37N 19 50W
Hvitsten 71 59 35N 10 42 E
Hwachon-chŏsuji 107 38 5N 127 50 E
Hwang Ho = Huang Ho, R. 107 36 50N 118 20 E
Hwekum 98 26 7N 95 22 E
Hyannis, Mass., U.S.A. 162 41 39N 70 17W
Hyannis, Nebr., U.S.A. 158 41 60N 101 45W
Hyargas Nuur 105 49 12N 93 34 E
Hyattsville 162 38 59N 76 55W
Hybo 72 61 49N 16 15 E
Hydaburg 147 55 15N 132 45W
Hyde, N.Z. 143 45 18 S 170 16 E
Hyde, U.K. 32 53 26N 2 6W
Hyde Park 162 41 47N 73 56W
Hyden 137 32 24 S 118 46 E
Hyderabad, India 96 17 10N 78 29 E
Hyderabad, Pak. 94 25 23N 68 36 E
Hyderabad □ 94 25 3N 68 24 E
Hyères 45 43 8N 6 9 E
Hyères, Is. d' 45 43 0N 6 28 E
Hyesan 107 41 20N 128 10 E
Hyland Post 139 57 40N 128 10W
Hyland, R. 152 59 52N 128 12W
Hylestad 71 59 6N 7 29 E
Hyllested 71 56 17N 10 46 E
Hyltebruk 73 56 59N 13 15 E
Hymia 95 33 40N 78 2 E
Hyndman Pk. 160 44 4N 114 0W
Hynish 34 56 27N 6 54W
Hynish B. 34 56 29N 6 40W
Hyōgo-ken □ 110 35 15N 135 0 E
Hyrum 160 41 35N 111 56W
Hysham 160 46 21N 107 11W
Hythe 29 51 4N 1 5 E
Hyūga 110 32 25N 131 35 E
Hyvinkä 75 60 38N 24 50 E

I

I Ho, R. 107 34 10N 118 4 E
I-n-Azaoua 119 20 45N 7 31 E
I-n-Échaïe 118 20 10N 2 5W
I-n-Gall 121 6 51N 7 1 E
I-n-Tabedog 118 19 54N 1 3 E
Iabès, Erg 118 27 30N 2 2W
Iaco, R. 174 10 25 S 70 30W
Iaçu 171 12 45 S 40 13W
Iakora 129 23 6 S 46 40 E
Ialomiţa □ 70 44 30N 27 30 E
Ianca 70 45 6N 27 29 E
Iar Connacht 39 53 20N 9 20W
Iara 70 46 31N 23 35 E
Iaşi □ 70 47 20N 27 0 E
Iaşi (Jassy) 70 47 10N 27 40 E
Iauaretê 174 0 30N 69 5W
Iaucdjovac, (Port Harrison) 149 58 25N 78 15W
Iba 103 15 22N 120 0 E
Ibadan 121 7 22N 3 58 E
Ibagué 174 4 27N 73 14W
Ibaiti 171 23 50 S 50 10W
Iballja 68 42 12N 20 0 E
Ibar, R. 63 43 15N 20 40 E
Ibara 110 34 36N 133 28 E

Ibaraki-ken □ Inhambane

Ibaraki-ken □ 111 36 10N 140 10 E
Ibararaki 111 34 49N 135 34 E
Ibarra 174 0 21N 78 7W
Ibba 123 4 49N 29 2 E
Ibba, Bahr el 123 5 30N 28 55 E
Ibbenbüren 48 52 16N 7 41 E
Ibembo 126 2 35N 23 35 E
Ibera, Laguna 172 28 30 S 57 9W
Iberian Peninsula 16 40 0N 5 0W
Iberville 150 45 19N 73 17W
Iberville, Lac d' 150 55 55N 73 15W
Ibi 121 8 15N 9 50 E
Ibiá 171 19 30 S 46 30W
Ibicaraí 171 14 51 S 39 36W
Ibicuí 171 14 51 S 39 59W
Ibicuy 172 33 55 S 59 10W
Ibioapaba, Serra da 170 20 14 S 40 25W
Ibipetuba 171 11 0 S 44 32W
Ibiracu 171 19 50 S 40 30W
Ibitiara 171 12 39 S 42 13W
Ibiza 59 38 54N 1 26 E
Ibiza, I. 59 39 0N 1 30 E
Iblei, Monti 65 37 15N 14 45 E
Ibo 127 12 22 S 40 32 E
Ibonma 103 3 22 S 133 31 E
Ibotirama 171 12 13 S 43 12W
Ibriktepe 68 41 2N 26 33 E
Ibshawâi 122 29 21N 30 40 E
Ibstock 28 52 42N 1 23W
Ibu 103 1 35N 127 25 E
Ibuki-Sanchi 111 35 25N 136 34 E
Ibŭneşti 70 46 45N 24 50 E
Iburg 48 52 10N 8 3 E
Ibusuki 110 31 12N 130 32 E
Ibwe Munyama 127 16 5 S 28 31 E
Ica 174 14 0 S 75 30W
Ica, R. 174 2 55 S 69 0W
Icabarú 174 4 20N 61 45W
Içana 174 1 21N 69 0W
Icatu 170 2 46 S 44 4W
Iceland, I. ■ 74 65 0N 19 0W
Icha 77 55 30N 156 0 E
Ichang 109 25 25N 112 55 E
Ich'ang 109 30 40N 111 20 E
Ichchapuram 96 19 10N 84 40 E
Icheng 109 32 16N 119 12 E
Ich'eng, Hupeh, China 109 31 43N 112 12 E
Ich'eng, Shansi, China 106 35 42N 111 40 E
Ichihara 111 35 28N 140 5 E
Ichikawa 111 35 44N 139 55 E
Ichilo, R. 174 16 30 S 64 45W
Ichinomiya, Gifu, Japan 111 35 18N 136 48 E
Ichinomiya, Kumamoto, Japan 110 32 58N 131 5 E
Ichinoseki 112 38 55N 141 8 E
Ichŏn 107 37 17N 127 27 E
Icht 118 29 6N 8 54W
Ichtegem 47 51 5N 3 1 E
Ich'uan 106 36 4N 110 6 E
Ich'un 105 47 42N 128 54 E
Ichün 106 35 23N 109 7 E
Ich'un, Heilungkiang, China 105 47 42N 128 54 E
Ich'un, Kiangsi, China 109 27 47N 114 22 E
Icó 170 6 24 S 38 51W
Icoraci 170 1 18 S 48 28W
Icy C. 12 70 25N 162 0W
Icy Str. 153 58 20N 135 30W
Ida Grove 158 42 20N 95 25W
Ida Valley 137 28 42 S 120 29 E
Idabel 159 33 53N 94 50W
Idaga Hamus 123 14 13N 39 35 E
Idah 121 6 10N 6 40 E
Idaho □ 160 44 10N 114 0W
Idaho City 160 43 50N 115 52W
Idaho Falls 160 43 30N 112 10W
Idaho Springs 160 39 49N 105 30W
Idanha-a-Nova 56 39 50N 7 15W
Idanre 121 7 8N 5 5 E
Idar-Oberstein 49 49 43N 7 19 E
Idd el Ghanam 117 11 30N 24 25 E
Iddan 91 6 10N 49 5 E
Idehan 119 27 10N 11 30 E
Idehan Marzūq 119 24 50N 13 51 E
Idelès 119 23 58N 5 53 E
Idfû 122 25 0N 32 49 E
Idhi Oros 69 35 15N 24 45 E
Idhra 69 37 20N 23 28 E
Idi 102 4 55N 97 45 E
Idi Amin Dada, L. 93 0 25 S 29 40 E
Idiofa 124 4 55 S 19 42 E
Idkerberget 72 60 22N 15 15 E
Idle 33 53 50N 1 45W
Idle, R. 33 53 27N 0 49W
Idmiston 28 51 8N 1 43W
Idna 90 31 34N 34 58 E
Idria 163 36 25N 120 41W
Idrija 63 46 0N 14 5 E
Idritsa 80 56 25N 28 57 E
Idstein 49 50 13N 8 17 E
Idsworth 29 50 56N 0 56W
Idutywa 125 32 8 S 28 18 E
Ieper 47 50 51N 2 53 E
Ierápetra 69 35 0N 25 44 E
Ierissós 68 40 22N 23 52 E
Ierissóu Kólpos 68 40 27N 23 57 E
Ierzu 64 39 48N 9 32 E
Ieshima-Shotō 110 34 40N 134 32 E
Iesi 63 43 32N 13 12 E
Ifach, Punta 59 38 38N 0 5 E
Ifanadiana 129 21 29 S 47 39 E
Ife 121 7 30N 4 31 E
Iférouâne 121 19 5N 8 35 E
Ifni 118 29 25N 10 10W
Ifon 121 6 58N 5 40 E
Iga 111 34 45N 136 10 E
Iganga 126 0 30N 33 28 E
Igarapava 171 20 3 S 47 47W
Igarapé Açu 170 1 4 S 47 33W
Igarapé-Mirim 170 1 59 S 48 58W
Igarka 77 67 30N 87 20 E
Igatimi 173 24 5 S 55 30W
Igatpuri 96 19 40N 73 35 E
Igbetti 121 8 44N 4 8 E
Igbo-Ora 121 7 10N 3 15 E
Igboho 121 8 40N 3 50 E
Iggesund 72 61 39N 17 10 E
Igherm 118 30 7N 8 18W
Ighil Izane 118 35 44N 0 31 E
Iglene 118 22 57N 4 58 E
Iglésias 64 39 19N 8 27 E
Igli 118 30 25N 2 12W
Iglino 84 54 50N 56 26 E
Igloolik Island 149 69 20N 81 30W
Igma 118 29 9N 6 11W
Igma, Gebel el 122 28 55N 34 0 E
Ignace 150 49 30N 91 40W
Igoshevo 81 59 25N 42 35 E
Igoumenitsa 68 39 32N 20 18 E
Igra 84 57 33N 53 7 E
Iguaçu, Cat. del 173 25 41N 54 26W
Iguaçu, R. 173 25 30 S 53 10W
Iguala 165 18 20N 99 40W
Igualada 58 41 37N 1 37 E
Iguape 171 24 43 S 47 33W
Iguape, R. 173 24 40 S 48 0W
Iguassu = Iguaçu 173 25 41N 54 26W
Iguatu 170 6 20 S 39 18W
Iguéla 124 2 0 S 9 16 E
Igumale 121 6 47N 7 55 E
Igunga □ 126 4 20 S 33 45 E
Ihiala 121 5 40N 6 55 E
Ihosy 129 22 24 S 46 8 E
Ihotry, L. 129 21 56 S 43 41 E
Ihsien, Anwhei, China 109 29 53N 117 57E
Ihsien, Hopeh, China 106 39 21N 115 29E
Ihsien, Liaoning, China 107 41 34N 121 15E
Ihsien, Shantung, China 107 37 11N 119 55E
Ihuang 109 27 32N 115 57 E
Ii 74 65 15N 25 30 E
Iida 111 35 35N 138 0 E
Iiey 138 18 53 S 141 12 E
Iijoki 74 65 20N 26 15 E
Iisalmi 74 63 32N 27 10 E
Iizuka 110 33 38N 130 42 E
Ijebu-Igbo 121 6 56N 4 1 E
Ijebu-Ode 121 6 47N 3 52 E
IJmuiden 46 52 28N 4 35 E
IJssel, R. 46 52 35N 5 50 E
IJsselmeer 46 52 45N 5 20 E
IJsselmuiden 46 52 34N 5 57 E
IJsselstein 46 52 1N 5 2 E
Ijuí, R. 173 27 58 S 55 20W
Ijūin 110 31 37N 130 24 E
IJzendijke 47 51 19N 3 37 E
IJzer, R. 47 51 9N 2 44 E
Ik, R. 84 55 55N 52 36 E
Ikamatua 141 42 15 S 171 41 E
Ikare 121 7 18N 5 40 E
Ikaria, I. 69 37 35N 26 10 E
Ikast 73 56 8N 9 10 E
Ikawa 111 35 13N 138 15 E
Ikeda 111 34 1N 133 48 E
Ikeja 121 6 28N 3 45 E
Ikela 124 1 0 S 23 35 E
Ikerre 121 7 25N 5 19 E
Ikhtiman 67 42 27N 23 48 E
Iki 110 33 45N 129 42 E
Iki-Kaikyō 110 33 40N 129 45 E
Ikimba L. 126 1 30 S 31 20 E
Ikire 121 7 10N 4 15 E
Ikirun 121 7 54N 4 40 E
Ikitsuki-Shima 110 33 23N 129 26 E
Ikole 121 7 40N 5 37 E
Ikom 121 6 0N 8 42 E
Ikopa, R. 129 17 45 S 46 40 E
Ikot Ekpene 121 5 12N 7 40 E
Ikungu 126 1 33 S 33 42 E
Ikuno 110 35 10N 134 48 E
Ila 121 8 0N 4 51 E
Ilam 95 26 58N 87 58 E
Ilan, China 105 46 14N 129 33 E
Ilan, Taiwan 109 24 45N 121 44 E
Ilanskiy 77 56 14N 96 3 E
Ilanz 51 46 46N 9 12 E
Ilaomita, R. 47 44 47N 27 0 E
Ilaro Agege 121 6 53N 3 3 E
Ilayangudi 97 9 34N 78 37 E
Ilbilbie 138 21 45 S 149 20 E
Ilchester 28 51 0N 2 41W
Ile-à-la Crosse 153 55 27N 107 53W
Ile-à-la-Crosse, Lac 153 55 40N 107 45W
Ile Bouchard, L' 42 47 7N 0 26 E
Ile de France □ 43 49 0N 2 20 E
Ilebo 124 4 17 S 20 47 E
Ileje □ 127 9 30 S 33 25 E
Ilek 84 51 32N 53 21 E
Ilek, R. 84 51 30N 53 22 E
Ilen R. 39 51 38N 9 19W
Ilero 121 8 0N 3 20 E
Ilesha, West-Central, Nigeria 121 7 37N 4 40 E
Ilesha, Western, Nigeria 121 8 57N 3 28E
Ilford 153 56 4N 95 35W
Ilfov □ 70 44 20N 26 0 E
Ilfracombe, Austral. 138 23 30 S 144 30 E
Ilfracombe, U.K. 30 51 13N 4 8W
Ilha Grande, Baia da 171 23 9S 44 30W
Ílhavo 56 40 33N 8 43W
Ilheus 171 14 49 S 39 2W
Ili 85 45 53N 77 10 E
Ilia 70 45 57N 22 40 E
Ilia □ 69 37 45N 21 35 E
Iliamna L. 147 59 35N 155 30W
Iliang, Yunnan, China 108 24 54N 103 9E
Iliang, Yunnan, China 108 27 35N 104 1E
Ilich 85 40 50N 68 27 E
Ilico 172 34 50 S 72 20W
Iliff 158 40 50N 103 3W
Ilíki 69 38 24N 23 15 E
Ilio Pt. 147 21 13N 157 16W
Iliodhrómia 68 39 12N 23 50 E
Ilion 162 43 0N 75 3W
Ilirska Bistrica 63 45 34N 14 14 E
Iliysk 76 44 10N 77 20 E
Ilkal 97 15 57N 76 8 E
Ilkeston 33 52 59N 1 19W
Ilkley 21 53 56N 1 49W
Illana B. 103 7 35N 123 45 E
Illapel 172 32 0 S 71 10W
'Illar 90 32 23N 35 7 E
Ille 44 42 40N 2 37 E
Ille-et-Vilaine □ 42 48 10N 1 30W
Iller, R. 49 47 53N 10 10 E
Illescás 56 40 8N 3 51W
Illig 91 7 47N 49 45 E
Illimani, Mte. 174 16 30 S 67 50W
Illinois □ 155 40 15N 89 30W
Illinois, R. 155 40 10N 90 20W
Illizi 119 26 31N 8 32 E
Illora 57 37 17N 3 53W
Ilmen, Oz. 80 58 15N 31 10 E
Ilmenau 48 50 41N 10 55 E
Ilminster 28 50 55N 2 56W
Ilo 174 17 40 S 71 20W
Ilobu 121 7 45N 4 25 E
Ilohuli Shan 105 51 20N 124 20 E
Iloilo 103 10 45N 122 33 E
Ilok 66 45 15N 19 20 E
Ilora 121 7 45N 3 50 E
Ilorin 121 8 30N 4 35 E
Ilovatka 81 50 30N 46 50 E
Ilovlya 83 49 15N 44 2 E
Ilovlya, R. 83 49 38N 44 20 E
Iłowa 54 51 30N 15 10 E
Ilubabor □ 123 7 25N 35 0 E
Ilukste 80 55 55N 26 20 E
Ilung 108 31 34N 106 24 E
Ilva Micá 70 47 17N 24 40 E
Ilwaki 103 7 55 S 126 30 E
Ilyichevsk 82 46 10N 30 35 E
Imabari 110 34 4N 133 0 E
Imadahane 118 32 8N 7 0W
Imaichi 111 36 6N 139 16 E
Imaloto, R. 129 23 10 S 45 15 E
Iman = Dalneretchensk 77 45 50N 133 40 E
Imari 110 33 15N 129 52 E
Imasa 122 18 0N 36 12 E
Imathia □ 68 40 30N 22 15 E
Imbâbah 122 30 5N 31 12 E
Imbler 160 45 31N 118 0W
Imbros = Imroz 68 40 10N 26 0 E
Imen 108 24 40N 102 9 E
Imeni Panfilova 85 43 23N 77 7 E
Imeni Poliny Osipenko 77 55 25N 136 29 E
Imeri, Serra 174 0 50N 65 25W
Imerimandroso 129 17 26 S 48 35 E
Imi (Hinna) 123 6 35N 42 30 E
Imi n'Tanoute 118 31 13N 8 51 E
Imienp'o 107 45 0N 128 16 E
Imishly 83 39 49N 48 4 E
Imiteg 118 29 43N 8 10W
Imlay 160 40 45N 118 9W
Immingham 33 53 37N 0 12W
Immokalee 157 26 25N 81 20W
Imo □ 121 5 15N 7 20 E
Imola 63 44 20N 11 42 E
Imotski 66 43 27N 17 21 E
Imperatriz 170 5 30 S 47 29W
Impéria 62 43 52N 8 0 E
Imperial, Can. 153 51 21N 105 28W
Imperial, Calif., U.S.A. 161 32 52N 115 34W
Imperial, Nebr., U.S.A. 158 40 38N 101 39W
Imperial Beach 163 32 35N 117 8W
Imperial Dam 161 32 50N 114 30W
Imperial Valley 163 32 55N 115 30W
Imperieuse Reef 136 17 36 S 118 50 E
Impfondo 124 1 40N 18 0 E
Imphal 98 24 48N 93 56 E
Imphy 43 46 56N 3 15 E
Imroz = Gökçeada 68 40 10N 26 0 E
Imst 52 47 15N 10 44 E
Imuruan B. 103 10 40N 119 10 E
In Belbel 118 27 55N 1 12 E
In Delimane 121 15 52N 1 31 E
In-Gall 121 16 51N 7 1 E
In Rhar 118 27 10N 1 59 E
In Salah 118 27 10N 2 32 E
In Tallak 121 16 19N 3 15 E
Ina 111 35 50N 138 0 E
Ina-Bonchi 111 35 45N 137 58 E
Inagh 39 52 53N 9 11W
Inajá 170 8 54 S 37 49W
Inangahua Junc. 143 41 52 S 171 59 E
Inanwatan 103 2 10 S 132 5 E
Iñapari 174 11 0 S 69 40W
Inari 74 68 54N 27 5 E
Inari, L. 74 69 0N 28 0 E
Inazawa 111 35 15N 136 47 E
Inca 58 39 43N 2 54 E
Incaguasi 172 29 12 S 71 5W
Ince 32 53 32N 2 38W
İnce Burnu 92 42 2N 35 0 E
Inch 39 52 42N 8 8W
Inch Br. 39 52 49N 9 6W
Inchard, Loch 36 58 28N 5 2W
Inchcape Rock 35 56 26N 2 24W
Inchigeelagh 39 51 50N 9 8W
Inchini 123 8 55N 37 37 E
Inchkeith, I. 35 56 2N 3 8W
Inchnadamph 36 58 9N 5 0W
Inch'ŏn 107 37 27N 126 40 E
Inchture 35 56 26N 3 8W
Incio 56 42 39N 7 21W
Incomáti, R. 129 25 15 S 32 35 E
Incudine, Mte. l' 45 41 50N 9 12 E
Inda Silase 123 14 10N 38 15 E
Indaal L. 34 55 44N 6 20W
Indalsälven 72 62 36N 17 30 E
Indaw 98 24 15N 96 5 E
Indbir 123 8 7N 37 52 E
Indefatigable, gasfield 19 53 20N 2 40 E
Independence, Calif., U.S.A. 163 36 51N 118 7W
Independence, Iowa, U.S.A. 158 42 27N 91 52W
Independence, Kans., U.S.A. 159 37 10N 95 50W
Independence, Mo., U.S.A. 158 39 3N 94 25W
Independence, Oreg., U.S.A. 160 44 53N 123 6W
Independence Fjord 12 82 10N 29 0W
Independence Mts. 160 41 30N 116 2W
Independência 170 5 23 S 40 19W
Independencia, La 165 16 31N 91 47W
Independenţa 70 45 25N 27 42 E
Inderborskly 83 48 30N 51 42 E
India ■ 87 20 0N 80 0 E
Indian Cabins 152 59 52N 117 2W
Indian Harbour 151 54 27N 57 13W
Indian Head 153 50 30N 103 35W
Indian House L. 151 56 30N 64 30W
Indian Lake 162 43 47N 74 16W
Indian Ocean 11 5 0 S 75 0 E
Indian River B. 162 38 36N 75 4W
Indiana 156 40 38N 79 9W
Indiana □ 156 40 0N 86 0W
Indianapolis 156 39 42N 86 10W
Indianola, Iowa, U.S.A. 158 41 20N 93 38W
Indianola, Miss., U.S.A. 159 33 27N 90 40W
Indianópolis 171 19 2 S 47 55 E
Indiapora 171 19 57 S 50 17W
Indiaroba 171 11 32 S 37 31W
Indiga 78 67 50N 48 50 E
Indigirka, R. 77 69 0N 147 0 E
Indija 66 45 6N 20 7 E
Indio 163 33 46N 116 15W
Indonesia ■ 102 5 0 S 115 0 E
Indore 94 22 42N 75 53 E
Indramaju 103 6 21 S 108 20 E
Indramaju, Tg. 103 6 20 S 108 20 E
Indravati, R. 96 19 0N 81 15 E
Indre □ 43 47 12N 1 39 E
Indre-et-Loire □ 42 47 12N 0 40 E
Indre, R. 42 47 2N 1 8 E
Indre Söndeled 71 58 46N 9 5 E
Indus, Mouth of the 94 24 00N 68 00 E
Indus, R. 94 28 40N 70 10 E
İnebolu 92 41 55N 33 40E
Infante, Kaap 128 34 27 S 20 51 E
Infantes 59 38 43N 3 1W
Infiernillo, Presa del 164 18 9N 102 0W
Infiesto 56 43 21N 5 21W
Ingá 171 7 17 S 35 36W
Ingatestone 29 51 40N 0 23W
Ingelmunster 47 50 56N 3 16 E
Ingende 124 0 12 S 18 57 E
Ingenio Santa Ana 172 27 25 S 65 40W
Ingesvang 73 56 10N 9 20 E
Ingham 138 18 43 S 146 10 E
Ingichka 85 39 47N 65 58 E
Ingleborough, mt. 32 54 11N 2 23W
Inglefield Land 143 78 30N 70 0W
Ingleton 32 54 9N 2 29W
Inglewood, Queensland, Austral. 139 28 25 S 151 8 E
Inglewood, Vic., Austral. 140 36 29 S 143 53 E
Inglewood, N.Z. 142 39 9 S 174 14 E
Inglewood, U.S.A. 163 33 58N 118 21W
Ingoldmells, Pt. 33 53 11N 0 21 E
Ingólfshöfði 74 63 48N 16 39W
Ingolstadt 49 48 45N 11 26 E
Ingomar 160 46 43N 107 37W
Ingonish 151 46 42N 60 18W
Ingore 120 12 24N 15 48W
Ingul, R. 82 47 30N 32 15 E
Ingulec 82 47 42N 33 4 E
Ingulets, R. 82 47 20N 33 20 E
Inguri, R. 83 42 58N 42 17 E
Inhaca, I. 129 26 1 S 32 57 E
Inhafenga 129 20 36 S 33 47 E
Inhambane 125 23 54 S 35 30 E

Inhambane □ **Itaueira**

Inhambane □ **129** 22 30S 34 20E
Inhambupe **171** 11 47S 38 21W
Inhaminga **127** 18 26S 35 0E
Inharrime **129** 24 30S 35 0E
Inharrime, R. **129** 24 30S 35 0E
Inhassoro **127** 21 50S 35 15E
Inhuma **170** 6 40S 41 42W
Inhumas **171** 16 22S 49 30W
Iniesta **59** 39 27N 1 45W
Ining, Kwangsi-Chuang, China **109** 25 8N 109 57E
Ining, Sinkiang-Uigur, China **105** 43 54N 81 21E
Inírida, R. **174** 3 0N 68 40W
Inishark **38** 53 38N 10 17W
Inishark I. **38** 53 38N 10 17W
Inishbofin I., Donegal, Ireland **38** 55 10N 8 10W
Inishbofin I., Galway, Ireland **38** 53 35N 10 12W
Inisheer **39** 53 3N 9 32W
Inishfree B. **38** 55 4N 8 20W
Inishkea Is. **38** 54 8N 10 10W
Inishmaan I. **39** 53 5N 9 35W
Inishmore, I. **39** 53 8N 9 45W
Inishmurray I. **38** 54 26N 8 40W
Inishowen Hd. **38** 55 14N 6 56W
Inishowen, Pen. **38** 55 14N 7 15W
Inishrush **38** 54 52N 6 32W
Inishtooskert I. **39** 52 10N 10 35W
Inishturk I. **38** 53 42N 10 8W
Inishvickillane **39** 52 3N 10 37W
Inistioge **39** 52 30N 7 5W
Injune **139** 25 46S 148 32E
Inkberrow **28** 52 13N 1 59W
Inklin **152** 58 56N 133 5W
Inklin, R. **152** 58 50N 133 10W
Inkom **160** 42 51N 112 7W
Inkpen Beacon **28** 51 22N 1 28W
Inle Aing **98** 20 30N 96 58E
Inn, R. **49** 48 35N 13 28E
Innamincka **139** 27 44S 140 46E
Innellan **34** 55 54N 4 58W
Inner Mongolia □ **106** 44 50N 117 40E
Inner Sound **36** 57 30N 5 55W
Innerleithen **35** 55 37N 3 4W
Innertkirchen **50** 46 43N 8 14E
Innetalling I. **150** 56 0N 79 0W
Innfield **38** 53 25N 6 50W
Inniscrone **38** 54 13N 69 0W
Innisfail, Austral. **138** 17 33S 146 5E
Innisfail, Can. **152** 52 0N 113 57W
Innishannon **39** 51 45N 8 40W
Inniskeen **38** 54 0N 6 35W
In'no-shima **110** 34 19N 133 10E
Innsbruck **52** 47 16N 11 23E
Ino **110** 33 33N 133 26E
Inocência **171** 19 47S 51 48W
Inongo **124** 1 35S 18 30E
Inosu **174** 12 22N 71 38W
Inoucdjouac (Port Harrison) **149** 58 27N 78 6W
Inowrocław **54** 52 50N 18 20E
Inpundong **107** 41 25N 126 34E
Inquisivi **174** 16 50S 66 45W
Ins **50** 47 1N 7 7E
Insch **37** 57 20N 2 39W
Inscription, C. **137** 25 29S 112 59E
Insein **98** 17 15N 96 0E
Însurăţei **70** 44 50N 27 40E
Intendente Alvear **172** 35 12S 63 32W
Interior **158** 43 46N 101 59W
Interlaken, Switz. **50** 46 41N 7 50E
Interlaken, U.S.A. **162** 42 37N 76 43W
International Falls **158** 48 36N 93 25W
Interview I. **101** 12 55N 92 42E
Inthanon, Mt. **101** 18 35N 98 29E
Intiyaco **172** 28 50S 60 0W
Intragna **51** 46 11N 8 42E
Inubō-Zaki **111** 35 42N 140 52E
Inútil, B. **176** 53 30S 70 15W
Inuvik **147** 68 16N 133 40W
Inuyama **111** 35 23N 136 56E
Inver B. **38** 54 35N 8 28W
Inverallochy **37** 57 40N 1 56W
Inveran, Ireland **39** 53 14N 9 28W
Inveran, U.K. **37** 57 58N 4 26W
Inveraray **34** 56 13N 5 5W
Inverbervie **37** 56 50N 2 17W
Invercargill **143** 46 24S 168 24E
Inverell **139** 29 45S 151 8E
Invergarry **37** 57 5N 4 48W
Invergordon **37** 57 41N 4 10W
Invergowrie **35** 56 29N 3 5W
Inverie **36** 57 2N 5 40W
Inverkeilor **37** 56 38N 2 33W
Inverkeithing **35** 56 2N 3 24W
Inverleigh **140** 38 6S 144 3E
Invermere **152** 50 30N 116 2W
Invermoriston **37** 57 13N 4 38W
Inverness, Can. **151** 46 15N 61 19W
Inverness, U.K. **37** 57 29N 4 12W
Inverness, U.S.A. **157** 28 50N 82 20W
Inverness (□) **26** 57 6N 4 40W
Invershiel **36** 57 13N 5 25W
Inverurie **37** 57 15N 2 21W
Inverway **136** 17 50S 129 38E
Investigator Group **136** 34 45S 134 20E
Investigator Str. **140** 35 30S 137 0E
Inyanga **127** 18 12S 32 40E
Inyangahi, mt. **127** 18 20S 32 20E
Inyantue **127** 18 30S 26 40E
Inyazura **127** 18 40S 31 40E
Inyo Range **161** 37 0N 118 0W
Inyokern **163** 35 37N 117 54W
Inywa **98** 22 4N 94 44E
Inza **81** 53 55N 46 25E
Inzell **49** 47 48N 12 15E
Inzer **84** 54 14N 57 34E
Inzhavino **81** 52 22N 42 23E
Ioánnina (Janinà) □ **68** 39 39N 20 57E
Iōhen **110** 32 58N 132 32E
Iola **159** 38 0N 95 20W
Ioma **135** 8 19S 147 52E
Ion Corvin **70** 44 7N 27 50E
Iona I. **34** 56 20N 6 25W
Ionava **80** 55 8N 24 12E
Ione, Calif., U.S.A. **163** 38 20N 121 0W
Ione, Wash., U.S.A. **160** 48 44N 117 29W
Ionia **156** 42 59N 85 7W
Ionian Is. = Ionioi Nisoi **69** 38 40N 20 0E
Ionian Sea **61** 37 30N 17 30E
Iónioi Nísoi **69** 38 40N 20 8E
Ioniškis **80** 56 13N 23 35E
Iori, R. **83** 41 12N 46 10E
Íos, I. **69** 36 41N 25 20E
Iowa □ **158** 42 18N 93 30W
Iowa City **158** 41 40N 91 35W
Iowa Falls **158** 42 30N 93 15W
Ipala **126** 4 30S 33 5E
Ipameri **171** 17 44S 48 9W
Ipanema **75** 9 48S 41 45W
Ipáti **69** 38 52N 22 14E
Ipatovo **83** 45 45N 42 50E
Ipel, R. **53** 48 10N 19 35E
Ipiales **174** 0 50N 77 37W
Ipiaú **171** 14 8S 39 44W
Ipin **108** 28 48N 104 33E
Ipinlang **108** 25 5N 101 58E
Ipirá **171** 12 10S 39 44W
Ipiros □ **68** 39 30N 20 30E
Ipixuna **174** 7 0S 71 40W
Ipoh **101** 4 35N 101 5E
Iporá **171** 16 28S 51 7W
Ippy **117** 6 5N 21 7E
Ipsárion Óros **68** 40 40N 24 40E
Ipswich, Austral. **139** 27 35S 152 46E
Ipswich, U.K. **29** 52 4N 1 9E
Ipswich, N.H., U.S.A. **162** 42 40N 70 50W
Ipswich, S.D., U.S.A. **158** 45 28N 99 20W
Ipu **170** 4 23S 40 44W
Ipueiras **170** 4 33S 40 43W
Ipupiara **171** 11 49S 42 37W
Iput, R. **80** 53 0N 32 10E
Iquique **174** 20 19S 70 5W
Iquitos **174** 3 45S 73 10W
Iracoubo **175** 5 30N 53 10W
Iráklia, I. **69** 36 50N 25 28E
Iráklion **69** 35 20N 25 12E
Iráklion □ **69** 35 10N 25 10E
Irako-Zaki **111** 34 35N 137 1E
Irala **173** 25 55S 54 35W
Iramba □ **126** 4 30S 34 30E
Iran ■ **93** 33 0N 53 0E
Iran, Pegunungan **102** 2 20N 114 50E
Iran, Plateau of **43** 33 00N 55 0E
Iranamadu Tank **97** 9 23N 80 29E
Iranshahr **93** 27 75N 60 40E
Irapa **174** 10 34N 62 35W
Irapuato **164** 20 40N 101 40W
Iraq ■ **92** 33 0N 44 0E
Irarrar, W. **118** 20 10N 1 30E
Irati **173** 25 25S 50 38W
Irbid **90** 32 35N 35 48E
Irbit **84** 57 41N 63 3E
Irchester **29** 52 17N 0 40W
Irebu **124** 0 40S 17 55E
Irecê **170** 11 18S 41 52W
Iregua, R. **58** 42 22N 2 24E
Ireland ■ **38** 53 0N 8 0W
Ireland's Eye **38** 53 25N 6 4W
Irele **121** 7 40N 5 40E
Iremel, Gora **84** 54 33N 58 50E
Iret **77** 60 10N 154 5E
Irgiz, Bol. **81** 52 10N 49 10E
Irharharene **119** 27 37N 7 30E
Irharrhar, O. **119** 27 30N 6 0E
Irhyangdong **107** 41 15N 129 30E
Iri **107** 35 59N 127 0E
Irian Jaya □ **103** 4 0S 137 0E
Iriba **124** 15 7N 22 15E
Irié **120** 8 15N 9 10W
Iriklinskiy **84** 51 39N 58 38E
Iringa **126** 7 48S 35 43E
Iringa □, Tanz. **126** 7 48S 35 43E
Iringa □, Tanz. **127** 9 0S 35 0E
Irinjalakuda **97** 10 21N 76 14E
Iriomote-Jima **112** 24 19N 123 48E
Iriona **166** 15 57N 85 11W
Irish Sea **32** 54 0N 5 0W
Irish Town **93** 40 55S 145 9E
Irkeshtam **85** 39 41N 73 55E
Irkutsk **77** 52 10N 104 20E
Irlam **32** 53 26N 2 27W
Irma **153** 52 55N 111 14W
Irmak **92** 39 58N 33 25E
Irō-Zaki **111** 34 36N 138 51E
Iroise **42** 48 15N 4 45W
Iron Baron **140** 33 3S 137 11E
Iron Gate = Porţile de Fier **70** 44 42N 22 30E
Iron Knob **140** 32 46S 137 8E
Iron, L. **38** 53 37N 7 34W
Iron Mountain **156** 45 49N 88 4W
Iron River **158** 46 6N 88 40W
Ironbridge **28** 52 38N 2 29W
Ironhurst **138** 18 5S 143 28E
Ironstone Kopje, Mt. **128** 25 17S 24 5E
Ironton, Mo., U.S.A. **159** 37 40N 90 40W
Ironton, Ohio, U.S.A. **156** 38 35N 82 40W
Ironwood **158** 46 30N 90 10W
Iroquois Falls **150** 48 46N 80 41W
Irpen **80** 50 30N 30 8E
Irrara Cr. **139** 29 35S 145 31E
Irrawaddy **98** 17 0N 95 0E
Irrawaddy □ **98** 17 0N 95 0E
Irrawaddy, R. **98** 15 50N 95 6E
Irsina **65** 40 45N 16 15E
Irt R. **32** 54 24N 3 25W
Irthing R. **35** 54 25N 2 48W
Irthlingborough **29** 52 20N 0 37W
Irtysh, R. **76** 53 36N 75 30E
Irumu **126** 1 32N 29 53E
Irún **58** 43 20N 1 52W
Irurzun **58** 42 55N 1 50W
Irvine, Can. **153** 49 57N 110 16W
Irvine, U.K. **34** 55 37N 4 40W
Irvine, U.S.A. **156** 37 42N 83 58W
Irvinestown **38** 54 28N 7 38W
Irwin, Pt. **137** 35 5S 116 55E
Irwin, R. **137** 29 15S 114 54E
Irymple **140** 34 14S 142 8E
Is-sur-Tille **43** 47 30N 5 10E
Isa **121** 13 14N 6 24E
Isaac, R. **138** 22 55S 149 20E
Isabel **158** 45 27N 101 22W
Isabela, Dom. Rep. **167** 19 58N 71 2W
Isabela, Pto Rico **147** 18 30N 67 01W
Isabela, Cord. **166** 13 30N 85 25W
Isabela, I. **164** 21 51N 105 55W
Isabella Ra. **136** 21 0S 121 4E
Ísafjarðardjúp **74** 66 10N 23 0W
Ísafjörður **74** 66 5N 23 9W
Isagarh **94** 24 48N 77 51E
Isahaya **110** 32 52N 130 2E
Isaka **126** 3 56S 32 59E
Isakly **84** 54 8N 51 32E
Isangi **124** 0 52N 24 10E
Isar, R. **49** 48 40N 12 30E
Isarco, R. **63** 46 40N 11 35E
Ísari **69** 37 22N 22 0E
Isbergues **43** 50 36N 2 24E
Isbiceni **70** 43 45N 24 40E
Ischia, I. **64** 40 45N 13 51E
Iscuandé **174** 2 28N 77 59W
Isdell, R. **136** 16 27S 124 51E
Ise **111** 34 25N 136 45E
Ise-Heiya **111** 34 40N 136 30E
Ise-Wan **111** 34 43N 136 43E
Isefjord **73** 55 53N 11 50E
Iseltwald **50** 46 43N 7 58E
Isenthal **51** 46 55N 8 34E
Iseo **62** 45 40N 10 3E
Iseo, L. di **62** 45 45N 10 3E
Iseramagazi **126** 4 37S 32 10E
Isère □ **45** 45 15N 5 40E
Isère, R. **44** 45 15N 5 30E
Iserlohn **48** 51 22N 7 40E
Isérnia **65** 41 35N 14 12E
Isesaki **111** 36 19N 139 12E
Iset, R. **84** 56 36N 66 24E
Iseyin **121** 8 0N 3 36E
Isfara **85** 40 7N 70 38E
Ishan **108** 24 30N 108 41E
Ishara **121** 6 40N 3 40E
Ishigaki **112** 24 20N 124 10E
Ishikari-Wan **112** 43 20N 141 20E
Ishikawa **112** 26 25N 127 48E
Ishikawa-ken □ **111** 36 30N 136 30E
Ishim **76** 56 10N 69 18E
Ishim, R. **76** 57 45N 71 10E
Ishimbay **84** 53 28N 56 2E
Ishinomaki **112** 38 32N 141 20E
Ishioka **111** 36 11N 140 16E
Ishizuchi-Yama **110** 33 45N 133 6E
Ishkashim **85** 36 44N 71 37E
Ishkuman **95** 36 30N 73 50E
Ishmi **68** 41 33N 19 34E
Ishpeming **156** 46 30N 87 40W
Ishua **121** 7 15N 5 50E
Ishui **107** 35 50N 118 32E
Ishurdi **98** 24 9N 89 3E
Isigny-sur-Mer **42** 49 19N 1 6W
Işik **82** 40 40N 32 35E
Isil Kul **76** 54 55N 71 16E
Isili **44** 39 45N 9 6E
Isiolo **126** 0 24N 37 33E
Isipingo **129** 30 00S 30 57E
Isipingo Beach **129** 30 00S 30 57E
Isiro **126** 2 53N 27 58E
Iskander **85** 41 36N 69 41E
İskenderun **92** 36 32N 36 10E
İskilip **82** 40 50N 34 20E
Iskut, R. **152** 56 45N 131 49W
Iskyr, R. **67** 43 35N 24 20E
Isla Cristina **57** 37 13N 7 17W
Isla, La **174** 6 51N 76 56W
Isla, R. **37** 56 32N 3 20W
Islamabad **94** 33 40N 73 0E
Islamkot **94** 24 42N 70 13E
Islampur **96** 17 2N 72 9E
Island Falls, Can. **150** 49 35N 81 20W
Island Falls, U.S.A. **151** 46 0N 68 25W
Island L. **153** 53 47N 94 25W
Island Lagoon **140** 31 30S 136 40E
Island Pt. **137** 30 20S 115 1E
Island Pond **156** 44 50N 71 50W
Island, R. **152** 60 25N 121 12W
Islands, B. of, Can. **151** 49 11N 58 15W
Islands, B. of, N.Z. **142** 35 20S 174 20E
Islay, I. **34** 55 46N 6 10W
Islay Sound **34** 55 45N 6 5W
Isle-Adam, L' **43** 49 6N 2 14E
Isle aux Morts **151** 47 35N 59 0W
Isle-Jourdain, L', Gers, France **44** 43 36N 1 5E
Isle-Jourdain, L', Vienne, France **42** 46 13N 0 31E
Isle, L', Tarn, France **44** 43 52N 1 49E
Isle, L', Vaucluse, France **45** 43 55N 5 3E
Isle of Whithorn **34** 54 42N 4 22W
Isle of Wight □ **28** 50 40N 1 20W
Isle Ornsay **36** 57 9N 5 50W
Isle Royale **158** 48 0N 88 50W
Isle-sur-la-Sorgue, L' **45** 43 55N 5 2E
Isle-sur-le-Doubs, L' **43** 47 26N 6 34E
Isle Vista **163** 34 27N 119 52W
Isleham **29** 52 21N 0 24E
Islet, L' **151** 47 4N 70 23W
Isleta **161** 34 58N 106 46W
Isleton **163** 38 10N 121 37W
Islip **28** 51 49N 1 12W
Ismail **82** 45 22N 28 46E
Ismâ'ilîya **122** 30 37N 32 18E
Ismay **158** 46 33N 104 44W
Isna **122** 25 17N 32 30E
Isogstalo **95** 34 15N 78 46E
Isola del Liri **64** 41 39N 13 32E
Isola della Scala **62** 45 16N 11 0E
Isola di Capo Rizzuto **65** 38 56N 17 5E
Isparta **92** 37 47N 30 30E
Isperikh **67** 43 43N 26 50E
Íspica **65** 36 47N 14 53E
Israel ■ **90** 32 0N 34 50E
Isseka **137** 28 22S 114 35E
Issia **120** 6 33N 6 33W
Issoire **44** 45 32N 3 15E
Issoudun **43** 46 57N 2 0E
Issyk-Kul, Ozero **85** 42 25N 77 15E
İstanbul **92** 41 0N 29 0E
Istmina **174** 5 10N 76 39W
Istok **66** 42 45N 20 24E
Istokpoga, L. **157** 27 22N 81 14W
Istra, U.S.S.R. **81** 55 55N 36 50E
Istra, Yugo. **63** 45 10N 14 0E
Istranca Dağlari **67** 41 48N 27 30E
Istres **45** 43 31N 4 59E
Istria = Istra **63** 45 10N 14 0E
Itá **172** 25 29N 57 21W
Itabaiana, Paraíba, Brazil **170** 7 18S 35 19W
Itabaiana, Sergipe, Brazil **170** 10 41S 37 26W
Itabaianinha **170** 11 16S 37 47W
Itaberaba **171** 12 32S 40 18W
Itaberai **171** 16 2S 49 48W
Itabira **171** 19 37S 43 13W
Itabirito **173** 20 15S 43 48W
Itabuna **171** 14 48S 39 16W
Itacaiunas, R. **170** 5 21S 49 8W
Itacajá **170** 8 19S 47 46W
Itaete **171** 13 0S 41 5W
Itaguaçu **171** 19 48S 40 51W
Itaguari, R. **171** 14 11S 44 40W
Itaguatins **170** 5 47S 47 29W
Itaim, R. **170** 7 2S 42 2W
Itainópolis **170** 7 24S 41 31W
Itaituba **175** 4 10S 55 50W
Itajaí **173** 27 0S 48 45W
Itajubá **173** 22 24S 45 30W
Itajuipe **171** 14 41S 39 22W
Itaka **127** 8 50S 32 49E
Itako **111** 35 56N 140 33E
Italy ■ **60** 42 0N 13 0E
Itamataré **170** 2 16S 46 24W
Itambacuri **171** 18 1S 41 42W
Itambé **171** 15 15S 40 37W
Itambe, mt. **170** 18 30S 43 15W
Itampolo **129** 24 41S 43 57E
Itanhaém **121** 24 9S 46 47W
Itanhém **171** 17 9S 40 20W
Itano **110** 34 1N 134 28E
Itapaci **171** 14 57S 49 34W
Itapagé **170** 3 41S 39 34W
Itaparica, I. de **171** 12 54S 38 42W
Itapebi **171** 15 56S 39 32W
Itapecerica **171** 20 28S 45 7W
Itapecuru-Mirim **170** 3 24S 44 20W
Itapecuru, R. **170** 3 20S 44 15W
Itaperuna **171** 21 10S 42 0W
Itapetinga **171** 15 15S 40 15W
Itapetininga **173** 23 36S 48 7W
Itapeva **173** 23 59S 48 59W
Itapicuru **170** 10 50S 38 40W
Itapicuru, R. **170** 5 40S 44 30W
Itapipoca **170** 3 30S 39 35W
Itapiúna **170** 4 30S 38 57W
Itaporanga **171** 7 18S 38 10W
Itapuá □ **173** 26 40S 55 40W
Itapuranga **171** 15 35S 49 59W
Itaquari **173** 20 12S 40 25W
Itaquatiana **174** 2 58S 58 30W
Itaquí **172** 29 0S 56 30W
Itararé **173** 24 6S 49 23W
Itarsi **94** 22 36N 77 51E
Itarumã **171** 18 42S 51 25W
Itati **172** 27 16S 58 15W
Itatira **170** 4 30S 39 37W
Itatuba **174** 5 40S 63 20W
Itaueira **170** 7 36S 43 2W

Itaueira, R Jedrzejów

Itaueira, R. 170 6 41 S 42 55W
Itaúna 171 20 4 S 44 34W
Itchen, R. 28 50 57N 1 20W
Itéa 69 38 25N 22 25 E
Ithaca 162 42 25N 76 30W
Ithaca = Itháki 69 38 25N 20 43 E
Itháki, I. 69 38 25N 20 40 E
Ithon R. 31 52 16N 3 23W
It'iaoshan 106 37 10N 104 2 E
Itinga 171 16 36 S 41 47W
Itiruçu 171 13 31 S 40 9W
Itiúba 171 10 43 S 39 51W
Ito 111 34 58N 139 5 E
Itonamas, R. 174 13 0 S 64 25W
Itsa 122 29 15N 30 40 E
Itsukaichi 110 34 22N 132 8 E
Itsuki 110 32 24N 130 50 E
Itteville 46 48 31N 2 21 E
Ittiri 64 40 38N 8 32 E
Itu, Brazil 173 23 10 S 47 15W
Itu, Hupeh, China 109 30 24N 111 26 E
Itu, Shantung, China 107 36 41N 118 28 E
Itu, Nigeria 121 5 10N 7 58 E
Ituaçu 171 13 50 S 41 18W
Ituango 174 7 4N 75 45W
Ituiutaba 171 19 0 S 49 25W
Itumbiara 171 18 20 S 49 10W
Ituna 153 51 10N 103 30W
It'ung 107 43 20N 125 17 E
Itunge Port 127 9 40 S 33 55 E
Itupiranga 170 5 9 S 49 20W
Iturama 171 19 44 S 50 11W
Iturbe 172 23 0 S 65 25W
Ituri, R. 126 1 45N 26 45 E
Iturup, Ostrov 77 45 0N 148 0 E
Ituverava 171 20 20 S 47 47W
Ituyuro, R. 172 22 40 S 63 50W
Itzehoe 48 53 56N 9 31 E
Ivalo 74 68 38N 27 35 E
Ivalojoki 74 68 30N 27 0 E
Ivanaj 68 42 17N 19 25 E
Ivanhoe, N.S.W., Austral. 140 32 56 S 144 20 E
Ivanhoe, N.T., Austral. 136 15 41 S 128 41 E
Ivanhoe, U.S.A. 163 36 23N 119 13W
Ivanhoe L. 153 60 25N 106 30W
Ivanió Grad 63 45 41N 16 25 E
Ivanjica 66 43 35N 20 12 E
Ivanjscie 63 46 12N 16 13 E
Ivankovskoye Vdkhr. 81 56 48N 36 55 E
Ivano-Frankovsk, (Stanislav) 80 49 0N 24 40 E
Ivanovka 84 52 34N 53 23 E
Ivanovo, Byelorussia, U.S.S.R. 80 52 7N 25 29 E
Ivanovo, R.S.F.S.R., U.S.S.R. 81 57 5N 41 0 E
Ivato 129 20 37 S 47 10 E
Ivaylovgrad 67 41 32N 26 8 E
Ivinghoe 29 51 50N 0 38W
Ivinheima, R. 173 21 48 S 54 15W
Iviza = Ibiza 59 39 0N 1 30 E
Ivohibe 129 22 31 S 46 57 E
Ivolândia 171 16 34 S 50 51W
Ivory Coast ■ 120 7 30N 5 0W
Ivösjön 73 56 8N 14 25 E
Ivrea 62 45 30N 7 52 E
Ivugivik, (N.D. d'Ivugivic) 149 62 24N 77 55W
Ivybridge 30 50 24N 3 56W
Iwahig 102 8 35N 117 32 E
Iwai-Jima 110 33 47N 131 58 E
Iwaki 112 37 3N 140 55 E
Iwakuni 110 34 15N 132 8 E
Iwami 110 35 32N 134 15 E
Iwamisawa 112 43 12N 141 46 E
Iwanai 112 42 58N 140 30 E
Iwanuma 112 38 7N 140 58 E
Iwase 110 36 21N 140 6 E
Iwata 111 34 49N 137 59 E
Iwate-ken □ 112 39 30N 141 30 E
Iwate-San 112 39 51N 141 0 E
Iwo 121 7 39N 4 9 E
Iwonicz-Zdroj 54 49 37N 21 47 E
Ixiamas 174 13 50 S 68 5W
Ixopo 129 30 11 S 30 5 E
Ixtepec 165 16 40N 95 10W
Ixtlán de Juárez 165 17 23N 96 28W
Ixtlán del Rio 164 21 5N 104 28W
Ixworth 29 52 18N 0 50 E
Iyang, Honan, China 106 34 9N 112 25 E
Iyang, Hunan, China 109 28 36N 112 20 E
Iyang, Kiangsi, China 109 28 23N 117 25 E
Iyo 110 33 45N 132 45 E
Iyo-mishima 110 33 58N 133 30 E
Iyo-Nada 110 33 40N 132 20 E
Izabal, L. 166 15 30N 89 10W
Izamal 165 20 56N 89 1W
Izberbash 83 42 35N 47 45 E
Izbica Kujawski 54 52 25N 18 30 E
Izegem 47 50 55N 3 12 E
Izgrev 67 43 36N 26 58 E
Izh, R. 84 55 58N 52 38 E
Izhevsk 84 56 51N 53 14 E
Izmail 82 45 22N 28 46 E
Izmir (Smyrna) 79 38 25N 27 8E
Izmit 92 40 45N 29 50E
Izola 63 45 32N 13 39 E
Izu-Hantō 111 34 45N 139 0 E
Izuhara 110 34 12N 129 17 E
Izumi 110 32 5N 130 22 E
Izumiotsu 111 34 30N 135 24 E
Izumisano 111 34 40N 135 43 E
Izumo 110 35 20N 132 55 E
Izyaslav 80 50 5N 25 50 E
Izyum 82 49 12N 37 28 E

J

Jaba 123 6 20N 35 7 E
Jaba' 90 32 20N 35 13 E
Jabaliya 90 31 32N 34 27 E
Jabalón, R. 59 38 45N 3 35W
Jabalpur 95 23 9N 79 58 E
Jablah 92 35 20N 36 0 E
Jablanac 63 44 42N 14 56 E
Jablonec 52 50 43N 15 10 E
Jablonica 53 48 37N 17 26 E
Jabłonowo 54 53 23N 19 10 E
Jaboatão 170 8 7 S 35 1W
Jaboticabal 173 21 15 S 48 17W
Jabukovac 66 44 22N 22 21 E
Jaburu 174 5 30 S 64 0W
Jaca 58 42 35N 0 33W
Jacala 165 21 1N 99 11W
Jacaré, R. 170 10 3 S 42 13W
Jacareí 173 23 20 S 46 0W
Jacarèzinho 173 23 5 S 50 0W
Jáchal 172 30 5 S 69 0W
Jáchymov 52 50 22N 12 55 E
Jacinto 171 16 10 S 40 17W
Jack Lane B. 151 55 45N 60 35W
Jackfish 150 48 45N 87 0W
Jackman 151 45 35N 70 17W
Jacksboro 159 33 14N 98 15W
Jackson, Austral. 139 26 39 S 149 39 E
Jackson, Ala., U.S.A. 157 31 32N 87 53W
Jackson, Calif., U.S.A. 159 37 25N 89 42W
Jackson, Ill., U.S.A. 163 38 25N 120 47W
Jackson, Ky., U.S.A. 156 37 35N 83 22W
Jackson, Mich., U.S.A. 156 42 18N 84 25W
Jackson, Minn., U.S.A. 158 43 35N 95 30W
Jackson, Miss., U.S.A. 159 32 20N 90 10W
Jackson, Ohio, U.S.A. 156 39 0N 82 40W
Jackson, Tenn., U.S.A. 157 35 40N 88 50W
Jackson, Wyo., U.S.A. 160 43 30N 110 49W
Jackson Bay, Can. 152 50 32N 125 57W
Jackson Bay, N.Z. 143 43 58 S 168 42 E
Jackson, C. 143 40 59 S 174 20 E
Jackson, L. 160 43 55N 110 40W
Jacksons 143 42 46 S 171 32 E
Jacksonville, Ala., U.S.A. 157 33 49N 85 45W
Jacksonville, Calif., U.S.A. 163 37 52N 120 24W
Jacksonville, Fla., U.S.A. 157 30 15N 81 38W
Jacksonville, Ill., U.S.A. 158 39 42N 90 15W
Jacksonville, N.C., U.S.A. 157 34 50N 77 29W
Jacksonville, Oreg., U.S.A. 160 42 13N 122 56W
Jacksonville, Tex., U.S.A. 159 31 58N 95 12W
Jacksonville Beach 157 30 19N 81 26W
Jacmel 167 18 20N 72 40W
Jacob Lake 161 36 45N 112 12W
Jacobabad 94 28 20N 68 29 E
Jacobeni 70 47 25N 25 20 E
Jacobina 170 11 11 S 40 30W
Jacob's Well 90 32 13N 35 13 E
Jacques Cartier, Mt. 151 48 57N 66 0W
Jacques Cartier Pass 151 49 50N 62 30W
Jacqueville 120 5 12N 4 25W
Jacuí, R. 173 30 2 S 51 15W
Jacuipe, R. 171 12 30 S 39 5W
Jacundá, R. 170 1 57 S 50 26W
Jade 48 53 22N 8 14 E
Jadebusen, B. 48 53 30N 8 15 E
Jadoigne 47 50 43N 4 52 E
Jadotville = Likasi 127 10 55 S 26 48 E
Jadovnik 66 43 20N 19 45 E
Jadraque 58 40 55N 2 55W
Jādū 119 32 0N 12 0 E
Jaén, Peru 174 5 25 S 78 40W
Jaén, Spain 57 37 44N 3 43W
Jaén □ 57 37 50N 3 30W
Jafène 118 20 35N 5 30W
Jaffa = Tel Aviv-Yafo 90 32 4N 34 48 E
Jaffa, C. 140 36 58 S 139 40 E
Jaffna 97 9 45N 80 2 E
Jaffrey 162 42 50N 72 4W
Jagadhri 94 30 10N 77 20 E
Jagadishpur 95 25 30N 84 21 E
Jagdalpur 96 19 3N 82 6 E
Jagersfontein 128 29 44 S 25 27 E
Jaghbub 117 29 42N 24 38 E
Jagraon 93 30 50N 75 25 E
Jagst, R. 49 49 13N 10 0 E
Jagtial 96 18 50N 79 0 E
Jaguaquara 171 13 32 S 39 58W
Jaguariaíva 173 24 10 S 49 50W
Jaguaribe 170 5 53 S 38 37W
Jaguaribe, R. 170 6 0 S 38 35W
Jaguaruana 170 4 50 S 37 47W
Jagüey 166 22 35N 81 7W
Jagungal, Mt. 141 36 8 S 148 22 E
Jahangirabad 94 28 19N 78 4 E
Jahrom 92 28 30N 53 31 E
Jaicós 170 7 21 S 41 8W
Jainti 98 26 45N 89 40 E
Jaintiapur 98 25 8N 92 7 E
Jaipur 94 27 0N 76 10 E
Jajarm 93 37 5N 56 20 E
Jajce 66 44 19N 17 17 E
Jajere 121 11 58N 11 25 E
Jajpur 96 20 53N 86 22 E
Jakarta 103 6 9 S 106 49 E
Jakobstad (Pietarsaari) 74 63 40N 22 43 E
Jakupica 66 41 45N 21 22 E
Jal 159 32 8N 103 8W
Jala 93 27 30N 62 40 E
Jalalabad, Afghan. 94 34 30N 70 29 E
Jalalabad, India 95 26 41N 79 42 E
Jalalpur Jattan 94 32 38N 74 19 E
Jalama 163 34 29N 120 29W
Jalapa, Guat. 166 14 45N 89 59W
Jalapa, Mexico 165 19 30N 96 50W
Jalas, Jabal al 92 27 30N 36 30 E
Jalaun 95 26 8N 79 25 E
Jales 171 20 16 S 50 33W
Jaleswar 95 26 38N 85 48 E
Jalgaon, Maharashtra, India 96 21 2N 76 31 E
Jalgaon, Maharashtra, India 96 21 0N 75 42 E
Jalhay 47 50 33N 5 58 E
Jalingo 121 8 55N 11 25 E
Jalisco □ 164 20 0N 104 0W
Jalkot 95 35 20N 73 24 E
Jallas, R. 56 42 57N 9 0W
Jallumba 140 36 55N 141 57 E
Jalna 96 19 48N 75 57 E
Jalón, R. 58 41 20N 1 40W
Jalpa 164 21 38N 102 58W
Jalpaiguri 98 26 32N 88 46 E
Jalq 93 27 35N 62 33 E
Jaluit I. 130 6 0N 169 30 E
Jamaari 121 11 44N 9 53 E
Jamaica, I. ■ 166 18 10N 77 30W
Jamalpur, Bangla. 98 24 52N 90 2 E
Jamalpur, India 95 25 18N 86 28 E
Jamalpurganj 95 23 2N 88 1 E
Jamanxim, R. 175 6 30 S 55 50W
Jambe 103 1 15 S 132 10 E
Jambes 47 50 27N 4 52 E
Jambi 102 1 38 S 103 30 E
Jambusar 94 22 3N 72 51 E
Jamdena, I. = Yamdena 103 7 45 S 131 20 E
James B. 150 53 30N 80 0W
James, R., Dak., U.S.A. 158 44 50N 98 0W
James, R., Va., U.S.A. 162 37 0N 76 27W
James Ranges 136 24 10 S 132 0 E
James Ross I. 13 63 58 S 50 94W
Jamestown, Austral. 140 33 10 S 138 32 E
Jamestown, S. Afr. 128 31 6 S 26 45 E
Jamestown, Ky., U.S.A. 156 37 0N 85 5W
Jamestown, N.D., U.S.A. 158 47 0N 98 30W
Jamestown, N.Y., U.S.A. 156 42 5N 79 18W
Jamestown, Tenn., U.S.A. 157 36 25N 85 0W
Jamestown, Va., U.S.A. 162 37 12N 76 46W
Jamiltepec 165 16 17N 97 49W
Jamkhandi 97 16 30N 75 15 E
Jamma'in 90 32 8N 35 12 E
Jammalamadugu 97 14 51N 78 25 E
Jammerbugt 73 57 15N 9 20 E
Jammu 94 32 43N 74 54 E
Jammu & Kashmir □ 95 34 25N 77 0 E
Jamnagar 94 22 30N 70 0 E
Jamner 96 20 45N 75 45 E
Jamoigne 47 49 41N 5 24 E
Jampur 94 29 39N 70 32 E
Jamrud 94 34 2N 71 24 E
Jamshedpur 95 22 44N 86 20 E
Jamtara 95 23 59N 86 41 E
Jämtlands län □ 72 62 40N 13 50 E
Jamuna, R. 98 23 51N 89 45 E
Jamurki 98 24 9N 90 2 E
Jan Kemp 128 27 55 S 24 51 E
Jan L. 153 54 56N 102 55W
Jan Mayen Is. 12 71 0N 11 0W
Janaúba 171 15 48 S 43 19W
Janaucu, I. 170 0 30N 50 10W
Jand 94 33 30N 72 0 E
Janda, Laguna de la 57 36 15N 5 45W
Jandaia 171 17 6 S 50 7W
Jandaq 92 34 3N 54 22 E
Jandola 94 32 20N 70 9 E
Jandowae 139 26 45 S 151 7 E
Jandrain-Jandrenouilles 47 50 40N 4 58 E
Jándula, R. 57 38 25N 3 55W
Jane Pk. 142 45 15 S 168 20 E
Janesville 158 42 39N 89 1W
Janga 121 10 5N 1 0W
Jangaon 96 17 44N 79 5 E
Janhtang Ga 98 26 32N 96 38 E
Jani Khel 93 32 45N 68 25 E
Janja 66 44 40N 19 17 E
Janjevo 66 42 35N 21 19 E
Janjina 66 42 58N 17 25 E
Janos 164 30 45N 108 10W
Jánoshalma 53 46 18N 19 21 E
Jánosháza 53 47 8N 17 12 E
Jánossomorja 53 47 47N 17 11 E
Janów 54 50 43N 22 30 E
Janów Lubelski 54 50 48N 22 23 E
Janów Podlaski 54 52 11N 23 11 E
Janowiec Wlkp. 54 52 45N 17 30 E
Januária 171 15 25 S 44 25W
Janub Dârfûr □ 123 11 0N 25 0 E
Janub Kordofân □ 123 12 0N 30 0 E
Janville 43 48 10N 1 50 E
Janzé 42 47 55N 1 28W
Jaop'ing 109 23 43N 117 0 E
Jaora 94 23 40N 75 10 E
Jaoyang 106 38 14N 115 44 E
Japan ■ 112 36 0N 136 0 E
Japan, Sea of 112 40 0N 135 0 E
Japan Trench 142 28 0N 145 0 E
Japara 103 6 30 S 110 40 E
Japen, I. = Yapen 103 1 50 S 136 0 E
Japero 103 4 59 S 137 11 E
Japurá 174 1 48 S 66 30W
Japurá, R. 174 3 8 S 64 46W
Jaque 174 7 27N 78 15W
Jaques Cartier, Détroit de 151 50 0N 63 30W
Jara, La 161 37 16N 106 0W
Jaraguá 171 15 45 S 49 20W
Jaraicejo 57 39 40N 5 49W
Jaraiz 56 40 4N 5 45W
Jarales 161 34 44N 106 51W
Jarama, R. 58 40 50N 3 20W
Jarandilla 56 40 8N 5 39W
Jaranwala 94 31 15N 73 20 E
Jarash 90 32 17N 35 54 E
Järbo 72 60 42N 16 38 E
Jarbridge 160 41 56N 115 27W
Jardim 172 21 28 S 56 9W
Jardin, R. 59 38 50N 2 10W
Jardines de la Reina, Is. 166 20 50N 78 50W
Jargalant = Hovd 105 48 1N 91 38 E
Jargeau 43 47 50N 2 7 E
Jarmen 48 53 56N 13 20 E
Järna, Kopp., Sweden 72 60 33N 14 26 E
Järna, Stockholm, Sweden 72 59 7N 17 35 E
Jarnac 44 45 40N 0 11W
Jarny 43 49 9N 5 53 E
Jarocin 54 51 59N 17 29 E
Jaroměr 52 50 22N 15 52 E
Jarosław 54 50 2N 22 42 E
Järpås 73 58 23N 12 57 E
Järpås 73 58 23N 12 57 E
Järpen 72 63 21N 13 26 E
Jarrahdale 137 32 24 S 116 5 E
Jarres, Plaine des 100 19 27N 103 10 E
Jarrow 35 54 58N 1 28W
Jarso 123 5 15N 37 30 E
Järved 72 63 16N 18 43 E
Jarvis I. 131 0 15 S 159 55W
Jarvornik 53 50 23N 17 2 E
Jarwa 95 27 45N 82 30 E
Jaša Tomić 66 45 26N 20 50 E
Jasien 54 51 46N 15 0 E
Jasin 101 2 20N 102 26 E
Jāsk 93 25 38N 57 45 E
Jasło 54 49 45N 21 30 E
Jasper, Can. 152 52 55N 118 5W
Jasper, Ala., U.S.A. 157 33 48N 87 16W
Jasper, Ark., U.S.A. 97 36 0N 93 10W
Jasper, Fla., U.S.A. 157 30 31N 82 58W
Jasper, La., U.S.A. 159 30 59N 93 58W
Jasper, S.D., U.S.A. 158 43 52N 96 22W
Jasper Nat. Park 152 52 50N 118 8W
Jasper Place 152 53 33N 113 25W
Jastrebarsko 63 45 41N 15 39 E
Jastrowie 54 53 26N 16 49 E
Jastrzebie Zdroj 54 49 57N 18 35 E
Jászapáti 53 47 32N 20 10 E
Jászárokszállás 53 47 39N 20 1 E
Jászberény 53 47 30N 19 55 E
Jászkiser 53 47 27N 20 20 E
Jászladány 53 47 23N 20 18 E
Jatai 171 17 50 S 51 45W
Jati 94 24 27N 68 19 E
Jatibarang 103 6 28 S 108 18 E
Jatinegara 103 6 13 S 106 52 E
Játiva 59 39 0N 0 32W
Jatobal 170 4 35 S 49 33W
Jatt 90 32 24N 35 2 E
Jaú 173 22 10 S 48 30W
Jau al Milah 91 15 15N 45 40 E
Jauche 47 50 41N 4 57 E
Jauja 174 11 45 S 75 30W
Jaunelgava 80 56 35N 25 0 E
Jaunpur 95 25 46N 82 44 E
Java = Jawa 103 7 0 S 110 0 E
Java Sea 102 4 35 S 107 15 E
Javadi Hills 97 12 40N 78 40 E
Jávea 59 38 48N 0 10 E
Javhlant = Ulyasutay 105 47 45N 96 49 E
Javla 96 17 18N 75 9 E
Javron 42 48 25N 0 25W
Jawa 103 7 0 S 110 0 E
Jawor 54 51 4N 16 11 E
Jaworzno 54 50 13N 19 22 E
Jay 159 33 17N 94 46W
Jayawijaya, Pengunungan 103 7 0 S 139 0 E
Jaydot 153 49 15N 110 15W
Jaynagar 99 26 43N 86 9 E
Jayton 159 33 17N 100 35W
Jazminal 164 24 56N 101 25W
Jean 161 35 47N 115 20W
Jean Marie River 152 61 32N 120 38W
Jean Rabel 167 19 50N 73 30W
Jeanerette 159 29 52N 91 38W
Jebba, Moroc. 118 35 11N 4 43W
Jebba, Nigeria 121 9 9N 4 48 E
Jebel 66 40 35N 21 15 E
Jebel Aulia 123 15 10N 32 31 E
Jebel Qerri 123 16 16N 32 50 E
Jedburgh 35 55 28N 2 33W
Jedlicze 54 49 43N 21 40 E
Jedlnia-Letnisko 54 51 25N 21 15 E
Jedrzejów 54 50 35N 20 15 E

Jedway Kaboudia, Rass

Jedway	152	52 17N	131 14W
Jeetze, R.	48	52 58N	11 6E
Jefferson, Iowa, U.S.A.	158	42 3N	94 25W
Jefferson, Tex., U.S.A.	159	32 45N	94 23W
Jefferson, Wis., U.S.A.	158	43 0N	88 49W
Jefferson City	157	36 8N	83 30W
Jefferson, Mt., Calif., U.S.A.	163	38 51N	117 0W
Jefferson, Mt., Oreg., U.S.A.	160	44 45N	121 50W
Jeffersonville	156	38 20N	85 42W
Jega	121	12 15N	4 23E
Jekabpils	80	56 29N	25 57E
Jelenia Góra	54	50 50N	15 45E
Jelenia Góra □	54	51 0N	15 30E
Jelgava	80	56 41N	22 49E
Jelica	66	43 50N	20 17E
Jelli	123	5 25N	31 45E
Jellicoe	150	49 40N	87 30W
Jelšava	53	48 37N	20 15E
Jemaja	103	3 5N	105 45E
Jemaluang	101	2 16N	103 52E
Jemappes	47	50 27N	3 54E
Jember	103	8 11S	113 41E
Jembongan, I.	102	6 45N	117 20E
Jemmapes = Azzaba	119	36 48N	7 6E
Jemnice	52	49 1N	15 34E
Jena, Ger.	48	50 56N	11 33E
Jena, U.S.A.	159	31 41N	92 7W
Jench'iu	106	38 43N	116 5E
Jendouba	119	36 29N	8 47E
Jenhochieh	108	26 29N	101 45E
Jenhsien	106	37 8N	114 37E
Jenhua	109	25 5N	113 45E
Jenhuai	108	27 53N	106 17E
Jenin	90	32 28N	35 18E
Jenkins	156	37 13N	82 41W
Jennings	159	30 10N	92 45W
Jennings, R.	152	59 38N	132 5W
Jenny	73	57 47N	16 35E
Jeparit	140	36 8S	142 1E
Jequié	171	13 51S	40 5W
Jequitaí, R.	171	17 4S	44 50W
Jequitinhonha	171	16 30S	41 0W
Jequitinhonha, R.	171	15 51S	38 53W
Jerada	118	34 40N	2 10W
Jerantut	101	3 56N	102 22E
Jérémie	167	18 40N	74 10W
Jeremoabo	170	10 4S	38 21W
Jerez de García Salinas	164	22 39N	103 0W
Jerez de la Frontera	57	36 41N	6 7W
Jerez de los Caballeros	57	38 20N	6 45W
Jerez, Punta	165	22 58N	97 40W
Jericho	138	23 38S	146 6E
Jericho = El Arīhā	90	31 52N	35 27E
Jerichow	48	52 30N	12 2E
Jerilderie	141	35 20S	145 41E
Jermyn	162	41 31N	75 31W
Jerome	161	34 50N	112 0W
Jersey City	162	40 41N	74 8W
Jersey, I.	42	49 13N	2 7W
Jersey Shore	156	41 17N	77 18W
Jerseyville	158	39 5N	90 20W
Jerumenha	171	7 5S	43 30W
Jerusalem	90	31 47N	35 10E
Jervaulx	33	54 19N	1 41W
Jervis B.	141	35 8S	150 46E
Jervis, C.	139	35 38S	138 6E
Jesenice	63	46 28N	14 3E
Jesenik	53	50 0N	17 8E
Jesenik (Frývaldov)	53	50 15N	17 11E
Jesenske	53	48 20N	20 10E
Jesselton = Kota Kinabalu	102	6 0N	116 12E
Jessnitz	48	51 42N	12 19E
Jessore	98	23 10N	89 10E
Jesup	157	31 30N	82 0W
Jesús Carranza	165	17 28N	95 1W
Jesús María	172	30 59S	64 5W
Jetmore	159	38 10N	99 57W
Jetpur	94	21 45N	70 10E
Jette	47	50 53N	4 20E
Jevnaker	71	60 15N	10 26E
Jewett	159	31 20N	96 8W
Jewett City	162	41 36N	72 0W
Jeypore	96	18 50N	82 38E
Jeziorany	54	53 58N	20 46E
J.F. Rodrigues	170	2 55S	50 20W
Jhajjar	94	28 37N	76 14E
Jhal Jhao	93	26 20N	65 35E
Jhalakati	98	22 39N	90 12E
Jhalawar	94	24 35N	76 10E
Jhang Maghiana	94	31 15N	72 15E
Jhansi	95	25 30N	78 36E
Jharia	95	23 45N	86 18E
Jharsaguda	99	21 50N	84 5E
Jharsuguda	96	21 50N	84 5E
Jhelum	94	33 0N	73 45E
Jhelum, R.	95	31 50N	72 10E
Jhunjhunu	94	28 10N	75 20E
Jiangshan	95	28 45N	118 37E
Jibão, Serra do	171	14 48S	45 0W
Jibiya	121	13 5N	7 12E
Jibou	70	47 15N	23 17E
Jicín	52	50 25N	15 20E
Jicarón, I.	166	7 10N	81 50W
Jiddah	92	21 29N	39 16E
Jido	99	29 2N	94 58E
Jifna	90	31 58N	35 13E
Jiggalong	136	23 24S	120 47E
Jihk'atse	107	29 15N	88 53E
Jihlava	52	49 28N	15 35E
Jihočeský □	52	49 8N	14 35E
Jihomoravský □	53	49 5N	16 30E
Jiht'u	105	33 27N	79 42E
Jijiga	91	9 20N	42 50E
Jijona	59	38 34N	0 30W
Jikamshi	121	12 12N	7 45E
Jiloca, R.	58	41 0N	1 20W
Jilové	52	49 52N	14 29E
Jim Jim Cr.	136	12 50S	132 32E
Jima	123	7 40N	36 55E
Jimbolia	66	45 47N	20 57E
Jimena de la Frontera	57	36 27N	5 24W
Jimenbuen	141	36 42S	148 53E
Jiménez	164	27 10N	105 0W
Jind	94	29 19N	76 16E
Jindabyne	141	36 25S	148 35E
Jindrichuv Hradeç	52	49 10N	15 2E
Jinja	126	0 25N	33 12E
Jinjang	101	3 13N	101 39E
Jinjini	120	7 20N	3 42W
Jinnah Barrage	93	32 58N	71 33E
Jinotega	166	13 6N	85 59W
Jinotepe	166	11 50N	86 10W
Jiparaná (Machado), R.	174	8 45S	62 20W
Jipijapa	174	1 0S	80 40W
Jiquilpán	164	19 57N	102 42W
Jisresh Shughur	92	35 49N	36 18E
Jitarning	137	32 48S	117 57E
Jitra	101	6 16N	100 25E
Jiu, R.	70	44 50N	23 20E
Jiuchin	109	25 53N	116 0E
Jiuli	108	24 6N	97 54E
Jizera, R.	52	50 21N	14 48E
Jizl Wadi	122	26 30N	38 0E
Jizō-zaki	110	35 34N	133 20E
Joaçaba	173	27 5S	51 31W
Joaima	171	16 39S	41 2W
João	170	2 46S	50 59W
João Amaro	171	12 46S	40 22W
João Câmara	170	5 32S	35 48W
João de Almeida	125	15 10S	13 50E
João Pessoa	170	7 10S	34 52W
João Pinheiro	171	17 45S	46 10W
Joaquim Távora	171	23 30S	49 58W
Joaquín V. González	172	25 10S	64 0W
Jobourg, Nez de	42	49 41N	1 57W
Joch'iang	105	39 2N	88 0E
Jódar	59	37 50N	3 21W
Jodhpur	94	26 23N	73 2E
Joe Batt's Arm	151	49 44N	54 10W
Joensuu	78	62 37N	29 49E
Joeuf	43	49 12N	6 1E
Jofane	125	21 15S	34 18E
Joggins	151	45 42N	64 27W
Jogjakarta = Yogyakarta	103	7 49S	110 22E
Jõhana	111	36 37N	136 57E
Johannesburg, S. Afr.	129	26 10S	28 8E
Johannesburg, U.S.A.	163	35 22N	117 38W
Johannisnäs	72	62 45N	16 15E
Johansfors, Halland, Sweden	73	56 50N	12 58E
Johansfors, Kronoberg, Sweden	73	56 42N	15 32E
John Days, R.	160	45 0N	120 0W
John o' Groats	37	58 39N	3 3W
Johnshaven	37	56 48N	2 20W
Johnson	159	37 35N	101 48W
Johnson City, N.Y., U.S.A.	162	42 7N	75 57W
Johnson City, Tenn., U.S.A.	157	36 18N	82 21W
Johnson City, Tex., U.S.A.	159	30 15N	98 24W
Johnson Cy.	156	42 9N	67 0W
Johnson Ra.	137	29 40S	119 15E
Johnsondale	163	35 58N	118 32W
Johnsons Crossing	152	60 29N	133 18W
Johnsonville	142	41 13S	174 48E
Johnston	31	51 45N	5 5W
Johnston Falls = Mambilima Falls	127	10 31S	28 45E
Johnston I.	131	17 10N	169 8E
Johnston Lakes	137	32 20S	120 45E
Johnston Ra.	137	29 40S	119 20E
Johnstone	34	55 50N	4 31W
Johnstone Str.	152	50 28N	126 0W
Johnstown, Ireland	39	52 46N	7 34W
Johnstown, N.Y., U.S.A.	162	43 1N	74 20W
Johnstown, Pa., U.S.A.	156	40 19N	78 53W
Johnstown Bridge	38	53 23N	6 53W
Johor □	101	2 5N	103 20E
Johor Baharu	101	1 28N	103 46E
Johor, S.	101	1 45N	103 47E
Joigny	43	48 0N	3 20E
Joinvile	173	26 15S	48 55E
Joinville	43	48 27N	5 10E
Joinville I.	13	63 15S	55 30W
Jojutla	165	18 37N	99 11W
Jokkmokk	74	66 35N	19 50E
Jökulsá á Brú	74	65 40N	14 16W
Jökulsá Fjöllum	74	65 30N	16 15W
Jökulsa R.	74	65 30N	16 15W
Jolan	163	35 58N	121 9W
Joliet	156	41 30N	88 0W
Joliette	150	46 3N	73 24W
Jolo I.	103	6 0N	121 0E
Jome, I.	103	1 16S	127 30E
Jönåker	73	58 44N	16 40E
Jönaker	73	58 44N	16 43E
Jones C.	150	54 33N	79 35W
Jones Sound	12	76 0N	89 0W
Jonesboro, Ark., U.S.A.	159	35 50N	90 45W
Jonesboro, Ill., U.S.A.	159	37 26N	89 18W
Jonesboro, La., U.S.A.	159	32 15N	92 41W
Jonesport	151	44 32N	67 38W
Jönköping	73	57 45N	14 10E
Jönköpings län □	75	57 30N	14 30E
Jonquière	151	48 27N	71 14W
Jonsberg	73	58 30N	16 48E
Jonsered	73	57 45N	12 10E
Jonzac	44	45 27N	0 28W
Joplin	159	37 0N	94 25W
Jordan, Phil.	103	10 41N	122 38E
Jordan, Mont., U.S.A.	160	47 25N	106 58W
Jordan, N.Y., U.S.A.	162	43 4N	76 29W
Jordan ■	92	31 0N	36 0E
Jordan, R.	90	32 10N	35 32E
Jordan Valley	160	43 0N	117 2W
Jordânia	171	15 45S	40 11W
Jordanów	54	49 41N	19 49E
Jorhat	98	26 45N	94 20E
Jörn	74	65 4N	20 1E
Jørpeland	71	59 3N	6 1E
Jorquera, R.	172	28 3S	69 58W
Jos	121	9 53N	8 51E
Jošanička Banja	66	43 24N	20 47E
José Batlle y OrdóPez	173	33 20S	55 10W
Josefow	54	52 10N	21 11E
Joseni	70	47 42N	25 29E
Joseph	160	45 27N	117 13W
Joseph Bonaparte G.	136	14 35S	128 50E
Joseph City	161	35 0N	110 16W
Joseph, Lac	151	52 45N	65 18W
Josephine, oilfield	19	58 35N	2 45E
Joshua Tree	163	34 8N	116 19W
Joshua Tree Nat. Mon.	163	33 56N	116 5W
Josselin	42	47 57N	2 33W
Jostedal	71	61 35N	7 15E
Jostedalsbre, Mt.	71	61 45N	7 0E
Jotunheimen	71	61 35N	8 25E
Jounieh	92	33 59N	35 30E
Jourdanton	159	28 54N	98 32W
Journe	46	52 58N	5 48E
Joussard	152	55 22N	115 57W
Joux, Lac de	50	46 39N	6 18E
Jouzjan □	93	36 10N	66 0E
Jovellanos	166	22 40N	81 10W
Jowai	98	25 26N	92 12E
Joyce's Country, dist.	38	53 32N	9 30W
Joyeuse	45	44 29N	4 16E
Jozini Dam	129	27 27S	32 7E
Ju Shui, R.	109	28 36N	116 4E
Juan Aldama	164	24 20N	103 23W
Juan Bautista	161	36 55N	121 33W
Juan Bautista Alberdi	172	34 26S	61 48W
Juan de Fuca Str.	160	48 15N	124 0W
Juan de Nova, I.	129	17 3S	42 45E
Juan Fernández, Arch. de	131	33 50S	80 0W
Juan José Castelli	172	25 57S	60 37W
Juan L. Lacaze	172	34 26S	57 25W
Juárez, Argent.	172	37 40S	59 43W
Juárez, Mexico	164	27 37N	100 44W
Juárez, Sierra de	164	32 0N	116 0W
Juatinga, Ponta de	171	23 17S	44 30W
Juàzeiro	170	9 30S	40 30W
Juàzeiro do Norte	170	7 10S	39 18W
Jûbâ	123	4 57N	31 35E
Juba, R.	91	1 30N	42 35E
Jubaila	92	24 55N	46 25E
Jûbâl	122	27 30N	34 0E
Jubbulpore = Jabalpur	95	23 9N	79 58E
Jübek	48	54 31N	9 24E
Jubga	83	44 19N	38 48E
Jubilee L.	137	29 0S	126 50E
Juby, C.	116	28 0N	12 59W
Júcar, R.	58	40 8N	2 13W
Júcaro	166	21 37N	78 51W
Juch'eng	109	25 32N	113 39E
Juchitán	165	16 27N	95 5W
Judaea = Yehuda	90	31 35N	34 57E
Judenburg	52	47 12N	14 38E
Judith Gap	160	46 48N	109 46W
Judith Pt.	162	41 20N	71 30W
Judith, R.	160	47 30N	109 30W
Juian	109	27 45N	120 38E
Juich'ang	109	29 40N	115 39E
Juigalpa	166	12 6N	85 26W
Juillac	44	45 20N	1 19E
Juist, I.	48	53 40N	7 0E
Juiz de Fora	171	21 43S	43 19W
Jujuy	172	24 10S	65 25W
Jujuy □	172	23 20S	65 40W
Jukao	109	32 24N	120 35E
Julesberg	158	41 0N	102 20W
Juli	174	16 10S	69 25W
Julia Cr.	138	20 0S	141 11E
Julia Creek	138	20 39S	141 44E
Juliaca	174	15 25S	70 10W
Julian	163	33 4N	116 38W
Julian Alps = Julijske Alpe	63	46 15N	14 1E
Julianakanaal	47	51 6N	5 52E
Julianehåb	12	60 43N	46 0W
Julianstown	38	53 40N	6 16W
Jülich	48	50 55N	6 20E
Julier P.	51	46 28N	9 32E
Julijske Alpe	63	46 15N	14 1E
Julimes	164	28 25N	105 27W
Jullundur	94	31 20N	75 40E
Jumbo	127	17 30S	30 58E
Jumento, Cayos	167	23 0N	75 40E
Jumet	47	50 27N	4 25E
Jumilla	59	38 28N	1 19W
Jumla	95	29 15N	82 13E
Jumna, R. = Yamuna	94	27 0N	78 30E
Junagadh	94	21 30N	70 30E
Junan	109	32 58N	114 31E
Junction, Tex., U.S.A.	159	30 29N	99 48W
Junction, Utah, U.S.A.	161	38 10N	112 15W
Junction B.	138	11 52S	133 55E
Junction City, Kans., U.S.A.	158	39 4N	96 55W
Junction City, Oreg., U.S.A.	160	44 20N	123 12W
Jundah	138	24 46S	143 2E
Jundiaí	173	23 10S	47 0W
Juneau	147	58 26N	134 30W
Junee	141	34 53S	147 35E
Jung Chiang, R.	108	23 25N	110 0E
Jungan	108	25 14N	109 23E
Jungch'ang	108	29 27N	105 33E
Jungch'eng	107	37 9N	122 23E
Jungchiang	108	25 56N	108 31E
Jungching	108	29 49N	102 55E
Jungfrau	50	46 32N	7 58E
Jungho	106	35 21N	110 32E
Junghsien, Kwangsi-Chuang, China	109	22 52N	110 33E
Junghsien, Szechwan, China	108	29 29N	104 22E
Junglinster	47	49 43N	6 15E
Jungshahi	94	24 52N	67 44E
Jungshui	108	24 14N	109 23E
Juniata, R.	162	40 30N	77 40W
Junín	172	34 33S	60 57W
Junín de los Andes	176	39 45S	71 0W
Junnar	96	19 12N	73 58E
Junquera, La	58	42 25N	2 53E
Junta, La	159	38 0N	103 30W
Juntura	160	43 44N	119 4W
Juparanã, Lagoa	171	19 35S	40 18W
Jupiter, R.	151	49 29N	63 37W
Juquiá	171	24 19S	47 38W
Jur, Nahr el	123	8 45N	29 0E
Jura	43	46 35N	6 5E
Jura □	43	46 47N	5 45E
Jura, I.	34	56 0N	5 50W
Jura, Paps of, mts.	34	55 55N	6 0W
Jura, Sd. of	34	55 57N	5 45W
Jura Suisse	50	47 10N	7 0E
Jurado	174	7 7N	77 46W
Jurby Hd.	32	54 23N	4 31W
Jurien B.	132	30 17S	115 0E
Jurilovca	70	44 46N	28 52W
Jurm	93	36 50N	70 45E
Juruá, R.	174	2 30S	66 0W
Juruena, R.	174	7 20S	58 3W
Juruti	175	2 9S	56 4W
Jushan	107	36 54N	121 30E
Jussey	43	47 50N	5 55E
Justo Daract	172	33 52S	65 12W
Jüterbog	48	51 59N	13 6E
Juticalpa	166	14 40N	85 50W
Jutland	16	56 0N	8 0E
Jutphaas	46	52 2N	5 6E
Jutung	109	32 19N	121 14E
Juvigny-sous-Andaine	42	48 32N	0 30W
Juvisy	43	48 43N	2 23E
Juwain	93	31 45N	61 30E
Juyüan	109	24 46N	113 16E
Juzennecourt	43	48 10N	5 0E
Jye-kundo	99	33 0N	96 50E
Jylhama	74	64 34N	26 40E
Jylland	73	56 15N	9 20E
Jylland (Jutland)	73	56 25N	9 30E
Jyväskylä	74	62 14N	25 44E

K

K. Sedili Besar	101	1 55N	104 5E
K2, Mt.	95	36 0N	77 0E
Ka Lae (South C.)	147	18 55N	155 41W
Kaaia, Mt.	147	21 31N	158 9W
Kaap die Goeie Hoop	128	34 24S	18 30E
Kaap Plato	128	28 30S	24 0E
Kaapkruis	128	21 43S	14 0E
Kaapstad = Cape Town	125	33 56S	18 27E
Kaatsheuvel	47	51 39N	5 2E
Kabaena, I.	103	5 15S	122 0E
Kabala	120	9 38N	11 37W
Kabale	126	1 15S	30 0E
Kabalo	126	6 0S	27 0E
Kabambare	126	4 41S	27 39E
Kabango	127	8 35S	28 30E
Kabanjahe	102	3 2N	98 27E
Kabara	120	16 40N	2 50W
Kabardinka	82	44 40N	37 57E
Kabardino-Balkar, A.S.S.R. □	83	43 30N	43 30E
Kabarega Falls	126	2 15N	31 38E
Kabasalan	103	7 47N	122 44E
Kabba	121	7 57N	6 3E
Kabe	110	34 31N	132 31E
Kabi	121	13 30N	12 35E
Kabin Buri	100	13 57N	101 43E
Kabinakagami L.	150	48 54N	84 25W
Kabinda	126	6 23S	24 28E
Kablungu, C.	135	6 20S	150 1E
Kabna	122	19 6N	32 40E
Kabompo	127	13 30S	24 14E
Kabompo, R.	127	13 50S	24 10E
Kabondo	127	8 58S	25 40E
Kabongo	126	7 22S	25 33E
Kabou	121	9 28N	0 55E
Kaboudia, Rass	119	35 13N	11 10E

Kabra Kandalakshkiyzaliv

Place	Page	Lat.	Long.
Kabra	**138**	23 25 S	150 25 E
Kabūd Gonbad	**93**	37 5 N	59 45 E
Kabuiri	**121**	11 30 N	13 30 E
Kabul	**94**	34 28 N	69 18 E
Kabul □	**93**	34 0 N	68 30 E
Kabul, R.	**94**	34 30 N	69 13 E
Kabunga	**126**	1 38 S	28 3 E
Kaburuang	**103**	3 50 N	126 30 E
Kabushiya	**123**	16 54 N	33 41 E
Kabwe	**127**	14 30 S	28 29 E
Kabwum	**135**	6 11 S	147 15 E
Kačanik	**66**	42 13 N	21 12 E
Kachanovo	**80**	57 25 N	27 38 E
Kachebera	**127**	13 56 S	32 50 E
Kachin □	**98**	26 0 N	97 0 E
Kachira, Lake	**126**	0 40 S	31 0 E
Kachiry	**76**	53 10 N	75 50 E
Kachisi	**123**	9 40 N	37 57 E
Kachkanar	**84**	58 42 N	59 33 E
Kachot	**101**	11 30 N	103 3 E
Kaçkar	**83**	40 45 N	41 30 E
Kadaingti	**98**	17 37 N	97 32 E
Kadan Kyun, I.	**101**	12 30 N	98 20 E
Kadanai, R.	**94**	32 0 N	66 10 E
Kadarkút	**53**	46 13 N	17 39 E
Kadayanallur	**97**	9 3 N	77 22 E
Kaddi	**121**	13 40 N	5 40 E
Kade	**121**	6 7 N	0 56 W
Kadgo, L.	**137**	25 30 S	125 30 E
Kadi	**94**	23 18 N	72 23 E
Kadina	**140**	34 0 S	137 43 E
Kadiri	**97**	14 12 N	78 13 E
* Kadiyevka	**83**	48 35 N	38 30 E
Kadoka	**158**	43 50 N	101 31 W
Kadom	**81**	54 37 N	42 24 E
Kaduna	**121**	10 30 N	7 21 E
Kaduna □	**121**	11 0 N	7 30 E
Kaduna, R.	**121**	10 5 N	8 10 E
Kadyoha	**120**	8 58 N	5 53 W
Kadzhi-Say	**85**	42 8 N	77 10 E
Kaedi	**120**	16 9 N	13 28 W
Kaelé	**121**	10 15 N	14 15 E
Kaena Pt.	**147**	21 35 N	158 17 W
Kaeng Khoï	**100**	14 35 N	101 0 E
Kaeo	**142**	35 6 S	173 49 E
Kaerh, China	**105**	31 45 N	80 22 E
Kaerh, Sudan	**123**	5 35 N	31 20 E
Kaesŏng	**107**	37 58 N	126 35 E
Kaf	**92**	31 25 N	37 20 E
Kafakumba	**124**	9 38 S	23 46 E
Kafan	**79**	39 18 N	46 15 E
Kafanchan	**121**	9 40 N	8 20 E
Kafareti	**121**	10 25 N	11 12 E
Kaffrine	**120**	14 8 N	15 36 W
Kafia Kingi	**117**	9 20 N	24 25 E
Kafinda	**127**	12 32 S	30 20 E
Kafirévs, Ákra	**69**	38 9 N	24 8 E
Kafiristan	**93**	35 0 N	70 30 E
Kafr Ana	**70**	32 2 N	34 48 E
Kafr 'Ein	**90**	32 3 N	35 7 E
Kafr el Dauwâr	**122**	31 8 N	30 8 E
Kafr Kama	**90**	32 44 N	35 26 E
Kafr Kannã	**90**	32 45 N	35 20 E
Kafr Malik	**90**	32 0 N	35 18 E
Kafr Mandã	**90**	32 49 N	35 15 E
Kafr Quaddum	**90**	32 14 N	35 7 E
Kafr Ra'i	**90**	32 23 N	35 9 E
Kafr Sir	**90**	33 19 N	35 23 E
Kafr Yasif	**90**	32 58 N	35 10 E
Kafue	**127**	15 46 S	28 9 E
Kafue Flats	**127**	15 32 S	27 0 E
Kafue Gorge	**127**	16 0 S	28 0 E
Kafue Hook	**127**	14 58 S	26 0 E
Kafue Nat. Park	**65**	15 30 S	25 40 E
Kafue, R.	**125**	15 30 S	26 0 E
Kafulwe	**127**	9 0 S	29 1 E
Kaga, Afghan.	**94**	34 14 N	70 10 E
Kaga, Japan	**111**	36 16 N	136 15 E
Kagamil I.	**147**	53 0 N	169 40 W
Kagan	**85**	39 43 N	64 33 E
Kagawa-ken □	**110**	34 15 N	134 0 E
Kagera R.	**126**	1 15 S	31 20 E
Kagoshima	**110**	31 36 N	130 40 E
Kagoshima-ken □	**110**	30 0 N	130 0 E
Kagoshima-Wan	**110**	31 0 N	130 40 E
Kagul	**82**	45 50 N	28 15 E
Kahajan, R.	**102**	2 10 S	114 0 E
Kahama	**126**	4 8 S	32 30 E
Kahama □	**126**	3 40 S	32 0 E
Kahang	**101**	2 12 N	103 32 E
Kahe	**126**	3 30 S	37 25 E
Kahemba	**124**	7 18 S	18 55 E
Kaherekoua Mts.	**143**	45 45 S	167 15 E
Kahniah, R.	**152**	58 15 N	120 55 W
Kahnuj	**93**	27 55 N	57 40 E
Kahoka	**158**	40 25 N	91 42 W
Kahoolawe, I.	**147**	20 33 N	156 35 W
Kahuku & Pt.	**147**	21 41 N	157 57 W
Kahulai	**147**	20 54 N	156 28 W
Kahurangi, Pt.	**143**	40 50 S	172 10 E
Kahuta	**94**	33 35 N	73 24 E
Kai Kai	**128**	19 52 S	21 15 E
Kai, Kepulauan	**103**	5 55 S	132 45 W
Kaiama	**121**	9 36 N	4 1 E
Kaiapit	**135**	6 18 S	146 18 E
Kaiapoi	**143**	42 24 S	172 40 E
Kaibara	**111**	35 8 N	135 5 E
K'aichien	**109**	23 45 N	111 47 E
K'aifeng	**106**	34 50 N	114 27 E
Kaihsien	**107**	40 25 N	122 25 E
K'aihsien	**108**	31 12 N	108 25 E
K'aihua	**109**	29 9 N	118 24 E
Kaiingveld	**128**	30 0 S	22 0 E
Kaikohe	**142**	35 25 S	173 49 E
Kaikoura	**143**	42 25 S	173 43 E
Kaikoura Pen.	**143**	42 25 S	173 43 E
Kaikoura Ra.	**143**	.41 59 S	173 41 E
Kailahun	**120**	8 18 N	10 39 W
Kailashahar	**98**	25 19 N	92 0 E
Kaili	**108**	26 32 N	107 57 E
K'ailu	**107**	43 35 N	121 12 E
Kailua	**147**	19 39 N	156 0 W
Kaimana	**103**	3 30 S	133 45 E
Kaimanawa Mts.	**142**	39 15 S	175 56 E
Kaimata	**143**	42 34 S	171 28 E
Kaimganj	**95**	27 33 N	79 24 E
Kaimon-Dake	**110**	31 11 N	130 32 E
Kaimur Hill	**95**	24 30 N	82 0 E
Kainan	**110**	34 9 N	135 12 E
Kainantu	**135**	6 18 S	145 52 E
Kaingaroa Forest	**142**	38 30 S	176 30 E
Kainji Res.	**121**	10 1 N	4 40 E
Kaipara Harb.	**142**	36 25 S	174 14 E
K'aip'ing	**109**	22 31 N	112 32 E
Kaipokok B.	**151**	54 54 N	59 47 W
Kairana	**94**	29 33 N	77 15 E
Kairiru, I.	**138**	3 20 S	143 20 E
Kaironi	**103**	0 47 S	133 40 E
Kairouan	**119**	35 45 N	10 5 E
Kairuku	**135**	8 51 S	146 35 E
Kaiserslautern	**49**	49 30 N	7 43 E
Kaitaia	**142**	35 8 S	173 17 E
Kaitangata	**143**	46 17 S	169 51 E
Kaithal	**94**	29 48 N	76 26 E
Kaitu, R.	**94**	33 20 N	70 20 E
Kaiwi Channel	**147**	21 13 N	157 30 W
K'aiyang	**108**	27 4 N	106 55 E
K'aiyüan, Liaoning, China	**107**	42 33 N	124 4 E
K'aiyüan, Yunnan, China	**108**	23 47 N	103 10 E
Kaiyuh Mts.	**147**	63 40 N	159 0 W
Kajaani	**74**	64 17 N	27 46 E
Kajabbi	**138**	20 0 S	140 1 E
Kajan, R.	**102**	2 40 N	116 40 E
Kajang	**101**	2 59 N	101 48 E
Kajeli	**103**	3 20 S	127 10 E
Kajiado	**126**	1 53 S	36 48 E
Kajiki	**110**	31 44 N	130 40 E
Kajo Kaji	**123**	3 58 N	31 40 E
Kajoa, I.	**103**	0 1 N	127 28 E
Kajuagung	**102**	32 8 S	104 46 E
Kakabeka Falls	**150**	48 24 N	89 37 W
Kakamas	**125**	28 45 S	20 33 E
Kakamega	**126**	0 20 N	34 46 E
Kakamega □	**126**	0 20 N	34 46 E
Kakamigahara	**111**	35 28 N	136 48 E
Kakanj	**66**	44 9 N	18 7 E
Kakanui Mts.	**143**	45 10 S	170 30 E
Kakapotahi	**143**	43 0 S	170 45 E
Kake, Japan	**110**	34 36 N	132 19 E
Kake, U.S.A.	**147**	57 0 N	134 0 W
Kakegawa	**111**	34 45 N	138 1 E
Kakhib	**83**	42 28 N	46 34 E
Kakhovskoye Vdkhr.	**82**	47 5 N	34 16 E
Kakia	**125**	24 48 S	23 22 E
Kakinada = Cocanada	**99**	16 50 N	82 11 E
Kakinada (Cocanada)	**96**	16 50 N	82 11 E
Kakisa L.	**152**	60 56 N	117 43 W
Kakisa, R.	**152**	61 3 N	117 10 W
Kakogawa	**110**	34 46 N	134 51 E
Kaktovik	**147**	70 8 N	143 50 W
Kakwa, R.	**152**	54 37 N	118 28 W
Kala	**121**	12 2 N	14 40 E
Kala Oya.	**97**	8 15 N	80 0 E
Kala Shank'ou	**95**	35 42 N	78 20 E
Kalaa-Kebira	**119**	35 59 N	10 32 E
Kalabagh	**94**	33 0 N	71 28 E
Kalabáka	**68**	39 42 N	21 39 E
Kalabo	**125**	14 58 S	22 33 E
Kalach	**81**	50 22 N	41 0 E
Kaladan, R.	**99**	21 30 N	92 45 E
Kalahari, Des.	**128**	24 0 S	22 0 E
Kalahari Gemsbok Nat. Pk.	**128**	26 0 S	20 30 E
Kalahasti	**97**	13 45 N	79 44 E
Kalai-Khumb	**85**	38 28 N	70 46 E
Kalaja e Turrës	**68**	41 10 N	19 28 E
Kalakamati	**129**	20 40 S	27 25 E
Kalakan	**77**	55 15 N	116 45 E
K'alak'unlun Shank'ou	**95**	35 33 N	77 46 E
Kalam	**95**	35 34 N	72 30 E
Kalama, U.S.A.	**160**	46 0 N	122 55 W
Kalama, Zaîre	**126**	2 52 S	28 35 E
Kalamariá	**68**	40 33 N	22 55 E
Kalamata	**69**	37 3 N	22 10 E
Kalamazoo	**156**	42 20 N	85 35 W
Kalamazoo, R.	**156**	42 40 N	86 12 W
Kalamb	**96**	18 3 N	74 48 E
Kalambo Falls	**127**	8 37 S	31 35 E
Kálamos, I.	**69**	38 37 N	20 55 E
Kalamoti	**69**	38 15 N	26 4 E
Kalamunda	**137**	32 0 S	116 0 E
Kalangadoo	**140**	37 34 S	140 41 E
Kalannie	**137**	30 22 S	117 5 E
Kalao, I.	**103**	7 21 S	121 0 E
Kalaotoa, I.	**103**	7 20 S	121 50 E
Kälarne	**72**	62 59 N	16 8 E
Kalárovo	**53**	47 54 N	18 0 E
Kalasin	**100**	16 26 N	103 30 E
Kalat	**93**	29 8 N	66 31 E
Kalat □	**93**	27 0 N	64 30 E
Kalat-i-Ghilzai	**93**	32 15 N	66 58 E
Kálathos (Calato)	**69**	36 9 N	28 8 E
Kalaupapa	**147**	21 12 N	156 59 W
Kalaus, R.	**83**	45 40 N	43 30 E
Kalávrita	**69**	38 3 N	22 8 E
Kalaw	**98**	20 37 N	96 35 E
Kalba	**120**	9 30 N	2 42 W
Kalbarri	**137**	27 40 S	114 10 E
Kaldhovd	**71**	60 5 N	8 20 E
Kalecik	**82**	40 4 N	33 26 E
Kalegauk Kyun	**99**	15 33 N	97 35 E
Kalehe	**126**	2 6 S	28 50 E
Kalema	**126**	1 12 S	31 55 E
Kalemie	**124**	5 55 S	29 9 E
Kalemyo	**98**	23 11 N	94 4 E
Kalety	**54**	50 35 N	18 52 E
Kalewa	**98**	22 41 N	95 32 E
Kálfafellsstaður	**74**	64 11 N	15 53 W
Kalgan = Changchiak'ou	**106**	40 50 N	114 53 E
Kalgoorlie	**137**	30 40 S	121 22 E
Kaliakra, Nos	**67**	43 21 N	28 30 E
Kalianda	**102**	5 50 S	105 45 E
Kalibo	**103**	11 43 N	122 22 E
Kaliganj Town	**98**	23 25 N	89 8 E
Kalima	**126**	2 33 S	26 32 E
Kalimantan Barat □	**102**	0 0	110 30 E
Kalimantan Selatan □	**102**	4 10 S	115 30 E
Kalimantan Tengah □	**102**	2 0 S	113 30 E
Kalimantan Timor □	**102**	1 30 N	116 30 E
Kálimnos, I.	**69**	37 0 N	27 0 E
Kalimpong	**95**	27 4 N	88 35 E
Kalinadi, R.	**97**	14 50 N	74 20 E
Kalinin	**81**	56 55 N	35 55 E
Kaliningrad	**80**	54 42 N	20 32 E
Kalinino	**83**	45 12 N	38 59 E
Kalininskoye	**85**	42 50 N	73 49 E
Kalinkovichi	**80**	52 12 N	29 20 E
Kalinovik	**66**	43 31 N	18 29 E
Kalipetrovo (Starčevo)	**67**	44 5 N	27 14 E
Kaliro	**126**	0 56 N	33 30 E
Kalirrákhi	**68**	40 40 N	24 35 E
Kalispell	**160**	48 10 N	114 22 W
Kalisz	**54**	51 45 N	18 8 E
Kalisz □	**54**	51 30 N	18 0 E
Kalisz Pom	**54**	53 17 N	15 55 E
Kaliua	**126**	5 5 S	31 48 E
Kaliveli Tank	**97**	12 5 N	79 50 E
Kalix R.	**74**	67 0 N	22 0 E
Kalka	**94**	30 56 N	76 57 E
Kalkaroo	**140**	31 12 S	143 54 E
Kalkaska	**150**	44 44 N	85 11 W
Kalkfeld	**128**	20 57 S	16 14 E
Kalkfontein	**128**	22 4 S	20 57 E
Kalkfontein Dam	**128**	29 30 S	24 15 E
Kalkrand	**128**	24 1 S	17 35 E
Kall L.	**72**	63 35 N	13 10 E
Kallakurichi	**97**	11 44 N	79 1 E
Kållandsö	**73**	58 40 N	13 5 E
Källby	**73**	58 30 N	13 8 E
Kallia	**86**	31 46 N	35 30 E
Kallidaikurichi	**97**	8 38 N	77 31 E
Kallinge	**73**	56 15 N	15 18 E
Kallithéa	**69**	37 55 N	23 41 E
Kallmeti	**68**	41 51 N	19 41 E
Kallonís, Kólpos	**69**	39 10 N	26 10 E
Kallsjön	**74**	63 38 N	13 0 E
Kalltorp	**73**	58 23 N	13 20 E
Kalmalo	**121**	13 40 N	5 20 E
Kalmar	**73**	56 40 N	16 20 E
Kalmar län □	**73**	57 25 N	16 15 E
Kalmar sund	**73**	56 40 N	16 25 E
Kalmthout	**47**	51 23 N	4 29 E
Kalmyk A.S.S.R. □	**83**	46 5 N	46 1 E
Kalmykovo	**83**	49 0 N	51 35 E
Kalna	**95**	23 13 N	88 25 E
Kalo	**135**	10 1 S	147 48 E
Kalocsa	**53**	46 32 N	19 0 E
Kalofer	**67**	42 37 N	24 59 E
Kalol, Gujarat, India	**94**	23 15 N	72 33 E
Kalol, Gujarat, India	**94**	22 37 N	73 31 E
Kalola	**127**	10 0 S	28 0 E
Kalolímnos	**69**	37 4 N	27 8 E
Kalomo	**127**	17 0 S	26 30 E
Kaloнerón	**69**	37 20 N	21 38 E
Kalpi	**95**	26 8 N	79 47 E
Kalrayan Hills	**97**	11 45 N	78 40 E
Kalsubai, Mt.	**96**	17 35 N	73 45 E
Kaltbrunn	**51**	47 13 N	9 2 E
Kaltungo	**121**	9 48 N	11 19 E
Kalu	**94**	25 5 N	67 39 E
Kaluga	**81**	54 35 N	36 10 E
Kalulushi	**127**	12 50 S	28 3 E
Kalundborg	**73**	55 41 N	11 5 E
Kalush	**80**	42 9 N	24 12 E
Kałuszyn	**54**	52 13 N	21 52 E
Kalutara	**97**	6 35 N	80 0 E
Kalwaria	**54**	49 53 N	19 41 E
Kalya	**84**	60 15 N	59 59 E
Kalyan, Austral.	**140**	34 55 S	139 49 E
Kalyan, India	**96**	20 30 N	74 3 E
Kalyani	**174**	17 53 N	76 59 E
Kalyazin	**81**	57 15 N	37 45 E
Kam Keut	**101**	18 20 N	104 48 E
Kama, Burma	**98**	22 10 N	95 10 E
Kama, Zaîre	**126**	3 30 S	27 5 E
Kama, R.	**84**	60 0 N	53 0 E
Kamachumu	**126**	1 37 S	31 37 E
Kamae	**110**	32 48 N	131 56 E
Kamaguenam	**121**	13 36 N	10 30 E
Kamaing	**98**	24 26 N	94 55 E
Kamaishi	**112**	39 20 N	142 0 E
Kamakura	**111**	35 19 N	139 33 E
Kamalia	**94**	30 44 N	72 42 E
Kamalino	**147**	21 50 N	160 14 W
Kamamaung	**98**	17 21 N	97 40 E
Kamango	**126**	0 40 N	29 52 E
Kamapanda	**127**	12 5 S	24 0 E
Kamaran	**91**	15 28 N	42 35 E
Kamashi	**85**	38 51 N	65 23 E
Kamativi	**127**	18 15 S	0 27 E
Kamba	**121**	11 50 N	3 45 E
Kambalda	**137**	31 10 S	121 37 E
Kambam	**97**	9 45 N	77 16 E
Kambar	**94**	27 37 N	68 1 E
Kambarka	**84**	56 15 N	54 11 E
Kambia	**120**	9 3 N	12 53 W
Kambolé	**127**	8 47 S	30 48 E
Kambove	**127**	10 51 S	26 33 E
Kamchatka, P-ov.	**77**	57 0 N	160 0 E
Kamde	**138**	8 0 S	140 58 E
Kamen	**76**	53 50 N	81 30 E
Kamen Kashirskiy	**80**	51 39 N	24 56 E
Kamenica	**66**	44 25 N	19 40 E
Kamenice	**52**	49 18 N	15 2 E
Kamenjak, Rt.	**63**	44 47 N	13 55 E
Kamenka, R.S.F.S.R., U.S.S.R.	**78**	65 58 N	44 0 E
Kamenka, R.S.F.S.R., U.S.S.R.	**81**	50 47 N	39 20 E
Kamenka Bugskaya	**80**	50 8 N	24 16 E
Kamenka Dneprovskaya	**82**	47 29 N	34 14 E
Kamensk	**76**	56 25 N	62 45 E
Kamensk Shakhtinskiy	**83**	48 23 N	40 20 E
Kamensk-Uralskiy	**84**	56 25 N	62 2 E
Kamenskiy	**81**	50 48 N	45 25 E
Kamenskoye	**77**	62 45 N	165 30 E
Kamenyak	**67**	43 24 N	26 57 E
Kamenz	**48**	51 17 N	14 7 E
Kameoka	**111**	35 0 N	135 35 E
Kames	**34**	55 53 N	5 15 W
Kameyama	**111**	34 51 N	126 27 E
Kami	**68**	42 17 N	20 18 E
Kami-Jima	**110**	32 27 N	130 20 E
Kami-koshiki-Jima	**110**	31 50 N	129 52 E
Kamiah	**160**	46 12 N	116 2 W
Kamien Krajenskie	**54**	53 32 N	17 32 E
Kamien Pomorski	**54**	53 57 N	14 43 E
Kamiensk	**54**	51 12 N	19 29 E
Kamiita	**110**	34 6 N	134 22 E
Kamilonísion	**69**	35 50 N	26 15 E
Kamilukuak, L.	**153**	62 22 N	101 40 W
Kamina	**127**	8 45 S	25 0 E
Kaminak L.	**153**	62 10 N	95 0 W
Kamioka	**111**	36 25 N	137 15 E
Kamituga Mungombe	**126**	3 2 S	28 10 E
Kamiyaku	**112**	30 25 N	130 30 E
Kamloops	**152**	50 40 N	120 20 W
Kamo	**143**	35 42 S	174 20 E
Kamogawa	**111**	35 5 N	140 5 E
Kamoke	**94**	32 4 N	74 4 E
Kamono	**124**	3 10 S	13 20 E
Kamp, R.	**52**	48 35 N	15 26 E
Kampala	**126**	0 20 N	32 30 E
Kampar	**101**	4 18 N	101 9 E
Kampar, R.	**102**	0 30 N	102 0 E
Kampen	**46**	52 33 N	5 53 E
Kamperland	**47**	51 34 N	3 43 E
Kamphaeng Phet	**100**	16 28 N	99 30 E
Kampolombo, L.	**127**	11 30 S	29 35 E
Kampong Ayer Puteh	**101**	4 15 N	103 10 E
Kampong Jerangau	**101**	4 50 N	103 10 E
Kampong Raja	**101**	5 45 N	102 35 E
Kampong Sedili Besar	**101**	1 56 N	104 8 E
Kampong To	**101**	6 3 N	101 13 E
Kampot	**101**	10 36 N	104 10 E
Kamptee	**94**	21 9 N	79 19 E
Kampti	**120**	10 7 N	3 25 W
Kampuchea ■ = Cambodia	**100**	12 15 N	105 0 E
Kamrau, Teluk	**103**	3 30 S	133 45 E
Kamsack	**153**	51 34 N	101 54 W
Kamskove Ustye	**81**	55 10 N	49 20 E
Kamskoye Vdkhr.	**78**	58 0 N	56 0 E
Kamuchawie L.	**153**	56 18 N	101 59 W
Kamui-Misaki	**112**	45 3 N	142 30 E
Kamyshin	**81**	50 10 N	45 30 E
Kamyshlov	**84**	56 50 N	62 43 E
Kamyzyak	**83**	46 4 N	48 10 E
Kan	**98**	20 53 N	93 49 E
Kan Chiang, R.	**109**	29 45 N	116 10 E
Kanaaupscow	**150**	54 2 N	76 30 W
Kanab	**161**	37 3 N	112 29 W
Kanab Creek	**161**	37 0 N	112 40 W
Kanaga I.	**147**	51 45 N	177 22 W
Kanagawa-ken □	**111**	35 20 N	139 20 E
Kanairiktok, R.	**151**	55 2 N	60 18 W
Kanakanak	**147**	59 0 N	158 58 W
Kanakapura	**97**	12 33 N	77 28 E
Kanália	**68**	39 30 N	22 53 E
Kananga	**124**	5 55 S	22 18 E
Kanarraville	**161**	37 34 N	113 12 W
Kanash	**81**	55 48 N	47 32 E
Kanawha, R.	**156**	39 40 N	82 0 W
Kanayis, Ras el	**122**	31 30 N	28 5 E
Kanazawa	**111**	36 30 N	136 38 E
Kanbalu	**98**	17 55 N	85 24 E
Kanchanaburi	**100**	14 8 N	99 31 E
Kanchenjunga, Mt.	**95**	27 50 N	88 10 E
Kanchipuram (Conjeeveram)	**97**	12 52 N	79 45 E
Kanchou	**109**	25 51 N	114 59 E
Kanch'üan	**106**	36 19 N	109 19 E
Kanda Kanda	**124**	6 52 S	23 48 E
Kandagach	**79**	49 20 N	57 15 E
Kandahar	**94**	31 32 N	65 30 E
Kandahar □	**94**	31 0 N	65 0 E
Kandalaksha	**78**	67 9 N	32 30 E
Kandalakshkiyzaliv	**78**	66 0 N	35 0 E

* *Renamed Stakhanov*

Kandalu **Kástron**

Name	Page	Lat.	Long.
Kandalu	**93**	29 55N	63 20 E
Kandangan	**102**	2 50 S	115 20 E
Kandanos	**69**	35 19N	23 44 E
Kandé	**121**	9 57N	1 53 E
Kandep	**135**	5 54 S	143 32 E
Kander, R.	**50**	46 33N	7 38 E
Kandersteg	**50**	46 30N	7 40 E
Kandewu	**127**	14 1 S	26 16 E
Kandhila	**69**	37 46N	22 22 E
Kandhkot	**94**	28 16N	69 8 E
Kandhla	**94**	29 18N	77 19 E
Kandi, Benin	**121**	11 7N	2 55 E
Kandi, India	**95**	23 58N	88 5 E
Kandinduna	**127**	13 58 S	24 19 E
Kandira	**92**	41 5N	30 10 E
Kandla	**94**	23 0N	70 10 E
Kandos	**141**	32 45 S	149 58 E
Kandrach	**93**	25 30N	65 30 E
Kandrian	**135**	6 14 S	149 37 E
Kandukur	**95**	15 12N	79 57 E
Kandy	**97**	7 18N	80 43 E
Kane	**156**	41 39N	78 53W
Kane Bassin	**12**	79 30N	68 0W
Kanel	**120**	13 18N	14 35W
Kaneohe	**147**	21 25N	157 48W
Kanevskaya	**83**	46 3N	39 3 E
Kanfanar	**63**	45 7N	13 50 E
Kang	**93**	30 55N	61 55 E
Kangaba	**120**	11 56N	8 25W
Kangar	**101**	6 27N	100 12 E
Kangaroo I.	**140**	35 45 S	137 0 E
Kangaroo Mts.	**138**	23 25 S	142 0 E
Kangavar	**92**	34 40N	48 0 E
Kangean, Kepulauan	**102**	6 55 S	115 23 E
Kangerdlugsuaé	**12**	68 10N	32 20W
Kanggye	**107**	41 0N	126 35 E
Kanggyŏng	**107**	36 10N	126 0 E
Kanghwa	**107**	37 45N	126 30 E
K'angkang	**108**	32 46N	101 3 E
Kangnŭng	**107**	37 45N	128 54 E
Kango	**124**	0 11N	10 5 E
K'angp'ing	**107**	43 45N	123 20 E
Kangpokpi	**98**	25 8N	93 58 E
K'angting	**108**	30 2N	102 0 E
Kangtissu Shan	**95**	31 0N	82 0 E
Kangto, Mt.	**99**	27 50N	92 35 E
Kangyao	**107**	44 15N	126 40 E
Kangyidaung	**98**	16 56N	94 54 E
Kanhangad	**97**	12 21N	74 58 E
Kanheri	**96**	19 13N	72 50 E
Kani, China	**99**	29 25N	95 25 E
Kani, Ivory C.	**120**	8 29N	6 36W
Kaniama	**126**	7 30 S	24 12 E
Kaniapiskau L.	**151**	54 10N	69 55W
Kaniapiskau, R.	**151**	57 40N	69 30 E
Kanibadam	**85**	40 17N	70 25 E
Kanin Nos, Mys	**78**	68 45N	43 20 E
Kanin, P-ov.	**78**	68 0N	45 0 E
Kanina	**68**	40 23N	19 30 E
Kaniva	**140**	36 22 S	141 18 E
Kanjiza	**66**	46 3N	20 4 E
Kanjut Sar	**95**	36 15N	75 25 E
Kankakee	**156**	41 6N	87 50W
Kankakee, R.	**156**	41 13N	87 0W
Kankan	**120**	10 30N	9 15W
Kanker	**96**	20 10N	81 40 E
Kankouchen	**107**	40 30N	119 27 E
Kanku	**106**	34 45N	105 12 E
Kankunskiy	**77**	57 37N	126 8 E
Kanmuri-Yama	**110**	34 30N	132 4 E
Kannabe	**110**	34 32N	133 23 E
Kannapolis	**157**	35 32N	80 37W
Kannauj	**95**	27 3N	79 26 E
Kannod	**93**	22 45N	76 40 E
Kano	**121**	12 2N	8 30 E
Kano □	**121**	12 30N	9 0 E
Kan'onji	**110**	34 7N	133 39 E
Kanoroba	**120**	9 7N	6 8W
Kanowit	**102**	2 14N	112 20 E
Kanowna	**137**	30 32 S	121 31 E
Kanoya	**110**	31 25N	130 50 E
Kanózuga	**54**	49 58N	22 25 E
Kanpetlet	**98**	21 10N	93 59 E
Kanpur	**95**	26 35N	80 20 E
Kansas □	**158**	38 40N	98 0W
Kansas City, Kans., U.S.A.	**158**	39 0N	94 40W
Kansas City, Mo., U.S.A.	**158**	39 3N	94 30W
Kansas, R.	**158**	39 15N	96 20W
Kansenia	**127**	10 20 S	26 0 E
Kansk	**77**	56 20N	95 37 E
Kansŏng	**107**	38 24N	128 30 E
Kansu □	**105**	35 30N	104 30 E
Kant	**85**	42 53N	74 51 E
Kant'angtzu	**106**	37 28N	104 33 E
Kantché	**121**	13 31N	8 30 E
Kantemirovka	**83**	49 43N	39 55 E
Kantharalak	**100**	14 39N	104 39 E
Kantishna	**147**	63 31N	151 5W
Kantō □	**111**	36 0N	140 0 E
Kantō-Heiya	**111**	36 0N	139 30 E
Kantō-Sanchi	**111**	35 50N	138 50 E
Kantu-long	**98**	19 57N	97 36 E
Kanturk	**39**	52 10N	8 55W
Kantzu	**108**	31 37N	100 0 E
Kanuma	**111**	36 44N	139 42 E
Kanus	**128**	27 50 S	18 39 E
Kanye	**128**	25 0 S	25 28 E
Kanyu	**128**	20 7 S	24 37 E
Kanyü	**107**	34 53N	119 9 E
Kanzene	**127**	10 30 S	25 12 E
Kanzi, Ras	**126**	7 1 S	39 33 E
Kaoan	**109**	28 25N	115 22 E
Kaochou	**109**	21 55N	110 52 E
Kaohofu	**109**	30 43N	116 49 E
Kaohsien	**108**	28 21N	104 31 E
Kaohsiung	**109**	22 35N	120 16 E
Kaok'eng	**109**	27 39N	114 4 E
Kaoko Otavi	**125**	18 12 S	13 45 E
Kaokoveld	**128**	19 0 S	13 0 E
Kaolack	**120**	14 5N	16 8W
Kaolan Shan	**109**	21 55N	113 15 E
Kaolikung Shan	**108**	26 0N	98 55 E
Kaomi	**107**	36 25N	119 45 E
Kaopao Hu	**109**	32 50N	119 15 E
Kaop'ing	**106**	35 48N	112 55 E
K'aoshant'un	**107**	44 25N	124 27 E
Kaot'ang	**106**	36 51N	116 13 E
Kaoyang	**106**	38 42N	115 47 E
Kaoyu	**109**	32 46N	119 32 E
Kaoyüan	**107**	37 7N	118 0 E
Kapaa	**147**	22 5N	159 19W
Kapadvanj	**94**	23 5N	73 0 E
Kapagere	**135**	9 46 S	147 42 E
Kapanga	**124**	8 30 S	22 40 E
Kapanovka	**83**	47 28N	46 50 E
Kapata	**127**	14 16 S	26 15 E
Kapellen	**47**	51 19N	4 25 E
Kapello, Ákra	**69**	36 9N	23 3 E
Kapema	**127**	10 45 S	28 22 E
Kapfenberg	**52**	47 26N	15 18 E
Kapiri Mposhi	**127**	13 59 S	28 43 E
Kapiskau	**150**	52 50N	82 1W
Kapiskau, R.	**150**	52 47N	81 55W
Kapit	**102**	2 0N	113 5 E
Kapiti I.	**142**	40 50 S	174 56 E
Kaplice	**52**	48 42N	14 30 E
Kapoe	**101**	9 34N	98 32 E
Kapoeta	**123**	4 50N	33 35 E
Kápolnásnyék	**53**	47 16N	18 41 E
Kaponga	**143**	39 29 S	174 9 E
Kapos, R.	**53**	46 30N	18 20 E
Kaposvár	**53**	46 25N	17 47 E
Kappeln	**48**	54 37N	9 56 E
Kapps	**128**	22 32 S	17 18 E
Kaprije	**63**	43 42N	15 43 E
Kaprijke	**47**	51 13N	3 38 E
Kapsan	**107**	41 4N	128 19 E
Kapsukas	**80**	54 33N	23 19 E
Kapuas Hulu, Pegunungan	**102**	1 30N	113 30 E
Kapuas, R.	**102**	0 20N	111 40 E
Kapuka	**127**	10 30 S	32 55 E
Kapulo	**127**	8 18 S	29 15 E
Kapunda	**140**	34 20 S	138 56 E
Kapurthala	**94**	31 23N	75 25 E
Kapuskasing	**150**	49 25N	82 30W
Kapuskasing, R.	**150**	49 49N	82 0W
Kapustin Yar	**83**	48 37N	45 40 E
Kaputar, Mt.	**139**	30 15 S	150 10 E
Kaputir	**126**	2 5N	35 28 E
Kapuvár	**53**	47 36N	17 1 E
Kara, Turkey	**69**	38 29N	26 19 E
Kara, U.S.S.R.	**76**	69 10N	65 25 E
Kara Bogaz Gol, Zaliv	**76**	41 0N	53 30 E
Kara Burun	**69**	38 41N	26 28 E
Kara, I.	**69**	36 58N	27 30 E
Kara Kalpak A.S.S.R. □	**76**	43 0N	60 0 E
Kara Kum	**76**	39 30N	60 0 E
Kara-Saki	**110**	34 41N	129 30 E
Kara Sea	**76**	75 0N	70 0 E
Kara Su	**85**	40 44N	72 53 E
Kara, Wadi	**122**	20 40N	42 0 E
Karabash	**84**	55 29N	60 14 E
Karabekaul	**85**	38 30N	64 8 E
Karabük	**82**	41 10N	32 30 E
Karabulak	**85**	44 54N	78 30 E
Karaburuni	**68**	40 25N	19 20 E
Karabutak	**84**	49 59N	60 14 E
Karachala	**83**	39 45N	48 53 E
Karachayevsk	**83**	43 50N	42 0 E
Karachev	**80**	53 10N	35 5 E
Karachi	**94**	24 53N	67 0 E
Karachi □	**94**	25 30N	67 0 E
Karad	**96**	17 15N	74 10 E
Karadeniz Boğazı	**92**	41 10N	29 5 E
Karadeniz Dağlari	**92**	41 30N	35 0 E
Karaga	**121**	9 58N	0 28W
Karagajly	**76**	49 26N	76 0 E
Karaganda	**76**	49 50N	73 0 E
Karaginskiy, Ostrov	**77**	58 45N	164 0 E
Karagwe □	**126**	2 0 S	31 0 E
Karaikal	**97**	10 59N	79 50 E
Karaikkudi	**97**	10 0N	78 45 E
Karaitivu I.	**97**	9 45N	79 52 E
Karaj	**93**	35 4N	51 0 E
Karak, Jordan	**90**	31 14N	35 40 E
Karak, Malay.	**101**	3 25N	102 2 E
Karakas	**76**	48 20N	83 30 E
Karakitang	**103**	3 14N	125 28 E
Karakobis	**128**	22 3 S	20 37 E
Karakoram	**95**	35 20N	76 0 E
Karakoram P. = K'alak'unlun Shank'ou	**95**	35 33N	77 46 E
Karakoram Pass	**93**	35 20N	78 0 E
Karakul, Tadzhik, S.S.R., U.S.S.R.	**85**	39 2N	73 33 E
Karakul, Uzbek S.S.R., U.S.S.R.	**85**	39 22N	63 50 E
Karakuldzha	**85**	40 39N	73 26 E
Karakulino	**84**	56 1N	53 43 E
Karalon	**77**	57 5N	115 50 E
Karaman	**92**	37 14N	33 13 E
Karambu	**102**	3 53 S	116 6 E
Karamea	**143**	41 14 S	172 6 E
Karamea Bight	**143**	41 22 S	171 40 E
Karamea, R.	**143**	41 13 S	172 26 E
Karamet Niyaz	**85**	37 45N	64 34 E
Karamoja □	**126**	3 0N	34 15 E
Karamsad	**94**	22 35N	72 50 E
Karanganjar	**103**	7 38 S	109 37 E
Karanja	**96**	20 29N	77 31 E
Karapoit	**142**	37 53 S	175 32 E
Karaşar	**82**	40 21N	31 55 E
Karasburg	**128**	28 0 S	18 44 E
Karasino	**76**	66 50N	86 50 E
Karasjok	**74**	69 27N	25 30 E
Karasuk	**76**	53 44N	78 2 E
Karasuk □	**126**	2 12N	35 15 E
Karasuyama	**111**	36 39N	140 9 E
Karatau	**85**	43 10N	70 28 E
Karatau, Khrebet	**85**	43 30N	69 30 E
Karativu, I.	**97**	8 22N	79 52 E
Karatiya	**90**	31 39N	34 43 E
Karatobe	**84**	49 44N	53 30 E
Karatoya, R.	**98**	24 7N	89 36 E
Karaturuk	**85**	43 35N	78 0 E
Karaul-Bazar	**85**	39 30N	64 48 E
Karauli	**94**	26 30N	77 4 E
Karavasta	**68**	40 53N	19 28 E
Karawa	**124**	3 18N	20 17 E
Karawanken	**52**	46 30N	14 40 E
Karazhal	**76**	48 2N	70 49 E
Karbala	**92**	32 47N	44 3 E
Kårböle	**72**	61 59N	15 22 E
Karcag	**53**	47 19N	21 1 E
Karcha, R.	**95**	34 15N	75 57 E
Kärda	**73**	57 10N	13 49 E
Kardeljevo	**66**	43 2N	17 27 E
Kardhámila	**69**	38 35N	26 5 E
Kardhitsa	**68**	39 23N	21 54 E
Kardhitsa □	**68**	39 15N	21 50 E
Kärdla	**80**	58 50N	22 40 E
Kareeberge	**128**	30 50 S	22 0 E
Kareima	**122**	18 30N	31 49 E
Karelian A.S.S.R. □	**78**	65 30N	32 30 E
Karema, P.N.G.	**135**	9 12 S	147 18 E
Karema, Tanz.	**126**	6 49 S	30 24 E
Karen	**101**	12 49N	92 53 E
Karganrud	**92**	37 55N	49 0 E
Kargapolye	**84**	55 57N	64 24 E
Kargasok	**76**	59 3N	80 53 E
Kargat	**76**	55 10N	80 15 E
Kargı	**82**	41 11N	34 30 E
Kargil	**95**	34 32N	76 12 E
Kargowa	**54**	52 5N	15 51 E
Karguéri	**121**	13 36N	10 30 E
Kariai	**69**	40 14N	24 19 E
Kariba	**127**	16 28 S	28 36 E
Kariba Dam	**125**	16 30 S	28 35 E
Kariba Gorge	**127**	16 30 S	28 35 E
Kariba Lake	**127**	16 40 S	28 25 E
Karibib	**128**	21 0 S	15 56 E
Karikal	**97**	10 59N	79 50 E
Karikkale	**92**	39 55N	33 30 E
Karimata, Kepulauan	**102**	1 40 S	109 0 E
Karimata, Selat	**102**	2 0 S	108 20 E
Karimnagar	**96**	18 26N	79 10 E
Karimundjawa, Kepulauan	**102**	5 50 S	110 30 E
Karin	**91**	10 50N	45 52 E
Káristos	**69**	38 1N	24 29 E
Karitane	**51**	45 38 S	170 39 E
Kariya	**111**	34 58N	137 1 E
Karkal	**97**	13 15N	74 56 E
Karkar I.	**135**	4 40 S	146 0 E
Karkinitskiy Zaliv	**82**	45 36N	32 35 E
Karkur	**90**	32 29N	34 57 E
Karkur Tohl	**122**	22 5N	25 5 E
Karl Libknekht	**80**	51 40N	35 45 E
Karl-Marx-Stadt	**48**	50 50N	12 55 E
Karl-Marx-Stadt □	**48**	50 45N	13 0 E
Karla, L = Voiviis, Limni	**68**	39 35N	22 45 E
Karlino	**54**	54 3N	15 53 E
Karlobag	**63**	44 32N	15 5 E
Karlovac	**63**	45 31N	15 36 E
Karlovka	**82**	49 29N	35 8 E
Karlovy Vary	**52**	50 13N	12 51 E
Karlsborg	**73**	58 33N	14 33 E
Karlshamn	**73**	56 10N	14 51 E
Karlskoga	**72**	59 22N	14 33 E
Karlskrona	**73**	56 10N	15 35 E
Karlsruhe	**49**	49 3N	8 23 E
Karlstad, Sweden	**72**	59 23N	13 30 E
Karlstad, U.S.A.	**158**	48 38N	96 30W
Karmøy	**71**	59 15N	5 15 E
Karnal	**94**	29 42N	77 2 E
Karnali, R.	**95**	29 0N	82 0 E
Karnaphuli Res.	**98**	22 40N	92 20 E
Karnataka □	**97**	13 15N	77 0 E
Karnes City	**159**	28 53N	97 53W
Karni	**120**	10 45N	2 40W
Karnische Alpen	**52**	46 36N	13 0 E
Karnobat	**67**	42 40N	27 0 E
Kärnten □	**52**	46 52N	13 30 E
Karo	**120**	12 16N	2 22W
Karoi	**127**	16 48 S	29 45 E
Karonga	**127**	9 57 S	33 55 E
Karoonda	**140**	35 1 S	139 59 E
Karos, Is.	**69**	36 54N	25 40 E
Karousâdhes	**68**	39 47N	19 45 E
Karpalund	**73**	56 4N	14 5 E
Kárpathos, I.	**69**	35 37N	27 10 E
Kárpathos, Stenón	**69**	36 0N	27 30 E
Karpinsk	**84**	59 45N	60 1 E
Karpogory	**78**	63 59N	44 27 E
Karrebaek	**73**	55 12N	11 39 E
Kars	**92**	40 40N	43 5 E
Karsakpay	**76**	47 55N	66 40 E
Karsha	**83**	49 45N	51 35 E
Karshi	**85**	38 53N	65 48 E
Karsun	**81**	54 14N	46 57 E
Kartál Óros	**68**	41 15N	25 13 E
Kartaly	**84**	53 3N	60 40 E
Kartapur	**94**	31 27N	75 32 E
Kartuzy	**54**	54 22N	18 10 E
Karuah	**141**	32 37 S	151 56 E
Karufa	**103**	3 50 S	133 20 E
Karumba	**138**	17 31 S	140 50 E
Karumo	**126**	2 25 S	32 50 E
Karumwa	**126**	3 12 S	32 38 E
Karungu	**126**	0 50 S	34 10 E
Karunjie	**136**	16 18 S	127 12 E
Karup	**73**	56 19N	9 10 E
Karur	**97**	10 59N	78 2 E
Karviná	**53**	49 53N	18 25 E
Karwar	**93**	14 55N	74 13 E
Karwi	**95**	25 12N	80 57 E
Kas Kong	**101**	11 27N	102 12 E
Kasache	**127**	13 25 S	34 20 E
Kasai	**110**	34 55N	134 52 E
Kasai Occidental □	**127**	6 30 S	22 30 E
Kasai Oriental □	**126**	5 0 S	24 30 E
Kasai, R.	**124**	8 20 S	22 0 E
Kasaji	**127**	10 25 S	23 27 E
Kasama, Japan	**111**	36 23N	140 16 E
Kasama, Zambia	**127**	10 16 S	31 9 E
Kasandong	**107**	41 18N	126 55 E
Kasane	**128**	17 34 S	24 50 E
Kasanga	**127**	8 30 S	31 10 E
Kasangulu	**124**	4 15 S	15 15 E
Kasaoka	**110**	34 30N	133 30 E
Kasaragod	**97**	12 30N	74 58 E
Kasat	**98**	15 56N	98 13 E
Kasba	**98**	25 51N	87 37 E
Kasba L.	**153**	60 20N	102 10W
Kasba Tadla	**118**	32 36N	6 17W
Kaschmar	**93**	35 16N	58 26 E
Kaseberga	**73**	55 24N	14 8 E
Kaseda	**110**	31 25N	130 19 E
Kasempa	**127**	13 30 S	25 44 E
Kasenga	**127**	10 20 S	28 45 E
Kasese	**126**	0 13N	30 3 E
Kasewa	**127**	14 28 S	28 53 E
Kasganj	**95**	27 48N	78 42 E
Kashabowie	**150**	48 40N	90 26W
Kashan	**93**	34 5N	51 30 E
Kashgar = K'oshin	**105**	39 29N	75 58 E
Kashihara	**111**	34 35N	135 37 E
Kashima, Ibaraki, Japan	**111**	35 58N	140 38 E
Kashima, Saga, Japan	**110**	33 7N	130 6 E
Kashima-Nada	**111**	36 0N	140 45 E
Kashimbo	**127**	11 12 S	26 19 E
Kashin	**81**	57 20N	37 36 E
Kashipur, Orissa, India	**96**	19 16N	83 3 E
Kashipur, Ut. P., India	**95**	29 15N	79 0 E
Kashira	**81**	54 45N	38 10 E
Kashiwa	**111**	35 52N	139 59 E
Kashiwazaki	**112**	37 22N	138 33 E
Kashkasu	**85**	39 54N	72 44 E
Kashmir □	**95**	32 44N	74 54 E
Kashmor	**94**	28 28N	69 32 E
Kashpirovka	**81**	53 0N	48 30 E
Kashum Tso	**99**	34 45N	86 0 E
Kashun Noerh	**105**	42 25N	101 0 E
Kasimov	**81**	54 55N	41 20 E
Kasing	**126**	6 15 S	26 58 E
Kaskaskia, R.	**158**	37 58N	89 57W
Kaskattama, R.	**153**	57 3N	90 4W
Kaskelan	**85**	43 20N	76 35 E
Kaskinen (Kaskö)	**74**	62 22N	21 15 E
Kaskö (Kaskinen)	**74**	62 22N	21 15 E
Kasli	**84**	55 53N	60 46 E
Kaslo	**152**	49 55N	117 0W
Kasmere L.	**153**	59 34N	101 10W
Kasonawedjo	**127**	1 50 S	137 41 E
Kasongo	**126**	4 30 S	26 33 E
Kasongo Lunda	**124**	6 35 S	17 0 E
Kásos, I.	**69**	35 20N	26 55 E
Kásos, Stenón	**69**	35 30N	26 30 E
Kaspi	**83**	41 54N	44 17 E
Kaspiysk	**83**	42 45N	47 40 E
Kaspiyskiy	**83**	45 22N	47 23 E
Kassab ed Doleib	**123**	13 30N	33 35 E
Kassaba	**122**	22 40N	29 55 E
Kassala	**123**	15 23N	36 26 E
Kassala □	**123**	15 20N	36 26 E
Kassan	**85**	39 2N	65 35 E
Kassandra	**68**	40 0N	23 30 E
Kassansay	**85**	41 15N	71 31 E
Kassel	**48**	51 19N	9 32 E
Kassinger	**122**	18 46N	31 51 E
Kassiopi	**80**	39 48N	19 55 E
Kassue	**103**	6 58 S	139 21 E
Kastamonu	**92**	41 25N	33 43 E
Kastav	**63**	45 22N	14 20 E
Kastélli	**69**	35 29N	23 38 E
Kastéllion	**69**	35 12N	25 20 E
Kastellorizon = Megiste	**61**	36 8N	29 34 E
Kastellou, Ákra	**69**	35 30N	27 15 E
Kasterlee	**47**	51 15N	4 59 E
Kastlösa	**73**	56 26N	16 25 E
Kastó, I.	**69**	38 35N	20 55 E
Kastóri	**69**	37 10N	22 17 E
Kastoria	**68**	40 30N	21 19 E
Kastoria □	**68**	40 30N	21 15 E
Kastorías	**68**	40 30N	21 20 E
Kastornoye	**81**	51 55N	38 2 E
Kástron	**68**	39 53N	25 8 E

Kastrosikiá Kerman

Kastrosikiá 69 39 6N 20 36 E
Kasugai 111 35 12N 136 59 E
Kasukabe 111 35 58N 139 49 E
Kasulu 126 4 37 S 30 5 E
Kasulu □ 126 4 37 S 30 5 E
Kasumi 110 35 38N 134 38 E
Kasumiga-Ura 111 36 0N 140 25 E
Kasumkent 83 41 47N 48 15 E
Kasungu 127 13 0 S 33 29 E
Kasur 94 31 5N 74 25 E
Kata 77 58 46N 102 40 E
Kataba 127 16 10 S 25 10 E
Katako Kombe 126 3 25 S 24 20 E
Katákolon 69 37 38N 21 19 E
Katale 126 4 52 S 31 7 E
Katalla 147 60 10N 144 35W
Katama 123 9 35N 38 36 E
Katamatite 141 36 6 S 145 41 E
Katanda 126 0 55 S 29 21 E
Katanga = Shaba 126 8 0 S 25 0 E
Katanghan □ 93 36 0N 69 0 E
Katangi 96 21 56N 79 50 E
Katangli 77 51 42N 143 14 E
Katanich 123 6 0N 33 40 E
Katanning 132 33 40 S 117 33 E
Katastári 69 37 50N 20 45 E
Katav Ivanovsk 84 54 45N 58 12 E
Katavi Swamps 126 6 50 S 31 10 E
Katerini 68 40 18N 22 37 E
Katesbridge 38 54 18N 6 8W
Katha 99 24 10N 96 30 E
Katherina, Gebel 122 28 30N 33 57 E
Katherine 136 14 27 S 132 20 E
Kathiawar, dist. 93 22 20N 71 0 E
Kathua 95 32 23N 75 30 E
Kati 120 12 41N 8 4W
Katiet 102 2 21 S 99 44 E
Katihar 95 25 34N 87 36 E
Katima Mulilo 125 17 28 S 24 13 E
Katima Mulilo Rapids 128 17 28 S 24 13 E
Katimbira 127 12 40 S 34 0 E
Katiola 120 8 10N 5 10W
Katkopberg 128 30 0 S 20 0 E
Katlanovo 66 41 52N 21 40 E
Katmai Nat. Monument 147 58 30N 155 0W
Katmai, vol. 147 58 20N 154 59W
Katmandu 95 27 45N 85 12 E
Kato Akhaïa 69 38 8N 21 33 E
Kato Stazros 68 40 39N 23 43 E
Katol 96 21 17N 78 38 E
Katompi 124 6 2 S 26 23 E
Katonga, R. 126 0 15N 31 50 E
Katoomba 141 33 41 S 150 19 E
Katowice 54 50 17N 19 5 E
Katowice □ 53 50 15N 19 0 E
Katrine L. 34 56 15N 4 30W
Katrineholm 72 59 9N 16 12 E
Katsepe 129 15 45 S 46 15 E
Katsina 121 7 10N 9 20 E
Katsina Ala, R. 121 6 52N 9 40 E
Katsumoto 110 33 51N 129 42 E
Katsuta 111 36 25N 140 31 E
Katsuura 111 35 15N 140 20 E
Katsuyama 111 36 3N 136 30 E
Kattakurgan 85 39 55N 66 15 E
Kattawaz 93 32 48N 68 23 E
Kattawaz-Urgun □ 93 32 10N 62 20 E
Kattegat 73 57 0N 11 20 E
Katumba 126 7 40 S 25 17 E
Katungu 126 2 55 S 40 3 E
Katwa 95 23 30N 89 25 E
Katwijk-aan-Zee 46 52 12N 4 24 E
Katy 54 51 2N 16 45 E
Kau Tao 101 10 6N 99 48 E
Kauai Chan. 147 21 45N 158 50W
Kauai, I. 147 19 30N 155 30W
Kaufakha 90 31 29N 34 40 E
Kaufbeuren 49 47 42N 10 37 E
Kaufman 159 32 35N 96 20W
Kaukauna 156 44 20N 88 13W
Kaukauveld 128 20 0 S 20 15 E
Kaukonen 74 67 31N 24 53 E
Kaulille 47 51 11N 5 31 E
Kauliranta 74 66 27N 23 41 E
Kaunas 80 54 54N 23 54 E
Kaunghein 98 25 41N 95 26 E
Kaupulehu 147 19 43N 155 53W
Kaura Namoda 121 12 37N 6 33 E
Kautokeino 74 69 0N 23 4 E
Kavacha 77 60 16N 169 51 E
Kavadarci 66 41 26N 22 3 E
Kavaja 68 41 11N 19 33 E
Kavali 97 14 55N 80 1 E
Kaválla 68 40 57N 24 28 E
Kaválla □ 68 41 05N 24 30 E
Kaválla Kólpos 68 40 50N 24 25 E
Kavanayén 174 5 38N 61 48W
Kavarna 67 43 26N 28 22 E
Kavieng 135 2 36 S 150 51 E
Kavkaz, Bolshoi 83 42 50N 44 0 E
Kavousi 69 35 7N 25 51 E
Kaw = Caux 175 4 30N 52 15W
Kawa 123 13 42N 32 34 E
Kawachi-Nagano 111 34 28N 135 31 E
Kawagoe 111 35 55N 139 29 E
Kawaguchi 111 35 52N 138 45 E
Kawaihae 147 20 3N 155 50W
Kawaihoa Pt. 147 21 47N 160 12W
Kawaikini, Mt. 147 22 0N 159 30W
Kawakawa 142 35 23 S 174 6 E
Kawama 127 9 30 S 28 30 E
Kawambwa 127 9 48 S 29 3 E
Kawanoe 110 34 1N 133 34 E
Kawarau 143 45 3 S 169 0 E
Kawardha 95 22 0N 81 17 E
Kawasaki 111 35 35N 138 42 E
Kawau I. 142 36 25 S 174 52 E
Kawene 150 48 45N 91 15W
Kawerau 142 38 7 S 176 42 E
Kawhia Harbour 142 38 5 S 174 51 E
Kawick Peak 163 37 58N 116 57W
Kawkareik 98 16 33N 98 14 E
Kawlin 98 23 47N 95 41 E
Kawnro 99 22 48N 99 8 E
Kawthaung 101 10 5N 98 36 E
Kawthoolei □ = Kawthuk 98 18 0N 97 30 E
Kawthuk □ 98 18 0N 97 30 E
Kawya 98 16 40N 97 50 E
Kay 84 59 57N 52 59 E
Kaya 121 13 25N 1 10W
Kayah □ 98 19 15N 97 15 E
Kayaho 107 43 5N 129 46 E
Kayak I. 147 60 0N 144 30W
Kayan 98 16 54N 96 34 E
Kayangulam 97 9 10N 76 33 E
Kaycee 160 43 45N 106 46W
Kayenta 161 36 46N 110 15W
Kayes 120 14 25N 11 30W
Kayima 120 8 54N 11 15W
Kayl 47 49 29N 6 2 E
Kayomba 127 13 11 S 24 2 E
Kayoro 121 11 0N 1 28W
Kayrakkumskoye Vdkhr. 85 40 20N 70 0 E
Kayrunnera 139 30 40 S 142 30 E
Kaysatskoye 83 49 47N 46 49 E
Kayseri 92 38 45N 35 30 E
Kaysville 160 41 2N 111 58W
Kazachinskoye 77 56 16N 107 36 E
Kazachye 77 70 52N 135 58 E
Kazakh S.S.R. □ 85 50 0N 58 0 E
Kazakhstan 84 51 11N 53 0 E
Kazan 81 55 48N 49 3 E
Kazan, R. 153 64 2N 95 30W
Kazanluk 67 42 38N 25 35 E
Kazanskaya 83 49 50N 40 30 E
Kazarman 85 41 24N 73 59 E
Kazatin 82 49 45N 28 50 E
Kazerun 93 29 38N 51 40 E
Kazhim 84 60 21N 51 33 E
Kazi Magomed 83 40 3N 49 0 E
Kazimierza Wielki 54 50 15N 20 30 E
Kazincbarcika 53 48 17N 20 36 E
Kazo 111 36 7N 139 36 E
Kaztalovka 83 49 47N 48 43 E
Kazu 98 25 27N 97 46 E
Kazumba 124 6 25 S 22 5 E
Kazvin 92 36 15N 50 0 E
Kazym, R. 76 63 40N 68 30 E
Kcynia 54 53 0N 17 30 E
Kė 120 13 58N 5 18W
Ke-hsi Mansam 98 21 56N 97 50 E
Ke-Macina 120 14 5N 5 20W
Kéa 69 37 35N 24 22 E
Kea 30 50 13N 5 4W
Kéa, I. 69 37 30N 24 22 E
Keaau 147 19 37N 155 3W
Keady 38 54 15N 6 42W
Keal, Loch na 34 56 30N 6 5W
Kealkill 39 51 45N 9 20W
Keams Canyon 161 35 53N 110 9W
Keanae 147 20 52N 156 9W
Kearney 158 40 45N 99 3W
Kearsage, Mt. 162 43 25N 71 51W
Keban 92 38 50N 38 50 E
Kebele 123 12 52N 40 40 E
Kebi 120 9 18N 6 37W
Kebili 119 33 47N 9 0 E
Kebkabiya 117 13 50N 24 0 E
Kebnekaise, mt. 74 67 54N 18 33 E
Kebock Hd. 36 58 1N 6 20W
Kebri Dehar 91 6 45N 44 17 E
Kebumen 103 7 42 S 109 40 E
Kecel 53 46 31N 19 16 E
Kechika, R. 152 59 41N 127 12W
Kecskemét 53 46 57N 19 35 E
Kedada 123 5 30N 35 58 E
Kedah □ 101 5 50N 100 40 E
Kedainiai 80 55 15N 23 57 E
Kedgwick 151 47 40N 67 20W
Kedia Hill 128 21 28 S 24 37 E
Kediri 103 7 51 S 112 1 E
Kédougou 120 12 35N 12 10W
Kedzierzyn 54 50 20N 18 12 E
Keefers 152 50 0N 121 40W
Keel 38 53 59N 10 2W
Keelby 33 53 34N 0 15W
Keele 32 53 0N 2 17W
Keele, R. 147 64 15N 127 0W
Keeler 163 36 29N 117 52W
Keeley L. 153 54 54N 108 8W
Keeling Is. = Cocos Is. 142 12 12 S 96 54 E
Keelung = Chilung 109 25 3N 121 45 E
Keen, Mt. 37 56 58N 2 54W
Keenagh 38 53 36N 7 50W
Keene, Calif., U.S.A. 163 35 13N 118 33W
Keene, N.H., U.S.A. 162 42 57N 72 17W
Keeper, Mt. 39 52 46N 8 17W
Keer-Weer, C. 138 14 0 S 141 32 E
Keerbergen 47 51 1N 4 38 E
Keeten Mastgat 47 51 36N 4 0 E
Keetmanshoop 128 26 35 S 18 8 E
Keewatin 158 47 23N 93 0W
Keewatin □ 153 63 20N 94 40W
Keewatin, R. 153 56 29N 100 46W
Kefa □ 123 6 55N 36 30 E
Kefallinía, I. 69 38 28N 20 30 E
Kefamenanu 103 9 28 S 124 38 E
Kefar Ata 90 32 48N 35 7 E
Kefar Etsyon 90 31 39N 35 7 E
Kefar Hasidim 90 32 47N 35 5 E
Kefar Hittim B. 90 32 48N 35 27 E
Kefar Nahum 90 32 54N 35 22 E
Kefar Sava 90 32 11N 34 54 E
Kefar Szold 90 33 11N 35 34 E
Kefar Vitkin 90 32 22N 34 53 E
Kefar Yehezqel 90 32 34N 35 22 E
Kefar Yona 90 32 20N 34 54 E
Kefar Zekharya 90 31 43N 34 57 E
Keffi 121 8 55N 7 43 E
Keflavík 74 64 2N 22 35W
Keg River 152 57 54N 117 7W
Kegalla 97 7 15N 80 21 E
Kegashka 151 50 14N 61 18W
Kegworth 28 52 50N 1 17W
Kehl 49 48 34N 7 50 E
Keighley 32 53 52N 1 54W
Keimaneigh, P. of 39 51 49N 9 17W
Keimoes 128 28 41 S 21 0 E
Keiss 37 58 33N 3 6W
Keïta 121 14 46N 5 56 E
Keith, Austral. 140 36 0 S 140 20 E
Keith, U.K. 37 57 33N 2 58W
Keith Arm 148 65 20N 122 15W
Kekaygyr 85 40 42N 75 32 E
Kekri 94 26 0N 75 10 E
Kël 77 69 30N 124 10 E
Kelamet 123 16 0N 38 20 E
Kelang 101 3 2N 101 26 E
Kelani Ganga, R. 97 6 58N 79 50 E
Kelantan □ 101 5 10N 102 0 E
Kelantan, R. 101 6 13N 102 14 E
Kělcyra 68 40 22N 20 12 E
Keld 32 54 24N 2 11W
Keles, R. 85 41 1N 68 37 E
Kelheim 49 48 58N 11 57 E
Kelibia 119 36 50N 11 3 E
Kellas 37 57 33N 3 23W
Kellé, Congo 124 0 8 S 14 38 E
Kellé, Niger 121 14 18N 10 10 E
Keller 160 48 2N 118 44W
Kellerberrin 137 31 36 S 117 38 E
Kellett C. 12 72 0N 126 0W
Kellogg 160 47 30N 116 5W
Kelloselkä 74 66 56N 28 53 E
Kells, Ireland 39 52 33N 7 18W
Kells, U.K. 38 54 48N 6 13W
Kells = Ceanannas Mor 38 53 42N 6 53W
Kells, Rhinns of 34 55 9N 4 22W
Kelmentsy 80 48 30N 26 50 E
Kélo 124 9 10N 15 45 E
Kelowna 152 49 50N 119 25W
Kelsale 29 52 15N 1 30 E
Kelsall 32 53 14N 2 44W
Kelsey Bay 152 50 25N 126 0W
Kelso, N.Z. 143 45 54 S 169 15 E
Kelso, U.K. 35 55 36N 2 27W
Kelso, U.S.A. 160 46 10N 122 57W
Keltemashat 85 42 25N 70 8 E
Keluang 101 2 3N 103 18 E
Kelvedon 29 51 50N 0 43 E
Kelvington 153 52 10N 103 30W
Kem 78 65 0N 34 38 E
Kem-Kem 118 30 40N 4 30W
Kem, R. 78 64 45N 32 20 E
Kema 103 1 22N 125 8 E
Kemah 92 39 32N 39 5 E
Kemano 152 53 35N 128 0W
Kemapyu 98 18 49N 97 19 E
Kemasik 101 4 25N 103 25 E
Kembolcha 123 11 29N 39 42 E
Kemenets-Podolskiy 82 48 40N 26 30 E
Kemerovo 76 55 20N 85 50 E
Kemi 74 65 44N 24 34 E
Kemi älv = Kemijoki 74 65 47N 24 32 E
Kemijärvi 74 66 43N 27 22 E
Kemijoki 74 65 47N 24 32 E
Kemmel 47 50 47N 2 50 E
Kemmerer 160 41 52N 110 30W
Kemmnay 37 57 14N 2 28W
Kemp Coast 13 69 0 S 55 0 E
Kemp L. 159 33 45N 99 15W
Kempsey, Austral. 141 31 1 S 152 50 E
Kempsey, U.K. 28 52 8N 2 11W
Kempston 29 52 7N 0 30W
Kempt, L. 150 47 25N 74 22W
Kempten 49 47 42N 10 18 E
Kemptville 150 45 0N 75 38W
Ken L. 35 55 0N 4 8W
Kenadsa 118 31 48N 2 26W
Kenai 147 60 35N 151 20W
Kenai Mts. 147 60 0N 150 0W
Kendal, Indon. 103 6 56 S 110 14 E
Kendal, U.K. 32 54 19N 2 44W
Kendall 141 31 35 S 152 44 E
Kendall, R. 138 14 4 S 141 35 E
Kendallville 156 41 25N 85 15W
Kendari 103 3 50 S 122 30 E
Kendawangan 102 2 32 S 110 17 E
Kende 121 11 30N 4 12 E
Kendenup 137 34 30 S 117 38 E
Kendrapara 96 20 35N 86 30 E
Kendrick 160 46 43N 116 41W
Kendriki Kai Dhitiki Makedhonia □ 68 40 30N 22 0 E
Kene Thao 100 17 44N 101 25 E
Kenema 120 7 50N 11 14W
Keng Kok 100 16 26N 105 12 E
Keng Tawng 98 20 45N 98 18 E
Keng Tung, Burma 99 21 0N 99 30 E
Keng Tung, Burma 99 21 0N 99 30 E
Kenge 124 4 50 S 16 55 E
Kengeja 126 5 26 S 39 45 E
Kengma 108 23 34N 99 24 E
Kenhardt 128 29 19 S 21 12 E
Kenilworth 28 52 22N 1 35W
Kenimekh 85 40 16N 65 7 E
Kéninkoumou 120 15 17N 12 18W
Kénitra (Port Lyautey) 118 34 15N 6 40W
Kenmare, Ireland 39 51 52N 9 35W
Kenmare, U.S.A. 158 48 40N 102 4W
Kenmare, R. 39 51 40N 10 0W
Kenmore 37 56 35N 4 0W
Kenn Reef 133 21 12 S 155 46 E
Kennebec 158 43 56N 99 54W
Kennedy 127 18 52 S 27 10 E
Kennedy, C. = Canaveral, C. 157 28 28N 80 31W
Kennedy, Mt. 148 60 19N 139 0W
Kennedy Ra. 137 24 45 S 115 10 E
Kennedy Taungdeik 99 23 35N 94 4 E
Kennet, R. 28 51 24N 1 7W
Kenneth Ra. 137 23 50 S 117 8 E
Kennett 159 36 7N 90 0W
Kennett Square 162 39 51N 75 43W
Kennewick 160 46 11N 119 2W
Kenninghall 29 52 26N 1 0 E
Kénogami 151 48 25N 71 15W
Kenogami, R. 150 51 6N 84 28W
Kenora 153 49 50N 94 35W
Kenosha 156 42 33N 87 48W
Kensington, Can. 151 46 28N 63 34W
Kensington, U.S.A. 158 39 48N 99 2W
Kensington Downs 138 22 31 S 144 19 E
Kent, Ohio, U.S.A. 156 41 8N 81 20W
Kent, Oreg., U.S.A. 160 45 11N 120 45W
Kent, Tex., U.S.A. 159 31 5N 104 12W
Kent □ 29 51 12N 0 40 E
Kent Gr. 138 39 30 S 147 20 E
Kent Pen. 148 68 30N 107 0W
Kent Pt. 162 38 50N 76 22W
Kent, Vale of 23 51 12N 0 30 E
Kentau 85 43 32N 68 36 E
Kentdale 137 34 54 S 117 3 E
Kentisbeare 30 50 51N 3 18W
Kentland 156 40 45N 87 25W
Kenton, U.K. 30 50 37N 3 28W
Kenton, U.S.A. 156 40 40N 83 35W
Kentucky 141 30 45 S 151 28 E
Kentucky □ 156 37 20N 85 0W
Kentucky Dam 156 37 2N 88 15W
Kentucky L. 157 36 0N 88 0W
Kentucky, R. 156 38 41N 85 11W
Kentville 151 45 6N 64 29W
Kentwood 159 31 0N 90 30W
Kenya ■ 126 2 20N 38 0 E
Kenya, Mt. 126 0 10 S 37 18 E
Keo Nena, Deo 100 18 23N 105 10 E
Keokuk 158 40 25N 91 24W
Kep, Camb. 101 10 29N 104 19 E
Kep, Viet. 100 21 24N 106 16 E
Kep-i-Gjuhëzës 68 40 28N 19 15 E
Kep-i-Palit 68 41 25N 19 21 E
Kep-i-Rodonit 68 41 32N 19 30 E
Kepi 103 6 32 S 139 19 E
Kepice 54 54 16N 16 51 E
Kepler Mts. 143 45 25 S 167 20 E
Kepno 54 51 18N 17 58 E
Keppel B. 133 23 21 S 150 55 E
Kepsut 92 39 40N 28 15 E
Kepuhi 147 22 13N 159 21W
Kepulauan, R. 103 5 30 S 139 0 E
Kepulauan Sunda, Ketjil Barat □ 102 8 50 S 117 30 E
Kepulauan Sunda, Ketjil Timor □ 103 9 30 S 122 0 E
Kerala □ 97 11 0N 76 15 E
Kerama-Shotō 112 26 12N 127 22 E
Keran 95 34 35N 73 59 E
Kerang 140 35 40 S 143 55 E
Keratéa 69 37 48N 23 58 E
Keraudren, C., Tas., Austral. 136 40 22 S 144 47 E
Keraudren, C., W. Austral., Austral. 138 19 58 S 119 45 E
Keravat 135 4 17 S 152 2 E
Keray 93 26 15N 57 30 E
Kerch 82 45 20N 36 20 E
Kerchinskiy Proliv 82 45 10N 36 30 E
Kerchoual 121 17 20N 0 20 E
Kerem Maharal 90 32 39N 34 59 E
Kerema 135 7 58 S 145 50 E
Keren 123 15 45N 38 28 E
Kerewan 120 13 35N 16 10W
Kerguelen I. 11 48 15 S 69 10 E
Kerhonkson 162 41 46N 74 11W
Keri 69 37 40N 20 49 E
Keri Kera 123 12 21N 32 37 E
Kericho 126 0 22 S 35 15 E
Kericho □ 126 0 30 S 35 15 E
Kerikeri 143 35 12 S 173 59 E
Kerinci 102 2 5 S 101 0 E
Kerkdriel 46 51 47N 5 20 E
Kerkenna, Iles 119 34 48N 11 1 E
Kerki 85 37 50N 65 12 E
Kérkira 68 39 38N 19 50 E
Kerkrade 47 50 53N 6 4 E
Kerma 122 19 33N 30 32 E
Kermadec Is. 130 31 8 S 175 16W
Kermān 93 30 15N 57 1 E
Kerman 163 36 43N 120 4W

Kermān □ **Killavullen**

Kermān □	93	30 0N	57 0 E
Kermanshah	92	34 23N	47 0 E
Kermanshah □	92	34 0N	46 30 E
Kerme Körfezi	69	36 55N	27 50 E
Kermen	67	42 30N	26 16 E
Kermit	159	31 56N	103 3W
Kern, R.	163	35 16N	119 18W
Kerns	51	46 54N	8 17 E
Kernville	163	35 45N	118 26W
Keroh	101	5 43N	101 1 E
Kerr, Pt.	142	34 25 S	173 5 E
Kerrera I.	34	56 24N	5 32W
Kerrobert	157	52 0N	109 11W
Kerrville	159	30 1N	99 8W
Kerry	31	52 28N	3 16W
Kerry □	39	52 7N	9 35W
Kerry Hd.	39	52 26N	9 56W
Kerrysdale	36	57 41N	5 39W
Kersa	123	9 28N	41 48 E
Kerstinbo	72	60 16N	16 58 E
Kerteminde	73	55 28N	10 39 E
Kertosono	103	7 38 S	112 9 E
Keru	123	15 40N	37 5 E
Kerulen, R.	105	48 48N	117 0 E
Kerzaz	118	29 29N	1 25W
Kerzers	50	46 59N	7 12 E
Kesagami L.	150	50 23N	80 15W
Kesagami, R.	150	51 4N	79 45W
Kesan	68	41 49N	26 38 E
Kesch, Piz	51	46 38N	9 53 E
Kesh	38	54 31N	7 43W
Keski Suomen □	74	62 45N	25 15 E
Kessel, Belg.	47	51 8N	4 38 E
Kessel, Neth.	47	51 17N	6 3 E
Kessel-Lo	47	50 53N	4 43 E
Kessingland	29	52 25N	1 41 E
Kestell	129	28 17 S	28 42 E
Kestenga	78	66 0N	31 50 E
Kesteren	46	51 56N	5 34 E
Keswick	32	54 35N	3 9W
Keszthely	53	46 50N	17 15 E
Keta	121	5 49N	1 0 E
Ketapang	102	1 55 S	110 0 E
Ketchikan	147	55 25N	131 40W
Ketchum	160	43 50N	114 27W
Kete Krachi	121	7 55N	0 1W
Ketef, Khalîg Umm el	122	23 40N	35 35 E
Ketelmeer	46	32 36N	5 46 E
Keti Bandar	94	24 8N	67 27 E
Ketri	94	28 1N	75 50 E
Ketrzyn	54	54 7N	21 22 E
Kettering	29	52 24N	0 44W
Kettla, Ness	36	60 3N	1 20W
Kettle Falls	160	48 41N	118 2W
Kettle Ness	33	54 32N	0 41W
Kettle, R.	153	56 23N	94 34W
Kettleman City	163	36 1N	119 58W
Kettlewell	32	54 8N	2 2W
Kety	54	49 51N	19 16 E
Kevin	160	48 45N	111 58W
Kewanee	158	41 18N	90 0W
Kewaunee	156	44 27N	87 30W
Keweenaw B.	156	46 56N	88 23W
Keweenaw Pen.	156	47 30N	88 0W
Keweenaw Pt.	156	47 26N	87 40W
Kexby	33	53 21N	0 41W
Key Harbour	150	45 50N	80 45W
Key, L.	38	54 0N	8 15W
Key West	166	24 40N	82 0W
Keyingham	33	53 42N	0 7W
Keyling Inlet	136	14 50 S	129 40 E
Keymer	29	50 55N	0 5W
Keynsham	28	51 25N	2 30W
Keynshamburg	127	19 15 S	29 40 E
Keyport	162	40 26N	74 12W
Keyser	156	39 26N	79 0W
Keystone, S.D., U.S.A.	158	43 54N	103 27W
Keystone, W. Va., U.S.A.	156	37 30N	81 30W
Keyworth	28	52 52N	1 8W
Kez	84	57 55N	53 46 E
Kezhma	77	59 15N	100 57 E
Kezmarok	53	49 10N	20 28 E
Khabarovo	76	69 30N	60 30 E
Khabarovsk	77	48 20N	135 0 E
Khachmas	83	41 31N	48 42 E
Khachraud	94	23 25N	75 20 E
Khadari, W. el	123	10 35N	26 16 E
Khadro	94	26 11N	68 50 E
Khadyzhensk	83	44 26N	39 32 E
Khadzhilyangar	95	35 45N	79 20 E
Khagaria	95	25 18N	86 32 E
Khaibar	92	25 38N	39 28 E
Khaibor	122	25 49N	39 16 E
Khaipur, Bahawalpur, Pak.	94	29 34N	72 17 E
Khaipur, Hyderabad, Pak.	94	27 32N	68 49 E
Khair	94	27 57N	77 46 E
Khairabad	95	27 33N	80 47 E
Khairagarh	95	21 27N	81 2 E
Khairpur	93	27 32N	68 49 E
Khairpur □	94	23 30N	69 8 E
Khakhea	125	24 48 S	23 22 E
Khalach	85	38 4N	64 52 E
Khalfallah	118	34 33N	0 16 E
Khalij-e-Fars □	93	28 20N	51 45 E
Khalilabad	95	26 48N	83 5 E
Khálki	68	39 36N	22 30 E
Khálki, I.	69	36 15N	27 35 E
Khalkidhiki □	68	40 25N	23 20 E
Khalkís	69	38 27N	23 42 E
Khalmer-Sede = Tazovskiy	76	67 30N	78 30 E
Khalmer Yu	76	67 58N	65 1 E
Khalturin	81	58 40N	48 50 E
Kham Kent	100	18 15N	104 43 E
Khamaria	96	23 10N	80 52 E
Khama's Country	128	21 45 S	26 30 E
Khamba Dzong	99	28 25N	88 30W
Khambhalia	94	22 14N	69 41 E
Khamgaon	96	20 42N	76 37 E
Khammam	96	17 11N	80 6 E
Khān Yūnis	90	31 21N	34 18 E
Khan Yunus	90	31 21N	34 18 E
Khanabad, Afghan.	93	36 45N	69 5 E
Khanabad, U.S.S.R.	85	40 59N	70 38 E
Khānaqin	92	34 23N	45 25 E
Khandrá	69	35 3N	26 8 E
Khandwa	96	21 49N	76 22 E
Khandyga	77	62 30N	134 50 E
Khanewal	94	30 20N	71 55 E
Khanga Sidi Nadji	119	34 50N	6 50 E
Khanh Duong	100	12 44N	108 44 E
* Khanh Hung	101	9 36N	105 58 E
Khaniá	69	35 30N	24 4 E
Khaniá □	69	35 0N	24 0 E
Khanion Kólpos	69	35 33N	23 55 E
Khanka, Oz.	76	45 0N	132 30 E
Khanna	94	30 42N	76 16 E
Khanpur	94	28 42N	70 35 E
Khantau	85	44 13N	73 48 E
Khanty-Mansiysk	76	61 0N	69 0 E
Khapalu	95	35 10N	76 20 E
Kharagpur	95	22 20N	87 25 E
Kharaij	122	21 25N	41 0 E
Kharan Kalat	93	28 34N	65 21 E
Kharanaq	93	32 20N	54 45 E
Kharda	96	18 40N	75 40 E
Khardung La	95	34 20N	77 43 E
Kharfa	92	22 0N	46 35 E
Kharg, Jazireh	92	29 15N	50 28 E
Khârga, El Wâhât el	122	25 0N	30 0 E
Khargon, India	93	21 45N	75 35 E
Khargon, India	96	21 45N	75 40 E
Kharit, Wadi el	122	24 5N	34 10 E
Kharkov	82	49 58N	36 20 E
Kharmanli	67	41 55N	25 55 E
Kharovsk	81	59 56N	40 13 E
Kharsaniya	92	27 10N	49 10 E
Khartoum = El Khartûm	123	15 31N	32 35 E
Khartoum □	123	16 0N	33 0 E
Khasab	93	26 14N	56 15 E
Khasavyurt	83	43 30N	46 40 E
Khasebake	128	20 42 S	24 29 E
Khash	93	28 15N	61 5 E
Khashm el Girba	123	14 59N	35 58 E
Khasi Hills	98	25 30N	91 30 E
Khaskovo	67	41 56N	25 30 E
Khatanga	77	72 0N	102 20 E
Khatanga, Zaliv	12	66 0N	112 0 E
Khatauli	94	29 17N	77 43 E
Khatyrchi	85	40 2N	65 58 E
Khatyrka	77	62 3N	175 15 E
Khavar □	92	37 20N	46 0 E
Khavast	85	40 10N	68 49 E
Khawa	122	29 45N	40 25 E
Khaydarken	85	39 57N	71 20 E
Khazzân Jabal el Awliyâ	123	15 24N	32 20 E
Khe Bo	100	19 8N	104 41 E
Khe Long	100	21 29N	104 46 E
Khed, Maharashtra, India	96	18 51N	73 56 E
Khed, Maharashtra, India	96	17 43N	73 27 E
Khed Brahma	93	24 7N	73 5 E
Khekra	94	28 52N	77 20 E
Khemarak Phouminville	101	11 37N	102 59 E
Khemis Miliana	118	36 11N	2 14 E
Khemisset	118	33 50N	6 1W
Khemmarat	100	16 10N	105 15 E
Khenchela	119	35 28N	7 11 E
Khenifra	118	32 58N	5 46W
Khenmarak Phouminville	102	11 40N	102 58 E
Kherrata	119	36 27N	5 13 E
Kherson	82	46 35N	32 35 E
Khersónisos Akrotíri	69	35 30N	24 10 E
Khetinsiring	99	32 54N	92 50 E
Khiliomódhion	69	37 48N	22 51 E
Khilok	77	51 30N	110 45 E
Khimki	81	55 50N	37 20 E
Khingan, mts.	86	47 0N	119 30 E
Khíos	69	38 27N	26 9 E
Khisar-Momina Banya	67	42 30N	24 44 E
Khiuma = Hiiumaa	80	58 50N	22 45 E
Khiva	76	41 30N	60 18 E
Khiyav	92	38 30N	47 45 E
Khlaouia	118	25 50N	6 32W
Khlong Khlung	100	16 12N	99 43 E
Khlong, R.	101	15 30N	98 50 E
Khmelnitsky	82	49 23N	27 0 E
Khmer Republic ■ = Cambodia	100	12 15N	105 0 E
Khoai, Hon	101	8 26N	104 50 E
Khodzhent	85	40 14N	69 37 E
Khoi	92	38 40N	45 0 E
Khojak P.	93	30 55N	66 30 E
Khok Kloi	101	8 17N	98 19 E
Khok Pho	101	6 43N	101 6 E
Khokholskiy	81	51 35N	38 50 E
Kholm	80	57 10N	31 15 E
Kholmsk	77	35 5N	139 48 E
Khomas Hochland	128	22 40 S	16 0 E
Khomayn	92	33 40N	50 7 E
Khomo	128	21 7 S	24 35 E
Khon Kaen	100	16 30N	102 47 E
Khong, Camb.	101	13 55N	105 56 E
Khong, Laos	100	14 7N	105 51 E
Khong, R., Laos	101	15 0N	106 50 E
Khong, R., Thai.	101	17 45N	104 20 E
Khong Sedone	100	15 34N	105 49 E
Khonh Hung (Soc Trang)	101	9 37N	105 50 E
Khonu	77	66 30N	143 25 E
Khoper, R.	81	52 0N	43 20 E
Khor el 'Atash	123	13 20N	34 15 E
Khóra	69	37 3N	21 42 E
Khóra Sfákion	69	35 15N	24 9 E
Khorasan □	93	34 0N	58 0 E
Khorat = Nakhon Ratchasima	100	14 59N	102 12 E
Khorat, Cao Nguyen	100	15 30N	102 50 E
Khorat Plat.	101	15 30N	102 50 E
Khorb el Ethel	118	28 44N	6 11W
Khorog	85	37 30N	71 36 E
Khorol	82	49 48N	33 15 E
Khorramabad	92	33 30N	48 25 E
Khorramshahr	92	30 29N	48 15 E
Khota Kota	127	12 55 S	34 15 E
Khotan = Hot'ien	105	37 7N	79 55 E
Khotin	82	48 31N	26 27 E
Khouribga	118	32 58N	6 50W
Khowai	98	24 5N	91 40 E
Khoyniki	80	51 54N	29 55 E
Khrami, R.	83	41 30N	44 30 E
Khrenovoye	81	51 4N	40 6 E
Khristianá, I.	69	36 14N	25 13 E
Khromtau	84	50 17N	58 27 E
Khtapodhiá, I.	69	37 24N	25 34 E
Khu Khan	100	14 42N	104 12 E
Khufaifiya	92	24 50N	44 35 E
Khugiani	94	31 28N	66 14 E
Khulna	98	22 45N	89 34 E
Khulna □	98	22 45N	89 35 E
Khulo	83	41 33N	42 19 E
Khunzakh	83	42 35N	46 42 E
Khur	93	32 55N	58 18 E
Khurai	94	24 3N	78 23 E
Khurais	92	24 55N	48 5 E
Khurja	94	28 15N	77 58 E
Khurma	92	21 58N	42 3 E
Khūryān Mūryān, Jazā 'ir	91	17 30N	55 58 E
Khush	93	32 55N	62 10 E
Khushab	94	32 20N	72 20 E
Khuzdar	94	27 52N	66 30 E
Khuzestan □	92	31 0N	50 0 E
Khvalynsk	81	52 30N	48 2 E
Khvatovka	81	52 24N	46 32 E
Khvor	93	33 45N	55 0 E
Khvormuj	93	28 40N	51 30 E
Khvoy	92	38 35N	45 0 E
Khvoynaya	80	58 49N	34 28 E
Khwaja Muhammad	93	36 0N	70 0 E
Khyber Pass	94	34 10N	71 8 E
Kiabukwa	127	8 40 S	24 48 E
Kiadho, R.	96	19 50N	76 55 E
Kiama	141	34 40 S	150 50 E
Kiamba	126	6 0N	124 40 E
Kiambi	126	7 15 S	28 0 E
Kiambu	126	1 8 S	36 50 E
Kiangsi □	109	27 20N	115 40 E
Kiangsu □	109	33 0N	119 50 E
Kiania	129	20 18 S	47 8 E
Kiaohsien = Chiaohsien	107	36 20N	120 0 E
Kibæk	73	56 2N	8 51 E
Kibanga Port	126	0 10 S	32 58 E
Kibangou	124	3 18 S	12 22 E
Kibara	126	2 8 S	33 30 E
Kibara, Mts.	126	8 25 S	27 10 E
Kibombo	126	3 57 S	25 53 E
Kibondo	126	3 35 S	30 45 E
Kibondo □	126	4 0 S	30 55 E
Kibumbu	126	3 32 S	29 45 E
Kibungu	126	2 10 S	30 32 E
Kibuye, Burundi	126	3 39 S	29 59 E
Kibuye, Rwanda	126	2 3 S	29 21 E
Kibwesa	126	6 30 S	29 58 E
Kibwezi	124	2 27 S	37 57 E
Kibworth Beauchamp	29	52 33N	0 59W
Kičevo	66	41 34N	20 59 E
Kichiga	77	59 50N	163 5 E
Kicking Horse Pass	152	51 27N	116 25W
Kidal	121	17 50N	1 22 E
Kidderminster	28	52 24N	2 13W
Kidete	126	6 25 S	37 17 E
Kidira	120	14 28N	12 13W
Kidlington	28	51 49N	1 18W
Kidnappers, C.	142	39 38 S	177 5 E
Kidsgrove	32	53 6N	2 15W
Kidston	138	18 52 S	144 8 E
Kidstones	32	54 15N	2 2W
Kidugalle	126	6 49 S	38 15 E
Kidwelly	31	51 44N	4 20W
Kiel	48	54 16N	10 8 E
Kiel Canal = Nord-Ostee-Kanal	48	54 15N	9 40 E
Kielce	54	50 58N	20 42 E
Kielce □	54	51 0N	20 40 E
Kielder	35	55 14N	2 35W
Kieldrecht	47	51 17N	4 11 E
Kieler Bucht	48	54 30N	10 30 E
Kien Binh	101	9 55N	105 19 E
Kien Hung	101	9 43N	105 17 E
Kien Tan	101	10 7N	105 17 E
Kienchwan	99	26 30N	99 45 E
Kienge	127	10 30 S	27 30 E
Kiessé	121	13 29N	4 1 E
Kieta	135	6 12 S	155 36 E
Kiev = Kiyev	80	50 30N	30 28 E
Kiffa	120	16 50N	11 15W
Kifisiá	69	38 4N	23 49 E
Kifissós, R.	69	38 30N	23 0 E
Kifri	92	34 45N	45 0 E
Kigali	126	1 5 S	30 4 E
Kigarama	126	1 1 S	31 50 E
Kigoma □	126	5 0 S	30 0 E
Kigoma-Ujiji	126	5 30 S	30 0 E
Kigomasha, Ras	126	4 58 S	38 58 E
Kihee	139	27 23 S	142 37 E
Kihikihi	142	38 2 S	175 22 E
Kii-Hantō	111	34 0N	135 45 E
Kii-Sanchi	111	34 20N	136 0 E
Kijik	147	60 20N	154 20W
Kikai-Jima	112	28 19N	129 58 E
Kikinda	66	45 50N	20 30 E
Kikládhes □	69	37 0N	25 0 E
Kikládhes, Is.	69	37 20N	24 30 E
Kikoira	141	33 59 S	146 40 E
Kikori	135	7 13 S	144 15 E
Kikori, R.	135	7 5 S	144 0 E
Kikuchi	110	32 59N	130 47 E
Kikwit	124	5 5 S	18 45 E
Kil	72	59 30N	13 20 E
Kilafors	72	61 14N	16 36 E
Kilakarai	97	9 12N	78 47 E
Kilauea	147	22 13N	159 25W
Kilauea Crater	147	19 24N	155 17W
Kilbaha	39	52 35N	9 51W
Kilbeggan	38	53 22N	7 30W
Kilbeheny	39	52 18N	8 13W
Kilbennan	38	53 33N	8 54W
Kilbirnie	34	55 46N	4 42W
Kilbrannan Sd.	34	55 40N	5 23W
Kilbride	39	52 56N	6 5W
Kilbrien	39	52 12N	7 40W
Kilbrittain	39	51 40N	8 42W
Kilbuck Mts.	147	60 30N	160 0W
Kilchberg	51	47 18N	8 33 E
Kilchoan	36	56 42N	6 8W
Kilcock	38	53 24N	6 40W
Kilcoe	39	51 33N	9 26W
Kilcogan	39	53 13N	8 52W
Kilconnell	39	53 20N	8 25W
Kilcoo	38	54 14N	6 1W
Kilcormac	39	53 11N	7 44W
Kilcoy	139	26 59 S	152 30 E
Kilcreggan	34	55 59N	4 50W
Kilcrohane	39	51 35N	9 44W
Kilcullen	39	53 8N	6 45W
Kilcurry	38	54 3N	6 26W
Kildare	39	53 10N	6 50W
Kildare □	39	53 10N	6 50W
Kildavin	39	52 41N	6 42W
Kildemo	39	52 37N	8 50W
Kildonan	37	58 10N	3 50W
Kildorrery	39	52 15N	8 25W
Kilembe	126	0 15N	30 3 E
Kilfenora	39	53 0N	9 13W
Kilfinan	34	55 57N	5 19W
Kilfinnane	39	52 21N	8 30W
Kilgarvan	39	51 54N	9 28W
Kilgore	159	32 22N	94 40W
Kilham	33	54 4N	0 22W
Kilian Qurghan	93	36 52N	78 3 E
Kilifi	126	3 40 S	39 48 E
Kilifi □	126	3 30 S	39 40 E
Kilimanjaro □	126	4 0 S	38 0 E
Kilimanjaro, Mt.	126	3 7 S	37 20 E
Kilinailau, Is.	135	4 45 S	155 20 E
Kilindini	126	4 4 S	39 40 E
Kilis	92	36 50N	37 10 E
Kiliya	82	45 28N	29 16 E
Kilju	107	40 57N	129 25 E
Kilkea	39	52 57N	6 55W
Kilkee	39	52 41N	9 40W
Kilkeel	38	54 4N	6 0W
Kilkelly	38	53 53N	8 50W
Kilkenny	39	52 40N	7 17W
Kilkenny □	39	52 35N	7 15W
Kilkerrin	38	52 32N	8 36W
Kilkhampton	30	50 53N	4 30W
Kilkieran	39	53 20N	9 45W
Kilkieran B.	38	53 18N	9 45W
Kilkis	68	40 58N	22 57 E
Kilkis □	68	41 5N	22 50 E
Kilkishen	39	52 49N	8 45W
Kilknock	38	53 42N	8 53W
Kill	39	52 11N	7 20W
Killadoon	38	53 44N	9 53W
Killadysert	39	52 40N	9 7W
Killala	38	54 13N	9 12W
Killala B.	38	54 20N	9 12W
Killaloe	39	52 48N	8 28W
Killam	152	52 47N	111 51W
Killane	39	53 20N	7 6W
Killard, Pt.	38	54 18N	5 31W
Killare	38	53 28N	7 34W
Killarney, Man., Can.	150	49 10N	99 40W
Killarney, Ont., Can.	153	45 55N	81 30W
Killarney, Ireland	39	52 2N	9 30W
Killarney, L's. of	39	52 0N	9 30W
Killary Harb.	38	53 38N	9 52W
Killashandra	38	54 1N	7 32W
Killashee	38	53 40N	7 52W
Killavally	38	53 22N	7 23W
Killavullen	39	52 8N	8 32W

*Renamed Soc Trang

Killchianaig	34	56 2N	5 48W
Killdeer, Can.	153	49 6N	106 22W
Killdeer, U.S.A.	158	47 26N	102 48W
Killeagh	39	51 56N	8 0W
Killean	34	55 38N	5 40W
Killeen	159	31 7N	97 45W
Killeenleigh	39	51 58N	8 49W
Killeigh	39	53 14N	7 27W
Killenaule	39	52 35N	7 40W
Killianspick	39	52 21N	7 18W
Killiecrankie P.	37	56 44N	3 46W
Killimor	39	53 10N	8 17W
Killin	34	56 28N	4 20W
Killiney	39	53 15N	6 8W
Killingdal	71	62 47N	11 26 E
Killinghall	33	54 1N	1 33W
Killini	69	37 55N	21 8 E
Killini, Mts.	69	37 54N	22 25 E
Killinick	39	52 15N	6 29W
Killorglin	39	52 6N	9 48W
Killough	38	54 16N	5 40W
Killtullagh	39	53 17N	8 37W
Killucan	38	53 30N	7 10W
Killurin	39	52 23N	6 35W
Killybegs	38	54 38N	8 26W
Killyleagh	38	54 24N	5 40W
Kilmacolm	34	55 54N	4 39W
Kilmacthomas	39	52 13N	7 27W
Kilmaganny	39	52 26N	7 20W
Kilmaine	38	53 33N	9 10W
Kilmaley	39	52 50N	9 11W
Kilmallock	39	52 22N	8 35W
Kilmaluag	36	57 40N	6 18W
Kilmanagh	39	52 38N	7 28W
Kilmarnock, U.K.	34	55 36N	4 30W
Kilmarnock, U.S.A.	162	37 43N	76 23W
Kilmartin	34	56 8N	5 29W
Kilmaurs	34	55 37N	4 33W
Kilmeaden	39	52 15N	7 15W
Kilmeedy	39	52 25N	8 55W
Kilmelford	34	56 16N	5 30W
Kilmez	84	56 58N	50 55 E
Kilmez, R.	84	56 58N	50 28 E
Kilmichael	39	51 49N	9 4W
Kilmichael Pt.	39	52 44N	6 8W
Kilmihill	39	52 44N	9 18W
Kilmore, Austral.	141	37 25 S	144 53 E
Kilmore, Ireland	39	52 12N	6 35W
Kilmore Quay	39	52 10N	6 36W
Kilmuir	37	57 44N	4 7W
Kilmurry	39	52 47N	9 30W
Kilmurvy	39	53 9N	9 46W
Kilnaleck	38	53 52N	7 21W
Kilninver	34	56 20N	5 30W
Kilombero □	127	8 0 S	37 0 E
Kilondo	127	9 45 S	34 20 E
Kilosa	126	6 48 S	37 0 E
Kilosa □	126	6 48 S	37 0 E
Kilpatrick	39	51 46N	8 42W
Kilrea	38	54 58N	6 34W
Kilrenny	35	56 15N	2 40W
Kilronan	39	53 8N	9 40W
Kilrush	39	52 39N	9 30W
Kilsby	28	52 20N	1 11W
Kilsheelan	39	52 23N	7 37W
Kilsmo	72	59 6N	15 35 E
Kilsyth	35	55 58N	4 3W
Kiltamagh	38	53 52N	9 0W
Kiltealy	39	52 34N	6 45W
Kiltegan	39	52 53N	6 35W
Kiltoom	38	53 30N	8 0W
Kilwa □	127	9 0 S	39 0 E
Kilwa Kisiwani	127	8 58 S	39 32 E
Kilwa Kivinje	127	8 45 S	39 25 E
Kilwa Masoko	127	8 55 S	39 30 E
Kilwinning	34	55 40N	4 41W
Kilworth	39	52 10N	8 15W
Kilworth, mts.	39	52 10N	8 15W
Kim	159	37 18N	103 20W
Kimamba	126	6 45 S	37 10 E
Kimba	140	33 8 S	136 23 E
Kimball, Nebr., U.S.A.	158	41 17N	103 20W
Kimball, S.D., U.S.A.	158	43 47N	98 57W
Kimbe	135	5 33 S	150 11 E
Kimbe B.	135	5 15 S	150 30 E
Kimberley, N.S.W., Austral.	140	32 50 S	141 4 E
Kimberley, W. Australia, Austral.	136	16 20 S	127 0 E
Kimberley, Can.	152	49 40N	115 59W
Kimberley, S. Afr.	128	28 43 S	24 46 E
Kimberley, dist.	132	16 20 S	127 0 E
Kimberley Downs	136	17 24 S	124 22 E
Kimberly	160	42 33N	114 25W
Kimbolton	29	52 17N	0 23W
Kimchŏn	107	36 11N	128 4 E
Kími	69	38 38N	24 6 E
Kimje	107	35 48N	126 45 E
Kimmeridge, oilfield	19	50 36N	2 6W
Kímolos	69	36 48N	24 37 E
Kímolos, I.	69	36 48N	24 35 E
Kimovsk	81	54 0N	38 29 E
Kimparana	120	12 48N	5 0W
Kimry	81	56 55N	37 15 E
Kimsquit	152	52 45N	126 57W
Kimstad	73	58 35N	15 58 E
Kinabalu, mt.	102	6 0N	116 0 E
Kínaros, I.	69	36 59N	26 15 E
Kinaskan L.	152	57 38N	130 8W
Kinawley	38	54 14N	7 40W
Kinbrace	37	58 16N	3 56W
Kincaid	153	49 40N	107 0W
Kincardine, Can.	150	44 10N	81 40W
Kincardine, Fife, U.K.	35	56 4N	3 43W
Kincardine, Highland, U.K.	37	57 52N	4 20W
Kincardine (□)	26	56 56N	2 28W
Kincraig	37	57 8N	3 57W
Kindersley	153	51 30N	109 10W
Kindia	120	10 0N	12 52W
Kindu	126	2 55 S	25 50 E
Kinel	84	53 15N	50 40 E
Kineshma	81	57 30N	42 5 E
Kinesi	126	1 25 S	33 50 E
Kineton	28	52 10N	1 30W
King and Queen	162	37 42N	76 50W
King City	163	36 11N	121 8W
King Cr.	138	24 35 S	139 30 E
King Edward, R.	136	14 14 S	126 35 E
King Frederick VI Land	12	63 0N	43 0W
King Frederick VIII Land	12	77 30N	25 0W
King George	162	38 15N	77 10W
King George B.	176	51 30 S	60 30W
King George I.	13	60 0 S	60 0W
King George Is.	149	53 40N	80 30W
King George Sd.	132	35 5 S	118 0 E
King I., Austral.	138	39 50 S	144 0 E
King I., Can.	152	52 10N	127 40W
King I. = Kadah Kyun	101	12 30N	98 20 E
King, L.	137	33 10 S	119 35 E
King Leopold Ranges	136	17 20 S	124 20 E
King, Mt.	138	25 10 S	147 30 E
King Sd.	136	16 50 S	123 20 E
King William I.	148	69 10N	97 25W
King William, L.	50	42 14 S	146 15 E
King William's Town	128	32 51 S	27 22 E
Kingairloch, dist.	36	56 37N	5 30W
Kingaroy	139	26 32 S	151 51 E
Kingarrow	38	54 55N	8 5W
Kingarth	34	55 45N	5 2W
Kingfisher	159	35 50N	97 55W
Kinghorn	35	56 4N	3 10W
Kingisepp	80	59 25N	28 40 E
Kingisepp (Kuressaare)	80	58 15N	22 15 E
Kingman, Ariz., U.S.A.	161	35 12N	114 2W
Kingman, Kans., U.S.A.	159	37 41N	96 9W
Kings B.	12	78 0N	15 0 E
Kings Canyon National Park	163	37 0N	118 35W
King's Lynn	29	52 45N	0 25 E
Kings Mountain	157	35 13N	81 20W
Kings Park	162	40 53N	73 16W
King's Peak	160	40 46N	110 27W
King's, R.	39	52 32N	7 12W
Kings, R.	163	36 10N	119 50W
King's Sutton	28	52 1N	1 16W
King's Worthy	28	51 6N	1 18W
Kingsbarns	35	56 18N	2 40W
Kingsbridge	30	50 17N	3 46W
Kingsburg	163	36 35N	119 36W
Kingsbury	28	52 33N	1 41W
Kingscote	140	35 33 S	137 31 E
Kingscourt	38	53 55N	6 48W
Kingskerswell	30	50 30N	3 34W
Kingsland	28	52 15N	2 49W
Kingsley	158	42 37N	95 58W
Kingsley Dam	158	41 20N	101 40W
Kingsport	157	36 33N	82 36W
Kingsteignton	30	50 32N	3 35W
Kingston, Can.	150	44 14N	76 30W
Kingston, Jamaica	166	18 0N	76 50W
Kingston, N.Z.	143	45 20 S	168 43 E
Kingston, U.K.	28	51 23N	1 40W
Kingston, N.Y., U.S.A.	162	41 55N	74 0W
Kingston, Pa., U.S.A.	162	41 19N	75 58W
Kingston, R.I., U.S.A.	162	41 29N	71 30W
Kingston South East	140	36 51 S	139 55 E
Kingston-upon-Thames	29	51 23N	0 20W
Kingstown, Austral.	141	30 29 S	151 6 E
Kingstown, St. Vinc.	167	13 10N	61 10W
Kingstree	157	33 40N	79 48W
Kingsville, Can.	150	42 2N	82 45W
Kingsville, U.S.A.	159	27 30N	97 53W
Kingswear	30	50 21N	3 33W
Kingswood	28	51 26N	2 31W
Kington	28	52 12N	3 2W
Kingtung	99	24 30N	100 50 E
Kingussie	37	47 5N	4 2W
Kinistino	153	52 57N	105 2W
Kinkala	124	4 18 S	14 49 E
Kinki □	111	35 0N	135 30 E
Kinleith	142	38 20 S	175 56 E
Kinloch, N.Z.	143	44 51 S	168 20 E
Kinloch, L. More, U.K.	37	58 17N	4 50W
Kinloch, Rhum, U.K.	36	57 0N	6 18W
Kinloch Rannoch	37	56 41N	4 12W
Kinlochbervie	36	58 28N	5 5W
Kinlochewe	36	57 37N	5 20W
Kinlochiel	36	56 52N	5 20W
Kinlochleven	36	56 42N	4 59W
Kinlochmoidart	36	56 47N	5 43W
Kinloss	37	57 38N	3 37W
Kinlough	38	54 27N	8 16W
Kinn	71	61 34N	4 45 E
Kinna	73	57 32N	12 42 E
Kinnaird	152	49 17N	117 39W
Kinnaird's Hd.	37	57 40N	2 0W
Kinnared	73	57 2N	13 7 E
Kinnegad	38	53 28N	7 8W
Kinneret	90	32 44N	35 34 E
Kinneret, Yam	90	32 45N	35 35 E
Kinneviken, B.	73	58 38N	18 20 E
Kinnitty	39	53 6N	7 44W
Kino	164	28 45N	111 59W
Kinoje, R.	150	52 8N	81 25W
Kinomoto	111	35 30N	136 13 E
Kinoni, C. Afr. Emp.	123	5 40N	26 10 E
Kinoni, Uganda	126	0 41 S	30 28 E
Kinping	101	22 56N	103 15 E
Kinrooi	47	51 9N	5 45 E
Kinross	35	56 13N	3 25W
Kinross (□)	26	56 13N	3 25W
Kinsale	39	51 42N	8 31W
Kinsale Harbour	39	51 40N	8 30W
Kinsale Head, gasfield	19	51 20N	8 0W
Kinsale Old Hd.	39	51 37N	8 32W
Kinsarvik	71	60 22N	6 43 E
Kinshasa	124	4 20 S	15 15 E
Kinsley	159	37 57N	99 30W
Kinston	157	35 18N	77 35W
Kintampo	121	8 5N	1 41W
Kintap	102	3 51 S	115 13 E
Kintaravay	36	58 4N	6 42W
Kintore	37	57 14N	2 20W
Kintore Ra.	137	23 15 S	128 47 E
Kintyre, Mull of	34	55 17N	5 4W
Kintyre, pen.	34	55 30N	5 35W
Kinu	98	22 46N	95 37 E
Kinu-Gawa, R.	111	35 36N	139 57 E
Kinushseo, R.	150	55 15N	83 45W
Kinuso	152	55 25N	115 25W
Kinvara	39	53 8N	8 57W
Kinyangiri	126	4 35 S	34 37 E
Kióni	69	38 27N	20 41 E
Kiosk	150	46 6N	78 53W
Kiowa, Kans., U.S.A.	159	37 3N	98 30W
Kiowa, Okla., U.S.A.	159	34 45N	95 50W
Kipahigan L.	153	55 20N	101 55W
Kipanga	126	6 15 S	35 20 E
Kiparissía	69	37 15N	21 40 E
Kiparissiakós Kólpos	69	37 25N	21 25 E
Kipawa Res. Prov. Park	150	47 0N	78 30W
Kipembawe	124	7 38 S	33 27 E
Kipengere Ra.	127	9 12 S	34 15 E
Kipili	126	7 28 S	30 32 E
Kipini	126	2 30 S	40 32 E
Kipling	153	50 6N	102 38W
Kipnuk	147	59 55N	164 7W
Kippen	34	56 8N	4 12W
Kippure, Mt.	39	53 11N	6 23W
Kipushi	127	11 48 S	27 12 E
Kir	124	1 29 S	19 25 E
Kirandul	96	18 33N	81 10 E
Kiratpur	94	29 32N	78 12 E
Kirchberg	50	47 5N	7 35 E
Kirchhain	48	50 49N	8 54 E
Kirchheim	49	48 38N	9 20 E
Kirchheim Bolanden	49	49 40N	8 0 E
Kirchschlag	53	47 30N	16 19 E
Kircubbin	38	54 30N	5 33W
Kirensk	77	57 50N	107 55 E
Kirgiz S.S.R. □	85	42 0N	75 0 E
Kirgiziya Steppe	79	50 0N	55 0 E
Kiri	124	1 29 S	19 25 E
Kiriburu	96	22 0N	85 0 E
Kirikkale	92	39 51N	33 32 E
Kirikopuni	142	35 50 S	174 1 E
Kirillov	81	59 51N	38 14 E
Kirin □	107	43 50N	125 45 E
Kirindi, R.	97	6 15N	81 20 E
Kirishi	80	51 28N	31 59 E
Kirishima-Yama	110	31 58N	130 55 E
Kiriwina Is. = Trobriand Is.	138	8 40 S	151 0 E
Kirk Michael	32	54 17N	4 35W
Kirkbean	35	54 56N	3 35W
Kirkbride	32	54 54N	3 13W
Kirkburton	33	53 36N	1 42W
Kirkby	32	53 29N	2 54W
Kirkby-in-Ashfield	33	53 6N	1 15W
Kirkby Lonsdale	32	54 13N	2 36W
Kirkby Malzeard	33	54 10N	1 38W
Kirkby Moorside	33	54 16N	0 56W
Kirkby Steven	32	54 27N	2 23W
Kirkby Thore	32	54 38N	2 34W
Kirkcaldy	35	56 7N	3 10W
Kirkcolm	34	54 59N	5 4W
Kirkconnel	35	55 23N	4 0W
Kirkcowan	34	54 53N	4 38W
Kirkcudbright	35	54 50N	4 3W
Kirkcudbright (□)	26	55 4N	4 0W
Kirkcudbright B.	35	54 46N	4 0W
Kirkeby	73	55 7N	8 33 E
Kirkee	96	18 34N	73 56 E
Kirkenær	71	60 27N	12 3 E
Kirkenes	74	69 40N	30 5 E
Kirkham	32	53 47N	2 52W
Kirkinner	34	54 59N	4 28W
Kirkintilloch	35	55 57N	4 10W
Kirkjubæjarklaustur	74	63 47N	18 4W
Kirkland, Ariz., U.S.A.	161	34 29N	112 46W
Kirkland, Wash., U.S.A.	160	47 40N	122 10W
Kirkland Lake	150	48 9N	80 2W
Kirklareli	67	41 44N	27 15 E
Kirkliston	35	55 55N	3 27W
Kirkliston Ra.	143	44 25 S	170 34 E
Kirkmichael	37	56 43N	3 31W
Kirkoswald	32	54 46N	2 41W
Kirkoswold	34	55 19N	4 48W
Kirkstone P.	32	54 29N	2 55W
Kirksville	158	40 8N	92 35W
Kirkuk	92	35 30N	44 21 E
Kirkwall	37	58 59N	2 59W
Kirkwhelpington	35	55 9N	2 0W
Kirkwood	128	33 22 S	25 15 E
Kirlampudi	96	17 12N	82 12 E
Kirn	49	49 46N	7 29 E
Kirov, R.S.F.S.R., U.S.S.R.	81	54 3N	34 12 E
Kirov, R.S.F.S.R., U.S.S.R.	84	58 35N	49 40 E
Kirovabad	83	40 45N	46 10 E
Kirovakan	83	41 0N	44 0 E
Kirovo	85	40 26N	70 36 E
Kirovo-Chepetsk	81	58 28N	50 0 E
Kirovograd	82	48 35N	32 20 E
Kirovsk, R.S.F.S.R., U.S.S.R.	78	67 48N	33 50 E
Kirovsk, Ukraine, U.S.S.R.	83	48 35N	38 30 E
Kirovski	83	45 51N	48 11 E
Kirovskiy	85	44 52N	78 12 E
Kirovskoye	85	42 39N	71 35 E
Kirriemuir, Can.	153	51 56N	110 20W
Kirriemuir, U.K.	37	56 41N	3 0W
Kirs	84	59 21N	52 14 E
Kirsanov	81	52 35N	42 40 E
Kirşehir	92	39 14N	34 5 E
Kirstonia	128	25 30 S	23 45 E
Kirtachi	121	12 52N	2 30 E
Kirthar Range	93	27 0N	67 0 E
Kirtling	29	52 11N	0 27 E
Kirtlington	28	51 54N	1 9W
Kirton	39	52 56N	0 3W
Kirton-in-Lindsey	33	53 29N	0 35W
Kiruna	74	67 52N	20 15 E
Kirundu	124	0 50 S	25 35 E
Kirup	137	33 40 S	115 50 E
Kiryū	111	36 24N	139 20 E
Kiryu	81	55 5N	46 45 E
Kirzhach	81	56 12N	38 50 E
Kisa	73	58 0N	15 39 E
Kisaga	126	4 30 S	34 23 E
Kisalaya	166	14 40N	84 3W
Kisámou, Kólpos	69	35 30N	23 38 E
Kisanga	126	2 30N	26 35 E
Kisangani	126	0 35N	25 15 E
Kisar, I.	103	8 5 S	127 10 E
Kisaran	102	2 47N	99 29 E
Kisarawe	126	6 53 S	39 0 E
Kisarawe □	126	7 3 S	39 0 E
Kisarazu	111	35 23N	139 55 E
Kisbér	53	47 30N	18 0 E
Kiselevsk	76	54 5N	86 6 E
Kishanganga, R.	95	34 50N	74 15 E
Kishanganj	95	26 3N	88 14 E
Kishangarh	94	27 50N	70 30 E
Kishi	121	9 1N	3 45 E
Kishinev	82	47 0N	28 50 E
Kishinoi	82	47 1N	28 50 E
Kishiwada	111	34 28N	135 22 E
Kishkeam	39	52 15N	9 12 E
Kishon	90	32 33N	35 12 E
Kishorganj	98	24 26N	90 40 E
Kishorn L.	36	57 22N	5 40W
Kishtwar	95	33 20N	75 48 E
Kisii	126	0 40 S	34 45 E
Kisii □	126	0 40 S	34 45 E
Kisiju	124	7 23 S	39 19 E
Kısır, Dağ	83	41 0N	43 5 E
Kisizi	126	1 0 S	29 58 E
Kiska I.	147	52 0N	177 30 E
Kiskatinaw, R.	152	56 8N	120 10W
Kiskittogisu L.	153	54 13N	98 20W
Kiskomárom = Zalakomár	53	46 33N	17 10 E
Kiskörös	53	46 37N	19 20 E
Kiskundorozsma	53	46 16N	20 5 E
Kiskunfelégyháza	53	46 42N	19 53 E
Kiskunhalas	53	46 28N	19 37 E
Kiskunmajsa	53	46 30N	19 48 E
Kislovodsk	83	43 50N	42 45 E
Kismayu	113	0 20 S	42 30 E
Kiso-Gawa, R.	111	35 2N	136 45 E
Kiso-Sammyaku	111	35 30N	137 45 E
Kisofukushima	111	35 52N	137 43 E
Kisoro	126	1 17 S	29 48 E
Kispest	53	47 27N	19 9 E
Kissidougou	120	9 5N	10 0W
Kissimmee	157	28 18N	81 22W
Kissimmee, R.	157	27 20N	81 0W
Kississing L.	153	55 34N	100 47W
Kistanje	63	43 58N	15 55 E
Kisterenye	53	48 3N	19 50 E
Kisújszállás	53	47 12N	20 50 E
Kisuki	110	35 17N	132 54 E
Kisumu	126	0 3 S	34 45 E
Kisvárda	53	48 14N	22 4 E
Kiswani	126	4 5 S	37 57 E
Kiswere	127	9 27 S	39 30 E
Kit Carson	158	38 48N	102 45W
Kita	120	13 5N	9 25W
Kita-Ura	111	36 0N	140 34 E
Kitab	85	39 7N	66 52 E
Kitakami, R.	112	38 25N	141 19 E
Kitakyūshū	110	33 50N	130 50 E
Kitale	126	1 0N	35 12 E
Kitami	112	43 48N	143 54 E
Kitangiri, L.	126	4 5 S	34 20 E
Kitano-Kaikyō	110	34 17N	134 58 E
Kitaya	127	10 38 S	40 8 E
Kitchener, Austral.	137	30 55 S	124 8 E
Kitchener, Can.	150	43 27N	80 29W
Kitchigami, R.	150	50 35N	78 5W
Kitega = Citega	126	3 30 S	29 58 E
Kiteto □	126	5 0 S	37 0 E
Kitgum Matidi	126	3 17N	32 52 E
Kíthira	69	36 9N	23 0 E
Kíthira, I.	69	36 15N	23 0 E
Kíthnos	69	37 26N	24 27 E

Kíthnos, I	Konstantinovski

Kithnos, I. 69 37 25N 24 25 E
Kitimat 152 54 3N 128 38W
Kitinen, R. 74 67 34N 26 40 E
Kitiyab 123 17 13N 33 35 E
Kitros 68 40 22N 22 34 E
Kitsuki 110 33 35N 131 37 E
Kittakittaooloo, L. 139 28 3 S 138 14 E
Kittanning 156 40 49N 79 30W
Kittatinny Mts. 162 41 0N 75 0W
Kittery 162 43 7N 70 42W
Kitui 126 1 17 S 38 0 E
Kitui □ 126 1 30 S 38 25 E
Kitwe 127 12 54 S 28 7 E
Kitzbühel 52 47 27N 12 24 E
Kitzingen 49 49 44N 10 9 E
Kivalina 147 67 45N 164 40W
Kivalo 74 66 18N 26 0 E
Kivarli 94 24 33N 72 46 E
Kivotós 68 40 13N 21 26 E
Kivu □ 126 3 10 S 27 0 E
Kivu, L. 126 1 48 S 29 0 E
Kiwai I. 135 8 35 S 143 30 E
Kiyev 80 50 30N 30 28 E
Kiyevskoye Vdkhr. 80 51 0N 30 0 E
Kizel 84 59 3N 57 40 E
Kiziguru 126 1 46 S 30 23 E
Kizil Jilga 95 35 26N 79 50 E
Kizil Kiya 76 40 20N 72 35 E
Kızılcahaman 82 40 30N 32 30 E
Kızılırmak 83 39 15N 36 0 E
Kizilskoye 84 52 44N 58 54 E
Kizimkazi 126 6 28 S 39 30 E
Kizlyar 83 43 51N 46 40 E
Kizyl-Arvat 76 38 58N 56 15 E
Kjellerup 73 56 17N 9 25 E
Klabat, Teluk 102 1 30 S 105 40 E
Kladanj 66 44 14N 18 42 E
Kladnica 66 43 23N 20 2 E
Kladno 52 50 10N 14 7 E
Kladovo 66 44 36N 22 33 E
Klaeng 100 12 47N 101 39 E
Klagenfurt 52 46 38N 14 20 E
Klagerup 73 55 36N 13 17 E
Klagshamn 73 55 32N 12 53 E
Klagstorp 73 55 22N 13 23 E
Klaipeda 80 55 43N 21 10 E
Klakring 73 55 42N 9 59 E
Klamath Falls 160 42 20N 121 50W
Klamath Mts. 160 41 20N 123 0W
Klamath, R. 160 41 40N 123 30W
Klang = Kelang 101 3 1N 101 33 E
Klangklang 98 22 41N 93 26 E
Klanjec 63 46 3N 15 45 E
Klappan, R. 152 58 0N 129 43W
Klarälven 72 60 32N 13 15 E
Klaten 103 7 43 S 110 36 E
Klatovy 52 49 23N 13 18 E
Klawak 152 55 35N 133 0W
Klawer 128 31 44 S 18 36 E
Klazienaveen 46 52 44N 7 0 E
Kłecko 54 52 38N 17 25 E
Kleczew 54 52 22N 18 9 E
Kleena Kleene 152 52 0N 124 50W
Klein 160 46 26N 108 31W
Klein-Karas 128 27 33 S 18 7 E
Klein Karoo 128 33 45 S 21 30 E
Kleine Gette, R. 47 50 51N 5 6 E
Kleine Nete, R. 47 51 12N 4 46 E
KlekovaCa, mt. 63 44 25N 16 32 E
Klemtu 152 52 35N 128 55W
Klenovec, Czech. 53 48 36N 19 54 E
Klenovec, Yugo. 66 31 32N 20 49 E
Klepp 71 59 48N 5 36 E
Klerksdorp 128 26 51 S 26 38 E
Kletnya 80 53 30N 33 2 E
Kletsk 80 53 5N 26 45 E
Kletskiy 83 49 20N 43 0 E
Kleve 48 51 46N 6 10 E
Klickitat 160 45 50N 12 10W
Klimovichi 80 53 36N 32 0 E
Klin 81 56 28N 36 48 E
Klinaklini, R. 152 51 21N 125 40W
Klinte 73 53 35N 10 12 E
Klintehamn 73 57 22N 18 12 E
Klintsey 80 52 50N 32 10 E
Klipplaat 128 33 0 S 24 22 E
Klisura 67 42 40N 24 28 E
Klitmøller 73 57 3N 8 30 E
Kljajićevo 66 45 45N 19 17 E
Ključ 63 44 32N 16 48 E
Kłobuck 54 50 55N 19 5 E
Kłodzko 54 50 28N 16 38 E
Kloetinge 47 51 30N 3 56 E
Klondike 147 64 0N 139 26W
Kloosterzande 47 51 22N 4 1 E
Klosi 68 41 28N 20 10 E
Klosterneuburg 53 48 18N 16 19 E
Klosters 51 46 52N 9 52 E
Kloten, Sweden 72 59 54N 15 19 E
Kloten, Switz. 51 47 27N 8 35 E
Klötze 48 52 38N 11 9 E
Klouto 121 6 57N 0 44 E
Klovborg 73 55 56N 9 30 E
Klövsjöfj, mt. 72 62 36N 13 57 E
Kluane, L. 147 61 15N 138 40W
Kluang = Keluang 101 1 59N 103 20 E
Kluczbork 54 50 58N 18 12 E
Klundert 47 51 40N 4 32 E
Klyuchevskaya, Guba 83 55 50N 160 30 E
Kmelnitski 80 49 23N 27 0 E
Knapdale, dist. 34 55 55N 5 30W
Knaresborough 33 54 1N 1 29W
Knebworth 29 51 52N 0 11W
Knee L., Man., Can. 153 55 3N 94 45W
Knee L., Sask., Can. 153 55 51N 107 0W
Knesselare 47 51 9N 3 26 E
Knezha 67 43 30N 23 56 E
Knic 66 43 53N 20 45 E
Knight Inlet 152 50 45N 125 40W
Knighton 31 52 21N 3 2W
Knights Ferry 163 37 50N 120 40W
Knight's Landing 160 38 50N 121 43W
Knin 63 44 1N 16 17 E
Knittelfeld 52 47 13N 14 51 E
Knjazevac 66 43 35N 22 18 E
Knob, C. 137 34 32 S 119 16 E
Knock 38 53 48N 8 55W
Knockananna 39 52 52N 6 34W
Knockhoy Mt. 39 51 49N 9 27W
Knocklayd Mt. 38 55 10N 6 15W
Knocklofty 39 52 20N 7 49W
Knockmahon 39 52 8N 7 21W
Knockmealdown Mts. 39 52 16N 8 0W
Knocknaskagh Mt. 39 52 7N 8 25W
Knokke 47 51 20N 3 17 E
Knott End 32 53 55N 3 0W
Knottingley 33 53 42N 1 15W
Knowle 28 52 23N 1 43W
Knox 156 41 18N 86 36W
Knox, C. 152 54 11N 133 5W
Knox City 159 33 26N 99 38W
Knox Coast 13 66 30 S 108 0 E
Knoxville, Iowa, U.S.A. 158 41 20N 93 5W
Knoxville, Pa., U.S.A. 157 41 57N 77 26W
Knoxville, Tenn., U.S.A. 157 35 58N 83 57W
Knoydart, dist. 36 57 3N 5 33W
Knurów 54 50 13N 18 38 E
Knutsford 32 53 18N 2 22W
Knutshø 71 62 18N 9 41 E
Knysna 128 34 2 S 23 2 E
Knyszyn 54 53 20N 22 56 E
Ko Chang 101 12 0N 102 20 E
Ko Ho, R. 109 32 58N 117 13 E
Ko Kha 100 18 11N 99 24 E
Ko Kut 101 11 40N 102 32 E
Ko Phangan 101 9 45N 100 10 E
Ko Phra Thong 101 9 6N 98 15 E
Kō-Saki 110 34 5N 129 13 E
Ko Samui 101 9 30N 100 0 E
Koartac (Notre Dame de Koartac) 149 61 5N 69 36 E
Koba, Aru, Indon. 103 6 37 S 134 37 E
Koba, Bangka, Indon. 102 2 26 S 106 14 E
Kobarid 63 46 15N 13 30 E
Kobayashi 110 31 56N 130 59 E
Kōbe 111 34 45N 135 10 E
Kobelyaki 82 49 11N 34 9 E
København 73 55 41N 12 34 E
Koblenz, Ger. 49 50 21N 7 36 E
Koblenz, Switz. 50 47 37N 8 14 E
Kobo 123 12 2N 39 56 E
Kobrin 80 52 15N 24 22 E
Kobroor, Kepulauan 103 6 10 S 134 30 E
Kobuchizawa 111 35 52N 138 19 E
Kobuk 147 66 55N 157 0W
Kobuk, R. 147 66 55N 157 0W
Kobuleti 83 41 55N 41 45 E
Kobylin 54 51 43N 17 12 E
Kobyłka 54 52 21N 21 10 E
Kobylkino 81 54 8N 43 46 E
Kobylnik 80 54 58N 26 39 E
Kočani 66 41 55N 22 25 E
Koçarli 69 37 45N 27 43 E
Koceljevo 66 44 28N 19 50 E
Kočevje 63 45 39N 14 50 E
Kochang 107 35 41N 127 55 E
Kochas 95 25 15N 83 56 E
Kōchi 110 33 30N 133 35 E
Kōchi-Heiya 110 33 28N 133 30 E
Kōchi-ken □ 110 33 40N 133 30 E
Kochiu 108 23 25N 103 7 E
Kochkor-Ata 85 41 1N 72 29 E
Kochkorka 85 42 13N 75 46 E
Kodaikanai 97 10 13N 77 32 E
Kodaira 111 35 44N 139 29 E
Koddiyar Bay 97 8 33N 81 15 E
Kodiak 147 57 30N 152 45W
Kodiak I. 147 57 30N 152 45W
Kodiang 101 6 21N 100 18 E
Kodinar 94 20 46N 70 46 E
Kodori, R. 83 43 0N 41 40 E
Koekelare 47 51 5N 2 59 E
K'oerch'inyuich-'iench'i 107 46 5N 122 5 E
Koerhmu 105 36 22N 94 55 E
Koersel 47 51 3N 5 17 E
Koes 125 26 0 S 19 15 E
Köflach 13 47 4N 15 4 E
Koforidua 121 6 3N 0 17W
Kōfu 111 35 40N 138 30 E
Koga 111 36 11N 139 43 E
Kogaluk, R. 151 56 12N 61 44W
Kogan 139 27 2 S 150 40 E
Kogin Baba 121 7 55N 11 35 E
Kogizman 92 40 5N 43 10 E
Kogon 121 11 20N 14 32W
Kogota 112 38 33N 141 3 E
Koh-i-Bab, mts. 93 34 30N 67 0 E
Koh-i-Khurd 94 33 30N 65 59 E
Koh-i-Mazar 94 32 30N 66 25 E
Kohat 94 33 40N 71 29 E
Kohima 98 25 35N 94 10 E
Kohler Ra. 13 77 0N 110 0W
Kohtla-Järve 80 59 20N 27 20 E
Kohukohu 142 36 31 S 173 38 E
Koindong 107 40 28N 126 18 E
Kojabuti 103 2 36 S 140 37 E
Kojetin 53 49 21N 17 20 E
Kojima 110 34 20N 133 38 E
Kōjo 110 34 33N 133 55 E
Kojō 107 38 58N 127 58 E
Kojonup 137 33 48 S 117 10 E
Kok Yangak 85 41 2N 73 12 E
Koka 122 20 5N 30 35 E
Kokand 85 40 30N 70 57 E
Kokanee Glacier Prov. Park 152 49 47N 117 10W
Kokas 103 2 42 S 132 26 E
Kokava 53 48 35N 19 50 E
Kokchetav 76 53 20N 69 10 E
Kokemäenjoki 75 61 32N 21 44 E
Kokemäenjoki = Kumo älv 75 61 32N 21 44 E
Kokhma 81 56 55N 41 18 E
Kokkola (Gamlakarleby) 74 63 50N 23 8 E
Koko, Mid-Western, Nigeria 121 6 5N 5 28 E
Koko, North-Western, Nigeria 121 11 28N 4 29 E
Koko Kyunzu 101 14 10N 93 25 E
Koko-Nor = Ch'ing Hai 105 37 0N 100 20 E
Koko Shili 99 35 20N 91 0 E
Kokoda 135 8 54 S 147 47 E
Kokolopozo 120 5 8N 6 5W
Kokomo 156 40 30N 86 6W
Kokopo 135 4 22 S 152 19 E
Kokoro 121 14 12N 0 55 E
Kokoura 77 71 35N 144 50 E
Koksan 107 38 46N 126 40 E
Koksengir, Gora 85 44 21N 65 6 E
Koksoak, R. 149 54 5N 64 10W
Kokstad 125 30 32 S 29 29 E
Kokubu 110 31 44N 130 46 E
Kola 78 68 45N 33 8 E
Kola, I. 103 5 35 S 134 30 E
Kola Pen. = Kolskiy P-ov. 78 67 30N 38 0 E
Kolagede 103 7 54 S 110 26 E
Kolahoi 95 34 12N 75 22 E
Kolahun 120 8 15N 10 4W
Kolaka 103 4 3 S 121 46 E
K'olamai 105 45 30N 84 55 E
K'olan 106 38 43N 111 32 E
Kolar 97 13 12N 78 15 E
Kolar Gold Fields 97 12 58N 78 16 E
Kolari 74 67 20N 23 48 E
Kolarovgrad 67 43 27N 26 42 E
Kolarovo 53 47 56N 18 0 E
Kolašin 66 42 50N 19 31 E
Kolayat 93 27 50N 72 50 E
Kolby 73 55 49N 10 33 E
Kolby Kås 73 55 48N 10 32 E
Kolchugino 81 56 17N 39 22 E
Kolda 120 12 55N 14 50W
Koldewey I. 12 77 0N 18 0W
Kolding 73 55 30N 9 29 E
Kole 124 3 16 S 22 42 E
Koléa 118 36 38N 2 46 E
•Kolepom, Pulau 103 8 0 S 138 30 E
Kölfors 72 62 9N 16 30 E
Kolguyev, Ostrov 78 69 20N 48 30 E
Kolham 46 53 11N 6 44 E
Kolhapur 96 16 43N 74 15 E
Kolia 120 9 46N 6 28W
Kolín 52 50 2N 15 9 E
Kolind 73 56 21N 10 34 E
Kölleda 48 51 11N 11 14 E
Kollegal 97 12 9N 77 9 E
Kolleru L. 96 16 40N 81 10 E
Kollum 46 53 17N 6 10 E
Kolmanskop 128 26 45 S 15 14 E
Köln 48 50 56N 6 58 E
Koło 54 52 14N 18 40 E
Kołobrzeg 54 54 10N 15 35 E
Kologriv 81 58 48N 44 25 E
Kolokani 120 13 35N 7 45W
Kolomna 81 55 8N 38 45 E
Kolomyya 82 48 31N 25 2 E
Kolondiéba 120 11 5N 6 54W
Kolonodale 103 2 3 S 121 25 E
Kolosib 98 24 15N 92 45 E
Kolpashevo 76 58 20N 83 5 E
Kolpino 80 59 44N 30 39 E
Kolpny 81 52 12N 37 10 E
Kolskiy Poluostrov 78 67 30N 38 0 E
Kolskiy Zaliv 78 69 23N 34 0 E
Koltubanovskiy 84 52 57N 52 2 E
Kolubara, R. 66 44 35N 20 15 E
Kolumna 54 51 36N 19 14 E
Koluszki 54 51 45N 19 46 E
Kolwezi 124 10 40 S 25 25 E
Kolyberovo 81 55 15N 38 40 E
Kolyma, R. 77 64 40N 153 0 E
Kolymskoye, Okhotsko 77 63 0N 157 0 E
Kôm Ombo 122 24 25N 32 52 E
Komagene 111 35 44N 137 58 E
Komaki 111 35 17N 136 55 E
Komandorskiye Ostrava 77 55 0N 167 0 E
Komárno 53 47 49N 18 5 E
Komárom 53 47 43N 18 7 E
Komárom □ 53 47 35N 18 20 E
Komarovo 80 58 38N 33 40 E
Komatsu 111 36 25 S 136 30 E
Komatsukima 110 34 0N 134 35 E
Kombissiri 121 12 4N 1 20W
Kombori 120 13 26N 3 56W
Kombóti 69 39 6N 21 5 E
Komen 63 45 49N 13 45 E
Komenda 121 5 4N 1 28W
Komi, A.S.S.R. □ 84 64 0N 55 0 E
Komiza 63 43 3N 16 11 E
Komló 53 46 15N 18 16 E
Kommamur Canal 97 16 0N 80 25 E
Kommunarsk 83 48 30N 38 45 E
Kommunizma, Pik 85 39 0N 72 2 E
Komnes 71 59 30N 9 55 E
Komodo 103 8 37 S 119 20 E
Komoé 120 5 12N 3 44W
Komono 124 3 15 S 13 20 E
Komoran, Pulau 103 8 18 S 138 45 E
Komoro 111 36 19N 138 26 E
Komorze 54 62 8N 17 38 E
Komotiri 68 41 9N 25 26 E
Kompong Bang 101 12 24N 104 40 E
Kompong Cham 101 11 54N 105 30 E
Kompong Chhnang 101 12 20N 104 35 E
Kompong Chikreng 100 13 5N 104 18 E
Kompong Kleang 101 13 6N 104 8 E
Kompong Luong 101 11 49N 104 48 E
Kompong Pranak 101 13 35N 104 55 E
Kompong Som 101 10 38N 103 30 E
Kompong Som, Chhung 101 10 50N 103 32 E
Kompong Speu 101 11 26N 104 32 E
Kompong Sralao 100 14 5N 105 46 E
Kompong Thom 100 12 35N 104 51 E
Kompong Trabeck, Camb. 100 13 6N 105 14 E
Kompong Trabeck, Camb. 101 11 9N 105 28 E
Kompong Trach, Camb. 101 11 25N 105 48 E
Kompong Trach, Camb. 118 10 34N 104 28 E
Kompong Tralach 101 11 54N 104 47 E
Komrat 82 46 18N 28 40 E
Komsberge 128 32 40 S 20 45 E
Komsomolabad 85 38 50N 69 55 E
Komsomolets 84 53 45N 62 2 E
Komsomolets, Ostrov 77 80 30N 95 0 E
Komsomolsk, R.S.F.S.R., U.S.S.R. 77 50 30N 137 0 E
Komsomolsk, Turkmen S.S.R., U.S.S.R. 85 39 2N 63 36 E
Komsomolskiy 81 53 30N 49 40 E
Kona, Niger 121 13 33N 8 3 E
Kona, Nigeria 121 8 58N 11 15 E
Konakovo 81 56 52N 36 45 E
Konam Dzong 99 29 5N 93 0 E
Konawa 159 34 59N 96 46W
Kondagaon 96 19 35N 81 35 E
Konde 126 4 57 S 39 45 E
Kondiá 68 39 52N 25 10 E
Kondinin 137 32 34 S 118 8 E
Kondoa 126 4 55 S 35 50 E
Kondoa □ 126 5 0 S 36 0 E
Kondratyevo 77 57 30N 98 30 E
Konduga 121 11 35N 13 26 E
Kong 120 8 54N 4 36W
Kong Christian IX.s Land 12 68 0N 36 0W
Kong Christian X.s Land 12 74 0N 29 0W
Kong Frederik VIII.s Land 12 78 30N 26 0W
Kong Frederik VI.s Kyst 12 63 0N 43 0W
Kong, Koh 101 11 20N 103 0 E
Kong Oscar Fjord 12 72 20N 24 0W
Kong, R. 100 13 32N 105 58 E
Konga 73 56 30N 15 6 E
Kongeå 73 55 24N 8 39 E
Kongju 107 36 30N 127 0 E
Konglu 98 27 13N 97 57 E
Kongolo 126 5 22 S 27 0 E
Kongoussi 121 13 19N 1 32W
Kongsberg 71 59 39N 9 39 E
Kongsvinger 71 60 12N 12 2 E
Kongsvoll 71 62 20N 9 36 E
Kongwa 126 6 11 S 36 26 E
Koni 127 10 40 S 27 11 E
Koni, Mts. 127 10 36 S 27 10 E
Koniecpol 54 50 46N 19 40 E
Königsberg = Kaliningrad 80 54 42N 20 32 E
Königslutter 48 52 14N 10 50 E
Königswusterhausen 48 52 19N 13 38 E
Konin 54 52 12N 18 15 E
Konin □ 54 52 15N 18 30 E
Konispol 68 39 42N 20 10 E
Kónitsa 68 40 5N 20 48 E
Köniz 50 46 56N 7 25 E
Konjic 66 43 42N 17 58 E
Konjice 63 46 20N 15 28 E
Konkouré, R. 120 10 30N 13 40W
Könnern 48 51 40N 11 45 E
Konnur 96 16 14N 74 49 E
Kono 120 8 30N 11 5W
Konoğlu 82 40 35N 31 50 E
Konolfingen 50 46 54N 7 38 E
Konongo 121 6 40N 1 15W
Konos 135 3 10 S 151 44 E
Konosha 78 61 0N 40 5 E
Kōnosu 111 36 3N 139 31 E
Konotop 80 51 12N 33 7 E
Konskaya, R. 82 47 30N 35 0 E
Konskie 54 51 15N 20 23 E
Konsmo 71 58 16N 7 23 E
Konstantinovka 82 48 32N 37 39 E
Konstantinovski, R.S.F.S.R., U.S.S.R. 81 57 45N 39 35 E

*Renamed Yos Sudarso, Pulau

Konstantinovski **Krokom**

Konstantinovski, R.S.F.S.R., U.S.S.R. **83** 47 33N 41 10 E
Konstantynów Łódzki **54** 51 45N 19 20 E
Konstanz **49** 47 39N 9 10 E
Kontagora **121** 10 23N 5 27 E
Kontich **47** 51 8N 4 26 E
Kontum **100** 14 24N 108 0 E
Kontum, Plat. du **100** 14 30N 108 0 E
Konya **92** 37 52N 32 35 E
Konyin **98** 22 58N 94 42 E
Konz Karthaus **49** 49 41N 6 36 E
Konza **124** 1 45 S 37 0 E
Konzhakovskiy Kamen, Gora **84** 59 38N 59 8 E
Koog **12** 52 27N 4 49 E
Kookynie **137** 29 17 S 121 22 E
Koolan I. **136** 16 0 S 123 45 E
Kooline **136** 22 57 S 116 20 E
Kooloonong **140** 34 48 S 143 10 E
Koolyanobbing **137** 30 48 S 119 36 E
Koolymilka P.O. **140** 30 58 S 136 32 E
Koondrook **140** 35 33 S 144 8 E
Koorawatha **141** 34 2 S 148 33 E
Koorda **137** 30 48 S 117 35 E
Kooskia **160** 46 9N 115 59W
Koostatak **153** 51 26N 97 26W
Kootenai, R. **160** 48 30N 115 30W
Kootenay L. **153** 49 45N 117 0W
Kootenay Nat. Park **152** 51 0N 116 0W
Kootingal **173** 31 1 S 151 3 E
Kopa **85** 43 31N 75 50 E
Kopaonik Planina **66** 43 10N 21 0 E
Kopargaon **96** 19 51N 74 28 E
Kópavogur **74** 64 6N 21 55W
Koper **63** 45 31N 13 44 E
Kopervik **71** 59 17N 5 17 E
Kopeysk **84** 55 7N 61 37 E
Kopi **139** 33 24 S 135 40 E
Köping **72** 59 31N 16 3 E
Kopiste **63** 42 48N 16 42 E
Kopliku **68** 42 15N 19 25 E
Köpmanholmen **72** 63 10N 18 35 E
Köpmannebro **73** 58 45N 12 30 E
Koppal **97** 15 23N 76 5 E
Koppang **71** 61 34N 11 3 E
Kopparberg **75** 59 52N 15 0 E
Kopparbergs län □ **147** 61 20N 14 15 E
Koppeh Dāgh **93** 38 0N 58 0 E
Kopperå **71** 63 24N 11 50 E
Kopperå **71** 63 24N 11 52 E
Koppio **140** 34 26 S 135 51 E
Koppom **72** 59 43N 12 10 E
Koprivlen **67** 41 36N 23 53 E
Koprivnica **63** 46 12N 16 45 E
Koprivshtitsa **67** 42 40N 24 19 E
Kopychintsy **80** 49 7N 25 58 E
Korab, mt. **66** 41 44N 20 40 E
Korakiána **68** 39 42N 19 45 E
Koraput **96** 18 50N 82 40 E
Korba **95** 22 20N 82 45 E
Korbach **48** 51 17N 8 50 E
Korbu, G. **101** 4 41N 101 18 E
Korça **68** 40 37N 20 50 E
Korça □ **68** 40 40N 20 50 E
Korčula **63** 42 57N 17 8 E
Korčula, I. **63** 42 57N 17 0 E
Korčulanski Kanal **63** 43 3N 16 40 E
Kordestān □ **92** 36 0N 47 0 E
Korea **107** 40 0N 127 0 E
Korea Bay **107** 39 0N 124 0 E
Korea, South ■ **107** 36 0N 128 0 E
Korea Strait **107** 34 0N 129 30 E
Koregaon **96** 17 40N 74 10 E
Korenevo **80** 51 27N 34 55 E
Korenovsk **83** 45 12N 39 22 E
Korets **80** 50 40N 27 5 E
Korgus **122** 19 16N 33 48 E
Korhogo **120** 9 29N 5 28W
Koribundu **120** 7 41N 11 46W
Koridina **139** 29 42 S 143 25 E
Korim **103** 0 58 S 136 10 E
Korinthia □ **69** 37 50N 22 35 E
Korinthiakós Kólpos **69** 38 16N 22 30 E
Kórinthos **69** 37 56N 22 55 E
Korioumé **120** 16 35N 3 0W
Kōriyama **112** 37 24N 140 23 E
Korkino **84** 54 54N 61 23 E
Körmend **53** 47 5N 16 35 E
Kornat, I. **63** 43 50N 15 20 E
Korneshty **82** 47 21N 28 1 E
Korneuburg **53** 48 20N 16 20 E
Korning **73** 56 30N 9 44 E
Kornsjø **71** 58 57N 11 39 E
Kornstad **71** 62 59N 7 27 E
Koro, Ivory C. **120** 8 32N 7 30W
Koro, Mali **120** 14 1N 2 58W
Koroba **135** 5 44 S 142 47 E
Korocha **81** 50 55N 37 30 E
Korogwe **124** 5 5 S 38 25 E
Korogwe □ **126** 5 0 S 38 20 E
Koroit **140** 38 18 S 142 24 E
Korong Vale **140** 36 22 S 143 45 E
Koróni **69** 36 48N 21 57 E
Korónia, Limni **68** 40 47N 23 37 E
Koronis **69** 37 12N 25 35 E
Koronowo **54** 53 19N 17 55 E
Koror **103** 7 20N 134 28 E
Körös, R. **53** 46 45N 20 20 E
Körōstarcsa **53** 46 53N 21 3 E
Korosten **80** 50 57N 28 25 E
Korotoyak **81** 51 1N 39 2 E
Korraraika, B. de **129** 17 45 S 43 57 E
Korsakov **77** 46 30N 142 42 E
Korshavn **71** 58 2N 7 0 E
Korshunovo **77** 58 37N 110 10 E
Korsör **73** 55 20N 11 9 E
Korsze **54** 54 11N 21 9 E
Kortemark **47** 51 2N 3 3 E
Kortessem **47** 50 52N 5 23 E
Korti **122** 18 0N 31 40 E
Kortrijk **47** 50 50N 3 17 E
Korumburra **141** 38 26 S 145 50 E
Korwai **94** 24 7N 78 5 E
Koryakskiy Khrebet **77** 61 0N 171 0 E
Koryŏng **107** 35 44N 128 15 E
Kos **69** 36 52N 27 19 E
Kos, I. **69** 36 50N 27 15 E
Kosa, Ethiopia **123** 7 50N 36 50 E
Kosa, U.S.S.R. **84** 59 56N 55 0 E
Kosa, R. **84** 60 11N 55 10 E
Kosaya Gora **81** 54 10N 37 30 E
Koschagy **79** 46 40N 54 0 E
Kosciusko **159** 33 3N 89 34W
Kosciusko, I. **152** 56 0N 133 40W
Kosciusko, Mt. **141** 36 27 S 148 16 E
Kösély, R. **53** 47 25N 21 30 E
Kosgi **96** 16 58N 77 43 E
Kosha **122** 20 50N 30 30 E
Koshigaya **111** 35 54N 139 48 E
K'oshih **105** 39 29N 75 58 E
K'oshihk'ot'engch'i **107** 43 17N 117 24 E
Koshiki-Rettō **110** 31 45N 129 49 E
Kōshoku **111** 36 38N 138 6 E
Koshtëbë **85** 41 5N 74 15 E
Kosi **94** 27 48N 77 29 E
Kosi-meer **129** 27 0 S 32 50 E
Košice **53** 48 42N 21 15 E
Kosjerič **66** 44 0N 19 55 E
Koslan **78** 63 28N 48 52 E
Kosŏng **107** 38 48N 128 24 E
Kosovska-Mitrovica **66** 42 54N 20 52 E
Kosścian **54** 52 5N 16 40 E
Kosścierzyna **54** 54 8N 17 59 E
Kosso **120** 5 3N 5 47W
Kostajnica **63** 45 17N 16 30 E
Kostanjevica **63** 45 51N 15 27 E
Kostelec **53** 50 14N 16 35 E
Kostenets **67** 42 15N 23 52 E
Koster **128** 25 52 s 26 54 E
Kōstî **123** 13 8N 32 43 E
Kostolac **66** 44 43N 21 15 E
Kostroma **81** 57 50N 41 58 E
Kostromskoye Vdkhr. **81** 57 52N 40 49 E
Kostrzyn **54** 52 24N 17 14 E
Kostyukovichi **80** 53 10N 32 4 E
Koszalin **54** 54 12N 16 8 E
Koszalin □ **54** 54 10N 16 10 E
Kőszeg **53** 47 23N 16 33 E
Kot Adu **94** 30 30N 71 0 E
Kot Moman **94** 32 13N 73 0 E
Kota **94** 25 14N 75 49 E
Kota Baharu **101** 6 7N 102 14 E
Kota Kinabalu **102** 6 0N 116 12 E
Kota-Kota = Khota Kota **127** 12 55 S 34 15 E
Kota Tinggi **101** 1 44N 103 53 E
Kotaagung **102** 5 38 S 104 29 E
Kotabaru **102** 3 20 S 116 20 E
Kotabumi **102** 4 49 S 104 46 E
Kotamobagu **103** 0 57N 124 31 E
Kotaneelee, R. **152** 60 11N 123 42W
Kotawaringin **102** 2 28 S 111 27 E
Kotchandpur **98** 23 24N 89 1 E
Kotcho L. **152** 59 7N 121 12W
Kotel **67** 42 52N 26 26 E
Kotelnich **81** 58 20N 48 10 E
Kotelnikovo **83** 47 45N 43 15 E
Kotelnyy, Ostrøv **77** 75 10N 139 0 E
Kothagudam **96** 17 30N 80 40 E
Kothapet **96** 19 21N 79 28 E
Köthen **48** 51 44N 11 59 E
Kothi **95** 24 45N 80 40 E
Kotiro **94** 26 17N 67 13 E
Kotka **75** 60 28N 26 58 E
Kotlas **78** 61 15N 47 0 E
Kotlenska Planina **67** 42 56N 26 30 E
Kotli **94** 33 30N 73 55 E
Kotmul **95** 35 32N 75 10 E
Kotohira **110** 34 11N 133 49 E
Kotonkoro **121** 11 3N 5 58 E
Kotor **66** 42 25N 18 47 E
Kotor Varoš **66** 44 38N 17 22 E
Kotoriba **63** 46 23N 16 48 E
Kotovo **81** 50 22N 44 45 E
Kotovsk **82** 47 55N 29 35 E
Kotputli **94** 27 43N 76 12 E
Kotri **94** 25 22N 68 22 E
Kotri, R. **96** 19 45N 80 35 E
Kótronas **69** 36 38N 22 29 E
Kötschach-Mauthen **52** 46 41N 13 1 E
Kottayam **97** 9 35N 76 33 E
Kottur **97** 10 34N 76 56 E
Kotturu **93** 14 45N 76 10 E
Kotuy, R. **77** 70 30N 103 0 E
Kotzebue **147** 66 50N 162 40W
Kotzebue Sd. **147** 66 30N 164 0W
Kouango **124** 5 0N 20 10 E
Koudekerke **47** 51 29N 3 33 E
Koudougou **120** 12 10N 2 20W
Koufonisi, I. **69** 34 56N 26 8 E
Koufonisia, I. **69** 36 57N 25 35 E
Kougaberge **128** 33 48 S 24 20 E
Kouibli **120** 7 15N 7 14W
Kouilou, R. **124** 4 10 S 12 5 E
Kouki **124** 7 22N 17 3 E
Koula Moutou **124** 1 15 S 12 25 E
Koulen **100** 13 50N 104 40 E
Koulikoro **120** 12 40N 7 50W
Koumala **138** 21 38 S 149 15 E
Koumankoun **120** 11 58N 6 6W
Koumbia, Guin. **120** 11 54N 13 40W
Koumbia, Upp. Vol. **120** 11 10N 3 50W
Koumboum **120** 10 25N 13 0W
Koumpenntoum **120** 13 59N 14 34W
Koumra **117** 8 50N 17 35 E
Koumradskiy **76** 47 20N 75 0 E
Koundara **120** 12 29N 13 18W
Kountze **159** 30 20N 94 22W
Koupangtzu **107** 41 22N 121 46 E
Koupéla **121** 12 11N 0 21 E
Kourizo, Passe de **119** 22 28N 15 27 E
Kouroussa **120** 10 45N 9 45W
Koussané **120** 14 53N 11 14W
Kousseri **117** 12 0N 14 55 E
Koutiala **120** 12 25N 5 35W
Kouto **120** 9 53N 6 25W
Kouvé **121** 6 25N 0 59 E
KovaCica **66** 45 5N 20 38 E
Kovel **80** 51 10N 24 20 E
Kovilpatti **97** 9 10N 77 50 E
Kovin **66** 44 44N 20 59 E
Kovrov **81** 56 25N 41 25 E
Kovur, Andhra Pradesh, India **96** 17 3N 81 39 E
Kovur, Andhra Pradesh, India **97** 14 30N 80 1 E
Kowal **54** 52 32N 19 7 E
Kowalewo Pomorskie **54** 53 10N 18 52 E
Kowkash **150** 50 20N 87 20W
Kowloon **109** 22 20N 114 15 E
Kowŏn **107** 39 26N 127 14 E
Kōyama **110** 31 20N 130 56 E
Koyan, Pegunungan **102** 3 15N 114 30 E
Koyang **106** 33 31N 116 11 E
Koytash **85** 40 11N 67 19 E
Koyuk **147** 64 55N 161 20W
Koyukuk, R. **147** 65 45N 156 30W
Koyulhisar **82** 40 20N 37 52 E
Koza **112** 26 19N 127 46 E
Kozan **92** 37 35N 35 50 E
Kozáni **68** 40 19N 21 47 E
Kozáni □ **68** 40 18N 21 45 E
Kozara, Mts. **63** 45 0N 17 0 E
Kozarac **63** 44 58N 16 48 E
Kozelsk **80** 54 2N 35 38 E
Kozhikode = Calicut **97** 11 15N 75 43 E
Kozhva **78** 65 10N 57 0 E
Koziegłowy **54** 50 37N 19 8 E
Kozje **63** 46 5N 15 35 E
Kozle **54** 50 20N 18 8 E
Kozlodui **67** 43 45N 23 42 E
Kozlovets **67** 43 30N 25 20 E
Kozmin **54** 51 48N 17 27 E
Kōzu-Shima **111** 34 13N 139 10 E
Kozuchów **54** 51 45N 15 31 E
Kpabia **121** 9 10N 0 20W
Kpandae **121** 8 30N 0 2W
Kpandu **121** 7 2N 0 18 E
Kpessi **121** 8 4N 1 16 E
Kra Buri **101** 10 22N 98 46 E
Kra, Isthmus of = Kra, Kho Khot **101** 10 15N 99 30 E
Kra, Kho Khot **101** 10 15N 99 30 E
Krabbendijke **47** 51 26N 4 7 E
Krabi **101** 8 4N 98 55 E
Kragan **103** 6 43 S 111 38 E
Kragerø **71** 58 52N 9 25 E
Kragujevac **66** 44 2N 20 56 E
Krajenka **54** 53 18N 16 59 E
Krakatau = Rakata, Pulau **102** 6 10 S 105 20 E
Krakor **100** 12 32N 104 12 E
Kraków **54** 50 4N 19 57 E
Kraków □ **53** 50 0N 20 0 E
Kraksaan **103** 7 43 S 113 23 E
Kraksmala **73** 57 2N 15 20 E
Kråkstad **71** 59 40N 10 50 E
Kråkstad **71** 59 39N 10 55 E
Kralanh **100** 13 35N 103 25 E
Králíky **53** 50 6N 16 45 E
Kraljevo **66** 43 44N 20 41 E
Kralovice **52** 49 59N 13 29 E
Králövsky Chlmec **53** 48 27N 22 0 E
Kralupy **52** 50 13N 14 20 E
Kramatorsk **82** 48 50N 37 30 E
Kramer **161** 35 0N 117 38W
Kramfors **72** 62 55N 17 48 E
Kramis, C. **118** 36 26N 0 45 E
Krångede **72** 63 9N 16 10 E
Krångede **72** 63 9N 16 6 E
Kraniá **68** 39 53N 21 18 E
Kranidhion **69** 37 20N 23 10 E
Kranj **63** 46 16N 14 22 E
Kranjska Gora **63** 46 29N 13 48 E
Kranzberg **128** 21 59 S 15 37 E
Krapina **63** 46 10N 15 52 E
Krapina, R. **63** 46 0N 15 55 E
Krapivna **81** 53 58N 37 10 E
Krapkowice **54** 50 29N 17 56 E
Kras Polyana **83** 43 40N 40 25 E
Krashyy Klyuch **84** 55 23N 56 39 E
Kraskino **77** 42 44N 130 48 E
Krāslāva **80** 55 52N 27 12 E
Kraslice **52** 50 19N 12 31 E
Krasnaya Gorbatka **81** 55 52N 41 45 E
Krasnik Fabryezny **54** 50 58N 22 11 E
Krasnoarmeisk **82** 48 18N 37 11 E
Krasnoarmeysk, R.S.F.S.R., U.S.S.R. **81** 50 32N 45 50 E
Krasnoarmeysk, R.S.F.S.R., U.S.S.R. **83** 48 30N 44 25 E
Krasnodar **83** 45 5N 38 50 E
Krasnodonetskaya **83** 48 5N 40 50 E
Krasnog Dardeiskoye **82** 45 32N 34 16 E
Krasnogorskiy **81** 56 10N 48 28 E
Krasnograd **82** 49 27N 35 27 E
Krasnogvardeysk **85** 39 46N 67 16 E
Krasnogvardeyskoye **83** 45 52N 41 33 E
Krasnoïarsk **77** 56 8N 93 0 E
Krasnokamsk **84** 58 4N 55 48 E
Krasnokutsk **80** 50 10N 34 50 E
Krasnoperekopsk **82** 46 0N 33 54 E
Krasnoselkupsk **76** 65 20N 82 10 E
Krasnoslobodsk **83** 48 42N 44 33 E
Krasnoturinsk **84** 59 46N 60 12 E
Krasnoufimsk **84** 56 57N 57 46 E
Krasnouralsk **84** 58 21N 60 3 E
Krasnousolskiy **84** 53 54N 56 27 E
Krasnovishersk **84** 60 23N 57 3 E
Krasnovodsk **79** 40 0N 52 52 E
Krasnoyarsk **77** 56 8N 93 0 E
Krasnoyarskiy **84** 51 58N 59 55 E
Krasnoye, Kal., U.S.S.R. **83** 46 16N 45 0 E
Krasnoye, R.S.F.S.R., U.S.S.R. **81** 59 15N 47 40 E
Krasnoye, Ukr., U.S.S.R. **80** 49 56N 24 42 E
Krasnozavodsk **81** 56 38N 38 16 E
Krasny Liman **82** 48 58N 37 50 E
Krasny Sulin **83** 47 52N 40 8 E
Krasnystaw **54** 50 57N 23 5 E
Krasnyy **80** 49 56N 24 42 E
Krasnyy Kholm, R.S.F.S.R., U.S.S.R. **81** 58 10N 37 10 E
Krasnyy Kholm, R.S.F.S.R., U.S.S.R. **84** 51 35N 54 9 E
Krasnyy Kut **81** 50 50N 47 0 E
Krasnyy Luch **83** 48 13N 39 0 E
Krasnyy Yar, Kal., U.S.S.R. **83** 46 43N 48 23 E
Krasnyy Yar, R.S.F.S.R., U.S.S.R. **81** 50 42N 44 45 E
Krasnyy Yar, R.S.F.S.R., U.S.S.R. **81** 53 30N 50 22 E
Krasnyyoskolskoye, Vdkhr. **82** 49 30N 37 30 E
Kraśnik **54** 50 55N 22 5 E
Kraszna, R. **53** 48 0N 22 20 E
Kratie **100** 12 32N 106 10 E
Kratke Ra. **135** 6 45 S 146 0 E
Kratovo **66** 42 6N 22 10 E
Kravanh, Chuor Phnum **101** 12 0N 103 32 E
Krawang **103** 6 19N 107 18 E
Krefeld **48** 51 20N 6 22 E
Kremaston, Limni **69** 38 52N 21 30 E
Kremenchug **82** 49 5N 33 25 E
Kremenchugskoye Vdkhr. **82** 49 20N 32 30 E
Kremenets **82** 50 8N 25 43 E
Kremenica **66** 40 55N 21 25 E
Kremennaya **82** 49 1N 38 10 E
Kremikovtsi **67** 42 46N 23 28 E
Kremmen **48** 52 45N 13 1 E
Kremmling **160** 40 10N 106 30W
Kremnica **53** 48 45N 18 50 E
Krems **52** 48 25N 15 36 E
Kremsmünster **52** 48 3N 14 8 E
Kretinga **80** 55 53N 21 15 E
Krettamia **118** 28 47N 3 27W
Krettsy **80** 58 15N 32 30 E
Kreuzlingen **51** 47 38N 9 10 E
Kribi **121** 2 57N 9 56 E
Krichem **67** 46 16N 24 28 E
Krichev **80** 53 45N 31 50 E
Kriens **51** 47 2N 8 17 E
Krim, mt. **63** 45 53N 14 30 E
Krimpen **46** 51 55N 4 34 E
Krionéri **69** 38 20N 21 35 E
Krishna, R. **96** 16 30N 77 0 E
Krishnagiri **97** 12 32N 78 16 E
Krishnanagar **95** 23 24N 88 33 E
Krishnaraja Sagara **97** 12 20N 76 30 E
Kristianopel **73** 56 12N 16 0 E
Kristiansand **71** 58 9N 8 1 E
Kristianstad **73** 56 2N 14 9 E
Kristianstad □ **75** 56 15N 14 0 E
Kristiansund **71** 63 7N 7 45 E
Kristiinankaupunki **74** 62 16N 21 21 E
Kristinehamn **72** 59 18N 14 13 E
Kristinestad **74** 62 16N 21 21 E
Kríti, I. **69** 35 15N 25 0 E
Kritsá **69** 35 10N 25 41 E
Kriva Palanka **66** 42 11N 22 19 E
Kriva, R. **66** 42 12N 22 18 E
Krivaja, R. **66** 44 15N 18 22 E
Krivelj **66** 44 8N 22 5 E
Krivoy Rog **82** 47 51N 33 20 E
Krizevci **63** 46 3N 16 32 E
Krk **63** 45 5N 14 36 E
Krk, I. **63** 45 8N 14 40 E
Krka, R. **63** 45 50N 15 30 E
Krkonoše **52** 50 50N 16 10 E
Krnov **53** 50 5N 17 40 E
Krobia **54** 51 47N 16 59 E
Kročehlavy **52** 50 8N 13 9 E
Kroeng Krai **101** 14 55N 98 30 E
Krokawo **54** 54 47N 18 9 E
Krokeai **69** 36 53N 22 32 E
Kroken, Norway **71** 58 57N 9 8 E
Kroken, Sweden **71** 59 2N 11 23 E
Krokom **72** 63 20N 14 30 E

Krolevets **Kuybyshevskoye Vdkhr**

Krolevets **80** 51 35N 33 20 E
Kroměříz **53** 49 18N 17 21 E
Krommenie **46** 52 30N 4 46 E
Krompachy **53** 48 54N 20 52 E
Kromy **80** 52 40N 35 48 E
Kronobergs län □ **73** 56 45N 14 30 E
Kronprins Harald Kyst **13** 70 0 S 35 1 E
Kronprins Olav Kyst **13** 69 0 S 42 0 E
Kronprinsesse Märtha Kyst **13** 73 30 S 10 0W
Kronshtadt **80** 60 5N 29 35 E
Kroonstad **125** 27 43 S 27 19 E
Kröpelin **48** 54 4N 11 48 E
Kropotkin **77** 45 25N 40 35 E
Kropp **48** 54 24N 9 32 E
Krósniewice **54** 52 15N 19 11 E
Krosno **54** 49 35N 21 56 E
Kroşno □ **54** 49 30N 22 0 E
Krosno Odrz **54** 52 3N 15 7 E
Krosścienko **54** 49 29N 20 25 E
Krotoszyn **54** 51 42N 17 23 E
Krotovka **84** 53 18N 51 10 E
Krraba **68** 41 13N 20 0 E
Krško **63** 45 57N 15 30 E
Krstač a, mt. **66** 42 57N 20 8 E
Kruger Nat. Pk. **129** 24 0 S 31 40 E
Krugersdorp **129** 26 5 S 27 46 E
Kruidfontein **128** 32 48 S 21 59 E
Kruiningen **47** 51 27N 4 2 E
Kruis, Kaap **128** 21 55 S 13 57 E
Kruishoutem **47** 50 54N 3 32 E
Kruisland **47** 51 34N 4 25 E
Kruja **68** 41 32N 19 46 E
Krulevshchina **80** 55 5N 27 45 E
Kruma **68** 42 37N 20 28 E
Krumovgrad **67** 41 29N 25 38 E
Krung Thep = Bangkok **100** 13 45N 100 35 E
Krupanj **66** 44 25N 19 22 E
Krupina **53** 48 22N 19 5 E
Krupinica, R. **53** 48 15N 19 5 E
Kruševac **66** 43 35N 21 28 E
Krušovo **66** 41 23N 21 19 E
Kruszwica **54** 52 40N 18 20 E
Kruzof I. **152** 57 10N 135 40W
Krylbo **72** 60 7N 16 15 E
Krymsk Abinsk **82** 44 50N 38 0 E
Krymskaya **82** 45 0N 34 0 E
Krynica **54** 49 25N 20 57 E
Krynica Morska **54** 54 23N 19 28 E
Krynki **54** 53 17N 23 43 E
Kryulyany **70** 47 12N 29 9 E
Krzepice **54** 50 58N 18 50 E
Krzeszowice **54** 50 8N 19 37 E
Krzywin **54** 51 58N 16 50 E
Krzyz **54** 52 52N 16 0 E
Ksabi, Alg. **118** 29 8N 0 58W
Ksabi, Moroc. **118** 32 51N 4 13W
Ksar Chellala **118** 35 13N 2 19 E
Ksar el Boukhari **118** 35 51N 2 52 E
Ksar el Kebir **118** 35 0N 6 0W
*Ksar es Souk **118** 31 58N 4 20W
Ksar Rhilane **119** 33 0N 9 39 E
Ksiba **118** 32 46N 6 0W
Ksour, Mts. des **118** 32 45N 0 30W
Kstovo **81** 56 12N 44 13 E
Kuachou **109** 32 14N 119 24 E
Kuala **102** 2 46N 105 47 E
Kuala Berang **101** 5 5N 103 1 E
Kuala Dungun **101** 4 45N 103 25 E
Kuala Kangsar **101** 4 46N 100 56 E
Kuala Kerai **101** 5 30N 102 12 E
Kuala Klawang **101** 2 56N 102 5 E
Kuala Kubu Baharu **101** 3 34N 101 39 E
Kuala Lipis **101** 4 10N 102 3 E
Kuala Lumpur **101** 3 9N 101 41 E
Kuala Marang **101** 5 12N 103 13 E
Kuala Nerang **101** 6 16N 100 37 E
Kuala Pilah **101** 2 45N 102 15 E
Kuala Rompin **101** 2 49N 103 29 E
Kuala Selangor **101** 3 20N 101 15 E
Kuala Terengganu **101** 5 20N 103 8 E
Kuala Trengganu **101** 5 20N 103 8 E
Kualakahi Chan **147** 22 2N 159 53W
Kualakapuas **102** 2 55 S 114 20 E
Kualakurun **102** 1 10 S 113 50 E
Kualapembuang, Indon. **102** 3 14 S 112 38 E
Kualapembuang, Indon. **102** 2 52 S 111 45 E
Kuanaan **107** 34 8N 119 24 E
Kuanch'eng **107** 40 39N 118 32 E
Kuandang **103** 0 56N 123 1 E
Kuangan **108** 30 30N 106 35 E
Kuangch'ang **109** 26 50N 116 15 E
Kuangchou **109** 23 12N 113 12 E
Kuangfeng **109** 28 26N 118 12 E
Kuanghan **108** 30 56N 104 15 E
Kuanghua **109** 32 22N 111 43 E
Kuangjao **107** 37 5N 118 25 E
Kuangling **106** 39 47N 114 10 E
Kuangnan **108** 24 3N 105 3 E
Kuangning **109** 23 40N 112 23 E
Kuangshi **109** 29 55N 115 25 E
Kuangshun **108** 26 5N 106 16 E
Kuangte **109** 30 54N 119 26 E
Kuangtse **109** 27 30N 117 24 E
Kuangwuch'eng **106** 37 49N 108 51 E
Kuangyüan **108** 32 22N 105 50 E
Kuanhsien **108** 31 0N 103 40 E
Kuanling **108** 25 55N 105 35 E
Kuanp'ing **109** 31 39N 110 16 E
Kuantan **101** 3 49N 103 20 E
Kuant'ao **106** 36 31N 115 16 E
Kuantaok'ou **106** 34 18N 111 1 E
K'uantien **107** 40 47N 124 43 E

*Renamed Ar Rachidya,

Kuanyang **109** 25 29N 111 9 E
Kuanyün **107** 34 17N 119 15 E
Kuaram **123** 12 25N 39 30 E
Kuba **83** 41 21N 48 32 E
Kubak **93** 27 10N 63 10 E
Kuban, R. **82** 45 5N 38 0 E
Kubenskoye, Oz. **81** 59 40N 39 25 E
Kuberle **83** 47 0N 42 20 E
Kubokawa **110** 33 12N 133 8 E
Kubor **135** 6 10 S 144 44 E
Kubrat **67** 43 49N 26 31 E
Kučevo **66** 44 30N 21 40 E
Kucha Gompa **95** 34 25N 76 56 E
Kuchaman **94** 27 13N 74 47 E
Kuch'ang **108** 24 58N 102 45 E
Kuchang **109** 28 37N 109 56 E
K'uche K'uerhlo **105** 41 43N 82 54 E
Kuchenspitze **49** 47 3N 10 14 E
Kuchiang **109** 27 11N 114 47 E
Kuching **102** 1 33N 110 25 E
Kuchinoerabu-Jima **112** 30 28N 130 11 E
Kuchinotsu **110** 32 36N 130 11 E
Kuçove = Qytet Stalin **68** 40 47N 19 57 E
Kud, R. **94** 26 30N 66 12 E
Kuda **93** 23 10N 71 15 E
Kudalier, R. **96** 18 20N 78 40 E
Kudamatsu **110** 34 0N 131 52 E
Kudara **85** 38 25N 72 39 E
Kudat **102** 6 55N 116 55 E
Kudremukh, Mt. **97** 13 15N 75 20 E
Kuduarra Well **136** 20 38 S 126 20 E
Kudus **103** 6 48 S 110 51 E
Kudymkar **84** 59 1N 54 39 E
Kuei Chiang, R. **109** 23 33N 111 18 E
Kueich'i **109** 28 17N 117 11 E
Kueich'ih **109** 30 42N 117 30 E
Kueichu **108** 26 25N 106 40 E
Kueihsien **108** 23 6N 109 36 E
Kueilin **109** 25 20N 110 18 E
Kueip'ing **108** 23 24N 110 5 E
Kueiting **108** 26 30N 107 17 E
Kueitung **109** 26 12N 114 0 E
Kueiyang, Hunan, China **109** 25 44N 112 43 E
Kueiyang, Kweichow, China **108** 26 35N 106 43 E
K'uerhlo **105** 41 44N 86 9 E
Kufra, El Wâhât el **117** 24 17N 23 15 E
Kufrinja **90** 32 20N 35 41 E
Kufstein **52** 47 35N 12 11 E
Kugmallit B. **147** 29 0N 134 0W
Kugong, I. **150** 56 18N 79 50W
Kūh-e-Alijuq **93** 31 30N 51 41 E
Kūh-e-Dinar **93** 30 10N 51 0 E
Kūh-e-Hazaran **93** 29 35N 57 20 E
Kūh-e-Jebel Barez **93** 29 0N 58 0 E
Kūh-e-Sorkh **93** 35 30N 58 45 E
Kūh-e-Taftan **93** 28 40N 61 0 E
Kūhak **93** 27 12N 63 10 E
Kūhha-ye-Bashakerd **93** 26 45N 59 0 E
Kūhha-ye Sabalān **93** 38 15N 47 45 E
Kuhnsdorf **52** 46 37N 14 38 E
Kuhpayeh **93** 32 44N 52 20 E
Kui Buri **101** 12 3N 99 52 E
Kuinre **46** 52 47N 5 51 E
Kuiseb, R. **125** 23 40 S 15 30 E
Kuiu I. **147** 56 40N 134 15W
Kujangdong **107** 39 57N 126 1 E
Kuji **112** 40 11N 141 46 E
Kujū-San **110** 33 5N 131 15 E
Kujukuri-Heiya **111** 35 45N 140 30 E
Kukavica, mt. **66** 42 48N 21 57 E
Kukawa **121** 12 58N 13 27 E
Kukerin **137** 33 13 S 118 0 E
Kukësi **68** 42 5N 20 20 E
Kukësi □ **68** 42 25N 20 15 E
Kukko **123** 8 26N 41 35 E
Kukmor **84** 56 11N 50 54 E
Kukup **101** 1 20N 103 27 E
K'uk'ushihli Shanmo **105** 35 20N 91 0 E
Kukvidze **81** 50 40N 43 15 E
Kula, Bulg. **66** 43 52N 22 36 E
Kula, Yugo. **66** 45 37N 19 32 E
Kulai **101** 1 44N 103 35 E
Kulal, Mt. **126** 2 42N 36 57 E
Kulaly, O. **83** 45 0N 50 0 E
Kulanak **85** 41 22N 75 30 E
Kulasekharapattanam **97** 8 20N 78 0 E
Kuldiga **80** 56 58N 21 59 E
Kuldja = Ining **105** 43 54N 81 21 E
Kuldu **123** 12 50N 28 30 E
Kulebaki **81** 55 22N 42 25 E
Kulen Vakuf **63** 44 35N 16 2 E
Kulgam **95** 33 36N 75 2 E
Kuli **83** 42 2N 46 12 E
Kulim **101** 5 22N 100 34 E
Kulin **137** 32 40 S 118 2 E
Kulja **137** 30 28 S 117 18 E
Küllük **69** 37 12N 27 36 E
Kulm **158** 46 22N 98 58W
K'uloch'akonnoerh **106** 43 25N 114 50 E
Kulsary **76** 46 59N 54 1 E
Kultay **83** 45 5N 51 40 E
Kulti **95** 23 43N 86 50 E
Kulu **93** 37 12N 115 2 E
Kulumadau **138** 9 15 S 152 50 E
K'ulunch'i **107** 42 44N 121 44 E
Kulunda **76** 52 45N 79 15 E
Kulungar **94** 34 0N 69 2 E
Kulwin **140** 35 0 S 142 42 E
Kulyab **85** 37 55N 69 50 E
Kum Tekei **76** 43 10N 79 30 E
Kuma **110** 33 39N 132 54 E
Kuma, R. **83** 44 55N 45 57 E
Kumaganum **121** 13 8N 10 38 E
Kumagaya **111** 36 9N 139 22 E
Kumak **84** 51 10N 60 8 E
Kumamoto **110** 32 45N 130 45 E
Kumamoto-ken □ **110** 32 30N 130 40 E
Kumano **111** 33 54N 136 5 E
Kumano-Nada **111** 33 47N 136 20 E
Kumanovo **66** 42 9N 21 42 E
Kumara **143** 42 37 S 171 12 E
Kumarkhali **98** 23 51N 89 15 E
Kumarl **137** 32 47 S 121 33 E
Kumasi **120** 6 41N 1 38W
Kumba **121** 4 36N 9 24 E
Kumbakonam **97** 10 58N 79 25 E
Kumbarilla **139** 27 15 S 150 55 E
Kumbo **121** 6 15N 10 36 E
Kumbukkan Oya **97** 6 35N 81 40 E
Kŭmchŏn **107** 38 10N 126 29 E
Kumdok **95** 33 32N 78 10 E
Kumeny **81** 58 10N 49 47 E
Kŭmhwa **107** 38 17N 127 28 E
Kumi **126** 1 30N 33 58 E
Kumkale **68** 40 30N 26 13 E
Kumla **72** 59 8N 15 10 E
Kumo **121** 10 1N 11 12 E
Kumon Bum **98** 26 30N 97 15 E
Kumotori-Yama **111** 35 51N 138 57 E
Kumta **97** 14 29N 74 32 E
Kumtorkala **83** 43 2N 46 50 E
Kumukahi, C. **147** 19 31N 154 49W
Kumusi, R. **135** 8 16 S 148 13 E
Kumylzhenskaya **83** 49 51N 42 38 E
Kunágota **53** 46 26N 21 3 E
Kunama **141** 35 35 S 148 4 E
Kunar **93** 34 30N 71 3 E
Kunashir, Ostrov **77** 44 0N 146 0 E
Kunch **95** 26 0N 79 10 E
Kunda **80** 59 30N 26 34 E
Kundiawa **135** 6 2 S 145 1 E
Kundip **137** 33 42 S 120 10 E
Kundla **94** 21 21N 71 25 E
Kunduz **93** 36 50N 68 50 E
Kunduz □ **93** 36 50N 68 50 E
Kunene, R. **128** 17 15 S 13 40 E
Kungala **139** 29 58 S 153 7 E
Kungälv **73** 57 53N 11 59 E
Kungan **109** 30 4N 112 12 E
Kungch'eng **109** 24 50N 110 49 E
K'ungch'iao Ho **105** 41 48N 86 47 E
Kŭngdong **107** 39 9N 126 5 E
Kungey Alatau, Khrebet **85** 42 50N 77 0 E
Kunghit I. **152** 52 6N 131 3W
Kungho **105** 36 28N 100 45 E
Kungka **108** 28 44N 100 22 E
Kungkuan **108** 21 51N 109 33 E
Kungrad **76** 43 6N 58 54 E
Kungsbacka **73** 57 30N 12 5 E
Kungshan **108** 27 41N 97 37 E
Kungt'an **108** 28 49N 108 38 E
Kungur **84** 57 25N 56 57 E
Kungurri **138** 21 3 S 148 46 E
Kungyangon **98** 16 27N 96 1 E
Kungyingtzu **107** 43 38N 121 0 E
Kunhar, R. **95** 35 0N 73 40 E
Kunhegyes **53** 47 22N 20 36 E
Kunimi-Dake **110** 32 33N 131 1 E
Kuningan **103** 6 59 S 108 29 E
Kunisaki **110** 33 33N 131 45 E
Kunlara **140** 34 54 S 139 55 E
Kunlong **98** 23 20N 98 50 E
Kunlun Shan **105** 36 0N 86 30 E
Kunmadaras **53** 47 28N 20 45 E
K'unming **108** 25 5N 102 40 E
Kunnamkulam **97** 10 38N 76 7 E
Kunrade **47** 50 53N 5 57 E
Kunsan **107** 35 59N 126 45 E
K'unshan **109** 31 22N 121 0 E
Kunszentmárton **53** 46 50N 20 20 E
Kununurra **136** 15 40 S 128 39 E
Kunwarara **138** 22 55 S 150 9 E
Kuohsien **106** 38 57N 112 46 E
Kuopio **74** 62 53N 27 35 E
Kuopion Lääni □ **74** 63 25N 27 10 E
Kupa, R. **63** 45 30N 16 10 E
Kupang **103** 10 19 S 123 39 E
Kupeik'ou **107** 40 42N 117 9 E
Kupiano **135** 10 4 S 148 14 E
Kupreanof I. **147** 56 50N 133 30W
Kupres **66** 44 1N 17 15 E
Kupyansk **82** 49 45N 37 35 E
Kupyansk-Uzlovoi **82** 49 52N 37 34 E
Kur, R. **98** 26 50N 91 0 E
Kura, R. **83** 40 20N 47 30 E
Kurahashi-Jima **110** 34 8N 132 31 E
Kuranda **138** 16 48 S 145 35 E
Kurandvad **96** 16 45N 74 39 E
Kurashiki **110** 34 40N 133 50 E
Kurayoshi **110** 35 26N 133 50 E
Kurday **85** 43 21N 74 59 E
Kurdistan, reg. **92** 37 30N 42 0 E
Kurduvadi **96** 18 8N 75 29 E
Kure **110** 34 14N 132 32 E
Kuressaare = Kingisepp **80** 58 15N 22 15 E
Kurgaldzhino **76** 50 35N 70 20 E
Kurgan, R.S.F.S.R., U.S.S.R. **77** 64 5N 172 50W
Kurgan, R.S.F.S.R., U.S.S.R. **84** 55 26N 65 18 E
Kurgan-Tyube **85** 37 50N 68 47 E
Kuria Muria I = Khy ryān Muryān J. **91** 17 30N 55 58 E
Kurichchi **97** 11 36N 77 35 E
Kuridala **138** 21 16 S 140 29 E
Kurigram **98** 25 49N 89 39 E
Kurihashi **111** 36 8N 139 42 E
Kuril Trench **142** 44 0N 153 0 E
Kurilskiye Ostrova **77** 45 0N 150 0 E
Kuring Kuru **128** 17 42 S 18 32 E
Kuringen **47** 50 56N 5 18 E
Kurino **110** 31 57N 130 43 E
KüRKkkuyu **68** 39 35N 26 27 E
Kurkur **122** 23 50N 32 0 E
Kurkûrah **119** 31 30N 20 1 E
Kurla **96** 19 5N 72 52 E
Kurlovski **81** 55 25N 40 40 E
Kurma **123** 13 55N 24 40 E
Kurmuk **123** 10 33N 34 21 E
Kurnalpi **137** 30 29 S 122 16 E
Kurnool **97** 15 45N 78 0 E
Kurobe-Gawe, R. **111** 36 55N 137 25 E
Kurogi **110** 33 12N 130 40 E
Kurovskoye **81** 55 35N 38 55 E
Kurow **143** 44 4 S 170 29 E
Kurrajong, N.S.W., Austral. **141** 33 33 S 150 42 E
Kurrajong, W.A., Austral. **137** 28 39 S 120 59 E
Kurram, R. **94** 33 30N 70 15 E
Kurri Kurri **141** 32 50 S 151 28 E
Kuršenai **80** 56 1N 23 3 E
Kurseong **95** 26 56N 88 18 E
Kursk **81** 51 42N 36 11 E
Kuršumlija **66** 43 9N 21 19 E
Kuršumlijska Banja **66** 43 3N 21 11 E
Kurtalon **92** 37 55N 41 40 E
Kurtamysh **84** 54 55N 64 27 E
Kurty, R. **85** 44 16N 76 42 E
Kuru (Chel), Bahr el **123** 8 10N 26 50 E
Kuruman **128** 27 28 S 23 28 E
Kurume **110** 33 15N 130 30 E
Kurunegala **97** 7 30N 80 18 E
Kurya **77** 61 15N 108 10 E
Kusa **84** 55 20N 59 29 E
Kuşadası **69** 37 52N 27 15 E
Kuşadası Körfezı **69** 37 56N 27 0 E
Kusatsu, Gumma, Japan **111** 36 37N 138 36 E
Kusatsu, Shiga, Japan **111** 34 58N 136 5 E
Kusawa L. **152** 60 20N 136 13W
Kusel **49** 49 31N 7 25 E
Kushchevskaya **83** 46 33N 39 35 E
Kushikino **110** 31 44N 130 16 E
Kushima **110** 31 29N 131 14 E
Kushimoto **111** 33 28N 135 47 E
Kushin **109** 32 12N 115 48 E
Kushiro **112** 43 0N 144 25 E
Kushiro, R. **112** 42 59N 144 23 E
Kushk **93** 34 55N 62 30 E
Kushka **76** 35 20N 62 18 E
Kushmurun **84** 52 27N 64 36 E
Kushmurun, Ozero **84** 52 40N 64 48 E
Kushnarenkovo **84** 55 6N 55 22 E
Kushol **95** 33 40N 76 36 E
Kushrabat **85** 40 18N 66 32 E
Kushtia **98** 23 55N 89 5 E
Kushum, R. **83** 50 40N 50 20 E
Kushva **84** 58 18N 59 45 E
Kuskokwim Bay **147** 59 50N 162 56W
Kuskokwim Mts. **147** 63 0N 156 0W
Kuskokwim, R. **147** 61 48N 157 0W
Küsnacht **51** 47 19N 8 15 E
Kussa **123** 4 9N 38 58 E
Küssnacht **51** 47 5N 8 26 E
Kustanay **84** 53 10N 63 35 E
Kusu **110** 33 16N 131 9 E
Kusung **108** 28 25N 105 12 E
Kut, Ko **101** 11 40N 102 35 E
Kutá Horq **52** 49 57N 15 16 E
Kutahya **92** 39 30N 30 2 E
Kutaisi **83** 42 19N 42 40 E
Kutaradja = Banda Aceh **102** 5 35N 95 20 E
Kutatjane **102** 3 45N 97 50 E
Kutch, G. of **94** 22 50N 69 15 E
Kutch, Rann of **94** 24 0N 70 0 E
Kut'ien **109** 26 36N 118 48 E
Kutina **63** 45 29N 16 48 E
Kutiyana **94** 21 36N 70 2 E
Kutjevo **66** 45 23N 17 55 E
Kutkai **98** 23 27N 97 56 E
Kutkashen **83** 40 58N 47 47 E
Kutná Hora **52** 49 57N 15 16 E
Kutno **54** 52 15N 19 23 E
Kuttabul **138** 21 5 S 148 48 E
Kutu **124** 2 40 S 18 11 E
Kutum **123** 14 20N 24 10 E
Kúty **53** 48 40N 17 3 E
Kuŭptong **107** 40 45N 126 1 E
Kuurne **47** 50 51N 3 18 E
Kuvandyk **84** 51 28N 57 21 E
Kuvasay **85** 40 18N 71 59 E
Kuvshinovo **80** 57 2N 34 11 E
Kuwait = Al Kuwayt **92** 29 30N 47 30 E
Kuwait ■ **92** 29 30N 47 30 E
Kuwana **111** 35 0N 136 43 E
Kuyang **106** 41 8N 110 1 E
Kuybyshev **81** 55 27N 78 19 E
Kuybyshevo, Ukraine S.S.R., U.S.S.R. **82** 47 25N 36 40 E
Kuybyshevo, Uzbek S.S.R., U.S.S.R. **85** 40 20N 71 15 E
Kuybyshevskiy **85** 37 52N 68 44 E
Kuybyshevskoye Vdkhr. **81** 55 2N 49 30 E

Kuyeh Ho, R Lambay I

Kuyeh Ho, R. 106 38 30N 110 44 E
Kuylyuk 85 41 14N 69 17 E
Kuyto, Oz. 78 64 40N 31 0 E
Kuyüan, Hopeh, China 106 41 34N 115 38 E
Kuyüan, Ningsia Hui, China 106 36 1N 106 17 E
Kuzhithura 97 8 18N 77 11 E
Kuzino 84 57 1N 59 27 E
Kuzmin 66 45 2N 19 25 E
Kuznetsk 81 53 12N 46 40 E
Kuzomen 78 66 22N 36 50 E
Kvænangen 74 69 55N 21 15 E
Kvam 71 61 40N 9 42 E
Kvamsøy 71 61 7N 6 28 E
Kvarken 74 63 30N 21 0 E
Kvarner 63 44 50N 14 10 E
Kvarnerič 63 44 43N 14 37 E
Kvarnsveden 72 60 32N 15 25 E
Kvarntorp 72 59 8N 15 17 E
Kvås 71 58 16N 7 14 E
Kvernes 71 63 1N 7 44 E
Kvillsfors 73 57 24N 15 29 E
Kvina, R. 71 58 43N 6 52 E
Kvinesdal 71 58 18N 6 59 E
Kviteseid 71 59 24N 8 29 E
Kwabhaca 129 30 51 S 29 0 E
Kwadacha, R. 152 57 28N 125 38W
Kwakhanai 128 21 39 S 21 16 E
Kwakoegron 175 5 25N 55 25W
Kwale, Kenya 126 4 15 S 39 31 E
Kwale, Nigeria 121 6 18N 5 28 E
Kwale □ 126 4 15 S 39 10 E
Kwamouth 124 3 9 S 16 20 E
Kwando, R. 128 16 48 S 22 45 E
Kwangdaeri 107 40 31N 127 32 E
Kwangju 107 35 9N 126 54 E
Kwangsi-Chuang A.R. □ 109 24 0N 109 0 E
Kwangtung □ 109 23 45N 114 0 E
Kwara □ 121 8 0N 5 0 E
Kwaraga 128 20 26 S 24 32 E
Kwataboahegan, R. 150 51 9N 80 50W
Kwatisore 103 3 7 S 139 59 E
Kweichow □ 108 27 20N 107 0 E
Kweiyang = Kueiyang 108 26 35N 106 43 E
Kwethluk 147 60 45N 161 34W
Kwidzyn 54 54 45N 18 58 E
Kwigillingok 147 59 50N 163 10W
Kwiguk 147 63 45N 164 35W
Kwikila 135 9 49 S 147 38 E
Kwimba □ 126 3 0 S 33 0 E
Kwinana 137 32 15 S 115 47 E
Kwitaba 126 3 56 S 29 39 E
Kya-in-Seikkyi 98 16 2N 98 8 E
Kyabe 117 9 30N 19 0 E
Kyabra Cr. 139 25 36 S 142 55 E
Kyabram 139 36 19 S 145 4 E
Kyaiklat 98 16 46N 96 52 E
Kyaikmaraw 98 16 23N 97 44 E
Kyaikthin 98 23 32N 95 40 E
Kyaikto 100 17 20N 97 3 E
Kyakhta 77 50 30N 106 25 E
Kyangin 98 18 20N 95 20 E
Kyaring Tso 99 31 5N 88 25 E
Kyaukhnyat 98 18 15N 97 31 E
Kyaukpadaung 99 20 52N 95 8 E
Kyaukpyu 99 19 28N 93 30 E
Kyaukse 98 21 36N 96 10 E
Kyauktaw 98 21 16N 96 44 E
Kyawkku 98 21 48N 96 56 E
Kyburz 163 38 47N 120 18W
Kybybolite 140 36 53 S 140 55 E
Kyegegwa 126 0 30N 31 0 E
Kyeintali 98 18 0N 94 29 E
Kyela □ 127 9 45 S 34 0 E
Kyenjojo 126 0 40N 30 37 E
Kyidaunggan 98 19 53N 96 12 E
Kyle Dam 127 20 15 S 31 0 E
Kyle, dist. 34 55 32N 4 25W
Kyle of Lochalsh 36 57 17N 5 43W
Kyleakin 36 57 16N 5 44W
Kyneton 140 37 10 S 144 29 E
Kynuna 138 21 37 S 141 55 E
Kyō-ga-Saki 111 35 45N 135 15 E
Kyoga, L. 126 1 35N 33 0 E
Kyogle 139 28 40 S 153 0 E
Kyongju 107 35 51N 129 14 E
Kyongpyaw 99 17 12N 95 10 E
Kyōngsōng 107 41 35N 129 36 E
Kyōto 111 35 0N 135 45 E
Kyōto-fu □ 111 35 15N 135 30 E
Kyrinia 92 35 20N 33 20 E
Kyritz 48 52 57N 12 25 E
Kyrkebyn 72 59 18N 13 3 E
Kyrping 71 59 45N 6 5 E
Kyshtym 84 55 42N 60 34 E
Kystatyam 77 67 20N 123 10 E
Kytalktakh 77 65 30N 123 40 E
Kytlym 84 59 30N 59 12 E
Kyu-hkok 98 24 4N 98 4 E
Kyulyunken 77 64 10N 137 5 E
Kyunhla 98 23 25N 95 15 E
Kyuquot 152 50 3N 127 25W
Kyuquot Sd. 83 50 0N 127 25W
Kyurdamir 83 40 25N 48 3 E
Kyūshū 110 33 0N 131 0 E
Kyūshū □ 110 33 0N 131 0 E
Kyūshū-Sanchi 110 32 45N 131 40 E
Kyustendil 66 42 25N 22 41 E
Kyusyur 77 70 39N 127 15 E
Kywong 141 34 58 S 146 44 E
Kyzyl 77 51 50N 94 30 E
Kyzyl-Kiya 85 40 16N 72 8 E
Kyzyl Orda 85 44 56N 65 30 E
Kyzyl Rabat 76 37 45N 74 55 E
Kyzylkum 84 42 30N 65 0 E
Kyzylsu, R. 85 39 11N 72 2 E
Kzyl-orda 85 44 48N 65 28 E

L

Laa 53 48 43N 16 23 E
Laage 48 53 55N 12 21 E
Laasphe 48 50 56N 8 23 E
Laau Pt. 147 21 57N 159 40W
Laba, R. 83 45 0N 40 30 E
Laban, Burma 98 25 52N 96 40 E
Laban, Ireland 39 53 8N 8 50W
Labasheeda 39 52 37N 9 15W
Labastide 44 43 28N 2 39 E
Labastide-Murat 44 44 39N 1 33 E
Labbézenga 121 15 2N 0 48 E
Labdah = Leptis Magna 119 32 40N 14 12 E
Labé 120 11 24N 12 16W
Labe, R. 52 50 3N 15 20 E
Laberec, R. 53 21 57N 49 7 E
Laberge, L. 152 61 11N 135 12W
Labin 63 45 5N 14 8 E
Labinsk 83 44 40N 40 48W
Labis 101 2 22N 103 2 E
Labiszyn 54 52 57N 17 54 E
Laboa 103 8 6 S 122 50 E
Laboe 48 54 25N 10 13 E
Labouheyre 44 44 13N 0 55W
Laboulaye 172 34 10 S 63 30W
Labrador City 151 52 57N 66 55W
Labrador, Coast of ■ 149 53 20N 61 0W
Labranzagrande 174 5 33N 72 34W
Lábrea 174 7 15 S 64 51W
Labrède 44 44 41N 0 32W
Labuan, I. 102 5 15N 115 38W
Labuha 103 0 30 S 127 30 E
Labuhan 103 6 26 S 105 50 E
Labuhanbajo 103 8 28 S 120 1 E
Labuissière 47 50 19N 4 11 E
Labuk, Telok 102 6 10N 117 50 E
Labutta 98 16 9N 94 46 E
Labytnangi 78 66 29N 66 40 E
Lac Allard 151 50 33N 63 24W
Lac Bouchette 151 48 16N 72 11W
Lac du Flambeau 158 46 1N 89 51W
Lac Édouard 151 47 40N 72 16W
Lac la Biche 152 54 45N 111 58W
Lac-Mégantic 151 45 35N 70 53W
Lac Seul 153 50 28N 92 0W
Lac Thien 100 12 25N 108 11 E
Lacanau, Étang de 44 44 58N 1 7W
Lacanau Médoc 44 44 59N 1 5W
Lacantum, R. 165 16 36N 90 40W
Lacara, R. 57 39 7N 6 25W
Lacaune 44 43 43N 2 40 E
Lacaune, Mts. de 44 43 43N 2 50 E
Laccadive Is. = Lakshadweep Is. 86 10 0N 72 30 E
Laceby 33 53 32N 0 10W
Lacepede B. 140 36 40 S 139 40 E
Lacepede Is. 136 16 55 S 122 0 E
Lacerdónia 127 18 3 S 35 35 E
Lachen, Sikkim 98 47 12N 8 51 E
Lachen, Switz. 51 47 12N 8 51 E
Lachi 94 33 25N 71 20 E
Lachine 150 45 30N 73 40W
Lachlan 139 42 50 S 147 3 E
Lachlan, R. 140 34 22 S 143 55 E
Lachmangarh 94 27 50N 75 4 E
Lachute 150 45 39N 74 21 E
Lackagh Hills 38 54 14N 8 0W
Lackawanna 156 42 49N 78 50W
Lackawaxen 162 41 29N 74 59W
Lacock 28 51 24N 2 8W
Lacombe 152 52 30N 113 44W
Lacona 162 43 37N 76 5W
Láconi 64 39 54N 9 4 E
Laconia 162 43 32N 71 30W
Lacq 44 43 25N 0 35W
Lacrosse 160 46 51N 117 58W
Ladainha 171 17 39 S 41 44W
Ladakh Ra. 95 34 0N 78 0 E
Ladder Hills 37 57 14N 3 13W
Ladhar Bheinn 36 57 5N 5 37W
Ladhon, R. 69 37 40N 21 50 E
Lâdik 82 40 57N 35 58 E
Ladismith 128 33 28 S 21 15 E
Lādiz 93 28 55N 61 15 E
Ladnun 94 27 38N 74 25 E
Ladock 30 50 19N 4 58W
Ladoga, L. = Ladozhskoye Oz. 78 61 15N 30 30 E
Ladon 43 48 0N 2 30 E
Ladozhskoye Ozero 76 61 15N 30 30 E
Ladrone Is. = Mariana Is. 130 17 0N 145 0 E
Lady Babbie 127 18 30 S 29 20 E
Lady Beatrix L. 150 5 20N 76 50W
Lady Edith Lagoon 136 20 36 S 126 47 E
Lady Grey 128 30 43 S 27 13 E
Ladybank 35 56 16N 3 8W
Ladybrand 128 29 9 S 27 29 E
Lady's I. Lake 39 52 12N 6 23W
Ladysmith, Can. 152 49 0N 123 49W
Ladysmith, S. Afr. 129 28 32 S 29 46 E
Ladysmith, U.S.A. 158 45 27N 91 4W
Lae 135 6 40 S 147 2 E
Laem Ngop 101 12 10N 102 26 E
Laem Pho 101 6 55N 101 19 E
Læsø 73 57 15N 10 53 E
Læsø Rende 73 57 20N 10 45 E
Lafayette, Colo., U.S.A. 158 40 0N 105 2W
Lafayette, Ga., U.S.A. 157 34 44N 85 15W
Lafayette, La., U.S.A. 159 30 18N 92 0W
Lafayette, Tenn., U.S.A. 157 36 35N 86 0W
Laferté 150 48 37N 78 48W
Laferte, R. 152 61 53N 117 44W
Laffan's Bridge 39 52 36N 7 45W
Lafia 121 8 30N 8 34 E
Lafiagi 121 8 52N 5 20 E
Lafleche 153 49 45N 106 40W
Lafon 123 5 5N 32 29 E
Laforest 150 47 4N 81 12W
Laforsen 72 61 56N 15 3 E
Lagaip, R. 135 5 4 S 141 52 E
Lagan 73 56 32N 12 58 E
Lagan, R. 38 54 35N 5 55W
Lagarfljót 74 65 40N 14 18W
Lagarto 170 10 54 S 37 41W
Lagarto, Serra do 173 23 0 S 57 15W
Lage, Ger. 48 52 0N 8 47 E
Lage, Spain 56 43 13N 9 0W
Lage-Mierde 47 51 25N 5 9 E
Lågen 71 61 29N 10 2 E
Lågen, R. 75 61 30N 10 20 E
Lägerdorf 48 53 53N 9 35 E
Lagg 34 56 57N 5 50W
Laggan, Grampian, U.K. 37 57 24N 3 6W
Laggan, Highland, U.K. 37 57 3N 4 48W
Laggan B. 34 55 40N 6 20W
Laggan L. 37 56 57N 4 30W
Laggers Pt. 139 30 52 S 153 4 E
Laghman □ 93 34 20N 70 0 E
Laghouat 118 33 50N 2 59 E
Laghy 38 54 37N 8 7W
Lagnieu 45 45 55N 5 20 E
Lagny 43 48 52N 2 40 E
Lago 65 39 9N 16 8 E
Lagôa 57 37 8N 8 27W
Lagoaça 56 41 11N 6 44W
Lagodekhi 83 41 50N 46 22 E
Lagónegro 65 40 8N 15 45 E
Lagonoy Gulf 103 13 50N 123 50 E
Lagos, Nigeria 121 6 25N 3 27 E
Lagos, Port. 57 37 5N 8 41W
Lagos de Moreno 164 21 21N 101 55W
Lagrange 136 14 13 S 125 46 E
Lagrange B. 136 18 38 S 121 42 E
Laguardia 58 42 33N 2 35W
Laguépie 44 44 8N 1 57 E
Laguna, Brazil 173 28 30 S 48 50W
Laguna, U.S.A. 161 35 3N 107 28W
Laguna Beach 163 33 31N 117 52W
Laguna Dam 161 32 55N 114 30W
Laguna de la Janda 57 36 15N 5 45W
Laguna Limpia 172 26 32 S 59 45W
Laguna Madre 165 27 0N 97 20W
Laguna Veneta 63 45 23N 12 25 E
Lagunas, Chile 172 21 0 S 69 45W
Lagunas, Peru 174 5 10 S 75 35W
Lagunillas 174 10 8N 71 16W
Lahad Datu 103 5 0N 118 30 E
Lahaina 147 20 52N 156 41W
Lahan Sai 100 14 25N 102 52 E
Lahanam 100 16 16N 105 16 E
Lahardaun 38 54 2N 9 20W
Laharpur 95 27 43N 80 56 E
Lahat 102 3 45 S 103 30 E
Lahe 98 19 18N 93 36 E
Lahewa 102 1 22N 97 12 E
Lahijan 93 37 10N 50 6 E
Lahn, R. 48 50 52N 8 35 E
Laholm 73 56 30N 13 2 E
Laholmsbukten 73 56 30N 12 45 E
Lahontan Res. 160 39 28N 118 58W
Lahore 94 31 32N 74 22 E
Lahore □ 94 31 55N 74 5 E
Lahpongsel 98 27 7N 98 25 E
Lahr 49 48 20N 7 52 E
Lahti 75 60 58N 25 40 E
Lai (Béhagle) 117 9 25N 16 30 E
Lai Chau 100 22 5N 103 3 E
Lai-hka 98 21 16N 97 40 E
Laiagam 135 5 33 S 143 30 E
Laian 109 32 27N 118 25 E
Laichou Wan 107 37 30N 119 30 E
Laidley 139 27 39 S 152 20 E
Laidon L. 37 56 40N 4 40W
Laifeng 108 29 31N 109 18 E
Laigle 42 48 46N 0 38 E
Laignes 43 47 50N 4 20 E
Laihsi 107 36 51N 120 30 E
Laikipia □ 126 0 30N 36 30 E
Laila 92 22 10N 46 40 E
Laillahue, Mt. 174 17 0 S 69 30W
Laingsburg 128 33 9 S 20 52 E
Laipin 108 23 42N 109 16 E
Lairg 37 58 1N 4 24W
Lais 102 3 35 S 102 0 E
Laishui 106 39 23N 115 42 E
Laiwu 107 36 12N 117 38 E
Laiyang 107 36 58N 120 40 E
Laiyüan 106 39 19N 114 41 E
Laja, R. 164 20 55N 100 46W
Lajes, Rio Grande d. N., Brazil 170 5 41 S 36 14W
Lajes, Sta. Catarina, Brazil 173 27 48 S 50 20W
Lajinha 171 20 9 S 41 37W
Lajkovac 66 44 27N 20 14 E
Lajosmizse 53 47 3N 19 32 E
Lak Sao 100 18 11N 104 59 E
Laka Chih 95 30 40N 81 10 E
Lakaband 94 31 2N 69 15 E
Lakar 103 8 15 S 128 17 E
Lake Alpine 163 38 29N 120 0W
Lake Andes 158 43 10N 98 32W
Lake Anse 156 46 42N 88 25W
Lake Arthur 159 30 8N 92 40W
Lake Brown 137 30 56 S 118 20 E
Lake Cargelligo 141 33 15 S 146 22 E
Lake Charles 159 31 10N 93 10W
Lake City, Colo, U.S.A. 161 38 3N 107 27W
Lake City, Fla., U.S.A. 157 30 10N 82 40W
Lake City, Iowa, U.S.A. 158 42 12N 94 42W
Lake City, Mich., U.S.A. 156 44 20N 85 10W
Lake City, Minn., U.S.A. 158 44 28N 92 21W
Lake City, S.C., U.S.A. 157 33 51N 79 44W
Lake Coleridge 143 43 17 S 171 30 E
Lake District 23 54 30N 3 10W
Lake George 162 43 25N 73 43W
Lake Grace 137 33 7 S 118 28 E
Lake Harbour 149 62 30N 69 50W
Lake Havasu City 161 34 25N 114 29W
Lake Hughes 163 34 41N 118 26W
Lake Isabella 163 35 38N 118 28W
Lake King 137 33 5 S 119 45 E
Lake Lenore 153 52 24N 104 59W
Lake Louise 152 51 30N 116 10W
Lake Mason 137 27 30 S 119 30 E
Lake Mead Nat. Rec. Area 161 36 0N 114 30W
Lake Mills 158 43 23N 93 33W
Lake Murray 135 6 48 S 141 29 E
Lake Nash 138 20 57 S 138 0 E
Lake of the Woods 155 49 0N 95 0W
Lake Pleasant 162 43 28N 74 25W
Lake Providence 159 32 49N 91 12W
Lake River 150 54 22N 82 31W
Lake Superior Prov. Park 150 47 45N 84 45W
Lake Tekapo 143 43 55 S 170 30 E
Lake Traverse 150 45 56N 78 4W
Lake Varley 137 32 48 S 119 30 E
Lake Village 159 33 20N 91 19W
Lake Wales 157 27 55N 81 32W
Lake Worth 157 26 36N 80 3W
Lakefield 150 44 25N 78 16W
Lakehurst 162 40 1N 74 19W
Lakeland 157 28 0N 82 0W
Lakenheath 29 52 25N 0 30 E
Lakes Entrance 141 37 50 S 148 0 E
Lakeside, Ariz., U.S.A. 161 34 12N 109 59W
Lakeside, Calif., U.S.A. 163 32 52N 116 55W
Lakeside, Nebr., U.S.A. 158 42 5N 102 24W
Lakeview, N.Y., U.S.A. 156 42 43N 78 57W
Lakeview, Oreg., U.S.A. 160 42 15N 120 22W
Lakewood, Calif., U.S.A. 163 33 51N 118 8W
Lakewood, N.J., U.S.A. 162 40 5N 74 13W
Lakhaniá 69 35 58N 27 54 E
Lákhi 69 35 24N 23 27 E
Lakhimpur 95 27 14N 94 7 E
Lakhipur, Assam, India 98 24 48N 93 0 E
Lakhipur, Assam, India 98 26 2N 90 18 E
Lakhonpheng 100 15 54N 105 34 E
Lakhpat 94 23 48N 68 47 E
Laki 74 64 4N 18 14W
Lakin 159 37 58N 101 18W
Lakitusaki, R. 150 54 21N 82 25W
Lakki 93 32 38N 70 50 E
Lakonía □ 69 36 55N 22 30 E
Lakonikós Kólpos 69 36 40N 22 40 E
Lakor, I. 103 8 15 S 128 17 E
Lakota, Ivory C. 120 5 50N 5 30W
Lakota, U.S.A. 158 48 0N 98 22W
Laksefjorden 74 70 45N 26 50 E
Lakselv 74 70 2N 24 56 E
Lakselvbukt 74 69 26N 19 40 E
Lakshadweep Is. 86 10 0N 72 30 E
Laksham 98 23 14N 91 8 E
Lakshmi Kantapur 95 22 5N 88 20 E
Lakshmipur 98 22 38N 88 16 E
Lakuramau 135 2 54 S 151 15 E
Lala Ghat 99 24 30N 92 40 E
Lala Musa 94 32 40N 73 57 E
Lalago 126 3 28 S 33 58 E
Lalapanzi 127 19 20 S 30 15 E
Lalganj 95 25 52N 85 13 E
Lalibala 123 12 8N 39 10 E
Lalin 107 45 14N 126 52 E
Lalín 56 42 40N 8 5W
Lalin Ho, R. 107 45 28N 125 43 E
Lalinde 44 44 50N 0 44 E
Lalitapur 99 26 36N 85 32 E
Lalitpur 95 24 42N 78 28 E
Lam 100 21 21N 106 31 E
Lam Pao Res. 100 16 50N 103 15 E
Lama Kara 121 9 30N 1 15 E
Lamaing 99 15 25N 97 53 E
Lamaipum 98 25 40N 97 57 E
Lamar, Colo., U.S.A. 158 38 9N 102 35W
Lamar, Mo., U.S.A. 159 37 30N 94 20W
Lamas 174 6 28 S 76 31W
Lamastre 45 44 59N 4 35 E
Lamaya 108 29 50N 99 56 E
Lamb Hd. 37 59 5N 2 32W
Lambach 52 48 6N 13 51 E
Lamballe 42 48 29N 2 31W
Lambaréné 124 0 20 S 10 12 E
Lambay I. 38 53 30N 6 0W

Lambayeque □ **Lawrenceville**

Lambayeque □ 174 6 45 S 80 0W
Lamberhurst 29 51 5N 0 21 E
Lambert 158 47 44N 104 39W
Lambert, C. 135 4 11 S 151 31 E
Lambert Land 12 79 12N 20 30W
Lambesc 45 43 39N 5 16 E
Lambeth 29 51 27N 0 7W
Lambi Kyun, (Sullivan I.) 101 10 50N 98 20 E
Lámbia 69 37 52N 21 53 E
Lambley 35 54 56N 2 30W
Lambon 135 4 45 S 152 48 E
Lambourn 28 51 31N 1 31W
Lambro, R. 62 45 18N 9 20 E
Lambs Hd. 39 51 44N 10 10W
Lame 121 10 27N 9 12 E
Lame Deer 160 45 45N 106 40W
Lamego 56 41 5N 7 52W
Lameque 151 47 45N 64 38W
Lameroo 140 35 19 S 140 33 E
Lamesa 159 32 45N 101 57W
Lamhult 73 57 12N 14 36 E
Lamia 69 38 55N 22 41 E
*Lamitan 103 6 40N 122 10 E
Lammermuir 35 55 50N 2 25W
Lammermuir Hills 35 55 50N 2 40W
Lamoille 160 40 47N 115 31W
Lamon Bay 103 14 30N 122 20 E
Lamont, Can. 152 53 46N 112 50W
Lamont, U.S.A. 163 35 15N 118 55W
Lampa 174 15 10 S 70 30W
Lampang 100 18 18N 99 31 E
Lampasas 159 31 5N 98 10W
Lampaul 42 48 28N 5 7W
Lampazos de Naranjo 164 27 2N 100 32W
Lampedusa, I. 60 35 36N 12 40 E
Lampeter 31 52 6N 4 6W
Lampione, I. 119 35 33N 12 20 E
Lampman 153 49 25N 102 50W
Lamprechtshausen 52 48 0N 12 58 E
Lampung 102 1 48 S 115 0 E
Lamu, Burma 98 19 14N 94 10 E
Lamu, Kenya 126 2 10 S 40 55 E
Lamy 161 35 30N 105 58W
Lan Tsan Kiang (Mekong) 87 18 0N 104 15 E
Lanai City 147 20 50N 156 56W
Lanai I. 147 20 50N 156 55W
Lanak La 95 34 27N 79 32 E
Lanaken 47 50 53N 5 39 E
Lanak'o Shank'ou = Lanak La 95 34 27N 79 32 E
Lanao, L. 103 7 52N 124 15 E
Lanark 35 55 40N 3 48W
Lanark (□) 26 55 37N 3 50W
Lancashire □ 32 53 40N 2 30W
Lancaster, Can. 151 45 17N 66 10W
Lancaster, U.K. 32 54 3N 2 48W
Lancaster, Calif., U.S.A. 163 34 47N 118 8W
Lancaster, Ky., U.S.A. 156 37 40N 84 40W
Lancaster, Pa., U.S.A. 162 40 4N 76 19W
Lancaster, S.C., U.S.A. 157 34 45N 80 47W
Lancaster, Va., U.S.A. 162 37 46N 76 28W
Lancaster, Wis., U.S.A. 158 42 48N 90 43W
Lancaster Sd. 12 74 13N 84 0W
Lancer 153 50 48N 108 53W
Lanchester 33 54 50N 1 44W
Lanch'i 109 29 11N 119 30 E
Lanchou 106 36 5N 103 55 E
Lanciano 63 42 15N 14 22 E
Lancing 29 50 49N 0 19W
Łancut 54 50 10N 22 20 E
Lancy 50 46 12N 6 8 E
Lándana 124 5 11 S 12 5 E
Landau 49 49 12N 8 7 E
Landeck 52 47 9N 10 34 E
Landen 47 50 45N 5 3 E
Lander, Austral. 136 20 25 S 132 0 E
Lander, U.S.A. 160 42 50N 108 49W
Landerneau 42 48 28N 4 17W
Landeryd 73 57 7N 13 15 E
Landes □ 44 43 57N 0 48W
Landes, Les 44 44 20N 1 0W
Landete 58 39 56N 1 25W
Landi Kotal 94 34 7N 71 6 E
Landivisiau 42 48 31N 4 6W
Landkey 30 51 2N 4 0W
Landor 137 25 10 S 117 0 E
Landquart 51 46 58N 9 32 E
Landquart, R. 51 46 50N 9 47 E
Landrecies 43 50 7N 3 40 E
Land's End, Can. 12 76 10N 123 0W
Land's End, U.K. 30 50 4N 5 43W
Landsberg 49 48 3N 10 52 E
Landsborough Cr. 138 22 28 S 144 35 E
Landsbro 73 57 24N 14 56 E
Landschaft 50 47 28N 7 40 E
Landshut 48 48 31N 12 10 E
Landskrona 73 56 53N 12 50 E
Landvetter 73 57 41N 12 17 E
Lane 73 58 25N 12 3 E
Laneffe 47 50 17N 4 35 E
Lanesboro 162 41 57N 75 34W
Lanesborough 38 53 40N 8 0W
Lanett 157 33 0N 85 15W
Lang Bay 152 49 17N 124 21W
Lang Qua 100 22 16N 104 27 E
Lang Shan 106 41 0N 106 20 E
Lang Suan 101 9 57N 99 4 E
Langaa 73 56 23N 9 51 E
Långadhás 68 40 46N 23 2 E
Langádhia 69 37 43N 22 1 E
Långan 72 63 19N 14 44 E

*Renamed Isabela

Langara I. 152 54 14N 133 1W
Langavat L. 36 58 4N 6 48W
Langchen Khambah (Sutlej) 95 31 25N 80 0 E
Langch'i 109 31 10N 119 10 E
Langchung 108 31 31N 105 58 E
Langdon 158 48 47N 98 24W
Langdorp 47 50 59N 4 52 E
Langeac 44 45 7N 3 29 E
Langeb, R. 122 17 28N 36 50 E
Langeberge, C. Prov., S. Afr. 128 28 15 S 22 33 E
Langeberge, C. Prov., S. Afr. 128 33 55 S 21 20 E
Langeland 73 54 56N 10 48 E
Langelands Bælt 73 54 55N 10 56 E
Langemark 47 50 55N 2 55 E
Langen 49 53 36N 8 36 E
Langenburg 153 50 51N 101 43W
Langeness 48 54 34N 8 35 E
Langenlois 52 48 29N 15 40 E
Langensalza 48 51 6N 10 40 E
Langenthal 50 47 13N 7 47 E
Langeoog 48 53 44N 7 33 E
Langeskov 73 55 22N 10 35 E
Langesund 71 59 0N 9 45 E
Langhem 73 57 36N 13 14 E
Länghem 73 57 36N 13 14 E
Langhirano 62 44 39N 10 16 E
Langholm 35 55 9N 2 59W
Langidoon 140 31 36 S 142 2 E
Langjökull 74 64 39N 20 12W
Langkawi I. 101 6 20N 99 45 E
Langkawi, P. 101 6 25N 99 45 E
Langkon 102 6 30N 116 40 E
Langk'ouhsü 109 26 8N 115 10 E
Langlade, Can. 150 48 14N 76 10W
Langlade, St. P. & M. 151 46 50N 56 20W
Langlo 139 26 26 S 146 5 E
Langlois 160 42 54N 124 26W
Langnau 50 46 56N 7 47 E
Langness 32 54 3N 4 37W
Langogne 44 44 43N 3 50 E
Langon 44 44 33N 0 16W
Langøya 74 68 45N 15 10 E
Langport 28 51 2N 2 51W
Langres 43 47 52N 5 20 E
Langres, Plateau de 43 47 45N 5 20 E
Langsa 102 4 30N 97 57 E
Långsele 72 63 12N 17 4 E
Långshyttan 72 60 27N 16 2 E
Langson 100 21 52N 106 42 E
Langstrothdale Chase 32 54 14N 2 13W
Langtai 108 26 6N 105 20 E
Langtao 98 27 15N 97 34 E
Langting 98 25 31N 93 7 E
Langtoft 29 52 42N 0 19W
Langtree 30 50 55N 4 11W
Langtry 159 29 50N 101 33W
Langu 101 6 53N 99 47 E
Languedoc □ 44 43 58N 3 22 E
Langwies 51 46 50N 9 44 E
Lanhsien 106 38 17N 111 38 E
Lanigan 153 51 51N 105 2W
Lank'ao 106 34 50N 114 49 E
Lanna 72 59 16N 14 56 E
Lannemezan 44 43 8N 0 23 E
Lannercost 138 18 35 S 146 0 E
Lannilis 42 48 35N 4 32W
Lannion 42 48 46N 3 29W
Lanouaille 44 45 24N 1 9 E
Lanp'ing 108 26 25N 99 24 E
Lansdale 162 40 14N 75 18W
Lansdowne 141 31 48 S 152 30 E
Lansdowne House 150 52 14N 87 53W
Lansford 162 40 48N 75 55W
Lanshan 109 25 18N 112 6 E
Lansing 156 42 47N 84 32W
Lanslebourg-Mont-Cenis 45 45 17N 6 52 E
Lanta Yai, Ko 101 7 35N 99 3 E
Lant'ien 106 34 3N 109 20 E
Lants'ang 108 22 40N 99 58 E
Lants'ang Chiang, R. 108 30 0N 98 0 E
Lantsien 99 32 4N 96 6 E
Lants'un 107 36 24N 120 10 E
Lantuna 103 8 19 S 124 8 E
Lanus 172 34 44 S 58 27W
Lanusei 64 39 53N 9 31 E
Lanzarote, I. 116 29 0N 13 40W
Lanzo Torinese 62 45 16N 7 29 E
Lao Bao 100 16 35N 106 30 E
Lao Cai 100 22 30N 103 57 E
Lao, R. 65 39 45N 15 45 E
Laoag 103 18 7N 120 34 E
Laoang 103 12 32N 125 8 E
Laoha Ho, R. 107 43 24N 120 39 E
Laois □ 39 53 0N 7 20W
Laon 43 49 33N 3 35 E
Laona 156 45 32N 88 41W
Laos ■ 100 17 45N 105 0 E
Lapa 173 25 46 S 49 44W
Lapalisse 44 46 15N 3 44 E
Laparan Cap, I. 103 6 0N 120 0 E
Lapeer 156 43 3N 83 20W
Lapford 30 50 52N 3 49W
Lapi □ 74 67 0N 27 0 E
Lapland = Lappland 74 68 7N 24 0 E
Laporte 162 41 27N 76 30W
Lapovo 66 44 10N 21 2 E
Lappland 74 68 7N 24 0 E
Laprida 172 37 34 S 60 45W
Laptev Sea 77 76 0N 125 0 E

Lapush 160 47 56N 124 33W
Lăpuşu, R. 70 47 25N 23 40 E
Lar 93 27 40N 54 14 E
Lara 140 38 2 S 144 26 E
Lara □ 174 10 10N 69 50W
Larabanga 120 9 16N 1 56W
Laracha 56 43 15N 8 35W
Larache 118 35 10N 6 5W
Laragh 39 53 0N 6 20W
Laragne-Montéglin 45 44 18N 5 49 E
Laramie 158 41 15N 105 29W
Laramie Mts. 158 42 0N 105 30W
Laranjeiras 170 10 48 S 37 10W
Laranjeiras do Sul 173 25 23 S 52 23W
Larantuka 103 8 5 S 122 55 E
Larap 103 14 18N 122 39 E
Larat, I. 103 7 0 S 132 0 E
Larbert 35 56 2N 3 50W
Lärbro 73 57 47N 18 50 E
Larch, R. 149 57 30N 71 0W
Lårdal 71 59 20N 8 25 E
Lårdal 71 59 25N 8 10 E
Larde 127 16 28 S 39 43 E
Larder Lake 150 48 5N 79 40W
Lárdhos, Akra 69 36 4N 28 10 E
Laredo, Spain 58 43 26N 3 28W
Laredo, U.S.A. 159 27 34N 99 29W
Laredo Sd. 152 52 30N 128 53W
Laren 46 52 16N 5 14 E
Largeau (Faya) 117 17 58N 19 6 E
Largentière 45 44 34N 4 18 E
Largs 34 55 48N 4 51W
Lari 62 43 34N 10 35 E
Lariang 103 1 35 S 119 25 E
Larimore 158 47 55N 97 35W
Larino 65 41 48N 14 54 E
Lárisa 68 39 38N 22 28 E
Lárisa □ 68 39 39N 22 24 E
Larkana 94 27 32N 68 2 E
Larkollen 71 59 20N 10 41 E
Larnaca 92 35 0N 33 35 E
Lárnax 92 35 0N 33 35 E
Larne 38 54 52N 5 50W
Larne L. 38 54 52N 5 50W
Larned 158 38 15N 99 10W
Laroch 36 56 40N 5 9W
Larochette 47 49 47N 6 13 E
Laroquebrou 44 44 58N 2 12 E
Larrey, Pt. 136 19 55 S 119 7 E
Larrimah 136 15 35 S 133 12 E
Larsen Ice Shelf 13 67 0 S 62 0W
Larteh 121 5 50N 0 5W
Laru 126 2 54N 24 25 E
Larvik 71 59 4N 10 0 E
Laryak 76 61 15N 80 0 E
Larzac, Causse du 44 44 0N 3 17 E
Las Animas 159 38 8N 103 18W
Las Anod 91 8 26N 47 19 E
Las Blancos 59 37 38N 0 49W
Las Bonitas 174 7 50N 65 40W
Las Brenãs 172 27 5 S 61 7W
Las Cabezas de San Juan 57 37 0N 5 58W
Las Cruces 161 32 25N 106 50W
Las Flores 172 36 0 S 59 0W
Las Heras, Mendoza, Argent. 173 32 51 S 68 49W
Las Heras, Santa Cruz, Argent. 176 46 30 S 69 0W
Las Huertas, Cabo de 59 38 22N 0 24W
Las Khoreh 91 11 4N 48 20 E
Las Lajas 176 38 30 S 70 25W
Las Lajitas 174 6 55N 65 39W
Las Lomitas 172 24 35 S 60 50W
Las Marismas 57 37 5N 6 20W
Las Mercedes 174 9 7N 66 24W
Las Navas de la Concepción 57 37 56N 5 30W
Las Navas de Tolosa 57 38 18N 3 38W
Las Palmas, Argent. 172 27 8 S 58 45W
Las Palmas, Canary Is. 116 28 10N 15 28W
Las Palmas □ 116 28 10N 15 28W
Las Piedras 173 34 35 S 56 20W
Las Plumas 176 43 40 S 67 15W
Las Rosas 172 32 30 S 61 40W
Las Tablas 166 7 49N 80 14W
Las Termas 172 27 29 S 64 52W
Las Tres Marías, Is. 164 20 12N 106 30W
Las Varillas 172 32 0 S 62 50W
Las Vegas, Nev., U.S.A. 161 36 10N 115 5W
Las Vegas, N.M., U.S.A. 161 35 35N 105 10W
Lascano 173 33 35 S 54 18W
Lascaux 44 45 5N 1 10 E
Lashburn 153 53 10N 109 40W
Lashio 98 22 56N 97 45 E
Lashkar 94 26 10N 78 10 E
Łasin 54 53 30N 19 2 E
Lasithi □ 69 35 5N 25 50 E
Lask 54 51 34N 19 8 E
Laskill 33 54 19N 1 6W
Laško 63 46 10N 15 16 E
Lassance 171 17 54 S 44 34W
Lassay 42 48 27N 0 30W
Lassen, Pk. 160 40 20N 121 0W
Lasswade 35 55 53N 3 8W
Last Mountain L. 153 51 5N 105 14W
Lastoursville 124 0 55 S 12 38 E
Lastovo 63 42 46N 16 55 E
Lastovo, I. 63 42 46N 16 55 E
Lastovski Kanal 63 42 50N 17 0 E
Lat Yao 100 15 45N 99 48 E
Latacunga 174 0 50 S 78 35W

Latakia = Al Ladhiqiya 92 35 30N 35 45 E
Latchford 150 47 20N 79 50W
Laterza 65 40 38N 16 47 E
Latham 137 29 44 S 116 20 E
Lathen 48 52 51N 7 21 E
Latheron 37 58 17N 3 20W
Lathrop Wells 163 36 39N 116 24W
Latiano 65 40 33N 17 43 E
Latina 64 41 26N 12 53 E
Latisana 63 45 47N 13 1 E
Latium = Lazio 63 42 0N 12 30 E
Laton 163 36 26N 119 41W
Latorica, R. 53 48 31N 22 0 E
Latouche 147 60 0N 148 0W
Latouche Treville, C. 136 18 27 S 121 49 E
Latrobe 138 38 8 S 146 44 E
Latrobe, Mt. 139 39 0 S 146 23 E
Latrónico 65 40 5N 16 0 E
Latrun 90 31 50N 34 58 E
Latur 96 18 25N 76 40 E
Latvia, S.S.R. □ 80 56 50N 24 0 E
Latzu 105 29 10N 87 45 E
Lauchhammer 48 51 35N 13 40 E
Laudal 71 58 15N 7 30 E
Lauder 35 55 43N 2 45W
Lauderdale 35 55 43N 2 44W
Lauenburg 48 53 23N 10 33 E
Läufelfingen 50 47 24N 7 52 E
Laufen 50 47 25N 7 30 E
Laugarbakki 74 65 20N 20 55W
Laugharne 31 51 45N 4 28W
Laujar 59 37 0N 2 54W
Launceston, Austral. 138 41 24 S 147 8 E
Launceston, U.K. 30 50 38N 4 21W
Laune, R. 39 52 5N 9 40W
Launglon Bok 101 13 50N 97 54 E
Laupheim 49 48 13N 9 53 E
Laura, Queens., Austral. 133 15 32 S 144 32 E
Laura, S.A., Austral. 140 33 10 S 138 18 E
Lauragh 39 51 46N 9 46W
Laureana di Borrello 65 38 28N 16 5 E
Laurel, Del., U.S.A. 162 38 33N 75 34W
Laurel, Md., U.S.A. 162 39 6N 76 51W
Laurel, Miss., U.S.A. 159 31 50N 89 0W
Laurel, Mont., U.S.A. 160 45 46N 108 49W
Laurencekirk 37 56 50N 2 30W
Laurencetown 39 53 14N 8 11W
Laurens 157 34 32N 82 2W
Laurentian Plat. 151 52 0N 70 0W
Laurentides, Parc Prov. des 151 47 45N 71 15W
Lauria 65 40 3N 15 50 E
Laurie I. 13 60 0 S 46 0W
Laurie L. 153 56 35N 101 57W
Laurieston 35 54 57N 4 2W
Laurinburg 157 34 50N 79 25W
Laurium 156 47 14N 88 26W
Lausanne 50 46 32N 6 38 E
Laut Kecil, Kepulauan 102 4 45 S 115 40 E
Laut, Kepulauan 102 4 45N 108 0 E
Lauterbach 48 50 39N 9 23 E
Lauterbrunnen 50 46 36N 7 55 E
Lauterecken 49 49 38N 7 35 E
Lauwe 47 50 47N 3 12 E
Lauwers 46 53 32N 6 23 E
Lauwers Zee 46 53 21N 6 13 E
Lauzon 151 46 48N 71 10W
Lava Hot Springs 160 42 38N 112 1W
Lavadores 56 42 14N 8 41W
Lavagna 62 44 18N 9 22 E
Laval 42 48 4N 0 48W
Lavalle 172 28 15 S 65 15W
Lavandou, Le 45 43 8N 6 22 E
Lávara 68 41 19N 26 22 E
Lavardac 44 44 12N 0 20 E
Lavaur 44 43 42N 1 49 E
Lavaux 50 46 30N 6 45 E
Lavaveix 44 46 5N 2 8 E
Lavelanet 44 42 57N 1 51 E
Lavello 65 41 4N 15 47 E
Lavendon 29 52 11N 0 39W
Lavenham 29 52 7N 0 48 E
Laverendrye Prov. Park 150 46 15N 17 15W
Laverne 159 36 43N 99 58W
Lavers Hill 140 38 40 S 143 25 E
Laverton 137 28 44 S 122 29 E
Lavi 90 32 47N 35 25 E
Lavik 71 61 6N 5 25 E
Lávkos 69 39 9N 23 14 E
Lavos 56 40 6N 8 49W
Lavras 173 21 20 S 45 0W
Lavre 57 38 46N 8 22W
Lavrentiya 77 65 35N 171 0W
Lávrion 69 37 40N 24 4 E
Lavumisa 129 27 20 S 31 55 E
Lawas 102 4 55N 115 40 E
Lawele 103 5 16 S 123 3 E
Lawers 35 56 31N 4 9W
Lawksawk 98 21 15N 96 52 E
Lawn Hill 138 18 36 S 138 33 E
Lawng Pit 99 26 45N 98 35 E
Lawra 120 10 39N 2 51W
Lawrence, Austral. 173 29 30 S 153 8 E
Lawrence, Kans., U.S.A. 158 39 0N 95 10W
Lawrence, Mass., U.S.A. 162 42 40N 71 9W
Lawrenceburg, Ind., U.S.A. 156 39 5N 84 50W
Lawrenceburg, Tenn., U.S.A. 157 35 12N 87 19W
Lawrenceville, Ga., U.S.A. 157 33 55N 83 59W

Lawrenceville **Lexington**

Lawrenceville, Pa., U.S.A. **162** 42 0N 77 8W
Laws **163** 37 24N 118 20W
Lawton **159** 34 33N 98 25W
Lawu Mt. **103** 7 40S 111 13E
Laxa **72** 59 0N 14 37E
Laxey **32** 54 15N 4 23W
Laxfield **29** 52 18N 1 23E
Laxford, L. **36** 58 25N 5 10W
Laxmeshwar **97** 15 9N 75 28E
Laysan I. **143** 25 30N 167 0W
Laytonville **160** 39 44N 123 29W
Laytown **38** 53 40N 6 15W
Laza **98** 26 30N 97 38E
Lazarevac **66** 44 23N 20 17E
Lazio □ **63** 42 10N 12 30E
Lazonby **32** 54 45N 2 42W
Łazy **54** 50 27N 19 24E
Łbzenica **54** 53 18N 17 15E
Lea **33** 53 22N 0 45W
Lea, R. **29** 51 40N 0 3W
Leach **101** 12 21N 103 46E
Lead **158** 44 20N 103 40W
Leadenham **33** 53 5N 0 33W
Leader **153** 50 50N 109 30W
Leadhills **35** 55 25N 3 47W
Leadville **161** 39 17N 106 23W
Leaf, R., Can. **149** 58 47N 70 4W
Leaf, R., U.S.A. **159** 31 45N 89 20W
Leakey **159** 29 45N 99 45W
Leaksville **157** 36 30N 79 49W
Lealui **125** 15 10S 23 2E
Leamington, Can. **150** 42 3N 82 36W
Leamington, N.Z. **130** 37 55S 175 29E
Leamington, U.K. **28** 52 18N 1 32W
Leamington, U.S.A. **160** 39 37N 112 17W
Leandro Norte Alem **173** 27 34S 55 15W
Leane L. **39** 52 2N 9 32W
Leaoto, Mt. **70** 45 20N 25 20E
Leap **39** 51 34N 9 11W
Learmonth **136** 22 40S 114 10E
Leask **153** 53 5N 106 45W
Leatherhead **29** 51 18N 0 20W
Leavenworth, Mo., U.S.A. **158** 39 25N 95 0W
Leavenworth, Wash., U.S.A. **160** 47 44N 120 37W
Łeba **54** 54 45N 17 32E
Lebak **103** 6 32N 124 5E
Lebane **66** 42 56N 21 44E
Lebanon, Ind., U.S.A. **156** 40 3N 86 55W
Lebanon, Kans., U.S.A. **158** 39 50N 98 35W
Lebanon, Ky., U.S.A. **156** 37 35N 85 15W
Lebanon, Mo., U.S.A. **159** 37 40N 92 40W
Lebanon, Oreg., U.S.A. **160** 44 31N 122 57W
Lebanon, Pa., U.S.A. **162** 40 20N 76 28W
Lebanon, Tenn., U.S.A. **157** 36 15N 86 20W
Lebanon ■ **92** 34 0N 36 0E
Lebbeke **47** 51 0N 4 8E
Lebec **163** 34 36N 118 59W
Lebedin **80** 50 35N 34 30E
Lebedyan **81** 53 0N 39 10E
Lebomboberge **129** 24 30S 32 0E
Łebork **54** 54 33N 17 46E
Lebrija **57** 36 53N 6 5W
Lebu **172** 37 40S 73 47W
Lecce **65** 40 20N 18 10E
Lecco **62** 45 50N 9 27E
Lecco, L. di. **62** 45 51N 9 22E
Lécera **58** 41 13N 0 43W
Lech **52** 47 13N 10 9E
Lech, R. **49** 48 45N 10 45E
Lechlade **28** 51 42N 1 40W
Lechtaler Alpen **52** 47 15N 10 30E
Lectoure **44** 43 56N 0 38E
Łeczyca **54** 52 5N 19 45E
Ledbury **28** 52 3N 2 25W
Lede **47** 50 58N 3 59E
Ledeberg **47** 51 2N 3 45E
Ledec **52** 49 41N 15 18E
Ledesma **56** 41 6N 5 59W
Leduc **152** 53 20N 113 30W
Ledyczek **54** 53 33N 16 59E
Lee, U.K. **28** 50 47N 1 11W
Lee, U.S.A. **160** 40 35N 115 36W
Lee Vining **163** 37 58N 119 7W
Leech L. **158** 47 9N 94 23W
Leedey **159** 35 53N 99 24W
Leeds, U.K. **33** 53 48N 1 34W
Leeds, U.S.A. **157** 33 32N 86 30W
Leek, Neth. **46** 53 10N 6 24E
Leek, U.K. **32** 53 7N 2 2W
Leende **47** 51 21N 5 33E
Leer **48** 53 13N 7 29E
Leerdam **46** 51 54N 5 6E
Leersum **46** 52 0N 5 26E
Leesburg **157** 28 47N 81 52W
Leeston **143** 43 45N 172 19E
Leesville **159** 31 12N 93 15W
Leeton **141** 34 23S 146 23E
Leeuwarden **46** 53 15N 5 48E
Leeuwin, C. **137** 34 20S 115 9E
Leeward Is. **167** 16 30N 63 30W
Lefors **159** 35 30N 100 50W
Lefroy, L. **137** 31 21S 121 40E
Legal **152** 53 55N 113 45W
Legendre I. **136** 20 22S 116 55E
Leghorn = Livorno **62** 43 32N 10 18E
Legion **127** 21 25S 28 30E
Legionowo **54** 52 25N 20 50E
Léglise **47** 49 48N 5 32E
Legnago **63** 45 10N 11 19E
Legnano **62** 45 35N 8 55E
Legnica **54** 51 12N 16 10E
Legnica □ **54** 51 30N 16 0E
Legoniel **38** 54 38N 6 0W
Legrad **63** 46 17N 16 51E
Legume **139** 28 20S 152 12E
Leh **95** 34 15N 77 35E
Lehi **160** 40 20N 112 0W
Lehighton **162** 40 50N 75 44W
Lehinch **39** 52 56N 9 21E
Lehliu **70** 44 29N 26 20E
Lehrte **48** 52 22N 9 58E
Lehua, I. **147** 22 1N 160 6W
Lehututu **128** 23 54S 21 55E
Lei Shui, R. **109** 26 56N 112 39E
Leiah **94** 30 58N 70 58E
Leibnitz **52** 46 47N 15 34E
Leicester **28** 52 39N 1 9W
Leicester □ **28** 52 40N 1 10W
Leichhardt, R. **133** 17 50S 139 49E
Leichhardt Ra. **138** 20 46S 147 40E
Leichou Chiang, R. **109** 20 52N 110 10E
Leichou Pantao **108** 20 40N 110 10E
Leiden **46** 52 9N 4 30E
Leiderdorp **46** 52 9N 4 32E
Leidschendam **46** 52 5N 4 24E
Leie, R. **47** 51 2N 3 45E
Leigh, Gr. Manch., U.K. **32** 53 29N 2 31W
Leigh, Here. & Worcs., U.K. **28** 52 10N 2 21W
Leigh Creek **140** 30 28S 138 24E
Leighlinbridge **39** 52 45N 7 2W
Leighton Buzzard **29** 51 55N 0 39W
Leignon **47** 50 16N 5 7E
Leiktho **98** 19 13N 96 35E
Leinster, Mt. **39** 52 38N 6 47W
Leinster, prov. **39** 53 0N 7 10W
Leintwardine **28** 52 22N 2 51W
Leipo **108** 28 15N 103 34E
Leipzig **48** 51 20N 12 23E
Leipzig □ **48** 51 20N 12 30E
Leiria **57** 39 46N 8 53W
Leiria □ **57** 39 46N 8 53W
Leisler, Mt. **136** 23 23S 129 30E
Leiston **29** 52 13N 1 35E
Leith **35** 55 59N 3 10W
Leith Hill **29** 51 10N 0 23W
Leitha, R. **53** 47 57N 17 5E
Leitholm **35** 55 42N 2 16W
Leitrim **38** 54 0N 8 5W
Leitrim □ **38** 54 8N 8 0W
Leiyang **109** 26 24N 112 51E
Leiza **58** 43 5N 1 55W
Lek, R. **46** 51 54N 4 38E
Lekáni **68** 41 10N 24 35E
Leke **47** 51 6N 2 54E
Lekhainá **69** 37 57N 21 16E
Lekkerkerk **46** 51 54N 4 41E
Leknice **61** 51 34N 14 45E
Leksula **103** 3 46S 126 31E
Leland **159** 33 25N 90 52W
Leland Lakes **153** 60 0N 110 59W
Lelant **30** 50 11N 5 26W
Leleque **176** 42 15S 71 0W
Lelu **98** 19 4N 95 30E
Lelystad **46** 52 30N 5 25E
Lema **121** 12 58N 4 13E
Lemagrut, mt. **123** 3 9S 35 22E
Leman Bank, gasfield **19** 53 5N 2 20E
Léman, Lac **50** 46 26N 6 30E
Lemelerveld **46** 52 26N 6 20E
Lemera **126** 3 0S 28 55E
Lemery **103** 13 58N 120 56E
Lemesós **92** 34 42N 33 1E
Lemgo **48** 52 2N 8 52E
Lemhi Ra. **160** 44 30N 113 30W
Lemmer **46** 52 51N 5 43E
Lemmon **158** 45 59N 102 10W
Lemon Grove **163** 32 45N 117 2W
Lemoore **163** 36 23N 119 46W
Lempdes **44** 45 22N 3 17E
Lemvig **73** 56 33N 8 20E
Lemyethna **98** 21 10N 95 52E
Lena, R. **77** 64 30N 127 0E
Lenadoon Pt. **38** 54 19N 9 3W
Lencloître **42** 46 50N 0 20E
Lençóis **171** 12 35S 41 43W
Lendalfoot **34** 55 12N 4 55W
Lendelede **47** 50 53N 3 16E
Lendinara **63** 45 4N 11 37E
Lene L. **38** 53 40N 7 12W
Lengau de Vaca, Punta **172** 30 14S 71 38W
Lenger **85** 42 12N 69 54E
Lengerich **48** 52 12N 7 50E
Lenggong **101** 5 6N 100 58E
Lengyeltóti **53** 46 40N 17 40E
Lenham **29** 51 14N 0 44E
Lenhovda **73** 57 0N 15 16E
Lenia **123** 4 10N 37 25E
Lenin **83** 48 20N 40 56E
Lenina, Pik **85** 39 20N 72 55E
Leninabad **85** 40 17N 69 37E
Leninakan **83** 41 0N 42 50E
Leningrad **80** 59 55N 30 20E
Leninogorsk, Kazakh S.S.R., U.S.S.R. **76** 50 20N 83 30E
Leninogorsk, R.S.F.S.R., U.S.S.R. **84** 54 36N 52 30E
Leninpol **85** 42 29N 71 55E
Leninsk, R.S.F.S.R., U.S.S.R. **83** 48 40N 45 15E
Leninsk, Uzbek S.S.R., U.S.S.R. **85** 40 38N 72 15E
Leninsk-Kuznetskiy **76** 55 10N 86 10E
Leninskaya **81** 56 7N 44 29E
Leninskoye, R.S.F.S.R., U.S.S.R. **77** 47 56N 132 38E
Leninskoye, R.S.F.S.R., U.S.S.R. **81** 58 23N 47 3E
Leninskoye, Uzbek S.S.R., U.S.S.R. **85** 41 45N 69 23E
Lenk **50** 46 27N 7 28E
Lenkoran **79** 39 45N 48 50E
Lenmalu **103** 1 58S 130 0E
Lennard, R. **136** 17 22S 124 20E
Lennox Hills **34** 56 3N 4 12W
Lennoxtown **34** 55 58N 4 14W
Leno **62** 45 24N 10 14E
Lenoir **157** 35 55N 81 36W
Lenoir City **157** 35 40N 84 20W
Lenora **158** 39 39N 100 1W
Lenore L. **153** 52 30N 104 59W
Lenox **162** 42 20N 73 18W
Lens, Belg. **47** 50 33N 3 54E
Lens, France **43** 50 26N 2 50E
Lens St. Remy **47** 50 39N 5 7E
Lensk (Mukhtuya) **77** 60 48N 114 55E
Lenskoye **82** 45 3N 34 1E
Lent **46** 51 52N 5 52E
Lentini **65** 37 18N 15 0E
Lenwood **163** 34 53N 117 7W
Lenzburg **50** 47 23N 8 11E
Lenzen **48** 53 6N 11 26E
Lenzerheide **51** 46 44N 9 34E
Léo **120** 11 3N 2 2W
Leoben **52** 47 22N 15 5E
Leola **158** 45 47N 98 58W
Leominster, U.K. **28** 52 15N 2 43W
Leominster, U.S.A. **162** 42 32N 71 45W
Léon **44** 43 53N 1 18W
León, Mexico **164** 21 7N 101 30W
León, Nic. **166** 12 20N 86 51W
León, Spain **56** 42 38N 5 34W
Leon **158** 40 40N 93 40W
León □ **56** 42 40N 5 55W
León, Montañas de **56** 42 30N 6 18W
Leonardtown **162** 38 19N 76 39W
Leonel, Mte. **50** 46 15N 8 5E
Leonforte **65** 37 39N 14 22E
Leongatha **141** 38 30S 145 58E
Leonidhion **69** 37 9N 22 52E
Leonora **137** 28 49S 121 19E
Leonora Downs **140** 32 29S 142 5E
Léopold II, Lac = Mai-Ndombe **124** 2 0S 18 0E
Leopoldina **173** 21 28S 42 40W
Leopoldo Bulhões **171** 16 37S 48 46W
Leopoldsburg **47** 51 7N 5 13E
Léopoldville = Kinshasa **124** 4 20S 15 15E
Leoti **158** 38 31N 101 19W
Leoville **153** 53 39N 107 33W
Lépa, L. do **128** 17 0S 19 0E
Lepe **57** 37 15N 7 12W
Lepel **80** 54 50N 28 40E
Lephin **36** 57 26N 6 43W
Lepikha **77** 64 45N 125 55E
Lépo, L. do **128** 17 0S 19 0E
Lepontine Alps **62** 46 22N 8 27E
Lepsény **53** 47 0N 18 15E
Leptis Magna **119** 32 40N 14 12E
Lequeitio **58** 43 20N 2 32W
Lerbäck **72** 58 56N 15 2E
Lercara Friddi **64** 37 42N 13 36E
Lerdo **164** 25 32N 103 32W
Léré **124** 9 39N 14 13E
Lere **121** 9 43N 9 18E
Leribe **129** 28 51S 28 3E
Lérici **62** 44 4N 9 48E
Lérida **58** 41 37N 0 39E
Lérida □ **58** 42 6N 1 0E
Lérins, Is. de **45** 43 31N 7 3E
Lerma **56** 42 0N 3 47W
Léros, I. **69** 37 10N 26 50E
Lérouville **43** 48 50N 5 30E
Lerrig **39** 52 22N 9 47W
Lerwick **36** 60 10N 1 10W
Les **70** 46 58N 21 50E
Lesbos, I. = Lésvos **69** 39 0N 26 20E
Lesbury **35** 55 25N 1 37W
Lésina, L. di **63** 41 53N 15 25E
Lesja **71** 62 7N 8 51E
Lesjaverk **71** 62 12N 8 34E
Lesko **54** 49 30N 22 23E
Leskov, I. **13** 56 0S 28 0W
Leskovac **68** 43 0N 21 58E
Leskovec **68** 40 10N 20 34E
Leslie, U.K. **35** 56 12N 3 12W
Leslie, U.S.A. **159** 35 50N 92 35W
Lesmahagow **35** 55 38N 3 55W
Lesna **54** 51 0N 15 15E
Lesneven **42** 48 35N 4 20W
Lesniča **66** 44 39N 19 20E
Lesnoy **84** 59 47N 52 9E
Lesnoye **80** 58 15N 35 31E
Lesotho ■ **129** 29 40S 28 0E
Lesozavodsk **77** 45 30N 133 20E
Lesparre-Médoc **44** 45 18N 0 57W
Lessay **42** 49 14N 1 30W
Lesse, R. **47** 50 15N 4 54E
Lesser Antilles **167** 12 30N 61 0W
Lesser Slave L. **152** 55 30N 115 25W
Lessines **47** 50 42N 3 50E
Lestock **153** 51 19N 103 59W
Lesuer I. **136** 13 50S 127 17E
Lesuma **128** 17 58S 25 12E
Lésvos, I. **69** 39 0N 26 20E
Leswalt **34** 54 56N 5 6W
Leszno **54** 51 50N 16 30E
Leszno □ **54** 51 45N 16 30E
Letchworth **29** 51 58N 0 13W
Letea, Ostrov **70** 45 18N 29 20E
Lethbridge **152** 49 45N 112 45W
Lethero **140** 33 33S 142 30E
Lethlhakeng **128** 24 0S 24 59E
Leti **103** 8 10S 127 40E
Leti, Kepulauan **103** 8 10S 128 0E
Letiahau, R. **128** 21 40S 23 30E
Leticia **174** 4 0S 70 0W
Letpadan **98** 17 45N 96 0E
Letpan **98** 19 28N 93 52E
Letsôk-aw-Kyun (Domel I.) **101** 11 30N 98 25E
Letterbreen **38** 54 18N 7 43W
Letterfrack **38** 53 33N 9 58W
Letterkenny **38** 54 57N 7 42W
Lettermacaward **38** 54 51N 8 18W
Lettermore I. **39** 53 18N 9 40W
Lettermullan **39** 53 15N 9 44W
Letterston **31** 51 56N 5 0W
Lettoch **37** 57 22N 3 30W
Leu **70** 44 10N 24 0E
Leucadia **163** 33 4N 117 18W
Leucate **44** 42 56N 3 3E
Leucate, Étang de **44** 42 50N 3 0E
Leuchars **35** 56 23N 2 53W
Leuk **50** 46 19N 7 37E
Leukerbad **50** 46 24N 7 36E
Leupegem **47** 50 50N 3 36E
Leuser, G. **102** 4 0N 96 51E
Leutkirch **49** 47 49N 10 1E
Leuven (Louvain) **47** 50 52N 4 42E
Leuze, Hainaut, Belg. **47** 50 36N 3 37E
Leuze, Namur, Belg. **47** 50 33N 4 54E
Lev Tolstoy **81** 53 13N 39 29E
Levádhia **69** 38 27N 22 54E
Levan **160** 39 37N 111 32W
Levanger **74** 63 45N 11 19E
Levani **68** 40 40N 19 28E
Lévanto **62** 44 10N 9 37E
Levanzo, I. **64** 38 0N 12 19E
Levelland **159** 33 38N 102 17W
Leven, Fife, U.K. **35** 56 12N 3 0W
Leven, Humb., U.K. **33** 53 54N 0 18W
Leven, Banc du **129** 12 30S 47 45E
Leven, L. **35** 56 12N 3 22W
Leven R. **33** 54 27N 1 15W
Levens **45** 43 50N 7 12E
Leveque C. **136** 16 20S 123 0E
Leverano **65** 40 16N 18 0E
Leverburgh **36** 57 46N 7 0W
Leverkusen **48** 51 2N 6 59E
Levet **43** 46 56N 2 22E
Levice **53** 48 13N 18 35E
Levick, Mt. **13** 75 0S 164 0E
Levico **63** 46 0N 11 18E
Levie **45** 41 40N 9 7E
Levier **43** 46 58N 6 8E
Levin **142** 40 37S 175 18E
Levis **151** 46 48N 71 9W
Levis, L. **152** 62 37N 117 58W
Levítha, I. **69** 37 0N 26 28E
Levittown, N.Y., U.S.A. **162** 40 41N 73 31W
Levittown, Pa., U.S.A. **162** 40 10N 74 51W
Levka **67** 41 52N 26 15E
Lévka, Mt. **69** 35 18N 24 3E
Levkás **69** 38 48N 20 43E
Levkás, I. **69** 38 40N 20 43E
Levkimmi **68** 39 25N 20 3E
Levkôsia = Nicosia **92** 35 10N 33 25E
Levoča **53** 48 59N 20 35E
Levroux **43** 47 0N 1 38E
Levski **67** 43 21N 25 10E
Levskigrad **67** 42 38N 24 47E
Lewe **98** 19 38N 96 7E
Lewellen **158** 41 22N 102 5W
Lewes, U.K. **29** 50 53N 0 2E
Lewes, U.S.A. **156** 38 45N 75 8W
Lewes, L. **148** 60 30N 134 20W
Lewin Brzeski **54** 50 45N 17 37E
Lewis, Butt of **36** 58 30N 6 12W
Lewis, I. **36** 58 10N 6 40W
Lewis, R. **160** 48 0N 113 15W
Lewis Ra. **136** 20 3S 128 50E
Lewisburg, Pa., U.S.A. **162** 40 57N 76 57W
Lewisburg, Tenn., U.S.A. **157** 35 29N 86 46W
Lewisham **29** 51 27N 0 1W
Lewisporte **151** 49 15N 55 3W
Lewiston, U.K. **37** 57 19N 4 30W
Lewiston, Idaho, U.S.A. **160** 45 58N 117 0W
Lewiston, Utah, U.S.A. **160** 42 0N 111 56W
Lewistown, Mont., U.S.A. **160** 47 0N 109 25W
Lewistown, Pa., U.S.A. **156** 40 37N 77 33W
Lexington, Ill., U.S.A. **158** 40 37N 88 47W
Lexington, Ky., U.S.A. **156** 38 6N 84 30W
Lexington, Md., U.S.A. **162** 38 16N 76 27W
Lexington, Miss., U.S.A. **159** 33 8N 90 2W
Lexington, Mo., U.S.A. **158** 39 7N 93 55W
Lexington, N.C., U.S.A. **157** 35 50N 80 13W
Lexington, Nebr., U.S.A. **158** 40 48N 99 45W
Lexington, N.Y., U.S.A. **162** 42 15N 74 22W
Lexington, Oreg., U.S.A. **160** 45 29N 119 46W

Lexington **Litija**

Lexington, Tenn., U.S.A. 157 35 38N 88 25W
Leyburn 33 54 19N 1 50W
Leyland 32 53 41N 2 42W
Leysdown on Sea 29 51 23N 0 57 E
Leysin 50 46 21N 7 0 E
Leyte, I. 103 11 0N 125 0 E
Lezay 44 46 17N 0 0 E
Lèze, R. 44 43 28N 1 25 E
Lezha 68 41 47N 19 42 E
Lézignan-Corbières 44 43 13N 2 43 E
Lezoux 44 45 49N 3 21 E
Lgov 80 51 42N 35 10 E
Lhanbryde 37 57 38N 3 12W
Lhariguo 99 30 29N 93 4 E
Lhasa 105 29 39N 91 6 E
Lhokseumawe 102 5 20N 97 10 E
Lhuntsi Dzong 98 27 39N 91 10 E
Li, Finland 74 65 20N 25 20 E
Li, Thai. 100 17 48N 98 57 E
Li Shui, R. 109 29 24N 112 1 E
Liádhoi, I. 69 36 50N 26 11 E
Liang Liang 103 5 58N 121 30 E
Liang Shan 108 23 42N 99 48 E
Lianga 103 8 38N 126 6 E
Liangch'eng, Inner Mongolia, China 106 40 26N 112 14 E
Liangch'eng, Shantung, China 107 35 35N 119 32 E
Lianghok'ou 108 29 10N 108 44 E
Lianghsiang 106 39 44N 116 8 E
Liangp'ing 108 30 41N 107 49 E
Liangpran, Gunong 102 1 0N 114 23 E
Liangtang 106 33 56N 106 12 E
Liao Ho, R. 107 40 39N 122 12 E
Liaoch'eng 106 36 26N 115 58 E
Liaochung 107 41 30N 122 42 E
Liaoning □ 107 41 15N 122 0 E
Liaotung Pantao 107 40 0N 122 22 E
Liaotung Wan 107 40 30N 121 30 E
Liaoyang 107 41 17N 123 11 E
Liaoyüan 107 42 55N 125 10 E
Liapádhes 68 39 42N 19 40 E
Liard, R. 152 61 51N 121 18W
Liari 94 25 37N 66 30 E
Libau = Liepaja 80 56 30N 21 0 E
Libby 160 48 20N 115 10W
Libenge 124 3 40N 18 55 E
Liberal, Kans., U.S.A. 159 37 4N 101 0W
Liberal, Mo., U.S.A. 159 37 35N 94 30W
Liberec 52 50 47N 15 7 E
Liberia 166 10 40N 85 30W
Liberia ■ 120 6 30N 9 30W
Libertad 174 8 20N 69 37W
Libertad, La 166 16 47N 90 7W
Liberty, Mo., U.S.A. 158 39 15N 94 24W
Liberty, N.Y., U.S.A. 162 41 48N 74 45W
Liberty, Pa., U.S.A. 162 41 34N 77 6W
Liberty, Tex., U.S.A. 159 30 5N 94 50W
Libiaz 53 50 7N 19 21 E
Libin 47 49 59N 5 15 E
Lîbîya, Sahrâ' 114 27 35N 25 0 E
Libohava 68 40 3N 20 10 E
Libourne 44 44 55N 0 14W
Libramont 47 49 55N 5 23 E
Librazhdi 68 41 12N 20 22 E
Libreville 124 0 25N 9 26 E
Libya ■ 117 28 30N 17 30 E
Libyan Plateau = Ed-Déffa 122 30 40N 26 30 E
Licantén 172 34 55 S 72 0W
Licata 64 37 6N 13 55 E
Lich'eng 106 36 59N 113 31 E
Lichfield 28 52 40N 1 50W
Lichiang 108 26 54N 100 12 E
Lichin 107 37 32N 118 20 E
Lichtaart 47 51 13N 4 55 E
Lichtenburg 128 26 8 S 26 8 E
Lichtenfels 49 50 7N 11 4 E
Lichtenvoorde 46 51 59N 6 34 E
Lichtervelde 47 51 2N 3 9 E
Lich'uan, Hupeh, China 109 30 18N 108 51 E
Lich'uan, Kiangsi, China 109 27 14N 116 51 E
Licosa, Punta 65 40 15N 14 53 E
Lida, U.S.A. 163 37 30N 117 30W
Lida, U.S.S.R. 80 53 53N 25 15 E
Lidhult 73 56 50N 13 27 E
Lidingö 73 59 22N 18 8 E
Lidköping 73 58 31N 13 14 E
Lido, Italy 63 45 25N 12 23 E
Lido, Niger 121 12 54N 3 44 E
Lido di Ostia 64 41 44N 12 14 E
Lidzbark 54 53 15N 19 49 E
Lidzbark Warminski 54 54 7N 20 34 E
Liebenwalde 48 52 51N 13 23 E
Lieberose 48 51 59N 14 18 E
Liebling 66 45 36N 21 20 E
Liechtenstein ■ 49 47 8N 9 35 E
Liederkerke 47 50 52N 4 5 E
Liège 47 50 38N 5 35 E
Liège □ 47 50 32N 5 35 E
Liegnitz = Legnica 54 51 12N 16 10 E
Liempde 47 51 35N 5 23 E
Lienart 126 3 3N 25 31 E
Lienartville 126 3 3N 25 31 E
Liench'eng 109 25 47N 116 48 E
Lienchiang, Fukien, China 109 26 11N 119 32 E
Lienchiang, Kwangtung, China 109 21 36N 110 16 E
Lienhsien 109 24 50N 112 23 E
Lienp'ing 109 24 22N 114 30 E
Lienshan, Kwangtung, China 109 24 37N 112 2 E
Lienshan, Yunnan, China 108 24 48N 97 54 E
Lienshankuan 107 40 58N 123 46 E
Lienshui 107 33 46N 119 18 E
Lienyüan 109 27 41N 111 40 E
Lienyünchiang 107 34 47N 119 30 E
Lienyünchiangshih 107 34 37N 119 13 E
Lienz 52 46 50N 12 46 E
Liepāja 80 56 30N 21 0 E
Lier 47 51 7N 4 34 E
Lierneux 47 50 17N 5 47 E
Lieshout 47 51 31N 5 36 E
Lieşta 70 45 38N 27 34 E
Liestal 50 47 29N 7 44 E
Lieşti 70 45 38N 27 34 E
Liévin 43 50 24N 2 47 E
Lièvre, R. 150 45 31N 75 26W
Liezen 52 47 34N 14 15 E
Liffey, R. 39 53 21N 6 20W
Lifford 38 54 50N 7 30W
Liffré 42 48 12N 1 30W
Lifjell 71 59 27N 8 45 E
Lightning Ridge 139 29 22 S 148 0 E
Lignano 63 45 42N 13 8 E
Ligny-er-Barrois 43 48 36N 5 20 E
Ligny-le-Châtel 43 47 54N 3 45 E
Ligoúrion 69 37 37N 23 2 E
Ligua, La 172 32 30 S 71 16W
Liguria □ 62 44 30N 9 0 E
Ligurian Sea 62 43 20N 9 0 E
Lihir Group 135 3 0 S 152 35 E
Lihou Reefs and Cays 138 17 25 S 151 40 E
Lihsien, Hopeh, China 106 38 29N 115 34 E
Lihsien, Hunan, China 109 29 38N 111 45 E
Lihsien, Kansu, China 106 34 11N 105 2 E
Lihsien, Szechwan, China 108 31 28N 103 17 E
Lihue 147 21 59N 159 24W
Lihwa 99 30 4N 100 18 E
Likasi 127 10 55 S 26 48 E
Likati 124 3 20N 24 0 E
Likhoslavl 80 57 12N 35 30 E
Likhovski 83 48 10N 40 10 E
Likoma I. 127 12 3 S 34 45 E
Likumburu 127 9 43 S 35 8 E
Liling 109 27 40N 113 30 E
Lill 47 51 15N 4 50 E
Lille 43 50 38N 3 3 E
Lille Bælt 73 55 30N 9 45 E
Lillebonne 42 49 30N 0 32 E
Lillehammer 71 61 8N 10 30 E
Lillers 43 50 35N 2 28 E
Lillesand 71 58 15N 8 23 E
Lillestrøm 71 59 58N 11 5 E
Lillian Point, Mt. 137 27 40 S 126 6 E
Lillo 58 39 45N 3 20W
Lillooet, R. 152 49 15N 121 57W
Lilongwe 127 14 0 S 33 48 E
Liloy 103 8 4N 122 39 E
Lilun 108 28 3N 100 27 E
Lim, R. 66 43 0N 19 40 E
Lima, Indon. 103 3 37 S 128 4 E
Lima, Peru 174 12 0 S 77 0W
Lima, Sweden 72 60 55N 13 20 E
Lima, Mont., U.S.A. 160 44 41N 112 38W
Lima, Ohio, U.S.A. 156 40 42N 84 5W
Lima, R. 56 41 50N 8 18W
Limanowa 54 49 42N 20 22 E
Limassol 92 34 42N 33 1 E
Limavady 38 55 3N 6 58W
Limavady □ 38 55 0N 6 55W
Limay Mahuida 172 37 10 S 66 45W
Limay, R. 176 39 40 S 69 45W
Limbang 102 4 42N 115 6 E
Limbara, Monti 64 40 50N 9 10 E
Limbdi 94 22 34N 71 51 E
Limbourg 47 50 37N 5 56 E
Limbourg □ 47 51 2N 5 25 E
Limbri 141 31 3 S 151 5 E
Limbunya 136 17 14 S 129 50 E
Limburg 49 50 22N 8 4 E
Limburg □ 47 51 20N 5 55 E
Limedsforsen 72 60 52N 13 25 E
Limeira 173 22 35 S 47 28W
Limenária 68 40 38N 24 32 E
Limerick 39 52 40N 8 38W
Limerick □ 39 52 30N 8 50W
Limerick Junction 39 52 30N 8 12W
Limestone, R. 153 56 31N 94 7W
Limfjorden 73 56 55N 9 0 E
Limia, R. 56 41 55N 8 8W
Limmared 73 57 34N 13 20 E
Limmat, R. 51 47 26N 8 20 E
Limmen 46 52 34N 4 42 E
Limmen Bight 138 14 40 S 135 35 E
Limmen Bight R. 138 15 7 S 135 44 E
Límni 69 38 43N 23 18 E
Límnos, I. 68 39 50N 25 5 E
Limoeiro 170 7 52 S 25 27W
Limoeiro do Norte 170 5 5 S 38 0W
Limoges 44 45 50N 1 15 E
Limón 167 10 0N 83 2W
Limon 158 39 18N 103 38W
Limone 62 44 12N 7 32 E
Limousin 44 46 0N 1 0 E
Limousin, Plateau de 44 46 0N 1 0 E
Limoux 44 43 4N 2 12 E
Limpopo, R. 129 23 15 S 32 5 E
Limpsfield 29 51 15N 0 1 E
Limu Ling, mts. 100 19 0N 109 20 E
Limuru 126 1 2 S 36 35 E
Lin 68 41 4N 20 38 E
Linan 109 30 13N 119 40 E
Linares 172 35 50 S 71 40W
Linàres 174 1 23N 77 31W
Linares, Mexico 165 24 50N 99 40W
Linares, Spain 59 38 10N 3 40W
Linares □ 172 36 0 S 71 0W
Linas Mte. 64 39 25N 8 38 E
Linchenchen 106 36 28N 110 0 E
Linch'eng 106 37 26N 114 34 E
Linch'i 106 35 46N 113 53 E
Linchiang 107 41 50N 126 55 E
Linchin 106 35 6N 110 33 E
Linch'ing 106 36 56N 115 45 E
Linch'ü 107 36 30N 118 32 E
Linch'uan 109 28 0N 116 20 E
Lincluden 35 55 5N 3 40W
Lincoln, Argent. 172 34 55N 61 30W
Lincoln, N.Z. 143 43 38 S 172 30 E
Lincoln, U.K. 33 53 14N 0 32W
Lincoln, Ill., U.S.A. 158 40 10N 89 20W
Lincoln, Kans., U.S.A. 158 39 6N 98 9W
Lincoln, Maine, U.S.A. 151 45 27N 68 29W
Lincoln, N. Mex., U.S.A. 161 33 30N 105 26W
Lincoln, Nebr., U.S.A. 158 40 50N 96 42W
Lincoln, N.H., U.S.A. 162 44 3N 71 40W
Lincoln □ 33 53 14N 0 32W
Lincoln Sea 12 84 0N 55 0W
Lincoln Wolds 33 53 20N 0 5W
Lincolnton 157 35 30N 81 15W
Lind, Austral. 138 18 58 S 144 30 E
Lind, U.S.A. 160 47 0N 118 33W
Lindale 32 54 14N 2 54W
Lindås 71 60 44N 5 10 E
Lindås, Norway 71 60 44N 5 9 E
Lindås, Sweden 73 56 38N 15 35 E
Lindau 49 47 33N 9 41 E
Linde 46 52 50N 6 57 E
Linden, Guyana 174 6 0N 58 10W
Linden, Calif., U.S.A. 163 38 1N 121 5W
Linden, Tex., U.S.A. 159 33 0N 94 20W
Lindenheuvel 47 50 59N 5 48 E
Lindenwold 162 39 49N 72 59W
Linderöd 73 55 56N 13 47 E
Linderödsåsen 73 55 53N 13 53 E
Lindesberg 72 59 36N 15 15 E
Lindesnes 71 57 58N 7 3 E
Lindfield 29 51 2N 0 5W
Lindi 127 9 58 S 39 38 E
Lindi □ 127 9 40 S 38 30 E
Lindi, R. 126 1 25N 25 50 E
Lindoso 56 41 52N 8 11W
Lindow 48 52 58N 12 58 E
Lindsay, Can. 150 44 22N 78 43W
Lindsay, Calif., U.S.A. 163 36 14N 119 6W
Lindsay, Okla., U.S.A. 159 34 51N 97 37W
Lindsborg 158 38 35N 97 40W
Línea de la Concepciõn, La 55 36 15N 5 23W
Línea de la Concepción, La 57 36 15N 5 23W
Linfen 106 36 5N 111 32 E
Lingakok 99 29 55N 87 38 E
Lingayer 103 16 1N 120 14 E
Lingayer G. 103 16 10N 120 15 E
Lingch'iu 106 39 28N 114 10 E
Lingch'uan, Kwangsi Chuang, China 109 25 25N 110 20 E
Lingch'uan, Shansi, China 106 35 46N 113 26 E
Lingen 48 52 32N 7 21 E
Lingfield 29 51 11N 0 1W
Lingga, Kepulauan 102 0 10 S 104 30 E
Linghed 72 60 48N 15 55 E
Linghsien, Hunan, China 109 26 26N 113 45 E
Linghsien, Shantung, China 106 37 21N 116 34 E
Lingle 158 42 10N 104 18W
Lingling 109 26 13N 111 37 E
Lingpi 107 33 33N 117 33 E
Lingshan 108 22 26N 109 17 E
Lingshih 106 36 51N 111 47 E
Lingshou 106 38 18N 114 22 E
Lingshui 100 18 27N 110 0 E
Lingt'ai 106 35 4N 107 37 E
Linguéré 120 15 25N 15 5W
Lingwu 106 38 5N 106 20 E
Lingyün 108 24 24N 106 31 E
Linh Cam 100 18 31N 105 31 E
Linhai 109 28 51N 121 7 E
Linhares 171 19 25 S 40 4W
Linho 106 40 50N 107 30 E
Linhsi 107 43 37N 118 8 E
Linhsia 105 35 36N 103 5 E
Linhsiang 109 29 29N 113 30 E
Linhsien 106 37 57N 110 57 E
Lini 107 35 5N 118 20 E
Linju 106 34 14N 112 45 E
Link 68 41 4N 20 38 E
Linkao 100 19 56N 109 42 E
Linkinhorne 30 50 31N 4 22W
Linköping 73 58 28N 15 36 E
Link'ou 107 45 18N 130 15 E
Linli 109 29 27N 111 39 E
Linlithgow 35 55 58N 3 38W
Linn, Mt. 160 40 0N 123 0W
Linney Head 31 51 37N 5 4W
Linnhe, L. 34 56 36N 5 25W
Linosa 119 35 51N 12 50 E
Lins 173 21 40 S 49 44W
Linshui 108 30 18N 106 55 E
Linslade 29 51 55N 0 40W
Lint'ao 106 35 20N 104 0 E
Linth, R. 49 46 54N 9 0 E
Linthal 51 46 54N 9 0 E
Lintlaw 153 52 4N 103 14W
Linton, Can. 151 47 15N 72 16W
Linton, U.K. 29 52 6N 0 19 E
Linton, Ind., U.S.A. 156 39 0N 87 10W
Linton, N. Dak., U.S.A. 158 46 21N 100 12W
Lints'ang 108 23 54N 100 0 E
Lint'ung 106 34 24N 109 13 E
Linville 139 26 50 S 152 11 E
Linwu 109 25 17N 112 33 E
Linxe 44 43 56N 1 13W
Linyanti, R. 128 18 10 S 24 10 E
Linyüan 107 41 18N 119 15 E
Linz, Austria 52 48 18N 14 18 E
Linz, Ger. 48 50 33N 7 18 E
Lion-d'Angers, Le 42 47 37N 0 43W
Lion, G. du 44 43 0N 4 0 E
Lioni 65 40 52N 15 10 E
Lion's Den 127 17 15 S 30 5 E
Lion's Head 150 44 58N 81 15W
Liozno 80 55 0N 30 50 E
Lipali 127 15 50 S 35 50 E
Lipari 65 38 26N 14 58 E
Lipari, Is. 65 38 40N 15 0 E
Lipetsk 81 52 45N 39 35 E
Lipiany 54 53 2N 14 58 E
Lip'ing 108 26 16N 109 8 E
Lipkany 82 48 14N 26 25 E
Lipljan 66 42 31N 21 7 E
Lipnik 53 49 32N 17 36 E
Lipno 54 52 49N 19 15 E
Lipo 108 25 25N 107 53 E
Lipova 66 46 8N 21 42 E
Lipovets 82 49 12N 29 1 E
Lippstadt 48 51 40N 8 19 E
Lipsco 54 51 10N 21 36 E
Lipscomb 159 36 16N 100 28W
Lipsko 54 51 9N 21 40 E
Lipsói, I. 69 37 19N 26 50 E
Liptovsky Svaty Milkula 53 49 6N 19 35 E
Liptrap C. 141 38 50 S 145 55 E
Lip'u 109 24 30N 110 23 E
Lira 126 2 17N 32 57 E
Liri, R. 64 41 25N 13 45 E
Liria 58 39 37N 0 35W
Lisala 124 2 12N 21 38 E
Lisbellaw 38 54 20N 7 32W
Lisboa 57 38 42N 9 10W
Lisboa □ 57 39 0N 9 12W
Lisbon 158 46 30N 97 46W
Lisbon = Lisboa 57 38 42N 9 10W
Lisburn 38 54 30N 6 9W
Lisburne, C. 147 68 50N 166 0W
Liscannor 39 52 57N 9 24W
Liscannor, B. 39 52 57N 9 24W
Liscarroll 39 52 15N 8 44W
Liscia, R. 64 41 5N 9 17 E
Liscomb 151 45 2N 62 0W
Lisdoonvarna 39 53 2N 9 18W
Lishe Ho, R. 108 24 18N 101 32 E
Lishih 106 37 30N 111 7 E
Lishu 107 43 20N 124 37 E
Lishuchen 107 45 5N 130 40 E
Lishui, Chekiang, China 109 28 27N 119 54 E
Lishui, Kiangsu, China 109 31 38N 119 2 E
Lisianski I. 130 25 30N 174 0W
Lisieux 42 49 10N 0 12 E
Lisichansk 83 48 55N 38 30 E
Liskeard 30 50 27N 4 29W
Lismore, N.S.W., Austral. 139 28 44 S 153 21 E
Lismore, Vic., Austral. 133 37 58 S 143 21 E
Lismore, Ireland 39 52 8N 7 58W
Lismore I. 34 56 30N 5 30W
Lisnacree 38 54 4N 6 5W
Lisnaskea 38 54 15N 7 27W
Liss 29 51 3N 0 53W
Lissatinning Bri. 39 51 55N 10 1W
Lisse 46 52 16N 4 33 E
Lisselton 39 52 30N 9 34W
Lissycasey 39 52 44N 9 12W
List 48 55 1N 8 26 E
Lista, Norway 71 58 7N 6 39 E
Lista, Sweden 75 59 19N 16 16 E
Lister, Mt. 13 78 0 S 162 0 E
Liston 139 28 39 S 152 6 E
Listowel, Can. 150 43 44N 80 58W
Listowel, Ireland 39 52 27N 9 30W
Listowel Dns. 139 25 10 S 145 12 E
Lit-et-Mixe 44 44 2N 1 15W
Lit'ang, Kwangsi-Chuang, China 108 23 11N 109 5 E
Lit'ang, Szechwan, China 108 30 4N 100 18 E
Litang 103 5 27N 118 31 E
Lit'ang Ho, R. 108 28 5N 101 28 E
Litcham 29 52 43N 0 49 E
Litchfield, Austral. 140 36 18 S 142 52 E
Litchfield, Conn., U.S.A. 162 41 44N 73 12W
Litchfield, Ill., U.S.A. 158 39 10N 89 40W
Litchfield, Minn., U.S.A. 158 45 5N 95 0W
Liteni 70 47 32N 26 32 E
Litherland 32 53 29N 3 0W
Lithgow 141 33 25 S 150 8 E
Lithinon, Ákra 69 34 55N 24 44 E
Lithuania S.S.R. □ 80 55 30N 24 0 E
Litija 63 46 3N 14 50 E

Lititz Londonderry

Lititz **162** 40 9N 76 18W
Litókhoron **68** 40 8N 22 34 E
Litoměrice **52** 50 33N 14 10 E
Litomysi **53** 49 52N 16 20 E
Litschau **52** 48 58N 15 4 E
Little Abaco I. **157** 26 50N 77 30W
Little Aden **91** 12 41N 45 6 E
Little America **13** 79 0N 160 0W
Little Andaman I. **101** 10 40N 92 15 E
Little Barrier I. **142** 36 12 S 175 8 E
Little Belt **72** 55 8N 9 55 E
Little Belt Mts. **160** 46 50N 111 0W
Little Blue, R. **158** 40 18N 97 45W
Little Bushman Land **128** 29 10 S 18 10 E
Little Cadotte, R. **152** 56 41N 117 6W
Little Cayman, I. **166** 19 41N 80 3W
Little Churchill, R. **153** 57 30N 95 22W
Little Coco I. **101** 14 0N 93 15 E
Little Colorado, R. **161** 36 0N 111 31W
Little Current **150** 45 55N 82 0W
Little Current, R. **150** 50 57N 84 36W
Little Egg Inlet **162** 39 30N 74 20W
Little Falls, Minn., U.S.A. **158** 45 58N 94 19W
Little Falls, N.Y., U.S.A. **162** 43 3N 74 50W
Lit. Grand Rapids **153** 52 0N 95 29W
Lit. Humbaldt, R. **160** 41 20N 117 27W
Lit. Inagua I. **167** 21 40N 73 50W
Little Lake **163** 35 58N 117 58W
Little Longlac **150** 49 42N 86 58W
Little Marais **158** 47 24N 91 8W
Little Mecatiná I. **151** 50 30N 59 25W
Little Minch **36** 57 35N 6 45W
Lit. Miquelon I. **151** 46 45N 56 25W
Lit. Missouri R. **158** 46 40N 103 50W
Little Namaqualand **128** 29 0 S 17 9 E
Little Ormes Hd. **31** 53 19N 3 47W
Little Ouse, R. **29** 52 25N 0 50 E
Little Para, R. **109** 34 47 S 138 25 E
Little Rann of Kutch **94** 23 25N 71 25 E
Little Red, R. **159** 35 40N 92 15W
Little River **143** 43 45 S 172 49 E
Little Rock **159** 34 41N 92 10W
Little Ruaha, R. **126** 7 50 S 35 30 E
Little Sable Pt. **156** 43 40N 86 32W
Little Scarcies, R. **125** 9 30N 12 25W
Little Sioux, R. **147** 42 20N 95 55W
Little Smoky **152** 54 44N 117 11W
Little Smoky River **152** 55 40N 117 38W
Little Snake, R. **160** 40 45N 108 15W
Little Wabash, R. **156** 38 40N 88 20W
Little Walsingham **29** 52 53N 0 51 E
Little Whale, R. **150** 55 50N 75 0W
Littleborough **32** 53 38N 2 8W
Littlefield **159** 33 57N 102 17W
Littlefork **158** 48 24N 93 35W
Littlehampton, Austral. **109** 35 3 S 138 52 E
Littlehampton, U.K. **29** 50 48N 0 32W
Littlemill **37** 57 31N 3 49W
Littleport **29** 52 27N 0 18 E
Littlestone-on-Sea **29** 50 59N 0 59 E
Littlestown **162** 39 45N 77 3W
Littleton Common **162** 42 32N 71 28W
Litu **108** 28 24N 101 16 E
Liuan **109** 31 45N 116 30 E
Liuch'eng **108** 24 39N 109 14 E
Liuchou **108** 24 15N 109 22 E
Liuchuang **107** 33 9N 120 18 E
Liuheng Tao **109** 29 43N 122 8 E
Liuho, Kiangsu, China **109** 32 20N 118 51 E
Liuho, Kirin, China **107** 42 16N 125 42 E
Liukou **107** 40 57N 118 18 E
Liuli **127** 11 3 S 34 38 E
Liupa **106** 33 40N 107 0 E
Liuwa Plain **125** 14 20 S 22 30 E
Liuyang **109** 28 9N 113 38 E
Livada **70** 47 52N 23 5 E
Livadherón **68** 40 2N 21 57 E
Livanovka **84** 52 6N 61 59 E
Livarot **42** 49 0N 0 9 E
Live Oak **157** 30 17N 83 0W
Liveringa **136** 18 3 S 124 10 E
Livermore **163** 37 41N 121 47W
Livermore, Mt. **159** 30 45N 104 8W
Liverpool, Austral. **141** 33 54 S 150 58 E
Liverpool, Can. **151** 44 5N 64 41W
Liverpool, U.K. **32** 53 25N 3 0W
Liverpool, U.S.A. **162** 43 6N 76 13W
Liverpool Bay, Can. **147** 70 0N 128 0W
Liverpool Bay, U.K. **23** 53 30N 3 20W
Liverpool Plains **141** 31 15 S 150 15 E
Liverpool Ra. **141** 31 50 S 150 30 E
Livingston, Guat. **166** 15 50N 88 50W
Livingston, U.K. **45** 55 52N 3 33W
Livingston, Calif., U.S.A. **163** 37 23N 120 43W
Livingston, Mont., U.S.A. **160** 45 40N 110 40W
Livingstone **159** 30 44N 94 54W
Livingstone Falls **126** 5 25 S 13 35 E
Livingstone I. **13** 63 0 S 60 15W
Livingstone (Maramba) **127** 17 46 S 25 52 E
Livingstone Memorial **127** 12 20 S 30 18 E
Livingstone Mts., N.Z. **143** 45 15 S 168 9 E
Livingstone Mts., Tanz. **127** 9 40 S 34 20 E
Livingstonia **127** 10 38 S 34 5 E
Livno **66** 43 50N 17 0 E
Livny **81** 52 30N 37 30 E
Livorno **62** 43 32N 10 18 E
Livramento **173** 30 55 S 55 30W
Livramento do Brumado **171** 13 39 S 41 50W
Livron-sur-Drôme **45** 44 46N 4 51 E
Liwale **127** 9 48 S 37 58 E
Liwale □ **127** 9 0 S 38 0 E
Liwale Chini **127** 9 40 S 38 0 E
Lixnaw **39** 52 24N 9 37W
Lixoúrion **69** 38 14N 20 24 E
Liyang **109** 31 22N 119 30 E
Lizard **30** 49 58N 5 10W
Lizard I. **138** 14 42 S 145 30 E
Lizard Pt. **30** 49 57N 5 11W
Lizarda **170** 9 36 S 46 41W
Lizzano **65** 40 23N 17 25 E
Ljig **66** 44 13N 20 18 E
Ljubija **63** 44 55N 16 35 E
Ljubinje **66** 42 58N 18 5 E
Ljubljana **63** 46 4N 14 33 E
Ljubno **63** 46 25N 14 46 E
Ljubovija **66** 44 11N 19 22 E
Ljubuški **66** 43 12N 17 34 E
Ljung **73** 58 1N 13 3 E
Ljungan **72** 62 18N 17 23 E
Ljungan, R. **74** 62 30N 14 30 E
Ljungaverk **72** 62 30N 16 5 E
Ljungby **73** 56 49N 13 55 E
Ljusdal **72** 61 46N 16 3 E
Ljusnan **72** 61 12N 17 8 E
Ljusnan, R. **75** 62 0N 15 20 E
Ljusne **72** 61 13N 17 7 E
Ljutomer **63** 46 31N 16 11 E
Lki **67** 41 28N 23 43 E
Llagostera **58** 41 50N 2 54 E
Llanaber **31** 52 45N 4 5W
Llanaelhaiarn **31** 52 59N 4 24W
Llanafan-fawr **31** 52 12N 3 29W
Llanarmon Dyffryn Ceiriog **31** 52 53N 3 15W
Llanarth **31** 52 12N 4 19W
Llanarthney **31** 51 51N 4 9W
Llanbedr **31** 52 40N 4 7W
Llanbedrog **31** 52 52N 4 29W
Llanberis **31** 53 7N 4 7W
Llanbister **31** 52 22N 3 19W
Llanbrynmair **31** 52 36N 3 19W
Llancanelo, Salina **172** 35 40 S 69 8W
Llandaff **31** 51 29N 3 13W
Llanddewi-Brefi **31** 52 11N 3 57W
Llandilo **31** 51 45N 4 0W
Llandogo **31** 51 44N 2 40W
Llandovery **31** 51 59N 3 49W
Llandrillo **31** 52 56N 3 27W
Llandrindod Wells **31** 52 15N 3 23W
Llandudno **31** 53 19N 3 51W
Llandybie **31** 51 49N 4 0W
Llandyfriog **31** 52 2N 4 26W
Llandygwydd **31** 52 3N 4 33W
Llandyrnog **31** 53 10N 3 19W
Llandyssul **31** 52 3N 4 20W
Llanelli **31** 51 41N 4 11W
Llanelltyd **31** 52 45N 3 54W
Llanenddwyn **31** 52 48N 4 7W
Llanerchymedd **31** 53 20N 4 22W
Llanes **56** 43 25N 4 50W
Llanfaelog **31** 53 13N 4 29W
Llanfair Caereinion **31** 52 39N 3 20W
Llanfair Talhaiarn **31** 53 13N 3 37W
Llanfairfechan **31** 53 15N 3 58W
Llanfechell **31** 52 23N 4 25W
Llanfyllin **31** 52 47N 3 17W
Llangadog **31** 51 56N 3 53W
Llangefni **31** 53 15N 4 20W
Llangelynin **31** 52 39N 4 7W
Llangennech **31** 51 41N 4 10W
Llangerniew **31** 53 12N 3 41W
Llangollen **31** 52 58N 3 10W
Llangranog **31** 52 11N 4 29W
Llangurig **31** 52 25N 3 36W
Llangynog **31** 52 50N 3 24W
Llanharan **31** 51 32N 3 28W
Llanidloes **31** 52 28N 3 31W
Llanilar **31** 52 22N 4 2W
Llanllyfni **31** 53 2N 4 18W
Llannor **31** 52 55N 4 25W
Llano Estacado **154** 34 0N 103 0W
Llano R. **159** 30 50N 99 0W
Llanon **31** 52 17N 4 9W
Llanos **174** 3 25N 71 35W
Llanpumpsaint **31** 51 56N 4 19W
Llanrhaedr-ym-Mochnant **31** 52 50N 3 18W
Llanrhidian **31** 51 36N 4 11W
Llanrhystyd **31** 52 19N 4 9W
Llanrwst **31** 53 8N 3 49W
Llansannan **31** 53 10N 3 35W
Llansawel **31** 52 0N 4 1W
Llanstephan **31** 51 46N 4 24W
Llanthony **31** 51 57N 3 2W
Llantrisant **31** 51 33N 3 22W
Llanuwchllyn **31** 52 52N 3 41W
Llanvihangel Crucorney **31** 51 53N 2 58W
Llanwenog **31** 52 6N 4 11W
Llanwrda **31** 51 58N 3 52W
Llanwrtyd Wells **31** 52 6N 3 39W
Llanyblodwel **28** 52 47N 3 8W
Llanybyther **31** 52 4N 4 10W
Llanymynech **28** 52 48N 3 6W
Llanystymdwy **31** 52 56N 4 17W
Llera **165** 23 19N 99 1W
Llerena **57** 38 17N 6 0W
Llethr Mt. **31** 52 47N 3 58W
Lleyn Peninsula **31** 52 55N 4 35W
Llico **172** 34 46 S 72 5W
Llobregat, R. **58** 41 19N 2 9 E
Lloret de Mar **58** 41 41N 2 53 E
Lloyd B. **138** 12 45 S 143 27 E
Lloyd Barrage **95** 27 46N 68 50 E
Lloyd L. **153** 57 22N 108 57W
Lloydminster **153** 53 20N 110 0W
Lluchmayor **59** 39 29N 2 53 E
Llullaillaco, volcán **172** 24 30 S 68 30W
Llwyngwril **31** 52 41N 4 6W
Llyswen **31** 52 2N 3 18W
Lo **47** 50 59N 2 45 E
Lo Ho, Honan, China **106** 34 48N 113 4 E
Lo Ho, Shensi, China **106** 34 41N 110 6 E
Lo, R. **100** 21 18N 105 25 E
Loa **161** 38 18N 111 46W
Loa, R. **172** 21 30 S 70 0W
Loan **109** 27 24N 115 49 E
Loanhead **35** 55 53N 3 10W
Loano **62** 44 8N 8 14 E
Loans **34** 55 33N 4 39W
Lobatse **125** 25 12 S 25 40 E
Löbau **48** 51 5N 14 42 E
Lobaye, R. **128** 4 30N 17 0 E
Lobbes **47** 50 21N 4 16 E
Lobenstein **48** 50 25N 11 39 E
Lobería **172** 38 10 S 58 40W
Łobez **54** 53 38N 15 39 E
Lobito **125** 12 18 S 13 35 E
Lobón, Canal de **57** 38 50N 6 55W
Lobos **172** 35 2 S 59 0W
Lobos, I. **164** 21 27N 97 13W
Lobos, Is. **168** 6 35 S 80 45W
Lobstick L. **151** 54 0N 65 12W
Lobva **84** 59 10N 60 30 E
Lobva, R. **84** 59 8N 60 48 E
Loc Binh **100** 21 46N 106 54 E
Loc Ninh **101** 11 50N 106 34 E
Locarno **51** 46 10N 8 47 E
Loch Raven Res. **162** 39 26N 76 33W
Lochaber **36** 56 55N 5 0W
Lochailort **36** 56 53N 5 40W
Lochaline **36** 56 32N 5 47W
Loch'ang **109** 25 10N 113 20 E
Lochans **34** 54 52N 5 1W
Lochboisdale **36** 57 10N 7 20W
Lochbuie **34** 56 21N 5 52W
Lochcarron **36** 57 25N 5 30W
Lochdonhead **34** 56 27N 5 40W
Loche L., La **153** 56 40N 109 30W
Loche, La **153** 56 29N 109 26W
Lochearnhead **34** 56 24N 4 19W
Lochem **46** 52 9N 6 26 E
Loch'eng **108** 24 47N 108 54 E
Loches **42** 47 7N 1 0 E
Lochgelly **35** 56 7N 3 18W
Lochgilphead **34** 56 2N 5 37W
Lochgoilhead **34** 56 10N 4 54W
Lochiang **108** 31 21N 104 28 E
Lochih **108** 30 18N 105 0 E
Loch'ing **109** 28 8N 120 57 E
Loch'ing Wan **109** 28 4N 121 5 E
Lochinver **36** 58 9N 5 15W
Lochlaggan Hotel **37** 56 59N 4 25W
Lochmaben **35** 55 8N 3 27W
Lochmaddy **36** 57 36N 7 10W
Lochnagar, Queens., Austral. **138** 24 34 S 144 52 E
Lochnagar, Queens., Austral. **138** 23 33 S 145 38 E
Lochnagar, Mt. **37** 56 57N 3 14W
Łochow **54** 52 33N 21 42 E
Lochranza **34** 55 42N 5 18W
Lochs Park, Reg. **36** 58 7N 6 33W
Loch'uan **106** 35 48N 109 35 E
Lochwinnoch **34** 55 47N 4 39W
Lochy, L. **37** 56 58N 4 55W
Lochy, R. **36** 56 52N 5 3W
Lock **139** 33 34 S 135 46 E
Lock Haven **156** 41 7N 77 31W
Lockeford **163** 38 10N 121 9W
Lockeport **151** 43 47N 65 4W
Lockerbie **35** 55 7N 3 21W
Lockhart, Austral. **141** 35 14 S 146 40 E
Lockhart, U.S.A. **159** 29 55N 97 40W
Lockhart, L. **137** 33 15 S 119 3 E
Lockington **140** 36 16 S 144 34 E
Lockport **156** 43 12N 78 42W
Locle, Le **50** 47 3N 6 44 E
Locminé **42** 47 54N 2 51W
Locri **65** 38 14N 16 14 E
Locronan **42** 48 7N 4 15W
Loctudy **42** 47 50N 4 12W
Lod **90** 31 57N 34 54 E
Lodalskåpa **71** 61 47N 7 13 E
Loddon **29** 52 32N 1 29 E
Lodève **44** 43 44N 3 19 E
Lodge Grass **160** 45 21N 107 27W
Lodgepole **158** 41 12N 102 40W
Lodgepole Cr. **158** 41 20N 104 30W
Lodhran **94** 29 32N 71 30 E
Lodi, Italy **62** 45 19N 9 30 E
Lodi, U.S.A. **163** 38 12N 121 16W
Lodja **124** 3 30 S 23 23 E
Lodji **103** 1 38 S 127 28 E
Lodosa **58** 42 25N 2 4W
Lodose **73** 58 5N 12 10 E
Lödöse **73** 58 2N 12 9 E
Lodwar **126** 3 10N 35 40 E
Łodz **54** 51 45N 19 27E
Łodz □ **54** 51 45N 19 27E
Loengo **126** 4 48 S 26 30 E
Lofer **52** 47 35N 12 41 E
Lofoten **74** 68 10N 13 0 E
Lofoten Is. **74** 68 30N 15 0 E
Lofsen **72** 62 7N 13 57 E
Loftahammar **73** 57 54N 16 41 E
Loftsdalen **72** 62 10N 13 20 E
Loftus **33** 54 33N 0 52W
Lofty Ra. **136** 24 15 S 119 30 E
Loga **121** 13 37N 3 14 E
Logan, Kans., U.S.A. **158** 39 23N 99 35W
Logan, Ohio, U.S.A. **156** 39 25N 82 22 E
Logan, Utah, U.S.A. **160** 41 45N 111 50W
Logan, Mt. **147** 60 41N 140 22W
Logan Pass **152** 48 41N 113 44W
Logansport **156** 31 58N 93 58W
Loganville **162** 39 51N 76 42W
Logo **123** 5 20N 30 18 E
Logo Dergo **123** 6 10N 29 18 E
Logroño **58** 42 28N 2 32W
*Logroño □ **58** 42 28N 2 27W
Logrosán **57** 39 20N 5 32W
Løgstør **73** 56 58N 9 14 E
Lohardaga **95** 23 27N 84 45 E
Loheia **91** 15 45N 42 40 E
Lohja **75** 60 12N 24 5 E
Loho **106** 33 33N 114 5 E
Lohr **49** 50 0N 9 35 E
Loikaw **98** 19 40N 97 17 E
Loimaa **75** 60 50N 23 5 E
Loir-et-Cher □ **43** 47 40N 1 20 E
Loire □ **45** 45 40N 4 5 E
Loire-Atlantique □ **42** 47 25N 1 40W
Loire, R. **42** 47 16N 2 10W
Loiret □ **43** 47 58N 2 10 E
Loitz **48** 53 58N 13 8 E
Loja, Ecuador **174** 3 59 S 79 16W
Loja, Spain **57** 37 10N 4 10W
Lojung **108** 24 27N 109 36 E
Loka **123** 4 13N 31 0 E
Lokandu **124** 2 30 S 25 45 E
Løken **71** 59 48N 11 29 E
Lokerane **128** 24 54 S 24 42 E
Lokeren **47** 51 6N 3 59 E
Lokhvitsa **80** 50 25N 33 18 E
Lokichokio **126** 4 19N 34 13 E
Lokitaung **124** 4 12N 35 48 E
Lokka **74** 67 49N 27 45 E
Løkken, Denmark **73** 57 22N 9 41 E
Løkken, Norway **71** 63 8N 9 45 E
Loknya **80** 56 49N 30 4 E
Lokobo **123** 4 20N 30 30 E
Lokoja **121** 7 47N 6 45 E
Lokolama **124** 2 35 S 19 50 E
Loktung **100** 18 41N 109 5 E
Lokuti **123** 4 21N 33 15 E
Lokwei **100** 19 12N 110 30 E
Lol **123** 5 28N 29 36 E
Lol, R. **123** 9 0N 28 10 E
Lola **120** 7 52N 8 29W
Lolibai, Gebel **123** 3 50N 33 50 E
Lolimi **123** 4 35N 34 0 E
Loliondo **124** 2 2 S 35 39 E
Lolland **73** 54 45N 11 30 E
Lollar **48** 50 39N 8 43 E
Lolo **160** 46 50N 114 8W
Lolodorf **121** 3 16N 10 49 E
Lolungchung **126** 30 43N 96 7 E
Lom **67** 43 48N 23 20 E
Lom Kao **100** 16 53N 101 14 E
Lom, R. **66** 43 45N 23 7 E
Lom Sak **100** 16 47N 101 15 E
Loma **160** 47 59N 110 29W
Loma Linda **163** 34 3N 117 16W
Lomami, R. **126** 1 0 S 24 40 E
Lomas de Zamóra **172** 34 45 S 58 25W
Lombadria **136** 16 31 S 122 54 E
Lombard **160** 46 7N 111 28W
Lombardia □ **62** 45 35N 9 45 E
Lombardy = Lombardia **62** 45 35N 9 45 E
Lombez **44** 43 29N 0 55 E
Lomblen, I. **103** 8 30 S 123 32 E
Lombok, I. **102** 8 35 S 116 20 E
Lomé **121** 6 9N 1 20 E
Lomela **124** 2 5 S 23 52 E
Lomela, R. **124** 1 30 S 22 50 E
Lomello **62** 45 11N 8 46 E
Lometa **159** 31 15N 98 25W
Lomie **124** 3 13N 13 38 E
Loming **123** 4 27N 33 40W
Lomma **73** 55 43N 13 6 E
Lomme, R. **47** 50 8N 5 10 E
Lommel **47** 51 14N 5 19 E
Lomond **152** 50 24N 112 36W
Lomond, gasfield **19** 57 18N 1 12 E
Lomond, L. **34** 56 8N 4 38W
Lomond, mt. **139** 30 0 S 151 45 E
Lomphat **101** 13 30N 106 59 E
Lompobatang, mt. **103** 5 24 S 119 56 E
Lompoc **163** 34 41N 120 32W
Lomsegga **71** 61 49N 8 21 E
Łomza **54** 53 10N 22 2 E
Łomza □ **54** 53 0N 22 30 E
Lonan **106** 34 6N 110 10 E
Lonavla **96** 18 46N 73 29 E
Loncoche **176** 39 20 S 72 50W
Londa **97** 15 30N 74 30 E
Londe, La **45** 43 8N 6 14 E
Londerzeel **47** 51 0N 4 19 E
Londiani **126** 0 10 S 35 33 E
Londinières **42** 49 50N 1 25 E
London, Can. **150** 43 0N 81 15W
London, U.K. **29** 51 30N 0 5W
London, Ky., U.S.A. **156** 37 11N 84 5W
London, Ohio, U.S.A. **156** 39 54N 83 28W
London □ **29** 51 30N 0 5W
Londonderry **38** 55 0N 7 20W

*Renamed La Rioja

Lugansk McIlwraith Ra

Lugansk = Voroshilovgrad 83 48 35N 39 29 E
Lugard's Falls 126 3 6 S 38 41 E
Lugela 127 16 25 S 36 43 E
Lugenda, R. 127 12 35 S 36 50 E
Lugh Ganana 91 3 48N 42 40 E
Lugnaquilla, Mt. 39 52 48N 6 28W
Lugnvik 72 62 56N 17 55 E
Lugo, Italy 63 44 25N 11 53 E
Lugo, Spain 56 43 2N 7 35W
Lugo □ 56 43 0N 7 30W
Lugoj 66 45 42N 21 57 E
Lugones 56 43 26N 5 50W
Lugovoy 76 43 0N 72 20 E
Lugovoye 85 42 55N 72 43 E
Lugwardine 28 52 4N 2 38W
Luhe, R. 48 53 7N 10 0 E
Luhsi, Yunan, China 108 24 31N 103 46 E
Luhsi, Yunnan, China 108 24 27N 98 36 E
Luhuo 108 31 24N 100 41 E
Lui 106 33 52N 115 28 E
Luiana 125 17 25 S 22 30W
Luichart L. 37 57 36N 4 43W
Luichow Pen. = Leichou Pantao 108 20 40N 110 5 E
Luing I. 34 56 15N 5 40W
Luino 62 46 0N 8 42 E
Luís 164 26 36N 109 11W
Luís Correia 170 3 0 S 41 35W
Luís Gomes 171 6 25 S 38 23W
Luís Gonçalves 170 5 37 S 50 25W
Luisa 124 7 40 S 22 30 E
Luiza 124 7 40 S 22 30 E
Luizi 126 6 0 S 27 25 E
Luján 172 34 45 S 59 5W
Lukanga Swamp 127 14 30 S 27 40 E
Lukenie, R. 124 3 0 S 18 50 E
Lukhisaral 95 27 11N 86 5 E
Lukolela 124 1 10 S 17 12 E
Lukosi 127 18 30 S 26 30 E
Lukovit 67 43 13N 24 11 E
Lukoyanov 81 55 2N 44 20 E
Lukuhu 108 27 46N 100 50 E
Lukulu 125 14 35 S 23 25 E
Lula 126 0 30N 25 10 E
Lule, R. 74 65 35N 22 10 E
Luleå 74 65 35N 22 10 E
Lüleburgaz 67 41 23N 27 28 E
Luliang 108 25 3N 103 39 E
Luling 159 29 45N 97 40W
Lulonga, R. 124 1 0N 19 0 E
Lulua, R. 124 6 30 S 22 50 E
Luluabourg = Kananga 124 5 55 S 22 18 E
Lulung 107 39 55N 118 57 E
Lumai 125 13 20 S 21 25 E
Lumajang 103 8 8 S 113 16 E
Lumbala, Angola 125 12 36 S 22 30 E
Lumbala, Angola 125 14 18 S 21 18 E
Lumberton, Miss., U.S.A. 159 31 4N 89 28W
Lumberton, N. Mex., U.S.A. 161 36 58N 106 57W
Lumberton, N.C., U.S.A. 157 34 37N 78 59W
Lumbres 43 50 40N 2 5 E
Lumbwa 126 0 12 S 35 28 E
Lumby 152 50 10N 118 50W
Lumding 98 25 46N 93 10 E
Lumege 125 11 45 S 20 50 E
Lumeyen 123 4 55N 33 28 E
Lumi 135 3 30 S 142 2 E
Lummen 47 50 59N 5 12 E
Lumphanan 37 57 8N 2 41W
Lumsden, N.Z. 143 45 44 S 168 27 E
Lumsden, U.K. 37 57 16N 2 51W
Lumut 101 4 13N 100 37 E
Lumut, Tg. 102 3 50 S 105 58 E
Lunan 108 24 47N 103 16 E
Lunan B. 37 56 40N 2 25W
Lunavada 94 23 8N 73 37 E
Lunca 70 47 22N 25 1 E
Lund, Norway 74 68 42N 18 9 E
Lund, Sweden 73 55 41N 13 12 E
Lund, U.S.A. 160 38 53N 115 0W
Lunda 124 9 40 S 20 12 E
Lundazi 125 12 20 S 33 7 E
Lunde 71 59 17N 9 5 E
Lunderskov 73 55 29N 9 19 E
Lundi, R. 127 21 15 S 31 25 E
Lundu 102 1 40N 109 50 E
Lundy, I. 30 51 10N 4 41W
Lune, R. 32 54 0N 2 51W
Lüneburg 48 53 15N 10 23 E
Lüneburg Heath = Lüneburger Heide 48 53 0N 10 0 E
Lüneburger Heide 48 53 0N 10 0 E
Lunel 45 43 39N 4 9 E
Lünen 48 51 36N 7 31 E
Lunenburg 151 44 22N 64 18W
Lunéville 43 48 36N 6 30 E
Lung Chiang, R. 108 24 30N 109 15 E
Lunga, R. 127 13 0 S 26 33 E
Lungan 108 23 11N 107 41 E
Lungch'ang 108 29 20N 105 19 E
Lungch'ih 108 29 25N 103 24 E
Lungchou 108 22 24N 106 50 E
Lungch'üan 109 28 5N 119 7 E
Lungch'uan, Kwangtung, China 109 24 6N 115 15 E
Lungch'uan, Yunnan, China 108 24 16N 97 58 E
Lungern 50 46 48N 8 10 E
Lungholt 74 63 35N 18 10 E
Lunghsi 106 35 3N 104 38 E
Lunghsien 106 34 47N 107 0 E
Lunghua 107 41 18N 117 42 E
Lunghui 109 27 18N 110 52 E
Lungi Airport 120 8 40N 16 47 E
Lungk'ou 107 37 42N 120 21 E
Lungkuan 106 40 45N 115 43 E
Lungkukang 108 32 18N 99 7 E
Lungleh 98 22 55N 92 45 E
Lungli 108 26 27N 106 58 E
Lunglin 108 24 43N 105 26 E
Lungling 108 24 38N 98 35 E
Lungmen 109 23 44N 114 15 E
Lungming 108 23 4N 107 14 E
Lungnan 109 24 54N 114 47 E
Lungngo 98 21 57N 93 36 E
Lungshan 108 29 27N 109 23 E
Lungsheng 109 25 48N 110 0 E
Lungte 106 35 38N 106 6 E
Lungyen 109 25 9N 117 0 E
Lungyu 109 29 2N 119 10 E
Luni 94 26 0N 73 6 E
Luni, R. 94 25 40N 72 20 E
Luninets 80 52 15N 27 0 E
Luning 163 38 30N 118 10W
Lunino 81 53 35N 45 6 E
Lunna Ness 36 60 27N 1 4W
Lunner 71 60 19N 10 35 E
Lunsemfwa Falls 127 14 30 S 29 6 E
Lunsemfwa, R. 127 14 50 S 30 10 E
Lunteren 46 52 5N 5 38 E
Luofu 126 0 1 S 29 15 E
Luozi 124 4 54 S 14 0 E
Lupeni 70 45 21N 23 13 E
Łupków 53 49 15N 22 4 E
Lupundu 127 14 18 S 26 45 E
Luque, Parag. 172 25 19 S 57 25W
Luque, Spain 57 37 35N 4 16W
Luray 156 38 39N 78 26W
Lure 43 47 40N 6 30 E
Luremo 124 8 30 S 17 50 E
Lurgainn L. 36 58 1N 5 15W
Lurgan 38 54 28N 6 20W
Luristan 92 33 20N 47 0 E
Lusaka 127 15 28 S 28 16 E
Lusambo 126 4 58 S 23 28 E
Luseland 153 52 5N 109 24W
Lushan, Honan, China 106 33 45N 113 10 E
Lushan, Kweichow, China 108 26 33N 107 58 E
Lushan, Szechwan, China 108 30 10N 102 59 E
Lushih 106 34 4N 110 2 E
Lushnja 68 40 55N 19 41 E
Lushoto 126 4 47 S 38 20 E
Lushoto □ 126 4 45 S 38 20 E
Lushui 108 25 51N 98 55 E
Lüshun 107 38 48N 121 16 E
Lusignan 44 46 26N 0 8 E
Lusigny-sur-Barse 43 48 16N 4 15 E
Lusk, Ireland 38 53 32N 6 10W
Lusk, U.S.A. 158 42 47N 104 27W
Luss 34 56 6N 4 40W
Lussac-les-Châteaux 44 46 24N 0 43 E
Lussanvira 171 20 42 S 51 7W
Lüta 107 38 55N 121 40 E
Luti 108 7 14 S 157 0 E
Luting 108 29 56N 102 12 E
Luton 29 51 53N 0 24W
Lutong 102 4 30N 114 0 E
Lutry 50 46 31N 6 42 E
Lutsk 80 50 50N 25 15 E
Lutterworth 28 52 28N 1 12W
Luverne 158 43 35N 96 12W
Luvua 127 8 48 S 25 17 E
Luwegu, R. 127 9 30 S 36 20 E
Luwingu, Mt. 124 10 15 S 30 2 E
Luwuk 103 10 0 S 122 40 E
Luxembourg 47 49 37N 6 9 E
Luxembourg □ 47 49 58N 5 30 E
Luxembourg ■ 47 50 0N 6 0 E
Luxeuil-les-Bains 43 47 49N 6 24 E
Luxor = El Uqsur 122 25 41N 32 38 E
Luy de Béarn, R. 44 43 39N 0 48W
Luy de France, R. 44 43 39N 0 48W
Luy, R. 44 43 39N 1 9W
Luyksgestel 47 51 17N 5 20 E
Luz, Brazil 171 19 48 S 45 40W
Luz, France 44 42 53N 0 1 E
Luzern 51 47 3N 8 18 E
Luzern □ 50 47 2N 7 55 E
Luzerne 162 41 17N 75 54W
Luziânia 171 16 20 S 48 0W
Luzilândia 170 3 28 S 42 22W
Luzon, I. 103 16 0N 121 0 E
Luzy 43 46 47N 3 58 E
Luzzi 65 39 28N 16 17 E
Lvov 80 49 40N 24 0 E
Lwówek 54 52 28N 16 10 E
Lwówek Śląski 54 51 7N 15 38 E
Lyakhovichi 80 53 2N 26 32 E
Lyakhovskiye, Ostrova 77 73 40N 141 0 E
Lyaki 83 40 34N 47 22 E
Lyall Mt. 142 45 16 S 167 32 E
* Lyallpur 94 31 30N 73 5 E
Lyalya, R. 84 59 9N 61 29 E
Lyaskovets 67 43 6N 25 44 E
Lybster 37 58 18N 3 16W
Lychen 48 53 13N 13 20 E
Lyckeby 73 56 12N 15 37 E
Lycksele 74 64 38N 18 40 E
Lydd 29 50 57N 0 56 E
Lydda = Lod 90 31 57N 34 54 E
*Renamed Faisalabad
Lydenburg 129 25 10 S 30 29 E
Lydford 30 50 38N 4 7W
Lydham 28 52 31N 2 59W
Lyell 143 41 48 S 172 4 E
Lyell I. 152 52 40N 131 35W
Lyell, oilfield 19 60 55N 1 12 E
Lyell Range 143 41 38 S 172 20 E
Lygnern 73 57 30N 12 15 E
Lykens 162 40 34N 76 42W
Lykling 71 59 42N 5 12 E
Lyman 160 41 24N 110 15W
Lyme Bay 23 50 36N 2 55W
Lyme Regis 30 50 44N 2 57W
Lyminge 29 51 7N 1 6 E
Lymington 28 50 46N 1 32W
Lymm 32 53 23N 2 30W
Lympne 29 51 4N 1 2 E
Lynchburg 156 37 23N 79 10W
Lynd, R. 138 16 28 S 143 18 E
Lynd Ra. 139 25 30 S 149 20 E
Lynden 160 48 56N 122 32W
Lyndhurst, N.S.W., Austral. 138 33 41 S 149 2 E
Lyndhurst, Queens., Austral. 138 19 12 S 144 20 E
Lyndhurst, S. Australia, Austral. 139 30 15 S 138 18 E
Lyndhurst, U.K. 28 50 53N 1 33W
Lyndon, R. 137 23 29 S 114 6 E
Lyneham 28 51 30N 1 57W
Lyngdal, Agder, Norway 71 58 8N 7 7 E
Lyngdal, Buskerud, Norway 71 59 54N 9 32 E
Lynher Reef 136 15 27 S 121 55 E
Lynmouth 30 51 14N 3 50W
Lynn 162 42 28N 70 57W
Lynn Canal 152 58 50N 135 20W
Lynn L. 153 56 30N 101 40W
Lynn Lake 153 56 51N 101 3W
Lynton 30 51 14N 3 50W
Lyntupy 80 55 4N 26 23 E
Lynx L. 153 62 25N 106 15W
Lyø 73 55 3N 10 9 E
Lyon 45 45 46N 4 50 E
Lyonnais 45 45 45N 4 15 E
Lyons, Colo., U.S.A. 158 40 17N 105 15W
Lyons, Ga., U.S.A. 157 32 10N 82 15W
Lyons, Kans., U.S.A. 158 38 24N 98 13W
Lyons, N.Y., U.S.A. 162 43 3N 77 0W
Lyons = Lyon 45 45 46N 4 50 E
Lyons Falls 162 43 37N 75 22W
Lyons, R. 137 25 2 S 115 9 E
Lyrestad 73 58 48N 14 4 E
Lysá 52 50 11N 14 51 E
Lysekil 73 58 17N 11 26 E
Lyskovo 81 56 0N 45 3 E
Lyss 50 47 4N 7 19 E
Lysva 84 58 07N 57 49 E
Lysvik 72 60 1N 13 9 E
Lytchett Minster 28 50 44N 2 3W
Lytham St. Anne's 32 53 45N 2 58W
Lythe 33 54 30N 0 40W
Lytle 159 29 14N 98 46W
Lyttelton 143 43 35 S 172 44 E
Lytton 152 50 13N 121 31W
Lyuban 80 59 16N 31 18 E
Lyubim 81 58 20N 40 50 E
Lyubimets 67 41 50N 26 5 E
Lyubomi 81 51 10N 24 2 E
Lyubotin 82 50 0N 36 4 E
Lyubytino 80 58 50N 33 16 E
Lyudinovo 80 53 52N 34 28 E

M

Ma, R. 100 19 47N 105 56 E
Ma'ad 90 32 37N 35 36 E
Maam Cross 38 53 28N 9 32W
Maamba 128 17 17 S 26 28 E
Ma'an 92 30 12N 35 44 E
Maanshan 109 31 40N 118 30 E
Maarheeze 47 51 19N 5 36 E
Maarianhamina 75 60 5N 19 55 E
Maarn 47 52 3N 5 22 E
Maarssen 46 52 9N 5 2 E
Maartensdijk 46 52 9N 5 10 E
Maas 38 54 49N 8 21W
Maas, R. 47 51 48N 4 55 E
Maasbracht 47 51 9N 5 54 E
Maasbree 47 51 22N 6 3 E
Maasdan 46 51 48N 4 34 E
Maasdijk 46 51 58N 4 13 E
Maaseik 47 51 6N 5 45 E
Maasin 102 10 5N 124 55 E
Maasland 46 51 57N 4 16 E
Maasniel 47 51 12N 6 1 E
Maassluis 47 51 56N 4 16 E
Maastricht 47 50 50N 5 40 E
Maatin-es-Sarra 117 21 45N 22 0 E
Maave 129 21 4 S 34 47 E
Mabein 98 23 29N 96 37 E
Mabel L. 152 50 35N 118 43W
Mabel, oilfield 19 58 6N 1 36 E
Mabenge 126 4 15N 24 12 E
Mablethorpe 33 53 21N 0 14 E
Mabrouk 121 19 29N 1 15W
Mabton 127 46 13N 120 1W
Mac Bac 101 9 46N 106 7 E
Mc Grath 147 62 58N 155 40W
Macachin 172 37 10 S 63 43W
Macadam Ra. 136 14 40 S 129 50 E
Macaé 173 22 20 S 41 55W
Macaguane 174 6 35N 71 43W
Macaiba 170 5 15 S 35 21W
Macajuba 171 12 9 S 40 22W
McAlester 159 34 57N 95 40W
Macamic 150 48 45N 79 0W
Macão 57 39 35N 7 59W
Macao = Macau ■ 109 22 16N 113 35 E
Macapá 175 0 5N 51 10W
Macarani 171 15 33 S 40 24W
Macarena, Serranía de la 174 2 45N 73 55W
Macarthur 140 38 5 S 142 0 E
McArthur, R. 136 16 45 S 136 0 E
McArthur River 138 16 27 S 137 7 E
Macau 170 5 0 S 36 40W
Macau ■ 109 22 16N 113 35 E
Macaúbas 171 13 2 S 42 42W
McBride 152 53 20N 120 10W
McCamey 159 31 8N 102 15W
McCammon 160 42 41N 112 11W
McCarthy 147 61 25N 143 0W
McCauley I. 152 53 40N 130 15W
Macclesfield 32 53 16N 2 9W
McClintock 153 57 50N 94 10W
McClintock Chan. 148 72 0N 102 0W
McClintock Ra., Mts. 136 18 44 S 127 38 E
McCloud 160 41 14N 122 5W
McCluer Gulf 103 2 20 S 133 0 E
McCluer I. 136 11 5 S 133 0 E
McClure, L. 163 37 35N 120 16W
McClusky 158 47 30N 100 31W
McComb 159 31 20N 90 30W
McConnell Creek 152 56 53N 126 30W
McCook 158 40 15N 100 35W
McCulloch 152 49 45N 119 15W
McCusker, R. 153 55 32N 108 39W
McDame 152 59 44N 128 59W
McDermitt 160 42 0N 117 45W
McDonald I. 11 54 0 S 73 0 E
Macdonald L. 137 23 30 S 129 0 E
Macdonald Ra. 136 15 35 S 124 50 E
Macdonnell Ranges 136 23 40 S 133 0 E
McDouall Peak 139 29 51 S 134 55 E
Macdougall L. 148 66 00N 98 27W
McDougalls Well 140 31 8 S 141 15 E
MacDowell L. 150 52 15N 92 45W
Macduff 37 57 40N 2 30W
Mace 150 48 55N 80 0W
Maceda 56 42 16N 7 39W
Macedo da Cavaleiros 124 11 25 S 16 45 E
Macedo de Cavaleiros 56 41 31N 6 57W
Macedonia = Makedonija 66 41 53N 21 40 E
Macedonia = Makhedonia 68 40 39N 22 0 E
Maceió 170 9 40 S 35 41W
Maceira 57 39 41N 8 55W
Macenta 120 8 35N 9 20W
Macerata 63 43 19N 13 28 E
McFarland 163 35 41N 119 14W
Macfarlane, L. 140 32 0 S 136 40 E
McFarlane, R. 153 59 12N 107 58W
McGehee 159 33 40N 91 25W
McGill 160 39 27N 114 50W
Macgillycuddy's Reeks, mts. 39 52 2N 9 45W
McGraw 162 42 35N 76 4W
MacGregor 153 49 57N 98 48W
McGregor, Iowa, U.S.A. 158 42 58N 91 15W
McGregor, Minn., U.S.A. 158 46 37N 93 17W
McGregor, R. 152 55 10N 122 0W
McGregor Ra. 139 27 0 S 142 45 E
Mach 93 29 50N 67 20 E
Machacalis 171 17 5 S 40 45W
Machachi 174 0 30 S 78 15W
Machado, R. = Jiparana 174 8 45 S 62 20W
Machagai 172 26 56 S 60 2W
Machakos 126 1 30 S 37 15 E
Machakos □ 126 1 30 S 37 15 E
Machala 174 3 10 S 79 50W
Machanga 129 20 59 S 35 0 E
Machar Marshes 123 9 28N 33 21 E
Machattie, L. 138 24 50 S 139 48 E
Machava 129 25 54 S 32 28 E
Machece 127 19 15 S 35 32 E
Machecoul 42 47 0N 1 49W
Machelen 47 50 55N 4 26 E
Mach'eng 109 31 11N 115 2 E
Mcherrah 118 27 0N 4 30W
Machevna 77 61 20N 172 20 E
Machezo, mt. 57 39 21N 4 20W
Machiang 108 26 30N 107 35 E
Mach'iaoho 107 44 41N 130 32 E
Machias 151 44 40N 67 34W
Machichaco, Cabo 58 43 28N 2 47W
Machichi, R. 153 57 3N 92 6W
Machida 111 35 28N 139 23 E
Machilipatnam 99 16 12N 81 12 E
Machilipatnam = Masulipatnam 96 16 12N 131 15 E
Machine, La 43 46 54N 3 27 E
Mchinja 127 9 44 S 39 45 E
Mchinji 127 13 47 S 32 58 E
Machiques 174 10 4N 72 34W
Machrihanish 34 55 25N 5 42W
Machupicchu 174 13 8 S 72 30W
Machynlleth 31 52 36N 3 51W
•Macias Nguema Biyoga 113 3 30N 8 40 E
McIlwraith Ra. 138 13 50 S 143 20 E
•Renamed Bioko

Macina Makgobistad

Macina 120 14 40N 4 50W
Macina, Canal de 120 13 50N 5 40W
McIntosh 158 45 57N 101 20W
McIntosh L. 153 55 11N 104 41W
MacIntosh Range, Mts. 137 24 45S 121 33E
Macintyre, R. 139 28 37S 149 40E
Macizo Galaico 56 42 30N 7 30W
Mackay, Austral. 138 21 8S 149 11E
Mackay, U.S.A. 160 43 58N 113 37W
Mackay, L. 136 22 30S 129 0E
Mackay, R. 152 57 10N 111 38W
McKay Ra. 137 23 0S 122 30E
McKeesport 156 40 21N 79 50W
Mackenzie 152 55 20N 123 05W
McKenzie 157 36 10N 88 31W
Mackenzie Bay 147 69 0N 137 30W
Mackenzie City = Linden 174 6 0N 58 10W
Mackenzie Highway 152 58 0N 117 15W
Mackenzie Mts. 147 64 0N 128 0W
Mackenzie Plains 143 44 10S 170 25W
Mackenzie, R., Austral. 138 23 38S 149 46E
Mackenzie, R., Can. 148 69 10N 134 20W
McKenzie, R. 160 44 2N 122 30W
•Mackenzie, Terr. 149 61 30N 144 30W
McKerrow L. 143 44 25S 168 5E
Mackinaw City 156 45 47N 84 44W
McKinlay 138 21 16S 141 18E
McKinlay, R. 138 20 50S 141 28E
McKinley, Mt. 147 63 10N 151 0W
McKinley Sea 12 84 0N 10 0W
McKinney 159 33 10N 96 40W
Mackinnon Road 126 3 40S 39 1E
Mackintosh Ra. 137 27 39S 125 32E
McKittrick 163 35 18N 119 39W
Mackmyra 72 60 40N 17 3E
Macksville 141 30 40S 152 56E
McLaren Vale 140 35 13S 138 31E
McLaughlin 158 45 50N 100 50W
Maclean 139 29 26S 153 16E
McLean 159 35 15N 100 35W
McLeansboro 158 38 5N 88 30W
Maclear 129 31 2S 28 23E
Macleay, R. 141 30 56S 153 0E
McLennan 152 55 42N 116 50W
MacLeod, B. 152 62 53N 110 0W
McLeod L. 137 24 9S 113 47E
McLeod, L. 137 24 50S 114 0E
MacLeod Lake 152 54 58N 123 0W
McIlwraith Ra., Mts. 138 13 43S 143 23E
McLoughlin, Mt. 160 42 30N 122 30W
McLure 152 51 2N 120 13W
McMillan L. 159 32 40N 104 20W
McMinnville, Oreg., U.S.A. 160 45 16N 123 11W
McMinnville, Tenn., U.S.A. 157 35 43N 85 45W
McMorran 153 51 19N 108 42W
McMurdo Sd. 13 77 0S 170 0E
McMurray = Fort McMurray 152 56 45N 111 27W
McNary 161 34 4N 109 53W
McNaughton L. 152 52 0N 118 10W
Macnean L. 38 54 19N 7 52W
MacNutt 153 51 5N 101 36W
Macodoene 129 23 32S 35 5E
Macomb 158 40 25N 90 40W
Macomer 64 40 16N 8 48E
Mâcon 45 46 19N 4 50E
Macon, Ga., U.S.A. 157 32 50N 83 37W
Macon, Miss., U.S.A. 157 33 7N 88 31W
Macon, Mo., U.S.A. 158 39 40N 92 26W
Macondo 125 12 37S 23 46E
Macosquink 38 55 5N 6 43W
Macossa 127 17 55S 33 56E
Macoun L. 153 56 32N 103 50W
Macovane 129 21 30S 35 0E
McPherson 158 38 25N 97 40W
McPherson Pk. 163 34 53N 119 53W
Macpherson Ra. 139 28 15S 153 15E
Macquarie Harbour 138 42 15S 145 15E
Macquarie Is. 130 50 0S 160 0E
Macquarie, R. 139 30 50S 147 30E
McRae, Mt. 136 22 17S 117 35E
MacRobertson Coast 13 68 30S 63 0E
Macroom 39 51 54N 8 57W
McSwyne's B. 38 54 37N 8 25W
Macu 174 0 25N 69 15W
Macugnaga 62 45 57N 7 58E
Macuirima 127 19 14S 35 5E
Macuiza 127 8 7S 34 29E
Macujer 174 0 24N 73 0W
Macumba, R. 133 27 11S 136 0E
Macuse 127 17 45S 37 17E
Macuspana 165 17 46N 92 36W
Macusse 128 17 48S 20 23E
Mácuzari, Presa 164 27 10N 109 10W
Macuze 127 17 45S 37 17E
Madā 'in Sālih 122 26 51N 37 58E
Madagali 121 10 56N 13 33E
Madagascar ■ 129 20 0S 47 0E
Madagascar, I. 129 20 0S 47 0E
Madam 120 7 58N 3 32W
Madama 119 22 0N 14 0E
Madame I. 151 45 30N 60 58W
Madanapalle 97 13 33N 78 34E
Madang 135 5 12S 145 49E
Madaoua 121 14 5N 6 27E
Madara 121 11 45N 10 35E
Madaripur 98 23 2N 90 15E
Madauk 98 17 56N 96 52E
Madawaska 150 45 30N 77 55W
Madawaska, R. 150 45 27N 76 21W

*Now part of Fort Smith □

Madaya 98 22 20N 96 10E
Madbar 123 6 17N 30 45E
Maddalena, I. 64 41 15N 9 23E
Maddalena, La 64 41 13N 9 25E
Maddaloni 65 41 4N 14 23E
Maddy, L. 36 57 36N 7 8W
Made 47 51 41N 4 49E
Madebele 123 12 30N 41 10E
Madeira, Is. 116 32 50N 17 0W
Madeira, R. 174 5 30S 61 20W
Madeleine, Is. de la 151 47 30N 61 40W
Madeley 28 52 38N 2 28W
Madely 32 52 59N 2 20W
Madenda 127 13 42S 35 1W
Madera 163 37 0N 120 1W
Madha 96 18 0N 75 55E
Madhubani 95 26 21N 86 7E
Madhumati, R. 98 22 53N 89 52E
Madhupur 126 24 18N 86 37E
Madhya Pradesh □ 94 21 50N 81 0E
Madi Opei 126 3 47N 33 5E
Madill 159 34 5N 96 49W
Madimba, Mozam. 127 4 58S 15 6E
Madimba, Zaïre 124 5 0S 15 0E
Madinat al Shaab 91 12 50N 45 0E
Madingou 124 4 10S 13 33E
Madirovalo 129 16 26S 46 32E
Madison, Fla., U.S.A. 157 30 29N 83 26W
Madison, Ind., U.S.A. 156 38 42N 85 20W
Madison, Nebr., U.S.A. 158 41 53N 97 25W
Madison, S.D., U.S.A. 158 44 0N 97 8W
Madison, Wis., U.S.A. 158 43 5N 89 25W
Madison City 158 43 5N 93 10W
Madison Junc. 160 44 42N 110 56W
Madison, R. 160 45 0N 111 48W
Madisonville 156 37 42N 87 30W
Madista 128 21 15S 25 6E
Madiun 103 7 38S 111 32E
Madol 123 9 3N 27 45E
Madona 80 56 53N 26 5E
Madonie, Le, Mts. 64 37 50N 13 50E
Madoonga 174 26 56S 117 35E
Madras, India 97 13 8N 80 19E
Madras, U.S.A. 160 44 40N 121 10W
Madras = Tamil Nadu □ 97 11 0N 77 0E
Madre de Dios, I. 176 50 20N 75 10W
Madre de Dios, R. 174 11 30S 67 30W
Madre del Sur, Sierra 165 17 30N 100 0W
Madre, Laguna 165 25 0N 97 30W
Madre Occidental, Sierra 164 27 0N 107 0W
Madre Oriental, Sierra 164 25 0N 100 0W
Madre, Sierra, Mexico 165 16 0N 93 0W
Madre, Sierra, Phil. 103 17 0N 122 0E
Madri 94 24 16N 73 32E
Madrid 56 40 25N 3 45W
Madrid □ 56 40 30N 3 45W
Madridejos 57 39 28N 3 33W
Madrigal de las Altas Torres 56 41 5N 5 0W
Madrona, Sierra 57 38 27N 4 16W
Madroñera 57 39 26N 5 42W
Madu 123 14 37N 26 4E
Madura Motel 137 31 55S 127 0E
Madura, Selat 103 7 30S 113 20E
Madurai 97 9 55N 78 10E
Madurantakam 97 12 30N 79 50E
Madurta 109 35 1S 138 44E
Maduru Oya 97 7 40N 81 7E
Madzhalis 83 42 9N 47 47E
Mae Chan 100 20 9N 99 52E
Mae Hong Son 100 19 16N 98 8E
Mae Khlong, R. 100 13 24N 100 0E
Mae Phrik 100 17 27N 99 7E
Mae Ramat 100 16 58N 98 31E
Mae Rim 100 18 54N 98 57E
Mae Sot 100 16 43N 98 34E
Mae Suai 100 19 39N 99 33E
Mae Tha 100 18 28N 99 8E
Maebaru 110 33 33N 130 12E
Maebashi 111 36 24N 139 4E
Maella 58 41 8N 0 7E
Maentwrog 31 52 57N 4 0W
Maerhk'ang 108 31 51N 102 28E
Mâeruş 70 45 53N 25 31E
Maesteg 31 51 36N 3 40W
Maestra, Sierra 166 20 15N 77 0W
Maestrazgo, Mts. del 58 40 30N 0 25W
Maevatanana 125 16 56N 46 49E
Ma'fan 119 25 56N 14 56E
Mafeking, Can. 153 52 40N 101 10W
•Mafeking, S. Afr. 128 25 50S 25 38E
Maféré 120 5 30N 3 2W
Mafeteng 128 29 51S 27 15E
Maffe 47 50 21N 5 19E
Maffra 141 37 53S 146 58E
Mafia □ 126 7 50S 39 45E
Mafia I. 126 7 45S 39 50E
Mafou 109 31 34N 115 15E
Mafra, Brazil 173 26 10N 50 0W
Mafra, Port. 57 38 55N 9 20W
Mafungabusi Plateau 127 18 30S 29 8E
Magadan 77 59 30N 151 0E
Magadi 126 1 54S 36 19E
Magadi, L. 126 1 54S 36 19E
Magaliesburg 129 26 1S 27 32E
Magallanes, Estrecho de 176 52 30S 75 0W
Magangué 174 9 14N 74 45W
Magaria 121 13 4N 9 5W
Magburaka 120 8 47N 12 0W
Magdal 90 32 51N 35 30E

*Renamed Mafikeng

Magdalen Is. = Madeleine, Is. de la 151 47 30N 61 40W
Magdalena, Argent. 172 35 5S 57 30W
Magdalena, Boliv. 174 13 13S 63 57W
Magdalena, Mexico 164 30 50N 112 0W
Magdalena, U.S.A. 161 34 10N 107 20W
Magdalena □ 174 10 0N 74 0W
Magdalena, B. 164 24 30N 112 10W
Magdalena, I. 164 24 40N 112 15W
Magdalena, Llano de la 164 25 0N 111 30W
Magdalena, mt. 102 4 25N 117 55E
Magdalena, R., Colomb. 174 8 30N 74 0W
Magdalena, R., Mexico 164 30 50N 112 0W
Magdeburg 48 52 8N 11 36E
Magdeburg □ 48 52 20N 11 40E
Magdelaine Cays 138 16 33S 150 18E
Magdiel 90 32 10N 34 54E
Magdub 123 13 42N 25 5E
Magee 159 31 53N 89 45W
Magee, I. 38 54 48N 5 44W
Magelang 103 7 29S 110 13E
Magellan's Str. 176 52 30S 75 0W
Magellan's Str. = Magallanes, Est. de 176 52 30S 75 0W
Magenta, Austral. 140 33 51S 143 34E
Magenta, Italy 62 45 28N 8 53E
Magenta, L. 137 33 30S 119 10E
Maggea 140 34 28S 140 2E
Maggia 51 46 15N 8 42E
Maggia, R. 51 46 18N 8 36E
Maggiorasca, Mt. 62 44 33N 9 29E
Maggiore, L. 62 46 0N 8 35E
Maghama 120 15 32N 12 57W
Maghar 90 32 54N 35 24E
Maghera 38 54 51N 6 40W
Magherafelt 38 54 44N 6 37W
Maghnia 118 34 50N 1 43W
Maghull 32 53 31N 2 56W
Magilligan 38 55 10N 6 53W
Magilligan Pt. 38 55 10N 6 58W
Magione 63 43 10N 12 12E
Maglaj 66 44 33N 18 7E
Magliano in Toscana 63 42 36N 11 18E
Máglie 65 40 8N 18 17E
Magnac-Laval 44 46 13N 1 11E
Magnetic Pole, 1976, (South) 13 68 48S 139 30E
Magnetic Pole, 1976(North) 12 76 12N 100 12W
Magnisia □ 69 39 24N 22 46E
Magnitogorsk 84 53 27N 59 4E
Magnolia, Ark., U.S.A. 159 33 18N 93 12W
Magnolia, Miss., U.S.A. 159 31 8N 90 28W
Magnor 71 59 56N 12 15E
Magnus, oilfield 19 61 40N 1 20E
Magny-en-Vexin 43 49 9N 1 47E
Màgoé 127 15 45S 31 42E
Magog 151 45 18N 72 9W
Magoro 126 1 45N 34 12E
Magosta = Famagusta 92 35 8N 33 55E
Magoye 127 16 1S 27 30E
Magpie L. 151 51 0N 64 40W
Magrath 152 49 25N 112 50W
Magro, R. 59 39 20N 0 45W
Magruder Mt. 163 37 25N 117 33W
Magrur, W. 123 16 5N 26 30E
Magu □ 126 2 45S 33 15E
Maguarinho, C. 170 0 15S 48 30W
Maguire's Bri. 38 54 18N 7 28W
Maguse L. 153 61 40N 95 10W
Maguse Pt. 153 61 20N 93 50W
Maguse River 153 61 20N 94 25W
Magwe 98 20 10N 95 0E
Maha Sarakham 100 16 12N 103 16E
Mahābād 92 36 50N 45 45E
Mahabaleshwar 96 17 58N 73 50E
Mahabarat Lekh 95 28 30N 82 0E
Mahabo 129 20 23S 44 40E
Mahad 96 18 6N 73 29E
Mahadeo Hills 94 22 20N 78 30E
Mahadeopur 96 18 48N 80 0E
Mahagi 126 2 20N 31 0E
Mahajamba, B. de la 129 15 24S 47 5E
Mahajamba, R. 129 17 0S 47 30E
Mahajan 94 28 48N 73 56E
Mahajilo, R. 129 19 30S 46 0E
Mahakam, R. 102 1 0N 114 40E
Mahalapye 128 23 1S 26 51E
Mahalla el Kubra 122 31 10N 31 0E
Mahallāt 93 33 55N 50 30E
Mahanadi R. 96 20 33N 85 0E
Mahanagh 38 53 31N 8 42W
Mahanoro 129 19 54S 48 48E
Mahanoy City 162 40 48N 76 10W
Maharashtra □ 96 19 30N 75 30E
Maharès 119 34 32N 10 29E
Mahari Mts. 126 6 20S 30 0E
Mahasolo 129 19 7S 46 22E
Mahaweli Ganga 97 8 0N 81 10E
Mahaxay 100 17 22N 105 48E
Mahboobabad 96 17 42N 80 2E
Mahbubnagar 96 16 45N 77 59E
Mahd Dhahab 92 25 55N 45 30E
Mahdia 119 35 28N 11 0E
Mahé 97 11 42N 75 34E
Mahe 95 33 10N 78 32E
Mahendra Giri, mt. 97 8 20N 77 30E
Mahendraganj 98 25 20N 89 45E
Mahenge 127 8 45S 36 35E
Maheno 143 45 10S 170 50E
Mahia Pen. 142 39 9S 177 55E
Mahirija 118 34 0N 3 16W

Mahlaing 98 21 6N 95 39E
Mahmiya 123 17 5N 33 50E
Mahmud Kot 94 30 16N 71 0E
Mahmudia 70 45 5N 29 5E
Mahnomen 158 47 22N 95 57W
Mahoba 95 25 15N 79 55E
Mahón 58 39 50N 4 18E
Mahone Bay 151 44 30N 64 20W
Mahopac 162 41 22N 73 45W
Mahsü 108 30 31N 100 19E
Mahukona 147 20 11N 155 52W
Mahuta 121 11 32N 4 58E
Mai-Ndombe, L. 124 2 0S 18 0E
Mai-Sai 100 20 20N 99 55E
Maibara 111 35 19N 136 17E
Maîche 43 47 16N 6 48E
Maicuru, R. 175 1 0S 54 30W
Máida 65 38 51N 16 21E
Maidan Khula 94 33 36N 69 50E
Maiden Bradley 28 51 9N 2 18W
Maiden Newton 28 50 46N 2 35W
Maidenhead 29 51 31N 0 42W
Maidi 123 16 20N 42 45E
Maidstone, Can. 153 53 5N 109 20W
Maidstone, U.K. 29 51 16N 0 31E
Maiduguri 121 12 0N 13 20E
Maignelay 43 49 32N 2 30E
Maigualida, Sierra 174 5 30N 65 10W
Maijdi 98 22 48N 91 10E
Maikala Ra. 96 22 0N 81 0E
Mailly-le-Camp 43 48 41N 4 12E
Mailsi 94 29 48N 72 15E
Maimana 93 35 53N 64 38E
Main Barrier Ra. 133 31 10S 141 20E
Main Centre 153 50 35N 107 21W
Main Coast Ra. 138 16 22S 145 10E
Main, R., Ger. 49 50 13N 11 0E
Main, R., U.K. 38 54 49N 6 20W
Mainburg 49 48 37N 11 49E
Maindargi 96 17 33N 74 21E
Maine 42 48 0N 0 0E
Maine □ 151 45 20N 69 0W
Maine-et-Loire □ 42 47 31N 0 30W
Maine, R. 39 52 10N 9 40W
Maïne-Soroa 121 13 13N 12 2E
Maingkwan 98 26 15N 96 45E
Mainit, L. 103 9 31N 125 30E
Mainkaing 98 24 48N 95 16E
Mainland, I., Orkneys, U.K. 37 59 0N 3 10W
Mainland, I., Shetlands, U.K. 36 60 15N 1 22W
Mainpuri 95 27 18N 79 4E
Maintenon 43 48 35N 1 35E
Maintirano 129 18 3S 44 1E
Mainvault 47 50 39N 3 43E
Mainz 49 50 0N 8 17E
Maipú 172 37 0S 58 0W
Maipures 174 5 11N 67 49W
Maiquetia 174 10 36N 66 57W
Maira, R. 62 44 29N 7 15E
Mairabari 98 26 30N 92 30E
Mairipotaba 171 17 18S 49 28W
Maisi 167 20 17N 74 9W
Maisi, C. 167 20 10N 74 10W
Maisse 43 48 24N 2 21E
Maissin 47 49 58N 5 10E
Maitland, N.S.W., Austral. 141 32 44S 151 36E
Maitland, S. Australia, Austral. 140 34 23S 137 40E
Maitland, L. 137 27 11S 121 3E
Maiyema 121 12 5N 4 25E
Maiz, Islas del 166 12 15N 83 4W
Maizuru 111 35 25N 135 22E
Majagual 174 8 33N 74 38W
Majalengka 103 6 55S 108 14E
Majd el Kurum 90 32 56N 35 15E
Majene 103 3 27S 118 57E
Majevica Planina 66 44 45N 18 50E
Maji 123 6 20N 35 30E
Major 153 51 52N 109 37W
Majorca, I. = Mallorca, I. 58 39 30N 3 0E
Majors Creek 141 35 33S 149 45E
Majunga 125 15 40S 46 25E
Majunga □ 129 17 0S 47 0E
Maka 120 13 40N 14 10W
Makak 121 3 36N 11 0E
Makale 103 3 6S 119 51E
Makamba 126 4 8S 29 49E
Makamik 150 48 45N 79 0W
Makapuu Hd. 147 21 19N 157 39W
Makarewa 143 46 20S 168 21E
Makari 124 12 35N 14 28E
Makarikari = Makgadikgadi 128 20 40S 25 45E
Makarovo 77 57 40N 107 45E
Makarska 66 43 20N 17 2E
Makaryev 81 57 52N 43 50E
Makasar = Ujung Pandang 103 5 10S 119 20E
Makasar, Selat 103 1 0S 118 20E
Makat 76 47 39N 53 19E
Makedhonia □ 68 40 39N 22 0E
Makedonija □ 66 41 53N 21 40E
Makena 147 20 39N 156 27W
Makeni 120 8 55N 12 5W
Maker 30 50 20N 4 10W
Makeyevka 82 48 0N 38 0E
Makgadikgadi 128 20 40S 25 45E
Makgadikgadi Salt Pans 128 20 40S 25 45E
Makgobistad 128 25 45S 25 12E

Makhachkala	83	43 0N	47 15 E
Makharadze	83	41 55N	42 2 E
Makian, I.	103	0 12N	127 20 E
†Makin, I.	130	3 30N	174 0 E
Makindu	124	2 7 S	37 40 E
Makinsk	76	52 37N	70 26 E
Makkah	122	21 30N	39 54 E
Makkovik	151	55 0N	59 10W
Makkum	46	53 3N	5 25 E
Maklakovo	77	58 16N	92 29 E
Makó	53	46 14N	20 33 E
Makokou	124	0 40N	12 50 E
Makongo	126	3 15N	26 17 E
Makoro	126	3 10N	29 59 E
Makoua	124	0 5 S	15 50 E
Maków Podhal	54	49 43N	19 45 E
Makrá, I.	69	36 15N	25 54 E
Makrai	93	22 2N	77 0 E
Makran	93	26 13N	61 30 E
Makran Coast Range	93	25 40N	4 0 E
Makrana	94	27 2N	74 46 E
Mákri	68	40 52N	25 40 E
Maksimkin Yar	76	58 58N	86 50 E
Maktar	119	35 48N	9 12 E
Mâkû	92	39 15N	44 31 E
Makuan	108	23 2N	104 24 E
Makum	98	27 30N	95 23 E
Makumbe	128	20 15 S	24 26 E
Makumbi	124	5 50 S	20 43 E
Makunda	128	22 30 S	20 7 E
Makurazaki	110	31 15N	130 20 E
Makurdi	120	7 43N	8 28 E
Makwassie	128	27 17 S	26 0 E
Mal	98	26 51N	86 45 E
Mal B.	39	52 50N	9 30W
Mal-i-Gjalicës së Lumës	68	42 2N	20 25 E
Mal i Gribës	68	40 17N	9 45 E
Mal i Nemërçkës	68	40 15N	20 15 E
Mal i Tomorit	68	40 42N	20 11 E
Mala Kapela	63	44 45N	15 30 E
Mala, Pta.	166	7 28N	80 2W
Malabang	103	7 36N	124 3 E
Malabar Coast	97	11 0N	75 0 E
Malacca = Melaka	101	2 15N	102 15 E
Malacca, Str. of	101	3 0N	101 0 E
Malacky	53	48 27N	17 0 E
Malad City	160	41 10N	112 20 E
Maladetta, Mt.	59	42 40N	0 30 E
Malafaburi	123	10 37N	40 30 E
Málaga, Colomb.	174	6 42N	72 44W
Málaga, Spain	57	36 43N	4 23W
Malaga	159	32 12N	104 2W
Málaga □	57	36 38N	4 58W
Malagarasi	126	5 5 S	30 50 E
Malagarasi, R.	126	3 50 S	30 30 E
Malagasy Rep. ■ = Madagascar ■	129	20 0 S	47 0 E
Malagón	57	39 11N	3 52W
Malagón, R.	57	37 40N	7 20W
Malahide	38	53 26N	6 10W
Malaimbandy	129	20 20 S	45 36 E
Malakâl	123	9 33N	31 50 E
Malakand	94	34 40N	71 55 E
Malakoff	159	32 10N	95 55W
Malakwa	152	50 55N	118 50W
Malamyzh	77	50 0N	136 50 E
Malang	103	7 59 S	112 35 E
Malanje	124	9 30 S	16 17 E
Mälaren	72	59 30N	17 10 E
Malargüe	172	35 40 S	69 30W
Malartic	150	48 9N	78 9W
Malatya	92	38 25N	38 20 E
Malawi ■	127	13 0 S	34 0 E
Malawi, L. (Lago Niassa)	127	12 30 S	34 30 E
Malay Pen.	101	7 25N	100 0 E
*Malaya □	101	4 0N	102 0 E
Malaya Belözerka	82	47 12N	34 56 E
Malaya Vishera	80	58 55N	32 25 E
Malaybalay	103	8 5N	125 15 E
Malayer	92	34 19N	48 51 E
Malaysia ■	102	5 0N	110 0 E
*Malaysia, Western □	101	5 0N	102 0 E
Malazgirt	92	39 10N	42 33 E
Malbaie, La	151	47 40N	70 10W
Malbon	138	21 5 S	140 17 E
Malbooma	139	30 41 S	134 11 E
Malbork	54	54 3N	19 10 E
Malca Dube	123	6 40N	41 52 E
Malchin	48	53 43N	12 44 E
Malchow	48	53 29N	12 25 E
Malcolm	137	28 51 S	121 25 E
Malcolm, Pt., S. Australia, Austral.	109	34 52 S	138 29 E
Malcolm, Pt., W. Australia, Austral.	137	33 48 S	123 45 E
Malczyce	54	51 14N	16 29 E
Maldegem	47	51 14N	3 26 E
Malden, Mass., U.S.A.	162	42 26N	71 5W
Malden, Mo., U.S.A.	159	36 35N	90 0W
Malden I.	143	4 3 S	155 1W
Maldive Is. ■	86	2 0N	73 0W
Maldon, Austral.	140	37 0 S	144 6 E
Maldon, U.K.	29	51 43N	0 41 E
Maldonado	173	35 0 S	55 0W
Maldonado, Punta	165	16 19N	98 35W
Malé	62	46 20N	10 55 E
Malé Karpaty	53	48 30N	17 20 E
Malea, Ákra	69	36 28N	23 7 E
Malegaon	96	20 30N	74 30 E
Malei	127	17 12 S	36 58 E
Malela	126	4 22 S	26 8 E
Malenge	127	12 40 S	26 42 E
Målerås	73	56 54N	15 34 E
Malerkotla	94	30 32N	75 58 E
Máles	69	36 6N	25 35 E
Malesherbes	43	48 15N	2 24 E
Maleske Planina	66	41 38N	23 7 E
Malestroit	42	47 49N	2 25W
Malfa	65	38 35N	14 50 E
Malgobek	83	43 30N	44 52 E
Malgomaj L.	74	64 40N	16 30 E
Malgrat	58	41 39N	2 46 E
Malham Tarn	32	54 6N	2 11W
Malhão, Sa. do	55	37 25N	8 0W
Malheur L.	160	43 19N	118 42W
Malheur, R.	160	43 55N	117 55W
Mali	120	12 10N	12 20W
Mali ■	121	15 0N	10 0W
Mali H Ka R.	98	25 42N	97 30 E
Mali Kanal	66	45 36N	19 24 E
Mali Kyun, I.	101	13 0N	98 20 E
Mali, R.	99	26 20N	97 40 E
Malibu	163	34 2N	118 41W
Malih, Nahr al	90	32 20N	35 29 E
Malik	103	0 39 S	123 16 E
Malili	103	2 42 S	121 23 E
Malimba, Mts.	126	7 30 S	29 30 E
Malin, Ireland	38	55 18N	7 16W
Malin, U.S.S.R.	80	50 46N	29 15 E
Malin Hd.	38	55 18N	7 16W
Malin Pen.	38	55 20N	7 17W
Malinau	102	3 35N	116 30 E
Malindi	126	3 12 S	40 5 E
Maling, Mt.	103	1 0N	121 0 E
Malingping	103	6 45 S	106 2 E
Malinyi	127	8 56 S	36 0 E
Maliqi	68	40 45N	20 48 E
Malita	103	6 19N	125 39 E
Malkapur, Maharashtra, India	96	16 57N	74 0W
Malkapur, Maharashtra, India	96	20 53N	76 17 E
Małkinia Grn.	54	52 42N	21 58 E
Malko Turnovo	67	41 59N	27 31 E
Mallacoota	141	37 40 S	149 40 E
Mallacoota Inlet	141	37 40 S	149 40 E
Mallaha	90	33 6N	35 35 E
Mallaig	36	57 0N	5 50W
Mallala	140	34 26 S	138 30 E
Mallawan	95	27 4N	80 12 E
Mallawi	122	27 44N	30 44 E
Mallemort	45	43 44N	5 11 E
Málles Venosta	62	46 42N	10 32 E
Mállia	69	35 17N	25 27 E
Mallina P.O.	136	20 53 S	118 2 E
Mallorca, I.	58	39 30N	3 0 E
Mallow	39	52 8N	8 40W
Malltraeth B.	31	53 7N	4 30W
Mallwyd	31	52 43N	3 41W
Malmbäck	73	57 34N	14 28 E
Malmberget	74	67 11N	20 40 E
Malmèdy	47	50 25N	6 2 E
Malmesbury, S. Afr.	128	33 28 S	18 41 E
Malmesbury, U.K.	28	51 35N	2 5W
Malmö	75	55 36N	12 59 E
Malmöhus län □	73	55 45N	13 30 E
Malmslätt	73	58 27N	15 33 E
Malmyzh	84	56 31N	50 41 E
Malmyzh Mozhga	81	56 35N	50 30 E
Malnaş	70	46 2N	25 49 E
Malo Konare	67	42 12N	24 24 E
Maloarkhangelsk	81	52 28N	36 30 E
Maloja	51	46 25N	9 35 E
Maloja Pass	51	46 23N	9 42 E
Malolos	103	14 50N	121 2 E
Malomalsk	84	58 45N	59 53 E
Malombe L.	127	14 40 S	35 15 E
Malomir	67	42 16N	26 30 E
Malone	156	44 50N	74 19W
Malorad	67	43 28N	23 41 E
Malorita	80	51 41N	24 3 E
Maloyaroslovets	81	55 2N	36 20 E
Malozemelskaya Tundra	78	67 0N	50 0 E
Malpartida	57	39 26N	6 30W
Malpas	32	53 3N	2 47W
Malpelo I.	174	4 3N	80 35W
Malpica	56	43 19N	8 50W
Malprabha, R.	97	15 40N	74 50 E
Malta, Brazil	170	6 54 S	37 31W
Malta, Idaho, U.S.A.	160	42 15N	113 50W
Malta, Mont., U.S.A.	160	48 20N	107 55W
Malta ■	64	35 50N	14 0 E
Maltahöhe	125	24 55 S	17 0 E
Maltby	33	53 25N	1 12W
Malters	50	47 3N	8 11 E
Malton	33	54 9N	0 48W
Maluku □	103	3 0 S	128 0 E
Maluku, Kepulauan	103	3 0 S	128 0 E
Malumfashi	121	11 48N	7 39 E
Malung, China	108	25 18N	103 20 E
Malung, Sweden	72	60 42N	13 44 E
Malvalli	97	12 28N	77 8 E
Malvan	97	16 2N	73 30 E
Malvern, U.K.	28	52 7N	2 19W
Malvern, U.S.A.	159	34 22N	92 50W
Malvern Hills	28	52 0N	2 19W
Malvern Wells	28	52 4N	2 19W
Malvérnia	129	22 6 S	31 42 E
Malvik	71	63 25N	10 40 E
Malvinas Is. = Falkland Is.	174	51 30 S	59 0W
Malya	126	3 5 S	33 38 E
Malybay	85	43 30N	78 25 E
Mama	77	58 18N	112 54 E
Mamadysh	81	55 44N	51 23 E
Mamaia	70	44 18N	28 37 E
Mamaku	142	38 5 S	176 8 E
Mamanguape	170	6 50 S	35 4W
Mamasa	103	2 55 S	119 20 E
Mambasa	126	1 22N	29 3 E
Mamberamo, R.	103	2 0 S	137 50 E
Mambilima Falls	127	10 31 S	28 45 E
Mambirima	127	11 25 S	27 33 E
Mambo	126	4 52 S	38 22 E
Mambrui	126	3 5 S	40 5 E
Mameigwess L.	150	52 35N	87 50W
Mamer	47	49 38N	6 2 E
Mamers	42	48 21N	0 22 E
Mamfe	121	5 50N	9 15 E
Mammamattawa	150	50 25N	84 23W
Mâmmola	65	38 23N	16 13 E
Mammoth	161	32 46N	110 43W
Mamoré, R.	175	9 55 S	65 20W
Mamou	120	10 15N	12 0W
Mampatá	120	11 54N	14 53W
Mampawah	102	0 30N	109 5 E
Mampong	121	7 6N	1 26W
Mamuju	103	2 50 S	118 50 E
Man	120	7 30N	7 40W
Man, I. of	32	54 15N	4 30W
Man Na	98	23 27N	97 19 E
Man O' War Peak	151	56 58N	61 40W
Man, R.	96	17 20N	75 0 E
Man Tun	98	23 2N	98 38 E
Mana, Fr. Gui.	175	5 45N	53 55W
Mana, U.S.A.	147	22 3N	159 45W
Mana, R.	123	6 20N	40 41 E
Måna, R.	71	59 55N	8 50 E
Manaar, Gulf of	97	8 30N	79 0 E
Manacacias, R.	174	4 23N	72 4W
Manacapuru	174	3 10 S	60 50W
Manacles, The	30	50 3N	5 5W
Manacor	58	39 32N	3 12 E
Manage	47	50 31N	4 15 E
Managua	166	12 0N	86 20W
Managua, L.	166	12 20N	86 30W
Manaia	142	39 33 S	174 8 E
Manakana	129	13 45 S	50 4 E
Manakara	129	22 8 S	48 1 E
Manakau Mt.	143	42 15 S	173 42 E
Manam I.	135	4 5 S	145 0 E
Manamāh, Al	93	26 11N	50 35 E
Manambao, R.	129	17 35 S	44 45 E
Manambato	129	13 43 S	49 7 E
Manambolo, R.	129	19 20 S	45 0 E
Manambolosy	129	16 2 S	49 40 E
Mananara	129	16 10 S	49 30 E
Mananara, R.	129	23 25 S	48 10 E
Mananjary	129	21 13 S	48 20 E
Manantenina	129	24 17 S	47 19 E
Manaos = Manaus	174	3 0 S	60 0W
Manapouri	143	45 34 S	167 39 E
Manapouri, L.	143	45 32 S	167 32 E
Manar, R.	96	18 50N	77 20 E
Manas, Gora	85	42 22N	71 2 E
Manas, R.	99	26 12N	90 40 E
Manasarowar, L.	105	30 45N	81 20 E
Manasarowar L.	105	30 45N	81 20 E
Manasir	93	24 30N	51 10 E
Manaslu, Mt.	95	28 33N	84 33 E
Manasquan	162	40 7N	74 3W
Manassa	161	37 12N	105 58W
Manassas	162	38 45N	77 28W
Manassu	105	44 18N	86 13 E
Manati	147	18 26N	66 29W
Manaung Kyun	98	18 45N	93 40 E
Manaus	174	3 0 S	60 0W
Manawan L.	153	55 24N	103 14W
Manawatu, R.	142	40 28 S	175 12 E
Manay	103	7 17N	126 33 E
Manby	33	53 22N	0 6 E
Mancelona	156	44 54N	85 5W
Mancha, La	59	39 10N	2 54W
Mancha Real	57	37 48N	3 39W
Manchaster, L.	108	27 29 S	152 46 E
Manche □	42	49 10N	1 20W
Manchester, U.K.	32	53 30N	2 15W
Manchester, Conn., U.S.A.	162	41 47N	72 30W
Manchester, Ga., U.S.A.	157	32 53N	84 32W
Manchester, Iowa, U.S.A.	158	42 28N	91 27W
Manchester, Ky., U.S.A.	156	38 40N	83 45W
Manchester, N.H., U.S.A.	162	42 58N	71 29W
Manchester, Pa., U.S.A.	162	40 4N	76 43W
Manchester, Vt., U.S.A.	162	43 10N	73 5W
Manchester L.	153	61 28N	107 29W
Manchouli	105	49 46N	117 24 E
Manchuria = Tung Pei	107	44 0N	126 0 E
Manciano	63	42 35N	11 30 E
Mancifa	123	6 53N	41 50 E
Mand, R.	93	28 20N	52 30 E
Manda, Chunya, Tanz.	127	6 51 S	32 29 E
Manda, Jombe, Tanz.	127	10 30 S	34 40 E
Mandabé	125	21 0 S	44 55 E
Mandaguari	173	23 32 S	51 42W
Mandah	106	44 27N	108 20 E
Mandal	71	58 2N	7 25 E
Mandalay	99	22 0N	96 10 E
Mandalay = Mandale	98	22 0N	96 10 E
Mandale	99	22 0N	96 10 E
Mandalgovi	106	45 45N	106 20 E
Mandali	92	33 52N	45 28 E
Mandalya Körfezi	69	37 15N	27 20 E
Mandan	158	46 50N	101 0W
Mandapeta	96	16 47N	81 56 E
Mandar, Teluk	103	3 35 S	119 4 E
Mandas	64	39 40N	9 8 E
Mandasaur	93	24 3N	75 8 E
Mandasor (Mandsaur)	94	24 3N	75 8 E
Mandawai (Katingan), R.	102	1 30 S	113 0 E
Mandelieu-la-Napoule	45	43 34N	6 57 E
Mandera	126	3 55N	41 42 E
Mandera □	126	3 30N	41 0 E
Manderfeld	47	50 20N	6 20 E
Mandi, India	94	31 39N	76 58 E
Mandi, Zambia	127	14 30 S	23 45 E
Mandimba	125	14 20 S	35 40 E
Mandioli	103	0 40 S	127 20 E
Mandla	95	22 39N	80 30 E
Mandø	73	55 18N	8 33 E
Mandoto	129	19 34 S	46 17 E
Mandoúdhion	69	38 48N	23 29 E
Mandra	94	33 23N	73 12 E
Mandráki	69	36 36N	27 11 E
Mandrase, R.	129	25 10 S	46 30 E
Mandritsara	129	15 50 S	48 49 E
Mandsaur (Mandasor)	94	24 3N	75 8 E
Mandurah	137	32 36 S	115 48 E
Mandúria	65	40 25N	17 38 E
Mandvi	96	22 51N	69 22 E
Mandya	97	12 30N	77 0 E
Mandzai	94	30 55N	67 6 E
Mané	121	12 59N	1 21W
Manea	29	52 29N	0 10 E
Maner, R.	97	18 30N	79 40 E
Maneroo	138	23 22 S	143 53 E
Maneroo Cr.	138	23 21 S	143 53 E
Manfalût	122	27 20N	30 52 E
Manfred	140	33 19 S	143 45 E
Manfredónia	65	41 40N	15 55 E
Manfredónia, G. di	65	41 30N	16 10 E
Manga, Brazil	171	14 46 S	43 56W
Manga, Upp. Vol.	121	11 40N	1 4W
Mangabeiras, Chapada das	170	10 0 S	46 30W
Mangahan	142	40 26 S	175 48 E
Mangalagiri	96	16 26N	80 36 E
Mangaldai	98	26 26N	92 2 E
Mangalia	70	43 50N	28 35 E
Mangalore, Austral.	141	36 56 S	145 10 E
Mangalore, India	97	12 55N	74 47 E
Manganeses	56	41 45N	5 43W
Mangaon	96	18 15N	73 20 E
Manger	71	60 38N	5 3W
Mangerton Mt.	39	51 59N	9 30W
Manggar	102	2 50 S	108 10 E
Manggawitu	103	4 8 S	133 32 E
Mangin Range	98	24 15N	95 45 E
Mangla Dam	95	33 32N	73 50 E
Manglaur	94	29 44N	77 49 E
Mangoche	125	14 25 S	35 16 E
Mangoky, R.	129	21 55 S	44 40 E
Mangole I.	103	1 50 S	125 55 E
Mangombe	126	1 20 S	26 48 E
Mangonui	142	35 1 S	173 32 E
Mangotsfield	28	51 29N	2 29W
Mangualde	56	40 38N	7 48W
Mangueigne	117	10 40N	21 5 E
Mangueira, Lagoa da	173	33 0 S	52 50W
Manguéni, Hamada	119	22 47N	12 56 E
Mangum	159	34 50N	99 30W
Mangyai	105	37 50N	91 38 E
Mangyshlak P-ov.	83	43 40N	52 30 E
Manhattan, Kans., U.S.A.	158	39 10N	96 40W
Manhattan, Nev., U.S.A.	163	38 31N	117 3W
Manhiça	129	25 23 S	32 49 E
Manhuaçu	171	20 15 S	42 2W
Manhui	106	41 1N	107 14 E
Manhumirim	171	20 22 S	41 57W
Mani	99	34 52N	87 11 E
Maní	174	4 49N	72 17W
Mania, R.	129	19 55 S	46 10 E
Maniago	63	46 11N	12 40 E
Manica	127	18 58 S	32 59 E
Manica e Sofala □	129	19 10 S	33 45 E
Manicaland □	127	19 0 S	32 30 E
Manicoré	174	6 0 S	61 10W
Manicouagan L.	151	51 25N	68 15W
Manicouagan, R.	151	49 30N	68 30W
Manifah	92	27 30N	49 0 E
Manifold	138	22 41 S	150 40 E
Manigotagan	153	51 6N	96 8W
Manigotagan L.	153	50 52N	95 37W
Manihiki I.	131	10 24 S	161 1W
Manika, Plat. de	127	10 0 S	25 5 E
Manikganj	98	23 52N	90 0 E
Manila, Phil.	103	14 40N	121 3 E
Manila, U.S.A.	160	41 0N	109 44W
Manila B.	103	14 0N	120 0 E
Manilla	141	30 45 S	150 43 E
Manimpé	120	14 11N	5 28W
Maningory	129	17 9 S	49 30 E
Manipur □	98	24 30N	94 0 E
Manipur, R.	98	23 45N	93 40 E
Manisa	92	38 38N	27 30 E
Manistee	156	44 15N	86 20W
Manistee, R.	156	44 15N	86 21W
Manistique	156	45 59N	86 18W
Manito L.	153	52 43N	109 43W
Manitoba □	153	55 30N	97 0W
Manitoba, L.	153	51 0N	98 45W
Manitou	153	49 15N	98 32W
Manitou I.	150	47 22N	87 30W

* *Renamed Peninsular Malaysia*
† *Renamed Butaritari*

Manitou Is Marosakoa

Manitou Is. 156 45 8N 86 0W
Manitou L., Ont., Can. 153 49 15N 93 0W
Manitou L., Qué., Can. 151 50 55N 65 17W
Manitoulin I. 150 45 40N 82 30W
Manitowaning 150 45 46N 81 49W
Manitowoc 156 44 8N 87 40W
Manizales 174 5 5N 75 32W
Manja 129 21 26S 44 20E
Manjacaze 125 24 45S 34 0E
Manjakandriana 129 18 55S 47 47E
Manjeri 97 11 7N 76 11E
Manjhand 94 25 50N 68 10E
Manjil 92 36 46N 49 30E
Manjimup 137 34 15S 116 6E
Manjra, R. 96 18 20N 77 20E
Mankaiana 129 26 38S 31 6E
Mankato, Kans., U.S.A. 158 39 49N 98 11W
Mankato, Minn., U.S.A. 158 44 8N 93 59W
Mankono 120 8 10N 6 10W
Mankota 153 49 25N 107 5W
Manlay 106 44 9N 106 50E
Manlleu 58 42 2N 2 17E
Manly, N.S.W., Austral. 141 33 48S 151 17E
Manly, Queens., Austral. 108 27 27S 153 11E
Manmad 96 20 18N 74 28E
Mann Ranges, Mts. 137 26 6S 130 5E
Manna 102 4 25S 102 55E
Mannahill 140 32 25S 140 0E
Mannar 97 9 1N 79 54E
Mannar, G. of 97 8 30N 79 0E
Mannar I. 97 9 5N 79 45E
Mannargudi 97 10 45N 79 32E
Männedorf 51 47 15N 8 43E
Mannheim 49 49 28N 8 29E
Manning, Can. 152 56 53N 117 39W
Manning, U.S.A. 157 33 40N 80 9W
Manning Prov. Park 152 49 5N 120 45W
Mannington 156 39 35N 80 25W
Manningtree 29 51 56N 1 3E
Mannu, C. 64 40 2N 8 24E
Mannu, R. 64 39 35N 8 56E
Mannum 140 34 57S 139 12E
Mano 120 8 3N 12 12W
Manokwari 103 0 54S 134 0E
Manolás 69 38 4N 21 21E
Manombo 129 22 57S 43 28E
Manono 124 7 15S 27 25E
Manorbier 31 51 38N 4 48W
Manorhamilton 38 54 19N 8 11W
Manosque 45 43 49N 5 47E
Manouane L. 151 50 45N 70 45W
Manpojin 107 41 6N 126 24E
Manresa 58 41 48N 1 50E
Mans, Le 42 48 0N 0 10E
Mansa, Gujarat, India 94 23 27N 72 45E
Mansa, Punjab, India 94 30 0N 75 27E
Mansa, Zambia 127 11 13S 28 55E
Mansel I. 149 62 0N 79 50W
Mansenra 94 34 20N 73 11E
Mansfield, Austral. 141 37 4S 146 6E
Mansfield, U.K. 33 53 8N 1 12W
Mansfield, La., U.S.A. 159 32 2N 93 40W
Mansfield, Mass., U.S.A. 162 42 2N 71 12W
Mansfield, Ohio, U.S.A. 156 40 45N 82 30W
Mansfield, Pa., U.S.A. 162 41 48N 77 4W
Mansfield, Wash., U.S.A. 160 47 51N 119 44W
Mansfield Woodhouse 33 53 11N 1 11W
Mansi 98 24 40N 95 44E
Mansidão 170 10 43S 44 2W
Mansilla de las Mulas 56 42 30N 5 25W
Mansle 44 45 52N 0 9E
Manso, R. 171 14 0S 52 0W
Mansôa 120 12 0N 15 20W
Manson Cr. 152 55 37N 124 25W
Mansoura, Djebel 119 36 1N 4 31E
Manta 174 1 0S 80 40W
Mantalingajan, Mt. 102 8 55N 117 45E
Mantare 126 2 42S 33 13E
Manteca 163 37 50N 121 12W
Mantecal 174 7 34N 69 17W
Mantekomu Hu 99 34 40N 89 0E
Mantena 171 18 47S 40 59W
Manteo 157 35 55N 75 41W
Mantes-la-Jolie 43 49 0N 1 41E
Manthani 96 18 40N 79 35E
Manthelan 42 47 9N 0 47E
Manti 160 39 23N 111 32W
Mantiqueira, Serra da 173 22 0S 44 0W
Manton, U.K. 29 52 37N 0 41W
Manton, U.S.A. 156 44 23N 85 25W
Mantorp 73 58 21N 15 20E
Mántova 62 45 10N 10 47E
Mänttä 74 62 0N 24 40E
Mantua = Mántova 62 45 10N 10 47E
Mantung 140 34 35S 140 3E
Manturova 81 58 10N 44 30E
Manu 174 12 10S 71 0W
Manucan 103 8 14N 123 3E
Manuel Alves Grande, R. 170 7 27S 47 35W
Manuel Alves, R. 171 11 19S 48 28W
Manui I. 103 3 35S 123 5E
Manukau 142 37 1S 174 55E
Manukau Harbour 142 37 3S 174 45E
Manunui 142 38 54S 175 21E
Manus I. 135 2 0S 147 0E
Manvi 97 15 57N 76 59E
Manville, R.I., U.S.A. 162 41 58N 71 28W
Manville, Wyo., U.S.A. 158 42 48N 104 36W
Manwath 96 19 19N 76 32E
Many 159 31 36N 93 28W
Manyane 128 23 21S 21 42E
Manyara L. 126 3 40S 35 50E
Manych-Gudilo, Oz. 83 46 24N 42 38E
Manych, R. 83 47 0N 41 15E
Manyonga, R. 126 4 5S 34 0E
Manyoni 126 5 45S 34 55E
Manyoni □ 126 6 30S 34 30E
Manzai 94 32 20N 70 15E
Manzala, Bahra el 122 31 10N 31 56E
Manzanares 59 39 0N 3 22W
Manzaneda, Cabeza de 56 42 12N 7 15W
Manzanillo, Cuba 166 20 20N 77 10W
Manzanillo, Mexico 164 19 0N 104 20W
Manzanillo, Pta. 166 9 30N 79 40W
Manzano Mts. 161 34 30N 106 45W
Manzini 129 26 30S 31 25E
Mao 117 14 4N 15 19E
Maohsing 107 45 31N 124 32E
Maoke, Pengunungan 102 3 40S 137 30E
Maolin 107 43 55N 123 25E
Maoming 109 21 39N 110 54E
Maopi T'ou 109 21 56N 120 43E
Maoping 109 30 51N 110 54E
Maowen 108 31 41N 103 52E
Mapastepec 165 15 26N 92 54W
Mapia, Kepulauan 103 0 50N 134 20E
Mapien 108 28 48N 103 39E
Mapimí 164 25 50N 103 31W
Mapimí, Bolsón de 164 27 30N 103 15W
Map'ing 109 31 36N 113 33E
Mapinga 126 6 40S 39 12E
Mapinhane 129 22 20S 35 0E
Maple Creek 153 49 55N 109 29W
Mapleton 160 44 4N 123 58W
Maplewood 158 38 33N 90 18W
Mappinga 109 34 58S 138 52E
Maprik 135 3 44S 143 3E
Mapuca 97 15 36N 73 46E
Mapuera, R. 174 0 30S 58 25W
Maputo 129 25 58S 32 32E
Maqnā 92 28 25N 34 50E
Maquela do Zombo 124 6 0S 15 15E
Maquinchao 176 41 15S 68 50W
Maquoketa 158 42 4N 90 40W
Mar Chiquita, L. 172 30 40S 62 50W
Mar del Plata 172 38 0S 57 30W
Mar Menor, L. 59 37 40N 0 45W
Mar, Reg. 37 57 11N 2 53W
Mar, Serra do 173 25 30S 49 0W
Mara, Bangla. 98 28 11N 94 7E
Mara, Tanz. 126 1 30S 34 32E
Mara □, Tanz. 126 1 45S 34 20E
Mara □, Tanz. 126 1 30S 34 32E
Maraã 174 1 43S 65 25W
Marabá 170 5 20S 49 5W
Maracá, I. de 170 2 10N 50 30W
Maracaibo 174 10 40N 71 37W
Maracaibo, Lago de 174 9 40N 71 30W
Maracaju 173 21 38S 55 9W
Maracanã 170 0 46S 47 27W
Maracás 171 13 26S 40 27W
Maracay 174 10 15N 67 36W
Marādah 119 29 4N 19 4E
Maradi 121 13 35N 8 10E
Maradun 121 12 35N 6 18E
Marāgheh 92 37 30N 46 12E
Maragogipe 171 12 46S 38 55W
Marajó, B. de 170 1 0S 48 30W
Marajó, Ilha de 170 1 0S 49 30W
Maralal 124 1 0N 36 38E
Maralinga 137 29 45S 131 15E
Marama 140 35 10S 140 10E
Marampa 120 8 45N 10 28W
Maramureş □ 70 47 45N 24 0E
Maran 101 3 35N 102 45E
Marana 161 32 30N 111 9W
Maranboy 136 14 40S 132 40E
Maranchón 58 41 6N 2 15W
Marand 92 38 30N 45 45E
Marandellas 127 18 5S 31 42E
Maranguape 170 3 55S 38 50W
Maranhão = São Luis 170 2 31S 44 16W
Maranhão □ 170 5 0S 46 0W
Marañón, R. 174 4 50S 75 35W
Marano, L. di 63 45 42N 13 13E
Maranoa R. 139 27 50S 148 37E
Maraş 92 37 37N 36 53E
Mărăşeşti 70 45 52N 27 5E
Maratea 65 39 59N 15 43E
Marateca 57 38 34N 8 40W
Marathókambos 69 37 43N 26 42E
Marathon, Austral. 138 20 51S 143 32E
Marathon, Can. 150 48 44N 86 23W
Marathón 69 38 11N 23 58E
Marathon, N.Y., U.S.A. 162 42 25N 76 3W
Marathon, Tex., U.S.A. 159 30 15N 103 15W
Maratua, I. 103 2 10N 118 35E
Maraú 171 14 6S 39 0W
Marazion 30 50 8N 5 29W
Marbat 91 17 0N 54 45E
Marbella 57 36 30N 4 57W
Marble Bar 136 21 9S 119 44E
Marble Falls 159 30 30N 98 15W
Marblehead 162 42 29N 70 51W
Marburg 48 50 49N 8 44E
Marby 72 63 7N 14 18E
Marcal, R. 53 47 21N 17 15E
Marcali 53 46 35N 17 25E
Marcaria 62 45 7N 10 34E
March 29 52 33N 0 5E
Marchand = Rommani 118 33 20N 6 40W
Marché 44 46 0N 1 20E
Marche □ 63 43 22N 13 10E
Marche-en-Famenne 47 50 14N 5 19E
Marchena 57 37 18N 5 23W
Marches = Marche 63 43 22N 13 10E
Marciana Marina 62 42 44N 10 12E
Marcianise 65 41 3N 14 16E
Marcigny 45 46 17N 4 2E
Marcillac-Vallon 44 44 29N 2 27E
Marcillat 44 46 12N 2 38E
Marcinelle 47 50 24N 4 26E
Marck 43 50 57N 1 57E
Marckolsheim 43 48 10N 7 30E
Marcos Juárez 172 32 42S 62 5W
Marcus I. 130 24 0N 153 45E
Mardan 94 34 20N 72 0E
Marden 28 52 7N 2 42W
Mardie 136 21 12S 115 59E
Mardin 92 37 20N 40 36E
Marechal Deodoro 170 9 43S 35 54W
Maree L. 36 57 40N 5 30W
Mareeba 138 16 59S 145 28E
Mareham le Fen 33 53 7N 0 3W
Marek 103 4 41S 120 24E
Marek = Stanke Dimitrov 66 42 27N 23 9E
Maremma 62 42 45N 11 15E
Maréna 120 14 0N 7 30W
Marenberg 63 46 38N 15 13E
Marengo 158 41 42N 92 5W
Marennes 126 45 49N 1 5W
Marenyi 126 4 22S 39 8E
Marerano 129 21 23S 44 52E
Marèttimo, I. 64 37 58N 12 5E
Mareuil-sur-Lay 44 46 32N 1 14W
Marfa 159 30 15N 104 0W
Marfleet 33 53 45N 0 15W
Margable 123 12 54N 42 38E
Margam 31 51 33N 3 45W
Marganets 82 47 40N 34 40E
Margao 97 14 12N 73 58E
Margaree Harbour 151 46 26N 61 8W
Margaret Bay 152 51 20N 127 20W
Margaret L. 152 58 56N 115 25W
Margaret, R. 136 12 57S 131 16E
Margaret River 137 33 57S 115 7E
Margarita, Isla de 174 11 0N 64 0W
Margarition 68 39 22N 20 26E
Margate, S. Afr. 129 30 50S 30 20E
Margate, U.K. 29 51 23N 1 24E
Margate City 162 39 20N 74 31W
Margelan 85 40 27N 71 42E
Margeride, Mts. de la 44 44 43N 3 38E
Margherita 98 27 16N 95 40E
Margherita di Savola 65 41 25N 16 5E
Marghita 70 47 22N 22 22E
Margonin 54 52 58N 17 5E
Margreten 47 50 49N 5 49E
Marguerite 152 52 30N 122 25W
Marhoum 118 34 27N 0 11W
Mari, A.S.S.R. □ 81 56 30N 48 0E
María Elena 172 22 18S 69 40W
María Grande 172 31 45S 59 55W
Maria, I. 138 14 52S 135 45E
Maria I. 138 42 35S 148 0E
Maria van Diemen, C. 142 34 29S 172 40E
Mariager 73 56 40N 10 0E
Mariager Fjord 73 56 42N 10 19E
Mariakani 126 3 50S 39 27E
Marian L. 152 63 0N 116 15W
Mariana 171 20 23S 43 25W
Mariana Is. 130 17 0N 145 0E
Mariana Trench 130 13 0N 145 0W
Marianao 166 23 8N 82 24W
Mariani 98 26 39N 94 19E
Marianna, Ark., U.S.A. 159 34 48N 90 48W
Marianna, Fla., U.S.A. 157 30 45N 85 15W
Mariannelund 73 57 37N 15 35E
Mariánské Lázně 52 49 57N 12 41E
Marias, R. 160 48 26N 111 40W
Mariato, Punta 166 7 12N 80 52W
Mariazell 52 47 47N 15 19E
Marib 91 15 25N 45 20E
Maribo 73 54 48N 11 30E
Maribor 63 46 36N 15 40E
Marico, R. 128 24 25S 26 30E
Maricopa, Ariz., U.S.A. 161 33 5N 112 2W
Maricopa, Calif., U.S.A. 163 35 7N 119 27W
Marîdî 123 4 55N 29 25E
Marîdî, W. 123 5 25N 29 21E
Marie Galante, I. 167 15 56N 61 16W
Mariecourt 149 61 30N 72 0W
Mariefred 72 59 15N 17 12E
Mariehamn (Maarianhamina) 75 60 5N 19 57E
Marienberg, Ger. 48 50 40N 13 10E
Marienberg, Neth. 47 52 30N 6 35E
Marienberg, P.N.G. 138 3 54S 144 10E
Marienbourg 47 50 6N 4 31E
Mariental 128 24 36S 18 0E
Mariestad 73 58 43N 13 50E
Marietta, Ga., U.S.A. 157 34 0N 84 30W
Marietta, Ohio, U.S.A. 156 39 27N 81 27W
Marignane 45 43 25N 5 13E
Mariinsk 76 56 10N 87 20E
Mariinskiy Posad 81 56 10N 47 45E
Marília 173 22 0S 50 0W
Marillana 136 22 37S 119 24E
Marín 56 42 23N 8 42W
Marina 163 36 41N 121 48W
Marina di Cirò 65 39 22N 17 8E
Mariña, La 56 43 30N 7 40W
Marina Plains 138 14 37S 143 57E
Marinduque, I. 103 13 25N 122 0E
Marine City 156 42 45N 82 29W
Marinel, Le 127 10 25S 25 17E
Marineo 64 37 57N 13 23E
Marinette, Ariz., U.S.A. 161 33 41N 112 16W
Marinette, Wis., U.S.A. 156 45 4N 87 40W
Maringá 173 23 35S 51 50W
Marinha Grande 57 39 45N 8 56W
Marino 109 35 3S 138 31E
Marino Rocks 109 35 3S 138 31E
Marion, Austral. 109 34 59S 138 33E
Marion, Ala., U.S.A. 157 32 33N 87 20W
Marion, Ill., U.S.A. 159 37 45N 88 55W
Marion, Ind., U.S.A. 156 40 35N 85 40W
Marion, Iowa, U.S.A. 158 42 2N 91 36W
Marion, Kans., U.S.A. 158 38 25N 97 2W
Marion, Mich., U.S.A. 156 44 7N 85 8W
Marion, N.C., U.S.A. 157 35 42N 82 0W
Marion, Ohio, U.S.A. 156 40 38N 83 8W
Marion, S.C., U.S.A. 157 34 11N 79 22W
Marion, Va., U.S.A. 157 36 51N 81 29W
Marion Bay 140 35 12S 136 59E
Marion, L. 157 33 30N 80 15W
Marion Reef 138 19 10S 152 17E
Maripa 174 7 26N 65 9W
Mariposa 163 37 31N 119 59W
Mariscal Estigarribia 172 22 3S 60 40W
Maritime Alps = Alpes Maritimes 62 44 10N 7 10E
Maritsa 67 42 1N 25 50E
Maritsá 69 36 22N 28 10E
Maritsa, R. 67 42 15N 24 0E
Mariyampole = Kapsukas 80 54 33N 23 19E
Marjan 93 32 5N 68 20E
Mark 34 55 2N 5 1W
Marka 122 18 14N 41 19E
Markapur 97 15 44N 79 19E
Markaryd 73 56 28N 13 35E
Marke 47 50 48N 3 14E
Marked Tree 159 35 35N 90 24W
Markelo 46 52 14N 6 30E
Markelsdorfer Huk 48 54 33N 11 0E
Marken 46 52 26N 5 12E
Markerwaard 46 52 33N 5 15E
Market Bosworth 28 52 37N 1 24W
Market Deeping 29 52 40N 0 20W
Market Drayton 32 52 55N 2 30W
Market Harborough 29 52 29N 0 55W
Market Lavington 28 51 17N 1 59W
Market Rasen 33 53 24N 0 20W
Market Weighton 33 53 52N 0 40W
Markethill 38 54 18N 6 31W
Markfield 28 52 42N 1 18W
Markham I. 12 84 0N 0 45W
Markham L. 153 62 30N 102 35W
Markham Mts. 13 83 0S 164 0E
Markham, R. 135 6 41S 147 2E
Marki 54 52 20N 21 2E
Markinch 35 56 12N 3 9W
Markleeville 163 38 42N 119 47W
Markoupoulon 69 37 53N 23 57E
Markovac 66 44 14N 21 7E
Markovo 77 64 40N 169 40E
Markoye 121 14 39N 0 2E
Marks 81 51 45N 46 50E
Marks Tey 29 51 53N 0 48E
Marksville 159 31 10N 92 2W
Markt Schwaben 49 48 14N 11 49E
Marktredwitz 49 50 1N 12 2E
Marlboro, Can. 152 53 30N 116 50W
Marlboro, U.S.A. 162 42 19N 71 33W
Marlboro, N.Y., U.S.A. 162 41 36N 73 58W
Marlborough, Austral. 138 22 46S 149 52E
Marlborough, U.K. 28 51 26N 1 44W
Marlborough □ 143 41 45S 173 33E
Marlborough Downs 28 51 25N 1 55W
Marle 43 49 43N 3 47E
Marlin 159 31 25N 96 50W
Marlow, Austral. 141 35 17S 149 55E
Marlow, Ger. 48 54 8N 12 34E
Marlow, U.K. 29 51 34N 0 47W
Marlow, U.S.A. 159 34 40N 97 58W
Marly-le-Grand 50 46 47N 7 10E
Marmagao 97 15 25N 73 56E
Marmande 44 44 30N 0 10E
Marmara denizi 92 40 45N 28 15E
Marmara, I. 82 40 35N 27 38E
Marmara, Sea of = Marmara denizi 92 40 45N 28 15E
Marmaris 92 36 50N 28 14E
Marmarth 158 46 21N 103 52W
Marmion L. 150 48 55N 91 30W
Marmion Mt. 137 29 16S 119 50E
Marmolada, Mte. 63 46 25N 11 55E
Marmolejo 57 38 3N 4 13W
Marmora 150 44 28N 77 41W
Marnay 43 47 20N 5 48E
Marne 48 53 57N 9 1E
Marne □ 43 49 0N 4 10E
Marne, R. 43 48 53N 4 25E
Marnhull 28 50 58N 2 20W
Maro 124 8 30N 19 0E
Maroa 174 2 43N 67 33W
Maroala 129 15 23S 47 59E
Maroantsetra 129 15 26S 49 44E
Marocco ■ 129 32 0N 5 50W
Maromandia 129 14 13S 48 5E
Maroni, R. 175 4 0N 52 0W
Marónia 68 40 53N 25 24E
Maroochydore 139 26 29S 153 5E
Maroona 140 37 27S 142 54E
Maros, R. 53 46 25N 20 20E
Marosakoa 129 15 26S 46 38E

Marostica Maya, R

Marostica	63	45 44N	11 40 E
Maroua	121	10 40N	14 20 E
Marovoay	129	16 6 S	46 39 E
Marple	32	53 23N	2 5W
Marquard	128	28 40 S	27 28 E
Marqueira	57	38 41N	9 9W
Marquesas Is. = Marquises	131	9 30 S	140 0W
Marquette	156	46 30N	87 21W
Marquise	43	50 50N	1 40 E
Marquises, Is.	131	9 30 S	140 0W
Marra	139	31 12 S	144 10 E
Marra, Gebet	123	7 20N	27 35 E
Marradi	63	44 5N	11 37 E
Marrakech	118	31 40N	8 0W
Marrat	92	25 0N	45 35 E
Marrawah	138	40 55 S	144 42 E
Marrecas, Serra das	170	9 0 S	41 0W
Marree	139	29 39 S	138 1 E
Marrimane	129	22 58 S	33 34 E
Marromeu	125	18 40 S	36 25 E
Marroqui, Punta	56	36 0N	5 37W
Marrowie Creek	141	33 23 S	145 40 E
Marrubane	127	18 0 S	37 0 E
Marrum	46	53 19N	5 48 E
Marrupa	127	13 8 S	37 30 E
Mars, Le	158	43 0N	96 0W
Marsa Susa (Apollonia)	117	32 52N	21 59 E
Marsabit	126	2 18N	38 0 E
Marsabit □	126	2 45N	37 45 E
Marsala	64	37 48N	12 25 E
Marsciano	63	42 54N	12 20 E
Marsden	141	33 47N	147 32 E
Marsdiep	46	52 58N	4 46 E
Marseillan	44	43 23N	3 31 E
Marseille	45	43 18N	5 23 E
Marseilles = Marseille	45	43 18N	5 23 E
Marsh I.	159	29 35N	91 50W
Marshall, Liberia	120	6 8N	10 22W
Marshall, Ark., U.S.A.	159	35 58N	92 40W
Marshall, Mich., U.S.A.	156	42 17N	84 59W
Marshall, Minn., U.S.A.	158	44 25N	95 45W
Marshall, Mo., U.S.A.	158	39 8N	93 15W
Marshall, Tex., U.S.A.	159	32 29N	94 20W
Marshall Is.	130	9 0N	171 0 E
Marshall, R.	138	22 59 S	136 59 E
Marshalltown	158	42 0N	93 0W
Marshfield, U.K.	28	51 27N	2 18W
Marshfield, Mo., U.S.A.	159	37 20N	92 58W
Marshfield, Wis., U.S.A.	158	44 42N	90 10W
Mársico Nuovo	65	40 26N	15 43 E
Marske by the sea	33	54 35N	1 0W
Märsta	72	59 37N	17 52 E
Marstal	73	54 51N	10 30 E
Marston Moor	33	53 58N	1 17W
Marstrand	73	57 53N	11 35 E
Mart	159	31 34N	96 51W
Marta, R.	63	42 18N	11 47 E
Martaban	98	16 30N	97 35 E
Martaban, G. of	98	15 40N	96 30 E
Martano	65	40 14N	18 18 E
Martapura	102	3 22 S	114 56 E
Marte	121	12 23N	13 46 E
Martebo	73	57 45N	18 30 E
Martelange	47	49 49N	5 43 E
Martés, Sierra	59	39 20N	1 0W
Marthaguy Creek	141	30 50 S	147 45 E
Martham	29	52 42N	1 38 E
Martha's Vineyard	162	41 25N	70 35W
Martigné Ferchaud	42	47 50N	1 20W
Martigny	50	46 6N	7 3 E
Martigues	45	43 24N	5 4 E
Martil	118	35 36N	5 15W
Martin, Czech.	53	49 6N	18 48 E
Martin, S.D., U.S.A.	158	43 11N	101 45W
Martin, Tenn., U.S.A.	159	36 23N	88 51W
Martin, L.	157	32 45N	85 50W
Martin, R.	58	41 2N	0 43W
Martina	51	46 53N	10 28 E
Martina Franca	65	40 42N	17 20 E
Martinborough	142	41 14 S	175 29 E
Martinez	163	38 1N	122 8W
Martinho Campos	171	19 20 S	45 13W
Martinique, I.	167	14 40N	61 0W
Martinique Passage	167	15 15N	61 0W
Martinon	69	38 25N	23 15 E
Martinópolis	173	22 11 S	51 12W
Martins	171	6 5 S	37 55W
Martinsberg	52	48 22N	15 9 E
Martinsburg	156	39 30N	77 57W
Martinsville, Ind., U.S.A.	156	39 29N	86 23W
Martinsville, Va., U.S.A.	157	36 41N	79 52W
Martley	28	52 14N	2 22W
Martock	28	50 58N	2 47W
Marton	142	40 4 S	175 23 E
Martorell	58	41 28N	1 56 E
Martos	57	37 44N	3 58W
Martre, La, L.	148	63 8N	117 16W
Martre, La, R.	148	63 0N	118 0W
Martuk	84	50 46N	56 31 E
Martuni	83	40 9N	45 10 E
Maru	121	12 22N	6 22 E
Marudi	102	4 10N	114 25 E
Maruf	93	31 30N	67 0 E
Marugame	110	34 15N	133 55 E
Maruggio	65	40 20N	17 33 E
Marui	135	4 4 S	143 2 E
Maruim	170	10 45 S	37 5W
Marulan	141	34 43 S	150 3 E
Marum	46	53 9N	6 16 E
Marunga	128	17 20 S	20 2 E
Marungu, Mts.	126	7 30 S	30 0 E
Maruoka	111	36 9N	136 16 E
Marvejols	44	44 33N	3 19 E
Marvine Mt.	161	38 44N	111 40W
Marwar	94	25 43N	73 45 E
Mary	76	37 40N	61 50 E
Mary Frances L.	153	63 19N	106 13W
Mary Kathleen	138	20 35 S	139 48 E
Maryborough, Queens., Austral.	139	25 31 S	152 37 E
Maryborough, Vic., Austral.	140	37 0 S	143 44 E
Maryets	81	56 17N	49 47 E
Maryfield	153	49 50N	101 35W
Marykirk	37	56 47N	2 30W
Maryland □	156	39 10N	76 40W
Maryland Jc.	127	12 45 S	30 31 E
Maryport	32	54 43N	3 30W
Mary's Harbour	151	52 18N	55 51W
Marystown	151	47 10N	55 10W
Marysvale	161	38 25N	112 17W
Marysville, Can.	152	49 35N	116 0W
Marysville, Calif., U.S.A.	160	39 14N	121 40W
Marysville, Kans., U.S.A.	158	39 50N	96 38W
Marysville, Ohio, U.S.A.	156	40 15N	83 20W
Marytavy	30	50 34N	4 6W
Maryvale	139	28 4 S	152 12 E
Maryville	157	35 50N	84 0W
Marywell	37	56 35N	2 31W
Marzo, Punta	174	6 50N	77 42W
Marzuq	119	25 53N	14 10 E
Masada = Mesada	90	31 20N	35 19 E
Masafa	127	13 50 S	27 30 E
Masai	101	1 29N	103 55 E
Masai Steppe	126	4 30 S	36 30 E
Masaka	126	0 21 S	31 45 E
Masakali	121	13 2N	12 32 E
Masalima, Kepulauan	102	5 10 S	116 50 E
Masamba	103	2 30 S	120 15 E
Masan	107	35 11N	128 32 E
Masanasa	59	39 25N	0 25W
Masandam, Ras	93	26 30N	56 30 E
Masasi	127	10 45 S	38 52 E
Masasi □	127	10 45 S	38 50 E
Masaya	166	12 0N	86 7W
Masba	121	10 35N	13 1 E
Mascara	118	35 26N	0 6 E
Mascota	164	20 30N	104 50W
Masela	103	8 9 S	129 51 E
Maseme	147	18 46 S	25 3 E
Maseru	128	29 18 S	27 30 E
Mashaba	127	20 2 S	30 29 E
Mashabih	92	25 35N	36 30 E
Masham	33	54 15N	1 40W
Mashan	108	23 44N	108 14 E
Masherbrum, mt.	95	35 38N	76 18 E
Mashhad	93	36 20N	59 35 E
Mashi	121	13 0N	7 54 E
Mashiki	110	32 51N	130 53 E
Mashki Chah	93	29 5N	62 30 E
Mashkode	150	47 2N	84 7W
Mashonaland, North, □	127	16 30 S	30 0 E
Mashonaland, South, □	127	18 0 S	31 30 E
Mashtagi	83	40 35N	50 0 E
Masi	74	69 26N	23 50 E
Masi-Manimba	124	4 40 S	18 5 E
Masindi	126	1 40N	31 43 E
Masindi Port	126	1 43N	32 2 E
Masirah	91	20 25N	58 50 E
Masisea	174	8 35 S	74 15W
Masisi	126	1 23 S	28 49 E
Masjed Solyman	92	31 55N	49 25 E
Mask, L.	38	53 36N	9 24W
Maski	97	15 56N	76 46 E
Maslen Nos	67	42 18N	27 48 E
Maslinica	63	43 24N	16 13 E
Masnou	58	41 28N	2 20 E
Masoala, C.	129	15 59 S	50 13 E
Masoarivo	129	19 3 S	44 19 E
Masohi	103	3 2 S	128 15 E
Masomeloka	129	20 17 S	48 37 E
Mason, Nev., U.S.A.	163	38 56N	119 8W
Mason, S.D., U.S.A.	158	45 12N	103 27W
Mason, Tex., U.S.A.	159	30 45N	99 15W
Mason B.	143	46 55 S	167 45 E
Mason City	160	48 0N	119 0W
Masqat	93	23 37N	58 36 E
Massa	62	44 2N	10 7 E
Massa Maríttima	62	43 3N	10 52 E
Massa, O.	118	30 0N	9 30W
Massachusetts □	162	42 25N	72 0W
Massachusetts B.	162	42 30N	70 0W
Massada	90	33 12N	35 45 E
Massafra	65	40 35N	17 8 E
Massaguet	124	12 28N	15 26 E
Massakory	117	13 0N	15 49 E
Massangena	129	21 34 S	33 0 E
Massapê	170	3 31 S	40 19W
Massarosa	62	43 53N	10 17 E
Massat	44	42 53N	1 21 E
Massava	84	60 40N	62 6 E
Massawa = Mitsiwa	123	15 35N	39 25 E
Massena	156	44 52N	74 55W
Massenya	117	11 30N	16 25 E
Masset	152	54 0N	132 0W
Massiac	44	45 15N	3 11 E
Massif Central	44	45 30N	2 21 E
Massillon	156	40 47N	81 30W
Massinga	125	23 15 S	35 22 E
Massingir	129	23 46 S	32 4 E
Mässlingen	98	62 42N	12 48 E
Massman	138	16 25 S	145 25 E
Masson I.	13	66 10 S	93 20 E
Mastaba	122	20 52N	39 30 E
Mastanli = Momchilgrad	21	41 33N	25 23 E
Masterton	142	40 56 S	175 39 E
Mástikho, Ákra	68	38 10N	26 2 E
Mastuj	95	36 20N	72 36 E
Mastung	93	29 50N	66 42 E
Mastura	122	23 7N	38 52 E
Masuda	110	34 40N	131 51 E
Masulipatam	96	16 12N	81 12 E
Maswa □	126	1 20 S	34 0 E
Mat, R.	68	41 40N	20 0 E
Mata de São João	171	12 31 S	38 17W
Matabeleland North □	127	20 0 S	28 0 E
Matabeleland South □	127	19 0 S	29 0 E
Mataboor	103	1 41 S	138 3 E
Matachel, R.	57	38 32N	6 0W
Matachewan	150	47 56N	80 39W
Matad	105	47 12N	115 29 E
Matadi	124	5 52 S	13 31 E
Matador	153	50 49N	107 56W
Matagalpa	166	13 10N	85 40W
Matagami	150	49 45N	77 34W
Matagami, L.	150	49 50N	77 40W
Matagorda	159	28 43N	96 0W
Matagorda, B.	159	28 30N	96 15W
Matagorda I.	159	28 10N	96 40W
Matak, P.	101	3 18N	106 16 E
Matakana	141	32 59 S	145 54 E
Matale	97	7 30N	80 44 E
Matam	120	15 34N	13 17W
Matamata	142	37 48 S	175 47 E
Matameye	121	13 26N	8 28 E
Matamoros, Campeche, Mexico	165	25 53N	97 30W
Matamoros, Coahuila, Mexico	164	25 45N	103 1W
Matamoros, Puebla, Mexico	165	18 2N	98 17W
Matamoros, Tamaulipas, Mexico	165	25 50N	97 30W
Matana, D.	103	2 30 S	121 25 E
Matandu, R.	127	8 35 S	39 40 E
Matane	151	48 50N	67 33W
Mat'ang, Szechwan, China	108	31 54N	102 55 E
Mat'ang, Yunnan, China	108	23 30N	104 4 E
Matankari	121	13 46N	4 1 E
Matanuska	148	61 38N	149 0W
Matanzá	174	7 22N	73 2W
Matanzas	166	23 0N	81 40W
Matapá, Ákra	69	36 22N	22 27 E
Matapedia	151	48 0N	66 59W
Matara	97	5 58N	80 30 E
Mataram	102	8 41 S	116 10 E
Matarani	174	16 50 S	72 10W
Mataranka	136	14 55 S	133 4 E
Mataró	58	41 32N	2 29 E
Matarraña, R.	58	40 55N	0 8 E
Mataruška Banja	66	43 40N	20 45 E
Matata	142	37 54 S	176 48 E
Matatiele	129	30 20 S	28 49 E
Mataura	143	46 11 S	168 51 E
Mataura, R.	143	45 49 S	168 44 E
Matehuala	164	23 40N	100 50W
Mateira	171	18 54 S	50 30W
Mateke Hills	127	21 48 S	31 0 E
Matélica	63	43 15N	13 0 E
Matera	65	40 40N	16 37 E
Mátészalka	53	47 58N	22 20 E
Matetsi	127	18 12 S	26 0 E
Mateur	119	37 0N	9 48 E
Mateyev Kurgan	83	47 35N	38 47 E
Matfors	72	62 21N	17 2 E
Matha	44	45 52N	0 20W
Matheson I.	153	51 45N	96 56W
Mathews	162	37 26N	76 19W
Mathias Pass	143	43 7 S	171 6 E
Mathis	159	28 4N	97 48W
Mathoura	141	35 50 S	144 55 E
Mathry	31	51 56N	5 6W
Mathura	94	27 30N	77 48 E
Mati	103	6 55N	126 15 E
Mati, R.	68	41 40N	20 0 E
Matías Romero	165	16 53N	95 2W
Matibane	127	14 49 S	40 45 E
Matien	109	32 55N	116 26 E
Matlock	33	53 8N	1 32W
Matmata	119	33 30N	9 59 E
Matna	123	13 49N	35 10 E
Mato Grosso □	175	14 0 S	55 0W
Mato Grosso, Planalto do	174	15 0 S	54 0W
Mato Verde	171	15 23 S	42 52W
Matochkin Shar	76	73 10N	56 40 E
Matong	135	5 36 S	151 50 E
Matopo Hills	127	20 36 S	28 20 E
Matopos	127	20 20 S	28 29 E
Matour	45	46 19N	4 29 E
Matozinhos	56	41 11N	8 42W
Matrah	93	23 37N	58 30 E
Matrûh	122	31 19N	27 9 E
Matsang Tsangpo (Brahmaputra), R.	99	29 25N	88 0 E
Matsena	121	13 5N	10 5 E
Matsesta	83	43 34N	39 44 E
Matsu Tao	109	26 9N	119 56 E
Matsubara	111	34 33N	135 34 E
Matsudo	111	35 47N	139 54 E
Matsue	110	35 25N	133 10 E
Matsumae	112	41 26N	140 7 E
Matsumoto	111	36 15N	138 0 E
Matsusaka	111	34 34N	136 32 E
Matsutō	111	36 31N	136 34 E
Matsuura	110	33 20N	129 49 E
Matsuyama	110	33 45N	132 45 E
Mattagami, R.	150	50 43N	81 29W
Mattancheri	97	9 50N	76 15 E
Mattawa	150	46 20N	78 45W
Mattawamkeag	151	45 30N	68 30W
Matterhorn, mt.	50	45 58N	7 39 E
Mattersburg	53	47 44N	16 24 E
Matthew Town	167	20 57N	73 40W
Matthew's Ridge	174	7 37N	60 10W
Mattice	150	49 40N	83 20W
Mattituck	162	40 58N	72 32W
Mattmar	72	63 18N	13 54 E
Mattoon	156	39 30N	88 20W
Matua	102	2 58 S	110 52 E
Matuba	129	24 28 S	32 49 E
Matucana	174	11 55 S	76 15W
Matun	94	33 22N	69 58 E
Maturin	174	9 45N	63 11W
Matutina	171	19 13 S	45 58W
Matzuzaki	111	34 43N	138 50 E
Mau-é-ele	129	24 18 S	34 2 E
Mau Escarpment	126	0 40 S	36 0 E
Mau Ranipur	95	25 16N	79 8 E
Mauagami, R.	150	49 30N	82 0W
Maubeuge	43	50 17N	3 57 E
Maubourguet	44	43 29N	0 1 E
Mauchline	34	55 31N	4 23W
Maud	37	57 30N	2 8W
Maud, Pt.	137	23 6 S	113 45 E
Maude	140	34 29 S	144 18 E
Maudheim	13	71 5 S	11 0W
Maudin Sun	99	16 0N	94 30 E
Maués	174	3 20 S	57 45W
Mauganj	99	24 50N	81 55 E
Maughold	32	54 18N	4 17W
Maughold Hd.	32	54 18N	4 17W
Maui I.	147	20 45N	156 20 E
Maulamyaing	99	16 30N	97 40 E
Maule □	172	36 5 S	72 30W
Mauleon	44	43 14N	0 54W
Maulvibazar	98	24 29N	91 42 E
Maum	38	53 31N	9 35W
Maumee	156	41 35N	83 40W
Maumee, R.	156	41 42N	83 28W
Maumere	103	8 38 S	122 13 E
Maumturk Mts.	38	53 32N	9 42W
Maun	128	20 0 S	23 26 E
Mauna Kea, Mt.	147	19 50N	155 28W
Mauna Loa, Mt.	147	19 50N	155 28W
Maunath Bhanjan	95	25 56N	83 33 E
Maungaturoto	142	36 6 S	174 23 E
Maungdow	98	21 14N	94 5 E
Maungmagan Is.	99	14 0 S	97 48 E
Maungmagan Kyunzu	101	14 0N	97 48 E
Maupin	160	45 12N	121 9W
Maure-de-Bretagne	42	47 53N	2 0W
Maureen, oilfield	19	58 5N	1 45 E
Maurepas L.	159	30 18N	90 35W
Maures, mts.	45	43 15N	6 15 E
Mauriac	44	45 13N	2 19 E
Maurice L.	137	29 30 S	131 0 E
Mauriceville	142	40 45 S	175 35 E
Maurienne	45	45 15N	6 20 E
Mauritania ■	116	20 50N	10 0W
Mauritius ■	11	20 0 S	57 0 E
Mauron	42	48 9N	2 18W
Maurs	44	44 43N	2 12 E
Maurthe, R.	43	48 47N	6 9 E
Mauston	158	43 48N	90 5W
Mauterndorf	52	47 9N	13 40 E
Mauvezin	44	43 44N	0 53 E
Mauzé-sur le Mignon	44	46 12N	0 41W
Mavelikara	97	9 14N	76 32 E
Mavinga	125	15 50 S	20 10 E
Mavli	94	24 45N	73 55 E
Mavqi'im	90	31 38N	34 32 E
Mavrova	68	40 26N	19 32 E
Mavuradonha Mts.	127	16 30 S	31 30 E
Mawa	126	2 45N	26 33 E
Mawana	94	29 6N	77 58 E
Mawand	94	29 33N	68 38 E
Mawer	153	50 46N	106 22W
Mawgan	30	50 4N	5 10W
Mawkmai	98	20 14N	97 50 E
Mawlaik	98	23 40N	94 26 E
Mawlawkho	98	17 50N	97 38 E
Mawson Base	13	67 30N	65 0 E
Max	158	47 50N	101 20W
Maxcanú	165	20 40N	90 10W
Maxhamish L.	152	59 50N	123 17W
Maxixe	129	23 54 S	35 17 E
Maxwellheugh	35	55 35N	2 23W
Maxwelltown	142	39 51 S	174 49 E
Maxwelton, Queens., Austral.	138	15 45 S	142 30 E
Maxwelton, Queens., Austral.	138	20 43 S	142 41 E
May Downs	138	22 38 S	148 55 E
May, I. of	35	56 11N	2 32W
May Nefalis	123	15 0N	38 12 E
May Pen	166	17 58N	77 15W
May River	135	4 19 S	141 58 E
Maya	58	43 12N	1 29W
Maya Gudo, Mt.	123	7 30N	37 8 E
Maya Mts.	165	16 30N	89 0W
Maya, R.	77	58 20N	135 0 E

Mayaguana Island Menglien

Place	Page	Lat.	Long.
Mayaguana Island	167	21 30N	72 44W
Mayagüez	147	18 12N	67 9W
Mayahi	121	13 58N	7 40 E
Mayals	58	41 22N	0 30 E
Mayang	108	27 53N	109 48 E
Mayanup	137	33 58 S	116 25 E
Mayapán	165	20 38N	89 27W
Mayarf	167	20 40N	75 39W
Mayarí	167	20 40N	75 41W
Mayavaram = Mayuram	97	11 3N	79 42 E
Maybell	160	40 30N	108 4W
Maybole	34	55 21N	4 41W
Maychew	123	12 50N	39 42 E
Maydena	138	42 45 S	146 39 E
Maydos	68	40 13N	26 20 E
Mayen	49	50 18N	7 10 E
Mayenne	42	48 20N	0 38W
Mayenne □	42	48 10N	0 40W
Mayer	161	34 28N	112 17W
Mayerthorpe	152	53 57N	115 8W
Mayfield, Derby., U.K.	33	53 1N	1 47W
Mayfield, E. Sussex, U.K.	29	51 1N	0 17 E
Mayfield, Ky., U.S.A.	157	36 45N	88 40W
Mayfield, N.Y., U.S.A.	162	43 6N	74 16W
Mayhill	161	32 58N	105 30W
Maykop	83	44 35N	40 25 E
Mayli-Say	85	41 17N	72 24 E
Maymyo	100	22 2N	96 28 E
Maynard	162	42 30N	71 33W
Maynard Hills	137	28 35 S	119 50 E
Mayne, Le, L.	151	57 5N	68 30W
Mayne, R.	138	23 40 S	142 10 E
Maynooth, Can.	150	45 14N	77 56W
Maynooth, Ireland	38	53 22N	6 38W
Mayo	147	63 38N	135 57W
Mayo □	139	53 47N	9 7W
Mayo Bridge	38	54 11N	6 13W
Mayo L.	147	63 45N	135 0W
Mayo, R.	164	26 45N	109 47W
Mayon, Mt.	103	13 15N	123 42 E
Mayor I.	142	37 16 S	176 17 E
Mayorga	56	42 10N	5 16W
Mays Landing	162	39 27N	74 44W
Mayskiy	83	43 47N	43 59 E
Mayson L.	153	57 55N	107 10W
Maysville	156	38 43N	84 16W
Mayu, I.	103	1 30N	126 30 E
Mayuram	97	11 3N	79 42 E
Mayville	158	47 30N	97 23W
Mayya	77	61 44N	130 18 E
Mazabuka	127	15 52 S	27 44 E
Mazagán = El Jadida	118	33 11N	8 17W
Mazagão	175	0 20 S	51 50W
Mazama	152	49 43N	120 8W
Mazamet	44	43 30N	2 20 E
Mazán	174	3 15 S	73 0W
Mazapil	164	24 38N	101 34W
Mazar-i-Sharif	93	36 41N	67 0 E
Mazar, O.	118	32 0N	1 38 E
Mazara del Vallo	64	37 40N	12 34 E
Mazarredo	176	47 10 S	66 50W
Mazarrón	59	37 38N	1 19W
Mazarrón, Golfo de	59	37 27N	1 19W
Mazaruni, R.	174	6 15N	60 0W
Mazatán	164	29 0N	110 8W
Mazatenango	166	14 35N	91 30W
Mazatlán	164	23 10N	106 30W
Māzhān	93	32 30N	59 0 E
Mazheikyai	80	56 20N	22 20 E
Mazinān	93	36 25N	56 48 E
Mazoe	127	17 28 S	30 58 E
Mazoe R.	125	16 45 S	32 30 E
Mazoi	127	16 42 S	33 7 E
Mazrûb	123	14 0N	29 20 E
Mazurian Lakes = Mazurski, Pojezierze	54	53 50N	21 0 E
Mazurski, Pojezierze	54	53 50N	21 0 E
Mazzarino	65	37 19N	14 12 E
Mbaba	120	14 59N	16 44W
Mbabane	129	26 18 S	31 6 E
Mbagne	120	16 6N	14 47W
M'bahiakro	120	7 33N	4 19W
M'Baiki	124	3 53N	18 1 E
Mbala	127	8 46 S	31 17 E
Mbale	126	1 8N	34 12 E
Mbalmayo	121	3 33N	11 33 E
Mbamba Bay	127	11 13 S	34 49 E
Mbandaka	124	0 1 S	18 18 E
Mbanga	121	4 30N	9 33 E
Mbanza Congo	124	6 18 S	14 16 E
Mbanza Ngungu	124	5 12 S	14 53 E
Mbarara	126	0 35 S	30 25 E
Mbatto	120	6 28N	4 22W
Mbenkuru, R.	127	9 25 S	39 50 E
Mberubu	121	6 10N	7 38 E
Mbesuma	127	10 0 S	32 2 E
Mbeya	127	8 54 S	33 29 E
Mbeya □	126	8 15 S	33 30 E
Mbia	123	6 15N	29 18 E
Mbimbi	127	13 25 S	23 2 E
Mbinga	127	10 50 S	35 0 E
Mbinga □	127	10 50 S	35 0 E
Mbini □	124	1 30N	10 0 E
Mbiti	123	5 42N	28 3 E
Mboki	123	5 19N	25 58 E
Mboro	120	15 9N	16 54W
Mboune	120	14 42N	13 34W
Mbour	120	14 22N	16 54W
Mbout	120	16 1N	12 38W
Mbozi □	127	9 0 S	32 50 E
Mbuji-Mayi	126	6 9 S	23 40 E
Mbulu	124	3 45 S	35 30 E
Mbulu □	126	3 52 S	35 33 E
Mbumbi	128	18 26 S	19 59 E
Mburucuyá	172	28 1 S	58 14W
M'chounech	119	34 57N	6 1 E
M'Clure Str., Can.	10	75 0N	118 0W
M'Clure Str., Can.	12	74 0N	120 0W
Mdennah	118	24 37N	6 0W
Mead L.	161	36 1N	114 44W
Meade, Can.	150	49 26N	83 51W
Meade, U.S.A.	159	37 18N	100 25W
Meadow	137	26 35 S	114 40 E
Meadow Lake	153	54 10N	108 26W
Meadow Lake Prov. Park	153	54 27N	109 0W
Meadville	156	41 39N	80 9W
Meaford	150	44 36N	80 35W
Mealfuarvonie, Mt.	37	57 15N	4 34W
Mealhada	56	40 22N	8 27W
Mealsgate	32	54 46N	3 14W
Mealy Mts.	151	53 10N	60 0W
Meander, R. = Menderes, Büyük	92	37 45N	27 40 E
Meander River	152	59 2N	117 42W
Meare's, C.	160	45 37N	124 0W
Mearim, R.	170	3 4 S	44 35W
Mearns, Howe of the	37	56 52N	2 26W
Measham	28	52 43N	1 30W
Meath □	38	53 32N	6 40W
Meath Park	153	53 27N	105 22W
Meatian	140	35 34 S	143 21 E
Meaulne	44	46 36N	2 28 E
Meaux	43	48 58N	2 50 E
Mecanhelas	127	15 12 S	35 54 E
Mecca	163	33 37N	116 3W
Mecca = Makkah	122	21 30N	39 54 E
Mechanicsburg	162	40 12N	77 0W
Mechanicville	162	42 54N	73 41W
Mechara	123	8 36N	40 20 E
Mechelen, Anvers, Belg.	47	51 2N	4 29 E
Mechelen, Limbourg, Belg.	47	50 58N	5 41 E
Méchéria	118	33 35N	0 18W
Mechernich	48	50 35N	6 39 E
Mechetinskaya	83	46 45N	40 32 E
Mecidiye	68	40 38N	26 32 E
Mecitözü	82	40 32N	35 25 E
Mecklenburg B.	48	54 20N	11 40 E
Meconta	127	14 59 S	39 50 E
Meda	56	40 57N	7 18W
Meda P.O.	136	17 22 S	123 59 E
Meda, R.	136	17 20 S	124 30 E
Medaguine	118	33 41N	3 26 E
Medak	96	18 1N	78 15 E
Medan	102	3 40N	98 38 E
Medanosa, Pta.	176	48 0 S	66 0W
Medawachchiya	97	8 30N	80 30 E
Meddouza, cap	118	32 33N	9 9W
Médéa	118	36 12N	2 50 E
Mededa	66	43 44N	19 15 E
Medeiros Neto	171	17 20 S	40 14W
Medel, Pic	51	46 37N	8 55 E
Medellín	174	6 15N	75 35W
Medemblik	46	52 46N	5 8 E
Meder	123	14 42N	40 44 E
Mederdra	120	17 0N	15 38W
Medford, Oreg., U.S.A.	160	42 20N	122 52W
Medford, Wis., U.S.A.	158	45 9N	90 21W
Medford Lakes	162	39 52N	74 48W
Medgidia	70	44 15N	28 19 E
Medi	123	5 4N	30 42 E
Media	162	39 55N	75 23W
Media Agua	172	31 58 S	68 25W
Media Luna	172	34 45 S	66 44W
Mediaş	70	46 9N	24 22 E
Medical Lake	160	47 41N	117 42W
Medicina	63	44 29N	11 38 E
Medicine Bow	160	41 56N	106 11W
Medicine Hat	153	50 0N	110 45W
Medicine Lake	158	48 30N	104 30W
Medicine Lodge	159	37 20N	98 37W
Medina, Brazil	171	16 15 S	41 29W
Medina, Colomb.	174	4 30N	73 21W
Medina, N.D., U.S.A.	158	46 57N	99 20W
Medina, N.Y., U.S.A.	156	43 15N	78 27W
Medina, Ohio, U.S.A.	156	41 9N	81 50W
Medina = Al Madīnah	92	24 35N	39 52 E
Medina de Rioseco	56	41 53N	5 3W
Medina del Campo	56	41 18N	4 55W
Medina L.	159	29 35N	98 58W
Medina, R.	159	29 10N	98 20W
Medina-Sidonia	57	36 28N	5 57W
Medinaceli	58	41 12N	2 30W
Mediterranean Sea	60	35 0N	15 0 E
Medjerda, O.	119	36 35N	8 30 E
Medkovets	67	43 37N	23 10 E
Medley	153	54 25N	110 16W
Mednogorsk	84	51 24N	57 37 E
Médoc	44	45 10N	0 56W
Medstead, Can.	153	53 19N	108 5W
Medstead, U.K.	28	51 7N	1 4W
Medulin	63	44 49N	13 55 E
Medveda	66	42 50N	21 32 E
Medveditsa, R.	81	50 30N	44 0 E
Medvedok	81	57 20N	50 1 E
Medvezhi, Ostrava	77	71 0N	161 0 E
Medvezhyegorsk	78	63 0N	34 25 E
Medway, R.	29	51 12N	0 23 E
Medyn	81	54 59N	35 56 E
Medzev	53	48 43N	20 55 E
Medzilaborce	53	49 17N	21 52 E
Meeandh	108	27 26 S	153 6 E
Meeberrie	137	26 57 S	116 0 E
Meekatharra	137	26 32 S	118 29 E
Meeker	160	40 1N	107 58W
Meelpaeg L.	151	48 18N	56 35W
Meeniyan	141	38 35 S	146 0 E
Meer	47	51 27N	4 45 E
Meerane	48	50 51N	12 30 E
Meerbeke	47	50 50N	4 3 E
Meerle	47	51 29N	4 48 E
Meerssen	47	50 53N	5 50 E
Meerut	94	29 1N	77 50 E
Meeteetsa	160	44 10N	108 56W
Meeuwen	47	51 6N	5 31 E
Mega	123	3 57N	38 30 E
Megálo Khorío	69	36 27N	27 24 E
Megálo Petalí, I.	69	38 0N	24 15 E
Megalópolis	69	37 25N	22 7 E
Meganísi, I.	69	38 39N	20 48 E
Mégantic	151	45 36N	70 56W
Mégara	69	37 58N	23 22 E
Megarine	119	33 14N	6 2 E
Megdhova, R.	69	39 10N	21 45 E
Megen	46	51 49N	5 34 E
Mégève	45	45 51N	6 37 E
Meghalaya □	98	25 50N	91 0 E
Meghalayap	99	25 40N	89 55 E
Meghezez, Mt.	123	9 18N	39 26 E
Meghna, R.	98	23 45N	90 40 E
Megiddo	90	32 36N	35 11 E
Mégiscane, L.	150	48 35N	75 55W
Megiste	61	36 8N	29 34 E
Mehadia	70	44 56N	22 23 E
Mehaigne, R.	47	50 32N	5 13 E
Mehaïguene, O.	118	32 20N	2 45 E
Meharry, Mt.	132	22 59 S	118 35 E
Mehedinti □	70	44 40N	22 45 E
Meheisa	122	19 38N	32 57 E
Mehndawal	95	26 58N	83 5 E
Mehsana	94	23 39N	72 26 E
Mehun-sur-Yèvre	43	47 10N	2 13 E
Mei Chiang, R.	109	24 24N	116 35 E
Meia Ponte, R.	171	18 32 S	49 36W
Meichuan	109	30 9N	115 33 E
Meidrim	31	51 51N	4 3W
Meiganga	124	6 20N	14 10 E
Meigh	38	54 8N	6 22W
Meihsien, Kwangtung, China	109	24 18N	116 7 E
Meihsien, Shensi, China	106	34 16N	107 42 E
Meijel	47	51 21N	5 53 E
Meiktila	98	21 0N	96 0 E
Meilen	51	47 16N	8 39 E
Meiningen	48	50 32N	10 25 E
Meio, R.	171	13 36 S	49 7W
Meira, Sierra de	56	43 15N	7 15W
Meiringen	50	46 43N	8 12 E
Meishan	108	30 3N	103 51 E
Meissen	48	51 10N	13 29 E
Meit'an	108	27 48N	107 28 E
Meithalun	90	32 21N	35 16 E
Méjean	44	44 15N	3 30 E
Mejillones	172	23 10 S	70 30W
Meka	137	27 25 S	116 48 E
Mekambo	124	1 2N	14 5 E
Mekdela	123	11 24N	39 10 E
Mekhtar	93	30 30N	69 15 E
Meklong = Samut Songkhram	101	13 24N	100 1 E
Meknès	118	33 57N	5 33W
Meko	121	7 27N	2 52 E
Mekong, R.	101	18 0N	104 15 E
Mekongga	103	3 50 S	121 30 E
Mekoryok	147	60 20N	166 20W
Melagiri Hills	97	12 20N	77 30 E
Melah, Sebkhet el	118	29 20N	1 30W
Melaka	101	2 15N	102 15 E
Melaka □	101	2 20N	102 15 E
Melalap	102	5 10N	116 5 E
Mélambes	69	35 8N	24 40 E
Melanesia	130	4 0 S	155 0 E
Melapalaiyam	97	8 39N	77 44 E
Melbost	36	58 12N	6 20W
Melbourn	29	52 5N	0 1 E
Melbourne, Austral.	141	37 50 S	145 0 E
Melbourne, U.K.	28	52 50N	1 25W
Melbourne, U.S.A.	157	28 13N	80 14W
Melcésine	62	45 46N	10 48 E
Melchor Múzquiz	164	27 50N	101 40W
Melchor Ocampo (San Pedro Ocampo)	164	24 52N	101 40W
Méldola	63	44 7N	12 3 E
Meldorf	48	54 5N	9 5 E
Mêle-sur-Sarthe, Le	42	48 31N	0 22 E
Melegnano	62	45 21N	9 20 E
Melekess = Dimitrovgrad	81	54 25N	49 33 E
Melenci	66	45 32N	20 20 E
Melenki	81	55 20N	41 37 E
Meleuz	84	52 58N	55 55 E
Melfi, Chad	117	11 0N	17 59 E
Melfi, Italy	65	41 0N	15 40 E
Melfort, Can.	153	52 50N	104 37W
Melfort, Zimb.	127	18 0 S	31 25 E
Melfort, Loch	34	56 13N	5 33W
Melgaço	56	42 7N	8 15W
Melgar de Fernamental	56	42 27N	4 17W
Melhus	71	63 17N	10 18 E
Melick	47	51 10N	6 1 E
Melide	51	45 57N	8 57 E
Meligalá	69	37 15N	21 59 E
Melilla	118	35 21N	2 57W
Melilot	42	31 22N	34 37 E
Melipilla	172	33 42 S	71 15W
Mélissa Óros	69	37 32N	26 4 E
Melita	153	49 15N	101 5W
Mélito di Porto Salvo	65	37 55N	15 47 E
Melitopol	82	46 50N	35 22 E
Melk	52	48 13N	15 20 E
Melksham	28	51 22N	2 9W
Mellan-Fryken	72	59 45N	13 10 E
Mellansel	74	63 25N	18 17 E
Melle, Belg.	47	51 0N	3 49 E
Melle, France	44	46 14N	0 10W
Melle, Ger.	48	52 12N	8 20 E
Mellégue, O.	119	36 32N	8 51 E
Mellen	158	46 19N	90 36W
Mellerud	73	58 41N	12 28 E
Mellette	158	45 11N	98 29W
Mellid	56	42 55N	8 1W
Mellish Reef	133	17 25 S	155 50 E
Mellit	123	14 15N	25 40 E
Mellon Charles	36	57 52N	5 37W
Melmerby	32	54 44N	2 35W
Melnik	67	40 58N	23 25 E
Mělník	52	50 22N	14 23 E
Melo	173	32 20 S	54 10W
Melolo	103	9 53 S	120 40 E
Melones Res.	163	37 57N	120 31W
Melouprey	100	13 48N	105 16 E
Melovoye	83	49 25N	40 5 E
Melrhir, Chott	119	34 25N	6 24 E
Melrose, N.S.W., Austral.	141	32 42 S	146 57 E
Melrose, W. Australia, Austral.	137	27 50 S	121 15 E
Melrose, U.K.	35	55 35N	2 44W
Melrose, U.S.A.	159	34 27N	103 33W
Mels	51	47 3N	9 25 E
Melsele	47	51 13N	4 17 E
Melsonby	33	54 28N	1 41W
Melstone	160	46 45N	108 0W
Melsungen	48	51 8N	9 34 E
Melton	29	52 51N	1 1 E
Melton Constable	29	52 52N	1 1 E
Melton Mowbray	29	52 46N	0 52W
Melun	43	48 32N	2 39 E
Melunga	128	17 15 S	16 22 E
Melur	97	10 2N	78 23 E
Melut	123	10 30N	32 20 E
Melvaig	36	57 48N	5 49W
Melvich	37	58 33N	3 55W
Melville	153	50 55N	102 50W
Melville B.	138	12 0 S	136 45 E
Melville, C.	138	14 11 S	144 30 E
Melville I., Austral.	136	11 30 S	131 0 E
Melville I., Can.	12	75 30N	111 0W
Melville, L., Newf., Can.	151	53 45N	59 40W
Melville, L., Newf., Can.	151	59 30N	53 40W
Melville Pen.	149	68 0N	84 0W
Melvin L.	38	54 26N	8 10W
Melvin, R.	152	59 11N	117 31W
Mélykút	53	46 11N	19 25 E
Memaliaj	68	40 25N	19 58 E
Memba	127	14 11 S	40 30 E
Memboro	103	9 30 S	119 30 E
Membrilla	59	38 59N	3 21W
Memel	129	27 38 S	29 36 E
Memel = Klaipeda	80	55 43N	21 10 E
Memmingen	49	47 59N	10 12 E
Memphis, Tenn., U.S.A.	159	35 7N	90 0W
Memphis, Tex., U.S.A.	159	34 45N	100 30W
Mena	159	34 40N	94 15W
Menai Bridge	31	53 14N	4 11W
Menai Strait	31	53 7N	4 20W
Ménaka	121	15 59N	2 18 E
Menaldum	46	53 13N	5 40 E
Menamurtee	140	31 25 S	143 11 E
Menarandra, R.	129	25 0 S	44 50 E
Menard	159	30 57N	99 58W
Menasha	156	44 13N	88 27W
Menate	102	0 12 S	112 47 E
Mendawai, R.	102	1 30 S	113 0 E
Mende	44	44 31N	3 30 E
Mendebo Mts.	123	7 0N	39 22 E
Mendenhall, C.	147	59 44N	166 10W
Menderes, R.	92	37 25N	28 45 E
Mendez	165	25 7N	98 34W
Mendhar	95	33 35N	74 10 E
Mendi, Ethiopia	123	9 47N	35 4 E
Mendi, P.N.G.	135	6 11 S	143 47 E
Mendip Hills	28	51 17N	2 40W
Mendlesham	29	52 15N	1 4 E
Mendocino	160	39 26N	123 50W
Mendong Gompa	95	31 16N	85 11 E
Mendota, Calif., U.S.A.	163	36 46N	120 24W
Mendota, Ill., U.S.A.	158	41 35N	89 5W
Mendoza	172	32 50 S	68 52W
Mendoza □	172	33 0 S	69 0W
Mendrisio	51	45 52N	8 59 E
Mene Grande	174	9 49N	70 56W
Menemen	92	38 18N	27 10 E
Menen	47	50 47N	3 7 E
Menfi	64	37 36N	12 57 E
Meng-pan	99	23 5N	100 19 E
Meng-so	101	22 33N	99 31 E
Meng-wang	99	22 17N	100 32 E
Meng Wang	101	22 18N	100 31 E
Mengch'eng	106	33 17N	116 34 E
Mengeš	63	46 24N	14 35 E
Menggala	102	4 20 S	105 15 E
Menghai	108	21 58N	100 28 E
Menghsien	106	34 55N	112 47 E
Mengibar	57	37 58N	3 48W
Mengla	108	21 28N	101 35 E
Menglien	108	22 21N	99 36 E

Mengoub Mikołajki

Place	Page	Lat.	Long.
Mengoub	118	29 49N	5 26W
Mengpolo	108	24 24N	99 14 E
Mengshan	109	24 12N	110 31 E
Mengting	108	23 33N	98 5 E
Mengtz = Mengtzu	108	23 25N	103 20 E
Mengtzu	108	23 25N	103 20 E
Mengyin	107	35 40N	117 55 E
Menihek L.	151	54 0N	67 0W
Menin	47	50 47N	3 7 E
Menindee	140	32 20N	142 25 E
Menindee, L.	140	32 20N	142 25 E
Meningie	140	35 43 S	139 20 E
Menkúng	99	28 38N	98 24 E
Menlo Park	163	37 27N	122 12W
Menominee	156	45 9N	87 39W
Menominee, R.	156	45 30N	87 50W
Menomonie	158	44 50N	91 54W
Menor, Mar	59	37 43N	0 48W
Menorca, I.	58	40 0N	4 0 E
Mentawai, Kepulauan	102	2 0 S	99 0 E
Mentekab	101	3 29N	102 21 E
Menton	45	43 50N	7 29 E
Menyamya	135	7 10 S	145 59 E
Menzel-Bourguiba	119	39 9N	9 49 E
Menzel Chaker	119	35 0N	10 26 E
Menzelinsk	84	55 53N	53 1 E
Menzies	137	29 40 S	120 58 E
Me'ona (Tarshiha)	90	33 1N	35 15 E
Meoqui	164	28 17N	105 29W
Mepaco	127	15 57 S	30 48 E
Meppel	47	52 42N	6 12 E
Meppen	48	52 41N	7 20 E
Mequinenza	58	41 22N	0 17 E
Mer Rouge	159	32 47N	91 48W
Merabéllou, Kólpos	69	35 10N	25 50 E
Merai	135	4 52 S	152 19 E
Merak	103	5 55 S	106 1 E
Meramangye, L.	137	28 25 S	132 13 E
Merano (Meran)	63	46 40N	11 10 E
Merate	62	45 42N	9 23 E
Merauke	103	8 29 S	140 24 E
Merbabu, Mt.	103	7 30 S	110 40 E
Merbein	140	34 10 S	142 2 E
Merca	91	1 48N	44 50 E
Mercadal	58	39 59N	4 5 E
Mercara	97	12 30N	75 45 E
Mercato Saraceno	63	43 57N	12 11 E
Merced	163	37 18N	120 30W
Merced Pk.	163	37 36N	119 24W
Merced, R.	163	37 21N	120 58W
Mercedes, Buenos Aires, Argent.	172	34 40 S	59 30W
Mercedes, Corrientes, Argent.	172	29 10 S	58 5W
Mercedes, San Luis, Argent.	172	33 5 S	65 21W
Mercedes, Uruguay	172	33 12 S	58 0W
Merceditas	172	28 20 S	70 35W
Mercer	142	37 16 S	175 5 E
Merchtem	47	50 58N	4 14 E
Mercy C.	149	65 0N	62 30W
Merdrignac	42	48 11N	2 27W
Mere, Belg.	47	50 55N	3 58 E
Mere, U.K.	28	51 5N	2 16W
Meredith C.	176	52 15 S	60 40W
Meredith, L.	159	35 30N	101 35W
Merei	70	45 7N	26 43 E
Merelbeke	47	51 0N	3 45 E
Meréville	43	48 20N	2 5 E
Merewa	123	7 40N	36 54 E
Mergenevo	84	49 56N	51 18 E
Mergenevskiy	83	49 59N	51 15 E
Mergui	101	12 30N	98 35 E
Mergui Arch. = Myeik Kyunzu	101	11 30N	97 30 E
Meribah	140	34 43 S	140 51 E
Mérida, Mexico	165	20 50N	89 40W
Mérida, Spain	57	38 55N	6 25W
Mérida, Venez.	174	8 36N	71 8W
Mérida □	174	8 30N	71 10W
Mérida, Cord. de	174	9 0N	71 0W
Meriden, U.K.	28	52 27N	1 36W
Meriden, U.S.A.	162	41 33N	72 47W
Meridian, Idaho, U.S.A.	160	43 41N	116 25W
Meridian, Miss., U.S.A.	157	32 20N	88 42W
Meridian, Tex., U.S.A.	159	31 55N	97 37W
Mering	49	48 15N	11 0 E
Merioneth (□)	26	52 49N	3 55W
Merirumã	175	1 15N	54 50W
Merke	85	42 52N	73 11 E
Merkel	159	32 30N	100 0W
Merkem	47	50 57N	2 51 E
Merksem	47	51 16N	4 25 E
Merksplas	47	51 22N	4 52 E
Merlebach	43	49 5N	6 52 E
Merlerault, Le	42	48 41N	0 16 E
Mermaid Mt.	108	27 29 S	152 49 E
Mermaid Reef	136	17 6 S	119 36 E
Mern	73	55 3N	12 3 E
Merowe	122	18 29N	31 46 E
Merredin	137	31 28 S	118 18 E
Merrick, Mt.	34	55 8N	4 30W
Merrill, Oregon, U.S.A.	160	42 2N	121 37W
Merrill, Wis., U.S.A.	158	45 11N	89 41W
Merrimack, R.	162	42 49N	70 49W
Merritt	152	50 10N	120 45W
Merriwa	141	32 6 S	150 22 E
Merriwagga	141	33 47 S	145 43 E
Merroe	137	27 53 S	117 50 E
Merry I.	150	55 29N	77 31W
Merrygoen	141	31 51 S	149 12 E
Merryville	159	30 47N	93 31W
Mersa Fatma	123	14 57N	40 17 E
Mersch	47	49 44N	6 7 E
Merse, dist.	35	55 40N	2 30W
Mersea I.	29	51 48N	0 55 E
Merseburg	48	51 20N	12 0 E
Mersey, R.	32	53 20N	2 56W
Merseyside □	32	53 25N	2 55W
Mersin	92	36 51N	34 36 E
Mersing	101	2 25N	103 50 E
Merta	94	26 39N	74 4 E
Mertert	47	49 43N	6 29 E
Merthyr Tydfil	31	51 45N	3 23W
Mértola	57	37 40N	7 40 E
Merton	29	51 25N	0 13W
Mertzig	47	49 51N	6 1 E
Mertzon	159	31 17N	100 48W
Méru	43	49 13N	2 8 E
Meru	126	0 3N	37 40 E
Meru □	126	0 3N	37 46 E
Meru, mt.	126	3 15 S	36 46 E
Merville	43	50 38N	2 38 E
Méry-sur-Seine	43	48 31N	3 54 E
Merzifon	82	40 53N	35 32 E
Merzig	49	49 26N	6 37 E
Merzouga, Erg Tin	119	24 0N	11 4 E
Mesa	161	33 20N	111 56W
Mesa, La, Colomb.	174	4 38N	74 28W
Mesa, La, Calif., U.S.A.	163	32 48N	117 5W
Mesa, La, N. Mex., U.S.A.	161	32 6N	106 48W
Mesach Mellet	119	24 30N	11 30 E
Mesada	90	31 20N	35 19 E
Mesagne	65	40 34N	17 48 E
Mesaras, Kólpos	69	35 6N	24 47 E
Meschede	48	51 20N	8 17 E
Mesfinto	123	13 30N	37 22 E
Mesgouez, L.	150	51 20N	75 0W
Meshchovsk	80	54 22N	35 17 E
Meshed = Mashhad	93	36 20N	59 35 E
Meshoppen	162	41 36N	76 3W
Mesick	156	44 24N	85 42W
Mesilinka, R.	152	56 6N	124 30W
Mesilla	161	32 20N	107 0W
Meslay-du-Maine	42	47 58N	0 33W
Mesocco	51	46 23N	9 12 E
Mesolóngion	69	38 27N	21 28 E
Mesopotamia, reg.	92	33 30N	44 0 E
Mesoraca	65	39 5N	16 47 E
Mésou Volímais	69	37 53N	27 35 E
Mess Cr.	152	57 55N	131 14W
Messac	42	47 49N	1 50W
Messad	118	34 8N	3 30 E
Méssaména	121	3 48N	12 49 E
Messancy	47	49 36N	5 49 E
Messeix	44	45 37N	2 33 E
Messina, Italy	65	38 10N	15 32 E
Messina, S. Afr.	129	22 20 S	30 12 E
Messina, Str. di	65	38 5N	15 35 E
Messini	69	37 4N	22 1 E
Messinia □	69	37 10N	22 0 E
Messiniakós, Kólpos	69	36 45N	22 5 E
Mestà, Akra	69	38 16N	25 53 E
Mesta, R.	67	41 30N	24 0 E
Mestanza	57	38 35N	4 4W
Město Teplá	52	49 59N	12 52 E
Mestre	63	45 30N	12 13 E
Mestre, Espigão	171	12 30 S	46 10W
Městys Zelezná Ruda	52	49 8N	13 15 E
Meta □	174	3 30N	73 0W
Meta, R.	174	6 20N	68 5W
Metagama	150	47 0N	81 55W
Metaline Falls	160	48 52N	117 22W
Metán	172	25 30 S	65 0W
Metauro, R.	63	43 45N	12 59 E
Metchosin	152	48 15N	123 37W
Metehara	123	8 58N	39 57 E
Metema	123	12 56N	36 13 E
Metengobalame	127	14 49 S	34 30 E
Méthana	69	37 35N	23 23 E
Metheringham	33	53 9N	0 22W
Methlick	37	57 26N	2 13W
Methóni	69	36 49N	21 42 E
Methuen, Mt.	136	15 54 S	124 44 E
Methven, N.Z.	143	43 38 S	171 40 E
Methven, U.K.	35	56 25N	3 35W
Methwin, Mt.	137	25 3 S	120 45 E
Methwold	29	52 30N	0 33 E
Methy L.	153	56 28N	109 30W
Metil	125	16 24 S	39 0 E
Metkovets	67	43 37N	23 10 E
Metkovió	66	43 6N	17 39 E
Metlakatla	147	55 10N	131 33W
Metlaoui	119	34 24N	8 24 E
Metlika	63	45 40N	15 20 E
Metowra	139	25 3 S	146 15 E
Metropolis	159	37 10N	88 47W
Métsovon	68	39 48N	21 12 E
Mettet	47	50 19N	4 41 E
Mettuppalaiyam	97	11 18N	76 59 E
Mettur	97	11 48N	77 47 E
Mettur Dam	95	11 45N	77 45 E
Metulla	90	33 17N	35 34 E
Metz	43	49 8N	6 10 E
Meulaboh	102	4 11N	96 3 E
Meulan	43	49 0N	1 52 E
Meung-sur-Loire	43	47 50N	1 40 E
Meureudu	102	5 19N	96 10 E
Meurthe-et-Moselle □	43	48 52N	6 0 E
Meuse □	43	49 8N	5 25 E
Meuse, R.	47	50 45N	5 41 E
Meuselwitz	48	51 3N	12 18 E
Mevagissey	30	50 16N	4 48W
Mevagissey Bay	30	50 15N	4 40W
Mexborough	33	53 29N	1 18W
Mexia	159	31 38N	96 32W
Mexiana, I.	170	0 0	49 30W
Mexicali	164	32 40N	115 30W
México	165	19 20N	99 10W
Mexico, Me., U.S.A.	156	44 35N	70 30W
Mexico, Mo., U.S.A.	158	39 10N	91 55W
Mexico, N.Y., U.S.A.	162	43 28N	76 18W
Mexico ■	164	20 0N	100 0W
México □	164	19 20N	99 10W
Mexico, G. of	165	25 0N	90 0W
Mey	37	58 38N	3 14W
Meyenburg	48	53 19N	12 15 E
Meymac	44	45 32N	2 10 E
Meyrargues	45	43 38N	5 32 E
Meyrueis	44	44 12N	3 27 E
Meyssac	44	45 3N	1 40 E
Mezdra	67	43 12N	23 35 E
Mèze	44	43 27N	3 36 E
Mezen	78	65 50N	44 20 E
Mezha, R.	80	55 50N	31 45 E
Mezhdurechenskiy	84	59 36N	65 56 E
Mezidon	42	49 5N	0 1W
Mézières	43	49 45N	4 42 E
Mézilhac	45	44 49N	4 21 E
Mézin	44	44 4N	0 16 E
Mezöberény	53	46 49N	21 3 E
Mezöfalva	53	46 55N	18 49 E
Mezöhegyes	53	46 19N	20 49 E
Mezokövácsháza	53	46 25N	20 57 E
Mezökövesd	53	47 49N	20 35 E
Mézos	44	44 5N	1 10W
Mezötúr	53	47 0N	20 41 E
Mezquital	164	23 29N	104 23W
Mezzolombardo	62	46 13N	11 5 E
Mgeta	127	8 22 S	38 6 E
Mglin	80	53 2N	32 50 E
Mhlaba Hills	127	18 30 S	30 30 E
Mhow	94	22 33N	75 50 E
Mi-Shima	110	34 46N	131 9 E
Miahuatlán	165	16 21N	96 36W
Miajadas	57	39 9N	5 54W
Mialar	94	26 15N	70 20 E
Miallo	138	16 28 S	145 22 E
Miami, Ariz., U.S.A.	161	33 25N	111 0W
Miami, Fla., U.S.A.	157	25 52N	80 15W
Miami, Tex., U.S.A.	159	35 44N	100 38W
Miami Beach	157	25 49N	80 6W
Miami, R.	156	39 20N	84 40W
Miamisburg	156	39 40N	84 11W
Miandowāb	92	37 0N	46 5 E
Miandrivazo	125	19 50 S	45 56 E
Miāneh	92	37 30N	47 40 E
Mianwali	94	32 38N	71 28 E
Miaoli	109	24 34N	120 48 E
Miarinarivo	129	18 57 S	46 55 E
Miass	84	54 59N	60 6 E
Miass, R.	84	56 6N	64 30 E
Miasteczko Kraj	54	53 7N	17 1 E
Miastko	54	54 0N	16 58 E
Mica Dam	152	52 5N	118 32W
Mica Res.	152	51 55N	118 00W
Michael, Mt.	135	6 27 S	145 22 E
Michalovce	29	48 44N	21 54 E
Micheldever	28	51 7N	1 17W
Michelson, Mt.	147	69 20N	144 20W
Michelstadt	49	49 40N	9 0 E
Michigan □	155	44 40N	85 40W
Michigan City	156	41 42N	86 56W
Michigan, L.	156	44 0N	87 0W
Michih	106	37 49N	110 7 E
Michikamau L.	151	54 0N	64 0W
Michipicoten	150	47 55N	84 55W
Michipicoten I.	150	47 40N	85 50W
Michoacan □	164	19 0N	102 0W
Michurin	67	42 9N	27 51 E
Michurinsk	81	52 58N	40 27 E
Mickle Fell	32	54 38N	2 16W
Mickleover	33	52 55N	1 32W
Mickleton, Oxon., U.K.	28	52 5N	1 45W
Mickleton, Yorks., U.K.	32	54 36N	2 3W
Miclere	138	22 34 S	147 32 E
Micronesia	130	17 0N	160 0 E
Micŭsasa	70	46 7N	24 7 E
Mid Calder	35	55 53N	3 23W
Mid Glamorgan □	31	51 40N	3 25W
Mid Yell	36	60 36N	1 5W
Midai, P.	101	3 0N	107 47 E
Midale	153	49 25N	103 20W
Midas	160	41 14N	116 56W
Middagsfjället	72	63 27N	12 19 E
Middelbeers	47	51 28N	5 15 E
Middelburg, Neth.	47	51 30N	3 36 E
Middelburg, C. Prov., S. Afr.	128	31 30 S	25 0 E
Middelburg, Trans., S. Afr.	129	25 49N	29 28 E
Middelfart	73	55 30N	9 43 E
Middelharnis	46	51 46N	4 10 E
Middelkerke	47	51 11N	2 49 E
Middelrode	47	51 41N	5 26 E
Middelveld	128	29 45 S	22 30 E
Middle Alkali L.	160	41 30N	120 3W
Middle Andaman I.	101	12 30N	92 30 E
Middle Brook	151	48 40N	54 20W
Middle I.	137	28 55 S	113 55 E
Middle River	162	39 19N	76 25W
Middle Zoy	28	51 5N	2 54W
Middleboro	162	41 49N	70 55W
Middleburg, N.Y., U.S.A.	162	42 36N	74 19W
Middleburg, Pa., U.S.A.	162	40 47N	77 3W
Middlebury	162	44 0N	73 9W
Middleham	33	54 17N	1 49W
Middlemarch	143	45 30 S	170 9 E
Middlemarsh	28	50 51N	2 29W
Middleport	156	39 0N	82 5W
Middlesbrough	33	54 35N	1 14W
Middlesex, Belize	165	17 2N	88 31W
Middlesex, U.S.A.	162	40 36N	74 30W
Middleton, Can.	151	44 57N	65 4W
Middleton, Gr. Manchester, U.K.	32	53 33N	2 12W
Middleton, Norfolk, U.K.	29	52 43N	0 29 E
Middleton Cheney	28	52 4N	1 17W
Middleton Cr.	138	22 35 S	141 51 E
Middleton I.	147	59 30N	146 28W
Middleton-in-Teesdale	32	54 38N	2 5W
Middleton in the Wolds	33	53 56N	0 35W
Middleton P.O.	138	22 22 S	141 32 E
Middletown, U.K.	38	54 18N	6 50W
Middletown, Conn., U.S.A.	162	41 37N	72 40W
Middletown, Del., U.S.A.	162	39 30N	84 21W
Middletown, N.Y., U.S.A.	162	41 28N	74 28W
Middletown, Pa., U.S.A.	162	40 12N	76 44W
Middlewich	32	53 12N	2 28W
Midelt	118	32 46N	4 44W
Midhurst, N.Z.	142	39 17 S	174 18 E
Midhurst, U.K.	29	50 59N	0 44W
Midi, Canal du	44	43 45N	1 21 E
Midi d'Ossau	58	42 50N	0 25W
Midland, Austral.	137	31 54 S	115 59 E
Midland, Can.	150	44 45N	79 50W
Midland, Mich., U.S.A.	156	43 37N	84 17W
Midland, Tex., U.S.A.	159	32 0N	102 3W
Midland Junc.	137	31 50 S	115 58 E
Midlands □	127	19 40 S	29 0 E
Midleton	39	51 52N	8 12W
Midlothian, Austral.	138	17 10 S	141 12 E
Midlothian, U.S.A.	159	32 30N	97 0W
Midlothian (□)	26	55 45N	3 15W
Midnapore	95	22 25N	87 21 E
Midongy du Sud	129	23 35 S	47 1 E
Midongy, Massif de	129	23 30 S	47 0 E
Midskog	73	58 56N	14 5 E
Midsomer Norton	28	51 17N	2 29W
Midvale	160	40 39N	111 58W
Midway Is.	130	28 13N	177 22W
Midwest	160	43 27N	106 11W
Midwolda	46	53 12N	6 52 E
Midzur	66	43 24N	22 40 E
Mie-ken □	111	34 30N	136 10 E
Miechów	54	50 21N	20 5 E
Miedzyborz	54	51 39N	17 24 E
Miedzychód	54	52 35N	15 53 E
Miedzylesie	54	50 41N	16 40 E
Miedzyrzec Podlaski	54	51 58N	22 45 E
Miedzyrzecz	54	52 26N	15 35 E
Miedzyzdroje	54	53 56N	14 26 E
Miejska Górka	54	51 39N	16 58 E
Miélan	44	43 27N	0 19 E
Mielelek	138	6 1 S	148 58 E
Mienchʼih	106	34 48N	111 40 E
Mienchu	108	31 22N	104 7 E
Mienga	128	17 12 S	19 48 E
Mienhsien	106	33 11N	106 36 E
Mienning	108	28 30N	102 10 E
Mienyang, Hupei, China	109	30 10N	113 20 E
Mienyang, Szechwan, China	108	31 28N	104 46 E
Miercurea Ciuc	70	46 21N	25 48 E
Mieres	56	43 18N	5 48W
Mierlo	47	51 27N	5 37 E
Mieso	123	9 15N	40 43 E
Mieszkowice	54	52 47N	14 30 E
Migdal	90	32 51N	35 30 E
Migdal Afeq	90	32 5N	34 58 E
Migennes	43	47 58N	3 31 E
Migliarino	63	44 54N	11 56 E
Miguel Alemán, Presa	165	18 15N	96 40W
Miguel Alves	170	4 11 S	42 55W
Miguel Calmon	170	11 26 S	40 36W
Mihara	110	34 24N	133 5 E
Mihara-Yama	111	34 43N	139 23 E
Mihsien	106	34 31N	113 22 E
Mii	108	26 50N	102 3 E
Mijares, R.	58	40 15N	0 50W
Mijas	57	36 36N	4 40W
Mijdrecht	46	52 13N	4 53 E
Mijilu	121	10 22N	13 19 E
Mikese	126	6 48 S	37 55 E
Mikha Tskhakaya	83	42 15N	42 7 E
Mikhailovgrad	67	43 27N	23 16 E
Mikhailovka	82	47 16N	35 27 E
Mikhaylov	81	54 20N	39 0 E
Mikhaylovka, Azerbaijan, U.S.S.R.	83	41 31N	48 52 E
Mikhaylovka, R.S.F.S.R., U.S.S.R.	81	50 3N	43 5 E
Mikhaylovski	84	56 27N	59 7 E
Mikhnevo	81	55 4N	37 59 E
Miki, Hyōgō, Japan	110	34 48N	134 59 E
Miki, Kagawa, Japan	110	34 12N	134 7 E
Mikinai	69	37 43N	22 46 E
Mikindani	127	10 15 S	40 2 E
Mikkeli	75	61 43N	27 25 E
Mikkeli □	74	62 0N	28 0 E
Mikkelin Lääni □	74	61 56N	28 0 E
Mikkwa, R.	152	58 25N	114 46W
Mikniya	123	17 0N	33 45 E
Mikołajki	54	53 49N	21 37 E

Mikoł Mjømna

Mikołów 53 50 10N 18 50E
Mikonos, I. 69 37 30N 25 25E
Mikrón Dhérion 68 41 19N 26 6E
Mikulov 53 48 48N 16 39E
Mikumi 126 7 26S 37 9E
Mikun 78 62 20N 50 0E
Mikuni 111 36 13N 136 9E
Mikuni-Tōge 111 36 50N 138 40E
Mikura-Jima 111 33 52N 139 36E
Mila 119 36 27N 6 16E
Milaca 158 45 45N 93 40W
Milagro 174 2 0S 79 30W
Milan, Mo., U.S.A. 158 40 10N 93 5W
Milan, Tenn., U.S.A. 157 35 55N 88 45W
Milan = Milano 62 45 28N 9 10E
Milang, S. Australia, Austral. 139 32 2S 139 10E
Milang, S. Australia, Austral. 140 35 24S 138 58E
Milange 127 16 3S 35 45E
Milano 62 45 28N 9 10E
Milâs 92 37 20N 27 50E
Milazzo 65 38 13N 15 13E
Milbank 158 45 17N 96 38W
Milborne Port 28 50 58N 2 28W
Milden 153 51 29N 107 32W
Mildenhall 29 52 20N 0 30E
Mildura 140 34 13S 142 9E
Miléai 68 39 20N 23 9E
Miles, Austral. 139 26 40S 150 23E
Miles, U.S.A. 159 31 39N 100 11W
Miles City 158 46 30N 105 50W
Milestone 153 49 59N 104 31W
Mileto 65 38 37N 16 3E
Miletto, Mte. 65 41 26N 14 23E
Mileura 137 26 22S 117 20E
Milevsko 52 49 27N 14 21E
Milford, Ireland 39 52 20N 8 52W
Milford, Conn., U.S.A. 162 41 13N 73 4W
Milford, Del., U.S.A. 162 38 52N 75 27W
Milford, Mass., U.S.A. 162 42 8N 71 30W
Milford, N.H., U.S.A. 162 42 50N 71 39W
Milford, Pa., U.S.A. 162 41 20N 74 47W
Milford, Utah, U.S.A. 161 38 20N 113 0W
Milford Haven 31 51 43N 5 2W
Milford Haven, B. 31 51 40N 5 10W
Milford on Sea 28 50 44N 1 36W
Milford Sd. 143 44 34S 167 47E
Milgun 137 25 6S 118 18E
Milh, Ras el 117 32 0N 24 55E
Miliana, Aïn Salah, Alg. 118 27 20N 2 32E
Miliana, Médéa, Alg. 118 36 12N 2 15E
Milicz 54 51 31N 17 19E
Miling 137 30 30S 116 17E
Militello in Val di Catánia 65 37 16N 14 46E
Milk, R. 160 48 40N 107 15W
Milk River 152 49 10N 112 5W
Mill 47 51 41N 5 48E
Mill City 160 44 45N 122 28W
Mill, I. 13 66 0S 101 30E
Mill Valley 163 37 54N 122 32W
Millau 44 44 8N 3 4E
Millbrook, U.K. 30 50 19N 4 12W
Millbrook, U.S.A. 162 41 47N 73 42W
Millbrook Res. 109 34 50S 138 49E
Mille Lacs, L. 158 46 10N 93 30W
Mille Lacs, L. des 150 48 45N 90 35W
Milledgeville 157 33 7N 83 15W
Millen 157 32 50N 81 57W
Miller 158 44 35N 98 59W
Millerovo 83 48 57N 40 28E
Miller's Flat 143 45 39S 169 23E
Millersburg 162 40 32N 76 58W
Millerton, N.Z. 143 41 39S 171 54E
Millerton, U.S.A. 162 41 57N 73 32W
Millerton, L. 163 37 0N 119 42W
Milleur Pt. 34 55 2N 5 5W
Millevaches, Plat. de 44 45 45N 2 0E
Millicent 140 37 34S 140 21E
Millingen 46 51 52N 6 2E
Millinocket 151 45 45N 68 45W
Millisle 38 54 38N 5 33W
Millmerran 139 27 53S 151 16E
Millom 32 54 13N 3 16W
Millport 34 55 45N 4 55W
Mills L. 152 61 30N 118 20W
Millsboro 162 38 36N 75 17W
Millstreet 39 52 4N 9 5W
Milltown, Galway, Ireland 38 53 37N 8 54W
Milltown, Kerry, Ireland 39 52 9N 9 42W
Milltown, U.K. 37 57 33N 4 48W
Milltown Malbay 39 52 51N 9 25W
Millville, N.J., U.S.A. 162 39 22N 75 0W
Millville, Pa., U.S.A. 162 41 7N 76 32W
Millwood Res. 159 33 45N 94 0W
Milly 43 48 24N 2 20E
Milly Milly 137 26 4S 116 43E
Milna 63 43 20N 16 28E
Milnathort 35 56 14N 3 25W
Milne Inlet 149 72 30N 80 0W
Milne, R. 138 21 10S 137 33E
Milngavie 34 55 57N 4 20W
Milnor 158 46 19N 97 29W
Milnthorpe 32 54 14N 2 47W
Milo, Can. 152 50 34N 112 53W
Milo, China 108 24 28N 103 23E
Milolii 147 22 8N 159 42W
Milos 69 36 44N 24 25E
Milos, I. 69 36 44N 24 25E
Milo evo 66 45 42N 20 20E
Miłoslaw 54 52 12N 17 32E
Milovaig 36 57 27N 6 45W
Milparinka P.O. 139 29 46S 141 57E
Miltenberg 49 49 41N 9 13E
Milton, N.Z. 143 46 7S 169 59E
Milton, Dumf. & Gall., U.K. 34 55 18N 4 50W
Milton, Hants., U.K. 28 50 45N 1 40W
Milton, Northants, U.K. 29 52 12N 0 55W
Milton, Calif., U.S.A. 163 38 3N 120 51W
Milton, Del., U.S.A. 162 38 47N 75 19W
Milton, Fla., U.S.A. 157 30 38N 87 0W
Milton, Pa., U.S.A. 162 41 0N 76 53W
Milton Abbot 30 50 35N 4 16W
Milton-Freewater 160 45 57N 118 24W
Milton Keynes 29 52 3N 0 42W
Milverton 28 51 2N 3 15W
Milwaukee 156 43 9N 87 58W
Milwaukie 160 45 27N 122 39W
Mim 120 6 57N 2 33W
Mimizan 44 44 12N 1 13W
Mimon 52 50 38N 14 43E
Mimoso 171 15 10S 48 5W
Min Chiang, R., China 105 28 48N 104 33E
Min Chiang, R., Fukien, China 109 26 5N 119 37E
Min Chiang, R., Szechwan, China 108 28 48N 104 33E
Min-Kush 85 41 4N 74 28E
Mina 161 38 21N 118 9W
Mina Pirquitas 172 22 40S 66 40W
Mina Saud 92 28 45N 48 20E
Minā'al Ahmadī 92 29 5N 48 10E
Mīnāb 93 27 10N 57 1E
Minago, R. 153 54 33N 98 13W
Minakami 111 36 49N 138 59E
Minaki 153 50 0N 94 40W
Minakuchi 111 34 58N 136 10E
Minamata 110 32 10N 130 30E
Minamitane 112 30 25N 130 54E
Minas Basin 151 45 20N 64 12W
Minas de Rio Tinto 57 37 42N 6 22W
Minas de San Quintín 57 38 49N 4 23W
Minas Gerais □ 171 18 50S 46 0W
Minas Novas 171 17 15S 42 36W
Minas, Sierra de las 166 15 9N 89 31W
Minatitlán 165 17 58N 94 35W
Minbu 98 20 10N 95 0E
Minbya 98 20 22N 93 16E
Mincha 140 36 1S 144 6E
Minch'in 106 38 42N 103 11E
Minch'ing 109 26 13N 118 51E
Minchinhampton 28 51 42N 2 10W
Mincio, R. 62 45 8N 10 55E
Mindanao, I. 103 8 0N 125 0E
*Mindanao Sea 103 9 0N 124 0E
Mindanao Trench 103 8 0N 128 0E
Mindelheim 49 48 4N 10 30E
Minden, Ger. 48 52 18N 8 54E
Minden, U.S.A. 159 32 40N 93 20W
Mindiptana 103 5 45S 140 22E
Mindon 98 19 21N 94 44E
Mindoro, I. 103 13 0N 121 0E
Mindoro Strait 103 12 30N 120 30E
Mindouli 124 4 12S 14 28E
Mine 110 34 12N 131 7E
Mine Hd. 39 52 0N 7 37W
Minehead 28 51 12N 3 29W
Mineola, N.Y., U.S.A. 162 40 45N 73 38W
Mineola, Tex., U.S.A. 159 32 40N 95 30W
Minera 31 53 3N 3 7W
Mineral King 163 36 27N 118 36W
Mineral Wells 159 32 50N 98 5W
Mineralnyye Vody 83 44 18N 43 15E
Minersville, Pa., U.S.A. 162 40 40N 76 17W
Minersville, Utah, U.S.A. 161 38 14N 112 58W
Minervino Murge 65 41 6N 16 4E
Minette 157 30 54N 87 43W
Minetto 162 43 24N 76 28W
Mingan 151 50 20N 64 0W
Mingary, Austral. 140 32 8S 140 45E
Mingary, U.K. 36 56 42N 6 5W
Mingch'i 109 26 24N 117 12E
Mingchiang 109 32 28N 114 8E
Mingechaur 83 40 52N 47 0E
Mingechaurskoye Vdkhr. 83 40 56N 47 20E
Mingela 138 19 52S 146 38E
Mingenew 137 29 12S 115 21E
Mingera Cr. 138 20 38S 138 10E
Mingin 98 22 50N 94 30E
Minginish, Dist. 36 57 14N 6 15W
Minglanilla 58 39 34N 1 38W
Mingulay I. 36 56 50N 7 40W
Minho □ 55 41 25N 8 20W
Minho, R. 55 41 58N 8 40W
Minhou 109 26 0N 119 18E
Minhow = Fuchou 109 26 5N 119 18E
Minhsien 106 34 26N 104 2E
Minidoka 160 42 47N 113 34W
Minigwal L. 137 29 31S 123 14E
Minilya 137 23 55S 114 0E
Minilya, R. 137 23 45S 114 0E
Mininera 140 37 37S 142 58E
Minióevo 66 43 42N 22 18E
Minipi, L. 151 52 25N 60 45W
Minj 135 5 54S 144 30E
Mink L. 152 61 54N 117 40W
Minlaton 140 34 45S 137 35E
Minna 121 9 37N 6 30E
Minneapolis, Kans., U.S.A. 158 39 11N 97 40W
Minneapolis, Minn., U.S.A. 158 44 58N 93 20W
Minnesota □ 158 46 40N 94 0W
Minnesund 71 60 23N 11 14E
Minnie Creek 137 24 3S 115 42E
Minnigaff 34 54 58N 4 30W
Minnitaki L. 150 49 47N 91 5W
Mino 111 35 32N 136 55E
Mino-Kamo 111 35 23N 137 2E
Mino-Mikawa-Kōgen 111 35 10N 137 30E
Miño, R. 56 41 58N 8 40W
Minobu 111 35 22N 138 26E
Minobu-Sanchi 111 35 14N 138 20E
Minorca = Menorca 58 40 0N 4 0E
Minore 141 32 14S 148 27E
Minot 158 48 10N 101 15W
Minquiers, Les 42 48 58N 2 8W
Minsen 48 53 43N 7 58E
Minsk 80 53 52N 27 30E
Minsk Mazowiecki 54 52 10N 21 33E
Minster 29 51 20N 1 20E
Minster-on-Sea 29 51 25N 0 50E
Minsterley 28 52 38N 2 56W
Mintaka Pass 93 37 0N 74 58E
Minthami 98 23 55N 94 16E
Mintlaw 37 57 32N 1 59W
Minto 147 64 55N 149 20W
Minto L. 150 48 0N 84 45W
Minton 153 49 10N 104 35W
Minturn 160 39 45N 106 25W
Minturno 64 41 15N 13 43E
Minûf 122 30 26N 30 52E
Minusinsk 77 53 50N 91 20E
Minutang 98 28 15N 96 30E
Minvoul 124 2 9N 12 8E
Minya Konka 108 29 34N 101 53E
Minyar 84 55 4N 57 33E
Minyip 140 36 29S 142 36E
Mionica 66 44 14N 20 6E
Mios Num, I. 103 1 30S 135 10E
Miquelon 151 47 3N 56 20W
Miquelon, St. Pierre et, □ 151 47 8N 56 24W
Mir-Bashir 83 40 11N 46 58E
Mira, Italy 63 45 26N 12 9E
Mira, Port. 56 40 26N 8 44W
Mira, R. 57 37 30N 8 30W
Mirabella Eclano 65 41 3N 14 59E
Miracema do Norte 170 9 33S 48 24W
Mirador 170 6 22S 44 22W
Miraflores 164 23 21N 109 45W
Miraj 96 16 50N 74 45E
Miram 138 21 15S 148 55E
Miram Shah 94 33 0N 70 0E
Miramar, Argent. 172 38 15S 57 50W
Miramar, Mozam. 129 23 50S 35 35E
Miramas 45 43 33N 4 59E
Mirambeau 44 45 23N 0 35W
Miramichi B. 151 47 15N 65 0W
Miramont-de-Guyenne 44 44 37N 0 21E
Miranda 175 20 10S 56 15W
Miranda de Ebro 58 42 41N 2 57W
Miranda do Corvo 56 40 6N 8 20W
Miranda do Douro 56 41 30N 6 16W
Mirando City 159 27 28N 98 59W
Mirandola 62 44 53N 11 2E
Mirandópolis 173 21 9S 51 6W
Mirango 127 13 32S 34 58E
Mirano 63 45 29N 12 6E
Miraporvos, I. 167 22 9N 74 30W
Mirassol 173 20 46S 49 28W
Mirboo North 141 38 24S 146 10E
Mirear, I. 122 23 15N 35 41E
Mirebeau, Côte d'Or, France 43 47 25N 5 20E
Mirebeau, Vienne, France 42 46 49N 0 10E
Mirecourt 43 48 20N 6 10E
Mirgorod 80 49 58N 33 50E
Miri 102 4 18N 114 0E
Miriam Vale 138 24 20S 151 33E
Mirim, Lagoa 173 32 45S 52 50W
Mirimire 174 11 10N 68 43W
Mirny 13 66 0S 95 0E
Mirnyy 77 62 33N 113 53E
Mirond L. 153 55 6N 102 47W
Mirosławiec 54 53 20N 16 5E
Mirpur 95 33 15N 73 50E
Mirpur Bibiwari 94 28 33N 67 44E
Mirpur Khas 94 25 30N 69 0E
Mirpur Sakro 94 24 33N 67 41E
Mirrool 141 34 19S 147 10E
Mirror 152 52 30N 113 7W
Mîrsani 70 44 1N 23 59E
Mirsk 54 50 58N 15 23E
Miryang 107 35 31N 128 44E
Mirzaani 83 41 24N 46 5E
Mirzapur 95 25 10N 82 45E
Misantla 165 19 56N 96 50W
Miscou I. 151 47 57N 64 31W
Misery, Mt. 108 34 52S 138 48E
Mish'ab, Ra'as al 92 28 15N 48 43E
Mishan 105 45 31N 132 2E
Mishawaka 156 41 40N 86 8W
Mishbih, Gebel 122 22 48N 34 38E
Mishima 111 35 10N 138 52E
Mishkino 84 55 20N 63 55E
Mishmar Aiyalon 90 31 52N 34 57E
Mishmar Ha' Emeq 90 32 37N 35 7E
Mishmar Ha Negev 90 31 22N 34 48E
Mishmar Ha Yarden 90 33 0N 35 56E
Mishmi Hills 98 29 0N 96 0E
Misilmeri 64 38 2N 13 25E
Misima I. 135 10 40S 152 45E
Misión, La 164 32 5N 116 50W
Misiones □, Argent. 173 27 0S 55 0W
Misiones □, Parag. 172 27 0S 56 0W
Miskin 93 23 44N 56 52E
Miskitos, Cayos 166 14 26N 82 50W
Miskolc 53 48 7N 20 50E
Misoke 126 0 42S 28 2E
Misoöl, I. 103 2 0S 130 0E
Misrātah 119 32 18N 15 3E
Missanabie 150 48 20N 84 6W
Missão Velha 170 7 15S 39 10W
Misserghin 118 35 44N 0 49W
Missinaibi L. 150 48 23N 83 40W
Missinaibi, R. 150 50 30N 82 40W
Mission, S.D., U.S.A. 158 43 21N 100 36W
Mission, Tex., U.S.A. 159 26 15N 98 30W
Mission City 152 49 10N 122 15W
Missisa L. 150 52 20N 85 7W
Missisagi 150 46 15N 83 9W
Mississippi, R. 159 35 30N 90 0W
Mississippi Sd. 159 30 25N 89 0W
Missoula 160 47 0N 114 0W
Missouri □ 158 38 25N 92 30W
Missouri, Little, R. 160 46 0N 111 35W
Missouri, R. 158 40 20N 95 40W
Mistake B. 153 62 8N 93 0W
Mistassini L. 150 51 0N 73 40W
Mistassini, R. 151 48 42N 72 20W
Mistastin L. 151 55 57N 63 20W
Mistatim 153 52 52N 103 22W
Mistelbach 53 48 34N 16 34E
Misterbianco 65 37 32N 15 0E
Misterton, Notts., U.K. 33 53 27N 0 49W
Misterton, Som., U.K. 28 50 51N 2 46W
Mistretta 65 37 56N 14 20E
Misty L. 153 58 53N 101 40W
Misugi 111 34 31N 136 16E
Misumi 110 32 37N 130 27E
Mît Ghamr 122 30 42N 31 12E
Mitaka 111 35 40N 139 33E
Mitan 85 40 0N 66 35E
Mitatib 123 15 59N 36 12E
Mitchel Troy 31 51 46N 2 45W
Mitcheldean 28 51 51N 2 29W
Mitchell, Austral. 139 26 29S 147 58E
Mitchell, Ind., U.S.A. 156 38 42N 86 25W
Mitchell, Nebr., U.S.A. 158 41 58N 103 45W
Mitchell, Oreg., U.S.A. 160 44 31N 120 8W
Mitchell, S.D., U.S.A. 158 43 40N 98 0W
Mitchell, Mt. 157 35 40N 82 20W
Mitchell, R. 138 15 12S 141 35E
Mitchelstown 39 52 16N 8 18W
Mitchelton 108 27 25S 152 59E
Mitha Tiwana 94 32 13N 72 6E
Míthimna 68 39 20N 26 12E
Mitiamo 140 36 12S 144 15E
Mitilini 69 39 6N 26 35E
Mitilíni = Lesvos 68 39 0N 26 20E
Mitilinoi 69 37 42N 26 56E
Mitla 165 16 55N 96 24W
Mito 111 36 20N 140 30E
Mitsinjo 129 16 1S 45 52E
Mitsiwa 123 15 35N 39 25E
Mitsiwa Channel 123 15 30N 40 0E
Mitsukaidō 111 36 1N 139 59E
Mittagong 141 34 28S 150 29E
Mittelland 50 46 50N 7 23E
Mittelland Kanal 48 52 23N 7 45E
Mittenwalde 48 52 16N 13 33E
Mittweida 48 50 59N 13 0E
Mitu 108 25 21N 100 32E
Mitú 174 1 8N 70 3W
Mituas 174 3 52N 68 49W
Mitumba 126 7 8S 31 2E
Mitumba, Chaîne des 126 10 0S 26 20E
Mitwaba 127 8 2N 27 17E
Mityana 126 0 23N 32 2E
Mitzick 124 0 45N 11 40E
Miura 111 35 12N 139 40E
Mius, R. 83 47 30N 39 0E
Mixteco, R. 165 18 11N 98 30W
Miyagi-Ken □ 112 38 15N 140 45E
Miyâh, W. el 122 25 10N 33 30E
Miyake-Jima 111 34 0N 139 30E
Miyako 112 39 40N 141 75E
Miyako-Jima 112 24 45N 125 20E
Miyakonojō 110 31 32N 131 5E
Miyanojō 110 31 54N 130 27E
Miyanoura-Dake 112 30 20N 130 26E
Miyata 110 33 49N 130 42E
Miyazaki 110 31 56N 131 30E
Miyazaki-ken □ 110 32 0N 131 30E
Miyazu 110 35 35N 135 10E
Miyet, Bahr el 92 31 30N 35 30E
Miyoshi 110 34 48N 132 51E
Miyün 106 40 22N 116 49E
Mizamis = Ozamiz 103 8 15N 123 50E
Mizdah 119 31 30N 13 0E
Mizen Hd., Cork, Ireland 39 51 27N 9 50W
Mizen Hd., Wick., Ireland 39 52 52N 6 4W
Mizil 70 44 59N 26 29E
Mizoram □ 98 23 0N 92 40E
Mizuho 111 35 6N 135 17E
Mizunami 111 35 22N 137 15E
Mjöbäck 73 57 28N 12 53E
Mjölby 73 58 20N 15 10E
Mjømna 71 60 55N 4 55E

*Renamed Bohol Sea

CIB

Mjörn Montcornet

Mjörn	**73**	57 55N	12 25 E
Mjøsa	**71**	60 40N	11 0 E
Mkata	**126**	5 45 S	38 20 E
Mkokotoni	**126**	5 55 S	39 15 E
Mkomazi	**126**	4 40 S	38 7 E
Mkulwe	**127**	8 37 S	32 20 E
Mkumbi, Ras	**126**	7 38 S	39 55 E
Mkushi	**127**	14 25 S	29 15 E
Mkushi River	**127**	13 40 S	29 30 E
Mkuze, R.	**129**	27 45 S	32 30 E
Mkwaya	**126**	6 17 S	35 40 E
Mladá Boleslav	**52**	50 27N	14 53 E
Mladenovac	**66**	44 28N	20 44 E
Mlala Hills	**126**	6 50 S	31 40 E
Mlange	**127**	16 2 S	35 33 E
Mlava, R.	**66**	44 35N	21 18 E
Mława	**54**	53 9N	20 25 E
Mlinište	**63**	44 15N	16 50 E
Mljet, I.	**66**	42 43N	17 30 E
Młynary	**54**	54 12N	19 46 E
Mme	**121**	6 18N	10 14 E
Mo, Hordaland, Norway	**71**	60 49N	5 48 E
Mo, Telemark, Norway	**71**	59 28N	7 50 E
Mo, Sweden	**72**	61 19N	16 47 E
Mo i Rana	**74**	66 15N	14 7 E
Moa, I.	**103**	8 0 S	128 0 E
Moa, R.	**120**	7 0N	11 40W
Moab	**161**	38 40N	109 35W
Moabi	**124**	2 24 S	10 59 E
Moalie Park	**139**	29 42 S	143 3 E
Moaña	**56**	42 18N	8 43W
Moanda	**124**	1 28 S	13 21 E
Moapo	**161**	36 45N	114 37W
Moate	**39**	53 25N	7 43W
Moba	**126**	7 0 S	29 48 E
Mobara	**111**	35 25N	140 18 E
Mobaye	**124**	4 25N	21 5 E
Mobayi	**124**	4 15N	21 8 E
Moberley	**158**	39 25N	92 25W
Moberly, R.	**152**	56 12N	120 55W
Mobert	**150**	48 41N	85 40W
Mobile	**157**	30 41N	88 3W
Mobile B.	**157**	30 30N	88 0W
Mobile, Pt.	**157**	30 15N	88 0W
Mobjack B.	**162**	37 16N	76 22W
Möborg	**73**	56 24N	8 21 E
Mobridge	**158**	45 40N	100 28W
Mobutu Sese Seko, L.	**126**	1 30N	31 0 E
Moc Chav	**100**	20 50N	104 38 E
Moc Hoa	**101**	10 46N	105 56 E
Mocabe Kasari	**127**	9 58 S	26 12 E
Mocajuba	**170**	2 35 S	49 30W
Moçambique	**127**	15 3 S	40 42 E
Moçambique □	**127**	14 45 S	38 30 E
Mocanaqua	**162**	41 9N	76 8W
Mochiang	**108**	23 25N	101 44 E
Mochiara Grove	**128**	20 43 S	21 50 E
Mochudi	**128**	24 27 S	26 7 E
Mocimboa da Praia	**127**	11 25 S	40 20 E
Mociu	**70**	46 46N	24 3 E
Möckeln	**73**	56 40N	14 15 E
Mockhorn I.	**162**	37 10N	75 52W
Moclips	**160**	47 14N	124 10W
Moçâmedes □	**128**	16 35 S	12 30 E
Mocoa	**174**	1 15N	76 45W
Mococa	**173**	21 28 S	47 0W
Mocorito	**164**	25 20N	108 0W
Moctezuma	**164**	30 12N	106 26W
Moctezuma, R.	**165**	21 59N	98 34W
Mocuba	**125**	16 54 S	37 25 E
Moda	**98**	24 22N	96 29 E
Modane	**45**	45 12N	6 40 E
Modasa	**94**	23 30N	73 21 E
Modave	**47**	50 27N	5 18 E
Modbury, Austral.	**109**	34 50 S	138 41 E
Modbury, U.K.	**30**	50 21N	3 53W
Modder, R.	**128**	28 50 S	24 50 E
Modderrivier	**128**	29 2 S	24 38 E
Módena	**62**	44 39N	10 55 E
Modena	**161**	37 55N	113 56W
Modesto	**163**	37 43N	121 0W
Módica	**65**	36 52N	14 45 E
Modigliana	**63**	44 9N	11 48 E
Modjokerto	**103**	7 29 S	112 25 E
Modlin	**54**	52 24N	20 41 E
Mödling	**53**	48 5N	16 17 E
Modo	**123**	5 31N	30 33 E
Modra	**53**	48 19N	17 20 E
Modreeny	**39**	52 57N	8 6W
Modriča	**66**	44 57N	18 17 E
Moe	**141**	38 12 S	146 19 E
Moebase	**127**	17 3 S	38 41 E
Moei, R.	**101**	17 25N	98 10 E
Moëlan-s-Mer	**42**	47 49N	3 38W
Moelfre	**31**	53 21N	4 15W
Moengo	**175**	5 45N	54 20W
Moergestel	**47**	51 33N	5 11 E
Moësa, R.	**51**	46 12N	9 10 E
Moffat	**35**	55 20N	3 27W
Moga	**94**	30 48N	75 8 E
Mogadiscio = Mogadishu	**91**	2 2N	45 25 E
Mogadishu	**91**	2 2N	45 25 E
Mogador = Essaouira	**118**	31 32N	9 42W
Mogadouro	**56**	41 22N	6 47W
Mogami-gawa, R.	**112**	38 45N	140 0 E
Mogaung	**98**	25 20N	97 0 E
Møgeltønder	**73**	54 57N	8 48 E
Mogente	**59**	38 52N	0 45W
Moggil	**108**	27 34 S	152 52 E
Mogho	**123**	4 54N	40 16 E
Mogi das Cruzes	**173**	23 45 S	46 20W
Mogi-Guaçu, R.	**173**	20 53 S	48 10W
Mogi-Mirim	**173**	22 20 S	47 0W
Mogielnica	**54**	51 42N	20 41 E
Mogilev	**80**	53 55N	30 18 E
Mogilev Podolskiy	**82**	48 20N	27 40 E
Mogilno	**54**	52 39N	17 55 E
Mogincual	**125**	15 35 S	40 25 E
Mogliano Veneto	**63**	45 33N	12 15 E
Mogocha	**77**	53 40N	119 50 E
Mogoi	**103**	1 55 S	133 10 E
Mogok	**98**	23 0N	96 40 E
Mogollon	**161**	33 25N	108 55W
Mogollon Mesa	**161**	43 40N	111 0W
Mogriguy	**141**	32 3 S	148 40 E
Moguer	**57**	37 15N	6 52W
Mogumber	**137**	31 2 S	116 3 E
Mohács	**53**	45 58N	18 41 E
Mohaka, R.	**142**	39 7 S	177 12 E
Mohall	**158**	48 46N	101 30W
Mohammadābād	**93**	37 30N	59 5 E
Mohammedia	**118**	33 44N	7 21W
Mohave Desert	**161**	35 0N	117 30W
Mohawk	**161**	32 45N	113 50W
Mohawk, R.	**162**	42 47N	73 42W
Moheda	**73**	57 1N	14 35 E
Mohembo	**125**	18 15 S	21 43 E
Moher, Cliffs of	**39**	52 58N	9 30W
Mohican, C.	**147**	60 10N	167 30W
Mohill	**38**	53 57N	7 52W
Möhne, R.	**48**	51 29N	8 10 E
Mohnyin	**98**	24 47N	96 22 E
Moholm	**73**	58 37N	14 5 E
Mohon	**43**	49 45N	4 44 E
Mohoro	**126**	8 6 S	39 8 E
Moia	**123**	5 3N	28 2 E
Moidart, L.	**36**	56 47N	5 40W
Moinabad	**96**	17 44N	77 16 E
Moineşti	**70**	46 28N	26 21 E
Mointy	**76**	47 40N	73 45 E
Moira	**38**	54 28N	6 16W
Moirais	**69**	35 4N	24 56 E
Moirans	**45**	45 20N	5 33 E
Moirans-en-Montagne	**45**	46 26N	5 43 E
Moisäkula	**80**	58 3N	24 38 E
Moisie	**151**	50 7N	66 1W
Moisie, R.	**151**	50 6N	66 5W
Moissac	**44**	44 7N	1 5 E
Moita	**57**	38 38N	8 58W
Mojácar	**59**	37 6N	1 55W
Mojados	**56**	41 26N	4 40W
Mojave	**163**	35 8N	118 8W
Mojave Desert	**163**	35 0N	116 30W
Mojo, Boliv.	**172**	21 48 S	65 33W
Mojo, Ethiopia	**123**	8 35N	39 5 E
Mojo, I.	**102**	8 10 S	117 40 E
Moju, R.	**170**	1 40 S	48 25W
Mokai	**142**	38 32 S	175 56 E
Mokambo	**127**	12 25 S	28 20 E
Mokameh	**95**	25 24N	85 55 E
Mokau, R.	**142**	38 35 S	174 55 E
Mokelumne Hill	**163**	38 18N	120 43W
Mokelumne, R.	**163**	38 23N	121 25W
Mokhós	**69**	35 16N	25 27 E
Mokhotlong	**126**	29 22 S	29 2 E
Mokihinui	**143**	41 33 S	171 58 E
Moknine	**119**	35 35N	10 58 E
Mokokchung	**99**	26 15N	94 30 E
Mokpalin	**98**	17 26N	96 53 E
Mokpo	**107**	34 50N	126 30 E
Mokra Gora	**66**	42 50N	20 30 E
Mokronog	**63**	45 57N	15 9 E
Moksha, R.	**81**	54 45N	43 40 E
Mokshan	**81**	52 25N	44 35 E
Mokta Spera	**120**	16 38N	9 6W
Moktama Kwe	**99**	15 40N	96 30 E
Mol	**47**	51 11N	5 5 E
Mola, C. de la	**58**	39 53N	4 20 E
Mola di Bari	**65**	41 3N	17 5 E
Moland	**71**	59 11N	8 6 E
Moláoi	**69**	36 49N	22 56 E
Molat, I.	**63**	44 15N	14 50 E
Molchanovo	**76**	57 40N	83 50 E
Mold	**31**	53 10N	3 10W
Moldava nad Bodvou	**53**	48 38N	21 0 E
Moldavia = Moldova	**70**	46 30N	27 0 E
Moldavian S.S.R. □	**82**	47 0N	28 0 E
Molde	**71**	62 45N	7 9 E
Moldotau, Khrebet	**85**	41 35N	75 0 E
Moldova	**70**	46 30N	27 0 E
Moldova Nouă	**70**	44 45N	21 41 E
Moldoveanu, mt.	**67**	45 36N	24 45 E
Mole Creek	**138**	41 32 S	146 24 E
Mole, R.	**29**	51 13N	0 15W
Molepolole	**125**	24 28 S	25 28 E
Moléson	**50**	46 33N	7 1 E
Molesworth	**143**	42 5 S	173 16 E
Molfetta	**65**	41 12N	16 35 E
Molina de Aragón	**58**	40 46N	1 52W
Moline	**158**	41 30N	90 30W
Molinella	**63**	44 38N	11 40 E
Molinos	**172**	25 28 S	66 15W
Moliro	**126**	8 12 S	30 30 E
Molise □	**63**	41 45N	14 30 E
Moliterno	**65**	40 14N	15 50 E
Mollahat	**98**	22 56N	89 48 E
Mölle	**73**	56 17N	12 31 E
Molledo	**56**	43 8N	4 6W
Mollendo	**174**	17 0 S	72 0W
Mollerin, L.	**137**	30 30 S	117 35 E
Mollerusa	**58**	41 37N	0 54 E
Mollina	**57**	37 8N	4 38W
Mölln	**48**	53 37N	10 41 E
Mollösund	**73**	58 4N	11 30 E
Mölltorp	**73**	58 30N	14 26 E
Mölndal	**73**	57 40N	12 3 E
Mölnlycke	**73**	57 40N	12 8 E
Molo	**98**	23 22N	96 53 E
Molochansk	**82**	47 15N	35 23 E
Molochaya, R.	**82**	47 0N	35 30 E
Molodechno	**80**	54 20N	26 50 E
Molokai, I.	**147**	21 8N	157 0W
Moloma, R.	**81**	59 0N	48 15 E
Molong	**141**	33 5 S	148 54 E
Molopo, R.	**125**	25 40 S	24 30 E
Mólos	**69**	38 47N	22 37 E
Molotov, Mys	**77**	81 10N	95 0 E
Moloundou	**124**	2 8N	15 15 E
Molsheim	**43**	48 33N	7 29 E
Molson L.	**153**	54 22N	95 32W
Molteno	**128**	31 22 S	26 22 E
Molu, I.	**103**	6 45 S	131 40 E
Molucca Sea	**103**	4 0 S	124 0 E
Moluccas = Maluku, Is.	**103**	1 0 S	127 0 E
Molusi	**128**	20 21 S	24 29 E
Moma, Mozam.	**127**	16 47 S	39 4 E
Moma, Zaïre	**126**	1 35 S	23 52 E
Momanga	**128**	18 7 S	21 41 E
Momba	**140**	30 58 S	143 30 E
Mombaça	**170**	15 43 S	48 43W
Mombasa	**126**	4 2 S	39 43 E
Mombetsu, Hokkaido, Japan	**112**	42 27N	142 4 E
Mombetsu, Hokkaido, Japan	**112**	44 21N	143 22 E
Mombuey	**56**	42 3N	6 20W
Momchilgrad	**67**	41 33N	25 23 E
Momi	**126**	1 42 S	27 0 E
Momignies	**47**	50 2N	4 10 E
Mompós	**174**	9 14N	74 26W
Møn	**73**	54 57N	12 15 E
Mon, R.	**99**	20 25N	94 30 E
Mona, Canal de la	**167**	18 30N	67 45W
Mona, I.	**167**	18 5N	67 54W
Mona Passage	**167**	18 0N	67 40W
Mona, Punta, C. Rica	**166**	9 37N	82 36W
Mona, Punta, Spain	**57**	36 43N	3 45W
Monach Is.	**36**	57 32N	7 40W
Monach, Sd. of	**36**	57 34N	7 26W
Monaco ■	**44**	43 46N	7 23 E
Monadhliath Mts.	**37**	57 10N	4 4W
Monadnock Mt.	**162**	42 52N	72 7W
Monagas □	**174**	9 20N	63 0W
Monaghan	**38**	54 15N	6 58W
Monaghan □	**38**	54 10N	7 0W
Monahans	**159**	31 35N	102 50W
Monapo	**127**	14 50 S	40 12 E
Monar For.	**36**	57 27N	5 10W
Monar L.	**36**	57 26N	5 8W
Monarch Mt.	**152**	51 55N	125 57W
Monasterevan	**39**	53 10N	7 5W
Monastier-sur-Gazeille, Le	**44**	44 57N	3 59 E
Monastir	**119**	35 50N	10 49 E
Monastyriska	**80**	49 8N	25 14 E
Monavullagh Mts.	**39**	52 14N	7 35W
Moncada	**58**	39 30N	0 24W
Moncalieri	**62**	45 0N	7 40 E
Moncalvo	**62**	45 3N	8 15 E
Moncarapacho	**57**	37 5N	7 46W
Moncayo, Sierra del	**58**	41 48N	1 50W
Mönchengladbach	**48**	51 12N	6 23 E
Monchique	**57**	37 19N	8 38W
Monchique, Sa. de,	**55**	37 18N	8 39W
Monclova	**164**	26 50N	101 30W
Monção	**56**	42 4N	8 27W
Moncontant	**42**	46 43N	0 36W
Moncontour	**42**	48 22N	2 38W
Moncton	**151**	46 7N	64 51W
Mondego, Cabo	**56**	40 11N	8 54W
Mondego, R.	**56**	40 28N	8 0W
Mondeodo	**103**	3 21 S	122 9 E
Mondolfo	**63**	43 45N	13 8 E
Mondoñedo	**56**	43 25N	7 23W
Mondoví	**62**	44 23N	7 56 E
Mondovi	**158**	44 37N	91 40W
Mondragon	**45**	44 13N	4 44 E
Mondragone	**64**	41 8N	13 52 E
Mondrain I.	**137**	34 9 S	122 14 E
Monduli □	**126**	3 0 S	36 0 E
Monemvasía	**69**	36 41N	23 3 E
Monessen	**156**	40 9N	79 50W
Monesterio	**57**	38 6N	6 15W
Monestier-de-Clermont	**45**	44 55N	5 38 E
Monet	**150**	48 10N	75 40W
Monêtier-les-Bains, Le	**45**	44 58N	6 30 E
Monett	**159**	36 55N	93 56W
Moneygall	**39**	52 54N	7 59W
Moneymore	**38**	54 42N	6 40W
Monfalcone	**63**	45 49N	13 32 E
Monflanquin	**44**	44 32N	0 47 E
Monforte	**57**	39 6N	7 25W
Monforte de Lemos	**56**	42 31N	7 33W
Mong Cai	**101**	21 27N	107 54 E
Möng Hsu	**99**	21 54N	98 30 E
Mong Hta	**98**	19 50N	98 35 E
Mong Ket	**98**	23 8N	98 22 E
Möng Kung	**98**	21 35N	97 35 E
Mong Kyawt	**98**	19 56N	98 45 E
Mong Lang	**101**	20 29N	97 52 E
Möng Nai	**98**	20 32N	97 55 E
Möng Pai	**98**	19 40N	97 15 E
Mong Pawk	**99**	22 4N	99 16 E
Mong Ping	**98**	21 22N	99 2 E
Mong Pu	**98**	20 55N	98 44 E
Mong Ton	**98**	20 25N	98 45 E
Mong Tung	**98**	22 2N	97 41 E
Mong Wa	**99**	21 26N	100 27 E
Mong Yai	**98**	22 28N	98 3 E
Mongalla	**123**	5 8N	31 55 E
Monger, L.	**137**	29 25 S	117 5 E
Monghyr	**95**	25 23N	86 30 E
Mongla	**98**	22 8N	89 35 E
Mongngaw	**98**	22 47N	96 59 E
Mongo	**117**	12 14N	18 43 E
Mongolia ■	**105**	47 0N	103 0 E
Mongonu	**121**	12 40N	13 32 E
Mongororo	**124**	12 22N	22 26 E
Mongoumba	**124**	3 33N	18 40 E
Mongpang	**101**	23 5N	100 25 E
Mongu	**125**	15 16 S	23 12 E
Mongua	**128**	16 43 S	15 20 E
Moniaive	**35**	55 11N	3 55W
Monifieth	**35**	56 30N	2 48W
Monistral-St.-Loire	**45**	45 17N	4 11 E
Monitor, Pk.	**163**	38 52N	116 35W
Monitor, Ra.	**163**	38 30N	116 45W
Monivea	**38**	53 22N	8 42W
Monk	**153**	47 7N	69 59W
Monkey Bay	**127**	14 7 S	35 1 E
Monkey River	**165**	16 22N	88 29W
Monki	**54**	53 23N	22 48 E
Monkira	**138**	24 46 S	140 30 E
Monkoto	**124**	1 38 S	20 35 E
Monmouth, U.K.	**31**	51 48N	2 43W
Monmouth, U.S.A.	**158**	40 50N	90 40W
Monmouth (□)	**26**	51 34N	3 5W
Monnow R.	**28**	51 54N	2 48W
Mono, L.	**163**	38 0N	119 9W
Mono, Punta del	**166**	12 0N	83 30W
Monolith	**163**	35 7N	118 22W
Monópoli	**65**	40 57N	17 18 E
Monor	**53**	47 21N	19 27 E
Monóvar	**59**	38 28N	0 53W
Monowai	**143**	45 53 S	167 25 E
Monowai, L.	**143**	45 53 S	167 25 E
Monreal del Campo	**58**	40 47N	1 20W
Monreale	**64**	38 6N	13 16 E
Monroe, La., U.S.A.	**159**	32 32N	92 4W
Monroe, Mich., U.S.A.	**156**	41 55N	83 26W
Monroe, N.C., U.S.A.	**157**	35 2N	80 37W
Monroe, Utah, U.S.A.	**161**	38 45N	111 39W
Monroe, Wis., U.S.A.	**158**	42 38N	89 40W
Monroe City	**158**	39 40N	91 40W
Monroeton	**162**	41 43N	76 29W
Monroeville	**157**	31 33N	87 15W
Monrovia, Liberia	**120**	6 18N	10 47W
Monrovia, U.S.A.	**161**	34 7N	118 1W
Mons	**47**	50 27N	3 58 E
Møns Klint	**73**	54 57N	12 33 E
Monsaraz	**57**	38 28N	7 22W
Monse	**103**	4 0 S	123 10 E
Monségur	**44**	44 38N	0 4 E
Monsélice	**63**	43 13N	11 45 E
Monster	**46**	52 1N	4 10 E
Mont-aux-Sources	**129**	28 44 S	28 52 E
Mont-de-Marsin	**44**	43 54N	0 31W
Mont d'Or, Tunnel	**43**	46 45N	6 18 E
Mont-Dore, Le	**44**	45 35N	2 50 E
Mont Joli	**151**	48 37N	68 10W
Mont Laurier	**150**	46 35N	75 30W
Mont Luis	**151**	42 31N	2 6 E
Mont St. Michel	**42**	48 40N	1 30W
Mont-sur-Marchienne	**47**	50 23N	4 24 E
Mont Tremblant Prov. Park	**150**	46 30N	74 30W
Montabaur	**48**	50 26N	7 49 E
Montacute	**109**	34 53 S	138 45 E
Montagnac	**44**	43 29N	3 28 E
Montagnana	**63**	45 13N	11 29 E
Montagu	**128**	33 45 S	20 8 E
Montagu, I.	**164**	58 30 S	26 15W
Montague, Can.	**151**	46 10N	62 39W
Montague, Calif., U.S.A.	**160**	41 47N	122 30W
Montague, Mass., U.S.A.	**162**	42 31N	72 33W
Montague, I.	**164**	31 40N	144 46W
Montague I.	**147**	60 0N	147 0W
Montague Ra.	**137**	29 15 S	119 30 E
Montague Sd.	**136**	14 28 S	125 20 E
Montaigu	**42**	46 59N	1 18W
Montalbán	**58**	40 50N	0 45W
Montalbano di Elicona	**65**	38 1N	15 0 E
Montalbano Iónico	**65**	40 17N	16 33 E
Montalbo	**58**	39 53N	2 42W
Montalcino	**63**	43 4N	11 30 E
Montalegre	**56**	41 49N	7 47W
Montalto di Castro	**63**	42 20N	11 36 E
Montalto Uffugo	**65**	39 25N	16 9 E
Montalvo	**163**	34 15N	119 12W
Montamarta	**56**	41 39N	5 49W
Montaña	**174**	6 0 S	73 0W
Montana	**50**	46 19N	7 29 E
Montana □	**154**	47 0N	110 0W
Montánchez	**57**	39 15N	6 8W
Montañita	**174**	1 30N	75 28W
Montargis	**43**	48 0N	2 43 E
Montauban	**44**	44 0N	1 21 E
Montauk	**162**	41 3N	71 57W
Montauk Pt.	**162**	41 4N	71 52W
Montbard	**43**	47 38N	4 20 E
Montbéliard	**43**	47 31N	6 48 E
Montblanch	**58**	41 23N	1 4 E
Montbrison	**45**	45 36N	4 3 E
Montcalm, Pic de	**44**	42 40N	1 25 E
Montceau-les-Mines	**43**	46 40N	4 23 E
Montchanin	**62**	46 47N	4 30 E
Montclair	**162**	40 53N	74 49W
Montcornet	**43**	49 40N	4 0 E

Montcuq Morvan, Mts. du

Montcuq 44 44 21N 1 13 E
Montdidier 43 49 38N 2 35 E
Monte Albán 165 17 2N 96 45W
Monte Alegre 175 2 0S 54 0W
Monte Alegre de Goiás 171 13 14S 47 10W
Monte Alegre de Minas 171 18 52S 48 52W
Monte Azul 171 15 9S 42 53W
Monte Bello Is. 136 20 30S 115 45 E
Monte Carlo 45 43 46N 7 23 E
Monte Carmelo 171 18 43S 47 29W
Monte Caseros 172 30 10S 57 50W
Monte Comán 172 34 40S 68 0W
Monte Cristi 167 19 52N 71 39W
Monte Libano 16 8 5N 75 29W
Monte Lindo, R. 172 25 30S 58 40W
Monte Quemado 172 25 53S 62 41W
Monte Redondo 56 39 53N 8 50W
Monte San Savino 63 43 20N 11 42 E
Monte Sant' Angelo 65 41 42N 15 59 E
Monte Santo, C. di 64 40 5N 9 42 E
Monte Visto 161 37 40N 106 8W
Monteagudo 173 27 14S 54 8W
Montealegre 59 38 48N 1 17W
Montebello 150 45 40N 74 55W
Montebelluna 63 45 47N 12 3 E
Montebourg 42 49 30N 1 20W
Montecastrilli 63 42 40N 12 30 E
Montecatini Terme 62 43 55N 10 48 E
Montecito 163 34 26N 119 40W
Montecristi 174 1 0S 80 40W
Montecristo, I. 62 42 20N 10 20 E
Montefalco 63 42 53N 12 38 E
Montefiascone 63 42 31N 12 2 E
Montefrío 57 37 20N 3 39W
Montegnée 47 50 38N 5 31 E
Montego B. 166 18 30N 78 0W
Montegranaro 63 43 13N 13 38 E
Monteiro 170 7 22S 37 38W
Monteith 140 35 11S 139 23 E
Montejicar 59 37 33N 3 30W
Montejinnie 136 16 40S 131 45 E
Montekomu Hu 99 34 40N 89 0 E
Montelibano 174 8 5N 75 29W
Montélimar 45 44 33N 4 45 E
Montella 65 40 50N 15 0 E
Montellano 57 36 59N 5 36W
Montello 158 43 49N 89 21W
Montelupo Fiorentino 62 43 44N 11 2 E
Montemór-o-Novo 57 38 40N 8 12W
Montemór-o-Velho 56 40 11N 8 40W
Montemorelos 165 25 11N 99 42W
Montendre 44 45 16N 0 26W
Montenegro 173 29 39S 51 29W
Montenegro □ 66 42 40N 19 20 E
Montenero di Bisaccia 63 42 0N 14 47 E
Montepuez 127 13 8S 38 59 E
Montepuez, R. 127 12 40S 40 15 E
Montepulciano 63 43 5N 11 46 E
Montereale 63 42 31N 13 13 E
Montereau 43 48 22N 2 57 E
Monterey 163 36 35N 121 57W
Monterey, B. 163 36 50N 121 55W
Montería 174 8 46N 75 53W
Monteros 172 27 11S 65 30W
Monterotondo 63 42 3N 12 36 E
Monterrey 164 25 40N 100 30W
Montes Altos 170 5 50S 47 4W
Montes Claros 171 16 30S 43 50W
Montes de Toledo 57 39 35N 4 30W
Montesano 160 47 0N 123 39W
Montesárchio 65 41 5N 14 37 E
Montescaglioso 65 40 34N 16 40 E
Montesilvano 63 42 30N 14 8 E
Montevarchi 63 43 30N 11 32 E
Monteverde 124 8 45S 16 45 E
Montevideo 173 34 50S 56 11W
Montezuma 158 41 32N 92 35W
Montfaucon, Haute-Loire, France 45 45 11N 4 20 E
Montfaucon, Meuse, France 43 49 16N 5 8 E
Montfort 47 51 7N 5 58 E
Montfort-l'Amaury 43 48 47N 1 49 E
Montfort-sur-Meu 42 48 8N 1 58W
Montgenèvre 45 44 56N 6 42 E
Montgomery, U.K. 31 52 34N 3 9W
Montgomery, Ala., U.S.A. 157 32 20N 86 20W
Montgomery, Pa., U.S.A. 162 41 10N 76 53W
Montgomery, W. Va., U.S.A. 156 38 9N 81 21W
Montgomery = Sahiwal 94 30 45N 73 8 E
Montgomery (□) 26 52 34N 3 9W
Montgomery Pass 163 37 58N 118 20W
Montguyon 44 45 12N 0 12W
Monthey 50 46 15N 6 56 E
Monticelli d'Ongina 62 45 3N 9 56 E
Monticello, Ark., U.S.A. 159 33 40N 91 48W
Monticello, Fla., U.S.A. 157 30 35N 83 50W
Monticello, Ind., U.S.A. 156 40 40N 86 45W
Monticello, Iowa, U.S.A. 158 42 18N 91 18W
Monticello, Ky., U.S.A. 157 36 52N 84 50W
Monticello, Minn., U.S.A. 158 45 17N 93 52W
Monticello, Miss., U.S.A. 159 31 35N 90 8W
Monticello, N.Y., U.S.A. 162 41 37N 74 42W
Monticello, Utah, U.S.A. 161 37 55N 109 27W
Montichiari 62 45 28N 10 29 E
Montieri 43 48 30N 4 45 E
Montignac 44 45 4N 1 10 E
Montignies-sur-Sambre 47 50 24N 4 29 E
Montigny-les-Metz 43 49 7N 6 10 E
Montigny-sur-Aube 43 47 57N 4 45 E
Montijo 57 38 52N 6 39W
Montijo, Presa de 57 38 55N 6 26W
Montilla 57 37 36N 4 40W
Montivideo 158 44 55N 95 40W
Montlhéry 43 48 39N 2 15 E
Montluçon 44 46 22N 2 36 E
Montmagny 151 46 58N 70 34W
Montmarault 53 46 11N 2 54 E
Montmartre 153 50 14N 103 27W
Montmédy 43 49 30N 5 20 E
Montmélian 45 45 30N 6 4 E
Montmirail 43 48 51N 3 30 E
Montmoreau-St.-Cybard 44 45 23N 0 8 E
Montmorency 151 46 53N 71 11W
Montmorillon 44 46 26N 0 50 E
Montmort 43 48 55N 3 49 E
Monto 138 24 52S 151 12 E
Montório al Vomano 63 42 35N 13 38 E
Montoro 57 38 1N 4 27W
Montour Falls 162 42 20N 76 51W
Montpelier, Idaho, U.S.A. 160 42 15N 111 29W
Montpelier, Ohio, U.S.A. 156 41 34N 84 40W
Montpelier, Vt., U.S.A. 156 44 15N 72 38W
Montpellier 44 43 37N 3 52 E
Montpezat-de-Quercy 44 44 15N 1 30 E
Montpon-Ménestrol 44 45 2N 0 11 E
Montréal, Can. 150 45 31N 73 34W
Montréal, France 44 43 13N 2 8 E
Montréal L. 153 54 20N 105 45W
Montreal Lake 153 54 3N 105 46W
Montredon-Labessonnié 44 43 45N 2 18 E
Montréjeau 44 43 6N 0 35 E
Montrésor 42 47 10N 1 10 E
Montreuil 43 50 27N 1 45 E
Montreuil-Bellay 42 47 8N 0 9W
Montreux 50 46 26N 6 55 E
Montrevault 42 47 17N 1 2W
Montrevel-en-Bresse 45 46 21N 5 8 E
Montrichard 42 47 20N 1 10 E
Montrose, U.K. 37 56 43N 2 28W
Montrose, Col., U.S.A. 161 38 30N 107 52W
Montrose, Pa., U.S.A. 162 41 50N 75 55W
Montrose, oilfield 19 57 20N 1 35 E
Montross 162 38 6N 76 50W
Monts, Pte des 151 49 27N 67 12W
Montsalvy 44 44 41N 2 30 E
Montsant, Sierra de 58 41 17N 0 1 E
Montsauche 43 47 13N 4 0 E
Montsech, Sierra del 58 42 0N 0 45 E
Montseny 58 42 29N 1 2 E
Montserrat, I. 167 16 40N 62 10W
Montserrat, mt. 58 41 36N 1 49 E
Montuenga 56 41 3N 4 38W
Montuiri 58 39 34N 2 59 E
Monveda 124 2 52N 21 30 E
Monymusk 37 57 13N 2 32W
Monyo 98 17 59N 95 30 E
Mônywa 98 22 7N 95 11 E
Monza 62 45 35N 9 15 E
Monze 127 16 17S 27 29 E
Monze, C. 94 24 47N 66 37 E
Monzón 58 41 52N 0 10 E
Mook 46 51 46N 5 54 E
Mo'oka 111 36 26N 140 1 E
Moolawatana 139 29 55S 139 45 E
Mooleulooloo 140 31 36S 140 32 E
Mooliabeenee 137 31 20S 116 2 E
Mooloogool 137 26 2S 119 5 E
Moomin, Cr. 139 29 44S 149 20 E
Moonah, R. 138 22 3S 138 33 E
Moonbeam 150 49 20N 82 10W
Mooncoin 39 52 18N 7 17W
Moonie 139 27 46S 150 20 E
Moonie, R. 139 27 45S 150 0 E
Moonta 140 34 6S 137 32 E
Moora 137 30 37S 115 58 E
Mooraberree 138 25 13S 140 54 E
Moorarie 137 25 56S 117 35 E
Moorcroft 158 44 17N 104 58W
Moore, L. 137 29 50S 117 35 E
Moore, R. 137 31 22S 115 30 E
Moore Reefs 138 16 0S 149 5 E
Moore River Native Settlement 137 31 1S 115 56 E
Moorebank 47 33 56S 150 56 E
Moorefield 156 39 5N 78 59W
Mooresville 157 35 36N 80 45W
Moorfoot Hills 35 55 44N 3 8W
Moorhead 158 47 0N 97 0W
Moorland 141 31 46S 152 38 E
Mooroopna 141 36 25S 145 22 E
Moorpark 163 34 17N 118 53W
Moorreesburg 128 33 6S 18 38 E
Moorslede 47 50 54N 3 4 E
Moosburg 49 48 28N 11 57 E
Moose Factory 150 51 20N 80 40W
Moose I. 153 51 42N 97 10W
Moose Jaw 153 50 24N 105 30W
Moose Jaw R. 153 50 34N 105 18W
Moose Lake, Can. 153 53 43N 100 20W
Moose Lake, U.S.A. 158 46 27N 92 48W
Moose Mountain Cr. 153 49 13N 102 12W
Moose Mtn. Prov. Park 153 49 48N 102 25W
Moose, R. 150 51 20N 80 25W
Moose River 150 50 48N 81 17W
Moosehead L. 151 45 40N 69 40W
Moosomin 153 50 9N 101 40W
Moosonee 150 51 17N 80 39W
Moosup 162 41 44N 71 52W
Mopeia 125 17 30S 35 40 E
Mopipi 128 21 6S 24 55 E
Mopoi 123 5 6N 26 54 E
Moppin 139 29 12S 146 45 E
Mopti 120 14 30N 4 0W
Moqatta 123 14 38N 35 50 E
Moquegua 174 17 15S 70 46W
Mór 53 47 25N 18 12 E
Móra 57 38 55N 8 10W
Mora, Sweden 72 61 2N 14 38 E
Mora, Minn., U.S.A. 158 45 52N 93 19W
Mora, N. Mex., U.S.A. 161 35 58N 105 21W
Mora de Ebro 58 41 6N 0 38 E
Mora de Rubielos 58 40 15N 0 45W
Mora la Nueva 58 41 7N 0 39 E
Morača, R. 66 42 40N 19 20 E
Morada Nova 170 5 7S 38 23W
Morada Nova de Minas 171 18 37S 45 22W
Moradabad 94 28 50N 78 50 E
Morafenobe 129 17 50S 44 53 E
Morag 54 53 55N 19 56 E
Moral de Calatrava 59 38 51N 3 33W
Moraleja 56 40 6N 6 43W
Morales 174 2 45N 76 38W
Moramanga 125 18 56S 48 12 E
Moran, Kans., U.S.A. 159 37 53N 94 35W
Moran, Wyo., U.S.A. 160 43 53N 110 37W
Morano Cálabro 65 39 51N 16 8 E
Morant Cays 166 17 22N 76 0W
Morant Pt. 166 17 55N 76 12W
Morar 36 56 58N 5 49W
Morar L. 36 56 57N 5 40W
Moratalla 59 38 14N 1 49W
Moratuwa 97 6 45N 79 55 E
Morava, R. 53 49 50N 16 50 E
Moravatío 164 19 51N 100 25W
Moravia, Iowa, U.S.A. 158 40 50N 92 50W
Moravia, N.Y., U.S.A. 162 42 43N 76 25W
Moravian Hts. = Ceskemoravská V. 52 49 30N 15 40 E
Moravica, R. 66 43 40N 20 8 E
Moravice, R. 53 49 50N 17 43 E
Moravița 66 45 17N 21 14 E
Moravska Trebová 53 49 45N 16 40 E
Moravské Budějovice 52 49 4N 15 49 E
Morawa 137 29 13S 116 0 E
Morawhanna 174 8 30N 59 40W
Moray (□) 26 57 32N 3 25W
Moray Firth 37 57 50N 3 30W
Morbach 49 49 48N 7 7 E
Morbegno 62 46 8N 9 34 E
Morbihan □ 42 47 55N 2 50W
Morcenx 44 44 0N 0 55W
Mordelles 42 48 5N 1 52W
Morden 153 49 15N 98 10W
Mordovian S.S.R.□ 81 54 20N 44 30 E
Mordovo 81 52 13N 40 50 E
More L. 37 58 18N 4 52W
Møre og Romsdal □ 71 63 0N 9 0 E
Morea 140 36 45S 141 18 E
Moreau, R. 158 45 15N 102 45W
Morebattle 35 55 30N 2 20W
Morecambe 32 54 5N 2 52W
Morecambe B. 32 54 7N 3 0W
Morecambe, gasfield 19 53 57N 3 40W
Moree 139 29 28S 149 54 E
Morehead, P.N.G. 135 8 41S 141 41 E
Morehead, U.S.A. 156 38 12N 83 22W
Morehead City 157 34 46N 76 44W
Moreira 174 0 34S 63 26W
Morelia 164 19 40N 101 11W
Morella, Austral. 138 23 0S 143 47 E
Morella, Spain 58 40 35N 0 2 E
Morelos 164 26 42N 107 40W
Morelos □ 165 18 40N 99 10W
Morena, Sierra 57 38 20N 4 0W
Morenci 161 33 7N 109 20W
Moreni 70 44 59N 25 36 E
Moreno 171 8 7S 35 6W
Mores, I. 157 26 15N 77 35W
Moresby I. 152 52 30N 131 40W
Morestel 45 45 40N 5 28 E
Moret 43 48 22N 2 48 E
Moreton B. 133 27 10S 153 10 E
Moreton, I. 139 27 10S 153 25 E
Moreton-in-Marsh 28 51 59N 1 42W
Moreton Telegraph Office 138 12 22S 142 30 E
Moretonhampstead 30 50 39N 3 45W
Moreuil 43 49 46N 2 30 E
Morez 45 46 31N 6 2 E
Morgan, Austral. 140 34 0S 139 35 E
Morgan, U.S.A. 160 41 3N 111 44W
Morgan City 159 29 40N 91 15W
Morgan Hill 163 37 8N 121 39W
Morganfield 156 37 40N 87 55W
Morganton 157 35 46N 81 48W
Morgantown 156 39 39N 79 58W
Morganville, Queens., Austral. 139 25 10S 152 0 E
Morganville, S. Australia, Austral. 140 33 10S 140 32 E
Morgat 42 48 15N 4 32 E
Morgenzon 129 26 45S 29 36 E
Morges 50 46 31N 6 29 E
Morhange 43 48 55N 6 38 E
Mori 62 45 51N 10 59 E
Morialmée 47 50 17N 4 30 E
Morialta Falls Reserve 109 34 54S 138 43 E
Moriarty 161 35 3N 106 2W
Morice L. 152 53 50N 127 40W
Morichal 174 2 10N 70 34W
Morichal Largo, R. 174 8 55N 63 0W
Moriguchi 111 34 44N 135 34 E
Moriki 121 12 52N 6 30 E
Morinville 152 53 49N 113 41W
Morioka 112 39 45N 141 8 E
Moris 164 28 8N 108 32W
Morisset 141 33 6S 151 30 E
Morkalla 140 34 23S 141 10 E
Morlaàs 44 43 21N 0 18W
Morlaix 42 48 36N 3 52W
Morlanwelz 47 50 28N 4 15 E
Morley 33 53 45N 1 36W
Mormanno 65 39 53N 15 59 E
Mormant 43 48 37N 2 52 E
Morney 139 25 22S 141 23 E
Morningside 108 27 28S 153 4 E
Mornington, Victoria, Austral. 141 38 15S 145 5 E
Mornington, W. Australia, Austral. 136 17 31S 126 6 E
Mornington, Ireland 38 53 42N 6 17W
Mornington I. 138 16 30S 139 30 E
Mornington, I. 176 49 50S 75 30W
Mórnos, R. 69 38 30N 22 0 E
Moro 123 10 50N 30 9 E
Moro G. 103 6 30N 123 0 E
Morobe 135 7 49S 147 38 E
Morocco ■ 118 32 0N 5 50W
Morococha 174 11 40S 76 5W
Morogoro 126 6 50S 37 40 E
Morogoro □ 126 8 0S 37 0 E
Morokweng 125 26 12S 23 45 E
Moroleón 164 20 8N 101 32W
Morombé 129 21 45S 43 22 E
Moron 172 34 39S 58 37W
Morón 166 22 0N 78 30W
Morón de Almazán 58 41 29N 2 27W
Morón de la Frontera 57 37 6N 5 28W
Morondava 129 20 17S 44 17 E
Morondo 120 8 57N 6 47W
Morongo Valley 163 34 3N 116 37W
Moronou 120 6 16N 4 59W
Morotai, I. 103 2 10N 128 30 E
Moroto 124 2 28N 34 42 E
Moroto Summit, Mt. 126 2 30N 34 43 E
Morozov (Bratan), mt. 67 42 30N 25 10 E
Morozovsk 83 48 25N 41 50 E
Morpeth 35 55 11N 1 41W
Morrelganj 98 22 28N 89 51 E
Morrilton 159 35 10N 92 45W
Morrinhos, Ceara, Brazil 170 3 14S 40 7W
Morrinhos, Minas Gerais, Brazil 171 17 45S 49 10W
Morrinsville 142 37 40S 175 32 E
Morris, Can. 153 49 25N 97 22W
Morris, Ill., U.S.A. 156 41 20N 88 20W
Morris, Minn., U.S.A. 158 45 33N 95 56W
Morris, N.Y., U.S.A. 162 42 33N 75 15W
Morris, Mt. 137 26 9S 131 4 E
Morrisburg 150 44 55N 75 7W
Morrison 158 41 47N 90 0W
Morristown, Ariz., U.S.A. 161 33 54N 112 45W
Morristown, N.J., U.S.A. 162 40 48N 74 30W
Morristown, S.D., U.S.A. 158 45 57N 101 44W
Morristown, Tenn., U.S.A. 157 36 18N 83 20W
Morrisville, N.Y., U.S.A. 162 42 54N 75 39W
Morrisville, Pa., U.S.A. 162 40 13N 74 47W
Morro Agudo 171 20 44S 48 4W
Morro Bay 163 35 27N 120 54W
Morro do Chapéu 171 11 33S 41 9W
Morro, Pta. 172 27 6S 71 0W
Morros 170 2 52S 44 3W
Morrosquillo, Golfo de 167 9 35N 75 40W
Morrum 73 56 12N 14 45 E
Morrumbene 125 23 31S 35 16 E
Mors 73 56 50N 8 45 E
Morshank 81 53 28N 41 50 E
Mörsil 72 63 19N 13 40 E
Mortagne, Charente Maritime, France 44 45 28N 0 49W
Mortagne, Orne, France 42 48 30N 0 32 E
Mortagne, Vendée, France 42 46 59N 0 57W
Mortagne-au-Perche 42 48 31N 0 33 E
Mortagne, R. 43 48 30N 6 30 E
Mortain 42 48 40N 0 57W
Mortara 62 45 15N 8 43 E
Morte Bay 30 51 10N 4 13W
Morte Pt. 30 51 13N 4 14W
Morteau 43 47 3N 6 35 E
Mortehoe 30 51 21N 4 12W
Morteros 172 30 50S 62 0W
Mortes, R. das 171 11 45S 50 44W
Mortimer's Cross 28 52 17N 2 50W
Mortlake 140 38 5S 142 50 E
Morton, Tex., U.S.A. 159 33 39N 102 49W
Morton, Wash., U.S.A. 160 46 33N 122 17W
Morton Fen 29 52 45N 0 23W
Mortsel 47 51 11N 4 27 E
Morundah 141 34 57S 146 19 E
Moruya 141 35 58N 150 3 E
Morvan, Mts. du 43 47 5N 4 0 E

Mukeiras Nabari

Mukeiras 91 13 59N 45 52E
Mukhtolovo 81 55 29N 43 15E
Mukinbudin 137 30 55S 118 5E
Mukombwe 127 15 48S 26 32E
Mukomuko 102 2 20S 101 10E
Mukomwenze 126 6 49S 27 15E
Mukry 85 37 54N 65 12E
Muktsar 94 30 30N 74 30E
Muktsar Bhatinda 94 30 15N 74 57E
Mukur 94 32 50N 67 50E
Mukutawa, R. 153 53 10N 97 24W
Mukwela 127 17 0S 26 40E
Mula 59 38 3N 1 33W
Mula, R. 96 19 16N 74 20E
Mulanay 103 13 30N 122 30E
Mulange 126 3 40S 27 10E
Mulatas, Arch. de las 166 6 51N 78 31W
Mulchén 172 37 45S 72 20W
Mulde, R. 48 50 55N 12 42E
Mule Creek 158 43 19N 104 8W
Muleba 126 1 50S 31 37E
Muleba □ 126 2 0S 31 30E
Mulegé 164 26 53N 112 1W
Mulegns 51 46 32N 9 38E
Mulengchen 107 44 32N 130 14E
Muleshoe 159 34 17N 102 42W
Mulga Valley 140 31 8S 141 3E
Mulgathing 139 30 15S 134 0E
Mulgrave 151 45 38N 61 31W
Mulgrave I. 135 10 5S 142 10E
Mulhacén 59 37 4N 3 20W
Mülheim 48 51 26N 6 53W
Mulhouse 43 47 40N 7 20E
Muli, China 99 28 21N 100 40E
Muli, China 108 27 50N 101 15E
Mull Head 37 59 23N 2 53W
Mull I. 34 56 27N 6 0W
Mull, Ross of, dist. 34 56 20N 6 15W
Mull, Sound of 34 56 30N 5 50W
Mullagh 39 53 13N 8 25W
Mullaghareirk Mts. 39 52 20N 9 10W
Mullaittvu 97 9 15N 80 55E
Mullardoch L. 36 57 30N 5 0W
Mullen 158 42 5N 101 0W
Mullengudgery 141 31 43S 147 29E
Mullens 156 37 34N 81 22W
Muller, Pegunungan 102 0 30N 113 30E
Muller Ra. 138 5 30S 143 0E
Mullet Pen. 38 54 10N 10 2W
Mullewa 137 28 29S 115 30E
Mullheim 49 47 48N 7 37E
Mulligan, R. 138 26 40S 139 0E
Mullin 159 31 33N 98 38W
Mullinahone 39 52 30N 7 31W
Mullinavat 39 52 23N 7 10W
Mullingar 38 53 31N 7 20W
Mullins 157 34 12N 79 15W
Mullion 30 50 1N 5 15W
Mullsjö 73 57 56N 13 55E
Mullumbimby 139 28 30S 153 30E
Mulobezi 127 16 45S 25 7E
Mulrany 38 53 54N 9 47W
Mulroy B. 38 55 15N 7 45W
Mulshi L. 96 18 30N 73 20E
Multai 96 21 39N 78 15E
Multan 94 30 15N 71 30E
Multan □ 94 30 29N 72 29E
Multrå 72 63 10N 17 24E
Mulumbe, Mts. 127 8 40S 27 30E
Mulungushi Dam 127 14 48S 28 48E
Mulvane 159 37 30N 97 15W
Mulwad 122 18 45N 30 39E
Mulwala 141 35 59S 146 0E
Mumbles 31 51 34N 4 0W
Mumbles Hd. 31 51 33N 4 0W
Mumbwa 125 15 0S 27 0E
Mumeng 135 7 1S 146 37E
Mumra 83 45 45N 47 41E
Mun 101 15 17N 103 0E
Mun, R. 100 15 19N 105 30E
Muna, I. 103 5 0S 122 30E
Muna Sotuta 165 20 29N 89 43W
Munawwar 95 32 47N 74 27E
Münchberg 49 50 11N 11 48E
Müncheberg 48 52 30N 14 9E
München 49 48 8N 11 33E
Munchen-Gladbach = Mönchengladbach 48 51 12N 6 23E
Muncho Lake 152 59 0N 125 50W
Munchŏn 107 39 14N 127 19E
Münchwilen 51 47 38N 8 59E
Muncie 156 40 10N 85 20W
Mundakayam 97 9 30N 76 32E
Mundala, Puncak 103 4 30S 141 0E
Mundare 152 53 35N 112 20W
Munday 159 33 26N 99 39W
Münden 48 51 25N 9 42E
Mundesley 29 52 53N 1 24E
Mundiwindi 136 23 47S 120 9E
Mundo Novo 171 11 50S 40 29W
Mundo, R. 59 38 30N 2 15W
Mundra 94 22 54N 69 26E
Mundrabilla 137 31 52S 127 51E
Munera 59 39 2N 2 29W
Muneru, R. 96 16 45N 80 3E
Mungallala 139 26 25S 147 34E
Mungallala Cr. 139 28 53S 147 5E
Mungana 138 17 8S 144 27E
Mungaoli 94 24 24N 78 7E
Mungari 127 17 12S 33 42E
Mungbere 124 2 36N 28 28E
Mungindi 139 28 58S 149 1E
Munhango 125 12 10S 18 38E
Munhango R. 125 11 30S 19 30E
Munich = München 49 48 8N 11 35E
Munising 156 46 25N 86 39W
Munjiye 122 18 47N 41 20W
Munka-Ljungby 73 56 16N 12 58E
Munkedal 73 58 28N 11 40E
Munkfors 72 59 50N 13 30E
Muñoz Gamero, Pen. 176 52 30S 73 5E
Munro 141 37 56S 147 11E
Munroe L. 153 59 13N 98 35W
Munsan 107 37 51N 126 48E
Munshiganj 98 23 33N 90 32E
Münsingen 50 46 52N 7 32E
Munster 43 48 2N 7 8E
Münster, Niedersachsen, Ger. 48 52 59N 10 5E
Münster, Nordrhein-Westfalen, Ger. 48 51 58N 7 37E
Münster, Switz. 51 46 30N 8 17E
Munster □ 39 52 20N 8 40W
Muntadgin 137 31 45S 118 33E
Muntele Mare 70 46 30N 23 12E
Muntok 102 2 5S 105 10E
Muon Pak Beng 101 19 51N 101 4E
Muong Beng 100 20 23N 101 46E
Muong Boum 100 22 24N 102 49E
Muong Er 100 20 49N 104 1E
Muong Hai 100 21 3N 101 49E
Muong Hiem 100 20 5N 103 22E
Muong Houn 100 20 8N 101 23E
Muong Hung 100 20 56N 103 53E
Muong Kau 100 15 6N 105 47E
Muong Khao 100 19 47N 103 29E
Muong Khoua 100 21 5N 102 31E
Muong La 101 20 52N 102 5E
Muong Liep 100 18 29N 101 40E
Muong May 100 14 49N 106 56E
Muong Ngeun 100 20 36N 101 3E
Muong Ngoi 100 20 43N 102 41E
Muong Nhie 100 22 12N 102 28E
Muong Nong 100 16 22N 106 30E
Muong Ou Tay 100 22 7N 101 48E
Muong Oua 100 18 18N 101 20E
Muong Pak Bang 100 19 54N 101 8E
Muong Penn 100 20 13N 103 52E
Muong Phalane 100 16 39N 105 34E
Muong Phieng 100 19 6N 101 32E
Muong Phine 100 16 32N 106 2E
Muong Sai 100 20 42N 101 59E
Muong Saiapoun 100 18 24N 101 31E
Muong Sen 100 19 24N 104 8E
Muong Sing 100 21 11N 101 9E
Muong Son 100 20 27N 103 19E
Muong Soui 100 19 33N 102 52E
Muong Va 100 21 53N 102 19E
Muong Xia 100 20 19N 104 50E
Muonio 74 67 57N 23 40E
Muonio älv 74 67 48N 23 25E
Muotathal 51 46 58N 8 46E
Muotohora 142 38 18S 177 40E
Mupa 125 16 5S 15 50E
Muqaddam, Wadi 123 17 0N 32 0E
Mur-de-Bretagne 42 48 12N 3 0W
Mur, R. 52 47 7N 13 55E
Mura, R. 63 46 37N 16 9E
Murallón, Cuerro 176 49 55S 73 30W
Muralto 51 46 11N 8 49E
Muranda 126 1 52S 29 20E
Murang'a 126 0 45S 37 9E
Murashi 81 59 30N 49 0E
Murat 44 45 7N 2 53E
Murau 52 47 6N 14 10E
Muravera 64 39 25N 9 35E
Murça 56 41 24N 7 28W
Murchison 143 41 49S 172 21E
Murchison Downs 137 26 45S 118 55E
Murchison Falls = Kabarega Falls 126 2 15N 31 38E
Murchison House 137 27 39S 114 14E
Murchison Mts. 143 45 13S 167 23E
Murchison, oilfield 19 61 25N 1 40E
Murchison, R. 137 26 45S 116 15E
Murchison Ra. 138 20 0S 134 10E
Murchison Rapids 127 15 55S 34 35E
Murcia 59 38 2N 1 10W
Murcia □ 59 37 50N 1 30W
Murdo 158 43 56N 100 43W
Murdoch Pt. 138 14 37S 144 55E
Murdock Hill 109 34 59S 138 55E
Mure, La 45 44 55N 5 48E
Mureş □ 70 46 45N 24 40E
Mureşul, R. 70 46 15N 20 13E
Muret 44 43 30N 1 20E
Murfatlar 70 44 10N 28 26E
Murfreesboro 157 35 50N 86 21W
Murg 51 47 8N 9 13E
Murgab 85 38 10N 73 59E
Murgeni 70 46 12N 28 1E
Murgenthal 50 47 16N 7 50E
Murgon 139 26 15S 151 54E
Murgoo 137 27 24S 116 28E
Muri 51 47 17N 8 21E
Muriaé 173 21 8S 42 23W
Murias de Paredes 56 42 52N 6 19W
Murici 170 9 19S 35 56W
Muriel Mine 127 17 14S 30 40E
Muritiba 171 12 55S 39 15W
Murits see 48 53 25N 12 40E
Murjo Mt. 103 6 36S 110 53E
Murka 126 3 27S 38 0E
Murmansk 78 68 57N 33 10E
Murmerwoude 46 53 18N 6 0E
Murnau 49 47 40N 11 11E
Muro, France 45 42 34N 8 54E
Muro, Spain 58 39 45N 3 3E
Muro, C. di 45 41 44N 8 37E
Muro Lucano 65 40 45N 15 30E
Murom 81 55 35N 42 3E
Muroran 112 42 25N 141 0E
Muros 56 42 45N 9 5W
Muros y de Noya, Ria de 56 42 45N 9 0W
Muroto 110 33 18N 134 9E
Muroto-Misaki 110 33 15N 134 10E
Murowana Gosślina 54 52 35N 17 0E
Murphy 160 43 11N 116 33W
Murphys 163 38 8N 120 28W
Murphysboro 159 37 50N 89 20W
Murrat 122 18 51N 29 33E
Murray, Ky., U.S.A. 157 36 40N 88 20W
Murray, Utah, U.S.A. 160 40 41N 111 58W
Murray Bridge 140 35 6S 139 14E
Murray Downs 138 21 4S 134 40E
Murray Harb. 151 46 0N 62 28W
Murray, L., P.N.G. 135 7 0S 141 35E
Murray, L., U.S.A. 157 34 8N 81 30W
Murray, R., S. Australia, Austral. 140 35 20S 139 22E
Murray, R., W. Australia, Austral. 133 32 33S 115 45E
Murray, R., Can. 152 56 11N 120 45W
Murraysburg 128 31 58S 23 47E
Murree 94 33 56N 73 28E
Murrieta 163 33 33N 117 13W
Murrin Murrin 137 28 50S 121 45E
Murrough 39 53 7N 9 18W
Murrumbidgee, R. 140 34 40S 143 0E
Murrumburrah 141 34 32S 148 22E
Murrurundi 141 31 42S 150 51E
Murshid 122 21 40N 31 10E
Murshidabad 95 24 11N 88 19E
Murska Sobota 63 46 39N 16 12E
Murtazapur 96 20 40N 77 25E
Murten 50 46 56N 6 7E
Murten-see 50 46 56N 7 4E
Murtle L. 152 52 8N 119 38W
Murtoa 140 36 35S 142 28E
Murton 33 54 51N 1 22W
Murtosa 56 40 44N 8 40W
Muru 123 6 36N 29 16E
Murungu 126 4 12S 31 10E
Murupara 142 38 28S 176 42E
Murwara 95 23 46N 80 28E
Murwillumbah 139 28 18S 153 27E
Mürz, R. 52 47 30N 15 25E
Mürzzuschlag 52 47 36N 15 41E
Muş 92 38 45N 41 30E
Musa, Gebel (Sinai) 122 28 32N 33 59E
Musa Khel 94 30 29N 69 52E
Musa Qala (Musa Kala) 93 32 20N 64 50E
Musa, R. 135 9 3S 148 55E
Musaffargarh 93 30 10N 71 10E
Musairik, Wadi 122 19 30N 43 10E
Musala, I. 102 1 41N 98 28E
Musalla, mt. 67 42 13N 23 37E
Musan 107 42 12N 129 12E
Musangu 127 10 28S 23 55E
Musasa 126 3 25S 31 30E
Musashino 111 35 42N 139 34E
Muscat = Masqat 93 23 37N 58 36E
Muscat & Oman = Oman 91 23 0N 58 0E
Muscatine 158 41 25N 91 5W
Musel 56 43 34N 5 42W
Musetula 127 14 28S 24 1E
Musgrave Ras. 137 26 0S 132 0E
Mushie 124 2 56S 17 4E
Mushin 121 6 32N 3 21E
Musi, R., India 96 17 10N 79 25E
Musi, R., Indon. 102 2 55S 103 40E
Muskeg, R. 152 60 20N 123 20W
Muskegon 156 43 15N 86 17W
Muskegon Hts. 156 43 12N 86 17W
Muskegon, R. 156 43 25N 86 0W
Muskogee 159 35 50N 95 25W
Muskwa, R. 152 58 47N 122 48W
Musmar 122 18 6N 35 40E
Musofu 127 13 30S 29 0E
Musoma 126 1 30S 33 48E
Musoma □ 126 1 50S 34 30E
Musquaro, L. 151 50 38N 61 5W
Musquodoboit Harbour 151 44 50N 63 9W
Mussau I. 135 1 30S 149 40E
Musselburgh 35 55 57N 3 3W
Musselkanaal 46 52 57N 7 0E
Musselshell, R. 160 46 30N 108 15W
Mussidan 44 45 2N 0 22E
Mussomeli 64 37 35N 13 43E
Musson 47 49 33N 5 42E
Mussooree 94 30 27N 78 6E
Mussuco 128 17 2S 19 3E
Mustafa Kemalpaşa 92 40 3N 28 25E
Mustajidda 92 26 30N 41 50E
Mustang 95 29 10N 83 55E
Mustapha, C. 119 36 55N 11 3E
Musters, L. 176 45 20S 69 25W
Musudan 107 40 50N 129 43E
Muswellbrook 141 32 16S 150 56E
Muszyna 53 49 22N 20 55E
Mût 122 25 28N 28 58E
Mut 92 36 40N 33 28E
Mutan Chiang, R. 107 46 18N 129 31E
Mutanchiang 107 44 40N 129 35E
Mutanda, Mozam. 129 21 0S 33 34E
Mutanda, Zambia 127 12 15S 26 13E
Muthill 35 56 20N 3 50W
Mutis 174 1 4N 77 25W
Mutooroo 140 32 26S 140 55E
Mutshatsha 127 10 35S 24 20E
Mutsu-Wan 112 41 5N 140 55E
Muttaburra 138 22 38S 144 29E
Muttama 141 34 46S 148 8E
Mutton Bay 151 50 50N 59 2W
Mutton I. 39 52 50N 9 31W
Mutuáli 127 14 55S 37 0E
Mutung 108 29 35N 106 51E
Mutunópolis 171 13 40S 49 15W
Muvatupusha 97 9 53N 76 35E
Muxima 124 9 25S 13 52E
Muy, Le 45 43 28N 6 34E
Muy Muy 166 12 39N 85 36W
Muya 77 56 27N 115 39E
Muyaga 126 3 14S 30 33E
Muyunkum, Peski 85 44 12N 71 0E
Muzaffarabad 95 34 25N 73 30E
Muzaffargarh 94 30 5N 71 14E
Muzaffarnagar 94 29 26N 77 40E
Muzaffarpur 95 26 7N 85 32E
Muzhi 76 65 25N 64 40E
Muzillac 42 47 35N 2 30W
Muzkol, Khrebet 85 38 22N 73 20E
Muzo 174 5 32N 74 6W
Muzon C. 152 54 40N 132 40W
Mvôlô 123 6 10N 29 53E
Mwadui 126 3 35S 33 40E
Mwandi Mission 127 17 30S 24 51E
Mwango 126 6 48S 24 12E
Mwanza, Katanga, Congo 126 7 55S 26 43E
Mwanza, Kwango, Congo 127 5 29S 17 43E
Mwanza, Malawi 126 16 58S 24 28E
Mwanza, Tanz. 126 2 30S 32 58E
Mwanza □ 126 2 0S 33 0E
Mwaya 126 9 32S 33 55E
Mweelrea, Mt. 38 53 37N 9 48W
Mweka 124 4 50S 21 40E
Mwenga 126 3 1S 28 21E
Mwepo 127 11 50S 26 10E
Mweru, L. 127 9 0S 29 0E
Mweza Range 127 21 0S 30 0E
Mwimbi 127 8 38S 31 39E
Mwinilunga 127 11 43S 24 25E
Mwinilunga, Mt. 127 11 43S 24 25E
My Tho 101 10 29N 106 23E
Mya, O. 119 30 46N 4 44E
Myadh 124 1 16N 13 10E
Myanaung 98 18 25N 95 10E
Myaungmya 98 16 30N 95 0E
Mybster 37 58 27N 3 24W
Myddfai 31 51 59N 3 47W
Myddle 28 52 49N 2 47W
Myerstown 162 40 22N 76 18W
Myingyan 98 21 30N 95 30E
Myitkyina 98 25 30N 97 26E
Myittha, R. 98 16 15N 94 34E
Myjava 53 48 41N 17 37E
Mylor 109 35 3S 138 46E
Mymensingh 98 24 45N 90 24E
Myndmere 158 46 23N 97 7W
Mynydd Bach, Hills 31 52 16N 4 6W
Mynydd Eppynt, Mts. 31 52 4N 3 30W
Mynydd Prescelly, mt. 31 51 57N 4 48W
Mynzhilgi, Gora 85 43 48N 68 51E
Myogi 101 21 24N 96 28E
Myrdal 71 60 43N 7 10E
Mýrdalsjökull 74 63 40N 19 6W
Myrrhee 136 36 46S 146 17E
Myrtle Beach 157 33 43N 78 50W
Myrtle Creek 160 43 0N 123 19W
Myrtle Point 160 43 0N 124 4W
Myrtleford 141 36 34S 146 44E
Myrtletown 108 27 23S 153 8E
Mysen 71 59 33N 11 20E
Myslenice 54 49 51N 19 57E
Myslibórz 54 52 55N 14 50E
Mysłowice 54 50 15N 19 12E
Mysore 97 12 17N 76 41E
Mysore □ = Karnataka 142 13 15N 77 0E
Mystic 162 41 21N 71 58W
Mystishchi 81 55 50N 37 50E
Myszkow 54 50 45N 19 22E
Mythen 51 47 2N 8 42E
Myton 160 40 10N 110 2W
Mývatn 74 65 36N 17 0W
Mze, R. 52 49 47N 12 50E
Mzimba 127 11 48S 33 33E
Mzuzu 127 11 30S 33 55E

N

N' Dioum 120 16 31N 14 39W
Na-lang 98 22 42N 97 33E
Na Noi 100 18 19N 100 43E
Na Phao 100 17 35N 105 44E
Na Sam 100 22 3N 106 37E
Na San 100 21 12N 104 2E
Naaldwijk 46 51 59N 4 13E
Naalehu 147 19 4N 155 35W
Na'am 123 9 42N 28 27E
Na'an 90 31 53N 34 52E
Naantali 75 60 29N 22 2E
Naarden 46 52 18N 5 9E
Naas 39 53 12N 6 40W
Nababeep 128 29 36S 17 46E
Nabadwip 95 23 34N 88 20E
Nabari 111 34 37N 136 5E

Nabas Nashville

Nabas 103 11 47N 122 6 E
Nabberu, L. 137 25 30S 120 30 E
•Naberezhnyye Chelny 84 55 42N 52 19 E
Nabesna 147 62 33N 143 10W
Nabeul 119 36 30N 10 51 E
Nabha 94 30 26N 76 14 E
Nabi Rubin 90 31 56N 34 44 E
Nabire 103 3 15S 136 27 E
Nabisar 94 25 8N 69 40 E
Nabispi, R. 151 50 14N 62 13W
Nabiswera 126 1 27N 32 15 E
Nablus = Nābulus 90 32 14N 35 15 E
Naboomspruit 129 24 32S 28 40 E
Nābulus 90 32 14N 35 15 E
Nabúri 127 16 53S 38 59 E
Nacala-Velha 127 14 32S 40 34 E
Nacaome 166 13 31N 87 30W
Nacaroa 127 14 22S 39 56 E
Naches 160 46 48N 120 49W
Nachikatsuura 111 33 33N 135 58 E
Nachingwea 127 10 49S 38 49 E
Nachingwea □ 127 10 30S 38 30 E
Nachna 94 27 34N 71 41 E
Náchod 53 50 25N 16 8 E
Nacimento Res. 163 35 46N 120 53W
Nacka 72 59 17N 18 12 E
Nackara 140 32 48S 139 12 E
Naco, Mexico 164 31 20N 109 56W
Naco, U.S.A. 161 31 24N 109 58W
Nacogdoches 159 31 33N 95 30W
Nácori Chico 164 29 39N 109 1W
Nacozari 164 30 30N 109 50W
Nadi 122 18 40N 33 41 E
Nadiad 94 22 41N 72 56 E
Nador 118 35 14N 2 58W
Nadushan 93 32 2N 53 35 E
Nadvornaya 80 48 40N 24 35 E
Nadym 76 63 35N 72 42 E
Nadym, R. 76 65 30N 73 0 E
Nærbø 71 58 40N 5 39 E
Næstved 73 55 13N 11 44 E
Nafada 121 11 8N 11 20 E
Näfels 51 47 6N 9 4 E
Nafferton 33 54 1N 0 24W
Naft Shāh 92 34 0N 45 30 E
Nafūd ad Dahy 92 22 0N 45 0 E
Nafūsah, Jabal 119 32 12N 12 30 E
Nag Hammâdi 122 26 2N 32 18 E
Naga 103 13 38N 123 15 E
Naga Hills 99 26 0N 94 30 E
Naga, Kreb en 118 24 12N 6 0W
Naga-Shima, Kagoshima, Japan 110 32 10N 130 9 E
Naga-Shima, Yamaguchi, Japan 110 33 55N 132 5 E
Nagagami, R. 150 49 40N 84 40W
Nagahama, Ehime, Japan 111 33 36N 132 29 E
Nagahama, Shiga, Japan 111 35 23N 136 16 E
Nagai Parkar 94 24 28N 70 46 E
Nagaland □ 98 26 0N 94 30 E
Nagambie 141 36 47S 145 10 E
Nagano 111 36 40N 138 10 E
Nagano-ken □ 111 36 15N 138 0 E
Nagaoka 112 37 27N 138 50 E
Nagappattinam 97 10 46N 79 51 E
Nagar Parkar 93 24 30N 70 35 E
Nagara-Gawa, R. 111 35 1N 136 43 E
Nagari Hills 97 15 30N 79 45 E
Nagarjuna Sagar 96 16 35N 79 17 E
Nagasaki 110 32 47N 129 50 E
Nagasaki-ken □ 110 32 50N 129 40 E
Nagato 110 34 19N 131 5 E
Nagaur 94 27 15N 73 45 E
Nagbhir 96 20 34N 79 42 E
Nagchu Dzong 99 31 22N 91 54 E
Nagercoil 97 8 12N 77 33 E
Nagina 95 29 30N 78 30 E
Nagineh 93 34 20N 57 15 E
Nagold 49 48 38N 8 40 E
Nagoorin 138 24 17S 151 15 E
Nagorsk 81 59 18N 50 48 E
Nagorum 126 4 1N 34 33 E
Nagoya 111 35 10N 136 50 E
Nagpur 96 21 8N 79 10 E
Nagrong 99 32 46N 84 16 E
Nagua 167 19 23N 69 50W
Nagyatád 53 46 14N 17 22 E
Nagyecsed 53 47 53N 22 24 E
Nagykanizsa 53 46 28N 17 0 E
Nagykörös 53 46 55N 19 48 E
Nagyléta 53 47 23N 21 55 E
Naha 112 26 13N 127 42 E
Nahalal 90 32 41N 35 12 E
Nahanni Butte 152 61 2N 123 20W
Nahanni Nat. Pk. 152 61 15N 125 0W
Naharayim 90 32 28N 35 33 E
Nahariyya 90 33 1N 35 5 E
Nahāvand 92 34 10N 48 30 E
Nahe, R. 49 49 48N 7 33 E
Nahf 90 32 56N 35 18 E
Nahîya, Wadi 122 27 37N 32 0 E
Nahlin 152 58 55N 131 38W
Nahud 122 18 12N 41 40 E
Naiapu 70 44 12N 25 47 E
Naicá 164 27 53N 105 31W
Naicam 153 52 30N 104 30W
Na'ifah 91 19 59N 50 46 E
Naila 49 50 19N 11 43 E
Nailsea 28 51 25N 2 44W
Nailsworth 28 51 41N 2 12W
Nain 151 56 34N 61 40W
Na'in 93 32 54N 53 0 E
Naini Tal 95 29 23N 79 30 E
Nainpur 93 22 30N 80 10 E
Naintré 42 46 46N 0 29 E
Naira, I. 103 4 28S 130 0 E
Nairn 37 57 35N 3 54W
Nairn (□) 26 57 28N 3 52W
Nairn R. 37 57 32N 3 58W
Nairobi 126 1 17S 36 48 E
Naivasha 126 0 40S 36 30 E
Naivasha □ 126 0 40S 36 30 E
Naivasha L. 126 0 48S 36 20 E
Najac 44 44 14N 1 58 E
Najafābād 93 32 40N 51 15 E
Najd 92 26 30N 42 0 E
Nájera 58 42 26N 2 48W
Najerilla, R. 58 42 15N 2 45W
Najibabad 94 29 40N 78 20 E
Najin 107 42 12N 130 15 E
Naju 107 35 3N 126 43 E
Naka-Gawa, R. 111 36 20N 140 36 E
Naka-no-Shima 112 29 51N 129 46 E
Nakalagba 126 2 50N 27 58 E
Nakama 110 33 56N 130 43 E
Nakaminato 111 36 21N 140 36 E
Nakamura 110 33 0N 133 0 E
Nakanai Mts. 135 5 40S 151 0 E
Nakano 111 36 45N 138 22 E
Nakanojō 111 36 35N 138 51 E
Nakatane 112 30 31N 130 57 E
Nakatsu 110 33 40N 131 15 E
Nakatsugawa 111 35 29N 137 30 E
Nakelele Pt. 147 21 2N 156 35W
Nakfa 123 16 40N 38 25 E
Nakhichevan, A.S.S.R. □ 79 39 14N 45 30 E
Nakhl 122 29 55N 33 43 E
Nakhl Mubarak 92 24 10N 38 10 E
Nakhodka 77 43 10N 132 45 E
Nakhon Nayok 100 14 12N 101 13 E
Nakhon Pathom 100 13 49N 100 3 E
Nakhon Phanom 100 17 23N 104 43 E
Nakhon Ratchasima (Khorat) 100 14 59N 102 12 E
Nakhon Sawan 100 15 35N 100 10 E
Nakhon Si Thammarat 100 8 29N 100 0 E
Nakhon Thai 100 17 17N 100 50 E
Nakina, B.C., Can. 152 59 12N 132 52W
Nakina, Ont., Can. 150 50 10N 86 40W
Nakło n. Noteoja 54 53 9N 17 38 E
Naknek 147 58 45N 157 0W
Nakodar 94 31 8N 75 31 E
Nakomis 127 39 19N 89 19W
Nakskov 73 54 50N 11 8 E
Näkten 72 62 48N 14 38 E
Naktong, R. 107 35 7N 128 57 E
Nakur 94 30 2N 77 32 E
Nakuru 126 0 15S 35 5 E
Nakuru □ 126 0 15S 35 5 E
Nakuru, L. 126 0 23S 36 5 E
Nakusp 152 50 20N 117 45W
Nal, R. 94 27 0N 65 50 E
Nalchik 83 43 30N 43 33 E
Nälden 72 63 21N 14 14 E
Näldsjön 72 63 25N 14 15 E
Nalerigu 121 10 35N 0 25W
Nalgonda 96 17 6N 79 15 E
Nalhati 95 24 17N 87 52 E
Nalinnes 47 50 19N 4 27 E
Nallamalai Hills 97 15 30N 78 50 E
Nalón, R. 56 43 35N 6 10W
Nālūt 119 31 54N 11 0 E
Nam Can 101 8 46N 104 59 E
Nam Dinh 100 20 25N 106 5 E
Nam Du, Hon 101 9 41N 104 21 E
'Nam', gasfields 19 53 17N 3 36 E
Nam Ngum 100 18 35N 102 34 E
'Nam', oilfield 19 54 50N 4 40 E
Nam-Phan 101 10 30N 106 0 E
Nam Phong 100 16 42N 102 52 E
Nam Tha 100 20 58N 101 30 E
Nam Tok 100 14 14N 99 4 E
Nam Tso = Namu Hu 105 30 45N 90 30 E
Namacurra 125 17 30S 36 50 E
Namakkal 97 11 13N 78 13 E
Namaland, Africa 128 26 0S 18 0 E
Namaland, S. Afr. 128 30 0S 18 0 E
Namangan 85 41 0N 71 40 E
Namapa 127 13 43S 39 50 E
Namasagali 126 1 2N 33 0 E
Namatanai 135 3 40S 152 29 E
Nambala 120 14 1N 5 58W
Namber 103 1 2S 134 57 E
Nambour 139 26 32S 152 58 E
Nambucca Heads 141 30 37S 153 0 E
Namcha Barwa 105 29 40N 95 10 E
Namche Bazar 95 27 51N 86 47 E
Namchonjŏm 107 38 15N 126 26 E
Namêche 47 50 28N 5 0 E
Namecund 127 14 54S 37 37 E
Nameh 102 2 34N 116 21 E
Nameponda 127 15 50S 39 50 E
Namerikawa 111 36 46N 137 20 E
Námestovo 53 49 24N 19 25 E
Nametil 127 15 40S 39 15 E
Náměšť nad Oslavou 53 49 12N 16 10 E
Namew L. 153 54 14N 101 56W
Namhsan 98 22 48N 97 42 E
Nami 101 6 2N 100 46 E
Namib Desert = Namib Woestyn 128 22 30S 15 0 E
Namib-Woestyn 128 22 30S 15 0 E
Namibia □ 128 22 0S 18 9 E
Namiquipa 164 29 15N 107 25W
Namja Pass 95 30 0N 82 25 E
Namkhan 98 23 50N 97 41 E
Namlea 103 3 10S 127 5 E
Namoi, R. 141 30 12S 149 30 E
Namous, O. 118 30 44N 0 18W
Nampa 160 43 40N 116 40W
Nampula 127 15 6S 39 7 E
Namrole 103 3 46S 126 46 E
Namsen 74 64 27N 11 42 E
Namsen, R. 74 64 40N 12 45 E
Namsos 74 64 28N 11 0 E
Namtu 98 23 5N 97 28 E
Namtumbo 127 10 30S 36 4 E
Namu 152 51 52N 127 41W
Namu Hu 105 30 45N 90 30 E
Namur 47 50 27N 4 52 E
Namur □ 47 50 17N 5 0 E
Namutoni 128 18 49S 16 55 E
Namwala 127 15 44S 26 30 E
Namwŏn 107 35 23N 127 23 E
Namysłow 54 51 6N 17 42 E
Nan 100 18 48N 100 46 E
Nan Ling 109 25 0N 112 30 E
Nan, R. 100 15 42N 100 9 E
Nan Shan 105 38 30N 99 0 E
Nana 70 44 17N 26 34 E
Nānā, W. 119 30 0N 15 24 E
Nanaimo 152 49 10N 124 0W
Nanam 107 41 44N 129 40 E
Nan'an 109 24 58N 118 23 E
Nanango 139 26 40S 152 0 E
Nanao 109 23 26N 117 1 E
Nanch'ang 109 28 40N 115 50 E
Nanchang, Fukien, China 109 24 26N 117 18 E
Nanchang, Hupei, China 109 31 47N 111 42 E
Nanch'eng 109 27 33N 116 35 E
Nancheng = Hanchung 106 33 10N 107 2 E
Nanchiang 108 32 21N 106 50 E
Nanchiao 108 22 2N 100 15 E
Nanchien 106 25 5N 100 30 E
Nanching 109 32 3N 118 47 E
Nanchishan Liehtao 108 27 28N 121 4 E
Nanch'uan 108 29 7N 107 16 E
Nanch'ung 108 30 50N 106 4 E
Nancy 43 48 42N 6 12 E
Nanda Devi, Mt. 95 30 30N 80 30 E
Nandan 110 34 10N 134 42 E
Nander 96 19 10N 77 20 E
Nandewar Ra. 139 30 15S 150 35 E
Nandi □ 126 0 15N 35 0 E
Nandikotkur 97 15 52N 78 18 E
Nandura 96 20 52N 76 25 E
Nandurbar 96 21 20N 74 15 E
Nandyal 97 15 30N 78 30 E
Nanfeng 109 27 10N 116 24 E
Nanga 137 26 7S 113 45 E
Nanga Eboko 121 4 41N 12 22 E
Nanga Parbat, mt. 95 35 10N 74 35 E
Nangade 127 11 5S 39 36 E
Nangapinoh 102 0 20S 111 14 E
Nangarhar □ 93 34 20N 70 0 E
Nangatajap 102 1 32S 110 34 E
Nangeya Mts. 126 3 30N 33 30 E
Nangis 43 48 33N 3 0 E
Nangodi 121 10 58N 0 42W
Nangola 120 12 41N 6 35W
Nangwarry 140 37 33S 140 48 E
Nanhsien 109 29 22N 112 25 E
Nanhsiung 109 25 10N 114 18 E
Nanhua 108 25 10N 101 20 E
Nanhui 109 31 3N 121 46 E
Nani Hu 109 31 10N 118 55 E
Nanjangud 97 12 6N 76 43 E
Nanjeko 127 5 31S 23 30 E
Nanjirinji 127 9 41S 39 5 E
Nankana Sahib 94 31 27N 73 38 E
Nank'ang 109 25 38N 114 45 E
Nanking = Nanching 109 32 5N 118 45 E
Nankoku 110 33 29N 133 38 E
Nankung 106 37 22N 115 20 E
Nanling 109 30 56N 118 19 E
Nannine 137 26 51S 118 18 E
Nanning 108 22 48N 108 20 E
Nannup 137 33 59S 115 48 E
Nanpa 108 32 13N 104 51 E
Nanp'an Chiang, R. 108 25 0N 106 11 E
Nanpara 95 27 52N 81 33 E
Nanp'i 106 38 4N 116 34 E
Nanp'ing, Fukien, China 109 26 38N 118 10 E
Nanp'ing, Hupeh, China 109 29 55N 112 2 E
Nanpu 108 31 19N 106 2 E
Nanripe 127 13 52S 38 52 E
Nansei-Shotō 112 26 0N 128 0 E
Nansen Sd. 12 81 0N 91 0W
Nansio 126 2 3S 33 4 E
Nanson 137 28 35S 114 45 E
Nant 44 44 1N 3 18 E
Nantes 42 47 12N 1 33W
Nanteuil-le-Haudouin 43 49 9N 2 48 E
Nantiat 44 46 1N 1 11 E
Nanticoke 162 41 12N 76 1W
Nanticoke, R. 162 38 16N 75 56W
Nanton, Can. 152 50 21N 113 46W
Nanton, China 108 24 59N 107 32 E
Nantua 45 46 10N 5 35 E
Nantucket 162 41 17N 70 6W
Nantucket I. 155 41 16N 70 3W
Nantucket Sd. 162 41 30N 70 15W
Nant'ung 109 32 0N 120 55 E
Nantwich 32 53 5N 2 31W
Nanuque 171 17 50S 40 21W
Nanutarra 136 22 32S 115 30 E
Nanyang 106 33 0N 112 32 E
Nan'yō 110 34 3N 131 49 E
Nanyüan 106 39 48N 116 24 E
Nanyuki 126 0 2N 37 4 E
Nao, C. de la 59 38 44N 0 14 E
Nao Chou Tao 109 20 55N 110 35 E
Nao, La, Cabo de 59 38 44N 0 14 E
Naococane L. 151 52 50N 70 45W
Naogaon 98 24 52N 88 52 E
Napa 163 38 18N 122 17W
Napa, R. 163 38 10N 122 19W
Napamute 147 61 30N 158 45W
Napanee 150 44 15N 77 0W
Napanoch 162 41 44N 74 2W
Nape 100 18 18N 105 6 E
Nape Pass = Keo Neua, Deo 100 18 23N 105 10 E
Napf 50 47 1N 7 56 E
Napiéolédougou 120 9 18N 5 35W
Napier 142 39 30S 176 56 E
Napier Broome B. 136 14 2S 126 37 E
Napier Downs 136 17 11S 124 36 E
Napier Pen. 138 12 4S 135 43 E
Naples 157 26 10N 81 45W
Naples = Nápoli 65 40 50N 14 5 E
Nap'o 108 23 44N 106 49 E
Napo □ 174 0 30S 77 0W
Napo, R. 174 3 5S 73 0W
Napoleon, N. Dak., U.S.A. 158 46 32N 99 49W
Napoleon, Ohio, U.S.A. 156 41 24N 84 7W
Nápoli 65 40 50N 14 5 E
Nápoli, G. di 65 40 40N 14 10 E
Napopo 126 4 15N 28 0 E
Napoule, La 45 43 31N 6 56 E
Nappa 32 53 58N 2 14W
Nappa Merrie 139 27 36S 141 7 E
Naqâda 122 25 53N 32 42 E
Nara, Japan 111 34 40N 135 49 E
Nara, Mali 120 15 25N 7 20W
Nara, Canal 94 26 0N 69 20 E
Nara-ken □ 111 34 30N 136 0 E
Nara Visa 159 35 39N 103 10W
Naracoorte 140 36 58S 140 45 E
Naradhan 141 33 34S 146 17 E
Narasapur 96 16 26N 81 50 E
Narasaropet 96 16 14N 80 4 E
Narathiwat 101 6 40N 101 55 E
Narayanganj 98 23 31N 90 33 E
Narayanpet 96 16 45N 77 30 E
Narberth 31 51 48N 4 45W
Narbonne 44 43 11N 3 0 E
Narborough 28 52 34N 1 12W
Narcea, R. 56 43 15N 6 30W
Nardò 65 40 10N 18 0 E
Nare Head 30 50 12N 4 55W
Narembeen 137 32 7S 118 17 E
Naretha 137 31 0S 124 45 E
Nari, R. 94 29 10N 67 50 E
Narin 93 36 5N 69 0 E
Narinda, B. de 129 14 55S 47 30 E
Narino □ 174 1 30N 78 0W
Narita 111 35 47N 140 19 E
Narmada, R. 94 22 40N 77 30 E
Narnaul 94 28 5N 76 11 E
Narni 63 42 30N 12 30 E
Naro, Ghana 120 10 22N 2 27W
Naro, Italy 64 37 18N 13 48 E
Naro Fominsk 81 55 23N 36 32 E
Narodnaya, G. 78 65 5N 60 0 E
Narok 126 1 20S 33 30 E
Narok □ 126 1 20S 33 30 E
Narón 56 43 32N 8 9W
Narooma 141 36 14S 150 4 E
Narowal 94 32 6N 74 52 E
Narrabri 139 30 19S 149 46 E
Narran, R. 139 28 37S 148 12 E
Narrandera 141 34 42S 146 31 E
Narraway, R. 152 55 44N 119 55W
Narrogin 137 32 58S 117 14 E
Narromine 141 32 12S 148 12 E
Narrows, str. 36 57 20N 6 5W
Narsampet 96 17 57N 79 58 E
Narsinghpur 95 22 54N 79 14 E
Naruto 110 34 11N 134 37 E
Narutō 111 35 36N 140 25 E
Naruto-Kaikyō 110 34 14N 134 39 E
Narva 80 59 10N 28 5 E
Narva, R. 80 59 10N 27 50 E
Narvik 74 68 28N 17 26 E
Narvskoye Vdkhr. 80 59 10N 28 5 E
Narwana 94 29 39N 76 6 E
Naryan-Mar 78 68 0N 53 0 E
Naryilco 139 28 37S 141 53 E
Narym 76 59 0N 81 58 E
Narymskoye 76 49 10N 84 15 E
Naryn 85 41 26N 75 58 E
Naryn, R. 85 40 52N 71 36 E
Nasa 74 66 29N 15 23 E
Nasa, mt. 74 66 32N 15 23 E
Nasarawa 121 8 32N 7 41 E
Naseby, N.Z. 143 45 1S 170 10 E
Naseby, U.K. 29 52 24N 0 59W
Naser, Buheirat en 122 23 0N 32 30 E
Nash Pt. 31 51 24N 3 34W
Nashua, Iowa, U.S.A. 158 42 55N 92 34W
Nashua, Mont., U.S.A. 160 48 10N 106 25W
Nashua, N.H., U.S.A. 162 42 50N 71 25W
Nashville, Ark., U.S.A. 159 33 56N 93 50W

*Renamed Brezhnev

Nashville Nevillé-Pont-Pierre

Nashville, Ga., U.S.A. 157 31 13N 83 15W
Nashville, Tenn., U.S.A. 157 36 12N 86 46W
Na ice 66 45 32N 18 4 E
Nasielsk 54 52 35N 20 50 E
Nasik 96 20 2N 73 50 E
Nasirabad, Bangla. 95 24 42N 90 30 E
Nasirabad, India 94 26 15N 74 45 E
Nasirabad, Pak. 96 28 25N 68 25 E
Naskaupi, R. 151 53 47N 60 51W
Naso 65 38 8N 14 46 E
Nass, R. 152 55 0N 129 40W
Nassau, Bahamas 166 25 0N 77 30W
Nassau, U.S.A. 162 42 30N 73 34W
Nassau, Bahía 176 55 20 S 68 0W
Nasser City = Kôm Ombo 122 24 25N 32 52 E
Nasser, L. = Naser, Buheiret en 122 23 0N 32 30 E
Nassian 120 7 58N 2 57W
Nässjö 73 57 38N 14 45 E
Nastopoka Is. 150 57 0N 77 0W
Näsum 73 56 10N 14 29 E
Näsviken 72 61 46N 16 52 E
Nata, Bots. 128 20 7 S 26 4 E
Nata, China 100 19 37N 109 17 E
Nata, Si Arab. 92 27 15N 48 35 E
Nata, Tanz. 125 2 0 S 34 25 E
Natagaima 174 3 37N 75 6W
Natal, Brazil 170 5 47 S 35 13W
Natal, Can. 152 49 43N 114 51W
Natal, Indon. 102 0 35N 99 0 E
Natal □ 129 28 30 S 30 30 E
Natalinci 66 44 15N 20 49 E
Natanz 93 33 30N 51 55 E
Natashquan 151 50 14N 61 46W
Natashquan Pt. 151 50 8N 61 40W
Natashquan, R. 151 50 7N 61 50W
Natchez 159 31 35N 91 25W
Natchitoches 159 31 47N 93 4W
Naters 50 46 19N 8 0 E
Nathalia 141 36 1 S 145 7 E
Nathdwara 94 24 55N 73 50 E
Natick 162 42 16N 71 19W
Natih 93 22 25N 56 30 E
Natimuk 140 36 42 S 142 0 E
Nation, R. 152 55 30N 123 32W
National City 163 32 45N 117 7W
National Mills 153 52 52N 101 40W
Natitingou 121 10 20N 1 26 E
Natividad, I. de 164 27 50N 115 10W
Natkyizin 101 14 57N 97 59 E
Natogyi 98 21 25N 95 39 E
Natoma 158 39 14N 99 0W
Natron L. 126 2 20 S 36 0 E
Natrûn, W. el. 122 30 25N 30 0 E
Natuna Besar, Kepulauan 101 4 0N 108 15 E
Natuna Selatan, Kepulauan 101 2 45N 109 0 E
Naturaliste, C. 132 33 32 S 115 0 E
Naturaliste C. 138 40 50 S 148 15 E
Naturaliste Channel 137 25 20 S 113 0 E
Natya 140 34 57 S 143 13 E
Nau 85 40 9N 69 22 E
Nau-Nau 128 18 57 S 21 4 E
Nau Qala 94 34 5N 68 5 E
Naubinway 150 46 7N 85 27W
Naucelle 44 44 13N 2 20 E
Nauders 52 46 54N 10 30 E
Nauen 48 52 36N 12 52 E
Naujoji Vilnia 80 54 48N 25 27 E
Naumburg 48 51 10N 11 48 E
Nauru I. 130 0 25N 166 0 E
Naurzum 84 51 32N 64 34 E
Naushahra 93 34 0N 72 0 E
Nauta 174 4 20 S 73 35W
Nautanwa 99 27 20N 83 25 E
Nautla 165 20 20N 96 50W
Nava 164 28 25N 100 46W
Nava del Rey 56 41 22N 5 6W
Navacerrada, Puerto de 56 40 47N 4 0W
Navahermosa 57 39 41N 4 28W
Navalcarnero 56 40 17N 4 5W
Navalmoral de la Mata 56 39 52N 5 16W
Navalvillar de Pela 57 39 9N 5 24W
Navan = An Uaimh 38 53 39N 6 40W
Navarino, I. 176 55 0 S 67 30W
Navarra □ 58 42 40N 1 40W
Navarre 44 43 15N 1 20 E
Navarreux 44 43 20N 0 47W
Navasota 159 30 20N 96 5W
Navassa I. 167 18 30N 75 0W
Nave 62 45 35N 10 17 E
Navenby 33 53 7N 0 32W
Naver L. 37 58 18N 4 20W
Naver, R. 37 58 34N 4 15W
Navia 56 43 24N 6 42W
Navia de Suarna 56 42 58N 6 59W
Navia, R. 56 43 15N 6 50W
Navidad 172 33 57 S 71 50W
Navlya 80 52 53N 34 15 E
Navoi 85 40 9N 65 22 E
Navojoa 164 27 0N 109 30W
Navolato 164 24 47N 107 42W
Navolok 78 62 33N 39 57 E
Návpaktos 69 38 23N 21 42 E
Návplion 69 37 33N 22 50 E
Navrongo 121 10 57N 0 58W
Navsari 96 20 57N 72 59 E
Nawa Kot 94 28 21N 71 24 E
Nawabganj 98 24 35N 81 14 E
Nawabganj, Bara Banki 95 26 56N 81 14 E
Nawabganj, Bareilly 95 28 32N 79 40 E
Nawabshah 94 26 15N 68 25 E
Nawada 95 24 50N 85 25 E
Nawakot 95 28 0N 85 10 E
Nawalgarh 96 27 50N 75 15 E
Nawansnahr 95 32 33N 74 48 E
Nawapara 95 20 52N 82 33 E
Nawi 122 18 32N 30 50 E
Nawng Hpa 98 21 52N 97 52 E
Náxos 69 37 8N 25 25 E
Náxos, I. 69 37 5N 25 30 E
Nay 44 43 10N 0 18W
Nay Band 93 27 20N 52 40 E
Naya 174 3 13N 77 22W
Naya, R. 174 3 13N 77 22W
Nayakhan 77 62 10N 159 0 E
Nayarit □ 164 22 0N 105 0W
Nayé 120 14 28N 12 12W
Nayung 108 26 50N 105 17 E
Nazaré, Bahia, Brazil 171 13 0 S 39 0W
Nazaré, Goiás, Brazil 170 6 23 S 47 40W
Nazaré, Port. 57 39 36N 9 4W
Nazaré Antônio de Jesus 171 13 2 S 39 0W
Nazaré da Mata 171 7 44 S 35 14W
Nazareth, Israel 90 32 42N 35 17 E
Nazareth, U.S.A. 162 40 44N 75 19W
Nazas 164 25 10N 104 0W
Nazas, R. 164 25 20N 104 4W
Naze 112 28 22N 129 27 E
Naze, The 29 51 43N 1 19 E
Nazeret 123 8 45N 39 15 E
Nazir Hat 98 22 35N 91 55 E
Nazko 152 53 1N 123 37W
Nazko, R. 152 53 7N 123 34W
Nchacoongo 129 24 20 S 35 9 E
Nchanga 127 12 30 S 27 49 E
Ncheu 127 14 50 S 34 37 E
Ndala 126 4 45 S 33 23 E
Ndali 121 9 50N 2 46 E
Ndareda 126 4 12 S 35 30 E
Ndélé 117 8 25N 20 36 E
Ndendeé 124 2 29 S 10 46 E
Ndjamena 117 12 4N 15 8 E
Ndjolé 124 0 10 S 10 45 E
Ndola 127 13 0 S 28 34 E
Ndoto Mts. 126 2 0N 37 0 E
Ndrhamcha, Sebkra de 120 18 30N 15 55W
Nduguti 126 4 18 S 34 41 E
NE Frt. Agency = Arun. Pradesh □ 98 28 0N 95 0 E
Nea 71 63 15N 11 0 E
Néa Epidhavros 69 37 40N 23 7 E
Néa Filippiás 68 39 12N 20 53W
Néa Kallikrátiá 68 40 21N 23 1 E
Néa Vissi 68 41 34N 26 33 E
Neagari 111 36 26N 136 25 E
Neagh, Lough 38 54 35N 6 25W
Neah Bay 160 48 25N 124 40W
Neale L. 137 24 15 S 130 0 E
Neamarrói 127 15 58 S 36 50 E
Neamţ □ 70 47 0N 26 20 E
Neápolis, Kozan, Greece 68 40 20N 21 24 E
Neápolis, Kriti, Greece 69 35 15N 25 36 E
Neápolis, Lakonia, Greece 69 36 27N 23 8 E
Near Is. 147 53 0N 172 0W
Neath 31 51 39N 3 49W
Neath, R. 23 51 46N 3 35W
Nebbou 121 11 9N 1 51W
Nebine Cr. 139 29 7 S 146 56 E
Nebo 138 21 42 S 148 42 E
Nebolchy 81 59 12N 32 58 E
Nebraska □ 158 41 30N 100 0W
Nebraska City 158 40 40N 95 52W
Necedah 158 44 2N 90 7W
Nechako, R. 152 53 30N 122 44W
Neches, R. 159 31 80N 94 20W
Neckar, R. 49 48 43N 9 15 E
Necochea 172 38 30 S 58 50W
Nectar Brook 140 32 43 S 137 57 E
Nedelišće 63 46 23N 16 22 E
Neder Rijn, R. 46 51 57N 6 2 E
Nederbrakel 47 50 48N 3 46 E
Nederlandsöy I. 71 62 20N 5 35 E
Nederweert 47 51 17N 5 45 E
Nedha, R. 69 37 25N 21 45 E
Nedroma 118 35 1N 1 45W
Nedstrand 71 59 21N 5 49 E
Neede 46 52 8N 6 37 E
Needham Market 29 52 9N 1 2 E
Needilup 137 33 55 S 118 45 E
Needles 161 34 50N 114 35W
Needles, Pt. 142 36 3 S 175 25 E
Needles, The 28 50 48N 1 19W
Ñeembucú □ 172 27 0 S 58 0W
Neemuch (Nimach) 94 24 30N 74 50 E
Neenah 156 44 10N 88 30W
Neepawa 153 50 20N 99 30W
Neer 47 51 16N 5 59 E
Neerheylissem 47 51 5N 5 42 E
Neeroeteren 47 50 44N 4 58 E
Neerpelt 47 51 13N 5 26 E
Nefta 119 33 53N 7 58 E
Neftah Sidi Boubekeur 118 35 1N 0 4 E
Neftegorsk 83 44 25N 39 45 E
Neftenbach 51 47 32N 8 41 E
Neftyannye Kamni 79 40 20N 50 55 E
Nefyn 31 52 57N 4 29W
Negapatam = Nagappattinam 97 10 46N 79 38 E
Negaunee 156 46 30N 87 36W
Negba 90 31 40N 34 41 E
Negele 123 5 20N 39 30 E
Negeri Sembilan □ 101 2 50N 102 10 E
Negev = Hanegev 90 30 50N 35 0 E
Negolu 70 45 48N 24 32 E
Negombo 97 7 12N 79 50 E
Negotin 66 44 16N 22 37 E
Negotino 66 41 29N 22 9 E
Negra, La 172 23 46 S 70 18W
Negra, Peña 56 42 11N 6 30W
Negra Pt. 103 18 40N 120 50 E
Negrais C. 98 16 0N 94 30 E
Negreira 56 42 54N 8 45W
Negreşti 70 46 50N 27 30 E
Négrine 119 34 30N 7 30 E
Negro, C. 118 35 40N 5 11W
Negro, R., Argent. 176 40 0 S 64 0W
Negro, R., Brazil 174 0 25 S 64 0W
Negro, R., Uruguay 173 32 30 S 55 30W
Negros, I. 103 10 0N 123 0 E
Negru Vodŭ 70 43 47N 28 21 E
Nehbandān 93 31 35N 60 5 E
Neheim-Hüsten 48 51 27N 7 58 E
Nehoiaşu 70 45 24N 26 20 E
Neichiang 108 29 35N 105 0 E
Neich'iu 106 37 17N 114 31 E
Neidpath 153 50 12N 107 20W
Neihart 160 47 0N 110 52W
Neihsiang 106 33 3N 111 53 E
Neilrex 141 31 44 S 149 20 E
Neilston 34 55 47N 4 27W
Neilton 160 47 24N 123 59W
Neira de Jusá 56 42 53N 7 14W
Neisse, R. 48 51 0N 15 0 E
Neiva 174 2 56N 75 18W
Nejanilini L. 153 59 33N 97 48W
Nejo 123 9 30N 35 28 E
Nekemte 123 9 4N 36 30 E
Nêkheb 122 25 10N 33 0 E
Neksø 73 55 4N 15 8 E
Nelas 56 40 32N 7 52W
Nelaug 71 58 39N 8 40 E
Nelgowrie 141 30 54 S 148 7 E
Nelia 138 20 39 S 142 12 E
Nelidovo 80 56 13N 32 49 E
Neligh 158 42 11N 98 2W
Nelkan 77 57 50N 136 15 E
Nellikuppam 97 11 46N 79 43 E
Nellore 97 14 27N 79 59 E
Nelma 77 47 30N 139 0 E
Nelson, Can. 152 49 30N 117 20W
Nelson, N.Z. 143 41 18 S 173 16 E
Nelson, U.K. 32 53 50N 2 14W
Nelson, Ariz., U.S.A. 161 35 35N 113 24W
Nelson, Nev., U.S.A. 161 35 46N 114 55W
Nelson □ 143 42 11 S 172 15 E
Nelson, C., Austral. 140 38 26 S 141 32 E
Nelson, C., P.N.G. 135 9 0 S 149 20 E
Nelson, Estrecho 176 51 30 S 75 0W
Nelson Forks 152 59 30N 124 0W
Nelson House 153 55 47N 98 51W
Nelson I. 147 60 40N 164 40W
Nelson L. 153 55 48N 100 7W
Nelson, R. 153 54 33N 98 2W
Nelspruit 126 25 29 S 30 59 E
Néma 120 16 40N 7 15W
Neman (Nemunas), R. 80 53 30N 25 10 E
Neméa 69 37 49N 22 40 E
Nemegos 150 47 40N 83 15W
Nemeiben L. 153 55 20N 105 20W
Nemira, Mt. 70 46 17N 26 19 E
Nemiscau 150 49 30N 111 15W
Nemours 43 48 16N 2 40 E
Nemunas, R. 80 55 25N 21 10 E
Nemuro 112 43 20N 145 35 E
Nemuro-Kaikyō 112 43 30N 145 30 E
Nemuy 77 55 40N 135 55 E
Nenagh 39 52 52N 8 11W
Nenana 147 64 30N 149 0W
Nenasi 101 3 9N 103 23 E
Nenchiang 105 49 11N 125 13 E
Nene, R. 29 52 38N 0 7 E
Neno 127 15 25 S 34 40 E
Nenusa, Kepulauan 103 4 45N 127 1 E
Neodesha 159 37 30N 95 37W
Néon Petritsi 68 41 16N 23 15 E
Neópolis 170 10 18 S 36 35W
Neosho 159 36 56N 94 28W
Neosho, R. 159 35 59N 95 10W
Nepal ■ 95 28 0N 84 30 E
Nepalganj 95 28 0N 81 40 E
Nephi 160 39 43N 111 52W
Nephin Beg Ra. 38 54 0N 9 40W
Nephin, Mt. 38 54 1N 9 21W
Nepomuk 52 49 29N 13 35 E
Neptune City 162 40 13N 74 4W
Néra, R. 66 44 52N 21 45 E
Nerac 44 44 19N 0 20 E
Nerchinsk 77 52 0N 116 39 E
Nerchinskiy Zavod 77 51 10N 119 30 E
Nereju 70 45 43N 26 43 E
Nerekhta 81 57 26N 40 38 E
Neret L. 151 54 45N 70 44W
Neretva, R. 66 43 30N 17 50 E
Neretvanski 66 43 7N 17 10 E
Neringa 80 55 21N 21 5 E
Nerja 57 36 43N 3 55W
Nerl, R. 81 56 30N 40 30 E
Nerokoúrou 69 35 29N 24 3 E
Nerpio 59 38 11N 2 16W
Nerva 57 37 42N 6 30W
Nes, Iceland 74 65 53N 17 24W
Nes, Neth. 46 53 26N 5 47 E
Nes Ziyyona 90 31 56N 34 48W
Nesbyen 71 60 34N 9 6 E
Nescopeck 162 41 3N 76 12W
Nesebyr 67 42 41N 27 46 E
Nesflaten 71 59 38N 6 48 E
Neskaupstaður 74 65 9N 13 42W
Nesland 71 59 31N 7 59 E
Neslandsvatn 71 58 57N 9 10 E
Nesle 43 49 45N 2 53 E
Nesodden 71 59 48N 10 40 E
Ness, dist. 36 58 27N 6 20W
Ness, Loch 37 57 15N 4 30W
Nesslau 51 47 14N 9 13 E
Neston 32 53 17N 3 3W
Nestórion Óros 68 40 24N 21 16 E
Néstos, R. 68 41 20N 24 35 E
Nesttun 71 60 19N 5 21 E
Nesvizh 80 53 14N 26 38 E
Netanya 90 32 20N 34 51 E
Nèthe, R. 47 51 5N 4 55 E
Netherdale 138 21 10 S 148 33 E
Netherlands ■ 47 52 0N 5 30 E
Netherlands Guiana = Surinam 170 4 0N 56 0W
Nethy Bridge 37 57 15N 3 40W
Netley 28 50 53N 1 21W
Netley Gap 28 32 43 S 139 59 E
Netley Marsh 28 50 55N 1 32W
Neto, R. 65 39 10N 16 58 E
Netrakong 98 24 53N 90 47 E
Nettancourt 43 48 51N 4 57 E
Nettilling L. 149 66 30N 71 0W
Nettlebed 29 51 34N 0 54W
Nettleham 33 53 15N 0 28W
Nettuno 64 41 29N 12 40 E
Netzahualcoyotl, Presa 165 17 10N 93 30W
Neu-Isenburg 49 50 3N 8 42 E
Neu Ulm 49 48 23N 10 2 E
Neubrandenburg 48 53 33N 13 17 E
Neubrandenburg □ 48 53 30N 13 20 E
Neubukow 48 54 1N 11 40 E
Neuburg 49 48 43N 11 11 E
Neuchâtel 50 47 0N 6 55 E
Neuchâtel □ 50 47 0N 6 55 E
Neuchâtel, Lac de 50 46 53N 6 50 E
Neudau 52 47 11N 16 6 E
Neuenegg 50 46 54N 7 18 E
Neuenhaus 48 52 30N 6 55 E
Neuf-Brisach 43 48 0N 7 30 E
Neufchâteau, Belg. 47 49 50N 5 25 E
Neufchâteau, France 43 48 21N 5 40 E
Neufchâtel 43 49 43N 1 30 E
Neufchâtel-sur-Aisne 43 49 26N 4 0 E
Neuhaus 48 53 16N 10 54 E
Neuhausen 51 47 41N 8 37 E
Neuilly-St. Front 43 49 10N 3 15 E
Neukalen 49 53 49N 12 48 E
Neumarkt 49 49 16N 11 28 E
Neumünster 48 54 4N 9 58 E
Neung-sur-Beuvron 43 47 30N 1 50 E
Neunkirchen, Austria 52 47 43N 16 4 E
Neunkirchen, Ger. 49 49 23N 7 6 E
Neuquén 176 38 0 S 68 0 E
Neuquén □ 172 38 0 S 69 50W
Neuruppin 48 52 56N 12 48 E
Neuse, R. 157 35 5N 77 40W
Neusiedl 53 47 57N 16 50 E
Neusiedler See 53 47 50N 16 47 E
Neuss 48 51 12N 6 39 E
Neussargues-Moissac 44 45 9N 3 1 E
Neustadt, Bay., Ger. 49 49 42N 12 10 E
Neustadt, Bay., Ger. 49 48 48N 11 47 E
Neustadt, Bay., Ger. 49 49 34N 10 37 E
Neustadt, Bay., Ger. 49 50 23N 11 0 E
Neustadt, Gera, Ger. 48 50 45N 11 43 E
Neustadt, Hessen, Ger. 48 50 51N 9 9 E
Neustadt, Niedersachsen, Ger. 48 52 30N 9 30 E
Neustadt, Potsdam, Ger. 48 52 50N 12 27 E
Neustadt, Rhld-Pfz., Ger. 49 49 21N 8 10 E
Neustadt, S.-Holst., Ger. 48 54 6N 10 49 E
Neustrelitz 48 53 22N 13 4 E
Neuveville, La 50 47 4N 7 6 E
Neuvic 44 45 23N 2 16 E
Neuville, Belg. 95 50 11N 4 32 E
Neuville, France 43 45 52N 4 51 E
Neuville-aux-Bois 43 48 4N 2 3 E
Neuvy-St.-Sépulchure 44 46 35N 1 48 E
Neuvy-sur-Barangeon 43 47 20N 2 15 E
Neuwerk, I. 48 53 55N 8 30 E
Neuwied 48 50 26N 7 29 E
Neva, R. 78 59 50N 30 30 E
Nevada 159 37 20N 94 40W
Nevada □ 160 39 20N 117 0W
Nevada City 163 39 20N 121 0W
Nevada de Sta. Marta, Sa. 174 10 55N 73 50W
Nevada, Sierra, Spain 59 37 3N 3 15W
Nevada, Sierra, U.S.A. 160 39 0N 120 30W
Nevado, Cerro 172 35 30 S 68 20W
Nevado de Colima, Mt. 164 19 35N 103 45W
Nevanka 77 56 45N 98 55 E
Nevasa 94 19 34N 75 0 E
Nevel 80 56 0N 29 55 E
Nevele 47 51 3N 3 28 E
Nevern 31 52 2N 4 49W
Nevers 43 47 0N 3 9 E
Nevertire 141 31 50 S 147 44 E
Neville 153 49 58N 107 39W
Nevillé-Pont-Pierre 42 47 33N 0 33 E

Nevinnomyssk Nîl el Abyad, Bahr

Nevinnomyssk 83 44 40N 42 0 E
Nevis I. 167 17 0N 62 30W
Nevis, L. 36 57 0N 5 43W
Nevlunghavn 71 58 58N 9 53 E
Nevoria 137 31 25 S 119 25 E
Nevrokop = Gotse Delchev 67 41 43N 23 46 E
Nevşehir 92 38 33N 34 40 E
Nevyansk 84 57 30N 60 13 E
New Abbey 35 54 59N 3 38W
New Aberdour 37 57 39N 2 12W
New Adawso 121 6 50N 0 2W
New Albany, Ind., U.S.A. 156 38 20N 85 50W
New Albany, Miss., U.S.A. 159 34 30N 89 0W
New Albany, Pa., U.S.A. 162 41 35N 76 28W
New Alresford 28 51 6N 1 10W
New Amsterdam 174 6 15N 57 30W
New Angledool 139 29 10 S 147 55 E
New Bedford 162 41 40N 70 52W
New Berlin, N.Y., U.S.A. 162 42 38N 75 20W
New Berlin, Pa., U.S.A. 162 40 50N 76 57W
New Bern 157 35 8N 77 3W
New Birmingham 39 52 36N 7 38W
New Boston 159 33 27N 94 21W
New Braunfels 159 29 43N 98 9W
New Brighton, N.Z. 143 43 29 S 172 43 E
New Brighton, U.K. 32 53 27N 3 2W
New Britain 162 41 41N 72 47W
New Britain, I. 135 5 50 S 150 20 E
New Brunswick 162 40 30N 74 28W
New Brunswick □ 151 46 50N 66 30W
New Buildings 38 54 57N 7 21W
New Bussa 121 9 53N 4 31 E
New Byrd 13 80 0 S 120 0W
New Caledonia, I. 130 21 0 S 165 0 E
New Castile = Castilla La Neuva 57 39 45N 3 20W
New Castle, Del., U.S.A. 162 39 40N 75 34W
New Castle, Ind., U.S.A. 156 39 55N 85 23W
New Castle, Pa., U.S.A. 156 41 0N 80 20W
New Chapel Cross 39 51 51N 10 12W
New City 162 41 8N 74 0W
New Cumnock 34 55 24N 4 13W
New Cuyama 163 34 57N 119 38W
New Deer 37 57 30N 2 10W
New Delhi 94 28 37N 77 13 E
New Denver 152 50 0N 117 25W
New England 158 46 36N 102 47W
New England Ra. 139 30 20 S 151 45 E
New Forest 28 50 53N 1 40W
New Freedom 162 39 44N 76 42W
New Galloway 35 55 4N 4 10W
New Glasgow 151 45 35N 62 36W
New Gretna 162 39 35N 74 28W
New Guinea, I. 135 4 0 S 136 0 E
New Hampshire □ 156 43 40N 71 40W
New Hampton 158 43 2N 92 20W
New Hanover 129 29 22 S 30 31 E
New Hanover I. 135 2 30 S 150 10 E
New Hartford 162 43 4N 75 18W
New Haven 162 41 20N 72 54W
New Hazelton 152 55 20N 127 30W
*New Hebrides, Is. 130 15 0 S 168 0 E
New Holland, U.K. 33 53 42N 0 22W
New Holland, U.S.A. 162 40 6N 76 5W
New Iberia 159 30 2N 91 54W
New Inn 39 53 5N 7 10W
New Ireland, I. 135 3 20 S 151 50 E
New Jersey □ 162 39 50N 74 10W
New Kensington 156 40 36N 79 43W
New Kent 162 37 31N 76 59W
New Lexington 156 39 40N 82 15W
New Liskeard 150 47 31N 79 41W
New London, Conn., U.S.A. 162 41 23N 72 8W
New London, Minn., U.S.A. 158 45 17N 94 55W
New London, Wis., U.S.A. 158 44 23N 88 43W
New Luce 34 54 57N 4 50W
New Madrid 159 36 40N 89 30W
New Meadows 160 45 0N 116 10W
New Mexico □ 154 34 30N 106 0W
New Milford, Conn., U.S.A. 162 41 35N 73 25W
New Milford, Pa., U.S.A. 162 41 50N 75 45W
New Mills 32 53 22N 2 0W
New Norcia 137 30 57 S 116 13 E
New Norfolk 138 42 46 S 147 2 E
New Orleans 159 30 0N 90 5W
New Oxford 162 39 52N 77 4W
New Philadelphia 156 40 29N 81 25W
New Pitsligo 37 57 35N 2 11W
New Plymouth, Bahamas 166 26 56N 77 20W
New Plymouth, N.Z. 142 39 4 S 174 5 E
New Point Comfort 162 37 18N 76 15W
New Providence I. 166 25 0N 77 30W
New Quay 31 52 13N 4 21W
New Radnor 31 52 15N 3 10W
New Richmond 158 45 6N 92 34W
New Roads 159 30 43N 91 30W
New Rockford 158 47 44N 99 7W
New Romney 29 50 59N 0 57 E
New Ross 39 52 24N 6 58W
New Rossington 33 53 30N 1 4W

* Renamed Vanuatu

New Salem 158 46 51N 101 25W
New Siberian Is. = Novosibirskiye Os. 77 75 0N 140 0 E
New Smyrna Beach 157 29 0N 80 50W
New South Wales □ 139 33 0 S 146 0 E
New Springs 137 25 49 S 120 1 E
New Tamale 121 9 10N 1 10W
New Tredegar 31 51 43N 3 15W
New Ulm 158 44 15N 94 30W
New Waterford 151 46 13N 60 4W
New Westminster 152 49 10N 122 52W
New York □ 156 42 40N 76 0W
New York City 162 40 45N 74 0W
New Zealand ■ 143 40 0 S 176 0 E
Newala 127 10 58 S 39 10 E
Newala □ 127 10 46 S 39 20 E
Newark, U.K. 33 53 6N 0 48W
Newark, Del., U.S.A. 162 39 42N 75 45W
Newark, N.J., U.S.A. 162 40 41N 74 12W
Newark, N.Y., U.S.A. 162 43 2N 77 10W
Newark, Ohio, U.S.A. 156 40 5N 82 30W
Newark Valley 162 42 14N 76 11W
Newberg 160 45 22N 123 0W
Newberry 156 46 20N 85 32W
Newberry Springs 163 34 50N 116 41W
Newbiggin-by-the-Sea 35 55 12N 1 31W
Newbigging 35 55 42N 3 33W
Newbliss 38 54 10N 7 8W
Newborough 31 53 10N 4 22W
Newbridge, Kildare, Ireland 39 53 11N 6 50W
Newbridge, Limerick, Ireland 38 52 33N 9 0W
Newbridge-on-Wye 31 52 13N 3 27W
Newbrook 152 54 24N 112 57W
Newburgh, Fife, U.K. 35 56 21N 3 15W
Newburgh, Grampian, U.K. 37 57 19N 2 0W
Newburgh, U.S.A. 162 41 30N 74 1W
Newburn 35 54 57N 1 45W
Newbury 28 51 24N 1 19W
Newburyport 162 42 48N 70 50W
Newby Bridge 32 54 16N 2 59W
Newbyth 37 57 35N 2 17W
Newcastle, Austral. 141 33 0 S 151 40 E
Newcastle, Can. 151 47 1N 65 38W
Newcastle, Ireland 39 53 5N 6 4W
Newcastle, S. Afr. 125 27 45 S 29 58 E
Newcastle, U.K. 38 54 13N 5 54W
Newcastle, U.S.A. 158 43 50N 104 12W
Newcastle Emlyn 31 52 2N 4 29W
Newcastle Ra. 136 15 45 S 130 15 E
Newcastle-under-Lyme 32 53 2N 2 15W
Newcastle-upon-Tyne 35 54 59N 1 37W
Newcastle Waters 136 17 30 S 133 28 E
Newcastle West 38 52 27N 9 3W
Newcastleton 35 55 10N 2 50W
Newchurch 31 52 9N 3 10W
Newdegate 137 33 6 S 119 0 E
Newe Etan 90 32 30N 35 32 E
Newe Sha'anan 90 32 47N 34 59 E
Newe Zohar 90 31 9N 35 21 E
Newell 158 44 48N 103 25W
Newenham, C. 147 58 40N 162 15W
Newent 28 51 56N 2 24W
Newfield, N.J., U.S.A. 162 39 33N 75 1W
Newfield, N.Y., U.S.A. 162 42 18N 76 33W
Newfound L. 162 43 40N 71 47W
Newfoundland 151 48 30N 56 0W
Newfoundland □ 151 48 28N 56 0W
Newhalem 152 48 41N 121 16W
Newhalen 147 59 40N 155 0W
Newhall 163 34 23N 118 32W
Newham 29 51 31N 0 2 E
Newhaven 29 50 47N 0 4 E
Newington, N. Kent, U.K. 29 51 21N 0 40 E
Newington, S. Kent, U.K. 29 51 5N 1 8 E
Newinn 39 52 28N 7 54W
Newkirk 159 36 52N 97 3W
Newlyn 30 50 6N 5 33W
Newlyn East 30 50 22N 5 3W
Newmachar 37 57 16N 2 11W
Newman 163 37 19N 121 1W
Newman, Mt. 137 23 20 S 119 34 E
Newmarket, Ireland 39 52 13N 9 0W
Newmarket, Lewis, U.K. 36 58 14N 6 24W
Newmarket, Suffolk, U.K. 29 52 15N 0 23 E
Newmarket, U.S.A. 162 43 4N 70 57W
Newmarket-on-Fergus 39 52 46N 8 54W
Newmill 37 57 34N 2 58W
Newmills 38 54 56N 7 49W
Newmilns 34 55 36N 4 20W
Newnan 157 33 22N 84 48W
Newnes 139 33 9 S 150 16 E
Newnham 28 51 48N 2 27W
Newport, Essex, U.K. 29 51 58N 0 13 E
Newport, Gwent, U.K. 31 51 35N 3 0W
Newport, I. of W., U.K. 28 50 42N 1 18W
Newport, Salop, U.K. 28 52 47N 2 22W
Newport, Ark., U.S.A. 159 35 38N 91 15W
Newport, Ky., U.S.A. 156 39 5N 84 23W
Newport, N.H., U.S.A. 162 43 23N 72 8W
Newport, Oreg., U.S.A. 160 44 41N 124 2W
Newport, R.I., U.S.A. 162 41 30N 71 19W
Newport, Tenn., U.S.A. 157 35 39N 83 12W
Newport, Wash., U.S.A. 160 48 11N 117 2W
Newport B. 38 53 52N 9 38W
Newport Beach 163 33 40N 117 58W
Newport News 162 37 2N 76 54W
Newport on Tay 35 56 27N 2 56W
Newport Pagnell 29 52 5N 0 42W
Newquay 30 50 24N 5 6W
Newry 38 54 10N 6 20W
Newry & Mourne □ 38 54 10N 6 15W
Newton, Iowa, U.S.A. 158 41 40N 93 3W
Newton, Kans., U.S.A. 159 38 2N 97 30W
Newton, Mass., U.S.A. 156 42 21N 71 10W
Newton, N.C., U.S.A. 157 35 42N 81 10W
Newton, N.J., U.S.A. 162 41 3N 74 46W
Newton, Texas, U.S.A. 159 30 54N 93 42W
Newton Abbot 30 50 32N 3 37W
Newton Arlosh 32 54 53N 3 15W
Newton-Aycliffe 33 54 36N 1 33W
Newton Boyd 139 29 45 S 152 16 E
Newton Ferrers 30 50 19N 4 3W
Newton le Willows 32 53 28N 3 27W
Newton St. Cyres 30 50 46N 3 35W
Newton Stewart 34 54 57N 4 30W
Newtonabbey □ 38 54 45N 6 0W
Newtongrange 35 55 52N 3 4W
Newtonhill 37 57 1N 20 52 E
Newtonmore 37 57 4N 4 7W
Newtown, Ireland 39 52 20N 8 47W
Newtown, Scot, U.K. 35 55 34N 2 38W
Newtown, Wales, U.K. 31 52 31N 3 19W
Newtown Crommelin 38 54 59N 6 13W
Newtown Cunningham 38 55 0N 7 32W
Newtown Forbes 38 53 46N 7 50W
Newtown Gore 38 54 3N 7 41W
Newtown Hamilton 38 54 12N 6 35W
Newtownabbey 38 54 40N 5 55W
Newtownards 38 54 37N 5 40W
Newtownbutler 38 54 12N 7 22W
Newtownmount-kennedy 39 53 5N 6 7W
Newtownstewart 38 54 43N 7 22W
Nexon 48 45 41N 1 10 E
Neya 81 58 21N 43 49 E
Neyland 31 51 43N 4 58W
Neyrīz 93 29 15N 54 55 E
Neyshābūr 93 36 10N 58 20 E
Neyyattinkara 97 8 26N 77 5 E
Nezhin 80 51 5N 31 55 E
Nezperce 160 46 13N 116 15W
Ngabang 102 0 30N 109 55 E
Ngaiphaipi 98 22 14N 93 15 E
Ngambé 121 5 48N 11 29 E
Ngami Depression 128 20 30 S 22 46 E
Ngamo 127 19 3 S 27 25 E
Ngandjuk 103 7 32 S 111 55 E
Ngao 100 18 46N 99 59 E
Ngaoundéré 124 7 15N 13 35 E
Ngapara 143 44 57 S 170 46 E
Ngara 126 2 29 S 30 40 E
Ngara □ 126 2 29 S 30 40 E
Ngaruawahia 142 37 42 S 175 11 E
Ngatapa 142 38 32 S 177 45 E
Ngathainggyaung 98 17 24N 95 5 E
Ngauruhoe, Mt. 142 39 13 S 175 45 E
Ngawi 103 7 24 S 111 26 E
Ngetera 121 12 40 S 12 46 E
Ngha Lo 101 21 33N 104 28 E
Nghia Lo 100 21 33N 104 28 E
Ngoma 127 13 8 S 33 45 E
Ngomahura 127 20 33 S 30 57 E
Ngomba 127 8 20 S 32 53 E
Ngonye Falls 128 16 35 S 23 30 E
Ngop 123 6 17N 30 9 E
Ngorkou 120 15 40N 3 41W
Ngorongoro 126 3 11 S 35 32 E
Ngozi 126 2 54 S 29 50 E
Ngudu 126 2 58 S 33 25 E
N'Guigrai 117 14 20N 13 20 E
Nguna, I. 100 17 26 S 168 21 E
Ngunga 126 3 37 S 33 37 E
Ngungu 143 6 15N 28 16 E
Ngunguru 94 35 37 S 174 30 E
Nguru 121 12 56N 10 29 E
Nguru Mts. 126 6 0 S 37 30 E
Nguyen Binh 100 22 39N 105 56 E
Ngwenya 129 26 5 S 31 7 E
Nha Trang 101 12 16N 109 10 E
Nhacoongo 129 24 18 S 35 14 E
Nhangutazi, Lago 129 24 0 S 34 30 E
Nhill 140 36 18 S 141 40 E
Nho Quan 100 20 18N 105 45 E
Nhulunbuy 138 12 10 S 136 45 E
Nia-nia 126 1 30N 27 40 E
Niafounké 120 16 0N 4 5W
Niagara 156 45 45N 88 0W
Niagara Falls, Can. 150 43 7N 79 5W
Niagara Falls, N. Amer. 150 43 5N 79 5W
Niah 102 3 58N 113 46 E
Niamey 121 13 27N 2 6 E
Nianforando 120 9 37N 10 36W
Nianfors 72 61 36N 16 46 E
Niangara 126 3 50N 27 50 E
Niantic 162 41 19N 72 12W
Nias, I. 102 1 0N 97 40 E
Niassa □ 127 13 30 S 36 0 E
Niassa, Lago 127 12 30 S 34 30 E
Nibbiano 62 44 54N 9 20 E
Nibe 73 56 59N 9 38 E
Nibong Tebal 101 5 10N 100 29 E
Nicaragua ■ 166 11 40N 85 30W
Nicaragua, Lago de 166 12 50N 85 30W
Nicastro 65 39 0N 16 18 E
Nice 45 43 42N 7 14 E
Niceville 157 30 30N 86 30W
Nichinan 110 31 38N 131 23 E
Nicholas, Chan. 166 23 30N 80 30W
Nicholasville 156 37 54N 84 31W
Nichols 162 42 1N 76 22W
Nicholson, Austral. 136 18 2 S 128 54 E
Nicholson, Can. 150 47 58N 83 47W
Nicholson, U.S.A. 162 41 37N 75 47W
Nicholson, R. 138 17 31 S 139 36 E
Nicholson Ra. 137 27 15 S 116 30 E
Nicobar Is. 86 9 0N 93 0 E
Nicoclí 174 8 26N 76 48W
Nicola 152 50 8N 120 40W
Nicolet 150 46 17N 72 35W
Nicolls Town 166 25 8N 78 0W
Nicosia, Cyprus 92 35 10N 33 25 E
Nicosia, Italy 65 37 45N 14 22 E
Nicótera 65 38 33N 15 57 E
Nicoya 166 10 9N 85 27W
Nicoya, Golfo de 166 10 0N 85 0W
Nicoya, Pen. de 166 9 45N 85 40W
Nidau 50 47 7N 7 15 E
Nidd, R. 33 54 1N 1 32W
Nidda 48 50 24N 9 2 E
Nidda, R. 49 50 25N 9 2 E
Nidderdale 33 54 5N 1 46W
Nidzica 54 53 25N 20 28 E
Niebüll 48 54 47N 8 49 E
Niederaula 48 50 48N 9 37 E
Niederbipp 50 47 16N 7 42 E
Niederbronn 43 48 57N 7 39 E
Niedere Tauern 93 47 18N 14 0 E
Niedermarsberg 48 51 28N 8 52 E
Niederösterreich □ 52 48 25N 15 40 E
Niedersachsen □ 48 54 45N 9 0 E
Niel 47 51 7N 4 20 E
Niellé 120 10 5N 5 38W
Niemba 126 5 58 S 28 24 E
Niemcza 54 50 42N 16 47 E
Niemodlin 54 50 38N 17 38 E
Niemur 140 35 17 S 144 9 E
Nienburg 48 52 38N 9 15 E
Niench'ingt'angkula Shan 105 30 10N 90 0 E
Niepołomice 54 50 3N 20 13 E
Niesen 50 46 38N 7 39 E
Niesky 48 51 18N 14 48 E
Nieszawa 54 52 52N 18 42 E
Nieuw Amsterdam 46 52 43N 6 52 E
Nieuw Beijerland 46 51 49N 4 20 E
Nieuw-Buinen 46 52 58N 6 56 E
Nieuw-Dordrecht 46 52 45N 6 59 E
Nieuw Hellevoet 46 51 51N 4 8 E
Nieuw Loosdrecht 46 52 12N 5 8 E
Nieuw Nickerie 175 6 0N 57 10W
Nieuw-Schoonebeek 46 52 39N 7 0 E
Nieuw-Vassemeer 47 51 34N 4 12 E
Nieuw-Vennep 46 52 16N 4 38 E
Nieuw-Weerdinge 46 52 51N 6 59 E
Nieuwe-Niedorp 46 52 44N 4 54 E
Nieuwe-Pekela 46 53 5N 6 58 E
Nieuwe-Schans 46 53 11N 7 12 E
Nieuwe-Tonge 47 51 43N 4 10 E
Nieuwendijk 46 51 46N 4 55 E
Nieuwerkerken 47 50 52N 5 12 E
Nieuwkoop 46 52 9N 4 48 E
Nieuwleusen 46 52 34N 6 17 E
Nieuwnamen 47 51 18N 4 9 E
Nieuwolda 46 53 15N 6 58 E
Nieuwpoort 47 51 8N 2 45 E
Nieuwveen 46 52 12N 4 46 E
Nieves 56 42 7N 8 26W
Nièvre □ 43 47 10N 5 40 E
Nigata 110 34 13N 132 39 E
Nigde 92 38 0N 34 40 E
Nigel 129 26 27 S 28 25 E
Niger □ 121 10 0N 5 0 E
Niger ■ 121 13 30N 10 0 E
Niger, R. 121 10 0N 4 40 E
Nigeria ■ 121 8 30N 8 0 E
Nigg B. 37 57 41N 4 5W
Nightcaps 143 45 57 S 168 14 E
Nigrita 68 40 56N 23 29 E
Nihtaur 94 29 27N 78 23 E
Nii-Jima 111 34 20N 139 15 E
Niigata 112 37 58N 139 0 E
Niigata-ken □ 112 37 15N 138 45 E
Niihama 110 33 55N 133 10 E
Niihau, I. 147 21 55N 160 10W
Niimi 110 34 59N 133 28 E
Níjar 59 36 53N 2 15W
Nijkerk 47 52 13N 5 30 E
Nijlen 47 51 10N 4 40 E
Nijmegen 47 51 50N 5 52 E
Nijverdal 46 52 22N 6 28 E
Nike 121 6 26N 7 29 E
Nikel 74 69 30N 30 5 E
Nikiniki 103 9 40 S 124 30 E
Nikitas 68 40 17N 23 34 E
Nikki 121 9 58N 3 21 E
Nikkō 111 36 45N 139 35 E
Nikolayev 82 46 58N 32 7 E
Nikolayevsk-na-Amur 77 53 40N 140 50 E
Nikolayevski 81 50 10N 45 35 E
Nikolsk 81 59 30N 45 28 E
Nikolski 147 53 0N 168 50W
Nikolskoye, Amur, U.S.S.R. 77 47 50N 131 5 E
Nikolskoye, Kamandorskiye, U.S.S.R. 77 55 12N 166 0 E
Nikopol, Bulg. 67 43 43N 24 54 E
Nikopol, U.S.S.R. 82 47 35N 34 25 E
Niksar 82 40 31N 37 2 E
Nīkshah 93 26 15N 60 10 E
Nik ió 66 42 50N 18 57 E
Nîl el Abyad, Bahr 123 9 30N 31 40 E

Nîl el Azraq □ N. Taranaki Bt

Nîl el Azraq □ 123 12 30N 34 30 E
Nîl el Azraq, Bahr 123 10 30N 35 0 E
Nîl, Nahr el 122 27 30N 30 30 E
Nila 103 8 24 S 120 29 E
Niland 161 33 16N 115 30W
Nile □ 126 2 0N 31 30 E
Nile Delta 122 31 40N 31 0 E
Nile, R. = Nîl, Nahr el 122 27 30N 30 30 E
Niles 156 41 8N 80 40W
Nilgiri Hills 97 11 30N 76 30 E
Nilo Peçanha 171 13 37 S 39 6W
Nilpena 140 30 58 S 138 20 E
Nimach = Neemuch 94 24 30N 74 50 E
Nimar 96 21 49N 76 22 E
Nimba, Mt. 120 7 39N 8 30W
Nimbahera 94 24 37N 74 45 E
Nîmes 45 43 50N 4 23 E
Nimfaíon, Ákra 68 40 5N 24 20 E
Nimingarra 132 20 31 S 119 55 E
Nimmitabel 141 36 29 S 149 15 E
Nimneryskiy 77 58 0N 125 10 E
Nimule 123 3 32N 32 3 E
Nimy 47 50 28N 3 57 E
Nin 63 44 16N 15 12 E
Nindigully 139 28 21 S 148 50 E
Ninemile 152 56 0N 130 7W
Ninemilehouse 39 52 28N 7 29W
Ninety Mile Beach 130 34 45 S 173 0 E
Ninety Mile Beach, The 133 38 15 S 147 24 E
Nineveh 92 36 25N 43 10 E
Ninfield 29 50 53N 0 26 E
Ningaloo 136 22 41 S 113 41 E
Ningan 107 44 23N 129 26 E
Ningch'eng 107 41 34N 119 20 E
Ningch'iang 106 32 49N 106 13 E
Ningchin 106 37 37N 114 55 E
Ningching Shan 108 31 45N 97 15 E
Ninghai 109 29 18N 121 25 E
Ninghsiang 109 28 15N 112 30 E
Ninghsien 106 35 35N 107 58 E
Ninghua 109 26 14N 116 36 E
Ningkang 109 26 45N 113 58 E
Ningkuo 109 30 38N 118 58 E
Ninglang 108 27 19N 100 53 E
Ningling 106 34 27N 115 19 E
Ningming 108 22 12N 107 5 E
Ningnan 108 27 7N 102 42 E
Ningpo 109 29 53N 121 33 E
Ningshan 106 33 12N 108 29 E
Ningsia Hui A.R. □ 106 37 45N 106 0 E
Ningte 109 26 45N 120 0 E
Ningtsin 99 29 44N 98 28 E
Ningtu 109 26 22N 115 48 E
Ningwu 106 29 2N 112 15 E
Ningyang, Fukien, China 109 25 44N 117 8 E
Ningyang, Shantung, China 106 35 46N 116 47 E
Ningyüan 109 25 36N 111 54 E
Ninh Binh 100 20 15N 105 55 E
Ninh Giang 100 20 44N 106 24 E
Ninh Hoa 100 12 30N 109 7 E
Ninh Ma 100 12 48N 109 21 E
Ninian, oilfield 19 60 42N 1 30 E
Ninove 47 50 51N 4 2 E
Nioaque 173 21 5 S 55 50W
Niobrara 158 42 48N 97 59W
Niobrara R. 158 42 30N 103 0W
Nioki 124 2 47 S 17 40 E
Niono 120 14 15N 6 0W
Nioro 120 15 30N 9 30W
Nioro du Rip 120 13 40N 15 50W
Nioro du Sahel 120 15 30N 9 30W
Niort 44 46 19N 0 29W
Niou 121 12 42N 2 1W
Nipa 135 6 9 S 143 29 E
Nipan 138 24 45 S 150 0 E
Nipani 96 16 20N 74 25 E
Nipawin 153 53 20N 104 0W
Nipawin Prov. Park 153 54 0N 104 37W
Nipigon 150 49 0N 88 17W
Nipigon, L. 150 49 50N 88 30W
Nipin, R. 153 55 46N 109 2W
Nipishish L. 151 54 12N 60 45W
Nipissing L. 150 46 20N 80 0W
Nipomo 163 35 4N 120 29W
Niquelândia 171 14 33 S 48 23W
Nira, R. 96 18 5N 74 25 E
Nirasaki 111 35 42N 138 27 E
Nirmal 96 19 3N 78 20 E
Nirmali 95 26 20N 86 35 E
Ni 66 43 19N 21 58 E
Nisa 57 39 30N 7 41W
Nisab 91 14 25N 46 29 E
Nišava, R. 66 43 20N 22 10 E
Niscemi 65 37 8N 14 21 E
Nishi-Sonogi-Hantō 110 32 55N 129 45 E
Nishinomiya 111 34 45N 135 20 E
Nishinoomote 112 30 43N 130 59 E
Nishio 111 34 52N 137 3 E
Nishiwaki 110 34 59N 134 48 E
Nísiros, I. 69 36 35N 27 12 E
Niskibi, R. 150 56 29N 88 9W
Nisko 54 50 35N 22 7 E
Nispen 47 51 29N 4 28 E
Nisporeny 70 47 4N 28 10 E
Nissafors 73 57 25N 13 37 E
Nissan 73 56 40N 12 51 E
Nissan I. 138 4 30 S 154 10 E
Nissedal 71 59 10N 8 30 E
Nisser 71 59 7N 8 28 E
Nissum Fjord 73 56 20N 8 11 E
Nistelrode 47 51 42N 5 34 E
Nisutlin, R. 152 60 14N 132 34W
Nitchequon 151 53 10N 70 58W
Niterói 173 22 52 S 43 0W
Nith, R. 35 55 20N 3 5W
Nithsdale 35 55 14N 3 50W
Niton 28 50 35N 1 14W
Nitra 53 48 19N 18 4 E
Nitra, R. 53 48 30N 18 7 E
Nitsa, R. 84 57 29N 64 33 E
Nittedal 71 60 1N 10 57 E
Niuchieh 108 27 47N 104 16 E
Niuchuang 107 40 58N 122 38 E
Niue I. (Savage I.) 130 19 2 S 169 54W
Niulan Chiang, R. 108 27 24N 103 9 E
Niut, Mt. 102 0 55N 109 30 E
Nivelles 47 50 35N 4 20 E
Nivernais 43 47 0N 3 40 E
Nixon, Nev., U.S.A. 160 39 54N 119 22W
Nixon, Tex., U.S.A. 159 29 17N 97 45W
Nizam Sagar 96 18 10N 77 58 E
Nizamabad 96 18 45N 78 7 E
Nizamghat 98 28 20N 95 45 E
Nizhanaya Tunguska 77 64 20N 93 0 E
Nizhiye Sergi 84 56 40N 59 18 E
Nizhne Kolymsk 77 68 40N 160 55 E
Nizhne-Vartovskoye 76 60 56N 76 38 E
Nizhneangarsk 77 56 0N 109 30 E
Nizhnegorskiy 82 45 27N 34 38 E
Nizhneudinsk 77 55 0N 99 20 E
Nizhniy Lomov 81 53 34N 43 38 E
Nizhniy Novgorod = Gorkiy 81 56 20N 44 0 E
Nizhniy Pyandzh 85 37 12N 68 35 E
Nizhniy Tagil 84 57 55N 59 57 E
Nizhny Salda 84 58 8N 60 42 E
Nizké Tatry 53 48 55N 20 0 E
Nizza Monferrato 62 44 46N 8 22 E
Njakwa 127 11 1 S 33 56 E
Njinjo 127 8 34 S 38 44 E
Njombe 124 9 20 S 34 50 E
Njombe □ 127 9 20 S 34 49 E
Njombe, R. 126 7 15 S 34 30 E
Nkambe 121 6 35N 10 40 E
Nkana 127 13 0 S 28 8 E
Nkawkaw 121 6 36N 0 49W
Nkhata Bay 124 11 33 S 34 16 E
Nkhota Kota 127 12 56 S 34 15 E
Nkongsamba 121 4 55N 9 55 E
Nkunka 127 14 57 S 25 58 E
Nkwanta 120 6 10N 2 10W
Nmai Pit, R. 99 25 30N 98 0 E
Nmai, R. 99 25 30N 98 0 E
Nmaushahra 95 33 11N 74 15 E
Nnewi 121 6 0N 6 59 E
Noakhali = Maijdi 98 22 50N 90 45 E
Noatak 147 67 32N 163 10W
Noatak, R. 147 68 0N 161 0W
Nobber 38 53 49N 6 45W
Nobeoka 110 32 36N 131 41 E
Nōbi-Heiya 111 35 15N 136 45 E
Noblejas 58 39 58N 3 26W
Noblesville 156 40 1N 85 59W
Noce, R. 62 46 22N 11 0 E
Nocera Inferiore 65 40 45N 14 37 E
Nocera Terinese 65 39 2N 16 9 E
Nocera Umbra 63 43 8N 12 47 E
Nochixtlán 165 17 28N 97 14W
Noci 65 40 47N 17 7 E
Nockatunga 139 27 42 S 142 42 E
Nocona 159 33 48N 97 45W
Nocrich 70 45 55N 24 26 E
Noda, Japan 111 35 56N 139 52 E
Noda, U.S.S.R. 77 47 30N 142 5 E
Noel 159 36 36N 94 29W
Nogales, Mexico 164 31 36N 94 29W
Nogales, U.S.A. 161 31 33N 115 50W
Nōgata 110 33 48N 130 54 E
Nogent-en-Bassigny 43 48 0N 5 20 E
Nogent-le-Rotrou 42 48 20N 0 50 E
Nogent-sur-Seine 43 48 30N 3 30 E
Noggerup 137 33 32 S 116 5 E
Noginsk, Moskva, U.S.S.R. 81 55 50N 38 25 E
Noginsk, Sib., U.S.S.R. 77 64 30N 90 50 E
Nogoa, R. 138 23 33 S 148 32 E
Nogoyá 172 32 24 S 59 48W
Nógrád □ 53 48 0N 19 30 E
Nogueira de Ramuin 56 42 21N 7 43W
Noguera Pallaresa, R. 58 42 15N 1 0 E
Noguera Ribagorzana, R. 58 42 15N 0 45 E
Nohar 94 29 11N 74 49 E
Noi, R. 101 14 50N 100 15 E
Noire, Mts. 42 48 11N 3 40W
Noirétable 44 45 48N 3 46 E
Noirmoutier 42 47 0N 2 15W
Noirmoutier, Î. de 42 46 58N 2 10W
Nojane 128 23 15 S 20 14 E
Nojima-Zaki 111 34 54N 139 53 E
Nok Kundi 93 28 50N 62 45 E
Nokaneng 128 19 47 S 22 17 E
Nokhtuysk 77 60 0N 117 45 E
Nokomis 153 51 35N 105 0W
Nokomis L. 153 57 0N 103 0W
Nokou 124 14 35N 14 47 E
Nol 73 57 56N 12 5 E
Nola, C. Afr. Emp. 124 3 35N 16 10 E
Nola, Italy 65 40 54N 14 29 E
Nolay 43 46 58N 4 35 E
Nolby 72 62 17N 17 26 E
Noli, C. di 62 44 12N 8 26 E
Nolinsk 84 57 28N 49 57 E
Noma Omuramba, R. 128 19 6 S 20 30 E
Noma-Saki 110 31 25N 130 7 E
Nomad 135 6 19 S 142 13 E
Noman L. 153 62 15N 108 55W
Nombre de Dios 166 9 34N 79 28W
Nome 147 64 30N 165 30W
Nomo-Zaki 110 32 35N 129 44 E
Nonacho L. 153 61 57N 109 28W
Nonancourt 42 48 47N 1 11 E
Nonant-le-Pin 42 48 42N 0 12 E
Nonda 138 20 40 S 142 28 E
Nong Chang 100 15 23N 99 51 E
Nong Het 100 19 29N 103 59 E
Nong Khae 101 14 29N 100 53 E
Nong Khai 100 17 50N 102 46 E
Nonoava 164 27 22N 106 38W
Nonopapa 147 21 50N 160 15W
Nonthaburi 100 13 51N 100 34 E
Nontron 44 45 31N 0 40 E
Noonamah 136 12 40 S 131 4 E
Noonan 158 48 51N 102 59W
Noondoo 139 28 35 S 148 30 E
Noonkanbah 102 18 30 S 124 50 E
Noord-Bergum 46 53 14N 6 1 E
Noord Brabant □ 47 51 40N 5 0 E
Noord Holland □ 46 52 30N 4 45 E
Noordbeveland 47 51 45N 3 50 E
Noordeloos 46 51 55N 4 56 E
Noordhollandsch Kanaal 46 52 55N 4 48 E
Noordhorn 46 53 16N 6 24 E
Noordoostpolder 46 52 45N 5 45 E
Noordwijk aan Zee 46 52 14N 4 26 E
Noordwijk-Binnen 46 52 14N 4 27 E
Noordwijkerhout 46 52 16N 4 30 E
'Noordwinning', gasfield 19 53 13N 3 10 E
Noordzee Kanaal 46 52 28N 4 35 E
Noorvik 147 66 50N 161 14W
Noorwolde 46 52 54N 6 8 E
Nootka 152 49 38N 126 38W
Nootka I. 152 49 40N 126 50W
Noqui 124 5 55 S 13 30 E
Nora, Ethiopia 123 16 6N 40 4 E
Nora, Sweden 72 59 32N 15 2 E
Noranda 150 48 20N 79 0W
Norberg 72 60 4N 15 56 E
Norbottens län □ 74 66 58N 20 0 E
Nórcia 63 42 50N 13 5 E
Norco 163 33 56N 117 33W
Nord □ 43 50 15N 3 30 E
Nord-Ostee Kanal 48 54 5N 9 15 E
Nord-Süd Kanal 48 53 0N 10 32 E
Nord-Trondelag Fylke □ 74 64 20N 12 0 E
Nordagutu 71 59 25N 9 20 E
Nordaustlandet 12 79 55N 23 0 E
Nordborg 73 55 5N 9 50 E
Nordby, Fanø, Denmark 73 55 27N 8 24 E
Nordby, Samsø, Denmark 73 55 58N 10 32 E
Norddal 71 62 15N 7 14 E
Norddalsfjord kpl. 71 61 39N 5 23 E
Norddeich 48 53 37N 7 10 E
Nordegg 152 52 29N 116 5W
Nordelph 29 52 34N 0 18 E
Norden 48 53 35N 7 12 E
Nordenham 48 53 29N 8 28 E
Norderhov 71 60 7N 10 17 E
Norderney 48 53 42N 7 9 E
Norderney, I. 48 53 42N 7 15 E
Nordfjord 71 61 55N 5 30 E
Nordfriesische Inseln 48 54 40N 8 20 E
Nordhausen 48 51 29N 10 47 E
Nordhorn 48 52 27N 7 4 E
Nordjyllands Amt □ 73 57 0N 10 0 E
Nordkapp, Norway 74 71 10N 25 44 E
Nordkapp, Svalb. 12 80 31N 20 0 E
Nordkinn 16 71 3N 28 0 E
Nordland Fylke □ 74 65 40N 13 0 E
Nördlingen 49 48 50N 10 30 E
Nordrhein-Westfalen □ 48 51 45N 7 30 E
Nordstrand, I. 48 54 27N 8 50 E
Nordvik 77 73 40N 110 57 E
Nore 71 60 10N 9 0 E
Nore R. 39 52 40N 7 20W
Noreena Cr. 136 22 20 S 120 25 E
Norefjell 71 60 16N 9 29 E
Norembega 150 48 59N 80 43W
Noresund 71 60 11N 9 37 E
Norfolk, Nebr., U.S.A. 158 42 3N 97 25W
Norfolk, Va., U.S.A. 156 36 52N 76 15W
Norfolk □ 29 52 39N 1 0 E
Norfolk Broads 29 52 30N 1 15 E
Norfolk I. 130 28 58 S 168 3 E
Norfork Res. 159 36 25N 92 0W
Norg 46 53 4N 6 28 E
Norham 35 55 44N 2 9W
Norilsk 77 69 20N 88 0 E
Norley 139 27 45 S 143 48 E
Normal 158 40 30N 89 0W
Norman 159 35 12N 97 30W
Norman, R. 138 19 20 S 142 35 E
Norman Wells 147 65 17N 126 45W
Normanby 142 39 32 S 174 18 E
Normanby I. 135 10 55 S 151 5 E
Normanby, R. 138 14 23 S 144 10 E
Normandie 42 48 45N 0 10 E
Normandie, Collines de 42 48 55N 0 45W
Normandin 150 48 49N 72 31W
Normandy = Normandie 42 48 45N 0 10 E
Normanhurst, Mt. 137 25 13 S 122 30 E
Normanton, Austral. 138 17 40 S 141 10 E
Normanton, U.K. 33 53 41N 1 26W
Normanville 140 35 27 S 138 18 E
Norna, Mt. 138 20 55 S 140 42 E
Nornalup 137 35 0 S 116 48 E
Norquay 153 51 53N 102 5W
Ñorquinco 176 41 51 S 70 55W
Norrahammar 73 57 43N 14 7 E
Norrbottens län □ 74 66 50N 18 0 E
Norrby 74 64 55N 18 15 E
Nørre Åby 73 55 27N 9 52 E
Nørre Nebel 73 55 47N 8 17 E
Nørresundby 73 57 5N 9 52 E
Norris 160 45 40N 111 48W
Norristown 162 40 9N 75 15W
Norrköping 73 58 37N 16 11 E
Norrland □ 74 66 50N 18 0 E
Norrtälje 72 59 46N 18 42 E
Norseman 137 32 8 S 121 43 E
Norsholm 73 58 31N 15 59 E
Norsk 77 52 30N 130 0 E
Norte de Santander □ 174 8 0N 73 0W
North Adams 162 42 42N 73 6W
North America 50 40 0N 70 0W
North Andaman I. 101 13 15N 92 40 E
North Atlantic Ocean 14 30 0N 50 0W
North Ballachulish 36 56 42N 5 9W
North Battleford 153 52 50N 108 17W
North Bay 150 46 20N 79 30W
North Belcher Is. 150 56 50N 79 50W
North Bend, Can. 152 49 50N 121 35W
North Bend, U.S.A. 160 43 28N 124 7W
North Bennington 162 42 56N 73 15W
North Berwick, U.K. 35 56 4N 2 44W
North Berwick, U.S.A. 162 43 18N 70 43W
North Br., Ashburton R. 143 43 30 S 171 30 E
North Buganda □ 126 1 0N 32 0 E
North Canadian, R. 159 36 48N 103 0W
North C., Antarct. 13 71 0N 166 0 E
North C., Can. 151 47 2N 60 20W
North, Cape 151 47 2N 60 25W
North C., N.Z. 142 34 23 S 173 4 E
North C., P.N.G. 135 2 32 S 150 50 E
North C., Spitsbergen 12 80 40N 20 0 E
North Caribou L. 150 52 50N 90 40W
North Carolina □ 157 35 30N 80 0W
North Cerney 28 51 45N 1 58W
North Channel, Br. Is. 34 55 0N 5 30W
North Channel, Can. 150 46 0N 83 0W
North Chicago 156 42 19N 87 50W
North Collingham 33 53 8N 0 46W
North Dakota □ 158 47 30N 100 0W
North Dandalup 137 32 30 S 116 2 E
N. Dorset Downs 28 50 50N 2 30W
North Down □ 38 54 40N 5 45W
North Downs 29 51 17N 0 30W
North East 162 39 36N 75 56W
North Eastern □ 126 1 30N 40 0 E
North Esk, R. 37 56 44N 2 25W
North European Plain 16 55 0N 20 0 E
N. Foreland, Pt. 29 51 22N 1 28 E
North Fork 163 37 14N 119 29W
N. Frisian Is. = Nordfr'sche Inseln 48 54 50N 8 20 E
N. Harris, dist. 36 58 0N 6 55W
North Henik L. 153 61 45N 97 40W
North Hill 30 50 33N 4 26W
North Horr 126 3 20N 37 8 E
North Hykeham 33 53 10N 0 35W
North I., Kenya 126 4 5N 36 5 E
North I., N.Z. 143 38 0 S 175 0 E
North Kamloops 152 50 40N 120 25W
North Kessock 37 57 30N 4 15W
North Knife L., Can. 153 58 0N 97 0W
North Knife L., Man., Can. 153 58 5N 97 5W
North Knife, R. 153 58 53N 94 45W
North Koel, R. 95 23 50N 84 5 E
North Korea ■ 105 40 0N 127 0 E
N. Lakhimpur 99 27 15N 94 10 E
N. Las Vegas 161 36 15N 115 6W
North Mara □ 126 1 20 S 34 20 E
North Minch 36 58 5N 5 55W
North Molton 30 51 3N 3 48W
North Nahanni, R. 152 62 15N 123 20W
North Ossetian A.S.S.R. □ 83 43 30N 44 30 E
North Palisade 163 37 6N 118 32W
North Petherton 28 51 6N 3 1W
North Platte 158 41 10N 100 50W
North Platte, R. 160 42 50N 106 50W
North Pt., Austral. 108 27 23 S 153 14 E
North Pt., Can. 151 47 5N 65 0W
North Pole 12 90 0N 0 0 E
North Portal 153 49 0N 102 33W
North Powder 160 45 2N 117 59W
North Queensferry 35 56 1N 3 22W
North Riding (□) 26 54 22N 1 30W
North Roe, dist. 36 60 40N 1 22W
North Ronaldsay, I. 37 59 20N 2 30W
North Sea 19 56 0N 4 0 E
North Sentinel, I. 101 11 35N 92 15 E
North Somercotes 33 53 28N 0 9 E
North Sound 39 53 10N 9 48W
North Sound, The 37 59 18N 2 45W
North Sporades = Voríai Sporádhes 69 39 0N 24 10 E
North Stradbroke I. 133 27 35 S 153 28 E
North Sunderland 35 55 35N 1 40W
North Sydney 151 46 12N 60 21W
North Syracuse 162 43 8N 76 7W
N. Taranaki Bt. 82 38 45 S 174 20 E

North Tawton Nyirbátor

North Tawton 30 50 48N 3 55W
North Thompson, R. 152 50 40N 120 20W
North Thoresby 33 53 27N 0 3W
North Tidworth 28 51 14N 1 40W
North Tolsta 36 58 21N 6 13W
N. Tonawanda 156 43 5N 78 50W
N. Truchas Pk. 161 36 0N 105 30W
North Twin I. 150 53 20N 80 0W
North Tyne, R. 35 54 59N 2 7W
North Uist I. 36 57 40N 7 15W
North Vancouver 152 49 25N 123 20W
North Vermilion 152 58 25N 116 0W
North Vernon 156 39 0N 85 35W
North Vietnam ■ 100 22 0N 105 0E
North Wabasca L. 152 56 0N 113 55W
North Walsham 29 52 49N 1 22E
North West C. 136 21 45S 114 9E
North West Highlands 36 57 35N 5 2W
North West River 151 53 30N 60 10W
North Western □ 127 13 30S 25 30E
North York Moors 33 54 25N 0 50W
North Yorkshire □ 33 54 15N 1 25W
Northallerton 33 54 20N 1 26W
Northam, Austral. 132 31 35S 116 42E
Northam, S. Afr. 137 24 55S 27 15E
Northam, U.K. 30 51 2N 4 13W
Northampton, Austral. 137 28 21S 114 33E
Northampton, U.K. 29 52 14N 0 54W
Northampton, Mass., U.S.A. 162 42 22N 72 39W
Northampton, Pa., U.S.A. 162 40 38N 75 24W
Northampton □ 29 52 16N 0 55W
Northampton Downs 138 24 35S 145 48E
Northbridge 162 42 12N 71 40W
Northcliffe 137 34 39S 116 7E
N.E. Land 12 80 0N 24 0E
N.E. Providence Chan. 166 26 0N 76 0W
Northeast Providence Channel 166 26 0N 76 0W
Northeim 48 51 42N 10 0E
Northern □, Malawi 127 11 0S 34 0E
Northern □, Uganda 126 3 5N 32 30E
Northern □, Zambia 127 10 30S 31 0E
Northern Circars 96 17 30N 82 30E
Northern Indian L. 153 57 20N 97 20W
Northern Ireland □ 38 54 45N 7 0W
Northern Light, L. 150 48 15N 90 39W
Northern Province □ 120 9 0S 11 30W
Northern Territory □ 136 16 0S 133 0E
Northfield, Minn., U.S.A. 158 44 37N 93 10W
Northfield, N.J., U.S.A. 162 39 22N 74 33W
Northfleet 29 51 26N 0 20E
Northiam 29 50 59N 0 39E
Northland □ 143 35 30S 173 30E
Northleach 28 51 49N 1 50W
Northome 158 47 53N 94 15W
Northop 31 53 13N 3 8W
Northport, Ala., U.S.A. 157 33 15N 87 35W
Northport, Mich., U.S.A. 156 45 8N 85 39W
Northport, N.Y., U.S.A. 162 40 53N 73 20W
Northport, Wash., U.S.A. 160 48 55N 117 48W
Northrepps 29 52 53N 1 20E
Northumberland □ 35 55 12N 2 0W
Northumberland, C. 140 38 5S 140 40E
Northumberland Is. 138 21 30S 149 50E
Northumberland Str. 151 46 20N 64 0W
Northville 162 43 13N 74 11W
Northway Junction 147 63 0N 141 55W
N.W. Providence Chan. 166 26 0N 78 0W
Northwest Terr. 148 65 0N 100 0W
N.W.Basin 137 25 45S 115 0E
Northwich 32 53 16N 2 30W
Northwold 29 52 33N 0 37E
Northwood, Iowa, U.S.A. 158 43 27N 93 12W
Northwood, N.D., U.S.A. 158 47 44N 97 30W
Norton, Rhod. 127 17 52S 30 40E
Norton, N. Yorks., U.K. 33 54 9N 0 48W
Norton, Suffolk, U.K. 29 52 15N 0 52E
Norton, U.S.A. 158 39 50N 100 0W
Norton B. 147 64 40N 162 0W
Norton Fitzwarren 28 51 1N 3 10W
Norton Sd. 147 64 0N 165 0W
Norton Summit 109 34 56S 138 43E
Nortorf 48 54 14N 9 47E
Norwalk, Calif., U.S.A. 163 33 54N 118 5W
Norwalk, Conn., U.S.A. 162 41 9N 73 25W
Norwalk, Ohio, U.S.A. 156 41 13N 82 38W
Norway 156 45 46N 87 57W
Norway ■ 74 67 0N 11 0E
Norway House 153 53 59N 97 50W
Norwegian Dependency 13 66 0N 15 0E
Norwegian Sea 14 66 0N 1 0E
Norwich, U.K. 29 52 38N 1 17E
Norwich, Conn., U.S.A. 162 41 33N 72 5W
Norwich, N.Y., U.S.A. 162 42 32N 75 30W
Norwood, Austral. 109 34 56S 138 39E
Norwood, U.S.A. 162 42 10N 71 10W
Noshiro 112 40 12N 140 0E
Noshiro, R. 112 40 15N 140 15E
Nosok 76 70 10N 82 20E
Nosovka 80 50 50N 31 30E
Nosratābād 93 29 55N 60 0E
Noss Hd. 37 58 29N 3 4W
Noss, I. of 36 60 8N 1 1W
Nossa Senhora da Glória 170 10 14S 37 25W
Nossa Senhora das Dores 170 10 29S 37 13W
Nossebro 73 58 12N 12 43E
Nossob 128 22 15S 17 48E
Nossob, R. 128 25 15S 20 30E
Nosy Bé, I. 125 13 25S 48 15E
Nosy Mitsio, I. 125 12 54S 48 36E
Nosy Varika 125 20 35S 48 32E
Notigi Dam 153 56 40N 99 10W
Notikewin 152 56 55N 117 50W
Notikewin, R. 152 56 59N 117 38W
Notios Evvoïkós Kólpos 69 38 20N 24 0E
Noto 65 36 52N 15 4E
Notò, G. di 65 36 50N 15 10E
Notodden 71 59 35N 9 17E
Notre Dame 151 46 18N 64 46W
Notre Dame B. 151 49 45N 55 30W
Notre Dame de Koartac 149 60 55N 69 40W
Notre Dame d'Ivugivic 149 62 20N 78 0W
Nottaway, R. 150 51 22N 78 55W
Nøtterøy 71 59 14N 10 24E
Nottingham 33 52 57N 1 10W
Nottingham □ 33 53 10N 1 0W
Nottoway, R. 156 37 0N 77 45W
Notwani, R. 128 24 14S 26 20E
Nouadhibou 116 21 0N 17 0W
Nouakchott 120 18 20N 15 50W
Nouméa 130 22 17S 166 30E
Noup Hd. 37 59 20N 3 2W
Noupoort 128 31 10S 24 57E
Nouveau Comptoir (Paint Hills) 150 53 0N 78 49W
Nouvelle Calédonie 142 21 0S 165 0E
Nouzonville 43 49 48N 4 44E
Nova-Annenskiy 81 50 32N 42 39E
Nová Bana 53 48 28N 18 39E
Nová Bystrice 52 49 2N 15 8E
Nova Chaves 124 10 50S 21 15E
Nova Cruz 170 6 28S 35 25W
Nova Era 171 19 45S 43 3W
Nova Esperança 173 23 8S 52 13W
Nova Friburgo 173 22 10S 42 30W
Nova Gaia 124 10 10S 17 35E
Nova Gradiška 66 45 17N 17 28E
Nova Granada 171 20 30S 49 20W
Nova Iguaçu 173 22 45S 43 28W
Nova Iorque 170 7 0S 44 5W
Nova Lamego 120 12 19N 14 11W
Nova Lima 173 19 59S 43 51W
Nova Lisboa = Huambo 125 12 42S 15 54E
Nova Lusitânia 127 19 50S 34 34E
Nova Mambone 129 21 0S 35 3E
Nova Mesto 63 45 47N 15 12E
Nova Paka 52 50 29N 15 30E
Nova Ponte 171 19 8S 47 41W
Nova Preixo 127 14 45S 36 22E
Nova Scotia □ 151 45 10N 63 0W
Nova Sofala 129 20 7S 34 48E
Nova Varoš 66 43 29N 19 48E
Nova Venécia 171 18 45S 40 24W
Nova Zagora 67 42 32N 25 59E
Novaci, Rumania 70 45 10N 23 42E
Novaci, Yugo. 66 41 5N 21 29E
Novaleksandrovskaya 83 45 29N 41 17E
Novalorque 171 6 48S 44 0W
Novara 62 45 27N 8 36E
Novato 163 38 6N 122 35W
Novaya Kakhovka 82 46 42N 33 27E
Novaya Ladoga 78 60 7N 32 16E
Novaya Lyalya 84 58 50N 60 35E
Novaya Sibir, O. 77 75 10N 150 0E
Novaya Zemlya 76 75 0N 56 0E
Novelda 59 38 24N 0 45W
Novellara 62 44 50N 10 43E
Noventa Vicentina 63 45 18N 11 30E
Novgorod 80 58 30N 31 25E
Novgorod Severskiy 80 52 2N 33 10E
Novgorod Volynski 80 50 38N 27 47E
Novi Bečej. 66 45 36N 20 10E
Novi Grad 63 45 19N 13 33E
Novi Knezeva 66 46 4N 20 8E
Novi Krichim 67 42 22N 24 31E
Novi Ligure 62 44 45N 8 47E
Novi-Pazar 67 43 25N 27 15E
Novi Pazar 66 43 12N 20 28E
Novi Sad 66 45 18N 19 52E
Novi Vinodolski 63 45 10N 14 48E
Novigrad 63 44 10N 15 32E
Noville 47 50 4N 5 46E
Novo Acôrdo 170 13 10S 46 48W
Nôvo Cruzeiro 171 17 29S 41 53W
Novo Freixo 127 14 49S 36 30E
Nôvo Hamburgo 173 29 37S 51 7W
Nôvo Horizonte 171 21 25S 49 10W
Novo Luso 103 4 3S 126 6E
Novo Redondo 124 11 10S 13 48E
Novo Selo 66 44 11N 22 47E
Novo-Sergiyevskiy 84 52 5N 53 38E
Novo-Zavidovskiy 81 56 32N 36 29E
Novoalekseyevka 84 50 8N 55 39E
Novoataysk 76 53 30N 84 0E
Novoazovsk 82 47 15N 38 4E
Novobelitsa 80 52 27N 31 2E
Novobogatinskoye 83 47 26N 51 17E
Novocherkassk 83 47 27N 40 5E
Novodevichye 81 53 37N 48 58E
Novograd Volynskiy 80 50 40N 27 35E
Novogrudok 80 53 40N 25 50E
Novokayakent 83 42 45N 42 52E
Novokazalinsk 76 45 40N 61 40E
Novokhopersk 81 51 5N 41 50E
Novokuybyshevsk 84 53 7N 49 58E
Novokuznetsk 76 54 0N 87 10E
Novomirgorod 82 48 57N 31 33E
Novomoskovsk, R.S.F.S.R., U.S.S.R. 81 54 5N 38 15E
Novomoskovsk, Ukrainian S.S.R., U.S.S.R. 81 48 33N 35 17E
Novoorsk 84 51 21N 59 2E
Novopolotsk 80 55 38N 28 37E
Novorossiysk 82 44 43N 37 52E
Novorzhev 80 57 3N 29 25E
Novoselitsa 82 48 14N 26 15E
Novoshakhtinsk 83 47 39N 39 58E
Novosibirsk 76 55 0N 83 5E
Novosibirskiye Ostrava 77 75 0N 140 0E
Novosil 81 52 58N 36 58E
Novosokolniki 80 56 33N 28 42E
Novotroitsk 84 51 10N 58 15E
Novotroitskoye 85 43 42N 73 46E
Novotulskiy 81 54 10N 37 36E
Novoukrainka 82 48 25N 31 30E
Novouzensk 81 50 32N 48 17E
Novovolynsk 80 50 45N 24 4E
Novovyatsk 84 58 24N 49 45E
Novozybkov 80 52 30N 32 0E
Novska 66 45 19N 17 0E
Novy Bug 82 47 34N 34 29E
Nový Bydzov 52 50 14N 15 29E
Novy Dwór Mazowiecki 54 52 26N 20 44E
Nový Jičín 53 49 15N 18 0E
Novyy Oskol 81 50 44N 37 55E
Novyy Port 76 67 40N 72 30E
Novyye Aneny 70 46 51N 29 13E
Now Shahr 93 36 40N 51 40E
Nowa Deba 54 50 26N 21 41E
Nowa Nowa 141 37 44S 148 3E
Nowa Skalmierzyce 54 51 43N 18 0E
Nowa Sól 54 51 48N 15 44E
Nowe 54 53 41N 18 44E
Nowe Miasteczko 54 51 42N 15 42E
Nowe Miasto 54 51 38N 20 34E
Nowe Miasto Lubawskie 54 53 27N 19 33E
Nowe Warpno 54 53 42N 14 18E
Nowen Hill 39 51 42N 9 15W
Nowendoc 141 31 32S 151 44E
Nowgong 98 26 20N 92 50E
Nowingi 140 34 33S 142 15E
Nowogard 54 53 41N 15 10E
Nowogród 54 53 14N 21 53E
Nowra 141 34 53S 150 35E
Nowthanna Mt. 137 27 0S 118 40E
Nowy Dwór 54 53 40N 23 0E
Nowy Korczyn 54 50 19N 20 48E
Nowy Sącz 54 49 40N 20 41E
Nowy Sącz □ 54 49 30N 20 30E
Nowy Staw 54 54 13N 19 2E
Nowy Targ 53 49 30N 20 2E
Nowy Tomyśl 54 52 19N 16 10E
Noxen 162 41 25N 76 4W
Noxon 160 48 0N 115 54W
Noya 56 42 48N 8 53W
Noyant 42 47 30N 0 6E
Noyers 43 47 40N 4 0E
Noyes, I. 152 55 30N 133 40W
Noyon 43 49 34N 3 0E
Nqiquinha 125 16 0S 21 25E
Nsa, O. en 119 32 23N 5 20E
Nsanje 127 16 55S 35 12E
Nsawam 121 5 50N 0 24W
Nsomba 127 10 45S 29 59E
Nsopzup 98 25 51N 97 30E
Nsukka 121 7 0N 7 50E
Nuanetsi 125 21 15S 30 48E
Nuanetsi, R. 127 21 10S 31 20E
Nuatja 121 7 0N 1 10E
Nuba Mts. = Nubāh, Jibālan 123 12 0N 31 0E
Nubāh, Jibālan 123 12 0N 31 0E
Nûbîya, Es Sahrâ En 122 21 30N 33 30E
Nuble □ 172 37 0S 72 0W
Nuboai 103 2 10S 136 30E
Nubra, R. 95 34 50N 77 25E
Nudgee 108 27 22S 153 5E
Nudgee Beach 108 27 21S 153 6E
Nûdlac 66 46 10N 20 50E
Nudo Ausangate, Mt. 174 13 45S 71 10W
Nudo de Vilcanota 174 14 30S 70 0W
Nueces, R. 159 28 18N 98 39W
Nueltin L. 153 60 30N 99 30W
Nuenen 47 51 29N 5 33E
Nueva Antioquia 174 6 5N 69 26W
Nueva Casas Grandes 164 30 25N 107 55W
Nueva Esparta □ 174 11 0N 64 0W
Nueva Gerona 166 21 53N 82 49W
Nueva Imperial 176 38 45S 72 58W
Nueva Palmira 172 33 52S 58 20W
Nueva Rosita 164 28 0N 101 20W
Nueva San Salvador 166 13 40N 89 25W
Nuéve de Julio 172 35 30S 61 0W
Nuevitas 166 21 30N 77 20W
Nuevo, Golfo 176 43 0S 64 30W
Nuevo Guerrero 165 26 34N 99 15W
Nuevo Laredo 165 27 30N 99 40W
Nuevo León □ 164 25 0N 100 0W
Nuevo Rocafuerte 174 0 55S 76 50W
Nugget Pt. 143 46 27S 169 50E
Nugrus Gebel 122 24 58N 39 34E
Nuhaka 142 39 3S 177 45E
Nuhurowa, I. 103 5 30S 132 45E
Nuits 43 47 10N 4 56E
Nuits-St.-Georges 43 47 10N 4 56E
Nukey Bluff, Mt. 132 32 32S 135 40E
Nukheila (Merga) 122 19 1N 26 21E
Nukus 76 42 20N 59 40E
Nuland 46 51 44N 5 26E
Nulato 147 64 40N 158 10W
Nules 58 39 51N 0 9W
Nullagine 136 21 53S 120 6E
Nullagine, R. 136 21 20S 120 20E
Nullarbor 137 31 28S 130 55E
Nullarbor Plain 137 30 45S 129 0E
Numalla, L. 139 28 43S 144 20E
Numan 121 9 29N 12 3E
Numansdorp 46 51 43N 4 26E
Numata 111 36 45N 139 4E
Numatinna, W. 123 6 38N 27 15E
Numazu 111 35 7N 138 51E
Numbulwar 138 14 15S 135 45E
Numfoor, I. 103 1 0S 134 50E
Numurkah 141 36 0S 145 26E
Nun, R. 105 47 30N 124 40E
Nunaksaluk, I. 151 55 49N 60 20W
Nundah 108 27 24S 152 54E
Nuneaton 28 52 32N 1 29W
Nungo 127 13 23S 37 43E
Nungwe 126 2 48S 32 2E
Nunivak I. 147 60 0N 166 0W
Nunkun, Mt. 95 33 57N 76 8E
Nunney 28 51 13N 2 20W
Nunspeet 46 52 21N 5 45E
Nuoro 64 40 20N 9 20E
Nûousa 68 40 42N 22 9E
Nuqayy, Jabal 119 23 11N 19 30E
Nuquí 174 5 42N 77 17W
Nurata 85 40 33N 65 41E
Nuratau, Khrebet 85 40 40N 66 30E
Nure, R. 62 44 40N 9 32E
Nuremburg = Nürnberg 49 49 26N 11 5E
Nuri 164 28 2N 109 22W
Nurina 137 30 44S 126 23E
Nuriootpa 140 34 27S 139 0E
Nurlat 84 54 29N 50 45E
Nürnberg 49 49 26N 11 5E
Nurrari Lakes 137 29 1S 130 5E
Nurri 64 39 43N 9 13E
Nusa Barung 103 8 22S 113 20E
Nusa Kambangan 103 7 47S 109 0E
Nusa Tenggara □ 102 7 30S 117 0E
Nusa Tenggara Barat 102 8 50S 117 30E
Nusa Tenggara Timur 103 9 30S 122 0E
Nushki 94 29 35N 65 65E
Nûsûud 70 47 19N 24 29E
Nutak 149 57 28N 61 52W
Nuth 47 50 55N 5 53E
Nutwood Downs 138 15 49S 134 10E
Nuwaiba 122 28 58N 34 40E
Nuwakot 95 28 10N 83 55E
Nuwara Eliya 97 6 58N 80 55E
Nuwefontein 128 28 1S 19 6E
Nuweveldberge 128 32 10S 21 45E
Nuyts Arch. 139 32 12S 133 20E
Nuyts, C. 137 32 2S 132 21E
Nuyts, Pt. 132 35 4S 116 38E
Nuzvid 96 16 47N 80 53E
NW Tor, oilfield 19 56 42N 3 13E
Nyaake (Webo) 120 4 52N 7 37W
Nyabing 137 33 30S 118 7E
Nyack 162 41 5N 73 57W
Nyadal 72 62 48N 17 59E
Nyagyn 76 62 8N 63 36E
Nyah West 140 35 11S 143 21E
Nyahanga 126 2 20S 33 37E
Nyahua 126 5 25S 33 23E
Nyahururu 126 0 2N 36 27E
Nyahururu Falls 126 0 2N 36 27E
Nyakanazi 126 3 2S 31 10E
Nyakasu 126 3 58S 30 6E
Nyakrom 121 5 40N 0 50W
Nyâlâ 123 12 2N 24 58E
Nyamandhlovu 127 19 55S 28 16E
Nyambiti 126 2 48S 33 27E
Nyamwaga 126 1 27S 34 33E
Nyandekwa 126 3 57S 32 32E
Nyanga, L. 137 29 57S 126 10E
Nyangana 128 18 0S 20 40E
Nyanguge 126 2 30S 33 12E
Nyangwena 127 15 18S 28 45E
Nyanji 127 14 25S 31 46E
Nyankpala 121 9 21N 0 58W
Nyanza, Burundi 126 4 21S 29 36E
Nyanza, Rwanda 126 2 20S 29 42E
Nyanza □ 126 0 10S 34 15E
Nyarling, R. 152 60 41N 113 23W
Nyasa, L. = Malawi, L. 127 12 0S 34 30E
Nyaunglebin 98 17 52N 96 42E
Nyazepetrovsk 84 56 3N 59 36E
Nyazwidzi, R. 127 19 35S 32 0E
Nyborg 73 55 18N 10 47E
Nybro 73 56 44N 15 55E
Nybster 37 58 34N 3 6W
Nyda 76 66 40N 73 10E
Nyenchen Tanglha Shan 99 30 30N 95 0E
Nyeri 126 0 23S 36 56E
Nyeri □ 126 0 25S 56 55E
Nyerol 123 8 41N 32 1E
Nyhem 72 62 54N 15 37E
Nyiel 123 6 9N 31 4E
Nyika Plat. 127 10 30S 36 0E
Nyilumba 127 10 30S 40 22E
Nyinahin 120 6 43N 2 3W
Nyirbátor 53 47 49N 22 9E

Nyíregyháza Oldmeldrum

Nyíregyháza 53 48 0N 21 47 E
Nykarleby (Uusikaarlepyy) 74 63 32N 22 31 E
Nykobing 73 54 56N 11 52 E
Nykøbing, Falster, Denmark 73 54 56N 11 52 E
Nykøbing, Mors, Denmark 73 56 48N 8 51 E
Nykøbing, Sjælland, Denmark 73 55 55N 11 40 E
Nyköbing 73 56 49N 8 50 E
Nyköping 73 58 45N 17 0 E
Nykroppa 72 59 37N 14 18 E
Nykvarn 72 59 11N 17 25 E
Nyland 72 63 1N 17 45 E
Nylstroom 129 24 42 S 28 22 E
Nymagee 141 32 7 S 146 20 E
Nymburk 52 50 10N 15 1 E
Nymindegab 73 55 50N 8 12 E
Nynäshamn 72 58 54N 17 57 E
Nyngan 141 31 30 S 147 8 E
Nyon 50 46 23N 6 14 E
Nyons 45 44 22N 5 10 E
Nyora 141 38 20 S 145 41 E
Nyord 73 55 4N 12 13 E
Nysa 54 50 40N 17 22 E
Nysa, R. 54 52 4N 14 46 E
Nyssa 160 43 56N 117 2W
Nysted 73 54 40N 11 44 E
Nytva 84 57 56N 55 20 E
Nyūgawa 110 33 56N 133 5 E
Nyunzu 126 5 57 S 27 58 E
Nyurba 77 63 17N 118 20 E
Nzega 126 4 10 S 33 12 E
Nzega □ 126 4 10 S 33 10 E
N'Zérékoré 120 7 49N 8 48W
Nzilo, Chutes de 127 10 18 S 25 27 E
Nzubuka 126 4 45 S 32 50 E

O

O-Shima, Fukuoka, Japan 110 33 54N 130 25 E
O-Shima, Nagasaki, Japan 110 33 29N 129 33 E
O-Shima, Shizuoka, Japan 111 34 44N 139 24 E
Oa, Mull of 34 55 35N 6 20W
Oa, The, Pen. 34 55 36N 6 17W
Oacoma 158 43 50N 99 26W
Oadby 28 52 37N 1 7W
Oahe 158 44 33N 100 29W
Oahe Dam 158 44 28N 100 25W
Oahe Res 158 45 30N 100 15W
Oahu I. 147 21 30N 158 0W
Oak Creek 160 40 15N 106 59W
Oak Harb. 160 48 20N 122 38W
Oak Lake 153 49 45N 100 45W
Oak Park 156 41 55N 87 45W
Oak Ridge 157 36 1N 84 5W
Oak View 163 34 24N 119 18W
Oakbank, S. Australia, Austral. 109 34 59 S 138 51 E
Oakbank, S. Australia, Austral. 140 33 4 S 140 33 E
Oakdale, Calif., U.S.A. 163 37 49N 120 56W
Oakdale, La., U.S.A. 159 30 50N 92 38W
Oakengates 28 52 42N 2 29W
Oakes 158 46 14N 98 4W
Oakesdale 160 47 11N 117 9W
Oakey 139 27 25 S 151 43 E
Oakham 29 52 40N 0 43W
Oakhill 156 38 0N 81 7W
Oakhurst 163 37 19N 119 40W
Oakland 163 37 50N 122 18W
Oakland City 156 38 20N 87 20W
Oaklands, N.S.W., Austral. 141 35 34 S 146 10 E
Oaklands, S. Australia, Austral. 109 35 1 S 138 32 E
Oakley 160 42 14N 113 55W
Oakley Creek 141 31 37 S 149 46 E
Oakover, R. 136 20 43 S 120 33 E
Oakridge 160 43 47N 122 31W
Oakwood 159 31 35N 95 47W
Oamaru 143 45 5 S 170 59 E
Oamishirasato 111 35 23N 140 18 E
Oarai 111 36 21N 140 40 E
Oasis, Calif., U.S.A. 163 33 28N 116 6W
Oasis, Nev., U.S.A. 163 37 29N 117 55W
Oates Coast 13 69 0 S 160 0 E
Oatman 161 35 1N 114 19W
Oaxaca 165 17 2N 96 40W
Oaxaca □ 165 17 0N 97 0W
Ob, R. 76 62 40N 66 0 E
Oba 150 49 4N 84 7W
Obala 121 4 9N 11 32 E
Obama, Eukui, Japan 111 35 30N 135 45 E
Obama, Nagasaki, Japan 110 32 43N 130 13 E
Oban, N.Z. 143 46 55 S 168 10 E
Oban, U.K. 34 56 25N 5 30W
Obatogamau L. 150 49 34N 74 26W
Obbia 91 5 25N 48 30 E
Obdam 46 52 41N 4 55 E
Obed 152 53 30N 117 10W
Obeh 93 34 28N 63 10 E
Ober-Aagau 50 47 10N 7 45 E
Obera 173 27 21 S 55 2W
Oberalppass 51 46 39N 8 35 E
Oberalpstock 51 46 45N 8 47 E
Oberammergau 49 47 35N 11 3 E
Oberdrauburg 52 46 44N 12 58 E
Oberengadin 51 46 35N 9 55 E
Oberentfelden 50 47 21N 8 2 E
Oberhausen 48 51 28N 6 50 E
Oberkirch 49 48 31N 8 5 E
Oberland 50 46 30N 7 30 E
Oberlin, Kans., U.S.A. 158 39 52N 100 31W
Oberlin, La., U.S.A. 159 30 42N 92 42W
Obernai 43 48 28N 7 30 E
Oberndorf 49 48 17N 8 35 E
Oberon 141 33 45 S 149 52 E
Oberösterreich □ 52 48 10N 14 0 E
Oberpfalzer Wald 49 49 30N 12 25 E
Oberseebach 51 48 53N 7 58 E
Obersiggenthal 51 47 29N 8 18 E
Oberstdorf 49 47 25N 10 16 E
Oberwil 50 47 32N 7 33 E
Obi, Kepulauan 103 1 30 S 127 30 E
Obiaruku 121 5 51N 6 9 E
Óbidos, Brazil 175 1 50 S 55 30W
Óbidos, Port. 57 39 19N 9 10W
Obihiro 112 42 25N 143 12 E
Obilnoye 83 47 32N 44 30 E
Obisfelde 48 52 27N 10 57 E
Objat 44 45 16N 1 24 E
Obluchye 77 49 10N 130 50 E
Obninsk 81 55 8N 36 13 E
Obo, C. Afr. Emp. 123 5 20N 26 32 E
Obo, Ethiopia 123 3 34N 38 52 E
Oboa, Mt. 126 1 45N 34 45 E
Obock 123 12 0N 43 20 E
Oborniki 54 52 39N 16 59 E
Oborniki Śl. 54 51 17N 16 53 E
Obot 123 4 32N 37 13 E
Obout 121 3 28N 11 47 E
Oboyan 81 51 20N 36 28 E
Obrenovac 66 44 40N 20 11 E
O'Briensbridge 39 52 46N 8 30W
Obrovac 63 44 11N 15 41 E
Observatory Inlet 152 55 25N 129 45W
Obshchi Syrt 16 52 0N 53 0 E
Obskaya Guba 76 70 0N 73 0 E
Obuasi 121 6 17N 1 40W
Obubra 121 6 8N 8 20 E
Obyachevo 84 60 20N 49 37 E
Obzor 67 42 50N 27 52 E
Ocala 157 29 11N 82 5W
Ocampo 164 28 9N 108 8W
Ocaña 58 39 55N 3 30W
Ocanomowoc 158 43 7N 88 30W
Ocate 159 36 12N 104 59W
Occidental, Cordillera 174 5 0N 76 0W
Ocean City, Md., U.S.A. 162 38 20N 75 5W
Ocean City, N.J., U.S.A. 162 39 18N 74 34W
Ocean Falls 152 52 25N 127 40W
Ocean I. 130 0 45 S 169 50 E
Ocean Park 160 46 30N 124 2W
Oceanlake 160 45 0N 124 0W
Oceano 163 35 6N 120 37W
Oceanside 163 33 13N 117 26W
Ochagavia 58 42 55N 1 5W
Ochakov 82 46 35N 31 30 E
Ochamchire 83 42 46N 41 32 E
Ochamps 47 49 56N 5 16 E
Och'eng 109 30 20N 114 51 E
Ocher 84 57 53N 54 42 E
Ochiai 110 35 1N 133 45 E
Ochil Hills 35 56 14N 3 40W
Ochiltree 35 55 26N 4 23W
Ochre River 153 51 4N 99 47W
Ochsenfurt 49 49 38N 10 3 E
Ocilla 157 31 35N 83 12W
Ockelbo 72 60 54N 16 45 E
Ocmulgee, R. 157 32 0N 83 19W
Ocna Mureş 70 46 23N 23 49 E
Ocna-Sibiului 70 45 52N 24 2 E
Ocnele Mari 70 45 8N 24 18 E
Oconee, R. 157 32 30N 82 55W
Oconto 156 44 52N 87 53W
Oconto Falls 156 44 52N 88 10W
Ocós 166 14 31N 92 11W
Ocosingo 165 18 4N 92 15W
Ocotal 166 13 41N 86 41W
Ocotlán 164 20 21N 102 42W
Ocquier 47 50 24N 5 24 E
Ocreza, R. 56 39 50N 7 35W
Ócsa 53 47 17N 19 15 E
Octave 161 34 10N 112 43W
Octeville 42 49 38N 1 40W
Octyabrskoy Revolyutsii, Os. 77 79 30N 97 0 E
Ocumare del Tuy 174 10 7N 66 46W
Ocussi 103 9 20 S 124 30 E
Oda, Ghana 121 5 50N 1 5W
Oda, Ehime, Japan 110 33 36N 132 53 E
Oda, Shimane, Japan 110 35 11N 132 30 E
Ödåkra 73 56 9N 12 45 E
Ödåkra 73 56 7N 12 45 E
Odanakumadona 128 20 55 S 24 46 E
Odáoahraun 74 65 5N 17 0W
Odate 112 40 16N 140 34 E
Odawara 111 35 20N 139 6 E
Odda 71 60 3N 6 35 E
Odder 73 55 58N 10 10 E
Oddobo 123 12 21N 42 6 E
Oddur 91 4 0N 43 35 E
Ödeborg 73 58 32N 11 58 E
Odei, R. 153 56 6N 96 54W
Odemira 57 37 35N 8 40W
Ödemiş 92 38 15N 28 0 E
Odense 73 55 22N 10 23 E
Odenton 162 39 5N 76 42W
Odenwald 48 49 18N 9 0 E
Oder, R. 48 53 0N 14 12 E
Oderzo 63 45 47N 12 29 E
Odessa, Del., U.S.A. 162 39 27N 75 40W
Odessa, Tex., U.S.A. 159 31 51N 102 23W
Odessa, Wash., U.S.A. 160 47 25N 118 35W
Odessa, U.S.S.R. 82 46 30N 30 45 E
Odiel, R. 57 37 30N 6 55W
Odienné 120 9 30N 7 34W
Odiham 29 51 16N 0 56W
Odin, gasfield 19 60 5N 2 10 E
Odoben 121 5 38N 0 56W
Odobeşti 70 45 43N 27 4 E
Odolanów 54 51 34N 17 40 E
O'Donnell 159 33 0N 101 48W
Odoorn 46 52 51N 6 51 E
Odorheiul Secuiesc 70 46 21N 25 21 E
Odoyevo 81 53 56N 36 42 E
Odra, R., Czech. 53 49 43N 17 47 E
Odra, R., Poland 54 52 40N 14 28 E
Odra, R., Spain 56 42 30N 4 15W
Odzaci 66 45 30N 19 17 E
Odzak 66 45 3N 18 18 E
Odzi 125 19 0 S 32 20 E
Oedelem 47 51 10N 3 21 E
Oegstgeest 46 52 11N 4 29 E
Oeiras, Brazil 170 7 0 S 42 8W
Oeiras, Port. 57 38 41N 9 18W
Oelrichs 158 43 11N 103 14W
Oelsnitz 48 50 24N 12 11 E
Oenpelli 136 12 20 S 133 4 E
Oensingen 50 47 17N 7 43 E
Oerhtossu, reg. 106 39 20N 108 30 E
Ofanto, R. 65 41 8N 15 50 E
Ofen Pass 51 46 37N 10 17 E
Offa 121 8 13N 4 42 E
Offaly □ 39 53 15N 7 30W
Offenbach 49 50 6N 8 46 E
Offenbeek 47 51 17N 6 5 E
Offenburg 126 48 27N 7 56 E
Offerdal 72 63 28N 14 0 E
Offida 63 42 56N 13 40 E
Offranville 42 49 52N 1 0 E
Ofidhousa, I. 69 36 33N 26 8 E
Ofotfjorden 74 68 27N 16 40 E
Oga-Hantō 111 39 58N 139 59 E
Ogahalla 150 50 6N 85 51W
Ōgaki 111 35 21N 136 37 E
Ogallala 158 41 12N 101 40W
Ogbomosho 121 8 1N 3 29 E
Ogden, Iowa, U.S.A. 158 42 3N 94 0W
Ogden, Utah, U.S.A. 160 41 13N 112 1W
Ogdensburg 156 44 40N 75 27W
Ogeechee, R. 157 32 30N 81 32W
Oglio, R. 62 45 15N 10 15 E
Ogmore 138 22 37 S 149 35 E
Ogmore, R. 31 51 29N 3 37W
Ogmore Vale 30 51 35N 3 32W
Ogna 71 58 31N 5 48 E
Ognon, R. 43 47 43N 6 32 E
Ogoja 121 6 38N 8 39 E
Ogoki 150 51 35N 86 0W
Ogoki L. 150 50 50N 87 10W
Ogoki, R. 150 51 38N 85 57W
Ogoki Res. 150 50 45N 88 15W
Ogooué, R. 124 1 0 S 10 0 E
Ogori 110 34 6N 131 24 E
Ogosta, R. 67 43 35N 23 35 E
Ogowe, R. = Ogooué, R. 124 1 0 S 10 0 E
Ograzden 66 41 30N 22 50 E
Ogrein 122 17 55N 34 50 E
Ogulin 63 45 16N 15 16 E
Ogun □ 121 7 0N 3 0 E
Oguni 110 33 4N 131 2 E
Oguta 121 5 44N 6 44 E
Ogwashi-Uku 121 6 15N 6 30 E
Ogwe 121 5 0N 7 14 E
Ohai 143 44 55 S 168 0 E
Ohakune 142 39 24 S 175 24 E
Ohara 111 35 15N 140 23 E
Ohau, L. 143 44 15 S 169 53 E
Ohaupo 142 37 56 S 175 20 E
Ohey 47 50 26N 5 8 E
O'Higgins □ 172 34 15 S 71 1W
Ohio □ 156 40 20N 83 0W
Ohio, R. 156 38 0N 86 0W
Ohiwa Harbour 142 37 59 S 177 10 E
Ohre, R. 52 50 10N 12 30 E
Ohrid 66 41 8N 20 52 E
Ohridsko, Jezero 66 41 8N 20 52 E
Ohrigstad 129 24 41 S 30 36 E
Öhringen 49 49 11N 9 31 E
Oi Ho 108 28 37N 98 16 E
Oignies 47 50 28N 3 0 E
Oil City 156 41 26N 79 40W
Oildale 163 35 25N 119 1W
Oilgate 39 52 25N 6 30W
Oinousa, I. 69 38 33N 26 14 E
Oirschot 47 51 30N 5 18 E
Oise □ 43 49 28N 2 30 E
Oise, R. 43 49 53N 3 50 E
Oisterwijk 47 51 35N 5 12 E
Oita 110 33 14N 131 36 E
Oita-ken □ 110 33 15N 131 30 E
Oiticica 170 5 3 S 41 5W
Ojai 163 34 28N 119 16W
Ojinaga 164 29 34N 104 25W
Ojocaliente 164 30 25N 106 30W
Ojos del Salado 172 27 0 S 68 40W
Oka, R. 81 56 20N 43 59 E
Okahandja 128 22 0 S 16 59 E
Okahukura 142 38 48N 175 14 E
Okaihau 142 35 19 S 173 36 E
Okakune 142 39 26 S 175 24 E
Okanagan L. 152 50 0N 119 30W
Okanogan 160 48 22N 119 35W
Okanogan, R. 160 48 40N 119 24W
Okány 53 46 52N 21 21 E
Okapa 135 6 38 S 145 39 E
Okaputa 128 20 5 S 17 0 E
Okara 94 30 50N 73 25 E
Okarito 143 43 15 S 170 9 E
Okato 142 39 12 S 173 53 E
Okaukuejo 125 19 10 S 16 0 E
Okavango, R. = Cubango, R. 125 16 15 S 18 0 E
Okavango Swamp 128 19 30 S 23 0 E
Okawa 110 33 9N 130 21 E
Okaya 111 36 0N 138 10 E
Okayama 110 34 40N 133 54 E
Okayama-ken □ 110 35 0N 133 50 E
Okazaki 111 34 57N 137 10 E
Oke-Iho 121 8 1N 3 18 E
Okeechobee 157 27 16N 80 46W
Okeechobee L. 157 27 0N 80 50W
Okefenokee Swamp 157 30 50N 82 15W
Okehampton 30 50 44N 4 1W
Okene 121 7 32N 6 11 E
Oker, R. 48 52 7N 10 34 E
Okha 77 53 40N 143 0 E
Ókhi Óros 69 38 5N 24 25 E
Okhotsk 77 59 20N 143 10 E
Okhotsk, Sea of 77 55 0N 145 0 E
Okhotskiy Perevoz 77 61 52N 135 35 E
Okhotsko Kolymskoy 77 63 0N 157 0 E
Oki-no-Shima 110 32 44N 132 33 E
Oki-Shotō 110 36 15N 133 15 E
Okiep 128 29 39 S 17 53 E
Okigwi 121 5 52N 7 20 E
Okija 121 5 54N 6 55 E
Okinawa-Jima 112 26 32N 128 0 E
Okinawa-Shotō 112 27 0N 128 0 E
Okinoerabu-Jima 112 27 21N 128 33 E
Okitipupa 121 6 31N 4 50 E
Oklahoma □ 159 35 20N 97 30W
Oklahoma City 159 35 25N 97 30W
Okmulgee 159 35 38N 96 0W
Oknitsa 82 48 25N 27 20 E
Okolo 126 2 37N 31 8 E
Okondeka 128 21 38 S 15 37 E
Okondja 124 0 35 S 13 45 E
Okonek 54 53 32N 16 51 E
Okrika 121 4 47N 7 4 E
Oksby 73 55 33N 8 8 E
Oktyabr 85 43 41N 77 12 E
Oktyabrskiy 84 54 28N 53 28 E
Okuchi 110 32 4N 130 37 E
Okulovka 80 58 19N 33 28 E
Okuru 143 43 55 S 168 55 E
Okushiri-Tō 112 42 15N 139 30 E
Okuta 121 9 14N 3 12 E
Okwa, R. 128 22 25 S 22 30 E
Okwoga 121 7 3N 7 42 E
Ola 159 35 2N 93 10W
Ólafsfjörður 74 66 4N 18 39W
Ólafsvík 74 64 53N 23 43W
Olancha 163 36 15N 118 1W
Olancha Pk. 163 36 15N 118 7W
Olanchito 167 15 30N 86 30W
Öland 73 56 45N 16 50 E
Olargues 44 43 34N 2 53 E
Olary 140 32 18 S 140 19 E
Olascoaga 172 35 15 S 60 39W
Olathe 158 38 50N 94 50W
Olavarría 172 36 55 S 60 20W
Oława 54 50 57N 17 20 E
Olbia 64 40 55N 9 30 E
Olbia, G. di 64 40 55N 9 35 E
Old Bahama Chan. 166 22 10N 77 30W
Old Baldy Pk = San Antonio, Mt. 163 34 17N 117 38W
Old Castile = Castilla la Vieja 56 41 55N 4 0W
Old Castle 38 53 46N 7 10W
Old Cork 138 22 57 S 142 0 E
Old Dale 163 34 8N 115 47W
Old Deer 37 57 30N 2 3W
Old Dongola 122 18 11N 30 44 E
Old Factory 150 52 36N 78 43W
Old Forge, N.J., U.S.A. 162 43 43N 74 58W
Old Forge, N.Y., U.S.A. 162 43 43N 74 58W
Old Forge, Pa., U.S.A. 162 41 20N 75 46W
Old Fort, R. 153 58 36N 110 24W
Old Harbor 147 57 12N 153 22W
Old Kilpatrick 34 55 56N 4 34W
Old Leake 33 53 2N 0 6 E
Old Leighlin 39 52 46N 7 2W
Old Man of Hoy 37 58 53N 3 25W
Old Point Comfort 162 37 0N 76 20W
Old Radnor 31 52 14N 3 7W
Old Serenje 127 13 7 S 30 45 E
Old Shinyanga 126 3 33 S 33 27 E
Old Town 151 45 0N 68 50W
Old Wives L. 153 50 5N 106 0W
Oldbury 28 52 30N 2 0W
Oldeani 126 3 22 S 35 35 E
Oldenburg, Niedersachsen, Ger. 48 53 10N 8 10 E
Oldenburg, S.-Holst, Ger. 48 54 16N 10 53 E
Oldenzaal 46 52 19N 6 53 E
Oldham 32 53 33N 2 8W
Oldman, R. 152 49 57N 111 42W
Oldmeldrum 37 57 20N 2 19W

Örkény Owen

Örkény	**53**	47 9N	19 26 E
Orkla	**71**	63 18N	9 51 E
Orkla, R.	**74**	63 18N	9 51 E
Orkney	**128**	26 42 S	26 40 E
Orkney □	**37**	59 0N	3 0W
Orkney Is.	**37**	59 0N	3 0W
Orland	**160**	39 46N	122 12W
Orlando	**157**	28 30N	81 25W
Orlando, C.d'	**65**	38 10N	14 43 E
Orléanais	**43**	48 0N	2 0 E
Orléans	**43**	47 54N	1 52 E
Orleans, I. d'	**156**	46 54N	70 58W
Orlice, R.	**52**	50 5N	16 10 E
Orlické Hory	**53**	50 15N	16 30 E
Orlov	**53**	49 17N	20 51 E
Orlov Gay	**81**	51 4N	48 19 E
Orlovat	**66**	45 14N	20 33 E
Ormara	**93**	25 16N	64 33 E
Ormea	**62**	44 9N	7 54 E
Ormesby St. Margaret	**29**	52 39N	1 42 E
Ormília	**68**	40 16N	23 33 E
Ormoc	**103**	11 0N	124 37 E
Ormond, N.Z.	**142**	38 33 S	177 56 E
Ormond, U.S.A.	**157**	29 13N	81 5W
Ormondville	**142**	40 5 S	176 19 E
Ormoz	**63**	46 25N	16 10 E
Ormskirk	**32**	53 35N	2 53W
Ornans	**43**	47 7N	6 10 E
Orne □	**42**	48 40N	0 0 E
Orneta	**54**	54 8N	20 9 E
Ørnhøj	**73**	56 13N	8 34 E
Ornö	**72**	59 4N	18 24 E
Örnsköldsvik	**72**	63 17N	18 40 E
Oro Grande	**163**	34 36N	117 20W
Oro, R.	**164**	26 8N	105 58W
Orocué	**174**	4 48N	71 20W
Orodo	**121**	5 34N	7 4 E
Orogrande	**161**	32 20N	106 4W
Orol	**56**	43 34N	7 39W
Oromocto	**151**	45 54N	66 29W
Oron, Israel	**90**	30 55N	35 1 E
Oron, Nigeria	**121**	4 48N	8 14 E
Oron, Switz.	**50**	46 34N	6 50 E
Oron, R.	**77**	69 21N	95 43 E
Oronsay I.	**34**	56 0N	6 14W
Oronsay, Pass of	**34**	56 0N	6 10W
Oropesa	**56**	39 57N	5 10W
Oroquieta	**103**	8 32N	123 44 E
Orori	**107**	40 1N	127 27 E
Orós	**170**	6 15 S	38 55W
Orosei, G. di	**64**	40 15N	9 40 E
Orosháza	**53**	46 32N	20 42 E
Orotukan	**77**	62 16N	151 42 E
Oroville, Calif., U.S.A.	**160**	39 31N	121 30W
Oroville, Wash., U.S.A.	**160**	48 58N	119 30W
Orowia	**143**	46 1 S	167 50 E
Orphir	**37**	58 56N	3 8W
Orrefors	**73**	56 50N	15 45 E
Orroroo	**140**	32 43 S	138 38 E
Orsa	**72**	61 7N	14 37 E
Orsara di Puglia	**65**	41 17N	15 16 E
Orsasjön	**72**	61 7N	14 37 E
Orsha	**80**	54 30N	30 25 E
Orsières	**50**	46 2N	7 9 E
Orsk	**84**	51 12N	58 34 E
Ørslev	**73**	55 23N	11 56 E
Orsogna	**63**	42 13N	14 17 E
Orşova	**70**	44 41N	22 25 E
Ørsted	**73**	56 30N	10 20 E
Orta, L. d'	**62**	45 48N	8 21 E
Orta Nova	**65**	41 20N	15 40 E
Orte	**63**	42 28N	12 23 E
Ortegal, C.	**56**	43 43N	7 52W
Orthez	**44**	43 29N	0 48W
Ortho	**47**	50 8N	5 37 E
Ortigueira	**56**	43 40N	7 50W
Ortles, mt.	**62**	46 31N	10 33 E
Orto, Tokay	**85**	42 20N	76 1 E
Ortón, R.	**174**	10 50 S	67 0W
Orton Tebay	**32**	54 28N	2 35W
Ortona	**63**	42 21N	14 24 E
Orune	**64**	40 25N	9 20 E
Oruro	**174**	18 0 S	67 19W
Orust	**73**	58 10N	11 40 E
Orůştie	**70**	45 50N	23 10 E
Oruzgan	**94**	32 30N	66 35 E
Orvault	**42**	47 17N	1 38 E
Orvieto	**63**	42 43N	12 8 E
Orwell	**162**	43 35N	75 60W
Orwell, R.	**29**	52 2N	1 12 E
Orwigsburg	**162**	40 38N	76 6W
Oryakhovo	**66**	43 40N	23 57 E
Orzinuovi	**62**	45 24N	9 55 E
Orzysz	**54**	53 50N	21 58 E
Os	**71**	60 9N	5 30 E
Osa	**84**	57 17N	55 26 E
Osa, Pen. de	**166**	8 0N	84 0W
Osage, Iowa, U.S.A.	**158**	43 15N	92 50W
Osage, Wyo., U.S.A.	**158**	43 59N	104 25W
Osage City	**158**	38 43N	95 51W
Osage, R.	**158**	38 15N	92 30W
Ōsaka	**111**	34 30N	135 30 E
Osaka-fu □	**111**	34 40N	135 30 E
Osaka-Wan	**111**	34 30N	135 18 E
Osan	**107**	37 11N	127 4 E
Osawatomie	**158**	38 30N	94 55W
Osborne	**158**	39 30N	98 45W
Osby	**73**	56 23N	13 59 E
Osceola, Ark., U.S.A.	**159**	35 40N	90 0W
Osceola, Iowa, U.S.A.	**158**	41 0N	93 20W
Oschatz	**48**	51 17N	13 8 E
Oschersleben	**48**	52 2N	11 13 E
Óschiri	**64**	40 43N	9 7 E
Osečina	**66**	44 23N	19 34 E
Ösel = Saaremaa	**80**	58 30N	22 30W
Osenovka	**66**	70 40N	120 50 E
Osëry	**81**	54 52N	38 28 E
Osh	**85**	40 37N	72 49 E
Oshan	**108**	24 11N	102 24 E
Oshawa	**150**	43 50N	78 45W
Oshikango	**128**	17 9 S	16 10 E
Oshima	**110**	33 11N	132 24 E
Oshkosh, Nebr., U.S.A.	**156**	41 27N	102 20W
Oshkosh, Wis., U.S.A.	**156**	44 3N	88 35W
Oshmyany	**80**	54 26N	25 58 E
Oshogbo	**121**	7 48N	4 37 E
Oshwe	**124**	3 25 S	19 28 E
Osica de Jos	**70**	44 14N	24 20 E
Osieczna	**54**	51 55N	16 40 E
Osijek	**66**	45 34N	18 41 E
Osilo	**64**	40 45N	8 41 E
Osimo	**63**	43 40N	13 30 E
Osintorf	**80**	54 34N	30 31 E
Osipovichi	**80**	53 25N	28 33 E
Oskaloosa	**158**	41 18N	92 40W
Oskarshamn	**73**	57 15N	16 27 E
Oskelaneo	**150**	48 5N	75 15W
Oskol, R.	**81**	50 20N	38 0 E
Oslo	**71**	59 55N	10 45 E
Oslob	**103**	9 31N	123 26 E
Oslofjorden	**71**	59 20N	10 35 E
Osmanabad	**96**	18 5N	76 10 E
Osmancık	**82**	40 45N	34 47 E
Osmand Ra.	**136**	17 10 S	128 45 E
Osmaniye	**92**	37 5N	36 10 E
Osmo	**72**	58 58N	17 55 E
Osmotherley	**33**	54 22N	1 18W
Osnabrück	**48**	52 16N	8 2 E
Osobláha	**53**	50 17N	17 44 E
Osolo	**71**	59 53N	10 52 E
Osona	**128**	22 3 S	16 59 E
Osorio	**173**	29 53 S	50 17W
Osorno, Chile	**176**	40 25 S	73 0W
Osorno, Spain	**56**	42 24N	4 22W
Osorno, Vol.	**176**	41 0N	72 30W
Osoyoos	**152**	49 0N	119 30W
Ospika, R.	**152**	56 20N	124 0W
Osprey Reef	**138**	13 52 S	146 36 E
Oss	**46**	51 46N	5 32 E
Ossa de Montiel	**59**	38 58N	2 45W
Ossa, Mt.	**138**	41 52 S	146 3 E
Ossa, Oros	**68**	39 47N	22 42 E
Ossabaw I.	**157**	31 45N	81 8W
Ossendrecht	**47**	51 24N	4 20 E
Ossett	**33**	53 40N	1 35W
Ossining	**162**	41 9N	73 50W
Ossipee	**162**	43 41N	71 9W
Ossno Lubuskie	**54**	52 28N	14 51 E
Ossokmanuan L.	**151**	53 25N	65 0W
Ossora	**77**	59 20N	163 13 E
Osświecim	**54**	50 2N	19 11 E
Ostashkov	**80**	57 4N	33 2 E
Oste, R.	**48**	53 30N	9 12 E
Ostend = Oostende	**47**	51 15N	2 50 E
Oster	**80**	50 57N	30 46 E
Osterburg	**48**	52 47N	11 44 E
Österby	**72**	60 13N	17 55 E
Österbymo	**73**	57 49N	15 15 E
Österdalälven	**72**	61 30N	13 45 E
Östergötlands Län □	**73**	58 35N	15 45 E
Osterholz-Scharmbeck	**48**	53 14N	8 48 E
Osterild	**73**	57 3N	8 50 E
Østerild	**73**	57 2N	8 51 E
Österkorsberga	**73**	57 18N	15 6 E
Ostermundigen	**50**	46 58N	7 30 E
Osterøya	**71**	60 32N	5 30 E
Östersund	**72**	63 10N	14 38 E
Østfold fylke □	**71**	59 25N	11 25 E
Ostfriesische Inseln	**48**	53 45N	7 15 E
Ostia Lido (Lido di Roma)	**64**	41 43N	12 17 E
Ostiglía	**63**	45 4N	11 9 E
Ostrava	**53**	49 51N	18 18 E
Ostrgrog	**54**	52 37N	16 33 E
Ostróda	**54**	53 42N	19 58 E
Ostrog	**80**	50 20N	26 30 E
Ostrogozhsk	**81**	50 55N	39 7 E
Ostrołeka	**54**	53 4N	21 38 E
Ostrołeka □	**54**	53 0N	21 30 E
Ostrov, Bulg.	**67**	43 40N	24 9 E
Ostrov, Rumania	**70**	44 6N	27 24 E
Ostrov, U.S.S.R.	**80**	57 25N	28 20 E
Ostrów Mazowiecka	**54**	52 50N	21 51 E
Ostrów Wielkopolski	**54**	51 36N	17 44 E
Ostrowiec-Swietokrzyski	**54**	50 55N	21 22 E
Ostrozac	**66**	43 43N	17 49 E
Ostrzeszów	**54**	51 25N	17 52 E
Ostseebad-Kühlungsborn	**48**	54 10N	11 40 E
Östsinni	**71**	60 53N	10 3 E
Ostuni	**65**	40 44N	17 34 E
Osum, R.	**67**	43 35N	25 0 E
Osumi-Hanto	**110**	31 20N	130 55 E
Osumi-Kaikyō	**112**	30 55N	130 50 E
Osumi, R.	**68**	40 40N	20 10 E
Osumi-Shoto	**112**	30 30N	130 40 E
Osuna	**57**	37 14N	5 8W
Oswaldtwistle	**32**	53 44N	2 27W
Oswego	**162**	43 29N	76 30W
Oswestry	**28**	52 52N	3 3W
Ota, Japan	**111**	35 11N	136 38 E
Ota, Japan	**111**	36 18N	139 22 E
Ota-Gawa	**110**	34 21N	132 18 E
Otago □	**143**	45 20 S	169 20 E
Otago Harb.	**143**	45 47 S	170 42 E
Otago Pen.	**143**	45 48 S	170 45 E
Otahuhu	**142**	36 56 S	174 51 E
Otake	**110**	34 12N	132 13 E
Otaki, Japan	**111**	35 17N	140 15 E
Otaki, N.Z.	**142**	40 45 S	175 10 E
Otane	**142**	39 54 S	176 39 E
Otar	**85**	43 32N	75 12 E
Otaru	**112**	43 10N	141 0 E
Otaru-Wan	**112**	43 25N	141 1 E
Otautau	**143**	46 9 S	168 1 E
Otava, R.	**52**	49 16N	13 32 E
Otavalo	**174**	0 20N	78 20W
Otavi	**128**	19 40 S	17 24 E
Otchinjau	**128**	16 30 S	13 56 E
Otelec	**66**	45 36N	20 50 E
Otero de Rey	**56**	43 6N	7 36W
Othello	**160**	46 53N	119 8W
Othonoí, I.	**68**	39 52N	19 22 E
Othris, Mt.	**69**	39 4N	22 42 E
Otira	**143**	42 49 S	171 35 E
Otira Gorge	**143**	42 53 S	171 33 E
Otis	**158**	40 12N	102 58W
Otjiwarongo	**128**	20 30 S	16 33 E
Otley	**33**	53 54N	1 41W
Otmuchow	**54**	50 28N	17 10 E
Otočac	**63**	44 53N	15 12 E
Otoineppu	**112**	44 44N	142 16 E
Otorohanga	**142**	38 12 S	175 14 E
Otoskwin, R.	**150**	52 13N	88 6W
Otosquen	**153**	53 17N	102 1W
Otoyo	**110**	33 43N	133 45 E
Otra	**71**	58 8N	8 1 E
Otranto	**65**	40 9N	18 28 E
Otranto, C.d'	**65**	40 7N	18 30 E
Otranto, Str. of	**65**	40 15N	18 40 E
Otrøy	**71**	62 43N	6 50 E
Otsuki	**111**	35 36N	138 57 E
Otta	**71**	61 46N	9 32 E
Ottapalam	**97**	10 46N	76 23 E
Ottawa, Can.	**150**	45 27N	75 42W
Ottawa, Ill., U.S.A.	**156**	41 20N	88 55W
Ottawa, Kans., U.S.A.	**158**	38 40N	95 10W
Ottawa Is.	**149**	59 35N	80 16W
Ottawa, R.	**150**	47 45N	78 35W
Ottélé	**121**	3 38N	11 19 E
Ottenby	**73**	56 15N	16 24 E
Otter L.	**153**	55 35N	104 39W
Otter R.	**30**	50 47N	3 12W
Otter Rapids, Ont., Can.	**150**	50 11N	81 39W
Otter Rapids, Sask., Can.	**153**	55 38N	104 44W
Otterburn	**35**	55 14N	2 12W
Otterndorf	**48**	53 47N	8 52 E
Otteröy, I.	**71**	62 45N	6 50 E
Ottersheim	**52**	48 21N	14 12 E
Otterup	**73**	55 30N	10 22 E
Ottery St. Mary	**30**	50 45N	3 16W
Ottignies	**47**	50 40N	4 33 E
Otto Beit Bridge	**127**	15 59 S	28 56 E
Ottosdal	**128**	26 46 S	25 59 E
Ottoshoop	**128**	25 45 S	26 58 E
Ottsjö	**72**	63 13N	13 2 E
Ottter Ferry	**34**	56 1N	5 20W
Ottumwa	**158**	41 0N	92 25W
Otu	**121**	8 14N	3 22 E
Otukpa (Al Owuho)	**121**	7 9N	7 41 E
Oturkpo	**121**	7 10N	8 15 E
Otway, Bahía	**176**	53 30 S	74 0W
Otway, C.	**140**	38 52 S	143 30 E
Otwock	**54**	52 5N	21 20 E
Ötz	**52**	47 13N	10 53 E
Otz, Fl.	**52**	47 13N	10 53 E
Ötz, R.	**52**	47 14N	10 50 E
Ötztaler Alpen	**52**	46 58N	11 0 E
Ou, Neua	**100**	22 18N	101 48 E
Ou, R.	**100**	20 4N	102 13 E
Ouachita Mts.	**159**	34 50N	94 30W
Ouachita, R.	**159**	33 0N	92 15W
Ouadane	**116**	20 50N	11 40W
Ouadda	**117**	8 15N	22 20 E
Ouagadougou	**121**	12 25N	1 30W
Ouahigouya	**120**	13 40N	2 25W
Ouahila	**118**	27 50N	5 0W
Ouahran = Oran	**118**	35 37N	0 39W
Oualâta	**121**	17 20N	6 55W
Ouallene	**118**	24 41N	1 11 E
Ouanda Djallé	**117**	8 55N	22 53 E
Ouango	**124**	4 19N	22 30 E
Ouargla	**119**	31 59N	5 25 E
Ouarkziz, Djebel	**118**	28 50N	8 0W
Ouarzazate	**118**	30 55N	6 55W
Ouatagouna	**121**	15 11N	0 43 E
Oubangi, R.	**124**	1 0N	17 50 E
Oubarakai, O.	**119**	27 20N	9 0 E
Ouche, R.	**43**	47 11N	5 10 E
Oud-Gastel	**47**	51 35N	4 28 E
Oud Turnhout	**47**	51 19N	5 0 E
Ouddorp	**46**	51 50N	3 57 E
Oude-Pekela	**46**	53 6N	7 0 E
Oude Rijn, R.	**46**	52 12N	4 24 E
Oudega	**46**	53 8N	6 0 E
Oudenaarde	**47**	50 50N	3 37 E
Oudenbosch	**47**	51 35N	4 32 E
Oudenburg	**47**	51 11N	3 1 E
Ouderkerk, Holl. Mérid., Neth.	**46**	51 56N	4 38 E
Ouderkerk, Utrecht, Neth.	**46**	52 18N	4 55 E
Oudeschild	**46**	53 2N	4 50 E
Oudewater	**46**	52 2N	4 52 E
Oudkarspel	**46**	52 43N	4 49 E
Oudon	**42**	47 22N	1 19W
Oudon, R.	**42**	47 47N	1 2W
Oudtshoorn	**128**	33 35 S	22 14 E
Oued Sbita	**118**	25 50N	5 2W
Ouellé	**120**	7 26N	4 1W
Ouessa	**120**	11 4N	2 47W
Ouessant, Île d'	**42**	48 28N	5 6W
Ouesso	**124**	1 37N	16 5 E
Ouezzane	**118**	34 51N	5 42W
Ouffet	**47**	50 26N	5 28 E
Oughter L.	**38**	54 2N	7 30W
Oughterard	**38**	53 26N	9 20W
Ougrée	**47**	50 36N	5 32 E
Ouidah	**121**	6 25N	2 0 E
Ouimet	**150**	48 43N	88 35W
Ouistreham	**42**	49 17N	0 18W
Ouj, R.	**118**	51 15N	29 45 E
Oujda □	**118**	33 18N	1 25W
Oujeft	**116**	20 2N	13 0W
Oulad Naïl, Mts. des	**118**	34 30N	3 30 E
Ouled Djellal	**119**	34 28N	5 2 E
Oulmès	**118**	33 17N	6 0W
Oulton	**29**	52 29N	1 40 E
Oulton Broad	**29**	52 28N	1 43 E
Oulu	**74**	65 1N	25 29 E
Oulu □	**74**	65 10N	27 20 E
Oulujärvi	**74**	64 25N	27 0 E
Oulujoki	**74**	64 45N	26 30 E
Oulun Lääni □	**74**	64 36N	27 20 E
Oulx	**62**	45 2N	6 49 E
Oum el Bouaghi	**119**	35 55N	7 6 E
Oum el Ksi	**118**	29 4N	6 59W
Oum-er-Rbia	**118**	32 30N	6 30W
Oum-er-Rbia, O.	**118**	32 30N	6 30W
Oumè	**120**	5 21N	5 27W
Ounane, Dj.	**119**	25 4N	7 10 E
Ounasjoki	**74**	66 31N	25 44 E
Oundle	**29**	52 28N	0 28W
Ounguati	**128**	21 54 S	15 46 E
Ounianga Kébir	**117**	19 4N	20 29 E
Ounlivou	**121**	7 20N	1 34 E
Our, R.	**47**	49 55N	6 5 E
Ouray	**161**	38 3N	107 48W
Oureg, Oued el	**118**	32 34N	2 10 E
Ourém	**170**	1 33 S	47 6W
Ouricuri	**170**	7 53 S	40 5W
Ourinhos	**173**	23 0 S	49 54W
Ourini	**117**	16 7N	22 25 E
Ourique	**57**	37 38N	8 16W
Ouro Fino	**173**	22 16 S	46 25W
Ouro Prêto	**173**	20 20 S	43 30W
Ouro Sogui	**120**	15 36N	13 19W
Oursi	**121**	14 41N	0 27W
Ourthe, R.	**47**	50 29N	5 35 E
Ouse	**138**	42 25 S	146 42 E
Ouse, R., Sussex, U.K.	**29**	50 58N	0 3 E
Ouse, R., Yorks., U.K.	**33**	54 3N	0 7 E
Oust	**44**	42 52N	1 13 E
Oust, R.	**42**	48 8N	2 49W
Out Skerries, Is.	**36**	60 25N	0 50W
Outardes, R.	**151**	50 0N	69 4W
Outer Hebrides, Is.	**36**	57 30N	7 40W
Outer I.	**151**	51 10N	58 35W
Outes	**56**	42 52N	8 55W
Outjo	**128**	20 5 S	16 7 E
Outlook, Can.	**153**	51 30N	107 0W
Outlook, U.S.A.	**158**	48 53N	104 46W
Outreau	**43**	50 40N	1 36 E
Outwell	**29**	52 36N	0 14 E
Ouyen	**140**	35 1 S	142 22 E
Ouzouer-le-Marché	**42**	47 54N	1 32 E
Ovada	**62**	44 39N	8 40 E
Ovalle	**172**	30 33 S	71 18W
Ovamboland = Owambo	**128**	17 20 S	16 30 E
Ovar	**56**	40 51N	8 40W
Ovejas	**174**	9 32N	75 14W
Ovens	**141**	36 35 S	146 46 E
Over Flakkee, I.	**47**	51 45N	4 5 E
Over Wallop	**28**	51 9N	1 35W
Overbister	**37**	59 16N	2 33W
Overdinkel	**46**	52 14N	7 2 E
Overflakkee	**46**	51 44N	4 10 E
Overijse	**47**	50 47N	4 32 E
Overijssel	**46**	50 46N	4 32 E
Overijssel □	**46**	52 25N	6 35 E
Overijsselsch Kanaal	**46**	52 31N	6 6 E
Överkalix	**74**	66 19N	22 50 E
Overpelt	**47**	51 12N	5 20 E
Overstand	**29**	52 55N	1 20W
Overton, Clwyd, U.K.	**31**	52 58N	2 56W
Overton, Hants, U.K.	**28**	51 14N	1 16W
Overton, U.S.A.	**161**	36 32N	114 31W
Övertorneå	**74**	66 23N	23 40 E
Overum	**73**	58 0N	16 20 E
Ovid, Colo., U.S.A.	**158**	41 0N	102 17W
Ovid, N.Y., U.S.A.	**162**	42 41N	76 49W
Ovidiopol	**82**	46 15N	30 30 E
Oviedo	**56**	43 25N	5 50W
Oviedo □	**56**	43 20N	6 0W
Oviken	**72**	63 0N	14 23 E
Oviksfjällen	**72**	63 0N	13 49 E
Övör Hangay □	**106**	45 0N	102 30 E
Ovoro	**121**	5 26N	7 16 E
Övre Sirdal	**71**	58 48N	6 43 E
Øvre Sirdal	**71**	58 48N	6 47 E
Ovruch	**80**	51 25N	28 45 E
Owaka	**143**	46 27 S	169 40 E
Owambo	**128**	17 20 S	16 30 E
Owasco L.	**162**	42 50N	76 31W
Owase	**111**	34 7N	136 5 E
Owatonna	**158**	44 3N	93 17W
Owego	**162**	42 6N	76 17W
Owel, L.	**38**	53 34N	7 24W
Owen	**140**	34 15 S	138 32 E

Owen Falls Pang-Yang

Owen Falls 126 0 30N 33 5 E
Owen Mt. 143 41 35 S 152 33 E
Owen Sound 150 44 35N 80 55W
Owen Stanley Range 135 8 30 S 147 0 E
Owendo 124 0 17N 9 30 E
Oweniny R. 38 54 13N 9 32W
Owenkillew R. 38 54 44N 7 15W
Owens L. 163 36 20N 118 0W
Owens, R. 163 36 32N 117 59W
Owensboro 156 37 40N 87 5W
Owensville 158 38 20N 91 30W
Owerri 121 5 29N 7 0 E
Owhango 142 39 51 S 175 20 E
Owl, R. 153 57 51N 92 44W
Owo 121 7 18N 5 30 E
Owosso 156 43 0N 84 10W
Owston Ferry 33 53 28N 0 47W
Owyhee 160 42 0N 116 3W
Owyhee, R. 160 43 10N 117 37W
Owyhee Res. 160 43 30N 117 30W
Ox Mts. 38 54 6N 9 0W
Oxberg 72 61 7N 14 11 E
Oxelösund 73 58 43N 17 15 E
Oxford, N.Z. 143 43 18 S 172 11 E
Oxford, U.K. 28 51 45N 1 15W
Oxford, Mass., U.S.A. 162 42 7N 71 52W
Oxford, Miss., U.S.A. 159 34 22N 89 30W
Oxford, N.C., U.S.A. 157 36 19N 78 36W
Oxford, N.Y., U.S.A. 162 42 27N 75 36W
Oxford, Ohio, U.S.A. 156 39 30N 84 40W
Oxford, Pa., U.S.A. 162 39 47N 75 59W
Oxford □ 28 51 45N 1 15W
Oxford L. 153 54 51N 95 37W
Oxilíthos 69 38 35N 24 7 E
Oxley 140 34 11 S 144 6 E
Oxley Cr. 108 27 35 S 153 0 E
Oxnard 163 34 10N 119 14W
Oya 102 2 55N 111 55 E
Oyabe 111 36 47N 136 56 E
Oyama 111 36 18N 139 48 E
Oyana 110 32 32N 130 18 E
Oyem 124 1 42N 11 43 E
Oyen 153 51 22N 110 28W
Øyeren 71 59 48N 11 14 E
Öyeren 71 59 50N 11 15 E
Oykel Bridge 37 57 58N 4 45W
Oykell, R. 37 57 55N 4 26W
Oymyakon 77 63 25N 143 10 E
Oyo 121 7 46N 3 56 E
Oyo □ 121 8 0N 3 30 E
Oyonnax 45 46 16N 5 40 E
Oyster B. 138 42 15 S 148 5 E
Öystese 71 60 22N 6 9 E
Øystese 71 60 24N 6 12 E
Oytal 85 42 54N 73 17 E
Ozamis (Mizamis) 103 8 15N 123 50 E
Ozark, Ala., U.S.A. 157 31 29N 85 39W
Ozark, Ark., U.S.A. 159 35 30N 93 50W
Ozark, Mo., U.S.A. 159 37 0N 93 15W
Ozark Plateau 159 37 20N 91 40W
Ozarks, L. of 158 38 10N 93 0W
Ózd 53 48 14N 20 15 E
Ozerhinsk 80 53 40N 27 7 E
Ozërnyy 84 51 8N 60 50 E
Ozieri 64 40 35N 9 0 E
Ozimek 54 50 41N 18 11 E
Ozona 159 30 43N 101 11W
Ozorków 54 51 57N 19 16 E
Ozren, Mt. 66 43 55N 18 29 E
Ozu 110 33 30N 132 33 E
Ozu Kumamoto 110 32 52N 130 52 E
Ozuluama 165 21 40N 97 50W
Ozun 70 45 47N 25 50 E

P

Pa 120 11 33N 3 19W
Pa-an 98 16 45N 97 40 E
Pa Mong Dam 100 18 0N 102 22 E
Pa Sak, R. 101 15 30N 101 0 E
Paal 47 51 2N 5 10 E
Paar, R. 49 48 42N 11 27 E
Paarl 128 33 45 S 18 56 E
Paatsi, R. 74 68 55N 29 0 E
Paauilo 147 20 3N 155 22W
Pab Hills 94 26 30N 66 45 E
Pabbay I. 36 57 46N 7 12W
Pabbay, Sd. of 36 57 45N 7 4W
Pabianice 54 51 40N 19 20 E
Pabna 98 24 1N 89 18 E
Pabo 126 2 56N 32 3 E
Pacajá, R. 170 1 56 S 50 50W
Pacajus 170 4 10 S 38 38W
Pacasmayo 174 7 20 S 79 35W
Pacaudière, La 43 46 11N 3 52 E
Paceco 64 37 59N 12 32 E
Pachhar 94 24 40N 77 42 E
Pachino 65 36 43N 15 4 E
Pacho 174 5 8N 74 10W
Pachora 96 20 38N 75 29 E
Pachpadra 93 25 58N 72 10 E
Pachuca 165 20 10N 98 40W
Pachung 108 31 58N 106 40 E
Pacific 152 54 48N 128 28W
Pacific Grove 163 36 38N 121 58W
Pacific Ocean 143 10 0N 140 0W
Pacifica 163 37 36N 122 30W
Packsaddle 140 30 36 S 141 58 E
Pacoh 152 53 0N 132 30W
Pacov 52 49 27N 15 0 E
Pacsa 53 46 44N 17 2 E
Pacuí, R. 171 16 46 S 45 1W
Pacy-sur-Eure 171 49 1N 1 23 E
Paczkow 54 50 28N 17 0 E
Padaido, Kepulauan 103 1 5 S 138 0 E
Padalarang 103 7 50 S 107 30 E
Padang 102 1 0 S 100 20 E
Padang, I. 102 1 0 S 100 10 E
Padangpanjang 102 0 30 S 100 20 E
Padangsidimpuan 102 1 30N 99 15 E
Padatchuang 98 19 41N 96 35 E
Padborg 73 54 49N 9 21 E
Paddock Wood 29 51 13N 0 24 E
Paddockwood 153 53 30N 105 30W
Paderborn 48 51 42N 8 44 E
Padesul 70 45 40N 22 22 E
Padiham 32 53 48N 2 20W
Padina 70 44 50N 27 8 E
Padlei 153 62 10N 97 5W
Padloping Island 149 67 0N 63 0W
Padma, R. 98 23 22N 90 32 E
Padmanabhapuram 97 8 16N 77 17 E
Pádova 63 45 24N 11 52 E
Padra 94 22 15N 73 7 E
Padrauna 95 26 54N 83 59 E
Padre I. 159 27 0N 97 20W
Padrón 56 42 41N 8 39W
Padstow 32 50 33N 4 57W
Padstow Bay 30 50 35N 4 58W
Padua = Pádova 63 45 24N 11 52 E
Paducah, Ky., U.S.A. 156 37 0N 88 40W
Paducah, Tex., U.S.A. 159 34 3N 100 16W
Padul 57 37 1N 3 38W
Padula 65 40 20N 15 40 E
Padwa 96 18 27N 82 37 E
Paekakariki 142 40 59 S 174 58 E
Paektu-san 107 42 0N 128 3 E
Paengaroa 142 37 49 S 176 29 E
Paengnyŏng Do 107 37 57N 124 40 E
Paeroa 142 37 23 S 175 41 E
Paesana 62 44 40N 7 18 E
Pag 63 44 27N 15 5 E
Pag, I. 63 44 50N 15 0 E
Paga 121 11 1N 1 8W
Pagadian 103 7 55N 123 30 E
Pagai Selatan, I. 102 3 0 S 100 15W
Pagai Utara, I. 102 2 35 S 100 0 E
Pagalu, I. 114 1 35 S 3 35 E
Pagaralam 102 4 0 S 103 17 E
Pagastikós Kólpos 68 39 15N 23 12 E
Pagatan 102 3 33 S 115 59 E
Page 158 47 11N 97 37W
Paglieta 63 42 10N 14 30 E
Pagnau 123 8 15N 34 7 E
Pagny-sur-Moselle 43 48 59N 6 2 E
Pagosa Springs 161 37 16N 107 4W
Pagwa River 150 50 2N 85 14W
Pahala 147 20 25N 156 0W
Pahang □ 101 3 40N 102 20 E
Pahang, R. 101 3 30N 103 9 E
Pahang, st. 101 3 30N 103 9 E
Pahiatua 142 40 27 S 175 50 E
Pahoa 147 19 30N 154 57W
Pahokee 157 26 50N 80 30W
Pahrump 161 36 15N 116 0W
Pahsien 106 39 10N 116 20 E
Pahsientung 107 43 11N 120 57 E
Pai 100 19 19N 98 27 E
Paia 147 20 54N 156 22W
Paible 36 57 35N 7 30W
Paich'eng 105 45 40N 122 52 E
Paich'i 109 28 2N 111 18 E
P'aichou 109 30 12N 113 56 E
Paicines 163 36 44N 121 17W
Paide 80 58 57N 25 31 E
Paignton 30 50 26N 3 33W
Paiho, China 109 32 49N 110 3 E
Paiho, Taiwan 109 23 21N 120 25 E
Paihok'ou 109 31 46N 110 13 E
Päijänne 75 61 30N 25 30 E
Pailin 101 12 46N 102 36 E
Pailolo Chan. 147 21 5N 156 42W
Paimbœuf 42 47 17N 2 0W
Paimboeuf 44 47 17N 2 2W
Paimpol 42 48 48N 3 4W
Painan 102 1 15 S 100 40 E
Painesville 156 41 42N 81 18W
Painiu 109 32 51N 112 10 E
Painscastle 31 52 7N 3 13W
Painswick 28 51 47N 2 11W
Paint I. 153 55 28N 97 57W
Painted Desert 161 36 40N 112 0W
Paintsville 156 37 50N 82 50W
Paipa 174 5 47N 73 7W
Paise 108 23 55N 106 28 E
Paisha 106 34 23N 112 32 E
Paisley, U.K. 34 55 51N 4 27W
Paisley, U.S.A. 160 42 43N 120 40W
Paita 174 5 5 S 81 0W
Paiva, R. 56 40 50N 7 55W
Paiyin 105 36 45N 104 4 E
Paiyü 99 31 12N 98 45 E
Paiyunopo 106 41 46N 109 58 E
Pajares 56 39 57N 1 48W
Pak Lay 100 18 15N 101 27 E
Pak Phanang 101 8 21N 100 12 E
Pak Sane 100 18 22N 103 39 E
Pak Song 100 15 11N 106 14 E
Pak Suong 100 19 58N 102 15 E
Pakala 97 13 29N 79 8 E
Pakanbaru 102 0 30N 101 15 E
Pakaraima, Sierra 174 6 0N 60 0W
Pakembe 127 13 3 S 29 58 E
Pakenham 141 38 6 S 145 30 E
Pakhoi = Peihai 108 21 30N 109 5 E
Pakhtakor 85 40 2N 65 46 E
Pakistan ■ 93 30 0N 70 0 E
Pakistan, East = Bangladesh ■ 99 24 0N 90 0 E
Pakkading 100 18 19N 103 59 E
Paknam = Samut Prakan 100 13 36N 100 36 E
P'ako 105 30 52N 81 19 E
Pakokku 98 21 30N 95 0 E
Pakpattan 94 30 25N 73 16 E
Pakrac 66 45 27N 17 12 E
Paks 53 46 38N 18 55 E
Pakse 100 15 5N 105 52 E
Paksikori 107 42 27N 130 31 E
Paktya □ 93 33 0N 69 15 E
Pakwach 126 2 28N 31 27 E
Pal 93 33 45N 79 33 E
Pala, Chad 117 9 25N 15 5 E
Pala, U.S.A. 163 33 22N 117 5W
Pala, Zaïre 126 6 45 S 29 30 E
Palabek 126 3 22N 32 33 E
Palacious 159 28 44N 96 12W
Palafrugell 58 41 55N 3 10 E
Palagiano 65 40 35N 17 0 E
Palagonia 65 37 20N 14 43 E
Palagruza 63 42 24N 16 15 E
Palaiókastron 69 35 12N 26 18 E
Palaiokhora 69 35 16N 23 39 E
Pálairos 69 38 45N 20 51 E
Palais, Le 42 47 20N 3 10W
Palakol 96 16 31N 81 46 E
Palam 96 19 0N 77 0 E
Palamás 68 39 26N 22 4 E
Palamós 58 41 50N 3 10 E
Palampur 94 32 10N 76 30 E
Palana, Austral. 138 39 45 S 147 55 E
Palana, U.S.S.R. 77 59 10N 160 10 E
Palanan 103 17 8N 122 29 E
Palandri 95 33 42N 73 40 E
Palanpur 94 24 10N 72 25 E
Palapye 128 22 30 S 27 7 E
Palar, R. 97 12 27N 80 13 E
Palas 95 35 4N 73 4 E
Palatka 157 29 40N 81 40W
• Palau Is. 130 7 30N 134 30 E
Palauig 103 15 26N 119 54 E
Palauk 101 13 10N 98 40 E
Palavas 44 43 32N 3 56 E
Palawan, I. 102 10 0N 119 0 E
Palayancottai 97 8 45N 77 45 E
Palazzo San Gervásio 65 40 53N 15 58 E
Palazzolo Acreide 65 37 4N 14 43 E
Paldiski 80 59 23N 24 9 E
Pale 66 43 50N 18 38 E
Palel 98 24 27N 94 2 E
Paleleh 103 1 10N 121 50 E
Palembang 102 3 0 S 104 50 E
Palencia 56 42 1N 4 34W
Palencia □ 56 42 31N 4 33W
Palermo, Colomb. 174 2 54N 75 26W
Palermo, Italy 64 38 8N 13 20 E
Palermo, U.S.A. 160 39 30N 121 37W
Palestine, Asia 90 32 0N 35 0 E
Palestine, U.S.A. 159 31 42N 95 35W
Palestrina 64 41 50N 12 52 E
Paletwa 98 21 30N 92 50 E
Palghat 97 10 46N 76 42 E
Palgrave 29 52 22N 1 7 E
Palgrave, Mt. 136 23 22 S 115 58 E
P'ali 105 27 45N 89 10 E
Pali 94 25 50N 73 20 E
Palik'un 105 43 35N 92 51 E
Palimé 121 6 57N 0 37 E
Palintaoch'i 107 43 59N 119 20 E
Palinuro, C. 65 40 1N 15 14 E
Palinyuch'i (Tapanshang) 107 43 40N 118 20 E
Palisade 158 40 35N 101 10W
Paliseul 47 49 54N 5 8 E
Palitana 94 21 32N 71 49 E
Palizada 165 18 18N 92 8W
Palizzi 65 37 58N 15 59 E
Palk Bay 97 9 30N 79 30 E
Palk Strait 97 10 0N 80 0 E
Palkonda 96 18 36N 83 48 E
Palkonda Ra. 97 13 50N 79 20 E
Pallasgreen 39 52 35N 8 22W
Pallaskenry 39 52 39N 8 53W
Pallasovka 81 50 4N 47 0 E
Palleru, R. 96 17 30N 79 40 E
Pallinup 137 34 0 S 117 55 E
Pallisa 126 1 12N 33 43 E
Palliser Bay 142 41 26 S 175 5 E
Palliser, C. 142 41 37 S 175 14 E
Pallu 94 28 59N 74 14 E
Palm Beach 157 26 46N 80 0W
Palm Desert 163 33 43N 116 22W
Palm Is. 138 18 40 S 146 35 E
Palm Springs 163 33 51N 116 35W
Palma, Canary Is. 116 28 40N 17 50W
Palma, Mozam. 127 10 46 S 40 29 E
Palma, Spain 58 39 33N 2 39 E
Palma, Bahia de 59 39 30N 2 39 E
Palma del Río 57 37 43N 5 17W
Palma di Montechiaro 64 37 12N 13 46 E
Palma, I. 116 28 45N 17 50W
Palma, La, Panama 166 8 15N 78 0W
Palma, La, Spain 57 37 21N 6 38W
Palma, R. 171 10 10N 71 50W
Palma Soriano 166 20 15N 76 0W
Palmanova 63 45 54N 13 18 E
Palmares 170 8 41 S 35 36W
Palmarito 174 7 37N 70 10W
Palmarola, I. 64 40 57N 12 50 E
Palmas 173 26 29 S 52 0W
Palmas, C. 120 4 27N 7 46W
Palmas de Monte Alto 171 14 16 S 43 10W
Pálmas, G. di 64 39 0N 8 30 E
Palmdale 163 34 36N 118 7W
Palmeira 171 25 25 S 50 0W
Palmeira dos Índios 170 9 25 S 36 37W
Palmeirais 170 12 31 S 41 34W
Palmeiras, R. 171 12 22 S 47 8W
Palmeirinhas, Pta. das 124 9 2 S 12 57 E
Palmela 57 38 32N 8 57W
Palmelo 171 17 20 S 48 27W
Palmer, Alaska, U.S.A. 147 61 35N 149 10W
Palmer, Mass., U.S.A. 162 42 9N 72 21W
Palmer Arch 13 64 15 S 65 0W
Palmer Lake 158 39 10N 104 52W
Palmer Pen. 13 73 0 S 60 0W
Palmer, R., N. Terr., Austral. 138 24 30 S 133 0 E
Palmer, R., Queens., Austral. 138 16 5 S 142 43 E
Palmerston 142 45 29 S 170 43 E
Palmerston, C. 133 21 32 S 149 29 E
Palmerston North 143 40 21 S 175 39 E
Palmerton 162 40 47N 75 36W
Palmetto 157 27 33N 82 33W
Palmi 65 38 21N 15 51 E
Palmira, Argent. 172 32 59 S 68 25W
Palmira, Colomb. 174 3 32N 76 16W
Palmyra, Mo., U.S.A. 158 39 45N 91 30W
Palmyra, N.J., U.S.A. 162 40 0N 75 1W
Palmyra, Pa., U.S.A. 162 40 18N 76 36W
Palmyra = Tadmor 92 34 30N 37 55 E
Palni 97 10 30N 77 30 E
Palni Hills 97 10 14N 77 33 E
Palo Alto 163 37 25N 122 8W
Palo del Colle 65 41 4N 16 43 E
Paloe 103 8 20 S 121 43 E
Paloma, La 172 30 35 S 71 0W
Palombara Sabina 63 42 4N 12 45 E
Palopo 103 3 0 S 120 16 E
Palos, Cabo de 59 37 38N 0 40W
Palos Verdes 163 33 48N 118 23W
Palos Verdes, Pt. 163 33 43N 118 26W
Palouse 160 46 59N 117 5W
Palparara 138 24 47 S 141 22 E
Pålsboda 73 59 3N 15 22 E
Palu, Indon. 103 1 0 S 119 59 E
Palu, Turkey 92 38 45N 40 0 E
Paluan 103 13 35N 120 29 E
Palwal 94 28 8N 77 19 E
Pama, China 108 24 9N 107 15 E
Pama, Upp. Vol. 121 11 19N 0 44 E
Pamanukan 103 6 16 S 107 49 E
Pamban I. 97 9 24N 79 35 E
Pamekasan 103 7 10 S 113 29 E
Pameungpeuk 103 7 38 S 107 44 E
Pamiench'eng 107 43 13N 124 2 E
Pamiers 44 43 7N 1 39 E
Pamir, R. 85 37 1N 72 41 E
Pamirs, Ra. 85 37 40N 73 0 E
Pamlico, R. 157 35 25N 76 40W
Pamlico Sd. 157 35 20N 76 0W
Pampa 159 35 35N 100 58W
Pampa de las Salinas 172 32 1 S 66 58W
Pampa, La □ 172 36 50 S 66 0W
Pampanua 103 4 22 S 120 14 E
Pamparato 62 44 16N 7 54 E
Pampas, Argent. 172 34 0 S 64 0W
Pampas, Peru 174 12 20 S 74 50W
Pamplona, Colomb. 174 7 23N 72 39W
Pamplona, Spain 58 42 48N 1 38W
Pampoenpoort 128 31 3 S 22 40 E
Pamunkey, R. 162 37 32N 76 50W
Pana 158 39 25N 89 0W
Panaca 161 37 51N 114 50W
Panagyurishte 67 42 49N 24 15 E
Panaitan, I. 103 6 35 S 105 10 E
Panaji (Panjim) 97 15 25N 73 50 E
Panamá 166 9 0N 79 25W
Panama ■ 166 8 48N 79 55W
Panama Canal 166 9 10N 79 56W
Panama Canal Zone 166 9 10N 79 56W
Panama City 157 30 10N 85 41W
Panamá, Golfo de 166 8 4N 79 20W
Panamint Mts. 161 36 15N 117 20W
Panamint Springs 163 36 20N 117 28W
Panão 174 9 55 S 75 55W
Panare 101 6 51N 101 30 E
Panarea, I. 65 38 38N 15 3 E
Panaro, R. 62 44 48N 11 5 E
Panarukan 103 7 40 S 113 52 E
Panay, G. 103 11 0N 122 30 E
Panay I. 103 11 10N 122 30 E
Pancake Ra. 161 38 30N 116 0W
Pančevo 66 44 52N 20 41 E
Panciu 70 45 54N 27 8 E
Pancorbo, Paso 58 42 32N 3 5W
Pandan 103 11 45N 122 10 E
Pandangpanjang 102 0 40 S 100 20 E
Pandeglang 103 6 25 S 106 0 E
Pandharpur 96 17 41N 75 20 E
Pandhurna 96 21 36N 78 35 E
Pandilla 58 41 32N 3 43W
Pando 173 34 30 S 56 0W
Pando, L. = Hope L. 139 28 24 S 139 18 E
Panevėžys 80 55 42N 24 25 E
Panfilov 76 44 30N 80 0 E
Panfilovo 81 50 25N 42 46 E
Pang-Long 99 23 11N 98 45 E
Pang-Yang 99 22 7N 98 48 E

*Renamed Belau

Panga Paulista

Panga 126 1 52N 26 18 E
Pangaion Óros 68 40 50N 24 0 E
Pangalanes, Canal des 129 22 48 S 47 50 E
Pangani 126 5 25 S 38 58 E
Pangani □ 126 5 25 S 39 0 E
Pangani, R. 126 4 40 S 37 50 E
Pangbourne 28 51 28N 1 5W
P'angchiang 106 42 50N 113 1 E
Pangfou 109 32 55N 117 25 E
Pangi 126 3 10 S 26 35 E
Pangkai 98 22 40N 97 31 E
Pangkalanberandan 102 4 1N 98 20 E
Pangkalansusu 102 4 2N 98 42 E
Pangkoh 102 3 5 S 114 8 E
Pangnirtung 149 66 0N 66 0W
Pangong Tso, L. 95 34 0N 78 20 E
Pangrango 103 6 46 S 107 1 E
Pangsau Pass 98 27 15N 96 10 E
Pangta 105 30 14N 97 24 E
Pangtara 98 20 57N 96 40 E
Panguitch 161 37 52N 112 30W
Pangutaran Group 103 6 18N 120 34 E
Panhandle 159 35 23N 101 23W
P'anhsien 108 25 46N 104 39 E
Pani Mines 94 22 29N 73 50 E
Panipat 94 29 25N 77 2 E
Panjal Range 94 32 30N 76 50 E
Panjgur 93 27 0N 64 5 E
Panjim = Panaji 93 15 25N 73 50 E
Panjinad Barrage 93 29 22N 71 15 E
Panjwai 94 31 26N 65 27 E
Pankadjene 103 4 46 S 119 34 E
Pankal Pinang 102 2 0 S 106 0 E
Pankshin 121 9 25N 9 25 E
P'anlung Chiang, R. 108 21 18N 105 25 E
Panmunjŏm 107 37 59N 126 38 E
Panna 95 24 40N 80 15 E
Panna Hills 95 24 40N 81 15 E
Pannuru 97 16 5N 80 34 E
Panorama 173 21 21 S 51 51W
Panruti 97 11 46N 79 35 E
P'anshan 107 41 12N 122 4 E
P'anshih 107 42 55N 126 3 E
Pant'anching 106 39 7N 103 52 E
Pantano 161 32 0N 110 32W
Pantar, I. 103 8 28 S 124 10 E
Pantelleria 64 36 52N 12 0 E
Pantelleria, I. 64 36 52N 12 0 E
Pantha 98 24 7N 94 17 E
Pantin Sakan 98 18 38N 97 33 E
Pantjo 103 8 42 S 118 40 E
Pantón 56 42 31N 7 37W
Pantukan 103 7 17N 125 58 E
Panuco 165 22 0N 98 25W
Panyam 121 9 27N 9 8 E
P'anyü 109 23 2N 113 20 E
Pão de AçIcar 171 9 45 S 37 26W
Paoan 109 22 32N 114 8 E
Paoch'eng 106 33 14N 106 56 E
Paochi 106 34 25N 107 11 E
Paochiatun 107 33 56N 120 12 E
Paoching 108 28 41N 109 35 E
Paok'ang 109 31 57N 111 20 E
Paokuot'u 107 42 20N 120 42 E
Páola 65 39 21N 16 2 E
Paola 158 38 36N 94 50W
Paonia 161 38 56N 107 37W
Paoshan, Shanghai, China 109 31 25N 121 29 E
Paoshan, Yunnan, China 105 25 7N 99 9 E
Paote 106 39 7N 111 13 E
Paoti 107 39 44N 117 18 E
Paoting 106 38 50N 115 30 E
Paot'ou 106 40 35N 110 3 E
Paoua 117 7 25N 16 30 E
Paoying 107 33 15N 119 20 E
Papá 53 47 22N 17 30 E
Papa Sd. 37 59 20N 2 56W
Papa, Sd. of 36 60 19N 1 40W
Papa Stour I. 36 60 20N 1 40W
Papa Stronsay I. 37 59 10N 2 37W
Papa Westray I. 37 59 20N 2 55W
Papagayo, Golfo de 166 10 4N 85 50W
Papagayo, R., Brazil 164 12 30 S 58 10W
Papagayo, R., Mexico 165 16 36N 99 43W
Papagni R. 97 14 10N 78 30 E
Papaikou 147 19 47N 155 6W
Papakura 142 37 4 S 174 59 E
Papaloapan, R. 164 18 2N 96 51W
Papantla 165 20 45N 97 21W
Papar 102 5 45N 116 0 E
Paparoa 142 36 6 S 174 16 E
Paparoa Range 143 42 5 S 171 35 E
Pápas, Ákra 69 38 13N 21 6 E
Papatoetoe 142 36 59 S 174 51 E
Papenburg 48 53 7N 7 25 E
Papien Chiang, R. (Da) 108 22 56N 101 47 E
Papigochic, R. 164 29 9N 109 40W
Paposo 172 25 0 S 70 30W
Paps, The, mts. 39 52 0N 9 15W
Papua, Gulf of 135 9 0 S 144 50 E
Papua New Guinea ■ 135 8 0 S 145 0 E
PapuCa 63 44 22N 15 30 E
Papudo 172 32 29 S 71 27W
Papuk, mts. 66 45 30N 17 30 E
Papun 98 18 0N 97 30 E
Pará = Belém 170 1 20 S 48 30W
Pará □ 175 3 20 S 52 0W
Parábita 65 40 3N 18 8 E
Paracatú 171 17 10 S 46 50W
Paracatu, R. 171 16 30 S 45 4W
Paracel Is. 102 16 49N 111 2 E
Parachilna 140 31 10 S 138 21 E
Parachinar 94 34 0N 70 5 E
Paracombe 109 34 51 S 138 47 E
Paracuru 170 3 24 S 39 4W
Paradas 57 37 18N 5 29W
Paradela 56 42 44N 7 37W
Paradip 95 20 15N 86 35 E
Paradise 160 47 27N 114 54W
Paradise, R. 151 53 27N 57 19W
Paradise Valley 160 41 30N 117 28W
Parado 103 8 42 S 118 30 E
Paradyz 54 51 19N 20 2 E
Parafield 109 34 47 S 138 38 E
Parafield Airport 109 34 48 S 138 38 E
Paragould 159 36 5N 90 30W
Paragua, La 174 6 50N 63 20W
Paragua, R. 174 6 30N 63 30W
Paraguaçu Paulista 173 22 22 S 50 35W
Paraguaçu, R. 171 12 45 S 38 54W
Paraguai, R. 174 16 0 S 57 52W
Paraguaipoa 174 11 21N 71 57W
Paraguana, Pen. de 174 12 0N 70 0W
Paraguarí 172 25 36 S 57 0W
Paraguarí □ 172 26 0 S 57 10W
Paraguay ■ 172 23 0 S 57 0W
Paraguay, R. 172 27 18 S 58 38W
Paraíba = Joéo Pessoa 164 7 10 S 35 0W
Paraiba □ 170 7 0 S 36 0W
Paraíba do Sul, R. 173 21 37 S 41 3W
Paraibano 171 6 30 S 44 1W
Parainen 75 60 18N 22 18 E
Paraiso 165 19 3 S 52 59W
Paraiso 165 18 24N 93 14W
Parakhino Paddubye 80 58 46N 33 10 E
Parakou 121 9 25N 2 40 E
Parakylia 140 30 24 S 136 25 E
Paralion-Astrous 69 37 25N 22 45 E
Paramagudi 97 9 31N 78 39 E
Paramaribo 175 5 50N 55 10W
Parambu 170 6 13 S 40 43W
Paramillo, Nudo del 174 7 4N 75 55W
Paramirim 171 13 26 S 42 15W
Paramirim, R. 171 11 34 S 43 18W
Paramithiá 68 39 30N 20 35 E
Paramushir, Ostrov 77 40 24N 156 0 E
Paran, N. 90 30 14N 34 48 E
Paraná 172 32 0 S 60 30W
Paranã 171 12 30 S 47 40W
Paraná □ 173 24 30 S 51 0W
Paraná, R. 172 33 43 S 59 15W
Paranã, R. 171 22 25 S 53 1W
Paranaguá 173 25 30 S 48 30W
Paranaíba, R. 171 18 0 S 49 12W
Paranapanema, R. 173 22 40 S 53 9W
Paranapiacaba, Serra do 173 24 31 S 48 35W
Paranavaí 173 23 4 S 52 28W
Parang, Jolo, Phil. 103 5 55N 120 54 E
Parang, Mindanao, Phil. 103 7 23N 124 16 E
Parangaba 170 3 45 S 38 33W
Paraóin 66 43 54N 21 27 E
Paraparanma 143 40 57 S 175 3 E
Parapóla, I. 69 36 55N 23 27 E
Paraspóri, Ákra 69 35 55N 27 15 E
Paratinga 171 12 40 S 43 10W
Paratoo 140 32 42 S 139 22 E
Parattah 138 42 22 S 147 23 E
Paraúna 171 17 2 S 50 26W
Paray-le-Monial 45 46 27N 4 7 E
Parbati, R. 94 25 51N 76 34 E
Parbatipur 98 25 39N 88 55 E
Parbhani 96 19 8N 76 52 E
Parchim 48 53 25N 11 50 E
Parczew 54 51 9N 22 52 E
Pardee Res. 163 38 16N 120 51W
Pardes Hanna 90 32 28N 34 57 E
Pardilla 56 41 33N 3 43W
Pardo, R., Bahia, Brazil 171 15 40 S 39 0W
Pardo, R., Mato Grosso, Brazil 171 21 0 S 53 25W
Pardo, R., Minas Gerais, Brazil 171 15 48 S 44 48W
Pardo, R., São Paulo, Brazil 171 20 45 S 48 0W
Pardubice 52 50 3N 15 45 E
Pare 103 7 43 S 112 12 E
Pare □ 126 4 10 S 38 0 E
Pare Mts. 126 4 0 S 37 45 E
Pare Pare 103 4 0 S 119 45 E
Parecis, Serra dos 174 13 0 S 60 0W
Paredes de Nava 56 42 9N 4 42W
Parelhas 170 6 41 S 36 39W
Paren 77 62 45N 163 0 E
Parengarenga Harbour 142 34 31 S 173 0 E
Parent 150 47 55N 74 35W
Parent, Lac. 150 48 31N 77 1W
Parentis-en-Born 44 44 21N 1 4W
Parepare 103 4 0 S 119 40 E
Parfino 80 57 59N 31 34 E
Parfuri 129 22 28 S 31 17 E
Paria, Golfo de 174 10 20N 62 0W
Paria, Pen. de 174 10 50N 62 30W
Pariaguán 174 8 51N 64 43W
Pariaman 102 0 47 S 100 11 E
Paricutín, Cerro 164 19 28N 102 15W
Parigi 103 0 50 S 120 5 E
Parika 174 6 50N 58 20W
Parima, Serra 174 2 30N 64 0W
Parinari 174 4 35 S 74 25W
Parincea 70 46 27N 27 9 E
Parîng, mt. 70 45 20N 23 37 E
Parintins 175 2 40 S 56 50W
Pariparit Kyun 99 14 55 S 93 45 E
Paris, Can. 150 43 12N 80 25W
Paris, France 43 48 50N 2 20 E
Paris, Idaho, U.S.A. 160 42 13N 111 30W
Paris, Ky., U.S.A. 156 38 12N 84 12W
Paris, Tenn., U.S.A. 157 36 20N 88 20W
Paris, Tex., U.S.A. 159 33 40N 95 30W
Parish 162 43 24N 76 9W
Pariti 103 9 55 S 123 30 E
Park City 160 40 42N 111 35W
Park Falls 158 45 58N 90 27 E
Park Range 160 40 0N 106 30W
Park Rapids 158 46 56N 95 0W
Park River 158 48 25N 97 17W
Park Rynie 129 30 25 S 30 35 E
Park View 161 36 45N 106 37W
Parkent 85 41 18N 69 40 E
Parker, Ariz., U.S.A. 161 34 8N 114 16W
Parker, S.D., U.S.A. 158 43 25N 97 7W
Parker Dam 161 34 13N 114 5W
Parkersburg 156 39 18N 81 31W
Parkerview 153 51 21N 103 18W
Parkes, A.C.T., Austral. 133 35 18 S 149 8 E
Parkes, N.S.W., Austral. 141 33 9 S 148 11 E
Parkfield 163 35 54N 120 26W
Parkhar 85 37 30N 69 34 E
Parknasilla 39 51 49N 9 50W
Parkside 153 53 10N 106 33W
Parkston 158 43 25N 98 0W
Parksville 152 49 20N 124 21W
Parkville 162 39 23N 76 33W
Parlakimedi 96 18 45N 84 5 E
Parma, Italy 62 44 50N 10 20 E
Parma, U.S.A. 160 43 49N 116 59W
Parna, R. 62 44 27N 10 3 E
Parnaguá 170 10 10 S 44 10W
Parnaiba, Piauí, Brazil 170 3 0 S 41 40W
Parnaiba, São Paulo, Brazil 170 19 34 S 51 14W
Parnaíba, R. 170 3 35 S 43 0W
Parnamirim 170 8 5 S 39 34W
Parnarama 170 5 41 S 43 6W
Parnassôs, mt. 69 38 17N 21 30 E
Parnassus 143 42 42 S 173 23 E
Párnis, mt. 69 38 14N 23 45 E
Párnon Óros 69 37 15N 22 45 E
Pärnu 80 58 12N 24 33 E
Parola 96 20 47N 75 7 E
Paroo Chan. 133 30 50 S 143 35 E
Paroo, R. 139 30 0 S 144 5 E
Paropamisus Range = Fīroz Kohi 93 34 45N 63 0 E
Páros 69 37 5N 25 9 E
Páros, I. 69 37 5N 25 12 E
Parowan 161 37 54N 112 56W
Parpaillon, mts. 45 44 30N 6 40 E
Parracombe 30 51 11N 3 55W
Parral 172 36 10 S 72 0W
Parramatta 141 33 48 S 151 1 E
Parramore I. 162 37 32N 75 39W
Parras 164 25 30N 102 20W
Parrett, R. 28 51 7N 2 58W
Parris I. 157 32 20N 80 30W
Parrsboro 151 45 30N 64 10W
Parry 153 49 47N 104 41W
Parry, C. 147 70 20N 123 38W
Parry Is. 12 77 0N 110 0W
Parry Sound 150 45 20N 80 0W
Parshall 158 47 56N 102 11W
Parsnip, R. 152 55 10N 123 2W
Parsons 159 37 20N 95 10W
Parsons Ra., Mts. 138 13 30 S 135 15 E
Partabpur 96 20 0N 80 42 E
Partanna 64 37 43N 12 51 E
Partapgarh 94 24 2N 74 40 E
Parthenay 42 46 38N 0 16W
Partille 73 57 48N 12 18 E
Partinico 64 38 3N 13 6 E
Partney 33 53 12N 0 7 E
Parton 32 54 34N 3 35W
Partry Mts. 38 53 40N 9 28W
Partur 96 19 40N 76 14 E
Paru, R. 175 0 20 S 53 30W
Parur 97 10 13N 76 14 E
Paruro 174 13 45 S 71 50W
Parvatipuram 96 18 50N 83 25 E
Parwan □ 93 35 0N 69 0 E
Påryd 73 56 34N 15 55 E
Parys 128 26 52 S 27 29 E
Parys, Mt. 31 53 23N 4 18W
Pas-de-Calais □ 43 50 30N 2 30 E
Pasadena, Calif., U.S.A. 163 34 5N 118 9W
Pasadena, Tex., U.S.A. 159 29 45N 95 14W
Pasaje 174 3 10 S 79 40W
Pasaje, R. 172 25 35 S 64 57W
Pascagoula 159 30 30N 88 30W
Pascagoula, R. 159 30 40N 88 35W
Paşcani 70 47 14N 26 45 E
Pasco 160 46 10N 119 0W
Pasco, Cerro de 174 10 45 S 76 10W
Pascoag 162 41 57N 71 42W
Pascoe, Mt. 137 27 25 S 120 40 E
Pasewalk 48 53 30N 14 0 E
Pasfield L. 153 58 24N 105 20W
Pasha, R. 80 60 20N 33 0 E
Pashiwari 95 34 40N 75 10 E
Pashiya 84 58 33N 58 26 E
Pashmakli = Smolyan 67 41 36N 24 38 E
Pasighat 98 28 4N 95 21 E
Pasir Mas 101 6 2N 102 8 E
Pasir Puteh 101 5 50N 102 24 E
Pasirian 103 8 13 S 113 8 E
Pasley, C. 137 33 52 S 123 35 E
Pasman I. 63 43 58N 15 20 E
Pasmore, R. 140 31 5 S 139 49 E
Pasni 93 25 15N 63 27 E
Paso de Indios 176 43 55 S 69 0W
Paso de los Libres 172 29 44 S 57 10W
Paso de los Toros 172 32 36 S 56 37W
Paso Robles 161 35 40N 120 45W
Paspebiac 151 48 3N 65 17W
Pasrur 94 32 16N 74 43 E
Passage East 39 52 15N 7 0W
Passage West 39 51 52N 8 20W
Passaic 162 40 50N 74 8W
Passau 49 48 34N 13 27 E
Passendale 47 50 54N 3 2 E
Passero, C. 65 36 42N 15 8 E
Passo Fundo 173 28 10 S 52 30W
Passos 171 20 45 S 46 37W
Passow 48 53 13N 14 3 E
Passwang 50 47 22N 7 41 E
Passy 43 45 55N 6 41 E
Pastaza, R. 174 2 45 S 76 50W
Pastek 54 54 3N 19 41 E
Pasto 174 1 13N 77 17W
Pasto Zootécnico do Cunene 128 16 20 S 15 20 E
Pastos Bons 170 6 36 S 44 5W
Pastrana 58 40 27N 2 53W
Pasuruan 103 7 40 S 112 53 E
Pasym 54 53 48N 20 49 E
Pásztó 53 47 52N 19 43 E
Patagonia, Argent. 176 45 0 S 69 0W
Patagonia, U.S.A. 161 31 35N 110 45W
Patan, India 93 23 54N 72 14 E
Patan, Gujarat, India 96 17 22N 73 48 E
Patan, Maharashtra, India 94 23 54N 72 14 E
Patan (Lalitapur) 99 27 40N 85 20 E
Pat'ang Szechwan 105 30 2N 98 58 E
Patani 103 0 20N 128 50 E
Pataohotzu 107 43 5N 127 33 E
Patapsco Res. 162 39 27N 76 55W
Pataudi 94 28 18N 76 48 E
Patay 43 48 2N 1 40 E
Patcham 29 50 52N 0 9W
Patchewollock 140 35 22 S 142 12 E
Patchogue 162 40 46N 73 1W
Patea 142 39 45 S 174 30 E
Pategi 121 8 50N 5 45 E
Pateley Bridge 33 54 5N 1 45W
Patensie 128 33 46 S 24 49 E
Paternò 65 37 34N 14 53 E
Paternoster, Kepulauan 102 7 5 S 118 15 E
Pateros 160 48 4N 119 58W
Paterson, Austral. 141 32 37 S 151 39 E
Paterson, U.S.A. 162 40 55N 74 10W
Paterson Inlet 143 46 56 S 168 12 E
Paterson Ra. 136 21 45 S 122 10 E
Paterswolde 46 53 9N 6 34 E
Pathankot 94 32 18N 75 45 E
Patharghata 98 22 2N 89 58 E
Pathfinder Res. 160 42 0N 107 0W
Pathiu 101 10 42N 99 19 E
Pathum Thani 100 14 1N 100 32 E
Páti 103 6 45 S 111 3 E
Patiala 94 30 23N 76 26 E
Patine Kouta 120 12 45N 13 45W
Patjitan 103 8 12 S 111 8 E
Patkai Bum 98 27 0N 95 30 E
Pátmos 69 37 21N 26 36 E
Pátmos, I. 69 37 21N 26 36 E
Patna, India 95 25 35N 85 18 E
Patna, U.K. 34 55 21N 4 30W
Patonga 126 2 45N 33 15 E
Patos 170 7 1 S 37 16W
Patos de Minas 171 18 35 S 46 32W
Patos, Lag. dos 173 31 20 S 51 0 E
Patosi 68 40 42N 19 38 E
Patquía 172 30 0 S 66 55W
Pátrai 69 38 14N 21 47 E
Pátraikos, Kólpos 69 38 17N 21 30 E
Patrick 32 54 13N 4 41W
Patrocínio 171 18 57 S 47 0W
Patta 126 2 10 S 41 0 E
Patta, I. 126 2 10 S 41 0 E
Pattada 64 40 35N 9 7 E
Pattanapuram 97 9 6N 76 33 E
Pattani 101 6 48N 101 15 E
Patten 151 45 59N 68 28W
Patterdale 32 54 33N 2 55W
Patterson, Calif., U.S.A. 163 37 30N 121 9W
Patterson, La., U.S.A. 159 29 44N 91 20W
Patterson, Mt. 163 38 29N 119 20W
Patti 94 31 17N 74 54 E
Patti Castroreale 65 38 8N 14 57 E
Pattoki 94 31 5N 73 52 E
Pattukkottai 97 10 25N 79 20 E
Patu 170 6 6 S 37 38W
Patuakhali 98 22 20N 90 25 E
Patuca, Punta 166 15 49N 84 14W
Patuca, R. 166 15 20N 84 40W
Patung 109 31 0N 110 30 E
Pâturages 47 50 25N 3 52 E
Patutahi 142 38 38 S 177 55 E
Pátzcuaro 164 19 30N 101 40W
Pau 44 43 19N 0 25W
Pau d' Arco 170 7 30 S 49 22W
Pau dos Ferros 170 6 7 S 38 10W
Pauillac 44 45 11N 0 46W
Pauini, R. 174 1 42 S 62 50W
Pauk 98 21 55N 94 30 E
Paul I. 151 56 30N 61 20W
Paulatuk 147 69 25N 124 0W
Paulhan 44 43 33N 3 28 E
Paulis = Isiro 126 2 53N 27 58 E
Paulista 170 7 57 S 34 53W

Paulistana **Perryton**

Paulistana	**170**	8 9S	41 9W
Paull	**33**	53 42N	0 12W
Paullina	**158**	42 55N	95 40W
Paulo A'onso	**170**	9 21S	38 15W
Paulo de Faria	**171**	20 2S	49 24W
Paulpietersburg	**129**	27 23S	30 50E
Paul's Valley	**159**	34 40N	97 17W
Pauma Valley	**163**	33 16N	116 58W
Paungde	**98**	18 29N	95 30E
Pauni	**96**	20 48N	79 40E
Pavelets	**81**	53 49N	39 14E
Pavia	**62**	45 10N	9 10E
Pavlikeni	**67**	43 14N	25 20E
Pavlodar	**76**	52 33N	77 0E
Pavlof Is.	**147**	55 30N	161 30W
Pavlograd	**82**	48 30N	35 52E
Pavlovo, Gorkiy, U.S.S.R.	**81**	55 58N	43 5E
Pavlovo, Yakut A.S.S.R., U.S.S.R.	**77**	63 5N	115 25E
Pavlovsk	**81**	50 26N	40 5E
Pavlovskaya	**83**	46 17N	39 47E
Pavlovskiy Posad	**81**	55 37N	38 42E
Pavullo nel Frignano	**62**	44 20N	10 50E
Pawahku	**98**	26 11N	98 40E
Pawhuska	**159**	36 40N	96 25W
Pawling	**162**	41 35N	73 37W
Pawnee	**159**	36 24N	96 50W
Pawnee City	**158**	40 8N	96 10W
Pawtucket	**162**	41 51N	71 22W
Paximádhia	**69**	35 0N	24 35E
Paxoi, I.	**68**	39 14N	20 12E
Paxton, Ill., U.S.A.	**156**	40 25N	88 0W
Paxton, Nebr., U.S.A.	**158**	41 12N	101 27W
Paya Bakri	**101**	2 3N	102 44E
Payakumbah	**102**	0 20S	100 35E
Payenhaot'e (Alashantsoch'i)	**106**	38 50N	105 32E
Payenk'ala Shan	**105**	34 20N	97 0E
Payerne	**50**	46 49N	6 56E
Payette	**160**	44 0N	117 0W
Paymogo	**57**	37 44N	7 21W
Payne L.	**149**	59 30N	74 30W
Payne, R.	**149**	60 0N	70 0W
Payneham	**109**	34 54S	138 39E
Paynes Find	**137**	29 15S	117 42E
Paynesville, Liberia	**120**	6 20N	10 45W
Paynesville, U.S.A.	**158**	45 21N	94 44W
Paysandú	**172**	32 19S	58 8W
Payson, Ariz., U.S.A.	**161**	34 17N	111 15W
Payson, Utah, U.S.A.	**160**	40 8N	111 41W
Paz, Bahía de la	**164**	24 15N	110 25W
Paz Centro, La	**166**	12 20N	86 41W
Paz, La, Entre Ríos, Argent.	**172**	30 50S	59 45W
Paz, La, San Luis, Argent.	**172**	33 30S	67 20W
Paz, La, Boliv.	**174**	16 20S	68 10W
Paz, La, Hond.	**166**	14 20N	87 47W
Paz, La, Mexico	**164**	24 10N	110 20W
Paz, La, Bahía de	**164**	24 20N	110 40W
Paz, R.	**166**	13 44N	90 10W
Pazar	**92**	41 10N	40 50E
Pazardzhik	**67**	42 12N	24 20E
Pazin	**63**	45 14N	13 56E
Pčinja, R.	**66**	42 0N	21 45E
Pe Ell	**160**	46 30N	123 18W
Peabody	**162**	42 31N	70 56W
Peace Point	**152**	59 7N	112 27W
Peace, R.	**152**	59 0N	111 25W
Peace River	**152**	56 15N	117 18W
Peace River Res.	**152**	55 40N	123 40W
Peacehaven	**29**	50 47N	0 1E
Peach Springs	**161**	35 36N	113 30W
Peak Downs	**138**	22 55S	148 0E
Peak Downs Mine	**138**	22 17S	148 11E
Peak Hill, N.S.W., Austral.	**141**	32 39S	148 11E
Peak Hill, W. A., Austral.	**137**	25 35S	118 43E
Peak Range	**138**	22 50S	148 20E
Peak, The	**32**	53 24N	1 53W
Peake	**140**	35 25S	140 0E
Peake Cr.	**139**	28 2S	136 7E
Peale Mt.	**161**	38 25N	109 12W
Pearblossom	**163**	34 30N	117 55W
Pearce	**161**	31 57N	109 56W
Pearl Banks	**97**	8 45N	79 45E
Pearl City	**147**	2 21N	158 0W
Pearl Harbor	**147**	21 20N	158 0W
Pearl, R.	**159**	31 50N	90 0W
Pearsall	**159**	28 55N	99 8W
Pearse I.	**152**	54 52N	130 14W
Peary Land	**12**	82 40N	33 0W
Pease, R.	**159**	34 18N	100 15W
Peasenhall	**29**	52 17N	1 24E
Pebane	**127**	17 10S	38 8E
Pebas	**174**	3 10S	71 55W
Pebble Beach	**163**	36 34N	121 57W
Peçanha	**171**	18 33S	42 34W
Péccioli	**62**	43 32N	10 43E
Pechea	**70**	45 36N	27 49E
Pechenezhin	**82**	48 30N	24 48E
Pechenga	**78**	69 30N	31 25E
Pechnezhskoye Vdkhr.	**81**	50 0N	36 50E
Pechora, R.	**78**	62 30N	56 30E
Pechorskaya Guba	**78**	68 40N	54 0E
Pechory	**80**	57 48N	27 40E
Pecica	**66**	46 10N	21 3E
Pečka	**66**	44 18N	19 33E
Pécora, C.	**64**	39 28N	8 23E
Pecos	**159**	31 25N	103 35W
Pecos, R.	**159**	31 22N	102 30W
Pecqueuse	**47**	48 39N	2 3E
Pécs	**53**	46 5N	18 15E
Pedasí	**166**	7 32N	80 3W
Peddapalli	**96**	18 40N	79 24E
Peddapuram	**96**	17 6N	82 5E
Peddavagu, R.	**96**	16 33N	79 8E
Pedder, L.	**138**	42 55S	146 10E
Pedernales	**167**	18 2N	71 44W
Pedirka	**139**	26 40S	135 14E
Pedjantan, I.	**102**	0 5S	106 15E
Pedra Azul	**171**	16 2S	41 17W
Pedra Grande, Recifes do	**171**	17 45S	38 58W
Pedras, Pta. de	**171**	7 38S	34 47W
Pedreiras	**170**	4 32S	44 40W
Pedrera, La	**174**	1 18S	69 43W
Pedro Afonso	**170**	9 0S	48 10W
Pedro Antonio Santos	**165**	18 54N	88 15W
Pedro Cays	**166**	17 5N	77 48W
Pedro Chico	**174**	1 4N	70 25W
Pedro de Valdivia	**172**	22 33S	69 38W
Pedro Juan Caballero	**173**	22 30S	55 40W
Pedro Muñoz	**59**	39 25N	2 56W
Pedrógão Grande	**56**	39 55N	8 0W
Peebinga	**140**	34 52S	140 57E
Peebles	**35**	55 40N	3 12W
Peebles (□)	**26**	55 37N	3 4W
Peekshill	**162**	41 18N	73 57W
Peel, Austral.	**139**	33 20S	149 38E
Peel, I. of Man	**32**	54 14N	4 40W
Peel Fell, mt.	**35**	55 17N	2 35W
Peel, R., Austral.	**141**	30 50S	150 29E
Peel, R., Can.	**147**	67 0N	135 0W
Peelwood	**141**	34 7S	149 27E
Peene, R.	**48**	53 53N	13 53E
Peera Peera Poolanna L.	**139**	26 30S	138 0E
Peers	**152**	53 40N	116 0W
Pegasus Bay	**143**	43 20S	173 10E
Peggau	**52**	47 12N	15 21E
Pego	**59**	38 51N	0 8W
Pegswood	**35**	55 12N	1 38W
Pegu	**99**	17 20N	96 29E
Pegu Yoma, mts.	**98**	19 0N	96 0E
Pegwell Bay	**29**	51 18N	1 22E
Pehčevo	**66**	41 41N	22 55E
Pehuajó	**172**	36 0S	62 0W
Pei Chiang, R.	**109**	23 12N	112 45E
Pei Wan	**107**	36 25N	120 45E
Peian	**105**	48 16N	126 36E
Peichen	**107**	41 38N	121 50E
Peichengchen	**107**	44 30N	123 27E
Peichiang	**109**	23 0N	120 0E
Peihai	**108**	21 30N	109 5E
P'eihsien, Kiangsu, China	**106**	34 44N	116 55E
P'eihsien, Kiangsu, China	**107**	34 20N	117 57E
Peiliu	**109**	22 45N	110 20E
Peine, Chile	**172**	23 45S	68 8W
Peine, Ger.	**48**	52 19N	10 12E
Peip'an Chiang, R.	**108**	25 0N	106 11E
Peip'ei	**105**	29 49N	106 27E
Peip'iao	**107**	41 48N	120 44E
Peip'ing	**106**	39 45N	116 25E
Peissenberg	**49**	47 48N	11 4E
Peitz	**48**	51 50N	14 23E
Peixe	**171**	12 0S	48 40W
Peixe, R.	**171**	21 31S	51 58W
Peize	**46**	53 9N	6 30E
Pek, R.	**66**	44 58N	21 55E
Pekalongan	**103**	6 53S	109 40E
Pekan	**101**	3 30N	103 25E
Pekin	**158**	40 35N	89 40W
Peking = Peip'ing	**106**	39 45N	116 25E
Pelabuhan Ratu, Teluk	**103**	7 5S	106 30E
Pelabuhanratu	**103**	7 0S	106 32E
Pélagos, I.	**68**	39 17N	24 4E
Pelagruza, Is.	**63**	42 24N	16 15E
Pelaihari	**102**	3 55S	114 45E
Pelczyce	**54**	53 3N	15 16E
Peleaga, mt.	**70**	45 22N	22 55E
Pelee I.	**150**	41 47N	82 40W
Pelée, Mt.	**167**	14 40N	61 0W
Pelee, Pt.	**150**	41 54N	82 31W
Pelekech, mt.	**126**	3 52N	35 8E
Peleng, I.	**103**	1 20S	123 30E
Pelham	**157**	31 5N	84 6W
Pelhrimov	**52**	49 24N	15 12E
Pelican	**147**	58 12N	136 28W
Pelican L.	**153**	52 28N	100 20W
Pelican Narrows	**153**	55 10N	102 56W
Pelican Portage	**152**	55 51N	113 0W
Pelican Rapids	**153**	52 45N	100 42W
Peligre, L. de	**167**	19 1N	71 58W
Pelkosenniemi	**74**	67 6N	27 28E
Pella	**158**	41 20N	93 0W
Pélla □	**68**	40 52N	22 0E
Péllaro	**65**	38 1N	15 40E
Pellworm, I.	**48**	54 30N	8 40E
Pelly Bay	**149**	68 0N	89 50W
Pelly L.	**148**	66 0N	102 0W
Pelly, R.	**147**	62 15N	133 30W
Peloponnese = Pelóponnisos	**69**	37 10N	22 0E
Pelopónnisos Kai Dhitiktí Iprotikí Ellas □	**69**	37 10N	22 0E
Peloritani, Monti	**65**	38 2N	15 15E
Peloro, C.	**65**	38 15N	15 40E
Pelorus Sound	**143**	40 59S	173 59E
Pelotas	**173**	31 42S	52 23W
Pelòvo	**67**	43 26N	24 17E
Pelvoux, Massif de	**45**	44 52N	6 20E
Pelym R.	**84**	59 39N	63 6E
Pemalang	**103**	6 53S	109 23E
Pematang Siantar	**102**	2 57N	99 5E
Pemba, Mozam.	**127**	12 58S	40 30E
Pemba, Zambia	**127**	16 30S	27 28E
Pemba Channel	**126**	5 0S	39 37E
Pemba, I.	**126**	5 0S	39 45E
Pemberton, Austral.	**137**	34 30S	116 0E
Pemberton, Can.	**152**	50 25N	122 50W
Pembina	**153**	48 58N	97 15W
Pembina, R.	**153**	49 0N	98 12W
Pembine	**156**	45 38N	87 59W
Pembrey	**31**	51 42N	4 17W
Pembroke, Can.	**150**	45 50N	77 7W
Pembroke, N.Z.	**143**	44 33S	169 9E
Pembroke, U.K.	**31**	51 41N	4 57W
Pembroke, U.S.A.	**157**	32 5N	81 32W
Pembroke (□)	**26**	51 40N	5 0W
Pembroke Dock	**31**	51 41N	4 57W
Pembury	**29**	51 8N	0 20E
Pen-y-Ghent	**32**	54 10N	2 15W
Pen-y-groes, Dyfed, U.K.	**31**	51 48N	4 3W
Pen-y-groes, Gwynedd, U.K.	**31**	53 3N	4 18W
Peñíscola	**58**	40 22N	0 24E
Peña de Francia, Sierra de	**56**	40 32N	6 10W
Peña Roya, mt.	**58**	40 24N	0 40W
Peña, Sierra de la	**58**	42 32N	0 45W
Penafiel	**56**	41 12N	8 17W
Peñafiel	**56**	41 35N	4 7W
Peñaflor	**57**	37 43N	5 21W
Peñalara, Pico	**56**	40 51N	3 57W
Penally	**31**	51 39N	4 44W
Penalva	**170**	3 18S	45 10W
Penamacôr	**56**	40 10N	7 10W
Penang = Pinang	**101**	5 25N	100 15E
Penápolis	**173**	21 30S	50 0W
Peñaranda de Bracamonte	**56**	40 53N	5 13W
Peñarroya-Pueblonuevo	**57**	38 19N	5 16W
Penarth	**31**	51 26N	3 11W
Peñas, C. de	**56**	43 42N	5 52W
Peñas de San Pedro	**59**	38 44N	2 0W
Peñas, G. de	**176**	47 0S	75 0W
Peñas, Pta.	**174**	11 17N	70 28W
Pench'i	**107**	41 20N	123 48E
Pencoed	**31**	51 31N	3 30W
Pend Oreille, L.	**160**	48 0N	116 30W
Pend Oreille, R.	**160**	49 4N	117 37W
Pendálofon	**68**	40 14N	21 12E
Pendeen	**30**	50 11N	5 39W
Pendelikón	**69**	38 5N	23 53E
Pendembu	**120**	9 7N	12 14W
Pendências	**170**	5 15S	36 43W
Pender B.	**136**	16 45S	122 42E
Pendine	**31**	51 44N	4 33W
Pendle Hill	**32**	53 53N	2 18W
Pendleton, Calif., U.S.A.	**163**	33 16N	117 23W
Pendleton, Oreg., U.S.A.	**160**	45 35N	118 50W
Pendzhikent	**85**	39 29N	67 37E
Penedo	**170**	10 15S	36 36W
Penetanguishene	**150**	44 50N	79 55W
Penfield	**109**	34 44S	138 38E
Pengalengan	**103**	7 9S	107 30E
P'engch'i	**108**	30 50N	105 42E
Penge, Kasai, Congo	**126**	5 30S	24 33E
Penge, Kivu, Congo	**126**	4 27S	28 25E
P'enghsien	**108**	30 59N	103 56E
P'enghu Liehtao	**109**	22 30N	119 30E
P'englai	**107**	37 49N	120 47E
P'engshui	**108**	29 19N	108 12E
P'engtse	**109**	29 53N	116 32E
Penguin	**138**	41 8S	146 6E
Penhalonga	**127**	18 52S	32 40E
Peniche	**57**	39 19N	9 22W
Penicuik	**35**	55 50N	3 14W
Penida, I.	**102**	8 45S	115 30E
Penistone	**33**	53 31N	1 38W
Penitentes, Serra dos	**170**	8 45S	46 20W
Penkridge	**28**	52 44N	2 8W
Penmachno	**31**	53 2N	3 47W
Penmaenmawr	**31**	53 16N	3 55W
Penmarch	**42**	47 49N	4 21W
Penmarch, Pte. de	**42**	47 48N	4 22W
Penn Yan	**162**	42 39N	77 7W
Pennabilli	**63**	43 50N	12 17E
Pennant	**153**	50 32N	108 14W
Penne	**63**	42 28N	13 56E
Penner, R.	**97**	14 50N	78 20E
Penneshaw	**140**	35 44S	137 56E
Pennines	**32**	54 50N	2 20W
Pennino, Mte.	**63**	43 6N	12 54E
Pennsburg	**162**	40 23N	75 30W
Pennsville	**162**	39 39N	75 31W
Pennsylvania □	**156**	40 50N	78 0W
Penny	**152**	53 51N	121 48W
Peno	**80**	57 2N	32 33E
Penola	**140**	37 25S	140 47E
Penong	**139**	31 59S	133 5E
Penonomé	**166**	8 31N	80 21W
Penpont	**35**	55 14N	3 49W
Penrhyn Is.	**131**	9 0S	150 30W
Penrith, Austral.	**141**	33 43S	150 38E
Penrith, U.K.	**32**	54 40N	2 45W
Penryn	**30**	50 10N	5 7W
Pensacola	**157**	30 30N	87 10W
Pensacola Mts.	**13**	84 0S	40 0W
Pense	**153**	50 25N	104 59W
Penshurst, Austral.	**140**	37 49S	142 20W
Penshurst, U.K.	**29**	51 10N	0 12E
Pentecoste	**170**	3 48S	37 17W
Penticton	**152**	49 30N	119 30W
Pentire Pt.	**30**	50 35N	4 57W
Pentland	**138**	20 32S	145 25E
Pentland Firth	**37**	58 43N	3 10W
Pentland Hills	**35**	55 48N	3 25W
Pentland Skerries	**37**	58 41N	2 53W
Pentraeth	**31**	53 17N	4 13W
Pentre Foelas	**31**	53 2N	3 41W
Penukonda	**97**	14 5N	77 38E
Penwortham	**32**	53 45N	2 44W
Penybont	**31**	52 17N	3 18W
Penylan L.	**153**	61 50N	106 20W
Penza	**81**	53 15N	45 5E
Penzance	**30**	50 7N	5 32W
Penzberg	**49**	47 46N	11 23E
Penzhinskaya Guba	**77**	61 30N	163 0E
Penzlin	**48**	53 32N	13 6E
Peó	**66**	42 40N	20 17E
Peoria, Ariz., U.S.A.	**161**	33 40N	112 15W
Peoria, Ill., U.S.A.	**158**	40 40N	89 40W
Pepacton Res.	**162**	42 5N	74 58W
Pepingen	**47**	50 46N	4 10E
Pepinster	**47**	50 34N	5 47E
Pepmbridge	**28**	52 13N	2 54W
Pepperwood	**160**	40 23N	124 0W
Peqini	**68**	41 4N	19 44E
Pera Hd.	**138**	12 55S	141 37E
Perabumilih	**102**	3 27S	104 15E
Perakhóra	**69**	38 2N	22 56E
Peraki, R.	**101**	5 10N	101 4E
Perales de Alfambra	**58**	40 38N	1 0W
Perales del Puerto	**56**	40 10N	6 40W
Peralta	**58**	42 21N	1 49W
Pérama	**69**	35 20N	24 22E
Perast	**66**	42 31N	18 47E
Percé	**151**	48 31N	64 13W
Perche	**42**	48 31N	1 1E
Perche, Collines de la	**42**	42 30N	2 5E
Percival Lakes	**136**	21 25S	125 0E
Percy	**42**	48 55N	1 11W
Percy Is.	**138**	21 39S	150 16E
Percyville	**138**	19 2S	143 45E
Perdido, Mte.	**58**	42 40N	0 50E
Pereira	**174**	4 49N	75 43W
Pereira Barreto	**171**	20 38S	51 7W
Pereira de Eóa	**128**	16 48S	15 50E
Perekerten	**140**	34 55S	143 40E
Perenjori	**137**	29 26S	116 16E
Pereslavi-Zelesskiy	**80**	56 45N	38 58E
Pereyaslav-Khmelnitskiy	**80**	50 3N	31 28E
Perez, I.	**165**	22 24N	89 42W
Perg	**52**	48 15N	14 38E
Pergamino	**172**	33 52S	60 30W
Pergine Valsugano	**63**	46 4N	11 15E
Pérgola	**63**	43 35N	12 50E
Perham	**158**	46 36N	95 36W
Perham Down Camp	**28**	51 14N	1 38W
Perhentian, Kepulauan	**101**	5 54N	102 42E
Peri, L.	**140**	30 45S	143 35E
Periam	**66**	46 2N	20 59E
Peribonca, L.	**151**	50 1N	71 10W
Péribonca, R.	**151**	48 45N	72 5W
Perico	**172**	24 20S	65 5W
Pericos	**164**	25 3N	107 42W
Périers	**42**	49 11N	1 25W
Périgord	**44**	45 0N	0 40E
Périgueux	**44**	45 10N	0 42E
Perija, Sierra de	**174**	9 30N	73 3W
Perim, I.	**91**	12 39N	43 25E
Peristera, I.	**69**	39 15N	23 58E
Peritoró	**170**	4 20S	44 18W
Periyakulam	**97**	10 5N	77 30E
Periyar, L.	**97**	9 25N	77 10E
Periyar, R.	**97**	10 15N	78 10E
Perkam, Tg.	**103**	1 35S	137 50E
Perkasie	**162**	40 22N	75 18W
Perkovió	**63**	43 41N	16 10E
Perlas, Arch. de las	**166**	8 41N	79 7W
Perlas, Punta de	**166**	11 30N	83 30W
Perleberg	**48**	53 5N	11 50E
Perlevka	**81**	51 56N	38 57E
Perlez	**66**	45 11N	20 22E
Perlis □	**101**	6 30N	100 15E
Perm (Molotov)	**84**	58 0N	57 10E
Përmeti	**68**	40 15N	20 21E
Pernambuco = Recife	**170**	8 0S	35 0W
Pernambuco □	**170**	8 0S	37 0W
Pernatty Lagoon	**140**	31 30S	137 12E
Peron, C.	**137**	25 30S	113 30E
Peron Is.	**136**	13 9S	130 4E
Peron Pen.	**137**	26 0S	113 10E
Péronne	**43**	49 55N	2 57E
Péronnes	**47**	50 27N	4 9E
Perosa Argentina	**62**	44 57N	7 11E
Perouse Str., La	**86**	45 40N	142 0E
Perow	**152**	54 35N	126 10W
Perpendicular Pt.	**139**	31 37S	152 52E
Perpignan	**44**	42 42N	2 53E
Perranporth	**30**	50 21N	5 9W
Perranzabuloe	**30**	50 18N	5 7W
Perris	**163**	33 47N	117 14W
Perros-Guirec	**42**	48 49N	3 28W
Perry, Fla., U.S.A.	**157**	30 9N	83 10W
Perry, Ga., U.S.A.	**157**	32 25N	83 41W
Perry, Iowa, U.S.A.	**158**	41 48N	94 5W
Perry, Maine, U.S.A.	**157**	44 59N	67 20W
Perry, Okla., U.S.A.	**159**	36 20N	97 20W
Perry, Mt.	**139**	25 12S	151 41E
Perryton	**159**	36 28N	100 48W

Perryville Ping, R

Perryville, Alas., U.S.A. 147 55 54N 159 10W
Perryville, Mo., U.S.A. 159 37 42N 89 50W
Persberg 72 59 47N 14 15 E
Persepolis 93 29 55N 52 50 E
Pershore 28 52 7N 2 4W
Persia = Iran 93 35 0N 50 0 E
Persian Gulf 93 27 0N 50 0 E
Perstorp 73 56 10N 13 25 E
Perth, Austral. 137 31 57 S 115 52 E
Perth, N.B., Can. 150 46 43N 67 42W
Perth, Ont., Can. 150 44 55N 76 15W
Perth, U.K. 35 56 24N 3 27W
Perth (□) 26 56 30N 4 0W
Perth Amboy 162 40 30N 74 25W
Perthus, Le 44 42 30N 2 53 E
Pertuis 45 43 42N 5 30 E
Pertuis Breton 44 46 17N 1 25W
Pertuis d'Antioche 44 46 6N 1 20W
Peru, Ill., U.S.A. 158 41 18N 89 12W
Peru, Ind., U.S.A. 156 40 42N 86 0W
Peru ■ 174 8 0 S 75 0W
Perúgia 63 43 6N 12 24 E
Perušić 63 44 40N 15 22 E
Péruwelz 47 50 31N 3 36 E
Pervomayskiy 81 53 20N 40 10 E
Pervouralsk 84 56 55N 60 0 E
Perwez 47 50 38N 4 48 E
Pésaro 63 43 55N 12 53 E
Pesca, La 165 23 46N 97 47W
Pescadores Is. (P'enghu Liehtao) 109 23 30N 119 30 E
Pescara 63 42 28N 14 13 E
Peschanokopskoye 83 46 14N 41 4 E
Péscia 62 43 54N 10 40 E
Pescina 63 42 0N 13 39 E
Peseux 50 46 59N 6 53 E
Peshawar 94 34 2N 71 37 E
Peshawar □ 94 35 0N 72 50 E
Peshkopia 68 41 41N 20 25 E
Peshovka 84 59 4N 52 22 E
Peshtera 67 42 2N 24 18 E
Peshtigo 156 45 4N 87 46W
Peski 81 51 14N 42 12 E
Peskovka 81 59 9N 52 28 E
Pêso da Régua 56 41 10N 7 47W
Pesqueira 170 8 20 S 36 42W
Pesquieria 164 29 23N 110 54W
Pesquieria, R. 164 25 54N 99 11W
Pessac 44 44 48N 0 37W
Pessoux 47 50 17N 5 11 E
Pest □ 53 47 29N 19 5 E
Pestovo 80 58 33N 35 18 E
Pestravka 81 52 28N 49 57 E
Pêta 69 39 10N 21 2 E
Petah Tiqwa 90 32 6N 34 53 E
Petalídhion, Khóra 69 36 57N 21 55 E
Petaling Jaya 101 3 4N 101 42 E
Petaluma 163 38 13N 122 39W
Petange 47 49 33N 5 55 E
Petatlán 164 17 31N 101 16W
Petauke 127 14 14 S 31 12 E
Petawawa 150 45 54N 77 17W
Petegem 47 50 59N 3 32 E
Petén Itza, Lago 166 16 58N 89 50W
Peter 1st, I. 13 69 0 S 91 0W
Peter Pond L. 153 55 55N 108 44W
Peterbell 150 48 36N 83 21W
Peterboro 162 42 55N 71 59W
Peterborough, S. Australia, Austral. 140 32 58 S 138 51 E
Peterborough, Victoria, Austral. 133 38 37 S 142 50 E
Peterborough, U.K. 29 52 35N 0 14W
Peterchurch 28 52 3N 2 57W
Peterculter 37 57 5N 2 18W
Peterhead 37 57 30N 1 49W
Peterlee 33 54 45N 1 18W
Petersburg, Alas., U.S.A. 152 56 50N 133 0W
Petersburg, Ind., U.S.A. 156 38 30N 87 15W
Petersburg, Va., U.S.A. 162 37 17N 77 26W
Petersburg, W. Va., U.S.A. 156 38 59N 79 10W
Petersfield 29 51 0N 0 56W
Peterswell 39 53 7N 8 46W
Petford 138 17 20 S 144 50 E
Petília Policastro 65 39 7N 16 48 E
Petit Bois I. 157 30 16N 88 25W
Petit Cap 151 48 58N 63 58W
Petit Goâve 167 18 27N 72 51W
Petit-Quevilly, Le 42 49 26N 1 0 E
Petitcodiac 151 45 57N 65 11W
Petite Saguenay 151 47 59N 70 1W
Petitsikapau, L. 151 54 37N 66 25W
Petlad 94 22 30N 72 45 E
Peto 165 20 10N 89 0W
Petone 142 41 13 S 174 53 E
Petoskey 150 45 22N 84 57W
Petra, Jordan 90 30 20N 35 22 E
Petra, Spain 58 39 37N 3 6 E
Petra, Ostrova 12 76 15N 118 30 E
Petralia 65 37 49N 14 4 E
Petrel 59 38 30N 0 46W
Petrich 67 41 24N 23 13 E
Petrijanec 63 46 23N 16 17 E
Petrikov 80 52 11N 28 29 E
Petrila 70 45 29N 23 29 E
Petrinja 63 45 28N 16 18 E
'Petroland', gasfield 19 53 35N 4 15 E
Petrolândia 170 9 5 S 38 20W
Petrolia 150 42 54N 82 9W
Petrolina 170 9 24 S 40 30W
Petropavlovsk 76 55 0N 69 0 E
Petropavlovsk-Kamchatskiy 77 53 16N 159 0 E
Petrópolis 173 22 33 S 43 9W
Petroşeni 70 45 28N 23 20 E
Petrova Gora 63 45 15N 15 45 E
Petrovac 66 42 13N 18 57 E
Petrovaradin 66 45 16N 19 55 E
Petrovsk 81 52 22N 45 19 E
Petrovsk-Zabaykalskiy 77 51 26N 108 30 E
Petrovskoye, R.S.F.S.R., U.S.S.R. 83 45 25N 42 58 E
Petrovskoye, R.S.F.S.R., U.S.S.R. 84 53 37N 56 23 E
Petrozavodsk 78 61 41N 34 20 E
Petrus Steyn 129 27 38 S 28 8 E
Petrusburg 128 29 4 S 25 26 E
Pettigo 38 54 32N 7 49W
Pettitts 141 34 56 S 148 10 E
Petworth 29 50 59N 0 37W
Peumo 172 34 21 S 71 19W
Peureulak 102 4 48N 97 45 E
Pevek 77 69 15N 171 0 E
Pevensey 29 50 49N 0 20 E
Pevensey Levels 29 50 50N 0 20 E
Peveragno 62 44 20N 7 37 E
Pewsey 28 51 20N 1 46W
Pewsey, Vale of 28 51 20N 1 46W
Peyrehorade 44 43 34N 1 7W
Peyruis 45 44 1N 5 56 E
Pézenas 44 43 28N 3 24 E
Pezinok 53 48 17N 17 17 E
Pfaffenhofen 49 48 31N 11 31 E
Pfäffikon 51 47 13N 8 46 E
Pfarrkirchen 49 48 25N 12 57 E
Pforzheim 49 48 53N 8 43 E
Pfungstadt 49 49 47N 8 36 E
Phagwara 93 31 10N 75 40 E
Phala 128 23 45 S 26 50 E
Phalodi 94 27 12N 72 24 E
Phalsbourg 43 48 46N 7 15 E
Phan 100 19 28N 99 43 E
Phan Rang 101 11 40N 109 9 E
Phan Thiet 101 11 1N 108 9 E
Phanat Nikhom 100 13 27N 101 11 E
Phangan, Ko 101 9 45N 100 0 E
Phangnga 101 8 28N 98 30 E
Phanh Bho Ho Chi Minh 101 10 58N 106 40 E
Phanom Dang Raek, mts. 100 14 45N 104 0 E
Phanom Sarakham 100 13 45N 101 21 E
Pharenda 95 27 5N 83 17 E
Phatthalung 101 7 39N 100 6 E
Phayao 100 19 11N 99 55 E
Phelps, N.Y., U.S.A. 162 42 57N 77 5W
Phelps, Wis., U.S.A. 158 46 2N 89 2W
Phelps L. 153 59 15N 103 15W
Phenix City 157 32 30N 85 0W
Phet Buri 100 13 1N 99 55 E
Phetchabun 100 16 25N 101 8 E
Phetchabun, Thiu Khao 100 16 0N 101 20 E
Phetchaburi 101 13 1N 99 55 E
Phi Phi, Ko 101 7 45N 98 46 E
Phiafay 100 14 48N 106 0 E
Phibun Mangsahan 100 15 14N 105 14 E
Phichai 100 17 22N 100 10 E
Phichit 100 16 26N 100 22 E
Philadelphia, Miss., U.S.A. 159 32 47N 89 5W
Philadelphia, Pa., U.S.A. 162 40 0N 75 10W
Philip 158 44 4N 101 42W
Philip Smith Mts. 147 68 0N 146 0W
Philippeville 47 50 12N 4 33 E
Philippi L. 138 24 20 S 138 55 E
Philippines ■ 103 12 0N 123 0 E
Philippolis 128 30 15 S 25 16 E
Philippopolis = Plovdiv 67 42 8N 24 44 E
Philipsburg 160 46 20N 113 21W
Philipstown 128 30 28 S 24 30 E
Phillip, I. 141 38 30 S 145 12 E
Phillips, Texas, U.S.A. 159 35 48N 101 17W
Phillips, Wis., U.S.A. 158 45 41N 90 22W
Phillips Ra. 136 16 53 S 125 50 E
Phillipsburg, Kans., U.S.A. 158 39 48N 99 20W
Phillipsburg, Penn., U.S.A. 162 40 43N 75 12W
Phillott 139 27 53 S 145 50 E
Philmont 162 42 14N 73 37W
Philomath 160 44 28N 123 21W
Phimai 100 15 13N 102 30 E
Phitsanulok 100 16 50N 100 12 E
Phnom Penh 101 11 33N 104 55 E
Phnom Thbeng 101 13 50N 104 56 E
Phoenicia 162 42 5N 74 14W
Phoenix, Ariz., U.S.A. 161 33 30N 112 10W
Phoenix, N.Y., U.S.A. 162 43 13N 76 18W
Phoenix Is. 130 3 30 S 172 0W
Phoenixville 162 40 12N 75 29W
Phon 100 15 49N 102 36 E
Phon Tiou 100 17 53N 104 37 E
Phong, R. 100 16 23N 102 56 E
Phong Saly 100 21 42N 102 9 E
Phong Tho 100 22 32N 103 21 E
Phongdo 99 30 14N 91 14 E
Phonhong 100 18 30N 102 25 E
Phonum 101 8 49N 98 48 E
Photharam 100 13 41N 99 51 E
Phra Chedi Sam Ong 100 15 16N 98 23 E
Phra Nakhon Si Ayutthaya 100 14 25N 100 30 E
Phra Thong, Ko 101 9 5N 98 17 E
Phrae 100 18 7N 100 9 E
Phrao 101 19 23N 99 15 E
Phrom Phiram 100 17 2N 100 12 E
Phu Dien 100 18 58N 105 31 E
Phu Doan 101 21 40N 105 10 E
Phu Loi 100 20 14N 103 14 E
Phu Ly (Ha Nam) 100 20 35N 105 50 E
Phu Qui 100 19 20N 105 20 E
Phu Tho 100 21 24N 105 13 E
Phuc Yen 100 21 16N 105 45 E
Phuket 100 8 0N 98 28 E
Phuket, Ko, I. 101 8 0N 98 22 E
Phulbari 98 21 52N 88 8 E
Phulera (Phalera) 94 26 52N 75 16 E
Phun Phin 101 9 7N 99 12 E
Phuoc Le (Baria) 101 10 39N 107 19 E
Piabia 138 25 12 S 152 45 E
Piacá 170 7 42 S 47 18W
Piacenza 62 45 2N 9 42 E
Piaçubaçu 170 10 24 S 36 25W
Piádena 62 45 8N 10 22 E
Pialba 139 25 20 S 152 45 E
Pian, Cr. 139 30 2 S 148 12 E
Piancó 171 7 12 S 37 57W
Pianella 63 42 24N 14 5 E
Piangil 140 35 5 S 143 20 E
Pianoro 63 44 20N 11 20 E
Pianosa, I., Puglia, Italy 63 42 12N 15 44 E
Pianosa, I., Toscana, Italy 62 42 36N 10 4 E
Piapot 153 49 59N 109 8W
Pias 57 38 1N 7 29W
Piaseczno 54 52 5N 21 2 E
Piassabussu 171 10 24 S 36 25W
Piastow 54 52 12N 20 48 E
Piatá 171 13 9 S 41 48W
Piatra Neamţ 70 46 56N 26 21 E
Piatra Olt 70 43 51N 25 9 E
Piauí □ 170 7 0 S 43 0W
Piaui, R. 170 6 38 S 42 42W
Piave, R. 63 45 50N 13 9 E
Piazza Ármerina 65 37 21N 14 20 E
Pibor Post 123 6 47N 33 3 E
Pibor, R. 123 7 1N 33 0 E
Pica 174 20 35 S 69 25W
Picard, Plaine de 43 50 0N 2 0 E
Picardie 43 50 0N 2 15 E
Picardy = Picardie 43 50 0N 2 15 E
Picayune 159 30 40N 89 40W
Piccadilly, Austral. 109 34 59 S 138 44 E
Piccadilly, Zambia 127 14 0 S 29 30 E
Picerno 65 40 40N 15 37 E
Pichiang 108 26 40N 98 53 E
Pichieh 108 27 20N 105 20 E
Pichilemu 172 34 22 S 72 9W
Pickerel L. 150 48 40N 91 25W
Pickering 33 54 15N 0 46W
Pickering, Vale of 33 54 0N 0 45W
Pickle Lake 150 51 30N 90 12W
Pico 16 38 28N 28 18W
Pico Truncado 176 46 40 S 68 10W
Picos 170 7 5 S 41 28W
Picos Ancares, Sierra de 56 42 51N 6 52W
Picquigny 43 49 56N 2 10 E
Picton, Austral. 141 34 12 S 150 34 E
Picton, Can. 150 44 1N 77 9W
Picton, N.Z. 143 41 18 S 174 3 E
Pictou 151 45 41N 62 42W
Picture Butte 152 49 55N 112 45W
Picuí 170 6 31 S 36 21W
Picún-Leufú 176 39 30 S 69 5W
Pidley 29 52 33N 0 4W
Pidurutalagala, mt. 97 7 10N 80 50 E
Piedad, La 164 20 20N 102 1W
Piedecuesta 174 6 59N 73 3W
Piedicavallo 62 45 41N 7 57 E
Piedmont 157 33 55N 85 39W
Piedmont = Piemonte 62 45 0N 7 30 E
Piedmont Plat. 157 34 0N 81 30W
Piedmonte d'Alife 65 41 22N 14 22 E
Piedra, R. 58 41 10N 1 45W
Piedrabuena 57 39 0N 4 10W
Piedrahita 56 40 28N 5 23W
Piedras Blancas Pt. 161 35 45N 121 18W
Piedras Negras 164 28 35N 100 35W
Piedras, R. de las 174 11 40 S 70 50W
Piemonte 62 45 0N 7 30 E
Piena 45 42 15N 8 34 E
Piensk 54 51 16N 15 2 E
Pier Millan 140 35 14 S 142 40 E
Pierce 160 46 46N 115 53W
Piería □ 68 40 13N 22 25 E
Pierowall 37 59 20N 3 0W
Pierre, France 43 46 54N 5 13 E
Pierre, U.S.A. 158 44 23N 100 20W
Pierrefeu 45 43 8N 6 9 E
Pierrefonds 43 49 20N 3 0 E
Pierrefontaine 43 47 14N 6 32 E
Pierrefort 44 44 55N 2 50 E
Pierrelatte 45 44 23N 4 43 E
Pieštany 155 48 35N 17 50 E
Piesting, R. 53 48 0N 16 19 E
Pieszyce 54 50 43N 16 33 E
Piet Retief 129 27 1 S 30 50 E
Pietarsaari 74 63 41N 22 40 E
Pietermaritzburg 129 29 35 S 30 25 E
Pietersburg 129 23 54 S 29 25 E
Pietraperzia 65 37 26N 14 8 E
Pietrasanta 62 43 57N 10 12 E
Pietrosu 70 47 12N 25 8 E
Pietrosul 70 47 35N 24 43 E
Pieve di Cadore 63 46 25N 12 22 E
Pieve di Teco 62 44 3N 7 54 E
Pievepélago 62 44 12N 10 35 E
Pigadhítsa 68 39 59N 21 23 E
Pigadia 69 35 30N 27 12 E
Pigeon I. 97 14 2N 74 20 E
Pigeon, R. 150 48 1N 89 42W
Piggott 159 36 20N 90 10W
Pigna 62 43 57N 7 40 E
Pigüé 172 37 36 S 62 25W
Pihani 95 27 36N 80 15 E
Pijnacker 46 52 1N 4 26 E
Pikalevo 80 59 37N 34 0 E
Pikes Peak 158 38 50N 105 10W
Pikesville 162 39 23N 76 44W
Piketberg 128 32 55 S 18 40 E
Pikeville 156 37 30N 82 30W
Pik'ochi 106 40 45N 111 17 E
Pikou 106 32 45N 105 22 E
Pikwitonei 153 55 35N 97 9W
Piła 54 53 10N 16 48 E
Piła □ 54 53 0N 17 0 E
Pila, mte. 59 38 16N 1 11W
Pilaia 68 40 32N 22 59 E
Pilani 94 28 22N 75 33 E
Pilão Arcado 170 10 9 S 42 26W
Pilar, Brazil 170 9 36 S 35 56W
Pilar, Parag. 172 26 50 S 58 10W
Pilas, I. 103 6 39N 121 37 E
Pilatus 51 46 59N 8 15 E
Pilbara Cr. 132 21 15 S 118 22 E
Pilbara Mining Centre 136 21 15 S 118 16 E
Pilcomayo, R. 172 25 21 S 57 42W
Pili 69 36 50N 27 15 E
Pilibhit 95 28 40N 79 50 E
Pilion, mt. 68 39 27N 23 7 E
Pilis 53 47 17N 19 35 E
Pilisvörösvár 53 47 38N 18 56 E
Pilkhawa 94 28 43N 77 42 E
Pilling 32 53 55N 2 54W
Pilltown 39 51 59N 7 49W
Pilos 69 36 55N 21 42 E
Pilot Mound 153 49 15N 98 54W
Pilot Point 159 33 26N 97 0W
Pilot Rock 160 45 30N 118 58W
Pilsen = Plzen 52 49 45N 13 22 E
Pilštanj 63 46 8N 15 39 E
Pilton 28 51 0N 2 35W
Piltown 39 52 22N 7 18W
Pilzno 54 50 0N 21 16 E
Pimba 140 31 18 S 136 46 E
Pimenta Bueno 174 11 35 S 61 10W
Pimentel 174 6 45 S 79 55W
Pimuacan, Rés. 151 49 45N 70 30W
Pina 58 41 29N 0 33W
Pinang, I. 101 5 25N 100 15 E
Pinar del Río 166 22 26N 83 40W
Pinawa 149 50 9N 95 50W
Pince C. 151 46 38N 53 45W
Pinchbeck 29 52 48N 0 9W
Pincher Creek 152 49 30N 113 57W
Pinchi L. 152 54 38N 124 30W
Pinch'uan 108 25 51N 100 34 E
Pinckneyville 158 38 5N 89 20W
Pincota 66 46 20N 21 45 E
Pind Dadan Khan 94 32 55N 73 47 E
Pindar 137 28 30 S 115 47 E
Pindaré Mirim 170 3 37 S 45 21W
Pindaré, R. 170 3 17 S 44 47W
Pindi Gheb 94 33 14N 72 12 E
Pindiga 121 9 58N 10 53 E
Pindobal 170 3 16 S 48 25W
Pindos Óros 68 40 0N 21 0 E
Pindus Mts. = Pindos Óros 68 40 0N 21 0 E
Pine 161 34 27N 111 30W
Pine Bluff 159 34 10N 92 0W
Pine, C. 151 46 37N 53 32W
Pine City 158 45 46N 93 0W
Pine Creek, N.T., Austral. 132 13 50 S 131 49 E
Pine Creek, Queens., Austral. 138 13 13 S 142 47 E
Pine Dock 153 51 38N 96 48W
Pine Falls 153 50 34N 96 11W
Pine Flat Res. 163 36 50N 119 20W
Pine Grove 162 40 33N 76 23W
Pine Hill 138 23 42 S 147 0 E
Pine, La 160 40 53N 80 45W
Pine Pass 152 55 25N 122 42W
Pine Point 152 60 50N 114 28W
Pine, R., Austral. 108 27 18 S 153 2 E
Pine, R., Can. 153 55 20N 107 38W
Pine Ridge, Austral. 141 31 10 S 147 30 E
Pine Ridge, U.S.A. 158 42 2N 102 35W
Pine River, Can. 153 51 45N 100 30W
Pine River, U.S.A. 158 46 40N 94 20W
Pine Valley 163 32 50N 116 32W
Pinecrest 163 38 12N 120 1W
Pinedale, Ariz., U.S.A. 161 34 23N 110 16W
Pinedale, Calif., U.S.A. 163 36 50N 119 48W
Pinega 52 64 45N 43 40 E
Pinega, R. 78 64 20N 43 0 E
Pinehill 138 23 38 S 146 57 E
Pinerolo 62 44 47N 7 21 E
Pineto 63 42 36N 14 4 E
Pinetop 161 34 10N 109 57W
Pinetown 129 29 48 S 30 54 E
Pinetree 158 43 42N 105 52W
Pineville, Ky., U.S.A. 157 36 42N 83 42W
Pineville, La., U.S.A. 159 31 22N 92 30W
Pinewood 153 48 45N 94 10W
Piney, Can. 153 49 5N 96 10W
Piney, France 43 48 22N 4 21 E
Ping, R. 100 15 42N 100 9 E

Pingaring **Polcura**

Pingaring **137** 32 40S 118 32E
P'ingch'ang **108** 31 33N 107 6E
P'ingchiang **109** 28 42N 113 35E
P'ingch'uan **107** 41 0N 118 36E
Pingelly **137** 32 29S 116 59E
P'ingho **109** 24 18N 117 2E
P'inghsiang, Kiangsi, China **109** 27 39N 113 50E
P'inghsiang, Kwangsi Chuang, China **108** 22 6N 106 44E
P'inghu **109** 30 38N 121 0E
P'ingi, Shantung, China **107** 35 30N 117 36E
P'ingi, Yünnan, China **108** 25 40N 104 14E
P'ingkuo **108** 23 20N 107 34E
P'ingli **108** 32 26N 109 22E
P'ingliang **105** 35 32N 106 50E
Pinglo, Kwangsi-Chuang, China **109** 24 30N 110 45E
Pinglo, Ningsia Hui, China **106** 38 58N 106 30E
P'inglu **106** 37 32N 112 14E
P'ingluch'eng **106** 39 46N 112 6E
P'ingnan, Fukien, China **109** 26 56N 119 3E
P'ingnan, Kwangsi-Chiang, China **109** 23 33N 110 23E
P'ingpa **108** 26 25N 106 15E
P'ingpien **108** 22 54N 103 40E
Pingrup **137** 33 32S 118 29E
P'ingt'an **109** 25 31N 119 47E
P'ingt'ang **108** 25 50N 107 19E
P'ingting **106** 37 48N 113 37E
P'ingt'ingshan **106** 33 43N 113 28E
P'ingtu **107** 36 47N 119 56E
P'ingtung **105** 22 38N 120 30E
Pingwu **105** 32 27N 104 25E
P'ingwu **108** 32 25N 104 36E
P'ingyang **109** 27 40N 120 33E
P'ingyangchen **107** 45 11N 131 15E
P'ingyao **106** 37 12N 112 10E
P'ingyin **106** 36 18N 116 26E
P'ingyüan, Kwangtung, China **109** 24 34N 115 54E
P'ingyüan, Ningsia Hui, China **106** 37 9N 116 25E
Pinhai **107** 34 0N 119 50E
Pinhal **173** 22 10S 46 46W
Pinheiro **170** 2 31S 45 5W
Pinhel **56** 40 18N 7 0W
Pinhoe **30** 50 44N 3 29W
Pinhsien, Heilung Kiang, China **107** 45 44N 127 27E
Pinhsien, Shensi, China **106** 35 10N 108 10E
Pini, I. **102** 0 10N 98 40E
Piniós, R., Ilia, Greece **69** 37 38N 21 20E
Piniós, R., Trikkala, Greece **68** 39 55N 22 10E
Pinjarra **137** 32 37S 115 52E
Pink, R. **153** 56 50N 103 50W
Pinkafeld **53** 47 22N 16 9E
Pinlebu **98** 24 5N 95 22E
Pinnacles, Austral. **137** 28 12S 120 26E
Pinnacles, U.S.A. **163** 36 33N 121 8W
Pinnaroo **140** 35 13S 140 56E
Pinon Hills **163** 34 26N 117 39W
Pinos **164** 22 20N 101 40W
Pinos, I. de **166** 21 40N 82 40W
Pinos, Mt **163** 34 49N 119 8W
Pinos Pt. **161** 36 50N 121 57W
Pinos Puente **57** 37 15N 3 45W
Pinotepa Nacional **165** 16 25N 97 55W
Pinrang **103** 3 46S 119 34E
Pinsk **80** 52 10N 26 8E
Pintados **174** 20 35S 69 40W
Pinto Butte Mt. **153** 49 22N 107 27W
Pintumba **137** 31 50S 132 18E
Pinwherry **34** 55 9N 4 50W
Pinyang **108** 23 17N 108 47E
Pinyug **78** 60 5N 48 0E
Pinzolo **62** 46 9N 10 45E
Pio XII **170** 3 53S 45 17W
Pioche **161** 38 0N 114 35W
Piombino **62** 42 54N 10 30E
Pioner, I. **77** 79 50N 92 0E
Pionki **54** 51 29N 21 28E
Piorini, L. **174** 3 15S 62 35W
Piotrków Trybunalski **54** 51 23N 19 43E
Piotrków Trybunalski □ **54** 51 30N 19 45E
Piove di Sacco **63** 45 18N 12 1E
Pip **93** 26 45N 60 10E
Pipar **94** 26 25N 73 31E
Pipariya **96** 22 45N 78 23E
Piper, oilfield **19** 58 30N 0 15E
Pipéri, I. **68** 39 20N 24 19E
Pipestone **158** 44 0N 96 20W
Pipestone Cr. **153** 53 37N 109 46W
Pipestone, R. **150** 52 53N 89 23W
Pipinas **172** 35 30S 57 19W
Pipiriki **142** 38 28S 175 5E
Pipmuacan Res. **151** 49 40N 70 25W
Pippingarra **136** 20 27S 118 42E
Pipriac **42** 47 49N 1 58W
Piqua **156** 40 10N 84 10W
Piquet Carneiro **171** 5 48S 39 25W
Piquiri, R. **173** 24 3S 54 14W
Piracanjuba **171** 17 18S 49 1W
Piracicaba **173** 22 45S 47 30W
Piracuruca **170** 3 50S 41 50W
Piræus = Piraiévs **69** 37 57N 23 42E
Piraiévs **69** 37 57N 23 42E
Piraiévs □ **69** 37 0N 23 30E
Piráino **65** 38 10N 14 52E
Pirajuí **173** 21 59S 49 29W
Piran (Pirano) **63** 45 31N 13 33E
Pirane **172** 25 25S 59 30W
Piranhas **170** 9 27S 37 46W
Pirapemas **170** 3 43S 44 14W
Pirapora **171** 17 20S 44 56W
Piratyin **80** 50 15N 32 25E
Pirbright **29** 51 17N 0 40W
Pirdop **67** 42 40N 24 10E
Pires do Rio **171** 17 18S 48 17W
Pirganj **98** 25 51S 88 24E
Pirgos, Ilia, Greece **69** 37 40N 21 27E
Pirgos, Messinia, Greece **69** 36 50N 22 16E
Pirgovo **67** 43 44N 25 43E
Piriac-sur-Mer **42** 47 22N 2 33W
Piribebuy **172** 25 26S 57 2W
Pirin Planina **67** 41 40N 23 30E
Pirineos, mts. **58** 42 40N 1 0E
Piripiri **170** 4 15S 41 46W
Piritu **174** 9 23N 69 12W
Pirmasens **49** 49 12N 7 30E
Pirna **48** 50 57N 13 57E
Pirojpur **98** 22 35N 90 1E
Pirot **66** 43 9N 22 39E
Pirsagat, R. **83** 40 15N 48 45E
Pirtleville **161** 31 25N 109 35W
Piru **163** 34 25N 118 48W
Piryí **69** 38 13N 25 59E
Pisa **62** 43 43N 10 23E
Pisa Ra. **143** 44 52S 169 12E
Pisagua **174** 19 40S 70 15W
Pisarovina **63** 45 35N 15 50E
Pisciotta **65** 40 7N 15 12E
Pisco **174** 13 50S 76 5W
Piscu **70** 45 30N 27 43E
Písek **52** 49 19N 14 10E
Pisham **108** 29 37N 106 13E
P'ishan **105** 37 38N 78 19E
Pishin Lora, R. **94** 30 15N 66 5E
Pising **103** 5 8S 121 53E
Pismo Beach **163** 35 9N 120 38W
Pissos **44** 44 19N 0 49W
Pisticci **65** 40 24N 16 33E
Pistoia **62** 43 57N 10 53E
Pistol B. **153** 62 25N 92 37W
Pisuerga, R. **56** 42 10N 4 15W
Pisz **54** 53 38N 21 49E
Pitalito **174** 1 51N 76 2W
Pitanga **171** 24 46S 51 44W
Pitangui **171** 19 40S 44 54E
Pitarpunga, L. **140** 34 24S 143 30E
Pitcairn I. **131** 25 5S 130 5W
Pite älv **74** 65 44N 20 50W
Piteå **74** 65 20N 21 25E
Piteşti **70** 44 52N 24 54E
Pithapuram **96** 17 10N 82 15E
Pithara **137** 30 20S 116 35E
Píthion **68** 41 24N 26 40W
Pithiviers **43** 48 10N 2 13E
Pitigliano **63** 42 38N 11 40E
Pitiquito **164** 30 42N 112 2W
Pitlochry **37** 56 43N 3 43W
Pitt I. **152** 53 30N 129 50W
Pittem **47** 51 1N 3 13E
Pittenweem **35** 56 13N 2 43W
Pittsburg, Calif., U.S.A. **163** 38 1N 121 50W
Pittsburg, Kans., U.S.A. **159** 37 21N 94 43W
Pittsburg, Tex., U.S.A. **159** 32 59N 94 58W
Pittsburgh **156** 40 25N 79 55W
Pittsfield, Ill., U.S.A. **158** 39 35N 90 46W
Pittsfield, N.H., U.S.A. **162** 43 17N 71 18W
Pittston **162** 41 19N 75 50W
Pittsworth **139** 27 41S 151 37E
Pituri, R. **138** 22 35S 138 30E
Pitzewo **107** 39 28N 122 30E
Piuí **171** 20 28S 45 58W
Pium **170** 10 27S 49 11W
Piura **174** 5 5S 80 45W
Piva, R. **66** 43 15N 18 50E
Pivijay **174** 10 28N 74 37W
Piwniczna **54** 49 27N 20 42E
Pixariá Óros **69** 38 42N 23 39E
Pixley **163** 35 58N 119 18W
Piyai **68** 39 17N 21 25E
Piyang **109** 32 50N 113 30E
Piz Bernina **49** 46 23N 9 45E
Pizarro **174** 4 58N 77 22W
Pizol **51** 46 57N 9 23E
Pizzo **65** 38 44N 16 10E
Placentia **151** 47 20N 54 0W
Placentia B. **151** 47 0N 54 40W
Placerville **160** 38 47N 120 51W
Placetas **166** 22 15N 79 44W
'Placid', gasfield **19** 53 25N 4 20E
Plačkovica, mts. **66** 41 45N 22 30E
Pladda, I. **34** 55 25N 5 7W
Plaffein **50** 46 45N 7 17E
Plain Dealing **159** 32 56N 93 41W
Plainfield **162** 40 37N 74 28W
Plains, Kans., U.S.A. **159** 37 20N 100 35W
Plains, Mont., U.S.A. **160** 47 27N 114 57W
Plains, Tex., U.S.A. **159** 33 11N 102 50W
Plainview, Nebr., U.S.A. **158** 42 25N 97 48W
Plainview, Tex., U.S.A. **159** 34 10N 101 40W
Plainville **158** 39 18N 99 19W
Plainwell **156** 42 28N 85 40W
Plaisance **44** 43 36N 0 3E
Pláka **68** 36 45N 24 26E
Plakhino **76** 67 45N 86 5E
Planá **52** 49 50N 12 44E
Plana Cays **167** 22 38N 73 30W
Planada **163** 37 18N 120 19W
Planaltina **171** 15 30S 47 45W
Plancoët **42** 48 32N 2 13W
Plandisśte **66** 45 16N 21 10E
Planeta Rica **174** 8 25N 75 36W
Planina, Slovenija, Yugo. **63** 45 47N 14 19E
Planina, Slovenija, Yugo. **63** 46 10N 15 12E
Plankinton **158** 43 45N 98 27W
Plano **159** 33 0N 96 45W
Plant City **157** 28 0N 82 15W
Plant, La **158** 45 11N 100 40W
Plaquemine **159** 30 20N 91 15W
Plasencia **56** 40 3N 6 8W
Plaški **63** 45 4N 15 22E
Plassen **72** 61 9N 12 30E
Plast **84** 54 22N 60 50E
Plaster Rock **151** 46 53N 67 22W
Plata, La, Argent. **172** 35 0S 57 55W
Plata, La, U.S.A. **162** 38 32N 76 59W
Plata, La, Río de **172** 35 0S 56 40W
Platani, R. **64** 37 28N 13 23E
Plateau **13** 70 55S 40 0E
Plateau □ **121** 9 0N 9 0E
Plateau du Coteau du Missouri **158** 47 9N 101 5W
Platí, Ákra **68** 40 27N 24 0E
Platinum **147** 59 2N 161 50W
Plato **174** 9 47N 74 47W
Platte **158** 43 28N 98 50W
Platte, Piz **51** 46 30N 9 35E
Platte, R. **158** 41 0N 98 0W
Platteville **158** 40 18N 104 47W
Plattling **49** 48 46N 12 53E
Plattsburgh **156** 44 41N 73 30W
Plattsmouth **158** 41 0N 96 0W
Plau **48** 53 27N 12 16E
Plauen **48** 50 29N 12 9E
Plav **66** 42 38N 19 57E
Plavnica **66** 42 10N 19 20E
Plavsk **81** 53 40N 37 18E
Playa Azul **164** 17 59N 102 24W
Playa de Castilla **57** 41 25N 0 12W
Playgreen L. **153** 54 0N 98 15W
Pleasant Bay **151** 46 51N 60 48W
Pleasant Hill **158** 38 48N 94 14W
Pleasant Hills **141** 35 28S 146 50E
Pleasant Mount **162** 41 44N 75 26W
Pleasant Pt. **143** 44 16S 171 9E
Pleasanton **159** 29 0N 98 30W
Pleasantville **162** 39 25N 74 30W
Pléaux **44** 45 8N 2 13E
Pleiku (Gia Lai) **101** 14 3N 108 0E
Plélan-le-Grand **42** 48 0N 2 7W
Plémet **42** 48 11N 2 36W
Pléneuf-Val-André **42** 48 35N 2 32W
Pleniţa **70** 44 14N 23 10E
Plenty, Bay of **142** 37 45S 177 0E
Plenty, R. **138** 23 25S 136 31E
Plentywood **158** 48 45N 104 35W
Plesetsk **78** 62 40N 40 10E
Plessisville **151** 46 14N 71 47W
Plestin-les-Grèves **42** 48 40N 3 39W
Pleszew **54** 51 53N 17 47E
Pleternica **66** 45 17N 17 48E
Pletipi L. **151** 51 44N 70 6W
Pleven **67** 43 26N 24 37E
Plevlja **66** 43 21N 19 21E
Płock **54** 52 32N 19 40E
Płock □ **54** 52 30N 19 45E
Plöcken Passo **63** 46 37N 12 57E
Plockton **36** 57 20N 5 40W
Ploegsteert **47** 50 44N 2 53E
Ploëmeur **42** 47 44N 3 26W
Ploërmel **42** 47 55N 2 26W
Ploieşti **70** 44 57N 26 5E
Plomárion **69** 38 58N 26 24E
Plomb du Cantal **44** 45 2N 2 48E
Plombières **43** 47 59N 6 27E
Plomin **63** 45 8N 14 10E
Plön **48** 54 8N 10 22E
Plöner See **48** 53 9N 15 5E
Plonge, Lac La **153** 55 8N 107 20W
Płonsk **54** 52 37N 20 21E
Płoty **54** 53 48N 15 18E
Plouay **42** 47 55N 3 21W
Ploudalmézeau **42** 48 34N 4 41W
Plougasnou **42** 48 42N 3 49W
Plouha **42** 48 41N 2 57W
Plouhinec **42** 48 0N 4 29W
Plovdiv **67** 42 8N 24 44E
Plum I. **162** 41 10N 72 12W
Plumbridge **38** 54 46N 7 15W
Plummer **160** 47 21N 116 59W
Plumtree **127** 20 27S 27 55E
Plunge **80** 55 53N 21 51E
Pluvigner **42** 47 46N 3 1W
Plymouth, U.K. **30** 50 23N 4 9W
Plymouth, Calif., U.S.A. **163** 38 29N 120 51W
Plymouth, Ind., U.S.A. **156** 41 20N 86 19W
Plymouth, Mass., U.S.A. **162** 41 58N 70 40W
Plymouth, N.C., U.S.A. **157** 35 54N 76 55W
Plymouth, N.H., U.S.A. **162** 43 44N 71 41W
Plymouth, Pa., U.S.A. **162** 41 17N 76 0W
Plymouth, Wis., U.S.A. **156** 43 42N 87 58W
Plymouth Sd. **30** 50 20N 4 10W
Plympton **30** 50 24N 4 2W
Plymstock **30** 50 22N 4 6W
Plynlimon = Pumlumon Fawr **31** 52 29N 3 47W
Plyussa **80** 47 40N 29 0E
Plyussa, R. **80** 58 40N 28 30E
Plzen **52** 49 45N 13 22E
Pniewy **54** 52 31N 16 16E
Pô **121** 11 14N 1 5W
Po Hai **107** 38 30N 119 0E
Po, R. **62** 45 0N 10 45E
Poai **106** 35 10N 113 4E
Pobé **121** 7 0N 2 38E
Pobedino **76** 49 51N 142 49E
Pobedy Pik **76** 40 45N 79 58E
Pobiedziska **54** 52 29N 17 19E
Pobla de Lillet, La **58** 42 16N 1 59E
Pobla de Segur **58** 42 15N 0 58E
Pobladura de Valle **56** 42 6N 5 44W
Pocahontas, Arkansas, U.S.A. **159** 37 18N 81 20W
Pocahontas, Iowa, U.S.A. **158** 42 41N 94 42W
Pocatello **160** 42 50N 112 25W
Pochep **80** 52 58N 33 15E
Pochinki **81** 54 41N 44 59E
Pochinok **80** 54 28N 32 29E
Pöchlarn **52** 48 12N 15 12E
Pochontas **152** 53 0N 117 51W
Pochutla **165** 15 50N 96 31W
Pocinhos **170** 7 4S 36 3W
Pocita Casas **164** 28 32N 111 6W
Pocklington **33** 53 56N 0 48W
Poções **171** 14 31S 40 21W
Pocomoke City **162** 38 4N 75 32W
Pocomoke, R. **162** 38 5N 75 34W
Poços de Caldas **173** 21 50S 46 45W
Pocrane **171** 19 37S 41 37W
PoC!tky **52** 49 15N 15 14E
Poddebice **54** 51 54N 18 58E
Poděbrady **52** 50 9N 15 8E
Podensac **44** 44 40N 0 22W
Podgorica = Titograd **66** 42 30N 19 19E
Podkamennaya Tunguska **77** 61 50N 90 26E
Podlapac **63** 44 45N 15 47E
Podmokly **52** 50 48N 14 10E
Podoleni **70** 46 46N 26 39E
Podolínec **53** 49 16N 20 31E
Podolsk **81** 55 25N 37 30E
Podor **120** 16 40N 14 50W
Podporozhy **78** 60 55N 34 2E
Podravska Slatina **66** 45 42N 17 45E
Podsreda **63** 45 42N 17 41E
Podu Turcului **70** 46 11N 27 25E
Podujevo **66** 42 54N 21 10E
Poel, I. **48** 54 0N 11 25E
Pofadder **128** 29 10S 19 22E
Pogamasing **150** 46 55N 81 50W
Poggiardo **65** 40 3N 18 21E
Poggibonsi **63** 43 27N 11 8E
Pogoanele **70** 44 55N 27 0E
Pogorzela **54** 51 50N 17 12E
Pogradeci **68** 40 57N 20 48E
Poh **103** 0 46S 122 51E
Pohang **107** 36 1N 129 23E
Pohorelá **53** 48 50N 20 2E
Pohorelice **53** 48 59N 16 31E
Pohorje, mts. **63** 46 30N 15 7E
Poiana Mare **70** 43 57N 23 5E
Poiana Ruscŭi, Munţii **70** 45 45N 22 25E
Pt. Augusta **140** 32 30S 137 50E
Point Baker **147** 56 20N 133 35W
Point Cloates **137** 22 40S 113 45E
Point Edward **150** 43 10N 82 30W
Point Fortin **167** 10 9N 61 46W
Point Hope **147** 68 20N 166 50W
Point Lay **147** 69 45N 163 10W
Point Pass **140** 34 5S 139 5E
Point Pedro **97** 9 50N 80 15E
Point Pleasant, N.J., U.S.A. **162** 40 5N 74 4W
Point Pleasant, W. Va., U.S.A. **156** 38 50N 82 7W
Point Reyes Nat. Seashore **163** 38 0N 122 58W
Point Rock **159** 31 30N 99 56W
Pointe-à-la Hache **159** 29 35N 89 55W
Pointe-à-Pitre **167** 16 10N 61 30W
Pointe-Noire **124** 4 48S 12 0E
Poirino **62** 44 55N 7 50E
Poisonbush Ra. **136** 22 30S 121 30E
Poissy **43** 48 55N 2 0E
Poitiers **42** 46 35N 0 20W
Poitou, Plaines du **44** 46 30N 0 1W
Poix **43** 49 47N 2 0E
Poix-Terron **43** 49 38N 4 38E
Pojoaque **161** 35 55N 106 0W
Pojuca **171** 12 21S 38 20W
Pokaran **93** 27 0N 71 50E
Pokataroo **139** 29 30S 148 34E
Poko, Sudan **123** 5 41N 31 55E
Poko, Zaïre **126** 3 7N 26 52E
Pok'ot'u **105** 48 46N 121 54E
Pokrovka **85** 42 20N 78 0E
Pokrovsk **77** 61 29N 129 6E
Pokrovsk-Uralskiy **84** 60 10N 59 49E
Pol **56** 43 9N 7 20W
Pola **80** 57 30N 32 0E
Pola de Allande **56** 43 16N 6 37W
Pola de Gordón, La **56** 42 51N 5 41W
Pola de Lena **56** 43 10N 5 49W
Pola de Siero **56** 43 24N 5 39W
Pola de Somiedo **56** 43 5N 6 15W
Polacca **161** 35 52N 110 25W
Polan **93** 25 30N 61 10E
Poland ■ **54** 52 0N 20 0E
Polanów **54** 54 7N 16 41E
Polar Bear Prov. Park **150** 54 30N 83 20W
Polcura **172** 37 10S 71 50W

Połcyn Zdrój
Portel

Połcyn Zdrój 54 53 47N 16 5 E
Polden Hills 28 51 7N 2 50W
Polegate 29 50 49N 0 15 E
Polessk 80 54 50N 21 8 E
Polesworth 28 52 37N 1 37W
Polevskoy 84 56 26N 60 11 E
Polewali, Sulawesi, Indon. 103 4 8 S 119 43 E
Polewali, Sulawesi, Indon. 103 3 21 S 119 31 E
Polgar 53 47 54N 21 6 E
Pŏlgyo-ri 107 34 51N 127 21 E
Poli 124 8 34N 12 54 E
Poliaigos, I. 69 36 45N 24 38 E
Policastro, Golfo di 65 39 55N 15 35 E
Police 54 53 33N 14 33 E
Polička 53 49 43N 16 15 E
Polignano a Mare 65 41 0N 17 12 E
Poligny 43 46 50N 5 42 E
Polikhnitas 69 39 4N 26 10 E
Polillo I. 103 14 56N 122 0 E
Polis 92 35 3N 32 30 E
Polistena 65 38 25N 16 4 E
Políyiros 68 40 23N 23 25 E
Polkowice 54 51 29N 16 3 E
Polla 65 40 31N 15 27 E
Pollachi 97 10 35N 77 0 E
Pollensa 58 39 54N 3 2 E
Pollensa, B. de 58 39 55N 3 5 E
Póllica 65 40 13N 15 3 E
Pollino, Mte. 65 39 54N 16 13 E
Pollock 158 45 58N 100 18W
Pollremon 38 53 40N 8 38W
Polna 80 58 31N 28 0 E
Polnovat 76 63 50N 66 5 E
Polo, Kwangtung, China 109 23 9N 114 17 E
Polo, S.-U., China 105 44 59N 81 57 E
Polo, U.S.A. 158 42 0N 89 38W
Pologi 82 47 29N 36 15 E
Polonnoye 80 50 6N 27 30 E
Polossu 108 31 12N 98 36 E
Polotsk 80 55 30N 28 50 E
Polperro 30 50 19N 4 31W
Polruan 30 50 17N 4 36W
Polski Trmbesh 67 43 20N 25 38 E
Polsko Kosovo 67 43 23N 25 38 E
Polson 160 47 45N 114 12W
Poltava 82 49 35N 34 35 E
Polur 97 12 32N 79 11 E
Polyarny 78 69 8N 33 20 E
Pomarance 62 43 18N 10 51 E
Pomarico 65 40 31N 16 33 E
Pomaro 164 18 20N 103 18W
Pombal, Brazil 170 6 55 S 37 50W
Pombal, Port. 56 39 55N 8 40W
Pómbia 69 35 0N 24 51 E
Pomeroy, U.K. 38 54 36N 6 56W
Pomeroy, Ohio, U.S.A. 156 39 0N 82 0W
Pomeroy, Wash., U.S.A. 160 46 30N 117 33W
Pomio 135 5 32 S 151 33 E
Pomona 163 34 2N 117 49W
Pomorie 67 42 26N 27 41 E
Pompano 157 26 12N 80 6W
Pompei 65 40 45N 14 30 E
Pompey 43 48 50N 6 2 E
Pompeys Pillar 160 46 0N 108 0W
Ponape I. 130 6 55N 158 10 E
Ponask, L. 150 54 0N 92 41W
Ponass L. 153 52 16N 103 58W
Ponca 158 42 38N 96 41W
Ponca City 159 36 40N 97 5W
Ponce 147 18 1N 66 37W
Ponchatoula 159 30 27N 90 25W
Poncheville, L. 150 50 10N 76 55W
Poncin 45 46 6N 5 25 E
Pond 163 35 43N 119 20W
Pond Inlet 149 72 30N 75 0W
Pondicherry 97 11 59N 79 50 E
Pondoland 129 31 10 S 29 30W
Pondooma 140 33 29 S 136 59 E
Pondrôme 47 50 6N 5 0 E
Ponds, I. of 151 53 27N 55 52W
Ponferrada 56 42 32N 6 35W
Pongaroa 142 40 33 S 176 15 E
Pôngo , Ponte de 127 19 0 S 34 0 E
Pongo, W. 123 8 0N 27 20 E
Poniatowa 54 51 11N 22 3 E
Poniec 54 51 48N 16 50 E
Ponnaiyar, R. 97 11 50N 79 45 E
Ponnani 97 10 45N 75 59 E
Ponnani, R. 97 10 45N 75 59 E
Ponneri 97 13 20N 80 15 E
Ponnyadaung 99 22 0N 94 10 E
Ponoi 78 67 0N 41 0 E
Ponoi, R. 78 67 10N 39 0 E
Ponoka 152 52 42N 113 40W
Ponomarevka 84 53 19N 54 8 E
Ponorogo 103 7 52 S 111 29 E
Pons, France 44 45 35N 0 34W
Pons, Spain 58 41 55N 1 12 E
Ponsul, R. 57 39 54N 8 45 E
Pont-à-Celles 47 50 30N 4 22 E
Pont-à-Mousson 43 45 54N 6 1 E
Pont Audemer 42 49 21N 0 30 E
Pont Aven 42 47 51N 3 47W
Pont Canavese 62 45 24N 7 33 E
Pont Château 42 47 26N 2 8W
Pont-de-Roide 43 47 23N 6 45 E
Pont-de-Salars 44 44 18N 2 44 E
Pont-de-Vaux 43 46 26N 4 56 E
Pont-de-Veyle 45 46 17N 4 53 E
Pont-l'Abbé 42 47 52N 4 15W
Pont Lafrance 151 47 40N 64 58W
Pont, Le 50 46 41N 6 20 E
Pont-l'Eveque 42 49 18N 0 11 E
Pont-St.-Esprit 45 44 16N 4 40 E
Pont-sur-Yonne 43 48 18N 3 10 E
Ponta de Pedras 170 1 23 S 48 52W
Ponta Grossa 173 25 0 S 50 10W
Ponta Pora 173 22 20 S 55 35W
Ponta São Sebastião 129 22 2 S 35 25 E
Pontacq 44 43 11N 0 8W
Pontailler 43 47 18N 5 24 E
Pontal, R. 170 9 8 S 40 12W
Pontalina 171 17 31 S 49 27W
Pontardawe 31 51 43N 3 51W
Pontardulais 31 51 42N 4 3W
Pontarlier 43 46 54N 6 20 E
Pontassieve 63 43 47N 11 25 E
Pontaubault 42 48 40N 1 20W
Pontaumur 44 45 52N 2 40 E
Pontcharra 45 45 26N 6 1 E
Pontchartrain, L. 159 30 12N 90 0W
Pontchâteau 42 47 25N 2 5W
Ponte Alta do Norte 170 10 45 S 47 34W
Ponte Alta, Serra do 171 19 42 S 47 40W
Ponte da Barca 56 41 48N 8 25W
Ponte de Sor 57 39 17N 7 57W
Ponte dell 'Olio 62 44 52N 9 39 E
Ponte di Legno 62 46 15N 10 30 E
Ponte do Lima 56 41 46N 8 35W
Ponte do Pungué 127 19 30 S 34 33 E
Ponte Leccia 45 42 28N 9 13 E
Ponte nell' Alpi 63 46 10N 12 18 E
Ponte Nova 173 20 25 S 42 54W
Ponte San Martino 62 45 36N 7 47 E
Ponte San Pietro 62 45 42N 9 35 E
Pontebba 63 46 30N 13 17 E
Pontecorvo 64 41 28N 13 40 E
Pontedera 62 43 40N 10 37 E
Pontefract 33 53 42N 1 19W
Ponteix 153 49 46N 107 29W
Ponteland 35 53 3N 1 45W
Pontelandolfo 65 41 17N 14 41 E
Pontemacassar Naikliu 103 9 30 S 123 58 E
Pontevedra 56 42 26N 8 40W
Pontevedra □ 56 42 25N 8 39W
Pontevedra, R. de 56 42 22N 8 45W
Pontevico 62 45 16N 10 6 E
Ponthierville = Ubundi 126 0 22 S 25 30 E
Pontiac, Ill., U.S.A. 158 40 50N 88 40W
Pontiac, Mich., U.S.A. 156 42 40N 83 20W
Pontian Kechil 101 1 29N 103 23 E
Pontianak 102 0 3 S 109 15 E
Pontine Is. = Ponziane, Isole 64 40 55N 13 0 E
Pontine Mts. = Karadeniz D. 92 41 30N 35 0 E
Pontínia 64 41 25N 13 2 E
Pontivy 42 48 5N 3 0W
Pontoise 43 49 3N 2 5 E
Ponton, R. 152 58 27N 116 11W
Pontorson 42 48 34N 1 30W
Pontrémoli 62 44 22N 9 52 E
Pontresina 51 46 29N 9 48 E
Pontrhydfendigaid 31 52 17N 3 50W
Pontrieux 28 48 42N 3 10W
Pontrilas 28 51 56N 2 53W
Ponts-de Cé, Les 42 47 25N 0 30W
Pontypool 31 51 42N 3 1W
Pontypridd 31 51 36N 3 21W
Ponza, I. 64 40 55N 12 57 E
Ponziane, Isole 64 40 55N 13 0 E
Poochera 139 32 43 S 134 51 E
Poole 28 50 42N 2 2W
Poole Harb. 28 50 41N 2 0W
Poolewe 36 57 45N 5 38W
Pooley Bridge 32 54 37N 2 49W
Pooley I. 152 52 45N 128 15W
Poonamallee 97 13 3N 80 10 E
Poona = Pune 96 18 29N 73 57 E
Pooncarie 140 33 22 S 142 31 E
Poonindie 140 34 34 S 135 54 E
Poopelloe, L. 140 31 40 S 144 0 E
Poopó, Lago de 174 18 30 S 67 35W
Poor Knights Is. 142 35 29 S 174 43 E
Pooraka 109 34 50 S 138 38 E
Poorman 147 64 5N 155 48W
Popai 108 22 13N 109 55 E
Popak 101 22 15N 109 56 E
Popakai, Austral. 170 32 12 S 141 46 E
Popakai, Surinam 170 3 20N 55 30W
Popanyinning 137 32 40 S 117 2 E
Popayán 174 2 27N 76 36W
Poperinge 47 50 51N 2 42 E
Popigay 77 71 55N 110 47 E
Popilta, L. 140 33 10 S 141 42 E
Popio, L. 140 33 10 S 141 52 E
Poplar 158 48 3N 105 9W
Poplar Bluff 159 36 45N 90 22W
Poplar, R., Man., Can. 153 53 0N 97 19W
Poplar, R., N.W.T., Can. 152 61 22N 121 52W
Poplarville 159 30 55N 89 30W
Popocatepetl, vol. 165 19 10N 98 40W
Popokabaka 124 5 49 S 16 40 E
Pópoli 63 42 12N 13 50 E
Popondetta 135 8 48 S 148 17 E
Popovača 63 45 30N 16 41 E
Popovo 67 43 21N 26 18 E
Poppel 47 51 27N 5 2 E
Poprád 53 49 3N 20 18 E
Poprád, R. 53 49 15N 20 30 E
Poquoson 162 37 7N 76 21W
Poradaha 98 23 51N 89 1 E
Porali, R. 94 27 15N 66 24 E
Porangahau 142 40 17 S 176 37 E
Porangatu 171 13 26 S 49 10W
Porbandar 94 21 44N 69 43 E
Porcher I. 152 53 50N 130 30W
Porcos, R. 171 12 42 S 45 7W
Porcuna 57 37 52N 4 11W
Porcupine, R., Can. 153 59 11N 104 46W
Porcupine, R., U.S.A. 147 67 0N 143 0W
Pordenone 63 45 58N 12 40 E
Pordim 67 43 23N 24 51 E
Pore 174 5 43N 72 0W
Poreč 63 45 14N 13 36 E
Porecatu 171 22 43 S 51 24W
Poretskoye 81 55 9N 46 21 E
Pori 75 61 29N 21 48 E
Porirua 142 41 8 S 174 52 E
Porjus 74 66 57N 19 50 E
Porkhov 80 57 45N 29 38 E
Porkkala 75 59 59N 24 26 E
Porlamar 174 10 57N 63 51W
Porlezza 62 46 2N 9 8 E
Porlock 28 51 13N 3 36W
Porlock B. 28 51 14N 3 37W
Porlock Hill 28 51 12N 3 40W
Porma, R. 56 42 45N 5 21W
Pornic 42 47 7N 2 5W
Poronaysk 77 49 20N 143 0 E
Pôros 69 37 30N 23 30 E
Pôros, I. 69 37 30N 23 30 E
Poroshiri-Dake 112 42 41N 142 52 E
Poroszló 53 47 39N 20 40 E
Poroto Mts. 127 9 0 S 33 30 E
Porraburdoo 137 23 15 S 117 28 E
Porrentruy 50 47 25N 7 6 E
Porreras 58 39 29N 3 2 E
Porsangen 74 70 40N 25 40 E
Porsgrunn 71 59 10N 9 40 E
Port 43 47 43N 6 4 E
Port Adelaide 140 34 46 S 138 30 E
Port Alberni 152 49 15N 124 50W
Port Albert 141 38 42 S 146 42 E
Port Albert Victor 94 21 0N 71 30 E
Port Alexander 147 56 13N 134 40W
Port Alfred, Can. 151 48 18N 70 53W
Port Alfred, S. Afr. 125 33 36 S 26 55 E
Port Alice 152 50 25N 127 25W
Port Allegany 156 41 49N 78 17W
Port Allen 159 30 30N 91 15W
Port Alma 138 23 38 S 150 53 E
Port Angeles 160 48 7N 123 30W
Port Antonio 166 18 10N 76 30W
Port Aransas 159 27 49N 97 4W
Port Arthur, Austral. 138 43 7 S 147 50 E
Port Arthur, U.S.A. 159 30 0N 94 0W
Port Arthur = Lüshun 107 38 51N 121 20 E
Port Arthur = Thunder Bay 150 48 25N 89 10W
Port Askaig 34 55 51N 6 8W
Port au Port B. 151 48 40N 58 50W
Port-au-Prince 167 18 40N 72 20W
Port Augusta West 140 32 29 S 137 47 E
Port Austin 150 44 3N 82 59W
Port aux Basques 151 47 32N 59 8W
Port Awanui 142 37 50 S 178 29 E
Port Bannatyne 34 55 51N 5 4W
Port Bell 126 0 18N 32 35 E
Port Bergé Vaovao 129 15 33 S 47 40 E
Port Blair 101 11 40N 92 30 E
Port Blandford 151 48 30N 53 50W
Port Bolivar 159 29 20N 94 40W
Port Bou 58 42 25N 3 9 E
Port Bouet 120 5 16N 4 57W
Port Bradshaw 138 12 30 S 137 0 E
Port Broughton 140 33 37 S 137 56 E
Port Burwell 150 42 40N 80 48W
Port Campbell 140 35 37 S 143 1 E
Port Canning 95 22 17N 88 48 E
Port Carlisle 32 54 56N 3 12W
Port-Cartier 151 50 10N 66 50W
Port Chalmers 143 45 49 S 170 30 E
Port Charlotte 34 55 44N 6 22W
Port Chester 162 41 0N 73 41W
Port Clements 152 53 40N 132 10W
Port Clinton 156 41 30N 83 0W
Port Colborne 150 42 50N 79 10W
Port Coquitlam 152 49 20N 122 45W
Port Curtis 138 24 0 S 151 34 E
Port Darwin, Austral. 136 12 24 S 130 45 E
Port Darwin, Falk. Is. 176 51 50 S 59 0W
Port Davey 138 43 16 S 145 55 E
Port-de-Bouc 45 43 24N 4 59 E
Port de Paix 167 19 50N 72 50W
Port Deposit 162 39 37N 76 5W
Port Dickson 101 2 30N 101 49 E
Port Dinorwic 31 53 11N 4 12W
Port Douglas 138 16 30 S 145 30 E
Port Edward 152 54 12N 130 10W
Port Elgin 150 44 25N 81 25W
Port Elizabeth 128 33 58 S 25 40 E
Port Ellen 34 55 38N 6 10W
Port Erin 32 54 5N 4 45W
Port Erroll 37 57 25N 1 50W
Port Essington 136 11 15 S 132 10 E
Port Étienne = Nouadhibou 116 21 0N 17 0W
Port Ewen 162 41 54N 73 59W
Port Fairy 140 38 22 S 142 12 E
Port Fitzroy 142 36 8 S 175 20 E
Port Fouâd = Bûr Fuad 122 31 15N 32 20 E
Port Francqui 124 4 17 S 20 47 E
Port-Gentil 124 0 47 S 8 40 E
Port Gibson 159 31 57N 91 0W
Port Glasgow 34 55 57N 4 40W
Port Gregory 137 27 40 S 114 0 E
Port Harcourt 121 4 40N 7 10 E
Port Hardy 152 50 41N 127 30W
Port Harrison 149 58 25N 78 15W
Port Hawkesbury 151 45 36N 61 22W
Port Hedland 136 20 25 S 118 35 E
Port Heiden 147 57 0N 158 40W
Port Hood 151 46 0N 61 32W
Port Hope 150 44 0N 78 20W
Port Hueneme 163 34 7N 119 12W
Port Huron 156 43 0N 82 28W
Port Isaac 30 50 35N 4 50W
Port Isaac B. 30 50 36N 4 50W
Port Isabel 159 26 12N 97 9W
Port Jackson 133 33 50 S 151 18 E
Port Jefferson 162 40 58N 73 5W
Port Jervis 162 41 22N 74 42W
Port Joinville 42 46 45N 2 23W
Port Kaituma 174 8 3N 59 58W
Port Katon 83 46 27N 38 56 E
Port Kelang 101 3 0N 101 23 E
Port Kembla 141 34 29 S 150 56 E
Port La Nouvelle 44 43 1N 3 3 E
Port Laoise 39 53 2N 7 20W
Port Lavaca 159 28 38N 96 38W
Port Leyden 162 43 35N 75 21W
Port Lincoln 140 34 42 S 135 52 E
Port Logan 34 54 42N 4 57W
Port Loko 120 8 48N 12 46W
Port Louis 42 47 42N 3 22W
Port Lyautey = Kenitra 118 34 15N 6 40W
Port Lyttelton 143 43 37N 172 50 E
Port Macdonnell 140 38 0 S 140 39 E
Port Macquarie 141 31 25 S 152 54 E
Port Maitland 151 44 0N 66 2W
Port Maria 166 18 25N 76 55W
Port Mellon 152 49 32N 123 31W
Port Menier 151 49 51N 64 15W
Port Morant 166 17 54N 76 19W
Port Moresby 135 9 24 S 147 8 E
Port Mouton 151 43 58N 64 50W
Port Musgrave 138 11 55 S 141 50 E
Port Navalo 42 47 34N 2 54W
Port Nelson 153 57 3N 92 36W
Port Nicholson 142 41 20 S 174 52 E
Port Nolloth 128 29 17 S 16 52 E
Port Norris 162 39 15N 75 2W
Port Nouveau-Quebec (George R.) 149 58 30N 65 50W
Port O'Connor 159 28 26N 96 24W
Port of Ness 36 58 29N 6 13W
Port of Spain 167 10 40N 61 20W
Port Orchard 160 47 31N 122 38W
Port Oxford 160 42 45N 124 28W
Port Pegasus 143 47 12 S 167 41 E
Port Perry 150 44 6N 78 56W
Port Phillip B. 139 38 10 S 144 50 E
Port Pirie 140 33 10 S 137 58 E
Port Pólnocny □ 54 54 25N 18 42 E
Port Radium = Echo Bay 148 66 10N 117 40W
Port Renfrew 152 48 30N 124 20W
Port Roper 138 14 45 S 134 47 E
Port Rowan 150 42 40N 80 30W
Port Royal 162 38 10N 77 12W
Port Safaga = Bûr Safâga 122 26 43N 33 57 E
Port Said = Bûr Sa'îd 122 31 16N 32 18 E
Port St. Joe 157 29 49N 85 20W
Port St. Johns = Umzimvubu 129 31 38 S 29 33 E
Port-St.-Louis 45 43 23N 4 50 E
Port St. Louis 129 13 7 S 48 48 E
Port-St.-Louis-du-Rhône 45 43 23N 4 49 E
Port St. Mary 32 54 5N 4 45W
Port St. Servain 151 51 21N 58 0W
Port Sanilac 150 43 26N 82 33W
Port Saunders 151 50 40N 57 18W
Port Shepstone 129 30 44 S 30 28 E
Port Simpson 152 54 30N 130 20W
Port Stanley 150 42 40N 81 10W
Port Sudan = Bôr Sûdân 122 19 32N 37 9 E
Port Sunlight 32 53 22N 3 0W
Port Talbot 31 51 35N 3 48W
Port Taufiq = Bûr Taufiq 122 29 54N 32 32 E
Port Townsend 160 48 7N 122 50W
Port-Vendres 44 42 32N 3 8 E
Port Victoria 140 34 30 S 137 29 E
Port Wakefield 140 34 12 S 138 10 E
Port Washington 156 43 25N 87 52W
Port Weld 101 4 50N 100 38 E
Port William 34 54 46N 4 35W
Portachuelo 174 17 10 S 63 20W
Portacloy 38 54 20N 9 48W
Portadown (Craigavon) 38 54 27N 6 26W
Portaferry 38 54 23N 5 32W
Portage, Can. 151 46 40N 64 5W
Portage, U.S.A. 158 43 31N 89 25W
Portage la Prairie 153 49 58N 98 18W
Portage Mt. Dam 152 56 0N 122 0W
Portageville 159 36 25N 89 40W
Portaguiran 36 58 15N 6 10W
Portalegre 57 39 19N 7 25W
Portalegre □ 57 39 20N 7 40W
Portales 159 34 12N 103 25W
Portarlington 39 53 10N 7 10W
Porte, La 156 41 40N 86 40W
Porteirinha 171 15 44 S 43 2W
Portel, Brazil 170 1 57 S 50 49W

Portel Prochowice

Portel, Port. 57 38 19N 7 41W
Porter L., N.W.T., Can. 153 61 41N 108 5W
Porter L., Sask., Can. 153 56 20N 107 20W
Porterville, S. Afr. 128 33 0S 18 57E
Porterville, U.S.A. 163 36 5N 119 0W
Portet 44 43 34N 0 11W
Porteynon 31 51 33N 4 13W
Portglenone 38 54 53N 6 30W
Portgordon 37 57 40N 3 1W
Porth Neigwl 31 52 48N 4 35W
Porth Neigwl, B. 31 52 48N 4 33W
Porthcawl 31 51 28N 3 42W
Porthill 160 49 0N 116 30W
Porthleven 30 50 5N 5 19W
Porthmadog 31 52 55N 4 13W
Portile de Fier 70 44 42N 22 30E
Portimão 57 37 8N 8 32W
Portishead 28 51 29N 2 46W
Portknockle 37 57 40N 2 52W
Portland, N.S.W., Austral. 141 33 20S 150 0E
Portland, Victoria, Austral. 140 38 20S 141 35E
Portland, Conn., U.S.A. 162 41 34N 72 39W
Portland, Me., U.S.A. 151 43 40N 70 15W
Portland, Mich., U.S.A. 156 42 52N 84 58W
Portland, Oreg., U.S.A. 160 45 35N 122 40W
Portland B. 140 38 15S 141 45E
Portland Bill 28 50 31N 2 27W
Portland, C. 133 40 46S 148 0E
Portland I. 142 39 20S 177 51E
Portland, I. of 28 50 32N 2 25W
Portland, Pa. 162 40 55N 75 6W
Portland Prom. 149 58 40N 78 33W
Portlaw 39 52 18N 7 20W
Portmagee 39 51 53N 10 22W
Portmahomack 37 57 50N 3 50W
Portmarnock 38 53 25N 6 10W
Portnacroish 34 56 34N 5 24W
Portnahaven 34 55 40N 6 30W
Porteuf 151 46 43N 71 55W
Pôrto, Brazil 170 3 54S 42 42W
Pôrto, Port. 56 41 8N 8 40W
Pôrto □ 56 41 8N 8 20W
Pôrto Alegre, Mato Grosso, Brazil 170 21 40S 53 30W
Pôrto Alegre, Rio Grande do Sul, Brazil 173 30 5S 51 3W
Porto Alexandre 128 15 55S 11 55E
Porto Amboim = Gunza 124 10 50S 13 50E
Porto Amelia = Pemba 127 12 58S 40 30E
Porto Argentera 62 44 15N 7 27E
Porto Azzurro 62 42 46N 10 24E
Porto Botte 64 39 3N 8 33E
Pôrto Calvo 171 9 4S 35 24W
Porto Civitanova 63 43 19N 13 44E
Pôrto da Fôlha 170 9 55S 37 17W
Pôrto de Moz 170 1 41S 52 22W
Pôrto de Pedras 170 9 10S 35 17W
Porto Empédocle 64 37 18N 13 30E
Pôrto Esperança 174 19 37S 57 29W
Pôrto Franco 170 6 20S 47 24W
Porto Garibaldi 63 44 41N 12 14E
Porto, G. de 45 42 17N 8 34E
Pôrto Lago 68 41 1N 25 6E
Porto Mendes 173 24 30S 54 15W
Porto Murtinho 174 21 45S 57 55W
Pôrto Nacional 170 10 40S 48 30W
Porto Novo, Benin 121 6 23N 2 42E
Porto Novo, India 97 11 30N 79 38E
Porto Recanati 63 43 26N 13 40E
Porto San Giorgio 63 43 11N 13 49E
Porto San Stéfano 68 42 26N 11 6E
Porto Santo, I. 116 33 45S 16 25W
Porto São José 173 22 43S 53 10W
Pôrto Seguro 171 16 26S 39 5W
Porto Tolle 63 44 57N 12 20E
Porto Tórres 64 40 50N 8 23E
Pôrto União 173 26 10S 51 10W
Pôrto Válter 174 8 5S 72 40W
Porto-Vecchio 45 41 35N 9 16E
Pôrto Velho 174 8 46S 63 54W
Portobelo 166 9 35N 79 42W
Portoferráio 62 42 50N 10 20E
Portogruaro 63 45 47N 12 50E
Portola 160 39 49N 120 28W
Portomaggiore 63 44 41N 11 47E
Porton Camp 28 51 8N 1 42W
Portoscuso 64 39 12N 8 22E
Portovénere 62 44 2N 9 50E
Portoviejo 174 1 0S 80 20W
Portpatrick 34 54 50N 5 7W
Portree 36 57 25N 6 11W
Portroe 39 52 53N 8 20W
Portrush 38 55 13N 6 40W
Portsall 42 48 37N 4 45W
Portsalon 38 55 12N 7 37W
Portskerra 37 58 35N 3 55W
Portslade 29 50 50N 0 11W
Portsmouth, Domin. 167 15 34N 61 27W
Portsmouth, U.K. 28 50 48N 1 6W
Portsmouth, N.H., U.S.A. 162 43 5N 70 45W
Portsmouth, Ohio, U.S.A. 156 38 45N 83 0W
Portsmouth, R.I., U.S.A. 162 41 35N 71 44W
Portsmouth, Va., U.S.A. 156 36 50N 76 20W
Portsoy 37 57 41N 2 41W
Portstewart 38 55 12N 6 43W
Porttipahta 74 68 5N 26 30E
Portugal ■ 56 40 0N 7 0W
Portugalete 58 43 19N 3 4W
Portuguesa □ 174 9 10N 69 15W
Portuguese Guinea = Guinea Bissau 120 12 0N 15 0W
Portuguese Timor ■ = Timor 103 8 0S 126 30E
Portumna 39 53 5N 8 12W
Porvenir 176 53 10S 70 30W
Porvoo 75 60 24N 25 40E
Porzuna 57 39 9N 4 9W
Posada, R. 64 40 40N 9 35E
Posadas, Argent. 173 27 30S 56 0W
Posadas, Spain 57 37 47N 5 11W
Poschiavo 51 46 19N 10 4E
Posets, mt. 58 42 39N 0 25E
Poshan 107 36 30N 117 50E
Posídhio, Ákra 68 39 57N 23 30E
Poso 103 1 20S 120 55E
Poso Colorado 172 23 30S 58 45W
Poso, D. 103 1 20S 120 55E
Posong 107 34 46N 129 5E
Posse 171 14 4S 46 18W
Possel 124 5 5N 19 10E
Possession I. 13 72 4S 172 0E
Pössneck 48 50 42N 11 34E
Possut'eng Hu 105 42 0N 87 0E
Post 159 33 13N 101 21W
Post Falls 160 47 50N 116 59W
Postavy 80 55 4N 26 58E
Postbridge 30 50 36N 3 54W
Poste-de-la-Baleine 30 50 36N 3 54W
Poste Maurice Cortier (Bidon 5) 118 22 14N 1 2E
Postiljon, Kepulauan 103 6 30S 118 50E
Postmasburg 128 28 18S 23 5E
Postojna 63 45 46N 14 12E
Potamós 69 39 38N 19 53E
Potchefstroom 125 26 41S 27 7E
Potcoava 70 44 30N 24 39E
Poté 171 17 49S 41 49W
Poteau 159 35 5N 94 37W
Poteet 159 29 4N 98 35W
Potelu, Lacul 70 43 44N 24 20E
Potenza 65 40 40N 15 50E
Potenza Picena 63 43 22N 13 37E
Poteriteri, L. 143 46 5S 167 10E
Potes 56 43 15N 4 42W
Potgietersrus 129 24 10S 29 3E
Poti 83 42 10N 41 38E
Potiraguá 171 15 36S 39 53W
Potiskum 121 11 39N 11 2E
Potlogi 70 44 34N 25 34E
Potomac, R. 162 38 0N 76 23W
Potosí 174 19 38S 65 50W
Potosí □ 174 20 31S 67 0W
Pot'ou 106 37 57N 116 39E
Potrerillos 172 26 20S 69 30W
Potros, Cerro del 172 28 32S 69 0W
Potsdam, Ger. 48 52 23N 13 4E
Potsdam, U.S.A. 156 44 40N 74 59W
Potsdam □ 48 52 40N 12 50E
Potter 158 41 15N 103 20W
Potter Heigham 29 52 44N 1 33E
Potterne 28 51 19N 2 0W
Potters Bar 29 51 42N 0 11W
Potterspury 29 52 5N 0 52W
Pottery Hill = Abu Ballas 122 24 26N 27 36E
Pottstown 162 40 17N 75 40W
Pottsville 162 40 39N 76 12W
Pottuvil 93 6 55N 81 50E
P'otzu 109 23 30N 120 25E
Pouancé 42 47 44N 1 10W
Pouce Coupé 152 55 40N 120 10W
Poughkeepsie 162 41 40N 73 57W
Pouilly 43 47 18N 2 57E
Poulaphouca Res. 39 53 8N 6 30W
Pouldu, Le 42 47 41N 3 36W
Poulsbo 160 47 45N 122 39W
Poultney 162 43 31N 73 14W
Poulton le Fylde 32 53 51N 2 59W
Poundstock 30 50 44N 4 34W
Pouso Alegre, Mato Grosso, Brazil 175 11 55S 57 0W
Pouso Alegre, Minas Gerais, Brazil 173 22 14S 45 57W
Pouzages 44 46 40N 0 50W
Povenets 78 62 50N 34 50E
Poverty Bay 142 38 43S 178 2E
Póvoa de Lanhosa 56 41 33N 8 15W
Póvoa de Varzim 56 41 25N 8 46W
Povorino 81 51 12N 42 28E
Powassan 150 46 5N 79 25W
Poway 163 32 58N 117 2W
Powder, R. 158 46 47N 105 12W
Powell 160 44 45N 108 45W
Powell Creek 136 18 6S 133 46E
Powell River 152 49 22N 125 31W
Powers, Mich., U.S.A. 156 45 40N 87 32W
Powers, Oreg., U.S.A. 160 42 53N 124 2W
Powers Lake 158 48 37N 102 38W
Powick 28 52 9N 2 15W
Powis, Vale of 23 52 40N 3 10W
Powys □ 31 52 20N 3 20W
P'oyang 109 29 1N 116 38E
Poyang Hu 109 29 10N 116 10E
Poyarkovo 77 49 36N 128 41E
Poyntzpass 38 54 17N 6 22W
Poysdorf 53 48 40N 16 37E
Poza de la Sal 58 42 35N 3 31W
Poza Rica 165 20 33N 97 27W
Pozarevac 66 44 35N 21 18E
Pozega 66 45 21N 17 41E
Pozhva 84 59 5N 56 5E
Poznan 54 52 25N 17 0E
Pozo 163 35 20N 120 24W
Pozo Alcón 59 37 42N 2 56W
Pozo Almonte 174 20 10S 69 50W
Pozoblanco 57 38 23N 4 51W
Pozzallo 65 36 44N 15 40E
Pra, R. 121 5 30N 1 38W
Prabuty 54 53 47N 19 15E
Prača 66 43 47N 18 43E
Prachatice 52 49 1N 14 0E
Prachin Buri 100 14 0N 101 25E
Prachuap Khiri Khan 101 11 49N 99 48E
Pradelles 44 44 46N 3 52E
Pradera 174 3 25N 76 15W
Prades 44 42 38N 2 23E
Prado 171 17 20S 39 13W
Prado del Rey 57 36 48N 5 33W
Præstø 73 55 8N 12 2E
Pragersko 63 46 27N 15 42E
Prague = Praha 52 50 5N 14 22E
Praha 52 50 5N 14 22E
Prahecq 44 46 19N 0 26W
Prahita, R. 97 19 0N 79 55E
Prahova □ 70 44 50N 25 50E
Prahova, R. 70 44 50N 25 50E
Prahova, Reg. 70 44 50N 25 50E
Prahovo 66 44 18N 22 39E
Praid 70 46 32N 25 10E
Prainha, Amazonas, Brazil 174 7 10S 60 30W
Prainha, Pará, Brazil 175 1 45S 53 30W
Prairie, Queens., Austral. 138 20 50S 144 35E
Prairie, S. Australia, Austral. 109 34 51S 138 49E
Prairie City 160 45 27N 118 44W
Prairie du Chien 158 43 1N 91 9W
Prairie, R. 159 34 45N 101 15W
Praja 102 8 39S 116 27E
Prajeczno 54 51 10N 19 0E
Pramánda 68 39 32N 21 8E
Pran Buri 100 12 23N 99 55E
Prang 121 8 1N 0 56W
Prapat 102 2 41N 98 58E
Praszka 54 51 32N 18 31E
Prata, Minas Gerais, Brazil 171 19 25S 49 0W
Prata, Pará, Brazil 170 1 10S 47 35W
Prática di Mare 64 41 40N 12 26E
Prato 62 43 53N 11 5E
Prátola Peligna 63 42 7N 13 51E
Pratovécchio 63 43 44N 11 43E
Prats-de-Molló 44 42 25N 2 27E
Pratt 159 37 40N 98 45W
Pratteln 50 47 31N 7 41E
Prättigau 51 46 56N 9 44E
Prattville 157 32 30N 86 28W
Pravara, R. 96 19 30N 74 28E
Pravdinsk 81 56 29N 43 28E
Pravia 56 43 30N 6 12W
Prawle Pt. 30 50 13N 3 41W
Pré-en-Pail 42 48 28N 0 12W
Pré St. Didier 62 45 45N 7 0E
Precordillera 172 30 0S 69 1W
Predáppio 63 44 7N 11 58E
Predazzo 63 46 19N 11 37E
Predejane 66 42 51N 22 9E
Preeceville 153 51 57N 102 40W
Prees 32 52 54N 2 40W
Preesall 32 53 55N 2 58W
Préfailles 42 47 9N 2 11W
Pregonero 174 8 1N 71 46W
Pregrada 63 46 11N 15 45E
Preko 63 44 7N 15 14E
Prelate 153 50 51N 109 24W
Prelog 63 46 18N 16 32E
Premier 152 56 4N 129 56W
Premier Downs 137 30 30S 126 30E
Premont 159 27 19N 91 8W
Premuda, I. 63 44 20N 14 36E
Prenj, mt. 66 43 33N 17 53E
Prenjasi 68 41 6N 20 32E
Prentice 158 45 31N 90 19W
Prenzlau 48 53 19N 13 51E
Prepansko Jezero 68 40 45N 21 0E
Preparis I. 99 14 55N 93 45E
Preparis North Channel 101 15 12N 93 40E
Preparis South Channel 101 14 36N 93 40E
Prerov 53 49 28N 17 27E
Prescot 32 53 27N 2 49W
Prescott, Can. 150 44 45N 75 30W
Prescott, Ariz., U.S.A. 161 34 35N 112 30W
Prescott, Ark., U.S.A. 159 33 49N 93 22W
Preservation Inlet 143 46 8S 166 35E
Preševo 66 42 19N 21 39E
Presho 158 43 56N 100 4W
Preshute 28 51 24N 1 45W
Presicce 65 39 53N 18 13E
Presidencia de la Plaza 172 27 0S 60 0W
Presidencia Roque Sáenz Peña 172 26 45S 60 30W
Presidente Dutra 164 5 15S 44 30W
Presidente Epitácio 171 21 46S 52 6W
Presidente Hayes □ 172 24 0S 59 0W
Presidente Hermes 174 11 0S 61 55W
Presidente Prudente 173 22 5S 51 25W
Presidente Rogue Saena Peña 172 34 33S 58 30W
Presidio, Mexico 164 29 29N 104 23W
Presidio, U.S.A. 159 29 30N 104 20W
Preslav 67 43 10N 26 52E
Prespa, L. = Prepansko Jezero 68 40 45N 21 0E
Prespa, mt. 67 41 44N 25 0E
Presque Isle 151 46 40N 68 0W
Prestatyn 31 53 20N 3 24W
Prestea 120 5 22N 2 7W
Presteigne 31 52 17N 3 0W
Preštice 52 49 34N 13 20E
Preston, Borders, U.K. 35 55 48N 2 18W
Preston, Dorset, U.K. 28 50 38N 2 26W
Preston, Lancs., U.K. 32 53 46N 2 42W
Preston, Idaho, U.S.A. 160 42 0N 112 0W
Preston, Minn., U.S.A. 158 43 39N 92 3W
Preston, Nev., U.S.A. 160 38 59N 115 2W
Preston, C. 136 20 51S 116 12E
Prestonpans 35 55 58N 3 0W
Prestwich 32 53 32N 2 18W
Prestwick 34 55 30N 4 38W
Prêto, R., Bahia 170 11 21S 43 52W
Pretoria 129 25 44S 28 12E
Prettyboy Res. 162 39 37N 76 43W
Preuilly-sur-Claise 42 46 51N 0 56E
Préveza 69 38 57N 20 47E
Préveza □ 68 39 20N 20 40E
Prey-Veng 101 11 35N 105 29E
Priazovskoye 82 46 22N 35 28E
Pribilov Is. 12 56 0N 170 0W
Priboj 66 43 35N 19 32E
Pribram 52 49 41N 14 2E
Price 160 39 40N 110 48W
Price I. 152 52 23N 128 41W
Prichalnaya 83 48 57N 44 33E
Priego 58 40 38N 2 21W
Priego de Córdoba 57 37 27N 4 12W
Priekule 80 57 27N 21 45E
Prieska 128 29 40S 22 42E
Priest Gully Cr. 108 27 29S 153 11E
Priest L. 160 48 30N 116 55W
Priest River 160 48 11N 117 0W
Priest Valley 163 36 10N 120 39W
Priestly 152 54 8N 125 20W
Prievidza 53 48 46N 18 36E
Prijedor 63 44 58N 16 41E
Prijepolje 66 43 27N 19 40E
Prilep 66 41 21N 21 37E
Priluki 80 50 30N 32 15E
Prime Seal I. 138 40 3S 147 43E
Primeira Cruz 170 2 30S 43 26W
Primorsko 67 42 15N 27 44E
Primorsko-Akhtarsk 82 46 2N 38 10E
Primrose L. 153 54 55N 109 45W
Prince Albert 153 53 15N 105 50W
Prince Albert Nat. Park 153 54 0N 106 25W
Prince Albert Pen. 148 72 30N 116 0W
Prince Alfred C. 12 74 20N 124 40W
Prince Charles I. 149 67 47N 76 12W
Prince Edward I. □. 151 44 2N 77 20W
Prince Edward Is. 11 45 15S 39 0E
Prince Frederick 162 38 33N 76 35W
Prince George 152 53 50N 122 50W
Prince of Wales, C. 147 65 50N 168 0W
Prince of Wales I. 147 73 0N 99 0W
Prince of Wales, I. 147 53 30N 131 30W
Prince of Wales Is. 135 10 40S 142 10E
Prince Patrick I. 12 77 0N 120 0W
Prince Regent Inlet 12 73 0N 90 0W
Prince Rupert 152 54 20N 130 20W
Prince William Sd. 147 60 20N 146 30W
Princenhage 47 51 9N 4 45E
Princes Risborough 29 51 43N 0 50W
Princesa Isabel 170 7 44S 38 0W
Princess Anne 162 38 12N 75 41W
Princess Charlotte B. 138 14 25S 144 0E
Princess Mary Ranges 136 15 30S 125 30E
Princess Royal I. 152 53 0N 128 40W
Princeton, Can. 152 49 27N 120 30W
Princeton, Ill., U.S.A. 158 41 25N 89 25W
Princeton, Ind., U.S.A. 156 38 20N 87 35W
Princeton, Ky., U.S.A. 156 37 6N 87 55W
Princeton, Mo., U.S.A. 158 40 23N 93 35W
Princeton, N.J., U.S.A. 162 40 18N 74 40W
Princeton, W. Va., U.S.A. 156 37 21N 81 8W
Princetown 30 50 33N 4 0W
Principe Chan. 152 53 28N 130 0W
Principe da Beira 174 12 20S 64 30W
Principe, I. de 114 1 37N 7 27E
Prineville 160 44 17N 120 57W
Prins Albert 128 33 12S 22 2E
Prins Harald Kyst 13 70 0S 35 1E
Prinzapolca 166 13 20N 83 35W
Prior, C. 56 43 34N 8 17W
Pripet Marshes = Polesye 80 52 0N 28 10E
Pripet, R. = Pripyat, R. 80 51 30N 30 0E
Pripyat, R. 80 51 30N 30 0E
Prislop, Pasul 70 47 37N 25 15E
Pristen 81 51 15N 12 40E
Priština 66 42 40N 21 13E
Pritchard 157 30 47N 88 5W
Pritzwalk 48 53 10N 12 11E
Privas 45 44 45N 4 37E
Priverno 64 41 29N 13 10E
Privolzhsk 81 57 9N 14 9E
Privolzhskaya Vozvyshennost 81 51 0N 46 0E
Privolzhskiy 81 51 25N 46 3E
Privolzhye 81 52 52N 48 33E
Privutnoye 83 47 12N 43 30E
Prizren 66 42 13N 20 45E
Prizzi 64 37 44N 13 24E
Prnjavor 66 44 52N 17 43E
Probolinggo 103 7 46S 113 13E
Probus 30 50 17N 4 55W
Prochowice 54 51 17N 16 20E

Procida, I Qattâra, Munkhafed el

Procida, I. 64 40 46N 14 0 E
Proctor 162 43 40N 73 2W
Proddatur 97 14 45N 78 30 E
Proença-a-Nova 57 39 45N 7 54W
Profondeville 47 50 23N 4 52 E
Progreso 165 21 20N 89 40W
Prokhladnyy 83 43 50N 44 2 E
Prokletije 68 42 30N 19 45 E
Prokopyevsk 76 54 0N 87 3 E
Prokuplje 66 43 16N 21 36 E
Proletarskaya 83 46 42N 41 50 E
Prome = Pyè 99 18 45N 95 30 E
Prophet, R. 152 58 48N 122 40W
Propriá 170 10 13 S 36 51W
Propriano 45 41 41N 8 52 E
Proserpine 138 20 21 S 148 36 E
Prospect, Austral. 109 34 53 S 138 36 E
Prospect, U.S.A. 162 43 18N 75 9W
Prosser 160 46 11N 119 52W
Prostějov 53 49 30N 17 9 E
Proston 139 26 14 S 151 32 E
Proszowice 54 50 13N 20 16 E
Protection 159 37 16N 99 30W
Próti, I. 69 37 5N 21 32 E
Provadija 67 43 12N 27 30 E
Proven 47 50 54N 2 40 E
Provence 45 43 40N 5 46 E
Providence, Ky., U.S.A. 156 37 25N 87 46W
Providence, R.I., U.S.A. 162 41 41N 71 15W
Providence Bay 150 45 41N 82 15W
Providence C. 143 45 59 S 166 29 E
Providence Mts. 161 35 0N 115 30W
Providencia 174 0 28 S 76 28W
Providencia, I. de 166 13 25N 81 26W
Provideniya 77 64 23N 173 18 E
Province Wellesley 101 5 15N 100 20 E
Provincetown 162 42 5N 70 11W
Provins 43 48 33N 3 15 E
Provo 160 40 16N 111 37W
Provost 153 52 25N 110 20W
Prozor 66 43 50N 17 34 E
Prudentópolis 171 25 12 S 50 57W
Prudhoe 35 54 57N 1 52W
Prudhoe Bay, Austral. 138 21 30 S 149 30W
Prudhoe Bay, U.S.A. 147 70 20N 148 20W
Prudhoe I. 138 21 23 S 149 45 E
Prudhoe Land 12 78 1N 65 0W
Prud'homme 153 52 20N 105 54W
Prudnik 54 50 20N 17 38 E
Prüm 49 50 14N 6 22 E
Pruszcz 54 54 17N 19 40 E
Pruszków 54 52 9N 20 49 E
Prut, R. 70 46 3N 28 10 E
Prvič, I. 63 44 55N 14 47 E
Prvomay 67 42 8N 25 17 E
Prydz B. 13 69 0 S 74 0 E
Pryor 159 36 17N 95 20W
Przasnysz 54 53 2N 20 45 E
Przedbórz 54 51 6N 19 53 E
Przedecz 54 52 20N 18 53 E
Przemyśl 54 49 50N 22 45 E
Przemyśl □ 54 80 0N 23 0 E
Przeworsk 54 50 6N 22 32 E
Przewóz 54 51 28N 14 57 E
Przhevalsk 85 42 30N 78 20 E
Przysucha 54 51 22N 20 38 E
Psakhná 69 38 34N 23 35 E
Psarà, I. 69 38 37N 25 38 E
Psathoúra, I. 68 39 30N 24 12 E
Psel, R. 82 49 25N 33 50 E
Pserimos, I. 69 36 56N 27 12 E
Pskem, R. 85 41 38N 70 1 E
Pskemskiy Khrebet 85 42 0N 70 45 E
Pskent 85 40 54N 69 20 E
Pskov 80 57 50N 28 25 E
Psunj, mt. 66 45 25N 17 19 E
Pszczyna 54 49 59N 18 58 E
Pteleón 69 39 3N 22 57 E
Ptich, R. 80 52 30N 28 45 E
Ptolemais 68 40 30N 21 43 E
Ptuj 63 46 28N 15 50 E
Ptujska Gora 63 46 23N 15 47 E
Pua 100 19 11N 100 55 E
Puán 172 37 30 S 63 0W
P'uan 108 25 47N 104 57 E
Puan 107 35 44N 126 7 E
Pubnico 151 43 47N 65 50W
Pucallpa 174 8 25 S 74 30W
P'uchen 107 37 21N 118 1 E
P'uch'eng 109 27 45N 118 47 E
Pucheni 70 45 12N 25 17 E
P'uch'i 109 29 43N 113 53 E
Pucisce 63 43 22N 16 43 E
Puck 54 54 45N 18 23 E
Puddletown 28 50 45N 2 21W
Pudsey 33 53 47N 1 40W
Pudukkottai 97 10 28N 78 47 E
Puebla 165 19 0N 98 10W
Puebla □ 165 18 30N 98 0W
Puebla de Alcocer 57 38 59N 5 14W
Puebla de Don Fadrique 59 37 58N 2 25W
Puebla de Don Rodrigo 57 39 5N 4 37W
Puebla de Guzmán 57 37 37N 7 15W
Puebla de los Infantes, La 57 37 47N 5 24W
Puebla de Montalbán, La 56 39 52N 4 22W
Puebla de Sanabria 56 42 4N 6 38W
Puebla de Trives 56 42 20N 7 10W
Puebla del Caramiñal 56 42 37N 8 56W
Puebla, La 58 39 50N 3 0 E
Pueblo 158 38 20N 104 40W
Pueblo Bonito 161 36 4N 107 57W
Pueblo Hundido 172 26 20 S 69 30W
Pueblo Nuevo 174 8 26N 71 26W
Pueblonuevo 55 38 16N 5 16W
Puelches 172 38 5 S 66 0W
Puelén 172 37 32 S 67 38W
Puente Alto 172 33 32 S 70 35W
Puente del Arzobispo 56 39 48N 5 10W
Puente Genil 57 37 22N 4 47W
Puente la Reina 58 42 40N 1 49W
Puentearas 56 42 10N 8 28W
Puentedeume 56 43 24N 8 10W
Puentes de García Rodríguez 56 43 27N 7 51W
Puerco, R. 161 35 10N 109 45W
Puerh 105 23 11N 100 56 E
P'uerh 108 23 5N 101 5 E
Puerhching 105 47 43N 86 53 E
Puerta, La 59 38 22N 2 45W
Puerto Aisén 176 45 10 S 73 0W
Puerto Angel 165 15 40N 96 29W
Puerto Arista 165 15 56N 93 48W
Puerto Armuelles 166 8 20N 83 10W
Puerto Ayacucho 174 5 40N 67 35W
Puerto Barrios 166 15 40N 88 40W
Puerto Bermejo 172 26 55 S 58 34W
Puerto Bermúdez 174 10 20 S 75 0W
Puerto Bolívar 174 3 10 S 79 55W
Puerto Cabello 174 10 28N 68 1W
Puerto Cabezas 166 14 0N 83 30W
Puerto Cabo Gracias a Dios 166 15 0N 83 10W
Puerto Capaz = Jebba 118 35 11N 4 43W
Puerto Carreño 174 6 12N 67 22W
Puerto Casado 172 22 19 S 57 56W
Puerto Castilla 166 16 0N 86 0W
Puerto Chicama 174 7 45 S 79 20W
Puerto Coig 176 50 54 S 69 15W
Puerto Columbia 174 10 59N 74 58W
Puerto Cortés, C. Rica 166 8 20N 82 20W
Puerto Cortés, Hond. 166 15 51N 88 0W
Puerto Cuemani 174 0 5N 73 21W
Puerto Cumarebo 174 11 29N 69 21W
Puerto de Cabras 116 28 40N 13 30W
Puerto de Morelos 165 20 49N 86 52W
Puerto de Santa María 57 36 36N 6 13W
Puerto Deseado 176 47 45 S 66 0W
Puerto Heath 174 12 25 S 68 45W
Puerto Huitoto 174 0 18N 74 3W
Puerto Juárez 165 21 11N 86 49W
Puerto La Cruz 174 10 13N 64 38W
Puerto Leguízamo 174 0 12 S 74 46W
Puerto Libertad 164 29 55N 112 41W
Puerto Limón, Meta, Colomb. 174 3 23N 73 30W
Puerto Limón, Putumayo, Colomb. 174 1 3N 76 30W
Puerto Lobos 176 42 0 S 65 3W
Puerto López 174 4 5N 72 58W
Puerto Lumbreras 59 37 34N 1 48W
Puerto Madryn 176 42 48 S 65 4W
Puerto Maldonado 174 12 30 S 69 10W
Puerto Manotí 166 21 22N 76 50W
Puerto Mazarrón 59 37 34N 1 15W
Puerto Mercedes 174 1 11N 72 53W
Puerto Montt 176 41 22 S 72 40W
Puerto Natales 176 51 45 S 72 25W
Puerto Nuevo 174 5 53N 69 56W
Puerto Ordaz 174 8 16N 62 44W
Puerto Padre 166 21 13N 76 35W
Puerto Páez 174 6 13N 67 28W
Puerto Peñasco 164 31 20N 113 33W
Puerto Pinasco 172 22 43 S 57 50W
Puerto Pirámides 176 42 35 S 64 20W
Puerto Plata 167 19 40N 70 45W
Puerto Princesa 94 9 44N 118 44 E
Puerto Quellón 176 43 7 S 73 37W
Puerto Quepos 166 9 29N 84 6W
Puerto Real 57 36 33N 6 12W
Puerto Rico 174 1 54N 75 10W
Puerto Rico ■ 147 18 15N 66 45W
Puerto Rico Trough 14 20 0N 63 0W
Puerto Sastre 172 22 25 S 57 55W
Puerto Suárez 174 18 58 S 57 52W
Puerto Tejada 174 3 14N 76 24W
Puerto Umbria 174 0 52N 76 33W
Puerto Vallarta 164 20 26N 105 15W
Puerto Villamizar 174 8 25N 72 30W
Puerto Wilches 174 7 21N 73 54W
Puertollano 57 38 43N 4 7W
Puertomarín 56 42 48N 7 37W
Pueyrredón, L. 176 47 20 S 72 0W
Puffin I., Ireland 39 51 50N 10 25W
Puffin I., U.K. 31 53 19N 4 1W
Pugachev 81 52 0N 48 55 E
Puge 126 4 45 S 33 11 E
Puget Sd. 160 47 15N 123 30W
Puget-Théniers 45 43 58N 6 53 E
Púglia 65 41 0N 16 30 E
Pugŏdong 107 42 5N 130 0 E
Pugu 126 6 55 S 39 4 E
Puha 142 38 30 S 177 50 E
P'uhsien 106 36 25N 110 4 E
Puhute Mesa 163 37 25N 116 50W
Pui 70 45 30N 23 4 E
Puieşti 70 46 25N 27 33 E
Puig Mayor, Mte. 58 39 49N 2 47 E
Puigcerdá 58 42 24N 1 50 E
Puigmal, Mt. 58 42 23N 2 7 E
Puisaye, Collines de 43 47 34N 3 28 E
Puiseaux 43 48 11N 2 30 E
Pujon-chosuji 107 40 35N 127 35 E
Puka 68 42 2N 19 53 E
Pukaki L. 143 44 4 S 170 1 E
Pukatawagan 153 55 45N 101 20W
Pukchin 107 40 12N 125 45 E
Pukchŏng 107 40 14N 128 18 E
Pukearuhe 142 38 55 S 174 31 E
Pukekohe 142 37 12 S 174 55 E
Puketeraki Ra. 143 42 58 S 172 13 E
Pukeuri 143 45 4 S 171 2 E
P'uko 108 27 27N 102 34 E
Pukoo 147 21 4N 156 48W
P'uk'ou 109 32 7N 118 43 E
Pula 64 39 0N 9 0 E
Pula (Pola) 63 44 54N 13 57 E
Pulaski, N.Y., U.S.A. 162 43 32N 76 9W
Pulaski, Tenn., U.S.A. 157 35 10N 87 0W
Pulaski, Va., U.S.A. 156 37 4N 80 49W
Pulawy 54 51 23N 21 59 E
Pulborough 29 50 58N 0 30W
Pulgaon 96 20 44N 78 21 E
Pulham Market 29 52 25N 1 15 E
Pulham St. Mary 29 52 25N 1 14 E
Pulicat, L. 97 13 40N 80 15 E
Puliyangudi 97 9 11N 77 24 E
Pullabooka 141 33 44 S 147 46 E
Pullen Cr. 108 27 33 S 152 54 E
Pullman 160 46 49N 117 10W
Pulmakong 121 11 2N 0 2 E
Pulog, Mt. 103 16 40N 120 50 E
Puloraja 102 4 55N 95 24 E
Pułtusk 54 52 43N 21 6 E
Pumlumon Fawr 31 52 29N 3 47W
Pumpsaint 31 52 3N 3 58W
Puna 174 19 45 S 65 28W
Puna de Atacama 172 25 0 S 67 0W
Puná, I. 174 2 55 S 80 5W
Punakha 98 27 42N 89 52 E
Punalur 97 9 0N 76 56 E
Punasar 94 27 6N 73 6 E
Punata 174 17 25 S 65 50W
Punch 95 33 48N 74 4 E
Pune 96 18 29N 73 57 E
Pungsan 107 40 50N 128 9 E
P'uning 109 23 19N 116 9 E
Punjab □ 94 31 0N 76 0 E
Punkatawagon 153 55 44N 101 20W
Puno 174 15 55 S 70 3W
Punt, La 51 46 35N 9 56 E
Punta Alta 176 38 53 S 62 4W
Punta Arenas 176 53 0 S 71 0W
Punta de Díaz 172 28 0 S 70 45W
Punta de Piedras 174 10 54N 64 6W
Punta del Lago Viedma 176 49 45 S 72 0W
Punta Gorda, Belize 165 16 10N 88 45W
Punta Gorda, U.S.A. 157 26 55N 82 0W
Punta Prieta 164 28 58N 114 17W
Puntabie 139 32 12 S 134 5 E
Puntarenas 166 10 0N 84 50W
Puntes de García Rodríguez 56 43 27N 7 50W
Punto Fijo 174 11 42N 70 13W
Punxsutawney 156 40 56N 79 0W
P'upei 108 22 16N 109 33 E
Puquio 174 14 45 S 74 10W
Pur, R. 76 65 30N 77 40 E
Purace, vol. 174 2 21N 76 23W
Puračić 66 44 33N 18 28 E
Purari, R. 135 7 49 S 145 0 E
Purbeck, Isle of 28 50 40N 2 5W
Purcell 159 35 0N 97 25W
Purchena Tetica 59 37 21N 2 21W
Purdy Is. 138 3 0 S 146 0 E
Purfleet 29 51 29N 0 15 E
Puri 96 19 50N 85 58 E
Purificación 174 3 51N 74 55W
Purísima, La 164 26 10N 112 4W
Purley 28 51 29N 1 4W
Purli 96 18 50N 76 35 E
Purmerend 47 52 30N 4 58 E
Purna, R. 96 19 55N 76 20 E
Purnea 95 25 45N 87 31 E
Pursat 101 12 34N 103 50 E
Puruey 174 7 35N 64 48W
Purukcahu 102 0 35 S 114 35 E
Purulia 95 23 17N 86 33 E
Purus, R. 174 5 25 S 64 0W
Purwakarta 103 6 35 S 107 29 E
Purwodadi, Jawa, Indon. 103 7 7 S 110 55 E
Purwodadi, Jawa, Indon. 103 7 51 S 110 0 E
Purworejo 103 7 43 S 110 2 E
Puryŏng 107 42 0N 129 43 E
Pus, R. 96 19 50N 77 45 E
Pusad 96 19 56N 77 36 E
Pusan 107 35 5N 129 0 E
Pushchino 77 54 20N 158 10 E
Pushkin 80 59 45N 30 25 E
Pushkino 81 51 16N 47 9 E
Puskitamika L. 150 49 20N 76 30W
Püspökladány 53 47 19N 21 6 E
Pussa 129 24 30 S 33 55 E
Pustoshka 80 56 11N 29 30 E
Puszczykowo 54 52 18N 16 49 E
Putahow L. 153 59 54N 100 40W
Putao 98 27 28N 97 30 E
Putaruru 142 38 2 S 175 50 E
Putbus 48 54 19N 13 29 E
Put'ehach'i 105 48 0N 122 43 E
Puţeni 70 45 49N 27 42 E
Puthein Myit, R. 99 15 56N 94 18 E
P'ut'ien 109 25 27N 118 59 E
Putignano 65 40 50N 17 5 E
P'uting 108 26 19N 105 45 E
Putlitz 48 53 15N 12 3 E
Putna 70 47 50N 25 33 E
Putna, R. 70 45 42N 27 26 E
Putnam 162 41 55N 71 55W
Putnok 53 48 18N 20 26 E
P'ut'o 109 29 58N 122 15 E
Putorana, Gory 77 69 0N 95 0 E
Putorino 142 39 4 S 177 9 E
Putta 47 51 4N 4 38 E
Puttalam 93 8 1N 79 55 E
Puttalam Lagoon 97 8 15N 79 45 E
Putte 47 51 22N 4 24 E
Putten 46 52 16N 5 36 E
Puttgarden 48 54 28N 11 15 E
Puttur 97 12 46N 75 12 E
Putty 141 32 57 S 150 42 E
Putumayo □ 174 1 30 S 70 0W
Putumayo, R. 174 1 30 S 70 0W
Putussibau, G. 102 0 45N 113 50 E
Pututahi 142 38 39 S 177 53 E
Puurs 47 51 5N 4 17 E
Puy-de-Dôme 44 45 46N 2 57 E
Puy-de-Dôme □ 44 45 47N 3 0 E
Puy-de-Sancy 44 45 32N 2 41 E
Puy Guillaume 44 45 57N 3 28 E
Puy, Le 44 45 3N 3 52 E
Puy l'Evêque 44 44 31N 1 9 E
Puyallup 160 47 10N 122 22W
P'uyang 106 35 41N 115 0 E
Puylaurens 44 43 35N 2 0 E
Puyôo 44 43 33N 0 56W
Pwalagu 121 10 38N 0 50W
Pwani □, Tanz. 126 7 0 S 39 0 E
Pwani □, Tanz. 126 7 0 S 39 30 E
Pweto 127 8 25 S 28 51 E
Pwinbyu 98 20 23N 94 40 E
Pwllheli 31 52 54N 4 26W
Pya Ozero 78 66 8N 31 22 E
Pyana, R. 81 55 30N 45 0 E
Pyandzh 85 37 14N 69 6 E
Pyandzh, R. 85 37 6N 68 20 E
Pyapon 98 16 5N 95 50 E
Pyasina, R. 77 72 30N 90 30 E
Pyatigorsk 83 44 2N 43 0 E
Pyatikhatki 82 48 28N 33 38 E
Pyaye 98 19 12N 95 10 E
Pyè 98 18 49N 95 13 E
Pyinbauk 98 19 10N 95 12 E
Pyinmana 98 19 45N 96 20 E
Pyŏktong 107 40 37N 125 26 E
Pyŏnggang 107 38 24N 127 17 E
Pyŏngtaek 107 37 1N 127 4 E
P'yŏngyang 107 39 0N 125 45 E
Pyote 159 31 34N 103 5W
Pyramid L. 160 40 0N 119 30W
Pyramid Pk. 163 36 25N 116 37W
Pyramids 122 29 58N 31 9 E
Pyrenees 44 42 45N 0 18 E
Pyrénées-Atlantiques □ 44 43 15N 1 0W
Pyrénées-Orientales □ 44 42 35N 2 26 E
Pyrzyce 54 53 10N 14 55 E
Pyshchug 81 58 57N 45 27 E
Pyshma, R. 84 57 8N 66 18 E
Pytalovo 80 57 5N 27 55 E
Python 127 17 56 S 29 10 E
Pyttegga 71 62 13N 7 42 E
Pyu 98 18 30N 96 35 E
Pyzdry 54 52 11N 17 42 E

Q

Qaar Zeitun 122 29 10N 25 48 E
Qabalon 90 32 8N 35 17 E
Qabatiya 90 32 25N 35 16 E
Qadam 93 32 55N 66 45 E
Qadhimah 92 22 20N 39 13 E
Qadian 94 31 51N 74 19 E
Qal at Shajwa 122 25 2N 38 57 E
Qala-i-Jadid (Spin Baldak) 94 31 1N 66 25 E
Qala-i-Kirta 93 32 15N 63 0 E
Qala Nau 93 35 0N 63 5 E
Qala Punja 93 37 0N 72 40 E
Qala Yangi 94 34 20N 66 30 E
Qal'at al Akhdhar 92 28 0N 37 10 E
Qal'at Saura 122 26 10N 38 40 E
Qal'eh Shaharak 93 34 10N 64 20 E
Qalqīlya 90 32 12N 34 58 E
Qalyûb 122 30 12N 31 11 E
Qam 90 32 36N 35 43 E
Qamar, Ghubbat al 91 16 20N 52 30 E
Qamruddin Karez 94 31 45N 68 20 E
Qana 90 33 12N 35 17 E
Qâra 122 29 38N 26 30 E
Qara Qash, R. 95 35 45N 78 45 E
Qara Tagh La = Kala Shank'ou 95 35 42N 78 20 E
Qarachuk 92 37 0N 42 2 E
Qarah 92 29 55N 40 3 E
Qardud 123 10 20N 29 56 E
Qarrasa 123 14 38N 32 5 E
Qarsa 123 9 28N 41 48 E
Qaşr Bū Hadi 119 31 1N 16 45 E
Qasr-e-Qand 93 26 15N 60 45 E
Qasr Farâfra 122 27 0N 28 1 E
Qastina 90 31 44N 34 45 E
Qatar ■ 93 25 30N 51 15 E
Qattâra 122 30 12N 27 3 E
Qattara Depression = Q. Munkhafed el 122 29 30N 27 30 E
Qattâra, Munkhafed el 122 29 30N 27 30 E

Qayen Rancharia

Qayen 93 33 40N 59 10 E
Qazvin 92 36 15N 50 0 E
Qena 122 26 10N 32 43 E
Qena, Wadi 122 26 57N 32 50 E
Qendrevca 68 40 20N 19 48 E
Qesari 90 32 30N 34 53 E
Qeshm 93 26 55N 56 10 E
Qeshm, I. 93 26 50N 56 0 E
Qila Safed 93 29 0N 61 30 E
Qila Saifulla 94 30 45N 68 17 E
Qiryat 'Anivim 90 31 49N 35 7 E
Qiryat Bialik 90 32 50N 35 5 E
Qiryat 'Eqron 90 31 52N 34 49 E
Qiryat Hayyim 90 32 49N 35 4 E
Qiryat Shemona 90 33 13N 35 35 E
Qiryat Yam 90 32 51N 35 4 E
Qishon, R. 90 32 42N 35 7 E
Qishran 122 20 14N 40 2 E
Qizan 123 16 57N 42 34 E
Qom 93 34 40N 51 0 E
Quabbin Res. 162 42 17N 72 21W
Quabbo 123 12 2N 39 56 E
Quackenbrück 48 52 40N 7 59 E
Quadring 33 52 53N 0 9W
Quainton 29 51 51N 0 53W
Quairading 137 32 0 S 117 21 E
Quakerstown 162 40 27N 75 20W
Qualeup 137 33 48 S 116 48 E
Quambatook 138 35 49 S 143 34 E
Quambone 141 30 57 S 147 53 E
Quan Long 101 9 7N 105 8 E
Quanan 159 34 20N 99 45W
Quandialla 141 34 1 S 147 47 E
Quang Nam 101 15 55N 108 15 E
Quang Ngai 101 15 13N 108 58 E
Quang Yen 100 21 3N 106 52 E
Quantock Hills, The 28 51 8N 3 10W
Quaraí 172 30 15 S 56 20W
Quarré les Tombes 43 47 21N 4 0 E
Quarryville 162 39 54N 76 10W
Quartu Sant' Elena 64 39 15N 9 10 E
Quartzsite 161 33 44N 114 16W
Quatsino 152 50 30N 127 40W
Quatsino Sd. 152 50 42N 127 58W
Qubab = Mishmar Aiyalon 90 31 52N 34 57 E
Qūchān 93 37 10N 58 27 E
Que Que 127 18 58 S 29 48 E
Queanbeyan 141 35 17 S 149 14 E
Québec 151 46 52N 71 13W
Québec □ 151 50 0N 70 0W
Quedlinburg 48 51 47N 11 9 E
Queen Alexandra Ra. 13 85 0 S 170 0 E
Queen Anne 162 38 55N 75 57W
Queen Bess Mt. 152 51 13N 124 35W
Queen Charlotte 152 53 15N 132 2W
Queen Charlotte Is. 152 53 20N 132 10W
Queen Charlotte Sd. 143 41 10 S 174 15 E
Queen Charlotte Str. 152 51 0N 128 0W
Queen Elizabeth Is. 10 78 0N 95 0W
Queen Elizabeth Nat. Pk. 126 0 0 S 30 0 E
Queen Mary Coast 13 70 0 S 95 0 E
Queen Maud G. 148 68 15N 102 30W
Queenborough 29 51 24N 0 46 E
Queen's Chan. 136 15 0 S 129 30 E
Queensbury 32 53 46N 1 50W
Queenscliff 138 38 16 S 144 39 E
Queensferry 35 56 0N 3 25W
Queensland □ 138 15 0 S 142 0 E
Queenstown, Austral. 138 42 4 S 145 35 E
Queenstown, N.Z. 143 45 1 S 168 40 E
Queenstown, S. Afr. 125 31 52 S 26 52 E
Queguay Grande, R. 172 32 9 S 58 9W
Queimadas 170 11 0 S 39 38W
Quela 124 9 10 S 16 56 E
Quelimane 127 17 53 S 36 58 E
Quemado, N. Mex., U.S.A. 161 34 17N 108 28W
Quemado, Tex., U.S.A. 159 28 58N 100 35W
Quemoy, I. = Chinmen Tao, I. 109 24 25N 118 25 E
Quemú-Quemú 172 36 3 S 63 36W
Quendale, B. of 36 59 53N 1 20W
Quequén 172 38 30 S 58 30W
Querein 123 13 30N 34 50 E
Querétaro 164 20 40N 100 23W
Querétaro □ 164 20 30N 100 30W
Querfurt 48 51 22N 11 33 E
Quesada 59 37 51N 3 4W
Quesnel 152 53 5N 122 30W
Quesnel L. 152 52 30N 121 20W
Quesnel, R. 152 52 58N 122 29W
Quest, Pte. 151 49 52N 64 40W
Questa 161 36 45N 105 35W
Questembert 42 47 40N 2 28W
Quetico 150 48 45N 90 55W
Quetico Prov. Park 150 48 30N 91 45W
Quetta 93 30 15N 66 55 E
Quetta □ 93 30 15N 66 55 E
Quezaltenango 166 14 40N 91 30W
Quezon City 103 14 38N 121 0 E
Qui Nhon 101 13 40N 109 13 E
Quiaca, La 172 22 5 S 65 35W
Quibaxi 124 8 24 S 14 27 E
Quibdó 174 5 42N 76 40W
Quiberon 42 47 29N 3 9W
Quíbor 174 9 56N 69 37W
Quick 152 54 36N 126 54W
Quickborn 48 53 42N 9 52 E
Quiet L. 152 61 5N 133 5W
Quiévrain 47 50 24N 3 41 E
Quiindy 172 25 58 S 57 14W
Quila 164 24 23N 107 13W
Quilán, C. 176 43 15 S 74 30W
Quilengues 125 14 12 S 14 12 E
Quilimarí 172 32 5 S 70 30W
Quilino 172 30 14 S 64 29W
Quillabamba 174 12 50 S 72 50W
Quillagua 172 21 40 S 69 40W
Quillaicillo 172 31 17 S 71 40W
Quillan 44 42 53N 2 10 E
Quillebeuf 42 49 28N 0 30 E
Quillota 172 32 54 S 71 16W
Quilmes 172 34 43 S 58 15W
Quilon 97 8 50N 76 38 E
Quilpie 139 26 35 S 144 11 E
Quilpué 172 33 5 S 71 33W
Quilty 39 52 50N 9 27W
Quilua 127 16 17 S 39 54 E
Quimilí 172 27 40 S 62 30W
Quimper 42 48 0N 4 9W
Quimperlé 42 47 53N 3 33W
Quin 39 52 50N 8 52W
Quinag 36 58 13N 5 5W
Quincy, Calif., U.S.A. 160 39 56N 121 0W
Quincy, Fla., U.S.A. 157 30 34N 84 34W
Quincy, Ill., U.S.A. 158 39 55N 91 20W
Quincy, Mass., U.S.A. 162 42 14N 71 0W
Quincy, Wash., U.S.A. 160 47 22N 119 56W
Quines 172 32 13 S 65 48W
Quinga 127 15 49 S 40 15 E
Quingey 43 47 7N 5 52 E
Quinhagak 147 59 45N 162 0W
Quintana de la Serena 57 38 45N 5 40W
Quintana Roo □ 165 19 0N 88 0W
Quintanar de la Orden 58 39 36N 3 5W
Quintanar de la Sierra 58 41 57N 2 55W
Quintanar del Rey 59 39 21N 1 56W
Quintero 172 32 45 S 71 30W
Quintin 42 48 26N 2 56W
Quinto 58 41 25N 0 32W
Quinyambie 139 30 15 S 141 0 E
Quípar, R. 59 37 58N 2 3W
Quirihue 172 36 15 S 72 35W
Quirindi 141 31 28 S 150 40 E
Quiriquire 174 9 59N 63 13W
Quiroga 56 42 28N 7 18W
Quirpon I. 151 51 32N 55 28W
Quisiro 174 10 53N 71 17W
Quissac 45 43 55N 4 0 E
Quissanga 127 12 24 S 40 28 E
Quitilipi 172 26 50 S 60 13W
Quitman, Ga., U.S.A. 157 30 49N 83 35W
Quitman, Miss., U.S.A. 157 32 2N 88 42W
Quitman, Tex., U.S.A. 159 32 48N 95 25W
Quito 174 0 15 S 78 35W
Quixadá 170 4 55 S 39 0W
Quixaxe 127 15 17 S 40 4 E
Quixeramobim 170 5 12 S 39 17W
Qul'ân, Jazâ'ir 122 24 22N 35 31 E
Qumran 90 31 43N 35 27 E
Quneitra 90 33 7N 35 48 E
Quoich L. 36 57 4N 5 20W
Quoile, R. 38 54 21N 5 40W
Quoin I. 136 14 54 S 129 32 E
Quoin Pt., N.Z. 143 46 19 S 170 11 E
Quoin Pt., S. Afr. 128 34 46 S 19 37 E
Quondong 140 33 6 S 140 18 E
Quorn, Austral. 140 32 25 S 138 0 E
Quorn, Can. 150 49 25N 90 55W
Quorndon 28 52 45N 1 10W
Qûs 122 25 55N 32 50 E
Quseir 122 26 7N 34 16 E
Qusra 90 32 5N 35 20 E
Quthing 129 30 25 S 27 36 E
Quynh Nhai 100 21 49N 103 33 E
Qytet Stalin (Kuçove) 68 40 47N 19 57 E

R

Ra, Ko 101 9 13N 98 16 E
Raa. 73 56 0N 12 45 E
Råa 73 56 0N 12 45 E
Raahana 90 32 12N 34 52 E
Raahe 74 64 40N 24 28 E
Raalte 46 52 23N 6 16 E
Raamsdonksveer 47 51 43N 4 52 E
Raasay I. 36 57 25N 6 4W
Raasay, Sd. of 36 57 30N 6 8W
Rab 63 44 45N 14 45 E
Rab, I. 63 44 45N 14 45 E
Raba 103 8 36 S 118 55 E
Rába, R. 54 47 38N 17 38 E
Rabaçal, R. 56 41 41N 7 15W
Rabah 121 13 5N 5 30 E
Rabai 126 3 50 S 39 31 E
Rabaraba 135 9 58 S 149 49 E
Rabastens 44 43 50N 1 43 E
Rabastens, Hautes Pyrénées 44 43 25N 0 10 E
Rabat 118 34 2N 6 48W
Rabaul 135 4 24 S 152 18 E
Rabbalshede 73 58 40N 11 27 E
Rabbit L. 153 47 0N 79 38W
Rabbit Lake 153 53 8N 107 46W
Rabbit, R. 152 59 41N 127 12W
Rabbitskin, R. 152 61 47N 120 42W
Rabigh 92 22 50N 39 5 E
Rabka 54 49 37N 19 59 E
Rača 66 44 14N 21 0 E
Răcale 65 39 57N 18 6 E
Racalmuto 64 37 25N 13 41 E
Racconigi 62 44 47N 7 41 E
Race, C. 151 46 40N 53 5W
Raceview 108 27 38 S 152 47 E
Rach Gia 101 10 5N 105 5 E
Raciaz 54 52 46N 20 10 E
Racibórz (Ratibor) 54 50 7N 18 18 E
Racine 156 42 41N 87 51W
Rackheath 29 52 41N 1 22 E
Rackwick 37 58 52N 3 23W
Radama, Is. 129 14 0 S 47 47 E
Radama, Presqu'ile d' 129 14 16 S 47 53 E
Radan, mt. 66 42 59N 21 29 E
Radbuza, R. 52 49 35N 13 5 E
Radcliffe, Gr. Manch., U.K. 32 53 35N 2 19W
Radcliffe, Notts., U.K. 33 52 57N 1 3W
Rade 71 59 21N 10 53 E
Radeburg 48 51 6N 13 45 E
Radeče 63 46 5N 15 14 E
Radekhov 80 50 25N 24 32 E
Radford 156 37 8N 80 32W
Radhanpur 94 23 50N 71 38 E
Radika, R. 66 41 38N 20 37 E
Radisson 153 52 30N 107 20W
Radium Hill 133 32 30 S 140 42 E
Radium Hot Springs 152 50 48N 116 12W
Radkow 54 50 30N 16 24 E
Radley 28 51 42N 1 14W
Radlin 54 50 3N 18 29 E
Radna 66 46 7N 21 41 E
Radnevo 67 42 17N 25 58 E
Radnice 52 49 51N 13 35 E
Radnor (□) 26 52 20N 3 20W
Radnor Forest 31 52 17N 3 10W
Radom 54 51 23N 21 12 E
Radom □ 54 51 30N 21 0 E
Radomir 66 42 37N 23 4 E
Radomsko 54 51 5N 19 28 E
Radomyshl 80 50 30N 29 12 E
Radomysl Wielki 54 50 14N 21 15 E
Radoszyce 54 51 4N 20 15 E
Radoviš 66 41 38N 22 28 E
Radovljica 63 46 22N 14 12 E
Radöy I. 71 60 40N 4 55 E
Radstadt 52 47 24N 13 28 E
Radstock 28 51 17N 2 25W
Radstock, C. 139 33 12 S 134 20 E
Raduša 66 42 7N 21 15 E
Radviliškis 80 55 49N 23 33 E
Radville 153 49 30N 104 15W
Radymno 54 49 59N 22 52 E
Radyr 31 51 32N 3 16W
Radzanów 54 52 56N 20 8 E
Radziejów 54 52 40N 18 30 E
Radzyn Chełminski 54 53 23N 18 55 E
Rae 152 62 50N 116 3W
Rae Bareli 95 26 18N 81 20 E
Rae Isthmus 149 66 40N 87 30W
Raeside, L. 137 29 20 S 122 0 E
Raetihi 142 39 25 S 175 17 E
Rafaela 172 31 10 S 61 30W
Rafah 122 31 18N 34 14 E
Rafai 126 4 59N 23 58 E
Raffadali 64 37 23N 13 29 E
Rafhā 92 29 35N 43 35 E
Rafid 90 32 57N 35 52 E
Rafsanjān 93 30 30N 56 5 E
Raft Pt. 136 16 4 S 124 26 E
Ragag 123 10 59N 24 40 E
Ragama 93 7 0N 79 50 E
Ragged Mt. 137 33 27 S 123 25 E
Raglan, Austral. 138 23 42 S 150 49 E
Raglan, N.Z. 142 37 55 S 174 55 E
Raglan, U.K. 31 51 46N 2 51W
Ragueneau 151 49 11N 68 18W
Ragunda 72 63 6N 16 23 E
Ragusa 65 36 56N 14 42 E
Raha 103 8 20 S 118 40 E
Rahad el Berdi 117 11 20N 23 40 E
Rahad, Nahr er 123 12 40N 35 30 E
Rahden 48 52 26N 8 36 E
Raheita 123 12 46N 43 4 E
Raheng = Tak 100 17 5N 99 10 E
Rahimyar Khan 94 28 30N 70 25 E
Rahotu 142 39 20 S 173 49 E
Raichur 96 16 10N 77 20 E
Raiganj 95 25 37N 88 10 E
Raigarh, Madhya Pradesh, India 96 21 56N 83 25 E
Raigarh, Orissa, India 96 19 51N 82 6 E
Raiis 92 23 33N 38 43 E
Raijua 103 10 37 S 121 36 E
Railton 138 41 25 S 146 28 E
Rainbow 140 35 55 S 142 0 E
Rainbow Lake 152 58 30N 119 23W
Rainham 29 51 22N 0 36 E
Rainier 160 46 4N 123 0W
Rainier, Mt. 160 46 50N 121 50W
Rainworth 33 53 8N 1 6W
Rainy L. 153 48 30N 92 30W
Rainy River 153 48 50N 94 30W
Raipur 96 21 17N 81 45 E
Raith 150 48 50N 90 0W
Raj Nandgaon 99 21 0N 81 0 E
Raja Empat, Kepulauan 103 0 30 S 129 40 E
Raja-Jooseppi 74 68 28N 28 29 E
Raja, Ujung 102 3 40N 96 25 E
Rajahmundry 96 17 1N 81 48 E
Rajang, R. 102 2 30N 113 30 E
Rajapalaiyarm 97 9 25N 77 35 E
Rajasthan □ 94 26 45N 73 30 E
Rajasthan Canal 94 30 31N 71 0 E
Rajauri 95 33 25N 74 21 E
Rajbari 98 23 47N 89 41 E
Rajgarh, Mad. P., India 94 24 2N 76 45 E
Rajgarh, Raj., India 94 28 40N 75 25 E
Rajgród 54 53 42N 22 42 E
Rajhenburg 63 46 1N 15 29 E
Rajkot 94 22 15N 70 56 E
Rajmahal Hills 95 24 30N 87 30 E
Rajnandgaon 96 21 5N 81 5 E
Rajojooseppi 74 68 25N 28 30 E
Rajpipla 96 21 50N 73 30 E
Rajpura 94 30 32N 76 32 E
Rajshahi 98 24 22N 88 39 E
Rajshahi □ 95 25 0N 89 0 E
Rakaia 143 43 45 S 172 1 E
Rakaia, R. 143 43 26 S 171 47 E
Rakan, Ras 93 26 10N 51 20 E
Rakaposhi 95 36 10N 74 0 E
Rakaposhi, mt. 93 36 20N 74 30 E
Rakha 122 18 25N 41 30 E
Rakhni 94 30 4N 69 56 E
Rakitovo 67 41 59N 24 5 E
Rakkestad 71 59 25N 11 21 E
Rakoniewice 54 52 10N 16 16 E
Rakops 128 21 1 S 24 28 E
Rákospalota 53 47 30N 19 5 E
Rakovica 63 44 59N 15 38 E
Rakovník 52 50 6N 13 42 E
Rakovski 67 42 21N 24 57 E
Raleigh, Can. 150 49 30N 92 5W
Raleigh, U.S.A. 150 35 46N 78 38W
Raleigh B. 157 34 50N 76 15W
Ralja 66 44 33N 20 34 E
Ralls 159 33 40N 101 20W
Ralston 162 41 30N 76 57W
Rām Allāh 90 31 55N 35 10 E
Ram Hd. 141 37 47 S 149 30 E
Ram, R. 152 62 1N 123 41W
Rama, Israel 90 32 56N 35 21 E
Rama, Nic. 166 12 9N 84 15W
Ramacca 65 37 24N 14 40 E
Ramachandrapuram 96 16 50N 82 4 E
Ramadi 92 33 28N 43 15 E
Ramales de la Victoria 58 43 15N 3 28W
Ramalho, Serra do 171 13 45 S 44 0W
Raman 101 6 29N 101 18 E
Ramanathapuram 97 9 25N 78 55 E
Ramanetaka, B. de 129 14 13 S 47 52 E
Ramas C. 97 15 5N 73 55 E
Ramat Gan 90 32 4N 34 48 E
Ramatlhabama 128 25 37 S 25 33 E
Ramban 95 33 14N 75 12 E
Rambervillers 43 48 20N 6 38 E
Rambipudji 103 8 12 S 113 37 E
Rambla, La 57 37 37N 4 45W
Rambouillet 43 48 40N 1 48 E
Rambre Kyun 98 19 0N 94 0 E
Ramdurg 97 15 58N 75 22 E
Rame Head 30 50 19N 4 14W
Ramechhap 95 27 25N 86 10 E
Ramelau, Mte. 103 8 55 S 126 22 E
Ramenskoye 81 55 32N 38 15 E
Ramgarh, Bihar, India 95 23 40N 85 35 E
Ramgarh, Rajasthan, India 94 27 16N 75 14 E
Ramgarh, Rajasthan, India 94 27 30N 70 36 E
Ramhormoz 92 31 15N 49 35 E
Ramla 90 31 55N 34 52 E
Ramlat Zalṭan 119 28 30N 19 30 E
Ramlu Mt. 123 13 32N 41 40 E
Ramme 73 56 30N 8 11 E
Rammun 90 31 55N 35 17 E
Ramna Stacks, Is. 36 60 40N 1 20W
Ramnad = Ramanathapuram 97 9 25N 78 55 E
Ramnagar 95 32 47N 75 18 E
Ramnäs 72 59 46N 16 12 E
Ramon 81 52 8N 39 21 E
Ramona 163 33 1N 116 56W
Ramor L. 38 53 50N 7 5W
Ramore 150 48 30N 80 25W
Ramos Arizpe 164 23 35N 100 59W
Ramos, R. 164 25 35N 105 3W
Ramoutsa 128 24 50 S 25 52 E
Rampart 147 65 0N 150 15W
Rampside 32 54 6N 3 10W
Rampur, H.P., India 94 31 26N 77 43 E
Rampur, M.P., India 94 23 25N 73 53 E
Rampur, Orissa, India 96 21 48N 83 58 E
Rampur, U.P., India 94 28 50N 79 5 E
Rampura 94 24 30N 75 27 E
Rampurhat 95 24 10N 87 50 E
Ramsbottom 32 53 36N 2 20W
Ramsbury 28 51 26N 1 37W
Ramsel 47 51 2N 4 50 E
Ramsele 74 63 31N 16 27 E
Ramsey, Can. 150 47 25N 82 20W
Ramsey, Cambs., U.K. 29 52 27N 0 6W
Ramsey, Essex, U.K. 29 51 55N 1 12 E
Ramsey, I. of M., U.K. 32 54 20N 4 21W
Ramsgate 29 51 20N 1 25 E
Ramshai 98 26 44N 88 51 E
Rämshyttan 72 60 17N 15 15 E
Ramsjö 72 62 11N 15 37 E
Ramtek 96 21 20N 79 15 E
Ramu, R. 135 4 0 S 144 41 E
Ramvik 72 62 49N 17 51 E
Ranaghat 95 23 15N 88 35 E
Ranahu 94 25 55N 69 45 E
Ranau 102 6 2N 116 40 E
Rancagua 172 34 10 S 70 50W
Rance 47 50 9N 4 16 E
Rance, R. 42 48 34N 1 59W
Rancharia 171 22 15 S 50 55W

Rancheria, R **Rennell Sd**

Rancheria, R.	**152**	60 13N	129 7W
Ranchester	**160**	44 57N	107 12W
Ranchi	**95**	23 19N	85 27E
Rancu	**70**	44 32N	24 15E
Rand	**141**	35 33S	146 32E
Randallstown	**162**	39 22N	76 48W
Randalstown	**38**	54 45N	6 20W
Randan	**44**	46 2N	3 21E
Randazzo	**65**	37 53N	14 56E
Randböl	**73**	55 43N	9 17E
Randers	**73**	56 29N	10 1E
Randers Fjord	**73**	56 37N	10 20E
Randfontein	**129**	26 8S	27 45E
Randolph, Mass., U.S.A.	**162**	42 10N	71 3W
Randolph, Utah, U.S.A.	**160**	41 43N	111 10W
Randolph, Vt., U.S.A.	**162**	43 55N	72 39W
Randsburg	**163**	35 26N	117 44W
Randsfjord	**71**	60 15N	10 25E
Råne älv	**74**	66 26N	21 10E
Råneå	**74**	65 53N	22 18E
Ranfurly	**143**	45 7S	170 6E
Rangae	**101**	6 19N	101 44E
Rangamati	**98**	22 38S	92 12E
Rangataua	**142**	39 26S	175 28E
Rangaunu B.	**142**	34 51S	173 15E
Rångedala	**73**	57 47N	13 9E
Rangeley	**156**	44 58N	70 33W
Rangely	**160**	40 3N	108 53W
Ranger	**159**	32 30N	98 42W
Rangia	**98**	26 15N	91 20E
Rangiora	**143**	43 19S	172 36E
Rangitaiki	**130**	38 52S	176 23E
Rangitaiki, R.	**142**	37 54S	176 49E
Rangitata, R.	**143**	43 45S	171 15E
Rangitikei, R.	**142**	40 17S	175 15E
Rangitoto Range	**142**	38 25S	175 35E
Rangkasbitung	**103**	6 22S	106 16E
Rangon	**99**	16 45N	96 20E
Rangon, R.	**99**	16 28N	96 40E
Rangoon	**98**	16 45N	96 20E
Rangpur	**98**	25 42N	89 22E
Rangsit	**100**	13 59N	100 37E
Ranibennur	**97**	14 35N	75 30E
Raniganj	**95**	23 40N	87 15E
Ranipet	**97**	12 56N	79 23E
Raniwara	**93**	24 50N	72 10E
Ranken, R.	**138**	20 31S	137 36E
Rankin	**159**	31 16N	101 56W
Rankin Inlet	**148**	62 30N	93 0W
Rankin's Springs	**141**	33 49S	146 14E
Rannes	**138**	24 6S	150 11E
Rannoch L.	**37**	56 41N	4 20W
Rannoch Moor	**34**	56 38N	4 48W
Rannoch Sta.	**37**	56 40N	4 32W
Ranobe, B. de	**129**	23 3S	43 33E
Ranohira	**129**	22 29S	45 24E
Ranomafana, Tamatave, Madag.	**129**	18 57S	48 50E
Ranomafana, Tuléar, Madag.	**129**	24 34S	47 0E
Ranong	**101**	9 56N	98 40E
Rantau	**102**	4 15N	98 5E
Rantauprapat	**102**	2 15N	99 50E
Rantemario	**103**	3 15S	119 57E
Rantis	**90**	32 4N	35 3E
Rantoul	**156**	40 18N	88 10W
Ranum	**73**	56 54N	9 14E
Ranwanlenau	**128**	19 37S	22 49E
Raon-l' Étape	**43**	48 24N	6 50E
Raoui, Erg er	**118**	29 0N	2 0W
Rapa Iti, I.	**131**	27 35S	144 20W
Rapallo	**62**	44 21N	9 12E
Rapang	**103**	3 45S	119 55E
Rāpch	**93**	25 40N	59 15E
Raphoe	**38**	54 52N	7 36W
Rapid City	**158**	44 0N	103 0W
Rapid, R.	**152**	59 15N	129 5W
Rapid River	**156**	45 55N	87 0W
Rapides des Joachims	**150**	46 13N	77 43W
Rapla	**80**	58 88N	24 52E
Rapness	**37**	59 15N	2 51W
Raposos	**171**	19 57S	43 48W
Rappahannock, R.	**162**	37 35N	76 17W
Rapperswil	**51**	47 14N	8 45E
Raqqa	**92**	36 0N	38 55E
Raquete	**127**	14 8S	38 13E
Raquette Lake	**162**	43 49N	74 40W
Rareagh	**38**	53 37N	8 37W
Rarotonga, I.	**131**	21 30S	160 0W
Ras al Khaima	**93**	25 50N	56 5E
Ra's Al-Unūf	**119**	30 25N	18 15E
Ra's at Tannurah	**92**	26 40N	50 10E
Ras Dashan, mt.	**123**	13 8N	37 45E
Ras el Ma	**118**	34 26N	0 50W
Ras Gharib	**122**	28 6N	33 18E
Ras Mallap	**122**	29 18N	32 50E
Rasa, Punta	**176**	40 50S	62 15W
Rasboda	**72**	60 8N	16 58E
Raseiniai	**80**	55 25N	23 5E
Rashad	**123**	11 55N	31 0E
Rashîd	**122**	31 21N	30 22E
Rashîd, Masabb	**122**	31 22N	30 17E
Rasht	**92**	37 20N	49 40E
Rasi Salai	**100**	15 20N	104 9E
Rasipuram	**97**	11 30N	78 25E
Raška	**66**	43 19N	20 39E
Raso, C.	**170**	1 50N	50 0W
Rason, L.	**137**	28 45S	124 25E
Raşova	**70**	44 15N	27 55E
Rasovo	**67**	43 42N	23 17E
Rasra	**95**	25 50N	83 50E
Rass el Oued	**119**	35 57N	5 2E
Rasskazovo	**81**	52 35N	41 50E
Rastatt	**49**	48 50N	8 12E
Rastu	**70**	43 53N	23 16E
Raszków	**54**	51 43N	17 40E
Rat Buri	**100**	13 30N	99 54E
Rat, Is.	**147**	51 50N	178 15E
Rat, R.	**152**	56 0N	99 30W
Rat River	**152**	61 7N	112 36W
Rätan	**72**	62 27N	14 33E
Ratangarh	**94**	28 5N	74 35E
Rath	**95**	25 36N	79 37E
Rath Luirc (Charleville)	**39**	52 21N	8 40W
Rathangan	**39**	53 13N	7 0W
Rathconrah	**38**	53 30N	7 32W
Rathcoole	**39**	53 17N	6 29W
Rathcormack	**39**	52 5N	8 19W
Rathdowney	**39**	52 52N	7 36W
Rathdrum, Ireland	**39**	52 57N	6 13W
Rathdrum, U.S.A.	**160**	47 50N	116 58W
Ratheclaung	**98**	20 29N	92 45E
Rathen	**37**	57 38N	1 58W
Rathenow	**48**	52 38N	12 23E
Rathfriland	**38**	54 12N	6 12W
Rathkeale	**39**	52 32N	8 57W
Rathkenny	**38**	53 45N	6 39W
Rathlin I.	**38**	55 18N	6 14W
Rathlin O'Birne I.	**38**	54 40N	8 50W
Rathmelton	**38**	55 3N	7 35W
Rathmolyon	**38**	53 30N	6 49W
Rathmore, Cork, Ireland	**39**	51 30N	9 21W
Rathmore, Kerry, Ireland	**39**	52 5N	9 12W
Rathmore, Kildare, Ireland	**39**	53 13N	6 35W
Rathmullen	**38**	55 6N	7 32W
Rathnure	**39**	52 30N	6 47W
Rathvilly	**72**	52 54N	6 42W
Ratlam	**94**	23 20N	75 0E
Ratnagiri	**96**	16 57N	73 18E
Ratnapura	**97**	6 40N	80 20E
Ratoath	**38**	53 30N	6 27W
Raton	**159**	37 0N	104 30W
Rattaphum	**101**	7 8N	100 16E
Ratten	**52**	47 28N	15 44E
Rattray	**37**	56 36N	3 20W
Rattray Hd.	**37**	57 38N	1 50W
Rättvik	**72**	60 52N	15 7E
Ratz, Mt.	**152**	57 23N	132 12W
Ratzeburg	**48**	53 41N	10 46E
Raub	**101**	3 47N	101 52E
Rauch	**172**	36 45S	59 5W
Raufarhöfn	**74**	66 27N	15 57W
Raufoss	**71**	60 44N	10 37E
Raukumara Ra.	**142**	38 5S	177 55E
Raul Soares	**171**	20 5S	42 22W
Rauland	**71**	59 43N	8 0E
Rauma	**75**	61 10N	21 30E
Rauma, R.	**71**	62 34N	7 43E
Raundal	**71**	60 40N	6 37E
Raunds	**29**	52 20N	0 32W
Raung, Mt.	**103**	8 8S	114 4E
Raurkela	**96**	22 14N	84 50E
Rava Russkaya	**80**	50 15N	23 42E
Ravanusa	**64**	37 16N	13 58E
Ravar	**93**	31 20N	56 51E
Ravels	**47**	51 22N	5 0E
Ravena	**162**	42 28N	73 49W
Ravenglass	**32**	54 21N	3 25W
Ravenna, Italy	**63**	44 28N	12 15E
Ravenna, U.S.A.	**158**	41 3N	98 58W
Ravensburg	**49**	47 48N	9 38E
Ravenshoe	**138**	17 37S	145 29E
Ravenstein	**46**	51 47N	5 39E
Ravensthorpe	**137**	33 35S	120 2E
Ravenstonedale	**32**	54 26N	2 26W
Ravenswood, Austral.	**138**	20 6S	146 54E
Ravenswood, U.S.A.	**156**	38 58N	81 47W
Ravensworth	**141**	32 26S	151 4E
Raventasón	**174**	6 10S	81 0W
Ravi, R.	**94**	31 0N	73 0E
Ravna Gora	**63**	45 24N	14 50E
Ravna Reka	**66**	43 59N	21 35E
Ravnstrup	**73**	56 27N	9 17E
Rawa Mazowiecka	**54**	51 46N	20 12E
Rawalpindi	**94**	33 38N	73 8E
Rawalpindi □	**93**	33 10N	72 50E
Rawāndūz	**92**	36 40N	44 30E
Rawang	**101**	3 20N	101 35E
Rawdon	**150**	46 3N	73 40W
Rawene	**142**	35 25S	173 32E
Rawicz	**54**	51 36N	16 52E
Rawlinna	**137**	30 58S	125 28E
Rawlins	**160**	41 50N	107 20W
Rawlinson Range	**137**	24 40S	128 30E
Rawmarsh	**33**	53 27N	1 20W
Rawson	**176**	43 15S	65 0W
Rawtenstall	**32**	53 42N	2 18W
Rawuya	**121**	12 10N	6 50E
Ray, N. Mex., U.S.A.	**159**	35 57N	104 8W
Ray, N.D., U.S.A.	**158**	48 21N	103 6W
Ray, C.	**151**	47 33N	59 15W
Ray Mts.	**147**	66 0N	152 10W
Rayachoti	**97**	14 4N	78 50E
Rayadrug	**97**	14 40N	76 50E
Rayagada	**96**	19 15N	83 20E
Raychikhinsk	**77**	49 46N	129 25E
Rayevskiy	**84**	54 4N	54 56E
Rayin	**93**	29 40N	57 22E
Rayleigh	**29**	51 36N	0 38E
Raymond, Can.	**152**	49 30N	112 35W
Raymond, Calif., U.S.A.	**163**	37 13N	119 54W
Raymond, Wash., U.S.A.	**160**	46 45N	123 48W
Raymond Terrace	**141**	32 45S	151 44E
Raymondville	**159**	26 30N	97 50W
Raymore	**153**	51 25N	104 31W
Rayne	**159**	30 16N	92 16W
Rayón	**164**	29 43N	110 35W
Rayong	**100**	12 40N	101 20E
Rayville	**159**	32 30N	91 45W
Raz, Pte. du	**42**	48 2N	4 47W
Razana	**66**	44 6N	19 55E
Razanj	**66**	43 40N	21 31E
Razdelna	**67**	43 13N	27 41E
Razelm, Lacul	**70**	44 50N	29 0E
Razgrad	**67**	43 33N	26 34E
Razlog	**67**	41 53N	23 28E
Razmak	**94**	32 45N	69 50E
Razole	**96**	16 56N	81 48E
Razor Back Mt.	**152**	51 32N	125 0W
Ré, Île de	**44**	46 12N	1 30W
Rea, L.	**39**	53 10N	8 32W
Reading, U.K.	**29**	51 27N	0 57W
Reading, U.S.A.	**162**	40 20N	75 53W
Realicó	**172**	35 0S	64 15W
Réalmont	**44**	43 48N	2 10E
Ream	**101**	10 34N	103 39E
Reata	**164**	26 8N	101 5W
Reay	**37**	58 33N	3 48W
Rebais	**43**	48 50N	3 10E
Rebecca L.	**137**	30 0S	122 30E
Rebi	**103**	5 30S	134 7E
Rebiana	**117**	24 12N	22 10E
Rebun-Tō	**112**	45 23N	141 2E
Recanati	**63**	43 24N	13 32E
Recaş	**66**	45 46N	21 30E
Recess	**38**	53 29N	9 4W
Recherche, Arch. of the	**137**	34 15S	122 50E
Rechitsa	**80**	52 13N	30 15E
Recht	**47**	50 20N	6 3E
Recife	**170**	8 0S	35 0W
Recklinghausen	**48**	51 36N	7 10E
Reconquista	**172**	29 10S	59 45W
Recreo	**172**	29 25S	65 10W
Reculver	**29**	51 22N	1 12E
Recz	**54**	53 16N	15 31E
Red B.	**38**	55 4N	6 2W
Red Bank	**162**	40 21N	74 4W
Red Bay	**151**	51 44N	56 25W
Red Bluff	**160**	40 11N	122 11W
Red Bluff L.	**159**	31 59N	103 58W
Red Cliffs	**140**	34 19S	142 11E
Red Cloud	**158**	40 8N	98 33W
Red Creek	**162**	43 14N	76 45W
Red Deer	**152**	52 20N	113 50W
Red Deer L.	**153**	52 55N	101 20W
Red Deer, R.	**152**	50 58N	110 0W
Red Deer R.	**153**	52 53N	101 1W
Red Dial	**32**	54 48N	3 9W
Red Hook	**162**	41 55N	73 53W
Red Indian L.	**151**	48 35N	57 0W
Red L.	**158**	48 0N	95 0W
Red Lake	**153**	51 1N	94 1W
Red Lake Falls	**158**	47 54N	96 30W
Red Lion	**162**	39 54N	76 36W
Red Lodge	**160**	45 10N	109 10W
Red Mountain	**163**	35 37N	117 38W
Red Oak	**158**	41 0N	95 10W
Red Point Rock	**137**	32 13S	127 32E
Red, R., Can.	**153**	50 24N	96 48W
Red, R., Minn., U.S.A.	**158**	48 10N	97 0W
Red, R., Tex., U.S.A.	**159**	33 57N	95 30W
Red, R. = Hong, R.	**100**	20 17N	106 34E
Red Rock	**150**	48 55N	88 15W
Red Rock, L.	**158**	41 30N	93 15W
Red Sea	**91**	25 0N	36 0E
Red Slate Mtn.	**163**	37 31N	118 52W
Red Sucker L	**153**	54 9N	93 40W
Red Tower Pass = Turnu Rosu P.	**70**	45 33N	24 17E
Red Wharf Bay	**31**	53 18N	4 10W
Red Wing	**158**	44 32N	92 35W
Reda	**54**	54 40N	18 19E
Rédange	**47**	49 46N	5 52E
Redbank	**108**	27 36S	152 52E
Redbridge	**29**	51 35N	0 7E
Redcar	**33**	54 37N	1 4W
Redcliff	**153**	50 10N	110 50W
Redcliffe	**139**	27 12S	153 0E
Redcliffe, Mt.	**137**	28 30S	121 30E
Redcliffs	**139**	34 16S	142 10E
Reddersburg	**128**	29 41S	26 10E
Redding	**160**	40 30N	122 25W
Redditch	**28**	52 18N	1 57W
Rede, R.	**35**	55 8N	2 12W
Redenção	**170**	4 13S	38 43W
Redesmouth	**35**	55 7N	2 12W
Redfield	**158**	45 0N	98 30W
Redhill	**29**	51 14N	0 10W
Redknife, R.	**152**	61 14N	119 22W
Redland	**37**	59 6N	3 4W
Redlands	**163**	34 0N	117 11W
Redlynch	**28**	50 59N	1 42W
Redmile	**33**	52 54N	0 48W
Redmire	**32**	54 19N	1 55W
Redmond, Austral.	**137**	34 55S	117 40E
Redmond, U.S.A.	**160**	44 19N	121 11W
Redon	**42**	47 40N	2 6W
Redonda, I.	**167**	16 58N	62 19W
Redondela	**56**	42 15N	8 38W
Redondo	**57**	38 39N	7 37W
Redondo Beach	**163**	33 52N	118 26W
Redrock Pt.	**152**	62 11N	115 2W
Redruth	**30**	50 14N	5 14W
Redvers	**153**	49 35N	101 40W
Redwater	**152**	53 55N	113 6W
Redwood City	**163**	37 30N	122 15W
Redwood Falls	**158**	44 30N	95 2W
Ree, L.	**38**	53 35N	8 0W
Reed City	**156**	43 52N	85 30W
Reed L.	**153**	54 38N	100 30W
Reed, Mt.	**151**	52 5N	68 5W
Reeder	**158**	47 7N	102 52W
Reedham	**29**	52 34N	1 33E
Reedley	**163**	36 36N	119 27W
Reedsburg	**158**	43 34N	90 5W
Reedsport	**160**	43 45N	124 4W
Reedy Creek	**140**	36 58S	140 2E
Reef Pt.	**142**	35 10S	173 5E
Reefton, N.S.W., Austral.	**141**	34 15S	147 27E
Reefton, S. Australia, Austral.	**109**	34 57S	138 55E
Reefton, N.Z.	**143**	42 6S	171 51E
Reepham	**29**	52 46N	1 6E
Reeth	**32**	54 23N	1 56W
Refsnes	**71**	61 9N	7 14E
Reftele	**73**	57 11N	13 35E
Refugio	**159**	28 18N	97 17W
Rega, R.	**54**	53 52N	15 16E
Regalbuto	**65**	37 40N	14 38E
Regar	**85**	38 30N	68 14E
Regavim	**90**	32 32N	35 2E
Regen	**49**	48 58N	13 9E
Regeneração	**170**	6 15S	42 41W
Regensburg	**49**	49 1N	12 7E
Regensdorf	**51**	47 26N	8 28E
Réggio di Calábria	**65**	38 7N	15 38E
Réggio nell' Emilia	**62**	44 42N	10 38E
Regina	**153**	50 30N	104 35W
Registan □	**93**	30 15N	65 0E
Registro	**173**	24 29S	47 49W
Reguengos de Monsaraz	**57**	38 25N	7 32W
Rehar	**95**	23 36N	82 52E
Rehoboth, Damaraland, Namibia	**128**	23 15S	17 4E
Rehoboth, Ovamboland, Namibia	**128**	17 55S	15 5E
Rehoboth Beach	**162**	38 43N	75 5W
Rehovot	**90**	31 54N	34 48E
Reichenbach, Ger.	**48**	50 36N	12 19E
Reichenbach, Switz.	**50**	46 38N	7 42E
Reid	**137**	30 49S	128 26E
Reid River	**138**	19 40S	146 48E
Reiden	**50**	47 14N	7 59E
Reidsville	**157**	36 21N	79 40W
Reigate	**29**	51 14N	0 11W
Reillo	**58**	39 54N	1 53W
Reims	**43**	49 15N	4 0E
Reina	**90**	32 43N	35 18E
Reina Adelaida, Arch.	**176**	52 20S	74 0W
Reinach, Aargau, Switz.	**50**	47 14N	8 11E
Reinach, Basel, Switz.	**50**	47 29N	7 35E
Reinbeck	**158**	42 18N	92 40W
Reindeer I.	**153**	52 30N	98 0W
Reindeer L.	**153**	57 15N	102 15W
Reindeer, R.	**153**	55 36N	103 11W
Reine, La	**150**	48 50N	79 30W
Reinga, C.	**142**	34 25S	172 43E
Reinosa	**56**	43 2N	4 15W
Reinosa, Paso	**56**	42 56N	4 10W
Reira	**123**	15 25N	34 50E
Reiss	**37**	58 29N	3 7W
Reisterstown	**162**	39 28N	76 50W
Reitdiep	**46**	53 20N	6 20E
Reitz	**129**	27 48S	28 29E
Reivilo	**128**	27 36S	24 8E
Rejmyra	**73**	58 50N	15 55E
Reka, R.	**63**	45 40N	14 0E
Rekovac	**66**	43 51N	21 3E
Remad, Ouedber	**118**	33 28N	1 20W
Remanso	**170**	9 41S	42 4W
Remarkable, Mt.	**140**	32 48S	138 10E
Rembang	**103**	6 42S	111 21E
Remchi	**118**	35 2N	1 26W
Remedios, Colomb.	**174**	7 2N	74 41W
Remedios, Panama	**166**	8 15N	81 50W
Remeshk	**93**	26 55N	58 50E
Remetea	**70**	46 45N	29 29E
Remich	**47**	49 32N	6 22E
Remiremont	**43**	48 0N	6 36E
Remo	**123**	6 48N	41 20E
Remontnoye	**83**	47 44N	43 37E
Remoulins	**45**	43 55N	4 35E
Remscheid	**48**	51 11N	7 12E
Remsen	**162**	43 19N	75 11W
Rena	**71**	61 8N	11 20E
Renda	**123**	14 30N	40 0E
Rende	**65**	39 19N	16 11E
Rendeux	**47**	50 14N	5 30E
Rendina	**69**	39 4N	21 58E
Rendsburg	**48**	54 18N	9 41E
Rene	**77**	66 2N	179 25W
Renee, oilfield	**19**	58 4N	0 16E
Renens	**50**	46 31N	6 34E
Renfrew, Can.	**150**	45 30N	76 40W
Renfrew, U.K.	**34**	55 52N	4 24W
Renfrew (□)	**26**	55 50N	4 30W
Rengat	**102**	0 30S	102 45E
Rengo	**172**	34 24S	70 50W
Reni	**82**	45 28N	28 15E
Renigunta	**97**	13 38N	79 30E
Renish Pt.	**36**	57 44N	6 59W
Renkum	**46**	51 58N	5 43E
Renmark	**140**	34 11S	140 43E
Rennell Sd.	**152**	53 23N	132 35W

Renner Springs Teleg. Off **Riverton**

Renner Springs Teleg. Off. 138 18 20 S 133 47 E
Rennes 42 48 7N 1 41W
Rennesøy 71 59 6N 5 43 E
Reno 160 39 30N 119 50W
Reno, R. 63 44 45N 11 40 E
Renovo 156 41 20N 77 47W
Rens 55 54 54N 9 5 E
Rensselaer, Ind., U.S.A. 156 41 0N 87 10W
Rensselaer, N.Y., U.S.A. 162 42 38N 73 41W
Rentería 58 43 19N 1 54W
Renton 160 47 30N 122 9W
Renwicktown 143 41 30 S 173 51 E
Réo 120 12 28N 2 35 E
Réole, La 44 44 35N 0 1W
Reotipur 95 25 33N 83 45 E
Repalle 97 16 2N 80 45 E
Répcelak 53 47 24N 17 1 E
Repton 28 52 50N 1 32W
Republic, Mich., U.S.A. 156 46 25N 87 59W
Republic, Wash., U.S.A. 160 48 38N 118 42W
Republican City 158 40 9N 99 20W
Republican, R. 158 40 0N 98 30W
Repulse B., Antarct. 13 64 30 S 99 30 E
Repulse B., Austral. 133 20 31 S 148 45 E
Repulse Bay 149 66 30N 86 30W
Requena, Peru 174 5 5 S 73 52W
Requena, Spain 59 39 30N 1 4W
Resele 72 63 20N 17 5 E
Resen 66 41 5N 21 0 E
Reserve, Can. 153 52 28N 102 39W
Reserve, U.S.A. 161 33 50N 108 54W
Resht = Rasht 92 37 20N 49 40 E
Resistencia 172 27 30 S 59 0W
Reşiţa 66 45 18N 21 53 E
Resko 54 53 47N 15 25 E
Resolution I., Can. 149 61 30N 65 0W
Resolution I., N.Z. 143 45 40 S 166 40 E
Resolven 31 51 43N 3 42W
Resplandes 170 6 17 S 45 13W
Resplendor 171 19 20 S 41 15W
Ressano Garcia 129 25 25 S 32 0 E
Rest Downs 141 31 48 S 146 21 E
Reston, Can. 153 49 33N 101 6W
Reston, U.K. 35 55 51N 2 11W
Restrepo 174 4 15N 73 33W
Reszel 54 54 4N 21 10 E
Retalhuleu 166 14 33N 91 46W
Reteag 70 47 10N 24 0 E
Retem, O. el 119 33 40N 0 40 E
Retenue, Lac de 127 11 0 S 27 0 E
Rethel 43 49 30N 4 20 E
Rethem 48 52 47N 9 25 E
Réthimnon 69 35 15N 24 40 E
Réthimnon □ 69 35 23N 24 28 E
Retie 47 51 16N 5 5 E
Rétiers 42 47 55N 1 25W
Retiro 172 35 59 S 71 47W
Retortillo 56 40 48N 6 21W
Rétság 53 47 58N 19 10 E
Reuland 47 50 12N 6 8 E
Réunion, Î. 11 22 0 S 56 0 E
Reus 58 41 10N 1 5 E
Reusel 47 51 21N 5 9 E
Reuss, R. 51 47 16N 8 24 E
Reuterstadt-Stavenhagen 48 53 41N 12 54 E
Reutlingen 49 48 28N 9 13 E
Reutte 52 47 29N 10 42 E
Reuver 47 51 17N 6 5 E
Revda 84 56 48N 59 57 E
Revel 44 43 28N 2 0 E
Revelganj 95 25 50N 84 40 E
Revelstoke 152 51 0N 118 0W
Revigny 43 48 50N 5 0 E
Revilla Gigedo, Is. de 131 18 40N 112 0W
Revillagigedo I. 152 55 50N 131 20W
Revin 43 49 55N 4 39 E
Revolyutsii, Pix 85 38 31N 72 21 E
Revuè, R. 127 19 30 S 33 35 E
Rewa 95 24 33N 81 25 E
Rewari 94 28 15N 76 40 E
Rex 147 64 10N 149 20W
Rexburg 160 43 45N 111 50W
Rey Bouba 117 8 40N 14 15 E
Rey Malabo 121 3 45N 8 50 E
Reyes, Pt. 163 37 59N 123 2W
Reykjahlið 74 65 40N 16 55W
Reykjanes 74 63 48N 22 40W
Reykjavík 74 64 10N 21 57 E
Reynolds 153 49 40N 95 55W
Reynolds Ra. 136 22 30 S 133 0 E
Reynosa 165 26 5N 98 18W
*Rezā'iyeh 92 37 40N 45 0 E
*Rezā'iyeh, Daryācheh-ye 92 37 30N 45 30 E
Rēzekne 80 56 30N 27 17 E
Rezh 84 57 23N 61 24 E
Rezina 70 47 45N 29 0 E
Rezovo 67 42 0N 28 0 E
Rgotina 67 44 1N 22 18 E
Rhaeadr Ogwen 31 53 8N 4 0W
Rharis, O. 119 26 30N 5 4 E
Rhayader 31 52 19N 3 30W
Rheden 46 52 0N 6 3 E
Rheidol, R. 31 52 25N 3 57W
Rhein 153 51 25N 102 15W
Rhein, R. 48 51 42N 6 20 E
Rheinbach 48 50 38N 6 54 E
Rheine 48 52 17N 7 25 E
Rheineck 51 47 28N 9 31 E
*Renamed Orumiyeh
Rheinfelden 50 47 32N 7 47 E
Rheinland-Pfalz □ 49 50 50N 7 0 E
Rheinsberg 48 53 6N 12 52 E
Rheinwaldhorn 51 46 30N 9 3 E
Rhenen 46 51 58N 5 33 E
Rheydt 48 51 10N 6 24 E
Rhin, R. 48 51 42N 6 20 E
Rhinau 43 48 19N 7 43 E
Rhine, R. = Rhein 47 51 42N 6 20 E
Rhinebeck 162 41 56N 73 55W
Rhinelander 158 45 38N 89 29W
Rhino Camp 126 3 0N 31 22 E
Rhisnes 47 50 31N 4 48 E
Rhiw 31 52 49N 4 37W
Rho 62 45 31N 9 2 E
Rhode Island □ 162 41 38N 71 37W
Rhodes = Ródhos 69 36 15N 28 10 E
Rhodes' Tomb 127 20 30 S 28 30 E
Rhodesia = Zimbabwe ■ 127 20 0 S 30 0 E
Rhodope Mts. = Rhodopi Planina 67 41 40N 24 20 E
Rhondda 31 51 39N 3 30W
Rhône □ 45 45 54N 4 35 E
Rhône, R. 45 43 28N 4 42 E
Rhos-on-Sea 31 53 18N 3 46W
Rhosllanerchrugog 31 53 3N 3 4W
Rhossilli 31 51 34N 4 18W
Rhu Coigach, C. 36 58 6N 5 27W
Rhuddlan 31 53 17N 3 28W
Rhum, I. 36 57 0N 6 20W
Rhyl 31 53 19N 3 29W
Rhymney 31 51 45N 3 17W
Rhynie 37 57 20N 2 50W
Ri-Aba 121 3 28N 8 40 E
Riachão 170 7 20 S 46 37W
Riachão do Jacuípe 171 11 48 S 39 21W
Riacho de Santana 171 13 37 S 42 57W
Rialma 171 15 18 S 49 34W
Rialto 163 34 6N 117 22W
Riang 98 27 31N 92 56 E
Riaño 56 42 59N 5 0W
Rians 45 43 37N 5 44 E
Riansares, R. 58 40 0N 3 0W
Riasi 95 33 10N 74 50 E
Riau □ 102 0 0 102 35 E
Riau, Kepulauan 102 0 30N 104 20 E
Riaza 58 41 18N 3 30W
Riaza, R. 58 41 16N 3 29W
Riba de Saelices 58 40 55N 2 18 E
Ribadavia 56 42 17N 8 8W
Ribadeo 56 43 35N 7 5W
Ribadesella 56 43 30N 5 7W
Ribamar 170 2 33 S 44 3W
Ribas 58 42 19N 2 15 E
Ribat 125 29 50N 60 55 E
Ribatejo □ 55 39 15N 8 30W
Ribble, R. 32 54 13N 2 20W
Ribe 73 55 19N 8 44 E
Ribe Amt □ 73 55 34N 8 30 E
Ribeauvillé 43 48 10N 7 20 E
Ribécourt 43 49 30N 2 55 E
Ribeira 56 42 36N 8 58W
Ribeira do Pombal 170 10 50 S 38 32W
Ribeirão Prêto 173 21 10 S 47 50W
Ribeiro Gonçalves 170 7 32 S 45 14W
Ribémont 43 49 47N 3 27 E
Ribera 64 37 30N 13 13 E
Ribérac 44 45 15N 0 20 E
Riberalta 174 11 0 S 66 0W
Ribnica 63 45 45N 14 45 E
Ribnitz-Dangarten 48 54 14N 12 24 E
Ričany 52 50 0N 14 40 E
Riccall 33 53 50N 1 4W
Riccarton 143 43 32 S 172 37 E
Riccia 65 41 30N 14 50 E
Riccione 63 44 0N 12 39 E
Rice Lake 158 45 30N 91 42W
Rich 118 32 16N 4 30W
Rich Hill 159 38 5N 94 22W
Richards B. 129 28 48 S 32 6 E
Richards Deep 15 25 0 S 73 0W
Richards L. 153 59 10N 107 10W
Richardson Mts. 143 44 49 S 168 34 E
Richardson, R. 153 58 25N 111 14W
Richardton 158 46 56N 102 22W
Riche, C. 137 34 36 S 118 47 E
Richelieu 42 47 0N 0 20 E
Richey 158 47 42N 105 5W
Richfield, Idaho, U.S.A. 160 43 2N 114 5W
Richfield, Utah, U.S.A. 161 38 50N 112 0W
Richfield Springs 162 42 51N 74 59W
Richibucto 151 46 42N 64 54W
Richland, Ga., U.S.A. 157 32 7N 84 40W
Richland, Oreg., U.S.A. 160 44 49N 117 9W
Richland, Wash., U.S.A. 160 46 15N 119 15W
Richland Center 158 43 21N 90 22W
Richlands 156 37 7N 81 49W
Richmond, N.S.W., Austral. 141 33 35 S 150 42 E
Richmond, Queens., Austral. 138 20 43 S 143 8 E
Richmond, N.Z. 143 41 4 S 173 12 E
Richmond, S. Afr. 125 29 51 S 30 18 E
Richmond, N. Yorks., U.K. 33 54 24N 1 43W
Richmond, Surrey, U.K. 29 51 28N 0 18W
Richmond, Calif., U.S.A. 163 38 0N 122 21W
Richmond, Ind., U.S.A. 156 39 50N 84 50W
Richmond, Ky., U.S.A. 156 37 40N 84 20W
Richmond, Mo., U.S.A. 158 39 15N 93 58W
Richmond, Tex., U.S.A. 159 29 32N 95 42W
Richmond, Va., U.S.A. 162 37 33N 77 27W
Richmond Gulf 150 56 20N 75 50W
Richmond, Mt. 143 41 32 S 173 22 E
Richmond, Ra. 139 29 0 S 152 45 E
Richmond Ra. 143 41 32 S 173 22 E
Richterswil 51 47 13N 8 43 E
Richton 157 31 23N 88 58W
Richwood 156 38 17N 80 32W
Rickmansworth 29 51 38N 0 28W
Ricla 58 41 31N 1 24W
Riddarhyttan 72 59 49N 15 33 E
Ridderkerk 46 51 52N 4 35 E
Riddes 50 46 11N 7 14 E
Ridgecrest 163 35 38N 117 40W
Ridgedale 153 53 0N 104 10W
Ridgefield 162 41 17N 73 30W
Ridgeland 157 32 30N 80 58W
Ridgelands 138 23 16 S 150 17 E
Ridgetown 150 42 26N 81 52W
Ridgewood 162 40 59N 74 7W
Ridgway 156 41 25N 78 43W
Riding Mt. Nat. Park 153 50 50N 100 0W
Ridley Mt. 137 33 12 S 122 7 E
Ridsdale 35 55 9N 2 8W
Ried 52 48 14N 13 30 E
Riehen 50 47 35N 7 39 E
Riel 47 51 31N 5 1 E
Rienne 47 50 0N 4 53 E
Rienza, R. 63 46 49N 11 47 E
Riesa 48 51 19N 13 19 E
Riesi 65 37 16N 14 4 E
Rietfontein 128 26 44 S 20 1 E
Rieti 63 42 23N 12 50 E
Rieupeyroux 44 44 19N 2 12 E
Rievaulx 33 54 16N 1 7W
Riez 45 43 49N 6 6 E
Rifle 160 39 40N 107 50W
Rifstangi 74 66 32N 16 12W
Rift Valley 126 0 20N 36 0 E
Rig Rig 117 14 13N 14 25 E
Riga 80 56 53N 24 8 E
Riga, G. of = Rīgas Jūras Līcis 80 57 40N 23 45 E
Rīgas Jūras Līcis 80 57 40N 23 45 E
Rigby 160 43 41N 111 58W
Riggins 160 45 29N 116 26W
Rignac 44 44 25N 2 16 E
Rigo 138 9 41 S 147 31 E
Rigolet 151 54 10N 58 23W
Riihimäki 75 60 45N 24 48 E
Riiser-Larsen halvøya 13 68 0 S 35 0 E
Riishiri-Tō 112 45 11N 141 15 E
Rijau 121 11 8N 5 17 E
Rijeka Crnojevica 66 42 24N 19 1 E
Rijeka (Fiume) 63 45 20N 14 21 E
Rijen 47 51 35N 4 55 E
Rijkevorsel 47 51 21N 4 46 E
Rijn, R. 47 52 5N 4 50 E
Rijnsberg 46 52 11N 4 27 E
Rijsbergen 47 51 31N 4 41 E
Rijssen 46 52 19N 6 30 E
Rijswijk 46 52 4N 4 22 E
Rike 123 10 50N 39 53 E
Rikita 123 5 5N 28 29 E
Rila 67 42 7N 23 7 E
Rila Planina 66 42 10N 23 30 E
Rillington 33 54 10N 0 41W
Rilly 43 49 11N 4 3 E
Rima 99 28 35N 97 5 E
Rima, R. 121 13 15N 5 15 E
Rimavská Sobota 53 48 22N 20 2 E
Rimbey 152 52 35N 114 15W
Rimbo 72 59 44N 18 21 E
Rimforsa 73 58 8N 15 42 E
Rimi 121 12 58N 7 43 E
Rímini 63 44 3N 12 33 E
Rîmna, R. 70 45 36N 27 3 E
Rîmnicu Sărat 70 45 26N 27 3 E
Rîmnicu Vîlcece 70 45 9N 24 21 E
Rimouski 151 48 27N 68 30W
Rinca 103 8 45 S 119 35 E
Rincón de Romos 164 22 14N 102 18W
Rinconada 172 22 26 S 66 10W
Ringarum 73 58 21N 16 26 E
Ringe 73 55 13N 10 28 E
Ringel Spitz 51 46 53N 9 19 E
Ringford 35 54 55N 4 3W
Ringim 121 12 13N 9 10 E
Ringkøbing 73 56 5N 8 15 E
Ringkøbing Amt □ 73 56 15N 8 30 E
Ringling 160 46 16N 110 56W
Ringmer 29 50 53N 0 5 E
Ringmoen 71 60 21N 10 6 E
Ringsaker 71 60 54N 10 45 E
Ringsend 38 55 2N 6 45W
Ringsjön L. 73 55 55N 13 30 E
Ringsted 73 55 25N 11 46 E
Ringvassøy 74 69 36N 19 15 E
Ringville 39 52 3N 7 37W
Ringwood 28 50 50N 1 48W
Rinia, I. 69 37 23N 25 13 E
Rinjani 65 8 20 S 116 30 E
Rinns, The, Reg. 34 54 52N 5 3W
Rintein 48 52 11N 9 3 E
Rio Arica 174 1 35 S 75 30W
Rio Branco 174 9 58 S 67 49W
Rio Branco 173 32 40 S 53 40W
Rio Brilhante 173 21 48 S 54 33W
Rio Chico 174 10 19N 65 59W
Rio Claro, Brazil 173 22 19 S 47 35W
Rio Claro, Trin 167 10 20N 61 25W
Río Colorado 176 39 0 S 64 0W
Río Cuarto 172 33 10 S 64 25W
Rio das Pedras 129 23 8 S 35 28 E
Rio de Contas 171 13 36 S 41 48W
Rio de Janeiro 173 23 0 S 43 12W
Rio de Janeiro □ 173 22 50 S 43 0W
Rio del Rey 121 4 42N 8 37 E
Rio do Prado 171 16 35 S 40 34W
Rio do Sul 173 27 95 S 49 37W
Río Gallegos 176 51 35 S 69 15W
Río Grande 176 53 50 S 67 45W
Rio Grande 173 32 0 S 52 20W
Río Grande, Mexico 164 23 50N 103 2W
Río Grande, Nic. 166 12 54N 83 33W
Rio Grande City 159 26 30N 91 55W
Río Grande del Norte, R. 154 26 0N 97 0W
Rio Grande do Norte □ 170 5 40 S 36 0W
Rio Grande do Sul □ 173 30 0 S 53 0W
Rio Grande, R. 161 37 47N 106 15W
Río Hato 166 8 22N 80 10W
Rio Lagartos 165 21 36N 88 10W
Rio Largo 171 9 28 S 35 50W
Rio Maior 57 39 19N 8 57W
Rio Marina 62 42 48N 10 25 E
Río Mulatos 174 19 40 S 66 50W
Río Muni □ = Mbini □ 124 1 30N 10 0 E
Rio Negro 173 26 0 S 50 0W
Río Oriente 166 22 17N 81 13W
Rio Pardo, Minas Gerais, Brazil 171 15 55 S 42 30W
Rio Pardo, Rio Grande do Sul, Brazil 173 30 0 S 52 30W
Rio Prêto, Serra do 171 13 29 S 39 55W
Rio, Punta del 59 36 49N 2 24W
Río Real 171 11 28 S 37 56W
Río Segundo 172 31 40 S 63 59W
Río Tercero 172 32 15 S 64 8W
Rio Tinto, Brazil 170 6 48 S 35 5W
Rio Tinto, Port. 56 41 11N 8 34W
Rio Verde 170 17 50 S 51 0W
Rio Verde 165 21 56N 99 59W
Rio Vista 163 38 11N 121 44W
Riobamba 174 1 50 S 78 45W
Riohacha 174 11 33N 72 55W
Rioja, La, Argent. 172 29 20 S 67 0W
Rioja, La, Spain 58 42 20N 2 20W
Rioja, La □ 172 29 30 S 67 0W
Riom 44 45 54N 3 7 E
Riom-és-Montagnes 44 45 17N 2 39 E
Rion-des-Landes 44 43 55N 0 56W
Rionegro 174 6 9N 75 22W
Rionero in Vúlture 65 40 55N 15 40 E
Rios 56 41 58N 7 16W
Riosucio, Caldas, Colomb. 174 5 30N 75 40W
Riosucio, Choco, Colomb. 174 7 27N 77 7W
Riou L. 153 59 7N 106 25W
Riparia, Dora, R. 62 45 7N 7 24 E
Ripatransone 63 43 0N 13 45 E
Ripley, Derby, U.K. 33 53 3N 1 24W
Ripley, N. Yorks, U.K. 33 54 3N 1 34W
Ripley, U.S.A. 159 35 43N 89 34W
Ripoll 58 42 15N 2 13 E
Ripon, Calif., U.S.A. 163 37 44N 121 7W
Ripon, Wis., U.S.A. 156 43 51N 88 50W
Riposto 65 37 44N 15 12 E
Risalpur 94 34 3N 71 59 E
Risan 66 42 32N 18 42 E
Risca 31 51 36N 3 6W
Riscle 44 43 39N 0 5W
Rishon Le Zion 90 31 58N 34 48 E
Rishpon 90 32 12N 34 49 E
Rishton 32 53 46N 2 26W
Riska 71 58 56N 5 52 E
Risle, R. 42 48 55N 0 41 E
Rîsnov 70 45 35N 25 27 E
Rison 159 33 57N 92 11W
Risør 71 58 43N 9 13 E
Ritchie's Archipelago 101 12 5N 94 0 E
Riti 121 7 57N 9 41 E
Ritzville 160 47 10N 118 21W
Riu 98 28 19N 95 3 E
Riva Bella Ouistreham 42 49 17N 0 18W
Riva del Garda 62 45 53N 10 50 E
Rivadavia, Buenos Aires, Argent. 172 35 29 S 62 59W
Rivadavia, Mendoza, Argent. 172 33 13 S 68 30W
Rivadavia, Salta, Argent. 172 24 5 S 63 0W
Rivadavia, Chile 172 29 50 S 70 35W
Rivarolo Canavese 62 45 20N 7 42 E
Rivas 166 11 30N 85 50W
Rive-de-Gier 45 45 32N 4 37 E
River Cess 120 5 30N 9 25W
Rivera 173 31 0 S 55 50W
Riverchapel 39 52 38N 6 14W
Riverdale 163 36 26N 119 52W
Riverhead 162 40 53N 72 40W
Riverhurst 153 50 55N 106 50W
Riverina 136 29 45 S 120 40 E
Riverina, dist. 133 35 30 S 145 20 E
Rivers 153 50 2N 100 14W
Rivers □ 121 5 0N 6 30 E
Rivers Inlet 152 51 40N 127 20W
Rivers, L. of the 153 49 49N 105 44W
Riversdal 128 34 7 S 21 15 E
Riverside, Calif., U.S.A. 163 34 0N 117 22W
Riverside, Wyo., U.S.A. 160 41 12N 106 57W
Riversleigh 138 19 5 S 138 48 E
Riverton, Austral. 140 34 10 S 138 46 E

Riverton **Ross and Cromarty (□)**

Riverton, Can.	**153**	51 5N	97 0W
Riverton, N.Z.	**143**	46 21S	168 0E
Riverton, U.S.A.	**160**	43 1N	108 27W
Riverview	**108**	27 36S	152 51E
Rives	**45**	45 21N	5 31E
Rivesaltes	**44**	42 47N	2 50E
Riviera	**62**	44 0N	8 30E
Rivière à Pierre	**151**	46 57N	72 12W
Rivière-au-Renard	**151**	48 59N	64 23W
Rivière Bleue	**151**	47 26N	69 2W
Rivière-du-Loup	**151**	47 50N	69 30W
Rivière Pontecôte	**151**	49 57N	67 1W
Rivoli	**62**	45 3N	7 31E
Rivoli B.	**140**	37 32S	140 3E
Rivungo	**128**	16 9S	21 51E
Riwaka	**143**	41 5S	172 59E
Rixensart	**47**	50 43N	4 32E
Riyadh = Ar Riyad	**92**	24 41N	46 42E
Rize	**92**	41 0N	40 30E
Rizzuto, C.	**65**	38 54N	17 5E
Rjukan	**71**	59 54N	8 33E
Roa, Norway	**71**	60 17N	10 37E
Roa, Spain	**56**	41 41N	3 56W
Road Town	**167**	18 27N	64 37W
Road Weedon	**28**	52 14N	1 6W
Roade	**29**	52 10N	0 53W
Roadhead	**32**	55 4N	2 44W
Roag, L.	**36**	58 10N	6 55W
Roan Antelope	**127**	13 2S	28 19E
Roanne	**45**	46 3N	4 4E
Roanoke, Ala., U.S.A.	**157**	33 9N	85 23W
Roanoke, Va., U.S.A.	**156**	37 19N	79 55W
Roanoke I.	**157**	35 55N	75 40W
Roanoke, R.	**157**	36 15N	77 20W
Roanoke Rapids	**157**	36 36N	77 42W
Roaringwater B.	**39**	51 30N	9 30W
Roatán	**166**	16 18N	86 35W
Robbins I.	**138**	40 42S	145 0E
Robe, R., Austral.	**136**	21 42S	116 15E
Robe, R., Ireland	**38**	53 38N	9 10W
Röbel	**48**	53 24N	12 37E
Robert Lee	**159**	31 55N	100 26W
Robert Pt.	**137**	32 34S	115 40E
Roberton	**35**	55 24N	2 53W
Roberts	**160**	43 44N	112 8W
Robertsganj	**95**	24 44N	83 12E
Robertson, Austral.	**132**	34 37S	150 36E
Robertson, S. Afr.	**128**	33 46S	19 50E
Robertson I.	**13**	68 0S	75 0W
Robertson Ra.	**136**	23 15S	121 0E
Robertsport	**120**	6 45N	11 26W
Robertstown, Austral.	**140**	33 58S	139 5E
Robertstown, Ireland	**39**	53 16N	6 50W
Roberval	**150**	48 32N	72 15W
Robeson Kanal	**12**	82 0N	61 30W
Robesonia	**162**	40 21N	76 8W
Robin Hood's B.	**33**	54 26N	0 31W
Robinson Crusoe I.	**143**	33 50S	78 30W
Robinson, R.	**138**	16 3S	137 16E
Robinson Ranges	**137**	25 40S	118 0E
Robinson River	**138**	16 45S	136 58E
Robinvale	**140**	34 40S	142 45E
Robla, La	**56**	42 50N	5 41W
Roblin	**153**	51 14N	101 21W
Roboré	**174**	18 10S	59 45W
Robson, Mt.	**152**	53 10N	119 10W
Robstown	**159**	27 47N	97 40W
Roca, C. da	**57**	38 40N	9 31W
Roca Partida, I.	**164**	19 1N	112 2W
Roçadas	**128**	16 45S	15 0E
Rocas, I.	**170**	4 0S	34 1W
Rocca d'Aspidé	**65**	40 27N	15 10E
Rocca San Casciano	**63**	44 3N	11 30E
Roccalbegna	**63**	42 47N	11 30E
Roccastrada	**63**	43 0N	11 10E
Rocella Iónica	**65**	38 20N	16 24E
Rocester	**32**	52 56N	1 50W
Rocha	**173**	34 30S	54 25W
Rochdale	**32**	53 36N	2 10W
Roche	**30**	50 24N	4 50W
Roche-Bernard, La	**42**	47 31N	2 19W
Roche-Canillac, La	**44**	45 12N	1 57E
Roche-en-Ardenne, La	**47**	50 11N	5 35E
Roche, La, France	**45**	46 4N	6 19E
Roche, La, Switz.	**50**	46 42N	7 7E
Roche-sur-Yon, La	**42**	46 40N	1 25W
Rochechouart	**44**	45 50N	0 49E
Rochefort, Belg.	**47**	50 9N	5 12E
Rochefort, France	**44**	45 56N	0 57W
Rochefort-en-Terre	**42**	47 42N	2 22W
Rochefoucauld, La	**44**	45 44N	0 24E
Rochelle	**158**	41 55N	89 5W
Rochelle, La	**44**	46 10N	1 9W
Rocher River	**152**	61 23N	112 44W
Rocherath	**47**	50 26N	6 18E
Rocheservière	**42**	46 57N	1 30W
Rochester, Austral.	**140**	36 22S	144 41E
Rochester, Can.	**152**	54 22N	113 27W
Rochester, Kent, U.K.	**29**	51 22N	0 30E
Rochester, Northum., U.K.	**35**	55 16N	2 16W
Rochester, Ind., U.S.A.	**156**	41 5N	86 15W
Rochester, Minn., U.S.A.	**158**	44 1N	92 28W
Rochester, N.H., U.S.A.	**162**	43 19N	70 57W
Rochester, N.Y., U.S.A.	**156**	43 10N	77 40W
Rochford	**29**	51 36N	0 42E
Rochfortbridge	**38**	53 25N	7 19W
Rociana	**57**	37 19N	6 35W
Rociu	**70**	44 43N	25 2E
Rock Flat	**141**	36 21S	149 13E
Rock Hall	**162**	39 8N	76 14W
Rock Hill	**157**	34 55N	81 2W
Rock Island	**158**	41 30N	90 35W
Rock Lake	**158**	48 50N	99 13W
Rock, R.	**152**	60 7N	127 7W
Rock Rapids	**158**	43 25N	96 10W
Rock River	**160**	41 49N	106 0W
Rock Sound	**166**	24 54N	76 12W
Rock Sprs., Ariz., U.S.A.	**161**	34 2N	112 11W
Rock Sprs., Mont., U.S.A.	**160**	46 55N	106 11W
Rock Sprs., Tex., U.S.A.	**159**	30 2N	100 11W
Rock Sprs., Wyo., U.S.A.	**160**	41 40N	109 10W
Rock Valley	**158**	43 10N	96 17W
Rockall I.	**16**	57 37N	13 42W
Rockanje	**46**	51 52N	4 4E
Rockcliffe	**32**	54 58N	3 0W
Rockcorry	**38**	54 7N	7 0W
Rockdale	**159**	30 40N	97 0W
Rockefeller Plat.	**13**	84 0S	130 0W
Rockford	**158**	42 20N	89 0W
Rockglen	**153**	49 11N	105 57W
Rockhampton	**138**	23 22S	150 32E
Rockhampton Downs	**138**	18 57S	135 10E
Rockhill	**39**	52 25N	8 44W
Rockingham, Austral.	**137**	32 15S	115 38E
Rockingham, U.K.	**29**	52 32N	0 43W
Rockingham B.	**138**	18 5S	146 10E
Rockingham For.	**29**	52 28N	0 42W
Rockland, Idaho, U.S.A.	**160**	42 37N	112 57W
Rockland, Me., U.S.A.	**151**	44 0N	69 0W
Rockland, Mich., U.S.A.	**158**	46 40N	89 10W
Rockmart	**157**	34 1N	85 2W
Rockmills	**39**	52 13N	8 25W
Rockport, Mass., U.S.A.	**162**	42 39N	70 36W
Rockport, Mo., U.S.A.	**158**	40 26N	95 30W
Rockport, Tex., U.S.A.	**159**	28 2N	97 3W
Rockville, Conn., U.S.A.	**162**	41 51N	72 27W
Rockville, Md., U.S.A.	**162**	39 7N	77 10W
Rockwall	**159**	32 55N	96 30W
Rockwell City	**158**	42 20N	94 35W
Rockwood	**157**	35 52N	84 40W
Rocky Ford	**158**	38 7N	103 45W
Rocky Gully	**137**	34 30S	117 0E
Rocky Lane	**152**	58 31N	116 22W
Rocky Mount	**157**	35 55N	77 48W
Rocky Mountain House	**152**	52 22N	114 55W
Rocky Mts.	**152**	55 0N	121 0W
Rocky Pt.	**137**	33 30S	123 57E
Rockyford	**152**	51 14N	113 10W
Rocroi	**43**	49 55N	4 30E
Rod	**93**	28 10N	63 5E
Roda, La, Albacete, Spain	**59**	39 13N	2 15W
Roda, La, Sevilla, Spain	**57**	37 12N	4 46W
Rødberg	**71**	60 17N	8 56E
Rødby	**73**	54 41N	11 23E
Rødby Havn	**73**	54 39N	11 22E
Roddickton	**151**	50 51N	56 8W
Rødding	**73**	55 23N	9 3E
Rødekro	**73**	55 4N	9 20E
Rodel	**36**	57 45N	6 57W
Roden	**46**	53 8N	6 26E
Rødenes	**71**	59 35N	11 34E
Rodenkirchen	**48**	53 24N	8 26E
Roderick I.	**152**	52 38N	128 22W
Rodez	**44**	44 21N	2 33E
Rodholívas	**68**	40 55N	24 0E
Rodhópi □	**68**	41 10N	25 30E
Ródhos	**69**	36 15N	28 10E
Ródhos, I.	**69**	36 15N	28 10E
Roding R.	**29**	51 31N	0 7E
Rödjenäs	**73**	57 33N	14 50E
Rodna	**70**	47 25N	24 50E
Rodney, C.	**142**	36 17S	174 50E
Rodniki	**81**	57 7N	41 37E
Rodriguez, I.	**11**	20 0S	65 0E
Roe, R.	**38**	55 0N	6 56W
Roebling	**162**	40 7N	74 45W
Roebourne	**136**	20 44S	117 9E
Roebuck B.	**136**	18 5S	122 20E
Roebuck Plains P.O.	**136**	17 56S	122 28E
Roelofarendsveen	**46**	52 12N	4 38E
Roer, R.	**47**	51 12N	5 59E
Roermond	**47**	51 12N	6 0E
Roes Welcome Sd.	**149**	65 0N	87 0W
Roeselare	**47**	50 57N	3 7E
Rœulx	**47**	50 31N	4 7E
Rogachev	**80**	53 8N	30 5E
Rogagua, L.	**174**	14 0S	66 50W
Rogaland fylke □	**75**	59 12N	6 20E
Rogans Seat, Mt.	**32**	54 25N	2 10W
Rogaóica	**66**	44 4N	19 40E
Rogaška Slatina	**63**	46 15N	15 42E
Rogate	**29**	51 0N	0 51W
Rogatec	**63**	46 15N	21 46E
Rogatin	**80**	29 24N	24 36E
Rogers	**159**	36 20N	94 0W
Rogers City	**156**	45 25N	83 49W
Rogerson	**160**	42 10N	114 40W
Rogersville	**157**	36 27N	83 1W
Roggan River	**151**	54 25N	79 32W
Roggel	**47**	51 16N	5 56E
Roggeveldberge	**128**	32 10S	20 10E
Roggiano Gravina	**65**	39 37N	16 9E
Rogliano, France	**45**	42 57N	9 30E
Rogliano, Italy	**65**	39 11N	16 20E
Rogoaguado, L.	**174**	13 0S	65 30W
Rogowo	**54**	52 43N	17 38E
Rogozno	**54**	52 45N	16 59E
Rogue, R.	**160**	42 30N	124 0W
Rohan	**42**	48 4N	2 45W
Rohnert Park	**163**	38 16N	122 40W
Rohrbach	**43**	49 3N	7 15E
Rohri	**94**	27 45N	68 51E
Rohri Canal	**94**	26 15N	68 27E
Rohtak	**94**	28 55N	76 43E
Roi Et	**100**	15 56N	103 40E
Roisel	**43**	49 58N	3 6E
Rojas	**172**	34 10S	60 45W
Rojo, C., Mexico	**165**	21 33N	97 20W
Rojo, C., W. Indies	**147**	17 56N	67 11W
Rokan, R.	**102**	1 30N	100 50E
Rokeby	**138**	13 39S	142 40E
Rokiskis	**80**	55 55N	25 35E
Rokitnoye	**81**	50 57N	35 56E
Rokycany	**52**	49 43N	13 35E
Rolândia	**173**	23 5S	52 0W
Røldal	**71**	59 47N	6 50E
Rolde	**46**	52 59N	6 39E
Rolette	**158**	48 42N	99 50W
Rolfstorp	**73**	57 11N	12 27E
Rolla, Kansas, U.S.A.	**159**	37 10N	101 40W
Rolla, Missouri, U.S.A.	**159**	38 0N	91 42W
Rolla, N. Dak., U.S.A.	**158**	48 50N	99 36W
Rollag	**71**	60 2N	9 18E
Rollands Plains	**141**	31 17S	152 42E
Rolle	**50**	46 28N	6 20E
Rolleston, Austral.	**138**	24 28S	148 35E
Rolleston, N.Z.	**143**	43 35S	172 24E
Rollingstone	**138**	19 2S	146 24E
Rom	**123**	9 54N	32 16E
Roma, Austral.	**139**	26 32S	148 49E
Roma, Italy	**64**	41 54N	12 30E
Roma, Sweden	**73**	57 32N	18 26E
Roman, Bulg.	**67**	43 8N	23 54E
Roman, Rumania	**70**	46 57N	26 55E
Romana, La	**167**	18 27N	68 57W
Romang, I.	**103**	7 30S	127 20E
Romania ■	**61**	46 0N	25 0E
Romanija planina	**66**	43 50N	18 45E
Romano, Cayo	**166**	22 0N	77 30W
Romano di Lombardia	**62**	45 32N	9 45E
Romanovka = Bessarabka	**82**	46 21N	28 51E
Romans	**62**	45 3N	5 3E
Romanshorn	**51**	47 33N	9 22E
Romanzof, C.	**147**	62 0N	165 50W
Rombo □	**126**	3 10S	37 30E
Rome, U.S.A.	**162**	41 51N	76 21W
Rome, Ga., U.S.A.	**157**	34 20N	85 0W
Rome, N.Y., U.S.A.	**162**	43 14N	75 29W
Rome = Roma	**64**	41 54N	12 30E
Romeleåsen	**73**	55 34N	13 33E
Romenây	**45**	46 30N	5 1E
Romeo	**151**	47 28N	57 4W
Romerike	**71**	60 7N	11 10E
Romilly	**43**	48 31N	3 44E
Romîni	**70**	44 59N	24 11E
Rommani	**118**	33 31N	6 40W
Romney	**156**	39 21N	78 45W
Romney Marsh	**29**	51 0N	1 0E
Romny	**80**	50 48N	33 28E
Rømø	**73**	55 10N	8 30E
Romodan	**80**	50 0N	33 15E
Romodanovo	**81**	54 26N	45 23E
Romont	**50**	46 42N	6 54E
Romorantin-Lanthenay	**43**	47 21N	1 45E
Romsdal, R.	**71**	62 25N	8 0E
Romsdalen	**74**	62 25N	7 50E
Romsey	**28**	51 0N	1 29W
Ron	**100**	17 53N	106 27E
Rona I.	**36**	57 33N	6 0W
Ronan	**160**	47 30N	114 11W
Ronas Hill	**36**	60 33N	1 25W
Ronay I.	**36**	57 30N	7 10W
Roncador Cay	**166**	13 40N	80 4W
Roncador, Serra do	**171**	12 30S	52 30W
Roncesvalles, Paso	**58**	43 1N	1 19W
Ronceverte	**156**	37 45N	80 28W
Ronciglione	**63**	42 18N	12 12E
Ronco, R.	**63**	44 26N	12 15E
Ronda	**57**	36 46N	5 12W
Ronda, Serranía de	**57**	36 44N	5 3W
Rondane	**71**	61 57N	9 50E
Rondón	**174**	6 17N	71 6W
Rondônia □	**174**	11 0S	63 0W
Rong, Koh	**101**	10 45N	103 15E
Ronge, La, Can.	**153**	55 5N	105 20W
Ronge, La, Sask., Can.	**153**	55 6N	105 17W
Ronge, Lac La	**153**	55 10N	105 0W
Rongotea	**142**	40 19S	175 25E
Rønne	**73**	55 6N	14 44E
Ronne Land	**13**	83 0S	70 0W
Ronneby	**73**	56 12N	15 17E
Ronsard, C.	**137**	24 46S	113 10E
Ronse	**47**	50 45N	3 35E
Roodepoort-Maraisburg	**125**	26 8S	27 52E
Roodeschool	**46**	53 25N	6 46E
Roof Butte	**161**	36 29N	109 5W
Roompot	**47**	51 37N	3 44E
Roorkee	**94**	29 52N	77 59E
Roosendaal	**47**	51 32N	4 29E
Roosevelt, Minn., U.S.A.	**158**	48 51N	95 2W
Roosevelt, Utah, U.S.A.	**160**	40 19N	110 1W
Roosevelt I.	**13**	79 0S	161 0W
Roosevelt, Mt.	**152**	58 20N	125 20W
Roosevelt Res.	**161**	33 46N	111 0W
Roosky	**38**	53 50N	7 55W
Ropczyce	**54**	50 4N	21 38E
Roper, R.	**138**	14 43S	135 27E
Ropesville	**159**	33 25N	102 10W
Ropsley	**33**	52 53N	0 31W
Roque Pérez	**172**	35 25S	59 24W
Roquefort	**44**	44 2N	0 20W
Roquefort-sur-Souizon	**44**	43 58N	2 59E
Roquemaure	**45**	44 3N	4 48E
Roquetas	**58**	40 50N	0 30E
Roquevaire	**45**	43 20N	5 36E
Roraima □	**174**	2 0N	61 30W
Roraima, Mt.	**174**	5 10N	60 40W
Rorketon	**153**	51 24N	99 35W
Røros	**71**	62 35N	11 23E
Rorschach	**51**	47 28N	9 30E
Rørvik	**74**	64 54N	11 15E
Rosa, U.S.A.	**160**	38 15N	122 16W
Rosa, Zambia	**127**	9 33S	31 15E
Rosa Brook	**137**	33 57S	115 10E
Rosa, C.	**119**	37 0N	8 16E
Rosa, Monte	**50**	45 57N	7 53E
Rosal	**56**	41 57N	8 51W
Rosal de la Frontera	**57**	37 59N	7 13W
Rosalia	**160**	47 26N	117 25W
Rosamund	**163**	34 52N	118 10W
Rosans	**45**	44 24N	5 29E
Rosario	**172**	33 0S	60 50W
Rosário, Maran., Brazil	**170**	3 0S	44 15W
Rosário, Rio Grande do Sul, Brazil	**176**	30 15S	55 0W
Rosario, Baja California, Mexico	**164**	30 0N	116 0W
Rosario, Durango, Mexico	**164**	26 30N	105 35W
Rosario, Sinaloa, Mexico	**164**	23 0N	106 0W
Rosario, Venez.	**174**	10 19N	72 19W
Rosario de la Frontera	**172**	25 50S	65 0W
Rosario de Lerma	**172**	24 59S	65 35W
Rosario del Tala	**172**	32 20S	59 10W
Rosário do Sul	**173**	30 15S	54 55W
Rosarito	**164**	28 38N	114 4W
Rosarno	**65**	38 29N	15 59E
Rosas	**58**	42 19N	3 10E
Rosas, G. de	**55**	42 10N	3 15E
Rosburgh	**143**	45 33S	169 19E
Roscoe	**162**	41 56N	74 55W
Roscoff	**42**	48 44N	4 0W
Roscommon, Ireland	**38**	53 38N	8 11W
Roscommon, U.S.A.	**156**	44 27N	84 35W
Roscommon □	**38**	53 40N	8 15W
Roscrea	**39**	52 58N	7 50W
Rose Blanche	**151**	47 38N	58 45W
Rose Harbour	**152**	52 15N	131 10W
Rose Ness	**37**	58 52N	2 50W
Rose Pt.	**152**	54 11N	131 39W
Rose, R.	**138**	14 16S	135 45E
Rose Valley	**153**	52 19N	103 49W
Roseau, Domin.	**167**	15 20N	61 30W
Roseau, U.S.A.	**158**	48 51N	95 46W
Rosebery	**138**	41 46S	145 33E
Rosebud, Austral.	**141**	38 21S	144 54E
Rosebud, U.S.A.	**159**	31 5N	97 0W
Roseburg	**160**	43 10N	123 10W
Rosedale, Austral.	**138**	24 38S	151 53E
Rosedale, U.S.A.	**159**	33 51N	91 0W
Rosedale Abbey	**33**	54 22N	0 51W
Rosée	**47**	50 14N	4 41E
Rosegreen	**39**	52 28N	7 51W
Rosehall	**37**	57 59N	4 36W
Rosehearty	**37**	57 42N	2 8W
Rosemarkie	**37**	57 35N	4 8W
Rosemary	**152**	50 46N	112 5W
Rosenallis	**39**	53 10N	7 25W
Rosenberg	**159**	29 30N	95 48W
Rosendaël	**43**	51 3N	2 24E
Rosenheim	**49**	47 51N	12 9E
Roseto degli Abruzzi	**63**	42 40N	14 2E
Rosetown	**153**	51 35N	108 3W
Rosetta = Rashîd	**122**	31 21N	30 22E
Roseville	**160**	38 46N	121 17W
Rosewood, N.S.W., Austral.	**141**	35 38S	147 52E
Rosewood, N.T., Austral.	**136**	16 28S	128 58E
Rosewood, Queens., Austral.	**139**	27 38S	152 36E
Rosh Haniqra, Kefar	**90**	33 5N	35 5E
Rosh Pinna	**90**	32 58N	35 32E
Rosh Ze'ira	**90**	31 14N	35 15E
Roshage C.	**73**	57 7N	8 35E
Rosières	**43**	48 36N	6 20E
Rosignano Marittimo	**62**	43 23N	10 28E
Rosignol	**174**	6 15N	57 30W
Roşiori-de-Vede	**70**	44 9N	25 0E
Rositsa	**67**	43 57N	27 57E
Rositsa, R.	**67**	43 10N	25 30E
Roskeeragh Pt.	**38**	54 22N	8 40W
Roskhill	**36**	57 24N	6 31W
Roskilde	**73**	55 38N	12 3E
Roskilde Amt □	**73**	55 35N	12 5E
Roskilde Fjord	**73**	55 50N	12 2E
Roskill, Mt.	**142**	36 55S	174 45E
Roslavl	**80**	53 57N	32 55E
Roslyn	**141**	34 29S	149 37E
Rosmaninhal	**57**	39 44N	7 5W
Røsnæs	**73**	55 44N	10 55E
Rosneath	**34**	56 1N	4 49W
Rosolini	**65**	36 49N	14 58E
Rosporden	**42**	47 57N	3 50W
Ross, Austral.	**138**	42 2S	147 30E
Ross, N.Z.	**143**	42 53S	170 49E
Ross, U.K.	**28**	51 55N	2 34W
Ross and Cromarty (□)	**26**	57 43N	4 50W

Ross Dependency **Sabang, O**

Ross Dependency 13 70 0S 170 5W
Ross I. 13 77 30S 168 0E
Ross Ice Shelf 13 80 0S 180 0W
Ross L. 160 48 50N 121 0W
Ross on Wye 28 51 55N 2 34W
Ross River, Austral. 138 19 15S 146 51E
Ross River, Can. 147 62 30N 131 30W
Ross Sea 13 74 0S 178 0E
Rossa 51 46 23N 9 8E
Rossall Pt. 32 53 55N 3 2W
Rossan Pt. 38 54 42N 8 47W
Rossano Cálabro 65 39 36N 16 39E
Rossburn 153 50 40N 100 49W
Rosscahill 38 53 23N 9 15W
Rosscarbery 39 51 39N 9 1W
Rosscarbery B. 39 51 32N 9 0W
Rossel I. 138 11 30S 154 30E
Rosses B. 38 55 2N 8 30W
Rosses Point 38 54 17N 8 34W
Rosses, The 38 55 2N 8 20W
Rossignol, L., N.S., Can. 151 44 12N 65 0W
Rossignol, L., Qué., Can. 150 52 43N 73 40W
Rossing 128 22 30S 14 50E
Rossland 152 49 6N 117 50W
Rosslare 39 52 17N 6 23W
Rosslau 48 51 52N 12 15E
Rosslea 38 54 15N 7 11W
Rosso 120 16 40N 15 45W
Rossosh 83 50 15N 39 20E
Rossport 150 48 50N 87 30W
Rossum 46 51 48N 5 20E
Røssvatnet 74 65 45N 14 5E
Rossville 138 15 48S 145 15E
Rosthern 153 52 40N 106 20W
Rostock 48 54 4N 12 9E
Rostock □ 48 54 10N 12 30E
Rostov, Don, U.S.S.R. 83 47 15N 39 45E
Rostov, Moskva, U.S.S.R. 81 57 14N 39 25E
Rostrenen 42 48 14N 3 21W
Rostrevor 38 54 7N 6 12W
Roswell 159 33 26N 104 32W
Rosyth 35 56 2N 3 26W
Rota 57 36 37N 6 20W
Rotälven 72 61 30N 14 10E
Rotan 159 32 52N 100 30W
Rotem 47 51 3N 5 45E
Rotenburg 48 53 6N 9 24E
Rothbury 35 55 19N 1 55W
Rothbury Forest 35 55 19N 1 50W
Rothenburg 51 47 6N 8 16E
Rothenburg ob der Tauber 49 49 21N 10 11E
Rother, R. 29 50 59N 0 40W
Rotherham 33 53 26N 1 21W
Rothes 37 57 31N 3 12W
Rothesay, Can. 151 45 23N 66 0W
Rothesay, U.K. 34 55 50N 5 3W
Rothhaar G., mts. 50 51 6N 8 10E
Rothienorman 37 57 24N 2 28W
Rothrist 50 47 18N 8 54E
Rothwell, Northants, U.K. 29 52 25N 0 48W
Rothwell, W. Yorks., U.K. 33 53 46N 1 29W
Roti, I. 103 10 50S 123 0E
Rotkop 128 26 44S 15 27E
Roto 141 33 0S 145 30E
Roto Aira L. 142 39 3S 175 55E
Rotoehu L. 142 38 1S 176 32E
Rotoiti L. 142 41 51S 172 49E
Rotoma L. 142 38 2S 176 35E
Rotondella 65 40 10N 16 30E
Rotoroa Lake 143 41 55S 172 39E
Rotorua 142 38 9S 176 16E
Rotorua, L. 142 38 5S 176 18E
Rotselaar 47 50 57N 4 42E
Rottal 37 56 48N 3 1W
Rotten, R. 50 46 18N 7 36E
Rottenburg 49 48 28N 8 56E
Rottenmann 52 47 31N 14 22E
Rotterdam 46 51 55N 4 30E
Rottingdean 29 50 48N 0 3W
Rottnest I. 137 32 0S 115 27E
Rottumeroog 46 53 33N 6 34E
Rottweil 49 48 9N 8 38E
Rotuma, I. 130 12 25S 177 5E
Roubaix 43 50 40N 3 10E
Roudnice 52 50 25N 14 15E
Rouen 42 49 27N 1 4E
Rouergue 45 44 20N 2 20E
Rough, gasfield 19 53 50N 0 27E
Rough Pt. 39 52 19N 10 0W
Rough Ridge 143 45 10S 169 55E
Rouillac 44 45 47N 0 4W
Rouleau 153 50 10N 104 56W
Round Mt. 139 30 26S 152 16E
Round Mountain 163 38 46N 117 3W
Roundstone 38 53 24N 9 55W
Roundup 160 46 25N 108 35W
Roundwood 39 53 4N 6 14W
Rourkela 95 22 14N 84 50E
Rousay, I. 37 59 10N 3 2W
Rousky 38 54 44N 7 10E
Rousse, L'Île 45 43 27N 8 57E
Roussillon 45 45 24N 4 49E
Rouveen 46 52 37N 6 11E
Rouxville 128 30 11S 26 50E
Rouyn 150 48 20N 79 0W
Rovaniemi 74 66 29N 25 41E
Rovato 62 45 34N 10 0E
Rovenki 83 48 5N 39 27E
Rovereto 62 45 53N 11 3E
Rovigo 63 45 4N 11 48E
Rovinari 70 46 56N 23 10E
Rovinj 63 45 18N 13 40E
Rovira 174 4 15N 75 20W
Rovno 80 50 40N 26 10E
Rovnoye 81 50 52N 46 3E
Rovuma, R. 127 11 30S 36 10E
Rowanburn 35 55 5N 2 54W
Rowena 139 29 48S 148 55E
Rowes 141 37 0S 149 6E
Rowley Shoals 136 17 40S 119 20E
Rowood 161 32 18N 112 54W
Rowrah 32 54 34N 3 26W
Roxa 120 11 15N 15 45W
Roxas 103 11 36N 122 49E
Roxboro 157 36 24N 78 59W
Roxborough Downs 138 22 20S 138 45E
Roxburgh, N.Z. 143 45 33S 169 19E
Roxburgh, U.K. 35 55 34N 2 30W
Roxburgh (□) 26 55 30N 2 30W
Roxby 33 53 38N 0 37W
Roxen 73 58 30N 15 40E
Roy 160 47 17N 109 0W
Roy Hill 136 22 37S 119 58E
Roy, Le 159 38 8N 95 35W
Roya, Peña 58 40 25N 0 40W
Royal Canal 38 53 29N 7 0W
Royal Oak 156 42 30N 83 5W
Royalla 141 35 30S 149 9E
Royan 44 45 37N 1 2W
Roybridge 37 56 53N 4 50W
Roye 43 47 40N 6 31E
Røyken 71 59 45N 10 23E
Royston 29 52 3N 0 1W
Royton 32 53 34N 2 7W
Rozaj 66 42 50N 20 15E
Rozan 54 52 52N 21 25E
Rozdol 80 49 30N 24 1E
Rozier, Le 44 44 13N 3 12E
Roznava 53 48 37N 20 35E
Rozoy 43 48 40N 2 56E
Rozoy-sur-Serre 43 49 40N 4 8E
Rozwadów 54 50 37N 22 2E
Rrësheni 68 41 47N 19 49E
Rtanj, mt. 66 43 45N 21 50W
Rtem, Oued el 119 33 40N 5 34E
Rtishchevo 81 52 35N 43 50E
Rúa 56 42 24N 7 6W
Ruacaná 128 17 20S 14 12E
Ruahine Ra. 142 39 55S 176 2E
Ruamahanga, R. 142 41 24S 175 8E
Ruapehu 142 39 17S 175 35E
Ruapuke I. 143 46 46S 168 31E
Ruatoria 142 37 55S 178 20E
Ruâus, W. 119 30 14N 15 0E
Ruawai 142 36 15S 173 59E
Rub 'al Khali 91 21 0N 51 0E
Rubeho, mts. 126 6 50S 36 25E
Rubery 28 52 24N 1 59W
Rubezhnoye 82 49 6N 38 25E
Rubha Ardvule C. 36 57 17N 7 32W
Rubha Hunish, C. 36 57 42N 6 20W
Rubh'an Dunain, C. 36 57 10N 6 20W
Rubiataba 171 15 8S 49 48W
Rubicone, R. 63 44 0N 12 20E
Rubim 171 16 23S 40 32W
Rubinéia 171 20 13S 51 2W
Rubino 120 6 4N 4 18W
Rubio 174 7 43N 72 22W
Rubona 126 0 29N 30 9E
Rubtsovsk 76 51 30N 80 50E
Ruby 147 64 40N 155 35W
Ruby L. 160 40 10N 115 28W
Ruby Mts. 160 40 30N 115 30W
Rubyvale 138 23 25S 147 45E
Rucava 80 56 9N 20 32E
Ruciane-Nida 54 53 40N 21 32E
RûcûSdia 66 44 59N 21 36E
Rud 71 60 1N 10 1E
Ruda 73 57 6N 16 7E
Ruda Slaska 53 50 16N 18 50E
Rudall 140 33 43S 136 17E
Rudbar 93 30 0N 62 30E
Ruden, I. 48 54 13N 13 47E
Rüdersdorf 48 52 28N 13 48E
Rudewa 127 10 7S 34 47E
Rudgwick 29 51 7N 0 54W
Rudkøbing 73 54 56N 10 41E
Rudna 54 51 30N 16 17E
Rudnichnyy 84 59 38N 52 26E
Rudnik, Bulg. 67 42 36N 27 30E
Rudnik, Yugo. 67 44 7N 20 35E
Rudnik, mt. 67 44 7N 20 35E
Rudnogorsk 77 57 15N 103 42E
Rudnya 80 54 55N 31 13E
Rudnyy 84 52 57N 63 7E
Rudo 66 43 41N 19 23E
Rudolstadt 48 50 44N 11 20E
Rudozem 67 41 29N 24 51E
Rudston 33 54 6N 0 19W
Rûducaneni 70 46 58N 27 54E
Rûdûuţi 70 47 50N 25 59E
Rudyard 156 46 14N 84 35E
Rue 43 50 15N 1 40E
Ruelle 44 45 41N 0 14E
Rufa'a 123 14 44N 33 32E
Ruffec Charente 44 46 2N 0 12W
Rufi 123 5 58N 30 18E
Rufiji □ 126 8 0S 38 30E
Rufiji, R. 124 7 50S 38 15E
Rufino 172 34 20S 62 50W
Rufisque 120 14 40N 17 15W
Rufunsa 127 15 4S 29 34E
Rugby, U.K. 28 52 23N 1 16W
Rugby, U.S.A. 158 48 21N 100 0W
Rugeley 28 52 47N 1 56W
Rügen, I. 48 54 22N 13 25E
Rugezi 126 2 6S 33 18E
Rugles 42 48 50N 0 40E
Ruhâma 90 31 31N 34 43E
Ruhea 98 26 10N 88 25E
Ruhengeri 126 1 30S 29 36E
Ruhla 48 50 53N 10 21E
Ruhland 48 51 27N 13 52E
Ruhr, R. 48 51 25N 7 15E
Ruhuhu, R. 127 10 15S 34 55E
Rui Barbosa 171 12 18S 40 27W
Ruidosa 159 29 59N 104 39W
Ruidoso 161 33 19N 105 39W
Ruinen 46 52 46N 6 21E
Ruinen A Kanaal 46 52 54N 7 8E
Ruinerwold 46 52 44N 6 15E
Ruj, mt. 66 42 52N 22 42E
Rujen, mt. 66 42 9N 22 30E
Ruk 94 27 50N 68 42E
Rukwa □, Tanz. 126 7 0S 31 30E
Rukwa □, Tanz. 126 7 0S 31 30E
Rukwa L. 126 7 50S 32 10E
Rulhieres, C. 136 13 56S 127 22E
Rulles 47 49 43N 5 32E
Rully 167 46 52N 4 44E
Rum Jungle 136 13 0S 130 59E
Ruma 66 45 8N 19 50E
Rumah 92 25 35N 47 10E
Rumania ■ 61 46 0N 25 0E
Rumbalara 138 25 20S 134 29E
Rumbek 123 6 54N 29 37E
Rumbeke 47 50 56N 3 10E
Rumburk 52 50 57N 14 32E
Rumelange 47 49 27N 6 2E
Rumford 156 44 30N 70 30W
Rumia 54 54 37N 18 25E
Rumilly 45 45 53N 5 56E
Rumney 31 51 32N 3 7W
Rumoi 112 43 56N 141 39W
Rumonge 126 3 59S 29 26E
Rumsey 152 51 51N 112 48W
Rumson 162 40 23N 74 0W
Rumula 138 16 35S 145 20E
Rumuruti 126 0 17N 36 32E
Runabay Hd. 38 55 10N 6 2W
Runanga 143 42 25S 171 15E
Runaway, C. 142 37 32S 178 2E
Runcorn, Austral. 108 27 36S 153 4E
Runcorn, U.K. 32 53 20N 2 44W
Rungwa 126 6 55S 33 32E
Rungwa, R. 126 7 15S 33 10E
Rungwe 127 9 11S 33 32E
Rungwe □ 127 9 25S 33 32E
Runka 121 12 28N 7 20E
Runn 72 60 30N 15 40E
Rupa 98 27 15N 92 30E
Rupar 94 31 2N 76 38E
Rupat, I. 102 1 45N 101 40E
Rupea 61 46 2N 25 13E
Rupert House = Fort Rupert 150 51 30N 78 40W
Rupert, R. 150 51 29N 78 45W
Rupsa 98 21 44N 87 20E
Rupununi, R. 175 3 30N 59 30W
Ruquka Gie La 99 31 35N 97 55E
Rurrenabaque 174 14 30S 67 32W
Rus, R. 58 39 30N 2 30W
Rusambo 127 16 30S 32 4E
Rusape 125 18 35S 32 8E
Ruschuk = Ruse 67 43 48N 25 59E
Ruse 67 43 48N 25 59E
Rusetu 70 44 57N 27 14E
Rush 38 53 31N 6 7W
Rushden 29 52 17N 0 37W
Rushford 158 43 48N 91 46W
Rushville, Ill., U.S.A. 158 40 6N 90 35W
Rushville, Ind., U.S.A. 156 39 38N 85 22W
Rushville, Nebr., U.S.A. 158 42 43N 102 35W
Rushworth 141 36 32S 145 1E
Rusken 73 57 15N 14 20E
Ruskington 33 53 5N 0 23W
Russas 171 4 56S 38 2W
Russell, Can. 153 50 50N 101 20W
Russell, N.Z. 142 35 16S 174 10E
Russell, U.S.A. 158 38 56N 98 55W
Russell L., Man., Can. 153 56 15N 101 30W
Russell L., N.W.T., Can. 152 63 5N 115 44W
Russellkonda 96 19 57N 84 42E
Russellville, Ala., U.S.A. 157 34 30N 87 44W
Russellville, Ark., U.S.A. 159 35 15N 93 0W
Russellville, Ky., U.S.A. 157 36 50N 86 50W
Russi 63 44 21N 12 1E
Russian Mission 147 61 45N 161 25W
Russian S.F.S.R. □ 77 62 0N 105 0E
Russkoye Ustie 12 71 0N 149 0E
Rust 53 47 49N 16 42E
Rustam 94 34 25N 72 13E
Rustam Shahr 94 26 58N 66 6E
Rustavi 83 40 45N 44 30E
Rustenburg 128 25 41S 27 14E
Ruston 159 32 30N 92 40W
Ruswil 50 47 5N 8 8E
Rutana 126 3 55S 30 0E
Rutba 92 33 4N 40 15E
Rute 57 37 19N 4 29W
Ruteng 103 8 26S 120 30E
Ruth 160 39 15N 115 1W
Ruth, oilfield 19 55 33N 4 55E
Rutherglen, Austral. 141 36 5S 146 29E
Rutherglen, U.K. 34 55 50N 4 11W
Ruthin 31 53 7N 3 20W
Ruthven 37 57 4N 4 2W
Ruthwell 35 55 0N 3 24W
Rüti 51 47 16N 8 51E
Rutigliano 65 41 1N 17 0E
Rutland 162 43 38N 73 0W
Rutland (□) 26 52 38N 0 40W
Rutland I. 101 11 25N 92 40E
Rutland Plains 138 15 38S 141 49E
Rutledge L. 153 61 33N 110 47W
Rutledge, R. 153 61 4N 112 0W
Rutshuru 126 1 13S 29 25E
Ruurlo 46 52 5N 6 24E
Ruvo di Púglia 65 41 7N 16 27E
Ruvu 126 6 49S 38 43E
Ruvu, R. 126 7 25S 38 15E
Ruvuma □ 127 10 20S 36 0E
Ruvuma, R. 127 11 30S 36 10E
Ruwaidha 92 23 40N 44 40E
Ruwandiz 92 36 40N 44 32E
Ruwenzori Mts. 126 0 30N 29 55E
Ruwenzori, mt. 126 0 30N 29 55E
Ruyigi 126 3 29S 30 15E
Ruzayevka 81 54 10N 45 0E
Ruzhevo Konare 67 42 23N 24 46E
Ruzomberok 53 49 3N 19 17E
Rwanda ■ 126 2 0S 30 0E
Ryaberg 73 56 47N 13 15E
Ryakhovo 67 44 0N 26 18E
Ryan, L. 34 55 0N 5 2W
Ryazan 81 54 50N 39 40E
Ryazhsk 81 53 45N 40 3E
Rybache 76 46 40N 81 20E
Rybachi Poluostrov 78 69 43N 32 0E
Rybachye 85 42 26N 76 12E
Rybinsk (Shcherbakov) 81 58 5N 38 50E
Rybinsk Vdkhr. 81 58 30N 38 0E
Rybnik 54 50 6N 18 32E
Rybnitsa 82 47 45N 29 0E
Rychwał 54 52 4N 18 10E
Ryd 73 56 27N 14 42E
Rydal 32 54 28N 2 59W
Ryde 28 50 44N 1 9W
Rydö 73 56 58N 13 10E
Rydsnäs 73 57 47N 15 9E
Rydułtowy 54 50 4N 18 23E
Rydzyna 54 51 47N 16 39E
Rye, Denmark 73 56 5N 9 45E
Rye, U.K. 29 50 57N 0 46E
Rye Patch Res. 160 40 45N 118 20W
Rye, R. 33 54 12N 0 53W
Ryegate 160 46 21N 109 27W
Ryhope 35 54 52N 1 22W
Rylsk 80 51 30N 34 51E
Rylstone 141 32 46S 149 58E
Rymanów 54 49 35N 21 51E
Ryn 54 53 57N 21 34E
Ryningsnäs 73 57 17N 15 58E
Ryōhaku-Sanchi 111 36 0N 136 49E
Rypin 54 53 3N 19 32E
Ryton, Tyne & Wear, U.K. 35 54 58N 1 44W
Ryton, Warwick, U.K. 28 52 23N 1 25W
Ryūgasaki 111 35 54N 140 11E
Ryūkyū Is. = Nansei-Shotō 112 26 0N 128 0E
Rzepin 54 52 20N 14 49E
Rzeszów 54 50 5N 21 58E
Rzeszów □ 54 50 0N 22 0E
Rzhev 80 56 20N 34 20E

S

s'-Hertogenbosch 47 51 42N 5 17E
Sa 100 18 34N 100 45E
Sa. da Canastra 125 19 30S 46 5W
Sa Dec 101 10 20N 105 46E
Sa-Koi 98 19 54N 97 3E
Sa'ad (Muharraga) 90 31 28N 34 33E
Sa'ādatabād 93 30 10N 53 5E
Saale, R. 48 51 25N 11 56E
Saaler Bodden 48 54 20N 12 25E
Saalfelden 70 47 26N 12 51E
Saalfield 48 50 39N 11 21E
Saane, R. 50 46 23N 7 18E
Saanen 50 46 29N 7 15E
Saar (Sarre), □ 43 49 20N 6 45E
Saarbrücken 49 49 15N 6 58E
Saarburg 49 49 36N 6 32E
Saaremaa 80 58 30N 22 30E
Saariselkä 74 68 16N 28 15E
Saarland □ 131 49 20N 6 45E
Saarlouis 49 49 19N 6 45E
Saas Fee 50 46 7N 7 56E
Saas-Grund 50 46 7N 7 57E
Saba I. 167 17 30N 63 10W
Sabac 66 44 48N 19 42E
Sabadell 58 41 28N 2 7E
Sabae 111 35 57N 136 11E
Sabagalel 102 1 36S 98 40E
Sabah □ 102 6 0N 117 0E
Sabak 100 3 46N 100 58E
Sábana de la Mar 167 19 7N 69 40W
Sábanalarga 174 10 38N 74 55W
Sabang, O. 102 5 50N 95 15E

Sabará St. Lawrence

Sabará	171	19 55 S	43 55W
Sabarania	103	2 5 S	138 18 E
Sabari, R.	96	18 0N	81 25 E
Sabastiya	90	32 17N	35 12 E
Sabaudia	64	41 17N	13 2 E
Sabderat	123	15 26N	36 42 E
Sabhah	119	27 9N	14 29 E
Sabie	129	25 4 S	30 48 E
Sabinal, Mexico	164	30 50N	107 25W
Sabinal, U.S.A.	159	29 20N	99 27W
Sabinal, Punta del	59	36 43N	2 44W
Sabinas	164	27 50N	101 10W
Sabinas Hidalgo	164	26 40N	100 10W
Sabinas, R.	164	27 37N	100 42W
Sabine	159	29 42N	93 54W
Sabine, R.	159	31 30N	93 35W
Sabinópolis	171	18 40 S	43 6W
Sabinov	53	49 6N	21 5 E
Sabirabad	83	40 0N	48 30 E
Sabkhat Tawurgha	119	31 48N	15 30 E
Sablayan	103	12 5N	120 50 E
Sable	42	47 50N	0 21W
Sable, C., Can.	151	43 29N	65 38W
Sable, C., U.S.A.	166	25 5N	81 0W
Sable I.	151	44 0N	60 0W
Sablé-sur-Sarthe	42	47 50N	0 20W
Sables-D'Olonne, Les	44	46 30N	1 45W
Saboeiro	170	6 32 S	39 54W
Sabor, R.	56	41 16N	7 10W
Sabou	120	12 1N	2 28W
Sabrātah	119	32 47N	12 29 E
Sabrina Coast	13	67 0 S	120 0 E
Sabugal	56	40 20N	7 5W
Sabzevar	93	36 15N	57 40 E
Sabzvaran	93	28 45N	57 50 E
Sac City	158	42 26N	95 0W
Sacandaga Res.	162	43 6N	74 16W
Sacedón	58	40 29N	2 41W
Sachigo, L.	150	53 50N	92 12W
Sachigo, R.	150	55 6N	88 58W
Sachinbulako	106	43 5N	111 47 E
Sachkhere	83	42 25N	43 28 E
Sachseln	51	46 52N	8 15 E
Sacile	63	45 58N	16 7 E
Säckingen	49	47 34N	7 56 E
Saco, Me., U.S.A.	162	43 30N	70 27W
Saco, Mont., U.S.A.	160	48 28N	107 19W
Sacquoy Hd.	37	59 12N	3 5W
Sacramento, Brazil	171	19 53 S	47 27W
Sacramento, U.S.A.	163	38 39N	121 30 E
Sacramento Mts.	161	32 30N	105 30W
Sacramento, R.	163	38 3N	121 56W
Sacratif, Cabo	59	36 42N	3 28W
Sacriston	33	54 49N	1 38W
Sada	56	43 22N	8 15W
Sada-Misaki-Hantō	110	33 22N	132 1 E
Sadaba	58	2 19N	1 12W
Sa'dani	124	5 58 S	38 35 E
Sadao	101	6 38N	100 26 E
Sadasivpet	96	17 38N	77 50 E
Sadberge	33	54 32N	1 30W
Sadd el Aali	122	24 5N	32 54 E
Saddell	34	55 31N	5 30W
Saddle, Hd.	38	54 0N	10 10W
Saddle, The	36	57 10N	5 27W
Sade	121	11 22N	10 45 E
Sadiba	128	18 53 S	23 1 E
Sadimi	127	9 25 S	23 32 E
Sado	112	38 0N	138 25 E
Sado, R.	57	38 10N	8 22W
Sadon, Burma	99	25 28N	98 0 E
Sadon, U.S.S.R.	83	42 52N	43 58 E
Sadri	94	24 28N	74 30 E
Saduya	98	27 50N	95 40 E
Sæby	73	57 21N	10 30 E
Saelices	58	39 55N	2 49W
Safâga	122	26 42N	34 0 E
Safaha	122	26 25N	39 0 E
Safaniya	92	28 5N	48 42 E
Safárikovo	53	48 25N	20 20 E
Safed Koh, Mts.	94	34 15N	64 0 E
Safford	61	32 54N	109 52W
Saffron Walden	29	52 2N	0 15 E
Safi, Jordan	90	31 2N	35 28 E
Safi, Moroc.	118	32 18N	9 14W
Safiah	42	31 27N	34 46 E
Safonovo	80	65 40N	47 50 E
Safranbolu	82	41 15N	32 34 E
Sag Harbor	162	40 59N	72 17W
Sag Sag	135	5 32 S	148 23 E
Saga, Indon.	103	2 40 S	132 55 E
Saga, Kōchi, Japan	110	33 5N	133 6 E
Saga, Saga, Japan	110	33 15N	130 16 E
Saga-ken □	110	33 15N	130 20 E
Sagâg	71	59 46N	5 25 E
Sagaing	98	23 30N	95 30 E
Sagaing □	98	22 0N	95 30 E
Sagala	120	14 9N	6 38W
Sagami-Nada	111	34 58N	139 23 E
Sagami-Wan	111	35 15N	139 25 E
Sagamihara	111	35 33N	139 25 E
Saganoseki	110	33 15N	131 53 E
Sagar	93	23 50N	78 50 E
Sagara, India	97	14 14N	75 6 E
Sagara, Japan	111	34 41N	138 12 E
Sagara, L.	126	5 20 S	31 0 E
Sagawa	110	33 28N	133 11 E
Sågen	72	60 17N	14 10 E
Sagil	105	50 20N	91 40 E
Saginaw	156	43 26N	83 55W
Saginaw B.	150	43 50N	83 40W
Sagleipie	45	45 25N	7 0 E
Saglouc (Sugluk)	149	62 30N	74 15W
Sagone	45	42 7N	8 42 E
Sagone, G. de	45	42 4N	8 40 E
Sagori	107	35 25N	126 49 E
Sagra, La, Mt.	59	38 0N	2 35W
Sagres	57	37 0N	8 58W
Sagu	98	20 13N	94 46 E
Sagua la Grande	166	22 50N	80 10W
Saguache	161	38 10N	106 4W
Saguenay, R.	151	48 22N	71 0W
Sagunto	58	39 42N	0 18W
Sahaba	122	18 57N	30 25 E
Sahagún, Colomb.	174	8 57N	75 27W
Sahagún, Spain	56	42 18N	5 2W
Saham	90	32 42N	35 46 E
Sahara	118	23 0N	5 0W
Saharanpur	94	29 58N	77 33 E
Saharien Atlas	118	34 9N	3 29 E
Sahasinaka	129	21 49 S	47 49 E
Sahaswan	95	28 5N	78 45 E
Sahel, Canal du	120	14 20N	6 0W
Sahibganj	95	25 12N	87 55 E
Sahiwal	94	30 45N	73 8 E
Sahl Arraba	90	37 26N	35 12 E
Sahtaneh, R.	152	59 2N	122 28W
Sahuaripa	164	29 30N	109 0W
Sahuarita	161	31 58N	110 59W
Sahuayo	164	20 4N	102 43W
Sahy	53	48 4N	18 55 E
Sai Buri	101	6 43N	101 39 E
Saibai I.	135	9 25 S	142 40 E
Sa'id Bundas	117	8 24N	24 48 E
Saïda	118	34 50N	0 11 E
Sa'idabad	93	29 30N	55 45 E
Saidapet	97	13 0N	80 15 E
Saidor	135	5 40 S	146 29 E
Saidu	95	34 50N	72 15 E
Säle	72	59 8N	12 55 E
Saighan	93	35 10N	67 55 E
Saignelégier	50	47 15N	7 0 E
Saignes	44	45 20N	2 31 E
Saigō	110	36 12N	133 20 E
Saigon = Phanh Bho Ho Chi Minh	101	10 58N	106 40 E
Saih-al-Malih	93	23 37N	58 31 E
Saihut	91	15 12N	51 10 E
Saijō, Ehima, Japan	110	33 55N	133 11 E
Saijō, Hiroshima, Japan	110	34 25N	132 45 E
Saikhoa Ghat	99	27 50N	95 40 E
Saiki	110	32 58N	131 57 E
Saillans	45	44 42N	5 12 E
Sailolof	103	1 7 S	130 46 E
Saima	107	40 59N	124 15 E
Saimaa, L.	78	61 15N	28 15 E
St. Abbs	35	55 54N	2 7W
St. Abb's Head	35	55 55N	2 10W
St. Aegyd	52	47 52N	15 33 E
St. Affrique	44	43 57N	2 53 E
St. Agnes	30	50 18N	5 13W
St. Agnes Hd.	30	50 19N	5 14W
St. Agnes I.	30	49 53N	6 20W
St.-Agrève	45	45 0N	4 23 E
St.-Aignan	42	47 16N	1 22 E
St. Albans, Austral.	138	24 43 S	139 56 E
St. Albans, Can.	151	47 51N	55 50W
St. Albans, U.K.	29	51 44N	0 19W
St. Albans, Vt., U.S.A.	156	44 49N	73 7W
St. Albans, W. Va., U.S.A.	156	38 21N	81 50W
St. Alban's Head	28	50 34N	2 3W
St. Albert	152	53 37N	113 40W
St. Amand	43	50 25N	3 6 E
St.-Amand-en-Puisaye	43	47 32N	3 5 E
St.-Amand-Mont-Rond	44	46 43N	2 30 E
St.-Amarin	43	47 54N	7 0 E
St.-Amour	45	46 26N	5 21 E
St. Andrā	52	46 46N	14 50 E
St. André, C.	129	16 11 S	44 27 E
St.-André-de-Cubzac	44	44 59N	0 26W
St. André de l'Eure	42	48 54N	1 16 E
St.-André-les-Alpes	45	43 58N	6 30 E
St. Andrews, Can.	151	47 45N	59 15W
St. Andrews, N.Z.	143	44 33 S	171 10 E
St. Andrews, U.K.	35	56 20N	2 48W
St. Ann B.	151	46 22N	60 25W
St. Anne	42	49 43N	2 11W
St. Anne's	32	53 45N	3 2W
St. Ann's	35	55 14N	3 28W
St. Ann's Bay	166	18 26N	77 15W
St. Ann's Hd.	31	51 41N	5 11W
St. Anthony, Can.	151	51 22N	55 35W
St. Anthony, U.S.A.	160	44 0N	111 49W
St.-Antonin-Noble-Val	44	44 10N	1 45 E
St. Arnaud	140	36 32 S	143 16 E
St. Arnaud Ra.	143	42 1 S	172 53 E
St. Arthur	151	47 47N	67 46W
St. Asaph	31	53 15N	3 27W
St. Astier	44	45 8N	0 31 E
St.-Aubin	50	46 54N	6 47 E
St.-Aubin-du-Cormier	42	48 15N	1 26W
St. Augustin	129	23 33 S	43 46 E
St-Augustin-Saguenay	151	51 13N	58 38W
St. Augustine	157	29 52N	81 20W
St. Austell	30	50 20N	4 48W
St.-Avold	43	49 6N	6 43 E
St. Barthélemy, I.	167	17 50N	62 50W
St. Bathans	143	44 53 S	170 0 E
St. Bathan's Mt.	143	44 45 S	169 45 E
St. Bees	32	54 29N	3 36W
St. Bee's Hd.	32	54 30N	3 38 E
St.-Benoît-du-Sault	44	46 26N	1 24 E
St. Bernard, Col du Grand	50	45 53N	7 11 E
St.-Blaise	50	47 1N	6 59 E
St. Blazey	32	50 22N	4 48W
St. Boniface	153	49 50N	97 10W
St. Bonnet	45	44 40N	6 5 E
St. Boswells	35	55 34N	2 39W
St.-Brévin-les-Pins	42	47 14N	2 10W
St. Briavels	28	51 44N	2 39W
St.-Brice-en-Coglès	42	48 25N	1 22W
St. Bride's	151	46 56N	54 10W
St. Bride's B.	31	51 48N	5 15W
St.-Brieuc	42	48 30N	2 46W
St. Budeaux	30	50 23N	4 10W
St. Buryan	30	50 4N	5 34W
St.-Calais	42	47 55N	0 45 E
St.-Cast	42	48 37N	2 18W
St. Catharines	150	43 10N	79 15W
St. Catherine's I.	157	31 35N	81 10W
St. Catherine's Pt.	28	50 34N	1 18W
St.-Céré	44	44 51N	1 54 E
St. Cergue	50	46 27N	6 10 E
St. Cernin	44	45 5N	2 25 E
St.-Chamond	45	45 28N	4 31 E
St. Charles, Ill., U.S.A.	156	41 55N	88 21W
St. Charles, Mo., U.S.A.	158	38 46N	90 30W
St.-Chély-d'Apcher	44	44 48N	3 17 E
St.-Chinian	44	43 25N	2 56 E
St. Christopher (St. Kitts)	167	17 20N	62 40W
St.-Ciers-sur-Gironde	44	45 17N	0 37W
St. Clair	162	40 42N	76 12W
St. Clair, L.	150	42 30N	82 45W
St.-Claud	44	45 54N	0 28 E
St. Claude	153	49 40N	98 20W
St.-Claude	45	46 22N	5 52 E
St. Clears	31	51 48N	4 30W
St.-Cloud	42	48 51N	2 12 E
St. Cloud, Fla., U.S.A.	157	28 15N	81 15W
St. Cloud, Minn., U.S.A.	158	45 30N	94 11W
St. Coeur de Marie	151	48 39N	71 43W
St. Columb Major	30	50 26N	4 56W
St. Combs	37	57 40N	1 55W
St. Cricq, C.	137	25 17 S	113 6 E
St. Croix Falls	158	45 18N	92 22W
St. Croix, I.	147	17 45N	64 45W
St. Croix, R.	158	45 20N	92 50W
St. Cyprien	44	42 37N	3 0 E
St.-Cyr	45	43 11N	5 43 E
St. Cyrus	36	56 47N	2 25W
St. David's, Can.	151	48 12N	58 52W
St. David's, U.K.	31	51 54N	5 16W
St. David's Head	31	51 54N	5 16W
St.-Denis	43	48 56N	2 22 E
St.-Denis-d'Orques	42	48 2N	0 17W
St. Dennis	30	50 23N	4 53W
St.-Dié	43	48 17N	6 56 E
St. Dizier	43	48 40N	5 0 E
St. Dogmaels	31	52 6N	4 42W
St. Dominick	30	50 28N	4 15W
St. Donats	31	51 23N	3 32W
St.-Egrève	45	45 14N	5 41 E
St. Elias, Mt.	147	60 20N	141 59W
St. Elias Mts.	147	59 30N	137 30W
St. Eloy	44	46 10N	2 51 E
St. Emilon	44	44 53N	0 9W
St. Endellion	30	50 33N	4 49W
St. Enoder	30	50 22N	4 57W
St. Erth	30	50 10N	5 26W
St. Étienne	45	45 27N	4 22 E
St.-Étienne-de-Tinée	45	44 16N	6 56 E
St. Eustatius I.	167	17 20N	63 0W
St. Félicien	150	48 40N	72 25W
St. Fergus	37	57 33N	1 50W
St. Fillans	35	56 25N	4 7W
St. Finian's B.	39	51 50N	10 22W
St. Fintan's	151	48 10N	58 50W
St.-Florent	45	42 41N	9 18 E
St.-Florent-sur-Cher	43	46 59N	2 15 E
St.-Florentin	43	48 0N	3 45 E
St.-Flour	44	45 2N	3 6 E
St.-Fons	45	45 42N	4 52 E
St. Francis	158	39 48N	101 47W
St. Francis C.	128	34 14 S	24 49 E
St. Francis, R.	159	32 25N	90 36W
St.-Fulgent	42	46 50N	1 10W
St. Gabriel de Brandon	150	46 17N	73 24W
St.-Gengoux-le-National	45	46 37N	4 40 E
St.-Geniez-d'Olt	44	44 27N	2 58 E
St. George, Austral.	139	28 1 S	148 41 E
St. George, Can.	151	45 11N	66 50W
St. George, P.N.G.	135	4 10 S	152 20 E
St. George, S.C., U.S.A.	157	33 13N	80 37W
St. George, Utah, U.S.A.	161	37 10N	113 35W
St. George, C., Can.	151	48 30N	59 16W
St. George, C., P.N.G.	135	4 49 S	152 53 E
St. George, C., U.S.A.	157	29 36N	85 2W
St. George Hd.	139	35 11 S	150 45 E
St. George Ra., Mts.	136	18 40 S	125 0 E
St. George West	153	50 33N	96 7W
St.-Georges	47	50 37N	4 20 E
St. George's	151	48 26N	58 31W
St. Georges, Qué., Can.	151	46 8N	70 40W
St. Georges, Quebec, Can.	150	46 42N	72 35W
St. Georges, Fr. Gui.	175	4 0N	52 0W
St. George's	167	12 5N	61 43W
St. George's B.	151	48 24N	58 53W
St. George's Channel	147	52 0N	6 0W
St. Georges-de-Didonne	44	45 36N	1 0W
St. Georges Head	141	35 12 S	150 42 E
St.-Gérard	47	50 21N	4 44 E
St. Germain	43	48 53N	2 5 E
St.-Germain-Lembron	44	45 27N	3 14 E
St.-Germain-de-Calberte	44	44 13N	3 48 E
St.-Germain-des-Fossés	44	46 12N	3 26 E
St.-Germain-du-Plain	43	46 42N	4 58 E
St.-Germain-Laval	45	45 50N	4 1 E
St. Germans	30	50 24N	4 19W
St. Gervais, Haute Savoie, France	45	45 53N	6 42 E
St. Gervais, Puy de Dôme, France	44	46 4N	2 50 E
St.-Gervais-les-Bains	43	45 53N	6 41 E
St.-Gildas, Pte. de	42	47 8N	2 14W
St.-Gilles	45	43 40N	4 26 E
St. Gilles Croix-de-Vie	42	46 41N	1 55W
St.-Gingolph	50	46 24N	6 48 E
St.-Girons	44	42 59N	1 8 E
St. Gla, L.	72	59 35N	12 30 E
St. Goar	49	50 31N	7 43 E
St. Gotthard P. = San Gottardo	51	46 33N	8 33 E
St. Govan's Hd.	31	51 35N	4 56W
St.-Guadens	44	43 6N	0 44 E
St.-Gualtier	42	46 39N	1 26 E
St.-Guénolé	42	47 49N	4 23W
St. Harmon	31	52 21N	3 29W
St. Heddinge	73	55 9N	12 26 E
St. Helena	160	38 29N	122 30W
St. Helena, I.	15	15 55 S	5 44W
St. Helenabaai	128	32 40 S	18 10 E
St. Helens, Austral.	138	41 20 S	148 15 E
St. Helens, I.o.W., U.K.	28	50 42N	1 6W
St. Helens, Merseyside, U.K.	32	53 28N	2 44W
St. Helens, U.S.A.	160	45 55N	122 50W
St. Helier	42	49 11N	2 6W
St. Hilaire	42	48 35N	1 7W
St. Hippolyte	43	47 20N	6 50 E
St. Hippolyte-du-Fort	44	43 58N	3 52 E
St.-Honoré	43	46 54N	3 50 E
St.-Hubert	47	50 2N	5 23 E
St. Hyacinthe	150	45 40N	72 58W
St. Ignace	156	45 53N	84 43W
St. Ignace I.	150	48 45N	88 0W
St. Ignatius	160	47 25N	114 2W
St.-Imier	50	47 9N	6 58 E
St. Issey	30	50 30N	4 55W
St. Ives, Cambs., U.K.	29	52 20N	0 5W
St. Ives, Cornwall, U.K.	30	50 13N	5 29W
St. Ives Bay	30	50 15N	5 27W
St.-James	42	48 31N	1 20W
St. James	158	43 57N	94 40W
St. James C.	152	51 55N	131 0W
St. Jean	150	45 20N	73 50W
St.-Jean	45	48 57N	3 1 E
St. Jean Baptiste	153	49 15N	97 20W
St. Jean, C.	124	1 5N	9 20 E
St.-Jean-de-Maurienne	45	45 16N	6 28 E
St.-Jean-de-Luz	44	43 23N	1 39W
St.-Jean-de-Monts	42	46 47N	2 4W
St.-Jean-du-Gard	44	44 7N	3 52 E
St.-Jean-en-Royans	45	45 1N	5 18 E
St.-Jean, L.	151	48 40N	72 0W
St. Jean-Port-Joli	151	47 15N	70 13W
St.-Jean, R.	151	50 17N	64 20W
St. Jérôme, Qué., Can.	150	45 47N	74 0W
St. Jérôme, Qué., Can.	151	48 26N	71 53W
St. John, Can.	151	45 20N	66 8W
St. John, Kans., U.S.A.	159	37 59N	98 45W
St. John, N.D., U.S.A.	158	48 58N	99 40W
St. John, C.	151	50 0N	55 32W
St. John, I.	147	18 20N	64 45W
St. John, R.	151	45 15N	66 4W
St. Johns	167	17 6N	61 51W
St. John's, Can.	151	47 35N	52 40W
St. John's, U.K.	32	54 13N	4 38W
St. Johns, Ariz., U.S.A.	161	34 31N	109 26W
St. Johns, Mich., U.S.A.	156	43 0N	84 38W
St. Johns Chapel	32	54 43N	2 10W
St. John's Pt., Ireland	38	54 35N	8 26W
St. John's Pt., U.K.	38	54 14N	5 40W
St. Johns, R.	157	30 20N	81 30W
St. Johnsbury	156	44 25N	72 1W
St. Johnston	38	54 56N	7 29W
St. Johnsville	162	43 0N	74 43W
St. Joseph, La., U.S.A.	159	31 55N	91 15W
St. Joseph, Mo., U.S.A.	158	39 40N	94 50W
St. Joseph, I.	150	46 12N	83 58W
St. Joseph, L.	150	51 10N	90 35W
St. Joseph, R.	156	42 7N	86 30W
St. Joseph's	156	42 5N	86 30W
St. Jovite	150	46 8N	74 38W
St. Juéry	44	43 55N	2 42 E
St. Julien	45	46 8N	6 5 E
St.-Julien-Chapteuil	45	45 2N	4 4 E
St. Julien du Sault	43	48 1N	3 17 E
St.-Junien	44	45 53N	0 55 E
St. Just	30	50 7N	5 41W
St.-Just-en-Chaussée	43	49 30N	2 25 E
St.-Just-en-Chevalet	44	45 55N	3 50 E
St.-Justin	44	43 59N	0 14W
St. Karlsö, I.	73	57 17N	17 58 E
St. Keverne	30	50 3N	5 5W
St. Kew	30	50 34N	4 48W
St. Kilda	143	45 53 S	170 31 E
St. Kilda, I.	23	57 40N	8 0W
St. Kitts-Nevis ■	167	17 20N	62 40W
St. Laurent	153	50 25N	97 58W
St.-Laurent-du-Pont	45	45 23N	5 45 E
St.-Laurent-en-Grandvaux	45	46 35N	5 45 E
St. Lawrence, Austral.	138	22 16 S	149 31 E
St. Lawrence, Can.	151	46 54N	55 23W

St. Lawrence, Gulf of

Sam Ngao

St. Lawrence, Gulf of 151 48 25N 62 0W
St. Lawrence, I. 147 63 0N 170 0W
St. Lawrence, R. 151 49 30N 66 0W
St.-Léger 47 49 37N 5 39E
St. Leonard 151 47 12N 67 58W
St.-Léonard-de-Noblat 44 45 49N 1 29E
St. Leonards 29 50 51N 0 34E
St. Levan 30 50 3N 5 36W
St Lewis, R. 151 52 26N 56 11W
St. Lin 150 45 44N 73 46W
St.-Lô 42 49 7N 1 5W
St. Louis, Senegal 120 16 8N 16 27W
St. Louis, Mich., U.S.A. 156 43 27N 84 38W
St. Louis, Mo., U.S.A. 158 38 40N 90 12W
St. Louis R. 158 47 15N 92 45W
St.-Loup-sur-Semouse 43 47 53N 6 16E
St. Lucia, C. 129 28 32S 32 29E
St. Lucia Channel 167 14 15N 61 0W
St. Lucia I. 167 14 0N 60 50W
St. Lucia, Lake 129 28 5S 32 30E
St. Lunaire-Griquet 151 51 31N 55 28W
St. Maarten, I. 167 18 0N 63 5W
St. Mabyn 30 50 30N 4 45W
St. Magnus B. 36 60 25N 1 35W
St.-Maixent-l'École 44 46 24N 0 12W
St.-Malo 42 48 39N 2 1W
St. Malo, G. de 42 48 50N 2 30W
St. Mandrier 45 43 4N 5 56E
St. Marc 167 19 10N 72 50W
St.-Marcellin 45 45 9N 5 20E
St. Marcouf, Îs. 42 49 30N 1 10W
St.-Mard 47 49 2N 2 42E
St. Margaret's-at-Cliffe 29 51 10N 1 23E
St. Margaret's Hope 37 58 49N 2 58W
St. Maries 160 47 17N 116 34W
St. Martin 43 50 42N 1 38E
St.-Martin, I. 167 18 0N 63 0W
St. Martin L. 153 51 40N 98 30W
St. Martin-Tende-Vésubie 45 44 4N 7 15E
St. Martins 151 45 22N 65 25W
St. Martin's I. 30 49 58N 6 16W
St. Martinsville 159 30 10N 91 50W
St.-Martory 44 43 9N 0 56E
St. Mary B. 151 46 50N 53 50W
St. Mary Bourne 28 51 16N 1 24W
St. Mary C. 120 13 24N 13 10E
St. Mary Is. 97 13 20N 74 35E
St. Mary, Mt. 135 8 8S 146 54E
St. Mary Pk. 140 31 32S 138 34E
St. Marys, N.S.W., Austral. 133 33 44S 150 49E
St. Marys, Tas., Austral. 138 41 32S 148 11E
St. Mary's, Can. 151 46 56N 53 34W
St. Mary's, U.K. 37 58 53N 2 55W
St. Mary's, Ohio, U.S.A. 156 40 33N 84 20W
St. Mary's, Pa., U.S.A. 156 41 30N 78 33W
St Marys Bay 151 44 25N 66 10W
St. Mary's, C. 151 46 50N 54 12W
St. Mary's I. 30 49 55N 6 17W
St. Mary's Pk. 133 31 30S 138 33E
St. Mary's Sd. 30 49 53N 6 19W
St. Mathews I. = Zadetkyi Kyun 101 10 0N 48 25E
St.-Mathieu, Pte. de 42 48 20N 4 45W
St. Matthias Grp. 135 1 30S 150 0E
St.-Maur-des-Fosses 43 48 48N 2 30E
St. Maurice 50 46 13N 7 0E
St. Maurice R. 150 47 20N 72 50W
St. Mawes 30 50 10N 5 1W
St.-Médard-de-Guizières 44 45 1N 0 4W
St.-Méen-le-Grand 42 48 11N 2 12W
St. Merryn 30 50 31N 4 58W
St. Michael 147 63 30N 162 30W
St. Michaels, Arizona, U.S.A. 161 35 45N 109 5W
St. Michaels, Maryland, U.S.A. 162 38 47N 76 14W
St. Michael's Mt. 30 50 7N 5 30W
St. Michel 45 45 15N 6 29E
St. Mihiel 43 48 54N 5 30E
St. Minver 30 50 34N 4 52W
St. Monans 35 56 13N 2 46W
St.-Nazaire 42 47 17N 2 12W
St. Neots 29 52 14N 0 16W
St.-Nicholas-de-Port 43 48 38N 6 18E
St. Niklaus 50 46 10N 7 49E
St. Ninian's, I. 36 59 59N 1 20W
St. Olaf 73 55 40N 14 12E
St.-Omer 43 50 45N 2 15E
St. Osyth 29 51 47N 1 4E
St. Ouen 43 48 50N 2 20E
St. Pacome 151 47 24N 69 58W
St. Palais 44 45 40N 1 8W
St. Pamphile 151 46 58N 69 48W
St.-Pardoux-la-Rivière 44 45 29N 0 45E
St. Pascal 151 47 32N 69 48W
St. Patrickswell 39 52 36N 8 43W
St. Paul, Can. 152 54 59N 111 17W
St. Paul, France 44 43 44N 1 3W
St. Paul, Minn., U.S.A. 158 44 54N 93 5W
St. Paul, Nebr., U.S.A. 158 41 15N 98 30W
St. Paul-de-Fenouillet 44 42 50N 2 28E
St. Paul, I., Atl. Oc. 14 0 50N 31 40W
St. Paul, I., Can. 151 47 12N 60 9W
St. Paul, I., Ind. Oc. 11 30 40S 77 34E
St. Paul's B. 151 49 48N 57 58W
St.-Peray 45 44 57N 4 50E
St.-Père-en-Retz 42 47 11N 2 2W
St. Peter 158 44 15N 93 57W
St. Peter Port 42 49 27N 2 31W
St. Peters, N.S., Can. 151 45 40N 60 53W
St. Peters, P.E.I., Can. 151 46 25N 62 35W
St. Petersburg 157 27 45N 82 40W
St.-Philbert-de-Grand-Lieu 42 47 2N 1 39W
St Pierre 151 46 40N 56 0W
St.-Pierre-d'Oleron 44 45 57N 1 19W
St.-Pierre-Eglise 42 49 40N 1 24W
St.-Pierre-en-Port 42 49 48N 0 30E
Saint-Pierre et Miquelon □ 151 46 55N 56 10W
St-Pierre, L. 150 46 12N 72 52W
St.-Pierre-le-Moûtier 43 46 47N 3 7E
St. Pierre-sur-Dives 42 49 2N 0 1W
St.-Pieters Leew 47 50 47N 4 16E
St. Pol 43 50 21N 2 20E
St.-Pol-de-Léon 42 48 41N 4 0W
St.-Pol-sur-Mer 43 51 1N 2 20E
St. Pons 44 43 30N 2 45E
St.-Pourçain-sur-Sioule 43 46 18N 3 18E
St.-Quay-Portrieux 42 48 39N 2 51W
St.-Quentin 43 49 50N 3 16E
St. Rambert-d'Albon 45 45 17N 1 35E
St.-Raphaël 45 43 25N 6 46E
St. Regis 160 47 20N 115 3W
St.-Rémy-de-Provence 45 43 48N 4 50E
St.-Renan 42 48 26N 4 37W
St.-Saëns 42 49 41N 1 16E
St.-Sauveur-en-Puisaye 43 47 37N 3 12E
St.-Sauveur-le-Vicomte 42 49 23N 1 32W
St. Savin 44 46 34N 0 50E
St.-Savinien 44 45 53N 0 42W
St. Sebastien, C. 129 12 26S 48 44E
St.-Seine-l'Abbaye 43 47 26N 4 47E
St. Sernin 44 43 54N 2 35E
St.-Servan-sur-Mer 42 48 38N 2 0E
St.-Sever-Calvados 42 48 50N 1 3W
St. Simeon 151 47 51N 69 54W
St. Stephen, Can. 151 45 16N 67 17W
St. Stephen, U.K. 30 50 20N 4 52W
St.-Sulpice 44 43 46N 1 41E
St.-Sulpice-Laurière 44 46 3N 1 29E
St. Teath 30 50 34N 4 45W
St.-Thegonnec 42 48 31N 3 57W
St. Thomas 150 42 45N 81 10W
St. Thomas, I. 147 18 21N 64 55W
St. Tite 150 46 45N 72 40W
St. Tropez 45 43 17N 6 38E
St. Troud 47 50 48N 5 10E
St. Tudwal's Is. 31 52 48N 4 28W
St. Tudy 30 50 33N 4 45W
St.-Vaast-la-Hougue 42 49 35N 1 17W
St. Valéry 43 50 10N 1 38E
St.-Valéry-en-Caux 42 49 52N 0 43E
St.-Vallier 45 45 11N 4 50E
St.-Vallier-de-Thiey 45 43 42N 6 51E
St.-Varent 42 46 53N 0 13W
St. Vincent 14 18 0N 26 1W
St. Vincent C. 125 21 58S 43 20E
St. Vincent, C. = São Vincente 57 37 0N 9 0W
St. Vincent-de-Tyrosse 44 43 39N 1 18W
St. Vincent, G. 140 35 0S 138 0E
St. Vincent, I. 167 13 10N 61 10W
St. Vincent Passage 167 13 30N 61 0W
St.-Vith 47 50 17N 6 9E
St.-Yrieux-la-Perche 44 45 31N 1 12E
Ste.-Adresse 42 49 31N 0 5E
Ste.-Agathe-des-Monts 150 46 3N 74 17W
Ste. Anne 167 14 26N 60 53W
Ste. Anne de Beaupré 151 47 2N 70 58W
Ste. Anne de Portneuf 151 48 38N 69 8W
Ste.-Anne-des-Monts 151 49 8N 66 30W
Ste. Benoîte 43 49 47N 3 30E
Ste. Cecile 151 47 56N 64 34W
Ste.-Croix 43 46 49N 6 34W
Ste.-Enimie 44 44 22N 3 26E
Ste.-Foy-la-Grande 44 44 50N 0 13E
Ste. Genevieve 158 37 59N 90 2W
Ste. Germaine 151 46 24N 70 24W
Ste.-Hermine 44 46 32N 1 4W
Ste.-Livrade-sur-Lot 44 44 24N 0 36E
Ste. Marguerite, R. 151 50 9N 66 36W
Ste. Marie 167 14 48N 61 1W
Ste.-Marie-aux-Mines 43 48 10N 7 12E
Ste. Marie, C. 129 25 36S 45 8E
Ste. Marie de la Madeleine 151 46 26N 71 0W
Ste. Marie, I. 129 16 50S 49 55E
Ste.-Maure-de-Touraine 42 47 7N 0 37E
Ste.-Maxime 45 43 19N 6 39E
Ste.-Menehould 43 49 5N 4 54E
Ste.-Mère-Église 42 49 24N 1 19W
Ste. Rose 167 16 20N 61 45W
Ste. Rose du lac 153 51 41N 99 30W
Ste. Teresa 172 33 33S 60 54W
Saintes 44 45 45N 0 37W
Saintes, I. des 167 15 50N 61 35W
Saintes-Maries-de-la-Mer 45 43 26N 4 26E
Saintes Maries, Les 45 43 27N 4 25E
Saintfield 38 54 28N 5 50W
Saintonge 44 45 40N 0 50W
Sairang 99 23 50N 92 45E
Sairecábur, Cerro 172 22 43S 67 54W
Saitama-ken □ 111 36 25N 137 0E
Saito 110 32 3N 131 18E
Sajama, Nevada 174 18 0S 68 55W
Sajan 66 45 50N 20 58E
Sajószentpéter 53 48 12N 20 44E
Sajum, mt. 95 33 20N 79 0E
Saka Ilkalat 93 27 20N 64 7E
Sakai 111 34 30N 135 30E
Sakaide 110 34 15N 133 56E
Sakaiminato 110 35 38N 133 11E
Sakaka 92 30 0N 40 8E
Sakami, L. 150 53 15N 76 45W
Sâkâne, 'Erg i-n 118 20 30N 1 30W
Sakania 127 12 43S 28 30E
Sakar, I. 138 5 30S 148 0E
Sakarya, R. 82 40 5N 31 0E
Sakata 112 36 38N 138 19E
Sakchu 107 40 23N 125 2E
Sakeny, R. 129 20 0S 45 25E
Sakété 121 6 40N 2 32E
Sakhalin, Ostrov 77 51 0N 143 0E
Sakhi Gopal 96 19 58N 85 50E
Sakhnin 90 32 52N 35 12E
Saki 82 45 16N 33 34E
Sakiai 80 54 59N 23 0E
Sakmara 84 52 0N 55 20E
Sakmara, R. 84 51 46N 55 1E
Sakołow Małopolski 54 50 10N 22 9E
Sakon Nakhon 100 17 10N 104 9E
Sakrand 94 26 10N 68 15E
Sakri 96 21 2N 74 40E
Sakskøbing 73 54 49N 11 39E
Saku 111 36 11N 138 31E
Sakuma 111 35 3N 137 56E
Sakurai 111 34 30N 135 51E
Sakuru 111 35 43N 140 14E
Säkylä 75 61 4N 22 20E
Sal, R. 83 47 25N 42 20E
Sal'a 53 48 10N 17 50E
Sala 72 59 58N 16 35E
Sala Consilina 65 40 23N 15 35E
Sala-y-Gomez, I. 131 26 28S 105 28W
Salaberry-de-Valleyfield 150 45 15N 74 8W
Salada, La 164 24 30N 111 30W
Saladas 172 28 15S 58 40W
Saladillo 172 35 40S 59 55W
Salado, R., Buenos Aires, Argent. 172 35 40S 58 10W
Salado, R., Santa Fe, Argent. 172 27 0S 63 40W
Salado, R., Mexico 164 26 52N 99 19W
Salaga 121 8 31N 0 31W
Salala, Liberia 120 6 42N 10 7W
Salala, Sudan 122 21 17N 36 16E
Salalah 91 16 56N 53 59E
Salama 90 32 3N 34 48E
Salamanca, Chile 172 32 0S 71 25W
Salamanca, Spain 56 40 58N 5 39W
Salamanca, U.S.A. 156 42 10N 78 42W
Salamanca □ 56 40 57N 5 40W
Salamaua 138 7 10S 147 0E
Salamina 174 5 25N 75 29W
Salamis 69 37 56N 23 30E
Salar de Atacama 176 23 30S 68 25W
Salar de Uyuni 174 20 30S 67 45W
Salard 70 47 12N 22 3E
Salas 56 43 25N 6 15W
Salas de los Infantes 58 42 2N 3 17W
Salavat 84 53 21N 55 55E
Salaverry 174 8 15S 79 0W
Salawe 126 3 17S 32 56E
Salayar, I. 103 6 15S 120 30E
Salazar, R. 58 42 45N 1 8W
Salbohed 72 59 55N 16 22E
Salbris 43 47 25N 2 3E
Salcia 70 43 56N 24 55E
Salcombe 30 50 14N 3 47W
Salcombe Regis 30 50 41N 3 11W
Saldaña 56 42 32N 4 48W
Saldanha 128 33 0S 17 58E
Saldanhabaai 128 33 6S 18 0E
Saldus 80 56 45N 22 37E
Sale 141 38 6S 147 6E
Salé 118 34 3N 6 48W
Sale 32 53 26N 2 19W
Saléa-koïra 121 16 54N 0 46W
Salebabu 103 3 45N 125 55E
Salehabad 93 35 40N 61 2E
Salekhard 76 66 30N 66 25E
Salem, India 97 11 40N 78 11E
Salem, Ind., U.S.A. 156 38 38N 86 16W
Salem, Mass., U.S.A. 162 42 29N 70 53W
Salem, Mo., U.S.A. 159 37 40N 91 30W
Salem, N.H., U.S.A. 162 42 47N 71 12W
Salem, N.J., U.S.A. 162 39 34N 75 29W
Salem, N.Y., U.S.A. 162 43 10N 73 20W
Salem, Ohio, U.S.A. 156 40 52N 80 50W
Salem, Oreg., U.S.A. 160 45 0N 123 0W
Salem, Va., U.S.A. 156 37 19N 80 8W
Salembu, Kepulauan 102 5 35S 114 30E
Salemi 64 37 49N 12 47E
Salen, Norway 75 64 41N 11 27E
Salen, Highland, U.K. 36 56 42N 5 48W
Salen, Strathclyde, U.K. 34 56 31N 5 57W
Salernes 45 43 34N 6 15E
Salerno 65 40 40N 14 44E
Salerno, G. di 65 40 35N 14 45E
Salfit 90 32 5N 35 11E
Salford 32 53 30N 2 17W
Salford Priors 28 52 10N 1 52W
Salgir, R. 82 45 30N 34 30E
Salgótarján 53 48 5N 19 47E
Salgueiro 170 8 4S 39 6W
Salies-de-Béarn 44 43 28N 0 56W
Salima 125 13 47S 34 28E
Salin 98 20 35N 94 40E
Salina 158 38 50N 97 40W
Salina Cruz 165 16 10N 95 10W
Salina, I. 65 38 35N 14 50E
Salina, La 174 10 22N 71 27W
Salinas, Brazil 171 16 20S 42 10W
Salinas, Chile 172 23 31S 69 29W
Salinas, Ecuador 174 2 10S 80 50W
Salinas, Mexico 164 23 37N 106 8W
Salinas, U.S.A. 163 36 40N 121 31W
Salinas Ambargasta 172 29 0S 65 30W
Salinas, B. de 166 11 4N 85 45W
Salinas, Cabo de 59 39 16N 3 4E
Salinas (de Hidalgo) 164 22 30N 101 40W
Salinas Grandes 172 30 0S 65 0W
Salinas, Pampa de las 172 31 58S 66 42W
Salinas, R., Mexico 165 16 28N 90 31W
Salinas, R., U.S.A. 163 36 45N 121 48W
Saline, R. 158 39 10N 99 5W
Salines-les-Bains 43 46 58N 5 52E
Salinópolis 170 0 40S 47 20W
Salir 57 37 14N 8 2W
Salisbury, Austral. 140 34 46S 138 40E
•Salisbury, Zimb. 127 17 50S 31 2E
Salisbury, U.K. 28 51 4N 1 48W
Salisbury, Md., U.S.A. 162 38 20N 75 38W
Salisbury, N.C., U.S.A. 157 35 42N 80 29W
Salisbury Plain 28 51 13N 1 50W
Salitre, R. 170 9 29S 40 39W
Salka 121 10 20N 4 58E
Salle, La 158 41 20N 89 5W
Sallent 58 41 49N 1 54E
Salles-Curan 44 44 11N 2 48E
Salling 73 56 40N 8 55E
Sallisaw 159 35 26N 94 45W
Sallom Junc. 122 19 23N 37 6E
Sally Gap, Mt. 39 53 7N 6 18W
Salmerón 58 40 33N 2 29W
Salmo 152 49 10N 117 20W
Salmon 160 45 12N 113 56W
Salmon Arm 152 50 40N 119 15W
Salmon Falls 160 42 55N 114 59W
Salmon Gums 137 32 59S 121 38E
Salmon, R., Can. 152 54 3N 122 40W
Salmon, R., U.S.A. 160 46 0N 116 30W
Salmon Res. 151 48 05N 56 00W
Salmon River Mts. 160 45 0N 114 30W
Salo 75 60 22N 23 3E
Salò 62 45 37N 10 32E
Salobreña 57 36 44N 3 35W
Salome 161 33 51N 113 37W
Salon-de-Provence 45 43 39N 5 6E
Salonica = Thessaloniki 68 40 38N 22 58E
Salonta 70 46 49N 21 42E
Salop □ 28 52 36N 2 45W
Salor, R. 57 39 39N 7 3W
Salou, Cabo 58 41 3N 1 10E
Salsacate 172 31 20S 65 5W
Salsaker 72 62 59N 18 20E
Salses 44 42 50N 2 55E
Salsette I. 96 19 5N 72 50E
Salsk 83 46 28N 41 30E
Salso, R. 65 37 6N 13 55E
Salsomaggiore 62 44 48N 9 59E
Salt 90 32 2N 35 43E
Salt Creek 140 36 8S 139 38E
Salt Creek Telegraph Office 139 36 0S 139 35E
Salt Fork R. 159 37 25N 98 40W
Salt Lake City 160 40 45N 111 58W
Salt, R., Can. 152 60 0N 112 25W
Salt, R., U.S.A. 161 33 50N 110 25W
Salt Range 94 32 30N 72 25E
Salta 172 24 47S 65 25W
Salta □ 172 24 48S 65 30W
Saltash 30 50 25N 4 13W
Saltburn by Sea 33 54 35N 0 58W
Saltcoats 34 55 38N 4 47W
Saltee Is. 39 52 7N 6 37W
Saltergate 33 54 20N 0 40W
Saltfjorden 74 67 15N 14 20E
Saltfleet 33 53 25N 0 11E
Saltfleetby 33 53 23N 0 10E
Salthill 39 53 15N 9 6W
Saltholm 73 55 38N 12 43E
Salthólmavík 74 65 24N 21 57W
Saltillo 164 25 30N 100 57W
Salto, Argent. 172 34 20S 60 15W
Salto, Uruguay 172 31 20S 57 59W
Salto □ 172 31 20S 57 59W
Salto Augusto, falls 172 8 30S 58 0W
Salto da Divisa 171 16 0S 39 57W
Salton City 163 33 21N 115 59W
Salton Sea 163 33 20N 115 50W
Saltpond 121 5 15N 1 3W
Saltsjöbaden 73 59 15N 18 20E
Saltspring 152 48 54N 123 37W
Saltwood 29 51 4N 1 5E
Saluda 162 37 36N 76 36W
Salula, R. 157 34 12N 81 45W
Salûm 122 31 31N 25 7E
Salûm, Khâlig el 122 31 30N 25 9E
Salur 96 18 27N 83 18E
Saluzzo 62 44 39N 7 29E
Salvador, Brazil 171 13 0S 38 30W
Salvador, Can. 153 52 10N 109 25W
Salvador ■ 164 13 50N 89 0W
Salvador, L. 159 29 46N 90 16W
Salvaterra 170 0 46S 48 31W
Salvaterra de Magos 57 39 1N 8 47W
Sálvora, Isla 56 42 30N 8 58W
Salwa 93 24 45N 50 55E
Salween, R. 98 16 31N 97 37E
Salza, R. 52 47 43N 15 0E
Salzach, R. 52 47 15N 12 25E
Salzburg 52 47 48N 13 2E
Salzgitter 48 52 2N 10 22E
Salzwedel 48 52 50N 11 11E
Sam Neua 100 20 29N 104 0E
Sam Ngao 100 17 18N 99 0E

*Renamed Harare

Sam Rayburn Res **San Quintín**

Sam Rayburn Res. 159 31 15N 94 20W
Sam Son 100 19 44N 105 54 E
Sam Ten 100 19 59N 104 38 E
Sama 84 60 12N 60 22 E
Sama de Langreo 56 43 18N 5 40W
Samales Group 103 6 0N 122 0 E
Samalkot 96 17 3N 82 13 E
Samâlût 122 28 20N 30 42 E
Samana 94 30 10N 76 13 E
Samana Cay 167 23 3N 73 45W
Samanco 174 9 10 S 78 30W
Samanga 127 8 20 S 39 13 E
Samangan 93 36 15N 67 40 E
Samangwa 126 4 23 S 24 10 E
Samani 112 42 7N 142 56 E
Samar, I. 103 12 0N 125 0 E
Samara, R. 84 53 10N 50 4 E
Samaria 135 10 39 S 150 41 E
Samaria = Shomron 90 32 15N 35 13 E
Samarkand 85 39 40N 67 0 E
Samarra 92 34 16N 43 55 E
Samastipur 95 25 50N 85 50 E
Samatan 44 43 29N 0 55 E
Samba, Kashmir 95 32 32N 75 10 E
Samba, Zaïre 126 4 38 S 26 22 E
Sambaiba 170 7 8 S 45 21W
Sambaina 129 19 37 S 47 8 E
Sambaise 65 38 58N 16 16 E
Sambalpur 96 21 28N 83 58 E
Sambas, S. 102 1 20N 109 20 E
Sambava 129 14 16 S 50 10 E
Sambawizi 127 18 24 S 26 13 E
Sambhal 95 28 35N 78 37 E
Sambhar 94 26 52N 75 10 E
Sambonifacio 62 45 24N 11 16 E
Sambor, Camb. 100 12 46N 106 0 E
Sambor, U.S.S.R. 80 49 30N 23 10 E
Sambre, R. 47 50 27N 4 52 E
Sambuca 64 37 39N 13 6 E
Samburu □ 126 1 10N 37 0 E
Sambusu 128 17 55 S 19 21 E
Samchŏk 107 37 30N 129 10 E
Samchonpo 107 34 54N 128 6 E
Same 126 4 2 S 37 38 E
Samedan 51 46 32N 9 52 E
Samer 43 50 38N 1 44 E
Samfya 127 11 16 S 29 31 E
Sámi 69 38 15N 20 39 E
Samna 122 25 12N 37 17 E
Samnager 71 60 23N 5 39 E
Samnaun 51 46 57N 10 22 E
Samnu 119 27 15N 14 55 E
Samo Alto 172 30 22 S 71 0W
Samoan Is. 10 14 0 S 171 0W
Samobor 63 45 47N 15 44 E
Samoëns 45 46 5N 6 45 E
Samoorombón, Bahía 172 36 5 S 57 20W
Samorogouan 120 11 21N 4 57W
Samos 56 42 44N 7 20W
Samoš 66 45 13N 20 49 E
Sámos, I. 69 37 45N 26 50 E
Samosir, P. 102 2 35N 98 50 E
Samothráki 68 40 28N 25 38 E
Samothráki, I. 68 40 25N 25 40 E
Sampa 120 8 0N 2 36W
Sampacho 172 33 20 S 64 50W
Sampang 103 7 11 S 113 13 E
Samper de Calanda 58 41 11N 04 2W
Sampford Courtenay 30 50 47N 3 58W
Sampit 102 2 20 S 113 0 E
Samra 92 25 35N 41 0 E
Samreboi 120 5 34N 7 28 E
Samrée 47 50 13N 5 39 E
Samrong, Camb. 100 14 15N 103 30 E
Samrong, Thai. 100 15 10N 100 40 E
Samsø 73 55 50N 10 35 E
Samsø Bælt 73 55 45N 10 45 E
Samsonovo 85 37 53N 65 15 E
Samsun 92 41 15N 36 15 E
Samsun Daği 69 37 45N 27 10 E
Samtredia 83 42 7N 42 24 E
Samui, Ko 101 9 30N 100 0 E
Samur, R. 83 41 30N 48 0 E
Samusole 127 10 2 S 24 0 E
Samut Prakan 100 13 32N 100 40 E
Samut Sakhon 100 13 31N 100 20 E
Samut Songkhram (Mekong) 100 13 24N 100 1 E
Samwari 94 28 5N 66 46 E
Samyo La 99 29 55N 84 46 E
San 120 13 15N 4 45W
San Adrián, C. de 56 43 21N 8 50W
San Adrián, G. de 56 43 21N 8 50W
San Agustín 174 1 53N 76 16W
San Agustín, C. 103 6 20N 126 13 E
San Agustín de Valle Fértil 172 30 35 S 67 30W
San Ambrosio, I. 131 26 35 S 79 30W
San Andreas 163 38 17N 120 39W
San Andrés, I. de 166 12 42N 81 46W
San Andres Mts. 161 33 0N 106 45W
San Andrés Tuxtla 165 18 30N 95 20W
San Angelo 159 31 30N 100 30W
San Anselmo 163 37 49N 122 34W
San Antonio, Belize 165 16 15N 89 2W
San Antonio, Chile 172 33 40 S 71 40W
San Antonio, N. Mex., U.S.A. 161 33 58N 106 57W
San Antonio, Tex., U.S.A. 159 29 30N 98 30W
San Antonio, Venez. 174 3 30N 66 44W
San Antonio Abad 59 38 59N 1 19 E
San Antonio, C., Argent. 172 36 15 S 56 40W
San Antonio, C., Cuba 166 21 50N 84 57W
San Antonio, C. de 59 38 48N 0 12 E
San Antonio de Caparo 174 7 35N 71 27W
San Antonio de los Baños 166 22 54N 82 31W
San Antonio de los Cobres 172 24 16 S 66 2W
San Antonio do Zaire 124 6 8 S 12 11 E
San Antonio, Mt. (Old Baldy Pk.) 163 34 17N 117 38W
San Antonio Oeste 176 40 40 S 65 0W
San Antonio, R. 159 28 30N 97 14W
San Ardo 163 36 1N 120 54W
San Bartolomeo in Galdo 65 41 23N 15 2 E
San Benedetto 62 45 2N 10 57 E
San Benedetto del Tronto 63 42 57N 13 52 E
San Benedicto, I. 164 19 18N 110 49W
San Benito 159 26 5N 97 32W
San Benito Mtn. 163 36 22N 120 37W
San Benito, R. 163 36 53N 121 50W
San Bernardino 163 34 7N 117 18W
San Bernardino, Paso del 51 46 28N 9 11 E
San Bernardo 172 33 40 S 70 50W
San Bernardo, I. de 174 9 45N 75 50W
San Blas 164 26 10N 108 40W
San Blas, C. 157 29 40N 85 25W
San Blas, Cord. de 166 9 15N 78 30W
San Borja 174 15 0 S 67 12W
San Buenaventura 164 27 5N 101 32W
San Buenaventura = Ventura 163 34 17N 119 18W
San Carlos, Argent. 172 33 50 S 69 0W
San Carlos, Mexico 164 29 0N 101 10W
San Carlos, Nic. 166 11 12N 84 50W
San Carlos, Phil. 103 10 29N 123 25 E
San Carlos, Uruguay 173 34 46 S 54 58W
San Carlos, U.S.A. 161 33 24N 110 27W
San Carlos, Amazonas, Venez. 174 1 55N 67 4W
San Carlos, Cojedes, Venez. 174 9 40N 68 36W
San Carlos de Bariloche 176 41 10 S 71 25W
San Carlos de la Rápita 58 40 37N 0 35 E
San Carlos del Zulia 174 9 1N 71 55W
San Carlos L. 161 33 20N 110 10W
San Carlos = Butuku-Luba 121 3 29N 8 33 E
San Cataldo 64 37 30N 13 58 E
San Celoni 58 41 42N 2 30 E
San Clemente, Chile 172 35 30 S 71 39W
San Clemente, Spain 59 39 24N 2 25W
San Clemente, U.S.A. 163 33 29N 117 45W
San Clemente I. 163 32 53N 118 30W
San Constanzo 63 43 46N 13 5 E
San Cristóbal, Argent. 172 30 20 S 61 10W
San Cristóbal, Dom. Rep. 167 18 25N 70 6W
San Cristóbal, Venez. 174 7 46N 72 14W
San Cristóbal de las Casas 165 16 50N 92 33W
San Damiano d'Asti 62 44 51N 8 4 E
San Daniel del Friuli 63 46 10N 13 0 E
San Demétrio Corone 65 39 34N 16 22 E
San Diego, Calif., U.S.A. 163 32 43N 117 10W
San Diego, Tex., U.S.A. 159 27 47N 98 15W
San Diego, C. 176 54 40 S 65 10W
San Diego de la Unión 164 21 28N 100 52W
San Donà di Piave 63 45 38N 12 34 E
San Elpídio a Mare 63 43 16N 13 41 E
San Estanislao 172 24 39 S 56 26W
San Esteban de Gormaz 58 41 34N 3 13W
San Felice sul Panaro 62 44 51N 11 9 E
San Felipe, Chile 172 32 43 S 70 50W
San Felipe, Mexico 164 31 0N 114 52W
San Felipe, Venez. 174 10 20N 68 44W
San Felipe, R. 163 33 12N 115 49W
San Feliu de Guixols 58 41 45N 3 1 E
San Feliu de Llobregat 58 41 23N 2 2 E
San Félix 174 8 20N 62 35W
San Felix, I. 131 26 30 S 80 0W
San Fernando, Chile 172 34 30 S 71 0W
San Fernando, Mexico 164 30 0N 115 10W
San Fernando, Luzon, Phil. 103 15 5N 120 37 E
San Fernando, Luzon, Phil. 103 16 40N 120 23 E
San Fernando, Spain 57 36 22N 6 17W
San Fernando, Trin 167 10 20N 61 30W
San Fernando, U.S.A. 163 34 15N 118 29W
San Fernando de Apure 174 7 54N 67 28W
San Fernando de Atabapo 174 4 3N 67 42W
San Fernando di Puglia 65 41 18N 16 5 E
San Fernando, R. 164 25 0N 99 0W
San Francisco, Córdoba, Argent. 172 31 30 S 62 5W
San Francisco, San Luis, Argent. 172 32 45 S 66 10W
San Francisco, U.S.A. 163 37 47N 122 30W
San Francisco de Macorís 167 19 19N 70 15W
San Francisco del Monte de Oro 172 32 36 S 66 8W
San Francisco del Oro 164 26 52N 105 50W
San Francisco Javier 59 38 40N 1 25 E
San Francisco, Paso de 172 35 40 S 70 24W
San Francisco, R. 161 33 30N 109 0W
San Francisco Solano, Pta. 174 6 18N 77 29W
San Francisville 159 30 48N 91 22W
San Fratello 65 38 1N 14 33 E
San Gabriel 174 0 36N 77 49W
San Gavino Monreale 64 39 33N 8 47 E
San German 147 18 5N 67 3W
San Gil 174 6 33N 73 8W
San Gimignano 62 43 28N 11 3 E
San Giórgio di Nogaro 63 45 50N 13 13 E
San Giórgio Iónico 65 40 27N 17 23 E
San Giovanni Bianco 62 45 52N 9 40 E
San Giovanni in Fiore 65 39 16N 16 42 E
San Giovanni in Persiceto 63 44 39N 11 12 E
San Giovanni Rotondo 65 41 41N 15 42 E
San Giovanni Valdarno 63 43 32N 11 30 E
San Giuliano Terme 62 43 45N 10 26 E
San Gorgonio Mtn. 163 34 7N 116 51W
San Gottardo, Paso del 51 46 33N 8 33 E
San Gregorio, Uruguay 173 32 37 S 55 40W
San Gregorio, U.S.A. 163 37 20N 122 23W
San Guiseppe Iato 64 37 37N 13 11 E
San Ignacio, Boliv. 174 16 20 S 60 55W
San Ignacio, Mexico 164 27 27N 112 51W
San Ignacio, Parag. 172 26 52 S 57 3W
San Ignacio, Laguna 164 26 50N 113 11W
San Ildefonso, C. 103 16 0N 122 10 E
San Isidro 172 34 29 S 58 31W
San Jacinto, Colomb. 174 9 50N 75 8W
San Jacinto, U.S.A. 163 33 47N 116 57W
San Javier, Misiones, Argent. 173 27 55 S 55 5W
San Javier, Santa Fe, Argent. 172 30 40 S 59 55W
San Javier, Boliv. 174 16 18 S 62 30W
San Javier, Chile 172 35 40 S 71 45W
San Javier, Spain 59 37 49N 0 50W
San Jerónimo, Sa. de 174 8 0N 75 50W
San Joaquin 163 36 36N 120 11W
San Joaquín 174 10 16N 67 47W
San Joaquin R. 163 38 4N 121 51W
San Joaquin Valley 163 37 0N 120 30W
San Jorge 172 31 54 S 61 50W
San Jorge, Bahía de 164 31 20N 113 20W
San Jorge, Golfo de 176 46 0 S 66 0W
San Jorge, G. de 58 40 50N 0 55W
San José, Boliv. 174 17 45 S 60 50W
San José, C. Rica 166 10 0N 84 2W
San José, Guat. 164 14 0N 90 50W
San José, Luzon, Phil. 103 15 45N 120 55 E
San José, Mindoro, Phil. 103 10 50N 122 5 E
San José, Spain 59 38 55N 1 18 E
San Jose, Calif., U.S.A. 163 37 20N 121 53W
San Jose, N. Mex., U.S.A. 159 35 26N 105 30W
San José Carpizo 165 19 26N 90 32W
San José de Feliciano 172 30 26 S 58 46W
San José de Jáchal 172 30 5 S 69 0W
San José de Mayo 172 34 27 S 56 27W
San José de Ocuné 174 4 15N 70 20W
San José del Cabo 164 23 0N 109 50W
San José del Guaviare 174 2 35N 72 38W
San José, I. 164 25 0N 110 50W
San Juan, Argent. 172 31 30 S 68 30W
San Juan, Antioquía, Colomb. 174 8 46N 76 32W
San Juan, Meta, Colomb. 174 3 26N 73 50W
San Juan, Dom. Rep. 147 18 49N 71 12W
San Juan, Coahuila, Mexico 164 29 34N 101 53W
San Juan, Jalisco, Mexico 164 21 20N 102 50W
San Juan, Querétaro, Mexico 164 20 25N 100 0W
San Juan, Phil. 103 8 35N 126 20 E
San Juan, Pto Rico 147 18 28N 66 37W
San Juan □ 172 31 9 S 69 0W
San Juan Bautista, Parag. 172 26 37 S 57 6W
San Juan Bautista, Spain 59 39 5N 1 31 E
San Juan Bautista, U.S.A. 163 36 51N 121 32W
San Juan, C. 147 18 23N 65 37W
San Juan Capistrano 163 33 29N 117 40W
San Juan de Guadalupe 164 24 38N 102 44W
San Juan de los Cayos 174 11 10N 68 25W
San Juan de los Morros 174 9 55N 67 21W
San Juan de Norte, B. de 166 11 30N 83 40W
San Juan del Norte 166 10 58N 83 40W
San Juan del Puerto 57 37 20N 6 50W
San Juan del Río 165 24 47N 104 27W
San Juan del Sur 166 11 20N 86 0W
San Juan Mts. 161 38 30N 108 30W
San Juan, Presa de 164 17 45N 95 15W
San Juan, R., Argent. 172 32 20 S 67 25W
San Juan, R., Colomb. 174 4 0N 77 20W
San Juan, R., Nic. 166 11 0N 84 30W
San Juan, R., Calif., U.S.A. 163 36 14N 121 9W
San Juan, R., Utah, U.S.A. 161 37 20N 110 20W
San Julián 176 49 15 S 68 0W
San Just, Sierra de 58 40 45N 0 41W
San Justo 172 30 55 S 60 30W
San Kamphaeng 100 18 45N 99 8 E
San Lázaro, C. 164 24 50N 112 18W
San Lázaro, Sa. de 164 23 25N 110 0W
San Leandro 163 37 40N 122 6W
San Leonardo 58 41 51N 3 5W
San Lorenzo, Argent. 172 32 45 S 60 45W
San Lorenzo, Ecuador 174 1 15N 78 50W
San Lorenzo, Parag. 172 25 20 S 57 32W
San Lorenzo, Venez. 174 9 47N 71 4W
San Lorenzo de la Parilla 58 39 51N 2 22W
San Lorenzo de Morunys 58 42 8N 1 35 E
San Lorenzo, I., Mexico 164 28 35N 112 50W
San Lorenzo, I., Peru 174 12 20 S 77 35W
San Lorenzo, Mt. 176 47 40 S 72 20W
San Lorenzo, R. 164 24 15N 107 24W
San Lucas, Boliv. 174 20 5 S 65 0W
San Lucas, Baja California S., Mexico 164 27 10N 112 14W
San Lucas, Baja California S., Mexico 164 22 53N 109 54W
San Lucas, U.S.A. 163 36 8N 121 1W
San Lucas, C. de 164 22 50N 110 0W
San Lucido 65 39 18N 16 3 E
San Luis, Argent. 172 33 20 S 66 20W
San Luis, Cuba 166 22 17N 83 46W
San Luis, Guat. 166 16 14N 89 27W
San Luis, U.S.A. 161 37 14N 105 26W
San Luis, Venez. 174 11 7N 69 42W
San Luis □ 172 34 0 S 66 0W
San Luis de la Loma 164 17 18N 100 55W
San Luis de la Paz 164 21 19N 100 32W
San Luis de Potosí 164 22 9N 100 59W
San Luis de Potosí □ 164 22 10N 101 0W
San Luis, I. 164 29 58N 114 26W
San Luis Obispo 161 35 21N 120 38W
San Luis Res. 163 37 4N 121 5W
San Luis Río Colorado 164 32 29N 114 48W
San Luis, Sierra de 172 37 25N 66 10W
San Marco Argentano 65 39 34N 16 8 E
San Marco dei Cavoti 65 41 20N 14 50 E
San Marco in Lámis 65 41 43N 15 38 E
San Marcos, Guat. 166 14 59N 91 52W
San Marcos, U.S.A. 159 29 53N 98 0W
San Marcos, I. 164 27 13N 112 6W
San Marino 63 43 56N 12 25 E
San Marino ■ 63 43 56N 12 25 E
San Martín, Argent. 172 33 5 S 68 28W
San Martín, Colomb. 174 3 42N 73 42W
San Martín de Valdeiglesias 56 40 21N 4 24W
San Martín, L. 176 48 50 S 72 50W
San Martino de Calvi 62 45 57N 9 41 E
San Mateo, Spain 58 40 28N 0 10 E
San Mateo, U.S.A. 163 37 32N 122 19W
San Matías 174 16 25 S 58 20W
San Matías, Golfo de 176 41 30 S 64 0W
San Miguel, El Sal. 166 13 30N 88 12W
San Miguel, Panama 166 8 27N 78 55W
San Miguel, Spain 59 39 3N 1 26 E
San Miguel, U.S.A. 163 35 45N 120 42W
San Miguel, Venez. 174 9 40N 65 11W
San Miguel de Salinas 59 37 59N 0 47W
San Miguel de Tucumán 172 26 50 S 65 20W
San Miguel del Monte 172 35 23 S 58 50W
San Miguel I. 163 34 2N 120 23W
San Miguel, R., Boliv. 174 16 0 S 62 45W
San Miguel, R., Ecuador/Ecuador 174 0 25N 76 30W
San Miniato 62 43 40N 10 50 E
San Narcisco 103 15 2N 120 3 E
San Nicolás de los Arroyas 172 33 17 S 60 10W
San Nicolas I. 154 33 16N 119 30W
San Onafre 163 33 22N 117 34W
San Onofre 174 9 44N 75 32W
San Pablo, Boliv. 172 21 43 S 66 38W
San Pablo, Colomb. 174 5 27N 70 56W
San Paolo di Civitate 65 41 44N 15 16 E
San Pedro, Buenos Aires, Argent. 173 33 43 S 59 45W
San Pedro, Jujuy, Argent. 172 24 12 S 64 55W
San Pedro, Chile 172 21 58 S 68 30W
San Pedro, Colomb. 174 4 56N 71 53W
San Pedro, Dom. Rep. 167 18 30N 69 18W
San Pedro, Ivory C. 120 4 50N 6 33W
San Pedro, Mexico 164 23 55N 110 17W
San Pedro □ 172 24 0 S 57 0W
San Pedro Channel 163 33 35N 118 25W
San Pedro de Arimena 174 4 37N 71 42W
San Pedro de Atacama 172 22 55 S 68 15W
San Pedro de Jujuy 172 24 12 S 64 55W
San Pedro de las Colonias 164 25 50N 102 59W
San Pedro de Lloc 174 7 15 S 79 28W
San Pedro del Norte 166 13 4N 84 33W
San Pedro del Paraná 172 26 43 S 56 13W
San Pedro del Pinatar 59 37 50N 0 50W
San Pedro Mártir, Sierra 164 31 0N 115 30W
San Pedro Mixtepec 165 16 2N 97 0W
San Pedro Ocampo = Melchor Ocampo 164 24 52N 101 40W
San Pedro, Pta. 172 25 30 S 70 38W
San Pedro, R., Chihuahua, Mexico 164 28 20N 106 10W
San Pedro, R., Michoacan, Mexico 164 19 23N 103 51W
San Pedro, R., Nayarit, Mexico 164 21 45N 105 30W
San Pedro, R., U.S.A. 161 32 45N 110 35W
San Pedro, Sierra de 57 39 18N 6 40W
San Pedro Sula 166 15 30N 88 0W
San Pedro Tututepec 165 16 9N 97 38W
San Pedro,Pta. 172 25 30 S 70 38W
San Pietro, I. 64 39 9N 8 17 E
San Pietro Vernotico 65 40 28N 18 0 E
San Quintín, Mexico 164 30 29N 115 57W

San Quintín Santiago

San Quintín, Phil. 103 16 1N 120 56 E
San, R. 54 50 25N 22 20 E
San Rafael, Argent. 172 34 40 S 68 30W
San Rafael, Colomb. 174 6 2N 69 45W
San Rafael, Calif., U.S.A. 163 38 0N 122 32W
San Rafael, N. Mex., U.S.A. 161 35 6N 107 58W
San Rafael, Venez. 174 10 42N 71 46W
San Rafael Mtn. 163 34 41N 119 52W
San Ramón de la Nueva Orán 172 23 10 S 64 20W
San Remo 62 43 48N 7 47 E
San Román, C. 174 12 12N 70 0W
San Roque, Argent. 172 28 15 S 58 45W
San Roque, Spain 57 36 17N 5 21W
San Rosendo 172 37 10 S 72 50W
San Saba 159 31 12N 98 45W
San Salvador 166 13 40N 89 20W
San Salvador de Jujuy 172 23 30 S 65 40W
San Salvador (Watlings) I. 167 24 0N 74 40W
San Sebastián, Argent. 176 53 10 S 68 30W
San Sebastián, Spain 58 43 17N 1 58W
San Sebastián, Venez. 174 9 57N 67 11W
San Serverino 63 43 13N 13 10 E
San Severo 63 41 41N 15 23 E
San Simeon 163 35 39N 121 11W
San Simon 161 32 14N 109 16W
San Stéfano di Cadore 63 46 34N 12 33 E
San Telmo 164 30 58N 116 6W
San Tiburcio 164 24 8N 101 32W
San Valentin, Mte. 176 46 30 S 73 30W
San Vicente de Alcántara 57 39 22N 7 8W
San Vicente de la Barquera 56 43 30N 4 29W
San Vicente del Caguán 174 2 7N 74 46W
San Vicenzo 93 43 9N 10 32 E
San Vito al Tagliamento 63 45 55N 12 50 E
San Vito, C. 64 38 11N 12 41 E
San Vito Chietino 63 42 19N 14 27 E
San Vito dei Normanni 65 40 40N 17 40 E
San Yanaro 174 2 47N 69 42W
San Ygnacio 159 27 6N 92 24W
San Ysidro 161 32 33N 117 5W
San'a 91 15 27N 44 12 E
Sana, R. 63 44 40N 16 43 E
Sanaba 120 12 25N 3 47W
Sanabria, La 56 42 0N 6 30W
Sanâfir 122 27 49N 34 37 E
Sanaga, R. 121 3 35N 9 38 E
Sanak I 147 53 30N 162 30W
Sanaloa, Presa 164 24 50N 107 20W
Sanana 103 2 5 S 125 50 E
Sanand 94 22 59N 72 25 E
Sanandaj 92 35 25N 47 7 E
Sanandita 172 21 40 S 63 35W
Sanary 45 43 7N 5 48 E
Sanawad 94 22 11N 76 5 E
Sanbe-San 110 35 6N 132 38 E
Sancergues 43 47 10N 2 54 E
Sancerre 43 47 20N 2 50 E
Sanch'a Ho 108 26 55N 106 6 E
Sanch'aho 107 44 59N 126 1 E
Sánchez 167 19 15N 69 36W
Sanchiang 108 25 22N 109 26 E
Sanchor 94 24 52N 71 49 E
Sanco, Pt. 103 8 15N 126 24 E
Sancoins 43 46 47N 2 55 E
Sancti-Spíritus 166 21 52N 79 33W
Sand Lake 150 47 46N 84 31W
Sand Point 147 55 20N 160 32W
Sand, R. 129 22 25 S 30 5 E
Sand Springs 159 36 12N 96 5W
Sanda 111 34 53N 135 14 E
Sanda I. 34 55 17N 5 35W
Sandah 122 20 35N 39 32 E
Sandakan 102 5 53N 118 10 E
Sandalwood 140 34 55 S 140 9 E
Sandan 101 12 46N 106 0 E
Sandanski 67 41 35N 23 16 E
Sandaré 120 14 40N 10 15W
Sanday I. 36 57 2N 6 30W
Sanday, I. 37 59 15N 2 30W
Sanday Sd. 37 59 11N 2 31W
Sandbach 32 53 9N 2 23W
Sandbank 34 55 58N 4 57W
Sande, Möre og Romsdal, Norway 71 62 15N 5 27 E
Sande, Sogn og Fjordane, Norway 71 61 20N 5 47 E
Sandefjord 71 59 10N 10 15 E
Sandeid 71 59 33N 5 52 E
Sanders 161 35 12N 109 25W
Sanderson 159 30 5N 102 30W
Sanderston 140 34 46 S 139 15 E
Sandfell 74 63 57N 16 48W
Sandfly L. 153 55 43N 106 6W
Sandgate, Austral. 139 27 18 S 153 3 E
Sandgate, U.K. 29 51 5N 1 9 E
Sandhammaren, C. 73 55 23N 14 14 E
Sandhead 34 54 48N 4 58W
Sandhurst 29 51 21N 0 48W
Sandia 174 14 10 S 69 30W
Sandikli 92 38 30N 30 20 E
Sandiman, Mt. 137 24 21 S 115 20 E
Sandnes 71 58 50N 5 45 E
Sandness 37 60 18N 1 38W
Sandoa 124 9 48 S 23 0 E
Sandomierz 54 50 40N 21 43 E
Sandona 174 1 17N 77 28W
Sandover, R. 138 21 43 S 136 32 E
Sandoway 99 18 20N 94 30 E
Sandown 28 50 39N 1 9W
Sandpoint 160 48 20N 116 40W
Sandray, I. 36 56 53N 7 30W
Sandringham 29 52 50N 0 30 E
Sandslån 72 63 2N 17 49 E
Sandspit 152 53 14N 131 49W
Sandston 162 37 31N 77 19W
Sandstone 137 27 59 S 119 16 E
Sandusky, Mich., U.S.A. 150 43 26N 82 50W
Sandusky, Ohio, U.S.A. 156 41 25N 82 40W
Sandveld 128 32 0 S 18 15 E
Sandvig, Denmark 73 55 18N 14 48 E
Sandvig, Sweden 72 55 32N 14 47 E
Sandvika 71 59 54N 10 29 E
Sandviken 72 60 38N 16 46 E
Sandwich 29 51 16N 1 21 E
Sandwich B., Can. 151 53 40N 57 15W
Sandwich B., S. Afr. 128 23 25 S 14 20 E
Sandwich, C. 138 18 14 S 146 18 E
Sandwich Group 13 57 0 S 27 0W
Sandwip Chan. 99 22 35N 91 35 E
Sandy 29 53 8N 0 18W
Sandy Bight 137 33 50 S 123 20 E
Sandy C., Queens., Austral. 139 24 42 S 153 15 E
Sandy C., Tas., Austral. 138 41 25 S 144 45 E
Sandy Cay 167 23 13N 75 18W
Sandy Cr. 160 42 20N 109 30W
Sandy L. 150 53 2N 93 0W
Sandy Lake 150 53 0N 93 15W
Sandy Narrows 153 55 5N 103 4W
Sanford, Fla., U.S.A. 157 28 45N 81 20W
Sanford, Me., U.S.A. 162 43 28N 70 47W
Sanford, N.C., U.S.A. 157 35 30N 79 10W
Sanford, Mt. 136 16 58 S 130 32 E
Sanford Mt. 148 62 30N 143 0W
Sanford, R. 137 27 22 S 115 53 E
Sang-i-Masha 94 33 16N 67 5 E
Sanga 127 12 22 S 35 21 E
Sanga, R. 124 1 0N 16 30 E
Sanga Tolon 77 61 50N 149 40 E
Sangamner 96 19 30N 74 15 E
Sangar, Afghan. 94 32 56N 65 30 E
Sangar, U.S.S.R. 77 63 55N 127 31 E
Sangar Sarcai 94 34 27N 70 35 E
Sangasanga 102 0 29 S 117 13 E
Sangchen La 99 31 30N 84 40 E
Sangchih 109 29 25N 109 30 E
Sange 126 6 58 S 84 40 E
Sangeang, I. 103 8 12 S 119 6 E
Sanger 163 36 47N 119 35W
Sangerhausen 48 51 28N 11 18 E
Sanggau 102 0 5N 110 30 E
Sangihe, Kep. 103 3 0N 126 0 E
Sangihe, P. 103 3 45N 125 30 E
Sangju 107 36 25N 128 10 E
Sangkan Ho 106 40 24N 115 19 E
Sangkapura 102 5 52 S 112 40 E
Sangkhla 100 15 7N 98 28 E
Sangli 96 16 55N 74 33 E
Sangmélina 121 2 57N 12 1 E
Sangonera, R. 59 37 39N 2 0W
Sangpang Bum 98 26 30N 95 50 E
Sangre de Cristo Mts. 159 37 0N 105 0W
Sangro, R. 63 42 10N 14 30 E
Sangudo 152 53 50N 114 54W
Sangüesa 58 42 37N 1 17W
Sanguinaires, I. 45 41 51N 8 36 E
Sanhala 120 10 3N 6 51W
Sanho 107 39 59N 117 4 E
Sani R. 100 13 32N 105 57 E
Sanish 158 48 0N 102 30W
Sanje 126 0 49 S 31 30 E
Sankaranayinarkovil 97 9 10N 77 35 E
Sankeshwar 96 16 23N 74 23 E
Sankosh, R. 98 26 24N 89 47 E
Sankt Andra 52 46 46N 14 50 E
Sankt Antönien 51 46 58N 9 48 E
Sankt Blasien 49 47 47N 8 7 E
Sankt Gallen 51 47 26N 9 22 E
Sankt Gallen □ 51 47 25N 9 22 E
Sankt Ingbert 49 49 16N 7 6 E
Sankt Johann 52 47 22N 13 12 E
Sankt Margrethen 51 47 28N 9 37 E
Sankt Moritz 51 46 30N 9 50 E
Sankt Olof 73 55 37N 14 8 E
Sankt Pölten 52 48 12N 15 38 E
Sankt Valentin 52 48 11N 14 33 E
Sankt Veit 52 46 54N 14 22 E
Sankt Wendel 49 49 27N 7 9 E
Sankt Wolfgang 52 47 43N 13 27 E
Sankuru, R. 124 4 17 S 20 25 E
Sanlúcar de Barrameda 57 37 26N 6 18W
Sanlucár la Mayor 57 37 26N 6 18W
Sanluri 64 39 35N 8 55 E
Sanmártin 70 46 19N 25 58 E
Sanmen 109 29 5N 121 35 E
Sanmenhsia 106 34 46N 111 30 E
Sanming 109 26 13N 117 35 E
Sannan 111 35 2N 135 1 E
Sannaspos 128 29 6 S 26 34 E
Sannicandro Gargánico 65 41 50N 15 34 E
Sânnicolaul-Maré 66 46 5N 20 39 E
Sannidal 71 58 55N 9 15 E
Sannieshof 128 26 30 S 25 47 E
Sano 111 36 19N 139 35 E
Sanok 54 49 35N 22 10 E
Sanokwelle 120 7 19N 8 38W
Sanpa 108 29 43N 99 33 E
Sanpah 139 30 32 S 141 12 E
Sanquhar 35 55 21N 3 56W
Sansanding Dam 120 13 37N 6 0W
Sansanné-Mango 121 10 20N 0 30 E
Sansepolcro 63 43 34N 12 8 E
Sanshui 109 23 11N 112 53 E
Sanski Most 63 44 46N 16 40 E
Sansui 108 26 57N 108 37 E
Sant' Ágata de Gati 65 41 6N 14 30 E
Sant' Ágata di Militello 65 38 2N 14 40 E
Santa Ana, Ecuador 174 1 10 S 80 20W
Santa Ana, El Sal. 166 14 0N 89 40W
Santa Ana, Mexico 164 30 31N 111 8W
Santa Ana, U.S.A. 163 33 48N 117 55W
Santa Ana, El Beni 174 13 50 S 65 40W
Sant' Ángelo Lodigiano 62 45 14N 9 25 E
Sant' Antíoco 64 39 2N 8 30 E
Sant' Antíoco, I. 64 39 2N 8 30 E
Sant' Arcángelo di Romagna 63 44 4N 12 26 E
Santa Bárbara, Brazil 171 16 0 S 59 0W
Santa Bárbara, Colomb. 174 5 53N 75 35W
Santa Barbara 166 14 53N 88 14W
Santa Bárbara, Mexico 164 26 48N 105 50W
Santa Bárbara, Spain 58 40 42N 0 29 E
Santa Barbara 163 34 25N 119 40W
Santa Bárbara 174 7 47N 71 10W
Santa Barbara Channel 163 34 20N 120 0W
Santa Barbara I. 163 33 29N 119 2W
Santa Barbara Is. 161 33 31N 119 0W
Santa Bárbara, Mt. 59 37 23N 2 50W
Santa Catalina 174 10 36N 75 17W
Santa Catalina, G. of 163 33 0N 118 0W
Santa Catalina, I., Mexico 164 25 40N 110 50W
Santa Catalina, I., U.S.A. 163 33 20N 118 30W
Santa Catarina □ 173 27 25 S 48 30W
Santa Catarina, I. de 173 27 30 S 48 40W
Santa Caterina 65 37 37N 14 1 E
Santa Cecília 173 26 56 S 50 27W
Santa Clara, Cuba 166 22 20N 80 0W
Santa Clara, Calif., U.S.A. 163 37 21N 122 0W
Santa Clara, Utah, U.S.A. 161 37 10N 113 38W
Santa Clara de Olimar 173 32 50 S 54 54W
Santa Clotilde 174 2 25 S 73 45W
Santa Coloma de Farnés 58 41 50N 2 39 E
Santa Coloma de Gramanet 58 41 27N 2 13 E
Santa Comba 56 43 2N 8 49W
Santa Croce Camerina 65 36 50N 14 30 E
Santa Cruz, Argent. 176 50 0 S 68 50W
Santa Cruz, Boliv. 174 17 43 S 63 10W
Santa Cruz, Brazil 170 7 57 S 36 12W
Santa Cruz, Canary Is. 116 28 29N 16 26W
Santa Cruz, Chile 172 34 38 S 71 27W
Santa Cruz, C. Rica 166 10 15N 85 41W
Santa Cruz, Phil. 103 14 20N 121 30 E
Santa Cruz, Calif., U.S.A. 163 36 55N 122 1W
Santa Cruz, N. Mexico, U.S.A. 161 35 59N 106 1W
Santa Cruz □ 174 17 43 S 63 10W
Santa Cruz Cabrália 171 16 17 S 39 2W
Santa Cruz de Barahona 167 18 12N 71 6W
Santa Cruz de Mudela 59 38 39N 3 28W
Santa Cruz de Tenerife □ 72 28 10N 17 20W
Santa Cruz del Norte 166 23 9N 81 55W
Santa Cruz del Retamar 56 40 8N 4 14W
Santa Cruz del Sur 166 20 50N 78 0W
Santa Cruz do Rio Pardo 173 22 54 S 49 37W
Santa Cruz do Sul 173 29 42 S 52 25W
Santa Cruz I. 154 34 0N 119 45W
Santa Cruz, Is. 130 10 30 S 166 0 E
Santa Cruz, R. 176 50 10 S 70 0W
Santa Elena, Argent. 172 30 58 S 59 47W
Santa Elena, Ecuador 174 2 16 S 80 52W
Santa Elena C. 167 10 54N 85 56W
Santa Enimie 44 44 24N 3 26 E
Sant' Eufémia, Golfo di 65 38 50N 16 10 E
Santa Eulalia 59 40 34N 1 20W
Santa Fe, Argent. 172 31 35 S 60 41W
Santa Fe, Spain 57 37 11N 3 43W
Santa Fe, U.S.A. 161 35 40N 106 0W
Santa Fé □ 172 31 50 S 60 55W
Santa Filomena 170 9 0 S 45 50W
Santa Genoveva, Mt. 164 23 18N 109 52W
Santa Groce di Magliano 65 41 43N 14 59 E
Santa Helena 170 2 14 S 45 18W
Santa Helena de Goiás 171 17 43 S 50 35W
Santa Inês 171 13 17 S 39 48W
Santa Inés, I. 176 54 0 S 73 0W
Santa Inés, Mt. 57 38 32N 5 37W
Santa Isabel, Argent. 172 36 10 S 67 0W
Santa Isabel, Brazil 171 13 45 S 56 30W
Santa Isabel = Rey Malabo 121 3 45N 8 50 E
Santa Isabel do Araguaia 170 6 7 S 48 19W
Santa Isabel, Pico 121 4 43N 8 49 E
Santa Juliana 171 19 19 S 47 32W
Santa Lucía, Corrientes, Argent. 172 28 58 S 59 5W
Santa Lucía, San Juan, Argent. 172 31 30 S 68 45W
Santa Lucía, Spain 59 37 35N 0 58W
Santa Lucia 172 34 27 S 56 24W
Santa Lucia Range 163 36 0N 121 20W
Santa Luzia 170 6 53 S 36 56W
Santa Magdalena, I. 164 24 50N 112 15W
Santa Margarita, Argent. 172 38 18 S 61 35W
Santa Margarita, U.S.A. 163 35 23N 120 37W
Santa Margarita, I. 164 24 30N 112 0W
Santa Margarita, R. 163 33 13N 117 23W
Santa Margherita 62 44 20N 9 11 E
Santa Maria, Argent. 172 26 40 S 66 0W
Santa Maria, Brazil 173 29 40 S 53 40W
Santa Maria 65 41 3N 14 29 E
Santa Maria 164 27 40N 114 40W
Santa Maria, Spain 58 39 39N 2 45 E
Santa Maria, Switz. 51 46 36N 10 25 E
Santa Maria, U.S.A. 163 34 58N 120 29W
Santa Maria, Zambia 127 11 5 S 29 58 E
Santa Maria, Bahía de 164 25 10N 108 40W
Santa Maria, Cabo de 57 36 39N 7 53W
Santa Maria da Vitória 171 13 24 S 44 12W
Santa Maria del Oro 164 25 30N 105 20W
Santa Maria di Leuca, C. 65 39 48N 18 20 E
Santa Maria do Suaçuí 171 18 12 S 42 25W
Santa Maria la Real de Nieva 56 41 4N 4 24W
Santa María, R. 164 31 0N 107 14W
Santa Marta, Colomb. 174 11 15N 74 13W
Santa Marta, Spain 57 38 37N 6 39W
Santa Marta Grande, C. 173 28 43 S 48 50W
Santa Marta, Ría de 56 43 44N 7 45W
Santa Marta, Sierra Nevada de 147 10 55N 73 50W
Santa Monica 163 34 0N 118 30W
Santa Napa 160 38 28N 122 45W
Santa Olalla, Huelva, Spain 57 37 54N 6 14W
Santa Olalla, Toledo, Spain 56 40 2N 4 25W
Sant' Onofrio 65 38 42N 16 10 E
Santa Paula 163 34 20N 119 2W
Santa Pola 59 38 13N 0 35W
Santa Quitéria 170 4 20 S 40 10W
Santa Rita, U.S.A. 161 32 50N 108 0W
Santa Rita, Guarico, Venez. 174 8 8N 66 16W
Santa Rita, Zulia, Venez. 174 10 32N 71 32W
Santa Rosa, La Pampa, Argent. 172 36 40 S 64 30W
Santa Rosa, San Luis, Argent. 172 32 30 S 65 10W
Santa Rosa, Boliv. 174 10 25 S 67 20W
Santa Rosa, Brazil 173 27 52 S 54 29W
Santa Rosa, Colomb. 174 3 32N 69 48W
Santa Rosa, Hond. 164 14 40N 89 0W
Santa Rosa, Calif., U.S.A. 163 38 26N 122 43W
Santa Rosa, N. Mexico, U.S.A. 159 34 58N 104 40W
Santa Rosa, Amazonas, Venez. 174 1 29N 66 55W
Santa Rosa, Apure, Venez. 174 6 37N 67 57W
Santa Rosa de Cabal 174 4 52N 75 38W
Santa Rosa de Copán 166 14 47N 88 46W
Santa Rosa de Osos 174 6 39N 75 28W
Santa Rosa de Río Primero 172 31 8 S 63 20W
Santa Rosa de Viterbo 174 5 53N 72 59W
Santa Rosa I., Calif., U.S.A. 163 34 0N 120 6W
Santa Rosa I., Fla., U.S.A. 157 30 23N 87 0W
Santa Rosa Mts. 160 41 45N 117 30W
Santa Rosalía 164 27 20N 112 30W
Santa Sofia 63 43 57N 11 55 E
Santa Sylvina 172 27 50 S 61 10W
Santa Tecla = Nueva San Salvador 164 13 40N 89 25W
Santa Teresa, Argent. 172 33 25 S 60 47W
Santa Teresa, Brazil 171 19 55 S 40 36W
Santa Teresa, Mexico 165 25 17N 97 51W
Santa Teresa, Venez. 174 4 43N 61 4W
Santa Teresa di Riva 65 37 58N 15 21 E
Santa Teresa Gallura 64 41 14N 9 12 E
Santa Teresinha 170 12 45 S 39 32W
Santa Vitória 171 18 50 S 50 8W
Santa Vitória do Palmar 173 33 32 S 53 25W
Santa Ynez 163 34 37N 120 5W
Santa Ynez, R. 163 34 37N 120 41W
Santa Ysabel 163 33 7N 116 40W
Sant'ai 108 31 5N 105 2 E
Santadi 64 39 5N 8 42 E
Santahar 98 24 48N 88 59 E
Santaluz 171 11 15 S 39 22W
Santana 171 13 2 S 44 5W
Santana, Coxilha de 173 30 50 S 55 35W
Santana do Ipanema 170 9 22 S 37 14W
Santana do Livramento 173 30 55 S 55 30W
Santander, Colomb. 174 3 1N 76 28W
Santander, Spain 56 43 27N 3 51W
Santander □ 56 43 25N 4 0W
Santander Jiménez 165 24 11N 98 29W
Santañy 59 39 20N 3 5 E
Santaquin 160 40 0N 111 51W
Santarém, Brazil 175 2 25 S 54 42W
Santarém, Port. 57 39 12N 8 42W
Santarém □ 57 39 10N 8 40W
Santaren Channel 166 24 0N 79 30W
Santèramo in Colle 65 40 48N 16 45 E
Santerno, R. 63 44 10N 11 38 E
Santhia 62 45 20N 8 10 E
Santiago, Brazil 173 29 11 S 54 52W
Santiago, Chile 172 33 24 S 70 50W
Santiago, Dom. Rep. 167 19 30N 70 40W

Santiago Sayville

Santiago, Panama 166 8 0N 81 0W
Santiago □ 172 33 30S 70 50W
Santiago de Compostela 56 42 52N 8 37W
Santiago de Cuba 166 20 0N 75 49W
Santiago del Estero 172 27 50S 64 15W
Santiago del Estero □ 172 27 50S 64 20W
Santiago do Cacém 57 38 1N 8 42W
Santiago Ixcuintla 164 21 50N 105 11W
Santiago Papasquiaro 164 25 0N 105 20W
Santiago, Punta de 121 3 12N 8 40E
Santiaguillo, L. de 164 24 50N 104 50W
Santillana del Mar 56 43 24N 4 6W
Santipur 95 23 17N 88 25E
Säntis 51 47 15N 9 22E
Santisteban del Puerto 59 38 17N 3 15W
Santo Amaro 171 12 30S 38 50W
Santo Anastácio 173 21 58S 51 39W
Santo André 173 23 39S 46 29W
Santo Ângelo 173 28 15S 54 15W
Santo Antonio 170 15 50S 56 0W
Santo Antônio de Jesus 171 12 58S 39 16W
Santo Antonio do Zaire 124 6 7S 12 20E
Santo Corazón 174 18 0S 58 45W
Santo Domingo, Dom. Rep. 167 18 30N 70 0W
Santo Domingo, Baja Calif. N., Mexico 164 30 43N 115 56W
Santo Domingo, Baja Calif. S., Mexico 164 25 32N 112 2W
Santo Domingo, Nic. 166 12 14N 84 59W
Santo Domingo de la Calzada 58 42 26N 2 27W
Santo Isabel do Morro 171 11 34S 50 40W
Santo Stéfano di Camastro 65 38 1N 14 22E
Santo Stino di Livenza 63 45 45N 12 40E
Santo Tirso 56 41 29N 8 18W
Santo Tomas 164 31 33N 116 24W
Santo Tomás 174 14 34S 72 30W
Santo Tomé 173 28 40S 56 5W
Santoña 56 43 29N 3 20W
Santos 173 24 0S 46 20W
Santos Dumont 173 22 55S 43 10W
Santos, Sierra de los 57 38 7N 5 12W
Santport 46 52 26N 4 39E
Santu 108 25 59N 107 52E
Sanur 90 32 22N 35 15E
Sanvignes-les-Mines 43 46 40N 4 18E
San'yō 110 34 2N 131 5E
Sanyuki-Sammyaku 110 34 5N 133 0E
Sanza Pombo 124 7 18S 15 56E
São Anastacio 173 22 0S 51 40W
São Bartolomeu de Messines 57 37 15N 8 17W
São Benedito 170 4 3S 40 53W
São Bento 170 2 42S 44 50W
São Bento do Norte 170 5 4S 36 2W
São Borja 173 28 45S 56 0W
São Bras d'Alportel 57 37 8N 7 58W
São Caitano 170 8 21S 36 6W
São Carlos 173 22 0S 47 50W
São Cristóvão 170 11 15S 37 15W
São Domingos, Brazil 171 13 25S 46 10W
São Domingos, Guin.-Biss. 170 12 22N 16 8W
São Domingos do Maranhão 170 5 42S 44 22W
São Félix, Bahia, Brazil 171 12 38S 38 58W
São Félix, Mato Grosso, Brazil 171 11 36S 50 39W
Sao Francisco 171 16 0S 44 50W
São Francisco do Maranhão 170 6 15S 42 52W
São Francisco do Sul 173 26 15S 48 36W
São Francisco, R. 170 10 30S 36 24W
São Gabriel 173 30 10S 54 30W
São Gabriel da Palha 171 18 47S 40 59W
São Gonçalo 173 22 48S 43 5W
São Gotardo 171 19 19S 46 3W
Sao Hill 127 8 20S 35 18E
São João da Boa Vista 173 22 0S 46 52W
São João da Pesqueira 56 41 8N 7 24W
São João da Ponte 171 15 56S 44 1W
São João del Rei 173 21 8S 44 15W
São João do Araguaia 170 5 23S 48 46W
São João do Paraíso 171 15 19S 42 1W
São João do Piauí 170 8 10S 42 15W
São João dos Patos 170 6 30S 43 42W
São João Evangelista 171 18 32S 42 45W
São Joaquim da Barra 171 20 35S 47 53W
São José, B. de 170 2 38S 44 4W
São José da Laje 170 9 1S 36 3W
São José de Mipibu 170 6 5S 35 15W
São José do Peixe 170 7 24S 42 34W
São José do Rio Prêto 173 20 50S 49 20W
São José dos Campos 173 23 7S 45 52W
São Leopoldo 173 29 50S 51 10W
São Lourenço, Mato Grosso, Brazil 173 16 30S 55 5W
São Lourenço, Minas Gerais, Brazil 171 22 7S 45 3W
São Lourenço, R. 175 16 40S 56 0W
São Luís do Curu 170 3 40S 39 14W
São Luís Gonzaga 173 28 25S 55 0W
São Luís (Maranhão) 170 2 39S 44 15W
Sao Marcelino 174 1 0N 67 12W
São Marcelino 174 1 0N 67 12W
São Marcos, B. de 170 2 0S 44 0W
São Marcos, R. 171 18 15S 47 37W
São Martinho 56 39 30N 9 8W
São Mateus 171 18 44S 39 50W
São Mateus, R. 171 18 35S 39 44W
São Miguel 16 37 33N 25 27W
São Miguel do Araguaia 171 13 19S 50 13W
São Miguel dos Campos 170 9 47S 36 5W
São Nicolau, R. 170 5 45S 42 2W
São Paulo 173 23 40S 46 50W
São Paulo □ 173 22 0S 49 0W
São Pedro do Piaui 171 5 56S 42 43W
São Pedro do Sul 56 40 46N 8 4W
São Rafael 170 5 47S 36 55W
São Raimundo das Mangabeiras 170 7 1S 45 29W
São Raimundo Nonato 170 9 1S 42 42W
São Romão, Amazonas, Brazil 174 5 53S 67 50W
São Romão, Minas Gerais, Brazil 171 16 22S 45 4W
São Roque, C. de 170 5 30S 35 10W
São Sebastião do Paraíso 173 20 54S 46 59W
São Sebastião, I. 173 23 50S 45 18W
São Simão 171 18 56S 50 30W
São Teotónio 57 37 30N 8 42W
São Tomé 170 5 58S 36 4W
São Tomé, C. de 173 22 0S 41 10W
São Tomé, I. 114 0 10N 7 0E
São Vicente 173 23 57S 46 23W
São Vicente, Cabo de 57 37 0N 9 0W
Saona, I. 167 18 10N 68 40W
Saône-et-Loire □ 43 46 25N 4 50E
Sâone, R. 43 46 25N 4 50E
Saonek 103 0 28S 130 47E
Saoura, O. 118 29 55N 1 50W
Sapai 68 41 2N 25 43E
Sapão, R. 170 11 1S 45 32W
Saparua, I. 103 3 33S 128 40E
Sapé 170 7 6S 35 13W
Sapele 121 5 50N 5 40E
Sapelo I. 157 31 28N 81 15W
Sapiéntza I. 69 36 33N 21 43E
Sapodnyy Sayan 77 52 30N 94 0E
Sapone 121 12 3N 1 35W
Saposoa 174 6 55S 76 30W
Sapozhok 81 53 59N 40 51E
Sappemeer 46 53 10N 6 48E
Sapporo 112 43 0N 141 15E
Sapri 65 40 5N 15 37E
Sapudi, I. 103 7 2S 114 17E
Sapulpa 159 36 0N 96 40W
Sapur 95 34 18N 74 27E
Saqota 123 12 40N 39 1E
Saqqez 92 36 15N 46 20E
Sar-i-Pul 93 36 10N 66 0E
Sar Planina 66 42 10N 21 0E
Sara 120 11 40N 3 53W
Sara Buri 100 14 30N 100 55E
Sarab 92 38 0N 47 30E
Sarada, R. 99 28 15N 80 30E
Saragossa = Zaragoza 58 41 39N 0 53W
Saraguro 174 3 35S 79 16W
Sarai 70 44 43N 28 10E
Saraipalli 96 21 20N 82 59E
Sarajevo 66 43 52N 18 26E
Saraktash 84 51 47N 56 22E
Saramati 98 25 44N 95 2E
Saran 122 19 35N 40 30E
Saran, G. 102 0 30S 111 25E
Saranac Lake 156 44 20N 74 10W
Saranda, Alb. 68 39 59N 19 55E
Saranda, Tanz. 126 5 45S 34 59E
Sarandí del Yi 173 33 18S 55 38W
Sarandí Grande 172 33 20S 55 50W
Sarangani B. 103 6 0N 125 13E
Sarangani Is. 103 5 25N 125 25E
Sarangarh 96 21 30N 82 57E
Saransk 81 54 10N 45 10E
Sarapul 84 56 28N 53 48E
Sarasota 157 27 10N 82 30W
Saratoga, Calif., U.S.A. 163 37 16N 122 2W
Saratoga, Wyo., U.S.A. 160 41 30N 106 56W
Saratoga Springs 162 43 5N 73 47W
Saratok 102 3 5S 110 50E
Saratov 81 51 30N 46 2E
Saravane 100 15 43N 106 25E
Sarawak □ 102 2 0N 113 0E
Saraya 120 12 50N 11 45W
Sarbaz 93 26 38N 61 19E
Sarbisheh 93 32 30N 59 40E
Sârbogârd 53 46 55N 18 40E
Sarca, R. 62 46 5N 10 45E
Sardalas 119 25 50N 10 54E
Sardarshahr 94 28 30N 74 29E
Sardegna, I. 64 39 57N 9 0E
Sardhana 94 29 9N 77 39E
Sardinata 174 8 5N 72 48W
Sardinia = Sardegna 64 39 57N 9 0E
Sardo 123 11 56N 41 14E
Sarektjåkkå 74 67 27N 17 43E
Sarengrad 66 45 14N 19 16E
Saréyamou 120 16 25N 3 10W
Sargasso Sea 14 27 0N 72 0W
Sargent 158 41 42N 99 24W
Sargodha 94 32 10N 72 40E
Sargodha □ 94 31 50N 72 0E
Sarh 117 9 5N 18 23E
Sarhro, Jebel 118 31 6N 5 0W
Sárí 93 36 30N 53 11E
Sária, I. 69 35 54N 27 17E
Sarichef C. 147 54 38N 164 59W
Sarida, R. 90 32 4N 35 3E
Sarikamiş 92 40 22N 42 35E
Sarikei 102 2 8N 111 30E
Sarina 138 21 22S 149 13E
Sarine, R. 50 46 32N 7 4E
Sariñena 58 41 47N 0 10W
Sarír Tibasti 119 22 50N 18 30E
Sarita 159 27 14N 90 49W
Sariwołn 107 38 31N 125 46E
Sariyer 67 41 10N 29 3E
Sark, I. 42 49 25N 2 20W
Sarkad 53 46 47N 21 17E
Sarlat-la-Canéda 44 44 54N 1 13E
Sarles 158 48 58N 98 57W
Sarmi 103 1 49S 138 38E
Särna 72 61 41N 12 58E
Sarnano 63 43 2N 13 17E
Sarnen 50 46 53N 8 13E
Sarnia 150 42 58N 82 23W
Sarno 65 40 48N 14 35E
Sarnowa 54 51 39N 16 53E
Sarny 80 51 17N 26 40E
Särö 73 57 31N 11 57E
Sarolangun 102 2 30S 102 30E
Saronikós Kólpos 69 37 45N 23 45E
Saros Körfezi 68 40 30N 26 15E
Sárospatak 53 48 18N 21 33E
Sarosul Romanesc 66 45 34N 21 43E
Sarpsborg 71 59 16N 11 12E
Sarracín 58 42 15N 3 45W
Sarralbe 43 48 55N 7 1E
Sarraz, La 50 46 38N 6 30E
Sarre, La 150 48 45N 79 15W
Sarre, R. 43 48 49N 7 0E
Sarre-Union 43 48 55N 7 4E
Sarrebourg 43 48 43N 7 3E
Sarreguemines 43 49 1N 7 4E
Sarriá 56 42 41N 7 29W
Sarrión 58 40 9N 0 49W
Sarro 120 13 40N 5 5W
Sarstedt 48 52 13N 9 50E
Sartène 45 41 38N 9 0E
Sarthe □ 42 47 58N 0 10E
Sarthe, R. 42 47 33N 0 31W
Sartilly 42 48 45N 1 28W
Sartynya 76 63 30N 62 50E
Sarum 122 21 11N 39 10E
Sarúr 93 23 17N 58 4E
Sárvár 53 47 15N 16 56E
Sarveston 93 29 20N 53 10E
Särvfjället 72 62 42N 13 30E
Sárviz, R. 53 46 40N 18 40E
Sary Ozek 85 44 22N 77 59E
Sary-Tash 85 39 44N 73 15E
Saryagach 85 41 27N 69 9E
Sarych, Mys. 82 44 25N 33 25E
Sarykolskiy Khrebet 85 38 30N 74 30E
Sarykopa, Ozero 84 50 22N 64 6E
Sarymoin, Ozero 84 51 36N 64 30E
Saryshagan 76 46 12N 73 48E
Sarzana 70 44 7N 9 57E
Sarzeau 42 47 31N 2 48W
Sas van Gent 47 51 14N 3 48E
Sasa 90 33 2N 35 23E
Sasabeneh 91 7 59N 44 43E
Sasaram 95 24 57N 84 5E
Sasayama 111 35 4N 135 13E
Sasca Montanŭ 66 44 41N 21 45E
Sasebo 110 33 10N 129 43E
Saser Mt. 95 34 50N 77 50E
Saskatchewan □ 153 54 40N 106 0W
Saskatchewan, R. 153 53 12N 99 16W
Saskatoon 153 52 10N 106 38W
Sasolburg 129 26 46S 27 49E
Sasovo 81 54 25N 41 55E
Sassandra 120 5 0N 6 8W
Sassandra, R. 120 5 0N 6 8W
Sássari 64 40 44N 8 33E
Sassenheim 46 52 14N 4 31E
Sassnitz 48 54 29N 13 39E
Sasso Marconi 63 44 22N 11 12E
Sassocorvaro 63 43 47N 12 30E
Sassoferrato 63 43 26N 12 51E
Sassuolo 62 44 31N 10 47E
Sástago 58 41 19N 0 21W
Sastown 120 4 45N 8 27W
Sasumua Dam 126 0 54S 36 46E
Sasyk, Ozero 70 45 45N 30 0E
Sasykkul 85 37 41N 73 11E
Sata-Misaki 110 30 59N 130 40E
Satadougou 120 12 40N 11 25W
Satanta 159 37 30N 101 0W
Satara 96 17 44N 73 58E
Satilla, R. 157 31 15N 81 50W
Satka 84 55 3N 59 1E
Satkania 98 22 4N 92 3E
Satkhira 98 22 43N 89 8E
Satmala Hills 96 20 15N 74 40E
Satna 95 24 35N 80 50E
Sator, mt. 63 44 11N 16 43E
Sátoraljaújhely 53 48 25N 21 41E
Satpura Ra. 94 21 40N 75 0E
Satrup 48 54 39N 9 38E
Satsuma-Hantō 110 31 25N 130 25E
Satsuna-Shotō 112 30 0N 130 0E
Sattahip 100 12 41N 100 54E
Sattenpalle 96 16 25N 80 6E
Satu Mare 70 47 46N 22 55E
Satui 102 3 50S 115 20E
Satumare □ 70 47 45N 23 0E
Satun 101 6 43N 100 2E
Saturnina, R. 174 12 15S 58 10W
Sauce 172 30 5S 58 46W
Sauceda 164 25 46N 101 19W
Saucillo 164 28 1N 105 17W
Sauda 71 59 38N 6 21E
Saúde 170 10 56S 40 24W
Sauðarkrókur 74 65 45N 19 40W
Saudi Arabia ■ 92 26 0N 44 0E
Sauerland 48 51 0N 8 0E
Saugerties 162 42 4N 73 58W
Saugues 44 44 58N 3 32E
Sauherad 71 59 25N 9 15E
Sauid el Amia 118 25 57N 6 8W
Saujon 44 45 41N 0 55W
Sauk Center 158 45 42N 94 56W
Sauk Rapids 158 45 35N 94 10W
Saulgau 49 48 4N 9 32E
Saulieu 43 47 17N 4 14E
Sault 45 44 6N 5 24E
Sault Ste. Marie, Can. 150 46 30N 84 20W
Sault Ste. Marie, U.S.A. 156 46 27N 84 22W
Saumlaki 103 7 55S 131 20E
Saumur 42 47 15N 0 5W
Saunders 152 52 58N 115 40W
Saunders C. 143 45 53S 170 45E
Saunders I. 13 57 30S 27 30W
Saunders Point, Mt. 137 27 52S 125 38E
Saundersfoot 31 51 43N 4 42W
Saurbær, Borgarfjarðarsýsla, Iceland 74 64 24N 21 35W
Saurbær, Eyjafjarðarsýsla, Iceland 74 65 27N 18 13W
Sauri 121 11 50N 6 44E
Sausalito 163 37 51N 122 29W
Sautatá 174 7 50N 77 4W
Sauveterre, B. 44 43 25N 0 57W
Sauzé-Vaussais 44 46 8N 0 8E
Savá 166 15 32N 86 15W
Sava 65 40 28N 17 32E
Sava, R. 63 44 40N 19 50E
Savage 158 47 43N 104 20W
Savalou 121 7 57N 2 4E
Savanah Downs 138 19 30S 141 30E
Savane 127 19 37S 35 8E
Savanna 158 42 5N 90 10W
Savanna la Mar 166 18 10N 78 10W
Savannah, Ga., U.S.A. 157 32 4N 81 4W
Savannah, Mo., U.S.A. 158 39 55N 94 46W
Savannah, Tenn., U.S.A. 157 35 12N 88 18W
Savannah Downs 138 19 28S 141 47E
Savannah, R. 157 33 0N 81 30W
Savannakhet 100 16 30N 104 49E
Savant L. 150 50 14N 90 6W
Savant Lake 150 50 30N 90 25W
Savantvadi 97 15 55N 73 54E
Savanur 97 14 59N 75 28E
Savda 96 21 9N 75 56E
Savé 121 8 2N 2 17E
Save R. 125 21 16S 34 0E
Saveh 92 35 2N 50 20E
Savelovo 81 56 51N 37 20E
Savelugu 121 9 38N 0 54W
Savenay 42 47 20N 1 55W
Saverdun 44 43 14N 1 34E
Saverne 43 48 39N 7 20E
Savièse 50 46 17N 7 22E
Savigliano 62 44 39N 7 40E
Savigny-sur-Braye 44 47 53N 0 49E
Saviñao 56 42 35N 7 38W
Savio, R. 63 43 58N 12 10E
Savnik 66 42 59N 19 10E
Savognin 51 46 36N 9 37E
Savoie □ 45 45 26N 6 35E
Savona 62 44 19N 8 29E
Savonlinna 78 61 55N 28 55E
Sävsjö 73 57 20N 14 40E
Sävsjøström 73 57 1N 15 25E
Sawahlunto 102 0 52S 100 52E
Sawai 103 3 0S 129 5E
Sawai Madhopur 94 26 0N 76 25E
Sawang Daen Din 100 17 28N 103 28E
Sawankhalok 100 17 19N 99 50E
Sawara 111 35 55N 140 30E
Sawatch Mts. 161 38 30N 106 30W
Sawbridgeworth 29 51 49N 0 10E
Sawdā, Jabal as 119 28 51N 15 12E
Sawel, Mt. 38 54 48N 7 5W
Sawfajjin, W. 119 31 46N 14 30E
Sawi 101 10 14N 99 5E
Sawmills 127 19 30S 28 2E
Sawston 29 52 7N 0 11E
Sawtry 29 52 26N 0 17W
Sawu, I. 103 10 35S 121 50E
Sawu Sea 103 9 30S 121 50E
Saxby, R. 138 18 25S 140 53E
Saxilby 33 53 16N 0 40W
Saxlingham Nethergate 29 52 33N 1 16E
Saxmundham 29 52 13N 1 29E
Saxon 50 46 9N 7 11E
Saxony, Lower = Niedersachsen 48 52 45N 9 0E
Say 121 13 8N 2 22E
Saya 121 9 30N 3 18E
Sayabec 151 48 35N 67 41W
Sayaboury 100 19 15N 101 45E
Sayán 174 11 0S 77 25W
Sayan, Vostochnyy 77 54 0N 96 0E
Sayan, Zapadnyy 77 52 30N 94 0E
Sayasan 83 42 56N 46 15E
Sayda 92 33 35N 35 25E
Sayhan Ovoo 106 45 27N 103 54E
Sayhandulaan 106 44 40N 109 1E
Saynshand 106 44 55N 110 11E
Sayō 110 34 59N 134 22E
Sayre, Okla., U.S.A. 159 35 20N 99 40W
Sayre, Pa., U.S.A. 162 42 0N 76 30W
Sayula 164 19 50N 103 40W
Sayville 162 40 45N 73 7W

Sazan **Semirara Is**

Sazan 68 40 30N 19 20 E
Sazin 95 35 35N 73 30 E
Sazlika, R. 67 42 15N 25 50 E
Sbeïtla 119 35 12N 9 7 E
Scaër 42 48 2N 3 42W
Scalasaig 34 56 4N 6 10W
Scalby 33 54 18N 0 26W
Scalby Ness 33 54 18N 0 25W
Scalea 65 39 49N 15 47 E
Scalloway 36 60 9N 1 16W
Scalpay, I., Inner Hebrides, U.K. 36 57 18N 6 0W
Scalpay, I., Outer Hebrides, U.K. 36 57 51N 6 40W
Scamblesby 33 53 17N 0 5W
Scammon Bay 147 62 0N 165 49W
Scandia 152 50 20N 112 0W
Scandiano 62 44 36N 10 40 E
Scandinavia 16 64 0N 12 0 E
Scansano 63 42 40N 11 20 E
Scapa Flow 37 58 52N 3 6W
Scarastovore 36 57 50N 7 2W
Scarba, I. 34 56 10N 5 42W
Scarborough, Trin 167 11 11N 60 42W
Scarborough, U.K. 33 54 17N 0 24W
Scargill 143 42 56 S 172 58 E
Scariff 39 52 55N 8 32W
Scariff I. 39 51 43N 10 15W
Scarinish 34 56 30N 6 48W
Scarning 29 52 40N 0 53W
Scarp, I. 36 58 1N 7 8W
Scarpe, R. 43 50 31N 3 27 E
Scarsdale 140 37 41 S 143 39 E
Scattery I. 39 52 37N 9 30W
Scavaig, L. 36 57 8N 6 10W
Scebeli, Uebi 91 2 0N 44 0 E
Scédro, I. 63 43 6N 16 43 E
Scenic 158 43 49N 102 32W
Schaal See 48 53 40N 10 57 E
Schaan 51 47 10N 9 31 E
Schaesberg 47 50 54N 6 0 E
Schaffen 47 51 0N 5 5 E
Schaffhausen 51 47 42N 8 39 E
Schaffhausen □ 51 47 42N 8 36 E
Schagen 47 52 49N 4 48 E
Schaghticoke 162 42 54N 73 35W
Schalkhaar 46 52 17N 6 12 E
Schalkwijk 46 52 0N 5 11 E
Schangnau 50 46 50N 7 47 E
Schänis 51 47 10N 9 3 E
Schärding 52 48 27N 13 27 E
Scharhörn, I. 48 53 58N 8 24 E
Scharnitz 52 47 23N 11 15 E
Scheessel 48 53 10N 9 33 E
Schefferville 151 54 48N 66 50W
Scheibbs 52 48 1N 15 9 E
Schelde, R. 47 51 10N 4 20 E
Scheldewindeke 47 50 56N 3 46 E
Schenectady 162 42 50N 73 58W
Schenevus 162 42 33N 74 50W
Scherfede 48 51 32N 9 2 E
Scherpenheuvel 47 50 58N 4 58 E
Scherpenisse 47 51 33N 4 6 E
Scherpenzeel 46 52 5N 5 30 E
Schesaplana 51 47 5N 9 43 E
Scheveningen 46 52 6N 4 16 E
Schichallion, Mt. 37 56 40N 4 6W
Schiedam 46 51 55N 4 25 E
Schiermonnikoog 46 53 29N 6 10 E
Schiermonnikoog, I. 46 53 30N 6 15 E
Schiers 51 47 58N 9 41 E
Schifferstadt 49 49 22N 8 23 E
Schifflange 47 49 30N 6 1 E
Schijndel 47 51 37N 5 27 E
Schiltigheim 43 48 35N 7 45 E
Schio 63 45 42N 11 21 E
Schipbeek 46 52 14N 6 10 E
Schipluiden 46 51 59N 4 19 E
Schirmeck 43 48 29N 7 12 E
Schladming 52 47 23N 13 41 E
Schlei, R. 48 54 45N 9 52 E
Schleiden 48 50 32N 6 26 E
Schleswig 48 54 32N 9 34 E
Schleswig-Holstein □ 48 54 10N 9 40 E
Schlieren 51 47 28N 8 27 E
Schlüchtern 49 50 20N 9 32 E
Schmalkalden 48 50 43N 10 28 E
Schmölin 48 50 54N 12 22 E
Schneeberg, Austria 52 47 53N 15 55 E
Schneeberg, Ger. 48 50 35N 12 39 E
Schoenberg 47 50 17N 6 16 E
Schofield 158 44 54N 89 39W
Schoharie 162 42 40N 74 19W
Schoharie, R. 162 42 56N 74 18W
Schönberg, Rostock, Ger. 48 53 50N 10 55 E
Schönberg, Schleswig-Holstein, Ger. 48 54 23N 10 20 E
Schönebeck 48 52 2N 11 42 E
Schönenwerd 50 47 23N 8 0 E
Schöningen 48 52 8N 10 57 E
Schoondijke 47 51 21N 3 33 E
Schoonebeek 46 52 39N 6 52 E
Schoonebeek, oilfield 19 52 45N 6 50 E
Schoonhoven 46 51 57N 4 51 E
Schoonoord 46 52 51N 6 46 E
Schoorl 46 52 42N 4 42 E
Schors 80 51 48N 31 56 E
Schortens 48 53 37N 7 51 E
Schoten 47 51 16N 4 30 E
Schouten, Kepulauan 103 1 0 S 136 0 E
Schouter I. 138 42 20 S 148 20 E
Schouwen, I. 47 51 43N 3 45 E
Schramberg 49 48 12N 8 24 E
Schrankogl 52 47 3N 11 7 E
Schreckhorn 50 46 36N 8 7 E
Schreiber 150 48 45N 87 20W
Schroon Lake 162 43 47N 73 46W
Schruns 52 47 5N 9 56 E
Schuler 153 50 20N 110 6W
Schuls 51 46 48N 10 18 E
Schumacher 150 48 30N 81 16W
Schüpfen 50 47 2N 7 24 E
Schüpfheim 50 46 57N 8 2 E
Schurz 163 38 57N 118 48W
Schuyler 158 41 30N 97 3W
Schuylerville 162 43 6N 73 35W
Schuylkill Haven 162 40 37N 76 11W
Schuylkill, R. 162 39 53N 75 12W
Schwabach 49 49 19N 11 3 E
Schwäbisch Gmünd 49 48 49N 9 48 E
Schwäbisch Hall 49 49 7N 9 45 E
Schwäbischer Alb 49 48 30N 9 30 E
Schwanden 51 47 1N 9 5 E
Schwarzach, R. 52 50 30N 11 30 E
Schwarzenberg 48 50 31N 12 49 E
Schwarzenburg 50 46 49N 7 20 E
Schwarzwald 49 48 0N 8 0 E
Schwaz 52 47 20N 11 44 E
Schwedt 48 53 4N 14 18 E
Schweinfurt 49 50 3N 10 12 E
Schweizer Mittelland 50 47 0N 7 15 E
Schweizer Reneke 128 27 11 S 25 18 E
Schwerin 48 53 37N 11 22 E
Schwerin □ 48 53 35N 11 20 E
Schweriner See 48 53 45N 11 26 E
Schwetzingen 49 49 22N 8 35 E
Schwyz 51 47 2N 8 39 E
Schwyz □ 51 47 2N 8 39 E
Sciacca 64 37 30N 13 3 E
Scicli 65 36 48N 14 41 E
Scie, La 151 49 57N 55 36W
Scillave 91 6 22N 44 32 E
Scilly, Isles of 30 49 55N 6 15W
Scinawa 54 51 25N 16 26 E
Scioto, R. 156 39 0N 83 0W
Scituate 162 42 12N 70 44W
Sclayn 47 50 29N 5 2 E
Scobey 158 48 47N 105 30W
Scole 29 52 22N 1 10 E
Scone 141 32 0 S 150 52 E
Scopwick 33 53 6N 0 24W
Scórdia 65 37 19N 14 50 E
Score Hd. 36 60 12N 1 5W
Scoresby Sund 12 70 20N 23 0W
Scorno, Punta dello 64 41 7N 8 23 E
Scotia, Calif., U.S.A. 160 40 36N 124 4W
Scotia, N.Y., U.S.A. 162 42 50N 73 58W
Scotia Sea 13 56 5 S 56 0W
Scotland 158 43 10N 97 45W
Scotland □ 51 57 0N 4 0W
Scotland Neck 157 36 6N 77 24W
Scott 13 77 0 S 165 0 E
Scott, C., Antarct. 13 71 30 S 168 0 E
Scott, C., Austral. 136 13 30 S 129 49 E
Scott City 158 38 30N 100 52W
Scott, I. 13 67 0 S 179 0 E
Scott Inlet 149 71 0N 71 0W
Scott Is. 152 50 48N 128 40W
Scott L. 153 59 55N 106 18W
Scott Reef 136 14 0 S 121 50 E
Scottburgh 129 30 15 S 30 47 E
Scottsbluff 158 41 55N 103 35W
Scottsboro 157 34 40N 86 0W
Scottsburg 156 38 40N 85 46W
Scottsdale 138 41 9 S 147 31 E
Scottsville 157 36 48N 86 10W
Scottville, Austral. 138 20 33 S 147 49 E
Scottville, U.S.A. 156 43 57N 86 18W
Scourie 36 58 20N 5 10W
Scousburgh 36 59 58N 1 20W
Scrabby 38 53 53N 7 32W
Scrabster 37 58 36N 3 31W
Scram, gasfield 19 52 55N 2 42 E
Scramoge 38 53 46N 8 4W
Scranton 162 41 22N 75 41W
Screebe Lodge 38 53 23N 9 33W
Screggan 42 53 15N 7 32W
Scremerston 35 55 44N 1 59W
Scridain, L. 34 56 23N 6 7W
Scunthorpe 33 53 35N 0 38W
Scuol 51 46 48N 10 17 E
Scusciuban 91 10 28N 50 5 E
SE Tor, oilfield 19 56 38N 3 27 E
Sea Isle City 162 39 9N 74 42W
Seabra 171 12 25 S 41 46W
Seabrook, L. 137 30 55 S 119 40 E
Seaford, Austral. 141 38 10 S 145 11 E
Seaford, U.K. 29 50 46N 0 8 E
Seaford, U.S.A. 162 38 37N 75 36W
Seaforth 150 43 35N 81 25W
Seaforth, L. 36 57 52N 6 36W
Seagraves 159 32 56N 102 30W
Seaham 35 54 51N 1 20W
Seahouses 35 55 35N 1 39W
Seal Cove 151 49 57N 56 22W
Seal L. 151 54 20N 61 30W
Seal, R. 153 58 50N 97 30W
Sealga, L. na 36 57 50N 5 18W
Sealy 159 29 46N 96 9W
Seamer 33 54 14N 0 27W
Sean, gasfield 19 53 13N 2 50 E
Searchlight 161 35 31N 114 55W
Searcy 159 35 15N 91 45W
Searles, L. 163 35 47N 117 17W
Seascale 32 54 24N 3 29W
Seaside, Calif., U.S.A. 163 36 37N 121 50W
Seaside, Oreg., U.S.A. 160 46 12N 121 55W
Seaside Park 162 39 55N 74 5W
Seaspray 141 38 25 S 147 15 E
Seaton, U.K. 30 50 42N 3 3W
Seaton, U.K. 32 54 40N 3 31W
Seaton Delaval 35 55 5N 1 33W
Seattle 160 47 41N 122 15W
Seaview Ra. 138 18 40 S 145 45 E
Seaward Kaikouras, Mts. 143 42 10 S 173 44 E
Sebago Lake 162 43 50N 70 35W
Sebastián Vizcaino, Bahia 164 28 0N 114 30W
Sebastopol 160 38 24N 122 49W
Sebastopol = Sevastopol 82 44 35N 33 30 E
Sebderat 123 15 26N 36 42 E
Sebdou 118 34 38N 1 19W
Sebeşului, Mţii. 70 45 56N 23 40 E
Sebewaing 156 43 45N 83 27W
Sebezh 80 56 14N 28 22 E
Sebi 120 15 50N 4 12W
Sebinkarahisar 82 40 22N 38 28 E
Sebiş 70 46 23N 22 13 E
Sebkra Azzel Mati 118 26 10N 0 43 E
Sebkra Mekerghene 118 26 21N 1 30 E
Sebou, Oued 118 34 16N 6 40W
Sebring 157 27 36N 81 47W
Sebta = Ceuta 118 35 52N 5 26W
Sebuku, I. 102 3 30 S 116 25 E
Sebuku, Teluk 102 4 0N 118 10 E
Sečanj 66 45 25N 20 47 E
Secchia, R. 62 44 30N 10 40 E
Sechelt 152 49 25N 123 42W
Sechura, Desierto de 174 6 0 S 80 30W
Seclin 43 50 33N 3 2 E
Secondigny 42 46 37N 0 26W
Sečovce 53 48 42N 21 40 E
Secretary I. 143 45 15 S 166 56 E
Secunderabad 96 17 28N 78 30 E
Seda, R. 57 39 6N 7 53W
Sedalia 158 38 40N 93 18W
Sedan, Austral. 140 34 34 S 139 19 E
Sedan, France 43 49 43N 4 57 E
Sedan, U.S.A. 159 37 10N 96 11W
Sedano 58 42 43N 3 49W
Sedbergh 32 54 20N 2 31W
Seddon 143 41 40 S 174 7 E
Seddonville 143 41 33 S 172 1 E
Sede Ya'aqov 90 32 43N 35 7 E
Sederberg, Mt. 128 32 22 S 19 7 E
Sedgefield 33 54 40N 1 27W
Sedgewick 152 52 48N 111 41W
Sedhiou 120 12 50N 15 30W
Sedičany 52 49 40N 14 25 E
Sedico 63 46 8N 12 6 E
Sedinenie 67 42 16N 24 33 E
Sedley 153 50 10N 104 0W
Sedom 90 31 5N 35 20 E
Sedova, Pik 76 73 20N 55 10 E
Sédrata 119 36 7N 7 31 E
Sedro Woolley 160 48 30N 122 15W
Sedrun 51 46 36N 8 47 E
Seduva 80 55 45N 23 45 E
Sedziszów Małapolski 54 50 5N 21 45 E
Seebad Ahlbeck 48 53 56N 14 10 E
Seefeld 52 47 19N 11 13 E
Seehausen 48 52 52N 11 43 E
Seeheim 128 26 32 S 17 52 E
Seekoe, R. 128 30 34 S 24 45 E
Seeland 50 47 0N 7 6 E
Seelaw 48 52 32N 14 22 E
Seend 28 51 20N 2 2W
Sées 42 48 38N 0 10 E
Seesen 48 51 53N 10 10 E
Sefadu 120 8 35N 10 58W
Séfeto 120 14 8N 9 49W
Sefrou 118 33 52N 4 52W
Sefton 143 43 15 S 172 41 E
Sefton Mt. 143 43 40 S 170 5 E
Sefuri-San 110 33 28N 130 18 E
Sefwi Bekwai 120 6 10N 2 25W
Seg-ozero 76 63 0N 33 10 E
Segamat 101 2 30N 102 50 E
Segarcea 70 44 6N 23 43 E
Segbwema 120 8 0N 11 0W
Segeston 31 51 41N 4 48W
Seget 103 1 24 S 130 58 E
Seggueur, O. 118 32 4N 2 4 E
Segid 123 16 55N 42 0 E
Segonzac 44 45 36N 0 14W
Segorbe 58 39 50N 0 30W
Ségou 120 13 30N 6 10W
Segovia 56 40 57N 4 10W
Segovia □ 56 40 55N 4 10W
Segré 42 47 40N 0 52W
Segre, R. 58 41 40N 0 43 E
Seguam 147 52 0N 172 30W
Seguam Pass. 147 53 0N 175 30W
Séguéla 120 7 55N 6 40W
Segula I. 147 52 0N 178 5W
Segundo 159 37 12N 104 50W
Segundo, R. 172 30 53 S 62 44W
Segura, R. 59 38 9N 0 40W
Segura, Sierra de 59 38 5N 2 45W
Sehithwa 125 20 30 S 22 30 E
Sehore 94 23 10N 77 5 E
Sehwan 94 26 28N 67 53 E
Seica Mare 70 46 1N 24 7 E
Seikpyu 98 20 54N 94 48 E
Seil, I. 34 56 17N 5 37W
Seilandsjøkelen 74 70 25N 23 16 E
Seiling 159 36 10N 99 5W
Seille, R. 45 46 31N 4 57 E
Seilles 47 50 30N 5 6 E
Sein, I. de 42 48 2N 4 52W
Seinäjoki 74 62 48N 22 43 E
Seine-Maritime □ 42 49 40N 1 0 E
Seine □ 43 49 0N 3 0 E
Seine-et-Marne □ 43 48 45N 3 0 E
Seine, R. 42 49 28N 0 15 E
Seine-Saint-Denis □ 43 48 58N 2 24 E
Seini 70 47 44N 23 21 E
Seistan 93 30 50N 61 0 E
Seiyala 122 22 57N 32 41 E
Sejal 174 2 45N 68 0W
Sejerby 73 55 54N 11 10 E
Sejerø 73 55 54N 11 15 E
Sejerø Bugt 73 55 53N 11 9 E
Seka 123 8 10N 36 52 E
Sekaju 102 2 58 S 103 58 E
Seke 126 3 20 S 33 31 E
Sekenke 126 4 18 S 34 11 E
Seki 111 35 29N 136 55 E
Sekigahara 111 35 22N 136 28 E
Sekiu 160 48 30N 124 29W
Sekkane, Erg in 118 20 30N 1 30W
Sekondi 120 5 2N 1 48W
Sekondi-Takoradi 120 5 0N 1 48W
Sekuma 128 24 36 S 23 57 E
Sela Dingay 123 9 58N 39 32 E
Selah 160 46 44N 120 30W
Selama 101 5 12N 100 42 E
Selangor □ 101 3 20N 101 30 E
Selargius 64 39 14N 9 14 E
Selaru, I. 103 8 18 S 131 0 E
Selat Bangka 102 2 30 S 105 30 E
Selawik 147 66 55N 160 10W
Selb 49 50 9N 12 9 E
Selborne 29 51 5N 0 55W
Selby, U.K. 33 53 47N 1 5W
Selby, U.S.A. 158 45 34N 99 55W
Selbyville 162 38 28N 75 13W
Selce 63 43 20N 16 50 E
Selden 158 39 24N 100 39W
Seldovia 147 59 30N 151 45W
Sele, R. 65 40 27N 15 0 E
Selenica 68 40 33N 19 39 E
Selenter See 48 54 19N 10 26 E
Selestat 43 48 10N 7 26 E
Selet 72 63 15N 15 45 E
Seletan, Tg. 102 4 10 S 114 40 E
Seletin 70 47 50N 25 12 E
Selevac 66 44 44N 20 52 E
Selfridge 158 46 3N 100 57W
Sélibaby 120 15 20N 12 15W
Seliger, Oz. 80 57 15N 33 0 E
Seligman 161 35 17N 112 56W
Selim, C. Afr. 126 5 31N 23 48 E
Selim, Turkey 83 40 15N 42 58 E
Selîma, El Wâhât el 122 21 28N 29 31 E
Selinda Spillway 128 18 35 S 23 10 E
Selinoûs 69 37 35N 21 37 E
Selinsgrove 162 40 48N 76 52W
Selipuk Gompa 95 31 23N 82 49 E
Selizharovo 80 57 1N 33 17 E
Selje 71 62 3N 5 22 E
Seljord 71 59 30N 8 40 E
Selkirk, Can. 153 50 10N 97 20W
Selkirk, U.K. 35 55 33N 2 50W
Selkirk (□) 26 55 30N 3 0W
Selkirk I. 153 53 20N 99 6W
Selkirk Mts. 152 51 15N 117 40W
Selles-sur-Cher 43 47 16N 1 33 E
Sellières 43 46 50N 5 32 E
Sells 161 31 57N 111 57W
Sellye 53 45 52N 17 51 E
Selma, Ala., U.S.A. 157 32 30N 87 0W
Selma, Calif., U.S.A. 163 36 39N 119 39W
Selma, N.C., U.S.A. 157 35 32N 78 15W
Selmer 157 35 9N 88 36W
Sélo, Óros 68 41 10N 126 0 E
Selongey 43 47 36N 5 10 E
Selowandoma Falls 127 21 15 S 31 50 E
Selpele 103 0 1 S 130 5 E
Selsey 29 50 44N 0 47W
Selsey Bill 29 50 44N 0 47W
Seltz 43 48 48N 8 4 E
Selu, I. 103 7 26 S 130 55 E
Selukwe 127 19 40 S 30 0 E
Sélune, R. 42 48 38N 1 22W
Selva, Argent. 172 29 50 S 62 0W
Selva, Spain 58 41 13N 1 8 E
Selva Beach, La 163 36 56N 121 51W
Selva, La 58 42 0N 2 45 E
Selvas 174 6 30 S 67 0W
Selwyn 133 21 30 S 140 29 E
Selwyn L. 153 60 0N 104 30W
Selwyn Mts. 147 63 0N 130 0W
Selwyn P.O. 138 21 32 S 140 30 E
Selwyn Ra. 138 21 10 S 140 0 E
Semani, R. 68 40 45N 19 50 E
Semarang 103 7 0 S 110 26 E
Sembabule 126 0 4 S 31 25 E
Semeih 123 12 43N 30 53 E
Semenov 81 56 43N 44 30 E
Semenovka 82 49 37N 33 2 E
Semeru, Mt. 103 8 4 S 113 3 E
Sémi 120 15 4N 13 41W
Semiluki 81 51 41N 39 10 E
Seminoe Res. 160 42 0N 107 0W
Seminole, Okla., U.S.A. 159 35 10N 96 45W
Seminole, Tex., U.S.A. 159 32 41N 102 38W
Semiozernoye 84 52 22N 64 8 E
Semipalatinsk 76 50 30N 80 10 E
Semirara Is. 103 12 0N 121 20 E

Semisopochnoi I Shawbost

Semisopochnoi I.	147	52 0N	179 40W
Semitau	102	0 29N	111 57 E
Semiyarskoye	76	50 55N	78 30 E
Semmering Pass.	52	47 41N	15 45 E
Semnan	93	35 55N	53 25 E
Semnan □	93	36 0N	54 0 E
Semois, R.	47	49 53N	4 44 E
Semporna	103	4 30N	118 33 E
Semuda	102	2 51 S	112 58 E
Semur-en-Auxois	43	47 30N	4 20 E
Sen. R.	101	13 45N	105 12 E
Sena Madureira	174	9 5 S	68 45W
Senador Pompeu	170	5 40 S	39 20W
Senai	101	1 38N	103 38 E
Senaja	102	6 49 S	117 2 E
Senanga	128	16 2 S	23 14 E
Senatobia	159	34 38N	89 57W
Sendafa	123	9 11N	39 3 E
Sendai, Kagoshima, Japan	110	31 50N	130 20 E
Sendai, Miyagi, Japan	112	38 15N	141 0 E
Sendamangalam	97	11 17N	78 17 E
Sendeling's Drift	128	28 12 S	16 52 E
Sendenhorst	48	51 50N	7 49 E
Sendurjana	96	21 32N	78 24 E
Senec	53	48 12N	17 23 E
Seneca, Oreg., U.S.A.	160	44 10N	119 2W
Seneca, S.C., U.S.A.	157	34 43N	82 59W
Seneca Falls	162	42 55N	76 50W
Seneca L.	162	42 40N	76 58W
Seneffe	47	50 32N	4 16 E
Senegal ■	120	14 30N	14 30W
Senegal, R.	120	16 30N	15 30W
Senekal	129	28 18 S	27 36 E
Senftenberg	48	51 30N	13 51 E
Senga Hill	127	9 19 S	31 11 E
Senge Khambab (Indus), R.	94	28 40N	70 10 E
Sengerema □	126	2 10 S	32 20 E
Sengiley	81	53 58N	48 54 E
Sengwa, R.	127	17 10 S	28 15 E
Senhor-do-Bonfim	170	10 30 S	40 10W
Senica	53	48 41N	17 25 E
Senigállia	63	43 42N	13 12 E
Seniku	98	25 32N	97 48 E
Senio, R.	63	44 18N	11 47 E
Senj	63	45 0N	14 58 E
Senja	74	69 25N	17 20 E
Senlis	43	49 13N	2 35 E
Senmonorom	100	12 27N	107 12 E
Sennâr	123	13 30N	33 35 E
Senne, R.	47	50 42N	4 13 E
Sennen	30	50 4N	5 42W
Senneterre	150	48 25N	77 15W
Senno	80	54 45N	29 58 E
Sennori	64	40 49N	8 36 E
Senny Bridge	31	51 57N	3 35W
Seno	100	16 41N	105 1 E
Senonches	42	48 34N	1 2 E
Senorbi	64	39 33N	9 8 E
Senoze e	63	45 43N	14 3 E
Sens	43	48 11N	3 15 E
Senta	66	45 55N	20 3 E
Sentein	44	42 53N	0 58 E
Senteny	126	5 17 S	25 42 E
Sentier, Le	51	46 37N	6 15 E
Sentinel	161	32 56N	113 13W
Sento Sé	170	9 40 S	41 18W
Sentolo	103	7 55 S	110 13 E
Senya Beraku	121	5 28N	0 31W
Seo de Urgel	58	42 22N	1 23 E
Seohara	95	29 15N	78 33 E
Seoni	95	22 5N	79 30 E
Seorinayan	96	21 45N	82 34 E
Separation Point	151	53 37N	57 25W
Seph, R.	33	54 17N	1 9W
Sepik, R.	135	3 49 S	144 30 E
Sepólno Krajenskie	54	53 26N	17 30 E
Sepone	100	16 45N	106 13 E
Sepopa	128	18 49 S	22 12 E
Sepopol	54	54 16N	21 2 E
Sepori	107	38 57N	127 25 E
Sept Îles	151	50 13N	66 22W
Septemvri	67	42 13N	24 6 E
Septimus	138	21 13 S	148 47 E
Sepúlveda	56	41 18N	3 45W
Sequeros	56	40 31N	6 2W
Sequim	160	48 3N	123 9W
Sequoia Nat. Park	163	36 30N	118 30W
Serafimovich	83	49 30N	42 50 E
Seraing	47	50 35N	5 32 E
Seraja	101	2 41N	108 35 E
Seram, I.	103	3 10 S	129 0 E
Serampore	95	22 44N	88 30 E
Serang	103	6 8 S	106 10 E
Serasan	101	2 31N	109 2 E
Serasan, I.	102	2 29N	109 4 E
Seravezza	62	43 59N	10 13 E
Serbia = Srbija	66	43 30N	21 0 E
Sercaia	70	45 49N	25 9 E
Serdo	123	11 56N	41 14 E
Serdobsk	81	52 28N	44 10 E
Seredka	80	58 12N	28 3 E
Seregno	62	45 40N	9 12 E
Seremban	101	2 43N	101 53 E
Serena, La, Chile	172	29 55 S	71 10W
Serena, La, Spain	57	38 45N	5 40W
Serengeti □	126	2 0 S	34 30 E
Serengeti Plain	126	2 40 S	35 0 E
Serenje	125	13 14 S	30 15 E
Sergach	81	55 30N	45 30 E
Serge, R.	58	42 5N	1 21 E
Sergievsk	81	54 0N	51 10 E
Sergipe □	170	10 30 S	37 30W
Seria	102	4 37N	114 30 E
Serian	102	1 10N	110 40 E
Seriate	62	45 42N	9 43 E
Sérifontaine	43	49 20N	1 45 E
Sérifos, I.	69	37 9N	24 30 E
Sérignan	44	43 17N	3 17 E
Serik	92	36 55N	31 10 E
Seringapatam Reef	136	13 38 S	122 5 E
Sermaize-les-Bains	43	48 47N	4 54 E
Sermata, I.	103	8 15 S	128 50 E
Sérmide	63	45 0N	11 17 E
Sernovdsk	76	61 20N	73 28 E
Sernovodsk	84	53 54N	51 16 E
Sero	120	14 42N	10 59W
Serón	59	37 20N	2 29W
Serós	58	41 27N	0 24 E
Serov	84	59 36N	60 35 E
Serowe	128	22 25 S	26 43 E
Serpa	57	37 57N	7 38 E
Serpeddi, Punta	64	39 19N	9 28 E
Serpentara	64	39 8N	9 38 E
Serpentine	137	32 23 S	115 58 E
Serpentine L.	137	28 30 S	129 10 E
Serpent's Mouth	174	10 0N	61 30W
Serpis, R.	59	38 45N	0 21W
Serpukhov	81	54 55N	37 28 E
Serra	171	20 7 S	40 18W
Serra Capriola	65	41 47N	15 12 E
Serra do Salitre	74	19 6 S	46 41W
Serra Talhada	170	7 59 S	38 18W
Serradilla	56	39 50N	6 9W
Sérrai □	68	41 5N	23 37 E
Serramanna	64	39 26N	8 56 E
Serrania de Cuenca	58	40 10N	1 50W
Serrat, C.	119	37 14N	9 10 E
Serres	45	44 26N	5 43 E
Serrezuela	172	30 40 S	65 20W
Serrinha	171	11 39 S	39 0W
Serrita	170	7 56 S	39 19W
Serro	171	18 37 S	43 23W
Sersale	65	39 1N	16 44 E
Sertã	56	39 48N	8 6W
Sertânia	170	8 5 S	37 20W
Sertanópolis	173	23 4 S	51 2W
Sertão	170	10 0 S	40 20W
Sertig	51	46 44N	9 52 E
Serua, P.	103	6 18 S	130 1 E
Serui	103	1 45 S	136 10 E
Serule	128	21 57 S	27 11 E
Sérvia	68	40 9N	21 58 E
Sesajap Lama	102	3 32N	117 11 E
Sese Is.	126	0 30 S	32 30 E
Sesepe	103	1 30 S	127 59 E
Sesfontein	128	19 7 S	13 39 E
Sesheke	128	17 29 S	24 13 E
Sesia, R.	62	45 35N	8 23 E
Sesimbra	57	38 28N	9 20W
Seskanore	38	54 31N	7 15W
Sessa Aurunca	64	41 14N	13 55 E
Sestao	58	43 18N	3 0W
Sesto S. Giovanni	62	45 32N	9 14 E
Sestri Levante	62	44 17N	9 22 E
Sestrières	62	44 58N	6 56 E
Sestrunj, I.	63	44 10N	15 0 E
Sestu	64	39 18N	9 6 E
Sesvenna	51	46 42N	10 25 E
Seta	108	32 20N	100 41 E
Setaka	110	33 9N	130 28 E
Setana	112	42 26N	139 51 E
Sète	44	43 25N	3 42 E
Sete Lagoas	171	19 27 S	44 16W
Sétif	119	36 9N	5 26 E
Seto	111	35 14N	137 6 E
Seto Naikai	110	34 20N	133 30 E
Setouchi	112	28 8N	129 19 E
Setsan	98	16 3N	95 23 E
Settat	118	33 0N	7 40W
Setté Cama	124	2 32 S	9 57 E
Séttimo Tor	62	45 9N	7 46 E
Setting L.	153	55 0N	98 38W
Settle	32	54 5N	2 18W
Settlement Pt.	157	26 40N	79 0W
Setto Calende	62	45 44N	8 37 E
Setúbal	57	38 30N	8 58W
Setúbal □	57	38 25N	8 35W
Setúbal, B. de	57	38 40N	8 56W
Seul L.	150	50 25N	92 30W
Seul Reservoir, Lac	150	50 25N	92 30W
Seulimeum	102	5 27N	95 15 E
Seuzach	51	47 32N	8 49 E
Sevastopol	82	44 35N	33 30 E
Sevelen	51	47 7N	9 30 E
Seven Emu	138	16 20 S	137 8 E
Seven Heads	39	51 35N	8 43W
Seven Hogs, Is.	39	52 20N	10 0W
Seven, R.	33	54 11N	0 51W
Seven Sisters	31	51 46N	3 43W
Seven Sisters, mt	152	54 56N	128 10W
Sevenoaks	29	51 16N	0 11 E
Sevenum	47	51 25N	6 2 E
Sever, R.	57	39 40N	7 32W
Sévérac-le-Chateau	44	44 20N	3 5 E
Severn Beach	28	51 34N	2 39W
Severn L.	150	53 54N	90 48W
Severn, R., Can.	150	56 2N	87 36W
Severn, R., U.K.	28	51 35N	2 38W
Severn Stoke	28	52 5N	2 13W
Severnaya Zemlya	77	79 0N	100 0 E
Severnyye Uvaly	78	58 0N	48 0 E
Severo-Kurilsk	77	50 40N	156 8 E
Severodonetsk	83	48 50N	38 30 E
Severodvinsk	78	64 27N	39 58 E
Severomoravsky □	53	49 38N	17 40 E
Severouralsk	84	60 9N	59 57 E
Sevier	161	38 39N	112 11W
Sevier L.	160	39 0N	113 20W
Sevier, R.	161	39 10N	112 50W
Sevilla, Colomb.	174	4 16N	75 57W
Sevilla, Spain	57	37 23N	6 0W
Sevilla □	57	37 0N	6 0W
Seville = Sevilla	57	37 23N	6 0W
Sevnica	63	46 2N	15 19 E
Sevsk	80	52 10N	34 30 E
Seward	147	60 0N	149 40W
Seward Pen.	147	65 0N	164 0W
Sewell	172	34 10 S	70 45W
Sewer	103	5 46 S	134 40 E
Sexbierum	46	53 13N	5 29 E
Sexsmith	152	55 21N	118 47W
Seychelles, Is.	11	5 0 S	56 0 E
Seyðisfjörður	74	65 16N	14 0W
Seym, R.	80	51 45N	35 0 E
Seymchan	77	62 40N	152 30 E
Seymour, Austral.	141	37 0 S	145 10 E
Seymour, Conn., U.S.A.	162	41 23N	73 5W
Seymour, Ind., U.S.A.	156	39 0N	85 50W
Seymour, Tex., U.S.A.	159	33 35N	99 18W
Seymour, Wis., U.S.A.	156	44 30N	88 20W
Seyne	45	44 21N	6 22 E
Seyne-sur-Mer, La	45	43 7N	5 52 E
Sezana	63	45 43N	13 41 E
Sézanne	43	48 40N	3 40 E
Sezze	64	41 30N	13 3 E
Sfântu Gheorghe	70	45 52N	25 48 E
Sfax	119	34 49N	10 48 E
Sgurr Mor	36	57 42N	5 0W
Sgurr na Ciche	36	57 0N	5 29W
Sgurr na Lapaich	36	57 23N	5 5W
Sha Ch'i, R.	109	26 35N	118 8 E
Shaartuz	85	37 16N	68 8 E
Shaba	126	8 0 S	25 0 E
Shaba Gamba	99	32 8N	88 55 E
Shaballe, R.	123	5 0N	44 0 E
Shabani	127	20 17 S	30 2 E
Shabbear	30	50 52N	4 12W
Shabla	67	43 31N	28 32 E
Shabogamo L.	151	48 40N	77 0W
Shabunda	126	2 40 S	27 16 E
Shackleton	13	78 30 S	36 1W
Shackleton Inlet	13	83 0 S	160 0 E
Shaddad	122	21 25N	40 2 E
Shadi	95	33 24N	77 14 E
Shadrinsk	84	56 5N	63 58 E
Shadwân	122	27 30N	34 0 E
Shaffa	121	10 30N	12 6 E
Shafter	163	35 32N	119 14W
Shaftesbury	28	51 0N	2 12W
Shag Pt.	143	45 29 S	170 52 E
Shagamu	121	6 51N	3 39 E
Shagram	95	36 24N	72 20 E
Shah Bunder	94	24 13N	67 50 E
Shahabad, And. P., India	96	17 10N	78 11 E
Shahabad, Punjab, India	94	30 10N	76 55 E
Shahabad, Raj., India	94	25 15N	77 11 E
Shahabad, Uttar Pradesh, India	95	27 36N	79 56 E
Shāhābād	93	37 40N	56 50 E
Shahada	96	21 33N	74 30 E
Shahapur	96	15 50N	74 34 E
Shāhbād	92	34 10N	46 30 E
Shahdād	93	30 30N	57 40 E
Shahdadkot	94	27 50N	67 55 E
Shahddpur	94	25 55N	68 35 E
Shahganj	95	26 3N	82 44 E
Shahgarh	93	27 15N	69 50 E
Shahhat (Cyrene)	117	32 40N	21 35 E
Shāhī	93	36 30N	52 55 E
Shahjahanpur	95	27 54N	79 57 E
Shaho	106	36 31N	114 35 E
Shahpur, Mad. P., India	94	22 12N	77 58 E
Shahpur, Mysore, India	97	16 40N	76 48 E
Shahpur, Iran	92	38 12N	44 45 E
Shahpur, Pak.	94	28 46N	68 27 E
Shahpura	95	23 10N	80 45 E
Shahr-e Babak	93	30 10N	55 20 E
Shahr Kord	93	32 15N	50 55 E
Shahraban	92	34 0N	45 0 E
Shahreza	93	32 0N	51 55 E
Shahrig	94	30 15N	67 40 E
Shahriza	93	32 0N	51 50 E
Shahrud	93	36 30N	55 0 E
Shahrukh	93	33 50N	60 10 E
Shahsavar	93	36 45N	51 12 E
Shahsien	109	26 25N	117 50 E
Shahuk'ou	106	40 20N	112 18 E
Shaibâra	123	25 26N	36 47 E
Shaikhabad	94	34 0N	68 45 E
Shaim	84	60 21N	64 10 E
Shajapur	94	23 20N	76 15 E
Shakargarh	94	32 17N	75 43 E
Shakawe	128	18 28 S	21 49 E
Shakhristan	85	39 47N	68 49 E
Shakhrisyabz	85	39 3N	66 50 E
Shakhty	83	47 40N	40 10 E
Shakhunya	81	57 40N	47 0 E
Shaki	121	8 41N	3 21 E
Shakopee	158	44 45N	93 30W
Shaktolik	147	64 30N	161 15W
Shala Lake	123	7 30N	38 30 E
Shaldon	30	50 32N	3 31W
Shalkar Karashatau, Ozero	84	50 26N	61 12 E
Shalkar Yega Kara, Ozero	84	50 45N	60 54 E
Sham, J. ash	93	23 10N	57 5 E
Shama	121	5 1N	1 42W
Shamâl Dâfû □	123	15 0N	25 0 E
Shamâl Kordofân □	123	15 0N	30 0 E
Shamar, Jabal	92	27 40N	41 0 E
Shamattawa	153	55 51N	92 5W
Shamattawa, R.	150	55 1N	85 23W
Shambe	123	7 2N	30 46 E
Shambu	123	9 32N	37 3 E
Shamgong Dzong	98	27 19N	90 35 E
Shamil, India	94	29 32N	77 18 E
Shamil, Iran	93	27 30N	56 55 E
Shamkhor	83	40 56N	46 0 E
Shamo, L.	123	5 45N	37 30 E
Shamokin	162	40 47N	76 33W
Shamrock	159	35 15N	100 15W
Shamva	125	17 20 S	31 32 E
Shan □	98	21 30N	98 30 E
Shanagolden	39	52 35N	9 6W
Shanan, R.	123	8 0N	40 20 E
Shanch'eng	109	31 45N	115 30 E
Shandon	163	35 39N	120 23W
Shandon Downs	138	17 45 S	134 50 E
Shanga	121	9 1N	5 2 E
Shangalowe	127	10 50 S	26 30 E
Shangani	127	19 1 S	28 51 E
Shangani, R.	127	18 35 S	27 45 E
Shangchih, (Chuho)	107	45 10N	127 59 E
Shangching	106	33 9N	110 2 E
Shangch'iu	105	34 26N	115 40 E
Shangch'uan Shan, I.	109	21 45N	112 45 E
Shanghai	109	31 10N	121 25 E
Shanghang	109	25 5N	116 30 E
Shangho	107	37 19N	117 9 E
Shanghsien	106	33 30N	109 58 E
Shangjao	109	28 25N	117 57 E
Shangkao	109	28 16N	114 50 E
Shanglin	108	23 26N	108 36 E
Shangnan	106	33 35N	110 49 E
Shangpanch'eng	107	40 50N	118 0 E
Shangshui	106	33 42N	114 34 E
Shangssu	108	22 10N	108 0 E
Shangtsai	106	33 15N	114 20 E
Shangtu	106	41 31N	113 35 E
Shangyu	109	25 59N	114 29 E
Shanhaikuan	107	40 2N	119 48 E
Shanhot'un	107	44 42N	127 12 E
Shanhsien	106	34 51N	116 9 E
Shani	121	10 14N	12 2 E
Shaniko	160	45 0N	120 15W
Shanklin	28	50 39N	1 9W
Shannon, Greenl.	12	75 10N	18 30W
Shannon, N.Z.	142	40 33 S	175 25 E
Shannon Airport	39	52 42N	8 57W
Shannon Bridge	39	53 17N	8 2W
Shannon I.	12	75 0N	18 0W
Shannon, Mouth of the	39	52 30N	9 55W
Shannon, R.	39	53 10N	8 10W
Shansi □	106	37 30N	112 15 E
Shantar, Ostrov Bolshoi	77	55 9N	137 40 E
Shant'ou	109	23 28N	116 40 E
Shantung □	105	36 0N	117 30 E
Shantung Pantao	107	37 5N	121 0 E
Shanyang	106	33 39N	110 2 E
Shanyin	106	39 34N	112 50 E
Shaohing	109	30 0N	120 32 E
Shaokuan	109	24 50N	113 35 E
Shaowu	109	27 25N	117 30 E
Shaoyang	109	27 10N	111 30 E
Shap	32	54 32N	2 40W
Shap'ing	109	22 46N	112 57 E
Shapinsay, I.	37	59 2N	2 50W
Shapinsay Sd.	37	59 0N	2 51W
Shaqra	92	25 15N	45 16 E
Sharafa (Ogr)	123	11 59N	27 7 E
Sharavati, R.	97	14 32N	74 0 E
Sharhjui	93	32 30N	67 22 E
Shari	92	27 20N	43 45 E
Sharjah	93	25 23N	55 26 E
Shark B., N. Territory, Austral.	132	11 20 S	130 35 E
Shark B., W. Australia, Austral.	137	25 55 S	113 32 E
Sharm el Sheikh	122	27 53N	34 15 E
Sharon, Mass., U.S.A.	162	42 5N	71 11W
Sharon, Pa., U.S.A.	156	41 18N	80 30W
Sharon, Plain of = Hasharon	90	32 12N	34 49 E
Sharon Springs	162	42 48N	74 37W
Sharp Pt.	138	10 58 S	142 43 E
Sharpe, L.	150	54 10N	93 21W
Sharpe L.	153	50 23N	95 30W
Sharpness	28	51 43N	2 28W
Sharya	81	58 12N	45 40 E
Shasha	123	6 29N	35 59 E
Shashemene	123	7 13N	38 33 E
Shashi	125	21 15 S	27 27 E
Shashi, R.	127	21 40 S	28 40 E
Shashih	109	30 19N	112 14 E
Shasta, Mt.	160	41 45N	122 0W
Shasta Res.	160	40 50N	122 15W
Shati	109	26 6N	114 51 E
Shatsk	81	54 0N	41 45 E
Shattuck	159	36 17N	99 55W
Shaumyani	83	41 13N	44 45 E
Shaunavon	153	49 35N	108 25W
Shaver Lake	163	37 9N	119 18W
Shaw I.	138	20 30 S	149 2 E
Shaw, R.	136	20 21 S	119 17 E
Shawan	105	44 21N	85 37 E
Shawangunk Mts.	162	41 40N	74 25W
Shawano	156	44 45N	88 38W
Shawbost	36	58 20N	6 40W

Shawbury Siddeburen

Shawbury 28 52 48N 2 40W
Shawinigan 150 46 35N 72 50W
Shawnee 159 35 15N 97 0W
Shaymak 85 37 33N 74 50E
Shaziz 99 33 10N 82 43E
Shchëkino 81 54 1N 37 28E
Shcherbakov = Rybinsk 81 58 5N 38 50E
Shchigri 81 51 55N 36 58E
Shchuchinsk 76 52 56N 70 12E
Shchuchye 84 55 12N 62 46E
Shchurovo 81 55 0N 38 51E
Shebekino 81 50 28N 37 0E
Shebele, Wabi 123 2 0N 44 0E
Sheboygan 156 43 46N 87 45W
Shechem 90 32 13N 35 21E
Shech'i 106 33 3N 112 57E
Shediac 151 46 14N 64 32W
Sheefry Hills 38 53 40N 9 40W
Sheelin, Lough 38 53 48N 7 20W
Sheep Haven 38 55 12N 7 55W
Sheeps Hd. 39 51 32N 9 50W
Sheerness 29 51 26N 0 47E
Sheet Harbour 151 44 56N 62 31W
Shefar'am 90 32 48N 35 10E
Shefeiya 90 32 35N 34 58E
Sheffield, U.K. 33 53 23N 1 28W
Sheffield, Ala., U.S.A. 157 34 45N 87 42W
Sheffield, Mass., U.S.A. 162 42 6N 73 23W
Sheffield, Tex., U.S.A. 159 30 42N 101 49W
Shefford 29 52 2N 0 20W
Shegaon 96 20 48N 76 59E
Sheho 153 51 35N 103 13W
Shehojele 123 10 40N 35 27E
Shehsien, Anhwei, China 109 29 52N 118 26E
Shehsien, Hopeh, China 106 36 33N 113 40E
Shehung 108 31 0N 105 12E
Shehy Mts. 39 51 47N 9 15W
Sheikhpura 95 25 9N 85 53E
Shek Hasan 123 13 5N 35 58E
Shekar Dzong 95 28 45N 87 0E
Shekhupura 94 31 42N 73 58E
Sheki 83 41 10N 47 5E
Sheksna, R. 81 59 30N 38 30E
Shelburne, N.S., Can. 151 43 47N 65 20W
Shelburne, Ont., Can. 150 44 4N 80 15W
Shelburne B. 133 11 50S 143 0E
Shelburne Falls 162 42 36N 72 45W
Shelby, Mich., U.S.A. 156 43 34N 86 27W
Shelby, Mont., U.S.A. 160 48 30N 111 59W
Shelby, N.C., U.S.A. 157 35 18N 81 34W
Shelbyville, Ill., U.S.A. 158 39 25N 88 45W
Shelbyville, Ind., U.S.A. 156 39 30N 85 42W
Shelbyville, Tenn., U.S.A. 157 35 30N 86 25W
Sheldon 158 43 6N 95 51W
Sheldon Point 147 62 30N 165 0W
Sheldrake 151 50 20N 64 51W
Shelikef, Str. 147 58 0N 154 0W
Shelikhova, Zaliv 77 59 30N 157 0E
Shell, L. 36 58 0N 6 28W
Shell Lake 153 53 19N 107 14W
Shell Lakes 137 29 20S 127 30E
Shellbrook 153 53 13N 106 24W
Shellharbour 141 34 31S 150 51E
Shelon, R. 80 58 10N 30 30E
Shelter Bay 151 50 30N 67 20W
Shelter I 162 41 5N 72 21W
Shelton, Conn., U.S.A. 162 41 18N 73 7W
Shelton, Wash., U.S.A. 160 47 15N 123 6W
Shemakha 83 40 50N 48 28E
Shenandoah, Iowa, U.S.A. 158 40 50N 95 25W
Shenandoah, Pa., U.S.A. 162 40 49N 76 13W
Shenandoah, Va., U.S.A. 156 38 30N 78 38W
Shenandoah, R. 156 38 30N 78 38W
Shencha 105 30 56N 88 38E
Shench'ih 106 39 8N 112 10E
Shenchingtzu 107 44 48N 124 32E
Shench'iu 106 33 26N 115 2E
Shencottah 97 8 59N 77 18E
Shendam 121 9 10N 9 30E
Shendî 123 16 46N 33 33E
Shendurni 96 20 39N 75 36E
Shenfield 29 51 39N 0 21E
Shengfang 106 39 5N 116 42E
Shëngjergji 68 41 2N 20 10E
Shëngjini 68 41 50N 19 35E
Shenmëria 68 42 7N 20 13E
Shenmu 106 38 54N 110 24E
Shensi □ 106 34 50N 109 25E
Shenton, Mt. 137 27 57S 123 22E
Shenyang 107 42 50N 123 25E
Sheopur Kalan 93 25 40N 76 40E
Shepetovka 80 50 10N 27 0E
Shephelah = Hashefela 90 31 30N 34 43E
Shepparton 141 36 23S 145 26E
Sheppey, I. of 29 51 23N 0 50E
Shepshed 28 52 47N 1 18W
Shepton Mallet 28 51 11N 2 31W
Sher Khan Qala 94 29 55N 66 10E
Sher Qila 95 36 7N 74 2E
Sherada 123 7 25N 36 30E
Sherborne 28 50 56N 2 31W
Sherborne St. John 28 51 18N 1 7W
Sherbro I. 120 7 30N 12 40W
Sherbrooke 151 45 8N 81 57W
Sherburn, N. Yorks., U.K. 33 54 12N 0 32W
Sherburn, N. Yorks., U.K. 33 53 47N 1 15W
Sherburne 162 42 41N 75 30W
Shercock 38 54 0N 6 54W
Sherda 119 20 7N 16 46E
Shere 29 51 13N 0 28W
Shereik 122 18 52N 33 40E
Sherfield English 28 51 1N 1 35W
Sheridan, Ark., U.S.A. 159 34 20N 92 25W
Sheridan, Col., U.S.A. 158 39 44N 105 3W
Sheridan, Wyo., U.S.A. 160 44 50N 107 0W
Sheriff Hutton 33 54 5N 1 0W
Sheriff Muir 35 56 12N 3 53W
Sheringham 29 52 56N 1 11E
Sherkin I. 39 51 38N 9 25W
Sherkot 95 29 22N 78 35E
Sherman 159 33 40N 96 35W
Sherpur 98 24 41N 89 25E
Sherridon 153 55 8N 101 5W
Sherston 28 51 35N 2 13W
Sherwood, N.D., U.S.A. 158 48 59N 101 36W
Sherwood, Tex., U.S.A. 159 31 18N 100 45W
Sherwood For. 33 53 5N 1 5W
Shesheke 125 17 14S 24 22E
Sheslay 152 58 17N 131 45W
Sheslay, R. 152 58 48N 132 5W
Shethanei L. 153 58 48N 97 50W
Shetland □ 36 60 30N 1 30W
Shetland Is. 36 60 30N 1 30W
Shevaroy Hills 97 11 58N 78 12E
Shevchenko 83 44 25N 51 20E
Shewa □ 123 9 33N 38 10E
Sheyenne 159 47 52N 99 8W
Sheyenne, R. 158 47 40N 98 15W
Shiant Is. 36 57 54N 6 20W
Shiant, Sd. of Scot. 36 57 54N 6 30W
Shibam 91 16 0N 48 36E
Shibata 112 37 57N 139 20E
Shiberghan □ 93 35 45N 66 0E
Shibetsu 112 44 10N 142 23E
Shibîn El Kôm 122 30 31N 30 55E
Shibogama L. 150 53 35N 88 15W
Shibukawa 111 36 29N 139 0E
Shibushi 110 31 25N 131 0E
Shibushi-Wan 110 31 24N 131 8E
Shickshinny 162 41 9N 76 9W
Shido 110 34 19N 134 10E
Shiel, L. 36 56 48N 5 32W
Shield, C. 138 13 20S 136 20E
Shieldaig 36 57 31N 5 39W
Shifnal 28 52 40N 2 23W
Shiga-ken □ 111 35 20N 136 0E
Shigaib 117 15 5N 23 35E
Shigaraki 111 34 57N 136 2E
Shihch'eng 109 26 19N 116 15E
Shihchiachuangi 106 38 2N 114 30E
Shihch'ien 108 27 30N 108 14E
Shihchiu Hu 109 31 28N 118 53E
Shihchu 108 30 4N 108 10E
Shihch'üan 106 33 3N 108 17E
Shihhsing 109 24 57N 114 4E
Shihku 108 26 52N 99 56E
Shihkuaikou 106 40 42N 110 20E
Shihlung 109 23 55N 113 35E
Shihmen 109 29 36N 111 23E
Shihmenchien 109 29 33N 116 47E
Shihmien 108 29 20N 102 28E
Shihping 108 27 2N 108 7E
Shihp'ing 108 23 43N 102 30E
Shihshou 109 29 43N 112 26E
Shihtai 109 30 22N 117 57E
Shihtien 108 24 44N 99 11E
Shiht'ouhotzu 107 44 52N 128 41E
Shihtsuishan 106 39 15N 106 50E
Shihtsung 108 24 51N 103 59E
Shiiba 110 32 29N 131 4E
Shijaku 68 41 21N 19 33E
Shikarpur, India 94 28 17N 78 7E
Shikarpur, Pak. 94 27 57N 68 39E
Shikine-Jima 111 34 19N 139 13E
Shikohabad 93 27 6N 78 38E
Shikoku 110 33 30N 133 30E
Shikoku □ 110 33 30N 133 30E
Shikoku-Sanchi 110 33 30N 133 30E
Shilbottle 35 55 23N 1 42W
Shilda 84 51 49N 59 47E
Shildon 33 54 37N 1 39W
Shilka 77 52 0N 115 55E
Shilka, R. 77 57 30N 93 18E
Shillelagh 39 52 46N 6 32W
Shillingstone 28 50 54N 2 15W
Shillington 162 40 18N 75 58W
Shillong 98 25 35N 91 53E
Shiloh 90 32 4N 35 10E
Shilovo 81 54 25N 40 57E
Shima-Hantō 111 34 22N 136 45E
Shimabara 110 32 48N 130 20E
Shimada 111 34 49N 138 19E
Shimane-Hantō 110 35 30N 133 0E
Shimane-ken □ 110 35 0N 132 30E
Shimenovsk 77 52 15N 127 30E
Shimizu 111 35 0N 138 30E
Shimo-Jima 110 32 15N 130 7E
Shimo-Koshiki-Jima 110 31 40N 129 43E
Shimoda 111 34 40N 138 57E
Shimodate 111 36 20N 139 55E
Shimoga 97 13 57N 75 32E
Shimoni 126 4 38S 39 20E
Shimonita 111 36 13N 138 47E
Shimonoseki 110 33 58N 131 0E
Shimotsuma 111 36 11N 139 58E
Shimpuru Rapids 128 17 45S 19 55E
Shimsha, R. 97 13 15N 76 54E
Shimsk 80 58 15N 30 50E
Shin Dand 93 33 12N 62 8E
Shin, L. 37 58 7N 4 30W
Shin, R. 37 58 0N 4 26W
Shin-Tone-Gawa 111 35 57N 140 27E
Shingbwiyang 98 26 41N 96 13E
Shingleton 150 46 33N 86 33W
Shingu 111 33 40N 135 55E
Shinji 110 35 24N 132 54E
Shinji Ko 110 35 26N 132 57E
Shinjō 112 38 46N 140 18E
Shinkafe 121 13 8N 6 29E
Shinminato 111 36 47N 137 4E
Shinonoi 111 36 35N 138 9E
Shinrone 39 53 0N 7 58W
Shinshiro 111 34 54N 137 30E
Shinyanga 126 3 45S 33 27E
Shinyanga □ 126 3 30S 33 30E
Shio-no-Misaki 111 33 25N 135 45E
Shiogama 112 38 19N 141 1E
Shiojiri 111 36 6N 137 58E
Ship I. 159 30 16N 88 55W
Ship Shoal I. 162 37 10N 75 45W
Shipbourne 29 51 13N 0 19E
Shipdham 29 52 38N 0 53E
Shipehenski Prokhod 67 42 39N 25 28E
Shipki La 93 31 45N 78 40E
Shipley 33 53 50N 1 47W
Shippegan 151 47 45N 64 45W
Shippensburg 156 40 4N 77 32W
Shiprock 161 36 51N 108 45W
Shipston-on-Stour 28 52 4N 1 38W
Shipton-under-Wychwood 28 51 51N 1 35W
Shir Kūh 93 31 45N 53 30E
Shirabad 85 37 40N 67 1E
Shirahama 111 33 41N 135 20E
Shirakawa 111 36 17N 136 56E
Shirane-San, Gumma, Japan 111 36 48N 139 22E
Shirane-San, Yamanashi, Japan 111 35 34N 138 9E
Shiraoi 112 42 33N 141 21E
Shirati 126 1 10S 34 0E
Shiraz 93 29 42N 52 30E
Shire, R. 127 16 30S 35 0E
Shirebrook 33 53 13N 1 11W
Shiresh 85 39 58N 70 59E
Shirinab, R. 94 29 30N 66 30E
Shiringushi 81 42 54N 53 56W
Shiriya-Zaki 112 41 25N 141 30E
Shirol 96 16 47N 74 41E
Shirpur 96 21 21N 74 57E
Shirvan 93 37 30N 57 50E
Shirwa L. = Chilwa L. 127 15 15S 35 40E
Shishmanova 67 42 58N 23 12E
Shishmaref 147 66 15N 166 10W
Shivali, (Sirkall) 97 11 15N 79 41E
Shivpuri 94 25 18N 77 42E
Shivta 90 30 53N 34 40E
Shiwele Ferry 127 11 25S 28 31E
Shiyata 122 29 25N 25 7E
Shizuoka 111 35 0N 138 30E
Shizuoka-ken □ 111 35 15N 138 40E
Shklov 80 54 10N 30 15E
Shkoder = Shkodra 68 42 6N 19 20E
Shkodra 68 42 6N 19 20E
Shkodra □ 68 42 5N 19 20E
Shkumbini, R. 68 41 5N 19 50E
Shmidt, O. 77 81 0N 91 0E
Shō Gawa, R. 111 36 47N 137 4E
Shoa Ghimirra, (Wota) 123 7 4N 35 51E
Shoal, C. 137 33 52S 121 10E
Shoal Lake 153 50 30N 100 35W
Shōbara 110 34 51N 133 1E
Shōdo-Shima 110 34 30N 134 15E
Shoeburyness 29 51 31N 0 49E
Shokpar 85 43 49N 74 21E
Sholapur 96 17 43N 75 56E
Shologontsy 77 66 13N 114 14E
Shomera 90 33 4N 35 17E
Shōmrōn 90 32 15N 35 13E
Shona I. 36 56 48N 5 50W
Shongopovi 161 35 49N 110 37W
Shoranur 97 10 46N 76 19E
Shorapur 96 16 31N 76 48E
Shoreham-by-Sea 29 50 50N 0 17W
Shortland I. 135 7 0S 155 45E
Shoshone, Calif., U.S.A. 163 35 58N 116 16W
Shoshone, Idaho, U.S.A. 160 43 0N 114 27W
Shoshone L. 160 44 0N 111 0W
Shoshone Mts. 160 39 30N 117 30W
Shoshong 125 22 56S 26 31E
Shoshoni 160 43 13N 108 5W
Shostka 80 51 57N 33 32E
Shotts 35 55 49N 3 47W
Shouch'ang 109 29 22N 119 13E
Shouhsien 109 32 35N 116 48E
Shoukuang 107 36 53N 118 42E
Shouning 109 27 26N 119 27E
Shouyang 106 37 59N 113 9E
Show Low 161 34 16N 110 0W
Shpola 82 49 1N 31 30E
Shreveport 159 32 30N 93 50W
Shrewsbury 28 52 42N 2 45W
Shrewton 28 51 11N 1 55W
Shrivardhan 96 18 10N 73 3E
Shrivenham 28 51 36N 1 39W
Shropshire □ 28 52 36N 2 45W
Shrule 38 53 32N 9 7W
Shuangch'eng 107 45 25N 126 20E
Shuangchiang 108 23 33N 99 45E
Shuangfeng 109 27 26N 112 10E
Shuangfeng Tao 109 26 35N 120 8E
Shuangkou 107 34 3N 117 34E
Shuangliao 105 43 31N 123 30E
Shuangpai 108 24 50N 101 36E
Shuangshantzu 107 40 21N 119 12E
Shuangyang 107 43 32N 125 40E
Shuangyashan 105 46 37N 131 22E
Shuch'eng 109 31 27N 116 57E
Shugden Gomba 99 29 35N 96 55E
Shuguri Falls 127 8 33S 37 22E
Shuich'eng 108 26 35N 104 54E
Shuichi 109 27 28N 118 21E
Shuiyeh 106 36 8N 114 6E
Shujalpur 94 23 43N 76 40E
Shulan 107 44 27N 126 57E
Shumagin Is. 147 55 0N 159 0W
Shumerlya 81 55 30N 46 10E
Shumikha 84 55 10N 63 15E
Shunan 109 29 37N 119 0E
Shunch'ang 109 26 48N 117 47E
Shungay 83 48 30N 46 45E
Shungnak 147 66 55N 157 10W
Shunning 99 24 35N 99 50E
Shunte 109 22 48N 113 17E
Shuohsien 106 39 19N 112 25E
Shupka Kunzang 95 34 22N 78 22E
Shuqra 91 13 22N 45 34E
Shur, R. 93 28 30N 55 0E
Shurab 85 40 3N 70 33E
Shurchi 85 37 59N 67 47E
Shurkhua 98 22 15N 93 38E
Shurma 84 56 58N 50 21E
Shusf 93 31 50N 60 5E
Shūshtar 92 32 0N 48 50E
Shuswap L. 152 50 55N 119 3W
Shuweika 90 32 20N 35 1E
Shuya 81 56 50N 41 28E
Shuyak I. 147 58 35N 152 30W
Shuzenji 111 34 58N 138 56E
Shwebo 98 22 30N 95 45E
Shwegu 98 18 49N 95 26E
Shwegun 98 17 9N 97 39E
Shweli Myit 99 23 45N 96 45E
Shweli, R. 99 23 45N 96 45E
Shwenyaung 98 20 46N 96 57E
Shyok 95 34 15N 78 5E
Shyok, R. 95 34 30N 78 15E
Si Chon 101 9 0N 99 54E
Si Kiang = Hsi Chiang, R. 39 22 20N 113 20E
Si Prachan 100 14 37N 100 9E
Si Racha 101 13 10N 100 56E
Siah 92 22 0N 47 0E
Siahan Range 93 27 30N 64 40E
Siaksriinderapura 102 0 51N 102 0E
Sialkot 94 32 32N 74 30E
Sialsuk 98 23 24N 92 45E
Siam 140 32 35S 136 41E
Siam, G. of 101 11 30N 101 0E
Siam = Thailand ■ 100 16 0N 102 0E
Sian = Hsian 106 34 17N 109 0E
Siantan, P. 101 3 10N 106 15E
Siareh 93 28 5N 60 20E
Siargao, I. 103 9 52N 126 3E
Siari 95 34 55N 76 40E
Siasi 103 5 34N 120 50E
Siassi 135 5 40S 147 51E
Siátista 68 40 15N 21 33E
Siau, I. 103 2 50N 125 25E
Siauliai 80 55 56N 23 15E
Siaya □ 126 0 0N 34 20E
Siazan 83 41 3N 48 7E
Sibâi, Gebel el 122 25 45N 34 10E
Sibari 65 39 47N 16 27E
Sibay 84 52 42N 58 39E
Sibaya, L. 129 27 20S 32 45E
Sibbald 153 51 24N 110 10W
Sibenik 63 43 48N 15 54E
Siberia 77 60 0N 100 0E
Siberut, I. 102 1 30S 99 0E
Sibi 94 29 30N 67 48E
Sibil 103 4 59S 140 35E
Sibiti 124 3 38S 13 19E
Sibiu 70 45 45N 24 9E
Sibiu □ 70 45 50N 24 15E
Sible Hedingham 29 51 58N 0 37E
Sibley, Iowa, U.S.A. 158 43 21N 95 43W
Sibley, La., U.S.A. 159 32 34N 93 16W
Sibolga 102 1 50N 98 45E
Sibret 47 49 58N 5 38E
Sibsagar 98 27 0N 94 36E
Sibsey 33 53 3N 0 1E
Sibuco 103 7 20N 122 10E
Sibuguey B. 103 7 50N 122 45E
Sibuko 103 7 20N 122 10E
Sibut 117 5 52N 19 10E
Sibutu, I. 102 4 45N 119 30E
Sibutu Passage 103 4 50N 120 0E
Sibuyan, I. 103 12 25N 122 40E
Sicamous 152 50 49N 119 0W
Sicapoo 103 18 9N 121 34E
Sicasica 154 17 20S 67 45W
Siccus, R. 140 31 42S 139 25E
Sicilia, Canale di 64 37 25N 12 30E
Sicilia, I. 65 37 30N 14 30E
Sicily = Sicilia 65 37 30N 14 30E
Sicuani 174 14 10S 71 10W
Siculiana 64 37 20N 13 23E
Sid 63 45 6N 19 16E
Sidamo □ 123 5 0N 37 50E
Sidaouet 121 18 34N 8 3E
Sidaradougou 120 10 42N 4 12W
Sidbury 30 50 43N 3 12W
Siddeburen 46 53 15N 6 52E

Siddipet Skaneateles

Siddipet	96	18 0N	79 0E
Sidensjo	72	63 20N	18 20E
Sidéradougou	120	10 42N	4 12W
Siderno Marina	65	38 16N	16 17E
Sidheros, Akra	69	35 19N	26 19E
Sidhirókastron	68	37 20N	21 46E
Sidhpur	94	23 56N	71 25E
Sîdi Abd el Rahman	122	30 55N	28 41E
Sîdi Barrâni	122	31 32N	25 58E
Sidi-Bel-Abbès	118	35 13N	0 10W
Sidi Bennour	118	32 40N	9 26W
Sidi Haneish	122	31 10N	27 35E
Sidi Ifni	118	29 29N	10 3W
Sidi Kacem	118	34 11N	5 40W
Sīdī Miftāh	119	31 8N	16 58E
Sidi Moussa, O.	118	33 0N	8 50W
Sidi Omar	122	31 24N	24 57E
Sīdī Yahya	119	30 55N	16 30E
Sidlaw Hills	35	56 32N	3 10W
Sidlesham	29	50 46N	0 46W
Sidmouth	30	50 40N	3 13W
Sidmouth, C.	138	13 25S	143 36E
Sidney, Can.	152	48 39N	123 24W
Sidney, Mont., U.S.A.	158	47 51N	104 7W
Sidney, N.Y., U.S.A.	162	42 18N	75 20W
Sidney, Ohio, U.S.A.	156	40 18N	84 6W
Sidoardjo	103	7 30S	112 46E
Sidoktaya	98	20 27N	94 15E
Sidon, (Saida)	92	33 38N	35 28E
Sidra, G. of = Khalīj Surt	61	31 40N	18 30E
Siedlce	54	52 10N	22 20E
Siedlce □	54	52 0N	22 0E
Siegburg	48	50 48N	7 12E
Siegen	48	50 52N	8 2E
Siem Pang	100	14 7N	106 23E
Siem Reap	100	13 20N	103 52E
Siena	63	43 20N	11 20E
Sieniawa	54	50 11N	22 38E
Sieradź	54	51 37N	18 41E
Sieradź □	54	51 30N	19 0E
Sieraków	54	52 39N	16 2E
Sierck-les-Bains	43	49 26N	6 20E
Sierpc	54	52 55N	19 43E
Sierpe, Bocas de la	174	10 0N	61 30W
Sierra Alta	58	40 31N	1 30W
Sierra Blanca	161	31 11N	105 17W
Sierra Blanca, mt.	161	33 20N	105 54W
Sierra City	160	39 34N	120 42W
Sierra Colorado	176	40 35S	67 50W
Sierra de Gädor	59	36 57N	2 45W
Sierra de Yeguas	57	37 7N	4 52W
Sierra Gorda	172	23 0S	69 15W
Sierra Leone ■	120	9 0N	12 0W
Sierra Majada	164	27 19N	103 42W
Sierre	50	46 17N	7 31E
Sífnos	69	37 0N	24 45E
Sifton	153	51 21N	100 8W
Sifton Pass	152	57 52N	126 15W
Sig	118	35 32N	0 12W
Sigaboy	103	6 39N	126 10E
Sigdal	71	60 4N	9 38E
Sigean	44	43 2N	2 58E
Sighetul Marmatiei	70	47 57N	23 52E
Sighişoara	70	46 12N	24 50E
Sighty Crag	35	55 8N	2 37W
Sigli	102	5 25N	96 0E
Siglufjörður	74	66 12N	18 55W
Sigma	103	11 29N	122 40E
Sigmaringen	49	48 5N	9 13E
Signakhi	83	40 52N	45 57E
Signau	50	46 56N	7 45E
Signy I.	13	60 45S	46 30W
Signy-l'Abbaye	43	49 40N	4 25E
Sigsig	174	3 0S	78 50W
Sigtuna	72	59 36N	17 44E
Sigüenza	58	41 3N	2 40W
Siguiri	120	11 31N	9 10W
Sigulda	80	57 10N	24 55E
Sigurd	161	38 57N	112 0W
Sihanoukville = Kompong Som	101	10 40N	103 30E
Si'ir	90	31 35N	35 9E
Siirt	92	37 57N	41 55E
Sijarira, Ra.	127	17 36S	27 45E
Sijsele	13	51 12N	3 20E
Sikandarabad	94	28 30N	77 39E
Sikandra Rao	93	27 43N	78 24E
Sikar	94	27 39N	75 10E
Sikasso	120	11 7N	5 35W
Sikerete	128	19 0S	20 48E
Sikeston	159	36 52N	89 35W
Sikhote Alin, Khrebet	77	46 0N	136 0E
Sikiá.	68	40 2N	23 56E
Sikinos, I.	69	36 40N	25 8E
Sikionia	69	38 0N	22 44E
Sikkani Chief, R.	152	57 47N	122 15W
Sikkim ■	98	27 50N	88 50E
Siklós	53	45 50N	18 19E
Sikoro	120	12 19N	7 8W
Sikqo	101	7 34N	99 21E
Sil, R.	56	42 23N	7 30W
Sila, La, Mts.	65	39 15N	16 35E
Silacayoapán	165	17 30N	98 9W
Silandro	62	46 38N	10 48E
Silat adh Dhahr	90	32 19N	35 11E
Silba	63	44 24N	14 41E
Silba, I.	63	44 24N	14 41E
Silchar	98	24 49N	92 48E
Silcox	153	57 12N	94 10W
Silenrieux	47	50 14N	4 27E
Siler City	157	35 44N	79 30W
Sileru, R.	96	18 0N	82 0E
Silesia = Slask	54	51 0N	16 30E
Silet	118	22 44N	4 37E
Silgarhi Doti	95	29 15N	82 0E
Silghat	98	26 35N	93 0E
Silifke	92	36 22N	33 58E
Siliguri	98	26 45N	88 25E
Siliqua	64	39 20N	8 49E
Silistra	67	44 6N	27 19E
Siljan, L.	72	60 55N	14 45E
Silkeborg	73	56 10N	9 32E
Sillajhuay, Cordillera	174	19 40S	68 40W
Sillé-le Guillaume	42	48 10N	0 8W
Silloth	32	54 53N	3 25W
Siloam Springs	159	36 15N	94 31W
Silogui	102	1 10S	98 46E
Silsbee	159	30 20N	94 8W
Silsden	32	53 55N	1 55W
Silute	80	55 21N	21 33E
Silva Porto = Bié	125	12 22S	16 55E
Silvaplana	51	46 28N	9 48E
Silver City, Calif., U.S.A.	160	36 19N	119 44W
Silver City, N. Mex., U.S.A.	161	32 50N	108 18W
Silver Cr., R.	160	43 30N	119 30W
Silver Creek	156	42 33N	79 9W
Silver L.	163	38 39N	120 6W
Silver Lake, Calif., U.S.A.	163	35 21N	116 7W
Silver Lake, Oreg., U.S.A.	160	43 9N	121 4W
Silver Springs	162	39 2N	77 3W
Silverhojden	72	60 2N	15 0E
Silvermine, Mts.	39	52 47N	8 15W
Silvermines	39	52 48N	8 15W
Silverpeak, Ra.	163	37 35N	117 45W
Silverstone	28	52 5N	1 3W
Silverton, Austral.	140	31 52S	141 10E
Silverton, U.K.	30	50 49N	3 29W
Silverton, Colo., U.S.A.	161	37 51N	107 45W
Silverton, Tex., U.S.A.	159	34 30N	101 16W
Silves	57	37 11N	8 26W
Silvia	174	2 37N	76 21W
Silvies, R.	160	43 57N	119 5W
Silvolde	46	51 55N	6 23E
Silvretta Gruppe	51	46 50N	10 6E
Silwa Bahari	122	24 45N	32 55E
Silwan	90	31 59N	35 15E
Silwani	93	23 18N	78 27E
Silz	52	47 16N	10 56E
Sim, C.	118	31 26N	9 51W
Simanggang	102	1 15N	111 25E
Simão Dias	170	10 44S	37 49W
Simard, L.	150	47 40N	78 40W
Simarun	93	31 16N	51 40E
Simba	126	1 41S	34 12E
Simbach	49	48 16N	13 3E
Simbo	126	4 51S	29 41E
Simcoe	150	42 50N	80 20W
Simcoe, L.	150	44 25N	79 20W
Simenga	77	62 50N	107 55E
Simeon	47	50 45N	5 36E
Simeulue, I.	102	2 45N	95 45E
Simferopol	82	44 55N	34 3E
Simi	69	36 35N	27 50E
Simi, I.	69	36 35N	27 50E
Simi Valley	163	34 16N	118 47W
Simikot	95	30 0N	81 50E
Simití	174	7 58N	73 57W
Simitli	66	41 52N	23 7E
Simla	94	31 2N	77 15E
Simleu-Silvaniei	70	47 17N	22 50E
Simme, R.	50	46 38N	7 25E
Simmern	48	49 59N	7 32E
Simmie	153	49 56N	108 6W
Simmler	163	35 21N	119 59W
Simões	170	7 30S	40 49W
Simojärvi	74	66 5N	27 10E
Simojoki	74	65 46N	25 15E
Simojovel	165	17 12N	92 38W
Simonette, R.	152	55 9N	118 15W
Simonsbath	28	51 8N	3 45W
Simonside, Mt.	35	55 17N	2 0W
Simonstown	128	34 14S	18 26E
Simontornya	53	46 45N	18 33E
Simpang	101	4 50N	100 40E
Simpleveld	47	50 50N	5 58E
Simplício Mendes	170	7 51S	41 54W
Simplon	50	46 12N	8 4E
Simplon Pass	50	46 15N	8 0E
Simplon Tunnel	50	46 15N	8 7E
Simpson Des.	138	25 0S	137 0E
Simpungdong	107	41 56N	129 29E
Simrishamn	73	55 33N	14 22E
Simsbury	162	41 52N	72 48W
Simunjan	102	1 25N	110 45E
Sîmŭrtin	70	46 19N	25 58E
Simushir, Ostrov	77	46 50N	152 30E
Sina, R.	97	18 25N	75 28E
Sinaai	47	51 9N	4 2E
Sinabang	102	2 30N	46 30E
Sinai = Es Sînâ'	122	29 0N	34 0E
Sinai, Mt. = Musa, G.	122	28 32N	33 59E
Sinaia	70	45 21N	25 38E
Sinaloa	164	25 50N	108 20W
Sinaloa □	164	25 0N	107 30W
Sinalunga	63	43 12N	11 43E
Sinamaica	174	11 5N	71 51W
Sînandrei	70	45 52N	21 13E
Sināwan	119	31 0N	10 30E
Sinbaung we	98	19 43N	95 10E
Sinbo	98	24 46N	97 3E
Sincé	174	9 15N	75 9W
Sincelejo	174	9 18N	75 24W
Sinchangni, Kor., N.	107	40 7N	128 28E
Sinchangni, Kor., N.	107	39 24N	126 8E
Sinclair	160	41 47N	107 35W
Sinclair Mills	152	54 5N	121 40W
Sinclair's B.	37	58 30N	3 0W
Sincorá, Serra do	171	13 30S	41 0W
Sind, R.	95	34 18N	75 0E
Sind Sagar Doab	94	32 0N	71 30E
Sinda	127	17 28S	25 51E
Sindal	73	57 28N	10 10E
Sindangan	103	8 10N	123 5E
Sindangbarang	103	7 27S	107 9E
Sindjai	103	5 0S	120 20E
Sinelnikovo	82	48 25N	35 30E
Sines	57	37 56N	8 51W
Sines, Cabo de	57	37 58N	8 53W
Sineu	58	39 39N	3 0E
Sinewit, Mt.	135	4 44S	152 2E
Sinfra	120	6 35N	5 56W
Sing Buri	100	14 53N	100 25E
Singa	123	13 10N	33 57E
Singanallurt	97	11 2N	77 1E
Singaparna	103	7 23S	108 4E
Singapore ■	101	1 17N	103 51E
Singapore, Straits of	101	1 15N	104 0E
Singaraja	102	8 15S	115 10E
Singen	49	47 45N	8 50E
Singida	126	4 49S	34 48E
Singida □	126	6 0S	34 30E
Singitikós, Kólpos	68	40 6N	24 0E
Singkaling Hkamti	98	26 0N	95 45E
Singkang	103	4 8S	120 1E
Singkawang	102	1 0N	109 5E
Singkep, I.	102	0 30S	104 20E
Singleton, Austral.	141	32 33S	151 10E
Singleton, U.K.	29	50 55N	0 45W
Singleton, Mt.	137	29 27S	117 15E
Singö	72	60 12N	18 45E
Singoli	94	25 0N	75 16E
Singora = Songkhla	101	7 12N	100 36E
Singosan	107	38 52N	127 25E
Sinhailian (Lienyünchiangshih)	107	34 31N	118 15E
Sinhung	107	40 11N	127 34E
Siniatsikon, Óros	68	40 25N	21 35E
Siniscóla	64	40 35N	9 40E
Sinj	63	43 42N	16 39E
Sinjajevina, Planina	66	42 57N	19 22E
Sinjil	90	32 3N	35 15E
Sinkat	122	18 55N	36 49E
Sinkiang-Uighur □	105	42 0N	86 0E
Sinmark	107	38 25N	126 14E
Sinnai Sardinia	64	39 18N	9 13E
Sinnar	96	19 48N	74 0E
Sinni, R.	65	40 6N	16 15E
Sînnicolau-Maré	70	46 5N	20 39E
Sinnûris	122	29 26N	30 31E
Sinoe, L.	70	44 35N	28 50E
Sinoia	127	17 20S	30 8E
Sinop	92	42 1N	35 11E
Sinop, R.	82	42 1N	35 2E
Sinpo	107	40 0N	128 13E
Sins	51	47 12N	8 24E
Sinskoye	77	61 8N	126 48E
Sint Annaland	47	51 36N	4 6E
Sint Annaparochie	46	53 16N	5 40E
Sint-Denijs	47	50 45N	3 23E
Sint Eustatius, I.	167	17 30N	62 59W
Sint-Genesius-Rode	47	50 45N	4 22E
Sint-Gillis-Waas	47	51 13N	4 6E
Sint-Huibrechts-Lille	47	51 13N	5 29E
Sint-Katelinje-Waver	47	51 5N	4 32E
Sint-Kruis	47	51 13N	3 15E
Sint-Laureins	47	51 14N	3 32E
Sint Maarten, I.	167	18 4N	63 4W
Sint-Michiels	47	51 11N	3 15E
Sint Nicolaasga	46	52 55N	5 45E
Sint Niklaas	47	51 10N	4 9E
Sint Oedenrode	47	51 35N	5 29E
Sint Pancras	46	52 40N	4 48E
Sint-Pauwels	47	51 11N	3 57E
Sint Philipsland	47	51 37N	4 10E
Sint Truiden	47	50 48N	5 12E
Sint Willebroad	47	51 33N	4 33E
Sîntana Ano	70	46 20N	21 30E
Sintang	102	0 5N	111 35E
Sintjohannesga	46	52 55N	5 52E
Sinton	159	28 1N	97 30W
Sintra	57	38 47N	9 25W
Sinŭiju	107	40 5N	124 24E
Sinuk	147	64 42N	166 22W
Sinyang = Hsinyang	109	32 10N	114 6E
Sinyukha, R.	82	48 31N	30 31E
Siófok	53	46 54N	18 4E
Sióma	128	16 25S	23 28E
Sion	50	46 14N	7 20E
Sion Mills	38	54 47N	7 29W
Sioua, El Wâhât es	122	29 10N	25 30E
Sioux City	158	42 32N	96 25W
Sioux Falls	158	43 35N	96 40W
Sioux Lookout	150	50 10N	91 50W
Sip Song Chaw Thai, reg.	100	21 30N	103 30E
Sipan	66	42 45N	17 52E
Sipera, I.	102	2 18S	99 40E
Sipiwesk L.	153	55 5N	97 35W
Sipul	138	5 50S	148 28E
Siquia, R.	166	12 30N	84 30W
Siquijor, I.	103	9 12N	123 45E
Siquirres	166	10 6N	83 30W
Siquisique	174	10 34N	69 42W
Sir Edward Pellew Group	138	15 40S	137 10E
Sir Graham Moore Is.	136	13 53S	126 34E
Sir Samuel Mt.	137	27 45S	120 40E
Sir Thomas, Mt.	137	27 10S	129 45E
Sira	97	13 41N	76 49E
Sira, R.	71	58 43N	6 40E
Siracusa	65	37 4N	15 17E
Sirajganj	95	24 25N	89 47E
Sirake	138	9 1S	141 2E
Sirakoro	120	12 41N	9 14W
Sirasso	120	9 16N	6 6W
Siret	70	47 55N	26 5E
Siret, R.	70	47 58N	26 5E
Siria	66	46 16N	21 38E
Sirinhaém	171	8 35S	35 7W
Sirkall (Shivali)	97	11 15N	79 41E
Sirna, I.	69	36 22N	26 42E
Sirnach	51	47 28N	8 59E
Sirohi	94	24 52N	72 53E
Siroki Brijeg	66	43 21N	17 36E
Sironj	94	24 5N	77 45E
Siros	69	37 28N	24 57E
Siros, I.	69	37 28N	24 57E
Sirretta Pk.	163	35 56N	118 19W
Sirsa	94	29 33N	75 4E
Sirsi	97	14 40N	74 49E
Siruela	57	38 58N	5 3W
Sisak	63	45 30N	16 21E
Sisaket	100	15 8N	104 23E
Sisante	59	39 25N	2 12W
Sisargas, Islas	56	43 21N	8 50W
Sishen	128	27 55S	22 59E
Sisipuk I.	153	55 40N	102 0W
Sisipuk L.	153	55 45N	101 50W
Sisophon	100	13 31N	102 59E
Sissach	50	47 27N	7 48E
Sisseton	158	45 43N	97 3W
Sissonne	43	49 34N	3 51E
Sistan-Baluchistan □	93	27 0N	62 0E
Sistema Central	56	40 40N	5 55W
Sistema Ibérico	58	41 0N	2 10W
Sisteron	45	44 12N	5 57E
Sisters	160	44 21N	121 32W
Sitamarhi	95	26 37N	85 30E
Sitapur	95	27 38N	80 45E
Siteki	129	26 32S	31 58E
Sitges	58	41 17N	1 47E
Sithoniá	68	40 0N	23 45E
Sitía	69	35 13N	26 6E
Sítio da Abadia	171	14 48S	46 16W
Sitka	147	57 9N	134 58W
Sitona	123	14 25N	37 23E
Sitoti	128	23 15S	23 40E
Sitra	122	28 40N	26 53E
Sittang Myit, R.	99	18 20N	96 45E
Sittang, R.	98	17 10N	96 58E
Sittard	47	51 0N	5 52E
Sittaung	98	24 10N	94 35E
Sittensen	48	53 17N	9 32E
Sittingbourne	29	51 20N	0 43E
Sittwe	99	20 15N	92 45E
Situbondo	103	7 45S	114 0E
Siuch'uan	109	26 20N	114 30E
Siuna	166	13 37N	84 45W
Sivaganga	97	9 50N	78 28E
Sivagiri	97	9 16N	77 26E
Sivakasi	97	9 24N	77 47E
Sivand	93	30 5N	52 55E
Sivas	92	39 43N	36 58E
Siverek	92	37 50N	39 25E
Sivrihisar	92	39 30N	31 35E
Sivry	47	50 10N	4 12E
Siwa	122	29 11N	25 31E
Siwalik Range	95	28 0N	83 0E
Siwan	95	26 13N	84 27E
Sixmile Cross	38	54 34N	7 7W
Sixmilebridge	39	52 45N	8 46W
Siyâl, Jazâ'ir	122	22 49N	36 6E
Siyana	94	28 37N	78 6E
Sizewell	29	52 13N	1 38E
Sjaelland	73	55 30N	11 30E
Sjaellands Odde	73	56 0N	11 15E
Själevad	72	63 18N	18 36E
Sjarinska Banja	66	42 45N	21 38E
Sjenica	66	43 16N	20 0E
Sjernaröy	71	59 15N	5 50E
Sjoa	71	61 41N	9 40E
Sjöbo	73	55 37N	13 45E
Sjöholt	71	62 27N	6 52E
Sjönsta	74	67 10N	16 3E
Sjösa	73	58 47N	17 4E
Skadovsk	82	46 17N	32 52E
Skælskör	73	55 16N	11 18E
Skagafjörður	74	65 54N	19 35W
Skagastölstindane, mt.	75	61 25N	8 10E
Skagen	75	68 37N	14 27E
Skagen, pt.	73	57 43N	10 35E
Skagern	72	59 0N	14 20E
Skagerrak	73	57 30N	9 0E
Skagway	147	59 30N	135 20W
Skaidi	74	70 26N	24 30E
Skala Podolskaya	82	48 50N	26 15E
Skalat	80	49 23N	25 55E
Skalbmierz	54	56 22N	12 30E
Skalderviken	73	56 22N	12 30E
Skalicd	53	48 50N	17 15E
Skallingen, Odde	73	55 32N	8 13E
Skalni Dol = Kamenyak	67	43 24N	26 57E
Skals	73	56 34N	9 24E
Skanderborg	73	56 2N	9 55E
Skaneateles	162	42 57N	76 26W

Skaneateles L Sollentuna

Skaneateles L. 162 42 51N 76 22W
Skånevik 71 59 43N 5 53 E
Skanninge 73 58 24N 15 5 E
Skanör 73 55 24N 12 50 E
Skanor 73 55 24N 12 50 E
Skantzoúra I. 69 39 5N 24 6 E
Skara 73 58 25N 13 30 E
Skaraborgs län □ 73 58 20N 13 30 E
Skarblacka 73 58 36N 15 50 E
Skardhö 71 62 30N 8 47 E
Skardu 95 35 20N 75 35 E
Skaresta 73 58 26N 16 22 E
Skarszewy 54 54 4N 18 25 E
Skarvane, Mt. 71 63 18N 11 27 E
Skarzysko Kamienna 54 51 7N 20 52 E
Skatöy 71 50 50N 9 30 E
Skattungbyn 72 61 10N 14 56 E
Skaw (Grenen) 73 57 46N 10 34 E
Skaw Taing 36 60 23N 0 57W
Skebo 72 59 58N 18 37 E
Skebokvarn 72 59 7N 16 45 E
Skeena Mts. 152 56 40N 128 30W
Skeena, R. 152 54 9N 130 5W
Skeggjastadir 74 66 3N 14 50W
Skegness 33 53 9N 0 20 E
Skeldon 174 6 0N 57 20W
Skellefte älv 74 65 30N 18 30 E
Skellefteå 74 64 45N 20 58 E
Skelleftehamn 74 64 41N 21 14 E
Skellig Rocks 39 51 47N 10 32W
Skellingthorpe 33 53 14N 0 37W
Skelmersdale 32 53 34N 2 49W
Skelmorlie 34 55 52N 4 53W
Skelton, Cleveland., U.K. 33 54 33N 0 59W
Skelton, Cumb., U.K. 32 54 42N 2 50W
Skender Vakuf 66 44 29N 17 22 E
Skene 73 57 30N 12 37 E
Skerries, Rks. 38 55 14N 6 40W
Skerries, The 31 53 27N 4 40W
Skhirra, La = Cekhira 119 34 20N 10 5 E
Skhíza, I. 69 36 41N 20 40 E
Skhoinoúsa, I. 69 36 53N 25 31 E
Ski 71 59 43N 10 52 E
Skíathos, I. 69 39 12N 23 30 E
Skibbereen 39 51 33N 9 16W
Skiddaw, Mt. 32 54 39N 3 9W
Skidegate, Inlet 48 53 20N 132 0W
Skien 71 59 12N 9 35 E
Skierniewice 54 51 58N 20 19 E
Skikda 119 36 50N 6 58 E
Skillingaryd 73 57 27N 14 5 E
Skillinge 73 55 30N 14 16 E
Skillingmark 72 59 48N 120 1 E
Skinari, Ákra 69 37 56N 20 40 E
Skipness 34 55 46N 5 20W
Skipsea 33 53 58N 0 13W
Skipton, Austral. 140 37 39 S 143 21 E
Skipton, U.K. 32 53 57N 2 1W
Skirild 73 55 58N 8 53 E
Skirmish Pt. 138 11 59 S 134 17 E
Skiropoúla, I. 69 38 50N 24 21 E
Skíros 69 38 55N 24 34 E
Skíros, I. 69 38 55N 24 34 E
Skivarp 73 55 26N 13 34 E
Skive 73 56 33N 9 2 E
Skjåk 71 61 52N 8 22 E
Skjálfandafljót 74 65 15N 17 25W
Skjálfandi 74 66 5N 17 30W
Skjeberg 71 59 12N 11 12 E
Skjern 73 55 57N 8 30 E
Skjönne 71 60 16N 9 1 E
Skoczów 54 49 49N 18 45 E
Skodje 71 62 30N 6 43 E
Skofja Loka 63 46 9N 14 19 E
Skoger 71 59 42N 10 16 E
Skoghall 72 59 20N 13 30 E
Skoghult 73 56 59N 15 55 E
Skokholm, I. 31 51 42N 5 16W
Skoki 54 52 40N 17 11 E
Skole 80 49 3N 23 30 E
Skomer, I. 31 51 44N 5 19W
Skonsberg 72 62 25N 17 21 E
Skópelos 69 39 9N 23 47 E
Skópelos, I. 69 39 9N 23 47 E
Skopin 81 53 55N 39 32 E
Skopje 66 42 1N 21 32 E
Skorcz 54 43 47N 18 30 E
Skorped 72 63 23N 17 55 E
Skotfoss 71 59 12N 9 30 E
Skoudas 80 56 21N 21 45 E
Skövde 75 58 15N 13 59 E
Skovorodino 77 54 0N 125 0 E
Skowhegan 151 44 49N 69 40W
Skowman 153 51 58N 99 35W
Skradin 63 43 52N 15 53 E
Skreanäs 73 56 52N 12 35 E
Skudeneshavn 71 59 10N 5 10 E
Skull 39 51 32N 9 40W
Skultorp 73 58 24N 13 51 E
Skulyany 82 47 19N 27 39 E
Skunk, R. 158 40 42N 91 7W
Skurup 73 55 28N 13 30 E
Skutskär 73 60 37N 17 25 E
Skvira 82 49 44N 29 32 E
Skwaner, Pegunungan 102 1 0 S 112 30 E
Skwierzyna 54 52 46N 15 30 E
Skye, I. 36 57 15N 6 10W
Skykomish 160 47 43N 121 16W
Skyros (Skíros), L. 69 38 52N 24 37 E
Slagelse 73 55 23N 11 19 E
Slagharen 46 52 37N 6 34 E
Slaidburn 32 53 57N 2 28W
Slaley 35 54 55N 2 4W
Slamannon 140 32 1 S 143 41 E
Slamet, G. 102 7 16 S 109 8 E
Slane 38 53 42N 6 32W
Slaney, R. 39 52 52N 6 45W
Slangerup 73 55 50N 12 11 E
Slănic 70 45 14N 25 58 E
Slankamen 66 45 8N 20 15 E
Slano 66 42 48N 17 53 E
Slantsy 80 59 7N 28 5 E
Slany 52 50 13N 14 6 E
Slask 54 51 25N 16 0 E
Slatbaken 73 58 28N 16 30 E
Slate Is. 150 48 40N 87 0W
Slatina 70 44 28N 24 22 E
Slatington 162 40 45N 75 37W
Slaton 159 33 27N 101 38W
Slave Coast 121 6 0N 2 30 E
Slave Lake 152 55 17N 114 50W
Slave Pt. 152 61 11N 114 56W
Slave, R. 152 61 18N 113 39W
Slavgorod 76 53 10N 78 50 E
Slavinja 66 43 14N 22 50 E
Slavkov (Austerlitz) 53 49 10N 16 52 E
Slavnoye 80 54 24N 29 15 E
Slavonski Brod 66 45 11N 18 0 E
Slavonski Pozega 66 45 20N 17 40 E
Slavuta 80 50 15N 27 2 E
Slavyans 82 48 55N 37 30 E
Slavyansk 82 45 15N 38 11 E
Sława 54 51 52N 16 2 E
Sławno 54 54 20N 16 41 E
Sławoborze 54 53 55N 15 42 E
Slea Hd. 39 52 7N 10 30W
Sleaford 33 53 0N 0 22W
Sleaford B. 139 34 55 S 135 45 E
Sleat, Pt. of 36 57 1N 6 0W
Sleat, Sd. of 36 57 5N 5 47W
Sledmere 33 54 4N 0 35W
Sleeper, Is. 149 56 50N 80 30W
Sleepers, The 149 58 30N 81 0W
Sleepy Eye 158 44 15N 94 45W
Sleidinge 47 51 8N 3 41 E
Sleights 33 54 27N 0 40W
Sleipner, gasfield 19 58 30N 1 48 E
Sleman 103 7 40 S 110 20 E
Slemmestad 71 59 47N 10 30 E
Slemon L. 152 63 13N 116 4W
Slesin 54 52 22N 18 14 E
Sletterhage, Kap 73 56 7N 10 31 E
Slide Mt. 162 42 0N 74 23W
Slidell 159 30 20N 89 48W
Sliedrecht 46 51 50N 4 45 E
Slieve Anierin 38 54 5N 7 58W
Slieve Aughty 39 53 4N 8 30W
Slieve Bernagh 39 52 50N 8 30W
Slieve Bloom 39 53 4N 7 40W
Slieve Callan 39 52 51N 9 16W
Slieve Donard 38 54 10N 5 57W
Slieve Felim 39 52 40N 8 20W
Slieve Gamph 38 54 6N 9 0W
Slieve Gullion 38 54 8N 6 26W
Slieve League 38 54 40N 8 42W
Slieve Mish 39 52 12N 9 50W
Slieve Miskish 39 51 40N 10 10W
Slieve More 38 54 1N 10 3W
Slieve Snaght 38 54 59N 8 7W
Slieve Tooey 38 54 46N 8 39W
Slievenamon Mt. 39 52 25N 7 37W
Sligachan 36 57 17N 6 10W
Sligo 38 54 17N 8 28W
Sligo □ 38 54 10N 8 35W
Sligo B. 38 54 20N 8 40W
Slikkerveer 46 51 53N 4 36 E
Slioch, mt. 36 57 40N 5 20W
Slipje 47 51 9N 2 51 E
Slite 75 57 42N 18 48 E
Sliven 67 42 42N 26 19 E
Slivnitsa 66 42 50N 23 0 E
Sljeme, mt. 63 45 57N 15 58 E
Słupsk □ 54 54 15N 17 30 E
Sloansville 162 42 45N 74 22W
Slobodskoy 84 58 40N 50 6 E
Slobozia, Ialomiţa, Rumania 70 44 34N 27 23 E
Slobozia, Valahia, Rumania 70 44 30N 25 14 E
Slocan 152 49 48N 117 28W
Slochteren 46 53 12N 6 48 E
Slochteren-Groningen, gasfield 19 53 10N 6 45 E
Slöinge 73 56 51N 12 42 E
Słomniki 54 50 16N 20 4 E
Slonim 80 53 4N 25 19 E
Slotermeer 46 52 55N 5 38 E
Slough 29 51 30N 0 35W
Sloughhouse 163 38 26N 121 12W
Slovakia □ 53 48 30N 19 0 E
Slovenia = Slovenija 63 45 58N 14 30 E
Slovenija □ 63 45 58N 14 30 E
Slovenska Bistrica 63 46 24N 15 35 E
Slovenske Krusnohorie 53 48 45N 20 0 E
Slovenské Rhudhorie 52 48 45N 19 0 E
Słubice 54 52 22N 14 35 E
Sluis 47 51 18N 3 23 E
Slunchev Bryag 67 42 40N 27 41 E
Slunj 63 45 6N 15 33 E
Słupca 54 52 15N 17 52 E
Słupsk 54 54 30N 17 3 E
Slurry 128 25 49 S 25 42 E
Slyne Hd. 38 53 25N 10 10W
Slyudyanka 77 51 40N 103 30 E
Smål-Taberg 73 57 42N 14 5 E
Smålandsfarvandet 73 55 10N 11 20 E
Smalandsstenar 73 57 9N 13 24 E
Smålandstarvandet 73 55 10N 11 20 E
Smalltree L. 153 61 0N 105 0W
Smallwood Reservoir 151 54 20N 63 10W
Smara 118 26 48N 11 31W
Smarje 63 46 15N 15 34 E
Smart Syndicate Dam 128 30 45 S 23 10 E
Smeaton 153 53 30N 105 49W
Smedberg 73 58 35N 12 0 E
Smederevo 66 44 40N 20 57 E
Smedstorp 73 55 38N 13 58 E
Smela 82 49 30N 32 0 E
Smerwick Harb. 39 52 12N 10 23W
Smethwick 28 52 29N 1 58W
Smidovich 77 48 36N 133 49 E
Smilde 46 52 58N 6 28 E
Smiley 153 51 38N 109 29W
Smilyan 67 41 29N 24 46 E
Smith 152 55 10N 114 0W
Smith Arm 152 66 15N 123 0W
Smith Center 158 39 50N 98 50W
Smith I. 162 38 0N 76 0W
Smith, R. 152 59 34N 126 30W
Smith Sund 12 78 30N 74 0W
Smithborough 38 54 13N 7 8W
Smithburne, R. 138 17 3 S 140 57 E
Smithers 152 54 45N 127 10W
Smithfield, U.K. 32 54 59N 2 51W
Smithfield, U.S.A. 157 35 31N 78 16W
Smith's Falls 150 44 55N 76 0W
Smithton, N.S.W., Austral. 139 31 0 S 152 48 E
Smithton, Tas., Austral. 138 40 53 S 145 6 E
Smithtown 141 30 58 S 152 56 E
Smithville 159 30 2N 97 12W
Smjörfjöll 74 65 30N 15 42W
Smoky Bay 139 32 22 S 133 56 E
Smoky Falls 150 50 4N 82 10W
Smoky Hill, R. 158 38 45N 98 0W
Smoky Lake 152 54 10N 112 30W
Smola 71 63 23N 8 3 E
Smolensk 80 54 45N 32 0 E
Smolikas, Óros 68 40 9N 20 58 E
Smolník 53 48 43N 20 44 E
Smolyan 67 41 36N 24 38 E
Smooth Rock Falls 150 49 17N 81 37W
Smoothstone L. 153 54 40N 106 50W
Smorgon 80 54 28N 26 24 E
Smulţi 70 45 57N 27 44 E
Smyadovo 67 43 2N 27 1 E
Smyrna 162 39 18N 75 36W
Smyrna = Izmir 92 38 25N 27 8 E
Snaefell 30 54 18N 4 26W
Snaefells Jökull 74 64 45N 23 25W
Snainton 33 54 14N 0 33W
Snaith 33 53 42N 1 1W
Snake I. 141 38 47 S 146 33 E
Snake L. 153 55 32N 106 35W
Snake, R. 160 46 31N 118 50W
Snake Ra., Mts. 160 39 0N 114 30W
Snake River Plain 160 43 13N 113 0W
Snap, The 36 60 35N 0 50W
Snape 29 52 11N 1 29 E
Snarum 71 60 1N 9 54 E
Snasahogarha 72 63 10N 12 20 E
Snedsted 73 56 55N 8 32 E
Sneek 46 53 2N 5 40 E
Sneeker-meer 46 53 2N 5 45 E
Sneem 39 51 50N 9 55W
Snejbjerg 73 56 8N 8 54 E
Snĕka 52 50 41N 15 50 E
Snelling 163 37 31N 120 26W
Snettisham 29 52 52N 0 30 E
Snezhnoye 83 48 0N 38 58 E
Sneznik, mt. 63 45 36N 14 35 E
Snigirevka 82 47 2N 32 35 E
Snina 53 49 0N 22 9 E
Snizort, L. 36 57 33N 6 28W
Snohetta 71 62 19N 9 16 E
Snohomish 160 47 53N 122 6W
Snonuten 71 59 31N 6 50 E
Snoul 101 12 4N 106 26 E
Snow Hill 162 38 10N 75 21W
Snow L. 153 54 52N 100 3W
Snowbird L. 153 60 45N 103 0W
Snowdon, Mt. 31 53 4N 4 8W
Snowdrift 153 62 24N 110 44W
Snowdrift, R. 153 62 24N 110 44W
Snowflake 161 34 30N 110 4W
Snowshoe 152 53 43N 121 0W
Snowtown 140 33 46 S 138 14 E
Snowville 160 41 59N 112 47W
Snowy Mt. 162 43 45N 74 26W
Snowy Mts. 141 36 30 S 148 20 E
Snowy, R. 141 37 46 S 148 30 E
Snug Corner 167 22 33N 73 52W
Snyder, Okla., U.S.A. 159 34 4N 99 0W
Snyder, Tex., U.S.A. 159 32 45N 100 57W
Soacha 174 4 35N 74 13W
Soahanina 129 18 42 S 44 13 E
Soalala 129 16 6 S 45 20 E
Soan, R. 94 33 20N 72 40 E
Soanierana-Ivongo 129 16 55 S 49 35 E
Soap Lake 160 47 29N 119 31W
Soay, I. 36 57 9N 6 13W
Soay Sd. 36 57 10N 6 15W
Sobat, Nahr 123 8 32N 32 40 E
Sobĕslav 52 49 16N 14 45 E
Sobhapur 94 22 47N 78 17 E
Sobinka 81 56 0N 40 0 E
Sobo-Yama 110 32 51N 131 16 E
Sobótka 54 50 54N 16 44 E
Sobrado 56 43 2N 8 2W
Sobral 170 3 50 S 40 30W
Sobreira Formosa 57 39 46N 7 51W
Soc Giang 100 22 54N 106 1 E
Soc Trang = Khonh Hung 101 9 37N 105 50 E
Soča, R. 63 46 20N 13 40 E
Socha 174 6 0N 72 41W
Sochaczew 54 52 15N 20 13 E
Soch'e 105 38 24N 77 20 E
Sochi 83 43 35N 39 40 E
Société, Is. de la 131 17 0 S 151 0W
Socompa, Portezuelo de 172 24 27 S 68 18W
Socorro 174 6 29N 73 16W
Socorro, I. 164 18 45N 110 58W
Socotra, I. 91 12 30N 54 0 E
Socúellmos 59 39 16N 2 47W
Soda Creek 152 52 25N 122 10W
Soda L. 161 35 7N 116 2W
Soda Plains 94 35 30N 79 0 E
Soda Springs 160 42 4N 111 40W
Sodankylä 74 67 29N 26 40 E
Söderfjärden 72 62 3N 17 25 E
Söderfors 72 60 23N 17 25 E
Söderhamn 72 61 18N 17 10 E
Söderköping 73 58 31N 16 35 E
Södermanlands län □ 72 59 10N 16 30 E
Södertälje 72 59 12N 17 50 E
Sodium 128 30 15 S 15 45 E
Sodo 123 7 0N 37 57 E
Södra Vi 73 57 45N 15 45 E
Sodrazica 63 45 45N 14 39 E
Sodus 162 43 13N 77 5W
Soekmekaar 129 23 30 S 29 55 E
Soest, Ger. 48 51 34N 8 7 E
Soest, Neth. 46 52 9N 5 19 E
Soestdijk 46 52 11N 5 17 E
Sofádhes 68 39 28N 22 4 E
Sofara 120 13 59N 4 9W
Sofia = Sofiya 67 42 45N 23 20 E
Sofia, R. 129 15 25 S 48 40 E
Sofievka 82 47 58N 34 14 E
Sofikón 69 37 47N 23 3 E
Sofila 67 42 45N 23 20 E
Sofiya 67 42 45N 23 20 E
Sogad 103 10 30N 125 0 E
Sogakofe 121 6 2N 0 39 E
Sogamoso 174 5 43N 72 56W
Sögel 48 52 50N 7 32 E
Sogeri 135 9 26 S 147 35 E
Sogipo 107 33 13N 126 34 E
Sogn og Fjordane fylke □ 71 61 40N 6 0 E
Sogndal 71 58 20N 6 15 E
Sogndalsfjøra 75 61 14N 7 5 E
Sognefjorden 71 61 10N 5 50 E
Sohâg 122 26 27N 31 43 E
Soham 29 52 20N 0 20 E
Sohano 135 5 22 S 154 37 E
Sŏhori 107 40 7N 128 23 E
Soignies 47 50 35N 4 5 E
Soira, Mt. 123 14 45N 39 30 E
Soissons 43 49 25N 3 19 E
Soitava, R. 53 49 30N 16 37 E
Sojat 94 25 55N 73 38 E
Sok, R. 84 53 24N 50 8 E
Sokal 80 50 31N 24 15 E
Söke 69 37 48N 27 28 E
Sokhós 68 40 48N 23 22 E
Sokhta Chinar 93 35 5N 67 35 E
Sokna 71 60 16N 9 50 E
Soknedal 71 62 57N 10 13 E
Soko Banja 66 43 40N 21 51 E
Sokodé 121 9 0N 1 11 E
Sokó'ka 54 53 25N 23 30 E
Sokol 81 59 30N 40 5 E
Sokolo 120 14 42N 6 8W
Sokolov 52 50 12N 12 40 E
Sokoł ó w Matopolski 53 50 12N 22 7 E
Sokoł ó w Podlaski 54 52 25N 22 15 E
Sokoto 121 13 2N 5 16 E
Sokoto □ 121 12 30N 5 0 E
Sokoto, R. 121 12 30N 6 10 E
Sokuluk 85 42 52N 74 18 E
Sol Iletsk 84 51 10N 55 0 E
Sola 71 58 53N 5 36 E
Sola, R. 126 49 38N 19 8 E
Solai 126 0 2N 36 12 E
Solana, La 59 38 59N 3 14W
Solano 103 16 25N 121 15 E
Solares 56 43 23N 3 43W
Solberga 73 57 45N 14 43 E
Solca 70 47 40N 25 50 E
Solec Kujawski 54 53 5N 18 14 E
Soledad, Colomb. 174 10 55N 74 46W
Soledad, U.S.A. 163 36 27N 121 16W
Soledad, Venez. 174 8 10N 63 34W
Solemint 163 34 25N 118 27W
Solent, The 28 50 45N 1 25W
Solenzara 45 41 53N 9 23 E
Solesmes 43 50 10N 3 30 E
Solfonn, Mt. 71 60 2N 6 57 E
Soligalich 81 59 5N 42 10 E
Solihull 28 52 26N 1 47W
Solikamsk 84 59 38N 56 50 E
Solila 129 21 25 S 46 37 E
Soliman 119 36 42N 10 30 E
Solimões, R. 174 2 15 S 66 30W
Solingen 48 51 10N 7 4 E
Sollas 36 57 39N 7 20W
Sollebrunn 73 58 8N 12 32 E
Sollefteå 72 63 12N 17 20 E
Sollentuna 72 59 26N 17 56 E

Soller Speer

Soller	**58**	39 43N	2 45E
Sollerön	**72**	60 54N	14 38E
Solna	**72**	59 22N	18 1E
Solnechnogorsk	**81**	56 10N	36 57E
Sölnkletten, Mt.	**71**	61 55N	10 18E
Sologne	**59**	47 40N	2 0E
Solojärg	**73**	56 50N	10 8E
Solok	**102**	0 55S	100 40E
Sololá	**166**	14 49N	91 10E
Solomon Is. ■	**135**	6 0S	155 0E
Solomon, N. Fork, R.	**158**	39 45N	99 0W
Solomon Sea	**135**	7 0S	150 0E
Solomon, S. Fork, R.	**158**	39 25N	99 12W
Solomon's Pools = Burak Sulayman	**90**	31 42N	35 7E
Solon Springs	**158**	46 19N	91 47W
Solonópole	**170**	5 44S	39 1W
Solor, I.	**103**	8 27S	123 0E
Solotcha	**81**	54 48N	39 53E
Solothurn	**50**	47 13N	7 32E
Solothurn □	**50**	47 18N	7 40E
Solotobe	**85**	44 37N	66 3E
Solsona	**58**	42 0N	1 31E
Solt	**53**	46 45N	19 1E
Solta, I.	**63**	43 24N	16 15E
Soltanabad	**93**	36 29N	58 5E
Soltaniyeh	**92**	36 20N	48 55E
Soltau	**48**	52 59N	9 50E
Soltsy	**80**	58 10N	30 10E
Solun	**105**	46 40N	120 40E
Solund	**71**	61 5N	4 50E
Solund I.	**71**	61 7N	4 50E
Solunska Glava	**66**	41 44N	21 31E
Solva	**31**	51 52N	5 12W
Solvang	**163**	34 36N	120 8W
Solvay	**162**	43 5N	76 17W
Solvesborg	**73**	56 5N	14 35E
Sölvesborg	**73**	56 5N	14 35E
Solway Firth	**32**	54 45N	3 38W
Solwezi	**127**	12 20S	26 21E
Somali Rep. ■	**91**	7 0N	47 0E
Somaliland	**123**	12 0N	43 0E
Sombe Dzong	**98**	27 13N	89 8E
Sombernon	**43**	47 20N	4 40E
Sombor	**66**	45 46N	19 17E
Sombrerete	**164**	23 40N	103 40W
Sombrero I.	**167**	18 30N	63 30W
Somerby	**29**	52 42N	0 49W
Someren	**47**	51 23N	5 42E
Somers	**160**	48 4N	114 18W
Somerset, Austral.	**138**	10 45S	142 25E
Somerset, Can.	**153**	49 25N	98 39W
Somerset, Colo., U.S.A.	**161**	38 55N	107 30W
Somerset, Ky., U.S.A.	**156**	37 5N	84 40W
Somerset, Mass., U.S.A.	**162**	41 45N	71 10W
Somerset □	**28**	51 9N	3 0W
Somerset East	**128**	32 42S	25 35E
Somerset, I.	**148**	73 30N	93 0W
Somerset West	**128**	34 8S	18 50E
Somersham	**29**	52 24N	0 0W
Somersworth	**162**	43 15N	70 51W
Somerton, U.K.	**28**	51 3N	2 45W
Somerton, U.S.A.	**161**	32 41N	114 47W
Somerville	**162**	40 34N	74 36W
Someş, R.	**70**	47 15N	23 45E
Someşul Mare, R.	**70**	47 18N	24 30E
Somma Lombardo	**62**	45 41N	8 42E
Somma Vesuviana	**65**	40 52N	14 23E
Sommariva	**139**	26 24S	146 36E
Sommatino	**65**	37 20N	14 0E
Somme □	**43**	50 0N	2 20E
Somme, B. de la	**42**	5 22N	1 30E
Sommelsdijk	**46**	51 46N	4 9E
Sommen	**73**	58 12N	15 0E
Sommen, L.	**73**	58 0N	15 15E
Sommepy-Tahure	**43**	49 15N	4 31E
Sömmerda	**48**	51 10N	11 8E
Sommersted	**73**	55 19N	9 18E
Sommesous	**43**	48 44N	4 12E
Sommières	**45**	43 47N	4 6E
Somogy □	**53**	46 19N	17 30E
Somogyszob	**53**	46 18N	17 20E
Somoto	**166**	13 28N	86 37W
Sompolno	**54**	52 26N	18 45E
Somport, Paso	**58**	42 48N	0 31W
Somport, Puerto de	**58**	42 48N	0 31W
Sompting	**29**	50 51N	0 20W
Son, Neth.	**47**	51 31N	5 30E
Son, Norway	**71**	59 32N	10 42E
Son, Spain	**56**	42 43N	8 58W
Son Hoa	**100**	13 2N	108 58E
Son La	**100**	21 20N	103 50E
Son Ma	**100**	15 3N	108 34E
Son Tay	**100**	21 8N	105 30E
Soná	**166**	8 0N	81 10W
Sonamarg	**95**	34 18N	75 21E
Sonamukhi	**95**	23 18N	87 27E
Sonamura	**98**	23 29N	91 15E
Sŏnchŏn	**107**	39 48N	124 55E
Soncino	**62**	45 24N	9 52E
Sondags, R.	**128**	32 10N	24 40E
Sóndala	**62**	46 20N	10 20E
Sondar	**95**	33 28N	75 56E
Sönder Hornum	**73**	56 32N	9 38E
Sønder Omme	**73**	55 50N	8 54E
Sønderborg	**73**	54 55N	9 49E
Sonderhausen	**48**	51 22N	10 50E
Sonderjyllands Amt □	**73**	55 10N	9 10E
Sondre Höland	**71**	59 44N	11 30E
Sondre Land	**71**	60 44N	10 21E
Söndre Stromfjord	**12**	66 30N	50 52W
Sóndrio	**62**	46 10N	9 53E
Sone	**127**	17 23S	34 55E
Sonepat	**94**	29 0N	77 5E
Sonepur	**96**	20 55N	83 50E
Song	**100**	18 28N	100 11E
Song Cau	**100**	13 20N	109 18E
Songa, R.	**71**	59 57N	7 30E
Sŏngchŏn	**107**	39 12N	126 15E
Songea	**127**	10 40S	35 40E
Songea □	**127**	10 30S	36 0E
Songeons	**43**	49 32N	1 50E
Songjin	**107**	40 40N	129 10E
Songjŏngni	**107**	35 8N	126 47E
Songkhla	**101**	7 13N	100 37E
Songnim	**107**	38 45N	125 39E
Songwe, Malawi	**127**	9 44S	33 58E
Songwe, Zaîre	**127**	3 20S	26 16E
Sonkel, Ozero	**85**	41 50N	75 12E
Sonkovo	**81**	57 50N	37 5E
Sonmiani	**94**	25 25N	66 40E
Sonning	**29**	51 28N	0 53W
Sonnino	**64**	41 25N	13 13E
Sono, R., Goias, Brazil	**170**	8 58S	48 11W
Sono, R., Minas Gerais, Brazil	**171**	17 2S	45 32W
Sonobe	**111**	35 6N	135 28E
Sonogno	**51**	46 22N	8 47E
Sonoma	**163**	38 17N	122 27W
Sonora, Calif., U.S.A.	**163**	37 59N	120 27W
Sonora, Texas, U.S.A.	**159**	30 33N	100 37W
Sonora □	**164**	28 0N	111 0W
Sonora P.	**160**	38 17N	119 35W
Sonora, R.	**164**	28 30N	111 33W
Sonoyta	**164**	31 51N	112 50W
Sŏnsan	**107**	36 14N	128 17E
Sonskyn	**128**	30 47S	26 28E
Sonsonate	**166**	13 43N	89 44W
Sonthofen	**49**	47 31N	10 16E
Soo Junction	**156**	46 20N	85 14W
Soochow = Suchou	**109**	31 15N	120 40E
Söonder Nissum	**73**	56 19N	8 11E
Sop Hao	**100**	20 33N	104 27E
Sop Prap	**100**	17 53N	99 20E
Sopi	**103**	2 40N	128 28E
Sopo, Nahr	**123**	8 40N	26 30E
Sopot, Poland	**54**	54 27N	18 31E
Sopot, Yugo.	**66**	44 29N	20 30E
Sopotnica	**66**	41 23N	21 13E
Sopron	**49**	47 41N	16 37E
Sop's Arm	**151**	49 46N	56 56W
Sör-Fron	**71**	61 35N	9 59E
Sor, R.	**57**	39 7N	9 52E
Sør-Rondane	**13**	72 0S	25 0E
Sør Trøndelag fylke □	**71**	63 0N	11 0E
Sora	**64**	41 45N	13 36E
Sorada	**96**	19 32N	84 45E
Sorah	**94**	27 13N	68 56E
Söråker	**72**	62 30N	17 32E
Sorano	**63**	42 40N	11 42E
Sorata	**174**	15 50S	68 50W
Sorbas	**59**	37 6N	2 7W
Sorbie	**34**	54 46N	4 26W
Sordale	**37**	58 33N	3 26W
Sordeval	**42**	48 44N	0 55W
Sorel	**150**	46 0N	73 10W
Sörenberg	**50**	46 50N	8 2E
Soresina	**62**	45 17N	9 51E
Sörfold	**74**	67 5N	14 20E
Sorgues	**45**	44 1N	4 53E
Soria	**58**	41 43N	2 32W
Soria □	**58**	41 46N	2 28W
Soriano	**172**	33 24S	58 19W
Soriano □	**176**	33 30S	58 0W
Sorisdale	**34**	56 40N	6 28W
Sorn	**34**	55 31N	4 18W
Sorø	**73**	55 26N	11 32E
Soro	**120**	10 9N	9 48W
Sorocaba	**173**	23 31S	47 35W
Sorochinsk	**84**	52 26N	53 10E
Soroki	**82**	48 8N	28 12E
Soroksár	**53**	47 24N	19 9E
Soron	**94**	27 55N	78 45E
Sorong	**103**	0 55S	131 15E
Sororoca	**174**	0 43N	61 31W
Soroti	**126**	1 43N	33 35E
Soröy Sundet	**74**	70 25N	23 0E
Soröya	**74**	70 35N	22 45E
Soroyane	**71**	62 25N	5 32E
Sorraia, R.	**57**	38 55N	8 35W
Sorrento, Austral.	**139**	38 22S	144 47E
Sorrento, Italy	**65**	40 38N	14 23E
Sorris Sorris	**128**	21 0S	14 46E
Sorsele	**74**	65 31N	17 30E
Sorso	**64**	40 50N	8 34E
Sorsogon	**103**	13 0N	124 0E
Sortat	**37**	58 32N	3 12W
Sortino	**65**	37 9N	15 1E
Sos	**58**	42 30N	1 13W
Sŏsan	**107**	36 47N	126 27E
Soscumica, L.	**150**	50 15N	77 27W
Sosdala	**73**	56 2N	13 41E
Sosna, R.	**81**	52 30N	38 0E
Sosnowiec	**54**	50 20N	19 10E
Sospel	**45**	43 52N	7 27E
Šoštanj	**63**	46 23N	15 4E
Sŏsura	**107**	42 16N	130 36E
Sosva	**84**	59 10N	61 50E
Sosva, R.	**84**	59 32N	62 20E
Soto la Marina, R.	**165**	23 40N	97 40W
Soto y Amío	**56**	42 46N	5 53W
Sotra I.	**71**	60 15N	5 0E
Sotteville	**42**	49 24N	1 5E
Souanké	**124**	2 10N	14 10E
Souderton	**162**	40 19N	75 19W
Soufi	**120**	15 13N	12 17W
Souflion	**68**	41 12N	26 18E
Soufrière	**167**	13 51N	61 4W
Soufrière, vol.	**167**	13 10N	61 10W
Sougne-Remouchamps	**47**	50 29N	5 42E
Souillac	**44**	44 53N	1 29E
Souk-Ahras	**119**	36 17N	7 57E
Souk el Arba du Rharb	**118**	34 50N	5 59W
Souk el Khemis	**119**	36 36N	8 58E
Soukhouma	**100**	14 38N	105 48E
Sŏul	**105**	37 31N	127 6E
Soulac-sur-Mer	**44**	45 30N	1 7W
Soultz	**43**	48 57N	7 52E
Soumagne	**47**	50 37N	5 44E
Sound, The	**75**	56 7N	12 30E
Soúnion, Ákra	**69**	37 37N	24 1E
Sour el Ghozlane	**119**	36 10N	3 45E
Sources, Mt. aux	**129**	28 45S	28 50E
Sourdeval	**42**	48 43N	0 55W
Soure, Brazil	**170**	0 35S	48 30W
Soure, Port.	**56**	40 4N	8 38W
Souris, Man., Can.	**153**	49 40N	100 20W
Souris, P.E.I., Can.	**151**	46 21N	62 15W
Souris, R.	**153**	49 40N	99 34W
Soúrpi	**69**	39 6N	22 54E
Sous, R.	**118**	30 31N	9 27W
Sousa	**170**	6 45S	38 10W
Sousel, Brazil	**170**	2 38S	52 29W
Sousel, Port.	**57**	38 57N	7 40W
Souss, O.	**118**	30 23N	8 24W
Sousse	**119**	35 50N	10 38E
Soustons	**44**	43 45N	1 19W
Souterraine, La	**44**	46 15N	1 30E
South Africa, Rep. of, ■	**125**	30 0S	25 0E
South Amboy	**162**	40 29N	74 17W
South America	**168**	10 0S	60 0W
South Auckland & Bay of Plenty □	**142**	38 30S	177 0E
South Aulatsivik I.	**151**	56 45N	61 30W
South Australia □	**136**	32 0S	139 0E
South Baldy, Mt.	**161**	34 6N	107 27W
South Bend, Indiana, U.S.A.	**156**	41 38N	86 20W
South Bend, Wash., U.S.A.	**160**	46 44N	123 52W
South Benfleet	**29**	51 33N	0 34E
South Blackwater	**138**	24 00S	148 35E
South Boston	**157**	36 42N	78 58W
South Br. Ashburton, R.	**143**	43 30S	171 15E
South Branch, Can.	**151**	47 55N	59 2W
South Branch, U.S.A.	**151**	44 30N	83 55W
South Brent	**30**	50 26N	3 50W
South Brook	**151**	49 26N	56 5W
South Buganda □	**126**	0 15S	31 30E
South Cape	**147**	18 58N	155 24E
South Carolina □	**157**	33 45N	81 0W
South Cave	**33**	53 46N	0 37W
South Charleston	**156**	38 20N	81 40W
South China Sea	**101**	7 0N	107 0E
South Dakota □	**158**	45 0N	100 0W
South Dell	**36**	58 28N	6 20W
South Dorset Downs	**28**	50 40N	2 26W
South Downs	**29**	50 53N	0 10W
South East C.	**138**	43 40S	146 50E
South East Is.	**137**	34 17S	123 30E
South Elkington	**33**	53 22N	0 5W
South Esk, R.	**37**	56 44N	3 3W
South Foreland	**29**	51 7N	1 23E
S. Fork, American, R.	**163**	38 45N	121 5W
South Fork, R.	**160**	47 54N	113 15W
South Gamboa	**164**	9 4N	79 40W
South Gate	**163**	33 57N	118 12W
South Georgia	**13**	54 30S	37 0W
South Glamorgan □	**31**	51 30N	3 20W
South Grafton	**139**	29 41S	152 47E
South Harris, district	**36**	56 51N	3 10W
South Haven	**156**	42 22N	86 20W
South Hayling	**29**	50 47N	0 56W
South Henik, L.	**153**	61 30N	97 30W
South Horr	**126**	2 12N	36 56E
South I., Kenya	**126**	2 35N	36 35E
South I., N.Z.	**143**	43 0S	170 0E
South Invercargill	**143**	46 26N	168 23E
South Kirby	**33**	53 35N	1 25W
South Knife, R.	**153**	58 55N	94 37W
S. Kolok	**101**	6 2N	101 58E
South Korea ■	**107**	36 0N	128 0E
S. Lembing	**101**	3 55N	103 3E
South Magnetic Pole	**13**	66 30S	139 30E
South Marsh Is.	**162**	38 6N	76 1W
South Milwaukee	**156**	42 50N	87 52W
South Molton	**30**	51 1N	3 50W
South Nahanni, R.	**152**	61 3N	123 21W
South Nesting B.	**36**	60 18N	1 5W
South Orkney Is.	**13**	63 0S	45 0W
South Pass	**160**	42 20N	108 58W
South Passage	**137**	26 07S	113 09E
S. Pétani	**101**	5 37N	100 30E
South Petherton	**28**	50 57N	2 49W
South Petherwin	**30**	50 35N	4 22W
South Pines	**157**	35 10N	79 25W
South Platte, R.	**158**	40 50N	102 45W
South Pt.	**151**	49 6N	62 11W
South Pole	**13**	90 0S	0 0E
South Porcupine	**150**	48 30N	81 12W
South Portland	**162**	43 38N	70 15W
South River, Can.	**150**	45 52N	79 29W
South River, U.S.A.	**162**	40 27N	74 23W
South Ronaldsay, I.	**37**	58 46N	2 58W
S. Sandwich Is.	**15**	57 0S	27 0W
South Saskatchewan, R.	**153**	53 15N	105 5W
South Sd.	**39**	53 4N	9 28W
South Seal, R.	**153**	58 48N	98 8W
South Sentinel, I.	**101**	11 1N	92 16E
South Shetland Is.	**13**	62 0S	59 0W
South Shields	**35**	54 59N	1 26W
South Sioux City	**158**	42 30N	96 30W
South Taranaki Bight	**142**	39 40S	174 5E
South Tawton	**30**	50 44N	3 55W
South Thompson, R.	**152**	50 40N	120 20W
South Twin I.	**150**	53 7N	79 52W
South Tyne, R.	**35**	54 46N	2 25W
South Uist, I.	**37**	57 4N	7 21W
South Ulvön, I.	**72**	63 0N	18 45E
South Walls, I.	**37**	58 45N	3 7W
South West Africa ■ = Namibia	**128**	22 0S	18 9E
South West C.	**138**	43 34S	146 3E
South West Cape	**143**	47 16S	167 31E
South Williamsport	**162**	41 14N	77 0W
South Yarmouth	**162**	41 35N	70 10W
South Yemen ■	**91**	15 0N	48 0E
South Yorkshire □	**33**	53 30N	1 20W
Southam	**28**	52 16N	1 24W
Southampton, Can.	**150**	44 30N	81 25W
Southampton, U.K.	**28**	50 54N	1 23W
Southampton, U.S.A.	**162**	40 54N	72 22W
Southampton I.	**149**	64 30N	84 0W
Southampton Water	**28**	50 52N	1 21W
Southborough	**29**	51 10N	0 15E
Southbridge, N.Z.	**143**	43 48S	172 16E
Southbridge, U.S.A.	**162**	42 4N	72 2W
Southeast C.	**147**	62 55N	169 40W
Southend, Can.	**153**	56 19N	103 14W
Southend, U.K.	**34**	55 18N	5 38W
Southend-on-Sea	**29**	51 32N	0 42E
Southern □, Malawi	**127**	15 0S	35 0E
Southern □, S. Leone	**120**	0 8N	12 30E
Southern □, Uganda	**122**	0 30S	30 30E
Southern □, Zambia	**127**	16 20S	26 20E
Southern Alps	**143**	43 41S	170 11E
Southern Cross	**137**	31 12S	119 15E
Southern Hills	**137**	32 15S	122 40E
Southern Indian L.	**153**	57 10N	98 30W
Southern Indian Lake	**153**	57 0N	99 0W
Southern Ocean	**13**	62 0S	160 0W
Southern Uplands	**35**	55 30N	3 3W
Southery	**29**	52 32N	0 23E
Southington	**162**	41 37N	72 53W
Southland □	**143**	45 51S	168 13E
Southminster	**29**	51 40N	0 51E
Southold	**162**	41 4N	72 26W
Southport, Austral.	**139**	27 58S	153 25E
Southport, U.K.	**32**	53 38N	3 1W
Southport, U.S.A.	**157**	33 55N	78 0W
Southwark	**29**	51 29N	0 5W
Southwell	**33**	53 4N	0 57W
Southwick	**29**	50 50N	0 14W
Southwold	**29**	52 19N	1 41E
Soutpansberge	**129**	23 0S	29 30E
Souvigny	**44**	46 33N	3 10E
Sovata	**70**	46 35N	25 3E
Sovetsk, Lithuania, U.S.S.R.	**80**	55 6N	21 50E
Sovetsk, R.S.F.S.R., U.S.S.R.	**81**	57 38N	48 53E
Sovetskaya Gavan	**77**	48 50N	140 0E
Sovicille	**63**	43 16N	11 12E
Sovra	**66**	42 44N	17 34E
Sowerby	**33**	54 13N	1 19W
Sōya-Misaki	**112**	45 30N	142 0E
Soyopa	**164**	28 41N	109 37W
Sozh, R.	**80**	53 50N	31 50E
Sozopol	**67**	42 23N	27 42E
Spa	**47**	50 29N	5 53E
Spain ■	**55**	40 0N	5 0W
Spakenburg	**46**	52 15N	5 22E
Spalding, Austral.	**140**	33 30S	138 37E
Spalding, U.K.	**29**	52 47N	0 9W
Spalding, U.S.A.	**158**	41 45N	98 27W
Spandet	**73**	55 15N	8 54E
Spånga	**72**	59 23N	17 55E
Spångenäs	**73**	57 36N	16 7E
Spangereid	**71**	58 3N	7 9E
Spaniard's Bay	**151**	47 38N	53 20W
Spanish	**150**	46 12N	82 20W
Spanish Fork	**160**	40 10N	111 37W
Spanish Pt.	**39**	52 51N	9 27W
Spanish Sahara □ = Western Sahara	**116**	25 0N	13 0W
Spanish Town	**166**	18 0N	77 20W
Sparkford	**28**	51 2N	2 33W
Sparrows Point	**162**	39 13N	76 29W
Sparta, Ga., U.S.A.	**157**	33 18N	82 59W
Sparta, N.J., U.S.A.	**162**	41 2N	74 38W
Sparta, Wis., U.S.A.	**158**	43 55N	91 10W
Sparta = Spárti	**69**	37 5N	22 25E
Spartanburg	**157**	35 0N	82 0W
Spartel, C.	**118**	35 47N	5 56W
Spárti	**69**	37 5N	22 25E
Spartivento, C., Calabria, Italy	**65**	37 56N	16 4E
Spartivento, C., Sard., Italy	**65**	38 52N	8 50E
Spas-Demensk	**80**	54 20N	34 0E
Spas-Klepiki	**81**	54 34N	40 2E
Spassk-Dalniy	**77**	44 40N	132 40E
Spassk-Ryazanskiy	**81**	54 30N	40 25E
Spatha Ákra.	**69**	35 42N	23 43E
Spatsizi, R.	**152**	57 42N	128 7W
Spean Bridge	**36**	56 53N	4 55W
Spearfish	**158**	44 32N	103 52W
Spearman	**159**	36 15N	101 10W
Speculator	**162**	43 30N	74 25W
Speed	**140**	35 21S	142 27E
Speer	**51**	47 12N	9 8E

Speers Stíra

Speers 153 52 43N 107 34W
Speightstown 167 13 15N 59 39W
Speke 32 53 21N 2 51W
Speke Gulf, L. Victoria 126 2 20S 32 50E
Spekholzerheide 47 50 51N 6 2E
Spelve, L. 34 56 22N 5 45W
Spenard 147 61 5N 149 50W
Spencer, Idaho, U.S.A. 160 44 18N 112 8W
Spencer, Iowa, U.S.A. 158 43 5N 95 3W
Spencer, Nebr., U.S.A. 158 42 52N 98 43W
Spencer, N.Y., U.S.A. 162 42 14N 76 30W
Spencer, W. Va., U.S.A. 156 38 47N 81 24W
Spencer B. 128 25 30S 14 47E
Spencer Bay 148 69 32N 93 32W
Spencer, C. 140 35 20S 136 45E
Spencer G. 140 34 0S 137 20E
Spences Bridge 152 50 25N 121 20W
Spennymoor 33 54 43N 1 35W
Spenser Mts. 143 42 15S 172 45E
Sperkhiós, R. 69 38 57N 22 3E
Sperrin Mts. 38 54 50N 7 0W
Spessart 49 50 0N 9 20E
Spetsai 69 37 16N 23 9E
Spétsai, I. 69 37 15N 23 10E
Spey B. 37 57 41N 3 0W
Spey Bay 37 57 39N 3 4W
Spey, R. 37 57 26N 3 25W
Speyer 49 49 19N 8 26E
Speyer, R. 41 49 18N 7 52E
Spezia = La Spézia 62 44 7N 9 49E
Spézia, La 62 44 8N 9 50E
Spezzano Albanese 65 39 41N 16 19E
Spiddal 39 53 14N 9 19W
Spiekeroog, I. 48 53 45N 7 42E
Spielfeld 63 46 43N 15 38E
Spiez 50 46 40N 7 40E
Spijk 46 53 24N 6 50E
Spijkenisse 46 51 51N 4 20E
Spili 69 35 13N 24 31E
Spilimbergo 63 46 7N 12 53E
Spillimacheen 152 51 6N 117 0W
Spilsby 33 53 10N 0 6E
Spin Baldak 93 31 3N 66 16E
Spinazzola 65 40 58N 16 5E
Spincourt 43 49 20N 5 39E
Spind 71 58 6N 6 53E
Spineni 70 44 43N 24 37E
Spirit Lake 160 47 56N 116 56W
Spirit River 152 55 45N 118 50W
Spiritwood 153 53 24N 107 33W
Spiš ská Nová Ves 53 48 58N 20 34E
Spiš ské Podhradie 53 49 0N 20 48E
Spit Pt. 136 20 4S 118 59E
Spithead 29 50 43N 0 56W
Spittal 52 46 48N 13 31E
Spitzbergen (Svalbard) 12 78 0N 17 0E
Split 63 43 31N 16 26E
Split L. 153 56 8N 96 15W
Splitski Kan 63 43 31N 16 20E
Splügen 51 46 34N 9 21E
Splügenpass 51 46 30N 9 20E
Spoffard 159 29 10N 100 27W
Spofforth 33 53 57N 1 28W
Spokane 160 47 45N 117 25W
Sponvika 71 59 7N 11 15E
Spooner 158 45 49N 91 51W
Sporádhes 69 37 0N 27 0E
Sporyy Navolok, M. 76 75 50N 68 40E
Spotswood 162 40 23N 74 23W
Spragge 150 46 15N 82 40W
Sprague 160 47 25N 117 59W
Sprague River 160 42 49N 121 31W
Spratly, I. 102 8 20N 112 0E
Spray 160 44 56N 119 46W
Spree, R. 48 52 23N 13 52E
Sprimont 47 50 30N 5 40E
Spring City, Pa., U.S.A. 162 40 11N 75 33W
Spring City, Utah, U.S.A. 160 39 31N 111 28W
Spring Grove 162 39 55N 76 56W
Spring Hill 141 33 23S 149 9E
Spring Mts. 161 36 20N 115 43W
Spring Valley, Minn., U.S.A. 158 43 40N 92 30W
Spring Valley, N.Y., U.S.A. 162 41 7N 74 4W
Springbok 128 29 42S 17 54E
Springburn 143 43 40S 171 32E
Springdale, Can. 151 49 30N 56 6W
Springdale, Ark., U.S.A. 159 36 10N 94 5W
Springdale, Wash., U.S.A. 160 48 1N 117 50W
Springe 48 52 12N 9 35E
Springerville 161 34 10N 109 16W
Springfield, N.Z. 143 43 19S 171 56E
Springfield, Colo., U.S.A. 159 37 26N 102 40W
Springfield, Ill., U.S.A. 158 39 48N 89 40W
Springfield, Mass., U.S.A. 162 42 8N 72 37W
Springfield, Mo., U.S.A. 159 37 15N 93 20W
Springfield, Ohio, U.S.A. 156 39 50N 83 48W
Springfield, Oreg., U.S.A. 160 44 2N 123 0W
Springfield, Tenn., U.S.A. 157 36 35N 86 55W
Springfield, Va., U.S.A. 162 38 45N 77 13W
Springfield, Vt., U.S.A. 162 43 20N 72 30W
Springfontein 128 30 15S 25 40E
Springhill 151 45 40N 64 4W
Springhouse 152 51 56N 122 7W
Springhurst 141 36 10S 146 31E
Springs 129 26 13S 28 25E
Springsure 138 24 8S 148 6E
Springvale, Queens., Austral. 138 23 33S 140 42E
Springvale, W. Australia, Austral. 136 17 48S 127 41E
Springvale, U.S.A. 162 43 28N 70 48W
Springville, Calif., U.S.A. 163 36 8N 118 49W
Springville, N.Y., U.S.A. 156 42 31N 78 41W
Springville, Utah, U.S.A. 160 40 14N 111 35W
Springwater 153 51 58N 108 23W
Sproatley 33 53 46N 0 9W
Spur 159 33 28N 100 50W
Spurn Hd. 33 53 34N 0 8E
Spuz 66 42 32N 19 10E
Spuzzum 152 49 37N 121 23W
Spydeberg 71 59 37N 11 4E
Squam L. 162 43 45N 71 32W
Squamish 152 49 45N 123 10W
Square Islands 151 52 47N 55 47W
Squillace, Golfo di 65 38 43N 16 35E
Squinzano 65 40 27N 18 1E
Squires, Mt. 137 26 14S 127 46E
Sragen 103 7 28S 110 59E
Srbac 66 45 7N 17 30E
Srbija □ 66 43 30N 21 0E
Srbobran 66 45 32N 19 48E
Sre Khtum 101 12 10N 106 52E
Sre Umbell 101 11 8N 103 46E
Srebrnica 66 44 10N 19 18E
Sredinyy Khrebet 77 57 0N 160 0E
Središce 63 46 24N 16 17E
Sredna Gora 67 42 40N 25 0E
Sredne Tambovskoye 77 50 55N 137 45E
Srednekolymsk 77 67 20N 154 40E
Srednevilyuysk 77 63 50N 123 5E
Sredni Rodopi 67 41 40N 24 45E
Sredniy Ural, mts. 166 59 0N 59 0E
Srem 54 52 6N 17 2E
Srepok, R. 100 13 33N 106 16E
Sretensk 77 52 10N 117 40E
Sri Lanka ■ 97 7 30N 80 50E
Sriharikota, I. 97 13 40N 81 30E
Srikakulam 96 18 14N 84 4E
Srinagar 95 34 12N 74 50E
Sripur 98 24 14N 90 30E
Srirangam 97 10 54N 78 42E
Srirangapatnam 97 12 26N 76 43E
Srivilliputtur 97 9 31N 77 40E
Šroda Wlkp. 54 52 15N 17 19E
Srpska Crnja 66 45 38N 20 44E
Srpska Itabej 66 45 35N 20 44E
Ssu Chiao 109 30 43N 122 28E
Ssuhsien 107 33 25N 117 54E
Ssuhui 109 23 20N 112 41E
Ssunan 108 27 56N 108 14E
Ssup'ing 105 43 10N 124 25E
Ssushui, Honan, China 106 34 51N 113 12E
Ssushui, Shantung, China 107 35 39N 117 15E
Ssutzuwangch'i 106 41 30N 111 37E
Staaten, R. 138 16 24S 141 17E
Stabroek 47 51 20N 4 22E
Stack's Mts. 39 52 20N 9 34W
Stad Delden 46 52 16N 6 43E
Stade 48 53 35N 9 31E
Staden 47 50 59N 3 1E
Staðarhólskirkja 74 65 23N 21 58W
Stadil 73 56 12N 8 12E
Städjan 72 61 56N 12 30E
Stadlandet 71 62 10N 5 10E
Stadsforsen 72 63 0N 16 45E
Stadskanaal 46 53 4N 6 48E
Stadthagen 48 52 20N 9 14E
Stadtlohn 48 51 59N 6 52E
Stadtroda 48 50 51N 11 44E
Stäfa 51 47 14N 8 45E
Stafafell 74 64 25N 14 52W
Staffa, I. 34 56 26N 6 21W
Stafford, U.K. 28 52 49N 2 9W
Stafford, Kansas, U.S.A. 159 38 0N 98 35W
Stafford, Va., U.S.A. 162 38 2S 77 30W
Stafford □ 28 52 53N 2 10W
Stafford Springs 162 41 58N 72 20W
Stagnone, I. 64 37 50N 12 28E
Staindrop 33 54 35N 1 49W
Staines 29 51 26N 0 30W
Stainforth 33 53 37N 0 59W
Stainmore For. 32 54 29N 2 5W
Stainton 33 53 17N 0 23W
Stainz 52 46 53N 15 17E
Staithes 33 54 33N 0 47W
Stakkroge 73 55 53N 8 51E
Stala 66 43 43N 21 28E
Stalbridge 28 50 57N 2 22W
Stalden 50 46 14N 7 52E
Stalham 29 52 46N 1 31E
Stalingrad = Volgograd 83 48 40N 44 25E
Staliniri = Tskhinvali 82 42 14N 44 1E
Stalino = Donetsky 82 48 0N 37 45E
Stalinogorsk = Novomoskovsk 81 54 5N 38 15E
Stallingborough 33 53 36N 0 11W
Stalowa Wola 54 50 34N 22 3E
Stalybridge 32 53 29N 1 56W
Stamford, Austral. 138 21 15S 143 46E
Stamford, U.K. 29 52 39N 0 29W
Stamford, Conn., U.S.A. 162 41 5N 73 30W
Stamford, N.Y., U.S.A. 162 42 25N 74 37W
Stamford, Tex., U.S.A. 159 32 58N 99 50W
Stamford Bridge 33 53 59N 0 53W
Stamfordham 35 55 3N 1 53W
Stampersgat 47 51 37N 4 26E
Stamps 159 33 22N 93 30W
Stanberry 158 40 12N 94 32W
Standerton 129 26 55S 29 13E
Standish, U.K. 32 53 35N 2 39W
Standish, U.S.A. 156 43 58N 83 57W
Standon 29 51 53N 0 2E
Stanford 160 47 11N 110 10W
Stanford on Teme 28 52 17N 2 26W
Stange Hedmark 71 60 43N 11 11E
Stanger 129 29 18S 31 21E
Stanhope, Austral. 141 36 27S 144 59E
Stanhope, U.K. 32 54 45N 2 0W
Staniŝic 53 45 53N 19 12E
Stanislaus, R. 163 37 40N 121 15W
Stanislav = Ivano-Frankovsk 80 49 0N 24 40E
Stanke Dimitrov 66 42 27N 23 9E
Stanley, Austral. 138 40 46S 145 19E
Stanley, N.B., Can. 151 46 20N 66 50W
Stanley, Sask., Can. 153 55 24N 104 22W
Stanley, Falk. Is. 176 51 40S 58 0W
Stanley, Durham, U.K. 33 54 53N 1 42W
Stanley, Tayside, U.K. 35 56 29N 3 28W
Stanley, Idaho, U.S.A. 160 44 10N 114 59W
Stanley, N.D., U.S.A. 158 48 20N 102 23W
Stanley, Wis., U.S.A. 158 44 57N 91 0W
Stanley Res. 97 11 50N 77 40E
Stanleyville = Kisangani 126 0 35N 25 15E
Stanlow 32 53 17N 2 52W
Stann Creek 165 17 0N 88 20W
Stannington 35 55 7N 1 41W
Stanovoy Khrebet 77 55 0N 130 0E
Stans 51 46 58N 8 21E
Stansmore Ra. 136 21 23S 128 33E
Stansted Mountfitchet 29 51 54N 0 13E
Stanthorpe 139 28 36S 151 59E
Stanton, Can. 147 69 45N 128 52W
Stanton, U.S.A. 159 32 8N 101 45W
Stantsiya Karshi 85 38 49N 65 47E
Stanwix 32 54 54N 2 56W
Staphorst 46 52 39N 6 12E
Stapleford 33 52 56N 1 16W
Staplehurst 29 51 9N 0 35E
Stapleton 158 41 30N 100 31W
Staporkow 54 51 9N 20 31E
Star City 153 52 55N 104 20W
Stara-minskaya 83 46 33N 39 0E
Stara Moravica 66 45 50N 19 30E
Stara Pazova 66 45 0N 20 10E
Stara Planina 67 43 15N 23 0E
Stara Zagora 67 42 26N 25 39E
Starachowice-Wierzbnik 54 51 3N 21 2E
Staraya Russa 80 57 58N 31 10E
Starbuck I. 131 5 37S 155 55W
Stargard 48 53 29N 13 19E
Stargard Szczecinski 54 53 20N 15 0E
Stari Bar 66 42 7N 19 13E
Stari Trg. 63 45 29N 15 7E
Staritsa 80 56 33N 35 0E
Starke 157 30 0N 82 10W
Starkville, Colo., U.S.A. 159 37 10N 104 31W
Starkville, Miss., U.S.A. 157 33 26N 88 48W
Starnberg 49 48 0N 11 20E
Starnberger See 49 48 0N 11 0E
Starobelsk 83 49 27N 39 0E
Starodub 80 52 30N 32 50E
Starogard 54 53 55N 18 30E
Start Bay 30 50 15N 3 35W
Start Pt., Devon, U.K. 30 50 13N 3 38W
Start Pt., Orkney, U.K. 37 59 17N 2 25W
Stary Sacz 54 49 33N 30 26E
Staryy Biryuzyak 83 44 46N 46 50E
Staryy Kheydzhan 77 60 0N 144 50E
Staryy Krym 82 44 48N 35 8E
Staryy Oskol 81 51 12N 37 55E
Stassfurt 48 51 51N 11 34E
State College 156 40 47N 77 49W
State Is. 150 48 40N 87 0W
Staten I. 162 40 35N 74 10W
Staten, I. = Los Estados, I. de 176 54 40S 64 0W
Statesboro 157 32 26N 81 46W
Statesville 157 35 48N 80 51W
Statfjord, oilfield 19 61 15N 1 50E
Stathelle 71 59 3N 9 41E
Stauffer 163 34 45N 119 3W
Staunton, U.K. 28 51 58N 2 19W
Staunton, Ill., U.S.A. 158 39 0N 89 49W
Staunton, Va., U.S.A. 156 38 7N 79 4W
Stavanger 71 58 57N 5 40E
Staveley, Cumbria, U.K. 32 54 24N 2 49W
Staveley, Derby, U.K. 33 53 16N 1 20W
Stavelot 47 50 23N 5 55E
Stavenisse 47 51 35N 4 1E
Staveren 46 52 53N 5 22E
Stavern 71 59 0N 10 1E
Stavfjord 71 61 30N 5 0E
Stavre 72 62 51N 15 19E
Stavropol 83 45 5N 42 0E
Stavroúpolis 68 41 12N 24 45E
Stavsjö 73 48 42N 16 30E
Stawell 140 37 5S 142 47E
Stawell, R. 138 20 38S 142 55E
Stawiszyn 54 51 56N 18 4E
Staxigoe 37 58 28N 3 2W
Steamboat Springs 160 40 30N 106 58W
Stebark 54 53 30N 20 10E
Stebleva 68 41 18N 20 33E
Steckborn 51 47 44N 8 59E
Steele 158 46 56N 99 52W
Steelton 162 40 17N 76 50W
Steelville 159 37 57N 91 21W
Steen, R. 152 59 35N 117 10W
Steen River 152 59 40N 117 12W
Steenbergen 47 51 35N 4 19E
Steenvoorde 43 50 48N 2 33E
Steenwijk 46 52 47N 6 7E
Steep Pt. 137 26 08S 113 8E
Steep Rock 153 51 30N 98 48W
Steep Rock Lake 150 48 50N 91 38W
Stefănesti 70 47 44N 27 15E
Stefanie L. = Chew Bahir 123 4 40N 30 50E
Steffisburg 50 46 47N 7 38E
Stefŭnesti 70 47 44N 27 15E
Stege 73 55 0N 12 18E
Steierdorf Anina 66 45 6N 21 51E
Steiermark □ 52 47 26N 15 0E
Steigerwald 49 49 45N 10 30E
Stein, Neth. 47 50 58N 5 45E
Stein, Switz. 51 47 40N 8 50E
Stein, U.K. 36 57 30N 6 35W
Steinbach 153 49 32N 96 40W
Steinfort 47 49 39N 5 55E
Steinheim 48 51 50N 9 6E
Steinkjer 74 63 59N 11 31E
Steinkopf 125 29 15S 17 48E
Stekene 47 51 12N 4 2E
Stella Land 128 26 45S 24 50E
Stellarton 151 45 32N 62 45W
Stellenbosch 128 33 58S 18 50E
Stellendam 46 51 49N 4 1E
Stelvio, Paso dello 51 46 32N 10 27E
Stemshaug 71 63 19N 8 44E
Stendal 48 52 36N 11 50E
Stene 47 51 12N 2 56E
Stenhousemuir 35 56 2N 3 46W
Stenmagle 73 55 49N 11 39E
Stenness, L., of 37 59 0N 3 15W
Stensele 74 65 3N 17 8E
Stenstorp 73 58 17N 13 45E
Stenungsund 73 58 6N 11 50E
Stepanakert 79 40 0N 46 25E
Stephan 158 48 30N 96 53W
Stephens Cr. 140 32 15S 141 55E
Stephens I., Can. 152 54 10N 130 45W
Stephens I., N.Z. 143 40 40S 174 1E
Stephenville, Can. 151 48 31N 58 30W
Stephenville, U.S.A. 159 32 12N 98 12W
Stepnica 54 53 38N 14 36E
Stepnoi = Elista 83 46 25N 44 17E
Stepnoye 84 54 4N 60 26E
Sterkstroom 128 31 32S 26 32E
Sterlego, Mys 12 80 30N 90 0E
Sterling, Colo., U.S.A. 158 40 40N 103 15W
Sterling, Ill., U.S.A. 158 41 45N 89 45W
Sterling, Kans., U.S.A. 158 38 17N 98 13W
Sterling City 159 31 50N 100 59W
Sterlitamak 84 53 40N 56 0E
Sternberg 48 53 42N 11 48E
Sternberk 53 49 45N 17 15E
Stettin = Szczecin 54 53 27N 14 27E
Stettiner Haff 48 53 50N 14 25E
Stettler 152 52 19N 112 40W
Steubenville 156 40 21N 80 39W
Stevenage 29 51 54N 0 11W
Stevens Port 158 44 32N 89 34W
Stevens Village 147 66 0N 149 10W
Stevenson L. 153 53 55N 95 9W
Stevenson, R. 136 46 15S 134 10E
Stevenston 34 55 38N 4 46W
Stevns Klint 73 55 17N 12 28E
Stewart 152 55 56N 129 57W
Stewart, C. 138 11 57S 134 45E
Stewart, I. 176 54 50S 71 30W
Stewart I. 143 46 58S 167 54E
Stewart River 147 63 19N 139 26W
Stewarton 34 55 40N 4 30W
Stewartstown 38 54 35N 6 40W
Stewiacke 151 45 9N 63 22W
Steyning 29 50 54N 0 19W
Steynsburg 128 31 15S 25 49E
Steyr 52 48 3N 14 25E
Steyr, R. 52 48 57N 14 15E
Steytlerville 128 33 17S 24 19E
Stia 63 43 48N 11 41E
Stiens 46 53 16N 5 46E
Stigler 159 35 19N 95 6W
Stigliano 65 40 24N 16 13E
Stigsnæs 73 55 13N 11 18E
Stigtomta 73 58 47N 16 48E
Stikine Mts. 148 59 30N 129 30W
Stikine, R. 147 58 0N 131 12W
Stilfontein 128 26 50S 26 50E
Stilis 69 38 55N 22 37E
Stillington 33 54 7N 1 5W
Stillwater, Minn., U.S.A. 158 45 3N 92 47W
Stillwater, N.Y., U.S.A. 162 42 55N 73 41W
Stillwater, Okla., U.S.A. 159 36 5N 97 3W
Stillwater Mts. 160 39 45N 118 6W
Stilwell 159 35 52N 94 36W
Stimfalias, L. 69 37 51N 22 27E
Stimson 150 48 58N 80 30W
Stinchar, R. 34 55 10N 4 50W
Stingray Pt. 162 37 35N 76 15W
Stip 66 41 42N 22 10E
Stiperstones Mt. 28 52 36N 2 57W
Stira 69 38 9N 24 14E

Stiring Wendel Sukkur

Stiring Wendel **43** 49 12N 6 57 E
Stirling, Austral. **138** 17 12 S 141 35 E
Stirling, Can. **152** 49 30N 112 30W
Stirling, N.Z. **143** 46 14 S 169 49 E
Stirling, U.K. **35** 56 17N 3 57W
Stirling (□) **26** 56 3N 4 10W
Stirling Ra. **137** 34 0 S 118 0 E
Stjárneborg **73** 57 53N 14 45 E
Stjarnsfors **72** 60 2N 13 45 E
Stjördalshalsen **71** 63 29N 10 51 E
Stobo **35** 55 38N 3 18W
Stoborough, oilfield **19** 50 38N 2 8W
Stockaryd **73** 57 19N 14 36 E
Stockbridge **28** 51 7N 1 30W
Stockerau **53** 48 24N 16 12 E
Stockett **160** 47 23N 111 7W
Stockholm **72** 59 20N 18 3 E
Stockholms län □ **72** 59 30N 18 20 E
Stockhorn **50** 46 42N 7 33 E
Stockport **32** 53 25N 2 11W
Stocksbridge **33** 53 30N 1 36W
Stockton, Austral. **141** 32 56 S 151 47 E
Stockton, Calif., U.S.A. **163** 38 0N 121 20W
Stockton, Kans., U.S.A. **158** 39 30N 99 20W
Stockton, Mo., U.S.A. **159** 37 40N 93 48W
Stockton-on-Tees **33** 54 34N 1 20W
Stockvik **72** 62 17N 17 23 E
Stoczek Łukowski **54** 51 58N 22 22 E
Stode **72** 62 28N 16 35 E
Stoer **36** 58 12N 5 20W
Stogovo, mts. **66** 41 31N 20 38 E
Stoke, N.Z. **143** 41 19N 173 14 E
Stoke, U.K. **29** 51 26N 0 41 E
Stoke Ferry **29** 52 34N 0 31 E
Stoke Fleming **30** 50 19N 3 36W
Stoke Mandeville **29** 51 46N 0 47W
Stoke Prior **28** 52 18N 2 5W
Stokenham **30** 50 15N 3 40W
Stokes Bay **150** 45 0N 81 22W
Stokes Pt. **138** 40 10 S 143 56 E
Stokes Ra. **136** 15 50 S 130 50 E
Stokesley **33** 54 27N 1 12W
Stokke **71** 59 13N 10 17 E
Stokkem **47** 51 1N 5 45 E
Stokken **71** 58 31N 8 53 E
Stokkseyri **74** 63 50N 20 58W
Stokksnes **74** 64 14N 14 58W
Stolac **66** 43 8N 17 59 E
Stolberg, Germ., E. **48** 51 33N 11 0 E
Stolberg, Germ., W. **48** 50 48N 6 13 E
Stolbovaya, R.S.F.S.R., U.S.S.R. **77** 64 50N 153 50 E
Stolbovaya, R.S.F.S.R., U.S.S.R. **81** 55 10N 37 32 E
Stolbtsy **80** 53 22N 26 43 E
Stolin **80** 51 53N 26 50 E
Stolnici **70** 44 31N 24 48 E
Stolwijk **46** 51 59N 4 47 E
Ston **66** 42 51N 17 43 E
Stone, Bucks., U.K. **29** 51 48N 0 52W
Stone, Stafford, U.K. **32** 52 55N 2 10W
Stone Harbor **162** 39 3N 74 45W
Stonecliffe **150** 46 13N 77 56W
Stonehaven **37** 56 58N 2 11W
Stonehenge, Austral. **138** 24 22 S 143 17 E
Stonehenge, U.K. **28** 51 9N 1 45W
Stonehouse, Glous., U.K. **28** 51 45N 2 18W
Stonehouse, Strathclyde, U.K. **35** 55 42N 4 0W
Stonewall **153** 50 10N 97 19W
Stongfjord **71** 61 28N 14 0 E
Stonham Aspall **29** 52 11N 1 7 E
Stony L. **153** 58 51N 98 40W
Stony Point **162** 41 14N 73 59W
Stony Rapids **153** 59 16N 105 50W
Stony River **147** 61 48N 156 48W
Stony Stratford **29** 52 4N 0 51W
Stony Tunguska = Tunguska, Nizhmaya **77** 64 0N 95 0 E
Stopnica **54** 50 27N 20 57 E
Stor Elvdal **71** 61 30N 11 1 E
Stora Borge Fjell, Mt. **48** 65 12N 14 0 E
Stora Gla **72** 59 30N 12 30 E
Stora Karlsö **73** 57 17N 17 59 E
Stora Lulevatten **74** 67 10N 19 30 E
Stora Sjøfallet **74** 67 29N 18 40 E
Storavan **74** 65 45N 18 10 E
Stord Leirvik, I. **71** 59 48N 5 27 E
Store Bælt **73** 55 20N 11 0 E
Store Creek **141** 32 54 S 149 6 E
Store Heddinge **73** 55 18N 12 23 E
Storen **71** 63 3N 10 18 E
Storfjorden **71** 62 25N 6 30 E
Storm B. **138** 43 10 S 147 30 E
Storm Lake **158** 42 35N 95 5W
Stormberg **125** 31 16 S 26 17 E
Stormsrivier **128** 33 59 S 23 52 E
Stornoway **36** 58 12N 6 23W
Storozhinets **82** 48 14 S 25 45 E
Storr, The, mt. **36** 57 30N 6 12W
Storrs **162** 41 48N 72 15W
Storsjö **72** 62 49N 13 5 E
Storsjöen, Hedmark, Norway **71** 60 20N 11 40 E
Storsjöen, Hedmark, Norway **71** 61 30N 11 14 E
Storsjön, Gavleborg, Sweden **72** 60 35N 16 45 E
Storsjön, Jämtland, Sweden **72** 62 50N 13 8 E
Storstroms Amt □ **73** 49 50N 11 45 E
Stort, R. **29** 51 50N 0 7 E
Storuman **74** 65 5N 17 10 E
Storuman, L. **74** 65 5N 17 10 E
Storvätteshagna, Mt. **72** 62 6N 12 30 E
Storvik **72** 60 35N 16 33 E
Stotfold **29** 52 2N 0 13W
Stoughton **153** 49 40N 103 0W
Stour, R., Dorset, U.K. **28** 50 48N 2 7W
Stour, R., Heref. & Worcs., U.K. **28** 52 25N 2 13W
Stour, R., Kent, U.K. **29** 51 15N 0 57 E
Stour, R., Suffolk, U.K. **29** 51 55N 1 5 E
Stourbridge **28** 52 28N 2 8W
Stourport **28** 52 21N 2 18W
Stout, L. **153** 52 0N 94 40W
Stove Pipe Wells Village **163** 36 35N 117 11W
Stow **35** 55 41N 2 50W
Stow Bardolph **29** 52 38N 0 24 E
Stow-on-the-Wold **28** 51 55N 1 42W
Stowmarket **29** 52 11N 1 0 E
Stowupland **29** 52 12N 1 3 E
Strabane **38** 54 50N 7 28W
Strabane □ **38** 54 45N 7 25W
Strachan **37** 57 1N 2 31W
Strachur **34** 56 10N 5 5W
Stracin **66** 42 13N 22 2 E
Stradbally, Kerry, Ireland **39** 52 15N 10 4W
Stradbally, Laoighis, Ireland **39** 53 2N 7 10W
Stradbally, Waterford, Ireland **39** 52 7N 7 28W
Stradbroke **29** 52 19N 1 16 E
Strade **38** 53 56N 9 8W
Stradella **62** 45 4N 9 20 E
Stradone **38** 54 0N 7 12W
Strahan **138** 42 9 S 145 20 E
Straldzha **67** 42 35N 26 40 E
Stralkonice **52** 49 15N 13 53 E
Stralsund **48** 54 17N 13 5 E
Strand, Hedmark, Norway **71** 61 18N 11 15 E
Strand, Rogaland, Norway **71** 59 3N 5 56 E
Strand, S. Afr. **128** 34 9 S 18 48 E
Stranda **71** 62 19N 6 58 E
Strandby **73** 56 47N 9 13 E
Strandebarm **71** 60 17N 6 0 E
Strandhill **38** 54 16N 8 34W
Strandvik **71** 60 9N 5 41 E
Strangford **38** 54 23N 5 34W
Strängnäs **72** 59 23N 17 8 E
Stranorlar **38** 54 58N 7 47W
Stranraer **34** 54 54N 5 0W
Strasbourg, Can. **153** 51 4N 104 55W
Strasbourg, France **43** 48 35N 7 42 E
Strasburg, Ger. **48** 53 30N 13 44 E
Strasburg, U.S.A. **158** 46 12N 101 9W
Strassen **47** 49 37N 6 4 E
Stratford, N.S.W., Austral. **141** 32 7 S 151 55 E
Stratford, Vic., Austral. **141** 37 59 S 147 7 E
Stratford, Can. **150** 43 23N 81 0W
Stratford, N.Z. **142** 39 20 S 174 19 E
Stratford, Calif., U.S.A. **163** 36 10N 119 49W
Stratford, Conn., U.S.A. **162** 41 13N 73 8W
Stratford, Tex., U.S.A. **159** 36 20N 102 3W
Stratford-on-Avon **28** 52 12N 1 42W
Stratford St. Mary **29** 51 58N 0 59 E
Strath Avon **37** 57 19N 3 23W
Strath Dearn **37** 57 20N 4 0W
Strath Earn **35** 56 20N 3 50W
Strath Glass **37** 57 20N 4 40W
Strath Naver **37** 58 24N 4 12W
Strath Spey **37** 57 15N 3 40W
Strathalbyn **140** 35 13 S 138 53 E
Strathaven **35** 55 40N 4 4W
Strathbogie, Dist. **37** 57 25N 2 45W
Strathclyde □ **34** 56 0N 4 50W
Strathcona Prov. Park **152** 49 38N 125 40W
Strathdon **37** 57 12N 3 4W
Strathkanaird **36** 57 58N 5 5W
Strathmore, Austral. **138** 17 50 S 142 35 E
Strathmore, Can. **152** 51 5N 113 25W
Strathmore, Highland, U.K. **37** 58 20N 4 40W
Strathmore, Tayside, U.K. **37** 56 40N 3 4W
Strathmore, U.S.A. **163** 36 9N 119 4W
Strathnaver **152** 53 20N 122 33W
Strathpeffer **37** 57 35N 4 32W
Strathroy **150** 42 58N 81 38W
Strathy **37** 58 30N 4 0W
Strathy Pt. **37** 58 35N 4 0W
Strathyre **34** 56 14N 4 20W
Stratmiglo Scot. **35** 56 16N 3 15W
Stratton, U.K. **30** 50 49N 4 31W
Stratton, U.S.A. **158** 39 20N 102 36W
Stratton St. Margaret **28** 51 35N 1 45W
Straubing **49** 48 53N 12 35 E
Straumnes **74** 66 26N 23 8W
Straumsnes Åsskard **71** 63 4N 8 2 E
Strausberg **48** 52 40N 13 52 E
Strawberry Res. **160** 40 0N 111 0W
Strawn **159** 32 36N 98 30W
Strážnice **53** 48 54N 17 19 E
Streaky B. **139** 32 51 S 134 18 E
Streaky Bay **139** 32 48 S 134 13 E
Streatley **28** 51 31N 1 9W
Streator **158** 41 9N 88 52W
Stredočeský □ **52** 49 55N 14 30 E
Stredoslovenský □ **53** 48 30N 19 15 E
Streé **47** 50 17N 4 18 E
Street **28** 51 7N 2 43W
Strehaia **70** 44 37N 23 10 E
Strelcha **67** 42 30N 24 19 E
Strelka **77** 58 5N 93 10 E
Streng, R. **100** 13 12N 103 37 E
Strengelvåg **74** 68 58N 15 11 E
Strensall **33** 54 3N 1 2W
Stretford **32** 53 27N 2 19W
Stretton **32** 53 21N 2 34W
Strezhevoy **76** 60 42N 77 34 E
Strezhnoye **76** 57 45N 84 2 E
Stribro **52** 49 44N 13 0 E
Strichen **37** 57 35N 2 5W
Strickland, R. **135** 7 35 S 141 36 E
Strijen **46** 51 45N 4 33 E
Strimón, R. **68** 41 0N 23 30 E
Strimonikós Kólpos **68** 40 33N 24 0 E
Striven, L. **34** 55 58N 5 9W
Strofadhes, I. **69** 37 15N 21 0 E
Strokestown **38** 53 47N 8 6W
Strom **71** 60 17N 11 44 E
Ström **72** 61 52N 17 20 E
Stroma, I. of **37** 58 40N 3 8W
Strombacka **72** 61 58N 16 44 E
Strómboli, I. **65** 38 48N 15 12 E
Stromeferry **36** 57 20N 5 33W
Stromemore **36** 57 22N 5 33W
Stromness **37** 58 58N 3 18W
Ströms Vattudal L. **74** 64 0N 15 30 E
Stromsberg **72** 60 28N 17 44 E
Strömsnäsbruk **73** 56 35N 13 45 E
Strömstad **72** 58 55N 11 15 E
Stromsund **74** 63 51N 15 35 E
Stronachlachar **34** 56 15N 4 35W
Strone **34** 55 59N 4 54W
Strôngoli **65** 39 16N 17 2 E
Stronsay Firth **37** 59 4N 2 50W
Stronsay, I. **37** 59 8N 2 38W
Strontian **36** 56 42N 5 32W
Strood **29** 51 23N 0 30 E
Stroove **38** 55 13N 6 57W
Stropkov **53** 49 13N 21 39 E
Stroud **28** 51 44N 2 12W
Stroud Road **141** 32 18 S 151 57 E
Stroudsberg **162** 40 59N 75 15W
Struer **73** 56 30N 8 35 E
Struga **66** 41 13N 20 44 E
Strugi Krasnye **80** 58 21N 28 51 E
Struma, R. **67** 41 50N 23 18 E
Strumble Hd. **31** 52 3N 5 6W
Strumica **66** 41 28N 22 41 E
Strumica, R. **66** 41 26N 27 46 E
Strusshamn **71** 60 24N 5 10 E
Struthers **150** 48 41N 85 51W
Struy **37** 57 25N 4 40W
Stryama **67** 42 16N 24 54 E
Stryi **80** 49 16N 23 48 E
Stryker **152** 48 40N 114 44W
Stryków **54** 51 55N 19 33 E
Strzegom **54** 50 58N 16 20 E
Strzelce Krajenskie **54** 52 52N 15 33 E
Strzelecki Creek **139** 29 37 S 139 59 E
Strzelin **54** 50 46N 17 2 E
Strzelno **54** 52 35N 18 9 E
Strzyzów **54** 49 52N 21 47 E
Stuart, Fla., U.S.A. **157** 27 11N 80 12W
Stuart, Nebr., U.S.A. **158** 42 39N 99 8W
Stuart I. **147** 63 55N 164 50W
Stuart L. **152** 54 30N 124 30W
Stuart Mts. **143** 45 2 S 167 39 E
Stuart, R. **152** 54 0N 123 35W
Stuart Range **139** 29 10 S 134 56 E
Stuart's Ra. **136** 29 10 S 135 0 E
Stubbekøbing **73** 54 53N 12 9 E
Stuben **52** 46 58N 10 31 E
Stuberhuk **48** 54 23N 11 18 E
Studholme Junc. **143** 44 42 S 171 9 E
Studland **28** 50 39N 1 58W
Studley **28** 52 16N 1 54W
Stugsund **72** 61 16N 17 18 E
Stugun **72** 63 10N 15 40 E
Stull, L. **153** 54 24N 92 34W
Stung-Treng **100** 13 31N 105 58 E
Stupart, R. **153** 56 0N 93 25W
Stupino **81** 54 57N 38 2 E
Sturgeon B. **153** 52 0N 97 50W
Sturgeon Bay **156** 44 52N 87 20W
Sturgeon Falls **150** 46 25N 79 57W
Sturgeon L., Alta., Can. **152** 55 6N 117 32W
Sturgeon L., Ont., Can. **150** 50 0N 90 45W
Sturgis, Mich., U.S.A. **156** 41 50N 85 25W
Sturgis, S.D., U.S.A. **158** 44 25N 103 30W
Sturko, I. **73** 56 5N 15 42 E
Sturminster Marshall **28** 50 48N 2 4W
Sturminster Newton **28** 50 56N 2 18W
Stúrovo **53** 47 48N 18 41 E
Sturt Cr. **136** 19 0 S 128 15 E
Sturt Creek **136** 19 0 S 128 15 E
Sturt, R. **136** 34 58 S 138 31 E
Sturton **33** 53 22N 0 39W
Sturts Meadows **140** 31 18 S 141 42 E
Stutterheim **128** 32 33 S 27 28 E
Stuttgart, Ger. **49** 48 46N 9 10 E
Stuttgart, U.S.A. **159** 34 30N 91 33W
Stuyvesant **162** 42 23N 73 45W
Stykkishólmur **74** 65 2N 22 40W
Styr, R. **80** 51 4N 25 20 E
Styria = Steiermark **52** 47 26N 15 0 E
Su-no-Saki **111** 34 58N 139 45 E
Suakin **122** 19 0N 37 20 E
Suan **107** 38 42N 126 22 E
Suaqui **164** 29 12N 109 41W
Suay Rieng **101** 11 9N 105 45 E
Subang **103** 7 30 S 107 45 E
Subansiri, R. **98** 26 48N 93 50 E
Subi **101** 2 55N 108 50 E
Subi, I. **102** 2 58N 108 50 E
Subiaco **63** 41 56N 13 5 E
Subotica **66** 46 6N 19 29 E
Success **153** 50 28N 108 6W
Suceava **70** 47 38N 26 16 E
Suceava □ **70** 47 37N 26 18 E
Suceava, R. **70** 47 38N 26 16 E
Sucha-Beskidzka **54** 49 44N 19 35 E
Suchan **54** 53 18N 15 18 E
Suchedniów **54** 51 3N 20 49 E
Such'i **109** 21 23N 110 16 E
Suchien **107** 33 58N 118 17 E
Suchil **164** 23 38N 103 55W
Suchitoto **166** 13 56N 89 0W
Suchou **109** 31 15N 120 40 E
Süchow = Hsüchou **107** 34 15N 117 10 E
Suchowola **54** 53 33N 23 3 E
Sucio, R. **174** 6 40N 77 0W
Suck, R. **39** 53 17N 8 10W
Suckling, Mt. **135** 9 43 S 148 59 E
Sucre, Boliv. **174** 19 0 S 65 15W
Sucre, Venez. **174** 10 25N 64 5W
Sucre □, Colomb. **174** 8 50N 75 40W
Sucre □, Venez. **174** 10 25N 63 30W
Súcueni **70** 47 20N 22 5 E
Sucunduri, R. **174** 6 20N 58 35W
SuCuraj **63** 43 10N 17 8 E
Sucuriju **170** 1 39N 49 57W
Sud-Ouest, Pte. du **151** 49 23N 63 36W
Sud, Pte. **151** 49 3N 62 14W
Suda, R. **81** 59 40N 36 30 E
Sudak **82** 44 51N 34 57 E
Sudan ■ **117** 15 0N 30 0 E
Sudan, The **114** 11 0N 9 0 E
Suday **81** 59 0N 43 15 E
Sudbury, Can. **150** 46 30N 81 0W
Sudbury, Derby, U.K. **33** 52 53N 1 43W
Sudbury, Suffolk, U.K. **29** 52 2N 0 44 E
Sûdd **123** 8 20N 29 30 E
Süderbrarup **48** 54 38N 9 47 E
Süderlügum **48** 54 50N 8 46 E
Sudetan Mts. = Sudety **53** 50 20N 16 45 E
Sudety **53** 50 20N 16 45 E
Sudi **127** 10 11 S 39 57 E
Sudirman, Pengunungan **103** 4 30N 137 0 E
Suditi **70** 44 35N 27 38 E
Sudogda **81** 55 55N 40 50 E
Sudr **122** 29 40N 32 42 E
Sudzha **80** 51 14N 34 25 E
Sueca **59** 39 12N 0 21W
Sueur, Le **158** 44 25N 93 52W
Suez = Suweis **122** 28 40N 33 0 E
Suf **90** 32 19N 35 49 E
Sufaina **92** 23 6N 40 44 E
Suffield **153** 50 12N 111 10W
Suffolk **156** 36 47N 76 33W
Suffolk □ **29** 52 16N 1 0 E
Suffolk, East, □ **29** 52 16N 1 10 E
Suffolk, West, □ **29** 52 16N 0 45 E
Sufi-Kurgan **85** 40 2N 73 30 E
Sufuk **93** 23 50N 51 50 E
Suga no-Sen **110** 35 25N 134 25 E
Sugag **70** 45 47N 23 37 E
Sugar City **158** 38 18N 103 38W
Sugarloaf Pt. **126** 32 22 S 152 30 E
Sugluk = Sagloue **149** 62 10N 75 40W
Sugny **47** 49 49N 4 54 E
Suhaia, L. **70** 43 45N 25 15 E
Suhãr **93** 24 20N 56 40 E
Suhbaatar **105** 46 54N 113 25 E
Suhl **48** 50 35N 10 40 E
Suhl □ **48** 50 37N 10 43 E
Suhr **50** 47 22N 8 5 E
Suhsien **106** 33 40N 117 0 E
Suhum **121** 6 5N 0 27W
Suian **109** 29 28N 118 44 E
Suica **66** 43 52N 17 11 E
Suich'ang **109** 28 36N 119 16 E
Suichiang **108** 28 40N 103 58 E
Suifenho **107** 44 30N 131 2 E
Suihsien **109** 31 41N 113 20 E
Suihua **98** 46 37N 127 0 E
Suilu **108** 22 20N 107 48 E
Suining, Hunan, China **108** 26 21N 110 0 E
Suining, Kiangsu, China **107** 33 54N 117 56 E
Suining, Szechwan, China **108** 30 31N 105 34 E
Suippes **43** 49 8N 4 30 E
Suir, R. **39** 52 31N 7 59W
Suita **111** 34 45N 135 32 E
Suiteh **106** 37 35N 110 5 E
Suiyang, Heilungkiang, China **107** 44 26N 130 51 E
Suiyang, Kweichow, China **108** 27 57N 107 11 E
Sujangarh **94** 27 42N 47 31 E
Sukabumi **103** 6 56 S 106 57 E
Sukadana **102** 1 10 S 110 0 E
Sukandja **102** 2 28 S 110 25 E
Sukarnapura = Jajapura **103** 2 28N 140 38 E
Sukarno, G. = Jaja, Puncak **103** 3 57 S 137 17 E
Sukchŏn **107** 39 22N 125 35 E
Sukhinichi **80** 54 8N 35 10 E
Sukhona, R. **78** 60 30N 45 0 E
Sukhothai **100** 17 1N 99 49 E
Sukhoy Log **84** 56 55N 62 1 E
Sukhumi **83** 43 0N 41 0 E
Sukkur **94** 27 50N 68 46 E

Sukkur Barrage
Sydra, G. of

Sukkur Barrage 93 27 50N 68 45 E
Sukma 96 18 24N 81 37 E
Sukovo 66 43 4N 22 37 E
Sukumo 110 32 56N 132 44 E
Sukunka, R. 152 55 45N 121 15W
Sul, Canal do 170 0 10 S 48 30W
Sula, Kepulauan 103 1 45 S 125 0 E
Sula, R. 80 50 0N 33 0 E
Sulaco, R. 166 15 2N 87 44W
Sulaiman Range 94 30 30N 69 50 E
Sulaimanke Headworks 94 30 27N 73 55 E
Sülaj □ 70 47 15N 23 0 E
Sulak, R. 83 43 20N 47 20 E
Sulam Tsor 90 33 4N 35 6 E
Sulawesi □ 103 2 0 S 120 0 E
Sulawesi, I. 103 2 0 S 120 0 E
Sulby 32 54 18N 4 29W
Sulechów 54 52 5N 15 40 E
Sulecin 54 52 26N 15 10 E
Sulejów 54 51 26N 19 53 E
Sulejówek 54 52 13N 21 17 E
Sulgen 51 47 33N 9 7 E
Sulima 120 6 58N 11 32W
Sulina 70 45 10N 29 40 E
Sulingen 48 52 41N 8 47 E
Sülişte 70 45 45N 23 56 E
Suliţa 70 47 39N 20 59 E
Sulitälma 74 67 17N 17 28 E
Sulitjelma 74 61 7N 16 8 E
Sułkowice 54 49 50N 19 49 E
Sullana 174 5 0 S 80 45W
Sullivan, Ill., U.S.A. 158 39 40N 88 40W
Sullivan, Ind., U.S.A. 156 39 5N 87 26W
Sullivan, Mo., U.S.A. 158 38 10N 91 10W
Sullivan Bay 152 50 55N 126 50W
Sullom Voe 36 60 30N 1 20W
Sully-sur-Loire 43 47 45N 2 20 E
Sulmierzyce 57 51 36N 17 30 E
Sulmona 63 42 3N 13 55 E
Sulo 105 39 25N 76 6 E
Sulphur, La., U.S.A. 159 30 20N 93 22W
Sulphur, Okla., U.S.A. 159 34 35N 97 0W
Sulphur Pt. 152 60 56N 114 48W
Sulphur Springs 159 33 5N 95 30W
Sulphur Springs, Cr. 159 32 50N 102 8W
Sultan 150 47 36N 82 47W
Sultanpur 95 26 18N 82 10 E
Sulu Arch. 103 6 0N 121 0 E
Sulu Sea 103 8 0N 120 0 E
Sululta 123 9 10N 38 43 E
Sulung Shan 108 31 30N 99 30 E
Suluq 119 31 44N 20 14 E
Sulyukta 85 39 56N 69 34 E
Sulzbach-Rosenburg 49 49 30N 11 46 E
Sumalata 103 1 0N 122 37 E
Sumampa 172 29 25 S 63 29W
Sumatera, I. 102 0 40N 100 20 E
Sumatera Selatan □ 102 3 30 S 104 0 E
Sumatera Tengah □ 102 1 0 S 100 0 E
Sumatera Utara □ 102 2 0N 99 0 E
Sumatra 160 46 45N 107 37W
Sumatra = Sumatera 102 0 40N 100 20 E
Sumba, I. 103 9 45 S 119 35 E
Sumba, Selat 103 9 0 S 118 40 E
Sumbawa 102 8 26 S 117 30 E
Sumbawa, I. 103 8 34 S 117 17 E
Sumbawanga □ 126 8 0 S 31 30 E
Sumbing, mt. 103 7 19 S 110 3 E
Sumburgh Hd. 36 59 52N 1 17W
Sumdo 95 35 6N 79 43 E
Sumé 170 7 39 S 36 55W
Sumedang 103 6 49 S 107 56 E
Sümeg 53 46 59N 17 20 E
Sumenep 103 7 3 S 113 51 E
Sumgait 83 40 34N 49 10 E
Sumisu-Jima 111 31 27N 140 3 E
Sumiswald 50 47 2N 7 44 E
Summer Is. 36 58 0N 5 27W
Summer L. 160 42 50N 120 50W
Summerhill 38 53 30N 6 44W
Summerland 152 49 32N 119 41W
Summerside 151 46 24N 63 47W
Summerville, Ga., U.S.A. 157 34 30N 85 20W
Summerville, S.C., U.S.A. 157 33 2N 80 11W
Summit, Can. 150 47 50N 72 20W
Summit, U.S.A. 147 63 20N 149 20W
Summit L. 152 54 20N 122 40W
Summit Pk. 161 37 20N 106 48W
Sumner, N.Z. 143 43 35 S 172 48 E
Sumner, U.S.A. 158 42 49N 92 7W
Sumner L. 143 42 42 S 172 15 E
Sumoto 110 34 21N 134 54 E
Sumperk 53 49 59N 17 0 E
Sumprabum 98 26 33N 97 4 E
Sumter 157 33 55N 80 10W
Sumy 80 50 57N 34 50 E
Sun City 163 33 41N 117 11W
Suna 126 5 23 S 34 48 E
Sunan 107 39 15N 125 40 E
Sunart, dist. 36 56 40N 5 40W
Sunart, L. 36 56 42N 5 43W
Sunburst 160 48 56N 111 59W
Sunbury, Austral. 141 37 35 S 144 44 E
Sunbury, U.S.A. 162 40 50N 76 46W
Sunchales 172 30 58 S 61 35W
Suncho Corral 172 27 55 S 63 14W
Sunchŏn 107 34 52N 127 31 E
Suncook 162 43 8N 71 27W
Sund 71 60 13N 5 10 E
Sunda Ketjil, Kepulauan 102 7 30 S 117 0 E
Sunda, Selat 102 6 20 S 105 30 E
Sundalsöra 71 62 40N 8 36 E
Sundance 158 44 27N 104 27W
Sundarbans, The 98 22 0N 89 0 E
Sundargarh 96 22 10N 84 5 E
Sunday Str. 136 16 25 S 123 18 E
Sundays, R. 128 32 10 S 24 40 E
Sundby 73 56 53N 8 40 E
Sundbyberg 72 59 22N 17 58 E
Sunderland, U.K. 35 54 54N 1 22W
Sunderland, U.S.A. 162 42 27N 72 36W
Sundre 152 51 49N 114 38W
Sundridge, Can. 150 45 45N 79 25W
Sundridge, U.K. 29 51 15N 0 10 E
Sunds 73 56 13N 9 1 E
Sundsjö 72 62 59N 15 9 E
Sundsvall 72 62 23N 17 17 E
Sung Hei 101 10 20N 106 2 E
Sungaipakning 102 1 19N 102 0 E
Sungaipenuh 102 2 1 S 101 20 E
Sungaitiram 102 0 45 S 117 8 E
Sungari, R. = Sunghua Chiang 107 44 30N 126 20 E
Sungch'i 109 27 2N 118 19 E
Sungchiang 109 31 2N 121 14 E
Sungei Lembing 101 2 53N 103 4 E
Sungei Patani 101 5 38N 100 29 E
Sungei Siput 101 4 51N 101 6 E
Sungfou 109 31 5N 114 42 E
Sungguminasa 103 5 17 S 119 30 E
Sunghsien 106 34 10N 112 10 E
Sunghua Chiang, R. 105 47 42N 132 30 E
Sungikai 123 12 20N 29 51 E
Sungk'an 108 28 33N 106 52 E
Sungming 108 25 22N 103 2 E
Sungpan 105 32 50N 103 20 E
Sungp'an 108 32 36N 103 36 E
Sungt'ao 108 28 12N 109 12 E
Sungtzu Hu 109 30 10N 111 45 E
Sungü 129 21 18 S 32 28 E
Sungurlu 82 40 12N 34 21 E
Sungyang 109 28 16N 119 29 E
Sunja 63 45 21N 16 35 E
Sunk Island 33 53 38N 0 7W
Sunkar, Gora 85 44 15N 73 50 E
Sunnäsbruk 72 61 10N 7 12 E
Sunne, Jamtland, Sweden 72 63 7N 14 25 E
Sunne, Varmland, Sweden 72 59 52N 13 12 E
Sunnfjord 71 61 25N 5 18 E
Sunnhordland 71 59 50N 5 30 E
Sunninghill 29 51 25N 0 40W
Sunnmöre 71 62 15N 6 30 E
Sunnyside, Utah, U.S.A. 160 39 40N 110 24W
Sunnyside, Wash., U.S.A. 160 46 24N 120 2W
Sunnyvale 163 37 23N 122 2W
Sunray 159 36 1N 101 47W
Sunshine 141 37 48 S 144 52 E
Sunson 121 9 35N 0 2W
Suntar 77 62 15N 117 30 E
Sunyani 120 7 21N 2 22W
Suō-Nada 110 33 50N 131 30 E
Suolahti 74 62 34N 25 52 E
Suonenjoki 74 62 37N 27 7 E
Supai 161 36 14N 112 44W
Supaul 95 26 10N 86 40 E
Supe 123 8 34N 35 35 E
Superior, Ariz., U.S.A. 161 33 19N 111 9W
Superior, Mont., U.S.A. 160 47 15N 114 57W
Superior, Nebr., U.S.A. 158 40 3N 98 2W
Superior, Wis., U.S.A. 158 46 45N 92 0W
Superior, L. 155 47 40N 87 0W
Supetar 63 43 25N 16 32 E
Suphan Buri 100 14 30N 100 10 E
Suprasśl 54 53 13N 23 19 E
Suq al Jumah 119 32 58N 13 12 E
Sūr, Leb. 90 33 19N 35 16 E
Sūr, Oman 93 22 34N 59 32 E
Sur, Pt. 163 36 18N 121 54W
Sura, R. 81 55 30N 46 20 E
Surab 94 28 25N 66 15 E
Surabaja = Surabaya 103 7 17 S 112 45 E
Surabaya 103 7 17 S 112 45 E
Surahammar 72 59 43N 16 13 E
Suraia 70 45 40N 27 25 E
Surakarta 103 7 35 S 110 48 E
Surakhany 83 40 13N 50 1 E
Surandai 97 8 58N 77 26 E
Surany 53 48 6N 18 10 E
Surat, Austral. 139 27 10 S 149 6 E
Surat, India 96 21 12N 72 55 E
Surat, Khalīj 119 31 40N 18 30 E
Surat Thani 101 9 6N 99 14 E
Suratgarh 94 29 18N 73 55 E
Surazh 80 53 5N 32 27 E
Surduc 70 47 15N 23 25 E
Surduc Pasul 70 45 21N 23 23 E
Surdulica 66 42 41N 22 11 E
Sûre, R. 47 49 51N 6 6 E
Surendranagar 94 22 45N 71 40 E
Surf 163 34 41N 120 36W
Surf Inlet 152 53 8N 128 50W
Surgères 44 46 7N 0 47W
Surhuisterveen 46 53 11N 6 10 E
Suri 95 23 50N 87 34 E
Surianu, mt. 70 45 33N 23 31 E
Suriapet 96 17 10N 79 40 E
Surif 90 31 40N 35 4 E
Surin 100 14 50N 103 34 E
Surin Nua, Ko 101 9 30N 97 55 E
Surinam ■ 175 4 0N 56 15W
Suriname, R. 170 4 30N 55 30W
Surkhandarya, R. 85 37 12N 67 20 E
Sŭrmasu 70 46 45N 25 13 E
Sürmene 83 41 0N 40 1 E
Surovikino 83 48 32N 42 55 E
Surprise L. 152 59 40N 133 15W
Surrey □ 29 51 16N 0 30W
Surry 162 37 8N 76 50W
Sursee 50 47 11N 8 6 E
Sursk 81 53 3N 45 40W
Surt 119 31 11N 16 46 E
Surt, Al Hammādah al 119 30 0N 17 50 E
Surtsey 74 63 20N 20 30W
Surubim 170 7 50 S 35 45W
Suruga-Wan 111 34 45N 138 30 E
Surup 103 6 27N 126 17 E
Surur 93 23 20N 58 10 E
Susa 62 45 8N 7 3 E
Susaa, R. 73 55 20N 11 42 E
Sušac, I. 63 42 46N 16 30 E
Susak, I. 63 44 30N 14 28 E
Susaki 110 33 22N 133 17 E
Susamyr 85 42 12N 73 58 E
Susamyrtau, Khrebet 85 42 8N 73 15 E
Susangerd 92 31 35N 48 20 E
Susanino 77 52 50N 140 14 E
Susanville 160 40 28N 120 40W
Susch 51 46 46N 10 5 E
Sušice 52 49 17N 13 30 E
Susquehanna Depot 162 41 55N 75 36W
Susquehanna, R. 156 41 50N 76 20W
Susques 172 23 35 S 66 25W
Sussex, Can. 151 45 45N 65 37W
Sussex, U.S.A. 162 41 12N 74 38W
Sussex (□) 26 50 55N 0 20W
Sussex, E. □ 29 51 0N 0 0 E
Sussex, W. □ 29 51 0N 0 30W
Susten Pass 51 46 43N 8 26 E
Susteren 47 51 4N 5 51 E
Sustut, R. 152 56 20N 127 30W
Susuman 77 62 47N 148 10 E
Susuna 103 3 20 S 133 25 E
Susung 109 30 9N 116 6 E
Susz 54 53 44N 19 20 E
Suţeşti 70 45 13N 27 27 E
Sutherland, Austral. 141 34 2 S 151 4 E
Sutherland, Can. 153 52 15N 106 40W
Sutherland, S. Afr. 125 32 33 S 20 40 E
Sutherland, U.S.A. 158 41 12N 101 11W
Sutherland (□) 26 58 10N 4 30W
Sutherland Falls 143 44 48 S 167 46 E
Sutherland Pt. 133 28 15 S 153 35 E
Sutherland Ra. 137 25 42 S 125 21 E
Sutherlin 160 43 28N 123 16W
Sutivan 63 43 23N 16 30 E
Sutlej, R. 94 30 0N 73 0 E
Sutter Creek 163 38 24N 120 48W
Sutterton 33 52 54N 0 8W
Sutton, N.Z. 143 45 34 S 170 8 E
Sutton, U.K. 29 51 22N 0 13W
Sutton, U.S.A. 158 40 40N 97 50W
Sutton Bridge 29 52 46N 0 12 E
Sutton Coldfield 28 52 33N 1 50W
Sutton Courtenay 28 51 39N 1 16W
Sutton-in-Ashfield 33 52 8N 1 16W
Sutton-on-Sea 33 53 18N 0 18 E
Sutton, R. 150 55 15N 83 45W
Sutton Scotney 28 51 9N 1 20W
Suttor, R. 138 20 36 S 147 2 E
Sutwik I. 147 56 35N 157 10W
Suva 143 17 40 S 178 8 E
Suva Gora 66 41 45N 21 3 E
Suva Planina 66 43 10N 22 5 E
Suva Reka 66 42 21N 20 50 E
Suvarov Is. 131 13 15 S 163 30W
Suvo Rudište 66 43 17N 20 49 E
Suvorovo 67 43 20N 27 35 E
Suwa 111 36 2N 138 8 E
Suwa-Ko 111 36 3N 138 5 E
Suwałki 54 54 8N 22 59 E
Suwałki □ 54 54 0N 22 30 E
Suwannaphum 100 15 33N 105 47 E
Suwannee, R. 157 30 0N 83 0W
Suwanose-Jima 112 29 38N 129 38 E
Suweis, El 122 29 58N 32 31 E
Suweis, Khalîg es 122 28 40N 33 0 E
Suweis, Qanâl es 122 31 0N 32 20 E
Suwŏn 107 37 17N 127 1 E
Suykbulak 84 50 25N 62 33 E
Suzak 85 44 9N 68 27 E
Suzaka 111 36 39N 138 19 E
Sŭzava, R. 52 49 50N 15 0 E
Suzdal 81 56 29N 40 26 E
Suze, La 42 47 54N 0 2 E
Suzuka 111 34 55N 136 36 E
Suzuka-Sam 111 35 5N 136 30 E
Suzzara 62 45 0N 10 45 E
Svalbard, Arctica 12 78 0N 17 0 E
Svalbard, Iceland 74 66 12N 15 43W
Svalöv 73 55 57N 13 8 E
Svanå 72 59 46N 15 23 E
Svanvik 74 69 38N 30 3 E
Svappavaari 74 67 40N 21 03 E
Svarstad 71 59 27N 9 56 E
Svartisen 74 66 40N 14 16 E
Svartvik 72 62 19N 17 24 E
Svatovo 82 49 35N 38 5 E
Svay Chek 100 13 48N 102 58 E
Svay Rieng 101 11 5N 105 48 E
Svealand □ 75 59 55N 15 0 E
Svedala 73 55 30N 13 15 E
Sveg 72 62 2N 14 21 E
Sveio 71 59 33N 5 23 E
Svelvik 71 59 37N 10 24 E
Svendborg 73 55 4N 10 35 E
Svene 71 59 45N 9 31 E
Svenljunga 73 57 29N 13 29 E
Svensbro 73 58 15N 13 52 E
Svenstavik 72 62 45N 14 26 E
Svenstrup 73 56 58N 9 50 E
Sverdlovsk 84 56 50N 60 30 E
Sverdrup Is. 12 79 0N 97 0W
Svetac 63 43 3N 15 43 E
Sveti Ivan Zelina 63 45 57N 16 16 E
Sveti Jurij 63 46 14N 15 24 E
Sveti Lenart 63 46 36N 15 48 E
Sveti Nikola 66 41 51N 21 56 E
Sveti Trojica 63 46 37N 15 33 E
Svetlogorsk 80 52 38N 29 46 E
Svetlograd 83 45 25N 42 58 E
Svetlovodsk 80 49 2N 33 13 E
Svetlyy 84 50 48N 60 51 E
Svetozarevo 66 44 0N 21 15 E
Svidnik 53 49 20N 21 37 E
Svilaja Pl. 63 43 49N 16 31 E
Svilajnac 66 44 15N 21 11 E
Svilengrad 67 41 49N 26 12 E
Svinö 73 55 6N 11 44 E
Svir, R. 78 61 2N 34 50 E
Svishov 67 43 36N 25 23 E
Svisloch 80 53 26N 24 2 E
Svitavy 53 49 47N 16 28 E
Svobodnyy 77 51 20N 128 0 E
Svoge 67 42 59N 23 23 E
Svolvær 74 68 15N 14 34 E
Svratka, R. 53 49 27N 16 12 E
Svrljig 66 43 25N 22 6 E
Swa 98 19 15N 96 17 E
Swabian Alps 49 48 30N 9 30 E
Swadlincote 28 52 47N 1 34W
Swaffham 29 52 38N 0 42 E
Swain Reefs 138 21 45 S 152 20 E
Swainsboro 157 32 38N 82 22W
Swakopmund 128 22 37 S 14 30 E
Swale, R. 34 54 18N 1 20W
Swallowfield 29 51 23N 0 56W
Swalmen 47 51 13N 6 2 E
Swan Hill 140 35 20 S 143 33 E
Swan Hills 152 54 42N 115 24W
Swan Islands 166 17 22N 83 57W
Swan L. 153 52 30N 100 50W
Swan Pt. 136 16 22 S 123 1 E
Swan, R. 132 32 3 S 115 35 E
Swan Reach 140 34 35 S 139 37 E
Swan River 153 52 10N 101 16W
Swanage 28 50 36N 1 59W
Swanlinbar 38 54 11N 7 42W
Swansea, Austral. 141 33 3 S 151 35 E
Swansea, U.K. 31 51 37N 3 57W
Swansea Bay 31 51 34N 3 55W
Swar, R. 95 35 15N 72 24 E
Swartberg 128 30 15 S 29 23 E
Swartberge 128 33 20 S 22 0 E
Swarte Bank, gasfield 19 53 27N 2 10 E
Swartruggens 128 25 39 S 26 42 E
Swarzedz 54 52 25N 17 4 E
Swastika 150 48 7N 80 6W
Swatow = Shant'ou 109 23 28N 116 40 E
Swatragh 38 54 55N 6 40W
Swaziland ■ 129 26 30 S 31 30 E
Sweden ■ 74 67 0N 15 0 E
Swedru 121 5 32N 0 41W
Sweet Home 160 44 26N 122 38W
Sweetwater, Nev., U.S.A. 163 38 27N 119 9W
Sweetwater, Tex., U.S.A. 159 32 30N 100 28W
Sweetwater, R. 160 42 31N 107 30W
Swellendam 128 34 1 S 20 26 E
Świdin 54 53 47N 15 49 E
Swidnica 54 50 50N 16 30 E
Świdnik 54 51 13N 22 39 E
Świebodzice 54 50 51N 16 20 E
Swiebodzin 54 52 15N 15 37 E
Swiecie 54 53 25N 18 30 E
Swietorkrzyskie, Góry 54 51 0N 20 30 E
Swift Current 153 50 20N 107 45W
Swiftcurrent Cr. 153 50 38N 107 44W
Swilly L. 38 55 12N 7 35W
Swilly, R. 38 54 56N 7 50W
Swindle, I. 152 52 30N 128 35W
Swindon 28 51 33N 1 47W
Swinemünde = Świnoujście 54 53 54N 14 16 E
Swineshead 33 57 57N 0 9W
Swinford 38 53 57N 8 57W
Świnoujście 54 53 54N 14 16 E
Swinton, Borders, U.K. 35 55 43N 2 14W
Swinton, Gr. Manch., U.K. 32 53 31N 2 21W
Swinton, S. Yorks., U.K. 33 53 28N 1 20W
Switzerland ■ 49 46 30N 8 0 E
Swona, I. 37 58 30N 3 3W
Swords 38 53 27N 6 15W
Syasstroy 80 60 5N 32 15 E
Sybil Pt. 39 52 12N 10 28W
Sychevka 80 55 45N 34 10 E
Syców 54 51 19N 17 40 E
Sydney, Austral. 141 33 53 S 151 10 E
Sydney, Can. 151 46 7N 60 7W
Sydney, U.S.A. 158 41 12N 103 0W
Sydney Mines 151 46 18N 60 15W
Sydproven 12 60 30N 45 35W
Sydra, G. of = Surt 61 31 40N 18 30 E

Syke Tambelan, Kepulauan

Syke 48 52 55N 8 50 E
Syktyvkar 78 61 45N 50 40 E
Sylacauga 157 33 10N 86 15W
Sylarna, Mt. 72 63 2N 12 11 E
Sylhet 98 24 54N 91 52 E
Sylt, I. 48 54 50N 8 20 E
Sylva, R. 84 58 0N 56 54 E
Sylvan Beach 162 43 12N 75 44W
Sylvan Lake 152 52 20N 114 10W
Sylvania 157 32 45N 81 37W
Sylvester 157 31 31N 83 50W
Sym 76 60 20N 87 50 E
Symington 35 55 35N 3 36W
Symón 164 24 42N 102 35W
Symonds Yat 28 51 50N 2 38W
Synnott Ra. 136 16 30 S 125 20 E
Syr Darya 76 45 0N 65 0 E
Syracuse, Kans., U.S.A. 159 38 0N 101 40W
Syracuse, N.Y., U.S.A. 162 43 4N 76 11W
Syrdarya 85 40 50N 68 40 E
Syria ■ 92 35 0N 38 0 E
Syriam 98 16 44N 96 19 E
Syrian Des. 92 31 30N 40 0 E
Sysert 84 56 29N 60 49 E
Syston 28 52 42N 1 5W
Syuldzhyukyor 77 63 25N 113 40 E
Syutkya, mt. 67 41 50N 24 16 E
Syzran 81 53 12N 48 30 E
Szabolcs-Szatmár □ 53 48 2N 21 45 E
Szamocin 54 53 2N 17 7 E
Szamotuły 54 52 35N 16 34 E
Szaraz, R. 53 46 28N 20 44 E
Szazhalombatta 53 47 20N 18 58 E
Szczara, R. 53 53 15N 25 10 E
Szczebrzeszyn 54 50 42N 22 59 E
Szczecin 54 53 27N 14 27 E
Szczecin □ 54 53 25N 14 32 E
Szczecinek 54 53 43N 16 41 E
Szczekocimy 54 50 38N 19 48 E
Szczrk 53 49 42N 19 1 E
Szczuczyn 54 53 36N 22 19 E
Szczytno 54 53 33N 21 0 E
Szechwan □ 109 30 15N 103 15 E
Szécsény 53 48 7N 19 30 E
Szeged 53 46 16N 20 10 E
Szeghalom 53 47 1N 21 10 E
Székesfehérvár 53 47 15N 18 25 E
Szekszárd 53 46 22N 18 42 E
Szendrö 53 48 24N 20 41 E
Szentendre 53 47 39N 19 4 E
Szentes 53 46 39N 20 21 E
Szentgotthárd 53 46 58N 16 19 E
Szentlörinc 53 46 3N 18 1 E
Szerencs 53 48 10N 21 12 E
Szeshui 33 34 50N 113 20 E
Szigetvár 53 46 3N 17 46 E
Szlichtyogowa 54 51 42N 16 15 E
Szob 53 47 48N 18 53 E
Szolnok 53 47 10N 20 15 E
Szolnok □ 53 47 15N 20 30 E
Szombathely 53 47 14N 16 38 E
Szprotawa 54 51 33N 15 35 E
Sztum 54 53 55N 19 1 E
Sztuto 54 54 20N 19 15 E
Sztutowo 54 54 20N 19 15 E
Szûrvas 53 46 50N 20 38 E
Szydłowiec 54 51 15N 20 51 E
Szypliszki 54 54 17N 23 2 E

T

't Harde 46 52 24N 5 54 E
't Zandt 46 53 22N 6 46 E
Ta-erh Po, L. 106 43 15N 116 35 E
Ta Khli Khok 100 15 18N 100 20 E
Ta Lai 101 11 24N 107 23 E
Taalintehdas 74 60 2N 22 30 E
Taan 107 45 30N 124 18 E
Taavetti 75 60 56N 27 32 E
Taba 92 26 55N 42 30 E
Tabacal 172 23 15 S 64 15W
Tabaco 103 13 22N 123 44 E
Tabagné 120 7 59N 3 4W
Tabar Is. 135 2 50 S 152 0 E
Tabarca, Isla de 59 38 17N 0 30W
Tabarka 119 36 56N 8 46 E
Tabarra 59 38 37N 1 44 E
Tabas, Khorasan, Iran 93 33 35N 56 55 E
Tabas, Khorasan, Iran 93 32 48N 60 12 E
Tabasará, Serranía de 166 8 35N 81 40W
Tabasco □ 165 17 45N 93 30W
Tabatinga 174 4 11 S 69 58W
Tabatinga, Serra da 170 10 30 S 44 0W
Tabayin 98 22 42N 95 20 E
Tabelbala, Kahal de 118 28 47N 2 0W
Taber 152 49 47N 112 8W
Taberg 162 43 18N 75 37W
Tabernas 59 37 4N 2 26W
Tabernas de Valldigna 59 39 5N 0 13W
Tabigha 90 32 53N 35 33 E
Tabira 170 7 35 S 37 33W
Tablas, I. 103 12 25N 122 2 E
Table B. 151 53 40N 56 25W
Table Mt. 128 34 0 S 18 22 E
Table Top, Mt. 138 23 24 S 147 11 E
Tableland 136 17 16 S 126 51 E
Tabletop, mt. 137 22 32 S 123 50 E
Tábor 52 49 25N 14 39 E
Tabor 90 32 42N 35 24 E
Tabora 126 5 2 S 32 57 E
Tabora □ 126 5 0 S 33 0 E
Tabory 84 58 31N 64 33 E
Tabou 120 4 30N 7 20W
Tabouda 118 34 44N 5 14W
Tabrīz 92 38 7N 46 20 E
Tabūk 92 28 30N 36 25 E
Täby 72 59 29N 18 4 E
Tacámbaro 164 19 14N 101 28W
Tacarigua, L. de 174 11 3N 68 25W
Tach'aitan 105 37 50N 95 18 E
T'ach'eng 105 46 45N 82 57 E
Tach'eng 106 38 35N 116 39 E
Tach'engtzu 107 41 44N 118 52 E
Tach'i 109 24 51N 121 14 E
Tachia 109 24 25N 120 28 E
Tachiai 108 23 44N 103 57 E
Tachibana-Wan 110 32 45N 130 7 E
Tachikawa 111 35 42N 139 25 E
Tach'in Ch'uan, R. 108 31 57N 102 11 E
Tach'ing Shan, mts. 106 40 50N 111 0 E
Tachira 174 8 7N 72 21W
Tachira □ 174 8 7N 72 15W
Tachov 52 49 47N 12 39 E
Tachu 108 30 45N 107 13 E
Tacina, R. 65 39 5N 16 51 E
Tacloban 103 11 15N 124 58 E
Tacna 174 18 0 S 70 20W
Tacoma 160 47 15N 122 30W
Tacuarembó 173 31 45 S 56 0W
Tacumshin L. 39 52 12N 6 28W
Tadcaster 33 53 53N 1 16W
Tademaït, Plateau du 118 28 30N 2 30 E
Tadent, O. 119 22 30N 7 0 E
Tadjerdjert, O. 119 26 0N 8 0W
Tadjerouna 118 33 31N 2 3 E
Tadjettaret, O. 119 22 0N 7 30W
Tadjmout, O. 118 25 37N 3 48 E
Tadjoura 123 11 50N 42 55 E
Tadjoura, Golfe de 123 11 50N 43 0 E
Tadley 28 51 21N 1 8W
Tadmor, N.Z. 143 41 27 S 172 45 E
Tadmor, Syria 92 34 30N 37 55 E
Tado 174 5 16N 76 32W
Tadotsu 110 34 16N 133 45 E
Tadoule L 153 58 36N 98 20W
Tadoussac 151 48 11N 69 42W
Tadzhik S.S.R. □ 85 35 30N 70 0 E
Taechŏnni 107 36 21N 126 36 E
Taegu 107 35 50N 128 37 E
Taegwandong 107 40 13N 125 12 E
Taejŏn 107 36 20N 127 28 E
Taerhhanmaoming-anlienhoch'i 106 41 50N 110 27 E
Taerhting 105 37 15N 92 36 E
Taf, R. 31 51 55N 4 36W
Tafalla 58 42 30N 1 41W
Tafang 108 27 10N 105 39 E
Tafar 123 6 52N 28 15 E
Tafas 90 32 44N 36 5 E
Tafassasset, O. 119 23 0N 9 11 E
Tafelbaai 128 33 35 S 18 25 E
Tafelney, C. 118 31 3N 9 51W
Tafermaar 103 6 47 S 134 10 E
Tafi Viejo 172 26 43 S 65 17W
Tafiré 120 9 4N 5 10W
Tafnidilt 118 28 47N 10 58W
Tafraout 118 29 50N 8 58W
Taft, Phil. 103 11 57N 125 30 E
Taft, Ala., U.S.A. 163 35 10N 119 28W
Taft, Tex., U.S.A. 159 27 58N 97 23W
Taga Dzong 98 27 5N 90 0 E
Taganrog 83 47 12N 38 50 E
Taganrogskiy Zaliv 82 47 0N 38 30 E
Tagant 120 18 20N 11 0W
Tagap Ga 98 26 56N 96 13 E
Tagbilaran 103 9 39N 123 51 E
Tage 135 6 19 S 143 20 E
Tággia 62 43 52N 7 50 E
Taghmon 39 52 19N 6 40W
Taghrīfat 119 29 5N 17 26 E
Taghzout 118 33 30N 4 49W
Tagish 152 60 19N 134 16W
Tagish L. 147 60 10N 134 20W
Tagliacozzo 63 42 4N 13 13 E
Tagliamento, R. 63 45 38N 13 5 E
Táglio di Po 63 45 0N 12 12 E
Tagomago, Isla de 59 39 2N 1 39 E
Tagua, La 174 0 3N 74 40W
Taguatinga 171 12 26 S 46 26W
Tagula 135 11 22 S 153 15 E
Tagula I. 135 11 30 S 153 30 E
Tagum (Hijo) 103 7 33N 125 53 E
Tagus = Tajo, R. 55 39 44N 5 50W
Tahahbala, I. 102 0 30 S 98 30 E
Tahakopa 143 46 30 S 169 23 E
Tahala 118 34 0N 4 28W
Tahan, Gunong 101 4 45N 102 25 E
Tahara 111 34 40N 137 16 E
Tahat Mt. 119 23 18N 5 21 E
Tāherī 93 27 43N 52 20 E
Tahiti, I. 131 17 37 S 149 27W
Tahoe 160 39 12N 120 9W
Tahoe, L. 160 39 0N 120 9W
Tahora 142 39 2 S 174 49 E
Tahoua 121 14 57N 5 16 E
Tahsien 108 31 17N 107 30 E
Tahsin 108 22 48N 107 23 E
Tahsinganling Shanmo 105 49 0N 122 0 E
Tahsingkou 107 43 23N 129 39 E
Tahsintien 107 37 37N 120 50 E
Tahsüeh Shan, mts. 108 31 15N 101 20 E
Tahta 122 26 44N 31 32 E
Tahulandang, I. 103 2 27N 125 23 E
Tahuna 103 3 45N 125 30 E
Tahung Shan, mts. 109 31 30N 112 50 E
Tai 108 30 41N 103 29 E
Taï 120 5 55N 7 30W
T'ai Hu 105 31 10N 120 0 E
Tai Shan 109 30 17N 122 10 E
T'aian 107 36 12N 117 7 E
T'aichiang 108 26 40N 108 19 E
T'aichou 109 32 22N 119 45 E
T'aichou Liehtao 109 28 30N 121 53 E
T'aichung 105 24 9N 120 37 E
T'aichunghsien 109 24 15N 120 35 E
Taieri, R. 143 46 3 S 170 12 E
Taiga Madema 119 23 46N 15 25 E
T'aihang Shan, mts. 106 35 40N 113 20 E
Taihape 142 39 41 S 175 48 E
T'aiho, Anhwei, China 109 33 10N 115 36 E
T'aiho, Kiangsi, China 109 26 50N 114 53 E
T'aihsien 109 32 17N 120 10 E
T'aihsing 109 32 10N 120 4 E
Taihu 109 30 30N 116 25 E
T'aik'ang 106 34 4N 114 52 E
Taikkyi 98 17 20N 96 0 E
T'aiku 106 37 23N 112 34 E
Tailem Bend 140 35 12 S 139 29 E
Tailfingen 49 48 15N 9 1 E
Taïma 92 27 35N 38 45 E
Taimyr = Taymyr 77 75 0N 100 0 E
Taimyr, Oz. 77 74 20N 102 0 E
Tain 37 57 49N 4 4W
T'ainan 109 23 0N 120 10 E
T'ainanhsien 109 23 21N 120 17 E
Tainaron, Akra 69 36 22N 22 27 E
Tainggya 98 17 49N 94 29 E
T'aining 109 26 55N 117 12 E
Taintignies 47 50 33N 3 22 E
Taiobeiras 171 15 49 S 42 14W
T'aipei 109 25 2N 121 30 E
T'aip'ing 109 30 18N 118 6 E
Taiping 101 4 51N 100 44 E
Taipu 170 5 37 S 35 36W
T'aip'ussuchi 106 41 55N 115 23 E
Taisha 110 35 24N 132 40 E
T'aishan 109 22 17N 112 43 E
Taishun 109 27 33N 119 43 E
Taita □ 126 4 0 S 38 30 E
Taita Hills 126 3 25 S 38 15 E
Taitao, Pen. de 176 46 30 S 75 0W
T'aitung 105 22 43N 121 4 E
Taivalkoski 74 65 33N 28 12 E
Taiwan (Formosa) ■ 109 23 30N 121 0 E
Taiwara 93 33 30N 64 24 E
Taïyetos Óros 69 37 0N 22 23 E
Taiyiba, Israel 90 32 36N 35 27 E
Taiyiba, Jordan 90 31 55N 35 17 E
T'aiyüan 106 37 55N 112 40 E
Ta'izz 91 13 43N 44 7 E
Tajapuru, Furo do 170 1 50 S 50 25W
Tajarhī 119 24 15N 14 46 E
Tajicaringa 164 23 15N 104 44W
Tajima 112 35 19N 135 8 E
Tajimi 111 35 19N 137 8 E
Tajimi Gifu 55 35 25N 137 5 E
Tajitos 164 30 58N 112 18W
Tajo, R. 57 40 35N 1 52W
Tajumulco, Volcán de 165 15 20N 91 50W
Tājūrā 119 32 51N 13 27 E
Tak 100 16 52N 99 8 E
Takachiho 110 32 42N 131 18 E
Takahashi 110 34 51N 133 39 E
Takaka 143 40 51 S 172 50 E
Takamatsu 110 34 20N 134 5 E
Takanabe 110 32 8N 131 30 E
Takaoka 111 36 40N 137 0 E
Takapau 142 40 2 S 176 21 E
Takapuna 142 36 47 S 174 47 E
Takasago 110 34 45N 134 48 E
Takasaki 111 36 20N 139 0 E
Takase 110 34 7N 133 48 E
Takatsuki 111 34 51N 135 37 E
Takaungu 126 3 38 S 39 52 E
Takawa 110 33 47N 130 51 E
Takayama 111 36 18N 137 11 E
Takayama-Bonchi 111 36 0N 137 18 E
Takefu 111 35 50N 136 10 E
Takehara 110 34 21N 132 55 E
Takeley 29 51 52N 0 16 E
Takeo, Camb. 101 10 59N 104 47 E
Takeo, Japan 110 33 12N 130 1 E
Tåkern 73 58 22N 14 45 E
Takestan 92 36 0N 49 50 E
Taketa 110 32 58N 131 24 E
Takh 95 33 6N 77 32 E
Takhman 101 11 29N 104 57 E
Taki 135 6 29 S 155 52 E
Takingeun 102 4 45N 96 50 E
Takla L. 152 55 15N 125 45W
Takla Landing 152 55 30N 125 50W
Takla Makan 105 39 0N 83 0 E
Takoradi 120 4 58N 1 55W
Taku, China 107 38 59N 117 41 E
Taku, Japan 110 33 18N 130 3 E
Taku, R. 152 58 30N 133 50W
Takuan 108 27 44N 103 53 E
Takum 121 7 18N 9 36 E
Takuma 110 34 13N 133 40 E
Takushan 107 39 55N 123 30 E
Tal-y-llyn 31 52 40N 3 44W
Tal-y-sarn 31 53 3N 4 12W
Tala, Uruguay 173 34 21 S 55 46W
Tala, U.S.S.R. 77 72 40N 113 30 E
Talach'in 106 36 42N 104 54 E
Talagante 172 33 40 S 70 50W
Talaint 118 29 37N 9 45W
Talak 121 18 0N 5 0 E
Talamanca, Cordillera de 166 9 20N 83 20W
Talara 174 4 30 S 81 10 E
Talas 85 42 45N 72 0 E
Talas, R. 85 44 0N 70 20 E
Talasea 135 5 20 S 150 2 E
Talasskiy, Khrebet 85 42 15N 72 0 E
Talata Mafara 121 12 38N 6 4 E
Talaud, Kepulauan 103 4 30N 127 10 E
Talavera de la Reina 56 39 55N 4 46W
Talawana 136 22 51 S 121 9 E
Talawgyi 98 25 4N 97 19 E
Talayan 103 6 52N 124 24 E
Talbot, C. 136 13 48 S 126 43 E
Talbragar, R. 141 32 5 S 149 15 E
Talca 172 35 20 S 71 46W
Talca □ 172 35 20 S 71 46W
Talcahuano 172 36 40 S 73 10W
Talcher 96 20 55N 85 3 E
Talcho 121 14 35N 3 22 E
Taldom 81 56 45N 37 29 E
Taldy Kurgan 76 45 10N 78 45 E
Taleqan □ 93 36 40N 69 30 E
Talesh, Kūlhā-Ye 92 39 0N 48 30 E
Talfit 90 32 5N 35 17 E
Talga, R. 136 21 2 S 119 51 E
Talgar 85 43 19N 77 15 E
Talgar, Pic 85 43 5N 77 20 E
Talgarth 31 51 59N 3 15W
Talguharai 122 18 19N 35 56 E
Talguppa 93 14 10N 74 45 E
Tali, Shensi, China 106 34 48N 109 48 E
Tali, Yunnan, China 108 25 45N 100 5 E
Tali Post 123 5 55N 30 44 E
Taliabu, I. 103 1 45 S 125 0 E
Taliang Shan 108 28 0N 103 0 E
Talibong, Ko 101 7 15N 99 23 E
Talihina 159 34 45N 95 1W
Talikoti 96 16 29N 76 17 E
Talimardzhan 85 38 23N 65 37 E
Taling Ho, R. 107 40 54N 121 38 E
Taling Sung 101 15 5N 99 11 E
Talitsa 84 57 0N 63 43 E
Taliwang 102 8 50 S 116 55 E
Talkeetna 147 62 20N 150 0W
Talkeetna Mts. 147 62 20N 149 0W
Tall 'Asūr 90 31 59N 35 77 E
Talla 122 28 5N 30 43 E
Talladale 36 57 41N 5 20W
Talladega 157 33 28N 86 2W
Tallahassee 157 30 25N 84 15W
Tallangatta 141 36 15 S 147 10 E
Tallarook 141 37 5 S 145 6 E
Tallåsen 72 61 52N 16 2 E
Tallawang 141 32 12 S 149 28 E
Tällberg 72 60 51N 15 2 E
Tallebung 141 32 42 S 146 34 E
Tallering Pk 137 28 6 S 115 37 E
Tallinn (Reval) 80 59 29N 24 58 E
Tallow 39 52 6N 8 0W
Tallowbridge 39 52 6N 8 1W
Tallulah 159 32 25N 91 12W
Talluza 90 32 17N 35 18 E
Talmage 153 49 46N 103 40W
Talmest 118 31 48N 9 21W
Talmont 44 46 27N 1 37W
Talnoye 82 48 57N 30 35 E
Taloda 96 21 34N 74 19 E
Talodi 123 10 35N 30 22 E
Talou Shan, mts. 108 28 20N 107 10 E
Talovaya 81 51 13N 40 38 E
Talpa de Allende 164 20 23N 104 51W
Talsarnau 31 52 54N 4 4W
Talsinnt 118 32 33N 3 27W
Taltal 172 25 23 S 70 40W
Taltson L. 153 61 30N 110 15W
Taltson R. 152 61 24N 112 46W
Talwood 139 28 29 S 149 29 E
Talyawalka Cr. 140 32 28 S 142 22 E
Talybont 31 52 29N 3 59W
Tam Chau 101 10 48N 105 12 E
Tam Ky 100 15 34N 108 29 E
Tam Quan 100 14 35N 109 3 E
Tama 158 41 56N 92 37W
Tama Abu, Pegunungan 102 3 10N 115 0 E
Tamala 137 26 35 S 113 40 E
Tamalameque 174 8 52N 73 49W
Tamale 121 9 22N 0 50W
Taman 82 45 14N 36 41 E
Tamana 110 32 58N 130 32 E
Tamanar 118 31 1N 9 46W
Tamano 110 34 35N 133 59 E
Tamanrasset 119 22 56N 5 30 E
Tamanrasset, O. 118 22 0N 2 0 E
Tamanthi 98 25 19N 95 17 E
Tamaqua 162 40 46N 75 58W
Tamar, R. 30 50 33N 4 15W
Támara 174 5 50N 72 10W
Tamarang 141 31 27 S 150 5 E
Tamarite de Litera 58 41 52N 0 25 E
Tamashima 110 34 32N 133 40 E
Tamási 53 46 40N 18 18 E
Tamaské 121 14 55N 5 55 E
Tamatave 129 18 10 S 49 25 E
Tamatave □ 129 18 0 S 49 0 E
Tamaulipas □ 165 24 0N 99 0W
Tamaulipas, Sierra de 165 23 30N 98 20W
Tamazula 164 24 55N 106 58W
Tamazunchale 165 21 16N 98 47W
Tambacounda 120 13 55N 13 45W
Tambai 123 16 32N 37 13 E
Tambelan, Kepulauan 102 1 0N 107 30 E

Tambellup **Taunton**

Tambellup 137 34 4S 117 37E
Tambo 138 24 54S 146 14E
Tambo de Mora 174 13 30S 76 20W
Tambohorano 129 17 30S 43 58E
Tambora, G. 102 8 12S 118 5E
Tamboritha, Mt. 141 37 31S 146 51E
Tambov 81 52 45N 41 20E
Tambre, R. 56 42 55N 8 30W
Tambuku, G. 103 7 8S 113 40E
Tamburâ 123 5 40N 27 25E
Tamchaket 120 17 25N 10 40W
Tamchok Khambab (Brahmaputra) 99 29 25N 88 0E
Tamdybulak 85 41 46N 64 36E
Tame 174 6 28N 71 44W
Tame, R. 28 52 43N 1 45W
Tamega, R. 56 41 12N 8 5W
Tamelelt 119 26 30N 6 14E
Tamenglong 98 25 0N 93 35E
Tamerfors 75 61 30N 23 50E
Tamerlanovka 85 42 36N 69 17E
Tamerton Foliot 30 50 25N 4 10W
Tamerza 119 34 23N 7 58E
Tamgak, Mts. 121 19 12N 8 35E
Tamiahua, Laguna de 165 21 30N 97 30W
Tamil Nadu □ 97 11 0N 77 0E
Tamines 47 50 26N 4 36E
Taming 106 36 20N 115 10E
Tamins 51 46 50N 9 24E
Tamluk 95 22 18N 87 58E
Tammisaari (Ekenäs) 75 60 0N 23 26E
Tammun' 90 32 18N 35 23E
Tamnaren 72 60 10N 17 25E
Tamou 121 12 45N 2 11E
Tampa 157 27 57N 82 30W
Tampa B. 157 27 40N 82 40W
Tampere 75 61 30N 23 50E
Tampico 165 22 20N 97 50W
Tampin 101 2 28N 102 13E
Tamri 118 30 49N 9 50W
Tamrida = Hadibu 91 12 35N 54 2E
Tamsagbulag 105 47 14N 117 21E
Tamsagout 118 24 5N 6 35W
Tamsalu 80 59 11N 26 8E
Tamsweg 52 47 7N 13 49E
Tamu 99 24 13N 94 12E
Tamuja, R. 57 39 33N 6 8W
Tamworth, Austral. 141 31 0S 150 58E
Tamworth, U.K. 28 52 38N 1 41W
Tamyang 107 35 19N 126 59E
Tan An 101 10 32N 106 25E
Tana 74 70 7N 28 5E
Tana Fd. 74 70 35N 28 30E
Tana, L. 123 13 5N 37 30E
Tana, R., Kenya 126 0 50S 39 45E
Tana, R., Norway 48 69 50N 26 0E
Tanabe 111 33 44N 135 22E
Tanabi 171 20 37S 49 37W
Tanacross 147 63 40N 143 30W
Tanafjorden 74 70 45N 28 25E
Tanagro, R. 65 40 35N 15 25E
Tanahdjampea, I. 103 7 10S 120 35E
Tanahgrogot 102 1 55S 116 15E
Tanahmasa, I. 102 0 5S 98 29E
Tanahmerah 103 6 0S 140 7E
Tanami 136 19 59S 129 43E
Tanami Des. 136 18 50S 132 0E
Tanana 147 65 10N 152 15W
Tanana, R. 147 64 25N 145 30W
Tananarive 129 18 55S 47 31E
Tananarive □ 129 19 0S 47 0E
Tananarive = Antananarivo 125 18 55S 47 31E
Tananger 71 58 57N 5 37E
Tanant 118 31 54N 6 56W
Tánaro, R. 62 44 9N 7 50E
Tanaunelia 64 40 42N 9 45E
Tanba-Sanchi 111 35 7N 135 48E
Tanbar 97 25 55S 142 0E
Tancarville 42 49 29N 0 28E
Tanchai 108 25 58N 107 49E
T'anch'eng 107 34 38N 118 21E
Tanda, U.P., India 95 26 33N 82 35E
Tanda, U.P., India 95 28 57N 78 56E
Tanda, Ivory C. 120 7 48N 3 10W
Tandag 103 9 4N 126 9E
Tandala 127 9 25S 34 15E
Tândârei 70 44 39N 27 40E
Tandil 172 37 15S 59 6W
Tandjungpandan 102 2 43S 107 38E
Tandlianwald 94 31 3N 73 9E
Tando Adam 94 25 45N 68 40E
Tandou L. 140 32 40S 142 5E
Tandragee 38 54 22N 6 23W
Tandsbyn 72 63 0N 14 45W
Tandur 96 19 11N 79 30E
Tane-ga-Shima 112 30 35N 130 59E
Taneatua 142 38 4S 177 1E
Tanen Range 101 19 40N 99 0E
Tanen Tong Dan, Burma 99 16 30N 98 30E
Tanen Tong Dan, Thai. 100 19 43N 98 30E
Taneytown 162 39 40N 77 10W
Tanezrouft 118 23 9N 0 11E
Tanfeng 106 33 45N 110 18E
Tang 38 53 31N 7 49W
Tang, Koh 101 10 16N 103 7E
Tang Krasang 101 12 34N 105 3E
Tang La 99 32 59N 92 17E
Tang Pass 99 32 59N 92 17E
Tanga 99 5 5S 39 2E
Tanga □ 126 5 20S 38 0E
Tanga Is. 135 3 20S 153 15E
Tangail 98 24 15N 89 55E
Tanganyika, L. 126 6 40S 30 0E
T'angch'i 109 29 3N 119 24E
Tanger 118 35 50N 5 49W
Tangerang 103 6 12S 106 39E
Tangerhütte 48 52 26N 11 50E
Tangermünde 48 52 32N 11 57E
T'angho 109 32 10N 112 20E
Tangier 162 37 49N 75 59W
Tangier = Tanger 118 35 50N 5 49W
Tangier I. 162 37 50N 76 0W
Tangier Sd. 162 38 3N 75 5W
Tangkak 101 2 18N 102 34E
T'angku 107 39 4N 117 45E
T'angkula Shanmo 98 33 0N 92 0E
Tanglha Shan 99 33 0N 90 0E
Tangorin P.O. 138 21 47S 144 12E
Tangra Tso 99 31 25N 85 30E
Tangshan 106 34 25N 116 24E
T'angshan 107 39 40N 118 10E
T'angt'ang 108 26 29N 104 12E
T'angt'ou 107 35 21N 118 32E
Tangt'u 109 31 34N 118 29E
Tanguiéta 121 10 40N 1 21E
Tangyang, Chekiang, China 109 29 17N 120 14E
Tangyang, Hupeh, China 109 30 50N 111 45E
Tangyen Ho, R. 108 28 55N 108 36E
Tanimbar, Kepulauan 103 7 30S 131 30E
Taning 106 36 32N 110 47E
Taniyama 110 31 31N 130 31E
Tanjay 103 9 30N 123 5E
Tanjore = Thanjavur 97 10 48N 79 12E
Tanjung 102 2 10S 115 25E
Tanjung Malim 101 3 42N 101 31E
Tanjungbalai 102 2 55N 99 44E
Tanjungbatu 102 2 23N 118 3E
Tanjungkarang 102 5 20S 105 10E
Tanjungpinang 102 1 5N 104 30E
Tanjungpriok 103 6 8S 106 55E
Tanjungredeb 102 2 9N 117 29E
Tanjungselor 102 2 55N 117 25E
Tank 94 32 14N 70 25E
Tankan Shan 109 22 3N 114 16E
Tanleng 108 30 2N 103 33E
Tanndalen 72 62 33N 12 18E
Tannin 150 49 40N 91 0W
Tannis B. 73 57 40N 10 15E
Tano, R. 120 6 0N 2 30W
Tanoumrout 119 23 2N 5 31E
Tanout 121 14 50N 8 55E
Tanquinho 171 12 42S 39 43W
Tanshui 109 25 10N 121 28E
Tanta 122 30 45N 30 57E
Tantan 118 28 29N 11 1W
Tantoyuca 165 21 21N 98 10W
Tantung 107 40 10N 124 23E
Tantura = Dor 90 32 37N 34 55E
Tanuku 96 16 45N 81 44E
Tanum 73 58 42N 11 20E
Tanunda 140 34 30S 139 0E
Tanur 97 11 1N 75 46E
Tanus 44 44 8N 2 19E
Tanworth 28 52 20N 1 50W
Tanzania ■ 126 6 40S 34 0E
Tanzawa-Sanchi 111 35 27N 139 0E
Tanzilla, R. 152 58 8N 130 43W
T'aoan 107 45 20N 122 50E
Taoch'eng 108 29 3N 100 10E
Taoerh Ho 107 45 42N 124 5E
Taofu 108 31 0N 101 9E
Taohsien 109 25 37N 111 24E
T'aohua Tao 109 29 48N 122 17E
T'aolo 106 38 45N 106 40E
Taormina 65 37 52N 15 16E
Taos 161 36 28N 105 35W
Taoudenni 118 22 40N 3 55W
Taoudrart, Adrar 118 24 25N 2 24E
Taounate 118 34 32N 4 41W
Taourirt, Alg. 118 26 37N 0 8E
Taourirt, Moroc. 118 34 20N 2 47W
Taouz 118 31 2N 4 0W
T'aoyüan, China 109 28 54N 111 29E
T'aoyüan, Taiwan 109 25 0N 121 4E
Tapa 80 59 15N 26 0E
Tapa Shan 108 31 45N 109 30E
Tapachula 165 14 54N 92 17W
Tapah 101 4 12N 101 15E
Tapajós, R. 175 4 30S 56 10W
Tapaktuan 102 3 30N 97 10E
Tapanui 143 45 56S 169 18E
Tapauá 174 5 40S 64 20W
Tapauá, R. 174 6 0S 65 40W
Tapeta 120 6 36N 8 52W
Taphan Hin 100 16 13N 100 16E
Tapia 56 43 34N 6 56W
Tapieh Shan, mts. 109 31 20N 115 30E
T'ap'ingchen 106 33 42N 111 44E
Tapini 135 8 19S 147 0E
Tápiószele 53 47 45N 19 55E
Tapiraí 171 19 52S 46 1W
Tapirapé, R. 170 10 41S 50 38W
Tapirapecó, Serra 174 1 10N 65 0W
Taplan 140 34 33S 140 52E
Tapolca 53 46 53N 17 29E
Tappahannock 162 37 56N 76 50W
Tapsing 99 30 22N 96 25E
Tapti, R. 96 21 25N 75 0E
Tapu 109 24 31N 116 41E
Tapuaenuku, Mt. 143 41 55S 173 50E
Tapul Group, Is. 103 5 35N 120 50E
Tapun 98 18 22N 95 27E
Taquara 173 29 36N 50 46W
Taquari, R. 173 18 10S 56 0W
Taquaritinga 171 21 24S 48 30W
Tara, Austral. 139 27 17S 150 31E
Tara, Japan 110 33 2N 130 11E
Tara, U.S.S.R. 76 56 55N 74 30E
Tara, Zambia 127 16 58S 26 45E
Tara-Dake 110 32 58N 130 6E
Tara, R. 66 43 10N 19 20E
Tarabagatay, Khrebet 77 48 0N 83 0E
Tarābulus, Leb. 92 34 31N 33 52E
Tarābulus, Libya 119 32 49N 13 7E
Taradale 142 39 33S 176 53E
Tarahouahout 119 22 47N 5 59E
Tarakan 102 3 20N 117 35E
Tarakit, Mt. 126 2 2N 35 10E
Taralga 141 34 26S 149 52E
Taramakau, R. 143 42 34S 171 8E
Tarana 141 33 31S 149 52E
Taranagar 94 28 43N 75 9E
Taranaki □ 142 39 5S 174 51E
Tarancón 58 40 1N 3 1W
Taranga 94 23 56N 72 43E
Taranga Hill 94 24 0N 72 40E
Taransay, I. 36 57 54N 7 0W
Taransay, Sd. of 36 57 52N 7 0W
Táranto 65 40 30N 17 11E
Táranto, G. di 65 40 0N 17 15E
Tarapacá 174 2 56S 69 46W
Tarapacá □ 172 20 45S 69 30W
Tarare 45 45 54N 4 26E
Tararua Range 142 40 45S 175 25E
Tarascon, Ariège, France 44 42 50N 1 37E
Tarascon, Bouches-du-Rhône, France 45 43 48N 4 39E
Tarashcha 82 49 30N 30 31E
Tarat, Bj. 119 26 4N 9 7E
Tarauacá 174 8 6S 70 48W
Tarauacá, R. 174 7 30S 70 30W
Taravo, R. 45 41 48N 8 52E
Tarawera 142 39 2S 176 36E
Tarawera L. 142 38 13S 176 27E
Tarawera Mt. 142 38 14S 176 32E
Tarazat, Massif de 119 20 2N 8 30E
Tarazona 58 41 55N 1 43W
Tarazona de la Mancha 59 39 16N 1 55W
Tarbat Ness 37 57 52N 3 48W
Tarbela Dam 94 34 0N 72 52E
Tarbert, Ireland 39 52 34N 9 22W
Tarbert, Strathclyde, U.K. 34 55 55N 5 25W
Tarbert, W. Isles, U.K. 36 57 54N 6 49W
Tarbert, L. E. 36 57 50N 6 45W
Tarbert, L. W., Strathclyde, U.K. 34 55 58N 5 30W
Tarbert, L. W., W. Isles, U.K. 36 57 55N 6 56W
Tarbes 44 43 15N 0 3E
Tarbet, Highland, U.K. 36 56 58N 5 38W
Tarbet, Strathclyde, U.K. 34 56 13N 4 44W
Tarbolton 34 55 30N 4 30W
Tarboro 157 35 55N 77 3W
Tarbrax 138 21 7S 142 26E
Tarbū 119 26 0N 15 5E
Tarcento 63 46 12N 13 12E
Tarcoola 139 30 44S 134 36E
Tarcoon 139 30 15S 146 35E
Tarcău, Munţii 70 46 39N 26 7E
Tardets-Sorholus 44 43 17N 0 52W
Taree 141 31 50S 152 30E
Tarentaise 45 45 30N 6 35E
Tarf Shaqq al Abd 122 26 50N 36 6E
Tarfa, Wadi el 122 28 16N 31 15E
Tarfaya 116 27 55N 12 55W
Targon 44 44 44N 0 16W
Targuist 118 34 59N 4 14W
Tarhbalt 118 30 48N 5 10W
Tarhit 118 30 58N 2 0W
Tarhūnah 119 32 15N 13 28E
Tari 135 5 54S 142 59E
Tarib, Wadi 122 18 30N 43 23E
Táriba 174 7 49N 72 13W
Tarifa 57 36 1N 5 36W
Tarija 172 21 30S 64 40W
Tarija □ 172 21 30S 63 30W
Tarim, R. 105 41 5N 86 40E
Tarime □ 126 1 15S 34 0E
Taringo Downs 141 32 13S 145 33E
Taritoe, R. 103 3 0S 138 5E
Tarka, R. 128 32 10S 26 0E
Tarkastad 128 32 0S 26 16E
Tarkhankut, Mys 82 45 25N 32 30E
Tarko Sale 76 64 55N 77 50E
Tarkwa 120 5 20N 2 0W
Tarlac 103 15 29N 120 35E
Tarland 37 57 8N 2 51W
Tarleton 32 53 41N 2 50W
Tarlsland 152 57 03N 111 40W
Tarlton Downs 138 22 40S 136 45E
Tarm 73 55 56N 8 31E
Tarma 174 11 25S 75 45W
Tarn □ 44 43 49N 2 8E
Tarn-et-Garonne □ 44 44 8N 1 20E
Tarn, R. 44 44 5N 1 2E
Tärna 74 65 45N 15 10E
Tarna, R. 53 48 0N 20 5E
Tårnby 73 55 37N 12 36E
Tarnobrzeg □ 54 50 40N 22 0E
Tarnów 54 50 3N 21 0E
Tarnów □ 54 50 0N 21 0E
Tarnowskie Góry 54 50 27N 18 54E
Táro, R. 62 44 37N 9 58E
Tarong 139 26 47S 151 51E
Taroom 139 25 36S 149 48E
Taroudannt 118 30 30N 8 52W
Tarp 48 54 40N 9 25E
Tarpon Springs 157 28 8N 82 42W
Tarporley 32 53 10N 2 42W
Tarquinia 63 42 15N 11 45E
Tarqumiyah 90 31 35N 35 1E
Tarragona 58 41 5N 1 17E
Tarragona □ 58 41 0N 1 0E
Tarrasa 58 41 26N 2 1E
Tárrega 58 41 39N 1 9E
Tarrytown 162 41 5N 73 52W
Tarshiha = Me'ona 90 33 1N 35 15E
Tarso Emissi 119 21 27N 18 36E
Tarso Ovrari 119 21 27N 17 27E
Tarsus 92 36 58N 34 55E
Tartagal 172 22 30S 63 50W
Tartan, oilfield 19 58 22N 0 5E
Tartas 44 43 50N 0 49W
Tartna Point 140 32 54S 142 24E
Tartu 80 58 25N 26 58E
Tartus 92 34 55N 35 55E
Tarumirim 171 19 16S 41 59W
Tarumizu 110 31 29N 130 42E
Tarussa 81 54 44N 37 10E
Tarutao, Ko 101 6 33N 99 40E
Tarutung 102 2 0N 99 0E
Tarves 37 57 22N 2 13W
Tarvisio 63 46 31N 13 35E
Tarz Ulli 119 25 46N 9 44E
Tas-Buget 85 44 46N 65 33E
Tasahku 98 27 33N 97 52E
Tasâwah 119 26 0N 13 37E
Taschereau 150 48 40N 78 40W
Taseko, R. 152 52 4N 123 9W
Tasgaon 96 17 2N 74 39E
Ta'shan 123 16 31N 42 33E
Tashauz 76 42 0N 59 20E
Tashet'ai 106 41 0N 109 21E
Tashi Chho Dzong 98 27 31N 89 45E
Tashihch'iao (Yingk'ou) 107 40 38N 122 30E
T'ashihk'uerhkan 85 37 47N 75 14E
Tashkent 85 41 20N 69 10E
Tashkumyr 85 41 40N 72 10E
Tashkurghan 93 36 45N 67 40E
Tashtagol 76 52 47N 87 53E
Tasikmalaya 103 7 18S 108 12E
Tasjön 74 64 15N 15 45E
Taşköpru 82 41 30N 34 15E
Tasman Bay 143 40 59S 173 25E
Tasman Glacier 143 43 45S 170 20E
Tasman, Mt. 143 43 34S 170 12E
Tasman Mts. 143 41 3S 172 25E
Tasman Pen. 138 43 10S 148 0E
Tasman, R. 143 43 48S 170 8E
Tasman Sea 142 36 0S 160 0E
Tasmania, I., □ 138 49 0S 146 30E
Tassil Tin-Rerhoh 118 20 5N 3 55E
Tassili n-Ajjer 119 25 47N 8 1E
Tassili-Oua-Ahaggar 119 20 41N 5 30E
Tasty 85 44 47N 69 7E
Tasu Sd. 152 52 47N 132 2W
Tata, Hung. 53 47 37N 18 19E
Tata, Moroc. 118 29 46N 7 50W
Tatabánya 53 47 32N 18 25E
Tatar A.S.S.R. □ 84 55 30N 51 30E
Tatarsk 76 55 20N 75 50E
*Tatarskiy Proliv 77 54 0N 141 0E
Tatebayashi 111 36 15N 139 32E
Tateshina-Yama 111 36 8N 138 11E
Tateyama 111 35 0N 139 50E
Tathlina L. 152 60 33N 117 39W
Tathra 141 36 44S 149 59E
Tat'ien, Fukien, China 109 25 42N 117 50E
Tat'ien, Szechwan, China 108 26 18N 101 45E
Tatinnai L. 153 60 55N 97 40W
Tatlayoka Lake 152 51 35N 124 24W
Tatnam, C. 153 57 16N 91 0W
Tato Ho, R. 108 31 25N 100 42E
Tatra = Tatry 54 49 20N 20 0E
Tatry 54 49 20N 20 0E
Tatsu 108 29 40N 105 45E
Tatsuno 110 34 52N 134 33E
Tatta 94 24 42N 67 55E
Tattenhall 32 53 7N 2 47W
Tatu Ho, R. 108 29 35N 103 47E
Tatuí 173 23 25S 48 0W
Tatum 159 33 16N 103 16W
Tat'ung, Anhwei, China 109 30 48N 117 44E
Tat'ung, Shansi, China 106 40 9N 113 19E
Tatura 141 36 29S 145 16E
Tatvan 92 37 28N 42 27E
Tauá 170 6 1S 40 26W
Taubaté 173 23 5S 45 30W
Tauberbischofsheim 49 49 37N 9 40E
Taucha 48 51 22N 12 31E
Tauern, mts. 52 47 15N 12 40E
Tauern-tunnel 52 47 0N 13 12E
Taufikia 123 9 24N 31 37E
Taumarunui 142 38 53S 175 15E
Taumaturgo 174 9 0S 73 50W
Taung 128 27 33S 24 47E
Taungdwingyi 98 20 1N 95 40E
Taunggyi 98 20 50N 97 0E
Taungtha 98 20 45N 94 50E
Taungup 98 18 51N 94 14E
Taungup Pass 98 18 40N 94 45E
Taungup Taunggya 99 18 20N 93 40E
Taunsa Barrage 95 31 0N 71 0E
Taunton, U.K. 28 51 1N 3 7W

*Renamed Sakhalinskiy Zalir

Taunton **Tetbury**

Taunton, U.S.A. 162 41 54N 71 6W
Taunus 49 50 15N 8 20 E
Taupo 142 38 41 S 176 7 E
Taupo, L. 142 38 46 S 175 55 E
Tauq 92 35 12N 44 29 E
Taurage 80 55 14N 22 28 E
Tauramena 174 5 1N 72 45W
Tauranga 142 37 35 S 176 11 E
Tauranga Harb. 142 37 30 S 176 5 E
Taureau, Lac 150 46 50N 73 40W
Tauri, R. 135 8 8 S 146 8 E
Taurianova 65 38 22N 16 1 E
Taurus Mts. = Toros Dağlari 92 37 0N 35 0 E
Táuste 58 41 58N 1 18W
Tauz 83 41 0N 45 40 E
Tavani 153 62 10N 93 30W
Tavannes 50 47 13N 7 12 E
Tavas 92 37 35N 29 8 E
Tavda 84 58 7N 65 8 E
Tavda, R. 84 59 30N 63 0 E
Taverny 43 49 2N 2 13 E
Taveta 124 3 31N 37 37 E
Taviche 165 16 38N 96 32W
Tavignano, R. 45 42 7N 9 33 E
Tavira 57 37 8N 7 40W
Tavistock 30 50 33N 4 9W
Tavolara, I. 64 40 55N 9 40 E
Távora, R. 56 41 0N 7 30W
Tavoy 101 14 7N 98 18 E
Tavoy, I. = Mali Kyun 99 13 0N 98 20 E
Taw, R. 30 50 58N 3 58W
Tawang 99 27 37N 91 50 E
Tawas City 156 44 16N 83 31W
Tawau 102 4 20N 117 55 E
Tawngche 98 26 34N 95 38 E
Tawnyinah 38 53 55N 8 45W
Tāworgha' 119 32 1N 15 2 E
Taxila 94 33 42N 72 52 E
Tay Bridge 35 56 28N 3 0W
Tay, Firth of 35 56 25N 3 8W
Tay, L., Austral. 137 32 55 S 120 48 E
Tay, L., U.K. 35 56 30N 4 10W
Tay Ninh 101 11 20N 106 5 E
Tay, R. 35 56 37N 3 38W
Tay Strath 37 56 38N 3 40W
Tayabamba 174 8 15 S 77 10W
Tayao 108 25 41N 101 18 E
Tayaparva La 95 31 35N 83 20 E
Tayeh 109 30 5N 114 57 E
Taylor, Can. 152 56 13N 120 40W
Taylor, Alaska, U.S.A. 147 65 40N 164 50W
Taylor, Pa., U.S.A. 162 41 23N 75 43W
Taylor, Tex., U.S.A. 159 30 30N 97 30W
Taylor, Mt. 143 43 30 S 171 20 E
Taylor Mt. 161 35 16N 107 50W
Taylorville 158 39 32N 89 20W
Taymyr, Oz. 77 74 50N 102 0 E
Taymyr, P-ov. 77 75 0N 100 0 E
Taynuilt 34 56 25N 5 15W
Tayport 34 56 27N 2 52W
Tayr Zebna 90 33 14N 35 23 E
Tayshet 77 55 58N 97 25 E
Tayside □ 35 56 25N 3 30W
Taytay 103 10 45N 119 30 E
Tayu 109 25 38N 114 9 E
Tayülo 105 29 13N 98 13 E
Tayung 109 29 8N 110 30 E
Taz, R. 76 65 40N 82 0 E
Taza 118 34 10N 4 0W
Taze 98 22 57N 95 24 E
Tazenakht 118 30 46N 7 3W
Tazin L. 153 59 44N 108 42W
Tazin, R. 153 60 26N 110 45W
Tazoult 119 35 29N 6 11 E
Tazovskiy 76 67 30N 78 30 E
Tbilisi (Tiflis) 83 41 50N 44 50 E
Tchad (Chad) ■ 117 12 30N 17 15 E
Tchad, Lac 117 13 30N 14 30 E
Tchaourou 121 8 58N 2 40 E
Tchentlo L. 152 55 15N 125 0W
Tchibanga 124 2 45 S 11 12 E
Tchin Tabaraden 121 15 58N 5 50 E
Tczew 54 54 8N 18 50 E
Te Anau L. 143 45 15 S 167 45 E
Te Araroa 142 37 39 S 178 25 E
Te Aroha 142 37 32 S 175 44 E
Te Awamutu 142 38 1 S 175 20 E
Te Horo 142 40 48 S 175 6 E
Te Kaha 142 37 44 S 177 44 E
Te Karaka 142 38 26 S 177 53 E
Te Kauwhata 142 37 25 S 175 9 E
Te Kinga 143 42 35 S 171 31 E
Te Kopuru 142 36 2 S 173 56 E
Te Kuiti 142 38 20 S 175 11 E
Te Puke 142 37 46 S 176 22 E
Te Waewae B. 143 46 13 S 167 33 E
Tea Tree 136 22 11 S 133 17 E
Teaca 70 46 55N 24 30 E
Teague 159 31 40N 96 20W
Tean 109 29 21N 115 42 E
Teangue 36 57 7N 5 52W
Teano 65 41 15N 14 1 E
Teapa 165 17 35N 92 56W
Teba 57 36 59N 4 55W
Tebay 32 54 25N 2 35W
Teberda 83 43 30N 43 54 E
Tébessa 119 35 22N 8 8 E
Tebicuary, R. 172 26 36 S 58 16W
Tebing Tinggi 102 3 38 S 102 1 E
Tébourba 119 36 49N 9 51 E
Téboursouk 119 36 29N 9 10 E
Tebulos 83 42 36N 45 25 E
Tecapa 163 35 51N 116 14W
Tecate 164 32 34N 116 38W
Techa, R. 84 56 13N 62 58 E
Tech'ang 108 27 22N 102 10 E
Techiang 108 28 19N 108 5 E
Techiman 120 7 35N 1 58W
Tech'in 108 28 30N 98 52 E
Tech'ing 109 23 8N 111 46 E
Techirghiol 70 44 4N 28 32 E
Techou 106 37 19N 116 19 E
Tecomán 164 18 55N 103 53W
Tecoripa 164 28 37N 109 57W
Tecuci 70 45 51N 27 27 E
Tecumseh 156 42 1N 83 59W
Tedavnet 38 54 19N 7 2W
Tedesa 123 5 10N 37 40 E
Tedzhen 76 37 23N 60 31 E
Tees B. 72 54 37N 1 10W
Tees, R. 33 54 36N 1 25W
Teesdale 32 54 37N 2 10W
Teesside 33 54 37N 1 13W
Tefé 174 3 25 S 64 50W
Tegal 103 6 52 S 109 8 E
Tegelen 47 51 20N 6 9 E
Teggiano 65 40 24N 15 32 E
Teghra 95 25 30N 85 34 E
Tegid, L. 31 52 53N 3 38W
Tegina 121 10 5N 6 11 E
Tegucigalpa 166 14 10N 87 0W
Tehachapi 163 35 11N 118 29W
Tehachapi Mts. 163 35 0N 118 40W
Tehamiyam 122 18 26N 36 45 E
Tehilla 122 17 42N 36 6 E
Têhini 120 9 39N 3 32W
Tehrān 93 35 44N 51 30 E
Tehrān □ 93 35 0N 49 30 E
Tehsing 109 28 54N 117 34 E
Tehua 109 25 30N 118 14 E
Tehuacán 165 18 20N 97 30W
Tehuantepec 165 16 10N 95 19W
Tehuantepec, Golfo de 165 15 50N 95 0W
Tehuantepec, Istmo de 165 17 0N 94 30W
Tehui 107 44 32N 125 42 E
Teich, Le 44 44 38N 0 59W
Teifi, R. 31 52 4N 4 14W
Teign, R. 30 50 41N 3 42W
Teignmouth 30 50 33N 3 30W
Teikovo 81 56 55N 40 30 E
Teil, Le 45 44 33N 4 40 E
Teilleul, Le 42 48 32N 0 53W
Teishyai 80 55 59N 22 14 E
Teiuş 70 46 12N 23 40 E
Teixeira 170 7 13 S 37 15W
Teixeira de Sousa = Luau 124 10 40 S 22 10 E
Teixeira Pinto 120 12 10N 13 55 E
Tejo, R. 57 39 15N 8 35W
Tejon Pass 163 34 49N 118 53W
Tejung 108 28 46N 99 19 E
Tekamah 158 41 48N 96 14W
Tekapo, L. 143 43 53 S 170 33 E
Tekax 165 20 20N 89 30W
Tekeli 85 44 50N 79 0 E
Tekeze, W. 123 13 50N 37 50 E
Tekija 66 44 42N 22 26 E
Tekirdağ 92 40 58N 27 30 E
Tekkali 96 18 43N 84 24 E
Teko 108 31 49N 98 40 E
Tekoa 160 47 19N 117 4W
Tekoulât, O. 118 22 30N 2 20 E
Tel Adashim 90 32 39N 35 17 E
Tel Aviv-Yafo 90 32 4N 34 48 E
Tel Hanan 90 32 47N 35 3 E
Tel Hazor 90 33 2N 35 2 E
Tel Lakhish 90 31 34N 34 51 E
Tel Malhata 90 31 13N 35 2 E
Tel Megiddo 90 32 35N 38 11 E
Tel Mond 90 32 15N 34 56 E
Tela 166 15 40N 87 28W
Télagh 118 34 51N 0 32W
Telanaipura = Jambi 102 1 38 S 103 30 E
Telavi 83 42 0N 45 30 E
Telciu 70 47 25N 24 24 E
Telefomin 135 5 10 S 141 40 E
Telega = Doftana 70 45 17N 25 45 E
Telegraph Cr. 152 58 0N 131 10W
Telekhany 80 52 30N 25 46 E
Telemark fylke □ 71 59 25N 8 30 E
Telén 172 36 15 S 65 31W
Teleneshty 70 47 35N 28 24 E
Teleño 56 42 23N 6 22W
Teleorman □ 70 44 0N 25 0 E
Teleorman, R. 70 44 15N 25 20 E
Teles Pires (São Manuel), R. 174 8 40 S 57 0W
Telescope Peak, Mt. 163 36 6N 117 7W
Teletaye 121 16 31N 1 30 E
Telford 28 52 42N 2 31W
Telfs 52 47 19N 11 4 E
Telgte 48 51 59N 7 46 E
Telichie 139 31 45 S 139 59 E
Télimélé 120 10 54N 13 2W
Telkwa 152 54 41N 126 56W
Tell 90 32 12N 35 12 E
Tell City 156 38 0N 86 44W
Teller 147 65 12N 166 24W
Tellicherry 97 11 45N 75 30 E
Tellin 47 50 5N 5 13 E
Telluride 161 37 58N 107 54W
Telok Anson 101 4 3N 101 0 E
Teloloapán 165 18 21N 99 51W
Telom, R. 101 4 20N 101 46 E
Telpos Iz. 78 63 35N 57 30 E
Telsen 176 42 30 S 66 50W
Teltow 48 52 24N 13 15 E
Telukbetung 102 5 29 S 105 17 E
Telukbutun 101 4 5N 108 7 E
Telukdalem 102 0 45N 97 50 E
Tema 121 5 41N 0 0 E
Temagami L. 150 47 0N 80 10W
Temanggung 103 7 18 S 110 10 E
Temapache 165 21 4N 97 38W
Temax 165 21 10N 88 50W
Tembe 126 0 30 S 28 25 E
Tembeling, R. 101 4 20N 102 23 E
Tembleque 58 39 41N 3 30W
Temblor Ra, mts. 163 35 30N 120 0W
Tembuland □ 129 31 35 S 28 0 E
Teme, R. 28 52 23N 2 15W
Temecula 163 33 26N 117 6W
Temelelt 118 31 50N 7 32W
Temerloh 101 3 27N 102 25 E
Temir Tau 76 53 10N 87 20 E
Temirtau 76 50 5N 72 56 E
Témiscaming 150 46 44N 79 5W
Temma 138 41 12 S 144 42 E
Temnikov 81 54 40N 43 11 E
Temo, R. 64 40 20N 8 30 E
Temora 141 34 30 S 147 30 E
Temosachic 164 28 58N 107 50W
Tempe, S. Afr. 161 29 1 S 26 13 E
Tempe, U.S.A. 161 33 26N 111 59W
Tempe Downs 136 24 22 S 132 24 E
Temperanceville 162 37 54N 75 33W
Tempestad 174 1 20 S 74 56W
Tempino 102 1 55 S 103 23 E
Témpio Pausania 64 40 53N 9 6 E
Temple 159 31 5N 97 28W
Temple B. 138 12 15 S 143 3 E
Temple Combe 28 51 0N 2 25W
Temple Ewell 29 51 9N 1 16W
Temple Sowerby 30 54 38N 2 33W
Templemore 39 52 48N 7 50W
Templenoe 39 51 52N 9 40W
Templeton, Austral. 138 18 30 S 142 30 E
Templeton, U.K. 31 51 46N 4 45W
Templeton, U.S.A. 163 35 33N 120 42W
Templeton, R. 138 21 0 S 138 40 E
Templeuve 47 50 39N 3 17 E
Templin 48 53 8N 13 31 E
Tempo 38 54 23N 7 28W
Tempoal 165 21 31N 98 23W
Temryuk 82 45 15N 37 11 E
Temse 47 51 7N 4 13 E
Temska, R. 66 43 17N 22 33 E
Temuco 176 38 50 S 72 50W
Temuka 143 44 14 S 171 17 E
Ten Boer 46 53 16N 6 42 E
Tena 174 0 59 S 77 49W
Tenabo 165 20 2N 90 12W
Tenaha 159 31 57N 94 15W
Tenali 96 16 15N 80 35 E
Tenancingo 165 19 0N 99 33W
Tenango 165 19 0N 99 40W
Tenasserim 100 12 6N 99 3 E
Tenasserim □ 100 14 0N 98 30 E
Tenay 45 45 55N 5 30 E
Tenbury 28 52 18N 2 35W
Tenby 31 51 40N 4 42W
Tenda 45 44 5N 7 34 E
Tenda, Col de 45 44 9N 7 32 E
Tendaho 123 11 39N 40 54 E
Tende 45 44 5N 7 35 E
Tendelti 123 13 1N 31 55 E
Tendjedi, Adrar 119 23 41N 7 32 E
Tendrara 118 33 3N 1 58W
Tendre, Mt. 50 46 35N 6 18 E
Teneida 122 25 30N 29 19 E
Ténéré 119 23 2N 16 0 E
Tenerife, I. 116 28 20N 16 40W
Ténès 118 36 31N 1 14 E
T'eng Ch'ung 99 25 9N 98 22 E
Teng, R. 101 20 30N 98 10 E
Tengah □ 103 2 0 S 122 0 E
Tengah Kepulauan 102 7 5 S 118 15 E
Tengchow = P'englai 107 37 49N 120 47 E
Tengch'uan 108 26 0N 100 4 E
Tengch'ung 108 25 2N 98 28 E
Tengfeng 106 34 27N 113 2 E
Tenggara □ 103 3 0 S 122 0 E
Tenggol, P. 101 4 48N 103 41 E
T'enghsien, Honan, China 109 32 41N 112 5 E
T'enghsien, Kwangsi Chuang, China 109 23 23N 110 54 E
T'enghsien, Shantung, China 105 35 8N 117 9 E
Tengiz, Ozero 76 50 30N 69 0 E
Tengko 99 32 30N 98 0 E
Tengk'o 108 32 32N 97 35 E
Tengk'ou 106 40 18N 106 59 E
Tenigerbad 51 46 42N 8 57 E
Tenille 157 32 58N 82 50W
Tenindewa 137 28 30 S 115 20 E
Tenkasi 97 8 55N 77 20 E
Tenke, Congo 127 11 22 S 26 40 E
Tenke, Zaïre 127 10 32 S 26 7 E
Tenkodogo 121 12 0N 0 10W
Tenna, R. 63 43 12N 13 43 E
Tennant Creek 136 19 30 S 134 0 E
'Tenneco', oilfield 19 54 6N 4 42 E
Tennessee □ 155 36 0N 86 30W
Tenneville 47 50 6N 5 32 E
Tennsift, Oued 118 32 3N 9 28W
Tenom 102 5 4N 115 38 E
Tenosique 165 17 30N 91 24W
Tenri 111 34 46N 135 55 E
Tenryū 111 34 52N 137 55 E
Tent L. 153 62 25N 107 54W
Tenterden 29 51 4N 0 42 E
Tenterfield 139 29 0 S 152 0 E
Teófilo Otôni 171 17 50 S 41 30W
Tepa 120 6 57N 2 30W
Tepalcatepec, R. 164 18 35N 101 59W
Tepao 108 23 21N 106 33 E
Tepehuanes 164 25 21N 105 44W
Tepetongo 164 22 28N 103 9W
Tepic 164 21 30N 104 54W
Tepi'ng 107 37 28N 116 67 E
Teploklyuchenka 85 42 30N 78 30 E
Tepoca, C. 164 29 20N 112 25W
Tequila 164 20 54N 103 47W
Ter Apel 46 52 53N 7 5 E
Ter, R. 58 42 0N 2 30 E
Téra 121 14 0N 0 57 E
Tera, R. 56 41 54N 5 44W
Téramo 63 42 40N 13 40 E
Terang 140 38 15 S 142 55 E
Terawhiti, C. 142 41 16 S 174 38 E
Terborg 46 51 56N 6 22 E
Tercan 92 39 50N 40 30 E
Terceira 16 38 43N 27 13W
Tercero, R. 172 32 58 S 61 47W
Terdal 96 16 33N 75 9 E
Terebovlya 80 49 18N 25 44 E
Teregova 70 45 10N 22 16 E
Terek-Say 85 41 30N 71 11 E
Terembone Cr. 139 30 25 S 148 50 E
Terengganu □ 101 4 55N 103 0 E
Tereshka, R. 81 52 0N 46 36 E
Teresina 170 5 2 S 42 45W
Terewah L. 139 29 52 S 147 35 E
Terezinha 174 0 44N 69 27W
Terges, R. 57 37 49N 7 41W
Tergnier 43 49 40N 3 17 E
Terhazza 118 23 45N 4 59W
Terheijden 47 51 38N 4 45 E
Teriang 101 3 15N 102 26 E
Terkezi 117 18 27N 21 40 E
Terlizzi 65 41 8N 16 32 E
Termas de Chillan 172 36 50 S 71 31W
Terme 82 41 11N 37 0 E
Termez 85 37 0N 67 15 E
Términi Imerese 43 37 59N 13 51 E
Términos, Laguna de 165 18 35N 91 30W
Termoli 63 42 0N 15 0 E
Termon 38 55 3N 7 50W
Termonfeckin 38 53 47N 6 15W
Tern, oilfield 19 61 17N 0 55 E
Ternate 103 0 45N 127 25 E
Terneuzen 47 51 20N 3 50 E
Terney 77 45 3N 136 37 E
Terni 63 42 34N 12 38 E
Ternitz 52 47 43N 16 2 E
Ternopol 80 49 30N 25 40 E
Terowie, N.S.W., Austral. 139 32 27 S 147 52 E
Terowie, Vic., Austral. 140 33 10 S 138 50 E
Terra Bella 163 35 58N 119 3W
Terra Nova B. 13 74 50 S 164 40 E
Terrace 152 54 30N 128 35W
Terrace Bay 150 48 47N 87 10W
Terracina 64 41 17N 13 12 E
Terralba 64 39 42N 8 38 E
Terranuova 63 43 38N 11 35 E
Terrasini Favarotta 64 38 10N 13 4 E
Terrasson 44 45 7N 1 19 E
Terrebonne B. 159 29 15N 90 28W
Terrecht 118 20 10N 0 10W
Terrell 159 32 44N 96 19W
Terrenceville 151 47 40N 54 44W
Terrick Terrick 138 24 44 S 145 5 E
Terry 158 46 47N 105 20W
Terryglass 39 53 3N 8 14W
Terryville 162 41 41N 73 1W
Terschelling, I. 46 53 25N 5 20 E
Terskey Alatau, Khrebet 85 41 50N 77 0 E
Terter, R. 83 40 5N 46 15 E
Teruel 58 40 22N 1 8W
Teruel □ 58 40 48N 1 0W
Tervel 67 43 45N 27 28 E
Tervola 74 66 6N 24 49 E
Teryaweyna L. 140 32 18 S 143 22 E
Tešanj 66 44 38N 17 59 E
Teseney 123 15 5N 36 42 E
Tesha, R. 81 55 32N 43 0 E
Teshio 112 44 53N 141 44 E
Teshio-Gawa, R. 112 44 53N 141 45 E
Tešica 66 43 27N 21 45 E
Tesiyn Gol, R. 105 50 28N 93 4 E
Teslin 147 60 10N 132 43W
Teslin L. 152 60 15N 132 57W
Teslin, R. 152 61 34N 134 35W
Teslió 66 44 37N 17 54 E
Teso □ = Eastern □ 126 1 50N 33 45 E
Tessalit 121 20 12N 1 0 E
Tessaoua 121 13 47N 7 56 E
Tessenderlo 47 51 4N 5 5 E
Tessier 153 51 48N 107 26W
Tessin 48 54 2N 12 28 E
Tessit 121 15 13N 0 18 E
Test, R. 28 51 7N 1 30W
Testa del Gargano 65 41 50N 16 10 E
Teste, La 44 44 37N 1 8W
Têt 53 47 30N 17 33 E
Tetachuck L. 152 53 18N 125 55W
Tetas, Pta. 172 23 31 S 70 38W
Tetbury 28 51 37N 2 9W

Tete **Tijibadok**

Tete 127 16 13S 33 33E
Tete □ 127 15 15S 32 40E
Teterev, R. 80 50 30N 29 30E
Teteringen 47 51 37N 4 49E
Teterow 48 53 45N 12 34E
Teteven 67 42 58N 24 17E
Tethull, R. 152 60 35N 112 12W
Tetiyev 82 49 22N 29 38E
Tetlin 147 63 14N 142 50W
Tetlin Junction 147 63 29N 142 55W
Tetney 33 53 30N 0 1W
Teton, R. 160 47 58N 111 0W
Tétouan 118 35 35N 5 21W
Tetovo 66 42 1N 21 2E
Tettenhall 28 52 35N 2 7W
Tetuán = Tétouan 118 35 30N 5 25W
Tetyukhe 77 44 45N 135 40E
Teuco, R. 172 25 30S 60 25W
Teufen 51 47 24N 9 23E
Teulada 64 38 59N 8 47E
Teulon 153 50 23N 97 16W
Tevere, R. 63 42 30N 12 20E
Teviot, R. 35 55 21N 2 51W
Teviotdale 35 55 25N 2 50W
Teviothead 35 55 19N 2 55W
Tewantin 139 26 27S 153 3E
Tewkesbury 28 51 59N 2 8W
Texada I. 152 49 40N 124 25W
Texarkana, Ark., U.S.A. 159 33 25N 94 0W
Texarkana, Tex., U.S.A. 159 33 25N 94 3W
Texas 139 28 49S 151 15E
Texas □ 159 31 40N 98 30W
Texas City 159 27 20N 95 20W
Texel, I. 46 53 5N 4 50E
Texhoma 159 36 32N 101 47W
Texline 159 36 26N 103 0W
Texoma L. 159 34 0N 96 38W
Teyang 108 31 8N 104 24E
Teykovo 81 56 55N 40 30E
Teynham 29 51 19N 0 50E
Teyr Zebna 90 33 14N 35 23E
Teza, R. 81 56 41N 41 45E
Tezin 94 34 24N 69 30E
Teziutlán 165 19 50N 97 30W
Tezpur 98 26 40N 92 45E
Tezzeron L. 152 54 43N 124 30W
Tha-anne, R. 153 60 31N 94 37W
Tha Deua, Laos 100 17 57N 102 38E
Tha Deua, Laos 100 19 26N 101 50E
Tha Nun 101 8 12N 98 17E
Tha Pia 100 17 48N 100 32E
Tha Rua 100 14 34N 100 44E
Tha Sala 101 8 40N 99 56E
Tha Song Yang 101 17 34N 97 55E
Thaba Putsoa, mt. 129 29 45S 28 0E
Thabana Ntlenyana, Mt. 129 29 30S 29 9E
Thabazimbi 129 24 40S 26 4E
Thabeikkyin 98 22 53N 95 59E
Thai Binh 100 20 27N 106 20E
Thai Muang 101 8 24N 98 16E
Thai Nguyen 100 21 35N 105 46E
Thailand (Siam) ■ 100 16 0N 102 0E
Thakhek 100 17 25N 104 45E
Thakurgaon 98 26 2N 88 28E
Thal 94 33 28N 70 33E
Thal Desert 93 31 0N 71 30E
Thala 119 35 35N 8 40E
Thala La 99 28 25N 97 23E
Thalabarivat 100 13 33N 105 57E
Thalkirch 51 46 39N 9 17E
Thallon 139 28 30S 148 57E
Thalwil 51 47 17N 8 35E
Thame 29 51 44N 0 58W
Thame, R. 29 51 52N 0 47W
Thames 142 37 7S 175 34E
Thames, Firth of 142 37 0S 175 25E
Thames, R., Can. 150 42 20N 82 25W
Thames, R., N.Z. 142 37 32S 175 45E
Thames, R., U.K. 28 51 30N 0 35E
Thames, R., U.S.A. 162 41 18N 72 9W
Thâmit, W. 119 30 51N 16 14E
Than Uyen 100 22 0N 103 54E
Thana 96 19 12N 72 59E
Thanbyuzayat 98 15 58N 97 44E
Thanesar 94 30 1N 76 52E
Thanet, I. of 29 51 21N 1 20E
Thang Binh 101 15 50N 108 20E
Thangoo P.O. 136 18 10S 122 22E
Thangool 138 24 29S 150 35E
Thanh Hoa 100 19 48N 105 46E
Thanh Hung 101 9 55N 105 43E
Thanh Thuy 100 22 55N 104 51E
Thanjavur (Tanjore) 97 10 48N 79 12E
Thanlwin myit, R. 99 20 0N 98 0E
Thann 43 47 48N 7 5E
Thaon 43 48 15N 6 25E
Thap Sakae 101 11 30N 99 37E
Thap Than 100 15 27N 99 54E
Thar (Great Indian) Desert 94 28 25N 72 0E
Tharad 94 24 30N 71 30E
Thargomindah 139 27 58S 143 46E
Tharrawaddy 98 17 38N 95 48E
Tharrawaw 98 17 41N 95 28E
Tharthār, Bahr ath 92 34 0N 43 0E
Thasopoúla, I. 68 40 49N 24 45E
Thásos 68 40 50N 24 50E
Thásos, I. 68 40 40N 24 40E
That Khe 100 22 16N 106 28E
Thatcham 28 51 24N 1 17W
Thatcher, Ariz., U.S.A. 161 32 54N 109 46W
Thatcher, Colo., U.S.A. 161 37 38N 104 6W
Thaton 98 16 55N 97 22E
Thau, Étang de 44 43 23N 3 36E
Thaungdut 98 24 30N 94 40E
Thaxted 29 51 57N 0 20E
Thayer 159 36 34N 91 34W
Thayetmyo 98 19 20N 95 18E
Thayngen 51 47 49N 8 43E
Thazi 99 21 0N 96 5E
The Alberga, R. 139 27 6S 135 33E
The Bight 167 24 19N 75 24W
The Corrong 139 36 0S 139 30E
The Dalles 160 45 40N 121 11W
The Diamantina 139 26 45S 139 30E
The English Company's Is. 138 11 50S 136 32E
The Entrance 141 33 21S 151 30E
The Four Archers 138 15 31S 135 22E
The Frome, R. 139 29 8S 137 54E
The Granites 136 20 35S 130 21E
The Great Divide 141 35 0S 149 17E
The Grenadines, Is. 167 12 30N 61 30W
The Hague (s'Gravenhage) 47 52 7N 7 14E
The Hamilton, R. 139 26 40S 135 19E
The Johnston Lakes 137 32 25S 120 30E
The Lake 167 21 5N 73 34W
The Loup 38 54 42N 6 32W
The Macumba, R. 139 27 52S 137 12E
The Neales, R. 139 28 8S 136 47E
The Oaks 141 34 3S 150 34E
The Officer, R. 137 27 46S 129 46E
The Pas 153 53 45N 101 15W
The Range 127 19 2S 31 2E
The Rock 141 35 15S 147 2E
The Salt Lake 139 30 6S 142 8E
The Stevenson, R. 139 27 6S 135 33E
The Thumbs, Mts. 143 43 35S 170 40E
The Warburton, R. 139 28 4S 137 28E
Theale 28 51 26N 1 5W
Thebes 122 25 40N 32 35E
Thedford 158 41 59N 100 31W
Theebine 139 25 57S 152 34E
Thekulthili L. 153 61 3N 110 0W
Thelma, oilfield 19 58 25N 1 18E
Thelon, R. 153 62 35N 104 3W
Thénezay 42 46 44N 0 2W
Thenon 44 45 9N 1 4E
Theodore 138 24 55S 150 3E
Thepha 101 6 52N 100 58E
Thérain, R. 43 49 15N 2 27E
Thermaïkos Kólpos 68 40 15N 22 45E
Thermopílai P. 69 38 48N 22 45E
Thermopolis 160 43 14N 108 10W
Thesprotía □ 68 39 27N 20 22E
Thessalía □ 68 39 30N 22 0E
Thessalon 150 46 20N 83 30W
Thessaloníki 68 40 38N 23 0E
Thessaloníki □ 68 40 45N 23 0E
Thessaly = Thessalía 68 39 30N 22 0E
Thetford 29 52 25N 0 44E
Thetford Mines 151 46 8N 71 18W
Theun, R. 100 18 19N 104 0E
Theunissen 128 28 26S 26 43E
Theux 47 50 32N 5 49E
Thevenard 139 32 9S 133 38E
Thiámis, R. 68 39 34N 20 18E
Thiberville 42 49 8N 0 27E
Thicket Portage 153 55 19N 97 42W
Thief River Falls 159 48 15N 96 10W
Thiel 120 14 55N 15 5W
Thiene 63 45 42N 11 29E
Thierache 43 49 51N 3 45E
Thiers 44 45 52N 3 33E
Thies 120 14 50N 16 51W
Thiet 123 7 37N 28 49E
Thika 126 1 1S 37 5E
Thika □ 126 1 1S 37 5E
Thille-Boubacar 120 16 31N 15 5W
Thillot, Le 43 47 53N 6 46E
Thimphu (Tashi Chho Dzong) 98 27 31N 89 45E
Þingvallavatn 74 64 11N 21 9W
Thionville 43 49 20N 6 10E
Thirá 69 36 23N 25 27E
Thirasiá, I. 69 36 26N 25 21E
Thirlmere, L. 32 54 32N 3 4W
Thirsk 33 54 15N 1 20W
Thisted 75 56 58N 8 40E
Thistle I. 140 35 0S 136 8E
Thistle, oilfield 19 61 20N 1 35E
Thitgy 98 18 15N 96 13E
Thitpokpin 98 19 24N 96 1E
Thiu Khao Phetchabun 101 16 20N 100 55E
Thívai 69 38 19N 23 19E
Thiviers 44 45 25N 0 54E
Thizy 45 46 2N 4 18E
Þjorsa 74 63 47N 20 48W
Thlewiaza, R., Man., Can. 153 59 43N 100 5W
Thlewiaza, R., N.W.T., Can. 153 60 29N 94 40W
Thmar Puok 100 13 57N 103 4E
Tho Vinh 100 19 16N 105 42E
Thoa, R. 153 60 31N 109 47W
Thoen 100 17 36N 99 12E
Thoeng 100 19 41N 100 12E
Thoissey 45 46 12N 4 48E
Tholdi 95 35 5N 76 6E
Tholen 47 51 32N 4 13E
Thomas, Okla., U.S.A. 159 35 48N 98 48W
Thomas, W. Va., U.S.A. 156 39 10N 79 30W
Thomas, L. 139 26 4S 137 58E
Thomas Street 38 53 27N 8 15W
Thomastown 39 52 32N 7 10W
Thomasville, Ala., U.S.A. 157 31 55N 87 42W
Thomasville, Fla., U.S.A. 157 30 50N 84 0W
Thomasville, N.C., U.S.A. 157 35 5N 80 4W
Thommen 47 50 14N 6 5E
Thompson, Can. 153 55 45N 97 52W
Thompson, U.S.A. 162 41 52N 75 31W
Thompson Falls 160 47 37N 115 26W
Thompson Landing 153 62 56N 110 40W
Thompson, R., Can. 152 50 15N 121 24W
Thompson, R., U.S.A. 158 39 46N 93 37W
Thompsons 161 39 0N 109 50W
Thompsonville 162 42 0N 72 37W
Thomson, R. 138 25 11S 142 53E
Thomson's Falls = Nyahururu Falls 126 0 2N 36 27E
Thon Buri 100 13 43N 100 29E
Thonburi 101 13 50N 100 36E
Thônes 45 45 54N 6 18E
Thongwa 98 16 45N 96 33E
Thonon-les-Bains 45 46 22N 6 29E
Thonze 98 17 38N 95 47E
Thorez 83 48 4N 38 34E
Þorlákshöfn 74 63 51N 21 22W
Thornaby on Tees 33 54 36N 1 19W
Thornborough 138 16 54S 145 2E
Thornbury, N.Z. 143 46 17S 168 9E
Thornbury, U.K. 28 51 36N 2 31W
Thorndon 29 52 16N 1 8E
Thorne, U.K. 33 53 36N 0 56W
Thorne, U.S.A. 163 38 36N 118 34W
Thorne Glacier 13 87 30N 150 0E
Thorney 29 52 37N 0 8W
Thornham 29 52 59N 0 35E
Thornhill 35 55 15N 3 46W
Thornthwaite 32 54 36N 3 13W
Thornton-Beresfield 141 32 50S 151 40E
Thornton Celveleys 32 53 52N 3 1W
Thornton Dale 33 54 14N 0 41W
Thorpe 29 52 38N 1 20E
Thorpe le Soken 29 51 50N 1 11E
Thouarcé 43 47 17N 0 30W
Thouin, C. 136 20 20S 118 10E
Thousand Oakes 163 34 10N 118 50W
Thrace = Thráki 68 41 10N 25 30E
Thráki 68 41 9N 25 30E
Thrakikón Pélagos 68 40 30N 25 0E
Thrapston 29 52 24N 0 32W
Three Bridges 29 51 7N 0 9W
Three Forks 160 45 5N 111 40W
Three Hills 152 51 43N 113 15W
Three Hummock I. 138 40 25S 144 55E
Three Kings Is. 142 34 10S 172 10E
Three Lakes 158 45 41N 89 10W
Three Pagodas P. 100 15 16N 98 23E
Three Points, C. 120 4 42N 2 6W
Three Rivers, Austral. 137 25 10S 119 5E
Three Rivers, Calif., U.S.A. 163 36 26N 118 54W
Three Rivers, Tex., U.S.A. 159 28 30N 98 10W
Three Sisters, Mt. 160 44 10N 121 52W
Threlkeld 32 54 37N 3 2W
Threshfield 32 54 5N 2 2W
Þ ó risvatn 74 64 50N 19 26W
Throssell, L. 137 27 27S 124 16E
Throssell Ra. 136 17 24S 126 4E
Þ ó rshöfn 74 66 12N 15 20W
Thrumster 37 58 24N 3 8W
Thuan Moa 101 8 58N 105 30E
Thubun Lakes 153 61 30N 112 0W
Thueyts 45 44 41N 4 9E
Thuillies 47 50 18N 4 20E
Thuin 47 50 20N 4 17E
Thuir 44 42 38N 2 45E
Thule 12 77 30N 69 0W
Thun 50 46 45N 7 38E
Thundelarra 137 28 53S 117 7E
Thunder B. 156 45 0N 83 20W
Thunder Bay 150 48 20N 89 0W
Thunder River 152 52 13N 119 20W
Thundulda 137 32 15S 126 3E
Thunersee 50 46 43N 7 39E
Thung Song 101 8 10N 99 40E
Thunkar 98 27 55N 91 0E
Thuong Tra 100 16 2N 107 42E
Thur, R. 51 47 32N 9 10E
Thurgau □ 51 47 34N 9 10E
Thüringer Wald 48 50 35N 11 0E
Thurlby 29 52 45N 0 21W
Thurles 39 52 40N 7 53W
Thurloo Downs 139 29 15S 143 30E
Thurmaston 28 52 40N 1 8W
Thurmont 162 39 37N 77 25W
Thurn P. 49 47 20N 12 15E
Thursby 32 54 40N 3 3W
Thursday I. 138 10 30S 142 3E
Thurso, Can. 150 45 36N 75 15W
Thurso, U.K. 37 58 34N 3 31W
Thurso, R. 37 58 36N 3 30W
Thurston I. 13 72 0S 100 0W
Thury-Harcourt 42 49 0N 0 30W
Thusis 51 46 42N 9 26E
Thutade L. 152 57 0N 126 55W
Thuy, Le 100 17 14N 106 49E
Thylungra 139 26 4S 143 28E
Thyolo 127 16 7S 35 5E
Thysville = Mbanza Ngungu 124 5 12S 14 53E
Ti-n-Amzi, O. 121 17 35N 4 20E
Ti-n-Barraouene, O. 121 18 40N 4 5E
Ti-n-Emensan 118 22 59N 4 45E
Ti-n-Geloulet 118 25 58N 4 2E
Ti-n-Medjerdam, O. 118 25 45N 1 30W
Ti-n-Tarabine, O. 119 21 37N 7 11E
Ti-n-Zaouaténe 118 48 55S 77 9W
Tia 141 31 10S 151 50E
Tiahualilo 164 26 20N 103 30W
Tianguá 170 3 44S 40 59W
Tiankoura 120 10 47N 3 17W
Tiaret (Tagdent) 118 35 28N 1 21E
Tiarra 141 32 46S 145 1E
Tiassalé 120 5 58N 4 57W
Tibagi 173 24 30S 50 24W
Tibagi, R. 173 22 47S 51 1W
Tibari 123 5 2N 31 48E
Tibati 121 6 22N 12 30E
Tiber = Tevere, R. 63 42 30N 12 20E
Tiber Res. 160 48 20N 111 15W
Tiberias 90 32 47N 35 32E
Tiberias, L. = Kinneret, Yam 90 32 49N 35 36E
Tibesti 119 21 0N 17 30E
Tibet 99 32 30N 86 0E
Tibet □ 105 32 30N 86 0E
Tibiri 121 13 34N 7 4E
Tibleş, mt. 70 47 32N 24 15E
Tibleş, Mţii 70 47 41N 24 6E
Tibnīn 90 33 12N 35 24E
Tibooburra 139 29 26S 142 1E
Tibro 73 58 28N 14 10E
Tibugá, Golfo de 174 5 45N 77 20W
Tiburón, I. 164 29 0N 112 30W
Ticehurst 29 51 2N 0 23E
Tichit 120 18 35N 9 20W
Ticino □ 51 46 20N 8 45E
Ticino, R. 62 45 23N 8 47E
Tickhill 33 53 25N 1 8W
Ticonderoga 162 43 50N 73 28W
Ticul 165 20 20N 89 50W
Tidaholm 73 58 12N 13 55E
Tiddim 98 23 20N 93 45E
Tideridjaouine, Adrar 118 23 0N 2 15E
Tideswell 33 53 17N 1 46W
Tidikelt 118 26 58N 1 30E
Tidjikdja 120 18 4N 11 35W
Tidore 103 0 40N 127 25E
Tidra, I. 120 19 45N 16 20W
Tiébélé 121 11 6N 0 59W
Tiébissou 120 7 9N 5 18W
Tiéboro 119 21 20N 17 7E
Tiefencastel 51 46 40N 9 33E
Tiego 120 12 6N 2 38E
T'iehling 107 42 17N 123 50E
Tiel 46 51 53N 5 26E
Tielt 47 51 0N 3 20E
Tien Shan 85 42 0N 80 0E
Tien Yen 100 21 20N 107 24E
T'iench'ang 107 32 41N 118 59E
T'ienchen 106 40 30N 114 6E
Tiench'eng 109 21 31N 111 18E
T'ienching 107 39 10N 117 15E
T'ienchu 108 26 55N 109 12E
T'iench'üan 108 30 4N 102 50E
T'ienchuangt'ai 107 40 49N 122 6E
Tienen 47 50 48N 4 57E
T'ienho 108 24 47N 108 42E
T'ienhsi 108 24 26N 106 5E
Tiénigbé 120 8 11N 5 43W
Tienkianghsien 69 30 25N 107 30E
T'ienlin 108 24 19N 106 15E
T'ienmen 109 30 37N 113 10E
T'ieno 108 25 9N 106 57E
Tienpai 109 21 30N 111 1E
T'ienshui 105 34 35N 105 15E
T'ient'ai 109 29 9N 121 2E
Tientsin = T'ienching 105 39 10N 117 15E
T'ientung 108 23 39N 107 8E
T'ienyang 108 23 43N 106 44E
Tierp 72 60 20N 17 30E
Tierra Alta 174 8 11N 76 4W
Tierra Amarilla 172 27 28S 70 18W
Tierra Colorada 165 17 10N 99 35W
Tierra de Barros 57 38 40N 6 30W
Tierra de Campos 56 42 10N 4 50W
Tierra del Fuego, I. Gr. de 176 54 0S 69 0W
Tiétar, R. 56 39 55N 5 50W
Tieté, R. 171 20 40S 51 35W
Tieyon 139 26 12S 133 52E
Tiffin 156 41 8N 83 10W
Tifi 123 6 12N 36 55E
Tiflèt 118 33 54N 6 20W
Tiflis = Tbilisi 83 41 50N 44 50E
Tifrah 90 31 19N 34 42E
Tifton 157 31 28N 83 32W
Tifu 103 3 39S 126 18E
Tigalda I. 147 54 9N 165 0W
Tighnabruaich 34 55 55N 5 13W
Tigil 77 58 0N 158 10E
Tignish 151 46 58N 64 2W
Tigre □ 123 13 35N 39 15E
Tigre, R. 174 3 30S 74 58W
Tigu 99 29 48N 91 38E
Tiguentourine 119 28 8N 8 58E
Tiguila 121 14 44N 1 50W
Tigveni 70 45 10N 24 31E
Tigyaing 98 23 45N 96 10E
Tîh, Gebel el 122 29 32N 33 26E
Tihodaine, Dunes de 119 25 15N 7 15E
Tîjî 119 32 0N 11 18E
Tijiamis 103 7 16S 108 29E
Tijibadok 103 6 53S 106 47E

Tijirit, O Tolox

Tijirit, O. 120 19 30N 6 15W
Tijuana 164 32 30N 117 3W
Tikal 166 17 2N 89 35W
Tikamgarh 95 24 44N 78 57 E
Tikan 138 5 58 S 149 2 E
Tikhoretsk 83 45 56N 40 5 E
Tikhvin 80 59 35N 33 30 E
Tikkadouine, Adrar 118 24 28N 1 30 E
Tiko 121 4 4N 9 20 E
Tikrit 92 34 35N 43 37 E
Tiksi 77 71 50N 129 0 E
Tilamuta 103 0 40N 122 15 E
Tilburg 47 51 31N 5 6 E
Tilbury, Can. 150 42 17N 84 23W
Tilbury, U.K. 29 51 27N 0 24 E
Tilcara 172 23 30 S 65 23W
Tilden 158 42 3N 97 45W
Tilemsès 121 15 37N 4 44 E
Tilemsi, Vallée du 121 17 42N 0 15 E
Tilghman 162 38 42N 76 20W
Tilhar 95 28 0N 79 45 E
Tilia, O. 118 27 32N 0 55 E
Tilichiki 77 61 0N 166 5 E
Tiligul, R. 82 47 35N 30 30 E
Tililane 118 27 49N 0 6W
Tilin 98 21 41N 94 6 E
Tilissos 69 38 15N 25 0 E
Till, R. 35 55 35N 2 3W
Tillabéri 121 14 7N 1 28 E
Tillamook 160 45 29N 123 55W
Tillberga 72 59 42N 16 39 E
Tilley 152 50 28N 111 38W
Tillia 121 16 8N 4 47 E
Tillicoultry 35 56 9N 3 44W
Tillsonburg 150 42 53N 80 44W
Tilmanstone 29 51 13N 1 18 E
Tilos, I. 69 36 27N 27 27 E
Tilpa 139 30 57 S 144 24 E
Tilrhemt 118 33 9N 3 22 E
Tilsit = Sovetsk 80 55 6N 21 50 E
Tilt, R. 37 56 50N 3 50W
Tilton 162 43 25N 71 36W
Timahoe 39 52 59N 7 12W
Timanskiy Kryazh 78 65 58N 50 5 E
Timaru 143 44 23 S 171 14 E
Timashevo 84 53 22N 51 9 E
Timashevsk 83 45 35N 39 0 E
Timau 126 0 4N 37 15 E
Timbákion 69 35 4N 24 45 E
Timbaúba 170 7 31 S 35 19W
Timbédra 120 16 17N 8 16W
Timber L. 158 45 29N 101 0W
Timber Mtn. 163 37 6N 116 28W
Timbío 174 2 20N 76 40W
Timbiquí 174 2 46N 77 42W
Timboon 140 38 30 S 142 58 E
Timbuktu = Tombouctou 120 16 50N 3 0W
Timdjaouine 118 21 47N 4 30 E
Timétrine Montagnes 121 19 25N 1 0W
Timfi Óros 68 39 59N 20 45 E
Timfristós, Óros 69 38 57N 21 50 E
Timhadite 118 33 15N 5 4W
Timimoun 118 29 14N 0 16 E
Timimoun, Sebkha de 118 28 50N 0 46 E
Timiris, C. 120 19 15N 16 30W
Timiş □ 66 45 40N 21 30 E
Timiş, R. 70 45 30N 21 0 E
Timişoara 66 45 43N 21 15 E
Timmins 150 48 28N 81 25W
Timmoudi 118 29 20N 1 8W
Timok, R. 66 44 10N 22 40 E
Timoleague 39 51 40N 8 51W
Timolin 39 52 59N 6 49W
Timon 170 5 8 S 42 52W
Timor □ 103 8 0 S 126 30 E
Timor, I. 103 9 0 S 125 0 E
Timor Sea 136 10 0 S 127 0 E
Timur □ 103 9 0 S 125 0 E
Tin Alkoum 119 24 30N 10 17 E
Tin Gornai 121 16 38N 0 38W
Tin Mtn. 163 36 54N 117 28W
Tina, Khalîg el 122 31 20N 32 42 E
Tinaca Pt. 103 5 30N 125 25 E
Tinaco 174 9 42N 68 26W
Tinafak, O. 119 27 10N 7 0W
Tinahely 39 52 48N 6 28W
Tinambacan 103 12 5N 124 32 E
Tinapagee 139 29 25 S 144 15 E
Tinaquillo 174 9 55N 68 18W
Tinaroo Falls 138 17 5 S 145 4 E
Tinca 70 46 46N 21 58 E
Tinchebray 42 48 47N 0 45W
Tindivanam 97 12 15N 79 35 E
Tindouf 118 27 50N 8 4W
Tindzhe Dzong 95 28 20N 88 8 E
Tineo 56 43 21N 6 27W
Tinerhir 118 31 29N 5 31W
Tinfouchi 118 28 58N 5 54W
T'ing Chiang, R. 109 24 24N 116 35 E
Tingan 100 19 42N 110 18 E
Tingch'u, R. 108 28 20N 99 12 E
Tingewick 28 51 59N 1 4W
Tinggi, Pulau, Is. 101 2 18N 104 7 E
Tinghai 109 30 0N 122 10 E
Tinghsi 106 35 33N 104 32 E
Tinghsiang 106 38 32N 112 59 E
Tinghsien 106 38 30N 115 0 E
Tingkawk Sakun 98 26 4N 96 44 E
Tingk'ouchen 106 39 48N 106 36 E
Tinglev 73 54 57N 9 13 E
Tingnan 109 24 47N 115 2 E
Tingo María 174 9 10 S 76 0W
Tingpien 106 37 36N 107 38 E
Tingshan 109 31 16N 119 51 E
Tingsryd 73 56 31N 15 0 E
Tingt'ao 106 35 4N 115 34 E
Tingvalla 73 58 47N 12 2 E
Tingyüan 109 32 32N 117 41 E
Tinh Bien 101 10 36N 104 57 E
Tinharé, I. de 171 13 30 S 38 58W
Tinié 121 14 17N 1 30W
Tinioulig, Sebkra 118 22 30N 6 45W
Tinjoub 118 29 45N 5 40W
Tinkurrin 137 32 59 S 117 46 E
Tinnia 172 27 0 S 62 45W
Tinnoset 71 59 45N 9 3 E
Tinnsjø 71 59 55N 8 54 E
Tinogasta 172 28 0 S 67 40W
Tinos 69 37 33N 25 8 E
Tiñoso, C. 59 37 32N 1 6W
Tinsukia 98 27 29N 95 26 E
Tintagel 30 50 40N 4 45W
Tintagel Hd. 30 50 40N 4 46W
Tintern 31 51 42N 2 41W
Tintern Abbey 39 52 14N 6 50W
Tintigny 47 49 41N 5 31 E
Tintina 172 27 2 S 62 45W
Tintinara 140 35 48 S 140 2 E
Tinto, R. 57 37 30N 5 33W
Tinui 142 40 52 S 176 5 E
Tinwald 143 43 55 S 171 43 E
Tioga 162 41 54N 77 9W
Tioman, I. 101 2 50N 104 10 E
Tioman, Pulau, Is. 101 2 50N 104 10 E
Tionaga 150 48 0N 82 0W
Tione di Trento 62 46 3N 10 44 E
Tior 123 6 26N 31 11 E
Tioulilin 118 27 1N 0 2W
Tipongpani 99 27 20N 95 55 E
Tipperary 39 52 28N 8 10W
Tipperary □ 39 52 37N 7 55W
Tipton, U.K. 28 52 32N 2 4W
Tipton, Calif., U.S.A. 163 36 3N 119 19W
Tipton, Ind., U.S.A. 156 40 17N 86 30W
Tipton, Iowa, U.S.A. 158 41 45N 91 12W
Tiptonville 159 36 22N 89 30W
Tiptree 29 51 48N 0 46 E
Tiptur 97 13 15N 76 26 E
Tira 90 32 14N 34 56 E
Tiracambu, Serra do 170 3 15 S 46 30W
Tirahart, O. 118 23 55N 2 0W
Tiran 93 32 45N 51 0 E
Tirân 122 27 56N 34 35 E
Tirana 68 41 18N 19 49 E
Tirana-Durrësi □ 68 41 35N 20 0 E
Tirano 62 46 13N 10 11 E
Tirarer, Mont 121 19 35N 1 10W
Tiraspol 82 46 55N 29 35 E
Tirat Carmel 90 32 46N 34 58 E
Tirat Tsevi 90 32 26N 35 31 E
Tirat Yehuda 90 32 1N 34 56 E
Tiratimine 118 25 56N 3 37 E
Tirdout 121 16 7N 1 5W
Tire 92 38 5N 27 50 E
Tirebolu 92 40 58N 38 45 E
Tiree, I. 34 56 31N 6 55W
Tiree, Passage of 34 56 30N 6 30W
Tîrgoviste 70 44 55N 25 27 E
Tîrgu Frumos 70 47 12N 27 2 E
Tîrgu-Jiu 70 45 5N 23 19 E
Tîrgu Mureş 70 46 31N 24 38 E
Tîrgu Neamţ 70 47 12N 26 25 E
Tîrgu Ocna 70 46 16N 26 39 E
Tîrgu Secuiesc 70 46 0N 26 10 E
Tirich Mir Mt. 93 36 15N 71 35 E
Tiriola 65 38 57N 16 32 E
Tiririca, Serra da 171 17 6 S 47 6W
Tirlyanskiy 84 54 14N 58 35 E
Tirna, R. 96 18 5N 76 30 E
Tîrnava = Botoroaga 70 44 8N 25 32 E
Tîrnava Mare, R. 70 46 15N 24 30 E
Tîrnava Mica, R. 70 46 17N 24 30 E
Tírnavos 68 39 45N 22 18 E
Tîrnova 70 45 23N 22 1 E
Tîrnŭveni 70 46 19N 24 13 E
Tirodi 96 21 35N 79 35 E
Tirol □ 52 47 3N 10 43 E
Tiros 171 19 0 S 45 58W
Tirschenreuth 49 49 51N 12 20 E
Tirso, L. 64 40 8N 8 56 E
Tirso, R. 64 40 33N 9 12 E
Tirstrup 73 56 18N 10 42 E
Tirua 142 38 25 S 174 40 E
Tiruchchirappalli 97 10 45N 78 45 E
Tiruchendur 97 8 30N 78 11 E
Tiruchengodu 97 11 23N 77 56 E
Tirumangalam 97 9 49N 77 58 E
Tirunelveli (Tinnevelly) 97 8 45N 77 45 E
Tirupati 97 13 45N 79 30 E
Tiruppattur 97 12 30N 78 30 E
Tiruppur 97 11 12N 77 22 E
Tiruturaipundi 97 10 32N 79 41 E
Tiruvadaimarudur 97 11 2N 79 27 E
Tiruvallar 97 13 9N 79 57 E
Tiruvannamalai 97 12 10N 79 12 E
Tiruvarur (Negapatam) 97 10 46N 79 38 E
Tiruvatipuram 97 12 39N 79 33 E
Tiruvottiyur 97 13 10N 80 22 E
Tisa, R. 66 45 30N 20 20 E
Tisdale 153 52 50N 104 0W
Tiseirhatène, Mares de 118 22 51N 9 30W
Tishomingo 159 34 14N 96 38W
Tisjön 72 60 56N 13 0 E
Tisnaren 72 58 58N 15 56 E
Tisno 63 44 45N 15 41 E
Tišnov 53 49 21N 16 25 E
Tisovec 53 48 41N 19 56 E
Tissemsilt 118 35 35N 1 50 E
Tissit, O. 119 27 28N 9 58W
Tissø 73 55 35N 11 18 E
Tista, R. 98 25 23N 89 43 E
Tisted 73 56 58N 8 40 E
Tisza, R. 53 47 38N 20 44 E
Tiszaföldvár 53 47 0N 20 14 E
Tiszafüred 53 47 38N 20 50 E
Tiszalök 53 48 0N 21 10 E
Tiszavasvári 53 47 58N 21 18 E
Tit, Alg. 118 27 0N 1 37 E
Tit, Alg. 119 23 0N 5 10 E
Tit-Ary 77 71 50N 126 30 E
Titaguas 58 39 53N 1 6W
Titahi Bay 142 41 6 S 174 50 E
Titai Damer 123 16 43N 37 25 E
Titchfield 28 50 51N 1 13W
Titel 66 45 29N 20 18 E
Tithwal 95 34 21N 73 50 E
Titicaca, L. 174 15 30 S 69 30W
Titilagarh 96 20 15N 83 5 E
Tititira Head 98 43 38 S 169 26 E
Titiwa 121 12 14N 12 53 E
Titlis 51 46 46N 8 27 E
Titograd 66 42 30N 19 19 E
Titov Veles 66 41 46N 21 47 E
Titova Korenica 63 44 45N 15 41 E
Titovo Uzice 66 43 55N 19 50 E
Titule 126 3 15N 25 31 E
Titumate 174 8 19N 77 5W
Titusville 156 41 35N 79 39W
Tiumpan Hd. 36 58 15N 6 10W
Tivaouane 120 14 56N 16 45W
Tivat 66 42 28N 18 43 E
Tiveden 73 58 50N 14 30 E
Tiverton 30 50 54N 3 30W
Tivoli 63 41 58N 12 45 E
Tiwi 93 22 45N 59 12 E
Tiyo 123 14 41N 40 57 E
Tizga 118 32 1N 5 9W
Tizi n'Isly 118 32 28N 5 47W
Tizi Ouzou 119 36 42N 4 3 E
Tizmín 165 21 0N 88 1W
Tiznados, R. 174 8 50N 67 50W
Tiznit 118 29 48N 9 45W
Tjalang 103 4 30N 95 43 E
Tjangkuang, Tg. 102 7 0 S 105 0 E
Tjareme, G. 103 6 55 S 108 27 E
Tjeggelvas 74 66 37N 17 45 E
Tjepu 103 7 12 S 111 31 E
Tjeukemeer 46 52 53N 5 48 E
Tjiandjur 103 6 51 S 107 7 E
Tjibatu 103 7 8 S 107 59 E
Tjikadjang 103 7 25 S 107 48 E
Tjimahi 103 6 53 S 107 33 E
Tjirebon = Cirebon 103 6 45 S 108 32 E
Tjöllong 71 59 6N 10 3 E
Tjöme 71 59 8N 10 26 E
Tjonger Kanaal 46 52 52N 6 52 E
Tjörn 73 58 0N 11 35 E
Tjörnes 74 66 12N 17 9W
Tjuls 73 57 30N 18 15 E
Tjurup 102 4 26 S 102 13 E
Tkibuli 83 42 26N 43 0 E
Tkvarcheli 83 42 47N 41 52 E
Tlacolula 165 16 57N 96 29W
Tlacotalpán 165 18 37N 95 40W
Tlaquepaque 164 20 39N 103 19W
Tlaxcala 165 19 20N 98 14W
Tlaxcala □ 165 19 30N 98 20W
Tlaxiaco 165 17 10N 97 40W
Tlell 152 53 34N 131 56W
Tlemcen 118 34 52N 1 15W
Tleta di Sidi Bouguedra 118 32 16N 8 58W
Tleta Sidi Bouguedra 118 32 16N 9 59W
Tlumach 80 48 46N 25 0 E
Tłuszcz 54 52 25N 21 25 E
Tlyarata 83 42 9N 46 26 E
Tmassah 119 26 19N 15 51 E
Tmisan 119 27 23N 13 30 E
To Bong 100 12 45N 109 16 E
T'o Chiang, R. 108 28 55N 105 33 E
To-Shima 111 34 31N 139 17 E
Toad, R. 152 59 25N 124 57W
Toay 172 36 50 S 64 30W
Toba 111 34 30N 136 45 E
Toba Kakar 94 31 30N 69 0 E
Toba, L. 102 2 40N 98 50 E
Toba Tek Singh 94 30 55N 72 25 E
Tobago, I. 167 11 10N 60 30W
Tobarra 59 38 35N 1 41W
Tobelo 103 1 25N 127 56 E
Tobercurry 38 54 3N 8 43W
Tobermore 38 54 49N 6 43W
Tobermorey 138 22 12 S 138 0 E
Tobermory, Can. 150 45 12N 81 40W
Tobermory, U.K. 34 56 37N 6 4W
Tobin, L. 136 21 45 S 125 49 E
Tobin L. 153 53 35N 103 30W
Toboali 102 3 0 S 106 25 E
Tobol 84 52 40N 62 39 E
Tobol, R. 84 58 10N 68 12 E
Toboli 103 0 38 S 120 12 E
Tobolsk 84 58 0N 68 10 E
Tobruk = Tubruq 117 32 7N 23 55 E
Tobyhanna 162 41 10N 75 15W
Tocantínia 170 9 33 S 48 22W
Tocantinópolis 170 6 20 S 47 25W
Tocantins, R. 170 14 30 S 49 0W
Tocca 157 34 6N 83 17W
Toce, R. 62 46 5N 8 29 E
Tochigi 111 36 25N 139 45 E
Tochigi-ken □ 111 36 45N 139 45 E
Tocina 57 37 37N 5 44W
Toconao 172 34 35N 83 19W
Toconhão, Serra do 171 14 30 S 47 46W
Tocópero 174 11 30N 69 16W
Tocopilla 172 22 5 S 70 10W
Tocumwal 141 35 45 S 145 31 E
Tocuyo, R. 174 10 50N 69 0W
Todd, R. 138 24 52 S 135 48 E
Toddington 29 51 57N 0 31W
Todeli 103 1 38 S 124 34 E
Todenyang 126 4 35N 35 56 E
Todi 63 42 47N 12 24 E
Tödi 51 46 48N 8 55 E
Todjo 103 1 20 S 121 15 E
Todmorden 32 53 43N 2 7W
Todos os Santos, Baía de 171 12 48 S 38 38W
Todos Santos 164 23 27N 110 13W
Todos Santos, Bahia de 164 31 48N 116 42W
Todtnau 49 47 50N 7 56 E
Toe Hd., Ireland 39 51 29N 9 13W
Toe Hd., U.K. 36 57 50N 7 10W
Toecé 121 11 50N 1 16W
Toetoes B. 143 46 42 S 168 41 E
Tofield 152 53 25N 112 40W
Tofino 152 49 11N 125 55W
Töfsingdalems National Park 72 62 15N 12 44 E
Tofta 73 57 11N 12 20 E
Toftlund 73 55 11N 9 2 E
Tōgane 111 35 33N 140 22 E
Togba 120 17 26N 10 25W
Toggenburg 51 47 16N 9 9 E
Togian, Kepulauan 103 0 20 S 121 50 E
Togliatti 81 53 37N 49 18 E
Togo ■ 121 6 15N 1 35 E
Toguzak, R. 84 54 3N 62 44 E
Tōhoku □ 112 39 50N 141 45 E
Toi 111 34 54N 134 47 E
Toinya 123 6 17N 29 46 E
Toiyabe Dome 163 38 51N 117 22W
Toiyabe, Ra. 163 39 10N 117 10W
Tōjō 110 34 53N 133 16 E
Tok, R. 84 52 46N 52 22 E
Tokaanu 142 38 58 S 175 46 E
Tokachi, R. 112 42 44N 143 42 E
Tokaj 53 48 8N 21 27 E
Tokala, G. 103 1 30 S 121 40 E
Tokanui 143 46 34 S 168 56 E
Tokarahi 143 44 56 S 170 39 E
Tokat 92 40 22N 36 35 E
Tŏkchŏn 107 39 45N 126 18 E
Tokelau Is. 130 9 0 S 172 0W
Toki 111 35 18N 137 8 E
Tokmak, Kirgizia, U.S.S.R. 84 42 55N 75 45 E
Tokmak, Ukraine, U.S.S.R. 82 47 16N 35 42 E
Toko Ra. 138 23 5 S 138 20 E
Tokomaru Bay 142 38 8 S 178 22 E
Tokombere 121 11 18N 3 30 E
Tókomlós 53 46 24N 20 45 E
Tokoname 111 34 53N 136 51 E
Tokong 101 5 27N 100 23 E
Tokoroa 142 38 20 S 175 50 E
Tokorozawa 111 35 47N 139 28 E
T'ok'ot'o 106 40 15N 111 12 E
Toktogul 85 41 50N 72 50 E
Tokuii 110 34 11N 131 42 E
Tokule 123 14 54N 38 26 E
Tokunoshima 112 27 56N 128 55 E
Tokushima 110 34 4N 134 34 E
Tokushima-ken □ 110 35 50N 134 30 E
Tokuyama 110 34 0N 131 50 E
Tōkyō 111 35 45N 139 45 E
Tōkyō-to □ 111 35 40N 139 30 E
Tōkyō-Wan 111 35 25N 139 47 E
Tolaerh 105 35 8N 81 33 E
Tolaga Bay 142 38 21 S 178 20 E
Tolageak 147 70 2N 162 50W
Tolbukhin 67 43 37N 27 49 E
Toledo, Spain 56 39 50N 4 2W
Toledo, Ohio, U.S.A. 156 41 37N 83 33W
Toledo, Oreg., U.S.A. 160 44 40N 123 59W
Toledo, Wash., U.S.A. 160 42 29N 122 58W
Toledo, Montes de 57 39 33N 4 20W
Tolentino 63 43 12N 13 17 E
Tolfino 152 49 6N 125 54W
Tolga, Alg. 119 34 46N 5 22 E
Tolga, Norway 71 62 26N 11 1 E
Tolima □ 174 3 45N 75 15W
Tolima, Vol. 174 4 40N 75 19W
Tolitoli 103 1 5N 120 50 E
Tolkamer 46 51 52N 6 6 E
Tolkmicko 54 54 19N 19 31 E
Tollarp 73 55 55N 13 58 E
Tollesbury 29 51 46N 0 51 E
Tolleson 161 33 29N 112 10W
Tollhouse 163 37 1N 119 24W
Tolmachevo 80 58 56N 29 57 E
Tolmezzo 63 46 23N 13 0 E
Tolmino 63 46 11N 13 45 E
Tolna 53 46 25N 18 48 E
Tolna □ 53 46 30N 18 30 E
Tolne 73 57 28N 10 20 E
Tolo 124 2 50 S 18 40 E
Tolo, Teluk 103 2 20 S 122 10 E
Tolokiwa I. 138 5 30 S 147 30 E
Tolon 121 9 26N 1 3W
Tolosa 58 43 8N 2 5W
Tolox 57 36 41N 4 54W

Tolsta Hd Tregnago

Tolsta Hd.	36	58 20N	6 10W
Toluca	165	19 20N	99 50W
Tolun	106	42 22N	116 30E
Tom Burke	129	23 5S	28 4E
Tomahawk	158	45 28N	89 40W
Tomakomai	112	42 38N	141 36E
Tomales	163	38 15N	122 53W
Tomales B.	163	38 15N	123 58W
Tomar	57	39 36N	8 25W
Tómaros Óros	68	39 29N	20 48E
Tomaszów Lubelski	54	50 29N	23 23E
Tomaszów Mazowiecki	54	51 30N	19 57E
Tomatin	37	57 20N	4 0W
Tomatlán	164	19 56N	105 15W
Tombé	123	5 53N	31 40E
Tombigbee, R.	157	32 0N	88 6W
Tombodor, Serra do	171	12 0S	41 30W
Tombouctou	120	16 50N	3 0W
Tombstone	161	31 40N	110 4W
Tomdoun	36	57 4N	5 2W
Tomé	172	36 36S	73 6W
Tomé-Açu	170	2 25S	48 9W
Tomelilla	73	55 33N	13 58E
Tomelloso	59	39 10N	3 2W
Tomingley	141	32 31S	148 16E
Tomini	103	0 30N	120 30E
Tomini, Teluk	103	0 10S	122 0E
Tominian	120	13 17N	4 35W
Tomiño	56	41 59N	8 46W
Tomintoul	37	57 15N	3 22W
Tomioka	111	36 15N	138 54E
Tomkinson Ranges	137	26 11S	129 5E
Tommot	77	58 50N	126 20E
Tomnavoulin	37	57 19N	3 18W
Tomnop Ta Suos	101	11 20N	104 15E
Tomo, Colomb.	174	2 38N	67 32W
Tomo, Japan	110	34 23N	133 23E
Tomobe	111	36 40N	140 41E
Toms Place	163	37 34N	118 41W
Toms River	162	39 59N	74 12W
Tomsk	76	56 30N	85 12E
Tomtabacken	73	57 30N	14 30E
Tonalá	165	16 8N	93 41W
Tonale, Passo del	62	46 15N	10 34E
Tonalea	161	36 17N	110 58W
Tonami	111	36 56N	136 58E
Tonantins	174	2 45S	67 45W
Tonasket	160	48 45N	119 30W
Tonawanda	156	43 0N	78 54W
Tonbridge	29	51 12N	0 18E
Tondano	103	1 35N	124 54E
Tondela	56	40 31N	8 5W
Tønder	73	54 58N	8 50E
Tondi	97	9 45N	79 4E
Tondi Kiwindi	121	14 28N	2 02E
Tondibi	121	16 39N	0 14W
Tone-Gawa, R.	111	35 44N	140 51E
Tone, R.	137	34 23S	116 25E
Tone R.	30	50 59N	3 15W
Tong	28	52 39N	2 18W
Tonga Is. ■	130	20 0S	173 0W
Tonga Trench	143	18 0S	175 0W
Tongaat	129	29 33S	31 9E
Tongala	141	36 14S	144 56E
Tongaland	129	27 0S	32 0E
Tongareva I	143	9 0S	158 0W
Tongariro, mt.	142	39 7S	175 50E
Tongchŏnni	107	39 50N	127 25E
Tongeren	47	50 47N	5 28E
Tongio	141	37 14S	147 44E
Tongjosŏn Man	107	39 30N	128 0E
Tongking = Bac-Phan	101	21 30N	105 0E
Tongking, G. of	101	20 0N	108 0E
Tongnae	107	35 12N	129 5E
Tongobory	129	23 32S	44 20E
Tongoy	172	30 25S	71 40W
Tongres = Tongeren	47	50 47N	5 28E
Tongsa Dzong	98	27 31N	90 31E
Tongue	37	58 29N	4 25W
Tongue, Kyle of	37	58 30N	4 30W
Tongue, R.	160	48 30N	106 30W
Tongyang	107	39 9N	126 53E
Tonj	123	7 20N	28 44E
Tonk	94	26 6N	75 54E
Tonkawa	159	36 44N	67 22W
Tonkin = Bac-Phan	100	22 0N	105 0E
Tonkin, G. of	100	20 0N	108 0E
Tonlé Sap	100	13 0N	104 0E
Tonnay-Charente	44	45 56N	0 55W
Tonneins	44	44 24N	0 20E
Tonnerre	43	47 51N	3 59E
Tönning	48	54 18N	8 57E
Tonopah	163	38 4N	117 12W
Tonoshō	110	34 29N	134 11E
Tonosí	166	7 20N	80 20W
Tonsberg	71	59 19N	10 25E
Tonstad	71	58 40N	6 45E
Tonto Basin	61	33 58N	111 15W
Tonyrefail	31	51 35N	3 26W
Tonzang	98	23 36N	93 42E
Tonzi	98	24 39N	94 57E
Tooele	160	40 30N	112 20W
Toolonda	140	36 58S	141 5E
Toombeolo	38	53 26N	9 52W
Toomevara	39	52 50N	8 2W
Toompine	139	27 15S	144 19E
Toongi	141	32 28S	148 30E
Toonpan	138	19 28S	146 48E
Toora	141	38 39S	146 23E
Toora-Khem	77	52 28N	96 9E
Toormore	39	51 31N	9 41W
Toowoomba	139	27 32S	151 56E
Top	93	34 15N	68 35E
Top Ozero	78	65 35N	32 0E
Topalu	70	44 31N	28 3E
Topaz	163	38 41N	119 30W
Topeka	158	39 3N	95 40W
Topki	76	55 25N	85 20E
Topla, R.	53	49 0N	21 36E
Topley	152	54 32N	126 5W
Toplica, R.	66	43 15N	21 30E
Toplița	70	46 55N	25 27E
Topocalma, Pta.	172	34 10S	72 2W
Topock	161	34 46N	114 29W
Topola	66	44 17N	20 32E
Topol'čany	53	48 35N	18 12E
Topoli	83	47 59N	51 45E
Topolnitsa, R.	67	42 21N	24 0E
Topolobampo	164	25 40N	109 10W
Topolovgrad	67	42 5N	26 20E
TopolvŭT Mare	66	45 46N	21 41E
Toppenish	160	46 27N	120 16W
Topsham	30	50 40N	3 27W
Topusko	63	45 18N	15 59E
Toquima, Ra.	163	39 0N	117 0W
Tor Bay, Austral.	137	35 5S	117 50E
Tor Bay, U.K.	23	50 26N	3 31W
Tor Ness	37	58 47N	3 18W
Tor, oilfield	19	56 40N	3 35E
Torá	58	41 49N	1 25E
Tora Kit	123	11 2N	32 30E
Torata	174	17 3S	70 1W
Torbat-e Heydarīyeh	93	35 15N	59 12E
Torbat-e Jām	93	35 8N	60 35E
Torbay, Can.	151	47 40N	52 42W
Torbay, U.K.	30	50 26N	3 31W
Torchin	80	50 45N	25 0E
Tordal	71	59 10N	8 45E
Tordesillas	56	41 30N	5 0W
Tordoya	56	43 6N	8 36W
Töre	74	65 55N	22 40E
Töreboda	73	58 41N	14 7E
Torfajökull	74	63 54N	19 0W
Torgau	48	51 32N	13 0E
Torgelow	48	53 40N	13 59E
Torhout	47	51 5N	3 7E
Tori	123	7 53N	33 35E
Torigni-sur-Vire	42	49 3N	0 58W
Torija	58	40 44N	3 2W
Torin	164	27 33N	110 5W
Toriñana, C.	56	43 3N	9 17W
Torino	62	45 4N	7 40E
Torit	123	4 20N	32 55E
Torkovichi	80	58 51N	30 30E
Tormac	66	45 30N	21 30E
Tormentine	151	46 6N	63 46W
Tormes, R.	56	41 7N	6 0W
Tornado Mt.	152	49 55N	114 40W
Tornby	73	57 32N	9 56E
Torne älv	74	65 50N	24 12E
Torneå = Tornio	74	65 50N	24 12E
Torness	37	57 18N	4 22W
Torneträsk	74	68 24N	19 15E
Tornio	74	65 50N	24 12E
Tornionjoki	74	65 50N	24 12E
Tornquist	172	38 0S	62 15W
Toro	56	41 35N	5 24W
Torö	73	58 48N	17 50E
Toro, Cerro del	172	29 0S	69 50W
Toro Pk.	163	33 34N	116 24W
Törökszentmjklés	53	47 11N	20 27E
Toronátos Kólpos	68	40 5N	23 30E
Toronto, Austral.	141	33 0S	151 30E
Toronto, Can.	150	43 39N	79 20W
Toronto, U.S.A.	156	40 27N	80 36W
Toronto, L.	164	27 40N	105 30W
Toropets	80	56 30N	31 40E
Tororo	126	0 45N	34 12E
Toros Dağlari	92	37 0N	35 0E
Torphins	37	57 7N	2 37W
Torpoint	30	50 23N	4 12W
Torpshammar	72	62 29N	16 20E
Torquay, Austral.	140	38 20S	144 19E
Torquay, Can.	153	49 9N	103 30W
Torquay, U.K.	30	50 27N	3 31W
Torquemada	56	42 2N	4 19W
Torralba de Calatrava	57	39 1N	3 44W
Torran Rocks	34	56 14N	6 24W
Torrance	163	33 50N	118 19W
Torrão	57	38 16N	8 11W
Torre Annunziata	64	40 45N	14 26E
Tôrre de Moncorvo	56	41 12N	7 8W
Torre del Greco	65	40 47N	14 22E
Torre del Mar	57	36 44N	4 6W
Torre-Pacheco	29	37 44N	0 57W
Torre Pellice	62	44 49N	7 13E
Torreblanca	58	40 14N	0 12E
Torrecampo	57	38 29N	4 41W
Torrecilla en Cameros	58	42 15N	2 38W
Torredembarra	58	41 9N	1 24W
Torredonjimeno	57	37 46N	3 57W
Torrejoncillo	56	39 54N	6 28W
Torrelaguna	58	40 50N	3 38W
Torrelavega	56	43 20N	4 5W
Torremaggiore	65	41 42N	15 17E
Torremolinos	57	36 38N	4 30W
Torrens Cr.	138	22 23S	145 9E
Torrens Creek	138	20 48S	145 3E
Torrens, L.	140	31 0S	137 50E
Torrente	59	39 27N	0 28W
Torrenueva	59	38 38N	3 22W
Torreón	164	25 33N	103 25W
Torreperogil	59	38 2N	3 17W
Torres, Mexico	164	28 46N	110 47W
Torres, Spain	56	41 6N	5 0W
Tôrres Novas	57	39 27N	8 33W
Torres Strait	135	9 50S	142 20E
Torres Vedras	57	39 5N	9 15W
Torrevieja	59	37 59N	0 42W
Torrey	161	38 12N	111 30W
Torridge, R.	30	50 51N	4 10W
Torridon	36	57 33N	5 34W
Torridon, L.	36	57 35N	5 50W
Torrijos	56	39 59N	4 18W
Törring	73	55 52N	9 29E
Torrington, Conn., U.S.A.	162	41 50N	73 9W
Torrington, Wyo., U.S.A.	158	42 5N	104 8W
Torroboll	37	58 0N	4 23W
Torroella de Montgri	58	42 2N	3 8E
Torrox	57	36 46N	3 57W
Torsås	73	56 24N	16 0E
Torsby	72	60 7N	13 0E
Torsjok	72	57 5N	34 55E
Torsö	73	58 48N	13 45E
Torthorwald	35	55 7N	3 30W
Tortola, I.	147	18 19N	65 0W
Tórtoles de Esgueva	56	41 49N	4 2W
Tortona	62	44 53N	8 54E
Tortoreto	63	42 50N	13 55E
Tortorici	65	38 2N	14 48E
Tortosa	58	40 49N	0 31E
Tortosa C.	58	40 41N	0 52E
Tortosendo	56	40 15N	7 31W
Tortue, I. de la	167	20 5N	72 57W
Tortuga, Isla la	167	11 8N	67 2W
Torud	93	35 25N	55 5E
Torugart, Pereval	85	40 32N	75 24E
Torun	54	53 0N	18 39E
Torup	73	56 57N	13 5E
Torvastad	71	59 23N	5 15E
Torver	32	54 20N	3 7W
Tory I.	38	55 17N	8 12W
Torysa, R.	53	48 50N	21 15E
Torzhok	80	57 5N	34 55E
Tosa	110	33 24N	133 23E
Tosa-shimizu	110	32 52N	132 58E
Tosa-Wan	110	33 15N	133 30E
Tosa-yamada	110	33 36N	133 38E
Toscaig	36	57 23N	5 49W
Toscana	62	43 30N	11 5E
Tosno	80	59 30N	30 58E
Töss, R.	51	47 32N	8 39E
Tossa	58	41 43N	2 56E
Tostado	172	29 15S	61 50W
Tostedt	48	53 17N	9 42E
Tosu	110	33 22N	130 31E
Toszek	54	50 27N	18 32E
Totak	71	59 40N	7 45E
Totana	59	37 45N	1 30W
Toten	71	60 37N	10 53E
Toteng	128	20 22S	22 58E
Tôtes	42	49 41N	1 3E
Totland	28	50 41N	1 32W
Totley	33	53 18N	1 32W
Totma	81	60 0N	42 40E
Totnes	30	50 26N	3 41W
Totonicapán	166	14 50N	91 20W
Totskoye	84	52 32N	52 45E
Tottenham	141	32 14S	147 21E
Totton	28	50 55N	1 29W
Tottori	110	35 30N	134 15E
Tottori-ken □	110	35 30N	134 12E
Touamotou, Archipel des	131	17 0S	144 0W
Touat	118	27 30N	0 30E
Touba	120	8 15N	7 40W
Toubkal, Djebel	118	31 0N	8 0W
Toubouai, Îles	131	25 0S	150 0W
Toucy	43	47 44N	3 15E
Tougan	120	13 11N	2 58W
Touggourt	119	33 10N	6 0E
Tougué	120	11 25N	11 50W
Toukmatine	119	24 49N	7 11E
Toul	43	48 40N	5 53E
Toulepleu	120	6 32N	8 24W
Toulon	45	43 10N	5 55E
Toulouse	44	43 37N	1 27E
Toummo	119	22 45N	14 8E
Toummo Dhoba	119	22 30N	14 31E
Toumodi	120	6 32N	5 4W
Tounan	109	23 41N	120 28E
Tounassine, Hamada	118	28 48N	5 0W
Toungoo	98	19 0N	96 30E
Touques, R.	42	49 22N	0 8E
Touquet, Le	43	50 30N	1 36E
Tour-du-Pin, La	45	45 33N	5 27E
Touraine	42	47 20N	0 30E
Tourane = Da Nang	100	16 4N	108 13E
Tourcoing	43	50 42N	3 10E
Tourcoingbam	121	13 23N	1 33W
Tournai	47	50 35N	3 25E
Tournan-en-Brie	43	48 44N	2 46E
Tournay	44	43 13N	0 13E
Tournon	45	45 4N	4 50E
Tournon-St.-Martin	42	46 45N	0 58E
Tournus	45	46 35N	4 54E
Touros	170	5 12S	35 28W
Tours	42	47 22N	0 40E
Touside, Pic	119	21 1N	16 18E
T'outaokou	107	42 44N	129 12E
Touwsrivier	128	33 20S	20 0E
Tovar	174	8 20N	71 46W
Tovarkovskiy	81	53 40N	38 5E
Tovdal	71	58 47N	8 10E
Tovdalselva	71	58 20N	8 16E
Towamba	141	37 6S	149 43E
Towanda	162	41 46N	76 30W
Towcester	29	52 7N	0 56W
Tower	158	47 49N	92 17W
Towerhill Cr.	138	22 28S	144 35E
Town Yetholm	35	55 33N	2 19W
Towner	158	48 25N	100 26W
Townsend	160	46 25N	111 32W
Townshend, C.	133	22 18S	150 30E
Townshend, I.	138	22 16S	150 31E
Townsville	138	19 15S	146 45E
Towson	162	39 26N	76 34W
Toyah	159	31 20N	103 48W
Toyahvale	159	30 58N	103 45W
Toyama	111	36 40N	137 15E
Toyama-ken □	111	36 45N	137 30E
Tōyō	110	33 26N	134 16E
Toyohashi	111	34 45N	137 25E
Toyokawa	111	34 48N	137 27E
Toyonaka	111	34 50N	135 28E
Toyooka	110	35 35N	134 55E
Toyota	111	35 3N	137 7E
Toyoura	110	34 6N	130 57E
Toytepa	85	41 3N	69 20E
Tozeur	119	33 56N	8 8E
Tra On	101	9 58N	105 55E
Trabancos, R.	56	41 0N	5 3E
Trabzon	92	41 0N	39 45E
Tracadie	151	47 30N	64 55W
Tracy, Calif., U.S.A.	163	37 46N	121 27W
Tracy, Minn., U.S.A.	158	44 12N	95 3W
Tradate	62	45 43N	8 54E
Trafalgar	141	38 14S	146 12E
Trafalgar, C.	57	36 10N	6 2W
Traghan	119	26 0N	14 30E
Traian	70	45 2N	28 15E
Trail	152	49 5N	117 40W
Trainor L.	152	60 24N	120 17W
Traipu	171	9 58S	37 1W
Tralee	39	52 16N	9 42W
Tralee B.	39	52 17N	9 55W
Tramelan	50	47 13N	7 7E
Tramore	39	52 10N	7 10W
Tramore B.	39	52 9N	7 10W
Tran Ninh, Cao Nguyen	100	19 30N	103 10E
Tranas	73	58 3N	14 59E
Tranås	73	55 37N	13 59E
Trancas	172	26 20S	65 20W
Tranche-sur-Mer, La	42	46 20N	1 27W
Trancoso	56	40 49N	7 21W
Tranebjerg	73	55 51N	10 36E
Tranemo	73	57 30N	13 20E
Tranent	35	55 57N	2 58W
Trang	101	7 33N	99 38E
Trangahy	129	19 7S	44 43E
Trangan, I.	103	6 40S	134 20E
Trangie	141	32 4S	148 0E
Trångsviken	72	63 19N	14 0E
Trani	65	41 17N	16 24E
Tranoroa	129	24 42S	45 4E
Tranquebar	97	11 1N	79 54E
Tranqueras	173	31 8S	56 0W
Trans Nzoia □	126	1 0N	35 0E
Transcona	153	49 50N	97 0W
Transilvania	70	46 19N	25 0E
Transkei □	129	32 15S	28 15E
Transtrand	72	61 6N	13 20E
Transvaal □	128	25 0S	29 0E
Transylvania = Transilvania	70	46 19N	25 0E
Transylvanian Alps	70	45 30N	25 0E
Trápani	64	38 1N	12 30E
Trappe Peak, Mt.	160	45 56N	114 29W
Traqowel	140	35 50S	144 0E
Traralgon	141	38 12S	146 34E
Traryd	73	56 35N	13 45E
Trarza □	120	17 30N	15 0W
Tras os Montes e Alto-Douro □	55	41 25N	7 20W
Trasacco	63	41 58N	13 30E
Trasimeno, L.	63	43 10N	12 5E
Träslöv	73	57 8N	12 21E
Trat	101	12 14N	102 33E
Traun	52	48 14N	14 15E
Traun-see	49	47 48N	13 45E
Traunstein	49	47 52N	12 40E
Tråvad	73	58 15N	13 5E
Traveller's L.	140	33 20S	142 0E
Travemünde	48	53 58N	10 52E
Travers, Mt.	143	42 1S	172 45E
Traverse City	156	44 45N	85 39W
Traverse I.	13	48 0S	28 0E
Travnik	66	44 17N	17 39E
Trawbreaga B.	38	55 20N	7 25W
Trawsfynydd	31	52 54N	3 55W
Trayning	137	31 7S	117 46E
Traynor	153	52 20N	108 32W
Trazo	56	43 0N	8 30W
Trbovlje	63	46 12N	15 5E
Trebbia, R.	62	44 52N	9 30E
Trebel, R.	48	54 0N	12 50E
Trebinje	66	42 44N	18 22E
Trebisacce	65	39 52N	16 32E
Trebišnica, R.	66	42 47N	18 8E
Trebišov	53	48 38N	21 41E
Trebizat	66	43 15N	17 30E
Trěbon	52	48 59N	14 48E
Trebujena	57	36 52N	6 11W
Trecate	62	45 29N	8 42E
Tredegar	31	51 47N	3 16W
Trefeglwys	31	52 31N	3 31W
Trefriw	31	53 9N	3 50W
Tregaron	31	52 14N	3 56W
Trégastel-Plage	42	48 49N	3 31W
Tregnago	63	45 31N	11 10E

Tregrasse Is Tullow

Tregrasse Is. **138** 17 41S 150 43E
Tréguier **42** 48 47N 3 16W
Trégunc **42** 47 51N 3 51W
Tregynon **31** 52 32N 3 19W
Treharris **31** 51 40N 3 17W
Treherne **153** 49 38N 98 42W
Tréia **63** 43 30N 13 20E
Treig, L. **37** 56 48N 4 42W
Treignac **44** 45 32N 1 48E
Treinta y Tres **173** 33 10S 54 50W
Treis **49** 50 9N 7 19E
Trekveid **128** 30 35S 19 45E
Trelde Næs **73** 55 38N 9 53E
Trelech **31** 51 56N 4 28W
Trelew **176** 43 10S 65 20W
Trélissac **44** 45 11N 0 47E
Trelleborg **73** 55 20N 13 10E
Trélon **43** 50 5N 4 6E
Tremadoc **31** 52 57N 4 9W
Tremadoc, Bay **31** 52 51N 4 18W
Tremblade, La **44** 45 46N 1 8W
Tremelo **47** 51 0N 4 42E
Trementina **159** 35 27N 105 30W
Tremiti, I. **63** 42 8N 15 30E
Tremonton **160** 41 45N 112 10W
Tremp **58** 42 10N 0 52E
Trenary **156** 46 12N 86 59W
Trenčin **53** 48 52N 18 4E
Trenche, R. **150** 47 46N 72 53W
Trenggalek **103** 8 5S 111 44E
Trenque Lauquen **172** 36 0S 62 45W
Trent, R. **33** 53 33N 0 44W
Trentham **32** 52 59N 2 12W
Trentino-Alto Adige □ **62** 46 5N 11 0E
Trento **62** 46 5N 11 8E
Trenton, Can. **150** 44 10N 77 40W
Trenton, Mo., U.S.A. **158** 40 5N 93 37W
Trenton, Nebr., U.S.A. **158** 40 14N 101 4W
Trenton, N.J., U.S.A. **162** 40 15N 74 41W
Trenton, Tenn., U.S.A. **159** 35 58N 88 57W
Trepassey **151** 46 43N 53 25W
Tréport, Le **42** 50 3N 1 20E
Treptow **48** 53 42N 13 15E
Trepuzzi **65** 40 26N 18 4E
Tres Arroyos **172** 38 20S 60 20W
Três Corações **173** 21 30S 45 30W
Três Lagoas **171** 20 50S 51 50W
Tres Marías, Is. **164** 21 25N 106 28W
Três Marias, Reprêsa **171** 18 12S 45 15W
Tres Montes, C. **176** 47 0S 75 35W
Tres Pinos **163** 36 48N 121 19W
Três Pontas **173** 21 23S 45 29W
Tres Puentes **172** 27 50S 70 15W
Três Puntas, C. **176** 47 0S 66 0W
Três Rios **173** 22 20S 43 30W
Tres Valles **165** 18 15N 96 8W
Tresco I. **30** 49 57N 6 20W
Treshnish Is. **34** 56 30N 6 25W
Treska, R. **66** 41 45N 21 11E
Treskavika Planina **66** 43 40N 18 20E
Trespaderne **58** 42 47N 3 24W
Tretower **31** 51 53N 3 11W
Trets **45** 43 27N 5 41E
Treuchtlingen **49** 48 58N 10 55E
Treuddyn **31** 53 7N 3 8W
Treuenbrietzen **48** 52 6N 12 51E
Treungen **75** 59 1N 8 31E
Treviglio **62** 45 31N 9 35E
Trevinca, Peña **56** 42 15N 6 46W
Treviso **63** 45 40N 12 15E
Trevose Hd. **30** 50 33N 5 3W
Trévoux **45** 45 57N 4 47E
Trgovište **66** 42 20N 22 10E
Triabunna **138** 42 30S 147 55E
Triánda **69** 36 25N 28 10E
Triang **101** 3 13N 102 27E
Triangle **162** 38 33N 77 20W
Triaucourt-en-Argonne **43** 48 59N 5 2E
Tribsees **48** 54 4N 12 46E
Tribulation, C. **138** 16 5S 145 29E
Tribune **158** 38 30N 101 45W
Tricárico **65** 40 37N 16 9E
Tricase **65** 39 56N 18 20E
Trichinopoly = Tiruchchirappalli **97** 10 45N 78 45E
Trichur **97** 10 30N 76 18E
Trida **141** 33 1S 145 1E
Trier **49** 49 45N 6 37E
Trieste **63** 45 39N 13 45E
Trieste, G. di **63** 45 37N 13 40E
Triggiano **65** 41 4N 16 58E
Triglav **63** 46 30N 13 45E
Trigno, R. **63** 41 55N 14 37E
Trigueros **57** 37 24N 6 50W
Trikeri **69** 39 6N 23 5E
Trikhonis, Límni **69** 38 34N 21 30E
Trikkala **68** 39 34N 21 47E
Trikkala □ **68** 39 41N 21 30E
Trikora, G. **103** 4 11S 138 0E
Trilj **63** 43 38N 16 42E
Trillick **38** 54 27N 7 30W
Trillo **58** 40 42N 2 35W
Trim **38** 53 34N 6 48W
Trimdon **33** 54 43N 1 23W
Trimley **29** 51 59N 1 19E
Trincomalee **97** 8 38N 81 15E
Trindade **171** 16 40S 49 30W
Trindade, I. **15** 20 20S 29 50W
Trinidad, Boliv. **174** 14 54S 64 50W
Trinidad, Colomb. **174** 5 25N 71 40W
Trinidad, Cuba **166** 21 40N 80 0W
Trinidad, Uruguay **172** 33 30S 56 50W
Trinidad, U.S.A. **159** 37 15N 104 30W
Trinidad & Tobago ■ **167** 10 30N 61 20W
Trinidad, I., Argent. **176** 39 10S 62 0W
Trinidad, I., S. Amer. **167** 10 30N 61 15W
Trinidad, R. **165** 17 49N 95 9W
Trinitápoli **65** 41 22N 16 5E
Trinity, Can. **151** 48 22N 53 29W
Trinity, U.S.A. **159** 30 50N 95 20W
Trinity B., Austral. **133** 16 30S 146 0E
Trinity B., Can. **151** 48 20N 53 10W
Trinity Mts. **159** 40 20N 118 50W
Trinity R. **159** 30 30N 95 0W
Trino **62** 45 10N 8 18E
Trion **157** 34 35N 85 18W
Trionto C. **65** 34 38N 16 47E
Triora **62** 44 0N 7 46E
Tripoli = Tarabulus **92** 34 31N 33 52E
Tripoli = Tarābulus **119** 32 49N 13 7E
Trípolis **69** 37 31N 22 25E
Tripp **158** 43 16N 97 58W
Tripura □ **98** 24 0N 92 0E
Trischen, I. **48** 54 3N 8 32E
Tristan da Cunha, I. **15** 37 6S 12 20W
Trivandrum **97** 8 31N 77 0E
Trivento **65** 41 48N 14 31E
Trnava **53** 48 23N 17 35E
Trobriand Is. **135** 8 30S 151 0E
Trochu **152** 51 50N 113 13W
Trodely I. **150** 52 15N 79 26W
Trogir **63** 43 32N 16 15E
Troglav, mt. **63** 43 56N 16 36E
Trögstad **71** 59 37N 11 16E
Tróia **65** 41 22N 15 19E
Troilus, L. **150** 50 50N 74 35W
Troina **65** 37 47N 14 34E
Trois Fourches, Cap des **118** 35 26N 2 58W
Trois Pistoles **151** 48 5N 69 10W
Trois-Rivières **150** 46 25N 72 40W
Troisvierges **47** 50 8N 6 0E
Troitsk **84** 54 10N 61 35E
Troitskiy **84** 55 29N 37 18E
Troitsko-Pechorsk **78** 62 40N 56 10E
Trölladyngja **74** 64 54N 17 15W
Trolladyngja **74** 64 49N 17 29W
Trollhättan **73** 58 17N 12 20E
Trollheimen **71** 62 46N 9 1E
Tromöy **71** 58 28N 8 53E
Troms fylke □ **74** 68 56N 19 0E
Tromsø **74** 69 40N 18 56E
Trona **163** 35 46N 117 23W
Tronador, Mt. **176** 41 53S 71 0W
Tröndelag, N. □ **74** 65 0N 12 0E
Tröndelag, S. □ **71** 62 0N 10 0E
Trondheim **71** 63 25N 10 25E
Trondheimsfjorden **74** 63 35N 10 30E
Trönninge **73** 56 38N 12 59E
Trönö **72** 61 22N 16 54E
Tronto, R. **63** 42 50N 13 46E
Troodos, mt. **128** 34 58N 32 55E
Troon **34** 55 33N 4 40W
Tropea **65** 38 40N 15 53E
Tropic **161** 37 44N 112 4W
Tropoja **68** 42 23N 20 10E
Trossachs, The **34** 56 14N 4 24W
Trostan Mt. **38** 55 4N 6 10W
Trostberg **49** 48 2N 12 33E
Trotternish, dist. **36** 57 32N 6 15W
Troup **159** 32 10N 95 3W
Troup Hd. **37** 57 41N 2 18W
Trout L., N.W. Terr., Can. **152** 60 40N 121 40W
Trout L., Ont., Can. **153** 51 20N 93 15W
Trout Lake **150** 46 10N 85 2W
Trout, R. **152** 61 19N 119 51W
Trout River **151** 49 29N 58 8W
Trout Run **162** 41 23N 77 3W
Trouville **42** 49 21N 0 5E
Trowbridge **28** 51 18N 2 12W
Troy, Turkey **92** 39 55N 26 20E
Troy, Alabama, U.S.A. **157** 31 50N 85 58W
Troy, Kans., U.S.A. **158** 39 47N 95 2W
Troy, Mo., U.S.A. **158** 38 56N 90 59W
Troy, Montana, U.S.A. **160** 48 30N 115 58W
Troy, N.Y., U.S.A. **162** 42 45N 73 39W
Troy, Ohio, U.S.A. **156** 40 0N 84 10W
Troy, Pa., U.S.A. **162** 41 47N 76 47W
Troyan **67** 42 57N 24 43E
Troyes **43** 48 19N 4 3E
Trpanj **66** 43 1N 17 15E
Trstena **53** 49 21N 19 37E
Trstenik **66** 43 36N 21 0E
Trubchevsk **80** 52 33N 33 47E
Truc Giang **101** 10 14N 106 22E
Trucial States = Utd. Arab Emirates **93** 24 0N 54 30E
Truckee **160** 39 20N 120 11W
Trujillo, Colomb. **174** 4 10N 76 19W
Trujillo, Hond. **166** 16 0N 86 0W
Trujillo, Peru **174** 8 0S 79 0W
Trujillo, Spain **57** 39 28N 5 55W
Trujillo, U.S.A. **159** 35 34N 104 44W
Trujillo, Venez. **174** 9 22N 70 26W
Truk Is. **131** 7 25N 151 46E
Trull **28** 50 58N 3 8W
Trumann **159** 35 42N 90 32W
Trumansburg **162** 42 33N 76 40W
Trumbull, Mt. **161** 36 25N 113 32W
Trumpington **29** 52 11N 0 6E
Trún **66** 42 51N 22 38E
Trun, France **42** 48 50N 0 2E
Trun, Switz. **51** 46 45N 8 59E
Trundle **141** 32 53S 147 42E
Trung-Phan, reg. **100** 16 0N 108 0E
Truro, Austral. **140** 34 24S 139 9E
Truro, Can. **151** 45 21N 63 14E
Truro, U.K. **30** 50 17N 5 2W
Trŭscŭu, Muntii **70** 46 14N 23 14E
Truskmore, mt. **38** 54 23N 8 20W
Truslove **137** 33 20S 121 45E
Trustrup **73** 56 20N 10 46E
Truth or Consequences **161** 33 9N 107 16W
Trutnov **52** 50 37N 15 54E
Truxton **162** 42 45N 76 2W
Truyère, R. **44** 44 38N 2 34E
Trwyn Cilan **31** 52 47N 4 31W
Tryavna **67** 42 54N 25 25E
Tryon **157** 35 15N 82 16W
Trzciarka **54** 53 3N 16 25E
Trzciel **54** 52 23N 15 50E
Trzcinsko-Zdroj **54** 52 58N 14 35E
Trzebiez **54** 53 38N 14 31E
Trzebinia **54** 50 11N 19 30E
Trzeblatów **54** 54 3N 15 18E
Trzebnica **54** 51 20N 17 1E
Trzemeszno **54** 52 33N 17 48E
Tržič **63** 46 22N 14 18E
Tsafriya **90** 31 59N 34 51E
Tsaidam **105** 37 0N 95 0E
Tsak'o **108** 31 56N 99 35E
Tsamandás **68** 39 46N 20 21E
Tsamkong = Chanchiang **109** 21 15N 110 20E
Tsana Dzong **99** 28 0N 91 55E
Tsanga **99** 30 43N 100 32E
Ts'angchi **108** 31 48N 105 57E
Ts'angchou **106** 38 10N 116 50E
Tsangpo **99** 29 40N 89 0E
Ts'angyüan **108** 23 9N 99 15E
Ts'ao Ho, R. **107** 40 32N 124 11E
Tsaochuang **107** 34 30N 117 49E
Tsaochwang **174** 35 11N 115 28E
Ts'aohsien **106** 34 50N 115 31E
Tsaoyang **109** 32 8N 112 42E
Tsaratanana **129** 16 47S 47 39E
Tsaratanana, Mt. de **129** 14 0S 49 0E
Tsarevo = Michurin **67** 42 9N 27 51E
Tsaring Nor **99** 34 40N 97 20E
Tsaritsáni **68** 39 53N 15 14E
Tsau **128** 20 8S 22 29E
Tsaukaib **128** 26 37S 15 39E
Tsebrikovo **82** 47 9N 30 10E
Ts'ehung **108** 25 2N 105 47E
Tselinograd **76** 51 10N 71 30E
Tsengch'eng **109** 23 17N 113 49E
Ts'enkung **108** 27 13N 108 45E
Tsetserleg **105** 47 36N 101 32E
Tshabong **128** 26 2S 22 29E
Tshane **125** 24 5S 21 54E
Tshela **124** 5 4S 13 0E
Tshesebe **129** 20 43S 27 32E
Tshhinvali **83** 42 14N 44 1E
Tshibeke **126** 2 40S 28 35E
Tshibinda **126** 2 23S 28 30E
Tshikapa **124** 6 17S 21 0E
Tshilenge **126** 6 12S 23 40E
Tshinsenda **127** 12 15N 28 0E
Tshofa **124** 5 8S 25 8E
Tshombe **129** 25 18S 45 29E
Tshwane **128** 22 24S 22 1E
Tsigara **128** 20 22S 25 54E
Tsihombe **125** 25 10S 45 41E
Tsilmamo **123** 6 1N 35 10E
Tsimlyansk **83** 47 45N 42 0E
Tsimlyanskoye Vdkhr. **83** 48 0N 43 0E
Tsinan = Chinan **106** 36 32N 117 0E
Tsineng **128** 27 05S 23 05E
Tsinga, mt. **68** 41 23N 24 44E
Tsinghai □ **105** 36 0N 96 0E
Tsingtao = Ch'ingtao **107** 36 5N 120 25E
Tsinjomitondraka **129** 15 40S 47 8E
Tsiroanomandidy **129** 18 46S 46 2E
Tsivilsk **81** 55 50N 47 25E
Tsivory **129** 24 4S 46 5E
Tskhinali **79** 42 22N 43 52E
Tso Chiang, R. **108** 22 52N 108 5E
Tso Morari, L. **95** 32 50N 78 20E
Tsochou **108** 22 36N 107 36E
Tsoch'üan **106** 37 3N 113 27E
Tsodilo Hill **128** 18 49S 21 43E
Tsogttsetsiy **106** 43 43N 105 35E
Tsokung **108** 29 55N 97 44E
Tsona Dzong **99** 28 0N 91 55E
Tsoshui **106** 33 40N 109 9E
Tsouhsien **106** 35 24N 116 58E
Tsu **111** 34 45N 136 25E
Tsu L. **152** 60 40N 111 52W
Tsuchiura **111** 36 12N 140 15E
Tsugaru-Kaikyō **112** 41 35N 141 0E
Tsukumi **110** 33 4N 131 52E
Tsukushi-Sanchi **110** 33 25N 130 30E
Tsumeb **128** 19 9S 17 44E
Tsumis **128** 23 39S 17 29E
Tsuna **110** 34 28N 134 56E
Ts'ungchiang **108** 25 45N 108 54E
Tsunhua **107** 40 12N 117 56E
Tsuni **108** 27 43N 106 52E
Tsuno-Shima **110** 34 21N 130 52E
Tsuru **111** 35 31N 138 57E
Tsuruga **111** 35 45N 136 2E
Tsuruga-Wan **111** 35 50N 136 3E
Tsurugi **111** 36 37N 136 37E
Tsurugi-San **110** 33 51N 134 6E
Tsurumi-Saki **110** 32 56N 132 5E
Tsuruoka **112** 38 44N 139 50E
Tsurusaki **110** 33 14N 131 41E
Tsushima **111** 35 10N 136 43E
Tsushima, I. **110** 34 20N 129 20E
Tsvetkovo **82** 49 15N 31 33E
Tu, R. **98** 22 50N 97 15E
Tua, R. **57** 41 19N 7 15W
Tuai **143** 38 47S 177 15E
Tuakau **142** 37 16S 174 59E
Tual **103** 5 30S 132 50E
Tuam **38** 53 30N 8 50W
Tuamarina **143** 41 25S 173 59E
Tuamgraney **39** 52 54N 8 32W
Tuamotu Arch = Touamotou **131** 17 0S 144 0W
Tuan **108** 23 59N 108 3E
T'uanch'i **108** 27 28N 107 7E
T'uanfeng **109** 30 38N 114 52E
Tuao **103** 17 47S 121 30E
Tuapse **83** 44 5N 39 10E
Tuatapere **143** 46 8S 167 41E
Tuath, Loch **34** 56 30N 6 15W
Tuba City **161** 36 8N 111 12W
Tubac **161** 31 45N 111 2W
Tubai Is. = Toubouai, Îles **131** 25 0S 150 0W
Tuban **102** 6 57S 112 4E
Tubarão **173** 28 30S 49 0W
Tubas **90** 32 20N 35 22E
Tubau **102** 3 10N 113 40E
Tubayq, Jabal at **122** 29 30N 27 30E
Tubbergen **46** 52 24N 6 48E
Tübingen **48** 48 31N 9 4E
Tubize **47** 50 42N 4 13E
Tubja, W. **122** 25 27N 38 55E
Tubruq, (Tobruk) **117** 32 7N 23 55E
Tubuai, Îles **131** 25 0S 150 0W
Tuc Trung **101** 11 1N 107 12E
Tucacas **174** 10 48N 68 19W
Tucano **170** 10 58S 38 48W
Tuch'ang **109** 29 15N 116 13E
T'uch'ang **109** 24 42N 121 25E
Tuchodi, R. **152** 58 17N 123 42W
Tuchola **54** 53 33N 17 52E
Tuchów **54** 49 54N 21 1E
T'uch'üan **107** 45 22N 121 41E
Tuckanarra **137** 27 8S 118 1E
Tuckernuck I. **162** 41 15N 70 17W
Tucson **161** 32 14N 110 59W
Tucumán **172** 26 50S 65 20W
Tucumán □ **172** 26 48S 66 2W
Tucumcari **159** 35 12N 103 45W
Tucupido **174** 9 17N 65 47W
Tucupita **174** 9 14N 62 3W
Tucuracas **174** 11 45N 72 22W
Tucuruí **170** 3 42S 49 27W
Tuczno **54** 53 13N 16 10E
Tudela **58** 42 4N 1 39W
Tudela de Duero **56** 41 37N 4 39W
Tudor, Lac **151** 55 50N 65 25W
Tudora **70** 47 31N 26 45E
Tudweiliog **31** 52 54N 4 37W
Tuella, R. **56** 41 50N 7 10W
Tuen **139** 28 33S 145 37E
Tueré, R. **170** 2 48S 50 59W
Tufi **135** 9 8S 149 19E
Tugidak I. **147** 56 30N 154 40W
Tuguegarao **103** 17 35N 121 42E
Tugur **77** 53 50N 136 45E
Tugwa **128** 17 27S 18 33E
Tukangbesi, Kepulauan **103** 6 0S 124 0E
Tukarak I. **150** 56 15N 78 45W
Tukobo **120** 5 1N 2 47W
Tükrah **119** 32 30N 20 37E
Tuku, mt. **123** 9 10N 36 43E
Tukums **80** 57 2N 23 3E
Tukuyu **127** 9 17S 33 35E
Tukzar **93** 35 55N 66 25E
Tula, Hidalgo, Mexico **165** 20 0N 99 20W
Tula, Tamaulipas, Mexico **165** 23 0N 99 40W
Tula, Nigeria **121** 9 51N 11 27E
Tula, U.S.S.R. **81** 54 13N 37 32E
Tulak **93** 33 55N 63 40E
Tulancingo **165** 20 5N 98 22W
Tulanssu **105** 36 52N 98 24E
Tulare **163** 36 15N 119 26W
Tulare Basin **163** 36 0N 119 48W
Tulare Lake **161** 36 0N 119 53W
Tularosa **161** 33 4N 106 1W
Tulbagh **128** 33 16S 19 6E
Tulcán **174** 0 48N 77 43W
Tulcea **70** 45 13N 28 46E
Tulcea □ **70** 45 0N 29 0E
Tulchin **82** 48 41N 28 55E
*Tuléar **129** 23 21S 43 40E
Tuléar □ **129 21 0S 45 0E
Tulemalu L. **153** 62 58N 99 25W
Tulgheş **70** 4 58N 25 45E
Tuli, Indon. **103** 1 24S 122 26E
Tuli, Zimb. **127** 21 58S 29 13E
Tuliuchen **106** 39 1N 116 54E
Tulkarm **90** 32 19N 35 10E
Tulla, Ireland **39** 52 53N 8 45W
Tulla, U.S.A. **159** 34 35N 101 44W
Tulla, L. **34** 56 33N 4 47W
Tullaghoge **38** 54 36N 6 43W
Tullaghought **39** 52 25N 7 22W
Tullahoma **157** 35 23N 86 12W
Tullamore, Austral. **141** 32 39S 147 36E
Tullamore, Ireland **39** 53 17N 7 30W
Tullaroan **39** 52 40N 7 27W
Tulle **44** 45 16N 0 47E
Tullibigeal **141** 33 25S 146 44E
Tullins **45** 45 18N 5 29E
Tulln **52** 48 20N 16 4E
Tullow **39** 52 48N 6 45W

*Renamed Toliara
**Renamed Toliara □

Tullus **Uddingston**

Tullus 123 11 7N 24 40 E
Tully, Austral. 138 17 56 S 145 55 E
Tully, Ireland 38 53 44N 8 9W
Tully, U.S.A. 162 42 48N 76 7W
Tully Cross 38 53 35N 9 59W
Tŭlmaciu 70 45 38N 24 19 E
Tulmaythah 117 32 40N 20 55 E
Tulmur 138 22 40 S 142 20 E
Tulnici 70 45 51N 26 38 E
Tulovo 67 42 33N 25 32 E
Tulsa 159 36 10N 96 0W
Tulsequah 152 58 39N 133 35W
Tulsk 38 53 47N 8 15W
Tulu Milki 123 9 55N 38 14 E
Tulu Welel, Mt. 123 8 56N 35 30 E
Tulua 174 4 6N 76 11W
T'ulufan 105 42 56N 89 10 E
Tulun 77 54 40N 100 10 E
Tulungagung 103 8 5 S 111 54 E
Tum 103 3 28 S 130 21 E
Tuma 81 55 10N 40 30 E
Tuma, R. 166 13 18N 84 50W
Tumaco 174 1 50N 78 45W
Tumatumari 174 5 20N 58 55W
Tumba 72 59 12N 17 48 E
Tumba, L. 124 0 50 S 18 0 E
Tumbarumba 141 35 44 S 148 0 E
Tumbaya 172 23 50 S 65 20W
Tumbes 174 3 30 S 80 20W
Tumbwa 127 11 25 S 27 15 E
Tumby B. 140 34 21 S 136 8 E
T'umen 107 42 55N 129 50 E
T'umen Kiang, R. 107 42 18N 130 41 E
Tumeremo 174 7 18N 61 30W
Tumiritinga 171 18 58 S 41 38W
Tumkur 97 13 18N 77 12 E
Tumleberg 73 58 16N 12 52 E
Tummel, L. 37 56 43N 3 55W
Tummel, R. 37 56 42N 4 5W
T'umot'eyuch'i 106 40 42N 111 8 E
Tump 93 26 7N 62 16 E
Tumpat 101 6 11N 102 10 E
Tumsar 96 21 26N 79 45 E
Tumu 120 10 56N 1 56W
Tumucumaque, Serra de 175 2 0N 55 0W
Tumut 141 35 16 S 148 13 E
Tumutuk 84 55 1N 53 19 E
Tumwater 160 47 0N 122 58W
Tuna, Pta. 147 17 59N 65 53W
Tunas de Zaza 166 21 39N 79 34W
Tunbridge Wells 29 51 7N 0 16 E
T'unch'i 105 29 50N 118 26 E
Tuncurry 141 32 9 S 152 29 E
Tunduru 127 11 0 S 37 25 E
Tunduru □ 127 11 5 S 37 22 E
Tundzha, R. 67 42 0N 26 35 E
Tune 71 59 16N 11 2 E
Tung Chiang, R. 109 22 55N 113 35 E
Tung-Pei 77 44 0N 126 0 E
Tunga La 99 29 0N 94 14 E
Tunga Pass 98 29 0N 94 14 E
Tunga, R. 97 13 42N 75 20 E
Tungabhadra Dam 97 15 21N 76 23 E
Tungabhadra, R. 97 15 30N 77 0 E
Tungachen 106 36 15N 165 12 E
Tungan 109 26 24N 111 17 E
T'ungan 109 24 44N 118 9 E
T'ungcheng, Anhwei, China 109 31 3N 116 58 E
T'ungcheng, Hupeh, China 109 29 15N 113 49 E
Tungch'i 108 28 43N 106 42 E
T'ungchiang, Heilungkiang, China 105 47 40N 132 30 E
T'ungchiang, Szechwan, China 108 31 56N 107 15 E
Tungchingch'eng 107 44 9N 129 7 E
Tungchuan 105 35 4N 109 2 E
T'ungch'uan 108 35 95N 109 5 E
Tungch'uan 108 26 9N 103 7 E
Tungfanghsien, (Paso) 100 18 50N 108 33 E
Tungfeng 107 42 40N 125 34 E
T'unghai 108 24 8N 102 43 E
Tunghai Tao 109 21 2N 110 25 E
Tunghsiang 109 28 14N 116 35 E
T'unghsien 105 39 45N 116 43 E
T'unghsin 106 37 9N 106 28 E
T'unghua 107 41 45N 126 0 E
Tungi 98 23 53N 90 24 E
T'ungjen 105 27 43N 109 10 E
Tungkan 108 23 22N 105 9 E
Tungkou 107 39 52N 124 8 E
Tungku 108 31 52N 100 14 E
T'ungku 109 28 32N 114 23 E
Tungkuan 109 23 0N 113 39 E
T'ungkuan 105 34 37N 110 27 E
Tungkuang 106 37 53N 116 32 E
Tungla 166 13 24N 84 15W
Tunglan 108 24 30N 107 23 E
T'ungliang 108 29 52N 106 2 E
T'ungliao 107 43 37N 122 16 E
Tungling 109 31 0N 117 54 E
Tungliu 109 30 13N 116 55 E
T'unglu 109 29 49N 119 40 E
Tungnafellsjökull 74 64 45N 17 55W
T'ungnan 108 30 14N 105 48 E
Tungning 107 44 3N 131 7 E
T'ungpai 109 32 22N 113 24 E
Tungp'ing 106 35 55N 116 18 E
Tungpu 99 31 42N 98 19 E
Tungshan 109 23 40N 117 31 E
Tungshih 109 24 12N 120 43 E
Tungsten, Can. 152 61 57N 128 16W
Tungsten, U.S.A. 160 40 50N 118 10W
Tungt'ai 109 32 50N 120 46 E
T'ungtao 108 26 21N 109 36 E
T'ungtien 108 26 40N 99 32 E
Tungt'ing Hu 109 29 18N 112 45 E
Tungtzu 108 28 8N 106 49 E
Tunguchumuch'inch'i 106 45 33N 116 50 E
Tunguska, Nizhmaya, R. 77 64 0N 95 0 E
Tunguska, Podkammenaya, R. 77 61 0N 98 0 E
T'ungwei 106 35 18N 105 10 E
T'ungyü 107 44 48N 123 6 E
Tunhua 107 43 20N 128 10 E
Tunhuang 105 40 10N 94 50 E
Tuni 96 17 22N 82 43 E
Tunia 174 2 41N 76 31W
Tunica 159 34 43N 90 23W
Tunis 119 36 50N 10 11 E
Tunis, Golfe de 119 37 0N 10 30 E
Tunisia ■ 119 33 30N 9 10 E
Tunja 174 5 40N 73 25W
Tunkhannock 162 41 32N 75 56W
T'unliu 106 36 19N 112 54 E
Tunnsjøen 74 64 45N 13 25 E
Tuno I. 73 55 58N 10 27 E
T'unpuli Shan 105 35 0N 89 30 E
Tunstall 29 52 7N 1 28 E
Tuntatuliag 147 60 20N 162 45W
Tunungayualuk I. 151 56 0N 61 0W
Tunuyán 172 33 55 S 69 0W
Tunuyán, R. 172 33 33 S 67 30W
Tuolumne 163 37 59N 120 16W
Tuolumne, R. 163 37 36N 121 13W
Tuoy-Khaya 77 62 32N 111 18 E
Tupã 173 21 57 S 50 28W
Tupaciguara 171 18 35 S 48 42W
Tuparro, R. 174 5 0N 68 40W
Tupelo 157 34 15N 88 42W
Tupik 77 54 26N 119 57 E
Tupinambaranas, I. 174 3 0 S 58 0W
Tupirama 170 8 58 S 48 12W
Tupiratins 170 8 23 S 48 8W
Tupiza 172 21 30 S 65 40W
Tupman 163 35 18N 119 21W
Tupper 152 55 32N 120 1W
Tupper L. 156 44 18N 74 30W
Tupungato, Cerro 172 33 15 S 69 50W
Tuque, La 150 47 30N 72 50W
Túquerres 174 1 5N 77 37W
Tur 90 31 47N 35 14 E
Tura, India 98 25 30N 90 16 E
Tura, U.S.S.R. 77 64 20N 99 30 E
Tura, R. 84 57 12N 66 56 E
Turaba, W. 122 21 15N 41 32 E
Turagua, Serranía 174 7 20N 64 35W
Turaiyur 97 11 9N 78 38 E
Turakina 142 40 3 S 175 16 E
Turakirae Hd. 142 41 26 S 174 56 E
Tūrān 93 35 45N 56 50 E
Turan 77 51 38N 101 40 E
Turbenthal 51 47 27N 8 51 E
Tureburg 72 59 30N 17 58 E
Turégano 56 41 9N 4 1W
Turek 54 52 3N 18 30 E
Turen 174 9 17N 69 6W
Turfan Depression 105 42 45N 89 0 E
Turgay 84 49 38N 63 30 E
Turgay, R. 84 48 1N 62 45 E
Tŭrgovishte 67 43 17N 26 38 E
Turgutlu 92 38 30N 27 48 E
Turhal 82 40 24N 36 19 E
Turia, R. 58 39 43N 1 0W
TuriaçI 170 1 40 S 45 28W
TuriaçI, R. 170 3 0 S 46 0W
Turigshih 100 18 42N 109 27 E
Turin = Torino 62 45 3N 7 40 E
Turin Taber 152 49 47N 112 24W
Turinsk 84 58 3N 63 42 E
Turkana □ 126 3 0N 35 30 E
Turkana, L. 80 4 10N 32 10 E
Turkestan 76 43 10N 68 10 E
Turkestanskiy, Khrebet 85 39 35N 69 0 E
Túrkeve 53 47 6N 20 44 E
Turkey ■ 92 39 0N 36 0 E
Turkey Creek P.O. 136 17 2 S 128 12 E
Turki 81 52 0N 43 15 E
Turkmen S.S.R. □ 85 39 0N 59 0 E
Turks Is. 167 21 20N 71 20W
Turks Island Passage 167 21 30N 71 20W
Turku (Åbo) 75 60 30N 22 19 E
Turku-Pori □ 75 60 27N 22 15 E
Turkwell, R. 126 2 30N 35 20 E
Turlock 163 37 30N 120 55W
Turnagain, C. 142 40 28 S 176 38 E
Turnagain, R. 152 59 12N 127 35W
Turnberry, Can. 153 53 25N 101 45W
Turnberry, U.K. 34 55 19N 4 50W
Turneffe Is. 165 17 20N 87 50W
Turner 160 48 52N 108 25W
Turner Pt. 138 11 47 S 133 32 E
Turner River 136 17 52 S 128 16 E
Turner Valley 152 50 40N 114 17W
Turners Falls 162 42 36N 72 34W
Turnhout 47 51 19N 4 57 E
Türnitz 52 47 55N 15 29 E
Turnor L. 153 56 35N 108 35W
Turnov 52 50 34N 15 10 E
Turnovo 67 43 5N 25 41 E
Turnovo □ 67 43 4N 25 39 E
Turnu Mǔgurele 70 43 46N 24 56 E
Turnu Roşu Pasul 70 45 33N 24 17 E
Turnu-Severin 70 44 39N 22 41 E
Turö 73 55 2N 10 40 E
Turon 159 37 48N 98 27W
Tuross Head 141 36 3 S 150 8 E
Turriff 37 57 32N 2 28W
Tursha 81 56 50N 47 45 E
Tursi 65 40 15N 16 27 E
Turtle Hd. I. 138 10 50 S 142 37 E
Turtle L., Can. 153 53 36N 108 38W
Turtle L., N.D., U.S.A. 158 47 30N 100 55W
Turtle L., Wis., U.S.A. 158 45 22N 92 10W
Turtleford 153 53 23N 108 57W
Turua 142 37 14 S 175 35 E
Turubah 92 28 20N 43 15 E
Turukhansk 77 65 50N 87 50 E
Turun ja Porin lääni □ 75 60 27N 22 15 E
Turzovka 53 49 25N 18 41 E
Tuscaloosa 157 33 13N 87 31W
Tuscánia 63 42 25N 11 53 E
Tuscany = Toscana 62 43 28N 11 15 E
Tuscola, Ill., U.S.A. 156 39 48N 88 15W
Tuscola, Tex., U.S.A. 159 32 15N 99 48W
Tuscumbia 157 34 42N 87 42W
Tushan 106 25 50N 107 33 E
Tushino 81 55 44N 37 29 E
Tuskar Rock 39 52 12N 6 10W
Tuskegee 157 32 24N 85 39W
Tŭşnad 70 47 30N 22 33 E
Tustna 71 63 10N 8 5 E
Tuszyn 54 51 36N 19 33 E
Tutaryd 73 56 54N 13 59 E
Tutbury 28 52 52N 1 41W
Tutikorin 97 8 50N 78 12 E
Tutin 66 43 0N 20 20 E
Tutóia 170 2 45 S 42 20W
Tutoko Mt. 143 44 35 S 168 1 E
Tutong 102 4 47N 114 34 E
Tutova, R. 70 46 20N 27 30 E
Tutrakan 67 44 2N 26 40 E
Tutshi L. 152 59 56N 134 30W
Tuttlingen 49 47 59N 8 50 E
Tutuaia 103 8 25 S 127 15 E
Tutye 140 35 12 S 141 29 E
Tuva, A.S.S.R. □ 77 51 30N 95 0 E
Tuxford 33 53 14N 0 52W
Tuxpan 165 20 50N 97 30W
Tuxtla Gutiérrez 165 16 50N 93 10W
Tuy 56 42 3N 8 39W
Tuy An 100 13 17N 109 16 E
Tuy Doc 101 12 15N 107 27 E
Tuy Hoa 100 13 5N 109 17 E
Tuy Phong 101 11 14N 108 43 E
Tuya L. 152 59 7N 130 35W
Tuyen Hoa 100 17 50N 106 10 E
Tuyen Quang 100 21 50N 105 10 E
Tuymazy 84 54 36N 53 42 E
Tuyun 108 26 15N 107 32 E
Tuz Gölü 92 38 45N 33 30 E
Tuz Khurmatli 92 34 52N 44 41 E
Tuz Khurmatu 92 34 50N 44 45 E
Tuzkan, Ozero 85 40 35N 67 28 E
Tuzla 66 44 34N 18 41 E
Tuzlov, R. 83 47 28N 39 45 E
Tvååker 73 57 4N 12 25 E
Tværsted 73 57 36N 10 12 E
Tvarskog 73 56 34N 16 0 E
Tved 73 56 12N 10 25 E
Tvedestrand 71 58 38N 8 58 E
Tveitsund 71 59 2N 8 31 E
Tvelt 71 60 30N 7 11 E
Tvyrditsa 67 42 42N 25 53 E
Twain Harte 163 38 2N 120 14W
Twardogóra 54 51 23N 17 28 E
Twatt 37 59 6N 3 15W
Tweed, R. 35 55 42N 2 10W
Tweede Exploërmond 46 52 55N 6 56 E
Tweedmouth 35 55 46N 2 1W
Tweedshaws 35 55 26N 3 29W
Tweedsmuir Prov. Park 152 52 55N 126 20W
Twello 46 52 14N 6 6 E
Twelve Pins 38 53 32N 9 50W
Twentynine Palms 163 34 10N 116 4W
Twillingate 151 49 42N 54 45W
Twin Bridges 160 45 33N 112 23W
Twin Falls 160 42 30N 114 30W
Twin Valley 158 47 18N 96 15W
Twinnge 98 21 58N 96 23 E
Twisp 160 48 21N 120 5W
Twistringen 48 52 48N 8 38 E
Two Harbors 158 47 1N 91 40W
Two Hills 152 53 43N 111 45W
Two Mile Borris 39 52 41N 7 43W
Two Rivers 156 44 10N 87 31W
Two Thumbs Ra. 143 43 45 S 170 44 E
Two Tree 138 18 25 S 140 3 E
Twofold B. 141 37 8 S 149 59 E
Twong 123 5 18N 28 29 E
Twyford, Berks., U.K. 29 51 29N 0 51W
Twyford, Hants., U.K. 28 51 1N 1 19W
Ty 73 56 27N 8 32 E
Tyborön 73 56 42N 8 12 E
Tychy 54 50 9N 18 59 E
Tyczyn 54 49 58N 22 2 E
Tydd St. Mary 29 52 45N 0 9 E
Tykocin 54 53 13N 22 46 E
Tyldal 71 62 8N 10 48 E
Tyldesley 32 53 31N 2 29W
Tyler, Minn., U.S.A. 158 44 18N 96 15W
Tyler, Tex., U.S.A. 159 44 18N 96 15W
Tylldal 71 62 7N 10 45 E
Tylösand 73 56 33N 12 40 E
Týn nad Vltavou 52 49 13N 14 26 E
Tynagh 39 53 10N 8 22W
Tyndall, Mt. 143 43 15 S 170 55 E
Tyndinskiy 77 55 10N 124 43 E
Tyndrum 34 56 26N 4 41W
Tyne & Wear □ 35 54 55N 1 35W
Tyne, R., Eng., U.K. 35 54 58N 1 28W
Tyne, R., Scot., U.K. 35 55 58N 2 45W
Tynemouth 35 55 1N 1 27W
Tynset 71 62 17N 10 47 E
Tyre = Sūr 90 33 19N 35 16 E
Tyrifjorden 71 60 2N 10 8 E
Tyringe 73 56 9N 13 35 E
Tyristrand 71 60 5N 10 5 E
Tyrnyauz 83 43 21N 42 45 E
Tyrol = Tirol 52 46 50N 11 20 E
Tyrone □ 38 54 40N 7 15W
Tyrone, Co. 38 54 40N 7 15W
Tyrrell Arm 153 62 27N 97 30W
Tyrrell, L. 140 35 20 S 142 50 E
Tyrrell L. 153 63 7N 105 27W
Tyrrell, R. 140 35 26 S 142 51 E
Tyrrhenian Sea 60 40 0N 12 30 E
Tysfjörden 74 68 10N 16 10 E
Tysmenitsa 80 48 58N 24 50 E
Tysnes 71 60 1N 5 30 E
Tyssedal 71 60 7N 6 35 E
Tystberga 73 58 51N 17 15 E
Tyulgan 84 52 22N 56 12 E
Tyumen 84 57 0N 65 18 E
Tyumen-Aryk 85 44 2N 67 1 E
Tyup 85 42 45N 78 20 E
Tyvoll 71 62 43N 11 21 E
Tywardreath 30 50 21N 4 40W
Tywi, R. 31 51 48N 4 20W
Tywyn 31 52 36N 4 5W
Tzaneen 129 23 47 S 30 9 E
Tzefa 90 31 7N 35 12 E
Tzermiadhes Neapolis 69 35 11N 25 29 E
Tzoumérka, Óros 68 39 30N 21 26 E
Tzu Shui, R. 109 29 2N 112 55 E
Tzuch'ang 106 37 12N 109 44 E
Tzuch'eng 107 36 39N 117 56 E
Tzuch'i 109 27 42N 116 58 E
Tz'uch'i 109 29 59N 121 14 E
Tzuchien 99 27 43N 98 34 E
Tzuchin 109 23 38N 115 10 E
Tzuchung 108 29 49N 104 55 E
Tz'uhsien 106 36 22N 114 23 E
Tzuhsing 109 25 58N 113 24 E
Tzukuei 105 31 0N 110 38 E
Tzukung 108 29 20N 104 50 E
Tz'uli 109 29 25N 111 6 E
Tzummarum 46 53 14N 5 32 E
Tzupo 105 36 49N 118 5 E
T'zuyang 108 32 31N 108 32 E
Tzuyang 108 30 7N 104 39 E
Tzuyün 108 25 45N 106 5 E

U

U Taphao 100 12 35N 101 0 E
Uad Erni, O. 118 26 30N 9 30W
Uainambi 174 1 43N 69 51W
Uanda 138 21 37 S 144 55 E
Uarsciek 91 2 28N 45 55 E
Uasadi-jidi, Sierra 174 4 54N 65 18W
Uasin □ 126 0 30N 35 20 E
Uassem 90 32 59N 36 2 E
Uato-Udo 103 4 3 S 126 6 E
Uatumã, R. 174 1 30 S 59 25W
Uauá 170 9 50 S 39 28W
Uaupés 174 0 8 S 67 5W
Uaxactún 166 17 25N 89 29W
Ub 66 44 28N 20 6 E
Ubá 173 21 0 S 43 0W
Ubaitaba 171 14 18 S 39 20W
Ubangi, R. = Oubangi 124 1 0N 17 50 E
Ubaté 174 5 19N 73 49W
Ubauro 94 28 15N 69 45 E
Ube 110 33 56N 131 15 E
Ubeda 58 38 3N 3 23W
Uberaba 171 19 50 S 47 55W
Uberlândia 171 19 0 S 48 20W
Ubiaja 121 6 41N 6 22 E
Ubolratna Phong, L. 100 16 45N 102 30 E
Ubombo 129 27 31 S 32 4 E
Ubon Ratchathani 100 15 15N 104 50 E
Ubondo 126 0 55 S 25 42 E
Ubort, R. 80 51 45N 28 30 E
Ubrique 57 36 41N 5 27W
Ubundi 126 0 22 S 25 30 E
Ucayali, R. 174 6 0 S 75 0W
Uccle 47 50 48N 4 22 E
Uchaly 84 54 19N 59 27 E
Uchi Lake 153 51 10N 92 40W
Uchiko 110 33 33N 132 39 E
Uchiura-Wan 112 42 25N 140 40 E
Uchte 48 52 29N 8 52 E
Uchterek 85 41 45N 73 12 E
Uckerath 48 50 44N 7 22 E
Uckfield 29 50 58N 0 6 E
Ucluelet 152 48 57N 125 32W
Ucolta 107 32 56 S 138 59 E
Ucuriş 70 46 41N 21 58 E
Uda, R. 77 54 42N 135 14 E
Udaipur 94 24 36N 73 44 E
Udaipur Garhi 95 27 0N 86 35 E
Udamalpet 97 10 35N 77 15 E
Udbina 63 44 31N 15 47 E
Uddeholm 72 60 1N 13 38 E
Uddel 46 52 15N 5 48 E
Uddevalla 73 58 21N 11 55 E
Uddingston 35 55 50N 4 3W

Uddjaur **Ust Kuyga**

Uddjaur 74 65 55N 17 50 E
Uden 47 51 40N 5 37 E
Udgir 96 18 25N 77 5 E
Udhampur 95 33 0N 75 5 E
Udi 121 6 23N 7 21 E
Udine 63 46 5N 13 10 E
Udine □ 63 46 3N 13 13 E
Udipi 97 13 25N 74 42 E
Udmurt, A.S.S.R. □ 84 57 30N 52 30 E
Udon Thani 100 17 29N 102 46 E
Udubo 121 11 52N 10 35 E
Udvoj Balken 67 42 50N 26 50 E
Udzungwa Range 127 11 15 S 35 10 E
Ueckermünde 48 53 45N 14 1 E
Ueda 111 36 24N 138 16 E
Uedineniya, Os. 12 78 0N 85 0 E
Uele, R. 124 3 50N 22 40 E
Uelen 77 66 10N 170 0W
Uelzen 48 53 0N 10 33 E
Ueno 111 34 53N 136 14 E
Uere, R. 124 3 45N 24 45 E
Uetendorf 50 46 47N 7 34 E
Ufa 84 54 45N 55 55 E
Ufa, R. 84 56 30N 58 10 E
Uffculme 30 50 45N 3 19W
Ufford 29 52 6N 1 22 E
Ugad R. 125 20 55 S 14 30 E
Ugalla, R. 126 6 0 S 32 0 E
Ugamas 128 28 0 S 19 41 E
Uganda ■ 126 2 0N 32 0 E
Ugborough 30 50 22N 3 53W
Ugchelen 46 52 11N 5 56 E
Ugento 65 39 55N 18 10 E
Ugep 121 5 53N 8 2 E
Ugie 129 31 10 S 28 13 E
Ugijar 59 36 58N 3 7W
Ugine 45 45 45N 6 25 E
Ugla 122 25 40N 37 42 E
Uglich 81 57 33N 38 13 E
Ugljane 63 43 35N 16 46 E
Ugra, R. 80 54 45N 35 30 E
Ugurchin 67 43 6N 24 26 E
Uh, R. 53 48 40N 22 0 E
Uherske Hradištĕ 53 49 4N 17 30 E
Uhersky Brod 53 49 1N 17 40 E
Uhrichsville 156 40 23N 81 22W
Uig, Lewis, U.K. 36 58 13N 7 1W
Uig, Skye, U.K. 36 57 35N 6 20W
Uinta Mts. 160 40 45N 110 30W
Uitenhage 128 33 40 S 25 28 E
Uitgeest 46 52 32N 4 43 E
Uithoorn 46 52 14N 4 50 E
Uithuizen 46 53 24N 6 41 E
Uitkerke 47 51 18N 3 9 E
Ujda = Oujda 118 34 45N 2 0W
Ujfehértó 53 47 49N 21 41 E
Ujh, R. 95 32 40N 75 30 E
Ujhani 95 28 0N 79 6 E
Uji 111 34 53N 135 48 E
Ujjain 94 23 9N 75 43 E
Újpest 53 47 22N 19 6 E
Ujszász 53 47 19N 20 7 E
Ujung Pandang 103 5 10 S 119 20 E
Uka 77 57 50N 162 0 E
Ukara I. 126 1 44 S 33 0 E
Ukehe 121 6 40N 7 24 E
Ukerewe □ 126 2 0 S 32 30 E
Ukerewe Is. 126 2 0 S 33 0 E
Ukholovo 81 54 47N 40 30 E
Ukhrul 98 25 10N 94 25 E
Ukhta 78 63 55N 54 0 E
Ukiah 160 39 10N 123 9W
Ukki Fort 95 33 28N 76 54 E
Ukmerge 80 55 15N 24 45 E
Ukraine S.S.R. □ 82 48 0N 35 0 E
Uksyanskoye 84 55 57N 63 1 E
Ukwi 128 23 29 S 20 30 E
Ulaanbaatar 105 47 55N 106 53 E
Ulaangom 105 49 58N 92 2 E
Ulak I. 147 51 24N 178 58W
Ulamambri 141 31 19 S 149 23 E
Ulamba 127 9 3 S 23 38 E
Ulan Bator = Ulaanbaatar 105 47 55N 106 53 E
Ulan Ude 77 52 0N 107 30 E
Ulanbel 85 44 50N 71 7 E
Ulanga □ 127 8 40 S 36 50 E
Ulanów 54 50 30N 22 16 E
Ulaya, Morogoro, Tanz. 126 7 3 S 36 55 E
Ulaya, Shinyanga, Tanz. 126 4 25 S 33 30 E
Ulbster 37 58 21N 3 9W
Ulceby Cross 33 53 14N 0 6 E
Ulcinj 66 41 58N 19 10 E
Ulco 128 28 21 S 24 15 E
Ulefoss 71 59 17N 9 16 E
Ulëza 68 41 46N 19 57 E
Ulfborg 73 56 16N 8 20 E
Ulft 46 51 53N 6 23 E
Ulhasnagar 96 19 15N 73 10 E
Ulinda 141 31 35 S 149 30 E
Uljma 66 45 2N 21 10 E
Ulla, R. 56 42 45N 8 30W
Ulladulla 141 35 21 S 150 29 E
Ullånger 72 62 58N 18 16 E
Ullapool 36 57 54N 5 10W
Ullared 73 57 8N 12 42 E
Ulldecona 58 40 36N 0 20 E
Ullswater, L. 32 54 35N 2 52W
Ullvättern, L. 72 59 30N 14 21 E
Ulm 49 48 23N 10 0 E
Ulmarra 139 29 37 S 153 4 E
Ulmeni 70 45 4N 46 40 E
Ulricehamn 73 57 46N 13 26 E
Ulrum 46 53 22N 6 20 E
Ulsberg 71 62 45N 9 59 E
Ulsfeinvik 71 62 21N 5 53 E
Ulster □ 38 54 45N 6 30W
Ulster Canal 38 54 15N 7 0W
Ulstrem 67 42 1N 26 27 E
Ultima 140 35 22 S 143 18 E
Ulubaria 95 22 31N 88 4 E
Ulugh Muztagh 99 36 40N 87 30 E
Uluguru Mts. 126 7 15 S 37 30 E
Ulva, I. 34 56 30N 6 12W
Ulvenhout 47 51 33N 4 48 E
Ulverston 32 54 13N 3 7W
Ulverstone 138 41 11 S 146 11 E
Ulvik 71 60 35N 6 54 E
Ulvo 73 56 40N 14 37 E
Ulya 77 59 10N 142 0 E
Ulyanovsk 81 54 25N 48 25 E
Ulyasutay 105 47 45N 96 49 E
Ulysses 159 37 39N 101 25W
Ulzio 62 45 2N 6 49 E
Um Qeis 90 32 40N 35 41 E
Umag 63 45 26N 13 31 E
Umala 174 17 25 S 68 5W
Uman 82 48 40N 30 12 E
Umánaé 12 70 40N 52 10W
Umánaé Fjord 10 70 40N 52 0W
Umaria 99 23 35N 80 50 E
Umarkhed 96 19 37N 77 38 E
Umarkot 93 25 15N 69 40 E
Umatilla 160 45 58N 119 17W
Umba 78 66 50N 34 20 E
Umbertide 63 43 18N 12 20 E
Umboi I. 135 5 40 S 148 0 E
Umbrella Mts. 143 45 35 S 169 5 E
Umbria □ 63 42 53N 12 30 E
Ume, R. 74 64 45N 18 30 E
Umeå 74 63 45N 20 20 E
Umera 103 0 12 S 129 30 E
Umfuli, R. 127 17 50 S 29 40 E
Umgusa 127 19 29 S 27 52 E
Umi 110 33 34N 130 30 E
Umiat 147 69 25N 152 20W
Umka 66 44 40N 20 19 E
Umkomaas 129 30 13 S 30 48 E
Umm al Aranib 119 26 10N 14 54 E
Umm al Qaiwain 93 25 30N 55 35 E
Umm Arda 123 15 17N 32 31 E
Umm az Zamul 93 22 35N 55 18 E
Umm Bel 123 13 35N 28 0 E
Umm Digulgulaya 123 10 28N 24 58 E
Umm Dubban 123 15 23N 32 52 E
Umm el Fahm 90 32 31N 35 9 E
Umm Hagar 123 14 20N 36 41 E
Umm Koweika 123 13 10N 32 16 E
Umm Lajj 92 25 0N 37 23 E
Umm Merwa 122 18 4N 32 30 E
Umm Qurein 123 16 3N 28 49 E
Umm Rumah 122 25 50N 36 30 E
Umm Ruwaba 123 12 50N 31 10 E
Umm Said 93 25 0N 51 40 E
Umm Sidr 123 14 29N 25 10 E
Ummanz I. 48 54 29N 13 9 E
Umnak. 147 53 20N 168 20W
Umnak I. 147 53 0N 168 0W
Umniati, R. 127 18 0 S 29 0 E
Umpang 101 16 3N 98 54 E
Umpqua, R. 160 43 30N 123 30W
Umrer 96 20 51N 79 18 E
Umreth 94 22 41N 73 4 E
Umshandige Dam 127 20 10 S 30 40 E
Umtali 127 18 58 S 32 38 E
Umtata 129 31 36 S 28 49 E
Umuahia-Ibeku 121 5 33N 7 29 E
Umvukwe Ra.. 127 16 45 S 30 45 E
Umvuma 127 19 16 S 30 30 E
Umzimvubu, R. 129 31 38 S 29 33 E
Umzingwane, R. 127 21 30 S 29 30 E
Umzinto 129 30 15 S 30 45 E
Una 94 20 46N 71 8 E
Una, Mt. 143 42 13 S 172 36 E
Una, R. 63 44 50N 16 15 E
Unac, R. 63 44 42N 16 15 E
Unadilla 162 42 20N 75 17W
Unalanaska I. 147 54 0N 164 30W
Uncastillo 58 42 21N 1 8W
Uncia 174 18 25 S 66 40W
Uncompahgce Pk., Mt. 161 38 5N 107 32W
Unden 73 58 45N 14 25 E
Underbool 140 35 10 S 141 51 E
Undersaker 72 63 19N 13 21 E
Undersvik 72 61 36N 16 20 E
Undredal 71 60 57N 7 6 E
Unecha 80 52 50N 32 37 E
Ungarie 141 33 38 S 146 56 E
Ungarra 140 34 12 S 136 2 E
Ungava B. 149 59 30N 67 30W
Ungava Pen. 50 60 0N 75 0W
Ungeny 82 47 11N 27 51 E
Unggi 105 42 16N 130 28 E
Ungwatiri 123 16 52N 36 10 E
Uni 84 56 44N 51 47 E
União 170 4 50 S 37 50W
União da Vitória 173 26 5 S 51 0W
União dos Palamares 170 9 10 S 36 2W
Uniejów 54 51 59N 18 46 E
Unije, I. 63 44 40N 14 15 E
Unimak I. 147 54 30N 164 30W
Unimak Pass. 148 53 30N 165 15W
Union, Mo., U.S.A. 158 38 25N 91 0W
Union, S.C., U.S.A. 157 34 49N 81 39W
Union City, N.J., U.S.A. 162 40 47N 74 5W
Union City, Ohio, U.S.A. 156 40 11N 84 49W
Union City, Pa., U.S.A. 156 41 53N 79 50W
Union Gap 157 46 38N 120 29W
Unión, La, Chile 176 40 10 S 73 0W
Unión, La, Colomb. 174 1 35N 77 5W
Unión, La, El Sal. 165 13 20N 87 50W
Union, La 164 17 58N 101 49W
Unión, La, Spain 59 37 38N 0 53W
Unión, La, Venez. 174 7 28N 67 53W
Union, Mt. 161 34 34N 112 21W
Union of Soviet Soc. Rep. ■ 77 47 0N 100 0 E
Union Springs 157 32 9N 85 44W
Uniondale Road 128 33 39 S 23 7 E
Uniontown 156 39 54N 79 45W
Unirea 70 44 15N 27 35 E
United Arab Emirates ■ 93 23 50N 54 0 E
United Arab Republic ■ 113 27 5N 30 0 E
United Kingdom ■ 27 55 0N 3 0W
United States of America ■ 155 37 0N 96 0W
Unity 153 52 30N 109 5W
Unjha 94 23 46N 72 24 E
Unnao 95 26 35N 80 30 E
Uno, Ilha 120 11 15N 16 13W
Unshin, R. 38 54 8N 8 26W
Unst, I. 36 60 50N 0 55W
Unstrut, R. 48 51 16N 11 29 E
Unter-Engadin 51 46 48N 10 20 E
Unterägeri 51 47 8N 8 36 E
Unterkulm 50 47 18N 8 7 E
Unterseen 50 46 41N 7 50 E
Unterwalden nid dem Wald □ 51 46 50N 8 25 E
Unterwalden ob dem Wald □ 51 46 55N 8 15 E
Unterwaldner Alpen 51 46 55N 8 15 E
Unterwasser 51 46 32N 8 21 E
Unturán, Sierra de 174 1 35N 64 40W
Unuk, R. 152 56 5N 131 3W
Unye 82 41 5N 37 15 E
Unzen-Dake 111 32 45N 130 17 E
Unzha 81 57 40N 44 8 E
Unzha, R. 81 58 0N 43 40 E
Uors 51 46 42N 9 12 E
Uozu 111 36 48N 137 24 E
Upa, R. 53 50 45N 16 15 E
Upal 123 6 56N 34 12 E
Upata 174 8 1N 62 24W
Upavon 28 51 17N 1 49W
Upemba, L. 127 8 30 S 26 20 E
Upernavik 12 72 49N 56 20W
Upington 128 28 25 S 21 15 E
Upleta 94 21 46N 70 16 E
Upolu Pt. 147 20 16N 155 52W
Upper Alkali Lake 160 41 47N 120 0W
Upper Arrow L. 152 50 30N 117 50W
Upper Austria = Oberösterreich 52 48 15N 14 10 E
Upper Chapel 31 52 3N 3 26W
Upper Foster L. 153 56 47N 105 20W
Upper Heyford 28 51 54N 1 16W
Upper Hutt 142 41 8 S 175 5 E
Upper Klamath L. 160 42 16N 121 55W
Upper L. Erne 38 54 14N 7 22W
Upper Lake 160 39 10N 122 55W
Upper Manilla 141 30 38 S 150 40 E
Upper Marlboro 162 38 49N 76 45W
Upper Musquodoboit 151 45 10N 62 58W
Upper Sandusky 156 40 50N 83 17W
Upper Volta ■ 120 12 0N 0 30W
Upperchurch 39 52 43N 8 2W
Upphärad 73 58 9N 12 19 E
Uppingham 29 52 36N 0 43W
Uppsala 72 59 53N 17 38 E
Uppsala län □ 72 60 0N 17 30 E
Upshi 95 33 48N 77 52 E
Upstart, C. 138 19 41 S 147 45 E
Upton, U.K. 32 53 14N 2 52W
Upton, U.S.A. 158 44 8N 104 35W
Upton-upon-Severn 28 52 4N 2 12W
Upwey 28 50 40N 2 29W
Ur 92 30 55N 46 25 E
Ura-Tyube 85 39 55N 69 1 E
Urabá, Golfo de 174 8 25N 76 53W
Uracará 174 2 20 S 57 50W
Urach 49 48 29N 9 25 E
Uraga-Suidō 111 35 13N 139 45 E
Urakawa 112 42 9N 142 47 E
Ural, Mt. 141 33 21 S 146 12 E
Ural Mts. = Uralskie Gory 78 60 0N 59 0 E
Ural, R. 84 49 0N 52 0W
Uralla 141 30 37 S 151 29 E
Uralsk 84 51 20N 51 20 E
Uralskie Gory 78 60 0N 59 0 E
Urambo 126 5 4 S 32 47 E
Urambo □ 126 5 0 S 32 0 E
Urana 141 35 15 S 146 21 E
Urandangi 138 21 32 S 138 14 E
Uranium City 153 59 34N 108 37W
Uraricaá, R. 174 3 20N 61 56W
Uravakonda 97 14 57N 77 12 E
Urawa 111 35 50N 139 40 E
Uray 76 60 5N 65 15 E
Urbana, Ill., U.S.A. 156 40 7N 88 12W
Urbana, Ohio, U.S.A. 156 40 9N 83 44W
Urbana, La 174 7 8N 66 56W
Urbánia 63 43 40N 12 31 E
Urbano Santos 170 3 12 S 43 23W
Urbel, R. 58 42 30N 3 49W
Urbino 63 43 43N 12 38 E
Urbión, Picos de 58 42 1N 2 52W
Urcos 174 13 30 S 71 30W
Urda, Spain 57 39 25N 3 43W
Urda, U.S.S.R. 83 48 52N 47 23 E
Urdinarrain 172 32 37 S 58 52W
Urdos 44 42 51N 0 35W
Urdzhar 76 47 5N 81 38 E
Ure, R. 33 54 20N 1 25W
Uren 81 57 35N 45 55 E
Ures 164 29 30N 110 30W
Ureshino 110 33 6N 129 59 E
Urfa 92 37 12N 38 50 E
Urfahr 52 48 19N 14 17 E
Urgench 76 41 40N 60 30 E
Urgun 93 32 55N 69 12 E
Urgut 85 39 23N 67 15 E
Uri 95 34 8N 74 2 E
Uri □ 51 46 43N 8 35 E
Uribante, R. 174 7 25N 71 50W
Uribe 174 3 13N 74 24W
Uribia 174 11 43N 72 16W
Urim 90 31 18N 34 32 E
Uriondo 172 21 41 S 64 41W
Urique 164 27 13N 107 55W
Urique, R. 164 26 29N 107 58W
Urirotstock 51 46 52N 8 32 E
Urk 46 52 39N 5 36 E
Urla 92 38 20N 26 55 E
Urlati 70 44 59N 26 15 E
Urlingford 39 52 43N 7 35W
Urmia, L. 92 37 30N 45 30 E
Urmia 92 37 40N 45 0 E
Urmston 32 53 28N 2 22W
Urner Alpen 51 46 45N 8 45 E
Uroševac 66 42 23N 21 10 E
Urrao 174 6 20N 76 11W
Urshult 73 56 31N 14 50 E
Urso 123 9 35N 41 33 E
Ursus 54 52 21N 20 53 E
Uruaca 171 15 30 S 49 41W
Uruaçu 171 14 30 S 49 10W
Uruapán 164 19 30N 102 0W
Urubamba 174 13 5 S 72 10W
Urubamba, R. 174 11 0 S 73 0W
Uruçuca 171 14 35 S 39 16W
Uruçuí 170 7 20 S 44 28W
Uruçuí Prêto, R. 170 7 20 S 44 38W
Uruçuí, Serra do 170 9 0 S 44 45W
Urucuia, R. 171 16 8 S 45 5W
Uruguai, R. 173 24 0 S 53 30W
Uruguaiana 172 29 50 S 57 0W
Uruguay ■ 172 32 30 S 55 30W
Uruguay, R. 172 28 0 S 56 0W
Urumchi = Wulumuchi 105 43 40N 87 50 E
Urup, I. 77 43 0N 151 0 E
Urup, R. 83 44 19N 41 30 E
Urutaí 171 17 28 S 48 12W
Uruyén 174 5 41N 62 25W
Uruzgan □ 93 33 30N 66 0 E
Uryupinsk 81 50 45N 42 3 E
Urzhum 81 57 10N 49 56 E
Urziceni 70 44 46N 26 42 E
Usa 110 33 31N 131 21 E
Usa, R. 78 66 20N 56 0 E
Uşak 92 38 43N 29 28 E
Usakos 128 22 0 S 15 31 E
Usambara Mts. 126 4 50 S 38 20 E
Usedom 48 53 50N 13 55 E
Useko 124 5 8 S 32 24 E
Usfan 122 21 58N 39 27 E
Ush-Tobe 76 45 16N 78 0 E
Ushakova, O. 12 82 0N 80 0 E
Ushant = Ouessant, Île d' 42 48 25N 5 5W
Ushashi 126 1 59 S 33 57 E
Ushat 123 7 59N 29 28 E
Ushibuka 110 32 11N 130 1 E
Ushuaia 176 54 50 S 68 23W
Ushumun 77 52 47N 126 32 E
Usk 31 51 42N 2 53W
Usk, R. 31 51 37N 2 56W
Uskedal 71 59 56N 5 53 E
Üsküdar 92 41 0N 29 5 E
Uslar 48 51 39N 9 39 E
Usman 81 52 5N 39 48 E
Usoga □ 126 0 5N 33 30 E
Usoke 126 5 7 S 32 19 E
Usolye Sibirskoye 77 52 40N 103 40 E
Usoro 121 5 33N 6 11 E
Uspallata, P. de 172 32 30 S 69 28W
Uspenskiy 76 48 50N 72 55 E
Usquert 46 53 24N 6 36 E
Ussel 44 45 32N 2 18 E
Ussuriysk 77 43 40N 131 50 E
Ust 52 50 41N 14 2 E
Ust Aldan = Batamay 77 63 30N 129 15 E
Ust Amginskoye = Khandyga 77 62 30N 134 50 E
Ust-Bolsheretsk 77 52 40N 156 30 E
Ust Buzulukskaya 81 50 8N 42 11 E
Ust Doneckij 83 47 35N 40 55 E
Ust Donetskiy 83 47 35N 40 55 E
Ust Ilga 77 55 5N 104 55 E
Ust Ilimpeya = Yukti 77 63 20N 105 0 E
Ust-Ilimsk 77 58 3N 102 39 E
Ust Ishim 76 57 45N 71 10 E
Ust Kamchatsk 77 56 10N 162 0 E
Ust Kamenogorsk 76 50 0N 82 20 E
Ust Karenga 77 54 40N 116 45 E
Ust Khayryuzova 77 57 15N 156 55 E
Ust Kut 77 56 50N 105 10 E
Ust Kuyga 77 70 1N 135 36 E

Ust Labinsk **Vatoloha, Mt**

Ust Labinsk **83** 45 15N 39 50 E
Ust Luga **80** 59 35N 28 26 E
Ust Maya **77** 60 30N 134 20 E
Ust Mil **77** 59 50N 133 0 E
Ust Nera **77** 64 35N 143 15 E
Ust Olenek **77** 73 0N 120 10 E
Ust-Omchug **77** 61 9N 149 38 E
Ust Port **76** 70 0N 84 10 E
Ust Tsilma **78** 65 25N 52 0 E
Ust-Tungir **77** 55 25N 120 15 E
Ust Urt = Ustyurt **76** 44 0N 55 0 E
Ust Usa **78** 66 0N 56 30 E
Ust-Uyskoye **84** 54 16N 63 54 E
Ust Vorkuta **76** 67 7N 63 35 E
Ustaoset **71** 60 30N 8 2 E
Ustaritz **44** 43 24N 1 27W
Uste **81** 59 35N 39 40 E
Uster **51** 47 22N 8 43 E
Ustí na Orlici **53** 49 58N 16 38 E
Ustí nad Labem **52** 50 41N 14 3 E
Ustica, I. **64** 38 42N 13 10 E
Ustka **54** 54 35N 16 55 E
Ustron **54** 49 45N 18 48 E
Ustrzyki Dolne **54** 49 27N 22 40 E
Ustye **77** 55 30N 97 30 E
Ustyurt, Plato **76** 44 0N 55 0 E
Ustyuzhna **81** 58 50N 36 32 E
Ušće **66** 43 43N 20 39 E
Usuki **110** 33 8N 131 49 E
Usulután **166** 13 25N 88 28W
Usumacinta, R. **165** 17 0N 91 0W
Usva **84** 58 41N 57 37 E
Uta **66** 45 24N 21 13 E
Utah □ **160** 39 30N 111 30W
Utah, L. **160** 40 10N 111 58W
Ute Cr. **159** 36 5N 103 45W
Utena **80** 55 27N 25 40 E
Ütersen **48** 53 40N 9 40 E
Utete **124** 8 0S 38 45 E
Uthai Thani **100** 15 22N 100 3 E
Uthal **94** 25 44N 66 40 E
Uthmaniyah **92** 25 5N 49 6 E
Utiariti **174** 13 0S 58 10W
Utica **162** 43 5N 75 18W
Utiel **58** 39 37N 1 11W
Utik L. **153** 55 15N 96 0W
Utikuma L. **152** 55 50N 115 30W
Utinga **171** 12 6S 41 5W
Uto **110** 32 41N 130 40 E
Utrecht, Neth. **46** 52 3N 5 8 E
Utrecht, S. Afr. **129** 27 38S 30 20 E
Utrecht □ **46** 52 6N 5 7 E
Utrera **57** 37 12N 5 48W
Utsjoki **74** 69 51N 26 59 E
Utsunomiya **111** 36 30N 139 50 E
Uttar Pradesh □ **95** 27 0N 80 0 E
Uttaradit **100** 17 36N 100 5 E
Uttersberg **72** 59 45N 15 39 E
Uttersley **73** 54 56N 11 11 E
Uttoxeter **32** 52 53N 1 50W
Utva, R. **84** 51 28N 52 40 E
Ütze **48** 52 28N 10 11 E
Uudenmaan lääni □ **75** 60 25N 25 0 E
Uusikaarlepyy **74** 63 32N 22 31 E
Uusikaupunki **75** 60 47N 21 25 E
Uva **84** 56 59N 52 13 E
Uvac, R. **66** 43 35N 19 40 E
Uvalde **159** 29 15N 99 48W
Uvarovo **81** 51 59N 42 14 E
Uvat **76** 59 5N 68 50 E
Uvelskiy **84** 54 26N 61 22 E
Uvinza **126** 5 5S 30 24 E
Uvira **126** 3 22S 29 3 E
Uvlova, R. **52** 49 34N 13 20 E
Uvs Nuur, L. **105** 50 20N 92 45 E
Uwa **110** 33 22N 132 31 E
Uwainhid **92** 24 50N 46 0 E
Uwajima **110** 33 10N 132 35 E
Uxmal **165** 20 22N 89 46W
Uyeasound **36** 60 42N 0 55W
Uyo **121** 5 1N 7 53 E
Uyu, R. **98** 24 51N 94 57 E
Uyuk **85** 43 36N 71 16 E
Uyuni **172** 20 35S 66 55W
Uyuni, Salar de **172** 20 10S 68 0W
Uzbekistan S.S.R. □ **85** 40 5N 65 0 E
Uzen, Bol. **81** 50 0N 49 30 E
Uzen, Mal. **81** 50 0N 48 30 E
Uzerche **44** 45 25N 1 35 E
Uzès **45** 44 1N 4 26 E
Uzgen **85** 40 46N 73 18 E
Uzh, R. **80** 51 15N 29 45 E
Uzhgorod **80** 48 36N 22 18 E
Uzlovaya **81** 54 0N 38 5 E
Uzun-Agach **85** 43 35N 76 20 E
Uzunköprü **67** 41 16N 26 43 E
Uzure **126** 4 40S 34 22 E
Uzwil **51** 47 26N 9 9 E

V

Vaal, R. **128** 27 40S 25 30 E
Vaaldam **129** 27 0S 28 14 E
Vaals **47** 50 46N 6 1 E
Vaalwater **129** 24 15S 28 8 E
Vaasa **74** 63 16N 21 35 E
Vaasan lääni □ **74** 63 2N 22 50 E
Vaassen **46** 52 17N 5 58 E
Vabre **44** 43 42N 2 24 E
Vác **53** 47 49N 19 10 E
Vacaria **173** 28 31S 50 52W
Vacaville **163** 38 21N 122 0W
Vach, R. **76** 60 56N 76 38 E
Vache, I.-à **167** 18 2N 73 35W
Väddö **72** 59 55N 18 50 E
Väderum **73** 57 32N 16 11 E
Vadnagar **94** 23 47N 72 40 E
Vado Ligure **62** 44 16N 8 26 E
Vadodara **94** 22 20N 73 10 E
Vadsø **74** 70 3N 29 50 E
Vadstena **73** 58 28N 14 54 E
Vaduz **51** 47 8N 9 31 E
Vaerøy, Nordland Fylke, Norway **74** 67 40N 12 40 E
Vaerøy, Sogn og Fjordane, Norway **71** 61 17N 4 45 E
Vagney **43** 48 1N 6 43 E
Vagnhärad **72** 58 57N 17 33 E
Vagos **56** 40 33N 8 42W
Vagsöy, I. **71** 62 0N 5 0 E
Váh, R. **53** 49 10N 18 20 E
Vaigach **76** 70 10N 59 0 E
Vaigai, R. **97** 9 47N 78 23 E
Vaiges **42** 48 2N 0 30W
Vaihingen **49** 48 44N 8 58 E
Vaihsel B. **13** 75 0S 35 0W
Vaijapur **96** 19 58N 74 45 E
Vaikam **97** 9 45N 76 25 E
Vaila I. **36** 60 12N 1 34W
Vailly Aisne **43** 49 25N 3 30 E
Vaippar, R. **97** 9 0N 78 25 E
Vaison **45** 44 14N 5 4 E
Vajpur **96** 21 24N 73 45 E
Vakarel **67** 42 35N 23 40 E
Vakhsh, R. **85** 37 6N 68 18 E
Vaksdal **71** 60 29N 5 45 E
Vál **53** 47 22N 18 40 E
Val d' Ajol, Le **43** 47 55N 6 30 E
Val-de-Marne □ **43** 48 45N 2 28 E
Val-d'Oise □ **43** 49 5N 2 0 E
Val d'Or **150** 48 7N 77 47W
Val Marie **153** 49 15N 107 45W
Val-St.-Germain **47** 48 34N 2 4 E
Valadares **56** 41 5N 8 38W
Valahia **70** 44 35N 25 0 E
Valais □ **50** 46 12N 7 45 E
Valais, Alpes du **50** 46 47N 7 30 E
Valandovo **66** 41 19N 22 34 E
Valasské MeziríU5 **53** 49 29N 17 59 E
Valaxa, I. **69** 38 50N 24 29 E
Valcheta **176** 40 40S 66 20W
Valdagno **63** 45 38N 11 18 E
Valdahon, Le **43** 47 8N 6 20 E
Valday **80** 57 58N 31 9 E
Valdayskaya Vozvyshennost **80** 57 0N 33 40 E
Valdeazogues, R. **57** 38 45N 4 55W
Valdemarsvik **73** 58 14N 16 40 E
Valdepeñas, Ciudad Real, Spain **57** 38 43N 3 25W
Valdepeñas, Jaén, Spain **57** 37 33N 3 47W
Valderaduey, R. **56** 42 30N 5 0W
Valderrobres **58** 40 53N 0 9 E
Valdes Pen. **176** 42 30S 63 45W
Valdez **147** 61 14N 146 10W
Valdivia **176** 39 50S 73 14W
Valdivia □ **176** 40 0S 73 0W
Valdivia, La **172** 34 43S 72 5W
Valdobbiádene **63** 45 53N 12 0 E
Valdosta **157** 30 50N 83 48W
Valdoviño **56** 43 36N 8 8W
Valdres **71** 60 55N 9 28 E
Vale, U.S.A. **160** 44 0N 117 15W
Vale, U.S.S.R. **83** 41 30N 42 58 E
Valea lui Mihai **70** 47 32N 22 11 E
Valença, Brazil **171** 13 20S 39 5W
Valença, Port. **56** 42 1N 8 34W
Valença do Piauí **170** 6 20S 41 45W
Valence **45** 44 57N 4 54 E
Valence-d'Agen **44** 44 8N 0 54 E
Valencia, Spain **59** 39 27N 0 23W
Valencia, Venez. **174** 10 11N 68 0W
Valencia □ **59** 39 20N 0 40W
Valencia, Albufera de **59** 39 20N 0 27W
Valencia de Alcántara **57** 39 25N 7 14W
Valencia de Don Juan **56** 42 17N 5 31W
Valencia des Ventoso **57** 38 15N 6 29W
Valencia, G. de **59** 39 30N 0 20 E
Valencia, L. de **167** 10 13N 67 40W
Valenciennes **43** 50 20N 3 34 E
Valensole **45** 43 50N 5 59 E
Valentia Hr. **39** 51 56N 10 17W
Valentia I. **39** 51 54N 10 22W
Valentine, Nebr., U.S.A. **158** 42 50N 100 35W
Valentine, Tex., U.S.A. **159** 30 36N 104 28W
Valenton **160** 48 45N 2 28 E
Valenza **62** 45 2N 8 39 E
Våler **71** 60 41N 11 50 E
Valera **174** 9 19N 70 37W
Valguarnera Caropepe **65** 37 30N 14 22 E
Valhall, oilfield **19** 56 17N 3 25 E
Valier **160** 48 15N 112 9W
Valinco, G. de **45** 41 40N 8 52 E
Valjevo **66** 44 18N 19 53 E
Valkeakoski **75** 61 16N 24 2 E
Valkenburg **47** 50 52N 5 50 E
Valkenswaard **47** 51 21N 5 29 E
Vall de Uxó **58** 40 49N 0 15W
Valla **72** 59 2N 16 20 E
Valladolid, Mexico **165** 20 30N 88 20W
Valladolid, Spain **56** 41 38N 4 43W
Valladolid □ **56** 41 38N 4 43W
Vallata **65** 41 3N 15 16 E
Valldalssæter **71** 59 56N 6 57 E
Valle **71** 59 13N 7 33 E
Valle d'Aosta □ **62** 45 45N 7 22 E
Valle de Arán **58** 42 50N 0 55 E
Valle de Cabuérniga **56** 43 14N 4 18W
Valle de la Pascua **174** 9 13N 66 0W
Valle de Santiago **164** 20 25N 101 15W
Valle de Zaragoza **164** 27 28N 105 49W
Valle del Cauca □ **174** 3 45N 76 30W
Valle Fértil, Sierra del **172** 30 20S 68 0W
Valle Hermosa **165** 25 35N 102 25 E
Valle Nacional **165** 17 47N 96 19W
Vallecas **56** 40 23N 3 41W
Valledupar **174** 10 29N 73 15W
Vallejo **163** 38 12N 122 15W
Vallenar **172** 28 30S 70 50W
Valleraugue **44** 44 6N 3 39 E
Vallet **42** 47 10N 1 15W
Valletta **60** 35 54N 14 30 E
Valley **31** 53 17N 4 31W
Valley Center **163** 33 13N 117 2W
Valley City **158** 46 57N 98 0W
Valley Falls **160** 42 33N 120 8W
Valley Okolona **159** 34 0N 88 45W
Valley Springs **163** 38 11N 120 50W
Valley View **162** 40 39N 76 33W
Valleyfield **150** 45 15N 74 8W
Valleyview **152** 55 5N 117 17W
Valli di Comácchio **63** 44 40N 12 15 E
Vallimanca, Arroyo **172** 35 40S 59 10W
Vallo della Lucánia **65** 40 14N 15 16 E
Vallon **45** 44 25N 4 23 E
Vallorbe **50** 46 42N 6 20 E
Valls **58** 41 18N 1 15 E
Vallsta **72** 61 31N 16 22 E
Valmaseda **58** 43 11N 3 12W
Valmiera **80** 57 37N 25 38 E
Valmont **42** 49 45N 0 30 E
Valmontone **64** 41 48N 12 55 E
Valmy **43** 49 5N 4 45 E
Valnera, Mte. **58** 43 9N 3 40W
Valognes **42** 49 30N 1 28W
Valona (Vlora) **68** 40 32N 19 28 E
Valongo **56** 40 37N 8 27W
Valpaços **56** 41 36N 7 17W
Valparaíso, Chile **172** 33 2S 71 40W
Valparaíso, Mexico **164** 22 50N 103 32W
Valparaiso **156** 41 27N 87 2W
Valparaíso □ **172** 33 2S 71 40W
Valpovo **66** 45 39N 18 25 E
Valréas **45** 44 24N 5 0 E
Vals **51** 46 39N 10 11 E
Vals-les-Bains **45** 44 42N 4 24 E
Vals, R. **128** 27 28S 26 52 E
Vals, Tanjung **103** 8 32S 137 32 E
Valsbaai **128** 34 15S 18 40 E
Valskog **72** 59 27N 15 57 E
Válta **68** 40 3N 23 25 E
Valtellina **62** 46 9N 10 2 E
Valverde del Camino **57** 37 35N 6 47W
Valverde del Fresno **56** 40 15N 6 51W
Valyiki **81** 50 10N 38 5 E
Vama **70** 47 34N 25 42 E
Vambarra Ra. **136** 15 13S 130 24 E
Vamdrup **50** 55 26N 9 10 E
Vammala **75** 61 20N 22 55 E
Vámos **69** 35 24N 24 13 E
Vamsadhara, R. **96** 18 22N 84 15 E
Van **92** 38 30N 43 20 E
Van Alstyne **159** 33 25N 96 36W
Van Bruyssel **151** 47 56N 72 9W
Van Buren, Can. **151** 47 10N 67 55W
Van Buren, Ark., U.S.A. **159** 35 28N 94 18W
Van Buren, Me., U.S.A. **157** 47 10N 68 1W
Van Buren, Mo., U.S.A. **159** 37 0N 91 0W
Van Canh **100** 13 37N 109 0 E
Van der Kloof Dam **128** 30 04S 24 40 E
Van Diemen, C., N.T., Austral. **136** 11 9S 130 24 E
Van Diemen, C., Queens., Austral. **138** 16 30S 139 46 E
Van Diemen G. **136** 11 45S 131 50 E
Van Gölü **92** 38 30N 43 0 E
Van Horn **161** 31 3N 104 55W
Van Ninn **100** 12 42N 109 14 E
Van Reenen P. **129** 28 22S 29 27 E
Van Tassell **158** 42 40N 104 3W
Van Tivu, I. **97** 8 51N 78 15 E
Van Wert **156** 40 52N 84 31W
Van Yen **100** 21 4N 104 42 E
Vanavara **77** 60 22N 102 16 E
Vancouver, Can. **152** 49 20N 123 10W
Vancouver, U.S.A. **160** 45 44N 122 41W
Vancouver, C. **137** 35 2S 118 11 E
Vancouver I. **152** 49 50N 126 0W
Vandalia, Ill., U.S.A. **158** 38 57N 89 4W
Vandalia, Mo., U.S.A. **158** 39 18N 91 30W
Vandeloos Bay **97** 8 0N 81 45 E
Vandenburg **163** 34 35N 120 44W
Vanderbijlpark **86** 26 42S 27 54 E
Vanderhoof **152** 54 0N 124 0W
Vanderlin I. **138** 15 44S 137 2 E
Vandyke **138** 24 10S 147 51 E
Vänern **73** 58 47N 13 30 E
Vänersborg **73** 58 26N 12 27 E
Vang Vieng **100** 18 58N 102 32 E
Vanga **126** 4 35S 39 12 E
Vangaindrano **129** 23 21S 47 36 E
Vanguard **153** 49 55N 107 20W
Vanier **150** 45 27N 75 40W
Vanimo **135** 2 42S 141 21 E
Vanivilasa Sagara **97** 13 45N 76 30 E
Vaniyambadi **97** 12 46N 78 44 E
Vankleek Hill **150** 45 32N 75 40W
Vanna **74** 70 6N 19 50 E
Vannas **74** 63 58N 19 48 E
Vannes **42** 47 40N 2 47W
Vanoise, Massif de la **45** 45 25N 6 40 E
Vanrhynsdorp **128** 31 36S 18 44 E
Vanrook **138** 16 57S 141 57 E
Vans, Les **45** 44 25N 4 7 E
Vansbro **72** 60 32N 14 15 E
Vanse **71** 58 6N 6 41 E
Vansittart B. **136** 14 3S 126 17 E
Vanthli **94** 21 28N 70 25 E
Vanua Levu, I. **130** 16 33S 178 8 E
Vanwyksvlei **128** 30 18S 21 49 E
Vanylven **71** 62 5N 5 33 E
Vapnyarka **82** 48 32N 28 45 E
Var □ **45** 43 27N 6 18 E
Vara **73** 58 16N 12 55 E
Varada, R. **97** 14 46N 75 15 E
Varades **42** 47 25N 1 1W
Varaita, R. **62** 44 35N 7 15 E
Varaldsöy **71** 60 6N 5 59 E
Varallo **62** 45 50N 8 13 E
Varanasi (Benares) **95** 25 22N 83 8 E
Varangerfjorden **74** 70 3N 29 25 E
Varazdin **63** 46 20N 16 20 E
Varazze **62** 44 21N 8 36 E
Varberg **73** 57 17N 12 20 E
Vardar, R. **66** 41 25N 22 20 E
Varde **73** 55 38N 8 29 E
Varde Å **73** 55 35N 8 19 E
Vardø **74** 70 23N 31 5 E
Varel **48** 53 23N 8 9 E
Varella, Mui **100** 12 54N 109 26 E
Varena **80** 54 12N 24 30 E
Värendseke **73** 57 4N 15 0 E
Varennes-sur-Allier **44** 49 12N 5 0 E
Vareš **66** 44 12N 18 23 E
Varese **62** 45 49N 8 50 E
Varese Ligure **62** 44 22N 9 33 E
Vårgårda **73** 58 2N 12 49 E
Vargem Bonita **171** 20 20S 46 22W
Vargem Grande **170** 3 33S 43 56W
Varginha **173** 21 33S 45 25W
Vargön **73** 58 22N 12 20 E
Varhaug **71** 58 37N 5 41 E
Varillas **172** 24 0S 70 10W
Varing **73** 58 30N 14 0 E
Värmdö, I. **72** 59 18N 18 45 E
Värmeln **72** 59 35N 13 0 E
Värmlands län □ **72** 59 45N 13 20 E
Varmlandssaby **72** 59 7N 14 15 E
Varna, Bulg. **67** 43 13N 27 56 E
Varna, U.S.S.R. **84** 53 24N 60 58 E
Varna, R. **96** 17 13N 73 50 E
Varnamo **73** 57 10N 14 3 E
Varnsdorf **52** 49 56N 14 38 E
Värö **73** 51 16N 12 15 E
Varpelev **73** 55 22N 12 17 E
Värsjö **73** 56 23N 13 27 E
Varsseveld **46** 51 56N 6 29 E
Varteig **71** 59 23N 11 12 E
Varto **92** 39 10N 41 28 E
Vartofta **73** 58 6N 13 40 E
Vartry Res. **39** 53 3N 6 12W
Varvarin **66** 43 43N 21 20 E
Varzaneh **93** 32 25N 52 40 E
Várzea Alegre **170** 6 47S 39 17W
Várzea da Palma **171** 17 36S 44 44W
Varzi **62** 44 50N 9 12 E
Varzo **62** 46 12N 8 15 E
Varzy **43** 47 22N 3 20 E
Vas □ **53** 47 10N 16 55 E
Vasa **74** 63 6N 21 38 E
Vasa Barris, R. **170** 11 10S 37 10W
Vásárosnamény **53** 48 9N 22 19 E
Väsby **73** 56 13N 12 37 E
Vascão, R. **57** 37 44N 8 15W
Vascongadas **58** 42 50N 2 45W
Vaşcǎu **70** 46 28N 22 30 E
Väse **72** 59 23N 13 52 E
Vasht = Khāsh **93** 28 20N 61 6 E
Vasil Levski **67** 43 23N 25 26 E
Vasilevichi **80** 52 15N 29 50 E
Vasilikón **69** 38 25N 23 40 E
Vasilkov **80** 50 7N 30 28 E
Vaslui **70** 46 38N 27 42 E
Vaslui □ **71** 46 30N 27 30 E
Väsman **72** 60 9N 15 5 E
Vassa **74** 63 6N 21 38 E
Vassar, Can. **153** 49 10N 95 55W
Vassar, U.S.A. **156** 43 23N 83 33W
Vast Silen, L. **72** 59 15N 12 15 E
Västerås **73** 59 37N 16 38 E
Västerbottens län □ **74** 64 58N 18 0 E
Västerdalälven **72** 60 50N 13 25 E
Västernorrlands län □ **72** 63 30N 17 40 E
Västervik **73** 57 43N 16 43 E
Västmanland □ **72** 59 55N 16 30 E
Vasto **63** 42 8N 14 40 E
Vasvár **53** 47 3N 16 47 E
Vatan **43** 47 4N 1 50 E
Vaternish Pt. **36** 57 36N 6 40W
Vatersay, I. **36** 56 55N 7 32W
Vathí **69** 37 46N 27 1 E
Váthia **69** 36 29N 22 29 E
Vatican City ■ **63** 41 54N 12 27 E
Vatin **66** 45 12N 21 20 E
Vatnajökull **74** 64 30N 16 48W
Vatnås **71** 59 58N 9 37 E
Vatne **71** 62 33N 6 38 E
Vatneyri **74** 65 35N 24 0W
Vatoloha, Mt. **129** 17 52S 47 48 E

Vatomandry Vijayadurg

Name	Page	Lat.	Long.
Vatomandry	**129**	19 20 S	48 59 E
Vatra-Dornei	**70**	47 22N	25 22 E
Vats	**71**	59 29N	5 45 E
Vättern, L.	**73**	58 25N	14 30 E
Vättis	**51**	46 55N	9 27 E
Vaucluse □	**45**	44 3N	5 10 E
Vaucouleurs	**43**	48 37N	5 40 E
Vaud □	**50**	46 35N	6 30 E
Vaughan	**161**	34 37N	105 12W
Vaughn	**160**	47 37N	111 36W
Vaulruz	**50**	46 38N	7 0 E
Vaupés □	**174**	1 0N	71 0W
Vaupés, R.	**174**	1 0N	71 0W
Vauvert	**45**	43 42N	4 17 E
Vauxhall	**152**	50 5N	112 9W
Vavincourt	**43**	48 49N	5 12 E
Vavoua	**120**	7 23N	6 29W
Vaxholm	**72**	59 25N	18 20 E
Växjö	**73**	56 52N	14 50 E
Vaygach, Ostrov	**76**	70 0N	60 0 E
Vaza Barris, R.	**171**	10 0 S	37 30W
Veadeiros	**171**	14 7 S	47 31W
Veagh L.	**38**	55 3N	7 57W
Vechta	**48**	52 47N	8 18 E
Vechte, R.	**46**	52 34N	6 6 E
Vecilla, La	**56**	42 51N	5 27W
Vecsés	**53**	47 26N	19 19 E
Vedaraniam	**97**	10 25N	79 50 E
Vedbæk	**73**	55 50N	12 33 E
Veddige	**73**	57 17N	12 20 E
Vedea, R.	**70**	44 0N	25 20 E
Vedelgem	**47**	51 7N	3 10 E
Vedia	**172**	34 30 S	61 31W
Vedra, Isla del	**59**	38 52N	1 12 E
Vedrin	**47**	50 30N	4 52 E
Veendam	**46**	53 5N	6 52 E
Veenendaal	**46**	52 2N	5 34 E
Veenwouden	**46**	53 14N	6 0 E
Veerle	**47**	51 4N	4 59 E
Vefsna	**74**	65 48N	13 10 E
Vega, Norway	**74**	65 40N	11 55 E
Vega, U.S.A.	**159**	35 18N	102 26W
Vega Baja	**147**	18 27N	66 23W
Vega Fd.	**74**	65 37N	12 0 E
Vega, I.	**74**	65 42N	11 50 E
Vega, La	**167**	19 20N	70 30W
Vegadeo	**56**	43 27N	7 4W
Vegesack	**48**	53 10N	8 38 E
Vegfjorden	**74**	65 37N	12 0 E
Veggerby	**73**	56 54N	9 39 E
Veggli	**71**	60 3N	9 9 E
Veghel	**47**	51 37N	5 32 E
Vegorritis, Limni	**68**	40 45N	21 45 E
Vegreville	**152**	53 30N	112 5W
Vegusdal	**71**	58 32N	8 10 E
Veii	**63**	42 0N	12 24 E
Veinticino de Mayo	**172**	38 0 S	67 40W
Veitch	**140**	34 39 S	140 31 E
Vejen	**73**	55 30N	9 9 E
Vejer de la Frontera	**57**	36 15N	5 59W
Vejle	**73**	55 43N	9 30 E
Vejle Amt □	**73**	55 2N	11 22 E
Vejle Fjord	**73**	55 40N	9 50 E
Vejlo	**73**	55 10N	11 45 E
Vela Luka	**63**	42 59N	16 44 E
Velanai I.	**97**	9 45N	79 45 E
Velarde	**161**	36 11N	106 1W
Velas, C.	**166**	10 21N	85 52W
Velasco	**159**	29 0N	95 20W
Velasco, Sierra de.	**172**	29 20 S	67 10W
Velay, Mts. du	**44**	45 0N	3 40 E
Velb	**46**	52 0N	5 59 E
Velddrif	**128**	32 42 S	18 11 E
Velden	**47**	51 25N	6 10 E
Veldhoven	**47**	51 24N	5 25 E
Veldwezelt	**47**	50 52N	5 38 E
Velebit Planina	**63**	44 50N	15 20 E
Velebitski Kanal	**63**	44 45N	14 55 E
Veleka, R.	**67**	42 4N	27 30 E
Velenje	**63**	46 23N	15 8 E
Velestinon	**68**	39 23N	22 43 E
Vélez	**174**	6 1N	73 41W
Velez	**66**	43 19N	18 2 E
Vélez Blanco	**57**	37 41N	2 5W
Vélez Málaga	**57**	36 48N	4 5W
Vélez Rubio	**59**	37 41N	2 5W
Velhas, R.	**171**	17 13 S	44 49W
Velika	**66**	45 27N	17 40 E
Velika Goricá	**63**	45 44N	16 5 E
Velika Kapela	**63**	45 10N	15 5 E
Velika Kladuša	**63**	45 11N	15 48 E
Velika Morava, R.	**66**	44 30N	21 9 E
Velika Plana	**66**	44 20N	21 1 E
Velikaya, R.	**80**	56 40N	28 40 E
Veliké Kapušany	**53**	48 34N	22 5 E
Velike Lašče	**63**	45 49N	14 45 E
Veliki Backa Kanal	**68**	45 45N	19 15 E
Veliki Jastrebac	**66**	43 25N	21 30 E
Veliki Ustyug	**78**	60 47N	46 20 E
Velikiye Luki	**80**	56 25N	30 32 E
Veliko Turnovo	**67**	43 5N	25 41 E
Velikonda Range	**97**	14 45N	79 10 E
Velikoye, Oz.	**81**	55 15N	40 0 E
Velingrad	**67**	42 4N	23 58 E
Velino, Mt.	**63**	42 10N	13 20 E
Velizh	**80**	55 30N	31 11 E
Velké Karlovice	**53**	49 20N	18 17 E
Velke Mezirici	**52**	49 21N	16 1 E
Velký ostrov Zitný	**53**	48 5N	17 20 E
Vellar, R.	**97**	11 30N	79 36 E
Velletri	**64**	41 43N	12 43 E
Velling	**73**	56 2N	8 20 E
Vellinge	**73**	55 29N	13 0 E
Vellir	**74**	65 55N	18 28W
Vellore	**97**	12 57N	79 10 E
Velsen-Noord	**46**	52 27N	4 40 E
Velsk	**78**	61 10N	42 5 E
Velten	**48**	52 40N	13 11 E
Veluwe Meer	**46**	52 24N	5 44 E
Velva	**158**	48 6N	100 56W
Velvendós	**68**	40 15N	22 6 E
Vem	**73**	56 21N	8 21 E
Vembanad Lake	**97**	9 36N	76 15 E
Veme	**71**	60 14N	10 7 E
Ven	**73**	55 55N	12 45 E
Vena	**73**	57 31N	16 0 E
Venado	**164**	22 50N	101 10W
Venado Tuerto	**172**	33 50 S	62 0W
Venafro	**65**	41 28N	14 3 E
Venarey-les-Laumes	**43**	47 32N	4 26 E
Venaria	**62**	45 12N	7 39 E
Venčane	**66**	44 24N	20 28 E
Vence	**45**	43 43N	7 6 E
Vendas Novas	**57**	38 39N	8 27W
Vendée	**42**	46 50N	1 35W
Vendée □	**44**	46 40N	1 20W
Vendée, Collines de	**42**	46 35N	0 45W
Vendée, R.	**42**	46 30N	0 45W
Vendeuvre-sur-Barse	**43**	48 14N	4 28 E
Vendôme	**42**	47 47N	1 3 E
Vendrell	**58**	41 10N	1 30 E
Vendsyssel	**73**	57 22N	10 0 E
Veneta, Laguna	**63**	45 19N	12 13 E
Venetie	**147**	67 0N	146 30W
Véneto □	**63**	45 30N	12 0 E
Venev	**81**	54 22N	38 17 E
Venézia	**63**	45 27N	12 20 E
Venézia, Golfo di	**63**	45 20N	13 0 E
Venezuela ■	**174**	8 0N	65 0W
Venezuela, Golfo de	**174**	11 30N	71 0W
Vengurla	**97**	15 53N	73 45 E
Vengurla Rocks	**97**	15 50N	73 22 E
Venice = Venézia	**63**	45 27N	12 20 E
Vénissieux	**45**	45 43N	4 53 E
Venjansjön	**72**	60 58N	14 2 E
Venkatagiri	**97**	14 0N	79 35 E
Venkatapuram	**96**	18 20N	80 30 E
Venlo	**47**	51 22N	6 11 E
Vennesla	**71**	58 15N	8 0 E
Venø, Is.	**73**	56 33N	8 38 E
Venraij	**47**	51 31N	6 0 E
Venta de Cardeña	**57**	38 16N	4 20W
Venta de San Rafael	**56**	40 42N	4 12W
Venta, La	**165**	18 8N	94 3W
Ventana, Punta de la	**164**	24 4N	109 48W
Ventersburg	**128**	28 7 S	27 9 E
Ventimiglia	**62**	43 50N	7 39 E
Ventnor	**28**	50 35N	1 12W
Ventotene, I.	**64**	40 48N	13 25 E
Ventry	**39**	52 8N	10 21W
Ventspils	**80**	57 25N	21 32 E
Ventuari, R.	**174**	5 20N	66 0W
Ventucopa	**163**	34 50N	119 29W
Ventura	**163**	34 16N	119 18W
Ventura, La	**164**	24 38N	100 54W
Venturosa, La	**174**	6 8N	68 48W
Venus B.	**141**	38 40 S	145 42 E
Veoy	**71**	62 45N	7 30 E
Veoy Is.	**71**	62 45N	7 30 E
Vera, Argent.	**172**	29 30 S	60 20W
Vera, Spain	**59**	37 15N	1 15W
Veracruz	**165**	19 10N	96 10W
Veracruz □	**165**	19 0N	96 15W
Veraval	**94**	20 53N	70 27 E
Verbánia	**62**	45 50N	8 55 E
Verbicaro	**65**	39 46N	15 54 E
Verbier	**50**	46 6N	7 13 E
Vercelli	**62**	45 19N	8 25 E
Verdalsøra	**74**	63 48N	11 30 E
Verde Grande, R.	**171**	16 13 S	43 49W
Verde Pequeno, R.	**171**	14 48 S	43 31W
Verde, R., Argent.	**176**	41 55 S	66 0W
Verde, R., Goiás, Brazil	**171**	18 1 S	50 14W
Verde, R., Goiás, Brazil	**171**	19 11 S	50 44W
Verde, R., Chihuahua, Mexico	**164**	26 59N	107 58W
Verde, R., Oaxaca, Mexico	**164**	15 59N	97 50W
Verde, R., Veracruz, Mexico	**165**	21 10N	102 50W
Verde, R., Parag.	**172**	23 9 S	57 37W
Verden	**48**	52 58N	9 18 E
Verdhikoúsa	**68**	39 47N	21 59 E
Verdigre	**158**	42 38N	98 0W
Verdon-sur-Mer, Le	**44**	45 33N	1 4W
Verdun	**43**	49 12N	5 24 E
Verdun-sur-le Doubs	**43**	46 54N	5 0 E
Vereeniging	**129**	26 38 S	27 57 E
Vérendrye, Parc Prov. de	**150**	47 20N	76 40W
Vereshchagino	**84**	58 5N	54 40 E
Verga, C.	**120**	10 30N	14 10W
Vergara	**58**	43 9N	2 28W
Vergato	**62**	44 18N	11 8 E
Vergemont	**138**	23 33 S	143 1 E
Vergemont Cr.	**138**	24 16 S	143 16 E
Vergt	**44**	45 2N	0 43 E
Verín	**56**	41 57N	7 27W
Veriña	**56**	43 32N	5 43W
Verkhnedvinsk	**80**	55 45N	27 58 E
Verkhneuralsk	**84**	53 53N	59 13 E
Verkhniy-Avzyan	**84**	53 32N	57 33 E
Verkhniy Baskunchak	**83**	48 5N	46 50 E
Verkhniy Tagil	**84**	57 22N	59 56 E
Verkhniy Ufaley	**84**	56 4N	60 14 E
Verkhniye Kigi	**84**	55 25N	58 37 E
Verkhnyaya Salda	**84**	58 2N	60 33 E
Verkhoturye	**84**	58 52N	60 48 E
Verkhovye	**81**	52 55N	37 15 E
Verkhoyansk	**77**	67 50N	133 50 E
Verkhoyanskiy Khrebet	**77**	66 0N	129 0 E
Verlo	**153**	50 19N	108 35W
Verma	**71**	62 21N	8 3 E
Vermenton	**43**	47 40N	3 42 E
Vermilion	**153**	53 20N	110 50W
Vermilion, B.	**159**	29 45N	91 55W
Vermilion Bay	**153**	49 50N	93 20W
Vermilion Chutes	**152**	58 22N	114 51W
Vermilion, R., Alta., Can.	**153**	53 22N	110 51W
Vermilion, R., Qué., Can.	**150**	47 38N	72 56W
Vermillion	**158**	42 50N	96 56W
Vermont □	**156**	43 40N	72 50W
Vern, oilfield	**19**	55 35N	4 45 E
Vernal	**160**	40 28N	109 35W
Vernalis	**163**	37 36N	121 17W
Vernayez	**50**	46 8N	7 3 E
Verner	**150**	46 25N	80 8W
Verneuil, Bois de	**50**	48 59N	1 59 E
Verneuil-sur-Avre	**42**	48 45N	0 55 E
Vernier	**50**	46 13N	6 5 E
Vernon, Can.	**152**	50 20N	119 15W
Vernon, France	**42**	49 5N	1 30 E
Vernon, U.S.A.	**159**	34 0N	99 15W
Vero Beach	**157**	27 39N	80 23W
Véroia	**68**	40 34N	22 18 E
Verolanuova	**62**	45 20N	10 5 E
Véroli	**64**	41 43N	13 24 E
Verona	**62**	45 27N	11 0 E
Veropol	**77**	66 0N	168 0 E
Verrieres, Les	**50**	46 55N	6 28 E
Versailles	**43**	48 48N	2 8 E
Versoix	**50**	46 17N	6 10 E
Vert, C.	**120**	14 45N	17 30W
Vertou	**42**	47 10N	1 28W
Vertus	**43**	48 54N	4 0 E
Verulam	**129**	29 38 S	31 2 E
Verviers	**47**	50 37N	5 52 E
Vervins	**43**	49 50N	3 53 E
Verwood, Can.	**153**	49 30N	105 40W
Verwood, U.K.	**28**	50 53N	1 53W
Veryan	**30**	50 13N	4 56W
Veryan Bay	**30**	50 12N	4 51W
Verzej	**63**	46 34N	16 13 E
Vesdre, R.	**47**	50 36N	6 0 E
Veselí nad Luznicí	**52**	49 12N	14 15 E
Veselie	**67**	42 18N	27 38 E
Veselovskoye Vdkhr.	**83**	47 0N	41 0 E
Veselyy Res.	**83**	47 0N	41 0 E
Veshenskaya	**83**	49 35N	41 44 E
Vesle, R.	**43**	49 17N	3 50 E
Veslyana, R.	**84**	60 20N	54 0 E
Vesoul	**43**	60 40N	6 11 E
Vessigebro	**73**	56 58N	12 40 E
Vest-Agder fylke □	**71**	58 30N	7 15 E
Vest Fjorden	**71**	68 0N	15 0 E
Vesta	**166**	9 43N	83 3W
Vestby	**71**	59 37N	10 45 E
Vester Hassing	**73**	57 4N	10 8 E
Vesterålen	**74**	68 45N	14 30 E
Vestersche Veld	**46**	52 52N	6 9 E
Vestfjorden	**74**	67 55N	14 0 E
Vestfold fylke □	**71**	59 15N	10 0 E
Vestmannaeyjar	**74**	63 27N	20 15W
Vestmarka	**71**	59 56N	11 59 E
Vestnes	**71**	62 39N	7 5 E
Vestone	**62**	45 43N	10 25 E
Vestsjaellands Amt □	**73**	55 30N	11 20 E
Vestspitsbergen	**12**	78 40N	17 0 E
Vestvågøy	**74**	68 18N	13 50 E
Vesuvio	**65**	40 50N	14 22 E
Vesuvius, Mt. = Vesuvio	**65**	40 50N	14 22 E
Veszprém	**53**	47 8N	17 57 E
Veszprém □	**53**	47 5N	17 55 E
Vésztö	**53**	46 55N	21 16 E
Vetapalam	**97**	15 47N	80 18 E
Vetlanda	**73**	57 24N	15 3 E
Vetluga	**81**	57 53N	45 45 E
Vetluzhskiy	**81**	57 17N	45 12 E
Vetovo	**67**	43 42N	26 16 E
Vetralia	**63**	42 20N	12 2 E
Vetren	**67**	42 15N	24 3 E
Vettore, Mte.	**63**	44 38N	7 5 E
Veurne	**47**	51 5N	2 40 E
Vevey	**50**	46 28N	6 51 E
Vévi	**68**	40 47N	21 38 E
Veys	**92**	31 30N	49 0 E
Vézelise	**43**	48 30N	6 5 E
Vezhen, mt.	**67**	42 50N	24 20 E
Vi Thanh	**101**	9 42N	105 26 E
Viacha	**174**	16 30 S	68 5W
Viadana	**62**	44 55N	10 30 E
Viana, Brazil	**170**	3 0 S	44 40W
Viana, Port.	**55**	38 20N	8 0W
Viana, Spain	**58**	42 31N	2 22W
Viana do Castelo	**56**	41 42N	8 50W
Vianden	**47**	49 56N	6 12 E
Vianen	**46**	51 59N	5 5 E
Vianna do Castelo □	**56**	41 50N	8 30W
Vianópolis	**171**	16 40 S	48 35W
Viar, R.	**56**	37 45N	5 54W
Viarèggio	**62**	43 52N	10 13 E
Vibank	**153**	50 20N	103 56W
Vibey, R.	**56**	42 21N	7 15 E
Vibo Valéntia	**65**	38 40N	16 5 E
Viborg	**73**	56 27N	9 23 E
Viborg Amt □	**73**	56 30N	9 20 E
Vic-en-Bigorre	**44**	43 24N	0 3 E
Vic-Fezensac	**44**	43 45N	0 18 E
Vic Fézensac	**44**	43 47N	0 19 E
Vic-sur-Cère	**44**	44 59N	2 38 E
Vic-sur-Seille	**43**	48 45N	6 33 E
Vicarstown	**39**	53 5N	7 7W
Vicenza	**63**	45 32N	11 31 E
Vich	**58**	41 58N	2 19 E
Vichada □	**174**	5 0N	69 30W
Vichuga	**81**	57 25N	41 55 E
Vichy	**44**	46 9N	3 26 E
Vickerstown	**32**	54 8N	3 17W
Vicksburg, Mich., U.S.A.	**156**	42 10N	85 30W
Vicksburg, Miss., U.S.A.	**159**	32 22N	90 56W
Vico, L. di	**63**	42 20N	12 10 E
Viçosa, Min. Ger., Brazil	**170**	20 45 S	42 53W
Viçosa, Pernambuco, Brazil	**170**	9 28 S	36 14W
Viçosa do Ceará	**170**	3 34 S	41 5W
Vicosoprano	**51**	46 22N	9 38 E
Victor	**158**	38 43N	105 7W
Victor Emanuel Ra.	**135**	5 20 S	142 15 E
Victor Harbour	**139**	35 30 S	138 37 E
Victoria, Argent.	**172**	32 40 S	60 10W
Victoria, Austral.	**138**	21 16 S	149 3 E
*Victoria, Camer.	**121**	4 1N	9 10 E
Victoria, Can.	**152**	48 30N	123 25W
Victoria, Chile	**176**	38 13 S	72 20W
Victoria, Guin.	**120**	10 50N	14 32W
Victoria, H. K.	**109**	22 25N	114 15 E
Victoria, Malay.	**102**	5 20N	115 20 E
Victoria, Tex., U.S.A.	**159**	28 50N	97 0W
Victoria, Va., U.S.A.	**158**	38 52N	99 8W
Victoria □, Austral.	**131**	37 0 S	144 0 E
Victoria □, Zimb.	**127**	21 0 S	31 30 E
Victoria Beach	**153**	50 40N	96 35W
Victoria de las Tunas	**166**	20 58N	76 59W
Victoria Falls	**127**	17 58 S	25 45 E
Victoria, Grand L.	**150**	47 31N	77 30W
Victoria Harbour	**150**	44 45N	79 45W
Victoria I.	**148**	71 0N	111 0W
Victoria, L., N.S.W., Austral.	**140**	33 57 S	141 15 E
Victoria, L., Vic., Austral.	**139**	38 2 S	147 34 E
Victoria, L., E. Afr.	**126**	1 0 S	33 0 E
Victoria, La	**174**	10 14N	67 20W
Victoria Ld.	**13**	75 0 S	160 0 E
Victoria, Mt., Burma	**98**	21 15N	93 55 E
Victoria, Mt., P.N.G.	**135**	8 55 S	147 32 E
Victoria Nile R.	**126**	2 25N	31 50 E
Victoria, R.	**136**	15 10 S	129 40 E
Victoria R. Downs	**136**	16 25 S	131 0 E
Victoria Ra.	**143**	42 12 S	172 7 E
Victoria Res.	**151**	48 20N	57 27W
Victoria Taungdeik	**99**	21 15N	93 55 E
Victoria West	**128**	31 25 S	23 4 E
Victoriaville	**151**	46 4N	71 56W
Victorica	**172**	36 20 S	65 30W
Victorino	**174**	2 48N	67 50W
Victorville	**163**	34 32N	117 18W
Vicuña	**172**	30 0 S	70 50W
Vicuña Mackenna	**172**	33 53 S	64 25W
Vidalia	**157**	32 13N	82 25W
Vidauban	**45**	43 25N	6 27 E
Videlv, R.	**71**	58 50N	8 32 E
Vidigueira	**57**	38 12N	7 48W
Vidin	**66**	43 59N	22 28 E
Vidio, Cabo	**56**	43 35N	6 14W
Vidisha (Bhilsa)	**94**	23 28N	77 53 E
Vidöstern	**73**	57 5N	14 0 E
Vidra	**70**	45 56N	26 55 E
Viduša, mts.	**66**	42 55N	18 21 E
Vidzy	**80**	54 40N	26 37 E
Viedma	**176**	40 50 S	63 0W
Viedma, L.	**176**	49 30 S	72 30W
Vieira	**56**	41 38N	8 8W
Viejo Canal de Bahama	**166**	22 10N	77 30W
Viella	**58**	42 43N	0 44 E
Vielsalm	**47**	50 17N	5 54 E
Vien Pou Kha	**101**	20 45N	101 5 E
Vienenburg	**48**	51 57N	10 35 E
Vieng Pou Kha	**100**	20 41N	101 4 E
Vienna, Illinois, U.S.A.	**159**	37 29N	88 54W
Vienna, Va., U.S.A.	**162**	38 54N	77 16W
Vienna = Wien	**53**	48 12N	16 22 E
Vienne	**45**	45 31N	4 53 E
Vienne □	**44**	45 53N	0 42 E
Vienne, R.	**42**	47 5N	0 30 E
Vientiane	**100**	17 58N	102 36 E
Vieques, I.	**147**	18 8N	65 25W
Vierlingsbeek	**47**	51 36N	6 1 E
Viersen	**48**	51 15N	6 23 E
Vierwaldstättersee	**51**	47 0N	8 30 E
Vierzon	**43**	47 13N	2 5 E
Vieux-Boucau-les-Bains	**44**	43 48N	1 23W
Vif	**45**	45 5N	5 41 E
Vigan	**103**	17 35N	120 28 E
Vigan, Le	**44**	44 0N	3 36 E
Vigevano	**62**	45 18N	8 50 E
Vigia	**170**	0 50 S	48 5W
Vigía Chico	**165**	19 46N	87 35W
Vignacourt	**43**	50 1N	2 15 E
Vignemale, Pic du	**44**	42 47N	0 10W
Vigneulles	**43**	48 59N	5 40 E
Vignola	**62**	44 29N	11 0 E
Vigo	**56**	42 12N	8 41W
Vigo, Ria de	**56**	42 15N	8 45W
Vihiers	**42**	47 10N	0 30W
Vijayadurg	**96**	16 30N	73 25 E

*Renamed Limbe

Vijayawada (Bezwada) Voitsberg

Vijayawada (Bezwada) 96 16 31N 80 39E
Vijfhuizen 46 52 22N 4 41E
Vikedal 71 59 30N 5 55E
Viken, L. 73 58 40N 10 2E
Vikersund 71 59 58N 10 2E
Viking 152 53 7N 111 50W
Viking, gasfield 19 53 30N 2 20E
Vikna 74 64 52N 10 57E
Vikramasingapuram 97 8 40N 76 47E
Viksjö 72 62 45N 17 26E
Vikulovo 76 56 50N 70 40E
Vila Alferes Chamusca 129 24 27S 33 0E
Vila Arriaga 125 14 35S 13 30E
Vila Bittencourt 174 1 20S 69 20W
Vila Cabral = Lichinga 127 13 13S 35 11E
Vila Caldas Xavier 127 14 28S 33 0E
Vila Coutinho 127 14 37S 34 19E
Vila da Maganja 127 17 18S 37 30E
Vila da Ponte 125 14 35S 16 40E
Vila de Aljustrel 125 13 30S 19 45E
Vila de João Belo = Xai-Xai 129 25 6S 33 31E
Vila de Liquica 103 8 40S 125 20E
Vila de Manica 125 18 58S 32 59E
Vila de Rei 57 39 41N 8 9W
Vila de Sena = Sena 127 17 25S 35 0E
Vila do Bispo 57 37 5N 8 53W
Vila do Conde 56 41 21N 8 45W
Vila Fontes 125 17 51S 35 24E
Vila Fontes Velha 127 17 51S 35 24E
Vila Franca de Xira 57 38 57N 8 59W
Vila Gamito 127 14 12S 33 0E
Vila General Machado 125 11 58S 17 22E
Vila Gomes da Costa 129 24 20S 33 37E
Vila Henrique de Carvalho = Lunda 124 9 40S 20 12E
Vila Junqueiro 127 15 25S 36 58E
Vila Luisa 129 25 45S 32 35E
Vila Luso = Moxico 125 11 53S 19 55E
Vila Machado 127 19 15S 34 14E
Vila Marechal Carmona = Uige 124 7 30S 14 40E
Vila Mariano Machado 125 13 3S 14 35E
Vila Moatize 127 16 11S 33 40E
Vila Mouzinho 127 14 48S 34 25E
Vila Murtinho 174 10 20S 65 20W
Vila Nova de Fozcôa 56 41 5N 7 9W
Vila Nova de Ourém 57 39 40N 8 35W
Vila Nova do Seles 125 11 35S 14 22E
Vila Novo de Gaia 56 41 4N 8 40W
Vila Paiva Couceiro 125 14 37S 14 40E
Vila Paiva de Andrada 127 18 37S 34 2E
Vila Pery = Chimoio 127 19 4S 33 30E
Vila Pouca de Aguiar 56 41 30N 7 38W
Vila Real 56 41 17N 7 48W
Vila Real de Santo Antonio 57 37 10N 7 28W
Vila Robert Williams 125 12 46S 15 30E
Vila Salazar, Angola 124 9 12S 14 48E
Vila Salazar, Indon. 103 5 25S 123 50E
Vila Teixeira da Silva 125 12 10S 15 50E
Vila Vasco da Gama 127 14 54S 32 14E
Vila Velha 173 20 20S 40 17W
Vila Verissimo Sarmento 124 8 15S 20 50E
Vila Viçosa 57 38 45N 7 27W
Vilaboa 56 42 21N 8 39W
Vilaine, R. 42 47 35N 2 10W
Vilanculos 129 22 1S 35 17E
Vilar Formosa 56 40 38N 6 45W
Vilareal □ 56 41 36N 7 35W
Vileyka 80 54 30N 27 0E
Vilhelmina 74 64 35N 16 39E
Vilhena 174 12 30S 60 0W
Viliga 77 60 2N 156 56E
Viliya, R. 80 54 57N 24 35E
Viljandi 80 58 28N 25 30E
Villa Abecia 172 21 0S 68 18W
Villa Ahumada 164 30 30N 106 40W
Villa Ana 172 28 28S 59 40W
Villa Ángela 172 27 34S 60 45W
Villa Bella 174 10 25S 65 30W
Villa Bens (Tarfaya) 116 27 55N 12 55W
Villa Cañas 172 34 0S 61 35W
Villa Cisneros = Dakhla 116 23 50N 15 53W
Villa Colón 172 31 38S 68 20W
Villa Constitución 172 33 15S 60 20W
Villa de Cura 174 10 2N 67 29W
Villa de María 172 30 0S 63 43W
Villa de Rosario 172 24 30S 57 35W
Villa Dolores 172 31 58S 65 15W
Villa Franca 172 26 14S 58 20W
Villa Frontera 164 26 56N 101 27W
Villa Guillermina 172 28 15S 59 29W
Villa Hayes 172 25 0S 57 20W
Villa Iris 172 38 12S 63 12W
Villa Julia Molina 167 19 5N 69 45W
Villa Madero 164 24 28N 104 10W
Villa María 172 32 20S 63 10W
Villa Mazán 172 28 40S 66 30W
Villa Mentes 172 21 10S 63 30W
Villa Minozzo 62 44 21N 10 30E
Villa Montes 172 21 10S 63 30W
Villa Ocampo, Argent. 172 28 30S 59 20W
Villa Ocampo, Mexico 164 26 29N 105 30W
Villa Ojo de Agua 172 29 30S 63 44W
Villa San Agustín 172 30 35S 67 30W
Villa San Giovanni 65 38 13N 15 38E
Villa San José 172 32 12S 58 15W
Villa San Martín 172 28 9S 64 9W
Villa Santina 63 46 25N 12 55E
Villa Unión 164 23 12N 106 14W
Villablino 56 42 57N 6 19W
Villabruzzi 91 3 3N 45 18E
Villacampo, Pantano de 56 41 31N 6 0W
Villacañas 58 39 38N 3 20W
Villacarlos 58 39 53N 4 17E
Villacarriedo 58 43 14N 3 48W
Villacarrillo 59 38 7N 3 3W
Villacastín 56 40 46N 4 25W
Villach 52 46 37N 13 51E
Villaciaro 64 39 27N 8 45E
Villada 56 42 15N 4 59W
Villadiego 56 42 31N 4 1W
Villadossóla 62 46 4N 8 16E
Villafeliche 58 41 10N 1 30W
Villafranca 58 42 17N 1 46W
Villafranca de los Barros 57 38 35N 6 18W
Villafranca de los Caballeros 59 39 26N 3 21W
Villafranca del Bierzo 56 42 38N 6 50W
Villafranca del Cid 58 40 26N 0 16W
Villafranca del Panadés 58 41 21N 1 40E
Villafranca di Verona 62 45 20N 10 51E
Villagarcía de Arosa 56 42 34N 8 46W
Villagrán 165 24 29N 99 29W
Villaguay 172 32 0S 58 45W
Villaharta 57 38 9N 4 54W
Villahermosa, Mexico 165 17 45N 92 50W
Villahermosa, Spain 59 38 46N 2 52W
Villaines-la-Juhel 42 48 21N 0 20W
Villajoyosa 59 38 30N 0 12W
Villalba 56 40 36N 3 59W
Villalba de Guardo 56 42 42N 4 49W
Villalón de Campos 56 42 5N 5 4W
Villalpando 56 41 51N 5 25W
Villaluenga 56 40 2N 3 54W
Villamañ!n 56 42 19N 5 35W
Villamartín 56 36 52N 5 38W
Villamayor 58 41 42N 0 43W
Villamblard 44 45 2N 0 32E
Villanova Monteleone 64 40 30N 8 28E
Villanueva, Colomb. 174 10 37N 72 59W
Villanueva, U.S.A. 161 35 16N 105 31W
Villanueva de Castellón 59 39 5N 0 31W
Villanueva de Córdoba 57 38 20N 4 38W
Villanueva de la Fuente 59 38 42N 2 42W
Villanueva de la Serena 57 38 59N 5 50W
Villanueva de la Sierra 56 40 12N 6 24W
Villanueva de los Castillejos 57 37 30N 7 15W
Villanueva del Arzobispo 59 38 10N 3 0W
Villanueva del Duque 57 38 20N 4 38W
Villanueva del Fresno 57 38 23N 7 10W
Villanueva y Geltrú 58 41 13N 1 40E
Villaodrid 56 43 20N 7 11W
Villaputzu 64 39 28N 9 33E
Villar del Arzobispo 58 39 44N 0 50W
Villar del Rey 57 39 7N 6 50W
Villarcayo 58 42 56N 3 34W
Villard 45 45 4N 5 33E
Villard-Bonnot 45 45 14N 5 53E
Villard-de-Lans 45 45 3N 5 33E
Villarino de los Aires 56 41 18N 6 23W
Villarosa 65 37 36N 14 9E
Villarramiel 56 42 2N 4 55W
Villarreal 58 39 55N 0 3W
Villarrica, Chile 176 39 15S 72 30W
Villarrica, Parag. 172 25 40S 56 30W
Villarrobledo 59 39 18N 2 36W
Villarroya de la Sierra 58 41 27N 1 46W
Villarrubia de los Ojos 59 39 14N 3 36W
Villars 45 46 0N 5 2E
Villarta de San Juan 59 39 15N 3 25W
Villasayas 58 41 24N 2 39W
Villaseca de los Gamitos 56 41 2N 6 7W
Villastar 58 40 17N 1 9W
Villatobas 58 39 54N 3 20W
Villavicencio, Argent. 172 32 28S 69 0W
Villavicencio, Colomb. 174 4 9N 73 37W
Villaviciosa 56 43 32N 5 27W
Villazón 172 22 0S 65 35W
Ville de Paris □ 43 48 50N 2 20E
Ville Marie 150 47 20N 79 30W
Ville Platte 159 30 45N 92 17W
Villedieu 42 48 50N 1 12W
Villefort 44 44 28N 3 56E
Villefranche 43 47 19N 146 0E
Villefranche-de-Lauragais 44 43 25N 1 44E
Villefranche-de-Rouergue 44 44 21N 2 2E
Villefranche-du-Périgord 44 44 38N 1 5E
Villefranche-sur-Saône 45 45 59N 4 43E
Villel 58 40 14N 1 12W
Villemaur 43 48 14N 3 40E
Villemur-sur-Tarn 44 43 51N 1 31E
Villena 59 38 39N 0 52W
Villenauxe 43 48 36N 3 30E
Villenave 44 44 46N 0 33W
Villeneuve, France 43 48 42N 2 25E
Villeneuve, Italy 62 45 40N 7 10E
Villeneuve, Switz. 50 46 24N 6 56E
Villeneuve-l'Archevèque 43 48 14N 3 32E
Villeneuve-lès-Avignon 45 43 57N 4 49E
Villeneuve-sur-Allier 44 46 40N 3 13E
Villeneuve-sur-Lot 44 44 24N 0 42E
Villeréal 44 44 38N 0 45E
Villers Bocage 42 49 3N 0 40W
Villers Bretonneux 43 49 50N 2 30E
Villers-Cotterets 43 49 15N 3 4E
Villers-Farlay 47 47 0N 5 45E
Villers-le-Bouillet 47 50 34N 5 15E
Villers-le-Gambon 47 50 11N 4 37E
Villers-sur-Mer 42 49 21N 0 2W
Villersexel 43 47 33N 6 26E
Villerslev 73 56 49N 8 29E
Villerupt 43 49 28N 5 55E
Villerville 42 49 26N 0 5E
Villiers 129 27 2S 28 36E
Villingen = Schwenningen 49 48 3N 8 29E
Villisca 158 40 55N 94 59W
Villupuram 97 11 59N 79 31E
Vilna 152 54 7N 111 55W
Vilnius 80 54 38N 25 25E
Vils 52 47 33N 10 37E
Vilsbiburg 49 48 27N 12 23E
Vilslev 73 55 24N 8 42E
Vilusi 66 42 44N 18 34E
Vilvoorde 47 50 56N 4 26E
Vilyuy, R. 77 63 58N 125 0E
Vilyuysk 77 63 40N 121 20E
Vimercate 62 45 38N 9 25E
Vimiosa 56 41 35N 6 13W
Vimmerby 73 57 40N 15 55E
Vimo 72 60 50N 14 20E
Vimoutiers 42 48 57N 0 10E
Vimperk 52 49 3N 13 46E
Viña del Mar 172 33 0S 71 30W
Vinaroz 58 40 30N 0 27E
Vincennes 156 38 42N 87 29W
Vincent 163 34 33N 118 11W
Vinchina 172 28 45S 68 15W
Vindel älv 74 64 20N 19 20E
Vindeln 74 64 12N 19 43E
Vinderup 73 56 29N 8 45E
Vindhya Ra. 94 22 50N 77 0E
Vinegar Hill 39 52 30N 6 28W
Vineland 162 39 30N 75 0W
Vinga 66 46 0N 21 14E
Vingnes 71 61 7N 10 26E
Vinh 100 18 45N 105 38E
Vinh Linh 100 17 4N 107 2E
Vinh Loi 101 9 20N 104 45E
Vinh Long 101 10 16N 105 57E
Vinh Yen 100 21 21N 105 35E
Vinhais 56 41 50N 7 0W
Vinica 63 45 28N 15 16E
Vinita 159 36 40N 95 12W
Vinkeveen 46 52 13N 4 56E
Vinkovci 66 45 19N 18 48E
Vinnitsa 82 49 15N 28 30E
Vinstra 71 61 37N 9 44E
Vinton, Iowa, U.S.A. 158 42 8N 92 1W
Vinton, La., U.S.A. 159 30 13N 93 35W
Vintu de Jos 70 46 0N 23 30E
Viöl 48 54 32N 9 12E
Violet Town 141 36 38S 145 42E
Vipava 63 45 51N 13 38E
Vipiteno 63 46 55N 11 25E
Viqueque 103 8 42S 126 30E
Vir 85 37 45N 72 5E
Vir, I. 63 44 17N 15 3E
Virac 103 13 30N 124 20E
Virachei 100 13 59N 106 49E
Virago Sd. 152 54 0N 132 42W
Virajpet 97 12 15N 75 50E
Viramgam 94 23 5N 72 0E
Virarajendrapet (Virajpet) 97 12 10N 75 50E
Viravanallur 97 8 40N 79 30E
Virden 153 49 50N 100 56W
Vire 42 48 50N 0 53W
Virgem da Lapa 171 16 49S 42 21W
Vírgenes, C. 176 52 19S 68 21W
Virgin Gorda, I. 147 18 45N 64 26W
Virgin Is. 147 18 40N 64 30W
Virgin, R., Can. 153 57 2N 108 17W
Virgin, R., U.S.A. 161 36 50N 114 10W
Virginia, Ireland 38 53 50N 7 5W
Virginia, S. Afr. 128 28 8S 26 55E
Virginia, U.S.A. 158 47 30N 92 32W
Virginia □ 156 37 45N 78 0W
Virginia Beach 156 36 54N 75 58W
Virginia City, Mont., U.S.A. 160 45 25N 111 58W
Virginia City, Nev., U.S.A. 160 39 19N 119 39W
Virginia Falls 152 61 38N 125 42W
Virginiatown 150 48 9N 79 36W
Virgins, C. 176 52 10S 68 30W
Virieu-le-Grand 45 45 51N 5 39E
Virje 66 46 4N 16 59E
Viroqua 158 43 33N 90 57W
Virovitica 66 45 51N 17 21E
Virpaza, R. 66 42 14N 19 6E
Virserum 73 57 20N 15 35E
Virton 47 49 35N 5 32E
Virtsu 80 58 32N 23 33E
Virudhunagar 97 9 30N 78 0E
Vis 63 43 0N 16 10E
Vis, I. 63 43 0N 16 10E
Vis Kanal 63 43 4N 16 5E
Visalia 163 36 25N 119 18W
Visayan Sea 103 11 30N 123 30E
Visby 73 57 37N 18 18E
Viscount Melville Sd. 12 74 10N 108 0W
Visé 47 50 44N 5 41E
Višegrad 66 43 47N 19 17E
Viseu, Brazil 170 1 10S 46 20W
Viseu, Port. 56 40 40N 7 55W
Vişeu 70 47 45N 24 25E
Viseu □ 56 40 40N 7 55W
Vishakhapatnam 96 17 45N 83 20E
Vishera, R. 84 59 55N 56 25E
Vishnupur 95 23 8N 87 20E
Visikoi I. 13 56 30S 26 40E
Visingsö 73 58 2N 14 20E
Viskafors 73 57 37N 12 50E
Vislanda 73 56 46N 14 30E
Vislinskil Zaliv (Zalew Wislany) 54 54 20N 19 50E
Visnagar 94 23 45N 72 32E
Višnja Gora 63 45 58N 14 45E
Viso del Marqués 59 38 32N 3 34W
Viso, Mte. 62 44 38N 7 5E
Visoko 66 43 58N 18 10E
Visp 50 46 17N 7 52E
Vispa, R. 50 46 9N 7 48E
Visselhovde 48 52 59N 9 36E
Vissoie 50 46 13N 7 36E
Vista 163 33 12N 117 14W
Vistonis, Limni 68 41 0N 25 7E
Vistula, R. = Wisła, R. 54 53 38N 18 47E
Vit, R. 67 43 30N 24 30E
Vitanje 63 46 40N 15 18E
Vitebsk 80 55 10N 30 15E
Viterbo 63 42 25N 12 8E
Viti Levu, I. 143 17 30S 177 30E
Vitiaz Str. 135 5 40S 147 10E
Vitigudino 56 41 1N 6 35W
Vitim 77 59 45N 112 25E
Vitim, R. 77 58 40N 112 50E
Vitína 69 37 40N 22 10E
Vitina 66 43 17N 17 29E
Vitória 171 20 20S 40 22W
Vitoria 58 42 50N 2 41W
Vitória da Conquista 171 14 51S 40 51W
Vitória de São Antão 170 8 10S 37 20W
Vitorino Friere 170 4 4S 45 10W
Vitré 42 48 8N 1 12W
Vitry-le-François 43 48 43N 4 33E
Vitsi, Mt. 68 40 40N 21 25E
Vittangi 74 67 41N 21 40E
Vitteaux 43 47 24N 4 30E
Vittel 43 48 12N 5 57E
Vittória 65 36 58N 14 30E
Vittório Véneto 63 45 59N 12 18E
Vitu Is. 135 4 50S 149 25E
Vivegnis 47 50 42N 5 39E
Viver 58 39 55N 0 36W
Vivero 56 43 39N 7 38W
Viviers 45 44 30N 4 40E
Vivonne, Austral. 140 35 59S 137 9E
Vivonne, France 44 46 36N 0 15E
Vivonne B. 140 35 59S 137 9E
Vivsta 72 62 30N 17 18E
Vizcaíno, Desierto de 164 27 40N 113 50W
Vizcaíno, Sierra 164 27 30N 114 0W
Vizcaya □ 58 43 15N 2 45W
Vizianagaram 96 18 6N 83 10E
Vizille 45 45 5N 5 46E
Vizinada 63 45 20N 13 46E
Viziru 70 45 0N 27 43E
Vizovice 53 49 12N 17 56E
Vizzini 65 37 9N 14 43E
Vlaardingen 46 51 55N 4 21E
Vladicin Han 66 42 42N 22 1E
Vladimir 81 56 0N 40 30E
Vladimir Volynskiy 80 50 50N 24 18E
Vladimirci 66 44 36N 19 45E
Vladimirovac 66 45 1N 20 53E
Vladimirovka, U.S.S.R. 83 44 37N 44 41E
Vladimirovka, U.S.S.R. 83 48 27N 46 5E
Vladimirovo 67 43 32N 23 22E
Vladislavovka 82 45 15N 35 15E
Vladivostok 82 43 10N 131 53E
Vlamertinge 47 50 51N 2 49E
Vlaming Head 137 21 48S 114 5E
Vlasenica 66 44 11N 18 59E
Vlasim 52 49 40N 14 53E
Vlasinsko Jezero 66 42 44N 22 37E
Vlašió, mt. 66 44 19N 17 37E
Vlasotinci 66 42 59N 22 7E
Vleuten 46 52 6N 5 1E
Vlieland, I. 46 53 30N 4 55E
Vliestroom 46 53 19N 5 8E
Vlijmen 47 51 42N 5 14E
Vlissingen 47 51 26N 3 34E
Vlora 68 40 32N 19 28E
Vlora □ 68 40 12N 20 0E
Vltava, R. 52 49 35N 14 10E
Vlŭdeasa, mt. 70 46 47N 22 50E
Vo Dat 101 11 9N 107 31E
Vobarno 62 45 38N 10 30E
Vočin 66 45 37N 17 33E
Vodice 63 43 47N 15 47E
Vodnany 52 49 9N 14 11E
Vodnjan 63 44 59N 13 52E
Voe 36 60 21N 1 15W
Voga 121 6 23N 1 30E
Vogelkop = Doberai, Jazirah 103 1 25S 133 0E
Vogelsberg 48 50 37N 9 30E
Voghera 62 44 59N 9 1E
Vohémar 129 13 25S 50 0E
Vohipeno 129 22 22S 47 51E
Voi 126 3 25S 38 32E
Void 43 48 40N 5 36E
Voil, L. 34 56 20N 4 25W
Voineşti, Iaşi, Rumania 70 47 5N 27 27E
Voineşti, Ploeşti, Rumania 70 45 5N 25 14E
Voiotía □ 69 38 20N 23 0E
Voiron 45 45 22N 5 35E
Voiseys B. 151 56 15N 61 50W
Voitsberg 52 47 3N 15 9E

Voiviis Limni, L

Walla Walla

Voiviis Limni, L. 68 39 30N 22 45 E
Vojens 73 55 16N 9 18 E
Vojmsjön 74 64 55N 16 40 E
Vojnió 63 45 19N 15 43 E
Vojvodina, Auton. Pokragina 66 45 20N 20 0 E
Vokhma 81 59 0N 46 45 E
Vokhma, R. 81 59 0N 46 44 E
Vokhtoga 81 58 46N 41 8 E
Volary 52 48 54N 13 52 E
Volborg 158 45 50N 105 44W
Volchansk 81 50 17N 36 58 E
Volchya, R. 82 48 0N 37 0 E
Volda 71 62 9N 6 5 E
Volendam 46 52 30N 5 4 E
Volga 81 57 58N 38 16 E
Volga Hts. = Privolzhskaya V.S. 79 51 0N 46 0 E
Volga, R. 83 52 20N 48 0 E
Volgodonsk 83 47 33N 42 5 E
Volgograd 83 48 40N 44 25 E
Volgogradskoye Vdkhr. 81 50 0N 45 20 E
Volgorechensk 81 57 28N 41 14 E
Volissós 69 38 29N 25 54 E
Volkerak 47 51 39N 4 18 E
Völkermarkt 52 46 39N 14 39 E
Volkhov 80 59 55N 32 15 E
Volkhov, R. 80 59 30N 32 0 E
Völklingen 49 49 15N 6 50 E
Volkovysk 80 53 9N 24 30 E
Volksrust 129 27 24 S 29 53 E
Vollenhove 46 52 40N 5 58 E
Volnovakha 82 47 35N 37 30 E
Volo 140 31 37 S 143 0 E
Volochayevka 77 48 40N 134 30 E
Volodary 81 56 12N 43 15 E
Vologda 81 59 25N 40 0 E
Volokolamsk 81 56 5N 36 0 E
Volokonovka 81 50 33N 37 58 E
Volontirovka 82 46 28N 29 28 E
Vólos 68 39 24N 22 59 E
Volosovo 80 59 27N 29 32 E
Volozhin 80 54 3N 26 30 E
Volsk 81 52 5N 47 28 E
Volstrup 73 57 19N 10 27 E
Volta, L. 121 7 30N 0 15 E
Volta, R. 121 8 0N 0 10W
Volta Redonda 173 22 31 S 44 5W
Voltaire, C. 136 14 16 S 125 35 E
Volterra 62 43 24N 10 50 E
Voltri 62 44 25N 8 43 E
Volturara Áppula 65 41 30N 15 2 E
Volturno, R. 65 41 18N 14 20 E
Volubilis 118 34 2N 5 33W
Vólvi, L. 68 40 40N 23 34 E
Volzhsk 81 55 57N 48 23 E
Volzhskiy 83 48 56N 44 46 E
Vondrozo 129 22 49 S 47 20 E
Vónitsa 69 38 53N 20 58 E
Voorburg 46 52 5N 4 24 E
Voorne Putten 46 51 52N 4 10 E
Voorst 46 52 10N 6 8 E
Voorthuizen 46 52 11N 5 36 E
Vopnafjörður 74 65 45N 14 40W
Vorarlberg □ 52 47 20N 10 0 E
Vóras Óros 68 40 57N 21 45 E
Vorbasse 73 55 39N 9 6 E
Vorden 46 52 6N 6 19 E
Vorderrheim, R. 51 46 49N 9 25 E
Vordingborg 73 55 0N 11 54 E
Voreppe 45 45 18N 5 39 E
Voríai Sporádhes 69 39 15N 23 30 E
Vórios Evvoïkós Kólpos 69 38 45N 23 15 E
Vorkuta 78 67 48N 64 20 E
Vorma 71 60 9N 11 27 E
Vorona, R. 81 52 0N 42 20 E
Voronezh, R.S.S.R., U.S.S.R. 81 51 40N 39 10 E
Voronezh, Ukraine, U.S.S.R. 80 51 47N 33 28 E
Voronezh, R. 81 52 30N 39 30 E
Vorontsovo-Aleksandrovskoïe = Zelenokumsk. 83 44 30N 44 1 E
Voroshilovgrad 83 48 38N 39 15 E
Voroshilovsk = Kommunarsk 83 48 3N 38 40 E
Vorovskoye 77 54 30N 155 50 E
Vorselaar 47 51 12N 4 46 E
Vorskla, R. 82 49 30N 34 31 E
Vorukh 85 39 52N 70 35 E
Vorupør 73 56 58N 8 22 E
Vosges 43 48 20N 7 10 E
Vosges □ 43 48 12N 6 20 E
Voskopoja 68 40 40N 20 33 E
Voskresensk 81 55 27N 38 31 E
Voskresenskoye 81 56 51N 45 30 E
Voss 71 60 38N 6 26 E
Vosselaar 47 51 19N 4 52 E
Vostok I. 131 10 5 S 152 23W
Vostotnyy Sayan 77 54 0N 96 0 E
Votice 52 49 38N 14 39 E
Votkinsk 84 57 0N 53 55 E
Votkinskoye Vdkhr. 78 57 30N 55 0 E
Vouga, R. 56 40 46N 8 10W
Voulte-sur-Rhône, La 45 44 48N 4 46 E
Vouvry 50 46 21N 6 21 E
Voúxa, Ákra 69 35 37N 20 32 E
Vouzela 56 40 43N 8 7W
Vouziers 43 49 22N 4 40 E
Voves 43 48 15N 1 38 E
Voxna 72 61 20N 15 30 E
Voy 37 59 1N 3 16W
Vozhe Oz. 78 60 45N 39 0 E
Vozhgaly 81 58 24N 50 1 E
Voznesensk 82 47 35N 31 15 E
Voznesenye 78 61 0N 35 45 E
Vráble 53 48 15N 18 16 E
Vrácevšnica 66 44 2N 20 34 E
Vrådal 71 59 20N 8 25 E
Vradiyevka 82 49 56N 30 38 E
Vraka 68 42 8N 19 28 E
Vrakhnéika 69 38 10N 21 40 E
Vrancea □ 70 45 50N 26 45 E
Vrancei, Munţi 70 46 0N 26 30 E
Vrangelja, Ostrov 77 71 0N 180 0 E
Vrangtjarn 72 62 14N 16 37 E
Vranica, mt. 66 43 59N 18 0 E
Vranje 66 42 34N 21 54 E
Vranjska Banja 66 42 34N 22 1 E
Vranov 53 48 53N 21 40 E
Vransko 63 46 17N 14 58 E
Vratsa 67 43 13N 23 30 E
Vratsa □ 67 43 30N 23 30 E
Vrbas 66 45 0N 17 27 E
Vrbas, R. 66 44 30N 17 10 E
Vrbnik 63 45 4N 14 32 E
Vrboviec 63 45 53N 16 28 E
Vrbovsko 63 45 24N 15 5 E
Vrchlabí 52 49 38N 15 37 E
Vrede 129 27 24 S 29 6 E
Vredefort 128 27 0 S 26 58 E
Vredenburg 128 32 51 S 18 0 E
Vredendal 128 31 41 S 18 35 E
Vreeswijk 46 52 1N 5 6 E
Vrena 73 58 54N 16 41 E
Vrgorac 66 43 12N 17 20 E
Vrhnika 63 45 58N 14 15 E
Vriddhachalam 97 11 30N 79 10 E
Vridi 120 5 15N 4 3W
Vridi Canal 120 5 15N 4 3W
Vries 46 53 5N 6 35 E
Vriezenveen 46 52 25N 6 38 E
Vrindaban 94 27 37N 77 40 E
Vrnograč 63 43 12N 17 20 E
Vrondádhes 69 38 25N 26 7 E
Vroomshoop 46 52 27N 6 34 E
Vrpolje 66 43 42N 16 1 E
Vršac 66 45 8N 21 18 E
Vršački Kanal 66 45 15N 21 0 E
Vrsheto 67 43 15N 23 23 E
Vryburg 128 26 55 S 24 45 E
Vryheid 129 27 54 S 30 47 E
Vsetin 53 49 20N 18 0 E
Vu Liet 100 18 43N 105 23 E
Vŭcha, R. 67 41 53N 24 26 E
Vučitrn 66 42 49N 20 59 E
Vught 47 51 38N 5 20 E
Vuka, R. 66 45 28N 18 30 E
Vukovar 66 45 21N 18 59 E
Vulcan, Can. 152 50 25N 113 15W
Vulcan, Rumania 70 45 23N 23 17 E
Vulcan, U.S.A. 156 45 46N 87 51W
Vŭlcani 66 46 0N 20 26 E
Vulcano, I. 65 38 25N 14 58 E
Vulchedrŭma 67 43 42N 23 16 E
Vulci 63 42 23N 11 37 E
Vŭleni 70 44 15N 24 45 E
Vulkaneshty 82 45 35N 28 30 E
Vunduzi, R. 127 18 0 S 33 45 E
Vung Tau 101 10 21N 107 4 E
Vûrbitsa 67 42 59N 26 40 E
Vutcani 70 46 26N 27 59 E
Vuyyuru 96 16 28N 80 50 E
Vvedenka 84 54 0N 63 53 E
Vyara 96 21 8N 73 28 E
Vyasniki 81 56 10N 42 10 E
Vyatka, R. 84 56 30N 51 0 E
Vyatskiye Polyany 84 56 5N 51 0 E
Vyazemskiy 77 47 32N 134 45 E
Vyazma 80 55 10N 34 15 E
Vyborg 78 60 43N 28 47 E
Vychegda R. 78 61 50N 52 30 E
Východné Beskydy 53 49 30N 22 0 E
Východočeský □ 52 50 20N 15 45 E
Východoslovenský □ 53 48 50N 21 0 E
Vyg-ozero 78 63 30N 34 0 E
Vyja, R. 81 41 53N 24 26 E
Vypin, I. 97 10 10N 76 15 E
Vyrnwy, L. 31 52 48N 3 30W
Vyrnwy, R. 31 52 43N 3 15W
Vyshniy Volochek 80 57 30N 34 30 E
Vyškov 53 49 17N 17 0 E
Vysoké Mýto 53 49 58N 16 23 E
Vysoké Tatry 53 49 30N 20 0 E
Vysokovsk 81 56 22N 36 30 E
Vysotsk 80 51 43N 26 32 E
Vyssi Brod 92 48 36N 14 20 E
Vytegra 52 61 15N 36 40 E

W

Wa 121 10 7N 2 25W
Waal, R. 46 51 59N 4 8 E
Waalwijk 47 51 42N 5 4 E
Waarschoot 47 51 10N 3 36 E
Waasmunster 47 51 6N 4 5 E
Wabag 135 5 32 S 143 53 E
Wabakimi L. 150 50 38N 89 45W
Wabana 151 47 40N 53 0W
Wabasca 152 55 57N 113 45W
Wabash 156 40 48N 85 46W
Wabash, R. 156 39 10N 87 30W
Wabawng 98 25 18N 97 46 E
Wabeno 156 45 25N 88 40W
Wabi Gestro, R. 123 6 0N 41 35 E
Wabi, R. 123 7 35N 40 5 E
Wabi Shaballe, R. 123 8 0N 40 45 E
Wabigoon, L. 153 49 44N 92 34W
Wabowden 153 54 55N 98 38W
Wabrzezno 54 53 16N 18 57 E
Wabuk Pt. 150 55 20N 85 5W
Wabush City 151 52 55N 66 52W
Wabuska 160 39 16N 119 13W
W.A.C. Bennett Dam 152 56 2N 122 6W
Wachapreague 162 37 36N 75 41W
Wachtebeke 47 51 11N 3 52 E
Waco 159 31 33N 97 5W
Waconichi, L. 150 50 8N 74 0W
Wad ar Rimsa 92 26 5N 41 30 E
Wad Ban Naqa 123 16 32N 33 9 E
Wad Banda 123 13 10N 27 50 E
Wad el Haddad 123 13 50N 33 30 E
Wad en Nau 123 14 10N 33 34 E
Wad Hamid 123 16 20N 32 45 E
Wâd Medanî 123 14 28N 33 30 E
Wad Thana 94 27 22N 66 23 E
Wadayama 110 35 19N 134 52 E
Waddān 119 29 9N 16 45 E
Waddān, Jabal 119 29 0N 16 15 E
Waddeneilanden 46 53 25N 5 10 E
Waddenzee 46 53 6N 5 10 E
Wadderin Hill 137 32 0 S 118 25 E
Waddesdon 29 51 50N 0 54W
Waddingham 33 53 28N 0 31W
Waddington 33 53 10N 0 31W
Waddington, Mt. 152 51 23N 125 15W
Waddinxveen 46 52 2N 4 40 E
Waddy Pt. 139 24 58 S 153 21 E
Wadebridge 30 50 31N 4 51W
Wadena, Can. 153 51 57N 103 38W
Wadena, U.S.A. 158 46 25N 95 2W
Wädenswil 51 47 14N 8 30 E
Wadesboro 157 35 2N 80 2W
Wadhams 152 51 30N 127 30W
Wadhurst 29 51 3N 0 21 E
Wadi 121 13 5N 11 40 E
Wādī ash Shāfi' 119 27 30N 15 0 E
Wādī Banī Walīd 119 31 49N 14 0 E
Wadi Gemâl 122 24 35N 35 10 E
Wadi Halfa 122 21 53N 31 19 E
Wadi Masila 91 16 30N 49 0 E
Wadi Sabha 92 23 50N 48 30 E
Wadlew 54 51 31N 19 23 E
Wadowice 54 49 52N 19 30 E
Wadsworth 160 39 44N 119 22W
Waegwan 107 35 59N 128 23 E
Waenfawr 31 53 7N 4 10W
Wafou Hu 109 32 19N 116 56 E
Wafra 92 28 33N 48 3 E
Wagenberg 47 51 40N 4 46 E
Wageningen 46 51 58N 5 40 E
Wager B. 149 65 26N 88 40W
Wager Bay 149 65 56N 90 49W
Wagga Wagga 141 35 7 S 147 24 E
Waghete 103 4 10 S 135 50 E
Wagin, Austral. 137 33 17 S 117 25 E
Wagin, Nigeria 137 12 42N 7 10 E
Wagon Mound 159 36 10N 105 0W
Wagoner 159 36 0N 95 20W
Wagrowiec 54 52 48N 17 19 E
Wah 94 33 45N 72 40 E
Wahai 103 2 48 S 129 35 E
Wahiawa 147 21 30N 158 2W
Wahnai 94 32 40N 65 50 E
Wahoo 158 41 15N 96 35W
Wahpeton 158 46 20N 96 35W
Wahratta 140 31 58 S 141 50 E
Wai 96 17 56N 73 57 E
Wai, Koh 101 9 55N 102 55 E
Waiai, R. 143 45 36 S 167 45 E
Waianae 147 21 25N 158 8W
Waiau 143 42 39 S 173 5 E
Waiau, R. 143 42 47 S 173 22 E
Waiawe Ganga 97 6 15N 81 0 E
Waibeem 103 0 30 S 132 50 E
Waiblingen 49 48 49N 9 20 E
Waidhofen, Niederösterreich, Austria 52 48 49N 15 17 E
Waidhofen, Niederösterreich, Austria 52 47 57N 14 46 E
Waigeo, I. 103 0 20 S 130 40 E
Waihao Downs 143 44 48 S 170 55 E
Waihao, R. 143 44 52 S 171 11 E
Waiheke Islands 142 36 48 S 175 6 E
Waihi 142 37 23 S 175 52 E
Waihola 143 46 1 S 170 8 E
Waihola L. 143 45 59 S 170 8 E
Waihou, R. 143 37 15 S 175 40 E
Waika 126 2 22 S 25 42 E
Waikabubak 103 9 45 S 119 25 E
Waikaka 143 45 55 S 169 1 E
Waikaoti 131 45 36 S 170 41 E
Waikare, L. 142 37 26 S 175 13 E
Waikaremoana 142 38 42 S 177 12 E
Waikaremoana L. 142 38 49 S 177 9 E
Waikari 143 42 58 S 172 41 E
Waikato, R. 142 37 23 S 174 43 E
Waikawa Harbour 143 46 39 S 169 9 E
Waikerie 140 34 9 S 140 0 E
Waikiekie 142 35 57 S 174 16 E
Waikokopu 142 39 3 S 177 52 E
Waikokopu Harb. 142 39 4 S 177 53 E
Waikouaiti 143 45 36 S 170 41 E
Wailuku 147 20 53N 156 26W
Waimakariri, R. 143 42 23 S 172 42 E
Waimangaroa 143 41 43 S 171 46 E
Waimanola 147 21 19N 157 43W
Waimarie 143 41 35 S 171 58 E
Waimarino 143 40 40 S 175 20 E
Waimate 143 44 53 S 171 3 E
Waimea 147 21 57N 159 39W
Waimea Plain 143 45 55 S 168 35 E
Waimes 47 50 25N 6 7 E
Wainfleet All Saints 33 53 7N 0 16 E
Wainganga, R. 96 21 0N 79 45 E
Waingapu 103 9 35 S 120 11 E
Waingmaw 98 25 21N 97 26 E
Wainiha 147 22 9N 159 34W
Wainuiomata 142 41 17 S 174 56 E
Wainwright, Can. 153 52 50N 110 50W
Wainwright, U.S.A. 147 70 39N 160 10W
Waiotapu 142 38 21 S 176 25 E
Waiouru 142 39 28 S 175 41 E
Waipahi 143 46 6 S 169 15 E
Waipahu 147 21 23N 158 1W
Waipapa Pt. 143 46 40 S 168 51 E
Waipara 143 43 3 S 172 46 E
Waipawa 142 39 56 S 176 38 E
Waipiro 142 38 2 S 176 22 E
Waipori 131 45 50 S 169 52 E
Waipu 142 35 59 S 174 29 E
Waipukurau 142 40 1 S 176 33 E
Wairakei 142 38 37 S 176 6 E
Wairarapa I. 142 41 14 S 175 15 E
Wairau, R. 143 41 32 S 174 7 E
Wairio 143 45 59 S 168 3 E
Wairoa 142 39 3 S 177 25 E
Wairoa, R. 142 36 5 S 173 59 E
Waitaki Plains 143 44 22 S 170 0 E
Waitaki, R. 143 44 23 S 169 55 E
Waitara 142 38 59 S 174 15 E
Waitchie 140 35 22 S 143 8 E
Waitoa 142 37 37 S 175 35 E
Waitotara 142 39 49 S 174 44 E
Waitsburg 160 46 15N 118 10W
Waiuku 142 37 15 S 174 45 E
Wajir 126 1 42N 40 20 E
Wajir □ 126 1 42N 40 20 E
Wakaia 143 45 44 S 168 51 E
Wakasa 110 35 20N 134 24 E
Wakasa-Wan 111 34 45N 135 30 E
Wakatipu, L. 143 45 5 S 168 33 E
Wakaw 153 52 39N 105 44W
Wakayama 111 34 15N 135 15 E
Wakayama-ken □ 111 33 50N 135 30 E
Wake 110 34 48N 134 8 E
Wake Forest 157 35 58N 78 30W
Wake I. 130 19 18N 166 36 E
Wakefield, N.Z. 143 41 24 S 173 5 E
Wakefield, U.K. 33 53 41N 1 31W
Wakefield, Mass., U.S.A. 162 42 30N 71 3W
Wakefield, Mich., U.S.A. 158 46 28N 89 53W
Wakema 98 16 40N 95 18 E
Wakhan □ 93 37 0N 73 0 E
Wakkanai 112 45 28N 141 35 E
Wakkerstroom 129 27 24 S 30 10 E
Wako 150 49 50N 91 22W
Wakool 140 35 28 S 144 23 E
Wakool, R. 140 35 5 S 143 33 E
Wakre 103 0 30 S 131 5 E
Waku 135 6 5 S 149 9 E
Wakuach L. 151 55 34N 67 32W
Walachia □ 70 44 40N 25 0 E
Walamba 127 13 30 S 28 42 E
Walberswick 29 52 18N 1 39 E
Wałbrzych 54 50 45N 16 18 E
Walbury Hill 28 51 22N 1 28W
Walcha 141 30 55 S 151 31 E
Walcha Road 141 30 55 S 151 24 E
Walcheren, I. 46 51 30N 3 35 E
Walcott 160 41 50N 106 55W
Walcz 54 53 17N 16 27 E
Wald 51 47 17N 8 56 E
Waldbröl 48 50 52N 7 36 E
Waldeck 48 51 12N 9 4 E
Walden, Colo., U.S.A. 160 40 47N 106 20W
Walden, N.Y., U.S.A. 162 41 32N 74 13W
Waldenburg 50 47 23N 7 45 E
Waldorf 162 38 37N 76 54W
Waldport 160 44 30N 124 2W
Waldron, Can. 153 50 53N 102 35W
Waldron, U.K. 29 50 56N 0 13 E
Waldron, U.S.A. 159 34 52N 94 4W
Waldshut 49 47 37N 8 12 E
Waldya 123 11 50N 39 34 E
Walebing 137 30 40 S 116 15 E
Walembele 120 10 30N 1 14W
Walensee 51 47 7N 9 13 E
Walenstadt 51 47 8N 9 19 E
Wales 147 65 38N 168 10W
Walewale 121 10 21N 0 50W
Walgett 133 30 0 S 148 5 E
Walhalla, Austral. 141 37 56 S 146 29 E
Walhalla, U.S.A. 153 48 55N 97 55W
Waliso 123 8 33N 38 1 E
Walkaway 137 28 59 S 114 48 E
Walker 158 47 4N 94 35W
Walker L., Man., Can. 153 54 42N 96 57W
Walker L., Qué., Can. 151 50 20N 67 11W
Walker L., U.S.A. 163 38 56N 118 46W
Walkerston 138 21 11 S 149 8 E
Wall 158 44 0N 102 14W
Walla Walla, Austral. 141 35 45 S 146 54 E
Walla Walla, U.S.A. 160 46 3N 118 25W

Wallabadah **Weaverham**

Wallabadah **138** 17 57 S 142 15 E
Wallace, Idaho, U.S.A. **160** 47 30N 116 0W
Wallace, N.C., U.S.A. **157** 34 50N 77 59W
Wallace, Nebr., U.S.A. **158** 40 51N 101 12W
Wallaceburg **150** 42 40N 82 23W
Wallacetown **143** 46 21 S 168 19 E
Wallachia = Valahia **70** 44 35N 25 0 E
Wallal **139** 26 32 S 146 7 E
Wallal Downs **136** 19 47 S 120 40 E
Wallambin, L. **137** 30 57 S 117 35 E
Wallaroo **140** 33 56 S 137 39 E
Wallasey **32** 53 26N 3 2W
Walldurn **49** 49 34N 9 23 E
Wallerawang **141** 33 25 S 150 4 E
Wallhallow **138** 17 50 S 135 50 E
Wallingford **162** 43 27N 72 50W
Wallis Arch. **142** 13 20 S 176 20 E
Wallisellen **51** 47 25N 8 36 E
Wallowa **160** 45 40N 117 35W
Wallowa, Mts. **160** 45 20N 117 30W
Walls **36** 60 14N 1 32W
Wallsend, Austral. **141** 32 55 S 151 40 E
Wallsend, U.K. **35** 54 59N 1 30W
Wallula **160** 46 3N 118 59W
Wallumbilla **139** 26 33 S 149 9 E
Walmer, S. Afr. **128** 33 57 S 25 35 E
Walmer, U.K. **29** 51 12N 1 23 E
Walmsley, L. **153** 63 25N 108 36W
Walney, Isle of **32** 54 5N 3 15W
Walnut Ridge **159** 36 7N 90 58W
Walpeup **140** 35 10 S 142 2 E
Walpole **29** 52 44N 0 13 E
Walsall **28** 52 36N 1 59W
Walsenburg **159** 37 42N 104 45W
Walsh, Austral. **138** 16 40 S 144 0 E
Walsh, U.S.A. **159** 37 28N 102 15W
Walsh, R. **138** 16 31 S 143 42 E
Walshoutem **47** 50 43N 5 4 E
Walsoken **29** 52 41N 0 12 E
Walsrode **48** 52 51N 9 37 E
Waltair **96** 17 44N 83 23 E
Walterboro **157** 32 53N 80 40W
Walters **159** 34 25N 98 20W
Waltershausen **48** 50 53N 10 33 E
Waltham, Can. **150** 45 57N 76 57W
Waltham, U.K. **29** 53 32N 0 6W
Waltham, U.S.A. **34** 42 22N 71 12W
Waltham Abbey **29** 51 40N 0 1 E
Waltham Forest **29** 51 37N 0 2 E
Waltham on the Wolds **29** 52 49N 0 48W
Waltman **160** 43 8N 107 15W
Walton **162** 42 12N 75 9W
Walton-le-Dale **32** 53 45N 2 41W
Walton-on-the-Naze **29** 51 52N 1 17 E
Walu **98** 23 54N 96 57 E
Walvis Ridge **15** 30 0 S 3 0 E
Walvisbaai **128** 23 0 S 14 28 E
Walwa **141** 35 59 S 147 44 E
Wamaza **126** 4 12 S 27 2 E
Wamba, Kenya **126** 0 58N 37 19 E
Wamba, Nigeria **126** 8 58N 8 34 E
Wamba, Zaïre **121** 2 10N 27 57 E
Wamego **158** 39 14N 96 22W
Wamena **103** 3 58 S 138 50 E
Wampo **99** 31 30N 86 38 E
Wamsasi **103** 3 27 S 126 7 E
Wan Hat **98** 20 14N 97 53 E
Wan Kinghao **98** 21 34N 98 17 E
Wan Lai-Kam **98** 21 21N 98 22 E
Wan Tup **98** 21 13N 98 42 E
Wana **94** 32 20N 69 32 E
Wanaaring **139** 29 38 S 144 0 E
Wanaka L. **143** 44 33 S 169 7 E
Wanan **109** 26 25N 114 50 E
Wanapiri **103** 4 30 S 135 50 E
Wanapitei **150** 46 30N 80 45W
Wanapitei L. **150** 46 45N 80 40W
Wanaque **162** 41 3N 74 17W
Wanbi **140** 34 46 S 140 17 E
Wanborough **28** 51 33N 1 40W
Wanch'eng **108** 22 51N 107 25 E
Wanch'üan **106** 35 26N 110 50 E
Wanch'uan **106** 40 50N 114 56 E
Wandanian **141** 35 6 S 150 30 E
Wanderer **127** 19 36 S 30 1 E
Wandiwash **97** 12 30N 79 30 E
Wandoan **139** 26 5 S 149 55 E
Wandre **47** 50 40N 5 39 E
Wandsworth **29** 51 28N 0 15W
Wanfercée-Baulet **47** 50 28N 4 35 E
Wanfuchuang **107** 40 10N 122 34 E
Wang Kai (Ghâbat el Arab) **123** 9 3N 29 23 E
Wang Noi **100** 14 13N 100 44 E
Wang, R. **100** 17 8N 99 2 E
Wang Saphung **100** 17 18N 101 46 E
Wang Thong **100** 16 50N 100 26 E
Wanga **126** 2 58N 29 12 E
Wangal **103** 6 8 S 134 9 E
Wanganella **141** 35 6 S 144 49 E
Wanganui **142** 39 35 S 175 3 E
Wanganui, R., N.I., N.Z. **142** 39 25 S 175 4 E
Wanganui, R., S.I., N.Z. **143** 43 3 S 170 26 E
Wangaratta **141** 36 21 S 146 19 E
Wangchiang **109** 30 7N 116 41 E
Wangch'ing **107** 43 14N 129 38 E
Wangdu Phodrang **98** 27 28N 89 54 E
Wangerooge I. **48** 53 47N 7 52 E
Wangi **126** 1 58 S 40 58 E
Wangiwangi, I. **103** 5 22 S 123 37 E
Wangmo **108** 25 14N 105 59 E
Wangts'ang **108** 32 12N 106 21 E
Wangtu **106** 38 42N 115 4 E
Wanhsien, Hopeh, China **106** 38 49N 115 7 E
Wanhsien, Kansu, China **105** 36 45N 107 24 E
Wankaner **94** 22 42N 71 0 E
Wanki Nat. Park **128** 19 0 S 26 30 E
Wankie **127** 18 18 S 26 30 E
Wankie □ **127** 18 18 S 26 30 E
Wanless **153** 54 11N 101 21W
Wanna Lakes **137** 28 30 S 128 27 E
Wannien **109** 28 40N 116 55 E
Wanon Niwar **100** 17 38N 103 46 E
Wanshengch'ang **108** 28 58N 106 55 E
Wanssum **47** 51 32N 6 5 E
Wanstead **143** 40 8 S 176 30 E
Wantage **28** 51 35N 1 25W
Wantsai **109** 28 5N 114 22 E
Wanyin **98** 20 23N 97 15 E
Wanyüan **108** 32 4N 108 5 E
Wanzarīk **119** 27 3N 13 30 E
Wanze **47** 50 32N 5 13 E
Wapakoneta **156** 40 35N 84 10W
Wapato **160** 46 30N 120 25W
Wapawekka L. **153** 54 55N 104 40W
Wapikopa L. **150** 42 50N 88 10W
Wapiti, R. **150** 55 5N 118 18W
Wappingers Fs. **162** 41 35N 73 56W
Wapsipinican, R. **158** 41 44N 90 19W
Warabi **111** 35 49N 139 41 E
Warandab **91** 7 20N 44 2 E
Warangal **96** 17 58N 79 45 E
Waratah **138** 41 30 S 145 30 E
Waratah B. **139** 38 54 S 146 5 E
Warboys **29** 52 25N 0 5W
Warburg **48** 51 29N 9 10 E
Warburton **141** 37 47 S 145 42 E
Warburton, R. **143** 27 30 S 138 30 E
Warburton Ra. **137** 25 55 S 126 28 E
Ward, Ireland **38** 53 25N 6 19W
Ward, N.Z. **143** 41 49 S 174 11 E
Ward Cove **152** 55 25N 132 10W
Ward Hunt, C. **135** 8 2 S 148 10 E
Ward Hunt Str. **135** 9 30 S 150 0 E
Ward Mtn. **163** 37 12N 118 54W
Ward, R. **139** 26 32 S 146 6 E
Warden **129** 27 50 S 29 0 E
Wardha **96** 20 45N 78 39 E
Wardha, R. **93** 19 57N 79 11 E
Wardington **28** 52 8N 1 17W
Wardle **32** 53 7N 2 35W
Wardlow **152** 50 56N 111 31W
Wardoan **133** 25 59 S 149 59 E
Wards River **141** 32 11 S 151 56 E
Ward's Stone, mt. **32** 54 2N 2 39W
Ware, Can. **152** 57 26N 125 41W
Ware, U.K. **29** 51 48N 0 2W
Ware, U.S.A. **162** 42 16N 72 15W
Waregem **47** 50 53N 3 27 E
Wareham, U.K. **28** 50 41N 2 8W
Wareham, U.S.A. **162** 41 45N 70 44W
Wareham, oilfield **19** 50 40N 2 8W
Waremme **47** 50 43N 5 15 E
Waren **48** 53 30N 12 41 E
Warendorf **48** 51 57N 8 0 E
Warialda **139** 29 29 S 150 33 E
Wariap **103** 1 30 S 134 5 E
Warin Chamrap **100** 15 12N 104 53 E
Wark **35** 55 5N 2 14W
Warkopi **103** 1 12 S 134 9 E
Warkworth, N.Z. **142** 36 24 S 174 41 E
Warkworth, U.K. **35** 55 22N 1 38W
Warley **28** 52 30N 2 0W
Warm Springs, Mont., U.S.A. **160** 46 11N 112 56W
Warm Springs, Nev., U.S.A. **161** 38 16N 116 32W
Warman **153** 52 19N 106 30W
Warmbad, Namibia **128** 19 14 S 13 51 E
Warmbad, Namibia **128** 28 25 S 18 42 E
Warmbad, S. Afr. **129** 24 51 S 28 19 E
Warmenhuizen **46** 52 43N 4 44 E
Warmeriville **43** 49 20N 4 13 E
Warminster **28** 51 12N 2 11W
Warmond **46** 52 12N 4 30 E
Warnambool Downs **138** 22 48 S 142 52 E
Warnemünde **48** 54 9N 12 5 E
Warner **152** 49 17N 112 12W
Warner Range, Mts. **160** 41 30N 120 20W
Warner Robins **157** 32 41N 83 36W
Warneton **47** 50 45N 2 57 E
Warnow, R. **48** 54 0N 12 9 E
Warnsveld **46** 52 8N 6 14 E
Waroona **137** 32 50 S 115 58 E
Warora **96** 20 14N 79 1 E
Warracknabeal **140** 36 9 S 142 26 E
Warragul **141** 38 10 S 145 58 E
Warrawaqine **136** 20 51 S 120 42 E
Warrayelu **123** 10 40N 39 28 E
Warrego, R. **139** 30 24 S 145 21 E
Warrego Ra. **138** 25 15 S 146 0 E
Warren, Austral. **141** 31 42 S 147 51 E
Warren, Ark., U.S.A. **159** 33 35N 92 3W
Warren, Pa., U.S.A. **156** 41 52N 79 10W
Warren, R.I., U.S.A. **156** 41 43N 71 19W
Warrenpoint **38** 54 7N 6 15W
Warrens Landing **153** 53 40N 98 0W
Warrensburg **158** 38 45N 93 45W
Warrenton, S. Afr. **128** 28 9 S 24 47 E
Warrenton, U.S.A. **160** 46 11N 123 59W
Warrenville **139** 25 48 S 147 22 E
Warri **121** 5 30N 5 41 E
Warrie **136** 22 12 S 119 40 E
Warrina **136** 28 12 S 135 50 E
Warrington, N.Z. **143** 45 43 S 170 35 E
Warrington, U.K. **32** 53 25N 2 38W
Warrington, U.S.A. **157** 30 22N 87 16W
Warrnambool **140** 38 25 S 142 30 E
Warroad **158** 49 0N 95 20W
Warsaw **156** 41 14N 85 50W
Warsaw = Warszawa **54** 52 13N 21 0 E
Warsop **33** 53 13N 1 9W
Warstein **48** 51 26N 8 20 E
Warszawa **54** 52 13N 21 0 E
Warszawa □ **54** 52 30N 17 0 E
Warta **54** 51 43N 18 38 E
Warta, R. **54** 52 40N 16 10 E
Waru **103** 3 30 S 130 36 E
Warud **96** 21 30N 78 16 E
Warwick, Austral. **139** 28 10 S 152 1 E
Warwick, U.K. **28** 52 17N 1 36W
Warwick, N.Y., U.S.A. **162** 41 16N 74 22W
Warwick, R.I., U.S.A. **162** 41 43N 71 25W
Warwick □ **28** 52 20N 1 30W
Wasa **152** 49 45N 115 50W
Wasatch, Mt., Ra. **160** 40 30N 111 15W
Wasbank **129** 28 15 S 30 9 E
Wasbister **37** 59 11N 3 2W
Wasco, Calif., U.S.A. **163** 35 37N 119 16W
Wasco, Oreg., U.S.A. **160** 45 45N 120 46W
Waseca **158** 44 3N 93 31W
Wasekamio L. **153** 56 45N 108 45W
Wash, The **33** 52 58N 0 20W
Washburn, N.D., U.S.A. **158** 47 23N 101 0W
Washburn, Wis., U.S.A. **158** 46 38N 90 55W
Washford **28** 51 9N 3 22W
Washington, U.K. **35** 54 55N 1 30W
Washington, D.C., U.S.A. **162** 38 52N 77 0W
Washington, Ga., U.S.A. **157** 33 45N 82 45W
Washington, Ind., U.S.A. **156** 38 40N 87 8W
Washington, Iowa, U.S.A. **158** 41 20N 91 45W
Washington, Miss., U.S.A. **158** 38 35N 91 20W
Washington, N.C., U.S.A. **157** 35 35N 77 1W
Washington, N.J., U.S.A. **162** 40 45N 74 59W
Washington, Ohio, U.S.A. **156** 39 34N 83 26W
Washington, Pa., U.S.A. **156** 40 10N 80 20W
Washington, Utah, U.S.A. **161** 37 10N 113 30W
Washington □ **160** 47 45N 120 30W
Washington Court House **156** 39 34N 83 26W
* Washington I., Pac. Oc. **131** 4 43N 160 25W
Washington I., U.S.A. **156** 45 24N 86 54W
Washington Mt. **156** 44 15N 71 18W
Washir **93** 32 15N 63 50 E
Wasian **103** 1 47 S 133 19 E
Wasilków **54** 53 12N 23 13 E
Wasior **103** 2 43 S 134 30 E
Waskaiowaka, L. **153** 56 33N 96 23W
Waskesiu Lake **153** 53 55N 106 5W
Wasm **122** 18 2N 41 32 E
Waspik **47** 51 41N 4 57 E
Wassen **51** 46 42N 8 36 E
Wassenaar **46** 52 8N 4 24 E
Wasserburg **49** 48 4N 12 15 E
Wassy **43** 48 30N 4 58 E
Wast Water, L. **32** 54 26N 3 18W
Waswanipi **150** 49 40N 75 59W
Waswanipi, L. **150** 49 35N 76 40W
Watangpone **103** 4 29 S 120 25 E
Wataroa **143** 43 18 S 170 24 E
Wataroa, R. **143** 43 7 S 170 16 E
Watawaha, P. **103** 6 30 S 122 20 E
Watchet **28** 51 10N 3 20W
Water Park Pt. **138** 22 56 S 150 47 E
Water Valley **159** 34 9N 89 38W
Waterberg, Namibia **128** 20 30 S 17 18 E
Waterberg, S. Afr. **129** 24 14 S 28 0 E
Waterberg, mt. **128** 20 26 S 17 13 E
Waterbury **162** 41 32N 73 0W
Waterbury L. **153** 58 10N 104 22W
Waterford, Ireland **39** 52 16N 7 8W
Waterford, S. Afr. **128** 33 6 S 25 0 E
Waterford, U.S.A. **163** 37 38N 120 46W
Waterford □ **39** 51 10N 7 40W
Waterford Harb. **39** 52 10N 6 58W
Watergate Bay **30** 50 26N 5 4W
Watergrasshill **39** 52 1N 8 20W
Waterhen L., Man., Can. **153** 52 10N 99 40W
Waterhen L., Sask., Can. **153** 54 28N 108 25W
Wateringen **46** 52 2N 4 16 E
Waterloo, Belg. **47** 50 43N 4 25 E
Waterloo, Can. **150** 43 30N 80 32W
Waterloo, S. Leone **120** 8 26N 13 8W
Waterloo, U.K. **32** 53 29N 3 2W
Waterloo, Ill., U.S.A. **158** 38 22N 90 6W
Waterloo, Iowa, U.S.A. **158** 42 27N 92 20W
Waterloo, N.Y., U.S.A. **162** 42 54N 76 53W
Watermeal-Boitsford **47** 50 48N 4 25 E
Watermeet **158** 46 15N 89 12W
Waternish **36** 57 32N 6 35W
Waterton Lakes Nat. Park **152** 49 5N 114 15W
Watertown, Conn., U.S.A. **162** 41 36N 73 7W
Watertown, N.Y., U.S.A. **162** 43 58N 75 57W
Watertown, S.D., U.S.A. **158** 44 57N 97 5W
Watertown, Wis., U.S.A. **158** 43 15N 88 45W
Waterval-Boven **129** 25 40 S 30 18 E
Waterville, Ireland **39** 51 49N 10 10W
Waterville, Me., U.S.A. **151** 44 35N 69 40W
Waterville, N.Y., U.S.A. **162** 42 56N 75 23W
Waterville, Wash., U.S.A. **160** 47 45N 120 1W
Watervliet, Belg. **47** 51 17N 3 38 E
Watervliet, U.S.A. **162** 42 46N 73 43W
Wates **103** 7 53 S 110 6 E
Watford **29** 51 38N 0 23W
Watford City **158** 47 50N 103 23W
Wath **33** 53 29N 1 20W
Wathaman, R. **153** 57 16N 102 59W
Watheroo **137** 30 15 S 116 0W
Watien **109** 32 45N 112 30 E
Wat'ing **106** 35 25N 106 46 E
Watkins Glen **162** 42 25N 76 55W
Watlings I. **167** 24 0N 74 35W
Watlington, Norfolk, U.K. **29** 52 40N 0 24 E
Watlington, Oxford, U.K. **29** 51 38N 1 0W
Watonga **159** 35 51N 98 24W
Watou **47** 50 51N 2 38 E
Watraba **139** 31 58 S 133 13 E
Watrous, Can. **153** 51 40N 105 25W
Watrous, U.S.A. **159** 35 50N 104 55W
Watsa **126** 3 4N 29 30 E
Watseka **156** 40 45N 87 45W
Watson, Austral. **137** 30 29 S 131 31 E
Watson, Can. **153** 52 10N 104 30W
Watson Lake **147** 60 6N 128 49W
Watsontown **162** 41 5N 76 52W
Watsonville **163** 36 55N 121 49W
Watten **37** 21 1 S 144 3 E
Wattenwil **50** 46 46N 7 30 E
Wattiwarriganna Cr. **139** 28 57 S 136 10 E
Watton **29** 52 35N 0 50 E
Wattwil **51** 47 18N 9 6 E
Watubela, Kepulauan **103** 4 28 S 131 54 E
Wau **135** 7 21 S 146 47 E
Waubach **47** 50 55N 6 3 E
Waubay **158** 45 42N 97 17W
Waubra **140** 37 21 S 143 39 E
Wauchope **141** 31 28 S 152 45 E
Wauchula **157** 27 35N 81 50W
Waugh **153** 49 40N 95 20W
Waukegan **156** 42 22N 87 54W
Waukesha **156** 43 0N 88 15W
Waukon **158** 43 14N 91 33W
Wauneta **158** 40 27N 101 25W
Waupaca **158** 44 22N 89 8W
Waupun **158** 43 38N 88 44W
Waurika **159** 34 12N 98 0W
Wausau **158** 44 57N 89 40W
Wautoma **158** 44 3N 89 20W
Wauwatosa **156** 43 6N 87 59W
Wave Hill **136** 17 32N 131 0 E
Waveney, R. **29** 52 24N 1 20 E
Waver R. **32** 54 50N 3 15W
Waverley **142** 39 46 S 174 37 E
Waverly, Iowa, U.S.A. **158** 42 40N 92 30W
Waverly, N.Y., U.S.A. **162** 42 0N 76 33W
Wavre **47** 50 43N 4 38 E
Wavreille **47** 50 7N 5 15 E
Wâw **123** 7 45N 28 1 E
Waw an Namus **119** 24 24N 18 11 E
Wawa, Can. **150** 47 59N 84 47W
Wawa, Nigeria **121** 9 54N 4 27 E
Wawa, Sudan **122** 20 30N 32 22 E
Wawanesa **153** 49 36N 99 40W
Wawoi, R. **135** 7 48 S 143 16 E
Wawona **163** 37 32N 119 39W
Waxahachie **159** 32 22N 96 53W
Waxweiler **49** 50 6N 6 22 E
Way, L. **137** 26 45 S 120 16 E
Wayabula Rau **103** 2 29N 128 17 E
Wayatinah **138** 42 19 S 146 27 E
Waycross **157** 31 12N 82 25W
Wayi **123** 5 8N 30 10 E
Wayne, Nebr., U.S.A. **158** 42 16N 97 0W
Wayne, W. Va., U.S.A. **156** 38 15N 82 27W
Waynesboro, Miss., U.S.A. **157** 31 40N 88 39W
Waynesboro, Pa., U.S.A. **156** 39 46N 77 32W
Waynesboro, Va., U.S.A. **156** 38 4N 78 57W
Waynesburg **156** 39 54N 80 12W
Waynesville **157** 35 31N 83 0W
Waynoka **159** 36 38N 98 53W
Waza **94** 33 22N 69 22 E
Wāzin **119** 31 58N 10 51 E
Wazirabad, Afghan. **93** 36 44N 66 47 E
Wazirabad, Pak. **94** 32 30N 74 8 E
We **102** 6 3N 95 56 E
Weald, The **29** 51 7N 0 9 E
Wear, R. **35** 54 55N 1 22W
Weardale **32** 54 45N 2 5W
Wearhead **32** 54 45N 2 14W
Weatherford, Okla., U.S.A. **159** 35 30N 98 45W
Weatherford, Tex., U.S.A. **159** 32 45N 97 48W
Weaver, R. **32** 53 17N 2 35W
Weaverham **32** 53 15N 2 30W

**Renamed Teraina*

Webb City **Whitby**

Webb City **159** 37 9N 94 30W
Weber **142** 40 24S 176 20E
Webera, Bale, Ethiopia **123** 6 29N 40 33E
Webera, Shewa, Ethiopia **123** 9 40N 39 0E
Webster, Mass., U.S.A. **162** 42 4N 71 54W
Webster, S.D., U.S.A. **158** 45 24N 97 33W
Webster, Wis., U.S.A. **158** 45 53N 92 25W
Webster City **158** 42 30N 93 50W
Webster Green **158** 38 38N 90 20W
Webster Springs **156** 38 30N 80 25W
Wecliniec **54** 51 18N 15 10E
Weda **103** 0 30N 127 50E
Weda, Teluk **103** 0 30N 127 50E
Weddell I. **176** 51 50S 61 0W
Weddell Sea **13** 72 30S 40 0W
Wedderburn **140** 36 20S 143 33E
Wedge I. **132** 30 50S 115 11E
Wedgeport **151** 43 44N 65 59W
Wedmore **28** 51 14N 2 50W
Wednesbury **28** 52 33N 2 1W
Wednesfield **28** 52 36N 2 3W
Wedza **127** 18 40S 31 33E
Wee Elwah **141** 32 2S 145 14E
Wee Waa **139** 30 11S 149 26E
Weed **160** 41 29N 122 22W
Weedsport **162** 43 3N 76 35W
Weemelah **139** 29 2S 149 7E
Weenen **129** 28 48S 30 7E
Weener **48** 53 10N 7 23E
Weert **47** 51 15N 5 43E
Weesen **51** 47 7N 9 4E
Weesp **46** 52 18N 5 2E
Weggis **51** 47 2N 8 26E
Wegierska-Gorka **54** 49 36N 19 7E
Wegorzewo **54** 54 13N 21 43E
Wegrów **54** 52 24N 22 0E
Wehl **46** 51 58N 6 13E
Wei Ho, R., Honan, China **106** 34 58N 113 32E
Wei Ho, R., Shensi, China **106** 34 38N 110 20E
Wei-si **99** 27 18N 99 18E
Weich'ang **107** 41 56N 117 34E
Weichou Tao **108** 21 3N 109 2E
Weich'uan **106** 34 19N 114 0E
Weida **48** 50 47N 12 3E
Weiden **49** 49 40N 12 10E
Weifang **107** 36 47N 119 10E
Weihai **107** 37 30N 122 10E
Weihsi **108** 27 18N 99 18E
Weihsin **108** 27 48N 105 5E
Weilburg **48** 50 28N 8 17E
Weilheim **49** 47 50N 11 9E
Weimar **48** 51 0N 11 20E
Weinan **106** 34 30N 109 35E
Weinfelden **51** 47 34N 9 6E
Weingarten **49** 47 49N 9 39E
Weinheim **49** 49 33N 8 40E
Weining **108** 26 50N 104 19E
Weipa **138** 12 24S 141 50E
Weir, R., Austral. **139** 28 20S 149 50E
Weir, R., Càn. **153** 56 54N 93 21W
Weir River **153** 56 49N 94 6W
Weisen **51** 46 42N 9 43E
Weiser **160** 44 10N 117 0W
Weishan, Shantung, China **107** 34 49N 47 6E
Weishan, Yunnan, China **108** 25 16N 100 21E
Weissenburg **49** 49 2N 10 58E
Weissenfels **48** 51 11N 11 58E
Weisshorn **50** 46 7N 7 43E
Weissmies **50** 46 8N 8 1E
Weisstannen **51** 46 59N 9 22E
Weisswasser **48** 51 30N 14 36E
Weiswampach **47** 50 8N 6 5E
Wéitra **52** 48 41N 14 54E
Weiyüan **106** 35 6N 104 14E
Weiyuan **106** 35 10N 104 20E
Weiz **52** 47 13N 15 39E
Wejherowo **54** 54 35N 18 12E
Wekusko **153** 54 45N 99 45W
Wekusko L. **153** 54 40N 99 50W
Welbourn Hill **139** 27 21S 134 6E
Welby **153** 50 33N 101 29W
Welch **156** 37 29N 81 36W
Welcome **138** 15 20S 144 40E
Weldon **35** 55 16N 1 46W
Welega □ **123** 9 25N 34 20E
Welford, Berks., U.K. **28** 51 28N 1 24W
Welford, Northampton, U.K. **28** 52 26N 1 5W
Welkenraedt **47** 50 39N 5 58E
Welkite **123** 8 15N 37 42E
Welkom **128** 28 0S 26 50E
Welland **150** 43 0N 79 10W
Welland, R. **29** 52 43N 0 10W
Wellen **47** 50 50N 5 21E
Wellesley Is. **138** 17 20S 139 30E
Wellin **47** 50 5N 5 6E
Wellingborough **29** 52 18N 0 41W
Wellington, Austral. **141** 32 35S 148 59E
Wellington, Can. **150** 43 57N 77 20W
Wellington, N.Z. **142** 41 19S 174 46E
Wellington, S. Afr. **128** 33 38S 18 57E
Wellington, U.K. **28** 50 58N 3 13W
Wellington, Col., U.S.A. **158** 40 43N 105 0W
Wellington, Kans., U.S.A. **159** 37 15N 97 25W
Wellington, Nev., U.S.A. **163** 38 47N 119 28W
Wellington, Okla., U.S.A. **159** 34 55N 100 13W
Wellington □ **143** 40 8S 175 36E
Wellington Bridge **39** 52 15N 6 45W
Wellington, I. **176** 49 30S 75 0W
Wellington, L. **141** 38 6S 147 20E
Wellington, Mt. **142** 36 55S 174 52E
Wellington (Telford) **28** 52 42N 2 31W
Wello, L. **137** 26 43S 123 10E
Wellow **28** 51 20N 2 22W
Wells, Norfolk, U.K. **29** 52 57N 0 51E
Wells, Somerset, U.K. **28** 51 12N 2 39W
Wells, Me., U.S.A. **162** 43 18N 70 35W
Wells, Minn., U.S.A. **158** 43 44N 93 45W
Wells, Nev., U.S.A. **160** 41 8N 115 0W
Wells, N.Y., U.S.A. **162** 43 24N 74 17W
Wells Gray Prov. Park **152** 52 30N 120 15W
Wells L. **137** 26 44S 123 15E
Wellsboro **156** 41 46N 77 20W
Wellsford **142** 36 16S 174 32E
Wellsville, Mo., U.S.A. **158** 39 4N 91 30W
Wellsville, N.Y., U.S.A. **156** 42 9N 77 53W
Wellsville, Ohio, U.S.A. **156** 40 36N 80 40W
Wellsville, Utah, U.S.A. **160** 41 35N 111 59W
Wellton **161** 32 46N 114 6W
Welmel, W. **123** 6 0N 40 20E
Welney **29** 52 31N 0 15E
Welo □ **123** 11 50N 39 48E
Wels **52** 48 9N 14 1E
Welshpool **31** 52 40N 3 9W
Welton **33** 53 19N 0 29W
Welwel **91** 7 5N 45 25E
Welwitschia **128** 20 16S 14 59E
Welwyn **153** 50 20N 101 30W
Welwyn Garden City **29** 51 49N 0 11W
Wem **28** 52 52N 2 45W
Wembere, R. **126** 4 45S 34 0E
Wembury **30** 50 19N 4 6W
Wemmel **47** 50 55N 4 18E
Wemyss Bay **34** 55 52N 4 54W
Wenatchee **160** 47 30N 120 17W
Wench'ang **100** 19 38N 110 42E
Wencheng **109** 27 48N 120 5E
Wenchi **120** 7 46N 2 8W
Wenchiang **108** 30 43N 103 56E
Wenchou **109** 28 1N 120 39E
Wench'uan **108** 31 28N 103 35E
Wendell **160** 42 50N 114 51W
Wendesi **103** 2 30S 134 10E
Wendo **123** 6 40N 38 27E
Wendover, U.K. **29** 51 46N 0 45W
Wendover, U.S.A. **160** 40 49N 114 1W
Wenduine **47** 51 18N 3 5E
Wengan **108** 27 0N 107 32E
Wengch'eng **109** 24 22N 113 50E
Wenge **126** 0 3N 24 0E
Wengen **50** 46 37N 7 55E
Wengniut'ech'i **107** 42 59N 118 48E
Wengpu **108** 32 55N 98 30E
Wengyüan **109** 24 21N 114 7E
Wenhsi **106** 35 23N 111 8E
Wenhsiang **106** 34 36N 110 34E
Wenhsien, Honan, China **106** 34 56N 113 4E
Wenhsien, Kansu, China **106** 58 0N 104 39E
Wenling **109** 28 22N 121 18E
Wenlock **138** 13 6S 142 58E
Wenlock Edge **23** 52 30N 2 43W
Wenlock, R. **133** 12 2S 141 55E
Wenshan **108** 23 22N 104 13E
Wenshang **106** 35 37N 116 33E
Wenshui, Kweichow, China **108** 28 27N 106 31E
Wenshui, Shansi, China **106** 37 25N 112 1E
Wensleydale **32** 54 18N 2 0W
Wensu **105** 41 15N 80 14E
Wenteng **107** 37 10N 122 0E
Wentworth **140** 34 2S 141 54E
Wentworth, Mt. **138** 24 12S 147 1E
Wenut **103** 3 11S 133 19E
Weobley **28** 52 9N 2 52W
Weott **160** 40 19N 123 56W
Wepener **128** 29 42S 27 3E
Werbomont **47** 50 23N 5 41E
Werda **128** 25 24S 23 15E
Werdau **48** 50 45N 12 20E
Werder, Ethiopia **91** 6 58N 45 1E
Werder, Ger. **48** 52 23N 12 56E
Werdohl **48** 51 15N 7 47E
Weri **103** 3 10S 132 30E
Werkendam **46** 51 50N 4 53E
Werne **48** 51 38N 7 38E
Wernigerode **48** 51 49N .0 45E
Werribee **140** 37 54S 144 40E
Werrimull **140** 34 25S 141 38E
Werrington **30** 50 31N 4 22W
Werris Creek **141** 31 18S 150 38E
Wersar **103** 1 30S 131 55E
Wertheim **49** 49 44N 9 32E
Wervershoof **46** 52 44N 5 10E
Wervik **47** 50 47N 3 3E
Wesel **48** 51 39N 6 34E
Weser, R. **48** 53 33N 8 30E
Wesiri **103** 7 30S 126 30E
Wesleyville **151** 49 8N 53 36W
Wessel, C. **138** 10 59S 136 46E
Wessel Is. **138** 11 10S 136 45E
Wesselburen **48** 54 11N 8 53E
Wessem **47** 51 11N 5 49E
Wessington **158** 44 30N 98 40W
Wessington Springs **158** 44 10N 98 35W
West **159** 31 50N 97 5W
West Auckland **33** 54 38N 1 42W
West B. **151** 45 53N 82 8W
West, B. **159** 29 5N 89 27W
West Baines, R. **136** 15 36S 129 58E
West Bend **156** 43 25N 88 10W
West Bengal □ **95** 25 0N 90 0E
West Branch **156** 44 16N 84 13W
West Bridgford **33** 52 56N 1 8W
West Bromwich **28** 52 32N 2 1W
West Burra, I. **36** 60 5N 1 21W
West Calder **35** 55 51N 3 34W
West Canada Cr. **162** 43 1N 74 58W
West Cape Howe **137** 35 8S 117 36E
West Chester **162** 39 58N 75 36W
West Coker **28** 50 55N 2 40W
West Columbia **159** 29 10N 95 38W
West Covina **163** 34 4N 117 54W
West Derry **162** 42 55N 71 19W
West Des Moines **158** 41 30N 93 45W
West End **166** 26 41N 78 58W
West Falkland Island **176** 51 30S 60 0W
West Fen **33** 53 5N 0 5W
West Frankfort **158** 37 56N 89 0W
West Glamorgan □ **31** 51 40N 3 55W
West Grinstead **29** 50 58N 0 19W
West Haddon **28** 52 21N 1 5W
West Harbour **131** 45 51S 170 33E
West Hartford **162** 41 45N 72 45W
West Haven **162** 41 18N 72 57W
West Hazleton **162** 40 58N 76 0W
West Helena **159** 34 30N 90 40W
West Hurley **162** 41 59N 74 7W
West Indies **158** 15 0N 70 0W
West Kilbride **34** 55 41N 4 50W
West Kirby **32** 53 22N 3 11W
West Lavington **28** 51 16N 1 59W
West Linton **35** 55 45N 3 24W
West Looe **30** 50 21N 4 29W
West Lulworth **28** 50 37N 2 14W
West Lunga, R. **127** 12 35S 24 45E
West Magpie R. **151** 51 2N 64 42W
West Malling **29** 51 16N 0 25E
West Memphis **159** 35 5N 90 3W
West Meon **28** 51 2N 1 3W
West Mersea **29** 51 46N 0 55E
West Midlands □ **28** 52 30N 1 55W
West Milton **162** 41 1N 76 50W
West Monroe **159** 32 32N 92 7W
West Nicholson **127** 21 2S 29 20E
West Pakistan = Pakistan **93** 27 0N 67 0W
West Palm Beach **157** 26 44N 80 3W
West Paris **101** 44 18N 70 30W
West Parley **28** 50 46N 1 52W
West Plains **159** 36 45N 91 50W
West Pt. **140** 35 1S 135 56E
West Point, Can. **151** 49 55N 64 30W
West Point, Jamaica **166** 18 14N 78 30W
West Point, Ga., U.S.A. **157** 32 54N 85 10W
West Point, Miss., U.S.A. **157** 33 36N 88 38W
West Point, Nebr., U.S.A. **158** 41 50N 96 43W
West Point, Va., U.S.A. **162** 37 35N 76 47W
West Pokot □ **126** 1 30N 35 40E
West, R. **162** 42 52N 72 33W
West Rasen **33** 53 23N 0 23W
West Reading **162** 40 20N 75 57W
West Riding (□) **26** 53 50N 1 30W
West Road R. **152** 53 18N 122 53W
West Rutland **162** 43 36N 73 3W
West Schelde = Westerschelde **47** 51 23N 3 50E
West Sole, gasfield **19** 53 40N 1 15E
West Spitsbergen **12** 78 40N 17 0E
West Sussex □ **29** 50 55N 0 30W
West-Terschelling **46** 53 22N 5 13E
West Virginia □ **156** 39 0N 18 0W
West-Vlaanderen □ **47** 51 0N 3 0E
West Walker, R. **163** 38 54N 119 9W
West Wittering **29** 50 44N 0 53W
West Wyalong **141** 33 56S 147 10E
West Yellowstone **160** 44 47N 111 4W
West York **162** 39 57N 76 46W
West Yorkshire □ **33** 53 45N 1 40W
Westall **139** 32 55S 134 4E
Westbank **152** 49 50N 119 25W
Westbourne **29** 50 53N 0 55W
Westbrook, Maine, U.S.A. **162** 43 40N 70 22W
Westbrook, Tex., U.S.A. **159** 32 25N 101 0W
Westbury, Austral. **138** 41 30S 146 51E
Westbury, Salop, U.K. **28** 52 40N 2 57W
Westbury, Wilts., U.K. **28** 51 16N 2 11W
Westbury-on-Severn **28** 51 49N 2 24W
Westby **158** 48 52N 104 3W
Westend **163** 35 42N 117 24W
Wester Ross, dist. **36** 57 37N 5 0W
Westerbork **46** 52 51N 6 37E
Westerham **29** 51 16N 0 5E
Westerland **48** 54 51N 8 20E
Western □, Kenya **126** 0 30N 34 30E
Western □, Uganda **126** 1 45N 31 30E
Western □, Zambia **127** 13 15N 27 30E
Western Australia □ **137** 25 0S 118 0E
Western Bay **151** 46 50N 52 30W
Western Germany ■ **48** 50 0N 8 0E
Western Ghats **97** 15 30N 74 30E
Western Is. □ **36** 57 40N 7 0W
Western River **140** 35 42S 136 56E
Western Samoa ■ **130** 14 0S 172 0W
Westernport **156** 30 30N 79 5W
Westerschelde, R. **47** 51 25N 4 0E
Westerstede **48** 51 15N 7 55E
Westervoort **46** 51 58N 5 59E
Westerwald, mts. **48** 50 39N 8 0E
Westfield, U.K. **29** 50 53N 0 30E
Westfield, U.S.A. **162** 42 9N 72 49W
Westgat **47** 51 39N 3 44E
Westhope **158** 48 55N 101 0W
Westhoughton **32** 53 34N 2 30W
Westkapelle, Belg. **47** 51 19N 3 19E
Westkapelle, Neth. **47** 51 31N 3 28E
Westland □ **143** 43 33S 169 59E
Westland Bight **143** 42 55S 170 5E
Westlock **152** 54 9N 113 55W
Westmalle **47** 51 18N 4 42E
Westmeath □ **38** 53 30N 7 30W
Westmine **137** 29 2S 116 8E
Westminster **162** 39 34S 77 1W
Westmorland **161** 33 2N 115 42W
Westmorland (□) **26** 54 28N 2 40W
Weston, Malay. **102** 5 10N 115 35E
Weston, U.K. **28** 52 51N 2 2W
Weston, Oreg., U.S.A. **160** 45 50N 118 30W
Weston, W. Va., U.S.A. **156** 39 3N 80 29W
Weston I. **150** 52 33N 79 36W
Weston-super-Mare **28** 51 20N 2 59W
Westport, Ireland **38** 53 44N 9 31W
Westport, N.Z. **143** 41 46S 171 37E
Westport, U.S.A. **160** 46 48N 124 4W
Westport B. **38** 53 48N 9 38W
Westray **153** 53 36N 101 24W
Westray Firth **37** 59 15N 3 0W
Westray, I. **37** 59 18N 3 0W
Westree **150** 47 26N 81 34W
Westruther **35** 55 45N 2 34W
Westview **152** 49 50N 124 31W
Westville, Ill., U.S.A. **156** 40 3N 87 36W
Westville, Okla., U.S.A. **159** 36 0N 94 33W
Westward Ho **30** 51 2N 4 16W
Westwood **160** 40 26N 121 0W
Wetar, I. **103** 7 30S 126 30E
Wetaskiwin **152** 52 55N 113 24W
Wetherby **33** 53 56N 1 23W
Wethersfield **162** 41 43N 72 40W
Wetlet **98** 21 13N 95 53E
Wettingen **51** 47 28N 8 20E
Wetwang **33** 54 2N 0 35W
Wetzikon **51** 47 19N 8 48E
Wetzlar **48** 50 33N 8 30E
Wevelgem **47** 50 49N 3 12E
Wewak **135** 3 38S 143 41E
Wewaka **159** 35 10N 96 35W
Wexford **39** 52 20N 6 28W
Wexford □ **39** 52 20N 6 25W
Wexford Harb. **39** 52 20N 6 25W
Wey, R. **29** 51 19N 0 29W
Weybourne **29** 52 57N 1 9E
Weybridge **29** 51 22N 0 28W
Weyburn **153** 49 40N 103 50W
Weyburn L. **152** 63 0N 117 59W
Weyer **52** 47 51N 14 40E
Weymouth, Can. **151** 44 30N 66 1W
Weymouth, U.K. **28** 50 36N 2 28W
Weymouth, U.S.A. **162** 42 13N 70 53W
Weymouth, C. **133** 12 37S 143 27E
Wezep **46** 52 28N 6 0E
Whakamaru **142** 38 23S 175 63E
Whakatane **142** 37 57S 177 1E
Whale Cove **148** 62 11N 92 36W
Whale Firth **36** 60 40N 1 10W
Whale, R. **151** 58 15N 67 40W
Whales **13** 78 0S 165 0W
Whaley Bridge **32** 53 20N 2 0W
Whalley **32** 53 49N 2 25W
Whalsay, I. **36** 60 22N 1 0W
Whalton **35** 55 7N 1 46W
Whangamomona **142** 39 8S 174 44E
Whangarei **142** 35 43S 174 21E
Whangarei Harbour **142** 35 45S 174 28E
Whangaroa **142** 35 4S 173 46E
Whangumata **142** 37 12S 175 53E
Whaplode **29** 52 42N 0 3W
Wharanui **143** 41 55S 174 6E
Wharfe, R. **33** 53 55N 1 30W
Wharfedale **31** 54 7N 2 4W
Wharton, N.J., U.S.A. **162** 40 53N 74 36W
Wharton, Tex., U.S.A. **159** 29 20N 96 6W
Whauphill **34** 54 48N 4 31W
Whayjonta **139** 29 40S 142 35E
Wheatland **158** 42 4N 105 58W
Wheatley Hill• **33** 54 45N 1 23W
Wheaton, Md., U.S.A. **162** 39 3N 77 3W
Wheaton, Minn., U.S.A. **158** 45 50N 96 29W
Wheeler, Oreg., U.S.A. **160** 45 45N 123 57W
Wheeler, Tex., U.S.A. **159** 35 29N 100 15W
Wheeler Peak, Mt. **160** 38 57N 114 15W
Wheeler, R. **153** 57 34N 104 15W
Wheeler Ridge **163** 35 0N 118 57W
Wheeling **156** 40 2N 80 41W
Whichham **32** 54 14N 3 22W
Whidbey I. **152** 48 15N 122 40W
Whidbey Is. **136** 34 30S 135 3E
Whiddy, I. **39** 51 41N 9 30W
Whimple **30** 50 46N 3 21W
Whipsnade **29** 51 51N 0 32W
Whiskey Gap **152** 49 0N 113 3W
Whiskey Jack L. **153** 58 23N 101 55W
Whissendine **29** 52 43N 0 46W
Whistleduck Cr. **138** 20 15S 135 18E
Whistler **157** 30 50N 88 10W
Whiston **32** 53 25N 2 45W
Whitburn **35** 55 52N 3 41W
Whitby **33** 54 29N 0 37W

Whitchurch

Winterberg

Whitchurch, U.K. **31** 51 32N 3 15W
Whitchurch, Devon, U.K. **30** 50 31N 4 7W
Whitchurch, Hants., U.K. **28** 51 14N 1 20W
Whitchurch, Here., U.K. **28** 51 51N 2 41W
Whitchurch, Salop, U.K. **32** 52 58N 2 42W
Whitcombe, Mt. **131** 43 12 S 171 0 E
Whitcombe, P. **131** 43 12 S 171 0 E
White B. **151** 50 0N 56 35W
White Bear Res. **151** 48 10N 57 05W
White Bird **160** 45 46N 116 21W
White Bridge **35** 57 11N 4 32W
White Butte **156** 46 23N 103 25W
White City **158** 38 50N 96 45W
White Cliffs, Austral. **140** 30 50 S 143 10 E
White Cliffs, N.Z. **143** 43 26 S 171 55 E
White Deer **159** 35 30N 101 8W
White Esk, R. **35** 55 14N 3 11W
White Hall **158** 39 25N 90 27W
White Haven **162** 41 3N 75 47W
White Horse Hill **28** 51 35N 1 35W
White I. **142** 37 30 S 177 13 E
White L., Austral. **136** 24 43 S 121 44 E
White L., U.S.A. **159** 29 45N 92 30W
White Mts. **163** 37 30N 118 15W
White Nile = Nîl el Abyad, Bahr **123** 9 30N 31 40 E
White Nile Dam **123** 15 24N 32 30 E
White Otter L. **150** 49 5N 91 55W
White Pass **147** 59 40N 135 3W
White Plains, Liberia **120** 6 28N 10 40W
White Plains, U.S.A. **162** 41 2N 73 44W
White, R., Ark., U.S.A. **159** 36 28N 93 55W
White, R., Colo., U.S.A. **160** 40 8N 108 52W
White, R., Ind., U.S.A. **156** 39 25N 86 30W
White, R., S.D., U.S.A. **158** 43 10N 102 52W
White River, Can. **150** 48 35N 85 20W
White River, S. Afr. **129** 25 20 S 31 00 E
White River, U.S.A. **158** 43 48N 100 5W
White River Junc. **162** 43 38N 72 20W
White Russia = Byelorussia, SSR **80** 53 30N 27 0 E
White Sea = Beloye More **78** 66 30N 38 0 E
White Sulphur Springs, Mont., U.S.A. **160** 46 35N 111 0W
White Sulphur Springs, W. Va., U.S.A. **160** 37 50N 80 16W
White Volta, R., (Volta Blanche) **121** 10 0N 1 0W
White Well **137** 31 25 S 131 3 E
Whiteadder Water, R. **35** 55 47N 2 20W
Whitecourt **152** 54 10N 115 45W
Whiteface **159** 33 35N 102 40W
Whitefish **160** 48 25N 114 22W
Whitefish L. **153** 62 41N 106 48W
Whitefish Pt. **156** 46 45N 85 0W
Whitegate, Clare, Ireland **39** 52 58N 8 24W
Whitegate, Cork, Ireland **39** 51 49N 8 15W
Whitegull, L. **151** 55 27N 64 17W
Whitehall, Ireland **39** 52 42N 7 2W
Whitehall, U.K. **37** 59 9N 2 36W
Whitehall, Mich., U.S.A. **156** 43 21N 86 20W
Whitehall, Mont., U.S.A. **160** 45 52N 112 4W
Whitehall, N.Y., U.S.A. **162** 43 32N 73 28W
Whitehall, Wis., U.S.A. **158** 44 20N 91 19W
Whitehaven **32** 54 33N 3 35W
Whitehead **38** 54 45N 5 42W
Whitehorse **147** 60 43N 135 3W
Whitehorse, Vale of **28** 51 37N 1 30W
Whitekirk **35** 56 2N 2 36W
Whiteman Ra. **135** 5 55 S 150 0 E
Whitemark **138** 40 7 S 148 3 E
Whitemouth **153** 49 57N 95 58W
Whiten Hd. **37** 58 34N 4 35W
Whitesail, L. **152** 53 35N 127 45W
Whitesand B. **30** 50 18N 4 20W
Whitesboro, N.Y., U.S.A. **162** 43 8N 75 20W
Whitesboro, Tex., U.S.A. **159** 33 40N 96 58W
Whiteshell Prov. Park **153** 50 0N 95 40W
Whitetail **158** 48 54N 105 15W
Whiteville **157** 34 20N 78 40W
Whitewater **156** 42 50N 88 45W
Whitewater Baldy, Mt. **161** 33 20N 108 44W
Whitewater L. **150** 50 50N 89 10W
Whitewood, Austral. **138** 21 28 S 143 30 E
Whitewood, Can. **153** 50 20N 102 20W
Whitfield **141** 36 42 S 146 24 E
Whithorn **162** 54 55N 4 25W
Whitianga **142** 36 47 S 175 41 E
Whitland **31** 51 49N 4 38W
Whitley Bay **35** 55 4N 1 28W
Whitman **162** 42 4N 70 55W
Whitmire **157** 34 33N 81 40W
Whitney **150** 45 31N 78 14W
Whitney, Mt. **163** 36 35N 118 14W
Whitney Pt. **162** 42 19N 75 59W
Whitstable **29** 51 21N 1 2 E
Whitsunday I. **138** 20 15 S 149 4 E
Whittier **147** 60 46N 148 48W
Whittington, Derby, U.K. **33** 53 17N 1 26W
Whittington, Salop, U.K. **28** 52 53N 3 0W
Whittle, C. **151** 50 11N 60 8W
Whittlesea **141** 37 27 S 145 9 E
Whittlesey **29** 52 34N 0 8W
Whittlesford **29** 52 6N 0 9 E
Whitton **33** 53 42N 0 39W
Whitwell, Derby, U.K. **33** 53 16N 1 11W
Whitwell, Isle of Wight, U.K. **28** 50 35N 1 19W
Whitwell, U.S.A. **157** 35 15N 85 30W
Whitwick **28** 52 45N 1 23W
Whitworth **32** 53 40N 2 11W
Whixley **33** 54 2N 1 19W
Wholdaia L. **153** 60 43N 104 20W
Whyalla **140** 33 2 S 137 30 E
Whyjonta **139** 29 41 S 142 28 E
Whyte Yarcowie **107** 33 13 S 138 54 E
Wiarton **150** 44 50N 81 10W
Wiawso **120** 6 10N 2 25W
Wiay I. **36** 57 24N 7 12W
Wiazow **54** 50 50N 17 10 E
Wibaux **158** 47 0N 104 13W
Wichian Buri **100** 15 39N 101 7 E
Wichita **159** 37 40N 97 29W
Wichita Falls **159** 33 57N 98 30W
Wick, Scot., U.K. **37** 58 26N 3 5W
Wick, Wales, U.K. **31** 51 24N 3 32W
Wick R. **37** 58 28N 3 14W
Wickenburg **161** 33 58N 112 45W
Wickepin **137** 32 50 S 117 30 E
Wickett **159** 31 37N 102 58W
Wickford **29** 51 37N 0 31 E
Wickham **28** 50 54N 1 11W
Wickham, C. **138** 39 35 S 143 57 E
Wickham Market **29** 52 9N 1 21 E
Wicklow **39** 53 0N 6 2W
Wicklow □ **39** 52 59N 6 25W
Wicklow Gap **39** 53 3N 6 23W
Wicklow Hd. **39** 52 59N 6 3W
Wicklow Mts. **39** 53 0N 6 30W
Wickwar **28** 51 35N 2 23W
Widawa **54** 51 27N 18 51 E
Widdrington **35** 55 15N 1 35W
Wide B. **138** 4 52 S 152 0 E
Wide Firth **37** 59 2N 3 0W
Widecombe **30** 50 34N 3 48W
Widemouth **30** 50 45N 4 34W
Widgiemooltha **137** 31 30 S 121 34 E
Widnes **32** 53 22N 2 44W
Wiek **48** 54 37N 13 17 E
Wielbark **54** 53 24N 20 55 E
Wielén **54** 52 53N 16 9 E
Wieliczka **54** 50 0N 20 5 E
Wielun **54** 51 15N 18 40 E
Wien **53** 48 12N 16 22 E
Wiener Neustadt **53** 47 49N 16 16 E
Wieprz, R., Koszalin, Poland **54** 54 26N 16 35 E
Wieprz, R., Lublin, Poland **54** 51 15N 22 50 E
Wierden **46** 52 22N 6 35 E
Wiers **47** 50 30N 3 32 E
Wieruszów **54** 51 19N 18 9 E
Wiesbaden **49** 50 7N 8 17 E
Wiesental **49** 49 15N 8 30 E
Wigan **32** 53 33N 2 38W
Wiggins, Colo., U.S.A. **158** 40 16N 104 3W
Wiggins, Miss., U.S.A. **159** 30 53N 89 9W
Wight, I. of **28** 50 40N 1 20W
Wigmore **28** 52 19N 2 51W
Wigston **28** 52 35N 1 6W
Wigton **32** 54 50N 3 9W
Wigtown **34** 54 52N 4 27W
Wigtown (□) **26** 54 53N 4 45W
Wigtown B. **34** 54 46N 4 15W
Wihéries **47** 50 23N 3 45 E
Wijangala **139** 33 57 S 148 59 E
Wijchen **46** 51 48N 5 44 E
Wijhe **46** 52 23N 6 8 E
Wijk bij Duurstede **46** 51 59N 5 21 E
Wil **51** 47 28N 9 3 E
Wilamowice **53** 49 55N 19 9 E
Wilangee **140** 31 28 S 141 20 E
Wilber **158** 40 34N 96 59W
Wilburton **159** 34 55N 95 15W
Wilcannia **140** 31 30 S 143 26 E
Wildbad **49** 48 44N 8 32 E
Wildervank **46** 53 5N 6 52 E
Wildeshausen **48** 52 54N 8 25 E
Wildhorn **50** 46 22N 7 21 E
Wildon **52** 46 52N 15 31 E
Wildrose, Calif., U.S.A. **163** 36 14N 117 11W
Wildrose, N. Dak., U.S.A. **158** 48 36N 103 17W
Wildspitze **52** 46 53N 10 53 E
Wildstrubel **50** 46 24N 7 32 E
Wildwood **162** 38 59N 74 46W
Wilgaroon **141** 30 52 S 145 42 E
Wilhelm II Coast **13** 67 0 S 90 0 E
Wilhelm Mt. **135** 5 50 S 145 1 E
Wilhelm-Pieck-Stadt Guben **48** 51 59N 14 48 E
Wilhelmina Kanaal **47** 51 36N 5 6 E
Wilhelmina, Mt. **175** 3 50N 56 30W
Wilhelmsburg, Austria **52** 48 6N 15 36 E
Wilhelmsburg, Ger. **48** 53 28N 10 1 E
Wilhelmshaven **48** 53 30N 8 9 E
Wilhelmstal **128** 21 58 S 16 21 E
Wilkes-Barre **162** 41 15N 75 52W
Wilkes Land **13** 69 0 S 120 0 E
Wilkesboro **157** 36 10N 81 9W
Wilkie **153** 52 27N 108 42W
Wilkinson Lakes **137** 29 40 S 132 39 E
Willamina **160** 45 9N 123 32W
Willamulka **140** 33 55 S 137 52 E
Willandra Billabong Creek **140** 33 22 S 145 52 E
Willapa, B. **160** 46 44N 124 0W
Willard, N. Mex., U.S.A. **161** 34 35N 106 1W
Willard, N.Y., U.S.A. **162** 42 40N 76 50W
Willard, Utah, U.S.A. **160** 41 28N 112 1W
Willaumez Pen. **138** 5 3 S 150 3 E
Willaura **140** 37 31 S 142 45 E
Willberforce, C. **138** 11 54 S 136 35 E
Willbriggie **141** 34 28 S 146 2 E
Willcox **161** 32 13N 109 53W
Willebroek **47** 51 4N 4 22 E
Willemstad **167** 12 5N 69 0W
Willenhall **28** 52 36N 2 3W
Willeroo **136** 15 14 S 131 37 E
Willesborough **29** 51 8N 0 55 E
Willet **162** 42 28N 75 55W
William Cr. **139** 28 58 S 136 22 E
William, Mt. **140** 37 17 S 142 35 E
William, R. **153** 59 8N 109 19W
Williambury **137** 23 45 S 115 12 E
Williams, Austral. **137** 33 2 S 116 52 E
Williams, U.S.A. **161** 35 16N 112 11W
Williams Lake **152** 52 2N 122 10W
Williamsburg, Ky., U.S.A. **157** 36 45N 84 10W
Williamsburg, Va., U.S.A. **162** 37 17N 76 44W
Williamsburg, Va., U.S.A. **162** 37 16N 79 43W
Williamson **156** 37 46N 82 17W
Williamsport **162** 41 18N 77 1W
Williamston **157** 35 50N 77 5W
Williamstown, Austral. **141** 37 51 S 144 52 E
Williamstown, Ireland **38** 53 41N 8 34W
Williamstown, Mass., U.S.A. **162** 42 43N 73 12W
Williamstown, N.Y., U.S.A. **162** 43 25N 75 53W
Williamstown, N.Y., U.S.A. **162** 43 25N 75 54W
Williamsville **159** 37 0N 90 33W
Willimantic **162** 41 45N 72 12W
Willingdon **29** 50 47N 0 17 E
Willis Group **138** 16 18 S 150 0 E
Willisau **50** 47 7N 8 0 E
Williston, S. Afr. **128** 31 20 S 20 53 E
Williston, Fla, U.S.A. **157** 29 25N 82 28W
Williston, N.D., U.S.A. **158** 48 10N 103 35W
Williston L. **152** 56 0N 124 0W
Williton **28** 51 9N 3 20W
Willits **160** 39 28N 123 17W
Willmar **158** 45 5N 95 0W
Willoughby **33** 53 14N 0 12 E
Willow Bunch **153** 49 20N 105 35W
Willow L. **152** 62 10N 119 8W
Willow Lake **158** 44 40N 97 40W
Willow River **152** 54 6N 122 28W
Willow Springs **159** 37 0N 92 0W
Willow Tree **141** 31 40 S 150 45 E
Willow Wall **107** 41 30N 120 40 E
Willowlake, R. **152** 62 42N 123 8W
Willowmore **128** 33 15 S 23 30 E
Willows, Austral. **138** 23 45 S 147 25 E
Willows, U.S.A. **160** 39 30N 122 10W
Wills Cr. **138** 22 43 S 140 2 E
Wills, L. **136** 21 25 S 128 51 E
Wills Pt. **159** 32 42N 95 57W
Willunga **140** 35 15 S 138 30 E
Wilmete **156** 42 6N 87 44W
Wilmington, Austral. **140** 32 39 S 138 7 E
Wilmington, U.K. **30** 50 46N 3 8W
Wilmington, Del., U.S.A. **162** 39 45N 75 32W
Wilmington, Ill., U.S.A. **156** 41 19N 88 10W
Wilmington, N.C., U.S.A. **157** 34 14N 77 54W
Wilmington, Ohio, U.S.A. **156** 39 29N 83 46W
Wilmington, Vt., U.S.A. **162** 42 52N 72 52W
Wilmslow **32** 53 19N 2 14W
Wilnecote **28** 52 36N 1 40W
Wilpena Cr. **140** 31 25 S 139 29 E
Wilrijk **47** 51 9N 4 22 E
Wilsall **160** 45 59N 110 4W
Wilson, U.S.A. **162** 40 41N 75 15W
Wilson, N.C., U.S.A. **157** 35 44N 77 54W
Wilson Bluff **137** 31 41 S 129 0 E
Wilson Inlet **137** 35 0 S 117 20 E
Wilson, Mt. **161** 37 55N 105 3W
Wilson, R., Queens., Austral. **139** 27 38 S 141 24 E
Wilson, R., W. Australia, Austral. **136** 16 48 S 128 16 E
Wilson's Promontory **141** 38 55 S 146 25 E
Wilster **48** 53 55N 9 23 E
Wilton, U.K. **28** 51 5N 1 52W
Wilton, U.S.A. **158** 47 12N 100 53W
Wilton, R. **138** 14 45 S 134 33 E
Wiltshire □ **28** 51 20N 2 0W
Wiltz **47** 49 57N 5 55 E
Wiluna **137** 26 36 S 120 14 E
Wimblington **29** 52 31N 0 5 E
Wimborne Minster **28** 50 48N 2 0W
Wimereux **43** 50 45N 1 37 E
Wimmera **133** 36 30 S 142 0 E
Wimmera, R. **140** 36 8 S 141 56 E
Winam G. **126** 0 20 S 34 15 E
Winburg **128** 28 30 S 27 2 E
Wincanton **28** 51 3N 2 24W
Winchelsea, Austral. **140** 38 10 S 144 1 E
Winchelsea, U.K. **29** 50 55N 0 43 E
Winchendon **162** 42 40N 72 3W
Winchester, N.Z. **143** 44 11 S 171 17 E
Winchester, U.K. **28** 51 4N 1 19W
Winchester, Conn., U.S.A. **162** 41 53N 73 9W
Winchester, Conn., U.S.A. **162** 41 55N 73 8W
Winchester, Idaho, U.S.A. **160** 46 11N 116 32W
Winchester, Ind., U.S.A. **156** 40 10N 84 56W
Winchester, Ky., U.S.A. **156** 38 0N 84 8W
Winchester, Mass., U.S.A. **162** 42 28N 71 10W
Winchester, N.H., U.S.A. **162** 42 47N 72 22W
Winchester, Tenn., U.S.A. **157** 35 11N 86 8W
Winchester, Va., U.S.A. **156** 39 14N 78 8W
Wind, R. **160** 43 30N 109 30W
Wind River Range, Mts. **160** 43 0N 109 30W
Windber **156** 40 14N 78 50W
Winder **157** 34 0N 83 40W
Windera **139** 26 17 S 151 51 E
Windermere **32** 54 24N 2 56W
Windermere, L. **32** 54 20N 2 57W
Windfall **152** 54 12N 116 13W
Windflower L. **152** 62 52N 118 30W
Windhoek **128** 22 35 S 17 4 E
Windischgarsten **52** 47 42N 14 21 E
Windmill Pt. **162** 37 35N 76 17W
Windom **158** 43 48N 95 3W
Windorah **138** 25 24 S 142 36 E
Window Rock **161** 35 47N 109 4W
Windrush, R. **28** 51 48N 1 35W
Windsor, Austral. **141** 33 37 S 150 50 E
Windsor, Newf., Can. **151** 48 57N 55 40W
Windsor, N.S., Can. **151** 44 59N 64 5W
Windsor, Ont., Can. **150** 42 18N 83 82W
Windsor, N.Z. **143** 44 59 S 170 49 E
Windsor, U.K. **29** 51 28N 0 36W
Windsor, Col., U.S.A. **158** 40 33N 104 55W
Windsor, Conn., U.S.A. **162** 41 50N 72 40W
Windsor, Miss., U.S.A. **158** 38 32N 93 31W
Windsor, N.Y., U.S.A. **162** 42 5N 75 37W
Windsor, Vt., U.S.A. **162** 43 30N 72 25W
Windsorton **128** 28 16 S 24 44 E
Windward Is. **167** 13 0N 63 0W
Windward Passage **167** 20 0N 74 0W
Windy L. **153** 60 20N 100 2W
Windygap **39** 52 28N 7 24W
Windygates **35** 56 12N 3 1W
Winefred L. **153** 55 30N 110 30W
Winejok **123** 9 1N 27 30 E
Winfield **159** 37 15N 97 0W
Wing **29** 51 54N 0 41W
Wingate Mts. **136** 14 25 S 130 40 E
Wingen **141** 31 54 S 150 54 E
Wingene **47** 51 3N 3 17 E
Wingham, Austral. **141** 31 48 S 152 22 E
Wingham, Can. **150** 43 55N 81 20W
Wingham, U.K. **29** 51 16N 1 12 E
Winifred **160** 47 30N 109 28W
Winisk **150** 55 20N 85 15W
Winisk L. **150** 52 55N 87 22W
Winisk, R. **150** 55 17N 85 5W
Wink **159** 31 49N 103 9W
Winkleigh **30** 50 49N 3 57W
Winkler **153** 49 15N 97 56W
Winklern **52** 46 52N 12 52 E
Winneba **121** 5 25N 0 36W
Winnebago **158** 43 43N 94 8W
Winnebago L. **156** 44 0N 88 20W
Winnecke Cr. **136** 18 35 S 131 34 E
Winnemucca **160** 41 0N 117 45W
Winnemucca, L. **160** 40 25N 19 21W
Winner **158** 43 23N 99 52W
Winnetka **156** 42 8N 87 46W
Winnett **160** 47 2N 108 28W
Winnfield **159** 31 57N 92 38W
Winnibigoshish L. **158** 47 25N 94 12W
Winning Pool **136** 23 9 S 114 30 E
Winnipeg **153** 49 50N 97 9W
Winnipeg Beach **153** 50 30N 96 58W
Winnipeg, L. **153** 52 0N 97 0W
Winnipeg, R. **153** 50 38N 96 19W
Winnipegosis **153** 51 39N 99 55W
Winnipegosis L. **153** 52 30N 100 0W
Winnipesaukee, L. **162** 43 38N 71 21W
Winnisquam L. **162** 43 33N 71 30W
Winnsboro, Lou, U.S.A. **159** 32 10N 91 41W
Winnsboro, S.C., U.S.A. **157** 34 23N 81 5W
Winnsboro, Tex., U.S.A. **158** 32 56N 95 15W
Winokapau, L. **151** 53 15N 62 50W
Winona, Miss., U.S.A. **159** 33 30N 89 42W
Winona, Wis., U.S.A. **158** 44 2N 91 45W
Winooski **156** 44 31N 73 11W
Winschoten **46** 53 9N 7 3 E
Winsen **48** 53 21N 10 11 E
Winsford **32** 53 12N 2 31W
Winslow, U.K. **29** 51 57N 0 52W
Winslow, U.S.A. **161** 35 2N 110 41W
Winstead **162** 41 55N 73 5W
Winster **33** 53 9N 1 42W
Winston-Salem **157** 36 7N 80 15W
Winsum **46** 53 20N 6 32 E
Winter Garden **157** 28 33N 81 35W
Winter Haven **157** 28 0N 81 42W
Winter Park **157** 28 34N 81 19W
Winterberg **48** 51 12N 8 30 E

Winterborne Abbas Yaapeet

Winterborne Abbas **28** 50 43N 2 30W
Winters **159** 31 58N 99 58W
Winterset **158** 41 18N 94 0W
Winterswijk **46** 51 58N 6 43E
Winterthur **51** 47 30N 8 44E
Winterton, Humberside, U.K. **33** 53 39N 0 37W
Winterton, Norfolk, U.K. **29** 52 43N 1 43E
Winthrop, Minn., U.S.A. **158** 44 31N 94 25W
Winthrop, Wash., U.S.A. **160** 48 27N 120 6W
Winton, Austral. **138** 22 24S 143 3E
Winton, N.Z. **143** 46 8S 168 20E
Winton, U.S.A. **157** 36 25N 76 58W
Wirksworth **33** 53 5N 1 34W
Wirral **23** 53 25N 3 0W
Wirraminna **140** 31 12S 136 13E
Wirrulla **139** 32 24S 134 31E
Wisbech **29** 52 39N 0 10E
Wisborough Green **29** 51 2N 0 30W
Wisconsin □ **158** 44 30N 90 0W
Wisconsin Dells **158** 43 38N 89 45W
Wisconsin, R. **158** 45 25N 89 45W
Wisconsin Rapids **158** 44 25N 89 50W
Wisdom **147** 45 36N 113 1W
Wiserman **147** 67 25N 150 15W
Wishaw **35** 55 46N 3 55W
Wishek **158** 46 20N 99 35W
Wiske, R. **33** 54 26N 1 27W
Wisła **53** 49 38N 18 53E
Wisła, R. **54** 53 38N 18 47E
Wisłok, R. **53** 50 7N 22 25E
Wisłoka, R. **53** 49 50N 21 28E
Wismar **48** 53 53N 11 23E
Wismar B. **48** 54 0N 11 15E
Wisner **158** 42 0N 96 46W
Wissant **43** 50 52N 1 40E
Wissembourg **43** 48 57N 7 57E
Wissenkerke **47** 51 35N 3 45E
Wistoka, R. **54** 49 50N 21 28E
Witbank **129** 25 51S 29 14E
Witchita **159** 37 40N 97 22W
Witchyburn **37** 57 37N 2 37W
Witdraai **128** 26 58S 20 48E
Witham **29** 51 48N 0 39E
Witham, R. **33** 53 3N 0 8W
Withern **33** 53 19N 0 9E
Withernsea **33** 53 43N 0 2W
Witkowo **54** 52 26N 17 45E
Witley **29** 51 9N 0 39W
Witmarsum **46** 53 6N 5 28E
Witney **28** 51 47N 1 29W
Witnossob, R. **128** 23 0S 18 40E
Wittdün **48** 54 38N 8 23E
Witten **48** 51 26N 7 19E
Wittenberg **48** 51 51N 12 39E
Wittenberge **48** 53 0N 11 44E
Wittenburg **48** 53 30N 11 4E
Wittenoom, W. Australia, Austral. **132** 22 15S 118 20E
Wittenoom, W. Australia, Austral. **136** 18 34S 128 51E
Wittersham **29** 51 1N 0 42E
Wittingen **48** 52 43N 10 43E
Wittlich **49** 50 0N 6 54E
Wittmund **48** 53 39N 7 35E
Wittow **48** 54 37N 13 21E
Wittstock **48** 53 10N 12 30E
Witzenhausen **48** 51 20N 9 50E
Wiveliscombe **28** 51 2N 3 20W
Wivenhoe **29** 51 51N 0 59E
Wiyeb, W. **123** 7 15N 40 15E
Wladyslawowo **54** 52 6N 18 28E
Wlen **160** 51 0N 15 39E
Wlingi **103** 8 5S 112 25E
Włocławek **54** 52 40N 19 3E
Włodawa **54** 51 33N 23 31E
Włoszczowa **54** 50 50N 19 55E
Woburn, U.K. **29** 51 59N 0 37W
Woburn, U.S.A. **162** 42 31N 71 7W
Woburn Sands **29** 51 1N 0 38W
Wodonga **141** 36 5S 146 50E
Wodzisław Sl. **54** 50 1N 18 26E
Woerden **46** 52 5N 4 54E
Woerht'ukou **106** 42 35N 112 19E
Woerth **43** 48 57N 7 45E
Woevre **43** 49 15N 5 45E
Wognum **46** 52 40N 5 1E
Wohlen **51** 47 21N 8 17E
Wokam, I. **103** 5 45S 134 28E
Wokha **98** 26 6N 94 16E
Woking, Can. **152** 55 35N 118 50W
Woking, U.K. **29** 51 18N 0 33W
Wokingham **29** 51 25N 0 50W
Wolbrom **54** 50 24N 19 45E
Woldegk **48** 53 27N 13 35E
Wolf Creek **160** 47 1N 112 2W
Wolf L. **152** 60 24N 133 42W
Wolf Point **158** 48 6N 105 40W
Wolf, R. **152** 60 17N 132 33W
Wolf Rock **30** 49 56N 5 50W
Wolfe I. **150** 44 7N 76 20W
Wolfeboro **162** 43 35N 71 12W
Wolfenbüttel **48** 52 10N 10 33E
Wolfenden **152** 52 0N 119 25W
Wolfheze **46** 52 0N 5 48E
Wolfram **138** 17 6S 145 0E
Wolf's Castle **31** 51 53N 4 57W
Wolfsberg **52** 46 50N 14 52E
Wolfsburg **48** 52 27N 10 49E
Wolgast **48** 54 3N 13 46E
Wolhusen **50** 47 4N 8 4E
Wolin **54** 53 40N 14 37E
Wollaston, Islas **176** 55 40S 67 30W
Wollaston L. **153** 58 7N 103 10W
Wollaston Pen. **148** 69 30N 115 0W
Wollogorang **138** 17 13S 137 57E
Wollongong **141** 34 25S 150 54E
Wolmaransstad **128** 27 12S 26 13E
Wolmirstedt **48** 52 15N 11 35E
Wołomin **54** 52 19N 21 15E
Wołow **54** 51 20N 16 38E
Wolseley, Austral. **140** 36 23S 140 54E
Wolseley, Can. **153** 50 25N 103 15W
Wolseley, S. Afr. **128** 33 26S 19 7E
Wolsingham **32** 54 44N 1 52W
Wolstenholme Sound **12** 74 30N 75 0W
Wolsztyn **54** 52 8N 16 5E
Wolvega **46** 52 52N 6 0E
Wolverhampton **28** 52 35N 2 6W
Wolverton **29** 52 3N 0 48W
Wolviston **33** 54 39N 1 25W
Wombera **123** 10 45N 35 49E
Wombwell **33** 53 31N 1 23W
Wommels **46** 53 6N 5 36E
Wonarah P.O. **138** 19 55S 136 20E
Wonboyn **141** 37 15S 149 55E
Wonck **47** 50 46N 5 38E
Wondai **139** 26 20S 151 49E
Wondelgem **47** 51 5N 3 44E
Wonder Gorge **127** 14 40S 29 0E
Wongalarroo L. **140** 31 32S 144 0E
Wongan **137** 30 51S 116 37E
Wongan Hills **137** 30 53S 116 42E
Wongawal **137** 25 5S 121 55E
Wonosari **103** 7 38S 110 36E
Wŏnsan **107** 39 11N 127 27E
Wonston **28** 51 9N 1 18W
Wonthaggi **141** 38 37S 145 37E
Wonyulgunna Hill, Mt. **137** 24 52S 119 44E
Woocalla **140** 31 42S 137 12E
Wood Buffalo Nat. Park **152** 56 28N 113 41W
Wood Green **138** 22 26S 134 12E
Wood Is. **136** 16 24S 123 19E
Wood L. **153** 55 17N 103 17W
Wood Lake **158** 42 38N 100 14W
Wood Mt. **153** 49 14N 106 30W
Woodah I. **138** 13 27S 136 10E
Woodanilling **137** 33 31S 117 24E
Woodbine **162** 39 14N 74 49W
Woodbourne **162** 41 46N 74 35W
Woodbridge **29** 52 6N 1 19E
Woodburn **139** 29 6S 153 23E
Woodbury, U.K. **30** 50 40N 3 24W
Woodbury, U.S.A. **162** 39 50N 75 9W
Woodchopper **147** 65 25N 143 30W
Wooden Bridge **39** 52 50N 6 13W
Woodend **140** 37 20N 144 33E
Woodford **39** 53 3N 8 23W
Woodfords **163** 38 47N 119 50W
Woodhall Spa. **33** 53 10N 0 12W
Woodham Ferrers **29** 51 40N 0 37E
Woodlake **163** 36 25N 119 6W
Woodland **160** 38 40N 121 50W
Woodlands **137** 24 46S 118 8E
Woodlark I. **135** 9 10S 152 50E
Woodley **29** 51 26N 0 54W
Woodpecker **152** 53 30N 122 40W
Woodplumpton **32** 53 47N 2 46W
Woodridge **153** 49 20N 96 9W
Woodroffe, Mt. **137** 26 20S 131 45E
Woodruff, Ariz., U.S.A. **161** 34 51N 110 1W
Woodruff, Utah, U.S.A. **160** 41 30N 111 4W
Woods, L., Austral. **138** 17 50S 133 30E
Woods, L., Can. **151** 54 30N 65 13W
Woods, Lake of the **153** 49 30N 94 30W
Woodside, S. Australia, Austral. **140** 34 58S 138 52E
Woodside, Victoria, Austral. **141** 38 31S 146 52E
Woodstock, N.S.W., Austral. **141** 33 45S 148 53E
Woodstock, Queens., Austral. **138** 19 35S 146 50E
Woodstock, W.A., Austral. **136** 21 41S 118 57E
Woodstock, N.B., Can. **151** 46 11N 67 37W
Woodstock, Ont., Can. **150** 43 10N 80 45W
Woodstock, U.K. **28** 51 51N 1 20W
Woodstock, Ill., U.S.A. **158** 42 17N 88 30W
Woodstock, Vt., U.S.A. **162** 43 37N 72 31W
Woodstown **162** 39 39N 75 20W
Woodville, N.Z. **142** 40 20S 175 53E
Woodville, U.S.A. **159** 30 45N 94 25W
Woodward **159** 36 24N 99 28W
Woodward, Mt. **137** 26 0S 131 0E
Woody **163** 35 42N 118 50W
Wookey **28** 51 13N 2 41W
Wookey Hole **28** 51 13N 2 41W
Wool **28** 50 41N 2 13W
Woolacombe **30** 51 10N 4 12W
Woolamai, C. **141** 38 30S 145 23E
Wooler **35** 55 33N 2 0W
Woolgangie **137** 31 12S 120 35E
Woolyeenyer, Mt. **137** 32 16S 121 47E
Woombye **139** 26 40S 152 55E
Woomera **140** 31 11S 136 47E
Woonona **141** 34 21S 150 54E
Woonsocket **162** 42 0N 71 30W
Woonsockett **158** 44 5N 98 15W
Wooramel **137** 25 45S 114 40E
Wooramel, R. **137** 25 30S 114 30E
Wooroloo **137** 31 48S 116 18E
Wooroorooka **139** 29 0S 145 41E
Wooster **156** 40 38N 81 55W
Wootton Bassett **28** 51 32N 1 55W
Wootton Wawen **28** 52 16N 1 47W
Worb **50** 46 56N 7 33E
Worcester, S. Afr. **125** 33 39S 19 27E
Worcester, U.K. **28** 52 12N 2 12W
Worcester, Mass., U.S.A. **162** 42 14N 71 49W
Worcester, N.Y., U.S.A. **162** 42 35N 74 45W
Worcestershire (□) **26** 52 13N 2 10W
Worfield **28** 52 34N 2 22W
Wörgl **52** 47 29N 12 3E
Worikambo **121** 10 43N 0 11W
Workington **32** 54 39N 3 34W
Worksop **33** 53 19N 1 9W
Workum **46** 52 59N 5 26E
Worland **160** 44 0N 107 59W
Wormerveer **46** 52 30N 4 46E
Wormhoudt **43** 50 52N 2 28E
Wormit **35** 56 26N 2 59W
Worms **49** 49 37N 8 21E
Worms Head **29** 51 33N 4 19W
Worplesdon **29** 51 16N 0 36W
Worsley **137** 33 15S 116 2E
Wortham, U.K. **29** 52 22N 1 3E
Wortham, U.S.A. **159** 31 48N 96 27W
Wörther See **52** 46 37N 14 19E
Worthing **29** 50 49N 0 21W
Worthington **158** 43 35N 95 30W
Wosi **103** 0 15S 128 0E
Wota (Shoa Ghimirra) **123** 7 4N 35 51E
Wotton-under-Edge **28** 51 37N 2 20W
Woubrugge **46** 52 10N 4 39E
Woudenberg **46** 52 5N 5 25E
Woudsend **46** 52 56N 5 38E
Wour **119** 21 14N 16 0E
Wouw **47** 51 31N 4 23E
Wowoni, I. **103** 4 5S 123 5E
Woy Woy **141** 33 30S 151 19E
Wragby **33** 53 17N 0 18W
Wrangell **147** 56 30N 132 25W
Wrangell, I. **152** 56 20N 132 10W
Wrangell Mts. **147** 61 40N 143 30W
Wrangle **33** 53 3N 0 9E
Wrath, C. **36** 58 38N 5 0W
Wray **158** 40 8N 102 18W
Wreck I. **162** 37 12N 75 48W
Wrekin, The, Mt. **28** 52 41N 2 35W
Wrens **157** 33 13N 82 23W
Wrentham **29** 52 24N 1 39E
Wrexham **31** 53 5N 3 0W
Wriezen **48** 52 43N 14 9E
Wright, Can. **152** 51 52N 121 40W
Wright, Phil. **103** 11 42N 125 2E
Wright, Mt. **151** 52 40N 67 25W
Wrightlington **28** 51 18N 2 16W
Wrightson, Mt. **161** 31 49N 110 56W
Wrightsville **162** 40 2N 76 32W
Wrightwood **163** 34 21N 117 38W
Wrigley **148** 63 16N 123 27W
Writtle **29** 51 44N 0 27E
Wrocław **54** 51 5N 17 5E
Wrocław □ **54** 51 0N 17 0E
Wronki **54** 52 41N 16 21E
Wrotham **29** 51 18N 0 20E
Wroughton **28** 51 31N 1 47W
Wroxham **29** 52 42N 1 23E
Września **54** 52 21N 17 36E
Wschowa **54** 51 48N 16 20E
Wu Chiang, R. **108** 29 42N 107 20E
Wu Shui, R. **109** 27 7N 109 57E
Wuan **106** 36 45N 114 2E
Wubin **137** 30 6S 116 37E
Wuch'ang, Heilungkiang, China **107** 44 55N 127 10E
Wuch'ang, Hupeh, China **109** 30 30N 114 15E
Wuch'eng **108** 30 48N 98 46E
Wuch'i **108** 31 28N 109 36E
Wuchiang **109** 31 10N 120 37E
Wuchih Shan, mts. **100** 18 45N 109 45E
Wuch'ing **107** 39 25N 117 7E
Wuchou **105** 23 33N 111 18E
Wuch'uan, Inner Mong., China **106** 41 8N 111 24E
Wuch'uan, Kwangsi-Chuang, China **109** 21 29N 110 49E
Wuch'uan, Kweichow, China **108** 28 30N 107 58E
Wuchung **106** 38 4N 106 12E
Wufeng **109** 30 12N 110 36E
Wuhan **109** 30 35N 114 15E
Wuho **107** 33 9N 117 53E
Wuhsi **105** 31 30N 120 20E
Wuhsiang **106** 36 50N 112 52E
Wuhsing **109** 30 49N 120 5E
Wuhsüan **108** 23 36N 109 39E
Wuhu **105** 31 18N 118 20E
Wuhu (Wou-tou) **109** 31 21N 118 30E
Wui, Anhwei, China **109** 28 53N 119 48E
Wui, Hopeh, China **106** 37 49N 115 54E
Wui Shan, mts. **105** 27 30N 117 30E
Wukang **109** 26 50N 110 15E
Wukari **121** 7 57N 9 42E
Wulachieh **107** 44 5N 126 27E
Wulanhaot'e **105** 46 5N 122 5E
Wulanpulang **106** 41 8N 110 56E
Wulehe **121** 3 42N 0 0E
Wuliang Shan, mts. **108** 24 0N 100 55E
Wuliaru, I. **103** 7 10S 131 0E
Wulien **107** 35 45N 119 12E
Wuluk'omushih Ling **105** 36 25N 87 25E
Wulumuchi **105** 43 40N 87 50E
Wulunku Ho, R. **105** 46 58N 87 28E
Wum **121** 6 40N 10 2E
Wuming **108** 23 11N 108 12E
Wuneba **123** 4 49N 30 22E
Wuning **109** 29 16N 115 0E
Wunnummin L. **150** 52 55N 89 10W
Wunsiedel **49** 50 2N 12 0E
Wunstorf **48** 52 26N 9 29E
Wuntho, Burma **98** 21 44N 96 2E
Wuntho, Burma **99** 23 55N 95 45E
Wupao **106** 37 35N 110 45E
Wup'ing **109** 25 9N 116 5E
Wuppertal, Ger. **48** 51 15N 7 8E
Wuppertal, S. Afr. **128** 32 13S 19 12E
Wurarga **137** 28 25S 116 15E
Würenlingen **51** 47 32N 8 16E
Wurung **138** 19 13S 140 38E
Würzburg **49** 49 46N 9 55E
Wurzen **48** 51 21N 12 45E
Wushan, Kansu, China **106** 34 42N 104 58E
Wushan, Szechwan, China **108** 31 3N 109 57E
Wushench'i **106** 38 57N 109 15E
Wustrow **48** 54 4N 11 33E
Wusu **105** 44 27N 84 37E
Wutai **106** 38 44N 113 18E
Wuti **107** 37 46N 117 39E
Wuting **108** 25 33N 102 26E
Wuting = Huimin **107** 37 32N 117 33E
Wuting Ho, R. **106** 37 8N 110 25E
Wut'ungch'iao **108** 29 24N 104 0E
Wutunghaolan **107** 42 49N 120 11E
Wuustwezel **47** 51 23N 4 36E
Wuwei, Anhwei, China **109** 31 22N 117 55E
Wuwei, Kansu, China **105** 37 55N 102 48E
Wuyang **106** 33 25N 113 36E
Wuyo **121** 10 23N 11 50E
Wuyüan, Inner Mong., China **106** 41 6N 108 16E
Wuyüan, Kiangsi, China **109** 29 17N 117 54E
Wuyün **105** 49 17N 129 40E
Wyaaba Cr. **138** 16 27S 141 35E
Wyalkatchem **137** 31 8S 117 22E
Wyalong **139** 33 54S 147 16E
Wyalusing **162** 41 40N 76 16W
Wyandotte **156** 42 14N 83 13W
Wyandra **139** 27 12S 145 56E
Wyangala Res. **141** 33 54S 149 0E
Wyara, L. **139** 28 42S 144 14E
Wych Farm, oilfield **19** 50 38N 2 2W
Wycheproof **140** 36 0N 143 17E
Wye **29** 51 11N 0 56E
Wye, R. **28** 52 0N 2 36W
Wyemandoo, Mt. **137** 28 28S 118 29E
Wyk **48** 54 41N 8 33E
Wylfa Hd. **31** 53 25N 4 28W
Wylye, R. **28** 51 8N 1 53W
Wymondham, Leicester, U.K. **29** 52 45N 0 42W
Wymondham, Norfolk, U.K. **29** 52 34N 1 7E
Wymore **158** 40 10N 97 8W
Wynberg **128** 34 2S 18 28E
Wynbring **139** 30 33S 133 32E
Wyndham, Austral. **136** 15 33S 128 3E
Wyndham, N.Z. **143** 46 20S 168 51E
Wynne **159** 35 15N 90 50W
Wynnstay **31** 52 36N 3 33W
Wynnum **139** 27 27S 153 9E
Wynyard **153** 51 45N 104 10W
Wyola, L. **137** 29 8S 130 17E
Wyoming □ **154** 42 48N 109 0W
Wyong **141** 33 14S 151 24E
Wyre Forest **28** 52 24N 2 24W
Wyre, I. **37** 59 7N 2 58W
Wyre, R. **37** 53 52N 2 57W
Wyrzysk **54** 53 10N 17 17E
Wysoka **54** 53 13N 17 2E
Wyszków **54** 52 36N 21 25E
Wyszogród **54** 52 23N 20 9E
Wytheville **156** 37 0N 81 3W

X

Xai-Xai **129** 25 6S 33 31E
Xambioá **170** 6 25S 48 40W
Xanten **48** 51 40N 6 27E
Xanthí **68** 41 10N 24 58E
Xanthí □ **68** 41 10N 24 58E
Xapuri **174** 10 35S 68 35W
Xau **128** 21 15S 24 44E
Xavantina **173** 21 15S 52 48W
Xenia **156** 39 42N 83 57W
Xieng Khouang **100** 19 17N 103 25E
Xilókastron **69** 38 4N 22 43E
Xinavane **129** 25 2S 32 47E
Xingu, R. **175** 2 25S 52 35W
Xiniás, L. **69** 39 2N 22 12E
Xique-Xique **170** 10 50S 42 40W
Xuan Loc **101** 10 56N 107 14E
Xuyen Moc **101** 10 34N 107 25E

Y

Ya 'Bud **90** 32 27N 35 10E
Yaamba **138** 23 8S 150 22E
Yaan **108** 30 0N 102 59E
Yaapeet **140** 35 45S 142 3E

Yabassi **Yorktown**

Yabassi 121 4 30N 9 57 E
Yabba North 141 36 13 S 145 42 E
Yabelo 123 4 57N 38 8 E
Yablanitsa 67 43 2N 24 5 E
Yablonovyy Khrebet 77 53 0N 114 0 E
Yabrīn 92 23 7N 48 52 E
Yach'i 108 27 35N 106 40 E
Yachiang 108 30 4N 101 7 E
Yacuiba 172 22 0 S 63 25W
Yadgir 96 16 45N 77 5 E
Yadkin, R. 157 36 15N 81 0W
Yadrin 81 55 57N 46 6 E
Yaeyama-Shotō 112 24 25N 124 0 E
Yagaba 121 10 14N 1 20W
Yagoua 124 10 20N 14 58 E
Yagur 90 32 45N 35 4 E
Yaha 101 6 29N 101 8 E
Yahk 152 49 6N 116 10W
Yahuma 124 1 0N 22 5 E
Yaihsien 100 18 14N 109 29 E
Yaizu 111 34 52N 138 20 E
Yajua 121 11 27N 12 49 E
Yakage 110 34 37N 133 35 E
Yakataga 147 60 5N 142 32W
Yakiang 99 30 4N 101 15 E
Yakima 160 46 42N 120 30W
Yakima, R. 160 47 0N 120 30W
Yako 120 12 59N 2 15W
Yakoruda 67 42 1N 23 29 E
Yakshur Bodya 84 57 11N 53 7 E
Yaku-Jima 112 30 20N 130 30 E
Yakut A.S.S.R. □ 77 62 0N 130 0 E
Yakutat 147 59 50N 139 44W
Yakutsk 77 62 5N 129 40 E
Yala 101 6 33N 101 18 E
Yalabusha, R. 159 33 53N 89 50W
Yalbalgo 137 25 10 S 114 45 E
Yalboroo 138 20 50 S 148 40 E
Yalgoo 137 28 16 S 116 39 E
Yalikavak 69 37 6N 27 18 E
Yalinga 117 6 20N 23 10 E
Yalkubul, Punta 165 21 32N 88 37W
Y'allaq, G. 122 30 21N 33 31 E
Yalleroi 138 24 3 S 145 42 E
Yallourn 141 38 10 S 146 18 E
Yalpukh, Oz. 70 45 30N 28 41 E
Yalta 82 44 30N 34 10 E
Yalu Chiang, R. 107 39 45N 124 20 E
Yalung Chiang, R. 105 26 35N 101 45 E
Yalutorovsk 76 56 30N 65 40 E
Yam Kinneret 90 32 49N 35 36 E
Yamada 110 33 43N 130 49 E
Yamaga 110 33 1N 130 41 E
Yamagata 112 38 15N 140 15 E
Yamagata-ken □ 112 38 30N 140 0 E
Yamagawa 110 31 12N 130 39 E
Yamaguchi 110 34 10N 131 32 E
Yamaguchi-ken □ 110 34 20N 131 40 E
Yamal, Poluostrov 76 71 0N 70 0 E
Yamana 92 24 5N 47 30 E
Yamanaka 111 36 15N 136 22 E
Yamanashi-ken □ 111 35 40N 138 40 E
Yamankhalinka 83 47 43N 49 21 E
Yamantau 78 54 20N 57 40 E
Yamantau, Gora 84 54 15N 58 6 E
Yamato 111 35 27N 139 25 E
Yamatotakada 111 34 31N 135 45 E
Yamazaki 110 35 0N 134 32 E
Yamba, N.S.W., Austral. 139 29 26 S 153 23 E
Yamba, S. Australia, Austral. 140 34 10 S 140 52 E
Yambah 138 23 10 S 133 50 E
Yâmbiô 123 4 35N 28 16 E
Yambol 67 42 30N 26 36 E
Yamdena 103 7 45 S 131 20 E
Yame 110 33 13N 130 35 E
Yamethin 98 20 29N 96 18 E
Yamil 121 12 53N 8 4 E
Yamma-Yamma L. 139 26 16 S 141 20 E
Yampa, R. 160 40 37N 108 0W
Yampi Sd. 136 16 8 S 123 38 E
Yampol 82 48 15N 28 15 E
Yamrat 121 10 11N 9 55 E
Yamrukohal, Mt. 67 42 44N 24 52 E
Yamun 90 32 29N 35 14 E
Yamuna (Jumna), R. 94 27 0N 78 30 E
Yan 121 10 5N 12 11 E
Yan Oya 97 9 0N 81 10 E
Yana, R. 77 69 0N 134 0 E
Yanac 140 36 8 S 141 25 E
Yanagawa 110 33 10N 130 24 E
Yanahara 110 34 58N 134 2 E
Yañam 96 16 47N 82 15 E
Yanaul 84 56 25N 55 0 E
Yanbu 'al Bahr 92 24 0N 38 5 E
Yancannia 139 30 12 S 142 35 E
Yanchep 137 31 30 S 115 45 E
Yanco 141 34 38 S 146 27 E
Yanco Cr. 141 35 14 S 145 35 E
Yandabome 138 7 1 S 145 46 E
Yandal 137 27 35 S 121 10 E
Yandanooka 137 29 18 S 115 29 E
Yandaran 138 24 43 S 152 6 E
Yandil 137 26 20 S 119 50 E
Yandoon 98 17 0N 95 40 E
Yanfolila 120 11 11N 8 9W
Yangambi 126 0 47N 24 20 E
Yangch'angtzukou 106 41 31N 109 1 E
Yangch'eng 106 35 32N 112 26 E
Yangchiang 109 21 55N 111 55 E
Yangchiaoch'iao 109 29 45N 112 45 E
Yangchiapa 106 42 6N 113 46 E
Yangchou 109 32 24N 119 26 E
Yangchoyung Hu 105 29 0N 90 40 E
Yangch'ü = T'aiyüan 106 37 55N 112 40 E
Yangch'üan 106 37 54N 113 36 E
Yangch'un 109 22 10N 111 47 E
Yanghsien 106 33 20N 107 30 E
Yanghsin 109 29 53N 115 10 E
Yangi-Yer 76 40 17N 68 48 E
Yangibazar 85 41 40N 70 53 E
Yangikishlak 85 40 25N 67 10 E
Yangiyul 85 41 0N 69 3 E
Yangku 106 36 8N 115 48 E
Yangliuch'ing 107 39 11N 117 9 E
Yangp'i 108 25 40N 100 0 E
Yangp'ing 109 31 13N 111 33 E
Yangp'ingkuan 106 33 2N 105 56 E
Yangshan 109 24 28N 112 38 E
Yangshuo 109 24 45N 110 24 E
Yangtze (Ch'ang Chiang) 109 1 48N 121 53 E
Yangyang 107 38 4N 128 38 E
Yangyüan 106 40 5N 114 12 E
Yanhee Res. 101 17 30N 98 45 E
Yanko Cr. 139 35 17 S 145 15 E
Yankton 158 42 55N 97 25W
Yanna 139 26 58 S 146 0 E
Yanonge 126 0 35N 24 38 E
Yantabulla 139 29 21 S 145 0 E
Yantra, R. 67 43 35N 25 37 E
Yany Kurgan 85 43 55N 67 15 E
Yao, Chad 117 12 56N 17 33 E
Yao, Japan 111 34 32N 135 36 E
Yao Yai, Ko 101 8 0N 98 35 E
Yaoan 108 25 32N 101 12 E
Yaoundé 121 3 50N 11 35 E
Yaowan 107 34 10N 118 3 E
Yap Is. 103 9 30N 138 10 E
Yapen 103 1 50 S 136 0 E
Yapen, Selat 103 1 20 S 136 10 E
Yapo, R. 174 0 30 S 77 0W
Yappar, R. 138 18 22 S 141 16 E
Yaqui, R. 164 28 28N 109 30W
Yar 84 58 14N 52 5 E
Yar-Sale 76 66 50N 70 50 E
Yaracuy □ 174 10 20N 68 45W
Yaraka 138 24 53 S 144 3 E
Yaransk 81 57 13N 47 56 E
Yaratishky 80 54 3N 25 52 E
Yarcombe 30 50 51N 3 6W
Yarda 117 18 35N 19 0 E
Yardea P.O. 139 32 23 S 135 32 E
Yare, R. 29 52 36N 1 28 E
Yarensk 78 61 10N 49 8 E
Yarfa 122 24 40N 38 35 E
Yarí, R. 174 1 0N 73 40W
Yaringa North 137 25 53 S 114 30 E
Yaringa South 137 26 3 S 114 28 E
Yarkand = Soch'e 105 38 24N 77 20 E
Yarkhun, R. 95 36 30N 72 45 E
Yarm 33 54 31N 1 21W
Yarmouth, Can. 151 43 53N 65 45W
Yarmouth, U.K. 28 50 42N 1 29W
Yaroslavl 81 57 35N 39 55 E
Yarra Yarra Lakes 137 29 40 S 115 45 E
Yarraden 138 14 28 S 143 15 E
Yarraloola 136 21 33 S 115 52 E
Yarram 141 38 29 S 146 40 E
Yarraman 139 26 50 S 152 0 E
Yarraman Cr. 139 26 46 S 152 1 E
Yarranvale 139 26 50 S 145 20 E
Yarras 141 31 25 S 152 20 E
Yarrawonga 141 36 0 S 146 0 E
Yarrow 35 55 32N 3 0W
Yarrowee, R. 140 38 18 S 144 30 E
Yarto 140 35 28 S 142 16 E
Yartsevo 77 60 20N 90 0 E
Yarumal 174 6 58N 75 24W
Yaselda, R. 80 52 26N 25 30 E
Yashi 121 12 23N 7 54 E
Yashiro-Jima 110 33 55N 132 15 E
Yasin 95 36 24N 73 15 E
Yasinovataya 82 48 7N 37 57 E
Yasinski, L. 150 53 16N 77 35W
Yasnogorsk 81 54 32N 37 38 E
Yasothon 100 15 50N 104 10 E
Yass 141 34 49 S 148 54 E
Yasugi 110 35 26N 133 15 E
Yas'ur 90 32 54N 35 10 E
Yatagan 69 37 20N 28 10 E
Yate 28 51 32N 2 26W
Yates Center 159 37 53N 95 45W
Yates Pt. 143 44 29 S 167 49 E
Yathkyed L. 153 62 40N 98 0W
Yathong 141 32 37 S 145 33 E
Yatsuo 111 36 34N 137 8 E
Yatsushiro 110 32 30N 130 40 E
Yatsushiro-Kai 110 32 30N 130 25 E
Yatta 90 31 27N 35 6 E
Yatta Plat. 126 2 0 S 38 0 E
Yattah 90 31 27N 35 6 E
Yatton 28 51 23N 2 50W
Yauyos 174 12 10 S 75 50W
Yaval 96 21 10N 75 42 E
Yavan 85 38 19N 69 2 E
Yavari R. 174 4 50 S 72 0W
Yavorov 80 49 55N 23 20 E
Yawatahama 110 33 27N 132 24 E
Yawri B. 120 8 22N 13 0W
Yaxley 29 52 31N 0 14W
Yazagyo 98 23 30N 94 6 E
Yazd (Yezd) 93 31 55N 54 27 E
Yazdan 93 33 30N 60 50 E
Yazoo City 159 32 48N 90 28W
Yazoo, R. 159 32 35N 90 50W
Ybbs 52 48 12N 15 4 E
Yding Skovhøj 75 55 59N 9 46 E
Yea 141 37 14 S 145 26 E
Yealering 137 32 36 S 117 36 E
Yealmpton 30 50 21N 4 0W
Yearinan 141 31 10 S 149 11 E
Yebbi-Souma 119 21 7N 17 54 E
Yebbigué 119 22 30N 17 30 E
Yebel Jarris Tighzert, O. 118 28 10N 9 37W
Yebyu 99 14 15N 98 13 E
Yechŏn 107 36 39N 128 27 E
Yecla 59 38 35N 1 5W
Yécora 164 28 20N 108 58W
Yedashe 98 17 24N 95 50 E
Yeddou 118 28 5N 9 2W
Yeeda River 136 17 31 S 123 38 E
Yeelanna 139 34 9 S 135 45 E
Yefremov 81 53 15N 38 3 E
Yegorlyk, R. 83 46 15N 41 30 E
Yegorlykskaya 83 46 5N 40 35 E
Yegoryevsk 81 55 27N 38 55 E
Yegros 172 26 20 S 56 25W
Yehchih 108 27 39N 99 0 E
Yehsien 106 33 37N 113 20 E
Yehud 90 32 3N 34 53 E
Yehuda, Midbar 90 31 35N 34 57 E
Yei 123 4 3N 30 40 E
Yei, Nahr 123 5 50N 30 20 E
Yelan 81 50 55N 43 43 E
Yelan Kolenovski 81 51 16N 40 45 E
Yelandur 97 12 6N 77 0 E
Yelanskoye 77 61 25N 128 0 E
Yelarbon 139 28 33 S 150 49 E
Yelatma 81 55 0N 41 52 E
Yelets 81 52 40N 38 30 E
Yelimané 120 15 9N 22 49 E
Yell, I. 36 60 35N 1 5W
Yell Sd. 36 60 33N 1 15W
Yellamanchilli (Elamanchili) 96 17 26N 82 50 E
Yellow Sea 105 35 0N 123 0 E
Yellowdine 137 31 17 S 119 40 E
Yellowhead P. 152 52 53N 118 25W
Yellowknife 152 62 27N 114 21W
Yellowknife, R. 152 62 31N 114 19W
Yellowstone L. 160 44 30N 110 20W
Yellowstone National Park 160 44 35N 110 0W
Yellowstone, R. 158 46 35N 105 45W
Yelnya 80 54 35N 33 15 E
Yelsk 80 51 50N 29 3 E
Yelvertoft 138 20 13 S 138 53 E
Yelwa 122 10 49N 8 41 E
Yemanzhelinsk 84 54 58N 61 18 E
Yemen ■ 91 15 0N 44 0 E
Yemen, South ■ 91 15 0N 48 0 E
Yen Bai 100 21 42N 104 52 E
Yenakiyevo 82 48 15N 38 5 E
Yenan 106 36 42N 109 25 E
Yenangyaung 98 20 30N 95 0 E
Yenanma 98 19 46N 96 48 E
Yenchang 106 36 44N 110 2 E
Yench'eng, Honan, China 106 33 37N 114 0 E
Yench'eng, Kiangsu, China 107 33 24N 120 10 E
Yench'i 105 42 4N 86 34 E
Yenchi 107 42 53N 129 31 E
Yench'ih 106 37 47N 107 24 E
Yenchihsien 107 42 46N 129 24 E
Yenchin 108 28 4N 104 14 E
Yench'ing 106 40 28N 115 58 E
Yenching 108 29 7N 98 33 E
Yenchou 105 35 40N 116 50 E
Yench'uan 106 36 52N 110 11 E
Yenda 141 34 13 S 146 14 E
Yendéré 120 10 12N 4 59W
Yendi 121 9 29N 0 1W
Yenfeng 108 25 52N 101 5 E
Yenho 108 28 35N 108 28 E
Yenhsing 108 25 22N 101 44 E
Yenisaía 68 41 1N 24 57 E
Yenisey, R. 76 68 0N 86 30 E
Yeniseysk 77 58 39N 92 4 E
Yeniseyskiy Zaliv 76 72 20N 81 0 E
Yenne 45 45 43N 5 44 E
Yenotyevka 83 47 15N 47 0 E
Yenpien 108 26 54N 101 34 E
Yenshan, Hopeh, China 107 38 3N 117 12 E
Yenshan, Yunnan, China 108 23 40N 104 22 E
Yenshou 107 45 27N 128 19 E
Yent'ai 107 37 35N 121 25 E
Yent'ing 108 31 19N 105 20 E
Yenyüan 108 27 25N 101 33 E
Yenyuka 77 58 20N 121 30 E
Yeo, L. 137 28 0 S 124 30 E
Yeo, R. 28 51 1N 2 46W
Yeola 96 20 0N 74 30 E
Yeotmal 96 20 20N 78 15 E
Yeoval 141 32 41 S 148 39 E
Yeovil 28 50 57N 2 38W
Yepes 56 39 55N 3 39W
Yeppoon 138 23 5 S 150 47 E
Yeráki 69 37 0N 22 42 E
Yerbogachen 77 61 16N 108 0 E
Yerevan 83 40 10N 44 20 E
Yerilla 137 29 24 S 121 47 E
Yerington 163 38 59N 119 10W
Yerla, R. 96 17 35N 74 30 E
Yermakovo 77 52 35N 126 20 E
Yermo 163 34 58N 116 50W
Yermolayevo 78 52 58N 56 12 E
Yerofey Pavlovich 77 54 0N 122 0 E
Yerseke 47 51 29N 4 3 E
Yershov 81 51 15N 48 27 E
Yerūshalayim 90 31 47N 35 10 E
Yerville 42 49 40N 0 53 E
Yes Tor, Mt. 30 50 41N 3 59W
Yesagyo 98 21 38N 95 14 E
Yesan 107 36 41N 126 51 E
Yeşilirmak 82 41 0N 36 40 E
Yeso 159 34 29N 104 87W
Yessentuki 83 44 0N 42 45 E
Yeste 59 38 22N 2 19W
Yeu, I. d' 42 46 42N 2 20W
Yevlakh 83 40 39N 47 7 E
Yevpatoriya 82 45 15N 33 20 E
Yevstratovskiy 81 50 11N 39 2 E
Yeya, R. 83 46 40N 39 0 E
Yeysk Staro 82 46 40N 38 12 E
Yhati 172 25 45 S 56 35W
Yhú 173 25 0 S 56 0W
Yi, R. 172 33 7 S 57 8W
Yiali, I. 69 36 41N 27 11 E
Yiáltra 69 38 51N 22 59 E
Yianisádhes, I. 69 35 20N 26 10 E
Yiannitsa 68 40 46N 22 24 E
Yibal 91 22 10N 56 8 E
Yidhá 68 40 35N 22 53 E
Yinchiang 108 27 58N 108 20 E
Yinch'uan 105 38 30N 106 20 E
Yindarlgooda, L. 137 30 40 S 121 52 E
Ying Ho, R. 109 32 30N 116 32 E
Yingch'eng 109 30 55N 113 33 E
Yingchiang 108 24 48N 98 5 E
Yinghsien 106 39 36N 113 12 E
Yingk'ou 107 40 38N 122 30 E
Yingp'an, Chiang, G. 108 21 20N 109 30 E
Yingp'anshan 108 27 56N 105 34 E
Yingshan, Hupeh, China 109 31 37N 113 46 E
Yingshan, Hupeh, China 109 30 50N 115 45 E
Yingshan, Szechwan, China 108 31 6N 106 35 E
Yingshang 109 32 36N 116 16 E
Yingtan 105 28 12N 117 0 E
Yingte 109 24 10N 113 24 E
Yinkanie 140 34 22 S 140 17 E
Yinmabin 99 22 10N 94 55 E
Yinnietharra 137 24 39 S 116 12 E
Yioúra, I. 68 39 23N 24 10 E
Yipang 101 22 15N 101 26 E
Yirga Alem 124 6 34N 38 29 E
Yíthion 69 36 46N 22 34 E
Yizre'el 90 32 34N 35 19 E
Ylitornio 74 66 19N 23 39 E
Ylivieska 74 64 4N 24 28 E
Yngaren 73 58 50N 16 35 E
Ynykchanskiy 77 60 15N 137 43 E
Yoakum 159 29 20N 97 10W
Yobuko 110 33 32N 129 54 E
Yog Pt. 103 13 55N 124 20 E
Yogyakarta 103 7 49 S 110 22 E
Yoho Nat. Park 152 51 25N 116 30W
Yojoa, L. de 166 14 53N 88 0W
Yŏju 107 37 20N 127 35 E
Yokadouma 124 3 35N 14 50 E
Yōkaichi 111 35 6N 136 12 E
Yōkaichiba 111 35 42N 140 33 E
Yokkaichi 111 35 0N 136 30 E
Yoko 121 5 50N 12 20 E
Yokohama 111 35 27N 139 39 E
Yokosuka 111 35 20N 139 40 E
Yokote 112 39 20N 140 30 E
Yola 121 9 10N 12 29 E
Yolaina, Cordillera de 166 11 30N 84 0W
Yom Mae Nam 101 15 15N 100 20 E
Yonago 110 35 25N 133 19 E
Yŏnan 107 37 55N 126 11 E
Yonezawa 112 37 57N 140 4 E
Yong Peng 101 2 0N 103 3 E
Yong Sata 101 7 8N 99 41 E
Yongampo 107 39 56N 124 23 E
Yŏngchon 107 35 58N 128 56 E
Yŏngdŏk 107 36 24N 129 22 E
Yŏngdŭngpo 107 37 31N 126 54 E
Yŏnghŭng 107 39 31N 127 18 E
Yŏngju 107 36 50N 128 40 E
Yŏngwŏl 107 37 11N 128 28 E
Yonibana 120 8 30N 12 19W
Yonker 153 52 40N 109 40W
Yonkers 162 40 57N 73 51W
Yonne □ 43 47 50N 3 40 E
Yonne, R. 43 48 23N 2 58 E
Yonov 121 7 33N 8 42 E
Yoqueam 90 32 40N 35 6 E
York, Austral. 137 31 52 S 116 47 E
York, U.K. 33 53 58N 1 7W
York, Ala., U.S.A. 157 32 30N 88 18W
York, Nebr., U.S.A. 158 40 55N 97 35W
York, Pa., U.S.A. 162 39 57N 76 43W
York, C. 138 10 42 S 142 31 E
York Factory 153 57 0N 92 18W
York Haven 162 40 7N 76 46W
York, Kap 12 75 55N 66 25W
York, R. 162 37 15N 76 23W
York Sd. 136 14 50 S 125 5 E
York, Vale of 23 54 15N 1 25W
Yorke Pen. 140 34 50 S 137 40 E
Yorkshire Wolds 33 54 0N 0 30W
Yorkton 153 51 11N 102 28W
Yorktown, Tex., U.S.A. 159 29 0N 97 29W

Yorktown Zell

Yorktown, Va., U.S.A. 162 37 14N 76 30W
Yornup 137 34 2S 116 10E
Yoro 166 15 9N 87 7W
Yosemite National Park 163 38 0N 119 30W
Yosemite Village 163 37 45N 119 35W
Yoshii 110 33 16N 129 46E
Yoshimatsu 110 32 0N 130 47E
Yoshkar Ola 81 56 49N 47 10E
Yōsu 107 34 47N 127 45E
Youanmi 137 28 37S 118 49E
Youbou 152 48 53N 124 13W
Youghal 39 51 58N 7 51W
Youghal B. 39 51 55N 7 50W
Youkounkoun 120 12 35N 13 11W
Young, Austral. 141 34 19S 148 18E
Young, Can. 153 51 47N 105 45W
Young, Uruguay 172 32 44S 57 36W
Young, U.S.A. 161 34 9N 110 56W
Young Ra. 143 44 10S 169 30E
Younghusband, L. 140 30 50S 136 5E
Younghusband Pen. 140 36 0S 139 25E
Youngstown, Can. 153 51 35N 111 10W
Youngstown, U.S.A. 156 41 7N 80 41W
Youssoufia 118 32 16N 8 31W
Yoweragabbie 137 28 14S 117 39E
Yowrie 141 36 17S 149 46E
Yoxall 28 52 45N 1 49W
Yoxford 29 52 16N 1 30E
Yozgat 92 39 51N 34 47E
Ypané, R. 172 23 29S 57 19W
Yport 42 49 45N 0 15E
Ypres 47 50 50N 2 52E
Ypsilanti 156 42 18N 83 40W
Yreka 160 41 44N 122 40W
Ysabel Chan. 135 2 0S 150 0E
Ysbyty Ystwyth 31 52 20N 3 50W
Ysleta 161 31 45N 106 24W
Yssingeaux 45 45 9N 4 8E
Ystad 73 55 26N 13 50E
Ystalyfera 31 51 46N 3 48W
Ystradgynlais 31 51 47N 3 45W
Ystwyth, R. 31 52 24N 4 2W
Ythan, R. 37 57 26N 2 12W
Ytre Adal 71 60 15N 10 14E
Ytterhogdal 72 62 12N 14 56E
Ytyk-Kel 77 62 20N 133 28E
Yü Chiang, R., China 105 22 50N 108 6E
Yü Chiang, R., China 108 22 50N 108 6E
Yu Shui, R. 108 28 37N 110 23E
Yüan Chiang, R. 109 29 0N 111 50E
Yüan Chiang, R (Hong.) 108 29 12N 111 43E
Yüanan 109 31 3N 111 34E
Yüanchiang, Hünan, China 109 28 50N 112 23E
Yüanchiang, Yunnan, China 108 23 40N 102 0E
Yüanch'ü 106 35 18N 111 41E
Yüanli 109 24 27N 120 39E
Yüanlin 109 23 45N 120 30E
Yuanling 109 28 30N 110 5E
Yüanmou 108 25 42N 101 32E
Yuanyang 108 23 10N 102 58E
Yüanyang 108 35 3N 113 57E
Yuat, R. 135 4 10S 143 52E
Yuba City 160 39 12N 121 37W
Yübari 112 43 4N 141 59E
Yübetsu 112 43 13N 144 5E
Yucatán □ 165 21 30N 86 30W
Yucatán Basin 14 20 0N 84 0W
Yucatán Channel 166 22 0N 86 30W
Yucca 161 34 56N 114 6W
Yucca Valley 163 34 8N 116 30W
Yücha 108 26 55N 101 24E
Yucheng 106 36 55N 116 40E
Yüch'i 108 24 25N 102 35E
Yuch'i 109 26 10N 118 11E
Yüchiang 109 28 24N 116 53E
Yüch'ien 109 30 12N 119 24E
Yüch'ing 108 27 13N 107 54E
Yudino 76 55 10N 67 55E
Yüehhsi, Anhwei, China 109 30 54N 116 22E
Yüehhsi, Szechwan, China 108 28 36N 102 35E
Yüehyang 109 29 20N 113 7E
Yuendumu 136 22 16S 131 49E
Yufu-Dake 110 33 17N 131 33E
Yugoslavia ■ 66 44 0N 20 0E
Yühsien 106 34 10N 113 30E
Yuhsien, Hunan, China 109 27 2N 113 20E
Yuhsien, Shansi, China 106 38 5N 113 24E
Yühuan Tao, I. 109 28 5N 121 15E
Yukan 109 28 43N 116 35E
Yukhnov 80 54 44N 35 15E
Yüki 111 36 18N 139 53E
Yukon □ 147 63 0N 135 0W
Yukon, R. 147 65 30N 150 0W
Yukti 77 63 20N 105 0E
Yukuhashi 110 33 44N 130 59E
Yule, R. 136 20 24S 118 12E
Yuli 122 9 44N 10 12E
Yülin 100 18 10N 109 31E
Yulin, Guangdong, China 109 22 36N 110 7E
Yulin, Shensi, China 105 38 15N 109 30E
Yuma, Ariz., U.S.A. 161 32 45N 114 37W
Yuma, Colo., U.S.A. 158 40 10N 102 43W
Yuma, B. de 167 18 20N 68 35W
Yumali 140 35 32S 139 45E
Yumbe 126 3 28N 31 15E
Yumbi 126 1 12S 26 15E
Yumbo 174 3 35N 76 28W
Yümenhsien 105 40 17N 97 12E
Yün Ho 107 33 16N 118 45E
Yun Ho 109 35 0N 117 0E
Yuna 137 28 20S 115 0E
Yünan 109 23 14N 111 31E
Yunaska I. 147 52 40N 170 40W
Yünch'eng, Shansi, China 106 35 1N 110 59E
Yünch'eng, Shantung, China 106 35 35N 115 56E
Yunfou 109 22 56N 112 2E
Yungan 109 25 50N 117 25E
Yungas 174 17 0S 66 0W
Yungay 172 37 10S 72 5W
Yungch'eng 106 33 56N 116 22E
Yungchi 106 34 52N 110 26E
Yungch'ing 106 39 19N 116 29E
Yungch'uan 108 20 22N 105 52E
Yungch'un 109 25 19N 118 17E
Yungfeng 109 27 20N 115 27E
Yungfu 109 24 59N 109 59E
Yungho 106 36 44N 110 39E
Yunghsin 109 16 55N 114 18E
Yunghsing 109 26 8N 113 6E
Yunghsiu 109 29 8N 115 42E
Yungjen 108 26 4N 101 42E
Yungk'ang, Chekiang, China 109 28 53N 120 2E
Yungk'ang, Kwangsi Chuang Aut. Region, China 108 22 48N 107 51E
Yungnien 106 36 49N 114 33E
Yungning, Kwangsi Chuang A. R., China 108 22 45N 108 29E
Yungning, Ningsia Hui A. R., China 106 38 18N 106 18E
Yungning, Yunnan, China 108 27 50N 100 40E
Yungningchai 106 36 35N 108 51E
Yungp'ing 108 25 25N 99 36E
Yungshan 108 28 11N 103 35E
Yungsheng 108 26 42N 100 45E
Yungshun, Hunan, China 108 29 3N 109 50E
Yungshun, Kwangsi Chuang, China 108 22 48N 108 55E
Yungt'ai 109 25 52N 118 55E
Yungteng 106 36 44N 103 24E
Yungting 109 24 49N 116 46E
Yunho = Lishui 109 28 6N 119 34E
Yünhsi 109 33 0N 110 22E
Yünhsiao 109 24 1N 117 15E
Yünhsien, Hupeh, China 105 32 50N 110 53E
Yünhsien, Yunnan, China 108 24 25N 100 6E
Yünlin 109 23 42N 120 31E
Yunling Shan, mts. 108 28 30N 98 50E
Yunlung 99 25 50N 99 25E
Yünmeng 109 31 1N 113 39E
Yunnan □ 108 25 0N 102 30E
Yunndaga 137 29 45S 121 0E
Yunomae 110 32 12N 130 59E
Yunotso 110 35 5N 132 21E
Yunquera de Henares 58 40 47N 3 11W
Yunta 140 32 34S 139 36E
Yünyang 108 30 55N 108 56E
Yüp'ing 108 27 14N 108 54E
Yupyongdong 107 41 49N 128 53E
Yur 77 59 52N 137 49E
Yurga 76 55 42N 84 51E
Yuria 84 59 22N 54 10E
Yuribei 76 71 20N 76 30E
Yurimaguas 174 5 55S 76 0W
Yurya 81 59 1N 49 13E
Yuryev Polskiy 81 56 30N 59 47E
Yuryevets 81 57 25N 43 2E
Yuryuzan 84 54 27N 58 28E
Yuscarán 166 13 58N 86 51W
Yusha, Jebel 90 32 4N 35 41E
Yüshan 109 28 40N 118 15E
Yüshanchen 108 29 31N 108 25E
Yushe 106 37 4N 112 58E
Yüshu 105 33 1N 96 44E
Yushu 107 44 46N 126 34E
Yüt'ai 106 35 2N 116 40E
Yüt'ien 107 39 53N 117 45E
Yütu 109 26 0N 115 24E
Yütz'u 106 37 42N 112 44E
Yüwang 106 37 9N 106 28E
Yuyang 108 28 44N 108 46E
Yüyang 109 30 12N 119 56E
Yüyao 109 30 3N 121 9E
Yuyao 109 30 0N 121 20E
Yuyu 105 40 20N 112 30E
Yuyü 106 40 10N 112 25E
Yüyuan 109 28 9N 121 11E
Yuzha 81 56 40N 42 10E
Yuzhno-Sakhalinsk 77 47 5N 142 5E
Yuzhno-Surkhanskoye Vodokhranilishehe 85 37 53N 67 42E
Yuzhno-Uralsk 84 54 26N 61 15E
Yuzhnyy Ural, mts. 84 53 0N 58 0E
Yvelines □ 43 48 40N 1 45E
Yverdon 50 46 47N 6 39E
Yvetot 42 49 37N 0 44E
Yvonand 50 46 48N 6 44E

Z

Za, O. 118 34 5N 2 30W
Zaalayskiy Khrebet 85 39 20N 73 0E
Zaamslag 47 51 19N 3 55E
Zaan, R. 46 52 25N 4 52E
Zaandam 47 52 26N 4 49E
Zab, Monts du 119 34 55N 5 0E
Zabalj, Yugo. 66 45 21N 20 5E
Zabalj, Yugo. 66 45 23N 20 5E
Zabari 66 44 22N 21 15E
Zabarjad 122 23 40N 36 12E
Zabaykalskiy 77 49 40N 117 10E
Zabkowice Slaskie 54 50 22N 19 17E
Zabljak 66 42 19N 19 10E
Zabludow 54 53 0N 23 19E
Zabno 54 50 9N 20 53E
Zābol 93 31 0N 61 25E
Zābolī 93 27 10N 61 35E
Zabré 121 11 12N 0 36W
Zabrze 54 50 24N 18 50E
Zacapa 166 14 59N 89 31W
Zacapu 164 19 50N 101 43W
Zacatecas 164 22 49N 102 34W
Zacatecas □ 164 23 30N 103 0W
Zacatecolua 166 13 29N 88 51W
Zacaultipán 165 20 39N 98 36W
Zacoalco 164 20 10N 103 40W
Zadar 63 44 8N 15 8E
Zadawa 121 11 33N 10 19E
Zadetkyi Kyun 101 10 0N 98 25E
Zadonsk 81 52 25N 38 56E
Zafed 90 32 58N 35 29E
Zafora, I. 69 36 5N 26 24E
Zafra 57 38 26N 6 30W
Zagan 54 51 39N 15 22E
Zagazig 122 30 40N 31 12E
Zaghouan 119 36 23N 10 10E
Zaglivérion 68 40 36N 23 15E
Zaglou 118 27 17N 0 3W
Zagnanado 121 7 18N 2 28E
Zagorá 68 39 27N 23 6E
Zagora 118 30 14N 5 51W
Zagórów 54 52 10N 17 54E
Zagorsk 81 56 20N 38 10E
Zagórz 54 49 30N 22 14E
Zagreb 63 45 50N 16 0E
Zāgros, Kudha-ye 93 33 45N 47 0E
Zagubica 66 44 15N 21 47E
Zaguinaso 120 10 1N 6 14W
Zāhedān 93 29 30N 60 50E
Zahirabad 96 17 43N 77 37E
Zahlah 92 33 52N 35 50E
Zahna 48 51 54N 12 47E
Zahrez Chergui 118 35 0N 3 30E
Zahrez Rharbi 118 34 50N 2 55E
Zailiyskiy Alatau, Khrebet 85 43 5N 77 0E
Zainsk 84 55 18N 52 4E
Zaïr 118 29 47N 5 51W
Zaïre, R. 124 1 30N 28 0E
Zaïre, Rep. of ■ 124 3 0S 23 0E
Zaječar 66 43 53N 22 18E
Zakamensk 77 50 23N 103 17E
Zakariya 90 31 43N 34 57E
Zakataly 83 41 38N 46 35E
Zakavkazye 83 42 0N 44 0E
Zakhu 92 37 10N 42 50E
Zákinthos 69 37 47N 20 54E
Zákinthos, I. 69 37 45N 27 45E
Zakopane 54 49 18N 19 57E
Zala □ 53 46 42N 16 50E
Zala, R. 53 46 53N 17 6E
Zalaegerszeg 53 46 53N 16 47E
Zalakomár 53 46 33N 17 10E
Zalalövö 53 46 51N 16 35E
Zalamea de la Serena 57 38 40N 5 38W
Zalamea la Real 57 37 41N 6 38W
Zalau 121 10 30N 8 58E
Zalazna 84 58 39N 52 31E
Zalec 63 46 16N 15 10E
Zaleshchiki 82 48 45N 25 45E
Zalewo 54 53 55N 19 41E
Zalingei 117 13 5N 23 10E
Zalţan, Jabal 119 28 46N 19 45E
Zaltbommel 46 51 48N 5 15E
Zalŭ 121 47 12N 23 5E
Zambeke 126 2 8N 25 17E
Zambèze, R. 127 18 46S 36 16E
Zambezi, R. 127 18 46S 36 16E
Zambezia □ 127 16 15S 37 30E
Zambia ■ 125 15 0S 28 0E
Zamboanga 103 6 59N 122 3E
Zambrano 174 9 45N 74 49W
Zametchino 81 53 30N 42 30E
Zamora, Mexico 164 20 0N 102 21W
Zamora, Spain 56 41 30N 5 45W
Zamora □ 56 41 30N 5 46W
Zamość 54 50 50N 23 22E
Zamuro, Sierra del 174 4 0N 62 30W
Zamzam, W. 119 31 0N 14 30E
Zan 121 9 26N 0 17W
Zanaga 124 2 48S 13 48E
Záncara, R. 58 39 20N 3 0W
Zandvoort 46 52 22N 4 32E
Zanesville 156 39 56N 82 2W
Zangue, R. 127 18 5S 35 10E
Zanjan 92 36 40N 48 35E
Zannone, I. 64 40 38N 13 2E
Zante = Zákinthos 69 37 47N 20 54E
Zanthus 137 31 2S 123 34E
Zanzibar 126 6 12S 39 12E
Zanzibar I. 126 6 12S 39 12E
Zanzūr 119 32 55N 13 1E
Zaouatalaz 119 24 57N 8 16E
* Zaouiet El Kahla 119 27 10N 6 40E
Zaouiet Reggane 118 26 32N 0 3E
Zapadna Morava, R. 66 43 50N 20 15E
Zapadnaya Dvina 80 56 15N 32 3E
Západné Beskydy 54 49 30N 19 0E
Západočeský □ 52 49 35N 13 0E
Západoslovenský □ 53 48 30N 17 30E
Zapala 176 39 0S 70 5W
Zapaleri, Cerro 172 22 49S 67 11W
Zapata 159 26 56N 92 17W
Zapatón, R. 57 39 0N 6 49W
Zaporozhye 82 47 50N 35 10E
Zapponeta 65 41 27N 15 57E
Zara 92 39 58N 37 43E
Zaragoza, Colomb. 174 7 30N 74 52W
Zaragoza, Coahuila, Mexico 164 28 30N 101 0W
Zaragoza, Nuevo León, Mexico 165 24 0N 99 36W
Zaragoza, Spain 58 41 39N 0 53W
Zaragoza □ 58 41 35N 1 0W
Zarand 93 30 46N 56 34E
Zarasai 80 55 40N 26 12E
Zarate 172 34 7S 59 0W
Zaraysk 81 54 48N 38 53E
Zaraza 174 9 21N 65 19W
Zarembo I. 152 56 20N 132 50W
Zari 73 13 8N 12 37E
Zaria 121 11 0N 7 40E
Zarisberge 128 24 30S 16 15E
Zarki 54 50 38N 19 21E
Zarnów 54 51 16N 20 9E
Zarnuqa 90 31 53N 34 47E
Zarów 54 50 56N 16 29E
Zarqa, R. 90 32 10N 35 37E
Zaruma 174 3 40S 79 30W
Zary 54 51 37N 15 10E
Zarza de Alange 57 38 49N 6 13W
Zarza de Granadilla 56 40 14N 6 3W
Zarza, La 57 37 42N 6 51W
Zarzaïtine 119 28 32N 9 5E
Zarzal 174 4 24N 76 4W
Zarzis 119 33 31N 11 2E
Zas 56 43 4N 8 53W
Zashiversk 77 67 25N 142 40E
Zaskar Mountains 95 33 15N 77 30E
Zaskar, R. 95 33 55N 77 2E
Zastron 128 30 18S 27 7E
Zatec 52 50 20N 13 32E
Zator 54 49 59N 19 28E
Zavala 66 42 50N 17 59E
Zavareh 93 33 35N 52 28E
Zaventem 47 50 53N 4 28E
Zavetnoye 83 47 13N 43 50E
Zavidovići 66 44 27N 18 13E
Zavitinsk 77 50 10N 129 20E
Zavodoski, I. 13 56 0S 27 45W
Zavolzhye 81 56 37N 43 18E
Zawadzkie 54 50 37N 18 28E
Zawidów 54 51 1N 15 1E
Zawiercie 54 50 30N 19 13E
Zâwyet Shammâs 122 31 30N 26 37E
Zâwyet Um el Rakham 122 31 18N 27 1E
Zâwyet Ungeila 122 31 23N 26 42E
Zayandeh, R. 93 32 35N 32 0E
Zayarsk 77 56 20N 102 55E
Zaysan 76 47 28N 84 52E
Zaysan, Oz. 76 48 0N 83 0E
Zãzamt, W. 119 30 29N 14 30E
Zazir, O. 119 22 0N 5 40E
Zázrivá 53 49 16N 19 7E
Zbarazh 80 49 43N 25 44E
Zbaszyn 54 52 14N 15 56E
Zbaszynek 54 52 16N 15 51E
Zblewo 54 53 56N 18 19E
Zdandijk 46 52 82N 4 49E
Zdolbunov 80 50 30N 26 15E
Zdrelo 66 44 16N 21 28E
Zdunska Wola 54 51 37N 18 59E
Zduny 54 51 39N 17 21E
Zeballos 152 49 59N 126 50W
Zebediela 129 24 20S 29 17E
Zedelgem 47 51 8N 3 8E
Zeebrugge 47 51 19N 3 12E
Zeehan 138 41 52S 145 25E
Zeeland 47 51 41N 5 40E
Zeeland □ 47 51 30N 3 50E
Ze'elim 90 31 13N 34 32E
Zeelst 47 51 25N 5 25E
Zeerust 128 25 31S 26 4E
Zefat 90 32 58N 35 29E
Zegdou 118 29 51N 4 53W
Zege 123 11 43N 37 18E
Zegelsem 47 50 49N 3 43E
Zegoua 120 10 32N 5 35W
Zehdenick 48 52 59N 13 20E
Zeil, Mt. 136 23 24S 132 23E
Zeila 91 11 15N 43 30E
Zeist 46 52 5N 5 15E
Zeita 90 32 23N 35 2E
Zeitz 48 51 3N 12 9E
Zele 47 51 4N 4 2E
Zelendolsk 81 55 55N 48 30E
Zelengora, mts. 66 43 22N 18 30E
Zelenika 66 42 27N 18 37E
Zelenogradsk 54 53 53N 20 29E
Zelenokumsk 83 44 30N 44 1E
Zelenovski 83 48 6N 50 45E
Zelhem 47 52 0N 6 21E
Zell 49 47 42N 7 50E

*Renamed Bordj Omar Driss

Zell am See	**52**	47 19N	12 47 E
Zella Mehlis	**48**	50 40N	10 41 E
Zelouane	**86**	35 1N	2 58W
Zelzate	**47**	51 13N	3 47 E
Zémio	**126**	5 2N	25 5 E
Zemmora	**118**	35 44N	0 51 E
Zemora, I.	**119**	37 5N	10 56 E
Zemoul, W.	**118**	29 15N	7 30W
Zemst	**47**	50 59N	4 28 E
Zemun	**66**	44 51N	20 25 E
Zenica	**66**	44 10N	17 57 E
Zenina	**118**	34 30N	2 37 E
Zentsūji	**110**	34 14N	133 47 E
Zepce	**66**	44 28N	18 2 E
Zeravshan	**85**	39 10N	68 39 E
Zeravshan, R.	**85**	39 32N	63 45 E
Zeravshanskiy, Khrebet	**85**	39 20N	69 0 E
Zerbst	**48**	51 59N	12 8 E
Zerhamra	**118**	29 58N	2 30W
Zerków	**54**	52 4N	17 32 E
Zermatt	**50**	46 2N	7 46 E
Zernez	**51**	46 42N	10 7 E
Zernograd	**83**	46 52N	40 11 E
Zeroud, O.	**119**	35 30N	9 30 E
Zerqani	**68**	41 30N	20 20 E
Zestafoni	**83**	42 6N	43 0 E
Zetel	**48**	53 33N	7 57 E
Zetland (□)	**26**	60 30N	0 15W
Zetten	**46**	51 56N	5 44 E
Zeulenroda	**48**	50 39N	12 0 E
Zeven	**48**	53 17N	9 19 E
Zevenaar	**46**	51 56N	6 5 E
Zevenbergen	**47**	51 38N	4 37 E
Zévio	**62**	45 23N	11 10 E
Zeya	**77**	54 2N	127 20 E
Zeya, R.	**77**	53 30N	127 0 E
Zeyse	**123**	5 44N	37 23W
Zeytin	**92**	37 53N	36 53 E
Zêzere, R.	**56**	40 0N	7 55W
Zgierz	**54**	51 45N	19 27 E
Zgorzelec	**54**	51 10N	15 0 E
Zhabinka	**80**	52 13N	24 2 E
Zhailma	**84**	51 30N	61 50 E
Zhalanash	**85**	43 3N	78 38 E
Zhamensk	**80**	54 37N	21 17 E
Zhanadarya	**85**	44 45N	64 40 E
Zhanatas	**76**	43 11N	81 18 E
Zharkol	**84**	49 57N	64 5 E
Zharkovskiy	**80**	55 56N	32 19 E
Zhashkov	**82**	49 15N	30 5 E
Zhdanov	**82**	47 5N	37 31 E
Zheleznogorsk-Ilimskiy	**77**	56 34N	104 8 E
Zherdevka	**81**	51 56N	41 21 E
Zhetykol, Ozero	**84**	51 2N	60 54 E
Zhigansk	**77**	66 35N	124 10 E
Zhigulevsk	**81**	53 28N	49 45 E
Zhirhovsk	**81**	50 57N	44 49 E
Zhitomir	**80**	50 20N	28 40 E
Zhizdra	**80**	53 45N	34 40 E
Zhlobin	**80**	52 55N	30 0 E
Zhmerinka	**82**	49 2N	28 10 E
Zhodino	**80**	54 5N	28 17 E
Zhovtnevoye	**82**	47 54N	32 2 E
Zhuantobe	**85**	43 43N	78 18 E
Zhukovka	**80**	53 35N	33 50 E
Zhupanovo	**77**	51 59N	15 9 E
Ziarat	**94**	30 25N	67 30 E
Zichem	**47**	51 2N	4 59 E
Ziebice	**54**	50 37N	17 2 E
Ziel, Mt.	**136**	23 20 S	132 30 E
Zielona Góra	**54**	51 57N	15 31 E
Zielona Góra □	**54**	51 57N	15 30 E
Zierikzee	**47**	51 40N	3 55 E
Ziesar	**48**	52 16N	12 19 E
Zifta	**122**	30 43N	31 14 E
Zigazinskiy	**84**	53 50N	57 20 E
Zigey	**117**	14 50N	15 50 E
Ziguinchor	**120**	12 25N	16 20W
Zihuatanejo	**164**	17 38N	101 33W
Zikhron Ya'Aqov	**90**	32 34N	34 56 E
Zile	**92**	40 15N	36 0 E
Zilfi	**92**	26 12N	44 52 E
Zilina	**53**	49 12N	18 42 E
Zillah	**119**	28 40N	17 41 E
Zillertaler Alpen	**52**	47 6N	11 45 E
Zima	**77**	54 0N	102 5 E
Zimane, Adrar in	**118**	22 10N	4 30 E
Zimapán	**165**	20 40N	99 20W
Zimba	**127**	17 20 S	26 25 E
Zimbabwe ■	**127**	20 16 S	31 0 E
Zimovniki	**83**	47 10N	42 25 E
Zinal	**50**	46 8N	7 38 E
Zinder	**121**	13 48N	9 0 E
Zinga	**127**	9 16 S	38 41 E
Zingem	**47**	50 54N	3 40 E
Zingst	**48**	54 24N	12 45 E
Zini, Yebel	**118**	28 0N	11 0W
Ziniaré	**121**	12 44N	1 10W
Zinjibar	**91**	13 5N	46 0 E
Zinkgruvan	**73**	58 50N	15 6 E
Zinnowitz	**48**	54 5N	13 54 E
Zion Nat. Park	**161**	37 25N	112 50W
Zipaquirá	**174**	5 0N	74 0W
Zippori	**90**	32 64N	35 16 E
Zirc	**53**	47 17N	17 42 E
Ziri	**63**	47 17N	11 14 E
Zirje, I.	**63**	43 39N	15 42 E
Zirl	**52**	47 17N	11 14 E
Zisterdorf	**53**	48 33N	16 45 E
Zitácuaro	**164**	19 20N	100 30W
Zitava, R.	**53**	48 14N	18 21 E
Zitiste	**66**	45 30N	2 32 E
Zitsa	**68**	39 47N	20 40 E
Zittau	**48**	50 54N	14 47 E
Zitundo	**129**	26 48 S	32 47 E
Zivinice	**66**	44 27N	18 36 E
Ziway, L.	**123**	8 0N	38 50 E
Ziz, Oued	**118**	31 40N	4 15W
Zizip	**92**	37 5N	37 50 E
Zlarin	**63**	43 42N	15 49 E
Zlatar	**63**	46 5N	16 3 E
Zlataritsa	**67**	43 2N	24 55 E
Zlatibor	**66**	43 45N	19 43 E
Zlatista	**67**	42 41N	24 7 E
Zlatna	**70**	46 8N	23 11 E
Zlatograd	**67**	41 22N	25 7 E
Zlatoust	**78**	55 10N	59 40 E
Zletovo	**66**	41 59N	22 17 E
Zlitan	**119**	32 25N	14 35 E
Złocieniec	**54**	53 30N	16 1 E
Złoczew	**54**	51 24N	18 35 E
Zlot	**66**	44 1N	22 0 E
Złotoryja	**54**	51 8N	15 55 E
Złotów	**54**	53 22N	17 2 E
Złoty Stok	**54**	50 27N	16 53 E
Zmeinogorsk	**76**	51 10N	82 13 E
Zmigród	**54**	51 28N	16 53 E
Zmiyev	**82**	49 45N	36 27 E
Znamenka	**82**	48 45N	32 30 E
Znin	**54**	52 51N	17 44 E
Znojmo	**52**	48 50N	16 2 E
Zoar	**128**	33 30 S	21 26 E
Zobia	**126**	3 0N	25 50 E
Zoetermeer	**46**	52 3N	4 30 E
Zofingen	**50**	47 17N	7 56 E
Zogno	**62**	45 49N	9 41 E
Zolder	**47**	51 1N	5 19 E
Zollikofen	**50**	47 0N	7 28 E
Zollikon	**51**	47 21N	8 34 E
Zolochev	**80**	49 45N	24 58 E
Zolotonosha	**82**	49 45N	32 5 E
Zomba	**127**	15 30 S	35 19 E
Zombi	**126**	3 35N	29 10 E
Zomergem	**47**	51 7N	3 33 E
Zongo	**124**	4 12N	18 0 E
Zonguldak	**82**	41 28N	31 50 E
Zonhoven	**47**	50 59N	5 23 E
Zorgo	**121**	12 22N	0 35W
Zorita	**57**	39 17N	5 39W
Zorleni	**70**	46 14N	27 44 E
Zornitsa	**67**	42 23N	26 58 E
Zorritos	**174**	3 50 S	80 40W
Zory	**54**	50 3N	18 44 E
Zorzor	**120**	7 46N	9 28W
Zossen	**48**	52 13N	13 28 E
Zottegam	**47**	50 52N	3 48 E
Zouar	**119**	20 30N	16 32 E
Zouérabe	**116**	22 35N	12 30W
Zousfana, O.	**118**	31 51N	1 30W
Zoutkamp	**46**	53 20N	6 18 E
Zqorzelec	**54**	51 9N	15 0 E
Zrenjanin	**66**	45 22N	20 23 E
Zuarungu	**121**	10 49N	0 52W
Zuba	**121**	9 11N	7 12 E
Zubair, Jazāir	**123**	15 0N	42 10 E
Zubia	**57**	37 8N	3 33W
Zubtsov	**80**	56 10N	34 34 E
Zueitina	**119**	30 58N	20 7 E
Zuénoula	**120**	7 34N	6 3W
Zuera	**58**	41 51N	0 49W
Zug	**51**	47 10N	8 31 E
Zug □	**51**	47 9N	8 35 E
Zugar	**123**	14 0N	42 40 E
Zugdidi	**83**	42 30N	41 48 E
Zugersee	**51**	47 7N	8 35 E
Zugspitze	**49**	47 25N	10 59 E
Zuid-Holland □	**46**	52 0N	4 35 E
Zuid-horn	**46**	53 15N	6 23 E
Zuidbeveland	**47**	51 30N	3 50 E
Zuidbroek	**46**	53 10N	6 52 E
Zuidelijk-Flevoland	**46**	52 22N	5 22 E
Zuidlaarder meer	**46**	53 8N	6 42 E
Zuidland	**46**	51 49N	4 15 E
Zuidlaren	**46**	53 6N	6 42 E
Zuidwolde	**46**	52 40N	6 26 E
Zújar	**59**	37 34N	2 50W
Zújar, Pantano del	**57**	38 55N	5 35W
Zújar, R.	**59**	38 30N	5 30 E
Zula	**123**	15 17N	39 40 E
Zulia □	**174**	10 0N	72 10W
Zülpich	**48**	50 41N	6 38 E
Zululand	**129**	43 19N	2 15W
Zumaya	**58**	43 19N	2 15W
Zumbo	**127**	15 35 S	30 26 E
Zummo	**121**	9 51N	12 59 E
Zumpango	**165**	19 48N	99 6W
Zundert	**47**	51 28N	4 39 E
Zungeru	**121**	9 48N	6 8 E
Zuni	**161**	35 7N	108 57W
Zupania	**66**	45 4N	18 43 E
Zur	**66**	42 13N	20 34 E
Zura	**84**	57 36N	53 24 E
Zūrandului	**70**	46 14N	22 7 E
Zürich	**51**	47 22N	8 32 E
Zürich □	**51**	47 26N	8 40 E
Zürichsee	**51**	47 18N	8 40 E
Zuromin	**54**	53 4N	19 57 E
Zuru	**121**	11 27N	5 4 E
Zurzach	**51**	47 35N	8 18 E
Zut, I.	**63**	43 52N	15 17 E
Zutendaal	**47**	50 56N	5 35 E
Zutphen	**46**	52 9N	6 12 E
Zuwárrah	**119**	32 58N	12 1 E
Zuyevka	**84**	58 27N	51 10 E
Zuzemberk	**63**	45 52N	14 56 E
Zvenigorodka	**82**	49 4N	30 56 E
Zverinogolovskoye	**84**	55 0N	62 30 E
Zvezdets	**67**	42 6N	27 26 E
Zvolen	**53**	48 33N	19 10 E
Zvonce	**66**	42 57N	22 34 E
Zvornik	**66**	44 26N	19 7 E
Zwaag	**46**	52 40N	5 4 E
Zwanenburg	**46**	52 23N	4 45 E
Zwarte Meer	**46**	52 38N	5 57 E
Zwarte Waler	**46**	52 39N	6 1 E
Zwartemeer	**46**	52 43N	7 2 E
Zwartsluis	**46**	52 39N	6 4 E
Zwedru (Tchien)	**120**	5 59N	8 15W
Zweibrücken	**49**	49 15N	7 20 E
Zwenkau	**48**	51 13N	12 19 E
Zwetti	**52**	48 35N	15 9 E
Zwickau	**48**	50 43N	12 30 E
Zwijnaarde	**47**	51 0N	3 43 E
Zwijndrecht, Belg.	**47**	51 13N	4 20 E
Zwijndrecht, Neth.	**46**	51 50N	4 39 E
Zwolle	**46**	52 31N	6 6 E
Zymoelz, R.	**152**	54 33N	128 31W
Zyrardów	**54**	52 3N	20 35 E
Zywiec	**54**	44 42N	19 12 E

Recent Place-Name Changes

The following place-name changes have recently occurred in Angola, Iran, Madagascar, Mozambique, Vietnam and Zimbabwe. The new names are given on the maps but the former names are in the index.

Angola

Former Name	New name
Ambrizete	Nzeto
Artur de Paiva	Capelongo
Bié	Kuito
Cassinga	Kassinga
Dundo	Luachimo
General Machado	Camacupa
João de Almeida	Chibia
Macedo do Cavaleiros	Andulo
Mariano Machado	Ganda
Moçâmedes	Namibe
Nova Redondo	Ngunza
Ongiva	Ngiva
Paiva Couceiro	Gambos
Robert Williams	Caála
Roçadas	Xangongo
San António do Zaïre	Soyo
Teixeira da Silva	Bailundo
Vila Ariaga	Bibala
Vila Marechal Carmona	Uíge

Iran

Former name	New name
Bandar-e Pahlaví	Bandar-e Anzalī
Bandar-e Shah	Bandar-e Torkeman
Bandar-e Shahpur	Bandar-e Khomeynī
Dehkhvareqan	Āzar Shahr
Dezh Shahpur	Marīvan
Kermanshah	Qahremānshahr
Khorramshahr	Khorramshahr (Khūnīnshahr)
Naft Shah	Naftshahr
Reza'iyeh	Orūmīyeh
Reza'iyeh, Daryacheh-ye	Orūmīyeh, Daryācheh-ye
Sar Eskand Khan	Āzarān
Shāhābād	Eslāmābād-e Gharb
Shāhī	Qā'emshahr
Shahpur	Salmās
Shahreza	Qomsheh
Shāhrud	Emāmrūd
Shahsavar	Tunekābon
Soltaniyeh	Saʿīdīyeh

Madagascar

Former name	New name
Ambre, C. de	Bobaomby, Tanjon'i
Ambre, Mt. d'	Ambohitra
Brickaville	Vohibinany
Chesterfield I.	Vestale, Toraka
Diégo Suarez	Antsirañana
Fénérive	Fenoarivo Atsinanana
Fort-Dauphin	Faradofay
Majunga	Mahajanga
Midongy du Sud	Midongy Atsimo
Ste. Marie, C.	Vohimena, T.'i
Ste. Marie, I.	Boraha, Nosy
Tamatave	Toamasina
Tuléar	Toliara

Mozambique

Former name	New name
Augusto Cardosa	Metangula
Entre Rios	Malema
Malvérnia	Chicualacuala
Mau-é-ele	Marão
Olivença	Lupilichi
Vila Alferes Chamusca	Guijá
Vila Caldas Xavier	Muende
Vila Coutinho	Ulonguè
Vila Fontes	Caia
Vila de Junqueiro	Gurué
Vila Luísa	Marracuene
Vila Paiva de Andrada	Gorongoza

Vietnam

Former name	New name
An Loc	Hon Quan
An Tuc	An Khe
Chau Phu	Chau Doc
Dien Bien Phu	Dien Bien
Hau Bon	Cheo Reo
Khanh Hung	Soc Trang
Kien Hung	Go Quao
Phuoc Le	Ba Ria
Quan Long	Ca Mau
Truc Giang	Ben Tre

Zimbabwe

Former name	New name
Balla Balla	Mbalabala
Belingwe	Mberengwa
Chipinga	Chipinge
Dett	Dete
Enkeldoorn	Chivhu
Essexvale	Esigodini
Fort Victoria	Masvingo
Gwelo	Gweru
Hartley	Chegutu
Gatooma	Kadoma
Inyazura	Nyazura
Marandellas	Marondera
Mashaba	Mashava
Melsetter	Chimanimani
Mrewa	Murewa
Mtoko	Mutoko
Nuanetsi	Mwenezi
Que Que	Kwekwe
Salisbury	Harare
Selukwe	Shurugwi
Shabani	Zvishavane
Sinoia	Chinhoyi
Somabula	Somabhula
Tjolotjo	Tsholotsho
Umvuma	Mvuma
Umtali	Mutare
Wankie	Hwange

Chinese Place-Names

The following list gives the Pin Yin nameform and the modified Wade-Giles nameform for the principal places in China. Pin Yin is officially approved by the Chinese and is gaining in use throughout the world. Wade-Giles is the transcription selected for the maps and index in this atlas and is still extensively used in the West.

Pin Yin	Wade-Giles	Pin Yin	Wade-Giles	Pin Yin	Wade-Giles
Anhui	Anhwei	Jiangxi	Kiangsi	Taizhou	T'aichou
Anqing	Anch'ing	Jiaxing	Chiahsing	Tandong	T'antung
Baoding	Paoting	Jilin	Chilin	Tanggula Shan	T'angkula Shanmo
Baoji	Paochi	Jinan	Chinan	Tian Shan	Tien Shan
Baotou	Paot'ou	Jingdezhen	Chingtechen	Tianjin	T'ienching
Bei'an	Peian	Jinhua	Chinhua	Tianshui	Tienshui
Beihai	Peihai	Jining	Chining	Tongchuan	Tungchwan
Beijing	Peip'ing	Jinxi	Chinhsi	Tonghua	T'unghua
Bengbu	Pangfou	Jinxian	Chinhsien	Tongling	Tungling
Benxi	Pench'i	Jinzhou	Chinchou	Ürümqi	Wulumuchi
Boshan	Poshan	Jiujiang	Chiuchiang	Wanxian	Wanhsien
Cangzhou	Ts'angchou	Jixi	Chihsi	Wenzhou	Wenchou
Changchi	Ch'angchih	Junggur Pendi	Dzungaria	Wutongqiao	Wut'ungchi'ao
Changchun	Ch'angch'un	Kashi	Kashgar	Wuxi	Wuhsi
Changde	Changt'e	Lanzhou	Lanchou	Wuzhou	Wuchou
Changsha	Ch'angsha	Lianyungan	Lienyünchiangshih	Xiaguan	Hsiakuan
Changshu	Ch'angshu	Liuzhou	Liuchou	Xiamen	Hsiamen
Changzhou	Ch'angchou	Lüda	Lüta	Xi'an	Hsian
Chengde	Ch'engte	Luoshan	Loshan	Xiangfan	Hsiangfan
Chengdu	Ch'engtu	Luoyang	Loyang	Xiangtan	Hsiangt'an
Chongqing	Ch'ungch'ing	Luzhou	Luchou	Xianyang	Hsienyang
Da Hinggan Ling	Tahsinganling Shanmo	Manzhouli	Manchouli	Xiao Hinggan Ling	Hsiaohsinganling Shanmo
Datong	Tat'ung	Meixian	Meihsien		
Dezhou	Techou	Mudanjiang	Mutanchiang	Xingtai	Hsingt'ai
Dongchuan	Tungch'uan	Nanchong	Nanch'ung	Xining	Hsinging
Duyun	Tuyün	Nanjing	Nanching	Xinjiang Uygur Zizhiqu	Singkiang-Uigur
Fujian	Fukien	Nantong	Nant'ung	Xinjin	Hsinchin
Fuxin	Fouhsinshin	Nanzhang	Nanch'ang	Xinxiang	Hsinhsiang
Fuzhou	Fuchou	Neijiang	Neichiang	Xuanhua	Hsüanhua
Gansu	Kansu	Ningbo	Ningpo	Xuchang	Hsüch'ang
Ganzhou	Kanchou	Ningxia Huizu Zizhiqu	Ningsia Hui	Xuzhou	Hsüchou
Gejiu	Kochiu	Pingdingshan	P'ingt'ingshan	Yangquan	Yangch'üan
Guangdong	Kwangtung	Pingxiang	P'inghsiang	Yangzhou	Yangchou
Guangxi Zhuangzu Zizhiqu	Kwangsi-Chuang	Qaidam Pendi	Tsaidam	Yanji	Yenchi
Guangzhou	Kuangchou	Qingdao	Ch'ingtao	Yanjin	Yench'eng
Guilin	Kueilin	Qinghai	Tsinghai	Yantai	Yent'ai
Guiyang	Kueiyang	Qingjiang	Ch'ingchiang	Yibin	Ipin
Guizhou	Kweichow	Qinhuangdao	Ch'inhuangtao	Yichang	Ich'ang
Hangzhou	Hangchou	Qiqihar	Ch'ich'ihaerh	Yingchuan	Yinch'uan
Harbin	Haerhpin	Quanzhou	Ch'üanchou	Yining	Ining
Hebei	Hopei	Rugao	Jukao	Yiyang	Iyang
Hebi	Haopi	Sanmenxia	Sanmenhsia	Yuci	Yutz'ü
Hechuan	Hoch'uan	Shaanxi	Shensi	Zaozhuang	Tsaochuang
Hefei	Hofei	Shandong	Shantung	Zhangjiakou	Changchiak'ou
Hegang	Haokang	Shangqiu	Shangch'iu	Zhangjiang	Chanchiang
Heilong Jiang	Heilungkiang	Shangrao	Shangjao	Zhangzhou	Changchou
Henan	Honan	Shanxi	Shansi	Zhao'an	Ch'aoan
Hohhot	Huhohaot'e	Shaoguan	Shaokuan	Zhejiang	Chekiang
Huaide	Huaite	Shaoxing	Shaohsing	Zhengzhou	Chengchou
Huangshi	Huangshih	Shijiazhuang	Shihchiachuangi	Zhenjiang	Chenchiang
Hubei	Hupei	Shizuishan	Shihtsuishan	Zhuhai	Chuhai
Jiamusi	Chiamussu	Shunde	Shunte	Zhuzhou	Chuchou
Ji'an	Chian	Sichuan	Szechwan	Zigong	Tzukung
Jiangmen	Chiangmen	Siping	Ssup'ing	Zunyi	Tsuni
Jiangsu	Kiangsu	Suxian	Suhsien		
		Suzhou	Suchou		

Geographical Terms

This is a list of some of the geographical words from foreign languages which are found in the place names on the maps and in the index. Each is followed by the language and the English meaning.

Afr. afrikaans
Alb. albanian
Amh. amharic
Ar. arabic
Ber. berber
Bulg. bulgarian
Bur. burmese

Chin. chinese
Cz. czechoslovakian
Dan. danish
Dut. dutch
Fin. finnish
Flem. flemish
Fr. french

Gae. gaelic
Ger. german
Gr. greek
Heb. hebrew
Hin. hindi
I.-C. indo-chinese
Ice. icelandic

It. italian
Jap. japanese
Kor. korean
Lapp. lappish
Lith. lithuanian
Mal. malay
Mong. mongolian

Nor. norwegian
Pash. pashto
Pers. persian
Pol. polish
Port. portuguese
Rum. rumanian
Russ. russian

Ser.-Cr. serbo-croat
Siam. siamese
Sin. sinhalese
Som. somali
Span. spanish
Swed. swedish
Tib. tibetan
Turk. turkish

A. (Ain) *Ar.* spring
–á *Ice.* river
a *Dan., Nor., Swed.* stream
–abad *Pers., Russ.* town
Abyad *Ar.* white
Ad. (Adrar) *Ar., Ber.* mountain
Ada, Adasi *Tur.* island
Addis *Amh.* new
Adrar *Ar., Ber.* mountain
Ạin *Ar.* spring
Ằkra *Gr.* cape
Akrotíri *Gr.* cape
Alb *Ger.* mountains
Albufera *Span.* lagoon
–ålen *Nor.* islands
Alpen *Ger.* mountain pastures
Alpes *Fr.* mountains
Alpi *It.* mountains
Alto *Port.* high
–älv, –älven *Swed.* stream, river
Amt *Dan.* first-order administrative division
Appennino *It.* mountain range
Arch. (Archipiélago) *Span.* archipelago
Arcipélago *It.* archipelago
Arq. (Arquipélago) *Port.* archipelago
Arr. (Arroyo) *Span.* stream
–Ảs, –åsen *Nor., Swed.* hill
Autonomna Oblast *Ser.-Cr.* autonomous region
Ayios *Gr.* island
Ayn *Ar.* well, waterhole

B(a). (Baía) *Port.* bay
B. (Baie) *Fr.* bay
B. (Bahía) *Span.* bay
B. (Ben) *Gae.* mountain
B. (Bir) *Ar.* well
B. (Bucht) *Ger.* bay
B. (Bugt.) *Dan.* bay
Baai, –baai *Afr.* bay
Bảb *Ar.* gate
Bảck, –bäcken *Swed.* stream
Back, backen, *Swed.* hill
Bad, –baden *Ger.* spa
Bădiya,-t *Ar.* desert
Baek´*Dan.* stream
Baelt *Dan.* strait
Bahía *Span.* bay
Bahr *Ar.* sea, river
Bahra *Ar.* lake
Baía *Port.* bay
Baie *Fr.* bay
Bajo, –a, *Span.* lower
Bakke *Nor.* hill
Bala *Pers.* upper
Baltă *Rum.* marsh, lake
Banc *Fr.* bank
Bander *Ar., Mal.* port
Bandar *Pers.* bay
Banja *Ser. Cr.* spa resort
Barat *Mal.* western
Barr. (Barrage) *Fr.* dam
Barracão *Port.* dam, waterfall
Bassin *Fr.* bay
Bayt *Heb.* house, village
Bazar *Hin.* market, bazaar
Be'er *Heb.* well
Beit *Heb.* village
Belo-, Belyy, Belaya,

Beloye, *Russ.* white
Ben *Gae.* mountain
Bender *Somal.* harbour
Berg,(e) –berg(e) *Afr.* mountain(s)
Berg, –berg *Ger.* mountain
–berg, –et *Nor., Swed.* hill, mountain, rock
Bet *Heb.* house, village
Bir, Blr *Ar.* well
Birket *Ar.* lake, bay, marsh
Bj. (Bordj) *Ar.* port
–bjerg *Dan.* hill, point
Boca *Span.* river mouth
Bodden *Ger.* bay, inlet
Bogaz, Boğaz, –ı *Tur.* strait
Boka *Ser.-Cr.* gulf, inlet
Bol. (Bolshoi) *Russ.* great, large
Bordj *Ar.* fort
–borg *Dan., Nor., Swed.* castle, fort
–botn *Nor.* valley floor
bouche(s) *Fr.* mouth
Br. (Burnu) *Tur.* cape
Bratul *Rum.* distributary stream
–breen *Nor.* glacier
–bruck *Ger.* bridge
–brunn *Swed.* well, spring
Bucht *Ger.* bay
Bugt, –bugt *Dan.* bay
Buheirat *Ar.* lake
Bukit *Mal.* hill
Bukten *Swed.* bay
–bulag *Mong.* spring
Bûr *Ar.* port
Burg. *Ar.* fort
Burg, –burg *Ger.* castle
Burnu *Tur.* cape
Burun *Tur.* cape
Butt *Gae.* promontory
–by *Dan., Nor., Swed.* town
–byen *Nor., Swed.* town

C. (Cabo) *Port., Span.* headland, cape
C. (Cap) *Fr.* cape
C. (Capo) *It.* cape
Cabeza *Span.* peak, hill
Camp *Port., Span.* land, field
Campo *Span.* plain
Campos *Span.* upland
Can. (Canal) *Fr., Span.* canal
Canale *It.* canal
Canalul *Ser.-Cr.* canal
Cao Nguyên *Thai.* plateau, tableland
Cap *Fr.* cape
Capo *It.* cape
Cataracta *Sp.* cataract
Cauce *Span.* intermittent stream
Causse *Fr.* upland (limestone)
Cayi *Tur.* river
Cayo(s) *Span.* rock(s), islet(s)
Cerro *Span.* hill, peak
Ch. (Chaîne(s)) *Fr.* mountain range(s)
Ch. (Chott) *Ar.* salt lake
Chaco *Span.* jungle
Chaîne(s) *Fr.* mountain range(s)
Chap. (Chapada) *Port.* hills, upland

Chapa *Span.* hills, upland
Chapada *Port.* hills, upland
Chaung *Bur.* stream, river
Chen *Chin.* market town
Ch'eng *Chin.* town
Chiang *Chin.* river
Ch'ih *Chin.* pool
Ch'ön *Kor.* river
–chōsuji *Kor.* reservoir
Chott *Ar.* salt lake, swamp
Chou *Chin.* district
Chu *Tib.* river
Chung *Chin.* middle
Chute *Fr.* waterfall
Co. (Cerro) *Span.* hill, peak
Coch. (Cochilla) *Port.* hills
Col *Fr., It.* Pass
Colline(s) *Fr.* hill(s)
Conca *It.* plain, basin
Cord. (Cordillera) *Span.* mountain chain
Costa *It., Span.* coast
Côte *Fr.* coast, slope, hill
Cuchillas *Spain* hills
Cu-Lao *I.-C.* island

D. (Dolok) *Mal.* mountain
Dágh *Pers.* mountain
Dağ(ı) *Tur.* mountain(s)
Dağları *Tur.* mountain range
Dake *Jap.* mountain
–dal *Nor.* valley
–dal, –e *Dan., Nor.* valley
–dal, –en *Swed.* valley, stream
Dalay *Mong.* sea, large lake
–dalir *Ice.* valley
–dalur *Ice.* valley
–damm, –en *Swed.* lake
Danau *Mal.* lake
Dao *I.-O.* island
Dar *Ar.* region
Darya *Russ.* river
Daryācheh *Pers.* marshy lake, lake
Dasht *Pers.* desert, steppe
Daung *Bur.* mountain, hill
Dayr *Ar.* depression, hill
Debre *Amh.* hill
Deli *Ser.-Cr.* mountain(s)
Denizi *Tur.* sea
Dépt. (Département) *Fr.* first-order administrative division
Desierto *Span.* desert
Dhar *Ar.* region, mountain chain
Dj. (Djebel) *Ar.* mountain
Dō *Jap., Kor.* island
Dong *Kor.* village, town
Dong *Thai.* jungle region
–dorf *Ger.* village
–dorp *Afr.* village
–drif *Afr.* ford
–dybet *Dan.* marine channel
Dzong *Tib.* town, settlement

Eil.-eiland(en) *Afr., Dut.* island(s)
–elv *Nor.* river
–'emeq *Heb.* plain, valley
'erg *Ar.* desert with dunes
Estrecho *Span.* strait
Estuario *Span.* estuary

Étang *Fr.* lagoon
–ey(jar) *Ice.* island(s)

F. (Fiume) *It.* river
F. Folyó *Hung.* river
Fd. (Fjord) *Nor.* Inlet of sea
–feld *Ger.* field
–fell *Ice.* mountain, hill
–feng *Chin.* mountain
Fiume *It.* river
Fj. (–fjell) *Nor.* mountain
–fjall *Ice.* mountain(s), hill(s)
–fjäll(et) *Swed.* hill(s), mountain(s), ridge
–fjällen *Swed.* mountains
–fjard(en) *Swed.* fjord, bay, lake
Fjeld *Dan.* mountain
–fjell *Nor.* mountain, rock
–fjord(en) *Nor.* inlet of sea
–fjorden *Dan.* bay, marine channel
–fjördur *Ice.* fjord
Fl. (Fleuve) *Fr.* river
Fl. (Fluss) *Ger.* river
–flói *Ice.* bay, marshy country
Fluss *Ger.* river
foce,–i *It.* mouth(s)
Folyó *Hung.* river
–fontein *Afr.* fountain, spring
–fors, –en, *Swed.* rapids, waterfall
Foss *Ice., Nor.* waterfall
–furt *Ger.* ford
Fylke *Nor.* first-order administrative division

G. (Gebel) *Ar.* mountain
G. (Gebirge) *Ger.* hills, mountains
G. (Golfe) *Fr.* gulf
G. (Golfo) *It.* gulf
G. (Gora) *Bulg., Russ., Ser.-Cr.* mountain
G. (Gunong) *Mal.* mountain
–gang *Kor.* river
Ganga *Hin., Sin.* river
–gat *Dan.* sound
–gau *Ger.* district
Gave *Fr.* stream
–gawa *Jap.* river
Geb. (Gebirge) *Ger.* hills, mountains
Gebel *Ar.* mountain
Geziret *Ar.* island
Ghat *Hin.* range of hills
Ghiol *Rum.* lake
Ghubbat *Ar.* bay, inlet
Gji *Alb.* bay
Gjol *Alb.* lagoon, lake
Gl. (Glava) *Ser.-Cr.* mountain, peak
Glen. *Gae.* valley
Gletscher *Ger.* glacier
Gobi *Mong.* desert
Gol *Mong.* river
Golfe *Fr.* gulf
Golfo *It., Span.* gulf
Gomba *Tib.* settlement
Gora *Bulg., Russ., Ser.-Cr.* mountain(s)
Góry *Pol., Russ.* mountain
Gölü *Tur.* lake
–gorod *Russ.* small town
Grad *Bulg., Russ., Ser-Cr.* town, city

Grada *Russ.* mountain range
Guba *Russ.* bay
–Guntō *Jap.* island group
Gunong *Mal.* mountain
Gură *Rum.* passage

H. Hadabat *Ar.* plateau
–hafen *Ger.* harbour, port
Haff *Ger.* bay
Hai *Chin.* sea
Haihsia *Chin.* strait
–hale *Dan.* spit, peninsula
Hals *Dan., Nor.* peninsula, isthmus
Halvø *Dan.* peninsula
Halvøya *Nor.* peninsula
Hămad, Hamada, *Ar.* stony desert, plain
–hamn *Swed., Nor.* harbour, anchorage
Hămūn *Ar.* plain
Hămūn *Pers.* low-lying marshy area
–Hantō *Jap.* peninsula
Harju *Fin.* hill
Hassi *Ar.* well
–haug *Nor.* hill
Hav *Swed.* gulf
Havet *Nor.* sea
–havn *Dan., Nor.* harbour
Hegyseg *Hung.* forest
Heide *Ger.* heath
Hi. (hassi) *Ar.* well
Ho *Chin.* river
–hø *Nor.* peak
Hochland *Afr.* highland
Hoek, –hoek *Afr., Dut.* cape
Höfn *Ice.* harbour, port
–hög, –en, –högar, –högarna *Swed.* hill(s), peak, mountain
Höhe *Ger.* hills
Holm *Dan.* island
–holm, –holme, –holzen, *Swed.* island
Hon *I.-C.* island
Hora *Cz.* mountain
–horn *Nor.* peak
Hory *Cz.* mountain range, forest
–hoved *Dan.* point, headland, peninsula
Hráun *Ice.* lava
–hsi *Chin.* mountain, stream
–hsiang *Chin.* village
–hsien *Chin.* district
Hu *Chin.* lake
Huk *Dan., Ger.* point
Huken *Nor.* head

I. (Île) *Fr.* island
I. (Ilha) *Port.* island
I. (Insel) *Ger.* island
I. (Isla) *Span.* island
I. (Isola) *It.* island
Idehan *Ar., Ber.* sandy plain
Île(s) *Fr.* island(s)
Ilha *Port.* island
Insel(n) *Ger.* island(s)
Irmak *Tur.* river
Is. (Inseln) *Ger.* islands
Is. (Islas) *Span.* islands
Is. (Isola) *It.* island
Isola, –e *It.* island(s)
Istmo *Span.* isthmus

J. (Jabal) *Ar.* mountain
J. (Jazira) *Ar.* island
J. (Jebel) *Ar.* mountain
J. (Jezioro) *Pol.* lake
Jabal *Ar.* mountain, range
–jaur *Swed.* lake
–järvi *Fin.* lake, bay, pond
Jasovir *Bulg.* reservoir
Jază'ir *Ar.* islands
Jazira *Ar.* island
Jazireh *Pers.* island
Jebel *Ar.* mountain
Jezero *Ser.-Cr.* lake
Jezioro *Pol.* lake
–Jima *Jap.* island
Jøkelen *Nor.* glacier
–joki *Fin.* stream
–jökull *Ice.* glacier
Jūras Līcis *Lat.* bay, gulf

K. (Kap) *Dan.* cape
K (Khalig) *Ar.* gulf
K. (Kiang) *Chin.* river
K. (Kuala) *Mal.* confluence, estuary
Kaap *Afr.* cape
Kai *Jap.* sea
Kaikyō *Jap.* strait
Kamennyy *Russ.* stony
Kampong *Mal.* village
Kan. (Kanal) *Ser.-Cr.* channel, canal
Kanaal *Dut., Flem.* canal
Kanal *Dan.* channel, gulf
Kanal *Ger., Swed.* canal, stream
kanal *Ser.-Cr.* channel, canal
Kang *Kor.* river, bay
Kangri *Tib.* mountain glacier
Kap *Dan., Ger.* cape
Kapp *Nor.* cape
Kas *I.-C.* island
–kaupstaður *Ice.* market town
–kaupunki *Fin.* town
Kavīr *Pers.* salt desert
Kébir *Ar.* great
Kéfar *Ar.* village, hamlet
–ken *Jap.* first-order administrative division
Kep *Alb.* cape
Kepulauan *Mal.* archipelago
Ketjil *Mal.* lesser, little
Khalig, Khalij *Ar.* gulf
khamba, –ldg *Tib.* source, spring
Khawr *Ar.* wadi
Khirbat *Ar.* ruins
Kho Khot *Thai.* isthmus
Khōr *Pers.* creek, estuary
Khrebet *Russ.* mountain range
Kiang *Chin.* river
–klint *Dan.* cliff
–Klintar *Swed.* hills
Kloof *Afr.* gorge
Knude *Dan.* point
Ko *Jap.* lake
Ko *Thai.* island
Kohi *Pash.* mountains
Kol *Russ.* lake
Kolymskoye *Russ.* mountain range
Kólpos *Gr., Tur.* gulf, bay
Kompong *Mal.* landing place
–kop *Afr.* hill

-köping Swed. market town
Körfezi Tur. gulf
Kosa Russ. spit
-koski Fin. cataract, rapids
-kraal Afr. native village
Krasnyy Russ. red
Kryash Russ. ridge, hills
Kuala Mal. confluence, estuary
kuan Chin. pass
Kuh –hha Pers. mountains
Kul Russ. lake
Kulle Swed. hill, shoal
Kum Russ. sandy desert
Kumpu Fin. hill
Kurgan Russ. mound
Kwe Bur. bay, gulf
Kyst Dan. coast
Kyun, –zu, –umya Bur. island(s)

L. (Lac) Fr. lake
L. (Lacul) Rum. lake
L. (Lago) It., Span. lake, lagoon
L. (Lagoa) Port. lagoon
L. (Límni) Gr. lake
L. (Loch) Gae. (lake, inlet)
L. (Lough) Gae. (lake, inlet)
La Tib. pass
La (Lagoa) Port. lagoon
-laagte Afr. watercourse
Läani Fin. first-order administrative division
Län Swed. first-order administrative division
Lac Fr. lake
Lacul Rum. lake, lagoon
Lago It., Span. lake, lagoon
Lagoa Port. lagoon
Laguna It., Span. lagoon, intermittent lake
Lagune Fr. lake
Lahti Fin. bay, gulf, cove
Lakhti Russ. bay, gulf
Lampi Fin. lake
Land Ger. first-order administrative division
-land Dan. region
-land Afr., Nor. land, province
Lido It. beach, shore
Liehtao Chin. islands
Lilla Swed. small
Límni Gr. lake
Ling Chin. mountain range, ice
Linna Fin. historical fort
Llano Span. prairie, plain
Loch Gae. (lake)
Lough Gae. (lake)
Lum Alb. river
Lund Dan. forest
-lund, –en Swed. wood(s)

M. (Maj, Mai) Alb. mountain, peak
M. (Mont) Fr. mountain peak
M. (Mys) Russ. cape
Madīna(h) Ar. town, city
Madiq Ar. strait
Maj Alb. peak
Mäki Fin. hill, hillside
Mal Alb. mountain
Mal Russ. little, small
Mal/a, –i, –o Ser.-Cr. small, little
Man Kor. bay
Mar Span. lagoon, sea
Mare Rum. great
Marisma Span. marsh
-mark Dan., Nor. land
Marsâ Ar. anchorage, bay, inlet
Masabb Ar. river mouth
Massif Fr. upland, plateau
Mato Port. forest
Mazar Pers. shrine, tomb
Meer Afr., Dut., Ger. lake sea

Mi., Mti. (Monti) It. mountains
Miao Chin. temple, shrine
Midbar Heb. wilderness
Mif. (Massif) Fr. upland, plateau
Misaki Jap. cape, point
-mo Nor., Swed. heath, island
-mon Swed. heath
Mong Bur. town
Mont Fr. hill, mountain
Montagna It. mountain
Montagne Fr. hill, mountain
Montaña Span. mountain
Monte It., Port., Span. mountain
Monti It. mountains
More Russ. sea
Mörön Hung. river
Mt. (Mont) Fr. mountain
Mt. (Monti) It. mountain
Mt. (Montaña) Span. mountain range
Mte. (Monte) It., Port., Span. mountain
Mţi. (Munţi) Rum. mountain
Mts. (Monts) Fr. mountains
Muang Mal. town
Mui Ar., I.-C. cape
Mull Gae. (promontory)
Mund, –mund Afr. mouth
Munkhafed Ar. depression
Munte Rum. mount
Munţi(i) Rum. mountain(s)
Muong Mal. village
Myit Bur. river
Myitwanya Bur. mouths of river
-mýri Ice. bog
Mys Russ. cape

N. (Nahal) Heb. river
Naes Dan. point, cape
Nafūd Ar. sandy desert
Nahal Heb. river
Nahr Ar. river, stream
Najd Ar. plateau, pass
Nakhon Thai. town
Nam I.-C. river
-nam Kor. south
-näs Swed. cape
-nes Ice., Nor. cape
Ness, –ness Gae. promontory, cape
Nez Fr. cape
-niemi Fin. cape, point, peninsula, island
Nizhne, –iy Russ. lower
Nizmennost Russ. plain, lowland
Nísos, Nisoi Gr. island(s)
Nor Chin. lake
Nor Tib. peak
Nos Bulg., Russ. cape, point
Nudo Span. mountain
Nuruu Mong. mountain range
Nuur Mong. lake

O. (Ostrov) Russ. island
O (Ouâdî, Oued) Ar. wadi
-ö Swed. island, peninsula, point
-öar, (–na) Swed. islands
Oblast Russ. administrative division
Öbor Mong. inner
Occidental Fr., Span. western
Odde Dan., Nor. point, peninsula, cape
Oji Alb. bay
Ojo Span. spring
Oki Jap. bay
-ön Swed. island peninsula
Ondör Mong. high, tall

-ör Swed. island, peninsula, point
Oraşul Rum. city
Ord Gae. point
Óri Gr. mountains
Oriental Span. eastern
Órmos Gr. bay
Óros Gr. mountain
Ort Ger. point, cape
Ostrov(a) Russ. island(s)
Otok(-i) Ser.-Cr. island(s)
Ouadi, –edi Ar. dry watercourse, wadi
Ouzan Pers. river
Ova (–si) Tur. plains, lowlands
-øy, (–a) Nor. island(s)
Oya Hin. point
Oya Sin. river
Oz. (Ozero, a) Russ. lake(s)

P. (Passo) It. pass
P. (Pasul) Rum. pass
P. (Pico) Span. peak
P. (Prokhod) Bulg. pass
-pää Fin. hill(s), mountain
Pahta Lapp. hill
Pampa, –s Span. plain(s) salt flat(s)
Pan. (Pantano) Span. Reservoir
Pantao Chin. peninsula
Parbat Urdu mountain
Pas Fr. gap
Paso Span. pass, marine channel
Pass Ger. pass
Passo It. pass
Pasul Rum. pass
Patam Hin. small village
Patna, –patnam Hin. small village
Pegunungan Mal. mountain, range
Pei, –pei Chin. north
Pélagos Gr. sea
Pen. (Península) Span. peninsula
Peña Span. rock, peak
Península Span. peninsula
Per. (Pereval) Russ. pass
Pertuis Fr. channel
Peski Russ. desert, sands
Phanom I.-C., Thai. mountain
Phnom I.-C. mountain
Phu I.-C. mountain
Pic Fr. peak
Pico(s) Span. peak(s)
Pik Russ. peak
Piz., pizzo It. peak
Pl. (Planina) Ser.-Cr. mountain, range
Plage Fr. beach
Plaine Fr. plain
Planalto Span. plateau
Planina Bulg., Ser.-Cr. mountain, range
Plat. (Plateau) Fr. level upland
Plato Russ. plateau
Playa Span. beach
P-ov. (Poluostrov) Russ. peninsula
Pointe Fr. point, cape
Pojezierze Pol. lakes plateau
Polder Dut. reclaimed farmland
-pólis Gr. city, town
Poluostrov Russ. peninsula
Połwysep Pol. peninsula
Pont Fr. bridge
Ponta Port. point, cape
Ponte It. bridge
Poort Afr. passage, gate
-poort Dut. port
Porta Port. pass
Portil, -e Rum. gate
Portillo Span. pass
Porto It. port
Porto Port., Span. port

Pot. (Potámi, Potamós) Gr. river
Poulo I.-C. island
Pr. (Průsmyk) Cz. pass
Pradesh Hin. state
Presa Span. reservoir
Presqu'île Fr. peninsula
Prokhod Bulg. pass
Proliv Russ. strait
Prusmyk Cz. pass
Pso. (Passo) It. pass
Pta. (Ponta) Port. point, cape
Pta. (Punta) It., Span. point, cape, peak
Pte. (Pointe) Fr. point cape
Puerto Span. port, pass
Puig Cat. peak
Pulau Mal. island
Puna Span. desert plateau
Punta It., Span. point, peak
Puy Fr. hill

Qal'at Ar. fort
Qanal Ar. canal
Qasr Ar. fort
Qiryat Heb. town
Qolleh Pers. mountain

Ramla Ar. sand
Rann Hin. swampy region
Rao I.-C. river
Ras Amh. cape, headland
Rãs Ar. cape, headland
Recife(s) Port. reef(s)
Reka Bulg., Cz., Russ. river
Repede Rum. rapids
Represa Port. dam
Reshteh Pers. mountain range
-Rettō Jap. group of islands
Ría Span. estuary, bay
Ribeirão Port. river
Rijeka Ser.-Cr. river
Rio Port. river
Río Span. river
Riv. (Riviera) It. coastal plain, coast, river
Rivier Afr. river
Riviera It. coast
Rivière Fr. river
Roche Fr. rock
Rog Russ. horn
-rück Ger. ridge
Rūd Pers. stream, river
Rudohorie Cz. ore mountains
Rzeka Pol. river

S. (Sungei) Mal. river
Sa. (Serra) It., Port. range of hills
Sa. (Sierra) Span. range of hills
-saari Fin. island
Sadd Ar. dam
Sagar, –ara Hin., Urdu lake
Saharã Ar. desert
Sahrã Ar. desert
Sa'id Ar. highland
Sakar Fin. mountain
-Saki Jap. point
Sal. (Salar) Span. salt pan
Salina(s) Span. salt flat(s)
-salmi Fin. strait, sound, lake, channel
Saltsjöbad Swed. resort
Sammyaku Jap. mountain, range
Samut Thai. gulf
-San Jap. hill, mountain
Sap. (Sapadno) Russ. west
Sasso It. mountain
Se, Sé I.-C. river
Sebkha, –kra Ar. salt flats
See Ger. lake
-see Ger. sea
-şehir Turk. town
Selat Mal. strait
-selkä Fin. bay, lake, sound, ridge, hills

Selva Span. forest, wood
Seno Span. bay, sound
Serír Ar. desert of small stones
Serra It., Port. range of hills
Serranía Span. mountains
Sev. (Severo) Russ. north
-shahr Pers. city, town
Shan Chin. hills, mountains, pass
Shan-mo Chin. mountain range
Shatt Ar. river
-Shima Jap. island
Shimãli Ar. northern
-Shotō Jap. group of islands
Shuik'u Chin. reservoir
Sierra Span. hill, range
Sjö, sjön Swed. lake, bay, sea
Sjøen Dan. sea
Skär Swed. island, rock, cape
Skog Nor. forest
-skog, –skogen Swed. wood(s)
-skov Dan. forest
Slieve Gae. range of hills
-sø Dan., Nor. lake
Sør Nor. south, southern
Solonchak Russ. salt lake, marsh
Souk Ar. market
Spitze Ger. peak, mountain
-spruit Afr. stream
-stad Afr., Nor., Swed. town
-stadt Ger. town
Staður Ice. town
Stausee Ger. reservoir
Step Russ. plain
Stenón Gr. strait, pass
Str. (Stretto) It. strait
-strand Dan., Nor. beach
-strede Nor. straits
Strelka Russ. spit
-strete Nor. straits
Stretto It. strait
Stroedet Dan. strait
-ström, –strömmen Swed. stream(s)
-stroom Afr. large river
Suidō Jap. strait, channel
Sûn Bur. cape
Sund Dan. sound
-sund, –sundet Swed. sound, estuary, inlet
-sund(et) Nor. sound
Sungai, –ei Mal. river
Sungei Mal. river
Sur Span. south, southern
Sveti Bulg. pass
Syd Dan., Swed. south

Tai –tai Chin. tower
Tal Mong. plain, steppe
-tal Ger. valley
Tall Ar. hills, hummocks
Tandjung Mal. cape, headland
Tao Chin. island
Tassili Ar. rocky plateau
Tau Russ. mountain, range
Taung Bur. mountain, south
Taunggya Bur. pass
Tělok I.-C., Mal. bay bight
Teluk Mal. bay, gulf
Tg. (Tandjung) Mal. cape, headland
-thal Ger. valley
Thok Tib. town
Tierra Span. land, country
-tind Nor. peak
Tjärn, –en, –et Swed. lake
Tong Nor. village, town
Tong Bur., Thai. mountain range
Tonle I.-C. large river, lake
-träsk Swed. bog, swamp
Tsangpo Tib. large river
Tso Tib. lake

Tsu Jap. entrance, bay
Tulur Ar. hill
T'un Chin. village
Tung Chin. east
Tunnel Fr. tunnel
Tunturi Fin. hill(s), mountain(s), ridge

Uad Ar. dry watercourse, wadi
Udjung Mal. cape
Udd, udde, udden Swed. point, peninsula
Uebi Somal. river
Us Mong. water
Ust Russ. river mouth
Uul Mong., Russ. mountain, range

V. (Volcán) Span. volcano
-vaara Fin. hill, mountain, ridge, peak
-våg Nor. bay
Val Fr., It. valley
Valea Rum. valley
-vall, –vallen Swed. mountain
Valle Span. valley
Vallée Fr. valley
Valli It. lake, lagoon
Väst Swed. west
-vatn Ice., Nor. lake
Vatten Swed. lake
Vdkhr. (Vodokhranilishche) Russ. reservoir
-ved, –veden Swed. range, hills
Veld, –veld Afr. field
Velik/a, –e, –i, –o Ser.Cr. large
-vesi Fin. water, lake, bay sound, strait
Vest Dan., Nor. west
Vf. (vîrful) Rum. peak, mountain
-vidda Nor. plateau
Vig Dan. bay, inlet, cove, lagoon, lake, bight
-vik, –vika, –viken Nor., Swed. bay, cove, gulf, inlet, lake
Vila Port. small town
Villa Span. town
Ville Fr. town
Vinh I.-C. bay
Vîrful Rum. peak, mountain
-vlei Afr. pond, pool
Vodokhranilishche Russ. reservoir
Vol. (Volcán) Span. volcano, mountain
Vorota Russ. gate
Vostochnyy Russ. eastern
Vozyshennost Russ. heights, uplands
Vrata Bulg. gate, pass
Vrchovina Cz. mountainous country
Vrchy Cz. mountain range
Vung I.-C. gulf
-vuori Fin. mountain, hill

W. (Wādī) Ar. dry watercourse
Wâhât Ar. oasis
Wald Ger. wood, forest
Wan Chin., Jap. bay
Webi Amh. river
Woestyn Afr. desert

Yam Heb. sea
Yang Chin. ocean
Yazovir Bulg. reservoir
Yoma Bur. mountain range
-yüan Chin. spring

-Zaki Jap. peninsula
Zalew Pol. lagoon, swamp
Zaliv Russ. bay
Zan Jap. mountain
Zatoka Pol. bay
Zee Dut. sea
Zemlya Russ. land, island(s)